ARCTIC OCEAN
Barents Sea
East Siberian Sea
Bering Strait
Bering Sea
Sea of Okhotsk
SVALBARD (NORWAY)
FINLAND
Helsinki
Tallinn
ESTONIA
Riga
LATVIA
LITHUANIA
Vilnius
Minsk
BELARUS
Moscow
RUSSIAN FEDERATION
Kyiv
UKRAINE
Bratislava
Budapest
HUNGARY
MOLDOVA
Chişinău
ROMANIA
Bucharest
SERBIA
BULGARIA
Sofia
Skopje
Tirana
ALBANIA
GREECE
Athens
Black Sea
GEORGIA
Tbilisi
ARMENIA
Yerevan
AZERBAIJAN
Baku
Ankara
TURKEY
Nicosia
CYPRUS
SYRIA
Beirut
LEBANON
Damascus
ISRAEL
Amman
JORDAN
Baghdad
IRAQ
Tehran
IRAN
Kuwait City
KUWAIT
BAHRAIN
Manama
QATAR
Doha
UAE
Abu Dhabi
Muscat
OMAN
Riyadh
SAUDI ARABIA
Red Sea
Cairo
EGYPT
PALESTINIAN AUTONOMOUS AREAS
Sirte
CHAD
Khartoum
SUDAN
ERITREA
Asmara
San'a
YEMEN
DJIBOUTI
Addis Ababa
ETHIOPIA
SOMALIA
Mogadishu
CENTRAL AFRICAN REPUBLIC
DEMOCRATIC REPUBLIC OF THE CONGO
Kinshasa
UGANDA
Kampala
KENYA
Nairobi
RWANDA
Kigali
BURUNDI
Bujumbura
TANZANIA
Dodoma
Dar es Salaam
Victoria
SEYCHELLES
Lubumbashi
ZAMBIA
Lusaka
MALAWI
Lilongwe
Moroni
COMOROS
MAYOTTE (FRANCE)
Harare
ZIMBABWE
MOZAMBIQUE
Mozambique Channel
MADAGASCAR
Antananarivo
MAURITIUS
Port Louis
RÉUNION (FRANCE)
BOTSWANA
Gaborone
Pretoria
Maputo
Mbabane
SWAZILAND
LESOTHO
Maseru
SOUTH AFRICA
Astana
KAZAKHSTAN
UZBEKISTAN
Tashkent
TURKMENISTAN
Asgabat
Bishkek
KYRGYZSTAN
Almaty
Dushanbe
TAJIKISTAN
AFGHANISTAN
Kabul
Islamabad
PAKISTAN
New Delhi
INDIA
NEPAL
Kathmandu
Thimphu
BHUTAN
BANGLADESH
Dhaka
Bay of Bengal
SRI LANKA
Colombo
Sri Jayawardenepura
MALDIVES
BRITISH INDIAN OCEAN TERRITORY (UNITED KINGDOM)
INDIAN OCEAN
Ulan Bator
MONGOLIA
PEOPLE'S REPUBLIC OF CHINA
Beijing
DEMOCRATIC PEOPLE'S REPUBLIC OF KOREA
Pyongyang
Seoul
REPUBLIC OF KOREA
Sea of Japan
JAPAN
Tokyo
East China Sea
Taipei
TAIWAN
MACAO (CHINA)
HONG KONG (CHINA)
MYANMAR
Pyinmana
Yangon
THAILAND
Bangkok
LAOS
Vientiane
Hanoi
VIET NAM
CAMBODIA
Phnom-Penh
South China Sea
Philippine Sea
Manila
PHILIPPINES
BRUNEI
Bandar Seri Begawan
Kuala Lumpur
Putrajaya
MALAYSIA
SINGAPORE
Jakarta
INDONESIA
Dili
TIMOR-LESTE
CHRISTMAS ISLAND (AUSTRALIA)
COCOS ISLANDS (AUSTRALIA)
PAPUA NEW GUINEA
Port Moresby
Honiara
SOLOMON ISLANDS
Coral Sea
VANUATU
Port Vila
NEW CALEDONIA (FRANCE)
FIJI
Suva
AUSTRALIA
Canberra
Tasman Sea
NEW ZEALAND
Wellington
NORFOLK ISLAND (AUSTRALIA)
NORTHERN MARIANA ISLANDS (USA)
GUAM (USA)
PALAU
FEDERATED STATES OF MICRONESIA
MARSHALL ISLANDS
NAURU
KIRIBATI
TUVALU
TOKELAU (NEW ZEALAND)
WALLIS AND FUTUNA ISLANDS (FRANCE)
SAMOA
AMERICAN SAMOA (USA)
NIUE (NZ)
TONGA
PACIFIC OCEAN
Tropic of Cancer
40°
80°
0°

The USA and Canada 2009

The USA and Canada 2009

11th Edition

Routledge
Taylor & Francis Group
LONDON AND NEW YORK

First published 1989
Eleventh Edition 2009

Albert House, 1–4 Singer Street, London EC2A 4BQ, United Kingdom
(Routledge is an imprint of the Taylor & Francis Group, an Informa business)

ISBN-13 978-1-85743-478-1
ISBN-10 1-85743-478-1
ISSN 0956-0904

Editors: Katie Dawson, Jacqueline West

Associate Editor: David Gruar

Statistics Editor: Philip McIntyre

Contributing Editors: Iain Frame, Jillian O'Brien

Assistant Editors: Kim Chamberlain, Laura Davis, Neil Higgins, Christopher Matthews, Simon Molony, Adrian Reynolds, Janine Tenzer, Anna Thomas, Amyas Varcoe, Gareth Vaughan

Series Editor: Joanne Maher

Typeset in New Century Schoolbook

Typeset by Data Standards Limited, Frome, Somerset

Printed and bound in Great Britain by Polestar Wheatons, Exeter

FOREWORD

The year 2009 looked set to be greeted with huge anticipation in the region encompassed by THE USA AND CANADA. In November 2008, as this edition went to press, the USA was the focus of world-wide attention when the country elected its first black President, the Democratic candidate Barack Obama. The lengthy campaign by Obama and his Republican rival John McCain achieved high levels of political engagement among the electorate, resulting in some of the highest voter participation rates ever recorded in the country. This phenomenon was attributable in part to increasing popular dissatisfaction with the Administration of George W. Bush, particularly the USA's ongoing military involvement in Iraq, and, latterly in the campaign, to the anticipated effects of the economic downturn. Moreover, the selection by the Democratic party of a black nominee—the first such candidate in a presidential election—lent the campaign, and the election itself, an air of historic significance. In congressional elections held concurrently the Democrats increased their majority in the House of Representatives and gained a majority in the Senate. The new Administration, which was to take office in January 2009, was likely to focus on policies aimed at mitigating the impact of the expected economic recession and on US foreign relations, particularly with the Middle East. Canadian Prime Minister Stephen J. Harper called a snap general election, which took place in mid-October 2008. Although his Conservative Party increased its representation in the federal Parliament, it failed to achieve the necessary number of seats to secure a majority. A similar minority Government under Harper seemed unlikely to produce any major policy changes during 2009. Meanwhile, developments throughout the region were expected to be strongly influenced by the global economic downturn in 2009.

This 11th edition of THE USA AND CANADA has been fully revised and updated. Part One is a General Survey, consisting of articles examining a number of issues common to the two countries, including the Security and Prosperity Partnership of North America, immigration policies in Canada and the USA, the North American agenda in the Pacific Rim, and environmental issues in the USA and Canada. Parts Two and Three, on the USA and Canada, respectively, follow a uniform model. An Introduction provides historical, geographical and demographic data on the country. The Essays provide wide-ranging expert analysis of political, economic and social affairs. A new article on the US electoral system offers a timely insight into the democratic processes of the world's largest economic and military superpower. Additional essays, new for this edition, provide a comprehensive analysis of significant developments in the region, including the US Farm Bill and the developing relationship with the emerging powers referred to as the BRICs. The Directory chapters are divided into three sections: Public Affairs, the Economy, and Society. Statistical information accompanies the extensive listings in each section. Finally, there is a chapter dedicated specifically to each of the States of the USA and the Provinces and Territories of Canada. This provides a geographical, historical and economic introduction to each federal unit, together with up-to-date government and legislature details.

The Editors would once again like to thank all the contributors for their articles and advice, and the various organizations that have assisted in the revision of statistical and directory material for this edition.

November 2008

ACKNOWLEDGEMENTS

The editors gratefully acknowledge the co-operation, interest and enthusiasm of all the authors who have contributed to this volume. We are also indebted to all the federal, state, provincial and territorial government departments, organizations, associations and companies in the USA and Canada, whose kind assistance in updating the 11th edition of THE USA AND CANADA is greatly appreciated.

This publication makes extensive use of statistical information published by the US Bureau of the Census and the US Department of Commerce and data provided by Statistics Canada. Statistics Canada information is used with the permission of Statistics Canada. Users are forbidden to copy the data and redisseminate them, in an original or modified form, for commercial purposes, without the expressed permission of Statistics Canada. Information on the availability of the wide range of data from Statistics Canada can be obtained from Statistics Canada's Regional Offices, its internet site, www.statcan.ca, or by telephoning (613) 951-8116. We acknowledge particular indebtedness to the US Bureau of the Census's *Statistical Abstract of the United States* and to the IMF's statistical database *International Financial Statistics*. Data on the Jewish population of US states were provided by the *American Jewish Year Book*, copyright the American Jewish Committee. Data on US newspapers per state were provided by Editor & Publisher Co, Inc's *Editor & Publisher International Year Book* (VNU Business Media). Data on US physicians per state were provided by the American Medical Association's (AMA) *Physician Characteristics and Distribution in the US* (annual), copyright the AMA. Data on dentists per US state were provided by the American Dental Association (ADA), Survey Center, *Distribution of Dentists in the United States by Region and State*, copyright the ADA. All statistics on health care in Canada were provided by Canadian Institute for Health Information (CIHI), copyright CIHI.

Our thanks for particular assistance go to Paul Bourgeois at Statistics Canada. Thanks are also owed to Michelle Haas at the AMA and Jennifer Seligy at CIHI. In addition, thanks are owed to Edward Oliver for drawing the maps included in the volume.

CONTENTS

THE CONTRIBUTORS

John Agnew. Professor of Geography at the University of California—Los Angeles.

Robert M. Bone. Emeritus Professor of Geography at the University of Saskatchewan.

Mark R. Brawley. Professor in the Department of Political Science at McGill University.

Keith Brownsey. Lecturer in the Department of Policy Studies at Mount Royal College, Alberta.

P. W. Daniels. Professor of Geography, Deputy Pro-Vice-Chancellor, and Co-Director of the Services and Enterprise Unit at the University of Birmingham.

Philip John Davies. Director of the David and Mary Eccles Centre for American Studies at the British Library and Emeritus Professor of American Studies at De Montfort University, Leicester.

Claude Denis. Professor in the School of Political Studies at the University of Ottawa.

David H. Dunn. Reader in International Studies in the Department of Political Science and International Studies at the University of Birmingham.

John W. Foster. Principal Researcher (Civil Society/Governance) at the North–South Institute, Ottawa, and Lecturer in the Department of Political Science at Carleton University, Ottawa.

Martin Griffiths. Associate Professor of International Relations in the Department of International Business and Asian Studies at Griffith University, Brisbane.

Milton C. Hallberg. Emeritus Professor of Agricultural Economics at the Pennsylvania State University.

Alan Hallsworth. Emeritus Professor and Reader in the School of Management at the University of Surrey, and Treasurer and Past President of the British Association for Canadian Studies.

Athanasios Hristoulas. Professor of International Relations at the Instituto Tecnológico Autónomo de México.

John Kramer. Professor of Sociology at the Pennsylvania State University.

David McKay. Professor of Government at the University of Essex.

Sandy Markwick. Writer and researcher specializing in North and South American Affairs.

Geoffrey Mercer. Reader in the School of Sociology and Social Policy at the University of Leeds.

Calum Paton. Professor of Health Policy in the School of Public Policy at Keele University.

Gillian Peele. Fellow and Tutor in Politics at Lady Margaret Hall, University of Oxford.

David Robertson. Professor of Politics, Fellow and Vice-Principal at St Hugh's College, University of Oxford.

EXPLANATORY NOTE ON STATISTICAL TABLES

In the tables contained in this volume, a dash (—) is to be taken to represent zero, while 0 is used to indicate less than one half-unit: for example, where the unit used is a thousand US dollars (US $'000), 0 represents less than $500.

ABBREVIATIONS

AB	Alberta
Adj.	Adjutant
Adm.	Admiral
admin	administration
admin.	administrative/Administrator
a.i.	ad interim
AIDS	acquired immunodeficiency syndrome
AK	Alaska
AL	Alabama
Alt.	Alternate
AM	Amplitude Modulation
Apt	Apartment
approx.	approximately
AR	Arkansas
asscn	association
assoc.	associate
asst	assistant
ATM	automatic teller machine
Att.	Attorney
attn	attention
Aug.	August
Avda	Avenida
Ave	Avenue
AZ	Arizona
BC	British Columbia
BQ	Bloc Québécois
Bd	Board
b/d	barrels per day
Bdwy	Broadway
Bldg	Building
Blvd	Boulevard
BRIC	Brazil, Russia, India, China
Brig.	Brigadier
BSE	Bovine spongiform encephalopathy
c.	circa
CA	California
cap.	capital
Capt.	Captain
CD-ROM	compact disc read-only memory
CEO	Chief Executive Officer
Chair.	Chairman, Chairwoman; Chairperson
c.i.f.	cost, insurance and freight
circ.	circulation
CJD	Creutzfeldt-Jakob disease
cnr	corner
Co	Company
CO	Colorado
c/o	care of
Col	Colonel
Col.	Colonia
Comm.	Commission
Commdr	Commander
Commr	Commissioner
COO	Chief Operating Officer
Corpn	Corporation
CP	Case Postale; Casilla Postal (Post Office Box)
Cres.	Crescent
Ct	Court
CT	Connecticut
Cttee	Committee
cu	cubic
cwt	hundredweight
DC	District of Columbia
DE	Delaware
Dec.	December
Dem.	Democratic; Democrat
Dep.	Deputy
Dept	Department
devt	development
DFL	Democratic-Farmer-Labor
Dir	Director
Div.	Division(al)
DNA	deoxyribonucleic acid
doz.	dozen
Dr	Doctor
Dr.	Drive
DR-CAFTA	Dominican Republic-Central American Free Trade Agreement
E	East(ern)
EC	European Community
Econ.	Economic(s)
Edif.	Edificio; Edifice (Building)
edn	edition
e.g.	exempli gratia (for example)
esq.	esquina (corner)
etc.	et cetera
EU	European Union
excl.	excluding
Exec.	Executive
f.	founded
FAO	Food and Agriculture Organization
Feb.	February
Fed.	Federal
FL	Florida
FM	frequency modulation
fmr	former
fmrly	formerly
Fri.	Friday
FRY	Federal Republic of Yugoslavia
FTA	Free Trade Agreement
GA	Georgia
GATT	General Agreement on Tariffs and Trade
GDP	gross domestic product
Gen.	General
GNI	gross national income
GNP	gross national product
Govt	Government
grt	gross registered ton(s)
GWh	gigawatt hours
ha	hectare(s)
HI	Hawaii
HIV	human immunodeficiency virus
hl	hectolitres
Hon.	Honorary
Hwy	Highway
IA	Iowa
ID	Idaho
i.e.	id est (that is to say)
IL	Illinois
IMF	International Monetary Fund
IN	Indiana
Inc	Incorporated
incl.	including
Ind.	Independent
Int.	International
IR	Independent Republican
irreg.	irregular
Jan.	January
Jr	Junior
Jt	Joint
km	kilometre(s)

KS	Kansas
kW	kilowatt(s)
kWh	kilowatt hours
KY	Kentucky
LA	Louisiana
lb	pound(s)
Lib.	Liberal
Lt, Lieut	Lieutenant
m	metre(s)
m.	million
MA	Massachusetts
Maj.	Major
Man.	Manager; Managing
MB	Manitoba
MD	Maryland
ME	Maine
mem.	member
MFN	most favoured nation
mfrs	manufacturers
MI	Michigan
MMT	methylcyclopentadienyl manganese tricarbonyl
MN	Minnesota
MO	Missouri
Mon.	Monday
MS	Mississippi
MT	Montana
MW	megawatt(s); medium wave
MWh	megawatt hours
N	North(ern)
n.a.	not available
Nat.	National
NAFTA	North American Free Trade Agreement
NASA	National Aeronautics and Space Administration
NATO	North Atlantic Treaty Organization
NB	New Brunswick
NC	North Carolina
ND	North Dakota
NDP	New Democratic Party
NE	Nebraska; North-east(ern)
NGO	non-governmental organization
n.i.e.	not included elsewhere
NH	New Hampshire
NJ	New Jersey
NL	Newfoundland and Labrador
NM	New Mexico
no.	number
Nov.	November
NS	Nova Scotia
NT	Northwest Territories
NU	Nunavut Territory
NV	Nevada
NW	North-west(ern)
nwt	net weight
NY	New York
Oct.	October
OECD	Organisation for Economic Co-operation and Development
OH	Ohio
OK	Oklahoma
ON	Ontario
OPEC	Organization of the Petroleum Exporting Countries
OR	Oregon
org.	organization
p.	page
PA	Pennsylvania
PCP	Progressive Conservative Party
PE	Prince Edward Island
Pkwy	Parkway
Pl.	Place
POB	Post Office Box
POD	Post Office Drawer
POS	point-of-sale
pp.	pages
Pres.	President
Prof.	Professor
publ.	publication; published
Publr	publisher
QC	Québec
q.v.	quod vide (to which refer)
R&D	research and development
Rd	Road
Ref.	Reform Party; Reform Party of Canada
reorg.	reorganized
Rep.	Republic; Representative
Repub.	Republican
Rev.	Reverend
RI	Rhode Island
Rm	Room
RR	Rural Route
Rt	Right
S	South(ern); San
Sat.	Saturday
SC	South Carolina; Social Credit
SD	South Dakota
SDR(s)	Special Drawing Right(s)
SE	South-east(ern)
Sec.	Secretary
Sept.	September
SK	Saskatchewan
Soc.	Society
sq	square (in measurements)
Sq.	Square
Sr	Senior
St	Street; Saint
Ste	Sainte
Sun.	Sunday
Supt	Superintendent
SW	South-west(ern)
tel.	telephone
Thur.	Thursday
TN	Tennessee
Treas.	Treasurer
Tue.	Tuesday
TV	television
TWh	terawatt hour
TX	Texas
UN	United Nations
US	United States
USA	United States of America
USSR	Union of Soviet Socialist Republics
UT	Utah
v.	versus (against)
VA	Virginia
VAT	value-added tax
VT	Vermont
W	West(ern)
WA	Washington (state)
Wed.	Wednesday
WI	Wisconsin
WTO	World Trade Organization
WV	West Virginia
WY	Wyoming
YT	Yukon Territory

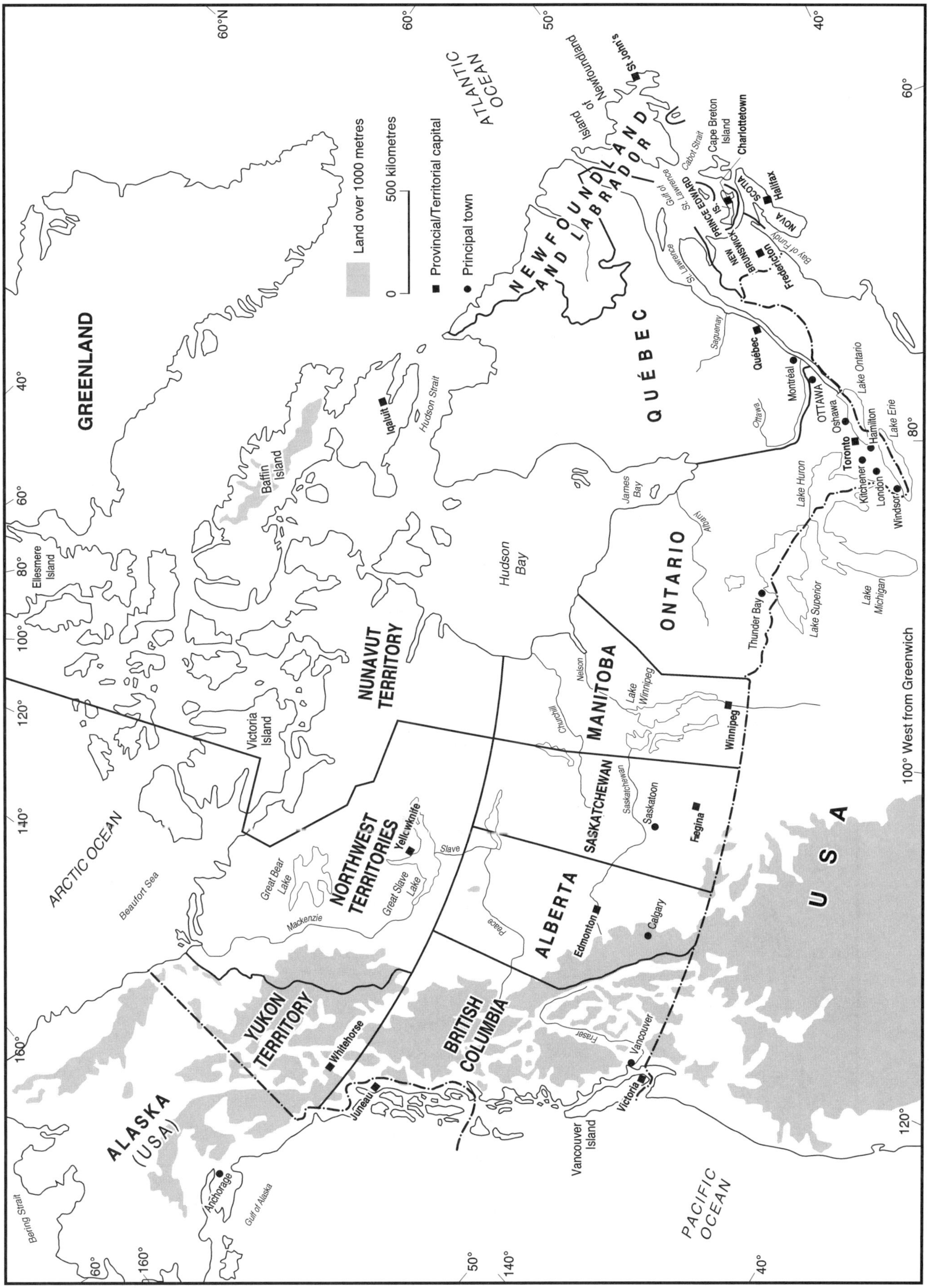

Land over 1000 metres
0
500 kilometres
Provincial/Territorial capital
Principal town
GREENLAND
Ellesmere Island
Baffin Island
Victoria Island
ARCTIC OCEAN
Beaufort Sea
ATLANTIC OCEAN
PACIFIC OCEAN
Hudson Bay
James Bay
Hudson Strait
Gulf of St. Lawrence
Cabot Strait
Bay of Fundy
Island of Newfoundland
Cape Breton Island
Bering Strait
Gulf of Alaska
Vancouver Island
NUNAVUT TERRITORY
NORTHWEST TERRITORIES
YUKON TERRITORY
BRITISH COLUMBIA
ALBERTA
SASKATCHEWAN
MANITOBA
ONTARIO
QUÉBEC
NEWFOUNDLAND AND LABRADOR
NEW BRUNSWICK
NOVA SCOTIA
PRINCE EDWARD IS.
ALASKA (USA)
USA
Iqaluit
Yellowknife
Whitehorse
Juneau
Anchorage
Victoria
Vancouver
Edmonton
Calgary
Saskatoon
Regina
Winnipeg
Thunder Bay
Toronto
OTTAWA
Oshawa
Hamilton
Kitchener
London
Windsor
Montréal
Québec
Fredericton
Charlottetown
Halifax
St. John's
Great Bear Lake
Great Slave Lake
Lake Winnipeg
Lake Superior
Lake Michigan
Lake Huron
Lake Erie
Lake Ontario
Mackenzie
Slave
Peace
Saskatchewan
Churchill
Nelson
Fraser
Albany
Ottawa
Saguenay
St. Lawrence
60°N
60°
50°
40°
160°
140°
120°
100°
80°
100° West from Greenwich

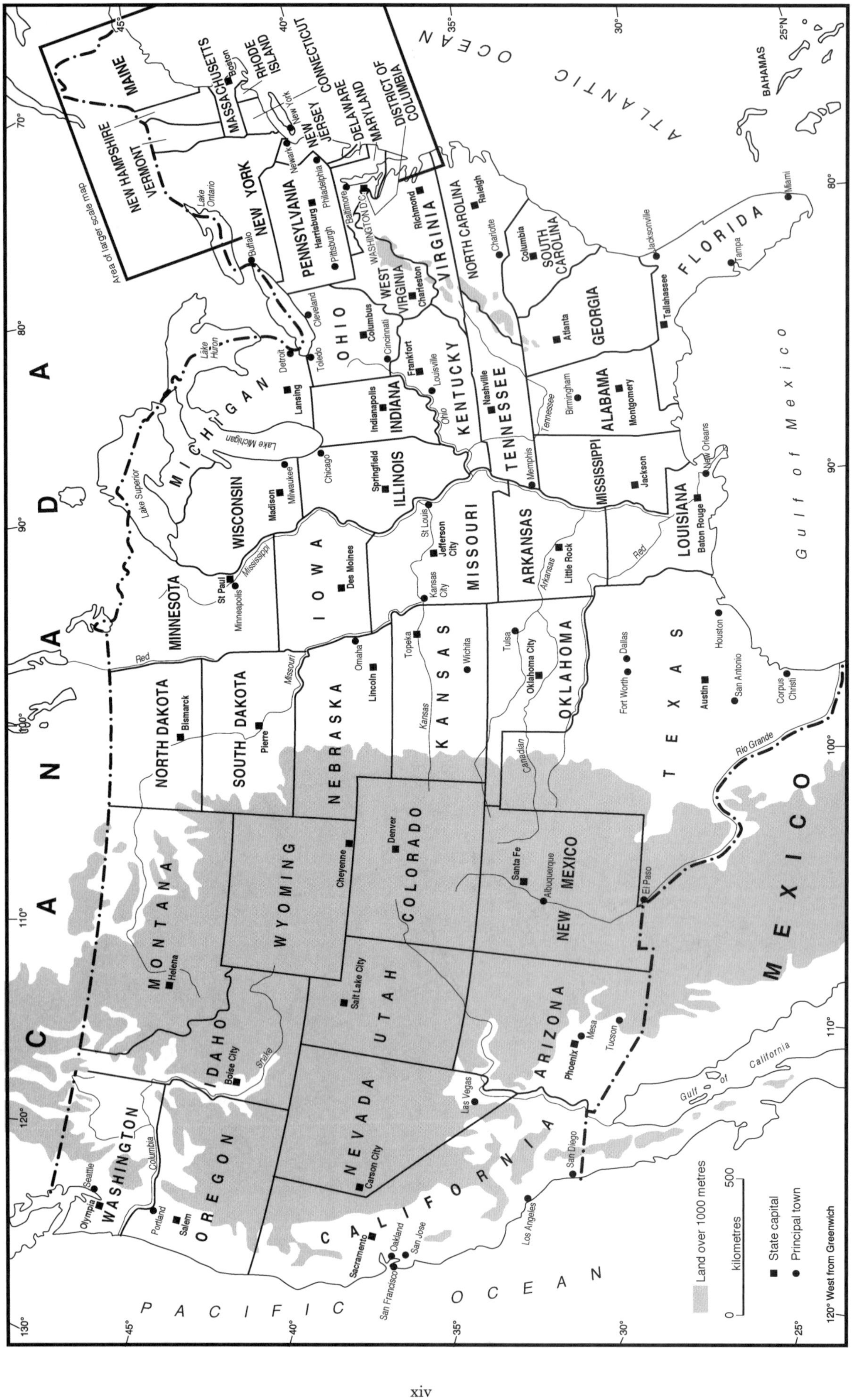

C A N A D A
M E X I C O
P A C I F I C O C E A N
A T L A N T I C O C E A N
G u l f o f M e x i c o
Gulf of California
BAHAMAS
Area of larger scale map
WASHINGTON
OREGON
CALIFORNIA
NEVADA
IDAHO
MONTANA
WYOMING
UTAH
ARIZONA
COLORADO
NEW MEXICO
NORTH DAKOTA
SOUTH DAKOTA
NEBRASKA
KANSAS
OKLAHOMA
TEXAS
MINNESOTA
IOWA
MISSOURI
ARKANSAS
LOUISIANA
WISCONSIN
ILLINOIS
MICHIGAN
INDIANA
OHIO
KENTUCKY
TENNESSEE
MISSISSIPPI
ALABAMA
GEORGIA
FLORIDA
SOUTH CAROLINA
NORTH CAROLINA
VIRGINIA
WEST VIRGINIA
PENNSYLVANIA
NEW YORK
VERMONT
NEW HAMPSHIRE
MAINE
MASSACHUSETTS
RHODE ISLAND
CONNECTICUT
NEW JERSEY
DELAWARE
MARYLAND
DISTRICT OF COLUMBIA
Olympia
Seattle
Portland
Salem
Sacramento
San Francisco
Oakland
San Jose
Los Angeles
San Diego
Carson City
Las Vegas
Boise City
Helena
Salt Lake City
Phoenix
Mesa
Tucson
Cheyenne
Denver
Santa Fe
Albuquerque
El Paso
Bismarck
Pierre
Lincoln
Omaha
Topeka
Wichita
Kansas City
Oklahoma City
Tulsa
Fort Worth
Dallas
Austin
San Antonio
Houston
Corpus Christi
St Paul
Minneapolis
Des Moines
Jefferson City
St Louis
Little Rock
Baton Rouge
New Orleans
Madison
Milwaukee
Chicago
Springfield
Jackson
Memphis
Nashville
Lansing
Detroit
Indianapolis
Louisville
Frankfort
Cincinnati
Columbus
Toledo
Cleveland
Charleston
Montgomery
Birmingham
Atlanta
Tallahassee
Jacksonville
Tampa
Miami
Columbia
Charlotte
Raleigh
Richmond
WASHINGTON D.C.
Baltimore
Pittsburgh
Harrisburg
Philadelphia
Newark
New York
Buffalo
Boston
Lake Superior
Lake Michigan
Lake Huron
Lake Ontario
Columbia
Snake
Missouri
Red
Kansas
Canadian
Arkansas
Mississippi
Ohio
Tennessee
Rio Grande
130°
120°
110°
100°
90°
80°
70°
45°
40°
35°
30°
25°
25°N
Land over 1000 metres
0 kilometres 500
State capital
Principal town
120° West from Greenwich

Land over 1000 metres
CANADA
MAINE
VERMONT
Augusta
Montpelier
NEW HAMPSHIRE
NEW YORK
Concord
Albany
Boston
MASSACHUSETTS
Hartford
Providence
PENNSYLVANIA
RHODE ISLAND
Newark
New York
CONNECTICUT
Harrisburg
Trenton
Philadelphia
NEW JERSEY
Baltimore
Dover
N
Annapolis
DELAWARE
MARYLAND
0
150
WASHINGTON, DC
DISTRICT OF COLUMBIA
kilometres

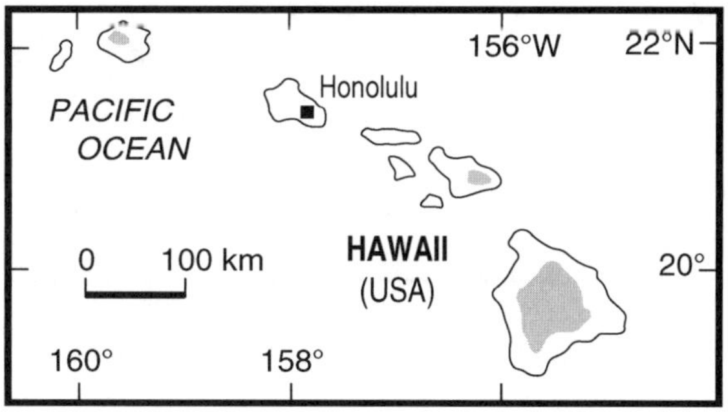
156°W
22°N
Honolulu
PACIFIC OCEAN
0
100 km
HAWAII (USA)
20°
160°
158°

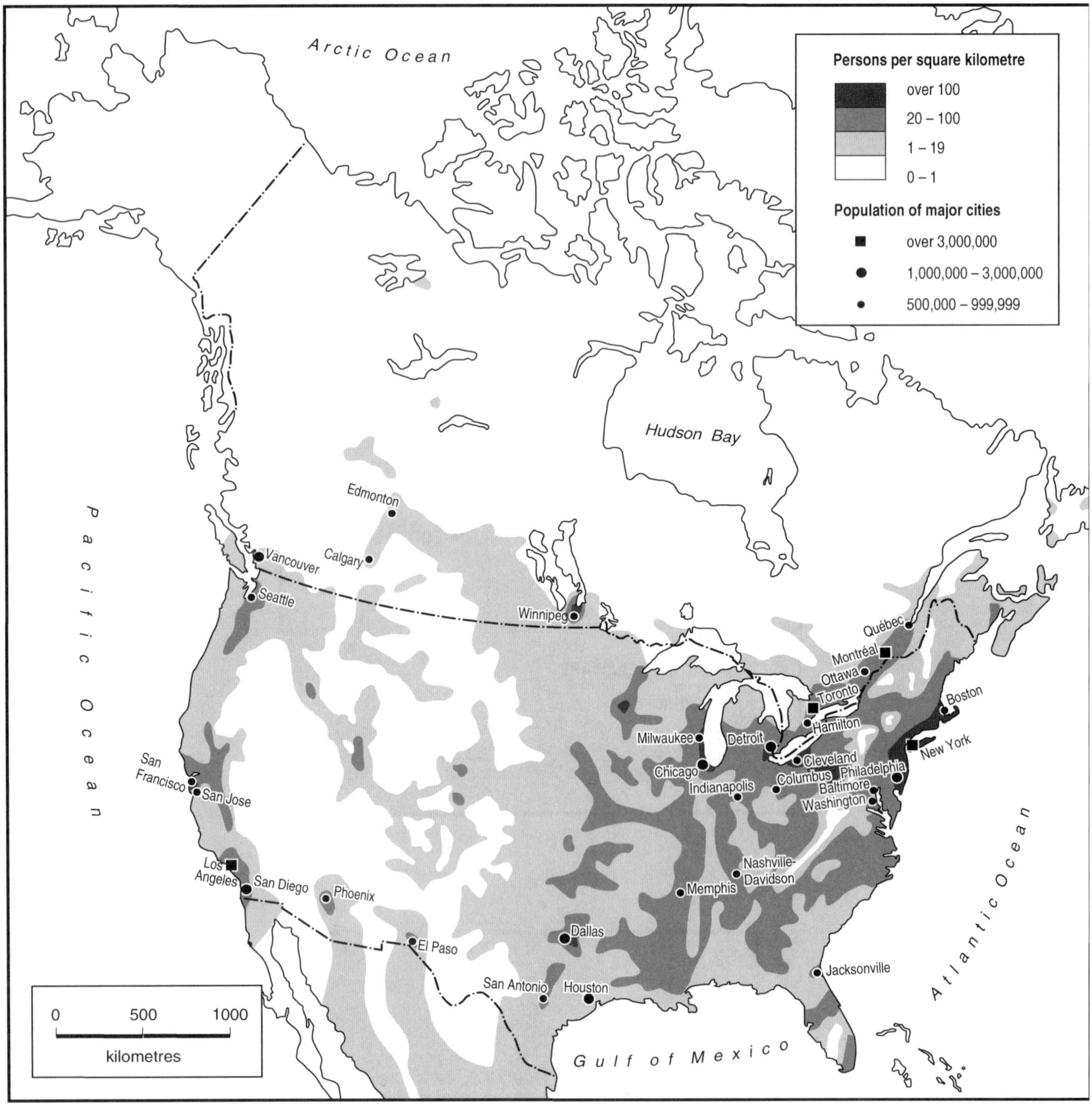

Density of Population in the USA and Canada

Part One

GENERAL SURVEY ON THE USA AND CANADA

IN QUESTION: NAFTA AND THE SECURITY AND PROSPERITY PARTNERSHIP

JOHN W. FOSTER

INTRODUCTION

The shape of trans-border governance in North America was under close scrutiny as two of the three North American Free Trade Agreement (NAFTA) partner countries entered federal elections late in 2008. In the USA the Democratic Party, considered more likely to dominate Congress and the new Administration, had called for renegotiation of NAFTA. In Canada, one of the three leading parties was also committed to such an agenda. In Mexico, the national debate over the future of public ownership of petroleum brought millions into the streets and into an unofficial national referendum.

At the same time the processes set in motion by the tri-lateral Security and Prosperity Partnership of North America (SPP) continued forward in such areas as regulatory harmonization and continental energy strategy. Further military arrangements beyond the scope of NAFTA and the SPP have brought Canada and Mexico further into US strategic dominance within a hemispheric context where the US-led 'war on terror' has led to further extension of its military presence.

The negative view of NAFTA and the SPP, which continued to dominate public opinion, had led corporate leaders with privileged access to the political chief executives to call for renewed efforts to convince the public of the benefits of the agreements. However, frustration with the limitations of progress had caused some, particularly the leadership of the Canadian Council of Chief Executives, to call for a shift in strategies for continental integration, putting priority on bilateral rather than trilateral approaches. Meanwhile, Democratic presidential hopeful Barack Obama indicated that while he would continue summit meetings with his Mexican and Canadian counterparts, the exclusive access for corporate leaders will end.

Civil society organizations, trade unions and environmentalists have been actively engaged in challenging these processes, and many hope that the opening to renegotiation of NAFTA will offer an opportunity to jettison pro-corporate elements like the investor-state provision. Academic and policy research centres and networks have multiplied initiatives to consider North American 'futures'. These debates, however, occur in an economic climate that is turbulent and insecure.

THE SECURITY AND PROSPERITY PARTNERSHIP

The SPP is an initiative or process of co-operation between the executive powers in Canada, Mexico and the USA, with which a privileged advisory body of powerful corporate leaders has been integrated. As the Congressional Research Service (CRS) points out, 'it is not a signed agreement or treaty and, therefore, contains no legally binding commitments or obligations . . . It is not a trade agreement and is distinct from the existing . . . NAFTA.'[1] 'It is a unique process in that the negotiations falling under its auspices occur at the bureaucratic level, rather than amongst traditional diplomats, and are informed by active consultation from the private sector.'[2]

Despite this lack of legislative or treaty quality, the SPP is widely ambitious. It seeks to 'energize' elements of NAFTA and its working groups are to 'consult with stakeholders; set specific, measurable, and achievable goals and implementation dates; and identify concrete steps the governments can take to achieve these goals'. Given its wide-ranging purview and its operational emphasis, and its lack of any parliamentary engagement, the Partnership has been identified by many as 'NAFTA Plus', 'NAFTA on steroids' or NAFTA in a post-11 September (2001) world. It is eliciting sharp criticism, particularly in Mexico and Canada.

The Partnership was initiated by the heads of government of Canada, Mexico and the USA at a summit meeting near Waco, Texas, in March 2005. The objectives of the SPP of North America were: enhanced sectoral co-operation, including energy, transportation, financial services and technology; a reduction in trade costs; and an improvement in environmental standards. This enhanced alliance was presented as an extension of NAFTA, in part a response to the increasing economic threat from Asia. Press coverage of the Waco meeting tended to be understated, and the far-reaching implications and the origins of the agreement were largely unexamined.

The Waco summit established a structure for trinational collaboration of the three executives. A series of trinational security working groups were established, convened by the US Secretary of Homeland Security and his Mexican and Canadian counterparts. Similarly, a series of prosperity working groups were co-ordinated by the US Secretary of Commerce and his counterparts. These working groups of civil servants were to report regularly to the chief political executives, through the trinational ministerial committees and a nine-minister follow-up group, in June 2005, September 2006, February 2007 and February 2008.

The SPP working groups established by the Waco agreement included issues such as: manufactured goods and sectoral and regional competitiveness; e-commerce and information and communications technology; energy; transportation; food and agriculture; environment; financial services; business facilitation; movement of goods; health; and security. The security agenda included related measures on cargo, maritime and aviation security and bioprotection, as well as the development and implementation of a North American traveller security strategy, involving enhanced intelligence-sharing and further 'smart border' measures. There was also a comprehensive strategy for combating transnational threats, including terrorism, organized crime, and drugs-, migrants- and contraband-trafficking. A series of border flow enhancement measures were also confirmed. Objectives for the next years were more ambitious: these included the development of a trilateral Regulatory Co-operation Framework, intended to reduce 'redundant testing and certification requirements' by 2007; a co-ordinated strategy on intellectual property protection by 2006; and a third round of liberalization of rules of origin by May of that year. Sectoral initiatives included a North American steel strategy, to be implemented through the North American Steel Trade Committee by 2006, the establishment of an Automotive Partnership Council of North America, and further energy co-operation. The June 2005 report set out the SPP's objective of 'making North America the best place to live': to this end it pledged to develop several clean water and air initiatives, protocols on cross-border health emergencies, and to improve information-sharing and examine possible common standards.

The SPP was further developed at a leadership summit in Cancún, Mexico, in March 2006. The three leaders continued several of the major themes of the Waco summit, including agreeing on the core of the Regulatory Co-operation Framework. They highlighted concern with pandemics and agreed on a Co-ordinating Body on Avian and Human Pandemic Influenza, which has begun work.

The Cancún summit resulted in a prioritization of five initiatives: increasing private sector engagement in the SPP through the North American Competitiveness Council (NACC—see below); advancing co-operation on avian and pandemic influenza management; ensuring a secure and sustainable energy supply through the North American Energy Security Initiative; developing a common approach to emergency management in all three countries; and contributing to smart and secure borders by increasing collaboration on standards and processes.[3]

In May 2006 the three countries reached further agreement on liberalization of rules of origin affecting over US $30,000m. in trilateral trade. A series of other bilateral and trilateral co-operation agreements—particularly relating to security concerns—have emerged, including a North American Aviation Trilateral on civil aviation security, a pilot programme on repatriation of Mexican nationals, and the Canada-USA Integrated Border Enforcement Team.

On 7 September 2006 the nine mandated ministers from the three countries conveyed their second SPP report to the three political chief executives. Divided into sections on prosperity and security, the report briefly outlined a series of task force, committee and other initiatives. The three Governments continue to pursue a North American Steel Strategy, although the substantive content thereof, apart from consultation and import-monitoring, is not explicit. The formation of a trilateral Automotive Partnership Council has been delayed, but work on compatible standards was proceeding as scheduled.

A number of other initiatives in manufacturing have been completed or are continuing, including facilitation of trade in medical devices; a single Canada-USA notification assessment for introduction of new chemical substances; three bilateral memorandums of understanding regarding exchange of information; public health and safety activities relating to consumer safety; and a possible collaboration on biotechnology, nanotechnology, building materials and an approach to emerging markets. Other themes include e-commerce, financial services, transportation, including facilitation of business aviation, border measures, clean air and water initiatives, common food safety standards and laboratory co-ordination.

In February 2007 the Ministerial Committees met in Ottawa, receiving reports from the various working groups and from the business council (NACC). In August the three chief political executives reconvened at a summit in Montebello, Québec, to evaluate progress and to meet with the NACC. This was followed nine months later by the final trinational summit of the Bush presidency in New Orleans, Louisiana.

MONTEBELLO, NEW ORLEANS, HARMONIZATION AND CONTINUED DISPUTE

The relatively high-profile August 2007 trinational summit in Montebello, Québec, was followed by a rather low-key 2008 summit held from 21–22 April in New Orleans, Louisiana, eight months on from the devastation caused by 'Hurricane Katrina'. As civil society observer Blair Redlin observed, the lead-up to the event, even in the approach of the NACC, was 'defensive'. The NACC noted: 'Unless we work together to turn around public misperceptions, other specific recommendations to improve North American competitiveness will become largely irrelevant. To the extent that NAFTA itself continues to be a target, efforts to "deepen the NAFTA" will be largely unsuccessful.'[4] There was a *fin de siècle* atmosphere attendant to the end of a very unpopular regime in Washington, the 'people's summit' response to the official meeting was rather subdued, and some commentators wondered how much life was left in the SPP, despite the fact that advances occurred on several fronts. Preliminary sectoral ministerial meetings had been held in February in Los Cabos, Mexico. The chief executives committed themselves to advance in the five areas cited in Montebello: regulatory harmonization to facilitate integrated production supply chains; smarter and more efficient and secure borders; energy and environment, including common North American technical standards; enhanced safety of food and other consumer products; and improved joint emergency response. However, the shift in Canadian business priorities from the NACC/SPP framework to a concentration on bilateral negotiations was explicit in business commentary.

One of the few remarkable events in New Orleans was a second trinational meeting of energy sector unions, following on from a pioneering event held in Montréal in August 2007. The gathering brought together more than 60 energy industry representatives and related organizations, including the anti-NAFTA coalitions from Canada, Québec, Mexico and the USA. They advanced a vision which was characterized by a recognition of the fundamental right of access to energy, but which also focused on specific actions, including how US and Canadian workers could assist Mexicans in resisting plans to privatize the national oil company, Petróleos Mexicanos (PEMEX).

The prospect of a significant political shift in the USA brought a tentativeness to discussions of the Security and Prosperity Initiative. However, the pace of integrative processes, which either predated or were enhanced by the SPP, continued on a number of fronts.

Regulatory 'Harmonization'

The significance of regulatory change is sometimes underestimated. One Canadian academic estimates that regulation represents about one-third of federal government activity. The trinational Regulatory Co-operation agreement permeated the Governments in diverse ways. The Governments committed to co-operate in all phases of the regulatory process, evaluating the processes with the objective of streamlining. They agreed to advance international private sector standards and eliminate 'redundant' public testing and certification. A Regulatory Co-operation Co-ordinating Committee was created to develop an annual work plan identifying priority areas for review. While no business figures were appointed to the Committee, the business leaders were asked to help with the work plan.

Labour analyst Teresa Healy comments that the business sector gained almost all that it desired in this regard, noting that the NACC's report to the leaders had recommended that 'regulators of each NAFTA country create simple regulations that make mandatory references to private sector international standards.' The implications of the NACC approach were in part spelled out in the Council's report, which touched on such items as a common standard for 'fortified' foods and the ending of 'duplication' in food safety audits. Thomas d'Aquino of the Canadian Council of Chief Executives (CCCE) commented: 'In Montebello, the three leaders—Canada's Stephen Harper, Mexico's Felipe Calderón and the United States' George W. Bush—delivered in full measure . . . they committed their officials to achieving closer regulatory co-operation in areas such as the chemical, automotive, transportation, and information and communications sectors.'

The regulatory 'reform' approach in the SPP links with other regulatory regime negotiations, particularly in the World Trade Organization and the General Agreement on Trade in Services, exciting considerable concern among environmental trade unions and education groups. It also links with the overall thrust to fast track energy integration. Canadian Minister of Natural Resources Gary Lunn is on record advocating a review of the 'entire regulatory process', including mining, hydroelectric generation, transmission lines, oil and gas projects. In particular, he highlighted his intention to accelerate a review of pipeline projects.

The effect of the regulatory review became more contentious in Canada after the Trade Committee hearings on the SPP in the Canadian House of Commons in 2007. Canadian regulations on pesticide residue levels on foods had been lowered to harmonize with US standards, provoking opposition outrage. Foreign affairs officials were unable to cite a case in the process where the USA and Mexico had revised their regulations to the higher Canadian level. The food regulation issue became highly charged in September 2008 with around a dozen deaths due to an outbreak of listeriosis, originating in tainted processed meat. This brought into the spotlight a slow and often intentionally obscure process, through which the Canadian inspection regime had been downgraded in personnel and budget, transferring more responsibility to industry self-inspection and reporting, matching the US pattern. The federal Minister of Agriculture was accused of knowingly misleading Parliament and the public, and the official opposition called for his resignation.

Food is perhaps the most visible and sensitive issue, but it is not the only area of change. Agreements at the Montebello summit moved the Canadian chemical regulatory regime away from the European model and into line with the USA. The US authorities used the SPP agreement to campaign actively against the European approach, which they argued put too much onus on industry.[5]

Dismantling Organized Marketing: the Wheat Board

The USA, in NAFTA negotiations and subsequent forums, has sought to dismantle the Canadian Wheat Board, which, as a monopoly, is a significant anomaly in the world grain trade, traditionally controlled by a handful of transnational companies, several of which—like ADM and Cargill—are based in the USA. As long as the Wheat Board remains a monopoly it is exempt under NAFTA, but as soon as private companies are allowed to compete with it, legal challenges to it will become more common, and also more likely to succeed. The Harper Government has similar aims to those of the US Administration, and has tried to undermine the Board with a number of strategems, only to encounter obstruction in the Canadian courts. At the time of writing, the Government had three bills in the Canadian House of Commons (C-39, C-46 and C-57), which sought to: remove the Canadian Grain Commission's authority in inspecting and regulating grain; permit barley producers to vote on the Wheat Board's role; and to revamp and reduce the farmer voters' list regarding the election of Wheat Board Directors.[6]

Intellectual Property

Canada has been under considerable pressure from industry and from the USA in several areas of intellectual property regulation. Pharmaceutical firms desired and received an extension to their monopoly rights on data exclusivity, thus complicating and delaying new generic copy production. Issues around intellectual property guarantees illustrate perhaps most clearly the narrow telescope through which public policy is viewed when the predominant influence is corporate. The Intellectual Property Action Strategy confirmed at the Montebello summit focused on piracy and counterfeit goods. The response to industry concerns was to commit a variety of law enforcement agencies to fighting infringement of intellectual property, involving 'new innovative border enforcement techniques'. Having the three leaders prioritize this corporate concern and commit the security apparatus at their disposal to its satisfaction, when an open debate, for example, over the impact of current intellectual property protections on such areas as access to medicines and health care costs might be of greater public benefit, demonstrates a tendency towards tunnel vision in the SPP process. Copyright law, principally an initiative to bring Canadian law into much greater conformity with US law (Bill C-61) was introduced in the Canadian House of Commons prior to the parliamentary recess of summer 2008.[7]

Borders

Perhaps the most marked frustration of the summits was in one of the key priority areas for business, namely that of the simplification and acceleration of border transit for goods.

The USA and Canada, over two years, were negotiating a 'pilot' project in pre-clearance of truck traffic, under the USA-Canada Shared Border Accord and the SPP. The proposal was that US Customs authorities would move inside Canada at Ontario's Peace Bridge over the Niagara River, with a related proposal of 'reverse inspections', in which the cross-border presence would be reciprocal. The bridge is the second busiest passenger crossing and the third busiest commercial crossing along the binational border, carrying an estimated US $20,000m. per year in trade, with nearly 6,000 trucks a day. The project was a high priority for the NACC and many manufacturers on both sides of the border.

In late April 2007 the US Department of Homeland Security announced that the USA was pulling out of the talks. Canada had objected to US fingerprinting on Canadian soil, which would conflict with the Canadian Charter of Rights. A US government source explained the US refusal to accept Canadian assurances that it would investigate any suspicious person thus: 'The Attorney-General's office really just wants to grab as much biometric information as it can.' In a letter to the Department, the US Chamber of Commerce joined many other business organizations expressing its 'disappointment' and urging both parties to renew the negotiations. 'It is,' the letter concluded, 'imperative that the heightened focus on security not impede the economic efficiencies created by the NAFTA.'[8]

At the Montebello summit proposals for emergency or disaster response were considered, in which the NACC sought commitments regarding critical infrastructure, the protection of property and the resumption of trade in emergency management, as well as a pecking order as to who would first gain mobility rights after an emergency. The North American Plan for Avian and Pandemic Influenza was the title of the emergency response agreed at the summit. The leaders noted that the plan 'extends beyond the health sector to include a co-ordinated approach to infrastructure protection, including the importance of business continuity planning and recognition of interdependencies among sectors.' Meanwhile, the SPP continued with a number of working groups dealing with border-facilitation issues, including a new USA-Mexico group on border facilitation, a new Canada-USA agreement on transport of dangerous goods, wireless communications, liberalized air cargo transport, etc. Ministries were asked to move to 'interoperable law enforcement models that promote seamless operations at the border'.

There are two concepts related to border facilitation worth noting: 'risk-based' management and 'pushing out the border'. 'Risk-based' management means defining people and goods as 'legitimate' or 'illegitimate'. It has led to 'no-fly' lists, now implemented by Canada as well as the USA. The Canadian 'passenger protect' list was instituted in June 2007 with no reference to Parliament. The privacy commissioners at the federal, provincial and territorial jurisdictions have called for its suspension, charging that the lists make 'secretive use of personal information in a way that will profoundly impact privacy and other related human rights such as freedom of association and expression and the right to mobility.' Sharing of extensive police databases, including many related to political activism and union activity, has already been initiated. 'Pushing out the border' refers to the desire to vet and clear incoming people and goods prior to their reaching continental shores. This has already had clear implications for Mexico, particularly as, in addition to the construction of the wall along the US southern frontier, Mexican security forces have been pressed into action to combat transit across the country's southern frontier with Guatemala and Belize. According to Mexican analyst Miguel Picard, 'gross violations of human rights occur daily' on this border. Stepping back from the details of arguments over travel documents, lists and clearances, a pattern emerges of a class- and commerce-based distribution of privileges at frontiers, in which the poor Guatemalan on the Chiapas border is at the bottom of the pyramid and the élite corporate manager with a special pass is at the top.

Softwood lumber

A symbol of the limitations of transnational co-operation is the bilateral dispute over softwood lumber, which the Harper Government attempted to close in 2006 but which continues to aggravate and undermine a number of Canadian producers, while transferring significant Canadian resources to US coffers. The bilateral agreement of October 2006 imposed quotas on Canadian producers as well as a 15% tax on exports. As Canadian analyst Bruce Campbell comments: "The deal implicitly accepted the US argument that Canadian governments were in fact subsidizing producers, when in fact all legal rulings found otherwise. Finally, it gave the US government the right to oversee any future changes in Canadian forest policies.'

The 'deal' did not satisfy the USA, however. In June 2008 the US Congress authorized border officials to conduct audits and issue fines to Canadian firms for non-compliance with the agreement. The effects of the continued US hostility to Canadian imports have been extremely negative on the industry in Canada, particularly on smaller competitors and their communities.[9]

ENERGY: THE HEART OF THE MATTER

One of the most important side effects of the ongoing US military occupation of Iraq and of increased insecurity in the region has been the re-orientation of US energy policy in a more continental direction, placing it in a militant national security framework, while increasing the strategic priority of Canadian and Mexican petroleum, and including electricity as well. The 2008 US presidential election campaign, in which both leading candidates pledged to reduce or end US dependency on foreign oil (while seemingly ignoring continental sources), promised to place more weight than ever on increasing supply, though even Republican candidate John McCain's mantra of 'drill, drill, drill' could not conceivably create the output necessary to bridge the gap between declining domestic production and escalating demand.

In the context, the election in 2006 of an oil patch-centred Conservative Government in Canada, and the emergence of Alberta-based tar sands reserves as one of the most important strategic reserves, has been prioritized since shortly after the terrorist attacks of September 2001. Prime Minister Harper repeatedly portrays Canada as an 'energy superpower'. The intention to complete NAFTA by drawing Mexico more thoroughly into US energy security strategies and finding ways to privatize Mexican petroleum has also gained priority.

The anchor of this new orientation was an article published in the US *Oil and Gas Journal* in December 2004, vaulting their estimates of Canadian reserves from 4,900m. barrels to 179,000m. barrels. These estimates were incorporated into those of the US Department of Energy. The significance of Canada's reserve estimates in the context of post-11 September 2001 US energy security concerns can hardly be overstated.

Canadian oil sands production stood at approximately 1m. barrels per day (b/d) in 2007. However, the USA's appetite is insatiable. In January 2006 one of the nine 'prosperity' working groups of the SPP, the North American Energy Working Group's (NAEWG) Oil Sands Expert Group, held a workshop in Houston, Texas. The meeting of 60 government and private industry representatives focused on the steps necessary to expand production to 5m. b/d, or even 5.5m. b/d, by 2025. The environmental cost of this prospect on rivers, forests and waste ponds, as well as the impact on dwindling natural gas supplies, promises to be monumental.

The NAEWG emerged from an announcement early in the Bush presidency, on 28 January 2001, of the formation of an Energy Policy Development Group under the authority of Vice-President Dick Cheney. Shortly thereafter, on 8 March, US Secretary of Energy Spencer Abraham met his Canadian and Mexican counterparts in Mexico City and announced the formation of the NAEWG. The Group published its first report in June 2002. It pre-dated the SPP and was simply incorporated into it after 2005. The NAEWG has spawned a series of subsidiary expert groups, whose members 'convene regularly', according to the official website, 'to build work plans and develop mutually beneficial deliverables, continuously identifying and implementing areas of co-operation within the continental energy market.'[10]

The extent to which an integrated energy strategy is in motion was summarized by current US Secretary of Energy Samuel W. Bodman in a September 2005 address to the CCCE: 'Since taking office in 2001, the Bush Administration has worked to achieve a fully integrated single North American market, one that will ... ensure a secure and reliable supply of energy ... Today, there are 35 cross-border natural gas pipelines, 22 oil and petroleum product pipelines, and 51 cross-border electric transmission lines that bind us together and increase the energy security of both our countries.' Bodman cited the NAEWG and the SPP as key elements of partnership, indicating that his department was in constant communication at all levels with Natural Resources Canada, 'exploring ways to expand cross-border infrastructure development and trade, and ... ensuring the continued security of our integrated systems.' Furthermore, he had met with five key provincial and territorial premiers.[11]

This agenda has been challenged from several quarters. Alberta-based Parklands Institute Director Gordon Laxer testified in April 2007 at the Canadian Parliamentary Standing Committee on International Trade that while the whole strategy was dedicated to ensuring US energy security, and keeping the US strategic reserves intact, Canada lacked an energy security policy, and that enquiries to the National Energy Board for information elicited nothing. While Canada exports more than 60% of its natural gas production and 70% of its oil to the USA, eastern Canada is dependent on imports from Algeria, Saudi Arabia and Iraq.

Union opposition is also extensive. A meeting of representatives of 19 unions from the energy sectors in the USA, Mexico and Canada in August 2007 produced a joint declaration questioning the whole strategy. The Communications, Energy and Paperworkers Union of Canada (CEP) has raised the issue of infrastructure and its impact on the economy and on jobs in detailed challenges at the National Energy Board and in the courts. The CEP argues that current pipeline projects, including the Keystone Pipeline which would transport raw bitumen to Illinois for processing, are not in the public interest because inadequate environmental impact scans have been undertaken, and because the project essentially transports processing jobs from Alberta to refineries in the USA.

Furthermore, even if the significant expansion of exports continues, it is argued that Canada has failed to secure adequate revenues in the form of royalties, taxes and other income. It is noted, for example, that while Norway has garnered over US $200,000m. for its reserve fund from petroleum, Alberta's Heritage Fund stands at a little over $12,000m. As nationalist cultural critic Prof. Robin Matthews exclaims, 'Canada is peculiar in the respect that it has a large class persistently determined to deny the Canadian right to Canadian wealth.'

A practical contrast to the Alberta approach was demonstrated in August 2007 when the Province of Newfoundland and Labrador, following a lengthy struggle with corporate investors, confirmed a deal for the development of the Hebron offshore field. The agreement moves the publicly owned Newfoundland and Labrador Hydro into a 4.9% equity share in a partnership with transnational oil firms, with enhanced revenues.

Critics in Canada base part of their opposition on the policy in Chapter Six of NAFTA, which carried over the bilateral free trade agreement (FTA) proportional sharing clause, from which Mexico remained exempt. According to John Dillon of the Ecumenical KAIROS coalition, if Canada should run short of petroleum, or decide to cut exploitation for environmental reasons, it could find itself trapped in this commitment to continue the same percentage of exports as established over the previous three years. Commentators from the Canadian Association of Petroleum Producers say the clause merely respects existing commercial contracts.

A further criticism of the extent to which Canada's policy is simply five-fold expansion of tar sands exploitation arises from its rapacious environmental effects. Essentially strip-mining the tar sands for bitumen consumes up to five barrels of fresh water to produce one barrel of synthetic crude. It also consumes immense quantities of natural gas and has affected almost 40,000 sq km of land.

The energy implications that run through the SPP are diverse and massive. The proposals are as much or more from industry as from government. 'Among the dozens of recommendations from business [the NACC] to the three governments', comments Fred Wilson, a Canadian union analyst, 'there are two pages of proposals on energy, including these recommendations dealing with Mexico:

A "Mexican domestic policy reform", which by 2010 would allow Mexican corporations to buy electricity directly from US producers.'

Also by 2010, to break up Mexico's national oil company, PEMEX, with its natural gas division to become a new corporation to be called GASMEX.

'By 2008, to put out "a benchmark analysis that illustrates PEMEX's operating and financial performance gaps".'

Wilson claimed these recommendations, among others, 'are aimed at dismantling Mexico's publicly owned and managed energy sector.'[12]

The trinational energy union meeting of 18 August 2007, which included significant participation of non-governmental, environmental, women's, church and development organizations, issued a joint solidarity statement in support of democratic, national development of North America's energy resources. The statement sums up the preoccupation of many of those who question the current agenda, and reads in part:

> 'Through the SPP and the North American Energy Working Group, the governments of Mexico, United States and Canada have formed an unprecedented collaboration with energy corporations to promote the continental integration of our energy industries and infrastructures. Nine working groups have been working intensively to integrate oil, natural gas, electricity, nuclear power, hydrocarbons, science and technology and regulatory agencies. While these

working groups bring together government, regulators and corporations at the highest level, they have excluded labour, environmentalists and civil society movements and circumvented the oversight of our elected legislatures. The SPP-corporate agenda of substituting continental corporate rule at the expense of national and local plans of development includes:

The complete integration of electricity grids between our countries and the continuing deregulation of electricity in each country to promote electricity generation for export.

The promotion of a continental integrated natural gas system and imports of liquefied natural gas to meet a continental shortage of natural gas which is expected within a short period of time.

The "streamlining" of regulatory processes and deregulation in each country for cross-border oil pipelines, including a five-fold increase in Canadian tar sands production, and continuing privatization of energy industries.

The direct intervention of the US to guarantee the security of energy installations.'

As Daniel Sullivan of the US Department of State told the Sub-Committee on the Western Hemisphere of the House Committee on Foreign Affairs, (31 July 2008), 'it would not be an exaggeration to say that the USA and Canada enjoy the largest bilateral energy relationship in the world ... These oil sands reserves are anchoring Canada as a pillar of hemispheric energy security.'[13]

As analyst Bruce Campbell comments: 'The main purpose of the SPP energy working group is to help reduce environmental and other regulatory barriers that stand in the way of tar sands development and the construction of the pipeline infrastructure necessary to transport oil to US markets.'[14] Thus, as the joint solidarity statement concludes, the issues it identified as well as 'other elements of the SPP-corporate energy agenda are unsustainable and sacrifice the needs of workers and communities in each country to the profits of energy corporations. This is an agenda that fails to address the need for each country to reduce greenhouse gas emissions, including a new round of far reaching goals after 2012. Nor does this corporate continental model of energy development respond to the needs of national economic development or recognize the primary role of energy industries for community economic development.'

In Canada there are renewed calls for abandonment of the elements of the bilateral and trilateral agreements which bind Canada to 'proportional sharing' of its production with the USA, and for the creation of a national energy strategy. Gordon Laxer of the Parkland Institute in Alberta and John Dillon of KAIROS have published a major study of the implications of the proportionality clause, with recommendations about how Canada might escape its grip.[15] With the USA increasingly looking to the tar sands as an answer to domestic petroleum deficits, some Canadians feel that the lack of a national energy policy should end. Former Alberta Conservative Premier, Peter Lougheed, among others, has begun to pose some long-overdue questions. Given Chinese and other interest in Canadian oil, does Canada not have a seller's advantage? Given the revenue potential, is not the current approach to tar sands development counter-productive? Furthermore, are Albertans and Canadians getting the revenue share for public purposes that could be secured? Canadian unions sent two ambassadors to Mexico in June 2008 to inform Mexicans of the negative effects of NAFTA's specific energy agreement for Canada, urging them to resist pressures to enter a similar pact.

In Mexico PEMEX, the world's sixth largest oil producer, has recorded the lowest output in ten years, and requires significant new investment. However, given increased oil prices, the company announced a stunning US $25,000m. in export revenues in the first half of 2008, a 52% increase from the same period in 2007. Mexico's government revenues are significantly dependent on PEMEX. Nevertheless, the Calderón Government pushed forward proposals for a staged privatization of the petroleum industry, which encountered massive resistance. The opposition Partido de la Revolución Democrática (Party of the Democratic Revolution—PRD) paralysed Congress with a two-week-long sit-in, preventing a quick vote on Calderón's proposals. Calderón's opponent, Andrés Manuel López Obrador, with significant community-level support, organized a three-stage national referendum on the proposals, spurring huge mobilization in the streets and at the voting posts. As the *Los Angeles Times* reported, many in Mexico recognize that PEMEX needs to change, but with oil at record prices 'it's hard, politically speaking, to convince people that they should share it with private companies.'[16]

WATER

Parallel to the issue of energy was the ongoing debate over water, particularly for Canada. This topic gained momentum as adverse global climate changes occurred rather more rapidly than anticipated. The ever-increasing appetite for water, together with droughts in the US South and Mid-West, and increased pollution throughout the continent, fed proposals to secure sources. It was forecast that the USA would increasingly press for large-scale water diversions from Canada.

Many scholars and activists made careful note of previously considered proposals such as the 'Grand' (Great Recycling and Northern Development) Canal, running from James Bay in Canada down to the US state of California, as well as the more recent idea for bulk water exports. The plan to export water in bulk from Newfoundland and Labrador to the US market was a pet project of former provincial Premier Roger Grimes. The plan was abandoned following substantial public opposition, but also because the projected royalty revenues were not as high as previously expected.

The issue of whether water is a 'tradeable' good continued to be contentious. Neither the bilateral US-Canadian FTA nor NAFTA settled the issue. In a September 2007 assessment prepared by the former co-chair of the International Joint Commission and the former Canadian federal government director of water planning and management, among others, warned: 'Make no mistake, Canada's water, through diversion, sale, trade or all of the above, is on the negotiating table in Canada/US relations ... The fate of our water resources is now dependent on shadowy discussions taking place under the aegis of the Security and Prosperity Partnership (SPP) ... The SPP, never subjected to legislative debate or approval, provides an ideal framework for negotiating away the rights to Canada's water.' Water would become, in the report's words, 'another cheap raw resource give-away much like oil'.

The Canadian report notes that a variety of academics, officials and think tanks have strongly advocated putting water up for sale. Attention has been focused on the work of the Washington-based Center for Strategic and International Studies (CSIS), which recently held a meeting with high-level officials and business representatives in Calgary, Alberta, to discuss water consumption, water transfers and artificial diversions of bulk water. The director of its North American Future 2025 project, Armand Peschard-Sverdrup, states: 'it's no secret the US is going to need water ... it's no secret that Canada is going to have an overabundance of water. At the end of the day there may have to be arrangements.'

As the Canadian report makes clear, the issue is not simply a matter of movement of water, but of the impact of any loss of water resources on manufacturing, resource-extraction and agricultural sectors. It points out that Canada lacks a full inventory of its own water resources, and an adequate assessment of the impact of currently planned tar sands development on water resources. One of the authors points out that Canada and the USA have roughly equivalent amounts of renewable water supplies, and that regional shortages should be dealt with by regional solutions.

The Canadian Government stated that it had 'no intention of entering into negotiations, behind closed doors or otherwise, regarding the issue of bulk water exports.' The leader of the Liberal Party, Stéphane Dion, argued that 'the Conservatives have failed to implement any strategy for the protection of our water resources', contrasting that with his party's position that 'opposes bulk water export, diversion or commodification'.[17]

A number of Canadian provincial governments have taken action to protect water resources, but a national policy is yet to surface. The authors of the recent Canadian report call for full public scrutiny of the SPP process, and call on the federal Government 'to make it clear to our NAFTA partners—formally informing the USA and Mexico that bulk water removals from Canada's major drainage basins will not be permitted and that the topic of water exports will be excluded from all future SPP or related discussions.'[18]

SECURITY

A separate chapter could be written examining the dynamics of the security elements of the SPP, and, indeed, in the overall relations of the three countries. Some elements, such as the Safe Third Country Agreement of 2002, which has limited refugee claimants' access to Canada, were reactions to the events of 11 September 2001, as was the Canada-USA 'Smart Border Declaration' of December 2001. 'Fundamental principles are at stake in these agreements,' points out security analyst, lawyer and author Maureen Webb, 'things like due process, presumption of innocence, the right to know the evidence against you and to respond, the right against unreasonable search and seizure, rights under data protection laws, rights of mobility and asylum rights.'

The key is a risk assessment and pre-emption approach. An illustrative example is the Automated Targeting System. In this, according to Webb, 'the State compiles a secret dossier on every individual and sorts the population according to secret criteria, assigning each person a 'risk score'. The individual has no recourse to challenge his risk rating, and he has no way of correcting any false or incomplete information about him. In fact, he will never know what information is being used against him, or even the criteria on which he has been judged a risk to the State.'

Webb points out that the implications are global: 'This is mass surveillance, and it's global in scope. Domestic systems feed into global ones and global systems—like biometric passports, the sharing of airline reservation system information, the interception of international banking records, and the interception of global communications, to name a few—feed into the domestic.'[19]

A related example is the provision in the 2001 Canadian Anti-Terrorism Act of the power to detain people without charges using 'preventive arrests'. This extends the more traditional provision that allows for a suspect to be arrested before an offence is committed, if there is a reasonable belief that the person in question is about to commit an offence. The Montebello summit might have been an opportunity to discuss some of the thorny issues on the security agenda. Prime Minister Harper was under pressure at home to raise outstanding bilateral security issues with President Bush; however, no progress was made.

SUMMITS: PUTTING THE MODEL IN QUESTION

Opposition activities around the summit in the small Québec riverside town of Montebello were lively, including a demonstration of several thousand people in front of the Canadian Parliament, a number of well-attended educational meetings, and 2,000–3,000 protesters, who gathered at the security cordon around the summit site itself. The protests were downplayed by the national leaders, although they enjoyed massive media attention. There were allegations, later proven, that some demonstrators were actually *agents provocateurs*, which, in turn, raised a question about whether the immense security deployment surrounding the summit was necessary, and whether the attempt to portray the protesters as violent was approved at the highest level. Overall, there was an official attempt to play down the event, trying to defuse suspicions of serious decision-making behind a well-armed security cordon. A number of journalists, perhaps expecting a 'big bang', agreed that the summit had resulted in little. The 2008 summit in New Orleans saw muted civil activity in the storm-ravaged city, and business and political leaders assured an increasingly sceptical press that there was good news. Any aggressive future proposals were curtailed by the imminent end of an incredibly unpopular US presidency.

Thus, a number of analysts foresaw a change of approach. US continental union advocate Prof. Robert Pastor pointed out, however, the last two gatherings were of three leaders with limited political capital: 'in essence, all three are running minority governments so there is little to expect in the way of progress.' Pastor was extremely critical of the summit's failure to deal with important issues, summed up when he commented on the process as a whole: 'It's not trying to do too much: it's trying to do too little. What we need is something more bold.'[20]

In a joint evaluation, Christopher Sands of the Hudson Institute in Washington, DC, and Greg Anderson of the University of Alberta, agreed that with the uneven follow-up to NAFTA, some sort of new arrangement was necessary to energize cross-border negotiations, and that it should be the SPP. 'With limited political capital to invest, Bush wanted negotiations to remain within the limits of executive branch authority for law enforcement, rule making, and regulation so that he did not need to secure congressional approval for a treaty or new implementing legislation.'

The problem Sands and Anderson outline was chiefly that of transparency: 'the technical nature of the talks, conducted with very little transparency, frustrates virtually all attempts to find out what is going on.' Critics on the Canadian left and US right are correct in their complaints, they conclude, because 'the structural flaws of the SPP are serious'. US leadership in correcting flaws is essential, but the Administration has done little, according to them. As James Travers of the *Toronto Star* concluded about such summits: 'It's a hazardous dynamic. Without the legitimacy or political checks and balances of formal structures, decisions are made behind closed doors that many outside consider too arbitrary and narrowly based to be democratic.'[21] Nevertheless, d'Aquino of the CCCE asked if Montebello was 'too much or not enough?', concluding that it was 'about just right'. As Robert Pastor pointed out, however, the Montebello meeting was a gathering of three world leaders with limited political capital.

A CORPORATE COUP D'ÉTAT?

A joint statement issued on the eve of the Montebello summit by the four nationally based civil society coalitions opposing the SPP (the Réseau Québécois sur l'Integration Continentale, the Red Mexicana de Acción Frente al Comercio Libre, the Alliance for Responsible Trade and Common Frontiers) called the government/corporate collaboration a corporate *coup d'état*.[22] The Waco agreement and the SPP symbolized a recovery of élite commercial and governmental momentum for deep integration that had been sidelined by the focus of attention on counter-terrorism. The events of 11 September 2001 prevented what appeared to be a conscious attempt by both the Mexican and US heads of state to bring about greater convergence in Mexican-US policies in areas such as migration and energy. In the case of Canada, the post-11 September emphasis was on bilateral relations, leading to changes in border policy, the hurried introduction of far-reaching security legislation and significant alterations in Canadian federal cabinet responsibilities. Previously launched proposals on deeper integration were, in part, pre-empted by harmonizing policy shifts, but, in general, were relaunched with greater vigour, taking into account the preoccupation with security.

The CCCE announced its approach in a January 2003 publication, 'Security and Prosperity: Toward a New Canada-United States Partnership in North America'. This prefigured not only the title, but much of the orientation of the inter-governmental SPP. Then, in April 2004 the CCCE published a comprehensive strategy for an overall bargain with the USA, 'New Frontiers: Building a 21st Century Canada-United States Partnership in North America'. The CCCE sought to engage the US Government and congressional leadership in its vision, its representatives visiting Washington, DC, in 2004 and undertaking a speaking tour of the USA. Many of its principal ideas were taken on by a so-called Independent Task Force on North America, sponsored by the US Council on Foreign Relations in association with the Consejo Mexicano de Asuntos Internacionales and the CCCE, which also provided a significant portion of the funding. For example, the Task Force recommended annual summit meetings, minister-led working groups, and the establishment of a North American Advisory

Council to explore new ideas for the region and provide a 'public voice for North America'. The initiative for 'deep integration', sponsored by the Canadian (largely, if not entirely, transnational in composition) business leadership and its academic and political allies at home and abroad, recaptured a measure of élite political consciousness and a place on the trinational intergovernmental agenda during 2005. The idea of a business advisory group given formal access to ministers and leaders was perhaps the most striking of the CCCE's ideas to win support at the Cancún trilateral summit in 2006.

Exclusive access: The North American Competitiveness Council

In June 2006 the North American Competitiveness Council (NACC) was launched, as agreed in Cancún, providing 'a voice and a formal role for the private sector', with a commitment to regular meetings with ministers and senior officials. It began with a meeting with the three trade ministers. The ministers committed to discussing priorities with NACC prior to the next meeting of the three national leaders in 2007.

The Council included chief executive officers of leading corporations from each country, including General Motors, Lockheed Martin, Walmart and Merck from the USA, and Bell Canada, Suncor, CN Rail, Power Corporation of Canada and Scotiabank from Canada. The CCCE acted as the Secretariat of the Canadian Section of the NACC, the US Section had a Secretariat composed jointly of the Council of the Americas and the US Chamber of Commerce, while the Instituto Mexicano para la Competividad acted as the Secretariat for the Mexican section.

The initial emphasis of the Council appeared to be on incremental change, rather than a 'big idea' for deep integration, and the SPP was a key vehicle. According to Canada's *Maclean's* magazine, Canadian executives focused on the facilitation of border transit, the US representatives on 'regulatory convergence' and the Mexicans on energy integration. The Council reported first to the trade ministers in October 2006, then to all the ministers in February 2007, and most recently was able to present its views and recommendations to the two Presidents and the Prime Minister at Montebello in August. The SPP sprang essentially from a multinational business proposal, and the integral involvement of corporate leaders in its ongoing governance was made permanent in Cancún and celebrated in Ottawa and Montebello. The NACC is essentially setting the agenda.

However, some argue that the issue of regulatory convergence, for example, is not only one of reducing trade-complicating differences between national regimes, but one that puts regulations at the whim of corporations themselves. And business could hardly be more content with the results to date. In his summation of the results of the 2007 Montebello summit, CCCE head d'Aquino commented, 'allow me to suggest that the SPP is achieving exactly what it is meant to achieve.'[23]

However, Jean-Yves LeFort, trade campaigner with the Council of Canadians, complains that 'while the SPP has formalized the power of large corporations by creating the North American Competitiveness Council (NACC), the Canadian public and civil society have been left out of these negotiations . . . Even our members of parliament have been excluded.' The NACC advised the ministers on their priorities for the 2006 and 2007 summits and was the only sectoral group to have a full formal meeting with them. While the Governments pledge meetings with 'other stakeholders', nothing remotely comparable to the access afforded to big business is apparent.

Change of approach

Despite their exclusive access to the political chief executives, the leadership of Canadian big business signalled a major shift of direction with regard to strategy for North American integration in 2008. In part this may simply be because of the impending need to deal with a new US administration, but it also seems to indicate frustration with trilateral approaches and a recognition of the relatively marginal importance of Mexico and Mexican priority concerns—like migration—for the Canadian business élite.

In the Simon Reisman lecture for 2008 d'Aquino called for a 'new big idea', a further stage in bilateral integration between the USA and Canada, where they 'will continue to nurture their independence as countries but . . . will achieve a level of economic and security cooperation unmatched by any two countries on earth.' He listed again the priority proposals of the business élite for such an agenda: a common external tariff, an electronically administered frontier between the two countries, common regulatory systems, etc. With apologies to the ambassador of Mexico who was present, d'Aquino argued the urgency of proceeding on a bilateral basis, in part to equip North America for the competition of India, the People's Republic of China and other emerging powers.[24] D'Aquino followed up with an address in June 2008 to the North American Forum in Washington, DC. He argued that North America was moving backwards, while the rest of the world advanced. Most egregious was the continued increase in complications at the border. He estimated 'a total of almost US $3,400m. in lost exports from what we refer to as the "thickening" of the Canada-United States border.' Every dollar wasted in queuing at the border is a 'dollar of disadvantage' when competing with the rest of the world.[25]

THE SPP IN CONTEXT

The SPP, as indicated above, is a process not a treaty. It exists alongside and as an operational extension of elements of NAFTA, as well as other bilateral agreements, particularly in the areas of military co-operation and foreign policy alliances which shape North American relations. The SPP represents a tactical shift on the part of business elements energizing an integration agenda, away from the so-called 'big bang' approach, to regulatory and operational executive co-ordination, which goes as far as possible without engaging legislative necessity.

Economic Climate

The US economic prospects looked bleaker in 2007, particularly with the threat of the collapse of the sub-prime mortgage industry. US deficits, the ongoing expense of military expenditures and the national debt continued to worry analysts. In Canada a significant shift continued, with more than 150,000 manufacturing jobs lost, largely in central Canada, during the mid-decade, though unemployment across the country was relatively low, and the demand for labour in the resource industries—largely in the west—increased. The relative weakness of the US dollar and the periodic rise of the Canadian dollar, to parity and beyond, increased the challenges for Canadian manufacturing exporters.

The melt-down of the sub-prime mortgage industry in the USA dominated economic news in 2008, with some direct and indirect repercussions for its neighbours' economies. Pressures to deal more effectively with a finance sector that seemed out of control following decades of de-regulation developed as the election campaign in the USA moved forward.

Military Dimensions: The Armouring of NAFTA

Prof. Michael Byers, formerly of Duke University, North Carolina, and now Canadian Research Chair at the University of British Columbia, argues that 'the integration of the Canadian and US military is not officially part of the SPP, but the SPP and the integration of the Canadian and US military are part of a larger project, and we need to address that larger project . . . There are people', he asserts, 'who want to transform the Canadian Forces into a miniature version of the US Marine Corps and want Canada to only choose missions that involve fighting shoulder-to-shoulder with the United States . . . The same people will tell you that peace-keeping is dead . . .'[26]

While the SPP comprises a significant range of arrangements affecting security, intelligence, policing, customs and military matters, and is one of a series of arrangements which align Mexico and Canada with US interests and foreign, commercial and refugee policies, there are separate, but nevertheless significant, military arrangements. Perhaps the most obvious is the membership of Canada and the USA in the North Atlantic Treaty Organization (NATO), and their bilateral North American Defense Organization (NORAD) agreement, from both of which Mexico is absent. However, Mexico, a country historically neutral in its international posture, is part of bilateral arrangements, including the Merida Initiative or 'Plan Mexico', which increasingly integrate it under the southern wing of the imperial eagle. This, in turn, should be placed in the context of hemispheric military planning on the part of the USA. Speaking to the June 2008 North American Forum, US Secretary of Defense Robert Gates, referring to threats like 'narco-terrorists', stressed the importance of hemisphere-wide links to 'safeguard gains in governance and free markets by enhancing relationships with our allies' militaries and defense ministries.' Key to this strategy is Colombia.[27]

The Bi-National Planning Group on Canada and the United States (CANUS) Enhanced Military Co-operation was one of the key agencies of aligning Canadian and US policy, reporting in March 2006. The preferred option was full integration of the armed forces of the two countries, with Canadian forces as part of a kind of expanded NORAD, in which ultimate control rested with the US military. Some initial steps have been taken towards this, including the expansion of NORAD to include shared maritime surveillance, such as monitoring of the Northwest Passage.

The Canada-US Civil Assistance Plan was signed on 14 February 2008. As military specialist journalist David Pugliese noted, 'the agreement paves the way for the militaries of either nation to send troops across the other's [borders] during an emergency.' Canada Command spokesman Commander David Scanlon was reassuring, saying the agreement was benign and simply sets the stage for collaboration if governments decide. The fact that the agreement was not announced by either the Harper Government nor the Canadian Forces raised concern by civil society groups like the Council of Canadians. Their staff discovered an announcement in the *Colorado Springs Gazette*, and raised concern about its intrusive potential.[28] Right-wing blogs and publications in the USA picked up the news and argued that the agreement lacked congressional approval and had dangerous implications for any community or group hit by an emergency.[29]

On the southern front, the Merida Initiative, which was eventually signed into law by President Bush on 30 June 2008, is justified as helping to 'address the corrosive threat of transnational crime'. Following the experience of Plan Colombia, however, and with an eye on wider US hemispheric strategy, Mexico-based NAFTA analyst Laura Carlsen terms it 'a regional security plan developed in the context of the SPP that bundles counter-narcotics, counter-terrorism, and border security measures into a new national security program for Mexico led by Washington.'[30]

As Carlsen comments, the SPP and the Merida Initiative are not only a significant threat to Mexican sovereignty, but impose on Mexico 'the security priorities of the United States at a time when those are very belligerent and aggressive throughout the world.' Canadian broadcaster Avi Lewis told the US show 'Democracy Now' that state department Undersecretary of State for Hemispheric Affairs Thomas Shannon said the SPP was about 'armouring NAFTA'. Lewis concludes: 'I think when you look at the intersection of the economic agenda, the cover of the war on drugs, the immigration and border hysteria underneath it, Plan Mexico represents exactly that, the armoring of NAFTA.'[31]

The 'armouring of NAFTA' is an element in a broader renewal of military attention on the hemisphere by the USA, echoed in its recent 'resurrection' of the Fourth Fleet for patrol duties off the coasts of Latin America. Venezuela's President Hugo Chávez Frías called it 'an act of war', clearly concerned about Venezuela's offshore oil operations. Undersecretary Shannon made a tour of Latin American capitals 'to allay leaders' fears'[32]. In an analysis of renewed US activity, Mexico-based John Ross notes that deep-sea petroleum deposits are a sensitive issue and a potential source of disputes between the USA and Mexico, as well as the USA and Brazil. Surprised at the relative lack of Mexican outrage at the Merida Initiative, Ross notes that the armed forces stand to benefit considerably from a US $1,400m. investment in rearmament: 'Indeed, just the need for spare parts will tie the Mexican military to the Pentagon for the life of the planes, helicopters, swift boats, and transport carriers Plan Mexico will buy.' Mexican armed forces personnel train at the Center for Strategic Forces in Fort Bragg, NC, and US Navy trainers provide courses for Mexicans in Veracruz and Manzanillo. Like US operations in many other zones, the Merida Initiative may also involve the employment of private mercenary groups, such as Blackwater.[33] The SPP brings together security and energy objectives.

Corporate Consolidation

Four years ago a leading Canadian business journalist, referring to estimates from the Royal Bank of Canada, pointed out that 62 of the country's largest companies have vanished though mergers or acquisitions since 2000. He termed it a 'hollowing out' of Canadian business, and also of the city of Toronto, where many of them had formerly established head offices. A further Royal Bank report documented the sale of 455 Canadian firms to foreign companies for a combined price of US $137,000m. between 2001 and 2006, second in value for the period only to Australia.

Four years later a wave of foreign—largely but not only US originated—takeovers led to a shudder of Canadian concern regarding 'hollowing out'. When aluminium producer Alcan, based in Montréal, was bought by Rio Tinto in July 2007, a former Québec industry minister stated 'when Alcan is sold to foreign interests, a part of Québec is also sold off to foreign interests.' The head office may remain in Montréal but most 'vital decisions' are likely to be transferred, 'leaving behind an empty shell'. The Alcan case was but one of a series of significant Canadian flagship enterprises that were sold in 2006–07, including Inco, Falconbridge, Algoma Steel, Stelco and Four Seasons Hotels.

Many in the business-funded 'think tanks', academic centres and business press were at pains to play down public concern, generally noting that Canadian businesses were active in buying firms overseas. The C. D. Howe Institute in Toronto argued, for example, that Canada should in fact take steps to be more open to foreign investment, integrating more thoroughly with global capital markets. However, this argument essentially misses the point. While the head of the Investment Industry Association of Canada dismissed concern as 'paranoia', the head of the Royal Bank of Canada referred to the 'dramatic impact' of the buy-outs and stated that Canada needed policies which would develop 'Canadian champions or Canadian industries'. As the Québec former minister concluded about Alcan, 'even though such a sale is bound to enrich a few individuals and many international speculators, it surely appears to be contrary to Canada's best interests.' Responding to growing concern, the Harper Government appointed a blue ribbon panel to review competition and foreign investment policy. In June 2008 they recommended a higher threshold of takeover investment necessary to provoke a review, lifting restrictions on foreign investment in banking, broadcasting and telecommunications, airlines, uranium and the cultural sector. They also sought to shift the emphasis from companies showing that a deal presented a 'net benefit to Canada' to the government being able to demonstrate that a takeover was against Canadian interest.[34]

Since the Canadian government's Investment Canada agency, which reviews foreign takeovers, was created in 1985 it approved every application up to the time of writing. Public reaction to the possible sale of the Canadian company MacDonald Dettwiler to a US firm (Alliant Techsystems) led the Conservative Minister of Industry, Jim Prentice, to deny the takeover, though this action is likely to be a one-off rather than a precedent. Canada's corporate evisceration was highlighted when the Australian chair of the world's largest mining corporation cited Canada as a worst-case scenario, it having become a 'branch office country' rather than possessing corporate leadership in the field. Canada has lost more mining head offices than any other country. Don Lindsay, head of Teck Cominco, Canada's largest base metals mining company, responded that 'as a Canadian, it hurts', going on to say that 'as a country we should be taking a different direction.'[35]

NAFTA, THE SPP AND INTEGRATION IN DEBATE IN THE USA: THE CAMPAIGN OF 2008

The SPP and NAFTA have faced increasing suspicion and some clear opposition in the USA. To a certain extent, this is part of the overall debate regarding free trade agreements, immigration and the accompanying fixation on security. 'In the US, protectionist attitudes are front and centre, ranging from the SPP's condemnation by state legislatures to its position as a target for CNN's Lou Dobbs' populist rhetoric, earning the distinction of potentially causing the "end (of) the United States as we know it".'[36]

Concern with lost jobs and 'offshore' subcontracting—long an issue in organized labour—has, in the last few years, been championed by a minority of media figures such as Lou Dobbs. It has tapped into the xenophobia of the far right, and connects with economic and social critiques of the trade regimes on the left. The election of a Democratic majority in both houses of the US Congress in 2006 led in turn to successful opposition to the bilateral agreement with Colombia in 2007 and 2008. In May 2007 congressional Democrats and the Bush Administration agreed to include a commitment in any foreign trade agreements to 'adopt, maintain and enforce' five fundamental International Labour Organization standards, together with the possibility of using trade sanctions to ensure them.[37] A number of contenders for the Democratic presidential nomination—Senators Joe Biden, Hillary Clinton and Chris Dodd—voted against the proposed Dominican Republic-Central American Free Trade Agreement, while John Edwards favoured closing down trade negotiations that have 'devastated America', and Barack Obama signalled an intention to rewrite NAFTA. Among Republicans, only John McCain, Mitt Romney and Sam Brownback could be counted on as clear supporters of trade agreements.[38]

The 2008 Democratic primaries in the 'rust belt' region of the Mid-West propelled NAFTA into the headlines. In the tight race between the final two Democratic candidates, Barack Obama and Hillary Clinton, each picked up the banner of NAFTA renegotiation. The trade unions and campaigning organizations like Citizens Trade Campaign elicited clearer commitments from each, and to some extent secured them. Clinton took the most detailed position, calling for integration of labour and environment guarantees within a reformed agreement rather than as addenda, and stating she 'would take out the ability of foreign companies to sue [the US Government] because of what we do to protect our workers.'[39] Obama, like Clinton, supported more adequate labour and environmental provisions and pledged to renegotiate with both Canada and Mexico. Both said they would use the threat of opting out to get 'terms more favorable to all America'.

Obama's primary case in Ohio was damaged when he called NAFTA a 'big mistake' in the 27 February Democratic debate in Ohio. It was later revealed that a senior economic advisor on his team, Austan Goolsbee, had held conversations on 8 February with the Canadian Consulate-General in Chicago indicating that Obama's threat to opt out was more 'political positioning' than policy. Clinton saw the opening and stated, 'I don't think people should come to Ohio and tell the people of Ohio one thing and then have your campaign tell a foreign government something else behind closed doors.'[40]

The issue of Canadian government complicity in the release of a memo from the Consulate-General which recounted the Goolsbee advice fed heated accusations in the Canadian Parliament, including that the Harper Conservatives were interfering in US politics and had contributed to Obama's defeat in the primary. This so-called 'NAFTA-gate' episode led to defensive denials and a pledge by the Canadian Prime Minister to appoint an independent investigator to get to the bottom of the memo's leak.[41]

Doubts about Obama's sincere desire to renegotiate the trade agreement were reiterated by commentators like Jagdish Bhagwati in the *Financial Times*, who stressed that 'Obama's free-trade credentials top Clinton's',[42] and pointed out that advisor Goolsbee taught at the Chicago Business School, itself 'a valuable source of free-trade advice over almost a decade'. When Obama appointed Jason Furman, a protégé of former Clinton economic chief Robert Rubin, as his economic policy director, it only fuelled more doubts. Union leaders pointed out that the Rubin-founded Hamilton Project which Furman headed had advocated free trade policies injurious to US workers.[43]

With Obama becoming the prospective Democratic nominee, his progressive supporters became 'increasingly concerned over [his] ideological torques, anxious to learn which NAFTA revisions [he] would actually pursue if elected.'[44] Obama's interview with *Fortune* on 18 June 2008 included references which seemed to echo the Canadian consular memo. Harsh references to NAFTA were perhaps rhetoric that 'gets overheated and amplified', he offered. He mentioned that he would not re-open the agreement unilaterally, and that he had just spoken with Prime Minister Harper, who had earlier called his threat a mistake.

While Republican nominee John McCain, himself a free trade advocate, accused Obama of 'flip-flopping' on free trade and NAFTA, less partisan assessments by the Council on Hemispheric Affairs and *Fortune* indicate that his position has been consistent, if rather too vague in some key aspects, like stating specifically how he would amend NAFTA. Obama has indicated that he would 'not sign any trade agreement as President that does not have protections for our environment and for American workers.' He has also indicated that in any trade negotiations 'our nation must address the dislocations caused by expanded global trade by maintaining workers' basic benefits and helping them retrain.' He would combat the outsourcing of jobs by ending tax breaks for companies that 'ship our jobs overseas', and give a federal income tax credit for 'patriot' employers who stay at home.[45] Obama summarizes his stance on NAFTA as follows:

> 'We must add binding obligations to the NAFTA agreement to protect the right to collective bargaining and other core labor standards recognized by the International Labor Organization. Similarly, we must add binding environmental standards so that companies from one country cannot gain an economic advantage by destroying the environment. And we should amend NAFTA to make clear that fair laws and regulations written to protect citizens in any of the three countries cannot be overridden simply at the request of foreign investors.'[46]

In June 2008 McCain, in a speech to the Economic Club of Toronto, renewed his firm commitment to NAFTA and to 'free trade'. He admitted that there can be negative impacts on US workers, and recommended unemployment insurance reforms and retraining programmes to respond to job losses. His two visits to Canada, including a short and unprecedented mid-campaign visit to Ottawa, may have added fuel to debate over NAFTA in Canada, whether he intended it or not. The élite Canadian business and political classes, who share virtually unanimous support for NAFTA, however, welcomed the visit and his enthusiasm for free trade, and happily turned out to dine with him in Ottawa.

Whatever the outcome of the November 2008 presidential election, the likelihood of a strong Democratic majority in Congress reinforces the close attention that will inevitably be given to the trade agenda. Indicative of some of the chief concerns is the Trade Reform, Accountability, Development and Employment (TRADE) act, launched on 8 June 2008 by Democratic congressional Representatives Sherrod Brown and Mike Michaud, accompanied by several prominent trade union leaders. The proposal would require: a full assessment of each existing agreement to evaluate its economic impact; a comparative analysis of wage trends in the USA and its major agreement partners; an analysis of agriculture and food-related outcomes; along with a number of other ambitious undertakings in terms of privatizations, disputes, human rights, etc.[47]

The contrast between the presidential contenders on trade is clear. The Democrats have responded to a 'growing sense of vulnerability' among 'blue collar' workers. Jared Bernstein, a senior economist at the liberal Economic Policy Institute, comments: 'there are qualified grounds for America's international trading partners to be more nervous about our commitment to new trade agreements than they have been 15 years ago.' Author Francis Fukuyama notes this shift: 'there is a structural change going on . . . most of the electorate believe the pendulum has swung too far in a *laissez-faire* direction in the last two decades. No successful candidate can ignore that.' Deputy US Secretary of State, John Negroponte, recognized this swing in his 17 June 2008 address to the North American Forum, noting citizens' concerns about 'their standards of living and . . . their children's prospects in the future', and what that would mean for the advocates of greater integration.[48]

DEBATE IN MEXICO

While debate in the USA focuses on job losses, border security and immigration, debate in Mexico has different dimensions. Mexican commentators noted that while press coverage of the 2007 trinational summit was limited in the USA, it was extensive in Mexico.

Perhaps the most profound difference in attitude is the point of view articulated by former diplomat Gustavo Iruegas. His emphasis has been principally on the security dimensions of the pact and implications for the historic orientation of Mexican foreign and security policy. Speaking in Ottawa on the eve of the Montebello meeting, he stated simply, 'Mexico has no enemies'. To become entangled in the SPP implicates Mexico as an enemy of US enemies, something which he believed Mexico was best advised to avoid. Further, the SPP has already led to increased militarization of the Mexican state and society. While it has a negative effect on Mexico's freedom of action internationally, the pact also has implications domestically, in terms of US intervention in Mexico's internal affairs, by what Iruegas terms 'Plan Mexico', a northern equivalent of the US anti-narco-trafficking 'Plan Colombia'.[49]

Analyst Miguel Picard of the Centro de Investigaciones Económicas y Política de Acción Comunitaria agrees with Iruegas that the SPP opens Mexico to greater US intervention, and makes both Canadian and Mexican borders potentially open to incursions by the US armed forces when there is a perceived terrorist threat. Picard notes that the SPP has avoided measures that 'recognize the importance of immigrant labor for the US and Canadian economies', as well as the vulnerability of this extensive labour pool. He comments that its provisions make future enhancement of the rights of first nations to natural resources and their lands more difficult.

However, Picard's most far-reaching criticisms of the SPP are that, first, the pact is, in the words of Mexican professor John Saxe-Fernandez, 'a battering ram to push forward "vertical integration" of Latin America' with the USA. Second, he states that the SPP is profoundly anti-democratic, avoiding all sectors but big business and bypassing democratic governmental bodies.[50]

NAFTA LIVES

The years of activity through the SPP may supersede some areas of NAFTA that were dormant or low priority, but the trade and investment agreement continues.

Commission

Prior to the Montebello summit the NAFTA Commission, composed of US Trade Representative Susan Schwab, Canadian Minister of International Trade David Emerson and Mexican Secretary of the Economy Eduardo Sojo Garza-Aldape, met in Vancouver, British Columbia, in mid-August 2007. The Commission agreed to develop a work plan to assess issues of competitiveness in a global context and to assess other trade agreements that each country had negotiated to identify meaningful differences. It followed up on a 2006 decision to evaluate the mandates of the various NAFTA working groups and committees. The Commission expressed pleasure with work on rules of origin begun in 2003. A first set of changes, affecting US $20,000m.-worth of trade, had been implemented in 2005, a further set affecting an estimated $15,000m. was implemented in 2006 and a third set, affecting $100,000m. in trilateral trade to be implemented in 2008, was agreed in Vancouver.

Chapter 11

Perhaps the single most controversial innovation in NAFTA is contained in Chapter 11 of the Agreement, which deals with investment. This section significantly reduces the ability of governments to condition foreign investment in order to ensure local benefit. It prohibits 'performance requirements' such as domestic content or purchasing regulations, technology transfer, etc. Chapter 11 seeks to protect the rights of investors against arbitrary state action, assuring compensation for expropriation and providing a process for resolving disputes. The most debated element of the NAFTA investment provisions is the 'investor state' mechanism. This provision allows investors to sue national governments for virtually any action that decreases their expected profits, alleging expropriation or 'measures tantamount to expropriation'. A government can take measures for public purposes, on a non-discriminatory basis, after due process of law, but only if it pays compensation to the foreign investor.

As of January 2008 there had been a total of 49 known investor claims: 18 against Canada, 14 against the USA and 17 against Mexico. There may, however, be additional claims that have not yet been made public.

The far-reaching impact of Chapter 11 and its usefulness to corporations interested in reducing regulation, as well as its original procedural secrecy and exclusivity, have stimulated considerable public criticism. Chapter 11 is seen by its critics as perhaps the most revolutionary aspect of the NAFTA trade and investment regime. Environmental policy analysts note that it threatens existing international environmental treaties and that, further, it has led politicians to refrain from implementing new environmental legislation.

An academic review of Chapter 11 concludes that it has altered the power relations between public (state) and private (investors) actors. Measures which theoretically might be taken to assert the public interest in the face of unwelcome decisions by tribunals, are ineffective. 'Rather, states have sanctioned a significant transfer of authority from public to private control. Essentially, a portion of national sovereignty is surrendered, not just to international entities, but to private ones.'[51]

Nevertheless, in 2007, one of the key cases before a Chapter 11 Tribunal set important limits on what a corporation might seek in terms of operations of the public sector: the ongoing case by United Parcel Service (UPS) against the Canadian postal service, Canada Post. In July 2002 the parties agreed that the dispute would be settled in public rather than through confidential hearings. Third parties, including the Council of Canadians, the Canadian Union of Postal Workers and the US Chamber of Commerce, won amicus standing. As one legal expert commented, 'I think a collective sigh of relief is being expressed in all three capitals: Mexico City, Washington and Ottawa.'[52] The core of the case was a challenge to a Crown corporation, Canada Post, based in the injury alleged from its operation of courier services in competition with UPS. There were also charges arising from the conditions applied to the Canadian Publication Assistance Program, which, according to Canada, fell under the cultural industries exception in NAFTA.

In what ways was the tribunal decision on *UPS v. Canada Post* precedent-setting? One of the amicus lawyers noted: 'It was the first investor-state claim to argue that delivery of public sector services, in this case by Canada Post, represented unfair competition for private companies providing similar services. The case was also the first of its type to target a cultural program . . . which supports Canadian publishers. It was the first as well to seek damages to a breach of worker rights under an ILO convention—not to the benefit of the workers directly harmed, but rather to compensate UPS for having to respect worker rights when Canada Post was relieved of this obligation. Fortunately, the UPS claims were rejected on all fronts.'

It is important to note that the tribunal decision does not exhaust all options open to UPS, and that it could request a judicial review of the award, or a state-to-state claim.[53]

An assessment of the difference in the US official approach to the investor-state issue in the negotiation of the US-Australian bilateral trade agreement notes that the USA retreated from the expected extension of the NAFTA Chapter 11 model. The assessment argues 'that between 2001 and 2004, the Office of the US Trade Representative moved away from a robust embrace of NAFTA-style Chapter 11 investor-state provisions. Part of this movement was a consequence of a generalized concern—which NAFTA government officials will freely admit in private—that those who negotiated NAFTA in the early 1990s did not anticipate that lawyers would . . . launch the kind of legal actions that generated such opposition in the late

1990s.' It continued, 'in the early 2000s, more "mainstream" groups added their voices to . . . opposition: state legislatures, cities, and mayors, all of whom had deep linkages to congressional delegations, and thus with more pronounced electoral implications.' The authors note that by putting confidence in national legal systems to deal with investment issues, the US-Australian free trade agreement provides a 'potent precedent' and a powerful argument of amendment of the NAFTA Chapter 11. This makes 'it very difficult to justify including NAFTA-style investor-state dispute settlement measures in future free trade agreements.' Obama and the Democratic platform appear to have taken this concern on board. However, pending any revision of NAFTA, the governments and peoples of Mexico, Canada and the USA remain saddled with Chapter 11 as negotiated.[54]

Current cases include several which are particularly controversial. A Canadian mining firm, Glamis Gold, is challenging Californian environmental regulations intended to limit negative environmental impacts and protect indigenous people's religious sites. Exxon-Mobil charges that Canadian guidelines requiring energy companies active in offshore exploitation to invest in research and development in Newfoundland and Labrador, are performance requirements inconsistent with NAFTA.[55]

Trade, Investment and Labour Mobility Agreement

In Canada there has begun an attempt to extend the sort of investment guarantees embodied in Chapter 11 to provincial and municipal level, through an inter-provincial scheme called the Trade, Investment and Labour Mobility Agreement (TILMA). Begun by British Columbia and Alberta, it has been considered by other provinces. The rationale for TILMA is that it would remove inter-provincial trade barriers, which are sometimes cited as an obstacle to a better business climate in Canada. A study by the Conference Board of Canada estimated, for example, that TILMA would increase Saskatchewan's GDP by US $291m. A counter-study by the Canadian Centre for Policy Alternatives, however, made a devastating critique of the Conference Board's methodology.

TILMA imposes a complete prohibition on all government measures that 'operate to restrict or impair' trade, investment or labour mobility unless exempted under the agreement. The definition for government includes not only all agencies of the provincial government, but school boards, municipalities and other publicly funded academic, health and social service entities. It offers private bodies who claim injury the opportunity to have it adjudicated by panels (not the courts) with a possible compensation of up to $5m. per case. As trade lawyer Steven Shrybman puts it, 'TILMA also expands the scope of foreign investor rights that can be asserted under NAFTA. Moreover, these rights are bestowed on US and Mexican investors without any reciprocal gains for BC or Alberta investors in the USA or Mexico.'

In August 2007 the then Saskatchewan Government announced it would not sign on to TILMA, citing 'the very broad scope of government measures that can be challenged by private interests and the strong enforcement measures in place in the deal.' The Nova Scotia Government, among others, continues to have the agreement under review.

The prospect that the TILMA might be superseded by a nation-wide Agreement on Internal Trade led to further debate in 2008. Business leaders told Québec's Premier Jean Charest, who hosted a 2008 meeting of provincial and territorial premiers—the Council of the Federation—that it was pleased with the premiers' consensus on 'an enforcement mechanism to resolve disputes, including a tiered approach to monetary penalties in the event of non-compliance.' Labour leaders responded that such a tribunal meant that 'premiers would abdicate significant authority to private interests.' The head of the Manitoba Federation of Labour noted that the proposed enhanced Agreement on Internal Trade would 'open the door for corporations who might want to challenge a province or a municipality's laws and regulations if they are deemed "barriers to trade". This would import into Canadian domestic affairs the measures that now exist under NAFTA.'[56]

Softwood Lumber

A long-term irritant in Canada–USA trade, that of US restrictions on Canadian softwood lumber exports, came to a climax of sorts in 2006. On 27 April the Harper Government announced that it had reached a 'framework' agreement with the Bush Administration to resolve the dispute. In response to a quite negative reaction among the Canadian industry, further adjustments were made and a legal text approved by the Canadian Minister of International Trade David Emerson, and the US Trade Representative, Susan Schwab. The Harper Government announced in August that it would introduce implementing legislation in the next session of Parliament and that it would treat it as a matter of confidence. Member of Parliament Peter Julian noted that Canadian taxpayers had invested over US $100m. in legal costs to win the NAFTA case, but the Government, in conceding, was giving $1,000m. to US competitors. Dominic Leblanc, a Liberal lawmaker and trade critic, argued that the federal Government should take advantage of legal victories in the dispute and persist through the courts until recovering 100% of the duties the USA had collected on Canadian softwood exports. The decision was also seen as a death knell for NAFTA. Robert Pastor argues that it weakened the overall agreement, hurting US interests in the long-term by making failure to adhere to the agreement more possible for all the parties.

The 2006 agreement, however, began to show severe strains when in August 2007 the USA announced that it was seeking binding arbitration at the London Court of International Arbitration, charging that Canada had broken the agreement by a 'surge' of low-price exports. A further critique of the accord was made by a US trade lawyer, Eliot Feldman, who noted that of the US $1,000m. of duties imposed on Canadian exports and retained by the USA, approximately $450m. remained under the control of the federal Government as a potential political 'pork barrel' fund, and $500m. under the control of the US lumber producers coalition, which was fighting Canadian imports. Julian, hearing Feldman's case, commented, 'So what you're saying is that we are not only providing money to the coalition to fight further legal victories, for further legal battles—giving half a billion dollars to them—but we're also providing money that may go to political purposes for the re-election of Republicans, many of whom have been the most adamant against allowing free trade in lumber. It is ridiculous.'[57]

SOCIAL CONSEQUENCES

The long-term social consequences of the implementation of the 'NAFTA model' have received relatively little journalistic or political attention. However, concern about growing inequality is surfacing in pre-electoral US debates and has been stressed in the Canadian parliamentary hearings on the SPP. Mexican analyst Michel Picard has documented, 'the Mexican people are the deal's big "losers". Mexicans now face greater unemployment, poverty and inequality than before the agreement began in 1994.' Furthermore, Mexico's population was not unique. In the USA, the wealthiest 1% increased their share of total income in the last decade of the 20th century from 12.5% to 17.8%. Recently accessed Canadian figures show that between 1989 and 2005 the lowest quintile of all family units saw their income fall by 11% and the next two quintiles lost 4% and 2%, respectively. Meanwhile, the top quintile share of total Canadian income increased by 16% to 46.9%. In summary, 80% of Canadian families have seen their income stagnate or fall during NAFTA's operation. NAFTA-style policies are benefiting those who need it least, and polarizing each of the three societies simultaneously.

Renewed concern with inequality animates elements of the electoral campaigns in the USA and Canada. The Democrats' talk of reforming the US tax code is a response, as is the emphasis on social equality characteristic of the New Democratic Party and its allies in Canada. Particular focus has been put on what the Washington-based Institute for Policy Studies calls 'Executive Excess'. *The Nation*, in its recent inequality issue, noted that the gap between the ultra rich and the poor is greater than the huge gap on the eve of the great depression. In

2006 the top 0.01% averaged 976 times more income than the USA's bottom 90%.[58]

Stephanie Golob of Baruch College, New York, confirms that one of the problems with NAFTA is that the agreement dealt solely with business interests, but did not promote a socially integrated system between the three countries that would spread the benefits to everyone.[59] Canadian political scientist Laura MacDonald of Carleton University notes 'the fact that the NAFTA era has been accompanied by ongoing polarization between rich and poor in the United States and Mexico (and, to a lesser extent in Canada) means that North American integration lacks a significant political constituency beyond the ranks of the rich.' US analyst Robert Pastor, agrees: the benefits of integration 'have not yielded a positive consensus in part because they have not been equitably shared with those who paid a price.'[60]

WAYS FORWARD

As is clear from the level of integration and executive collaboration in such areas as regulatory 'reform' and energy market integration, the SPP is a far-reaching process which permeates far below the flags of official sovereignty. At the same time, it is clearly not enough for a number of organizations. The business-funded Fraser Institute of Vancouver, for example, looks forward to a customs union, a common security perimeter with pre-clearance of outside goods, harmonized biometric checks on people, common security criteria, a single North American defence arrangement building up from the NORAD model, and a combined air, space, sea and land binational command structure.

Several quiet binational and trinational processes beyond the official SPP are advancing common agendas in 2007, notably the North American Future 2025 Project of the CSIS in Washington, DC. It brings together academic, government, industry and other experts in a series of discussions dealing with the future of, *inter alia*: North American labour mobility, energy, the environment, security, competitiveness, border infrastructure and logistics. The North American Forum, co-chaired by former US Secretary of State George Schultz, former Alberta Premier Peter Lougheed and former Mexican Secretary of Finance Pedro Aspe continued its fourth annual forum in Washington in June, 2008, hearing from US Secretary of Defense Robert Gates, Deputy Secretary of State John Negroponte, Canadian ambassador to the USA, Michael Wilson, and Mexican Secretary of Transportation and Communications Luis Tellez Kuenzler, among others. Among its objectives was 'to introduce the key issues to the incoming administration, Congress'.[61] The Norman Paterson School of International Affairs and the Centre for Trade Policy and Law at Ottawa's Carleton University, with an eye to the prospect of a new administration in Washington, are spearheading a further examination of Canada-US relations in 2008. They intend to develop a strategy document on effective Canadian engagement of the next US administration.[62]

The Council of Canadians, one of the major opponents of the CSIS agenda, charges that this style of closed-door limited élite policy planning is a fundamental threat to democracy, and contends that, through the SPP, the USA is attempting to stake a security claim to almost every aspect of Canadian life—'from our food and roads to our pipelines and telecommunications networks. Creating a Fortress North America will not make Canadians safer.'[63]

THE DEMOCRATIC CHALLENGE

The lack of participation and/or review by legislatures in the three countries is stark. In the Canadian Parliament, Peter Julian secured an initial series of hearings on the SPP in 2007. These were closely fought and it was unclear whether or not they would continue and whether the demand of a number of witnesses for a full parliamentary debate would be met. Julian, US Democratic Congresswoman Marcy Kaptur and Mexican counterparts have organized two rounds of trinational parliamentary consultations to seek a 'people's' approach to North American integration. However, congressional oversight of the SPP has yet to be asserted in either the USA or Mexico, and has hardly existed in the Canadian parliamentary session that ended in September 2008. The implications of the SPP go beyond what legislative hearings can offer. Teresa Healy comments that evidence is beginning to emerge 'that not only has there been no legislative review of the SPP ... but the judicial branch of government is being undermined as well. Instead it is the executive level of both government and business which is working with police and security forces to define this next stage in North American integration.' The nature of this approach is quite vulgar. As the Chairman of the US section of the NACC, Ron Covais, told *Maclean's* magazine in 2006: 'The guidance from the ministers was, "tell us what we need to do and we'll make it happen", and that rather than going through the legislative process in any country, the Security and Prosperity Partnership must be implemented in incremental changes by executive agencies, bureaucrats and regulators. We've decided not to recommend any things that would require legislative changes, because we won't get anywhere.'[64]

Among those arguing for a much more aggressive approach towards changing the alleged lack of transparency within the SPP is Washington-based academic Robert Pastor. He argues that critics have made the leaders 'timid', refusing to address 'big issues'. In a major article in the July/August 2008 edition of *Foreign Affairs* he argues for a new US 'good neighbour' policy, far more ambitious than his characterization of the SPP as a 'North American game of Scrabble with intergovernmental committees meeting periodically to spell new acronyms that purport to be initiatives.' He notes that border delays have increased since the terrorist attacks of September 2001, that despite great growth in trade transport infrastructure has lacked investment and Mexican trucks still face obstacles at the border, rules of origin are still time-consuming complications and migration is still a profound irritant. He advocates agreement on consolidated efficiencies, such as a single North American drugs-testing and certification agency. Pastor argues for a Marshall Plan-style initiative, eliminating rules of origin, securing a continental perimeter and creating a North American investment fund to stimulate infrastructural enhancement and integration, bringing southern Mexico more fully into the North-American economy with the three heads of government committed to 'building a new consciousness, a new way of thinking about one's neighbours and the continental agenda.'[65]

Pastor favours bringing academics, environmentalists, unions, the media, and state- and provincial-level legislators into the process. After more than a decade of NAFTA the context has shifted, and North America needs to address a world in which Chinese and Indian manufacturers and commercial interests in general are major players. As Anderson and Sands agree, the complaint that many sectors with an interest in the future of North America are closed out of the meetings is 'reasonable, and should be met'. Like Pastor, they advise opening the process up to non-governmental organizations and citizen groups. However, they conclude: 'The leaders have two chances left to fix the SPP. The first best chance was at Montebello, but the leaders took no action to make the SPP more transparent, or to reach out to Congress or the special interests. A second chance may come when the United States hosts next year and Bush may choose this opportunity to repair his North American legacy. Finally, in 2009, a new US President is likely to see the value in the negotiations, but either revamp the SPP or replace it with a new, better designed process.'

A strong riposte comes from Laura Carlsen, who argues in a July 3 2008 article that 'North America Doesn't Exist'. Carlsen maintains that élites have tried to convince their citizens that they have a shared future in one common path, 'the assumption that just one road leads to the fulfillment of everyone's goals.' She calls this 'absurd and dangerous', NAFTA 'constitutes a roadmap for U.S. regional hegemony', and the SPP is simply an arrangement for maximization of corporate profit among a superpower and two subordinates. She argues that the commonality of interests which is assumed by the élites is artificial. The North America of NAFTA and the SPP is a pilot project in the maximization of profit, not a community or commonality. Mexico, for example, has been split in two. Carlsen argues that the 'bloc' does not exist, but there are alliances among community organizations in the three countries, there are overlapping lives and avenues of mutual support for diverse objectives. She argues for a moratorium on the SPP, and for a cessation of the extension of NAFTA-style provisions through other trade, investment and intellectual property agreements. Any future proposals for North America should arise from citizens' networks and the community level. 'Citizens,' she argues, 'have the right and the obligation to know about and participate in mapping the future, and when they do it's likely to look far different from the future mapped for us by corporate and government leaders behind the closed doors of the Security and Prosperity Partnership.'[66]

The fundamental democratic challenge represented by the SPP structure and process, i.e. executive fiat advised by corporate leadership, is not really comprehended in Pastor's or Anderson and Sands' proposals for process reform. In one sense, the process is already transparent, as the three heads of state listen to corporate chief executive officers and mandate a goodly portion of the advised initiatives. The broad range of citizens' interest is hardly to be typified as 'special interests'. The marginalization of democratic legislatures in all three countries is not adequately dealt with by briefings or 'consultations'. So far communication strategies which pillory the opposition or minimize far-reaching processes of change may have succeeded. However, the heavy-handed intervention of police *agents provocateurs* at the Montebello summit publicized the SPP in a way that few blogs have succeeded in doing, and raised fundamental challenges about the securitization and well-guarded 'closed doors' of high-level negotiation, as well as the marginalization of democratic processes.

One of the most striking aspects of public opinion in the USA and Canada about NAFTA is the extent and persistence of opposition given the almost homogenous élite support for both NAFTA and the SPP that exists among party and business élites, constantly reinforced by supportive media. An Angus Reid survey released on 21 July 2008 indicated that only 'one in fourteen Canadians believes their country has been the main beneficiary' and a majority are calling for renegotiation. Only 18% believe Canada should continue with NAFTA under the current terms.[67] In the USA a Pew Research Centre survey published on 1 May 2008 discovered that 48% of Americans consider free trade agreements like NAFTA negatively while only 35% are positive. More than 50% of Americans consider that such agreements depress wages. A Rasmussen poll published on 20 June 2008 showed that 56% of Americans want NAFTA renegotiated, including 49% of Republican voters.[68]

The opposition is diverse and has quite a different profile in each of the three countries, although the four-member alliance of opposition coalitions has been re-energized by the challenge of the SPP. Attention in the USA has been stimulated by pre-election political debates around NAFTA. The coalitions have had experience with 'broader' strategies, first with initiatives on labour and environmental side-agreements in the 1990s, which split the initial NAFTA opposition forces, at least in the USA, then with 'insider' strategies utilized by the Summit of the Americas processes around the proposed Free Trade Area of the Americas (FTAA). In the latter case the official attempts to divide the opposition did not succeed and the FTAA failed.

The opposition has the challenge of suggesting alternatives beyond the issue of negotiating process. Demands for transparency and/or access do not a programme make. Should, for example, a US presidential victor establish a clear commitment to revise or rescind NAFTA and set aside the SPP, what proposals would opposition forces bring forward to inform the reform or post-NAFTA road forward? The Minneapolis-based Institute for Agriculture and Trade Policy has organized two civil society conferences, one in the Mid-West and one in Washington, to stimulate debate about the way forward. Food sovereignty and security, migration and workers' rights, environment and energy security are among the themes explored. Despite élite consensus resisting any thought of NAFTA renegotiation, the Canadian Centre for Policy Alternatives argues that progressive Canadians should develop a response to the possibility that the new US administration may re-open the agreement. As author Bruce Campbell puts it, 'The items Obama put on the table—environmental and labour protections and investor rights—could benefit people in all three countries if they succeed in rebalancing power relations between corporations and citizens, between private interests and the public good.'[69]

Political columnist Lawrence Martin told readers of the *Globe and Mail* that the 'era of limitless integration draws to a welcome close . . . The era of wholesale dependency is over . . . leaving public policy to catch up to the new times.'[70] What visions of North American futures might emerge if the political space was created? Transparency must be first: an end to closed door SPP negotiations, the full participation of parliaments and the public. The sorts of initiatives that the popular networks have urged since the trilateral summits began: income and tax policies that move toward equality instead of polarization, green industrial strategies, universal public quality health care, etc. The seeds of vision and programme may be extant among social forums, trade unions, church networks and environmental advocates, but the debate has just begun.

ENDNOTES

1 M. Angeles Villareal and Jennifer E. Lake, 'Security and Prosperity Partnership of North America: An Overview and Selected Issues', *CRS Report for Congress*, No. RS22701, 2 August 2007.

2 Andrew F. Cooper and Kelly Jackson, 'Montebello was More than a Slumber Party', *Embassy*, 22 August 2007.

3 Villareal and Lake, 'Security and Prosperity Partnership of North America'.

4 'Meeting the Global Challenge', North American Competitiveness Council report. As cited in Blair Redlin, 'SPP/NAFTA Boosters on the Defensive in New Orleans', April 28 2008. Posted on Rabble TV: <http://www.rabble.ca/news_full_story.shtml?x=70667>.

5 Bruce Campbell, 'Harper and NAFTA Plus: Deep Integration By Stealth', in *The Harper Record*, ed. by Teresa Healy. Ottawa, ON, Canadian Centre for Policy Alternatives, 2008.

6 *Ibid.*

7 *Ibid.*

8 Redlin, 'SPP/NAFTA Boosters on the Defensive in New Orleans'.

9 Campbell, 'Harper and the NAFTA'.

10 'North America: The Energy Picture II', Appendix 2. The North American Energy Working Group, Natural Resources Canada, 2006. Available from: <http://www2.nrcan.gc.ca/es/es/NA-enrgpic2006/p09-e.htm>.

11 Remarks prepared for Secretary of Energy Samuel W. Bodman, 12 September 2005. US Department of Energy, Office of Public Affairs, and Canadian Council of Chief Executives.

12 Fred Wilson, 'Mexican Jellybeans', Communications, Energy and Paperworkers Union of Canada weblog, 29 August 2007. Available from: <blogs.cep.ca/en/node/50>.

13 Daniel S. Sullivan, 'Energy Issues in the Western Hemisphere'. Statement before the Subcommittee on the Western Hemisphere of the House Committee on Foreign Affairs, US Department of State, 31 July 2008.

14 Campbell, 'Harper and the NAFTA'.

15 Gordon Laxer and John Dillon, 'Over a Barrel: Exiting from NAFTA's Proportionality Clause', Parkland Institute/Canadian Centre for Policy Alternatives, May 2008.

16 Marla Dickerson, 'Mexico's capital, 9 states vote on nation's oil industry', *Los Angeles Times*, 28 July 2008.

17 'Strong and Free: The Liberal Blueprint for the North American Leaders Summit at Montebello', Liberal Party of Canada, 17 August 2007.

18 Andrew Nikiforuk, Adèle Hurley and Ralph Pentland, 'Sold down the river', *Ottawa Citizen*, 10 September 2007.

19 Maureen Webb, 'Risk Scoring and the National Insecurity State', *Counterpunch*, 7 December 2006.

20 Don Butler, 'Broaden debate on North American integration: expert', *Ottawa Citizen*, 5 June 2007.

21 James Travers, 'Summits fall short on problem solving', *Toronto Star*, 23 August 2007.

22 'A coup d'état lies behind the "Three Amigos" SPP Summit', press release issued by Common Frontiers et al., 17 August 2007.

23 Thomas d'Aquino, 'Too Much, or Not Enough? The Montebello Summit in Perspective', The Canadian Council of Chief Executives, 29 August 2007.

[24] Thomas d'Aquino, 'Reaching for the Top: Strategic Imperatives for Canada in a Transforming Global Economy', the Simon Reisman Honorary Lecture, 27 March 2008.

[25] Thomas d'Aquino, 'Rekindling the Spirit of 1993: Forging a New Path Forward for North America', notes for remarks to the North American Forum, 17 June 2008.

[26] Michael Byers, 'SPP is built around secrecy and US military command—law expert', *The Harper Index*, 20 August 2007. Available from: <http://www.harperindex.ca/ViewArticle.cfm?-Ref=0081>.

[27] Robert M. Gates, speech at the North American Forum, 16 June 2008. Available from: <http://www.defenselink.mil/speeches/speech.aspx?speechid=1257>.

[28] David Pugliese, 'Canada, U.S. agree to use each other's troops in civil emergencies', Canwest News Service, 22 February 2008.

[29] Jerome R. Corsi, 'Premeditated Merger: North American Army created without OK by Congress', WorldNetDaily website, 24 February 2008. Available from: <http://www.worldnetdaily.com/index.php?fa=PAGE.view&pageID=57228>.

[30] Laura Carlsen, 'North America Doesn't Exist', 3 July 2008. Available from: <http://www.counterpunch.org/carlsen07082008.html>.

[31] Stuart Trew, 'Plan Mexico, SPP about "armouring NAFTA", says Avi Lewis', Integrate This website, 1 August 2008. Available from: <http://www.canadians.org/integratethis/insecurity/2008/Aug-1.html>.

[32] John Ross, 'Fourth Fleet Steams South: Return of the Gunboat', Pacific Free Press website, 1 August 2008. Available from: <http://pacificfreepress.com/content/view/2898/81/>.

[33] *Ibid.*

[34] 'Compete to Win', Competition Policy Review Panel report, June 2008. Available from: <http://www.ic.gc.ca/epic/site/cprp-gepmc.nsf/en/home>.

[35] Andy Hoffman, 'Setting an example—to avoid', *Globe and Mail*, 22 July 2008.

[36] Cooper and Jackson, 'Montebello was More than a Slumber Party'.

[37] 'Trade and labour standards—A dubious deal', *Economist*, 17 May 2007.

[38] Neil Reynolds, 'U.S. protectionists, 14; free traders, three', *Globe and Mail*, 29 August 2007.

[39] 'Clinton, Obama Pledge to Withdraw From NAFTA Unless Renegotiated', *Inside US Trade*, 29 February 2008.

[40] Mark Drajem, 'Clinton Criticizes Obama over Canadian-Nafta Memo (Update 2)', Bloomberg website, 3 March 2008.

[41] Prime Minister Harper appointed an arm of his office, the Privy Council Office, to investigate, and they, predictably, found no fault on the part of his chief of staff, Ian Brodie, who had been associated with the release of the offending memo. Les Whittington, 'Brodie role cited in leak report: Harper aide didn't disclose classified information, probe finds, but incident stemmed from incorrect assumption he made', *Toronto Star*, 23 May 2008.

[42] Jagdish Bhagwati, 'Obama's free-trade credentials top Clinton's', *Financial Times*, 3 March 2008.

[43] Louis Uchitelle, 'Union Critical of Obama's Top Economics Aide', *New York Times*, 12 June 2008 and Teddy Davis, James Gerber, and Gregory Wallace, 'Obama Economic Advisor Draws Fire On Left', ABC News website, 10 June 2008. The latter points out that Obama addressed the 2006 launch of the Hamilton Project.

[44] Maggie Airriess, 'Obama on NAFTA: Name This "Change We Can Believe In"', Council on Hemispheric Affairs, 29 July 2008.

[45] *Ibid.*

[46] As reproduced in 'Presidential Candidates on Trade', Americas Policy Program Policy Report, 13 March 2008. Available from: <http://americas.irc-online.org/am/5065>.

[47] H.R. 6180, TRADE Act of 2008.

[48] James Politi and Edward Luce, 'Democrats toughen anti-trade rhetoric', *Financial Times*, 7 May 2008.

[49] Gustavo Iruegas, 'Integracion por sometimiento', *La Jornada*, 7 September 2007.

[50] Miguel Pickard, 'Ten Easy Questions and Ten Tougher Ones Regarding the SPPAN (Security and Prosperity Partnership of North America)', *Bulletins of the Centro de Investigaciones Económicas y Política de Acción Comunitaria*, No. 541, 17 August 2007.

[51] Stephen McBride, 'Reconfiguring Sovereignty: NAFTA Chapter 11 Dispute Settlement Procedures and the Issue of Public-Private Authority', *Canadian Journal of Political Science*, Vol. 39, No. 4, December 2006.

[52] Steven Chase, 'Canada Post NAFTA win sets precedent', *Globe and Mail*, 14 June 2007.

[53] Steven Shrybman, Memorandum re: United Parcel Service (UPS) v. Canada. Toronto, ON, Sack Goldblatt Mitchell LLP, 27 June 2007.

[54] Ann Capling and Kim Nossal, 'The Rise and Fall of Chapter 11: Investor-State Dispute Mechanisms in the North American Free Trade Agreement and the Australian-United States Free Trade Agreement', paper prepared for the Oceanic Conference on International Studies, Australian National University, Canberra, 14–16 July 2004.

[55] Scott Sinclair, 'NAFTA Chapter 11 Investor-State Disputes', Analysis section, Canadian Centre for Policy Alternatives, January 2008.

[56] 'The Agreement on Internal Trade puts Quebec Model in Jeopardy', press release issued by presidents of regional labour federations, 17 July 2008.

[57] Elliot J. Feldman, 'Turning trade deal into Republican ammo? Softwood deal pours $450 straight into White House, says U.S. lawyer', The Tyee website, 29 August 2006.

[58] 'Plutocracy reborn', *The Nation*, 30 June 2008.

[59] Lee Berthiaume, 'There's Nothing Quick or Easy About NAFTA', *Embassy*, 13 June 2007.

[60] Robert A. Pastor, 'The Future of North America: Replacing a Bad Neighbor Policy', *Foreign Affairs*. Vol. 87, No. 4, July/August 2008.

[61] North American Forum detailed agenda, June 2008.

[62] 'Blueprint for Canada-US Engagement under a New Administration', Carleton University, Centre for Trade Policy and Law, NPSIA-CTPL Canada-US Project. Information available from: <http://www.carleton.ca/ctpl/>.

[63] 'Backgrounder: The North American Future 2025 Project', Council of Canadians, 2007.

[64] 'Backgrounder: the North American Competitiveness Council'., Council of Canadians, February 2007.

[65] Pastor, 'The Future of North America: Replacing a Bad Neighbor Policy'.

[66] Carlsen, 'North America Doesn't Exist'.

[67] 'Canadian Majority Wants to Renegotiate the Terms of NAFTA', published by Angus Reid Strategies, 21 July 2008.

[68] Campbell, 'Harper and the NAFTA'.

[69] Campbell, 'Harper and the NAFTA'.

[70] Lawrence Martin, 'North America's era of limitless integration draws to a welcome close', *Globe and Mail*, 3 June 2008.

THE EMERGENCE OF CHINA: THE NEW CHALLENGE TO NORTH AMERICA FROM THE PACIFIC RIM

Prof. JOHN AGNEW

It was widely anticipated that 2008 would be the 'coming out' year for the People's Republic of China. As host country of the Olympic Games for the first time, the Chinese Government turned the event into an opportunity to herald the country's ascension within the world economy. These Games were not just about rebuilding and showcasing the capital Beijing, but about announcing the appearance of a new great power on the world stage. This was an episode of significant import, not only because China was in self-imposed exile from the international community from 1949 until the late 1970s, but also because it signalled the advent of a much more self-confident orientation to the rest of the world. For all its ambiguities, in particular whether this emergence represents a new threat or a welcome departure, it is the end result of a lengthy cultivation of China's possible re-entry into the world economy by North Americans of all economic and political stripes. The promise of a China fully integrated into the world economy in fact dates back to the US attempt to 'open up' China for US trade in the 19th century. US governments and businesses gambled that what mattered in the relationship across the Pacific was trade. Moreover, the belief was that such trade would always advantage the North American side. However, cashing in on this gamble has long been frustrated by the recalcitrance of Chinese and other Asian governments in following US imperatives. Asian governments, particularly those of Japan and China, have always managed to make 'opening up' suit their own aims better than those of the USA. In particular, they have shown that US-type institutions and 'culture' are not prerequisites for economic growth and prosperity. Since the 1970s China has overcome a prior history of ravenous European and Japanese colonialism to become a major independent force in the world economy. It is now a full member of the World Trade Organization (WTO) and one of North America's main trading partners. Japan is the world's second major economic power, after the USA. It is a major trading partner of the USA, the main source of finance for US trade and government deficits, and the most significant sponsor of economic growth elsewhere in Asia. A vast east and south-east Asian trade and finance network and economically effective governments have extended the pattern of economic growth to other parts of the Pacific Rim, such as the Republic of Korea (South Korea), Taiwan, Singapore, Hong Kong and, increasingly, Malaysia and Thailand.

Yet, this very success illustrates the wisdom of taking more care about what one wishes for. The Pacific Rim in general and China in particular are increasingly seen in the USA and Canada as challenging North American centrality in the world economy. In the 20th century the USA fought a world war against Japan and wars in Korea and Indo-China because the region was seen as crucial to US global interests. As a resource-based economy with a history of limited export markets, Canada has long looked to East Asia to diversify its economy away from dependence on the USA and Western Europe. What is new, however, is the extent to which the 'Pacific Rim' now figures in one way or another in just about every debate about the economic and political future of North America. Rather than simply a market for North American resources and products or a destination for capital investment, China, alongside Japan, is becoming a driving force within the world economy. This is not exactly what 19th century, or more recent, US governments and businesses had in mind.

Defining the Pacific Rim is not self-evident. In terms of the contemporary geographical expression for what was historically 'Greater China', it is usually taken to mean the Asian side of the Pacific, excluding the USA, Canada, Russia, Australia and New Zealand. However, this huge region has several tiers. There is Japan, which is by far the most economically developed economy, but is almost entirely reliant on foreign sources of raw materials and has had a history of empire in Asia still fresh in Asian popular memory. There is the still nominally communist People's Republic of China, with a huge population and developing at a rapid rate (particularly in its coastal provinces) but still a relatively poor country in terms of the standard of living of most of its population. Along with China, it is the so-called 'Newly Industrializing Countries' (NICs), however, that lie at the core of the idea of the Pacific Rim and the hopes and fears for an emerging 'Pacific Century'. These are such countries as South Korea, Taiwan, Hong Kong and Singapore, but, increasingly, the category is expanded to include such second-wave 'NICs' as Thailand, the Philippines, Malaysia and Indonesia. All these have growing market economies, but lag behind Japan and the other countries (often referred to as the 'big tiger and the tiger cubs'). Finally, there are the other still-communist states of Viet Nam, Cambodia, Laos and the Democratic People's Republic of Korea (North Korea), all with largely centrally planned economies, but different degrees of openness to the world economy: Viet Nam leads the way along the path pioneered by China, while North Korea is still largely unreformed with very limited trade and foreign investment. So, to write of the 'Pacific Rim' as if it were an economically homogenous and politically meaningful region is doubly problematic. Not only does it refer entirely to the Asian side, it also includes within it Japan (with an annual gross national income—GNI—per head of US $32,710 in 2007, on an international purchasing power parity, PPP, basis), China (annual GNI per head on a PPP basis of $8,100 in 2007) and Laos ($2,300) with very different transpacific relationships and political-economic trajectories in each case. Nevertheless, the term has come into common usage in North America, not least because it draws attention to the emergence of the Pacific realm as a vital focus for US and Canadian national trade and security policies.

The current vision of a serious geopolitical challenge from China, based on systematic political-economic links between North America and the Pacific Rim, is driven by four factors. The first is the demographic heft of the Pacific Rim. Japan apart, with the world's most aged population because of hostility to immigration and low rate of natural increase, the Rim's ratio of dependants (those under 15 and over 65) to working-age population fell in 1965–2001 from 80% to 55%. By 2015 the ratio will reach a low of 49%, with many of the countries (e.g. Indonesia) much lower. By contrast, in North America the ratio will continue to rise as the population ages. This is Asia's 'demographic dividend'. Not only does it signal the development of a vast and vibrant labour force with lower expenses than those countries faced with ageing populations, such as the so-called 'baby boomer' generation in post-war USA, but it also augurs a massive expansion in consumption. US businesses see huge profits in both lowering production costs and capturing consumption by investing in the region. In 2003 China passed the USA as the world's major recipient of foreign direct investment (US $60,300m. in 2005). Unless China moves quickly beyond providing cheap economic inputs, however, other countries, such as India, are waiting in the wings to attract business as Chinese wage rates rise and the country starts to lose its primary competitive advantage. Much media hype about China's economy is still based on the promise of what China can become rather than what it has thus far achieved. Exports accounted for 40% of China's gross domestic product (GDP) in 2005, but since 2001 consumer demand has become an increasingly important part of total economic growth. If this continues, then China will truly become a motor of the world economy rather than simply an export 'platform' for richer countries.

The second factor is that the economic growth of the region is as yet based to a considerable extent on exports of manufactures to North America (and, to a degree, elsewhere). Trade across the Pacific is the most open and multilateral of all trade around the world, particularly that between China and the

NICs, on the one hand, and North America, on the other. There have been far fewer restraints on trade, for example, than characterized by North American-European trade. Transpacific trade represents perhaps the best example of the externally oriented economic growth that globalization images of the current world economy tend to celebrate.

A third factor is financial. The region has huge capital, as well as labour, surpluses. Not only are the Rim's savings rates extremely high (close to 40% of GDP in China), most countries have also run current account surpluses (mainly because of high trade surpluses) and thus accumulate US dollars. Asian central banks hold the world's largest foreign exchange reserves. Because regional capital markets (with the exception of Japan, Hong Kong and Singapore) are underdeveloped, many of the dollars end up back in the USA, where they currently fund about one-half of the huge US current account deficit (and, once again, through Treasury bonds, after three years of grace, the growing US federal government debt), but then return to Asia in the form of portfolio and foreign direct investment.

Fourth, and finally, although China and Japan are both potential geopolitical challengers to the USA, neither currently seems bent on converting its economic strength into posing a security threat to the USA on either side of the Pacific. Tensions between China and Taiwan (its so-called 'renegade province') declined significantly between 2006 and 2008, not least because of the defeat of Taiwan's ruling pro-independence party and President in the 2008 legislative and presidential elections. In addition, although China, Japan and South Korea have had different views from the US Administration of President George W. Bush (2001–) about how to deal with the military threat posed by North Korea, the Bush Administration has recently moved towards greater accommodation of their viewpoint and the strength of cross-Pacific economic ties is widely seen as limiting the potential for open conflict. Whether this might continue indefinitely, particularly in the face of US economic problems that were continuing during 2008 and a desire on the part of the Government of China to translate its economic growth (presumably one decreasingly reliant on US export markets) into increased global political influence, is another matter entirely. Rising nationalism in China, Japan and South Korea reflects both the end of the Cold War that cemented countries into a larger global conflict and the failure to resolve longstanding territorial and regional disputes over Korean reunification, Japanese 'guilt' over the Second World War and Taiwan's continuing conflict with mainland China. However this nationalism plays itself out, there are a number of reasons for thinking that the balance of power across the Pacific has begun to shift, to the detriment of the North American side.

CHINA'S CHALLENGE

Access to China's presumably gargantuan market has long been the prize most celebrated by the US idea of opening up China. As the seat of Asia's longest lasting and largest empire, China has always cast a spell over North Americans, both because of its potential economic capacity and the failure of the European colonial powers completely to redirect it to their ends. The goal of the US 'open door policy' initially articulated in the mid-19th century was always to make China available for US trade and investment. From 1949 until the 1970s, when there was something of a *rapprochement* between the Governments of China and the USA, this remained largely a hope rather than a realizable goal. Not surprisingly, given the longstanding animosity between the two countries after the Communist accession to power in China in 1949, China has also been regarded as a possible 'threat', or challenge, to US initiatives in Asia. Now a nuclear power with the world's largest population, China still can be portrayed in this light. Recurrent spying scandals in the USA and continuing disputes over the managed exchange rate of the Chinese yuan (renminbi) against the US dollar, the huge US trade deficit with China and the US Congress's rejection of the purchase of US corporate assets by Chinese state-owned companies suggest that China's possible emergence as a political competitor to the USA is very much still an element in transpacific perceptions. The two conceptions of China—as hope and as threat—remained in tension in the late 20th and early 21st century, with different US administrations implementing policies more in one direction and some pushing more in the other. The language of threat underwent something of a revival in the first year of the Bush Administration, in 2001, after years of military containment, but economic *rapprochement*, during the presidency of his predecessor, Bill Clinton (1993–2001). However, following the 11 September terrorist attacks, the Bush Administration essentially reversed its China policy. Terrorism was now seen as the USA's primary strategic threat. Indeed, China has become an ally in the global 'war on terror', notwithstanding Chinese opposition to US attempts to incorporate the war against the regime of Saddam Hussain in Iraq into that wider conflict.

In reality, therefore, the USA and Canada have mainly chosen to embrace China since US President Richard Nixon (1969–74) made his epochal trip to China in 1972. After the death of Mao Zedong, the historic leader of Chinese Communism, in 1976, China underwent rapid economic reform. Although Chinese national statistics on economic growth are unreliable, if some exaggerated claims are discounted, the pace of national economic growth since 1978 still has been truly remarkable. From 1978 to 2007 the country's GDP per head, measured on a PPP basis, increased by an average rate of 6.7% per year. Much of this growth has relied on three forces: a dramatic liberalization of government controls over agriculture and manufacturing industry; massive foreign direct investment; and export-oriented trade. Institutionally, the country remains dominated by the Communist Party and the People's Liberation Army, but economically, private entrepreneurship and a form of state-mandated capitalism have replaced central economic planning. By 2006 China accounted for about 12% of total world exports, from close to 0% in the mid-1970s, third globally behind the USA and Germany. Very quickly China has become the new 'workshop of the world', dominating entire sectors of manufacturing industry that used to be widely scattered around the industrialized world. This has led to charges that China (or, more accurately, multinational companies and their Chinese partners) have actively 'deindustrialized' many other countries, not least the USA. Thus, the world's largest retail chain of stores, Wal-Mart, increasingly relies on Chinese factories to supply many of its products and 80% of all toys sold in the USA in 2007 were manufactured in China. This dependence, however, is mutual. If the USA and Canada increasingly rely on China-based manufacturers, those suppliers are also subject to pressures when, for example, as in mid-2007, the safety of many foodstuffs and toys imported from China became a matter of concern in North America. The lack of enforcement of intellectual property rights and patent recognition in China has also long been a sore point among North American and European high tech, film, and media industries even, as industrial 'piracy', based on the absence of regulation, has boosted Chinese exports. Overall, export-based growth has turned China into a major consumer of imported raw materials (particularly petroleum and iron ore), further tying the country into the world economy. At the same time, of course, this also makes China a major competitor with the USA and others in the trade of world commodities, particularly as the Chinese Government prefers to enter into long-term contracts with suppliers (often such dubious regimes as those in Sudan and Zimbabwe), rather than rely on world markets. With the incorporation of Hong Kong into China in 1997 ('one nation, two systems'), China has also become a major financial power, with active stock markets, major banking assets and growing consumer finance (credit cards, etc.), not just in Hong Kong but in other cities too.

The currency, the yuan, however, remains largely convertible only on the current, not the capital, account (thus keeping out international hedge funds and other currency traders), which protected China from the worst effects of the Asian financial crisis of 1997–98, but which has also restricted attempts fully to open up China's capital markets. In 2007 some capital account convertibility was allowed through Hong Kong, but under close state supervision. Of all China's markets—labour, goods, services, capital—the last is the only one still mainly monopolized by the central government. The banking system has a major problem, with non-performing (unrepaid) loans estimated at US $900,000m. in 2006, more than the rest of Asia combined. Such a figure reflected the problems of state-owned industries being given loans to stem their losses and the shielding of banks from competition. Indeed, the lack of political and institutional reform to match economic development is increasingly seen as setting limits to the continuation of the current achievements of the Chinese economic 'miracle'. Recent efforts to reform the banking sector have involved using foreign exchange reserves to recapitalize banks in order to make them attractive partners for foreign investors and using government funds to pay off unpaid loans. Whether these efforts will succeed remains to be seen. Indeed, the drag of the state sector on the economy is still considerable. China's growth is obviously enormous, given the overall scale of the country, but it is by no means exceptional compared with other Asian countries. For example, during their most rapid periods of economic growth, Japan had an annual average growth rate of 8.2% (1950–73) and South Korea, in 1962–90, had an annual average rate of economic expansion of 7.6%. The rhetoric about China's 'incredible' growth is often well ahead of the reality—the average annual rate of economic growth between 1978 and 2007 was 6.7%.

This Chinese 'miracle', however, has had dramatic positive effects in raising the standard of living of at least a substantial minority of the population and in relaxing the draconian work camp character of the old Maoist economy. It also has a darker side. Overwhelmingly, the economic growth has been concentrated geographically in the coastal region and around Beijing. Linkages to Hong Kong and Taiwan (notwithstanding the state of war that nominally exists in the latter case and that was heightened by the approval in March 2005 of a Chinese law promising the use of force if Taiwan were formally to declare independent statehood) have prompted much of the growth of financial and production networks behind Chinese economic development. Taiwanese companies are the single largest foreign direct investors in China. Ironically, in this most centralized of polities, much of the economic growth has been stimulated at the periphery by external contacts. The net effect has been to neglect the interior, where many of the heavy industries and the state-owned sector tend to predominate in industrial employment. The sorry condition of many recent construction projects, particularly schools—as revealed in the aftermath of the earthquake in Sichuan in May 2008, when more than 1,000 schools were reportedly destroyed or damaged—is symptomatic of this neglect (and the massive corruption in the building sector). Agriculture has also been drained of investment and a vast rural to urban migration has produced urban sprawl and tenuous living conditions for many of those on the move. In the absence of much government regulation of the negative environmental effects of rapid industrialization, predictions of widespread environmental degradation and, even, collapse, have become increasingly common. High levels of air and water pollution have certainly led to more limited improvements in overall population health and life expectancy than recent rates of economic growth could lead one to expect. Preparations for the August 2008 Olympic Games included restrictions on vehicle usage and factory closures in order to improve, at least temporarily, the appalling air quality of the capital city.

Perhaps even more important than the frequent inefficiency and lack of vision of government, the relationship between state and market in China is also an unstable one. The continued political dominance of the Communist Party, along with the abandonment of its recognizably 'communist' policies, makes for a high degree of uncertainty about the enforcement of rules in the absence of anything like a rule of law and an independent judiciary. Many people in Hong Kong reasonably worry that in becoming a Special Administrative Region of China in 1997, Hong Kong abandoned an undemocratic but predictable British colonialism for a system inherently arbitrary and at the service of the 'communist' élite (a very Chinese communist-style version of 'crony capitalism'), rather than the mass of the population or those in favour of extending and guaranteeing basic human rights. Regulating the economy through administrative measures, such as rules, approvals and warnings, and not so much through monetary and fiscal policy, also seems to have led to a disconnection between planning, on the one hand, and the increasingly privatized economy, on the other. Thus, what can be called 'capitalist authoritarianism' appears inherently fragile. Not only is it subject to an internal legitimation crisis as the benefits of growth accumulate increasingly in fewer hands (as witnessed by the recent rapid rise of popular discontent in the form of strikes, demonstrations and riots), it is also vulnerable to external shocks that it is ill-equipped to handle institutionally, as China opens up increasingly to the world economy, as it must do having joined the WTO in 2001. This was manifested in the move, under pressure from the US Government, to loosen the yuan's 'peg' to the US dollar in July 2005. The continuing suppression of the demands of ethnic Tibetans for greater political autonomy and those of religious minorities for open recognition makes for difficult relationships with many other countries, not least Canada and many of the countries of the European Union (EU). All told, therefore, China is still some way from a stable or regularized relationship with the world economy in general, and the Pacific realm in particular.

THE JAPANESE RETREAT

In the 1980s Japan was widely viewed as the coming power in the world economy and in relation to the USA. However, the Japanese economic experience in the 1990s led to a reduction in expectations. If in the 1980s Japan was seen as the likely challenger to US global hegemony, by the mid-2000s this vision had all but disappeared. The US occupation of Japan after the Second World War, the pacifist Constitution the USA imposed and the frequently raw hostility of other Asians to the failure of Japan's post-War leaders to acknowledge the brutality of Japanese colonialism in Korea, China and elsewhere, all put significant restraints on the possibility of translating Japanese economic capacity into geopolitical clout. In 2005 the issue of new Japanese school history textbooks ignoring the brutality of Japan's occupation of China and Korea brought renewed attention throughout Asia to the stubborn resistance of powerful elements in Japan to rehabilitating the poor reputation of the country in much of the rest of the continent. At the same time, Japan is no longer seen even as much of an economic 'threat' by the USA, although complaints about Japanese 'protectionism' are still legion. However, this does not mean that its role in the Pacific realm is necessarily simply a benign one. Its recent economic woes could have widespread effects both regionally and globally. Although GDP growth recovered in 2002–07 following a 0.4% contraction in the economy in 2001 (the worst economic performance since the early 1950s), the net trend since 1990 has been lacklustre at best. Indeed, the Japanese economy has become the byword for stagnation, both with regard to overall economic performance and to the response of the Government to the malaise. Starting in inflated real estate, banking and finance sectors, deflation spread into the economy at large, draining vitality from a once vibrant and powerful economy. Of course, Japan remains the world's second largest economy, its high savings and relative underconsumption supporting the USA's low-savings, high-debt economy. Japanese goods are still highly valued in world markets and the national balance of payments remains in surplus. A reasonably robust recovery fuelled by the revival of exports, particularly in motor vehicles and electronics, seemed to be under way by 2006. In 2004 the annual economic growth rate had improved to 2.3%. Japanese manufacturing businesses have also undergone a major international expansion, integrating plants in Asia, Europe and North America into production chains that have their headquarters in Japan. In this respect, the Japanese economy is truly internationalized in ways that it was not only 20 years ago.

However, Japan is as yet the only major developed country since the Second World War to experience chronic deflation. Between 1989 and 2003 well over US $10,000,000m. was wiped off the national assets as real estate and stock prices collapsed, leading to an average annual increase in consumer prices of just 0.4% in 1990–2005. Unemployment has steadily increased as firms have either abandoned 'lifetime' employment or been forced out of business. Along with the dramatic increase in the number of retirees, as the population ages and finally using their savings for consumption, the increase in unemployment over the 1990s led to a steep decline in the rate of household saving. The root of the national economic problem lay in the country's private and public debt load arising from the collapse of real estate and finance. In the 1990s public debt increased by nearly 70% of GDP and the amount owed by businesses in trouble or actually bankrupt approached an additional 50% of GDP. What has made the problem less visible than it might otherwise have been is that the debt is mainly domestic, or owed within the country. This does not mean, however, that it can be solved any more easily than if the money was owed to foreign creditors. It does mean that the profligate USA may not be able to rely much longer on prudent Japanese savers, as those savers become spenders. What savings they had would plug the holes in the Japanese financial system before they become available for export across the Pacific. In addition, as the Japanese Government attempts to encourage exports by lowering the value of the yen against the US dollar, there is the danger of triggering competitive devaluations with neighbouring countries still recovering from the monetary crisis of 1997–98 and undermining economic growth in the region as a whole.

Why did this chronic deflation occur and why has nothing much seemingly been done about it? The two questions are not unrelated. Many of the banks' problem loans and much of the public sector debt, not to say the inflationary 'bubble' of real estate in the 1980s, can be traced to the political dominance of the so-called *doken kokka* or 'construction state'. This is the triangular relationship between the Ministry of Finance (in particular, its Trust Fund Bureau) and a major faction in the dominant political party (the Liberal-Democratic Party), the banks and the construction industry. The interests served are widely scattered geographically and not readily open to reform. Initially geared in post-War Japan to ensuring that sufficient funds were available to invest in infrastructure—highways, dams, bridges, city development, etc.—this system has taken on a life of its own, guaranteeing hefty returns to the interests involved, but effectively bankrupting the country in return. At the same time, the banks involved in funding many financially questionable construction projects have been protected from significant reform by the close political relationship they enjoyed with the dominant political party. So, nothing much can be done about Japan's major economic problem without changing the way Japan does politics. One positive sign in 2006 was the beginning of an attempt at breaking up and privatizing the state-owned post office, whose savings bank unit has been both a major source of funds for the Government and a vote-gathering machine for long-dominant factions of the Liberal-Democratic Party. That party has itself suffered recent setbacks, not least loss of control of the upper house of Parliament in 2007 to the political opposition. However, this reflected disaffection by rural voters concerned about attempts at reforming the public works economy more than a positive response to reform of an increasingly problematic national political economy. Whether this augurs a trend towards more democratic or more populist-nationalist politics is still entirely open to question. What is much clearer is that Japan's persistent deflation is no longer simply a domestic problem. It has major implications for the world economy as a whole, particularly given low levels of growth in Europe and the incredible increase in US current account and federal government deficits, beginning in 2002–03. Lowered Japanese growth and fewer Japanese savings means less is available to bail out other countries, particularly the greatest borrower of them all: the USA. Recent acrimony over the details of a bilateral trade pact between the USA and South Korea suggest that the relationship between the two countries will not quickly return to the seeming consensus characteristic of the Cold War period.

THE HERMIT KINGDOM AND THE 'ROGUE' STATE

The two parts of the Korean peninsula, once unified in the so-called 'Hermit Kingdom', have followed totally different trajectories over the past 50 years since the end of the Korean War in 1953. If the South has developed from an authoritarian capitalism towards a much more democratic one, the North has only deepened its isolation following the collapse of the USSR and the economic transformation of China, its erstwhile sponsors and supporters. Indeed, if, by the mid-1990s, South Korea had appeared to have graduated into the ranks of the developed world, North Korea has become so detached from the world economy that its Government must barter when it negotiates over the rewards it seeks in return for abandoning its programme for constructing long-range missiles with nuclear warheads. If South Korea is also the darling of the US financial press for its aggressive response to the 1997–98 financial crisis that threatened to destroy its economy, then North Korea is the quintessential 'rogue' state, an original member of President George W. Bush's 'axis of evil' along with Iraq and Iran, apparently determined to continue with its programme of developing and testing nuclear bombs to the dismay of most of the rest of the world. The Korean peninsula, therefore, contains within it two different challenges to a North American agenda in the Pacific Rim: a recovering South Korean economy with a more politically independent Government and a domestically, internationally and possibly militarily reckless, but undoubtedly economically feckless, North Korea

In 1997 South Korea came to the brink of national bankruptcy. Of all of the NICs (thus excluding Thailand, Indonesia and the Philippines, which were even more badly affected), it was South Korea that suffered the most from the so-called Asian financial crisis. Some Koreans have compared the magnitude of the economic shock of 1997–98 to the Korean War. Be this as it may, the depreciation of the currency, the won, highlighted the inefficiencies of the economy, particularly the proliferation of non-performing loans. This led to a rapid reform of the banking system and the sale of under-performing assets to both Korean and foreign interests. The relationship between the banks and the *chaebol*, or export-oriented conglomerates, has been transformed from all too comfortable to much more independent. Consumer credit and foreign direct investment have both expanded significantly. This dramatic change in economic policy demanded an equally revolutionary shift in politics. Under the leadership of Kim Dae-Jung (1998–2003) and his successor, Roh Moo-Hyun (2003–2008), South Korea's Government went from being a manager of corporate interests under the military thrall of the USA to an arbiter of various interests with a much more independent policy towards North Korea. This new attitude included instructing the military to prepare contingency plans for the possible withdrawal of US troops from the peninsula and entertaining the real possibility of reunification with the North. So, even as the South Korean Government successfully managed a serious economic crisis, it also embarked on a new foreign policy that caused more than a little consternation in US government circles.

At much the same time, North Korea has been sending conflicting messages about its military intentions towards the South, its other neighbours, and the USA. On the one hand, it has engaged in high-profile exchanges with South Korea, the USA and Japan, opening up debate over issues such as unification of families divided since the Korean War, establishing road and rail links with the South, sending athletes to sporting games in the South, enacting a series of economic reforms and admitting to the abductions of Japanese citizens in the 1970s and 1980s. On the other hand, the Government restarted its programme for making highly enriched uranium (and conducted a high-profile test of a nuclear bomb in October 2006) and has test-fired missiles provocatively into the Sea of Japan. Although fear of a pre-emptive attack, such as that of the USA against the Iraqi regime of Saddam Hussain in 2003, could well have been an incentive for recommencing a weapons programme that the North had promised to abandon in 1994, it was more likely that the goal was to gain some leverage in achieving recognition from the USA and acquiring access to food resources after a series of disastrous harvests and widespread famine and hunger in the country in the late 1990s. Although this approach did not initially elicit a very positive response from the US Administration, in mid-2003, partly because of worries about the increasing division between the USA and South Korea over how to deal with the North, the US Government agreed to attempt to negotiate a possible resolution through six-party talks (the two Koreas, Russia, China, the USA and Japan), brokered primarily by China and South Korea. In August 2004 the Bush Administration appeared, however, to contradict its 'carrot and stick' approach to North Korea by announcing that a major element of the 'stick', the US army units stationed in South Korea, would be removed, under a planned redeployment of US forces around the world. Renewed talks over North Korea's nuclear weapons programme began in mid-2005 and by mid-2007 brought agreement from North Korea to denuclearize militarily in response to a set of US commitments to remove sanctions and help with the development of civilian nuclear power. Since then an agreement to destroy the plant that produces weapon-grade uranium has been struck. A meeting between US Secretary of State Condoleezza Rice and her North Koraen counterpart in July 2008 perhaps signalled an imminent 'normalization' of diplomatic relations. Explicitly, therefore, after years of refusal to do so, the Bush Administration has recognized the legitimacy of the North Korean regime, and retreated from the confrontational policy associated with its previous 'axis of evil' rhetoric.

TIGERS LOSING THEIR STRIPES?

If, since the 1990s, China has been the wonder economy of Asia, in the 1980s it had been the NICs, particularly South Korea, Taiwan, Singapore and Hong Kong; however, other developing economies, such as Thailand, Malaysia, Indonesia and the Philippines, had also attracted admiration. Although initially associated with labour-intensive production for export in manufacturing sectors such as clothing, shoes, consumer durables and electronic assembly, by the late 1980s the original NICs had made a transition to greater involvement in services, particularly in banking and finance, and were on the threshold of admission to the 'club' of the world's most developed countries. For example, Taiwan had a standard of living higher than that of Greece or Portugal and South Korea had a diversified economy on a par with any in the world. Success was based, depending on which theorist one preferred, on protection of infant industries, government allocation of credit, openness to the world economy, quiescent industrial relations as a result of traditions of filial piety and assorted Confucian traditions conducive to accepting social hierarchies, and existing infrastructure developed under colonialism. Whatever the precise source of their rapid growth, the NICs delivered a blow to much conventional wisdom about economic development. They challenged the so-called radical view that economic development outside a limited 'core' of the world economy was impossible because of built-in structural dependency. They also suggested that some regions (and cultural and environmental contexts) are more conducive to development than others, thus challenging the agnosticism of conventional economists about such factors.

In 1997–98 these economies faced their most serious test to date. All open economies with fully convertible currencies under floating exchange rates are vulnerable to speculative pressures if, in the judgement of holders of the currency (including investors in banks and stocks), the economy is likely to see reversals in profitability in the near future. In the absence of capital controls, holders of the currency will convert their holdings into safer or 'harder' currencies and thus stimulate a run on the currency as its value falls against these harder currencies. This, in turn, stimulates a withdrawal of foreign investment and a flight of capital. The Asian crisis began with a run on the Thai baht in July 1997. This was followed by similar crises throughout the region. Only China, with a currency fixed against the US dollar and with capital controls in place, Taiwan with vast US dollar reserves and a strong presence in a still-growing US information technology and telecommunications economy, and Hong Kong, because of its role as a financial centre, managed to avoid the worst of the crisis. Thailand, Malaysia, Indonesia, the Philippines, South Korea and Singapore were all affected, with South Korea and Indonesia suffering the most. The extent to which each economy suffered depended on the robustness of the country's financial system, particularly the debt ratios of major banks, the transparency of bank operations, and the profitability of economies that relied mostly on the efficient use of the factors of production (particularly labour) rather than on their own technological innovation. Behind the deepening crisis lay the failure of global institutions such as the IMF to identify and treat what was wrong (inflation and spending on welfare services were definitely not the problems even though that tended to be the assumption of the European and US liberal economists who ran the IMF). Other factors behind the crisis, just as important, were the 'crony capitalism' that led state and private banks to lend too easily to companies with close ties to the state and to the relatives of presidents, and the positions of foreign governments, particularly that of the USA, which failed to note how the absence of capital controls and other governmental levers had exacerbated the crisis.

That this was entirely an 'Asian' crisis is clearly doubtful. Much of the withdrawn investment emanated from well beyond Asia. Many of the actors involved likewise could be thought of as living locally, but acting globally. It is only 'Asian' to the extent that the crisis began in Asia and many of its most negative effects were concentrated there. Even then, there were important exceptions, as noted previously. In responding to the crisis, Governments followed different strategies, mainly involving how to deal with large numbers of bad loans. In South Korea, an aggressive 'fire sale' of bad loans allowed for a rapid and fairly robust recovery. In Indonesia, to take the opposite pole of response, little progress was made in dealing with the politicized loan-making that originally caused the problems. Large segments of the economy were simply nationalized, but the non-performing assets did not improve their performance. Of course, Indonesia was also adversely affected by a number of distinctive political problems: from separatism in New Guinea and Sumatra, to the rise of a militant Islamist faction. Governments also adopted distinctive ways of articulating the nature of the crisis and why it struck. In Malaysia, for example, the then Prime Minister, Dr Mahathir bin Mohamad, tended to portray the crisis as part of a continuing struggle with colonialism, even though since independence from British rule in the 1960s Malaysia chose to participate in global capitalism in its own way. It was not simply imposed. Mahathir's policy of introducing capital controls in response to the crisis suggests that the discursive reaction is not entirely rhetorical. In Singapore, by way of contrast, leading politicians presented the crisis as an 'earthquake' or 'typhoon'. In other words, it was a force of nature that could not be prevented, only survived. Not surprisingly, Singapore's dominant self-representation is as a seat of global capitalism, not as one of its victims. Although the worst of the crisis had passed by 2003, the memory of its dramatic effects had become part of the psyche of the region. If it raised doubts about the virtues of untrammelled economic openness and the power asymmetry of the Pacific realm with the US Government and the IMF as unhelpful taskmasters, it has not thus far kindled anything like a singular response in terms of inward-biased economic management, or a turning away from the path of export-based economic development. The Malaysian decision of 21 July 2005 immediately to follow the Chinese Government in switching from a US dollar 'peg' to a managed 'float' against a basket of currencies perhaps indicates the degree to which China, rather than the USA or the IMF, was becoming a new macroeconomic bellwether for the region.

A REVERSAL OF THE CHALLENGE ACROSS THE PACIFIC?

By 2008 transpacific relations had recovered from the crisis of 1997–98, although not without continuing, if lessening, uncertainties with respect to North Korea, Chinese conflict with Taiwan (and the US and Japanese commitment to supporting Taiwan in the event of Chinese attack) and the ability of US consumer demand to stimulate export-based growth in the Pacific Rim. However, North Korea certainly does not seem to have generated the irrational irritation within the US Government that Iraq did, perhaps because of the sobering fact that North Korea has proved that it does, in fact, have weapons of mass destruction, although it currently appears to lack the means to deploy them internationally. Notwithstanding Chinese sabre-rattling and US military hawks' dire predictions about the threat of imminent invasion from the mainland,

Taiwan was increasingly marginalized internationally and yet also increasingly integrated with the mainland's economy. Direct airline flights to and from the mainland began in 2008. With the exception of the Philippines and Indonesia, export growth had also largely recovered across the region. The only blots on this cheery scenario were the diminished, if slowly recovering, economic vitality of Japan and the rise of an assertive China, less willing than Japan has been to follow US direction. However, even here the reliance of China on US export markets, the linkage of the yuan (and many other Asian currencies, albeit reduced after July 2005 with the move to a basket of currencies for setting its exchange rate) to the US dollar and the heavy dependence of Chinese economic growth on foreign direct investment (from Taiwan, the USA, the ethnic Chinese diaspora and Japan) limited the possibilities of independent action. Without doubt, China can be often seriously overrated as both an economic and a political actor at the global level. At least during the darkest days of the Cold War, when Maoism reigned in China, the country was, as the late Gerald Segal (see Select Bibliography) once put it, 'a beacon for many in the developing world. China now is a beacon for no one, and, indeed, an ally to no one. No other supposedly great power is as bereft of friends.' The Chinese Government's recent cultivation of governments in resource-rich African countries such as Zimbabwe and the Sudan, and its resistance to US attempts at trying to isolate such governments because of their fixing of elections or sponsorship of either genocide or terrorism could suggest a somewhat more malignant form of Segal's standard. Whatever this signifies for the long term, however, the Chinese challenge would seem set to continue much as it is at present for some time, with US governments irritated at their inability to persuade the Chinese Government into a significant devaluation of the yuan against the US dollar, but without, because of their dependence on Chinese (and Japanese) central bank financing to finance the US federal deficit, having much leverage to coerce them into doing so. If China is not yet a global power, then the USA shows increasing signs of being a fading one, at least in relation to its economic relationship with East Asia, even if the stocks and flows of trade and investment continue much as they were.

From a second viewpoint, however, the recent past may augur a more profound adjustment in relations across the Pacific, at least as seen from the USA's perspective. Two trends suggest a possible fundamental shift in the economic and political orientation of the Pacific Rim. First, although the USA is still a major exporter to all parts of the developed world, it has increasingly abandoned its adherence to the global trade system symbolized by the WTO. In sponsoring a range of regional trading blocs and bilateral deals, from the North American Free Trade Agreement to the now-stalled Free Trade Area of the Americas, recent US administrations have invited a response in like terms. As a result, the Asia-Pacific region, long the stronghold of the most open trade globally, was heading towards a fracture between its western and eastern halves. For example, China was actively pursuing the goal of free trade areas in South-East and North-East Asia. As a direct response, Japan has announced an end to its commitment to multilateral trade. Indeed, China and Japan seem set to co-operate increasingly at the expense of the USA whatever their differences over the history of Japanese colonialism in China. This is partly a reaction to recent US trade and financial policies. However, it is also a result of the significant increase in overall Chinese-Japanese trade, as the trade of both with the USA (except for China's exports to the USA) declines in relative terms. Between 1996 and 2003, for example, Japan's imports from the USA declined from US \$75,408m. to about \$59,995m., while imports from China increased from \$32,922m. to \$75,469m. By 2005 21% of Japan's imports were from China, compared with only 12.4% from the USA.

This 'Asian Fusion', as the economist Fred Bergsten (see Select Bibliography) calls it, is not restricted to China and Japan. Most of the countries in the Pacific Rim have been reorienting their trade relations towards increased intraregional ties at the expense of transpacific ones in the aftermath of the 1997–98 crisis. Japan's response to the crisis had been to propose active financial intervention through a massive loan to the worst affected countries. Vetoed by the then US Secretary of the Treasury, Lawrence Summers, this positive, if ultimately abortive, response by Japan has brought about a profound rethinking in the Asia-Pacific region about the relative weight to place on the USA and Japan as responsible partners in trade and financial policy. Thus, along with the development of the EU, moves towards a regional economic bloc in the Asia-Pacific region seem to portend a multipolarization of the world economy. Even if this trend delivers something rather less institutionalized than the EU, and the central role of family business networks and multilayered subcontracting as the agents of regional economic integration strongly suggest so, its advent does not augur well for the North American position in the Pacific Rim.

Second, the groundwork for the current relationship across the Pacific was carried out during the Cold War, with many of the trade, financial and diplomatic links across the Pacific underwritten by US military security guarantees in the face of the Soviet 'threat'. However, the Cold War also divided what had long been a Chinese-centred geopolitical region, with China and some other states marginalized by the USA and some firmly supported by it. With the end of the Cold War, the US security guarantees no longer make much sense and the geopolitical division within the region is rapidly receding. Indeed, from one point of view, a relatively benign Chinese hegemony is returning to the region, with many of its neighbouring states (save for Japan and Taiwan) largely accommodating of this development. Consequently, the political leverage of the USA in the Pacific Rim is now much less than it once was, notwithstanding the absolute superiority in military power that the USA now has at a world scale. What remains to be seen is whether governments in the region can successfully manage the range of problems they face in such a way that they do not remain hostages to fortune in the way they were during the economic crisis of 1997–98.

On balance, therefore, the challenge from China in particular and the Pacific Rim more generally to the longstanding North American ascendancy across the Pacific appears to be building. Relative power and economic interdependence both point this way, even if each counsels a different response from the other side of the ocean. Quite what will happen, however, depends as much on how ideas about China's global role evolve inside China as on projecting forward current economic and political trends. Ironically, the most negative scenarios of the rise of a more hostile China are more the result of a shift in US government policy than of any current challenge from China or other Asian countries to US pre-eminence in the Pacific Rim. US governments have become increasingly unilateral in their behaviour within a global system largely built on multilateral initiatives and institutions. The genius of that system, in terms of US hegemony, was to rely on at least the appearance of shared governance, connivance and mutual benefit. Indeed, the nature of the ties within the Pacific realm is a monument to the success of that endeavour. However, beginning with the Viet Nam War in the 1960s and US abrogation of the Bretton Woods Agreement in 1971, and accelerating with the end of the Cold War in the late 1980s and the US declaration of the global 'war on terror' in 2001, US governments have attempted to solve their domestic and foreign policy problems by increasing recourse to heavy-handed and unilateral monetary, fiscal and military measures. Although this may well maintain the illusion of US hegemony, that hegemony will be increasingly hollow if ultimately all it does is undermine the very political-economic system that the USA had previously succeeded in building across the Pacific. Confronting China directly does not really respond to a Chinese challenge that in actuality results from the peculiar conditions (labelled with the term 'authoritarian capitalism') under which China opened up to the world economy, conditions that work against the pro-US geopolitical 'one-way street' that the opening up of China was originally supposed to entail. As contemporary China shows, hegemony can have ironic outcomes when the hegemon forgets why its hegemony worked in the first place.

SELECT BIBLIOGRAPHY

Agnew, J. A. *Hegemony: The New Shape of Global Power*. Philadelphia, PA, Temple University Press, 2005.

Bergsten, C. F. 'America's Two-Front Economic Conflict', in *Foreign Affairs*, March/April, pp. 16–27, 2001.

Bowles, P., and Wang, B. 'Flowers and Criticism: The Political Economy of the Renminbi Debate', in *Review of International Political Economy*, 13/2, pp. 233–57, 2006.

Curtis, G. L. *The Logic of Japanese Politics: Leaders, Institutions, and the Limits of Change.* New York, NY, Columbia University Press, 1999.

Dickson, B. J. *Red Capitalists in China: The Party, Private Entrepreneurs, and Prospects for Political Change*. New York, NY, Cambridge University Press, 2004.

Economy, E. C. 'The Great Leap Backward?', in *Foreign Affairs*, September/October, pp. 38–59, 2007.

Gat, A. 'The Return of Authoritarian Great Powers', in *Foreign Affairs*, July/August, pp. 59–69, 2007.

Goldstein, M. and Lardy, N. R. (Eds). *Debating China's Exchange Rate Policy*. Washington, DC, Peterson Instiute for International Economics, 2008.

Kurlantzick, J. *Charm Offensive: How China's Soft Power is Transforming the World*. New Haven, CT, Yale University Press, 2008.

Lampton, D. M. *Same Bed, Different Dreams: Managing US–China Relations, 1989–2000*. Berkeley and Los Angeles, CA, University of California Press, 2001.

Legro, J. W. 'What China Will Want: The Future Intentions of a Rising Power', in *Perspectives in Politics*, 5/3, pp. 515–35, 2007.

McGregor, R. 'Renminbi Revaluation: Aim is to Allow Greater Flexibility While Still Keeping Firm Control', in *Financial Times*, 22 July 2005.

Overholt, W. H. *Asia, America, and the Transformation of Geopolitics*. New York, NY, Cambridge University Press, 2007.

Pei, M. *China's Trapped Transition: The Limits of Developmental Autocracy*. Cambridge, MA, Harvard University Press, 2006.

Sakakibara, E. *Structural Reform in Japan: Breaking the Iron Triangle*. Washington, DC, Brookings Institution Press, 2003.

Segal, G. 'Does China Matter?', in *Foreign Affairs*, 78/5, September/October, pp. 24–36, 1999.

IMMIGRATION AND NATION BUILDING: POLICY AND PRACTICE IN THE USA AND CANADA

GEOFFREY MERCER

The USA and Canada have been two of the world's largest immigrant 'receiving' countries for more than 150 years. This has been crucial to each country's nation-building. Policy decisions about the desired number and characteristics of newcomers have been influenced by economic and political interests, population targets and preferred socio-cultural identity. Over the period since the end of the Second World War international migration, fuelled by major refugee crises, escalated to historically high levels. Furthermore, in the 1960s both countries began to dismantle their discriminatory, Eurocentric admission policies, leading to a substantial rise in the proportion of immigrants from countries in Asia and Latin America. These trends attracted growing public and media discussion about the 'costs' as well as the 'benefits' of contemporary immigration and the 'new' immigrants to the host society. Governments intensified efforts to identify more efficient and effective ways to manage the admissions process, amid concerns about 'unauthorized' immigration and the rising international competition for individuals with specific skills, associated latterly with the shift to a 'knowledge-based' economy. Additionally, the terrorist attacks of 11 September 2001 on the USA projected national security issues to centre-stage in debates on immigration policy and practice.

HISTORICAL TRENDS

The flow of immigrants into the USA developed rapidly in the first half of the 19th century, whereas total arrivals to Canada at its Confederation in 1867 were modest in comparison. The scale and character of migration reflected conditions in the 'sending' countries, as well as the demand and opportunities within the 'receiving' nations. In the second half of the 19th century governments and key economic interests across Europe generally encouraged emigration among their 'surplus' masses. At the same time the agricultural and business sectors in North America actively sought cheap labour and homesteaders, with a widespread assumption that national economic growth depended on an expanding population and domestic markets. These factors sustained an upward decennial trend, while allowing for annual fluctuations, with striking rises in the 1880s and, most dramatically of all, through the early years of the 20th century. Over 13m. people entered the USA between 1900 and 1914, with a high point of 1,285,349 in 1907, when the overall population was almost 90m. In the same period immigration to Canada also increased significantly, to almost 3m., peaking at 400,870 entrants in 1913. Given that its entire population was little more than 7m., this constituted a much higher per-head immigrant rate than in the USA.

The onset of the First World War brought a sharp decline in immigration. Admissions to Canada fell from 150,484 in 1914 to 33,665 in the following year, and those entering the USA dropped from 1.2m. to 326,700. As economic conditions improved in the 1920s, so numbers increased again, if unevenly, with 164,993 immigrants admitted to Canada in 1929, and 279,678 to the USA. However, the Depression of the 1930s and the outbreak of the Second World War resulted in migration plummeting to its lowest point since the early 19th century. In 1942 there were only 7,596 immigrants to Canada, while entrants to the USA reached a low point of 23,725 in 1943. Conversely, emigration grew to such an extent that there was actually a net outflow of people from both countries.

After 1945 there was a return to higher immigration, with mounting optimism about economic recovery and renewed enthusiasm among Europeans to migrate. Between 1946 and 1959 annual totals averaged 222,440 to the USA and 135,794 to Canada. During the 1960s the average annual movement of documented (legal) immigrants to the USA rose to 330,000, and continued upwards to 440,000 in the 1970s, 730,000 in the 1980s, 900,000 in the 1990s, and more than 1m. in the first decade of the 21st century. The total intake of immigrants to the USA was 33.6m. between 1946 and 2007. In comparison, 10.1m. immigrants entered Canada during these years, with a much later surge in the decennial average: 141,000 in the 1960s, 144,000 in the 1970s, 133,000 in the 1980s, then jumping to 221,000 in the 1990s and moving on to 239,000 in the first decade of the 21st century (as measured before 2008). Annual admissions reflected prevailing economic conditions at least until the mid-1980s, when a longer-term view of immigration aims and population growth gained the ascendancy. Census data indicated that immigrant numbers in Canada grew from 15% of the total population to 19% between 1951 and 2006. In contrast, the USA's foreign-born inhabitants declined from 15% in 1910 to less than 5% by 1970, before climbing back to 12.5% in 2006.

REDUCING DISCRIMINATORY BARRIERS

Historically, this increase in immigration to North America was complemented by an openly discriminatory admissions policy. The USA introduced a series of restrictive measures from the mid-1870s that excluded entrants on racial, political, moral, medical and educational grounds. These culminated in the draconian 'Quota Acts' during the 1920s, which imposed an annual cap on immigration from non-Western countries and instituted a preference system based on their proportion within the US population. This ensured a prolonged European dominance, even if the early preponderance of migrants from Germany, the United Kingdom and Ireland gave way to those from Italy, Austria-Hungary and Russia, with Germany and the United Kingdom re-emerging as important sources after the Second World War. Besides this, around 2m. people migrated across the border from Canada to the USA in the first four decades of the 20th century, while a portent of subsequent trends was the appearance of Mexico among the foremost countries of origin in the 1920s.

An equally marked preference for European 'immigrant stock' underscored the Canadian policy prejudice against other nationalities well into the 20th century. The Immigration Act 1952 reinforced the discretionary powers vested in government ministers and officials to admit displaced persons and refugees, and the beneficiaries were overwhelmingly from Europe. The broad intention was that policies should encourage economic development and a rise in population without awakening public anxieties that migration would undermine the country's traditional way of life, 'ethnic' balance and absorptive capacity.

Then, in the early 1960s, the international context started to change appreciably. Poorer, often newly independent, states increasingly challenged global economic and political inequalities and the lack of positive action by richer, industrialized Western countries. A series of civil conflicts and natural disasters in Asia, Africa and Latin America emphasized the barriers to population movement. Within North America, the demand for migrants persisted at the same time as minority ethnic groups campaigned fiercely against discrimination and for their civil rights. The outcome was growing pressure on governments to dismantle their racist immigration policies.

Canada was the first of the large immigrant receiving countries to start overturning its selection procedures in 1962, but formulation of an alternative system was delayed until the appearance of the 1967 Immigration Regulations. These identified three 'classes' of immigrant: independent applicants, sponsored dependants and nominated relatives. Unlike its southern neighbour, Canada introduced a points system for selecting independent class members. Successful applicants had to achieve a minimum score based on education and skills, occupation, existence of prearranged employment, personal characteristics, age and fluency in English or French. Individuals qualifying for the new hybrid category of 'nominated relatives' were also expected to satisfy the 'meritocratic' criteria. Nevertheless, there was continuing criticism of the lack of legal scrutiny of the selection process and the Government responded by setting up the Immigration Appeal Board in 1969.

These alterations paved the way for a new Immigration Act in 1976. It stressed the social, economic and humanitarian dimensions of immigration policy by differentiating three new categories of immigrant: family class, comprising the immediate family and dependent children of a Canadian citizen or permanent resident sponsor; independent or economic class, chosen via the points system (and, from 1982, 'assisted relatives' sponsored by a family member in Canada); and refugees, defined in line with the 1951 UN Refugee Convention, plus other 'designated classes' authorized in times of crisis. The Act amended the points formula without entirely removing the discretion granted to the minister and officials in administering immigration regulations and procedures. Extra government assistance was promised to facilitate the settlement of new entrants.

The USA's response to charges of selection bias was contained in the Immigration and Nationality Act (INA) 1965. This represented a major policy shift, replacing the inequitable national quotas on immigrants with a 'first come, first served' approach. The INA outlined an expansionary programme, with a 'permeable cap' of 290,000 immigrants (visas issued) each year and a ceiling of 20,000 from any single country. The overall figure applied to two 'preference' groups: family members (spouses, children, parents and siblings) of US citizens or US permanent residents; and individuals with desired labour market skills and training. The family reunification category comprised about 80% of the total. The INA also recognized two classes outside the numerical limits: immediate relatives of US citizens; and a second, miscellaneous group. As with Canadian legislation, it confirmed other entrenched grounds for refusing entry such as: ill-health, if it led to 'excessive' demands on health or social services; inadequate means of support; and involvement in criminal activity or terrorism.

BALANCING EXPANSION AND REGULATION

The expansionary course contained in the INA was not without its critics, with congressional inquiries into the level and composition of inflows, chiefly in respect of refugees, and the large number of undocumented (illegal) immigrants. A new Immigration Act in 1990 substantially raised immigrant targets to a (permeable cap) maximum of 675,000, bringing it more in line with current practice. Within this annual ceiling, family-sponsored preferences were set at 480,000 (71%) and employment-based preferences at 140,000 (21%). The remaining 55,000 (8%) places went to a new category of 'diversity immigrants', with successful applicants drawn on a random basis from a postal lottery. Only nationals of countries with fewer than 50,000 numerically limited admissions over the previous five years were eligible, although 5,000 diversity visas were transferred to the Nicaraguan Adjustment and Central American Relief Act programme in 1999. Besides this, single country limits for family-sponsored and employment preference immigrants were set at 7% of total immigration, with dependent areas limited to a 2% maximum.

The 1990 Act also broadened the list of categories exempt from the numerical limit on preference and diversity visas to encompass: immediate relatives of US citizens; refugees (aliens unable to return to their own country for fear of persecution) and 'asylees' (who make an asylum claim on arrival in the USA); certain parolees (aliens permitted entry on urgent humanitarian grounds or because of 'significant public benefit') from the USSR and Indo-China; cancellation of removal cases; and undocumented migrants whose status was adjusted under the 1986 Immigration Reform and Control Act. From 1990 most newcomers were classified as immediate relatives and family preference. In 2007, of the 1,052,415 individuals who became legal residents, 66% were located in one of the two family reunification groups (compared with 63% in 2005), 15% were employment preference (13% in 2005), 13% were refugees and asylum seekers (17% in 2005) and 4% (similar to 2005) fell into the 'diversity' category.

In Canada, policy-makers shifted their priorities more directly in response to immediate economic conditions and the country's perceived 'absorptive capacity'. Thus, the 1982 Immigration Report stressed that rising unemployment and the need to protect 'jobs for Canadians' justified restrictions. Annual targets were lowered and regulations altered to limit entry to those with prearranged, approved employment, with parallel adjustments to the points system. As a result, admissions fell to 84,335 in 1985, their lowest level for 40 years. Yet, following signs of an economic recovery, entrants almost doubled to 161,537 in 1988, with the Government praising 'the significant contribution immigrants make to Canada's economic well-being by giving impetus to capital expansion, job creation for Canadians and consumer demand for Canadian goods and services'. This was reinforced by a commitment to raise annual immigration to 1% of the total population (equivalent to 310,000 admissions in 2001) to counter the predicted long-term consequences of a reduced birth rate. In practice, successive governments favoured more modest expansion (in the range of 0.6%–0.7% of the overall population in 1996–2001), on the grounds that anything larger would outrun the country's ability to 'absorb and settle immigrants'. All the same, current immigration by the mid-2000s comprised around 60% of the national population increase, only slightly below the US figure.

Again, Canada's selection criteria, reinforced by the 1993 Immigration Act, became much more focused on recruiting individuals with desired labour market experience and qualifications. The proportion of 'economic/independent class' immigrants grew from 30% in 1976 to 61% in 2001, but dropped back to 55% in 2007, while over the same period the family class proportion nose-dived from 62% to 28%. The Immigration and Refugee Protection Act of 2001 reinforced the labour market priority by accentuating an applicant's flexible/transferable skills. In more humanitarian mode, it removed the option to deny entry on the grounds of ill health and the likely high cost to the health care system. Family class membership was widened and encouragement given to those who had entered on temporary visas to transfer to permanent resident status once they had demonstrated their capacity to integrate economically, as with the Live-in-Caregiver Programme that allowed applications for permanent status after two years' residence.

A notable development since the 1980s was the heightened international competition for immigrants with business skills and capital. Canada allocated places for wealthy entrepreneurs and investors (and their families) promising to create 10 full-time jobs by investing C $1m., or $500,000 if moving to a high unemployment area. In the USA, the 1990 Immigration Act revised the 'employment based' category to target similar individuals. The terms of the Canadian scheme were modified several times during the 1990s to create a lower tier of investment or job creation target. Data on the 7,593 investors granted entry before 1992 indicated that they had brought in $1,500m., with a sizeable share going to disadvantaged regions. In 2007 only 581 'entrepreneurs' were admitted, compared with 1,609 in 2001, whereas the recruitment of 'investors' was above the 2001 admissions figure: 2,024, compared with 1,767.

Another issue confronting both countries was how to determine the appropriate balance between federal and state/provincial powers and responsibilities for immigration. In the USA, the long-term trend was to reduce local 'excesses' and inconsistencies in implementing immigration policies. However, in the last quarter of the 20th century, continuing centralization was challenged by state and local interests arguing for an enhanced say (and financial aid) in respect to immigrants. In Canada, the 1976 Immigration Act set out new arrangements for the planning, management and monitoring of immigration policy, and publication of an annual report with target numbers. It required consultation on immigration plans and stressed provincial participation. This was crucial to Québec, where control over immigration was regarded as necessary to maintain its distinctive political, economic and cultural position vis-à-vis the rest of the country. In 1978 a federal-provincial accord granted Québec its own, discretionary, points-based system for choosing immigrants, but within national targets set by the federal Government—an extended arrangement was agreed in 1991. Immigration was permitted to rise to 5% above its proportion of the Canadian population, although, in the short term, entry in Québec was held down because of public unease in the province. The scope of federal funding was expanded to the organization and delivery of linguistic and cultural integration programmes. A new category of 'Provincial/Territorial Nominees' was introduced in 1996 to prioritize regional needs, such as labour market shortages. Despite apprehension about the potential for 'selection wars' between provinces, the government target of 1,400 immigrants in 2001 soared, with actual admissions (including family members) rising quickly from 477 to 17,095 between 1999 and 2007.

Amid wider political demands to contain public expenditure, attempts were made to recoup some of the costs of administering immigration with a large hike in the fee for processing applications. Other measures lengthened the financial obligations of those supporting immigrants (to 10 years in the USA) and made these legally enforceable. The US Illegal Immigration Reform and Immigrant Responsibility Act 1996 also required that the sponsor's household income was at least 125% over the poverty line and added to that of the immigrant when determining welfare eligibility. The ongoing criticism of the delays and abuses in processing immigrants generated many instances of administrative 'fine tuning'. For instance, in Canada, the 1993 Immigration Act outlined three 'streams', with different limits on applications and the time for processing applications. It moved towards longer-term planning in 1990 by introducing five-year immigration plans—an approach amplified in the 2001 Immigration and Refugee Protection Act, which consolidated the multi-year planning cycle system, along with a new system for processing refugees.

A major and distinctive preoccupation of US policy became the scale of undocumented immigration, both unauthorized entrants and temporary visitors who overstayed, with Census estimates in 2000 that there were about 7m. unauthorized immigrants. Most attention focused on Mexicans crossing the permeable southern border, often providing a crucial source of cheap labour, mainly in agriculture in the south-western states. The first notable legislative response was the Immigration Reform and Control Act (IRCA) in 1986. It allowed undocumented immigrants to transfer to permanent resident status if they had lived in the USA for five years, or worked in 'perishable' agriculture for at least 90 days. Over 2.6m. unauthorized workers took advantage of these provisions between 1989 and 1992. At the same time the onus was placed on employers to confirm the citizenship or work eligibility of employees, with penalties introduced for those who hired undocumented migrants. A still more robust border enforcement strategy was launched in the early 1990s, leading to the Illegal Immigration Reform and Immigrant Responsibility Act 1996, bolstered by much higher federal funding for the Immigration and Naturalization Service (INS). Even so, recent calculations indicated a continuing high annual average of 800,000 unauthorized immigrants between 2002 and 2006.

CONSTRUCTING A REFUGEE POLICY

In the immediate post-1945 years both countries espoused a humanitarian approach towards refugees, albeit constrained by pragmatic domestic and foreign policy interests. Action was mostly reactive to acute crises, with large quantities of displaced persons and refugees admitted from the USSR and Eastern Europe.

Canada played an important part in the UN Convention to regulate the legal status of refuges in 1951, though it was not until 1969 that it signed the Geneva Convention and Protocol on the Status of Refugees, primarily because it regarded itself as a country of resettlement rather first asylum. The 1976 Immigration Act finally conferred a separate administrative status on refugees and lengthened the UN Convention eligibility criteria to cover specific 'Designated Classes'. Initially, these spotlighted Indo-China, 'Latin American Political Prisoners and Oppressed Persons' and 'East-European Self-Exiled Persons'. Other countries were incorporated later and special programmes introduced for people displaced by social conflicts and natural disasters. In an attempt to allow more administrative flexibility, the Designated Classes were replaced in 1997 by two new categories: country of asylum (where the claimant is not in their home country); and country of source.

The original intention was that most refugees would be selected abroad with set quotas, but the size and complexity of international migration frustrated hopes of an ordered processing system. Revised regulations in 1978 incorporated a refugee sponsorship plan that was immediately tested by the large exodus of refugees at the end of the Viet Nam war. The scheme called for a greater participation by the voluntary sector and the general public. A refugee family could be assisted by a group of five or more Canadian citizens or permanent residents, who were over 18 years old and lived in 'the expected community of settlement', or by eligible corporations. The sponsoring group had to give a written undertaking to support the refugee and accompanying dependants for one year. More generally, the system proved inadequate to cope with the unexpected growth in people claiming refugee status on arrival in Canada, and only an administrative review in 1986 reduced the huge backlog by awarding landed status to over 26,000 applicants. Thereafter, changes were introduced to accelerate the processing of applications, penalize those assisting illegal immigrants and strengthen deportation procedures.

Attempts to emphasize 'front-end screening' practices, including a 'safe third country' provision that would deny asylum for anyone travelling to Canada through a country with a good human rights record, foundered because of a lack of agreement on a list of 'safe' countries (notably whether this should contain the USA). At the same time legal appeals escalated, particularly after the Supreme Court decided that refugee claimants were covered by the Canadian Charter of Rights and Freedoms. Due process concerns resulted in the Immigration and Refugee Board (IRB) assuming responsibility for appeals in 1988. The Immigration and Refugee Protection Act 2001 reiterated the humanitarian dimension to refugee policy and stressed measures to accelerate decision-making on applications and faster referrals to the IRB. It also endorsed stricter controls towards those deemed a threat to national security.

Relative to its size, Canada developed one of the world's largest refugee programmes, with an annual average of 24,000 entrants from the 1980s, but noteworthy for periodic, large-scale movements—Ugandan Asians in the 1960s, Vietnamese in the mid- to late 1970s and those from the former Yugoslavia in the 1990s. The current main countries of last permanent residence in the 2000s included Colombia, Afghanistan, Pakistan, the People's Republic of China and Sri Lanka. Refugees as a proportion of all immigrants peaked in 1980 (at 28%), while over the 15 years before 2007 annual totals ranged between 20,400 and 35,800—equivalent to 9%–14% of all immigrants.

A similar trajectory characterized US policy. In the aftermath of the Second World War there was no formal provision for refugees, even in the Immigration and Nationality Act 1952. Instead, the USA resorted to specific legislation (such as the Displaced Persons Act 1948 and the Refugee Relief Act 1953) that resulted in the admission of over 600,000 Eastern Europeans by 1956. After the Soviet invasion of Hungary in 1956 widespread use was made of the Attorney-General's parole authority, which required Congress to intervene (e.g. the Hungarian Refugee Act 1957), to enable individuals to become permanent residents. This encompassed massive inflows from individual countries (such as Cuba and Viet Nam) that directly contrasted with the numerical and country limits imposed by INA. Initially, a refugee was defined as someone fleeing communist or communist-dominated countries, or the Middle East, but this became less tenable after the end of the Cold War. It had not been until the 1980 Refugee Act that the USA had had a statutory definition of 'refugee', in line with the UN Convention, that was geographically and politically neutral. This was extended to cover designated individuals within their country of origin. Regardless of these adjustments, the ascription of refugee status proved controversial. Executive and congressional views differed on whether those fleeing Haiti and Cuba in the 1990s were victims of political oppression or basically seeking economic advancement. More recently, in the 2000s, individuals at threat of 'coercive population control' (such as compulsory abortion and sterilization) have become eligible for refugee status.

As well as the criteria specified in INA, the US Refugee Program contained a three-fold priority system (P-1, P-2 and P-3) for processing applications. P-1 comprised those (typically individuals) regarded as under most threat of persecution and urgent need of resettlement (as determined by the UN High Commissioner for Refugees or the Department of State); P-2 covered 'approved' refugee groups, defined by the Department of State as in especial need of resettlement—in 2004 only Cubans, those from the former USSR, Vietnamese and certain minorities from Iran and Kenya qualified, with new groups inserted subsequently; P-3 focused on family members of refugees from specified national groups, containing, since 2004, those from Myanmar (Burma), Burundians, Colombians, Iranians, Liberians, Somalis and Sudanese. Conversely, various measures denied entry to those who had belonged to a criminal organization, been engaged in terrorist activities or acted as a senior government official in a country with a record of human rights abuses. The growth in international trafficking of migrants to North America prompted the design of enhanced measures for the surveillance and policing of applicants.

Allowing for the difficulties in predicting refugee movements, the President, in consultation with Congress, is required to set an annual (fiscal year) ceiling on refugee admissions. This fell from a high of 231,700 in 1981 before returning to 142,000 in 1992 and then dropping to 70,000 after 2002, largely because the quantity being resettled from South-East Asia and the former USSR was greatly reduced. The average for the period 1997–2000 was around 90% of the authorized limit, but this tumbled to 40% in 2002, before rising to 59% in 2006. Between 1996 and 2005 43% of refugees were from Europe, twice the proportion from both Asia and Africa, while plan targets in 2006 subdivided as follows: Africa (20,000), East Asia (15,000), Near East/South Asia (5,000), Europe/Central Asia (15,000), Latin America/Caribbean (5,000) and unallocated (10,000). Regional limits can be adjusted, with action targeted at nationals from Central American countries since the 1990s. Notwithstanding these fluctuations, the USA remained the largest recipient country of international refugees.

RECENT IMMIGRANTS AND SETTLEMENT PATTERNS

The reduction of discriminatory barriers in the 1960s triggered a radical shift in the national origins of immigrants. During the 1950s over two-thirds of (documented) newcomers to the USA came from Europe or Canada, one-quarter from Latin America and 6% from Asia. In 1951–60 53% arrived from Europe (with 19% from Germany, 8% from the United Kingdom and 7% from Italy), 6% from Asia, 40% from the Americas (15% from Canada, 12% from Mexico and 5% from Caribbean countries) and only 1% from Africa and Oceania combined. By the 1990s Latin America (including Mexico), Asia and the Caribbean emerged as the largest sources of immigrants. In 2007 the leading countries of birth of new legal permanent residents were: Mexico (14.1%), the People's Republic of China (7.3%), India (6.2%) and Colombia (3.2%), with 36.4% from Asia, 9% from Africa, 11.3% from the Caribbean, 10.1% from South America, 5.3% from Central America and 11.5% from Europe. The foreign-born proportion constituted 12.5% of the whole US population, more than three times the 1970 figure and the highest level for 70 years (for further details see Part Two, The USA, Introduction, Area and Population tables). In addition, INS estimated that 70% of the 5m. undocumented migrants in the USA in 1996 came from seven Latin American countries, primarily Mexico.

There was a corresponding transformation in the national background of immigrants to Canada. Among pre-1961 arrivals, around 26% were from the United Kingdom, just over 63% from other European countries and 5% from the USA, whereas in the 1980s the combined proportion from these countries descended below 30%, declining again to under 20% at the end of the century. By 2000 the annual intake of those from the United Kingdom entrants had fallen to only 2%. Conversely, migrants from Asian and Pacific countries comprised less than 5% in the 1950s, but over 50% in the late 1960s. This momentum was maintained into the 21st century, with Asian countries (notably the People's Republic of China, India, Pakistan and the Philippines) comprising one-half of the leading 10 sources (for further details see Part Three, Canada, Introduction, Area and Population tables). Across North America, immigration over the past two decades produced greater diversity in religious affiliation, with a growing minority of Buddhists, Hindus, Muslims and Sikhs, and fewer Roman Catholics and Protestants among Christian groups.

In terms of settlement patterns, the historical pattern of uneven dispersal within North America remained entrenched. In the USA, 68% of foreign-born people located in six states that contained only 40% of the national population: California (29%), New York (11%), Florida and Texas (each 9%), New Jersey (5%) and Illinois (4%). Moreover, most immigrants lived in a large metropolitan area. Los Angeles and New York had the largest number (each in excess of 5m.), whereas Miami contained the highest percentage (40%), compared with 30% in Los Angeles, 29% in San Francisco and 25% in New York. Overall, metropolitan areas contained 59% of all immigrants, but only 31% of the whole population as a whole.

Equally, in Canada, almost 90% of immigrants in 2001 lived in just three provinces—Ontario (56%), British Columbia (19%) and Québec (13%)—with 73% concentrated in three metropolitan urban areas: Toronto, Vancouver and Montréal. Immigrants comprised 18% of Canada's population in 2001, but 44% of those living in Toronto, the highest percentage in North America, and 38% of the population of Vancouver. Indeed, in 2001 50% of all new immigrants settled in Toronto, before falling to 39% in 2006. This uneven pattern of immigrant settlement led to sharp contrasts between urban areas. For example, Toronto and Halifax (Nova Scotia) demonstrated a broadly similar ethnic composition in 1951, with roughly 75% of British origin, yet by 2001 Toronto's population composition was transformed by the arrival of new immigrants, unlike that of Halifax.

This spawned initiatives to distribute immigrants away from the main metropolitan receiving areas. In Canada, intergovernmental collaboration underpinned efforts to restrict the movement of new entrants in the first three years after their arrival. As an illustration, a range of incentives such as employment opportunities were introduced in Québec, to divert immigrants away from Montréal, facilitated by a regional framework of settlement organizations. In 2006 the proportion of new immigrants resident in the three big cities went down to 69%, but some of the redistribution entailed a growth in surrounding municipalities. However, more also settled in a 'second tier' of metropolises, such as Calgary, Ottawa-Gatineau, Edmonton and Winnipeg.

Likewise, in the USA, the general pattern of immigrant settlement continued to accentuate differences between metropolitan centres and the small town and rural hinterland. Both 'established' 20th-century foreign-born groups, such as those born in Mexico, and 'recent' examples, such as those from China and India, gravitated overwhelmingly towards traditional 'gateway' states. This accentuated the concentration of immigrants in cities such as New York, Los Angeles (with 16.5% of all Mexican-born residents) and Chicago. None the less, there were signs from the late 1990s of a widening in immigrant settlement patterns to 'new' gateway states, ranging from Georgia and North Carolina to Nebraska and Ohio, and/or metropolitan areas, such as Atlanta, Dallas-Fort Worth and Las Vegas. Another set of metropolitan areas, such as Sacramento, Minneapolis and Seattle, were reborn as immigrant destinations.

Immigrant settlement choices were further influenced by the late-20th century restructuring of the US and Canadian economies. This included fundamental modifications of large metropolitan areas, with a slump in manufacturing and the growth of a knowledge- and service-based economy, leading to the dispersal of commercial and office space from city centres to the suburbs. There was a corresponding diversion of immigrant settlement away from inner city neighbourhoods. Yet, these emerging gateways, whether suburban or metropolitan, typically had few community and public institutional structures geared to dealing with significant levels of immigration from Asia, Latin America and Eastern Europe. This exacerbated anxieties about the impact of immigrants on schools, the local economy and work places, and the perceived demands on public expenditure.

IMMIGRATION AND NATIONAL SECURITY

The terrorist attacks of 11 September 2001 (9/11) cast an immediate shadow over immigration policy and practice. In the immediate aftermath, several thousand people, primarily from Arab or mainly Muslim countries, were held in the USA on technical immigration violations. Existing measures to enforce border security, to improve the screening of immigrants and refugees and to gather intelligence information were enlarged in the US Patriot Act 2001 and the US Enhanced Border Security and Visa Entry Reform Act 2002. There was a substantial growth in funding for the INS and allied agencies.

The identification of 'undefended' borders as a basic weakness in the 'war on terror' underscored a 'smart and secure borders' agreement with Canada in December 2001 and Mexico in March 2002. In the same year, to minimize so-called 'asylum shopping' (whereby individuals move from one country to another until they gain admission), Canada and the USA drafted a 'safe third country' agreement (whereby refugee claimants must seek protection in the country of first arrival). An Asylum Annex was appended in 2003 to allow sharing of information on refugee claimants. National security fears were also the pre-eminent motivation for absorbing the INS into an enlarged Department of Homeland Security in 2003. As the total of aliens apprehended in the USA escalated, predominantly along the south-west border, both New Mexico and Arizona declared a state of emergency to target illegal entrants. In 2004 the Department of Homeland Security announced that undocumented immigrants detained in selected border areas within a fortnight of their arrival would be liable to 'expedited removal'. The 2004 Intelligence Reform and Terrorist Prevention Act introduced extra surveillance measures, and these were reinforced in the Real ID Act of 2005, which introduced new standards for state-issued drivers' licences and identification (ID) cards, as well as stricter asylum regulations.

National security issues merged with disquiet over the extent of illegal immigration to prioritize development of a comprehensive entry- and exit-tracking system, or a 'virtual border fence', together with the vetting and monitoring of temporary workers, students and visitors. An immediate response to the 9/11 attacks was a temporary halt in processing refugee claimants, leading to a drastic fall in admissions from 68,925 in 2001 to 26,839 in 2002, although numbers rose back to 41,150 in 2006, with a world-wide growth in refugees. Overall, legal immigration to the USA plunged by one-third between 2002 and 2003, from 1,063,732 to 705,827, before recovering to 1,266,264 in 2006. Against this background, there was a flurry of congressional initiatives, but agreement on the future direction of immigration policy proved elusive, reflecting the gulf between competing arguments and interests over the best way to balance immigration, economic growth, civil liberties and national security. The failure of the Economic Opportunity and Immigration Reform Bill in the Senate in June 2007 effectively ended any prospect of comprehensive reforms before the election of a new President in 2008.

In Canada, the Immigration and Refugee Protection Act 2001 sought a different way forward, both upgrading the screening of refugee claimants and rationalizing detention and deportation procedures. Significantly, undocumented migration was lower down the political agenda, but a Ministry of Public Safety and Emergency-Preparedness was set up in 2003 to improve co-ordination of border security, intelligence-gathering and immigration enforcement functions. This was supplemented by a rise in border officers deployed at home and abroad, along with new surveillance systems, such as biometric screening. Total refugee admissions (government and private-sponsored), but excluding 'humanitarian and compassionate' cases, jumped to 35,776 in 2005, their highest point since 1992, but declined to 27,956 in 2007, or 11.8% of all immigrants, with not quite one-half of the cases reaching a final decision being successful. Legislation enacted in 2008 gave fresh momentum to reducing the large backlog (over 900,000) in applications by allowing greater flexibility in dealing with those with prioritized skills or qualifications, and removing the obligation to process all applications. This was reflected in a new 'Canadian Experience Class', designed as an added incentive to persuade temporary foreign workers with desired qualifications and experience to apply for permanent residence from within Canada.

IMMIGRANT INTEGRATION: MELTING POT AND MULTICULTURALISM

How far were those admitted integrated into the host society? The classic American myth characterized the immigrant experience as akin to a 'melting pot', with a progressive assimilation, perhaps extending into the second generation, across key areas such as socio-economic position, residential location, language and inter-marriage. Empirical studies typically presented a contrary picture that emphasized significant variation across foreign-born groups in the degree, character and timing of social inclusion and acceptance. These were associated with the impact of diverse barriers (structural, institutional and cultural), akin to the discrimination against black slaves and their descendants. Historically, immigrants to Canada were expected to accept the dominant British (or francophone in Québec) institutions and culture, but in 1971 the federal Government formally embraced multiculturalism and affirmed the value of an inclusive citizenship that preserved important elements of (immigrant) cultures. Critics challenged the notion of 'hyphenated' Canadianism on the grounds that it undermined a common national identity or moral community. Multiculturalism created fundamental difficulties in Québec, which retained a strong commitment to a 'national' (francophone) culture and identity, and among the founding Aboriginal Nations, who felt relegated to one among many ethnic minorities.

What is more, recent 'visible' immigrants experienced greater structural barriers to social inclusion than earlier cohorts. There was ample evidence of institutional bias, from the labour market to social welfare. In the USA, the average income of immigrants was 20% below that of established residents in the 1990s, whereas in 1960 the immigrants earned slightly more. Non-citizens were denied access to specific occupations and areas of public sector (principally federal) employment. These encompassed restrictions on employment licensing to prevent over-supply in some professions and states. In comparison, the private sector was more equitable, with Congress designating exceptions such as jobs connected to government contracts and national security. Likewise, in Canada, in the early 1980s two-thirds of skilled workers had above-average incomes within one year of admission, but by the mid-1990s only 4% achieved this. Subsequent data reported lower income and higher unemployment rates among those arriving in 1992–2004 compared with the rest of the population.

The contrasting experiences in the labour market among immigrant groups have been related to very different levels of educational qualification. Around 60% of Mexican-born immigrants to the USA had not graduated from high school, or its equivalent, compared to 32% of all foreign-born individuals aged five years or older. While the Mexican-born employment rate was higher than that of the whole foreign-born population, the proportion in management and the professions was much lower. In contrast, nearly three-quarters of Indian immigrants aged 25 years and over had a university degree, and their higher than average employment rate contained a high representation in information technology (IT) occupations and managerial and professional posts relative to all the foreign-born. There have been complaints about the lack of recognition of foreign credentials, but a striking feature of post-1995 immigrants to Canada was their higher than average educational qualifications, with more than one-third holding a university degree. Conversely, less well-qualified 'visible' groups experienced restricted opportunities, with higher unemployment rates and underemployment. More generally, the preference for new immigrants to settle near to others from a similar background replicated the experiences of previous foreign-born cohorts, leading to a growth of 'ethnic' businesses, services and cultural organizations. Beyond this, some comparative studies of immigrants to North America indicated that those going to the USA experienced relatively longer segregation, in poorer ethnic neighbourhoods, and lower access to public institutional aid.

General public reactions across the 'host' populations in North America expressed doubts about the benefits of current immigration for existing residents and seemed more preoccupied with the problems and disadvantages generated. There was a heightened belief that governments had lost control of immigration, with too many people entering or staying illegally, making 'bogus' refugee claims and too prone to 'abuse' support mechanisms rather than seek economic advancement. Such attitudes were illustrated by the acrimonious arguments around US social welfare policy, with claims that immigrants drew disproportionately on public assistance programmes. As a result, state governments complained that they were expected to pay too much towards basic social services for undocumented immigrants. The 1996 Welfare Reform Act was the first piece of US legislation since the 1930s to deny resident (rather than undocumented) immigrants access to social welfare benefits. Extra penalties on unauthorized immigrants were introduced, requiring that they wait five years after 'regularizing' their status before becoming eligible for major federal programmes such as food stamps, Temporary Aid to Families and Medicaid. Even so, attempts by individual states such as Florida and California to follow suit were denied. In California, popular alarm about the burden of providing public services to migrants led to state voters passing Proposition 187 in 1994. This refused undocumented immigrants and their children access to basic welfare and education services, and required state and local government employees to check client identity prior to providing a service. Proposition 187 illustrated the significant hostility to current immigration policies, but the courts rejected attempts by state governments to exclude undocumented immigrants from public education.

The focus on international terrorism, and the possible support base among immigrants, raised fears of a populist backlash against predominantly Muslim groups. In the USA, unease over security merged with attempts to restrict unauthorized immigration and its impact on local communities. The Illegal Immigrant Relief Act 2006 acted as a spur to local government initiatives to require employers, landlords and the police to check for unauthorized immigrants. Measures were introduced in every state to regulate immigrants, with 182 enacted in 43 states in 2007. These mostly focused on employment and driver's licences and forms of ID, but also extended into health, education, welfare benefits and voting, although, as with earlier legislation, the legality of such measures was challenged. Contrary responses ranged from local disquiet about the financial consequences of driving away immigrants to initiatives seeking greater accommodation, such as offering municipal ID cards to all residents.

At the same time there has been acceptance across North America of the importance of achieving 'sustainable diversity'. In the USA, there was a tradition of private and voluntary support services, as well as those provided by minority ethnic communities themselves, that resulted in considerable variation in the scope and impact of these local initiatives. Canada, which long prided itself on having more programmes to assist new immigrants, increased federal funding of cultural and language integration programmes, with complementary interventions by provincial governments. This emphasized the contribution of all levels of government, and private and voluntary institutions, to countering exclusionary barriers and facilitating economic, political and social integration. It presumed much greater intergovernmental collaboration and the involvement of municipal governments, which had key local responsibilities in such areas as urban planning, education, transport and housing, but lacked the financial resources to make a larger or more sustained input. The emphasis on multiculturalism underpinned an Action Plan to fight racism and educate Canadians 'about the many valuable contributions [that] newcomers make and by helping to build truly welcoming communities', as well as the celebration of diversity in ethnic festivals. Critics claimed that too little had been done to confront the sources of institutional and structural discrimination. Despite this, surveys of immigrant attitudes suggested that immigrants living in North America were broadly positive, with only 9% of recent entrants to Canada reporting that they were not satisfied with their lives.

REVIEW

There were ongoing policy deliberations in the USA and Canada about the most appropriate level of immigration, the selection criteria and the proper balance between the long-term interests and priorities of the 'host' country (such as population and economic growth) and the short-term (principally labour market) conditions. Still, both nations were committed to what in international terms are relatively high levels of entry and, furthermore, developed an impressive humanitarian record of admitting refugees from around the world.

The overwhelming preoccupation was to secure the receiving country's competitive interest, with little consideration of the impact on source nations. In the 21st century, against a background of significant global population movements, the USA and Canada reinforced their efforts to recruit migrants with the desired labour market skills and experience amid rising global competition. Immigration was favoured as a means of countering an ageing population and achieving the required proportion of 'productive' members of the work-force. Additionally, there was a continuing search for ways to administer the very complex system of processing potential immigrants more efficiently. Once people were admitted, there was a growing acceptance among governments that the settlement and integration of immigrants required more funding and active promotion. Yet, the pursuit of 'sustainable diversity' in population terms attracted vocal public criticism. This was compounded in the USA by the high number of illegal immigrants, with concerns over their segregation from mainstream society and disputes about what support should be provided by local communities in terms of, for example, education and health care. After the 2001 terrorist attacks disputes about national security and individual rights vied with economic and social arguments in evaluating the impact of immigration. Even if anti-immigrant views were not always translated into policy practice, in a period when the 'benefits' of immigration were downplayed and the 'costs' accentuated, Canada's multicultural society and the USA's cherished position as a 'nation of immigrants' were under intense scrutiny.

SELECT BIBLIOGRAPHY

Beach, C. M., Green, A. G., and Reitz, J. G. (Eds). *Canadian Immigration Policy for the 21st Century*. Montréal, QC, and Kingston, ON, McGill-Queen's University Press, 2003.

Biles, J., Burstein, M., and Frideres, J. (Eds). *Immigration and Integration in Canada in the Twenty-first Century*. Kingston, ON, Queen's School of Policy Studies and Metropolis, 2008.

Castro, M. J. (Ed.). *Free Markets, Open Societies, Closed Borders?* Miami, FL, North–South Center Press, 1999.

Citizenship and Immigration Canada (CIC). *Facts and Figures 2007: Immigration Overview—Permanent and Temporary Residents*. Ottawa, ON, CIC, 2008.

DeSipio, L., and de la Garza, R. O. *Making Americans, Remaking America*. Boulder, CO, Westview Press, 1998.

Meissner, D., Meyers, D. W., Papademetriou, D. G., and Fix, M. *Immigration and America's Future: A New Chapter*. Washington, DC, Migration Policy Institute, 2006.

Singer, A., Hardwick, S. W., and Brettell, C. B. *Twenty-First Century Gateways: Immigrant Incorporation in Suburban America*. Washington, DC, Brookings Institution Press, 2008.

US Department of Homeland Security. *2006 Yearbook of Immigration Statistics*. Washington, DC, US Government Printing Office, 2007.

ENVIRONMENTAL ISSUES IN NORTH AMERICA

Dr ROBERT M. BONE

OVERVIEW

North Americans once believed that their part of planet Earth was so vast and pristine that human activities could never harm their natural world. The rush to develop the abundant resources in North America came with little thought for the environment. Over the centuries, the hidden costs of development revealed themselves in the fouling of the land. By the 1970s, both Americans and Canadians realized that such a belief was wrong. The first sign of a shift in society's attitude toward the environment came in the 1960s, with the publication of Rachel Carson's *Silent Spring*. Gradually, the myth that North America's ecosystems could easily withstand the pressures from loosely regulated economic activities gave way to a more realistic view of sustainable development. Sustainable development is defined by the impact of human activities causing minimum damage to the environment. Furthermore, sustainable development requires that, when human activities are completed, the air, land and water in an industrial region are returned to their pre-development state. In accordance with the principles of sustainable development, governments have passed legislation to mitigate industrial, rural and urban impacts on the environment as well as holding industry responsible for returning the site to its original state. Still, more needs to be done, including tangible action on global warming. Without state intervention in the marketplace, the environment will not be afforded adequate protection. For instance, air pollution caused largely by fumes from motor vehicle exhaust and smoke from coal-burning power plants represents a growing health issue in the major cities of North America. Similarly, vast sources of water are threatened by industries that dump toxic wastes into streams and lakes, as well as by farmers who are using increasing amounts of chemicals to produce crops and to control insects and weeds. In both cases, these chemical residues have seeped into the hydrological system. A different type of ground pollution comes from increasing volumes of urban waste.

Are there solutions to these environmental challenges? Garrett Hardin holds out little hope. In his 1968 article, 'Tragedy of the Commons' (see Select Bibliography, below), Hardin sees the conflict leading to the eventual destruction of the North American environment. Other scientists argue that Hardin is far too pessimistic. They believe that a combination of technological advances and stricter government regulation will limit and, in some cases, even reverse negative human impacts on the environment. However, political solutions are not easy to reach. The 1997 Kyoto Protocol, for example, represented an attempt by advanced industrial countries to curb emissions of greenhouse gases. Yet the world's greatest producer of greenhouse gases, the USA, signed neither this Protocol nor the 2007 Bali Road Map. The USA did, however, reduce greenhouse emissions through its Clear Skies and Global Climate Change initiatives. By contrast, Canada signed the Protocol, but rejected the Bali Road Map. Unlike the USA, however, Canada has made little progress in reducing its greenhouse emissions. In 2006, the newly elected minority Conservative Government in Canada distanced itself from the Kyoto commitments and in its 2007 budget, the federal administration turned to 'made in Canada' solutions that develop technologies to reduce emissions. One approach falls along the lines of the Weyburn Project (see below), while others are to encourage ethanol and biodiesel production, to promote greater use of urban transit systems and to clean up contaminated sediments in the Great Lakes basin.

This discussion begins with an assessment of the two great polluters—motor vehicles and coal-burning thermal electricity plants—followed by an analysis of strategies to reduce these and other industrial emissions. This is followed by an examination of five major environmental issues (global warming, climate change, air pollution, water pollution, and urban waste), three trans-boundary regions (Alaska, the Great Lakes and the Arctic Ocean) and two trans-boundary regions.

THE TWO GREAT POLLUTERS

Motor vehicles and coal-burning thermal electricity plants represent the two greatest polluters in North America. Both are concentrated in large urban centres and together they generate smog which is a mixture of smoke and sulphur dioxide. A solution may be at hand for reducing pollution from motor vehicles. In 2008, record high petroleum prices caused consumers to shift to smaller, more efficient cars and thus forced the automotive industry to reduce its production of trucks and SUVs. Consequently, General Motors plans to close one SUV and three truck manufacturing plants in 2009: one in Canada, two in the USA and one in Mexico. A second way to reduce pollution from vehicles is to shift urban drivers to public transport systems, while a third way is the use of renewable fuels which produce fewer greenhouse gases. Production of renewable fuels was expected to increase significantly in North America because of legislation introduced by the Canadian and US Governments that requires gasoline to contain a certain percentage of ethanol. Such a gasoline mixture and bio-diesel have the potential significantly to reduce automobile emissions of carbon dioxide and other gases. However, the recent rise in corn and grain prices and the emergence of a global food shortage may delay such developments. Finally, innovative research may greatly diminish motor vehicle emissions by making 'plug-in' hybrids, electric cars and fuel-cell vehicles a reality. The net result will create cleaner and healthier air around these cities.

Coal-burning plants provide much-needed energy for North American industry and cities. Densely populated areas like New England in the USA and southern Ontario in Canada are energy-deficient regions. While coal-fired thermal plants continue to produce much of their electricity at relatively low cost, both regions are concerned about air pollution and have sought to limit sulphur dioxide emissions either by shifting to other fuels to generate electricity or by installing scrubbers in coal stacks and thereby removing sulphur from the smoke.

STRATEGIES TO REDUCE POLLUTION

Canada and the USA want to reduce the emission of greenhouse gases. Polls indicate that most North Americans favour a reduction in greenhouse gas emissions. However, the problem is, 'who should pay—industrial polluters, consumers using the polluting products, or both?' In 2006 greenhouse gas emissions in the USA declined slightly (by 1.3%), but greenhouse gas emissions continued to increase in Canada. Canada's emissions have been increasing, largely due to the expansion of oil sands production in Alberta and almost all of that production is shipped to the USA. Both US and Canadian Governments are examining strategies to reduce greenhouse emissions. Two prominent strategies under consideration are a carbon tax and cap-and-trade system. The challenges facing the Governments of their implementation are cost, potential negative impact on the economy, the willingness of citizens to accept higher costs for fossil fuels and slower (or even negative) economic growth. The advantage is that North America could dramatically reduce pollution and, at the same time, control greenhouse gas emissions.

A carbon tax by increasing the cost of fossil fuels, in theory at least, leads to a reduction in the consumption of fossil fuels and thereby diminishes the emissions of greenhouse gases to the atmosphere. The recent rapid increase in petrol prices in 2008 had such an effect and thus supports this theory. A carbon tax affects the consumer directly and, by causing pain in the consumer's wallet, this tax has three immediate effects. First, higher prices for fossil fuels have already caused consumers to shift away from using them or to consume smaller quantities. Second, since new taxes are never popular with the general population, the level of acceptance of a carbon tax will provide a measure of public support. Third, higher petrol prices affect the transportation industry, thus causing prices for food and other consumer goods to increase. So far, national governments in

North America have considered but have not implemented a carbon tax. However, a regional government has proceeded. On July 1, 2008, the province of British Columbia became the first jurisdiction in North America to introduce a consumer-based carbon tax. The British Columbia carbon tax applies to all fossil fuels, including petrol, diesel, natural gas, coal, propane, and home heating fuel. Since the programme is revenue-neutral, all money collected through the new tax will be returned through a package of tax cuts and credits. The initial reactions are mixed. Environmentalists are lauding the British Columbian Government for daring to take such a progressive stance on the environment. Most motorists, however, are finding the higher costs hard to accept, especially those in the transportation business and those living in remote areas. The problem for the consumer is that higher prices have taken effect immediately, while income tax reductions will not take effect until the following year. Whether or not the carbon tax proves acceptable to British Columbian voters will be carefully watched by other political parties, but especially by the federal Liberal Party that has proposed a national carbon tax and by the next President of the USA.

Governments are attracted to a cap-and-trade market system that assigns a cost to polluting. The cost is initially borne by the industrial polluter but is eventually passed on to the consumer. However, by directly taxing polluting industries, such firms have a financial incentive to reduce emissions. Cap-and-trade systems work by identifying greenhouse gas emitting industries, setting a cap on total emissions, distributing emissions allowances to industries which fall under the cap, and requiring heavy polluters to pay for emissions above their cap. This is achieved by purchasing extra allowances in the marketplace where the price of emissions allowances is established. Industries whose emissions are less than their cap sell their surplus in the marketplace. While a cap-and-trade system has much merit, regional differences pose several serious problems. One is that the fossil fuel industry which is concentrated in a few jurisdictions will bear the brunt of the cost, and higher production costs could hurt the regional economy. Another is that states or provinces with a large fossil fuel industry fear a transfer of wealth to less polluting states or provinces because of the need for their heavy polluting industries to buy 'pollution credits' in states or provinces which do not have such industries. Moreover, the cap-and-trade market system is complicated and in this case, its operation would be expensive.

Not surprisingly, progress to enact cap-and-trade legislation has been slow. For instance, in June 2008, the US Senate rejected the Lieberman-Warner bill, known as America's Climate Security Act. This bill included a cap-and-trade system. In the same year, Canada's federal Government rejected the idea of a national cap-and-trade system partly because of the potential negative political fallout. Alberta and other oil-producing provinces strongly oppose such a system while non oil-producing provinces, such as Ontario and Quebec, are calling for precisely such a system.

The first substantial step in establishing a cap-and-trade system will take place in 2009 in the north-eastern USA (Connecticut, Delaware, Maine, Maryland, New Hampshire, New Jersey, New York and Vermont). However, this regional system is restricted to coal-burning power plants in these eight US states.

Beyond these two strategies, efforts are underway to make more effective use of renewable energy and to find other ways of reducing greenhouse emissions. Substituting renewable fuels for fossil fuels is an innovative approach to decreasing greenhouse gas and toxic emissions. While hydroelectric power is the leading source of non-fossil energy, geothermal, wind and solar energy offer other approaches. These forms of energy have the potential to produce large amounts of clean power but so far are much more expensive than conventional forms of energy. Storing carbon dioxide in the Earth's crust is another experimental approach. The Weyburn Project is one of the most promising experiments. This international project represents an innovative method to dispose of carbon dioxide produced by a lignite-fired gasification plant. By means of a 320-km pipeline, the liquefied carbon dioxide is transported from the US gasification plant to an oilfield in Canada. The injection of carbon dioxide into the Williston Basin oilfield accomplishes two goals. First, a liquefied version of carbon dioxide is stored underground, thereby reducing the release of this gas into the atmosphere. Second, the injection of carbon dioxide greatly increases the recovery of petroleum. The technology associated with this experimental project might be used in other regions of North America and the rest of the world.

GLOBAL WARMING

Global warming represents a major potential threat to North America. The effects of global warming would be to cause North America's natural zones to shift northward. Under this scenario, the geographic extent of the Arctic would be greatly reduced because the greatest increases in annual temperatures would take place in high (more northerly) latitudes as the loss of snow cover would result in the heating of the land (the so-called albedo effect). With a reduced period of snow cover, solar energy would be able to warm the ground in high latitudes more effectively and thus cause temperatures in the atmosphere to increase more rapidly than in lower latitudes (closer to the equator). For this reason, global warming could see the Arctic ecosystem retreating and possibly disappearing. Across the northern hemisphere, glaciers, polar bears and permafrost could be phenomena of the past. In lower latitudes, existing ecosystems would be less affected, but turbulent and stormy weather is predicted to become more common in eastern North America, with a greater frequency and ferocity of tropical storms such as hurricanes and tornadoes. In sharp contrast, the interior of the continent, which is predicted to see hotter and drier weather, may face droughts more frequently.

The economic consequences of global warming for North America would be far-reaching. Some consequences would be favourable; many others would not. Most impact would affect the Arctic and sub-Arctic more than the temperate areas of North America. For example, the ice-free shipping season in Hudson Bay would be greatly extended and the opening of commercial shipping in the Arctic Ocean could become a reality. River and sea transportation would greatly benefit from longer navigation seasons. The Great Lakes and the St Lawrence River, for instance, would be ice-free year-round, while the Arctic Ocean would be sufficiently free of ice in the summer to permit ocean shipping through the Northwest Passage. A likely negative consequence, however, is that, with a rising sea level due to melting ice, flooding of coastal towns and cities could take place. Then, too, global warming could thaw the permanently frozen ground known as permafrost. Melting of the ice in permafrost could cause massive ground subsidence, resulting in an irregular relief referred to by physical geographers as thermo-karst topography. Such subsidence could disrupt transportation and pipeline systems, and play havoc with foundations for buildings, bridges and other human-made structures. Conversely, longer and warmer summers would see agricultural activities take place further north, although grain agriculture on the Great Plains might be subject to greater risk of drought and California's water shortage would become more acute. Forest fires could become more common, especially along the Pacific Coast and in the Boreal Forest. In 2008 California, for example, had a record number of wild fires.

Scientists know that global temperatures are rising and that this increase began shortly after the beginning of the Industrial Revolution. The primary factor causing this recent warming is the increase of emissions of greenhouse gases from the burning of greater amounts of fossil fuels. The major natural greenhouse gases are water vapour, carbon dioxide, methane and ozone. Human activity has resulted in increased levels of greenhouse gases in the atmosphere. The three main sources of greenhouse gases owing to human activity in North America are the burning of fossil fuels, the deforestation of the boreal forest, and intensive livestock farming.

While most scientists believe that global warming is under way, the Canadian and US Governments have been slow to react. Canada did sign the Kyoto Protocol, but Ottawa responded half-heartedly to the accord. The USA refused to sign this agreement to reduce greenhouse gas emissions;

because its Government feared that such action would slow the growth of the US economy. The Climate Change Conference in Bali (December 2007) sought an action plan that would replace the Kyoto Protocol targets for reducing greenhouse emission which expires in 2012. With 180 countries represented, the conference culminated in the adoption of the Bali Road Map, which is a timetable for after 2012 (a post-Kyoto Agreement). While the USA and Canada (along with China, India, Russia and other countries) did not support the concept of binding targets at Bali, it was widely hoped that an agreement will be reached at the December 2009 United Nations Climate Change Conference in Denmark.

CLIMATE CHANGE

Measuring climate change is not a simple matter. Climate is usually defined as the 'average weather' over a long span of time ranging from hundreds to thousands of years. Over such periods the world's great ecosystems were formed. Even so, the global climate has varied. For instance, over the last millennium, the climate has warmed, cooled and is warming again. Scientists have reconstructed past climate variations but the reason for these natural changes is not clear. During the Medieval Warm Period, which lasted from around 1000 to 1400, the climate became milder. The Medieval Warm Period was followed by the Little Ice Age, which occurred between about 1450 and 1850. Since then the world has entered another warming period. The difference is that the current warming cycle may be caused by the burning of fossil fuels

A prominent scientific body, the Intergovernmental Panel on Climate Change, has played a lead role in assessing global climate change. The Panel, established in 1988 by the World Meteorological Organization and the UN Environment Programme, has produced a comprehensive assessment on climate change every five years beginning in 1991. These scientists argue that the current warming period is associated with the Industrial Revolution, which, through the burning of coal and other fossil fuels, has added more and more carbon dioxide to the atmosphere. Carbon dioxide is one of the greenhouse gases that traps solar energy within the atmosphere. The Panel calculated that the global average surface temperature has increased by 0.6°C since the late 19th century and that the 1990s was the warmest decade in the previous 100 years. Furthermore, the Panel predicts rapid increases in world temperatures over the next 100 years, with rises in the global temperature taking place within the range of 1.7°C to 4.2°C.

While the physics of global warming in the greenhouse model are elementary, the actual process of climate change is extremely complex and remains unclear. Global warming seems inevitable, but other events might diminish the amount of solar energy reaching the earth's surface. For example, a massive volcanic eruption, by releasing huge amounts of dust into the air, could reflect significant amounts of incoming solar energy to outer space and thereby chill the world's climate for a short period of time. In 1883 the greatest eruption ever recorded took place at the Krakatau (Krakatoa) volcano near the island of Java (now in Indonesia). Huge amounts of volcanic dust flowed into the atmosphere, thus reducing the amount of sunlight reaching the surface of the earth. In the year following this catastrophic eruption, global temperatures were lowered by as much as 1.2°C. From 1844 to 1899 weather patterns were chaotic and temperatures cool, causing crop failures around the world. However, weather patterns and temperatures then recovered and resumed their previous patterns.

AIR POLLUTION

Besides increasing global temperatures, the burning of fossil fuels places huge quantities of dust and gases into the air, especially in large urban centres. In fact, air pollution represents a growing and serious health problem. Air pollution is the presence in the atmosphere of one or more contaminants in such quantity and for such duration that it is harmful to human health. The worst cases of air pollution are associated with large urban centres. Often, it takes the form of smog. Urban air contamination is caused by the discharge of harmful substances from vehicles (carbon dioxide) and thermal coal plants (sulphur dioxide). Motor vehicles account for over one-half of urban air pollution.

Nature also can pollute the atmosphere. Natural sources often come from volcanoes. Volcanic dust affects large geographic areas and may even affect the entire globe. In 1980 the eruption of Mount St Helens in Washington State, USA, sent up a massive ash cloud, which grew to 18 km in 15 minutes and spread across North America in three days. Although most of the ash fell within 500 km of the mountain, finer ash circled the earth for 15 days and minute particles still remain in the atmosphere.

Attempts to deal with air pollution focus on reducing emissions from motor vehicles and coal-burning thermal plants. Other efforts urge the use of other forms of energy to produce electricity. These efforts are discussed more fully in the section on global warming. Finally, environmentally friendly innovations, while playing a minor role in air pollution reduction, represent a positive sign. For example, 'green roofs' on buildings in major cities are credited with cooling down those buildings in the summer and thus reducing the demand for electricity needed for air conditioning.

Acid rain is another form of air pollution. In this case, the atmosphere has absorbed large amounts of acidic substances such as sulphur dioxide. Precipitation then takes on an unusually acidic chemical composition, which has already had a harmful impact on forests and lakes in eastern North America. Acidity levels are described in terms of the pH factor, which measures the acidity or alkalinity of a substance on a scale from 0 to 14, with 0 being extremely acidic and 14 being extremely alkaline. The average pH of normal rainfall is 5.6, making it slightly acidic. Acid rain, however, has a pH of 2.4 or less. At this pH level, acid rain is a serious environmental problem in many parts of the world, including eastern Canada.

Most acid rain results from the chemicals derived from the burning of fossil fuels in industrial plants and from car exhaust fumes. Sulphur dioxide and nitrogen oxides are emitted in the smoke from coal-burning plants, while car engines are particularly prolific producers of nitrogen oxides. Acid rain is created when oxides of sulphur and nitrogen change chemically as they dissolve in water vapour in the atmosphere and then return to earth as tiny droplets with high concentrations of sulphuric acid and nitric acid.

The most visible impact of acid rain is in urban areas where it slowly corrodes limestone buildings and defaces marble sculptures. Less visible, but just as destructive, are the effects of acid rain on forests, lakes and soils. In eastern Canada and the USA acid rain damaged many forests and caused a sharp decline in fish stocks in many lakes. The problem of acid rain is compounded by the fact that pollutants emitted from coal-burning electrical power plants in the Great Lakes area of the USA and Canada fall as acid rain, thus affecting the forests, lakes and soil of the north-eastern part of North America.

With the recognition of the negative impact of acid rain on the environment, federal and local governments urged measures to reduce the phenomenon. In 1991 Canada and the USA signed a bilateral Air Quality Agreement and, a few years later, New England governors and premiers from eastern Canada agreed on an Acid Rain Action Plan, which co-ordinated efforts to reduce acid rain. Progress was made and human health and the environment benefited significantly. The main methods included reducing sulphur emissions at coal-burning power plants, substituting natural gas for coal at power plants and introducing 'scrubbing' in existing coal-burning thermal facilities. Natural gas has little or no sulphur; hence emissions of sulphur dioxide are either greatly reduced or eliminated.

WATER POLLUTION

Water may become the most valuable natural resource in the 21st century. Pollution of water bodies represents a major challenge to this resource and to the human population who require drinking water. Agriculture and industry discharged a variety of chemicals into lakes and rivers. Even in minute amounts these chemicals are harmful to human, plant and animal life. A wide variety of toxic pesticides and polychlorinated phenols (PCBs) represents a serious health hazard.

How do these poisonous substances enter such bodies of water? North Americans use hundreds of chemicals each day in the home, in agriculture and industry. Urban residents use chemicals in washing, eating, house-cleaning, gardening and driving. Household products containing chemicals are often flushed into the sewer system, which eventually joins a natural water body. Modern farmers are heavy users of chemicals. Oil sands projects in Alberta use huge quantities of water to extract the oil and, in doing so, dispose of toxic sludge in tailing ponds. Farmers fertilize their crops and apply pesticides to kill weeds and insects. Inevitably, the residue of fertilizers and pesticides drains into lakes and rivers. Intensive livestock farming has become a major threat to the rural environment. Huge cattle and hog-barn operations are among the worst offenders. These enterprises produce vast quantities of animal waste that threaten both surface and subsoil water. For example, the practice of holding animal waste in slurry lagoons increases the risk of the waste finding its way into the groundwater. Many lagoons are merely dug-out holes in the ground, without impervious linings. Sometimes the toxic wastes seep into the ground table, with disastrous results for those depending on drinking water from wells. While most livestock operators and industrial firms now treat their waste effluence before discharging it into lakes and rivers, industry remains one of the major sources of water pollution. For example, the disposal of toxic effluence into lagoons can contaminate groundwater supplies for residents in the region. After such a disaster, the only solution is an expensive one, namely that water from a distant well has to replace the local supply.

URBAN WASTES

As North American cities grow, the problem of disposing of urban waste becomes more complicated. Large cities have long ago filled nearby land dumps. City governments face a difficult problem and all solutions are expensive. Many cities have had to seek other alternatives for the disposal of their waste products. One solution is to find a land dump site some distance from the urban centre. Toronto, Ontario, a Canadian city with a population of nearly 5m., provides an example of such an approach. After Toronto filled its local dump sites, the city arranged to ship its waste products to the neighbouring US state of Michigan. Toronto's waste disposal contract with Michigan is in effect until 2010, although many, particularly in the USA, are seeking options to end the contract sooner. The process of shipping Toronto's waste to another country has resulted in many problems and complaints, such as security concerns about the border crossings, opposition from Michigan residents and concerns about the pollution generated by thousands of diesel-powered trucks travelling to and from Michigan every day.

Another solution is to recycle some urban wastes and, in this way, to minimize the waste destined for the garbage dump site. Minimizing solutions to urban waste begin with urban residents and their civic leaders becoming more aware of the interrelationship between their waste and their environment. Waste reduction is then seen as self-interest. Progress is occurring—urban residents have taken to composting organic wastes, and cities have instituted special paper, bottles and tin cans collection systems and then recycled them into useful products.

THE GREAT ALASKAN DEBATE: CARIBOU, WILDERNESS AND PETROLEUM

A classic clash between the environment and industry is taking place in a remote region in the US state of Alaska. The struggle is over land in the Arctic National Wildlife Refuge (ANWR). The ANWR comprises 7.7m. ha of protected land in the north-east of Alaska, with the potential of recoverable oil and gas reserves perhaps rivalling those at Alaska's Prudhoe Bay oilfield. Should this arctic refuge remain a wilderness or should industry be permitted to search for petroleum? Those in the USA have two points of view. One is that the Refuge represents a US Serengeti, where million-year-old ecological rhythms exist. A second perspective is that this Refuge is the last frontier for oil exploration in mainland USA. The ANWR remains at the centre of state, national and international debate over petroleum exploration in the region. The Refuge includes the calving grounds of the Porcupine caribou herd, upon which the Gwich'in Athabascan people in both Alaska and the adjacent areas of Canada depend for subsistence. The Gwich'in are among those who oppose oil development in the ANWR. However, proponents of petroleum exploration, including residents of the Inupiat Inuit (Eskimo) village of Kaktovik, who will benefit from such exploration, maintain that oil exploration and development can take place without negative environmental impact. Complicating matters, the US and Canadian Governments signed an agreement in 1987 to protect the environment and the Porcupine caribou herd. This caribou herd, named for the Porcupine River of the region, regularly migrates across the international boundary between Canada and the USA. Pressure is mounting because of US concerns about secure petroleum supplies. In 2006 President George W. Bush approved energy companies being allowed the opportunity to search for crude petroleum and natural gas on 8m. acres (over 3.2m. ha) in Alaska's western Arctic region. By July 2008 no petroleum discoveries had been announced. However, Congress is under strain because of the soaring price of oil and no less than 17 bills are pending that called for the opening of the coastal plain of ANWR to oil and gas development. Most of these will come to a vote in late 2008.

THE ARCTIC OCEAN

The Arctic Ocean is truly an international sea. Both Canada and the USA border this ice-bound sea, but so do Russia, Norway and the Danish dependency of Greenland. The Arctic Ocean has unique physical and biological properties. Three unique features are its seasonality of light, its year-round existing ice cover and its life forms that are highly adapted in their life history, ecology and physiology to the extreme and seasonal conditions of their environment. The Arctic Ocean's location between Europe and Asia translates into the shortest potential ocean route between the two continents. In the mid-19th century the search for the Northwest Passage was thwarted by difficult ice conditions. Since then the global climate has warmed and predictions abound that the Northwest Passage will soon become ice-free during the summer months, and Arctic sea passage will become a reality. As discussed earlier, climate warming will affect more northerly latitudes most and, therefore, the Arctic Ocean is also the area where the impact of climate change might be most strongly experienced.

The Arctic Ocean contains vast petroleum reserves. Alaska produces about 8% of US petroleum production from offshore oilfields in the Beaufort Sea of the Arctic Ocean. Canada too has vast oil reserves, which have yet to be developed. Petroleum production in the Arctic is not without environmental risks. Scientists are concerned that an oil spill in the frigid Arctic waters would be extremely difficult to contain and to remove. One of the problems unique to the Arctic Ocean is that the difficulty of access to an offshore drilling rig is compounded by varying ice conditions. During the winter offshore drilling rigs are accessible by ice roads, but shore ice quickly melts in the summer, limiting access to sea transportation. Should a 'blow-out' occur while exploring for petroleum, getting the equipment necessary for stemming the flow to the well would take time, thus allowing huge amounts of oil to leak into the Arctic Ocean.

THE GREAT LAKES

The Great Lakes are the largest system of fresh surface water on earth, containing roughly 18% of the world supply. Lakes Superior, Michigan, Huron, Erie and Ontario contain about 23,000 cu km of water, covering a total area of 244,000 sq km. The Great Lakes are a product of the last ice age, when some 20,000 years ago the Laurentide ice sheet gouged and scraped the soil and bedrock from this area and, some 8,000 years later, meltwaters from the sheet began to fill the great depressions.

The area surrounding the Great Lakes is home to 35m. people, many of whom live in large cities such as Chicago (Illinois), Detroit (Michigan), Toronto (Ontario) and Montréal (Québec). The Great Lakes are also an integral part of the St

Lawrence Seaway. Thus, sea transportation, agriculture and industry pose a threat to the environmental well-being of the Great Lakes. This huge body of water is sensitive to the invasion of foreign species and to the effects of a wide range of pollutants. At least 160 new species have migrated into the Great Lakes. Many have come as unwanted passengers on the foreign ships sailing along the St Lawrence Seaway and on the Great Lakes. Zebra mussels and sea lamprey have had a negative impact on the domestic fishery. Over 360 chemical compounds have been identified in the Great Lakes, many being persistent toxic chemicals—alkylated lead, benzopyrene, DDT, mercury and mirex—potentially dangerous to humans and already destructive to the aquatic ecosystems. For example, various species of fish now suffer from tumours and lesions, and their reproductive capacities are decreasing. Populations of fish-consuming birds and mammals also seem to be on the decline. Of the 10 most highly valued species of fish in Lake Ontario, seven have now almost totally vanished.

The sources of pollution include the run-off of soils and farm chemicals from agricultural lands, the waste from cities and toxic discharges from industry. The large surface area of the lakes also makes them vulnerable to direct atmospheric pollutants that fall with rain or snow and as dust on the lake surface.

Physical characteristics vary across the basin. To the north the climate is cold and the terrain dominated by the Canadian Shield, granite bedrock consisting of ancient Precambrian rocks under a generally thin layer of acidic soils. Here the northern coniferous forest provides the foundation for a forest economy. To the south the climate is much warmer and the soils both deep and fertile. The original deciduous forest has been replaced by farmland, transportation routes and sprawling urban development.

Lake Erie is the shallowest of the five lakes, making it the most vulnerable lake to human pollution. Lake Erie also receives the greatest amount of human pollution of all the lakes, because it is surrounded by extensive levels of urbanization and intensive crop and livestock activities. The lake receives run-off from the agricultural area of south-western Ontario and, on the US side, from parts of Ohio, Indiana and Michigan. Twenty metropolitan areas with populations of over 50,000 are located within the Lake Erie basin. Although the area of the lake is about 26,000 sq km, the average depth is only about 19 m.

With the Great Lakes lying between Canada and the USA, governments at national and local levels face immense challenges, including water pollution, consumption, diversions, lake levels and shoreline management. The two national Governments have recognized these challenges and, in 1972, the Great Lakes Water Quality Agreement was signed. The Agreement—renewed in 1978—remains in effect today. The bilateral arrangement expresses the ongoing commitment of Canada and the USA to restore and maintain the chemical, physical and biological integrity of the Great Lakes basin ecosystem. The Agreement created the International Joint Commission, which is charged with reviewing and evaluating programmes designed to restore the natural integrity of the Great Lakes. The two respective federal agencies charged with conducting the programmes are Environment Canada and the US Environmental Protection Agency. The forging of a political will by Canada and the USA offers the hope that the natural integrity of the Great Lakes will be preserved for future generations. The challenges involved in this task are considerable.

CONCLUSION

North Americans are struggling to find a balance between economic development and a sustainable environment. Sustainable development might provide the answer. The New World remains a home to wilderness areas and wildlife, but, as the conflict between the environment and petroleum exploration in Alaska demonstrates, national interests threaten to trump ecological concerns. However, some progress toward balanced development, which requires that economic activities take place within a framework of environmental management, is occurring. Government regulations can provide the 'teeth' behind environmental management agencies. Canada and the USA have worked together to reduce acid rain and to restore the environmental integrity of the Great Lakes. While much work remains to be done, political co-operation has forged a powerful tool for addressing trans-border environmental matters. Global warming remains an issue receiving inadequate political attention in both Canada and the USA, despite the potential threat that it poses to the region and to the world. North America, but particularly the USA, should play a leadership role at the 2009 UN Climate Change Conference in Denmark.

SELECT BIBLIOGRAPHY

Carson, R. *Silent Spring*. Boston, MA, Houghton Mifflin, 1962.

Hardin, G. 'Tragedy of the Commons', in *Science*, Vol. 162, 13 December 1968, p. 1243.

Intergovernmental Panel on Climate Change. *Third Assessment Report. Climate Change 2001: Impacts, Adaptation and Vulnerability*. Cambridge, Cambridge University Press, 2001.

Part Two

THE UNITED STATES OF AMERICA

INTRODUCTION

THE USA: A CHRONOLOGY SINCE COLONIZATION

1492: Christopher Columbus, a Genoese navigator in the service of Spain, landed in the present-day Bahamas, marking the discovery of the 'New World' by Europeans.

1499: The voyage of the Italian explorer Amerigo Vespucci, on behalf of the Spanish Crown, resulted in America being so named.

1565: The Spanish explorer Pedro Menéndez de Aviles established the first permanent European settlement on the mainland of the modern USA, at St Augustine, now in Florida.

1585: Sir Walter Raleigh led the first English attempt to colonize 'Virginia'—an unsuccessful settlement on Roanoke island, off the coast of what became North Carolina.

1607: The first permanent English settlement was established at Jamestown, now in Virginia.

1614–26: Dutch settlers established the colony of 'New Netherlands', with fur-trading posts at Fort Orange (now Albany) and on Manhattan Island at New Amsterdam.

1619: The first representative assembly in American history, the House of Burgesses, met in Jamestown.

1620: The Puritan 'Pilgrim Fathers', sailing from England in the *Mayflower,* settled at Plymouth, now in Massachusetts.

1630: The foundation by a group of wealthy Puritans of the colony of Massachusetts Bay marked the beginning of the large-scale colonization of 'New England'.

1643: The first confederation of the American colonies was a defensive association of Connecticut, Massachusetts Bay and New Plymouth against the Dutch, French and the native Indians (Amerindians).

1655: New Sweden, a territory around the Delaware estuary settled by Swedes and Finns almost 20 years previously, was conquered by the Dutch and incorporated into New Netherlands.

1667: The Treaty of Breda ended the Second Anglo–Dutch War and confirmed the acquisition of New Netherlands by the English (British) King, Charles II; both the colony and the city of New Amsterdam were renamed New York, in honour of the Duke of York (brother of the British monarch).

1682: The lower Mississippi country was claimed for France and named Louisiana (the administrative centre of New Orleans was founded in 1718).

1740–41: Vitus Bering, a Danish captain employed by Russia, sailed to Alaska and the Aleutian Islands.

1754–63: The French and Indian War (in Europe, starting in 1756, it was known as the Seven-Years War): the United Kingdom gained control over French Canada and that part of Louisiana lying east of the Mississippi River, while the western part was ceded to Spain; Spain, in turn, surrendered Florida to the British.

1773: Massachusetts citizens occupied three ships in Boston harbour and threw overboard their cargoes of tea, in protest at another tax imposition by the British authorities.

1774: The first so-called Continental Congress of colonial delegates, meeting in Philadelphia, Pennsylvania, as the Congress of the United Colonies or States of America, voted for a number of anti-British measures.

1775: Forces of the 13 colonies, under the command of George Washington, entered into battle with the British army.

1776: The Declaration of Independence by the Congress of the United States of America was adopted.

1781: The Articles of Confederation and Perpetual Union, drafted in the Continental Congress of 1777, entered into effect. The surrender of British forces at Yorktown, Virginia, marked the end of serious military engagement, except for continued conflict between the United Kingdom and the European supporters of American independence, France and Spain.

1783: By signing the Treaty of Paris, the United Kingdom formally recognized the independence of the USA and ceded it all British American territorial claims south of Canada and west to the Mississippi, except for Florida, which was returned to Spain.

1787: A constitutional convention met in Philadelphia to revise the Articles of Confederation; they drafted a Constitution of the United States, which was ratified by Delaware, Pennsylvania and New Jersey during the same year.

1788: Georgia, Connecticut, Massachusetts, Maryland, South Carolina, New Hampshire, Virginia and New York ratified the Constitution; the ninth state ratification (that of New Hampshire) established the Constitution.

1789: George Washington was elected to be the first President of the USA in February; the Constitution came into effect in March; the first Congress met in New York City in April; the Supreme Court was created in September. North Carolina ratified the Constitution and was admitted to the Union.

1790: Rhode Island ratified the Constitution and became the last of the 13 original states to be admitted to the Union. Philadelphia became the temporary capital of the USA.

1791: The 10 original amendments to the Constitution (Bill of Rights) came into effect. Vermont was admitted to the Union.

1792: Kentucky was admitted to the Union.

1795: The 11th Amendment to the Constitution was ratified.

1796: Tennessee was admitted to the Union.

1797: John Adams, a Federalist like his predecessor, became the second President of the USA.

1800: The French ruler, Napoleon Bonaparte, secured the return of Louisiana from Spain. Federal government moved from Philadelphia to the newly created capital of Washington, District of Columbia (DC).

1801: Thomas Jefferson was installed as President.

1803: The Supreme Court established the power of judicial review in *Marbury v. Madison.* Napoleon sold all French possessions on the North American mainland to the USA for US $15m., under the Louisiana Purchase, thereby doubling US territory. Ohio was admitted to the Union.

1804: The 12th Amendment to the Constitution was ratified.

1809: James Madison became President.

1812: Louisiana was admitted to the Union.

1812–14: The War of 1812 with the United Kingdom: the USA failed to drive the British out of North America; the Capitol and the White House, in Washington, DC, were burnt in a British incursion; but, distracted by its war with France, the United Kingdom was content to agree the demilitarization of the Great Lakes and, otherwise, with the *status quo ante* in the concluding Treaty of Ghent.

1815: A US fleet ended the problem of piracy on the Barbary Coast of North Africa.

1816: Indiana was admitted to the Union.

1817: James Monroe assumed the presidency. Mississippi was admitted to the Union.

1818: Illinois was admitted to the Union.

1819: Spain sold Florida to the USA for US $5m. Alabama was admitted to the Union.

1820: The so-called Missouri Compromise legislation permitted slavery in Missouri, but outlawed it in areas west of the Mississippi River and north of a line extending from the southern boundary of Missouri. Maine separated from Massachusetts and was admitted to the Union.

1821: Missouri was admitted to the Union.

1823: President Monroe espoused the principle of no European intervention in the Americas, the so-called Monroe Doctrine.

1824: John Quincy Adams, the National Republican candidate, was elected to the presidency, ending the Democratic-Republican hold on the office (since 1801).

1828: The Democratic-Republican Party became the Democratic Party and its candidate, Andrew Jackson, won the presidential election.

1836: Arkansas was admitted to the Union. Texas declared its independence from Mexico, and the Texan army defeated the Mexican forces at San Jacinto.

1837: Martin Van Buren became President. Michigan was admitted to the Union.

1841: President William Henry Harrison, a Whig, died after 31 days in office, to be succeeded by John Tyler.

1842: The Seminole Indians of Florida were sent to Oklahoma, having fought US forces since 1835. The US–Canadian border in Maine and Minnesota was fixed by the Webster-Ashburton Treaty.

1845: James Polk assumed the presidency. Florida was admitted to the Union. Texas was also admitted, after Texans voted for annexation to the USA.

1846: The western US–Canadian boundary was fixed at the 49th parallel (49°N). Iowa was admitted to the Union.

1846–48: The Mexican War ended with Mexico ceding vast territories and claims, which not only included Texas and California (widely settled from the USA), but also present-day Arizona, Nevada, New Mexico and Utah, and parts of Colorado, Oklahoma and Wyoming, by the Treaty of Guadalupe Hidalgo.

1848: Wisconsin was admitted to the Union. Zachary Taylor, a hero of the Mexican War, was elected to the presidency for the Whigs.

1850: President Taylor died, to be succeeded by Millard Fillmore. California was admitted to the Union, with slavery outlawed, but New Mexico and Utah were made territories without a decision on slavery, under the so-called Compromise of 1850.

1853: Franklin Pierce became President.

1854: The Republican Party was founded.

1857: James Buchanan became President.

1858: Minnesota was admitted to the Union.

1859: Slavery abolitionists, led by John Brown, captured the US Armory at Harper's Ferry (then in Virginia); the Armory was recaptured by US Marines and Brown was hanged for treason. Oregon was admitted to the Union.

1860: Abraham Lincoln was the first Republican to be elected President. South Carolina became the first state to secede from the Union, citing the abolition-of-slavery issue.

1861: The secessionist Confederate States of America was founded by Alabama, Florida, Georgia, Louisiana, Mississippi, South Carolina and Texas, and later joined by Arkansas, North Carolina, Tennessee and Virginia. The first major battle of the Civil War was fought at Bull Run. Kansas was admitted to the Union.

1863: Lincoln's Emancipation Proclamation came into effect, 'freeing all slaves in areas still in rebellion'. By the middle of the year the Unionists controlled the entire Mississippi River. West Virginia, the part of Virginia that had stayed loyal, was admitted to the Union.

1864: Unionist troops marched through Georgia, led by Gen. William T. Sherman, taking Atlanta and Savannah. Nevada was admitted to the Union.

1865: The surrender of Gen. Robert E. Lee's Confederate troops in Virginia, at the Appomattox Court House, on 9 April marked the effective end of the Civil War (the last Confederate forces surrendered in May). President Lincoln was assassinated in April, to be succeeded by Andrew Johnson (a Democrat who had been nominated for the vice-presidency by the Republicans in the election of the previous year). Slavery was finally abolished by the 13th Amendment to the Constitution.

1867: The Russian Empire sold Alaska to the USA for US $7.2m. Nebraska was admitted to the Union.

1868: The 14th Amendment to the Constitution was ratified.

1869: Ulysses S. Grant, the leading Unionist general of the Civil War, became President.

1870: The 15th Amendment to the Constitution was ratified.

1872: Full civil rights were restored to Southern citizens, barring 500 Confederate leaders.

1876: Col George A. Custer was defeated in the Sioux Indian War, at the Battle of the Little Big Horn, Montana. Colorado was admitted to the Union.

1877: Neither of the main candidates having received the requisite number of Electoral College votes, Congress awarded the presidency to the Republican, Rutherford B. Hayes, although he had gained fewer votes, after the Republicans promised to end Reconstruction in the South.

1881: President James A. Garfield, who had taken office in March, was shot in July and died in September, to be succeeded by Chester A. Arthur.

1885: Grover Cleveland became President.

1889: Benjamin Harrison took office as President. North Dakota, South Dakota, Montana and Washington were admitted to the Union.

1890: The Battle of Wounded Knee, South Dakota, was the last major conflict between Indian (Sioux) and US troops. Idaho and Wyoming were admitted to the Union.

1892: Grover Cleveland was re-elected to the presidency.

1896: The Supreme Court approved racial segregation under the 'separate but equal' doctrine. Utah was admitted to the Union. William McKinley was elected to the presidency.

1898: The USA defeated Spain in war and acquired Guam, the Philippines and Puerto Rico. Hawaii, previously an independent republic, was annexed by the USA.

1901: President McKinley was shot in September and died eight days later; he was succeeded by Theodore Roosevelt.

1903: A treaty with the newly independent country of Panama provided for the construction of a transisthmian canal (opened in 1914).

1907: Oklahoma was admitted to the Union.

1909: William H. Taft became President.

1912: New Mexico and Arizona were admitted to the Union. Woodrow Wilson was elected to the presidency.

1913: The 16th (introducing income tax) and 17th Amendments to the Constitution were ratified.

1914: President Wilson proclaimed US neutrality in the First World War.

1916: The USA purchased the Danish West Indies (now the US Virgin Islands) for US $25m. The first woman was elected to Congress.

1917: The USA declared war on Germany on 6 April; conscription was introduced.

1918: Over 1m. US troops were in Europe by July; the 'Great War' ended with the surrender of Germany in November.

1919: The Prohibition of alcoholic beverages was introduced by the 18th Amendment to the Constitution.

1920: US membership of the League of Nations was blocked by the Senate. Women received the right to vote under the 19th Amendment to the Constitution. Warren G. Harding was elected to the presidency.

1921: The national quota system was introduced to restrict immigration.

1923: President Harding died and was replaced by Calvin Coolidge.

1924: All Indians were made citizens by Congress. The first woman governor was elected, in Texas.

1929: Herbert Hoover became President. The 'Stock Market Crash' marked the beginning of the Great Depression, an economic recession which lasted for most of the 1930s.

1933: President Franklin D. Roosevelt took office and appointed the first woman to the cabinet; he was the first Democratic President since Wilson. The 'New Deal' domestic legislation was passed by Congress. Isolationist policy was confirmed by the declaration that the USA would not become militarily involved in affairs of western hemisphere nations. The 20th Amendment and the 21st Amendment (the repeal of Prohibition) to the Constitution were ratified.

1939: President Roosevelt declared US neutrality in the Second World War.

1941: The USA entered the Second World War following the Japanese attack on Pearl Harbor, Hawaii.

1942: The USA inflicted the first major defeat on Japan at the Battle of Midway, in June; US and British forces invaded North Africa in November.

1943: The USA and its Allies invaded Italy in September.

1944: US and Allied forces invaded northern Europe in June; US forces landed in the Philippines in October.

1945: President Roosevelt died in April, having won an unprecedented fourth term of office in the election of the previous year; he was succeeded by Harry S Truman. US forces landed on Iwo Jima and Okinawa, Japan, in February and April, respectively; war with Germany ended on 7 May; the explosion of the first atomic bomb took place in July at Alamogordo, New Mexico, and atomic bombs were dropped on the Japanese cities of Hiroshima (6 August) and Nagasaki (9 August); Japan surrendered on 15 August; US forces moved into Korea, replacing the Japanese, in September. The United Nations (UN) Charter was signed in San Francisco, California, in June.

1946: The Philippines was granted independence by the USA.

1947: The granting of aid to Greece and Turkey, to combat Communist insurgency, occasioned the announcement of the so-called Truman Doctrine, which became central to the US foreign policy of 'containment'. Aid under the Marshall Plan (European Reconstruction Program, proposed by George Marshall, the Secretary of State) began for nine European countries.

1948: The Organization of American States (OAS) was created.

1949: US troops withdrew from Korea, which was split politically along the line dividing the zones of occupation. The North Atlantic Treaty Organization (NATO) was created, committing the USA to the defence of Western Europe.

1950: The production of the hydrogen bomb was authorized by President Truman. The USA answered a UN request for peacekeeping troops to be sent to Korea after the Communist regime of the North invaded the South.

1951: The 22nd Amendment to the Constitution formally limited a President to two terms of office.

1953: Dwight D. Eisenhower assumed the presidency for the Republicans. The Korean conflict was declared to be over.

1954: Senator Joseph McCarthy led hearings into alleged Communist influence in the US Army. The Supreme Court ruled, in *Brown v. Board of Education of Topeka,* that 'separate educational facilities are inherently unequal' and, therefore, that the 'separate but equal' doctrine was in violation of the 14th Amendment to the Constitution.

1955: The USA began to provide military-adviser assistance to the South Vietnamese army, to help it against the Communist regime in the North of Viet Nam.

1958: *Explorer 1,* the first US earth satellite, was launched.

1959: Alaska and Hawaii were admitted to the Union, as the 49th and 50th states.

1961: John F. Kennedy, a Democrat, became President. There was an unsuccessful attempt to overthrow the Cuban premier, Fidel Castro, in the 'Bay of Pigs' invasion by US-armed and US-directed Cuban exiles. US military advisers in Viet Nam were authorized to fight with the units they were training. The 23rd Amendment to the Constitution was ratified.

1962: The Cuban Missile Crisis abated when the Soviet leader, Nikita Khrushchev, agreed to withdraw nuclear missiles from Cuba, following a US naval blockade of the island.

1963: The Partial Test Ban Treaty, signed by the USSR, the United Kingdom and the USA, confined nuclear-explosives testing to underground sites. On 22 November President Kennedy was assassinated in Dallas, Texas, and was succeeded by Lyndon B. Johnson.

1964: The Civil Rights Act banned discrimination in places of public accommodation and in employment. The Tonkin Resolution of Congress authorized presidential action in Viet Nam following reports of a North Vietnamese attack on two US destroyers. The 24th Amendment to the Constitution was ratified.

1965: President Johnson ordered bombing raids on North Viet Nam. The Voting Rights Act banned the use of tests and other devices to deny the right to vote to certain minority groups. The national-origins quota system for immigration was abolished.

1966: Medicare and Medicaid, which provided some state welfare support for health care for the elderly and the poor, were introduced.

1967: The 25th Amendment to the Constitution was ratified. Domestic opposition to the undeclared war in Viet Nam increased.

1968: The US public's perception of the physical and financial costs of war in Viet Nam prompted President Johnson to propose cease-fire negotiations (at this time more than 500,000 US troops were in Viet Nam); the policy of Vietnamization was announced, by which the South Vietnamese would gradually assume the entire fighting role. Martin Luther King, Jr, and Senator Robert Kennedy were assassinated, in April and June, respectively.

1969: Richard Nixon, a Republican, became President. US forces began the withdrawal from Viet Nam. Neil Armstrong became the first man to step on to the Moon.

1970–71: The USA organized invasions into Cambodia and Laos to interrupt North Vietnamese supply lines.

1971: The voting age was lowered to 18 years by the 26th Amendment to the Constitution.

1972: President Nixon visited both the People's Republic of China and the USSR; the Strategic Arms Limitation Treaty was signed with the USSR. In Viet Nam the USA had withdrawn all combat troops by August, but continued to supply military assistance to South Viet Nam, notably air support; peace negotiations failed. Five men were arrested following a break-in at the offices of the Democratic National Committee in the Watergate complex, Washington, DC.

1973: The Watergate hearings began. Vice-President Spiro Agnew resigned over charges of tax evasion. An embargo was imposed on petroleum exports to the USA by Arab petroleum-producing nations following the outbreak of Arab–Israeli war.

1974: The House of Representatives Judiciary Committee opened impeachment hearings against President Nixon in May, and in July recommended three articles of impeachment against him. Nixon resigned the presidency in August and received an unconditional pardon from his successor, Gerald Ford, in September.

1975: The North Vietnamese launched an offensive in January; the remaining US personnel were evacuated and the South Vietnamese regime surrendered in April.

1976: The Democratic candidate, Jimmy Carter, was elected to the presidency.

1978: The Senate agreed to new treaties with Panama, which gave complete control over the Canal to that country by December 1999.

1979: A major accident at the Three Mile Island nuclear power-station, Pennsylvania, caused a radical alteration in attitudes to nuclear energy in the USA. Militant Islamic fundamentalist students took 63 US citizens hostage in the US embassy in Iran.

1980: Embargoes were placed on the sale of grain and advanced-technology products to the USSR following the Soviet invasion of Afghanistan. The Mount St Helens volcano in the state of Washington erupted.

1981: Following agreement on the return of US $8,000m. in frozen assets to Iran, the US hostages were released on the day of inauguration of a new US President, Ronald Reagan, a Republican. The first reusable spacecraft, the Space Shuttle, was launched.

1983: US Marines and Rangers participated in the invasion of Grenada, to overthrow a Marxist regime.

1984: The first woman chosen as a vice-presidential candidate in the election was Geraldine Ferraro for the Democrats (President Reagan, for the Republicans, was re-elected).

1986: The USA bombed Tripoli and Benghazi, Libya, claiming retaliation for terrorist attacks. The 'Iran-Contra' affair emerged, involving secret military sales to Iran and the use of the resulting funds, illegally, for the support of right-wing guerrilla forces in Central America.

1987: The USA and the USSR signed the Intermediate Nuclear Forces Treaty, providing for some arms limitation.

1989: George Bush, previously the Vice-President, became President. Following increasing tensions, the USA invaded Panama, restoring the authority of democratic government and bringing the Panamanian dictator, Gen. Manuel Noriega, to the USA to be tried on drugs-trafficking charges.

1990: The Treaty on Conventional Forces in Europe was signed by members of NATO and the Soviet alliance system, the Warsaw Pact. Economic sanctions were imposed against Iraq following its invasion of Kuwait.

1991: 'Operation Desert Storm' by US-led multinational forces resulted in the routing of Iraqi forces and the restoration of sovereign government to Kuwait. The USA and the USSR signed the Strategic Arms Reduction Treaty; the dissolution of the USSR in December marked the final end of the Cold War.

1992: The 27th Amendment to the Constitution, on increases in congressional rates of pay, was ratified, almost two centuries after its first proposal. The USA deployed 28,000 troops to Somalia to restore order and facilitate distribution of food supplies.

1993: In January Bill Clinton, a Democrat, was inaugurated as President.

1994: The North American Free Trade Agreement (NAFTA), negotiated with Canada and Mexico, took effect. In the November elections the Republicans gained control of both chambers of Congress for the first time since 1953.

1995: The detonation of a bomb outside a federal office in Oklahoma City caused 169 deaths and concern about the activities of right-wing militias. An *impasse* in budget negotiations between the executive and the legislature culminated in the temporary suspension of most federal government operations in November. US-sponsored peace negotiations at Dayton, Ohio, led to a settlement in the conflicts in the former Yugoslavia, notably of the civil war in Bosnia and Herzegovina.

1996: Relations with Canada, Mexico and the countries of the European Union were impaired by the enactment of the Helms-Burton proposals, which were described as extra-territorial legislation because they penalized foreign investment in Cuba. A strong economy ensured the re-election of President Clinton.

1997: An agreement was reached between the executive and the legislature on balanced budget legislation and, following the use of the presidential veto to remove three of the 79 measures, was enacted. Substantial US military forces were dispatched to the Persian (Arabian) Gulf region after the Iraqi Government demanded the removal of all US inspectors working with the UN Special Commission (UNSCOM) investigating weapons of mass destruction allegedly held by Iraq.

1998: The House of Representatives voted to commence an impeachment inquiry against President Clinton following the publication of a report that accused him of 11 offences of perjury and obstruction of justice in connection with his relationship with a White House intern. In the November elections the Republicans retained control of Congress. Deadly bomb attacks on US embassy buildings in Kenya and Tanzania were followed by US air missile attacks on targets in Sudan and Afghanistan, said to be operational centres for Osama bin Laden, a fugitive Saudi-born Islamist activist whom the USA believed to be responsible for the attacks.

1999: The Senate acquitted President Clinton on the articles of impeachment.

2000: George W. Bush, a Republican, was declared President-elect—one month after the presidential election and with a minority of the national popular vote—after the Supreme Court halted the manual recount of disputed ballots in Florida.

2001: On 11 September the worst ever terrorist attack on US territory took place when two hijacked passenger aeroplanes were flown into the World Trade Center in New York, and one hijacked passenger aeroplane attacked the Pentagon in Washington, DC. A fourth hijacked aeroplane crashed in Pennsylvania. The total death toll was put at 2,752, including 266 passengers and crew (and the hijackers) on the four aircraft, 190 at the Pentagon and the remainder in New York. The hijackings were believed to be the work of the militant Islamist al-Qa'ida (Base) organization, linked to bin Laden, whom the Afghan Government refused to hand over to the US authorities. In early October an international military campaign was launched against Afghanistan, led by the USA. Meanwhile, legislation ostensibly designed to combat terrorism gave wide-ranging powers to the Government to investigate citizens and non-citizens alike.

2002: In his State of the Union address in January, President Bush described Iran, Iraq and North Korea as an 'axis of evil' that supported international terrorism and sought to develop weapons of mass destruction. As a result of US-led pressure, in November the UN resolved to compel the Iraqi Government to declare all biological, chemical and other weapons of mass destruction and to comply with the UN Monitoring, Verification and Inspection Commission (UNMOVIC). After elections, the Republicans assumed control of the Senate and increased their majority in the House of Representatives.

2003: In February the USA, together with the United Kingdom and Spain, failed to secure a second UN resolution threatening Iraq with serious consequences if it failed to comply with UNMOVIC. The USA, the United Kingdom and Spain subsequently gave Iraqi President Saddam Hussain an ultimatum to leave Iraq. On 20 March US and British forces launched 'Operation Iraqi Freedom'. Within three weeks the regime had fallen; senior members of the regime were captured or killed in subsequent months, including Saddam Hussain.

2004: In April the publication of photographs of US soldiers abusing prisoners at the Abu Ghraib prison in Baghdad, Iraq, prompted the criminal prosecution of soldiers implicated in the scandal. Diplomatic relations were officially re-established with Libya for the first time since 1981. In October investigators finally reported that there were no weapons stockpiles in Iraq, but that Saddam Hussain had intended to redevelop the weapons programmes. In November President Bush was re-elected for a second term and the Republicans also retained control of both houses of Congress.

2005: In April the Senate approved John Negroponte as the first Director of National Intelligence, a cabinet-level post responsible for co-ordinating the security activities of 15 different agencies. In late August a state of emergency was declared in 13 states in the wake of 'Hurricane Katrina'. In September the Chief Justice of the Supreme Court, William Rehnquist, died; John G. Roberts, Jr, was sworn in as his successor. In December Secretary of State Condoleezza Rice confirmed that the Central Intelligence Agency (CIA) was engaged in the practice of 'extraordinary rendition', whereby suspected terrorists were secretly transported, without extradition, to be interrogated in countries where torture was condoned.

2006: In February a report by the UN Commission on Human Rights concluded that interrogators at the US naval base in Guantánamo Bay in Cuba, where suspected terrorists had been imprisoned since early 2002, had used methods that amounted to torture; the report urged the closure of the prison. In March Congress renewed the 2001 anti-terrorist legislation following amendments designed to strengthen civil liberties. In May Moroccan-born Zacarias Moussaoui was sentenced to life imprisonment for his part in the terrorist attacks of 11 September 2001; he remained the only person to stand trial for the attacks. In late June the Supreme Court ruled that military tribunals convened to try detainees at Guantánamo Bay were illegal. In November elections the Republicans lost control of both houses of Congress; the party's poor performance was partly attributed to the unpopularity of the ongoing war in Iraq. Immediately following the poll Secretary of Defense Donald H. Rumsfeld resigned; he was replaced by Robert M. Gates.

2007: In April the Supreme Court upheld the constitutionality of federal legislation enacted in 2003 restricting the right to abortion, reflecting its more conservative composition following recent appointments. In August Alberto Gonzales announced that he would resign (effective mid-September) as Attorney-General, after much controversy since his 2005 appointment and more recent allegations of bias and of misleading Congress. The September testimony to Congress of Gen. David Petraeus and Ambassador Ryan Crocker, the US military and civilian heads in Iraq, claimed sufficient success in the policy of a 'surge' in troop numbers (160,000 in 2007, 30,000 more than the previous year) to permit beginning troop withdrawals from the end of the year. In October former Vice-President Al Gore, Bush's principal opponent in the disputed 2000 presidential election, was awarded the Nobel Peace Prize for his efforts in drawing attention to environmental concerns (along with the UN's Intergovernmental Panel on Climate Change). Michael B. Mukasey was sworn in as the new Attorney-General in early November, despite concerns from some Democratic senators arising from his failure explicitly to classify 'waterboarding' (simulated drowning) as torture.

2008: In February charges were brought by the US Government against six prisoners being held in Guantánamo Bay, relating to their alleged involvement in the 2001 attacks. In early March President Bush vetoed legislation restricting 'harsh interrogation' techniques—widely regarded as a euphemism for torture—already approved by Congress, claiming that such 'specialized interrogation procedures' were of proven effectiveness and should remain available to the CIA. In the same month Housing and Urban Development Secretary Alphonso Jackson announced his resignation, amid an ongoing FBI investigation into allegations of favouritism in awarding housing contracts; Steven C. Preston was sworn in as his successor in June. Also in March details emerged of a federal investigation into a prostitution ring that implicated the Democratic Governor of New York, Eliot Spitzer, who subsequently tendered his resignation. The approval by the Senate in June of a further US $162,000m. in funding for military operations in Iraq and Afghanistan elicited criticism from some Democratic members of Congress, as the legislation did not include a timetable for the withdrawal of US troops from Iraq. In the midst of an economic downturn in the USA, President Bush approved legislation in July that allowed for the allocation of $300,000m. to enable those who were facing difficulties in meeting mortgage repayments to take advantage of fixed-rate loans. In a further effort to alleviate problems in the housing market, in September the US Government assumed control of the Federal National Mortgage Association (Fannie Mae) and the Federal Home Loan Mortgage Corporation (Freddie Mac), which financed or guaranteed almost one-half of all mortgages in the country. On 4 November the Democratic candidate, Barack Obama, defeated the Republican John McCain in the presidential election, obtaining an estimated 52.5% of popular votes cast; the Democrats also increased their representation in both houses of Congress.

PRESIDENTS OF THE USA

April 1789–March 1797: George Washington (Federalist).

March 1797–March 1801: John Adams (Federalist).

March 1801–March 1809: Thomas Jefferson (Democratic-Republican).

March 1809–March 1817: James Madison (Democratic-Republican).

March 1817–March 1825: James Monroe (Democratic-Republican).

March 1825–March 1829: John Quincy Adams (National Republican).

March 1829–March 1837: Andrew Jackson (Democrat).

March 1837–March 1841: Martin Van Buren (Democrat).

March 1841–April 1841: William Henry Harrison (Whig).

April 1841–March 1845: John Tyler (Whig).

March 1845–March 1849: James Knox Polk (Democrat).

March 1849–July 1850: Zachery Taylor (Whig).

July 1850–March 1853: Millard Fillmore (Whig).

March 1853–March 1857: Franklin Pierce (Democrat).

March 1857–March 1861: James Buchanan (Democrat).

March 1861–April 1865: Abraham Lincoln (Republican).

April 1865–March 1869: Andrew Johnson*.

March 1869–March 1877: Ulysses Simpson (Hiram Ulysses) Grant (Republican).

March 1877–March 1881: Rutherford Birchard Hayes (Republican).

March 1881–September 1881: James Abram Garfield (Republican).

September 1881–March 1885: Chester Alan Arthur (Republican).

March 1885–March 1889: Grover Cleveland (Democrat).

March 1889–March 1893: Benjamin Harrison (Republican).

March 1893–March 1897: Grover Cleveland (Democrat).

March 1897–September 1901: William McKinley (Republican).

September 1901–March 1909: Theodore Roosevelt (Republican).

March 1909–March 1913: William Howard Taft (Republican).

March 1913–March 1921: Woodrow Wilson (Democrat).

March 1921–August 1923: Warren Gamaliel Harding (Republican).

August 1923–March 1929: Calvin Coolidge (Republican).

March 1929–March 1933: Herbert Clark Hoover (Republican).

March 1933–April 1945: Franklin Delano Roosevelt (Democrat).

April 1945–January 1953: Harry S. Truman (Democrat).

January 1953–January 1961: Dwight David Eisenhower (Republican).

January 1961–November 1963: John Fitzgerald Kennedy (Democrat).

November 1963–January 1969: Lyndon Baines Johnson (Democrat).

January 1969–August 1974: Richard Milhous Nixon (Republican).

August 1974–January 1977: Gerald Rudolph Ford (Republican).

January 1977–January 1981: Jimmy (James Earl) Carter (Democrat).

January 1981–January 1989: Ronald Wilson Reagan (Republican).

January 1989–January 1993: George Bush (Republican).

January 1993–January 2001: Bill (William Jefferson) Clinton (Democrat).

January 2001–January 2009: George W. Bush (Republican).

January 2009–: Barack Obama (Democrat).

* Andrew Johnson, a Democrat, was nominated Vice-President by the Republicans and elected with Lincoln on a 'National Unity' ticket; he succeeded to the presidency on Lincoln's assassination.

AREA AND POPULATION

(Source, unless otherwise indicated: US Bureau of the Census, Department of Commerce, Washington, DC 20233.)

Area, Population and Density*

HISTORICAL SUMMARY
(census results)

	Population	Population per sq mile of land area	Area (sq miles)		
			Total	Land	Water
2 August 1790	3,929,214	4.5	891,364	864,746	24,065
4 August 1800	5,308,483	6.1	891,364	864,746	24,065
6 August 1810	7,239,881	4.3	1,722,685	1,681,828	34,175
7 August 1820	9,638,453	5.5	1,792,552	1,749,462	38,544
1 June 1830	12,866,020	7.4	1,792,552	1,749,462	38,544
1 June 1840	17,069,453	9.8	1,792,552	1,749,462	38,544
1 June 1850	23,191,876	7.9	2,991,655	2,940,042	52,705
1 June 1860	31,443,321	10.6	3,021,295	2,969,640	52,747
1 June 1870	39,818,449†	13.4	3,021,295	2,969,640	52,747
1 June 1880	50,155,783	16.9	3,021,295	2,969,640	52,747
1 June 1890	62,947,714	21.2	3,021,295	2,969,640	52,747
1 June 1900	75,994,575	25.6	3,021,295	2,969,834	52,553
15 April 1910	91,972,266	31.0	3,021,295	2,969,565	52,822
1 January 1920	105,710,620	35.6	3,021,295	2,969,451	52,936
1 April 1930	122,775,046	41.2	3,021,295	2,977,128	45,259
1 April 1940	131,669,275	44.2	3,021,295	2,977,128	45,259
1 April 1950	151,325,798	42.6	3,618,770	3,552,206	63,005
1 April 1960	179,323,175	50.6	3,618,770	3,540,911	74,212
1 April 1970	203,302,031	57.4	3,618,770	3,540,023	78,444
1 April 1980	226,542,199	64.0	3,618,770	3,539,289	79,481
1 April 1990	248,718,302	70.3	3,717,796‡	3,536,278	181,518‡
1 April 2000	281,421,906	79.6	3,794,083‡	3,537,438	256,645‡

* Area figures represent area on indicated date including in some cases considerable areas not then organized or settled, and not covered by the census. Total area figures for 1790 to 1970 have been recalculated on the basis of the remeasurement of states and counties for the 1980 census, but not on the basis of the 1990 census. The land and water area figures for past censuses have not been adjusted and are not strictly comparable with the total area data for comparable dates because the land areas were derived from different base data, and these values are known to have changed with the construction of reservoirs, draining of lakes, etc. Density figures are based on land area measurements as reported in earlier censuses.

† Revised to include adjustments for underenumeration in southern states; unrevised number is 38,558,371 (13.0 per square mile).

‡ Comprises or includes Great Lakes, inland, and coastal water. Also included for 2000 are territorial waters. Data for prior years cover inland water only.

STATES
(census of 1 April 2000)

State	Area (sq miles) Land	Water	Total	Population	Population per sq mile of land area
Alabama	50,744	1,675	52,419	4,447,100	87.6
Alaska	571,951	91,316	663,267	626,932	1.1
Arizona	113,635	364	113,998	5,130,632	45.2
Arkansas	52,068	1,110	53,179	2,673,400	51.3
California	155,959	7,736	163,696	33,871,648	217.2
Colorado	103,718	376	104,094	4,301,261	41.5
Connecticut	4,845	699	5,543	3,405,565	702.9
Delaware	1,954	536	2,489	783,600	401.1
District of Columbia	61	7	68	572,059	9,316.4
Florida	53,927	11,828	65,755	15,982,378	296.4
Georgia	57,906	1,519	59,425	8,186,453	141.4
Hawaii	6,423	4,508	10,931	1,211,537	188.6
Idaho	82,747	823	83,570	1,293,953	15.6
Illinois	55,584	2,331	57,914	12,419,293	223.4
Indiana	35,867	551	36,418	6,080,485	169.5
Iowa	55,869	402	56,272	2,926,324	52.4
Kansas	81,815	462	82,277	2,688,418	32.9
Kentucky	39,728	681	40,409	4,041,769	101.7
Louisiana	43,562	8,278	51,840	4,468,976	102.6
Maine	30,862	4,523	35,385	1,274,923	41.3
Maryland	9,774	2,633	12,407	5,296,486	541.9
Massachusetts	7,840	2,715	10,555	6,349,097	809.8
Michigan	56,804	39,912	96,716	9,938,444	175.0
Minnesota	79,610	7,329	86,939	4,919,479	61.8
Mississippi	46,907	1,523	48,430	2,844,658	60.6
Missouri	68,886	818	69,704	5,595,211	81.2
Montana	145,552	1,490	147,042	902,195	6.2
Nebraska	76,872	481	77,354	1,711,263	22.3
Nevada	109,826	735	110,561	1,998,257	18.2
New Hampshire	8,968	382	9,350	1,235,786	137.8
New Jersey	7,417	1,304	8,721	8,414,350	1,134.4
New Mexico	121,356	234	121,589	1,819,046	15.0
New York	47,214	7,342	54,556	18,976,457	401.9
North Carolina	48,711	5,108	53,819	8,049,313	165.2
North Dakota	68,976	1,724	70,700	642,200	9.3
Ohio	40,948	3,877	44,825	11,353,140	277.3
Oklahoma	68,667	1,231	69,898	3,450,654	50.3
Oregon	95,997	2,384	98,381	3,421,399	35.6
Pennsylvania	44,817	1,239	46,055	12,281,054	274.0
Rhode Island	1,045	500	1,545	1,048,319	1,003.2
South Carolina	30,109	1,911	32,020	4,012,012	133.2
South Dakota	75,885	1,232	77,116	754,844	9.9
Tennessee	41,217	926	42,143	5,689,283	138.0
Texas	261,797	6,784	268,581	20,851,820	79.6
Utah	82,144	2,755	84,899	2,233,169	27.2
Vermont	9,250	365	9,614	608,827	65.8
Virginia	39,594	3,180	42,774	7,078,515	178.8
Washington	66,544	4,756	71,300	5,894,121	88.6
West Virginia	24,078	152	24,230	1,808,344	75.1
Wisconsin	54,310	11,188	65,498	5,363,675	98.8
Wyoming	97,100	713	97,814	493,782	5.1
Total	3,537,438	256,645	3,794,083	281,421,906	79.6

Population by State and Race

(census of 1 April 2000, '000 persons)

State	White	White Hispanic	Black	Asian and Pacific Islander	American Indian, Eskimo, Aleut	Some other race	Two or more races	Other Hispanic*	Total
Alabama	3,126	37	1,156	33	22	29	44	76	4,447
Alaska	424	11	22	28	98	10	34	26	627
Arizona	3,274	599	159	99	256	597	147	1,296	5,131
Arkansas	2,100	38	419	22	18	40	36	87	2,673
California	15,817	4,353	2,264	3,814	333	5,682	1,608	10,967	33,872
Colorado	3,203	357	165	100	44	310	122	736	4,301
Connecticut	2,639	142	310	84	10	147	75	320	3,406
Delaware	568	17	151	17	3	16	13	37	784
District of Columbia	159	17	343	16	2	22	13	45	572
Florida	10,459	2,007	2,336	275	54	477	376	2,683	15,982
Georgia	5,129	199	2,350	177	22	196	114	435	8,186
Hawaii	277	17	22	618	4	15	259	88	1,212
Idaho	1,139	38	5	13	18	55	26	102	1,294
Illinois	8,424	701	1,877	428	31	723	235	1,530	12,419
Indiana	5,219	101	510	61	16	98	76	215	6,080
Iowa	2,710	38	62	38	9	37	32	82	2,926
Kansas	2,234	80	154	48	25	91	56	188	2,688
Kentucky	3,608	33	296	31	9	23	42	60	4,042
Louisiana	2,794	62	1,452	56	25	31	48	108	4,469
Maine	1,230	6	7	9	7	3	13	9	1,275
Maryland	3,287	105	1,477	213	15	96	104	228	5,296
Massachusetts	5,198	169	343	241	15	237	146	429	6,349
Michigan	7,807	159	1,413	179	58	130	192	324	9,938
Minnesota	4,337	63	172	144	55	66	83	143	4,919
Mississippi	1,728	18	1,034	19	12	14	20	40	2,845
Missouri	4,686	62	629	65	25	46	82	119	5,595
Montana	808	9	3	5	56	5	16	18	902
Nebraska	1,494	39	69	23	15	48	24	94	1,711
Nevada	1,303	199	135	99	26	159	76	394	1,998
New Hampshire	1,175	12	9	16	3	7	13	20	1,236
New Jersey	5,557	547	1,142	484	19	451	214	1,117	8,414
New Mexico	813	401	34	21	173	310	66	765	1,819
New York	11,761	1,133	3,014	1,054	82	1,342	590	2,868	18,976
North Carolina	5,647	158	1,738	118	100	187	103	379	8,049
North Dakota	589	4	4	4	31	3	7	8	642
Ohio	9,538	107	1,301	135	24	89	158	217	11,353
Oklahoma	2,556	72	261	49	273	83	156	179	3,451
Oregon	2,858	104	56	109	45	145	105	275	3,421
Pennsylvania	10,322	162	1,225	223	18	188	142	394	12,281
Rhode Island	858	33	47	24	5	53	28	91	1,048
South Carolina	2,652	43	1,185	38	14	40	40	95	4,012
South Dakota	665	5	5	5	62	4	10	11	755
Tennessee	4,506	57	933	59	15	56	63	124	5,689
Texas	10,933	3,866	2,405	577	118	2,438	515	6,670	20,852
Utah	1,904	89	18	52	30	93	47	202	2,233
Vermont	585	4	3	5	2	1	7	6	609
Virginia	4,966	154	1,390	265	21	139	143	330	7,079
Washington	4,652	169	190	346	93	229	214	442	5,894
West Virginia	1,710	9	57	10	4	3	16	12	1,808
Wisconsin	4,682	88	304	90	47	85	67	193	5,364
Wyoming	439	16	4	3	11	12	9	32	494
Total	194,553	16,908	34,658	10,642	2,476	15,359	6,826	35,306	281,422

* Comprises non-white Hispanic population. Those identifying themselves thus are included in the Black, Asian and Pacific Islander and Native American categories. Therefore, this category does not form part of the state total.

Population by State and Age*

(census of 1 April 2000, '000 persons)

State	Under 20 years	20 to 34 years	35 to 64 years	65 years and over	Total†
Alabama	1,256	910	1,701	580	4,447
Alaska	208	129	236	53	627
Arizona	1,518	1,106	1,839	668	5,131
Arkansas	761	534	1,004	374	2,673
California	10,235	7,610	12,431	3,596	33,872
Colorado	1,225	970	1,690	416	4,301
Connecticut	926	639	1,370	470	3,406
Delaware	218	161	303	102	784
District of Columbia	136	154	213	70	572
Florida	4,049	3,012	6,114	2,808	15,982
Georgia	2,415	1,891	3,095	785	8,186
Hawaii	327	255	469	161	1,212
Idaho	414	263	471	146	1,294
Illinois	3,606	2,663	4,651	1,500	12,419
Indiana	1,763	1,257	2,307	753	6,080
Iowa	828	567	1,095	436	2,926
Kansas	798	539	995	356	2,688
Kentucky	1,114	851	1,572	505	4,042
Louisiana	1,368	927	1,657	517	4,469
Maine	335	227	529	183	1,275
Maryland	1,493	1,063	2,142	599	5,296
Massachusetts	1,675	1,331	2,483	860	6,349
Michigan	2,884	2,006	3,829	1,219	9,938
Minnesota	1,435	996	1,895	594	4,919
Mississippi	873	595	1,033	344	2,845
Missouri	1,594	1,108	2,137	755	5,595
Montana	257	162	362	121	902
Nebraska	504	344	631	232	1,711
Nevada	562	437	781	219	1,998
New Hampshire	344	229	515	148	1,236
New Jersey	2,284	1,669	3,348	1,113	8,414
New Mexico	565	355	687	212	1,819
New York	5,211	4,002	7,315	2,448	18,976
North Carolina	2,193	1,791	3,096	969	8,049
North Dakota	183	127	237	94	642
Ohio	3,216	2,249	4,381	1,508	11,353
Oklahoma	1,002	699	1,294	456	3,451
Oregon	944	701	1,338	438	3,421
Pennsylvania	3,271	2,307	4,785	1,919	12,281
Rhode Island	283	212	401	152	1,048
South Carolina	1,136	843	1,548	485	4,012
South Dakota	227	144	275	108	755
Tennessee	1,561	1,202	2,223	703	5,689
Texas	6,546	4,701	7,532	2,073	20,852
Utah	811	552	680	190	2,233
Vermont	166	112	253	78	609
Virginia	1,937	1,518	2,832	792	7,079
Washington	1,683	1,231	2,318	662	5,894
West Virginia	455	349	728	277	1,808
Wisconsin	1,532	1,063	2,066	703	5,364
Wyoming	145	93	197	58	494
Total	80,472	58,856	107,084	35,008	281,422

* Excludes Armed Forces personnel stationed abroad.
† May not equal the sum of the individual categories owing to rounding.

Immigration

(year ending 30 September, '000 persons)

Country of birth	1981–90	1991–2000	2004	2005	2006	2007
Europe	705.6	1,311.4	133.2	176.5	164.2	120.8
Bosnia and Herzegovina	n.a.	39.1*	10.6	14.1	3.8	1.6
Poland	97.4	169.6	14.3	15.4	17.1	10.4
Russia	84.0†	128.0*	17.4	18.1	13.2	9.4
Ukraine	n.a.	141.3*	14.2	22.7	17.1	11.0
United Kingdom	142.1	135.8	14.9	19.8	17.2	14.5
Asia	2,817.4	2,892.2	334.5	400.1	422.3	383.5
Bangladesh	15.2	66.0	8.1	11.5	14.6	12.1
China, People's Republic	388.8‡	424.6	55.5	69.9	87.3	76.7
India	261.9	383.3	70.2	84.7	61.4	65.4
Iran	154.8	112.6	10.4	13.9	13.9	10.5
Korea, Republic	338.8	171.3	19.8	26.6	24.4	22.4
Pakistan	61.3	124.6	12.1	14.9	17.4	13.5
Philippines	495.3	505.6	57.8	60.7	74.6	72.6
Viet Nam	401.4	421.1	31.5	32.8	30.7	28.7
North America, Central America and the Caribbean	3,125.0	3,917.4	342.5	345.6	414.1	339.4
Canada	119.2	137.6	15.6	21.9	18.2	15.5
Cuba	159.2	180.9	20.5	36.3	45.6	29.1
Dominican Republic	251.8	340.9	30.5	27.5	38.1	28.0
El Salvador	214.6	217.4	29.8	21.4	31.8	21.1
Guatemala	87.9	103.1	18.9	16.8	24.1	17.9
Haiti	140.2	181.8	14.2	14.5	22.2	30.4
Jamaica	213.8	173.5	14.4	18.3	25.0	19.4
Mexico	1,653.3	2,251.4	175.4	161.4	173.7	148.6
Nicaragua	44.1	97.7	4.0	3.3	4.1	3.7
South America	455.9	539.9	72.1	103.1	138.0	106.5
Brazil	23.7	52.3	10.6	16.7	17.9	14.3
Colombia	124.4	131.0	18.8	25.6	43.1	33.2
Ecuador	56.0	76.4	8.6	11.6	17.5	12.2
Peru	64.4	105.7	11.8	15.7	21.7	17.7
Africa	192.3	383.0	66.4	85.1	117.4	94.7
Nigeria	35.3	67.3	9.4	10.6	13.5	12.4
Total (incl. others)	7,338.1	9,095.4	957.9	1,122.3	1,266.1	1,052.4

* Figure for 1992–2000.
† USSR figure.
‡ Includes Taiwan.

Sources: US Immigration and Naturalization Service, US Department of Justice, *Statistical Yearbook*, and US Department of Homeland Security, *Yearbook of Immigration Statistics*.

ESSAYS

ESSAYS ON PUBLIC AFFAIRS

THE CONSTITUTIONAL STRUCTURE OF THE USA

Prof. DAVID McKAY

INTRODUCTION

Compared with other constitutional systems, that of the USA has a number of unusual and, in some respects, unique, features. The first of these is its longevity, with neither the wording of the US Constitution nor the basic political relations it laid down changing a great deal after its ratification in June 1788. It has been amended on just 17 occasions (exclusive of the amendments contained in the Bill of Rights—see below), and early 21st century US politics remains dominated by the federal system and the separation of powers, which were initially laid down by the Constitution.

A second notable characteristic of the system lies in the unusual and extensive powers granted to Congress, the national legislature. Few constitutions give their assemblies or parliaments such wide-ranging powers; in even fewer are executives so constrained by legislators in terms of the routine exercise of power.

A third feature is the high esteem in which the country's population holds its Constitution. This has applied virtually throughout the history of the republic. Even during the Civil War of 1861–65 the Confederate states believed that the federal Government had violated the Constitution's prescription for federalism—the document itself was not the target of their grievances. Certainly at the beginning of the 21st century it was almost impossible to find a significant social or economic group that believed the Constitution should be abolished, replaced or changed in any fundamental sense. One possible exception was the right-wing militia and survivalist groups, the activities of which attracted so much attention in the 1990s. Even their main contention, however, seemed to be that the federal Government had exceeded its constitutional powers, rather than a belief that the Constitution as such was not legitimate.

THE LEGISLATURE

Article I of the Constitution is devoted to Congress, and in this respect the legislature was assigned pre-eminence over other institutions. The powers given to Congress were carefully defined: they include the power to tax and spend, to declare war, to regulate commerce between the states, to ratify treaties and to confirm appointments to the executive branch of government. Originally only the House of Representatives was to be elected directly by the people; the Senate, the upper house, was to assume the status of a more deliberative body, with two senators from each state being chosen indirectly by the individual state legislatures, to serve a six-year term. (The election of senators by direct popular vote was introduced by the 17th Amendment, ratified in 1913.) The House of Representatives was considered to be the 'people's' assembly; representatives were elected for just two years and the House was given special powers over those areas of public policy that were so central to the grievances of colonial America—taxation and spending, and the power to raise armies and declare war.

The 55 state delegates, or Founding Fathers, who drafted the US Constitution wanted to achieve a balance between popular representation (the apportionment of seats in the House of Representatives was, and is, proportional to population, with a minimum of one representative per state) and territorial representation (two senators were to be elected from each state, irrespective of its population). Most legislation (see below) may be introduced in either house of Congress, and bills must be passed by both before being presented to the President for approval. However, each house had independent sources of political power in addition to their joint sources: only the House of Representatives might originate bills for raising revenue, while the Senate was given special powers to ratify foreign treaties and to confirm executive appointments (and, therefore, an enhanced responsibility for exercising checks upon the executive branch). Congress was also given the power to impeach the President and other senior officials for 'high crimes and misdemeanours'. As was demonstrated in 1998 and early 1999 when President Bill Clinton was impeached, the House actually impeaches (that is, formally decides that a case against the President exists) and the Senate tries the case. In Clinton's case, the House impeached but the Senate acquitted. Indeed, no President has been successfully convicted following an impeachment trial, although Richard Nixon (1969–74), had he not resigned in August 1974, would almost certainly have been impeached and convicted.

THE EXECUTIVE

Article II of the Constitution defines the power of the executive, all of which was vested in the President. The most passionate debates among the framers of the Constitution concerned the relationship between the legislature and the executive. They were determined to prevent the possibility of the abuse of power by the chief executive—a direct consequence of their perception of the conduct of the Government of the British King, George III. However, the experience of very weak central authority, as provided for under the Articles of Confederation (which were the basis of government in 1781–89), indicated the need for a stronger national executive. The eventual solution was a system of separation of powers, designed, through a system of safeguards or 'checks and balances', to prevent one branch from usurping the power of the other. Thus, the President was given the executive power as well as being designated Commander-in-Chief of the armed forces, and he had the authority to recommend to Congress 'such measures as he shall judge necessary and expedient' in a 'state of the union' address made 'from time to time' (by convention given annually), but senior appointments were subject to the 'advice and consent of the Senate'. The Senate must also approve all foreign treaties by a two-thirds' majority, and war could only be declared by Congress.

The President was given the power to veto any bill passed by Congress, although the presidential veto could itself be set aside by a two-thirds' majority of a quorum in both the House of Representatives and the Senate. The presidency's powers were thus constrained by having only limited authority over the crucial law-making process. Moreover, the presidential constituency was a national one, whereas those of members of the House of Representatives were essentially local and those of senators state-wide.

The Founding Fathers were cautious about vesting too much power in the mass of the population. This was reflected in the original provisions for the indirect election of senators and also in the creation of an Electoral College responsible for electing the President. Each state was to appoint 'a number of electors, equal to the whole number of Senators and Representatives to which the State may be entitled in the Congress', the method by which each state did so being determined by its legislature. Whereas it was intended that the Electoral College would comprise wise and senior citizens who would exercise an independent choice, the development of political groups and parties meant that electors became increasingly partisan. Eventually, during the early 19th century, the states voted to allow the electorate to choose Electoral College members, with this system resulting in a de facto direct election of the US President and Vice-President. The Electoral College system has been much criticized, mainly because, in almost all states, legislatures have deemed that its members are chosen on a simple plurality system. Thus, a presidential candidate who wins the popular vote by whatever margin in a state wins all of the Electoral College seats. It was this system that made the ballot in Florida in the 2000 presidential election so crucial. In the event, George W. Bush won Florida's Electoral College votes, and thus the election, because the Supreme Court decided that further recounts would not be in the public interest. The 2000 result was also notable because, although Bush won a majority of votes in the Electoral College, he recorded fewer popular votes than his opponent Al Gore. Although beset with such anomalies, it is unlikely that the system will be reformed because each of the alternatives is opposed by one grouping or another (each house of Congress and/or a majority of the state legislatures), which would block a constitutional amendment.

THE JUDICIARY

The system of checks and balances was extended to the judicial branch. While all judicial power was vested in the US Supreme Court (Article III), responsibility for nominating its members was held by the President alone. Congress, in turn, might regulate the appellate jurisdiction of the Court, and the Senate must confirm all presidential appointments. Until the last part of the 20th century nominations to the Supreme Court were relatively uncontroversial, but, with the increase in importance of the role of the Court, they have taken on a highly political complexion. For example, in 2005 two vacancies on the Court occurred, thus giving President Bush the opportunity to shift the Court's political position to the right. He subsequently did so by nominating Samuel A. Alito, Jr, and John G. Roberts, Jr, to the Court, both of whom were confirmed by the Senate. The Constitution was highly ambiguous on the question of judicial review, or whether the Supreme Court had the power to determine what was, and what was not, compatible with the Constitution. This power was, however, established as early as 1803 in the case of *Marbury v. Madison*. Thereafter, it was the Court's responsibility to review acts of Congress, presidential decisions, and the actions of state and local government in order to determine their constitutionality. Although used sparingly, this power had a profound impact in dealing with such diverse issues as presidential powers, including the power of Commander-in-Chief, the separation of powers, civil rights and liberties, abortion and federal-state relations.

FEDERALISM

A further distinguishing feature of the US constitutional system is its federalism, or the notion that sovereignty is shared between the federal and state levels of government. In fact very little is mentioned about federalism in the Constitution, as very little is guaranteed to the states (they are assured of equal representation in the Senate, territorial integrity, a republican form of government, and protection against invasion and domestic violence). The 10th Amendment, however, guaranteed that 'the powers not delegated to the United States by the Constitution, nor prohibited by it to the States, are reserved to the States respectively, or to the people'. In other words, anything not specifically assigned as a federal responsibility in the Constitution is assumed to be a state responsibility. As in the case of judicial power, the problem is caused by the fact that the Constitution says very little about which level of government is responsible for which functional policy area. Foreign affairs and certain aspects of economic policy (printing and coining money, for example) are clearly federal tasks, but, beyond that, much ambiguity remains. As will be discussed later, the USA clearly retained a federal system of government, but while each state maintained a separate legal system and a structure of political institutions, the federal Government gradually assumed greater domestic policy responsibilities in relation to the states.

CONSTITUTIONAL AMENDMENTS

The Founding Fathers imposed upon the Constitution a very cumbersome amendment process, which required the agreement of more than a simple majority of elected officials at several levels in the system. The most commonly used method of amendment was proposal by a two-thirds' vote in both houses of Congress, followed by ratification by three-quarters of all state legislatures.

In December 1791, less than four years after ratification of the original seven Articles, 10 amendments came into effect that collectively are known as the Bill of Rights. These 10 provisions guaranteed basic liberties (of religion, speech, press, association, assembly and petition) and freedom from arbitrary government action (such as freedom from search and seizure, the right to trial by jury and due process of law) and were added at the insistence of those states that feared the new federal Government might threaten the rights of citizens.

Of the 17 amendments adopted after the ratification of the Bill of Rights, the most important are those affecting elections. In most cases these either extended the suffrage or introduced elections to particular institutions. Hence, the 15th Amendment (ratified in February 1870) extended the right to vote—at least in theory—to all races; the 17th (April 1913) provided for the popular election of senators; the 19th (August 1920) extended voting to women; and the 23rd (March 1961) awarded three Electoral College votes to the District of Columbia. The 24th Amendment (January 1964) abolished payment of the poll tax as a requirement for voting in federal elections and the 26th (June 1971) lowered the voting age to 18 years. Of the remaining amendments, two (the 18th and the 21st) were devoted to the adoption and rejection of 'Prohibition' (a legal ban on the manufacture, transportation or trade in alcoholic beverages or 'intoxicating liquor'). Only four others can be deemed to have had a lasting effect on the substance of policy and on the powers of the federal Government. The 13th Amendment (December 1865) abolished slavery, while the 14th (July 1868) extended the due process of law as expressed in the Bill of Rights to apply to the states as well as to the federal Government. (In practice, this was not implemented fully until the 1950s and 1960s.) The 16th Amendment (February 1913) established a graduated national income tax, and the 22nd (February 1951) limited Presidents to a maximum of eight years in office, or two full terms. (This could be up to 10 years if a President came into office no more than half-way through a term, as did Lyndon Johnson in 1963, although Johnson chose not to stand for re-election in 1968.)

CONSTITUTIONAL CHANGES BY INTERPRETATION

In general, interpretation, rather than amendment, of the US Constitution brought about many more far-reaching changes. All constitutions are subject to changes by interpretation, but that of the USA was more flexible than most—partly because the document is both short and, in places, quite vague. Four major processes of interpretative change can be identified.

The Rise of Federal Power

However measured, the federal Government played a much more dominant role in the system than that envisaged by the Founding Fathers. As the 20th century progressed, state and local governments were increasingly in receipt of federal aid to help finance a wide range of services. While it was originally envisaged that almost all domestic functions of government would be performed by the states and localities, a combination of factors—such as fiscal stress, the need to achieve some degree of equality in the provision of services and the increasing complexity of society—increased the role of the federal Government. This also applied to civil liberties and civil rights—from the 1940s both were subject to federalizing or nationalizing trends as the Supreme Court insisted on the application of national standards. Each state retained considerable autonomy in such areas as education, land-use planning, law enforcement and the administration of justice, but there were few legal limits on how far the federal Government could extend its influence into these areas. During the last quarter of the 20th century some powers were returned to the states, especially in the general area of welfare and social policy and, notably, capital punishment. However, the federal Government remains the main focus of public policy in the USA in a wide range of areas. Most US citizens also perceive the federal Government as the 'government of last resort' in a range of policy areas and following natural disasters. Hence, in the provision of basic services such as health care, citizens expect help from the federal authorities, and in such disasters as 'Hurricane Katrina' in 2005 it was the federal Government that was the main provider of assistance and reconstruction. Likewise, the federal Government acted decisively in 2008 to rescue the financial markets from collapse. Similarly, if things go wrong with the federal Government's policies or the public's perceptions of those policies, then voters are quick to punish Presidents in subsequent elections. This often applies in economic policy or in the conduct of foreign wars. Hence, George Bush, Sr, was defeated in 1992 partly because he was held responsible for economic recession. Likewise, his son was punished in the 2006 mid-term elections mainly because of a perceived mishandling of the war in Iraq.

The Rise of Executive Power

The executive branch, with the President at its apex, became much more powerful than originally intended. While the ascendancy of executives over legislatures is common to all democracies, it was especially noteworthy in the US context because of the very considerable constitutional autonomy of Congress. Presidents, however, were able to assert their ascendancy, if not their dominance, over Congress for a number of reasons. As the USA acquired vast overseas responsibilities and a major defence capability, so the President, as Commander-in-Chief, assumed responsibility for military and foreign policy. While it could be assumed that such power was always intended, the scale of these responsibilities increased immeasurably from the 1930s. With the onset of economic depression in the late 1920s, following the rapid industrialization of the country, the federal Government was also expected to be responsible for managing the economy. After the Second World War the crucial function of keeping the economy growing at something approaching full employment was added to the federal authorities' responsibilities. While Congress played some role here, the major part of the task fell to the executive branch and to the presidency, with the result that the US population tended to expect the presidency to take policy initiatives—and to assume responsibility for the outcome of the latter. A general increase in the size and complexity of government apparatus also added to the executive branch's responsibilities. Access to detailed information, available to those responsible for the implementation of policy, gave the executive a clear advantage over Congress. Partly as a result of these developments, certainly in the latter part of the 20th century the President had become the chief legislator—it was the President's programme, not that of Congress, that determined the national policy agenda. This said, there have been occasions when Congress has taken back the role of chief legislator, as was the case in 1994 when the Republicans recaptured Congress. However, their ability to set the agenda was limited by bicameralism and the presidential veto.

With the end of the Cold War, it might have been expected that executive power would wane as the USA's international responsibilities, not least the maintenance of a nuclear deterrent, receded in importance. However, the declaration by the Administration of President George W. Bush (2001–) of a global 'war against terror' following the attacks on New York and Washington, DC, on 11 September 2001, provoked the very opposite: an increase in the powers of the President and his Administration in relation to Congress. The reactive, emergency nature of the fight against terrorism required quick decision-making and the use of police and military power. Only the executive can perform these functions. Hence, the passage of the 'Patriot' Act (Uniting and Strengthening America by Providing the Appropriate Tools Required to Intercept and Obstruct Terrorism—PATRIOT—Act) in late 2001, the creation in November 2002 of the Department of Homeland Security (the cabinet-rank successor to the Office of Homeland Security, established in late 2001), as well as the military invasions of Afghanistan in 2001 and Iraq in 2003, all represented a significant enhancement of executive power. Moreover, as the war in Iraq progressed, so the President's power increased as he appealed to Congress and to the US people on the grounds that opposition to the President undermined the 'war on terror' in general. Only when that 'war' was seen to go badly wrong in 2006 and 2007 was the President's power base eroded. In addition, domestic pressures often force even conservative Presidents to wield increased executive power. Such was the case with President Bush, who increased federal spending on health care and emergency assistance to state and local governments, and, in 2008, executed a massive rescue of financial institutions.

The Democratization of US Politics

The spread of mass democracy was, of course, related to formal changes in the Constitution, but the democratization of US politics went much further than these changes imply. Increasingly, both the President and Congress were expected to respond quickly and appropriately to the people's will. This 'electoral connection' was much stronger than in most comparable countries, partly because the USA developed a more populist political culture, but also because the society was highly individualist in its values. Individual voters expected a great deal from individual senators, representatives and Presidents, and so the pressures on elected officials to 'perform' were very great. This was demonstrated in 2006, when an unpopular President lost control of both houses of Congress in the November mid-term elections.

The Growing Protection of Individual Rights

Until the 20th century the Supreme Court failed to interpret the Bill of Rights and the 14th Amendment (which guarantees all citizens the equal protection of the law) in ways that extended protection to state laws. Hence, the civil rights and liberties of groups such as Southern blacks were violated with relative impunity. From the 1940s, however, the Supreme Court extended these constitutional guarantees to all laws enforceable within the USA. In addition, the Supreme Court increasingly insisted that, under federal law, the rights of individuals often take precedence over those of the state (or of the federal Government). As a result, while protection was not completely guaranteed, freedom of speech, assembly and religion was better protected in the USA than in most comparable countries. Citizens also had considerable access to the affairs of government. Following the terrorist attacks on the USA of 11 September 2001 concerns were raised that individual rights would take second place to the defence of the national interest. Such fears are almost certainly justified; indeed, the USA has a history of reordering its priorities in this way, as the internment of the Japanese Americans following the Second World War and the McCarthyite 'red scare' period in the 1950s demonstrated. More recently, the 2001 Patriot Act sanctioned government intelligence-gathering of the sort that would not have been considered constitutional in earlier eras. However, the system contains so many checks and balances that retreats from the protection of individual freedom are usually reversed in the longer term. Indeed, from 2005 legal challenges to some provisions of the Patriot Act were raised—although it may be several years before their outcome is known.

THE US CONSTITUTIONAL SYSTEM: AN ASSESSMENT

For almost all of its history, into the present day, the USA enjoyed relative domestic political stability. Indeed, after the Civil War no threat to the US regime emanated from domestic political movements. Few democracies experienced such a long period of stability. The achievement is all the more remarkable when it is remembered that the USA experienced truly dramatic changes over the course of its history—it was transformed by immigration, industrialization, centralization and territorial expansion. Indeed, the building of the 'New Society' was founded on the bringing together of diverse peoples, whether defined in national, religious, linguistic, ethnic or racial terms. This being accepted, critics point to a number of features of the constitutional structure, which could put the USA at a disadvantage in relation to some other developed nations. Of these, two in particular dominated—the separation of powers and the federal system.

The Separation of Powers

The weakness of political parties in the USA, and the fact that Congress and the President were elected by completely different constituencies, meant that the executive and legislative branches of government had little obligation to act in harmony. In the modern period (from the election to the presidency of Franklin D. Roosevelt in 1932) there were, indeed, few occasions when these two branches worked easily together. The early 'New Deal' period (1933–35), the Second World War and the 'Great Society' period (1964–66) are conspicuous as exceptions. It may be argued that before the USA acquired its massive global responsibilities and became the effective economic locomotive of the world economy, this lack of co-operation was an affordable cost for the working of a healthy democracy. By the early 1990s, however, critics were arguing that the system so inhibited efficient policy-making that the USA was at a disadvantage in relation to other countries. Planning a national budget, for example, must involve both executive and legislature. However, there was little incentive for individual representatives and senators to put the national or public interest (i.e. balancing the budget) before the interests of their constituents. This problem was compounded by the fact that as the power of political parties diminished and political behaviour became more personalized, so the link between members of Congress and constituents was strengthened. Finally, by the late 1990s divided government (when one of the two main political parties controls the presidency and the other Congress) appeared to have become the norm in US politics. Between 1995 and 2001, for example, the Republicans controlled Congress, but there was a Democratic President, Bill Clinton. His successor, George W. Bush, enjoyed just a few months of unified government until one Republican senator, James W. Jeffords of Vermont, declared himself an Independent and consequently gave the Democrats a narrow majority. In the subsequent 2002 mid-term elections, the Republicans regained control of the Senate, but with a narrow majority. The party increased this majority in the November 2004 elections only to lose control of both houses of Congress in 2006. Hence, by early 2007 divided government had returned, and given the waning fortunes of the Republicans, it seemed unlikely that they would control both branches of government for some time to come.

A further problem associated with the constitutional separation of powers was the relative isolation of the executive branch. Unlike most parliamentary systems, there was no collective responsibility among prominent members of the executive: all executive power was vested in the President, who alone bore responsibility for the operations of a vast federal bureaucracy. Nor was there the sort of party peer-group review which, in the Japanese and British systems, for example, acted as something of a check on the suitability and qualifications of cabinet members and other top officials. Instead, Presidents relied more on networks of personal contacts when staffing the executive branch. As a result, the potential for errors and the placing of inappropriate men and women in key positions was probably higher in the USA than elsewhere. (The fact that the President is also head of state compounds this problem, since heads of state are traditionally held to be 'above politics'.)

Hence, during the second half of his first term in office, and even more so during his second term, President George W. Bush and his Cabinet increasingly became the focus of political attention with respect to his interventionist foreign policy stance, his handling of natural disasters and, particularly from 2007, in the general area of economic management. Whatever the intrinsic merits of these policies, the President became ever more exposed by national and international setbacks. In such a context, Presidents are now almost always obliged to pursue strategies that carry with them high risks, not least the prospect of defeat either for them or their party at the next election.

Finally, the institution of judicial review attracted many critics. By the beginning of the 21st century the Supreme Court was expected to deliberate on the constitutionality of a wide range of issues: from banking deregulation to abortion, and from civil rights to genetic engineering. Unlike comparable courts in other countries, the US Supreme Court's function was actually to make policy, rather than merely to clarify the law or to state whether Congress, the presidency or the states had acted beyond the law. Critics of judicial review put forward the argument that Congress and the President should assume the main responsibility for law-making.

Federalism and Political Fragmentation

A second major problem concerned the division of the country into 50 states (up from 48 in 1959 with the addition of Alaska and Hawaii), among which there was much inequality of size, population and wealth. As already noted, although the federal Government increasingly intervened in the affairs of the states, they retained considerable de facto autonomy and variety in the policy-making sphere. As a result, there were great disparities in such areas as labour law, the penal system (particularly over the vexed question of capital punishment), levels of taxation and environmental protection. Critics argued that, whether the main reason is justice, economic efficiency or protection from environmental pollution and global warming, there was an urgent need for national standards. This was not so much a legal as a political problem: although neither Congress nor the presidency was inhibited by the courts from insisting on national standards, they tended either to be very sensitive to pressures from the states or to be committed ideologically to some degree of decentralization. However, events such as 'Hurricane Katrina' in August 2005 force Presidents to face up to the inability of some states (and especially poor states such as Louisiana) to cope with such large-scale natural disasters. This obliges Presidents greatly to increase the federal role. Similarly, in September 2008 the federal Government was obliged to rescue the insurance company America International Group, Inc (AIG) partly because there is no federal regulation of the insurance industry. Instead, the 50 states separately regulate the industry. Conversely, the policy experience of some states such as California, which have pursued aggressive policies to combat global warming, served as an example to a Bush Administration that was reluctant to take a lead on this issue.

Conclusion

Each of these apparent disadvantages of the US constitutional structure had, however, a corresponding advantage. The separation of powers has, at least historically, ultimately prevented the concentration of power in just one branch of government. While the system of checks and balances may not have encouraged the development of the most efficient policy-making procedures, it did increase accountability, thus preventing the federal Government from making large and serious mistakes. Judicial review took the courts into unknown policy-making territory, but it also provided the US population with a decision-making reference point that at least appeared to be above the highly politicized world of presidency and legislature. Finally, while federalism may have encouraged inconsistencies and anomalies in public policy, it also provided for more variety and for responsive government at a level more directly involving the electorate.

Ultimately, the success of the US constitutional system must be judged in relation to that of other political systems. By this measure it has been broadly successful. Even at the beginning of the 21st century almost all of its diverse citizenry supported it, while for almost 220 years it had existed with the minimum of amendment. This intrinsic support was demonstrated following the terrorist attacks of 11 September 2001. Initially, at least, all sections of US society supported the federal Government in its determination to 'win' the global 'war on terror'. Few doubts were expressed at the capacity of the political system to respond effectively, and this in the context of an Administration whose chief executive had been originally elected by the narrowest of margins in a bitter and contested election. At the same time, the subsequent military interventions in Afghanistan and Iraq, and the general conduct of US foreign policy in the Middle East, demonstrated just how exposed US Presidents are to a critical public and legislature. In the longer term, Presidents are usually constrained by these forces, which can result in major changes in public policy.

US POLITICS AND GOVERNMENT

GILLIAN PEELE

Presidential campaigns in the USA inevitably take on the character of a marathon as the primary season elides into the summer party Conventions and then into the formal campaign proper. In 2008 the gruelling nature of the contest was more than normally apparent. On the Democratic side the long and bitter battle between Senators Hillary Clinton and Barack Obama ended with Obama's nomination and his choice of the veteran politician Senator Joe Biden as his running mate. The nomination of Obama—the first by any major US party of an African American—was itself of enormous symbolic significance, and reflected his ability to mobilize the enthusiasm of many different sections of US society and to capture the mood for change. On the Republican side, the nomination of Senator John McCain pitted an independent-minded, somewhat maverick 72-year-old against the youthful Obama. McCain's age inevitably created more than the usual interest in the selection of his vice-presidential candidate. When he tapped a little-known female politician, Sarah Palin, as his choice, the scene was set for an election which would emphasize the ideological and cultural divisions in US society. Palin, the Governor of Alaska, was closely identified with the values of the Republicans' core far-right conservative constituency. She was a strong opponent of abortion, a believer in 'creationism' and an enthusiastic supporter of hunting with guns. This choice (made before the Republicans scaled down their Convention because of the threat to New Orleans from 'Hurricane Gustav') triggered an immediate and massive increase in donations from conservative sources and signalled that, whatever else, the 2008 contest would be both tight and bitterly fought.

Even without the excitement of the Democratic primaries and the ideological passion generated by McCain's vice-presidential choice, US politics and government in 2008 had been increasingly dominated by what would happen to public policy once George W. Bush left office in January 2009. Such speculation is natural at the end of a two-term presidency, as interest shifts from a so-called 'lame-duck' President to the prospect of a new White House. Yet, even though such analysis is important, it is equally necessary to remember how substantially the USA had been changed during the eight years of the Bush Administration. Whoever won in November 2008 would find himself more than usually constrained by his predecessor's legacy in foreign and domestic policy, not least the continuing US military occupation of Iraq and the deteriorating economic performance of the USA.

Looking back on the Bush presidency reveals a series of extraordinary fluctuations in political circumstance, and the transformation of his presidency from a domestic to a war administration. Bush's contested legitimacy and lacklustre early period in office were, of course, all but forgotten after the terrorist attacks on New York and Washington, DC on 11 September 2001, which immediately redefined his agenda and gave him a new popularity and freedom of manoeuvre. After an electoral victory in November 2004 he theoretically had the necessary political capital to pursue his priorities in a second term, but Bush soon found himself confronting a series of challenges, the most unexpected of which was the devastation wrought by 'Hurricane Katrina' in the south of the country in August 2005. That natural disaster focused attention not just on the President himself, but also on the structure of federal government, the weaknesses of state and city governments and the domestic policies pursued by the Bush Administration in recent years. The US commitment to rebuilding Iraq continued to frustrate the Government and the public alike, depressing presidential poll ratings and further adding to the political constraints on Bush's freedom of action. In addition, more general issues, such as corruption, immigration and, more recently, the failing economy, created a general climate of opposition to the incumbent President. For, powerful though the office of the US President is, both the constitutional framework and the political system impose strong checks on the executive, checks that do not always operate predictably. Bush may have tried to circumvent those checks by asserting a strong unilateralist theory of the presidential role, but the Constitution grants other institutions important countervailing powers.

As the Bush presidency entered its final months the political landscape had become increasingly unfavourable to him. The mid-term elections of November 2006 saw major Democratic gains and the loss of Republican control of both chambers of Congress. Nor did the President have much political capital left: by August 2008 his personal approval ratings hovered around 29%, with an overwhelming majority of 65% or more saying they disapproved of his performance. Not merely were these figures the worst recorded for an incumbent, they contrasted starkly with the support he had enjoyed immediately after the events of 11 September 2001.

THE CONSTITUTIONAL FRAMEWORK

The significance attached to the Constitution in US political life is profound. The document itself, which came into effect in 1789, has been amended very little since then, despite the enormous changes that have engulfed the USA. It is a relatively short document, with just seven Articles and 27 Amendments, the most recent, concerning congressional salaries, in 1992. Yet it contains important principles that continue to exert enormous influence on the way US government and politics operate. The separation of powers is embodied in the way the executive (the presidency), the legislature (Congress) and the judicial system work, diffusing, rather than centralizing, authority and making the policy-making process a much more complex and tortuous one than in unified systems such as the United Kingdom. The idea that government is limited has slowed the expansion of the federal Government into many policy areas. Although new federal government regulatory activity generally has been granted constitutional approval since the 1930s, novel uses of governmental power may still be contested in the courts. The fact that the system is a federal one, where power is divided between the federal level and the individual states, remains an important reality. Part of the difficulty of responding to natural disasters of the magnitude of 'Hurricane Katrina' was that authority and responsibility is shared between different levels of government—federal, state and local—and in this, as in many policy areas, co-ordination can be a major problem.

Since the 1930s, when the state and local levels of government were unable to cope with the economic depression, the federal Government has expanded its authority. However, recent Republican Administrations have urged that greater protection should be given to the states in the state-federal relationship, and the judiciary has reflected that preference. Thus, Supreme Court decisions such as the 1995 *Lopez v. US* case have underlined the continuing relevance of the federal dimension of the US Constitution. (That decision overturned legislation designed to restrict carrying guns near schools because there was no constitutional authority for it.) Most importantly, for the citizens of the USA, the Constitution protects certain key civil liberties, such as freedom of speech, equal protection and due process, although it also notoriously protects rights such as the right to bear arms, which can seem anomalous in a modern society. The sensitivity to civil liberties issues has an extensive impact on the role of government and the ability of Congress to regulate aspects of the political process. The constitutional restrictions on any legislation that abridges freedom of speech, for example, makes the regulation of campaign finance in the USA difficult.

Some have argued that the emphasis on civil liberties weakens the ability of the USA to protect itself. Following the terrorist attacks of 11 September 2001, Congress quickly approved the so-called 'Patriot Act' (Uniting and Strengthening America by Providing the Appropriate Tools Required to Intercept and Obstruct Terrorism Act of 2001), which gave important new powers to domestic intelligence agencies and removed many of the existing checks on executive power in that area. Although many observers saw this legislation as necessary to fight the threat posed by terrorism, others saw it as a disproportionate response and one that would inflict long-term constitutional damage on the USA. Although President Bush urged renewal of the legislation in 2005, the Senate was concerned to introduce more civil liberties safeguards into the legislation and renewal was delayed until 2006 when a new version of the legislation was eventually approved. President Bush has incurred criticism from those who suspect him of promoting an agenda of extending presidential power, including a highly dangerous claim to have the power to hold people suspected of being a threat to national security without recourse to the courts. In two landmark cases in 2004 (*Rasul v. Bush* and *Al Odah v. US*) the Supreme Court found that detainees at the US naval base at Guantánamo Bay, Cuba, did have the right to challenge their confinement by bringing suits in US courts. The burden of interpreting the Constitution is placed on the federal courts, especially the Supreme Court. Although judicial review is not explicitly mentioned in the Constitution, from 1803 (when the Court decided *Marbury v. Madison*) the Supreme Court has been the body that has had to resolve crucial issues affecting the political system. Sometimes these issues have concerned the powers of the different political institutions. An example of this was the *Clinton v. New York* decision in 1998, when the Court decided that the Line Item Veto Act of 1996 was unconstitutional. The President was deprived of the power to remove items of proposed legislation without vetoing the whole bill (especially useful if a bill appears to contain unnecessary, or 'pork barrel' expenditure). Many state Governors have a line item veto and use it on legislation sent up to them from their state legislatures. Civil liberties issues form an enormously significant part of the Supreme Court's agenda. Landmark judicial decisions on segregation in the 1950s, on electoral reapportionment in the 1960s and on abortion in 1973 generated extensive political controversy and had widespread political repercussions. In 2008, to the delight of gun owners, the Supreme Court ruled in a 5-4 decision (*District of Columbia v. Heller*) that a range of gun-control laws were contrary to the Second Amendment's guarantee of the right to bear arms.

The centrality of the Court and the Constitution in US political life has two important consequences. Firstly, many issues which would elsewhere be handled by the political branches of government, find their way into the legal system in the USA. Pressure groups and parties use litigation as a regular political strategy and see the courts as a crucial arena for pursuing their agendas. Secondly, there is intense interest in the kind of judicial appointments that a US presidential aspirant would make. From 2001 this became a very real issue for liberals and women, who feared that the Bush Administration would oversee a return to the conservative nominees favoured by Presidents Ronald Reagan (1981–89) and George Bush, Sr (1989–93). President George W. Bush's efforts to expand executive power and further his own conservative agenda made the question of the character of the US judiciary a particularly salient one in the 2004 elections, as it was widely anticipated that a second term would give Bush the power to reshape the Supreme Court. So it proved, when in July 2005 Associate Justice Sandra Day O'Connor announced her retirement and in September Chief Justice William Rehnquist died. President Bush's eventual choice as O'Connor's replacement on the bench was John G. Roberts, Jr, a District of Columbia Court of Appeals judge, but he later successfully nominated Roberts for the vacant Chief Justiceship. Samuel A. Alito, Jr, later filled the remaining vacancy. Both new appointments appeared to tilt the Court in a more conservative direction, a direction confirmed in 2007 when the Court issued rulings upholding the Partial Birth Abortion Ban Act of 2003 (*Gonzales v. Carhart* and *Gonzales v. Planned Parenthood*).

CONGRESS

The US legislature (Congress) is a remarkably powerful body. Whereas legislatures in many, if not most, political systems have lost power to the executive, the US Congress continues to exercise significant influence over a range of policy issues, including budgetary matters, appointments and foreign policy. In form it is a bicameral legislature with a Senate comprising 100 members (two from each state) and a 435-member House of Representatives, composed according to population. The Senate is elected for a six-year term with one-third of its members retiring every two years. The House is re-elected as a whole every two years.

The two chambers operate very differently from each other. The Senate (which is the more prestigious body) is highly individualistic in its ethos. There are few procedural restraints and indeed the 'filibuster' (a procedural device for delaying voting on a measure) is an important tool that any minority can exploit for obstructing business. Leadership has to be exercised with subtlety in a chamber that prefers to work by consensus. The Constitution gives the Senate important powers in relation to foreign policy through the requirement that it gives its 'advice and consent' to treaties. This power means that a treaty that fails to get the necessary two-thirds' majority in the Senate will fail. Several Presidents have found their powers over foreign policy-making frustrated by the Senate. For example, the 1919 Versailles Treaty that President Woodrow Wilson (1913–21) concluded at the end of the First World War was never ratified. The 1979 Strategic Arms Limitation Treaty (SALT II), while signed by President Jimmy Carter (1977–81), was never ratified by the Senate, which would almost certainly have rejected it. The 1994 North American Free Trade Agreement (NAFTA) secured Senate approval by the narrowest of margins. The Senate must also give its consent to presidential appointments—cabinet officers, ambassadors and the like. Furthermore, and crucially, the Senate must approve all federal judicial nominations.

Although the approval of the Senate for treaties and for presidential appointments could never be taken for granted, in many ways the process of securing Senate confirmation has become more complex in recent years. Judicial appointments became an object of intense political scrutiny from the Reagan presidency, when it was feared that greater consideration was being given to the ideological leanings of nominees than to their legal qualifications. In 1986 President Reagan's nomination of Robert Bork to the Supreme Court was rejected by the Senate because of the nominee's conservative views, particularly on the sensitive issue of abortion. More generally, the increased frequency of divided government (when one party controls the presidency and another the Senate and/or the House) has made confirmation of appointments more difficult to achieve (so too has the close partisan balance in the Senate in recent elections). As a result, when making appointments Presidents increasingly have to consider their nominees' capacity to achieve confirmation, as well as their inherent merits for the job in question. In 2005 President Bush's nomination of John Bolton to be the USA's Permanent Representative to the UN was blocked by a Senate filibuster; Bolton's appointment was secured only by using the President's congressional recess appointment powers, which allowed Bush to bypass Senate confirmation.

By contrast with the Senate, the House of Representatives is more organized and more partisan. The locus of power and leadership in the House fluctuated considerably over the 20th century. At the end of the 19th century and in the early years of the 20th century there was a strong Speaker system, epitomized by the speakerships of Thomas Brackett ('Czar') Reed (1889–91 and 1895–99) and Joseph Gurney ('Uncle Joe') Cannon (1903–11). Cannon's autocratic use of power led to a revolt against him and the centralized system gave way to a strong committee system whose chairs were, at least until the 1970s, virtually sovereign in their own spheres. These committee barons, whose positions were gained by long service and seniority, strongly influenced the legislative process; as a result, they were able to control the congressional agenda. With the party assertion of control over committee chairs and the creation of a greater role for subcommittees in the 1970s, power became more dispersed. However, in the 1980s Speaker Jim Wright provided a new model of assertive partisan leadership in the House. When Newt Gingrich led the Republicans in the House to victory in the 1994 mid-term elections, he further strengthened a blend of personalized and strong partisan leadership built around the office of Speaker. Although Gingrich resigned as Speaker following the 1998 mid-term elections and the Republicans in the House adopted a more collegial leadership, he left a legacy of heightened partisanship in the organization of the House, which entailed strengthened prerogatives for the majority party and reduced powers for the minority. That atmosphere of bitter antagonism between the parties has continued under the speakership of Nancy Pelosi, who became the Democratic leader in the House when her party regained control in November 2006.

Members of both the Senate and the House are intensely sensitive to local constituency pressures. The link between the congressman or congresswoman and the district he or she represents is especially strong because the size of districts is sufficiently small to make them homogenous. When the time comes for reapportionment, the parties will do everything they can to preserve their own safe seats and, as a result, the majority of House seats are either solidly Democratic or solidly Republican.

The committee system in both the House and the Senate is structured to maximize expertise and to respond to members' interests. Committees and their chairs dominate the congressional legislative process and committees have historically often proved unresponsive to majority sentiment. Also the committee system frequently serves as a mechanism for promoting the special interests of members, often by the passage of so-called 'pork barrel' legislation, which particularly benefits a member's constituency. Under Newt Gingrich's speakership the House introduced a rule which forbade committee chairs in the House from serving more than three consecutive terms, a rule which the Democrats maintained when they regained control in 2007.

Party organization and leadership in the two chambers is slightly different, and it varies a little between the major parties. In the House the Speaker enjoys a powerful position, combining the role of majority leader and presiding officer. The Democrats are organized through the Democratic Caucus while the Republicans are organized through the Republican Conference. In the 110th Congress, elected in November 2006, the Democratic Steering and Policy Committee makes committee assignments for the majority party while the Republic Steering Committee performs this role for the minority. Both parties have separate fund-raising arms: the National Republican Congressional Committee for the Republican congress members and the Democratic Congressional Campaign Committee for House Democrats. In the Senate, where there is no strong presiding officer analogous to the Speaker in the House, the effective power belongs to the Senate Majority Leader, who is responsible for working with the committees on legislation and scheduling debate on business as well as being his party's primary spokesman in the Senate. The Republican and Democratic Parties each provide a whip in the Senate and both parties also elect a Chairman of the Conference, which is the policy-making body within each party. Both parties in the Senate, as in the House, also have campaign committees that manage the increasingly onerous task of electoral fund-raising for their respective parties.

The US legislative process is complex and tortuous. At every stage there are multiple opportunities for amendment and delay. The influence on Congress of interest groups means that controversial measures usually have to survive sustained and well-funded opposition campaigns. It is much easier to prevent change than to effect it. Even if a bill is passed by both the Senate and the House and signed, rather than vetoed, by the President, it may still be subject to legal challenges in the courts.

THE PRESIDENT

Under the US Constitution, executive power is concentrated in one person: the President. In order to avoid the kind of oppression that the Founding Fathers thought had come to mark British government in the 18th century, legislative and executive power were separated. The President could not sit in Congress. The President was to be indirectly elected for a four-year term through an Electoral College. It was informally understood that Presidents would serve no more than two terms in office, but after Franklin D. Roosevelt (1933–45) defied the convention and succeeded in being elected for four successive terms, a constitutional amendment was brought forward to limit presidential tenure formally. From 1951, when the 22nd Amendment was ratified, no President may serve more than two terms in office. The method of indirect election (through an Electoral College, composed of electoral votes from each state, the number of votes being equal to the number of senators and congressmen allocated to that state) made some concessions to population, but protected the smallest states. The survival of the Electoral College is controversial. In 2000 Al Gore, the Democratic nominee in the presidential election, won the popular vote but lost the Electoral College vote. In 2004, however, George W. Bush defeated John Kerry, gaining 50.6% of the popular vote to Kerry's 48.1%, an advantage which, although slight, translated into a 286 to 252 margin in the Electoral College. For all its defects it is unlikely that constitutional change to the presidential electoral system will be forthcoming because the Electoral College system gives smaller states a larger voice in the electoral process and also because the method of amending the Constitution makes change difficult. It is, however, likely that there will be changes to some aspects of the electoral system, especially as states are trying to hold their primaries ever earlier in the electoral season, a tactic which in the 2008 election resulted in Michigan and Florida being stripped of delegates.

Presidents can be removed from office only by impeachment, a process which involves the House of Representatives voting articles of impeachment and the Senate trying them. The process is cumbersome, surrounded with ambiguity and rarely used. The decision to impeach President Bill Clinton (1993–2001) because of his attempt to conceal an affair with an intern was widely seen as an inappropriate political strategy against a Democratic President by a Republican Congress. The failure to secure a conviction in that instance suggests that the impeachment weapon will be used even more rarely in future.

Initially, the President had only a limited political role. He was given a number of powers but many of them had to be exercised in conjunction with Congress. In the 19th century Presidents, for the most part, adopted a stewardship role. Over the 20th century the presidency became more active in its role. From the presidency of Franklin D. Roosevelt it became assumed that the President would provide dynamic leadership in the US system, including legislative leadership.

The expectation of strong presidential leadership continues in the 21st century. A variety of factors, including structural ones, however, have made it increasingly difficult for Presidents to deliver successful and effective leadership. The separation of powers means that although Presidents can propose legislation, the decision to approve it resides with Congress. Thus, President Clinton's major first-term project, health care reform, was not supported by Congress. Congress is responsive to different and more sectional forces from that of the President. The President alone has a national constituency, but he has to work with a Congress that has a series of specific constituency concerns. The changing power structure of Congress makes the task of legislative liaison much more complex than in an earlier period when the legislature had only a few power-brokers with whom the President could bargain.

Although the Constitution envisaged that the President and Congress would share foreign policy powers, the period after 1945 saw the President becoming the dominant force in this arena, not least because of the advent of nuclear weapons. As Commander-in-Chief, the President has the power to commit troops to a combat zone, but the power to declare war belongs to Congress. In practice, when an emergency occurs Congress is likely to defer to the President, who acquires enhanced status in a national emergency. However, Congress also would be likely to try to maintain some supervisory powers over military engagement in order to avoid a repetition of the Viet Nam scenario, in which the USA was increasingly locked into an unpopular and unwinnable war. The passage of the War Powers Resolution in 1973 underlined congressional determination to rein in presidential war-making powers. This so-called 'tug of war' between the executive and legislative branches over the conduct of foreign policy was seen again in mid-2002 when it was reported that President Bush believed he had the legal power to invade Iraq without congressional approval (although, in October Congress approved a resolution authorizing the President to use military force against Iraq).

In domestic matters Presidents have always found their ability to set policy constrained by Congress. Individual Presidents must devise strategies to deal with the specific situations they find themselves in. For Presidents facing a Congress controlled by an opposition party, one strategy often has been to rely on the prerogatives of the presidency (for example, the power to make executive orders) and to try to avoid needing congressional support. This so-called 'executive strategy' was used by President Richard Nixon (1969–74), although it was also to some extent discredited by his abuse of power revealed by the Watergate affair. President Reagan used the powers of the presidency to appoint to key bureaucratic and judicial positions systematically in an attempt to counter congressional opposition. President George W. Bush has made substantial use of executive orders and also reasserted a strong doctrine of executive privilege in what many see as an attempt to strengthen the presidency within the political system or, as critics allege, to recreate a new 'imperial presidency'. Other Presidents have carefully exploited their relationship with public opinion to try to achieve their goals. Certainly, newly elected Presidents will attempt to capitalize on their mandate to achieve key elements in their programme quickly, before their electoral support declines. Presidents are usually at their strongest when their electoral mandate is fresh. George W. Bush was, to some extent, an exception to this rule. The contested circumstances of his election in late 2000 meant that his mandate was weak and the first few months of his presidency saw a decline in his poll ratings. The terrorist attacks on the USA of 11 September 2001 transformed this situation, however, and the level of popular support for him rose dramatically immediately after. The successful invasion of Iraq in 2003 initially further enhanced presidential popularity. However, the difficulties encountered in establishing stable government in Iraq following the overthrow of Saddam Hussain, as well as extensive criticism of Bush's motives for invading Iraq in the first place, undermined the President's position in 2004, although he nevertheless secured a second term in office in November. Since his re-election, President Bush's popularity ratings have fallen precipitously, however. They fell to 33% in May 2006, before recovering slightly, to 40%, by the middle of the year, but by September 2008 they had slipped again to around 30%.

One aspect of the presidential role that seemed to be sidelined was the management of the executive branch. There were few government departments in 1787 and even in 1900 the bureaucracy in Washington, DC, was limited. The expansion of government during the 20th century created a labyrinthine executive structure. As of September 2008 President Bush's Cabinet contained (in addition to the President and Vice-President) the heads of 15 cabinet-level departments. Cabinet-level rank had also been given to five other key administrators—the Administrator of the Environmental Protection Agency, the US Trade Representative, the Director of the Office of Management and Budget, the Director of the Office of National Drug Control Policy and the Chief of Staff to the President.

In addition, there are numerous executive agencies that operate with a substantial degree of bureaucratic autonomy. The President has his own dedicated personal staff and a prestigious bureaucracy in the Executive Office of the President, formed in the 1930s to support the expanding role of the presidency under Franklin D. Roosevelt. The proliferation of departments and agencies produces frequent turf battles. New departments may be created from time to time, although cabinet-level reorganization is generally unpopular with client groups and needs congressional approval. In November 2002 Congress, after much delay, approved President Bush's proposal to upgrade the newly created Office of Homeland Security to a cabinet-level department. This Department, under the direction of Michael Chertoff from 2005, was widely criticized in September of that year for its failure to respond adequately to the damage across the southern states caused by 'Hurricane Katrina'. As in many other Western countries, the last decade or so has seen renewed efforts to control the expansion of government through public-sector reform measures such as the Gore Commission and the 1993 Government Performance and Results Act.

Although much of the US federal bureaucracy is recruited on a merit system, there are also a substantial number of political appointees. These political appointees go down perhaps four layers in the administrative structure and in theory ensure that within a new Administration the highest policy-making cadres are responsive to the President. In practice, the process of filling so many vacancies in a new Administration is difficult and time-consuming; many positions are still vacant at the end of a President's first year in office.

THE STATES AND SUB-NATIONAL GOVERNMENT

The USA is a federal system with power divided between the Government and the federal district and the 50 states. Each state has its own distinctive character and there is a good deal of variety in the constitutional structures of the states concerning such matters as the extent of the Governor's powers and the size of the state legislature. There are also extensive policy differences between the states in such areas as taxation, environmental policy, criminal law and penal policy, education, and health and welfare. Most of the services that US citizens use on a daily basis are the responsibility of the state or local government rather than the federal Government; in recent years polls have consistently recorded greater feelings of support by citizens for state and local, as opposed to national, government. This increased legitimacy for state-level government has reinforced a drive to rebalance the federal system so that states can exercise relatively greater power and autonomy in relation to federal government. Nevertheless, President Bush, despite his earlier experience as a Governor of Texas, has introduced initiatives that many see as weakening state government. These include important legislation in the field of education (the No Child Left Behind Act of 2002), which gave the federal Government new and highly controversial powers over US schools.

POLITICAL PARTIES AND ELECTORAL COMPETITION

The USA has a very large number of offices that are filled by competitive election. These offices range from the federal offices (membership of the Senate, the House and the ultimate prize of the presidency) to a range of state and local offices (including membership of school boards and some state judgeships). The increasingly important position of state Governor is a major elective office. Although many of the Founding Fathers distrusted political parties, party organization emerged to contest elections early in the life of the Republic. Although the basis of the party system has changed fundamentally since the early years of the Republic it has broadly remained a two-party system. Initially, party competition revolved around antagonism between the Federalists and Jeffersonian Republicans. This party system gave way to a contest between Whigs and Democrats. Finally, in the late 1850s the newly formed Republican Party and the Democrats became the main contestants for political power.

Although party competition in the early 21st century is still between the Democratic and Republican Parties, the character of the two coalitions changed markedly in the last century. Today, both parties are broad coalitions: of liberals, blue-collar workers and trade unions, together with many organized ethnic minorities, especially black and Latino Americans, in the case of the Democrats, and of more conservative groups, business and the religious right, in the case of the Republicans. The balance between the two major parties is at present very close. In the 2004 legislative election the Republicans strengthened their control of the House (securing 231 seats out of 435) and in the Senate where they won 55 of the 100 seats. However, in mid-2006 Democrats seized control of both the House and the Senate, winning 233 seats in the lower chamber compared with the Republicans' 202. Democrats enjoy a much narrower advantage in the Senate, where their two-seat majority is the result of the election of two Independents, Bernie Sanders (Vermont) and Joe Lieberman (Connecticut) who ally with them.

The USA is overwhelmingly a two-party system, but there is substantial variety in the style of competition between the parties and, indeed, in the character of the parties at the state level. A Democrat in Maine is not the same as a Democrat in Mississippi. Although the Democratic and Republican Parties dominate the party system, occasionally third parties and Independents can be successful at the state and federal level. Thus, in 1992 Ross Perot took 19% of the popular vote in the presidential election, the best score for a third party since 1912. In 2000 Ralph Nader's Green Party (which campaigns on environmentalist and consumer issues), although it took only 2.7% of the popular vote, had an impact both on Gore's campaigning tactics and the result of the presidential vote in closely fought states. However, that level of support was not maintained in 2004 and Nader was not seen as likely to have any major impact in the 2008 campaign.

PARTY ORGANIZATION

The electoral system itself has a marked impact on the US style of government. Parties are loosely organized and lacking in cohesion by comparison with many European parties. The use of the primary to choose candidates means that party élites have relatively little influence over who is to represent them. (This is also true to some extent at the congressional level; thus, in 2006 Senator Joe Lieberman lost the Democrats' Senate primary contest in Connecticut to Ned Lamont over his pro-war stance, although he then won the seat as an Independent Democrat.) The rise of the primary after 1968 as a method of presidential selection also had the effect of reducing the role of the national party convention and allowing a successful presidential candidate to feel that he or she could operate independently of the party. The tendency of candidates to choose their own campaign managers, policy consultants and electoral strategies has further fragmented the cohesiveness of US parties and increased the costs of campaigns. While in recent years national party committees have, to a large extent, reasserted their role as providers of services to candidates, US parties have no monopoly over the processes of candidate selection and campaigning.

PRESSURE GROUPS AND SOCIAL MOVEMENTS

The size and diversity of the USA as well as its democratic political culture have combined to promote pressure group organization. The range and variety of organized groups of every kind have expanded in recent years, leading some critics to suggest that the USA has replaced pluralism with hyper-pluralism. Some observers have suggested that so powerful are these groups in the political process that they are creating an impasse in Congress. There has also been concern about the ethics of some pressure group activity, and in the 110th Congress there were efforts to strengthen legislative codes of conduct and ethical training. Of particular interest in recent years has been the growth of so-called 'identity politics', which is based on such characteristics as ethnic identity, gender and sexual preference. In terms of the operation of US politics, the key point is that pressure groups have multiple opportunities to influence the political process at the federal and state level. They can support political candidates financially through the operation of political action committees (PACs) and they may become aligned with a political party. Thus, US trade unions have tended to be overwhelmingly supportive of the Democrats, although in 2005 the defection of two major unions from the American Federation of Labor and Congress of Industrial Organizations (AFL-CIO) was seen as potentially damaging for the Democrats. The Republicans have tended, by contrast, to secure the support of business and the religious right, and such single-issue groups as the anti-abortion movement are aligned with the Republicans.

DIRECT DEMOCRACY

One increasingly salient feature of US politics is the movement towards direct democracy at the state level. The initiative, referendum and recall are now a regular part of the political processes of many, but not all, US states. Direct democracy is widely used, for example, in the politically significant and powerful state of California where in October 2003 Governor Gray Davis lost a recall election, and was replaced by the actor Arnold Schwarzenegger. The introduction of these instruments of direct democracy is associated with the wave of progressive reforms at the turn of the 19th century, when a number of states introduced measures to broaden citizen participation in government. Although the operation of direct democracy occasioned little controversy for much of the 20th century, from the 1970s there was a resurgence of interest in direct democracy and an increase in recourse to initiatives and referendums. The kinds of issues that may generate referendums are various, but typical are tax increases and such moral questions as homosexual rights (particularly gay marriage bans), abortion and access to physician-assisted suicide. The advantage of direct democracy is that it promotes citizen involvement in government and allows the electorate a greater voice in the policies that will affect them. The disadvantage is that it encourages sporadic and unpredictable law-making and may lead to the tyranny by the majority over vulnerable minorities. Success in an initiative and referendum campaign also requires large sums of money to be spent, so that in practice it is easier for wealthy and well-organized groups to set the agenda.

CONCLUSION

The political system of the USA has adapted over its 230-year history to cope with the enormous changes in the size and composition of the country, as well as industrialization and the transformation of the USA's world role. In particular, the role and scope of government have grown beyond anything that the Founding Fathers could have envisaged. Within the governmental structure itself the presidency has become a much more assertive institution, some would say at the expense of the country's Madisonian (after President James Madison, 1809–17) constitutional philosophy. For others, an invigoration of executive power is essential if the President is to be capable of providing leadership, not just for the USA, but more recently for the world as a whole. Political parties and pressure groups have been altered by rapid and extensive changes in technology and communications. That the structure should have proved sufficiently flexible to accommodate these changes is a testament both to the genius of those who wrote the original Constitution and to the ingenuity and resourcefulness of the population itself.

US DOMESTIC POLITICS: PROBLEMS AND PROSPECTS

Prof. DAVID McKAY

Compared with many political systems, the US system of governance is widely recognized as complex, fragmented, and in many respects inefficient. This is particularly so in domestic politics, where the institutional and politically pluralistic character of the system is most apparent. The purpose of this essay is to explain why this is so with a special emphasis on the experience of recent Administrations, and in particular that of President George W. Bush (2001–09). (Hereafter, all references to President Bush will be to George W. Bush, unless otherwise stated.)

This essay will dwell on three institutional themes that demonstrate the problems associated with pluralism: the separation of powers, presidential power and federalism. In addition, the essay will analyse the interaction between these themes and four contemporary issues: taxing and spending, financial regulation, income security and emergency management.

THE SEPARATION OF POWERS

The separation of powers, and in particular the separation of legislative power in Congress from executive power in the presidency, has always been the most distinctive feature of the US political system. During most of the 19th and early 20th centuries Presidents were, except in times of war and national emergency, relatively passive figures. Most legislation was initiated and passed by Congress. All this changed under the presidency of Franklin D. Roosevelt (1933–45), when a pattern was set that was to last until the late 1960s. In this period Presidents set the national agenda and Congress reacted to it. It was not that Congress was compliant or passive (although in foreign policy it often was), but more that it increasingly saw its role in terms of modifying and occasionally vetoing presidential initiatives. In the crucial area of civil rights, the entrenched power of legislators from certain southern states ensured that no meaningful legislation was passed until 1964. However, in a wide range of other areas, including the centrally important question of taxation and spending, Presidents set the agenda and Congress reacted.

This was also the era of unified government. Only twice (in 1947–49 and 1955–59) was control of Congress in the hands of a different party from that of the President. Indeed, the Democrats dominated Congress throughout this period and the Republicans controlled the presidency for just eight years (in 1953–61). However, with the election of Richard Nixon in 1968 the pattern was broken. Since then, divided government has been the norm. Indeed, unified government has prevailed for only just over 10 years in this period (in 1977–81, 1993–95, part of 2001, and 2003–07), although for the first six years of the presidency of Ronald Reagan (1981–89) the Republicans controlled the Senate. The mid-term elections of 2002, in which the Republicans regained control of the Senate, as well as maintaining a House majority, initiated a new period of unified government that continued following the presidential and legislative elections of November 2004, only to be broken yet again with the mid-term elections of 2006 when the Democrats regained control of both houses. Indeed, the results were notable because the Democrats were able to overcome the much vaunted 'incumbency advantage' enjoyed by the Republicans. With a 51 (including two Independents who vote with the Democrats) to 49 advantage in the Senate and a 232 to 202 advantage in the House of Representatives, the Democrats were poised to make life very difficult for the Republicans in the remaining two years of the Bush presidency.

Until 1994 some sort of pattern within divided government seemed to prevail. The Democrats controlled the House of Representatives, while the Senate and the presidency were more competitive. However, the 1994 mid-term elections produced what was at the time considered a political earthquake: the Republicans won 230 seats in the House of Representatives, compared with the Democrats' 204 (the remaining seat was won by an Independent candidate), while in the Senate the Republicans secured 53 seats, compared with the 47 won by the Democrats. The Republicans have controlled the House ever since, although in May 2001 they lost control of the Senate when Republican senator James W. Jeffords of Vermont declared himself an Independent, thus giving the Democrats a majority of one. The parliamentary rules in both chambers mean that whichever party has a majority controls the leadership and committee chairs. The majority party does, therefore, have substantial agenda-setting powers. The Republicans regained control of the Senate in the 2002 mid-term elections and increased their majority in the 2004 elections only to lose control of both houses in 2006.

While there is some academic disagreement both over the origins and the consequences of divided government, nobody disputes that it gives the impression of combative and conflictive politics. It has also led to two important developments, both of which are relevant to the presidency of George W. Bush. First, Congress currently sets the domestic policy agenda in ways that were very rare before 1970. When it comes to budgets, taxation and financial regulation, Congress now often produces real alternatives to the President's programme. Sometimes these alternatives are rooted in the ideological differences between the two main parties; sometimes the conflicts are more technical in nature (as with campaign finance reform—see essay on Reforming Campaign Finance in the 21st Century). The differences, however, are real and thus elevate the question of reconciling presidential and congressional positions to the top of the agenda. Second, divided government can lead to political impasse. Graphic examples of what some commentators call 'gridlock' were the partial shutdowns of the federal Government that occurred during the Reagan (1981–89) and Clinton (1993–2001) presidencies following the House's failure to agree on the annual federal budget. In the case of the Clinton shutdown, in late 1995, the resulting dislocation was substantial. During 2007 something approaching an impasse emerged over the conduct of the ongoing US-led war in Iraq. Congressional Democrats insisted on a clear timetable for withdrawal of US troops while President Bush was intent on maintaining troop levels at a high level in order to ensure steady progress against the Iraqi insurgents. In 2008 the federal Government's bail out of distressed financial institutions was implemented only after emergency negotiations with a Congress itself intent on providing some relief for hard-pressed homeowners.

Only under the most exceptional circumstances does Congress agree to accede to the President's demands without some sort of fight. One such exception occurred following the terrorist attacks of 11 September 2001, when both houses of Congress unanimously approved the so-called 'Patriot Act' (Uniting and Strengthening America by Providing the Appropriate Tools Required to Intercept and Obstruct Terrorism—PATRIOT—Act of 2001, see below), which gave the federal Government wide-ranging new powers of investigation and surveillance. The Republicans regained control of the Senate following the November 2002 mid-term elections and Congress duly passed the President's proposals for hefty tax reductions in early 2003. In 2001–03 Congress proved to be unusually compliant with the President's wishes, partly because of the emergency nature of the times, but also because both the Bush Administration and Congress remained convinced that tax reductions would stimulate the economy and therefore increase net tax revenue. However, even before the Democrats' triumph in the 2006 mid-term elections, politics was returning to normal, with major disagreements between Congress and the President emerging in such areas as immigration and stem cell research.

The basic problem with the separation of powers is that, under the US Constitution, the constituencies responsible for the election of the President, the House and the Senate are all quite different and often vote at different times. The President's national constituency means that, notwithstanding the vagaries of the Electoral College, successful candidates have to appeal to the broad mass of the US people every four years.

Senators have to appeal to state constituencies, but only once every six years, with one-third elected every two years. With the states varying in the size of their population—from around 500,000 in Wyoming to almost 36m. in California—the motives and incentives of senators differ from state to state. Finally, the greater a state's population, the greater the number of members of the House that it elects every two years (every state is guaranteed at least one representative, however small the population). Representatives, therefore, have to be closely in tune with the needs of their constituents.

Compounding this complex picture is the peculiar nature of US political parties. Both the Democratic and Republican Parties are highly decentralized, and in many respects are coalitions of diverse interests rather than unified, hierarchical organizations. In recent years, however, there has been something of a resurgence of party unity, at least in the Republican Party. Ideologically, the Republicans have always been a party of the right; but over the last few decades what was a small but important centrist (and on some issues even liberal) grouping concentrated in the north-east, and in New England in particular, has diminished in importance. This was well demonstrated by the decision of Senator Jeffords to reassign himself as an Independent in May 2001. The Republican Party is now much more solidly identified with big business, low taxation and the agenda of the Christian right than ever before. In 2000 there were few qualms about nominating George W. Bush as the Republican presidential candidate. By contrast, those on the right of the party had serious doubts about the nomination of George Bush, Sr, in 1988 and 1992 and Bob Dole in 1996, both of whom were ideologically centrist rather than on the right. Hence, in Congress party unity among the Republicans has increased significantly, and in response Democrats have often united in opposition to Republican policies. Significantly, the Democrats are not as unified behind the Democrat agenda—they remain a loose coalition of interests and ideas—but they come together to oppose what they see as an unacceptable Republican programme in Congress. These developments have been aggravated by the fact that House seats are highly uncompetitive. The vast majority are safe Democratic or Republican constituencies, in the main because state legislatures have manipulated the boundaries of constituencies to make them safe for the incumbent party. Known as 'gerrymandering', this practice is so widespread that most sitting members of the House can adopt quite extreme policy positions without fear of being defeated in an election. This was amply demonstrated in 2004 when there were probably no more than 20 competitive House seats out of a total of 435. In the event, the Republicans made a modest gain of three seats. The only occasion when the 'out' party is likely to make significant inroads into the incumbent majority is when dramatic changes in national politics overwhelm local incumbents' advantage. This happened in 1994 when the Republicans swept the Democrats from power. Similar conditions applied in 2006 with an unpopular President fighting what many voters saw as an unwinnable war (in Iraq), but the incumbency advantage kept the Democratic majorities to relatively modest proportions.

PRESIDENTIAL POWER AND DOMESTIC POLITICS

The problems of the separation of powers are rooted not only in the existence of distinct constituencies for the election of members of Congress and the presidency, but also in the fact that the US Constitution assigns power jointly to executive and legislature. Hence, the legislative or law-making power is assigned to Congress, but the President is also instructed 'from time to time to give to the Congress information on the state of the union, and recommend to their consideration such measures as he shall judge necessary and expedient' (Article II, Section 3). Presidents can also, of course, veto acts of Congress (which can only be overturned by a two-thirds' majority in both houses). As indicated earlier, by the middle of the last century it was broadly accepted that Presidents would be the main source of public policy—indeed, they would become the *de facto* chief legislators. This is amply demonstrated by the labels attached to Presidents' programmes during the middle of the 20th century: Roosevelt's 'New Deal', Harry S Truman's 'Fair Deal', John F. Kennedy's 'New Frontier' and Lyndon B. Johnson's 'Great Society'. With the exception of the first few years of the Reagan presidency, however, no President since has been associated with a coherent and comprehensive domestic programme. This relates not only to the role of Congress in the context of divided government, but to broader problems associated with presidential domestic policy-making in the late 20th and early 21st centuries. Four of these problems are of paramount importance: the selection of presidential candidates and its impact on leadership; presidential use of staff and cabinet members; appointments to the Supreme Court; and the search for ideological coherence in an increasingly complex and media-influenced society.

Selection and Leadership

Until the 1970s myriad state and local party organizations, whose delegates met at national conventions, effectively selected presidential candidates. Since then voters have effectively replaced the parties by means of the primary election system. These intra-party nominating elections have placed great premium on individual candidates' ability to build personal organizations, raise money and use the media (especially television and the internet) effectively. As a result, presidential candidates must have the time, personal resources (it is a distinct advantage to be personally wealthy or have wealthy backers) and the public appeal to survive the long and arduous primary season. Successful candidates must, therefore, appeal to the media and be good campaigners. Experience in government and close peer group review of the suitability of candidates is much less important than it used to be. With the exception of George Bush, Sr, none of the recent Presidents—Jimmy Carter, Reagan, Clinton, George W. Bush—had any experience of national government on taking office. Their immediate predecessors—Roosevelt, Truman, Dwight Eisenhower, Kennedy, Johnson, Richard Nixon and Gerald Ford—all had experience of elected or appointed office at a national level. The 2008 presidential election proved an exception to this trend, with the two contenders for the office, Barack Obama and John McCain, both having strong party ties and experience of national office.

While the absence of national experience may not always have been a disadvantage, it has led many commentators to conclude that some recent Presidents are more skilled at campaigning for office than they are at governing. Clinton is usually cited as the prime example of this characteristic. In addition, Presidents with weak party ties have found it difficult to appoint cabinet members and suitable staffers to fill the many federal bureaucratic and judicial posts. In the past this job was greatly facilitated by the strong local party organizations that had secured the successful candidates' nominations. This was a particular problem for Presidents Carter and Clinton, neither of whom was able to use Democratic Party connections to good effect.

Appointments

This relates to more general problems associated with staffing the presidency. Three levels of officials are subject to presidential appointment (some with the advice and consent of the Senate). Presidents have to appoint members of the White House staff and members of their Cabinet, as well as the many thousands of positions in the federal bureaucracy and judiciary. Most controversy surrounds the White House staff. No recent President has been free of accusations that inappropriate people have been appointed or that some have exceeded their authority. Many Chiefs of Staff have had to resign for wrongdoing or incompetence, including Donald Regan in the second Reagan presidency, John Sununu in Bush, Sr's term of office, Mack McClarty in the Clinton presidency and Andrew Card in 2006 during Bush, Jr's second term of office. In addition, most recent Presidents have come to rely in part on individuals with little or no official status, including First Ladies (notably Nancy Reagan and Hillary Clinton) or old friends, confidants and mentors (Dick Morris in Clinton's case and Karl Rove and the extended Bush family in the case of George W. Bush). When, as has been the case with all recent Presidents, there is no coherent domestic policy agenda informed by party ideology, these confidants have tended to play the role of media 'spin doctors' advising on how best to improve poll ratings, rather than on the quality of public policy.

Cabinet members are often less controversial, usually because they wield much less power. Constitutionally, the President is not obliged to hold cabinet meetings or to heed individual cabinet members' advice. Most of the time they pay little attention to the Cabinet. This is especially true in domestic policy. In recent years few domestic cabinet incumbents have held great power or are even known to the general public. Notable exceptions are often Attorneys-General, who have to deal with the complex moral and individual rights issues that divide the public. Such was the case with Clinton's Attorney-General, Janet Reno, who was extremely unpopular with those on the political right, and with Bush's chief legal officer during his first term in office, John Ashcroft, who was equally unpopular with those on the left. Ashcroft's successor in Bush's second term, Alberto Gonzales, was unpopular not only over alleged ideological bias, but also because he was widely perceived as incompetent. He subsequently resigned in August 2007.

In foreign policy, however, cabinet members are more visible and more powerful. This is particularly true during periods of national emergency. During and after the Second World War such figures as Secretaries of State Gen. George Marshall and John Foster Dulles became internationally renowned figures. More recently, US intervention in Afghanistan (in 2001–) and Iraq (in 2003–) elevated the status of Secretaries of State Colin Powell and Condoleezza Rice and Bush's first Secretary of Defense, Donald Rumsfeld. Indeed, given that President Bush was largely unconcerned with the detail of policy, these and other officials were key players in both formulating and implementing US anti-terrorist and foreign policy strategies. In addition, Dick Cheney, President Bush's Vice-President, played an unusually prominent role in foreign policy, in part because of the President's inexperience in this area, and because Cheney had served in three previous Administrations, including as Secretary of Defense in 1989–92. Following President Bush's electoral victory in 2004 changes were made to the foreign policy team that indicated a potential increase in presidential control over the detail of policy. Most notably, national security adviser Condoleezza Rice was promoted to Secretary of State. Rice had been fiercely loyal to President Bush and was therefore more likely accurately to reflect his views when determining foreign policy. In November 2006 the controversial Secretary of Defense Donald Rumsfeld resigned and was replaced by the more accommodating figure of Robert Gates.

Appointments to the Supreme Court

Appointments to the Supreme Court can have a crucial influence on domestic policy, as was shown with the civil rights revolution in the 1950s and 1960s when a liberal Court extended civil rights to African-Americans in a wide area of public policy. Presidential appointments to the Court can be very important, therefore. As was widely expected with eight of the nine justices over 65 years old, in 2005 President Bush was given the opportunity to nominate two new justices to the Supreme Court. After an unusually long period of stability on the Court (eight years, the longest period without a change in 180 years), the President was thus given an opportunity to change the ideological complexion of the Court. In mid-2005 Justice Sandra Day O'Connor resigned on grounds of ill health and in late July the President nominated US Circuit Judge John G. Roberts, Jr, to the bench. Roberts was known as a moderate conservative with a long and honourable pedigree as a lawyer, first as an appellate attorney and more recently as a member of the influential US Court of Appeals for the District of Columbia. Although some Democrats vowed to fight the nomination, opposition was muted and the nomination process was pre-empted by the death of Chief Justice William Rehnquist in September. Bush withdrew Robert's original nomination and instead named him as the prospective Chief Justice. On 29 September the Senate voted 78 to 22 in favour of his appointment. As Rehnquist was identified with the conservative wing of the Court, on the face of it his replacement by Roberts changed little. As a result, the person nominated to replace O'Connor became pivotal, for she had often acted as the swing vote on the Court, sometimes taking a liberal position and sometimes a conservative one. Bush's eventual choice of White House Counsel Harriet Miers shocked the whole political establishment, for Miers had no experience as a judge and little experience as a senior lawyer. Conservatives were more outraged than liberals because they had no way of knowing whether she would be loyal to the conservative agenda on issues such as abortion and same-sex marriage. During preliminary Senate hearings into her nomination, Miers revealed scant knowledge of constitutional law and the nomination was hastily withdrawn in late October.

The President acted quickly to nominate Samuel A. Alito, Jr, to the vacancy. In stark contract to Miers, Alito had very extensive judicial experience, having served as a US Appeals Court justice since 1990. He also had clear conservative credentials and immediately won the support of Congressional Republicans and leading conservative interest groups. Democrats, however, vowed to fight the nomination and if necessary to block it through the use of Senate parliamentary rules. In the event, however, Alito's nomination was confirmed on 31 January 2006 by a 58 to 42 majority (only one Republican Senator voted against confirmation). In his decision-making Alito proved to be a loyal member of the conservative bloc on the Court, thus giving President Bush an effective 5–4 majority on a range of important issues.

Presidents and Ideology: the Search for Coherent Domestic Programmes

Perhaps the most important development in US politics and society over the last 40 years or so has been the blurring of traditional class and regional distinctions, and the emergence of much more complex issues that make the business of forging winning political coalitions more difficult. Two refinements to this theme compound the problem. First, the decline of class and regional alignments has affected the Democrats much more than the Republicans. Until the 1970s the Democrats were very much the party of the south, but also of blue-collar industrial workers in the north and elsewhere. Now they are no longer the dominant southern party and the traditional industrial working class has declined in numbers and influence. At the same time, the Democrats have not been replaced by the Republicans as the majority party in terms of voter identification. Instead, support for the parties is about evenly divided, some groups—ethnic minorities and working women—largely supporting the Democrats, while others—older white males, for example—support the Republicans. In effect, although the Republicans have won Congress and the presidency on several occasions, they have never been able to establish the sort of dominance enjoyed by the Democrats during the mid-20th century. They have a solid core of support in the south, the mountain states of the Midwest and among ideologically committed conservatives, but continue to compete with the Democrats for the middle ground in most of the country. This is why both Bush (in 2000 and in 2004) and the Republican presidential candidate in the 1996 election, Bob Dole, were eager to label themselves as 'compassionate conservatives' who care about the needy and disadvantaged members of society. In 2008 John McCain adopted a slightly different stance, while still claiming to represent the 'ordinary voter' and distancing himself from the 'big interests' in Washington.

These electoral alignments make it inordinately difficult for Presidents to create successful coalitions over the longer term. As a result, in domestic policy at least, all Presidents now appeal to the public on what political scientists call 'valence issues', or issues over which there can, by definition, be no disagreement. Among these are a balanced budget, economic prosperity and affordable health care for all US citizens, and resoluteness in the face of terrorism. Of course, Presidents and the parties differ over the means by which these objectives can be met. However, most US politicians are reluctant to enunciate precise details for fear of offending one group or another.

The same dilemmas apply to the so-called 'conscience issues', such as abortion and prayers in public schools. Because many voters hold very firm opinions on these issues, politicians are often reluctant to provide blanket endorsement or condemnation for fear of alienating sections of voters, although President

Bush was more prepared to declare a rightist position here than either his father or Bob Dole. This was particularly apparent in his second term when moral issues, such as the right of homosexuals to marry and the ethical status of stem cell research played a prominent role in politics. In March 2005 the President made a firm commitment to the 'right to life' when he persuaded Congress to change the law in order to permit a further judicial appeal on behalf of the seriously brain-damaged Terri Schiavo, whose husband insisted that she be allowed to die. In the event the Supreme Court rejected the appeal and Terri Schiavo's feeding tube was removed. In September 2006 Bush vetoed a measure by the House of Representatives that would have permitted federal funding of stem cell research. Congress failed to overturn this veto.

In sum, in spite of some exceptions, Presidents find it very difficult to pursue coherent and consistent programmes in the domestic policy area. The temptation is always to avoid firm commitments and to fall back on appeals to valence issues or policy statements over which there can be no real disagreement. As will be discussed later, this makes the business of domestic policy-making exceedingly difficult. It may also contribute to the declining trust in government that is such a prominent feature of the US political scene. Some commentators noted that, following his re-election in 2004, President Bush would have the opportunity to pursue his conservative domestic policy agenda unconstrained by Congress, the courts or electoral pressures. However, none of the structural constraints inherent in the US system had disappeared. Congress was much less compliant than in his first term, particularly on such questions as immigration reform, which was eventually rejected by Congress in 2007, and public opinion continued to express itself through the media and interest groups in ways that limited the President's ambitions. After the 2006 mid-term results, of course, the President faced a Democrat-controlled Congress implacably opposed to his programmes. In 2008 the US Treasury/Federal Reserve plan to bail out ailing banks was accepted only after the Democratic Congress exacted important compromises in the proposed bill.

FEDERALISM: STATE VERSUS FEDERAL POWER

Both Presidents and Congress are further restricted by the institution of federalism. From its very inception the US Republic has been characterized by a division of powers between the federal Government and the states. However, the Constitution is imprecise on the question of the exact division of responsibilities between the two levels. The 10th Amendment of the Constitution—'The powers not delegated to the United States by the Constitution, nor prohibited by it to the states, are reserved to the states respectively, or to the people'—assumes that all those powers not given to the federal Government are reserved to the states. However, what is assigned to the federal level is highly ambiguous and has changed considerably over time. In recent years most of the debate has centred on the imposition of national standards in economic and social life, and the Supreme Court has been the main arbiter on this issue. Generally speaking, federal or national standards move the country in a liberal direction, while maintaining state autonomy preserves those states' policies that are conservative (although, it must be said, many states also adopt liberal policy positions). Until 1937 the Supreme Court generally favoured state over federal law in such areas as occupational safety and health, the regulation of financial institutions and social welfare. Between 1937 and the 1970s the Court consistently supported federal over state law. This was, of course, the period when liberal federal Governments were legislating in a wide range of areas to establish and to improve national standards in almost every aspect of social and economic life, from civil rights to environmental protection, to minimum wage legislation to welfare. In addition, liberal Courts established their own precedents to set new, generally liberal, national standards in such areas as capital punishment, abortion and civil rights and liberties. From the 1970s onwards the pendulum swung again, this time back towards the states. This, in part, reflects a more conservative Supreme Court, but also represents a general shift to the right in US politics. Hence, during the 1970s the Supreme Court returned to the states the power to impose capital punishment. Later, in the 1990s, the Court limited the federal Government's power to require states to dispose of nuclear waste and to require states to create gun-free zones around public schools.

While these and other decisions represent the general trend, exceptions exist. For example, in 2002 the Supreme Court ruled that juveniles and the mentally ill were exempt from state-imposed capital offences; in 2003 the Court declared a Texas law outlawing sodomy to be unconstitutional. What all this demonstrates is just how powerful the Court can be when deciding the proper relations between the states and the federal Government. Presidents and other federal officials may want to impose national standards, or indeed to champion states' rights, but an activist Supreme Court can easily thwart their best intentions. The crucial role of the Supreme Court was highlighted in 2005 when two vacancies occurred following the resignation of Justice Sandra Day O'Connor in July and the death of Chief Justice William Rehnquist in September. President Bush nominated a moderate conservative, John G. Roberts, Jr, to replace Rehnquist and the dominating issue in the Senate's judicial committee's confirmation process was the judge's position on state versus federal power. With the abortion issue, for example, the conservative stance was to overturn the 1973 *Roe v. Wade* ruling that established a constitutional right to abortion in the first three months of pregnancy, effectively sanctioning abortion in every state. If the federal ruling was struck down, state governments would have the power to ban abortion.

The constitutional and political autonomy of the states has other important implications for US domestic policy. By pursuing their own policies, the states can partly thwart national policy and even lead it in new directions. In automobile safety and emission controls, for example, California pioneered the use of unleaded gasoline and air bags. So large is the Californian car market that other states followed and eventually Congress set a national policy. In 2002 the Californian legislature passed a law requiring a radical reduction in the emission of 'greenhouse' gases from vehicles. Although strongly opposed by the Bush Administration, the new law had a 'demonstration effect' on other states, which duly followed suit. Eventually, Congress may be forced to accept national standards in this area. The same applies to universal medical coverage, where by 2007 several states, including Massachusetts and Oregon, had legislated to produce universal programmes.

In some areas, notably education and law enforcement, the federal Government simply does not have the scope to affect the direction of public policy to a great extent. Almost all elementary, secondary and higher education is funded by state and local government (or privately). Almost all law enforcement in the USA is locally funded. President Bush may have proposed new educational programmes, such as the 'No Child Left Behind' Act, which mandated scholastic testing for schoolchildren, although the impact of any federal action was limited by the devolved nature of school funding. Even if federal funding were greatly increased the federal Government would continue to rely on state and local governments for the implementation of programmes.

Federalism also limits the scope of federal economic policy (in addition to the role of the Supreme Court, as discussed above). As noted previously, the states and localities are responsible for most public services. They control vast budgets and employ millions of people. Unlike the federal Government, however, all states except Vermont are constitutionally prohibited from running budget deficits. State governments cannot, therefore, use the deficit device to compensate for fluctuations in the business cycle or in the volatile flow of revenue from sales and income taxes. Often, however they accumulate large short-term deficits, as many states did in 2001–05 and again after 2007. As a result, states such as California had to implement painful expenditure reductions in order to help bring their budgets back into balance. The trials and tribulations of state finances have important consequences for national politics. Cuts in education, transport and other budgets affect large numbers of voters and increase pressures for federal aid and assistance. While these had been heeded in the past, they failed to impress a Bush Administration that was generally hostile to increases in federal spending.

TAXATION AND SPENDING

No issue dominates domestic politics more than taxation and spending. This is not only for the obvious reason that taxes and budgets help to determine the level and quality of service in other policy areas; it is also because taxes and how they are spent have a special place in US history and political culture. Americans have always been suspicious of governments that tax and spend freely, which is why in the Constitution the power of the purse was specifically assigned to a House of Representatives elected every two years by popular majority. Few politicians openly advocate increases in taxation. Furthermore, those that do are usually punished at the polls. Instead, politicians stress the virtues of low taxation and limited government, and this is more than rhetoric. As a percentage of gross domestic product (GDP), the US Government spends less than any comparable country (around 33%), with the federal Government responsible for just 20%. Of course, given the size of the US economy these figures still amount to vast sums in absolute terms.

This issue is further complicated by the institutional context of fiscal policy. Traditionally, Presidents have produced the annual budget and Congress has responded with a modified version of its own. Usually this involved members of Congress defending the congressional Priority Development Assistance Fund (the so-called 'pork barrel') or protecting federal programmes with positive income and employment consequences for constituents. While this remains the very stuff of budgetary politics, in recent decades Congress has tried to deal with the budget as a unified whole. To this end, Budget Committees have been created in both houses to complement the work of the appropriations committees. Divided government and party politics have also played their part. During the Reagan and Bush, Sr, Administrations, congressional Democrat majorities in one or both houses generally favoured higher domestic spending in relation to presidential proposals. During the later Clinton years the dynamics were reversed: Republicans in Congress attempted to reduce presidential spending plans. In the area of defence policy spending the dynamic changed again, with Republicans generally supportive of increased appropriations and Democrats opposed to them. Following the terrorist attacks of 11 September 2001, a period of unity on this and other issues prevailed. However, it was to be short-lived. By early 2002 Democrats and Republicans had assumed opposing positions once again on both defence and domestic programme expenditure. And while congressional Republicans showed an unusual eagerness to comply with Bush's spending plans, both during his first term in office and in the first year of his second term, this had all but evaporated by 2006 when many fiscally conservative Republicans expressed their strong disapproval at what they saw as the profligate spending policies of the President.

The salience of budgetary politics did, of course, increase greatly with the emergence of substantial budget deficits in the 1970s. By the mid-1980s this issue dominated domestic politics and this was to remain the case thereafter. Fundamentally, the problem was a result of the reluctance of US politicians to increase taxes while also being reluctant to cut programmes that would benefit their constituents directly. Divided government undoubtedly compounded the dilemma. It was not until a felicitous combination of circumstances during the 1990s that the problem seemed to have been solved. A booming economy with its attendant increase in tax receipts, combined with Republican control of Congress, resulted in increased revenue and controlled spending. By 1998 the deficit was eliminated and the focus of domestic politics shifted to how best to spend the budget surplus. Predictably, Democrats favoured increased spending on social programmes while the Republicans favoured reduced taxation.

Much to the surprise of many commentators, the fiscal deficit narrowed sharply in 2004–07, to an estimated US $354,245m., or 2.6% of GDP, in 2007 (estimate as of mid-2007), compared with $412,727m. in 2004 (3.6% of GDP). While representing an improvement, the deficit remained a substantial figure and battles between the Republicans and Democrats and both the taxation and spending side of the budget were brought into even sharper relief. Given that the tax cuts achieved by 2007 were politically sacrosanct, all this greatly increased the pressures on President Bush to contain spending. In fact, however, the President was unusually profligate for a Republican. Social security (pension), education, farm subsidy and homeland security spending all rose under the Bush Administration. Together with the substantially increased costs associated with the financial bail-outs in 2008 (see below), this resulted in the budget deficit rising to more than $500,000m. by the last quarter of 2008 (equivalent to around 4% of GDP).

FINANCIAL REGULATION

Since the Great Depression of the 1930s, the US Government has been active in regulating financial institutions from the stock market to banks and mortgage credit providers. Regulations appeared to work well until the 1980s when a wave of deregulation instituted by the Reagan Administration led to mainly localized problems by the end of the decade. At that time a number of savings and loans banks—essentially institutions established to help people save and to finance house purchases, often referred to as thrifts—found themselves in difficulties. Following deregulation they expanded into new areas such as commercial property where the risks were high and many were tempted into imprudent lending practices. In the event, the federal Government rescued the savings and loans banks through the establishment of a Resolution Trust Corporation, which bought up the assets of the failed thrifts with US $160,000m. appropriated by Congress. This crisis was, however, nothing compared with the collapse of credit finance in 2007–08. Following a period of very rapid appreciation in house prices between 2000 and 2006, the housing market collapsed in many parts of the country after 2007. The decline in house prices was worse even than that experienced during the Great Depression, reaching nearly 15% in the year to March 2008. This cycle of 'boom and bust' was fuelled in part by very low interest rates after 2001, but in the main by unregulated and often corrupt mortgage-lending practices. In the upper Mid-West and other parts of the country poorer homeowners were misled into signing apparently cheap remortgage arrangements with low initial payments that ballooned after a few years. The result was a rapid rise in bank repossessions after 2007. In California and Florida the problem was rather different. Here rapid price increases spurred massive building programmes. New buyers took out 'jumbo' loans, again at an initially low cost, only for them subsequently to rise rapidly. When the inevitable crash happened there was a large oversupply of new houses together with many homeowners burdened with negative equity. Spiralling foreclosures followed. The 'sub-prime' crisis escalated into an international problem when US banks sold on billions of dollars worth of 'bad' mortgages to financial institutions throughout the world. The effect of the crisis on US politics was profound. First, it helped to plunge the economy into recession; second, it spurred the President and Congress into adopting a variety of rescue policies, including bailing out the insurance giant American International Group, Inc. (AIG), the investment bank Bear Sterns and the federally-mandated mortgage lenders Fannie Mae and Freddie Mac; and third, it revealed the weaknesses inherent in federal regulation of the banking sector. As a result, Congress passed a series of new regulations to be implemented in late 2008 and 2009.

INCOME SECURITY

In no area are the pressures on the budget greater than in social security. For Americans, social security has a special status. Introduced in 1935 and greatly modified and expanded ever since, it covers old age pensions, and disability and widows' benefits. Citizens believe that as they (and their employers) have contributed to it through payroll taxes, it is a right or entitlement. Social security contributions are kept in a trust fund that is separated from the general budget in accounting terms. No such arrangement applies to Medicare (the state health care programme for those over 65 and certain categories of disabled people). In recent years much concern has been expressed about the actuarial viability of the fund. With an ageing population and longer life expectancy it is predicted that by about 2025 the fund will begin to diminish and eventually disappear. Soaring Medicare costs will add to the budgetary burden represented by social support for the elderly. (By 2007 social security and Medicare accounted for an estimated 35.2% of all federal spending.)

However, neither political party has dared to address this problem. Instead, most of the debate has focused on how to achieve better value for money in both health and social security. Even the Republicans have avoided any direct challenge to the prevailing system, although in 1981 President Reagan briefly considered a major overhaul of social security. In the Medicare programme, which has the largest cost increases, both parties in Congress are committed to some expansion of benefits in the area of prescription drugs, the cost of which is only partly covered by existing Medicare legislation. In 2003 President Bush succeeded in gaining congressional approval for a massive increase in Medicare cover by extending drugs prescription benefits for older US citizens. In August of that year he also pledged that Medicare and social security would be protected in future budgets. The President also promised extensive social security reform as part of his second-term programme. In part, this meant privatization of at least elements of the social security system; however, in the event, this was not achieved during Bush's second term, largely owing to the political protection afforded to social security, even in a Republican-dominated Congress.

In marked contrast to social security, welfare provision is politically unpopular. In US parlance, welfare applies to non-contributory income support for the needy. It also involves Medicaid, the programme of health care for certain low-income categories. Both welfare and Medicaid are funded from general taxation, and in contrast to social security the states play a major role in both programmes. Medicaid probably presents more political difficulties than welfare. Medicaid costs have been increasing rapidly over many years and now represent around 8% of the federal budget, yet politicians are reluctant to be seen to reduce funding for a programme that benefits children in poorer families and the elderly poor. The main hope is that the reform of welfare in the 1990s will have had the effect of removing many families from Medicaid eligibility. To understand how this might be, it is necessary to understand the objectives of the reforms as embodied in the 1996 Personal Responsibility and Work Opportunity Reconciliation Act. This law replaced legislation dating from the 1930s with a welfare programme entitled Temporary Assistance for Needy Families (TANF). From 1997 TANF was to be administered entirely by the states, with the help of federal block grants. States were also given incentives to reduce the number of recipients of TANF, almost all of whom were required to work or receive job training within specified periods. Limited childcare assistance was also available. Thus, TANF was very much a 'workfare' programme. It received broad political support from Democrats and Republicans alike. By early 2007 TANF appeared to have transformed welfare provision in the USA, with the number of recipients falling to just over 4.1m. in the first quarter—a reduction of 66% since the programme started in 1996. While impressive, these figures had been achieved in the context of a booming economy when jobs were relatively plentiful. Moreover, welfare numbers among the most disadvantaged group—African-Americans living in urban areas—declined only slowly and many of the newly working poor remained eligible for Medicaid benefits given their low-income levels. In addition, the Bush Administration was committed to subsidizing 'faith-based initiatives', providing federal funding for religious charities that organized welfare and housing schemes and other services.

HOMELAND SECURITY

Many of the institutional and political problems associated with domestic policy in the USA were well demonstrated by the response to the 'war on terror', including the implementation of the Patriot Act and the operations of the Department of Homeland Security. Just 45 days after the terrorist attacks of 11 September 2001 the US Congress passed the Patriot Act by overwhelming majorities in both houses (356 to 66 in the House and 98 to one in the Senate). Given the common accusations that the legislative process was slow and cumbersome, the speed at which it passed through Congress was remarkable. On 23 October Congressman James Sensenbrenner introduced the Act and then sent it to nine major committees, where it was approved. The next day it was presented to the Senate, where it was promptly passed and sent to the President, who immediately signed it into law. Admittedly, other versions had been discussed since early October, but the legislative timetable was nevertheless astonishingly short. In effect, the Act gave federal law enforcement authorities extensive new powers to investigate anyone thought to be engaging in terrorism or associated with those engaging in terrorism. The Act has been widely viewed as a threat to civil liberties, mainly because there are few safeguards against federal surveillance and investigations.

The Department of Homeland Security was created in a somewhat less frenzied environment. In late September 2001 the Bush Administration established the Office of Homeland Security, under Thomas J. Ridge (later replaced by Michael Chertoff), to develop and implement a strategy to prevent future terrorist attacks against the USA. In June 2002 the President proposed upgrading the office to a federal Department, and in November that measure was duly approved by both houses of Congress. The creation of the Department of Homeland Security was the biggest single administrative reorganization of the federal Government since the creation of the Department of Defense after the Second World War. A number of existing agencies were absorbed by it, including the US Coast Guard, the Secret Service, the Immigration and Naturalization Service and the US Customs Service. With more than 190,000 employees and an estimated budget of US $50,500m. in fiscal year 2009, the Department of Homeland Security was one of the largest departments in the federal Government. As remarkable was the fact that the budget was a huge increase on the $17,600m. allocated to the equivalent departments in 2002. Thus, the supposedly fiscally conservative Republican Administration presided over a massive increase in the size of the federal domestic budget.

The main criticism levelled at the agency was that it represented another bureaucratic behemoth that was likely to use resources inefficiently. Although the new Department appeared to be a rationalization of the myriad existing security and immigration agencies, it would prove very difficult to change existing bureaucratic cultures and to achieve effective co-ordination between different functions. Critics claimed that the new Department would duplicate many functions and greatly increase the cost of internal security. Federal funding was greatly increased, but even more expensive would be the unfunded mandates that the Homeland Security Act (by which the Department was created) imposed on state governments. Henceforth, states would be required to collect data on individuals and help to police immigration without any additional federal aid.

In addition, although there were provisions in the law for the protection of individual freedoms, many civil liberties groups were concerned that centralized data banks would be used for purposes other than national security concerns. Critics claimed that new legislation might even damage the economy by limiting the activities of foreign firms in the USA and by greatly reducing the number of visas issued to foreign nationals wishing to study and work in the country.

The passage of the Patriot Act and the Homeland Security Act was, of course, rushed through Congress in the aftermath of a national emergency, and many of the new Department's deficiencies would be resolved over the coming years. In the mean time, however, homeland security operations were likely to be limited by bureaucratic complexity, congressional infighting over the funding of its constituent agencies, judicial review of its actions, and inconsistent application of its directives by state governments. Nothing illustrated this problem more graphically than the Government's response to the devastation in Louisiana and Mississippi caused by 'Hurricane Katrina' in August 2005. The Federal Emergency Management Agency (FEMA) had been placed within the new Department of Homeland Security, effectively downgrading it from an independent agency to a sub-unit of homeland security. Most commentators agreed that in both funding and leadership, FEMA had been assigned a lower priority in the business of responding to natural disasters than the Department of Homeland Security's brief to co-ordinate the domestic side of the 'war on terror'. Add to this the problems inherent in co-ordinating federal, state and local authorities during an emergency and the very serious management failures associated with the authorities' response to 'Hurricane Katrina' can be appreciated. The reaction of the Bush Administration after the disaster was to increase FEMA funding and generally assign the Agency a higher priority. By 2008 most commentators agreed that emergency management systems had improved—as illustrated by the more effective response to 'Hurricane Ike', which struck Texas in September of that year.

CONCLUSION

It is in the domestic arena that US politics is at its most complicated. Politicians in general, and Presidents in particular, usually find it much easier to deal with foreign and defence policy—although as the wars in Viet Nam and Iraq show, there are major exceptions to this generalization. It is for this reason that every recent President has found himself increasingly involved in foreign affairs as his term has progressed. In the case of President Bush, of course, this was not a matter of choice. However, as noted earlier, outside exceptional times domestic events will eventually dominate the policy agenda, as they did following the events of September 2001, the 'Hurricane Katrina' disaster in 2005 and the financial collapse in 2008. Sometimes these events seriously undermine presidential popularity and even destroy re-election chances. This was the case with George Bush, Sr, whose 90% approval ratings at the time of the first conflict in the Persian (Arabian) Gulf in 1991 evaporated in less than a year. In the context of economic recession, Bush suffered the ignominy of being defeated as a sitting President in 1992. His son avoided a similar fate in 2004 in part because security questions and the President's pursual of a 'war on terror' diverted voters' attentions away from the domestic policy agenda, although in the wake of 'Hurricane Katrina' Bush's approval ratings sank to around 40%. By 2007, and following a major defeat in the 2006 mid-term elections, the President's approval ratings had fallen to around 30%, in the context of continuing worries about high oil prices and the fallout from the ongoing war in Iraq.

The separation of powers, often compounded by divided government and federalism, make it very difficult for Presidents to forge successful coalitions. At the same time, the US people expect a great deal from a federal Government that is not always able successfully to implement policies. When disappointed, as they have been repeatedly over recent years, voters lose faith in both politicians and political institutions. For these reasons, domestic politics in the USA have assumed a conflictive and highly volatile character, and no political leader is assured of success. In order to keep winning elections, leaders are obliged to keep campaigning and to keep making promises even when they know that honouring them may be difficult or even politically impossible. These problems may be temporarily overcome in an emergency, such as the events of 11 September 2001 and its aftermath; however, domestic problems always eventually return to haunt Presidents and Congresses alike.

FROM UNIPOLARITY TO AMERICAN REALISM: US FOREIGN POLICY UNDER GEORGE W. BUSH

DAVID HASTINGS DUNN

INTRODUCTION

Eight years ago, in the 2000 presidential election, Al Gore won the popular vote but it was George W. Bush, by a twist of fate and the majority decision of the US Supreme Court, who was delivered the presidency. On such a flimsy basis the fate of nations was decided. The repercussions of this event have impacted upon not just Iraq and Afghanistan but also, and perhaps most obviously, the USA itself, for President Bush has presided over the biggest loss of international influence, respect, prestige and power in US history. When Bush assumed office in January 2001 US power seemed unassailable. According to Charles Krauthammer, the Cold War had given way not to a multipolar international system but to a unipolar one where 'The center of world power is the unchallenged superpower, the United States, attended by its Western allies.'[1] In 2002 Krauthammer reiterated the point, arguing that the USA 'is dominant by every measure: military, economic, technological, diplomatic, cultural, even linguistic'.[2] In political and policy debate the dominant question was what this situation of unipolarity meant for the international system and how the new President would use the powerful position in which the USA found itself. Eight years later, as Bush prepares to leave office, the picture is a very different one. Having inherited a country at peace and with a budget surplus, Bush will bequeath a country embroiled in two wars and with a projected budget deficit for 2009 of US $438,000m.[3] From a surplus that represented 2.5% of the USA's gross domestic product (GDP) the Bush Administration created a deficit of 3% of GDP, what Fareed Zakaria terms 'a $4 trillion hit on the country's balance sheet.'[4] Bush also presided over the largest crisis in the US banking sector since the Great Depression and failed to prevent a global economic downturn as a result of the 'sub-prime' mortgage crisis, stemming from low-income borrowers' inability to meet repayment obligations on lending. Bush was without doubt the least fiscally responsible President in US history. Furthermore, the long-term trends look equally gloomy. According to the Chairman of the US National Intelligence Council, Dr Thomas Fingar, the preliminary findings of the Council's report, 'Global Trends 2025: A Transformed World', show that while the USA will remain the preeminent power in the international system in the years ahead, US leadership is eroding 'at an accelerating pace' in 'political, economic and arguably, cultural arenas.' The report acknowledges that the USA will remain the world's superior military power but also states that this will 'be the least significant' asset since 'nobody is going to attack us with conventional force.'[5] The report also predicts the continuing decline in influence of the UN and World Bank and the inability of the USA or any other great power to dictate the new global structures needed to govern the international system in the years ahead. While one reason for these predictions is acknowledged to be the growth of the People's Republic of China, India and other developing powers, another is the legacy of the Administration of George W. Bush.

The foreign policy record of the Bush Administration is at best a mixed one. To his credit Bush has massively increased US aid to Africa and to the funding of victims of HIV/AIDS in particular. During his first two years in office Bush spent less than US $1m. on HIV/AIDS programmes globally but in 2008 spending is expected to total $6,000m., most of it in Africa.[6] Bush has also adopted a series of pragmatic policies towards the rise of China and India and has successfully avoided the pressure from some commentators to treat China as a strategic rival on the global political scene. Despite being poorly planned, badly implemented and unnecessarily antagonistic to many parts of the world, the global 'war on terror' has also prevented any further successful terrorist attacks on the US mainland. As Edward Luttwak has argued, 'the global jihadi mobilisation, triggered by post-9/11 enthusiasm for Osama bin Laden, was stopped before it could gain any momentum by all that Bush set in motion: the destruction of al-Qaeda training bases in Afghanistan, the killing or capture of most of its operatives, and, most importantly, the conversion of Muslim governments from the support of jihad to its repression.'[7] Such achievements, however, are eclipsed in any evaluation of the Bush presidency by the catalogue of other foreign policy issues on which the Administration is usually judged to be found wanting. Initially, the Bush foreign policy was characterized by its assertive unilateralism, seeking to abandon its commitments to the Anti-Ballistic Missile Treaty and Comprehensive Nuclear Test-Ban Treaty, and its obligations to reduce global climate change under the Kyoto Protocol. At the end of the Administration discussions between the USA and countries in Eastern Europe regarding missile defence bases is in large part responsible for a marked deterioration of relations between the USA and Russia, particularly after the USA announced such an agreement with Poland in August 2008; the number of states that have tested or are developing nuclear weapons has increased; and the prospect of global environmental catastrophe has been brought closer by the astonishing attitude of the Bush Administration towards global warming. Initially, the Bush Administration denied the evidence of the scientific community about the impact of human activity on climate change and then, since it accepted it, has been in avoidance of its need to take responsible measures to address the problem while disrupting the efforts of others to do so.

In articulating a foreign policy response to the terrorist attacks on the USA in September 2001, the Bush Administration also formulated a foreign policy vision that was eventually to lead by its own logic to the invasion of Iraq in 2003 and to subsequent US embroilment there that has continued into 2008. It was a foreign policy vision, as will be explained below, which took as its basic premise the military, economic and normative pre-eminence of the USA in the international system and its ability to dictate the terms of global interactions to the rest of the world. Taking unipolarity as a given, however, proved a costly foreign policy adventure for the Bush Administration and an examination of US foreign policy at the end of his second term is a powerful illustration of the dangers of this hubristic approach.

This is most obviously the case with regard to the situation in Iraq, where some 140,000 US troops remain stationed more than five years after the invasion and where the death toll of US soldiers killed mounts daily, surpassing 4,000 deaths in 2008.[8] The reduction in troop levels promised after the implementation of the 'surge' in numbers in 2007 has so far failed to materialize. Although the Iraqi Government has provisionally suggested that all US combat personnel could leave the country by 2011, there is every prospect that large numbers of US military forces will be stationed in Iraq for many years to come for security and training purposes. While considerable improvements have been made in the security situation in Iraq during 2008, it is important to view these in their proper context. What is often attributed in a blanket term to the 'surge' is actually the consequence of a number of related factors. Most important of these was the formation of Awakening Councils from 2005 by local Sunni groups who, after previously fighting US and Iraqi government forces and permitting the operations of the al-Qa'ida (Base) organization, now allied themselves with the US military. A second factor was the consequence of the 'ethnic cleansing' that had taken place in Iraq as each sectarian group evicted its enemies from rival areas. The Iraqi Red Crescent Organization estimates that 280,000 families have fled their homes in a complex migration within Iraq to avoid sectarian violence. In Baghdad alone there are nearly 170,000 families, accounting for half a million people, who have fled their homes. Nationally the pattern has been for Sunnis generally to move north and west, Shi'as to move south, and Christians to move to the far north.[9] An additional 3m. Iraqis have also fled the country, mostly to Jordan and other neighbouring states. The effect of this de facto division of Iraq on a sectarian basis has been a reduction in inter-community violence. The third factor was the greater success of the US military at counter-insurgency operations using better intelligence, and an improved understanding of and respect for the local Iraqi population.[10] The additional troop numbers provided by the 'surge' also helped as part of this overall process. However, what these improvements have not yet done is provide the basis for sustained progress among the rival political factions in Iraq sufficient to suggest a stable political future for the country. Thus, while a certain amount of stability is returning to Iraq and the number of US soldiers and ordinary Iraqi citizens being killed on a daily basis is now much lower than it was, the country remains deeply divided and extremely violent. An indication of the fragility of the recent improved security situation can be gleaned from the fact that the recent cease-fire agreements are 'extremely decentralized: more than 200 tribal and regional groups have reached individual agreements with the United States to stand down from fighting' and, as a result, some future conflict among these parties is considered by many observers to be 'inevitable'.[11]

Looking at the US invasion in its wider strategic context is also illustrative. The justifications for the invasion of Iraq were many, varied and contested, but they included the need to remove the threat to the region posed by Saddam Hussain's programmes for the development of weapons of mass destruction; the need to bring democracy to Iraq; the need to re-establish the authority of the UN; and the need to spread stability to the Middle East. The absence of weapons of mass destruction nullified the first rationale; the future of Iraq as a unitary state has been exacerbated by the establishment of a democratic system that operates on ethnic and religious grounds and has yet to establish its full legitimacy on a national basis; the mandate of the UN was seriously damaged by a war conducted without its authority and which it was unable to prevent. The stability of the Middle East is also now more precarious than before the invasion and Iran's role is greatly enhanced as a result of the collapse of Iraq as a regional balance to its rising power. More broadly still the US military has lost credibility by its failure to quell its enemies and bring order to Iraq. Diplomatically, the USA has lost respect and moral authority by its decision to invade Iraq in 2003, and the occupation of the country by US troops has limited the USA's political capacity as well as its legitimacy for foreign policy initiatives elsewhere.

The invasion of Georgian territory by Russian troops in August 2008 in response to the ill-advised attempt by Georgian President Mikheil Saakashvili forcibly to re-establish rule over the breakaway province of South Ossetia was a case study of the legacy of the US invasion of Iraq. By initiating military action without ostensible provocation, without UN authority or without sound legal justification, the USA set a precedent for the Russian Government to justify its actions in South Ossetia, Abkhazia and Georgia as defensive and reasonable. Given that Georgian army troops fired on Russian peace-keeping forces in South Ossetia, it has been argued that the Russian military action was effected with greater justification than was the US invasion of Iraq. Certainly, appeals to the UN in respect of the rules and norms of non-intervention and of the need to respect state sovereignty and national integrity have much less authority in the wake of the invasion of Iraq. Preoccupied with Iraq and Afghanistan, the USA was also remarkably mute in its response to the Russian action, leaving the diplomacy to effect a cease-fire and deferring to French President Nicolas Sarkozy in his role as President of the Council of the European Union.

Although the situation is Iraq has improved in 2008, the opposite is true with regard to Afghanistan. Since 2005 the country has been the site of intense war-fighting between the USA and its North Atlantic Treaty Organization (NATO) allies on the one hand and the Taliban and regional warlords on the other; in the last year this fighting has become more severe, with the total number of US soldiers killed in Afghanistan reaching 500 in July 2008.[12] The scale and intensity of these engagements, together with the number of allied casualties, is higher than at any time since the invasion began in 2001. As a result there are now more US soldiers in Afghanistan than at any time since 2001 and there are plans to increase the US deployment by 4,500 troops in early 2009 by redeploying them from Iraq.[13] Even though they are now joined by 20,000 NATO troops in the International Security Assistance Force (ISAF) and 76,000 troops of the reconstructed Afghan army, there are parts of the country that remain the domain of the resurgent Taliban forces.[14] What in 2001 looked like a quick and decisive military victory has become a failing and festering political sore. Al-Qa'ida leader Osama bin Laden remains at large, the Taliban are as yet undefeated and the political and economic reconstruction of Afghanistan has only recently been fully engaged. In 2003 the USA spent US $737m. on reconstruction and equipping the Afghan army whereas in 2007 spending had risen to $10,000m. The USA's frustration in fighting the Taliban, who are able to retreat back to safe havens in the tribal areas of Pakistan, has also raised the prospect of confrontation between the USA and Pakistan over this issue. In July 2008 President Bush authorized US forces to pursue fleeing Taliban fighters into Pakistan if necessary. This policy has angered the Pakistani army, who have already fired on US helicopters operating in Pakistani airspace. The potential for these clashes to escalate is real, as is the withdrawal of the co-operation of the Pakistani army in hunting down the Taliban fighters. How this difficult situation can be resolved in a way that addresses the issue of safe havens in Pakistan is unclear and will be a high priority for the new administration.

While the situations in Afghanistan and Iraq are serious and ongoing challenges for US foreign policy in both their consumption of resources and their resistance to solution, they also represent policy failures in a number of other respects. After the September 2001 attacks the NATO alliance invoked its Article 5 obligation that an attack on one was an attack on all. It did so partly out of solidarity and partly in an effort to persuade the USA to engage its new enemies multilaterally. The Department of Defense's response in Secretary of Defense Donald Rumsfeld's famous words was that 'The mission must determine the coalition. The coalition must not determine the mission.' In other words, the USA would accept contributions of forces only on its terms. It alone would determine the way to engage with its enemies. In 2003, with the US army fully stretched in Iraq, the USA handed control of part of Afghanistan to NATO control through the ISAF. The USA has been unsuccessful in persuading NATO members, either privately or publicly, to supply an additional force of 2,500 troops and supporting helicopters and transport aircraft for this operation.[15] The tardiness of the European allies to supply forces at the US behest is in marked contrast to the spirit of 2001. As French Senator Serge Vinçon observed in 2006, 'The fight against terrorism united all the nations five years ago, but today, things are not going as well as what we had expected'. Former US ambassador to NATO Bob Hunter was more candid, stating that 'Some Europeans are hiding behind the Iraq issue and the public's unhappiness with the U.S. in order to shirk their own responsibilities in Afghanistan.'[16] Thus, while the USA's belated recognition of the need for a multilateral approach in Afghanistan and elsewhere was generally regarded as an improvement on the unilateralism of the previous period, it was also clear that much international goodwill and sympathy had been squandered in the intervening years.

The USA's embrace of a more multilateral approach, particularly since Condoleezza Rice became Secretary of State in 2005, has also been evident in US policy towards Iran and the Democratic People's Republic of Korea (North Korea), as part of a co-ordinated international effort to prevent both states breaching their anti-proliferation commitments. Despite these efforts, however, the USA and the international community more broadly have been conspicuous in their failure to build a consensus on an approach to this deviant behaviour. In the wake of the Iraq invasion, it is clear that the USA lacks the goodwill, respect, authority, legitimacy and power, of persuasion or otherwise, either to pressure these 'rogue' states or to build a coalition to do so in an effective manner. Thus, while its more exuberant phase of so-called 'cowboy' diplomacy may be over in some respects, its legacy is a formidable obstacle to its new and more consensual approach.[17] While the new-found willingness displayed throughout 2008 to engage in direct diplomatic contact with Iran and North Korea in order to advance the political process in both sets of nuclear negotiations was to be welcomed, there was also a widespread recognition that these policies came rather too late in the tenure of the Bush Administration to make much difference. Having failed to effect change by the exercise of its unilateral power, the USA's embrace of multilateralism was widely seen as an admission of powerlessness in the face of the intransigence of these recalcitrant regimes. While Rice has sought to rebrand this pragmatism with the title 'American Realism' and to afford to it the veneer of intellectual coherence, the reality is that US foreign policy in the second half of the Bush Administration is lacking in consistence and application.[18]

Thus, although the USA has reverted to a more traditional diplomatic approach in its dealings with Afghanistan, North Korea and Iran, the same cannot be said of its response to the Israeli invasion of Lebanon in July 2006. The Bush Administration's response to this serious outbreak of hostilities in the crucially important Middle East region marked a significant shift from the USA's traditional foreign policy approach. Rather than seeking to play an 'honest broker' role, the USA was clearly seen to take sides. It made it abundantly clear that it supported the Israeli action against the radical Shi'a Hezbollah organization in southern Lebanon as part of the ongoing 'war on terror'. While doing this provided diplomatic cover for Israel at the UN for actions that many states saw as a disproportionate response to Hezbollah provocation, it also confirmed for many in the region and beyond their suspicion of and dislike for the USA. For the Bush Administration, Israel's attempt to destroy Hezbollah militarily was a justified use of force against an Iranian-backed terrorist organization. That Israel failed in this quest, however, being forced to agree to a UN peace-keeping force in southern Lebanon as a guarantor of its security, represented another political and policy defeat for the USA in the region. Having supported Israel, the USA reaped greater hostility from within the region without the benefit of Hezbollah or Iran being cowed. The action also undermined the USA's claim to support the newly democratic Government in Lebanon, leaving both that administration and Bush's democracy promotion plans damaged as a result.

In many respects, the international environment that faced the Bush Administration in 2006 was what former Secretary of State Madeline Albright described as 'the perfect storm', with many individual crises according at the same time in a way that undermined governmental ability to resolve them either individually or collectively. It was a sentiment shared by Richard N. Haass, a former senior Bush administration official and President of the US Council on Foreign Relations. According to Haass, 'I am hard-pressed to think of any other moment in modern times where there have been so many challenges facing this country simultaneously.'[19] Not surprisingly, these charges are strenuously denied by the Bush Administration, which is keen to disaggregate the challenges that it faces and to stress the measures that it is taking in each policy area to deal with these issues. Nevertheless, it is undeniable that in recent years a number of issues have come together to present a significant challenge for US foreign policy. Iran remains defiant of UN efforts to curb its nuclear proliferation transgressions and claims to be engaged in uranium enrichment on an industrial scale. The Bush Administration's condemnation of its role within Iraq reflects its confidence that Iran is arming and financing the Shi'a insurgency that is killing so many Iraqi civilians and US soldiers. Despite progress on its nuclear weapons programmes, in September 2007 it emerged that North Korea, in a major escalation of its proliferation activities, was supplying nuclear material to Syria; in the previous year the country had tested an intercontinental ballistic missile designed to reach the USA.[20]

Notwithstanding the progress made in the situation in Iraq, the scenario in the Middle East more broadly is becoming progressively more unstable. The Syrian nuclear programme in particular is a warring development. Not only does its destruction by Israeli warplanes increase the prospect of war between these two states, but the purposes, plans and ownership of the Syrian programme provoke many real and potential insecurities and fears. The USA's international affairs are so problematic that this issue in general, and Iraq in particular, has dominated the political agenda in Washington. With the loss of both houses of Congress in the November 2006 mid-term elections, the Bush Administration seems incapable of progressing either significant domestic legislation or meaningful foreign policy direction. To understand why this state of affairs has come about, why the Administration's critics consider the USA so ill-prepared to deal with these challenges and how it arrived at this point it is necessary to examine the strategy adopted by the Bush Administration in the aftermath of 11 September 2001. For the USA's current international situation is, in large part, the consequence of the application of the 'Bush doctrine'. Accordingly this essay seeks to focus on the fundamentals of the Bush Administration's strategy. It does this by analysing the thinking behind the shift towards the strategy of pre-eminence and pre-emption and then looks at the application of that strategy in practice. It shows how the Bush doctrine was formed with Iraq in mind and that it has little to offer in relation to the challenges presented by North Korea, Iran and Syria. As such, it shows how the USA arrived at the 'perfect storm' in its foreign policy by its pursuit of the Bush doctrine and how it still adheres to this way of thinking as the Bush Administration enters its final year of office.

TOWARDS THE 'BUSH DOCTRINE'

If the controversy surrounding the war in Iraq is without precedent domestically and internationally, then so are the events that led the USA to this point. Not only were the events of 11 September 2001 uniquely barbaric, they were also unequalled in the effect they had on the US psyche. While the loss of life was great, the loss of the USA's sense of invulnerability was even greater. The collective sense of incomprehension was heightened by the fact that this enemy 'made no demands, gave no warning and left no explanation.'[21] It was an attack that struck at the very essence of the USA's sense of itself as both a nation and a superpower. It is partly for this reason that the USA's efforts to eliminate this threat quickly came to dominate all its external relations. From the outset, President Bush characterized the nature of the conflict as a 'war' and declared that the enemy was 'terror'. He also declared that the nature of the conflict would be unlike any other that the USA had faced. It would be considerable and complex and would have a variety of levels. These would include attacking the sources of funding of the terrorist network, preventing the proliferation of the component materials for weapons of mass destruction, as well as the use of military force against terrorists, their supporters and their allies.

At a political level it also required a series of changes in the USA's international engagement. The most immediately obvious manifestation of these changes was the re-engagement of the USA with the international system in its entirety, something that had been missing from US foreign policy for much of the 1990s. Given the nature of the enemy that the USA now faced, the Bush Administration turned its attention to issues that it had showed no inclination to engage with before 11 September. It also found it necessary to reorder its priorities in certain key bilateral relationships, most notably with Pakistan, in order to build an effective international coalition in response to the attacks. Indeed, in its response to the new threat the USA showed a level of international engagement not seen since the end of the Cold War. This re-engagement centred around a new focus on the global 'war on terror'. President Bush's comment that 'we have found our mission and our moment' aptly captured the personal and national priority that the new situation demanded.

The third reaction, which took slightly longer to formulate, was the development of a new strategic doctrine for the USA in both theory and practice. Initially formulated and announced through a series of speeches over the year, these ideas were distilled into the National Security Strategy of the United States of America 2002 (NSS 2002), which was presented to Congress on 20 September 2002; an updated version of the strategy document of the same name was published in 2006. This document was both a blueprint for the type of international order that the US Government envisaged and for the terms and conditions by which the country would be engaged in the international system. This essay will focus on this strategy as the guiding principle of the Bush Administration's foreign policy approach, both in theory and in the impact of the application of the NSS 2002 in the invasion of Iraq, and on what effect the consequences of this policy have had on the Bush Administration's new strategic doctrine, and thus the USA's global role.

A NEW GEOPOLITICAL STRATEGY: THE BUSH DOCTRINE IN THEORY

Probably the most significant change to result from the terrorist attacks on the USA has been the formulation of a new strategic doctrine by the Bush Administration. Although crystallized as a foreign policy issue by its practical application in the pre-emptive use of military force against Iraq, the issue and its implications are much broader and more significant than even this radical policy. For over 50 years the USA relied on a combination of containment and deterrence as the guiding principle of its geopolitical approach. It was this strategy that successfully won the Cold War and it was this approach that was applied to Iraq after the Gulf conflict in 1991 by successive Administrations, including, initially, that of George W. Bush. Containment, however, was a reactive and multilateral strategy that was framed in a period when US power was balanced by a rival superpower, the USSR. At the start of the 21st century the geopolitical position of the USA is very different, and it is in these circumstances and in the context of the global 'war on terror', that this new doctrine has been forged. It could be distinguished from previous US strategies in three important ways: its focus on pre-emption, its hegemonic aspirations and its unilateralism. While all three elements had an enhanced prominence in the new doctrine, they all had their antecedence in previous policy debates.

Pre-emption

Although the adoption of a policy that actively espoused pre-emptive military action to remove capabilities or regimes that threaten the USA was a significant change in policy, it was not actually a new idea. Throughout the Cold War there were various attempts made to break away from the constraints and risks that the containment doctrine involved. President Dwight Eisenhower (1953–61) announced in 1954 his 'rollback doctrine' (which sought to 'roll back' the 'Iron Curtain', that is, overthrow communist regimes in Eastern Europe), only to abandon Hungary to its fate in 1956 when that country put this policy to the test. Faced with the risk of confrontation with the USSR, which had invaded Hungary, the Eisenhower Administration reverted to the safety and security of containment. The Reagan Administration (1981–89) sought, in its nuclear policy options, pre-emptive contingencies for fighting a limited nuclear war with the USSR. Similarly Reagan's enthusiasm for both his Strategic Defense Initiative and, later, for radical arms control proposals, reflected his desire to escape US reliance on nuclear deterrence.[22] Despite his support for these policies, however, deterrence remained US strategy. In the post-Cold War era the Administration of Bill Clinton (1993–2001) took a small step towards a pre-emption policy in 1993 with the announcement of the Counter-Proliferation Initiative. As part of this policy development the Department of Defense called for the capability to 'delay, disrupt or deny the deployment of weapons of mass destruction, and to disrupt or destroy the supporting infrastructure for weapons of mass destruction and missile capabilities.'[23] Importantly, however, this initiative aimed to provide a military capability. It did not propose the elevation of pre-emption to the forefront of US foreign policy as a declaratory strategy.

Interestingly, the adoption of the pre-emption strategy was not the immediate response of the Bush Administration to the September 2001 terrorist attacks. In his congressional address on 20 September 2001 President Bush declared that the new grand purpose for US policy was 'ending terrorism'. The switch to preventing the accumulation of weapons of mass destruction 'in the hands of irresponsible states' was a policy developed gradually during 2002.[24] Its logic was based on the inability to deter the new type of adversary. 'In the Cold War', the NSS 2002 states, 'weapons of mass destruction were considered weapons of last resort whose use risked the destruction of those who used them. Today, our enemies see weapons of mass destruction as weapons of choice', with the result that the 'United States can no longer solely rely on a reactive posture as we have in the past. The inability to deter a potential attacker, the immediacy of today's threats, and the magnitude of potential harm that could be caused by our adversaries' choice of weapons, do not permit that option. We cannot let our enemies strike first.'[25] The way in which the USA viewed its own nuclear weapons was also revised in light of this new doctrine. The Bush Administration's Nuclear Posture Review added 'rogue' states to the list of potential targets and removed its pledge not to attack non-nuclear states.

Support for the idea of pre-emption was in part the product of the successful use of military force in both Afghanistan and Kosovo. For the USA, these missions developed 'a profound optimism that we can do it—we can invade a country halfway round the world and bring about a reasonable settlement.'[26] It was also a strategy that was developed with a target state in mind: Iraq. It was partly in that context that the strategy was initially judged favourably by members of Congress and the public alike. For many observers, however, there remained serious concerns about its implications both in general terms and with regard to Iraq in particular. Critics were concerned as to the wider implications of this policy. If pre-emption was legitimate for the USA then why not for India against Pakistan, or vice versa, or Israel against Iran or Syria, or any other number of possible scenarios. Concern was also expressed as to the limits of this policy. If Iraq followed Afghanistan then which state would be next after Iraq and where would the policy end, given the US Administration's long list of 'rogue' states? Furthermore, there were also fears about how this doctrine would affect the integrity of the USA's long-standing alliance relationships. While some allies, such as the United Kingdom, were supportive of the Bush Administration's approach, others, such as Germany and France, were much more critical. With regard to Iraq in particular there was concern that a pre-emptive attack without demonstrable evidence of an imminent attack would be in material breach of international law. For the critics, the USA and its allies had failed to prove a link between Iraq and the attacks of 11 September that would justify self-defence, nor had they provided evidence of a clear and present danger to the USA or its allies.

Pre-Eminence

Though less widely reported, an equally important aspect of the new Bush doctrine was its statement that the USA would not permit any state to close the military lead that it established after the collapse of the USSR. 'Our forces will be strong enough to dissuade potential adversaries from pursuing a military build-up in hopes of surpassing, or equaling, the power of the United States.' Given that US military spending accounts for 40% of global military expenditure, more than the next 20 largest spenders combined, as a statement of fact this was unremarkable. As a political aspiration, however, it illustrated how the USA viewed the world and its place in it. As a policy statement it had much in common with the 1992 Defence Planning Guidance Document, known as the 'No Rivals', draft which declared, 'Our first objective is to prevent the re-emergence of a new rival... Our strategy must now refocus on precluding the emergence of any potential future global competitor.'[27] This document was dismissed at the time as unworkable, unaffordable and unsupportable. To the current Administration, however, these objectives seem manageable. It is for this reason that the NSS 2002 sets out a world role that is proactive in its advocacy of what it called 'a distinctly American internationalism that reflects the union of our values and our interests. The aim of this strategy is to help make the world not just safer but better. Our goals on the path to progress are clear: political and economic freedom, peaceful relations with other states, and respect for human dignity.' It is a strategy that commits the USA to champion free markets, free trade, democracy and human rights. The mechanisms it identified for this purpose are supportive allies, increased but conditional foreign aid and unrestrained military might. More specifically it pledges to 'defend the peace by fighting terrorists and tyrants... preserve the peace by building good relations among the great powers... [and] extend the peace by encouraging free and open societies on every continent.' The universalism of this last point marks a deliberate departure from previous US policy, especially in relation to the Middle East. This point was reinforced by a further pledge to support 'moderate and modern government, especially in the Muslim world'. In doing this the Administration was signalling its plans for the democratic transformation of the Middle East, demonstrating the potentially far-reaching implications of this new strategy.

Unilateralism

The third and related aspect of NSS 2002 was its insistence that 'While the United States will constantly strive to enlist the support of the international community, we will not hesitate to act alone, if necessary, to exercise our right of self-defense'. Taken together with the new strategy's criticism of previous efforts to prevent weapons proliferation through arms control, it was clear that, for the Bush Administration, traditional multilateralism was a poor guarantee of US security. This approach was one of the most consistent themes in the foreign policy of the Bush Administration. Not only did it view international agreements as ineffective in their contribution to US national security, but by placing limits on the USA's freedom to act they were also counter-productive. Thus, President Bush opposed the International Criminal Court as he rejected the idea that others could potentially stand in judgment over US citizens. The Government also refused to ratify the so-called 'Ottawa Declarations' on landmines.[28] Similarly, the Comprehensive Nuclear Test-Ban Treaty was opposed as both an inadequate safeguard against proliferation and as a hindrance to the USA's development and maintenance of its nuclear arsenal. The Biological Weapons (and Toxins) Convention was also rejected on these terms, with the additional rationale that the USA's economic security would be threatened if intrusive inspection provisions were to allow foreigners into US pharmaceutical plants. And perhaps most notoriously, the Bush Administration refused to ratify the Kyoto Protocol because the proposals affected the USA—which created 25% of the world's greenhouse gasses from under 5% of the world's population, making it the largest polluter country—more than any other country.

While there was much speculation after the terrorist attacks that the USA would be forced to curb its unilateralist instincts in order to gain international support, the opposite was evident. A wounded USA approached international politics with an indignant self-righteousness. Its perception of external threat strengthened its willingness to use its unique position of power within the international system to solve its problems unilaterally. Where it did act in concert with its allies it was clear that this 'multilateralism' coincided with the US agenda. In 2001 President Bush rejected the Kyoto Protocol declaring, 'We will not do anything that harms our economy, because first things first, are the people who live in America. That's my priority'.[29] Faced with physical threats to the USA, this approach has been repeated and amplified. If the Kyoto Protocol could be viewed as the Bush Administration's rejection of the established means of global governance, then the Bush doctrine is the application of that approach to international security. Indeed, even before 11 September Condoleezza Rice, then Assistant to the President for National Security Affairs, argued that 'it is not isolationist to suggest that the United States has a special role in the world and should not adhere to every international convention and agreement that someone thinks to propose.'[30] The NSS 2002 document and the 2006 document alike are infused with this argument. Because the USA was the ultimate guardian of the international system, US strength must not be limited by international constraints. It was a sentiment based on the premise that 'overwhelming American power is good not just for the United States but for the world.'[31] Thus, it followed that US power must not be constrained in the same way as lesser powers lest this hinder the USA's freedom of action because, as Rice put it, 'America's pursuit of the national interest will create conditions that promote freedom, markets, and peace.'[32] Having established the parameters of the Bush doctrine in theory this essay will now analyse how the Administration has applied its logic to US foreign policy.

THE BUSH DOCTRINE IN PRACTICE: THE 'AXIS OF EVIL' AND THE WAR IN IRAQ

The 'Axis of Evil'

The response of the Bush Administration to the terrorist attacks of September 2001 evolved gradually in response to both events and internal debates within the Government. The rapid and apparently conclusive use of force in Afghanistan had a bearing on the overall debate. Despite predictions of a long and difficult campaign, the military action was concluded within two months, with the defeat of the Taliban in December 2001 and the establishment of a new interim Government. It was a success that emboldened the Administration and convinced it of the need to address the problem of 'rogue states' as a means of pursuing the global 'war on terror'. The decision to target Afghanistan was also consistent with Bush's announcement that he would make no distinction between terrorists and the states that harboured them. As the US historian Walter Lafeber argued, 'conceptualizing the chase so it centered on specific states and regimes... made both the military and the public relations jobs easier.'[33] Targeting states that are vulnerable to conventional military forces was also reassuring to the US people that the Administration had the means to protect them against this new threat. For the Bush Administration, however, the logic linking the two was compelling and simple. An enemy that sought weapons of mass destruction had attacked the USA. At the same time, there were states that were enemies of the USA, which were seeking to build weapons of mass destruction and were known to have armed terrorist groups in the past. In such circumstances, it argued, it would be foolish either to wait for a positive connection between these two enemies to be proved or until after such an attack had occurred. As President Bush said, 'We will not wait for the authors of mass murder to gain the weapons of mass destruction. We act now, because we must lift this dark threat from our age and save generations to come.'[34] In his January 2002 State of the Union address President Bush identified three such 'rogue' regimes as comprising an 'axis of evil': Iran, Iraq and North Korea. All three states had a record of supporting terrorism and had embarked on programmes to build weapons of mass destruction, including nuclear weapons and the long-range ballistic missiles to deliver them. All three were accordingly warned to desist from such activity or face serious consequences.

Although described as an 'axis of evil', the Bush Administration soon made clear that there was a hierarchy of concern within the group. While North Korea was the most advanced in building both nuclear weapons and the ability to deliver them over several hundred miles, the Bush Administration was initially encouraged by the way in which the North Korean Government acted following 11 September 2001. In the year after the terrorist attacks North Korea announced that it was extending its moratorium on missile testing and that it would allow International Atomic Energy Agency (IAEA) inspectors into the country to examine its nuclear programme. The North Koreans eventually appeared willing to honour their part of the deal reached with the Clinton Administration in 1994, in which North Korea agreed to suspend its nuclear programme and export its spent reactor fuel in exchange for two much-needed proliferation-resistant light-water reactors and fuel oil. Iran, by contrast, was regarded as being some years off its potential development of a nuclear capability and had been similarly supportive of the USA in its 'war on terror', especially in Afghanistan. Indeed, its unexpected mention in the same category as Iraq and North Korea was greatly resented by the Iranian Government and was responsible for a major set-back in US-Iranian relations. With regard to Iraq, however, as later became evident from reported deliberations within the Bush Government, the terrorist attacks of September 2001 were regarded at a very early stage as a potential opportunity to remove Saddam Hussain from power.

IRAQ: A TARGET IDENTIFIED

Among the 'axis of evil' states Iraq was seen by the Bush Administration as the obvious target of choice. With Saddam Hussain gone, it was argued, Iran would feel more secure and thus be able to develop towards its own 'velvet revolution'. North Korea, it was hoped, would learn the lessons of Iraq's military defeat and act to avoid the same fate. More broadly, it was reasoned that with Iraq liberated, the benefits of a post-Saddam Hussain Gulf would spread to include other states, including Iran, Syria, Lebanon and Saudi Arabia. The prime justification that was used to target Iraq, however, was not the threat or opportunity that it presented, but its non-compliance with a series of outstanding UN resolutions concerning its production of weapons of mass destruction. For the Bush Administration this approach had two benefits. First, its genuine concern with weapons of mass destruction was one that was shared by the US public.[35] Second, Iraq's non-compliance provided a diplomatic mechanism to pressure Iraq to comply with the demands of the international community or face the consequences in a similar way that it did in 1991. Saddam Hussain's 'decade of defiance' of the UN made it easier to make a case against Iraq than would otherwise have been the case simply because of its 'rogue state' status in the USA. Thus, rather paradoxically, Iraq became the US Government's target of choice not because it was an immediate threat but because it was immediately vulnerable. Twelve years of sanctions and no military modernization during the period following the decimation of its army in 1991 meant that war, when it came, was guaranteed to be one-sided. The only possible force equalizer that Iraq possessed was the recourse to chemical or biological munitions. Interestingly, this was a threat that the USA regarded as manageable and the war was fought in the context of that threat. Saddam Hussain's regime also had virtually no allies and his continued defiance of the UN in the face of the concerted efforts of the international community left him with little sympathy among the governments of the region. The Bush Administration's expectations about how US forces would be greeted after the fall of the regime and about how easily Iraq could be transformed at little cost into a model secular, democratic Middle Eastern state also informed its focus on Iraq. However, above all, the pretext of removing Saddam Hussain as an act of enforcement of UN resolutions rather than the decapitation of a hostile state made Iraq the perfect test and exemplar of the new US doctrine.

A POST-INVASION ANALYSIS

In retrospect, the events leading to the invasion of Iraq demonstrated the extent and the limits of US power at the start of the 21st century. They also showed a willingness of the USA to act multilaterally if the international community was willing to follow its lead on its terms, and a corresponding willingness to strike out on its own in pursuit of its own agenda if that support was not forthcoming. In 2003 the USA was able to set the agenda on Iraq but was unable to dictate fully how the international community should respond to the problem. Its threat of force succeeded in placing Iraq at the top of the international agenda, compelling both the international community and Saddam Hussain to confront the implications of Iraq's continued defiance of the UN. Having built its case against Iraq on its continued possession of weapons of mass destruction, however, and having used the UN as a mechanism to confront Saddam Hussain, the USA became tied to this process. Thus, when Iraq readmitted the UN weapons inspectors in November 2002 the momentum towards military action was slowed. The partial compliance by Iraq wrongfooted the Bush Administration, which had clearly not planned for a protracted and ambiguous response to the UN Security Council's Resolution 1441.[36] Iraq's limited concessions also divided the international community between those, led by France, who saw the UN inspection regime as a sufficient mechanism to contain and disarm Iraq, and those, led by the USA, who believed Iraq's failure to comply fully with Resolution 1441 was sufficient justification for immediate military action. From this point, what had been a remarkable diplomatic achievement turned into the most significant international dispute of the post-Second World War period. The USA's military deployment to the region, which previously had been seen as an effective inducement to Iraqi compliance, began to be viewed as both an indication of intent and a driver of policy. While France and others demanded that the inspections route be given time to work, the USA was perceived to be driven by the logic of attacking Iraq in accordance with climatic and electoral timetables. The desire to use the assembled military force before the desert heat made fighting impossible, together with the need to complete the task of removing Saddam Hussain before the start of a presidential election year led many critics to question whether the USA was simply using the UN as a pretext for regime change. For the US Government, however, Iraq's failure to comply with the UN was enough to act. Resolution 1441 deliberately put the onus on Iraq to provide evidence of the abandonment of its weapons of mass destruction programme. Iraq's failure to provide this was, for Washington, indicative of deception.

Although determined not to allow the UN inspection process to remove the pressure on Iraq, the Bush Administration still pursued the matter through the UN. While the Security Council had approved Resolution 1441 and the threat of force that it implied, its members were not, however, prepared to endorse the resort to force on the US timetable. Having established a new inspection regime, the majority of the Security Council wanted to allow a reasonable time to test the claims of the Iraqi regime that it no longer had weapons of mass destruction. France led the opposition to US diplomacy at the UN and effectively undercut US and British efforts to move towards a vote on this issue by announcing in advance that it would veto a second resolution under 'any circumstances'. France was joined in opposition to the immediate use of military force against Iraq by fellow Security Council members Russia and Germany. Although united in their desire to pressure Iraq into compliance with the UN, their disagreement about the appropriate and legitimate timing of this action was to prove insurmountable. In their opposition to the USA on a matter of such international importance, France and Germany were acting in a manner that was unprecedented in the post-War period. As such, the significance of this development was greater than its impact on the USA's Iraq policy. For, while primarily about Iraq, the diplomatic opposition that materialized in late 2002 and early 2003 was influenced by a broader concern about US foreign policy. Certainly, the Bush Administration's earlier unilateralism had built up no reserves of goodwill to draw upon within the international community. Furthermore, the publication of the NSS 2002 was seen as a further provocation against the established norms of international behaviour. As James Rubin observed, 'If gaining support for action against Iraq was truly Washington's highest priority in the fall of 2002, it is hard to imagine a more counterproductive step than to initiate a debate over whether the United States has the right to attack whomever it wants, whenever it deems it necessary.'[37] The USA was asserting by pronouncement and by deed that it would act to defend its security in a way that it defined as necessary and that it could not be stopped by the international community. The actions of France, supported by Germany and Russia, however, served to show the USA that in acting in this way it could not expect the automatic support of the international community. In choosing to do so anyway, as the Bush Administration did, its erstwhile allies made it clear that the venture that the USA had undertaken was now its alone to resolve. Just as the diplomacy on the road to war had showed the possibilities and limitations of US political power, so the war and occupation of Iraq showed the possibilities and limitations of US military force.

THE LEGACY OF INVASION AND OCCUPATION

As if an indicator of things to come, the USA's military plans suffered a set-back at the outset of the conflict when the Turkish parliament refused the use of its territory as a transit route and a launching point for an attack on northern Iraq. The decision had considerable military consequences for 'Operation Iraqi Freedom' and was the first of many examples of bad planning based on unsound assumptions. The invasion had been planned as a classic pincer movement forcing the Iraqi army to fight on two fronts. Without the Fourth Infantry Division coming down from the north, the most difficult area, the 'Sunni triangle', including Saddam Hussain's hometown of Tikrit, was of necessity dealt with last by the forces coming up from the south, rather than first as had been planned. According to *Time* magazine, this meant that 'Iraqi fighters loyal to Saddam left Baghdad and went home, where, motivated by nationalism and tribal loyalties, they could regroup and plan attacks on American forces.'[38] Another consequence of the Turkish refusal was that the US invading force that actually conducted the fighting in Iraq was much smaller than planned. Secretary of Defense Rumsfeld had already provoked controversy by deploying a much smaller force to the region than some strategists thought prudent, and was then denied the northern contingent of his invasion force by the Turkish decision. Under these conditions the US-led coalition's victory was all the more remarkable a military achievement, not least for the speed with which it was achieved. Within this triumph, however, lay the seeds of problems ahead. Without its northern division the invasion became much more of a decapitation operation based on Baghdad than had been envisaged. Furthermore, the rapid defeat of the regular Iraqi army left the coalition lines of supply stretched and severely vulnerable to attack from irregular forces. More significantly still, the invading forces lacked the troops necessary to detain and disarm Iraqi fighters or to maintain security in the cities. The Department of Defense had expected large sections of the Iraqi army to surrender to the coalition and had planned to use these units for policing and reconstruction. In the event this simply did not happen. In addition, the Iraqi government authority collapsed, leaving the US and British forces, already stretched thin, to do everything from guarding banks to hunting down guerrillas.[39] This situation was hindered further by Saddam Hussain's decision to empty Iraq's prisons of 100,000 convicts on the eve of the war, and by the widespread looting that followed the fall of Baghdad. While the military campaign had proved easier than expected, with no reported use of weapons of mass destruction and no attempt to drag Israel into the war as had been feared, the post-Saddam phase was to prove much more difficult than the USA had predicted or planned for.

On 1 May 2003 President Bush, in what was seen as a victory speech, on an aircraft carrier off the coast of California, declared an end to 'major combat operations'. While this may have been an accurate description of the intensive military conflict, it was true only for that part of the war. In the months and now years since that date the security situation in Iraq has progressively worsened. The immediate security situation in Iraq was not helped by the decision of the US Administrator of the Coalition Provisional Authority (CPA), L. Paul Bremmer, to disband the Iraqi army in May as part of the process of eradicating the influence of the Arab Baath Socialist Party. This move was counterproductive in two ways. First, it put thousands of disgruntled armed men onto the streets with no pay and no reason to support the US troops. Second, it dissolved a potentially useful auxiliary force for maintaining order in Iraq. In his defence, Bremmer argued that he was only institutionalizing what had already happened on the ground where the Iraqi army had effectively gone home.[40] Nevertheless, it was a decision quickly regretted and plans were instituted to create a new militia force of some 250,000 men to fulfil this role. Some 125,000 men were trained and in operation by the time of the January 2005 elections. The security situation in Iraq, however, has deteriorated gradually but significantly over the period of the occupation. The failure of the occupation force to deliver on their promises and the Iraqis' high expectations has resulted in loss of support, control and what little security there was. One grim manifestation of this situation is that by September 2008 more than 4,157 US service personnel had been killed in Iraq—more than the number killed in all US conflicts since Viet Nam combined—and more than 30,000 had been injured. The number of Iraqi civilians killed was estimated in September 2008 to be between 87,534 and 95,533.[41] These numbers give some indication of the scale and the intensity of the insurgency, which now dominates and, to a degree, paralyses Iraq.

While the period immediately after the fall of Baghdad was characterized by a general state of lawlessness and looting, what developed after was much worse. The forces that were most liberated by the US invasion were not the desires for modernity and democracy but their polar opposites, those of religious and tribal rivalry, Islamic fanaticism and Arab/Iraqi nationalism. It seems that the USA was not alone in seeing Iraq, post-Saddam Hussain, as a model for radical change in the Middle East. In the absence of any effective central authority, Iraq, like an unwashed petri dish, cultivated a number of parasitic pathogens, such as private armies and militias, an influx of foreign Jihadist fighters and opportunist criminal groups. These forces filled the power vacuum in the country for a number of reasons. First, the number of occupying troops, even under the 'surge', is far too small to police the country effectively. The 'surge', which is only sustainable for a short period and was being scaled back during 2008, only returned the USA back to its 2003 troop levels, of 150,000–160,000. A much larger force of at least twice that size would be necessary effectively to police a country the size of Iraq. Because the USA does not have that large an army the US strategy was predicated on working with the civil and military instruments of the Iraqi state. In the absence of these or supporting allied peace-keeping forces the task has proved too demanding for the relatively small US force. While a larger army would have intimidated and deterred the local population the small US presence has proved a tempting target for ambush for those keen to bloody the foreign occupiers widely regarded as an illegitimate invading force. The results of a poll conducted in 2007 showed that some 57% of Iraqis expressed support for attacks on coalition forces.[42] Second, the USA initially refused to admit that it was fighting an insurgency war, choosing to believe instead that the opposition was composed of 'dead-enders' from the previous regime who would soon be either caught, killed or co-opted by the new regime. By doing so, the US authorities failed to appreciate the scale and the dynamic nature of the problem they faced. This view only grudgingly began to change after Saddam Hussain was captured in December 2003 and the insurgency continued unaffected. This view also became untenable when it became clear that the insurgency was also coming from members of the Shi'a community, not just the Sunni community, to which Saddam Hussain belonged. Indeed, much of the violence took on a sectarian character as Sunnis killed Shi'as and vice versa in an attempt to influence the eventual political shape of Iraq. Third, the impact of the prisoner abuse scandal that emerged from April 2004 was a grave blow to the reputation of the US forces and the USA as a whole in Iraq. The fact that these misdeeds had also been photographed and released added further to the impact of the outrage. These images were played and replayed throughout the Arab world as evidence both of the supposed wickedness of the US army and the moral bankruptcy of Western culture. For a mission that was supposed to bring liberation, the rule of law and modernity, these pictures, which showed inhumane incarceration, torture and perverted humiliation, could not have been more damaging. The apparent lack of urgency with which these complaints were dealt with by the US Administration did little to convince Iraqis that the US leaders were as outraged by this affair as they ought to have been. The recent dispute over the role of private security companies operating in Iraq, apparently above Iraqi law, also has the potential to be further source of resentment against the US presence.[43] A final reason for the growth of instability in Iraq has been the failure to progress the rebuilding of the country's key infrastructure on a scale commensurate with the need or the investment allocated. Of the US $22,000m. allocated by Congress, much was wasted through misallocation, fraud and corruption or else went unspent owing to the poor security situation.[44] Indeed, in mid-2004 the Administration sought congressional approval to reallocate $3,000m. from the reconstruction budget to the security budget in recognition that the former cannot be accomplished until the latter is achieved. Only now, in mid-2008, with the improvement in the security situation and the willingness of the USA to fund government-run enterprises, is the situation in Iraq starting to show some signs of recovery.

Despite these obvious set-backs some progress has been made in Iraq in a series of political landmarks. In June 2004 sovereignty was handed over from the CPA and a new interim Iraqi Government was sworn in. More meaningful still was the highly symbolic election of a provisional Government in January 2005, which was given the task of drafting a new constitution. This was approved in a referendum in October, paving the way for the election in December of a new Government. Reconciling the different interests and views of Iraq's rivalling factions, however, has not proved easy. The former dominant Sunnis largely boycotted the election, leaving the majority Shi'as and Kurds to draft the new Constitution. The willingness of the Sunnis to accept these new realities through both the endorsement of the Constitution and its subsequent operation will largely determine the fate of Iraq. So far none of these politically momentous steps has been enough to quell the violence and Prime Minister Nuri al-Maliki is only slowly gaining sufficient support to be regarded as a leader with any real legitimacy.

Despite the very serious security situation in the country, progress elsewhere has been made. There are now more schools, hospitals and clinics open in Iraq than ever before, and in most of the country's 18 provinces the security situation is contained: the handover of Anbar province to the control of the Iraqi security forces in mid-2008 was a major milestone in this process. Among commentators, however, there is still considerable scepticism as to whether a functioning unitary state can be created out of the wreckage that was left at the end of the Saddam regime. What is becoming clearer now is the extent to which Saddam Hussain himself, brutal dictator that he was, was losing control of parts of Iraq, especially the south, and that 20 years of international isolation and 12 years of sanctions had done immense damage to the infrastructure and basic fabric of the country. Thus, a corollary of Iraq's military vulnerability, which the USA seems not to have accounted for, was its physical and psychological decrepitness and fragility as a unitary state. It was vulnerable not just to US military decapitation but also to political turmoil, internecine fighting and protracted instability. The USA's failure to appreciate this situation should be added to its list of intelligence and political failures. As a consequence there is now much less talk about Iraq being a model of secular democracy for the rest of the Middle East. Indeed, in most analyses expectations are being set much lower.

NORTH KOREA

Another victim of the conflict in Iraq was the USA's improving relationship with North Korea. While relations had been developing after September 2001, the invasion of Iraq resulted in a reversal of that process as the North Korean Government began to fear that it would be the next target of a US pre-emptive attack. This was, in part, a reaction to the open debate in Washington, both inside and outside the Administration, about the desirability of regime change in North Korea and the best way to achieve this. In an apparent effort to deter the USA from such a course, in October 2001 North Korea admitted to having a secret nuclear weapons programme in violation of the 1994 agreement. As punishment, the USA and its allies suspended promised oil shipments, which in turn led North Korea to reactivate its shelved nuclear weapons-making facilities, to announce its withdrawal from the nuclear Non-Proliferation Treaty (NPT), to deport UN monitors and to threaten to sell its plutonium to the highest bidder.[45] The communist regime also demanded bilateral talks with the USA to negotiate a non-aggression pact between the two countries. The USA declined this last demand, refusing to be coerced into direct talks and guarantees. Relations between the North Korean Government and the US Administration remained at crisis point thereafter. (North Korea's testing of a nuclear device in October 2006 represented a new low in relations.) The Bush Administration's response to the deteriorating relations was to orchestrate a regional diplomatic forum in Beijing, China. Consisting of China, Russia, Japan, North Korea, the Republic of Korea (South Korea) and the USA, this forum was an attempt to internationalize the response to the North's nuclear provocations in an effort both to reassure the North Korean Government and to pressure it into a new agreement over its atomic facilities. It was also intended to involve all the major regional powers in diplomacy to ensure their support for whatever action was necessary to contain North Korea's rogue activity. Unless the USA was seen to have exhausted all reasonable diplomatic measures it would not receive support from the UN nor regionally for further action. North Korea also seemed to be exploiting the USA's difficulties in Iraq, calculating that, in this context, the Bush Administration was unlikely to escalate the crisis.

While the multi-party negotiations on the future of Korea were intended by the USA to pressure the North Korean authorities to adopt a more flexible negotiating position, their effect, it could be argued, was most obvious in softening the USA's approach to the talks. An initial breakthrough was made in September 2003 when the USA agreed to the sequencing of rewards to the North in return for nuclear compliance, rather than insisting on complete nuclear disarmament first, its initial position. Then, in September 2004 a further apparent breakthrough was made when the USA conceded the possibility of re-establishing diplomatic relations with North Korea and the possibility that the North could be given a civilian nuclear reactor 'at an appropriate time.'[46] Immediately after agreeing to dismantle is nuclear weapons programme in return for these concessions, however, the North Korean Government announced a series of conditions and interpretations that rendered the putative agreement worthless. Its negotiating approach, it seemed, was to pocket every concession, while engaging its interlocutors in talks without any serious prospect of acceding to international demands with regards to its nuclear weapons programmes. Further concessions were made by the USA during 2007, with the Bush Administration agreeing to bilateral diplomatic contact with North Korea. The visit by US negotiator Christopher Hill was the first in five years by a senior US official and was accompanied by the further concession of freeing US $25m. in funds previously frozen by the USA under suspicion that it came from counterfeiting activities. After the North Korean Government agreed to the partial destruction of its plutonium-producing power plant in 2008, the USA announced its intention to remove North Korea from its State Sponsors of Terrorism list, and implemented the removal in October. Difficulties remain, however, over the sequencing of these actions and the resulting rewards, and over the USA's eventual demands for the documentation and destruction of the North Korean nuclear weapons programme. The concessions by the Bush Administration were aimed at advancing the prospects of a new deal preventing further nuclear proliferation by the North Korean Government, but were also an admission that the US Administration's more coercive approach had failed to deliver the desired results.[47]

Such moves are acutely embarrassing for the Bush Administration, since it came to office extremely critical of its predecessor for pursing a remarkably similar approach. Bush was critical of the Clinton Administration's 1994 agreement with North Korea for rewarding bad behaviour and for being unverifiable and yet it finds itself making concession after concession towards the Clinton Administration's position in the absence of any obvious policy alternative. It is an approach that recognizes the difficulty of dealing with a country that the Central Intelligence Agency estimates has the capacity to build between six and eight nuclear devices.[48] As such, North Korea is the most difficult of the 'axis' states to coerce militarily. A war on the Korean peninsular would risk the destruction of much of South Korea even without the resort to weapons of mass destruction, as much of North Korea's 1m.-strong army is stationed close to the border and within artillery range of the South Korean capital, Seoul.[49] Given North Korea's previous non-compliance with the 1994 agreement and the difficulty of negotiating with a regime that often issues contradictory statements the prospects for a sustainable long-term agreement with North Korea remain uncertain. What is clear, however, is that progress on the issue of North Korea's nuclear programme has been possible through the multilateral diplomatic route, while previous attempts to coerce the Government were totally without success.

IRAN

In the 2006 version of the NSS the Administration explained that 'We may face no greater challenge from a single country than from Iran.'[50] Indeed, in many ways, from support for terrorism and for Shi'a factions in Iraq and in its nuclear ambitions, Iran was a major irritant to US foreign policy. It initially warranted inclusion in the 'axis of evil' because of its pursuit of weapons of mass destruction and its support for terrorism. In 2002 the USA announced that Iran was developing a long-range missile, the Shabab III, with assistance from North Korea, and that its nuclear programme was considered to be some five years away from the production of a bomb. It has also been linked to the supply of weapons to Palestinians in the West Bank and the Gaza Strip and provision of financial support to the militant Islamist organization the Islamic Resistance Movement (Hamas) and, with more lethal recent consequences, to Hezbollah in southern Lebanon. While these facts were a major cause for concern in the USA, the Bush Administration was initially encouraged by internal developments within Iran such as evidence of debate about its foreign policy direction. Its decision to categorize Iran as part of the 'axis of evil' and its subsequent invasion of Iraq succeeded in strengthening considerably the position of the conservative nationalists in Iran, culminating in the election of a new hardline President, Mahmoud Ahmadinejad, in June 2005. The argument that the replacement of Saddam Hussain with a more benign regime might induce neighbouring Iran to abandon its nuclear ambitions and to seek new commercial opportunities in a reformed Middle East was not borne out by events. Indeed, the opposite effect seemed apparent. Geopolitically, Iran was the clearest beneficiary of the US invasion of Iraq. Not only does the fragmentation of Iraq into feuding semi-autonomous provinces deprive the region of its historic counterweight to Iran, but the creation within Iraq of a Shi'a-dominated province considerably increased Iranian influence within the country.[51]

The disadvantage of this change in Iran's situation is its increasing sense of vulnerability within the region to the threat of attack from the US military in pursuit of regime change on the Iraqi model. These fears were fuelled by discussion about precisely such a policy option in Washington in the immediate aftermath of the fall of Baghdad.[52] The fact that Iran is now surrounded by US military forces, in Afghanistan, Iraq, Kuwait and Qatar, has added to this perception of threat. Such concerns are likely to have reinforced Iran's motivation, although vigorously denied, to become a nuclear weapons state. While Iran claims that its extensive nuclear programme is for commercial and peaceful purposes, it does not seem plausible that an oil rich state would build a nuclear infrastructure of this scale and type purely for electricity. Of even greater concern has been its record of obfuscation and deceit in its dealing with the IAEA. Over the last four years the IAEA has repeatedly attempted to make Iran comply with the provisions of the NPT, of which it is a signatory. The IAEA has also insisted that Iran agree to an Additional Protocol allowing 'anytime, anywhere inspections' to ensure that its declared activities match its actions. International concern with Iran's nuclear programme, as represented by the IAEA's negotiations, involves the Iranian Government's plans to build a uranium-enrichment capability. With such a facility Iran could produce enough uranium perfectly legally under the IAEA safeguards, announce its withdrawal from the NPT, and then quickly build its own nuclear arsenal. Given its dubious need for nuclear energy and past deception there is widespread suspicion of Iran's motivation. The USA, for its part, argues that Iran's past deceptions mean that it should forfeit the right to such a civil nuclear programme. European efforts in the form of an initiative by the United Kingdom, France and Germany to induce Iran to give up its uranium-enrichment facilities in return for improved trade relations and development assistance, including the transfer of technologies for its civil nuclear programme, have ultimately proved unsuccessful. As a result, the IAEA reported Iran to the UN Security Council for its 'failures and breaches' of its international obligations and a deadline for compliance with the Security Council was set for 31 August 2006. As this deadline passed further efforts were made to re-engage Iran in diplomatic efforts to prevent its nuclear programme. These efforts in the face of such intransigence, however, serve only to show the collective reluctance of the international community to take these breaches seriously. While the USA regarded the failure of the European diplomatic effort as inevitable, it supported every effort to facilitate a negotiated agreement. Support on the Security Council from

China, a major consumer of Iranian oil, and from Russia, engaged in the sale of nuclear technology to Iran, seem likely to prevent any meaningful sanction being applied to Iran. Russia's current mood of belligerence towards the West makes this even more unlikely. As a result of this diplomatic impasse the USA is quietly building a 'coalition of the willing' composed of states who will join the USA in applying economic sanctions against Iran. There is already evidence that the USA is co-ordinating international efforts to restrict financial services to Iran in an effort to pressure the Government to comply with its international obligations. During his visit to Europe in June 2008 President Bush persuaded the EU to impose new sanctions on Iran if it failed to honour its international obligations on uranium enrichment. As an act of solidarity with European diplomatic pressure on Iran and to demonstrate Washington's seriousness with regard to the issues, the USA sent a formal diplomatic representative, Undersecretary of State for Political Affairs William Burns, to the multiparty talks with the Iranian Government concerning the nuclear issues. While demonstrating its renewed support for diplomacy, however, the presence of Burns at these meetings failed to extract further concessions from Iran. US participation in the 'dual track' negotiations—diplomatic engagement backed by the threat of sanctions—was intended to be an indication of the new American Realism. In 2007 the USA announced major arms deals with both Saudi Arabia and Israel worth over US $50,000m., which were widely seen as part of a strategy to contain Iran's regional ambitions.[53] Such responses are less than optimum, but reflect the USA's willingness to plan for every contingency with regard to the Iranian challenge.

In the absence of a diplomatic solution the USA has also indicated that 'all options are on the table', including military force, to deal with the nuclear threat that it perceives is emanating from Iran.[54] In reality, however, despite the exaltation of pre-emption as a strategic doctrine by the Bush Administration, in the wake of the Iraq war the scope for military pressure on Iran has been considerably reduced. Indeed, in some ways a more co-operative relationship with Iran would be preferable for the USA in order to reduce Iran's scope for mischief in Iraq. In recognition of this, and as part of Condoleezza Rice's American Realism approach, in May 2007 US diplomats held their first direct bilateral discussions with their Iranian counterparts in 28 years, specifically and solely on the subject of Iraq; however, little substantive progress was achieved. Indeed, since then the situation has deteriorated, with Iran continuing to support Shi'a elements within Iraq, including Hojatoleslam Muqtada as-Sadr and Grand Ayatollah Ali as-Sistani, the most influential cleric in Iraq. Furthermore, in August the USA took the unusual step of naming Iran's Revolutionary Guard Corps a 'specially designated global terrorist' organization for its role in fomenting and supporting sectarian violence in Iraq. This decision coincided with the order to US troops in Iraq that Iranian forces operating inside that country were now to be regarded as legitimate targets.[55]

Dealing with Iran, then, in both its nuclear ambitions, in its relationship with Iraq and in its activities in the region is a significant and important challenge for the USA. It is a challenge to which the Bush Administration's NSS does not seem to have a ready solution. This does not mean, however, that the USA has entirely ruled out a pre-emptive (i.e. preventive) strike against Iran's nuclear facilities, either directly or through an ally.[56] That is certainly the interpretation that has been drawn from the USA's sale in 2005 to Israel of 500 high-ordinance, bunker-busting bombs with the capacity to penetrate six feet of concrete.[57] While such moves are widely seen as controversial, especially within the region, they are most likely designed to deter Iran from further proliferation and to create military options in extremis rather than being motivated by any actual military intent, on the part of the USA at least. The fact that Iran's nuclear facilities are concealed, dispersed, duplicated and hardened means that a military strike could not be certain of destroying its nuclear infrastructure. Such an undertaking would also be highly reliant on military intelligence and this would be regarded highly sceptically in the wake of the war in Iraq. Thus, in the absence of a viable military pre-emptive option for either regime change or disarmament, the USA must content itself with 'soft' power efforts to effect change, such as the Voice of America's new Persian language service and the threat of co-ordinated sanctions with the EU and Japan.

SYRIA

Although not initially included in the Administration's 'axis of evil', Syria has long been regarded as a 'rogue' state by the USA. Following the events of 11 September 2001, however, relations improved as Syria made efforts to show that it was with the USA rather than against it in its global 'war on terror'. To this end, the Syrian Government shared intelligence about al-Qa'ida and other terrorist organizations it had been tracking. In return, the Bush Administration temporarily discarded its accusations of Syrian support for militant Islamist groups such as Hezbollah, Hamas and Islamic Jihad.[58] Following the invasion of Iraq, however, relations worsened considerably, with the USA issuing direct threats to Syria over accusations that it was helping both Saddam Hussain's regime (by supplying military equipment) and assisting Islamist militants seeking to fight against US troops. Although Syria strenuously denied these allegations, it could be that the invasion of Iraq led to a change in policy. For Thomas Friedman, the Syrians 'are so convinced that they are next on the Bush hit parade that they have been easing the entry of anti-U.S. guerrillas into Iraq—because the more preoccupied the U.S. is there, the less likely it is to invade Syria.'[59] Whatever the motivation, Syria's perceived failure to stop this flow of Islamic fighters into Iraq led to a hardening of the USA's position towards Syria. The Administration has indicated its support for congressional efforts to impose diplomatic and economic sanctions against Syria. This congressional initiative called for a range of measures, including: freezing Syrian assets in US banks; a ban on US exports except food and medicines; restrictions on Syrian diplomats and reduced diplomatic contact; a ban on business investment; and a ban on Syrian airlines in US airspace. Linked to these threats were calls for an end to support for terrorist groups, particularly in Lebanon, and the production of evidence proving that the country was not developing medium- and long-range missiles and chemical and biological weapons.[60] Such threats of force or sanctions, however, have proved unsuccessful in inducing Syria to modify its behaviour. Syria's decision to procure nuclear materials from North Korea is likely to contribute to a still further deterioration in relations. Indeed, the Israeli decision to bomb the Syrian facility where the North Korean nuclear material was being installed was taken with the full approval of the USA. While the USA seems powerless to change the behaviour of Syria, the logic of its own doctrine, as applied by Israel, has the potential for an escalation in the crisis with no obvious resolution.

CONCLUSION

Despite the valiant efforts of Secretary of State Condoleezza Rice to frame a more pragmatic foreign policy for the Bush Administration, that of American Realism—where multilateral diplomacy and internationally orchestrated negotiation replaces the threat of coercion or isolation—US foreign policy remains locked into the pattern of responses adopted in the aftermath of the terrorist attacks of 2001. Immediately following those attacks the USA re-engaged in international politics on a global scale. It did so in a way that re-evaluated its relations with many states in the context of the global 'war on terror'. The test of whether states were 'with us or against us' set the tone for an approach that was less tolerant of states that were potential threats to the USA and less concerned with other considerations than it was in dealing with terrorism in its international affairs. In setting out the NSS 2002 the Bush Administration laid out what has become known as the Bush doctrine, a strategy for preserving the USA's security through what amounts to a combination of pre-emption, pre-eminence and unilateralism. It was a strategy premised to a large extent on the assumption that the post-Cold War world was a unipolar one in which US power was unbound and unconstrained.[61] In adopting this strategy it was also signalling a greater willingness to wield its diplomatic and military power in pursuit of its perceived threats to its security. What this meant in practice was a multi-faceted pursuit of the 'war on terror' as the main priority of US diplomacy. It has required intensive and extensive collaboration in intelligence, financial regulation, judicial co-ordination and counter-proliferation. It also involved the use of military force in Afghanistan against the Taliban and al-Qa'ida. The USA also embarked upon a concerted effort to make the international community take more seriously the proliferation threats presented by North Korea and Iraq. In these aspects of policy the USA was met with broad international support and understanding. Where this support reached its limits, however, was over the urgency and severity of the Iraqi threat and the appropriate response that this situation required. The failure of the USA to muster support for military action from the international community as a whole, but to pursue regime change nevertheless, was an action with grievous consequences, not only for Iraq and the Middle East, but also for the international support that the USA had mustered. More broadly still, the consequences of the USA's invasion of Iraq have forced the virtual abandonment of the Bush doctrine in all but name as the bold approach adopted in 2002 has shown itself to offer no solutions to the problems that the Administration now confronts.

Almost all of the assumptions that the Bush Administration made in its decision to invade Iraq have been proved wrong by subsequent events. Internationally, the failure to find weapons of mass destruction means that the occupation continues to be opposed as illegitimate and illegal. In Iraq itself civil disorder, insurgency and nascent civil war have meant that the US army was not able to leave after six weeks as was planned, and was instead committed there in large numbers for the foreseeable future. While significant improvements in the security situation in Iraq have been made over the last two years, the situation remains violent, fragile, unstable and deeply divided. The creation of a model democratic, secular Iraq that the Administration envisaged as the product of its invasion has now been effectively abandoned. Instead, the Bush Administration will pass on to its successor the task of stabilizing Iraq sufficiently to reduce the number of US troops committed there from 2011 onwards in a way that satisfies the US public and the people and Government of Iraq, and does not compromise regional security. This is no easy task and no small legacy.

Not only is the USA's Iraq policy the single largest foreign policy failure of the Bush Administration to date, it is also a clear indictment of the overall doctrine of which it is a part. Indeed, it is ironic that a strategy that was framed largely with Iraq in mind should be so completely undone by its application to that country. The implications of the Iraq invasion for US foreign policy more broadly, however, are very considerable. The most immediate effect is to act as a constraint on the Administration's policy options in that Iraq is consuming the USA's economic, military and political resources on a grand scale. The cost in money (US $10,000m. a month), military personnel (4,157 US military deaths at September 2008) and political credibility (President Bush's approval rating is consistently around 34%) mean that the Bush Administration's capacity for any further radical foreign policy activity is severely limited. Indeed, the faulty assumptions on which 'Operation Iraq Freedom' were built and justified have not only diminished US popular support for the war in Iraq, but have undermined its support for the pursuit of the 'war on terror' and international engagement in general.[62] Any future call for pre-emptive military action based on secret intelligence material will face such a test of credibility that it is difficult to envision circumstances where it would be made. For this reason alone the USA's approach to the challenges presented by Iran and North Korea is of necessity being handled differently. The difficult and indefinite commitment to the establishment of security in Iraq has also tamed the 'hawkish elements' in the Bush Administration. The excited talk about which 'rogue' state was next that gripped US political circles immediately after the fall of Baghdad quickly subsided once the scale of the task in Iraq became ever more apparent. That is not to say, however, that the USA's ability pre-emptively to destroy the nuclear infrastructure of Iran or North Korea was militarily limited. Such options remained technical possibilities, especially through the use of air power, although this option could not be certain of destroying all stocks and facilities and was widely regarded as lacking credibility as a result. Politically, however, the difficulty generating domestic, congressional and international support all but rule this out in normal circumstances. Even if a technical 'pre-emptive strike' were possible, if such action led to large-scale conflict the USA would also find itself militarily stretched without the support of major allies. For these reasons a change in methods is noticeable from the Bush Administration. In its approach to Syria the main instrument available is that of sanctions. Over North Korea the Administration has engaged the regional powers in a multilateral diplomatic initiative to share the pressure on the Korean Government and the responsibility of further action should it be necessary. It has also met directly with North Korean diplomats for the first time in five years. With regard to Iran, too, the USA has allowed the UN and the EU to take prominent roles in outlining what is acceptable within Iran's treaty obligations. Despite this apparent abandonment of the Bush doctrine, however, there has been no change in rhetoric from the Bush Administration about the availability of pre-emption as a policy option in the USA's new strategy. It could be argued that the USA's support for Israel in its 2006 invasion of southern Lebanon was an endorsement of preventive war by proxy. The same can be said of the US endorsement of the Israeli attack on Syria in September 2007. And yet Condoleezza Rice, by her stewardship of US diplomacy and her attempt to reformulate this as American Realism, has tried to move beyond the 'strategy of pre-emption' and with it the unilateralism and hegemonic rhetoric of 'pre-eminence' that constituted the basis of the Bush doctrine. This in large part is a belated recognition that this strategy is now empty of practical political content over the major political challenges facing the Administration. Indeed, it must also be added that the legacy of the political failure of this doctrine as applied to Iraq is the major obstacle to the further application of this strategy in pursuit of the USA's foreign policy goals. This is evident in the USA's relations with the Middle East, the UN and NATO, and in pursuit of the 'war on terror' more broadly.

For the Middle East, like Iraq, US policy has created more difficulties than apparent solutions. The stated goal of transforming and democratizing the Middle East has had the effect of heightening the pervading sense of insecurity of both existing regimes and the region as a whole. Nor have the nuclear crisis with Iran and the worsening diplomatic relationship between the USA and Syria provided an international environment conducive to the advancement of the Israeli-Palestinian peace process. Indeed, the invasion of Iraq provided the precedent for Israel's attack against Syria, marking a 30-year low in relations between those countries. The election victory of Hamas in early 2006 stalled the Middle East peace process for the foreseeable future. While Condoleezza Rice is energetic in her efforts to forge a new settlement of the Palestinian question, the USA's ability to broker a deal is so diminished that these efforts show little prospect of success. For all its talk of spreading democracy, the USA refuses to recognize, fund or negotiate with a party that openly supports terrorism and calls for the destruction of Israel. The invasion of southern Lebanon by Israel in response to Hezbollah atrocities in 2006 has set the peace process back further. While all these events demonstrate the necessity of diplomatic progress on this question, at the same time they make it more difficult and less likely. At this point in the presidential cycle the Bush Administration has no leverage to effect any progress on this or any other substantive foreign policy issue. All of the major protagonists in these intractable issues are now waiting to engage with the next occupant of the White House.

Despite the best efforts of Condoleezza Rice to develop a new approach to the USA's international engagements, the Bush Administration cannot easily shed the encumbrance that its decision to invade Iraq has become. As well as being damaging to the reputation of the USA, this decision was also damaging to the institutions of the international system as a whole, the consequences of which continue to be felt. Most obviously, the role and credibility of the UN and the principle of collective defence for which it stood were diminished by this action. In an unusually candid statement to the special session of the UN General Assembly in September 2003, the UN Secretary-General, Kofi Annan, expressed his concern that the action 'could set precedents that resulted in a proliferation of the unilateral and lawless use of force, with or without credible justification...This logic [he continued] represents a fundamental challenge to the principles on which, however imperfectly, world peace and stability have rested for at least 58 years.' Annan's words were no exaggeration. The US action in seeking UN authority to confront Iraq and then ignoring the clear wishes of the international community in pressing ahead with military action to its own timetable demonstrated a cynical attitude towards the organization. The USA's post-war desire to prevent the internationalization of the governance of Iraq through the UN could be seen as a further example of its distrust of the organization's competence and a denial of its authority. For the USA it appeared that multilateral organizations and approaches were only useful when they served US purposes. The effect of such action was to damage the UN and the principles for which it stands without offering any alternative system of world order. For while the USA may believe itself capable of meeting its own security needs, the crises in Iran and North Korea and, indeed, Iraq showed the limitations of this approach. Russia's invasion of Georgia in 2008 was only the most recent manifestation of the application of force to solve a foreign policy crisis in a world in which the taboos on such behaviour have been weakened as a consequence of the Bush Administration's foreign policy.

The US-led invasion of Iraq was also gravely damaging to transatlantic relations for similar reasons. The NATO alliance was meant to represent more than a system of collective defence. It was also a political community with a mission for the export of security. Thus, when several of its principal members disagree so publicly and profoundly over an issue of such import, then it cannot fail to inflict collateral damage on the alliance. The integrity of NATO as an alliance had already been challenged by the way in which the USA responded to the invocation of its Article 5 (which states than an attack against one NATO member was an attack against all NATO members), following the terrorist attacks. Despite the political effort expended by the Germans and others to pledge forces to the USA to fight in Afghanistan, the Bush Administration declined to use NATO *qua* NATO, choosing instead allies and capabilities on an ad hoc basis. For this episode to be followed by the diplomatic opposition of several NATO allies, including France and Germany, to a US-led invasion of Iraq, was to plunge transatlantic relations into their worst crisis of the post-Second World War period. While relations subsequently improved to such an extent that NATO took over responsibility for the security of part of Afghanistan in mid-2003, the refusal of the European allies to resource this operation to the extent requested by the US military commander of NATO was an indication of a less than unified approach to the challenges faced.

In formulating the Bush doctrine the US Administration hoped that its policy of pre-emption would induce 'rogue' states to curtail their errant action in fear of US coercion. The opposite effect, however, seems to have occurred. For both North Korea and Iran, the attack on Iraq seemed to have strengthened their desire to obtain nuclear weapons as a deterrent. Similarly, Syria's fear of a US attack, rather than discouraging it from 'rogue' activity, might be behind its efforts to destabilize Iraq and perhaps its own nuclear ambitions. As a result, it seems that even Condoleezza Rice's Department of State has concluded that the Bush doctrine has not been able adequately to address the problems with which the USA has been confronted in the last years of the Bush Administration. In agreeing to direct negotiations with North Korea and Iran, in offering and endorsing strategies that employ incentives rather than just threats, the USA has progressed a long way from the strident and demanding diplomacy of the previous policy of the Bush Administration. To suggest that this new American Realism is anything other than the realization of the failure of the previous policy, however, would be a cruel self-delusion. For while these new approaches are to be welcomed in both their substance and their tone, their prospects of success are limited by the nature of their advocates. In enacting these policies now the Bush Administration is widely regarded as pursuing a policy that is half-hearted and lacking in ambition.[63] It is also one that is being pursued too late to make a significant difference since the Bush Administration is not able to actuate any meaningful leverage on the parties and has very little credibility on the world stage. The only positive legacy of the new American Realism may be to speed the end of the disastrous foreign policy of George Bush and pave the way for a period of renewal in the country's international engagements under the 44th President of the USA.

ENDNOTES

1 Charles Krauthammer, 'The Unipolar Moment', *Foreign Affairs*, Vol. 70, No. 1, Winter 1990–91.

2 Charles Krauthammer, 'The Unipolar Moment Revisited', *National Interest*, Vol. 70, Winter 2002, p. 7.

3 See <http://news.bbc.co.uk/1/hi/business/7607872.stm> [Accessed 14 October 2008].

4 Fareed Zakaria, 'What Bush Got Right', *Newsweek*, 9 August 2008.

5 Joby Warrick and Walter Pincus, 'Reduced Dominance is Predicted for U.S.', *Washington Post*, 10 September 2008.

6 Zakaria, 'What Bush Got Right'.

7 Edward Luttwak, 'A Truman for Our Times', *Prospect*, Issue 149, August 2008. Available from: <http://www.prospect-magazine.co.uk/article_details.php?id=10309> [Accessed 14 October 2008].

8 See <http://icasualties.org/oif/> [Accessed 14 October 2008].

9 James Glanz and Alissa J. Rubin, 'Migration Reshapes Iraq's Sectarian Landscape', *New York Times*, 19 September 2007.

10 See Bob Woodward, 'Why Did Violence Plummet? It Wasn't Just the Surge', *Washington Post*, 8 September 2008.

11 Stephen Biddle, Michael O'Hanlon, and Kenneth M. Pollack, 'Not Quite Ready to Go Home', *New York Times*, 5 August 2008.

12 Kirk Semple and Andrew W. Lehren, '500: Deadly U.S. Milestone in Afghan War', *New York Times*, 7 August 2008.

13 Ann Scott Tyson, 'Taliban's Gains Forestall U.S. Troop Reductions in Afghanistan', *Washington Post*, 22 September 2006.

14 *Ibid.*

15 Molly Moor and John Ward Anderson, 'NATO Faces Growing Hurdle as Call For Troops Falls Short', *Washington Post*, 18 September 2006.

16 *Ibid.*

17 Mike Allen and Romesh Ratnesar, 'The End of Cowboy Diplomacy', *Time*, 17 July 2006.

18 See Condoleezza Rice, 'Rethinking the National Interest: American Realism for a New World', *Foreign Affairs*, July–August 2008.

19 Michael Abramowitz and Robin Wright, 'A Driven President Faces a World of Crisis', *Washington Post*, 6 July 2006.

20 Uzi Mahaimi, Sarah Baxter and Michael Sheridan, 'Commando raid snatches nuclear clues', *The Sunday Times*, 23 September 2007.

21 'This is war', *The Sunday Times*, 16 September 2001.

22 See Lawrence Freedman, *The Evolution of Nuclear Strategy*. London, Macmillan, 1989, Chapter 11.

23 See Wyn Q. Bowen and David H. Dunn, *American Security Policy in the 1990s: Beyond Containment*. Aldershot, Dartmouth, 1996, Chapter 5.

24 Nicholas Lemann, 'The Next World Order', *New Yorker*, 25 August 2002.

25 The National Security Strategy of the United States, 2002 (NSS, 2002), cited in full in the *New York Times*, 20 September 2002, p. 6.

26 Philip Gordon, cited by Gerard Baker, 'Missing in Action', *Financial Times*, 1–2 February 2003.

27 Richard N. Haass, *The Reluctant Sheriff: The United States after the Cold War*. New York, Council on Foreign Relations, 1997, p. 53.

28 This was seen as an impediment to the flexibility of the US military.

29 James Graff, 'Bad Air Over Kyoto', *Time*, 19 April 2001, p. 18.

30 *Ibid.*

31 Charles Krauthammer, 'The Bush Doctrine: ABM, Kyoto, and the New American Unilateralism', *Weekly Standard*, Vol. 6, No. 36, 4 June 2001, pp. 6–8.

32 Condoleezza Rice, 'Promoting the National Interest', *Foreign Affairs*, Vol. 79, No. 1, January–February 2000, p. 47.

33 Walter LaFeber, 'The Bush Doctrine', *Diplomatic History*, Vol. 26, No. 4, Fall 2002, p. 547.

34 Anton LaGuardia, 'Time for all nations to act', *Daily Telegraph*, 7 November 2001.

35 See David H. Dunn, 'Myths, Motivations and "Misunderestimations": The Bush Administration and Iraq', *International Affairs*, Vol. 79, No. 2, March 2003, pp. 279–298.

36 Steven R. Weisman, 'A Long, Winding Road to a Diplomatic Dead End', *New York Times*, 17 March 2003.

37 James P. Rubin, 'Stumbling into War', *Foreign Affairs*, Vol. 82, No. 5, September–October 2003, p. 5.

38 Michael Elliot, 'So, What Went Wrong', *Time*, 6 October 2003, p. 28.

39 *Ibid*.

40 L. Paul Bremmer III with Malcolm McConnell, *My Year in Iraq: The Struggle to Build a Future of Hope*. New York, Simon & Schuster, 2006.

41 There is no official Iraqi body count. See <http://www.-iraqbodycount.org/>. See also <http://icasualties.org/oif/Iraqi-Deaths.aspx> [accessed 16 September 2008].

42 Editorial, 'Telling it like it isn't', *Guardian*, 11 September 2007.

43 Sabrina Tavernise and James Glanz, 'Iraqi Report Says Blackwater Guards Fired First', *New York Times*, 19 September 2007.

44 Romesh Ratesar, 'Can This War Be Won?', *Time*, 4 October 2004, p. 32.

45 Tracy McVeigh, 'North Korea and the US "on a slide towards conflict"', *Observer*, 6 April 2003.

46 Richard Spencer, 'North Korea already rocking the boat', *Telegraph*, 21 September 2005.

47 Norimitsu Onishi and David E. Sanger, 'U.S. Holds Direct Talks in North Korea on Arms', *New York Times*, 21 June 2007.

48 Nazila Fathi and David E. Sanger, 'Iran Warns Against Referral of Nuclear Issue to the U.N.', *New York Times*, 21 September 2005.

49 Michael R. Gordon, 'In Bush's "Axis of Evil", Why Iraq Stands Out', *New York Times*, 9 September 2002.

50 The National Security Strategy of the United States, 2002 (NSS 2002), op. cit.

51 Richard Beeston, 'Two years on, Iran is the only clear winner of war on Saddam', *The Times*, 23 September 2005.

52 David H. Dunn, '"Real men want to go to Tehran": Bush, pre-emption and the Iranian nuclear challenge', *International Affairs*, Vol. 83, No. 1, January 2007.

53 David S. Cloud, 'U.S. Set to Offer Huge Arms Deal to Saudi Arabia', *New York Times*, 28 July 2007.

54 'Bush to Iran: All Options on Table', *Boston Herald*, 13 August 2005.

55 Robin Wright, 'Iranian Unit to be Labeled "Terrorist"', *Washington Post*, 15 August 2007.

56 Craig S. Smith, 'Iran Moves Toward Enriching Uranium', *New York Times*, 22 September 2004.

57 *Ibid*.

58 Neil MacFarquhar, 'Syrian Official Says Relations With U.S. Plunge to New Low', *New York Times*, 12 October 2003.

59 Thomas L. Friedman, 'Long Spoon Diplomacy', *New York Times*, 9 October 2003.

60 Carl Hulse, 'Panel Approves Sanctions on Syria With White House Support', *New York Times*, 9 October 2003.

61 See Ivo H. Daalder and James M. Lindsay, *America Unbound: The Bush Revolution in Foreign Policy*, Washington, Brookings Institution, 2003.

62 See Frank Rich, 'One War Lost, Another to Go', *New York Times*, 20 November 2005.

63 Zakaria, 'What Bush Got Right'.

DEPENDENT, ADDICTED AND DELUDED: ENERGY SECURITY AND US FOREIGN POLICY

DAVID HASTINGS DUNN

INTRODUCTION

In December 2007 the US Congress passed into law the Energy Independence and Security Act, a piece of legislation which had taken years to reach this stage and which offered the first new efficiency standards for the US motor vehicle to be passed since 1975. Such is the pace of change in this significant area, however, that the bill has already been overtaken by events. Designed to tackle the USA's predilection for large inefficient vehicles, the legislation was brought into force just as that relationship began to founder. From mid-2007 the steady rise in the price of petroleum had a dramatic effect on the cost of petrol in the USA and, as a result, pushed energy policy to near the top of the political agenda. Two sets of consequences have resulted from these price increases. First, there was a change in consumption patterns, and second, energy policy rose in salience as a political issue. In mid-2007 the price of petrol reached a level that US consumers considered painfully expensive. As the US journalist Charles Krauthammer wryly observed, 'At $3 a gallon, Americans just grin and bear it . . . keep driving like crazy. At $4, it is a world transformed. Americans become rational creatures. Mass transit ridership is at a 50-year high. Driving is down 4% . . . Hybrids and compacts are flying off the lots. SUV sales are in free fall.'[1] The impact of petroleum prices reaching US $145 a barrel and petrol reaching $4.11 a gallon was indeed severe. As prices peaked in July 2007 petroleum consumption fell by 6% to its lowest level in five years, and, according to the Federal Highway Administration, the number of miles driven dropped the most since 1979. Compared with the previous June, US motorists drove 12,200m. fewer miles.[2] Nor was this reaction confined to the USA alone, for it was estimated that petroleum consumption in industrialized countries, which account for 60% of global petroleum demand, could fall by 1.3m. barrels per day (b/d) in 2008, the steepest decline since 1982.[3] The global airline industry has also lost money every year (bar one) since 2000. As a result of this energy crisis the big three car manufacturers (Ford, General Motors and Toyota) were forced to halt production of sports utility vehicles (SUVs) and other 'gas-guzzling' vehicles. In September 2008 Ford announced that its sales had dropped by 34%, partly as a result of the credit crisis, which had also affected US consumers as the economy took a downward turn.[4] Consequently, in the latter half of 2008 car sales in the USA were at a 10-year low.[5] The second consequence of this crisis is that energy policy has become a significant issue in US national and local politics. In both the presidential and congressional elections in 2008 energy policy and energy security have become divisive and contentious topics for all candidates and for both parties.

An unexpected consequence of this crisis has been that the passage of the Energy Independence and Security Act is now regarded as having been somewhat overtaken by events. The new energy efficiency standards demanded by the Act require a fleet-wide average of at least 35 miles per gallon (mpg) by 2020, a 40% increase over the previous average of 25 mpg. With the radical drop in demand for high-consuming vehicles, however, the price of petroleum seems set to achieve such changes much earlier, as consumers switch to smaller, more efficient vehicles. Other features of the Act, such as plans to phase out the incandescent light bulb by 2012, a requirement that all new federal government buildings be 'carbon neutral' by 2030, and tax breaks for biofuel production, while significant achievements in themselves, also seem parsimonious amid the new urgency that has gripped the debate.[6]

The issue most debated in the run-up to the 2008 elections was whether, and to what extent, the USA could wean itself off its reliance on foreign petroleum. In a sense this electoral debate was a popular manifestation of the political debate that President George W. Bush had highlighted in his 2006 and 2007 State of the Union Addresses, when he declared that 'we have a serious problem: America is addicted to oil, which is often imported from unstable parts of the world'.[7] For the Bush

Administration this was an issue involving more than just the rising price of petroleum. For Bush it was increasingly a political as well as an economic issue. The problem is not simply that the USA is the largest petroleum importer in the world, bringing in 13.5m. barrels per day (mbd), which accounts for 63.5% of the total US daily consumption of 20.6 mbd.[8] Rather, it is that for the first time since the oil crises of the 1970s the USA has begun to sense its economic and societal vulnerability at the hands of the oil-producing states in an increasingly unstable Middle East. In 2007 the costs and consequences of that dependence began to be felt by most Americans. The control of prices and supply lay outside US hands and the high prices paid for the petroleum flowed into states not all of whom were regarded as stable or friendly powers. As a result, both presidential candidates, Senators Barack Obama and John McCain, pledged to end US dependence on Middle Eastern and Venezuelan petroleum within 10 years of their coming to power. McCain promised to build 45 new nuclear power plants by 2030 if he were elected, while Obama vowed to implement a comprehensive energy programme incorporating nuclear, wind, solar and hydrothermal sources of energy.[9] Controversially, both candidates also changed their position regarding the use of domestic sources of fossil fuels.

For 25 years Congress has imposed a moratorium on drilling for petroleum and gas off the Pacific and Atlantic seaboards and in the Gulf of Mexico. There has also been a ban on the exploitation of the Arctic National Wildlife Refuge in Alaska (see below). While both presidential candidates had previously supported all these bans, during the electoral campaign both moved to support petroleum and gas exploitation off the coasts of the 48 mainland continental states of the USA. This shift, which was also adopted by the Democrats in Congress, was in response to intense lobbying from the oil industry and to changes in public opinion that took place in 2007. McCain made the move first, with the exhortation 'Drill, baby, drill', and, to avoid any electoral advantage in November 2008, all parties and many candidates followed suit. Congressional Democrats attempted to limit the damage of their concession by passing a bill allowing drilling only up to 50 miles from the coast and by tying their consent to many other energy saving and investing programmes. While this bill was passed by the House in September, the Republicans in the Senate, who were keen to exploit the electoral differences between their own enthusiasm to drill and the Democrats' environmental concerns, prevented its passage into law.[10] While the desire to exploit the petroleum and gas resources off the US coast is popular and is an idea now much more likely to be developed, there has been much less willingness in the political debate to address the fact that this move would actually have very little impact on US energy policy and security. Indeed, according to the US Government's Energy Information Administration, the exploitation of this domestic petroleum and gas would not come on stream until 2020 and would not reach peak production until 2030, and that even then 'Because oil prices are determined on the international market . . . any impact on average wellhead prices is expected to be insignificant.'[11] Thus, what was being presented to the US electorate in November 2008 by some candidates as a solution to high petroleum prices and dependence on foreign fuel sources was actually predicted to make little difference to the US fuel situation in the long term and was frankly doing little more than fostering a delusional belief.

ENERGY POLICY AND FOREIGN POLICY

Despite the rising costs of energy and the attempts at national level to raise the profile of energy security as an issue, the relationship between the USA's consumption habits and the energy policy debates remain fraught. This is especially the case in relation to the question of the USA's dependency on petroleum and the country's foreign policy. For some observers this relationship is rather complex, while for others it remains a simple one. In the opinion of the latter party, the USA's involvement and interventions in the Middle East can be explained by its dependence on that region's energy supplies. Accordingly, the Gulf conflicts of 1991 and 2003 can best be explained as the USA going to war to protect its access to cheap petroleum and to safeguard the profits of US oil companies. Not only was this view the rallying cry of the old Iraqi regime but it was also widespread, particularly on the left, in Europe, the USA itself and internationally. The appeal of such explanations is their apparent simplicity. Did not President Bush and Vice President Dick Cheney have backgrounds in the oil industry? Did not these companies contribute to their election campaign? Does not Iraq have potentially huge reserves of crude oil which would help ease the pressures of growing demand and reliance on Saudi Arabia? Is not the USA becoming ever more reliant on oil from the Persian (Arabian) Gulf for its energy needs? And once the fighting started did not the invading forces first secure the oil wells and pumping stations? Part of the appeal of this explanation was the opposition's failure to be persuaded by the official case that the Bush Administration presented for its action, namely the security threat that Iraq presented regionally and globally if it were allowed to develop weapons of mass destruction.[12] This, in turn, was predicated on a failure to appreciate how much the terrorist attacks of 11 September 2001 have affected the USA and altered its tolerance of states that are openly hostile to it and contemptuous of its concerns regarding the proliferation of such weapons. This much is evident in Paul Rogers's evaluation of the role of petroleum in US foreign policy. For Rogers, 'There is a deep and pervading recognition at the heart of the Bush administration that *the most significant vulnerability for the US* is its steadily growing dependence on Gulf oil.'[13] What is evident from this statement and in this approach is a complete failure to appreciate how seriously the USA takes the threat of another major terrorist attack on the country and how much the 'war on terror' has come to dominate Washington's foreign policy priorities since the September 2001 attacks. At a broader level, this approach demonstrates a willingness to emphasize material explanations for foreign policy actions, i.e. 'it's all about oil', at the expense of ideational ones rooted in the loss of a sense of invulnerability or the desire to spread its conception of freedom. However, to argue that these materialist motivations do not offer a plausible explanation for US actions in 1991 or 2003 is not to dismiss the significance of petroleum in US foreign policy altogether. Indeed, Rogers and others have a point when they stress that the Bush Administration was acutely aware that it was becoming increasingly dependent on imported petroleum, particularly from the Persian Gulf. That is not to say that dependence dictates policy towards the Middle East or elsewhere. Rather, it is to recognize that access to the free flow of fuel oil is a vital interest of the world economy and, as such, that there is an energy dimension to many foreign policy considerations.

This dimension can become manifest in a number of different ways. As far as the US-led invasion of Iraq is concerned, the possibility of a benign government in Baghdad bringing its petroleum reserves to the world market was undoubtedly one argument used in the case for 'regime change'. It offers no explanation by itself, however, as to why the USA abandoned 12 years of containment of Iraq to topple Saddam Hussain when it did. Nor does it explain why the USA led this international action when it is far less dependent on Middle Eastern oil as a percentage of its energy needs than are the People's Republic of China, most of Europe and Japan. The energy dimension is also much more complex than simply the USA's access to cheap oil. It is also a factor in the country's foreign relations with China and India, in that the exclusion of both of these geostrategic rivals from the strictures of the 1997 Kyoto Protocol on climate change (which seeks to reduce global carbon emissions by 2012) was one of the reasons why the Bush Administration refused to participate in this treaty. The USA's ability to bring international pressure on Iran over its development of a nuclear programme is also complicated by the fact that China and India are major purchasers of Iranian oil and are thus reluctant to agree to the imposition of UN sanctions against Iran. Oil is also used as a foreign policy instrument by the USA, as is evident by the recent threat to impose oil sanctions on Sudan in response to the Sudanese regime's conduct in the Darfur region of that country. Petroleum is also a factor in US foreign policy towards Africa, Central Asia and Latin America, as will be analysed below.

Indeed, it is the purpose of this essay to demonstrate the extent and the implications of the USA's dependence on oil and the influence that this dependence has on US foreign policy. The essay argues that to understand US foreign policy with regard to the politics of energy security, you must first of all understand the USA itself. It does this first of all by analysing the extent of the USA's cultural dependence on oil, and then it looks in turn at its strategic dependence. Finally, it looks at the ways and the extent to which the USA's attempt to mitigate the impact of these dependencies shape its foreign policy, and the difficulties and limitations which result from its efforts at finding alternative sources of supply.

CULTURAL DEPENDENCE

The development of the USA as a modern industrial power is inextricably linked to its relationship with, and indeed its dependence on, petroleum. The exploitation of its indigenous oil supplies, most notably by John D. Rockefeller's Standard Oil Company, was what fuelled the 19th century transformation of the USA from an agrarian to an industrial economy. Even today, oil accounts for 40% of the USA's energy needs.[14] In the 20th century, as the USA's economy and prosperity grew, its economic dependence on oil was matched by a cultural reliance on that commodity, primarily through its growing reliance on the motor car. This dependence is not only practical but also political. It is practical in the sense that how and where US citizens live and work has been shaped by a dependence on the car more than in any other society, with the result that the USA is now a completely car-dependent state. The scale on which US cities and other communities are planned and the relative paucity of public transport means that car ownership, or at least access, is almost universal. Without cars, travel to work and to the shops would be impossible in all but a few major cities. The dependence is also political in the sense that the car has come to represent individual freedom of movement, the idea of outdoor living and the frontier. Cars are also seen as statements of individual wealth and are viewed as items of personal security. Prior to the ongoing energy crisis, the growing trend towards ownership of SUVs, which accounted for 27.2% of 'light-duty vehicle use' in the first half of 2004, was fuelled by the belief that they were safer than conventional cars.[15] In a country where more than 42,000 people are killed in traffic accidents each year, this was not an unreasonable motive for this trend. SUV ownership on this scale, despite their poor fuel economy, was facilitated by the relatively cheap price of petrol in the USA. Tax on petrol has remained a small fraction of what it is in other industrial countries. Politicians' avoidance of heavy taxes on gasoline demonstrates a recognition of the car's necessity and its symbolism. The result of this love affair with the car is a culture dependent on cheap fuel. US citizens like big cars such as SUVs and V-8s and they routinely drive long distances, covering more miles per head every year (until the downturn in 2007).[16] In addition to this, they also use low-cost internal flights without any consideration that oil is both a finite and a problematic resource. A consequence of this relationship, combined with a growing economy and an expanding population, is that the USA's thirst for ever more oil is set to rise steadily.

The USA is the world's largest consumer of petroleum, accounting for more than one-quarter of global demand, even though its citizens constitute less than 5% of the world's population. Furthermore, the US Department of Energy (DoE) projects that US energy consumption will increase by 1.5% annually from 2000 to 2020 and that petroleum's share of that energy mix will increase slightly, from 39.4% in 2000 to 39.7% in 2020.[17] The USA is fortunate among the leading industrial powers in that it can supply a very large proportion of its energy requirements from domestic sources, having large supplies of coal, oil and natural gas, as well as an extensive nuclear power system. Indeed, for 2000 the DoE calculated that 73% of US consumption was met through domestic energy production.[18] Despite plans to increase production from domestic sources by about 20% over the next two decades, however, if present trends persist energy consumption will continue to rise faster than the rate of production. Consequently, the USA will have to import an ever larger proportion of its energy needs and become increasingly reliant on foreign sources of energy. This reliance is most acute in the case of oil, with domestic production projected to decline at an average annual rate of 0.2% for the next 20 years.[19] This projected gap between domestic production and consumption will need to be filled by imported oil. In the mid-2000s the USA imported 53% of its petroleum requirements, but that figure was forecast to grow to 62% by 2020. If these predictions are realized, the USA's intake of imported oil will have increased by some 50%, from 24.4m. b/d to 37.1m. b/d.[20]

Interestingly, between 2000 and 2006 the USA accounted for 12.5% of the increase in global demand for petroleum, whereas China accounted for 32%. As a result of high oil prices causing domestic booms at home, the Organization of the Petroleum Exporting Countries (OPEC) countries' share of this increase is rising at two-and-a-half times the average and accounted for 22% of the increase.[21] It is this global demand, magnified by a shortage of global refining capacity—together with war and instability in the Middle East—which has helped to raise the price of oil internationally in recent years. In this context, the thirst for oil created by the USA's economy and culture will continue to make energy supply a pressing issue in US foreign policy.

STRATEGIC DEPENDENCE

While the strategic importance of oil in international politics grew steadily throughout the 20th century, for the USA its significance was marked dramatically in 1941 with the Japanese attack on Pearl Harbor. For this attack was a direct response to the imposition against Japan of a complete oil embargo by the USA in protest at the Japanese Government's policies in China. Faced with economic strangulation, Japan chose to go to war with the USA, an action that the USA had not anticipated. From this moment onwards the USA has never underestimated the strategic significance of oil.

Since the end of the Second World War the USA's strategic dependence on petroleum has taken three forms. The most obvious of these is its reliance on oil in the three end-user sectors of its own domestic economy: residential and commercial, industrial, and transportation. While the first two sectors have shown some ability to move away from their dependence on fuel oil, the demand from the transportation sector has grown continuously.[22] The USA's second form of dependence is the reliance of its principal trading partners and allies on petroleum. This was of particular importance during the Cold War, when the threat from the Soviet bloc to allied oil supplies was considered to be a real and present danger; however, it is still a factor that shapes US geostrategic calculations. A third, related dependence is that of the world economy as a whole on the continuous supply of cheap oil. Given the interconnectedness of the USA to the world economy and its trading relationships with the other industrial powers, these states' dependence on oil represents a strategic dependence for the USA. Thus, rather paradoxically, even though the USA is less dependent on foreign oil than are other countries, its allies' dependence on petroleum is, in turn, the USA's dependence. This is especially the case in relation to the Persian Gulf, which is the largest and most important global source of petroleum, accounting for two-thirds of known world oil reserves. For, while oil from the Persian Gulf accounts for only 10% of total consumption in the USA, 30% of Europe's oil and nearly 80% of Japan's oil comes from the Gulf.[23] Yet despite its relative lack of direct dependence on Persian Gulf oil, it is the USA which assumes the role of ensuring the stability and thus the continued flow of cheap petroleum from the region. This is the case for historical and geopolitical reasons. Historically, it was the USA at the end of the Second World War that pledged its support to Saudi Arabia in return for privileged access to the kingdom's oil. As the United Kingdom and France relinquished their colonial ties to the Gulf, it was the USA that extended its influence in the region by providing security assistance to the Shah of Iran and the leaders of Kuwait, Bahrain and the United Arab Emirates. These relationships were developed in the context of the geopolitical competition of the Cold War, when the USA assumed the role of protecting the oil supply of the 'free world', but the commitments undertaken were against internal as well as external enemies. In support of these policies, the USA has also supplied large quantities of weapons and ammunition to the Gulf states, some of which have become the USA's biggest customers for military equipment. Saudi Arabia alone allocates 35%–45% of its considerable national budget to military expenditure, with most of this being spent in the USA.[24] Most recently, in 2007 the USA announced major arms deals worth more than US $50,000m. with both Saudi Arabia and Israel, which were widely considered as part of a US strategy to contain Iran's regional ambitions.[25]

Following the British military withdrawal from the Persian Gulf in 1971, the USA has gradually expanded its military presence in and around the region. Given the local sensitivity to the presence of US forces, most US deployments have been in East Africa and on the Indian Ocean island of Diego Garcia even though their focus has been on the Gulf. As well as ensuring the stable flow of cheap petroleum, these deployments are also designed to protect the USA's other interests in the region. The strategic significance of the Persian Gulf is such that the USA has an interest in preventing any potentially hostile state from gaining control over the region and its resources, and using such control to dictate its terms to the international community.[26] Military access to and through the Persian Gulf is also important to the USA owing to its geographical proximity to the Middle East, Central and South Asia and East Africa. As Kenneth Pollack observes, 'If the United States were denied access to the Persian Gulf, its ability to influence events in many other key regions of the world would be greatly diminished.'[27] For this reason the USA has long indicated that it would not allow such a situation to develop. The most explicit statement to this effect was issued in 1980, following the invasion of Afghanistan by the USSR in December 1979, which had followed the Islamic Revolution in Iran earlier that year. Fearing that the Soviets would continue their expansion into the Middle East, the USA announced what was to become known as the 'Carter Doctrine'. This stated that 'any attempt by any outside force to gain control of the Persian Gulf region will be regarded as an assault on the vital interests of the United States of America, and such an assault will be repelled by all means necessary, including military force'.[28] While this doctrine was precise in its public identification of the threat to repel 'outside force', the concept applied equally, if less publicly, to internal and regional threats. It is now known that the USA actively considered the use of military force to seize Arab oilfields in 1973 in response to the oil embargo, and would have done so as a last resort had the crisis continued.[29] President Ronald Reagan (1981–88) hinted at similar action in 1981, stating that 'Saudi Arabia, we will not permit to be an Iran'.[30] The promulgation of the Carter Doctrine was accompanied by the creation of the Rapid Reaction Force, which was later expanded to become Central Command, as a way of implementing this commitment. It was these forces that were subsequently used to enforce the Doctrine. The first military commitment was defensive in nature, to protect Kuwaiti oil tankers, reregistered under the US flag, from attack by Iranian missiles and gunboats during the Iran–Iraq War of 1980–88. The second, the expulsion of Iraqi forces from Kuwait during the Gulf conflict of 1991, however, saw the implementation of the Carter Doctrine in its pristine form. Although this war received its legitimacy and legality from its defence of Kuwaiti sovereignty, its strategic importance was also a motivating influence on the USA and the multinational coalition. As US Secretary of State James Baker stated at the time, as well as protecting Kuwaiti independence, it was also about 'our way of life'. The conclusion of the Gulf conflict, with Saddam Hussain remaining in power in Iraq—and thus still a potential threat to neighbouring states—led to a massive increase in the US military presence in the region. The UN mandate concerning Kuwait had sanctioned Iraq's expulsion from Kuwaiti territory but not the removal of the perpetrator or the threat. Thus, the need to contain Iraq (and also Iran) led the USA to step up its military commitment to the area with increased air force and naval deployments and the prepositioning of large numbers of ground forces.[31] Airbases in Turkey and Saudi Arabia were used by US forces as a means of enforcing the 'no-fly' zones in northern and southern Iraq between 1991 and 2003. These forces in the region were also used in late 2001 during the US-led campaign against al-Qa'ida and the Taliban regime in Afghanistan, and in 2003 provided the basis of the offensive operation for the coalition's invasion of Iraq.

The USA's approach towards its strategic dependence on petroleum from the Persian Gulf has not been without its cost and its critics, however. The cost of the military deployments that the USA makes to the Gulf, which amount to thousands of millions of dollars, is the most obvious price being paid as a result of this policy, a cost that is not accounted for in the per-barrel price of 'cheap' Gulf oil.[32] Indeed, according to one study, if the US $49,100m. annual cost of defending the Persian Gulf were added to fuel prices, petrol at the pumps would increase by $1.17, or to a total of $5.28 if all hidden costs were added.[33] The fact that the USA's defence burden in the Gulf is not shared by its major industrial allies is an added cost of this policy, both in dollars and in terms of legitimacy. Perhaps more important, however, is the cost that this approach has on the USA's reputation in the Middle East. While one might have expected the extension of US military protection to the region to have been welcomed by its population, the very opposite has occurred. This is the case for a variety of reasons. The continued isolation of Iraq as a result of the sanctions regime imposed against that country in 1990–2003 was largely viewed in the Arab world as being responsible for the immense suffering of the Iraqi people, while the continued bombing of Iraq by allied forces in support of the 'no-fly' zones was widely seen as punitive and illegitimate.[34] The presence of US military personnel in Saudi Arabia, which facilitated this policy, was another source of regional resentment against the USA. This presence was seen by many Muslims as an unwelcome intrusion by 'infidels' onto the territory of Islam's most sacred sites, Medina and Mecca. Not only did this stoke anti-US sentiment, but it was also damaging to the Saudi royal family's legitimacy as the keepers of the holy places. Moreover, the USA's uncritical support for the autocratic monarchies of the Gulf region has also been damaging to the country's reputation. Such support, according to Mamoun Fandy, 'undermines US policy by demonstrating the hypocrisy in American rhetoric about democracy and human rights and weakens the regimes by creating the perception among Gulf subjects that their countries are being ruled in the interests of an outside power'.[35] This problem is particularly acute in Saudi Arabia, where growing numbers of young people are also resentful of the USA because of its close ties to Israel and its perceived anti-Islamic bias.[36] It was against this background that Osama bin Laden was able to recruit many of his supporters and to raise funds to finance the operations of his al-Qa'ida organization. According to one former US Central Intelligence Agency (CIA) official, bin Laden's popularity in Saudi Arabia is such that if there were an election now, he would win 'by a landslide'.[37] It is indeed ironic that the USA deployed forces to Saudi Arabia in 1991 to defend the kingdom against a possible Iraqi invasion, yet the very act of containing Iraq led to popular resentment of the USA in Saudi Arabia and the Middle East region more generally. This, in turn, led to the growth of al-Qa'ida and, ultimately, to the attacks of 11 September 2001, when 15 of the 19 hijackers were of Saudi descent. The need to remove this source of resentment was a contributing argument for regime change in Baghdad, which, once achieved, allowed the USA to remove its forces from Saudi Arabia. Rather than this dissipating the resentment, however, the US-led occupation of Iraq created even more widespread anti-US sentiment in the Middle East. Much to the embarrassment of the Bush Administration, this fact was even recognized by the US intelligence community's National Intelligence Estimate for 2006, which 'says that the Iraq war has made the overall terrorism problem worse'.[38]

As a result of this troubled background, the USA's relationship with Saudi Arabia is now an extremely problematic one. This is particularly the case given the multiplicity of issues at stake. At its most fundamental level, Saudi Arabia is a vitally important ally for the USA in its relations with the Middle East and also with regard to US energy policy. In this role, relations with the ruling élite are good and Saudi Arabia is a force for stability. Not only is it the largest single producer of crude petroleum and petroleum products in the world, providing 13.1% of global output in 2006, but it is also a significant contributor to oil price stability. With the world's largest excess production capacity, Saudi Arabia acts to stabilize and control the price of oil by increasing or decreasing output as required, thus protecting the world economy from strategic shocks. Given projected US and international demand for oil, Saudi Arabia has also been identified as the only country with the potential capacity to meet the growing demand for future supply. According to the US Department of Energy, Saudi Arabia's net petroleum output would have to double over the next two decades, from 11.4m. b/d to 23.1m. b/d to satisfy anticipated world demand.[39] With China's oil requirements increasing by 50% on a year-on-year basis, these figures may even be a conservative estimate. For such a demand to be met by Saudi Arabia, however, would be no small order. An increase of 11.7m. b/d is the equivalent of the current combined oil production output of the USA and Canada, and would require an enormous investment to overcome the technical and logistical problems involved. The best means of achieving this growth, according to the US petroleum industry, would be to persuade Saudi Arabia to open up its oil industry to massive international investment. The reluctance of the Saudi royal family to do this, however, is expected to be considerable. Not only would this mean a reversal of the nationalization of US oil holdings that took place in the 1970s, but it also comes at a time when other issues are negatively influencing relations between the Saudi and US Governments. For the Saudi royal family there is a growing realization that its connections with the US Administration are viewed increasingly in a negative light, both domestically and regionally. Meanwhile, the events of 11 September 2001 convinced the USA that, despite the strategic role played by Saudi Arabia in world energy markets, it could not ignore the security implications of the tensions within the Saudi state. Indeed, Saudi Arabia's lack of democracy or any form of participatory politics has resulted in political opposition being channelled into religious extremism or acts of terrorism being perpetrated against the Government or its US allies. Nor has the Saudi Government's response to these developments been helpful. By clamping down and arresting advocates of democracy and domestic critics, the Government has blocked a legitimate route of political protest. Moreover, the regime's efforts to placate its religious critics by making large payments to Islamic charities has had the effect of funding its mortal enemies. As Michael Klare points out, 'by giving money to charities controlled by extremists, the royal family has unwittingly channelled funds to al-Qa'ida and other anti-monarchy, anti-American terrorist organizations'.[40] It is for this reason that the USA has insisted that Saudi Arabia take a tougher line with its own militant Islamists, and why, at a strategic level, the USA has called for the transformation of the Middle East by means of the region's rulers embracing democracy and human rights. While reassuring its allies in the Middle East that such change may be slow and gradual, this policy represents a fundamental shift in the way in which US foreign policy has been conducted towards Saudi Arabia and the other Gulf states over the past 50 years. How the management of these changes can be achieved through US policy without damaging that part of the relationship which is needed to maintain and increase the supply of cheap petroleum to the world economy will be an enduring test for US leaders in the years ahead.

MANAGING THE STRATEGIC VULNERABILITY OF OIL DEPENDENCE

The unfortunate consequence of the USA's cultural and strategic dependence on petroleum is the vulnerability that this presents to actions and events that threaten the global supply of oil. This problem is only made worse by the high correlation that exists globally between oil wealth and political violence, instability and authoritarianism. Nor are these factors unrelated.[41] Oil wealth tends to impede the development of values and institutions that are vital for open, market-based economies and political institutions, such as property rights, the rule of law, civil liberties and political participation.[42] This is the case because the oil wealth flows to the élites who control the 'rents' for these natural resources, rewarding them for being in power rather than for creating the conditions for order, stability and prosperity. As Nancy Birdsall and Arvind Subramanian observe, in many countries: 'The state is relieved of the pressure to tax and has no incentive to promote the protection of property rights as a way of creating wealth.' As for the country's citizens, because they are not taxed, they have little incentive and no effective mechanism by which to hold the Government accountable.[43] As a result of this 'resource curse' many oil-rich countries are characterized by authoritarian regimes where state power is unchecked and where there are no effective mechanisms for participation or accountability. This often leads to vast disparities in wealth, with large sections of the populations living in poverty: 12 of the 34 less-developed countries that derive 30% of their total export revenue from petroleum and gas have a daily income per head of less than US $1.50, and up to one-half of their populations live on less than $1 a day. Moreover, more than two-thirds of these 34 states are not democratic.[44] Such poverty and resentment without a means for expression through the political process often finds expression in violence and civil disorder. For example, Nigeria—the USA's fifth leading supplier of crude petroleum—has suffered six successful coups and four failed ones, the assassination of two leaders and 30 years of military rule.[45] Angola, Venezuela, Colombia, Equatorial Guinea and Gabon have all suffered a similar degree of turmoil and conflict over the control and distribution of oil wealth and the political power that it brings. While the oil-rich states of the Persian Gulf have so far managed to avoid a high degree of domestic political violence as a result of their oil wealth, they have suffered the lack of developed political and civil institutions that characterize other 'petro-states'. The rise of al-Qa'ida in Saudi Arabia and the growing incidence of political violence and dissent there, however, suggests that the Middle East is not immune from this pattern of events. For the USA, both as a large consumer of petroleum and as the guardian of the global economy, these correlations are important in emphasizing the troubled nature of its oil dependency. It is a correlation with which the USA is all too familiar, having suffered as a consequence of this dependence in the past.

In the 1970s two oil crises brought about by disruptions in the supply of petroleum from the Middle East had a major impact on the US and world economies. Following the Yom Kippur War of 1973, the Arab members of OPEC persuaded the organization to mount a boycott of the USA and other countries in response to their support for Israel in the conflict. Although the embargo was never watertight and was only imposed for a few months, its effects had a lasting impact on the energy sector. As part of the crisis and in order to increase their revenues, OPEC reduced oil production by 25% and quadrupled the price of oil from US $3 to $12 per barrel.[46] The result was a massive shift in wealth from the industrialized countries to the Arab world and a major downturn in the global economy. Ironically, however, since much of this new-found oil wealth was invested in the global economy, the recession that followed the crisis also affected Arab investments adversely. It was for this reason that many Gulf states began to appreciate their mutual interest in low and stable oil prices. The second oil shock followed the Islamic Revolution in Iran in 1979, when petroleum output decreased from 5.25m. b/d in 1978 to 1.3m. b/d in 1980—a fall of 75%.[47] The increase in demand for oil produced by the Western economic recovery that began in 1979, together with the reduction of supply following the outbreak of the Iran–Iraq War in 1980, caused a further series of oil price rises. Only with increased global oil production was the effect of this second crisis mitigated, with prices stabilizing in 1985 at a level 20% higher than they were in 1974.[48]

The potential for similar oil crises disrupting the US and global economies has decreased since the 1970s episodes, for a number of reasons. The first change since the 1970s is that producers no longer sell directly to customers and are therefore no longer in the position of being able to punish them individually. Today much of OPEC's clout is removed because petroleum is sold on an international market mediated by numerous middlemen and futures traders, with the result, according to energy policy expert William Hogan, that 'they can't cut off our oil supply, they can only cut off oil supply', and that because this is 'a very blunt political weapon . . . they have stopped using it as a weapon'.[49] Since, relatively speaking, the services sector has increased as a proportion of the US economy and manufacturing has declined, the US economy is also less dependent on oil as a percentage of gross domestic product (GDP) spending: just 3% of GDP in 1999, compared with 8% in 1980.[50] Despite its reduced direct vulnerability, however, the USA's position in the global economy means that higher oil prices for countries like China, Thailand or the Republic of Korea will also affect the USA. Those countries that now manufacture goods for the US economy will pass on the costs of higher oil prices to the US consumer, but only indirectly, and they may be forced to absorb some of those costs in the process. The result of successive price rises in the petroleum market has also had three beneficial effects. First, it has reduced the USA's energy consumption: between 1979 and 1985—the period of the steepest rise in oil prices—GDP grew by 16%, while total oil consumption fell by 15% and Gulf imports by 87%.[51] Second, these price hikes encouraged new competitors to enter the global market, resulting in periods of oversupply and subsequent falls in oil prices. In the 1990s, for example, 60 nations increased their oil production and are now supplying the USA.[52] Third, it encouraged energy companies to explore and discover new oil resources. While in the 1970s global reserves were estimated at 650,000m. barrels, the use of new sensors and advanced probes has meant that reserves are now judged to be more than 1,000,000m. barrels.[53]

Despite these changes to the international oil markets, the USA's dependence on foreign supplies of petroleum is an issue of increasing political saliency in the domestic debate. This much was made evident by the urgency with which the Bush Administration sought to address the issue on taking office in 2001. The National Energy Policy Development Group (NEPDG) reported in May of that year that the USA faced the possibility of 'the worst energy crisis since the 1970s' as a consequence of several related factors. Dwindling domestic supplies of oil and gas, an antiquated power grid and the heavy burden of government regulation were all identified as problems. The NEPDG report also warned that the USA was overly dependent on one source of energy—oil—and that it was reliant on production from too few regions, notably the Middle East. All the proposals recommended in the report were controversial. However, the plans to relax government regulations on the power industry and to permit exploitation of the Arctic National Wildlife Refuge in Alaska were the issues that provoked the most domestic debate. The former was controversial as it was seen as a payback to the energy companies that had been major contributors to President Bush's election campaign. The latter is controversial because it threatens the environmental destruction of one of the last untouched areas in the USA. Opinion polls consistently demonstrate large-scale opposition to such a plan.[54] This is not least because the oil reserves in Alaska would produce less than 0.3% of world output.[55] Thus, its contribution would be very small as a proportion of domestic demand—reducing imports by only 5%—and, as a result, the environmental cost, it is argued, would not be worth the benefit. The oil companies have also thus far shown little interest in exploiting this potential source of oil since the extraction and transportation costs of such a venture would not be cost-effective at current market conditions. A further factor in this debate is the vulnerability, and thus the security, of this oil supply. Exploitation would be reliant on the 800-mile Trans-Alaskan Pipeline System, which would be unserviceable in winter and which the US army has declared to be indefensible. For this reason the former CIA Director James Woolsey has argued that the pipeline would become 'the fattest energy-terrorist target in the country', thus making the whole project a non-starter.[56]

Attracting less public debate but no less controversial among the Bush Administration's plans was the identified need to reduce the USA's dependence on Middle Eastern oil, an issue with considerable foreign policy implications.[57] The NEPDG report identified the USA's need to diversify its sources of supply in order to ensure energy security. Diversification has been a long-standing goal of US energy policy as a way of safeguarding security of supply. Since the terrorist attacks of 2001, however, it has acquired an added sense of urgency. As Woolsey rather colourfully states, 'Relying for 13% of US oil supply on the pathological predators and vulnerable autocrats of the Mideast—home of at least two-thirds of the world's reserves—is a tragedy waiting to happen.'[58] The Bush Administration's approach was controversial, however, not because it sought diversity of supply as such, but because of its stated aim of encouraging oil imports from 'friendly' producers, such as Russia, in order to replace oil imports to the USA from the Middle East. This approach was problematic, according to Anthony Cordesman, because 'the policy acts as if the rest of the world didn't exist'.[59] That is to say that it ignored the fact that oil is a fungible commodity; it will flow to the highest bidder in the global market place. Therefore, even if the USA did not import any oil from the Middle East, it would still be vulnerable to disruptions of oil supplies from that region to the other consumers of petroleum such as China, Japan, Germany and India, who would scramble to buy the available supply and thus push up prices everywhere. As Gawdat Bahgat explains, the Bush Administration's policy was 'misplaced' because 'who sells and who buys a barrel of oil is less important than the availability of enough supplies to all consumers. Petroleum reserves are what count and Saudi reserves are indispensable for US and world needs'.[60] Furthermore, if the USA bought more of its oil from alternative sources to the Middle East, it would increase the dependence of other countries on this source since at present global production is only slightly ahead of global demand. Thus, if a crisis did affect Middle Eastern oil supplies, the impact on those countries and on the world economy might be even more severe.[61] It is also unclear how other oil-dependent countries might react if the USA were successful in reducing its dependence on oil from the Middle East. Petroleum from the Persian Gulf might become a sought after commodity in the international oil markets if its supply was genuinely seen as more secure, creating increased demand and thus a price premium for this oil. Alternatively, it could increase other countries' dependence on oil from countries such as Iran and Saudi Arabia, which would make them more beholden to these states in political terms. This is already evident in the economic dependence of China and Iran and the Chinese Government's subsequent reluctance to sanction Iran over its nuclear 'delinquency'.

Despite these criticisms of the Bush Administration's approach, oil diversification remained its first principle of energy policy. The policy was not only motivated by replacing the USA's oil supply, however, but it also aimed to increase total global supply as a means of improving energy security. An additional benefit of developing new sources and new supplies to the market would be to lessen the influence of OPEC and thus exert a downward pressure on prices. The impact of this approach to energy policy was already apparent in US foreign policy. Oil was a component in the improved relationship between the US and Russian Governments, with a new 'energy partnership' agreement being signed in May 2002. Russia had made considerable efforts to present itself as a reliable source of energy supplies to the global economy, in return for allowing US and European oil companies to provide large amounts of financial resources to the Russian energy industry. European companies had led the way in this investment, with British Petroleum (BP) and the Royal Dutch/Shell group investing heavily in oil and gas, and US companies such as ExxonMobil following on with heavy involvement in developments on Sakhalin Island and in Eastern Siberia.[62] Other developments included the underwriting of loans to Russian oil companies by the US Export-Import Bank to buy US equipment and services; the direct importation of Russian crude oil into the US market and its purchase for the first time by the US Strategic Petroleum Reserve.[63] There was also a great deal of excitement concerning the extent of the petroleum and gas reserves that may be present in Russia. Oil expert Paul Collison, for example, was of the opinion that 'by the end of the decade Russia will be proven to have 50% more hydrocarbon reserves than Saudi Arabia has today'.[64]

ALTERNATIVE SOURCES OF SUPPLY

Russia

Although much has been made of this new relationship between the world's largest consumer and the second largest producer of petroleum, there are many reasons as to why

Russia may not replace the Middle East as a major supplier of oil to the USA. Although Russia's oil production briefly overtook that of Saudi Arabia in 2002, this was mainly as a result of the latter working at full capacity while the former deliberately kept a proportion of its capacity idle in order to regulate world supply. Russian petroleum is also much more expensive to produce than oil from the Persian Gulf. The location of Russian oil is a major factor in this for a number of reasons. Exploration and extraction in inhospitable environments is always difficult and the land area involved is four times larger than that in the Persian Gulf. Transportation costs are also considerable and the pipelines that carry the oil are a source of bottlenecks and vulnerability. Russia is currently able to export less than one-half of the oil that it produces as a consequence of its Soviet-era infrastructure.[65] Its pipelines also transport the oil to Russia's traditional market, Europe, whereas shipping it to the USA is much more expensive. Much of this infrastructure is in a decrepit state and thus in need of substantial investment. Even with the construction of new pipelines, Russia would be unlikely to keep up with current production and demand.[66] This level of output is also a potential problem in that Russian production is not being matched by active exploration and the discovery of new sources. The result could be the depletion of existing stocks, with a period of bust following the boom years unless new fields are developed and the lives of old ones are extended. All this again requires substantially more investment than is currently forthcoming. One reason for this is the uncertain nature of Russia's business environment and indeed the integrity of the legal system. The creeping renationalization of the oil industry that some commentators detect in the policies of President Vladimir Putin and the recent problems encountered by the Russian oil company Yukos (whose Chief Executive, Mikhail Khodorkovsky, was arrested on charges of tax evasion and fraud in 2003) do not engender confidence among potential investors.[67] Indeed, following the Russian invasion of Georgia in August 2008, the Russian stock market crashed to levels from which a few months later it had yet to recover. The sharp deterioration in relations between Russia and the USA following this diplomatic crisis vividly demonstrated the unpredictable and problematic nature of reliance on Russian energy supplies.

The Caspian Basin

Similar efforts at source diversification have been pursued by the USA with regard to the other former Soviet republics of the Caspian Sea Basin. Azerbaijan, Kazakhstan, Turkmenistan and Uzbekistan were the subject of considerable diplomatic attention from the USA throughout the 1990s, in an effort to open up these countries to investment and exploration by US companies. Central to these initiatives was also the routing of oil pipelines to ensure that oil is transported in a way that is accessible for the US market. Specifically, the USA was concerned to prevent Caspian pipelines from being routed through either Russia or Iran for political reasons, and thus backed a construction route from the Azerbaijani capital, Baku, to Ceyhan in Turkey via Georgia. Similar problems beset these countries as are found in Russia; however, there are often significant infrastructural problems and the need for substantial investment is complicated by a political climate in which such undertakings are high-risk ventures. As well as the poor human rights record of most of these states, there is the added problem of militant separatist groups in Georgia and Chechnya that pose a threat to the region's long pipelines and pumping stations. Georgia's territorial disputes with Russia over Abkhazia and South Ossetia are another source of instability in this region, as the military clashes over these enclaves demonstrated in August 2008. As a result, according to Klare, 'The Caucasus and Central Asia are no more stable than the Persian Gulf, and developing the Caspian as an alternative source of energy is pointless if its outflow of oil and gas cannot be secured.'[68] Conscious of these considerations, the USA has sought to maintain the military bases that it established in Kyrgyzstan and Tajikistan in late 2001 for the US-led military campaign in Afghanistan. (The US airbase in Uzbekistan was closed in November 2005.) The USA also now conducts annual military exercises in the region and has deployed training forces in Georgia to assist with counter-insurgency measures. The latter, however, were cited by Russia as one of the provocations for its military incursion into Georgian territory in August 2008. This again demonstrates the problematic nature of increased reliance on this region for energy supplies.

Africa

The USA's renewed foreign policy interest in Africa also has a strong oil dimension. Currently Africa provides 15% of US crude petroleum imports, but that figure has been estimated to rise to 25% within the next decade.[69] It is also estimated that one-quarter of the new, non-Persian Gulf oil that comes onto the world market in the next five years will be from sub-Saharan Africa. African petroleum also has a number of distinct advantages for the USA. It tends to be of a high quality and low in sulphur, which makes it attractive to US refiners. The transportation and logistics are also easier for the USA, being on the Atlantic Rim, just 4,500 miles from the eastern coast of the USA, with an unobstructed sea route to US ports. Of all the sub-Saharan African oil-producing countries, only Nigeria and Angola are members of OPEC (Angola having joined in January 2007).[70] Thus, countries such as Gabon, Chad, Equatorial Guinea, and São Tomé and Príncipe—all potentially strong oil producers—are free to produce without production limits, exerting price pressures on the traditional producers. While much is made of the potential for African petroleum, however, it cannot substitute or replace the role of the Persian Gulf in the global energy market. Total African reserves are estimated at about 77,000m. barrels, while those in the Middle East are around 686,000m. barrels.[71] Africa also has its share of problems associated with other oil-producing areas. Like most African states, Nigeria, the continent's largest producer, lacks the finance to fund the expansion in production necessary to develop its oil assets, yet it is also reluctant to allow investment by outside firms. Corruption, theft and industrial relations disputes are also common in Africa's oil industries. While the Bush Administration was keen to address these problems by pressing for change in its relations with African governments, it was also conscious not to be seen to be too close to regimes that had a poor human rights record and a low level of accountability and legitimacy. The systematic theft of oil wealth over the years in many of these countries, resulting in high levels of absolute poverty, has created an unstable political climate in many 'petro-states'. As a result, according to Timothy Burn of *The Washington Times*, 'Militant protesters in West Africa often aim their wrath at Western oil companies, accusing them of exploiting Africa's oil wealth while their nations struggle under poverty.'[72] The fact that 60%–80% of that wealth goes to local government élites is often overlooked in the process of identifying a foreign political scapegoat. The USA's approach towards the region as a potential source of resource diversification needs to be tempered by wider security considerations. Given that the oil-rich areas of West Africa are predominantly Muslim, the USA is aware that the region is a potential target for the recruiting efforts of the al-Qa'ida network. Indeed, Gen. James Jones, head of US European Command, warned of the need for the USA to 'engage more in that theatre', lest its ungoverned regions 'could become terrorist breeding grounds'.[73] Given Africa's growing strategic significance, in February 2007 the US Department of Defense announced its intention to establish a new military command for Africa (the US Africa Command or AFRICOM) by September 2008. This controversial decision was taken despite the realization that a US military presence in Africa could be counterproductive if it were perceived as propping up unpopular regimes or primarily defending the interests of Western oil companies.[74] The symbolism of this deployment would need to be handled extremely carefully to avoid the accusation of a new colonialism. In Africa, as in the successor states of the USSR, diversification of oil supply is far from unproblematic for the USA.

Latin America

The Bush Administration was also keen to develop oil supplies closer to the US market in Latin America. Venezuela is the third largest supplier to the USA (after Saudi Arabia and Canada), Mexico is fourth and Colombia seventh. US policy towards this region is designed to facilitate the expansion of oil exports to the USA, and US officials have identified Mexico and Venezuela as countries with the potential greatly to increase their exports. According to President Bush's National Energy Policy report, Mexico's 'large reserve base, approximately 25% larger than our own proven reserves, makes [it] ... a likely source of increased oil production over the next decade', while 'Venezuelan success in making heavy oil deposits commercially viable suggests that they will contribute substantially to the diversity of global energy supply, and to our own energy supply over the medium- to long-term'.[75] The US Administration's ability to put these plans into operation, however, may be frustrated by resistance to increased participation by US oil companies in their domestic oil industries aimed at increasing production. In both these countries and elsewhere in the region, legal and constitutional barriers have been erected to protect the domestic oil and gas supplies from what is seen as the predatory role of foreign involvement. Security of supply is also a problem in Latin America, particularly for Colombia (which is the ninth largest supplier of crude oil to the USA) where frequent attacks on its 500-mile-long oil pipeline—an average of five per day at the peak of the guerrillas' activities—have had a major impact on supply. Indeed, the US Government has invested US $100m. in counter-insurgency aid under its 'Plan Colombia' policy to prevent major oil companies from leaving the country.[76] In Venezuela, the anti-US rhetoric and erratic policies of President Hugo Chávez Frías and his political opponents are another cause for concern. For these reasons US ambitions for increased oil production from Latin America may prove as elusive as the other superficially attractive sources of oil diversification.

Iraq

Iraq's petroleum reserves provide a potential source of diversification from US reliance on Saudi Arabian oil, but obviously not from Persian Gulf oil more generally. Indeed, for some commentators oil was the most important motivation for the US-led invasion of Iraq in March 2003. For Paul Rogers, 'if Iraq produced rice or oranges instead of oil, there would be no great concern ... The bottom line with Iraq is oil'. Rogers believes that the conflict in Iraq 'ensures the security of Iraqi oil for the long term, it limits dependence on a potentially unstable Saudi Arabia and it ... makes it abundantly clear to Iran that the United States is the controlling power in the region.'[77] While the USA was aware that Iraq post-Saddam Hussain offered the potential for a variety of strategic benefits, including the possibility of significantly increased oil production in the longer term, this was not the principal reason for the invasion. Certainly the USA was concerned, as Vice-President Cheney warned, that Iraq might 'seek domination of the entire Middle East' and 'take control of a great portion of the world's energy supplies', but this regional threat had been present for at least a decade. What had changed was not the demand for oil, as some suggest, but the context of the global 'war on terror'. Indeed, although Iraq's petroleum reserves are believed to be the second largest in the world, with a value of US $3,400,000m. (at $25 per barrel), its actual output is relatively small. What is under the ground is one thing, but how easily it can be brought to the surface and distributed is quite another. This is especially true of Iraq, which has the lowest yield of any major producer, amounting to 0.8% of potential output, or less than 3% of global output, due to the geology of the oilfields and the technology available to exploit it.[78] Such is the dilapidated state of the Iraq oil industry that it will take years of sustained investment before any return is possible. According to industry experts, at least $40,000m. will need to be invested to increase production from some 2.5m. b/d today (which yields $23,000m. per year) to 4.2m. b/d–6m. b/d. Thus, significant money would need to be spent before any relatively modest increases in revenue would be possible. Given Iraq's debts of over $100,000m. (excluding war reparations owed to Iran and Kuwait) and the need for investment in infrastructure and the establishment of democratic institutions, this may not be a priority.[79] As Daniel Yergin argues in *The Washington Post*, 'No US administration would launch so momentous a campaign just to facilitate a handful of oil development contracts and a moderate increase in supply—half a decade from now.'[80] Indeed, the USA has also made it clear that all petroleum revenues will be used for the reconstruction of Iraq and, although some reconstruction contracts have gone to US firms, this is not unexpected given that these are funded by the US taxpayer as part of the $87,000m. budget approved by Congress. In the short term, the security situation in Iraq is such that very little infrastructural repairs or work to develop the oil industry is likely or even possible in the immediate future. Even pre-war levels of oil production have been affected by the violence, with oil output regularly suspended as a consequence of attacks by insurgents. According to recent figures, Iraq produced between 0.8m. b/d and 1.3m. b/d less petroleum in 2005 than it did before the US-led invasion in 2003.[81] As a result, the idea of Iraq replacing Saudi Arabia as a more stable and secure source of oil does not seem to be a likely prospect.

Another security issue resulting from the USA's high dependence on oil in its economy is the environmental impact of this consumption and its associated political costs. As well as being the world's largest user of oil, the USA is also the largest polluter, producing 25% of the world's 'greenhouse gases' from less than 5% of the world's population. Furthermore, US energy-related carbon dioxide emissions are set to exceed 2,000m. metric tons of carbon (7,500m. tons of gas) by 2020, an increase of 33% above 2000 levels.[82] Not only is this a serious problem as far as climate change is concerned, but it also represents a diplomatic and political problem for the USA. In diplomatic terms, President Bush's rejection of the Kyoto Protocol on climate change cost the USA much credibility as an internationally responsible global power. In political terms, it has also suffered considerably in the court of international public opinion. Not only does the USA's non-participation matter in its own right as the largest polluter, but the US Government's lack of endorsement is a serious blow to the effectiveness of the regime as a whole, both on its own terms and as a basis for future agreements. The fact that the Bush Administration offered no alternatives to the Kyoto Protocol as a means of addressing this real and growing global problem was widely seen as an indictment both of its foreign policy and of the USA's claims to an international leadership role.

CONCLUSIONS

The USA's cultural and strategic dependence on oil is substantial and growing. Thirty years ago the country was virtually self-sufficient in petroleum, but it now imports more than 60% of its oil needs. While most of this originates from Canada and Mexico, a steadily increasing proportion comes from the Middle East. The USA's desire to reduce this specific dependency through a policy of diversification of supply has had an influence on many aspects of its foreign policy. In its relations with Russia and the newly independent states of Central Asia, as well as relations with West Africa and Latin America, diversification of oil supply has been a contributing factor to the USA's foreign policy and diplomatic engagement. The extent of the 'oil factor' in these relationships varies, and is dependent on the wider strategic relationship and how important individual states are viewed in this strategic context. Since the terrorist attacks of 11 September 2001 that context has largely been shaped by the USA's execution of a 'war on terror'. The Bush Administration's policy of diversification of oil supply to the US economy was roundly and rightly criticized for its focus on US dependence on Persian Gulf oil in isolation to the global dependence on energy from this region. In defence of US policy, however, it could be argued that the pursuit of diversification had the concurrent benefit of bringing new supplies to the world market, thereby lessening the pace of the increasing dependence on the Gulf—albeit in a small way—and depressing price inflation.

Nevertheless, the most important and controversial aspect of the relationship between US foreign policy and oil remains the Middle East. It is important for several reasons. First, in its own right, as the Middle East is the site of up to 70% of the world's known petroleum reserves. While this is less important for the USA as a direct consumer of Gulf oil than it is for the other industrial and industrializing powers, it is an important strategic issue given overall US energy consumption and the dependence of the USA on the smooth running of the global economy. Second, it is important because this region is also the main theatre of the 'war on terror', being the location for the US-led coalition's military action in Afghanistan and Iraq and the origin of the ideas, finance and personnel behind much of the terrorism itself. As such, the Middle East has replaced Europe as the main focus for US foreign policy, with political reform and democratization of the region becoming strategic goals of US policy. A third and related aspect of this relationship is the widespread accusation that US foreign policy towards the region in general, and Iraq in particular, is motivated by a desire to control the region's oil interests. While there are many reasons to dispute this crude analysis of the relationship, the fact that this view is so widespread, both in the Middle East and internationally, makes the perception a problem for US foreign policy towards the region. A fourth reason is the oil dependence of some of the other great powers, and the resultant impact that this has on the ability of the US Administration to apply diplomatic pressure on regimes such as that in Iran with regard to its alleged nuclear transgressions. The combination of these four factors means that oil security has become a complex and complicating factor in all of the USA's dealings with the Middle East. As the source of an increasing percentage of the world's growing energy demands, the Persian Gulf is the subject of US pressures to allow international involvement to develop and exploit these resources. As it is deemed to be the regional source of international terrorism, the Middle East has become the focus for the USA's 'forward strategy' for the 'transformation' of the region to allow greater political participation and individual rights and freedoms. In Iraq, the USA is committed to restoring internal security, civil order and the establishment of a democratic and benign regional power in the Middle East. In fulfilling this mission the US Administration must combat the widespread suspicion in Iraq and the region generally that its motives are self-interested and concern only the country's petroleum and gas reserves. The success of the USA in achieving this mission is of vital importance to its overall foreign policy goals in the Middle East, since failure to establish security and order in Iraq could mean that the net effect of removing Saddam Hussain from power would be profoundly to destabilize the entire region. Irrespective of how much the 'oil factor' motivated the USA's reasons for invading Iraq in 2003, Iraq has become a major factor in the security of oil supplies from the Middle East region as a whole as a result of the ongoing conflict there.

In the longer term, the USA's dependence on overseas sources of petroleum, both directly and indirectly through the dependence of the global economy, will continue to be a source of foreign policy vulnerability. Most immediately and problematically, its dependence on the Middle East complicates its task of pursuing the global 'war on terror'. In the long term the thirst for energy supplies from newly industrializing powers such as China and India is also likely to result in energy security becoming an issue in relations with these states. This may manifest itself as an issue with China over the disputed sovereignty of the South China Seas—an area believed to be rich in energy supplies—or in competition for energy supplies elsewhere in the world. Given the global dependence on Middle Eastern oil, it is also likely that the USA's ability to dominate policy towards this region will not go unchallenged by such states, especially if it is perceived as having a negative influence on energy supplies to the region. Differences in policy approach towards the Middle East are already apparent between the USA and its European allies. Similar differences may emerge as issues in relations with other energy-dependent states.

More broadly still, the USA's vast consumption of natural resources, including oil, has meant that it has spectacularly failed to address the threat to its security presented by global climate change. The USA has thus forfeited its ability to set the terms of the international regimes which need to be established to deal with this real and growing problem. When China and India eventually outstrip the USA in the production of 'greenhouse gases', as they are predicted to do, the ability of the USA to influence a regime to effect global reductions will necessarily involve trade-offs between other aspects of its power. Whether a market-based approach to global environmental futures can be made workable or not will require the USA and the other industrial countries to absorb some form of costs to effect change in this policy area. At present there is no evident political willingness to address this issue or indeed the expected gap between projected consumption and production trends by concerted efforts to reduce energy demand. Despite the USA's insistence on market-based solutions to the problem of global warming, there is no evident willingness to use taxation on petrol to reflect the true costs of oil consumption and dependence. Nor has Congress thus far proved able to overcome the objections of the oil companies and motor manufacturers to changing the consumption regulation for new vehicles beyond the levels set in 1975. Moreover, while alternative energy sources are being researched in the USA, there is no strategic policy to develop and introduce these technologies, and no tax incentives to do so, despite the rhetoric of President Bush and the efforts of reform-minded legislators. As a result, the USA—as the largest economy, the largest consumer of petroleum and gas, and the country that wastes most energy in its per-head consumption—will remain the most vulnerable to its strategic and cultural dependence on oil, with the influence on its foreign policy that this implies. Despite Bush's rhetorical embrace of the notion that the USA was 'addicted to oil' (in a speech in 2006), he subsequently showed no serious leadership in addressing ways significantly to reduce that addiction. As a self-confessed former alcoholic, he must know that recognizing addiction is an important first step to recovery, but without the next steps it is an insufficient and inadequate response to a dangerous and escalating hydrocarbon habit.

ENDNOTES

[1] Charles Krauthammer, 'At $4, Everybody Gets Rational', *Washington Post*, 6 June 2008.

[2] 'Stepping off the Gas', Editorial, *Washington Post*, 4 Sept. 2008.

[3] Jad Mouawad, 'Falling Oil Price Is a Positive Note Amid Turmoil', *New York Times*, 3 Oct. 2008.

[4] *Ibid.*

[5] Bill Vlasic, 'Car sales In America at 10 year low', *New York Times*, 2 July 2008.

[6] 'Fact Sheet: Energy Independence and Security Act of 2007'. See <www.whitehouse.gov/news/releases/2007/12/20071219-1.html> Accessed 25 Sept. 2008.

[7] 'President Bush Delivers State of the Union Address', 31 January 2006. See <www.whitehouse.gov/news/releases/2006/01/print/20060131-10.html> Accessed 28 Sept. 2008.

[8] See Ariel Cohen, 'Reducing US Dependence on Middle East Oil', Backgrounder No. 1926, April 2006, The Heritage Foundation. See <www.heritage.org/Research/Features/NationalSecurity/bg1926.cfm>. Accessed 2 Sept. 2006.

[9] Gail Collins, 'The Energy Drill', *New York Times*, 7 August 2008.

[10] Carl Hulse, 'Democrats Reluctantly Embrace Offshore Drilling', *New York Times*, 12 Sept. 2008.

[11] See 'Impacts of Increased Access to Oil and Natural Gas Resources in the Lower 48 Federal Outer Continental Shelf', Energy Information Agency, <www.eia.doe.gov/oiaf/aeo/otheranalysis/ongr.html>. Accessed 6 Oct. 2008.

[12] For an explanation of the US invasion of Iraq see David Hastings Dunn, 'Myths, Motivations and "Misunderestimations": The Bush Administration and Iraq', *International Affairs*, March 2003.

[13] Cited in Fred Pearce, 'Over a barrel?', *New Scientist*, 29 Jan. 2003, emphasis added. See <www.newscientist.com/article/dn3327-over-a-barrel.html>. Accessed 14 Sept. 2003.

[14] Irene Gendzier, 'Oil, Iraq and US Foreign policy in the Middle East', *Situation Analysis*, Issue 2, Spring 2003, p. 19.

[15] Ironically, occupants of SUVs are 11% more likely to die in an accident than people in cars due the higher probability of them rolling over and the less stringent safety standards that apply to the 'light truck' category in which they fall. Danny Hakim, 'Safety Gap Grows Wider Between SUV's and Cars', *New York Times*, 17 Aug. 2004.

[16] Owen Gutfreund, 'Driving Takes its Toll', *New York Times*, 4 Sept. 2004.

[17] Energy Information Administration, *International Energy Outlook 2002*, Washington, DC: US Government Printing Office (USGPO), 2002, p. 28. Cited by Gawdat Bahgat, 'The New Geopolitics of Oil: The United States, Saudi Arabia, and Russia', in *Orbis*, Vol. 47, No. 3, Summer 2003, p. 447.

[18] Michael T. Klare, 'Global Petro-Politics: The Foreign Policy Implications of the Bush Administration's Energy Plan', in *American Foreign Policy 04/05* (Annual Editions), Guilford, CT, McGraw-Hill/Dushkin, 2004, p. 161.

[19] Bahgat, op. cit, p. 448.

[20] Klare, op. cit, p. 161.

[21] Javier Blas and Ed Crooks, 'Growing share of cartel crude consumed by its own member nations', *Financial Times*, 11 Sept. 2007.

[22] Bahgat, op. cit, p. 448.

[23] Mamoun Fandy, 'US Oil Policy in the Middle East', *Foreign Policy In Focus*, Jan. 1997, p. 1. See <www.fpif.org/briefs/vol2/v2n4oil.html> Accessed 20 Aug. 2004.

[24] Fandy, op. cit, p. 1.

[25] David Cloud, 'US Set to offer Huge Arms Deal to Saudi Arabia', *New York Times*, 28 July 2007.

[26] Kenneth M. Pollack, 'Securing the Gulf', *Foreign Affairs*, July/Aug. 2003.

[27] *Ibid.*

[28] Quoted in Jimmy Carter, *Keeping Faith*, London, Collins, 1983, p. 473.

[29] Lizette Alvarez, 'Britain Says US Planned to Seize Oil in '73 Crisis', *New York Times*, 2 Jan. 2004.

[30] Cited by Barry Rubin, 'The Reagan Administration and the Middle East', in Oye, Lieber and Rothchild (eds), *Eagle Defiant: United States Foreign Policy in the 1980s*, Boston, MA, Little Brown and Co, 1983, pp. 375–76.

[31] Klare, op. cit, p. 162.

[32] Fandy, op. cit, p. 2.

[33] 'The Hidden Cost of Imported Oil: a National Defense Council Foundation Report', 30 October 2003. See <www.iags.org/n1030034.htm>. Accessed 6 Oct. 2008.

[34] Fandy, op. cit, p. 3.

[35] *Ibid.*

[36] Klare, op. cit. p. 162.

[37] Oliver Morgan, 'What If . . .', *The Observer*, 6 June 2004.

[38] Mark Mazzetti, 'Spy Agencies Say Iraq War Worsens Terrorism Threat', *New York Times*, 24 Sept. 2006.

[39] Klare, op. cit, p. 162. This section draws upon the work of Michael Klare, as cited.

[40] Michael T. Klare, 'The Deadly Nexus: Oil, Terrorism, and America's National Security', *Current History*, Dec. 2002, p. 418.

[41] The definitive study on this connection is Terry Lynn Karl's, *The Paradox of Plenty: Oil Booms and Petro-States*, Berkley, CA, University of California Press, 1997.

[42] Nancy Birdsall and Arvind Subramanian, 'Saving Iraq from its Oil', *Foreign Affairs*, Vol. 83. No. 4, July 2004, p. 77.

[43] *Ibid.*, p. 81.

[44] *Ibid.*, p. 77.

[45] *Ibid.*, p. 82.

[46] Jay M. Shafritz, Phil Williams, and Ronald S. Calinger, *The Dictionary of 20th Century World Politics*, New York, Henry Holt, 1993, p. 503.

[47] Morgan, op. cit.

[48] Gerald Segal, *Guide to the World Today*, London, Simon and Schuster, 1988, p. 68.

[49] Cited by Tony Emerson, 'The Thirst For Oil', *Newsweek*, 8–15 April 2002, p. 34.

[50] *Ibid.* For the global economy the figures are slightly different, calculated at 7.6% of GDP in 1979 and 2% now. Philip Coggan, 'Why you shouldn't let high oil prices get you down', *Financial Times*, 7–8 August 2004.

[51] R. James Woolsey, Amory B. Lovins, and L. Hunter Lovins, 'Energy Security: It takes more than drilling', *Christian Science Monitor*, 29 March 2002.

[52] See 'Event Summary: Global Challenges for US Energy Policy: Economic, Environmental, and Security Risks', 5 March 2004, at <www.brook.edu/comm/op-ed/20040305environment.htm> Accessed 5 Sept. 2004.

[53] Coggan, op. cit.

[54] Felicity Barringer, 'Bush Record: New Priorities in Environment', *New York Times*, 14 Sept. 2004.

[55] 'Dangerous Addiction: Ending America's Oil Dependence', National Resources Defense Council Report. See <www.nrdc.org/air/transportation/oilsecurity/execsum.asp> Accessed 9 Sept. 2004.

[56] Woolsey, *et al*, op. cit.

[57] Klare, 'Global Petro-Politics', op. cit, p. 160.

[58] Woolsey, *et al*, op. cit.

[59] Emerson, op. cit, p. 34.

[60] Bahgat, op. cit, p. 449.

[61] As Woolsey notes, 'I don't think the problem is resolved by the United States buying less oil in the Middle East and having other people buying more from them. That's a particularly stupid decision. Solutions that point towards changing the pattern of oil consumption in that way don't deserve the time of day.' R. James Woolsey cited in 'Event Summary: Global Challenges for US Energy Policy', op. cit.

[62] Bahgat, op. cit, p. 452.

[63] *Ibid.*

[64] Conal Walsh, 'West looks to Russia for a crisis solution', *The Observer*, 6 June 2004.

[65] Noam Scheiber, 'Where the Oil is', *New York Times*, 10 Nov. 2004.

[66] See 'Event Summary: Global Challenges for US Energy Policy', op. cit.

[67] See Walsh and Bahgat, p. 453.

[68] Klare, 'Global Petro-Politics', op. cit, p. 163.

[69] James Dao, 'In Quietly Courting Africa, US Likes the Dowry: Oil', *New York Times*, 19 Sept. 2004.

[70] Timothy Burn, 'Hunt for "new" oil', *Washington Times*, 28 Sept. 2003.

[71] Burn, op. cit, p.4.

[72] Burn, op. cit, p. 5.

[73] Burn, op. cit, p.7.

[74] Walter Pincus, 'US Africa Command Brings New Concerns', *Washington Post*, 28 May 2007.

[75] Cited by Klare in 'Global Petro-Politics', op. cit.

[76] Scheiber, op. cit.

[77] Paul Rogers, 'Iran: the next target?', 20 Jan. 2003, <www.opendemocracy.net/node/930>. Accessed 9 Sept. 2004.

[78] John Tatom, 'Iraqi oil is not America's objective', *Financial Times*, 17 Feb. 2003.

[79] 'All about oil?', *The Economist*, 25 Feb. 2003, p. 70.

[80] Daniel Yergin, 'A Crude View of the Crisis in Iraq', *Washington Post*, 8 Dec. 2002.

[81] See Ariel Cohen, op. cit, citing US Department of Energy, 'Iraq: Oil', Energy Information Administration Country Analysis Briefs, December 2005.

[82] .'The US Energy Outlook as of 2001', part of the Annual Energy Outlook 2001 Report, published by the US Department of Energy. See <www.eia.doe.gov/emeu/aer/eh/frame.html> Accessed 13 Sept. 2004.

US DEFENCE POLICY

Prof. DAVID ROBERTSON

INTRODUCTION

In some ways it could be argued that the USA does not have a defence policy at the moment. There are three related reasons as to why one might hold this view. The first is that the country is actually fighting a war and, as with strategy in general, policy seldom outlasts the first shock of action. Most of the intellectual energy of the USA's defence 'intelligentsia', as well as the resources of its military structures, are so absorbed in the global 'war on terror' that there is little left to craft a cohesive and sustainable general defence policy. The second principal reason, following directly from the first, is that the cost of current operations—in financial and military stock terms, as well as in manpower—is so enormous that no investment is being made to support any new long-term policy. Finally—and partially independent of the first two reasons—the recent Secretary of Defense, Donald Rumsfeld, had been fighting a war of his own against the established interests of the armed services, to overhaul radically both military structure and thinking, and, after nearly seven years, appeared to be no nearer victory. At the same time the imposition of Rumsfeld's immediate strategic views on the military made it extremely difficult for his senior commanders to pursue the war in ways that they understood.

Rumsfeld's replacement in December 2006 was Robert M. Gates, who became the 22nd Secretary of Defense (the office stems from an early Cold War reorganization of the US military defence structure). Most of Gates' experience has been in intelligence work—he was not only the Director of the Central Intelligence Agency (CIA) in 1991–93, but actually worked his way up to that post during a 27-year career in the Agency, the only person ever to achieve such a feat. As such, he probably brings a perspective to defence planning quite unlike either his predecessors or the professional military. This perspective ought to make it easier to craft sensitive policy within the boundaries of the global 'war on terror', and in particular within the context of the Iraq problem. It is far too early as yet to be sure of this. The whole defence policy position on Iraq is so highly politicized, particularly in an election year, that it would be difficult for it to be brought within a cohesive national defence policy. This, of course, is typical of defence policy—general plans and strategic calculations are ever held hostage to immediate crises and political commitments. The politics of the 2008 election campaign have probably made it inevitable that some form of major US troop withdrawal will take place from Iraq within the next two years. How complete this will be cannot be assessed, however. Probably a sizeable force, in the order of the continued commitment in the Republic of Korea (South Korea) more than half a century after the Korean War, will remain for decades. If anything, increasing requirements for US troops to be stationed in Afghanistan will offset part of the national benefit to any such withdrawal.

What had happened from early in the presidency of George W. Bush (2001–) was that Secretary of Defense Rumsfeld came into office determined radically to restructure the USA's defence posture: in this respect he was like Robert McNamara, his counterpart in the Administrations of John F. Kennedy (1961–63) and Lyndon B. Johnson (1963–69). Rumsfeld's ambitions and his own analysis of what needed to be changed were so out of tune with the military establishment that he saw the members of this establishment as having very little to contribute to the formulation of this new policy, and thus he turned them into political enemies almost overnight. This would have made the development and implementation of his policy extremely difficult at the best of times. However, the terrorist attacks of 11 September 2001 came soon after Rumsfeld started this campaign, and, as suggested, distracted everyone and made such a huge demand on resources that progress on the new policy became virtually impossible. In much the same way, of course, escalation of the conflict in Viet Nam continually dogged McNamara's attempts to design efficient and cost-effective defence policy. However, McNamara did manage to control the nuclear policy of the country. Rumsfeld arguably achieved no real change, but much disruption.

As Secretary of Defense, Rumsfeld exercised a virtually unprecedented intervention on operational matters, especially in Iraq, in which the spirit of his new policy ambitions thwarted the professional military's attempt to apply old policy ideas. The result can only be described as a mess. Probably never before in recent US history had so many senior officers in retirement (a retirement often entered earlier than they had planned) come out so vociferously against the political leadership of the Department of Defense. Moreover, opposition not only came from retired officers. At one stage the army leadership refused unconditionally to submit its budget plans to the Secretary of Defense, and attempted an independent campaign in Congress to have its financial demands accepted, in conflict with the overall departmental budget.

There has been an even deeper and more general problem about creating a defence policy at this time in US history. With the current US Administration due to be replaced in early 2009, a new defence policy is inevitable, and if the Democrats take over the White House it is likely to cause a major reform of defence thinking. Defence policies are long-term plans for the security of a nation, and depend as much on broad foreign policy, even domestic policy, goals as they do on technical assessment by military professionals. Defence policy is ideological in the sense that it can only grow from far deeper national consensuses on the posture that the country should hold towards the world community. In this sense US defence policy has always been exactly that: a defence policy. Defence in this sense involves: first, ensuring the physical safety of the nation; and second, protecting genuine national interests abroad. In the 19th century, for example, this meant two things: protecting the white population from the native Americans as settlers moved west; and protecting the merchant navy, and commerce more generally, from foreign naval threats. In view of this, it was possible to construct a simple defence policy, which, given that the internal security threat was weak and short-lived, essentially meant that the USA should have a strong navy. During the first half of the 20th century the protection of external vital interests broadened somewhat with the realization that international stability was probably worth investing in to an extent. Thus, the USA's very late intervention in the First World War did not fundamentally change the idea of a purely defensive defence policy. (Politically, it should be remembered that US intervention had a good deal to do with protection against German submarine attacks on US ships.) Even the massive intervention in world conflict undertaken in the Second World War was as much a matter of protecting national trading interests against Japanese expansionism as it was the use of force in Europe for more broadly value-laden aims.

Of course, this highly defensive orientation did not last into the second half of the 20th century. The stalemate in Europe along the frontier created by the further eastward penetration of US and British forces and the furthest westward penetration of Russian forces partitioned Europe and led to the Cold War and the development of the North Atlantic Treaty Organization (NATO) and the Warsaw Pact. The basic logic of defence policy remained, however. No one could pretend that the USA's interests would not be crucially affected if the whole of the European continent became communist. Whatever the inner truths of the cause of the Cold War may be, and however historians may apportion relative guilt for the ensuing 40 years of mutual suspicion and fear between the USA and the USSR, the core beliefs of US policy-makers were simple: the country was threatened in utterly crucial ways by an alliance thought to be dedicated to damaging it and its own allies. It was, above all, an era of conflicting nation-states and coalition blocs. The only difference between the geopolitics of the period from 1945 to 1990 and any previous period of European history was that the ideological conflict was so complete that the familiar method of seeking security through the balance of power between essentially similar states changed into a frozen bipolar balance. At no point in this entire period could the USA see itself as alone and beleaguered in a generally hostile world. The sheer fact of the Cold War made its allies easy to manage—they saw the USA as crucial to their own security, and accepted, willingly or otherwise, its leadership. Yet nor can the USA plausibly be accused of expansionist aims of its own—it might see enemies where others were less sure, but it had neither the intention nor the desire to do anything but protect itself and its friends from such aims. In short, the Cold War was not, from the US side in any case, an evangelical enterprise of exporting its own values.

It is this that has changed. The USA is no longer content to defend itself and its friends from an identifiable set of potentially hostile countries. In any ordinary terms, the USA and its overseas interests are now less threatened than they have been since before 1917. There is undeniably a small-scale threat of a sort from which the USA has hitherto been immune—terrorist attacks inside its borders. This is a shock to US citizens, though something that their European allies have long been used to. It has great political resonance, but is essentially trivial as a problem around which to design a defence policy. And yet the political leaders of US defence see things very differently. A single quotation from the Secretary of Defense's preface to the latest *Quadrennial Defense Review*, published in February 2006, serves to demonstrate this: 'Now in the fifth year of this global war, the ideas and proposals in this document are provided as a roadmap for change, leading to victory.'

The problem with this shift in emphasis from an essentially passive 'defence' model to an active model—which contemplates intervention across the world even where the USA's interests are not directly at stake—is that it provides very little basis for constructing a general defence policy. (Interestingly, the same document refers to a shift from a 'threat-based' policy to a 'capabilities-based policy'; that is, preparing the USA to defend against any possible challenge, rather than ones identified as coming from nations with the ambition to hurt the USA.) Nor does it really allow for structuring the defence machine, except that the one safe guess is that the military will need more of almost everything. To attempt to construct a defence policy against this background would be difficult at any time. To do so while the country sees itself at war is virtually impossible. Consider, if this sounds strange, the following simple question: What was the United Kingdom's defence policy in 1943? In 1933, six years before the start of the Second World War, the country had a policy, but in 1943 the only intelligent answer to the policy question would be 'to win the war we're in'.

Again, recent electoral politics may alter the situation. Even if the Republicans win the presidency, it seems almost inevitable that the neo-conservative shift in foreign and defence policy outlined above will be eroded, if not completely reversed. Yet while this may happen at an official level, it will take some time to remove the structural changes it has brought about in the military apparatus. One example will suffice. In 2007 the Department of Defense announced a reorganization to create an Africa Command alongside, and of equal status to, the long-term command structure which recognizes the Pacific Rim (Pacific Command), Europe (European Command), Latin America (Southern Command), the Middle East (Central Command) and North America (Northern Command) as the basis both for defence policy-making and future potential combat command structures. Widespread opposition to this change in Africa itself demonstrates, unfairly or otherwise, that suspicions of US intention to continue the export of its values at the point of a gun will take years to eradicate. It will help to understand the current problems if we look briefly at a simpler period in US military history, namely the Cold War.

US DEFENCE POLICY, 1945–90

Arguably, the USA did not have a fully fledged defence policy until the Cold War, that is, until sometime in the late 1940s. Very rapidly after the end of the Second World War relations between the two real victors, the USA and the USSR, descended into what came to be known as the Cold War. There were two reasons for this. First, technological change, most notably the development of nuclear weapons and long-range bombers, meant that the USA could no longer regard itself as immune to attack at home. Second, an extended conception of national interest now led the USA to feel that it needed to protect friendly countries from third party attack not, as in the past, after the event of invasion, but on a permanent basis. The so-called Truman Doctrine, unveiled in 1947, stated that the USA would now aid democratic countries against both internal and external enemies. At this stage they were referring to the USSR, subsequently joined by the People's Republic of China, which US foreign policy analysts were convinced were part of an international conspiracy to overthrow capitalist democracies everywhere. The USA's own interests, therefore, were at stake in distant places where their two main enemies were thought to be active. This included not only Western Europe, directly faced by Soviet military might, but at that stage South Korea, which had been attacked by the communist Democratic People's Republic of Korea (North Korea) in 1950.

From this point onwards all the ingredients of defence policy had to be worked out with all its interconnections. At the risk of over-simplification, one can see defence policy as having the following six components:

general ideological presuppositions;
identification of the enemy;
strategic aims;
war fighting theory (military doctrine);
consequent procurement policy;
manpower policy.

Many other similar lists could be drawn up, all of which would focus on the fact that the first task when formulating a defence policy is to understand the world and its threats, after which the enemy must be identified. Once this has been established, it has to be decided how to prevent the perceived foe from causing harm. The next step in the process is to decide how to effect this prevention. This latter step is where issues become complex and interrelated as it involves theories about how combat should be engaged, which technology should be used and how many troops, and of what sort, would be required. There is no single line of causality here, however, and value judgements, influenced by sometimes quite separate political preferences, come into consideration. A very over-simplified example will serve. In the 1950s one might choose to fight in Europe either with a very large army equipped with relatively simple and cheap low-technology weapons, as, essentially, did the USSR. Or one might prefer a small, highly technological army, relying on a superior scientific and industrial base to make up for lower troop numbers. A number of different factors had to be taken into account here. Could the country maintain conscription, or was this politically unfeasible? Could it afford a large army, given the level of military manpower costs for professional soldiers? (Conscripts are cheap, but ineffective when required to use high technology weapons without adequate training.) How would any of these answers work with the allies? Even the USA could not manage an entirely 'go it alone' policy, and thus for the first time in its history found itself having to 'manage' an alliance. All of these and many more questions had to be answered, and they had to be answered theoretically, as there was little or no evidence or experience on which to base planning and, therefore, policy. Mistakes made out of ignorance could prove extremely costly.

The Second World War provided many examples of pre-war theory leading to the wrong arms procurement policy. The United Kingdom's air defence policy was nearly fatally weak because the ministry responsible for it was committed to a theory that 'the bomber would always get through', leading to an inadequate procurement for Fighter Command and near defeat in the Battle of Britain. Germany, on the other hand, not expecting to engage in strategic bombardment, had put all its effort into army co-operation bombers, which were ill-equipped for the bombardment of London. Both the United Kingdom and the USA had failed to believe those who preached that the superiority of air attack made classical battleships redundant, and therefore lost battleships and were late in developing aircraft carriers.

If similar mistakes were made in the 1950s they could have had catastrophic results because there was, by this time, a new element that any defence policy had to take into consideration, namely the advent of nuclear weapons. The immediate impact of this new dimension was to suggest that future wars might be far too short to allow anyone's industrial base to compensate for theoretical mistakes made in peacetime planning. By the late 1950s the USA had, after a number of false starts and hesitations, designed its first fully fledged defence policy, which, with some change in detail, remained in place for almost 40 years. The main components (and the contrasts with today are marked) were:

An ideology which saw the world in terms of an inevitable struggle for supremacy between two entire systems—communism and capitalist democracy. Now the USA sees itself faced with a much more amorphous opposition, which is also seen as irrational and therefore incapable of any negotiated stalemate.

The identification of both the USSR and China as jointly and separately the threat against which US interests had to be defended. Now no single nation-state represents the enemy, but instead a multi-headed hydra, only contingently connected to any state.

A strategic aim based on both factors above, which foresaw the need to fight more than one major war simultaneously. (Originally defined as two-and-a-half major wars, the Korean campaign and later the Viet Nam War highlighted the fact that 'proxy' wars where the USA saw itself fighting against agents of its superpower enemies had to be factored in.) The entire idea of measuring force against expected wars has had to be abandoned.

A war fighting theory, which was originally one of nuclear deterrence supported by the capacity to fight highly technological conventional wars under the 'nuclear umbrella'. This also increasingly involved a preparedness to use limited nuclear strikes, described as 'theatre' or 'battlefield' weapons, along with conventional forces. War fighting theory now stresses the need for light and rapidly deployable conventional forces. Yet it is also committed to a fallback position of traditional heavy forces, and still retains a reliance on nuclear weapons.

A very heavy investment in military technology, including maintaining surplus industrial capacity for 'surge' production if, or when, a real war broke out. The shape of necessary economic and industrial underpinnings is currently a matter of hot debate.

A reliance after the Viet Nam War on a purely voluntary, and therefore expensive, manpower structure for the armed forces. This was partly the consequence of the huge political pressure the military—faced with heavy casualties—came under to conscript soldiers to fight in Viet Nam, and partly resulted from the difficulty experienced in training a short-service conscript army to the levels required for the war-fighting doctrine that had been adopted. The military currently sees itself as overstretched, relies heavily on reserves and is openly talking about the difficulty of maintaining the all-volunteer force concept.

As an example of the interrelatedness of all components in the defence policy equation we can consider the most important aspect of nuclear policy: that the USA's early monopoly on nuclear weapons did not last very long. The USSR had exploded an atomic device by 1949 (only four years after the USA had used them to end the war in the Pacific) and a full-scale nuclear weapon by 1954. Before 1954 US defence policy had not fully adapted to the implications of nuclear warfare. Operational plans up to the mid-1950s treated nuclear weapons merely as very big conventional bombs, and the plans were based on all-out strategic bombardment of the USSR by the combined US armed forces. No retaliation that could not be controlled by conventional air defences was anticipated. While the USA would not willingly use these weapons, it was not realized that they could not safely be used. The arrival of a roughly equal Soviet nuclear capacity coincided with the design stages of the intercontinental ballistic missile, against which there could be no defence. The first use of such an armoury became impossible, and this left a major hole in US thinking, particularly once it had been realized that the USSR intended to maintain in Eastern Europe a huge conventional military force, which the USA and its NATO allies were unwilling to match because of its expense. The official policy had been to use the much weaker NATO ground forces, especially those dedicated to the defence of West Berlin, Germany, as a 'tripwire'. They were there to put up an initial defence so that any attacker would have to make its intentions quite plain. However, they were not expected to win any battles. Instead, immediate massive nuclear retaliation would be brought down on the Soviet forces and their homeland. This was all that NATO could convince itself to afford. A standing army and air force large enough to participate in a drawn-out campaign against the Warsaw Treaty Organization, as the USSR and its allies were known, would be vastly more expensive than the provision, almost entirely by the USA itself, of huge nuclear forces.

Large-scale Soviet intercontinental ballistic missile forces made this scenario impossible, and the USA was obliged to conceive a nuclear policy that was purely a deterrent. Effectively, nuclear weapons, or other strategic weapons capable of attacking the USSR or the USA, existed simply to prevent the other side from using them, and thus defence policy became a stand-off. This stand-off could, in a sense, be precisely calculated, and the results of the calculation were known as Mutual Assured Destruction, or, as an acronym, the much lampooned 'MAD'. The logic was that the USA needed a strategic force capable of taking a major first strike from the USSR, after which it would still be in possession of sufficient capabilities to inflict unacceptable damage on the Soviet territory. For convenience, unacceptable damage was defined as the destruction of 30% of the population and 70% of the industrial capacity—a figure which happened to fit a cost effectiveness point on a planning graph, and which gave a precise size for the needed US armoury. As technology developed (including the creation of more accurate missiles and more invulnerable systems such as submarine-launched ballistic missiles), the equations could be re-run and different scenarios could be calculated for other requirements. This included negotiations towards a reduction in force levels at international conferences, such as occurred at the various stages of the Strategic Arms Limitation Talks in the 1970s and 1980s. Nuclear strategy has never quite settled down since this period. The USA certainly retains a large nuclear arsenal, but it has found it more useful to refit many of its missiles and delivery systems for precision conventional roles. There has been continued talk about, and investment in, strategic defence—what used to be called Anti-Ballistic Missile (ABM) technologies—but no widespread deployment or successful systems. If anything, the emphasis in nuclear policy has been on attempting to prevent other nations from developing weapons of mass destruction rather than on enhancing US capacity.

Many further elements of defence policy could be quite precisely calculated given these basics. It is the sudden lack of this ability to calculate, owing to the shift of underlying logic to the defence policy, which has caused most of the current problems. Before 1990, however, it was relatively easy. For example, while it was impossible to keep any army in Europe which could immediately defend against a Soviet conventional attack, use of reserves might make it possible for the USA to come to the aid of its European allies given time. The calculations suggested that the USA could afford a standing force in Europe, which, with the aid of the European members of NATO, could hold back a Soviet attack for 10 days; this was acknowledged as sufficient time in which to mobilize reserves and transport reinforcements across the Atlantic, given some reliance on smaller and more limited 'battlefield' or 'theatre' nuclear weapons. Hence recruitment and training, as well as deployment and equipment policies, all fell into place. All such complex policies were subject to endogenous shocks by technological change and altered behaviour by the assumed enemy. Thus, for example, a whole new chapter in NATO–Warsaw Treaty Organization relations, and therefore US defence policy, was opened in the late 1970s simply because the USSR decided to modernize its own 'theatre' nuclear weapons. This occurred just as President Ronald Reagan took office in the USA in 1981, beginning the final arms race of the Cold War. Even the USA's economy ultimately found the cost of maintaining the original posture—the ability to fight two-and-a-half conventional wars simultaneously—to be prohibitive. Steadily, this was scaled down: towards the end of the Cold War the target had become one-and-a-half wars—essentially a major war in Europe and a secondary conflict in Asia. However, the pressure on the USSR was far greater, and suddenly, long before defence policy-makers expected or could begin to reconsider, the Cold War was essentially over. At this point US defence policy collapsed.

US DEFENCE POLICY BETWEEN THE COLD WAR AND 2000

If one examines the check list of components suggested earlier, one can see the problem for policy-makers that occupied US Administrations up to the early years of George W. Bush's presidency.

General ideological presuppositions: how does the world work when there is only one superpower, but when, at the same time, war breaks out in several different places, above all in the former Yugoslavia and in the Middle East?

Identification of the enemy: there is no longer an enemy, but there remain numerous countries with which the USA might have to engage in combat. Nevertheless, at this stage it is still actual potential enemy countries which the USA sees as the problem. Yet, since the enemy has gone away, the old allies in NATO can no longer be relied on automatically to support the USA. The idea of 'defence burden sharing', by which the USA could count on major Western European countries spending around 3% of their gross domestic product each year towards a common defence purpose, has collapsed.

Strategic aims: what were they? To protect the USA and its interests, of course. But against what and whom?

War fighting theory (military doctrine): the only certainty was that warfare would not be like the heavy tank battles and possible small nuclear strikes for which the USA had trained. But how should the USA fight this unnamed battle?

Consequent procurement policy: technological marvels continued to be produced, but were they going to be appropriate for the unknown battle?

Manpower policy: with nuclear weapons no longer making up for manpower shortages, what size army did the USA need, and what size could it afford?

The politics of the 1990s and the end of the Cold War all played into these considerations. However much the US Administrations observed a need to maintain military capacity, the inability to point to any clear threat made it impossible to ignore the political demand for what came to be known as the 'Peace Dividend'—that is, a reduction in military expenditure.

The size of the original decrease in military expenditure is shown in Table 1.

Table 1. Items of the US Defence Budget
(US $ million at constant 2006 prices, federal years)

	1990	2000	2006
Military personnel	137,449	91,684	111,286
Operation and maintenance	135,028	129,859	148,437
Procurement	107,492	60,947	78,041
Research, development, testing and evaluation	49,252	43,383	69,356
Military construction	6,929	5,743	7,809
Family housing	4,228	3,936	4,242
Total (incl. other items)	439,984	341,779	421,116

Source: adapted from the Department of Defense's *Annual Report to the President and the Congress*, 2006.

Compared with 1985, the height of President Reagan's arms race against the USSR, by the end of the 20th century total defence expenditure in real terms had fallen by more than 30%. The procurement element fell to only 40% of Reagan's figure, and even now is barely 50% of the 1985 high. That the military personnel figure showed a smaller decline itself reveals much about manpower costs. Even in 2006, five years after the 2001 terrorist attacks, the expenditure on personnel was only 80% of the 1985 figure. These expenditures are ongoing and a major element is a combination of the generous pensions and health care benefits for service personnel and their families, which continue to be paid after the period of service has been completed. One indicator of the real costs of recruitment is that the money spent on family housing, at US $4,242m. in 2006, is virtually the same as in 1985, for a much smaller troop strength. This element is beginning to be a serious strain on the defence budget. The new defence posture requires such heavy troop deployment and increases the risk that all troops must face that re-recruitment has become very difficult. Thus far, the Department of Defense has attempted to deal with the problem by massively increasing the recruitment drive. An extra 3,000 recruiters were employed in 2005. In addition, very large financial incentives are being given to troops to sign up for second and subsequent tours of duty—some of the highest are in excess of $100,000. If one adds the inevitable increases in death and injury payouts, the actual cost per soldier of employment is escalating. One recent estimate is that it takes an average of $112,000 to maintain one service member on active duty for one year. Part of the problem is that both pay and other terms have had to improve to help recruitment, so that between 2000 and 2004 the manpower compensation costs for active duty forces rose by 29%, to a total of $158,000m. The report from which this is drawn suggests that an extra 200,000 personnel would have to be recruited to allow continued deployment at the current level. The US Congress considered imposing restrictions on how long anyone could be required to serve on active duty, restrictions which the Department of Defense viewed as unattainable. A Democrat majority in both houses of Congress might enforce such a change in the next few years, requiring either a reduction in commitment or even more expensive manpower increases. Some such movement has already occurred. According to the Department of Defense's budget plans for 2009, the army will increase by 65,000 and the Marine Corps by 5,000—at a total increase in manpower budget costs of $20,500m., most of the increase being intended to extend the period between deployments. The problem of estimating the total defence costs is made worse by uncertainty about just how much money initially authorized by Congress will in fact be appropriated. For example, the budget plan quoted from above has a total cost of $515,400m.—with an extra $70,000m. being requested as 'an emergency allowance for the Global War on Terror'—but goes on to say that details will be given to Congress when actual deployments are known.

This adds to the very considerable costs of this part of the defence budget without necessarily giving much defence value at any one time. There had, in fact, been a major reduction in the number of uniformed personnel who could be deployed by 2000. In the mid-1990s, that is, after the first Gulf War, the intention had been to reduce the US armed forces to a total of 1.4m. servicemen (from 2.2m. in 1988). A direct quotation from the 1995 Secretary of Defense's *Report to Congress* demonstrates how the Administration of the time was congratulating itself on reducing the size of the USA's military might:

> The Department plans to continue the force and personnel drawdown as initiated in previous years. The Army will reduce from 24 divisions during FY 1992 to 20 divisions by FY 1995 (12 active and 8 Reserve component). The Navy's Battle Force ships will decrease in number from 467 in FY 1992 to 373 in FY 1995. Included in the totals is a reduction of one aircraft carrier, bringing the total to 11 active and one Reserve aircraft carriers. The Marine Corps will maintain its three active and one Reserve divisions. By the end of FY 1995, the Air Force will have reduced to about 21 fighter wing equivalents (13 active and 8 Reserve component) from 29 fighter wing equivalents in FY 1992. Other U.S. attack/fighter air forces will include 10 active and one Reserve Navy carrier wings and three active and one Reserve Marine Corps wings. Strategic bombers will be decreased from 209 in FY 1992 to 141 by the end of FY 1995. The Air Force will also reduce the number of intercontinental ballistic missiles from 930 in FY 1992 to 585 by the end of FY 1995.

These reductions were made in the context of a dramatic downsizing of defence plans for sustainable combat. The concept of fighting even one major war was dismissed. Now the target was to be able to engage in two 'major regional conflicts' (MRCs).

MAJOR REGIONAL CONFLICTS

The idea of structuring military forces on the basis of predictable conflict continued, with modification, to be the essence of defence planning until quite recently. These conflicts were defined in the following quotation, again from the Secretary of Defense's Report to Congress in 1995:

> The United States' strategy of engagement and enlargement requires forces which are able, in concert with regional allies, to fight and win two MRCs which occur nearly simultaneously. In contrast to the days of the Cold War, when the focus of military planning was on winning a large-scale war in Europe, the most likely scenarios today focus defense planning on fighting and winning regional conflicts on the scale of the 1991 Gulf War or a potential conflict in Korea. Because the timing and location of these regional conflicts are uncertain, the bulk of U.S. forces needed normally will not be in theater prior to the outbreak of conflict. Although in areas of high interests and high threat, some equipment is prepositioned and troops are forward deployed, most U.S. forces will deploy from their home bases. Therefore, U.S. defense planning must focus on ensuring that selected forces can quickly project power from the United States into regions important to its interests to defeat hostile regional powers. Often in these MRCs, the United States will be fighting as the leader of a coalition, with allies and friends providing some support and combat forces. In fact, the DoD [Department of Defense] assumes that regional allies will fight along with U.S. forces. It is also expected that other friends and allies from beyond the crisis area will contribute forces to any MRC. However, U.S. forces must be sized and structured to preserve the flexibility and the capability to act without them, if necessary.

Two things should be noted: the overt expectation of having to rely on allies, along with some barely hidden doubts as to the reliability of these allies, and the Department of Defense's own contrast with the Cold War period. The only hangover from that period is the continuing commitment to a more or less full-blooded conventional war in Korea. Admittedly, diplomatic successes in this theatre may allow a small further drawdown of US troops there. North Korea has, of course, in recent years become even more of a concern for US policy-makers, but the issue, a nuclear threat, is ironically not relevant in manpower assessment.

The only obvious change in the hardware side envisaged in this defence review was the emphasis on what was technically known as the 'power projection' need. This remained a major problem for the USA as it had not successfully built up its capacity with sufficient speed to ship large numbers of men and large amounts of equipment to the areas where they wished to intervene. No military forces are ever really adequately equipped in this logistical aspect. The reason is simple: generals and admirals are almost exclusively men who have risen through the relatively glamorous combat units of their services—they have commanded armoured divisions, fighter or bomber wings, destroyer squadrons or aircraft carriers. They have very little personal interest in the necessary but mundane fleet replenishment ships, heavy cargo planes or supply transport companies. Furthermore, military procurement budgets are arrived at competitively. That is to say that each service competes for the biggest possible share of an overall defence budget, as opposed to a neutral arbiter from outside defining the tasks and then allotting them rationally to functional purposes. The budgets never grant sufficient funds to satisfy each of the separate services, especially as each service is competing to be the most important. Competition is for roles as much as for hardware or manpower. Each service wants to make itself as capable as possible of carrying out any task that the nation might need. Given all of this, no one in a senior position in any of the services will allot much of their funding to the routine logistics and transport capacities.

Inter-service rivalry is rife in all modern departments of defence, but it has had a peculiarly important role in the USA, despite periodic congressional attempts to force co-operation and 'joint service thinking'. Indeed, one of the things that recommended the MAD policy to Robert McNamara, who introduced the policy in the 1960s, was that it was a way of controlling the endless demands from all three services to be the USA's main nuclear force. Each service employs its own team of congressional lobbyists to campaign among congressmen for its pet projects during the budgetary cycle. During the Cold War the tasks could be relatively easily allotted in a rational manner among the three main services, the army, navy and air force. However, now that the classic battlefield or naval campaign is no longer relevant, no service has any obvious claim to carry out any specific set of tasks—all are needed, but they are needed only in a co-operative and unified way. Thus, controlling the separate service demands and holding down their ambitions and rivalries has become both more necessary and more difficult for the Secretary of Defense than ever before. This was perhaps the single major task Donald Rumsfeld set himself in 2000, and was probably the area in which he was least successful.

The most obvious missing part of defence policy towards the end of the 20th century was, of course, the nuclear dimension, and this has two quite separate components. The nuclear enemy has, more or less, disappeared. However, from the perspective of the defence planner, the single, well-equipped enemy—the USSR—was in many ways easier to handle than what they now fear, which is nuclear proliferation either to previously non-nuclear states or to non-state actors, most commonly labelled 'terrorists'. There is in fact a further distinction to be drawn. There is, on the one hand, a concern about otherwise non-threatening states like India and Pakistan obtaining nuclear weapons. However, the real fear, as has been shown by the USA's and Europe's diplomatic activity in 2004–08, is that what US thinkers sometimes call 'rogue states', such as Iran, may obtain them. The thinking is that Iran—and in the past Libya—might use such weapons to aid terrorist or other pan-national campaigns against the USA, not simply in pursuit of their own regional power struggles. Iran continues to this day to be such a concern, but it has been joined by North Korea. Either way the USA remained convinced that some form of threat, albeit a very 'formless' threat, continued to exist in the nuclear world. This led to the retention of a very sizeable strategic nuclear capacity, largely in the hands of the navy's submarine squadrons. There is little difference in such thinking, or in the relevant budgetary appropriations, between the immediate post-Cold War period and the most recent policy formulations. The other dimension is that of defence against a ballistic missile attack. President Reagan's Strategic Defense Initiative, popularly known as 'Star Wars', attracted much attention and not a little scorn in the mid- and late 1980s, but interest has, in recent years, largely dropped away. However, the programme has never been shut down, and even under the Administration of President Bill Clinton continued to command sizeable funding. Table 2 demonstrates funding figures for three years: 1990, in the middle of the Republican Administration of George Bush, Sr; 2000, the last year for which President Clinton was responsible; and 2005. The relative sizes of these requirements have not changed since then.

Table 2. Expenditure on Anti-missile Defence
(US $ million at constant 2005 prices)

1990	2000	2005
6,680	4,100	9,000

Source: adapted from the Missile Defense Agency's *Ballistic Missile Defense Historical Funding*.

As the table demonstrates, President Clinton did reduce the programme's expenditure, but left a non-negligible activity. What is really noteworthy, though very seldom commented on, is the size of President George W. Bush's funding once the full threat of terrorist activities had been noted. Expenditure of US $9,000m. far exceeded that of any other year since the programme's inception.

The prevailing situation in the mid-1990s was thus: the plans made at that time controlled defence expenditure until at least 2001, because defence budgetary cycles are inevitably long—it can take 15 years from inception before a new weapons system is in operation. It is common to see the change in the 21st century as a consequence of the 11 September 2001 terrorist attacks on the USA and of the campaign to oust the regime of Saddam Hussain in Iraq in 2003, but in fact the politics of the changes pre-date these events. Clinton's defence reductions may have been unavoidable given both his own policy priorities and public expectations of the 'Peace Dividend'; certainly they were in line with the downward trend in other NATO countries since the early 1990s. They were, none the less, deeply unpopular among the right wing in US politics, and above all in the military, which some commentators believe to have become politicized in a way previously unknown in US history. Military history and sociology might well have predicted the latter development. Military organizations that have seen their prime *raison d'être* vanish, as the US military did after the Cold War, become anxious about their status, and indeed their livelihoods, and deeply resent 'downsizing'. What angered the US military and the political right even more about budget, procurement and troop level reductions was the fact that the US military has had greater demands placed upon it since 1990 than at any other time since the Viet Nam War, with troops involved not only in the Gulf War and in the former Yugoslavia, but in several other places, most notably in Somalia. (Interestingly, this is not really highlighted by casualty figures; although 147 US troops were killed in the Gulf War, only another four were killed prior to 2001, while during the 1980s there were at least 81 deaths in combat situations.) There is little doubt that the military were stretched, however, in terms of deployment over this period. In 2000 there were 12,000 troops deployed in potentially dangerous roles in the former Yugoslavia, mainly in Bosnia and Herzegovina and Croatia, as well as the long-term commitment to Western Europe, with 70,000 troops in Germany alone, and a further 37,000 troops stationed in South Korea. This overstretch has increased exponentially since the invasion of Iraq and the continuing need for troops in Afghanistan.

President George W. Bush entered office in 2001 committed to increasing defence expenditure. His inaugural address contained the ringing commitment that 'we will build our defenses beyond challenge, lest weakness invite challenge'. The first major and detailed policy statement of the new Administration was the Secretary of Defense's Report to Congress for 2002. The events of September 2001 had influenced the statement, although the plans were clearly not merely a rushed response to that event. The Report represented the first serious attempt to construct an overall defence policy for the new uncertain role of the sole remaining superpower. Clinton's defence policy in the 1990s was largely reactive, and, as has been indicated, was still set in terms of a specified number of wars, though now less major ones, in which the USA would be engaged. Thus, in 2002 four major policy goals were identified:

assuring allies and friends;
dissuading future military competition;
deterring threats and coercion against US interests;
if deterrence fails, decisively defeating any adversary.

Deterrence had clearly resurfaced as a major concept, allied to something which was really deterrence in another guise, namely 'dissuasion'. This last referred to managing the whole gamut of training, research and doctrinal thinking, etc., in such a way as maximally to 'dissuade other countries from initiating future military competitions'. What is really innovative, and deserves the full title of a defence policy, is an unusually clear account of how the USA intends to go about thinking about its military needs. The US Government termed this a 'capabilities-based' approach, and it is intended to circumnavigate the problem of not having an identifiable enemy much of the time. A fuller quotation is required to give the full flavour of the approach:

> The new U.S. defense strategy is built around the concept of shifting to a 'capabilities-based' approach to defense. That concept reflects the fact that the U.S. cannot know with confidence what nation, combination of nations, or non-state actors will pose threats to vital U.S. interests or those of our allies and friends decades from now. It is possible, however, to anticipate the capabilities that an adversary might employ to coerce its neighbors, deter the U.S. from acting in defence of its allies and friends, or directly attack the U.S. or its deployed forces. A capabilities-based model—one that focuses more on how an adversary might fight than on whom the adversary might be and where a war might occur—broadens the strategic perspective. It requires identifying capabilities that U.S. military forces will need to deter and defeat adversaries who will rely on surprise, deception, and asymmetric warfare to achieve their objectives. Because such adversaries are looking for U.S. military vulnerabilities and building capabilities to exploit them, the Department is shoring up potential weak spots (e.g., by strengthening our information protection capabilities and developing countermeasures to anti-access threats) to close off such avenues of attack.

Whether it is feasible to plan like this time alone will tell, but the idea is essentially that a country calculates how exactly it might come under attack, and defends against those possibilities. In the past the theory, more or less throughout the world, had been to establish where the attack might originate, identify what they could and would be prepared to do, and defend against this 'threat assessment'. Although certainly not invented solely as a response to the September 2001 terrorist attacks, it is a policy better able, in principle, to cope with such unexpected, 'out of the box' attacks. There are elements of the past still, indeed eagerly, included. So we hear that 'the new U.S. defense strategy restores the emphasis once placed on defending the United States and its land, sea, air, and space approaches'. In fact, defending the USA in this sense has not been necessary since the 19th century. The clear meaning of the policy is to prepare the USA for intervention anywhere—the capabilities in question are the potential capabilities of countries which may challenge US interests in a non territorial way.

The problem with the 'capabilities-based' approach is an obvious one: if it were to be carried out thoroughly, it would be horrendously expensive and would produce a society continually concerned about risk whatever the actual world situation. It would only make sense, if at all, given a perception of the world as innately hostile to the USA. It is also a policy tailored towards the military, and towards those in favour of military procurement, because there is no obvious level at which one can set military assets. The 1995 Defense Policy statement discussed earlier set specific targets—the ability to fight two more or less simultaneous MRCs. This allowed the Department of Defense precisely to quantify its needs:

> Detailed analyses of possible future MRCs suggest that the following forces will be adequate to successfully fight and win a single MRC, assuming that DoD continues to make critical programmed enhancements to the capabilities of these forces and their supporting assets. 5 Army divisions; 10 Air Force fighter wing equivalents; up to 100 Air Force heavy bombers; 4–5 Navy aircraft carrier battle groups; 1–2 Marine Expeditionary Forces; Special operations forces.

Although the 2002 Report listed the forces it aimed to build up, they were not, and could not be, calculated against a specific need. The strength of the total US military in 2002 is shown in Table 3. At this stage it was clearly assessed as barely adequate.

Table 3. Reported US Military Capability, 2002

Army	
Divisions (active/National Guard)	10/8
Heavy Armored Cavalry/Light Cavalry Regiments	1/1
Enhanced separate brigades (National Guard)	15
Navy	
Aircraft carriers	12
Carrier air wings (active/reserve)	10/1
Amphibious ready groups	12
Attack submarines	55
Surface combatants (active/reserve)	108/8
Combat logistic force ships	33
Maritime patrol and reconnaissance air wings (active/reserve)	4/1
Helicopter anti-submarine light wings	2

Air Force	
Active fighter squadrons	46
Reserve fighter squadrons	38
Reserve air defense squadrons	4
Bombers (combat-coded)	112
Marine Corps	
Divisions (active/reserve)	3/1
Air wings (active/reserve)	3/1
Force service support groups (active/reserve)	3/1

Source: adapted from the Department of Defense's *Annual Report to the President and the Congress*, 2004.

This does not look enormously different from any similar table for the last 10–15 years, and the only real difference has been in the increased use of reserve forces and the period of time that US troops have been deployed abroad. However, the current Administration has taken a much tougher stance with the military in one respect: it was noticeable during the Iraq campaign that the Secretary of Defense, Donald Rumsfeld, himself was far more involved than previous practice (and arguably constitutional theory) would have predicted. In particular, Rumsfeld was known to have insisted on much lighter troop strengths for the invasion of Iraq than the military leaders thought were adequate. In retrospect he was proved to be right, of course, as far as the conduct of the conflict itself was concerned. This brings us to the main single problem facing the new style US defence policy, one that goes back to the basics in terms of war fighting theory and procurement and manpower needs. None of the conflicts in which the USA has been involved since the end of the Cold War can really be seen to have tested its defence capacity for the new century, because in all of them the USA has been able to fight very nearly a conventional war, and one, until the end of the actual major combat period in Iraq, which resulted in a very small number of US fatalities. From the invasion of Iraq in March 2003 until 30 April (the official end of 'major combat operations') the USA lost 139 people, 109 of these being defined as losses caused by hostile action, roughly the same figure as the country lost in the 1991 Gulf conflict. However, between 1 May 2003 and 30 September 2005 the USA lost a further 1,761 people to hostile action. By September 2006 this had risen to at least 2,700 deaths, and by September 2007 the figure stood at 3,332. At the time of writing the figure stands at over 4,000, though the partial success of the so-called 'surge' strategy has led to a marked fall in the recent monthly casualty rate. Thus the rate of US military deaths for July 2008 was 86% lower than the rate for July 2007, and indeed lower than earlier months in 2008.

That nearly 700 troops died in 2007 was itself a consequence of the US troop 'surge' between February and June of that year, by which 30,000 extra US troops were despatched to Iraq in an attempt to quell the various insurgencies. In contrast, the death rate in the much smaller war in Afghanistan is increasing, from fewer than 100 US military deaths per year up to 2006 to 117 in 2007 and 142 thus far in 2008. With the Department of Defense recently turning its attention to this theatre, and British calls for a 'surge' of up to 30,000 allied troops in the area, this increase can only continue.

The casualty rate in Iraq is by some distance the highest rate experienced by the US military since its campaign in Viet Nam. Until the post-war duties in Iraq, the USA had been allowed to fight extremely traditional conventional wars where its armoured ground forces and high technology air forces were essentially invulnerable. Where, as in Kosovo and elsewhere in the former Yugoslavia, ground combat was needed, it was almost entirely carried out by allied ground forces. This is actually in keeping with the Nixon Doctrine, pronounced in 1972, that while the USA would continue to come to its allies' assistance as promised in the 1947 Truman Doctrine, it would henceforth do this with naval and air resources, and not risk US lives in ground combat. This applied to a very large extent even in the post-11 September 2001 military actions in Afghanistan. Indeed, despite extensive news coverage of US forces on the ground, most of their activity was relatively safe air support, and casualties were minimal.

However, this is not the warfare for which the USA has to prepare. US defence policy must be aimed specifically at the sort of situation it is now facing—an extended, drawn out, low technology campaign to pacify elements of a mass population. It is the sort of conflict in which the French and British armies excelled during the 19th century, often described as the army being 'a colonial gendarmerie'. Most probably such a war cannot successfully be fought at all nowadays, because the equivalent of the under-armed and ignorant tribesmen are not particularly lightly armed, are not ignorant and have much more powerful ideologies in their support than used to be the case. There is no sign that the new and sophisticated intellectual framework of the Department of Defense's capabilities-based assessment can cope with this.

In part, the problem relates to the key element in the list of those components that comprise or drive defence policy: the ideological element. Essentially, the aim of US defence policy has changed in a way that makes the label of 'defence' policy only partly relevant. Certainly the terrorist attacks on New York and Washington, DC, reintroduced the idea of actually defending the homeland against direct attack, and considerable funding continues to go towards the Department of Homeland Security. Very little of this, however, involves the organized military. Although the continental USA may no longer be safe, it is still not vulnerable to the sort of attack that the ordinary units of the army, the air force or the navy are competent to handle. There are exceptions, naturally. The air force now has the added responsibility of providing some degree of combat air patrol capacity to cope with a repeat of the hijacked airliner attacks of 11 September 2001, but this is a trivial duty against its overall tasks and budget. Similarly, the navy has some additional duties in patrolling the coast line, but the USA already has a sizeable paramilitary force (the Coast Guard) to handle such matters. Defence policy has changed its nature because the US 'war on terror' is, to a large extent, an ideological struggle with the aim of spreading a Western conception of democracy throughout the world. This is not to say that the USA will invade countries just because it disapproves of their political regime; however, if such a country gives sufficient cause in any other way—threatening a neighbour, developing weapons of which the USA disapproves, hosting anti-US forces and movements that might be involved in terrorist activities—it may be attacked. The attack, if it comes, will not be limited to removing the specific threat, but may broaden into a 'regime change' policy, that is, the deliverance into democracy of the people from whatever government offended the USA. As long as this policy continues in force, and it is difficult to see how any future administration can unilaterally call an end to the 'war on terror', the USA's defence posture will need to change. There is no substitute in such a war for large infantry forces, relatively lightly armed but very well trained, and with first-rate intelligence and communications capacities. In the old English parlance, such activity is 'in the aid of the civil power', although with the added complexity there will probably be no legitimate or stable civil power to help. Prior to the end of the Second World War, in preparation for defeating the Germans and occupying Germany, US and allied forces invested heavily in training specialist 'military government' teams. No such teams were prepared for the 2003 campaign in Iraq, still less in the involvement in Afghanistan. Similar teams will have to become a regular part of US defence policy if it is to continue along the lines to which the current Administration is committed.

DEFENCE POLICY SINCE 2002

The chosen date of 2002 is based on the fact that the major statement of defence policy nowadays is contained in a *Quadrennial Defense Review*, the first of which was issued in 2002. At this stage the war in Iraq had not started. Its replacement, published in February 2006, came not only after the US-led invasion of Iraq, but after three years of post-invasion experience. There has been no further major policy statement since the 2006 *Review,* though it is inevitable that an incoming administration in 2009 will issue one—regardless of which party occupies the White House. As noted above, 95% of all deaths in Iraq come from this post-invasion period. Indeed, the

Table 4. Recent US Defence Expenditure
(US $ million at constant 2006 prices, federal years)

	1985	1990	2000	2002	2003	2004	2005	2006
Army	134,933	122,067	86,525	95,618	130,790	160,739	102,529	98,460
Navy	171,404	149,587	104,098	113,166	133,972	130,603	122,176	125,413
Air Force	168,690	137,631	96,821	110,278	134,971	131,862	120,091	127,408
Total	499,428	439,984	341,779	384,511	473,734	495,889	411,255	421,116

Source: adapted from the Department of Defense's *Annual Report to the President and the Congress*, 2005.

Table 5. % Real Growth in Recent US Defence Expenditure

	1990	2000	2002	2003	2004	2005	2006
Army	–2.1	3.5	7.7	36.8	22.9	–36.2	–4.0
Navy	–0.7	2.7	4.2	18.4	–2.5	–6.5	2.6
Air Force	–4.5	–0.8	9.2	22.4	–2.3	–8.9	6.1
Total	–2.1	1.6	8.5	23.2	4.7	–17.1	2.4

Source: adapted from the Department of Defense's *Annual Report to the President and the Congress*, 2005.

troop levels in Iraq are now higher than during the invasion itself, with an average of 130,000 troops deployed at any one time. In terms of the non-financial cost, it should be remembered that more than 60% of all US army personnel have now served in Iraq, with approximately 40% of those having served more than one tour of duty. With this as a measure of strain, the following tables showing recent US defence expenditure and real growth in this expenditure make a crucial point. The point is that expenditure for 2006 on the army, which bears the brunt of the activities in Iraq, actually shows a decline of 4% compared with the previous year, following on from a massive decrease, of 36.2%, in 2004/05. The actual daily costs of fighting in Iraq are not factored into the budget—they are paid for from a special congressional budget authority, and are truly staggering. None the less, the idea that one can reduce expenditure on routine training and maintenance activities while fighting a war explains why the professional military, and especially the army, are in constant conflict with the civilian leadership of the Department of Defense. There may be little choice for the President, given that the total cost of the war in Iraq had reached US $380,000m. by 2006, and that expenditure there increased by 20% in that year. However, clearly no major defence policy review, especially one intended to make the military capable of more, rather than less, foreign activity, can be undertaken meaningfully while the budget figures remain as in this table.

Even the quickest of readings of the *Quadrennial Defense Review* shows just how ambitious the armchair theory of defence has now become. It sets out four crucial primary tasks: defeating terrorist networks; defending the homeland in depth; shaping the choices of countries at strategic crossroads; and preventing hostile states and non-state actors from acquiring or using weapons of mass destruction.

The first task is itself a potentially endless drain on resources and, even worse, leads to no obvious method for structuring or training and deploying military force. It is the third task, 'shaping the choices of countries at strategic crossroads', which is both the most difficult and the most worrying for those outside the USA. It is in fact a code phrase for being prepared to intervene in any country where the USA decides to support one side against another in internal politics. (Moreover, this task actually embraces the final one, because the only ultimate means of preventing a country from developing weapons of mass destruction capacity is to invade it.) A fuller description of the ambitions of the *Quadrennial Defense Review* are given slightly later in the document. The defence policy requires US forces, under the label 'Conduct and Win Conventional Campaigns' to have two modes:

(1) Steady-state—deter inter-state coercion or aggression through forward deployed forces, enable partners through theatre security co-operation and conduct presence missions. These activities include day-to-day presence missions, military-to-military exchanges, combined exercises, security co-operation activities and normal increases in readiness during the seasonal exercises of potential adversaries;

(2) Surge—wage two nearly simultaneous conventional campaigns (or one conventional campaign if already engaged in a large-scale, long-duration irregular campaign), while selectively reinforcing deterrence against opportunistic acts of aggression. Be prepared in one of the two campaigns to remove a hostile regime, destroy its military capacity and set conditions for the transition to, or for the restoration of, civil society.

The problems inherent in these goals are fairly evident. First, there is a firm commitment to permanent forward deployment. As 50% of US troop strength is already deployed abroad, this means that even withdrawal from Iraq and Afghanistan would require a heavy and continued overseas deployment as part of what is described as 'steady state'. Admittedly, this will not be as demanding a call of resources as the long-term commitment to European-based troops was during the Cold War, but at that stage there was no equivalent to the second paragraph, the 'surge' planning. In fact the surge requirements are less than clear, starting with the question of what can be meant by 'nearly simultaneous'. In the first *Quadrennial Defense Review* Rumsfeld prided himself on having abandoned the outmoded 'one-and-a-half war' baseline. In fact the new formulation is very probably much more demanding. All of this is to be achieved without major increases in troop strengths, and with no increase in baseline military expenditure. What increases there may be in the baseline are supposed to go towards investment in new technologies and in support strengths. Ideally, such new investment would be achieved by actually cutting current structures—reducing the size of the navy by one Carrier Battle Group, for example, abolishing at least two army divisions and reducing current generation procurement. The strategies outlined in the 2006 *Review* are not feasible unless either the USA reverts to some form of conscription or it returns defence expenditure to a Cold War level. This is not a policy statement as such; rather, it is a list of aims, targets and statements of intent. For the time being there is no defence policy, or—which is the same thing—the defence policy inherited by President Bush struggles on beneath the overwhelming preoccupation of fighting a war that drains resources and energies.

Exactly what the new defence policy is, few, if any, now know. Nor can many people envisage quite what the policy could become. What is clear is that US defence policy from 2009 will depend both on the result of the presidential election in November 2008 and on the way in which the electoral campaigns are fought. As the Democratic campaign has clearly put Senator Barack Obama's opposition to the war in Iraq at the forefront, change may well be more abrupt and wide-ranging than one might otherwise have expected. In particular, it seems likely that defence policy will become subordinate to foreign policy to an extent greater than has been the case for the last few years. A second factor likely to affect defence policy is the global economic situation, especially given the huge sums added to the US national debt by current relief programmes for the financial sector. Defence will be in more intense competition for federal expenditure than it has been. In all years since 2002 defence has amounted to more than 50% of federal expenditure, and was as high as 58% in the estimates for 2008. Not since the late Cold War days has this been the case. None the less, caution is needed in interpreting such data. The truth is that, as a total drain on the national resources, President Bush's policies have not, historically speaking, been especially high. Although defence expenditure as a percentage of GDP has been slightly over 4% since 2004, and had been lower for a decade prior to that date, it had only dropped below 4% in 1995, and before then had never been below 5.5% during the entire Cold War. Thus, the USA could clearly afford to continue with Bush's level of expenditure if the federal Government so wished.

THE US ELECTORAL SYSTEM

PHILIP DAVIES

ELECTION DAY

Candidates and voters knew a long time in advance that Election Day 2008 would come on Tuesday, 4 November. National legislation determines that election days for political office in the federal government of the USA take place on the Tuesday after the first Monday in November of an election year. The terms of office are set, by the Constitution of the USA, at four years for the presidency, six years for US senators and two years for members of the House of Representatives. Since the passage in 1951 of the 22nd Amendment to the Constitution, Presidents have been limited to two terms in office, but federal legislators are not similarly term limited.

One consequence of this firmly established legal scaffolding is that candidates can plan campaigns well in advance, attempting to fit their strategy to the fixed timetable of US elections. There are, nevertheless, many unpredictable factors on the campaign trail, and only a small proportion of those who sketch out election strategies months and even years in advance will make it to office. An obstacle course of selection procedures, primaries, caucuses and conventions has to be negotiated. Running for election requires funds, and, if donations dry up, campaigns falter. A candidate may attract a loyal following willing to invest in the campaign, but still find that their campaign messages do not appeal to the varied groups that make up their potential constituencies. Candidates may fade under the intense media coverage that can be brought to bear on modern campaigns.

The route to political office may be complex, but on Election Day scores of millions of US citizens are presented with choices that will impact on the conduct of politics in their nation, state and local community. At the time of writing, the processes for deciding who will be on the ballot in all races remains unfinished in most states, but a good idea of the decisions put in the hands of voters can be gained by looking back four years to the previous presidential election year.

Leicester, Vermont, is a town of fewer than 1,000 people on the western side of Green Mountain State Forest, close to the birthplace of Stephen A. Douglas, the 19th century politician whose debates with Abraham Lincoln have an iconic place in the history of US electoral democracy. The general election ballot presented plenty of choices to voters of this town in November 2004. There were six teams vying for the offices of President and Vice-President of the USA. Six candidates had made the ballot to challenge for election to the US Senate from Vermont. Four candidates were listed for Representative to the US Congress. Also on the ballot were six candidates for Governor of Vermont, four options to vote for Lieutenant-Governor, three for the state's Auditor of Accounts, six for Vermont Attorney-General, four for the two state Senate seats up for election and two candidates for state Representative. Three further offices appeared on this ballot. Just one candidate name each was printed in the boxes for State Treasurer, Secretary of State and High Bailiff (whose duty, according to the office of Secretary of State, 'if the need should arise, is to arrest the sheriff because of some criminal or other problem' and to serve 'as an interim sheriff while the real sheriff is confined'. Those who turned out had no obligation to vote in all the races, so positive abstention was an option.

A conscientious Leicester voter, not abstaining in any of these races, had 746,496 different voting combinations available in casting his or her vote. If this wholly committed voter considered abstention as an alternative to any of the choices, then potentially millions of different patterns could be made with the machines in the voting booth. Furthermore, the choices available on the ballot in Leicester came not only from the Democratic and Republican parties, but also from candidates listed as Libertarian, Socialist Worker, Liberty Union, Marijuana, Vermont Green and Progressive, as well as a number of independents. Voters unhappy with any candidate might legitimately write in the name of an alternative. Candidates have, on occasion, campaigned for and won election on the write-in vote.

This is not an untypical ballot in its presentation of a variety of options at different levels of government. Different states and localities adopt different practices within the USA's federal system, and in some places the offices up for election may include such offices as judges, registrars of deeds, registrars of wills, sheriffs, constables, justices of the peace, school directors and board members, and university regents. Many ballots also include various forms of referendum. These may request an opinion on proposed amendments to the state constitution or to a local government charter. In some states citizens can put legislative proposals on the ballot for a public vote, and some require that local governments put any spending plans that would involve the government in major borrowing to the vote—effectively requiring the electorate to vote for or against the prospective tax burden.

It could be argued that the US ballot presents a burdensome amount of choice. However, Jane Walmsley's opinion, in her light-hearted but very perceptive book, *Brit-think, Ameri-think*, is quite persuasive. 'Choice—lots of it—is ... dear to the American heart', she says; the 'right to substitute a tossed salad for french fries is enshrined in the Constitution.' Certainly there is a cultural and systemic commitment to individualism in the USA that helps underpin an electoral system of such comprehensiveness and complexity. While the result may be a ballot that requires a curious level of dedication truly to be an enjoyable experience, proposals to simplify the process and reduce the number of voting opportunities available are doomed to suspicion and failure. Furthermore, such a formidable ballot has the potential to imbue the voter with a genuine sense of the drama and occasion that is part and parcel of taking part in the democratic process.

THE CONSTITUTIONAL BACKGROUND

The Founding Fathers who met in Philadelphia, Pennsylvania, in 1787 to consider the future form of their national government did not face the problem of constructing a constitution for the United States totally devoid of precedent. The USA lays claim to have the first written national constitution in the world, but those men were well aware of the power and value of earlier political documents. They accepted the merits of English common law and they examined England's history and practice in order to adopt valuable elements of its political forms and traditions. In addition, they could learn from the colonial experience.

The early settlement of the colonies was accomplished by a wide variety of wealthy entrepreneurs, religious dissidents, ex-convicts and others driven to life overseas by personal needs. These groups sometimes established their own dominance over particular areas or, on occasion, learned to live and mix with other settlers. Nominally under the control of the authorities in London, the British capital, the distance and slow communications meant that these colonies developed to some extent independently of the direct influence of the central Government. At times this freedom of development had unfortunate consequences: abuse of power by landowners and their representatives was well known; religious intolerance divided some communities; and the southern colonies gradually enshrined African-American slavery in their statutes.

At the same time there was experimentation with new political forms. On 30 July 1619 the Virginia Assembly, made up of 22 burgesses, was elected to represent the local planters in meetings with the royally appointed Governor and his council. All men aged 17 years and over were eligible to vote. Just over one year later, on 11 November 1620, the *Mayflower* anchored in the harbour of Cape Cod, off what is now Provincetown, Massachusetts. Having strayed off course during a rough transatlantic passage, these colonists were well outside any legal jurisdiction. In response to this legal limbo, the 41 men on board agreed and signed the Mayflower Compact, a document outlining a form of majoritarian government to be used until a permanent structure could be created.

Between then and the War of Independence there were to be many more examples of at least partial self-determination. The colonies developed their own forms of administration, consultative assemblies were set up, the law was enforced with the help of local juries and ideas of civil rights were discussed and, to a limited degree, implemented. These were not exercises in radical democracy by modern standards, but they set the direction towards a time when political structures could be organized by citizens of their own free will, through the election of their peers to direct policy, under the guidance of a form enshrined in the laws.

The issue of representation was central in the manoeuvring that preceded the American War of Independence. 'No Taxation Without Representation' shifted from political demand to battle cry in the face of British intractability. The Declaration of Independence proclaimed that all men were 'created equal', that they had certain 'unalienable Rights' and that 'whenever any Form of Government becomes destructive of these ends, it is the Right of the People to alter or abolish it'. The early attempt at national government, the Articles of Confederation (1781), proved too weak and the members of the Philadelphia Convention called to amend the Articles instead undertook the daunting task of designing a system that responded to both the radical demands of the revolution and the pragmatic operation of a nation state. The delegates debated all aspects of government institutions, appointment and election. Terms of office, forms of election and the extent of, and limits on, popular control, all formed part of this debate.

While there appeared to be a general feeling that the new United States Government should be held accountable for its actions, and should govern only with the consent of the governed, there were broad differences as to how this accountability should be effected and by whom. In the event, a relatively small percentage of the population had the vote immediately after the adoption of the Constitution. Women were generally excluded from the franchise, although in some states that had other hurdles, such as property ownership, a few women could vote. Religious barriers were erected by some states, and the main reference to black Americans in these early days was in the contemporary debates over slavery, a condition as far distant from enfranchisement as could be imagined. The legal bedrock of these limitations was gradually eroded by changes in the laws and the Constitution over the next two centuries.

To the Founding Fathers of 1787, even an electorate limited to qualified white males seemed broad, and the proponents of this degree of democratic involvement clashed with those who feared 'the mob'. Compromise resulted in a national election system where only US Representatives were elected directly 'every second Year by the People' (Article 1, Section 2, Clause 1). US Senators were to be chosen for their six-year terms 'from each State, chosen by the Legislature thereof' (Article 1, Section 3, Clause 1), with one-third of Senate members coming up for election every two years. The President and Vice-President were given four-year terms, and were further isolated from direct public control by the invention of an Electoral College, which was given the responsibility for choosing the nation's executive officers. The members of this College were, in turn, to be chosen in a manner prescribed by the state legislatures, thereby creating a kind of 'three-tier democracy' that remains a complicating factor in the quadrennial race for the White House.

The qualifications needed by citizens in order to vote were set by the individual states, although Congress has retained the right to pass laws regulating the conduct of federal elections, and over time there has been a move towards more uniform qualifications for voting. The different terms of office and the staggering of elections meant that the government would be receiving regular indications of public, or at least state legislative, opinion. However, radical response to swings of public mood would be moderated by the fact that at no time would all national government politicians face election simultaneously.

These constitutional mechanisms form the basis of the rights of the contemporary US electorate. Nevertheless, there have been many changes since the Constitution was ratified. Organizational changes to do with elections and office-holding have prompted four amendments to the Constitution. The clumsy operation of the presidential election of 1800 led to a redesign instituted in 1804 by the 12th Amendment. The 20th Amendment, ratified in 1933, moved the starting dates for presidential and congressional terms of office to the January following the elections. The 22nd Amendment (1951) limited Presidents to two elected terms of office and the 25th (1967) attempted to deal with the problem of succession and transfer of authority in the executive branch.

A further seven amendments are wholly or partly concerned with the extension and protection of the right to vote. The 14th and 15th, passed in the aftermath of the Civil War, contain an inclusive definition of US citizenship ('all persons born or naturalized in the United States') and guarantee the right to vote regardless of 'race, color, or previous condition of servitude'. In 1913 the 17th Amendment introduced the direct election of US senators throughout the nation, and the 19th (1920) extended the vote to all women. Direct election of senators was already operating in effect, and women were already voting in some states, but these practices were not confirmed and protected nationally until enshrined in the US Constitution.

Washington, DC, is a federal district, not part of any state, which left all of this city's electorate in the anomalous position of being unable to vote in any elections to the federal government until the 23rd Amendment (1961) gave Washington, DC, a place in the presidential Electoral College. The 24th Amendment (1964) abolished the imposition of a poll tax as a qualification for voting, thereby eliminating one of the few remaining vestiges of state attempts to reduce the electoral participation of African-American and poor people. The most recent extension of the franchise was by the 26th Amendment (1971), which reduced the voting age to 18 years.

POLITICAL PARTIES, PRIMARIES AND PR

While the legal and constitutional framework of US elections continues to show clearly the handiwork of the authors of the Constitution, the Founding Fathers would find some elements of the modern campaign unrecognizable. The modern political party is a very different animal to any 18th century political organization, but certainly the colonial and early national politicians of North America were familiar with political organizations, which already existed in the United Kingdom, and with groups of like-minded, politically aware individuals who took part in the debates of the day in America. Such 'factions' were often viewed with suspicion, with special concern expressed by some that a faction might exert overbearing dominance through skilful strategy or through demagoguery.

Some of the most influential early voices in America spoke out against party politics. In the contemporary so-called Federalist Papers, James Madison promoted support for the new Constitution as a defence against the development of large national political 'factions'. In the same important series of essays, Alexander Hamilton listed 'party opposition' as a motive comparable to 'Ambition, avarice, [and] personal animosity', and whenever he returned to the topic it was to say something in the vein of his comment that 'it will rarely happen that the advancement of public service will be the primary object either of party victories or of party negotiations'. George Washington did not change his opinion even after eight years as President, using his farewell address to warn his listeners 'in the most solemn manner against the baneful effects of the spirit of party generally'. US political parties developed, nevertheless, if hesitatingly at first and subject to considerable transformations over time. However, there has remained within the US polity much public suspicion that the discipline implicit in party politics makes an uncomfortable fit with the individualistic ideals of the American way.

The modern Democratic Party traces its origins at least to the presidential election of 1828, when the successful candidacy of Andrew Jackson consolidated the position of the party at a time when the USA was emerging from an early national period of very indistinct party politics. Other parties emerged, won office and then waned in the 19th century, until the Republican Party was founded in Ripon, Wisconsin in 1854, built on the foundation of a variety of groups, but depending for much of its starting talent on the recently collapsed Whig Party. Republican success came quickly, when Abraham Lincoln took the presidency in 1860.

Since the mid-19th century candidates from other political parties have occasionally won seats in the US Congress, and at state and local level, and there have been brief periods when other parties have shown regional strength and potential, but no other party has emerged to challenge the duopoly of authority exerted by the Republicans and Democrats. In 2008, apart from one independent in the US Senate, all national offices were held by these two parties. Every state governorship and all the state legislatures were controlled by these two parties, with the exception of Nebraska, which by state law has a non-partisan state legislature. Some minor party and independent candidates are elected to local and state offices, but in general Democrats and Republicans occupy almost all partisan elected offices in the USA.

With the emergence of political parties came the trappings of party organization, and a more centralized and strategic approach to gaining office and delivering policy. Party conventions originated with a minor party in the 1830s, but were quickly adopted by the Democrats and others as a way of solidifying the national authority of the party and of providing a forum where regional and ideological factions could compromise on their differences in the interest of gaining political power.

Partisan political slogans were soon in evidence during elections; campaign literature appeared promoting the virtues of favoured candidates and giving a negative interpretation of the actions, ideas and characters of opponents. The early means of political communication included almost anything that might be turned to carrying a slogan or image, with printed materials and newspapers featuring heavily; electoral competition was turning into an expensive business. The 1896 campaign for William McKinley was reputed to have mailed or given out 200m. pieces of campaign literature in almost a dozen different languages in order successfully to connect the candidate with the multinational electorate of the *fin de siècle* USA.

With the entry into electioneering of electronic media—radio in the 1920s and television in the 1950s—the opportunities for candidates and parties to speak directly to voters grew exponentially, and the expense of doing so also increased at a startling rate. The first million-dollar presidential campaign was that of Republican James A. Garfield, in 1880; in the pre-television age spending rose steadily but gradually. In 1948 the Republican and Democratic campaigns together spent less than $5m., but spending doubled by 1952, and doubled again by 1960, when the Kennedy and Nixon campaigns spent about $10m. each. When Nixon ran again, in 1968, his campaign cost $25m.; the total spent by Nixon, his Democratic opponent, Hubert Humphrey, and third-party candidate, George Wallace, approached $44 million.

Suspicions have always existed that the rapidly increasing expenditure on campaigning potentially gives large contributors unfair political advantage and the opportunity to buy advancement for themselves and their interests. Congress has sometimes tried to tackle such problems through legislation. The Federal Election Campaign Act of 1971, amended in 1974, 1976 and 1979, provided the foundation of campaign finance legislation in the past generation, and has recently been augmented by the Bipartisan Campaign Reform Act of 2002. This legislation certainly affects the nature of campaigning and campaign fund-raising, but has made little impact on the steady rise of election expenditure, with 2008 set to be a record year, and aggregate presidential election spending certain to exceed the billion-dollar ($1,000m.) mark.

THE ROAD TO THE WHITE HOUSE

The modern presidential candidate is a political entrepreneur in a highly competitive environment. The political parties manage a nomination system that draws hopefuls into intra-party combat to become the official candidate. The primary season consists of a series of state-level contests taking the competition to party loyalists around the nation, but that in its turn is a political and logistic challenge so considerable that the pre-primary period of planning and activities has become very extended in recent elections.

Given the fixed timetable of US elections, hopefuls for office have a firm, if skeletal, structure on which to hang alternative strategic plans. Campaign planning is said to start the day after any election, as those ambitious to be the next, or even the next but one, in the White House consult with their closest supporters about the potential opportunities in four or more years, and the way in which their career might map to fit. Developing that cadre of close support into an election winning network is one important part of the process.

Personal wealth is not a prerequisite for a presidential candidate, but the 'log cabin to White House' image is more powerful rhetoric than historical reality. While the parents of Lincoln and Garfield may have brought up their young families in log cabins, even most 18th and 19th century presidents enjoyed more palatial surroundings in their youth. It is nevertheless fair to say that presidential candidates have come from backgrounds covering a wide spectrum of social status. For some scions of financial and political dynasties, such as Franklin Roosevelt, John F. Kennedy and both Presidents Bush, the economic and political advantages stemming from their backgrounds have helped them on their way to electoral success. However, other presidents, such as Richard Nixon, Ronald Reagan, Gerald Ford and Bill Clinton, were born into families of very modest means and forged business, military and political careers that attracted financial and electoral support from a broad constituency of supporters en route to the White House.

The official contest to gain the nomination to run for President as the official candidate of a major political party most obviously starts early in election year with the first state-level caucuses and primaries. In order to be considered in these contests, hopefuls for the nomination will have had to register some months before, in the autumn of the previous year, and the most well organized and better funded contestants will have been making appearances and placing some paid advertising in these critical early states for some time. For recent presidential elections, campaign activity has been noted on the ground in the early states from the early summer of the year before the election, while the run-up to the 2008 election was longer than ever, with both major parties' hopefuls engaging in advertising, campaigning and televised debates on a scale not previously seen before the election year itself.

There may have been a very specific reason for the early outbreak of the 2008 campaign for the presidency. Most US presidential elections feature either an incumbent President, or an incumbent or former Vice-President, in the race. Vice-Presidents do not have a particularly high success rate in elections, but they tend to do well in nomination races. The presence of Presidents and Vice-Presidents in the contest may reduce the extent of competition in the primary stages. The 2008 election was the first since 1952 when neither a President nor a Vice-President would be a nominee; if one discounts the rather inconsequential campaign of Alben Barkley in 1952, it could be seen as the first primary campaign not to feature a

President or Vice-President since 1928. With no such distractions, the stage was set for a wide variety of potential candidates to contend for their party's nomination in 2008.

Quite clearly, the behind-the-scenes preparation for these activities will have been under discussion considerably prior to any public manifestation of the campaign, and the 2008 election seemed to demand an earlier start than usual even for recent elections. The received wisdom was that, once the formal primary campaign opened, the competition might be short-lived. The primary season had become increasingly 'front-loaded' as many states moved their contests to an earlier date, hoping to gain more influence in the process and more media coverage. As states crowded to the early stages, it appeared increasingly likely that the nominees would be decided in an intense and very expensive early multi-state blitz of primaries and caucuses. This scenario would not allow the slow emergence of a successful candidate that a more traditional, months-long presidential primary season had hitherto facilitated. Instead, it demanded a significant war-chest and high levels of name recognition very early in the electoral process, threatening to demote all campaigns without this capacity to the status of also-rans. Leading presidential hopefuls in 2007 were already spending at between three and five times the then record-breaking pace of their predecessors at similar stages of the previous two campaigns. In this rarefied atmosphere, several plausible candidacies were launched and wound up months before any votes had been cast in even the most preliminary straw polls.

The USA is a federal nation, and its presidential election is built with its federal nature in mind. The processes of voting and participating, and the organizing of the mechanisms of the election, all take place at the state level. The general election depends on the tallies in individual states, filtered through the Electoral College system. However, political parties too are federal structures, and their nomination processes are also federalized. Hopefuls are, at this stage, competing against others within their own party—Democrat against Democrat, Republican against Republican—to become that party's officially nominated candidate in the presidential election. In pursuit of this ambition they must campaign for support in the presidential primaries and caucuses that take place across the nation, and which send delegates to the national conventions where the nominations officially take place. There are, in addition, a small proportion of 'super delegates', made up mainly of officials holding elected office for the party.

Primaries are elections in which eligible voters express their preference as to which of the hopefuls they would like to see as the official nominee of the party. Caucuses, which are less widely used, are meetings of eligible voters for the same purpose. Primaries and caucuses may be used in combination in some states, and occasionally interface with local and state conventions before a particular state's nomination preferences can be said to be firm. The precise pattern of primary elections, caucuses and conventions used, along with the timing, rules for registration of candidates and political parties and other logistics are all decided at state level. Any serious candidate for the presidency needs to employ a staff keenly aware of this complex and changing federal patchwork, and the winding road to the nomination that results.

By tradition this season of primaries and caucuses opens formally with the New Hampshire primary and the Iowa caucuses. In recent elections, this start has generally been around early February of election year, running through to the final state contests in June. In 2008 so many states wished to have an early place in the process that Iowa moved its caucus to 3 January and there was very significant action from the very beginning. The season of primaries and caucuses provides a hard test for any campaign organization, and the field of candidates tends to reduce as the weaker campaigns run out of resources. In 2008 Joe Biden and Chris Dodd pulled out of the Democratic race for the presidency immediately after the first caucus, and the trail was littered with expired candidacies from that point.

The first official primary season contests, the Iowa caucus and the New Hampshire primary, attract international media coverage. In spite of the fact that these states are not representative samples of the US electorate, the results there can have massive significance, at least in winnowing the field of candidates, if not necessarily in pinpointing the eventual victors. It is important in such high-profile times to manage public expectations well.

In 2008 there were high expectations that the Democratic Senator from New York and former First Lady, Hillary Clinton, would be the front runner, albeit hampered by controversies that dogged the Clinton presidency. Senator Clinton's second-place finish in Iowa behind the 'freshman' US Senator from Illinois, Barack Obama, came as a shock to her campaign. The Obama camp gained publicity, and a substantial fund-raising boost, from its success. The Clinton campaign regrouped and went on to a slim victory in the 8 January New Hampshire primary, followed by Obama wins in Nevada and South Carolina later in the month. John Edwards remained in the race briefly, but it rapidly became clear that he was firmly in third place. On 5 February, which became known as 'Super Tuesday', 23 states and districts held simultaneous primaries and caucuses. Obama took 13 of these and Clinton won 10, indicating that the Democrats were hosting a tough two-horse contest. However, Obama came out of the first stage of the primary season with a small lead over Clinton and, while Clinton had significant state victories through the spring, Obama always remained slightly in the lead. It was not clear until the final primaries on 3 June, and with super delegates increasingly declaring their voting intentions, that Obama would take the nomination at the Democratic National Convention.

There was no clear front runner in the Republican camp as the primary season opened. John McCain had been thought the strongest in 2007, but his campaign appeared to falter as the formal stage began. Iowa was not natural territory for McCain, and his camp had carefully reduced any expectation of him featuring there at all, so that his 12% of the vote seemed quite a reasonable result. Mike Huckabee came first in the Republican race in Iowa, supported by a strong conservative and Christian fundamentalist vote that would be unlikely to propel him to the nomination or to general election victory. McCain won in New Hampshire, then a third Republican hopeful, Mitt Romney, took a couple of states. Rudi Giuliani never recovered from delaying his formal entry into the race until after these initial contests, and the three other leaders, McCain, Huckabee and Romney, looked set for a long season of contests. However, while Super Tuesday gave victories to all three, it indicated broadest support for McCain. While he may not have been most liked by a majority of Republican voters, he appeared to incite less negative reaction than either of the others, and Republicans seemed ready to compromise on him as a candidate that they thought might win the election, even in an unpromising year for Republicans. Romney withdrew from the contest on 9 February and Huckabee followed suit on 4 March, leaving the nomination open for Senator McCain.

Preconceptions that the nomination races would be decided quickly were not fulfilled, but, with close contests taking longer than expected, the early predictions that this campaign would be the most expensive ever were fulfilled. The Center for Responsive Politics calculated that by the end of July 2008 the Obama campaign had already spent over $323m. and the McCain campaign over $141m. Some of the hopefuls had also spent heavily: Clinton over $234m.; Romney over $107m.; Edwards and Giuliani over $114m. between them. That aggregated to almost $1,100m. for all the presidential hopefuls together, even before the costs of the party conventions and the general election were incurred.

Spending at that rate requires a businesslike, even industrial, approach, but it is not difficult to understand. The USA has a population exceeding 300m., spread over 50 states, some of which are thousands of miles apart. The campaigns need not only to communicate with their voters, but to make sure that they are registered to vote (a substantial proportion of the eligible electorate is not) and that they turn out to vote in their different states, both in primary and general elections. The main means of communication is the electronic media. The internet is playing an increasingly important part, and attracting appropriate campaign investment, but still thousands of television advertisements are used as the campaigns try to get their message across, in competition not only with other political campaigns, but with all the other well financed corporate advertising that fills the American airwaves. Campaigning in the US context is a big operation and demands heavy investment.

The campaigns are, therefore, faced with a huge fund-raising requirement, and there is a rigid legal context for this effort. Candidates and political parties can only raise money from individuals or from specified categories of political committees. The vast majority of presidential campaign money comes from individual donors. In 2008 no individual donor could give more than $2,300 to a candidate for any election. Up to the end of June 2008 over one-half of Obama's funding had been raised in contributions of less than $200 each. To raise the totals that current presidential campaigns demand in this way requires hundreds of thousands of donations to be made to major candidates, totalling millions of separate contributions for all candidates.

Hopefuls in the primary season may also call on the federal Government for funding. Those who raise a threshold amount of $100,000 by collecting $5,000 in 20 different states in amounts no greater than $250 can apply for matching funds from the federal Government; most campaigns have done this since the possibility was first introduced in 1976. However, accepting federal matching funds also involves contracting to limit primary spending to a figure that in 2008 was around $50m. Increasingly, the major contestants have felt that the acceptance of the spending limit was too great a handicap and have opted instead to raise all their own funds.

The primary season culminates in the National Conventions, generally held at the end of the summer of election year. Once quadrennial meetings where regional and ideological factions within the parties would thrash out compromises on policy and candidacies, these have increasingly become vehicles for showcasing a nominee whose victory is already clear. They also present one of the few opportunities for direct corporate and union expenditure on the campaigns. The federal Government in 2008 granted nearly $17m. to each of the two major political parties to support the conventions, but private donors were estimated by the Campaign Finance Institute to be donating in excess of $112m. The Institute also calculated that 173 corporations that were donating to the conventions' costs had made over $180m. in federal election contributions since 2005 and had incurred over $1,300m. in federal lobbying expenditures over the same period.

Thousands of delegates, officials, journalists and observers attend the conventions. The parties attempt to generate a positive public image with which to launch their general election campaigns. In 2008 the Democratic convention in Denver, Colorado, saw the party engaged in a major and public attempt to heal the wounds of a long and difficult primary contest, heightened by the fact that it pitched against each other hopefuls who could become the nation's first major party female or African-American candidate. Speeches by Hillary Clinton and Bill Clinton, and Senator Clinton's staged, but nevertheless dramatic, intervention in the nomination voting, were clear and powerful attempts to maintain Democratic unity behind Obama even in the face of disappointment for those who so much wanted a woman as President.

The Republican convention in Minneapolis, Minnesota, opened with a similarly powerful, if more unexpected, strategic gamble, when McCain named 44-year-old Governor Sarah Palin of Alaska as his running mate. While this solidified the image of his candidacy as one of reforming Republicans, it also balanced his age (72) with her youth, and may have been an attempt to reach out to disaffected 'Clintonistas'. Obama's vice-presidential choice also had elements of balance: Joe Biden's 36 years of Washington, DC, experience and his foreign policy expertise countering Obama's youth and wholly domestic experience.

After the conventions the campaigns were back on the streets and back in the states. The Electoral College system gives each state an electoral vote value that is equal to the number of members the state has in the federal Senate and House of Representatives, with the District of Columbia also having three electoral votes. This gives a national total of 538. An absolute majority, 270 votes or more, is required for victory. Several small states, like the District of Columbia, have only three electoral votes each, while the biggest states, such as California (55 votes), Texas (33) and New York (31), have many times more.

Campaigns use polling and existing electoral data to categorize states into winnable, unwinnable and marginal groups, and concentrate their resources accordingly. While it did not happen in 2008, the choice of a vice-presidential candidate from a large marginal state can be one such resource. For the most part, it is the deployment of campaign expenditure, staffing, volunteers and advertising to those marginal states where there might be significant potential return in electoral votes that is key to the decision-making in this final stage of the campaign. Massive polling resources will be devoted to maintaining a watch on marginal and near-marginal states, in order to detect and respond to any shifts in opinion. Communities for whom the candidate's policies have a special appeal will be tracked, mapped and assessed for their significance in this exercise in political geography.

The multi-state context of the general election has many similarities to that of the primary season, but while the primaries are spread over months, the general election takes place in all the states on the same day. The financing of this stage of the campaign is even more extreme than that of the nomination process. The federal Government offers the nominees of the two major parties a grant that in 2008 was $84.1m., but this would come with a requirement that the candidate campaigns accept no private donations to their general election fund and observe federal campaign expenditure limits. In 2008 Obama became the first candidate since the 1976 introduction of this grant to refuse the federal funds, preferring instead to raise his own money and to run a campaign unfettered by federal limits on his campaign spending.

All but two of the states deliver their electoral votes en bloc to the candidate who wins the public vote in that state, however small the local margin of victory. Campaign headquarters keeps a constant tally of those states that they think that they are likely to win, and their total electoral vote, always with an eye to the magic winning number of 270. In spite of the large funds expended, there are states in the nation, firmly in one camp or the other, that may hardly notice that an election is going on, as the candidates concentrate their effort and spending in those states that are most contestable, just occasionally straying into other locations to boost the morale of their loyalists or to provide a frisson of anxiety to their opponent.

Famously, in the 2000 election, this system resulted in George W. Bush gaining more electoral votes, and winning the presidential election, when Al Gore had gained about 550,000 more of the popular votes cast nation-wide. The fact that Bush's victory in the key state of Florida was so small that it took a decision by the Supreme Court to complete the election certainly increased the pain that Democrats felt at this loss. Nevertheless, the broad national acceptance of the result, once the political and legal avenues had been exhausted, testifies to the widespread acceptance of the presidential election system, with all its complications.

THE JUDICIAL SYSTEM OF THE USA

Prof. JOHN KRAMER

INTRODUCTION

The USA has a dual system of federal and state courts. This arrangement derives from the Constitution of 1789, under which the federal Government was created to 'form a more perfect Union' of the existing states. Both the federal and state systems have court structures with areas of autonomous jurisdiction and areas where there is dual or joint jurisdiction. There are 50 state court systems and a federal court system that includes courts for the territories of the US Virgin Islands, Guam, American Samoa and the Northern Mariana Islands. In addition, the District of Columbia and the Commonwealth of Puerto Rico have court systems similar to those in the states. This myriad of court systems provides the organizational home for the US judiciary. This court system is complex, due to the complexity of the laws that the courts enforce, the organizational structure of each of these court systems and the fact that many criminal and civil cases may be heard under either the federal or state system.

This essay provides an overview of the US judicial system, focusing on the jurisdiction of the courts (i.e. their power to decide a dispute), the organization of the court structures and procedures for selection of the judges. Each of these is important in developing an understanding of the formal and informal decisions that characterize decision-making in the US court and judicial system. Finally, four areas of development and controversy are reviewed: the growth of federalism, the movement towards 'merit selection' of judges, the sentencing reform movement and the growth of problem-oriented courts.

THE STRUCTURE OF THE US FEDERAL JUDICIAL SYSTEM

The US Constitution, in Article III, provides that 'The judicial power of the United States shall be vested in one Supreme Court, and in such inferior courts as the Congress may from time to time ordain and establish'. Congress wasted no time in exercising its authority to create inferior courts. Indeed, Congress's first proposed bill undertook to design a court structure and rekindled the debate heard earlier at the Constitutional Convention of 1787 between Federalists and Anti-Federalists. The Anti-Federalists feared that a system of federal courts would diminish individual freedoms, and preferred a system of state courts and a Supreme Court with very limited jurisdiction, allowing it only to hear cases appealed from state courts. Federalists advocated a stronger federal court system. The Judiciary Act of 1789 was written in the context of the development of the first 10 amendments to the Constitution that in 1791 became the Bill of Rights. For the Anti-Federalists the Bill of Rights was important in defining individual rights and limiting the power of the Government. The Anti-Federalists' imprint on the Judiciary Act of 1891 was reflected in limiting the venue (i.e. geographical jurisdiction) of the US District Courts to state lines and in requiring that district judges be residents of the district. This ensured that state jurisdictional lines were reinforced through the establishment of the federal courts and that judges were citizens of the state in which they were appointed. Furthermore, over the years the Anti-Federalists attempted to limit federal criminal and civil jurisdiction, leaving proceedings to state jurisdiction.

Despite limited federal jurisdiction, a rise in federal litigation during the 19th century increased pressure for expansion of the federal courts. Ultimately, this pressure on the Supreme Court resulted in the Court of Appeals Act of 1891, which created intermediate courts of appeal called Circuit Courts. These were intended to hear appeals from the US District Courts, thereby reducing case load pressure on the Supreme Court. Also, over the years issues arose that resulted in the creation of speciality courts such as the Court of Veterans Appeals, the Tax Court, the Court of International Trade and Bankruptcy Courts.

The resulting organizational structure of the federal courts is a unified pyramid, at the bottom of which are the US Magistrate Courts. These courts are parallel to municipal or justice of the peace courts at the state level. The responsibilities of the Magistrate Courts are to adjudicate minor offences, including federal misdemeanours (Class A misdemeanours), as well as many civil cases; to issue search warrants; to hold detention hearings; and to conduct preliminary hearings. The bulk of federal magistrates' responsibilities are preliminary proceedings. The selection of federal magistrates is carried out by District Court judges, and magistrates are appointed for eight-year terms. The duties performed by federal magistrates has more then doubled since 1990, and in 2007 involved 948,086 actions. The major component of federal magistrate cases is criminal; in 2007 federal magistrates adjudicated 9,154 Class A misdemeanours and 91,571 petty offences. Bankruptcy judges are also hired by District Court judges and preside over all bankruptcy proceedings; appeals from bankruptcy proceedings go to the District Court or to a panel of bankruptcy judges.

The 94 courts of general jurisdiction at the federal level are the Federal District Courts. These District Courts are located across the 50 states, the District of Columbia, and US territories. Twenty-six states comprise a single district, while others have between two and four districts. Federal District Court judges receive lifetime appointments from the President of the USA, subject to the confirmation of the US Senate. This means that they have jurisdiction over all federal felonies and federal civil cases (limited to claims involving at least US $75,000).

The intermediate courts of appeals are the 12 Circuit Courts. As with the District Courts, Circuit Court judges are appointed by the President with the advice and consent of the Senate, and appointments are for life. The judges of the Circuit Courts reflect the priorities of the Presidents who appointed them as well as the changing character of the legal profession. For example, of the appointments of President Lyndon B. Johnson (1963–69) only 2.5% were female, whereas women constituted 22.4% of appointments by George W. Bush (during 2001–07) and 32.2% of those appointed by Bill Clinton (1993–2000). Appointments of ethnic minorities further reflect presidential agendas. While the vast majority of appointments by all Presidents from Johnson to Bush have been white, Presidents have varied considerably in their appointment of black judges. Under all administrations from Johnson's to that of Gerald Ford (1974–77), no blacks were appointed; however, 16.1% of Jimmy Carter's appointments (1977–81) were black, whereas this fell to only 1.3% under Ronald Reagan (1981–89). More recently, Presidents Clinton and Bush have returned to relatively high levels of black appointments, with 13.1% and 12.2%, respectively.

STRUCTURE OF STATE COURTS

The state courts exhibit such diversity of organization, jurisdiction and venue across the country that attempting to describe them runs the risk of confusing the reader. Even the Supreme Court label has not passed on to all states. For example, in New York the court of general jurisdiction is the Supreme Court, while the highest appellate court, analogous to the Supreme Court in other jurisdictions, is the Court of Appeals. However, although there is great diversity among the state court systems, they all have minor courts of limited jurisdiction where the venue may be townships or cities. These minor courts are analogous to the Magistrate Courts in the federal system. Furthermore, all states have one or more courts with jurisdictions equivalent to that of the Federal District Courts, in which civil and criminal cases not adjudicated by the lower courts are heard. In Pennsylvania, for example, these are Courts of Common Pleas and their venue is by county; in New York these are called the Supreme Courts.

Most state systems also have intermediate courts of appeal analogous to the federal Circuit Courts. In Pennsylvania there are two intermediate courts, the Superior Court taking jurisdiction on appeals for all criminal and most civil cases and the Commonwealth Court having jurisdiction over challenges to state agency regulations. The highest court in most state systems is, like the federal Supreme Court, also called the Supreme Court.

Thus, the federal and state systems have many structural similarities, notwithstanding details such as the variations in titles and jurisdiction. However, in the selection and tenure of judges the states vary considerably from the federal judiciary. Also, the mode of selection varies in some cases between the lower courts and appellate courts with state-wide jurisdiction. Table 1 below presents the mode of selection for state courts of general jurisdiction.

In 22 states these judges are selected by elections, while 16 use the so-called 'merit selection' process. Merit selection, also called the 'Missouri plan' after the first state to adopt the model, involves a nominating commission recruiting and selecting a limited number of qualified candidates and presenting those names to the Governor for nomination.

Judicial elections have been the focus of reform efforts, due to concerns regarding the quality of judges willing to run for election as well as doubts over whether popularly elected judges can be independent and fair. In 2002 the *New York Times* refused to endorse any candidates running for judicial positions, declaring that 'to endorse particular candidates might mislead voters into thinking that they have a real say in choosing judges, which is decidedly not the case. In practice, this year's crop of judges has already been determined by the political insiders in the city's five boroughs who exercise tight control over which individuals get to run on the Democratic Party line, thereby ensuring their election in this overwhelmingly Democratic metropolis.' (Quoted in Mayer 2006.) While party politics dominates in some jurisdictions, in others, such as in Illinois, the elections are open to whomever meets the minimum qualifications, and elections may be determined by name or position on the ballot. As Martin Mayer observes, 'women vote for women; short names outpoll long names; and Irish names have an edge over all others'.

DUAL JURISDICTION: NEXUS OF STATE AND FEDERAL COURTS

Dual jurisdiction between federal and state laws leaves the decision as to where a case will be brought to local law enforcement. This can depend on who wants credit for the arrest and prosecution, where the most appropriate sanction would be available or who initiated the case. In criminal case processing, offences such as drugs-related offences, bank robbery or carjacking can be prosecuted at the federal or state level. Thus, there is dual jurisdiction for these offences and there can be double prosecution if so desired, because the principle of double jeopardy (which prevents retrials by the same government for the same offence—*Bartkus v. Illinois*, 1958) does not apply between different legal jurisdictions. Consequently, if an offender was prosecuted in state court for a bank robbery and found not guilty, the alleged offender could be retried in a federal court without violating double jeopardy. On the civil side there is dual jurisdiction for suits of at least US $75,000, allowing the plaintiff to decide where to bring the case.

There are instances where the laws conflict, although, in general, the laws between federal and state jurisdiction are very similar; however, often the penalties vary, with the general assumption that federal penalties are more severe. An example of a conflict in the law occurs where states such as California have legalized medical marijuana use whereas federal law defines such behaviour as illegal. Thus, individuals in California possessing marijuana for medical use would not be in violation of state statute but could be arrested and prosecuted federally.

CONTEMPORARY ISSUES IN US COURTS

The US courts and judiciary have been the focus of considerable interest, criticism and change during the past four decades, resulting in several movements. One movement has been to extend the reach of the federal government by developing federal laws to cover what historically were viewed as state issues. The second development centres on the selection of judges, and specifically concerns the ability of the courts to function independently and fairly when so many state judges are elected. The most noteworthy change in the US courts over the recent past is sentencing reform: this movement has links to the independence and fairness of the judiciary in sentencing, but is also connected to a perception that judges contributed to the dramatic rise in crime in the 1970s and 1980s as a result of their leniency. Finally, the judiciary has undertaken self-reform through the development of 'problem-solving' courts to deal with issues such as drug abuse and domestic violence.

Federalism

The historical legal dominance of the states has been diminishing over the past 70 years; however, while the federalism movement has strengthened, the states still control the majority of criminal and civil cases. Two key ways in which Congress and the executive branch of government have expanded the federalism movement are through legislating new criminal statutes and through financial incentives to stimulate state action.

A 1995 US Supreme Court decision in *United States v. Lopez* reversed Lopez's conviction for gun possession under a federal statute, thereby creating gun-free school zones. Lopez had been sentenced to six months' incarceration, but the Supreme Court ruled that the US Congress had no authority to outlaw guns in schools, thus reserving this jurisdiction to state courts. Conversely, the US Congress has extended the reach of federal jurisdiction or influenced state standards through various mechanisms. For example, when carjacking received national attention in the early 1990s and many states were creating anti-carjacking legislation, federal legislation was also initiated. However, the challenge was how to legitimize federal jurisdiction. This was creatively done by defining the offence as: 'Whoever, with the intent to cause death or serious bodily harm takes a motor vehicle that has been transported, shipped, or received in interstate or foreign commerce...' (18 USC section 2119). By limiting the jurisdiction to cases involving vehicles that had been engaged in interstate commerce, Congress was able to federalize an offence that had historically been left to state jurisdiction. The reason for Congress to federalize the offence is not clear, but it probably reflects the importance of the politics of crime at the end of the 20th century in the USA. As David Garland (2001) argues: 'The politicization of crime control has transformed the structure of relationships that connects the political process and the institutions of criminal justice. Legislators are becoming more "hands on", more directive, more concerned to subject penal decision-making to the discipline of party politics and short-term political calculation.' Katherine Beckett and Theodore Sasson (2004), supporting Garland's view, concluded: 'Over the past three decades, politicians have kept the issues of crime and drug abuse at the top of the national agenda and framed the issues in ways that suggest a need for a harsher and more expansive system of criminal justice'. The federal carjacking legislation allowed Congress to benefit politically from increased crime control in an arena traditionally left to state jurisdiction.

The tough penalties attached to the federal carjacking offence illustrate perhaps the major thrust of legislation influencing the courts during the last three decades of the 20th century. Mandatory minimum penalties for crimes including drugs offences, so-called 'three-strikes' offences and driving under the influence of alcohol, as well as the adoption of sentencing guidelines in many states, reflect attempts to use legislation to control sentencing decisions by the courts and often to increase the severity of penalties. Members of Congress and state legislators have publicly criticized the leniency of the judiciary when sentencing and have used the national concern about crime and the fear of crime to take tough stands on sentencing.

Judicial Selection

Judicial selection is one of the most controversial judicial issues in the USA. In Table 1 it was noted that many states still use popular elections to select judges. Elections have become much more politicized and expensive over the past two decades, reinforcing the belief that the judicial selection process needs reform. The American Judicature Society has been a leading advocate of merit selection. The perceived problem was illustrated by an article in the *New York Times* in August 2008, which reported that immigration judges selected by the Bush Administration had been vetted for political affiliation before being appointed. This politicization of hiring went beyond judges and included hiring in the Justice Department. Applicants were asked about political beliefs, and their contributions to political campaigns were reviewed. These judges are not confirmed by the Senate but are civil service positions, and civil service laws require that they be hired on the basis of merit using politically neutral criteria. According to the *New York Times*, 'among the judges selected were a member of the 2000 Bush-Cheney Florida recount team, people who worked for Republican lawmakers and a former Republican state officer in Illinois backed by Karl Rove, at the time the White House political adviser.'

Federal appointments to the District Court and Circuit Court benches have been historically politicized as well. President Carter attempted to distance politics from the selection process for Circuit Court judges by forming the US Circuit Judge Nominating Commission in 1977. Its mission was to select judges on the basis of professional merit and to diversify the court by seeking women and minority members. The Commission was composed of 13 panels with one panel for each circuit (except for the Fifth and the Ninth, which had two panels each because of their size). The panels were to publicize the vacancy, screen and interview candidates, and then make recommendations to the President. A study by Larry Berkson, Susan Carbon and Alan Neff (1979) concluded that panellists tended to have Democratic affiliation and that most of the 74 candidates recommended by the Commission were white male Democrats. Some 15% of the candidates were women or minorities and only 14% were Republicans. Despite the apparent politicalization of the Commission, the idea of a commission to identify and review candidates has had some legacy, with several senators using commissions to make recommendations for federal judicial appointments. The American Judicature Society recommends that bipartisan commissions be used by state senators to review and identify qualified candidates of diverse backgrounds to recommend to the President.

The selection of state judges, as indicated above, ranges widely across the states, but the selection of judges through elections has been the source of most concern in terms of the qualifications and independence of those elected. Historically, before independence judges were appointed by the King, and the first colonies continued this mode of selecting judges; however, gradually states began to reject the appointment of judges because of the view that property owners controlled the judiciary. In 1846 the New York Constitutional Convention adopted an electoral system, and, by the outbreak of the Civil War in 1861, 24 of the 34 states had an elected judiciary. The next judicial selection movement was towards non-partisan elections. This movement was relatively short-lived as voters found party labels helpful in choosing between candidates; none the less, 13 states still hold non-partisan elections today. However, criticism of judicial elections grew, and in 1906 Roscoe Pound told the American Bar Association that judicial involvement in politics had 'almost destroyed the traditional respect for the bench'. In 1937 the American Bar Association endorsed merit selection, and in 1940 Missouri began the movement to improve the selection of the judiciary by adopting this method.

Currently 21 states elect members of their highest court while in 24 states the Governor appoints these judges with the advice of nominating commissions. The cost of being elected to a state-wide judicial position is extremely expensive and raises serious concerns whether those most qualified to be judges will subject themselves to campaigning, and, for those who do campaign, whether their independence will be lost. In Pennsylvania a candidate for the state's Supreme Court office won election with the help of television advertisements showing the candidate slamming a gaol door shut. This advertisement played on the public's 'tough on crime' agenda, but also confirmed the general view that the public understands little about the role of the state's Supreme Court.

Texas and New York are two states that have recently undertaken reform efforts. Texas has been the subject of perhaps the greatest scrutiny nation-wide regarding its selection of judges. In 1987 the *Wall Street Journal* raised concerns about the integrity of the Texas Supreme Court after it denied an appeal from the lower court regarding a ruling on a case between two petroleum companies, Pennzoil and Texaco, which favoured Pennzoil. Both companies had made campaign contributions to the justices running for the Supreme Court, but Pennzoil had given much more. In response, proposals for the introduction of merit selection in Texas gained support. However, political compromises resulted in the comprehensive merit selection reform being restricted to just the appellate courts, and then, amid concerns from various fronts and lack of strong gubernatorial support, the legislation died. It was not until 1995 that Texas was able to enact the Judicial Campaign Fairness Act, which limited individual contributions to US $5,000 for state-wide candidates.

New York's experience contrasts with the relatively modest reform in Texas. Again, the context was a set of particularly controversial and expensive elections in the early 1970s, which resulted in a coalition in favour of reform that included the Governor, the Senate leadership and the chief judge of the highest court in the state. The 1977 law introducing merit selection for the appellate courts abolished the election of these judges and replaced it with a Commission on Judicial Nomination that was to recommend seven candidates for each position to the Governor. The 12-member Commission comprises four members appointed by the Governor, four appointed by the Chief Judge of the Court of Appeals, and one each appointed by the President Pro Tempore of the Senate, the Speaker of the Assembly, and the minority leadership in both legislative chambers. Of the Governor's appointments, only two may be from the same political party and only two may be members of the bar. The nominee selected by the Governor is then subject to confirmation by the Senate. Those who desire another term must reapply to the Commission.

Sentencing Reform

The 1970s was a period of severe challenge to the discretion of judges in the USA. In 1973 Judge Marvin Frankel criticized the legal foundation of the judiciary's discretion when sentencing and labelled it 'lawlessness'. Judge Frankel's challenge highlighted gross disparity in the sentencing of similarly situated defendants. In a country with a history of slavery and disparate treatment of racial minorities this was generally viewed as racial disparity. However, this was not the only criticism of the judiciary that was emerging. A second theme, as crime rates increased from the mid-1960s, was that judges were sentencing too leniently, thereby encouraging crime. Consequently, crime and sentencing emerged as politically linked issues, and numerous reforms were proposed.

The US federal and state courts had various forms of indeterminate sentencing formats in the early 1970s. The indeterminate sentence provided the judge with the responsibility of determining whether the offender should be incarcerated, and, if so, a minimum and a maximum sentence. For imprisonment sentences the judge's role ended at this point, as the decision on the prisoner's release date was made by a parole board. Appellate courts also had a 'hands off' policy for the sentencing judge. While the elements of the offence had to be proven 'beyond a reasonable doubt', the standard of proof required at sentencing was preponderance of the evidence, and, with no requirement for judicial statements giving the reasons for the sentence to be presented for appellate review, challenges to the evidence at sentencing were rare. Indeed, the Supreme Court ruled in *Williams v. New York* (1949) that the sentencing judge should not be constrained by 'rigid adherence to restrictive rules of evidence properly applicable to the trial'.

There were three basic models of sentencing reform considered in the USA, all of which focused on constraining judicial discretion in order to increase the severity of penalties and

Table 1: Initial Selection of State Judges in Courts of General Jurisdiction

Merit Selection Nominating Commission	Gubernatorial (G) or Legislative (L) Appointment	Partisan Election	Nonpartisan Election	Combined Methods
Alaska	California (G)	Alabama	Arkansas	Arizona
Colorado	Maine (G)	Illinois	Georgia	Florida
Connecticut	New Hampshire (G)	Louisiana	Idaho	Indiana
Delaware	New Jersey (G)	Michagan	Kentucky	Kansas
District of Columbia	South Carolina (L)	Ohio	Minnesota	Missouri
Hawaii	Virginia (L)	Pennsylvania	Mississippi	New York
Iowa		Texas	Montana	Oklahoma
Maryland		West Virginia	Nevada	South Dakota
Massachusetts			North Carolina	Tennessee
Nebraska			North Dakota	
New Hampshire			Oregon	
New Mexico			Washington	
Rhode Island			Wisconsin	
Utah				
Vermont				
Wyoming				

Source: American Judicature Society, *Judicial Selection in the United States: A Compendium of Provisions* (internet ajs.org/js/judicialselectioncharts.pdf), 25 January 2005.

decrease disparity. The first of these, mandatory minimum sentences, primarily focused on leniency by restricting the most lenient sentence a judge could give an offender. A common, almost universal, target for mandatory minimums was drugs offences. For example, the US Congress introduced mandatory minimum gaol terms of five years for trafficking in five grams of 'crack' cocaine or 500 grams of powder cocaine. This meant that if the defendant was convicted of trafficking cocaine and, at sentencing, the court found by a preponderance of the evidence that the defendant possessed with intent to deliver five grams of cocaine and that this cocaine was in the form of 'crack,' then the judge was to sentence the defendant to imprisonment of at least five years.

The two other models of sentencing reform focused, in general, more on the issue of sentencing disparity then sentencing severity: these were determinate sentencing and sentencing guidelines. Determinate sentences were 'flat' sentences established by legislation with general guidelines for the length of incarceration. For example, the sentencing reform enacted in 1976 in California abolished the indeterminate sentence and the parole board that made the release decision. Only a few states adopted this reform model, the last being North Carolina in 1980.

In 1978, following the suggestions of Judge Frankel, Minnesota and Pennsylvania enacted legislation to create sentencing commissions to write sentencing guidelines. The sentencing guideline reform model focuses primarily on sentencing disparity, but it can also be used to increase sentencing severity, as was the case under the Pennsylvania and federal sentencing guidelines. Guidelines are used in 20 states and the District of Columbia, and were considered but rejected in Canada. With the exception of Ohio, guideline systems employ a sentencing matrix that combines the seriousness of the offence with the offender's criminal history. Typically, a range is given within which the judge must sentence in order to conform to the guidelines, with the presumptive sentence being the midpoint of this range. A sentence outside the range constitutes a departure sentence and requires the judge to provide written justification for such a departure. The prosecutor or the defence can generally appeal against the sentence. The base for US state guideline systems is the offence of conviction; however, in some states the guidelines adjust the ranking of the offence depending on factors that are not a part of the conviction offence. For example, Pennsylvania's guidelines rank the seriousness of drugs offences according to the type and weight of the drugs.

The US federal sentencing guidelines adopted in 1987 departed from the state models in several ways, but most importantly in terms of the number of factors incorporated into the offence severity measure. The US commission developed guidelines that relied on the conviction offence to establish the statutory maximum but then incorporated many factors that were not part of the conviction offence into the offence severity measure. The federal guidelines called these sentencing factors 'relevant conduct' to reflect the fact that judges in the past used this information in sentencing and that they were 'relevant' under the guideline systems as well. For example, if an offender was convicted of robbery, the guideline manual directed the court to give the offender a base offence level of 20 as a result of the conviction offence. However, the guideline calculation does not end there as it does with most state guideline systems. Rather, the federal guidelines require the court to add to the base offence level according to factors such as victim injury, extent of financial loss and use of a weapon. These detailed enhancements create very complex guidelines, but they also mean that relevant conduct factors, rather than the elements of the crime, often dominate the sentence recommendation. Not surprisingly, challenges to the use of these sentence enhancements were forthcoming. In *United States v. Watts* (1997) the US Supreme Court upheld relevant conduct enhancements that were based on factors for which the defendant had been acquitted.

However, while *Watts* sustained the relevant conduct enhancements, a potentially conflicting sequence of decisions was emerging that would need to be reconciled. This change began with *Apprendi v. New Jersey* (2000). In this case the Supreme Court reviewed a New Jersey statue that increased the statutory maximum if the offence was based on bias. The Supreme Court ruled that 'any fact that increases the penalty for a crime beyond the prescribed statutory maximum must be submitted to a jury, and proved beyond a reasonable doubt'. The Court extended *Apprendi* in *Ring v. Arizona* (2002), in which it ruled that any fact making an offender eligible for the death penalty must be presented to a jury for proof beyond a reasonable doubt, justifying the ruling under *Apprendi* based on the fact that death goes beyond the statutory maximum prison term.

In *Blakely v. Washington* (2004) the Supreme Court was confronted with the challenge as to whether the legal arguments in *Apprendi* would apply to Washington's sentencing guidelines, which were legislatively adopted, required consideration, and imposed strict criteria that were to be met before the judge could depart from the guidelines. The facts of the case involved the defendant kidnapping his estranged wife at knifepoint, placing her in a wooden box, driving her across the state border, and forcing their 13-year-old son to follow in another car. Washington's guideline range for this offence was 49–53 months' incarceration. The judge held a sentencing hearing and determined that there were such aggravating factors as to sentence Blakely to 90 months rather than within the guideline range. Despite the fact that the sentence was within the statutory maximum for the conviction offence, the Court ruled that under determinate sentencing systems such as those used in Washington, facts that are used to depart above the guidelines must be presented to a jury and proved beyond a reasonable doubt. To those states and the federal system that had adopted sentencing guidelines and abolished the indeterminate sentence in favour of a determinate or flat system, this was a surprising ruling.

United States v. Booker (2005) applied *Blakely* to the federal guidelines, ruling that the relevant conduct so central to the federal guidelines was subject to the *Blakely* decision. In a remedial decision, those in the minority debated whether to rule the federal guidelines invalid; however, the court's opinion (written by Justice Stephen G. Breyer, who had been a member of the original sentencing commission that wrote the guidelines) ruled that the guidelines were advisory rather than mandatory, thereby keeping them in effect. As a result, the many state sentencing guideline systems that established determinate and tight constraints on judicial discretion, as well as the federal guidelines, have been ruled advisory. By reducing the status of the guideline recommendations, judicial discretion has to some extent been restored: judges must still consider the guidelines, but need not necessarily conform to them.

The sentencing reform movement started as an attack on disparity, but resulted in judges opening for public consideration issues such as the factors to be considered at sentencing and the standard of proof for those factors. Sentencing reform has slowed in the last few years due to criticism of the complexity of the federal guidelines and a lowering crime rate. It remains unclear whether the 2005 Supreme Court decision will strengthen or weaken the movement.

Problem-solving Courts

In the context of significant criticism and reforms that reduced judicial discretion and emphasized punishment over rehabilitation, the courts began to re-examine their role in coping with crime. While legislatures were writing mandatory sentencing laws for drugs offenders, judges began a movement to revitalize rehabilitation and allow an active role for judges in the process through the creation of problem-solving courts. The first drug court was opened in Dade County, Florida, in 1989, and by 2004 there were approximately 1,200 drug courts. Drug courts—and similar courts dealing with offences such as driving under the influence of alcohol and domestic violence—are called problem-solving courts because they respond to a social problem, such as drug abuse, and the crime generated as part of that problem, by combining the sanctioning powers of the court with the treatment resources of the community and the criminal justice system.

There are several key elements to these problem-solving courts. First, they have resuscitated rehabilitation as a major focus of judicial sentences. Second, they have changed the role of the judge from decision maker at sentencing to decision maker and enforcer of the court's order. Third, the judge has become a manager of the network of treatment providers for defendants. Fourth, the judge has taken on a long-term connection with the defendant, where the drug abuse problem is viewed as requiring a long, sustained monitoring of the defendant by the judge as he or she deals with drug dependence.

These courts are not without their critics, including Judge Morris Hoffman, a state judge in Denver, Colorado. Hoffman argues that drug courts are ineffective, have undermined the traditional role of the judge and have drawn into the courts offenders who previously would not have entered the criminal justice system. Perhaps his harshest criticism is that the courts are changing the judicial role into a combination of judicial, legislative and executive roles in their attempts to achieve social ends. However, despite these concerns the number of drug courts and other problem-solving courts is growing very rapidly. Research has suggested that the effectiveness of drug courts has been mixed. None the less, analysis of 23 drug court programmes by the General Accountability Office in 2005 reported lower rearrest and reconviction rates for programme participants than in comparison groups.

CONCLUSION

The USA has an adversarial system in which judges are, in theory, independent, while defence and plaintiffs or prosecutors argue the case before a jury. In reality, the US courts tend to process cases through negotiation rather trials, by means of an informal system of civil settlements and negotiated criminal pleas. This is demonstrated by the fact that less than 5% of criminal cases go to trial. Despite this 'invisible' reality of court processing, the system of US justice has faced four very important developments: the expansion of federal jurisdiction; the replacement of judicial elections with merit selection; commission-developed sentencing guidelines and Supreme Court-induced attention regarding the standard of proof at sentencing; and the emergence of problem-oriented courts. In some respects these changes in the US courts have aspects of convergence and conflicts. In terms of convergence, merit selection attempts to improve the quality of judicial recruitment and decision-making, while problem-oriented courts provide judges with greater discretion and a broader judicial role. On the other hand, sentencing reform was intended to reduce judicial discretion, while the problem-oriented courts expand it.

REFERENCES

Adult Drug Courts: Evidence Indicates Recidivism Reductions and Mixed Results for Other Outcomes. Washington, DC, General Accountability Office, 2005.

Becker, D., and Reddick, M. *Judicial Selection Reform: Examples for Six States*. Chicago, IL, American Judicature Society, 2003.

Beckett, K., and Sasson, T. *The Politics of Injustice: Crime and Punishment in America*. Thousand Oaks, CA, Sage Publications, 2004.

Berkson, L. C., and Caufield, R. *Judicial Selection in the United States: A Special Report*. Chicago, IL, American Judicature Society, 2004.

Berkson, L., Carbon, S., and Neff, A. 'A study of the U.S. circuit judge nominating commission: Findings, conclusions and recommendations'. *Judicature* 63/3, pp. 105-129, 1979.

Bureau of Justice Statistics. *Sourcebook of Criminal Justice Statistics*. Washington, DC, US Department of Justice, 2008.

Canadian Sentencing Commission. *Sentencing Reform: A Canadian Approach*. Ottawa, Canadian Government Publishing Centre, 1987.

Federalism, State Sovereignty, and the Constitution: Basis and Limits of Congressional Power. Washington, DC, Congressional Research Service, 2008.

Frase, R. 'The Apprendi-Blakely cases: The sentencing reform counter-revolution?' *Criminology and Public Policy* 6/3, pp. 403-432, 2007.

Garland, D. *The Culture of Control: Crime and Social Order in Contemporary Society*. Chicago, IL, University of Chicago Press, 2001.

Hoffman, M. B. 'The Denver Drug Court and its unintended consequences'. In Nolan, J. L., Jr. (Ed.). *Drug Courts in Theory and in Practice*. New York, Aldine De Gruyter, 2002.

Mayer, M. *The Judges*. New York, St. Martin's Press, 2006.

Neubauer, D. *America's Courts and the Criminal Justice System*. Belmont, CA, Thomson Wadsworth, 9th edn, 2008.

Cases

Williams v. New York, 337 US 241 (1949).

Bartkus v. Illinois, 355 US 281 (1958).

United States v. Lopez, 514 US 549 (1995).

United States v. Watts, 519 US 148 (1997).

Apprendi v. New Jersey, 530 US 466 (2000).

Ring v. Arizona, 536 US 584 (2002).

Blakely v. Washington, 542 US 296 (2004).

United States v. Booker, 543 US 220 (2005).

THE ROLE OF RELIGION IN US POLITICS

GILLIAN PEELE

INTRODUCTION

One of the most distinctive features of American society and politics is the role played by religion. Although the USA is formally committed by the Constitution to a separation of church and state, it remains a country where religion plays a vigorous and subtly changing role in its public life, and in shaping the attitudes of its citizens. In many respects, the contribution of religious organizations has been highly positive, reinforcing a strong tradition of philanthropy, for example. More recently, however, it has also seemed culturally divisive, as secular and religious Americans have found themselves at odds over a range of issues, from the status of scientific knowledge to ethical beliefs on such questions as homosexuality and abortion. Inevitably, these cultural frictions have profoundly affected the conduct of policy not just in the domestic arena but also in the field of foreign policy.

Although the contemporary form of debates about the role of religion in the USA is relatively new, religion has always been a major factor in the USA's development. That religion should have played a highly significant part in shaping US history is not perhaps surprising. The quest for religious freedom was one of the key factors drawing settlers to the colonies. A variety of religious groups and sects (including Anglicans, Baptists, Methodists, Calvinists, Congregationalists, Quakers, Roman Catholics, and many smaller sects) flourished in an atmosphere which, while it did not rule out sectarian rivalry and intolerance, was not dominated by a single church. Furthermore, even before the War of Independence (1775–83) the US colonies had experienced the emotional power of religion in the form of the religious revival movement, known as the first 'Great Awakening', which spread across the colonies in the 1740s. Such revivalist episodes were repeated in the 19th and 20th centuries in a way that generated radical redrawings of the US religious map. What remains surprising, however, is the extent to which religion has continued to play a formative and controversial role in US politics. Indeed, the USA stands out as a country where religion remains an important force both in the private life of individual citizens and in the national public consciousness, in marked contrast to the secularist trends in most other advanced democracies. (For example, in the first decade of the 21st century some 40% of Americans believed that the world was created by God in the last 10,000 years, a belief which prompts many to political activism in order to build a society in which they feel comfortable.)

To some extent, this continuing vitality of religion in American life reflects the country's distinctive historical, sociological and political development, especially the waves of immigration that brought the country a rich diversity of religious belief. However, although the contemporary vibrancy of US religion owes much to demography, it also reflects the more recent appreciation by political strategists of the importance of faith in shaping attitudes and voting behaviour. This essay will first look briefly at the spectrum of religious belief in the USA in the early 21st century. It will then examine the constitutional position of religion in US public life and the dilemmas that the USA has faced in its accommodation of religious belief, before moving on to look at some of the different ways in which religion shapes the conduct of politics, through its effect on voting patterns and partisan alignment, including the 2008 campaigns. It will also examine the impact of religion on public policy, especially the contentious issues of education and the public schools, as well as moral and social issues, including abortion, gay marriage and stem cell research, as well as at the attempts of President George W. Bush (2000–) to use his presidency to solidify the support of religious groups behind the Republican Party. Finally, the essay will return to the problems presented by the role of religion within the complex and fluid social mix that is the USA in the 21st century.

THE DIVERSITY OF RELIGIOUS BELIEF IN THE USA

From its conception, opportunity for freedom of worship in the USA produced a multiplicity of denominations, sects and religious groupings. Although some states had formally established churches or dominant churches, even by 1776 the variety of religious groups, including Puritans, Roman Catholics, Baptists, Quakers and Jews, reflected the New World's freedom from the orthodoxy of most European countries. After 1776 two additional factors added greatly to this mix. First, the religious culture of the USA generated new religious groups, such as the Church of Jesus Christ of Latter-day Saints (Mormons). These native-grown sects proved highly popular: the Mormons, for example, could claim 1.7% of American adults in 2008 according to that year's Pew Religious Landscape Survey, and have also spread their influence well beyond the USA. Second, the size, federal structure, organizational independence and ethnic heterogeneity of the country as it developed encouraged congregations to reflect their different constituencies. Thus, black US churches developed a distinctive style and organization—for example, the long-established African Methodist Episcopal Church and the African Methodist Episcopal Zion Church. There were, and remain, marked differences of theology and style within some nominally united denominations.

In 2008 the USA had a diverse array of religious groupings—perhaps as many as 1,600—and very probably more than any other single country. That diversity extended well beyond the basically Protestant Christian traditions of the early Republic to include not merely members of the Roman Catholic Church (who constituted nearly 25% of the whole) and Orthodox Christians, but many groups and congregations outside the Christian tradition. The US census does not include any questions about religious belief, but an excellent overview of the role of religion in the USA can be gained from the regular surveys of the population undertaken by academics and journalists, and by specialist religious research institutes and data collectors (for example, by the Pew Foundation and the Hartford Institute for Religious Research), as well as from regular publications such as the *Yearbook of the American and Canadian Churches*. These studies and publications provide detailed evidence not just about the spectrum of religious affiliation in the USA, but also about such issues as church attendance and the relevance of religion to the daily lives of Americans.

What is immediately striking about such surveys is that although the percentage of respondents who are non-believers or religiously unaffiliated—some 16%, an increase from about 8% in the 1980s—is growing, it still seems relatively small by comparison with many European countries. The USA remains an overwhelmingly Christian society (put by most surveys between 71% and 76% of the population), although one where, in recent years (particularly following the liberalization of immigration with the introduction of the Immigration and Nationality Act in 1965), new arrivals to the USA from outside Europe have added their own distinctive elements to the US religious mosaic. As a result, there has been a strengthening of religions outside the Christian tradition. Of course there has long been an important Jewish presence in the USA (which Pew reckoned to be about 1.7% of the population in 2008). However, more recently, the Muslim population has increased, and, although the figures are disputed (with some estimates going as high as 6m.), there is general agreement that Muslims are one of the fastest growing groups within the country. In addition to the Muslim population (0.6% according to Pew in 2008), other prominent non-Christian groups include Hindus (about 0.4% of the population) and Buddhists (about 0.7%). It should also be noted that there were small but growing numbers of Bahá'i groups, and indeed of neo-pagans. There has also been the consequent development of physical buildings for worship (mosques and temples) and of networks of support and lobbying so characteristic of the more established churches. This process of bringing new religions to the USA of course echoes the way in which the great waves of immigration in the 19th and early 20th century brought significant numbers of Roman Catholics and Jews to the USA, diluting the Protestant cultural hegemony.

One further point should be noted: Americans show a marked willingness to switch denominations. Indeed, the 2008 Pew Landscape Survey found that more than a quarter of adult Americans had left the faith of their childhood, often opting for a more personal style of religion than that offered by the traditional mainstream churches. If switches of allegiance within Protestant denominations are included then a startling 44% of the American population has shifted affiliation.

This fluidity of religious affiliation is but one feature of a picture which is far from static. Four other aspects of the dynamic character of the USA's religious diversity should also be borne in mind in analysing the changing picture of belief in the USA. The first is that religious adherence is not uniform across the country: certain churches are much stronger in some areas of the country than in others. Thus, evangelical and fundamentalist sects historically have been important in the south and remain more prevalent there than elsewhere. Roman Catholicism and Judaism are more prevalent in the north-east and large cities. Roman Catholicism, while dominant in the north-east, is as yet relatively under-represented in the south, although Catholicism in the south-west is growing as a result both of internal migration and Latino immigration. (Indeed, immigration primarily from Latin America is the only reason that Roman Catholicism is continuing to grow; without that new immigration there would be a nation-wide decline similar to that among mainstream Protestant churches.) The newer denomination of Mormonism is strong in Utah and the surrounding western states. The so-called 'mega-churches' are strong in the sun belt states.

Secondly, the pattern of growth of some churches is much faster than in others. Specifically, many have noted the tendency for the mainstream and liberal Protestant churches—especially Episcopalians, Methodists and Presbyterians—to be in decline, while the evangelical churches and those fundamentalist churches that place more emphasis on the literal word of the Bible and are more conservative in theology have seen sharp increases in numbers. Although there are variations in how such churches are defined, the Pew 2008 survey confirms this trend. In 2008 it reckoned that the mainstream Protestant churches accounted for 18.1% and the evangelical Protestant churches had 26.3% of the adult population as members. (The Pentecostal and charismatic movements have been a driving force in the growth of a distinctive form of Protestant Christianity in the USA, and the Assemblies of God are one of the fastest growing Protestant denominations.) Moreover, whereas Roman Catholics were once a minority of the population, they now comprise the biggest single group, and the Protestant proportion of the population has already fallen below 50%, according to some polls (for instance, Harris, 2000 and Walsh, 2005).

Thirdly, religious groupings in the USA are shaped by and, in turn, shape US culture; that is, they are conditioned by the democratic, individualist and capitalist culture in which they exist. Even the Roman Catholic Church, with its strong emphasis on authority, has found it necessary to adapt to the USA's highly democratic environment. The highly successful exploitation of media developments by pastors such as Billy Graham and the late Jerry Falwell reflect the entrepreneurship that has always been part of US religion. The 'mega-churches'—for example Rick Warren's Saddleback Church in Lake Forest, CA and Bill Hybels' Willow Creek Community Church in Chicago, IL—are important adaptations of religious organizational provision to the contemporary American cultural context. Churches and religious groups form political organizations and networks akin to other interest groups. Thus, individual churches have their own organizations, which range from groups such as the Islamic Society of North America or the National Council of Churches to more specific groups representing a particular religious or political position, such as the American Family Association.

There is, thus, much internal dissent within denominations, some of it over doctrine and theology, and some of it over political and social issues. Very recently, for example, the question of whether same-sex unions should be blessed and whether gay or lesbian candidates should be accepted for ordination have occasioned significant divisions, not only in the Episcopal Church but also in other Protestant and Jewish denominations. Similarly, the ordination of women, while now accepted in all but two or three dioceses of the Episcopal Church (where women have been ordained since 1974), remains a divisive issue among Roman Catholics. Support for female ordination among individual US Catholics stands in marked contrast to the Pope's refusal to allow it. The issue is also divisive for many Jewish groups (where Reform and Conservative groups accept female rabbis, but the Orthodox tradition does not).

Finally, church affiliation in the USA is not necessarily a formal matter: Americans regularly state that they attend church, believe in God and that religion makes a difference to their lives. Certainly, Americans give significant amounts of money to their churches and other religious organizations: in 2004 religious organizations were the largest recipients of philanthropic money, receiving some US $88,000m. from a total of $250,000m.

THE CONSTITUTIONAL POSITION

Many of the American colonies, when founded, reflected Puritan opposition to the established (Anglican) Church in England. Although some states retained established churches until long after independence, the new land was seen as a haven for minority sects, usually Protestant. (Maryland, a state which offered tolerance to Roman Catholics, was the exception.) By the time of the drafting of the US Constitution in 1787 it was clear that no single church or denomination could claim hegemony and that government and religion would need to be separated at the federal level.

The US Constitution reflects the Founding Fathers' belief that their new republic should protect freedom of worship and avoid having any established church. However, the degree of strictness of the separation between church and state has changed over time and the courts (and politicians) have adopted different attitudes to what the Constitution required. In practice, until very recently the USA was assumed to be not merely an overwhelmingly Christian country, but an overwhelmingly Protestant one. Until John F. Kennedy won the presidency in 1960, no Roman Catholic had been elected to the country's highest office, and none since (John Kerry in 2004 was only the third Roman Catholic to run for the presidency as a major party candidate). Anti-Catholicism and anti-Semitism marked much of 20th century US history.

The Constitution's provisions on religion are contained in three clauses—the 'religious test' clause of Article VI ('no religious test shall ever be required as a qualification to any office or public trust under the United States') and the 'no establishment' and 'free exercise' clauses of the First Amendment ('Congress shall make no law respecting establishment of religion, or prohibiting the free exercise thereof'). How these clauses have been interpreted over the years has, however, varied considerably. Initially, these clauses were interpreted to mean that no religion should be favoured at the federal level; however, in the post-1945 period, as a result of legal cases brought by minority sects and religious objectors, the courts made a much more systematic effort to develop a coherent jurisprudence on the relationship between church and state.

There is, of course, a paradox about US attitudes to religion. For, whereas the Constitution enjoins separation of church and state, religion pervades the symbolism and rhetoric of US public life: the coinage declares 'in God we trust'; the pledge of allegiance has, since 1954, contained the words 'under God'; politicians regularly invoke religion in their speeches. (President George W. Bush's second inaugural speech in 2005 was so suffused with religious references and symbols that even sympathetic observers thought it went too far.)

In the post-Second World War period the Supreme Court struggled with the issue of the implications of the Establishment Clause for religious observance in public institutions. In

1962 (in *Engel v. Vitale*) the Supreme Court banned prayer in public schools. In that landmark case, the Court stated that the 'Constitution's prohibition against laws respecting an establishment of religion must at least mean in this country that it is no part of the business of government to compose official prayers for any group of American people for reading as part of a religious program carried out by government.' The same logic was applied to strike down a moment of silence in Alabama schools in 1985 (*Wallace v. Jaffree*), clergy participation in graduation ceremonies in Rhode Island (*Lee v. Weissman*, 1992) and calls for student-led prayers on the football pitch in Texas (*Santa Fe v. Doe*, 2000). However, the courts upheld a 2002 Virginia statute for a minute of silence which had no religious intention. This secularization of the classroom was not, of course, universally welcomed. For some parents the move prompted transfer to the private school system—to both fee-paying Christian schools and to education at home, which became increasingly popular, especially in the wake of school integration.

School prayer was not the only issue relating to the separation of church and state to be decided by the courts. In 1971 *Lemon v. Kurtzman*, one of a group of cases involving state aid to religious schools, established that it was unconstitutional for the state to pay a proportion of the salaries of teachers who worked in parochial schools. Thereafter, the so-called 'Lemon test' has been used to establish if a law is in violation of the First Amendment (in that, intentionally or not, that law has the effect of establishing a religion). The 'Lemon test' has three elements: to be constitutional a law must not have been approved with the intention of favouring a religious purpose; it must neither advance nor inhibit religion; and it must not result in any unnecessary entanglement of the government with religion.

Recently, the scope of the Establishment Clause was once again the subject of litigation in relation to the pledge of allegiance. The pledge of allegiance has been regularly subject to constitutional objection from Jehovah's Witnesses and other minorities. In 1940 the *Minersville School District v. Gobitis* case found that a school could expel two Jehovah's Witnesses who had refused to salute the flag; however, in 1943 the Court effectively overruled this (*West Virginia Board of Education v. Barnette*).

The concern with terrorism that followed the attacks on New York and Washington, DC, in September 2001 was accompanied by an increase in overt patriotism, which inevitably puts religious and political dissidents at a disadvantage. Some states (such as Tennessee) passed new legislation requiring a recitation of the pledge of allegiance in schools and other public places, prompting litigation from civil liberties groups. In a 2004 case (*Elk Grove Unified School District v. Newdow*), which reached the Supreme Court, an atheist objected to the recital of the pledge of allegiance at his daughter's school. Although the Court dismissed the case on narrow grounds of standing, it is likely that the prevailing atmosphere will produce further such cases.

Maintaining freedom of speech for unpopular minorities is especially difficult in wartime or when the nation feels under attack. Thus, a poll in July 2003 found that 44% of the US public believed that Islam was more likely than other religions to encourage violence among its believers, a shift in public perception which represented a marked increase in hostility towards Islam after the events of 11 September 2001. By 2005 this figure had fallen back to 36%, although the 2005 poll found marked differences of opinion between other religious groups about Islam, with white evangelical Protestants likely to be more unfavourable to Islam than white Roman Catholics and mainstream Protestants (see *Pew Forum on Religion and Public Life*, 24 July 2003, and *Pew Forum*, 26 July 2005).

The Supreme Court's interpretation of the First Amendment raises many general issues of key significance for US culture: to what extent does the constitutional separation of church and state require the elimination of religious symbols from public life? If prayer is removed from schools should religious displays be removed from public places? May religious groups use public facilities? And to what extent should the state acknowledge specifically Christian holidays such as Christmas and Easter, as opposed to Islamic or Jewish or Hindu ones? Such difficult questions have occasioned different responses. Although it has sometimes seemed that the trend of Supreme Court thinking in the early part of the post-1945 period was towards stripping all religious association from US public life, by the early 21st century there was much more support for a multi-faith pluralism, which incorporates many different religions into US public life and ceremonies. For some religious groups, however, the important battle is to resist secular humanism, which many conservative Christians see as threatening the USA through control of public schools and other national institutions. That approach, which has informed much Republican thinking in recent years, found some constitutional support when the Supreme Court in June 2007 ruled that taxpayers did not have the right to challenge the authority of the executive branch in relation to its decision (under George W. Bush) to establish the Office of Faith-Based Community Initiatives (*Hein v. Freedom From Religion Foundation*).

RELIGION AND PUBLIC POLICY

The school prayer and pledge of allegiance cases were highly controversial and the courts' efforts to protect the rights of dissenters often go against the grain of public opinion. Issues of cultural and religious significance have, of course, divided Americans since the foundation of the Republic. The writings of Charles Darwin on evolution met with massive resistance from religious fundamentalists—a resistance which lasted into the 21st century. Opposition to Darwinism was especially marked in the South, where Tennessee's law against the teaching of evolution led to the famous *Tennessee v. Scopes* trial of 1925. Hostility to the theory of evolution has taken a new turn in recent times. Since the 1970s there have been concerted efforts by opponents of the doctrine of evolution (mainly conservative Christians) to ensure that evolution and 'creationism' (the belief that human life and the universe were created by God) are given equal time in schools and that evolution is described as a hypothesis rather than an overwhelmingly accepted scientific theory. There has also been an enormous investment of effort on the part of conservative religious groups in developing 'creationism' as an alternative to scientific ideas of evolution. More recently still, the so-called 'theory of intelligent design' has been developed in an effort to fight against teaching evolution in public schools. A statement by then President George W. Bush in August 2005 indicated his support for this theory, further angering scientists who were already critical of his Administration's approach to scientific issues in public policy.

Inevitably, much of the debate about the role of religion in US public life will focus on education. One fascinating recent development has been the realization that Charter schools (schools that are publicly funded but independently administered) could be established to serve distinct social communities. The Tarek ibn Ziyad academy was established in Minnesota to serve the needs of Islamic students while more recently, in 2007, the Ben Gamla Charter school was established in Florida to cater for students who wanted to be educated in a way that recognized their Hebrew culture. On one level such schools cater for the cultural needs of the USA's minority communities. On another level they seem to threaten the role of publicly funded schools as integrative mechanisms for diverse communities. Apart from the battle for control of the schools and what is taught in them, much of the religious and cultural clashes in the USA of recent years have turned on so-called 'family issues', where conservative Christians (and others) have fought to maintain the supremacy of traditional values in such areas as the role of women, abortion and sexuality.

Undoubtedly, the issue that has most divided Americans since the 1970s is abortion. Prior to 1973 most states banned or restricted access to abortion, but many churches had no explicit position on the issue (with the notable exception of the Roman Catholic Church). After the 1973 *Roe v. Wade* supreme court decision (which established a constitutional right to abortion in the first trimester of pregnancy, but allowed regulation of the right thereafter), the abortion issue became highly politicized and the so-called 'right to life' movement became a significant part of the increasingly strong conservative coalition. Supporters of abortion rights found they had to organize with other civil rights groups to defend the substance of the 1973 decision. The administrations of Ronald Reagan (1981–89) and George Bush, Sr (1989–93) saw several attempts to challenge *Roe v. Wade* and restrict abortion rights; however, despite an increasingly conservative Supreme Court, the substantive right remained in force. Nevertheless, in a series of cases the power of state governments to control the provision of abortion (through requirements such as parental notification and waiting periods) was acknowledged. Furthermore, in *Planned Parenthood of Eastern Pennsylvania v. Casey* (1992), the trimester framework of the *Roe v. Wade* decision (which divided a pregnancy into three-month periods) was overturned, although the substantive constitutional right was upheld.

The most recent efforts of abortion opponents have turned not so much on abortion *per se*, but on late terminations and so-called partial birth abortion. There have also been continuing efforts to restrict legal abortion—for instance by imposing parental notification laws. And some states have tried to outlaw it altogether. Thus South Dakota's legislature passed an outright prohibition on abortion, but this was later defeated in a referendum in November 2006. President George W. Bush (in addition to making his support for the 'right to life' movement clear through such initiatives as proclaiming a Life Day) signed into law the 2003 Partial Birth Abortion Act; however, it was held to be unconstitutional by a number of state courts. In 2007 the Supreme Court reviewed the constitutionality of late term abortions and in two cases upheld the federal Partial Birth Abortion Act by a 5–4 majority. This decision was widely seen as defining the character of the Court of new Chief Justice John G. Roberts, Jr, and sent out clear signals of increasing hostility to abortion on the part of the Court. President Bush's support for the anti-abortion lobby had been signalled by a number of initiatives during his presidency, including his support for the Unborn Victims of Violence Act 2004, which made anyone who killed or injured a pregnant woman guilty of crimes against two individuals, further reinforcing support for the approach that the foetus should be regarded as a living being. Early in his presidency George W. Bush also modified the guidelines on funding for embryonic stem cell research, effectively reducing the money available for scientific research that might produce advances towards treating such diseases as Alzheimer's, diabetes, heart failure and Parkinson's. Bush's argument was that there was a moral boundary that a Government should not cross in experimentation on human embryos, even if those embryos would otherwise be discarded. He also argued that there were enough stem cell lines already available from human embryos, from animal material and umbilical placenta material, without using more human embryos for research. This position, although it enjoyed some support from the right, evoked strong criticism from the scientific community, the general public and from celebrities such as Nancy Reagan, who was a prominent supporter of research into Alzheimer's disease (from which her late husband, President Reagan, suffered). It also evoked criticism within the Republican Party: Bill Frist, the Senate Majority Leader from 2003–06, and a heart surgeon, was openly hostile to President Bush's views. Nevertheless, proposed congressional legislation to lift the restrictions on stem cell research occasioned Bush's first presidential veto in July 2006. Meanwhile, some state governments, such as California and Missouri, made their own efforts to circumvent the ban. However, as was noted in the aftermath of the Bush veto on efforts to lift the restrictions, some of the controversy might be diluted if new advances to obtain single stem cells without killing the embryo proved successful. Similarly, there was optimism about the ability of scientists to use stem cells derived from adult human beings rather than embryos.

President Bush's first term in office in fact marked a new stage in the relationship between religion and politics in the USA. It also heralded a new cultural and electoral bonding between the Republican Party and conservative moral and religious values. For much of the 20th century there was a clear association between Protestantism and the Republican Party, and between other religions (especially Catholicism and Judaism) and the Democratic Party. The 'New Deal' alignment of Franklin D. Roosevelt's presidency (1933–45) cemented this division. More recently, however, the relationship has eroded. Social mobility in the latter half of the 20th century broke down the allegiance of Roman Catholics to the Democratic Party, but so too did the rise on the political agenda of social issues such as abortion. In the 21st century the division is not so much between Roman Catholics and Protestants, but between conservative and traditionalist religious groups and more liberal ones.

The Republican Party has itself been transformed by the mobilization of conservative Christians, although debate continues both about the strength and the desirability of its relationship with the Christian right. Recently serious splits have emerged within the evangelical community about political priorities, with many younger evangelicals displaying a more liberal approach to social issues such as homosexuality, and increasing concern with environmental issues, especially global warming, and world poverty. Moreover, a new generation of evangelicals such as Joel Hunter has promoted an agenda which is politically much more liberal than that associated with individuals such as Jerry Falwell or Pat Robertson.

The mobilization of religious conservatives which began in the 1970s had been prompted both by threats to the charitable status of Christian schools and a broad agenda of social and family policy concerns. Organizational efforts continued through the 1980s and 1990s, becoming politically more visible and successful. Originally spearheaded by pressure groups outside the formal organization of the Republican Party (such as Jerry Falwell's 'Moral Majority'), this first wave of activism faded as the Reagan presidency wore on. A key turning point was the Rev. Pat Robertson's 1988 bid for the presidency. At that point the recruitment and politicization of conservative Christians entered a new stage and passed from the fringe to the mainstream of American politics. The catalyst for this change was a more pragmatic and broadly based organization, the Christian Coalition, masterminded by its political director Ralph Reed. Reed turned the Christian Coalition into a major force within the Republican movement in 1989. Unlike earlier religious right organizations, the Christian Coalition developed a strong grass roots base and made a determined effort to cross sectarian boundaries. Increasingly, religion became a significant factor at every level of politics, and it was one of the best predictors of the vote in the choice of President in the 2000 election, despite suggestions that its significance had waned. In 2004 religious affiliation and attitudes to social issues were again highlighted as decisive factors in securing George W. Bush's victory. However, since then the unity of the religious right has been under strain and some critics such as E. J. Dionne have pronounced it dead.

Religion did indeed play an important and highly controversial role in the George W. Bush presidency, shaping much of his political philosophy and personal life. His rhetoric was laced with religious references and appeared also to be a strong factor in his selection of appointees, including his judicial nominations. President Bush also intended religion to play a greater role in the policy process: on taking office in 2000, he established the Office of Faith-Based and Community Initiatives to galvanize the involvement of churches in providing social welfare programmes and to make federal grants available to faith communities. This initiative had only mixed success, and had to be effected by presidential executive orders rather than by legislation. Religious belief also strongly affected President Bush's perception of foreign policy. He projected a vision of the world as a struggle between good and evil, rejecting the pragmatic *realpolitik* that characterized the approach both of his father and of his predecessor, Bill Clinton (1993–2001). Like many conservative Christians, he strongly supported the state of Israel and Zionism, a position which was, if anything, strengthened by events since the onset of the anti-terrorism policy that has dominated US strategy since September 2001.

This strategy has provoked a mixed response from a public whose attitudes to the separation of church and state are not always consistent and certainly not immutable. Earlier, although many Presidents had kept their religious beliefs private, thinking perhaps that religion was likely to be as divisive as it was unifying, much prominence was given to President Jimmy Carter's (1974–77) religious commitment, although he combined evangelical faith with liberal views. President Reagan was aware of the political significance of the mobilization of conservative Christians and he claimed to have been 'born again'. A poll taken in August 2004 found Americans comfortable with a President who talks about his religious beliefs (indeed, an astonishing 70% said a President should have strong religious beliefs), but much less comfortable with churches endorsing candidates or mobilizing voters. An overwhelming majority, the same poll found, thought it proper to display the Ten Commandments on a court building, an issue which had caused deep controversy in 2004. But by August 2008, for the first time since the Pew Forum began asking the question in 1996, a slim majority (52%) of the public said that churches should keep out of politics. And much of the change had come from Republicans whose opposition to religious involvement in politics had increased in recent months. The situation is obviously a fluid one and, although the gap is narrowing, Republicans are still more likely than Democrats to be supportive of a closer link between religion and politics.

RELIGION AND VOTING BEHAVIOUR

One of the reasons why President George W. Bush and contemporary Republican strategists have placed so much public emphasis on their religious beliefs may have been based on personal ideology and principles. In seeking to move away from a liberal, secular policy paradigm to one that relies explicitly on a conservative philosophy they naturally sought support from religion and religious organizations. However, it is also the case that religion has an impact on voting behaviour and that religious groups have come to form a core part of the new Republican constituency. Just how important religion is in determining voting is open to debate, but the results of the 2000 and 2004 elections provide plausible evidence for the claim that it has become a major factor in US politics.

There have always been differences of partisanship between religious groups. As noted earlier, traditionally established sections of US society (especially white Protestants) aligned with the Republican Party, while outsider groups—Roman Catholics and Jews—favoured the Democratic Party. Evangelicals and fundamentalists were slow to become involved in electoral politics, but by the late 1970s there were many signs that the Republicans had begun to appreciate their potential political significance. Of course the evangelical world is a large and diverse one, and not all evangelicals and fundamentalists are sympathetic to the right. Some, such as Jim Wallis (who founded 'Soujourners' in 1971), remain committed to left-of-centre values based on social justice and world peace. There is, as mentioned earlier, increasing evidence of divisions within the evangelical community, reflecting generational shifts and changes in ideological focus. There are strong indications that the evangelical community is now divided about how it engages with politics. Of particular importance here are evangelical leaders who are keen to distance themselves from the religious right and to emphasize issues such as poverty and the environment. Clearly also the opposition to same sex marriage within the USA seems to be shifting, and younger Americans appear much less opposed to the idea than the generation preceding them. (Same sex marriage is legal in Massachusetts and California, while other states such as Vermont, New Hampshire, New Jersey and Connecticut grant same sex couples the right to civil unions, which confer the same legal rights as marriage.) That said, it remains to be seen how far new priorities within the evangelical movement will translate into a change of voting patterns or partisan preference. Since the 1970s Republicans have successfully strengthened conservative Christian identification with their party by hammering traditional social, moral and foreign policy issues and the association is not going to be easily undone.

Some observers have suggested that it is not so much the religion to which people are affiliated that shapes voting behaviour, but rather the level of a voter's commitment to religion as measured by church attendance. Green and Silk examined the 2000 vote and found that while Bush predictably gathered strong support from the Christian right in 2000, he was also very popular among all-white Protestant groups and among regular mass-going Roman Catholics. His Democratic opponent in 2000, Al Gore, by contrast, did well among minority faiths and minority ethnic groups. Thus, in 2000 he was well-supported by black Protestants, Jews and Latino Catholics. During his first Administration, Bush attempted to build up a strong religious base for himself and the Republican Party. As well as appealing to his core white Protestant constituency, he also tried to use religious and faith-based issues to appeal to ethnic minorities traditionally more associated with the Democratic camp.

The results of the 2004 presidential election found religion to be a continuing and highly important factor. Bush gained the overwhelming support (78% of their vote) of the evangelical Protestants, but performed less well among mainstream Protestants. He secured a surprising amount of support from Latino Protestants and managed to lure a small section of black American voters from the Democratic camp. Some of this new support was perhaps owing to issues such as gay marriage, to which Bush made plain his opposition by supporting a constitutional amendment designed to confine marriage to heterosexual couples. Bush also gained a majority of non-Latino Roman Catholics. His 2004 Democratic opponent, John Kerry, by contrast, received support from most black Protestants, from non-believers and from modernist, liberal and mainstream Protestants. The religious divide remained significant in the 2006 mid-term elections. Although a post-election survey for the Pew Research Center found people in most religious groups happy that the Democrats had won both Houses, white evangelicals were evenly divided in their enthusiasm for the new political landscape. Interestingly, the white evangelicals in 2006 identified 'values issues' such as abortion and marriage as more important than the ongoing US-led war in Iraq. This was in stark contract with the rest of the country, which saw the war as one of the major issues facing the USA, and where there is an increasing percentage in favour of withdrawing US troops.

The 2008 presidential election season saw some initial suggestions that this pattern might be changing. Firstly, as was frequently noted, there was no clear or obvious candidate for the religious right. On the Republican side John McCain (a former Episcopalian turned Southern Baptist) was perceived by many as a moderate, although his pro-life views make him acceptable to many social conservatives. Once nominated, though, McCain took care to emphasize his support for the status of marriage and his opposition to abortion so that by August 2008 was there were signs that he had solidified the Republican Party's base of white evangelicals. His selection of Sarah Palin as his vice-presidential running mate delighted this core constituency. As a 'creationist', ardent opponent of abortion and gun-control, and as a regular worshipper at a Pentecostal church, she more than compensated for McCain's apparent aloofness from the religious right. Secondly, the Republican Party could not assume it was the only candidate reaching out to religious voters. Senator Obama, an adherent of the United Church of Christ, has also been courting the 'values vote' which proved so important in 2004, and to white evangelicals in particular. He has thus emphasized his religious commitment while at the same time being careful not to alienate liberals on such issues as abortion, which Obama takes to be a private issue. His choice of Joseph Biden, a Roman Catholic, as his running mate cannot hurt his support with this important religious group. But what is evident is how both candidates have identified Christians as a key constituency to court, appearing together at a religious forum hosted by 'mega-church' pastor Rick Warren. The candidates used Warren's forum to project their own distinct appeals to the religious voters of America. Warren's own celebrity reflects another important trend in American religion, the rise of so-called 'mega-churches', which are largely evangelical and predominantly a phenomenon of the southern states of Texas, California, Georgia and Florida. There are about 400 or so of these churches, which are distinguished both by their size—they regularly have a congregation of 2,000 or more—and by their ability to provide a range of religious, social and recreational activities.

CONCLUSION

What has been called the 'religion gap' has become extremely important in US politics, polarizing different religious groups against each other (although, as has been noted, the faultlines often run through formal denominational labels). Although George W. Bush represented a new stage in the Republican Party's relationship with the religious right, there are strong signs that other religious voices are more likely to be heard in the new post-Bush era. It is likely that the evangelical community will display increasing diversity in its political stance, perhaps diluting the extent to which it can automatically be counted as an ally of the Republican right, and the Democrats may re-establish their appeal to religious voters. The importance of this new competitiveness is not merely the sheer size of the evangelical community—reckoned by some to be about 30m. strong—but also the appeal of evangelicalism, which seems especially powerful in its ability to reach younger Americans. Political strategists will have their eyes on future voters as well as current ones. On the other hand, as already discussed, the Republicans reasserted their claim to this constituency through the nomination of Sarah Palin as the 2008 vice-presidential candidate. At the same time doubts about too close an involvement between religion and political life have grown recently, as has the number of Americans for whom religion is apparently not important.

Such changes underline the fluidity of American opinion. Religion is a powerful factor, shaping political and social attitudes, but Americans feel able to select the form and style of religion which suits them personally and, for the most part, do not feel locked into a particular religious adherence. New organizational developments such as the 'mega-churches' provide different opportunities for religious expression and involvement. Above all, the problem of the rapidly changing demography of the USA remains. President Bush's vision of the US creed was very much a Christian one, and a conservative Christian one at that. As the population of the USA becomes more religiously diverse in the 21st century, its public philosophy will need to accommodate the change. It is probable that only a stricter neutrality and a rediscovery of the merits of Thomas Jefferson's (1801–09) 'wall of separation' between church and state can produce an environment in which people of all religions and none feel equally comfortable. It is also unclear how far the religious-based doubts over stem cell research, or related issues such as cloning, will be able to withstand the social and economic pressure of those seeking to advance biotechnological research and development. Much will doubtless depend on the character and religious beliefs of the next President; at the time of writing the candidate for the Republican nomination for the 2008 presidential election seemed an unlikely spokesman for the religious right, whatever his other political credentials. However, even if the next occupant of the White House is less obviously committed to a particular religious vision than his immediate predecessor, it seems inevitable that religious issues, identities and influence will continue to structure political debate in the USA for many years to come.

Bibliographic References

Adherents, Inc. <www.adherents.com>

Banerjee, N., 'Americans Changing Faiths at Rising Rates, Report Finds', in *New York Times*, February 25 2008.

Dionne E.J., *Souled Out: Reclaiming Faith and Politics After the Religious Right*. Princeton, NJ, Princeton University Press, 2008.

Eck, D., 'The Multireligious Public Square', in Gerber, M., and Walkowitz, R. (Eds). *One Nation Under God? Religion and American Culture*. New York, NY, Routledge, 1999.

Fitzgerald, Frances, 'The New Evangelicals', in *The New Yorker*, 30 June 2008.

Grammich, C., 'Many Faiths of Many Religions: Continuities and Changes Among Religious Adherents Across US Counties', in *Rand Labor and Population Working Paper*. Santa Monica, CA, 2004.

Green, J., and Silk, M., 'The New Religion Gap', in *Religion in The News*, (Special Supplement), Fall 2003. Hartford, CT, The Leonard E. Greenberg Center for the Study of Religion in Public Life Trinity College, 2003.

Harris Poll, *Religious Affiliation Year 2000*. Hartford Institute for Religious Research. <www.adherents.com/rel_USA.html>

McLaren, A., 'The Ethical and Social Considerations of Stem Cell Research', in *Nature*, 1 November 2001, Vol. 414.

Pew Forum on Religion and Public Life: Religious Landscape Study, February 2008. Washington, DC, <pewforum.org>

Pew Forum on Religion and Public Life: Religion and Politics, 'More Question Religion's Role in Politics', August 21 2008. Washington, DC, <pewforum.org>

Popper, N., 'Chartering a New Course', in *Wall Street Journal*, New York, 31 August 2007.

Smith G., Keeter, S., and Green, J., 'Religious Groups React to the 2006 Election', in *Pew Research Center Publications*, 27 November 2006, Washington, DC.

Walsh, A., 'Protestants in decline', in *Religion in the News*, Winter 2005, Vol. 7, No 3. The Leonard E. Greenberg Center for the Study of Religion in Public Life, Trinity College, Hartford, CT.

Wallis, J., *God's Politics: Why the Right Gets It Wrong and the Left Doesn't Get It*. Oxford, Lion Hudson, 2006.

Yearbook of the American and Canadian Churches. New York, National Council of Churches of the USA, annual.

AMBIVALENT ENGAGEMENT: THE USA AND INTERNATIONAL ORGANIZATIONS

MARTIN GRIFFITHS

Since the terrorist attacks on the USA of 11 September 2001 and the proclamation of a 'war on terror' by the Administration of George W. Bush (2001–), it has become conventional wisdom to characterize US foreign policy in terms of a radical shift away from multilateral co-operation with other states towards a more unilateral stance. The clearest example of this shift was the 2003 invasion of Iraq in the absence of explicit authority from the UN Security Council. Other examples include the US refusal to support the International Criminal Court or ratify the Kyoto Protocol to regulate climate change, and its lack of effort to strengthen a variety of multilateral arms control treaties and conventions, including the Anti-Ballistic Missile Treaty and the Non-Proliferation Treaty. As this survey will demonstrate, however, the situation is more complex than conventional wisdom suggests. The term 'ambivalent engagement' is a more appropriate description of the contemporary relationship between the USA and key international organizations. On the one hand, the USA remains unwilling to be bound by rules and organizations that limit its freedom of action in the short term, particularly on security issues. On the other hand, it is increasingly apparent that global challenges—from terrorism and proliferation to climate change and poverty—require international co-operation. No single government, however powerful, is capable of solving these challenges alone. Moreover, there is a pervasive sense that progress is sorely needed on a variety of international issues under a new administration. On the economic front, multilateral trade talks and the fight to eradicate poverty have stalled. On the security front, the search for peace in the Middle East remains elusive, and the situation in Iraq is central to this condition. Global nuclear non-proliferation is being undermined by the poor relationship between the USA and Iran and ongoing frustration with the Democratic People's Republic of Korea (North Korea), while efforts to address perhaps the greatest long-term challenge, global climate change, are similarly impeded. Nevertheless, within these challenges and complexities lie opportunities for the USA to find common ground and to forge common cause with the international community. Especially by working with and helping to direct the UN, the USA still has an opportunity to take a leading role in responding to the great global challenges of the next century. This survey begins with the USA's relationship with the UN, and then considers its relationship with the North Atlantic Treaty Organization (NATO) and the European Union (EU). Third, it examines the USA's relationship with the key international organizations for managing the global economy: the IMF, the World Bank and the World Trade Organization (WTO). Finally, the survey concludes with an overview of the key challenges confronting the new US President when he takes office in 2009.

THE USA AND THE UN

The advantage of working through the UN is three-fold: burden-sharing, effectiveness and reputation. First, it is far cheaper for the USA to share the costs and burdens of global governance than it is to bear them alone. Most US taxpayer dollars spent through the UN and other major multilateral institutions are leveraged three-fold or more. For example, the US Government Accountability Office has argued that UN peace-keeping is at least eight times less expensive than fielding US forces. The UN's peace-keeping missions (which have grown to include some 100,000 troops) now bring a collective armed force—second in size only to the USA—to some of the most conflict-ridden areas in the world, places where the USA has a stake, but does not want to commit its own troops. Similar multipliers are found in refugee assistance, global health, food assistance and disaster relief. Second, the global effort to eliminate poverty and reach the UN Millennium Development Goals will never be successful without broad public and private efforts or without effective global norms and institutions. Similarly, the urgency of climate change demands a global effort of unprecedented diplomacy and economic co-operation. Third, at a time when every measure shows that global opinion of the USA has been flagging, improving its relationship with the UN would contribute substantially to the improved status of the USA world-wide. The UN is the world's stage, and US priorities and actions at the UN have real consequence. Fulfilling its financial commitments to the UN and making every effort to play a constructive role there will go a long way toward alleviating the surge of anti-US sentiment that has surfaced over the last five years.

Since assuming his position as Secretary-General of the UN Ban Ki-Moon has brought a fresh perspective to the organization. After being selected with the support of the USA and with the unanimous endorsement of the membership of the UN, the new Secretary-General identified the following priorities for his tenure: restoring a spirit of co-operation among the UN member states, encouraging peace in the Middle East, curtailing proliferation of weapons of mass destruction in places such as North Korea and Iran, stopping the conflict in Darfur (Sudan), breaking the logjam surrounding UN reform efforts, and engaging the UN more aggressively in the issues of energy and climate change. The new Secretary-General also demonstrated his understanding of the importance of a strong relationship between the UN and its largest financial contributor, the USA. The departure of US Ambassador to the UN John Bolton in 2007, and the quick confirmation and arrival of Zalmay Khalilzad as his successor was indicative of improved relations between the UN and the USA.

A number of definitive steps have been taken to consolidate a new spirit of co-operation between the USA and the UN, and to accelerate the process of reform within the UN. In 2007 the General Assembly approved plans to improve UN financial tracking and information technology systems, new ethics and financial disclosure regulations were established, and the UN created the Central Emergency Response Fund, the Peace-building Commission and the Democracy Fund to provide money for 125 projects in support of civil society and democracy around the globe. The Human Rights Commission was abolished and replaced by the Human Rights Council. Finally, the UN has been pressing ahead with a plan to streamline and consolidate UN field operations in five pilot countries, and is hopeful that this so-called 'one UN' approach to delivering services will save hundreds of millions of dollars and improve outcomes in the field—where UN services count most. Unfortunately, some of the more ambitious structural reform efforts, especially involving changes in the budget and personnel systems, were stalled in 2008. These significant reform issues need to be resumed and are a priority for the current Secretary-General and key Member States. None of these changes, however, will occur without persistent, diplomatic leadership from the USA.

Hovering behind many of the reform efforts is the awkward issue of Security Council reform. The US push for reforms in 2007 and 2008 excluded this major issue from the overall UN reform umbrella. Consequently, many members of the UN often perceived the drive for reform as an effort to curtail the General Assembly without addressing issues related to the Security Council. In fact, the USA had good reason to be satisfied with the performance of the existing Security Council once it overcame the unpleasantness about invading Iraq in 2003. Over the next five years the Council proved to be quite co-operative in rallying to press Syrian forces to withdraw from Lebanon and to install a peace-keeping force in Darfur, and even approved a US occupation regime in Iraq (in the process turning over to it the large unspent balances in the oil-for-food accounts and lifting the embargo on the sale of Iraqi oil). There was not, therefore, much that the USA needed from the Security Council reform process, or at least nothing that would outweigh US officials' wariness of what might come out of a UN negotiating process. In particular, almost every reform proposal emanating from the General Assembly would so expand the Council's membership as to dilute the US voice and, according to the USA, make the Council more unworkable than it already was. Similarly, improved US relations with the UN remained handicapped by a lack of US commitment on a number of fronts.

The USA continues to be a reluctant financial contributor to the UN, although the situation is far from the dark days of the late 1990s, during which the USA was more than US $1,000m. in arrears at the UN. Unfortunately, the underlying problem remains. The USA now has about $770m. in structural arrears at the UN. However, in early 2008 the General Assembly adopted a new, two-year budget of $4,000m.. The USA had objected to the inclusion of $7m. for a further World Conference against Racism—the USA considered that the original event, which took place in 2001, was biased in its proceedings against Israel—but finally approved the new financial arrangements. Furthermore, the USA provides little support for UN peace-keeping structures. UN peace-keeping has expanded to record levels because of Security Council requests in recent years. The Department of Peacekeeping Operations (DPKO) is over-stretched, under-staffed and in need of new mechanisms to facilitate flexibility and deployments for missions such as that to Darfur. The USA does not generally provide troops for UN peace-keeping forces but it could do a great deal more to enhance DPKO operations—whether that is in helping to streamline managerial structures in New York or in providing advice on intelligence or doctrine development. Similarly, US support for UN efforts to deal with climate change remains weak. In 1992 the US Senate ratified the basic climate treaty (The Framework Convention on Climate Change) and led the negotiations for the first steps toward implementation (The 1997 Kyoto Protocol). Little has happened in the last 10 years, while the scientific evidence has solidified, global carbon markets have grown, and an increasing number of US companies are asking for decisions and long-term predictability for a carbon-constrained economy. As the home of the Climate Convention, the Intergovernmental Panel on Climate Change, and a number of diverse agency actions and norm-setting requirements, the UN will be a major factor in the needed international negotiations, and Ban Ki-Moon has identified the climate issue as an important priority.

THE USA, NATO AND THE EU

In the 21st century NATO leaders confront a far different security landscape than the one faced by the founding fathers of the alliance. Those leaders established NATO in 1949 to defend Western Europe against Soviet military power. The USA, as the most powerful member of the alliance by far, came to dominate the transatlantic relationship, both politically and militarily. When the USSR unexpectedly collapsed, the instability generated in Central and Eastern Europe reminded European allies of the importance of maintaining the transatlantic alliance as a hedge against an uncertain future. The USA, for its part, had no desire to abandon the primary instrument through which it exercised influence in Europe, which remained vital to its long-term security interests.

NATO endured, but the disappearance of the Soviet threat gave the European allies, most of whom were also members of the EU, the political freedom to accelerate their goal of pursuing ever-closer European integration through the EU. As part of this process, the EU began to construct a distinctive security and defence personality of its own, a development that raised growing concerns within US federal government circles that the EU might one day compete with NATO. This has generated friction between NATO and the EU, as well as between the USA and its European allies over the respective roles of the two organizations. While some of its European allies have been working to establish an autonomous security capacity within the EU, the USA has been pulling in the opposite direction, seeking new roles and missions for the alliance as the NATO enlargement process began to wind down. The attacks on the USA on 11 September 2001 demonstrated that the most important security threats to NATO members originated from outside Europe and that NATO was poorly equipped to handle them. Although NATO invoked Article 5 for the first time in its history in the wake of the terrorist attacks and allies came forward with offers of military support for the subsequent military operation in Afghanistan, the USA found that European allies had little useful to offer. US rejection of most of the offers ruffled allied feathers and raised questions about the relevance of a military alliance where only one member could project significant expeditionary military power.

The US response to this issue was two-fold. The first was to persuade European allies to pool their limited resources to establish a single, multinational, European-based NATO Response Force (NRF), trained and equipped to US standards, that would be able to deploy quickly and fight effectively alongside US forces. The second response was to persuade allies that NATO needed to extend its mandate beyond the traditional borders of Europe. The two initiatives were adopted without controversy at a summit in Prague, Czech Republic, in November 2002. Despite the crisis in transatlantic relations brought about by the US invasion of Iraq in 2003, little damage was done to the Prague agenda. Indeed, in the immediate aftermath of the crisis, NATO agreed to assume command of the peace-keeping operation in Afghanistan, the first 'out-of-area' operation in the history of the alliance.

Afghanistan and the NRF have dominated the NATO agenda ever since. Under persistent US pressure, the allies have agreed to the expansion of the peace-keeping force from Kabul into the provinces, most recently into the former Taliban heartland of southern Afghanistan, where NATO peace-keeping operations are being tested seriously. Although increasing Taliban attacks have made peace-making operations highly dangerous, the allies have steadfastly resisted US efforts to get them involved in US-led 'Operation Enduring Freedom' counter-terrorism operations, which would put their forces even more seriously in harm's way. Meanwhile, progress in developing the NRF has been hampered by the continuing inability of European allies to devote the resources required to acquire key logistical capabilities, such as strategic airlift, or to train and equip sufficient numbers of combat troops to US standards, despite the force being declared fully operational in 2006.

Although these post-11 September US initiatives have met with mixed success, the crisis atmosphere that characterized the period leading up to the invasion of Iraq has faded. NATO has even undertaken a modest training mission in Iraq. The primary faultline at NATO now is of older and more familiar vintage: the long-standing struggle between the USA, concerned as always to maintain strong US influence in Europe through NATO, and France, just as determined to minimize that influence without actually breaking the transatlantic link. France is prepared to use NATO in what it regards as appropriate circumstances. That country has pressed for greater autonomy and opposed US efforts to strengthen NATO or move it in directions that the French Government believes are more properly the province of the EU. This has precipitated a tug of war both within the EU and within NATO.

Although France is not without allies, most EU-member NATO allies seek a middle road. This reflects an enduring commitment to maintain close relations with the USA, despite the absence of any palpable military threat to their security. Yet, just as they are unwilling to go as far as the French would like, they are similarly disinclined to go as far as the USA would like in finding new roles and missions for the alliance, particularly if they conflict with EU prerogatives, or in funding the NRF. Not surprisingly, Franco-US disagreement over the proper roles of NATO and the EU has complicated relations between the two organizations. Despite their overlapping mandates and the fact that they have 19 members in common, there is only minimal systematic interaction, very little transparency, and less co-ordination. For the most part, this has precipitated little direct conflict because each organization has tended to focus on different missions. NATO has focused on larger-scale and more difficult peace-keeping operations, while the EU has taken on much smaller-scale or more settled peace-keeping activities.

Over the past two years the USA has continued to press an ever more ambitious agenda on NATO. In Afghanistan the USA has been steadily pressuring allies to broaden the risk they are willing to shoulder in conducting peace-keeping operations. To boost the flagging NRF, the US Government is urging European allies to support a strategic airlift initiative that would provide the air transport and other logistical resources needed to help reduce the NRF's dependence on the USA. The USA has also been proposing that NATO expand its contacts with non-European Western allies, such as Japan, Australia and South Korea, which would give the alliance an even more global focus. The Bush Administration has also supported the appeal for enhanced political discussion at NATO. Finally, the USA is pressing NATO to assume a more substantial role in the Middle East and Africa by seeking to establish military training centres. Taken together, these initiatives represent an ambitious vision of an increasingly globally focused alliance undertaking a progressively wider range of potential issues, activities and missions, led by the USA.

If these trends are clear, the prospects for the future are not. US ambitions for NATO clearly conflict with French ambitions for the EU. Furthermore, even though most EU/NATO members find themselves caught in the middle, the current nature of NATO-EU relations suggests continuing difficulties ahead, to the detriment of both organizations and of transatlantic relations more generally. The extent to which the US Government can shape the alliance may depend as much on US preferences as it does on how far the NATO allies are prepared to allow. Similarly, for the EU, the availability of resources, not just ambition, will have a profound effect on the kind of security and defence role the organization can play in the future. NATO and the EU are fundamentally different kinds of organizations. NATO is a defence alliance whereas the EU has some of the trappings of a supranational state. As part of a defence alliance, NATO members agree to defend each other in the event of an attack, while EU members pledge to surrender various aspects of their national sovereignty across the full spectrum of governance, involving foreign and domestic issues. In foreign affairs, the EU mandate extends well beyond that of NATO. The EU routinely employs special representatives to act diplomatically on behalf of the organization, most prominently in Bosnia and Herzegovina, where the EU High Representative plays a critical role in national politics, something NATO has never done. Despite the recent rejection of the EU Constitution in two member states, which indefinitely stalled the latest attempt at further formal integration, it is reasonable to expect that the EU will continue to play an active, perhaps increasingly active, diplomatic role in world affairs.

It is difficult to envision NATO assuming this kind of role, at least to anywhere near the same extent. Expanding the range of political issues to be discussed at NATO is one thing; undertaking diplomatic initiatives under a NATO flag is quite another. This would require the USA to subordinate its diplomatic freedom of action to political oversight by NATO, something it has never been willing to do, given the constraints this would place on US flexibility, particularly on critical international issues such as the Middle East. Should the USA decide to pursue selected diplomatic initiatives through NATO none the less, prospects for success would be uncertain at best. Sympathetic EU members of NATO might be persuaded to assent, depending on the issue, while others might welcome the opportunity to constrain what they perceive to be unilateralist US tendencies.

The same fate could also await any US effort to encourage NATO to play a leading role in addressing security issues that are not primarily military in nature, such as terrorism or energy security. With respect to military capabilities and operations, the traditional lifeblood of NATO, the dynamics are reversed. European allies do not have the military capacity to undertake anything more than small-scale peace-keeping and peace-enforcement operations. For larger-scale operations they are dependent on geographical proximity and, at least for the time being, NATO planning and operational assets. This relative weakness is one key reason why the EU has gravitated toward more civilian-orientated rule of law operations, where they have been able to develop modest capabilities and are relatively stronger. Given US concerns over EU ambitions, ironically only one factor is likely to lead to significant improvement in European military capabilities for the foreseeable future: US persuasion of its European allies to expend the resources necessary to make the NRF a success.

The situation is considerably more complicated with respect to major combat operations. Here, the question is not simply whether the NRF will become a viable expeditionary force or even whether the USA is prepared to ferry European allies to the battlefield. The real question is whether the USA would choose to fight a major conflict on the scale of that in Afghanistan or Iraq under a NATO flag. Recent history suggests not. The USA is able to exercise much more control and freedom of action over major combat operations by working through 'coalitions of the willing' than within the heavily bureaucratized NATO structure.

The USA could choose, however, to work through NATO, either as a general policy or in specific cases where the advantages of operating under a NATO banner seem to outweigh the disadvantages. An example of the latter might be situations in which NATO cover is deemed desirable to give legitimacy to operations that cannot achieve UN sanction due to Russian or Chinese opposition. Although EU members of NATO, France included, would probably welcome a US decision to use NATO for major combat operations, the suspicion that the NRF will never be used in this way may be one reason why most European allies are not prepared to devote resources to it. Yet, even if NATO faces an uncertain future as a vehicle for conducting major combat operations, it still has an important role to play militarily, not only as a mechanism for mounting high-end peace-keeping and peace-enforcement operations, but also through its emphasis on interoperability and the habits of working, planning and exercising together that it inculcates in its members and partners. These habits have proven to be of vital importance in producing the successful coalitions of the willing that have characterized major US combat operations since the Arabian (Persian) Gulf War.

Ultimately, the future of the NATO alliance itself is of most concern to the USA. The glue that holds the alliance together today is unquestionably weaker than it was during the Cold War. As the situation in Iraq clearly demonstrated, European allies are more willing to oppose the USA on issues of critical importance to the USA than ever before. Yet, the cohesion remains, as the events following the attacks of 11 September markedly showed and as developments in Afghanistan demonstrate, however fitfully, even today. Although France and its supporters habitually may seek to keep US ambitions for NATO under restraint, if the USA were to make clear that NATO was its default setting for all major military operations, combat included, European allies might be more prepared to expend more on the NRF or invest in the organization more generally. As noted above, the USA has very good reasons not to use NATO as its default option, but it must then live with the consequences.

The real problem is that the USA does not really know what it wants from NATO. It continues to perceive the alliance through what is essentially a Cold War prism, as the key mechanism through which the USA attempts to project influence in Europe. The successes of the NATO enlargement process, which addressed genuine security concerns among newly freed former Communist states, and of NATO involvement in the Balkans have only helped to sustain this perception. Current US efforts to give NATO a more global reach also reflect the same perception of NATO pre-eminence, with the alliance moving beyond its European core to embrace the wider world. It is undeniably a grand vision, but it is also clearly at odds with reality. The notion of giving pride of place to a military alliance made sense during the Cold War, but it does not make sense today when the most critical threats are more varied and diffuse. NATO is of limited use as a diplomatic actor, which is why the USA has never really used it in this capacity. Other vehicles and partners are preferred for US diplomatic activity, the EU increasingly among them, and this is unlikely to change. Even in the military sphere, NATO is no longer the primary instrument of choice and has, at best, only a circumscribed, if still important, role to play.

Despite all these problems, it should be remembered that the economic relationship between the EU and the USA remains one of the main features of the global economy. Transatlantic integration is broader and deeper than between any other major political regions in the world. The EU and the USA account for 40% of global merchandise trade and 45% of world trade in services. The combined European and US economies account for nearly two-thirds of world gross domestic product (GDP). The partnership is the single most important driver of global economic growth, trade and prosperity, and bilateral economic ties are growing every year. Headlines and policy debates frequently focus on a minor part of the economic relationship, such as trade disputes. However, in reality the overwhelming majority of bilateral trade between the USA and the EU (over US $2,000m. per day in 2008) is not open to dispute. Moreover, merchandise trade constitutes a relatively small portion of transatlantic economic activity, less than 20%. Foreign affiliate sales (i.e. trade between parent companies, affiliates and suppliers across the Atlantic) are more than five times larger. The EU's total investment stake in the US economy today exceeds $1,700,000m., accounting for nearly 75% of all foreign investment in the USA. The EU is also a large supplier of capital for the US economy and (with the People's Republic of China and Japan) helps to finance the US Government's budget deficit.

MANAGING THE GLOBAL ECONOMY

Over the past few years the USA has played a major role in pushing for reforms at the IMF and the World Bank in the wake of a series of financial crises in the late 1990s affecting Mexico, East Asia, Russia, Argentina and Turkey, although it remains to be seen whether these organizations can still play a central role in managing the global economy. They all confront grave challenges. For example, the IMF has lost its role as the world's central banker and suffers from a mismatch between aspiration and authority. Demand for its resources is declining rapidly. In 2003 Thailand finished paying off its obligations two years ahead of schedule, while in 2004 Russia prepaid its US $3,300m. debt to the IMF. Then, in December 2005 and January 2006, Argentina and Brazil announced their decision to repay their entire debt to the Fund ($9,800m. and $15,500m. respectively). Pakistan has said that it is seeking to reduce its dependence on the Fund; Ukraine, the fourth largest debtor, has declined any further assistance; and Serbia has announced that it would not increase its borrowings. In 2007 just six countries had stand-by arrangements—the lowest number since 1975. The volume of lending rebounded in 2008, but almost entirely because of a $10,000m. loan package to Turkey.

Several factors have contributed to the development of alternative mechanisms to execute particular IMF functions, which can be grouped into three areas: surveillance, lending and technical assistance. Perhaps the most important factor has been the rapid growth of financial markets, and especially bond markets, which in turn has driven the expansion of institutions that monitor and conduct continuous market surveillance, notably rating agencies and other private and governmental institutions that track financial conditions. A second factor has been an equally impressive expansion in regional co-operation and integration. The third development, closely related to the above, has been modern communications technology, which has brought about a multiplication in the volume, access and speed of information, enormously facilitating surveillance by non-official actors.

For some time there has been broad consensus on the need to reform the IMF. Ideas for reform cover virtually every aspect of the Fund, from its surveillance role to its role in debt management and emergency lending, the nature of its advice and the roles it needs to add or discard, and its governance. The USA has been instrumental in pressing for increased transparency and accountability within the IMF. In addition, it initiated the creation of the Financial Stability Forum to promote information exchange among IMF members. However, the most important and urgent issue currently confronting the international monetary system and the IMF is the huge imbalance in major national economies and exchange rates. The global current account deficit of the USA is very large (nearing an annual rate of US $800,000m., almost 7% of its GDP), and its small reduction in 2007–2008 reflects the broader slowdown in the US economy. Equally, the global current account surplus of China is growing to approximately 6% of China's GDP. A number of other Asian countries—most notably Japan but also Korea, Taiwan, Hong Kong, Singapore, and Malaysia—are also running substantial global surpluses that are the counterparts of the US global deficit.

In the long term, the USA must lead the correction of these imbalances by raising its rate of national saving so that it will not be so reliant on inflows of foreign capital, which it must now borrow at the rate of US $5,000m. every day. Ongoing current account deficits generate enormous pressures for trade protection (which are now being realized rapidly, especially against China) as well as huge international financial risks. Another essential element of the global correction will be a further large decline in the exchange rate of the US dollar, probably by at least 20% on a trade-weighted average against the currencies of the USA's major trading partners. The dollar has already declined substantially against the currencies that float freely in the exchange markets, notably the euro, pound sterling, Swiss franc, Canadian dollar, and Australian dollar. The next phase of the US dollar's decline needs to take place against the currencies of the East Asian countries that are running the world's largest surpluses and have the world's fastest growth rates, but which have intervened massively in the exchange markets to limit their currency appreciation far below what market forces would have produced. China is the key country. Its surplus is now the largest among the major Asian economies as a share of its economy. The need for appreciation of the Asian currencies is particularly acute from a US standpoint now that the euro, which had risen 65% against the dollar between late 2000 and 2006, is under downward pressure as a result of the rejection of a new constitution for the EU.

In recent years the IMF has been making a more forceful effort to bring the global imbalances back under control. It has been vocally pushing the USA to initiate actions that would reduce its external deficits. Likewise, it has been urging the Europeans to implement structural reforms to accelerate the growth of domestic demand in their economies in order to offset the adverse impact they will experience from the declines in their trade surpluses that are an essential counterpart of the reduction in US deficits. Without much stronger support from the Group of Seven (G7) industrialized countries, however, there is little that the Fund can do to achieve such policy alterations. It should also be remembered that while the US President nominates the World Bank President, traditionally the head of the IMF is a European.

While the main function of the IMF is macroeconomic stability, its second function is to support its sister organization, the World Bank, and its mission of promoting economic development. The Bank pursues this objective through lending, the production of research and economic analysis and the provision of policy advice and technical assistance. It is a large organization employing some 10,000 development professionals (including economists, educators, environmental scientists, financial analysts, anthropologists, engineers and many others) from over 140 countries. Three-quarters of its employees work in its headquarters in Washington, DC, and the rest work in the Bank's 109 'country offices'. Under pressure from the USA, and in tandem with the IMF, in recent years the Bank has emphasized its role in promoting a 'good governance' agenda for the developing world. While by no means a new topic in the area of economic development, the issue of good governance has been given new impetus by five important factors. First, the issue is a response to the development failures in the 1980s, in particular the difficult experience with and mixed record of structural adjustment programmes. Second, it is a recognition of the failure of command economies and the emergence of consensus within the World Bank on the relative efficacy of export-orientated development strategies. Third, the rise of pro-democracy movements in Africa and other parts of the developing world has been accompanied by demand for good governance and more responsive forms of government as a rallying point. Fourth, there has been growing concern that widespread corruption is siphoning away both domestic and external resources of developing states. And fifth, the phenomenal increase in globalization has generated strong imperatives for sound domestic policy environments and economic management.

There is consensus that good governance should build on effective states, mobilized civil societies and efficient private sectors, three factors necessary for sustained development. Effective states create an enabling political and legal environment for equitable economic growth. Active and vibrant civil societies mobilize individuals, groups and communities, facilitate political and social interaction, help to generate social capital, and foster societal cohesion and stability. Productive private sectors generate jobs and income. There is also consensus that the key elements of good governance include accountability, transparency, combating corruption, participatory governance and an enabling legal/judicial framework.

Although the good governance agenda has wide support in the international community, there are some major differences between the USA and other Bank member states over development issues. British Prime Minister Gordon Brown has called for rich countries to increase their aid to the poorest states. In contrast, the USA places more emphasis on increasing aid efficiency rather than the volume of aid. This has complicated ongoing efforts for debt relief. While the United Kingdom would like to cancel all IMF and World Bank debt for all very poor countries, with donor countries increasing their contributions to the World Bank to fund the Bank's debt reduction, the USA believes that the World Bank can fund its own debt relief by refraining from providing loans to such countries and moving to grant-based assistance with tighter performance requirements.

Perhaps the greatest challenges confronting the USA and international organizations can be found in the trade arena, where there is a real crisis of multilateralism. Over the last 50 years states have played a major role in spurring the growth of trade. Multilateral and regional negotiations and unilateral policy decisions to reduce barriers and increase market access have provided a generally conducive international environment for trade expansion, although non-tariff barriers and subsidies have become more important since the 1970s. The various rounds of the General Agreement on Tariffs and Trade (GATT) reduced tariff levels significantly in the developed world and, more recently, many developing countries have also embraced trade liberalization. Mercantilist policies, however, continue to be attractive to developing countries in Asia and those willing to emulate them. The replacement of the GATT by the WTO in 1995 bolstered the freer trade cause, with the dispute settlement system an important new development. In theory, settlement underscores the rule of law and helps to make the trading system more secure and predictable. Critics argue, however, that the process takes too long. States may be well aware that they are transgressing WTO rules, but also know that by the time a dispute is settled, they will have provided critical leeway or support for their businesses. Power politics still shapes the system. The potential animosity generated by disputes also runs the risk of undermining the whole system, although the WTO leaves it to the victor of a settlement to impose sanctions. There is no provision for enforcement if the aggrieved party declines to act.

Difficult and acrimonious negotiations continue to plague the WTO system, partly because the scope of international trade negotiations has expanded enormously over the last decade and partly because of the newly found assertiveness of the major developing countries. The very success of post-war negotiations is also a factor: as trade barriers fell the trade agenda has shifted into sensitive areas of economies, not as amenable to easy negotiation. The multilateral trade agenda has gone beyond opening trade to global market integration through the convergence of national market regulation. This has a major impact on developing countries as they seek to catch up with the developed world, with restrictions on industry policies limiting their development options. The USA has pushed for the liberalization of services, trade and investment. Nevertheless, economic subsidies to attract investment remain prevalent in all countries. In 2008 the Doha Round, which began in 2001 in Doha, Qatar, with the aim of incorporating development into the WTO agenda, became deadlocked over agricultural trade, and ultimately failed to deliver any consensus in July 2008.

As WTO negotiations have faltered, regional trade agreements (RTAs) have proliferated. While the multilateral system spreads the benefits of liberalization on a non-discriminatory basis, RTAs generally restrict the benefits of liberalization to participants. By 2008 contracting parties had notified the WTO of nearly 400 RTAs. According to the WTO guidelines, RTAs are supposed to facilitate trade between the parties and not to raise barriers to trade for other WTO members. However, a major concern is that RTAs make states less willing to spend time and effort on multilateral negotiations. Many liberal supporters of freer trade are also critical, arguing that RTAs lead to a confusion of trade agreements with different standards.

THE CHALLENGE OF INTERNATIONAL ORDER

Although international order and the existing power structure should be kept analytically separate, any viable international order is bound to reflect the prevailing power structure. Thus, for international order to be effective, it has to be developed in co-operation with the USA as much as possible. Institutions lack the potency to equalize power disparities; they can only mitigate them. In addition, institutions that lack supranational authority need leading states to bolster collective action, making enforcement towards aggressors or free riders effective. At the same time, the strongest state also needs to legitimize the exercise of its power. In this context it is important to recognize the difference between power and authority. Authority is a relationship between two or more actors in which one actor or a subset of actors possesses some decision-making power over some specific issue and is regarded by other actors as being in legitimate possession of such power. Authority is a structure of shared perceptions of legitimacy, to be distinguished from notions of coercion, control and permission. Authority is located somewhere between negotiation, a process of compliance characterized by bargaining, and coercion, where compliance results more from fear of the consequences of non-compliance. Understood as a relationship, authority only exists when it is both exercised and complied with.

Legitimacy plays an important role in this context, providing the avenue of social control through which authority is able to operate, distinct from both self-interest and coercion. It instils a belief in actors that a rule or institution ought to be recognized and adhered to. As one would expect from its close relationship with authority, legitimacy operates on two levels. First, it functions at an individual level to internalize perceptions of self-interest, and thus promotes a behavioural response of an actor to an external rule or institution. Second, it also has a cumulative effect upon the strategic environment, potentially constituting the landscape within which actors pursue their interests. In international relations the inclination of the lesser powers to accept the right of the strongest to make far-reaching decisions with implications for many other countries will critically depend on the willingness of the strongest to be constrained by international norms, and to take the views of others into account. The more the strongest powers are prepared to involve other countries in their decisions, the more legitimate and effective these decisions will be.

In short, there is in the quest for international order no other direction but to seek to strengthen and at the same time reform the existing family of global organizations, regimes and informal arrangements. This is true regardless of whether the institutions in place are aimed at promoting co-operation in a wide range of policy domains (such as the UN) or on specific policy domains (such as the WTO). Contemporary global governance is not about creating new powerful institutions. Rather, it is about enhancing the coherence, effectiveness, and legitimacy of the existing ones, about identifying and filling the gaps in the multilateral institutional and regulatory architecture and, finally, about imagining new institutions where they are needed.

The notion of coherence refers to the degree to which international institutions are interlocked, and their missions are mutually reinforcing or supportive. According to this description, one of the glaring weaknesses of the UN system is the lack of coherence between the operations of the UN Security Council and important economic and financial institutions such as the WTO, the World Bank and the IMF. Strategies of conflict prevention and peace-building require a co-ordinated approach to security and economic development. The reality, however, is that the Security Council has no leverage over economic aid and financial rescue programs, while decision-making over these programmes is often completely out of touch with security considerations. Decision-making on international economic matters, particularly in the areas of finance and trade, has long left the UN. The meaning of the second yardstick, effectiveness, is quite simple: institutions must be able to do what they say, and powerful enough to enforce the decisions they have made. The third criterion, legitimacy, raises serious problems.

At the national level, there is legitimacy to the extent that people accept the right of political authorities to make binding decisions. The acceptance by the people also includes the rules and procedures according to which those decisions are taken. But who is supposed to accept and obey decisions at the global level? Is one only to think of national governments or should one also consider non-state actors and even ordinary people? In spite of vague ideas that circulate about the creation of a world assembly or a forum for civil society allowing for direct participation of world citizens, the only practical way to enhance the legitimacy of any system of global governance seems to be to look for a more balanced and equitable representation of countries in international bodies (first and foremost the composition of the UN Security Council) whose decisions affect their vital interests. While the reform of the Security Council is long overdue it is rather premature, if not inappropriate, to discuss democratic blueprints as models for global governance in a world where dozens of countries are still under the yoke of authoritarian regimes. There is much to say, though, for making international decision-making more transparent and accountable to a wider group of countries than those represented in international bodies with limited membership (such the UN Security Council) or weighted voting (such as the IMF and World Bank).

Similarly, it makes sense to create channels to international organizations for non-governmental organizations to state their case and enter into dialogue with representatives of governmental organizations at the global level. Under the present circumstances, however, priority has to be given to enhancing the effectiveness of multilateral institutions. After all, the general acceptance of these institutions depends not only on the possibilities for governments and world citizens to influence international policies, but also on the ability of institutions to impose solutions that address people's concerns. In many capitals there is growing awareness of the need to strengthen multilateral institutions. In a world of global threats, global markets and global media, our security and prosperity increasingly depend on an effective multilateral system. Several approaches may be taken to strengthen the present multilateral system. But none of them will be successful unless the USA commits itself to the project.

CONCLUSION

Any serious attempt to transform the present international system towards more effective forms of multilateralism must recognize the reality of US pre-eminence in global affairs. Anti-Americanism is, obviously, not conducive to the promotion of such a recognition, despite the role of the US Government in facilitating anti-Americanism as a result of its foreign policy over the past five years. The same sense of realism makes one understand that the USA, as a power with unsurpassed military and economic weight, might claim to have a certain leeway in how it operates internationally. The historical record suggests that stronger powers have a natural aversion to being restrained by weaker states, especially if these weaker states take the moral high ground with the knowledge that they are not being called upon to bear the costs of sustaining international order. It remains an interesting point of debate whether a unipolar power structure, which largely characterizes the current distribution of military resources in the world, is conducive to the pursuit of international order. The nature of the political regime of the strongest power in place should be taken as an important variable in the political equation. However justified the criticism of US policies and whatever the shortcomings of the USA's polity, it is a cause for some comfort that today's pre-eminent power is, still, a democracy. History has shown the ugly face of the alternatives. As for the UN, it is hard to imagine circumstances where the world organization would be capable of preserving international peace and security in opposition to the USA. It is the member states that determine the margins of political relevance of the world organization, not supranational bureaucrats, non-governmental organizations or eminent personalities. This explains why proposals for reforming the UN are either radical but futile or attainable but unimaginative.

If the problem of international order today is basically the problem of managing US power, what road should be taken? It is not this chapter's conclusion that because the UN cannot work without the USA fully behind it, the world organization can only be relevant if it is the USA's tool. Obviously, the USA cannot be allowed to take the law into its own hands. The view that US leaders can be trusted to use a monopoly of power has never been shared outside the USA. To the extent that the country is still ill at ease with the entanglements and complexities of multilateral institutions, it is essential that the next US administration rediscovers the potential value of these institutions as a source of international legitimacy as well as the opportunities they may offer to share burdens with friendly states that believe in the virtues of multilateral co-operation. A new commitment by the USA to multilateralism looks less like a chimera than is often suggested. The combined weight of persuasion by others who share the USA's security concerns and the force of circumstances pointing to the limits of US power may be stronger than the impact of anti-internationalist belief systems in the USA. The exercise of power that is not rooted in legitimacy involves political costs that are likely to rise prohibitively as campaigns to enforce democracy and modernization meet firm local resistance. The situation in Iraq should be a clear case in point. In exchange for international support, both diplomatic and material, the USA must accept the obligation to respect some basic rules concerning the rule of military force, such as circumscribing the right of self-defence and adhering to the principles of humanitarian law and proportionality.

Although in the more distant future China and perhaps India may pose the most serious challenge to US power, in the short term Europe is in the best position to moderate the worst impulses of the USA. While the EU cannot match the USA in terms of military capabilities, the experience with supporting nascent democracies demonstrates that the Union has something to offer the USA that it clearly needs: an extensive arsenal of civilian foreign policy tools. The magnitude of the task ahead can hardly be exaggerated: restoring US interest in achieving a transatlantic consensus on the appropriate response to major security threats while at the same time granting Europeans a louder voice in the alliance. European governments can only substantiate their claim to equality vis-à-vis the USA if they are prepared to take their full share in the common burdens. Equally, the effectiveness of the UN system depends on linking US power with international legitimacy. Just as important, a wide gulf exists between decision-making on traditional peace and security concerns in the Security Council and on financial and economic affairs in the boards of the World Bank and IMF. This fragmentation ignores the inter-relationship of the problems involved. Finally, priority should also be given to fostering a culture of anticipation of crises rather than one of reaction.

GUIDING GLOBAL SHIFTS: CURRENT AND FUTURE US RELATIONS WITH THE BRICS

MARK R. BRAWLEY

INTRODUCTION

The emergence of rising regional powers, collectively referred to as the BRICs (Brazil, Russia, India and the People's Republic of China), heralds change in the international political economy.[1] These countries have the potential to spark upheavals in the way global political and economic relations are conducted. As they grow economically, they will surely desire alterations in existing political and economic practices and institutions. Some fear this puts them on a collision course with the current dominant power, the USA. Such thinking prompted some US analysts to propose concessions to the BRICs; other analysts think it might be better to confront or pressure the BRICs now, while the USA still wields great influence.

To assess current US attitudes towards the BRICs, as well as weigh these options, it is first useful to assess the points of leverage the USA actually holds. It is then important to consider why any rising economic powers might wish to change the current international order, and think about when such issues will arise. Despite fearful depictions often delivered by the media, the USA may have greater economic influence over several of these countries than apparent at first glance; it may be quite capable of shaping future relations between itself and these rising powers. While the USA clearly holds the military edge over any one of these states today, and that advantage will stretch well into the future, it lacks the ability to pressure them into policy change through military threats. If anything, the economic rise of the BRICs will enable some of them to consider rivalling the US militarily in the future. By looking more closely at the economic and political ties between the USA and the BRICs, we can get a better idea of the more subtle ways the

USA will be able to influence relations with these rising regional powers through contemporary policies.

CURRENT ECONOMIC TIES

The USA is currently the single largest economy in the international system, placing it at the centre of many trade and financial networks. Economic links with each of the BRICs vary considerably, however. Trade between the USA and China has been booming, and China holds a substantial amount of financial instruments denominated in the dollar. At the other end of the spectrum, Russia and the USA have not developed such close economic ties. US economic relations with Brazil and India are closer, but remain much smaller in value than those between the USA and China. Suggestions by experts in international security that the USA and China will inevitably confront each other in the mid-21st century simply because they will be the two largest economies therefore need to be rethought. While the two countries will have the greatest capabilities to threaten each other, that alone should not condemn them to be political competitors. China would have the greatest ability to confront the USA's dominant military and political position, but would it have the motivation to mount such a challenge? To answer that question, we need to consider how their economies have been growing, and note the degree of interdependence and complementarity between the USA and China. Russia's economic recovery, relatively ignored by Western analysts in recent years, will eventually enable it to play the role of a global power again; its rebound has not been linked to the US economy. Russia's return to 'great power' status may therefore contain more dangerous elements for the future.

China's economic rise grabs most of the headlines these days, because the numbers generated are staggering.[2] In their projections of economic growth up to the mid-21st century, the Goldman Sachs analysts who coined the term 'BRICs' expect China's economy potentially to overtake that of the USA in terms of gross national product (GNP). (There are many important assumptions in that projection, of course, and that does not mean China will reach the same level of output per caput as the USA.) China's growth has been largely driven by internal factors, sparked by liberalization of the domestic economy. China's trade with the rest of the world has certainly blossomed. It ranked third among states in terms of the value of its exports in 2006, accounting for 8.0% of the world total.[3] It also ranked third in terms of the value of its imports, with 6.4% of the world total. Its bilateral trade with the USA in 2006 placed it third on the list of origin of US imports and fifth as the destination for US exports. The balance was massively in China's favour, but to evaluate how much each one needs the other, it is important to think about what is being traded, and how easily each can find alternative relationships.

China's exports to the USA in 2006 equalled US $305,800m. Conversely, China imported much less from the USA in terms of value ($55,200m. that same year). Chinese exports to the USA are notoriously labour-intensive: these products are competitive in the US market because their production requires a significant amount of labour, and wages are low in China compared to the USA. Since China does not import much directly from the USA, its continued bilateral trade surplus has allowed it to amass large foreign exchange reserves, much of them in US currency. This pattern is likely to continue into the future.

The figures describing India's economic rise are almost as impressive. The same projections that suggested that China's economy would rival that of the USA in size by the mid-21st century placed India's in third position—surpassing that of established industrial powers such as Japan or Germany. India's economic boom has been driven by both internal and external economic liberalization. India's imports and exports increased steadily since the early 1990s. In 2006 India ranked 28th on the list of world exporters and 17th on the list of exporters. The USA does not figure prominently in India's trade picture, however. India was the 14th largest source of US imports, accounting for only 1.2% of the goods imported by the USA in that year. India ranked 16th in terms of destinations for US goods, accounting for only 1.0% of total US exports. As with Chinese goods, India's manufactured exports are also quite labour-intensive, but the widespread knowledge of English, coupled with a sizable educated class, has enabled Indian firms to make inroads into the international services sector. These activities reach into several different markets, not simply the American. Indian manufactured goods exports to the USA in 2006 were valued at US $23,000m., while its exports to the European Union (EU) were $28,000m. India has not relied as heavily on a single market, nor has it attained the same sustained bilateral trade surplus with the USA. As a result, the country's foreign exchange holdings are much more diversified than China's. In both cases, the scale of the domestic markets needs to be kept in mind: growth generated from domestic sources builds its own momentum, and trade, while important, remains only one factor among many driving the economic rise of both India and China.

Brazil turned to market liberalizations earlier than India, as it emerged from the debt crisis of the 1980s. Exports figured prominently in its growth. The USA was an important market for it then and continues to be so today. Brazil's exports to the USA were valued at US $28,000m. in 2006, and its imports at $19,200m., placing its bilateral relationship in the same range as that between the USA and India. The US Government nurtured this economic relationship precisely because it wanted Brazilians to earn US dollars through trade so that Brazil could pay its way out of debt. Brazil therefore received preferential access to the US market for a number of its export items. Today Brazil's exports go to many other destinations (with exports of $32,900m. to the EU in 2006, for example). Unlike India or China, Brazil has been deeply involved in leading the creation of a successful regional trading bloc, the Southern Common Market (Mercado Común del Sur—Mercosur), which may give it additional options in the future. As a destination for US goods, Brazil ranks ninth, accounting for 1.9% in 2006. Nonetheless, Brazil remains firmly tied to US financial markets.

As mentioned above, Russian-US economic ties look quite different from the other bilateral relationships just described. Exports of raw materials fuel Russia's current economic boom—most especially sales of petroleum and natural gas. These raw material exports flow overwhelmingly to Europe, not to the USA. Russian goods sold to the USA in 2006 were below the value of any other BRIC exports, at only US $20,700m. (or 1.1% of total US imports). In comparison, Russia exported $148,700m. in goods to the EU. American exports to Russia were valued at a meagre $4,700m., placing Russia 26th on the list of destinations for US goods. These two countries simply do not have the same trade ties with each other as the USA has with Brazil, India or China. Financial patterns mirror the trade patterns. Russia holds a much more balanced portfolio, with euro-denominated instruments playing a significant role.

If we consider what this means for the future, the USA and China have a mutually beneficial relationship developing. If anything, China needs the USA more than the USA needs China. Were the trade relationship between the two severed for some reason, China would be forced to find an alternative destination for its labour-intensive exports. There are no true possibilities promising the same scale and wealth as the US market. Only two currently come close—the EU and Japan—and neither does as much business with China as does the USA. (China's exports to the EU in 2006 equalled US $240,500m., while its exports to Japan were valued at $118,600m.) It is unlikely that either the EU or Japan would be able or willing to absorb an additional quantity of labour-intensive Chinese goods equivalent to even one-half the US market. On the other hand, if the USA denied its market to Chinese goods, the Americans would merely need to find a different market for a much smaller portion of its exports, and then new supplies of cheap labour-intensive imports—and there would be many countries willing to fill that role. Moreover, despite the large value of those imports, Chinese goods still only accounted for 15.9% of all US merchandise imports in 2006.

Perhaps surprisingly, China might have more ability to flex its economic muscles in finance rather than trade. China may hold economic leverage against the USA because of its foreign exchange reserves. Overall, the IMF estimates that the BRICs hold around 60% of their foreign exchange reserves in US dollars, although this percentage varies across each of the four.[4] China's large holdings of dollars (or dollar-denominated financial instruments, including US Government-issued bonds) may give it the ability to pressure any US Administration on specific issues; on the other hand, a precipitous drop in the value of the US dollar reduces the value of the wealth the Chinese have accumulated over the years, so any such action against the dollar would hurt themselves as well as the Americans.

Brazil and India also have mutually positive economic ties with the USA. Like China, each produces little that the USA could not find in other places. The USA serves as a very important destination for their exports too, though both have developed more diversified markets for their goods than China. Brazil may be quite sensitive to US economic pressures, because of its financial ties, while India would be less vulnerable to any economic threats from the USA. On the other hand, India has the potential to develop much greater economic ties with the USA in terms of both trade and financial links. The relations between these two emerging economies and the US markets are largely positive, and look to remain that way.

Among the BRICs, Russia clearly has the greatest economic autonomy from the USA now; Russia's willingness to dispute US policies towards Eastern Europe, as well as to throw its weight around in the Caucasus and Central Asia (as when it fought a brief war with Georgia in 2008), reflect Russia's independence from US pressures. As a major source of energy supplies to Europe, and an important holder of euros, Russia has the potential to use its economic leverage to foster division between the USA and its traditional European allies. Whether the ties between Europe and Russia develop into mutually beneficial links, or simply place Russia in a position to threaten to cut off energy supplies to the EU, cannot yet be known. Perhaps more importantly, any emerging rivalry between the euro and the dollar may open up an opportunity for Russia to exacerbate turmoil in currency markets, to the disadvantage of the USA.

China's economic path may therefore give it the best capabilities for rivalling the USA politically some day, but the sources of that economic trajectory may also be driving it ever closer to shared interests with the USA. Russia, on the other hand, is growing economically outside US influence, and independent of US interests. India and Brazil have economic ties to the USA, but are also linked to other major economies, most especially the EU. None of the BRICs accounted for more than 5.3% of total US exports in 2006, and together they only accounted for 8.7%—less than the USA exported to Mexico alone. China is a critical source of US imports, and together the BRICs make up just below 20% of the country's total imports; but these goods can be produced elsewhere. The USA can afford to live without the BRICs, but the reverse is not true.

CURRENT POLITICAL TIES

Historically, the USA held close political ties with only one of the BRICs: Brazil. Its relations with India were wary, although these have warmed since the terrorist attacks of 11 September 2001. Its relations with Russia and China remain tainted by the past. Cold War rivalries have not been forgotten, and both Russia and China believe that their interests are not respected often enough in global affairs. The historical patterns need not continue into the future, but altering those patterns may prove quite difficult.

Brazil has quietly been a consistent, if relatively silent, supporter of US policies. Brazil and the USA have not had to deal with many direct political disputes. Brazil has refrained from interfering in the affairs of other countries in its region, and it has resolutely sought to carve out its own foreign policy priorities separate from those emanating from Washington, DC. This has allowed it to remain independent, yet maintain relatively strong bilateral ties with the USA over the years. There is little reason to expect conflicts to develop between these two; if anything, the rise of external powers might drive them closer together.

The Cold War had a profound and perhaps unnatural effect on relations between the USA and India. India strove to find a third path during the Cold War, standing outside either the Soviet or the US blocs. It led challenges to the US-led international economic institutions (especially in the 1970s), and took up political positions that reflected interests at variance with the USA. When India felt threatened by China (and when the People's Republic drew close to Pakistan), it developed strategic ties with the USSR. This naturally heightened friction with the USA. Economic changes initiated in the 1980s and early 1990s helped pull the two countries closer together, though the USA and India disagreed over policies towards Afghanistan. The end of the Cold War created an atmosphere in which the two could put aside some of these differences. As a long-standing democracy that was liberalizing its economy, India finally found common ground with the USA. Their interests and policies were moving to a more natural convergence. The events of 11 September 2001 accelerated this process, since the attacks shone a light on shared perspectives. India still seeks greater voice in a number of international institutions, and does not always feel recognized as a great power by the USA, but the underlying shared belief in democracy should help these two countries maintain positive ties into the future.

The attacks of September 2001 appeared at first to push the USA and Russia more closely together as well. Russia has had its own internal struggles with Islamist groups, though these are intimately intertwined with ethnic nationalism. President Vladimir Putin's Government tried to place Russia's struggle against Chechen rebels under the vast umbrella of the USA's global 'war on terror'. Russia's handling of Chechnya, however, clashed with US ideas about the way to respond to such problems. Moreover, US attitudes regarding the eastward expansion of the North Atlantic Treaty Organization (NATO) troubled Russia; the US military presence in Iraq, Afghanistan, and in Central Asia more broadly, fuelled Russian fears. Russian aspirations include a reassertion of power over the country's regional neighbours, many of whom have sought support from the USA or the EU. The fighting between Russia and Georgia that broke out in August 2008 is a reminder that Russia can and will assert its military might. It is also a reminder that Russian leaders believe their country has a privileged position in Asia and Eastern Europe; they have also proven willing to use an aggressive foreign policy to gain additional legitimacy with their constituents. With democratic institutions and practices rapidly eroding, an increasingly belligerent foreign policy towards its immediate neighbours, and antagonistic rhetoric aimed at other major powers, Russian relations with the USA seem destined for more trouble.

Some of the same potential may exist in US-Chinese relations. Of the four BRICs, China remains the least democratic. There are signs of a political relaxation, yet at the same time the continued internal social upheavals that come with rapid economic progress may plant the seeds of political problems. Worse still, Chinese citizens expect continued economic improvement; what will happen if those desires are frustrated by a slowdown of the world economy? How then would the Chinese leadership react? A political crackdown or reassertion of centralized leadership might easily sour political relations with the USA. In terms of its foreign policy concerns, China's attitudes towards its neighbours (including major US allies such as Japan and the Republic of Korea) or its own internal/external issue (Taiwan) could easily ensnare the USA. It might not take so much to trigger colder relations between the USA and the People's Republic. Thus while the USA and China enjoy amicable relations today, there are potentially perilous times ahead.

WHAT CAN THE USA DO TO SHAPE THE FUTURE?

The USA holds a dominant position in the international system for the moment, but everyone recognizes that this position cannot be maintained forever. The EU already has an economy as large and as rich as that of the USA; China and India will also rise to roughly the same scale (measured in GNP) in a few decades. None of these rising economies will be as rich as the USA, hence the complementarities in their production described above will undoubtedly continue. What strategies can the USA employ in its efforts to shape the future world political economy?

Advice flows from several well-established schools of thought in international relations: realism, liberalism and institutionalism. Scholars employing each of these approaches view the world in a particular way, which guides their thinking. Each set of scholars plays a prominent role in US academia, and thus has influence over policy-making. US foreign policy has historically been a blend of these approaches—often a very uneasy mix, in fact. Such tensions will undoubtedly persist, since the rise of the BRICs sets important challenges on the road ahead, and each of these three approaches to international relations leads to quite different suggestions for US policy.

Realists believe that the essence of international relations is competition.[5] Realists focus on sovereign states as the key actors in international affairs; as sovereign actors, states refuse to be constrained by anything but the power of other states. Because power is the key asset for defending and extending one's own interest in the international arena, the rise of several new regional or even global powers leads realists to fearful conclusions about the future. In an international system with poorly developed governance structures, sovereign states may always choose to settle their disputes by force of arms. Peace comes through deterring other states from pursuing that option.

Given US dominance over the last half-century, the current international order largely (but not completely) reflects what the USA has wanted. US realists worry that countries with new-found strength will express their desires to alter the status quo. This is partly driven by long-held realist arguments about the past. When the distribution of power in the international system has changed rapidly, wars have often resulted. In order to defend American interests (and the status quo), realists have urged the USA to implement policies that slow down the economic and/or military rise of rivals. (This is one reason why the USA has tried to halt the spread of weapons of mass destruction: such weaponry offsets the military edge the USA holds in conventional power.)

There are a few obvious problems with trying to implement the realists' advice. First, the USA cannot do much to prevent the economic rise of the BRICs. Trade is important to several of them, and the USA could hurt China (and Brazil) in particular through some sort of sanctions. But the BRICs are forging ahead because of their domestic economic transitions. External sanctions will not stop their growth, only temporarily slow it down. Sanctions would certainly sour their relations with the USA, ensuring that they would view the country as an enemy. Second, the realists cannot isolate which of these powers will pose the greatest threat to the USA. The USA cannot possibly hope to prevent the rise of all of the BRICs. That leaves the realists with one meaningful suggestion: the USA should position itself to deter any aggressive BRIC from opting to use force to overturn the international status quo. Deterrence can be achieved by amassing sufficient strength to defend the status quo through harnessing internal resources or finding external assistance. In the first instance, the USA should continue to invest in its own military forces. In the second, it should form alliances, possibly even with some of the BRICs themselves. This may be easy enough to do when the time comes, given the geographic proximity of Russia, India and China. Those three are likely to feel threatened by each other as their capabilities grow, and will probably have immediate interests in dispute as they seek to exert greater influence internationally. The clearest realist advice would be for the USA to wait for such troubles to arise, then play these countries off each other.

The liberal perspective arose because some international relations experts believed that the realists had overemphasized the importance of power and competition.[6] Instead of assuming that states always seek power, liberals argue for the need to look inside states to understand what they desire from the international system. States will seek goals set by domestic political decisions—and these goals may often be mutually beneficial. If China primarily seeks further economic welfare, then it will prefer to continue to participate in a US-led international political economy, regardless of its size. This same thinking helps explain why the EU remains a close ally of the USA even though the two are of similar size and capability in economic terms: the two generally share a vision of what the global political economy should look like.

If challenges to US interests are only likely to arise when other states have not only enough military power to consider waging a conflict (as the realists think), but also intensely desire different goals, liberals see other ways to influence the future beyond the realists' advice. Liberals suggest that US foreign policy needs to target the internal politics of the BRICs. Shaping the BRICs' domestic politics will shape the desires these rising regional powers voice in the future. With judicious exertions today, the USA could convince the BRICs to want to participate in a US-led international order. This advice harks back to earlier US foreign policy efforts, originating more than a century ago, when the USA sought to promote democracy abroad.

There are problems with instituting liberal policy recommendations, too, however. One of the key liberal insights has been that democracies maintain peaceful relations with each other. Yet, in practice, it has not been easy to support democratization abroad. Among the BRICs, democracy is firmly rooted in India and Brazil; it is failing in Russia (with precious little the USA can do about it), and has hardly established itself in China. So while the aims of liberal policy are clear, the means are not. Alternatively, liberals would argue that the USA can create important political and economic communities within the BRICs that would view the USA (and the US-led international order) favourably. US economic openness, and the development of important bilateral ties described above, means that this is de facto US policy. It even suggests success, at least with Brazil, India and China, but not with Russia.

The last important group of scholars giving policy advice in the USA adheres to institutionalism.[7] The institutionalists also criticize the realists for being overly concerned with competition, and for missing important ways that international affairs centre on co-operation in pursuit of mutually beneficial goals. The key for institutionalists, in contrast to liberals, is the presence of international rules, norms and organizations that support joint decision-making. According to institutionalist theory, states will not need to compete for resources if their desires can be met through better international political mechanisms. To avoid future conflicts with the BRICs, US policy therefore needs to reform and modify current international organizations, institutions and practices, in ways that will give the BRICs greater say in how things are run. While such measures might involve compromises on the part of the USA, they would hopefully ensure that the BRICs would have a stake in the international order, and therefore defend it rather than seek to overturn it.

The difficulty here lies in strategies for reforming established international institutions or creating new ones. The UN (or more specifically the UN Security Council) still reflects the distribution of power and interests when it was formed over half a century ago. Russia and China have veto powers on the Security Council, making it somewhat unworkable; adding two additional veto holders would make its functioning problematic indeed. Giving permanent seats with veto powers to Brazil and India while not providing similar arrangements to Japan or Germany would also be problematic.[8] Removing the power to veto from the United Kingdom and France would also be difficult—although they might settle for a single EU right to exercise a veto. Reform of other institutions (the Group of Eight—G8—industrialized nations, the IMF, the World Bank and so forth) appears equally problematic, since in each, other countries besides the BRICs seek greater influence, and those currently on top are unlikely to concede their privileged positions willingly.

A different strategy, already being explored and developed, would be to create new international institutions that overlap with existing ones. These would empower the voices of the BRICs. The best known might be the Group of 20 (G-20), a group of economically developed and developing states that meets routinely to discuss global economic affairs. The G-20 was created deliberately to overlap with the G8 but encompass a wider range of actors, including Brazil, China and India.[9] Thus, while the G8 nations may continue with their agenda, the dominant economic actors are exposed to the concerns and interests of other states. New international institutions such as the G-20 give the BRICs more input on global governance, just as institutionalists recommend. The weakness in this approach, however, comes from having numerous international organizations with similar jurisdictions. This introduces additional complications to international politics, including conflict between decisions made in different forums, as well as disputes between states over which forum takes precedence. If powerful states need to co-operate to deal with a common problem, but differ in their choice of appropriate setting for handling the issue, this may delay or even prevent a joint solution from emerging. More institutionalization of international affairs may not always be better.

Given the plurality of views among US experts, in addition to the challenges involved in implementing any one of these recommendations successfully, what should we expect the USA to do about its relations with the BRICs? Expect a little bit of each approach.[10] US policy will support or promote democratization in Russia and China, however meekly. US political and economic policies will try to create and nurture groups within the BRICs that will support favourable ties with the USA. The USA may not lead reform of existing international organizations, but it will remain open to alternative views being voiced through new institutions. Even with these efforts, the economic rise of the BRICs will enable any one of them to consider challenging the international status quo through political or even military measures. If that happens, the USA will still be prepared to engage in arms races and to form alliances with other major powers to face any potential threats. In that sense, the future players in world affairs may be different, but some parts of the games they engage in will look familiar.

CONCLUSIONS

Although some analysts see a bleak future ahead, as rising economic powers emerge to be global players, the current dominant power still has options for shaping how world affairs will unfold. Power will undoubtedly be more equally distributed in the future. Brazil, Russia, India and China will all take on greater roles in the international economy. Their economic rise gives them the option of converting some of their resources into political or military power. We know the likely paths these states will probably follow in their economic development. Remaining questions centre on how they will use their newfound capabilities. Will they want to change the international order substantially? How will they pursue their interests? How will they act towards the USA?

The USA itself has the means to shape how this future will unfold. It maintains positive economic and political ties with Brazil and India, and there is the potential for these ties to strengthen over time. To the extent that China's economic rise is based on trade and international investment, its ascendance is inexorably linked to shared interests with the USA. These three major powers are moving forward by engaging the global economic system that the USA helped design, create and maintain. Russia too has engaged that international economy, but has not found direct ties to the USA; moreover, its financial resources will enable it to drive a wedge between the USA and its European allies, should the Russians so desire. As Russia slips further away from democratic rule, it seems more and more likely to be a future threat to American interests.

Americans can implement three complementary strategies for reinforcing the current trends binding the BRICs to them, or at least making the BRICs more satisfied actors within the current international order. First, following the recommendations of institutionalists, the USA can encourage reform of existing international institutions to give the BRICs a greater stake in global governance. The USA should also consider where and when new international forums can be created, reflecting the current and future distribution of political and economic power. Second, following the recommendations of liberalism, the USA can promote the creation and stabilization of democratic institutions in China and Russia, respectively, and extend continued support to democratic rule in Brazil and India. The USA can also aim to create and support important groups within the BRICs that will seek to maintain ties with the USA, by finding and enhancing political economic projects that create mutually beneficial situations. This means enhancing trade and other forms of international economic intercourse in ways that distribute gains to all parties involved.

Finally, the USA needs to resist taking negative actions towards any of these states; following the realists' advice, the USA should accept that the distribution of power in the system will change. The trick for US policy makers will be to balance these states against one another. In some ways this may not be difficult, to the extent that these powers view each other as possible threats. If the three Asian powers fear one another, the USA should be able to find willing allies, building powerful coalitions in defence of an international order, isolating and deterring the most threatening of the BRICs. The international political economy of the mid-21st century may not look so different from the one we now live in—though the roll call of major powers will have substantially changed.

ENDNOTES

1 See Dominic Wilson and Roopa Purushothaman, 'Dreaming With BRICs: the Path to 2050', *Global Economics Papers* No. 99. New York, Goldman Sachs, 2003.

2 Ibid.; also see Albert Keidel, 'China Succeeding Beyond Expectations', unpublished paper, presented to the Atlantic Council of the United States, January 2006, internet <www.acus.org/docs/0601-China_Succeeding_Beyond_Expectations.pdf>.

3 All trade statistics refer to 2006 and are taken from World Trade Organization, *International trade statistics 2007*, internet <www.wto.org/english/res_e/statis_e/its2007_e/its07_world_trade_dev_e.htm>.

4 See 'Perspectives on the Global Economic Landscape and the Role of the Dollar', Address by John Lipsky, First Deputy Managing Director, IMF, 22 July 2008, internet <www.imf.org/external/np/speeches/2008/072208.htm>.

5 Famous US realist authors include Kenneth Waltz, Stephen Krasner and John Mearsheimer.

6 One of the more prominent US liberal scholars is Andrew Moravcsik; others include Bruce Russett and many of the people working within international political economy.

7 Prominent US institutionalist scholars include Robert Keohane and Lisa Martin.

8 None the less, at September 2008 Canada seemed poised to support such an effort. Canada's diplomatic strategies have long emphasized multilateralism and the promotion of international institutions as key tools in international governance.

9 Here, Canada took the initiative to create this body, and to give it a meaningful voice in global affairs.

10 To see how a US international relations expert uses the three together to understand the past, see G. John Ikenberry, *After Victory: Institutions, Strategic Restraint, and the Rebuilding of Order after Major Wars*. Princeton, Princeton University Press, 2001.

SELECT BIBLIOGRAPHY (PUBLIC AFFAIRS)

Domestic Politics

Aberbach, J., and Rockman, B. *In the Web of Politics*. Washington, DC, The Brookings Institution, 2000.

Ackerman, B. *The Failure of the Founding Fathers: Jefferson, Marshall, and the Rise of Presidential Democracy*. Cambridge, MA, Harvard University Press, 2005.

Ayres, G., and Oshinsky, S. *American Passages: A History of the United States*. Orlando, FL, Harcourt Inc, 2000.

Barone, M., and Cohen, R. *The Almanac of American Politics, 2006*. Washington, DC, National Journal Group, 2005.

Berlet, C., and Lyons, M. *Right-Wing Popularism in America: Too Close for Comfort*. New York, Guildford Press, 2000.

Bimber, B., and Davis, R. *Campaigning Online: The Internet in US Elections*. New York, Oxford University Press, 2003.

Black, A., Koopman, D. L., and Ryden, D. K. *Of Little Faith: The Politics of George W. Bush's Faith-Based Initiatives*. Georgetown University Press, 2004.

Blumenthal, S. *How Bush Rules: Chronicles of a Radical Regime*. Princeton, NJ, Princeton University Press, 2006.

Bodenhamer, D. J., and Ely, J. W. (Eds). *The Bill of Rights in Modern America*. Bloomington, IN, University of Indiana Press, 2008.

Bormann, N. *National Missile Defence and the Politics of US Identity: A Poststructural Critique*. Manchester, Manchester University Press, 2008.

Brogan, H. *History of the United States*. London, Penguin, 1985.

Buell, E. H., and Sigelman, L. *Attack Politics: Negativity in Presidential Campaigns Since 1960*. Lawrence, KS, University of Kansas Press, 2008.

Burns, J. M. *Running Alone: Presidential Leadership from JFK to Bush II—Why It Has Failed and How We Can Fix It*. New York, Basic Books, 2006.

Campbell, C., Rockman, B. A., and Rudalevige, A. *The George W. Bush Legacy*. Washington, DC, CQ Press, 2007.

Campbell, J. E. 'The Curious and Close Presidential Election of 2000', in Crotty, W. (Ed.). *America's Choice 2000*. Boulder, CO, Westview Press, 2001.

Cannon, L., and Cannon, C. M. *Reagan's Disciple: George W Bush's Troubled Quest for a Presidential Legacy*. New York, Public Affairs, 2008.

Ceaser, J. W., and Busch, A. E. *The Perfect Tie: The True Story of the 2000 Presidential Election*. Lanham, MD, Rowman & Littlefield Publrs, Inc, 2001.

Cole, D., and Dempsey, J. *Terrorism and the Constitution: Sacrificing Civil Liberties in the Name of National Security*, 2nd edn. New York, New Press, 2002.

Congressional Quarterly. *Almanac*. Washington, DC, Congressional Quarterly Inc.

Crotty, W. (Ed.). *America's Choice 2000*. Boulder, CO, Westview Press, 2001.

Currinder, M. *Money in the House: Campaign Funds and Congressional Party Politics*. Boulder, CO, Westview Press, 2008.

Davis, R. *Electing Justice: Fixing the Supreme Court Nomination Process*. New York, Oxford University Press, 2005.

Denton, R. E., Jr (Ed.). *The 2000 Presidential Campaign: A Communication Perspective*. Westport, CT, Greenwood Press, 2002.

Dionne, E. J., and Kristol, W. (Eds). *Bush v Gore. The Court Cases and Commentary*. Washington, DC, Brookings Institution, 2001.

Dionne, E. J., Pomper, G. M., and Mayer, W. G. (Eds). *The Election of 2000: Reports and Interpretations*. Chatham, NJ, Chatham House Publrs, 2001.

Edsall, T. B. *Building Red America: The New Conservative Coalition and the Drive for Permanent Power*. New York, Basic Books, 2006.

Fabbrini, S. *America and its Critics: Virtues and Vices of the Democratic Hyperpower*. Cambridge, Polity Press, 2008.

Farrard, M. *The Framing of the Constitution of the United States*. New Haven, CT, Yale University Press, 1913.

Ferguson, T. *Golden Rule: The Investment Theory of Party Competition and the Logic of Money-Driven Political Systems*. Chicago, IL, Chicago University Press, 1995.

Fleming, B. *Why Liberals and Conservatives Clash: A View from Annapolis*. Abingdon, Routledge, 2006.

Foner, E. *Reconstruction: America's Unfinished Revolution, 1863–1877 (New American Nation Series)*. New York, HarperCollins, 1989.

Friedman, L. M. *A History of American Law*. New York, Simon & Schuster Inc, 1975.

Gilbert, M. *The Routledge Atlas of American History*. 4th edn. New York, Routledge, 2005.

Gonzalez, M. G., and Delgado, R. *The Politics of Fear: How Republicans Use Money, Race and the Media to Win*. Boulder, CO, Paradigm Publrs, 2006.

Grant, A. *The American Political Process*, 7th edn. New York, Routledge, 2003.

Green, J. C., and Coffey, D. J. (Eds). *The State of the Parties*. Lanham, MD, Rowman and Littlefield, 2006.

Greene, J. R. *The Presidency of George Bush (Senior)*. Kansas City, KS, University Press of Kansas, 2000.

Greenfield, J. *'Oh, Waiter! One Order of Crow': Inside the Strangest Presidential Election Finishes in American History*. Itasca, IL, Putnam Publishing Group, 2001.

Greenstein, F. I. *The Presidential Difference: Leadership Style from FDR to Clinton*. New York, Free Press, 2000.

The George W. Bush Presidency: An Early Assessment. Baltimore, MD, Johns Hopkins University Press, 2003.

Griffiths, R. M. *Religion and Politics in the Contemporary United States*. Baltimore, MD, Johns Hopkins University Press, 2008.

Hall, K. J. (Ed.). *The Oxford Companion to the Supreme Court of the United States*. New York, Oxford University Press, 2nd edn, 2005.

Hartz, L. *The Liberal Tradition in America*. New York, Harcourt Brace, 1955.

Heclo, H., Bane, M. J., Kazin, M., and Wolfe, A. *Christianity and American Democracy*. Cambridge, MA, Harvard University Press, 2007.

Herman, E., and Chomsky, N. *Manufacturing Consent: The Political Economy of the Mass Media*. New York, Pantheon, 2002.

Houston, J. *Criminal Justice and the Policy Process*. Lanham, MD, University Press of America, 2008.

Jillson, C. *American Government: Political Change and Institutional Development*, 4th edn. New York, Routledge, 2007.

Johnson, J. W. *Historic US Court Cases*. Abingdon, Routledge, 2001.

Judis, J. B. *The Paradox of American Democracy. Elites, Special Interests, and the Public Trust*. New York, Routledge, 2001.

Kernell, S. *The Logic of American Politics*. Washington, DC, CQ Press, 2003.

King D. *Making Americans: Immigration, Race and the Makings of the Diverse Democracy*. Cambridge, MA, Harvard University Press, 2000.

Koszczuk, J., and Stern H. (Eds). *CQ's Politics in America 2006: The 109th Congress*. Washington, DC, CQ Press, 2005.

Landy, M., and Milkis, S. M. (Eds). *American Government: Balancing Democracy and Rights*. Cambridge, Cambridge University Press, 2008.

Lipset, S. M., and Marks, G. *It Didn't Happen Here: Why Socialism Failed in the United States*. New York, W. W. Norton & Co Inc, 2000.

Loomis, B. A. (Ed.). *Esteemed Colleagues: Civility and Deliberation in the US Senate*. Washington, DC, Brookings Institution, 2000.

McCloskey, R. G. *The American Supreme Court*, 4th edn. Chicago, IL, University of Chicago Press, 2004.

McKay, D. *American Politics and Society*, 5th edn. Oxford and New York, Blackwell Publrs, 2001.

Politics and Power in the United States, 2nd edn. Harmondsworth, Penguin Books Ltd, 1993.

McKay, D., Houghton D., and Wroe, A. *Controversies in American Politics*. Oxford, Blackwell Publrs, 2002.

Mattson, K. *When America Was Great: The Fighting Faith of Liberalism in Post-War America*. Abingdon, Routledge, 2006.

Meyer, W. J. (Ed.) *In Pursuit of the White House 2000: How We Choose Our Presidential Nominees*, 2nd edn. Chatham, NJ, Chatham House Publrs, 2000.

Miller, M. C. *The Bush Dyslexicon: The Sayings of President Dubya*. New York, Bantam Books, 2001.

Nelson, M. (Ed.). *The Presidency and the Political System*, 8th edn. Washington, DC, Congressional Quarterly Books, 2005.

Guide to the Presidency. Abingdon, Routledge, 2001.

O'Connor, K. *Essentials of American Government: Continuity and Change*. New York, Longman, 2005.

O'Hanlon, M. E., *et al*. *Protecting the American Homeland: One Year On*, 2nd edn. Washington, DC, Brookings Institution Press, 2003.

Peele, G., Bailey, C. J., Cain. B., and Peters, B. G. (Eds). *Developments in American Politics 5*. London, Palgrave, 2006.

Polsby, N. *How Congress Evolves: Strategies and Structures in United States Politics*. Oxford, Oxford University Press, 2004.

Rapoport, R. B., and Stone, W. *Three's a Crowd: The Dynamic of Third Parties, Ross Perot, and Republican Resurgence*. Ann Arbor, MI, University of Michigan Press, 2006.

Rosen, J. *The Supreme Court: The Personalities and Rivalries that Defined America*. New York, Times Books, 2007.

Rozell, M. J. *Media Power, Media Politics*. Lanham, MD, Rowman & Littlefield Publrs, Inc, 2003.

Rudalevige, A. *The New Imperial Presidency: Renewing Presidential Power after Watergate*, 2nd edn. Ann Arbor, MI, University of Michigan Press, 2006.

Ryden, D. K. (Ed.). *The US Supreme Court and the Electoral Process*, 2nd edn. Washington, DC, Georgetown University Press, 2002.

Schickler, E. *Disjointed Pluralism: Institutional Innovation and the Development of the US Congress*. Princeton, NJ, Princeton University Press, 2001.

Shapiro, R. Y., Kumar, M. J., and Jacobs, L. R. (Eds). *Presidential Power: Forging the Presidency for the 21st Century*. New York, Columbia University Press, 2000.

Sheldon, C. H., and Mank, L. S. *Choosing Justice: The Recruitment of State and Federal Judges*. Pullman, WA, Washington State University Press, 1997.

Stevenson, C. A. *SECDEF: The Nearly Impossible Job of Secretary of Defense*, 2nd edn. Dulles, VA, Potomac Books Inc, 2007.

The 9/11 Commission Report: Final Report of the National Commission on Terrorist Attacks on the United States. New York, W. W. Norton & Co Inc, 2005.

Toplin, R. B. *Radical Conservatism: The Right's Political Religion*. Lawrence, KS, University Press of Kansas, 2006.

Vanfossen, P. J., and Berson, M. J. (Eds). *The Electronic Republic: The Impact of Technology on Education for Citizenship*. West Lafayette, IN, Purdue University Press, 2008.

Vile, J. R. *A Companion to the US Constitution and its Amendments*. Westport, CT, Praeger Publrs, 2001.

Wilentz, S. *The Rise of American Democracy: Jefferson to Lincoln*. New York, Norton, 2005.

Yuill, K. L. *Richard Nixon and the Rise of Affirmative Action*. Lanham, MD, Rowman and Littlefield, 2006.

Zimmerman, J. F. *Contemporary American Federalism*. New York, New York State University Press, 2008.

The International Role of the USA

Astor, G. *Presidents at War: From Truman to Bush, The Gathering of Military Power to Our Commander in Chief*. Hoboken, NJ, John Wiley and Sons, 2006.

Bacevich, A. J. *American Empire: The Realities and Consequences of US Diplomacy*. Cambridge, MA, Harvard University Press, 2002.

Brewer, S. *Borders and Bridges: A History of US-Latin American Relations*. Westport, CT, Praeger, 2006.

Brooks, S. G., and Wohlforth, W. C. *World Out of Balance: International Relations and the Challenge of American Primacy*. Princeton, NJ, Princeton University Press, 2008.

Brune, L. *Chronological History of US Foreign Relations*, 2nd edn. New York, Routledge, 2002.

Byman, D. L., and Waxman, M. *The Dynamics of Coercion. American Foreign Policy and the Limits of Military Might (RAND Studies in Policy Analysis)*. Cambridge, Cambridge University Press, 2002.

Cameron, F. *US Foreign Policy after the Cold War*. Abingdon, Routledge, 2005.

Chomsky, N. *Deterring Democracy*, 2nd edn. New York, Vintage Books, 2006.

Chomsky, N. and Achar, G. *Perilous Power: The Middle East and US Foreign Policy*. Boulder, CO, Paradigm Publrs, 2006.

Clarke, R. A. *Against All Enemies: Inside America's War on Terror*. New York, Free Press, 2004.

Cooley, J. *Unholy Wars: Afghanistan, America and International Terrorism*. London, Pluto Press, 2001.

Cox, M., and Stokes, D. *US Foreign Policy*. Oxford, Oxford University Press, 2008.

Dobson, A. P., and Marsh, S. *US Foreign Policy Since 1945*. Abingdon, Routledge, 2006.

Forsythe, D. P., McMahon, P. C., and Wedeman, A. (Eds). *American Foreign Policy in a Globalized World*. Abingdon, Routledge, 2006.

Fukuyama, F. (Ed.). *Nation Building: Beyond Afghanistan and Iraq*. Baltimore, MD, Johns Hopkins University Press, 2006.

Gurtov, M. *Superpower on Crusade: The Bush Doctrine in US Foreign Policy*. Boulder, CO, Lynne Rienner Publishers, 2006.

Harris, P. (Ed.). *The Environment, International Relations and US Foreign Policy*. Washington, DC, Georgetown University Press, 2001.

Holsti, O. *Making American Foreign Policy*. Abingdon, Routledge, 2006.

Hossein-Zadeh, I. *The Political Economy of U.S. Militarism*. New York, Palgrave Macmillan, 2006.

Ikenberry, G. J. *Liberal Order and Imperial Ambition: Essays on American Power and International Order*. Cambridge, Polity Press, 2006.

Ilger, T. L. *Hard Power, Soft Power and the Future of Transatlantic Relations*. Aldershot, Ashgate Publishing, 2006.

Kagan, R. *Paradise and Power: America and Europe in the New World Order*. New York, Knopf, 2003.

Kane, J. *Between Virtue and Power: The Persistent Moral Dilemma of US Foreign Policy*. New Haven, CT, Yale University Press, 2008.

Kiracofe, C. A. *Dark Crusade: Christian Zionism and US Foreign Policy*. London, I. B. Tauris, 2008.

Kolko, G. *The United States Confronts the World*. Boulder, CO, Lynne Rienner Publrs, 2006.

LaFeber, W. *The American Age: United States Foreign Policy at Home and Abroad since 1750*. New York, W. W. Norton & Co Inc, 1989.

Loveman, B. (Ed.). *Addicted to Failure: US Security Policy in Latin America and the Andean Region*. Lanham, MD, Rowman and Littlefield, 2006.

McEvoy-Levy, S. *American Exceptionalism and US Foreign Policy: Public Diplomacy at the end of the Cold War*. New York, St Martin's Press, 2001.

MacKinnon, M. G. *The Evolution of US Peacekeeping Policy Under Clinton: A Fairweather Friend?* London, Frank Cass & Co Ltd, 1999.

Maingot, A., and Lozano, W. *The United States and the Caribbean*. New York, Routledge, 2003.

Mazza, J. *Don't Disturb the Neighbours. The US and Democracy in Mexico*. New York, Routledge, 2001.

Morley, M., and Petras, J. *Empire or Republic?* New York, Routledge, 2001.

Nau, H. R. *At Home Abroad: Identity and Power in American Foreign Policy (Cornell Studies in Political Economy)*. Ithaca, NY, Cornell University Press, 2002.

Newsom, D. D. *The Imperial Mantle: The United States, Decolonization, and the Third World*. Bloomington, IN, Indiana University Press, 2001.

Nugent, W. *Habits of Empire: A History of American Expansion*. New York, Knopf, 2008.

O'Connor, B., and Griffiths, M. (Eds). *The Rise of Anti-Americanism*. Abingdon, Routledge, 2005.

Odum, W. E. *Fixing Intelligence For A More Secure America*. New Haven, CT, Yale University Press, 2004.

Palmer, B. *The 25-Year War: America's Military Role in Vietnam*. New York, Simon & Schuster Inc, 1984.

Pillar, P. *Terrorism and US Foreign Policy*. Washington, DC, Brookings Institution, 2001.

Prins, G. *The Heart of War: On Power, Conflict and Obligation in the 21st Century*. Abingdon, Routledge, 2004.

Ramsey, M. D. *The Constitution's Text in Foreign Affairs*. Cambridge, MA, Harvard University Press, 2007.

Ryan, D. *US Foreign Policy in World History*. Abingdon, Routledge, 2000.

Smith, J. *The United States and Latin America*. New York, Routledge, 2005.

Sweig, J. *Friendly Fire: Anti-Americanism Gone Global, and What To Do About It*. New York, Public Affairs, 2006.

Thomas, M. *American Policy Towards Israel: The Power and Limits of Beliefs*. Abingdon, Routledge, 2007.

Tomes, R. R. *US Defense Strategy from Vietnam to Operation Iraqi Freedom: Military Innovation and the New American Way of War, 1973–2003*. New York, Routledge, 2006.

Ullman, H. *Unfinished Business: Afghanistan, the Middle East, and Beyond—Defusing the Dangers that Threaten America's Security*. Sacramento, CA, Citadel Press, 2003.

Warnock, J. W. *Creating a Failed State: The US and Canada in Afghanistan*. Winnipeg, MB, Fernwood Publishing Co Ltd, 2008.

Weaver, G. R., and Mendelson, A. *America's Mid-Life Crisis: The Future of a Troubled Superpower*. Boston, MA, Intercultural Press, 2008.

Weiner, T. *Legacy of Ashes: The History of the CIA*. New York, Doubleday Publishing, 2007.

Weitz, R. *Revitalizing US-Russian Security Cooperation*. Abingdon, Routledge, 2005.

Woodward, B. *Bush At War*. New York, Simon and Schuster, Inc, 2003.

ESSAYS ON US ECONOMIC AND SOCIAL AFFAIRS

ECONOMIC OVERVIEW

Prof. DAVID McKAY

INTRODUCTION

In 2008 the US economy remained the world's largest. While the difference between the USA and its leading competitors narrowed steadily up to the early 1990s, thereafter the US economy's position relative to Japan and the countries of the European Union (EU) was maintained, although it declined relative to the Chinese and Indian economies. By 2008 the gross domestic product (GDP) of the US economy had grown to US $13,800,000m., while, according to the Organisation for Economic Co-operation and Development (OECD), in the same year the GDP of Japan was $4,300,000m. and that of the People's Republic of China $6,900,000m. At one point in the early 1990s the Japanese economy was close to two-thirds the size of that of the USA. This was, however, when the Japanese currency, the yen, was particularly strong; it then depreciated by over 50% through the 1990s. Few doubt that the US economy will continue to dominate world economic financial affairs. US population growth remains high for a developed country. The populations of the next two largest rich country economies, Japan and Germany, are stagnating or even declining. During the 1990s and early 2000s US growth outstripped that of both countries. All this accepted, most commentators agree that, political disruptions aside, in the longer term the People's Republic of China and India are likely to become major competitors to the USA, although in the shorter term the EU will remain the major competing trading bloc. Unfortunately, estimating the true size of the Chinese and Indian economies is problematical. In 2007 the World Bank downgraded the reported size of both economies, arguing that previous figures were largely guesswork. Even so, by that year China remained in second place globally, with its GDP estimated at around $6,000,000m.

After the end of the Second World War in 1945 the US economy underwent a number of major transitions, of which two stand out: the shift away from agriculture, extractive and manufacturing industries and towards the services sector; and the increasing interdependence with other economies. Interdependence, by definition, accompanied the erosion of what, from 1945 to 1965, was accepted as a US economic hegemony. Until 1965 the USA and the multilateral institutions under its control effectively dictated the terms of world trade. Thereafter, however, a number of developed and newly developing countries asserted independent economic power. While initially this presented the USA with a number of new economic challenges, by the last years of the 20th century the USA has been able to exploit this new competitive environment to good effect. However, since 2000, with the collapse of the high-technology stock market, revelations about the veracity of company accounts, an overvalued housing market and the subsequent banking crash of 2008, together with rapidly increasing petroleum prices, the USA once again began to appear vulnerable to the vagaries of economic change.

This overview will begin with a brief review of US economic performance after 1945, emphasizing trends in GDP and productivity growth and changes in employment and inflation. Further sections will focus on income and poverty, investment and savings, foreign trade, government finances and economic management, research and development, regulation and deregulation, and trade unions and industrial relations.

THE US ECONOMY IN PERSPECTIVE

Between 1900 and 1988 the USA achieved average annual growth in gross national income (GNI) of 3.1%. Of the leading industrial nations, only Canada and Japan experienced a higher growth rate over this period. Measured in per-head terms, growth was not so rapid (1.7% per year, compared with 3.0% for Japan and 2.7% for the Federal Republic of Germany—West Germany), although it must be noted that the population grew more quickly in the USA during this period than was the case in most comparable countries. Between 1948 and 1973 US economic growth was generally slow in comparison with other nations; the economy expanded at an average rate of 3.7% per year, compared with 9.1% for Japan, 7.0% for West Germany and 5.3% for France. Only the economy of the United Kingdom, among the leading industrial nations, grew more slowly, at an average annual rate of 3.0%. However, after 1981 the rate of growth in the USA recovered to surpass that of most competing nations. During the 1980s the US economy expanded at an average annual rate of 3.0%, while growth in West Germany decreased to an average of 1.8% per year, as did that of France. Japan alone outpaced the USA, recording a 3.8% average annual growth rate. Most countries experienced a serious decline during the early 1990s; between 1990 and 1992 the US economy slowed to an average annual growth rate of just 0.5%. However, in 1992–2000 US economic performance was considered to be one of the best among the countries of OECD. In this period the US economy grew at an average rate of 3.9% per year, compared with an average of 1.7% for the countries of the EU (including the reunited Germany) and just 0.4% for Japan. In 2000–05, however, the economy faltered, with average annual growth falling to just 2.7%, increasing to 2.9% by 2006, only to sink once again to an estimated 2.0% in 2007. Moreover, the USA's record deteriorated compared with the overall rate of the so-called Group of Eight leading industrialized countries (G8—comprising Canada, France, Germany, Italy, Japan, the United Kingdom, the USA and Russia) at a projected 2.0% in 2008. After the terrorist attacks on the USA on 11 September 2001 the economy had come close to entering a recession. However, the downturn was, in historical terms, small, and a slow if erratic recovery followed. The events of 2007–08 were of a different order, however, as the so-called 'credit crunch' led to several bank failures and bail-outs. The resulting economic dislocation dragged both the US and many other economies into recession.

In a broader historical perspective, the entire post-Second World War period was one of rapid economic expansion. Pre-war the USA had been more adversely affected by the Great Depression of the 1930s than had most comparable countries; between 1930 and 1938 the economy grew at an average rate of just 0.4% per year, compared with Japan (6.3%), Germany (4.4%) and the United Kingdom (2.2%). During the 1930s serious mistakes in financial management contributed to a very low level of economic activity. The federal Government reduced the money supply and increased taxation between 1929 and 1933, thereby aggravating deflationary trends. In addition, a number of protectionist measures were enacted, which provoked retaliation by other nations and led to a sharp decline in world trade. Not until the mid-1930s were corrective policies adopted, but it was the rearmament policies of the late 1930s and early 1940s that facilitated recovery to full capacity. Given the difficulties encountered during these years, it is misleading to talk of the 1948–73 period in terms of anything but success.

After the Second World War political leaders were determined to avoid the mistakes of the past and, accordingly, designed an economic strategy intended to keep both the USA and other capitalist economies operating at, or near, full capacity. Three broad policies were adopted. First, the USA was designated leader of the world economy, a role effectively abandoned by the United Kingdom in 1931, when it ceased the free convertibility of sterling into gold. At the US-hosted conference of international economists in Bretton Woods, New Hampshire, in 1944 the USA pledged to maintain the convertibility of the dollar into gold, at a rate of US $35 per troy oz. The United Kingdom eventually agreed to join the USA in providing a reserve currency by facilitating the free convertibility of pounds sterling into US dollars. It was decided that a system of fixed exchange rates would be adopted by the capitalist economies, underpinned by the dollar. Only when an economy's currency was grossly under- or over-valued would a formal revaluation of the currency occur. A new multilateral institution, the IMF, would provide loans to help prevent national economies from having to impose devaluation, or in order to assist in adjustments following devaluation.

Second, the USA was also the foremost among the leading economies in cultivating a policy of free international trade. The General Agreement on Tariffs and Trade (GATT, now the World Trade Organization—WTO) was signed in 1948 by all the leading economic powers in order to facilitate successive rounds of tariff reductions. The ultimate objective was a completely open international trading system. The so-called 'beggar my neighbour' policies of the 1930s would be avoided, because the US economy, by far the largest, would take the lead in permitting goods from protected markets to be sold in the country. Finally, in the sphere of domestic economic policy, the USA formally adopted Keynesian demand management through the passage of the 1946 Full Employment Act. The federal Government was, therefore, committed to pursuing a policy of maintaining near-full employment by stimulating the economy in the event of a period of deflation and serious under-utilization of capacity (in accordance with the theories of the influential British economist John Maynard Keynes, 1883–1946).

Few dispute that these policies were successful. From the late 1940s to the late 1960s the US economy grew steadily. Recessions were relatively mild (the deepest occurring in 1958) and were in no way comparable with earlier economic declines. In addition to a stable domestic and international environment, the USA was able to take advantage of major advances in technology, which led directly to a rapid increase in productivity. Uniquely among the major economies, US productivity growth accelerated during the 1940s. In 1938 the six other large economies had productivity levels averaging 57% of the US figure; by 1950 this figure had declined to 43%.

If 1977 is taken as the base year and given the value of 100, in 1947 US output per hour in the business sector was 44.9. Productivity improved steadily until 1977. In the following three years, however, productivity declined, to a low of 99.3 in 1979. From 1979 to 1999 growth in total factor productivity averaged 0.6% per year, but from 1994 to 2004 it reached an impressive average of 4.3% per year.

From an international perspective, US post-war performance appears less impressive. Between 1960 and 1973 average annual growth in US total factor productivity was 1.5%, compared with 6.3% for Japan, 4.8% for Italy, 3.9% for France, 2.6% for Germany and 1.9% for the United Kingdom. The USA continued to experience restricted growth in comparison with these countries during the difficult 1973–80 period. However, after 1979 its comparative position improved. From 1979 to 2000 both Germany and Canada suffered lower productivity growth than the USA, and the difference in growth between the USA and Japan was reduced to an average of just 0.7% per year. By the 1990s US growth was far in excess of Japan's—a trend that continued until 2002. Of all the major economies, the USA achieved the greatest productivity growth during the 1990s and early 2000s. However, after 2002 US productivity growth, although still impressive, was matched by some competing economies, especially in manufacturing. For the period 1996—2007 the US Bureau of Labor Statistics recorded an annual increase in US manufacturing output per hour of 72.7%, compared with 46.2% in Japan, 51.3% in Germany and 51.8% in the United Kingdom. In terms of rates of inflation and unemployment, the post-Second World War years can be divided into three periods. Between 1950 and 1970 low levels of inflation and unemployment were recorded. In 1965, for example, the rate of inflation (the annual change in the consumer price index) was 1.9%, while unemployment totalled 4.5% of the labour force. During these years unemployment levels tended to fluctuate more than inflation, for, although the US economic strategy was broadly Keynesian, the trade-off between unemployment and inflation differed from other countries. Generally, US politicians and officials were more willing to accept higher levels of unemployment (up to 5%–6% of the work-force) than were their counterparts in Europe or Japan. Despite these variations, the period remained, in general, one of price and employment stability.

By the late 1960s, however, there were signs of strain in both the domestic and international economies. Commodity prices increased, and, partly because of the expenditure on the Viet Nam war, the domestic economy experienced excessive growth. In addition, a dollar shortage was replaced by a dollar surplus, as the demand for dollars declined.

These problems were acknowledged during the early 1970s by the effective abandonment, in 1973, of the Bretton Woods system of fixed exchange rates. The value of the dollar consequently fluctuated according to market forces. However, the most significant dislocation in the post-Second World War economic order came in the form of increased commodity prices. The Arab–Israeli war of October 1973 and the rise of the Organization of the Petroleum Exporting Countries (OPEC) led to an immediate quadrupling of petroleum prices. Other commodity prices also rose sharply, following a period of rapid economic growth in most of the industrialized countries during the early 1970s. As a result, many economies experienced a combination of relatively high rates of inflation and low economic growth (so-called 'stagflation'), with very disruptive consequences for employment and productivity. A further externally induced shock to the economy occurred in 1979–80 with the Iranian Revolution.

While the US economy did not regain its full strength until the early 1980s, its recovery then was quite comprehensive. Output, productivity and employment rose, while inflation fell—at least initially. Interestingly, in terms of employment, the US recovery was more solidly based than that of other countries. Between 1981 and 1987 civilian unemployment increased by 3.2% in France, 3.1% in Germany, 1.8% in Italy and 0.7% in Japan, but declined by 2.0% in the United Kingdom and 1.4% in the USA. This trend accelerated thereafter, especially when the USA is compared with the countries of the EU. In June 2002, when the US economy was officially in recession, the unemployment rate was just 5.9%, compared with 9.1% in France, 9.0% in Italy, 9.8% in Germany and 7.5% in Canada. Even in Japan, which had long experienced very low levels of officially defined unemployment, the rate, at 5.4%, was only slightly lower than that in the USA, while in the United Kingdom the rate was 5.2%. To explain the success of the USA in this area, commentators pointed to the country's flexible labour market, lower wage increases and less generous social benefits. By 2005 the unemployment rate had declined to 5.1%, but in 2008, amid increasing economic dislocation, it had increased to 6.1%.

The US inflation record after 1989 was also generally satisfactory. Between 1990 and 2004 the increase in consumer prices averaged 2.7% per year, compared with 3.1% in the United Kingdom, 2.7% in Germany, 2.3% in France and less than 1.0% in Japan. In the case of Japan, however, the country was recognized by some economists to be in a damaging deflationary spiral. In general, the US economy performed well in comparative terms from the early 1990s, and the global recession affected the USA only mildly until the events of 2001, when economic activity slowed perceptibly. Recovery thereafter was slow, but significantly better than some of the gloomier projections in 2001 and 2002. However, by 2006 the spectre of inflation returned when, in response to an annualized inflation rate of 3.2%, the US Federal Reserve Bank raised interest rates, only to reduce them radically when the credit crisis hit. Even so, increasing petroleum and food costs caused price inflation to accelerate once again, reaching 5.6% by mid-2008.

By late 2008, therefore, the US economy was experiencing a range of problems, including rising unemployment and inflation, as well as serious difficulties induced by drastic reductions in the availability of credit.

INCOME AND POVERTY

Between 1948 and 1973 the standard of living in the USA improved steadily, with real disposable family income increasing by an average of 2.4% per year. The wealthiest 20% of families enjoyed an average annual improvement of 3.1% and the least wealthy 20% an increase of 2.9%. However, during the later decades of the 20th century, while the wealthy continued to prosper, the relative position of the poorest 20% deteriorated. By 2004 it was estimated that this group were 3.8% poorer (in real terms) than they were in 1978. None the less, in absolute terms, most US citizens remain well off.

The economic declines of the 1970s and early 1980s accounted, in part, for the position of the poor. Lower-income workers and those at the margin of the labour force are more affected by fluctuations in growth rates than are other groups. Welfare benefits also reached their highest level during the late 1970s and, in response to a more hostile economic environment, employers reduced their real wages across a wide front. This was reflected in the data for earnings from this period. In constant 1977 dollars, earnings declined from US $5.10 per hour in all industries in 1975 to $4.83 in 1982. This general trend continued until the early 1990s, although some recovery in earnings was discernible from 1994. From 1994 to 2004 average annual compensation per employee increased by 5.6%, compared with less than 2.5% in 1991–93. By 2007 the average hourly earnings for production workers were $17.35, compared with $12.47 in 1997 (Bureau of Labor Statistics).

The USA uses an official measure of poverty, adjustable for family size and local cost of living. In 2008 it was US $21,203 for a family of four. The number of families living in poverty declined steadily from over 22.2% of the total in 1960 to 11.4% in 1978. In the following decades, however, the figure increased, reaching 15.1% in 1993, although by 1999 the figure had fallen sharply, to 11.8%; by 2008 it had increased to 12.8%, however. Families headed by females were greatly over-represented among this group; in 2008 28.5% of all female-headed families were living in poverty. Very generally, while the number of people living in poverty fluctuates with changes in the business cycle, certain social groups and, especially, minority families are caught in a cycle of poverty from which it is difficult to escape. This said, the welfare reforms introduced in 1996 reduced the number of families dependent on state aid, although 12 years later the full effects of the reforms had yet to be tested in the context of a serious economic downturn.

As far as the distribution of wealth is concerned, the USA displayed greater inequalities than most comparable countries from the 1970s onwards. In 2005 the richest 1% of the population received 21.8% of all pre-tax income—a much higher figure than for comparable countries such as Germany and Japan, and one that had increased steadily since the 1980s. While inequalities have not been reduced, family incomes have increased for all social groups, as a result of an increase in the number of employed. By 2008 the median annual family income had increased to US $61,500, one of the highest figures anywhere in the world.

Another area where the USA is distinctive is health care, for, although some 15% of GDP is devoted to health, 46.9m. US citizens had no health insurance in 2008 (US Census Bureau figures). Instead, they have to rely on charity and a range of government programmes such as Medicare and Medicaid. In 2007 26.6% of all Americans were fully or partly covered by such programmes—a small decline from the previous year.

INVESTMENT AND SAVINGS

As has already been suggested, US productivity growth was relatively high until the early 1970s, reflecting the high levels of investment. After 1973, however, investment growth declined. Most commentators agree that this was a direct result of higher inflation and (partly owing to inflation) of higher effective tax rates. The incentive to save and invest fell during these years, and the result was lower output and productivity levels. Furthermore, distortions in the tax code, in addition to inflation, diverted investment away from manufacturing industry and towards speculative residential and commercial development. Although economists disagreed about the magnitude of the disincentive effects of inflation and higher effective tax rates, they estimated that, in combination, they reduced overall investment by between 20% and 50% over this period. The rate of growth of net non-residential stock of capital per worker declined from 2.2% between 1966 and 1973 to 1.4% in 1973–81.

During the 1980s economic growth was fuelled both by further investment in property-based development and by high levels of government spending. Most economists were critical of this trend, predicting that a sharp adjustment would be necessary later in the decade. In the event, the so-called 'property bubble' (a continual increase in property prices, which had mainly affected the south and west of the country) burst at the end of the decade, and prices fell sharply as a consequence. Many savings and loan banks (or 'thrifts', as they were known) failed, and the federal Government was obliged to pay financial compensation to numerous investors. At the same time, significant efforts were made to reduce the federal budget deficit. Economists were also concerned at the persistently low household-savings ratio in the USA. In 1991 this was 4.1%, compared with 14.6% in Japan and 11.2% in Germany.

However, the very low—and sometimes negative—savings rate, which persisted through to the beginning of the 21st century (it became negative for the first time in the second quarter of 2005 and by the second quarter of 2007 it was –1.1%), did not seem to have a consistently detrimental effect on investment. Indeed, during the early 2000s the USA experienced an investment boom that reaped large improvements in productivity (by the second quarter of 2005 non-residential fixed investment had increased to 8.4% per year). Most commentators agree that this was the result of the falling price of capital goods and of consistently low interest rate levels. The dramatic recovery of US investment and productivity changed the nature of the debate on the role of the Government in the economy. Until the 1980s many US economists and politicians (especially those on the political left) argued that in order to compete with Japan and Europe the USA needed an industrial policy or active intervention by the Government to channel investment into growth industries. By the mid-1990s such options were rejected not only in the USA but also in all OECD countries. Instead, virtually all politicians and economists believed that the market was the best arbiter of the quantity and quality of industrial investment. In other words, the 'American model' of the free-market economy was preferred to the Japanese and French models of state intervention.

As noted, the collapse of the high-technology stocks in 2000 and then the terrorist attacks of 11 September 2001 damaged confidence in the economy and led to a prolonged decline of share prices on the US and foreign stock markets. These problems were compounded by revelations of illegal accounting practices in US companies such as Enron Corporation and WorldCom. Consequently, as a result of poor returns on stocks and interest rates remaining very low by historical standards, savings rates fell. Instead, many US citizens invested in real estate and other tangible assets. Unfortunately this diversion of money into residential real estate developed into a gigantic bubble and when Federal Reserve raised interest rates from a low of 1.0% in 2004 to 5.25% in July 2006 the bubble was pricked. Indeed, by mid-2007 excessive lending in the 'sub-prime' mortgage market had led to a full scale crisis with a number of lending institutions facing bankruptcy. By 2008 the federal Government was obliged to intervene to save a number of institutions including mortgage providers Fannie Mae and Freddie Mac as well as the major insurance company AIG. In addition all of the major investment banks either failed or were taken over or converted into commercial banks. With house prices in free fall the Federal Reserve reduced interest rates rapidly and the federal Government was obliged to create a plan to buy up the 'toxic' debts held by distressed banks.

At the time of writing it is uncertain how this crisis will play out, but the effective collapse of the deregulated 'American model' of financial management seemed sure to lead to serious economic dislocation and recession.

FOREIGN TRADE

Until the early 1960s, as has been indicated, the USA experienced few, if any, problems in foreign economic policy. Indeed, the major concern in the 1950s was the dollar shortage, which often worked to the advantage, rather than the disadvantage, of the USA. Following this period, however, three interrelated difficulties arose, none of which seemed likely to be completely resolved in the short term. First, the USA acquired a sizeable external trade deficit. Second, the subject of protectionism reappeared on the political agenda. Third, the value of the dollar fluctuated considerably, in ways that aggravated the first two problems.

Between 1960 and 1983 the current account of the USA's balance of payments was approximately in equilibrium. Deficits were recorded in the early and late 1970s, but these were relatively low. During the 1980s the trade deficit gradually increased, reaching US $159,560m., according to the IMF, in 1987. Some recovery occurred during the early 1990s, but thereafter the trade deficit generally rose, reaching $832,250m. in 2006.

It is difficult to determine precisely why the USA has a trade imbalance, as a number of factors confuse the issue. For example, the exchange rate for the dollar does not always adjust as it would in a free-market situation. Strictly speaking, the exchange rate should adapt automatically to eliminate surpluses or deficits on the current trading account, but market imperfections often prevent this. During 1990–92, for instance, the dollar fell in relation to other currencies, as the authorities pursued a low interest-rate policy to speed the recovery of the economy. Meanwhile, European countries kept their interest rates high, in order to control the inflationary effects of German unification. Later, these countries were obliged to follow the German lead as members of the Exchange Rate Mechanism of the European Monetary System. As a result, US goods decreased in price, which, in turn, helped to adjust the trade deficit.

By the late 1990s the situation had changed again. US interest rates were maintained at a relatively high level to keep a check on domestic inflation. As a result, the dollar appreciated rapidly in relation to the European currencies (except for sterling) and the Japanese yen. The price of US goods rose and the trade deficit increased. In response to these problems, the Group of Seven (G7) leading industrialized countries (from June 1999 known as the G8 following the inclusion of Russia) from the mid-1980s onwards attempted to co-ordinate their central banks' activities, in order to keep the value of the dollar down at a level that reflected the true trading position of the USA. These attempts were generally unsuccessful, mainly because domestic economic and political factors intervened to undermine international co-operation. This was apparent in 2001 when, despite a US economic slowdown, the dollar remained stubbornly strong, making imported goods relatively cheap and thus aggravating the trade deficit. It was not until 2002, when revelations of artificially inflated profits by US corporations affected market confidence, that the value of the dollar began to decline. In 2003 and 2004 very low US interest rates resulted in further dollar depreciation, especially against the euro, although a temporary recovery occurred in 2005 as the Federal Reserve resumed an upward interest rate trend, which continued into 2006 and 2007. By 2008, however, the dollar came under pressure once again and in the context of rapidly increasing oil prices the trade deficit rose steeply once more.

An increasingly volatile international trading environment at the beginning of the 21st century raised, once again, the question of trade barriers and protectionism. Until 1934 the USA was a protectionist state, the original impulse for tariffs being the need to protect the economy from cheap British goods. In contrast, after the Second World War the USA became one of the strongest advocates of free trade and led successive rounds of tariff reductions via the GATT mechanism. Tariff levels were reduced from a high of 20% in 1934 to 5% by 1992. However, from the 1970s onwards domestic pressures for a return to limited protectionism grew. Older industrial areas, producing such items as motor vehicles, textiles and steel, became concerned about competition from other countries and, in particular, from Japan. In the 1992 presidential election the independent candidate Ross Perot proposed a limited form of protection for US goods and won 19% of the votes cast. Congress only narrowly passed the so-called Uruguay Round of tariff reductions under GATT in early 1993, after almost seven years of negotiations. However, the rapid economic recovery of the following years meant that the issue receded in political importance. Protectionist sentiment remained to some degree, especially in the Midwest and the industrial north, but as long as employment continued to be held at relatively high levels this seemed unlikely seriously to affect public policy.

A further important development was the advent of the North American Free Trade Agreement (NAFTA) in 1994. The Agreement was signed by the USA, Canada and Mexico and was designed to eliminate tariff and non-tariff barriers between the three countries and, generally, to encourage trade and investment in the NAFTA region. However, there were fears in the USA that jobs could be 'exported' to the low-cost Mexican labour market, and NAFTA appeared likely to become more controversial should a recession in the economy increase unemployment.

With the election of President George W. Bush in 2000, trade issues again returned to the centre of the political stage. The new President adopted an unusually nationalistic approach to the protection of US business interests and clashed with the EU and other trading partners in areas such as protection for farmers and the US steel industry. In March 2002 the Government imposed tariffs on steel imported from the EU, Russia and Japan, among other countries (Canada, Mexico and some developing countries were exempt); the measure was taken as a response to cheap exports from those countries, which the USA claimed were damaging the domestic steel industry. The countries affected appealed to the WTO to overturn the decision and demanded compensation from the USA. Eventually, in 2004 the USA abandoned the tariff. While these trade skirmishes were significant in the sense that they represented a new nationalism on the part of US trade policy, the Bush Administration remained officially committed to free trade in most areas. Indeed, in 2005 President Bush pledged that his aim was to abolish all trade barriers and he made this pledge even as the old conflicts resurfaced between the USA and the EU over such issues as agriculture and aerospace subsidies. In July the US Congress narrowly voted to ratify the Dominican Republic-Central American Free Trade Agreement. One of the main disputes in trade negotiations has been the extent to which tariff negotiations can benefit developing countries. Generally, the USA is seen as placing free trade before protection for fragile developing economies. Indeed, this was the main reason for the collapse of the Doha Round of tariff reductions in 2006. By 2008 the trade issue had been conflated with the question of immigration, with many politicians resisting immigration reform (including an amnesty for illegal workers) on the grounds that it would threaten US jobs. During the 2008 presidential campaign the question of preserving American jobs returned to the centre of the stage with both the Republican candidate John McCain and his Democrat rival Barack Obama adopting cautious stances on the question of open foreign trade.

GOVERNMENT FINANCES AND ECONOMIC MANAGEMENT

Historically, the USA was a fiscally conservative country. Taxes were traditionally held low, budgets balanced and the role of government limited. Even in 2008 government expenditure as a percentage of GDP was significantly lower in the USA than in comparable countries. In that year government spending (federal, state and local) accounted for an estimated 37.1% of GDP in the USA, compared with 52.5% in France, 44.5% in Germany and 45.0% in the United Kingdom. Even in Japan, which traditionally had a small public sector, the figure had risen to 38.3%, as the Japanese Government increased public expenditure to encourage economic growth (all figures from OECD).

Nevertheless, government spending increased rapidly after 1929, from the equivalent of 10% of GDP to more than 30% in 1960. The pattern of government expenditure in the USA was slightly different from comparable countries. Generally, defence spending was higher, although as a percentage of total federal government outlays it declined from over 20% in 1993 to 15.5% in 2000. However, following the Bush Administration's declaration of 'war on terror' following the attacks on New York and Washington, DC, in September 2001, this figure increased to 19.9% in 2004. As a percentage of GDP, defence spending decreased from 6.2% in 1986 to an estimated 4.8% in 2008. However, spending on social security and medical care increased sharply in the 1990s, in line with other countries. Payments for individuals on such items as pensions, unemployment benefits, medical care and welfare constituted more than 60% of all federal outlays in 2008, equivalent to some 13.8% of GDP. Debt interest, grants to state and local governments and other grants accounted for the difference.

On the income side, individual income taxes provided 42% of federal revenue in 2006, social insurance taxes and contributions 37.9% and corporation income taxes 11.9% (figures from the 2008 Budget of the USA). Borrowing and excise taxes largely made up the remainder. Generally, compared with other countries, the US federal Government raised a higher percentage of revenue from income taxes than from indirect taxes, although state governments used sales taxes as their main source of revenue.

As regards the functioning of the economy, debates over government finances at the beginning of the 21st century focused on three major areas: the level of spending, including the general level of taxation needed to finance expenditure; the level of the budget surplus or deficit; and the degree of spending on social security and medical care. As indicated, the general levels of government spending in the USA were not extreme, in comparative terms. Nevertheless, most US taxpayers believed that they were too high. Tax and expenditure reductions dominated the agenda of the two Administrations of President Ronald Reagan (1981–89), and in 1981 the largest tax reduction measure in US history, the Economic Recovery Tax Act, was passed. Some US $162,000m. was removed from the revenue side of national income and expenditure, corporate and individual income taxes were reduced, as were the highest marginal rates. Throughout the 1980s the Administration sought to reduce domestic spending, but it was loath to decrease expenditure on defence. Simultaneously, the Democrat-dominated Congress proved reluctant to reduce social spending. Thus, taxes were lowered, but spending continued to increase, and the outcome was a rapidly expanding federal deficit. In 1986 the deficit was an unprecedented $221,200m., although as a percentage of GDP the highest point was reached in 1983, at 6.1%. During the recession of the early 1990s the deficit grew again, but by 1997 it had been reduced to around $22,000m., or just 0.3% of GDP. In the following year the deficit turned to surplus and by 2000 the USA enjoyed a substantial federal surplus, amounting to 2.4% of GDP. Overall debt (that accumulated through history) fell to 61% of GDP—a decrease of almost 15% over the previous seven years. Three factors were prominent in effecting this improvement. First, in 1991 and 1993 Congress passed major deficit-reduction legislation, which involved reducing expenditure and increasing taxation. The Administration of President George Bush, Sr (1989–93), sponsored the 1991 measure and incurred considerable political costs as a result; his defeat in 1992 is at least partly attributable to his failure to fulfil his 1988 campaign promise not to increase taxes. Second, as has already been noted, defence spending was reduced substantially in real terms. Third, and most importantly, from 1992 the US economy experienced a steady upward growth trend, the longest sustained expansion of the 20th century. As a result, tax revenues became buoyant and the size of the deficit decreased, with a surplus achieved in 1998. By the end of 1999 the debate on federal finances had changed from concern to reduce the deficit to conflicts over how to spend the surplus. Generally, the Democrats favoured social spending, while the Republicans, under President George W. Bush (2001–), supported tax cuts. In the event, in May 2001 Congress approved legislation providing for a $1,350,000m. reduction in taxes. However, by 2002 the debate had changed again. The economic downturn quickly turned the budget surplus into an initially small deficit (of $157,797m.), which had widened by 2004 into a deficit of $412,727m., equivalent to 3.6% of GDP. The Bush Administration remained convinced, however, that the deficit was temporary and continued to favour tax cuts in the belief that the fundamentals of government finance were good and that economic recovery would be aided by tax reductions. In other words, the Bush Administration believed that the deficit would soon dissipate and that rapid economic growth would soon return government finances to a healthy state. Many economists and the Congressional Budget Office disagreed, maintaining that the deficit was structural and would eventually have to be addressed through tax increases and/or expenditure reductions. Events were also to conspire against the President's assumptions as the after-effects of 'Hurricane Katrina' in August 2005 obliged the federal Government not only to ask Congress for over $50,000m. in federal aid, but also had the effect of greatly increasing Medicaid and welfare payments to the victims of the disaster. Notwithstanding, increasing growth in the economy and the consequent increase in tax revenues led to some amelioration of the deficit during 2005, to $318,346m., equivalent to 2.6% of GDP. However, following the credit crisis of 2007 and 2008 the budget deficit increased sharply as the economy slowed and federal spending on the bail-out of financial institutions soared. By the end of that year it was estimated that the deficit would reach $407,000m. or over 3% GDP (Congressional Budget Office estimate, September 2008).

Monetary policy in the USA during the early years of the 21st century was much more insulated from democratic pressures than was fiscal policy. A federally organized 'central' bank, the Federal Reserve, was responsible for controlling the money supply and setting interest rates. The Chairman of the Federal Reserve Board of Governors was, thus, a very powerful figure in the general area of monetary policy and, although appointed by the President, was widely recognized as independent. In the 1990s the incumbent Chairman, Alan Greenspan, proved particularly strict in his attempts to control inflation. Perceiving that prices on the stock market were increasing too rapidly, as in the first half of 1997, for instance, comments by Greenspan were sufficient for the markets to adjust downwards. Later, as the economy slowed in 2000, 2001 and 2003 he implemented a number of interest rate cuts that played some part in warding off recession. Following the terrorist attacks on the USA in September 2001, and the resulting further slowdown of the economy, by 2003 the Federal Reserve's benchmark interest rate had been reduced to 1%, its lowest rate for 40 years. None the less, the recovery was slow and low rates were encouraging consumers to borrow, especially to finance the purchase of residential property. Many economists believed that this might lead to a real estate 'bubble', which, if burst, could cause lasting damage to the economy. By 2004 economic growth had resumed again, and by July 2006 the Federal Reserve had increased the rate to 5.25% in the context of accelerating inflation. Fears of the real estate bubble were confirmed in 2007 and 2008 when many 'sub-prime' lenders found themselves in serious financial difficulty. Mortgage defaults increased and liquidity in the financial sector declined sharply, leading to fears of a recession. In response the Federal Reserve reduced interest rates to 2% by mid-2008.

RESEARCH AND DEVELOPMENT

The USA has invested more in absolute terms on research and development than any other country in recent years, spending more in 2005, for example, than France, Germany and the United Kingdom combined. Expressed as a percentage of GDP, total expenditure on research and development was an estimated 2.68% in 2005 compared with 1.84% in the EU-27 (Eurostat). However, a substantial proportion of US research and development expenditure (18% in 2004) continued to be dedicated to defence-related projects. Civilian research expenditure was, as a percentage of GDP, higher in Japan and Germany than in the USA.

The federal Government funded some 25.6% of total research in 2004, compared with 67.2% by industry, 2.8% by the universities and 3.1% by other non-profit institutions. The USA was generally recognized as the world leader in scientific discovery and in the development and application of scientific achievements. However, until the early 1990s many commentators claimed that the quality of US research was compromised by an over-reliance on defence-related research. Concern was also expressed that some of the more innovative applied research was taking place in Japan, which in 2005 spent 3.18% of GDP on research. Despite a continued dependence on defence-related research—which increased further after the terrorist attacks of September 2001—in certain crucial areas such as genetics, computer hardware and software and aerospace engineering, the US lead remained unquestioned in 2008.

REGULATION AND DEREGULATION

In all the modern industrial countries economic regulation was an important economic and political issue during the 20th century, and this was particularly true of the USA. Two broad areas of economic activity were covered by regulation: those activities associated with market imperfections and/or market failure, and those concerned with monopoly and oligopoly. The former was often labelled 'social regulation' and the latter 'economic regulation'. In the later part of the 20th century and the early 21st century both Democratic and Republican Administrations were active in both these areas, but there were major differences in their approaches, primarily in the area of social regulation.

Social regulation is designed to compensate for what economists call negative 'externalities', or those adverse consequences of economic activity that commerce and industry have no incentive to correct. In these cases the Government must intervene to do what the market will not or cannot do, by providing such benefits as environmental protection, occupational and health regulation and the regulation of financial institutions. From the mid-1960s there was a sharp increase in social regulation, which, according to the critics, came to constitute a burden on the economy. Certainly the Reagan and Bush, Sr, Administrations believed this to be the case, and made strenuous efforts to ease regulation on industry and commerce. There was, however, little evidence to suggest that the USA was at a competitive disadvantage because of burdensome social regulation. In the broad area of labour-market policies, including worker security, health benefits, unemployment compensation and trade union rights, the USA was much less stringently regulated than most European countries. On environmental and consumer protection issues it had broadly similar laws to those used by its economic competitors.

Economic regulation was a less controversial, but no less important, issue. In this area debate concentrated on the extent to which industries regulated by law should be required to operate in a more competitive environment. Until the 1970s regulations designed to protect the public interest often resulted in advantages for special interests. Hence telephone companies, airlines, trucking firms and railroads all enjoyed the benefits of price and/or route 'fixing', with ensuing higher profits. From the 1970s, however, Congress legislated to remove many of the advantages, and passenger and cargo air transport, telephone services, broadcasting, long-distance bus services, petroleum-refining and natural gas supplies were all deregulated. Studies on the resulting benefits varied in their conclusions, but few disputed that there were substantial net benefits for the economy, and for consumers, in such areas as air transport and energy.

During the 1990s deregulation moved one stage further towards the privatization of public services. Most of the privatizations occurred at state and local level, but in the late 1990s a number of federal government agencies and services were considered possible candidates for privatization, including the postal service and the National Aeronautics and Space Administration (NASA). As might be expected, the Bush Administration that took office in January 2001 generally favoured the interests of business over those of the environment, consumers and employees. This was evident in a number of decisions, in areas ranging from employment law to the granting of freer access to extractive industries to develop federal land.

In summary, at the beginning of the 21st century public policy in the USA regarding regulation was subject to conflicting pressures. On the one hand, the free-market ethos was very well established, as was demonstrated by the support for economic regulation and opposition to social regulation. On the other hand, public interest groups demanded stronger social regulatory laws. Conflict between these groups and producer interests seemed likely to remain a politically salient issue well into the 21st century, especially where issues of affirmative action and environmental and consumer protection were concerned. The continuing refusal by the Bush Administration to sign up to the terms of the Kyoto Protocol on climate change received much criticism, domestically and internationally. Indeed many individual US states (and in particular California) have adopted stricter emission controls than those required by the federal Government.

One final area of regulation, which caused severe problems for policy-makers in the 1990s and 2000s, concerned financial institutions. From the 1930s onwards a framework of legislation was created to protect investors and savers from the vagaries of economic dislocation and recession. Most of these laws provided federally guaranteed insurance for depositors at banks and savings and loans institutions. Until the 1990s few changes in the regulation of these banks and institutions were made; their day-to-day operation was regulated under state rather than federal law, with resulting wide variations. During the first years of the Reagan presidency the few remaining restrictions on savings and loans operations were removed, thus encouraging investment in high-risk commercial and residential property developments. Simultaneously, however, the incomes of these operations remained linked to fixed-interest mortgages. As interest rates rose, the difference between income and expenditures widened, leading to widespread insolvencies. By 1991 some US $155,000m. in federal insurance costs had been incurred, and the Federal Deposit Insurance Corporation Improvement Act was passed in that year, in an attempt to improve regulation in the future. By 1997 the savings and loans banks had returned to their original role of providing mortgages for homebuyers, and most of the accumulated debts were cleared. However, in the early 2000s the framework of regulatory law governing the accounting and reporting procedures of corporations came under intense scrutiny when it was revealed that accountants and corporations had colluded in inflating the profits of companies such as Enron and WorldCom. The Bush Administration's policy in this area was to apply existing law more stringently rather than to adopt new laws, as favoured by most Democrats, in order to hold corporate leaders more accountable to shareholders and employees.

This topic returned to centre stage in 2007 following the collapse of the real estate bubble in 'sub-prime' mortgages. It became apparent that the lending practices of many lending institutions had been less than prudent. As a result calls for stricter federal regulation of lending standards became vocal, and reached a crescendo in 2008 with the collapse of many banks and the giant insurance firm, AIG. Federal bail-outs of distressed banks and a plan for a government buy out of 'toxic' debts held by banks were proposed. As a result of these events the regulatory framework in which financial institutions had to operate was strengthened considerably.

TRADE UNIONS AND INDUSTRIAL RELATIONS

In 2008 only 12.6% of US wage and salary workers were unionized—the lowest figure for any large industrial country and a considerable decline from the 1945 figure of 36%. In the private sector the figure was even lower—a mere 8%, although fully 40% of public sector workers were unionized. As might be expected, trade union membership was concentrated in the older manufacturing industries, in extractive industries and, in particular, among government workers. Among the most notable unions were the United Automobile, Aerospace and Agricultural Implement Workers of America, the United Food and Commercial Workers International Union, the Service Employees' International Union (SEIU), the International Brotherhood of Teamsters and the American Federation of State, County and Municipal Employees (AFSCME). It is interesting to note that the most rapidly growing unions are found in the services sector (the AFSCME and the SEIU) and generally represent lower-paid, low-skill, often female, labour. Although relatively few workers are members of unions, a very rapidly expanding labour force has led to large numbers of workers organizing unions. Indeed, in 1999 more than 600,000 workers formed trade unions at previously unorganized plants and work places.

Most labour union activity was regulated at state level. Federal law provided a basic framework and allowed free collective bargaining; however, the individual states decided on whether a closed or union shop was permitted. Generally, the southern and western states had more restrictive laws and the northern and eastern states had laws more sympathetic to the unions.

Strike activity or industrial disruption declined steadily from the 1970s, as the price of labour fell and the industrial structure changed. This pattern was in line with the trends in other industrialized countries. A minimum-wage law existed, but this was set at a comparatively low level and adjusted for local cost of living. Most observers agree that the labour market in the USA is flexible and worker security low.

CONCLUSIONS

The most striking aspect of the US economy in 2008 was the serious dislocation caused by the panic in the financial markets and the resulting uncertainty for the health of the whole economy. This crisis represented a major change from the pre-2007 period. During the 1970s and, again, during the early 1990s both domestic and foreign commentators were quick to criticize what were perceived to be structural problems, including low savings and investment rates, 'deindustrialization' and declining improvements in productivity. However, the objective performance of the economy in the 1990s was significantly better than that of Japan and that of most of the countries of the EU. As measured by growth and employment, the US economy remained very strong. Indeed, from the late 1990s other countries attempted to adopt the 'American model', introducing flexible labour laws and investment in knowledge-intensive industries. Not until late 2000 did a serious downturn occur as the stock market growth of the late 1990s, fed by the frenzied growth of internet and high-technology shares, proved unsustainable. Worries about the trade deficit, continuing low savings rates, corporate greed and high levels of personal indebtedness persisted. Following the September 2001 terrorist attacks the economy again contracted, although from mid-2002 a gradual recovery began. In addition, some recovery in stock prices took place from 2003 and continued through mid-2007, although only to the levels achieved some six years earlier. By then, however, some economists expressed concern at the continued high level of personal indebtedness among US consumers, and in particular home owners, and at the burgeoning trade deficit. Concern was also expressed that many Americans had over-borrowed on their homes and with rising interest rates were increasingly unable to meet their mortgage payments. By late 2008 the collapse of the financial markets heralded an economic recession. So, although the USA remained the economic 'locomotive' of the industrialized world it was facing serious structural problems whose resolution required sound economic management over the medium to long term.

AGRICULTURE: HISTORY, TRENDS AND RECENT DEVELOPMENTS

Prof. MILTON C. HALLBERG

BRIEF HISTORY

The social and economic structure of colonial America (1497–1763), essentially on what is now the east coast of the USA, was predominantly agricultural, and its rural economy was, for the most part, one of self-sufficiency. While the plantation system determined the economy of the Southern colonies, here, as elsewhere, highly versatile, small farms were the rule rather than the exception. Exports of tobacco, cotton, rice and indigo were significant, although inadequate transportation facilities and the scarcity of metallic money were obstacles to expansion of colonial trade. Indian corn (maize) was the universal crop in the early years, but wheat, rye, barley, oats, buckwheat and peas also became important as time went on. Tobacco-growing occurred in Virginia, Maryland and North Carolina and was the staple crop of the South. Cotton, rice and indigo production occurred on a lesser scale and primarily in South Carolina.

Agriculture throughout the colonies was stimulated during the War of Independence period (1763–89) as demand for food and fibres was enhanced. Indigo production ceased as imperial bounties were imposed. Strong overseas demand for tobacco, rice and cotton, however, encouraged increased production of these Southern crops. At the outbreak of war, wool production in the colonies was stimulated by non-importation agreements. The exodus of the loyalist Tories during the course of the War of Independence (also known as the Revolutionary War) allowed for the dissolution of many large estates and brought about the demise of the feudal system in America. This set the stage for a policy of colonization and land sale following the War that favoured the small farmer.

In 1800, just prior to the Louisiana Purchase and the entry of Ohio and states to the west into the Union, there were 335,000 farms in the USA farming 68,675,000 acres (27,792,000 ha). The number of farms increased steeply as the interior of the USA was developed and as various measures were adopted to ensure that family farming was a vital part of this development process. The Homestead Act of 1862, for example, enabled homesteaders to claim a 160-acre (65-ha) parcel of unclaimed land for a filing fee of US $18. This Act remained in effect until 1976.

Between 1810 and 1840, in response to the growth of a home market, eastern farmers shifted from self-sufficiency to commercialized agriculture. Higher prices for grains after 1845 owing to conditions in Europe, together with the coming of the canals and railroads, further encouraged occupation of the prairies and contributed to a steep increase in the number of farms. At the beginning of the American Civil War there were 2.5m. farms in the USA farming 407,500,000 acres (164,909,000 ha).

While the process of western development was still unfolding, canals and railroads enabled farmers on rich, virgin, western soil to ship their produce to eastern markets. As a consequence, eastern farmers were forced to specialize in milk, butter, cheese, potatoes, vegetables, fruit and hay, which, by reason of perishability or bulk, escaped western competition and enjoyed a ready market in the expanding nearby urban centres.

Despite rivalry from the Northwest, the South continued as the principal centre of commercial agriculture up to the time of the Civil War. Tobacco production diminished somewhat after 1850. Cotton became the crop of choice in the South and was the principal source of the South's pre-eminence. Rice, hemp, flax and sugar achieved considerable success in various parts of the South, but it was cotton, particularly on the western lands of the South, that predominated.

Following the Civil War a variety of changes occurred that were so momentous in their ramifications and consequences that, taken together, they are frequently referred to as the

'Agricultural Revolution'. These changes included, the passing of the public domain into private ownership by means of liberal land policies; completion of the westward movement of settlement; the invention and popularization of improved farm implements and machinery; extension and development of transport facilities (particularly railroads); the migration of specialized industries from the farm to the factory; the expansion of domestic and foreign markets; the establishment of agencies for the promotion of scientific knowledge relating to agriculture; and the development of political organizations and actions by farmers in an effort to improve their relative economic position.

Agricultural output increased at the rate of about 3% per year after the Civil War, and by 1900 the number of farms had increased to 5.7m. Agricultural products accounted for the vast majority of the value of US exports. Between 1900 and 1925, however, growth in farm output slowed to less than 1% per year, as the land frontier started to close. This brought about the longest sustained increase in agricultural prices relative to the general price level since the Civil War. Rising food prices made clear to many the consequences of lagging productivity growth in agriculture during the first quarter of the 20th century. Public concern was manifest in greater emphasis on resource development and conservation, and in increased allocation of public funds for research and education designed to increase the rate of productivity.

Agriculture again resumed its prominence as a major contributor to national economic growth during the 1920s. The replacement of horses and mules by tractors and the release of land formerly used to produce feed for horses and mules for the production of food and fibre proceeded rapidly even during the Great Depression. By the beginning of the Second World War agriculture was in a position to release a substantial flow of labour to the non-farm sector and once again to achieve rapid increases in farm output.

At the beginning of the 19th century 72% of the nation's gainfully employed workers were employed in farming, 66% of the total population was in agriculture and nearly 50% of the nation's gross domestic product (GDP) was generated on farms. Today, a little more than 2% of the gainfully employed workers in the USA are employed in agriculture, farm families make up about 1.5% of the total US population and only about 1% of the national GDP originates in agriculture. While agriculture is unquestionably an important sector, supplying food to consumers at home and abroad, it is no longer the most important sector economically and no longer the hub of economic activity in the country. Specialization and the rapid development of the industrial sector, rather than the decline of the agricultural sector, are responsible for these developments. Nevertheless, a variety of significant adjustments occurred in US agriculture during the period following the Great Depression and the Second World War. The remainder of this essay provides a brief overview of the current structure of the US agricultural sector, reviews the adjustments the sector has made since the Second World War as well as legislative approaches to promote further adjustments, offers a brief discussion of the implications of these adjustments, and provides a survey of emerging new issues important to the sector.

CURRENT STRUCTURE

At present the vast majority of US farm output is generated on the largest farms. According to the 2002 Census of Agriculture, nearly 48% of the market value of agricultural products sold in the USA came from the largest 1.3% of farms, and nearly 90% came from the largest 14.6% of farms. Some 67% of all US farms are operated by full owners, 26% by part owners and the remainder by full tenants.

Of the 2.1m. farms in the USA, according to the 2002 Census of Agriculture, 90% were operated by individual/family proprietors, 6% by family partnerships and 3% by family-held corporations. A mere 0.3% were operated by non-family corporations and 0.8% by agricultural co-operatives, estates and trusts, and other institutions such as prisons. The average age of the farm operator in the USA was 55.3 years—up from 48.3 years in 1949.

The US agricultural sector is highly diversified. In 2006 beef generated the largest percentage of cash receipts (20.5%), followed by feed grains (11.7%), poultry and eggs (11.5%), dairy products (9.8%), vegetables (7.5%), soybeans (7.1%), fruit (7.1%), and greenhouse and nursery products (7.1%).

California led the country in milk production in 2006 with 21.4% of the total supply, followed by Wisconsin with 12.9%, New York with 6.6% and Pennsylvania with 5.9%. Dairy farming, though, is concentrated in the north-eastern and lake states. Climate and soil in these regions are best suited to raising grains and forage needed for the dairy enterprise and for providing pasture for dairy cattle. States in these parts of the USA cannot compete with other regions for feed grains, food grains or oilseeds grown on a commercial scale.

Broiler (chicken) production is important in Maine, Delaware and Maryland.

The major tobacco-producing states are Virginia, Kentucky, Tennessee and North Carolina. Peanuts, cattle, hog (pig) and dairy production are also important in these four states.

The south-eastern states concentrate on beef and broiler production, although fruits, vegetables and peanuts are also important to this region. Florida is a major producer of citrus fruits, winter vegetables and sugar cane. Cotton production is important in Alabama, Georgia and South Carolina.

In the delta states of Arkansas, Louisiana and Mississippi the principal cash crops are soybeans and cotton. Rice, corn and sugar cane are also grown here. With improved pastures, livestock production has gained in importance in these states in recent years. This is also a significant broiler-producing region.

The 'cornbelt' (Ohio, Indiana, Illinois, Iowa and Missouri) has rich soil and a good climate for corn and soybean production, as well as other feed grains. Cattle, hogs and dairy are also important agricultural enterprises in this region.

The northern and southern plains region, extending from Canada to Mexico, is restricted for agricultural use by low rainfall in the west and south and by cold winters and short growing seasons in the north. The majority of the USA's winter and spring wheat is produced in this region. Other small grains, sorghum, hay and forage crops form the basis for raising cattle. Cotton is a major crop in the southern part of this region.

The mountain states are more diversified. Vast areas of this region are suited to cattle-grazing. Wheat is important in the northern parts. Irrigation in the valleys provides the basis for such crops as hay, sugar beets, potatoes, fruits and vegetables. Dairy farming is also important in Idaho and New Mexico.

Farmers in Washington and Oregon specialize in raising wheat, fruit and potatoes. As noted earlier, California leads the nation in milk production, and vegetables, fruit and cotton production are also important in the state. Hawaii is a major producer of sugar cane and pineapples. Alaska's principal commodities are dairy products and greenhouse and nursery products.

TRENDS AND ADJUSTMENTS IN AGRICULTURE

The First World War and the Great Depression certainly had dramatic effects on the US agricultural sector. Most of the more significant trends in US agriculture, however, occurred subsequent to the Second World War. This is the period of major substitutions of capital, machinery and other non-farm inputs for labour, the period of strongest growth in farm productivity and the period of major changes in farm numbers and farm size.

Number of Farms and Farm Size

In 2006 there were just over 2m. farms in the USA—37% of the number of farms in 1950 and 31% of the peak number of farms in 1935. The vast majority of farms in the USA are relatively small. In fact, by the latest Census of Agriculture definition, a farm is any place that has US $1,000 or more of gross sales of farm products per year. Over 67% of US farms have annual gross sales of less than $25,000, and 84% have annual gross sales of less than $100,000. Only 16% of farms have annual gross sales of $100,000 or more, but these farms generate nearly 80% of aggregate farm output. In recent years, US farmers have received, on average, a net income of slightly more than 20% of gross farm income. With a net income margin of 20%, farms with even $100,000 of gross income annually hardly generate enough cash income from farming alone to provide a lifestyle for a family of two or three people on a par with that enjoyed by most US families. Clearly, the commercial farm providing full-time employment for the farm operator needs a gross income of well over $100,000 per year.

Between the Great Depression and 1979, there was a seven-fold increase in average farm size, as measured by real gross income per farm. There was a reduction in the rate of growth of farm size in the last two decades of the 20th century. This reduction in large part is attributable to the economic recession in agriculture in the late 1980s and early 1990s, which discouraged farmer purchases of new and bigger machines and investments in other growth-enhancing activities.

The farms with annual gross sales of farm products of US $20,000 or less mentioned above are in no sense viable commercial businesses capable of supporting a family. They should more properly be considered 'rural residences' or 'hobby farms'. They earn most of their income from non-farm occupations—jobs held by one or more family members. Most farm programme payments are distributed in proportion to sales of 'program commodities'. Thus the operators of these smaller farms receive little financial support from the government programmes available to farmers. Many lose money on farming operations. Yet the families on these farms are typically not financially distressed, earning substantial incomes from their non-farm occupations. On average, these families earn more than the median family income of all households in the USA.

Land Use

Land in farms in the USA has declined by more than 22% from an historical peak of slightly more than 1,200m. acres (486m. ha) in the early 1950s. This decline is primarily owing to, land bid away from agriculture by urban, industrial, highway and airport uses; land made idle by conservation programmes and by public policies aimed at reducing 'surplus' agricultural production; and land 'abandoned' because it was no longer profitable in agricultural or any other use. It is interesting to observe that, while total farm acreage declined significantly from the 1950s, real agricultural output increased nearly three-fold between 1950 and 2006, and the real value of agricultural exports increased about seven times over this same period.

The proportion of farm acreage planted to crops harvested has remained quite stable since 1950. Similarly, the proportion of acreage devoted to wheat and the major feed grains has changed very little since 1950. Oat acreage declined as machine power substituted for animal power. Cotton acreage declined slightly through the mid-1980s, as the demand for cotton decreased, but had a slight resurgence through the 1990s, as consumers have shown a preference for cotton fibre over synthetic fibres. Soybean acreage increased significantly in the 1950s and 1960s, as the demand for protein feed increased and as soybeans became a more popular crop. Sugar acreage increased only slightly. Tobacco acreage has decreased by 80% since 1950. Peanut acreage remained quite stable after 1950.

The proportion of total cash receipts from farming derived from the various crop and livestock enterprises showed remarkable stability from 1950 until the start of the 2000s.

Labour Use

Total employment in agriculture declined by 70% and the number of hired farm workers declined by 66% between 1950 and 2006. Obviously there was substantial substitution of the relatively cheaper capital and machinery inputs for the relatively more expensive labour input. Furthermore, by the start of the 21st century agricultural labour was much more mobile than it was during the 1950s and 1960s, when, for various reasons (e.g. lack of non-farm jobs, farm labourers' lack of skills, and racial discrimination), many farm workers were trapped in agriculture.

Capital Use

Gross capital expenditures per farm on buildings and land, machinery and equipment and motor vehicles in agriculture stood at US $828 in 1950 and peaked at $8,971 in 1979. Farmers had overcapitalized by the late 1970s to the point of getting into serious financial difficulty, as demand for agricultural output fell, farm-commodity prices fell and interest rates remained high. In response, capital use declined sharply over the following decade—to $4,077 per farm by 1986. From 1986 onward, however, gross capital expenditures per farm have again risen fairly steeply, reaching $11,397 in 2006.

Machinery and Chemical Use

As indicated above, there was a steep decline in labour use and a corresponding steep increase in machinery and chemical use in the second half of the 20th century. The total number of tractors per 100 acres (40 ha) planted continued to increase during the 1950s and 1960s as horses and mules were replaced by tractor power. Total tractor horsepower used per 100 acres planted nearly quadrupled over the 1950–86 period. From the mid-1980s tractor horsepower used per 100 acres planted declined slightly as incentives for farm enlargements diminished.

Nitrogen usage per-acre increased 10-fold between 1950 and the early 1970s. Potash usage per-acre increased about six-fold between 1950 and 1980. Phosphate usage per-acre also increased from 1950, but on a much less dramatic scale—about a three-fold increase between 1950 and the early 1970s. After the early 1970s, nitrogen use continued to increase, but at a much slower rate, phosphate use declined slightly and, from 1980, potash use levelled off. Various factors were responsible for the change in fertilizer use in recent years, including improved fertilizer-use recommendations, better fertilizer management practices and increased concerns about the environmental impacts of chemical use.

The real value of pesticide use per acre increased 10-fold after 1950. There was a slowdown in pesticide use during the early and mid-1980s, in response to the energy crisis of that period and earlier, but this was followed by a steep rise in pesticide use through the 1990s. More recently, there has been a slowdown in pesticide use per acre.

Prices Received and Prices Paid

Real prices received by US farmers for all farm commodities declined dramatically after 1950. For the major crop and livestock enterprises there was a brief interruption in the mid-1970s as export demand surged, but the decline resumed following the late 1970s. For fruits and vegetables, there was a largely uninterrupted decline in real prices received after 1950.

Real prices paid by US farmers, by contrast, decreased only slightly and, in fact, were somewhat higher during the 1970s and early 1980s than in the 1950s and 1960s. Nevertheless, the ratio of prices received to prices paid has fallen steadily over the entire 1950 to 2006 period. Farmers from the USA experienced an extended period described as a price-cost 'squeeze' from 1950, tempered only by an increase in agricultural productivity.

Productivity

There are various ways by which to measure agricultural productivity and they all indicate significant productivity growth in US agriculture since 1950. People fed per farm worker increased from a mere 15 in 1950 to 106 in 2006. The ratio of the index of total agricultural output to the index of total agricultural inputs—total factor productivity—increased from 41 in 1950 to 112 in 2006. Finally, productivity increases can be measured by examining individual crop and animal yield increases. In every case yields are up significantly, with the greatest yield increases observed in corn and milk production. Corn yields in the USA increased from an average of 38 bushels per acre in 1950 to an average of 149 bushels per acre in 2006. Milk production in the USA increased from an average of 5,273 lbs per cow in 1950 to an average of 20,059 lbs per cow in

2006. Rather large yield increases were also observed in sorghum, wheat, rice, peanut, cotton and egg production.

Agricultural Exports and Imports

Agricultural exports became a smaller proportion of total US exports in the decades after 1950 (from 28% in 1950 to 8% in 2006), but, historically, exports have been of key importance to the US agricultural sector. Farmers in the USA produce far more wheat, feed grains, rice, oilseeds, cotton and tobacco, for example, than US consumers will take off the market at prices near or above cost of production. It is crucial for these farmers, then, that their production, in excess of domestic needs, be sold in foreign markets.

The value of agricultural exports as a percentage of cash receipts from farm marketings stood at 30% at the turn of the 20th century, but plummeted to 4% by 1940 as a result of the protectionist policies of many countries during and following the First World War. This percentage rose gradually to 16% in 1964 and then sharply to the present 26%–30% in response to more favourable world trade developments. A significant development of the 1970s was a devaluation of the US dollar and, subsequently, permission to allow the US dollar to be openly traded on the world currency markets. Foreign demand for food outstripped foreign supply, making food-importing countries increasingly dependent on the USA as residual supplier. Following 1980 and continuing into the early 1990s, however, there was a relative decline in the value of exports of wheat and feed grains as world prices fell and as other regions of the world increased production of these commodities. The export situation improved by the mid-1990s, so that US agricultural exports as a percentage of cash receipts from farming again climbed back to the 26%–30% level by 2000.

The USA is the world's dominant exporter of feed grains. It accounts for 25%–30% of the world's exports of wheat, 45%–50% of the world's exports of soybeans, 20% of the world's exports of rice and 40% of the world's exports of cotton.

The largest markets for US agricultural exports are Canada, Japan, Mexico, the European Union (EU), and the People's Republic of China, in that order. Levels of agricultural exports to Japan were relatively stagnant into the early 2000s, while the relative importance of agricultural exports to the EU has diminished significantly and steadily since 1950, from 50% of US agricultural exports in that year to 11% of US agricultural exports in 2006. The growth markets for the last decades of the 20th century were Mexico and other Latin American countries, Canada, South-East Asia, Hong Kong, the Republic of Korea and Taiwan. In view of the USA's recent interest in negotiating a free trade agreement with Central America and the Dominican Republic (the Dominican Republic-Central American Free Trade Agreement—DR-CAFTA) it is interesting to note that, in 2006, US agricultural exports destined for Central America and the Caribbean amounted to only 2.5% and 3.0%, respectively, of total US agricultural exports.

Imports of agricultural products as a percentage of total US imports have declined sharply over the years, from over 50% in 1900 and 45% in 1950 to 3.5% in 2006. Nevertheless, the value of agricultural imports per head in the USA has increased steadily since the late 1960s. The mix of agricultural imports also changed considerably after 1950. A larger proportion of the value of US agricultural imports now consists of animal products, vegetable products and fruit products. Coffee, sugar and complements now constitute a much smaller proportion of total agricultural imports. Dairy product imports increased slightly as a proportion of the total, but these are severely restricted by tight import controls.

The USA had a strong incentive for reducing barriers to free trade in agricultural products and it acted accordingly. The USA participates actively in World Trade Organization (WTO) negotiations toward lowering trade barriers. The current round of negotiations—the Doha Round—was launched in November of 2001 and is still in process, although talks were stalled in August 2008. In addition, successive governments have in recent years aggressively sought bilateral and multilateral trade agreements designed to foster freer trade. In 1989, for example, a free trade agreement between the USA and Canada came into effect, followed in 1994 by the advent of the North American Free Trade Agreement (NAFTA) between the USA, Canada and Mexico. In August 2005 US President George W. Bush signed into law DR-CAFTA, which was designed to encourage free trade in agricultural products between the USA, five Central American countries (El Salvador, Guatemala, Honduras, Nicaragua and Costa Rica) and the Dominican Republic. DR-CAFTA and several other trade agreements, already in effect or being contemplated, were intended to eliminate non-tariff barriers to trade and gradually to eliminate tariffs within 15 years. Unfortunately, a wide range of agricultural products would continue to be protected by rather prohibitive tariff rate quotas under DR-CAFTA, and sugar-producing countries in Central America would still not have access to the US sugar market. Finally, the USA and the Republic of Korea initiated discussions on the KORUS Free Trade Agreement in May 2006. Agreement was reached and signed by the two administrations in June 2007 but in late 2008 it was still to be ratified by the respective Governments. When implemented, it will expand trade and investment flows between the two countries. In agriculture, it will create new export opportunities for American farmers and ranchers by eliminating and phasing out tariffs and quotas on a broad range of products. Under the agreement, roughly $1,910m., or 64%, of the Republic of Korea's agricultural imports from the USA will be immediately duty-free. Most remaining tariffs and quotas will be phased out over the first 10 years the agreement is in force.

TRENDS IN FOOD CONSUMPTION AND MARKETING

Food Marketing Costs

Middlemen are often criticized for contributing to the plight of farmers when economic conditions in agriculture are not favourable to farmers. The implication is that middlemen exact an excessive part of the consumer's food dollar in profits and/or processing inefficiencies, resulting in lower consumption of food and, therefore, lower demand for farm commodities than would otherwise be the case. There is little support for this argument, however.

Farmers' share of the consumer's food dollar is certainly low, ranging from a high of 33% in meats to a low of 6% in cereal and bakery products. Furthermore, between 1950 and 2006 it has declined steadily in every major food product category except processed fruits and vegetables. This decline, for the most part, underscores the fact that consumers are demanding, and processors and retailers are supplying more and more services in the form of more convenient packaging and pre-processing. In large part this can be attributed to the fact that the people of the USA have increasingly had less time to prepare food in the home, so they are interested in purchasing as many additional services as possible along with the basic food product. Ultimately, the demand for agricultural products has increased even though the farmers' share of the consumer's food dollar has declined.

Food Consumption

Significant changes also occurred in food consumption, owing to changes in the composition and behaviour of the USA's food consumers. The proportion of personal consumption expenditures spent on food declined continuously from 1950 to 2006. In 2006 US consumers spent an estimated 12% of their personal consumption expenditures on food (excluding alcoholic beverages)—the lowest of any country in the world. An even more striking trend is the proportion of food expenditures spent on food away from home—in restaurants, fast-food facilities and food service centres. The upward trend of the latter, from 17.6% in 1950 to nearly 42% in 2006, has been apparent over the entire period, but the steepest rise occurred after 1974.

Changes in per-head consumption over time are due to several factors, including changing product prices, changing income levels of consumers, the changing age distribution of the population, and changing consumer tastes and preferences. Real per-head disposable income more than doubled between 1950 and 2006, which certainly led to an increase in food consumption. Declining real prices for food also led to some increased consumption. In recent years, however, consumers have become more and more concerned about cholesterol levels, leading to a reduction in per-head consumption of animal products. The changing age distribution of the population over the last 30 years or so of the 20th century, the growth of single-parent families and the increase in the number of dual-income families also had a marked effect on per-head consumption of various food products.

In response to these changes, consumption of food away from home grew in importance, while consumption of food at home diminished in importance; per-head consumption of poultry meat increased steadily after 1950; per-head consumption of pork and all milk declined steadily until the very end of the 20th century; per-head consumption of beef declined from the 1970s; and per-head consumption of fresh fruits and vegetables increased from the 1970s. Carbonated soft drinks have become much more popular, while per-head consumption of coffee and fluid milk has declined.

Food-processing and Distribution

Although a significant proportion of US agricultural production is exported to foreign countries, the majority of this production is consumed domestically. Much of this production is first processed into final goods that consumers (at home as well as abroad) are willing to purchase. Farmers market a small amount of the commodities they produce direct to consumers, but the vast majority of commodities are sold to food packers or processors. Food wholesalers buy from food packers or processors and distribute to retail food stores and to eating and drinking establishments or other food service centres.

As has been the case in farming, food-processing and distribution firms have been getting larger in size and smaller in number since 1950. Volume of production increased consistent with the needs of a growing population, and productivity of the food-processing industries rose significantly. While the overall performance of the food-processing and retailing industries was enhanced, the decline in the number of operators meant that there were fewer handlers to which farmers could sell their produce. Food-processing, wholesaling and retailing firms are thus becoming larger at the expense of small local firms that are no longer able to compete. These larger firms do not depend solely on any one production area for raw materials. Rather, they obtain their supplies anywhere they can get the volume and quality necessary to support a nation-wide or region-wide marketing programme. With ready access to markets thus reduced, small-scale producers for local markets are at a serious competitive disadvantage.

As food-processing establishments get larger their owners seek farm products from areas that can supply the volume needed to sustain their size of business. In turn, local farm produce is often overlooked, not because it cannot be produced as efficiently as in other regions, but simply because it is not produced in the volume needed by processors. For a production activity to be viable in a particular area, it must be undertaken on a large enough scale for provision of the processing capacity to be economically justifiable. It must also be undertaken on a large enough scale for processors to find it economical to buy from local producers.

GOVERNMENT POLICY FOR AGRICULTURE

Most early legislation affecting US agriculture was directed at expanding food production for a growing nation and for developing the country so it could sustain growth. Agrarian fundamentalism, expressed most clearly by Thomas Jefferson, who argued that 'those who labour in the earth are the chosen people of God', shaped this development process and had a very profound impact on the nature of farming that evolved. Small, family-oriented farm units were deemed to be the most appropriate units with which to effect an egalitarian, agrarian society. Various acts passed by Congress in the formative years and prior to the Great Depression represented formalization of this agrarian policy. The land resource was viewed as the nation's source of material well-being. Rights to this resource were to be reserved for private individuals of the chosen agrarian structure rather than for monopolistic units more typical of the industrial sector. Private interests should guide resource allocation and landownership decisions, not public interests as reflected through the regulatory process. Farmers were not expected to need nor warrant income assistance from government.

In the 1920s, however, an alternative view emerged. Following the First World War there was a rapid and severe decline in agricultural prices as export demand for agricultural products plummeted. The situation persisted for the next decade or so while at the same time non-agricultural prices and wages remained relatively rigid. The result was a widening divergence between farm and non-farm incomes throughout the Great Depression. The Agricultural Marketing Act of 1929 was the first legislative measure aimed at providing farmers income assistance. This Act was not highly effective, however. It relied, in large part, on a Farm Board, the objective of which was to facilitate the effective merchandising of agricultural commodities in interstate and foreign competition.

The real beginning of compensation policy for agriculture is more properly assigned to the Agricultural Adjustment Act of 1933. Under this Act, farmers were permitted to enter into contracts with the Secretary of Agriculture to reduce production of surplus commodities in return for direct payments financed by taxes levied on processors of those commodities. The federal Government was required to make mandatory price-support loans on certain 'basic' commodities, and could spend money to expand markets or remove surpluses. The overriding objective of this measure was to restore the purchasing power of 'basic' agricultural commodities to the 1909–14 level by aligning productive capacity to market requirements. The 'basic' commodities defined by this Act were corn, cotton, rice, tobacco, wheat, milk and hogs.

The production control provisions of the 1933 Act were declared unconstitutional in 1936, owing to the contractual relation between farmers and the Government and because the Act attempted to finance the programme through the collection of processor taxes. It was replaced with the Soil Conservation and Domestic Allotment Act of 1936, which, with modifications, remained the basis of agricultural price-support and production-adjustment legislation through to the end of the 20th century. This Act changed the emphasis from price supports to income supports, and it replaced payments for acreage adjustment with payments for shifting acreage from soil-depleting to soil-conserving crops.

Surpluses continued to accumulate, however, so Congress passed the Agricultural Adjustment Act of 1938. This Act initiated mandatory non-recourse loans for corn, wheat and cotton producers and provided for marketing quotas if approved in a referendum of producers. It also introduced the concept of 'parity' prices for farmers. Parity prices were designed to give a unit of commodity the same purchasing power it had in the 'golden years' of agriculture (1910–14). Parity prices were the major determinants of support prices for crops until the early 1960s and for dairy products until the early 1980s.

During the early and mid-1940s policy shifted to encouraging production of farm commodities needed to meet wartime and post-war demands. Later, downward pressure on farm prices prompted the Agricultural Act of 1949, which set non-recourse loan rates at between 75% and 90% of parity. Prices were supported with non-recourse loans and direct government purchases of surplus commodities. This Act also established a permanent price-support programme for milk following a period of piecemeal extensions of wartime and earlier programmes for dairy.

During the 1950s surpluses again developed. Two legislative attempts were made to deal with these surpluses. The Agricultural and Trade Development Assistance Act of 1954 (the so-called 'PL 480' Act) was enacted to stimulate foreign demand, and the Soil Bank Program established by the Agricultural Act of 1956 was created to take a significant amount of cropland out of production for up to 10 years.

Beginning in 1963, and continuing into the early 1970s, the major focus of policy for feed grains was on non-recourse loan rates set at or near world prices, direct price-support payments and cropland diversion payments. In 1970 a set-aside acreage-reduction programme replaced the acreage-diversion programme in the hope of giving farmers more flexibility of choice.

The Agriculture and Consumer Protection Act of 1973 represented a step in the direction of a more market-orientated policy. World demand for US farm products was at an all-time high, farm product prices were quite favourable to farmers, and government cost of the farm programmes was minimal. Thus, a different approach to farm programmes was sought. Support prices based on parity calculations were replaced with target prices based on cost-of-production considerations. Income support was implemented with deficiency payments calculated as the difference between target prices and the maximum of non-recourse loan rates or market prices.

Legislation in 1985 and 1990 continued the major provisions of the previous measure, although the close association between target prices and cost of production was relaxed in favour of target prices set at levels more consistent with market conditions. Authority for implementing acreage-reduction, set-aside and paid land-diversion programmes was maintained. A Conservation Reserve Program designed to take 40m.–45m. acres (16m.–18m. ha) of marginal land out of production for a period of 10 to 15 years was instituted by the 1985 legislation. It also instituted a Conservation Compliance provision requiring any farmer who receives any programme benefits to have a farm conservation plan that meets specified environmental standards. A series of programmes designed to enhance exports of surplus agricultural commodities was also introduced during this period.

The Federal Agriculture Improvement and Reform Act of 1996 provided for significant changes in US agricultural policy until 2002. This legislation removed the link between income-support payments and farm prices by providing annual 'production-flexibility' contract payments. The contracts required participating producers to comply with existing conservation proposals. The Conservation Reserve Program was retained, but acreage-idling programmes were eliminated and farmers were given much greater flexibility in planting decisions on contract acres. Farmers were, for example, granted the freedom to plant any crop on contract acres except fruits and vegetables. It was anticipated that producers would come to rely more heavily on the market as a guide to production decisions. As payments would be fixed rather than related to the level of market prices, it was also anticipated that producers would bear greater income risk.

The Farm Security and Rural Investment Act of 2002, governing agricultural programmes until 2007, continued some of the directions of the 1996 Act, but promised more, not less, income support to producers of major commodities. It provided income support to producers of the major commodities via direct payments at payment rates specified in the legislation; counter-cyclical payments when the effective commodity price was lower than a target price specified in the legislation; and marketing loans at loan rates specified in the legislation. Direct payments replaced production-flexibility contract payments of the previous legislation. Counter-cyclical payments were new and were intended to provide an income 'safety net' for farmers. Marketing loan provisions were extended to wool, mohair, honey, small chickpeas, lentils and dry peas. Dairy price supports were reintroduced at a legislated level, and a dairy income-support programme was introduced providing monthly direct payments when the Class I (fluid grade) milk price was less than an amount specified in the legislation. The peanut marketing quota programme was replaced by a quota 'buy out' programme. Peanuts were treated in a similar way to other crops in the programme, with direct payments, counter-cyclical payments and marketing loans. Sugar was subject to a tariff-rate quota system and price-support loans. The major conservation programmes were maintained and a new Conservation Security Program was introduced that paid producers to adopt or maintain practices that preserved soil, water and/or wildlife habitat. Limits were put on payments to farm operations as a means of targeting benefits and reducing commodity programme costs. The Act required the Secretary of Agriculture, 'to the maximum extent practicable', to make adjustments to domestic commodity programme expenditures in order to avoid exceeding permitted WTO quotas.

The Food, Conservation and Energy Act of 2008 generally extends current policy aimed at supporting incomes of producers of the major commodities. It provides support for 25 different commodities, representing one-third of gross farm sales, including maize, wheat, soybeans, minor oilseeds, rice, cotton, sugar, peanuts, grain sorghum, barley, oats, wool, mohair, honey, dry peas, lentils, small chickpeas, and dairy products. Moreover, it recommends higher target prices for wheat, soybeans, barley, oats and minor oilseeds, and higher loan rates for wheat, barley, oats, minor oilseeds and sugar.

The new legislation sets specific price support levels for butter, cheese and non-fat dry milk, and extends the Milk Income Loss Contract Program, which provides payments to dairy producers when milk prices fall below a specified level. It also increases the amount of milk eligible for payments under this programme, and establishes a payment trigger for contract payments that can increase when feed prices are high. It re-establishes the Dairy Forward Pricing Program, allowing dairy producers to enter into forward contracts with milk handlers, thereby assisting dairy producers in risk management.

The new farm bill also provides for a Conservation Stewardship Program, which for the first time links federal payments for farmers to environmental improvements. Finally, this legislation initiates a new programme known as the Average Crop Revenue Election (ACRE). This is a revenue guarantee programme which provides payments to participating producers for a commodity when the actual state revenue for that commodity is less than the revenue guarantee.

The overriding objective of government policy for agriculture from the 1930s to the present was to support and stabilize prices of agricultural commodities. The instruments of this policy were non-recourse loans, support prices, government purchases of surpluses, target prices and deficiency payments, marketing orders, import quotas, export subsidies and acreage-reduction programmes.

Overall, these programmes increased returns to producers and somewhat reduced farm income variability. Direct payments to farmers over the years included deficiency payments made in cash, cash or in-kind payments made to farmers for reducing or diverting cropland acres, annual transition payments, disaster payments and miscellaneous payments such as wool price-support (incentive) payments and dairy diversion and 'buy out' payments. Government payments to farmers as a percentage of net farm income from all sources (including direct government payments and off-farm income) averaged 1.4% in 1950, 3.5% in 1960, 11.9% in 1970, 2.8% in 1980, 9.4% in 1990, 15.4% in 2000 and 9.0% in 2006. Clearly, the relative importance of government payments to farmers has varied greatly over the years, but overall it has been a significant factor in US agriculture. In general, the benefits were concentrated among the largest producers and became capitalized into land values, so that landowners' wealth was enhanced. Different sectors experienced different payment rates, but producers of feed grains, wheat, rice, cotton and milk benefited handsomely.

The supply management tools that have been implemented over the years were effective in preventing price-depressing crop surpluses and, therefore, in helping to maintain farm incomes without incurring the huge federal costs associated with government purchase and storage programmes. Until 1996 these programmes resulted in the idling of significant crop acreages at various times—10% to 15% of the total cropland through the 1960s and early 1970s, and over 20% in 1983. The percentage has fluctuated with variations in US production relative to world demand. More recently, efforts have been made to base farm policy on direct government payments, in order to reduce economic inefficiencies owing to misdirection of resources and price distortions.

IMPLICATIONS OF TRENDS AND EMERGING ISSUES

Farm Size and Structure

The key to understanding the trends in number and size of farms over the last 50 years is the new technology available to and adopted by farmers: machines to replace human and animal power; new plant and animal varieties; hybrid seed; new and improved fertilizers, pesticides and herbicides; new and improved feed additives; genetically improved livestock and poultry; new sources of information for farmer decision-making; new and improved managerial techniques; and availability of affordable computers for on-farm use, among others.

When innovative farmers adopt new technology and farm commodity prices remain unchanged, net profits rise, as total revenue per unit of production increases more than does total cost per unit of production. In the early stages of new-technology use, not enough farmers use the new technology to cause significant changes in total quantity marketed or in market price of the farm commodity. Over time, however, as other farmers find that their neighbours' profit levels rise, they too adopt this new technology in an effort to increase profits. In the longer term, when a majority of all farmers adopt the technology and the market adjusts to the increased production efficiency and greater aggregate quantity marketed, the market price of the farm commodity falls. Buyers of the farm product are unwilling to purchase, at past high prices, the increased quantity of the commodity that farmers are now placing on the market. Thus, market price falls in order to encourage buyers of farm produce to purchase all of the greater quantity that farmers in the aggregate are now placing on the market.

In the longer term, then, aggregate production increases and market price falls. All this, in turn, means that farmer profits per unit of production also fall in the longer term. With lower per-unit profits and, thus, lower aggregate farm income, even the most efficient farmers find it impossible to survive unless they can expand the size of their operation or in some other way increase family income. Thus, farmers continually face the choice of getting out of farming, getting into an alternative enterprise or enlarging their operation.

All this leads directly to a reduction in farm numbers and to an increase in the average size of those farms remaining. Owing to the reduced farm commodity prices and reduced profit rates per unit of output in the longer term, at least some of the smaller or less competitive farmers can expect to be forced out of business, because they will not be able to generate the volume of farm produce and thus aggregate farm income necessary to provide a standard of living satisfactory to the farm family. The farm family now barely managing on a 200-acre grain farm or with a 50-cow dairy herd will not be able to generate enough income from that farm to maintain the farm family's standard of living after the majority of other US farmers have adopted the new technology and after the market finds a new, lower equilibrium price.

All this is reflected in a decline in farm numbers from a peak of 6.8m. in 1935 to the current low of just over 2m., and to an increase in average farm size, measured in real gross income per farm (gross income per farm deflated by an index of general prices in the US economy), from US $17,700 in 1929 to almost $130,000 today. We are likely to see further declines in farm numbers and increases in farm size in the future, although these changes may not be as dramatic as was observed over the past seven decades. Clearly, also, we are likely to see a higher percentage of US farms falling into the smaller size categories over time unless the criteria for defining a farm changes (see section above on Number of Farms and Farm Size).

Specialization and Integration

Today US farms are not only larger than their pre-Second World War counterparts, they are highly specialized. Most grain farms raise few, if any, animals and sell practically all of their produce off-farm, while most livestock farms concentrate on a single livestock enterprise and purchase the majority of their feed inputs from other farmers or from commercial sources. In addition, there are specialized fruit and vegetable farms.

Although most agricultural produce is still sold on the open market, contracting by large corporations with farmers has in recent years been a significant and growing part of the production and marketing of broilers, turkeys, eggs, hogs and milk. Most sugar beets and sugar cane, as well as many fruits and vegetables for processing, are also produced under contract. Marketing contracts are verbal or written agreements between a contractor and a grower setting a price and establishing an outlet for the commodity before harvest. Production contracts specify in detail the production inputs supplied by the contractor, the quality and quantity of the commodity and the amount of compensation the grower will receive for services rendered. Under such arrangements, processors seek to guarantee a stable quantity and quality of product needed to meet consumers' demands, while farmers seek to minimize the price risk and the risk associated with finding a market for their produce. It is estimated that about one-third of the value of all crops and livestock in the USA is now produced or marketed under contract. Specialization on farms and the fewer and larger food-processing firms have both played a role in the increased importance of contracting.

Farm-family Well-being

One way to assess the impact of the trends just reviewed on farm-family well-being is to examine the ratio of net farm income from farm sources (including government payments) per farm household to disposable personal income per US household over the last two centuries. Such a comparison reveals that farm households were considerably disadvantaged relative to all US households for most of the period, lost ground from 1800 and into the period of the Great Depression, and then gained ground up to 1999. Specifically, this ratio averaged between 40% and 60% through the first half of the 1800s, dropped to a low of 20%–25% during the 1920s and 1930s, recovered again through the 1960s, fluctuated widely during the volatile 1970s and 1980s, rose to between 50% and 60% during the 1990s and remained at more or less this level thereafter.

A more satisfactory procedure would be to compare the mean money income of all US households to the aggregate of net farm income per farm household from farm sources, government payments per farm household and off-farm income per farm household. While these data are only available from 1950, they tell an interesting and useful story. An important conclusion is that, when all sources of farm-family monetary income are accounted for, the income of farm households has, on average, been well above that of the general population since 1985.

We also find that the gap between money incomes of farm and non-farm households appears to have been closed as of about 1970. Government payments to farmers have been a help, but have not been significant in closing the gap. Off-farm income of farm families has been a most significant factor in closing this gap.

Although many farm families have always been engaged in some amount of off-farm work, this practice has become increasingly important since the 1950s—even more so in the last two or three decades of the 20th century, as the frequency of two-wage earners among farm families increased. According to the Census of Agriculture, 23% of farm operators worked 200 or more days off-farm in 1949. This percentage increased steadily, so that by 2002 39% of farm operators worked 200 or more days off-farm. Off-farm income of farm families as a percentage of total money and non-money income of farm families from all sources (including direct government payments and off-farm income) averaged 27% in 1950, 37% in 1960, 46% in 1970, 47% in 1980, 47% in 1990, 55% in 2000 and 51% in 2006. The distribution of off-farm income by farms in different sales categories is not available for the entire 1950–2006 period. From the data that is available, however, it is clear that most of the off-farm income is earned by families on small farms. Furthermore, it is clear that the majority of farm families no longer depend primarily on farming for their livelihood. Hence, developmental or rural-industrial policy aimed at preserving off-farm jobs for farmers and their families is now more important to many farm families than is traditional farm price and income policy.

Green Issues

Concerns regarding conservation of the land resource has from time to time informed policy agenda. Soil erosion is of concern for a variety of reasons. It reduces on-farm productivity and hence farm profits. It imposes costs on society by relocating topsoil where it is not wanted and by carrying nitrates and phosphates into underground and surface water. Moreover, it imposes costs on future generations in the form of reduced soil productivity.

Farmers, driven by the desire to maximize profits, are not motivated to use soil-conserving practices because the costs associated with using such practices exceed the returns. Thus, considerations beyond the marketplace must be brought to bear on allocation decisions and farming practices. The Food Security Act of 1985 introduced penalties to encourage less pollution in the form of making farmers who plant programme commodities on highly erodible land ineligible for programme benefits. The Conservation Reserve Program (CRP) of the same act provides long-term rental payments to farmers who voluntarily take highly erodible land out of production. Farmers are also provided with technical assistance and cost-sharing to encourage the use of soil conservation practices. The Environmental Quality Incentives Program (EQIP), provided by the 2002 Farm Bill, for example, offers financial and technical assistance to help livestock and crop producers implement soil, water, and related natural resource conservation practices on working lands. EQIP contracts provide incentive payments and cost sharing for a maximum of 10 years. The Conservation Security Program (CSP), established under the 2002 Farm Act, provides payments to farmers to reward good conservation performance and encourage the implementation and maintenance of conservation practices on working lands. To participate, producers must develop a conservation plan identifying the resources and practices to be covered under the programme. The CSP contracts provide a 'stewardship' payment based on the level of existing conservation effort and an 'enhancement' payment for implementing additional practices designated in the conservation plan.

Conservation programmes over the last seven decades have certainly contributed to a reduction in soil erosion. Nevertheless, it can be said that land conservation has been a much more important issue to policy makers when incomes in the farm sector were depressed and when agricultural surpluses were excessive.

Policy concerning development and use of the nation's water resource was initially governed by a commitment to the expansion of agriculture and consistent with the adopted agrarian structure. Farmers were granted priority over other members of society to the use of this resource. However, water use in the West, where natural rainfall is insufficient to sustain crop and some livestock production, is now a major issue. Subsidized irrigation encourages overuse of water which in turn causes water mining of the underground aquifers, soil subsidence, and salinity as well as the increased cost of mining additional water. Subsidized irrigation contributes at least in part to the generation of surplus agricultural commodities and brings about adjustments in other regions of the country where irrigation-dependent crops can also be grown without irrigation. To date, little concern has been given to water conservation. However, since water will be a vital resource for the future, agriculture's contribution to ensuring a supply of water for other uses will be critical in the years ahead.

Science has generally been viewed as the path to human betterment. Few policy-makers questioned the wisdom of using new technologies, such as pesticides that are harmful to the environment, fertilizers that lead to pollution of underground and surface water, machines that compact the soil, management practices that lead to soil erosion and so on. The use of chemical-based inputs (pesticides and commercial fertilizers) has been spurred on by two factors: the continuing quest by farmers for technologies that maximize their profits and the desire to increase yields on fewer acres, in response to the acreage restriction programmes of farm policy designed to reduce farm surpluses. The social costs associated with the use of these chemical-based inputs is of obvious concern. To date policy-makers have done little to limit the use of these inputs.

Recently, there have been calls for new priorities in agricultural policy that would not only recognize protection of the environment, but contribute to remediation of greenhouse gas emissions (methane) from livestock enterprises, carbon sequestration through crop and land management, improved water and air quality, enhanced wildlife populations, and preservation of open spaces. Not only are questions being asked about the price and income policy enacted by Congress for agriculture, but the market system itself is regarded as having shortcomings in the way it allocates resources. Some argue that the private market encourages resource exploitation rather than resource stewardship, and that it favours individual interests over both the short- and long-term interests of society as a whole.

Biofuel Production and Food Prices

A topic receiving considerable interest in the past few years is biofuel production. Ethanol can be made from maize, barley, sorghum, wheat, sugar cane, and sugar beet. Substantial research is currently ongoing into the feasibility of producing cellulosic ethanol from straw, stover, wood chips, and grasses. Biodiesel is most typically made from oilseed crops such as soybeans and canola, or from animal fats and recycled cooking oils. A major objective of biofuel production is to help make the nation more self-sufficient in energy production while, at the same time, reducing the emission of greenhouse gases (GHG). Ethanol based on sugar cane—the main feedstock used in Brazil—reduces GHG emissions by 80% or more over the entire production and use cycle, in comparison to emissions from fossil fuels. This percentage falls to less than 30% when ethanol is made from maize, which is the main feedstock used in the USA.

In addition to providing a renewable source of energy and environmental improvement, other objectives of biofuel production include creating new demand for agricultural products, stimulating regional development, and contributing to enhanced economic activity.

The USA and Brazil produce nearly one-half and one-third, respectively, of the world's ethanol, while the European Union accounts for about 60% of global biodiesel production. The Organization for Economic Co-operation and Development expects ethanol output in the USA, Brazil, and China to double over the course of the next decade. The amount of oilseeds used in the European Union for biofuels is expected to double during the same period.

While the objectives are laudable, the results of biofuel production are still subject to uncertainties and criticism. Most production chains for biofuels have costs per unit of fuel energy significantly above those for the fossil fuels they aim to replace. Despite the rapid increase in crude oil prices, and hence the costs for fossil fuels, the cost disadvantage of biofuels has widened in the past few years as agricultural commodity prices and thus the costs of biofuel feedstock have soared (OECD indicates that world prices of maize, wheat and vegetable oils increased by 86%, 110% and 91%, respectively, between 2004 and 2007).

Hence, biofuel production is highly dependent on support from public policy. Three primary forms of support are provided. These comprise, first, budgetary support (either in the form of tax concessions to refineries, retailers or users, or as direct support to biomass supply), biofuel production, or infrastructure for biofuel users. The USA, for example, currently provides a US $0.51 per gallon tax refund for blenders of ethanol and $1.00 per gallon for producers of biodiesel from vegetable oils and animal fat. Second, the use of mandates requiring biofuels to represent a minimum share or quantity in the fuel sold at the pump. Third trade restrictions in the form of import tariffs and duties, which protect the less cost-efficient domestic biofuel industry from competition from lower-cost foreign suppliers. The US tariff on ethanol is currently 2.5% and in addition there is a $0.54 per gallon duty on imported ethanol.

Overall, the outlook for biofuels will depend on a number of factors, including the future price of oil, the availability of low-cost feedstocks, sustained commitment through supportive government policy, technological breakthroughs that could reduce the cost of second-generation biofuels, and competition from unconventional fossil fuel alternatives (such as oil sands and heavy crude petroleum, conversion of coal to oil, and drilling for oil in remote areas or deeper waters).

The sale of by-products also contributes to the financial viability of biofuels. Dried distillers' grain, a by-product of corn ethanol production, can be used as a protein-rich livestock feed additive. Sale of this by-product can add as much as 10%–15% to ethanol producers' incomes. Carbon dioxide, usually released into the atmosphere, is captured by some ethanol plants and sold for use in the food and beverage sector. Bagasse, left over from pressing sugar cane, can be burned to provide heat for distillation and electric power. Glycerine, a byproduct of biodiesel production, has a wide number of pharmaceutical, food-processing, and feed applications.

There are, however, disadvantages to biofuel production, which are of particular concern to net food importing countries, as well as for the urban poor, including the increased demand for food crops caused by increased biofuel production and the resulting increase in food prices world-wide. According to the International Monetary Fund, world food prices rose by 10% in 2006 and by another 25% in 2007 owing to increases in maize, wheat, and soybean prices, prompted by growing demand for biofuels. Livestock producers in the USA are facing increased costs for maize and other feed, which may translate into higher retail meat prices. Higher feedstock prices caused by increased biofuel production will certainly benefit feedstock producers. However, it will mean extra costs and lower incomes for farmers who need the feedstock for animal feed. Furthermore, increased demand for biofuels is causing fundamental changes in agricultural markets that could drive up world prices for many farm products. Temporary factors such as droughts in wheat-growing regions and low stocks explain the recent increases in farm commodity prices. The resultant reduction in crop surpluses and decline in export subsidies are contributing factors. Of even more importance, however, is the growing use of cereals, sugar, oilseed and vegetable oils to produce biofuels. This is underpinning crop prices and, indirectly through higher animal feed costs, also the prices for livestock products.

CONCLUSIONS

A variety of significant changes took place in US agriculture during the 20th century. Specialization, productivity growth, adoption of capital-intensive production methods, changes in trade policy and policy directly affecting prices and production choices, changes in institutional structure and changes in the relationship between farmers and the marketing sector, have all played a role in shaping the sector throughout the last century. There are fewer and larger farms today than there were at the beginning of the 20th century. The sector is highly dependent upon international markets. There is increasing concern about the environmental impact of production practices and about the impact of food production on human health.

It is likely that US farms will continue to decline in number and to grow larger in size as agricultural productivity continues unabated. Multilateral and bilateral trade negotiations will continue to be important to the sector. Environmental concerns and food safety issues are likely to continue to play an important role in the 21st century. Finally, pressure will no doubt continue for governmental support for farmers in the form of income support and risk management practices as the sector continues to face unstable prices and incomes, despite WTO efforts to reduce agricultural subsidies.

References

The text of this paper draws heavily from the following sources:

Everett, E. E. 'American Agriculture The First 300 Years', in *Farmers in a Changing World, 1940 Yearbook of Agriculture*. Washington, DC, US Dept of Agriculture.

Hallberg, M. C. *Policy for American Agriculture: Choices and Consequences*. Ames, IA, Iowa State University Press, 1992.

Economic Trends in US Agriculture and Food Systems Since World War II. Ames, IA, Iowa State University Press, 2001.

Kose, M. A., Rebucci, A., and Schipke. A. 'Macroeconomic Implications of CAFTA-DR', in *Central America: Global Integration and Regional Cooperation*. International Monetary Fund Occasional Paper 243. Washington, DC, July 2005.

Von Lampe, Martin. 'Economic Assessment of Biofuel Support Policies', in *OECD Trade and Agriculture Directorate*. July, 2008.

Westcott, P. C., Young, E., and Price, J. M. 'The 2002 Farm Act: Provisions and Implications for Commodity Markets', in *Agriculture Information Bulletin Number 778*. Washington, DC, US Dept of Agriculture, November 2002.

THE FOOD, CONSERVATION AND ENERGY ACT OF 2008—THE US FARM BILL

MILTON C. HALLBERG

Government programmes for agriculture in the USA have an impact, not only on farming and rural areas, but also on the country's food supply, the cost of food to consumers, natural resources and the environment, international trade, and hunger at home and abroad. Everyone in the USA, and millions elsewhere, are affected in some way by these programmes. Authority for the US Department of Agriculture (USDA) to operate farm programmes comes from three permanent laws: the Agricultural Adjustment Act of 1938, the Agricultural Act of 1949 and the Commodity Credit Corporation Charter Act of 1948. The objective of these laws is to stabilize and support farm incomes by shifting some of the risks of farming to the federal Government in order to maintain the economic health of the nation's farm sector and to ensure that it remains globally competitive. Congress amends these laws periodically with multi-year omnibus farm bills to reflect current market conditions, budget constraints and constituent preferences. Since 1965 these omnibus farm bills have generally had a lifespan of five years. If new legislation were not adopted to supersede expiring laws, out-of-date permanent legislation would again reign. The result would be substantially higher costs for the US taxpayer and greater subsidies for US farmers. Thus, there is every incentive for Congress to enact new legislation.

In some years securing approval of a new farm bill is a relatively straightforward task. In other years, however, legislators and the Administration have a difficult time agreeing among themselves and with each other on acceptable legislation. Such was the case when Congress crafted legislation with which to replace the Farm Security and Rural Investment Act of 2002. After several extensions of the 2002 legislation and an override of the President's veto, on 18 June 2008 Congress enacted a new farm bill—the Food, Conservation and Energy Act of 2008—which was to guide federal policy for the agricultural sector until 2012.

Citizens from a variety of areas, backgrounds and vocations help to shape each new farm bill. The formal process used by administrators and legislators (i.e. the 'official participants') to develop and enact this legislation is well recognized (see Hallberg, *Policy for American Agriculture: Choices and Con-*

sequences). However, there are also a large number of 'unofficial participants' active in the policy-making process, all of whom have their own individual agendas. First, there are many farm organizations. Some of these organizations represent all farmers in the USA or all farmers in a wide geographic region of the nation, while others represent farmers of a single commodity. However, farmers producing different commodities do not necessarily share the same policy objectives, so there can be conflict within and between farm organizations. There are also organizations that represent consumers, environmentalists, conservationists, grain dealers and input suppliers. These latter groups clearly do not have compatible interests, nor interests that are necessarily shared by farmers. The Food, Conservation and Energy Act of 2008 must therefore be viewed in light of these conflicting interests and as something of a compromise, as legislators and the Administration attempt to fulfil the desires of their constituents.

OVERVIEW

This essay outlines some of the more significant features of the Food, Conservation and Energy Act of 2008 (commonly referred to as the 2008 Farm Bill). Of primary interest are policy for the farm commodity programmes—i.e. price supports, loan rates, commodities supported and payment limitations—and conservation and energy provisions. The Bill continued many of the commodity programmes initiated under previous farm legislation, adjusting payment levels and eligibility, while introducing both a new crop revenue election programme and a permanent disaster assistant programme. However, the 2008 Farm Bill comprises 15 titles described in a 683-page document. It covers several areas that are not detailed in this essay, including: farmland protection and natural resource stewardship; food assistance and agricultural development efforts abroad; foreign trade; food stamps, domestic food distribution and local nutrition; rural economic development; research on various topics related to the agricultural and food sector; sustainability of forests; marketing of farm products; crop insurance and disaster assistance programmes; and initiatives for attracting and retaining 'beginning' and socially disadvantaged farmers.

New titles provided increased funding for horticultural crops and organic agriculture and for the livestock and poultry sector. A credit title authorized new conservation loans, and the forestry title included provisions for emergency private forest restoration. Benefits and eligibility were expanded for the Food Stamp Program, which was renamed the Supplemental Nutrition Assistance Program in October 2008. The Fresh Fruit and Vegetable Program and farmers' market and food distribution programmes were to receive increased funding. The trade title terminated some export assistance programmes, while continuing and expanding market development programmes. Funding for international food assistance was also increased. Co-ordination of agricultural research, education and extension programmes was to be reorganized through a new National Institute of Food and Agriculture; most research funding was to be competitively awarded.

FARM COMMODITY PROGRAMMES

Eligible Commodities

The objective of farm commodity programmes is to stabilize and support farm incomes by transferring some of the risks arising from short-term market price instability and longer-term resource adjustments to the federal Government. The overriding goal is to preserve the economic strength of the farm sector so that it remains internationally competitive in the production of food and fibre. Critics argue that the farm commodity programmes enacted distort world production and trade, result in large subsidies to individuals that become capitalized into land prices and rents—thus raising the cost of production—and produce benefits that are concentrated among a relatively small number of commodities produced on a small number of large farms. Supporters of farm commodity programmes do not disagree entirely, but maintain that they are necessary to balance distortions created by other countries, and to maintain the economic health of rural communities. Furthermore, supporters claim that targeting subsidies at small, inefficient farms would encourage inefficient food and fibre production since small farms cannot produce bulk commodities as efficiently as large farms.

The 2008 Farm Bill provided support for nearly two dozen farm commodities, which collectively accounted for nearly one-third of the total cash receipts from farming. The commodities eligible for support under the legislation were wheat, corn, grain sorghum, barley, oats, upland cotton, rice, pulse crops (dry peas, lentils and chickpeas), peanuts, soybeans and other oilseeds (sunflower seed, rapeseed, canola, safflower, flaxseed, mustard seed, crambe and sesame seed). For all but the pulse crops, farmers receive direct payments tied to historical production, as well as counter-cyclical payments that increase when market prices are low. Also, for all of the above commodities as well as cotton, wool, mohair and honey, eligible farmers may be eligible for marketing loans when market prices are low.

Dairy prices are supported indirectly through federal purchases of non-fat dry milk, butter and cheese. Milk producers received a Milk Income Loss Contract (MILC—see below) payment when prices fall below a target price established by the legislation.

Sugar support is indirect through import quotas and domestic 'marketing allotments'. No direct payments are made to sugar growers or to sugar processors.

Producers of the remaining agricultural commodities—meats, poultry, fruits, vegetables, nuts, hay and nursery products—which account for over 60% of the cash receipts from farming, receive no direct support of any kind.

Direct Payments and Planting Flexibility

Direct payments are fixed annual payments per unit of production based on historical output. They do not vary with current market prices or yields and rates are established by the legislation (see table below). A farm is eligible for direct payments on its 'base acres'—the historical average of its planting area for the relevant commodity—at the 'direct payment yield', which is the historical average of the farm's actual yields. The percentage of base acres on which direct payments were to be made under the 2008 Farm Bill was 83.3%, down from 85% under the previous Bill. This percentage would increase to 85% again for the 2012 crop year to maintain a higher baseline for the next farm bill.

A farmer is not obligated to grow the covered commodity in order to receive a direct payment for that commodity. For example, he or she may plant soybeans on corn base acres and receive the direct payment for corn. The rationale for this planting flexibility is to allow farmers to respond to market signals when choosing a crop to plant. The farmer may not, however, plant fruits, vegetables or wild rice on corn base acres and receive the direct payment for corn. This restriction is intended to protect growers of these unsubsidized crops from competition from those growing subsidized crops. A pilot programme scheduled to begin in 2009 was to relax this restriction somewhat for processed fruits and vegetables.

Counter-Cyclical Payments

Counter-cyclical payments compensate farmers for the difference between a crop's target price (as established by the legislation and shown in the table below) and a lower effective market price, which is defined as the direct payment rate plus the higher of (a) the national season-average market price or (b) the national loan rate. With this payment, farmers are compensated for low market prices down to the loan rate. Below this price the marketing loan programme is activated, while above this price no payment is made. As with direct payments, counter-cyclical payments are proportional to a farm's base acres and do not depend upon current production.

The 2008 Farm Bill adjusted target prices for counter-cyclical payments and extended support under this programme to new commodities. Target prices for wheat, sorghum, barley, oats, soybeans and other oilseeds were maintained at the level set by the 2002 Farm Bill for the

Direct Payment Rates, Target Prices for Counter-Cyclical Payments and Non-recourse Loan Rates through the Life of the 2008 Farm Bill (US $)

	Direct Payment Rates	Target Prices for Counter-cyclical Payments		Non-recourse Loan Rates	
	2009–12	2009	2010	2009	2010–12
Wheat (bushels)	0.52	3.92	4.17	2.75	2.94
Corn (bushels)	0.28	2.63	2.63	1.95	1.95
Grain sorghum (bushels)	0.35	2.57	2.63	1.95	1.95
Barley (bushels)	0.24	2.24	2.63	1.85	1.85
Oats (bushels)	0.02	1.44	1.79	1.33	1.39
Upland cotton (lb)	0.07	0.71	0.71	0.52	0.52
Rice (cwt)	2.35	10.50	10.50	6.50	6.50
Peanuts (short tons)	36.00	495.00	495.00	355.00	355.00
Soybeans (bushels)	0.44	5.80	6.00	5.00	5.00
Other oilseeds (cwt)	0.80	10.10	12.68	9.30	10.09
Dry peas (cwt)	—	8.32	8.32	5.40	5.40
Lentils (cwt)	—	12.81	12.81	11.28	11.28
Small chickpeas (cwt)	—	10.36	10.36	7.43	7.43
Large chickpeas (cwt)	—	12.81	12.81	11.28	11.28
Wool, graded (lb)	—	—	—	1.00	1.15
Mohair (lb)	—	—	—	4.20	4.20
Honey (lb)	—	—	—	0.60	0.60

2008–09 crop years and increased for subsequent crop years. Target prices were decreased for cotton and left unchanged for corn, rice and peanuts. Dry peas, lentils and chickpeas were added to the list of commodities eligible for support from the 2009 crop year onwards.

Marketing Loans and Loan Deficiency Payments

Marketing loans are non-recourse loans that farmers can obtain by pledging their harvested commodity as collateral. 'Non-recourse' means that the collateral can be forfeited at the end of the term of the loan with no penalty. The Government can take no recourse against the borrower beyond accepting the commodity as full settlement of the loan even if the market price is less than the loan rate.

As an alternative to taking out a non-recourse loan, a farmer may opt for a loan deficiency payment. Under this arrangement, the farmer is allowed to sell his grain in response to market signals without putting his commodity under loan, while still receiving the price benefit of the loan programme via a cash payment.

National-level loan prices were established by the 2008 Farm Bill (see table below). USDA adjusts the average loan rate to local loan rates to reflect spatial differences in markets and transportation.

Commodities eligible for marketing loans include all of those eligible for direct and counter-cyclical payments, as well as extra-long staple cotton, wool, mohair and honey. Extra-long staple cotton is not eligible for loan deficiency payments. The 2008 Farm Bill increased the loan rate for wheat, barley, oats, minor oilseeds, wool, honey, cane sugar and beet sugar, decreased the loan rate for dry peas and lentils, and added large chickpeas to the eligible list for the 2009 crop year.

Average Crop Revenue Election (ACRE)

The 2008 Farm Bill introduced a new programme, the Average Crop Revenue Election (ACRE). This is a revenue guarantee programme, which provides participating producers payments for a commodity when the actual state revenue for that commodity is less than the revenue guarantee. To receive an ACRE payment, two conditions must be met: (1) the actual state revenue for a supported crop must be less than the state-level revenue guarantee amount, and (2) an individual farm's actual revenue for a supported crop must be less than the farm's benchmark revenue.

The state-level revenue guarantee amount and the individual farm benchmark revenue are determined as the product of a guaranteed price with a guaranteed level of production. Benchmark or guaranteed yields at the state and farm levels are averages of the three middle years of the most recent five-year period. Price guarantees are averages of the higher of (a) the marketing year price, or (b) the marketing loan rate as specified under ACRE for the most recent two years. The revenue guarantee is 90% of the product of the average benchmark yield and the price guarantee.

If the two conditions indicated above are met, an individual farmer will receive an ACRE payment that is based on the state-level difference between actual revenue and the ACRE guarantee per acre, multiplied by 83.3% of the farm's planted acreage, but assessed proportionately according to the individual farm's yield history compared with the state's yield history. The maximum payment rate is 25% of the ACRE guarantee.

Beginning with the 2009 crop year, farmers would be able to choose the counter-cyclical payment programme of the new revenue-based ACRE programme. Participants in ACRE would continue to receive direct payments, but at a 20% reduced rate. Participants in ACRE would also continue to be eligible for non-recourse marketing loans and loan deficiency payments, but with a 30% lower loan rate. Participants in ACRE, however, would not be eligible for traditional counter-cyclical payments and, having elected to participate in ACRE, would not be permitted to revert back to the traditional counter-cyclical payment programme for the remainder of the period covered by the 2008 Farm Bill. ACRE was to be available for the same crops as counter-cyclical payments, but would be based on planted acres rather than on base acres.

Sugar Programme

The 2008 Farm Bill reauthorized the non-recourse loan programme for sugar, with loan rates specified in the legislation. There is no price support programme for sugar, but the sugar programme is designed to guarantee the minimum price received by growers of sugar cane and sugar beets, and by the firms that process these crops into refined sugar. To accomplish this, USDA limits the amount of sugar that processors can sell domestically under 'marketing allotments' and restricts imports. USDA is required to operate the sugar programme on a 'no-cost' basis. This means that USDA must regulate the US sugar supply using allotments, import quotas and related measures such that domestic market prices do not fall below guaranteed minimum price levels. These are set out in law as specific loan rates, which serve as the basis from which USDA derives effective support levels. If the market price is below the support level when a sugar price support loan becomes due, its non-recourse feature means that a processor can forfeit sugar to USDA as collateral for the loan in fulfilment of its repayment obligation.

Dairy Programmes

The 2008 Farm Bill provided authority for two major policy tools used by USDA to support the prices and incomes received by dairy farmers: the Dairy Product Price Support Program (previously known as the Milk Price Support Program) and the MILC Program. It also permanently established the Dairy

Forward Pricing Program, allowing dairy producers to enter into forward contracts with milk handlers, which had been introduced as a pilot programme by special legislation adopted in 2000. A fourth policy tool is the Federal Milk Marketing Order Program, which obliges dairy processors to pay producers a minimum price for farm milk depending on its end use. This programme is permanently authorized by independent legislation, which does not require periodic reauthorization.

As regards the Dairy Product Price Support Program, previous legislation authorized the support of the price received by farmers for milk at US $9.90 per cwt. In order to achieve this support level, a standing offer existed whereby USDA would purchase surplus manufactured dairy products (butter, non-fat dry milk and cheese) from processors at prices that were administratively established by the Department. Whenever market prices fell to the support level, processors would generally decide to sell surplus product to the Government rather than to the marketplace. Consequently, the Government's purchase prices for manufactured dairy products usually served as a floor to the market price, which, in turn, indirectly supported the farm price of milk at $9.90 per cwt.

The 2008 Farm Bill extended the Dairy Product Price Support Program until 2012, but modified the programme so that it would directly support the prices of manufactured dairy products at mandated levels. Although the 2008 law did not specifically state that the overall support price for milk would be US $9.90 per cwt, the mandated product prices were such that the farm price of milk would effectively be supported at that level. The law allowed USDA temporarily to reduce the mandated support prices when government purchases of the products exceeded a specified level. Also, USDA could sell inventoried dairy products at prevailing market prices when the selling price was 120% or more of the supported price.

Under previous legislation, dairy farmers nation-wide were eligible for a federal payment through the MILC Program whenever the minimum monthly market price for farm milk used for fluid consumption in Boston, Massachusetts, fell below US $16.94 per cwt. Eligible farmers then received a payment equal to 34% of the difference between the $16.94 target price and the lower monthly market price. These payments were limited to the first 2.4m. lb of milk produced per dairy operation per year—the equivalent of a 130-cow dairy operation.

The 2008 Farm Bill reauthorized the MILC Program with some modifications. First, the payment percentage was to increase to 45% from October 2008 until August 2012, after which it would revert to 34%. Second, the payment quantity limit was to be raised to 2.985m. lb—the equivalent of a 160-cow dairy operation—between October 2008 and August 2012, after which it would decline again to the 2.4m. lb level. These reversions were intended to minimize long-term budget outlays. Third, the target price of US $16.94 would be adjusted upward when feed prices exceeded a certain threshold. In any month that the average feed cost (as determined by a formula currently used by USDA to calculate dairy feed costs) rose above $7.35 per cwt, the $16.94 target price would be increased by 45% of the difference between the monthly feed cost and $7.35. In any month that the dairy feed cost was less than or equal to $7.35 per cwt, the target price would be $13.69 per cwt.

The Dairy Forward Pricing Program allowed dairy farmers and co-operatives voluntarily to enter into forward contracts with milk handlers, thereby assisting dairy farmers in risk management. Such a contract was a cash transaction in which a seller agreed to deliver a specific commodity to a buyer at some point in the future at a mutually agreed price. Any payments made by milk handlers under the contract were deemed to satisfy the minimum price requirements of federal milk marketing orders. This programme applied only to milk purchased for manufactured products.

PAYMENT LIMITS

Under the 2008 Farm Bill, the annual limit on payments to a person was US $105,000 for direct and counter-cyclical payments combined. This amount could be effectively doubled for a sole proprietor's farm if he or she had a spouse. There were no limits on marketing loan payments.

If the three-year average of non-farm adjusted gross income (AGI) exceeded US $500,000, no programme benefits would be allowed, i.e. no direct payments, no counter-cyclical payments and no marketing loan payments. If the three-year average of farm AGI exceeded $750,000, then no direct payments would be permitted, but counter-cyclical and marketing loan payments would be available.

The 2008 Farm Bill eliminated direct, counter-cyclical and ACRE payments to farms with fewer than 10 base acres of all crops, with the exception of farms owned by socially disadvantaged farmers or those with limited resources.

Finally, the 2008 Farm Bill required USDA to reconcile the social security numbers of programme recipients with a social security database twice a year. This was to ensure that programme beneficiaries were still alive, and that estates did not continue to qualify beyond a reasonable period.

CONSERVATION PROGRAMMES

The Conservation Reserve Program (CRP) provides technical and financial assistance to eligible farmers and ranchers to address soil, water and related natural resource concerns with regard to their land in an environmentally beneficial manner and to comply with federal, state and tribal environmental laws. It is aimed at curbing soil erosion, protecting the USA's ability to produce food and fibre, reducing sedimentation in streams and lakes, improving water quality, establishing wildlife habitat, and enhancing forest and wetland resources. It encourages farmers to convert highly erodible cropland and other environmentally sensitive acreage into vegetative cover. Farmers receive an annual rental payment for the term of a multi-year contract. Contracts are for a minimum of 10 years and a maximum of 15 years. Cost-sharing is offered to promote the establishment of the vegetative cover practices. Land that has been cropped in four of the six years preceding 2008 is eligible for CRP assistance.

The Wetlands Reserve Program (WRP) is a voluntary programme offering landowners the opportunity to protect, restore and enhance wetlands on their property, primarily with the aim of providing wildlife habitat. More specifically, under this programme USDA is permitted to purchase long-term or permanent easements and to provide technical support and cost-sharing payments up to US $50,000 per year to those who agree to restore wetlands. (An easement separates certain land use rights—primarily development as non-agricultural land—and conveys them to another party.) The WRP thus allows landowners to establish long-term conservation and wildlife practices and protection.

The Grassland Reserve Program (GRP) is similar to the WRP, but applies to grassland, rangeland, pastureland and shrubland. The GRP aims to conserve vulnerable grasslands by preventing their conversion to cropland or other uses and by helping to maintain viable ranching operations.

Succeeding the Conservation Security Program, the Conservation Stewardship Program (CSP) is a new voluntary programme that provides financial and technical assistance to producers who practice good stewardship on their agricultural lands. Eligible land includes private cropland, pastureland, prairie, improved pasture and rangeland, and incidental forested land with a cropping history of four out of the six years preceding June 2008. Land under CRP, WRP or GRP contracts is not eligible for this programme. Under the 2008 Farm Bill, USDA is directed to enrol 12.77m. acres per year into the CSP at an average cost of US $18 per acre per year.

The Farmland Protection Program (FPP) is a voluntary programme that helps farmers to keep their land in agricultural use. The programme provides matching funds to state, local or tribal government entities and non-governmental organizations (NGOs) with existing farmland protection programmes to purchase conservation easements. The aim of the FPP is to protect between 170,000 and 340,000 acres of farmland. The Farm Bill 2008 mandated US $743m. in funding for the programme until 2012. Commonly referred to as a 'purchase of development rights' programme, the FPP compensates landowners for voluntarily limiting future development on their land. Landowners retain many property rights, including the right to farm according to the provisions specified in the easement. The programme enables landowners to sell development rights on their land to a government agency or NGO, such as a land trust, while retaining full ownership.

To participate, landowners submit applications to the entities authorized to purchase easements and agree to limit the use of their land for non-agricultural purposes. The value of the conservation easement is usually determined through a professional appraisal. A qualified, professional appraiser assesses the difference between the fair market value of the property, often using comparable sales, and its restricted value under the easement.

The Environmental Quality Incentives Program (EQIP) offers technical assistance and incentive and cost-sharing payments to participants implementing structural and management conservation practices on eligible agricultural land. Persons who are engaged in livestock or agricultural production on eligible land may participate in the programme. EQIP activities are carried out according to a plan of operation, developed in conjunction with the producer, that identifies the appropriate conservation practice or practices to address the resource concerns. The practices are subject to technical standards adapted for local conditions by USDA's Natural Resources Conservation Service (NRCS). NRCS is the primary federal agency that works with private landowners to help them to conserve, maintain and improve their natural resources.

EQIP may share up to 75% of the costs of certain conservation practices. Incentive payments may be provided for up to three years to encourage producers to introduce management practices that they may not otherwise employ. However, producers with limited resources and 'beginning' farmers and ranchers may be eligible for cost-sharing payments of up to 90%. Farmers and ranchers may elect to use a certified third-party provider for technical assistance. An individual or entity may not receive, directly or indirectly, cost-sharing or incentive payments that, in the aggregate, exceed US $450,000 for all EQIP contracts agreed during the term of the 2008 Farm Bill.

ENERGY

Previous legislation included several provisions for encouraging the production, use and development of renewable energy sources. The 2008 Farm Bill continued and expanded funding for most of these programmes. It mandated nearly US $2,000m. in funding and authorized the provision of an additional $1,000m. until 2012 for a variety of programmes, including the testing and labelling of bio-based products; loan guarantees for the development, construction and retrofitting of biofuel refineries; and the promotion of energy efficiency and renewable energy development for agricultural producers and rural businesses. In addition, it offered new programmes to encourage renewable energy use by biofuel refineries, the introduction of renewable energy systems, energy efficiency improvements, rural energy self-sufficiency, the development of new feed stocks and the use of forest and woody biomass for energy production. Finally, it included a number of tax provisions, including several related to biofuels. Among these were a temporary tax credit for the production of cellulosic biofuels, a reduction in the tax credit for ethanol from 51 cents a gallon to 45 cents a gallon, and an extension of the duty of 54 cents a gallon on ethanol imported for fuel use until 2010.

References

Hallberg, M. C. *Policy for American Agriculture: Choices and Consequences*. Ames, IA, Iowa State University Press, 1992.

Harris, W., Lubben, B., Novak, J., and Sanders, L. 'The Food, Conservation and Energy Act of 2008: Summary and Possible Consequences'. Paper prepared for the Extension National Farm Bill Train the Trainer Conference, Kansas City, MO, 8 and 9 July 2008.

Monke, J. *Farm Commodity Programs in the 2008 Farm Bill*. Washington, DC, Congressional Research Service, 23 July 2008.

US Department of Agriculture Economic Research Service. '2008 Farm Bill Side-By-Side'. See www.ers.usda.gov/FarmBill/2008.

SERVICE INDUSTRIES: CENTRAL TO THE US ECONOMY

Prof. P. W. DANIELS

INTRODUCTION

The service sector was the 'engine room' of the world's biggest economy at the beginning of the 21st century and there was every reason to suggest that the so-called 'third sector' would be equally, or even more, important throughout the century. While key policy-makers and some academic observers have clung to the view that manufacturing industries are essential for the health of the domestic economy and the international competitiveness of the USA, the inexorable shift towards service industries continued unabated. Although manufacturing industries are an important driver of growth in a diverse economy, they increasingly rely on inputs from services. This symbiotic relationship may even be service-led, with intangible assets, such as design skills, often considered to be more valuable than tangible assets. In the so-called 'knowledge-based' or 'new' economy that dominates current thinking about economic agendas, it is becoming increasingly difficult to distinguish between services and manufacturing in the traditional sense. However, there are attributes that make services distinctive from goods. Services cannot be performed without some form of relationship between a producer and a consumer. Many services cannot be stored and retained for later use in the way typical of many goods, although some, such as a consultancy report, may have a 'shelf life' extending beyond the initial implementation of the advice provided to the client. Services such as plumbing, carpentry or a manicure involve some form of material change to an object or an individual consumer, while others involve consumption (such as fast food) that promotes a sense of well-being or satisfaction. Many services are embodied in the persons producing or delivering them; such human value added comes in numerous forms, ranging from the technical knowledge of a car mechanic to the specialized expertise of a heart surgeon.

US statisticians have yet to compile a classification of economic activities that adequately reflects the blurring of the boundaries between the major economic sectors. The US Census Bureau has, however, moved away from classifying businesses by industry groups based on the production process to a more detailed classification of service-producing activities (the North American Industry Classification System—NAICS). Service industries are now divided into seven sectors: information; professional, scientific and technical services; administrative, support, waste management and remediation services; educational services; health care and social assistance; arts, entertainment and recreation; and other services (except public administration). Most of these sectors service businesses that did not exist when earlier classifications were compiled. Thus, the category of professional, scientific and technical services covers businesses providing specialized business and personal services and identifies 47 industries, of which 28 are new (such as interpretation and translation, environmental consulting and interior design services). The information sector incorporates 34 industries, of which the majority are new, such as database publishers, cable television programme distributors and, in a 2007 revision, internet service providers. The Census Bureau statistics cover employment, payroll, receipts, profits and capital investment for these and other service industries. Analysis of the structure and functioning of the US service economy is now much improved, although still not as comprehensive as it could be.

New types of service businesses and the accompanying changes to US markets and society have also generated new or emerging occupations. Long-established occupations, such as secretarial work, have altered as the use of information and communications technology (ICT), including voicemail and interactive voice response systems, has become ubiquitous. Clerical work has been upgraded to the level of administrative assistance, while new service occupations, such as convention managers, web masters, technicians and co-ordinators, environmental engineers and job coaches, have emerged. Certain services have also shaped occupational demand. Professional and business services had the largest number of seasonally adjusted job openings at March 2008, making it one of three types of services (the others being education and health services, and accommodation and food services) to have been consistently in this position since 2000.

DIVERSIFICATION AND SPECIALIZATION OF SERVICES IN THE USA

The diversification of service-producing activities in the US economy was a response to several influences. There was a tendency for all firms across all sectors of the economy, most notably in manufacturing, to outsource everything other than core functions. This stimulated demand for a wide range of specialized or niche services that supply knowledge—other things being equal—of superior quality to those produced internally. Large companies were most likely to utilize outsourced services, especially for ICT, human resources, sales and marketing, and finance. Completely new services, such as data warehousing and data-mining services, which provide corporate clients with customer and market profiles, have also encouraged the outsourcing process. ICT has also spawned new industries, such as interactive multimedia systems for business applications and home use, online health care advice and support, or routine legal advice services.

It is also necessary, in an increasingly knowledge- and information-based economy, which relies heavily on human capital, to invest and reinvest in education and training services; the need for life-long learning and occupational flexibility is vital to the contemporary labour process. The nature of work is also changing, partly because of the impact of ICT and partly owing to social and welfare pressures to balance work with other activities. Combine this with higher living standards and extensive media-driven information about the numerous alternative ways of using leisure and other time, and there is increased demand for travel, recreation and entertainment services both within and beyond the USA (moderated in the aftermath of the terrorist attacks on New York and Washington, DC, in September 2001 but now recovering steadily). The net worth of US households was almost 5.6 times disposable income in 2006, an increase from a ratio below five during most of the 1980s. The population of the USA is also 'greying'; an estimated 30.4% will be aged over 55 by 2025. This has not only raised demand for health, social welfare and residential care services—health care consumption has doubled since 1970, to more than 15% of gross domestic product (GDP) in 2005—but it has also stimulated innovation in the supply of services such as long-term care insurance, so-called 'reverse' mortgages (which do not have to be paid back until the person dies or moves home), seniors-oriented travel options or savings schemes, and new medical and dental services aimed at the needs of the elderly.

SERVICES AND THE 'NEW' ECONOMY

Developments in ICT and the expansion of service-producing industries underpinned the notion of what was variously described as the 'new', 'digital', 'e-' or 'now' economy. The US media also referred to the 'information technology revolution' and the 'internet age' in an attempt to capture the pivotal contribution of ICT to accelerating the US economy's rate of output and of productivity growth. Financial services, business services, wholesale trade, communications and insurance accounted for more than 50% of US investment in computers in the late 1990s. ICT investment (encompassing computers and peripheral equipment, software and communications equipment) by financial services increased from US $16,000m. in 1990 to more than $65,000m. in 2000. Wholesale services and retail trade services more than matched this trend, investing almost $75,000m. in 1999 alone. These expenditures have been encouraged by a steady fall in the price of computer and communications hardware, as well as in the charges levied by national and international telecommunications services. Not surprisingly, such large-scale ICT investments by service firms increased the numbers of those employed in computer systems design and related services from approximately 1m. people in 1995 to almost 4m. people in 2004.

The most debated issue about ICT was whether it created improvements in the productivity of service-producing industries. From the early 1960s, when computers and data-processing equipment became relatively widespread, there was little to suggest that productivity was being enhanced. Part of the problem had been, and still was, the difficulty in measuring the productivity of certain service industries using conventional methods. For example, how could the output of management consultants be measured and their productivity be computed? The widespread introduction of automatic teller machines (ATMs) by retail banks reduced customer queuing time and allowed the completion of transactions outside bank business hours and at weekends; also, by using computer-assisted verification systems, customers could use ATMs virtually anywhere in the world to obtain local currency. However, how this could be incorporated into a productivity measure for an individual bank employee or for a bank as a whole remained problematic.

The difficulty of quantifying the impact of ICT on productivity was compounded by the rapid pace of its development. Nevertheless, US statistical agencies have made some progress towards resolving the productivity measurement problem for service-producing industries. In 1999, for example, a new measure of the output of the banking industry that focused on the benefits to consumers of services such as ATMs was incorporated into the national accounts. The Bureau of Labor Statistics also began to publish price indices for some types of business services, although in 2008 they remained far from comprehensive.

Recent evidence does, however, signal a productivity boost to the US economy as a consequence of the link between innovations in ICT and their widespread adoption by the service-producing sectors. In 1989–95 and 1995–98 value added per worker employed in the service sector improved by a rather modest, but notable, 0.3%, which was exceeded by individual activities such as finance, insurance and real estate (1.3%), retail trade (4.8%) and wholesale trade (6.4%). Among all other service providers, labour productivity rose in 2002 in six of the 11 industries for which measures were available. The strongest growth occurred in tax preparation services and photofinishing, at 17.8% and 16.1%, respectively. In 2004 labour productivity increases were recorded by more than two-thirds of the 31 service-producing activities measured by the Bureau of Labor Statistics, with seven sectors recording increases of more than 10%. Productivity rose in the three largest service-producing sectors: by 7.8% in automotive repair, by 5.3% in commercial banking and by 5.7% in travel accommodations.

As a general rule, it seemed that the increase in productivity was the result of higher investment in the service sector motivated by developments in ICT—notwithstanding the many other influences on service sector productivity, such as the level of output, efficient utilization of capacity, managerial skills and the characteristics and effort of the work-force. However, service-producing industries that tended to be more ICT intensive accrued the largest gains in productivity. Communication services and brokerage firms exhibited formidable gains that were not a consequence of job cuts, but of higher output per worker. Other service industries, such as wholesale and retail trade, increased productivity, even though their employment growth was modest. While the impact of ICT on the US service economy was clear to see, it did not mean that the concepts and analysis of change used for the 'old' economy had somehow been erased by the advent of the 'new' economy. Perhaps ICT had simply become pervasive, in much the same way that the telegraph, then the telephone and later the facsimile machine transformed the speed of communication and collapsed time and space as the US settlement frontier moved west during the 19th century and consolidated during the 20th century.

E-Commerce

The upward productivity trend was expected to continue as savings accrued, for example, from the use of the internet for services (now commonly described as 'B2B'—business-to-business) e-commerce (93% of the total for 2001). With the broadband penetration rate exceeding 80% of active internet users in February 2007, the USA was an e-business-friendly environment. Buyers obtained product information online and then completed the transfer of ownership offline, in stores, in sales offices, or via telephone or fax. Customer relations constituted another component of e-business, including direct marketing by e-mail and numerous customer self-service transactions and after-sale processes and services, such as assistance in operating and maintaining technical products, requests for changes in service, updating records, transferring funds, and viewing the status of transactions, orders and deliveries. This represents a much larger share of business in service firms that sell primarily to other service firms. The USA was the world leader for e-commerce innovation that involved the transformation of key business processes through the use of internet technology. It has been claimed that the use of e-commerce by intermediate services (rather than the final services to consumers, such as retailing or health care) could increase annual gross domestic product (GDP) by 0.25%. First, the automation of internal processing procedures reduced paperwork costs. Second, B2B reduced inventory costs (facilitating so-called 'just-in-time' inventory control). Third, B2B increased the scope for removing the so-called 'middleman' (wholesalers) and, fourth, the internet reduced input prices by squeezing out monopoly rents from producers of inputs. Fifth, e-business facilitated the linking of management teams across the USA and therefore reduced the demand for travel. Finally, it facilitated the improvement of customer services, partly through the unprecedented opportunties for e-businesses to gather and process information about their customers (data-mining).

The internet simultaneously increased accessibility to information and knowledge by and for businesses and the private consumer. This, in turn, stimulated demand for, and the supply of, new service-producing industries as well as contributing to improvements in productivity. According to the International Telecommunications Union, in 2005 some 23% of world-wide internet users were located in the USA. More than 88% of the highest income households (those earning US $75,000 or more per year) in the USA already had a personal computer in 2000, and even in the lowest income households (those earning $25,000 or less per year) the penetration (28%) was twice the level for equivalent households in, for example, Japan or France. The USA also led the world in the use of secure servers for e-commerce; in July 2002 the USA had 37.5 secure servers per 100,000 inhabitants, far more than competitor economies such as Canada (25.0), the United Kingdom (17.1) or Japan (5.6). However, in terms of broadband penetration (42.9m. lines in 2005) the USA was placed only 12th in the world.

E-commerce's most significant impact was on the service-producing industries, especially those that primarily transmit information (postal services, communications, radio and television) and those that produce it (finance, entertainment, travel agencies and stockbrokers). Electronically delivered products, such as software, travel services, entertainment and finance, were leading players. E-commerce continued to grow gradually with merchant wholesalers relying more on it than retailers or advanced activities such as business and professional services. B2B e-commerce accounted for the majority (93%) of the total using proprietory Electronic Data Interchange (EDI) systems. Although retailers' e-commerce sales (business-to-consumer—B2C) increased by 22% between 2005 and 2006, they represented a very modest 2.7% of total US retail sales (at US $107,000m.). Almost all retail e-sales in 2006 were undertaken by non-store retailers and motor vehicles and parts dealers. The e-sales of selected service industries (excluding retail) amounted to $114,000m. in 2006, which was a rise of 14.9% over 2005, but still contributed only 1.8% of the total revenues of these industries. E-commerce was still modest when compared with the use of direct marketing via post, telephone and newspapers, perhaps because of ongoing concerns about the security of payments via the internet and the privacy of personal data (for B2C e-commerce), or the enduring attraction of 'traditional' suburban malls and other outlets. Retail e-sales were expected to increase steadily to $219,000m. in 2010, but would still represent a small share of total retail sales, which in 2006, for example, were worth $3,900,000m. While e-commerce offers considerable potential benefits in terms of reduced automobile travel, congestion and air pollution, it may well become just another transaction channel for US retailers and consumers, rather than the dominant mode of conducting business.

SERVICES, GDP AND EMPLOYMENT

A number of measures, such as GDP and employment, can be used to convey the scale of services in the US economy. In 2005 the private service-producing industries accounted for almost two-thirds of current dollar GDP, compared with the goods-producing sector, which accounted for less than 25%. Service-producing industries grew by 7.0% in 2004–05. Overall, the sector accounted for four-fifths of the growth in real GDP during the same period. One-third of this real GDP growth was attributed to the real estate, rental and leasing industry group and professional and business services, while the finance and insurance industry group made only a limited contribution to sectoral growth in 2005. ICT-producing industries' GDP, which include information and data-processing services as well as computer systems design and related services, increased by 5.6% in 2005, less than one-half of the growth in the previous year. Although comprising only a 4.1% share of GDP, these industries accounted for 10.0% of real GDP growth in 2005.

The other important index of structural change in the US economy is employment in services. Between 1997 and April 2008 employment creation in the USA was concentrated in the service-producing sector; employment in primary activities and manufacturing decreased year-on-year, leaving 100% of net employment growth accounted for by services. Service-producing industries constitute the largest sector, accounting for almost 84% of private establishments in the third quarter of 2007 and over 84% of all employment in April 2008. Employment in the US economy (employees on non-farm payrolls by industry) as a whole increased by 12.2 between 1997 and 2008, but increased by some 15.9% in the service-providing industries division, growing to an estimated 116.2m. employees in April 2008. With about 12.4% of all establishments and 13.3% of employment in service-providing industries, the retail trade division is a major sector, with an estimated 15.4m. employees in April 2008, an increase of 5.7% since 1997. The US Bureau of Labor Statistics identifies financial activities as the median division that represented 10% of all establishments in 2007 and 7.6% of service-providing employment (the industry increased by 15.6% from 1997, to reach an all-time high of more than 8.2m. employees in 2008). The wholesale trade division incorporated 7.2% of establishments in 2007, when it accounted for 4.2% of employment in service-producing industries. Although transportation and warehousing are vital to the efficient day-to-day functioning of the US economy, they comprised a relatively small division, representing approximately 2.6% of all establishments in 2007 and approximately 3.9% of employment in 2008. Finally, employment in the government sector, which included groups such as postal workers and teachers, totalled 22.2m. in 2007. The sector expanded by 12.5% in 1997–2007. Most of the growth took place at state and local level; US federal employment had grown only slowly since 1997.

By 2014 most of the industries expected to be among the 10 fastest growing in terms of wage and salary employment are service-producing. For example, management, scientific and technical consulting services are used as an intermediate input by many industries and are projected to grow as more companies hire consultants for projects related to planning and logistics, compliance with environmental regulations, employee benefits, or compliance with workplace health and safety regulations. Below-average productivity growth and expanding business reliance on temporary help services and employment placement agencies as a way of matching their employment inputs as closely as possible with business cycles also placed employment services in the top 10. Although not in the leading 10, computer systems design and related services purchased as an intermediate input or as an investment will also continue to grow rapidly as the expansion of corporate intranets, an increased need for remote access (for home-based service businesses, for example), and the rising importance of security requirements remain prominent.

The successful record of employment creation by US service businesses reflects a number of factors. Although the widespread adoption of ICT has been shown to raise the productivity of some service industries, limits remain to the achievable improvements. This is especially the case for labour-intensive industries, such as personal services, so that, relative to US manufacturing, the overall productivity growth of the service-producing industries continued to lag and underwrote demand for more labour for any given rate of output growth. The income elasticity of services is also greater than that for goods and, as real incomes continued to increase in the USA, at least prior to the sharp contraction in credit markets in 2007–08, commonly referred to as the 'credit crunch', there was faster growth in demand for service industries' output. Outsourcing of service-related functions by manufacturing and service enterprises has already been identified as a driver of increased demand, while practices such as 24-hour trading by convenience retailers, or the demand for flexible, but often relatively low-paid jobs in the retail and convenience foods sectors, used primarily by students looking to finance their way through university education, also helped to maintain the higher growth rates of service-producing employment.

Service-producing activities have also been a relatively stable source of employment. In all of the service-producing divisions the rate of unemployment declined following the end of the recession of the early 1990s. While the national unemployment rate was 5.5% in June 2008, two service divisions exceeded this level—leisure and hospitality (8.9%) and professional and business services (6.2%)—with retail and wholesale trade just below, at 5.1%. In mid-2008 the lowest rates of unemployment were in financial activities (3.4%) and educational and health services (3.4%). Historically, service-producing industries were less prone to the effects of cyclical changes in the wider economy than manufacturing industries, but more recent evidence suggests that they are cyclical, some more so than others. Health services were the most countercyclical (i.e. they were immune to the effects of recession), along with legal, social, private education, and amusement/recreation services. Cyclical services included engineering and management services, personal services, automotive services, and business and professional services, in which jobs peaked in September 2000 (16.6m.) before decreasing—especially around the time of September 2001—to 16.0m., recovering thereafter, to reach an average of 18.0m. in 2007. During an economic recession consumers are more likely to defer the purchase of a durable good rather than the purchase of a service. Personal consumption accounted for some 70% of GDP in 2007, of which services had accounted for around 55%–60% for at least 15 years, so that any slowdown would have a consequent effect on related employment. The fact that the service sector is no longer exempt from a contraction in the economy was illustrated in late 2007 and 2008, when serious problems caused by the 'credit crunch' in the markets for housing mortgage finance caused property prices to fall and household wealth to decrease, affecting demand for real estate, consumer finance, recreation and tourism, and hospitality services. Thus, within professional and business services, 59,000 jobs in employment services were lost in June 2008, notably in temporary help services. Such declines in service sector employment were unprecedented since the expansion of the US economy in the 1990s ground to a halt. Nevertheless, the lower capital intensity of most service industries also reduced their exposure to the effects of fluctuating interest rates so that, as a group, they generally remained less cyclical. It was also the case that international demand for US services was more consistent than the demand for goods and this contributed to the relative stability of domestic employment in the service-producing industries.

A Service Occupation Perspective

A focus on employment by division or sector somewhat understates the penetration of service-type jobs into the US economy at large. This is better conveyed by examining occupations, for which a broad distinction can be made between white-collar (non-production) and blue-collar (production) jobs. Using a new Standard Occupational Classification System for US employment and wage estimates, the predominance of white-collar occupations is clear: almost 17.3% (23.3m.) of workers were engaged in office and administrative support occupations in 2007, followed by sales and related occupations (10.6%, or 14.3m.). While blue-collar occupations employed just 7.7% (10.4m.) of the 134.4m. people in employment in 2007 (farm and non-farm wage and salary), white-collar occupations, such as health care practitioners and health care support workers (10.3m.), computer and mathematical science occupations (3.2m.), and food preparation and serving related occupations (11.3m.), were very significant groups in their own right. As a rough estimate, in 2007 some 87% of US employees were engaged in white-collar occupations.

The momentum of the structural shift in US industry and occupations towards the service sector, which began during the 1990s, was expected to continue during the first decade of the 21st century. The Bureau of Labor Statistics published industry and occupation projections in 2004 showing that service occupations would continue to be the dominant source of job growth. Professional and related occupations, for example, were projected to increase by almost 6.1m. between 2004 and 2014. Other groups projected to grow faster than average were office and administrative support occupations and management, business and financial occupations; many of these occupations were knowledge- and information-intensive and required the use of advanced telecommunications and computing technology.

Low Wages versus High Wages in Services

One of the consequences of this massive shift in employment towards service-producing industries, and to white-collar work in particular, is the scope for routine work, low levels of remuneration, and limited potential for career advancement. This presumption is encouraged by the 'visibility' of jobs in areas such as retailing, hotels or some aspects of entertainment and tourism-related services, but contradicted to a degree by an average hourly remuneration of almost US $23 for white-collar workers compared with $16 for blue-collar workers. In 2008 there were a number of service-related occupations in which median hourly earnings for more than one-half of the workers were below the mean; examples included food service, personal service and protective service occupations. Mean hourly wages of $8–$11 per hour were well below the national average (of $19.56 per hour). Of the occupations with hourly earnings in the highest 10%, the majority were associated with professional and executive occupations. For the lowest 10% of occupations, average hourly earnings ranged from $6.50 to $10.60, including such service-related occupations as waiters and waitresses (with an average hourly rate of $8.93), bartenders ($9.49) and dishwashers ($8.20), prominent. The low rates of pay for some of these groups were slightly misleading, however, because gratuities were not included in the data. The wide range of cross-occupation compensation should not be allowed to disguise wide within-occupation disparities; in the case of professional and technical occupations, for example, the highest paid occupation received 757% more than the lowest paid occupation.

On the surface, the gap between well and poorly paid service-related occupations in the USA remains wide, but the balance has been slowly shifting towards high-wage service occupations. The rise of knowledge and information as key factors of production has been reflected in a high rate of growth of related occupations that attract the highest remuneration rates, such as executive, administrative and managerial, professional and some sales occupations. As a general rule, low-wage work grew more slowly after 1993. By 2008 more than one-half of all service-producing jobs provided rewards that exceeded the median wage; most new jobs will be similarly distributed. Therefore, it should not be surprising that average service sector remuneration was moving upwards as employers competed for the best qualified and most skilled workers to ensure that their businesses continued to prosper in competitive US domestic and international services markets.

SERVICES AND SPATIAL DEVELOPMENT

Ongoing change in the size and structure of the service-producing sector of the US economy had an impact on the economic geography of the country. It was widely established that the shift to more knowledge- and information-intensive service industries had been accompanied by a tendency for these activities not only to congregate disproportionately in metropolitan areas but also to revitalize many of the country's urban centres. Data from the 2000 US Census showed that cities that had populations greater than 100,000 in 1990 were more likely to have industry profiles dominated by wholesale and retail trade, or finance, insurance and real estate. These cities had also grown much faster than those cities with a large manufacturing base. Cities with more than 90% of the work-force employed in services increased their population by an average of 13.3%, compared with 6.3% for cities with less than 80% of the work-force employed in services, while those with the highest levels of skilled human capital (more than 25% college-educated) also demonstrated the highest population growth rates. Other research has noted that the response of services to labour market characteristics was broadly similar for large and medium-sized US metropolitan areas when compared with the difference between large and small metropolitan areas. Manufacturing concentration, low labour quality and a perception of higher wages were deterrents to growth in services, whereas localization economies (the concentration in one location of firms in a single industry—economies may arise from sharing common infrastructure, creating demand for certain specialized services that would not otherwise be viable) and high-order labour (occupations that usually require higher education qualifications or specialized, often knowledge-based, skills) were significant determinants of the expansion of certain types of service employment in metropolitan areas. These features generally favoured larger cities; those that created, accessed and utilized human capital gained a competitive advantage. This was reinforced in a study of the US health care economy published in 2003: cities and regions with the greatest health care resources, such as the top five (Boston, New York, Philadelphia, Chicago and Los Angeles), would be the big economic winners over the next 20 years or more.

Although the attacks on the World Trade Center on 11 September 2001 seriously affected some leading financial services and other firms, New York remained the US service city par excellence. In 2005 it was still struggling to fend off a prolonged recession that had started in 2001, and nowhere was this more evident than in Manhattan. There were job losses in key global (as distinct from local) economic activities; 45% occurred in financial services, especially commercial banking and securities brokerage, 28% were in professional, scientific and technical services, and 28% in information services. By mid-2006 New York, and Manhattan in particular, had yet to recover to the level of service-based activity characteristic of the period prior to 11 September 2001. However, the city certainly retained the most dynamic and innovative advanced financial, business and professional services complex in the USA. Manhattan was the location for the headquarters of the majority of the top 10 US advertising firms, five of the leading management consulting firms, three of the five largest US accounting firms and one of the largest concentrations of US and international commercial banks in the world. Its status was probably even higher if the role of these firms was measured in terms of their share of global fee income or their specialization in corporate and investment services. The concentration of financial, business and professional services in Manhattan had significant positive consequences for other activities, such as the demand for other services (entertainment, restaurants, etc.) and the attraction of the New York City region for corporate and middle-market headquarters. Many of these advanced services exported their output, not only to the rest of the USA, but also globally, and were a major source of tax and other revenues for New York and the wider region. Other prominent US service cities included Chicago, Los Angeles, Washington, DC (dominated by services linked in various ways to national government functions, which provided a very large proportion of employment), Atlanta and Boston.

There were also regional variations in the expansion or decline of service-producing activities within the USA. The historical economic hegemony of the industrial belt of the north-east had been partially displaced by the 'sunbelt' regions in the south and west. This created problems for the nine-state north-east economic region (Connecticut, Maine, Massachusetts, New Hampshire, New Jersey, New York, Pennsylvania, Rhode Island and Vermont), where there was a sharp decline in the traditional manufacturing employment base of textiles, defence, fisheries and agriculture—especially between 1980 and 1990. This has yet to be counterbalanced by employment growth in, for example, the newer business services sector. Despite a region-wide economic recovery since the early 1990s, many parts of the north-east, including smaller urban centres and towns previously dependent on single major employers, were bypassed. However, the region was extremely well positioned to take advantage of the new service economy: it had the highest concentration of institutions of higher education in the USA, with 489 colleges and universities at the beginning of 2000; basic and applied research were the required ingredients for the development of new services and ways of working; and Route 128 outside Boston had a world-class concentration of information technology (IT) and electronics firms. As biotechnology, medical instrumentation, software development, telecommunications and other knowledge-based industries expanded, higher education institutions created links with the fast-growing number of small firms with new ideas and technologies. Colleges and universities were also anchor institutions for their local communities, generating demand for services (and goods) as well as capital and technical assistance, which supported economic renewal.

The changing geography of US service industries was also evidenced by a shift from metropolitan to non-metropolitan areas. Business and professional services led the way, although the absolute share of the non-metropolitan areas is still relatively modest. The changes took two forms: relocation and expansion in the smaller communities (edge cities) near to large metropolitan areas such as Atlanta, Seattle and Chicago; or higher relative growth in rural counties distant from the well-established metropolitan service agglomerations. A study of the factors explaining decentralization of knowledge- and information-intensive activities, such as business or computer services, to the suburbs or edge cities, rather than to remote rural counties in the USA, found that agglomeration economies, local incomes, and the size and growth of service and government markets were all statistically significant determinants of location behaviour. Communities in remote rural counties could not match these requirements, especially if factors such as proximity to executive housing, suburban office rents, availability of suitable office space for lease, or the availability of a female labour force were included in the analysis. These would have confirmed even more strongly the attraction of the suburbs over remote rural counties for service industries relocating from the central cities.

A combination of demographic changes and the developments in ICT introduced some interesting trends in the supply of higher order producer services. Improved life expectancy, early retirement and an increased proportion of households with large retirement income or personal wealth spawned single-owner or micro-businesses that provided high-value, knowledge-intensive services. Many of these were located in remote rural communities that, in reality, were just as attuned to the national or international economy as any US metropolitan area, owing to the access facilitated by ICT. Similar opportunities existed for younger professionals and others who lost their jobs as a result of corporate downsizing or who decided to supply their specialist knowledge and skills on a self-employed basis. Provided that the ICT infrastructure was available, these individuals could take advantage of lower land or housing costs in rural communities while also enjoying a quality of life that, for many, was far superior to that found in the major service agglomerations. The terms 'high fliers' and 'lone eagles' have been coined for these two groups of mainly service workers that have transformed the economic health of small communities in states with high quality environmental amenities such as Utah, Idaho, Colorado and New Mexico. However, rural parts more widely did continue to lag behind their metropolitan counterparts in capturing the best slice of the service sector—high-skill, high-wage jobs. Even though during the 1990s rural earnings from service-producing industries rose annually by 3.5%, they still fell behind equivalent growth in metropolitan areas. The difference was largely owing to producer service industries, which accounted for only 9% of earnings, although rural earnings growth in recreation and consumer services did outpace the growth in the cities.

Inter-regional Trade in Services

By the very nature of the knowledge-intensive services offered by 'lone eagles' and 'high fliers', it was unlikely that their output would be consumed locally. There was, for example, only very limited demand in the rural counties for high-level management consultancy advice so that much of the output of these services, and indeed much of that originating in metropolitan centres, was, of necessity, traded between localities and regions across the USA. This contradicted the long-held view that service-producing industries were non-basic: they functioned in the local or regional economy as support for the basic goods-related activities that were engaged in inter-regional trade. The latter were supposed to be the source of the revenues (taxes and employee incomes) that stimulated the demand for services.

The fact that services, in their own right, could also perform a basic role in regional development has been illustrated in a number of US studies over the last 20 years. These demonstrated the scope for a more positive attitude towards the restructuring of the economy towards services: they offered new opportunities for the economic development of towns and cities, and a realistic way of compensating for the declining share of manufacturing—especially as the adoption of ICT facilitated interaction between places and regions, from the very smallest to the very largest. In broad terms, producer (or intermediate) services, such as advertising, architectural design, computing, research and development, real estate, management consulting or transport services, were more export-orientated than consumer services, such as retail banking, food stores or equipment rental services, which relied for a larger proportion of their revenues on sales to local clients. Overall, inter-regional service trade was considerable, at around 35% of the total sales of service-producing industries, and rising. While the indirect role of services in regional development should not be overlooked, it was clear that their direct or basic contribution was also significant.

US SERVICES IN THE GLOBAL ECONOMY

The importance of service-producing industries to the domestic economic scene was matched by their contribution to the international dimension of the US economy. Some 65% of US services sales to foreign markets in 2005 were via foreign affiliates of US companies. The value of exports of services was about 43% of the value of goods exports for 2005, but while there had been a long-standing deficit in the latter, trade in private services had been notable for a surplus every year since 1970. In 2007, according to the Bureau of Economic Analysis, there was a positive services trade balance of US $119,115m., compared with a huge $819,373m. deficit for goods. The performance of services reflected the significant competive advantage of many US service-producing activities, including financial services, insurance, telecommunications services, advertising, computer and information services, management consulting, research and development services, legal, accounting and other professional services, among others. Travel and tourism accounted for 19.5% of service exports in 2007, with other private services (including business and professional services) accounting for a massive 45.0%. Over one-half of the surplus was therefore created by 'other private services'. US service firms had been able to accrue significant home country advantages as a result of servicing a large, geographically extensive and increasingly demanding US market before addressing the challenges of supplying services in new, and sometimes very different, international markets. The United Kingdom (11.8%) and Japan (10.2%) were the main destinations for US private service exports in 2007, with the former also the principal source (12.0%) of US service imports; the USA achieved service trade surpluses with almost all its major trading partners.

Regulatory restrictions or controls on the cross-border movement of skilled personnel, for example, made it difficult for some services, such as legal and other professional services or hotel services, to operate in other countries. There was, therefore, a need to establish a commercial presence via foreign direct investment (FDI). The industries with the fastest growing FDI (outward stock) during the last decade have included public utilities, communications, car rental, business, and financial (excluding banking) services. Sales of private services by non-bank majority-owned foreign affiliates of US companies in 2005 exceeded US $574,664m., continuing a tendency to move ahead of revenues from cross-border exports ($332,000m. in 2004) in evidence since the second half of the 1990s. Overseas service-producing activities were also increasingly involved in FDI in the USA. The securities and communications industries experienced the most rapid growth in inbound foreign investment stock in the 1990s, but data for 2005 showed that information services, wholesale trade, financial services (except depository institutions) and insurance were very prominent. Manufacturing accounted for just 37% of inward investment to the USA in 2005. The outlook for services trade and FDI will depend on three factors: the strength of the US economy as measured by the growth of real GDP; the growth rate of major trading partners; and the international value of the US dollar. From early 2002 the growth of the US economy was slower than expected, with a risk of recession by the end of 2008, reflecting domestic factors (including the repercussions of the events of September 2001 and the credit crisis of 2007–08) and wider global trends. The size of the services trade surplus contracted between 2000 and 2003, but improved thereafter. Service export growth began to recover after 2003, but recent growth has slowed as a result of domestic uncertainties, as well as a global slowdown caused by sharp increases in food, crude petroleum and other energy prices.

A frequently used method for achieving a foreign, as well as a domestic, presence was through mergers and acquisitions (M&A). US and European Union service-producing firms accounted for over 80% of global M&A during the 1990s. The formidable dynamism of M&A in the service sector was explained largely by the series of consolidations and privatizations that followed deregulation (for example, in air transport). The telecommunications and transportation industries, following deregulation and liberalization earlier in the decade, experienced a significant increase in M&A, stimulated by both the traditional strategic considerations of cost savings and economies of scale and by the need to accumulate the large financial resources required to cover the very high costs of acquiring third generation mobile telephone licences in Europe. Services M&A tend to affect different sectors at different times; thus, in 2005 it increased dramatically among media and information services, reaching levels not seen since 2000. The year saw 525 deals completed, totalling US $56,000m. in value, across 11 media sectors. Major media companies, led by key sectors such as exhibitions and conferences, marketing and interactive services and online media services, pursued growth through acquisitions as mass changes in media consumption led them to invest in digital technology. Diversified media companies, such as Gannett, New York Times, Dow Jones and News Corporation, were rapidly acquiring fast growing online content and delivery channels to offset pressure on their traditional media products.

The Importance of Deregulation and Liberalization of Trade in Services

Given its prominence in international traded services and investment, the USA was an influential voice within the North American Free Trade Agreement (NAFTA—signed in 1992 with Canada and Mexico) and in the negotiations embraced by the General Agreement on Trade in Services (GATS—established in 1995). The GATS framework functions under the umbrella of the World Trade Organization (WTO) and seeks trade in services obligations for specific sectors, such as telecommunications or financial services, from signatories to 'most-favoured nation' status, national treatment, or market access agreements.

Progress on actual liberalization as opposed to modes of negotiation was very slow, with many of the developing countries reluctant to make more flexible commitments on services in the belief that these would enable some US service-producing industries, which had already achieved higher productivity levels than their international competitors, to capitalize further on their competitive advantage. Most of the multilateral agreements to date had retained the status quo so that new barriers or regulations that would discourage trade in the relevant services would not be introduced. Forecasts suggest that comprehensive trade liberalization in services would boost global GDP by some 4%–6% and long-term global growth by 5%. During the Doha Round of negotiations, which included services, the USA lobbied for deeper liberalization in professional services, air transport services, telecommunications, financial services (banks, insurance and securities firms), entertainment, tourism and education. In mid-2008 the impasse that had dogged the Round for more than a year seemed to have eased marginally, at least as regards services. A ministerial-level 'signalling conference' on services, which was intended to encourage some major economies, such as the USA, clearly to demonstrate their intention to offer improved commitments, was held in July, although the resulting proposals had still to be translated into agreements, while disagreements on agriculture remained unresolved. Apart from the reluctance of fast-growing emerging economies to grant access to US service-providers, another major impediment to service agreements between the USA and partners like Brazil, India and the People's Republic of China was its own domestic regulation of services, such as telecommunications, banking and insurance. US banking regulation, for example, involved the separate but overlapping jurisdictions of the federal Government and the 50 states, three federal regulators (the Federal Reserve System, the Federal Deposit Insurance Corporation and the Office of the Comptroller of the Currency) and other categories of depository institutions (savings and loans, savings banks and credit unions). There were signs during 2008 that the US position on trade in services was softening a little, since the national economy will lose out if there is no resolution to the deep-seated difficulties that have hampered services trade negotiations for many years.

The Vulnerabilities of the US Service Economy

There was a general consensus that service industries survive downturns in the economy better than manufacturing industries. However, the repercussions of the terrorist attacks of September 2001 adversely affected large swathes of the US service economy. This included not just the more obvious activities, such as airline and tourism-related services, but also insurance, freight, customs and immigration, and security services. For some of these it was a case of more careful scrutiny of passengers that imposed delays and additional costs for the individuals and corporations affected. In the case of the US insurance industry (as well as overseas insurers providing cover for corporations and others in the USA) a re-evaluation of attitudes towards risk and the calculation of the costs to clients of providing appropriate levels of cover was necessary. From 2002 most of the major insurance companies were wrestling with massive claims, both actual and potential (depending on the outcome of litigation that might take years or the fact that the health consequences for the insured survivors of the September 2001 terrorist attacks might not become apparent for 10–20 years), which could threaten their very existence as viable businesses.

The impact of the events of 11 September 2001 on some service industries was less obvious than for others. Perhaps the most closely documented were the travails of US airline services, which, owing to a booming US economy during the second half of the 1990s, witnessed rapid increases in passenger volumes and profitable operations in a competitive and deregulated marketplace. The civil aviation industry accounted for 5.2% of national GDP in 2000. A mild economic recession from early 2001 posed questions about the sustainability of airline services' growth and signs of retrenchment were emerging: the attacks of 11 September accelerated an emerging trend. Losses of US $3,000m. for 2001 had been predicted before the attacks; these were immediately revised to $7,000m. as revenue passenger miles, both domestic and international, fell by 35%–40% during September and October 2001. Every region of the USA was affected, but revenues declined most where the economic recession hit hardest and where travel alternatives were well established—notably in the north-east. The airline companies responded by reducing their schedules by 15% during the fourth quarter of 2001. The airlines also reduced the number of new aircraft on order, thus triggering further economic malaise in other industries and regions. Job growth among US airline companies was impressive in the late 1990s, but few were able to avoid staff reductions after September 2001; United Airlines and US Airways announced staff cuts of 20% and 24%, respectively. By mid-2002 overall job losses were estimated at 95,000. Although passenger numbers showed some signs of recovery in 2002, this was not enough to prevent US Airways filing for bankruptcy protection in August of that year, followed by United Airlines in December. All the major US carriers posted massive first-quarter losses in 2003 as they continued to struggle with sluggish demand for travel (both domestic and international) and declining revenues. The five largest carriers lost a total of $3,500m. during the first three months of the year. The ongoing conflict in Iraq from early 2003 and the SARS (Severe Acute Respiratory Syndrome) epidemic during that year created further uncertainty in an operating environment that was already extremely difficult. A study published in August 2002 noted that 45% of US service industry CEOs did not expect profit growth until well into 2003; this was probably overoptimistic because of steep rises in fuel costs and the impact of 'Hurricane Katrina' in 2005.

Nevertheless, passenger numbers and load factors recovered steadily; US airlines carried 307.9m. scheduled domestic and international passengers during the first five months of 2007, 1.8% more than during the same period in 2006. Although the operating environment remained challenging, the outlook was encouraging, but the sharp rise in aviation (and other) fuel prices in early 2008 was a major economic shock, possibly greater than that which followed the September 2001 attacks. US airlines expended nearly 50% more on jet fuel in 2008 (US $61,000m.) than they did in 2007 ($41,000m.) and many passenger and freight carriers had to adapt quickly in order to survive. They did this by drastically reducing flight schedules well into 2009, with fewer daily flights to many cities (for example, Portland, Maine, and Colorado Springs, Colorado), and by withdrawing scheduled flights to regional airports such as Lexington, Kentucky, and Idaho Falls, Idaho.

The fluctuating demand for US air services was reflected in, among other things, reduced demand for tourism-related travel. For example, there were important links between air travel and the prospects of the cruise industry. Much of the activity centred on ports such as Miami, Anchorage, Long Beach, San Francisco, New Orleans, New York and Boston. Apart from directly and indirectly supporting some 330,346 jobs in 2005, the cruise industry contributed to the tourism economy by way, for example, of local port-user fees, head taxes and surcharges, purchase of supplies and services such as pilots, tugboat services, waste disposal services, fuel supply services, and hotel, restaurant and retail services. However, the fortunes of the US cruise industry were intimately linked to the airline industry; it was the second largest purchaser of US airline tickets (over US $2,100m. in 2000) and was highly dependent on the airlines for assembling its passengers at the appropriate departure ports. Lowered confidence in air travel and reductions in route coverage, frequency and capacity were all unexpected obstacles to a recovery in the aftermath of September 2001. Following robust growth in 2004, passenger growth at US ports was slightly lower, at 6.3%, in 2005. Consequently, the growth in total industry spending (of $16,180m.) declined to 10% in 2005, but because the growth in spending exceeded the growth in embarcations, total expenditures by the industry (by cruise lines and passengers) on a per passenger basis increased from $1,553 in 2004 to $1,667 in 2005. This certainly helped to create significant employment, income and other economic benefits.

International travel (excluding Canada and Mexico) into the USA decreased by 15% in 2001 and by 10% in 2002, although there were signs of recovery during the fourth quarter of 2002. The volume of international tourist arrivals achieved in the first quarter of 2000 (5,545,137) was not yet matched in the first quarter of 2007 (4,893,413) or in the first quarter of 2008 (5,384,961). Total overseas arrivals to the USA in the first quarter of 2007 were almost 12% lower compared with the first quarter of 2000 and were only 4.6% higher than in 2005. This would have a significant impact on the tourist economies of key destinations such as Las Vegas, Miami or New York. Prior to 11 September 2001 tourism in the city of New York was worth US $25,000m. annually (equivalent to $3,100 for every resident). The industry supported 282,000 jobs directly and indirectly and produced more than $3,000m. in city, state and federal tax revenues. Tourism services expanded as steadily as the business, professional and financial services that are the other pillars of the New York economy. However, in the month immediately after 11 September it was estimated that visitor spending fell by more than $270m., with the consequences felt by hotels, restaurants (30 closed permanently) and the city's cultural institutions, theatres and attractions. A large proportion of the services firms affected were small and would find it hardest to stave off the effects of marked reductions in demand. Moreover, not only were contractions experienced in tourism in the city, but the primary driver of its economy, its financial, insurance and real estate services (approximately 14% of the city's work-force), also suffered significant short-term disruption and longer-term uncertainty. Following the destruction of the World Trade Center many financial firms relocated from the city (some 50,000 jobs were relocated outside Manhattan, many in New Jersey). There was doubt as to whether these companies would return. Some have already done so, but those that did not follow would threaten the critical mass of the New York financial, insurance and real estate sector, as well as sending 'ripple' effects through the rest of the economy as a consequence of lower tax revenues or reduced demand for the commercial office space, restaurant, hotel and numerous other services that are part of its world-class corporate complex.

There are also other ways in which US service industries looked vulnerable during the first decade of the 21st century. The problems encountered by professional service companies following the disclosure of questionable accountancy practices by major US enterprises, such as Enron Corporation, WorldCom and Tyco International, gave rise to concerns about the adequacy of the corporate regulatory environment in the USA, especially the relationships between big corporations and their advisers (many of which were service firms). These were addressed by the Sarbanes-Oxley Act (also known as the Public Company Accounting Reform and Investor Protection Act) of 2002, but the scandals undermined the reputation of the industry upon which many leading US service firms traded so successfully, both within and beyond the national market. Consequently, this made them vulnerable to mergers and takeovers from rival firms in other major markets such as Europe, and may eventually translate into a slowdown in growth for US international service exports, as the United Kingdom, which offers a relatively less rigorous regulatory environment, becomes even more attractive to US service firms, and an increase in imports.

The demand for a whole range of services, from financial to travel and tourism, was significantly affected by the 'sub-prime' mortgage crisis in 2007–08, which began in the USA and ultimately had far-reaching impacts on the global economy and the market for services. This crisis, in which a boom in house prices became unsustainable and foreclosures began to escalate among high-risk (sub-prime) borrowers, resulted in major losses for banks and other financial institutions. This, in turn, led the financial institutions to offer fewer housing and other loans at higher rates of interest, with the net effect of creating downward pressure on US economic growth because of declining investment by consumers and businesses. The consequences for service industries were manifold; between mid-2007 and May 2008 US financial institutions laid off some 43,000 workers, with major companies such as Merrill Lynch announcing the termination of 2,900 jobs by the end of 2008, joined by others such as Bear Stearns (who reported some 14,000 job losses), Washington Mutual (3,000) and Wachovia (500). Far from being a source of stability within the US economy, service industries became a source of instability and uncertainty, with the potential for further job losses, declining incomes and changes in consumer spending behaviour.

Services were also implicated in the growing concern in the USA over the movement of business functions overseas. The types of services vulnerable to 'offshoring' tended to be those that were capable of being performed at a distance and transacted using ICT, such as software programming and design, accounting and payroll operations, call centres, paralegal services or records management. 'Offshoring' is the practice, by companies or government entities, of replacing services previously produced domestically within the USA with services produced abroad. Advances in ICT and improvements in the management of business processes, coupled with a large pool of educated workers in other countries, allowed companies to move service work 'offshore' as part of the ongoing process of globalization. This was not a new phenomenon; it was previously primarily confined to manufacturing, but from about 2002 it became evident that a growing number of white-collar jobs in the USA were also being displaced as service firms chose suppliers or invested in new facilities in the Philippines, Ireland, the Caribbean, India or the People's Republic of China. One estimate suggested that some 340,000 office and administrative, business, financial, sales and management jobs would be moved 'offshore' annually between 2000 and 2015, resulting in growing anxiety about the effects on the economy, work-force, consumer privacy and national security. However, this would amount to only 0.3% of total non-farm employment. The veracity of this and other estimates was difficult to judge; official trade and other statistics lagged behind the process, although early indications from the Bureau of Labor Statistics were that between 2001 and 2004 the loss of service jobs was approximately 240,000, or less than one-third of the equivalent figures for manufacturing.

It is unlikely that the 'offshoring' of US service jobs would cease because of a groundswell of public and political opposition. The internet and high-speed/high-capacity data-transfer networks transformed the ability of US-based service firms to use their capital resources in a more cost-effective manner than previously. However, the process of 'offshoring' was not only about the cost advantages of sub-contracting call-centre services or software production to countries such as India; the quality and reliability of the services delivered were also enhanced. Such globalization of service production should be seen as an opportunity for US services rather than a threat. Businesses that outsource could concentrate on what they did best, releasing resources for the development of innovative services that made use of the high skill levels in the USA. Such an international division of service labour was nothing new; the key was to ensure that investment was made in high-quality education and training in the USA in order that major service firms could capitalize on their core competencies, leaving less-skilled, lower-remunerated service tasks to producers in other parts of the world. It is also important to note that 'offshoring' by US service businesses was counterbalanced by inward flows of service jobs, usually by transnational service corporations that were attracted by the quality of US infrastructure, the knowledge and skills of its labour force, and an environment that was conducive to doing business.

IN A COMPLICATED STATE: HEALTH AND WELFARE POLICY IN THE USA

Prof. CALUM PATON

INTRODUCTION: US IDEOLOGIES AND POLITICAL ECONOMY IN HEALTH AND WELFARE POLICY

The mainstream ideologies in the USA, which affect the mores of the nation (and which provide a general political backdrop to the context in which health and social welfare policy are made at the beginning of the 21st century), are neo-liberalism and conservatism. Recently, the USA became more polarized between conservatism and liberalism than at any time perhaps since the 'New Deal' welfare programme implemented under President Franklin Roosevelt (1933–45) in the 1930s. While until recently there was a perceived conservative hegemony, the nation-wide split illustrated by the presidential election result in 2004 shows that, while George W. Bush clearly regained the presidency for the Republicans, Democratic candidate John Kerry attracted a high popular vote in an increased turn-out. In the new popular orthodoxy, the USA's east and west coasts are liberal (excepting the south), while the heartlands that lie between are conservative. How the 2008 contest for the presidency between the Democrat Barack Obama and the Republican John McCain will affect health and welfare policy remains to be seen.

The conservative/liberal divide is reasonably well-mirrored by the Republican/Democrat divide (unlike in the earlier part of the 20th century when conservative Democrats and liberal Republicans were both salient, not least because party affiliation was to a large extent based upon the political, social and racial map of the USA). There are still conservative Democrats, but they tend to reflect the class and social structure of the areas they represent, along with a nation-wide conservative political economy, rather than the earlier North/South/West divisions.

Neo-liberalism refers to the compromises liberalism has made with a conservative political economy in order to remain politically viable; however, in the case of conservatism, the prefix 'neo' is eschewed as a generalization for two reasons. First, the term 'neo-conservatism' has been co-opted as a label for the messianic approach to global affairs that wishes to export 'US democracy-lite' around the globe (itself a misunderstanding of the original neo-conservatives' stance on foreign affairs—see below). Second, conservatism in the US sense (entailing free markets, market forces in what remains of the public sector and individualism—minimizing progressive state action) has been strengthened, not compromised in recent years, at the level of social and cultural ideology.

Health and Welfare

In the case of health care and welfare programmes, the nature of the Republican/Democrat division is not always a good indicator of the parties' respective policies. Some of the 'new Republicans' are blue-collar workers with anxieties about health care and its costs. Meanwhile, some of the Democrats' policies are only incrementally different from those of the Republicans, although in 2007 the main Democratic presidential contenders stressed the need for public regulation to achieve universal health care. One of President George W. Bush's (2001–) remaining claims to be a moderate (that is, a high-spending) Republican is actually in the field of health care. In general terms, his record on 'government spending and deficits bears resemblance to that of President Ronald Reagan's (1981–89). While preaching the virtues of financial orthodoxy he has, in practice, been a 'super-Keynesian'—albeit a right-wing one—with high defence spending and 'special programmes' for supporters comprising part of the package. Indeed, John McCain has campaigned on a platform of fiscal orthodoxy which is, in effect, a repudiation of the Bush approach.

As regards welfare reform, the landmark legislation of recent years was the Personal Responsibility and Work Opportunities Reconciliation Act, signed into law by Bush's predecessor, Bill Clinton (1993–2001), in 1996. This represented a neo-liberal/conservative compromise and formed the basis for the approach of the next significant revision of welfare, signed by Bush in early 2006 (the Deficit Reduction Act, which reauthorized the Temporary Assistance to Needy Families programme). Clinton's Act had, of course, reflected federal political realities from 1994 to 2000 (a Democratic President, but both chambers of Congress controlled by the Republicans). However, the legislation also symbolized moves 'from welfare to workfare' elsewhere in the developed world, irrespective of whether the party of the right or left was in power.

Especially from the early 1990s, traditional liberalism declined, while neo-liberalism resembled conservatism in its scepticism towards government spending and (particularly) the taxation necessary to fund it. 'Big Government' was no longer on the agenda (Osborne and Gaebler, 1993—see Select Bibliography, Social Affairs), and mainstream Democrats expressed increasing interest in making limited government work better. The new orthodoxy was concerned with 'freeing up' bureaucracy. By the late 1990s neo-liberalism was conservative: President Clinton's platform for his second term—and his actions when re-elected—were geared to defending Medicare (the health care programme for those over 65 years of age and certain categories of disabled people) and social security against the right's attrition. For example, he proposed to use budget surpluses (general revenues) to try to solve the alleged fiscal crisis of Medicare (seen by many as a contributory programme within social security). This reflected liberal difficulty in mobilizing 'middle America' in defence of social programmes, making liberalism seem 'conservative' in the sense of holding onto the past—resisting an ebbing tide rather than taking the lead for the future. Theda Skocpol in *The Missing Middle* (see Select Bibliography, Social Affairs) has suggested that the mainstream USA has an interest in social programmes to aid families, employment and children, but that 'left-of-centre' political programmes have not adequately articulated this.

It would, nevertheless, be fair to describe the US executive's health policy proposals under President Bush as neo-conservative, rather than just conservative, as long as the term is used carefully. The term neo-conservative is overused and therefore ambiguous. In foreign affairs, the neo-conservatives of the mid-20th century believed in (limited) foreign intervention and strength vis-à-vis the USSR, yet curbed pretensions for the USA's role in the world. The conservative academic and former government adviser Samuel P. Huntington conforms to these beliefs. The term neo-conservatism has its origins in the messianic world of (lapsed) Marxists, who, in their disillusionment with the USSR, also abandoned their leftist creed. They moved to the right of the political spectrum, bypassing in the process US liberalism—especially in its international form of working through international institutions and coalitions on the basis of consensus and 'détente', where possible. It thus refers in foreign affairs to the world-wide (but partial) promulgation of 'democracy and freedom US-style', often on a unilateral basis—and may therefore be seen as the other side of the coin of Republican 'isolationism'. In effect, neo-conservatives come from the tradition of US 'exceptionalism' (the former Marxists, as well as traditional liberal theorists of US exceptionalism such as Louis Hartz, came to see the values of the USA as special when they became disillusioned with the USSR), an ideology that rejects both the left and European conservatism. It engages with European liberalism in the sense of individualism and capitalism but emphasizes the unique setting of the USA, both domestically ('the endless frontier') and internationally. Regarding the latter, the difference is that the USA's global role—the imperial role, as both left and right may perceive it—reinforces a messianic creed: a serious version of the Scots' humorous 'here's tae us—wha's like us'.

Consequently, neo-conservatism has become capitalist liberalism 'at the point of a gun'. It thus firmly eschews US liberalism if the latter means, as it does in conventional US political discourse, the alternative to US conservatism, which is a bundle of contradictions: capitalist but protectionist (i.e. 'national capitalist'); individualist but socially illiberal; and alternatively isolationist (e.g. Bush prior to the terrorist attacks of 11 September 2001 on New York and Washington, DC) and unilaterally interventionist (common to both traditional conservatism and neo-conservatism).

In domestic policy, however, neo-conservatism still has some affinity with its roots as an engagement with, albeit mostly rejection of, the left (i.e. the changing views of former socialists who came to reject 1960s US liberalism's allegedly 'big state'—one might say, a state of high ambition but low autonomy from traditional social practice and dominant social interests). This engagement consists domestically of its attempt at least to consider social justice—or rather social protection—rather than to relegate it, as does traditional 'right-wing conservatism', even if that consideration leads to a rejection of traditional statism.

Social protection is now to be pursued in a market context rather than statist context, yet may call for state steering, and even regulation, which is opposed to the minimalist stance of traditional US conservatism. That is, just as neo-liberalism has taken conservatism on board, neo-conservatism has taken liberalism on board. This is especially true in health policy (at least, in Bush's rhetoric and parts of his spending record) and in education, which are both viewed as the foundation of opportunity in the 'competition state' (Jessop, 2002).

That said, it is nevertheless true that—even where Bush's proposals were for the expansion of Medicare (for example, extension of the availability of prescription drugs—see below), or the transformation of social security and, in particular, pensions—the policy direction was conservative. Bush's basic assumption—that social security is in crisis owing to its unaffordability—has been powerfully challenged (Marmor and Mashaw, 2006). If we look not just at senior citizens but at the total 'social security' population (including those under 20 years of age), the picture is a different one.

In addition, reforming social security by diminishing what Europeans call solidarity (that is, protecting the poor as well as giving a reasonable rate of return to better-off workers who contribute more) ultimately leads to a 'receive as you pay' welfare state, which leaves the poorest dependent upon tax-funded, means-tested programmes, charity, or nothing at all. President Bush's proposals for pension reform were resoundingly defeated in 2007 as his so-called 'lame duck' presidency neared its end; however, their ethos was one of diminishing solidarity.

Thus, we can trace similarities between conservatism and neo-liberalism, and/or between Republicans and Democrats, in terms of aspects of health and welfare policy. However, we should not ignore the ideological divide between those who seek more individualistic and market-driven initiatives and those who seek to preserve or extend social solidarity.

Far from being an unaffordable luxury in a cut-throat era of global capitalism, social security and public health insurance are the economic and social adhesives that make market capitalism viable, as Marmor and Mashaw suggest.

US Ideology in General and Particular: The Line from US Exceptionalism to Health Care in 2008

US (as opposed to European or classical) liberalism consists of a belief in government intervention to help the poor. Unlike European social democracy or British 'Old Labour', it does not generally involve notions of public ownership, public provision or even 'corporatism', whereby social partners (employers and employees) work with the state. Instead, it is concerned with the provision of greater equality of opportunity and the avoidance of domination of the economy by monopolistic and special interests. US conservatism consists of a belief in unfettered markets and a *laissez-faire* approach to social policy. Emphasis on voluntaristic and private solutions to social problems is strong in this ideology. To that extent, the earlier policy of President George Bush, Sr (1989–93), of using private and religious sources for social welfare provision, was well within traditional US conservatism. US conservatism generally lacks the paternalistic strand evident in certain European variants. Thus, the concept of, for example, a national health service is unpalatable to US conservatives in a way that it is not to many mainstream British conservatives. On the other hand, the so-called 'New Right' believes in 'moralistic' diktat on issues like abortion, and is generally illiberal (if liberalism means personal choice regarding lifestyle), with the exception of its libertarian strand.

The conservative coalition in the USA, particularly following the terrorist attacks of 11 September 2001, showed signs of the greater influence of the moralistic forces of the so-called 'sunbelt' states (the southern tier of US states), which are often allied to the naked self-interest expressed in anti-environmentalism and protectionism when it suits the USA. However, this may also have the effect that conservatism, as economic laissez-faire, combined with a good dose of social libertarianism, is against the spirit of the age. Indeed, such an ideology is often perceived as 'liberal' in today's USA, especially given liberalism's much lesser identification (post-Clinton) with 'Big Government' and economic planning. In the 21st century conservatism may be becoming 'USA first' on the basis of the often religious nationalism of the world's only superpower, which, paradoxically, perceives itself as under attack in all senses, but also on the basis of economic protectionism, which unites certain categories of employer and worker.

In this environment, the 'compassionate conservatism' of President George W. Bush can be seen as rhetoric, as a creed that is difficult to classify by European standards, or as a political response to cross-cutting constituencies implied by the analysis in the previous paragraph. In Europe, compassionate conservatism might conjure up images of moderation and 'centrism'. In the USA, however, a compassionate conservative may be a Christian fundamentalist with extreme right-wing views on many social issues, a 'populist conservative' on economic and employment/welfare issues, or both. That is, using Lowi's (1964; 1997) or Paton's (1990) typologies of US public policy, there are four dimensions of policy: redistributive (Lowi) and/or social and economic planning (Paton); distributive (Lowi); regulatory (Lowi) and/or 'formal rights' (Paton); and (right-wing) moralistic (Lowi). Bush's neo-conservatism is moralistic, anti-regulatory (in theory), yet interventionist, in terms of certain rights, which include (limited) extensions of access to social programmes. If we accept former US Speaker of the House of Representatives Tip O'Neill's dictum that 'all politics is local', of course, then both Republicans and Democrats may be found talking free trade yet enacting protectionism when it suits. Indeed, the aspiration behind protectionism may not always be unworthy: the challenge is to develop international agreement on such matters.

Of course, ideologically based attitudes to the health care system (and health care reform), and to the welfare and pensions system, may be significant. Greater reliance on voluntary provision may appeal on religious grounds to the right and on economic grounds to both libertarians and parts of the business lobby; and new programmes emphasize market mechanisms rather than state planning. Political deadlock at the national level meant delays in the implementation of health care reform in the first two years of Bush's first term in office, but there were more opportunities from 2003 onwards, given unified Republican control of the executive and both houses of Congress, in the context of greater partisanship in recent years. (Although such unity should not be overstated: note the attempt of the legislature to pare back President Bush's proposed US $15,000m. AIDS programme for Africa in July 2003.) Between 2003 and 2006 there were two significant health initiatives: Medicare reform (or rather, extension, allowing 'compassionate conservative' to be more than rhetoric) and the 'Health Savings Account' policy.

With the 2008 presidential election approaching, there were numerous proposals for 'universal healthcare' from leading Democrat presidential contenders John Edwards, Hillary Clinton and Barack Obama. These proposals, however, started with pre-existing private health care schemes. The uninsured would be covered mainly by extending the reach of existing programmes, increasing continuity for those who change employment, mandating business to 'play or pay' (offer insurance to their workers or pay into a fund for those without it), and expanding government programmes for those still left without coverage. Edwards was the first candidate to propose a substantial proposal for national health insurance. Clinton's chastening experience in 1993/94 as head of her husband's presidential task-force to develop national health insurance legislation caused her to be more cautious this time around, until Obama's success against her in the primaries and caucuses led her to occupy a more populist, 'liberal' (i.e. left-of-centre) stance, with a more radical approach to reforming health care, including more comprehensive national health insurance. Her original caution was for tactical reasons in two senses: to avoid being presented by her detractors as replicating a failed strategy; and to give the proposal more of a chance of receiving approval in Congress, where integrated social reform is very difficult to pass. The four main eras of attempted health reform over the last century or so—the progressive era at the end of the 19th century; the 'New Deal' of the 1930s; Harry S. Truman's reform attempts after the Second World War; and President Richard Nixon's (1969–74) proposed legislation in the early 1970s (Marmor, 2007)—serve to demonstrate the structural, institutional and ideological difficulties of passing such legislation (Paton, 1990), even when there is a majority in favour of it, at least initially.

Following Obama's victory over Clinton in the race for the 2008 Democratic presidential nomination, it is possible to compare the Democratic (Obama) approach with the Republican (McCain) approach. Indeed, they are both typical of their parties on this issue, so it is more useful to do so now than when presidential candidates are outliers on the issue—as Clinton (to the left) would have been, and as was Bush (also to the left on this issue, though less perceptibly).

As ever, there is a gap between the aspirations or policies of presidential candidates and the stuff of congressional practice and realism. (See below for the main congressional bills of recent years—although there was no major enactment.)

Welfare reform in recent years has consisted mainly of a more restrictive version of the 1996 Act signed by Bill Clinton, signed into law by President Bush in February 2006. The Bush Administration made pensions reform ('the cost of the social security system') a major part of its prospectus for its second term; however, by 2006 significant reform was stymied both by disagreement in society and in Congress about the nature (and scale) of reform, and (perhaps more significantly) by the President's waning authority. In the last years of Bush's presidency, his (mostly conservative) welfare reform ambitions fell victim to Democratic ascendancy in Congress, and his status as a so-called 'lame duck' President was enhanced by several factors: the political fallout from the continued US military occupation of Iraq; the public perception that he was out of step with changing opinion on issues like climate change; and the continuing deterioration of the economy from May 2008 onwards.

Nevertheless, the spectrum of opinion, running from liberalism to conservatism, is both narrower and more right-wing in mainstream US politics. With the 'Clintonization' of the Democratic Party in the 1990s, it could further be argued that there was a greater rapprochement between pragmatic liberalism and neo-conservatism, evidenced by the appointment of leading conservative Democrats to significant economic portfolios in the first-term Cabinet of President Clinton, and even Republicans in his second Administration. Other sources of convergence between liberalism and conservatism in US health care included the generally acknowledged need for a corporate rationalization of the health care system to allow national priorities and (slightly) greater equity to be rendered compatible with cost control, and the move from welfare to workfare noted above.

Clinton's health proposals during the 1992 presidential election campaign found initial support in the business community, as well as among the traditional Democratic constituency, on the grounds that cost control was also necessary to control the costs to businesses of providing extremely expensive health care to their employees. This coalition soon vanished, however (Paton, 1997), as perceptions of crisis proved as fleeting as ever in a land where normal politics is manufactured as optimism, and as swathes of the insurance industry mobilized against the proposed legislation. Furthermore, cost control in health care in the USA has been addressed in different ways. The Clinton Plan of 1993/94 really did offer a European-style national health insurance—albeit with more genuflection to the pro-market right than the European social model.

However, the most powerful source of attempted cost control has been through managed care. Managed care refers to protocols or regulation regarding how care is delivered and to whom. Democrats had been happy to support this as long as it was incorporated in wider system reform. This might be at individual state level, as in Oregon, where the 'Oregon Plan' meant giving more people access to a more strictly defined health care basket (see below for further details). Or it might mean extending the (limited) benefits of Medicaid (the health care programme for certain low-income categories) to a wider population, controlling costs through 'managed care'. Interestingly, in the 1992 presidential election, Clinton had supported managed care (such as Health Maintenance Organizations—HMOs), whereas his predecessor, President Bush, Sr, had opposed it on the grounds that it restricted liberties (while failing to propose a means whereby the poor might have such 'liberties').

Nevertheless, by the end of Clinton's period in office the wheel had come full circle. Indeed, by the end of its first term, managed care had become a political liability for the Bush Administration, to the extent that it was associated with it at all. As managed care meant that ordinary US citizens (the middle classes and working poor) had more strictly regulated access to health benefits and care, there was a backlash against it. Furthermore, it was Democrats who championed this backlash. Republicans typically took the 'pro-business' stance that managed care was a good means of preventing health care costs from rising even further (considering that most US health care is employer-paid, or co-paid). Thus, Republicans generally supported general business rather than the traditional health care private 'fee for service' lobby. This trend has been accentuated in the partisan stances on health policy from 2003, with both Republicans and Democrats seeking to extend Medicare for prescription drugs, albeit in different ways.

The main thing to remember is that US health care is, in the main, privately provided and financed. Different cadres of employee are afforded different benefits: good benefits are a recruitment incentive for skilled, scarce workers; and it can be easier to fire the poorer or less skilled and rehire others than to 'invest in them' through generous—or, indeed, any—health care benefits.

Thus, in the USA, the 'health care state' (Moran, 1999) is a complicated one. It reflects the individualist ideology, corporate domination of congressional politics and the fragmentation of the USA's state institutions (Paton, 1990). Of course, it also reflects the more internationally shared phenomenon of increased (even internet-driven) consumerism, declining deference to doctors, the need to support health care industries as part of global competition, and the effect of globalization upon domestic politics. This last factor reinforces a 'low tax, low spending' culture, already strong in the USA; even poor or insecure workers seem to have to choose this strategy for themselves rather than greater socialization. When one's income is falling in real terms (true of the average and poorer

US worker), lower taxes to offset this seem attractive, and, of course, businesses and rich individuals threaten relocation if high taxes prevail.

Health care is an investment as well as a consumption. In the USA both are handled privately, and equity (defined as equality of access to quality health care on the basis of need, not money) is less important. The state 'sweeps up' and also gives tax initiatives to investment, but not universally. It therefore fulfils the function of providing both 'social expenses' and 'social investment' (O'Connor, 1976).

Compared with Europe, however, in the USA the state's role is much less geared towards providing, or regulating for, universal access to a comprehensive package of health care. Significantly, some European health care systems are becoming more differentiated (for example, Italy has introduced more private payment for enhanced), and by the early 2000s there was evidence that the 'US influence on Europe may be growing. The opposite was true in the 1960s and 1970s, the heyday of modern US liberalism, which, in part, looked to European social democracy as a model. This was not an unequivocal picture, however, as some other European systems (such as France) were becoming more standardized.

However, the ideological influence of US health care abroad is probably accentuated by the fact that, at the micro level, close attention is paid to US 'quality initiatives' related to managed care. The British Government has intermittently sought to learn lessons from managed care in general, and from both Kaiser Permanente (a large, private sector HMO) and the Veterans Administration (a public sector HMO), in particular.

Yet the origins of managed care should be remembered. Ironically, managed care, in its modern context, is the USA's means of rationalizing the health care system to ensure that the privileges of private health care providers (whether doctors or companies) are rendered compatible with cost control. Cost control, to US citizens, raises the spectre of cuts and worries about quality, so managed care must have 'quality assurance' mechanisms. Nevertheless, managed care has not been accompanied by health care reform that would enable universal access to the finance required for care.

Whereas in Europe the state has generally supplanted the market in either providing, or regulating, health care, or both, in the USA the forces for corporate rationalization in health care have been privately led in recent decades, and have been a response to economic concerns, particularly on the part of business, at health care costs.

MAJOR INFLUENCES ON HEALTH AND WELFARE POLICY

The Political Structure

The US political structure involves, firstly, federalism (primarily, the division of governmental responsibility between the national government and the various state governments) and, secondly, a separation of powers between the presidency, Congress and the judiciary, especially the federal Supreme Court. These two basic features make a considerable amount of consensus and co-operation necessary for national health and welfare, or social security, programmes to be effected. Social planning, as understood in Europe, is difficult to organize in the USA, and health and welfare policy tends to lead to a complex mosaic of programmes provided for the benefit of separate social groups, rather than to nationally provided uniform services.

The two most significant periods of social reform in the 20th century that spawned health and welfare programmes were President Roosevelt's New Deal in the 1930s and the 'Great Society' under President Lyndon Johnson (1963–69) in the mid-1960s. The Social Security Act of 1935 was a landmark piece of legislation during the time of the New Deal. In a US context social security refers primarily to protection in old age (i.e., pensions), but also to protection from the consequences of unemployment. (In the United Kingdom, renaming the Department of Social Security the Department of Work and Pensions indicated a similar 'narrowing down' of what social security means.) The Social Security Act, and successor legislation, generally has wider social legitimacy, however, than among the 'elderly lobbies', and both social security and Medicare are still attacked by right-wing politicians at their peril. President Clinton realized this in 1996 when regrouping to emphasize the defence of these programmes in his second term, helping to put the Republicans, who had won control of Congress in 1994, onto the defensive (albeit with an intrinsically defensive programme). In the early 21st century, many of the initiatives to privatize pensions from the right of politics may be seen in ideological, rather than solely economic, terms: as attempts to detach 'middle, working America' from the 'underclass', to focus welfare provision upon the latter and to reform and restrict a more sectarian 'social security'.

The 89th Congress of 1965–66 is credited with being the most liberal Congress of the 20th century, certainly since the New Deal. In political terms, the New Deal Coalition was the left-of-centre coalition of particular groups—workers, rural interests and the public sector, in particular—that supported government intervention to provide health and welfare programmes. A reaction to the economic depression of the late 1920s and early 1930s, the formation of the New Deal Coalition represented a major realignment in US politics—the voting patterns of various classes and social groups underwent significant change, rather than a mere temporary adjustment in the usual manner. It was not until the late 1980s that the New Deal Coalition was widely acknowledged to be in final decline. The Democratic ascendancy in Congress was complete from the late 1950s—with the exception of temporary Republican control of the Senate in the early 1980s—until 1994. This was despite Republican domination of the presidency from Nixon's first term in 1969 until Bush, Sr's electoral defeat in November 1992 (the exception being Jimmy Carter in 1977–81). Moreover, the 1992 election of Bill Clinton had not led to greater harmony between President and Congress, as some expected. However, conflict between the Democratic Clinton and Republican 'Young Turks', under the leadership of Newt Gingrich, the Speaker of the House of Representatives, was centred more around personalities and personal vindictiveness than a great ideological divide. The Republicans took control of Congress in 1994, and their 'Contract with America' was based on extreme right-wing policy, not least in its proposed virtual abolition of welfare. The Republicans retained Congress in 1996, but their ideological ascendancy was somewhat neutralized by Clinton's re-election. President Clinton had, as introduced above, successfully portrayed their social policy as adversely affecting ordinary US citizens who relied on the 'middle-class welfare state'.

George W. Bush, elected to the presidency in 2000, was hailed as a 'compassionate conservative'. Yet his initial actions suggested a traditional right-wing agenda (on foreign affairs, the environment, and, most significantly for present purposes, tax cuts). His health proposals in the electoral campaign had been minimal, consisting mainly of tax incentives for private care rather than addressing the 'key issue'—that of the failure of Medicare to cover prescription drugs, increasingly significant in the USA as elsewhere in providing the hope of (expensive) cures for, among other conditions, multiple sclerosis, AIDS, and even influenza. However, by 2003 there was progress on both extensions to the Medicare programme and on the vexed issue of financing for long-term care, a move that could potentially impoverish the middle classes as well as the poor (as in many countries). In 2004 Bush faced public scepticism about his Medicare drug reforms. With Bush's re-election to the presidency in November 2004, and a Republican majority in both houses of Congress returned in the concurrently held legislative ballot, many of the features responsible for inaction in federal health policy remained. This was despite the unified Republican control of executive and legislative power, indicating that problems in passing domestic policy are a structural feature of the US political system, rather than contingent upon current political configurations.

This is not to be deterministic or fatalistic about the possibility of 'surprise'. Crisis can produce action through (for example) congressional 'special measures' (to approve legislation more comprehensively or quickly). In 1992, for example, President Clinton had hoped that either middle-class unease with employment-related health care or the threat of recession would build a larger popular coalition than usual for substantial reform in this area. Ultimately, however, this was not the case. Or rather, the issue was too transitory to overcome more deep-seated structural features of US politics (Paton, 1990), and specifically within Congress (Mann and Ornstein, Eds, 1995).

Fiscal Politics

A massive budget deficit in the USA had significant implications for health and welfare policy until the 1990s. Yet, by the end of the 1990s surpluses were available as a result of the 'Clinton boom'. In 2001 President Bush supported demands for low taxes to offset recession, and in May of that year Congress passed legislation for a US $1,350,000m. tax cut. Tax-cutting remained an executive priority, but—as President Reagan discovered in the 1980s—there was resistance from Congress in 2003, both Democrats and Republicans, not least owing to the legislature's continued subscription to balanced-budget legislation against the backdrop of such presidential 'supply-side economics' (i.e., reverse Keynesianism). The US state has had difficulties co-ordinating social and economic priorities; the macroeconomic consequences tend to be rationalized as virtuous rather than just necessary, in a theory christened 'voodoo economics' by Bush, Sr, in 1980. It is then left to the Federal Reserve (the national bank) to use monetary policy to enhance or correct the consequences, depending upon its stance on political economy at the time.

By 2008 the budget deficit after two Bush presidencies had outstripped the Reagan mega-deficit. This time around, however, differences in the international price of intergovernmental lending had allowed it to continue longer—with long-term bonds at lower interest-rates. Whereas, during the Reagan era, the cost of borrowing at high interest rates had brought 'hot' money into the USA, raising the value of the US dollar to nearly one pound sterling, this time around the pound was worth nearly two dollars, and the effect on exports from the USA was less serious. By 2008, however, the irresponsible lending practices of US- and British-based banks were coming home to roost.

The universal phenomenon whereby public expenditure is popular, yet taxation to finance it is not, is considerably increased in the USA by the fragmented way in which welfare policy is produced. This fragmentation contributed to a widespread perception that liberal policies were unaffordable; a conservative reaction against policies of, for example, the 1960s and early 1970s was evident. A contrast with other countries may be instructive. In the United Kingdom, for example, the National Health Service (NHS) was a centrally planned and budgeted service, characterized by strict cost control as well as by attempts at social equity. In the USA, however, liberal reforms attempted to spread the benefits of expensive private provision of health care to hitherto excluded or disadvantaged groups, such as those who previously had inadequate or nonexistent health insurance. As a result, liberal reforms were seen as unaffordable. By the 1990s ideas for rationing in health care became accepted on the liberal, as well as the conservative, side of the political spectrum. During the 1992 presidential election campaign Clinton supported the 'Oregon approach'. This sought to consult the public on health care priorities within limited budgets, in order to cover more of the poor for fewer treatments, rather than a more limited Medicaid population for more treatments (see below). In that sense, liberal reforms might be more affordable—although, arguably, at the cost of being less liberal. On ethical grounds, such 'rationing' may be, in fact, denial to the poor of care that is available to those who do not rely on public programmes for health care. There were also concerns regarding 'health fascism', whereby reactionary public opinion leads to treatments being denied on the grounds of social morality rather than medical ethics (for example, for patients with AIDS).

Common to the Republican presidencies of Richard Nixon, Gerald Ford and Ronald Reagan was the belief that, instead of spending money on specific health and welfare programmes themselves (so-called 'categorical' programmes), the federal Government ought to make block grants to the states, which would then have the responsibility for allocating resources for specific purposes. A more recent current of thought, prevalent by the 1990s, argued that as well as, or instead of, this approach, the federal Government ought to take more direct responsibility for health and welfare programmes as a means of cost control and stricter public management. President Bush, Sr, as well as Bill Clinton (then Governor of Arkansas), were forced to design a 'health proposal' during the 1992 presidential election campaign—somewhat ironically following four years of relative inaction in the realm of national health policy. The Bush plan sought to redistribute money saved from charitable care to the uninsured poor, in the form of limited vouchers for care for the 'nearly poor', who could buy themselves into Medicaid and other health care programmes. The Clinton programme, however, consisted of a more national approach mandating (eventual) universal coverage, with cost control achieved through 'managed competition', which involved competing HMOs.

In 1994 the Clinton health plan failed, for a number of reasons. First, it was a complex plan. Second and relatedly, it sought to appease conservatives without succeeding in so doing. As a result, it combined complex elements of 'managed competition' with regulations to promote equity. It was described by opponents as bureaucratic—perhaps a more populist approach could have attacked the plutocratic private insurance industry and proposed Canadian-style health insurance, given the (temporary) mood of insecurity. Even that was unlikely, given that the sense of insecurity was based on fear of job losses and, therefore (in the US system), loss of health insurance. When the economy improved the Republicans in Congress had less reason to compromise with President Clinton. They chose to fight him with determined obstruction rather than by centrist responsibility.

Health and welfare policies can, of course, be seen as investments in the economic future of a country, as well as attempts at social justice and equity. Given this fact, it is perhaps not surprising that, for example, US health care benefits were often based in the workplace. Thus, firms were investing in their workers, with government help or tax incentives to do so, rather than the state investing in both the productive and unproductive. US health and welfare policy was, therefore, a complex amalgam, not only of different specific programmes for specific groups, but also representing different social needs. It provided legitimacy for the existing social order, it invested in the future and it co-ordinated the pieces into a whole that was both manageable and fiscally controllable. The most interesting controversies in US health and welfare policy in the 1990s were informed by this last imperative. For example, health management reforms were seeking cost control in firms' health plans by directing clinical care through protocols—so-called 'managed care'.

HEALTH PROGRAMMES

US health care relies on the private sector for both provision and finance to a greater extent than the health care systems of other developed Western countries. Private insurance was the basis of the financing system, while private hospitals, whether non-profit or for-profit, were that of the system of provision. In considering the government's role in financing health care it is important to look at both overt government programmes and tax allowances for individuals and groups. The main government programmes were Medicare (Parts A and B, dealing with hospitals and ambulatory care, respectively) for those over 65 years of age and for certain categories of disabled people, and Medicaid for certain low-income categories. Medicare is more broadly financed than Medicaid, but consists basically of federally purchased private insurance. Medicaid's costs were shared between the federal Government and the states, with the federal contribution depending upon a number of factors, primarily, each state's willingness to spend and various indicators of need for health care in the various states. Individuals and companies received tax allowances for the purchase of private health insurance or membership in health programmes such as an HMO (see below), and even in 1985 it was estimated that the cost to the Treasury of this was greater than the total cost of the Medicaid programme.

Current and Recent Health Policy and Policy Proposals

In 2008 the Obama presidential plan for health consisted of guaranteed eligibility for all Americans, on the basis of comprehensive benefits similar to those enjoyed by the Federal Employees Health Benefits Program (FEHBP). It was not a publicly financed or publicly provided system that was proposed, but a publicly regulated structure embracing existing employer-financed schemes and other programmes. It proposed a 'national health insurance exchange' for individuals who wished to purchase a private insurance plan, essentially regulating the private insurance industry in the interests of equity and cost-control. It would also subsidize the costs of employer-funded 'catastrophic costs' if employers' savings were passed onto individuals in lower premiums. People could change job without altering or jeopardizing their insurance policy (so-called 'portability', a major problem in the USA, and one which has been increasingly highlighted since the 1990s, in the absence of more radical public-oriented reform). The plan also emphasized public and preventive health. Obama's record since 2003 as a senator focused on health insurance for children—later an important part of his presidential plan.

John McCain's plan stressed individuals and privatization. It was essentially based upon tax deductions for individuals and 'health savings accounts' and, as such, was similar to the Bush model (see below). Regarding access by those finding difficulty with coverage, he would work with state governors to develop best practice, including a non-profit corporation to contract with insurers to provide coverage for those who had been denied it. Joining other state 'pools' he also emphasized 'portability'. It is worth noting that, while Hillary Clinton stressed her intention to provide help to individuals using the tax system, this was via tax credits (i.e. actual allocations, not just deductions) so that families who did not pay tax could also be helped. Otherwise it was similar to Obama's, although with detailed differences.

When considering leading congressional health care bills from 2005 to 2007, three categories can be noted: 'fundamental reform' (by US standards); expansions of existing public insurance programmes; and the strengthening of employer-based health insurance.

In the first category were bills suggesting the use of Medicare as the basis for expansion (i.e. public programmes) involving the Democratic Representatives Fortney Pete Stark and John Dingell, and Senator Edward Kennedy; Senator Ronald Wyden's bill to create a regional insurance exchange; federal state partnerships; and the Bush approach of tax deductions. These proposals varied in terms of coverage, comprehensiveness and their sources (e.g. Medicare). Costs varied according to the extent and source of coverage, efficiency measures and the extent of premium subsidies—for instance, the Stark bill ('Americare') would have increased federal spending by US $154,500m. in 2007; but the effect on public spending in the short term would have been offset by savings in the long term. Senator Wyden's proposed 'healthy Americans act' would have made savings over time by incorporating existing employer expenditure in a federal programme.

More modest proposals would allow buy-in to Medicare or Medicaid by certain population groups, as advocated by Stark and Dingell, or would promote coverage for children (as favoured by Senator John Kerry)—both examples of public expansion. The Republican Representative Frank Pallone proposed the use of the private sector as the basis for expansion, requiring companies with 50 or more workers to offer and contribute to comprehensive health insurance for employees and their dependents (affecting about 12m. people.)

It is important to note that the same legislators will sponsor different bills of different scale and scope, reflecting both political pragmatism and the difficulty of getting such reforms passed. By July 2008 Senate committees were holding 'stakeholder meetings', including Edward Kennedy's staff at the Senate Committee on Health, Education, Labour and Pensions. As a prominent Obama supporter, Kennedy was keen to build consensus. In the House, however, Democrats on the Subcommittee on Health of the Committee on Ways and Means were allegedly less enamoured of this approach, implying that seeking to incorporate many interests could stifle reform. In an election year, Republicans do not generally join bipartisan fora to seek consensus, concentrating more on supporting their presidential candidate, in this case John McCain.

It should be remembered that this type of committee preparation for something resembling national health insurance has been going on for 40 years, since the inception of Medicare/Medicaid in 1965. It could be argued that far-reaching legislation is unlikely at the best of times, especially in the absence of bipartisan compromise and with the co-option of external interests through whatever means necessary; the US political structure and culture mean that simply having a majority is not always enough. Meanwhile, within the radical wing of politics, the Green Party had criticized the plans of both Obama and Clinton for doing more for insurance and so-called 'big pharma' (the collective term for large pharmaceutical companies) than for the American people with their subsidies and incentives.

President Bush's Medicare Prescription Drug, Improvement and Modernization Act of 2003 added to the benefits covered by Medicare, principally through the reimbursement of prescription drugs. A criticism was that it prohibited the import of cheaper drugs from Canada and elsewhere, as a result of lobbying by the drugs industry (which also prohibited the Government from using Medicare's purchasing power to regulate or lower prices). The Medicare Act was also criticized for its so-called 'doughnut hole' of uncovered costs. Incremental reforms to Medicare and Medicaid have been the hallmark of policy proposals and enactments over recent years. The 2003 Medicare Drug Law made less clear the distinctions between Medicare (hitherto a wholly federal, i.e., national, programme) and Medicaid (by origin, a states' programme with federal matching funds). From 1 January 2006 Medicaid was to provide drugs coverage for citizens dually eligible for both Medicare and Medicaid. Incidentally, some state governments rejected plans for their increased contribution to drugs benefits under the 2003 law (see below). In particular, New Hampshire challenged the constitutionality of the 2003 Act.

The 2003 Medicare Prescription Drug Law was also opposed by the drugs industry and by small business organizations, which might have been expected to be in favour of the emphasis placed upon business-led purchasing groups with which the elderly would enrol. However, the organizations viewed the proposals as costly and bureaucratic, despite the approach of avoiding traditional government programmes. One can note a parallel with the opposition to the Clinton Plan from the insurance industry (see below), for which concessions to both the private sector generally, and the insurance industry in particular, never seem to be enough in US politics.

Health Savings Accounts

Health Savings Accounts were created by the Medicare Act of 2003. Their aim was to 'help individuals save for future qualified medical and retiree health expenses on a tax-free basis'. They were especially geared to help individuals with 'High Deductible Health Plans', which mandated that the individual had to pay at least the first US $1,050 of any claim. The accompanying regulations and restrictions were complex and, overall, the policy represented an 'individualist' rather than 'statist' attempt to address under-coverage in the health-care system. The policy was also much less redistributionist than health care reform might have been. For example, there were no income limits on who might contribute, and subscribing individuals could not be claimed as dependent on other policies. Furthermore, children could not be covered while spouses could. There was also a clause that denied eligibility if state policies reduced the impact of 'high-deductible' policies through state-wide health benefits. Meanwhile, employee contributions were only allowable if they were balanced by a 'salary reduction agreement'.

The Health Care Legacy

Health care was traditionally provided in private, non-profit hospitals for secondary care, and through private 'office physicians' for primary and less-specialized care. The rise of the for-profit private hospital in the USA was a phenomenon of the

1980s, when many non-profit institutions were being taken over by the for-profit sector. In general, a 'rationalization' of the health care system seemed to be occurring through the economic imperative of financial solvency. Problems of cost escalation asserted themselves significantly, however, and in the 1990s rationalization remained an aspiration rather than an achievement. Just as devolution of responsibility for health care to the states has fitted in with both Republican ideology and (less often) Democratic populism, there is less adherence to the idea of publicly financed health care in the USA.

Ideologically, it is more common to believe that health care is a personal or familial responsibility. Where help for the poor is necessary, it is then more common to believe in general cash transfers, rather than publicly financed health care, although the former are difficult to arrange politically. In Europe, most systems carry out means-testing at the point of revenue generation for health care, whether by direct taxation, as in the United Kingdom and other 'Beveridge' systems (so called after the Beveridge Report of 1942, which formed the basis of much of the social legislation on which the British welfare state was founded), or by regulating payments to sickness funds or private insurers, as in the 'Bismarckian' social insurance systems (which originated in Germany in the 1880s). However, in the USA, means testing is at the point of receipt of care, with very strict means testing for receipt of the often less-than-generous Medicaid provisions. This means that, even for expensive or 'high technology' care, the better-off sections of society seek private arrangements, whereas in Europe they will often 'buy in' to state systems out of economic rationality rather than just ideology.

BALANCING COSTS WITH ACCESS

The two most significant characteristics of US health care are costs, which continue to rise, and the need to increase equity of and access to the health care system. Innovations in US health policy were geared to cost control, especially those made by the federal Government for its own programmes.

In 2003 high costs continued to dominate the sense of 'crisis'. It can be pointed out that high spending on health care is deliberate in that special interests, both consumer and provider, benefit from organizing health care in the US way—i.e., by sectional programmes—and that politicians both encourage and deprecate it. Nevertheless, in 2002 the Congressional Budget Office predicted that Medicare, which cost US $342,000m. in 2005, would cost an estimated $500,000m. in 2012. Many of the new costs are related to drugs. Overall, public health care accounts for only an estimated 40% of the total health care costs in the USA, but in absolute terms it accounts for more real spending per head than the British NHS.

By 2005 the core problems in US health care remained rapidly-rising costs, especially (Medicare) drug costs, and a growth in the number of uninsured. Spending per head on health care rose from US $4,670 in 2000 to $6,167 in 2004. The cost of prescription drugs increased by 13.8% in 2001 and by around 10% in 2002 and 2003. Regarding coverage, 43.6m. people were uninsured for the 2003 calendar year, and, even more strikingly, 81.8m. people under 65 years of age were uninsured for all or part of 2002–03. Of these, four-fifths were in working families, and one-quarter were middle class. Minority races were disproportionately represented, but one-half of the total were non-Hispanic whites. Loss of insurance owing to job loss or job change (i.e. 'between jobs') was, as ever, a significant issue. The proportion of workers covered by their employers fell from 52% in 2002 to 45% in 2003, with workers paying an annual average of $2,352 in 2004.

By 2008 things were even worse. A report in *Health Affairs* (an academic journal with strong links to practice) in June reported that 25.2m. people aged 19–64 years were under-insured, an increase of 60% from nearly 16m. in 2003. This brought the number of uninsured and under-insured adults in the USA to 42%.

In the 1970s, following the enactment of Medicare and Medicaid in 1965, it was widely perceived that, in order to control costs, a rationalization of the health care system would be necessary to provide affordable access to the system for the disadvantaged. Thus, in 1974, with bipartisan support, the National Health Planning and Resources Development Act was passed; this was intended to delegate responsibility to Health Systems Agencies (HSAs), working in co-operation with state governments, both to restrict unnecessary expansion and to direct funds to under-served areas. However, the HSAs were dominated by coalitions of providers and consumers, who preferred to allow as much expansion as possible rather than to plan. The failure of planning to achieve its ambitiously stated goals, let alone to mobilize new resources for the under-insured and under-served communities, was the consequence of expecting too much of the US political system, which is not geared to the demands of such programmes. As a result, planning became discredited, and most health care policy analysts in the 1980s preferred to rely on the open market rather than on planning.

A more significant policy sponsored by the federal Government in the 1970s was reflected in a series of HMO acts and amendments. The HMO seeks to provide a cost-effective alternative to fee-for-service medicine, whereby a private doctor is paid a fee for every item of service provided. Private fee-for-service medicine has been considered expensive, in that the consumer and provider have an incentive to overcharge a third-party payer, namely the insurer. The HMO seeks to merge the roles of insurer and provider. An individual pays a premium to join an HMO, for a year in most cases, and the HMO will then be financially liable to provide the necessary care (with exclusions perhaps stipulated) as required. Some companies subscribe to an HMO on behalf of their employees. HMOs did not expand as much as the federal Government had hoped during the 1970s, because interventionist legislation demanded that HMOs, if they were to receive federal subsidies, must not charge higher premiums to the poorer and sicker, and that they must accept all applications. This formula, however, meant that HMOs could not survive such regulation without corresponding financial support. In the 1980s, gradually freed from the details of federal regulation, HMOs flourished as a major feature of private corporate health care. HMOs have generally become freer to turn away people considered bad risks, or to charge them higher membership premiums. In the early 1980s the annual rate of growth of HMOs reached about 25%, and by 1991 about 34m. US citizens belonged to an HMO. By that time the rate of expansion seemed to be slowing a little, as HMOs faced bankruptcy on a greater scale than earlier in the decade.

Some HMOs employ all their staff directly and provide their health care through directly owned institutions such as hospitals. These are generally considered to be 40% cheaper than the traditional fee-for-service health care sector. Other HMOs neither own all their own facilities nor employ all their own doctors and other medical workers; instead, they contract with group practices of doctors to provide health care by paying them a capitation fee for each patient registered. This is the so-called 'Group' HMO model. Finally, some HMOs merely engage traditional fee-for-service doctors to provide for the patients who are registered with them. It is this type of HMO that has the least impressive record in controlling costs.

Additionally, HMOs, as the best-known form of managed care, varied with regard to their generosity of coverage. They became identified with corporate enterprises quoted on the US Stock Exchange, rather than the impetus to socialization of their progenitors in the 1990s. Big monopolistic or oligopolistic 'managed care organizations' swallowed up independent providers in localities; and big, monopsonistic health-insurance plans incorporated such organizations (or dealt with them cosily). Thus, managed care became tainted—the poor had always had to put up with it, but middle America was outraged.

In June 2004 the US Supreme Court ruled that patients could not sue managed care organizations for damages arguably related to denial of care, or 'rationing'. Ironically, the state of Texas had authorized patients to do so for denial of care, and President Bush had boasted of his support for this principle in 2000. Yet his Administration opposed allowing this in its deposition to the Supreme Court. As a result of the Court's decision, 10 states had laws invalidated, and managed care became even more unpopular.

The federal Government has been seeking to control costs directly as well by stimulating new forms of provision, both in the public and private sectors. A system of Diagnosis Related Groups (DRGs) has been instituted, whereby the fees payable by the federal Government for Medicare patients are dependent upon the diagnosis: the scheme operates, effectively, as a national system of price regulation. Seen as a much-needed response to the escalating costs of the health care system, DRGs were sponsored by a Republican Administration and received bipartisan support.

It seemed that by the mid-1980s cost control in the US health care system was beginning to take effect. However, costs began to grow rapidly again in the late 1980s, with about 21% of US gross domestic product (GDP) going to health care by 2004. Compare this 21% with around 7% in the United Kingdom (of a GDP per head that was, moreover, less than three-quarters that of the USA) and figures ranging from 8%–12% in the other major Western European countries, Canada and the countries of Australasia. As well as the overall cost problems, particular price regulations are beginning to have obvious consequences, particularly where the poor and uninsured are concerned. Hitherto they have relied on charitable care, especially in public and charitable hospitals (such as the major city hospitals), which has been subsidized from the surplus gained from conventional paying patients. However, regulatory-based limitations on reimbursement are restricting the capacity to do this, as surpluses are diminished. As a result, charitable care for the poor is being thrust even more firmly towards the federal Government. The same dynamics are evident with medical education. This is creating a paradoxical position for the Government: as the logical consequences of political fragmentation unfold, manifested in an inability to co-ordinate the health care system and provide a coherent national health care policy, a stronger federal role may, at last, emerge.

When Medicare and Medicaid were authorized in 1965, through amendments to the Social Security Act, they were in fact a compromise, as liberal reformers had sought a system of national health insurance. It is generally agreed that 1974 was the last year when any enactment of national health insurance, or at least its passage by Congress, was even a remote possibility. However, as inequity worsens within the system, the issue is reborn at times when economic insecurity brings a wider coalition to support reform (out of self-interest rather than social conscience).

Nationally, the provision and financing of health care for lower-income groups varies significantly. Some states are relatively generous, for example, Massachusetts and New Jersey, while others provide very little for their poor populations. An extreme example of the latter is found in Arizona, which declined to participate in the Medicaid programme at all, and only provided health care for some of its indigent population in the 1980s, when the opportunity to buy them into relatively cheap prepaid health care schemes arose. The Clinton Plan, developed by a health care 'task force' in 1993–94, argued for 'managed competition', whereby employees would be encouraged or forced to join HMOs through new financing organizations called Health Alliances, which would see providers directly controlled by special types of insurance companies. States and the federal Government would have a regulatory role in ensuring the acceptability of the competing, participating HMOs. This would be achieved through buying agents—the Health Alliances—bargaining on behalf of enrolees for contracts between competing HMOs. In theory, costs would, therefore, be driven downwards. The establishment of a federal National Health Board was a further proposal. This would oversee the system and disburse funds. The system would be unlikely to be egalitarian in the US political context, in that poor people would join the poorer HMOs, whereas the rich would be able to opt into excellent and expensive health care. Clinton also sought cost control through the mechanism of overall controls on health care expenditure by the various states. The means of doing this were unclear during the campaign. The main problem is that any national health plan is likely to remove the 'middle man' of the private insurance industry, a fact likely to make implementing a meaningful national health plan very difficult for any US President. President Clinton's proposed health care reforms failed in Congress even before the Republicans achieved majorities in both houses at the end of 1994.

The recurrent themes in US health policy were, therefore, the search for equity and greater access by the poor and uninsured, and—much more politically dominant—cost control by a variety of mechanisms. These ranged from national regulation through managed care, to competing HMOs, which, it was believed, would reduce costs both through competition and through financial incentives within the HMO. To these concerns could be added the strength of the 'elderly lobby'. The 'health care state' (Moran, 1999) is characterized by the influence of both the state upon health care and of health care issues upon the state. The elderly affect both strands of influence: they are politically strong and therefore can condition health priorities; and their political strength means that health care reformers seek to improve access generally by building upon the more popular Medicare rather than the less popular Medicaid.

Overall, US health care policy has been characterized by the dominant traits of US politics. However, this has created such complexity that a stronger co-ordinating role for federal Government may emerge, less as a point of political controversy than as an acknowledged need on both sides of the political spectrum. In 1997 President Clinton established the Advisory Commission on Consumer Rights and Quality, to examine complaints by the medical profession and consumers about managed care medical insurance. Managed care reduces employers' medical-insurance costs but, it is claimed by many, at the cost of the quality of care offered. In the United Kingdom a lot of positive attention is given to the best managed care (as in Kaiser, or the Veterans Administration) but the other side of the picture is often forgotten.

The innovation in US health care that attracted the most international attention in the 1990s was the 'Oregon Plan'. The Oregon Basic Health Services Plan was devised to address rising health care costs (with an implication that there is a need for rationing) and a possible expansion of health care for the uninsured. The state of Oregon sought to expand Medicaid and health insurance to people without coverage, so that all poor people in the state would be eligible—360,000 people, as opposed to the 240,000 previously covered by Medicaid. The most controversial element of the plan was the decision not to cover some medical procedures and to consult the public on what these should be. The plan sought to do five basic things: to extend medical eligibility from those people earning 50% of the income defined as the Federal Poverty Level to all those below the Federal Poverty Level; to set a public policy process for defining basic health care provision for Medicaid clients; to mandate that all employers should provide universal health care coverage for employees and their dependants at least equal to that coverage provided under the Medicaid programme; to establish an insurance pool for 'medically uninsurables'; and, finally, to protect providers against prosecution or civil liability for not providing services that the Oregon legislature had chosen not to fund.

As stated above, the idea was to cover more people for less cost. As in all public rationing procedures, there is a potential conflict between expert technical judgements, about which procedures best produce 'health gain', and consumer opinion: the two may not produce the same judgements. The first list of priorities produced under the 'Oregon formula' aroused criticism and was eventually rejected in the legislature. The Oregon Health Service Commission, therefore, had redesigned the formula by February 1991 and the plan awaited federal approval. This was granted by the Clinton Administration in early 1993 for a five-year trial period. Certain services would be excluded from cover, but 568 out of a list of 688 medical services would be covered. It was thought implementation of the plan might be delayed or blocked because of lawsuits brought against it. In the end, an amended version was accepted.

It can be argued, validly, that rationing for the poor alone is inequitable, as it means denying to one section of society care that is available through conventional medical insurance to the better-off. Furthermore, social choice in the field of health care priorities may produce dubious ethical, if not overtly reactionary, judgements. 'Rationing' has become a well-established term in international health care, and it is argued that where expectations outstrip resources it is inevitable. However, given the huge expenditure nationally on health care in the USA, it is an open question as to whether the kind of rationing for public health care proposed by Oregon is necessary. Rationing may, furthermore, divert attention from the need for redistribution and a genuine national health-insurance policy. Finally, the future for health policy will depend on how the economy performs and how business provides (or fails to provide) health benefits. If 'middle America' feels insecure, there may be a new push for health reform.

THE BUSH AGENDA IN THE SECOND TERM

By 2004 there was something of a consensus between the two main parties on the key theme of health reform, although they had very different approaches to implementation. Given the likely lack of implementation at federal level, despite stated policy, emphasis was placed upon state policies and local initiatives, not least in quality improvement. The debate was less about whether there should be national health insurance and more about which mechanism to use to count more people into effective programmes (such as Medicare) and control costs for business. Additionally, the long-term care 'time bomb' continued to tick—quality for those who were covered varied wildly, while the problem of equity and affordability for those who were not covered remained a major issue. State policies ranged from universal coverage in Massachusetts to pooling of risks in Maine, and in California firms of more than 50 employees were mandated by a 2003 ballot to provide health benefits. In 2004 the Bush electoral platform stressed Health Savings Accounts; tax credits for the uninsured (up to a ceiling of US $3,000 per family); further increases in the State Children's Health Insurance Program; and the promotion of 'associations' of the uninsured to pool risks, while avoiding 'Big Government'.

The first proposed health care legislation of President Bush's second term, in 2005, addressed the vexed question of medical malpractice suits. These threatened to put out of business some medical specialists (such as obstetricians), through the punitive costs of malpractice insurance. Class actions were to be banned. The Republicans, in the 13 years between the two Bush presidencies, have changed the emphasis slightly from the (paying) individual consumer's rights to the viability and cost of the system as a whole—although the latter has raised concerns over quality, with the Democrats calling for regulation and the Republicans seeing an opportunity for competition.

SOCIAL SECURITY, PENSIONS AND WELFARE

Welfare

In contrast to the position in many Western European countries, federal social security is only temporarily available after the loss of a job in the USA—although in 2008 proposed reforms in England were following this example. Different states and localities have varying types and levels of protection for the needy, the disabled and the unemployed. There is no national 'safety net' of the type found in developed welfare states.

The most fundamental disagreement over policy for income maintenance has been whether transfers to the poor ought to be 'in cash' or 'in kind'. In general, 'old Democrats' supported categorical programmes that provide specific benefits, sometimes in kind; the food stamp is an example of the latter. Republicans have tended to support cash transfers, in line with the ideology of letting the market work after the necessary redistribution of income. However, as with so many issues in social welfare policy, there is no clear party (or indeed left–right) division on matters such as these. Economists sometimes favour cash transfers on the grounds that they do not distort pricing in the market place in the same way as can the free provision of specific goods. However, if it is to be believed that an item constitutes a basic right—as many believe with health care, for example—specific provision of that item may be logical policy.

As is true in many countries, there are three main objectives to be met in designing a coherent policy for income maintenance. The policy must protect the poorest members of society and raise the incomes of those below the poverty line; the cost must be affordable to central government; and it must not institute perverse or bad incentives, such as those associated with the so-called 'poverty trap' and 'unemployment trap'. It is difficult to meet all three objectives. Poverty and unemployment traps can ensue when individuals lose benefits and/or become susceptible to tax when they raise their income or find a job, but actually have a lower disposable income as a result of having gained employment or their gross income having been increased otherwise. A means of evading such traps is to introduce a sliding scale whereby, as income increases, benefit or income support is only removed gradually. However, the more generous the protection (through the income floor guaranteed by the Government) and the more gradual the operation of the sliding scale, the more expensive the programme is overall. Accompanying administrative difficulties, expense rather than coherence, is the reason why sudden or total loss of benefits on reaching a certain threshold is commonplace. The Aid to Families with Dependent Children (AFDC) programme has been significant, helping in particular single-parent (usually mother) families, since the 'Great Society' legislation of the 1960s. In 1981, however, the Omnibus Budget Reconciliation Act (the 'cuts' in welfare during the early stages of the Reagan Administration) reduced AFDC, denying aid to single mothers who had found work. This created an unemployment and poverty trap.

An idea that has attracted liberals and conservatives, Democrats and Republicans alike, as a means of avoiding such traps, is the concept of the 'negative income tax' (supported variously in the latter half of the 20th century by free-market economist Professor Milton Friedman and Democratic Senator Professor Daniel Patrick Moynihan). This is a means of unifying the welfare and taxation systems, whereby, below a certain threshold a subsidy is received according to a formula, but above that threshold tax is paid according to the same formula. Conservatives have been attracted to it because it avoids government-controlled categorical programmes; liberals because, if adequately funded, it can achieve redistribution of money to the lowest income groups. A major initiative in the 1970s to seek to mobilize this (theoretical) consensus was the Family Assistance Program, devised in the Nixon Administration (Nixon being a moderate Republican in much of his domestic legislation, it should be noted, quite contrary to his traditional public image). It was voted down in the Senate Finance Committee, however, and was widely agreed to be the victim of opposition from both liberal Democrats antagonistic to Nixon initiatives and conservative Republicans antagonistic to redistributive policies.

Social Security

As noted above, the Social Security Act of 1935 provided the framework for today's social security (pensions and certain other protections). The 1996 Welfare Reform Law (referred to above as the 1996 Act) helped 4.7m. Americans to move from welfare-dependency to self-sufficiency by 2000 (a reduction of the welfare caseload by 54% since 1996). At that time, liberals generally were fearful that the Act would be a failure, but by 2000 child poverty had fallen by 25% and the earnings of the poorest 40% of claimants had doubled. Nevertheless, under the new rules state support was denied to up to 1m. people; most women leaving welfare (the salient category was single-parent families) took up low-paid, unskilled jobs; and one-half of those still on welfare are neither looking for work nor in education or training. After 2000, moreover, the child poverty rate rose again by 10% and the economic downturn from 2001 lowered one-half of the earnings gain for the poorest 40%. In 2006 more than one-half of those eligible for social security, significantly, did not receive benefit. Mark Greenberg, of the Center for American Progress, claimed that 'we now simply have a system that provides less help in times when people are without work'. In 2005 welfare had its first comprehensive overhaul in a decade. This reform led to tightened eligibility rules, increased numbers for whom work was a necessity, and a stricter monitoring of welfare recipients. Some think this reform went too far. Representative Ruth Kagi, Chairwoman of the

House Committee on Children and Family Services, commented that 'Congress stripped the spirit of the 1996 law which gave states great flexibility... in exchange for a limit on funds'.

Pensions

The insolvency of the social security system has been the 'big scare' of the US (and others') welfare state at the beginning of the 21st century. It has, of course, been noted above that this may be a 'moral panic' rather than a real crisis. For one-third of Americans older than 65 years of age, social security represents 90% of their income. The Bush Administration argued that in 1950 there were 16 workers for every social security beneficiary, whereas in 2006 there were 3.3. The imminent retirement (by 2008) of the 'baby boomer' generation is also seen as a fiscal threat—although arguably there is now less pressure on government expenditure at the other end of the life cycle. Bush argues that if the social security burden is not addressed now, the system will be bankrupt by 2041. Whatever the viability of social security, the scare is useful for right-wing reformers who wish to discredit social security and more solidaristic models of welfare. For those who wish to 'act in response to crisis', the options, as elsewhere, are: a reduction in benefits for the wealthy (i.e., means-testing); an indexation of benefits to prices not wages (i.e., increasing differentials between the working and the retired); an increase in the statutory retirement age; or incentives to reduce early retirement. Notably, increased statutory contributions are not part of the Bush Administration's policy agenda: a major aim is to convert the contributions of younger workers into Personal Retirement Accounts, that is, the so-called privatization of pensions. This is arguably part of a 'New Right' agenda (see above). However, the President has seen any radical initiative on this issue stymied.

In 2006 the Senate approved the Pensions Protection Act unamended from the House of Representatives. This promoted stricter regulation of pensions, to protect 'final payment plans', and also allowed the transfer of pension assets for health-care costs. It was supported by the powerful United Automobile, Aerospace and Agricultural Implement Workers of America (UAW) trade union, as well as by the business sector. This was in spite of the Act containing the threat that, while existing pension holders would be protected, 'defined contribution' plans might be closed to new employees as a kind of perverse response by employers.

In summary, welfare legislation signed into law in 1996 introduced dramatic changes in US social policy and, effectively ended 60 years of federally guaranteed welfare payments. The law allowed each state to set its own welfare rules, although some basic criteria had to be met: within two years of claiming welfare at least one-half of adult recipients must be back in employment and, over the course of a lifetime, a person may only claim welfare for a maximum of five years. The food-stamp programme remained under the control of the federal Government.

Overall, however, it can be argued that 'the missing middle' (Skocpol, 2000) has been neglected in designing welfare reform that combines greater equity with incentives to work, and creates a social coalition based on 'investment in the future', communitarian spirit and enlightened self-interest. Whether such an ideal can be born in the era of capitalist globalization and against the backdrop of US individualism is a moot point. The challenge was to combine security for the working poor and unemployed with incentives to work (in a manner that does not force people into employment when they legitimately do not wish to be so, for instance, in the case of some single parents, and some of the disabled). In the USA, President Clinton used the term 'the third way' to refer to a mix of market and government in reforming welfare. Yet, in essence there is a convergence between Republicans and Democrats around 'workfare' programmes, which require work or job training to be taking place before a claimant can qualify for welfare or income support. It is more a question of how much work is needed in order to claim benefits that divides the parties. In the last years of the Bush Administration, as noted above, welfare reforms have been off the agenda. It remains to be seen what the new presidency and congress will bring after 2008.

CONCLUSION

US social policy, including health and welfare, has recently been dominated by neo-liberal and conservative ideologies. Neo-liberalism is essentially a restrained and modified version of liberalism, which is, furthermore, less hostile to the market; neo-conservatism generally entails the view that the objectives of social policy should not necessarily be shunned, but should be achieved through an amalgam of market mechanisms and voluntary action, rather than by government intervention on the 1960s model. Neo-conservatism should not be confused with what is termed the 'New Right', which refers to social and cultural conservatives whose main policy agenda concerns emotive social issues, such as prayer in schools and abortion, and which is identified with a strong anti-libertarianism. Both ideologies stress cost-effectiveness more than traditional liberalism. This is also in reaction to the perception that welfare expenditure reached high proportions during the 'Great Society' of the 1960s, yet that welfare programmes had a low overall level of cost-effectiveness.

Furthermore, the new conservative coalition that produced Republican domination combines a number of interests: traditional east coast and Midwestern conservatives; the new economic right wing, identified with the 'sunbelt' states, supply-side economics, the virtual extinction of corporate income tax and a belief in a minimal government role in regulating domestic policy; and the former Democratic, poorly paid or welfare-dependent white working class, as well as middle-class conservative former Democrats of the South. The old Civil War divide is gone. It is in this context that reassessment of health and welfare policy ought to be understood. Much confusion in policy is based on an inability to achieve consensus among liberals or among conservatives, let alone between both camps. Conservatives, in general, wish to see a return of power to the states. Ironically, in early US history it was progressives and reformers who believed in giving greater power to the states, as a protection of direct democracy. By the 1960s, however, the federal Government was seen by liberals as the best source of protection for the disadvantaged.

President Bush's election in 2000 provided a renewed conservative thrust, but without much of a national mandate. However, in 2004 Bush gained his unequivocal mandate. The newly elected President of 2001, who had barely travelled abroad and who concentrated on the domestic agenda, was, in 2006, understandably, a President with a focus on national security, seeking to unravel the consequences of US behaviour around the world since the Second World War, and take a messianic, neo-conservative route to a US-style capitalist global democracy. However, as far as health was concerned, he was probably obeying the structural dictates of US domestic policy-making: incrementalism, with its institutional bias towards conservatism, does work (Paton, 1990); do not make strong demands on Congress; and try to combine cohesion within the party while not eschewing bipartisanship (Schick, in Mann and Ornstein, 1995).

Political tradition in the USA has a significant bearing on welfare policy. Unlike in Western Europe, where ideologies divide countries, there is an 'American creed'. This creed consists of a set of political ideals (whether compatible or not), including liberty and equality (of opportunity), democracy and the rule of law, government by the majority and respect for minority rights. Conflict arises in promoting the means to achieve these various ideals, particularly during idealistic periods of reform in the country's history. It is fair to cite both the New Deal of the 1930s and the Great Society legislation of the 1960s as examples of idealistic reforming periods. The decline of traditional liberalism, involving traditional 1930s- and 1960s-style programmes, has encouraged an increased use of the market even where redistributive welfare policy is accepted. Even if the political climate changes, a new welfare agenda is not likely to be characterized by government-dominated centralism. This is not to deny that there is a radical and, indeed, moralistic component to US politics which has implications for welfare policy. However, it remains to be seen what effect this will have upon public policy in future years, especially in light of the 'Clintonization' of the Democratic Party, whereby the Democratic Party represents the non-rich 'middle American', rather than the specific constituencies of the underprivileged.

Finally, both liberals and conservatives can agree that a major challenge is the co-ordination of health and welfare programmes. For example, the USA spends over US $100,000m. per year on programmes related to disability (including both national and state programmes). However, these programmes are unco-ordinated: for example, some imply that the disabled should work and join the mainstream, whereas others seem to advocate their retirement and segregation from the rest of the population. As with much of health and welfare policy in the USA, each programme represents a specific, 'single-issue' regulatory solution to a problem unique to its time and, in aggregate, each fails to meet contemporary needs in an effective manner. The challenge acknowledged by most politicians is how to make health and welfare programmes more effective without actually dismantling them.

DIVERSITY AND EQUALITY IN THE USA

GILLIAN PEELE

Whatever the outcome of the 2008 US presidential election, the contest will stand out as the first in which an African American successfully sought the nomination of his party and where his nearest rival in the race to carry the Democratic Party banner was a woman. If the Barack Obama and Hillary Clinton candidacies have been seen as important milestones on the road to ethnic and gender equality in the USA, the controversies surrounding them also underline the extent to which the electorate is not so much a collection of individual voters but a mosaic of diverse groups and identities, each with very different collective strengths and political agendas. Furthermore, the 2008 election has focused attention on the continuing fight by disadvantaged groups in American society to realize the Constitution's promise of equality and on the importance of symbolism in its public life. In this significant sense the USA remains a country where the noble aspiration of equality for individuals is often frustrated by deep economic, social and political inequalities.

THE PURSUIT OF EQUALITY

The demand for constitutional and, indeed, for broader political equality has been a continuing thread in the history and politics of the USA. However, the meaning of equality—and how best to achieve it—has been sharply contested at different points in the country's political development. This pursuit of equality within the US political system was made especially contentious by the large number of self-conscious minorities who claimed the protection of the Constitution and the courts, as well as the political branches of the governmental system. Different groups within the USA's highly pluralistic society, especially, but not exclusively, ethnic groups, thus sought the protection of the law against discrimination; however, they sometimes also sought from Congress and the executive branch special measures (such as affirmative-action policies) to advance their political and economic status.

Individuals too have looked to the Constitution and the courts to protect a range of civil liberties, including freedom of speech, freedom of religion and, more controversially, the right to bear arms. Crucial to the USA's constitutional tradition was a belief in limited government and government under law. The US political system was thus marked by two distinctive features: its vibrant pluralism created a system of political competition in which a multitude of interest groups have mobilized to shape public policy and values; and US constitutional law and practice provided principles for protecting minority rights and reconciling the many conflicts between minority groups and between majority and minority preferences.

Civil liberties and minority rights are themes that remained highly salient as the 2008 presidential election loomed and the Bush presidency entered its final phase. The climate for the protection of civil rights and civil liberties, indeed for the celebration of social diversity, had been changed both by the Bush Administration's own conservative instincts and by the 2001 terrorist attacks and the subsequent declaration of a global 'war on terror'. The terrorist attacks on New York and Washington, DC, in 2001 (as well as the subsequent campaign to oust the regime of Saddam Hussain in Iraq and the occupation of that country) inevitably placed a strain on the USA's cultural pluralism in a way that especially affected minority groups such as Muslims and Arabs.

The immediate response of Congress to the 2001 terrorist attacks was legislation—the so-called 'Patriot Act' (Uniting and Strengthening America by Providing the Appropriate Tools Required to Intercept and Obstruct Terrorism—PATRIOT—Act of 2001)—which was signed into law in October 2001 and renewed after much debate in 2006. Under this legislation, which complemented other statutes such as the Foreign Intelligence Surveillance Act, wide-ranging powers were given to the Government to conduct surveillance activities on citizens and non-citizens alike, and the grounds for deeming an alien inadmissible to the USA or deporting an alien were expanded. What especially concerned observers, however, was the extent to which the legislation allowed large numbers of non-citizens to be called in for questioning by federal authorities, owing to their religious and ethnic background, their associations or their national origin. There was also concern about the extent to which the Act allowed the federal Government access to a range of personal records, including medical notes and library borrowings. Thus, the period since the passage of the 2001 legislation has seen an increasingly intense debate (joined by such important pressure groups as the American Civil Liberties Union—ACLU) over the erosion of civil liberties in the USA and over the best measures to protect the country against the new species of terrorism.

In this essay we assess the evolution of the debate on civil liberties, constitutionalism and equality in the USA in an attempt to capture the changing character of the US political culture. The essay looks first at the way in which US society has been forged by immigration and at the tensions created by ethnic diversity and by the immigration issue itself. The essay then examines the current size and political agenda of the different ethnic groups, before moving on to consider the strategies of groups that mobilize around non-ethnic factors, such as gender, religion and sexual orientation, as well as key issues facing various minorities in the USA. In this context the essay examines the changing political strategies of these groups (including affirmative action) in their bid for greater equality, and assesses their response to a political climate that has been profoundly changed not just by the Bush Administration and its global 'war on terror', but by the experience of starkly deteriorating economic conditions.

IMMIGRATION, PLURALISM AND NATIVISM

To say that the USA is marked by pluralism is to highlight the various distinctive sub-groups within the USA and the extent to which political identities have been shaped by such key divisions as ethnicity and religion. Many of the ethnic divisions of US society are the product of the waves of immigration that have been a regular feature of US history. Despite spasmodic efforts to restrict entry into the USA (for example, in 1921 and 1924), the promise of a new life in the USA has always been a powerful magnet for migrants wishing to escape political persecution or simply to improve their economic lot. Over the course of the 20th century the population of the USA nearly quadrupled, from 76m. people in 1900 to 281m. at the census of 2000. (Just how quickly the population was rising could also be gleaned from the fact that, according to the US Census Bureau, by 2006 the estimated US population was 299m.) The 2000 census showed that the US population had increased by 32.7m. in the last decade of the 20th century alone. The extent to which immigration remained a factor in shaping the contemporary composition of the USA can be gauged also from the fact that in 2000 some 10% of the population was foreign-born. The distribution of population has changed markedly over the last century. Whereas in 1900 the most populous states were New York, Pennsylvania, Illinois, Ohio and Missouri, by 2000 the five most populous states were California, Texas, New York, Florida and Illinois. This movement has created a new dynamic, making these growth states politically, economically and culturally more important in the nation as a whole.

Although immigration has always been an acknowledged feature of US life, it has regularly been a topic of fierce political controversy. The symbolism of the Statue of Liberty, Emma Lazarus's welcoming lines and the image of the golden door through which the immigrants passed on Ellis Island may be familiar elements of the political culture, yet the reality of the relationship between the USA's immigrants and the host community was often one of conflict rather than harmony. Immigrants were variously accused of posing a political threat to the USA because of their enduring loyalties to their own country, of threatening economic prosperity and providing a source of cheap labour, and of threatening US identity. There was violence against ethnic minorities in the 19th century and extensive discrimination against them, especially regarding employment. Changes in the character of immigration from the 1880s tended to produce harsh reactions from the host community and the expression of nativist sentiment. This backlash reflected a shift in the source of immigration as the majority of new arrivals came not from Northern Europe but from Southern and Eastern Europe. Similarly, following the liberalization of the immigration laws in 1965 there was a massive influx of new immigration, which generated a heated public debate. Immigration after 1965 literally changed the face of the USA, as this new migration came primarily from Asia, Latin America and the Caribbean. Its impact on US identity was profound because not only did it create greater diversity within the USA, but it also begat a new demography in which non-Hispanic white citizens (who as late as the 1970s constituted nearly 90% of the population) would become a minority (an estimated 46%) by 2050.

In addition to legal immigration, there has also been the phenomenon of illegal immigration. This was the product both of the difficulty of policing the USA's extensive border with Mexico and of the need for cheap labour in various sectors of the US economy, not least agriculture, food preparation, construction and domestic service. In 2006 the Pew Hispanic Center in Washington, DC, calculated that the unauthorized population of the USA in March of that year was 11.5m.–12m. (Passel, 2006—see Bibliographic References). From time to time illegal aliens have been granted an amnesty, as occurred under the Immigration Reform and Control Act of 1986. This legislation, *inter alia*, also made it an offence to hire an illegal immigrant.

The terrorist attacks of 11 September 2001 and the subsequent 'war on terror' have transformed the debate about immigration. Public support for immigration control increased and a much harsher attitude towards illegal immigration and the enforcement of the law was adopted. In 2005 the House of Representatives approved legislation that sought to introduce much more draconian criminal penalties for illegal immigrants and those who aided them. There was also a project to construct a wall along the US–Mexican border. The new legislation provoked demonstrations across the USA in March and April 2006. The Senate, by contrast, adopted a more measured approach—the Comprehensive Immigration Reform Act, which placed less emphasis on criminalization and enforcement and left open the possibility that some long-term illegal aliens could become US citizens. Both chambers planned to hold further hearings on the issue later in the year. The widely supported protests against the lower chamber's effort to criminalize illegal immigration highlighted the extent to which the immigration debate had entered a new phase and was unlikely to disappear from the national agenda. On the other hand, groups such as the Federation for American Immigration Reform (FAIR) were also active in trying to limit immigration and especially to prevent amnesties for illegal immigrants.

The states most affected by illegal immigration, particularly California and Texas, have frequently experienced political campaigns designed to reduce illegal immigration and to restrict the rights of access to welfare and education. In California, for example, two referendum campaigns in recent years, Proposition 187 and Proposition 227, were directed at illegal immigrants and their rights to welfare. However, since the onset of the 'war on terror', immigration has become a national issue and one where a variety of groups were likely to mobilize. Past debates about immigration have seen some paradoxical alliances. For example, the business sector, although often identified with more conservative values in the USA, was generally pro-immigrant, seeing in the perpetual renewal of the USA both an expanding market and expanding source of labour. Organized labour, by contrast, although frequently identified with liberal and progressive values in the 20th century was often deeply hostile to immigration. In the 19th century trade unions mobilized behind restrictions based on colour and ethnicity, and until quite recently (2000) they were hostile to illegal immigration and unwilling to take any interest in the conditions under which such immigrants were employed. The south was generally more hostile to immigration than the north-east.

By 2007 the immigration debate had taken on a different character, with organizations such as FAIR being joined by groups such as the Coalition for Immigration Security, as well as many mainstream politicians in demanding stricter enforcement of immigration laws. Meanwhile, those minority groups especially affected by reform proposals, particularly Hispanics and their representative groups, such as the National Council of la Raza, saw the issue as threatening their civil rights: such a threat required a strengthening of their presence in the political arena.

THE CHANGING MOSAIC: ETHNIC DIVERSITY IN THE 21ST CENTURY

The contemporary immigration debate highlights the extent to which the USA's fluid demography raises questions both about US identity and about the balance of political and social power in the future. Before attempting to explore further the position of the USA's ethnic sub-groups it is necessary to identify them. This task is no easy matter since race and ethnicity throw up a host of complexities. Does it, for example, make sense to treat Latinos or Hispanics as a single group when they include people originating from many different parts of the world, ranging from Europe to Mexico, South America and the Caribbean? (Latino and Hispanic are interchangeable terms, though Latino is probably more widely used. The 2000 census used the category of Latino for the first time, allowing respondents of Spanish, Hispanic or Latino origin to identify themselves as of Mexican, Puerto Rican, Cuban or other Spanish/Hispanic/Latino origin.) Alterations to the decennial census format meant that ethnicity was recognized not as an objective or scientific category, but as a matter of personal identity. Respondents therefore assigned themselves to an ethnic group. In 2000, for the first time also, the census allowed Americans to define themselves in terms of more than one racial identity and just over 2% took this option. Indeed, the whole terminology of race and ethnicity is itself controversial and terms that groups are happy to use in one generation may become suspect in another.

The most recent population projections emphasize not merely the continuing cultural and ethnic diversity of the country but marked changes in the relative status of different groups and in the nation's age structure. In 2008 it was projected that ethnic minorities, now roughly one-third of the US population would become the majority in 2042, while in 2050 they would comprise 54% of the country's population. Ethnic minority children would account for more than one-half of all children as early as 2023. The non-Hispanic, white population is projected to grow only very slightly (from 199.8m. to 203.3m.) between 2008 and 2050, bringing its share of total population down to 46% in 2050 from 66% today. The Hispanic population is expected to triple between 2008 and 2050, increasing its share of the total population from 15% to 30%. Put slightly differently, by 2050 nearly one in three Americans will be Hispanic, making Hispanics by far the country's largest minority. By contrast today's black minority population would grow only slightly, from 14% in 2008 to 15% in 2050. The number of Americans of Asian origin is also projected to grow from today's 15.5m. to 40.6m., increasing as a percentage of the population from 5.1% to 9.2%. The representation of American Indian and Native Alaskans is expected to grow slightly from 1.6% of the total population to 2%.

These changes in the ethnic composition of the USA will have a profound effect on the country's cultural identity, not least because of language. But by the middle of the 21st century the USA will also have a very different age structure as by that time the proportion of the population of working age is projected to have decreased from 63% to 57%.

Native Americans

Of course, not all ethnic minorities within the USA are the product of immigration. Some minority groups, such as the African American population, were largely the product of slavery. Other minorities, such as Native Indians and Alaskans, were the original inhabitants of the lands settled by the US colonists. Native American and Alaskan people who predated the arrival of European settlers were badly treated for much of US history and were for a long time denied citizenship. Such legislation as the Indian Removal Act (1830) and the Dawes Act (1887) reflected the urge to appropriate Indian lands and to eradicate native culture. In the 20th century it appeared that the Native Indian population might die out altogether as a result of government mistreatment and neglect. From the 1970s, however, government policy and the courts became more enlightened, recognizing property rights and the distinctive cultural heritage of the Indians. The 1974 Indian Self-Determination and Education Assistance Act marked a change in public attitude, and over the last quarter of the 20th century there was both a steady natural increase and a marked rise in the numbers claiming tribal ancestry. Accompanying this rise was a growth in political awareness among Native Americans. Figures from the 2000 census indicated that there were about 2.5m. persons (0.9% of the population) claiming exclusively Native American ancestry. In comparison, in 1993, according to official figures, there were 2.2m. Native Americans, of whom just over one-half lived on or adjacent to special reservations. (As with other ethnic groups, the percentage of the population identified as Native American or Alaskan would be increased if those claiming this identity as one of a number of racial memberships were added to those identifying solely with those categories.)

The American Indian and native Alaskan population was not evenly distributed and five states with the largest percentage of Native American populations were located west of the Mississippi River. California, however, had the largest absolute number of American Indians (314,000), although this constituted a relatively small percentage of the state's population. In California, where American Indians ran over 50 casinos, their political role as donors became controversial in the 2003 gubernatorial recall election, when the Republican candidate, Arnold Schwarzenegger, attacked Indian involvement in the campaign of Cruz Bustamente, one of the Democratic candidates.

The place of Native Americans in the wider society of the USA received sustained attention in September 2004 with the opening of the National Museum of the American Indian in Washington, DC. Alongside the celebrations, however, there was criticism that many Native Americans still lived at the margins of the country's economic and political life and that the Native American community was especially marked by poor health (including high rates of diabetes, mental illness and alcoholism) and health care provision, a lack of clean living conditions and political impotence. There has also been concern recently about a rise in anti-Indian sentiment in some states, such as Montana. The National Congress of American Indians is the major organization dedicated to the protection of this minority, through defence of its sovereign areas and promotion of its general welfare. Initiatives such as a renewed Indian Health Care Improvement Act and a project designed to monitor the voting process in areas with high percentages of Native Americans represented two items of the political agenda for Native Americans. There have also been efforts by the National Collegiate Athletic Association and individual colleges to ban the use of American Indian nicknames and mascots in sports competitions, a practice which Native Indians find demeaning. Nevertheless, Native Americans remain disadvantaged in US society largely because their distinctive problems have, thus far, been sheltered from general public awareness.

Black Americans

Although slavery was formally abolished in 1865, the African American community had to endure a long period of constitutionally sanctioned segregation. Violence and discrimination, especially in the south, meant that until the 1960s at least the status of the black minority within the USA was difficult to reconcile with the country's claims to be a democracy. In 1954, however, the death knell of segregation was sounded in the *Brown v. Board of Education* case (which declared racial segregation in public schools to be unconstitutional). Thereafter, the Supreme Court increasingly exercised strict judicial scrutiny of laws that discriminated on the basis of race, colour or national origin.

The mobilization of black groups in the civil rights organizations of the 1950s and 1960s produced one of the USA's most significant social movements, led to the dismantling of formal segregation in the south and heightened awareness of de facto segregation and inequality outside the southern states. Producing substantive political and social equality, however, proved rather more difficult than removing the formal segregation. On almost every measure—employment, income levels, wealth, health and education—the USA's black community appears disadvantaged in comparison with white Americans. In 2007, for example, the unemployment rate among black Americans was 8.3%, more than twice that for whites. Census Bureau health insurance statistics published in 2008 showed that 19.5% of the African American population was without health insurance compared with 10.4% of non-Hispanic whites. Although figures on homelessness are difficult to obtain, a 2004 study of the urban poor by the US Conference of Mayors found that 42% of the urban homeless were African Americans. There was a startling disparity in life expectance of 30 years between black and white Americans in 2008 (Doyle, 2008). Such inequalities, though no longer the product of explicit discrimination, reflect complex social patterns and structural inequities in the USA, and are always likely to increase when the economy contracts or when sudden crises—such as that in the US housing market as evidenced from 2007—occur. Unsurprisingly, such inequality has meant that black Americans have become an increasingly important part of the Democratic coalition.

In the early 21st century there was a hint that black American support for the Democratic Party was showing signs of becoming less monolithic and President Bush scored some success in attempting to woo black voters on moral issues. Nevertheless, the Republican Party remained vulnerable to charges that its social and economic policies disadvantaged black Americans. Furthermore, the Bush Administration's tardy response to the effects of 'Hurricane Katrina' in New Orleans, Louisiana, in August 2005 provoked accusations that the race of the victims was a factor. During the campaign for the Democratic presidential nomination black Americans became increasingly enthusiastic about Barack Obama, an African American candidate.

In Congress African Americans have become an important representative force of their community's interests. In the 110th Congress (2006–08) there were 43 African Americans—42 in the House of Representatives and one (Obama) in the Senate.

Latinos

The Hispanic or Latino population was the product of a number of factors. Among these was the territorial expansion of the USA during the 19th century, which incorporated areas with a Spanish-speaking population. More recently, however, the Latino population has been extended by immigration, both legal and illegal, as large numbers of newcomers from Central and South America and the Caribbean entered the USA. The balance within the USA's Latino population is overwhelmingly weighted towards Mexicans, of whom there were an estimated 20,600m. in the USA in 2000, constituting 58% of the country's Latino population.

Language barriers have proved a major factor in preventing Latinos from integrating fully into US life. Some states have attempted to remedy the difficulties that some Latinos experience, particularly in education, by providing mother tongue education; however, this too has become a source of controversy, provoking efforts, particularly at state level, to make English the official language.

Hispanics have increased as a percentage of the school population and constituted 19.8% of all public school pupils in 2005–06, compared with 12.7% in 1993–94. Despite decades of effort to create equality in educational experience, recent studies have revealed an increasing pattern of isolation of ethnic minorities within US schools. Thus, a 2007 study by the Pew Hispanic Center found that three in 10 Hispanics in 2005–06 were attending schools that were 'nearly all minority' in composition, a category defined as a school with fewer than 5% of white pupils (Fry, 2007). On other additional measures Hispanics suffer from some of the inequalities that also affect African Americans—in access to health care, employment and housing.

The ability of Hispanics to wield political influence has been weakened by a tendency not to register for or to vote in elections. But as the fastest growing minority (and one strategically located in a number of swing states) the electoral potential of the Hispanic vote is enormous. Not surprisingly, President Bush was keen to detach the Hispanic vote from its Democratic loyalty, and to some extent his efforts yielded fruit. Yet by 2008 the Pew Hispanic Center was recording that 57% of Hispanic voters were inclined to vote for the Democratic Party as opposed to 23% who were more likely to vote for the Republican Party. During the course of the 2008 campaign there was speculation that hostility between black and Hispanic interests might cause some Hispanics to abstain if Obama secured the Democratic nomination.

Asian Americans

The Asian population expanded significantly in the post-1965 period. The earliest Asian communities in the USA were the result of hiring indentured Chinese labour to work on the construction of the railways. The 19th and early 20th centuries also witnessed some Japanese immigration. Both the Chinese and Japanese communities were objects of suspicion, not least because they were seen as difficult to assimilate into the US mainstream. The fact that these minorities were not of European origin generated hostility and legislative action against them, including laws to prevent entry and laws to prevent the ownership of property, such as the California land laws of 1913 and 1920. During the Second World War the USA's Japanese community became the object of suspicion, and more than 100,000 Japanese Americans, the majority of them US citizens, were interned without proper judicial procedures, simply because of their Japanese descent. Although in 1988 the US Government issued an apology to these Americans of Japanese extraction and awarded them retrospective compensation, the episode underlined the extent to which formal constitutional guarantees could be eroded in time of national emergency.

The more recent post-1965 Asian population (which included immigrants from Korea, Taiwan, Viet Nam, Cambodia and the Philippines) has further increased the US Asian population and, as noted earlier, it is set to rise to 9.2% of the total population by 2050.

NON-ETHNIC GROUPS

Ethnicity is not, of course, the only source of identity or dividing factor in US politics. Religion, gender and sexual identity are all important factors that have given rise to political mobilization and claims for equality and have forced the courts to attempt to determine the extent to which the same considerations of equal protection that apply to ethnic minorities apply to minorities based on religion, gender and sexual orientation. Similarly, Congress took the mandate for equality to apply to groups such as the disabled and the elderly, and passed legislation that protected against discrimination.

Religion

Religion has always been an important factor in US social life. The latter half of the 20th century witnessed a huge increase in the variety of religious practice in the USA and an enhanced awareness of the significance of religion in the political system. The diversity of the US religious scene can in part be explained by the early tolerance of non-conformity in the country and by the First Amendment's guarantees of the free exercise of religion and the prohibition against any federal establishment of religion. Immigration in the late 19th and early 20th centuries gave the USA a significant Jewish population. Post-1965 immigration also changed the USA's religious mix so that by the early years of the 21st century the USA had large numbers of adherents to religions outside the Judaeo-Christian tradition, including Hindus, Buddhists and Muslims.

Although the census no longer includes a question on religion, demographic change in the religious composition of the USA is closely monitored by academics and politicians, who know that religious adherents can be mobilized in the political arena. Traditionally, Jewish Americans formed an important part of the Democratic coalition. Today the Muslim community is seen as having electoral leverage. In 2004 it was reported that a coalition of Muslim interest groups had combined to put pressure on presidential candidates George W. Bush and John Kerry over the discrimination that American Muslims were experiencing and their concerns about civil liberties in the wake of the 'war on terror'. In 2000 American Muslims (who are seen to be acting as a coherent bloc) endorsed the candidacy of Bush; however, in 2004 they lent their support to the Democratic camp.

Many of Bush's social policy initiatives were aimed at shoring up the religious right's support for the Republican Party. The rise of the religious right reflects a general politicization of religion in the USA in the second half of the 20th century. This development could be attributed to at least three factors. First, there was the desire of the more conservative religious groups—evangelicals and fundamentalists—including those not previously much involved in direct political action, to organize in defence of their lifestyle and against permissiveness and secularism. Second, there was the search by political entrepreneurs, particularly those on the right, for support from religious groups and churches on issues such as abortion. Third, there was the impact of high-profile personalities, such as the late Jerry Falwell, who were able to exploit the media and new technology to communicate their message. By the late 1990s, for example, the Christian right had become a powerful, if divisive, force within the Republican Party.

The agenda of many right-of-centre religious groups brought them into direct conflict with other minorities, such as homosexuals, over the extent to which the law should protect privacy or enforce morality. It also produced a new set of questions for the courts, as Republicans and conservatives became more supportive of organized religion within the USA and indeed wanted to give it a greater role, for example by using faith-based groups to provide welfare services.

The political influence of religious groups is no longer as straightforward as it once was. First, the evangelical community is displaying greater diversity, not least because some of its leaders and younger members are anxious to distance themselves from any automatic alliance with the Republicans. Second, Americans generally have become more sceptical about the wisdom of a close relationship between religion and politics. Third, in 2008 all the presidential candidates seemed keen to gather the support of religious voters, thereby creating greater competition and ensuring that the Republican Party could not assume an advantage in this respect.

Gender

Although it might seem odd to count women as a minority group, when women form a majority of the population (in 2006 women continued to outnumber men very slightly in the US population as a whole), gender remains an important division in US society. Certainly, women's groups have been especially successful at using strategies and remedies devised primarily to counter discrimination against black Americans, and the courts and Congress generally looked with suspicion at discrimination based on gender. Thus, when Congress passed its ground-breaking Civil Rights Act of 1964, gender was included as one of the prohibited forms of discrimination and Title IX of the Educational Amendments of 1972 provided the Government with the important sanction of withholding funds from educational institutions that discriminated on grounds of gender. Affirmative-action strategies have been used by women as a way of redressing discrimination against them, especially in the professions and higher education.

Women were not granted the vote until 1920 and the passage of the 19th Amendment did not by itself produce anything like political equality for women, who continued to face a range of barriers in the workplace and in the political system. Indeed, it was not until the 1960s that there was any substantial mobilization of women or the emergence of a feminist movement; nor was there much evidence of a distinct female perception of politics. From the 1970s, however, the issue of women's rights became an important one and evidence of a gender difference in politics accumulated. By the 2000 presidential election, opinion polls were finding a full 10-point difference between men's and women's support for the Democratic candidate, Al Gore. By the 1980s women had also begun to acquire significant positions in national and state politics, mainly, but not exclusively, in the Democratic Party. In 1984 Geraldine Ferraro ran as the first female vice-presidential candidate and in 1997 Madeleine Albright became the first female Secretary of State. In 2004 Condoleezza Rice became the second female to occupy that post. In 2007–08 Hillary Clinton executed a resilient and formidable campaign for the Democratic presidential nomination. Although ultimately defeated by Barack Obama, she appealed strongly to many traditional Democratic constituencies such as the working class and the unions as well as to women and certain ethnic minority groups, notably Hispanics. Republican presidential nominee John McCain selected Sarah Palin as his running mate in 2008, a decision that was designed to appeal not merely to conservative and religious groups but also to women.

The representation of women in Congress has also increased substantially over recent years. In the 110th Congress, elected in 2006, there were 16 women in the Senate and 71 women in the House (together with three delegates without voting rights). Furthermore, one of the most powerful congressional leadership positions, that of Speaker of the House, is occupied by a woman, Nancy Pelosi. In addition, in 2008 eight of the state governors were women.

There are a variety of groups organized to protect women's rights in the USA. Some, such as the National Organization of Women (NOW) and the National Women's Political Caucus (NWPC), are firmly in the liberal and Democratic camp. Others, such as the League of Women Voters, are scrupulously bipartisan. There is also a range of specialist groups, such as the Women's Legal Defense Fund, which was founded in 1971 to promote legal equality for women. Other groups, such as EMILY's list (Early Money Is Like Yeast) and The WISH List (Women in the Senate and the House), are devoted to increasing the number of women in Congress.

Until the 1980s the women's movement had placed the passage of a constitutional amendment to secure equal rights high on its agenda. The development of a reaction against feminism in the 1980s as a result of the mobilization of the new right caused the amendment to founder in the ratification process and polarized the debate on women's issues. The pressure groups working on women's issues thus found themselves facing a fight on two fronts in the 1980s and 1990s. First, they had to prevent the loss of gains made in the 1960s and 1970s and, second, they had to build coalitions to secure improvements in such policy areas as child care.

A particular cause of concern among women was the right to reproductive freedom and, specifically, the right to secure an abortion. Although the Supreme Court had enunciated such a right in *Roe v. Wade* (1973), the opposition to abortion grew in political strength and there was frequent legal testing of the limits of the *Roe v. Wade* ruling. The Supreme Court majority for upholding the 1973 decision narrowed in the 1980s and 1990s as a result of conservative appointments to the Court, but the 1973 decision was not reversed. Instead, subsequent decisions allowed greater freedom to state governments to regulate the provision of abortion, although regulation must not undermine the exercise of the right itself. The occurrence of two vacancies in the Supreme Court in mid-2005 reignited the battle over abortion. Many liberal women's groups were deeply opposed to the appointment of John G. Roberts, Jr, as Chief Justice, as Roberts had expressed doubts about the constitutionality of the right to privacy, a key component of abortion rights. The anti-abortion campaign has witnessed an increasing use of violence, especially by picketing and even bombing abortion clinics and attacking staff. Legislation has been passed (the Freedom of Access to Clinic Entrances Act) to curb such activity and tough sentences have been passed on anti-abortion activists who employ violent tactics.

The agenda of feminist groups has been impeded by the more conservative climate of the USA in recent years. The election to the presidency in 2000 of George W. Bush signalled a serious reversal for them and there was significant opposition among women to the first term appointment of John Ashcroft as Bush's Attorney-General because of the former's stance on abortion and related issues.

The most recent abortion battles have focused on the partial-birth abortions. Congress approved (and Bush signed) legislation to proscribe such abortions in 2003, but there was immediate constitutional challenge to the legislation in a number of states, not least because it seemed to run contrary to the Supreme Court decision in the 2000 *Stenberg v. Carhart* case. In June 2004 the legislation was struck down by a federal district judge in California. In 2007 the Supreme Court upheld the legislation in two cases (*Gonzales v. Carhart* and *Gonzales v. Planned Parenthood*), which were viewed as possible signals that the *Roe v. Wade* ruling might be reviewed.

Sexual Orientation

The growth of the gay liberation movement in the 1960s made groupings based on sexual orientation a powerful force, especially in some areas of the country such as San Francisco. In the 1970s the goal of the lesbian and gay rights movement was primarily to achieve legal equality for homosexuals in such fields as property rights and employment. The shift from a liberal and permissive environment to one of conservatism in the 1980s put the gay movement on the defensive. The spread of AIDS and HIV gave the gay movement a new agenda, which increasingly centred on health care issues. The liberal orientation of homosexual pressure groups made it inevitable that they would overwhelmingly align with the Democratic Party, although a gay Republican group (the Log Cabin group, which dates from 1993) was active and well-funded. Although President Bill Clinton (1993–2001) was sympathetic to gay rights, the Bush Administration has been increasingly hostile. In June 2003 the Department of Justice under John Ashcroft became publicly embroiled in a controversy over whether its officials could mark Gay Pride Week in an awards ceremony at the Department. Initially, the Department appeared to have banned the ceremony, but subsequently allowed it. The issue had symbolic significance, given the signal that such a ban would have sent about civil rights and discrimination. In 2004 the Republican Party included opposition to gay marriage in its electoral platform, echoing President Bush's endorsement of a constitutional ban forbidding same-sex marriage. As a result, the Log Cabin group refused to endorse President Bush for re-election. The emphasis on traditional morality formed part of an electoral strategy designed to solidify key Republican supporters. It was not entirely clear what electoral effect the issue has but polls indicate that the majority of voters, while opposed to gay marriage, were willing to accept same-sex civil unions.

The courts have been cautious about extending constitutional protection to homosexuals. In *Romer v. Evans* (1996) the Supreme Court, however, did strike down a state constitutional amendment designed to prevent the state giving homosexuals protection against discrimination. Furthermore, in 2003, in the landmark case of *Lawrence v. Texas*, the Supreme Court, on equal protection grounds, struck down all anti-sodomy laws across the USA.

Willingness to recognize same-sex marriage and same-sex civil partnerships varies across the USA. Two states, Massachusetts and California, permit same-sex marriage while a growing number recognize same-sex civil partnerships, which allow same-sex couples the same rights as heterosexual couples. However, many other states have passed constitutional amendments confining marriage to unions between a man and a woman.

Disability

Disabled people were another group whose claims to equality were increasingly couched in the language of civil rights and the claims of non-discrimination implicit in the Constitution. The Americans with Disabilities Act 1990 provided wide-ranging protections to disabled people by putting an obligation on employers and government and educational institutions, for example, to ensure that, as far as possible, disabled people would be able to have access to all facilities.

Age

Senior citizens in many Western countries have organized themselves into powerful pressure groups. In the USA such groups as the American Association of Retired People (AARP) became highly successful advocates of such issues as health care, social security and Medicare. This development was not perhaps surprising as older citizens had the time and, perhaps, the money with which to pursue political objectives. It was also important to note the growth in the number of retirees and the elderly. It was estimated that, while in 2005 there were 36.8m. people aged 65 years and over in the USA (about 12% of the population), by 2030 one in five of the population would be over the age of 65. In the USA, although the Supreme Court has resisted treating age as a suspect classification, there are a number of legislative protections against age discrimination.

Affirmative Action

Minority groups determined to improve their position within US society promoted their cause on many fronts, using very different strategies at different levels of the US political system. Coalition-building and lobbying worked well in Congress. Almost all pressure groups kept a legal team to push test cases or defend litigation that might damage their interests. The tactics employed by groups would, of course, depend on the particular agenda at any time. In recent years one of the techniques originally used to promote minority interests—affirmative action—itself has become the object of extensive and bitter litigation. Affirmative action, first used in the 1960s, was a strategy by which government could do more than simply eliminate discrimination against minorities, especially black Americans. Government, through education programmes, could give hitherto disadvantaged groups a preference in a way that would aim to compensate for past discrimination. Such programmes proliferated at all levels of US life—federal, state and private—and involved educational admissions, employment and promotion, contracts and business financing.

Initially, these programmes were applauded as part of the effort to produce greater equality. During the 1970s, however, opponents of affirmative action began to argue that affirmative-action programmes were constitutionally obnoxious because, by definition, they discriminated on the basis of race. Such opponents were not simply to be found on the right. Civil libertarians who remembered the quotas against Jewish citizens opposed them, as did many black Americans who were, in theory, the beneficiaries of such programmes (Supreme Court Justice Clarence Thomas, for example, was a vehement opponent of affirmative action). A series of cases in the 1970s and 1980s attacked the foundations of the strategy, and in *Adarand Constructors, Inc v. Pena* (1995) the Supreme Court declared that all affirmative-action programmes should be subject to strict judicial review. However, the Court has not been entirely hostile to the intention behind affirmative action, and in 2003, when many conservatives (including the Bush Administration) were looking to the Court to strike a further blow against affirmative action, it upheld much of the affirmative-action programme run at the University of Michigan's law school and its College of Literature, Science and the Arts (*Grutter v. Bollinger* and *Gratz and Hamacher v. Bollinger*).

CONCLUSION

The USA is, and always has been, an 'unfinished' society in the sense that its openness to immigration and its diversity continually throw up new patterns of politics and new conflicts. The period since 1965 has been one of mass immigration, in many ways more profoundly unsettling than that of the late 19th and early 20th centuries. This was because of the character of the new immigration and because it came at a time when cultural divisions have produced new political fault lines within the USA. The events of 11 September 2001 and the controversial responses to them added further fuel to the already volatile politics of the USA. Thus, for some critics the post-11 September period justified an increase in nationalism, which involved strengthening the country's defences even at the expense of its tradition of sensitivity to minorities and to civil liberties. For other critics, the Bush Administration appears to be exploiting the fear of terrorism to strengthen the executive and is condoning a new ethnic and racial intolerance. Certainly, the immigration issue is unlikely to disappear and its salience itself causes divisions in US society and is disturbing for recent arrivals.

The 2008 presidential election has added a new dimension to the debate. Taking place as it does against a background of economic downturn and considerable unease about the conduct of the war with Iraq, the conditions appear to be favourable to a change of direction and party control of the White House. For many observers the nomination of Barack Obama offers a possibility of a new unity, transcending ethnic and other divisions. Yet at the same time it is possible that the divisions in American society, including the deeply embedded ones of ethnicity, will mobilize opposition to him. If so, it can be expected that the politics of the USA in the immediate future will become increasingly difficult to manage and that its social climate will become ever more beset by conflict.

Bibliographic References

Doyle, L. 'American Inequality Highlighted by 30-year Gap in Life Expectancy', in *The Independent*. London, 17 July 2008.

Fry, R. *The Changing Racial and Ethnic Composition of US Public Schools*. Washington, DC, Pew Hispanic Center, 2007.

Passel, J. S. *Size and Characteristics of the Unauthorized Migrant Population in the US*. Washington, DC, Pew Hispanic Center, 2006.

US Census Bureau. 'An older and more diverse nation by mid-century'. Washington, DC, 14 August 2008.

SELECT BIBLIOGRAPHY (ECONOMIC AFFAIRS)

Bordo, M. D. (Ed.). *The Defining Moment: The Great Depression and the American Economy in the Twentieth Century (National Bureau of Economic Research Project Report)*. Chicago, IL, University of Chicago Press, 1998.

Brenner, R. *The Boom and the Bubble: The US Economy Today*. London, Verso, 2002.

Caiden, N., and Wildavsky, A. B. *The New Politics of the Budgetary Process*, 4th edn. New York, Addison-Wesley, 2000.

Clarkson, K. W., and Muris, T. J. (Eds). *The Federal Trade Commission Since 1970: Economic Regulation and Bureaucratic Behavior*. Cambridge, Cambridge University Press, 2008.

Clement, N. C. (Ed.). *North American Integration: Theory and Practice*. Cheltenham, Edward Elgar Publishing, 2000.

Cohen, J. E. *Politics and Economic Policy in the United States*. Boston, MA, Houghton, Mifflin College, 2000.

Congressional Quarterly. *Congress and the Nation*, Vols 1–6 (1945–84). Washington, DC.

Congressional Quarterly Almanac, various dates. Washington, DC.

Crystal, J. *Unwanted Company: Foreign Investment in American Industries*. Ithaca, NY, Cornell University Press, 2003.

Davis, M. *Prisoners of the American Dream: Politics and Economy in the History of the US Working Class*. London, Verso Books, 2000.

Economic Report of the President. Washington, DC, Government Printing Office, annual.

Energy Information Administration (US Department of Energy). *Monthly Energy Review*. Washington, DC, Government Printing Office.

Annual Energy Outlook. Washington, DC, Government Printing Office.

Renewable Energy Annual. Washington, DC, Government Printing Office.

Freeman, R. B. *America Works: Thoughts on the Exceptional U.S. Labor Market*. New York, Russell Sage Foundation, 2008.

Garten, H. A. *US Financial Regulation and the Level Playing Field (International Political Economy)*. New York, St Martin's Press, 2001.

Geisst, C. R. *Wall Street—A History: From its Beginnings to the Fall of Enron*, 2nd edn. New York, Oxford University Press, 2004.

Gordon, J. S. *An Empire of Wealth: The Epic History of American Economic Power*. New York, HarperCollins, 2004.

Gosling, J. J. *Politics and the American Economy*. Reading, MA, Addison-Wesley, 1999.

Budgetary Politics in American Governments. New York, Routledge, 2001.

Hakes, J. *A Declaration of Energy Independence: How Freedom from Foreign Oil Can Improve National Security, Our Economy and the Environment*. Hoboken, NJ, John Wiley, 2008

Hallberg, M. C. *Economic Trends in US Agriculture and Food Systems Since World War II*. Ames, IA, Iowa State University Press, 2001.

Hamilton, S. *Trucking Country: The Road to America's Wal-Mart Economy*. Princeton, NJ, Princeton University Press, 2008.

Henning, C. R. *Accountability and Oversight of US Exchange Rate Policy*. Washington, DC, Peterson Institute for International Economics, 2008.

Hetzel, R. L. *The Monetary Policy of the Federal Reserve: A History*. Cambridge, Cambridge University Press, 2008.

Hughes, J., and Cain, L. P. *American Economic History*, 6th edn. Boston, MA, Addison Wesley, 2002.

International Monetary Fund. *International Financial Statistics*. Washington, DC, monthly.

United States of America: Article IV Consultation—Staff Report; Staff Statement; and Public Information Notice on the Executive Board Discussion. Washington, DC, annual.

World Economic Outlook. Washington, DC, annual.

Jansson, B. S. *The Sixteen-Trillion-Dollar Mistake*. New York, Columbia University Press, 2001.

Karrier, T. *Great Experiments in American Economic Policy: From Kennedy to Reagan*. Westport, CT, Praeger Publishing, 1999.

Killick, J. *The United States and European Reconstruction, 1945–1960*. Keele, Edinburgh University Press, 1997.

Lal, D. *In Defense of Empires*. Washington, DC, American Enterprise Institute, 2002.

Lauck, J. *American Agriculture and the Problem of Monopoly: The Political Economy of Grain Belt Farming 1953–1980*. Lincoln, NE, University of Nebraska Press, 2000.

Lazonick, W. (Ed.). *American Corporate Economy: Critical Perspectives on Business and Management*. Abingdon, Routledge, 2002.

Lichtenstein, N. (Ed.). *Wal-Mart: The Face of Twenty-First Century Capitalism*. New York, New Press, 2005.

Light, P. C. *The True Size of Government*. Washington, DC, Brookings Institution Press, 1999.

The New Public Service. Washington, DC, Brookings Institution Press, 1999.

Pressure To Grow. Policy Brief No. 65. Washington, DC, Brookings Institution, October 2000.

Lindsey, B. *The Age of Abundance*. London, Collins, 2008.

Litan, R. E., and Rivlin, A. M. *Beyond the Dot.coms. The Economic Promise of the Internet*. Washington, DC, Brookings Institution Press, 2001.

Lundestad, G. *Empire by Integration: The United States and European Integration, 1945–1997*. Oxford, Oxford University Press, 1998.

MacArthur, J. R. *The Selling of 'Free Trade': NAFTA, Washington and the Subversion of American Democracy*. Berkeley, CA, University of California Press, 2001.

Magnuson, J. *Mindful Economics: How the US Economy Works, Why It Matters and How It Could Be Different*. New York, Seven Stories Press, 2008.

Mahoney, A. V. *Federal Research and Development Budgeting and Priorities*. Hauppage, NY, Nova Science, 2008.

Makhijani, A. *Carbon-Free and Nuclear-Free: A Roadmap for US Energy Policy*. Muskegon, MI, RDR Books, 2008.

Mann, C. L. *Is the US Trade Deficit Sustainable?* Washington, DC, Institute for International Economics, 1999.

Is the Current Account Deficit Sustainable? Washington, DC, Institute for Finance and Development, 2000.

Marable, M., Ness, I., and Wilson, J. (Eds). *Race and Labor Matters in the New US Economy*. Lanham, MD, Rowman & Littlefield Publrs, Inc, 2006.

Maynard, M. *The End of Detroit: How the Big Three Lost Their Grip on the American Market*. New York, Doubleday Publishing, 2003.

Morris, C. R. *Apart at the Seams: The Collapse of Private Pension and Health Care Protections*. New York, Century Foundation, 2006.

National Governor Association/National Association of State Budget Officers. *The Fiscal Survey of the States*. Washington, DC, May 2002.

Naylor, R. T. *Satanic Purses: Money, Myth and Misinformation in the War on Terror*. Montréal, McGill-Queen's University Press, 2008.

O'Hanlon, M. E. *Defense Policy Choices for the Bush Administration*, 2nd edn. Washington, DC, Brookings Institution Press, 2002.

Oliver, M., and Shapiro, T. *Black Wealth / White Wealth: A New Perspective on Racial Inequality*. Abingdon, Routledge, 2006.

Organisation for Economic Co-operation and Development. *Economic Outlook*. Paris, 2 a year.

The United States, Economic Surveys. Paris, annual.

Palazzolo, D. J. *Done Deal? The Politics of the 1997 Budget Agreement*. New York, Chatham House Publrs, 2000.

Panitch, L., and Konings, M. (Eds). *American Empire and the Political Economy of Global Finance*. New York, Palgrave Macmillan, 2008.

Partnoy, F. *Infectious Greed: How Deceit and Risk Corrupted the Financial Markets*. London, Profile Books, 2003.

Peláez, C. M., and Peláez, C. A. *The Global Recession Risk: Dollar Devaluation and the World Economy*. New York, Palgrave Macmillan, 2007.

Powers, T. C. *Leakage: The Bleeding of the American Economy*. New Canaan, CT, Benchmark Publications Inc, 1996.

Reich, R. B. *Supercapitalism: The Battle for Democracy in an Age of Big Business*. Cambridge, Icon Books, 2008.

Reischauer, R., *et al*. *Setting National Priorities: Budget Choices for the Next Century*. Washington, DC, Brookings Institution, 1996.

Richards, L. *Union-Free America: Workers and Antiunion Culture*. Champaign, IL, University of Illinois Press, 2008.

Samuels, W. J. *Research in the History of Economic Thought and Methodology, Vol. 18: American Economics*, London, JAI Press, 2000.

Sato, R., and Wachtel, P. (Eds). *Trade Friction and Foreign Policy: Problems and Prospects of Japan and the United States*. Cambridge, Cambridge University Press, 2008.

Schick, A. *The Federal Budget: Politics, Policy, Process*, revised edn. Washington, DC, Brookings Institution, 2000.

Seabrooke, L. *US Power in International Finance: The Victory of Dividends (International Political Economy Series)*. New York, St Martin's Press, 2001.

Seavoy, R. *An Economic History of the United States*. Abingdon, Routledge, 2006.

Sedjo, R. A. *Perspectives on Sustainable Resources in America*. Baltimore, MD, Johns Hopkins University Press, 2008.

Soderberg, N., and Katulis, B. *The Prosperity Agenda: What the World Wants from America—and What We Want in Return*. Hoboken, NJ, John Wiley Press, 2008.

Spiliotes, C. J. *Vicious Cycle: Presidential Decision Making in the American Political Economy*. College Park, TX, Texas A&M University Press, 2002.

Stein, H. *Presidential Economics: The Making of Economic Policy from Roosevelt to Reagan and Beyond*. New York, Touchstone Books, 1994.

Swartz, M., with Watkins, S. *Power Failure: The Rise and Fall of Enron*. London, Aurum Press, 2003.

US Advisory Commission on Intergovernmental Relations. *Significant Aspects of Fiscal Federalism, 2000–2001*. Washington, DC, Government Printing Office, 2001.

US Bureau of the Census. *Annual Survey of Manufactures*. Washington, DC, Government Printing Office, annual.

US Bureau of Economic Analysis. *Survey of Current Business*. Washington, DC, monthly.

US Congressional Budget Office. *Statistical Abstract of the United States*. Washington, DC, Government Printing Office, annual.

US Department of Agriculture. *Agricultural Statistics*. Washington, DC, Government Printing Office, annual.

Crop Production Reports. Washington, DC, Government Printing Office, monthly and annual.

Economic Indicators of the Farm Sector. Washington, DC, Government Printing Office, 5 a year.

World Grain Situation and Outlook. Washington, DC, Government Printing Office, annual.

World Oilseed Situation and Market Highlights. Washington, DC, Government Printing Office, annual.

US Department of Commerce. *Fisheries of the United States*. Washington, DC, Government Printing Office, annual.

US Department of Energy—see Energy Information Administration.

US Department of the Interior, Bureau of Mines. *Minerals Year Book*. Washington, DC, Government Printing Office, annual (two vols).

US International Trade Administration. *US Industrial Outlook*. Washington, DC, Government Printing Office, annual.

US Office of Management and Budget. *Budget of the US Government, Fiscal Year 2003*. Washington, DC, US Government Printing Office, 2002; www.whitehouse.gov/OMB.

Historical Tables, Budget of the US Government, Fiscal Year 2003. Washington, DC, 2002; www.whitehouse.gov/OMB.

US Office of Personnel Management. *The Fact Book. Federal Civilian Workforce Statistics*. Washington, DC, 2001.

Demographic Profile of the Federal Workforce. Washington, DC, Federal Civilian Workforce Statistics, 2001.

Employment and Trends as of November 2001. Washington, DC, Federal Civilian Workforce Statistics, 2002.

Veeser, C. *A World Safe for Capitalism: Dollar Diplomacy and America's Rise to Global Power*. New York, Columbia University Press, 2002.

Walton, G., and Rockoff, H. *History of the American Economy with Economic Applications*. Cincinnati, OH, South-Western College Publishing, 2004.

Wendel, H. F. *State Profiles: The Population and Economy of Each US State*. Lanham, MD, Bernan, 2002.

The White House. *Financial Report of the United States: The Official Annual White House Report*. Nashville, TN, Nelson Current, 2006.

Wolff, E. N. *Top Heavy: The Increasing Inequality of Wealth in America and What Can Be Done About It*, 2nd edn. New York, New Press, 2002.

Woodward, B. *Maestro: Alan Greenspan and the American Economic Boom*. London, Simon and Schuster, 2000.

Wu, J. *Frontiers in Resource and Rural Economics*. Baltimore, MD, Johns Hopkins University Press, 2008.

SELECT BIBLIOGRAPHY (SOCIAL AFFAIRS)

Ahlstrom, S. E. *A Religious History of the American People*, 2 vols. New Haven, CT, Yale University Press, 1972.

Alex-Assensoh, Y., and Hanks, L. (Eds). *Black and Multiracial Politics in America*. New York, New York University Press, 2000.

Altenbaugh, R. *The Teacher's Voice: A Social History of Teaching in 20th Century America*. New York, Routledge, 1992.

Barone, M. *The New Americans*. Washington, DC, Regnery Publishing Inc, 2001.

Bayor, R. H. *Race and Ethnicity in America: A Concise History*. New York, Columbia University Press, 2003.

Beauregard, R. A. *When America Became Suburban*. Minneapolis, MN, Universty of Minnesota Press, 2006.

Becker, P. C. *A Statistical Portrait of the United States: Social Conditions and Trends*, 2nd edn. Lanham, MD, Bernan, 2002.

Bodnar, J. *The Transplanted: A History of Immigrants in Urban America*. Bloomington, IN, Indiana University Press, 1985.

Braverman, H. *Labour and Monopoly Capital*, 25th anniversary edn. New York, Monthly Review Press, 1998.

Buenker, J. D., and Ratman, L. A. *Multiculturalism in the United States: A Comparative Guide to Acculturation and Ethnicity*. London, Greenwood Press, 1992.

Buff, R. *Immigrant Rights in the Shadows of Citizenship*. New York, New York University Press, 2008.

Burke, S., *et al* (Eds). *Social Security and Medicare*. Washington, DC, Brookings Institution, 2000.

Cochran, C. E. *American Public Policy: An Introduction*. New York, St Martin's Press, 1993.

Cohen, C. L., and Boyer, P. S. (Eds). *Religion and the Culture of Print in Modern America*. Madison, WI, University of Wisconsin Press, 2008.

Colgrove, J., Markowitz, G., and Rosner, D. (Eds). *The Contested Boundaries of American Public Health*. Piscataway, NJ, Rutgers University Press, 2008.

Corbett, M., and Corbett, J. M. *Politics and Religion in the United States*. New York, Garland Publrs, 1999.

Davies, P. J. (Ed.). *An American Quarter Century*. Manchester and New York, Manchester University Press, 1995.

Davies, P. J., and Waldstein, F. J. (Eds). *Political Issues in America: The 1990s Revisited*, 2nd edn. Manchester and New York, Manchester University Press, 1996.

Davis, T. J. *Race Relations in America: A Reference Guide with Primary Documents*. Oxford, Greenwood Press, 2006.

D'Innocenzo, M. *Immigration and Ethnicity: 'Melting Pot' or 'Salad Bowl'*. London, Greenwood Press, 1992.

Eck, D. *A New Religious America*. San Francisco, CA, Harper-San Francisco, 2001.

Egan, M., and Crane, J. *Natural Protest: Essays on the History of American Environmentalism*. New York, Routledge, 2008.

Engle, R., and Miller, T. L. (Eds). *The American Stage: Social and Economic Issues from the Colonial Period to the Present*. Cambridge, Cambridge University Press, 1996.

Erie, S. P. *Rainbow's End: Irish-Americans and the Dilemmas of Urban Machine Politics, 1840–1985*. Berkeley, CA, University of California Press, 1988.

Feingold, H. L. *Zion in America: the Jewish Experience from Colonial Times to the Present New York*. Mineola, NY, Dover Publications, 2002.

Gabaccia, D. R., and Leach, C. W. (Eds). *Immigrant Life in the US: Multidisciplinary Perspectives*. Abingdon, Routledge, 2003.

Garcia, F. C. (Ed.). *Pursuing Power: Latinos and the Political System*. Notre Dame, IN, University of Notre Dame Press, 1997.

Garcia, J. A. *Latino Politics in America: Community, Culture and Interests*. Lanham, MD, Rowman and Littlefield, 2003.

Garcia, M. T. *Mexican Americans*. New Haven, CT, Yale University Press, 1989.

De Genova, N. (Ed.). *Racial Transformations: Latinos and Asians Remaking the United States*. Durham, NC, Duke University Press, 2006.

Gentile, E. *God's Democracy: American Religion After September 11*. Westport, CT, Greenwood Publishing Group, Inc., 2008.

Gerstle, G. *American Crucible: Race and Nation in the Twentieth Century*. Princeton, NJ, Princeton University Press, 2001.

Gottlieb, S. E. *Morality Imposed: The Rehnquist Court and Liberty in America*. New York, New York University Press, 2000.

Guerrero, A. *Silence at Boalt Hall: The Dismantling of Affirmative Action*. Berkeley, CA, University of California Press, 2002.

Gutierrez, D. G. *Walls and Mirrors: Mexican Americans, Mexican Immigrants and the Politics of Ethnicity*. Berkeley, CA, and London, University of California Press, 1995.

Hacker, A. *Two Nations: Black and White, Separate, Hostile, Unequal*, revised edn New York, Scribner, 2003.

Haddad, Y. Y., and Esposito, J. *Muslims on the Americanization Path*. New York, Oxford University Press, 2000.

Halliwell, M., and Morley, C. *American Thought and Culture in the 21st Century*. Edinburgh, Edinburgh University Press, 2008.

Heinz, W. R. *From Education to Work: Cross National Perspectives*. Cambridge, Cambridge University Press, 2008.

Heyck, D. *Barrios and Borders: Cultures of Latinos and Latinas in the United States*. New York, Routledge, 1994.

Jansson, B. *The Reluctant Welfare State—A History of American Social Welfare Policies*. Pacific Grove, CA, Brooks/Cole Publishing, 1993.

Jencks, C., and Peterson, P. E. (Eds). *The Urban Underclass*. Washington, DC, Brookings Institution, 1991.

Johnson, H. B. *The American Dream and the Power of Wealth*. Abingdon, Routledge, 2006.

Karim, J. *American Muslim Women: Negotiating Race, Class, and Gender Within the Ummah*. New York, New York University Press, 2008.

Katz, M. B., and Stern, M. J. *One Nation Divisible: What America Was and What It Is Becoming*. New York, Russell Sage Foundation Publications, 2006.

Kilty, K. M. (Ed.). *The Promise of Welfare Reform: Political Rhetoric and the Reality of Poverty in the Twenty-First Century*. Birmingham, Haworth Press Inc, 2006.

Kohut, A., *et al*. *The Diminishing Divide: Religion's Changing Role in American Life*. Washington, DC, Brookings Institution, 2000.

Kruse, K., and Sugrue, T. J. (Eds). *The New Suburban History*. Chicago, IL, University of Chicago Press, 2006.

Lambart, F. *The Founding Fathers and the Place of Religion in America*. Princeton, NJ, Princeton University Press, 2003.

Lewis-Colman, D. M. *Race Against Liberalism: Black Workers and the UAW in Detroit*. Champaign, IL, University of Illinois Press, 2008.

Lieberman, R. C. *Shifting the Color Line: Race and the American Welfare State*. Cambridge, MA, Harvard University Press, 2001.

Marger, M. *Race and Ethnic Relations. American and Global Perspectives*, 5th edn. London, Wadsworth, 2000.

Marmor, T. R. 'Universal Health Insurance 2007', in *Dissent*, Summer 2007. dissentmagazine.org.

Marmor, T. R., and Mashaw, J. L. 'Understanding Social Insurance: Fairness, Affordability, and the "Modernization" of Social Security and Medicare', in *Health Affairs*, 21 March 2006, Web Exclusive.

Melling, P. *Fundamentalism in America*. New York, Routledge, 1999.

Michael, J. *Identity and the Failure of America: From Thomas Jefferson to the War on Terror*. Minneapolis, MN, University of Minnesota Press, 2008.

Min, P. G. (Ed.). *Asian Americans: Contemporary Trends and Issues*. New York, Sage Publications, 1995.

Mass Migration to the United States: Classical and Contemporary Periods. Walnut Creek, CA, Altamira, 2002.

Moran, M. *Governing the Health Care State*. Manchester, Manchester University Press, 1999.

Moreno, P. D. *Black Americans and Organized Labor: A New History*. Baton Rouge, LA, Louisiana State University Press, 2006.

Nagel, J. *American Indian Ethnic Renewal: Red Power and the Resurgence of Identity and Culture*. New York, Oxford University Press, 1996.

National Urban League. *The State of Black America 2000: Blacks in the New Millennium*. Washington, DC, National Urban League, 2001.

Newton, L. *Illegal, Alien, or Immigrant: The Politics of Immigration Reform*. New York, New York University Press, 2008.

Nolt, S. M. *A History of the Amish*. Intercourse, PA, Good Books, 2004.

Ono, K., and Pham, V. *Asian Americans and the Media*. Cambridge, Polity Press, 2008.

Osborne, D., and Gaebler, T. *Reinventing Government: How the Entrepreneurial Spirit is Transforming the Public Sector*, revised edn. New York, Penguin Books, 1993.

Painter, N. I. *Creating Black Americans: African American History and its Meanings, 1619 to the Present*. Oxford, Oxford University Press, 2005.

Parrillo, V. N. *Diversity in America*. Thousand Oaks, CA, Pine Forge Press, 2008.

Paton, C. *US Health Politics: Public Policy and Political Theory*. Aldershot, Avebury, 1990.

Paton, C., in Altenstetter, C., and Bjorkman, J. (Eds). *Health Policy Reform, National Variations and Globalization*. London, Macmillan Publrs, and New York, St Martin's Press, 1997.

Pedraza, S. *Origins and Destinies: Immigration, Race and Ethnicity in America*. Belmont, CA, Wadsworth, 1995.

Perlman, J. *Italians Then, Mexicans Now*. New York, Russell Sage Foundation Publications, 2005.

Pien, P., Conway, M., and Wong, J. *The Politics of Asian Americans: Diversity and Community*. Abingdon, Routledge, 2004.

Prothero, S. *A Nation of Religions: The Politics of Pluralism in Multireligious America*. Chapel Hill, NC, University of North Carolina Press, 2006.

Raab, S. *The Five Families: The Rise, Decline and Resurgence of America's Most Powerful Mafia Families*. London, Robson Books, 2006.

Raphael, M. L. *Judaism in America (Columbia Contemporary American Religion Series)*. New York, Columbia University Press, 2003.

Reed, U., and Waters, M. C. *The New Americans: A Guide to Immigration Since 1965*. Cambridge, MA, Harvard University Press, 2007.

Roberts, G. K., and Steadman, P. *American Cities and Technology. Wilderness to Wired City*. Abingdon, Routledge, 1999.

Robinson, C. J. *Black Movements in America*. New York, Routledge, 1997.

Robinson, R., and Steiner, A. *Managed Health Care*. Buckingham, Open University Press, 1998.

Rose, P. I. *They and We: Racial and Ethnic Relations in the United States*. Boulder, CO, Paradigm Publrs, 2006.

Schaefer, R. T. *Race and Ethnicity in the United States*. Upper Saddle River, NJ, Prentice Hall, 2008.

Schama, S. *The American Future: A History*. London, Bodley Head, 2008.

Schulman, G. M. *American Prophecy: Race and Redemption in American Political Culture*. Minneapolis, MN, University of Minnesota Press, 2008.

Sen, R. *The Accidental American: Immigration and Citizenship in the Age of Globalization*. San Francisco, CA, Berrett-Koehler, 2008.

Skerry, P. *Counting on the Census? Race, Group Identity and the Evasion of Politics*. Washington, DC, Brookings Institution, 2000.

Skocpol, T. *Boomerang: Health Care Reform and the Turn Against Government*. New York, W. W. Norton, 1997.

The Missing Middle: Working Families and the Future of American Social Policy. New York, W. W. Norton, 2001.

Smith, J. *Islam in America*. New York, Columbia University Press, 1999.

Statistical Abstract of the United States: 2006. Washington, DC, Government Printing Office, 2006.

Tate, K. *Black Faces in the Mirror: African Americans and their Representation in the United States Congress*. Princeton, NJ, Princeton University Press, 2003.

Teixeira, R. (Ed.). *Red, Blue and Purple America: The Future of Election Demographics*. Washington, DC, Brookings Institute Press, 2008.

Thernstrom, S. and J. (Eds). *America Black and White: One Nation, Indivisible*. New York, Simon and Schuster, 1997.

Thomas, G. *Race and Ethnicity in America: Meeting the Challenge in the 21st Century*. New York, Routledge, 1995.

Veccoli, R. J., and Sinke, S. M. (Eds). *A Century of European Migrations, 1830–1930*. Urbana, IL, University of Illinois Press, 1991.

Walch, T. (Ed.). *Immigrant America: European Ethnicity in the United States*. New York, and London, Garland, 1994.

Whitt, J. *Women in American Journalism: A New History*. Champaign, IL, University of Illinois Press, 2008.

Wucker, M. *Lock Out: Why America Keeps Getting Immigration Wrong when Our Prosperity Depends on Getting It Right*. New York, Public Affairs, 2006.

Wunder, J. R. *Native American Sovereignty*. New York, and London, Garland, 1999.

DIRECTORY

DIRECTORY ON PUBLIC AFFAIRS

GOVERNMENT

THE CONSTITUTION OF THE USA

(Came into effect 4 March 1789)

Preamble

We, the people of the United States, in order to form a more perfect Union, establish justice, insure domestic tranquillity, provide for the common defence, promote the general welfare, and secure the blessings of liberty to ourselves and our posterity, do ordain and establish this Constitution for the United States of America.

Article I

SECTION 1

All legislative powers herein granted shall be vested in a Congress of the United States, which shall consist of a Senate and House of Representatives.

SECTION 2

1. The House of Representatives shall be composed of members chosen every second year by the people of the several States and the electors in each State shall have the qualifications requisite for electors of the most numerous branch of the State Legislature.

2. No person shall be a Representative who shall not have attained to the age of 25 years and been seven years a citizen of the United States and who shall not, when elected, be an inhabitant of that State in which he shall be chosen.

3. Representatives and direct taxes shall be apportioned among the several States which may be included within this Union according to their respective numbers, which shall be determined by adding to the whole number of free persons, including those bound to service for a term of years, and excluding Indians not taxed, three-fifths of all other persons. The actual enumeration shall be made within three years after the first meeting of the Congress of the United States, and within every subsequent term of 10 years, in such manner as they shall by law direct. The number of Representatives shall not exceed one for every 30,000, but each State shall have at least one Representative; and until such enumeration shall be made, the State of New Hampshire shall be entitled to choose 3; Massachusetts 8; Rhode Island and Providence Plantations 1; Connecticut 5; New York 6; New Jersey 4; Pennsylvania 8; Delaware 1; Maryland 6; Virginia 10; North Carolina 5; South Carolina 5; and Georgia 3.*

4. When vacancies happen in the representation from any State, the Executive Authority thereof shall issue writs of election to fill such vacancies.

5. The House of Representatives shall choose their Speaker and other officers and shall have the sole power of impeachment.

SECTION 3

1. The Senate of the United States shall be composed of two Senators from each State, chosen by the Legislature thereof, for six years; and each Senator shall have one vote.

2. Immediately after they shall be assembled in consequence of the first election, they shall be divided as equally as may be into three classes. The seats of the Senators of the first class shall be vacated at the expiration of the second year, of the second class at the expiration of the fourth year, and of the third class at the expiration of the sixth year, so that one-third may be chosen every second year, and if vacancies happen by resignation, or otherwise, during the recess of the Legislature of any State, the Executive thereof may make temporary appointments until the next meeting of the Legislature, which shall then fill such vacancies.

3. No person shall be a Senator who shall not have attained to the age of 30 years, and been nine years a citizen of the United States, and who shall not, when elected, be an inhabitant of that State for which he shall be chosen.

4. The Vice-President of the United States shall be President of the Senate, but shall have no vote, unless they be equally divided.

5. The Senate shall choose their other officers, and also a President *pro tempore,* in the absence of the Vice-President, or when he shall exercise the office of the President of the United States.

6. The Senate shall have the sole power to try all impeachments. When sitting for that purpose, they shall be on oath or affirmation. When the President of the United States is tried, the Chief Justice shall preside; and no person shall be convicted without the concurrence of two-thirds of the members present.

7. Judgment of case of impeachment shall not extend further than to removal from office, and disqualification to hold and enjoy any office of honour, trust, or profit under the United States; but the party convicted shall nevertheless be liable and subject to indictment, trial, judgment, and punishment, according to law.

SECTION 4

1. The times, places and manner of holding elections for Senators and Representatives shall be prescribed in each State by the Legislature thereof; but the Congress may at any time by law make or alter such regulations, except as to places of choosing Senators.

2. The Congress shall assemble at least once in every year, and such meeting shall be on the first Monday in December, unless they shall by law appoint a different day.

SECTION 5

1. Each House shall be the judge of the elections, returns, and qualifications of its own members, and a majority of each shall constitute a quorum to do business; but a smaller number may adjourn from day to day, and may be authorized to compel the attendance of absent members in such manner and under such penalties as each House may provide.

2. Each House may determine the rules of its proceedings, punish its members for disorderly behaviour, and, with the concurrence of two-thirds, expel a member.

3. Each House shall keep a journal of its proceedings, and from time to time publish the same, excepting such parts as may in their judgement require secrecy; and the yeas and nays of the members of either House on any question shall, at the desire of one-fifth of those present, be entered on the journal.

4. Neither House, during the session of Congress shall, without the consent of the other, adjourn for more than three days, nor to any other place than that in which the two Houses shall be sitting.

SECTION 6

1. The Senators and Representatives shall receive a compensation for their services, to be ascertained by law, and paid out of the Treasury of the United States. They shall in all cases, except treason, felony, and breach of the peace, be privileged from arrest during their attendance at the session of their respective Houses, and in going to and returning from the same; and for any speech or debate in either House they shall not be questioned in any other place.

2. No Senator or Representative shall, during the time for which he was elected, be appointed to any civil office under the authority of the United States which shall have been created, or the emoluments whereof shall have been increased during such time; and no person holding any office under the United States shall be a member of either House during his continuance in office.

SECTION 7

1. All bills for raising revenue shall originate in the House of Representatives, but the Senate may propose or concur with amendments, as on other bills.

2. Every bill which shall have passed the House of Representatives and the Senate shall, before it becomes a law, be presented to the President of the United States; if he approve, he shall sign it, but if not he shall return it, with his objections to that House in which it shall have originated, who shall enter the objections at large on their journal and proceed to reconsider it. If after such reconsideration two-thirds of that House shall agree to pass the bill, it shall be sent,

* See Amendment XIV.

together with the objections, to the other House, by which it shall likewise be reconsidered; and if approved by two-thirds of that House it shall become a law. But in such cases the votes of both Houses shall be determined by yeas and nays, and the names of the persons voting for and against the bill be entered on the journal of each House respectively. If any bill shall not be returned by the President within 10 days (Sundays excepted) after it shall have been presented to him, the same shall be a law in like manner as if he had signed it, unless the Congress by their adjournment prevent its return; in which case it shall not be a law.

3. Every order, resolution, or vote to which the concurrence of the Senate and House of Representatives may be necessary (except on a question of adjournment) shall be presented to the President of the United States, and before the same shall take effect shall be approved by him, or being disapproved by him, shall be repassed by two-thirds of the Senate and the House of Representatives, according to the rules and limitations prescribed in the case of a bill.

SECTION 8

The Congress shall have power:

1. To lay and collect taxes, duties, imposts, and excises, to pay the debts and provide for the common defence and general welfare of the United States; but all duties, imposts, and excises shall be uniform throughout the United States;
2. To borrow money on the credit of the United States;
3. To regulate commerce with foreign nations; and among the several States and with the Indian tribes;
4. To establish a uniform rule of naturalization and uniform laws on the subject of bankruptcies throughout the United States;
5. To coin money, regulate the value thereof, and of foreign coin, and fix the standard of weights and measures;
6. To provide for the punishment of counterfeiting the securities and current coin of the United States;
7. To establish post-offices and post-roads;
8. To promote the progress of science and useful arts by securing for limited times to authors and inventors the exclusive right to their respective writings and discoveries;
9. To constitute tribunals inferior to the Supreme Court;
10. To define and punish piracies and felonies committed on the high seas, and offences against the law of nations;
11. To declare war, grant letters of marque and reprisal, and make rules concerning captures on land and water;
12. To raise and support armies, but no appropriation of money to that use shall be for a longer term than two years;
13. To provide and maintain a navy;
14. To make rules for the government and regulation of the land and naval forces;
15. To provide for calling forth the militia to execute the laws of the Union, suppress insurrections, and repel invasions;
16. To provide for organizing, arming and disciplining the militia, and for governing such part of them as may be employed in the service of the United States, reserving to the States respectively the appointment of the officers, and the authority of training the militia according to the discipline prescribed by Congress;
17. To exercise exclusive legislation in all cases whatsoever over such district (not exceeding 10 miles square) as may, by cession of particular States and the acceptance of Congress, become the seat of Government of the United States and to exercise like authority over all places purchased by the consent of the Legislature of the State in which the same shall be, for the erection of forts, magazines, arsenals, dry-docks, and other needful buildings;
18. To make all laws which shall be necessary and proper for carrying into execution the foregoing powers and all other powers vested by this Constitution in the Government of the United States, or in any department or officer thereof.

SECTION 9

1. The migration or importation of such persons as any of the States now existing shall think proper to admit shall not be prohibited by the Congress prior to the year 1808, but a tax or duty may be imposed on such importations, not exceeding 10 dollars for each person.
2. The privilege of the writ of habeas corpus shall not be suspended, unless when in cases of rebellion or invasion the public safety may require it.
3. No bill or attainder or *ex post facto* law shall be passed.
4. No capitation or other direct tax shall be laid, unless in proportion to the census or enumeration hereinbefore directed to be taken.
5. No tax or duty shall be laid on articles exported from any State.
6. No preference shall be given by any regulation of commerce or revenue to the ports of one State over those of another, nor shall vessels bound to or from one State be obliged to enter, clear, or pay duties to another.
7. No money shall be drawn from the Treasury but in consequence of appropriations made by law; and a regular statement and account of the receipts and expenditures of all public money shall be published from time to time.
8. No title of nobility shall be granted by the United States. And no person holding any office of profit or trust under them shall, without the consent of the Congress, accept of any present, emolument, office, or title of any kind whatever from any king, prince, or foreign state.

SECTION 10

1. No State shall enter into any treaty, alliance or confederation, grant letters of marque and reprisal, coin money, emit bills of credit, make anything but gold and silver coin a tender in payment of debts, pass any bill of attainder, *ex post facto* law, or law impairing the obligation of contracts, or grant any title of nobility.
2. No State shall, without the consent of the Congress, lay any imposts or duties on imports or exports, except what may be absolutely necessary for executing its inspection laws, and the net produce of all duties and imposts, laid by any State on imports or exports, shall be for the use of the Treasury of the United States; and all such laws shall be subject to the revision and control of the Congress.
3. No State shall, without the consent of Congress, lay any duty of tonnage, keep troops or ships of war in time of peace, enter into agreement or compact with another State, or with a foreign power, or engage in war, unless actually invaded, or in such imminent danger as will not admit of delay.

Article II

SECTION 1

The Executive power shall be vested in a President of the United States of America. He shall hold his office during the term of four years, and, together with the Vice-President chosen for the same term, be elected as follows:

Each State shall appoint, in such manner as the Legislature thereof may direct, a number of electors equal to the whole number of Senators and Representatives to which the State may be entitled in the Congress; but no Senator or Representative or person holding an office of trust or profit under the United States shall be appointed an elector;

The electors shall meet in their respective States and vote by ballot for two persons, of whom one at least shall not be an inhabitant of the same State with themselves. And they shall make a list of all the persons voted for, and of the number of votes for each, which list they shall sign and certify and transmit, sealed, to the seat of the Government of the United States, directed to the President of the Senate. The President of the Senate shall, in the presence of the Senate and House of Representatives, open all the certificates, and the votes shall then be counted. The person having the greatest number of votes shall be the President, if such number be a majority of the whole number of electors appointed, and if there be more than one who have such a majority, and have an equal number of votes, then the House of Representatives shall immediately choose by ballot one of them for President; and if no person have a majority, then from the five highest on the list the said House shall in like manner choose the President. But in choosing the President, the vote shall be taken by States, the representation from each State having one vote. A quorum, for this purpose, shall consist of a member or members from two-thirds of the States, and a majority of all the States shall be necessary to a choice. In every case, after the choice of the President, the person having the greatest number of votes of the electors shall be the Vice-President. But if there should remain two or more who have equal votes, the Senate shall choose from them by ballot the Vice-President;[†]

The Congress may determine the time of choosing the electors and the day on which they shall give their votes, which day shall be the same throughout the United States;

No person except a natural born citizen, or a citizen of the United States, at the time of the adoption of this Constitution, shall be eligible to the office of President; neither shall any person be eligible to that office who shall not have attained to the age of 35 years and been 14 years a resident within the United States;

In case of the removal of the President from office, or of his death, resignation, or inability to discharge the powers and duties of the said office, the same shall devolve on the Vice-President, and the Congress may by law provide for the case of removal, death, resignation, or inability, both of the President and Vice-President, declaring what

† This clause is superseded by Amendment XII.

officer shall then act as President, and such officer shall act accordingly until the disability be removed or a President shall be elected;‡

The President shall, at stated times, receive for his services a compensation which shall neither be increased nor diminished during the period for which he shall have been elected, and he shall not receive within that period any other emolument from the United States, or any of them;

Before he enter on the execution of his office he shall take the following oath or affirmation:

'I do solemnly swear (or affirm) that I will faithfully execute the office of President of the United States, and will, to the best of my ability, preserve, protect, and defend the Constitution of the United States.'

SECTION 2

1. The President shall be Commander-in-Chief of the Army and Navy of the United States, and of the militia of the several States when called into the actual service of the United States; he may require the opinion, in writing, of the principal officer in each of the executive departments upon any subject relating to the duties of their respective offices, and he shall have the power to grant reprieves and pardons for offences against the United States except in cases of impeachment.

2. He shall have power, by and with the advice and consent of the Senate, to make treaties, provided two-thirds of the Senators present concur; and he shall nominate, and by and with the advice and consent of the Senate, shall appoint ambassadors, other public ministers and consuls, judges of the Supreme Court, and all other officers of the United States whose appointments are not herein otherwise provided for, and which shall be established by law; but the Congress may by law vest the appointment of such inferior officers as they think proper in the President alone, in the courts of law, or in the heads of departments.

3. The President shall have power to fill up all vacancies that may happen during the recess of the Senate by granting commissions, which shall expire at the end of their next session.

SECTION 3

He shall from time to time give to the Congress information of the state of the Union, and recommend to their consideration such measures as he shall judge necessary and expedient; he may, on extraordinary occasions, convene both Houses, or either of them, and in case of disagreement between them with respect to the time of adjournment, he may adjourn them to such time as he shall think proper; he shall receive ambassadors and other public ministers; he shall take care that the laws be faithfully executed, and shall commission all the officers of the United States.

SECTION 4

The President, Vice-President, and all civil officers of the United States shall be removed from office on impeachment for, and conviction of, treason, bribery or other high crimes and misdemeanours.

Article III

SECTION 1

The judicial power of the United States shall be vested in one Supreme Court, and in such inferior courts as the Congress may from time to time ordain and establish. The judges, both of the Supreme and inferior courts, shall hold their offices during good behaviour, and shall at stated times receive for their services a compensation which shall not be diminished during their continuance in office.

SECTION 2

1. The judicial power shall extend to all cases in law and equity arising under this Constitution, the laws of the United States, and treaties made, or which shall be made, under their authority; to all cases affecting ambassadors, other public ministers and consuls; to all cases of admiralty and maritime jurisdiction; to controversies to which the United States shall be a party; to controversies between two or more States, between a State and citizens of another State, between citizens of different States, between citizens of the same State claiming lands under grants of different States, and between a State, or the citizens thereof, and foreign States, citizens, or subjects.

2. In all cases affecting ambassadors, other public ministers, and consuls, and those in which a State shall be party, the Supreme Court shall have original jurisdiction. In all the other cases before mentioned the Supreme Court shall have appellate jurisdiction both as to law and fact, with such exceptions and under such regulations as the Congress shall make.

3. The trial of all crimes, except in cases of impeachment, shall be by jury, and such trials shall be held in the State where the said crimes shall have been committed; but when not committed within any State the trial shall be at such place or places as the Congress may by law have directed.

SECTION 3

1. Treason against the United States shall consist only in levying war against them, or in adhering to their enemies, giving them aid and comfort. No person shall be convicted of treason unless on the testimony of two witnesses to the same overt act, or on confession in open court.

2. The Congress shall have power to declare the punishment of treason, but no attainder of treason shall work corruption of blood or forfeiture except during the life of the person attained.

Article IV

SECTION 1

Full faith and credit shall be given in each State to the public acts, records, and judicial proceedings of every other State. And the Congress may by general laws prescribe the manner in which such acts, records, and proceedings shall be proved, and the effect thereof.

SECTION 2

1. The citizens of each State shall be entitled to all privileges and immunities of citizens in the several States.

2. A person charged in any State with treason, felony, or other crime, who shall flee from justice, and be found in another State, shall, on demand of the Executive authority of the State from which he fled, be delivered up, to be removed to the State having jurisdiction of the crime.

3. No person held to service or labour in one State, under the laws thereof, escaping into another shall, in consequence of any law or regulation therein, be discharged from such service or labour, but shall be delivered up on claim of the party to whom such service or labour may be due.

SECTION 3

1. New States may be admitted by the Congress into this Union; but no new State shall be formed or erected within the jurisdiction of any other State, nor any State be formed by the junction of two or more States, or parts of States, without the consent of the Legislatures of the States concerned, as well as of the Congress.

2. The Congress shall have the power to dispose of and make all needful rules and regulations respecting the territory or other property belonging to the United States; and nothing in this Constitution shall be so construed as to prejudice any claims of the United States, or of any particular State.

SECTION 4

The United States shall guarantee to every State in this Union a republican form of government, and shall protect each of them against invasion, and on application of the Legislature, or of the Executive (when the Legislature cannot be convened) against domestic violence.

Article V

The Congress, whenever two-thirds of both Houses shall deem it necessary, shall propose amendments to this Constitution, or, on the application of the Legislature of two-thirds of the several States, shall call a convention for proposing amendments, which, in either case, shall be valid to all intents and purposes, as part of this Constitution, when ratified by the Legislatures of three-fourths of the several States, or by conventions in three-fourths thereof, as the one or the other mode of ratification may be proposed by the Congress, provided that no amendment which may be made prior to the year 1808 shall in any manner affect the first and fourth clauses in the Ninth Section of the First Article; and that no State, without its consent, shall be deprived of its equal suffrage in the Senate.

Article VI

1. All debts contracted and engagements entered into before the adoption of this Constitution shall be as valid against the United States under this Constitution as under the Confederation.

2. This Constitution and the laws of the United States which shall be made in pursuance thereof and all treaties made, or which shall be

‡ This clause is amended by Amendments XX and XXV.

made, under the authority of the United States, shall be the supreme law of the land, and the judges in every State shall be bound thereby, anything in the Constitution or laws of any State to the contrary notwithstanding.

3. The Senators and Representatives before mentioned, and the members of the several State Legislatures, and all executives and judicial officers, both of the United States and of the several States, shall be bound by oath or affirmation to support this Constitution; but no religious test shall ever be required as a qualification to any office or public trust under the United States.

Article VII

The ratification of the Conventions of nine States shall be sufficient for the establishment of this Constitution between the States so ratifying the same.

Amendments to the Constitution

Ten Original Amendments, ratified 15 December 1791:

AMENDMENT I

Congress shall make no law respecting an establishment of religion, or prohibiting the free exercise thereof; or abridging the freedom of speech or of the Press; or the right of the people peaceably to assemble and to petition the Government for a redress of grievances.

AMENDMENT II

A well-regulated militia being necessary to the security of a free State, the right of the people to keep and bear arms shall not be infringed.

AMENDMENT III

No soldier shall, in time of peace, be quartered in any house without the consent of the owner, nor in time of war, but in a manner to be prescribed by law.

AMENDMENT IV

The right of the people to be secure in their persons, houses, papers, and effects, against unreasonable searches and seizures, shall not be violated, and no warrants shall issue but upon probable cause, supported by oath or affirmation, and particularly describing the place to be searched, and the persons or things to be seized.

AMENDMENT V

No person shall be held to answer for a capital or otherwise infamous crime unless on a presentment or indictment of a Grand Jury, except in cases arising in the land or naval forces, or in the militia, when in actual service, in time of war or public danger; nor shall any person be subject for the same offence to be twice put in jeopardy of life or limb; nor shall be compelled in any criminal case to be a witness against himself, nor be deprived of life, liberty, or property, without due process of law; nor shall private property be taken for public use without just compensation.

AMENDMENT VI

In all criminal prosecutions, the accused shall enjoy the right to a speedy and public trial, by an impartial jury of the State and district wherein the crime shall have been committed, which districts shall have been previously ascertained by law, and to be informed of the nature and cause of the accusation; to be confronted with the witnesses against him; to have compulsory process for obtaining witnesses in his favour, and to have the assistance of counsel for his defence.

AMENDMENT VII

In suits at common law, where the value in controversy shall exceed 20 dollars, the right of trial by jury shall be preserved, and no fact tried by a jury shall be otherwise re-examined in any court of the United States than according to the rules of the common law.

AMENDMENT VIII

Excessive bail shall not be required, nor excessive fines imposed, nor cruel and unusual punishments inflicted.

AMENDMENT IX

The enumeration in the Constitution of certain rights shall not be construed to deny or disparage others retained by the people.

AMENDMENT X

The powers not delegated to the United States by the Constitution, nor prohibited by it to the States, are reserved to the States respectively, or to the people.

Subsequent Amendments:

AMENDMENT XI
(ratified 7 February 1795)

The judicial power of the United States shall not be construed to extend to any suit in law or equity, commenced or prosecuted against one of the United States, by citizens of another State, or by citizens or subjects of any foreign State.

AMENDMENT XII
(ratified 15 June 1804)

The Electors shall meet in their respective States, and vote by ballot for President and Vice-President, one of whom at least shall not be an inhabitant of the same State with themselves; they shall name in their ballots the person voted for as President, and in distinct ballots the person voted for as Vice-President; and they shall make distinct lists of all persons voted for as President, and of all persons voted for as Vice-President, and of the number of votes for each, which list they shall sign and certify, and transmit, sealed, to the seat of the Government of the United States, directed to the President of the Senate; the President of the Senate shall, in the presence of the Senate and House of Representatives, open all the certificates and the votes shall then be counted; the person having the greatest number of votes for President shall be the President, if such number be a majority of the whole number of Electors appointed; and if no person have such a majority, then from the persons having the highest numbers, not exceeding three, on the list of those voted for as President, the House of Representatives shall choose immediately, by ballot, the President. But in choosing the President, the votes shall be taken by States, the representation from each State having one vote; a quorum for this purpose shall consist of a member or members from two-thirds of the States, and a majority of all the States shall be necessary to a choice. And if the House of Representatives shall not choose a President, whenever the right of choice shall devolve upon them, before the fourth day of March next following, then the Vice-President shall act as President, as in the case of the death or other constitutional disability of the President. The person having the greatest number of votes as Vice-President shall be the Vice-President, if such number be a majority of the whole number of Electors appointed, and if no person have a majority, then, from the two highest numbers on the list, the Senate shall choose the Vice-President; a quorum for the purpose shall consist of two-thirds of the whole number of Senators, and a majority of the whole number shall be necessary to a choice. But no person constitutionally ineligible to the office of President shall be eligible to that of Vice-President of the United States.

AMENDMENT XIII
(ratified 6 December 1865)

1. Neither slavery nor involuntary servitude, except as a punishment for crime whereof the party shall have been duly convicted, shall exist within the United States, or any place subject to their jurisdiction.

2. Congress shall have the power to enforce this article by appropriate legislation.

AMENDMENT XIV
(ratified 9 July 1868)

1. All persons born or naturalized in the United States, and subject to the jurisdiction thereof, are citizens of the United States and of the State wherein they reside. No State shall make or enforce any law which shall abridge the privileges or immunities of citizens of the United States, nor shall any State deprive any person of life, liberty, or property without due process of law, nor deny to any person within its jurisdiction the equal protection of the laws.

2. Representatives shall be apportioned among the several States according to their respective numbers, counting the whole number of persons in each State excluding Indians not taxed. But when the right to vote at any election for the choice of Electors for President and Vice-President of the United States, Representatives in Congress, the executive and judicial officers of a State, or the members of the Legislature thereof, is denied to any of the male inhabitants of such State, being 21 years of age, and citizens of the United States, or in any way abridged, except for participation in rebellion, or other crime, the basis of representation therein shall be reduced in the proportion which the number of such male citizens shall bear to the whole number of male citizens 21 years of age in such State.

3. No person shall be a Senator or Representative in Congress, or Elector of President and Vice-President, or hold any office, civil or

military, under the United States, or under any State, who, having previously taken an oath as a member of Congress or as an officer of the United States, or as a member of any State Legislature, or as an executive or judicial officer of any State, to support the Constitution of the United States, shall have engaged in insurrection or rebellion against the same, or given aid and comfort to the enemies thereof. But Congress may, by vote of two-thirds of each House, remove such disability.

4. The validity of the public debt of the United States, authorized by law, including debts incurred for payment of pensions and bounties for services in suppressing insurrection and rebellion, shall not be questioned. But neither the United States nor any State shall assume or pay any debt or obligation incurred in aid of insurrection or rebellion against the United States, or any claim for the loss or emancipation of any slave; but all such debts, obligations, and claims shall be held illegal and void.

5. The Congress shall have power to enforce, by appropriate legislation, the provisions of this article.

AMENDMENT XV
(ratified 3 February 1870)

1. The right of the citizens of the United States to vote shall not be denied or abridged by the United States or by any State on account of race, colour, or previous condition of servitude.

2. The Congress shall have power to enforce this article by appropriate legislation.

AMENDMENT XVI
(ratified 3 February 1913)

The Congress shall have power to lay and collect taxes on incomes, from whatever source derived, without apportionment among the several States, and without regard to any census or enumeration.

AMENDMENT XVII
(ratified 8 April 1913)

1. The Senate of the United States shall be composed of two Senators from each State, elected by the people thereof for six years; and each Senator shall have one vote. The electors in each State shall have the qualifications requisite for electors of the most numerous branch of the State Legislature.

2. When vacancies happen in the representation of any State in the Senate, the executive authority of such State shall issue writs of election to fill such vacancies: Provided that the Legislature of any State may empower the Executive thereof to make temporary appointments until the people fill the vacancies by election as the Legislature may direct.

3. This amendment shall not be so construed as to affect the election or term of any Senator chosen before it becomes valid as part of the Constitution.

AMENDMENT XVIII
(ratified 16 January 1919§)

1. After one year from the ratification of this article the manufacture, sale, or transportation of intoxicating liquors within, the importation thereof into, or the exportation thereof from the United States, and all territory subject to the jurisdiction thereof for beverage purposes is hereby prohibited.

2. The Congress and the several States shall have concurrent power to enforce this article by appropriate legislation.

3. This article shall be inoperative unless it shall have been ratified as an amendment to the Constitution by the Legislatures of the several States, as provided in the Constitution, within seven years from the date of the submission hereof to the States by the Congress.

AMENDMENT XIX
(ratified 18 August 1920)

1. The right of citizens of the United States to vote shall not be denied or abridged by the United States or by any State on account of sex.

2. Congress shall have power, by appropriate legislation, to enforce the provisions of this article.

AMENDMENT XX
(ratified 23 January 1933)

Section 1

The terms of the President and Vice-President shall end at noon on the 20th day of January, and the terms of Senators and Representatives at noon on the third day of January, of the years in which such terms would have ended if this article had not been ratified; and the terms of their successors shall then begin.

Section 2

The Congress shall assemble at least once in every year, and such meetings shall begin at noon on the third day of January, unless they shall by law appoint a different day.

Section 3

If, at the time fixed for the beginning of the term of the President, the President elect shall have died, the Vice-President elect shall become President. If a President shall not have been chosen before the time fixed for the beginning of his term, or if the President elect shall have failed to qualify, then the Vice-President elect shall act as President until a President shall have qualified; and the Congress may by law provide for the case wherein neither a President elect nor a Vice-President elect shall have qualified, declaring who shall then act as President, or the manner in which one who is to act shall be selected, and such person shall act accordingly until a President or Vice-President shall have qualified.

Section 4

The Congress may by law provide for the case of the death of any of the persons from whom the House of Representatives may choose a President whenever the right of choice shall have devolved upon them, and for the case of the death of any of the persons from whom the Senate may choose a Vice-President whenever the right of choice shall have devolved upon them.

Section 5

Sections 1 and 2 shall take effect on the 15th day of October following the ratification of this article.

Section 6

This article shall be inoperative unless it shall have been ratified as an amendment to the Constitution by the legislature of three-fourths of the several States within seven years from the date of its submission.

AMENDMENT XXI
(ratified 5 December 1933)

Section 1

The 18th article of amendment to the Constitution of the United States is hereby repealed.

Section 2

The transportation or importation into any State, Territory or Possession of the United States for delivery or use therein of intoxicating liquors, in violation of the laws thereof, is hereby prohibited.

Section 3

This article shall be inoperative unless it shall have been ratified as an amendment to the Constitution by conventions in the several States, as provided in the Constitution, within seven years from the date of the submission hereof to the States by the Congress.

AMENDMENT XXII
(ratified 27 February 1951)

1. No person shall be elected to the office of President more than twice, and no person who has held the office of President, or acted as President, for more than two years of a term to which some other person was elected President shall be elected to the office of President more than once. But this article shall not apply to any person holding the office of President when this Article was proposed by Congress, and shall not prevent any person who may be holding the office of President, or acting as President, during the term within which this Article becomes operative from holding the office of President or acting as President during the remainder of such term.

2. This article shall be inoperative unless it shall have been ratified as an amendment to the Constitution by the Legislatures of three-fourths of the several States within seven years from the date of its submission to the States by the Congress.

AMENDMENT XXIII
(ratified 29 March 1961)

Section 1

The District constituting the seat of Government of the United States shall appoint in such manner as the Congress may direct:

A number of electors of President and Vice-President equal to the whole number of Senators and Representatives in Congress to which the District would be entitled if it were a State, but in no event more than the least populous State; they shall be in addition to those

§ Repealed by Amendment XXI.

appointed by the States, but they shall be considered, for the purposes of the election of President and Vice-President, to be electors appointed by a State; and they shall meet in the District and perform such duties as provided by the 12th article of amendment.

Section 2

The Congress shall have power to enforce this article by appropriate legislation.

AMENDMENT XXIV
(ratified 23 January 1964)

Section 1

The right of citizens of the United States to vote in any primary or other election for President or Vice-President, for electors for President or Vice-President, or for Senator or Representative in Congress, shall not be denied or abridged by the United States or any State by reason of failure to pay any poll tax or other tax.

Section 2

The Congress shall have power to enforce this article by appropriate legislation.

AMENDMENT XXV
(ratified 10 February 1967)

Section 1

In case of the removal of the President from office or of his death or resignation, the Vice-President shall become President.

Section 2

Whenever there is a vacancy in the office of the Vice-President, the President shall nominate a Vice-President who shall take office upon confirmation by a majority vote of both Houses of Congress.

Section 3

Whenever the President transmits to the President *pro tempore* of the Senate and the Speaker of the House of Representatives his written declaration that he is unable to discharge the powers and duties of his office, and until he transmits to them a written declaration to the contrary, such powers and duties shall be discharged by the Vice-President as Acting President.

Section 4

Whenever the Vice-President and a majority of either the principal officers of the executive departments or of such other body as Congress may by law provide, transmit to the President *pro tempore* of the Senate and the Speaker of the House of Representatives their written declaration that the President is unable to discharge the powers and duties of his office, the Vice-President shall immediately assume the powers and duties of the office as Acting President.

Thereafter, when the President transmits to the President *pro tempore* of the Senate and the Speaker of the House of Representatives his written declaration that no inability exists, he shall resume the powers and duties of his office unless the Vice-President and a majority of either the principal officers of the executive department or of such other body as Congress may by law provide, transmit within four days to the President *pro tempore* of the Senate and the Speaker of the House of Representatives their written declaration that the President is unable to discharge the powers and duties of his office. Thereupon Congress shall decide the issue, assembling within 48 hours for that purpose if not in session. If the Congress, within 21 days after receipt of the latter written declaration, or, if Congress is not in session, within 21 days after Congress is required to assemble, determines by two-thirds vote of both Houses that the President is unable to discharge the powers and duties of his office, the Vice-President shall continue to discharge the same as Acting President; otherwise, the President shall resume the powers and duties of his office.

AMENDMENT XXVI
(ratified 1 July 1971)

Section 1

The right of citizens of the United States, who are 18 years of age or older, to vote shall not be denied or abridged by the United States or by any State on account of age.

Section 2

The Congress shall have power to enforce this article by appropriate legislation.

AMENDMENT XXVII
(ratified 7 May 1992)

No law, varying the compensation for the services of the Senators and Representatives, shall take effect, until an election of Representatives shall have intervened.

FEDERAL EXECUTIVE

Head of State

President: GEORGE W. BUSH (took office 20 January 2001; re-elected 2 November 2004).

Vice-President: RICHARD B. CHENEY.

President-elect: BARACK OBAMA (scheduled to take office 20 January 2009).

The Federal Cabinet

(October 2008)

Secretary of State: Dr CONDOLEEZZA RICE.

Secretary of the Treasury: HENRY M. PAULSON, Jr.

Secretary of Defense: ROBERT M. GATES.

Attorney-General: MICHAEL B. MUKASEY.

Secretary of the Interior: DIRK KEMPTHORNE.

Secretary of Agriculture: EDWARD SCHAFER.

Secretary of Commerce: CARLOS GUTIERREZ.

Secretary of Labor: ELAINE L. CHAO.

Secretary of Health and Human Services: MICHAEL O. LEAVITT.

Secretary of Homeland Security: MICHAEL CHERTOFF.

Secretary of Housing and Urban Development: STEVEN C. PRESTON.

Secretary of Transportation: MARY E. PETERS.

Secretary of Energy: SAMUEL W. BODMAN.

Secretary of Education: MARGARET SPELLINGS.

Secretary of Veterans Affairs: Dr JAMES PEAKE.

OFFICIALS WITH CABINET RANK

Vice-President: RICHARD B. CHENEY.

Chief of Staff to the President: JOSHUA B. BOLTEN.

Director of the Office of Management and Budget: JIM NUSSLE.

US Trade Representative: SUSAN C. SCHWAB.

Administrator of the Environmental Protection Agency: STEPHEN L. JOHNSON.

Director of the Office of National Drug Control Policy: JOHN P. WALTERS.

Director of National Intelligence: Adm. MIKE MCCONNELL.

Presidential Election, 4 November 2008, preliminary results

	Popular votes	% of Popular votes	Electoral College votes
Barack Obama (Democrat)	64,058,618	52.47	364
John McCain (Republican)	56,499,923	46.28	162
Others*	1,534,627	1.26	—
Total	122,093,168	100.00	538†

* Including write-in candidates, etc.
† The outcome of 12 Electoral College votes remained undecided.

Government Departments

Department of Agriculture: 1400 Independence Ave, SW, Washington, DC 20250; tel. (202) 720-5539; fax (202) 720-9997; e-mail ann.hamilton@usda.gov; internet www.usda.gov; f. 1889.

Department of Commerce: 1401 Constitution Ave, NW, Washington, DC 20230; tel. (202) 482-2000; e-mail cgutierrez@doc.gov; internet www.commerce.gov; f. 1913.

Department of Defense: 1400 Defense Pentagon, Washington, DC 20301; tel. (703) 428-0711; fax (703) 428-1982; internet www.defenselink.mil; f. 1947.

Department of Education: 400 Maryland Ave, SW, Washington, DC 20202; tel. (202) 401-2000; fax (202) 401-0596; internet www.ed.gov; f. 1979.

Department of Energy: Forrestal Bldg, 1000 Independence Ave, SW, Washington, DC 20585; tel. (202) 586-5000; fax (202) 586-4403; e-mail the.secretary@hq.doe.gov; internet www.energy.gov; f. 1977.

Department of Health and Human Services: 200 Independence Ave, SW, Washington, DC 20201; tel. (202) 619-0257; internet www.os.dhhs.gov; f. 1980.

Department of Homeland Security: 1600 Pennsylvania Ave, NW, Washington, DC 20528; tel. (202) 282-8000; e-mail john.minnick@dhs.gov; internet www.dhs.gov; f. 2002.

Department of Housing and Urban Development: 451 Seventh St, SW, Washington, DC 20410; tel. (202) 708-1112; fax (202) 708-0299; internet www.hud.gov; f. 1965.

Department of the Interior: 1849 C St, NW, Washington, DC 20240; tel. (202) 208-3100; fax (202) 208-5048; internet www.doi.gov; f. 1849.

Department of Justice: 950 Pennsylvania Ave, NW, Washington, DC 20530-0001; tel. (202) 514-2000; fax (202) 307-6777; e-mail askdoj@usdoj.gov; internet www.usdoj.gov; f. 1870; incl. the Office of the Attorney-Gen.

Department of Labor: Frances Perkins Bldg, 200 Constitution Ave, NW, Washington, DC 20210; tel. (202) 693-6000; fax (202) 693-6111; internet www.dol.gov; f. 1913.

Department of State: 2201 C St, NW, Washington, DC 20520; tel. (202) 647-4000; fax (202) 647-6738; internet www.state.gov; f. 1789.

Department of Transportation: 1200 New Jersey Ave, SE, Washington, DC 20590; tel. (202) 366-4000; fax (202) 366-7202; e-mail dot.comments@dot.gov; internet www.dot.gov; f. 1967.

Department of the Treasury: 1500 Pennsylvania Ave, NW, Washington, DC 20220; tel. (202) 622-2000; fax (202) 622-6415; internet www.ustreas.gov; f. 1789.

Department of Veterans Affairs: 810 Vermont Ave, NW, Washington, DC 20420; tel. (202) 273-6000; internet www.va.gov; f. 1989.

Executive Office of the President

The White House Office: 1600 Pennsylvania Ave, NW, Washington, DC 20500; tel. (202) 456-1414; fax (202) 456-2461; e-mail vice_president@whitehouse.gov; internet www.whitehouse.gov; co-ordinates activities relating to the President's immediate office; Chief of Staff to the Pres. JOSHUA B. BOLTEN.

Central Intelligence Agency: Office of Public Affairs, Washington, DC 20505; tel. (703) 482-0623; fax (703) 482-1739; internet www.cia.gov; f. 1947; Dir Gen. MICHAEL HAYDEN.

Council of Economic Advisers: Eisenhower Executive Office Bldg, 17th St and Pennsylvania Ave, NW, Washington, DC 20502; tel. (202) 395-5042; fax (202) 395-6958; internet www.whitehouse.gov/cea; f. 1946; Chair. Dr EDWARD P. LAZEAR.

Council on Environmental Quality: 722 Jackson Pl., Washington, DC 20503; tel. (202) 395-5750; fax (202) 456-6546; internet www.whitehouse.gov/ceq; f. 1969; Chair. JAMES L. CONNAUGHTON.

Homeland Security Council: Washington, DC; internet www.whitehouse.gov/hsc; f. 2001; Asst to the Pres. for Homeland Security and Counter-Terrorism KEN WAINSTEIN.

National Security Council: Eisenhower Executive Office Bldg, 17th St and Pennsylvania Ave, NW, Washington, DC 20504; tel. (202) 456-9371; internet www.whitehouse.gov/nsc; f. 1947; Asst to the Pres. for Nat. Security Affairs STEPHEN J. HADLEY.

Office of Administration: Eisenhower Executive Office Bldg, 17th St and Pennsylvania Ave, NW, Washington, DC 20503; tel. (202) 395-7235; fax (202) 456-6512; internet www.whitehouse.gov/oa; f. 1977; Dir (vacant).

Office of Faith-Based and Community Initiatives: The White House, Washington, DC 20502; tel. (202) 456-6708; fax (202) 456-7019; internet www.fbci.gov; f. 2001; Dir JAY F. HEIN.

Office of Management and Budget: 725 17th St and Pennsylvania Ave, NW Washington, DC 20503; tel. (202) 395-3080; fax (202) 395-3888; internet www.whitehouse.gov/omb; Dir JIM NUSSLE.

Office of National AIDS Policy: The White House, Rm 464 EEOB, Washington, DC 20502; tel. (202) 456-7320; fax (202) 456-7315; internet www.whitehouse.gov/onap/aids.html; Dir CAROL THOMPSON.

Office of National Drug Control Policy: POB 6000, Rockville, MD 20849-6000; tel. (202) 395-6700; fax (301) 519-5212; internet www.whitehousedrugpolicy.gov; f. 1988; Dir JOHN P. WALTERS.

Office of Policy Development: Executive Office of the President, 1600 Pennsylvania Ave, NW, Washington, DC 20500; tel. (202) 456-6515; fax (202) 456-2878; internet www.whitehouse.gov/dpc; f. 1970; composed of the Domestic Policy Council (f. 1993) and the Nat. Economic Council; Asst to the Pres. for Economic Policy and Dir of the Nat. Economic Council KARL ZINSMEISTER.

Office of Science and Technology Policy: 725 17th St, Rm 5228, NW, Washington, DC, 20502; tel. (202) 456-7116; fax (202) 456-6021; e-mail info@ostp.gov; internet www.ostp.gov; f. 1976; Dir JOHN H. MARBURGER, III.

Office of the United States Trade Representative: Winder Bldg, 600 17th St, NW, Washington, DC 20508; tel. (202) 395-3230; fax (202) 395-4549; e-mail contactustr@ustr.eop.gov; internet www.ustr.gov; f. 1963; US Trade Rep. SUSAN C. SCHWAB.

United States Mission to the United Nations: 799 United Nations Plaza, New York, NY 10017; tel. (212) 415-4404; fax (212) 415-4303; e-mail usa@un.int; internet www.un.int/usa; US Ambassador to the United Nations Dr ZALMAY KHALILZAD.

USA Freedom Corps: 1600 Pennsylvania Ave, NW, Washington, DC 20500; e-mail info@usafreedomcorps.gov; internet www.usafreedomcorps.gov; f. 2002; Dir ALISON T. YOUNG (acting).

White House Military Office: Executive Office of the President, 1600 Pennsylvania Ave, NW, Washington, DC 20500; internet www.whitehouse.gov/whmo; areas of responsibility incl. Camp David (f. 1942) and Air Force One (f. 1962); Dir Rear-Adm. RAYMOND A. SPICER.

Selected Federal Agencies

The following agencies are part of government departments and are responsible for overseeing activities within the scope of ordinary legislation:

Federal Aviation Administration: 800 Independence Ave, SW, Washington, DC 20591; tel. (202) 366-4000; fax (202) 267-5047; internet www.faa.gov; f. 1958; part of the Dept of Transportation; regulates civil aviation, promotes safety in the air and assists in devt of an effective national airport system; Admin. ROBERT A. STURGELL (designate).

Federal Emergency Management Agency: Federal Center Plaza, 500 C St, SW, Washington, DC 20472; tel. (202) 646-4600; fax (202) 646-2531; internet www.fema.gov; f. 1979; part of the Dept of Homeland Security; Admin. R. DAVID PAULISON.

Federal Energy Regulatory Commission (FERC): 888 First St, NE, Washington, DC 20426; tel. (202) 502-8004; e-mail customer@ferc.gov; internet www.ferc.gov; independent regulatory commission; Chair. JOSEPH T. KELLIHER.

Federal Highway Administration (FHWA): 400 Seventh St, SW, Washington, DC 20590; tel. (202) 366-0604; internet www.fhwa.dot.gov; part of the Dept of Transportation; implements federal highway policy and promotes road safety; Admin. THOMAS J. MADISON, Jr.

Federal Railroad Administration: Dept of Transportation, 1200 New Jersey Ave, SE, Washington, DC 20590; tel. (202) 493-6000; fax (202) 493-6009; internet www.fra.dot.gov; f. 1966; part of the Dept of Transportation; formulates federal railway policies and administers and enforces safety regulations; Admin. JOSEPH H. BOARDMAN.

Food and Drug Administration (FDA): 5600 Fishers Lane, Rockville, MD 20857; internet www.fda.gov; part of the Dept of Health and Human Services; Commr ANDREW C. VON ESCHENBACH.

Ginnie Mae (Government National Mortgage Association): 451 Seventh St, Rm B-133, SW, Washington, DC 20410-9000; tel. (202) 708-1535; fax (202) 485-0206; internet www.ginniemae.gov; f. 1968; part of the Dept of Housing and Urban Devt; Pres. JOSEPH J. MURIN.

Government Accountability Office: 441 G St, NW, Washington, DC 20548; tel. (202) 512-3000; e-mail contact@gao.gov; internet www.gao.gov; fmrly the Gen. Accounting Office; Comptroller-Gen. GENE L. DODARO (acting).

National Highway Traffic Safety Administration (NHTSA): 1200 New Jersey Ave, SE, West Bldg, Washington, DC 20590; tel. (202) 366-9550; e-mail webmaster@nhtsa.dot.gov; internet www.nhtsa.dot.gov; f. 1970; part of the Dept of Transportation; Admin. DAVID KELLY (acting).

National Park Service: 2120 North Central Ave, Phoenix, AZ 85004; tel. (602) 794-3804; internet www.nps.gov; f. 1916; part of the Dept of the Interior; Dir MARY A. BOMAR.

National Security Agency/Central Security Service (NSA/CSS): 9800 Savage Rd, STE 6248, Fort George G. Meade, MD

20755-6272; tel. (301) 688-6524; fax (301) 688-6198; e-mail nsapao@nsa.gov; internet www.nsa.gov; part of the Dept of Defense and Office of the Dir of Nat. Intelligence; Dir Lt-Gen. KEITH B. ALEXANDER.

Office of Thrift Supervision (OTS): 1700 G St, NW, Washington, DC 20552; tel. (202) 906-6000; fax (202) 906-7755; e-mail public.info@ots.treas.gov; internet www.ots.treas.gov; f. 1989; part of the Dept of the Treasury; Dir JOHN M. REICH.

Patent and Trademark Office (USPTO): Madison Bldgs, 600 Dulany St, POB 1450, Alexandria, VA 22313-1450; tel. (571) 272-7000; fax (571) 273-0099; e-mail usptoinfo@uspto.gov; internet www.uspto.gov; part of the Dept of Commerce; Dir JON W. DUDAS.

United States Customs and Border Protection (CBP): 1300 Pennsylvania Ave, NW, Washington, DC 20229; tel. (202) 354-1000; internet www.customs.treas.gov; f. 1789; part of the Dept of the Treasury; Commr W. RALPH BASHAM.

United States Drug Enforcement Administration (DEA): Information Services Section (CPI), 2401 Jefferson Davis Hwy, Alexandria, VA 22301; tel. (202) 307-7363; fax (202) 307-4778; internet www.dea.gov; f. 1973; part of the Dept of Justice; Admin. MICHELE LEONHART (acting).

United States Fish and Wildlife Service: 1849 C St, NW, Washington, DC 20240; e-mail contact@fws.gov; internet www.fws.gov; f. 1871; part of the Dept of the Interior; Dir H. DALE HALL.

United States Government Printing Office: 732 North Capitol St, NW, Washington, DC 20401; tel. (202) 512-1957; e-mail contactcenter@gpo.gov; internet www.gpo.gov; f. 1860; part of the Office of Congressional and Public Affairs; Public Printer and CEO ROBERT CHARLES TAPELLA.

USDA Forest Service: 1400 Independence Ave, SW, Washington, DC 20250-0003; tel. (202) 205-8333; e-mail webmaster@fs.fed.us; internet www.fs.fed.us; f. 1905; part of the Dept of Agriculture; Chief ABIGAIL R. KIMBELL.

Independent Agencies

The following agencies were created by Congress in order to oversee activities outside the scope of ordinary legislation:

Advisory Council on Historic Preservation: 1100 Pennsylvania Ave, NW, Suite 803, Old Post Office Bldg, Washington, DC 20004; tel. (202) 606-8503; e-mail achp@achp.gov; internet www.achp.gov; f. 1966; Exec. Dir JOHN M. FOWLER.

African Development Foundation: 1400 I St, NW, Suite 1000, Washington, DC 20005-2248; tel. (202) 673-3916; fax (202) 673-3810; e-mail info@adf.gov; internet www.adf.gov; Pres. and CEO LLOYD O. PIERSON.

American Battle Monuments Commission: Courthouse Plaza II, Suite 500, 2300 Clarendon Blvd, Arlington, VA 22201-3367; tel. (703) 696-6900; fax (703) 696-6666; e-mail info@abmc.gov; internet www.abmc.gov; f. 1923; Chair. Gen. (retd) FREDERICK M. FRANKS, Jr; Sec. and CEO Brig.-Gen. (retd) JOHN W. NICHOLSON.

Appalachian Regional Commission: 1666 Connecticut Ave, NW, Washington, DC 20009-1068; tel. (202) 884-7700; fax (202) 884-7682; e-mail info@arc.gov; internet www.arc.gov; f. 1965; Fed. Co-Chair. ANNE B. POPE; Alt. Fed. Co-Chair. RICHARD J. PELTZ.

Commission on Civil Rights: 624 Ninth St, NW, Washington, DC 20425; tel. (202) 376-7700; fax (202) 376-8116; e-mail publications@usccr.gov; internet www.usccr.gov; f. 1957; Chair. GERALD A. REYNOLDS; Staff Dir MARTIN DANNENFELSER.

Commission of Fine Arts: National Bldg Museum, Suite 312, 401 F St, NW, Washington, DC 20001-2728; tel. (202) 504-2200; fax (202) 504-2195; e-mail staff@cfa.gov; internet www.cfa.gov; f. 1910; Chair. EARL A. POWELL, III.

Commodity Futures Trading Commission (CFTC): 3 Lafayette Centre, 1155 21st St, NW, Washington, DC 20581; tel. (202) 418-5000; fax (202) 418-5521; e-mail oea@cftc.gov; internet www.cftc.gov; f. 1974; Chair. WALTER LUKKEN (acting).

Corporation for National and Community Service (CNS): 1201 New York Ave, NW, Washington, DC 20525; tel. (202) 606-5000; fax (202) 565-2799; e-mail info@cns.gov; internet www.nationalservice.gov; Chair. STEPHEN GOLDSMITH; CEO DAVID EISNER; Inspector-Gen. GERALD WALPIN.

Defense Nuclear Facilities Safety Board: 625 Indiana Ave, Suite 700, NW, Washington, DC 20004-2901; tel. (202) 694-7000; fax (202) 208-6518; e-mail mailbox@dnfsb.gov; internet www.dnfsb.gov; f. 1988; Chair. Dr A. J. EGGENBERGER.

Environmental Protection Agency: Ariel Rios Bldg, 1200 Pennsylvania Ave, NW, Washington, DC 20460; tel. (202) 564-4700; internet www.epa.gov; f. 1970; Admin. STEPHEN L. JOHNSON.

Equal Employment Opportunity Commission: 1801 L St, NW, POB 7033, Washington, DC 20507; tel. (202) 663-4900; fax (202) 663-4494; e-mail info@ask.eeoc.gov; internet www.eeoc.gov; f. 1965; Chair. NAOMI C. EARP.

Export-Import Bank of the United States (Ex-Im Bank): see Finance—Banking.

Farm Credit Administration (FCA): 1501 Farm Credit Dr., McLean, VA 22102-5090; tel. (703) 883-4000; fax (703) 790-3260; e-mail info-line@fca.gov; internet www.fca.gov; f. 1933; Chair. and CEO LELAND A. STROM.

Federal Communications Commission (FCC): 445 12th St, SW, Washington, DC 20554; tel. (202) 418-0200; fax (202) 418-0232; e-mail fccinfo@fcc.gov; internet www.fcc.gov; f. 1934; regulates inter-state and foreign communications by radio, television, wire and cable; Chair. KEVIN J. MARTIN.

Federal Deposit Insurance Corporation (FDIC): 550 17th St, NW, Washington, DC 20429; tel. (202) 736-0000; e-mail publicinfo@fdic.gov; internet www.fdic.gov; f. 1933; Chair. SHEILA C. BAIR; Dir THOMAS J. CURRY.

Federal Election Commission: 999 E St, NW, Washington, DC 20463; tel. (202) 694-1100; fax (202) 219-3880; e-mail webmaster@fec.gov; internet www.fec.gov; f. 1975; independent; Chair. DAVID M. MASON.

Federal Housing Finance Board: 1625 I St, NW, 4th Floor, Washington, DC 20006-4001; tel. (202) 408-2500; fax (202) 408-1435; e-mail fhfb@fhfb.gov; internet www.fhfb.gov; Chair. RONALD A. ROSENFELD.

Federal Labor Relations Authority (FLRA): 1400 K St, 4th Floor, NW, Washington, DC 20005; tel. (202) 218-7945; fax (202) 482-6635; e-mail jcrumpacker@flra.gov; internet www.flra.gov; f. 1978; Chair. (vacant).

Federal Maritime Commission: see Transport—Ocean Shipping.

Federal Mediation and Conciliation Service: 2100 K St, NW, Washington, DC 20427; tel. (202) 606-8100; fax (202) 606-4251; internet www.fmcs.gov; f. 1947; Dir ARTHUR F. ROSENFELD.

Federal Reserve System: see Finance—Banking.

Federal Retirement Thrift Investment Board (FRTIB): 1250 H St, NW, Washington, DC 20005; tel. (202) 942-1600; fax (202) 942-1676; internet www.frtib.gov; f. 1986; Exec. Dir GREGORY T. LONG.

Federal Trade Commission: 600 Pennsylvania, NW, Washington, DC 20580; tel. (202) 326-2222; fax (202) 326-2396; internet www.ftc.gov; f. 1914; Chair. WILLIAM E. KOVACIC.

General Services Administration: 1800 F St, NW, Washington, DC 20405; tel. (202) 501-1231; fax (202) 501-1489; internet www.gsa.gov; f. 1949; Admin. JIM WILLIAMS (acting).

Inter-American Foundation: 901 North Stuart St, 10th Floor, Arlington, VA 22203; tel. (703) 306-4319; fax (703) 306-4365; e-mail info@iaf.gov; internet www.iaf.gov; f. 1969; provides grants to non-governmental and community-based orgs in Latin America and the Caribbean; Chair. ROGER W. WALLACE.

Medicare Payment Advisory Commission (MedPAC): 601 New Jersey Ave, NW, Suite 9000, Washington, DC 2001; tel. (202) 220-3700; fax (202) 220-3759; e-mail webmaster@medpac.gov; internet www.medpac.gov; Chair. GLENN M. HACKBARTH.

Merit Systems Protection Board: 1615 M St, NW, Washington, DC 20419; tel. (202) 653-7200; fax (202) 653-7130; e-mail mspb@mspb.gov; internet www.mspb.gov; f. 1979; Chair. NEIL A. G. MCPHIE.

National Aeronautics and Space Administration (NASA): 300 E St, SW, Washington, DC 20546; tel. (202) 358-0000; fax (202) 358-3251; e-mail info-center@hq.nasa.gov; internet www.nasa.gov; f. 1958; Admin. MICHAEL D. GRIFFIN.

National Archives and Records Administration: 8601 Adelphi Rd, College Park, MD 20740-6001; tel. (301) 837-1600; fax (301) 837-3218; internet www.archives.gov; f. 1934; Archivist of the United States Prof. ALLEN WEINSTEIN.

National Capital Planning Commission: 401 Ninth St, NW, Suite 500, Washington, DC 20004; tel. (202) 482-7200; fax (202) 482-7272; e-mail info@ncpc.gov; internet www.ncpc.gov; f. 1924; Chair. JOHN V. COGBILL, III.

National Commission on Libraries and Information Science: 1800 M St, NW, Suite 350, North Tower, Washington, DC 20036-5841; tel. (202) 606-9200; fax (202) 606-9203; e-mail info@nclis.gov; internet www.nclis.gov; f. 1970; Chair. C. BETH FITZSIMMONS.

National Council on Disability: 1331 F St, NW, Suite 850, Washington, DC 20004-1107; tel. (202) 272-2004; fax (202) 272-2022; e-mail ncd@ncd.gov; internet www.ncd.gov; f. 1978; Chair. JOHN R. VAUGHN.

National Credit Union Administration: 1775 Duke St, Alexandria, VA 22314-3428; tel. (703) 518-6330; fax (703) 518-6409; e-mail pacamail@ncua.gov; internet www.ncua.gov; f. 1970; Chair. MICHAEL E. FRYZEL.

National Endowment for the Arts: 1100 Pennsylvania Ave, NW, Washington, DC 20506-0001; tel. (202) 682-5400; fax (202) 682-5611; e-mail webmgr@arts.endow.gov; internet www.arts.gov; f. 1965; Chair. DANA GIOIA.

National Endowment for the Humanities: 1100 Pennsylvania Ave, NW, Rm 503, Washington, DC 20506; tel. (202) 606-8310; e-mail info@neh.gov; internet www.neh.gov; f. 1965; Chair. BRUCE COLE.

National Labor Relations Board: 1099 14th St, NW, Washington, DC 20570-0001; tel. (202) 273-1991; fax (202) 273-1789; internet www.nlrb.gov; f. 1935; Chair. PETER C. SCHAUMBER.

National Mediation Board (NMB): 1301 K St, NW, Suite 250 East, Washington, DC 20005-7011; tel. (202) 692-5010; fax (202) 523-5080; internet www.nmb.gov; f. 1934; Chair. READ VAN DE WATER.

National Science Foundation (NSF): 4201 Wilson Blvd, Arlington, VA 22230; tel. (703) 292-5111; e-mail info@nsf.gov; internet www.nsf.gov; f. 1950; supports basic scientific and engineering research and education; Dir Dr ARDEN L. BEMENT, Jr.

National Transportation Safety Board: see Transport.

Nuclear Regulatory Commission (NRC): Office of Public Affairs, Washington, DC 20555; tel. (301) 415-8200; e-mail opa@nrc.gov; internet www.nrc.gov; Chair. DALE E. KLEIN.

Occupational Safety and Health Review Commission (OSHRC): 1120 20th St, 9th Floor, NW, Washington, DC 20036-3457; tel. (202) 606-5398; fax (202) 606-5052; internet www.oshrc.gov; f. 1970; Chair. HORACE A. THOMPSON.

Office of Government Ethics: 1201 New York Ave, NW, Suite 500, Washington, DC 20005-3917; tel. (202) 482-9300; fax (202) 482-9237; e-mail contactoge@oge.gov; internet www.usoge.gov; f. 1978; Dir ROBERT I. CUSICK.

Office of Personnel Management (OPM): Theodore Roosevelt Federal Bldg, 1900 E St, NW, Washington, DC 20415; tel. (202) 606-1800; fax (202) 606-2573; e-mail general@opm.gov; internet www.opm.gov; f. 1979; Dir MICHAEL W. HAGER (acting).

Office of Special Counsel: 1730 M St, NW, Suite 300, Washington, DC 20036-4505; tel. (202) 254-3600; fax (202) 653-5151; internet www.osc.gov; Special Counsel SCOTT J. BLOCH.

Peace Corps: Paul D. Coverdell Peace Corps HQ, 1111 20th St, NW, Washington, DC 20526; tel. (202) 692-2100; fax (202) 692-2101; e-mail webmaster@peacecorps.gov; internet www.peacecorps.gov; f. 1961; Dir RONALD A. TSCHETTER.

Pension Benefit Guaranty Corporation: 1200 K St, NW, Suite 12201, Washington, DC 20005-4026; tel. (202) 326-4010; fax (202) 326-4016; e-mail webmaster@pbgc.gov; internet www.pbgc.gov; f. 1974; Dir CHARLES E. F. MILLARD.

Postal Rate Commission: 901 New York Ave, NW, Suite 200, NW, Washington, DC 20268-0001; tel. (202) 789-6800; fax (202) 789-6886; e-mail prc-webmaster@prc.gov; internet www.prc.gov; f. 1970; Chair. DAN G. BLAIR.

Railroad Retirement Board: 844 North Rush St, Chicago, IL 60611-2092; tel. (312) 751-4777; fax (312) 751-7154; e-mail opa@rrb.gov; internet www.rrb.gov; f. 1935; Chair. MICHAEL S. SCHWARTZ.

Securities and Exchange Commission: Station Pl., 100 F St, NE, Washington, DC 20549; tel. (202) 942-8088; fax (202) 942-9646; e-mail help@sec.gov; internet www.sec.gov; f. 1935; Chair. CHRISTOPHER COX.

Selective Service System: 1515 Wilson Blvd, Arlington, VA 22209-2425; tel. (703) 605-4100; fax (703) 605-4106; e-mail information@sss.gov; internet www.sss.gov; f. 1940; Dir WILLIAM A. CHATFIELD.

Small Business Administration: 409 Third St, SW, Washington, DC 20416; tel. (202) 205-6650; fax (202) 205-6802; internet www.sba.gov; f. 1953; Admin. SANDY K. BARUAH (acting).

Smithsonian Institution: 1000 Jefferson Dr., SW, Washington, DC 20560-0001; tel. (202) 633-1000; e-mail info@si.edu; internet www.si.edu; f. 1846; Sec. G. WAYNE CLOUGH.

Social Security Administration: Office of Public Inquiries, Windsor Park Bldg, 6401 Security Blvd, Baltimore, MD 21235-0001; tel. (410) 965-3120; fax (410) 966-1463; internet www.ssa.gov; Commr MICHAEL J. ASTRUE.

Tennessee Valley Authority: 400 West Summit Hill Dr., Knoxville, TN 37902-1499; tel. (865) 632-2101; e-mail tvainfo@tva.gov; internet www.tva.gov; f. 1933; CEO and Pres. TOM KILGORE.

United States Agency for International Development (USAID): Ronald Reagan Bldg, 1300 Pennsylvania Ave, NW, Washington, DC 20523-0016; tel. (202) 712-4810; fax (202) 216-3524; e-mail pinquiries@usaid.gov; internet www.usaid.gov; f. 1961; Admin. HENRIETTA HOLSMAN FORE.

United States Consumer Product Safety Commission: 4330 East-West Hwy, Bethesda, MD 20814-4408; tel. (301) 504-7923; fax (301) 504-0124; e-mail info@cpsc.gov; internet www.cpsc.gov; f. 1972; Chair. NANCY NORD (acting); Commr THOMAS H. MOORE; Exec. Dir PATSY SEMPLE.

United States International Trade Commission: 500 E St, SW, Washington, DC 20436; tel. (202) 205-2000; fax (202) 205-2798; e-mail webmaster@usitc.gov; internet www.usitc.gov; f. 1916; Chair. SHARA L. ARANOFF.

United States Postal Service: 475 L'Enfant Plaza, SW, Washington, DC 20260-0010; tel. (202) 268-2000; fax (202) 268-4860; internet www.usps.com; f. 1970; Postmaster-Gen. and CEO JOHN (JACK) E. POTTER.

United States Trade and Development Agency (USTDA): 1000 Wilson Blvd, Suite 1600, Arlington, VA 22209-3901; tel. (703) 875-4357; fax (703) 875-4009; e-mail info@ustda.gov; internet www.ustda.gov; f. 1961; Dir LARRY W. WALTHER.

PRESIDENTIAL ELECTIONS

Popular Votes Cast for President, by State

('000, by major political party. Sources: Office of the Clerk of the House of Representatives, internet clerkweb.house.gov, and www.nytimes.com.)

	2004			2008 (preliminary)		
	Rep.	Dem.	Others*	Dem.	Rep.	Others†
Alabama	1,176	694	13	812	1,264	16
Alaska	191	111	11	80	136	5
Arizona	1,104	894	15	853	1,014	22
Arkansas	573	470	12	418	633	13
California	5,510	6,746	118	6,219	3,777	188
Colorado	1,101	1,002	26	1,109	967	31
Connecticut	694	858	28	944	606	18
Delaware	172	200	3	247	152	5
District of Columbia	21	203	3	210	15	1
Florida	3,965	3,584	62	4,104	3,909	60
Georgia	1,914	1,366	21	2,022	1,811	28
Hawaii	194	232	3	299	111	7
Idaho	409	181	8	401	235	15
Illinois	2,346	2,892	36	3,293	1,976	70
Indiana	1,479	969	19	1,367	1,341	29
Iowa	752	742	12	818	678	20
Kansas	736	435	16	500	686	21
Kentucky	1,069	713	14	747	1,043	26
Louisiana	1,102	820	21	781	1,148	29
Maine	330	397	14	390	272	13
Maryland	1,025	1,334	31	1,409	873	30
Massachusetts	1,071	1,804	53	1,891	1,104	53
Michigan	2,314	2,479	46	2,868	2,044	81
Minnesota	1,347	1,445	37	1,573	1,275	52
Mississippi	673	458	9	518	684	10
Missouri	1,456	1,259	16	1,437	1,443	37
Montana	266	174	11	230	242	15
Nebraska	513	254	11	316	439	12
Nevada	419	397	14	532	412	21
New Hampshire	331	341	7	362	295	6
New Jersey	1,670	1,911	30	2,074	1,541	39
New Mexico	377	371	8	454	334	10
New York	2,807	4,181	461	4,357	2,573	80
North Carolina	1,961	1,526	14	2,123	2,109	25
North Dakota	197	111	5	141	169	6
Ohio	2,860	2,741	27	2,674	2,470	84
Oklahoma	960	504	—	502	960	—
Oregon	867	943	27	785	583	29
Pennsylvania	2,794	2,938	38	3,185	2,584	61
Rhode Island	169	260	8	275	152	7
South Carolina	938	662	18	842	1,009	25
South Dakota	233	149	6	171	203	8
Tennessee	1,384	1,036	16	1,081	1,470	23
Texas	4,527	2,833	51	3,521	4,468	56
Utah	664	241	22	302	555	20
Vermont	121	184	7	202	95	5
Virginia	1,717	1,455	24	1,793	1,637	31
Washington	1,305	1,510	43	1,118	784	33
West Virginia	424	327	5	301	394	12
Wisconsin	1,478	1,490	30	1,670	1,258	37
Wyoming	168	71	5	80	161	5
Total‡	61,873	58,895	1,583	64,043	56,498	1,535

* Including write-in candidates, etc. Others also include Independent candidates and candidates from the Libertarian Party, the Constitution Party, the Green Party, the Reform Party, the Populist Party and the Independence Party.

† Including write-in candidates, etc. Others also include Independent candidates and candidates from the Green Party, the Libertarian Party and the Constitution Party.

‡ Totals may not equal the sum of their parts owing to rounding.

FEDERAL LEGISLATURE (CONGRESS)

The Senate

(internet www.senate.gov; results at November 2008)

The Senate comprises 100 members. Senators' terms are for six years, one-third of the Senate being elected every two years.

President of the Senate: Vice-President RICHARD B. CHENEY.

President Pro Tempore: ROBERT C. BYRD.

Majority Leader: HARRY M. REID.

Minority Leader: MITCH MCCONNELL.

Democrats: 55 seats.

Republicans: 40 seats.

Independents: 2 seats.

Undecided: 3 seats.

MEMBERS

(with political party and year in which term expires—on 3 January in all cases. Senators elected in 2008 were scheduled to take office on 3 January 2009.)

Alabama		
Jeff Sessions	Rep.	2015
Richard C. Shelby	Rep.	2011
Alaska		
Lisa Murkowski	Rep.	2011
Undecided		2015
Arizona		
Jon Kyl	Rep.	2013
John McCain	Rep.	2011
Arkansas		
Mark L. Pryor	Dem.	2015
Blanche L. Lincoln	Dem.	2011
California		
Dianne Feinstein	Dem.	2013
Barbara Boxer	Dem.	2011
Colorado		
Ken Salazar	Dem.	2011
Mark Udall	Dem.	2015
Connecticut		
Joe I. Lieberman	Ind.	2013
Chris J. Dodd	Dem.	2011
Delaware		
Thomas R. Carper	Dem.	2013
Joseph R. Biden, Jr	Dem.	2015
Florida		
Bill Nelson	Dem.	2013
Mel Martinez	Rep.	2011
Georgia		
Johnny Isakson	Rep.	2011
Undecided		2015
Hawaii		
Daniel K. Akaka	Dem.	2013
Daniel K. Inouye	Dem.	2011
Idaho		
James Risch	Rep.	2015
Michael Crapo	Rep.	2011
Illinois		
Richard J. Durbin	Dem.	2015
Barack Obama	Dem.	2011
Indiana		
Richard G. Lugar	Rep.	2013
Evan Bayh	Dem.	2011
Iowa		
Tom Harkin	Dem.	2015
Chuck Grassley	Rep.	2011
Kansas		
Pat Roberts	Rep.	2015
Sam Brownback	Rep.	2011
Kentucky		
Mitch McConnell	Rep.	2015
Jim Bunning	Rep.	2011
Louisiana		
Mary L. Landrieu	Dem.	2015
David Vitter	Rep.	2011
Maine		
Olympia J. Snowe	Rep.	2013
Susan M. Collins	Rep.	2015
Maryland		
Ben L. Cardin	Dem.	2013
Barbara A. Mikulski	Dem.	2011
Massachusetts		
Edward M. Kennedy	Dem.	2013
John F. Kerry	Dem.	2015
Michigan		
Debbie Stabenow	Dem.	2013
Carl Levin	Dem.	2015
Minnesota		
Amy Klobuchar	Dem.	2013
Undecided		2015
Mississippi		
Roger Wicker	Rep.	2013
Thad Cochran	Rep.	2015
Missouri		
Claire McCaskill	Dem.	2013
Christopher S. Bond	Rep.	2011
Montana		
Jon Tester	Dem.	2013
Max Baucus	Dem.	2015
Nebraska		
E. Ben Nelson	Dem.	2013
Mike Johanns	Rep.	2015
Nevada		
John E. Ensign	Rep.	2013
Harry M. Reid	Dem.	2011
New Hampshire		
Jeanne Shaheen	Dem.	2015
Judd Gregg	Rep.	2011
New Jersey		
Robert Menéndez	Dem.	2013
Frank R. Lautenberg	Dem.	2015
New Mexico		
Jeff Bingaman	Dem.	2013
Robert Udall	Dem.	2015
New York		
Hillary Rodham Clinton	Dem.	2013
Charles E. Schumer	Dem.	2011
North Carolina		
Kay Hagan	Dem.	2015
Richard Burr	Rep.	2011
North Dakota		
Kent Conrad	Dem.	2013
Byron L. Dorgan	Dem.	2011
Ohio		
Sherrod Brown	Dem.	2013
George V. Voinovich	Rep.	2011
Oklahoma		
James M. Inhofe	Rep.	2015
Tom Coburn	Rep.	2011
Oregon		
Gordon H. Smith	Rep.	2015
Ronald L. Wyden	Dem.	2011
Pennsylvania		
Robert P. Casey, Jr	Dem.	2013
Arlen Specter	Rep.	2011
Rhode Island		
Sheldon Whitehouse, II	Dem.	2013
Jack Reed	Dem.	2015
South Carolina		
Lindsey Graham	Rep.	2015
Jim DeMint	Rep.	2011
South Dakota		
Tim Johnson	Dem.	2015
John Thune	Rep.	2011
Tennessee		
Robert P. Corker	Rep.	2013

Lamar Alexander	Rep.	2015
Texas		
Kay Bailey Hutchison	Rep.	2013
John Cornyn	Rep.	2015
Utah		
Orrin G. Hatch	Rep.	2013
Bob F. Bennett	Rep.	2011
Vermont		
Bernard Sanders	Ind.	2013
Patrick J. Leahy	Dem.	2011
Virginia		
James H. Webb, Jr	Dem.	2013
Mark R. Warner	Dem.	2015
Washington		
Maria Cantwell	Dem.	2013
Patty Murray	Dem.	2011
West Virginia		
Robert C. Byrd	Dem.	2013
John D. (Jay) Rockefeller, IV	Dem.	2015
Wisconsin		
Herb Kohl	Dem.	2013
Russell D. Feingold	Dem.	2011
Wyoming		
Dr John Barrosso	Rep.	2013
Mike B. Enzi	Rep.	2015

The House of Representatives

(internet www.house.gov; results at November 2008)

A new House of Representatives, comprising 435 members, is elected every two years.

Speaker: Nancy Pelosi.

Majority Leader: Steny H. Hoyer.

Minority Leader: John Boehner.

Democrats: 235 seats.

Republicans: 199 seats.

Undecided: 1 seat.

MEMBERS

(with political party, listed in District order. Representatives were scheduled to take office on 3 January 2009.)

District		*Party*
	Alabama	
1	Jo Bonner	Rep.
2	Bobby Bright, Sr	Dem.
3	Michael D. Rogers	Rep.
4	Robert B. Aderholt	Rep.
5	Parker Griffith	Dem.
6	Spencer Bachus	Rep.
7	Artur Davis	Dem.
	Alaska	
At Large	Undecided	
	Arizona	
1	Ann Kirkpatrick	Dem.
2	Trent Franks	Rep.
3	John Shadegg	Rep.
4	Ed Pastor	Dem.
5	Harry Mitchell	Dem.
6	Jeff Flake	Rep.
7	Raul Grijalva	Dem.
8	Gabrielle Giffords	Dem.
	Arkansas	
1	Marion Berry	Dem.
2	Vic Snyder	Dem.
3	John Boozman	Rep.
4	Mike Ross	Dem.
	California	
1	Mike Thompson	Dem.
2	Wally Herger	Rep.
3	Dan E. Lungren	Rep.
4	Undecided	
5	Doris O. Matsui	Dem.
6	Lynn C. Woolsey	Dem.
7	George Miller	Dem.
8	Nancy Pelosi	Dem.

District—continued		*Party*
9	Barbara Lee	Dem.
10	Ellen O. Tauscher	Dem.
11	Jerry McNerney	Dem.
12	Jackie Speier	Dem.
13	Fortney Pete Stark	Dem.
14	Anna G. Eshoo	Dem.
15	Mike M. Honda	Dem.
16	Zoe Lofgren	Dem.
17	Sam Farr	Dem.
18	Dennis A. Cardoza	Dem.
19	George P. Radanovich	Rep.
20	Jim Costa	Dem.
21	Devin Nunes	Rep.
22	Kevin McCarthy	Rep.
23	Lois Capps	Dem.
24	Elton Gallegly	Rep.
25	Howard P. McKeon	Rep.
26	David Dreier	Rep.
27	Brad Sherman	Dem.
28	Howard L. Berman	Dem.
29	Adam B. Schiff	Dem.
30	Henry A. Waxman	Dem.
31	Xavier Becerra	Dem.
32	Hilda L. Solis	Dem.
33	Diane E. Watson	Dem.
34	Lucille Roybal-Allard	Dem.
35	Maxine Waters	Dem.
36	Jane Harman	Dem.
37	Laura Richardson	Dem.
38	Grace F. Napolitano	Dem.
39	Linda T. Sánchez	Dem.
40	Edward R. Royce	Rep.
41	Jerry Lewis	Rep.
42	Gary G. Miller	Rep.
43	Joe E. Baca	Dem.
44	Ken Calvert	Rep.
45	Mary Bono	Rep.
46	Dana Rohrabacher	Rep.
47	Loretta K. O. Sanchez	Dem.
48	John Campbell	Rep.
49	Darrell E. Issa	Rep.
50	Brian P. Bilbray	Rep.
51	Bob Filner	Dem.
52	Duncan Hunter	Rep.
53	Susan A. Davis	Dem.
	Colorado	
1	Diana DeGette	Dem.
2	Jared Polis	Dem.
3	John T. Salazar	Dem.
4	Betsy Markey	Dem.
5	Doug Lamborn	Rep.
6	Michael Coffman	Rep.
7	Ed Perlmutter	Dem.
	Connecticut	
1	John B. Larson	Dem.
2	Joseph D. Courtney	Dem.
3	Rosa L. DeLauro	Dem.
4	James Himes	Dem.
5	Chris Murphy	Dem.
	Delaware	
At Large	Michael N. Castle	Rep.
	Florida	
1	Jeff Miller	Rep.
2	Allen Boyd	Dem.
3	Corrine Brown	Dem.
4	Ander Crenshaw	Rep.
5	Ginny Brown-Waite	Rep.
6	Clifford B. Stearns	Rep.
7	John L. Mica	Rep.
8	Alan Grayson	Dem.
9	Michael Bilirakis	Rep.
10	C. W. Bill Young	Rep.
11	Kathy Castor	Dem.
12	Adam H. Putnam	Rep.
13	Vern Buchanan	Rep.
14	Connie Mack	Rep.
15	Bill Posey	Rep.
16	Tom Rooney	Rep.
17	Kendrick B. Meek	Dem.
18	Ileana Ros-Lehtinen	Rep.
19	Robert Wexler	Dem.
20	Debbie Wasserman Schultz	Dem.

District—continued		*Party*
21	Lincoln Diaz-Balart	Rep.
22	Ron Klein	Dem.
23	Alcee L. Hastings	Dem.
24	Suzanne Kosmas	Dem.
25	Mario Diaz-Balart	Rep.
	Georgia	
1	Jack Kingston	Rep.
2	Sanford D. Bishop, Jr	Dem.
3	Lynn A. Westmoreland	Rep.
4	Henry C. Johnson, Jr	Dem.
5	John Lewis	Dem.
6	Tom Price	Rep.
7	John Linder	Rep.
8	Jim Marshall	Dem.
9	Nathan Deal	Rep.
10	Paul Broun	Rep.
11	Phil Gingrey	Rep.
12	John Barrow	Dem.
13	David Scott	Dem.
	Hawaii	
1	Neil Abercrombie	Dem.
2	Mazie K. Hirono	Dem.
	Idaho	
1	Walter Minnick	Dem.
2	Michael K. Simpson	Rep.
	Illinois	
1	Bobby L. Rush	Dem.
2	Jesse L. Jackson, Jr	Dem.
3	Daniel Lipinski	Dem.
4	Luis V. Gutierrez	Dem.
5	Rahm Emanuel	Dem.
6	Peter Roskam	Rep.
7	Danny K. Davis	Dem.
8	Melissa L. Bean	Dem.
9	Janice D. Schakowsky	Dem.
10	Mark S. Kirk	Rep.
11	Deborah Halvorson	Dem.
12	Jerry F. Costello	Dem.
13	Judy Biggert	Rep.
14	Bill Foster	Dem.
15	Timothy V. Johnson	Rep.
16	Donald Manzullo	Rep.
17	Phil Hare	Dem.
18	Aaron Schock	Rep.
19	John M. Shimkus	Rep.
	Indiana	
1	Peter J. Visclosky	Dem.
2	Joe Donnelly	Dem.
3	Mark E. Souder	Rep.
4	Steve Buyer	Rep.
5	Dan L. Burton	Rep.
6	Mike Pence	Rep.
7	André Carson	Dem.
8	Brad Ellsworth	Dem.
9	Baron Hill	Dem.
	Iowa	
1	Bruce L. Braley	Dem.
2	Dave Loebsack	Dem.
3	Leonard L. Boswell	Dem.
4	Tom Latham	Rep.
5	Steve King	Rep.
	Kansas	
1	Jerry Moran	Rep.
2	Lynn Jenkins	Rep.
3	Dennis Moore	Dem.
4	Todd Tiahrt	Rep.
	Kentucky	
1	Edward Whitfield	Rep.
2	Ron Lewis	Rep.
3	John Yarmuth	Dem.
4	Geoff Davis	Rep.
5	Harold Rogers	Rep.
6	Ben Chandler	Dem.
	Louisiana	
1	Steve Scalise	Rep.
2	Undecided	
3	Charlie Melancon	Dem.
4	Undecided	
5	Rodney Alexander	Rep.
6	Bill Cassidy	Rep.
7	Charles Boustany, Jr	Rep.
	Maine	
1	Chellie Pingree	Dem.
2	Michael H. Michaud	Dem.
	Maryland	
1	Frank Kratovil	Dem.
2	C. A. Dutch Ruppersberger	Dem.
3	Paul S. Sarbanes	Dem.
4	Donna F. Edwards	Dem.
5	Steny H. Hoyer	Dem.
6	Roscoe G. Bartlett	Rep.
7	Elijah E. Cummings	Dem.
8	Chris Van Hollen	Dem.
	Massachusetts	
1	John W. Olver	Dem.
2	Richard E. Neal	Dem.
3	James P. McGovern	Dem.
4	Barney Frank	Dem.
5	Niki Tsongas	Dem.
6	John F. Tierney	Dem.
7	Edward J. Markey	Dem.
8	Michael E. Capuano	Dem.
9	Stephen F. Lynch	Dem.
10	William D. Delahunt	Dem.
	Michigan	
1	Bart Stupak	Dem.
2	Peter Hoekstra	Rep.
3	Vernon J. Ehlers	Rep.
4	Dave Camp	Rep.
5	Dale E. Kildee	Dem.
6	Fred Upton	Rep.
7	Mark Hamilton Schauer	Dem.
8	Mike Rogers	Rep.
9	Gary Peters	Dem.
10	Candice S. Miller	Rep.
11	Thaddeus G. McCotter	Rep.
12	Sander M. Levin	Dem.
13	Carolyn Cheeks Kilpatrick	Dem.
14	John Conyers, Jr	Dem.
15	John D. Dingell	Dem.
	Minnesota	
1	Tim Walz	Dem.
2	John Kline	Rep.
3	Erik Paulsen	Rep.
4	Betty McCollum	Dem.
5	Keith Ellison	Dem.
6	Michele Bachmann	Rep.
7	Collin C. Peterson	Dem.
8	James L. Oberstar	Dem.
	Mississippi	
1	Travis W. Childers	Dem.
2	Bennie G. Thompson	Dem.
3	Gregg Harper	Rep.
4	Gene Taylor	Dem.
	Missouri	
1	William Lacy Clay	Dem.
2	W. Todd Akin	Rep.
3	Russ Carnahan	Dem.
4	Ike Skelton	Dem.
5	Emanuel Cleaver	Dem.
6	Samuel B. Graves, Jr	Rep.
7	Roy Blunt	Rep.
8	Jo Ann Emerson	Rep.
9	Blaine Luetkemeyer	Rep.
	Montana	
At Large	Dennis R. Rehberg	Rep.
	Nebraska	
1	Jeff Fortenberry	Rep.
2	Lee Terry	Rep.
3	Adrian Smith	Rep.
	Nevada	
1	Shelley Berkley	Dem.
2	Dean Heller	Rep.
3	Alice Titus	Dem.
	New Hampshire	
1	Carol Shea-Porter	Dem.
2	Paul Hodes	Dem.

District—continued		Party
	New Jersey	
1	Robert E. Andrews	Dem.
2	Frank A. LoBiondo	Rep.
3	John Adler	Dem.
4	Christopher H. Smith	Rep.
5	Scott Garrett	Rep.
6	Frank Pallone, Jr	Dem.
7	Leonard Lance	Rep.
8	William J. Pascrell, Jr	Dem.
9	Steven R. Rothman	Dem.
10	Donald M. Payne	Dem.
11	Rodney P. Frelinghuysen	Rep.
12	Rush D. Holt	Dem.
13	Albio Sires	Dem.
	New Mexico	
1	Martin Heinrich	Dem.
2	Harry Teague	Dem.
3	Ben Lujan, Jr	Dem.
	New York	
1	Tim H. Bishop	Dem.
2	Steve Israel	Dem.
3	Peter T. King	Rep.
4	Carolyn McCarthy	Dem.
5	Gary L. Ackerman	Dem.
6	Gregory W. Meeks	Dem.
7	Joseph Crowley	Dem.
8	Jerrold L. Nadler	Dem.
9	Anthony D. Weiner	Dem.
10	Edolphus Towns	Dem.
11	Yvette D. Clarke	Dem.
12	Nydia M. Velázquez	Dem.
13	Michael McMahon	Dem.
14	Carolyn B. Maloney	Dem.
15	Charles B. Rangel	Dem.
16	José E. Serrano	Dem.
17	Eliot L. Engel	Dem.
18	Nita M. Lowey	Dem.
19	John Hall	Dem.
20	Kirsten Gillibrand	Dem.
21	Paul Tonko	Dem.
22	Maurice D. Hinchey	Dem.
23	John M. McHugh	Rep.
24	Michael A. Arcuri	Dem.
25	Dan Maffei	Dem.
26	Christopher Lee	Rep.
27	Brian M. Higgins	Dem.
28	Louise M. Slaughter	Dem.
29	Eric Massa	Dem.
	North Carolina	
1	George K. Butterfield	Dem.
2	Bob Etheridge	Dem.
3	Walter B. Jones, Jr	Rep.
4	David E. Price	Dem.
5	Virginia Foxx	Rep.
6	Howard Coble	Rep.
7	Mike McIntyre	Dem.
8	Larry Kissell	Dem.
9	Sue W. Myrick	Rep.
10	Patrick T. McHenry	Rep.
11	Heath Shuler	Dem.
12	Mel L. Watt	Dem.
13	Brad Miller	Dem.
	North Dakota	
At Large	Earl Pomeroy	Dem.
	Ohio	
1	Steven Driehaus	Dem.
2	Jean Schmidt	Rep.
3	Michael R. Turner	Rep.
4	Jim Jordan	Rep.
5	Robert E. Latta	Rep.
6	Charlie Wilson	Dem.
7	Steve Austria	Rep.
8	John A. Boehner	Rep.
9	Marcy Kaptur	Dem.
10	Dennis J. Kucinich	Dem.
11	Marcia Fudge	Dem.
12	Patrick J. Tiberi	Rep.
13	Betty Sutton	Dem.
14	Undecided	
15	Deborah D. Pryce	Rep.
16	John Boccieri	Dem.

District—continued		Party
17	Tim Ryan	Dem.
18	Zack Space	Dem.
	Oklahoma	
1	John Sullivan	Rep.
2	Dan Boren	Dem.
3	Frank D. Lucas	Rep.
4	Tom Cole	Rep.
5	Mary Fallin	Rep.
	Oregon	
1	David Wu	Dem.
2	Greg Walden	Rep.
3	Earl Blumenauer	Dem.
4	Peter A. DeFazio	Dem.
5	Kurt Schrader	Dem.
	Pennsylvania	
1	Robert A. Brady	Dem.
2	Chaka Fattah	Dem.
3	Kathy Dahlkemper	Dem.
4	Jason Altmire	Dem.
5	Glenn Thompson	Rep.
6	Jim Gerlach	Rep.
7	Joe Sestak	Dem.
8	Patrick Murphy	Dem.
9	Bill Shuster	Rep.
10	Christopher Carney	Dem.
11	Paul E. Kanjorski	Dem.
12	John P. Murtha	Dem.
13	Allyson Y. Schwartz	Dem.
14	Michael F. Doyle	Dem.
15	Charles W. Dent	Rep.
16	Joseph R. Pitts	Rep.
17	Tim Holden	Dem.
18	Timothy F. Murphy	Rep.
19	Todd R. Platts	Rep.
	Rhode Island	
1	Patrick J. Kennedy	Dem.
2	James R. Langevin	Dem.
	South Carolina	
1	Henry E. Brown, Jr	Rep.
2	Joe D. Wilson	Rep.
3	J. Gresham Barrett	Rep.
4	Bob Inglis	Rep.
5	John M. Spratt, Jr	Dem.
6	James E. Clyburn	Dem.
	South Dakota	
At Large	Stephanie Herseth Sandlin	Dem.
	Tennessee	
1	David Roe	Rep.
2	John J. Duncan, Jr	Rep.
3	Zach Wamp	Rep.
4	Lincoln Davis	Dem.
5	Jim Cooper	Dem.
6	Bart Gordon	Dem.
7	Marsha Blackburn	Rep.
8	John S. Tanner	Dem.
9	Stephen I. Cohen	Dem.
	Texas	
1	Louie Gohmert	Rep.
2	Ted Poe	Rep.
3	Sam Johnson	Rep.
4	Ralph M. Hall	Rep.
5	Jeb Hensarling	Rep.
6	Joe Barton	Rep.
7	John A. Culberson	Rep.
8	Kevin Brady	Rep.
9	Al Green	Dem.
10	Michael T. McCaul	Rep.
11	K. Mike Conaway	Rep.
12	Kay Granger	Rep.
13	William M. Thornberry	Rep.
14	Ron Paul	Rep.
15	Rubén Hinojosa	Dem.
16	Silvestre Reyes	Dem.
17	Chet Edwards	Dem.
18	Sheila Jackson-Lee	Dem.
19	Randy Neugebauer	Rep.
20	Charles A. Gonzalez	Dem.
21	Lamar Smith	Rep.
22	Pete Olson	Dem.
23	Ciro D. Rodriguez	Dem.

District—continued		*Party*
24	Kenny Marchant	Rep.
25	Lloyd Doggett	Dem.
26	Michael C. Burgess	Rep.
27	Solomon P. Ortiz	Dem.
28	Henry Cuellar	Dem.
29	Gene Green	Dem.
30	Eddie Bernice Johnson	Dem.
31	John R. Carter	Rep.
32	Pete Sessions	Rep.
	Utah	
1	Rob Bishop	Rep.
2	Jim Matheson	Dem.
3	Jason Chaffetz	Rep.
	Vermont	
At Large	Peter Welch	Dem.
	Virginia	
1	Robert J. Wittman	Rep.
2	Glen Nye III	Dem.
3	Bobby C. Scott	Dem.
4	J. Randy Forbes	Rep.
5	Undecided	
6	Robert W. Goodlatte	Rep.
7	Eric I. Cantor	Rep.
8	James P. Moran, Jr	Dem.
9	Rick Boucher	Dem.
10	Frank R. Wolf	Rep.
11	Gerald Connolly	Dem.

District—continued		*Party*
	Washington	
1	Jay Inslee	Dem.
2	Rick Larsen	Dem.
3	Brian Baird	Dem.
4	Richard Hastings	Rep.
5	Cathy McMorris Rodgers	Rep.
6	Norman D. Dicks	Dem.
7	Jim McDermott	Dem.
8	David G. Reichert	Rep.
9	Adam Smith	Dem.
	West Virginia	
1	Alan B. Mollohan	Dem.
2	Shelley Moore Capito	Rep.
3	Nick J. Rahall, II	Dem.
	Wisconsin	
1	Paul Ryan	Rep.
2	Tammy Baldwin	Dem.
3	Ron Kind	Dem.
4	Gwen S. Moore	Dem.
5	F. James Sensenbrenner, Jr	Rep.
6	Thomas E. Petri	Rep.
7	David R. Obey	Dem.
8	Steven Kagen	Dem.
	Wyoming	
At Large	Cynthia Lummis	Rep.

FEDERAL BUDGET

(Sources: Office of Management and Budget, Executive Office of the President; Financial Management Service, US Department of the Treasury.)

REVENUE
(US $ '000 million, year ending 30 September)*

	2007	2008†	2009†
Individual income taxes	1,163.5	1,169.0	1,250.4
Corporation income taxes	370.2	309.3	304.1
Social insurance taxes and contributions	869.6	901.2	931.5
Excise taxes	65.1	68.1	67.8
Estate and gift taxes	26.0	28.4	26.1
Customs duties and fees	26.0	27.7	28.3
Miscellaneous receipts	47.8	49.3	43.3
Total	2,568.2	2,552.9	2,651.4

* Including social security receipts, which are extrabudgetary.
† Mid-session estimates published in July 2008.

EXPENDITURE
(US $ '000 million, year ending 30 September)*

	2007	2008†	2009†
National defence	552.6	605.7	682.1
International affairs	28.5	32.4	39.9
General science, space research and technology	25.6	27.6	29.1
Energy	–0.9	1.3	3.4
Natural resources and environment	31.8	34.3	35.8
Agriculture	17.7	19.4	20.9
Commerce and housing credit	0.5	12.0	16.0
Transportation	72.9	78.9	83.6
Community and regional development	29.6	25.5	23.9
Education, training, employment and social services	91.7	93.2	89.3
Health	266.4	284.9	301.4
Medicare	375.4	392.5	411.9
Income security	366.0	435.7	431.3
Social security	586.2	615.8	656.1
Veterans' benefits and services	72.8	85.8	94.1
Administration of justice	41.2	45.8	51.2
General government	17.5	20.0	22.0
Allowances	—	—	–0.5
Net interest	237.1	231.8	228.0
Undistributed offsetting receipts	–82.2	–100.2	–86.2
Total	2,730.2	2,942.4	3,133.2

* Including social security and Postal Service outlays, which are extrabudgetary.
† Mid-session estimates published in July 2008.

STATE GOVERNMENTS

Votes Cast for US Senators, by State

('000, by major political party. Sources: Office of the Clerk of the House of Representatives, internet clerkweb.house.gov/elections, and www.nytimes.com.)

	2004		2006		2008 (preliminary)	
	Dem.	Rep.	Dem.	Rep.	Dem.	Rep.
Alabama	595	1,242	—	—	751	1,302
Alaska	140	150	—	—	103	106
Arizona	405	1,505	664	814	—	—
Arkansas	581	458	—	—	798	—
California	6,956	4,556	5,076	2,991	—	—
Colorado	1,081	981	—	—	1,065	890
Connecticut	945	458	451	109	—	—
Delaware	—	—	171	70	257	141
Florida	3,590	3,673	2,891	1,826	—	—
Georgia	1,288	1,865	—	—	1,728	1,841
Hawaii	314	87	210	126	—	—
Idaho	—	500	—	—	219	370
Illinois	3,597	1,390	—	—	2,844	1,476
Indiana	1,496	904	—	1,172	—	—
Iowa	412	1,038	—	—	931	556
Kansas	310	781	—	—	430	712
Kentucky	851	874	—	—	840	945
Louisiana	542	943	—	—	986	867
Maine	—	—	113	406	259	409
Maryland	1,505	783	966	787	—	—
Massachusetts	—	—	1,501	661	1,960	923
Michigan	—	—	2,151	1,560	3,034	1,639
Minnesota	—	—	1,279	836	1,211	1,212
Mississippi	—	—	213	388	447	720
Missouri	1,158	1,518	1,055	1,007	—	—
Montana	—	—	200	196	346	129
Nebraska	—	—	378	214	304	439
Nevada	495	285	239	323	—	—
New Hampshire	222	435	—	—	338	292
New Jersey	—	—	58	42	1,824	1,395
New Mexico	—	—	394	164	485	307
New York	4,385	1,625	2,699	1,213	—	—
North Carolina	1,633	1,791	—	—	2,226	1,868
North Dakota	212	99	150	64	—	—
Ohio	1,961	3,464	2,257	1,761	—	—
Oklahoma	597	763	—	—	528	763
Oregon	1,129	565	—	—	729	715
Pennsylvania	2,334	2,925	2,393	1,685	—	—
Rhode Island	—	—	206	179	296	107
South Carolina	704	857	—	—	774	1,051
South Dakota	193	198	—	—	238	143
Tennessee	—	—	880	930	763	1,572
Texas	—	—	1,555	2,662	3,384	4,327
Utah	259	626	177	356	—	—
Vermont	2,173	75	—	85	—	—
Virginia	—	—	1,176	1,166	2,190	1,176
Washington	1,550	1,205	1,185	832	—	—
West Virginia	—	—	159	47	444	253
Wisconsin	1,633	1,301	1,439	630	—	—
Wyoming	—	—	58	135	59	184

Votes Cast for US Representatives, by State

('000, by major political party. Sources: Office of the Clerk of the House of Representatives, internet clerk.house.gov/members/electionInfo, and www.cnn.com.)

	2004		2006		2008 (preliminary)	
	Dem.	Rep.	Dem.	Rep.	Dem.	Rep.
Alabama	708	1,080	502	628	497	635
Alaska	67	213	94	133		
Arizona	598	1,128	627	771	874	768
Arkansas*	426	358	457	306	—	—
California	6,224	5,031	4,720	3,314	4,782	3,072
Colorado	995	992	833	624	1,094	892
Connecticut	786	630	649	420	928	481
Delaware	106	246	98	144	146	235
Florida*	2,212	3,319	1,600	2,183	3,276	3,825
Georgia	1,141	1,820	932	1,138	1,388	1,776
Hawaii	262	148	220	118	294	76
Idaho	171	401	177	248	259	376
Illinois	2,675	2,272	1,986	1,443	2,843	1,902
Indiana	999	1,382	812	832	1,383	1,236
Iowa	625	823	493	522	749	694
Kansas	387	724	369	459	457	676
Kentucky	602	1,017	602	612	760	777
Louisiana*	478	780	309	580	323	516
Maine	418	283	351	163	392	249
Maryland	1,311	896	1,099	547	1,459	692
Massachusetts	2,060	435	1,632	199	851	316
Michigan	2,242	2,289	1,923	1,625	2,285	2,110
Minnesota	1,400	1,236	1,153	925	1,611	1,069
Mississippi	335	659	260	304	686	498
Missouri	1,193	1,430	992	1,049	1,168	1,310
Montana	146	286	159	239	155	307
Nebraska	231	515	262	334	251	494
Nevada	334	421	288	260	456	383
New Hampshire	244	396	209	190	343	273
New Jersey	1,515	1,721	1,208	903	1,636	1,395
New Mexico	385	358	313	248	439	310
New York	3,457	2,209	2,538	1,160	3,802	1,930
North Carolina	1,670	1,743	1,027	914	2,271	1,883
North Dakota	185	126	143	75	194	118
Ohio	2,515	2,650	2,082	1,870	2,560	2,398
Oklahoma	389	875	373	518	598	708
Oregon	952	762	766	557	438	378
Pennsylvania	2,478	2,565	2,229	1,732	2,887	2,455
Rhode Island	279	113	265	42	282	109
South Carolina	486	913	473	600	898	981
South Dakota	208	179	230	98	256	123
Tennessee	1,032	1,161	861	800	619	970
Texas	2,714	4,013	1,831	2,094	2,701	3,045
Utah	362	520	244	292	365	470
Vermont	22	74	140	117	—	—
Virginia	1,023	1,817	947	1,223	1,269	1,494
Washington	1,609	1,095	1,244	798	1,109	762
West Virginia	415	303	264	191	243	212
Wisconsin	1,368	1,381	1,003	1,040	1,157	998
Wyoming	100	132	92	93	128	104

* State law does not require tabulation of votes for unopposed candidates.

Votes Cast for State Governors, by State

('000, by major political party. Sources: www.cnn.com, www.washingtonpost.com and www.nytimes.com.)

	2004		2006		2008 (preliminary)	
	Dem.	Rep.	Dem.	Rep.	Dem.	Rep.
Alabama	—	—	519	717	—	—
Alaska	—	—	84	100	—	—
Arizona	—	—	728	405	—	—
Arkansas	—	—	419	309	—	—
California	—	—	2,702	3,868	—	—
Colorado	—	—	780	566	—	—
Connecticut	—	—	398	710	—	—
Delaware	186	167	—	—	267	127
Florida	—	—	2,152	2,487	—	—
Georgia	—	—	796	1,203	—	—
Hawaii	—	—	122	215	—	—
Idaho	—	—	198	236	—	—
Illinois	—	—	1,677	1,332	—	—
Indiana	1,106	1,299	—	—	1,558	1,078
Iowa	—	—	565	465	—	—
Kansas	—	—	481	337	—	—
Kentucky†	—	—	—	—	—	—
Louisiana‡	—	—	—	—	—	—
Maine	—	—	207	165	—	—
Maryland	—	—	875	757	—	—
Massachusetts	—	—	1,230	780	—	—
Michigan	—	—	2,140	1,606	—	—
Minnesota	—	—	1,008	1,030	—	—
Mississippi§	—	—	—	—	—	—
Missouri	1,296	1,380	—	—	1,675	1,134
Montana	221	202	—	—	317	158
Nebraska	—	—	141	431	—	—
Nevada	—	—	255	278	—	—
New Hampshire	340	326	298	105	448	177
New Jersey‖	—	—	—	—	—	—
New Mexico	—	—	374	170	—	—
New York	—	—	2,883	1,218	—	—
North Carolina	1,879	1,469	—	—	2,104	1,967
North Dakota	85	220	—	—	74	235
Ohio	—	—	2,307	1,407	—	—
Oklahoma	—	—	616	310	—	—
Oregon	—	—	652	551	—	—
Pennsylvania	—	—	2,432	1,599	—	—
Rhode Island	—	—	189	197	—	—
South Carolina	—	—	485	597	—	—
South Dakota	—	—	121	207	—	—
Tennessee	—	—	1,244	540	—	—
Texas	—	—	1,310	1,715	—	—
Utah	347	465	—	—	173	682
Vermont	117	181	107	149	62	161
Virginia¶	—	—	—	—	—	—
Washington	980	966	—	—	1,033	884
West Virginia	466	251	—	—	489	180
Wisconsin	—	—	1,137	976	—	—
Wyoming	—	—	135	58	—	—

† In November 2007 the Democratic candidate, Steve Beshear, won the governorship, with 619,552 votes.
‡ In November 2007 the Republican candidate, Bobby Jindal, won the governorship, with 699,275 votes.
§ In November 2007 the Republican candidate, Haley R. Barbour, won the governorship, with 430,807 votes.
‖ In November 2005 the Democratic candidate, Jon S. Corzine, won the governorship, with 1,224,551 votes.
¶ In November 2005 the Democratic candidate, Timothy M. Kaine, won the governorship, with 1,025,942 votes.

State and Local Government Finances

SUMMARY

(Note: Figures are in $ million and refer to fiscal years*. Sources: Governments Division, Bureau of the Census, US Department of Commerce, *Survey of Government Finances.*)

Revenue	2003/04	2004/05	2005/06
From federal government	425,683	438,432	452,233
From state and local governments	2,009,401	2,090,480	2,284,309
General revenue from own sources	1,464,058	1,588,292	1,733,785
Taxes	1,010,277	1,099,200	1,195,254
Property	318,242	335,981	359,109
Sales and gross receipts	360,629	384,383	412,114
Individual income	215,215	242,273	268,599
Corporation income	33,716	43,138	52,931
Other	82,475	93,425	102,500
Charges and miscellaneous	453,781	489,093	538,531
Utility and liquor stores	114,054	119,607	131,642
Insurance trust revenue	431,289	382,580	418,881
Employee retirement	365,265	316,576	352,521
Unemployment compensation	38,362	35,367	36,989
Other	27,662	30,637	29,372
Total	2,435,084	2,528,912	2,736,542

Expenditure	2003/04	2004/05	2005/06
General expenditure	1,903,194	2,017,039	2,128,450
Education	655,361	689,057	727,967
Elementary and secondary	452,055	473,406	500,528
Institutions of higher education	173,086	182,146	191,758
Other	30,220	33,505	35,681
Libraries	9,201	9,797	10,497
Public welfare	335,257	362,932	370,325
Hospitals	96,551	103,404	110,455
Health	63,125	66,971	71,110
Social insurance administration	4,679	4,340	4,614
Veterans' services	1,504	1,183	992
Highways	118,179	124,602	135,412
Other transportations	23,780	23,267	24,050
Police	69,707	74,727	79,066
Fire protection	28,330	31,439	34,167
Correction	56,521	59,151	62,667
Protective inspection	11,498	12,890	13,655
Natural resources	23,299	25,057	25,482
Parks and recreation	30,467	31,941	34,769
Housing and community development	37,221	39,969	41,980
Sewerage	35,535	36,599	39,220
Solid waste management	20,373	21,469	22,679
Financial administration	36,163	36,519	37,441
Judicial and legal services	32,993	34,991	36,823
General public buildings	11,763	11,858	12,103
Other government administration	19,823	22,945	24,968
Interest on general debt	81,723	81,119	85,660
Other and unallocable	100,143	106,195	115,844
Utility and liquor stores	159,732	160,682	174,679
Insurance trust expenditure	197,405	195,588	203,958
Unemployment compensation	43,278	29,849	28,097
Employee retirement	137,537	145,796	156,180
Other	16,590	19,943	19,681
Total†	2,265,051	2,373,309	2,507,086

* Figures refer to the fiscal year of individual state governments, normally ending 30 June, or, in the case of the following exceptions, ending on some date within the previous 12 months: the state government of Texas and Texas school districts (31 August); the state governments of Alabama and Michigan, all local governments in the District of Columbia and Alabama school districts (30 September); all state and local governments of New York (31 March).

† Including intergovernmental expenditure ($ million): 4,721 in 2003/04; 4,617 in 2004/05; 6,504 in 2005/06.

REVENUE, EXPENDITURE AND DEBT, BY STATE
(fiscal year 2005/06*, $ million)

	Revenue							
	General revenue							
	From federal government	From taxes	Charges, etc.	Total	Other revenue†	Total revenue	Debt outstanding	Total expenditure
Alabama	7,692	12,768	9,126	29,586	6,111	35,697	22,310	35,276
Alaska	2,406	3,665	4,952	11,023	2,224	13,247	9,449	10,788
Arizona	8,818	19,940	7,724	36,483	8,841	45,324	34,655	42,763
Arkansas	4,529	8,747	3,927	17,203	3,595	20,798	11,815	18,503
California	56,402	163,749	72,898	293,049	111,492	404,541	299,534	365,041
Colorado	5,333	17,224	10,074	32,631	8,525	41,158	39,932	37,107
Connecticut	4,596	19,872	4,476	28,944	4,610	33,554	32,228	31,502
Delaware	1,241	3,618	2,357	7,217	1,251	8,467	6,087	8,292
District of Columbia	3,060	4,545	1,565	9,171	1,905	11,075	8,020	10,091
Florida	23,674	66,695	33,266	123,635	27,989	151,624	119,674	140,638
Georgia	11,405	31,025	13,377	55,807	9,500	65,307	42,086	63,053
Hawaii	2,010	6,199	2,258	10,467	1,532	11,999	9,504	11,018
Idaho	1,963	4,503	2,391	8,856	1,933	10,850	4,442	9,330
Illinois	15,946	52,144	19,379	87,470	20,568	108,037	110,788	100,995
Indiana	7,493	22,950	15,395	45,838	5,224	51,062	34,347	44,033
Iowa	4,511	10,256	5,873	20,641	4,200	24,840	13,806	23,102
Kansas	3,484	10,452	4,398	18,334	3,268	21,602	19,907	20,295
Kentucky	6,746	13,558	6,010	26,315	4,838	31,152	32,480	29,514
Louisiana	10,038	15,724	7,781	33,543	6,186	39,729	24,733	35,314
Maine	2,692	5,806	2,042	10,540	1,160	11,700	7,473	10,713
Maryland	7,882	25,789	8,161	41,832	6,535	48,367	30,673	44,280
Massachusetts	9,740	30,636	11,873	52,249	14,354	66,603	86,940	61,910
Michigan	13,967	36,017	18,260	68,243	20,217	88,461	70,825	77,016
Minnesota	7,209	22,491	9,680	39,380	9,450	48,830	36,618	44,820
Mississippi	7,379	8,180	4,658	20,217	3,798	24,015	11,161	22,109
Missouri	8,619	18,312	8,580	35,510	8,690	44,201	33,957	39,551
Montana	2,031	3,020	1,678	6,729	1,290	8,019	5,787	6,948
Nebraska	2,618	6,875	3,426	12,919	4,087	17,006	9,336	15,320
Nevada	2,392	9,764	4,421	16,578	3,786	20,363	20,581	18,818
New Hampshire	1,652	4,517	1,923	8,092	1,288	9,380	9,952	9,030
New Jersey	11,746	47,308	14,334	73,388	12,129	85,517	79,281	82,928
New Mexico	4,090	6,974	4,307	15,372	3,081	18,452	10,707	16,404
New York	43,914	123,661	42,067	209,641	56,621	266,263	241,407	240,996
North Carolina	13,239	30,013	13,947	57,199	10,280	67,479	43,938	64,330
North Dakota	1,299	2,368	1,276	4,943	829	5,772	3,486	4,926
Ohio	18,051	43,247	19,707	81,005	26,489	107,494	63,658	97,514
Oklahoma	5,409	11,257	5,783	22,449	4,362	26,811	15,244	23,967
Oregon	5,418	12,403	7,758	25,579	10,570	36,149	26,919	30,549
Pennsylvania	18,114	49,063	20,312	87,489	21,811	109,300	106,042	104,228
Rhode Island	2,179	4,680	1,679	8,538	1,733	10,271	8,945	9,667
South Carolina	6,769	12,444	9,663	28,877	5,800	34,676	32,159	34,234
South Dakota	1,383	2,241	1,212	4,836	1,226	6,062	4,560	5,210
Tennessee	8,663	17,240	10,143	36,046	11,210	47,256	27,931	44,399
Texas	31,080	75,732	38,068	144,881	32,039	176,919	165,572	160,532
Utah	3,518	8,283	4,992	16,793	3,988	20,781	15,327	18,527
Vermont	1,355	2,753	1,004	5,112	620	5,732	3,854	5,390
Virginia	7,135	30,059	14,086	51,280	10,367	61,647	46,388	55,853
Washington	8,785	25,169	12,070	46,024	17,031	63,055	56,655	56,588
West Virginia	3,390	5,882	3,400	12,672	12,672	14,044	8,937	12,387
Wisconsin	7,125	22,300	8,945	38,370	9,597	47,967	38,834	45,316
Wyoming	2,045	3,136	1,846	7,027	858	7,885	1,947	5,972
Total	452,233	1,195,254	538,531	2,186,018	550,524	2,736,542	2,200,892	2,507,086

* See previous table for details.
† Comprising utility revenue, liquor store revenue and insurance trust revenue.

POLITICAL ORGANIZATIONS

Communist Party USA (CPUSA): 235 West 23rd St, 7th Floor, New York, NY 10011; tel. (212) 989-4994; fax (212) 229-1713; e-mail cpusa@cpusa.org; internet www.cpusa.org; f. 1919; mems in all 50 states, organized in over 40 states; Nat. Chair. SAM WEBB; Exec. Vice-Chair. JARVIS TYNER.

Constitution Party: 23 North Lime St, Lancaster, PA 17602; tel. (717) 390-1993; fax (717) 299-5115; internet www.constitutionparty.com; f. 1992 as the US Taxpayers Party; present name adopted in 1999; working to restore constitutionally limited govt; Nat. Chair. JAMES N. CLYMER.

Democratic National Committee: 430 South Capitol St, SE, Washington, DC 20003; tel. (202) 863-8000; fax (202) 863-8174; internet www.democrats.org; f. 1848; Nat. Chair. HOWARD DEAN; Sec. ALICE TRAVIS GERMOND; Treas. ANDREW TOBIAS.

Democratic Socialists of America (DSA): 75 Maiden Lane, Suite 505, New York, NY 10038; tel. (212) 727-8610; fax (212) 608-6955; e-mail dsa@dsausa.org; internet www.dsausa.org; f. 1983 by merger of the Democratic Socialist Organizing Committee (f. 1972) and New American Movement (f. 1972); mem. of the Socialist International; Nat. Dir FRANK LLEWELLYN.

The Green Party of the United States: POB 57065, Washington, DC 20037; tel. (202) 319-7191; fax (202) 319-7193; e-mail info@gp.org; internet www.gp.org; f. 2001; Sec. HOLLY HART; Treas. JODY GRAGE.

Libertarian Party: 2600 Virginia Ave, NW, Suite 200, Washington, DC 20037; tel. (202) 333-0008; fax (202) 333-0072; e-mail info@lp.org; internet www.lp.org; f. 1971; advocates individual freedom, smaller govt and fewer taxes; Exec. Dir ROBERT KRAUS (acting).

New Federalist Party: 760 Lilian Way, Apt 6, Los Angeles, CA 90038; tel. (213) 464-5468; e-mail new_federalists@yahoo.com; internet www.geocities.com/new_federalists; f. 1975; aims to promote the principles of Alexander Hamilton; 38 state groups, 76 local groups.

Prohibition National Committee: POB 2635, Denver, CO 80201; tel. (303) 237-4947; e-mail umalcohol@aol.com; internet www.prohibition.org; f. 1869; opposes the manufacture and sale of alcoholic drinks; opposes abortion, drug abuse and euthanasia; Nat. Chair. GENE AMONDSON; Nat. Sec. PAUL B. SCOTT.

La Raza Unida Party (Partido Nacional La Raza Unida): 483 Fifth St, POB 13, San Fernando, CA 91340; tel. (818) 365-6534; e-mail pnlrunm@yahoo.com; internet larazaunida.tripod.com; f. 1970; aims to achieve self-determination and greater govt representation for Latinos through electoral processes; four state groups, 100 local groups; Nat. Chair. XENARO G. AYALA.

Reform Party of the USA: POB 3236, Abilene, TX 79604; tel. (325) 672-2575; e-mail info@reformparty.org; internet www.reformparty.org; f. 1996; advocates reform of political system and ethical govt; Nat. Chair. CHARLES FOSTER; Sec. DIONE ORMOND.

Republican National Committee: 310 First St, SE, Washington, DC 20003; tel. (202) 863-8500; fax (202) 863-8820; e-mail info@gop.com; internet www.rnc.org; f. 1854; Chair. Nat. Cttee MIKE DUNCAN; Co-Chair. JO ANN DAVIDSON.

Social Democrats, USA: POB 5307, Johnston, PA 15904; tel. (814) 410-2542; e-mail info@socialdemocratsusa.org; internet www.socialdemocratsusa.org; f. 1972 following split from the Socialist Party of America (f. 1901); Pres. DAVID JESSUP; Nat. Vice-Chair. NORMAN HILL.

Socialist Labor Party: POB 218, Mountain View, CA 94042-0218; e-mail socialists@slp.org; internet www.slp.org; f. 1876 as the Workingmen's Party; present name adopted in 1877; advocates collective ownership and democratic control of all industries and services through industrial unions; Nat. Sec. ROBERT BILLS.

Socialist Party USA: A. J. Muste Bldg, 339 Lafayette St, Suite 303, New York, NY 10012; tel. and fax (212) 982-4586; e-mail natsec@sp-usa.org; internet www.sp-usa.org; f. 1972 following split from the Socialist Party of the USA (f. 1901); Co-Chairs ANDREA PASON, JERRY LEVY; Nat. Sec. GREG PASON; 1,800 mems.

Socialist Workers Party: 306 West 37th St, 10th Floor, New York, NY 10018; tel. (212) 736-2540; fax (212) 244-4274; e-mail swpno@mac.com; f. 1938; communist; Nat. Sec. JACK BARNES.

DIPLOMATIC REPRESENTATION IN THE USA

OVERSEAS REPRESENTATION IN THE USA

Embassies and Consulates-General

AFGHANISTAN

Embassy: 2341 Wyoming Ave, NW, Washington, DC 20008; tel. (202) 483-6410; fax (202) 483-6488; e-mail info@embassyofafghanistan.org; internet www.embassyofafghanistan.org; Ambassador SAID TAYEB JAWAD.

Consulate-General, Los Angeles: Suite 300, 11040 Santa Monica Blvd, Los Angeles, CA 90025; tel. (310) 473-6583; fax (310) 473-6775; e-mail afghanconsulate@hotmail.com; Consul-Gen. ATIQULLAH ATIFMAL.

Consulate-General, New York: 11th Floor, 360 Lexington Ave, New York, NY 10017; tel. (212) 972-2276; fax (212) 972-9046; e-mail afghancons@aol.com; Consul-Gen. MOHAMED SADIQ DAUDZAI.

ALBANIA

Embassy: 2100 S St, NW, Washington, DC 20008; tel. (202) 223-4942; fax (202) 628-7342; e-mail embassy.washington@mfa.gov.al; Ambassador ALEKSANDER SALLABANDA.

ALGERIA

Embassy: 2118 Kalorama Rd, NW, Washington, DC 20008; tel. (202) 265-2800; fax (202) 667-2174; e-mail ambalg2004@yahoo.com; internet www.algeria-us.org; Ambassador AMINE KHERBI.

ANDORRA

Embassy: 2 United Nations Plaza, 25th Floor, New York, NY 10017; tel. (212) 750-8064; fax (212) 750-6630; Ambassador CARLES FONT-ROSSELL.

ANGOLA

Embassy: 2100–08 16th St, NW, Washington, DC 20009; tel. (202) 785-1156; fax (202) 822-9049; e-mail angola@angola.org; internet www.angola.org; Ambassador JOSEFINA PERPETUA PITRA DIAKITÉ.

Consulate-General, New York: 866 United Nations Plaza, Suite 552, New York, NY 10017; tel. (212) 980-9615; fax (212) 980-9606; e-mail lealcordeiro@angolamissionun.org; Consul-Gen. JULIA MACHADO.

Consulate-General, Houston: 3040 Post Oak Blvd, Suite 780, Houston, TX 77056; tel. (713) 212-3840; fax (713) 212-3841; e-mail info@angola-consulate.org; internet www.angola-consulate.org; Consul-Gen. SIMÃO M. PEDRO.

ANTIGUA AND BARBUDA

Embassy: OECS Bldg, 3216 New Mexico Ave, NW, Washington, DC 20016; tel. (202) 362-5122; fax (202) 362-5225; e-mail embantbar@aol.com; Ambassador DEBORAH MAE LOVELL.

Consulate-General, Miami: 25 South East Second Ave, Suite 300, Miami, FL 33131; tel. (305) 381-6762; fax (305) 381-7908; e-mail cganubar@bellsouth.net; Consul-Gen. IAN E. ANDERSON SWEENEY.

ARGENTINA

Embassy: 1600 New Hampshire Ave, NW, Washington, DC 20009; tel. (202) 238-6400; fax (202) 332-3171; internet www.embassyofargentina.us; Ambassador HÉCTOR MARCOS TIMERMAN.

Consulate-General, Los Angeles: 5055 Wilshire Blvd, Suite 210, Los Angeles, CA 90036; tel. (213) 954-9155; fax (213) 934-9076; e-mail arconsul@pacbell.net; internet www.consuladoargentino-losangeles.org; Consul-Gen. JORGE T. LAPSENSON.

Consulate-General, Miami: 1101 Brickell Ave, Suite 500, Torre Norte, Miami, FL 33131; tel. (305) 373-1889; fax (305) 371-1598; e-mail info@consuladoargentinoenmiami.org; internet www.consuladoargentinoenmiami.org; Consul-Gen. (vacant).

Consulate-General, Atlanta: 245 Peachtree Center Ave, Suite 2101, Atlanta, GA 30303; tel. (404) 880-0805; fax (404) 880-0806; e-mail catla@bellsouth.net; internet www.consuladoargentinoatlanta.org; Consul-Gen. POMPEYO CARLOS LAYOS.

Consulate-General, Chicago: 205 North Michigan Ave, Suite 4208/9, Chicago, IL 60601; tel. (312) 819-2606; fax (312) 819-2612; e-mail argcchic@aol.com; Consul-Gen. ERNESTO M. PAZ.

Consulate-General, New York: 12 West 56th St, New York, NY 10019; tel. (212) 603-0400; fax (212) 541-7746; e-mail cnyor@mrecic.gov.ar; internet www.congenargentinany.com; Consul-Gen. (vacant).

Consulate-General, Houston: 3050 Post Oak Blvd, Suite 1625, Houston, TX 77056; tel. (713) 871-8935; fax (713) 871-0639; e-mail chous_ar@hotmail.com; Consul-Gen. RICARDO A. GAUTHIER.

ARMENIA

Embassy: 2225 R St, NW, Washington, DC 20008; tel. (202) 319-1976; fax (202) 319-2982; e-mail armpublic@speakeasy.net; internet www.armeniaemb.org; Ambassador TATOUL MARKARIAN.

Consulate-General, Los Angeles: 50 North La Cienaga Blvd, Suite 210, Beverly Hills, CA 90211; tel. (310) 657-6102; fax (310) 657-6419; e-mail armconla@aol.com; Consul-Gen. GAGIK KIRAKOSIAN.

AUSTRALIA

Embassy: 1601 Massachusetts Ave, NW, Washington, DC 20036-2273; tel. (202) 797-3000; fax (202) 797-3168; e-mail publicaffairsdc@gmail.com; internet www.usa.embassy.gov.au; Ambassador DENNIS RICHARDSON.

Consulate-General, Los Angeles: Century Plaza Towers, 31st Floor, 2029 Century Park East, Los Angeles, CA 90067-3121; tel. (310) 229-2300; fax (310) 229-2380; internet www.losangeles.consulate.gov.au; Consul-Gen. INNES WILLOX.

Consulate-General, San Francisco: 575 Market St, Suite 1800, San Francisco, CA 94105-2815; tel. (415) 536-1970; fax (415) 536-1982; Consul-Gen. DAVID A. LAWSON.

Consulate-General, Atlanta: Atlanta Financial Center, Suite 1140, 3353 Peachtree Rd, NE, Atlanta, GA 30326; tel. (404) 760-3400; fax (404) 760-3401; Consul-Gen. AMANDA M. HODGES.

Consulate-General, Honolulu: 1000 Bishop St, Penthouse, Honolulu, HI 96813; tel. (808) 524-5050; fax (808) 531-5142; Consul-Gen. DAVID BINNS.

Consulate-General, Chicago: 123 North Wacker Dr., Suite 1330, Chicago, IL 60606; tel. (312) 419-1480; fax (312) 419-1499; Consul-Gen. ROBERT E. CHARLES.

Consulate-General, New York: 150 East 42nd St, 34th Floor, New York, NY 10017-5612; tel. (212) 351-6500; fax (212) 351-6501; e-mail consular@australianyc.org; internet www.australianyc.org; Consul-Gen. JOHN W. OLSEN.

AUSTRIA

Embassy: 3524 International Ct, NW, Washington, DC 20008-3022; tel. (202) 895-6700; fax (202) 895-6750; e-mail austroinfo@austria.org; internet www.austria.org; Ambassador Dr EVA NOWOTNY.

Consulate-General, Los Angeles: 11859 Wilshire Blvd, Suite 501, Los Angeles, CA 90025; tel. (310) 444-9310; fax (310) 477-9897; e-mail los-angeles-gk@bmaa.gv.at; internet www.austria-la.org; Consul-Gen. MARTIN WEISS.

Consulate-General, Chicago: Wrigley Bldg, Suite 707, 400 North Michigan Ave, Chicago, IL 60611; tel. (312) 222-1515; fax (312) 222-4113; e-mail chicago-gk@bmeia.gv.at; internet www.austria-chicago.org; Consul-Gen. ROBERT ZISCHG.

Consulate-General, New York: 31 East 69th St, New York, NY 10021; tel. (212) 737-6400; fax (212) 585-1992; e-mail info@austria-ny.org; internet www.austria-ny.org; Consul-Gen. Dr BRIGITTA M. BLAHA.

AZERBAIJAN

Embassy: 2741 34th St, NW, Washington, DC 20008; tel. (202) 337-3500; fax (202) 337-5911; e-mail azerbaijan@azembassy.com; internet www.azembassy.com; Ambassador YASHAR ALIYEV.

Consulate-General, Los Angeles: 11766 Wilshire Blvd, Suite 1410, Los Angeles, CA 90025; tel. (310) 444-9101; fax (310) 477-4860; e-mail office@azconsulatela.org; internet www.azconsulatela.org; Consul-Gen. ELIN SULEYMANOV.

BAHAMAS

Embassy: 2220 Massachusetts Ave, NW, Washington, DC 20008; tel. (202) 319-2660; fax (202) 319-2668; e-mail bahemb@aol.com; Ambassador CORNELIUS A. SMITH.

Consulate-General, Miami: Ingraham Bldg, 25 Second Ave, SE, Miami, FL 33131; tel. (305) 373-6295; fax (305) 373-6312; e-mail bcgmia@bellsouth.net; Consul-Gen. ALMA A. ADAMS.

Consulate-General, New York: 231 East 46th St, New York, NY 10017; tel. (212) 421-6420; fax (212) 759-2135; e-mail ebethel@bahamasny.com; Consul-Gen. ELDRED EDISON BETHEL.

BAHRAIN

Embassy: 3502 International Dr., NW, Washington, DC 20008; tel. (202) 342-1111; fax (202) 362-2192; e-mail ambsecretary@bahrainembassy.org; internet www.bahrainembassy.org; Ambassador HOUDA ERZA EBRAHIM NONOO.

Consulate-General, New York: 866 Second Ave, 14th Floor, New York, NY 10017; tel. (212) 223-6200; fax (212) 319-0687; Consul-Gen. BASSAM AL MARZOOK (acting).

BANGLADESH

Embassy: 3510 International Dr., NW, Washington, DC 20008; tel. (202) 244-0183; fax (202) 244-2771; e-mail bdootwash@bangladoot.org; internet www.bangladoot.org; Ambassador M. HUMAYUN KABIR.

Consulate-General, Los Angeles: 4201 Wilshire Blvd, Suite 605, Los Angeles, CA 90010; tel. (310) 932-0100; fax (310) 932-9703; e-mail bcgla@earthlink.net; internet www.bangladeshconsulatela.com; Consul-Gen. MOHAMMED ABU ZAFAR.

Consulate-General, New York: 211 East 43rd St, Suite 502, New York, NY 10017; tel. (212) 599-6767; fax (212) 682-9211; e-mail contact@bdcgny.org; internet www.bdcgny.org; Consul-Gen. SHAMSUL HAQUE.

BARBADOS

Embassy: 2144 Wyoming Ave, NW, Washington, DC 20008; tel. (202) 939-9200; fax (202) 332-7467; e-mail washington@foreign.gov.bb; Ambassador MICHAEL IAN KING.

Consulate-General, Miami: 150 Alhambra Circle, Suite 1270, Coral Gables, Miami, FL 33134; tel. (305) 442-1994; fax (305) 567-2844; e-mail miami@foreign.gov.bb; Consul-Gen. COLIN MAYERS.

Consulate-General, New York: 800 Second Ave, 2nd Floor, New York, NY 10017; tel. (212) 867-8431; fax (212) 986-1030; e-mail newyork@foreign.gov.bb; Consul-Gen. LENNOX PRICE.

BELARUS

Embassy: 1619 New Hampshire Ave, NW, Washington, DC 20009; tel. (202) 986-1604; fax (202) 986-1805; e-mail usa@belarusembassy.org; internet www.belarusembassy.org; Ambassador MIKHAIL KHVOSTOV.

Consulate-General, New York: 708 Third Ave, 21st Floor, New York, NY 10017; tel. (212) 682-5392; fax (212) 682-5491; e-mail gcny@belembassy.org; internet www.belarusconsul.org; Consul-Gen. NIKOLAI LEPESHKO.

BELGIUM

Embassy: 3330 Garfield St, NW, Washington, DC 20008; tel. (202) 333-6900; fax (202) 333-3079; e-mail washington@diplobel.org; internet www.diplobel.us; Ambassador DOMINIQUE STRUYE DE SWIELANDE.

Consulate-General, Los Angeles: 6100 Wilshire Blvd, Suite 1200, Los Angeles, CA 90048; tel. (323) 857-1244; fax (323) 936-2564; e-mail losangeles@diplobel.org; internet www.diplomatie.be/losangeles; Consul-Gen. GEERT CRIEL.

Consulate-General, New York: 1065 Ave of the Americas, 22nd Floor, New York, NY 10018; tel. (212) 586-5110; fax (212) 582-9657; e-mail newyork@diplobel.org; internet www.diplomatie.be/newyork; Consul-Gen. RENILDE LOECKX-DROZDIAK.

BELIZE

Embassy: 2535 Massachusetts Ave, NW, Washington, DC 20008; tel. (202) 332-9636; fax (202) 332-6888; e-mail ebwreception@aol.com; internet www.embassyofbelize.org; Ambassador NESTOR MENDEZ.

Consulate-General, Los Angeles: 5825 West Sunset Blvd, Suite 206, Hollywood, CA 90028; tel. (323) 469-7343; fax (323) 469-7346; e-mail belizeconsul@earthlink.net; internet belizeconsulatela.org; Consul-Gen. ROY G. YOUNG.

BENIN

Embassy: 2124 Kalorama Rd, NW, Washington, DC 20008; tel. (202) 232-6656; fax (202) 265-1996; e-mail info@beninembassyus.org; internet www.beninembassy.us; Ambassador CYRILLE OGUIN.

BHUTAN

Consulate-General, New York: 2 United Nations Plaza, 27th Floor, New York, NY 10017; tel. (212) 826-1919; fax (212) 826-2998; Consul-Gen. SANGYE RINCHHEN.

BOLIVIA

Embassy: 3014 Massachusetts Ave, NW, Washington, DC 20008; tel. (202) 483-4410; fax (202) 328-3712; e-mail webmaster@bolivia-usa.org; internet www.bolivia-usa.org; Chargé d'affaires a.i. ERIKA DUEÑAS.

Consulate-General, San Francisco: 870 Market St, Suite 518, San Francisco, CA 94112; tel. (415) 765-6821; fax (419) 765-6826; e-mail conicsf@pacbell.net; Consul-Gen. DENIS GALEANO.

Consulate-General, Washington, DC: 4420 Connecticut Ave, NW, Suite 2, Washington, DC 20008; tel. (202) 232-4828; fax (202) 232-8017; e-mail consulgeneral@bolivia-usa.org; Consul-Gen. OSWALDO CUEVAS GAETE.

Consulate-General, Miami: 9100 South Dadeland Blvd, Suite 406, Miami, FL 33156; tel. (305) 358-6303; fax (305) 358-6305; e-mail consbolmia@attglobal.net; Consul-Gen. JAVIER RAMIRO CUSICANQUI FORTÚN.

Consulate-General, New York: 211 East 43rd St, Suite 702, New York, NY 10017; tel. (212) 687-0530; fax (212) 687-0532; e-mail coliviannyork@verizon.net; Consul-Gen. JORGE E. HEREDIA CAVERO.

BOSNIA AND HERZEGOVINA

Embassy: 2109 E St, NW, Washington, DC 20037; tel. (202) 337-1500; fax (202) 337-1502; e-mail info@bhembassy.org; internet www.bhembassy.org; Ambassador Dr BISERA TURKOVIĆ.

Consulate-General, Chicago: 737 North Michigan Ave, Suite 820, Chicago, IL 60611; tel. (312) 951-1245; fax (312) 951-1043; Consul-Gen. FILOMENA NIKOLIĆ.

Consulate-General, New York: 866 United Nations Plaza, Suite 580, New York, NY 10017; tel. (212) 593-1042; fax (212) 593-0843.

BOTSWANA

Embassy: 1531–33 New Hampshire Ave, NW, Washington, DC 20036; tel. (202) 244-4990; fax (202) 244-4164; e-mail cratsiripe@gov.bw; internet www.botswanaembassy.org; Ambassador LAPOLOGANG CAESAR LEKOA.

BRAZIL

Embassy: 3006 Massachusetts Ave, NW, Washington, DC 20008; tel. (202) 238-2700; fax (202) 238-2827; e-mail webmaster@brasilemb.org; internet www.brasilemb.org; Ambassador ANTONIO DE AGUIAR PATRIOTA.

Consulate-General, Los Angeles: 8484 Wilshire Blvd, Suite 711-730, Los Angeles, CA 90211; tel. (213) 651-2664; fax (213) 651-1274; e-mail consbrasla@earthlink.net; internet www.brazilian-consulate.org; Consul-Gen. THEREZA M. MACHADO QUINTELLA.

Consulate-General, San Francisco: 300 Montgomery St, Suite 900, San Francisco, CA 94104; tel. (415) 981-8170; fax (415) 981-4931; e-mail brazilsf@brazilsf.org; internet www.brazilsf.org; Consul-Gen. MAURICIO EDUARDO CORTES COSTA.

Consulate-General, Miami: 80 South West Eighth St, 26th Floor, Miami, FL 33130-3004; tel. (305) 285-6200; fax (305) 285-6240; e-mail consbras@brazilmiami.org; internet www.brazilmiami.org; Consul-Gen. JOÃO ALMINO DE SOUZA, Filho.

Consulate-General, Chicago: 401 North Michigan Ave, Suite 1850, Chicago, IL 60611; tel. (312) 464-0244; fax (312) 464-0299; e-mail central@brazilconsulatechicago.org; internet www.brazilconsulatechicago.org; Consul-Gen. RICARDO L. VIANA DE CARVALHO.

Consulate-General, Boston: The Statler Bldg, Suite 1420, 20 Park Plaza, Boston, MA 02116; tel. (617) 542-4000; fax (617) 542-4318; e-mail cgbos@consulatebrazil.org; internet www.consulatebrazil.org; Consul-Gen. MARIO E. SAADE.

Consulate-General, New York: 1185 Ave of the Americas, 21st Floor, New York, NY 10036-2601; tel. (917) 777-7777; fax (212) 827-0225; e-mail consulado@brazilny.org; internet www.brazilny.org; Consul-Gen. JOSÉ ALFREDO GRAÇA LIMA.

Consulate-General, Houston: 1233 West Loop South, Park Tower North, Suite 1150, Houston, TX 77027; tel. (713) 961-3063; fax (713) 961-3070; e-mail consbras@brazilhouston.org; internet www.brazilhouston.org; Consul-Gen. ANTONIO JOSÉ REZENDE DE CASTRO.

BRUNEI

Embassy: 3520 International Ct, NW, Washington, DC 20008; tel. (202) 237-1838; fax (202) 885-0560; e-mail info@bruneiembassy.org; internet www.bruneiembassy.org; Chargé d'affaires a.i. ANGELA SHIM.

BULGARIA

Embassy: 1621 22nd St, NW, Washington, DC 20008; tel. (202) 387-0174; fax (202) 234-7973; e-mail office@bulgaria-embassy.org; internet www.bulgaria-embassy.org; Ambassador ELENA POPTODOROVA.

Consulate-General, Los Angeles: 11766 Wilshire Blvd, Suite 440, Los Angeles, CA 90025; tel. (310) 478-6700; fax (310) 478-6277; e-mail bglaconsulate@adelphia.net; internet users.adelphia.net/~consulgeneral; Consul-Gen. IVO GUEORGUIEV MOUSKOUROV.

Consulate-General, Chicago: 737 North Michigan Ave, Suite 2105, Chicago, IL 60611-6647; tel. (312) 867-1904; fax (312) 867-1905; e-mail consul@bgconsulchicago.net; internet www.bgconsulchicago.net; Consul-Gen. IVAN IORDANOV SOTIROV.

Consulate-General, New York: 121 East 62nd St, New York, NY 10021; tel. (212) 935-4646; fax (212) 319-5955; e-mail consul@consulbulgaria-ny.org; internet www.consulbulgaria-ny.org; Consul-Gen. NIKOLAY MILKOV.

BURKINA FASO

Embassy: 2340 Massachusetts Ave, NW, Washington, DC 20008; tel. (202) 332-5577; fax (202) 667-1882; e-mail ambawdc@verizon.net; internet www.burkinaembassy-usa.org; Ambassador PARMANGA ERNEST YONLI.

BURUNDI

Embassy: 2233 Wisconsin Ave, NW, Suite 212, Washington, DC 20007; tel. (202) 342-2574; fax (202) 342-2578; e-mail burundiembassy@erols.com; internet www.burundiembassy-usa.org; Ambassador CELESTIN NIYONGABO.

CAMBODIA

Embassy: 4530 16th St, NW, Washington, DC 20011; tel. (202) 726-7742; fax (202) 726-8381; e-mail ambassador_office@embassyofcambodia.org; internet www.embassyofcambodia.org; Ambassador SEREYWATH EK.

CAMEROON

Embassy: 2349 Massachusetts Ave, NW, Washington, DC 20008; tel. (202) 265-8790; fax (202) 387-3826; e-mail cdm@ambacam-usa.org; internet www.ambacam-usa.org; Ambassador JOSEPH FOE-ATANGANA.

CANADA

Embassy: 501 Pennsylvania Ave, NW, Washington, DC 20001; tel. (202) 682-1740; fax (202) 682-7701; e-mail webmaster@canadianembassy.org; internet www.canadianembassy.org; Ambassador MICHAEL WILSON.

Consulate-General, Los Angeles: 550 Hope St South, 9th Floor, Los Angeles, CA 90071-2627; tel. (213) 346-2700; fax (213) 620-8827; e-mail lngls@international.gc.ca; internet www.losangeles.gc.ca; Consul-Gen. DAVID FRANSEN.

Consulate-General, San Francisco: 580 California St, 14th Floor, San Francisco, CA 94104; tel. (415) 834-3180; fax (415) 834-3189; e-mail sfran@international.gc.ca; internet www.sanfrancisco.gc.ca; Consul-Gen. MARC LEPAGE.

Consulate-General, Denver: 1625 Broadway, Suite 2600, Denver, CO 80202; tel. (303) 626-0640; fax (303) 572-1158; e-mail denvr_g@international.gc.ca; internet www.denver.gc.ca; Consul-Gen. DALE EISLER.

Consulate-General, Miami: 200 South Biscayne Blvd, Suite 1600, Miami, FL 33131; tel. (305) 579-1600; fax (305) 374-6774; e-mail miami-td@international.gc.ca; internet www.miami.gc.ca; Consul-Gen. MARCY GROSSMAN.

Consulate-General, Atlanta: 1175 Peachtree St, 100 Colony Sq., Suite 1700, 1175 St, NE, Atlanta, GA 30361-6205; tel. (404) 532-2000; fax (404) 532-2050; e-mail atnta-td@international.gc.ca; internet www.atlanta.gc.ca; Consul-Gen. BRIAN OAK.

Consulate-General, Chicago: 2 Prudential Plaza, 180 North Stetson Ave, Suite 2400, Chicago, IL 60601; tel. (312) 616-1860; fax (312) 616-1878; e-mail chcgo@international.gc.ca; Consul-Gen. GEORGE RIOUX.

Consulate-General, Boston: 3 Copley Pl., Suite 400, Boston, MA 02116; tel. (617) 262-3760; fax (617) 262-3415; e-mail bostn@international.gc.ca; internet www.boston.gc.ca; Consul-Gen. NEIL LEBLANC.

Consulate-General, Detroit: 600 Renaissance Center, Suite 1100, Detroit, MI 48243-1798; tel. (313) 567-2340; fax (313) 567-2164; e-mail dtrot@international.gc.ca; internet www.detroit.gc.ca; Consul-Gen. ROBERT NOBLE.

Consulate-General, Minneapolis: 701 South Fourth Ave, Suite 901, Minneapolis, MN 55415-1899; tel. (612) 333-4641; fax (612) 332-4061; e-mail mnpls@international.gc.ca; internet www.minneapolis.gc.ca; Consul-Gen. MARTIN LOKEN.

Consulate-General, Buffalo: 3000 HSBC Center, Buffalo, NY 14203-2884; tel. (716) 858-9500; fax (716) 852-4340; e-mail bfalo@international.gc.ca; internet www.buffalo.gc.ca; Consul-Gen. STEPHEN BRERETON.

Consulate-General, New York: 1251 Ave of the Americas, New York, NY 10020-1175; tel. (212) 596-1628; fax (212) 596-1790; e-mail cngny@international.gc.ca; internet www.canada-ny.org; Consul-Gen. DANIEL SULLIVAN.

Consulate-General, Dallas: St Paul Pl., 750 North St Paul St, Suite 1700, Dallas, TX 75201; tel. (214) 922-9806; fax (214) 922-9815; e-mail dalas-td@international.gc.ca; internet www.dallas.gc.ca; Consul-Gen. NORRIS PETTIS.

Consulate-General, Seattle: 1501 Fourth Ave, Suite 600, Seattle, WA 98101; tel. (206) 443-1777; fax (206) 443-9662; e-mail seatl-td@international.gc.ca; internet www.seattle.gc.ca; Consul-Gen. PETER LLOYD.

CAPE VERDE

Embassy: 3415 Massachusetts Ave, NW, Washington, DC 20007; tel. (202) 965-6820; fax (202) 965-1207; e-mail ambacvus@sysnet.net; internet www.virtualcapeverde.net; Ambassador MARIA DE FATIMA LIMA DA VEIGA.

Consulate-General, Boston: 607 Boylston St, Boston, MA 02116; tel. (617) 353-0014; Consul-Gen. MARÍA DE JESÚS VEIGA MASCARENHAS.

CENTRAL AFRICAN REPUBLIC

Embassy: 1618 22nd St, NW, Washington, DC 20008; tel. (202) 483-7800; fax (202) 332-9893; Ambassador EMMANUEL TOUABOY.

CHAD

Embassy: 2002 R St, NW, Washington, DC 20009; tel. (202) 462-4009; fax (202) 265-1937; internet chadembassy-usa.org; Ambassador MAHAMOUD ADAM BÉCHIR.

CHILE

Embassy: 1732 Massachusetts Ave, NW, Washington, DC 20036; tel. (202) 785-1746; fax (202) 887-5579; e-mail embassy@embassyofchile.org; internet www.chile-usa.org; Ambassador MARIANO FERNÁNDEZ AMUNATEGUI.

Consulate-General, Los Angeles: 6100 Wilshire Blvd, Suite 1240, Los Angeles, CA 90048; tel. (323) 933-3697; fax (323) 933-3842; e-mail cgchilela@aol.com; Consul-Gen. JOSÉ MANUEL LIRA.

Consulate-General, San Francisco: 870 Market St, Suite 1058, CA 94102; tel. (415) 982-7662; fax (415) 982-2384; e-mail cgsfchile@sbcglobal.net; Consul-Gen. CÉSAR ALBERTO RUÍZ AMUSSEN.

Consulate-General, Miami: 800 Brickell Ave, Suite 1230, Miami, FL 33131; tel. (305) 373-8623; fax (305) 379-6613; e-mail consuladochilemiami@yahoo.com; Consul-Gen. SAMUEL FERNÁNDEZ ILLANES.

Consulate-General, Chicago: 875 North Michigan Ave, Suite 3352, Chicago, IL 60611; tel. (312) 654-8780; fax (312) 654-8948; e-mail cgchicus@ameritech.net; Consul-Gen. JOSÉ M. CRUZ.

Consulate-General, New York: 866 United Nations Plaza, Suite 601, New York, NY 10017-1862; tel. (212) 980-3366; fax (212) 888-5288; e-mail admin@chileny.com; internet www.chileny.com; Consul-Gen. BENJAMIN CONCHA GAZMURI.

Consulate-General, Philadelphia: Public Ledger Bldg, Suite 1030, Sixth and Chestnut Sts, Philadelphia, PA 19106; tel. (215) 829-9520; fax (215) 829-0594; e-mail cnfilaus@infionline.net; Consul-Gen. JOSÉ LUIS MORALES MOLYNEUX.

Consulate-General, Houston: 1300 Post Oak Blvd, Suite 1130, Houston, TX 77056; tel. (713) 621-5853; fax (713) 621-8672; e-mail conchihous@aol.com; internet consuladodechilehouston.net; Consul-Gen. RICARDO ORTIZ VIDAL.

CHINA, PEOPLE'S REPUBLIC

Embassy: 2300 Connecticut Ave, NW, Washington, DC 20008; tel. (202) 328-2500; fax (202) 588-0032; e-mail chinaembassy_us@fmprc.gov.cn; internet www.china-embassy.org; Ambassador ZHOU WENZHONG.

Consulate-General, Los Angeles: 443 Shatto Pl., Los Angeles, CA 90020; tel. (213) 380-3105; fax (213) 380-1961; e-mail webmaster@chinaconsulatela.org; internet losangeles.china-consulate.org; Consul-Gen. ZHANG YUN.

Consulate-General, San Francisco: 1450 Laguna St, San Francisco, CA 94115; tel. (415) 674-2905; fax (415) 563-0494; e-mail chinasonsul_san_us@mfa.gov.cn; internet www.chinaconsulatesf.org; Consul-Gen. GAO ZHANSHENG.

Consulate-General, Chicago: 100 West Erie St, Chicago, IL 60610; tel. (312) 803-0095; fax (312) 803-0110; e-mail chinaconsul_chi_us@mfa.gov.cn; internet www.chinaconsulatechicago.org; Consul-Gen. PING HUANG.

Consulate-General, New York: 520 12th Ave, New York, NY 10036; tel. (212) 244-9456; fax (212) 502-0258; e-mail chinaconsul_ny_us@mfa.gov.cn; internet www.nyconsulate.prchina.org; Consul-Gen. LIU BIWEI.

Consulate-General, Houston: 3417 Montrose Blvd, Houston, TX 77006; tel. (713) 520-1462; fax (713) 521-3064; e-mail info@chinahouston.org; internet www.chinahouston.org; Consul-Gen. QIAO HONG.

COLOMBIA

Embassy: 2118 Leroy Pl., NW, Washington, DC 20008; tel. (202) 387-8338; fax (202) 232-8643; e-mail embassyofcolombia@colombiaemb.org; internet www.colombiaemb.org; Ambassador CAROLINA BARCO ISAKSON.

Consulate-General, Los Angeles: 8383 Wilshire Blvd, Suite 420, Beverly Hills, CA 90211; tel. (323) 653-9863; fax (323) 653-2964; e-mail consul@conangeles.org; internet www.conangeles.org; Consul-Gen. GABRIEL JAIME RESTREPO MARIN.

Consulate-General, San Francisco: 595 Market St, Suite 2130, San Francisco, CA 94105; tel. (415) 495-7195; fax (415) 777-3731; e-mail colombia@pacbell.net; Consul-Gen. JOSÉ MIGUEL CASTIBLANO MUÑOZ.

Consulate-General, Miami: 280 Aragón Ave, Coral Gables, Miami, FL 33134; tel. (305) 448-5558; fax (305) 441-9537; e-mail ciquejas@minrelext.gov.co; internet www.consuladodecolombia.com; Consul-Gen. LUIS IGNACIO GUZMÁN.

Consulate-General, Atlanta: 5901 Peachtree-Dunwoody Rd, Suite 375, GA 30328; tel. (770) 668-0451; fax (770) 668-0763; e-mail consulco@bellsouth.net; internet www.consuladodecolombiaatlanta.com; Consul-Gen. CAMILO DE BEDOUT HERRERA.

Consulate-General, Chicago: 500 North Michigan Ave, Suite 2040, Chicago, IL 60611; tel. (312) 923-1196; fax (312) 923-1197; e-mail conchicago@consulcolombia.us; internet www.consulcolombia.us; Consul-Gen. PAULINA GÓMEZ BORDA.

Consulate-General, New York: 10 East 46th St, New York, NY 10017; tel. (212) 798-9000; fax (212) 972-1725; e-mail cocolny@nosotros.com; internet www.consuladodecolombiany.com; Consul-Gen. FRANCISCO NOGUERA ROCHA.

Consulate-General, Houston: 2400 Augusta Dr., Suite 400, Houston, TX 77057; tel. (713) 527-8919; fax (713) 529-3395; e-mail infoconsulado@colhouston.org; internet www.colhouston.org; Consul-Gen. MARÍA CRISTINA CHIROLLA.

COMOROS

Embassy: 336 East 45th St, 2nd Floor, New York, NY 10017; tel. (212) 972-8010; fax (212) 983-4712; e-mail comun@undp.org; Ambassador MOHAMED TOIHIRI.

CONGO, DEMOCRATIC REPUBLIC

Embassy: 1726 M St, NW, Suite 601, Washington, DC 20036; tel. (202) 234-7690; fax (202) 234-2609; Ambassador FAIDA MITIFU.

CONGO, REPUBLIC

Embassy: 4891 Colorado Ave, NW, Washington, DC 20011; tel. (202) 726-5500; fax (202) 726-1860; e-mail info@embassyofcongo.org; Ambassador SERGE MOMBOULI.

COSTA RICA

Embassy: 2114 S St, NW, Washington, DC 20008; tel. (202) 234-2945; fax (202) 265-4795; e-mail embassy@costarica-embassy.org; internet www.costarica-embassy.org; Ambassador TOMÁS DUEÑAS.

Consulate-General, Los Angeles: 1605 West Olympic Blvd, Suite 400, Los Angeles, CA 90015; tel. (213) 380-7915; fax (213) 380-5639; e-mail costaricaconsulatela@hotmail.com; Consul-Gen. XINIA VARGAS MORA.

Consulate-General, Washington, DC: 2112 S St, NW, Washington, DC 20008; tel. (202) 328-6628; fax (202) 234-6950; e-mail consulate@costarica-embassy.org; Consul-Gen. ROLANDO M. GUTIÉRREZ.

Consulate-General, Miami: 1101 Bricknell Ave, Suite 704-S, Miami, FL 33131; tel. (305) 871-7487; fax (305) 871-0860; e-mail consulate_mia@costarica-embassy.org; Consul LORENA SÁNCHEZ.

Consulate-General, Atlanta: 1870 The Exchange, Suite 100, Atlanta, GA 30339; tel. (770) 951-7025; fax (770) 951-7073; e-mail consulate_ga@costarica-embassy.org; Consul-Gen. MANUEL DOBLES.

Consulate-General, Chicago: 203 North Wabash Ave, Suite 1312, Chicago, IL 60601; tel. (312) 263-2772; fax (312) 263-5807; e-mail crcchi@sbcglobal.net; Consul-Gen. ANELENA SOLEY LORIA.

Consulate-General, New York: 225 West 34th St, Suite 1202, New York, NY 10122; tel. (212) 509-3066; fax (212) 509-3068; e-mail costaricaconsul@yahoo.com; Consul-Gen. LAURA PIZARRO.

Consulate-General, Houston: 3000 Wilcrest, Suite 112, Houston, TX 77042; tel. (713) 266-0484; fax (713) 266-1527; e-mail consulatecr@sbcglobal.net; Consul-Gen. SERGIO ALONSO VALVERDE ALPIZAR.

CÔTE D'IVOIRE

Embassy: 2424 Massachusetts Ave, NW Washington, DC 200078; tel. (202) 797-0300; fax (202) 462-9444; Ambassador CHARLES KOFFI.

CROATIA

Embassy: 2343 Massachusetts Ave, NW, Washington, DC 20008-2803; tel. (202) 588-5899; fax (202) 588-8936; e-mail public@croatiaemb.org; internet www.croatiaemb.org; Ambassador KOLINDA GRABAR-KITAROVIĆ.

Consulate-General, Los Angeles: 11766 Wilshire Blvd, Suite 1250, Los Angeles, CA 90025; tel. (310) 477-1009; fax (310) 477-1866; e-mail crocons.la@mvpei.hr; Consul-Gen. ANTE BARBIR.

Consulate-General, Chicago: 737 North Michigan Ave, Suite 1030, Chicago, IL 60611; tel. (312) 482-9902; fax (312) 482-9987; e-mail chicago@mvpei.hr; Consul-Gen. MARICA MATKOVIĆ.

Consulate-General, New York: 369 Lexington Ave, 11th Floor, POB 4951, New York, NY 10017; tel. (212) 599-3066; fax (212) 599-3106; e-mail croatian.consulate@verizon.net; Consul-Gen. PETAR LJUBIČIĆ.

CUBA

Interests section in the Embassy of Switzerland: 2639 16th St, NW, Washington, DC 20009; tel. (202) 797-8518; fax (202) 797-8521; e-mail Informacion1@sicuw.org; internet embacu.cubaminrex.cu/sicw; Counsellor JORGE ALBERTO BOLAÑOS SUÁREZ.

CYPRUS

Embassy: 2211 R St, NW, Washington, DC 20008; tel. (202) 462-5772; fax (202) 462-0632; internet www.cyprusembassy.net; Ambassador ANDREAS KAKOURIS.

Consulate-General, New York: 13 East 40th St, New York, NY 10016; tel. (212) 686-6016; fax (212) 686-3660; e-mail consulgenofcyprus@earthlink.net; Consul-Gen. ANDREAS PANAYIOTOU.

CZECH REPUBLIC

Embassy: 3900 Spring of Freedom St, NW, Washington, DC 20008; tel. (202) 274-9100; fax (202) 966-8540; e-mail washington@embassy.mzv.cz; internet www.mzv.cz/washington; Ambassador PETR KOLAR.

Consulate-General, Los Angeles: 10990 Wilshire Blvd, Suite 1100, Los Angeles, CA 90024-4879; tel. (310) 473-0889; fax (310) 473-9813; e-mail losangeles@embassy.mzv.cz; internet www.mfa.cz/losangeles; Consul-Gen. DANIEL KUMERMANN.

Consulate-General, Chicago: 205 North Michigan Ave, Suite 1680, Chicago, IL 60601; tel. (312) 861-1037; fax (312) 861-1944; e-mail chicago@embassy.mzv.cz; internet www.mfa.cz/chicago; Consul-Gen. MAREK SKOLIL.

Consulate-General, New York: 321 East 73rd St, New York, NY 10021; tel. (646) 422-3344; fax (646) 422-3311; e-mail newyork@embassy.mzv.cz; internet www.mfa.cz/newyork; Consul-Gen. ELIŠKA ŽIGOVÁ.

DENMARK

Embassy: 3200 Whitehaven St, NW, Washington, DC 20008-3616; tel. (202) 234-4300; fax (202) 328-1470; e-mail wasamb@um.dk; internet www.ambwashington.um.dk; Ambassador FRIIS ARNE PETERSEN.

Consulate-General, Chicago: 211 East Ontario, Suite 1800, Chicago, IL 60611-3242; tel. (312) 787-8780; fax (312) 787-8744; e-mail hktord@um.dk; internet www.gkchicago.um.dk; Consul-Gen. MADS MIKKELSEN.

Consulate-General, New York: 1 Dag Hammerskjöld Plaza, 885 Second Ave, 18th Floor, New York, NY 10017-2201; tel. (212) 223-4545; fax (212) 754-1904; e-mail nycgkl@um.dk; internet www.gknewyork.um.dk; Consul-Gen. TORBEN ANTONIO GETTERMAN.

DJIBOUTI

Embassy: 1156 15th St, NW, Suite 515, Washington, DC 20005; tel. (202) 331-0270; fax (202) 331-0302; Ambassador ROBLÉ OLHAYE.

DOMINICA

Embassy: OECS Bldg, 3216 New Mexico Ave, NW, Washington, DC 20016; tel. (202) 364-6781; fax (202) 364-6791; e-mail embdomdc@aol.com; Chargé d'affaires a.i. JUDITH ANN ROLLE.

Consulate-General, New York: 820 Second Ave, Suite 900, New York, NY 10017; tel. (212) 599-8478; fax (212) 661-0979; e-mail domun@onecommonwealth.org; Consul-Gen. ZILPHA THEODORE (acting).

DOMINICAN REPUBLIC

Embassy: 1715 22nd St, NW, Washington, DC 20008; tel. (202) 332-6280; fax (202) 265-8057; e-mail embassy@us.serex.gov.do; internet www.domrep.org; Ambassador FLAVIO D. ESPINAL.

Consulate-General, Sun Valley: 9001 Laurel Canyon Blvd, Suite 204, Sun Valley, CA 91352; tel. (818) 504-6605; Consul-Gen. CELESTE JIMÉNEZ PEÑA DE AMARANTE.

Consulate-General, Chicago: 25 East Washington St, Suite 1400, Chicago, IL 60602; tel. (312) 469-8350; fax (312) 469-8386; Consul-Gen. GISSELLE D. CASTILLO VEREMIS.

Consulate-General, New Orleans: World Trade Center, Suite 2100, 2 Canal St, New Orleans, LA 70130; tel. (504) 522-1843; fax (504) 522-1007; e-mail codonos@bellsouth.net; Consul-Gen. JOAQUÍN A. BALAGUER RICARDO.

Consulate-General, Boston: The Statler Bldg, Suite 601, 20 Park Plaza, Boston, MA 02116; tel. (617) 482-2101; fax (617) 482-8133; Consul-Gen. DOMINICO CABRAL ABAD.

Consulate-General, New York: 1501 Broadway, Suite 410, New York, NY 10036; tel. (212) 768-2480; fax (212) 768-2677; e-mail admny.consul@verizon.net; internet consuladord-ny.org; Consul-Gen. RAFAEL EDUARDO SELMAN HASBUN.

ECUADOR

Embassy: 2535 15th St, NW, Washington, DC 20009; tel. (202) 234-7200; fax (202) 667-3482; e-mail embassy@ecuador.org; internet www.ecuador.org; Ambassador LUIS BENIGNO GALLEGOS CHIRIBOGA.

Consulate-General, Los Angeles: 8484 Wilshire Blvd, Suite 540, Beverly Hills, CA 90211; tel. (323) 658-5146; fax (323) 658-1198; e-mail coneclac@aol.com; Consul-Gen. EDDIE RAINIERO BEDÓN ORBE.

Consulate-General, San Francisco: 235 Montgomery St, Suite 944, San Francisco, CA 94104; tel. (415) 982-1819; fax (415) 982-1833; e-mail sfconsul@aol.com; Consul-Gen. JUAN MIGUEL LEORO ALMEIDA.

Consulate-General, Miami: 1101 Brickell Ave, Suite M-102, Miami, FL 33131; tel. (305) 373-8520; fax (305) 539-8313; Consul-Gen. JUAN CARLOS TOLEDO GRADIN.

Consulate-General, Chicago: 30 South Michigan Ave, Suite 204, Chicago, IL 60603; tel. (312) 338-1003; fax (312) 338-1004; e-mail conchiec@aol.com; Consul-Gen. Dr FERNANDO CHAVES.

Consulate-General, Newark: 400 Market St, 4th Floor, Newark, NJ 07105; tel. (973) 344-8837; fax (973) 344-0008; e-mail cecunewjersey@mmrree.gov.ec; internet www.consuladoecuadornj.com; Consul-Gen. JESSICA N. ESCALA MACCAFERRI.

Consulate-General, New York: 800 Second Ave, Suite 600, New York, NY 10017; tel. (212) 808-0170; fax (212) 808-0188; e-mail cecunewyork@mmrree.gov.ec; internet www.consulecuadornewyork.com; Consul-Gen. JORGE WASHINGTON LÓPEZ AMAYA.

Consulate-General, Houston: 4200 Westheimer Rd, Suite 218, Houston, TX 77027; tel. (713) 572-8731; fax (713) 572-8732; e-mail consultx@houtx.net; Consul-Gen. VERÓNICA PEÑA MONTERO.

EGYPT

Embassy: 3521 International Ct, NW, Washington, DC 20008; tel. (202) 895-5400; fax (202) 244-4319; e-mail embassy@egyptembassy.net; internet www.egyptembassy.net; Ambassador SAMEH SHOUKRY.

Consulate-General, San Francisco: 3001 Pacific Ave, San Francisco, CA 94115; tel. (415) 346-9700; fax (415) 346-9480; e-mail egypt@egy2000.com; internet www.egy2000.com; Consul-Gen. HESHAM ELNAKIB.

Consulate-General, Chicago: 500 North Michigan Ave, Suite 1900, Chicago, IL 60611; tel. (312) 828-9162; fax (312) 828-9167; internet www.eg2002.net; Consul-Gen. HODA A. M. GOUDA.

Consulate-General, New York: 1110 Second Ave, Suite 201, New York, NY 10022; tel. (212) 759-7120; fax (212) 308-7643; e-mail info@egyptnyc.net; internet www.egyptnyc.net; Consul-Gen. SHERIF R. ELKHOLY.

EL SALVADOR

Embassy: 1400 16th St, NW, Suite 100, Washington, DC 20036; tel. (202) 265-9671; fax (202) 232-3763; e-mail correo@elsalvador.org; internet www.elsalvador.org; Ambassador RENÉ ANTONIO LEÓN RODRÍGUEZ.

Consulate-General, Nogales: 840 North Grand Ave, Suite 3, Nogales, AZ 85621; tel. (520) 287-3381; fax (520) 287-2521; Consul-Gen. LEOCADIO JOSÉ J. CHACÓN.

Consulate-General, Los Angeles: 3450 Wilshire Blvd, Suite 250, Los Angeles, CA 90010; tel. (213) 383-5776; fax (213) 383-8599; Consul-Gen. HÉCTOR H. HERRERA.

Consulate-General, San Francisco: 507 Polk St, Suite 280, San Francisco, CA 94102; tel. (415) 771-8524; fax (415) 771-8522; Consul-Gen. JOSÉ RAFAEL A. CARBALLO LACAYO.

Consulate-General, Santa Ana: 203 North Golden Circle Dr., Suite 103, Santa Ana, CA 92705; tel. (714) 972-8105; fax (714) 972-8376; Consul-Gen. (vacant).

Consulate-General, Washington, DC: 1724 20th St, NW, Washington, DC 20009; tel. (202) 331-4032; fax (202) 331-4036; Consul-Gen. ANA MARGARITA CHÁVEZ ESCOBAR.

Consulate-General, Miami: 2600 Douglas Rd, Suite 104, Coral Gables, Miami, FL 33134; tel. (305) 774-0840; fax (305) 774-0850; Consul-Gen. LUIS M. BRITO.

Consulate-General, Duluth: 3505 Duluth Park Lane, Suite 320, Duluth, GA 30096; tel. (770) 623-8891; Consul-Gen. ASDRÚBAL AGUILAR ZEPEDA.

Consulate-General, Chicago: 104 South Michigan Ave, Suite 816, Chicago, IL 60603; tel. (312) 332-1393; fax (312) 332-4446; Consul-Gen. PATRICIA MAZA-PITTSFORD.

Consulate-General, Boston: 20 Meridian St, 4th Floor, East Boston, MA 02128; tel. (617) 567-8484; fax (617) 567-8686; Consul-Gen. ROXANA PATRICIA ABREGO.

Consulate-General, Las Vegas: 765 North Nellis Blvd, Suite C-5, Las Vegas, NV 89110; tel. (702) 437-5337; fax (702) 437-5336; Consul-Gen. OSCAR BENAVIDES GUTIÉRREZ.

Consulate-General, Brentwood: 1090 Suffolk Ave, Brentwood, NY 11717; tel. (631) 273-1355; fax (631) 273-2559; Consul-Gen. OSCAR E. LANDAVERDE CONTRERAS.

Consulate-General, New York: 46 Park Ave, New York, NY 10016; tel. (212) 889-3608; fax (212) 679-2835; Consul-Gen. LORENA SOL DE POOL.

Consulate-General, Dallas: Oakbrook Plaza, 1555 West Mockingbird Lane, Suite 216, Dallas, TX 75235; tel. (214) 637-1018; fax (214) 637-1106; Consul-Gen. MARIO R. HERNÁNDEZ.

Consulate-General, Houston: 1702 Hillendahl Blvd, Houston, TX 77055; tel. (713) 270-6239; fax (713) 270-9683; Consul-Gen. LUIS E. CARRANZA.

EQUATORIAL GUINEA

Embassy: 2020 16th St, NW, Washington, DC 20009; tel. (202) 518-5700; fax (202) 518-5252; Ambassador PURIFICACIÓN ANGUE ONDO.

ERITREA

Embassy: 1708 New Hampshire Ave, NW, Washington, DC 20009; tel. (202) 319-1991; fax (202) 319-1304; Ambassador GHIRMAI GHEBREMARIAM.

Consulate-General, San Francisco: 409 13th St, 14th Floor, Oakland, CA 94621; tel. (510) 986-1991; Consul-Gen. AHMED MOHAMMED IMAN.

ESTONIA

Embassy: 2131 Massachusetts Ave, NW, Washington, DC 20008; tel. (202) 588-0101; fax (202) 588-0108; e-mail info@estemb.org; internet www.estemb.org; Ambassador VÄINO REINART.

Consulate-General, New York: 3 Dag Hammarskjöld Plaza, Suite 6B, 305 East 47th St, New York, NY 10017-2001; tel. (212) 883-0636; fax (212) 883-0648; e-mail nyconsulate@mfa.ee; internet www.nyc.estemb.org; Consul-Gen. JAANUS KIRIKMÄE.

ETHIOPIA

Embassy: 3506 International Dr., NW, Washington, DC 20008; tel. (202) 364-1200; fax (202) 587-0195; e-mail info@ethiopianembassy.org; internet www.ethiopianembassy.org; Ambassador Dr SAMUEL ASSEFA.

Consulate-General, Los Angeles: 3460 Wilshire Blvd, Suite 308, Los Angeles, CA 90010; tel. (213) 365-6651; fax (213) 365-6670; e-mail info@ethioconsulate-la.org; internet www.ethioconsulate-la.org; Consul-Gen. Ato TAYE ATSKE SELASSIE.

FIJI

Embassy: 2000 M St, NW, Suite 710, Washington, DC 20036; tel. (202) 466-8320; fax (202) 466-8325; e-mail info@fijiembassydc.com; internet www.fijiembassy.org; Chargé d'affaires a.i. PENIJAMINI R. TUIKUBULAU LOMALOMA.

FINLAND

Embassy: 3301 Massachusetts Ave, NW, Washington, DC 20008; tel. (202) 298-5800; fax (202) 298-6030; e-mail sanomat.was@formin.fi; internet www.finland.org; Ambassador PEKKA LINTU.

Consulate-General, Los Angeles: 1801 Century Park East, Suite 2100, Los Angeles, CA 90067-2323; tel. (310) 203-9903; fax (310) 203-9186; e-mail info@finlandla.org; internet www.finlandla.org; Consul-Gen. MANU VIRTAMO.

Consulate-General, New York: 866 United Nations Plaza, Suite 250, New York, NY 10017; tel. (212) 750-4400; fax (212) 750-4418; e-mail consulate.nyc@formin.fi; internet www.finland.org; Consul-Gen. RITVA JOLKKONEN.

FRANCE

Embassy: 4101 Reservoir Rd, NW, Washington, DC 20007; tel. (202) 944-6000; fax (202) 944-6166; e-mail info@ambafrance-us.org; internet www.ambafrance-us.org; Ambassador PIERRE VIMONT.

Consulate-General, Los Angeles: 10390 Santa Monica Blvd, Suite 410, Los Angeles, CA 90025; tel. (310) 235-3200; fax (310) 479-4813; e-mail press-info@consulfrance-losangeles.org; internet www.consulfrance-losangeles.org; Consul-Gen. DAVID MARTINON.

Consulate-General, San Francisco: 540 Bush St, San Francisco, CA 94108; tel. (415) 397-4330; fax (415) 433-8357; e-mail presse-info@consulfrance-sanfrancisco.org; internet www.consulfrance-sanfrancisco.org; Consul-Gen. PIERRE-FRANÇOIS MOURIER.

Consulate-General, Miami: Suite 1050, Espirito Santo Plaza, 1395 Brickell Ave, Miami, FL 33131; tel. (305) 403-4150; fax (305) 403-4151; e-mail presse@consulfrance-miami.org; internet www.consulfrance-miami.org; Consul-Gen. PHILIPPE VINOGRADOFF.

Consulate-General, Atlanta: Prominence in Buckhead, Suite 1840, 3475 Piedmont Rd, NE, Atlanta, GA 30305; tel. (404) 495-1660; fax (404) 495-1661; e-mail info@consulfrance-atlanta.org; internet www.consulfrance-atlanta.org; Consul-Gen. PHILIPPE ARDANAZ.

Consulate-General, Chicago: 205 North Michigan Ave, Suite 3700, Chicago, IL 60601; tel. (312) 327-5200; fax (312) 327-5201; e-mail contact@consulfrance-chicago.org; internet www.consulfrance-chicago.org; Consul-Gen. JEAN-BAPTISTE MAIN DE BOISSIERE.

Consulate-General, New Orleans: Amoco Bldg, Suite 1340, Poydras St, New Orleans, LA 70112; tel. (504) 569-2870; fax (504) 569-2871; e-mail info@consulfrance-nouvelleorleans.org; internet www.consulfrance-nouvelleorleans.org; Consul-Gen. OLIVIER BROCHENIN.

Consulate-General, Boston: 31 St James Ave, Suite 750, Boston, MA 02116; tel. (617) 832-4400; fax (617) 542-8054; e-mail consulat@consulfrance-boston.org; internet www.consulfrance-boston.org; Consul-Gen. FRANÇOIS GAUTHIER.

Consulate-General, New York: 934 Fifth Ave, New York, NY 10021; tel. (212) 606-3600; fax (212) 606-3620; e-mail info@consulfrance-newyork.org; internet www.consulfrance-newyork.org; Consul-Gen. GUY YELDA.

Consulate-General, Houston: 777 Post Oak Blvd, Suite 600, Houston, TX 77056; tel. (713) 572-2799; fax (713) 572-2911; e-mail info@consulfrance-houston.org; internet www.consulfrance-houston.org; Consul-Gen. PIERRE GRANDJOUAN.

GABON

Embassy: 2034 20th St, NW, Washington, DC 20009; tel. (202) 797-1000; fax (202) 332-0668; Ambassador CARLOS BOUNGOU.

THE GAMBIA

Embassy: 1156 15th St, NW, Suite 905, Washington, DC 20005-2076; tel. (202) 785-1399; fax (202) 785-1430; Chargé d'affaires a.i. ABDUL RAHMAN COLE.

GEORGIA

Embassy: 1101 15th St, NW, Suite 602, Washington, DC 20005; tel. (202) 387-9151; fax (202) 393-4537; e-mail embgeorgiausa@yahoo.com; internet www.georgiaemb.org; Ambassador VASIL SIKHARULIDZE.

GERMANY

Embassy: 4645 Reservoir Rd, NW, Washington, DC 20007-1998; tel. (202) 298-4000; fax (202) 298-4249; internet www.germany.info; Ambassador KLAUS SCHARIOTH.

Consulate-General, Los Angeles: 6222 Wilshire Blvd, Suite 500, Los Angeles, CA 90048; tel. (323) 930-2703; fax (323) 930-2805; e-mail losangeles@germany.info; internet www.germany-info.org/losangeles; Consul-Gen. Dr CHRISTIAN STOCKS.

Consulate-General, San Francisco: 1960 Jackson St, San Francisco, CA 94109; tel. (415) 775-1061; fax (415) 775-0187; e-mail sanfrancisco@germanconsulate.org; internet www.sanfrancisco.diplo.de; Consul-Gen. ROLF SCHÜTTE.

Consulate-General, Miami: 100 North Biscayne Blvd, Suite 2200, Miami, FL 33132; tel. (305) 358-0290; fax (305) 358-0307; e-mail miami@germany.info; internet www.miami.diplo.de; Consul-Gen. KLAUS H. D. RANNER.

Consulate-General, Atlanta: Marquis Two Tower, Suite 901, 285 Peachtree Center Ave, NE, Atlanta, GA 30303-1221; tel. (404) 659-4760; fax (404) 577-2719; e-mail atlanta@germany.info; internet www.germany-info.org/atlanta; Consul-Gen. Dr LUTZ HERMANN GÖRGENS.

Consulate-General, Chicago: 676 North Michigan Ave, Suite 3200, Chicago, IL 60611; tel. (312) 202-0480; fax (312) 202-0466; internet www.germany.info/chicago; Consul-Gen. WOLFGANG DRAUTZ.

Consulate-General, Boston: 3 Copley Pl., Suite 500, Boston, MA 02116; tel. (617) 369-4900; fax (617) 369-4940; e-mail info@bost.diplo.de; internet www.germany-info.org/boston; Consul-Gen. FRIEDRICH LUDWIG LOEHR.

Consulate-General, New York: 871 United Nations Plaza, New York, NY 10017; tel. (212) 610-9700; fax (212) 610-9702; e-mail german-consulate-ku@nyct.net; internet www.germanconsulate.org/newyork; Consul-Gen. Dr HORST FREITAG.

Consulate-General, Houston: 1330 Post Oak Blvd, Suite 1850, Houston, TX 77056; tel. (713) 627-7770; fax (713) 627-0506; e-mail info@germanconsulatehouston.org; internet www.germanconsulatehouston.org; Consul-Gen. RAINER MÜNZEL.

GHANA

Embassy: 3512 International Dr., NW, Washington, DC 20008; tel. (202) 686-4520; fax (202) 686-4527; e-mail info@ghanaembassy.org; internet www.ghanaembassy.org; Ambassador Dr KWAME BAWUAH-EDUSEI.

Consulate-General, New York: 19 East 47th St, New York, NY 10017; tel. (212) 832-1300; fax (212) 751-6743; internet www.ghanaconsulatenewyork.org; Consul-Gen. OBENG GYAN BUSIA.

GREECE

Embassy: 2221 Massachusetts Ave, NW, Washington, DC 20008; tel. (202) 939-1300; fax (202) 939-1324; e-mail greece@greekembassy.org; internet www.greekembassy.org; Ambassador ALEXANDROS P. MALLIAS.

Consulate-General, Los Angeles: 12424 Wilshire Blvd, Suite 800, Los Angeles, CA 90025; tel. (310) 826-5555; fax (310) 826-8670; e-mail lagr@greekembassy.org; internet www.greekembassy.org/losangeles; Consul-Gen. DIMITRIS CARAMITSOS-TZIRAS.

Consulate-General, San Francisco: 2441 Gough St, San Francisco, CA 94123; tel. (415) 775-2102; fax (415) 776-6815; e-mail sfgr@greekembassy.org; internet www.greekembassy.org/consular/san_francisco; Consul-Gen. XENIA STEFANIDOU.

Consulate-General, Tampa: 601 Bayshore Blvd, Suite 800, Tampa, FL 33606; tel. (813) 865-0200; fax (813) 865-0206; e-mail grgencon.tam@mfa.gr; internet www.greekembassy.org/tampa; Consul-Gen. ANDREAS PSYCHARIS.

Consulate-General, Chicago: 650 North St Clair St, Chicago, IL 60611; tel. (312) 335-3915; fax (312) 335-3958; e-mail chicago@greekembassy.org; internet www.greekembassy.org/consular/chicago; Consul-Gen. ALIKI HADJI.

Consulate-General, Boston: 86 Beacon St, Boston, MA 02115; tel. (617) 523-0100; fax (617) 523-0511; e-mail boston@greekembassy.org; internet www.greekembassy.org/consular/boston; Consul-Gen. CONSTANTINOS ORPHANIDES.

Consulate-General, New York: 69 East 79th St, New York, NY 10021; tel. (212) 988-5500; fax (212) 734-8492; e-mail nycons@greekembassy.org; internet www.greekembassy.org/consular/newyork; Consul-Gen. AGHI BALTA.

GRENADA

Embassy: 1701 New Hampshire Ave, NW, Washington, DC 20009; tel. (202) 265-2561; fax (202) 265-2468; e-mail grenada@oas.org; internet www.grenadaembassyusa.org; Ambassador DENIS G. ANTOINE.

Consulate-General, New York: 800 Second Ave, Suite 400-K, New York, NY 10017; tel. (212) 599-0301; fax (212) 599-1540; e-mail cgny@grenadaconsulate.org; internet www.grenadaconsulate.org; Consul-Gen. DERRICK JAMES.

GUATEMALA

Embassy: 2220 R St, NW, Washington, DC 20008; tel. (202) 745-4952; fax (202) 745-1908; e-mail info@guatemala-embassy.org; internet www.guatemala-embassy.org; Ambassador FRANCISCO VILLAGRÁN DE LEÓN.

Consulate-General, Phoenix: 4747 North 7th Street, Suite 410, Phoenix, AZ 85014; tel. (602) 200-3660; fax (602) 200-3661; e-mail consguatearizona@minex.gob.gt; Consul-Gen. OSCAR ADOLFO PADILLA LAM.

Consulate-General, Los Angeles: 1605 West Olympic Blvd, Suite 422, Los Angeles, CA 90015; tel. (213) 365-9251; fax (213) 365-9245; e-mail conslosangeles@minex.gob.gt; Consul-Gen. MILTON E. ALVAREZ VELA.

Consulate-General, San Francisco: 785 Market St, Suite 400, San Francisco, CA 94103; tel. (415) 896-9181; fax (415) 896-9186; e-mail conssanfrancisco@minex.gob.gt; internet sfconsulguate.org; Consul-Gen. ANA PATRICIA RAMÍREZ M..

Consulate-General, Denver: 820 16th St, Suite 615, Denver, CO 80202; tel. (415) 788-5651; fax (415) 788-5653; e-mail consdenver@minex.gob.gt; Consul-Gen. ALFREDO VÁSQUEZ RIVERA.

Consulate-General, Miami: 1101 Brickell Ave, Suite 1003-S, Miami, FL 33131; tel. (305) 679-9945; fax (305) 679-9983; e-mail consmiami@minex.gob.gt; Consul-Gen. JULIA BEATRIZ ILLESCAS PUTZEYS.

Consulate-General, Atlanta: 2750 Buford Way, Suite 135, Atlanta, GA 30324; tel. (404) 320-8804; fax (404) 320-8806; e-mail consatlanta@minex.gob.gt; Consul-Gen. HUGO HAROLDO HUN ARCHILA.

Consulate-General, Chicago: 203 North Wabash Ave, Suite 910, Chicago, IL 60601; tel. (312) 332-1587; fax (312) 332-4256; e-mail conschicago@minex.gob.gt; internet www.consulguatechicago.org; Consul-Gen. GUSTAVO A. LÓPEZ CALDERÓN.

Consulate-General, New York: 57 Park Ave, New York, NY 10016; tel. (212) 686-3837; fax (212) 447-6947; e-mail consnewyork@minex.gob.gt; Consul-Gen. ROSA MARÍA MÉRIDA DE MORA.

Consulate-General, Providence: 754 Branch Ave, Suite 201, Providence, RI 02904; tel. (303) 629-9210; fax (303) 629-9211; e-mail consrhodeisland@minex.gob.gt; Consul-Gen. CARLOS ENRIQUE AVILA SANDOVAL.

Consulate-General, Houston: 3013 Fountainview, Suite 210, Houston, TX 77057; tel. (713) 953-9531; fax (713) 953-9383; e-mail conshouston@minex.gob.gt; Consul-Gen. JOSÉ BARILLAS TRENNERT.

GUINEA

Embassy: 2112 Leroy Pl., NW, Washington, DC 20008; tel. (202) 986-4300; fax (202) 986-3800; Ambassador MORY KARAMOKO KABA.

GUINEA-BISSAU

Embassy: 15929 Yukon Lane, Rockville, MD; tel. and fax (301) 947-3958; Ambassador (vacant).

GUYANA

Embassy: 2490 Tracy Pl., NW, Washington, DC 20008; tel. (202) 265-6900; fax (202) 232-1297; e-mail guyanaembassydc@verizon.net; Ambassador BAYNEY KARRAN.

Consulate-General, New York: 370 7th Ave, Suite 402, New York, NY 10001; tel. (212) 947-5110; fax (212) 947-5163; Consul-Gen. BRENTNOLD FITZPATRICK EVANS.

HAITI

Embassy: 2311 Massachusetts Ave, Washington, DC 20008; tel. (202) 332-4090; fax (202) 745-7215; e-mail embassy@haiti.org; internet www.haiti.org; Ambassador RAYMOND A. JOSEPH.

Consulate-General, Miami: Ingraham Bldg, 259 South West 13th St, Miami, FL 33131; tel. (305) 859-2003; fax (305) 854-7441; Consul JEAN BERNARD R. LATORTUE.

Consulate-General, Chicago: 11 East Adams St, Suite 1400, Chicago, IL 60603; tel. (312) 922-4004; fax (312) 922-7122; e-mail chicago@haitianconsulate.org; internet haitianconsulate.org; Consul LESLIE L. CONDÉ.

Consulate-General, Boston: 545 Boylston St, Suite 201, Boston, MA 02116; tel. (617) 266-3660; fax (617) 266-4060; e-mail info@consulathaitiboston.com; Consul JEAN ROLAND ELIE.

Consulate-General, New York: 271 Madison Ave, 5th Floor, New York, NY 10016; tel. (212) 697-9767; fax (212) 681-6991; e-mail contact@haitianconsulate-nyc.org; internet www.haitianconsulate-nyc.org; Consul-Gen. FÉLIX AUGUSTIN.

HOLY SEE

Apostolic Nunciature: 3339 Massachusetts Ave, NW, Washington, DC 20008; tel. (202) 333-7121; fax (202) 337-4036; Apostolic Nuncio Most Rev. PIETRO SAMBI (Titular Archbishop of Bellicastrum).

HONDURAS

Embassy: 3007 Tilden St, NW, Suite 4-M, Washington, DC 20008; tel. (202) 966-7702; fax (202) 966-9751; e-mail embassy@hondurasemb.org; internet www.hondurasemb.org; Ambassador ROBERTO FLORES BERMÚDEZ.

Consulate-General, Phoenix: 4040 East McDowell, Suite 305, Phoenix, AZ 85008; tel. (602) 273-0173; fax (602) 273-0547; Consul-Gen. NORA I. MONTOYA TORRES.

Consulate-General, Los Angeles: 3550 Wilshire Blvd, Suite 410, Los Angeles, CA 90010; tel. (213) 383-9244; fax (213) 383-9306; e-mail consulla@aol.com; Consul-Gen. VIVIAN VERONICA PANTING GALO.

Consulate-General, San Francisco: 870 Market St, Suite 875, San Francisco, CA 94102; tel. (415) 392-0076; fax (415) 392-6726; Consul-Gen. FRANCISCO ALONSO VENEGAS.

Consulate-General, Miami: 7171 Coral Way, Suite 309, Miami, FL 33155; tel. (305) 269-9399; fax (305) 269-9445; e-mail honmiami@bridge.net; Consul-Gen. FERNANDO AGURCIA.

Consulate-General, Atlanta: 600 Houze Way, Suite 3-A, Roswell, GA 30076; tel. (770) 234-9560; e-mail honconat@bellsouth.net; Consul-Gen. ROSA DE PINEDA.

Consulate-General, Chicago: 4439 West Fullerton Ave, Chicago, IL 60639; tel. (773) 342-8281; fax (773) 342-8293; e-mail consulchicago@yahoo.com; Consul-Gen. JOSÉ ERASMO MONTALVÁN.

Consulate-General, New Orleans: 2 Canal St, Suite 1641, New Orleans, LA 70130; tel. (504) 522-3118; fax (504) 523-0544; e-mail jvcalhoun@aol.com; Consul-Gen. ENA LILIANA CASTRO.

Consulate-General, New York: 35 West 35th St, 6th Floor, New York, NY 10001; tel. (212) 714-9450; fax (212) 714-9453; e-mail hondurasconsuladonyc@hotmail.com; Consul-Gen. CARMEN BELINDA MARTÍNEZ.

Consulate-General, Houston: 5433 Westheimer Rd, Suite 325, Houston TX 77401; tel. (713) 667-4693; fax (713) 667-4284; e-mail cnhnhouston@sbcglobal.net; Consul-Gen. LASTENIA PINEDA DE MEDINA.

HUNGARY

Embassy: 3910 Shoemaker St, NW, Washington, DC 20008; tel. (202) 362-6730; fax (202) 966-8135; e-mail informacio.was@kum.hu; internet www.huembwas.org; Ambassador Dr FERENC SOMOGYI.

Consulate-General, Los Angeles: 11766 Wilshire Blvd, Suite 410, Los Angeles, CA 90025; tel. (310) 473-9344; fax (310) 479-6443; e-mail huconlos@mpowercom.net; Consul-Gen. BALÁZS BOKOR.

Consulate-General, Chicago: 600 North State St, Chicago, IL 60610; tel. (312) 943-3800; Consul-Gen. Dr ISTVÁN MEZEI.

Consulate-General, New York: 223 East 52nd St, New York, NY 10022; tel. (212) 752-0669; fax (212) 755-5986; e-mail nyf.missions@kum.hu; Consul-Gen. VIKTOR POLGÁR.

ICELAND

Embassy: 1156 15th St, NW, Suite 1200, Washington, DC 20005; tel. (202) 265-6653; fax (202) 265-6656; e-mail icemb.wash@utn.stjr.is; internet www.iceland.org/us; Ambassador ALBERT JÓNSSON.

Consulate-General, New York: 800 Third Ave, 36th Floor, New York, NY 10022; tel. (212) 593-2700; fax (212) 593-6263; e-mail con.newyork@mfa.is; internet www.iceland.org/us/nyc; Consul-Gen. MAGNÚS GÚSTAFSSON.

INDIA

Embassy: 2107 Massachusetts Ave, NW, Washington, DC 20008; tel. (202) 939-7000; fax (202) 265-4351; e-mail info2@indiagov.org; internet www.indianembassy.org; Ambassador RONEN SEN.

Consulate-General, San Francisco: 540 Arguello Blvd, San Francisco, CA 94118; tel. (415) 668-0662; fax (415) 668-7968; e-mail info@cgisf.org; internet www.cgisf.org; Consul-Gen. B. S. PRAKASH.

Consulate-General, Chicago: NBC Tower Bldg, Suite 850, 455 North Cityfront Plaza Dr., Chicago, IL 60611; tel. (312) 595-0405; fax (312) 595-0416; internet chicago.indianconsulate.com; Consul-Gen. ASHOK KUMAR ATTRI.

Consulate-General, New York: New India House, 3 East 64th St, New York, NY 10021; tel. (212) 774-0600; fax (212) 861-3788; e-mail cpv@indiacgny.org; internet www.indiacgny.org; Consul-Gen. PRABHU DAYAL.

Consulate-General, Houston: 1990 Post Oak Blvd, Suite 600, Houston, TX 77056; tel. (713) 626-2148; fax (713) 626-2450; e-mail cgi-hou@swbell.net; internet www.cgihouston.org; Consul-Gen. SHASHISHEKAR M. GAVAI.

INDONESIA

Embassy: 2020 Massachusetts Ave, NW, Washington, DC 20036; tel. (202) 775-5200; fax (202) 775-5365; internet www.embassyofindonesia.org; Ambassador SUDJADNAN PARNOHADININGRAT.

Consulate-General, Los Angeles: 3457 Wilshire Blvd, Los Angeles, CA 90010; tel. (213) 383-5126; fax (213) 487-3971; e-mail kjri@kjri-la.net; internet www.kjri-la.net; Consul-Gen. SUBIJAKSONO SUJONO.

Consulate-General, San Francisco: 1111 Columbus Ave, San Francisco, CA 94133; tel. (415) 474-9571; fax (415) 441-4320; e-mail sanfrancisco@kjrisfo.net; internet www.kjrisfo.org; Consul-Gen. YUDHISTIRANTO SUNGADI.

Consulate-General, Chicago: 211 West Wacker Dr., 8th Floor, Chicago, IL 60606; tel. (312) 920-1880; fax (312) 920-1881; e-mail consular@indonesiachicago.org; internet www.indonesiachicago.org; Consul-Gen. HIDAYAT KARTA HADIMAJA.

Consulate-General, New York: 5 East 68th St, New York, NY 10065; tel. (212) 879-0600; fax (212) 570-6206; e-mail information@indonesianewyork.org; internet www.indonesianewyork.org; Consul-Gen. TRIE EDI MULYANI.

Consulate-General, Houston: 10900 Richmond Ave, Houston, TX 77042; tel. (713) 785-1691; fax (713) 780-9644; e-mail kjrihouston@prodigy.net; internet www.kjri-houston.net; Consul-Gen. KRIA FAHMI PASARIBU.

IRAN

Interests section in the Embassy of Pakistan: 2209 Wisconsin Ave, NW, Washington, DC 20007; tel. (202) 965-4990; fax (202) 965-1073; e-mail requests@daftar.org; internet www.daftar.org; Dir FARIBORZ JAHANSOOZAN.

IRAQ

Embassy: 1801 P St, NW, Washington, DC 20036; tel. (202) 483-7500; fax (202) 462-5066; e-mail admin@iraqiembassy.us; internet www.iraqiembassy.us; Ambassador SAMIR SHAKIR MAHMOOD AS-SUMAIDAIE.

IRELAND

Embassy: 2234 Massachusetts Ave, NW, Washington, DC 20008; tel. (202) 462-3939; fax (202) 232-5993; e-mail embirlus@aol.com; internet www.irelandemb.org; Ambassador MICHAEL COLLINS.

Consulate-General, San Francisco: 100 Pine St, Suite 3350, San Francisco, CA 94111; tel. (415) 392-4214; fax (415) 392-0885; e-mail sanfrancongen@dfa.ie; internet www.consulateofirelandsanfrancisco.org; Consul-Gen. GERRY STAUNTON.

Consulate-General, Chicago: 400 North Michigan Ave, Suite 911, Chicago, IL 60611; tel. (312) 337-1868; fax (312) 337-1954; e-mail chicagocongen@dfa.ie; internet www.irishconsulate.org; Consul-Gen. MARTIN ROUINE.

Consulate-General, Boston: 535 Boylston St, Boston, MA 02116; tel. (617) 267-9330; fax (617) 267-6375; e-mail irlcons@aol.com; Consul-Gen. DAVID BARRY.

Consulate-General, New York: 345 Park Ave, New York, NY 10154-0037; tel. (212) 319-2555; fax (212) 980-9475; e-mail congenny@aol.com; Consul-Gen. NIALL ANTHONY BURGESS.

ISRAEL

Embassy: 3514 International Dr., NW, Washington, DC 20008; tel. (202) 364-5500; fax (202) 364-5560; e-mail info@israelemb.org; internet www.israelemb.org; Ambassador SALLAI MERIDOR.

Consulate-General, Los Angeles: 6380 Wilshire Blvd, Suite 1700, Los Angeles, CA 90048; tel. (323) 852-5500; fax (323) 852-5555; e-mail info@losangeles.mfa.gov.il; internet www.israelemb.org/la; Consul-Gen. JACOB DAYAN.

Consulate-General, San Francisco: 456 Montgomery St, Suite 2100, San Francisco, CA 94104; tel. (415) 844-7500; fax (415) 844-7555; e-mail sf@isrealiconsulate.org; internet www.israeliconsulate.org; Consul-Gen. DAVID AKOV.

Consulate-General, Miami: 100 North Biscayne Blvd, Suite 1800, Miami, FL 33132; tel. (305) 925-9400; fax (305) 925-9455; e-mail info@miami.mfa.gov.il; internet miami.mfa.gov.il; Consul-Gen. OFER BAVLY.

Consulate-General, Atlanta: 1100 Spring St, Suite 440, Atlanta, GA 30309-2823; tel. (404) 487-6500; fax (404) 487-6555; e-mail Atlanta@israel.org; internet atlanta.mfa.gov.il; Consul-Gen. REDA MANSOUR.

Consulate-General, Chicago: 111 East Wacker Dr., Suite 1308, Chicago, IL 60601; tel. (312) 297-4800; fax (312) 297-4855; e-mail contactus@chicago.mfa.gov.il; internet chicago.mfa.gov.il; Consul-Gen. ORLI GIL.

Consulate-General, Boston: 20 Park Plaza, Suite 1020, Boston, MA 02116; tel. (617) 535-0200; fax (617) 535-0255; e-mail information@boston.mfa.gov.il; internet www.israelboston.org; Consul-Gen. NADAV TAMIR.

Consulate-General, New York: 800 Second Ave, New York, NY 10017; tel. (212) 499-5300; fax (212) 499-5477; e-mail newyork@israel.org; internet www.israelfm.org; Consul-Gen. ASAF SHARIV.

Consulate-General, Philadelphia: 230 South 15th St, Philadelphia, 8th Floor, PA 19102; tel. (215) 546-5556; fax (215) 545-3986; e-mail info@philadelphia.mfa.gov.il; internet philadelphia.mfa.gov.il; Consul-Gen. DANIEL KUTNER.

Consulate-General, Houston: 24 Greenway Plaza, Suite 1500, Houston, TX 77046; tel. (713) 627-3780; fax (713) 627-0149; e-mail consular.dep@houston.mfa.gov.il; internet houston.mfa.gov.il; Consul-Gen. ASHER YARDEN.

ITALY

Embassy: 3000 Whitehaven St, NW, Washington, DC 20008; tel. (202) 612-4400; fax (202) 518-2154; e-mail stampa.washington@esteri.it; internet www.ambwashingtondc.esteri.it; Ambassador GIOVANNI CASTELLANETA.

Consulate-General, Los Angeles: 12400 Wilshire Blvd, Suite 300, Los Angeles, CA 90025; tel. (310) 820-0622; fax (310) 820-0727; e-mail consolato.losangeles@esteri.it; internet www.conslosangeles.esteri.it; Consul-Gen. NICOLA FAGANELLO.

Consulate-General, San Francisco: 2590 Webster St, San Francisco, CA 94115; tel. (415) 931-4924; fax (415) 931-7205; Consul-Gen. FABRIZIO MARCELLI.

Consulate-General, Miami: 4000 Ponce de Leon Blvd, Suite 590, Coral Gables, Miami, FL 33146; tel. (305) 374-6322; fax (305) 374-7945; e-mail italianconsulate.miami@esteri.it; internet www.consmiami.esteri.it; Consul-Gen. MARCO ROCCA.

Consulate-General, Chicago: 500 North Michigan Ave, Suite 1850, Chicago, IL 60611; tel. (312) 467-1550; fax (312) 467-1335; e-mail italcons.chicago@esteri.it; internet www.conschicago.esteri.it; Consul-Gen. ALESSANDRO MOTTA.

Consulate-General, Boston: 1600 Atlantic Ave, 17th Floor, Boston, MA 02210; tel. (617) 722-9201; fax (617) 722-9407; e-mail archivio.boston@esteri.it; internet www.consboston.esteri.it; Consul-Gen. LIBORIO STELLINO.

Consulate-General, New York: 690 Park Ave, New York, NY 10021-5044; tel. (212) 439-8600; fax (212) 249-4945; e-mail info.newyork@esteri.it; internet www.consnewyork.esteri.it; Consul-Gen. FRANCESCO MARIA TALÒ.

Consulate-General, Philadelphia: Public Ledger Bldg, Suite 1026, 150 South Sixth St, Philadelphia, PA 19106-3470; tel. (215) 592-7329; fax (215) 592-9808; e-mail consolato.filadelfia@esteri.it; internet www.consfiladelfia.esteri.it; Consul-Gen. STEFANO MISTRETTA.

Consulate-General, Houston: 1300 Post Oak Blvd, Suite 660, Houston, TX 77056; tel. (713) 850-7520; fax (713) 850-9113; e-mail italcons.houston@esteri.it; internet www.conshouston.esteri.it; Consul-Gen. CRISTIANO MAGGIPINTO.

JAMAICA

Embassy: 1520 New Hampshire Ave, NW, Washington, DC 20036; tel. (202) 452-0660; fax (202) 452-0081; e-mail dcm@jamaicaembassy.org; internet www.jamaicaembassy.org; Ambassador ANTHONY JOHNSON.

Consulate-General, Miami: Ingraham Bldg, Suite 609, 25 Second Ave, SE, Miami, FL 33131; tel. (305) 374-8431; fax (305) 577-4970; e-mail jamconmi@bellsouth.net; internet www.jamaicacgmiami.org; Consul-Gen. CLEMENT P. R. ALLICOCK.

Consulate-General, New York: 767 Third Ave, 3rd Floor, New York, NY 10017; tel. (212) 935-9000; fax (212) 935-7507; Consul-Gen. Dr BASIL K. BRYAN.

JAPAN

Embassy: 2520 Massachusetts Ave, NW, Washington, DC 20008-2869; tel. (202) 238-6700; fax (202) 328-2187; e-mail jicc@embjapan.org; internet www.us.emb-japan.go.jp; Ambassador ICHIRO FUJISAKI.

Consulate-General, Los Angeles: 350 South Grand Ave, Suite 1700, Los Angeles, CA 90071; tel. (213) 617-6700; fax (213) 617-6727; internet www.la.us.emb-japan.go.jp; Consul-Gen. JUNICHI IHARA.

Consulate-General, San Francisco: 50 Fremont St, Suite 2300, San Francisco, CA 94105; tel. (415) 777-3533; fax (415) 974-3660; e-mail con-e@cgjsf.org; internet www.sf.us.emb-japan.go.jp; Consul-Gen. YASUMASA NAGAMINE.

Consulate-General, Denver: 1225 17th St, Suite 3000, Denver, CO 80202; tel. (303) 534-1151; fax (303) 534-3393; e-mail cgjd-pr@qwest.net; internet www.denver.us.emb-japan.go.jp; Consul-Gen. KAZUAKI KUBO.

Consulate-General, Miami: Brickell Bay View Center, Suite 3200, 80 Southwest Eighth St, Miami, FL 33130; tel. (305) 530-9090; fax (305) 530-0950; e-mail info@cgjmia.org; internet www.miami.us.emb-japan.go.jp; Consul-Gen. HIROSHI YAMAGUCHI.

Consulate-General, Atlanta: 3500 Lennox Rd, Suite 1600, Atlanta, GA 30326; tel. (404) 240-4300; fax (404) 240-4311; e-mail info@cgjapanatlanta.org; internet www.japanatlanta.org; Consul-Gen. SHOJI OGAWA.

Consulate-General, Honolulu: 1742 Nuuanu Ave, Honolulu, HI 96817-3294; tel. (808) 543-3111; fax (808) 543-3170; internet www.honolulu.us.emb-japan.go.jp; Consul-Gen. TOSHIO KUNIKATA.

Consulate-General, Chicago: Chicago Olympia Center, Suite 1100, 737 North Michigan Ave, Chicago, IL 60611; tel. (312) 280-0400; fax (312) 280-9568; e-mail cgjconsular@webkddi.com; internet www.chicago.us.emb-japan.go.jp; Consul-Gen. GEORGE HISAEDA.

Consulate-General, Boston: Federal Reserve Plaza, 14th Floor, 600 Atlantic Ave, Boston, MA 02210; tel. (617) 973-9772; fax (617) 542-1329; internet www.boston.us.emb-japan.go.jp; Consul-Gen. YOICHI SUZUKI.

Consulate-General, Detroit: 400 Renaissance Center, Suite 1600, Detroit, MI 48243; tel. (313) 567-0120; fax (313) 567-0274; internet www.detroit.us.emb-japan.go.jp; Consul-Gen. TAMOTSU SHINOTSUKA.

Consulate-General, New York: 299 Park Ave, 19th Floor, New York, NY 10171; tel. (212) 371-8222; fax (212) 371-1294; e-mail inquiry@ny.cgj.org; internet www.ny.us.emb-japan.go.jp; Consul-Gen. MOTOATSU SAKURAI.

Consulate-General, Portland: Wells Fargo Center, Suite 2700, 1300 Fifth Ave, SW, Portland, OR 97201; tel. (503) 221-1811; fax (503) 224-8936; e-mail cgegawa@cgjpdx.org; internet www.portland.us.emb-japan.go.jp; Consul-Gen. AKIO EGAWA.

Consulate-General, Nashville: 1801 West End Ave, Suite 900, Nashville, TN 37203; tel. (615) 340-4300; fax (615) 340-4311; e-mail info@cgjnashville.org; internet www.nashville.us.emb-japan.go.jp; Consul-Gen. KOICHI FUNAYAMA.

Consulate-General, Houston: 2 Houston Center, Suite 3000, 909 Fannin St, Houston, TX 77002; tel. (713) 652-2977; fax (713) 651-7822; e-mail info@cgjhou.org; internet www.houston.us.emb-japan.go.jp; Consul-Gen. TSUTOMU OSAWA.

Consulate-General, Seattle: 601 Union St, Suite 500, Seattle, WA 98101; tel. (206) 682-9107; fax (206) 624-9097; e-mail info@cgjapansea.org; internet www.seattle.us.emb-japan.go.jp; Consul-Gen. MITSUNORI NAMBA.

JORDAN

Embassy: 3504 International Dr., NW, Washington, DC 20008; tel. (202) 966-2664; fax (202) 966-3110; e-mail hkjembassydc@jordanembassyus.org; internet www.jordanembassyus.org; Ambassador HRH Prince ZEID RA'AD AL-HUSSEIN.

KAZAKHSTAN

Embassy: 1401 16th St, NW, Washington, DC 20036; tel. (202) 232-5488; fax (202) 232-5845; e-mail zakh.embusa@verizon.net; internet www.kazakhembus.com; Ambassador ERLAN A. IDRISSOV.

KENYA

Embassy: 2249 R St, NW, Washington, DC 20008; tel. (202) 387-6101; fax (202) 462-3829; e-mail information@kenyaembassy.com; internet www.kenyaembassy.com; Ambassador PETER N. R. O. OGEGO.

Consulate-General, Los Angeles: Park Mile Plaza, Mezzanine Floor, 4801 Wilshire Blvd, Los Angeles, CA 90010; tel. (323) 939-2408; fax (323) 939-2412; e-mail losangeles@kenyaembassy.com; Consul-Gen. MARY NYAMBURA KAMAU.

Consulate-General, New York: 866 United Nations Plaza, Suite 4016, New York, NY 10017; tel. (212) 421-4741; fax (212) 486-1985; e-mail newyorkconsulate@kenyaembassy.com; Consul CHARLES MANTHI MUENDO.

KOREA, REPUBLIC

Embassy: 2450 Massachusetts Ave, NW, Washington, DC 20008; tel. (202) 939-5600; fax (202) 387-0250; e-mail webmaster@dynamic-korea.com; internet www.koreaembassy.org; Ambassador TAE-SIK LEE.

Consulate-General, Los Angeles: 3243 Wilshire Blvd, Los Angeles, CA 90010; tel. (213) 385-9300; fax (213) 385-1849; e-mail consul-la@mofat.go.kr; internet www.koreanconsulatela.org; Consul-Gen. BYUNG-HYO CHOI.

Consulate-General, San Francisco: 3500 Clay St, San Francisco, CA 94118; tel. (415) 921-2251; fax (415) 921-5946; e-mail consularsf@mofat.go.kr; internet usa-sanfrancisco.mofat.go.kr; Consul-Gen. BON-WOO KOO.

Consulate-General, Atlanta: International Tower, Suite 500, 229 Peachtree St, NE, Atlanta, GA 30303; tel. (404) 522-1611; fax (404) 521-3169; internet www.koreanconsul.org; Consul-Gen. KWANG-JAE LEE.

Consulate-General, Honolulu: 2756 Pali Hwy, Honolulu, HI 96817; tel. (808) 595-6109; fax (808) 595-3046; e-mail consulatehi@mofat.go.kr; internet usa-honolulu.mofat.go.kr; Consul-Gen. BONG-JOO KIM.

Consulate-General, Chicago: 455 North City Front Plaza Dr. NBC Tower, Suite 2700, Chicago, IL 60611; tel. (312) 822-9485; fax

(312) 822-9849; e-mail chicago@mofat.go.kr; internet www.chicagoconsulate.org; Consul-Gen. SUNG-HWAN SON.

Consulate-General, Boston: 1 Gateway Center, Suite 251, 300 Washington St, Boston, MA 02458; tel. (617) 641-2830; fax (617) 641-2831; e-mail kcgboston@mofat.go.kr; internet www.kcgboston.org; Consul-Gen. JOO-SEOK KIM.

Consulate-General, New York: 335 East 45th St, 4th Floor, New York, NY 10017; tel. (646) 674-6000; fax (646) 674-6023; e-mail info@koreanconsulate.org; internet www.koreanconsulate.org; Consul-Gen. KYUNG-KEUN KIM.

Consulate-General, Houston: 1990 Post Oak Blvd, Suite 1250, Houston, TX 77056; tel. (713) 961-0186; fax (713) 961-3340; e-mail con-hu@mofat.go.kr; internet www.koreahouston.org; Consul-Gen. JUNG-KEUN KIM.

Consulate-General, Seattle: 2033 Sixth Ave, Suite 1125, Seattle, WA 98121; tel. (206) 441-1011; fax (206) 441-7912; e-mail koreanconsulate@yahoo.com; internet usa-seattle.mofat.go.kr; Consul-Gen. HAR-YONG LEE.

KUWAIT

Embassy: 2600 Virginia Ave, NW, Suite 404, Washington, DC 20037; tel. (202) 338-0211; fax (202) 338-0957; e-mail kio@kuwait-info.org; Ambassador Sheikh JABER AL-AHMED AL-SABAH.

Consulate-General, Los Angeles: 1801 Ave of the Stars, Suite 1010, Los Angeles, CA 90067; tel. (310) 556-0300; fax (310) 556-0400; e-mail info@kuwaitconsulate.org; internet kuwaitconsulate.org; Consul-Gen. MUHYEE ALDEEN RASHEED AL-FELAIJ.

KYRGYZSTAN

Embassy: 2360 Massachusetts Ave, NW, Washington, DC 20008; tel. (202) 449-9822; fax (202) 386-7550; e-mail consul@kgembassy.org; internet www.kgembassy.org; Ambassador ZAMIRA BEKSULTANOVNA SYDYKOVA.

LAOS

Embassy: 2222 S St, NW, Washington, DC 20008; tel. (202) 332-6416; fax (202) 332-4923; e-mail laoemb@verizon.net; internet www.laoembassy.com; Ambassador PHIANE PHILAKONE.

LATVIA

Embassy: 2306 Massachusetts Ave, NW, Washington, DC 20008; tel. (202) 328-2840; fax (202) 328-2860; e-mail embassy.usa@mfa.gov.lv; internet www.latvia-usa.org; Ambassador ANDREJS PILDEGOVICS.

LEBANON

Embassy: 2560 28th St, NW, Washington, DC 20008; tel. (202) 939-6300; fax (202) 939-6324; e-mail info@lebanonembassyus.org; internet www.lebanonembassyus.org; Ambassador ANTOINE CHEDID.

Consulate-General, Los Angeles: 660 South Figueroa St, Suite 1050, Los Angeles, CA 90017; tel. (213) 243-0999; fax (213) 612-5070; e-mail consuloflebanon@sbcglobal.net; Consul-Gen. FADI HAJJ ALI.

Consulate-General, Detroit: New Center One Bldg, 3031 West Grand Blvd, Suite 560, Detroit, MI 48202; tel. (313) 758-0753; fax (313) 758-0756; e-mail info@lebconsdet.org; internet www.lebconsdet.org; Consul-Gen. BASHIR TAWK.

Consulate-General, New York: 9 East 76th St, New York, NY 10021; tel. (212) 744-7905; fax (212) 794-1510; e-mail lebconsny@aol.com; internet www.lebconsny.org; Consul-Gen. ANTOINE AZZAM.

LESOTHO

Embassy: 2511 Massachusetts Ave, NW, Washington, DC 20008; tel. (202) 797-5533; fax (202) 234-6815; e-mail lesothoembassy@verizon.net; internet www.lesothoemb-usa.gov.ls; Ambassador DAVID MOHLOMI RANTEKOA.

LIBERIA

Embassy: 5201 16th St, NW, Washington, DC 20011; tel. (202) 723-0437; fax (202) 723-0436; e-mail info@embassyofliberia.org; internet www.embassyofliberia.org; Ambassador NATHANIEL BARNES.

Consulate-General, New York: 866 United Nations Plaza, Suite 478, New York, NY 10017; tel. (212) 687-1025; fax (212) 599-3189; e-mail info@liberiaconsulate.com; internet www.liberiaconsulate.com; Consul-Gen. JEFF GONGOER DWANA.

LIBYA

Liaison Office: 2600 Virginia Ave, NW, Suite 705, Washington, DC 20037; tel. (202) 944-9601; fax (202) 944-9606; e-mail libya@libyanbureau-dc.org; internet libyanbureau-dc.org; Chief of Office ALI SULEIMAN AUJALI.

LIECHTENSTEIN

Embassy: 888 17th St, NW, Suite 1250, Washington, DC 20006; tel. (202) 331-0590; fax (202) 331-3221; e-mail tamara.brunhart@was.rep.llv.li; internet www.liechtenstein.li; Ambassador CLAUDIA FRITSCHE.

LITHUANIA

Embassy: 2300 Clarendon Blvd, Suite 302, Arlington, VA 22201; tel. (202) 234-5860; fax (202) 328-0466; e-mail info@ltembassyus.org; internet www.ltembassyus.org; Ambassador AUDRIUS BRUZGA.

Consulate-General, Chicago: 211 East Ontario St, Suite 1500, Chicago, IL 60611; tel. (312) 397-0382; fax (312) 397-0385; e-mail admin@ltconschi.org; internet www.konsulatas.org; Consul-Gen. ARVYDAS DAUNORAVICIUS.

Consulate-General, New York: 420 Fifth Ave, 3rd Floor, New York, NY 10018; tel. (212) 354-7849; fax (212) 354-7911; e-mail kons.niujorkas@urm.lt; internet www.ltconsny.org; Consul-Gen. JONAS PASLAUSKAS.

LUXEMBOURG

Embassy: 2200 Massachusetts Ave, NW, Washington, DC 20008; tel. (202) 265-4171; fax (202) 328-8270; e-mail washington.info@mae.etat.lu; internet www.luxembourg-usa.org; Ambassador JEAN-PAUL SENNINGER.

Consulate-General, San Francisco: 1 Sansome St, Suite 830, San Francisco, CA 94104; tel. (415) 788-0816; fax (415) 788-0985; e-mail info@luxembourgsf.com; internet www.luxembourgsf.com; Consul-Gen. GEORGES FABER.

Consulate-General, New York: 17 Beekman Pl., New York, NY 10022; tel. (212) 888-6664; fax (212) 888-6116; e-mail newyork.cg@mae.etat.lu; internet www.luxembourgnyc.org; Consul-Gen. FRANÇOIS KNAFF.

MACEDONIA, FORMER YUGOSLAV REPUBLIC

Embassy: 2129 Wyoming Ave, Washington, DC 20008; tel. (202) 667-0501; fax (202) 667-2131; e-mail usoffice@macedonianembassy.org; internet www.macedonianembassy.org; Ambassador Dr ZORAN JOLEVSKI.

Consulate-General, Detroit: 2000 Town Center, Suite 1130, Southfield, Detroit, MI 48075; tel. (248) 354-5537; fax (248) 354-5538; e-mail detroit@mfa.gov.mk; Consul-Gen. JORDAN VESELINOV.

MADAGASCAR

Embassy: 2374 Massachusetts Ave, NW, Washington, DC 20008; tel. (202) 265-5525; fax (202) 265-3034; e-mail malagasy@embassy.org; Ambassador JOCELYN RADIFERA.

MALAWI

Embassy: 1029 Vermont Ave, NW, Suite 1000, Washington, DC 20005; tel. (202) 721-0270; fax (202) 721-0288; e-mail malawidc@aol.com; internet www.malawiembassy-dc.org; Ambassador HAWA NDILOWE.

MALAYSIA

Embassy: 3516 International Ct, NW, Washington, DC 20008; tel. (202) 572-9700; fax (202) 572-9882; e-mail malwashdc@kln.gov.my; internet www.kln.gov.my/perwakilan/washington; Chargé d'affaires a.i. ILANGO KARUPPANNAN.

Consulate-General, Los Angeles: 550 South Hope St, Suite 400, Los Angeles, CA 90071-1203; tel. (213) 892-1238; fax (213) 892-9031; e-mail info@malaysianconsulatela.com; internet www.malaysianconsulatela.com; Consul-Gen. NORMAN MUHAMAD.

Consulate-General, New York: 313 East 43rd St, New York, NY 10017; tel. (212) 490-2722; fax (212) 490-2049; e-mail malnycg@kln.gov.my; Consul-Gen. MOHAMAD SADIK BIN KETHERGANY.

MALDIVES

Embassy: 1111 19th St, NW, Suite 211, Washington, DC 20036; tel. (202) 463-6901; fax (202) 463-6905; e-mail info@maldivesembassy.us; internet www.maldivesembassy.us; Ambassador MOHAMED HUSSAIN MANIKU.

MALI

Embassy: 2130 R St, NW, Washington, DC 20008; tel. (202) 332-2249; fax (202) 332-6603; e-mail infos@maliembassy.us; internet www.maliembassy.us; Ambassador ABDOULAYE DIOP.

MALTA

Embassy: 2017 Connecticut Ave, NW, Washington, DC 20008; tel. (202) 462-3611; fax (202) 387-5470; e-mail maltaembassy.washington@gov.mt; Ambassador MARK MICELI-FARRUGIA.

MARSHALL ISLANDS

Embassy: 2433 Massachusetts Ave, NW, Washington, DC 20008; tel. (202) 234-5414; fax (202) 232-3236; e-mail info@rmiembassyus.org; internet www.rmiembassyus.org; Chargé d'affaires a.i. CHARLES A. PAUL.

Consulate-General, Honolulu: 1888 Lusitana St, Suite 301, Honolulu, HI 96813; tel. (808) 545-7767; fax (808) 545-7211; Consul-Gen. PHILIP ANUNGAR.

MAURITANIA

Embassy: 2129 Leroy Pl., NW, Washington, DC 20008; tel. (202) 232-5700; fax (202) 319-2623; e-mail info@mauritaniembassy-usa.org; Ambassador IBRAHIMA DIA.

MAURITIUS

Embassy: 4301 Connecticut Ave, NW, Suite 441, Washington, DC 20008; tel. (202) 244-1491; fax (202) 966-0983; e-mail mauritius.embassy@prodigy.net; Ambassador KEERTEECOOMAR RUHEE.

MEXICO

Embassy: 1911 Pennsylvania Ave, NW, Washington, DC 20006; tel. (202) 728-1600; fax (202) 728-1698; internet www.embassyofmexico.org; Ambassador ARTURO SARUKHAN CASAMITJANA.

Consulate-General, Nogales: 571 North Grand Ave, Nogales, AZ 85621; tel. (520) 287-2521; fax (520) 287-3175; e-mail consulmex2@mchsi.com; internet portal.sre.gob.mx/nogales; Consul-Gen. BEATRIZ LÓPEZ GARGALLO.

Consulate-General, Phoenix: 1990 West Camelback Rd, Suite 110, Phoenix, AZ 85015; tel. (602) 242-7398; fax (602) 242-2957; e-mail contactenos@consulmexphoenix.phxcoxmail.com; internet www.sre.gob.mx/phoenix; Consul-Gen. CARLOS FLORES VIZCARRA.

Consulate-General, Los Angeles: 2401 West Sixth St, Los Angeles, CA 90057; tel. (213) 351-6800; fax (213) 389-9186; e-mail lapublico@sre.gob.mx; internet www.sre.gob.mx/losangeles; Consul-Gen. JUAN MARCOS GUTIÉRREZ GONZÁLEZ.

Consulate-General, Sacramento: 1010 Eighth St, Sacramento, CA 95814; tel. (916) 441-3287; fax (916) 441-3147; e-mail sacramento@sre.gob.mx; internet portal.sre.gob.mx/sacramento; Consul-Gen. ALEJANDRA MARÍA GABRIELA BOLOGNA ZUBIKARAI.

Consulate-General, San Diego: 1549 India St, San Diego, CA 92101; tel. (619) 231-8414; fax (619) 231-4802; e-mail info@consulmexsd.org; internet portal.sre.gob.mx/sandiego; Consul-Gen. MARÍA DE LOS REMEDIOS GÓMEZ ARNAU.

Consulate-General, San Francisco: 532 Folsom St, San Francisco, CA 94102; tel. (415) 354-1700; fax (415) 495-3971; e-mail consfrancisco@sre.gob.mx; internet www.sre.gob.mx/sanfrancisco; Consul-Gen. CARLOS FÉLIX CORONA.

Consulate-General, San Jose: 540 North First St, San Jose, CA 95112; tel. (408) 294-3414; fax (408) 294-4506; e-mail consjose@sre.gob.mx; internet www.consulmexsj.com; Consul-Gen. DAVID FIGUEROA ORTEGA.

Consulate-General, Denver: 5350 Leetsdale Dr., Suite 100, Denver, CO 80206; tel. (303) 331-1110; fax (303) 331-0169; e-mail informacion@consulmex-denver.com; internet www.consulmex-denver.com; internet www.consulmex-denver.com; Consul-Gen. EDUARDO ARNAL PALOMERA.

Consulate-General, Miami: 5975 South West 72nd St, Suite 301, Miami, FL 33143; tel. (786) 268-4900; fax (786) 268-4895; e-mail info@mexicomiami.org; internet www.sre.gob.mx/miami; Consul-Gen. JUAN MIGUEL GUTIÉRREZ TINOCO.

Consulate-General, Atlanta: 2600 Apple Valley Rd, Atlanta, GA 30319; tel. (404) 266-2233; fax (404) 266-2302; e-mail information@consulmexatlanta.org; internet www.consulmexatlanta.org; Consul-Gen. SALVADOR DE LARA RANGEL.

Consulate-General, Chicago: 204 South Ashland Ave, Chicago, IL 60607; tel. (312) 855-1380; fax (312) 491-9072; e-mail info@consulmexchicago.com; internet www.consulmexchicago.com; Consul-Gen. MANUEL RODRÍGUEZ ARRIAGA.

Consulate-General, Boston: 20 Park Plaza, Suite 506, 20 Park Plaza, Boston, MA 02116; tel. (617) 426-4181; fax (617) 695-1957; e-mail cmxboston@conversent.net; internet www.sre.gob.mx/boston; Consul-Gen. (vacant).

Consulate-General, New York: 27 East 39th St, New York, NY 10016; tel. (212) 217-6400; fax (212) 217-6493; e-mail webmaster@consulmexny.org; internet www.sre.gob.mx/nuevayork; Consul-Gen. RUBÉN BELTRÁN GUERRERO.

Consulate-General, Austin: 800 Brazos St, Suite 330, Austin, TX 78701; tel. (512) 478-2866; fax (512) 478-8008; e-mail austin@sre.gob.mx; internet www.sre.gob.mx/austin; Consul-Gen. ROSALBA OJEDA Y CÁRDENAS.

Consulate-General, Dallas: 8855 North Stemmons Freeway, Dallas, TX 75247; tel. (214) 252-9250; fax (214) 630-3511; e-mail info@consulmexdallas.com; internet www.sre.gob.mx/dallas; Consul-Gen. ENRIQUE HUBBARD URREA.

Consulate-General, El Paso: 910 East San Antonio St, El Paso, TX 79901; tel. (915) 532-5540; fax (915) 532-7163; e-mail consulmexepa@elp.rr.co; internet www.sre.gob.mx/elpaso; Consul-Gen. ROBERTO RODRÍGUEZ HERNÁNDEZ.

Consulate-General, Houston: 4507 San Jacinto St, Houston, TX 77044; tel. (713) 271-6800; fax (713) 271-3201; e-mail conhouston@wt.net; internet www.sre.gob.mx/houston; Consul-Gen. CARLOS I. GONZÁLEZ MAGALLÓN.

Consulate-General, Laredo: 1612 Farragut St, Laredo, TX 78040; tel. (956) 723-0990; internet www.sre.gob.mx/laredo; Consul-Gen. MIGUEL ANGEL ISIDRO RODRÍGUEZ.

Consulate-General, San Antonio: 127 Navarro St, San Antonio, TX 78205; tel. (210) 227-9145; fax (210) 227-1817; e-mail info@consulmexsat.org; internet portal.sre.gob.mx/sanantonio; Consul-Gen. ARMANDO ORTIZ ROCHA.

MICRONESIA, FEDERATED STATES

Embassy: 1725 N St, NW, Washington, DC 20036; tel. (202) 223-4383; fax (202) 223-4391; e-mail firstsecretary@fsmembassydc.org; internet www.fsmembassydc.org; Ambassador YOSIWO P. GEORGE.

Consulate-General, Honolulu: 3049 Ualena St, Suite 904, Honolulu, HI 96819; tel. (808) 836-4775; fax (808) 836-6896; e-mail fsmcghnl@aol.com; Consul-Gen. AKILLINO SUSAIA.

MOLDOVA

Embassy: 2101 S St, NW, Washington, DC 20008; tel. (202) 667-1130; fax (202) 667-1204; e-mail washington@mfa.md; internet www.embassyrm.org; Ambassador NICOLAE CHIRTOACA.

MONACO

Embassy: 2314 Wyoming Ave, NW, Washington, DC 20008; tel. (202) 234-1530; fax (202) 552-5778; e-mail embassy@monaco-usa.org; internet www.monaco-usa.org; Ambassador GILLES ALEXANDRE NOGHÈS.

Consulate-General, New York: 565 Fifth Ave, 23rd Floor, New York, NY 10017; tel. (212) 286-0500; fax (212) 286-1574; e-mail info@monaco-consulate.com; internet www.monaco-consulate.com; Consul-Gen. MAGUY J. MACCARIO-DOYLE.

MONGOLIA

Embassy: 2833 M St, NW, Washington, DC 20007; tel. (202) 333-7117; fax (202) 298-9227; e-mail esyam@mongolianembassy.us; internet www.mongolianembassy.us; Ambassador KHASBAZAR BEKHBAT.

MONTENEGRO

Embassy: 1610 New Hampshire Ave, NW, Washington, DC 20009; tel. (202) 234-6108; fax (202) 234-6109; Ambassador MIODRAG VLAHOVIĆ.

Consulate-General, New York: 801 Second Ave, Suite 7, New York, NY 10017; tel. (212) 661-5400; fax (212) 661-5466; e-mail office@montenegroconsulatenewyork.info; Consul-Gen. BRANKO MILIĆ.

MOROCCO

Embassy: 1601 21st St, NW, Washington, DC 20009; tel. (202) 462-7980; fax (202) 265-0161; e-mail fmehdi@embassyofmorocco.us; Ambassador AZIZ MEKOUAR.

Consulate-General, New York: 10 East 40th St, New York, NY 10016; tel. (212) 758-2625; fax (212) 779-7441; e-mail info@moroccanconsulate.com; internet www.moroccanconsulate.com; Consul-Gen. MOHAMED KARMOUNE.

MOZAMBIQUE

Embassy: 1525 New Hampshire Ave, NW, Washington, DC 20036; tel. (202) 293-7146; fax (202) 835-9245; e-mail embamoc@aol.com; internet www.embamoc-usa.org; Ambassador ARMANDO ALEXANDRE PANGUENE.

MYANMAR

Embassy: 2300 S St, NW, Washington, DC 20008-4089; tel. (202) 332-9044; fax (202) 332-9046; Chargé d'affaires a.i. MYINT LWIN.

Consulate-General, New York: 10 East 77th St, New York, NY 10021; tel. (212) 535-1310; fax (212) 737-2421; Consul-Gen. (vacant).

NAMIBIA

Embassy: 1605 New Hampshire Ave, NW, Washington, DC 20009; tel. (202) 986-0540; fax (202) 986-0443; e-mail info@namibianembassyusa.org; internet www.namibianembassyusa.org; Ambassador PATRICK NANDAGO.

NAURU

Embassy: 800 Second Ave, New York, NY 10017; tel. (212) 937-0074; fax (212) 937-0079; Ambassador MARLENE MOSES.

NEPAL

Embassy: 2131 Leroy Pl., NW, Washington, DC 20008; tel. (202) 667-4550; fax (202) 667-5534; e-mail info@nepalembassyusa.org; internet www.nepalembassyusa.org; Ambassador SURESH CHANDRA CHALISE.

Consulate-General, New York: 820 Second Ave, Suite 17-B, New York, NY 10017; tel. (212) 370-3988; fax (212) 953-2038; e-mail nepal@un.int; Consul DURGA B. SUBEDI.

NETHERLANDS

Embassy: 4200 Linnean Ave, NW, Washington, DC 20008; tel. (202) 244-5300; fax (202) 362-3430; e-mail was@minbuza.nl; internet www.netherlands-embassy.org; Ambassador REGINA JONES-BOS.

Consulate-General, Los Angeles: 11766 Wilshire Blvd, Suite 1150, Los Angeles, CA 90025; tel. (310) 268-1598; fax (310) 312-0989; e-mail los@minbuza.nl; internet www.ncla.org; Consul-Gen. MADELIEN A. J. DE PLANQUE.

Consulate-General, Miami: 701 Brickell Ave, 5th Floor, Miami, FL 33131; tel. (786) 866-0480; fax (786) 866-0497; e-mail mia@minbuza.nl; internet www.cgmiami.org; Consul-Gen. LUCITA C. G. MOENIR ALAM.

Consulate-General, Chicago: 303 East Wacker Dr., Suite 2600, Chicago, IL 60601; tel. (312) 856-0110; fax (312) 856-9218; e-mail chi@minbuza.nl; internet www.cgchicago.org; Consul-Gen. DIRK WILLEM SCHIFF.

Consulate-General, New York: 1 Rockefeller Plaza, 11th Floor, New York, NY 10020-2094; tel. (212) 246-1429; fax (212) 333-3603; e-mail nlgovnyc@spacelab.net; internet www.cgny.org; Consul-Gen. HUGO GAJUS SCHELTEMA.

NEW ZEALAND

Embassy: 37 Observatory Circle, NW, Washington, DC 20008; tel. (202) 328-4800; fax (202) 667-5227; e-mail info@nzemb.org; internet www.nzembassy.com; Ambassador ROY FERGUSON.

Consulate-General, Los Angeles: 2425 Olympic Blvd, Suite 600E, Santa Monica, CA 90404; tel. (310) 566-6555; fax (310) 566-6556; e-mail contact@nzcgla.com; internet www.nzcgla.com; Consul-Gen. JOHN R. MATAIRA.

Consulate-General, New York: 222 East 41st St, Suite 2510, New York, NY 10017; tel. (212) 832-4038; fax (212) 832-7602; Consul CHRISTOPHER TOZER.

NICARAGUA

Embassy: 1627 New Hampshire Ave, NW, Washington, DC 20009; tel. (202) 939-6570; fax (202) 939-6545; e-mail info@embanic.org; Ambassador ARTURO JOSÉ CRUZ SEQUEIRA.

Consulate-General, Los Angeles: 3500 Wilshire Blvd, Suite 200, Los Angeles, CA 90010; tel. (213) 252-1170; fax (213) 252-1177; e-mail carloscarrion_5@hotmail.com; Consul-Gen. CARLOS JOSÉ CARRIÓN CORONEL.

Consulate-General, San Francisco: 870 Market St, Suite 1050, San Francisco, CA 94102; tel. (415) 765-6821; fax (415) 765-6826; e-mail conicsf@pacbell.net; Consul MAYRA CENTENO GADEA.

Consulate-General, Miami: 8532 South West Eighth St, Suite 270, Miami, FL 33144; tel. (305) 265-1415; fax (305) 265-1780; e-mail contactenos@consuladonicamiami.com; internet www.consuladonicamiami.com; Consul-Gen. LUIS ALBERTO MARTÍNEZ.

Consulate-General, New York: 820 Second Ave, Suite 802, New York, NY 10017; tel. (212) 983-1981; fax (212) 989-5528; e-mail eliseonum@aol.com; Consul CÉSAR MERCADO.

Consulate-General, Houston: 6300 Hillcrof, Suite 250, Houston, TX 77081; tel. (713) 789-2762; fax (713) 789-3164; e-mail ma.mercedesbeck@sbcglobal.net; Consul MICHAEL JOHN CORDÚA.

NIGER

Embassy: 2204 R St, NW, Washington, DC 20008; tel. (202) 483-4224; fax (202) 683-3169; e-mail ambassadeniger@hotmail.com; internet www.nigerembassyusa.org; Ambassador AMINATA DJIBRILLA MAIGA TOURÉ.

NIGERIA

Embassy: 3519 International Ct, NW, Washington, DC 20008; tel. (202) 986-8400; fax (202) 362-6541; e-mail babalola@nigeriaembassyusa.org; internet www.nigeriaembassyusa.org; Ambassador OLUWOLE ROTIMI.

Consulate-General, Atlanta: 8060 Roswell Rd, Dunwoody, Atlanta, GA 30350; tel. (770) 394-5745; fax (770) 394-4671; e-mail info@nigeria-consulate-atl.org; internet www.nigeria-consulate-atl.org; Hon. Consul-Gen. C. N. OKAFOR.

Consulate-General, New York: 828 Second Ave, New York, NY 10017; tel. (212) 808-0301; fax (212) 682-4789; e-mail cgnny@nigeriahouse.com; internet www.nigeriahouse.com; Consul-Gen. IBRAHIM AUWALU.

NORWAY

Embassy: 2720 34th St, NW, Washington, DC 20008-2714; tel. (202) 333-6000; fax (202) 337-0870; e-mail emb.washington@mfa.no; internet www.norway.org; Ambassador WEGGER CHRISTIAN STRØMMEN.

Consulate-General, San Francisco: 20 California St, 6th Floor, San Francisco, CA 94111-4830; tel. (415) 986-0766; fax (415) 986-3318; e-mail cgsfo@mfa.no; internet www.norway.org/sanfrancisco; Consul-Gen. STEN ARNE ROSNES.

Consulate-General, New York: 825 Third Ave, 38th Floor, New York, NY 10022-7584; tel. (212) 421-7333; fax (212) 754-0583; e-mail cg.newyork@mfa.no; internet www.norway.org/newyork; Consul-Gen. SISSEL BREIE.

Consulate-General, Houston: 2777 Allen Parkway, Suite 1185, Houston, TX 77019-2123; tel. (713) 521-2900; fax (713) 521-9648; e-mail cg.houston@mfa.no; internet www.norway.org/houston; Consul-Gen. LASSE SIGURD SEIM.

OMAN

Embassy: 2535 Belmont Rd, NW, Washington, DC 20008; tel. (202) 387-1980; fax (202) 745-4933; Ambassador HUNAINA SULTAN AHMED AL-MUGHAIRY.

PAKISTAN

Embassy: 3517 International Ct, NW, Washington, DC 20008; tel. (202) 243-6500; fax (202) 387-0484; e-mail info@embassyofpakistanusa.org; internet www.embassyofpakistanusa.org; Ambassador HUSAIN HAQQANI.

Consulate-General, Los Angeles: 10850 Wilshire Blvd, Suite 1250, Los Angeles, CA 90024; tel. (310) 441-5114; fax (310) 474-4871; e-mail info@pakconsulatela.org; internet www.pakconsulatela.org; Consul-Gen. SYED IBNE ABBAS.

Consulate-General, Chicago: 333 North Michigan Ave, Suite 728, Chicago, IL 60601; tel. (312) 781-1831; fax (312) 781-1838; e-mail parepchicago@yahoo.com; Consul-Gen. Dr AMAN RASHID.

Consulate-General, New York: 12 East 65th St, New York, NY 10021; tel. (212) 879-5800; fax (212) 517-6987; e-mail info@pakistanconsulateny.org; internet www.pakistanconsulateny.org; Consul-Gen. M. MOHSIN RAZI.

Consulate-General, Houston: 11850 Jones Rd, Houston, TX 77070; tel. (281) 890-2223; fax (281) 890-1433; e-mail consulate@pakistanconsulatehouston.org; internet www.pakistanconsulatehouston.org; Consul-Gen. MOHAMMAD AQIL NADEEM.

PALAU

Embassy: 1700 Pennsylvania Ave, NW, Suite 400, Washington, DC 20006; tel. (202) 452-6814; fax (202) 452-6281; e-mail info@palauembassy.com; internet www.palauembassy.com; Ambassador HERSEY KYOTA.

PANAMA

Embassy: 2862 McGill Terrace, NW, Washington, DC 20008; tel. (202) 483-1407; fax (202) 483-8413; e-mail info@embassyofpanama.org; internet www.embassyofpanama.org; Ambassador FEDERICO A. HUMBERT ARIAS.

Consulate-General, San Diego: 402 West Broadway Way, Suite 670, San Diego, CA 92101; tel. (619) 235-4441; fax (619) 235-4442; e-mail secpanconwest@sbcglobal.net; Consul-Gen. EDUARDO ARANGO ARIAS.

Consulate-General, Miami: 5757 Blue Lagoon Dr., Suite 320, Miami, FL 33126; tel. (305) 447-3700; fax (305) 447-4142; e-mail ptymia@bellsouth.net; Consul-Gen. ALBERTO GONZÁLEZ ABADÍA.

Consulate-General, Tampa: 2211 East Third Ave, Tampa, FL 33605; tel. (813) 283-0063; fax (813) 283-0064; e-mail consuladopanama@aol.com; Consul-Gen. FERNANDO NÚÑEZ FABREGA.

Consulate-General, New Orleans: World Trade Center Bldg, Suite 2424, 2 Canal St, New Orleans, LA 70130; tel. (504) 525-3458; fax (504) 524-8960; e-mail consulgeneral@consulateofpanama.com; Consul-Gen. ERICH A. RODRÍGUEZ TEJEIRA.

Consulate-General, New York: 1212 Ave of the Americas, 6th Floor, New York, NY 10036; tel. (212) 840-2450; fax (212) 840-2469; e-mail vbonilla@nyconsul.com; internet www.nyconsul.com; Consul-Gen. ROBERTO PASCUAL.

Consulate-General, Philadelphia: 124 Chestnut St, Philadelphia, PA 19106; tel. (215) 574-2994; fax (215) 574-4225; e-mail panama@foreignconsulate.com; Consul-Gen. GEORGIA ATHANASOPULOS.

Consulate-General, Houston: 24 Greenway Plaza, Suite 1307, Houston, TX 77046; tel. (713) 622-4451; fax (713) 622-4468; e-mail panama3@conpahouston.com; internet www.conpahouston.com; Consul-Gen. ADSINAR R. CAJAR.

PAPUA NEW GUINEA

Embassy: 1779 Massachusetts Ave, NW, Suite 805, Washington, DC 20036; tel. (202) 745-3680; fax (202) 745-3679; e-mail info@pngembassy.org; internet www.pngembassy.org; Ambassador EVAN J. PAKI.

PARAGUAY

Embassy: 2400 Massachusetts Ave, NW, Washington, DC 20008; tel. (202) 483-6960; fax (202) 234-4508; e-mail secretaria@embaparusa.gov.py; internet www.embaparusa.gov.py; Ambassador JAMES SPALDING HELLMERS.

Consulate-General, Los Angeles: 6033 West Century Blvd, Suite 985, Los Angeles, CA 90045; tel. (310) 417-9500; fax (310) 417-9520; e-mail consulpar@sbcglobal.net; internet www.paraguayconsulatela.com; Consul-Gen. SERGIO ADRIÁN BESTARD.

Consulate-General, Miami: 25 South East Second Ave, Suite 705, Miami, FL 33154; tel. (305) 374-9090; fax (305) 374-5522; e-mail paraguay@bellsouth.net; internet www.paraguaymiami.org; Consul-Gen. CARLOS A. ORTIZ BAREIRO.

Consulate-General, New York: 211 East 43rd St, Suite 2101, New York, NY 10017; tel. (212) 682-9441; fax (212) 682-9443; e-mail consulparny@aol.com; Consul-Gen. JUAN A. BAIARDI QUESNEL.

PERU

Embassy: 1700 Massachusetts Ave, NW, Washington, DC 20036; tel. (202) 833-9860; fax (202) 659-8124; e-mail webadmin@embassyofperu.us; internet www.peruvianembassy.us; Ambassador FELIPE ORTIZ DE ZEVALLOS MADUENO.

Consulate-General, Los Angeles: 3450 Wilshire Blvd, Suite 800, Los Angeles, CA 90010; tel. (213) 252-5910; fax (213) 252-8130; e-mail conperla@mpowercom.net; Consul-Gen. ALBERTO MASSA MURAZZI.

Consulate-General, San Francisco: 870 Market St, Suite 1067, San Francisco, CA 94102; tel. (415) 362-5185; fax (415) 362-2836; e-mail conpersfco@aol.com; Consul-Gen. NICOLÁS A. RONCAGLIOLO HIGUERAS.

Consulate-General, Denver: 1001 South Monaco Pkwy, Suite 210, Denver, CO 80224; tel. (303) 355-8555; e-mail conper_denver@consuladoperu.net; Consul-Gen. MARÍA SUSANA LANDAVERI PORTURAS.

Consulate-General, Hartford: 250D Main St, Suite D, Hartford, CT; tel. (860) 548-0266; fax (860) 548-0094; e-mail conperhartford@aol.com; Consul-Gen. JOSÉ ARSENIO BENZAQUEN PEREA.

Consulate-General, Miami: 444 Brickell Ave, Suite M-135, Miami, FL 33131; tel. (305) 374-1305; fax (305) 381-6027; e-mail informacion@consulado-peru.com; internet www.consulado-peru.com; Consul-Gen. JORGE ROMÁN MOREY.

Consulate-General, Chicago: 180 North Michigan Ave, Suite 1830, Chicago, IL 60601; tel. (312) 782-1599; fax (312) 704-6969; e-mail conperchig@aol.com; internet www.consuladodelperuenchicago.tk; Consul-Gen. JOSÉ EDUARDO CHAVARRI GARCÍA.

Consulate-General, Boston: 20 Park Plaza, Suite 511, Boston, MA 02116; tel. (617) 338-2227; fax (617) 338-2742; e-mail consuladogeneral@conperboston.com; Consul-Gen. ALBERTO AURELIO VALENCIA CARLO.

Consulate-General, Paterson: Broadway Bank Bldg, Suite 1221, 100 Hamilton Plaza, Paterson, NJ 07505; tel. (973) 278-3324; fax (973) 278-0254; e-mail consultas@conpernj.org; Consul-Gen. JOSÉ ANTONIO GARCÍA TORRES.

Consulate-General, New York: 241 East 49th St, New York, NY 10017; tel. (212) 481-7419; fax (646) 735-3866; e-mail userperu12@aol.com; Consul-Gen. HELÍ ADELFO PELÁEZ CASTRO.

Consulate-General, Houston: 5177 Richmond Ave, Suite 695, Houston, TX 77056; tel. (713) 355-9517; fax (713) 355-9377; e-mail conperu@sbcglobal.net; Consul-Gen. CARLOS R. POLO.

PHILIPPINES

Embassy: 1600 Massachusetts Ave, NW, Washington, DC 20036; tel. (202) 467-9300; fax (202) 467-9417; e-mail info@philippineembassy-usa.org; internet www.philippineembassy-usa.org; Ambassador WILLY C. GAA.

Consulate-General, Los Angeles: 3600 Wilshire Blvd, Suite 500, Los Angeles, CA 90010; tel. (213) 639-0980; fax (213) 639-0990; e-mail losangelespcg@earthlink.net; internet www.philippineconsulatela.org; Consul-Gen. MARY JO BERNARDO ARAGON.

Consulate-General, San Francisco: 447 Sutter St, 6th Floor, San Francisco, CA 94108; tel. (415) 433-6666; fax (415) 421-2641; e-mail sanfranciscopcg2004@yahoo.com; internet www.philippineconsulate-sf.org; Consul-Gen. MARCIANO A. PAYNOR, Jr.

Consulate-General, Honolulu: 2433 Pali Hwy, Honolulu, HI 96817; tel. (808) 595-6316; fax (808) 595-2581; e-mail honolulu@hawaii.rr.com; Consul-Gen. ARIEL Y. ABADILLA.

Consulate-General, Chicago: 30 North Michigan Ave, Suite 2100, Chicago, IL 60602; tel. (312) 332-6458; fax (312) 332-3657; e-mail chicagopcg@sbcglobal.net; internet www.chicagopcg.com; Consul-Gen. BLESILA C. CABRERA.

Consulate-General, New York: Philippine Center, 556 Fifth Ave, New York, NY 10036-5095; tel. (212) 764-1330; fax (212) 382-1146; e-mail newyork@pcgny.net; internet www.pcgny.net; Consul-Gen. CECILIA B. REBONG.

POLAND

Embassy: 2640 16th St, NW, Washington, DC 20009; tel. (202) 234-3800; fax (202) 328-6271; e-mail dcm@polemb.us; internet www.polandembassy.org; Ambassador ROBERT KUPIECKI.

Consulate-General, Los Angeles: 12400 Wilshire Blvd, Suite 555, Los Angeles, CA 90025; tel. (310) 442-8500; fax (310) 442-8515; e-mail consulplla@consulplla.org; internet www.losangeleskg.polemb.net; Consul-Gen. PAULINA KAPUŚCIŃSKA.

Consulate-General, Chicago: 820 N. Orleans St, Suite 335, Chicago, IL 60610-1695; tel. (312) 337-8166; fax (312) 337-7841; e-mail polcon@interaccess.com; internet www.polishconsulatechicago.org; Consul-Gen. ZYGMUNT MATYNIA.

Consulate-General, New York: 233 Madison Ave, New York, NY 10016; tel. (212) 561-8160; fax (646) 237-2105; e-mail kgrpny@polishconsulateny.org; internet www.polandconsulateny.com; Consul-Gen. KRZYSZTOF W. KASPRZYK.

PORTUGAL

Embassy: 2012 Massachusetts Ave, NW, Washington, DC 20036; tel. (202) 328-8610; fax (202) 462-3726; internet www.embassyportugal-us.org; Ambassador JOÃO DE VALLERA.

Consulate-General, San Francisco: 3298 Washington St, San Francisco, CA 94115; tel. (415) 346-3400; fax (415) 346-1440; e-mail congenportugal@cgsfr.dgaccp.pt; Consul-Gen. ANTÓNIO JOSÉ ALVES DE CARVALHO.

Consulate-General, Boston: 1 Exeter Plaza, 7th Floor, Boston, MA 02116; tel. (617) 536-8740; fax (617) 536-2503; e-mail mail@cgbos.dgaccp.pt; Consul-Gen. MARIA MANUELA FREITAS BAIROS.

Consulate-General, Newark: The Legal Center, 1 Riverfront Plaza, Main Floor, Newark, NJ 07102; tel. (973) 643-4200; fax (973) 643-3900; e-mail mail@cnnew.dgaccp.pt; Consul-Gen. FRANCISCO DUARTE AZEVEDO.

Consulate-General, New York: 590 Fifth Ave, 3rd Floor, New York, NY 10036; tel. (212) 221-3165; fax (212) 221-3462; e-mail mail@cgnyk.dgaccp.pt; Consul-Gen. ALEXANDRE M. GALVÃO MEXIA DE ALMEIDA FERNANDES.

QATAR

Embassy: 2555 M St, NW, Washington, DC 20037; tel. (202) 274-1603; fax (202) 237-0061; e-mail info@qatarembassy.net; internet www.qatarembassy.net; Ambassador ALI BIN FAHAD AL-HAJRI.

Consulate-General, Houston: 1990 Post Oak Blvd, Suite 810, Houston, TX 77056; tel. (713) 355-8221; fax (713) 355-8184; Consul-Gen. ABDULLA AL-MEDADI.

ROMANIA

Embassy: 1607 23rd St, NW, Washington, DC 20008; tel. (202) 232-4747; fax (202) 232-4748; e-mail info@roembus.org; internet www.roembus.org; Ambassador ADRIAN COSMIN VIERITA.

Consulate-General, Los Angeles: 11766 Wilshire Blvd, Suite 560, Los Angeles, CA 90025; tel. (310) 444-0043; fax (310) 445-0043; e-mail consulat@consulateromania.net; internet www.consulateromania.net; Consul MIRCEA C. GHENEA.

Consulate-General, Chicago: 737 North Michigan Ave, Suite 1170, Chicago, IL 60611; tel. (312) 573-1315; fax (312) 573-9771; e-mail office@roconschicago.org; internet www.roconschicago.org; Consul-Gen. LUCIAN LEUŞTEAN.

Consulate-General, New York: 200 East 38th St, New York, NY 10016; tel. (212) 682-9122; fax (212) 972-8463; e-mail office@romconsny.org; internet newyork.mae.ro; Consul-Gen. PIETRO LUCIAN PAVONI.

RUSSIA

Embassy: 2650 Wisconsin Ave, NW, Washington, DC 20007; tel. (202) 298-5700; fax (202) 298-5735; internet www.russianembassy.org; Ambassador SERGEY I. KISLYAK.

Consulate-General, San Francisco: 2790 Green St, San Francisco, CA 94123; tel. (415) 928-6878; fax (415) 929-0306; e-mail consulsf@sbcglobal.net; internet www.consulrussia.org; Consul-Gen. VLADIMIR N. VINOKUROV.

Consulate-General, New York: 9 East 91st St, New York, NY 10128; tel. (212) 348-0926; fax (212) 831-9162; e-mail mail@ruscon.org; internet www.ruscon.org; Consul-Gen. SERGEY V. GARMONIN.

Consulate-General, Houston: 1333 West Loop South, Suite 1300, Houston, TX 77027; tel. (713) 337-3300; fax (713) 337-3305; e-mail info@rusconshouston.org; internet www.rusconshouston.org; Consul-Gen. NIKOLAY Y. BABICH.

Consulate-General, Seattle: 2323 Westin Bldg, 23rd Floor, 2001 Sixth Ave, Seattle, WA 98121; tel. (206) 728-1910; fax (206) 728-1871; e-mail consul@seanet.com; internet www.netconsul.org; Consul-Gen. VLADIMIR I. VOLNOV.

RWANDA

Embassy: 1714 New Hampshire Ave, NW, Washington, DC 20009; tel. (202) 232-2882; fax (202) 232-4544; e-mail rwandaembassy@rwandaembassy.org; internet www.rwandaembassy.org; Ambassador JAMES KIMONYO.

SAINT CHRISTOPHER AND NEVIS

Embassy: OECS Bldg, 3216 New Mexico Ave, NW, Washington, DC 20016; tel. (202) 686-2636; fax (202) 686-5740; e-mail info@embskn.com; internet www.embassy.gov.kn; Ambassador Dr IZBEN CORDINAL WILLIAMS.

Consulate-General, Los Angeles: 1762 Westwood Blvd, Suite 420, Los Angeles, CA 90024; tel. (310) 691-5208; fax (310) 694-8239; Consul-Gen. BASSAM ALGHANIM.

Consulate-General, New York: 412–414 East 75th St, 5th Floor, New York, NY 10021; tel. (212) 535-1234; fax (212) 535-5521; e-mail sknconsulgeneral@aol.com; Consul-Gen. KUTAYBA YUSUF ALGHANIM.

SAINT LUCIA

Embassy: OECS Bldg, 3216 New Mexico Ave, NW, Washington, DC 20016; tel. (202) 364-6792; fax (202) 364-6723; e-mail eofsaintlu@aol.com; Ambassador MICHAEL LOUIS.

Consulate-General, Miami: 1101 Brickell Ave, Suite 1602, Miami, FL 33131; Consul-Gen. KENT MARCEL PRESTON HIPPOLYTE.

Consulate-General, New York: 800 Second Ave, Suite 400J, New York, NY 10017; tel. (212) 697-9360; fax (212) 697-4993; e-mail slumission@aol.com; Deputy Consul-Gen. HUBERT EMMANUEL.

SAINT VINCENT AND THE GRENADINES

Embassy: OECS Bldg, 3216 New Mexico Ave, NW, Washington, DC 20016; tel. (202) 364-6730; fax (202) 364-6736; e-mail mail@embsvg.com; internet www.embsvg.com; Ambassador LA CELIA PRINCE.

Consulate-General, New York: 801 Second Ave, 21st Floor, New York, NY 10017; tel. (212) 687-4490; e-mail svgconny@aol.com; Consul-Gen. COSMUS E. COZIER.

SAMOA

Embassy: 800 Second Ave, Suite 400D, New York, NY 10017; tel. (212) 599-6196; fax (212) 599-0797; e-mail samoa@un.int; Ambassador ALI'IOAIGA FETURI ELISAIA.

SÃO TOMÉ AND PRÍNCIPE

Embassy: 1211 Connecticut Ave, NW, Suite 300, Washington, DC 20036; tel. (202) 775-2075; fax (202) 775-2077; e-mail embstpusa@verizon.net; Ambassador OVIDIO MANUEL BARBOSA PEQUENO.

SAUDI ARABIA

Embassy: 601 New Hampshire Ave, NW, Washington, DC 20037; tel. (202) 342-3800; fax (202) 944-5983; e-mail info@saudiembassy.net; internet www.saudiembassy.net; Ambassador ADEL BIN AHMED AL-JUBEIR.

Consulate-General, Los Angeles: 2045 Sawtelle Blvd, Suite 480, Los Angeles, CA 90025; tel. (310) 479-6000; fax (310) 479-2752; Consul-Gen. ABDULLAH S. A. AL-HARTHI.

Consulate-General, New York: 866 United Nations Plaza, Suite 480, New York, NY 10017; tel. (212) 752-2740; fax (212) 688-2719; e-mail usnycon@mofa.gov.sa; Consul-Gen. ABDULRAHMAN M. GDAIA.

Consulate-General, Houston: 5718 Westheimer Rd, Suite 1500, Houston, TX 77057; tel. (713) 785-5577; fax (713) 785-1163; e-mail ustxcon@mofa.gov.sa; Consul-Gen. ABDULRAHMAN AL-SHAYA.

SENEGAL

Embassy: 2112 Wyoming Ave, NW, Washington, DC 20008; tel. (202) 234-0540; fax (202) 332-6315; Ambassador Dr AMADOU LAMINE BA.

Consulate-General, New York: 271 West 125th St, Suite 412/415, New York, NY 10127; tel. (917) 493-8950; fax (917) 493-8953; e-mail cgsny05@yahoo.com; Consul-Gen. CHEIKH NIANG.

SERBIA

Embassy: 2134 Kalorama St, NW, Washington, DC 20008; tel. (202) 332-0333; fax (202) 332-3933; e-mail info@serbiaembusa.org; internet www.serbiaembusa.org; Ambassador Dr IVAN VUJAČIĆ.

Consulate-General, Chicago: 201 East Ohio St, Suite 200, Chicago, IL 60611; tel. (312) 670-6707; fax (312) 670-6787; e-mail info@scgchicago.org; internet www.scgchicago.org; Consul-Gen. DESKO NIKITOVIĆ.

Consulate-General, New York: 62 West 45th Street, 7th Floor, New York, NY 10036; tel. (212) 596-4241; fax (212) 596-4363; e-mail consulategeneralserbia@verizon.net; Consul-Gen. SLOBODAN NENADOVIĆ.

SEYCHELLES

Embassy: 800 Second Ave, Suite 400C, New York, NY 10017; tel. (212) 972-1785; fax (212) 972-1786; Ambassador RONALD JEAN JUMEAU.

SIERRA LEONE

Embassy: 1701 19th St, NW, Washington, DC 20009; tel. (202) 939-9261; fax (202) 483-1793; e-mail info@embassyofsierraleone.net; internet www.embassyofsierraleone.org; Ambassador BOCKARI KORTU STEVENS.

SINGAPORE

Embassy: 3501 International Pl., NW, Washington, DC 20008; tel. (202) 537-3100; fax (202) 537-0876; e-mail singemb_was@sgmfa.gov.sg; internet www.mfa.gov.sg/washington; Ambassador HENG CHEE CHAN.

Consulate-General, San Francisco: 595 Market St, Suite 2450, San Francisco, CA 94105; tel. (415) 543-4775; fax (415) 543-4788; e-mail singcg_sfo@sgmfa.gov.sg; internet www.mfa.gov.sg/sanfrancisco; Consul-Gen. JEE SEE HENG.

SLOVAKIA

Embassy: 3523 International Ct, NW, Washington, DC 20008; tel. (202) 237-1054; fax (202) 237-6438; e-mail information@slovakembassy-us.org; internet www.slovakembassy-us.org; Chargé d'affaires a.i. ANDREJ DROBA.

Consulate-General, Los Angeles: 10940 Wilshire Blvd, Suite 2030, Los Angeles, CA 90024; tel. (310) 209-1253; fax (310) 209-1261; Consul-Gen. FRANTISEK HUDAK.

Consulate-General, New York: 801 Second Ave, 12th Floor, New York, NY 10017; tel. (212) 286-8434; fax (212) 286-8439; e-mail cg.newyork@mzv.sk; internet www.mzv.sk/cgnewyork; Consul-Gen. IGOR POKOJNY.

SLOVENIA

Embassy: 2410 California St, NW, Washington, DC 20008; tel. (202) 386-6601; fax (202) 386-6633; e-mail vwa@gov.si; internet washington.embassy.si; Chargé d'affaires a.i. MIRIAM MOZGAN.

Consulate-General, New York: 600 Third Ave, 21st Floor, New York, NY 10016; tel. (212) 370-3006; fax (212) 370-3581; e-mail kny@gov.si; Consul-Gen. ALENKA SUHADOLNIK.

Consulate-General, Cleveland: 55 Public Sq., Suite 945, Cleveland, OH 44113; tel. (216) 589-9220; fax (216) 589-9210; e-mail kcl@gov.si; internet cleveland.consulate.si; Consul-Gen. ZVONE ZIGON.

SOLOMON ISLANDS

Embassy: 800 Second Ave, Suite 400L, New York, NY 10017; tel. (212) 599-6192; fax (212) 661-8925; e-mail simny@solomons.com; Ambassador COLLIN DAVID BECK.

SOUTH AFRICA

Embassy: 3051 Massachusetts Ave, NW, Washington, DC 20008; tel. (202) 232-4400; fax (202) 244-1607; e-mail info@saembassy.org; internet www.saembassy.org; Ambassador WELILE NHLAPO.

Consulate-General, Los Angeles: 6300 Wilshire Blvd, Suite 600, Los Angeles, CA 90048; tel. (323) 651-0902; fax (323) 651-5969; e-mail info.losangeles@foreign.gov.za; internet www.link2southafrica.com; Consul-Gen. JEANETTE T. NDHLOVU.

Consulate-General, Chicago: 200 South Michigan Ave, Suite 600, Chicago, IL 60604; tel. (312) 939-7929; fax (312) 939-0344; e-mail sacgpolchicago@sacg.xohost.com; Consul-Gen. PEARL NOMVUME MAGAQA.

Consulate-General, New York: 333 East 38th St, 9th Floor, New York, NY 10016; tel. (212) 213-4880; fax (212) 213-0102; e-mail sacg@southafrica-newyork.net; internet www.southafrica-newyork.net; Consul-Gen. FIKILE S. MAGUBANE.

SPAIN

Embassy: 2375 Pennsylvania Ave, NW, Washington, DC 20037; tel. (202) 452-0100; fax (202) 833-5670; e-mail emb.washington@maec.es; internet www.maec.es/embajadas/washington; Ambassador JORGE DEZCALLAR DE MAZARREDO.

Consulate-General, Los Angeles: 5055 Wilshire Blvd, Suite 860, Los Angeles, CA 90036; tel. (323) 938-0158; fax (323) 938-2502; e-mail cog.losangeles@mae.es; internet www.maec.es/consulados/losangeles; Consul-Gen. INOCENCIO F. ARIAS LLAMAS.

Consulate-General, San Francisco: 1405 Sutter St, San Francisco, CA 94109-5417; tel. (415) 922-2995; fax (415) 931-9706; e-mail conspsfo@mail.mae.es; internet www.maec.es/consulados/sanfrancisco; Consul-Gen. D. MANUEL PRADAS ROMANÍ.

Consulate-General, Washington, DC: 2375 Pennsylvania Ave, NW, Washington, DC 20037; tel. (202) 728-2330; fax (202) 728-2302; e-mail cog.washington@mae.es; internet www.maec.es/consulados/washington; Consul-Gen. ALVARO DE SALAS GIMÉNEZ DE AZCÁRATE.

Consulate-General, Miami: 2655 Le Jeune Rd, Suite 203, Coral Gables, Miami, FL 33134; tel. (305) 446-5511; fax (305) 446-0585; e-mail cog.miami@mae.es; internet www.maec.es/consulados/miami; Consul-Gen. SANTIAGO CABANAS ANSORENA.

Consulate-General, Chicago: 180 North Michigan Ave, Suite 1500, Chicago, IL 60601; tel. (312) 782-4588; fax (312) 782-1635; e-mail conspainchicago@sbcglobal.net; internet www.maec.es/consulados/chicago; Consul-Gen. Dr FRANCISCO JAVIER RUPÉREZ RUBIO.

Consulate-General, New Orleans: World Trade Center, Rm 2102, 2 Canal St, New Orleans, LA 70130; tel. (504) 525-4951; fax (504) 525-4955; e-mail conspneworleans@correo.mae.es; internet www.maec.es/consulados/nuevaorleans; Consul-Gen. DANIEL CHAMORRO GARCÍA.

Consulate-General, Boston: 31 St James Ave, Suite 905, Boston, MA 02116; tel. (617) 536-2506; fax (617) 536-8512; e-mail cog.boston@mae.es; internet www.maec.es/consulados/boston; Consul-Gen. CARLOS ROBLES.

Consulate-General, New York: 150 58th St East, 30th–31st Floors, New York, NY 10155; tel. (212) 355-4080; fax (212) 644-3751; e-mail cog.nuevayork@mae.es; internet www.maec.es/consulados/nuevayork; Consul-Gen. JUAN MANUEL EGEA IBÁÑEZ.

Consulate-General, Houston: 1800 Bering Dr., Suite 660, Houston, TX 77057; tel. (713) 783-6200; fax (713) 783-6166; e-mail cog.houston@maec.es; Consul-Gen. MIGUEL ANGEL FERNÁNDEZ DE MAZARAMBROZ BERNABEU.

SRI LANKA

Embassy: 2148 Wyoming Ave, NW, Washington, DC 20008; tel. (202) 483-4025; fax (202) 232-7181; e-mail slembassy@slembassyusa.org; internet www.slembassyusa.org; Ambassador JALIYA WICKRAMASURIYA.

Consulate-General, Los Angeles: 3250 Wilshire Blvd, Suite 1405, Los Angeles, CA 90010; tel. (323) 387-0210; fax (323) 387-0216; e-mail lacongen@sbcglobal.net; internet www.srilankaconsulatela.com; Consul-Gen. ANANDA WICKRAMASINGHE.

SUDAN

Embassy: 2210 Massachusetts Ave, NW, Washington, DC 20008; tel. (202) 338-8565; fax (202) 667-2406; internet www.sudanembassy.org; Chargé d'affaires a.i. AKEC KHOC ACIEW KHOC.

SURINAME

Embassy: 4301 Connecticut Ave, NW, Suite 460, Washington, DC 20008; tel. (202) 244-7488; fax (202) 244-5878; e-mail embsur@erols.com; internet www.surinameembassy.org; Ambassador JACQUES R. C. KROSS.

Consulate-General, Miami: 6303 Blue Lagoon Dr., Suite 325, Miami, FL 33126; tel. (305) 265-4655; fax (305) 265-4599; e-mail surcgmia@bellsouth.net; internet www.scgmia.com; Consul-Gen. MOHAMED RAKIEB KHUDABUX.

SWAZILAND

Embassy: 1712 New Hampshire Ave, NW, Washington, DC 20009; tel. (202) 234-5002; fax (202) 234-8254; e-mail embassy@swaziland-usa.com; internet www.swazilandembassyus.com; Ambassador EPHRAIM MANDLENKOSI M. HLOPHE.

SWEDEN

Embassy: 2900 K St, NW, Washington, DC 20007; tel. (202) 467-2600; fax (202) 467-2699; e-mail ambassaden.washington@foreign.ministry.se; internet www.swedenabroad.com/washington; Ambassador JONAS HAFSTRÖM.

Consulate-General, Los Angeles: 10940 Wilshire Blvd, Suite 700, Los Angeles, CA 90024; tel. (310) 445-4008; fax (310) 473-2229; e-mail consularinfola@foreign.ministry.se; internet www.swedishoffices.org; Consul-Gen. NINA ERSMAN.

Consulate-General, New York: 1 Dag Hammarskjöld Plaza, 885 Second Ave, 45th Floor, New York, NY 10017-2201; tel. (212) 583-2550; fax (212) 583-2599; e-mail generalkonsulat.new-york@foreign.ministry.se; internet www.swedennewyork.com; Consul-Gen. ULF HJERTONSSON.

SWITZERLAND

Embassy: 2900 Cathedral Ave, NW, Washington, DC 20008; tel. (202) 745-7900; fax (202) 387-2564; e-mail was.vertretung@edaadmin.ch; internet www.swissemb.org; Ambassador URS JOHANN ZISWILER.

Consulate-General, Los Angeles: 11766 Wilshire Blvd, Suite 1400, Los Angeles, CA 90025; tel. (310) 575-1145; fax (310) 575-1982; e-mail los.vertretung@eda.admin.ch; Consul-Gen. BRIGITTA SCHOCH DETTWEILER.

Consulate-General, San Francisco: 456 Montgomery St, Suite 1500, San Francisco, CA 94104-1233; tel. (415) 788-2272; fax (415) 788-1402; e-mail sfr.vertretung@eda.admin.ch; Consul-Gen. JEAN-FRANÇOIS LICHTENSTERN.

Consulate-General, Atlanta: 1349 West Peachtree St, Suite 1000, Atlanta, GA 30309; tel. (404) 870-2000; fax (404) 870-2011; e-mail atl.vertretung@eda.admin.ch; Consul-Gen. ULRICH HUNN.

Consulate-General, Chicago: 737 North Michigan Ave, Suite 2301, Chicago, IL 60611; tel. (312) 915-0061; fax (312) 915-0388; e-mail chi.vertretung@eda.admin.ch; Consul-Gen. GIAMBATTISTA MONDADA.

Consulate-General, New York: 633 Third Ave, 30th Floor, New York, NY 10017-6706; tel. (212) 599-5700; fax (212) 599-4266; e-mail nyc.vertretung@eda.admin.ch; Consul-Gen. CHRISTOPH BUBB.

SYRIA

Embassy: 2215 Wyoming Ave, NW, Washington, DC 20008; tel. (202) 232-6313; fax (202) 234-9548; e-mail info@syrembassy.net; internet www.syrianembassy.us; Ambassador Dr IMAD MOUSTAPHA.

TAJIKISTAN

Embassy: 1005 New Hampshire Ave, NW, Washington, DC 20037; tel. (202) 223-6090; fax (202) 223-6091; e-mail tajikistan@verizon.net; internet www.tjus.org; Ambassador ABDUJABBOR SHIRINOV.

TANZANIA

Embassy: 2139 R St, NW, Washington, DC 20008; tel. (202) 939-6125; fax (202) 797-7408; e-mail ubalozi@tanzaniaembassy-us.org; internet www.tanzaniaembassy-us.org; Ambassador OMBENI SEFUE.

THAILAND

Embassy: 1024 Wisconsin Ave, NW, Suite 401, Washington, DC 20007; tel. (202) 944-3600; fax (202) 944-3611; e-mail info@thaiembdc.org; internet www.thaiembdc.org; Chargé d'affaires a.i. DAMRONG KRAIKRUAN.

Consulate-General, Los Angeles: 611 North Larchmont Blvd, 2nd Floor, Los Angeles, CA 90004; tel. (323) 962-9574; fax (323) 962-2128; e-mail thai-la@mindspring.com; internet www.thai-la.net; Consul-Gen. JUKR BOON LONG.

Consulate-General, Chicago: 700 North Rush St, Chicago, IL 60611; tel. (312) 664-3129; fax (312) 664-3230; e-mail thaichicago@ameritech.net; internet www.thaichicago.net; Consul-Gen. NARONG SASITORN.

Consulate-General, New York: 351 East 52nd St, New York, NY 10022; tel. (212) 754-1770; fax (212) 754-1907; e-mail thainycg@aol.com; internet www.thaiconsulnewyork.com; Consul-Gen. VIPAWAN NIPATAKUSOL.

TIMOR-LESTE

Embassy: 3415 Massachusetts Ave, NW, Washington, DC 20007; tel. (202) 965-1515; fax (202) 965-1517; e-mail embtlus@earthlink.net; Chargé d'affaires a.i. JORGE CAMEO.

TOGO

Embassy: 2208 Massachusetts Ave, NW, Washington, DC 20008; tel. (202) 234-4212; fax (202) 232-3190; Chargé d'affaires a.i. T. H. LOREMPO LANDJERGUE.

TONGA

Embassy: 250 East 51st St, New York, NY 10022; tel. (917) 369-1025; fax (917) 369-1024; Ambassador FEKITAMOELOA 'UTOIKAMANU.

Consulate-General, San Francisco: 360 Post St, Suite 604, San Francisco, CA 94108; tel. (415) 781-0365; fax (415) 781-3964; e-mail consulategeneraloftonga@gmail.com; internet tongaconsul.com; Consul-Gen. JAMES CECIL COCKER.

TRINIDAD AND TOBAGO

Embassy: 1708 Massachusetts Ave, NW, Washington, DC 20036-1975; tel. (202) 467-6490; fax (202) 785-3130; e-mail info@ttembwash.com; internet www.bordeglobal.com/ttembassy; Ambassador GLENDA MOREAN-PHILLIP.

Consulate-General, Miami: 1000 Brickell Ave, Suite 800, Miami, FL 33131-3047; tel. (305) 374-2199; fax (305) 374-3199; e-mail ttmiami@worldnet.att.net; internet www.ttcgmiami.com; Consul-Gen. GERARD P. GREENE.

Consulate-General, New York: 475 Fifth Ave, 4th Floor, New York, NY 10017-7700; tel. (212) 682-7272; fax (212) 986-2146; e-mail consulate@ttcgny.com; Consul-Gen. Dr HAROLD HAMPDEN ROBERTSON.

TUNISIA

Embassy: 1515 Massachusetts Ave, NW, Washington, DC 20005; tel. (202) 862-1850; fax (202) 862-1858; Chargé d'affaires a.i. TAREK BEN YOUSSEF.

TURKEY

Embassy: 2525 Massachusetts Ave, NW, Washington, DC 20008; tel. (202) 612-6700; fax (202) 612-6744; e-mail contact@turkishembassy.org; internet www.turkishembassy.org; Ambassador NABI ŞENSOY.

Consulate-General, Los Angeles: 6300 Wilshire Blvd, Suite 2010, Los Angeles, CA 90048; tel. (323) 655-8832; fax (323) 655-8681; e-mail turkcgla@pacbell.net; internet www.turkiye.net/lacg; Consul-Gen. RIZA HAKAN TEKIN.

Consulate-General, Chicago: 360 North Michigan Ave, Suite 1405, Chicago, IL 60601-3858; tel. (312) 263-0644; fax (312) 263-1449; e-mail trchicago@mfa.gov.tr; Consul-Gen. UĞUR KENAN IPEK.

Consulate-General, New York: 821 United Nations Plaza, 5th Floor, New York, NY 10017; tel. (212) 949-0160; fax (212) 983-1283; e-mail tcbkny@broadview.net; Consul-Gen. MEHMET SAMSAR.

Consulate-General, Houston: 1990 Post Oak Blvd, Suite 1300, Houston, TX 77056; tel. (713) 622-5849; fax (713) 623-6639; e-mail turcon@sbcglobal.net; Consul-Gen. ATILA UZER.

TURKMENISTAN

Embassy: 2207 Massachusetts Ave, NW, Washington, DC 20008; tel. (202) 588-1500; fax (202) 588-0697; e-mail turkmen@mindspring.com; internet www.turkmenistanembassy.org; Ambassador MERET BAIRAMOVICH ORAZOV.

UGANDA

Embassy: 5911 16th St, NW, Washington, DC 20011; tel. (202) 726-7100; fax (202) 726-1727; e-mail info@ugandaembassyus.org; internet www.ugandaembassy.com; Ambassador PEREZI KARUKUBIRO KAMUNANWIRE.

UKRAINE

Embassy: 3350 M St, NW, Washington, DC 20007; tel. (202) 333-0606; fax (202) 333-0817; internet www.mfa.gov.ua/usa; Ambassador OLEH SHAMSHUR.

Consulate-General, San Francisco: 530 Bush St, Suite 402, San Francisco, CA 94108-3623; tel. (415) 398-4974; fax (415) 398-5039; e-mail consulate@ukrainesf.com; internet www.ukrainesf.com; Consul-Gen. MYKOLA TOCHYTSKYI.

Consulate-General, Chicago: 10 East Huron St, Chicago, IL 60611; tel. (312) 642-4388; fax (312) 642-4385; e-mail ukrchicago@sbcglobal.net; internet www.ukrchicago.com; Consul-Gen. (vacant).

Consulate-General, New York: 240 East 49th St, New York, NY 10017; tel. (212) 371-5690; fax (212) 371-5547; e-mail gc_usn@mfa.gov.ua; internet www.ukrconsul.org; Consul-Gen. MYKOLA KYRYCHENKO.

UNITED ARAB EMIRATES

Embassy: 3422 International Ct, NW, Washington, DC 20037; tel. (202) 243-2400; fax (202) 243-2432; e-mail info@uaeembassy-usa.org; internet uae-embassy.org; Ambassador YOUSEF AL OTAIBA.

UNITED KINGDOM

Embassy: 3100 Massachusetts Ave, NW, Washington, DC 20008; tel. (202) 588-6500; fax (202) 588-7870; e-mail washi@fco.gov.uk; internet www.britainusa.com; Ambassador Sir NIGEL SHEINWALD.

Consulate-General, Los Angeles: 11766 Wilshire Blvd, Suite 1200, Los Angeles, CA 90025-6540; tel. (310) 481-0031; fax (310) 481-2960; e-mail mail@britishconsulatela.com; internet www.britainusa.com/la; Consul-Gen. BOB PEIRCE.

Consulate-General, San Francisco: 1 Sansome St, Suite 850, San Francisco, CA 94104; tel. (415) 617-1300; fax (415) 434-2018; internet www.britainusa.com/sf; Consul-Gen. JULIAN EVANS.

Consulate-General, Miami: 1001 Brickell Bay Dr., Suite 2800, Miami, FL 33131; tel. (305) 374-3500; Consul-Gen. KEITH ALLAN.

Consulate-General, Atlanta: Georgia Pacific Center, Suite 3400, 133 Peachtree St, NE, Atlanta, GA 30303; tel. (404) 954-7700; fax (404) 954-7702; e-mail britishconsulategeneral@fco.gov.uk; internet www.britainusa.com/atlanta; Consul-Gen. MARTIN RICKERD.

Consulate-General, Chicago: Wrigley Bldg, 13th Floor, 400 North Michigan Ave, Chicago, IL 60611; tel. (312) 970-3800; fax (312) 970-3852; internet www.britainusa.com/chicago; Consul-Gen. JAMES CLARK.

Consulate-General, Cambridge: 1 Memorial Dr., Suite 1500, Cambridge, MA 02142; tel. (617) 245-4500; fax (617) 621-0220; e-mail british.boston@fco.gov.uk; internet www.britainusa.com/boston; Consul-Gen. PHIL BUDDEN.

Consulate-General, New York: 845 Third Ave, New York, NY 10022; tel. (212) 745-0200; fax (212) 754-3062; internet www.britainusa.com/ny; Consul-Gen. Sir ALAN COLLINS.

Consulate-General, Houston: Wells Fargo Plaza Bldg, Suite 1900, 1000 Louisiana, Houston, TX 77002; tel. (713) 659-6270; fax (713) 659-7094; internet www.britainusa.com/houston; Consul-Gen. PAUL LYNCH.

URUGUAY

Embassy: 1913 I St, NW, 3rd Floor, Washington, DC 20006; tel. (202) 331-1313; fax (202) 331-8142; e-mail uruwashi@uruwashi.org; internet www.uruwashi.org; Ambassador CARLOS A. GIANELLI DEROIS.

Consulate-General, Los Angeles: 429 Santa Monica Blvd, Suite 400, Los Angeles, CA 90401; tel. (310) 394-5777; fax (310) 394-5140; e-mail consulado@conurula.org; Consul-Gen. ENRIQUE E. LOEDEL.

Consulate-General, Miami: 1077 Ponce de Leon Blvd, Suite B, Coral Gables, Miami, FL 33134; tel. (305) 443-9764; fax (305) 443-7802; e-mail consulado@uruguaymiami.org; Consul-Gen. MANUEL G. VIEIRA MEROLA.

Consulate-General, Chicago: 875 North Michigan Ave, Suite 1422, Chicago, IL 60611; tel. (312) 642-3430; fax (312) 642-3470; e-mail conuruchi@aol.com; internet www.uruguaychicago.org; Consul-Gen. Dr BORIS EDUARDO SVETOGORSKY MARINO.

Consulate-General, New York: 420 Madison Ave (48th and 49th Sts), 6th Floor, New York, NY 10017; tel. (212) 753-8191; fax (212) 753-1603; e-mail conuruyork@conuruyork.org; internet www.conuruyork.org; Consul-Gen. ADRIANA LISSIDINI DOTTI.

UZBEKISTAN

Embassy: 1746 Massachusetts Ave, NW, Washington, DC 20036; tel. (202) 887-5300; fax (202) 293-6804; e-mail info@uzbekistan.org; internet www.uzbekistan.org; Ambassador ABDULAZIZ KHAFIZOVICH KAMILOV.

Consulate-General, New York: 801 Second Ave, 20th Floor, New York, NY 10017; tel. (212) 754-7403; fax (212) 838-9812; e-mail info@uzbekconsulny.org; internet www.uzbekconsulny.org; Consul-Gen. KHASAN IKRAMOV.

VENEZUELA

Embassy: 1099 30th St, NW, Washington, DC 20007; tel. (202) 342-2214; fax (202) 342-6820; e-mail apaiva@embavenez-us.org; internet www.embavenez-us.org; Chargé d'affaires a.i. ANGELO SANTOS.

Consulate-General, San Francisco: 311 California St, Suite 620, San Francisco, CA 94104; tel. (415) 347-3323; fax (415) 955-1970; e-mail cven.sanfrancisco@gmail.com; internet sanfrancisco.embavenez-us.org; Consul-Gen. MARTÍN SÁNCHEZ.

Consulate-General, Miami: 1101 Brickell Ave, Suite 901, Miami, FL 33131; tel. (305) 577-4214; fax (305) 372-5167; e-mail conmiami@consuve.net; internet 68.153.95.162; Consul-Gen. ANTONIO JOSÉ HERNÁNDEZ BORGO.

Consulate-General, Chicago: 20 North Wacker Dr., Suite 1925, Chicago, IL 60606; tel. (312) 236-9655; fax (312) 580-1010; e-mail ven.chicago@gmail.com; internet chicago.embavenez-us.org; Consul-Gen. JESÚS RODRÍGUEZ ESPINOZA (acting).

Consulate-General, New Orleans: World Trade Center, Suite 2300, 2 Canal St, New Orleans, LA 70130; tel. (504) 522-3284; fax (504) 522-7092; e-mail info@neworleans.embavenez-us.org; internet neworleans.embavenez-us.org; Consul-Gen. JORGE GUERRERO.

Consulate-General, Boston: 545 Boylston St, 3rd Floor, Boston, MA 02116; tel. (617) 266-9368; fax (617) 266-2350; e-mail consulado@boston.embavenez-us.org; internet boston.embavenez-us.org; Consul-Gen. CARLOS OSORIO (acting).

Consulate-General, New York: 7 East 51st St, New York, NY 10022; tel. (212) 826-1660; fax (212) 644-7471; e-mail info@consulado-ny.gov.ve; internet newyork.embavenez-us.org; Consul-Gen. LEONOR C. OSORIO GRANADO.

Consulate-General, Houston: 2401 Fountain View Dr., Suite 220, Houston, TX 77057; tel. (713) 974-0028; fax (713) 974-1413; e-mail consulvzla@aol.com; internet www.consuvenezhouston.org; Consul-Gen. ANTONIO R. PADRINO QUINTERO.

VIET NAM

Embassy: 1233 20th St, NW, Suite 400, Washington, DC 20036; tel. (202) 861-0737; fax (202) 861-0917; e-mail info@vietnamembassy.us; internet www.vietnamembassy-usa.org; Ambassador LE CONG PHUNG.

Consulate-General, San Francisco: 1700 California St, Suite 430, San Francisco, CA 94109; tel. (415) 922-1577; fax (415) 922-1848; e-mail info@vietnamconsulate-ca.org; internet www.vietnamconsulate-ca.org; Consul-Gen. LE QUOC HUNG.

YEMEN

Embassy: 2319 Wyoming Ave, NW, Washington, DC 20008; tel. (202) 965-4760; fax (202) 337-2017; e-mail information@yemenembassy.org; internet www.yemenembassy.org; Ambassador ABDULWAHAB A. AL-HAJJRI.

ZAMBIA

Embassy: 2419 Massachusetts Ave, NW, Washington, DC 20008; tel. (202) 265-9717; fax (202) 265-9718; e-mail embzambia@aol.com; internet www.zambiaembassy.org; Ambassador Dr INONGE MBIKUSITA LEWANIKA.

ZIMBABWE

Embassy: 1608 New Hampshire Ave, NW, Washington, DC 20009; tel. (202) 332-7100; fax (202) 483-9326; e-mail info@zimbabwe-embassy.us; internet www.zimbabwe-embassy.us; Ambassador Dr MACHIVENYIKA TOBIAS MAPURANGA.

US REPRESENTATION ABROAD

Embassies

(All diplomatic offices listed below are embassies, unless otherwise indicated.)

Afghanistan: The Great Masoud Rd, Kabul; tel. (20) 2300436; fax (20) 2301364; e-mail usambassadorkabul@state.gov; internet kabul.usembassy.gov; Ambassador WILLIAM BRAUCHER WOOD.

Albania: Rruga Elbasanit 103, Rm 2921, POB 100, Tirana; tel. (4) 247285; fax (4) 232222; e-mail tiranausconsulate@state.gov; internet tirana.usembassy.gov; Ambassador JOHN L. WITHERS, II.

Algeria: 4 Chemin Cheikh Bachir El-Ibrahimi, BP 549, 16000 Alger-Gare, Algiers; tel. (770) 08-20-20; fax (21) 60-73-35; e-mail algiers_webmaster@state.gov; internet algiers.usembassy.gov; Ambassador DAVID D. PEARCE.

Angola: Rua Houari Boumedienne 32, Miramar, CP 6468, Luanda; tel. (2) 222641000; fax (2) 222641232; e-mail consularluanda@state.gov; internet luanda.usembassy.gov; Ambassador DAN MOZENA.

Argentina: Colombia 4300, Palermo, C1425GMN Buenos Aires; tel. (11) 5777-4533; fax (11) 5777-4240; e-mail buenosairesirc@state.gov; internet argentina.usembassy.gov; Ambassador EARL A. WAYNE.

Armenia: 0082 Yerevan, American Ave 1; tel. (1) 46-47-00; fax (1) 46-47-42; e-mail usinfo@usa.am; internet yerevan.usembassy.gov; Ambassador MARIE L. YOVANOVITCH.

Australia: Moonah Pl., Yarralumla, ACT 2600; tel. (2) 6214-5600; fax (2) 6214-5970; e-mail info@usembassy-australia.state.gov; internet canberra.usembassy.gov; Ambassador ROBERT D. MCCALLUM, Jr.

Austria: 1090 Vienna, Boltzmanngasse 16; tel. (1) 313-39-0; fax (1) 310-06-82; e-mail embassy@usembassy.at; internet www.usembassy.at; Ambassador DAVID F. GIRARD-DICARLO.

Azerbaijan: 83 Azadlyg Prospecti, 1007 Baku; tel. (12) 498-03-35; fax (12) 465-66-71; e-mail consularbaku@state.gov; internet azerbaijan.usembassy.gov; Ambassador ANNE E. DERSE.

Bahamas: Mosmar Bldg, Queen St, POB N-8197, Nassau; tel. 322-1181; fax 328-7838; e-mail embnas@state.gov; internet nassau.usembassy.gov; Ambassador NED SIEGEL.

Bahrain: Bldg 979, Rd 3119, Block 331, POB 26431, Zinj, Manama; tel. 17242700; fax 17270547; e-mail ManamaConsular@state.gov; internet manama.usembassy.gov; Ambassador J. ADAM ERELI.

Bangladesh: Diplomatic Enclave, Madani Ave, Baridhara, POB 323, Dhaka 1212; tel. (2) 8855500; fax (2) 8823744; e-mail dhakapa@state.gov; internet dhaka.usembassy.gov; Ambassador JAMES F. MORIARTY.

Barbados: Wildey Business Park, Wildey, St Michael 14006, POB 302, Bridgetown 11000; tel. 436-4950; fax 429-5316; e-mail lynchjh@state.gov; internet bridgetown.usembassy.gov; Ambassador MARY M. OURISMAN (also serves Antigua and Barbuda, Dominica, Grenada, Saint Christopher and Nevis, Saint Lucia and Saint Vincent and the Grenadines).

Belarus: 220002 Minsk, vul. Starovilenskaya 46; tel. (17) 210-12-83; fax (17) 234-78-53; e-mail webmaster@usembassy.minsk.by; internet belarus.usembassy.gov; Chargé d'affaires a.i. JONATHAN MOORE.

Belgium: 27 blvd du Régent, 1000 Brussels; tel. (2) 508-21-11; fax (2) 511-27-25; e-mail uscitizenbrussels@state.gov; internet belgium.usembassy.gov; Ambassador SAM FOX.

Belize: Floral Park Rd, Belmopan, Cayo; tel. 822-4011; fax 822-4012; e-mail embbelize@state.gov; internet belize.usembassy.gov; Ambassador ROBERT J. DIETER.

Benin: Carré 125, Rue Caporal Anani Bernard, 01 BP 2012, Cotonou; tel. 21-30-06-50; fax 21-30-03-84; e-mail consularcotono@state.gov; internet cotonou.usembassy.gov; Ambassador GAYLEATHA B. BROWN.

Bolivia: Avda Arce 2780, Casilla 425, La Paz; tel. (2) 216-8000; fax (2) 216-8111; e-mail consularlapaz@state.gov; internet bolivia.usembassy.gov; Chargé d'affaires a.i. KRISHNA R. URS.

Bosnia and Herzegovina: 71000 Sarajevo, Alipašina 43; tel. (33) 445700; fax (33) 659722; e-mail bhopa@state.gov; internet sarajevo.usembassy.gov; Ambassador CHARLES L. ENGLISH.

Botswana: Embassy Enclave, (off Khama Cres.), POB 90, Gaborone; tel. 3953982; fax 3956947; e-mail consulargaboro@state.gov; internet gaborone.usembassy.gov; Ambassador KATHERINE H. CANAVAN.

Brazil: SES, Av. das Nações, Quadra 801, Lote 03, 70403-900 Brasília, DF; tel. (61) 3312-7000; fax (61) 3312-7676; e-mail contact@embaixadaamericana.org.br; internet www.embaixada-americana.org.br; Ambassador CLIFFORD M. SOBEL.

Brunei: Teck Guan Plaza, 3rd Floor, Jalan Sultan, POB 2991, Bandar Seri Begawan BS 8811; tel. (2) 220384; fax (2) 225293; e-mail amembassy_bsb@state.gov; internet bandar.usembassy.gov; Ambassador WILLIAM E. TODD.

Bulgaria: 1407 Sofia, 16 Kozyak St; tel. (2) 937-51-00; fax (2) 937-53-20; e-mail sofia@usembassy.bg; internet sofia.usembassy.gov; Ambassador NANCY E. MCELDOWNEY.

Burkina Faso: 622 ave Raoul Follereau, Koulouba, Secteur 4, Ouagadougou 01; tel. 50-30-67-23; fax 50-31-23-68; e-mail amembouaga@state.gov; internet ouagadougou.usembassy.gov; Ambassador JEANINE JACKSON.

Burundi: Ave des Etats-Unis, BP 1720, Bujumbura; tel. 22223454; fax 22222926; internet burundi.usembassy.gov; Ambassador PATRICIA N. MOLLER.

Cambodia: 1 St 96, Sangkat Wat Phnom, Phnom-Penh; tel. (23) 728000; fax (23) 728600; e-mail traysm@state.gov; internet phnompenh.usembassy.gov; Chargé d'affaires a.i. PIPER ANNE WIND CAMPBELL.

Cameroon: Ave Rosa Parks, BP 817, Yaoundé; tel. and fax 2220-1500; e-mail consularyaound@state.gov; internet yaounde.usembassy.gov; Ambassador JANET E. GARVEY (also serves Equatorial Guinea).

Canada: 490 Sussex Dr., POB 866, Station B, Ottawa, ON K1N 1G8; tel. (613) 238-5335; fax (613) 688-3082; e-mail ottawareference@state.gov; internet canada.usembassy.gov; Ambassador DAVID HORTON WILKINS.

Cape Verde: 6 Rua Abilio Macedo, CP 201, Praia, Santiago; tel. 260-8900; fax 261-1355; internet praia.usembassy.gov; Ambassador MARIANNE M. MYLES.

Chad: Ave Félix Eboué, BP 413, N'Djamena; tel. 51-70-09; fax 51-56-54; e-mail consularndjame@state.gov; internet ndjamena.usembassy.gov; Ambassador LOUIS JOHN NIGRO, Jr.

Chile: Avda Andrés Bello 2800, Las Condes, Santiago; tel. (2) 330-3000; fax (2) 330-3710; e-mail infousa@state.gov; internet santiago.usembassy.gov; Ambassador PAUL E. SIMONS.

China, People's Republic: 3 Xiu Shui Bei Jie, Beijing 100600; tel. (10) 65323831; fax (10) 65322039; e-mail ircacee@state.gov; internet beijing.usembassy-china.org.cn; Ambassador CLARK T. RANDT, Jr.

Colombia: Calle 24-bis, No 48–50, Apdo Aéreo 3831, Bogotá, DC; tel. (1) 315-0811; fax (1) 315-2197; e-mail webb@state.gov; internet bogota.usembassy.gov; Ambassador WILLIAM BROWNFIELD.

Congo, Democratic Republic: 310 ave des Aviateurs, BP 697, Kinshasa; tel. 815560151; fax 815560175; e-mail usembassykinshasa@state.gov; internet kinshasa.usembassy.gov; Ambassador WILLIAM GARVELINK.

Congo, Republic: BDEAC Bldg, 4th Floor, Blvd de la Révolution, Brazzaville; tel. 81-14-81; e-mail greggcf@state.gov; internet brazzaville.usembassy.gov; Ambassador ALAN W. EASTHAM.

Costa Rica: Calle 120, Avda 0, Pavas, Apdo 920-1200, San José; tel. 519-2000; fax 519-2305; e-mail irc@usembassy.or.cr; internet sanjose.usembassy.gov; Ambassador PETER CIANCHETTE.

Côte d'Ivoire: 5 rue Jesse Owens, 01 BP 1712, Abidjan 01; tel. 22-49-40-00; fax 22-49-43-23; e-mail abjpress@state.gov; internet abidjan.usembassy.gov; Ambassador WANDA L. NESBITT.

Croatia: 10010 Zagreb, Thomasa Jeffersona 2; tel. (1) 6612200; fax (1) 6612373; e-mail irc@usembassy.hr; internet zagreb.usembassy.gov; Ambassador ROBERT A. BRADTKE.

Cuba (US Interests Section): c/o Embassy of Switzerland, Calzada entre L y M, Vedado, Havana; tel. (7) 833-3551; fax (7) 66-2095; e-mail irchavana@state.gov; internet havana.usinterestsection.gov; Principal Officer JONATHAN D. FARRAR.

Cyprus: POB 24536, 7 Ploutarchou, Engomi, 2407 Nicosia; tel. 22393939; fax 22780944; e-mail info@americanembassy.org.cy; internet www.americanembassy.org.cy; Ambassador FRANK CHARLES URBANCIC, Jr.

Czech Republic: Tržiště 15, 118 01 Prague 1; tel. (2) 57022000; fax (2) 57022809; e-mail consprague@state.gov; internet prague.usembassy.gov; Ambassador RICHARD W. GRABER.

Denmark: Dag Hammarskjölds Allé 24, 2100 Copenhagen Ø; tel. 33-41-71-00; fax 35-43-02-23; e-mail copenhagenirc@state.gov; internet denmark.usembassy.gov; Ambassador JAMES P. CAIN.

Djibouti: Villa Plateau du Serpent, blvd du Maréchal Joffre, BP 185, Djibouti; tel. 353995; fax 353940; e-mail linchangcod@state.gov; internet djibouti.usembassy.gov; Ambassador W. STUART SYMINGTON, IV.

Dominican Republic: César Nicolás Pensón, esq. Leopoldo Navarro, Santo Domingo, DN; tel. 221-2171; fax 686-7437; e-mail usis.ic@codetel.net.do; internet www.usemb.gov.do; Ambassador P. ROBERT FANNIN.

Ecuador: Avda 12 de Octubre y Patria 120, Quito; tel. (2) 256-2890; fax (2) 250-2052; e-mail contacto.usembuio@state.gov; internet ecuador.usembassy.gov; Ambassador HEATHER M. HODGES.

Egypt: 5 Tawfik Diab St, Garden City, Cairo; tel. (2) 7973300; fax (2) 7973200; e-mail consularcairo@state.gov; internet cairo.usembassy.gov; Ambassador MARGARET SCOBEY.

El Salvador: Final Blvd Santa Elena Sur, Antiguo Cuscatlán, La Libertad, San Salvador; tel. 234-2483; fax 278-5522; e-mail congensansal@state.gov; internet sansalvador.usembassy.gov; Ambassador CHARLES L. GLAZER.

Eritrea: 179 Ala St, POB 211, Asmara; tel. (1) 120004; fax (1) 127584; e-mail usembassyasmara@state.gov; internet eritrea.usembassy.gov; Ambassador RONALD K. MCMULLEN.

Estonia: Kentmanni 20, Tallinn 15099; tel. 668-8100; fax 668-8134; e-mail usasaatkond@state.gov; internet estonia.usembassy.gov; Ambassador STANLEY DAVIS PHILLIPS.

Ethiopia: Entoto St, POB 1014, Addis Ababa; tel. (1) 5174000; fax (1) 5174001; e-mail pasaddis@state.gov; internet addisababa.usembassy.gov; Ambassador DONALD Y. YAMAMOTO.

Fiji: 31 Loftus St, POB 218, Suva; tel. 3314466; fax 3308685; e-mail usembsuva@gmail.com; internet suva.usembassy.gov; Chargé d'affaires a.i. RICHARD PRUETT (also serves Kiribati, Nauru, Tonga and Tuvalu).

Finland: Itäinen puistotie 14B, 00140 Helsinki; tel. (9) 616250; fax (9) 174681; e-mail webmaster@usembassy.fi; internet finland.usembassy.gov; Ambassador BARBARA MCCONNELL BARRETT.

France: 2 ave Gabriel, 75382 Paris Cédex 08; tel. 1-43-12-22-22; fax 1-42-66-97-83; e-mail irc@amb-usa.fr; internet france.usembassy.gov; Ambassador CRAIG R. STAPLETON.

Gabon: Blvd du Bord de Mer, BP 4000, Libreville; tel. 01-76-20-03; fax 01-74-55-07; e-mail usembassylibreville@state.gov; internet libreville.usembassy.gov; Ambassador EUNICE S. REDDICK (also serves São Tomé and Príncipe).

The Gambia: The White House, Kairaba Ave, Fajara, PMB 19, Banjul; tel. 439-2856; fax 439-2475; e-mail consularbanjul@state.gov; internet www.usembassybanjul.gm; Ambassador BARRY LEON WELLS.

Georgia: 11 George Balanchine St, Tbilisi 0131; tel. (32) 27-70-00; fax (32) 53-23-10; e-mail consulate-tbilisi@state.gov; internet georgia.usembassy.gov; Ambassador JOHN F. TEFFT.

Germany: Pariser Platz 2, 10117 Berlin; tel. (30) 2385174; fax (30) 83051215; e-mail acsberlin@state.gov; internet berlin.usembassy.gov; Ambassador WILLIAM R. TIMKEN, Jr.

Ghana: 24 Fourth Circular Rd, Cantonments, POB 194, Accra; tel. (21) 741000; fax (21) 741775; e-mail consulateaccra@state.gov; internet accra.usembassy.gov; Ambassador DONALD G. TEITELBAUM.

Greece: Leoforos Vassilissis Sofias 91, 10160 Athens; tel. (210) 7212951; fax (210) 7292858; e-mail athensamemb@state.gov; internet athens.usembassy.gov; Ambassador DANIEL V. SPECKHARD.

Guatemala: Avda de la Reforma 7–01, Zona 10, Guatemala City; tel. 2326-4000; fax 2326-4654; e-mail amembassyguatemala@hotmail.com; internet guatemala.usembassy.gov; Ambassador STEPHEN GEORGE MCFARLAND.

Guinea: Transversale 2, BP 603, Conakry; tel. 30-42-08-61; fax 30-42-08-73; e-mail consularconakr@state.gov; internet conakry.usembassy.gov; Ambassador PHILLIP CARTER, III.

Guyana: 100 Young and Duke Sts, Kingston, POB 10507 Georgetown; tel. 225-4900; fax 225-8497; e-mail consulargeorge@state.gov; internet georgetown.usembassy.gov; Chargé d'affaires a.i. KAREN L. WILLIAMS.

Haiti: Tabarre 41, Route de Tabarre, Port-au-Prince; tel. 2229-8000; fax 2229-8028; e-mail acspap@state.gov; internet portauprince.usembassy.gov; Ambassador JANET A. SANDERSON.

Holy See: 26 via delle Terme Deciane, 00153 Rome; tel. (06) 46743425; fax (06) 46743425; e-mail vaticaninfo@mail.usembassy.it; internet vatican.usembassy.it; Ambassador MARY ANN GLENDON.

Honduras: Avda La Paz, Apdo 3453, Tegucigalpa; tel. 236-9320; fax 236-9037; e-mail ircinfo@pd.state.gov; internet honduras.usembassy.gov; Ambassador HUGO LLORENS.

Hungary: Szabadság tér 12, 1054 Budapest; tel. (1) 475-4400; fax (1) 475-4764; e-mail infousa@usembassy.hu; internet hungary.usembassy.gov; Ambassador APRIL H. FOLEY, III.

Iceland: Laufásvegur 21, Reykjavík 101; tel. 5629100; fax 5629139; e-mail reykjavikpublicaffairs@state.gov; internet reykjavik.usembassy.gov; Ambassador CAROL VAN VOORST.

India: Shantipath, Chanakyapuri, New Delhi 110 021; tel. (11) 24198000; fax (11) 24190017; e-mail ndcentral@state.gov; internet newdelhi.usembassy.gov; Ambassador DAVID C. MULFORD.

Indonesia: Jalan Medan Merdeka Selatan 4–5, Jakarta 10110; tel. (21) 34359000; fax (21) 34359922; e-mail info@usembassyjakarta.org; internet www.usembassyjakarta.org; Ambassador CAMERON R. HUME.

Iraq: APO AE 09316, Baghdad; tel. (1) 703-3437604; e-mail BaghdadPressOffice@state.gov; internet iraq.usembassy.gov; Ambassador RYAN CROCKER.

Ireland: 42 Elgin Rd, Ballsbridge, Dublin 4; tel. (1) 6688777; fax (1) 6689946; e-mail ircdublin@state.gov; internet dublin.usembassy.gov; Ambassador THOMAS C. FOLEY.

Israel: 71 Rehov Hayarkon, Tel-Aviv 63903; tel. 3-5197575; fax 3-5173227; e-mail ac5@bezeqint.net; internet telaviv.usembassy.gov; Ambassador JAMES B. CUNNINGHAM.

Italy: Via Vittorio Veneto 121, 00187 Rome; tel. (06) 46741; fax (06) 4882672; e-mail ircrome@usembassy.it; internet rome.usembassy.gov; Ambassador RONALD P. SPOGLI.

Jamaica: 142 Old Hope Rd, Kingston 6; tel. 702-6000; fax 935-6019; e-mail opakgn@state.gov; internet kingston.usembassy.gov; Ambassador BRENDA L. JOHNSON.

Japan: 1-10-5, Akasaka, Minato-ku, Tokyo 107-8420; tel. (3) 3224-5000; fax (3) 3505-1862; e-mail ustkyecn@ppp.bekkoame.or.jp; internet tokyo.usembassy.gov; Ambassador JOHN T. (TOM) SCHIEFFER.

Jordan: POB 354, Amman 11118; tel. (6) 5906000; fax (6) 5920121; e-mail webmasterjordan@state.gov; internet amman.usembassy.gov; Ambassador ROBERT S. BEECROFT.

Kazakhstan: 010010 Astana, Ak Bulak 4/23–22, Bldg 3; tel. (717) 270-21-00; fax (717) 234-08-90; e-mail info@usembassy.kz; internet www.usembassy.kz; Ambassador RICHARD E. HOAGLAND.

Kenya: United Nations Ave, Village Market, POB 606, 00621 Nairobi; tel. (20) 3636000; fax (20) 3633410; e-mail ircnairobi@state.gov; internet nairobi.usembassy.gov; Ambassador MICHAEL E. RANNEBERGER.

Korea, Republic (South Korea): 32 Sejongno, Jongno-gu, Seoul 110-710; tel. (2) 397-4114; fax (2) 725-8543; e-mail ircseoul@state.gov; internet seoul.usembassy.gov; Ambassador KATHLEEN STEPHENS.

Kosovo: 10000 Prishtina, Arbëri, Nazim Hikmet 30; tel. (38) 593000; fax (38) 549890; e-mail papristina@state.gov; internet pristina.usembassy.gov; Ambassador TINA S. KAIDANOW.

Kuwait: Bayan, Area 14, Al-Masjed Al-Aqsa St, POB 77, Safat 13001, Kuwait City; tel. 2591001; fax 5380282; e-mail paskuwaitm@state.gov; internet kuwait.usembassy.gov; Ambassador DEBORAH K. JONES.

Kyrgyzstan: 720016 Bishkek, Pr. Mira 171; tel. (312) 55-12-41; fax (312) 55-12-64; e-mail consularbishkek@state.gov; internet kyrgyz.usembassy.gov; Ambassador TATIANA C. GFOELLER.

Laos: 19 rue Bartholonie, BP 114, Vientiane; tel. (21) 267000; fax (21) 267074; e-mail consularvienti@state.gov; internet vientiane.usembassy.gov; Ambassador RAVIC R. HUSO.

Latvia: Raiņa bulv. 7, Rīga 1510; tel. 703-6200; fax 782-0047; e-mail pas@usembassy.lv; internet riga.usembassy.gov; Ambassador CHARLES W. LARSON, Jr.

Lebanon: POB 70-840, Antélias, Aoucar, Beirut; tel. (4) 542600; fax (4) 544136; e-mail PASBeirut@State.Gov; internet lebanon.usembassy.gov; Ambassador MICHELE J. SISON.

Lesotho: 254 Kingsway, POB 333, Maseru 100; tel. 22312666; fax 22310116; e-mail infomaseru@state.gov; internet maseru.usembassy.gov; Ambassador ROBERT B. NOLAN.

Liberia: 111 United Nations Dr., Mamba Point, POB 98, Monrovia; tel. 226370; fax 226148; e-mail consularmonrovia@state.gov; internet monrovia.usembassy.gov; Ambassador LINDA THOMAS-GREENFIELD.

Lithuania: 03106 Akmenų 6, Vilnius; tel. (526) 65500; fax (526) 65510; e-mail webemailvilnius@state.gov; internet vilnius.usembassy.gov; Ambassador JOHN A. CLOUD, Jr.

Luxembourg: 22 blvd Emmanuel Servais, 2535 Luxembourg; tel. 46-01-23; fax 46-14-01; e-mail paluxembourg@state.gov; internet luxembourg.usembassy.gov; Ambassador ANN L. WAGNER.

Macedonia, former Yugoslav republic: Bul. Ilinden, BB 1000 Skopje; tel. (2) 3116180; fax (2) 3117103; e-mail consularskopje@state.gov; internet skopje.usembassy.gov; Ambassador PHILIP T. REEKER.

Madagascar: 14 rue Rainitovo, Antsahavola, BP 620, 101 Antananarivo; tel. (20) 2221257; fax (20) 2234539; e-mail uswebmaster@usmission.mg; internet www.usmission.mg; Ambassador R. NIELS MARQUARDT.

Malawi: 16 Jomo Kenyatta Rd, POB 30016, Lilongwe 3; tel. 1773166; fax 1770471; e-mail consularlilongwe@state.gov; internet lilongwe.usembassy.gov; Ambassador PETER W. BODDE.

Malaysia: 376 Jalan Tun Razak, POB 10035, 50400 Kuala Lumpur; tel. (3) 21685000; fax (3) 21485801; e-mail klconsular@state.gov; internet malaysia.usembassy.gov; Ambassador JAMES KEITH.

Mali: ACI 2000, rue 243, porte 297, Bamako; tel. 270-23-00; fax 270-24-79; e-mail consularbamako@state.gov; internet mali.usembassy.gov; Ambassador GILLIAN A. MILOVANOVIĆ.

Malta: Development House, 3rd Floor, St Anne St, Floriana VLT 01POB 535, Valletta; tel. 25614000; fax 21243229; e-mail usembmalta@state.gov; internet malta.usembassy.gov; Ambassador MOLLY W. BORDONARO.

Marshall Islands: POB 1379, Majuro, MH 96960; tel. (247) 4011; fax (247) 4012; e-mail publicmajuro@state.gov; internet majuro.usembassy.gov; Ambassador CLYDE BISHOP.

Mauritania: 288 rue 41-100 (rue Abdallaye), BP 222, Nouakchott; tel. 525-26-60; fax 525-15-92; e-mail tayebho@state.gov; internet mauritania.usembassy.gov; Ambassador MARK M. BOULWARE.

Mauritius: Rogers House, 4th Floor, President John F. Kennedy Ave, POB 544, Port Louis; tel. 202-4400; fax 208-9534; e-mail usembass@intnet.mu; internet mauritius.usembassy.gov; Ambassador CESAR CABRERA (also serves Comoros and Seychelles).

Mexico: Paseo de la Reforma 305, Col. Cuauhtémoc, 06500 México, DF; tel. (55) 5080-2000; fax (55) 5511-9980; e-mail embeuamx@state.gov; internet mexico.usembassy.gov; Ambassador ANTONIO O. GARZA, Jr.

Micronesia, Federated States: POB 1286, Pohnpei, Kolonia FM 96941; tel. 320-2187; fax 320-2186; e-mail usembassy@mail.fm; internet kolonia.usembassy.gov; Ambassador MIRIAM HUGHES.

Moldova: 2009 Chişinău, str. Mateevici 103; tel. (22) 40-83-00; fax (22) 23-30-44; e-mail ircchisinau@state.gov; internet chisinau.usembassy.gov; Ambassador ASIF CHAUDHRY.

Mongolia: Ikh Toyruu 59/1, CPO Box 1021, Ulan Bator; tel. 329095; fax 320776; e-mail receptionist@usembassy.mn; internet mongolia.usembassy.gov; Ambassador MARK C. MINTON.

Montenegro: 81000 Podgorica, Ljubljanska bb; tel. (81) 225417; fax (81) 241358; e-mail podgorica@state.gov; internet podgorica.usembassy.gov; Ambassador RODERICK W. MOORE.

Morocco: 2 ave Marrakech el-Fassi, 1000 Rabat; tel. (3) 7762265; fax (3) 7765661; e-mail ircrabat@pd.state.gov; internet www.usembassy.ma; Ambassador THOMAS T. RILEY.

Mozambique: Avda Kenneth Kaunda 193, CP 783, Maputo; tel. 21492797; fax 21490114; e-mail maputoirc@state.gov; internet maputo.usembassy.gov; Ambassador WILLIAM R. STEIGER.

Myanmar: 110 University Ave, Kamayut Township, Yangon; tel. (1) 536509; fax (1) 650306; e-mail consularrangoo@state.gov; internet rangoon.usembassy.gov; Chargé d'affaires a.i. LARRY M. DINGER.

Namibia: 14 Lossen St, Ausspannplatz, Private Bag 12029, Windhoek 9000; tel. (61) 2958500; fax (61) 2958603; e-mail windhoek@pd.state.gov; internet windhoek.usembassy.gov; Ambassador GAIL DENISSE MATHIEU.

Nepal: Maharajgunj, POB 295, Kathmandu; tel. (1) 4007200; fax (1) 4007281; e-mail usembktm@state.gov; internet nepal.usembassy.gov; Ambassador NANCY POWELL.

Netherlands: Lange Voorhout 102, 2514 EJ, The Hague; tel. (70) 3102209; fax (70) 3102307; e-mail ircthehague@state.gov; internet thehague.usembassy.gov; Ambassador JAMES B. CULBERTSON.

New Zealand: 29 Fitzherbert Terrace, POB 1190, Thorndon, Wellington; tel. (4) 462-6000; fax (4) 499-0490; internet wellington.usembassy.gov; Ambassador WILLIAM P. MCCORMICK SWINDELLS (also serves Samoa).

Nicaragua: Km 5.5, Carretera Sur, Apdo 327, Managua; tel. (2) 52-7100; fax (2) 52-7304; e-mail consularmanagua@state.gov; internet managua.usembassy.gov; Ambassador ROBERT J. CALLAHAN.

Niger: rue des Ambassadeurs, BP 11201, Niamey; tel. 20-73-31-69; fax 20-73-55-60; e-mail niameypasn@state.gov; internet niamey.usembassy.gov; Ambassador BERNADETTE M. ALLEN.

Nigeria: Plot 1075, Diplomatic Dr., Central District Area, Abuja; tel. (9) 4614000; fax (9) 4614036; e-mail pasinfoabuja@state.gov; internet abuja.usembassy.gov; Ambassador ROBIN RENEE SANDERS.

Norway: Henrik Ibsens Gate 48, 0244 Oslo; tel. 22-44-85-50; fax 22-56-27-51; e-mail osloirc@state.gov; internet www.usa.no; Ambassador BENSON K. WHITNEY.

Oman: PC 115 Madinat Al Sultan Qaboos, POB 202, Muscat; tel. 24643400; fax 24699771; e-mail answersom@state.gov; internet oman.usembassy.gov; Ambassador GARY A. GRAPPO.

Pakistan: Diplomatic Enclave, Ramna 5, POB 1048, Islamabad; tel. (51) 2080000; fax (51) 2276427; e-mail webmasterisb@state.gov; internet islamabad.usembassy.gov; Ambassador ANNE W. PATTERSON.

Panama: Avda Demetrio Basilio Lakas 783, Clayton, Panamá; tel. 207-7000; fax 317-5568; e-mail panamaweb@state.gov; internet panama.usembassy.gov; Ambassador BARBARA J. STEPHENSON.

Papua New Guinea: Douglas St, POB 1492, Port Moresby; tel. 3211455; fax 3200637; e-mail png@state.gov; internet portmoresby.usembassy.gov; Ambassador LESLIE V. ROWE (also serves Solomon Islands and Vanuatu).

Paraguay: Avda Mariscal López 1776, Casilla 402, Asunción; tel. (21) 21-3715; fax (21) 21-3728; e-mail paraguayusembassy@state.gov; internet paraguay.usembassy.gov; Ambassador LILIANA AYALDE.

Peru: Avda La Encalada, Cuadra 17 s/n, Surco, Lima 33; tel. (1) 4343000; fax (1) 6182397; internet lima.usembassy.gov; Ambassador P. MICHAEL MCKINLEY.

Philippines: 1201 Roxas Blvd, Ermita 1000, Manila; tel. (2) 3012000; fax (2) 3012017; e-mail manila@pd.state.gov; internet manila.usembassy.gov; Ambassador KIRSTIE A. KENNY.

Poland: Al. Ujazdowskie 29–31, 00-540 Warsaw; tel. (22) 5042000; fax (22) 5042688; e-mail warsawmedia@state.gov; internet poland .usembassy.gov; Ambassador VICTOR H. ASHE.

Portugal: Avda das Forças Armadas (Sete Rios), 1649-044 Lisbon; Apdo 43033, 1601-301 Lisbon; tel. (21) 7273300; fax (21) 7269109; e-mail lisbonweb@state.gov; internet portugal.usembassy.gov; Ambassador THOMAS F. STEPHENSON.

Qatar: 22nd February St, Al-Luqta district, POB 2399, Doha; tel. 4884101; fax 4884298; e-mail pasdoha@state.gov; internet qatar .usembassy.gov; Ambassador JOSEPH E. LEBARON.

Romania: Str. Tudor Arghezi 7–9, 70132 Bucharest; tel. (1) 2003300; fax (1) 2003442; e-mail acsbucharest@state.gov; internet bucharest.usembassy.gov; Ambassador NICHOLAS F. TAUBMAN.

Russia: B. Devyatinskii per. 8, 121099 Moscow; tel. (495) 728-50-00; fax (495) 728-50-90; e-mail moscowwebm@state.gov; internet moscow.usembassy.gov; Ambassador JOHN R. BEYRLE.

Rwanda: 2657 Ave de la Gendarmerie, BP 28, Kacyiru, Kigali; tel. 596400; fax 596771; e-mail kigaliembassy@state.gov; internet kigali .usembassy.gov; Chargé d'affaires a.i. CHERYL J. SIM.

Samoa: ACB House, 5th Floor, Matafele, POB 3430, Apia; tel. 21436; fax 22030; e-mail amembapia@state.gov; internet samoa.usembassy .gov; Ambassador WILLIAM P. MCCORMICK (resident in New Zealand).

Saudi Arabia: POB 94309, Riyadh 11693; tel. (1) 488-3800; fax (1) 488-7360; e-mail usembriyadhwebsite@state.gov; internet riyadh .usembassy.gov; Ambassador FORD M. FRAKER.

Senegal: Ave Jean XXIII/rue Kléber, BP 49, Dakar; tel. 829-21-00; fax 822-29-91; e-mail consulardakar@state.gov; internet dakar .usembassy.gov; Ambassador MARCIA S. BERNICAT (also serves Guinea-Bissau).

Serbia: Kneza Miloša 50, 11000 Belgrade; tel. (11) 3619344; fax (11) 3615489; e-mail consularbelgrd@state.gov; internet belgrade .usembassy.gov; Ambassador CAMERON MUNTER.

Sierra Leone: Hill Station, Freetown; tel. (22) 515000; fax (22) 515355; e-mail taylorjb2@state.gov; internet freetown.usembassy .gov; Ambassador JUNE CARTER PERRY.

Singapore: 27 Napier Rd, Singapore 258508; tel. 64769100; fax 64769340; e-mail singaporeusembassy@state.gov; internet singapore.usembassy.gov; Ambassador PATRICIA L. HERBOLD.

Slovakia: Hviezdoslavovo nám 4, 814 99 Bratislava; tel. (2) 5443-3338; fax (2) 5441-8861; e-mail consulbratislava@state.gov; internet slovakia.usembassy.gov; Ambassador VINCENT OBSITNIK.

Slovenia: Prešernova 31, 1000 Ljubljana; tel. (1) 2005500; fax (1) 2005555; e-mail usembassyljubljana@state.gov; internet www .usembassy.si; Ambassador YOUSIF BOUTROUS GHAFARI.

South Africa: 877 Pretorius St, Pretoria 0083, POB 9536, Pretoria 0001; tel. (12) 4314000; fax (12) 3422299; e-mail embassypretoria@ state.gov; internet southafrica.usembassy.gov; Ambassador ERIC M. BOST.

Spain: Calle Serrano 75, 28006 Madrid; tel. (91) 5872200; fax (91) 5872303; e-mail amemb@embusa.es; internet madrid.usembassy .gov; Ambassador EDUARDO AGUIRRE, Jr (also serves Andorra).

Sri Lanka: 210 Galle Rd, POB 106, Colombo 3; tel. (1) 2498500; fax (1) 2437345; e-mail consularcolombo@state.gov; internet colombo .usembassy.gov; Ambassador ROBERT O. BLAKE, Jr (also serves Maldives).

Sudan: Shari'a Ali Abdul Latif, POB 699, Khartoum; tel. (183) 774701; fax (183) 774611; e-mail gameelisa@state.gov; internet khartoum.usembassy.gov; Chargé d'affaires ALBERTO M. FERNANDEZ.

Suriname: Dr Sophie Redmondstraat 129, POB 1821, Paramaribo; tel. 472900; fax 425690; e-mail djaminsc@state.gov; internet paramaribo.usembassy.gov; Ambassador LISA B. SCHREIBER HUGHES.

Swaziland: 2350 Mbabane Pl., Mbabane; tel. 4042445; fax 4042059; e-mail jsdlamini@usembassy.org.sz; internet mbabane.usembassy .gov; Ambassador MAURICE S. PARKER.

Sweden: Dag Hammarskjölds Väg 31, SE-115 89 Stockholm; tel. (8) 783-53-00; fax (8) 661-19-64; e-mail stockholmweb@state.gov; internet stockholm.usembassy.gov; Ambassador MICHAEL WOOD.

Switzerland: Sulgeneckstr. 19, 3007 Bern; tel. 313577011; fax 313577344; e-mail bernacs@state.gov; internet bern.usembassy .gov; Ambassador PETER R. CONEWAY (also serves Liechtenstein).

Syria: rue al-Mansour 2, BP 29, Abou Roumaneh, Damascus; tel. (11) 33914444; fax (11) 33913999; e-mail damasweb-query@state .gov; internet damascus.usembassy.gov; Chargé d'affaires a.i. MAURA CONNELLY.

Tajikistan: 109-A Ismoili Somoni Ave, 734019 Dushanbe; tel. (372) 29-20-00; fax (372) 29-20-50; e-mail usembassydushanbe@state.gov; internet dushanbe.usembassy.gov; Ambassador TRACEY A. JACOBSON.

Tanzania: 686 Old Bagamoyo Rd, Msasani, POB 9123, Dar es Salaam; tel. (22) 2668001; fax (22) 2668238; e-mail consulardx@ state.gov; internet tanzania.usembassy.gov; Ambassador MARK A. GREEN.

Thailand: 95 Wireless Rd, Patumwan, Bangkok 10330; tel. (2) 205-4192; fax (2) 650-8921; e-mail bangkokpd@state.gov; internet bangkok.usembassy.gov; Ambassador ERIC G. JOHN.

Timor-Leste: Avda de Portugal, Praia dos Coqueiros, Dili; tel. (390) 3324684; fax (390) 3313206; e-mail larsonta@state.gov; internet timor-leste.usembassy.gov; Ambassador HANS G. KLEMM.

Togo: Blvd Eyadema, BP 852, Lomé; tel. 261-54-70; fax 261-55-01; e-mail lomeirc@pd.state.gov; internet lome.usembassy.gov; Ambassador DAVID B. DUNN.

Trinidad and Tobago: 15 Queen's Park West, POB 752, Port of Spain; tel. 622-6371; fax 822-5905; e-mail ircpos@state.gov; internet trinidad.usembassy.gov; Ambassador Dr ROY L. AUSTIN.

Tunisia: Zone Nord-Est des Berges du Lac, Nord de Tunis, 1053 Tunis; tel. (71) 107-000; fax (71) 107-090; e-mail consulartunis@state .gov; internet tunisia.usembassy.gov; Ambassador ROBERT F. GODEC.

Turkey: Atatürk Bul. 110, 06540 Kavaklidere, Ankara 06100; tel. (312) 4555555; fax (312) 4670019; e-mail webmaster_ankara@state .gov; internet ankara.usembassy.gov; Ambassador ROSS L. WILSON.

Turkmenistan: ul. 1984 9 (ul. Pushkina), 744000 Ashgabat; tel. (12) 35-00-45; fax (12) 39-26-14; e-mail consularashgab@state.gov; internet turkmenistan.usembassy.gov; Chargé d'affaires a.i. SYLVIA R. CURRAN.

Uganda: Plot 1577, Ggaba Rd, POB 7007, Kampala; tel. (41) 259795; fax (41) 259794; e-mail kampalawebcontact@state.gov; internet kampala.usembassy.gov; Ambassador STEVEN A. BROWNING.

Ukraine: 01901 Kyiv, vul. Yu. Kotsyubynskoho 10; tel. (44) 490-40-00; fax (44) 490-40-85; e-mail irc@usembassy.kiev.ua; internet kiev .usembassy.gov; Ambassador WILLIAM B. TAYLOR, Jr.

United Arab Emirates: Al-Sudan St, POB 4009, Abu Dhabi; tel. (2) 4142200; fax (2) 4142241; e-mail webmasterabudhabi@state.gov; internet uae.usembassy.gov; Ambassador RICHARD OLSON.

United Kingdom: 24–32 Grosvenor Sq., London W1A 1AE; tel. (20) 7499-9000; fax (20) 7629-9124; internet london.embassy.gov; Ambassador ROBERT H. TUTTLE.

Uruguay: Lauro Muller 1776, Montevideo 11200; tel. (2) 4187777; fax (2) 4188611; e-mail ircmvd@state.gov; internet uruguay .usembassy.gov; Ambassador FRANK E. BAXTER.

Uzbekistan: ul. Moyqorghon 3, 5th Block, Yunusobod District, 100093 Tashkent; tel. (71) 120-54-50; fax (71) 120-63-35; e-mail consulartashkent@state.gov; internet www.usembassy.uz; Ambassador RICHARD B. NORLAND.

Venezuela: Calle F con Calle Suapure, Urb. Colinas de Valle Arriba, Caracas 1080; tel. (212) 975-6411; fax (212) 975-9429; e-mail embajada@state.gov; internet caracas.usembassy.gov; Chargé d'affaires a.i. JOHN CAULFIELD.

Viet Nam: 7 Lang Ha, Ba Dinh District, Hanoi; tel. (4) 772-1500; fax (4) 850-5010; e-mail irchanoi@state.gov; internet hanoi.usembassy .gov; Ambassador MICHAEL W. MICHALAK.

Yemen: Sa'awan St, POB 22347, Sana'a; tel. (1) 7552000; fax (1) 303182; e-mail ircsanaa@state.gov; internet yemen.usembassy.gov; Ambassador STEPHEN A. SECHE.

Zambia: Cnr Independence and United Nations Aves, POB 31617, 10101 Lusaka; tel. (1) 250955; fax (1) 252225; e-mail irclusaka@state .gov; internet zambia.usembassy.gov; Chargé d'affaires a.i. MICHAEL KOPLOVSKY.

Zimbabwe: 172 Herbert Chitepo Ave, POB 3340, Harare; tel. (4) 250593; fax (4) 796488; e-mail hararepas@state.gov; internet harare .usembassy.gov; Ambassador JAMES D. MCGEE.

JUDICIAL SYSTEMS OF THE USA

THE FEDERAL JUDICIAL SYSTEM

Supreme Court of the United States

(Supreme Court Bldg, 1 First St, NE, Washington, DC 20543; tel. (202) 479-3211; fax (202) 479-2971; internet www.supremecourtus.gov)

The Supreme Court is the only Federal Court established by the Constitution. It is the highest court in the nation, comprising a Chief Justice and eight Associate Justices. Appointments, which are for life or until voluntary retirement, are made by the President, subject to confirmation by the US Senate.

Chief Justice: JOHN G. ROBERTS, Jr (appointed 2005).

Associate Justices: JOHN PAUL STEVENS (1975), ANTONIN SCALIA (1986), ANTHONY M. KENNEDY (1988), DAVID H. SOUTER (1990), CLARENCE THOMAS (1991), RUTH BADER GINSBURG (1993), STEPHEN G. BREYER (1994), SAMUEL A. ALITO, Jr (2006).

US Courts of Appeal

(Administrative Office of the US Courts, Washington, DC 20544; tel. (202) 502-2600; internet www.uscourts.gov)

The USA is divided into 12 judicial circuits, in each of which there is one Court of Appeals. The Court of Appeals for the Federal Circuit has nation-wide specialized jurisdiction.

Federal Courts hear cases involving federal law, cases involving participants from more than one state, crimes committed in more than one state and civil or corporate cases that cross state lines. Federal District Courts, of which there are 94, are the courts of first instance for most federal suits.

Federal Circuit: PAUL R. MICHEL (Chief Judge), PAULINE NEWMAN, HALDANE ROBERT MAYER, ALAN D. LOURIE, RANDALL R. RADER, ALVIN A. SCHALL, WILLIAM CURTIS BRYSON, ARTHUR J. GAJARSA, RICHARD LINN, TIMOTHY B. DYK, SHARON PROST, KIMBERLEY MOORE.

District of Columbia Circuit: DAVID B. SENTELLE (Chief Judge), DOUGLAS H. GINSBURG, KAREN LECRAFT HENDERSON, A. RAYMOND RANDOLPH, JUDITH W. ROGERS, DAVID S. TATEL, MERRICK B. GARLAND, JANICE ROGERS BROWN, THOMAS B. GRIFFITH, BRETT M. KAVANAUGH.

First Circuit (Maine, Massachusetts, New Hampshire, Rhode Island, Puerto Rico): SANDRA L. LYNCH (Chief Judge), JUAN R. TORRUELLA, MICHAEL BOUDIN, KERMIT V. LIPEZ, JEFFREY R. HOWARD.

Second Circuit (Connecticut, New York, Vermont): DENNIS JACOBS (Chief Judge), GUIDO CALABRESI, JOSÉ A. CABRANES, CHESTER J. STRAUB, ROSEMARY S. POOLER, ROBERT D. SACK, SONIA SOTOMAYOR, ROBERT A. KATZMANN, BARRINGTON D. PARKER, REENA RAGGI, RICHARD C. WESLEY, PETER W. HALL, DEBRA ANN LIVINGSTON.

Third Circuit (Delaware, New Jersey, Pennsylvania, Virgin Islands): ANTHONY J. SCIRICA (Chief Judge), DOLORES K. SLOVITER, THEODORE A. MCKEE, MARJORIE O. RENDELL, MARYANNE TRUMP BARRY, THOMAS L. AMBRO, JULIO M. FUENTES, D. BROOKS SMITH, D. MICHAEL FISHER, MICHAEL A. CHAGARES, KENT A. JORDAN, THOMAS M. HARDIMAN.

Fourth Circuit (Maryland, North Carolina, South Carolina, Virginia, West Virginia): KAREN J. WILLIAMS (Chief Judge), J. HARVIE WILKINSON, III, PAUL V. NIEMEYER, M. BLANE MICHAEL, DIANA GRIBBON MOTZ, WILLIAM B. TRAXLER, Jr, ROBERT B. KING, ROGER L. GREGORY, DENNIS W. SHEDD, ALLYSON K. DUNCAN, G. STEVEN AGEE.

Fifth Circuit (Louisiana, Mississippi, Texas): EDITH H. JONES (Chief Judge), CAROLYN DINEEN KING, E. GRADY JOLLY, W. EUGENE DAVIS, JERRY E. SMITH, JACQUES L. WIENER, Jr, RHESA H. BARKSDALE, EMILIO M. GARZA, FORTUNATO P. BENAVIDES, CARL E. STEWART, JAMES L. DENNIS, EDITH BROWN CLEMENT, EDWARD C. PRADO, PRISCILLA R. OWEN, JENNIFER W. ELROD, LESLIE SOUTHWICK, CATHARINA HAYNES.

Sixth Circuit (Kentucky, Michigan, Ohio, Tennessee): DANNY J. BOGGS (Chief Judge), BOYCE F. MARTIN, Jr, ALICE M. BATCHELDER, MARTHA CRAIG DAUGHTREY, KAREN NELSON MOORE, RANSEY GUY COLE, Jr, ERIC L. CLAY, RONALD LEE GILMAN, JULIA SMITH GIBBONS, JOHN M. ROGERS, JEFFREY S. SUTTON, DEBORAH L. COOK, DAVID W. MCKEAGUE, RICHARD ALLEN GRIFFIN, RAYMOND M. KETHLEDGE, HELENE N. WHITE.

Seventh Circuit (Illinois, Indiana, Wisconsin): FRANK H. EASTERBROOK (Chief Judge), WILLIAM J. BAUER, RICHARD D. CUDAHY, RICHARD A. POSNER, JOHN L. COFFEY, JOEL M. FLAUM, KENNETH F. RIPPLE, DANIEL A. MANION, MICHAEL S. KANNE, ILANA DIAMOND ROVNER, DIANE P. WOOD, TERENCE T. EVANS, ANN CLAIRE WILLIAMS, DIANE S. SYKES, JOHN D. TINDER.

Eighth Circuit (Arkansas, Iowa, Minnesota, Missouri, Nebraska, North Dakota, South Dakota): JAMES B. LOKEN (Chief Judge), ROGER L. WOLLMAN, DIANA E. MURPHY, KERMIT E. BYE, WILLIAM J. RILEY, MICHAEL J. MELLOY, LAVENSKI R. SMITH, STEVEN M. COLLOTON, RAYMOND W. GRUENDER, DUANE BENTON, BOBBY E. SHEPHERD.

Ninth Circuit (Alaska, Arizona, California, Guam, Hawaii, Idaho, Montana, Nevada, Northern Mariana Islands, Oregon, Washington): ALEX KOZINSKI (Chief Judge), MARY M. SCHROEDER, HARRY PREGERSON, STEPHEN REINHARDT, DIARMUID F. O'SCANNLAIN, PAMELA ANN RYMER, ANDREW J. KLEINFELD, MICHAEL DALY HAWKINS, SIDNEY R. THOMAS, BARRY G. SILVERMAN, SUSAN P. GRABER, M. MARGARET MCKEOWN, KIM MCLANE WARDLAW, WILLIAM A. FLETCHER, RAYMOND C. FISHER, RONALD M. GOULD, RICHARD A. PAEZ, MARSHA S. BERZON, RICHARD C. TALLMAN, JOHNNIE B. RAWLINSON, RICHARD R. CLIFTON, JAY S. BYBEE, CONSUELO M. CALLAHAN, CARLOS T. BEA, MILAN D. SMITH, Jr, SANDRA S. IKUTA, N. RANDY SMITH.

Tenth Circuit (Colorado, Kansas, New Mexico, Oklahoma, Utah, Wyoming): ROBERT H. HENRY (Chief Judge), DEANELL REECE TACHA, PAUL J. KELLY, MARY BECK BRISCOE, CARLOS F. LUCERO, MICHAEL R. MURPHY, HARRIS L. HARTZ, TERRENCE L. O'BRIEN, MICHAEL W. MCCONNELL, TIMOTHY M. TYMKOVICH, NEIL M. GORSUCH, JEROME A. HOLMES.

Eleventh Circuit (Alabama, Florida, Georgia): J. L. EDMONSON (Chief Judge), GERALD B. TJOFLAT, R. LANIER ANDERSON, STANLEY F. BIRCH, Jr, JOEL F. DUBINA, SUSAN H. BLACK, EDWARD E. CARNES, ROSEMARY BARKETT, FRANK M. HULL, STANLEY MARCUS, CHARLES R. WILSON, WILLIAM H. PRYOR, Jr.

United States Federal District Courts

There are 94 Federal District Courts, with at least one in each state, and one each in the District of Columbia and the US External Territories of Guam, the Northern Mariana Islands, Puerto Rico and the US Virgin Islands. They are the courts of first instance for most federal suits. Although federal in their jurisdiction, these courts are listed by state (see below). The Federal District Courts handle bankruptcy cases, over which they have exclusive jurisdiction. Bankruptcy cases cannot be filed in state court.

United States Court of Federal Claims

(717 Madison Pl., NW, Washington, DC 20005; tel. (202) 357 6400; fax (202) 219-9593; internet www.uscfc.uscourts.gov)

Judges: EDWARD J. DAMICH (Chief Judge), CHRISTINE ODELL COOK MILLER, MARIAN BLANK HORN, FRANCIS M. ALLEGRA, LAWRENCE M. BASKIR, LYNN J. BUSH, NANCY B. FIRESTONE, EMILY C. HEWITT, LAWRENCE J. BLOCK, MARY ELLEN COSTER WILLIAMS, CHARLES F. LETTOW, SUSAN G. BRADEN, VICTOR J. WOLSKI, GEORGE W. MILLER, THOMAS C. WHEELER, MARGARET M. SWEENEY.

United States Court of International Trade

(1 Federal Plaza, New York, NY 10278-0001; tel. (212) 264-2800; fax (212) 264-1085; internet www.cit.uscourts.gov)

Judges: JANE A. RESTANI (Chief Judge), GREGORY W. CARMAN, DONALD C. POGUE, EVAN J. WALLACH, JUDITH M. BARZILAY, DELISSA A. RIDGWAY, RICHARD K. EATON, TIMOTHY C. STANCEU, LEO M. GORDON.

United States Tax Court

(400 Second St, NW, Washington, DC 20217; tel. (202) 521-0700; internet www.ustaxcourt.gov)

Judges: JOHN O. COLVIN (Chief Judge), MARY ANN COHEN, MAURICE B. FOLEY, JOSEPH H. GALE, JOSEPH R. GOEKE, DAVID GUSTAFSON, HARRY A. HAINES, JAMES S. HALPERN, MARK V. HOLMES, DIANE L. KROUPA, L. PAIGE MARVEL, RICHARD T. MORRISON, ELIZABETH C. PARIS, MICHAEL B. THORNTON, JUAN F. VASQUEZ, THOMAS B. WELLS, ROBERT A. WHERRY, Jr.

STATE JUDICIAL SYSTEMS

Alabama

FEDERAL COURTS

Alabama is in the Eleventh Circuit of the US Courts of Appeals. There are US District Courts at Birmingham, Montgomery and Mobile.

US District Courts

Middle: POB 711, Montgomery, AL 36101-0711; tel. (334) 954-3600; internet www.almd.uscourts.gov; Judges Mark E. Fuller (Chief Judge), Myron H. Thompson, W. Keith Watkins.

Northern: Hugo L. Black US Courthouse, 1729 Fifth Ave North, Birmingham, AL 35203; tel. (205) 278-1700; internet www.alnd.uscourts.gov; Judges Sharon Lovelace Blackburn (Chief Judge), U. W. Clemon, C. Lynwood Smith, Jr, Inge P. Johnson, Karon O. Bowdre, L. Scott Coogler, R. David Proctor, Virginia Emerson Hopkins.

Southern: US Courthouse, 113 St Joseph St, Mobile, AL 36602; tel. (251) 690-2371; fax (251) 694-4297; e-mail information@alsd.uscourts.gov; internet www.als.uscourts.gov; Judges Callie V. S. Granade (Chief Judge), William H. Steele, Kristi K. DuBose.

STATE COURTS

The state Supreme Court has nine justices, including the chief justice. All justices are elected at-large to serve staggered six-year terms. The state courts of appeals are the Court of Criminal Appeals and the Court of Civil Appeals, both of which have five judges serving six-year terms.

Supreme Court: 300 Dexter Ave, Montgomery, AL 36104-3741; tel. (334) 242-4609; fax (334) 242-4483; internet www.judicial.state.al.us/supreme.cfm; Justices Sue Bell Cobb (Chief Justice), Harold Frend See, Jr, Champ Lyons, Jr, Thomas A. Woodall, Lyn Stuart, Patricia M. Smith, Michael F. Bolin, Thomas Parker, Glen Murdock.

Alaska

FEDERAL COURTS

Alaska is in the Ninth Circuit of the US Courts of Appeals. There is a US District Court at Anchorage.

US District Court: Federal Bldg and US Courthouse, 222 West Seventh Ave, Anchorage, AK 99513; tel. (907) 677-6100; fax (907) 677-6180; internet www.akd.uscourts.gov; Judges John W. Sedwick (Chief Judge), Ralph R. Beistline, Timothy M. Burgess.

STATE COURTS

The state Supreme Court has five justices, including the chief justice. The justices are selected at-large and, once their appointments have been ratified by the electorate, serve a 10-year term of office. The chief justice is selected by the court to serve a three-year term. The state Court of Appeals has three judges, who serve for terms of eight years.

Supreme Court: Boney Memorial US Courthouse, 303 K St, Anchorage, AK 99501-2084; tel. (907) 264-0618; e-mail supreme_court@appellate.courts.state.ak.us; internet www.state.ak.us/courts/ctinfo.htm; Justices Dana Fabe (Chief Justice), Warren W. Matthews, Robert L. Eastaugh, Walter L. Carpeneti, Daniel E. Winfree.

Arizona

FEDERAL COURTS

Arizona is in the Ninth Circuit of the US Courts of Appeals. US District Courts operate in Phoenix and Tucson.

US District Courts: Sandra Day O'Connor US Courthouse, 401 West Washington St, Phoenix, AZ 85003-2118; tel. (602) 322-7200; internet www.azd.uscourts.gov; Evo A. DeConcini US Courthouse, 405 West Congress St, Suite 1500, Tucson, AZ 85701-5010; tel. (520) 205-4200; Judges John McCarthy Roll (Chief Judge), Susan R. Bolton, David G. Campbell, Frederick J. Martone, Mary H. Murguia, Roslyn O. Silver, James A. Teilborg, Neil V. Wake, David C. Bury, Raner C. Collins, Cindy K. Jorgenson, Frank R. Zapata, G. Murray Snow.

STATE COURTS

The state Supreme Court has five justices, including the chief justice. Justices are appointed by the governor and serve six-year terms of office. The justices select one of their number as chief justice and he or she serves a five-year term of office. The state Court of Appeals has 22 judges, all of whom serve six-year terms of office.

Supreme Court: 1501 West Washington, Phoenix, AZ 85007; tel. (602) 452-3545; e-mail info@supreme.sp.state.az.us; internet www.supreme.state.az.us; Justices Ruth V. McGregor (Chief Justice), Rebecca White Berch (Vice-Chief Justice), Michael D. Ryan, Andrew D. Hurwitz, W. Scott Bales.

Arkansas

FEDERAL COURTS

Arkansas is in the Eighth Circuit of the US Courts of Appeals. There are US District Courts at Little Rock and Fort Smith.

US District Courts

Eastern: US Courthouse, 500 West Capitol Ave, Little Rock, AR 72201-3325; tel. (501) 604-5351; fax (501) 604-5321; internet www.are.uscourts.gov; Judges J. Leon Holmes (Chief Judge), Susan Webber Wright, G. Thomas Eisele, William Roy Wilson, Jr, James M. Moody, Brian S. Miller.

Western: 1038 Isaac C. Parker Federal Bldg, 30 South Sixth St, Fort Smith, AR 72901; POB 1547, Fort Smith, AR 72902; tel. (479) 783-6833; fax (479) 783-6308; e-mail fsm_info@arwd.uscourts.gov; internet www.arwd.uscourts.gov; Judges Jimm Larry Hendren (Chief Judge), Harry F. Barnes, Robert T. Dawson.

STATE COURTS

The state Supreme Court has seven justices, including the chief justice, who is chosen by popular election and serves a term of eight years. The remaining justices, who also serve eight-year terms, are selected at-large. The state Court of Appeals has 12 judges serving terms of eight years.

Supreme Court: 120 Justice Bldg, 625 Marshall St, Little Rock, AR 72201; tel. (501) 682-9400; fax (501) 682-9410; internet courts.state.ar.us/courts/sc.html; Justices James Hannah (Chief Justice), Annabel Clinton Imber, Donald L. Corbin, Robert L. Brown, Jim Gunter, Paul E. Danielson, Elana Cunningham Wills.

California

FEDERAL COURTS

California is in the Ninth Circuit of the US Courts of Appeals. There are US District Courts in San Francisco, Sacramento, Los Angeles and San Diego.

US District Courts

Central: US Courthouse, 312 North Spring St, Los Angeles, CA 90012; tel. (213) 894-1565; fax (213) 894-6860; internet www.cacd.uscourts.gov; Judges Alicemarie Huber Stotler (Chief Judge), Percy Anderson, Cormac J. Carney, David O. Carter, Audrey B. Collins, Florence-Marie Cooper, Valerie Baker Fairbank, Gary A. Feess, Dale S. Fischer, Andrew J Guilford, Philip S. Gutierrez, George H. King, R. Gary Klausner, Stephen G. Larson, A. Howard Matz, Margaret M. Morrow, S. James Otero, Virginia A. Phillips, Dean D. Pregerson, Manuel L. Real, George P. Schiavelli, James V. Selna, Christina A. Snyder, John F. Walter, Stephen V. Wilson, Otis D. Wright, II, George H. Wu.

Eastern: US Courthouse, 501 I St, Sacramento, CA 95814; tel. (916) 930-4000; internet www.caed.uscourts.gov; Judges Garland E. Burrell, Jr (Chief Judge), Frank C. Damrell, Jr, Morrison C. England, Jr, John A. Mendez, Oliver W. Wagner, Anthony W. Ishii, Lawrence J. O'Neill.

Northern: Federal Bldg, 450 Golden Gate Ave, POB 36060, San Francisco, CA 94102; tel. (415) 522-2000; fax (415) 522-2176; internet www.cand.uscourts.gov; Judges Vaughn R. Walker (Chief Judge), William Alsup, Saundra Brown Armstrong, Charles R. Breyer, Maxine M. Chesney, Jeremy Fogel, Phyllis J. Hamilton, Susan Illston, Marilyn Hall Patel, James Ware, Jeffrey S. White, Ronald M. Whyte, Claudia Wilken.

Southern: 880 Front St, San Diego, CA 92101-8900; tel. (619) 557-5600; internet www.casd.uscourts.gov; Judges Irma E. Gonzalez (Chief Judge), Michael M. Anello, Roger T. Benitez, Larry A. Burns, William Q. Hayes, John A. Houston, Napoleon A. Jones, Jr,

Marilyn L. Huff , M. James Lorenz, Jeffrey T. Miller, Barry Ted Moskowitz, Dana M. Sabraw, Thomas J. Whelan.

STATE COURTS

The state Supreme Court has seven justices, including the chief justice. All appointments are made by the governor, confirmed by the Commission on Judicial Appointments and ratified by the electorate at the next election. Justices serve 12-year terms of office. The state Court of Appeals has 105 judges, who also serve 12-year terms of office.

Supreme Court: 350 McAllister St, San Francisco, CA 94102-4797; tel. (415) 865-7000; internet www.courtinfo.ca.gov/courts/supreme; Justices Ronald M. George (Chief Justice), Joyce L. Kennard, Kathryn M. Werdegar, Ming W. Chin, Marvin R. Baxter, Carlos R. Moreno, Carol A. Corrigan.

Colorado

FEDERAL COURTS

Colorado is in the Tenth Circuit of the US Courts of Appeals. The US District Court is at Denver.

US District Court: Alfred A. Arraj US Courthouse, 901 19th St, Denver, CO 80294; tel. (303) 844-3433; internet www.cod.uscourts.gov; Judges Edward W. Nottingham, Jr (Chief Judge), Wiley Y. Daniel, Marcia S. Krieger, Robert E. Blackburn, Christine M. Arguello, Philip A. Brimmer.

STATE COURTS

The state Supreme Court has seven justices, including the chief justice. The justices, who are elected at-large and appointed by the governor to serve 10-year terms of office, choose one of their number as chief justice to serve a term according to the pleasure of the Court. The state Court of Appeals has 19 judges, who serve terms of eight years.

Supreme Court: Colorado State Judicial Bldg, 4th Floor, 2 East 14th Ave, Denver, CO 80203; tel. (303) 837-3790; fax (303) 861-7429; internet www.coloradosupremecourt.com; Justices Mary Mullarkey (Chief Justice), Gregory J. Hobbs, Jr, Alex J. Martinez, Michael L. Bender, Nancy E. Rice, Nathan B. Coats, Allison Eid.

Connecticut

FEDERAL COURTS

Connecticut is in the Second Circuit of the US Courts of Appeals. The US District Court is at New Haven.

US District Court: US Courthouse, 141 Church St, New Haven, CT 06510; tel. (203) 773-2140; fax (203) 773-2334; internet www.ctd.uscourts.gov; Judges Robert N. Chatigny (Chief Judge), Janet Bond Arterton, Vanessa L. Bryant, Christopher F. Droney, Janet C. Hall, Mark R. Kravitz, Alvin W. Thompson, Stefan R. Underhill.

STATE COURTS

The state Supreme Court has seven justices, including the chief justice, serving eight-year terms of office; they are nominated by the governor and appointed by the General Assembly. The state Appellate Court has 10 judges, who serve eight-year terms of office.

Supreme Court: Supreme Court Bldg, 231 Capitol Ave, Hartford, CT 06106; tel. (860) 757-2200; internet www.jud.state.ct.us/external/supapp; Justices Chase T. Rogers (Chief Justice), Flemming L. Norcott, Jr, Joette Katz, Richard N. Palmer, Peter T. Zarella, Christine S. Vertefeuille, Barry R. Schaller.

Delaware

FEDERAL COURTS

Delaware is in the Third Circuit of the US Courts of Appeals. The US District Court is at Wilmington.

US District Court: J. Caleb Boggs Federal Bldg, 844 North King St, Wilmington, DE 19801; tel. (302) 573-6170; internet www.ded.uscourts.gov; Judges Gregory M. Sleet (Chief Judge), Joseph J. Farnan, Jr, Sue L. Robinson.

STATE COURTS

The state Supreme Court has five justices, including the chief justice. All the justices, selected at-large, are appointed by the governor with the consent of the Senate and serve terms of 12 years.

Supreme Court: Carvel State Office Bldg, 820 North French St, 11th Floor, Wilmington, DE 19801; tel. (302) 577-8425; fax (302) 577-3702; internet courts.state.de.us/supreme; Justices Myron T. Steele (Chief Justice), Jack B. Jacobs, Randy J. Holland, Henry duPont Ridgely, Carolyn Berger.

District of Columbia

FEDERAL COURTS

The District of Columbia constitutes a separate circuit of the US Courts of Appeals. There is also a US District Court in Washington.

US District Court: E. Barrett Prettyman US Courthouse, 333 Constitution Ave, NW, Washington, DC 20001; tel. (202) 354-3000; fax (202) 354-3023; internet www.dcd.uscourts.gov; Judges Royce C. Lamberth (Chief Judge), Thomas F. Hogan, Paul L. Friedman, Ricardo M. Urbina, Emmet G. Sullivan, James Robertson, Colleen Kollar-Kotelly, Henry Harold Kennedy, Jr, Richard W. Roberts, Ellen Segal Huvelle, Reggie B. Walton, John D. Bates, Richard J. Leon, Rosemary M. Collyer.

DISTRICT OF COLUMBIA COURTS

The District of Columbia's Court of Appeals has nine judges, including the chief justice, and functions as the court of last resort. Judges are selected at-large and serve for a term of 15 years; all District of Columbia judges are nominated by the President of the USA, from a list submitted by the District of Columbia Judicial Nominating Commission, and appointed with the consent of the US Senate. The chief justice is similarly appointed to serve a four-year term of office. In the general trial court, the Superior Court, criminal cases are prosecuted by the US Attorney's Office, a division of the federal Department of Justice.

Court of Appeals: 500 Indiana Ave, 6th Floor, Rm 6000, NW, Washington, DC 20001; tel. (202) 879-1010; internet www.dcappeals.gov; Judges Eric T. Washington (Chief Judge), Michael W. Farrell, Vanessa Ruiz, Inez Smith Reid, Stephen H. Glickman, Noël Anketell Kramer, John R. Fisher, Anna Blackburne-Rigsby, Phyllis D. Thompson.

Florida

FEDERAL COURTS

Florida is in the Eleventh Circuit of the US Courts of Appeals. US District Courts are situated in Tallahassee, Orlando and Miami.

US District Courts

Middle: US Courthouse, 401 West Central Blvd, Suite 1200, Orlando, FL 32801-0120; tel. (407) 835-4200; fax (407) 835-4207; internet www.flmd.uscourts.gov; Judges Anne C. Conway (Chief Judge), Henry Lee Adams, Jr, Timothy J. Corrigan, John Antoon, II, Gregory A. Presnell, Elizabeth A. Kovachevich, Steven D. Merryday, Susan C. Bucklew, Richard A. Lazzara, James D. Whittemore, James S. Moody, Jr, John E. Steele, Virginia Covington, Marcia Morales Howard, Mary Stenson Scriven.

Northern: US Courthouse, 111 North Adams St, Tallahassee, FL 32301-7730; tel. (850) 521-3501; fax (850) 521-3550; internet www.flnd.uscourts.gov; Judges Robert L. Hinkle (Chief Judge), Stephan P. Mickle, John Richard Smoak, Jr, Margaret Catherine Rodgers.

Southern: Wilkie D. Ferguson, Jr US Courthouse, 400 North Miami Ave, 8th Floor, Miami, FL 33128; tel. (305) 523-5100; internet www.flsd.uscourts.gov; Judges Federico A. Moreno (Chief Judge), William J. Zloch, Donald L. Graham, K. Michael Moore, Ursula Ungaro, Daniel T. K. Hurley, Joan A. Lenard, Donald M. Middlebrooks, Alan S. Gold, William P. Dimitrouleas, Patricia A. Seitz, Adalberto Jordan, Paul C. Huck, Kenneth A. Marra, José E. Martinez, Cecilia M. Altonaga, James I. Cohn, Marcia G. Cooke.

STATE COURTS

The state Supreme Court has seven justices, including the chief justice. The justices, who are selected at-large by the governor, on the advice of the Judicial Nominating Commission, serve terms of six years. The chief justice is chosen by the Court and serves a two-year term of office. There is a District Court of Appeals, which has 63 judges serving six-year terms of office. Judges of both these Courts may seek election to subsequent terms of office at the general election preceding the expiration of their existing term of office.

Supreme Court: 500 South Duval St, Tallahassee, FL 32399-1927; tel. (850) 488-0125; fax (850) 488-0156; internet www.flcourts.org; Justices Peggy A. Quince (Chief Justice), R. Fred Lewis, Charles T. Wells, Harry Lee Anstead, Barbara J. Pariente, Charles T. Canady, Ricky Polston.

Georgia

FEDERAL COURTS

Georgia is in the Eleventh Circuit of the US Courts of Appeals. There are US District Courts at Atlanta, Macon and Savannah.

US District Courts

Middle: William A. Bootle Federal Bldg, 475 Mulberry St, POB 128, Macon, GA 31202; tel. (478) 752-3497; fax (478) 752-3496; e-mail info@gamd.uscourts.gov; internet www.gamd.uscourts.gov; Judges HUGH LAWSON (Chief Judge), W. LOUIS SANDS, CLAY D. LAND, C. ASHLEY ROYAL.

Northern: Richard B. Russell Federal Bldg and Courthouse, 75 Spring St, SW, Atlanta, GA 30303-3361; tel. (404) 215-1660; internet www.gand.uscourts.gov; Judges JACK T. CAMP (Chief Judge), HAROLD L. MURPHY, ORINDA D. EVANS, JULIE E. CARNES, CLARENCE COOPER, THOMAS W. THRASH, Jr, RICHARD W. STORY, CHARLES A. PANNELL, Jr, BEVERLY B. MARTIN, WILLIAM S. DUFFEY, Jr, TIMOTHY C. BATTEN, Sr.

Southern: US Courthouse, 125 Bull St, Savannah, POB 8286, GA 31401; tel. (912) 650-4020; fax (912) 650-4029; internet www.gas.uscourts.gov; Judges WILLIAM THEODORE MOORE, Jr (Chief Judge), JAMES RANDAL HALL, LISA GODBEY WOOD.

STATE COURTS

The state Supreme Court has seven justices, including the chief justice. The justices are elected at-large and serve for terms of six years. The chief justice is appointed by the Court and serves a four-year term of office. The state Court of Appeals has 12 judges, who hold office for six years.

Supreme Court: 244 Washington St, SW, Rm 572, Atlanta, GA 30334; tel. (404) 656-3470; fax (404) 656-2253; e-mail scinfo@gasupreme.us; internet www.gasupreme.us; Justices LEAH WARD SEARS (Chief Justice), ROBERT BENHAM, CAROL W. HUNSTEIN, GEORGE H. CARLEY, HUGH P. THOMPSON, P. HARRIS HINES, HAROLD D. MELTON.

Hawaii

FEDERAL COURTS

Hawaii is in the Ninth Circuit of the US Courts of Appeals. There is a US District Court in Honolulu.

US District Court: US Courthouse, 300 Ala Moana Blvd, Honolulu, HI 96850; tel. (808) 541-1300; fax (808) 541-1303; internet www.hid.uscourts.gov; Judges HELEN W. GILLMOR (Chief Judge), DAVID ALAN EZRA, SUSAN OKI MOLLWAY, J. MICHAEL SEABRIGHT.

STATE COURTS

The state Supreme Court has five justices, including the chief justice. All the justices, chosen at-large, are appointed by the governor on the advice of the Senate and serve for terms of 10 years. The state has an Intermediate Court of Appeals, with six judges serving 10-year terms of office.

Supreme Court: Ali'iolani Hale, 417 South King St, Honolulu, HI 96813-2902; tel. (808) 539-4919; fax (808) 539-4928; internet www.courts.state.hi.us; Justices RONALD T. Y. MOON (Chief Justice), STEVEN H. LEVINSON, PAULA A. NAKAYAMA, SIMEON R. ACOBA, Jr, JAMES E. DUFFY, Jr.

Idaho

FEDERAL COURTS

Idaho is in the Ninth Circuit of the US Courts of Appeals. There is a US District Court at Boise.

US District Court: James A. McClure Federal Bldg and US Courthouse, 550 West Fort St, Rm 400, Boise, ID 83724; tel. (208) 334-1361; fax (208) 334-9362; internet www.id.uscourts.gov; Judges B. LYNN WINMILL (Chief Judge), EDWARD J. LODGE.

STATE COURTS

The state Supreme Court has five justices, including the chief justice. Justices are elected at-large and serve terms of office of six years; the chief justice is appointed by the Court and serves a four-year term of office. The state Court of Appeals has three judges, elected to serve six-year terms of office.

Supreme Court: 451 West State St, Boise, ID 83720; POB 83720, Boise, ID 83720-0101; tel. (208) 334-2246; internet www.isc.idaho.gov; Justices DANIEL T. EISMANN (Chief Justice), WARREN E. JONES, ROGER S. BURDICK, JAMES T. JONES, JOEL D. HORTON.

Illinois

FEDERAL COURTS

Illinois is in the Seventh Circuit of the US Courts of Appeals. There are US District Courts situated in Chicago, Springfield and East St Louis.

US District Courts

Central: 151 US Courthouse, 600 East Monroe St, Springfield, IL 62701; tel. (217) 492-4020; fax (217) 492-4028; internet www.ilcd.uscourts.gov; Judges MICHAEL P. MCCUSKEY (Chief Judge), JOE BILLY MCDADE, MICHAEL M. MIHM, JEANNE E. SCOTT.

Northern: Everett McKinley Dirksen Bldg, 219 South Dearborn St, Chicago, IL 60604; tel. (312) 435-5670; internet www.ilnd.uscourts.gov; Judges JAMES F. HOLDERMAN (Chief Judge), WAYNE R. ANDERSEN, ELAINE E. BUCKLO, RUBEN CASTILLO, DAVID H. COAR, JOHN W. DARRAH, SAMUEL DER-YEGHIAYAN, ROBERT M. DOW, Jr, MARK FILIP, ROBERT W. GETTLEMAN, JOAN B. GOTTSCHALL, RONALD A. GUZMAN, WILLIAM J. HIBBLER, FREDERICK J. KAPALA, VIRGINIA M. KENDALL, MATTHEW F. KENNELLY, JOAN HUMPHREY LEFKOW, BLANCHE M. MANNING, CHARLES R. NORGLE, Sr, REBECCA R. PALLMEYER, AMY J. ST EVE, JAMES B. ZAGEL.

Southern: Melvin Price Federal Courthouse, 750 Missouri Ave, East St Louis, IL 62201; tel. (618) 482-9371; fax (618) 482-9383; internet www.ilsd.uscourts.gov; Judges DAVID R. HERNDON (Chief Judge), G. PATRICK MURPHY, J. PHIL GILBERT, MICHAEL J. REAGAN.

STATE COURTS

The state Supreme Court has seven justices, including the chief justice. The justices are elected by judicial district and serve 10-year terms of office. The Court in turn elects one of its number as chief justice for a term of three years. The state Appellate Court has 54 judges, who serve 10-year terms of office.

Supreme Court: Supreme Court Bldg, 200 East Capitol, Springfield, IL 62701; tel. (217) 782-2035; internet www.state.il.us/court/supremecourt; Justices THOMAS R. FITZGERALD (Chief Justice), ROBERT R. THOMAS, CHARLES E. FREEMAN, THOMAS L. KILBRIDE, RITA B. GARMAN, LLOYD A. KARMEIER, ANNE M. BURKE.

Indiana

FEDERAL COURTS

Indiana is in the Seventh Circuit of the US Courts of Appeals. There are US District Courts at South Bend and Indianapolis.

US District Courts

Northern: US District Court, 204 South Main St, Rm 102, South Bend, IN 46601; tel. (574) 246-8000; fax (574) 246-8002; internet www.innd.uscourts.gov; Judges ROBERT MILLER, Jr (Chief Judge), PHILIP P. SIMON, THERESA SPRINGMANN, JOSEPH VAN BOKKELEN.

Southern: US Courthouse, 46 East Ohio St, Room 105, Indianapolis, IN 46204; tel. (317) 229-3700; fax (317) 229-3959; internet www.insd.uscourts.gov; Judges DAVID F. HAMILTON (Chief Judge), SARAH EVANS BARKER, LARRY J. MCKINNEY, WILLIAM T. LAWRENCE, RICHARD L. YOUNG.

STATE COURTS

The state Supreme Court has five justices, including the chief justice, who are appointed by the governor on the advice of the Judicial Nominating Commission. The chief justice is chosen by the Judicial Nominating Commission from the serving Supreme Court judges, and serves a five-year term. The state Court of Appeals has 15 judges. Judges in both courts serve for two years, and then for a further 10 years if they are approved by referendum.

Supreme Court: 315 Indiana State House, Indianapolis, IN 46204; tel. (317) 232-1930; fax (317) 232-8372; internet www.in.gov/judiciary/supreme; Justices RANDALL T. SHEPARD (Chief Justice), THEODORE R. BOEHM, ROBERT D. RUCKER, FRANK SULLIVAN, Jr, BRENT E. DICKSON.

Iowa

FEDERAL COURTS

Iowa is located in the Eighth Circuit of the US Courts of Appeals. There are US District Courts at Cedar Rapids and Des Moines.

US District Courts

Northern: Federal Bldg, 101 First St, SE, Cedar Rapids, IA 52401; tel. (319) 286-2300; internet www.iand.uscourts.gov; Judges LINDA R. READE (Chief Judge), MARK W. BENNETT.

Southern: US Courthouse, 123 East Walnut St, Rm 300, POB 9344, Des Moines, IA 50306-9344; tel. (515) 284-6248; fax (515) 284-6418; internet www.iasd.uscourts.gov; Judges ROBERT W. PRATT (Chief Judge), JAMES E. GRITZNER, JOHN A. JARVEY.

STATE COURTS

The state Supreme Court consists of seven justices, including a chief justice. The justices, who are chosen at-large, are appointed by the governor from lists submitted by nominating commissions, and serve terms of eight years. Once they have served for at least one year, justices' appointments must be ratified by voters at the next general election. The justices select one of their number as chief justice, who then serves for the remainder of the term. The state Court of Appeals has nine judges serving six-year terms of office.

Supreme Court: Iowa Judicial Branch Bldg, 1111 East Court Ave, Des Moines, IA 50319; tel. (515) 281-5174; internet www.judicial .state.ia.us; Justices MARSHA K. TERNUS (Chief Justice), MARK S. CADY, MICHAEL J. STREIT, DAVID S. WIGGINS, DARYL L. HECHT, BRENT R. APPEL, DAVID L. BAKER.

Kansas

FEDERAL COURTS

Kansas is in the Tenth Circuit of the US Courts of Appeals. Wichita is the seat of the US District Court.

US District Court: Robert J. Dole US Courthouse, 500 State Ave, Kansas City, KS 66101; tel. (913) 551-6719; e-mail ksd_clerks_kansascity@ksd.uscourts.gov; internet www.ksd .uscourts.gov; Judges KATHRYN HOEFER VRATIL (Chief Judge), JOHN WATSON LUNGSTRUM, MONTI L. BELOT, J. THOMAS MARTEN, CARLOS MURGUIA, JULIE A. ROBINSON, ERIC F. MELGREN.

STATE COURTS

The state Supreme Court has seven justices, including the chief justice. All justices are appointed by the governor from names submitted by the Supreme Court Nominating Commission. When justices have served at least one year in office voters may approve their retention at the next general election. Thereafter they serve for six years. The most senior justice is appointed as chief justice. The state Court of Appeals has 12 judges; appointments are as for Supreme Court judges, with election to serve a four-year term after an initial one-year term of service.

Supreme Court: Kansas Judicial Center, 301 South West 10th Ave, Topeka, KS 66612-1507; tel. (785) 296-2256; fax (785) 296-7076; e-mail info@kscourts.org; internet www.kscourts.org/ supreme-court; Justices KAY MCFARLAND (Chief Justice), ROBERT E. DAVIS, LAWTON R. NUSS, MARLA J. LUCKERT, ERIC S. ROSEN, CAROL A. BEIER, LEE A. JOHNSON.

Kentucky

FEDERAL COURTS

Kentucky belongs to the Sixth Circuit of the US Courts of Appeals. US District Courts are located in Lexington and Louisville.

US District Courts

Eastern: 206 US Courthouse, 101 Barr St, Lexington, KY 40507; tel. (859) 233-2503; fax (859) 233-2470; internet www.kyed.uscourts.gov; Judges JENNIFER B. COFFMAN (Chief Judge), KAREN K. CALDWELL, DANNY C. REEVES, DAVID L. BUNNING, GREGORY F. VAN TATENHOVE, AMUL R. THAPAR.

Western: Gene Snyder US Courthouse, 601 West Broadway, Louisville, KY 40202; tel. (502) 625-3500; fax (502) 625-3880; internet www .kywd.uscourts.gov; Judges JOHN GILPIN HEYBURN, II (Chief Judge), CHARLES R. SIMPSON, III, THOMAS B. RUSSELL, JOSEPH H. MCKINLEY, Jr, JENNIFER B. COFFMAN.

STATE COURTS

The state Supreme Court has seven justices, including a chief justice. The justices are elected from court districts for terms of eight years; they then choose one of their number to serve a four-year term as chief justice. The Court of Appeals has 14 judges, who are also elected to serve eight-year terms of office.

Supreme Court: 700 Capitol Ave, Capitol Bldg, Frankfort, KY 40601; tel. (502) 564-4720; internet www.kycourts.net/supreme/ sc_main.shtm; Justices JOHN D. MINTON, Jr (Chief Justice), BILL CUNNINGHAM, DANIEL J. VENTERS, LISABETH HUGHES ABRAMSON, MARY C. NOBLE, WIL SCHRODER, WILL T. SCOTT.

Louisiana

FEDERAL COURTS

Louisiana is in the Fifth Circuit of the US Courts of Appeals. There are US District Courts in New Orleans, Baton Rouge and Shreveport.

US District Courts

Eastern: 500 Poydras St, New Orleans, LA 70130; tel. (504) 589-7650; fax (504) 589-7697; internet www.laed.uscourts.gov; Judges SARAH S. VANCE (Chief Judge), HELEN G. BERRIGAN, JAY C. ZAINEY, IVAN L. R. LEMELLE, MARTIN L. C. FELDMAN, LANCE M. AFRICK, CARL J. BARBIER, STANWOOD R. DUVAL, Jr, ELDON E. FALLON, KURT D. ENGLEHARDT, MARY ANN VIAL LEMMON, G. THOMAS PORTEOUS, Jr.

Middle: Russell B. Long Federal Bldg, Suite 139, 777 Florida St, Baton Rouge, LA 70801; tel. (225) 389-3500; fax (225) 389-3501; internet www.lamd.uscourts.gov; Judges RALPH E. TYSON (Chief Judge), JAMES J. BRADY.

Western: 800 Lafayette St, Suite 2100, Lafayette, LA 70501; tel. (337) 593-5000; fax (337) 593-5027; internet www.lawd.uscourts.gov; Judges RICHARD T. HAIK (Chief Judge), REBECCA F. DOHERTY, TUCKER L. MELANÇON, ROBERT GILLESPIE JAMES, DEE D. DRELL, S. MAURICE HICKS, Jr, PATRICIA MINALDI.

STATE COURTS

The state Supreme Court has seven justices, including the chief justice, and an appointed justice. The justices are elected from seven supreme-court districts for staggered 10-year terms. The chief justice is chosen by seniority of service. The state Court of Appeals has 54 judges, also elected to serve 10-year terms. Louisiana is the only US state to have a judicial system founded on Roman Law (based on the Code Napoléon), with judgments made by interpretation of existing statutes and code law, as opposed to Common Law, which is founded on legal precedent. In practice, however, the conduct of court proceedings in Louisiana differs little from that in other states.

Supreme Court: Supreme Court Bldg, 400 Royal St, Suite 4200, New Orleans, LA 70130; tel. (504) 310-2300; fax (504) 310-2325; internet www.lasc.org; Justices PASCAL F. CALOGERO, Jr (Chief Justice), JEFFREY P. VICTORY, JEANNETTE THERIOT KNOLL, CHET D. TRAYLOR, CATHERINE D. KIMBALL, JOHN L. WEIMAR, BERNETTE J. JOHNSON.

Maine

FEDERAL COURTS

Maine is in the First Circuit of the US Courts of Appeals. There is a US District Court in Portland.

US District Court: 156 Federal St, Portland, ME 04101; tel. (207) 780-3356; internet www.med.uscourts.gov; Judges GEORGE Z. SINGAL (Chief Judge), DAVID BROCK HORNBY, JOHN A. WOODCOCK, Jr.

STATE COURTS

Maine has a Supreme Judicial Court with seven justices, including a chief justice. All the justices, selected at-large, are appointed by the governor with the consent of the Senate and serve terms of seven years.

Supreme Judicial Court: 142 Federal St, POB 368, Portland, ME 04112-0368; tel. (207) 822-4286; fax (207) 287-4641; internet www .courts.state.me.us; Justices LEIGH INGALLS SAUFLEY (Chief Justice), ROBERT W. CLIFFORD, DONALD G. ALEXANDER, JON D. LEVY, WARREN M. SILVER, ANDREW M. MEAD, ELLEN A. GORMAN.

Maryland

FEDERAL COURTS

Maryland is in the Fourth Circuit of the US Courts of Appeals. There is a US District Court at Baltimore.

US District Court: US Courthouse, 101 West Lombard St, Baltimore, MD 21201; tel. (410) 962-2600; internet www.mdd.uscourts .gov; Judge BENSON EVERETT LEGG (Chief Judge), RICHARD D. BENNETT, CATHERINE C. BLAKE, DEBORAH K. CHASANOW, ANDRE M. DAVIS, PETER J. MESSITTE, J. FREDERICK MOTZ, WILLIAM D. QUARLES, Jr, ROGER W. TITUS, ALEXANDER WILLIAMS, Jr.

STATE COURTS

The Maryland state court of last resort is the Court of Appeals. There are seven justices, including the chief justice. Justices are nominated by the Judicial Nominating Commission and appointed by the governor with the consent of the Senate. The appointment of justices has to be ratified by the electorate after a minimum of one year of service. Maryland's intermediate appellate court is the Court of Special Appeals, which has 13 judges nominated and ratified in a way similar to that for judges of the Court of Appeals. All judges in the state serve 10-year terms of office.

Court of Appeals: Robert C. Murphy Courts of Appeal Bldg, 361 Rowe Blvd, Annapolis, MD 21401; tel. (410) 260-1500; internet www.courts.state.md.us/coappeals; Judges ROBERT M. BELL (Chief Judge), GLENN T. HARRELL, Jr, LYNNE A. BATTAGLIA, CLAYTON GREENE, Jr, JOSEPH F. MURPHY, Jr, SALLY D. ATKINS, MARY ELLEN BARBERA.

Massachusetts

FEDERAL COURTS

Massachusetts is in the First Circuit of the US Courts of Appeals. There is a US District Court in Boston.

US District Court: John Joseph Moakley US Courthouse, 1 Courthouse Way, Boston, MA 02210; tel. (617) 748-9152; fax (617) 748-9096; internet www.mad.uscourts.gov; Judges MARK L. WOLF (Chief Judge), JOSEPH L. TAURO, RYA W. ZOBEL, WILLIAM G. YOUNG, DOUGLAS P. WOODLOCK, NATHANIEL M. GORTON, RICHARD G. STEARNS, REGINALD C. LINDSAY, PATTI B. SARIS, NANCY GERTNER, MICHAEL A. PONSOR, GEORGE A. O'TOOLE, Jr, F. DENNIS SAYLOR, IV.

STATE COURTS

Massachusetts has a Supreme Judicial Court with seven justices, including a chief justice. The chief justice and other justices are appointed by the governor with the advice and consent of the Governor's Council. They are selected at-large and may hold office until reaching the age of 70. The state Appeals Court has 25 statutory judges, who may also remain in office until attaining the age of 70.

Supreme Judicial Court: John Adams Courthouse, 1 Pemberton Sq., Boston, MA 02108; tel. (617) 557-1114; fax (617) 742-1807; internet www.mass.gov/courts/sjc; Justices MARGARET H. MARSHALL (Chief Justice), ROBERT J. CORDY, JUDITH A. COWIN, JOHN M. GREANEY, MARGOT BOTSFORD, FRANCIS X. SPINA, RODERICK L. IRELAND.

Michigan

FEDERAL COURTS

Michigan is in the Sixth Circuit of the US Courts of Appeals. US District Courts are located in Detroit and Grand Rapids.

US District Courts

Eastern: Theodore Levin US Courthouse, 231 West Lafayette Blvd, Detroit, MI 48226; tel. (313) 234-5000; fax (313) 234-5393; internet www.mied.uscourts.gov; Judges BERNARD A. FRIEDMAN (Chief Judge), GERALD E. ROSEN, ROBERT H. CLELAND, NANCY G. EDMUNDS, DENISE PAGE HOOD, PAUL D. BORMAN, ARTHUR J. TARNOW, GEORGE C. STEEH, VICTORIA A. ROBERTS, MARIANNE O. BATTANI, DAVID M. LAWSON, SEAN FRANCIS COX, THOMAS LAMSON LUDINGTON, STEPHEN JOSEPH MURPHY, III.

Western: 399 Federal Bldg, 110 Michigan St, NW, Grand Rapids, MI 49503; tel. (616) 456-2381; fax (616) 456-2066; internet www.miwd.uscourts.gov; Judges PAUL L. MALONEY (Chief Judge), ROBERT HOLMES BELL, GORDON J. QUIST, ROBERT J. JONKER, JANET T. NEFF.

STATE COURTS

The state Supreme Court has seven justices, including the chief justice. Justices are elected at-large and serve eight-year terms of office; the chief justice is elected by members of the Court and the position is held for two years. The state Court of Appeals has 28 judges, who are elected to serve six-year terms of office.

Supreme Court: Michigan Hall of Justice, 925 West Ottawa St, POB 30052, Lansing, MI 48913; POB 30052, Lansing, MI 48909; tel. (517) 373-0130; fax (517) 373-7517; internet courts.michigan.gov/supremecourt; Justices CLIFFORD W. TAYLOR (Chief Justice), MAURA D. CORRIGAN, MICHAEL F. CAVANAGH, ELIZABETH A. WEAVER, MARILYN KELLY, ROBERT P. YOUNG, Jr, STEPHEN J. MARKMAN.

Minnesota

FEDERAL COURTS

Minnesota is in the Eighth Circuit of the US Courts of Appeals. The US District Court operates in St Paul, Minneapolis, Duluth and Fergus Falls.

US District Court: 202 US Courthouse, 300 South Fourth St, Minneapolis, MN 55415; tel. (612) 664-5000; fax (612) 664-5033; internet www.mnd.uscourts.gov; Judges MICHAEL J. DAVIS (Chief Judge), JAMES M. ROSENBAUM, JOHN R. TUNHEIM, ANN D. MONTGOMERY, DONOVAN FRANK, JOAN N. ERICKSEN, PATRICK J. SCHILTZ.

STATE COURTS

The state Supreme Court has seven justices, including a chief justice. The justices are elected at-large for six-year terms. The chief justice is elected popularly to hold office for the remainder of the term. The state Court of Appeals has 16 judges, who are also elected to serve terms of six years.

Supreme Court: Minnesota Judicial Center, 25 Rev. Dr Martin Luther King Jr Blvd, St Paul, MN 55155; tel. (651) 297-7650; internet www.courts.state.mn.us; Justices ERIC J. MAGNUSON (Chief Justice), ALAN C. PAGE, PAUL H. ANDERSON, HELEN M. MEYER, G. BARRY ANDERSON, LORIE SKJERVEN GILDEA, CHRISTOPHER J. DIETZEN.

Mississippi

FEDERAL COURTS

Mississippi is in the Fifth Circuit of the US Courts of Appeals. There are US District Courts in Oxford and Jackson.

US District Courts

Northern: Federal Bldg, 911 Jackson Ave, Rm 369, Oxford, MS 38655; tel. (662) 234-1971; fax (662) 236-5210; e-mail ecf_Information@msnd.uscourts.gov; internet www.msnd.uscourts.gov; Judges MICHAEL P. MILLS (Chief Judge), W. ALLEN PEPPER, Jr, SHARION AYCOCK.

Southern: 316 James O. Eastland US Courthouse, 245 East Capitol St, Jackson, MS 39201; tel. (601) 965-4439; internet www.mssd.uscourts.gov; Judges HENRY T. WINGATE (Chief Judge), LOUIS GUIROLA, Jr, KEITH STARRETT, DANIEL P. JORDAN, III, SUL OZERDEN.

STATE COURTS

The state Supreme Court has nine justices, who are elected by district and serve for eight years. The most senior justice is appointed as chief justice. The state Court of Appeals has 10 judges.

Supreme Court: Gartin Justice Bldg, 450 High St, Jackson, MS 39201; POB 249, Jackson, MS 39205; tel. (601) 359-3694; fax (601) 359-2407; internet www.mssc.state.ms.us; Justices JAMES W. SMITH, Jr (Chief Justice), WILLIAM L. WALLER, Jr, OLIVER E. DIAZ, Jr, CHARLES D. (CHUCK) EASLEY, GEORGE C. CARLSON, Jr, JAMES E. GRAVES, Jr, JESS H. DICKINSON, MICHAEL K. RANDOLPH, ANN H. LAMAR.

Missouri

FEDERAL COURTS

Missouri is in the Eighth Circuit of the US Courts of Appeals. There are US District Courts in St Louis and Kansas City.

US District Courts

Eastern: Thomas F. Eagleton US Courthouse, 111 South 10th St, Rm 3300, St Louis, MO 63102; tel. (314) 244-7900; fax (314) 244-7909; internet www.moed.uscourts.gov; Judges CAROL E. JACKSON (Chief Judge), JEAN C. HAMILTON, CHARLES A. SHAW, CATHERINE D. PERRY, E. RICHARD WEBBER, Jr, RODNEY W. SIPPEL, HENRY E. AUTREY, STEPHEN N. LIMBAUGH, Jr.

Western: Charles Evans Whittaker US Courthouse, 400 East Ninth St, Kansas City, MO 64106; tel. (816) 512-5000; fax (816) 512-5078; e-mail dchelp@mow.uscourts.gov; internet www.mow.uscourts.gov; Judges FERNANDO J. GAITAN, Jr (Chief Judge), GARY A. FENNER, ORTRIE D. SMITH, NANETTE K. LAUGHREY, RICHARD E. DORR, DAVID GREGORY KAYS.

STATE COURTS

The state Supreme Court has seven justices, including a chief justice. The justices, who serve 12-year terms of office, are chosen at-large by the governor on the advice of a judicial commission. After an initial term of one year their appointment must be ratified by the electorate. The justices select one of their number to act as chief justice for a term of two years. The Court of Appeals has 32 judges, who also serve terms of 12 years.

Supreme Court: POB 150, Jefferson City, MO 65102; tel. (573) 751-4144; fax (573) 751-7514; internet www.courts.mo.gov; Justices LAURA DENVIR STITH (Chief Justice), MARY RHODES RUSSELL, MICHAEL A. WOLFF, WILLIAM RAY PRICE, Jr, RICHARD B. TEITELMAN, PATRICIA BRECKENRIDGE.

Montana

FEDERAL COURTS

Montana is in the Ninth Circuit of the US Courts of Appeals. There is a US District Court at Billings.

US District Court: James F. Battin Federal Courthouse, 316 North 26th St, Billings, MT 59101; tel. (406) 247-7000; fax (406) 247-7008; internet www.mtd.uscourts.gov; Judges RICHARD F. CEBULL (Chief Judge), DONALD W. MOLLOY, SAM E. HADDON.

STATE COURTS

The state Supreme Court has seven justices, including the chief justice, who are elected at-large to serve eight-year terms of office.

Supreme Court: Justice Bldg, 215 North Sanders, POB 203001, Helena, MT 59620-3001; tel. (406) 444-5490; fax (406) 444-3274; internet www.montanacourts.org/supreme; Justices KARLA M. GRAY (Chief Justice), JAMES (JIM) C. NELSON, W. WILLIAM LEAPHEART, JOHN WARNER, PATRICIA O'BRIEN COTTER, JAMES A. RICE, BRIAN MORRIS.

Nebraska

FEDERAL COURTS

Nebraska is in the Eighth Circuit of the US Courts of Appeals. There is a US District Court in Omaha and a District Court office in Lincoln.

US District Court: Roman L. Hruska US Courthouse, 111 South 18th Plaza, Omaha, NE 68102; tel. (402) 661-7350; fax (402) 661-7387; internet www.ned.uscourts.gov; Judges JOSEPH FRANCIS BATAILLON (Chief Judge), RICHARD GEORGE KOPF, LAURIE SMITH CAMP.

STATE COURTS

The state Supreme Court has seven justices, including a chief justice. Justices are initially appointed by the governor to serve for a three-year term, after which they must run for retention in the next general election. Following approval by the voters, justices serve a six-year term of office. All justices are selected from, and voted upon, by district, except the chief justice, who is chosen state-wide. The Court of Appeals has six judges, who are subject to the same terms of selection and retention as the judges of the Supreme Court.

Supreme Court: 2413 State Capitol Bldg, POB 98910, Lincoln, NE 68509; tel. (402) 471-3731; fax (402) 471-3480; internet www.supremecourt.ne.gov; Justices MICHAEL G. HEAVICAN (Chief Justice), LINDSEY MILLER-LERMAN, WILLIAM M. CONNOLLY, JOHN F. WRIGHT, KENNETH C. STEPHAN, MICHAEL MCCORMACK, JOHN M. GERRARD.

Nevada

FEDERAL COURTS

Nevada is in the Ninth Circuit of the US Courts of Appeals. There is a District Court in Las Vegas.

US District Court: Lloyd D. George US Courthouse, 333 Las Vegas Blvd South, Las Vegas, NV 89101; tel. (702) 464-5400; fax (702) 464-5457; internet www.nvd.uscourts.gov; Judges ROGER L. HUNT (Chief Judge), PHILIP M. PRO, LARRY R. HICKS, KENT J. DAWSON, JAMES C. MAHAN, ROBERT C. JONES, BRIAN EDWARD SANDOVAL.

STATE COURTS

The state Supreme Court has seven justices, including the chief justice, who are elected at-large and serve terms of six years. The chief justice is selected according to seniority of service and retains the position for one to two years.

Supreme Court: 201 South Carson St, Carson City, NV 89701-4702; tel. (775) 684-1600; e-mail nvscclerk@nvcourts.state.nv.us; internet www.nvsupremecourt.us; Justices MARK GIBBONS (Chief Justice), A. WILLIAM MAUPIN, NANCY M. SAITTA, MICHAEL A. CHERRY, MICHAEL L. DOUGLAS, JAMES W. HARDESTY, RON D. PARRAGUIRRE.

New Hampshire

FEDERAL COURTS

New Hampshire is in the First Circuit of the US Courts of Appeals. There is a US District Court in Concord.

US District Court: 110 Warren B. Rudman US Courthouse, 55 Pleasant St, Concord, NH 03301; tel. (603) 225-1423; internet www.nhd.uscourts.gov; Judges STEVEN JAMES MCAULIFFE (Chief Judge), PAUL JAMES BARBADORO, JOSEPH N. LAPLANTE.

STATE COURTS

The state Supreme Court has five justices, including a chief justice. The chief justice and all other justices, selected at-large, are appointed by the governor with the consent of the Executive Council and may hold office until reaching the age of 70.

Supreme Court: Supreme Court Bldg, 1 Charles Doe Dr., Concord, NH 03301; tel. (603) 271-2646; internet www.courts.state.nh.us/supreme; Justices JOHN T. BRODERICK, Jr (Chief Justice), LINDA S. DALIANIS, RICHARD E. GALWAY, JAMES E. DUGGAN, GARY E. HICKS.

New Jersey

FEDERAL COURTS

New Jersey is in the Third Circuit of the US Courts of Appeals. There is a US District Court at Newark.

US District Court: Martin Luther King, Jr Federal Bldg and US Courthouse, Rm 4015, 50 Walnut St, Newark, NJ 07101; tel. (973) 645-3730; internet www.njd.uscourts.gov; Judges GARRETT E. BROWN, Jr (Chief Judge), MARY LITTLE COOPER, JEROME B. SIMANDLE, DENNIS M. CAVANAUGH, JOSEPH A. GREENAWAY, Jr, KATHARINE S. HAYDEN, FAITH S. HOCHBERG, JOSÉ L. LINARES, WILLIAM J. MARTINI, JOEL A. PISANO, STANLEY R. CHESLER, ROBERT B. KUGLER, FREDA L. WOLFSON, RENEE MARIE BUMB, NOEL LAWRENCE HILLMAN, PETER G. SHERIDAN, SUSAN DAVIS WIGENTON.

STATE COURTS

The state Supreme Court has seven justices, including the chief justice. All justices, including the chief justice, are appointed by the governor with the consent of the Senate and serve terms of seven years. The Appellate Division of the Superior Court has 35 judges, who also serve seven-year terms of office.

Supreme Court: Richard J. Hughes Justice Complex, 25 West Market St, POB 970, Trenton, NJ 08625-0970; tel. (609) 292-4837; fax (609) 396-9056; internet www.judiciary.state.nj.us/supreme/index.htm; Justices STUART RABNER (Chief Justice), VIRGINIA A. LONG, ROBERTO A. RIVERA-SOTO, JAYNEE LAVECCHIA, HELEN E. HOENS, BARRY T. ALBIN, JOHN E. WALLACE, Jr.

New Mexico

FEDERAL COURTS

New Mexico is in the Tenth Circuit of the US Courts of Appeals. There is a US District Court in Albuquerque.

US District Court: 270 US Courthouse, 333 Lomas Blvd, NW, Albuquerque, NM 87102; tel. (505) 348-2000; fax (505) 348-2028; e-mail cmecf@nmcourt.fed.us; internet www.nmcourt.fed.us; Judges MARTHA VÁZQUEZ (Chief Judge), BRUCE D. BLACK, M. CHRISTINA ARMIJO, ROBERT C. BRACK, JAMES O. BROWNING, JUDITH C. HERRERA, WILLIAM P. JOHNSON.

STATE COURTS

The state Supreme Court has five justices, including a chief justice. The justices, who are elected at-large, serve terms of eight years. They elect one of their number to serve a two-year term as chief justice. The Court of Appeals has 10 judges, also elected to serve eight-year terms of office.

Supreme Court: 237 Don Gaspar Ave, Santa Fe, NM 87501; tel. (505) 827-4860; fax (505) 827-4837; internet nmsupremecourt.nmcourts.gov; Justices EDWARD L. CHÁVEZ (Chief Justice), PATRICIO M. SERNA, PETRA JIMENEZ MAES, RICHARD C. BOSSON, CHARLES W. DANIELS.

New York

FEDERAL COURTS

New York is in the Second Circuit of the US Courts of Appeals. There are US District Courts in Syracuse, Brooklyn, New York City (Manhattan) and Buffalo.

US District Courts

Eastern: US Courthouse, 225 Cadman Plaza East, Brooklyn, NY 11201; tel. (718) 613-2600; fax (718) 260-2264; internet www.nyed.uscourts.gov; Judges RAYMOND J. DEARIE (Chief Judge), CAROL BAGLEY AMON, JOSEPH FRANK BIANCO, BRIAN MARK COGAN, SANDRA J. FEUERSTEIN, NICHOLAS G. GARAUFIS, NINA GERSHON, JOHN GLEESON, DORA L. IRIZARRY, KIYO A. MATSUMOTO, ROSLYNN R. MAUSKOPF, ALLYNE R. ROSS, JOANNA SEYBERT, SANDRA L. TOWNES, ERIC NICHOLAS VITALIANO.

Northern: US District Courthouse, 100 South Clinton St, POB 7367, Syracuse, NY 13261-7367; tel. (315) 234-8500; fax (315) 234-8501; internet www.nynd.uscourts.gov; Judges NORMAN A. MORDUE (Chief Judge), DAVID N. HURD, GARY L. SHARPE, GLENN T. SUDDABY.

Southern: Daniel Patrick Moynihan US Courthouse, 500 Pearl St, New York, NY 10007-1312; tel. (212) 805-0136; internet www.nysd.uscourts.gov; Judges KIMBA M. WOOD (Chief Judge), DEBORAH A. BATTS, RICHARD M. BERMAN, NAOMI REICE BUCHWALD, P. KEVIN CASTEL, DENNY CHIN, DENISE L. COTE, PAUL A. CROTTY, GEORGE B. DANIELS, PAUL G. GARDEPHE, ALVIN K. HELLERSTEIN, RICHARD J. HOLWELL, BARBARA S. JONES, LEWIS A. KAPLAN, KENNETH M. KARAS, JOHN G. KOELTL, GERARD E. LYNCH, VICTOR MARRERO, COLLEEN MCMAHON, WILLIAM H. PAULEY, III, LORETTA A. PRESKA, JED S. RAKOFF, STEPHEN C. ROBINSON, SHIRA A. SCHEINDLIN, SIDNEY H. STEIN, RICHARD J. SULLIVAN, LAURA TAYLOR SWAIN.

Western: US Courthouse, 68 Court St, Buffalo, NY 14202; tel. (716) 551-4211; fax (716) 551-4850; internet www.nywd.uscourts.gov; Judges RICHARD J. ARCARA (Chief Judge), DAVID G. LARIMER, WILLIAM M. SKRETNY, CHARLES J. SIRAGUSA.

STATE COURTS

The highest state court is the Court of Appeals. This has seven judges, including the chief judge, who serve terms of 14 years. The Appellate Division of the Supreme Court has 55 justices, who serve five-year terms of office. Judges of the Court of Appeals and of the Appellate Division are appointed by the governor on the advice of, and with the consent of, the Senate. There is an upper age-limit of 70 years for judges in New York.

Court of Appeals: Court of Appeals Hall, 20 Eagle St, Albany, NY 12207-1095; tel. (518) 455-7711; internet www.courts.state.ny.us/ctapps; Judges JUDITH S. KAYE (Chief Judge), THEODORE T. JONES, CARMEN BEAUCHAMP CIPARICK, VICTORIA A. GRAFFEO, SUSAN P. READ, ROBERT S. SMITH, EUGENE F. PIGOTT, Jr.

North Carolina

FEDERAL COURTS

North Carolina is in the Fourth Circuit of the US Courts of Appeals. There are US District Courts in Raleigh, Greensboro and Charlotte.

US District Courts

Eastern: Terry Sanford Federal Bldg, 310 New Bern Ave, Raleigh, NC 27601; tel. (919) 645-1700; fax (919) 645-1750; internet www.nced.uscourts.gov; Judges LOUISE W. FLANAGAN (Chief Judge), TERRENCE W. BOYLE, JAMES C. DEVER, III.

Middle: 324 West Market St, Rm 401, Greensboro, NC 27401; tel. (336) 332-6000; fax (336) 332-6060; internet www.ncmd.uscourts.gov; Judges JAMES A. BEATY, Jr (Chief Judge), NORWOOD CARLTON TILLEY, Jr, WILLIAM LINDSAY OSTEEN, THOMAS D. SCHROEDER.

Western: Charles R. Jones Federal Bldg, 401 West Trade St, Rm 210, Charlotte, NC 28202; tel. (704) 350-7400; fax (704) 344-6703; internet www.ncwd.uscourts.gov; Judges ROBERT J. CONRAD, Jr (Chief Judge), RICHARD LESLEY VOORHEES, LACY H. THORNBURG, FRANK D. WHITNEY, MARTIN K. REINDINGER.

STATE COURTS

The state Supreme Court has seven justices, including the chief justice. All justices, including the chief justice, are elected at-large and serve terms of eight years. The state Court of Appeals has 15 judges, who are also elected to serve terms of eight years.

Supreme Court: 2 East Morgan St, Raleigh, NC 27601; tel. (919) 831-5700; fax (919) 733-0105; internet www.nccourts.org/courts/appellate/supreme; Justices SARAH E. PARKER (Chief Justice), MARK D. MARTIN, ROBERT H. EDMUNDS, Jr, EDWARD THOMAS BRADY, PAUL MARTIN NEWBY, PATRICIA TIMMONS-GOODSON, ROBIN E. HUDSON.

North Dakota

FEDERAL COURTS

North Dakota is in the Eighth Circuit of the US Courts of Appeals. The US District Courts are in Bismarck and Fargo.

US District Court: US Courthouse, 220 East Rosser Ave, POB 1193, Bismarck, ND 58502; tel. (701) 530-2300; fax (701) 530-2312; internet www.ndd.uscourts.gov; Judges DANIEL L. HOVLAND (Chief Judge), RALPH R. ERICKSON.

STATE COURTS

The state Supreme Court has five justices, including the chief justice, who are elected at-large and serve 10-year terms. The chief justice is selected by the Supreme and District Court judges and serves a five-year term.

Supreme Court: State Capitol Bldg, 1st Floor, Dept 180, 600 East Blvd Ave, Bismarck, ND 58505-0530; tel. (701) 328-2221; fax (701) 328-4480; internet www.ndcourts.com; Justices GERALD W. VANDEWALLE (Chief Justice), DALE V. SANDSTROM, MARY MUEHLEN MARING, CAROL RONNING KAPSNER, DANIEL J. CROTHERS.

Ohio

FEDERAL COURTS

Ohio is in the Sixth Circuit of the US Courts of Appeals. There are US District Courts in Cleveland and Columbus.

US District Courts

Northern: Carl B. Stokes US Courthouse, 801 West Superior Ave, Cleveland, OH 44113-1830; tel. (216) 357-7000; fax (216) 522-2140; internet www.ohnd.uscourts.gov; Judges JAMES G. CARR (Chief Judge), JOHN R. ADAMS, CHRISTOPHER A. BOYKO, PETER C. ECONOMUS, PATRICIA A. GAUGHAN, JAMES S. GWIN, SARA LIOI, DONALD C. NUGENT, SOLOMON OLIVER, Jr, KATHLEEN M. O'MALLEY, DAN A. POLSTER, JACK ZOUHARY.

Southern: 260 Joseph P. Kinneary US Courthouse, 85 Marconi Blvd, Columbus, OH 43215; tel. (614) 719-3000; fax (614) 719-3500; internet www.ohsd.uscourts.gov; Judges SANDRA S. BECKWITH (Chief Judge), SUSAN J. DLOTT, EDMUND A. SARGUS, Jr, ALGENON L. MARBLEY, THOMAS M. ROSE, GREGORY L. FROST, MICHAEL H. WATSON, MICHAEL R. BARRETT.

STATE COURTS

The state Supreme Court has seven justices, including a chief justice. All justices, including the chief justice, are elected at-large for terms of six years. The state Court of Appeals has 68 judges, all of whom also serve six-year terms of office.

Supreme Court: 65 South Front St, Columbus, OH 43215-3431; tel. (614) 387-9000; internet www.supremecourtofohio.gov; Justices THOMAS J. MOYER (Chief Justice), PAUL E. PFEIFER, EVELYN LUNDBERG STRATTON, MAUREEN O'CONNOR, TERRENCE O'DONNELL, JUDITH ANN LANZINGER, ROBERT R. CUPP.

Oklahoma

FEDERAL COURTS

Oklahoma is in the Tenth Circuit of the US Courts of Appeals. There are US District Courts in Tulsa, Muskogee and Oklahoma City.

US District Courts

Eastern: US Courthouse, 101 North Fifth St, Muskogee, OK 74401; tel. (918) 684-7920; fax (918) 684-7902; internet www.oked.uscourts.gov; Judges JAMES H. PAYNE (Chief Judge), RONALD A. WHITE.

Northern: US Courthouse, 333 West Fourth St, Tulsa, OK 74103; tel. (918) 699-4700; fax (918) 699-4756; internet www.oknd.uscourts.gov; Judges CLAIRE V. EAGAN (Chief Judge), JAMES H. PAYNE, TERRY C. KERN, GREGORY K. FRIZELL.

Western: US Courthouse, Rm 1210, 200 North West Fourth St, Oklahoma City, OK 73102; tel. (405) 609-5000; fax (405) 609-5099; internet www.okwd.uscourts.gov; Judges ROBIN J. CAUTHRON (Chief Judge), DAVID L. RUSSELL, TIMOTHY D. DEGIUSTI, VICKI MILES-LAGRANGE, STEPHEN P. FRIOT, JOE HEATON.

STATE COURTS

Oklahoma shares the distinction with Texas of having twin state courts of last resort: ultimate appellate jurisdiction resides with the Supreme Court in civil cases, and with the Court of Criminal Appeals in criminal cases. Judges are appointed by district to the Supreme Court and Court of Criminal Appeals by the governor, from lists of three submitted by the Judicial Nominating Commission. They serve six-year terms. At the general election following completion of at least one year's service, and every six years after appointment, judges must be confirmed in office by the electorate. The chief justice of the Supreme Court and the presiding judge of the Court of Criminal Appeals are elected by the members of each court to serve two-year terms of office. The Court of Civil Appeals has 12 judges, who are elected to serve six-year terms.

Supreme Court: State Capitol Bldg, 2nd Floor, Oklahoma City, OK 73105; tel. (405) 521-3845; internet www.oscn.net/oscn/schome/start.htm; Justices JAMES R. WINCHESTER (Chief Justice), JAMES E. EDMONDSON (Vice-Chief Justice), JOHN F. REIF, STEVEN W. TAYLOR, MARIAN P. OPALA, YVONNE KAUGER, TOM COLBERT, RUDOLPH HARGRAVE, JOSEPH M. WATT.

Court of Criminal Appeals: 230 State Capitol Bldg, Oklahoma City, OK 73105; tel. (405) 521-2156; internet www.occa.state.ok.us; Judges GARY L. LUMPKIN (Presiding Judge), CHARLES A. JOHNSON (Vice-Presiding Judge), ARLENE JOHNSON, DAVID B. LEWIS, CHARLES S. CHAPEL.

Oregon

FEDERAL COURTS

Oregon is in the Ninth Circuit of the US Courts of Appeals. There is a US District Court in Portland.

US District Court: 740 Mark O. Hatfield US Courthouse, 1000 South West Third Ave, Portland, OR 97204-2902; tel. (503) 326-8000; fax (503) 326-8010; e-mail info@ord.uscourts.gov; internet www.ord.uscourts.gov; Judges ANCER LEE HAGGERTY (Chief Judge), ANN L. AIKEN, GARR M. KING, ANNA J. BROWN, MICHAEL R. HOGAN, MICHAEL W. MOSMAN.

STATE COURTS

The state Supreme Court has seven justices, including a chief justice. Justices are elected at-large to serve terms of six years. They elect one of their number as chief justice. Oregon has a Court of Appeals, with 10 judges elected to serve six-year terms of office, and a Tax Court, which has a single judge also serving a term of six years. The Tax Court consists of two divisions—the Magistrate Division and the Regular Division.

Supreme Court: 1163 State St, Salem, OR 97301-2563; tel. (503) 986-5555; fax (503) 986-5730; e-mail ojd.info@ojd.state.or.us; internet www.ojd.state.or.us/courts/supreme; Justices PAUL J. DEMUNIZ (Chief Justice), THOMAS A. BALMER, ROBERT D. DURHAM, W. MICHAEL GILLETTE, RIVES KISTLER, VIRGINIA L. LINDER, MARTHA L. WALTERS.

Pennsylvania

FEDERAL COURTS

Pennsylvania is in the Third Circuit of the US Courts of Appeals. There are US District Courts in Philadelphia, Scranton and Pittsburgh.

US District Courts

Eastern: US Courthouse, Rm 2609, 601 Market St, Philadelphia, PA 19106-1797; tel. (215) 597-7704; fax (215) 597-6390; internet www.paed.uscourts.gov; Judges HARVEY BARTLE, III (Chief Judge), JAMES T. GILES, STEWART DALZELL, JOHN R. PADOVA, J. CURTIS JOYNER, EDUARDO C. ROBRENO, ANITA B. BRODY, BRUCE W. KAUFFMAN, MARY A. MCLAUGHLIN, PETRESE B. TUCKER, BERLE M. SCHILLER, R. BARCLAY SURRICK, LEGROME D. DAVIS, CYNTHIA M. RUFE, MICHAEL M. BAYLSON, TIMOTHY J. SAVAGE, JAMES KNOLL GARDNER, GENE E. K. PRATTER, LAWRENCE F. STENGEL, PAUL S. DIAMOND, JUAN R. SANCHEZ, THOMAS M. GOLDEN, JOEL HARVEY SLOMSKY.

Middle: William J. Nealon Federal Bldg and US Courthouse, 235 North Washington Ave, POB 1148, Scranton, PA 18501; tel. (570) 207-5600; fax (570) 207-5650; e-mail mdpacourt@pamd.uscourts.gov; internet www.pamd.uscourts.gov; Judges YVETTE KANE (Chief Judge), THOMAS I. VANASKIE, A. RICHARD CAPUTO, CHRISTOPHER C. CONNER, JAMES M. MUNLEY, JOHN E. JONES, III.

Western: US Post Office and Courthouse, Seventh Ave and Grant St, Pittsburgh, PA 15219; tel. (412) 208-7500; fax (412) 208-7530; internet www.pawd.uscourts.gov; Judges DONETTA W. AMBROSE (Chief Judge), GARY L. LANCASTER, ARTHUR J. SCHWAB, DAVID STEWART CERCONE, JOY FLOWERS CONTI, NORA BARRY FISCHER, TERRENCE F. MCVERRY, KIM R. GIBSON, SEAN J. MCLAUGHLIN.

STATE COURTS

The state Supreme Court has seven justices, who are elected at-large to serve 10-year terms of office. The longest-serving justice is appointed as chief justice. The Superior Court, the state intermediate appellate court, has 15 judges, also elected to serve 10-year terms of office. The other court of appeal, the Commonwealth Court, which has jurisdiction over civil cases involving the state, has nine judges serving 10-year terms of office.

Supreme Court: City Hall, Rm 468, Philadelphia, PA 19107; tel. (215) 560-2608; internet www.courts.state.pa.us/Index/Supreme/indexSupreme.asp; Justices RONALD D. CASTILLE (Chief Justice), THOMAS G. SAYLOR, J. MICHAEL EAKIN, MAX BAER, DEBRA TODD, SEUMAS P. MCCAFFERY, JANE CUTLER GREENSPAN.

Rhode Island

FEDERAL COURTS

Rhode Island is in the First Circuit of the US Courts of Appeals. There is a US District Court at Providence.

US District Court: Federal Bldg and US Courthouse, 1 Exchange Terrace, Providence, RI 02903; tel. (401) 752-7200; fax (401) 752-7247; internet www.rid.uscourts.gov; Judges MARY M. LISI (Chief Judge), WILLIAM E. SMITH.

STATE COURTS

The state Supreme Court is composed of five justices, including the chief justice. All Supreme Court justices are elected by the state legislature and hold office for life.

Supreme Court: Frank Licht Judicial Complex, 250 Benefit St, Providence, RI 02903; tel. (401) 222-3272; fax (401) 222-3599; internet www.courts.ri.gov; Justices FRANK J. WILLIAMS (Chief Justice), MAUREEN MCKENNA GOLDBERG, FRANCIS X. FLAHERTY, PAUL A. SUTTELL, WILLIAM P. ROBINSON, III.

South Carolina

FEDERAL COURTS

South Carolina is in the Fourth Circuit of the US Courts of Appeals. There is a US District Court in Columbia.

US District Court: Matthew J. Perry, Jr US Courthouse, 901 Richland St, Columbia, SC 29201; tel. (803) 765-5816; fax (803) 765-5960; internet www.scd.uscourts.gov; Judges DAVID C. NORTON (Chief Judge), JOSEPH F. ANDERSON, Jr, G. ROSS ANDERSON, Jr, HENRY M. HERLONG, Jr, CAMERON MCGOWAN CURRIE, PATRICK M. DUFFY, MARGARET B. SEYMOUR, TERRY L. WOOTEN, HENRY F. FLOYD, R. BRYAN HARWELL, Jr.

STATE COURTS

The state Supreme Court has five justices, including the chief justice, who serve terms of 10 years. Justices are elected by the General Assembly (the state legislature) from names submitted by the Judiciary Committee of the legislature. The state Court of Appeals has nine judges, elected by the General Assembly to serve six-year terms of office.

Supreme Court: POB 11330, Columbia, SC 29211; tel. (803) 734-1080; fax (803) 734-1499; internet www.judicial.state.sc.us/supreme; Justices JEAN HOEFER TOAL (Chief Justice), JOHN H. WALLER, Jr, COSTA M. PLEICONES, DONALD W. BEATTY, JOHN W. KITTREDGE.

South Dakota

FEDERAL COURTS

South Dakota is in the Eighth Circuit of the US Courts of Appeals. There is a US District Court in Sioux Falls, with divisions in Rapid City and Pierre.

US District Court: 128 US Courthouse, 400 South Phillips Ave, Sioux Falls, SD 57104; tel. (605) 330-6600; fax (605) 330-6601; internet www.sdd.uscourts.gov; Judges KAREN ELIZABETH SCHREIER (Chief Judge), CHARLES B. KORNMANN, LAWRENCE L. PIERSOL, RICHARD H. BATTEY.

STATE COURTS

The state Supreme Court has five justices, including a chief justice. Justices, selected by district, are initially appointed by the governor on the advice of the Judicial Qualifications Commission to serve a three-year term. Thereafter, they must seek retention in the next general election. Following approval by the voters, justices serve an eight-year term of office. The justices elect one of their number to a four-year term as chief justice.

Supreme Court: 500 East Capitol Ave, Pierre, SD 57501; tel. (605) 773-3511; fax (605) 773-6128; internet www.sdjudicial.com; Justices DAVID GILBERTSON (Chief Justice), RICHARD W. SABERS, JOHN K. KONENKAMP, STEPHEN ZINTER, JUDITH MEIERHENRY.

Tennessee

FEDERAL COURTS

Tennessee is in the Sixth Circuit of the US Courts of Appeals. There are US District Courts in Knoxville, Nashville and Memphis.

US District Courts

Eastern: 130 Howard H. Baker, Jr US Courthouse, 800 Market St, Suite 130, Knoxville, TN 37902; tel. (865) 545-4228; fax (865) 545-4228; internet www.tned.uscourts.gov; Judges CURTIS L. COLLIER (Chief Judge), HENRY S. MATTICE, Jr, THOMAS W. PHILLIPS, THOMAS A. VARLAN, J. RONNIE GREER.

Middle: US Courthouse, 801 Broadway, Nashville, TN 37203; tel. (615) 736-5498; fax (615) 736-7488; internet www.tnmd.uscourts.gov; Judges TODD J. CAMPBELL (Chief Judge), ALETA ARTHUR TRAUGER, WILLIAM J. HAYNES, Jr.

Western: Federal Bldg, Rm 242, 167 North Main St, Memphis, TN 38103; tel. (901) 495-1200; fax (901) 495-1250; internet www.tnwd.uscourts.gov; Judges JON PHIPPS MCCALLA (Chief Judge), BERNICE B. DONALD, SAMUEL H. MAYS, Jr, J. DANIEL BREEN, S. THOMAS ANDERSON.

STATE COURTS

The state Supreme Court has five justices, including the chief justice, who are elected at-large and serve eight-year terms of office. The chief justice is elected by members of the Court and holds office for 18 months. The state Court of Appeals has 12 judges and the Court of Criminal Appeals has 12 judges, all of whom serve eight-year terms. The judges are initially appointed by the governor, from lists of three submitted by the Appellate Court Nominating Commission, but they must seek election at subsequent general elections.

Supreme Court: Supreme Court Bldg, 401 Seventh Ave North, Nashville, TN 37219-1407; tel. (615) 741-1529; internet www.tsc.state.tn.us; Justices JANICE M. HOLDER (Chief Justice), CORNELIA A. CLARK, GARY R. WADE, WILLIAM C. KOCH, Jr, SHARON G. LEE.

Texas

FEDERAL COURTS

Texas is in the Fifth Circuit of the US Courts of Appeals. There are US District Courts in Dallas, Houston, Tyler and San Antonio.

US District Courts

Eastern: William M. Steger Federal Bldg and US Courthouse, 211 West Ferguson St, Tyler, TX 75702; tel. (903) 590-1000; fax (903) 590-1015; internet www.txed.uscourts.gov; Judges THAD HEARTFIELD (Chief Judge), RICHARD A. SCHELL, DAVID FOLSOM, LEONARD E. DAVIS, JOHN T. WARD, RONALD H. CLARK, MARCIA A. CRONE, MICHAEL H. SCHNEIDER.

Northern: US Courthouse, Rm 1452, 1100 Commerce St, Dallas, TX 75242; tel. (214) 753-2200; internet www.txnd.uscourts.gov; Judges SIDNEY A. FITZWATER (Chief Judge), MARY LOU ROBINSON, SAM R. CUMMINGS, JOHN H. MCBRYDE, JORGE A. SOLIS, TERRY R. MEANS, SAM A. LINDSAY, BARBARA M. G. LYNN, DAVID C. GODBEY, ED KINKEADE, JANE BOYLE, REED O'CONNOR.

Southern: Bob Casey US Courthouse, 515 Rusk Ave, Houston, TX 77002; tel. (713) 250-5500; e-mail info@www.txs.uscourts.gov; internet www.txs.uscourts.gov; Judges HAYDEN W. HEAD, Jr (Chief Judge), MICAELA ALVAREZ, NANCY F. ATLAS, RANDY CRANE, KEITH P. ELLISON, VANESSA D. GILMORE, ANDREW S. HANEN, MELINDA HARMON, RICARDO H. HINOJOSA, KENNETH M. HOYT, LYNN NETTLETON HUGHES, JANIS GRAHAM JACK, GEORGE P. KAZEN, Jr, SAMUEL B. KENT, SIMEON TIMOTHY LAKE, III, GRAY HAMPTON MILLER, JOHN D. RAINEY, LEE H. ROSENTHAL, HILDA G. TAGLE.

Western: John H. Wood, Jr Federal Courthouse, 655 East Durango Blvd, San Antonio, TX 78206; tel. (210) 472-6550; internet www.txwd.uscourts.gov; Judges WALTER S. SMITH, Jr (Chief Judge), SAM SPARKS, W. ROYAL FURGESON, FRED BIERY, ORLANDO L. GARCIA, DAVID BRIONES, ALIA M. LUDLUM, ROBERT A. JUNELL, LEE YEAKEL, KATHLEEN CARDONE , FRANK MONTALVO, XAVIER RODRIGUEZ, PHILIP R. MARTINEZ.

STATE COURTS

Texas, like Oklahoma, has a state Supreme Court and a Court of Criminal Appeals, each having nine judges. All judges, including the chief justice of the Supreme Court and the presiding judge of the Court of Criminal Appeals, are popularly elected at-large to staggered six-year terms. The Courts of Appeals have 80 judges, all of whom serve six-year terms.

Supreme Court: 201 West 14th St, Rm 104, POB 12248, Austin, TX 78711; tel. (512) 463-1312; fax (512) 463-1365; internet www.supreme.courts.state.tx.us; Justices WALLACE B. JEFFERSON (Chief Justice), DON R. WILLETT, HARRIET O'NEILL, DAVID MEDINA, PAUL W. GREEN, NATHAN L. HECHT, DALE WAINWRIGHT, PHIL JOHNSON, SCOTT A. BRISTER.

Court of Criminal Appeals: Capitol Station, POB 12308, Austin, TX 78711; 201 West 14th St, Rm 106, Austin, TX 78701; tel. (512) 463-1551; fax (512) 463-7061; internet www.cca.courts.state.tx.us; Judges SHARON KELLER (Presiding Judge), LAWRENCE E. MEYERS, TOM PRICE, PAUL WOMACK, CHERYL JOHNSON, MICHAEL KEASLER, BARBARA PARKER HERVEY, CHARLES HOLCOMB, CATHY COCHRAN.

Utah

FEDERAL COURTS

Utah is in the Tenth Circuit of the US Courts of Appeals. There is a US District Court in Salt Lake City.

US District Court: Frank E. Moss US Courthouse, 350 South Main St, Salt Lake City, UT 84101-2180; tel. (801) 524-6100; fax (801) 526-1175; internet www.utd.uscourts.gov; Judges TENA CAMPBELL (Chief Judge), DEE BENSON, DALE A. KIMBALL, TED STEWART.

STATE COURTS

The state Supreme Court has five justices, including the chief justice. Justices are appointed by the governor with the consent of the Senate. After an initial three-year term their appointment must be ratified by voters at the next general election; thereafter terms last for 10 years. The chief justice is elected by the members of the Court to serve a four-year term of office. The state Court of Appeals has seven judges, who serve six-year terms.

Supreme Court: 450 South State, POB 140210, Salt Lake City, UT 84114-0210; tel. (801) 238-7974; fax (801) 578-3999; internet www.utcourts.gov/courts/sup; Justices CHRISTINE M. DURHAM (Chief Justice), MATTHEW B. DURRANT (Assoc. Chief Justice), JILL N. PARRISH, RONALD E. NEHRING, MICHAEL J. WILKINS.

Vermont

FEDERAL COURTS

Vermont is in the Second Circuit of the US Courts of Appeals. There is a US District Court in Burlington.

US District Court: US Post Office and Courthouse, Rm 506, 11 Elmwood Ave, POB 945, Burlington, VT 05402-0945; tel. (802) 951-6301; internet www.vtd.uscourts.gov; Judges WILLIAM K. SESSIONS, III (Chief Judge), J. GARVAN MURTHA.

STATE COURTS

Vermont's Supreme Court has five justices, including the chief justice. All justices are nominated by the Judicial Nominating Board and are appointed by the governor to six-year terms, subject to confirmation by the state Senate.

Supreme Court: 109 State St, Montpelier, VT 05609-0701; tel. (802) 828-3278; fax (802) 828-4750; internet www.vermontjudiciary.org/courts/supreme/index.htm; Justices PAUL REIBER (Chief Justice), JOHN A. DOOLEY, III, DENISE R. JOHNSON, MARILYN S. SKOGLUND, BRIAN BURGESS.

Virginia

FEDERAL COURTS

Virginia belongs to the Fourth Circuit of the US Courts of Appeals. There are US District Courts in Alexandria and Roanoke.

US District Courts

Eastern: Albert V. Bryan, Sr US Courthouse, 401 Courthouse Sq., Alexandria, VA 22314; tel. (703) 299-2100; fax (703) 299-2109; internet www.vaed.uscourts.gov; Judges JAMES R. SPENCER (Chief Judge), HENRY E. HUDSON, LEONIE M. BRINKEMA, GERALD BRUCE LEE, REBECCA BEACH SMITH, RAYMOND A. JACKSON, JEROME B. FRIEDMAN, MARK S. DAVIS, LIAM O'GRADY, ANTHONY JOHN TRENGA.

Western: POB 1234, Roanoke, VA 24006; Richard H. Poff Federal Bldg, 210 Franklin Rd, POB 1234, SW, Roanoke, VA 24011; tel. (540) 857-5100; fax (540) 857-5110; internet www.vawd.uscourts.gov; Judges JAMES P. JONES (Chief Judge), SAMUEL G. WILSON, NORMAN K. MOON, GLEN E. CONRAD.

STATE COURTS

The state Supreme Court has seven justices, including the chief justice, who are elected at-large by the legislature and serve 12-year terms of office. The longest-serving justice is appointed as chief justice. The state Court of Appeals has 11 judges, who are similarly elected to serve for eight years.

Supreme Court: 100 North Ninth St, 5th Floor, POB 1315, Richmond, VA 23219; tel. (804) 786-2251; internet www.courts.state.va.us/scv/home.html; Justices LEROY ROUNTREE HASSELL, Sr (Chief Justice), ELIZABETH B. LACY, BARBARA MILANO KEENAN, LAWRENCE L. KOONTZ, Jr, CYNTHIA D. KINSER, DONALD W. LEMONS, G. STEVEN AGEE, LEROY F. MILLETTE, Jr.

Washington

FEDERAL COURTS

Washington is in the Ninth Circuit of the US Court of Appeals. There are US District Courts in Spokane and Seattle.

US District Courts

Eastern: Thomas S. Foley US Courthouse, 920 West Riverside Ave, POB 1493, Spokane, WA 99210; tel. (509) 458-3400; fax (509) 458-3420; internet www.waed.uscourts.gov; Judges ROBERT H. WHALEY (Chief Judge), LONNY R. SUKO, EDWARD F. SHEA.

Western: 700 Stewart St, Seattle, WA 98101; tel. (260) 370-8400; internet www.wawd.uscourts.gov; Judges ROBERT S. LASNIK (Chief Judge), BARBARA J. ROTHSTEIN, RICARDO S. MARTINEZ, MARSHA J. PECHMAN, RONALD B. LEIGHTON, JAMES L. ROBART, BENJAMIN H. SETTLE, RICHARD A. JONES.

STATE COURTS

The state Supreme Court consists of nine justices, including a chief justice. Justices are popularly elected at-large for staggered terms of six years. The chief justice, serving a two-year term of office, is the most senior justice who has not previously held that position. The state Court of Appeals has 22 judges, who are also elected to serve terms of six years.

Supreme Court: 415 12th Ave, SW, POB 40929, Olympia, WA 98504-0929; tel. (360) 357-2077; e-mail supreme@courts.wa.gov; internet www.courts.wa.gov; Justices GERRY L. ALEXANDER (Chief Justice), CHARLES W. JOHNSON (Assoc. Chief Justice), TOM CHAMBERS, MARY E. FAIRHURST, JAMES M. JOHNSON, BARBARA MADSEN, SUSAN OWENS, RICHARD B. SANDERS, DEBRA L. STEPHENS.

West Virginia

FEDERAL COURTS

West Virginia is in the Fourth Circuit of the US Courts of Appeals. There are US District Courts in Elkins and Charleston.

US District Courts

Northern: US Courthouse, 500 West Pike St, POB 2808, Clarksburg, WV 26302; tel. (304) 622-8513; fax (304) 623-4551; internet www.wvnd.uscourts.gov; Judges JOHN P. BAILEY, Jr (Chief Judge), IRENE M. KEELEY.

Southern: Robert C. Byrd US Courthouse, 300 East Virginia St, Charleston, WV 25301; tel. (304) 347-3000; internet www.wvsd.uscourts.gov; Judges JOSEPH ROBERT GOODWIN (Chief Judge), JOHN THOMAS COPENHAVER, Jr, DAVID A. FABER, ROBERT C. CHAMBERS, THOMAS E. JOHNSTON.

STATE COURTS

The state Supreme Court of Appeals has five justices, including the chief justice, who are elected to serve 12-year terms of office. The chief justice is appointed according to seniority of service and holds office for one year.

Supreme Court of Appeals: Capitol Complex, Bldg 1, Rm E-318, Charleston, WV 25305; tel. (304) 558-2601; fax (304) 558-3815; internet www.state.wv.us/wvsca; Justices ELLIOT E. MAYNARD (Chief Justice), ROBIN JEAN DAVIS, JOSEPH P. ALBRIGHT, LARRY V. STARCHER, BRENT D. BENJAMIN.

Wisconsin

FEDERAL COURTS

Wisconsin is in the Seventh Circuit of the US Courts of Appeals. There are US District Courts at Milwaukee and Madison.

US District Courts

Eastern: 362 US Courthouse, 517 East Wisconsin Ave, Milwaukee, WI 53202; tel. (414) 297-3372; fax (414) 297-3203; internet www.wied.uscourts.gov; Judges RUDOLPH T. RANDA (Chief Judge), J. P. STADTMUELLER, CHARLES N. CLEVERT, Jr, LYNN ADELMAN, WILLIAM C. GRIESBACH.

Western: US Courthouse, 120 North Henry St, Rm 320, POB 432, Madison, WI 53701-0432; tel. (608) 264-5156; fax (608) 264-5925; internet www.wiwd.uscourts.gov; Judges BARBARA B. CRABB (Chief Judge), JOHN C. SHABAZ.

STATE COURTS

The state Supreme Court has seven justices, including a chief justice. Justices are elected at-large for terms of 10 years. The most senior justice serves as chief justice for the remainder of the term. The state Court of Appeals has 16 judges serving six-year terms of office.

Supreme Court: 16 East State Capitol, POB 1688, Madison, WI 53701-1688; tel. (608) 266-1880; fax (608) 261-8299; internet www.wicourts.gov; Justices SHIRLEY S. ABRAHAMSON (Chief Justice), ANN WALSH BRADLEY, N. PATRICK CROOKS, DAVID T. PROSSER, Jr, PATIENCE D. ROGGENSACK, ANNETTE K. ZIEGLER, MICHAEL J. GABLEMAN.

Wyoming

FEDERAL COURTS

Wyoming is in the Tenth Circuit of the US Courts of Appeals. There is a US District Court in Cheyenne.

US District Court: 2120 Capitol Ave, Cheyenne, WY 82001-3658; tel. (307) 433-2120; fax (307) 433-2152; internet www.wyd.uscourts.gov; Judges WILLIAM F. DOWNES (Chief Judge), ALAN B. JOHNSON.

STATE COURTS

The state Supreme Court has five justices, including the chief justice. Justices, selected at-large, are appointed by the governor, from a list submitted by the Judicial Nominating Commission; appointments must be ratified by the voters at the next general election. Upon election, justices serve eight-year terms. The chief justice is elected by the members of the Court and holds office for two years.

Supreme Court: Wyoming Supreme Court Bldg, 2301 Capitol Ave, Cheyenne, WY 82001; tel. (307) 777-7316; fax (307) 777-6129; e-mail jpacheco@courts.state.wy.us; internet courts.state.wy.us; Justices BARTON R. VOIGT (Chief Justice), MICHAEL GOLDEN, MARILYN S. KITE, WILLIAM U. HILL, E. JAMES BURKE.

DIRECTORY ON THE ECONOMY

NATIONAL ECONOMIC INDICATORS

Currency and Exchange Rates

(Source: IMF, *International Financial Statistics*, unless otherwise indicated.)

MONETARY UNITS

100 cents = 1 United States dollar (US $).

DENOMINATIONS

Coins: 1, 5, 10, 25 and 50 cents; 1 dollar.

Notes: 1, 2, 5, 10, 20, 50 and 100 dollars.

INTERNATIONAL VALUE OF THE DOLLAR

Average Exchange Rates
(units of foreign currency equivalent to US $1)

	2005	2006	2007
Canada (dollar)	1.2118	1.1344	1.0741
Euro Area (euro)	0.8041	0.7971	0.7306
Japan (yen)	110.2180	116.2990	117.7540
United Kingdom (pound sterling)	0.5500	0.5435	0.4998

Foreign Currency Equivalents
(30 May 2008)

Canada: US $10 = C $9.9420; C $1,000 = US $1,005.8338.

Euro Area: US $10 = €6.4483; €1,000 = US $1,550.8011.

Japan: US $10 = ¥1,056.6000; ¥1,000 = US $9.4643.

United Kingdom: US $10 = £5.0671; £1,000 sterling = US $1,973.4998.

CURRENCY AND COIN IN CIRCULATION

($ million at end of June)

	2006	2007	2008
Total	797,131.3	812,760.5	826,313.9

Source: Financial Management Service, US Department of the Treasury.

INTERNATIONAL RESERVES

($ million at 31 December)

	2005	2006	2007
US gold stock	11,040	11,040	11,040
IMF Special Drawing Rights	8,210	8,870	9,480
Reserve position in the IMF	8,040	5,040	4,240
Foreign exchange	37,840	40,940	45,800
Total	65,130	65,890	70,560

Note: Figures are rounded to nearest $10m.

Cost of Living

(Consumer Price Index for all urban consumers, average of monthly figures; base: 1982–84 = 100, unless otherwise indicated)

	2005	2006	2007
Food and beverages	191.2	195.7	203.0
Housing	195.7	203.2	209.6
Shelter	224.4	232.1	240.6
Fuels and utilities	179.0	194.7	200.6
Furnishings and operations	126.1	127.0	126.9
Clothing	119.5	119.5	119.0
Transport	173.9	180.9	184.7
Medical care	323.2	336.2	351.1
Recreation*	109.4	110.9	111.4
Education and communication*	113.7	116.8	119.6
Other goods and services	313.4	321.7	333.3
All items	195.3	201.6	207.3

* Base: December 1997 = 100.
Source: Bureau of Labor Statistics, US Department of Labor.

National Accounts

(Source: Bureau of Economic Analysis, US Department of Commerce.)

NATIONAL INCOME AND PRODUCT
($'000 million at current prices, revised figures)

	2005	2006	2007
Compensation of employees	7,037.2	7,440.4	7,819.4
Operating surplus	2,974.9	3,350.6	3,386.0
Domestic factor incomes	10,012.1	10,791.0	11,205.4
Consumption of fixed capital	1,612.0	1,623.9	1,720.5
Statistical discrepancy	–71.2	–163.0	–81.4
Gross domestic product (GDP) at factor cost	11,552.9	12,251.9	12,844.5
Taxes on production and imports	928.2	976.2	1,015.5
Less Subsidies on production and imports	59.3	49.7	52.3
GDP in purchasers' values	12,421.9	13,178.4	13,807.5
Factor income received from abroad	573.5	725.4	861.7
Less Factor income paid abroad	480.5	647.1	759.3
Gross national product (GNP)	12,514.9	13,256.6	13,910.0
Less Consumption of fixed capital	1,612.0	1,623.9	1,720.5
Net national product	10,902.9	11,632.7	12,189.5
Statistical discrepancy	71.2	163.0	81.4
National income in market prices	10,974.0	11,795.7	12,270.9

EXPENDITURE ON GROSS DOMESTIC PRODUCT
($'000 million at current prices, revised figures)

	2005	2006	2007
Government final consumption expenditure	2,355.3	2,508.1	2,674.8
Private final consumption expenditure	8,694.1	9,207.2	9,710.2
Increase in stocks	43.3	49.3	–3.6
Gross fixed investment	2,042.8	2,171.1	2,134.0
Total domestic expenditure	13,135.5	13,935.7	14,515.4
Exports of goods and services	1,311.5	1,480.8	1,662.4
Less Imports of goods and services	2,025.1	2,238.1	2,370.2
GDP in purchasers' values	12,421.9	13,178.4	13,807.5
GDP at constant 2000 prices	10,989.5	11,294.8	11,523.9

GROSS DOMESTIC PRODUCT BY ECONOMIC ACTIVITY*
($'000 million at current prices, preliminary figures)

	2005	2006	2007
Private industries	10,861.5	11,556.0	12,103.8
Agriculture, forestry, fishing and hunting	128.8	125.4	161.4
Agriculture	100.9	95.7	n.a.
Forestry, fishing and related activities	27.9	29.7	n.a.
Mining	225.7	262.4	275.8
Electricity, gas and water	249.5	273.4	295.9
Construction	607.9	630.0	562.6
Manufacturing	1,483.9	1,549.7	1,615.8
Wholesale trade	723.7	762.2	799.1
Retail trade	812.7	848.0	886.5
Transport and storage	358.5	385.4	403.5
Information	570.5	598.8	645.3
Finance and insurance	982.5	1,093.7	1,113.6
Real estate and rental and leasing	1,566.5	1,662.8	1,747.1
Professional and business services	1,453.2	1,560.9	1,684.2
Professional, scientific and technical services	851.9	925.3	1,003.1
Management of companies and enterprises	234.9	242.1	261.7
Administrative and waste management services	366.4	393.5	419.4
Education	113.9	120.9	129.4
Health care and social assistance	847.6	901.4	961.3
Arts, entertainment and recreation	117.4	126.2	131.1
Hotels and restaurants	331.0	353.6	374.5
Other private services	288.1	301.1	316.6
Government	1,568.7	1,649.4	1,741.0
Federal	502.6	526.4	547.1
General government	438.9	458.6	n.a.
Government enterprises	63.7	67.8	n.a.
State and local	1,066.1	1,122.9	1,193.9
General government	987.0	1,042.9	n.a.
Government enterprises	79.1	80.0	n.a.
NIPA reconciliation item	3.7	–10.7	–3.4
GDP in purchasers' values	12,433.9	13,194.7	13,841.3

* The distribution is based on the 1997 North American Industry Classification System (NAICS), which differs from ISIC.

Balance of Payments

($ million, rounded figures)

	2005	2006	2007
Exports of goods f.o.b.	898,460	1,026,850	1,153,270
Imports of goods f.o.b.	–1,681,810	–1,861,410	–1,964,590
Trade balance	–783,350	–834,550	–811,330
Exports of services	384,610	418,850	475,090
Imports of services	–315,630	–342,820	–372,280
Balance on goods and services	–714,370	–758,520	–708,520
Other income received	505,490	650,450	782,230
Other income paid	–457,430	–613,820	–707,920
Balance on goods, services and income	–666,310	–721,890	–634,200
Current transfers received	18,610	24,420	23,060
Current transfers paid	–107,140	–114,010	–127,500
Current balance	–754,850	–811,490	–738,640
Capital account (net)	–4,060	–3,910	–2,320
Direct investment abroad	7,660	–235,360	–335,420
Direct investment from abroad	109,000	180,580	204,420
Portfolio investment assets	–203,430	–426,090	–233,650
Portfolio investment liabilities	832,040	1,017,440	976,570
Financial derivatives liabilities	—	28,760	22,350
Other investment assets	–245,200	–396,100	–637,140
Other investment liabilities	263,200	661,570	682,710
Net errors and omissions	–18,460	–17,800	61,250
Overall balance	–14,100	–2,390	130

Source: IMF, *International Financial Statistics*.

Economically Active Population

NON-FARM PAYROLL EMPLOYMENT
('000 persons, estimates, July 2008, preliminary)

	A	B	C	D	E	F	G†	H	**Total**
Alabama	12.8	113.9	289.6	398.1	101.1	208.6	512.7	371.4	2,008.2
Alaska	15.2	20.5	21.5	69.9	15.5	37.0	85.1	77.6	342.3
Arizona	12.7	192.6	177.9	513.1	176.9	308.9	798.9	389.6	2,570.6
Arkansas	10.3	57.1	182.8	248.9	54.2	155.3	289.2	197.1	1,194.9
California	27.6	832.2	1,447.3	2,892.4	871.5	1,684.0	4,855.6	2,446.1	15,056.7
Colorado	29.0	171.6	144.3	434.8	159.3	248.1	820.3	366.2	2,373.6
Connecticut	0.8	71.9	188.9	306.7	144.5	290.2	459.0	233.9	1,695.9
Delaware*	—	27.3	32.3	83.8	46.1	59.3	131.7	59.9	440.4
District of Columbia*	—	12.8	1.6	27.5	28.3	98.2	301.6	247.6	717.6
Florida	6.3	515.9	364.7	1,578.9	534.4	1,027.5	2,727.6	1,052.0	7,807.3
Georgia	11.3	213.1	411.1	886.7	227.5	460.0	1,244.4	654.8	4,108.9
Hawaii*	—	39.5	15.0	117.6	29.6	74.4	222.5	117.8	616.4
Idaho	5.2	51.4	63.3	132.4	32.6	75.5	183.1	114.0	657.5
Illinois	10.2	277.4	670.1	1,218.1	401.1	784.5	1,826.5	824.3	6,012.3
Indiana	7.2	156.6	523.3	583.8	140.0	392.9	740.6	393.3	2,937.7
Iowa	2.3	78.5	230.4	310.3	104.7	196.6	359.1	230.9	1,512.8
Kansas	9.7	69.3	186.7	263.8	74.4	172.2	360.0	238.7	1,374.8
Kentucky	22.2	90.2	247.8	392.0	93.7	239.8	468.6	322.5	1,876.8
Louisiana	51.3	138.3	157.1	385.0	96.8	251.6	499.9	357.6	1,937.6
Maine	2.7	32.1	59.1	128.0	33.3	115.9	163.9	92.1	627.1
Maryland*	—	193.3	128.1	477.1	157.1	382.3	840.2	470.4	2,648.5
Massachusetts	1.7	142.7	289.8	567.8	226.4	626.1	1,041.3	403.9	3,299.7
Michigan	7.8	165.5	572.1	782.7	208.6	597.0	1,239.1	578.5	4,151.3
Minnesota	6.3	127.9	338.3	530.2	182.2	433.8	769.9	395.0	2,783.6
Mississippi	9.8	58.8	162.6	226.5	46.7	125.4	273.6	236.9	1,140.3
Missouri	5.2	152.7	285.8	548.2	166.1	388.6	816.5	406.0	2,769.1
Montana	8.6	34.1	20.7	95.0	22.4	59.6	133.8	83.3	457.5
Nebraska*	—	54.3	101.1	206.6	71.3	133.0	250.0	156.8	973.1
Nevada	12.3	122.2	50.7	234.6	62.5	95.1	545.1	154.2	1,276.7
New Hampshire	1.2	29.6	77.4	144.5	39.6	105.0	178.9	84.0	660.2
New Jersey	1.7	173.2	302.1	871.2	269.0	586.7	1,260.5	624.3	4,088.7
New Mexico	19.9	60.7	35.2	146.6	35.0	111.9	247.6	189.8	846.7
New York	7.0	367.6	535.7	1,516.6	732.7	1,582.5	2,549.7	1,487.1	8,778.9
North Carolina	7.0	258.8	520.3	779.5	214.3	531.7	1,188.5	630.3	4,130.4
North Dakota	5.7	22.1	26.2	77.9	20.0	52.0	87.9	65.0	356.8
Ohio	12.4	233.0	758.8	1,047.7	301.2	786.9	1,514.1	755.8	5,409.9
Oklahoma	52.1	76.0	151.0	289.3	84.6	194.1	420.8	299.7	1,567.6
Oregon	8.6	99.5	197.9	342.6	105.3	214.7	481.7	275.0	1,725.3
Pennsylvania	22.2	273.5	645.8	1,120.5	332.7	1,072.0	1,630.0	687.8	5,784.5
Rhode Island	0.2	22.3	45.7	77.0	33.4	96.3	144.4	59.8	479.1
South Carolina	4.3	113.9	243.9	375.0	109.1	205.8	574.0	315.6	1,941.6
South Dakota*	—	26.6	43.7	82.7	31.9	60.9	99.7	73.0	418.5
Tennessee	—	140.4	368.1	609.0	142.2	356.8	753.3	404.0	2,773.8
Texas	223.0	676.6	928.1	2,143.7	656.1	1,283.8	2,982.4	1,669.1	10,562.8
Utah	11.8	95.5	128.5	249.0	74.3	142.1	353.2	196.0	1,250.4
Vermont	0.9	18.0	35.7	58.9	13.3	57.4	73.6	44.3	302.1
Virginia	10.8	240.0	274.8	665.0	194.0	410.4	1,305.7	673.1	3,773.8
Washington	8.4	211.9	301.6	558.9	153.8	344.6	872.2	519.7	2,971.1
West Virginia	30.4	39.4	57.4	141.7	29.6	115.1	205.4	140.4	759.5
Wisconsin	3.9	133.4	497.4	540.2	165.7	405.0	753.4	390.0	2,889.0
Wyoming	29.1	30.7	9.8	57.4	11.9	23.9	75.7	63.8	302.3

* Construction (B) includes natural resources and mining.
† Other services (G) comprises professional and business services, leisure and hospitality, information and other services.
Note: A = Natural resources and mining; B = Construction; C = Manufacturing; D = Trade, transportation and public utilities; E = Financial activities; F = Education and health services; G = Other services; H = Government.
Source: US Bureau of Labor Statistics.

AGRICULTURE, FORESTRY AND FISHING

Land Use

(Source: National Agricultural Statistics Service, US Department of Agriculture.)

HISTORICAL SUMMARY
(million acres)

	1982	1987	1992	1997*	1997†	2002
Cropland	445	443	435	431	445	434
Harvested cropland	326	282	296	309	319	303
Cropland used only for pasture	65	65	67	64	66	61
Other cropland	54	96	73	57	60	71
Forestland	87	80	74	71	77	76
Other pastureland and rangeland	418	410	411	397	398	395
Buildings, roads, ponds, wasteland, etc.	36	31	25	32	34	33
Total farmland area	987	964	946	932	955	938
Total land area	2,265	2,265	2,263	2,263	2,263	2,264

* Original results.
† Includes adjustment for undercoverage.
Note: The 2002 Census of Agriculture introduced new methodology to account for all farms in the USA. To provide comparable data, 1997 data published with the 2002 results were reweighted for undercoverage.

Net Farm Income

(Source: Economic Research Service, US Department of Agriculture.)

VALUE ADDED TO US ECONOMY BY AGRICULTURAL SECTOR
($ '000 million)

	2006	2007	2008*
Final crop output	119.2	150.8	188.8
Food grains	9.1	12.8	20.4
Feed crops	29.4	42.5	63.8
Cotton	5.6	6.2	5.6
Oil crops	18.5	22.6	33.3
Fruit and tree nuts	17.2	17.8	19.2
Vegetables	18.5	20.0	21.3
Other crops	24.3	25.1	26.1
Home consumption	0.1	0.1	0.1
Adjustment	–3.5	3.8	–1.0
Final animal output	119.0	138.1	146.1
Meat animals	63.6	65.0	68.3
Dairy products	23.4	35.4	35.9
Poultry and eggs	26.5	32.6	36.9
Miscellaneous	4.8	4.9	5.0
Home consumption	0.3	0.3	0.4
Adjustment	0.5	–0.1	–0.3
Services and Forestry	38.4	40.3	42.3
Machine hire and work	2.7	2.5	2.9
Forest products sold	2.5	2.4	2.4
Other farm income	12.3	11.8	12.2
Imputed rent of farms	20.9	23.6	24.9
Final agricultural output	276.6	329.2	377.3
Less Intermediate outlays	153.6	171.4	207.1
Farm origin	61.0	68.8	81.8
Manufactured inputs	37.5	43.7	59.5
Other expenses	55.2	58.9	65.8
Net government transactions	6.2	1.5	2.4
Gross value added	129.2	159.3	172.6
Less Capital consumption	26.1	26.9	28.4
Less Factor payments	44.6	45.7	48.5
Net farm income	58.5	86.8	95.7

* Forecasts.

Production of Principal Crops*

(Source: National Agricultural Statistics Service, US Department of Agriculture. Note: Weights given in tons refer to the US 'short' ton, equivalent to 0.9072 of a metric ton.)

SUMMARY
(processing and fresh usage, quantity in '000 cwt unless otherwise specified)

	2005		2006		2007	
	Quantity	Value ($ '000)	Quantity	Value ($ '000)	Quantity	Value ($ '000)
Wheat ('000 bushels)	2,104,690	7,171,441	1,812,036	7,710,014	2,066,722	13,669,482
Corn for grain ('000 bushels)	11,114,082	22,198,472	10,534,868	32,094,586	13,073,893	52,090,108
Barley ('000 bushels)	211,896	527,633	180,165	498,691	211,825	851,682
Sorghum for grain ('000 bushels)	392,933	737,038	277,538	885,394	504,993	1,950,936
Rice	223,235	1,741,721	193,736	1,982,696	197,456	2,273,955
Hay ('000 tons)	151,017	12,584,783	142,336	13,791,407	150,304	16,960,936
Cotton (480-lb nwt bales)	23,890	5,695,217	21,588	5,013,238	19,207	5,196,688
Cottonseed ('000 tons)	8,172	779,500	7,348	814,151	6,589	1,060,760
Peanuts ('000 lb)	4,869,860	843,435	3,464,250	612,798	3,740,650	762,646
Soybeans ('000 bushels)	3,063,237	17,269,138	3,188,247	20,415,948	2,585,207	26,752,197
Tobacco ('000 lb)	645,015	1,059,324	727,347	1,210,978	779,899	1,310,900
Sugar beet ('000 tons)	27,433	1,193,151	34,064	1,506,985	31,912	1,265,382
Sugar cane ('000 tons)	26,606	754,529	29,564	897,435	29,969	858,896
Potatoes	423,926	2,991,495	441,348	3,225,871	446,807	3,197,746
Broccoli	19,940	569,703	20,200	673,950	20,363	736,849
Onions	73,504	848,798	73,177	1,056,969	78,882	819,809
Strawberries	23,221	1,395,724	24,040	1,519,960	24,994	1,745,609

PRODUCTION OF PRINCIPAL CROPS BY STATE
(2007)

	Wheat ('000 bushels)	Corn for grain ('000 bushels)	Barley ('000 bushels)	Hay ('000 tons)	Sorghum for grain ('000 bushels)	Soybeans ('000 bushels)
Alabama	3,440	22,120	—	1,360	270	3,780
Arizona	8,260	4,255	3,795	2,227	1,995	—
Arkansas	28,700	99,120	—	3,022	20,210	100,440
California	26,325	36,000	2,400	9,422	990	—
Colorado	95,520	150,520	7,250	4,385	5,550	—
Connecticut	—	—	—	115	—	—
Delaware	3,740	17,945	1,482	29	—	3,480
Florida	513	3,325	—	780	—	288
Georgia	9,200	58,500	—	1,206	2,070	8,250
Idaho	83,675	17,325	44,000	5,430	—	—
Illinois	50,730	2,283,750	—	1,916	6,237	350,450
Indiana	21,090	987,350	—	1,544	—	210,600
Iowa	1,400	2,368,350	—	5,570	—	438,780
Kansas	283,800	518,000	624	6,370	212,000	84,150
Kentucky	12,250	175,440	105	4,140	1,080	28,080
Louisiana	11,880	120,450	—	1,200	23,765	24,780
Maine	—	—	1,190	261	—	—
Maryland	11,560	46,865	2,856	462	—	10,260
Massachusetts	—	—	—	152	—	—
Michigan	35,100	291,400	728	2,880	—	67,860
Minnesota	80,430	1,138,800	6,160	4,660	—	252,150
Mississippi	18,480	141,000	—	1,870	9,430	56,800
Missouri	37,840	461,500	—	7,528	10,080	168,350
Montana	149,820	5,510	31,680	5,145	—	—
Nebraska	84,280	1,472,000	—	6,298	23,520	190,385
Nevada	1,300	—	90	1,670	—	—
New Hampshire	—	—	—	85	—	—
New Jersey	1,428	10,250	136	206	—	2,449
New Mexico	7,800	9,625	506	1,550	3,000	—
New York	4,420	69,850	742	2,700	—	7,714
North Carolina	20,000	102,000	—	1,050	540	28,560
North Dakota	300,050	272,600	77,840	5,191	—	104,650
Ohio	45,990	541,500	150	2,931	—	194,110
Oklahoma	98,000	39,150	—	7,044	12,760	4,200
Oregon	46,785	6,825	2,491	2,960	—	—
Pennsylvania	8,990	125,440	3,066	4,200	168	17,220
Rhode Island	—	—	—	16	—	—
South Carolina	4,185	37,000	—	561	238	8,075
South Dakota	147,516	544,500	1,160	7,543	8,060	133,560
Tennessee	10,660	83,210	—	2,443	1,330	17,460
Texas	140,600	296,000	—	15,330	161,700	3,034
Utah	6,420	3,256	1,716	2,667	—	—
Vermont	—	—	—	410	—	—
Virginia	13,120	34,425	2,130	2,489	—	12,960

—*continued*	Wheat ('000 bushels)	Corn for grain ('000 bushels)	Barley ('000 bushels)	Hay ('000 tons)	Sorghum for grain ('000 bushels)	Soybeans ('000 bushels)
Washington	128,722	25,200	13,500	3,461	—	—
West Virginia	348	2,997	—	923	—	462
Wisconsin	18,910	442,800	1,311	4,515	—	51,870
Wyoming	3,445	7,740	4,717	2,387	—	—
Total	2,066,722	13,073,893	211,825	150,304	504,993	2,585,207

* A bushel is equivalent to 60 lb (27.2 kg) for wheat and soybeans; 56 lb (25.4 kg) for corn and sorghum; 48 lb (21.8 kg) for barley.
Note: Figures exclude production in Alaska. Production of all crops specified in the second table was nil in District of Columbia and Hawaii.

Livestock and Poultry on Farms

SUMMARY
('000 head)

	2003	2004	2005	2006	2007
Cattle	96,100	94,888	95,438	96,702	97,003
Goats	2,530*	2,525*	2,715	2,837	2,934
Pigs	59,554	60,444	60,975	61,449	61,860
Sheep	6,321	6,105	6,135	6,230	6,165
Chickens	1,920,000†	1,985,000*	2,035,000*	2,050,000*	2,050,000*
Turkeys	270,000*	263,207	252,053	261,960	271,676

* FAO estimate.
† Unofficial figure.
Source: FAO.

Livestock Products

SUMMARY
('000 metric tons)

	2003	2004	2005	2006	2007
Cattle meat	12,039	11,181	11,243	11,910	12,044
Pig meat	9,056	9,313	9,383	9,550	9,953
Chicken meat	14,696	15,286	15,869	15,870	16,000*
Sheep meat	92†	90	85	84	83
Turkey meat	2,529	3,128	3,151	3,260	3,397

* FAO estimate.
† Unofficial figure.
Source: FAO.

Forestry

ROUNDWOOD REMOVALS
('000 cu metres)

	2002	2003	2004	2005	2006
Sawlogs and veneer logs	234,578	230,012	247,958	253,636	256,036
Pulp wood	161,391	166,596	161,168	160,815	162,808
Other industrial wood	8,989	9,005	9,005	9,005	9,005
Fuel wood	43,042	42,900	43,608	43,891	44,769
Total	448,000	448,513	461,739	467,347	472,618

Source: FAO.

SAWNWOOD PRODUCTION
('000 cu metres)

	2002	2003	2004	2005	2006
Coniferous	60,913	61,190	66,428	69,187	65,549
Broadleaved	27,730	24,969	26,640	27,833	27,467
Total	88,643	86,159	93,067	97,020	93,016

Source: FAO.

Fishing

(Source: National Marine Fisheries Service, US Department of Commerce.)

SUMMARY
(principal species, million lb, live weight, preliminary figures)*

	2005	2006	2007
Pacific cod	548.7	518.7	488.3
Pacific hake (whiting)	569.4	570.5	455.3
Atlantic menhaden	428.2	405.4	475.1
Gulf menhaden	815.5	901.4	1,006.6
Walleye pollock	3,411.3	3,400.8	3,066.2
Pink (humpback) salmon	494.6	221.8	457.5
Total fish (incl. others)	8,462.5	8,287.3	8,210.8
Crabs	299.1	339.9	284.8
Shrimps	260.9	320.2	231.6
Other shellfish, molluscs, etc.	684.8	535.6	504.7
Total catch	9,707.3	9,483.0	9,231.8

* Figures refer to the total catch (excl. weight of mollusc shells) by US flag vessels, wherever landed.

Selected Agricultural, Forestry and Fisheries Organizations

AACC International: 3340 Pilot Knob Rd, St Paul, MN 55121-2097; tel. (651) 454-7250; fax (651) 454-0766; e-mail aacc@scisoc.org; internet www.aaccnet.org; fmrly American Asscn of Cereal Chemists; asscn of cereal specialists; 3,000 mems; Pres. Robert Hamer; Chair. Bernard L. Bruinsma.

Agricultural Research Service (ARS): Jamie L. Whitten Bldg, 1400 Independence Ave, SW, Whittenburg, Washington, DC 20250; tel. (202) 720-3656; fax (202) 720-5427; e-mail eknipling@ars.usda.gov; internet www.ars.usda.gov; f. 1953; research br. of federal Dept of Agriculture; Admin. Dr Edward B. Knipling.

American Angus Association: 3201 Frederick Ave, St Joseph, MO 64506; tel. (816) 383-5100; fax (816) 233-9703; e-mail angus@angus.org; internet www.angus.org; f. 1883; 32,000 mems; Pres. Paul H. Hill; CEO Bryce F. Schumann.

American Brahman Breeders Association (ABBA): 3003 South Loop West, Suite 140, Houston, TX 77054; tel. (713) 349-0854; fax (713) 349-9795; e-mail abba@brahman.org; internet www.brahman.org; f. 1924; 1,700 mems; Exec. Vice-Pres. Dr Chris Shivers.

American Butter Institute (ABI): 2101 Wilson Blvd, Suite 400, Arlington, VA 22201; tel. (703) 243-5630; fax (703) 841-9328; e-mail aminer@nmpf.org; internet www.butterinstitute.org; f. 1908; 31 mem. orgs; Exec. Dir Jerome J. Kozak.

American Cheese Society (ACS): 304 West Liberty St, Suite 201, Louisville, KY 40202; tel. (502) 583-3783; fax (502) 589-3602; e-mail acs@hqtrs.com; internet www.cheesesociety.org; f. 1982; 1,400 mems; Pres. David Gremmels; Exec. Dir Marci Wilson.

American Council for Food Safety and Quality: 710 Striker Ave, Sacramento, CA 95834; tel. (916) 561-5900; fax (916) 561-5910; e-mail merlej@dfaofca.com; internet www.dfaofca.com; f. 1908; agricultural asscn (dried fruit and tree nuts); 51 mems; Pres. and CEO Merle Jacobs.

American Egg Board (AEB): 1460 Renaissance Dr., Suite 301, Park Ridge, IL 60068-1340; tel. (847) 296-7043; fax (847) 296-7007; e-mail aeb@aeb.org; internet www.aeb.org; f. 1976; 750 mems; Chair Wayne Mooney; Pres. and CEO Joanne Ivy.

American Farm Bureau Federation (FB): 600 Maryland Ave, SW, Suite 1000W, Washington, DC 20024; tel. (202) 406-3600; fax (202) 406-3602; e-mail webmaster@fb.org; internet www.fb.org; f. 1919; 50 mem. states and Puerto Rico; Pres. Bob Stallman; Exec. Vice-Pres. Richard Newpher.

American Farmland Trust: 1200 18th St, NW, Suite 800, Washington, DC 20036; tel. (202) 331-7300; fax (202) 659-8339; e-mail info@farmland.org; internet www.farmland.org; f. 1980; Chair. John Winthrop, Jr.

American Feed Industry Association (AFIA): 1501 Wilson Blvd, Suite 1100, Arlington, VA 22209; tel. (703) 524-0810; fax (703) 524-1921; e-mail afia@afia.org; internet www.afia.org; represents animal feed and pet food industries; 690 mems; Pres. and CEO Joel Newman.

American Fisheries Society (AFS): 5410 Grosvenor Lane, Suite 110, Bethesda, MD 20814-2199; tel. (301) 897-8616; fax (301) 897-8096; e-mail franzin@shaw.ca; internet www.fisheries.org; f. 1870; 9,200 mems; Pres. Bill Franzin; Exec. Dir Ghassan (Gus) N. Rassam.

American Forest & Paper Association (AF&PA): 1111 19th St, NW, Suite 800, Washington, DC 20036; tel. (202) 463-2700; e-mail info@afandpa.org; internet www.afandpa.org; f. 1993; more than 175 mems; Pres. and CEO Donna Harman.

American Forests: 734 15th St, NW, Suite 800, POB 2000, Washington, DC 20005-1013; tel. (202) 737-1944; fax (202) 737-2457; e-mail info@amfor.org; internet www.americanforests.org; f. 1875; fmrly American Forestry Asscn; 100,000 mems; Chair. Caroline Gabel; Exec. Dir Deborah Gangloff.

American Guernsey Association (AGA): 7614 Slate Ridge Blvd, POB 666, Reynoldsburg, OH 43068-0666; tel. (614) 864-2409; fax (614) 864-5614; e-mail info@usguernsey.com; internet www.usguernsey.com; f. 1877; 2,000 mems; Pres. Dale Jensen; Exec. Sec.-Treas. Seth Johnson.

American Hereford Association (AHA): 1501 Wyandotte, POB 014059, Kansas City, MO 64101; tel. (816) 842-3757; fax (816) 842-6931; e-mail aha@hereford.org; internet www.hereford.org; f. 1881; 19,000 mems; Pres. Jack Evans; Exec. Vice-Pres. Craig Huffhines.

American International Charolais Association (AICA): 11700 NW Plaza Circle, POB 20247, Kansas City, MO 64153; tel. (816) 464-5977; fax (816) 464-5759; e-mail etnranch@midrivers.com; internet www.charolaisusa.com; f. 1957; more than 3,500 mems; Pres. Lee Eaton.

American Jersey Cattle Association (AJCA): 6486 East Main St, Reynoldsburg, OH 43068-2362; tel. (614) 861-3636; fax (614) 861-8040; e-mail pengland@usjersey.com; internet www.usjersey.com; f. 1868; services to improve and promote Jersey cattle and Jersey milk; Exec. Sec. and CEO Neal Smith.

American Lumber Standard Committee, Inc (ALSC): POB 210, Germantown, MD 20875-0210; tel. (301) 972-1700; fax (301) 540-8004; e-mail alsc@alsc.org; internet www.alsc.org; f. 1941; Pres. TOM SEARLES.

American Meat Institute: 1150 Connecticut Ave, NW, 12th Floor, Washington, DC 20036; tel. (202) 587-4200; fax (202) 587-4300; e-mail webmaster@meatami.com; internet www.meatami.com; f. 1906; 1,100 mems; Pres. DAVID MINIAT.

American Peanut Council (APC): 1500 King St, Suite 301, Alexandria, VA 22314; tel. (703) 838-9500; fax (703) 838-9508; e-mail info@peanutsusa.com; internet www.peanutsusa.com; f. 1997; 250 mems; Pres. PATRICK ARCHER.

American Seed Trade Association (ASTA): 225 Reinekers Lane, Suite 650, Alexandria, VA 22314-2875; tel. (703) 837-8140; fax (703) 837-9365; internet www.amseed.com; f. 1883; 850 mem. cos; Chair. KELLY KEITHLY.

American Sheep Industry Association (ASI): 9785 Maroon Circle, Suite 360, Centennial, CO 80112; tel. (303) 771-3500; fax (303) 771-8200; e-mail info@sheepusa.org; internet www.sheepusa .org; f. 1989; 69,000 mems, 40 mem. orgs; Pres. BURDELL JOHNSON.

American Society of Agricultural and Biological Engineers (ASABE): 2950 Niles Rd, St Joseph, MI 49085; tel. (269) 429-0300; fax (269) 429-3852; e-mail hq@asabe.org; internet www.asabe.org; f. 1907; fmrly American Society of Agricultural Engineers; 9,000 mems world-wide; Exec. Vice-Pres. MELISSA MOORE.

American Society of Farm Managers and Rural Appraisers (ASFMRA): 950 South Cherry St, Suite 508, Denver, CO 80246-2664; tel. (303) 758-3513; fax (303) 758-0190; internet www.asfmra .org; f. 1929; 3,000 mems; Pres. STEVE RUNYAN.

American Soybean Association (ASA): 12125 Woodcrest Executive Dr., Suite 100, St Louis, MO 63141-5009; tel. (800) 688-7692; fax (314) 576-2786; e-mail membership@soy.org; internet www .soygrowers.com; f. 1920; 27,000 mems; Pres. JOHN HOFFMAN; CEO STEPHEN CENSKY.

American Sugar Alliance: 2111 Wilson Blvd, Suite 600, Arlington, VA 22201; tel. (703) 351-5055; fax (703) 351-6698; e-mail info@ sugaralliance.org; internet www.sugaralliance.org; national coalition of sugar-cane and sugar-beet farmers, processors, refiners, suppliers and workers; Chair. LUTHER MARKWART; Exec. Dir VICKIE R. MYERS.

American Sugarbeet Growers Association (AGSA): 1156 15th St, NW, Suite 1101, Washington, DC 20005; tel. (202) 833-2398; fax (202) 833-2962; e-mail info@americansugarbeet.org; internet www .americansugarbeet.org; f. 1975; 21 mem. asscns; Exec. Vice-Pres. LUTHER MARKWART.

Animal Agricultural Alliance: POB 9522, Arlington, VA 22209; tel. (703) 562-5160; e-mail info@animalagalliance.org; internet www .animalagalliance.org; f. 2001; represents producers and producer orgs, suppliers, packer-processors, private industry and retailers; Chair. CLIFF BECKER; Exec.Vice-Pres. KAY JOHNSON-SMITH.

Beefmaster Breeders United (BBU): 6800 Park Ten Blvd, Suite 290 West, San Antonio, TX 78213; tel. (512) 732-3132; fax (512) 732-7711; e-mail wschronk@beefmasters.org; internet www.beefmasters .org; f. 1961; 7,000 mems; Exec. Vice-Pres. WENDELL SCHRONK.

Brown Swiss Cattle Breeders' Association of the USA (BSA): 800 Pleasant St, Beloit, WI 53511-5456; tel. (608) 365-4474; fax (608) 365-5577; e-mail info@brownswissusa.com; internet www .brownswissusa.com; f. 1880; 882 active mems; Pres. CHARLES VOELKER; Exec. Sec. DAVID J. KENDALL.

California Redwood Association (CRA): 405 Enfrente Dr., Suite 200, Novato, CA 94949; tel. (415) 382-0662; fax (415) 382-8531; e-mail info@calredwood.org; internet www.calredwood.org; f. 1916; 7 mem. orgs; Pres. CHARLIE JOURDAIN.

Commodity Markets Council (CMC): 1300 L St, NW, Suite 1020, Washington, DC 20005; tel. (202) 842-0400; fax (202) 789-7223; e-mail mwalter@cmcmarkets.org; internet www.cmcmarkets.org; f. 1930 as the National Grain Trade Council; reformed as two separate entities, CMC and the Transportation, Elevator and Grain Merchants Asscn, in 2006; 34 mems; Chair. THOMAS J. ERICKSON; Pres. MIKE WALTER.

Transportation, Elevator, & Grain Merchants Association (TEGMA): POB 26426 Kansas City, MO 64196; tel. (816) 628-1231; fax (816) 628-1905; e-mail bob.petersen@tegma.org; internet www.tegma.org; f. 2006 following the dissolution of the National Grain Trade Council; promotes efficiency, competitiveness and safety of handling and transportation of North American grain and grain products; 30 mems; Chair. MIKE MANDL; Pres. BOB PETERSEN.

Corn Refiners' Association (CRA): 1701 Pennsylvania Ave, Suite 950, Washington, DC 20006; tel. (202) 331-1634; fax (202) 331-2054; e-mail contacts@corn.org; internet www.corn.org; f. 1913; Pres. AUDRAE ERICKSON.

CropLife America (CLA): 1156 15th St, NW, Suite 400, Washington, DC 20005; tel. (202) 296-1585; fax (202) 463-0474; e-mail webmaster@croplifeamerica.org; internet www.croplifeamerica.org; f. 1933; fmrly American Crop Protection Asscn; name changed as above 2002; 80 mems; Pres. and CEO JAY VROOM.

Dairy Farmers of America (DFA): 10220 North Ambassador Dr., Kansas City, MO 64153; tel. (816) 801-6455; fax (816) 801-6456; e-mail webmail@dfamilk.com; internet www.dfamilk.com; f. 1998; 18,000 mems; Pres. and CEO RICK SMITH; Chair. TOM CAMERLO.

Farm Service Agency (FSA): 1400 Independence Ave, SW, Washington, DC 20250-0506; tel. (202) 720-7807; e-mail webmaster@wdc.usda.gov; internet www.fsa.usda.gov; br. of federal Dept of Agriculture; Admin. TERESA LASSETER.

The Fertilizer Institute (TFI): Union Center Plaza, 820 First St, NE, Suite 430, Washington, DC 20002; tel. (202) 962-0490; fax (202) 962-0577; e-mail webmaster@tfi.org; internet www.tfi.org; f. 1883 as National Fertilizer Association; adopted current name 1969; *c.* 300 mem. orgs; Pres. FORD B. WEST.

Forest Products Society (FPS): 2801 Marshall Ct, Madison, WI 53705-2295; tel. (608) 231-1361; fax (608) 231-2152; e-mail webmaster@forestprod.org; internet www.forestprod.org; f. 1947; Pres. ANTHONY WETHERSPOON.

Forest Resources Association Inc (FRA): 600 Jefferson Plaza, Suite 350, Rockville, MD 20852-1150; tel. (301) 838-9385; fax (301) 838-9481; e-mail rl@forestresources.org; internet www .forestresources.org; f. 1934; 1,300 mems; Chair. DAVE LIEBETREU; Pres. RICHARD LEWIS.

Henry A. Wallace Beltsville Agricultural Research Center (BARC): Bldg 003 BARC-WEST, Rm 223, Bldg 3, 10300 Baltimore Blvd, Beltsville, MD 20705; tel. (301) 504-6078; fax (301) 504-5863; e-mail joseph.spence@ars.usda.gov; internet www.ba.ars.usda.gov; linked to the federal Agricultural Research Service; Dir JOSEPH SPENCE.

Holstein Association USA, Inc: 1 Holstein Pl., POB 808, Brattleboro, VT 05302-0808; tel. (802) 254-4551; fax (802) 254-8251; e-mail info@holstein.com; internet www.holsteinusa.com; f. 1885; 35,000 mems; CEO JOHN M. MEYER.

International Dairy Foods Association (IDFA): 1250 H St, NW, Suite 900, Washington, DC 20005; tel. (202) 737-4332; fax (202) 331-7820; e-mail membership@idfa.org; internet www.idfa.org; f. 1908; umbrella asscn encompassing the Milk Industry Foundation, the Nat. Cheese Institute and the Int. Ice Cream Asscn; over 550 mem. cos; Chair. BRIAN HAUGH.

Irrigation Association (IA): 6540 Arlington Blvd, Falls Church, VA 22042-6638; tel. (703) 536-7080; fax (703) 536-7019; e-mail deborah@irrigation.org; internet www.irrigation.org; f. 1949; 2,000 mems; Exec. Dir DEBORAH M. HAMLIN.

Livestock Marketing Association (LMA): 10510 North West Ambassador Dr., Kansas City, MO 64153; tel. (816) 891-0502; fax (816) 891-7926; e-mail lmainfo@lmaweb.com; internet www.lmaweb .com; f. 1947; 1,350 mems; Pres. BOBBY SMITH; Chair. JIM SANTOMASO.

National Agri-Marketing Association (NAMA): 11020 King St, Suite 205, Overland Park, KS 66210; tel. (913) 491-6500; fax (913) 491-6502; e-mail agrimktg@nama.org; internet www.nama.org; f. 1957; 3,500 mems world-wide; Exec. Vice-Pres. and CEO JENNIFER PICKETT.

National Association of Animal Breeders (NAAB): POB 1033, Columbia, MO 65205; tel. (573) 445-4406; fax (573) 446-2279; e-mail naab-css@naab-css.org; internet www.naab-css.org; f. 1946; *c.* 30 mem. orgs; Chair. AL KUCK.

National Association of State Departments of Agriculture (NASDA): 1156 15th St, NW, Suite 1020, Washington, DC 20005; tel. (202) 296-9680; fax (202) 296-9686; e-mail nasda@nasda.org; internet www.nasda.org; f. 1945; 22 affiliates; Exec. Dir STEPHEN HATERIUS.

National Association of Wheat Growers (NAWG): 412 Second St, NE, Suite 300, Washington, DC 20002-4993; tel. (202) 547-7800; fax (202) 546-2638; e-mail wheatworld@wheatworld.org; internet www.wheatworld.org; f. 1950; 20 affiliated mem. states; CEO DAREN COPPOCK.

National Cattlemen's Beef Association (NCBA): 9110 East Nichols Ave, Suite 300, Centennial, CO 80112; tel. (303) 694-0305; fax (303) 694-7372; e-mail tstokes@beef.org; internet www.beefusa .org; f. 1898; 33,000 mems, plus 44 cattle asscns and 50 breed and industry asscns; Pres. ANDY GROSETA; CEO TERRY L. STOKES.

National Cherry Growers and Industries Foundation (NCGIF): 2667 Reed Rd, Hood River, OR 97031-9609; tel. (541) 386-5761; fax (541) 386-3191; e-mail nickerson9@embarqmail.com; internet www.nationalcherries.com; f. 1946; Admin. DANA BRANSON.

National Chicken Council (NCC): 1015 15th St, NW, Suite 930, Washington, DC 20005-2622; tel. (202) 296-2622; fax (202) 293-4005; e-mail ncc@chickenusa.org; internet www.nationalchickencouncil

.com; f. 1954; fmrly known as Nat. Broiler Council; name changed as above 1999; Pres. GEORGE B. WATTS.

National Corn Growers Association (NCGA): 632 Cepi Dr., Chesterfield, MO 63005; tel. (636) 733-9004; fax (636) 733-9005; e-mail corninfo@ncga.com; internet www.ncga.com; f. 1957; 32,300 mems; Pres. RON LITTERER; Chair. KEN MCCAULEY.

National Cotton Council of America (NCC): 1918 North Pkwy, Memphis, TN 38112-5000; tel. (901) 274-9030; fax (901) 725-0510; internet www.cotton.org; f. 1938; 25,000 mems; Pres. and CEO MARK D. LANGE; Chair. LARRY R. MCCLENDON, Jr.

National Council of Agricultural Employers (NCAE): 1112 16th St, NW, Suite 920, Washington, DC 20036; tel. (202) 728-0300; fax (202) 728-0303; e-mail hughes@ncaeonline.org; internet www.ncaeonline.org; f. 1964; Exec. Vice-Pres. FRANK GASPERINI.

National Dairy Council (NDC): 10255 West Higgins Rd, Suite 900, Rosemount, IL 60018; tel. (847) 803-2000; fax (847) 803-2077; e-mail ndc@dairyinformation.com; internet www.nationaldairycouncil.org; f. 1915; 600 mems.

National Farmers (NFO): 528 Billy Sunday Rd, Ames, IA 50010; tel. (800) 247-2110; e-mail nfo@nfo.org; internet www.nfo.org; f. 1955; c. 35,000 mems; Pres. PAUL OLSON.

National Farmers Union (NFU): 5619 DTC Pkwy, Suite 300, Greenwood Village, CO 80011-3136; tel. (303) 337-5500; fax (303) 771-1770; e-mail dave.frederickson@nfu.org; internet www.nfu.org; f. 1902; 250,000 mems; Pres. TOM BUIS.

National Fisheries Institute (NFI): 7918 Jones Branch Dr., Suite 700, McLean, VA 22102; tel. (703) 752-8880; fax (703) 752-7583; e-mail contact@nfi.org; internet www.aboutseafood.com; f. 1945; 350 mems; Pres. JOHN CONNELLY.

National Grain and Feed Association (NGFA): 1250 Eye St, NW, Suite 1003, Washington, DC 20005-3922; tel. (202) 289-0873; fax (202) 289-5388; e-mail ngfa@ngfa.org; internet www.ngfa.org; over 1,000 mem. cos; Chair. RONALD D. OLSON.

National Grange (The National Grange of the Order of Patrons of Husbandry): 1616 H St, NW, Washington, DC 20006-4999; tel. (202) 628-3507; fax (202) 347-1091; e-mail info@nationalgrange.org; internet www.nationalgrange.org; f. 1867; concerned with improving the economic and social position of the rural population; 300,000 mems; Pres. ED LUTTRELL.

National Hardwood Lumber Association (NHLA): 6830 Raleigh LaGrange Rd, POB 34518, Memphis, TN 38184-0518; tel. (901) 377-1818; fax (901) 382-6415; e-mail info@nhla.com; internet www.nhla.com; f. 1898; 1,800 mem. orgs; Pres. JIM HOWARD.

National Livestock Producers' Association (NLPA): 660 Southpointe Ct, Suite 314, Colorado Springs, CO 80906; tel. (719) 538-8843; fax (719) 538-8847; e-mail nlpa@nlpa.org; internet www.nlpa.org; f. 1921; Chair. JACK HANSON; Pres. and CEO R. SCOTT STEWART.

National Milk Producers Federation (NMPF): 2101 Wilson Blvd, Suite 400, Arlington, VA 22201; tel. (703) 243-6111; fax (703) 841-9328; e-mail info@nmpf.org; internet www.nmpf.org; f. 1916; Pres. and CEO JERRY KOZAK.

National Peanut Board: 2839 Paces Ferry Rd, Suite 210, Atlanta, GA 30339; tel. (678) 424-5750; fax (678) 424-5751; e-mail peanuts@nationalpeanutboard.org; internet www.nationalpeanutboard.org; f. 2000; Chair WES SHANNON.

National Pork Producers Council (NPPC): 10664 Justin Dr., Urbandale, IA 50322; tel. (515) 278-8012; fax (515) 278-8011; e-mail warnerd@nppc.org; internet www.nppc.org; f. 1954; 44 affiliated asscns; Pres. BRYAN BLACK.

National Potato Council (NPC): 1300 L St, NW, Suite 910, Washington, DC 20005; tel. (202) 682-9456; fax (202) 682-0333; e-mail spudinfo@nationalpotatocouncil.org; internet www.nationalpotatocouncil.org; f. 1948; Pres. RICHARD POLATIS; Exec. Vice-Pres. and CEO JOHN KEELING.

National Renderers Association, Inc (NRA): 801 North Fairfax St, Suite 205, Alexandria, VA 22314; tel. (703) 683-0155; fax (703) 683-2626; e-mail renderers@nationalrenderers.com; internet nationalrenderers.org; Pres. THOMAS M. COOK.

National Swine Registry (NSR): 1769 US 52 West, POB 2417, West Lafayette, IN 47996; tel. (765) 463-3594; fax (765) 497-2959; e-mail nsr@nationalswine.com; internet www.nationalswine.com; f. 1994; fmrly American Yorkshire Club; 2,000 mems; CEO DARRELL D. ANDERSON.

National Turkey Federation (NTF): 1225 New York Ave, NW, Suite 400, Washington, DC 20005; tel. (202) 898-0100; fax (202) 898-0203; e-mail info@turkeyfed.org; internet www.eatturkey.com; f. 1939; 310 mem. cos; Chair. PAUL HILL; Pres. JOEL BRANDENBERGER.

North American Limousin Foundation (NALF): 7383 S. Alton Way, Suite 100, Centennial, CO 80112-2339; tel. (303) 220-1693; fax (303) 220-1884; e-mail limousin@nalf.org; internet www.nalf.org; f. 1968; 4,000 mems; Exec. Vice-Pres. KENT ANDERSON.

North American Meat Processors Association (NAMP): 1910 Association Dr., Reston, VA 20191; tel. (703) 758-1900; fax (703) 758-8001; e-mail info@namp.com; internet www.namp.com; f. 1942; Exec. Dir PHILIP KIMBALL.

North American Millers' Association (NAMA): 600 Maryland Ave, SW, Suite 825 West, Washington, DC 20024; tel. (202) 484-2200; fax (202) 488-7416; e-mail generalinfo@namamillers.org; internet www.namamillers.org; f. 1998; 48 mems and 28 assoc. mems; Chair. RICK L. SCHWEIN; Pres. BETSY FAGA.

Northwest Horticultural Council (NHC): 105 South 18th St, Suite 105, Yakima, WA 98901; tel. (509) 453-3193; fax (509) 457-7615; e-mail general@nwhort.org; internet www.nwhort.org; f. 1947; Pres. CHRISTIAN SCHLECT.

R-CALF USA (R-CALF United Stockgrowers of America): POB 30715, Billings, MT 59107; tel. (406) 252-2516; fax (406) 252-3176; e-mail webmaster@r-calfusa.com; internet www.r-calfusa.com; f. 1998; represents US cattle producers on trade and marketing issues; 18,000 mems in 47 states; CEO BILL BULLARD.

Rural Coalition: 1012 14th St, NW, Suite 1100, Washington, DC 20005; tel. (202) 628-7160; fax (202) 628-7165; e-mail ruralco@ruralco.org; internet www.ruralco.org; Exec. Dir LORETTE PICCIANO; Chair. JOHN ZIPPERT.

Southern Forest Products Association (SFPA): 2900 Indiana Ave, Kenner, LA 70065-4605; tel. (504) 443-4464; fax (504) 443-6612; e-mail mail@spfa.org; internet www.sfpa.org; f. 1915; c. 180 mem. orgs; Pres. DIGGES MORGAN.

Sugar Association, Inc: 1101 15th St, NW, Suite 600, Washington, DC 20005; tel. (202) 785-1122; fax (202) 785-5019; e-mail sugar@sugar.org; internet www.sugar.org; f. 1947; fmrly Sugar Research Foundation; 13 mem. cos; Pres. and CEO ANDREW BRISCOE.

Supima Association of America (Supima): 4141 East Broadway Rd, Phoenix, AZ 85040; tel. (602) 437-1364; fax (602) 437-0143; e-mail info@supima.com; internet www.supimacotton.org; f. 1954; 2,300 mems; Chair. JEFF ELDER.

United Egg Producers (UEP): 1720 Windward Concourse, Suite 230, Alpharetta, GA 30005; tel. (770) 360-9220; fax (770) 360-7058; e-mail patricia@unitedegg.com; internet www.unitedegg.org; f. 1968; 5 mem. orgs; Pres. and CEO GENE GREGORY.

United Fresh Fruit & Vegetable Association: 1901 Pennsylvania Ave, NW, Suite 1100, Washington, DC 20006; tel. (202) 303-3400; fax (202) 303-3433; e-mail united@unitedfresh.org; internet www.unitedfresh.org; f. 1904; 1,300 mems; Pres. and CEO THOMAS E. STENZEL; Pres. TOM STENZEL.

United Soybean Board (USB): 16640 Chesterfield Grove Rd, Suite 130, Chesterfield, MO 63005-1429; tel. (636) 530-1577; fax (636) 530-1560; e-mail jbecherer@unitedsoybean.com; internet www.unitedsoybean.org; Chair. IKE BOUDREAUX; CEO JOHN BECHERER.

United States Apple Association (USApple): 8233 Old Courthouse Rd, Suite 200, Vienna, VA 22182; tel. (703) 442-8850; fax (703) 790-0845; e-mail sschaffer@usapple.org; internet www.usapple.org; 40 affiliated asscns and over 400 mem. cos; Pres. and CEO NANCY E. FOSTER.

United States Hide, Skin and Leather Association (USHSLA): 1150 Connecticut Ave, NW, Washington, DC 20036; tel. (202) 584-4261; fax (202) 587-4303; e-mail jreddington@meatami.com; internet www.ushsla.org; division of the American Meat Institute since 1990; 40 regular and 20 assoc. mems; Chair. ED GODSALVE; Pres. JOHN REDDINGTON.

US Poultry and Egg Association (USPOULTRY): 1530 Cooledge Rd, Tucker, GA 30084-7303; tel. (770) 493-9401; fax (770) 493-9257; e-mail jstarkey@poultryegg.org; internet www.poultryegg.org; f. 1947; Pres. JOHN STARKEY; Chair. BILL BRADLEY.

USA Rice Federation (USA Rice): 4301 North Fairfax Dr., Suite 425, Arlington, VA 22203; tel. (703) 236-2300; fax (703) 236-2301; e-mail riceinfo@usarice.com; internet www.usarice.com; orgs include USA Rice Council, Rice Millers' Asscn and US Rice Producers' Group; mem. councils in 6 states; Chair. JAMIE WARSHAW; Pres. and CEO BETSY WARD.

Western Wood Products Association (WWPA): 522 South West Fifth Ave, Suite 500, Portland, OR 97204-2122; tel. (503) 224-3930; fax (503) 224-3934; e-mail info@wwpa.org; internet www2.wwpa.org; f. 1964; 120 mem. orgs; Chair. DUANE VAAGEN; Pres. and CEO MICHAEL O'HALLORAN.

In addition, there are four regional agricultural export organizations: Food Export USA-Northeast (www.foodexportusa.org); Mid-America Agri-Trade Council (www.foodexport.org); Southern United States Trade Association (www.susta.org); and Western US Agricultural Trade Association (www.wusata.org). For further details, see External Trade Organizations.

MINING

Mineral Fuels

(Source: Energy Information Administration, US Department of Energy.)

SUMMARY
(million short tons, unless otherwise indicated)

	2005		2006		2007	
	Quantity	Value ($ '000 million)	Quantity	Value ($ '000 million)	Quantity	Value ($ '000 million)
Coal:						
Bituminous	571.2	21.0	561.6	22.1	534.9*	21.8*
Sub-bituminous	474.7	4.1	515.3	5.1	530.6*	5.8*
Lignite	83.9	1.1	84.2	1.2	78.5*	1.2*
Anthracite	1.7	0.0	1.5	0.0	1.6*	0.0*
Total	1,131.5	26.7	1,162.7	29.3	1,145.6*	29.1*
Crude oil (million barrels)	1,890.1	95.0	1,862.3	111.2	1,848.5	123.0
Natural gas (marketed, '000 million cu ft)	18,927	139	19,382	124	20,151	129

* Estimate.
Note: For values, totals may not be equal to the sum of components, owing to rounding.

Metals

(Source: US Geological Survey, US Department of the Interior.)

SUMMARY
('000 metric tons, unless otherwise indicated)

	2004		2005		2006	
	Quantity	Value ($ million)	Quantity	Value ($ million)	Quantity	Value ($ million)
Copper*	1,160	3,420	1,140	4,360	1,200	8,310
Gold (metric tons)*	258	3,400	256	3,670	252	4,910
Iron ore (shipments)	54,900	2,080	53,200	2,370	52,700	2,840
Lead*	430	523	426	574	419	715
Molybdenum†	42.0	1,420	58.0	3,660	59.9	3,040
Palladium metal (metric tons)†	13.7	102	13.3	87	14.4	150
Platinum metal (metric tons)†	4.0	110	3.9	113	4.3	158
Silver (metric tons)*	1,250	268	1,230	289	1,140	425
Zinc*	715	827	720	1,070	699	2,450

* Recoverable content of ores.
† Content of ore and concentrate.

Non-Metallic Minerals (Excluding Fuels)

(Source: US Geological Survey, US Department of the Interior.)

SUMMARY
('000 metric tons, unless otherwise indicated)

	2004		2005		2006	
	Quantity	Value ($ million)	Quantity	Value ($ million)	Quantity	Value ($ million)
Boron minerals	1,120	626	1,150	713	n.a.*	n.a.*
Bromine	222	191	226	168	243	339
Cement:						
masonry	5,000	585†	5,420	679†	5,400	743†
Portland	92,400	7,110†	93,900	8,360†	92,800	9,230†
Clays:						
Bentonite	4,060	179	4,710	215	4,940	234
Common	24,600	174	24,300	176	24,200	243
Fuller's earth	3,260	329	2,730	275	2,540	243
Kaolin	7,760	945	7,800	860	7,470	980
Diatomite	620	177	653	179	799	176
Gypsum (crude)	17,200	124	21,100	158	21,100	192
Helium:						
crude (million cu metres)	57	78	42	63	41	66
grade A (million cu metres)	130	299	133	336	139	395
Lime	20	1,370	20	1,500	21	1,700
Phosphate rock (marketable)	35,800	995	36,100	1,070	30,100	919
Potash	2,700	340	2,500	410	2,400	410
Salt	45,000	1,270	45,000	1,310	44,300	1,370
Sand and gravel:						
construction	1,240,000	6,590	1,280,000	7,500	1,320,000	8,540
industrial	29,700	685	30,600	752	31,700	807
Soda ash	11,000	770	11,000	968	11,000	1,170
Stone, crushed	1,630,000	9,890	1,700,000	12,400	1,720,000	13,800

* Withheld owing to confidentiality restrictions.
† Estimate.

Selected Mining Organizations

American Coal Ash Association (ACAA): 15200 East Girard Ave, Suite 3050, Aurora, CO 80014; tel. (720) 870-7897; fax (720)870-7889; e-mail info@acaa-usa.org; internet www.acaa-usa.org; Exec. Dir (vacant).

American Coal Council (ACC): 1101 Pennsylvania Ave, NW, Suite 600, Washington, DC 20004; tel. (202)756-4540; fax (202) 231-6581; e-mail info@americancoalcouncil.org; internet www.americancoalcouncil.org; f. 1982; CEO JANET GELLICI.

American Coke and Coal Chemicals Institute (ACCCI): 1140 Connecticut Ave NW, Suite 705, Washington, DC 20036; tel. (202) 452-7198; fax (202) 463-6573; e-mail information@accci.org; internet www.accci.org; f. 1944; 50 mem. cos; Pres. BRUCE STEINER; Chair. CHARLES STEWART.

American Institute of Professional Geologists (AIPG): 1400 West 122nd Ave, Suite 250, Westminster, CO 80234; tel. (303) 412-6205; fax (303) 253-9220; e-mail aipg@aipg.org; internet www.aipg.org; f. 1963; over 5,000 mems; Pres. DAN J. ST. GERMAIN.

American Petroleum Institute (API): 1220 L St NW, Washington, DC 20005-4070; tel. (202) 682-8000; e-mail mediacenter@api.org; internet www.api.org; f. 1919; 400 corporate mems; Pres. and CEO RED CAVANEY; Vice-Pres. and Dir JIM CRAIG.

China Clay Producers Association (CCPA): 113 Arkwright Landing, Macon, GA 31210; tel. (478) 757-1211; fax (478) 757-1949; e-mail info@georgiamining.org; internet www.kaolin.com; f. 1978; 4 mem. cos; Exec. Vice-Pres. LEE LEMKE.

Coal Exporters' Association of the US, Inc: 1130 17th St, NW, Washington, DC 20036; tel. (202) 463-2666; fax (202) 833-9636; e-mail eschlecht@nma.org; f. 1945; 35 mems; Exec. Dir MOYA PHELLEPS.

Copper Development Association, Inc (CDA): 260 Madison Ave, New York, NY 10016; tel. (212) 251-7200; fax (212) 251-7234; e-mail questions@cda.copper.org; internet www.copper.org; f. 1962; 65 mems; Pres. and CEO ANDREW G. KIRETA, Sr.

Industrial Minerals Association—North America (IMA—NA): 2011 Pennsylvania Ave NW, Suite 301, Washington, DC 20006; tel. (202) 457-0200; fax (202) 457-0287; e-mail info@ima-na.org; internet www.ima-na.org; f. 2002; Pres. MARK G. ELLIS.

Mining and Metallurgical Society of America (MMSA): POB 810, Boulder, CO 80306-0810; tel. (303) 444-6032; e-mail contactmmsa@mmsa.net; internet www.mmsa.net; f. 1908; 340 mems; Exec. Dir BETTY L. GIBBS; Pres. ROBERT V. WASHNOCK.

The National Coal Council (NCC): 1730 M St, NW, Suite 907, Washington, DC 20036; tel. (202) 223-1191; fax (202) 223-9031; e-mail rabeck@nationalcoalcouncil.org; internet www.nationalcoalcouncil.org; advisory committee to federal Sec. of Energy; Exec. Vice-Pres. and COO ROBERT A. BECK.

National Mining Association (NMA): 101 Constitution Ave, NW, Suite 500 East, Washington, DC 20001-2133; tel. (202) 463-2600; fax (202) 463-2666; e-mail craulston@nma.org; internet www.nma.org; f. 1995; over 325 mem. cos; Pres. and CEO HAROLD P. QUINN.

National Sand, Stone and Gravel Association (NSSGA): 1605 King St, Alexandria, VA 22314; tel. (703) 525-8788; e-mail info@nssga.org; internet www.nssga.org; f. 2000; Pres. and CEO JENNIFER JOY WILSON.

Northwest Mining Association (NWMA): 10 North Post St, Suite 220, Spokane, WA 99201; tel. (509) 624-1158; fax (509) 623-1241; e-mail nwma_info@nwma.org; internet www.nwma.org; f. 1895; 1,800 mems; Exec. Dir LAURA E. SKAER.

Offshore Operators' Committee (OOC): 1 Lakeway, 3900 Causeway Blvd, Suite 700, Metairie, LA 70002; tel. (504) 934-2159; fax (985) 795-9766; e-mail info@offshoreoperators.com; internet www.offshoreoperators.com; 70 operating and 25 service mems; environmental consultancy; Exec. Dir ALLAN J. VERRET.

Pennsylvania Coal Association (PCA): 212 North Third St, Suite 102, Harrisburg, PA 17101; tel. (717) 233-7909; fax (717) 231-7610; e-mail pacoal1@aol.com; 160 mems; Pres. GEORGE L. ELLIS.

The Perlite Institute, Inc: 4305 North Sixth St, Suite A, Harrisburg, PA 17110; tel. (717) 238-9723; fax (717) 238-9985; e-mail info@perlite.org; internet www.perlite.org; f. 1949; 56 mem. cos; Pres. ROGER SMITH.

The Silver Institute: 1200 G St, NW, Suite 800, Washington, DC 20005; tel. (202) 835-0185; fax (202) 835-0155; e-mail info@silverinstitute.org; internet www.silverinstitute.org; f. 1971; 30 mems; Pres. ROBERT QUARTERMAN; Exec. Dir MICHAEL DIRIENZO.

Society for Mining, Metallurgy, and Exploration, Inc (SME): 8307 Shaffer Pkwy, POB 277002, Littleton, CO 80127-4102; tel. (303) 973-9550; fax (303) 973-3845; e-mail cs@smenet.org; internet www.smenet.org; f. 1871; mem. soc. of AIME; 11,500 mems; Pres. GEORGE W. LUXBACHER; Exec. Dir DAVE KANAGY.

Society of Exploration Geophysicists (SEG): POB 702740, Tulsa, OK 74170-2740; tel. (918) 497-5500; fax (918) 497-5557; e-mail web@seg.org; internet www.seg.org; f. 1930; over 29,000 mems; Pres. FRED AMINZADEH; Exec. Dir MARY FLEMING.

Society of Mineral Analysts (SMA): POB 404, Lewiston, ID 83501; tel. (208) 799-3286; e-mail services@sma-online.org; internet www.sma-online.org; f. 1986; 300 mems; Man. Sec. PATRICK BRAUN.

Solution Mining Research Institute (SMRI): 105 Apple Valley Circle, Clarks Summit, PA 18411; tel. (570) 585-8092; fax (570) 585-8091; e-mail smri@solutionmining.org; internet www.solutionmining.org; f. 1958; conducts educational conferences, sponsors research; over 100 mem. orgs and cos; Exec. Dir JOHN VOIGT; Pres. ROGER BLAIR.

INDUSTRY

Manufacturing Production

(Source: Bureau of the Census, US Department of Commerce, *Annual Survey of Manufactures*.)

SUMMARY
($ million)

	2005		2006	
	Value added by manufacture	Total value of shipments	Value added by manufacture	Total value of shipments
Food and related products	234,662	532,402	233,741	537,787
Beverages and tobacco	81,161	124,086	79,595	124,693
Textile-mill products, unmade	18,585	42,328	17,220	38,795
Textile-mill products, made-up articles (excl. apparel)	15,935	35,022	15,115	33,220
Apparel	16,071	31,401	15,909	30,462
Lumber and wood products	44,752	112,095	44,432	112,404
Paper and allied products	75,346	161,928	80,601	170,361
Printing and publishing	58,794	96,922	60,380	99,688
Petroleum and coal products	117,986	475,787	133,994	548,955
Petroleum refining	105,227	445,642	119,866	514,839
Chemical and allied products	331,694	610,873	350,786	657,748
Pharmaceutical and medicine	127,639	169,226	137,928	184,636
Rubber and miscellaneous plastic products	96,162	200,304	99,528	211,345
Stone, clay and glass products	65,032	114,849	72,024	126,015
Primary metal industries	75,541	203,263	83,542	232,558
Iron and steel foundries	31,173	83,369	34,407	93,328
Fabricated metal products	155,801	289,432	169,381	317,223
Machinery	143,472	302,650	154,369	326,430
Agriculture, construction and mining machinery	28,908	69,504	32,454	77,268
Engine, turbine and power transmission equipment	14,170	39,588	15,221	42,234
Computer and electronic products	227,061	372,882	230,262	390,776
Computer and peripheral equipment	34,004	65,005	34,947	67,325
Communications equipment	31,760	58,914	36,888	70,174
Navigational, measuring, medical and control instruments	73,258	111,984	75,838	119,036
Electrical equipment and appliances	54,742	111,977	57,758	120,038
Transportation equipment	256,558	690,743	260,380	698,349
Motor vehicles	67,606	261,844	61,031	232,453
Motor vehicle parts	81,290	206,106	80,497	202,285
Aerospace products and parts	72,090	137,282	75,387	142,387
Furniture and related products	46,512	84,181	26,191	48,915
Miscellaneous manufacturing	91,564	142,770	55,858	78,372
Medical equipment and supplies	52,443	74,223	55,858	78,372
Total (incl. others)	2,210,349	4,742,077	2,305,589	5,019,963

SELECTED INDUSTRIES BY STATE
(industry groups with 950 employees or more, value of shipments in 2006, $ million)

	Food and related products	Beverages and tobacco	Lumber and wood products	Paper and allied products	Printing and publishing
Alabama	7,746	784	4,839	7,595	581
Alaska	1,925	—	—	—	—
Arizona	3,234	904	1,696	992	816
Arkansas	14,203	—	3,142	4,519	499
California	55,798	17,452	7,532	9,248	9,750
Colorado	6,368	3,632	745	497	1,515
Connecticut	2,816	—	251	1,700	1,401
Delaware	1,944	—	—	—	—
Florida	10,844	5,531	3,701	3,979	2,930
Georgia	19,940	3,853	5,398	10,084	2,976
Hawaii	986	—	—	—	182
Idaho	4,485	—	2,215	812	187
Illinois	31,766	2,716	1,514	6,069	6,995
Indiana	14,247	2,261	3,434	3,424	3,061
Iowa	26,593	740	1,979	1,522	1,690
Kansas	15,997	—	369	757	1,526
Kentucky	7,954	2,473	2,155	4,816	1,987
Louisiana	6,962	583	2,214	4,907	371
Maine	1,842	—	1,150	3,476	330
Maryland	6,341	1,031	1,166	1,328	1,973
Massachusetts	6,549	1,778	768	3,267	2,365
Michigan	11,203	2,377	2,534	4,965	2,731
Minnesota	17,712	698	3,643	5,428	4,913
Mississippi	5,241	—	2,919	2,451	365
Missouri	14,159	2,538	1,238	4,579	2,649
Montana	725	—	956	—	—
Nebraska	21,123	—	452	483	686
Nevada	1,190	—	338	—	610
New Hampshire	880	—	599	415	596
New Jersey	9,349	1,845	810	3,241	4,161
New Mexico	1,598	—	230	—	—
New York	14,822	3,384	1,717	5,059	5,726
North Carolina	16,213	28,772	5,969	5,711	2,056
North Dakota	2,484	—	357	—	—
Ohio	21,083	4,154	2,784	7,422	5,005
Oklahoma	5,503	739	452	2,269	518
Oregon	6,451	703	8,991	3,306	1,035
Pennsylvania	27,275	3,485	5,401	10,935	6,794
Rhode Island	546	—	—	257	204
South Carolina	4,308	—	2,496	6,341	886
South Dakota	2,832	—	295	—	157
Tennessee	14,120	4,064	2,900	5,002	2,811
Texas	34,098	6,798	5,557	6,389	5,105
Utah	4,801	—	496	1,028	985
Vermont	1,717	—	416	—	206
Virginia	11,517	12,479	4,189	4,311	2,585
Washington	11,044	1,600	4,900	5,617	1,146
West Virginia	756	—	1,887	—	526
Wisconsin	26,266	1,827	5,167	13,802	5,575
Total†	537,787	124,093	112,404	170,301	99,088

* Figure withheld to avoid disclosing data of individual companies; data are included in higher level totals.
† Totals may not be equal to the sum of components owing to incomplete data and rounding.

SELECTED INDUSTRIES BY STATE—CONTINUED
(industry groups with 950 employees or more, value of shipments in 2006, $ million)

	Petroleum and coal products	Chemical and allied products	Rubber and miscellaneous plastic products	Stone, clay and glass products	Primary metal industries	Fabricated metal products
Alabama	5,377	10,780	3,845	2,202	10,617	5,714
Arizona	—	2,196	1,724	3,149	2,000	3,914
Arkansas	—	3,320	4,092	1,137	6,449	4,146
California	68,746	36,922	16,394	12,729	7,322	27,178
Colorado	—	3,089	992	2,268	957	2,675
Connecticut	—	8,794	1,620	737	1,420	6,001
Delaware	—	10,297	534	305	—	414
Florida	930	9,237	3,628	8,191	1,540	8,083
Georgia	1,781	12,497	7,891	5,349	2,976	6,907
Hawaii	—	—	—	322	—	—
Idaho	—	987	307	272	—	673
Illinois	29,490	32,343	14,221	4,692	13,097	21,161
Indiana	11,995	20,831	9,897	4,230	28,716	14,610
Iowa	—	14,390	3,692	2,228	5,065	4,262
Kansas	9,014	4,645	3,213	1,610	519	2,970
Kentucky	n.a.*	11,224	4,598	2,455	12,393	4,977
Louisiana	95,053	53,782	1,100	1,223	1,142	4,525
Maine	—	—	632	242	—	960
Maryland	—	7,599	1,732	1,685	1,561	2,600
Massachusetts	—	10,509	3,788	1,373	1,424	6,662
Michigan	4,082	12,391	10,175	4,328	9,449	15,369
Minnesota	10,019	3,702	3,188	2,275	1,625	8,568
Mississippi	11,244	5,184	2,605	873	1,878	2,667
Missouri	1,026	13,997	4,642	2,659	3,554	6,232
Montana	—	—	—	—	—	213
Nebraska	—	2,556	1,261	762	698	1,974
Nevada	—	503	935	1,489	415	1,120
New Hampshire	—	399	755	737	440	1,988
New Jersey	19,835	29,205	4,953	3,308	2,729	5,758
New Mexico	—	—	252	582	—	422
New York	983	41,548	5,833	4,483	8,197	9,958
North Carolina	608	39,462	9,971	4,098	4,028	9,318
North Dakota	—	—	249—	—	—	421
Ohio	16,261	25,231	17,758	6,050	24,777	29,028
Oklahoma	15,675	2,538	3,640	2,021	1,833	5,237
Oregon	—	2,042	1,361	1,164	3,122	2,984
Pennsylvania	25,490	33,044	10,815	6,184	25,988	19,028
Rhode Island	—	3,033	756	—	452	1,758
South Carolina	—	13,981	7,893	2,649	5,025	5,566
South Dakota	—	—	273	296	—	622
Tennessee	4,763	13,428	7,048	3,160	6,858	7,764
Texas	143,077	131,128	14,282	10,900	15,311	24,679
Utah	5,281	1,896	1,555	1,435	3,132	2,414
Vermont	—	—	302	306	—	467
Virginia	—	8,098	6,290	2,815	2,663	4,396
Washington	17,098	1,806	2,647	2,173	2,710	4,494
West Virginia	—	7,114	821	787	3,542	2,283
Wisconsin	—	8,256	6,862	3,012	5,102	13,507
Wyoming	—	1,709	—	—	—	228
Total†	548,955	657,748	211,345	126,015	232,558	317,223

* Figure withheld to avoid disclosing data of individual companies; data are included in higher level totals.
† Totals may not be equal to the sum of components owing to incomplete data and rounding.

SELECTED INDUSTRIES BY STATE—CONTINUED
(industry groups with 950 employees or more, value of shipments in 2006, $ million)

	Machinery and equipment	Computer and electronic products	Electrical equipment and appliances	Transportation equipment	Furniture and related products	Miscellaneous manufacturing
Alabama	3,943	4,372	2,092	22,166	2,385	1,239
Arizona	1,559	11,265	509	11,894	1,198	1,946
Arkansas	3,374	1,176	3,830	5,261	834	881
California	19,134	80,991	7,776	40,825	8,661	24,212
Colorado	2,104	5,558	394	2,736	731	2,437
Connecticut	4,725	4,009	2,165	11,474	422	3,058
Delaware	—	653	—	2,608	271	417
Florida	5,210	15,006	1,507	6,402	2,288	7,454
Georgia	8,574	2,643	5,880	18,637	2,309	3,409
Hawaii	—	—	—	—	—	122
Idaho	471	2,943	—	530	250	248
Illinois	30,047	10,043	7,500	20,326	2,746	6,284
Indiana	13,583	5,282	3,595	55,873	4,616	7,149
Iowa	16,646	2,169	3,445	3,949	1,674	783
Kansas	4,993	2,541	1,019	17,050	700	744
Kentucky	5,395	2,987	3,191	35,466	824	1,235
Louisiana	2,314	n.a.*	268	7,460	247	818
Maine	481	911	—	2,394	189	297
Maryland	3,418	5,967	304	1,501	896	1,059
Massachusetts	7,102	21,511	2,531	3,783	1,016	7,090
Michigan	17,959	4,103	2,112	100,075	7,811	3,055
Minnesota	8,955	13,048	3,884	5,839	1,807	5,911
Mississippi	2,888	614	2,955	8,510	3,986	587
Missouri	7,265	1,762	3,577	29,330	1,690	1,935
Montana	299	—	—	—	—	208
Nebraska	3,441	1,064	1,273	2,271	573	1,507
Nevada	430	892	—	274	522	3,225
New Hampshire	2,312	3,515	1,246	509	153	1,341
New Jersey	3,520	6,903	2,346	760	1,205	5,507
New Mexico	299	6,363	298	506	n.a.*	923
New York	11,850	13,264	3,772	11,591	3,233	9,935
North Carolina	11,243	14,957	6,315	16,756	7,393	3,608
North Dakota	3,091	568	—	418	117	—
Ohio	18,815	8,629	9,265	76,397	4,273	5,511
Oklahoma	6,986	1,261	997	4,801	400	740
Oregon	3,273	23,378	592	4,148	1,017	1,212
Pennsylvania	13,460	9,190	5,444	14,590	3,606	7,126
Rhode Island	746	781	1,636	375	226	2,241
South Carolina	7,786	2,768	4,077	16,078	952	1,644
South Dakota	1,671	920	—	772	287	1,524
Tennessee	9,097	13,955	4,763	32,159	2,485	3,657
Texas	29,191	48,760	6,035	31,507	4,212	7,207
Utah	1,243	2,562	769	3,937	1,405	3,035
Vermont	716	4,479	347	262	268	469
Virginia	4,349	3,445	2,408	13,730	2,716	1,483
Washington	4,499	10,665	723	30,892	1,094	1,799
West Virginia	633	—	—	2,734	—	395
Wisconsin	16,924	12,250	8,277	18,501	2,591	3,492
Total†	326,430	390,776	120,038	698,349	86,749	150,349

* Figure withheld to avoid disclosing data of individual companies; data are included in higher level totals.
† Totals may not be equal to the sum of components owing to incomplete data and rounding.

Chambers of Commerce

NATIONAL ORGANIZATIONS

American Chamber of Commerce Executives (ACCE): 4875 Eisenhower Ave, Suite 250, Alexandria, VA 22304; tel. (703) 998-0072; fax (703) 212-9512; e-mail info-central@acce.org; internet www.acce.org; f. 1914; Pres. and CEO MICHAEL FLEMING.

Latin Chamber of Commerce of the USA (CAMACOL): 1417 West Flagler St, Third Floor, Miami, FL 33135; tel. (305) 642-3870; fax (305) 642-0653; e-mail hgasca@camacol.org; internet www.camacol.org; f. 1965; 1,800 mems; Exec. Dir WILLIAM ALEXANDER.

United States Council for International Business (USCIB): 1212 Ave of the Americas, New York, NY 10036; tel. (212) 354-4480; fax (212) 575-0327; e-mail info@uscib.org; internet www.uscib.org; f. 1945; US affiliate of Int. Chamber of Commerce; Chair. WILLIAM G. PARRETT.

US Chamber of Commerce: 1615 H St, NW, Washington, DC 20062-2000; tel. (202) 659-6000; fax (202) 463-5836; internet www.uschamber.com; f. 1912; mems: c. 3m. cos; over 100 US chambers of commerce in 91 countries; Pres. and CEO THOMAS J. DONOHUE; Chair. DONALD J. SHEPARD.

STATE ORGANIZATIONS

Alabama

Business Council of Alabama (BCA): 2 North Jackson St, POB 76, Montgomery, AL 36101-0076; tel. (334) 834-6000; fax (334) 262-7371; e-mail kimberly@bcatoday.org; internet www.bcatoday.org; c. 5,000 mems; Pres. and CEO WILLIAM J. CANARY.

Alaska

Alaska State Chamber of Commerce: 217 Second St, Suite 201, Juneau, AK 99801-1298; tel. (907) 586-2323; fax (907) 463-5515; e-mail info@alaskachamber.com; internet www.alaskachamber.com; Chair. WENDY LINDSKOOG; Pres. WAYNE STEPHENS.

Arizona

Arizona Chamber of Commerce: 1850 North Central Ave, Suite 1010, Phoenix, AZ 85004; tel. (602) 248-9172; fax (602) 265-1262; e-mail info@azchamber.com; internet www.azchamber.com; Chair. RICHARD M. HANNON; Pres. and CEO GLENN HAMER.

Arkansas

Arkansas State Chamber of Commerce/Associated Industries of Arkansas, Inc (ASCC/AIA): 1200 West Capitol Ave, POB 3645, Little Rock, AR 72203-3645; tel. (501) 374-2222; fax (501) 372-2722; e-mail rzook@arkansasstatechamber.com; internet statechamber-aia.dina.org; Pres. and CEO RANDY ZOOK.

California

California Chamber of Commerce (CalChamber): 1215 K St, Suite 1400, POB 1736, Sacramento, CA 95812-1736; tel. (916) 444-6670; fax (916) 325-1272; e-mail information@calchamber.com; internet www.calchamber.com; f. 1890; Pres. and CEO ALLAN ZAREMBERG.

Colorado

Colorado Office of Economic Development and International Trade (OED&IT): 1625 Broadway, Suite 2700, Denver, CO 80202; tel. (303) 892-3840; fax (303) 892-3848; e-mail brian.vogt@state.co.us; internet www.advancecolorado.com; Dir DON ELLIMAN.

Connecticut

Connecticut Business and Industry Association (CBIA): 350 Church St, Hartford, CT 06103-1126; tel. (860) 244-1900; fax (860) 278-8562; e-mail andrewsn@cbia.com; internet www.cbia.com; 10,000 mem. cos; Pres. and CEO JOHN R. RATHGEBER.

Delaware

Delaware State Chamber of Commerce: 1201 North Orange St, Suite 200, POB 671, Wilmington, DE 19899-0671; tel. (302) 655-7221; fax (302) 654-0691; e-mail aturochy@dscc.com; internet www.dscc.com; Pres. and CEO JAMES A. WOLFE.

District of Columbia

Greater Washington Board of Trade: Sun Trust Conference Center, Suite 200, 1725 I St, NW, Washington, DC 20006; tel. (202) 857-5900; fax (202) 223-2648; e-mail info@bot.org; internet www.bot.org; 1,000 mem. cos; Chair.-elect JOHN M. KANE; Pres. JIM DINEGAR.

Florida

Florida Chamber of Commerce: 136 South Bronough St, POB 11309, Tallahassee, FL 32302-3309; tel. (850) 521-1200; fax (850) 521-1219; e-mail info@flchamber.com; internet www.flchamber.com; c. 139,000 mem. cos; Pres. and CEO MARK A. WILSON.

Georgia

Georgia Chamber of Commerce: 233 Peachtree St, NE, Suite 2000, Atlanta, GA 30303-1564; tel. (404) 223-2264; fax (404) 223-2290; e-mail communications@gachamber.org; internet www.gachamber.com; over 4,000 mems; Pres. and CEO GEORGE M. ISRAEL, III.

Hawaii

The Chamber of Commerce of Hawaii: 1132 Bishop St, Suite 402, Honolulu, HI 96813; tel. (808) 545-4300; fax (808) 545-4369; e-mail info@cochawaii.org; internet www.cochawaii.com; over 1,100 mem. cos; Pres. and CEO JIM TOLLEFSON.

Idaho

Idaho Association of Commerce and Industry (IACI): 225 North Ninth St, Suite 230, POB 389, Boise, ID 83701-0389; tel. (208) 343-1849; fax (208) 338-5623; e-mail alabeau@iaci.org; internet www.iaci.org; Pres. ALEX S. LABEAU.

Illinois

Illinois Chamber of Commerce: 215 East Adams St, Springfield, IL 62701; tel. (217) 522-5512; fax (217) 522-5518; e-mail dmccarver@ilchamber.org; internet www.ilchamber.org; Pres. and CEO DOUGLAS L. WHITLEY.

Indiana

Indiana Chamber of Commerce: 115 West Washington St, Suite 850 S, Indianapolis, IN 46204-3420; tel. (317) 264-3110; fax (317) 264-6855; e-mail inchamber@indianachamber.com; internet www.indianachamber.com; f. 1922; c. 4,900 mem. cos; Pres. KEVIN BRINEGAR.

Iowa

Association of Business and Industry (ABI): 904 Walnut St, Suite 100, Des Moines, IA 50309-3503; tel. (515) 280-8000; fax (515) 244-8907; e-mail abi@iowaabi.org; internet www.iowaabi.org; 1,300 mem. cos; Pres. MICHAEL RALSTON.

Kansas

The Kansas Chamber of Commerce: 835 South West Topeka Blvd, Topeka, KS 66612-1671; tel. (785) 357-6321; fax (785) 357-4732; e-mail info@kansaschamber.org; internet www.kansaschamber.org; over 10,000 mem. cos; Pres. and CEO AMY J. BLANKENBILLER.

Kentucky

Kentucky Chamber of Commerce: 464 Chenault Rd, Frankfort, KY 40601; tel. (502) 695-4700; fax (502) 695-6824; e-mail kcc@kychamber.com; internet www.kychamber.com; over 7,000 mem. cos; Pres. and CEO DAVE ADKISSON.

Louisiana

Louisiana Association of Business and Industry (LABI): 3113 Valley Creek Dr., POB 80258, Baton Rouge, LA 70898-0258; tel. (225) 928-5388; fax (225) 929-6054; e-mail jouanar@labi.org; internet www.labi.org; Pres. DANIEL L. JUNEAU.

New Orleans Board of Trade: 316 Board of Trade Pl., New Orleans, LA 70130; tel. (504) 525-3271; fax (504) 525-9039; e-mail nobot@bellsouth.net; internet www.nobot.org; f. 1880; Exec. Dir BRETT BOURGEOIS.

Maine

Maine State Chamber of Commerce: 7 University Dr., Augusta, ME 04330-9412; tel. (207) 623-4568; fax (207) 622-7723; e-mail pfournier@mainechamber.org; internet www.mainechamber.org; 5,000 mem. cos; Pres. DANA F. CONNORS.

Maryland

Maryland Chamber of Commerce: 60 West St, Suite 100, Annapolis, MD 21401; tel. (410) 269-0642; fax (410) 269-5247; e-mail mcc@mdchamber.org; internet www.mdchamber.org; c. 860 mem. cos; Pres. and CEO KATHLEEN T. SNYDER.

Massachusetts

The Massachusetts Association of Chamber of Commerce Executives (MACCE): c/o Marlborough Regional Chamber of Commerce, 11 Florence St, Marlborough, MA 01752; tel. (508) 485-7746; fax (508) 481-1819; e-mail sleeber@marlboroughchamber.org; internet www.macce.org; Pres. WILLIAM K. PIERCEY.

Michigan

Michigan Chamber of Commerce: 600 South Walnut St, Lansing, MI 48933; tel. (517) 371-2100; fax (517) 371-7224; e-mail info@michamber.com; internet www.michamber.com; c. 6,300 mems; Pres. and CEO RICHARD K. STUDLEY.

Minnesota

Minnesota Chamber of Commerce: 400 Robert St North, Suite 1500, St Paul, MN 55101; tel. (651) 292-4650; fax (651) 292-4656; e-mail mail@mnchamber.com; internet www.mnchamber.com; more than 2,600 mem. cos; Pres. DAVID OLSON.

Mississippi

Mississippi Economic Council (MEC): 248 East Capitol St, Suite 940, Jackson, MS 39201; tel. (601) 969-0022; fax (601) 353-0247; e-mail bwilson@mec.ms; internet www.msmec.com; c. 9,000 mems; f. 1949; Chair. BLAKE WILSON.

Missouri

Missouri Chamber of Commerce and Industry: 428 East Capitol Ave, POB 149, Jefferson City, MO 65101; tel. (573) 634-3511; fax (573) 634-8855; e-mail kbuschmann@mochamber.com; internet www.mochamber.org; over 3,000 mems; Pres. and CEO DANIEL P. MEHAN.

Montana

Montana Chamber of Commerce: 900 Gibbon St, POB 1730, Helena, MT 59624-1730; tel. (406) 442-2405; fax (406) 442-2409; e-mail schaefer@3rivers.net; internet www.montanachamber.com; over 700 mem. cos; Pres. and CEO WEBB BROWN.

Nebraska

Nebraska Chamber of Commerce and Industry: 1320 Lincoln Mall, Suite 201, POB 95128, Lincoln, NE 68509-5128; tel. (402) 474-4422; fax (402) 474-5681; e-mail nechamber@nechamber.com;

internet www.nechamber.com; over 2,000 mems; Pres. Barry L. Kennedy.

New Hampshire

Business and Industry Association of New Hampshire (BIA): 122 North Main St, Concord, NH 03301-4918; tel. (603) 224-5388; fax (603) 224-2872; e-mail arupp@nhbia.org; internet www.nhbia.org; 400 mem. cos; Pres. and CEO Jim Roche.

New Jersey

New Jersey State Chamber of Commerce: 216 West State St, Trenton, NJ 08608-1002; tel. (609) 989-7888; fax (609) 989-9696; e-mail kevin@njchamber.com; internet www.njchamber.com; Pres. Joan Verplanck.

New Mexico

Association of Commerce and Industry of New Mexico (ACI): 2201 Buena Vista Dr., South East, Suite 410, Albuquerque, NM 87106; tel. (505) 842-0644; fax (505) 842-0734; e-mail dscott@aci-nm.org; internet www.aci-nm.org; Pres. and CEO Beverlee J. McClure.

New York

The Business Council of New York State, Inc: The Schuler Bldg, 152 Washington Ave, Albany, New York 12210-2289; tel. (518) 465-7511; fax (518) 465-4389; e-mail mike.moran@bcnys.org; internet www.bcnys.org; Pres. and CEO Kenneth Adams.

North Carolina

North Carolina Citizens for Business and Industry (NCCBI): 701 Corporate Center Dr., Suite 400, Raleigh, NC 27607; tel. (919) 836-1400; fax (919) 836-1425; e-mail info@ncchamber.net; internet www.ncchamber.net; 2,000 mem. cos; Pres. and CEO S. Lewis Ebert.

North Dakota

Greater North Dakota Chamber of Commerce: 2000 Schafer St, POB 2639, Bismarck, ND 58502-2639; tel. (701) 222-0929; fax (701) 222-1611; e-mail ndchamber@ndchamber.com; internet www.ndchamber.com; c. 1,100 mem. cos; Pres. David MacIver.

Ohio

Ohio Chamber of Commerce: 230 East Town St, POB 15159, Columbus, OH 43215-0159; tel. (614) 228-4201; fax (614) 228-6403; e-mail occ@ohiochamber.com; internet www.ohiochamber.com; Pres. and CEO Andrew E. Doehrel.

Oklahoma

The State Chamber (Oklahoma's Association of Business and Industry): 330 North East 10th St, Oklahoma City, OK 73104-3220; tel. (405) 235-3669; fax (405) 235-3670; e-mail info@okstatechamber.com; internet www.okstatechamber.com; over 2,000 mem. cos in 25 states; Pres. and CEO Richard P. Rush.

Oregon

Associated Oregon Industries (AOI): 1149 Court St, NE, Salem, OR 97301-4030; tel. (503) 588-0050; fax (503) 588-0052; e-mail aoi@aoi.org; internet www.aoi.org; Pres. and CEO Jay M. Clemens.

Pennsylvania

Pennsylvania Chamber of Business and Industry: 1 Commerce Sq., 417 Walnut St, Harrisburg, PA 17101-1902; tel. and fax (717) 225-3252; fax (717) 255-3298; e-mail info@pachamber.org; internet www.pachamber.org; Pres. Floyd W. Warner.

Rhode Island

Central Rhode Island Chamber of Commerce: 3288 Post Rd, Warwick, RI 02886; tel. (401) 732-1100; fax (401) 732-1107; e-mail info@centralrichamber.com; internet www.centralrichamber.com; Pres. and CEO Lauren E. I. Slocum.

South Carolina

South Carolina Chamber of Commerce: 1201 Main St, Suite 1700, Columbia, SC 29201-3254; tel. (803) 799-4601; e-mail chamber@scchamber.net; internet www.scchamber.net; 5,000 mems; Pres. and CEO S. Hunter Howard, Jr.

South Dakota

South Dakota Chamber of Commerce and Industry: Commerce Center, Suite 304, 200 North Phillips Ave, Sioux Falls, SD 57104; tel. (605) 335-6060; fax (605) 331-2536; e-mail contactus@sdchamber.biz; internet www.sdchamber.biz; Pres. David Owen.

Tennessee

Tennessee Chamber of Commerce and Industry: 611 Commerce St, Suite 3030, Nashville, TN 37203-3742; tel. (615) 256-5141; fax (615) 256-6726; e-mail info@tnchamber.org; internet www.tnchamber.org; over 1,000 mem. cos; Pres. Deborah K. Woolley.

Texas

Texas Association of Business (TAB): 1209 Nueces St, POB 2989, Austin, TX 78701-1209; tel. (512) 477-6721; fax (512) 477-0836; e-mail rtraywick@txbiz.org; internet www.txbiz.org; f. 1995; Pres. and CEO Bill Hammond.

Vermont

Vermont Chamber of Commerce: 751 Granger Rd-Berlin, Barre, VT 05641; tel. (802) 223-3443; fax (802) 223-4257; e-mail info@vtchamber.com; internet www.vtchamber.com; 1,600 mem. cos; Pres. Duane Marsh.

Virginia

Virginia Chamber of Commerce: 9 South Fifth St, Richmond, VA 23219-3890; tel. (804) 644-1607; fax (804) 783-6112; e-mail cmiracle@vachamber.com; internet www.vachamber.com; Pres. and CEO Hugh Keogh.

Washington

Association of Washington Business (AWB): POB 658, 1414 Cherry St, SE, Olympia, WA 98507-0658; tel. (360) 943-1600; fax (360) 943-5811; e-mail jocelynm@awb.org; internet www.awb.org; over 6,700 mem. cos; Pres. Don C. Brunell.

West Virginia

West Virginia Chamber of Commerce: 1624 Kanawha Blvd E, Charleston, WV 25311; tel. (304) 342-1115; fax (304) 342-1130; e-mail forjobs@wvchamber.com; internet www.wvchamber.com; Pres. and CEO Stephen G. Roberts.

Wisconsin

Wisconsin Manufacturers and Commerce: 501 East Washington Ave, POB 352, Madison, WI 53703-2944; tel. (608) 258-3400; fax (608) 258-3413; e-mail wmc@wmc.org; internet www.wmc.org; c. 4,000 mems; Pres. Jim Haney.

Wyoming

Wyoming Chamber of Commerce Executives (WCCE): POB 301, Wheatland, WY 82201; tel. (307) 322-3977; e-mail wcce@wyomingwireless.com; internet www.wyomingchambers.com; represents 25 local chambers; Dir Candy Wright.

Industrial and Employers' Organizations

AGRICULTURE AND HORTICULTURE

(see Selected Agricultural, Forestry and Fisheries Organizations)

CHEMICALS AND PHARMACEUTICALS

American Chemistry Council (ACC): 1300 Wilson Blvd, Arlington, VA 22209; tel. (703) 741-5000; fax (703) 741-6000; e-mail helpline@americanchemistry.com; internet www.americanchemistry.com; f. 1872; incl. the Plastics Division and Chlorine Chemistry Division; 136 mems; Pres. and CEO Cal Dooley; Sec. Dell Perelman.

American Pharmacists Association (APhA): 1100 15th St, NW, Suite 400, Washington, DC 20005-1707; tel. (202) 628-4410; fax (202) 783-2351; e-mail scorbitt@aphanet.org; internet www.pharmacist.com; f. 1852; over 60,000 mems; Pres. Timothy L. Tucker; Exec. Vice-Pres. and CEO John A. Gans.

Consumer Healthcare Products Association (CHPA): 900 19th St, NW, Suite 700, Washington, DC 20006; tel. (202) 429-9260; fax (202) 223-6835; e-mail efunderburk@chpa-info.org; internet www.chpa-info.org; f. 1881; 170 mem. and assoc. mem. cos; Pres. Lynda A. Suydam.

Consumer Specialty Products Association (CSPA): 900 17th St, NW, Suite 300, Washington, DC 20006; tel. (202) 872-8110; fax (202) 872-8114; e-mail info@cspa.org; internet www.cspa.org; f. 1914; fmrly Chemical Specialities Manufacturers Assn; over 250 mems; Pres. Christopher Cathcart.

Drug, Chemical and Associated Technologies Association, Inc (DCAT): 1 Washington Blvd, Suite 7, Robbinsville, NJ 08691; tel. (609) 448-1000; fax (609) 448-1944; e-mail info@dcat.org; internet www.dcat.org; f. 1890; fmrly Drug, Chemical and Allied Trades Asscn; name changed as above in 2003; 350 mems; Exec. Dir MARGARET M. TIMONY.

The Fertilizer Institute (TFI): see Selected Agricultural, Forestry and Fisheries Organizations.

National Community Pharmacists Association (NCPA): 100 Daingerfield Rd, Alexandria, VA 22314; tel. (703) 683-8200; fax (703) 683-3619; e-mail info@ncpanet.org; internet www.ncpanet.org; f. 1898; fmrly Nat. Asscn of Retail Druggists; 25,000 mems; Pres. STEPHEN L. GIROUX; Chair., Exec. Committee JOSEPH H. HARMISON.

Personal Care Products Council: 1101 17th St, NW, Suite 300, Washington, DC 20036-4702; tel. (202) 331-1770; fax (202) 331-1969; internet www.personalcarecouncil.org; f. 1894; fmrly Cosmetic, Toiletry and Fragrance Asscn (CTFA); adopted current name 2007; 600 mem. cos; Pres. and CEO PAMELA G. BAILEY.

Pharmaceutical Research & Manufacturers of America (PhRMA): 950 F St, NW, Suite 900, Washington, DC 20004; tel. (202) 835-3400; fax (202) 835-3414; internet www.phrma.org; f. 1958; 67 mems; Pres. WILLIAM TAUZIN.

Soap and Detergent Association (SDA): 1500 K St, NW, Suite 300, Washington, DC, 20005; tel. (202) 347-2900; fax (202) 347-4110; e-mail info@cleaning101.com; internet www.cleaning101.com; f. 1926; 110 mems; Pres. and CEO ERNIE ROSENBERG.

Synthetic Organic Chemical Manufacturers' Association (SOCMA): 1850 M St, NW, Suite 700, Washington, DC 20036-5810; tel. (202) 721-4100; fax (202) 296-8120; e-mail info@socma.com; internet www.socma.com; f. 1921; 275 mem. cos; Chair. CHARLES HINNANT.

CONSTRUCTION

(see also Electricity, and Engineering and Machinery)

American Institute of Constructors (AIC): POB 26334, Alexandria, VA 22314; tel. (703) 683-4999; fax (703) 683-5480; e-mail admin@aicnet.org; internet www.aicnet.org; f. 1971; 1,600 mems; Pres. STEVE BYRNE.

Associated Builders and Contractors, Inc (ABC): 4250 North Fairfax Dr., 9th Floor, Arlington, VA 22203-1607; tel. (703) 812-2000; e-mail gotquestions@abc.org; internet www.abc.org; f. 1950; 24,000 mems; Pres. and CEO M. KIRK PICKEREL.

Associated General Contractors of America (AGC) (AGC of America): 2300 Wilson Blvd, Suite 400, Arlington, VA 22201; tel. (703) 548-3118; fax (703) 548-3119; e-mail info@agc.org; internet www.agc.org; f. 1918; 33,000 mems; Pres. DOUGLAS E. BARNHART; CEO STEPHEN E. SANDHERR.

Associated Specialty Contractors, Inc (ASC): 3 Bethesda Metro Center, Suite 1100, Bethesda, MD 20814-5372; tel. (301) 657-3110; fax (301) 215-4500; e-mail dgw@necanet.org; internet www.assoc-spec-con.org; f. 1955; 9 mem. asscns; Pres. DANIEL G. WALTER.

Building Stone Institute (BSI): 551 Tollgate Rd, Suite C, Elgin, IL 60123; tel. (847) 695-0170; fax (847) 695-0174; e-mail margie@buildingstoneinstitute.org; internet www.buildingstoneinstitute.org; f. 1919; 400 mems; Pres. ROBERT BARDEN; Exec. Vice-Pres. MARGIE LECHOWICZ.

Construction Specifications Institute (CSI): 99 Canal Center Plaza, Suite 300, Alexandria, VA 22314-1588; tel. (703) 684-0300; fax (703) 684-8436; e-mail csi@csinet.org; internet www.csinet.org; f. 1948; over 16,000 mems; Pres. GILMAN K. M. HU; Exec. Dir and CEO WALTER T. MARLOWE.

Mechanical Contractors Association of America, Inc (MCAA): 1385 Piccard Dr., Rockville, MD 20850-4340; tel. (301) 869-5800; fax (301) 990-9690; e-mail mcaainfo@mcaa.org; internet www.mcaa.org; f. 1889; 2,500 mems; Exec. Vice-Pres. and CEO JOHN R. GENTILLE.

National Association of Home Builders of the US (NAHB): 1201 15th St, NW, Washington, DC 20005; tel. (202) 266-8200; fax (202) 266-8400; internet www.nahb.org; f. 1942; 800 mem. asscns, 220,000 mems; Pres. SANDY J. DUNN; Exec. Vice-Pres. and CEO GERALD M. HOWARD.

National Association of Plumbing-Heating-Cooling Contractors (PHCC): 180 South Washington St, POB 6808, Falls Church, VA 22046; tel. (703) 237-8100; fax (703) 237-7442; e-mail naphcc@naphcc.org; internet www.phccweb.org; f. 1883; 4,000 mems; Pres. JIM FINLEY; Exec. Vice-Pres. IKE CASEY.

National Ready Mixed Concrete Association (NRMCA): 900 Spring St, Silver Spring, MD 20910; tel. (301) 587-1400; fax (301) 585-4219; e-mail info@nrmca.org; internet www.nrmca.org; f. 1930; 1,000 mems; Chair. FRANK CRADDOCK; Pres. ROBERT GARBINI.

National Tile Contractors Association (NTCA): POB 13629, Jackson, MS 39236; tel. (601) 939-2071; fax (601) 932-6117; internet www.tile-assn.com; f. 1947; Exec. Dir BART BETTIGA.

Tile Council of North America Inc (TCNA): 100 Clemson Research Blvd, Anderson, SC 29625; tel. (864) 646-8453; fax (864) 646-2821; e-mail literature@tileusa.com; internet www.tileusa.com; f. 1945 as Tile Council of America; adopted current name in 2003; 130 mems; Exec. Dir ERIC ASTRACHAN.

US Green Building Council (USGBC): 1015 18th St, NW, Suite 508, Washington, DC 20036; tel. (202) 828-7422; fax (202) 828-5110; e-mail info@usgbc.org; internet www.usgbc.org; over 6,400 mem. orgs; Pres. and CEO S. RICHARD FEDRIZZI; Chair. REBECCA L. FLORA.

ELECTRICITY

(see also Construction, Electronics and Technology, and Engineering and Machinery)

Edison Electric Institute (EEI): 701 Pennsylvania Ave, NW, Washington, DC 20004-2696; tel. (202) 508-5000; e-mail feedback@eei.org; internet www.eei.org; f. 1933; mems: 190 investor-owned electric utility cos, more than 65 int. affiliates; mems generate 70% of electricity produced by US utilities; Chair. DAVID M. RATCLIFFE.

National Association of Electrical Distributors (NAED): 1181 Corporate Lake Dr., St Louis, MO 63132; tel. (314) 991-9000; fax (314) 991-3060; e-mail info@naed.org; internet www.naed.org; f. 1908; 2,900 mems; Pres. TOM NABER.

National Electrical Contractors Association (NECA): 3 Bethesda Metro Center, Suite 1100, Bethesda, MD 20814-5372; tel. (301) 657-3110; fax (301) 215-4500; internet www.necanet.org; f. 1901; 4,200 mems; Pres. MILNER IRVIN; CEO JOHN M. GRAU.

National Electrical Manufacturers Association (NEMA): 1300 North 17th St, Suite 1752, Rosslyn, VA 22209; tel. (703) 841-3200; fax (703) 841-5900; e-mail webmaster@nema.org; internet www.nema.org; f. 1926; 430 mem. cos; Pres. and CEO EVAN R. GADDIS.

ELECTRONICS AND TECHNOLOGY

AeA: 5201 Great America Pkwy, Suite 400, Santa Clara, CA 95054; tel. (408) 987-4200; fax (408) 987-4298; e-mail csc@aeanet.org; internet www.aeanet.org; f. 1943; fmrly American Electronics Asscn; 2,500 mem. cos; Pres. and CEO CHRISTOPHER HANSEN.

Electronic Industries Alliance: 2500 Wilson Blvd, Arlington, VA 22201-3834; tel. (703) 907-7500; fax (703) 907-7501; internet www.eia.org; f. 1924; 1,300 mem. cos; Pres. MATHEW FLANIGAN (acting).

Institute of Electrical and Electronics Engineers, Inc (IEEE): 445 Hoes Lane, Piscataway, NJ 08854-4141; tel. (732) 981-0060; fax (732) 981-1721; e-mail staff-director@ieee.org; internet www.ieee.org; f. 1963; more than 375,000 mems world-wide; Pres. and CEO Dr LEWIS M. TERMAN; Pres.-elect Dr JOHN R. VIG.

IPC (Association Connecting Electronics Industries): 3000 Lakeside Dr., Suite 309, Bannockburn, IL 60015; tel. (847) 615-7100; fax (847) 615-7105; e-mail mcgude@ipc.org; internet www.ipc.org; f. 1957; Chair. NILESH S. NAIK; Pres. and CEO DENNY MCGUIRK.

Telecommunications Industry Association (TIA): 2500 Wilson Blvd, Suite 300, Arlington, VA 22201; tel. (703) 907-7700; fax (703) 907-7727; e-mail tia@tiaonline.org; internet www.tiaonline.org; f. 1988; Pres. GRANT E. SEIFFERT.

ENGINEERING AND MACHINERY

(see also Electricity, Construction and Transport)

Air-Conditioning, Heating and Refrigeration Institute (AHRI): 2111 Wilson Blvd, Suite 500, Arlington, VA 22201; tel. (703) 524-8800; fax (703) 528-3816; e-mail ahri@ahrinet.org; internet www.ahrinet.org; f. 2007 by merger of the Air-Conditioning and Refrigeration Institute (ARI) and the Gas Appliance Mfrs Asscn (GAMA); 220 mems; Chair. C. DAVID MYERS; CEO JACK KLIMP.

American Council of Engineering Companies (ACEC): 1015 15th St, NW, 8th Floor, Washington, DC 20005-2605; tel. (202) 347-7474; fax (202) 898-0068; e-mail acec@acec.org; internet www.acec.org; f. 1905; 5,700 mem. cos; Chair. JOHN F. HENNESSY, III; Pres. and CEO DAVID A. RAYMOND.

American Institute of Chemical Engineers (AIChE): 3 Park Ave, New York, NY 10016-5991; tel. (203) 702-7660; fax (203) 775-5177; e-mail fiob@aiche.org; internet www.aiche.org; f. 1908; over 46,000 mems world-wide; Pres. DALE L. KEAIRNS; Exec. Dir JOHN A. SOFRANKO.

American Institute of Mining, Metallurgical and Petroleum Engineers, Inc: 8307 Shaffer Pkwy, Littleton, CO 80127-4012; tel. (303) 948-4255; fax (303) 948-4260; e-mail aime@aimehq.org; internet www.aimehq.org; f. 1871; five constituent socs representing 100,000 mems; Pres. MICHAEL KARMIS; Exec. Dir J. RICK ROLATER.

American Society of Civil Engineers (ASCE): 1801 Alexander Bell Dr., Reston, VA 20191-4400; tel. (703) 295-6300; fax (703) 295-6222; e-mail webmaster@asce.org; internet www.asce.org; f. 1852; over 133,000 mems; Pres. DAVID G. MONGAN; Exec. Dir PATRICK J. NATALE.

American Society of Heating, Refrigerating and Air-Conditioning Engineers (ASHRAE): 1791 Tullie Circle, NE, Atlanta, GA 30329; tel. (404) 636-8400; fax (404) 321-5478; e-mail ashrae@ashrae.org; internet www.ashrae.org; f. 1894; 55,000 mems; Pres. WILLIAM HARRISON.

American Society of Naval Engineers, Inc: 1452 Duke St, Alexandria, VA 22314-3458; tel. (703) 836-6727; fax (703) 836-7491; e-mail asnehq@navalengineers.org; internet www.navalengineers.org; f. 1888; 6,000 mems; Exec. Dir Capt. (retd) DENNIS K. KRUSE.

AMT (The Association for Manufacturing Technology): 7901 Westpark Dr., McLean, VA 22102-4206; tel. (703) 893-2900; fax (703) 893-1151; e-mail amt@amtonline.org; internet www.amtonline.org; f. 1902; 370 mems; Pres. JOHN B. BYRD, III.

Association of Coastal Engineers (ACE): c/o Patricia Ehrman, 2770 North West 43rd St, Suite B, Applied Technology and Management Inc, Gainesville, FL 32606; e-mail hugo@coastharborenq.com; internet www.coastalengineers.org; f. 1999; Exec. Sec. PATRICIA EHRMAN.

Association of Home Appliance Manufacturers (AHAM): 1111 19th St, NW, Suite 402, Washington, DC 20036; tel. (202) 872-5955; fax (202) 872-9354; e-mail info@aham.org; internet www.aham.org; f. 1915; Pres. JOSEPH M. MCGUIRE.

Manufacturers Alliance/MAPI, Inc: 1600 Wilson Blvd, Suite 1100, Arlington, VA 22209-2411; tel. (703) 841-9000; fax (703) 841-9514; e-mail info@mapi.net; internet www.mapi.net; f. 1933; 500 mem. cos; Pres. and CEO THOMAS J. DUESTERBERG.

National Center for Manufacturing Sciences (NCMS): 3025 Boardwalk, Ann Arbor, MI 48108-3230; tel. (734) 995-0300; fax (734) 995-1150; internet www.ncms.org; f. 1986; Pres. and CEO RICHARD B. JARMAN.

Petroleum Equipment Institute (PEI): POB 2380, Tulsa, OK 74101-2380; tel. (918) 494-9696; fax (918) 491-9895; e-mail info@pei.org; internet www.pei.org; f. 1951; over 1,600 mems world-wide; Exec. Vice-Pres. ROBERT N. RENKES.

SAE International (Society of Automotive Engineers): 400 Commonwealth Dr., Warrendale, PA 15096-0001; tel. (724) 776-4841; fax (724) 776-0790; e-mail customerservice@sae.org; internet www.sae.org; f. 1905; over 90,000 mems world-wide; Pres.-elect JAMES E. SMITH.

Society of Manufacturing Engineers (SME): 1 SME Dr., Dearborn, MI 48121; tel. (313) 271-1500; fax (313) 425-3401; e-mail service@sme.org; internet www.sme.org; f. 1932; Pres. NEIL A. DUFFIE.

Society of Naval Architects and Marine Engineers (SNAME): 601 Pavonia Ave, Suite 400, Jersey City, NJ 07306-2907; tel. (201) 798-4800; fax (201) 798-4975; e-mail ccali-poutre@sname.org; internet www.sname.org; f. 1893; over 10,000 mems; Pres. Adm. (retd) ROBERT E. KRAMEK; Exec. Dir PHILIP B. KIMBALL.

United Engineering Foundation (UEF): POB 70, Mount Vernon, VA 22121-0070; tel. (973) 244-2328; fax (973) 882-5155; e-mail engfnd@aol.com; internet www.uefoundation.org; f. 1914; umbrella org. of engineering socs, incl. ASME International, the Institute of Electrical and Electronics Engineers and the American Institute of Chemical Engineers; Pres. ROBERT C. FREAS; Exec. Dir Dr DAVID L. BELDEN.

FISHERIES

(see Selected Agricultural, Forestry and Fisheries Organizations)

FOOD AND BEVERAGES

(see also Selected Agricultural, Forestry and Fisheries Organizations)

American Bakers Association (ABA): 1350 I St, NW, Suite 700, Washington, DC 20005-3300; tel. (202) 789-0300; fax (202) 898-1164; e-mail info@americanbakers.org; internet www.americanbakers.org; f. 1897; Pres. and CEO ROBB MACKIE.

American Beverage Association (ABA): 1101 16th St, NW, Washington, DC 20036-4803; tel. (202) 463-6732; fax (202) 659-5349; e-mail info@ameribev.org; internet www.ameribev.org; f. 1919; fmrly Nat. Soft Drink Asscn; 1,700 mems; Pres. and CEO SUSAN K. NEELY.

Distilled Spirits Council of the US, Inc (DISCUS): 1250 Eye St, NW, Suite 400, Washington, DC 20005; tel. (202) 628-3544; internet www.discus.org; f. 1973; 12 active mems and 23 affiliates; Pres. and CEO Dr. PETER H. CRESSY.

Food Marketing Institute (FMI): 2345 Crystal Dr., Suite 800, Arlington, VA 22202; tel. (202) 452-8444; fax (202) 429-4519; e-mail fmi@fmi.org; internet www.fmi.org; f. 1977; 1,500 mems; Pres. and CEO TIMOTHY M. HAMMONDS.

Foodservice Sales and Marketing Association (FSMA): 9192 Red Branch Rd, Suite 200, Columbia, MD 21045; tel. (410) 715-6672; fax (410) 997-9387; e-mail info@fsmaonline.com; internet www.fsmaonline.com; f. 2003; Pres. and CEO RICK ABRAHAM.

Grocery Manufacturers of America, Inc (GMA): 1350 I St, NW, Suite 300, Washington, DC 20005; tel. (202) 639-5900; fax (202) 639-5932; e-mail info@gmaonline.org; internet www.gmaonline.org; f. 1908; over 185 mems; Pres. and CEO C. MANLY MOLPUS (acting).

International Foodservice Distributors Association (IFDA): 1410 Spring Hill Rd, Suite 210, McLean, VA 22102; tel. (703) 532-9400; fax (703) 538-4673; internet www.ifdaonline.org; f. 1906; over 140 mems; Pres. and CEO MARK ALLEN.

National Beer Wholesalers Association (NBWA): 1101 King St, Suite 600, Alexandria, VA 22314-2944; tel. (703) 683-4300; fax (703) 683-8965; e-mail info@nbwa.org; internet www.nbwa.org; f. 1938; 2,750 mem. distributor cos; Pres. CRAIG A. PURSER.

National Confectioners Association of the US (NCA): 8320 Old Courthouse Rd, Suite 300, Vienna, VA 22182; tel. (703) 790-5750; fax (703) 790-5752; e-mail info@candyusa.com; internet www.candyusa.com; f. 1884; includes Chocolate Mfrs Asscn; 340 mems; Pres. LAWRENCE T. GRAHAM.

National Frozen and Refrigerated Foods Association (NFRA): 4755 Linglestown Rd, Suite 300, POB 6069, Harrisburg, PA 17112; tel. (717) 657-8601; fax (717) 657-9862; e-mail info@nfraweb.org; internet www.nfraweb.org; f. 1945; over 400 mem. cos; Pres. and CEO NEVIN B. MONTGOMERY.

National Grocers Association (NGA): 1005 North Glebe Rd, Suite 250, Arlington, VA 22201-5758; tel. (703) 516-0700; fax (703) 516-0115; e-mail info@nationalgrocers.org; internet www.nationalgrocers.org; f. 1982; 3,000 mems; Pres. and CEO THOMAS K. ZAUCHA.

National Meat Association (NMA): NMA East: 1400 16th St, NW, Suite 400, Washington, DC 20036; tel. (202) 667-2108; NMA West: 1970 Broadway, Suite 825, Oakland, CA 94612; tel. (510) 763-1533; fax (510) 763-6186; e-mail staff@nmaonline.org; internet www.nmaonline.org; f. 1946; over 600 mems; Chair. JIM MAXEY.

US Dairy Export Council (USDEC): 2101 Wilson Blvd, Suite 400, Arlington, VA 22201-3061; tel. (703) 528-3049; fax (703) 528-3705; e-mail info@usdec.org; internet www.usdec.org; f. 1995; 86 mems; Pres. THOMAS M. SUBER.

Wine and Spirits Wholesalers of America, Inc (WSWA): 805 15th St, NW, Suite 430, Washington, DC 20005; tel. (202) 371-9792; fax (202) 789-2405; e-mail katrina@wswa.org; internet www.wswa.org; f. 1943; c. 450 mem. cos; Pres. and CEO CRAIG WOLF.

IRON AND STEEL

(see also Selected Mining Organizations)

American Hardware Manufacturers Association (AHMA): 801 North Plaza Dr., Schaumburg, IL 60173-4977; tel. (847) 605-1025; fax (847) 605-1030; e-mail info@ahma.org; internet www.ahma.org; f. 1901; 500 mems; Pres. and CEO TIMOTHY S. FARRELL; Vice-Chair. WILLIAM P. FARRELL.

American Institute of Steel Construction (AISC): 1 East Wacker Dr., Suite 700, Chicago, IL 60601-1802; tel. (312) 670-2400; fax (312) 670-5403; internet www.aisc.org; f. 1921; Pres. ROGER E. FERCH.

American Iron and Steel Institute (AISI): 1140 Connecticut Ave, NW, Suite 705, Washington, DC 20036; tel. (202) 452-7100; e-mail webmaster@steel.org; internet www.steel.org; f. 1908; 32 mem. cos and 125 assoc. and affiliated mems; Chair. KEITH E. BUSSE; Pres. and CEO THOMAS J. GIBSON.

Steel Founders' Society of America (SFSA): 780 McArdle Dr., Unit G, Crystal Lake, IL 60014; tel. (815) 455-8240; fax (815) 455-8241; e-mail monroe@sfsa.org; internet www.sfsa.org; f. 1902; 80 mems; Exec. Vice-Pres. RAYMOND W. MONROE.

Steel Manufacturers Association (SMA): 1150 Connecticut Ave, NW, Suite 715, Washington, DC 20036; tel. (202) 296-1515; fax (202) 296-2506; e-mail stuart@steelnet.org; internet www.steelnet.org; 39 North American mem. cos and six mem. cos world-wide, as well as 107 assoc. mem. cos; Pres. THOMAS A. DANJCZEK.

LEATHER

(see also Textiles)

Leather Industries of America (LIA): 3050 K St, NW, Suite 400, Washington, DC 20007; tel. (202) 342-8497; fax (202) 342-8583; e-mail info@leatherusa.com; internet www.leatherusa.com; f. 1917; 64 mems; Pres. JOHN WITTENBORN.

Travel Goods Association (TGA): 5 Vaughn Dr., Suite 105, Princeton, NJ 08540; tel. (609) 720-1200; fax (609) 720-0620; e-mail info@travel-goods.org; internet www.travel-goods.org; f. 1938; 400 mems; Pres. MICHELE MARINI PITTENGER.

LUMBER

(see also Paper and Selected Agricultural, Forestry and Fisheries Organizations)

APA–The Engineered Wood Association: 7011 South 19th St, Tacoma, WA 98466-5333; tel. (253) 565-6600; fax (253) 565-7265; e-mail help@apawood.org; internet www.apawood.org; f. 1933 as Douglas Fir Plywood Asscn; later became American Plywood Asscn; adopted current name 1994; 109 mems; Pres. DENNIS HARDMAN.

National Lumber and Building Material Dealers Association (NLBMDA): 2025 M Street, NW, Suite 800, Washington, DC 20036-3309; tel. (202) 367-1169; fax (202) 367-2169; e-mail info@dealer.org; internet www.dealer.org; f. 1915; 20 mem. orgs, representing 8,000 cos; Pres. and CEO MICHAEL O'BRIEN.

National Wooden Pallet and Container Association (NWPCA): 1421 Prince St, Suite 340, Alexandria, VA 22314-2805; tel. (703) 519-6104; fax (703) 519-4720; e-mail bscholnick@palletcentral.com; internet www.palletcentral.com; f. 1946; Pres. and CEO BRUCE N. SCHOLNICK.

North American Wholesale Lumber Association (NAWLA): 3601 Algonquin Rd, Suite 400, Rolling Meadows, IL 60008; tel. (847) 870-7470; fax (847) 870-0201; e-mail info@lumber.org; internet www.lumber.org; f. 1893; over 650 mems; Pres. and CEO NICHOLAS R. KENT.

Wood Products Manufacturers Association (WPMA): 175 State Rd East, POB 761, Westminster, MA 01473-0761; tel. (978) 874-5445; fax (978) 874-9946; e-mail woodprod@wpma.org; internet www.wpma.org; f. 1929; 664 mems; Pres. MAGGIE BRIGHAM; Exec. Dir PHILIP A. BIBEAU.

METALS

(see also Iron and Steel, and Selected Mining Organizations)

Aluminum Association, Inc: 1525 Wilson Blvd, Suite 600, Arlington, VA 22209; tel. (703) 358-2960; fax (703) 358-2961; e-mail lwilson@aluminum.org; internet www.aluminum.org; f. 1933; 82 mems; Pres. J. STEPHEN LARKIN.

American Zinc Association (AZA): 2025 M St, NW, Suite 800, Washington, DC 20036; tel. (202) 367-1151; fax (202) 367-2232; e-mail zincinfo@zinc.org; internet www.zinc.org; f. 1990; 10 regular mems, 14 affiliates; Exec. Dir GEORGE VARY.

ASM International: 9639 Kinsman Rd, Materials Park, OH 44073-0002; tel. (440) 338-5151; fax (440) 338-4634; e-mail customerservice@asminternational.org; internet asmcommunity.asminternational.org; f. 1913; fmrly the American Society for Materials; 40,000 mems world-wide; Man. Dir STANLEY C. THEOBALD.

Copper Development Association, Inc (CDA): 260 Madison Ave, New York, NY 10016; tel. (212) 251-7200; fax (212) 251-7234; e-mail questions@cda.copper.org; internet www.copper.org; f. 1962; 65 mems; Pres. and CEO ANDREW G. KIRETA, Sr.

Fabricators and Manufacturers Association, International (FMA): 833 Featherstone Rd, Rockford, IL 61107; tel. (815) 399-8775; fax (815) 484-7701; e-mail info@fmanet.org; internet www.fmanet.org; f. 1970; 2,100 mems; Pres. and CEO GERALD M. SHANKEL.

Manufacturing Jewelers and Suppliers of America, Inc (MJSA): 45 Royal Little Dr., Providence, RI 02904; tel. (401) 274-3840; fax (401) 274-0265; e-mail info@mjsa.org; internet www.mjsa.org; f. 1903; 1,800 mems; Chair. ALAN BELL; COO JAMES K. MCCARTY.

Metal Powder Industries Federation (MPIF): 105 College Rd East, 1st Floor, Princeton, NJ 08540-6692; tel. (609) 452-7700; fax (609) 987-8523; e-mail info@mpif.org; internet www.mpif.org; f. 1944; 6 feds of 300 corp. mems; Exec. Dir and CEO C. JAMES TROMBINO.

PAPER

(see also Lumber)

Association of Independent Corrugated Converters (AICC): 113 South West St, POB 25708, Alexandria, VA 22313; tel. (703) 836-2422; fax (703) 836-2795; e-mail info@aiccbox.org; internet www.aiccbox.org; mems: 603 box-makers, 480 associates; Chair. BRAD MORPHY; Pres. A. STEPHEN YOUNG.

North American Packaging Association (NAPA): 113 South West St, 3rd Floor, Alexandria, VA 22314; tel. (703) 684-2212; fax (703) 683-6920; e-mail info@paperbox.org; internet www.paperbox.org; f. 2006 by merger of National Paper Box Asscn and Canadian Paperboard Packaging Asscn; Pres. SCOTT MILLER.

NPTA Alliance: 401 North Michigan Ave, Chicago, Illinois IL 60611-4267; tel. (312) 321-4092; fax (312) 673-6736; e-mail newell@gonpta.com; internet www.gonpta.com; f. 1903; fmrly Nat. Paper Trade Asscn, Inc; restructured Sept. 2007 to operate under management of SmithBucklin Corpn; 2,000 mems; Chair. THOMAS G. KADIEN; CEO NEWELL HOLT.

Paperboard Packaging Council (PPC): 1350 Main St, Suite 1508, Springfield, MA 01103-1628; tel. (413) 686-9191; fax (413) 747-7777; e-mail paperboardpackaging@ppcnet.org; internet www.ppcnet.org; f. 1967; Pres. BEN MARKENS.

PETROLEUM AND FUEL

American Association of Petroleum Geologists (AAPG): 125 West 15th St, POB 979, Tulsa, OK 74101-0979; tel. (918) 584-2555; fax (918) 560-2694; e-mail postmaster@aapg.org; internet www.aapg.org; f. 1917; 30,000 mems world-wide; Exec. Dir RICHARD D. FRITZ.

American Association of Petroleum Landmen (AAPL): 4100 Fossil Creek Blvd, Fort Worth, TX 76137-2791; tel. (817) 847-7700; fax (817) 847-7704; e-mail aapl@landman.org; internet www.landman.org; f. 1955; 7,000 mems and 43 affiliated asscns; Pres. MARSHALL E. LOCHAUSEN.

American Petroleum Institute (API): 1220 L St NW, Washington, DC 20005-4070; tel. (202) 682-8000; e-mail mediacenter@api.org; internet www.api.org; f. 1919; 400 corporate mems; Pres. and CEO RED CAVANEY; Vice-Pres. and Dir JIM CRAIG.

Association of Diesel Specialists (ADS): 10 Laboratory Dr., POB 13966, Research Triangle Park, NC 27709-3966; tel. (919) 406-8804; fax (919) 406-1306; e-mail info@diesel.org; internet www.diesel.org; more than 700 corp. and individual mems; Exec. Dir DAVID FEHLING.

Independent Petroleum Association of America (IPAA): 1201 15th St, NW, Suite 300, Washington, DC 20005; tel. (202) 857-4722; fax (202) 857-4799; e-mail webmaster@ipaa.org; internet www.ipaa.org; f. 1929; 6,000 mems; Pres. BARRY RUSSELL.

National Ocean Industries Association (NOIA): 1120 G St, NW, Suite 900, Washington, DC 20005; tel. (202) 347-6900; fax (202) 347-8650; e-mail mkearns@noia.org; internet www.noia.org; f. 1972; over 300 mem. cos; Pres. TOM FRY.

National Petrochemical and Refiners' Association (NPRA): 1667 K Street, NW, Suite 700, Washington, DC 20006; tel. (202) 457-0480; fax (202) 457-0486; e-mail info@npra.org; internet www.npradc.org; f. 1902; over 450 mems; Pres. CHARLES T. DREVNA.

Petroleum Marketers Association of America (PMAA): 1901 North Fort Myer Dr., Suite 500, Arlington, VA 22209-1604; tel. (703) 351-8000; fax (703) 351-9160; e-mail info@pmaa.org; internet www.pmaa.org; 45 mem. asscns; Pres. DANIEL F. GILLIGAN.

Western States Petroleum Association (WSPA): 1415 L St, Suite 600, Sacramento, CA 95814; tel. (916) 498-7750; fax (916) 444-5745; internet www.wspa.org; f. 1907; 30 mem. cos; Pres. JOSEPH SPARANO.

PRINTING AND PUBLISHING

(see also Publishers)

Association for the Suppliers of Printing, Publishing and Converting Technologies (NPES): 1899 Preston White Dr., Reston, VA 22091-4367; tel. (703) 264-7200; fax (703) 620-0994; e-mail npes@npes.org; internet www.npes.org; f. 1933; over 400 mem. cos; Pres. RALPH J. NAPPI.

Binding Industries Association International (BIA): 200 Deer Run Rd, Sewickley, PA 15143-2600; tel. (412) 259-1806; fax (412) 259-1800; e-mail jgoldstein@piagatf.org; internet www.bindingindustries.com; f. 1955; 90 mems; Exec. Dir JUSTIN GOLDSTEIN.

National Association of Printing Ink Manufacturers (NAPIM): 581 Main St, 5th Floor, Woodbridge, NJ 07095; tel. (732) 855-1525; fax (732) 855-1838; e-mail napim@napim.org; internet www.napim.org; f. 1917; Exec. Dir JAMES E. COLEMAN.

National Association for Printing Leadership (NAPL): 75 West Century Rd, Paramus, NJ 07652-1408; tel. (201) 634-9600; e-mail information@napl.org; internet www.napl.org; f. 1933; 150 assoc. mems; Pres. and CEO JOSEPH P. TRUNCALE.

Printing Industries of America, Inc/Graphic Arts Information Network (PIA/GATF): 200 Deer Run Rd, Sewickley, PA 15143; tel. (412) 741-6861; fax (412) 741-2311; e-mail gain@piagatf.org; internet www.gain.net; f. 1887 (PIA), 1924 (GATF); consolidated operations in 1999; 12,000 mems; Chair. JANET GREEN; Pres. and CEO MICHAEL MAKIN.

PUBLIC UTILITIES

American Gas Association (AGA): 400 North Capitol St, NW, Suite 400, Washington, DC 20001; tel. (202) 824-7000; fax (202) 824-7115; e-mail khardardt@aga.org; internet www.aga.org; f. 1918; 202 mem. cos; Pres. and CEO DAVID N. PARKER.

American Public Gas Association (APGA): 201 Massachusetts Ave, NE, Suite C-4, Washington, DC 20002; tel. (202) 464-2742; fax (202) 464-0246; e-mail kgomez@apga.org; internet www.apga.org; f. 1961; over 650 mem. utilities; Chair. MIKE COMSTOCK; Pres. and CEO BERT KALISCH.

American Public Power Association (APPA): 1875 Connecticut Ave, NW, Suite 1200, Washington, DC 20009-5715; tel. (202) 467-2900; fax (202) 467-2910; e-mail mrufe@appanet.org; internet www.appanet.org; f. 1940; over 2,000 mem. utilities; Chair. MAUDE GRANTHAM-RICHARDS.

American Public Works Association (APWA): 2345 Grand Blvd, Suite 700, Kansas City, MO 64108-2625; tel. (816) 472-6100; fax (816) 472-1610; e-mail apwa@apwa.net; internet www.apwa.net; f. 1937; 29,000 mems; Exec. Dir PETER B. KING.

RUBBER

Rubber Manufacturers Association (RMA): 1400 K St, NW, Suite 900, Washington, DC 20005-2043; tel. (202) 682-4800; e-mail info@rma.org; internet www.rma.org; f. 1915; over 100 mem. cos; Pres. and CEO CHARLES A. CANNON.

Rubber Pavements Association (RPA): 1801 South Jentilly Lane, Suite A-2, Tempe, AZ 85281-5738; tel. (480) 517-9944; fax (480) 517-9959; e-mail donnac@rubberpavements.org; internet www.rubberpavements.org; f. 1985; Pres. MICHAEL HOAG.

STONE, CLAY AND GLASS PRODUCTS

(see also Selected Mining Organizations)

Glass Association of North America (GANA): 2945 South West Wanamaker Dr., Suite A, Topeka, KS 66614-5321; tel. (785) 271-0208; fax (785) 271-0166; e-mail gana@glasswebsite.com; internet www.glasswebsite.com; f. 1994; 208 mems; Exec. Vice-Pres. WILLIAM M. YANEK.

National Glass Association (NGA): 8200 Greensboro Dr., Suite 302, McLean, VA 22102-3881; tel. (703) 342-5642; fax (703) 442-0630; e-mail administration@glass.org; internet www.glass.org; f. 1948; c. 4,000 mem. cos; Pres. and CEO PHILIP J. JAMES.

TEXTILES

American Apparel and Footwear Association (AAFA): 1601 North Kent St, Suite 1200, Arlington, VA 22209; tel. (703) 524-1864; fax (703) 522-6741; e-mail mrust@apparelandfootwear.org; internet www.apparelandfootwear.org; f. 2000 following merger of American Apparel and Manufacturers Asscn and Footwear Industries of America; Pres. and CEO KEVIN M. BURKE.

American Fiber Manufacturers Association, Inc (AFMA): 1530 Wilson Blvd, NW, Suite 690, Arlington, VA 22209; tel. (703) 875-0432; fax (703) 875-0907; e-mail afma@afma.org; internet www.fibersource.com; f. 1933; 34 mems; Pres. PAUL T. O'DAY.

National Council of Textile Organizations (NCTO): 910 17th St, NW, Suite 1020, Washington, DC 20006; tel. (202) 822-8028; fax (202) 822-8029; e-mail info@ncto.org; internet www.ncto.org; f. 2004; Pres. CASS JOHNSON.

National Textile Association (NTA): 6 Beacon St, Suite 1125, Boston, MA 02108-3812; tel. (617) 542-8220; fax (617) 542-2199; e-mail info@nationaltextile.org; internet www.nationaltextile.org; f. 1854; fmrly Northern Textile Asscn and Knitted Textile Asscn; adopted current name in 2002; over 200 mems; Pres. KARL SPILHAUS.

TOBACCO

Tobacco Associates, Inc: 8452 Holly Leaf Dr., McLean, VA 22102-2225; tel. (703) 821-1255; fax (703) 821-1511; e-mail taw@tobaccoassociatesinc.org; internet www.tobaccoassociatesinc.org; f. 1947; Pres. KIRK WAYNE.

Tobacco Merchants Association of the United States (TMA): POB 8019, Princeton, NJ 08543-8019; tel. (609) 275-4900; fax (609) 275-8379; e-mail tma@tma.org; internet www.tma.org; f. 1915; 170 mems; Pres. FARRELL DELMAN.

TRANSPORT

Aerospace Industries Association of America, Inc (AIA): 1000 Wilson Blvd, Suite 1700, Arlington, VA 22209-3928; tel. (703) 358-1000; fax (703) 358-1012; e-mail matt.grimison@aia-aerospace.org; internet www.aia-aerospace.org; f. 1919; 107 mems and 183 assoc. mems; Pres. and CEO MARION C. BLAKEY.

Air Transport Association of America, Inc (ATA): see Transport—Civil Aviation.

Alliance of Automobile Manufacturers (Auto Alliance): 1401 Eye St, NW, Suite 900, Washington, DC 20005; tel. (202) 326-5500; fax (202) 326-5598; internet www.autoalliance.org; f. 1999; asscn of 10 car and light truck mfrs; Pres. and CEO DAVE MCCURDY.

American Bus Association (ABA): see Transport—Roads.

American International Automobile Dealers' Association (AIADA): 211 North Union St, Suite 300, Alexandria, VA 22314; tel. (703) 519-7800; fax (703) 519-7810; e-mail goaiada@aiada.org; internet www.aiada.org; f. 1970; 11,000 mems; Chair. JAMES HUDSON.

American Public Transportation Association (APTA): 1666 K St, NW, Suite 1100, Washington, DC 20006; tel. (202) 496-4800; fax (202) 496-4321; e-mail info@apta.com; internet www.apta.com; f. 1882; 1,600 mems; Pres. WILLIAM W. MILLAR.

American Railway Engineering and Maintenance-of-Way Association (AREMA): see Transport—Railways.

American Short Line and Regional Railroad Association (ASLRRA): see Transport—Railways.

American Trucking Associations (ATA): see Transport—Roads.

Association of American Railroads (AAR): see Transport—Railways.

National Air Transportation Association (NATA): see Transport—Civil Aviation.

National Automobile Dealers Association (NADA): 8400 Westpark Dr., McLean, VA 22102-3522; tel. (703) 821-7000; e-mail nadainfo@nada.org; internet www.nada.org; f. 1917; over 19,700 mems; Pres. PHILLIP D. BRADY.

Owner/Operator Independent Drivers' Association (OOIDA): see Transport—Roads.

Shipbuilders Council of America (SCA): 1455 F St, NW, Suite 225, Washington, DC 20005; tel. (202) 347-5462; fax (202) 347-5464; e-mail ibennitt@dc.bjllp.com; internet www.shipbuilders.org; f. 1921; absorbed the American Waterways Shipyard Conference (f. 1976) in 1999; 36 mem. cos and 25 affiliate mems; Pres. MATTHEW PAXTON.

MISCELLANEOUS

American Advertising Federation (AAF): 1101 Vermont Ave, NW, Suite 500, Washington, DC 20005-6306; tel. (202) 898-0089; fax (202) 898-0159; e-mail aaf@aaf.org; internet www.aaf.org; f. 1967; 50,000 mems, 130 corp. mems; Pres. and CEO WALLACE S. SNYDER.

American Association of Exporters and Importers (AAEI): 1050 17th St, NW, Suite 810, Washington, DC 20036; tel. (202) 857-8009; fax (202) 857-7843; e-mail hq@aaei.org; internet www.aaei.org; f. 1921; 1,200 mems; Pres. and CEO HALLOCK NORTHCOTT.

American Marketing Association (AMA): 311 South Wacker Dr., Suite 5800, Chicago, IL 60606; tel. (312) 542-9000; fax (312) 542-9001; e-mail info@ama.org; internet www.marketingpower.com; f. 1937; 38,000 mems; Chair. TOM KINNEAR; CEO DENNIS L. DUNLAP.

American Society of Association Executives (ASAE): ASAE and the Center for Association Leadership, 1575 I St, NW, Washington, DC 20005-1103; tel. (202) 626-2798; fax (202) 371-8825; e-mail pr@asaecenter.org; internet www.asaenet.org; f. 1920; over 22,000 mems; Pres. and CEO JOHN H. GRAHAM.

Association of Equipment Manufacturers (AEM): 6737 West Washington St, Suite 2400, Milwaukee, WI 53214-5647; tel. (414) 272-0943; fax (414) 272-1170; internet www.aem.org; f. 2002; Pres. DENNIS SLATER.

Institute for Supply Management (ISM): 2055 East Centennial Circle, POB 22160, Tempe, AZ 85285-2160; tel. (408) 752-6276; fax (408) 752-7890; e-mail pnovak@ism.ws; internet www.ism.ws; f. 1915; 40,000 mems; CEO PAUL NOVAK.

Material Handling Industry of America: 8720 Red Oak Blvd, Suite 201, Charlotte, NC 28217-3992; tel. (704) 676-1190; fax (704) 676-1199; e-mail vwheeler@mhia.org; internet www.mhia.org; f. 1946; *c.* 780 mem. corpns world-wide; CEO JOHN B. NOFSINGER.

Motion Picture Association of America, Inc (MPAA): 1600 Eye St, NW, Washington, DC 20006; tel. (202) 293-1966; fax (202)296-7410; internet www.mpaa.org; f. 1922; Chair. and CEO DAN GLICKMAN.

National Association of Manufacturers (NAM): 1331 Pennsylvania Ave, NW, Suite 600, Washington, DC 20004-1790; tel. (202) 637-3000; fax (202) 637-3182; e-mail manufacturing@nam.org; internet www.nam.org; f. 1895; 14,000 mems; Pres. and CEO JOHN ENGLER.

National Association of Realtors (NAR): 430 North Michigan Ave, Suite 500, Chicago, IL 60611-4087; fax (312) 329-8960; e-mail infocentral@realtors.org; internet www.realtor.org; f. 1908; 1.3m. mems; Pres. RICHARD F. GAYLORD.

National Cooperative Business Association (NCBA): 1401 New York Ave, NW, Suite 1100, Washington, DC 20005-2160; tel. (202) 638-6222; fax (202) 638-1374; e-mail ncba@ncba.coop; internet www.ncba.org; f. 1916; 450 mems; Pres. and CEO PAUL HAZEN.

National Retail Federation (NRF): 325 Seventh St, NW, Suite 1100, Washington, DC 20004-2802; tel. (202) 783-7941; fax (202) 737-2849; e-mail mullint@nrf.com; internet www.nrf.com; f. 1911; merged with American Retail Federation in 1990 and incorporated Apparel Retailers of America in 1995; mems: more than 100 state, nat. and trade orgs; Chair. MYRON E. ULLMAN, III; Pres. and CEO TRACY MULLIN.

Trade Unions

In 2007 there were approximately 15.7m. union members in the USA, representing 12.1% of wage and salary workers. Union membership was more prevalent among government workers (35.9%) than private sector employees (7.5%). However, total union membership has gradually declined since 1983, when it stood at 20.1%.

Many trade unions based in the USA have members throughout North America. Approximately 28% of Canada's trade union members belong to unions having headquarters in the USA.

American Federation of Labor and Congress of Industrial Organizations (AFL-CIO): 815 16th St, NW, Washington, DC 20006; tel. (202) 637-5000; fax (202) 637-5058; internet www.aflcio.org; f. 1955; Pres. JOHN J. SWEENEY; Sec.-Treas. RICHARD L. TRUMKA; 56 affiliated unions with total membership of 10.5m. (2008).

AFL-CIO AFFILIATES
(with 50,000 members and over)

Air Line Pilots' Association (ALPA): 1625 Massachusetts Ave, NW, Washington, DC 20036; tel. (703) 689-2270; internet www.alpa.org; f. 1931; Pres. Capt. JOHN PRATER; First Vice-Pres. Capt. PAUL RICE; 53,000 mems.

Amalgamated Transit Union: 5025 Wisconsin Ave, NW, Washington, DC 20016; tel. (202) 537-1645; fax (202) 244-7824; e-mail dispatch@atu.org; internet www.atu.org; f. 1892; Int. Pres. WARREN S. GEORGE; 185,000 mems.

American Federation of Government Employees: 80 F St, NW, Washington, DC 20001; tel. (202) 639-6419; fax (202) 639-6441; e-mail communications@afge.org; internet www.afge.org; f. 1932; Nat. Pres. JOHN GAGE; 600,000 mems.

American Federation of Musicians of the United States and Canada: Paramount Bldg, Suite 600, 1501 Broadway, New York, NY 10036; tel. (212) 869-1330; fax (212) 764-6134; e-mail naglieri@afm.org; internet www.afm.org; f. 1896; Pres. THOMAS F. LEE; Sec.-Treas. SAM FOLIO; 90,000 mems.

American Federation of State, County and Municipal Employees: 1625 L St, NW, Washington, DC 20036-5687; tel. (202) 429-1000; fax (202) 429-1293; internet www.afscme.org; f. 1936; Pres. GERALD W. MCENTEE; Sec.-Treas. WILLIAM LUCY; 1.4m. mems.

American Federation of Teachers (AFT-AFL-CIO): 555 New Jersey Ave, NW, Washington, DC 20001; tel. (202) 879-4400; fax (202) 879-4556; internet www.aft.org; f. 1916; Pres. RANDI WEINGARTEN; Sec.-Treas. ANTONIA CORTESE; 1.4m. mems (2008).

American Federation of Television and Radio Artists: 260 Madison Ave, 7th Floor, New York, NY 10016-2401; tel. (212) 532-0800; fax (212) 532-2242; internet www.aftra.org; f. 1937; Pres. ROBERTA REARDON; Nat. Exec. Dir KIM ROBERTS HEDGPETH; 70,000 mems.

American Postal Workers' Union: 1300 L St, NW, Washington, DC 20005; tel. (202) 842-4200; fax (202) 842-4297; internet www.apwu.org; f. 1971; Pres. WILLIAM BURRUS; 332,000 mems.

Bakery, Confectionery, Tobacco Workers' and Grain Millers International Union: 10401 Connecticut Ave, Kensington, MD 20895; tel. (301) 933-8600; fax (301) 946-8452; internet www.bctgm.org; f. 1886; Int. Pres. FRANK HURT; Sec.-Treas. DAVID B. DURKEE; 120,000 mems (2006).

California School Employees' Association (CSEA): 2045 Lundy Ave, POB 640, San Jose, CA 95131; tel. (408) 473-1000; fax (408) 954-0948; e-mail fpolito@csea.com; internet www.csea.com; f. 1927; Pres. ROB FECKNER; Dir FRANK POLITO; 230,000 mems.

Communications Workers of America: 501 Third St, NW, Washington, DC 20001; tel. (202) 434-1100; fax (202) 434-1279; internet www.cwa-union.org; f. 1939; Pres. LARRY COHEN; Sec.-Treas. JEFFREY A. RECHENBACH; 740,000 mems (2006).

Glass Molders, Pottery, Plastics & Allied Workers International Union (AFL-CIO, CLC): 608 East Baltimore Pike, POB 607, Media, PA 19063-0607; tel. (610) 565-5051; fax (610) 565-0983; e-mail gmpiu@gmpiu.org; internet www.gmpiu.org; f. 1842; Pres. JOHN P. RYAN; Sec.-Treas. BRUCE R. SMITH; 51,000 mems.

International Alliance of Theatrical Stage Employees, Moving Picture Technicians, Artists and Allied Crafts of the US, its Territories and Canada (IATSE): 1430 Broadway, 20th Floor, New York, NY 10018; tel. (212) 730-1770; fax (212) 730-7809; e-mail webmaster@iatse-intl.org; internet www.iatse-intl.org; f. 1893; Int. Pres. MATTHEW D. LOEB; Gen. Sec.-Treas. JAMES B. WOOD; 110,000 mems.

International Association of Bridge, Structural, Ornamental and Reinforcing Iron Workers: 1750 New York Ave, NW, Suite 400, Washington, DC 20006; tel. (202) 383-4800; fax (202) 638-4856; e-mail iwmagazine@iwintl.org; internet www.ironworkers.org; f. 1896; Gen. Pres. JOSEPH HUNT; Gen. Sec. MICHAEL A. FITZPATRICK; 140,000 mems.

International Association of Fire Fighters: 1750 New York Ave, NW, Washington, DC 20006-5395; tel. (202) 737-8484; fax (202) 737-8418; internet www.iaff.org; f. 1918; Gen. Pres. HAROLD SCHAITBERGER; Sec.-Treas. VINCENT J. BOLLON; 290,000 mems.

International Association of Machinists and Aerospace Workers (IAM): 9000 Machinists Pl., Upper Malrboro, MD 20772-2687; tel. (301) 967-4500; fax (301) 967-4588; e-mail websteward@goiam.org; internet www.iamaw.org; f. 1888; Int. Pres. R. THOMAS BUFFENBARGER; Gen. Sec.-Treas. WARREN L. MART; 730,000 mems (2006).

International Brotherhood of Boilermakers, Iron Ship Builders, Blacksmiths, Forgers and Helpers: 753 State Ave, Suite 570, Kansas City, KS 66101; tel. (913) 371-2640; fax (913) 281-8101; e-mail tracy.buck@boilermakers.org; internet www.boilermakers.org; f. 1880; Int. Pres. NEWTON B. JONES; Int. Sec.-Treas. WILLIAM T. CREEDEN; 100,000 mems.

International Brotherhood of Electrical Workers: 900 Seventh St, NW, Washington, DC 20001; tel. (202) 833-7000; fax (202) 728-7676; e-mail glenn_perusek@ibew.org; internet www.ibew.org; f. 1891; Pres. EDWIN D. HILL; Sec.-Treas. LINDELL K. LEE; 750,000 mems.

International Federation of Professional and Technical Engineers (IFPTE): 501 3rd Street, NW, Suite 701, Washington, DC 20001; tel. (202) 239-4880; fax (202) 239-4881; e-mail gjunemann@ifpte.org; internet www.ifpte.org; f. 1918; Pres. GREGORY J. JUNEMANN; Sec.-Treas. PAUL SHEARON; 75,000 mems.

International Longshoremen's Association: 17 Battery Pl., Suite 930, New York, NY 10004; tel. (212) 425-1200; fax (212) 425-2928; e-mail jmcnamara@ilaunion.org; internet www.ilaunion.org; f. 1892; Pres. RICHARD P. HUGHES, Jr; Sec.-Treas. ROBERT E. GLEASON; 65,000 mems.

International Union of Bricklayers and Allied Craftworkers: 620 F Street, NW, Washington, DC 20004; tel. (202) 783-3788; fax (202) 393-0219; e-mail askbac@bacweb.org; internet www.bacweb.org; f. 1865; Pres. JOHN J. FLYNN; Sec.-Treas. JAMES BOLAND; 100,000 mems (1999).

International Union of Operating Engineers: 1125 17th St, NW, Washington, DC 20036; tel. (202) 429-9100; fax (202) 778-2616; f. 1896; Gen. Pres. VINCENT J. GIBLIN; Gen. Sec.-Treas. CHRISTOPHER HANLEY; 400,000 mems (2006).

International Union of Painters and Allied Trades: 1750 New York Ave, NW, 8th Floor, Washington, DC 20006; tel. (202) 637-0700; fax (202) 637-0771; e-mail mail@iupat.org; internet www.iupat.org; f. 1887; Gen. Pres. JAMES A. WILLIAMS; Gen. Sec.-Treas. GEORGE GALIS; 140,000 mems.

International Union of Police Associations: 1549 Ringling Blvd, Suite 600, Sarasota, FL 34236; tel. (941) 487-2560; fax (941) 487-2570; e-mail iupa@iupa.org; internet www.iupa.org; Pres. SAMUEL A. CABRAL; Sec.-Treas. TIMOTHY A. SCOTT; 80,400 mems (2002).

Marine Engineers' Beneficial Association (MEBA): 444 North Capitol St, NW, Suite 800, Washington, DC 20001; tel. (202) 638-5355; fax (202) 638-5369; e-mail mebahq@d1meba.org; internet www.d1meba.org; f. 1875; Pres. DON KEEFE; Sec.-Treas. BILL VAN LOO; 50,000 mems.

National Association of Letter Carriers (NALC): 100 Indiana Ave, NW, Washington, DC 20001-2144; tel. (202) 393-4695; fax (202) 737-1540; e-mail nalcinf@nalc.org; internet www.nalc.org; f. 1889; Pres. WILLIAM H. YOUNG; Sec.-Treas. JANE E. BROENDEL; 300,058 mems (2006).

Office and Professional Employees International Union: 265 West 14th St, Suite 610, New York, NY 10011; tel. (212) 675-3210; fax (212) 727-3466; internet www.opeiu.org; f. 1945; Int. Pres. MICHAEL GOODWIN; Sec.-Treas. NANCY WOHLFORTH; 125,000 mems.

Screen Actors Guild: 5757 Wilshire Blvd, Los Angeles, CA 90036-3600; tel. (323) 954-1600; fax (323) 549-6656; internet www.sag.org; f. 1933; Pres. ALAN ROSENBERG; Sec.-Treas. CONNIE STEVENS; 120,000 mems (Feb. 2006).

Seafarers International Union of North America: 5201 Auth Way, Camp Springs, MD 20746; tel. (301) 899-0675; fax (301) 899-7355; e-mail webmaster@seafarers.org; internet www.seafarers.org; f. 1938; Pres. MICHAEL SACCO; Sec.-Treas. DAVID W. HEINDEL; 80,000 mems.

Sheet Metal Workers' International Association: 1750 New York Ave, NW, Washington, DC 20006; tel. (202) 783-5880; fax (202) 662-0894; e-mail info@smwia.org; internet www.smwia.org; f. 1888; Gen. Pres. MICHAEL J. SULLIVAN; Gen. Sec.-Treas. JOSEPH J. NIGRO; 150,000 mems (1999).

Transport Workers' Union of America (TWU): 1700 Broadway, 2nd Floor, New York, NY 10019; e-mail mailbox@twu.org; internet www.twu.org; f. 1934; Int. Pres. JAMES C. LITTLE; Sec.-Treas. JOSEPH C. GORDON; 135,000 mems.

United American Nurses (UAN): 8515 Georgia Ave, Suite 400, Silver Spring, MD 20910-3492; tel. (301) 628-5118; fax (301) 628-5347; e-mail uaninfo@uannurse.org; internet www.uannurse.org; f. 1999; also affiliated to the American Nurses Asscn; Pres. ANN CONVERSO; Sec.-Treas. JEAN ROSS; 104,000 mems.

United Association of Journeymen and Apprentices of the Plumbing and Pipe Fitting Industry of the United States and Canada: 901 Massachusetts Ave, NW, Washington, DC 20001; tel. (202) 628-5823; fax (202) 628-5024; internet www.ua.org; f. 1889; Pres. WILLIAM P. HITE; Sec.-Treas. PATRICK PERNO; 304,000 mems (1999).

United Automobile, Aerospace and Agricultural Implement Workers of America (UAW): Solidarity House, 8000 East Jefferson Ave, Detroit, MI 48214; tel. (313) 926-5000; fax (313) 823-6016; internet www.uaw.org; f. 1935; Pres. RON GETTELFINGER; Sec.-Treas. ELIZABETH BUNN; 640,000 active mems (2006).

United Mine Workers of America (UMWA): 8315 Lee Highway, Fairfax, VA 22031; tel. (703) 208-7200; internet www.umwa.org; f. 1890; Int. Pres. CECIL E. ROBERTS; Sec.-Treas. DANIEL J. KANE; 130,000 mems (1999).

United Steel, Paper and Forestry, Rubber, Manufacturing, Energy, Allied Industrial and Service Workers International Union (USW) (United Steelworkers): 5 Gateway Center, Pittsburgh, PA 15222; tel. (412) 562-2400; fax (412) 562-2445; e-mail webmaster@usw.org; internet www.usw.org; f. 1936; incorporated PACE International Union in 2005 and Independent Steelworkers Union in 2007; announced agreement in July 2008 to merge with Unite (United Kingdom) to create Workers Uniting; represents workers in the USA, Canada and the Caribbean; Int. Pres. LEO W. GERARD; Sec.-Treas. JAMES D. ENGLISH; 850,000 mems (2007).

United Transportation Union (UTU): 14600 Detroit Ave, Cleveland, OH 44107-4250; tel. (216) 228-9400; fax (216) 228-5755; e-mail pr@utu.org; internet www.utu.org; f. 1969; formed strategic alliance with USW in July 2006; Pres. MALCOLM B. FUTHEY; Gen. Sec. and Treas. KIM N. THOMPSON; 125,000 mems.

Utility Workers Union of America, AFL-CIO: 815 16th St, NW, Washington, DC 20006; tel. (202) 974-8200; fax (202) 974-8201; e-mail rfarley@aflcio.org; internet www.uwua.net; f. 1945; Pres. D. MICHAEL LANGFORD; Sec.-Treas. GARY M. RUFFNER; 50,000 mems (2008).

INDEPENDENT UNIONS

(with 50,000 members and over)

American Nurses Association: 8515 Georgia Ave, Suite 400, Silver Spring, MD 20910; tel. (301) 628-5000; fax (301) 628-5001; e-mail ana@ana.org; internet www.nursingworld.org; f. 1896; Pres. REBECCA M. PATTON; 54 constituent mem. state asscns comprising 2.9m. mems.

Change to Win: 1900 L St, NW, Suite 900, Washington, DC 20036; tel. (202) 721-0660; fax (202) 721-0661; e-mail info@changetowin.org; internet www.changetowin.org; f. 2005 following split in the AFL-CIO; Int. Pres. JOSEPH HANSEN; Sec.-Treas. EDGAR ROMNEY.

Affiliates with 50,000 mems and over include:

International Brotherhood of Teamsters: 25 Louisiana Ave, NW, Washington, DC 20001; tel. (202) 624-6800; fax (202) 624-6918; internet www.teamster.org; f. 1903; withdrew from AFL-CIO in 2005; Pres. JAMES P. HOFFA; Gen. Sec.-Treas. C. THOMAS KEEGEL; 1.4m. mems.

Laborers' International Union of North America: 905 16th St, NW, Washington, DC 20006; tel. (202) 737-8320; fax (202) 737-2754; e-mail rgreer@liuna.org; internet www.liuna.org; f. 1903; Pres. TERENCE M. O'SULLIVAN; Gen. Sec.-Treas. ARMAND E. SABATONI; 820,000 mems (2003).

Service Employees' International Union (SEIU): 1313 L St, NW, Washington, DC 20005; tel. (202) 898-3200; fax (202) 898-3304; internet www.seiu.org; f. 1921; withdrew from AFL-CIO in 2005; Pres. ANDREW L. STERN; Sec.-Treas. ANNA BURGER; c. 2m. mems.

UNITE HERE: 275 Seventh Ave, New York, NY 10001-6708; tel. (212) 265-7000; e-mail esharfstein@unitehere.org; internet www.unitehere.org; f. 2004 by merger of the Union of Needletrades, Industrial and Textile Employees (UNITE—f. 1995) and Hotel Employees and Restaurant Employees Int. Union (HERE—f. 1891); Gen. Pres. BRUCE S. RAYNOR; Pres. (Hospitality Industries) JOHN W. WILHELM; c. 450,000 mems.

United Brotherhood of Carpenters and Joiners of America: 101 Constitution Ave, NW, Washington, DC 20001; tel. (202) 546-6206; fax (202) 543-5724; internet www.carpenters.org; f. 1881; withdrew from AFL-CIO in 2001; Pres. DOUGLAS J. MCCARRON; Sec.-Treas. ANDRIS J. SILINS; 520,000 mems (2006).

United Food and Commercial Workers International Union: 1775 K St, NW, Washington, DC 20006; tel. (202) 223-3111; internet www.ufcw.org; f. 1979; Int. Pres. JOSEPH T. HANSEN; Int. Sec.-Treas. ANTHONY M. PERRONE; 1.3m. mems.

Fraternal Order of Police: 701 Marriott Dr., Nashville, TN 37214; tel. (615) 399-0900; fax (615) 399-0400; e-mail pyoes@fop.net; internet www.fop.net; Nat. Pres. CHUCK CANTERBURY; Nat. Sec. PATRICK YOES; 325,000 mems.

International Longshore and Warehouse Union: 1188 Franklin St, 4th Floor, San Francisco, CA 94109-6800; tel. (415) 775-0533; fax (415) 775-1302; e-mail info@ilwu.org; internet www.ilwu.org; f. 1937; Pres. ROBERT MCELLRATH; Sec.-Treas. WILLIAM ADAMS; 59,500 mems (2006).

National Education Association of the United States: 1201 16th St, NW, Washington, DC 20036-3290; tel. (202) 833-4000; fax (202) 822-7974; internet www.nea.org; f. 1857; Pres. DENNIS VAN ROEKEL; Sec.-Treas. REBECCA PRINGLE; 3.2m. mems.

National Rural Letter Carriers' Association: 1630 Duke St, 4th Floor, Alexandria, VA 22314-3465; tel. (703) 684-5545; fax (703) 548-8735; internet www.nrlca.org; f. 1903; Pres. DON CANTRIEL; Sec.-Treas. CLIFFORD D. DAILING; 98,000 mems (1999).

National Treasury Employees Union: 1750 H St, NW, Washington, DC 20006; tel. (202) 572-5500; fax (202) 572-5644; internet www.nteu.org; f. 1938; Nat. Pres. COLLEEN M. KELLEY; 150,000 mems.

ENERGY

INTRODUCTION

In 1960 the USA consumed 40% of world energy production, but by 2005 this share had declined to under 21.8%, i.e., 100.7 quadrillion ('000,000,000 million) British thermal units (Btu). In terms of shares of total energy production, coal, natural gas and petroleum provided a preliminary 33.2%, 28.0% and 15.3%, respectively, in 2007; the remainder was accounted for chiefly by nuclear power and renewable sources (principally biofuels—wood and waste—and hydro). In terms of share of total consumption, however, petroleum products had a clear lead, at a preliminary 39.2%, over natural gas and coal, at 23.3% and 22.4%, respectively. In 2007, according to preliminary figures, the USA produced domestically only 70.6% of its total energy consumption requirements. In that year residential and commercial uses accounted for a preliminary 39.6% of the total energy consumed, with the share of industry totalling 31.8%, and transport accounting for 28.6%.

The electricity-supply and -generating industry is diverse in nature, with ownership divided between federal and state authorities, municipal systems, rural co-operatives and the private sector. In 2005 there were an estimated 3,170 traditional electric utilities and a further 2,110 non-utility power producers. Privately owned utility companies represented 8% of the total number of electric utilities but more than three-quarters of electric utility generating capacity. Eight regional reliability councils and the North American Electric Reliability Corporation handle supply co-ordination across the USA and Canada.

From 1960 alternative sources of electricity generation, particularly nuclear power and hydropower, became increasingly important. The Three Mile Island (Pennsylvania) accident in 1979, together with escalating costs, delivered a serious reverse to nuclear power-plant expansion plans. Nevertheless, in 2007 gross production of nuclear electricity represented a preliminary 11.7% of total energy production. Renewable energy (biofuels, hydroelectric, geothermal, wind and solar) production accounted for 9.5% in the same year. In 2005 the USA accounted for an estimated 21.1% of the world's carbon dioxide emissions from energy consumption, compared to 24.5% in 2000.

Domestic consumption and expenditure on energy varies considerably between regions of the USA. The overall per-head consumption of energy in the USA in 2005 was 339.2m. Btu. The states with the highest energy consumption per head were Alaska (1,193.9m. Btu), Wyoming (911.9m. Btu) and Louisiana (803.7m. Btu), while those with the lowest consumption per head were Rhode Island (213.3m. Btu), New York (217.0m. Btu) and California (232.3m. Btu). In 2005 the average price of retail electricity sold to the residential sector was US $27.68 per million Btu, while that of natural gas was $12.34 per million Btu.

The Federal Energy Regulatory Commission, part of the Department of Energy, controlled the rates and charges current in many parts of the energy industry, including the transmission and sale of gas, and the transportation of petroleum. The Commission was responsible for supervising the deregulation of the electricity market, which commenced in 1998, and California was the first state to move to a free market system. The Nuclear Regulatory Commission is independent of the Department of Energy, and licenses and regulates the nuclear energy sector.

In August 2005 the US Congress approved the Energy Policy Act of 2005, intended better to manage the country's energy needs through increased oil and gas production, as well as through the promotion of energy efficiency, the modernization of the country's electricity grid and the development of environmentally friendly sources of energy, such as wave and wind power. There were also plans to increase the use of nuclear power. According to preliminary estimates, US carbon dioxide emissions decreased by 1.8% in 2006 (compared to an average annual increase of 1.4% in energy-related carbon dioxide emissions during 1990–2005). The reduction was attributed to higher fuel prices and milder weather conditions in 2006, among other factors.

STATISTICS

Energy Production and Consumption, by Major Source

('000,000,000 million British thermal units)

	2003	2004	2005	2006	2007*
Total production†	70.264	70.384	69.647	71.025	71.713
Fossil fuels	56.157	55.914	55.056	55.940	56.499
Coal	22.094	22.852	23.185	23.790	23.480
Natural gas (dry)	19.691	19.093	18.574	18.993	19.817
Petroleum‡	12.026	11.503	10.963	10.801	10.802
Nuclear (electric)	7.959	8.222	8.160	8.214	8.415
Renewable§	6.149	6.248	6.431	6.872	6.800
Total consumption	98.209	100.351	100.506	99.856	101.600

* Preliminary figures.

† Totals may not be equal to the sum of component parts, owing to rounding.

‡ Includes crude petroleum (crude oil) and lease condensate.

§ End-use consumption, and electric utility and non-utility electricity net generation.

Source: US Energy Information Administration.

Net Generation of Electricity, by Energy Source

('000 million kilowatt-hours)

	2003	2004	2005	2006	2007*
Fossil fuels	2,758.6	2,825.0	2,910.0	2,884.4	2,994.9
Coal	1,973.7	1,978.6	2,013.2	1,990.9	2,020.6
Natural gas (dry)	649.9	708.9	758.0	813.0	893.2
Other gases†	15.6	16.8	16.3	16.1	15.4
Petroleum	119.4	120.8	122.5	64.4	65.7
Nuclear (electric)	763.7	788.5	782.0	787.2	806.5
Renewable	355.3	351.0	357.5	385.7	351.3
Hydroelectric pumped storage	–8.5	–8.5	–6.6	–6.6	–7.0
Other sources	14.0	14.5	12.5	14.0	13.8
Total	3,883.2	3,970.6	4,055.4	4,064.7	4,159.5

* Preliminary figures.

† Includes blast furnace gas, propane gas and other manufactured and waste gases derived from fossil fuels.

Source: US Energy Information Administration.

Energy Consumption by States, 2005

(British thermal units—Btu)

	Consumption ('000,000m. Btu)*	Consumption per head (m. Btu)
Texas	11,558.3	506.0
California	8,359.8	232.3
Florida	4,563.3	257.3
New York	4,179.5	217.0
Illinois	4,121.5	324.0
Ohio	4,081.6	356.2
Pennsylvania	4,050.2	327.5
Louisiana	3,613.0	803.7
Georgia	3,173.0	348.4
Michigan	3,166.5	313.3
Indiana	2,904.7	464.2
North Carolina	2,732.0	314.8
New Jersey	2,728.6	315.2
Virginia	2,610.2	345.4
Tennessee	2,338.8	390.5
Alabama	2,119.0	466.8
Washington	2,058.8	328.3
Kentucky	1,970.1	472.3
Missouri	1,914.7	330.8
Wisconsin	1,861.8	336.0
Minnesota	1,852.2	362.2
South Carolina	1,694.3	398.2
Massachusetts	1,561.8	242.9
Maryland	1,555.2	279.1
Oklahoma	1,550.7	438.6
Arizona	1,479.7	248.6
Colorado	1,425.7	305.1
Iowa	1,227.8	415.4
Mississippi	1,182.3	407.6
Arkansas	1,135.1	409.5
Oregon	1,095.7	301.8
Kansas	1,031.8	376.4
Connecticut	900.2	258.2
Alaska	799.2	1,193.9
West Virginia	793.9	439.7
Utah	756.7	302.1
Nevada	727.8	302.1
New Mexico	675.0	352.3
Nebraska	654.9	373.0
Idaho	503.2	352.9
Maine	482.4	367.6
Wyoming	461.9	911.9
Montana	419.4	448.2
North Dakota	412.2	648.1
New Hampshire	335.4	257.4
Hawaii	333.4	263.0
Delaware	312.6	371.9
South Dakota	273.5	350.6
Rhode Island	227.6	213.3
District of Columbia	190.4	327.0
Vermont	167.0	269.5
Total	100,368.6†	339.2

* Ranked in descending order of total consumption; rankings based on unrounded data.

† Includes 44,200,000m. Btu of coal coke net imports.

Source: US Energy Information Administration.

NATIONAL ENERGY ORGANIZATIONS AND CO-ORDINATING BODIES

American Council for an Energy-Efficient Economy: 1001 Connecticut Ave, NW, Suite 801, Washington, DC 20036; tel. (202) 507-4000; fax (202) 429-2248; e-mail info@aceee.org; internet www .aceee.org; f. 1980; promotes economic prosperity and a cleaner environment through energy efficiency; Chair. CARL BLUMSTEIN.

American Nuclear Society: 555 North Kensington Ave, La Grange Park, IL 60526; tel. (708) 352-6611; fax (708) 352-0499; internet www .ans.org; f. 1954; around 11,000 mems; Pres. WILLIAM E. BURCHILL; Exec. Dir HARRY A. BRADLEY.

Association of Energy Engineers (AEE): 4025 Pleasantdale Rd, Suite 420, Atlanta, GA 30340; tel. (770) 447-5083; fax (770) 446-3969; e-mail info@aeecenter.org; internet www.aeecenter.org; f. 1977; 8,500 mems; Pres. Dr L. J. GROBLER; Exec. Dir ALBERT THUMANN.

Biomass Energy Research Association: 901 D St, Suite 100, Washington, DC 20024; tel. (410) 953-6202; fax (410) 290-0377; e-mail beraorg@yahoo.com; internet beraonline.org; f. 1982; 200 mems; Pres., Treas. and Dir JOAN PELLEGRINO.

Bonneville Power Administration: 905 North East 11th Ave, Portland, OR 97208-3621; tel. (503) 230-7334; e-mail comment@bpa .gov; internet www.bpa.gov; f. 1937; federal agency, part of the Department of Energy; wholesale distribution from hydro, nuclear and wind sources; covers Idaho, Montana, Oregon and Washington; Admin. STEPHEN J. WRIGHT.

Consumer Energy Council of America Research Foundation (CECA Solutions): 2737 Devonshire Pl., NW, Suite 102, Washington, DC 20036; tel. (202) 659-0404; fax (202) 659-0407; e-mail outreach@ cecarf.org; internet www.cecarf.org; f. 1973; non-profit org; 70 mems; Chair. RICHARD GOSS; Pres. ELLEN BERMAN.

Environmental Protection Agency: see Federal Executive—Independent Agencies.

Fusion Power Associates: 2 Professional Dr., Suite 249, Gaithersburg, MD 20879; tel. (301) 258-0545; fax (301) 975-9869; e-mail fpa@ compuserve.com; internet fusionpower.org; f. 1979; 400 mems; Chair. GERALD NAVRATIL; Pres. Dr STEPHEN O. DEAN.

Institute of Nuclear Power Operations: 1100 Circle 75 Pkwy, Suite 1500, Atlanta, GA 30339; tel. (404) 953-3600; e-mail esh-infocenter@eh.doe.gov; internet www.inpo.info; f. 1979; electric utilities operating nuclear power-plants; 101 mems; Pres. and CEO JAMES O. ELLIS, Jr.

National Council on Radiation Protection and Measurements: 7910 Woodmont Ave, Suite 400, Bethesda, MD 20814-3095; tel. (301) 657-2652; fax (301) 907-8768; e-mail schauer@ ncrponline.org; internet www.ncrp.com; f. 1928; 100 mems; Pres. THOMAS S. TENFORDE; Exec. Dir DAVID A. SCHAUER.

National Hydropower Association: 1 Massachusetts Ave, NW, Suite 850, Washington, DC 20001; tel. (202) 682-1700; fax (202) 682-9478; e-mail help@hydro.org; internet www.hydro.org; f. 1983; over 140 mems; Pres. RICK MILLER; Exec. Dir LINDA CHURCH CIOCCI.

National Old Timers' Association of the Energy Industry: 601 Veterans Memorial Hwy, Hauppauge, NY 11787; tel. (631) 360-0200; fax (516) 431-9850; e-mail m-fuel@comcast.net; internet www.notaei .org; f. 1926; 1,000 mems; Chair. JOHN M. SIBARIUM.

North American Electric Reliability Corpn (NERC): 116–390 Village Blvd, Princeton, NJ 08540-5731; tel. (609) 452-8060; fax (609) 452-9550; e-mail info@nerc.com; internet www.nerc.com; f. 1968 as National Electric Reliability Council; ensures the reliability of bulk electric power supply in North America and enforces reliability standards; Chair. RICHARD DROUIN; Pres. and CEO RICHARD P. SERGEL.

Nuclear Energy Institute: 1176 I St, NW, Suite 400, Washington, DC 20006-3708; tel. (202) 739-8000; fax (202) 785-4019; e-mail webmasterp@nei.org; internet www.nei.org; f. 1994; over 315 mems in 14 countries; Pres. and CEO Adm. FRANK L. BOWMAN.

Nuclear Regulatory Commission (NRC): Office of Public Affairs, Washington, DC 20555; tel. (301) 415-8200; e-mail opa@nrc.gov; internet www.nrc.gov; f. 1975; independent federal licensing and regulatory body; Chair. DALE E. KLEIN.

Professional Reactor Operator Society (PROS): POB 484, Byron, IL 61010-0484; e-mail webmaster@nucpros.com; internet nucpros.com; f. 1981; 875 mems; Pres. CARL M. GRAY.

Renewable Fuels Association (RFA): 1 Massachusetts Ave, NW, Suite 820, Washington, DC 20001; tel. (202) 289-3835; fax (202) 289-

7519; e-mail info@ethanolrfa.org; internet www.ethanolrfa.org; f. 1981; 113 mems; Pres. and CEO BOB DINNEEN; Chair. CHRIS STANDLEE.

Southeastern Power Administration: 1116 Athens Tech Rd, Elberton, GA 30635-6711; tel. (706) 213-3800; fax (706) 213-3884; e-mail info2@sepa.doe.gov; internet www.sepa.doe.gov; covers Alabama, Florida, Georgia, Illinois, Kentucky, Mississippi, North Carolina, South Carolina, Tennessee, Virginia and West Virginia; f. 1950; Admin. JON C. WORTHINGTON.

Southern States Energy Board: 6325 Amherst Ct, Norcross, GA 30092; tel. (770) 242-7712; fax (770) 242-0421; e-mail sseb@sseb.org; internet www.sseb.org; covers Alabama, Arkansas, Florida, Georgia, Kentucky, Louisiana, Maryland, Mississippi, Missouri, North Carolina, Oklahoma, South Carolina, Tennessee, Texas, Virginia and West Virginia; Chair. SONNY PERDUE, III.

Southwestern Power Administration: 1 West Third St, Tulsa, OK 74103-3502; tel. (918) 595-6600; fax (918) 595-6656; e-mail info@swpa.gov; internet www.swpa.gov; f. 1943; covers Arkansas, Kansas, Louisiana, Missouri, Oklahoma and Texas; Admin. MICHAEL DIEHL.

US Department of Energy: Forrestal Bldg, 1000 Independence Ave, SW, Washington, DC 20585-0001; tel. (202) 586-5000; fax (202) 586-4403; e-mail the.secretary@hq.doe.gov; internet www.doe.gov; f. 1977; provides the framework for a comprehensive and balanced national energy plan through the co-ordination and administration of the energy functions of the federal govt; responsible for long-term, high-risk research and development of energy technology, energy conservation, the nuclear-weapons programme, energy regulatory programmes and a central energy data collection and analysis programme; Sec. SAMUEL W. BODMAN.

Federal Energy Regulatory Commission: 888 First St, NE, Washington, DC 20426; tel. (202) 502-6088; e-mail customer@ferc.gov; internet www.ferc.gov; Chair. JOSEPH T. KELLIHER.

National Energy Technology Laboratory: 626 Cochrans Mill Rd, POB 10940, Pittsburgh, PA 15236-0940; tel. (412) 386-6000; fax (412) 386-4604; e-mail anna@netl.doe.gov; internet www.netl.doe.gov; laboratory conducting research into fossil fuel energy programmes; Dir CARL O. BAUER.

Office of Nuclear Energy: 1000 Independence Ave, SW, Washington, DC 20585-1290; tel. (202) 586-6450; fax (202) 586-8353; e-mail contact.ne@nuclear.energy.gov; internet www.nuclear.gov; Asst Sec. DENNIS R. SPURGEON.

US Energy Association: 1300 Pennsylvania Ave, NW, Suite 550, Washington, DC 20004; tel. (202) 312-1230; fax (202) 682-1682; e-mail bworthington@usea.org; internet www.usea.org; f. 1924; 160 mems; Exec. Dir BARRY K. WORTHINGTON; Chair. PETER J. ROBERTSON; Vice-Chair. TIMOTHY STATTON.

Western Area Power Administration: 12155 Alameda Pkwy, POB 281213, Lakewood, CO 80228-8213; tel. (720) 962-7000; fax (720) 962-7200; e-mail corpcomm@wapa.gov; internet www.wapa.gov; covers Arizona, California, Colorado, Iowa, Kansas, Minnesota, Montana, Nebraska, Nevada, New Mexico, North Dakota, South Dakota, Texas, Utah and Wyoming; Admin. TIMOTHY J. MEEKS.

Western Interstate Energy Board: 1600 Broadway, Suite 1700, Denver, CO 80202; tel. (303) 573-8910; fax (303) 534-7309; e-mail dlarson@westgov.org; internet www.westgov.org/wieb; covers Arizona, California, Colorado, Idaho, Montana, Nebraska, Nevada, New Mexico, Oregon, Utah, Washington and Wyoming; Chair. TONY USIBELLI.

ELECTRICITY

Alaska Power and Telephone Co (AP&T): 193 Otto St, POB 3222, Port Townsend, WA 98368; tel. (360) 385-1733; fax (360) 385-5177; e-mail apt@aptalaska.com; internet www.aptalaska.com; f. 1957; electric power distribution and local telephone communications; Pres. and CEO ROBERT GRIMM.

Allegheny Energy: 800 Cabin Hill Dr., Greensburg, PA 15601-1689; tel. (724) 838-6196; e-mail webmaster@alleghenyenergy.com; internet www.alleghenyenergy.com; main subsidiaries: Allegheny Energy Supply (conventional thermal generation), Allegheny Power (distribution); Pres., Chair. and CEO PAUL J. EVANSON.

Alliant Energy: 4902 North Biltmore Lane, POB 77007, Madison, WI 53707-1007; tel. (800) 255-4268; fax (608) 458-0100; e-mail customercare@alliantenergy.com; internet www.alliantenergy.com; conventional thermal and hydro generation; electricity and gas distribution; Pres., Chair. and CEO WILLIAM D. HARVEY.

Ameren Corpn: 1 Ameren Plaza, 1901 Chouteau Ave, POB 66149, St Louis, MO 63103; tel. (314) 621-6071; fax (314) 554-4075; internet www.ameren.com; Pres., Chair. and CEO GARY L. RAINWATER; owns four operating cos:.

AmerenCILCO: Peoria, IL; tel. (309) 672-5252; fax (309) 677-5025; e-mail cilcosolutionscenter@ameren.com; f. 1913 as Central Illinois Light Co.

AmerenCIPS: 607 East Adams St, Springfield, IL 62739; tel. (888) 789-2477; fax (877) 226-3736; e-mail IL-eCommerce@ameren.com; f. 1902 as Central Illinois Public Service Co Inc; present name adopted in 2000; CEO GARY L. RAINWATER.

AmerenIP: 500 27th St South, Decatur, IL 62525; tel. (800) 755-5000; fax (217) 425-4161; f. 1923; fmrly known as Illinois Power Co, acquired by Ameren from Dynegy in 2004; conventional thermal generation; Pres. LARRY F. ALTENBAUMER.

AmerenUE: 1 Ameren Plaza, 1901 Chouteau Ave, POB 66149, St Louis, MO 63166-6149; tel. (314) 342-1111; fax (314) 206-0485; e-mail solutionscenter@ameren.com; f. 1902 as Union Electric Co; CEO GARY L. RAINWATER.

American Electric Power (AEP): 1 Riverside Plaza, Columbus, OH 43215-2372; tel. (614) 716-1000; e-mail jsloat@aep.com; internet www.aep.com; f. 1906 as the American Gas and Electricity Co; present name adopted 1958; electricity supplier to Arkansas, Indiana, Kentucky, Louisiana, Michigan, Ohio, Oklahoma, Tennessee, Texas, Virginia and West Virginia; Pres., Chair. and CEO MICHAEL G. MORRIS.

American Public Power Association: 2301 M St, NW, 3rd Floor, Washington, DC 20037-1484; tel. (202) 467-2900; fax (202) 467-2910; e-mail mrufe@appanet.org; internet www.appanet.org; f. 1940; asscn of local publicly owned electric utilities; c. 2,000 mems; Chair. MAUDE GRANTHAM-RICHARDS; CEO MARK CRISSOM.

American Transmission Co (ATC): POB 47, Waukesha, WI 53187-0047; tel. (262) 506-6700; e-mail info@atcllc.com; internet www.atcllc.com; f. 2001; provides electric transmission service in Michigan, Wisconsin and Illinois; Pres. and CEO JOSÉ M. DELGADO.

Association of Edison Illuminating Cos: 600 North 18th St, POB 2641, Birmingham, AL 35291-0992; tel. (205) 257-2530; fax (205) 257-2540; e-mail aeicdir@bellsouth.net; internet www.aeic.org; f. 1885; mems comprise 78 investor-owned public utilities; Pres. RICHARD R. GRIGG; Exec. Dir EARL B. PARSONS, Jr.

Consolidated Edison Co of New York (conEdison): 4 Irving Pl., New York, NY 10003; tel. (212) 460-4600; fax (212) 475-0734; e-mail customerservice@coned.com; internet www.coned.com; conventional, thermal and nuclear generation; distributes electricity and gas; Chair. and CEO KEVIN BURKE.

Constellation Energy Group: 100 Constellation Way, Baltimore, MD 21202; tel. (410) 470-2800; e-mail communications@constellation.com; internet www.constellation.com; generation and distribution of electricity; Pres., Chair. and CEO MAYO A. SHATTUCK, III

Baltimore Gas and Electric Co (BGE): 39 West Lexington St, Baltimore, MD 21201; tel. (410) 685-0123; fax (410) 712-9323; e-mail corporate.communications@bge.com; internet www.bge.com; nuclear generation; Pres. and CEO KENNETH W. DEFONTES, Jr.

Constellation NewEnergy: 750 East Pratt St, 14th Floor, Baltimore, MD 21202; tel. (410) 783-2800; internet www.newenergy.com; f. 1995 as NewEnergy Ventures; changed name to above in 2002; provides electricity and gas to businesses; Pres. MICHAEL P. KAGAN.

Consumers Energy Co: 1 Energy Plaza, Jackson, MI 49201; tel. (517) 788-0550; internet www.consumersenergy.com; principal subsidiary of CMS Energy; generation and distribution of electric power; Pres. and COO JOHN G. RUSSELL.

Dayton Power and Light Co (DP&L): POB 1247, Dayton, OH 45401-1247; tel. (937) 331-3900; e-mail info@waytogo.com; internet www.waytogo.com; subsidiary of DPL, Inc; conventional thermal generation; distributes electricity and gas; f. 1911; Pres. and CEO PAUL M. BARBAS.

Dominion Resources: 120 Tredegar St, Richmond, VA 23219; POB 26532, Richmond, VA 23261; tel. (804) 819-2000; fax (804) 819-2232; e-mail investor.relations@dom.com; internet www.dom.com; generation and distribution of electric power, and natural gas production; Pres., Chair. and CEO THOMAS F. FARRELL, II.

DTE Energy: 2000 Second Ave, Detroit, MI 48226; tel. (313) 235-5555; internet www.dteenergy.com; f. 1903; main subsidiaries: Detroit Energy (conventional thermal and nuclear generation), Michigan Consolidated Gas Co (MichCon—natural gas distribution);

Chair. and CEO ANTHONY F. EARLEY, Jr; Pres. and COO GERARD M. ANDERSON.

Duke Energy: 526 South Church St, Charlotte, NC 28202-1904; tel. (704) 382-3853; fax (704) 382-3814; internet www.duke-energy.com; conventional thermal, hydro and nuclear generation; merged with Cinergy Corpn in 2006; Pres., Chair and CEO JAMES E. ROGERS.

Edison Electric Institute: 701 Pennsylvania Ave, NW, Washington, DC 2004-2696; tel. (202) 508-5000; fax (202) 508-5759; internet www.eei.org; f. 1933; mems comprise 184 investor-owned electric utility cos in the USA and 63 foreign mems; Chair. JAMES E. ROGERS; Pres. THOMAS R. KUHN.

Energy East Corpn: 52 Farm View Dr., New Gloucester, ME 04260-5116; tel. (207) 688-6300; internet www.energyeast.com; acquired by Iberdrola (Spain) in Sept. 2008; Pres., Chair. and CEO WESLEY W. VON SCHACK.

Central Maine Power Co: 88 Edison Dr., Augusta, ME 04336; tel. (207) 623-3521; fax (207) 623-5908; e-mail customer.service@cmpco.com; internet www.cmpco.com; 590,000 customers; Pres. SARA J. BURNS.

New York State Electric and Gas Corpn (NYSEG): Corporate Dr., Kirkwood Industrial Park, POB 5224, Binghampton, NY 13902-5224; tel. (607) 762-5900; fax (607) 762-8499; internet www.nyseg.com; conventional thermal generation; 1.1m. customers; Pres. JAMES P. LAURITO.

Rochester Gas and Electric Corpn (RG&E): 89 East Ave, Rochester, NY 14649-0001; internet www.rge.com; 657,000 customers; Pres. JAMES P. LAURITO.

Energy Telecommunications and Electrical Association (ENTELEC): 5005 West Royal Lane, Suite 190, Irving, TX 75063; tel. (888) 503-8700; fax (972) 915-6040; e-mail blaine@entelec.org; internet www.entelec.org; f. 1928 as the Petroleum Industry Electrical Asscn; changed name as above in 1978; 170 mems; Pres. GREG VAUGHN; Exec. Man. BLAINE SISKE.

Entergy Corpn: 639 Loyola Ave, New Orleans, LA 70161; tel. (504) 576-4000; fax (504) 576-4001; internet www.entergy.com; electricity production and distribution; Chair. and CEO J. WAYNE LEONARD; Pres. and COO RICHARD SMITH.

E.ON US: 220 West Main St, Louisville, KY 40202; tel. (502) 589-1444; internet www.eon-us.com; f. 1990 as LG&E Energy Corpn; changed name as above in 2005; wholly owned subsidiary of E.ON AG (Germany); Chair., Pres. and CEO VICTOR A. STAFFIERI.

Kentucky Utilities Co (KU): 1 Quality St, Lexington, KY 40507; internet www.eon-us.com/ku; f. 1912; conventional thermal generation; 485,253 customers (2008).

Louisville Gas and Electric Co (LG&E): 220 West Main St, Louisville, KY 40202; internet www.eon-us.com/lge; f. 1913; conventional thermal generation; 384,139 electricity customers, 312,146 gas customers (2008).

Exelon Corpn: 10 South Dearborn St, 48th Floor, Chicago, IL 60603; POB 805398, Chicago, IL 60680-5398; tel. (800) 483-3220; internet www.exeloncorp.com; Pres., Chair. and CEO JOHN W. ROWE.

Commonwealth Edison (ComEd): POB 805379 Chicago, IL 60680-5379; tel. (800) 334-7661; internet www.exeloncorp.com/ourcompanies/comed; Chair. and CEO FRANK M. CLARK.

PECO Energy: 2301 Market St, POB 8699, Philadelphia, PA 19101; tel. (800) 494-4000; internet www.exeloncorp.com/ourcompanies/peco; Pres. and CEO DENIS P. O'BRIEN.

FirstEnergy Corpn: 76 South Main St, Akron, OH 44308-1890; tel. (330) 384-5798; tel. (330) 761-4204; internet www.firstenergycorp.com; f. 1997 by merger of the Ohio Edison Co (f. 1930) and Centerior Energy Corpn (f. 1986); merged with GPU, Inc (f. 1996) in 2001; 4.5m. customers; Pres. and CEO ANTHONY J. ALEXANDER.

Comprises seven operating cos:

Cleveland Electric Illuminating Co (The Illuminating Company): Brecksville, OH; 741,000 customers.

Jersey Central Power and Light (JCP&L): Morristown, NJ; 1m. customers.

Metropolitan Edison (Met-Ed): Reading, PA; 495,000 customers.

Ohio Edison: 76 Main St South, Akron, OH 44308; tel. (216) 384-5100; conventional thermal generation; 1m. customers.

Pennsylvania Electric Co (Penelec): Erie, PA; 580,000 customers.

Pennsylvania Power Co: 1 East Washington St, POB 891, New Castle, PA 16103; tel. (742) 652-5531; fax (742) 656-5433; fmrly Pennsylvania Power Co; 138,000 customers.

Toledo Edison: 300 Madison Ave, Toledo, OH 43652; tel. (419) 259-5000; conventional thermal and nuclear generation; 303,000 customers.

FPL Group, Inc: 700 Universe Blvd, POB 14000, Juno Beach, FL 33408-0420; tel. (305) 442-8770; internet www.fplgroup.com; Chair. and CEO LEWIS HAY, III; Pres. and COO JAMES L. ROBO.

Florida Power and Light Co, Inc: POB 025576, Miami, FL 33102; POB 025576, Miami, FL 33102; tel. (305) 442-8770; internet www.fpl.com; conventional thermal and nuclear generation; 4.3m. customers; Pres. ARMANDO J. OLIVERA.

FPL Energy: 700 Universe Blvd, POB 14000, Juno Beach, FL 33408-0420; tel. (561) 691-7171; internet www.fplenergy.com; generation from renewable sources; Pres. F. MITCHELL DAVIDSON.

GE Energy: 4200 Wildwood Pkwy, Atlanta, GA 30339; tel. (678) 844-6948; e-mail dennis1.murphy@ge.com; internet www.gepower.com; Pres. and CEO JOHN KRENICKI, Jr.

Hawaiian Electric Co, Inc (HECO): 900 Richards St, Honolulu, HI 96813; tel. (808) 543-7972; internet www.heco.com; subsidiary of Hawaiian Electric Industries, Inc; conventional thermal generation; Chair. CONSTANCE H. LAU; Pres. and CEO T. MICHAEL MAY.

Hoosier Energy: 7398 North State Rd 37, POB 908, Bloomington, IN 47404-0908; tel. (812) 876-2021; fax (812) 876-3476; e-mail webmaster@hepn.com; internet www.hepn.com; generation and transmission co-operative; Pres. and CEO J. STEVEN SMITH; Chair. EUGENE ROBERTS.

Idaho Power Co: 1221 Idaho St West, Boise, ID 83702; tel. (208) 388-2200; internet www.idahopower.com; f. 1989; subsidiary of IDACORP, Inc; hydro and thermal generation; 481,651 customers (2007); Pres. and CEO J. LAMONT KEEN.

Indianapolis Power and Light Co: 1 Monument Circle, POB 1595, Indianapolis, IN 46206; tel. (317) 261-8222; e-mail customerservices@aes.com; internet www.iplpower.com; f. 1926; conventional thermal generation; acquired by AES in 2001; Pres. and CEO ANN MURTLOW.

Integrys Energy Group: POB 19001, Green Bay, WI 54307-9001; tel. (800) 450-7260; internet www.wisconsinpublicservice.com; fmrly Wisconsin Public Service Corpn; adopted current name in 2007; conventional thermal, hydro and nuclear generation; distributes electricity and gas; Chair., Pres. and CEO LARRY L. WEYERS.

Long Island Power Authority (LIPA): 333 Earle Ovington Blvd, Uniondale, NY 11553; tel. (516) 222-3417; internet www.lipower.org; corporate municipal electric service, acquired Long Island Lighting Co in 1998; Pres. and CEO KEVIN S. LAW; Chair. JAMES L. LAROCCA.

Los Angeles Department of Water and Power: 111 North Hope St, Room 1555-H, 15th Floor, POB 51111, Los Angeles, CA 90051-0100; tel. (213) 481-5411; e-mail ccenter@ladwp.com; internet www.ladwp.com; municipal water and electric service; Gen. Man. and CEO H. DAVID NAHAI; Pres. NICK PATSAOURAS.

MidAmerican Energy Co: 666 Grand Ave, POB 657, Des Moines, IA 50306-0657; tel. (515) 281-2785; fax (515) 2424236; e-mail info@midamerican.com; internet www.midamericanenergy.com; 1.4m. customers (2008); Chair. and CEO DAVID L. SOKOL; Pres. GREGORY E. ABEL.

PacifiCorp: 825 Multnomah St, Suite 2000, NE, Portland, OR 97232; tel. (503) 813-5000; e-mail customerservice@pacificorp.com; internet www.pacificorp.com; 2 operating cos, Pacific Power and Rocky Mountain Power; conventional thermal and hydro generation; 1.7m customers (2008); acquired by MidAmerican Energy Co in 2006; Chair. and CEO GREGORY E. ABEL; Pres. ROB LASICH.

Minnkota Power Cooperative, Inc: 1822 Mill Rd, POB 13200, Grand Forks, ND 58208-3200; tel. (701) 795-4000; fax (701) 795-4214; e-mail minnkota@minnkota.com; internet www.minnkota.com; regional generation and transmission co-operative; Pres. and CEO DAVID LOER.

National Grid: 25 Research Dr., Westborough, MA 01582; tel. (508) 389-2000; internet www.nationalgridus.com; wholly owned subsidiary of National Grid PLC (United Kingdom); distributes electricity; Chair. Sir JOHN PARKER; CEO STEVE HOLLIDAY.

National Rural Electric Co-operative Association: 4301 Wilson Blvd, Arlington, VA 22203; tel. (703) 907-5500; e-mail patrick.lavigne@nreca.coop; internet www.nreca.org; f. 1942; operates rural electric co-operative systems and public power distribution in 47 states; 900 mems; CEO GLENN ENGLISH.

New York Power Authority: 123 Main St, White Plains, NY 10601-3170; tel. (914) 681-6200; e-mail info@nypa.gov; internet www.nypa.gov; Chair. FRANK S. MCCULLOUGH, Jr; Pres. and CEO ROGER B. KELLEY.

NiSource, Inc: 801 East 86th Ave, Merrillville, IN 46410; tel. (219) 647-5990; e-mail questions@nisource.com; internet www.nisource.com; distributes electricity, natural gas and water; Chair. IAN M. ROLLAND; Pres. and CEO ROBERT C. SKAGGS, Jr

Northern Indiana Public Service Co (NIPSCO): 801 East 86th Ave, Merrillville, IN 46410; tel. (800) 464-7726; e-mail nipscoquestions@nisource.com; internet www.nipsco.nisource

.com; conventional thermal and hydro generation; distributes electricity and gas; Pres. MARK MAASSEL.

Northern Utilities, Inc: 801 East 86th Ave, Merillville, IN 46410; tel. (207) 647-5128; internet www.northernutilities.com; Pres. STEPHEN H. BRYANT.

Northeast Utilities System: POB 270, Hartford, CT 06141-0270; tel. (800) 286-5000; internet www.nu.com; f. 1966; Pres., Chair. and CEO CHARLES W. SHIVERY.

Connecticut Light and Power Co, Inc: POB 270, Hartford, CT 06141-0270; tel. (860) 286-2000; internet www.cl-p.com; distributes electricity to 1.2m. customers; Pres. and COO RAYMOND P. NECCI.

Public Service Co of New Hampshire: POB 330, Manchester, NH 03105-0330; tel. (800) 662-7764; e-mail psnhreq@psnh.com; internet www.psnh.com; Pres. and COO GARY A. LONG.

Western Massachusetts Electric Co: 1 Federal St, STCC Technology Park, Bldg 111, Springfield, MA 01105; WMECO Customer Service Center, POB 2010, West Springfield, MA 01090-2010; tel. (413) 781-4300; fax (413) 787-9352; internet www.wmeco.com; f. 1942 following merger with the Turners Falls Power and Electric Co, United Electric Light Co and Pittsfield Electric Co; Pres. and COO RODNEY O. POWELL.

Yankee Gas: 107 Selden St, Berlin, CT 06037; tel. (800) 989-0900; e-mail customerservice@yankeegas.com; internet www.yankeegas.com; 196,000 customers; Pres. and COO RAYMOND P. NECCI.

Northern California Power Agency: 651 Commerce Dr., Roseville, CA 95678-6420; tel. (916) 781-3636; fax (916) 783-7693; internet www.ncpa.com; f. 1968; asscn of public power cos; conventional thermal, hydro and geothermal generation; 15 mems; Gen. Man. JAMES H. POPE.

NorthWestern Energy Corpn: 3010 West 69th St, Sioux Falls, SD 57108; tel. (605) 978-2900; internet www.northwesternenergy.com; f. 1923 as NorthWestern Public Service; name changed as above in 2002; distributes electricity and natural gas; Chair. Dr E. LINN DRAPER, Jr.

NRG Energy, Inc: 211 Carnegie Center, Princeton, NJ 08540-6213; tel. (609) 524-4500; fax (609) 524-4501; internet www.nrgenergy.com; f. 1989; wholesale power generation; Pres. and CEO DAVID CRANE.

NSTAR: 1 NSTAR Way, Westwood, MA 02090; tel. (781) 441-8338; e-mail customer_service@nstar.com; internet www.nstaronline.com; fmrly Boston Edison Co; conventional thermal and nuclear generation; 1.4m. customers; Pres., Chair. and CEO THOMAS J. MAY.

OG&E Electric Services: POB 24990, Oklahoma City, OK 73126-0040; tel. (405) 272-9741; e-mail custcaredept@oge.com; internet www.oge.com; conventional thermal generation; 735,000 customers; Pres., Chair. and CEO PETER B. DELANEY.

Pacific Gas and Electric Co: 1 Market St, San Francisco, CA 94105-1126; tel. (415) 267-7000; internet www.pge.com; conventional thermal, hydro and nuclear generation; distributes electricity and gas; Chair. PETER A. DARBEE; Pres. and CEO WILLIAM T. MORROW.

Pennsylvania Power and Light Corpn (PPL): 2 North Ninth St, Allentown, PA 18101-1179; tel. (610) 774-4124; fax (610) 774-5106; internet www.pplweb.com; conventional thermal, hydro and nuclear generation; Pres., Chair. and CEO JAMES H. MILLER.

Portland General Electric Co: 121 Salmon St, SW, POB 4438, Portland, OR 97204; tel. (503) 464-7458; fax (503) 464-2236; e-mail investors@pgn.com; internet www.portlandgeneral.com; conventional thermal, hydro and nuclear generation; Pres. and CEO PEGGY FOWLER.

Potomac Electric Power Co (PEPCO): 701 Ninth St, NW, Washington, DC 20068; tel. (202) 872-2000; e-mail rshainey@pepcoholdings.com; internet www.pepco.com; wholly owned subsidiary of Pepco Holdings, Inc; conventional thermal generation; Pres., Chair. and CEO DENNIS R. WRAASE.

Progress Energy, Inc: 410 South Wilmington St, Raleigh, NC 27601; tel. (919) 508-5400; internet www.progress-energy.com; electric power generation and distribution; 3m. customers in North Carolina, South Carolina and Florida; Chair., Pres. and CEO WILLIAM D. JOHNSON.

Public Service Co of New Mexico (PNM): POB 349, Albuquerque, NM 87103-0349; tel. (505) 241-2700; internet www.pnm.com; f. 1917 as Albuquerque Gas and Electric Co; conventional thermal and nuclear generation; distributes electricity and gas; Pres., Chair. and CEO JEFFREY E. STERBA.

Puget Sound Energy (PSE): 10885 Fourth St, NE, Bellevue, WA 98009-9734; tel. (425) 452-1234; e-mail customercare@pse.com; internet www.pse.com; f. 1997 by merger of the Puget Sound Power and Light Co and Washington Energy Co; distributes electricity and natural gas; Pres., Chair. and CEO STEPHEN P. REYNOLDS.

Reliant Energy, Inc: POB 3765, Houston, TX 77253-3765; tel. (713) 207-7777; fax (713) 488-5925; internet www.reliantenergy.com; Pres. and CEO MARK M. JACOBS.

San Diego Gas and Electric Co: 8326 Century Park, POB 129831, San Diego, CA 92112-9831; tel. (619) 696-2000; internet www.sdge.com; conventional thermal and nuclear generation; electricity and gas distribution; Pres. DEBRA L. REED.

Scana Corpn: Palmetto Center, 1426 Main St, Columbia, SC 29218; tel. (803) 217-9000; internet www.scana.com; conventional thermal generation; Pres., Chair. and CEO WILLIAM B. TIMMERMAN.

South Carolina Electric and Gas Co: 1426 Main St, Columbia, SC 29218; tel. (800) 251-7234; internet www.sceg.com; conventional thermal and nuclear generation; distributes electricity and gas; Pres. and COO KEVIN B. MARSH.

Southern Co: 30 Ivan Allen Jr Blvd, NW, Atlanta, GA 30308; tel. (404) 506-5000; internet www.southerncompany.com; conventional thermal generation; Pres., Chair. and CEO DAVID M. RADCLIFFE.

Alabama Power Co: 600 North 18th St, Birmingham, AL 35291; tel. (205) 257-2318; internet www.alabamapower.com; Pres. and CEO CHARLES D. MCCRARY.

Georgia Power Co: 241 Ralph McGill Blvd, NE, Atlanta, GA 30308; tel. (404) 506-6526; internet www.georgiapower.com; conventional thermal, hydro and nuclear generation; Pres. and CEO MICHAEL D. GARRETT.

Gulf Power Co: 1 Energy Pl., Pensacola, FL 32520; tel. (800) 225-5797; internet www.gulfpower.com; Pres. and CEO SUSAN N. STORY.

Mississippi Power Co: 2992 West Beach Blvd, Gulfport, MS 39501; tel. (228) 864-1211; internet www.mississipipower.com; Pres. and CEO ANTHONY J. TOPAZI.

Tampa Electric: POB 111, Tampa, FL 33601-0111; tel. (813) 228-1111; internet www.tampaelectric.com; f. 1899; subsidiary of Teco Energy; conventional thermal generation; Chair. and CEO SHERRILL W. HUDSON; Pres. CHARLES R. BLACK.

Trans-Elect, Inc: 4800 Montgomery Lane, Suite 940, Bethesda, MD 20814; tel. (240) 483-4179; fax (301) 652-5580; e-mail pmccoy@trans-elect.com; internet www.trans-elect.com; independent transmission co; Pres. PAUL D. MCCOY; CEO ROBERT L. MITCHELL.

TXU Corpn: Energy Plaza, 1601 Bryan St, Dallas, TX 75201; tel. (214) 812-4600; e-mail businessgroup@txu.com; internet www.txu.com; f. 1945 as Texas Utilities Co; changed name as above in 1999; conventional thermal and nuclear generation; distributes electricity; Chair. and CEO JIM BURKE.

Wisconsin Energy Corpn: 231 West Michigan St, Milwaukee, WI 53203; tel. (414) 221-2345; e-mail barry.mcnulty@we-energies.com; internet www.wisconsinenergy.com; conventional thermal, hydro and nuclear generation; distributes electricity and gas; Pres., Chair. and CEO GALE E. KLAPPA.

Xcel Energy: 414 Nicollet Mall, Minneapolis, MN 55401-1993; tel. (612) 330-5500; internet www.xcelenergy.com; conventional thermal, hydro and nuclear generation; distributes electricity and natural gas to 5.1m. customers; operations in 8 states; Pres., Chair. and CEO RICHARD C. KELLY.

OIL AND GAS ASSOCIATIONS

American Association of Petroleum Geologists (AAPG): see Industrial and Employers' Organizations—Petroleum and Fuel.

American Association of Professional Landmen (AAPL): see Industrial and Employers' Organizations—Petroleum and Fuel.

American Gas Association (AGA): 400 North Capitol St, NW, Suite 400, Washington, DC 20001; tel. (202) 824-7000; fax (202) 824-7115; e-mail ccussimanio@aga.org; internet www.aga.org; f. 1918; represents 197 local utility cos; Pres. and CEO DAVID N. PARKER.

American Petroleum Institute (API): see Industrial and Employers' Organizations—Petroleum and Fuel.

American Public Gas Association (APGA): 201 Massachusetts Ave, NE, Suite C-4, Washington, DC 20002; tel. (202) 464-2742; fax

(202) 464-0246; e-mail mhager@apga.org; internet www.apga.org; f. 1961; promotes efficiency among public gas systems; 650 mems; Pres. and CEO BERT KALISCH.

American Society of Gas Engineers (ASGE): 2805 Barranca Pkwy, Irvine, CA 92606; tel. (949) 733-4304; fax (949) 733-4320; e-mail asgecge@sbcglobal.net; internet www.asge-national.org; f. 1954; 550 mems; Pres. DANTE CANTAL; Exec. Dir JERRY MOORE.

Association of Desk and Derrick Clubs (ADDC): 5153 East 51st St, Suite 107, Tulsa, OK 74135; tel. (918) 622-1749; fax (918) 622-1675; e-mail adotulsa@swbell.net; internet www.addc.org; f. 1951; *c.* 2,500 mems in 61 clubs throughout USA and Canada; employees in the petroleum, energy and allied industries; Pres. SHERYL MINEAR.

Association of Diesel Specialists (ADS): see Industrial and Employers' Organizations—Petroleum and Fuel.

Association of Oil Pipe Lines (AOPL): 1808 Eye St, NW, Washington, DC 20006; tel. (202) 408-7970; fax (202) 280-1949; e-mail rdobre@aopl.org; internet www.aopl.org; f. 1947; 49 mems; Pres. and CEO SHIRLEY J. NEFF.

Colorado Oil and Gas Association: 1660 Lincoln St, Suite 2710, Denver, CO 80264; tel. (303) 861-0362; fax (303) 861-0373; e-mail info@coga.org; internet www.coga.org; f. 1984; Pres. MEG COLLINS; Chair. JAY STILL.

Distribution Contractors Association (DCA): 101 Renner Rd West, Suite 250, Richardson, TX 75082-2024; tel. (972) 680-0261; fax (972) 680-0461; e-mail dca@dca-online.org; internet www.dca-online.org; f. 1961; 110 mems; Pres. ANTHONY R. DEUSENBERRY; Exec. Vice-Pres. DENNIS J. KENNEDY.

Gas Processors Association (GPA): 6526 East 60th St, Tulsa, OK 74145; tel. (918) 493-3872; fax (918) 493-3875; e-mail gpa@gasprocessors.com; internet www.gasprocessors.org; f. 1921; 123 mems; Pres. BOB DUNN; Exec. Dir MARK SUTTON.

Gas Processors Suppliers Association (GPSA): 6526 East 60th St, Tulsa, OK 74145; tel. (918) 493-3872; fax (918) 493-3875; e-mail msutton@gasprocessors.com; internet gpsa.gasprocessors.com; f. 1927 as Natural Gasoline Supply Men's Asscn; present name adopted in 1974; 350 mems; Pres. CHUCK DEWEES; Sec. MARK SUTTON.

Gas Technology Institute: 1700 South Mount Prospect Rd, Des Plaines, IL 60018; tel. (847) 768-0500; fax (847) 768-0501; e-mail businessdevelopmentinfo@gastechnology.org; internet www.gastechnology.org; f. 1976; fmrly Gas Research Institute; 175 mems; Chair. and CEO MARY JANE MCCARTNEY.

Illinois Oil and Gas Association (IOGA): POB 788, Mount Vernon, IL 62864; tel. (618) 242-2857; fax (618) 242-3418; e-mail diane@ioga.com; internet www.ioga.com; Pres. BRAD GESELL; Exec. Vice-Pres. BRAD RICHARDS.

Independent Petroleum Association of America (IPAA): see Industrial and Employers' Organizations—Petroleum and Fuel.

Interstate Natural Gas Association of America (INGAA): 10 G St, NE, Suite 700, Washington, DC 20002; tel. (202) 216-5900; fax (202) 216-0870; e-mail dsanta@ingaa.org; internet www.ingaa.org; f. 1944; transporters of natural gas; 29 mems; Pres. DONALD F. SANTA, Jr.

Liaison Committee of Co-operating Oil and Gas Associations: 105 South Bdwy, Suite 500, Wichita, KS 67202; tel. (316) 263-7297; fax (316) 263-3021; f. 1957; 25 mem. orgs; Chair. LARRY O. HULSEY.

Louisiana Mid-Continent Oil and Gas Association: 801 North Blvd, Suite 201, Baton Rouge, LA 70802; tel. (225) 387-3205; fax (225) 344-5502; e-mail info@lmoga.com; internet www.lmoga.com; Pres. CHRIS JOHN.

Louisiana Oil and Gas Association (LOGA): POB 4069, Baton Rouge, LA 70821-4069; tel. (800) 443-1433; e-mail cece@loga.la; internet www.loga.la; f. 1992; Chair. RAYMOND J. LASSEIGNE; Pres. DON G. BRIGGS.

Mid-Continent Oil and Gas Association of Oklahoma: 6701 North Bdwy, Suite 300, Oklahoma City, OK 73116; tel. (405) 843-5741; internet www.okmoga.com; f. 1919; Pres. MICHAEL H. BERNARD.

National Petrochemical and Refiners Association (NPRA): see Industrial and Employers' Organizations—Petroleum and Fuel.

National Propane Gas Association (NPGA): 1150 17th St, Suite 310, NW, Washington, DC 20036-4623; tel. (202) 466-7200; fax (202) 466-7205; e-mail tdavis@npga.org; internet www.npga.org; f. 1931; fmrly National LP-Gas Asscn; 3,500 mems; Chair. MALCOLM W. BARRETT; Pres. and CEO RICHARD R. ROLDAN.

Natural Gas Supply Association (NGSA): see Industrial and Employers' Organizations—Petroleum and Fuel.

Ohio Oil and Gas Association (OOGA): 1718 Columbus Rd, SW, POB 535, Granville, OH 43023-0535; tel. (740) 587-0444; fax (740) 587-0446; e-mail info@ooga.org; internet www.ooga.org; f. 1947; Pres. JAMES R. SMAIL; Exec. Vice-Pres. THOMAS E. STEWART.

Petroleum Marketers Association of America (PMAA): see Industrial and Employers' Organizations—Petroleum and Fuel.

Society of Independent Gasoline Marketers of America (SIGMA): 11495 Sunset Hills Rd, Suite 215, Reston, VA 20190-5213; tel. (703) 709-7000; fax (703) 709-7007; e-mail sigma@sigma.org; internet www.sigma.org; f. 1958; *c.* 250 mems; Pres. PAUL D. REID; Exec. Vice-Pres. KENNETH A. DOYLE.

Tennessee Oil and Gas Association (TOGA): 750 Old Hickory Blvd, Suite 150–152, Brentwood, TN 37027; tel. (615) 371-6137; fax (615) 599-1806; e-mail bgoodwin@tennoil.com; internet www.tennoil.com; f. 1971; Pres. SCOTT GILBERT.

Texas Alliance of Energy Producers: 719 Scott Ave, Suite 930, Wichita Falls, TX 76301; tel. (940) 723-4131; fax (940) 723-4132; e-mail texasalliance@texasalliance.org; internet www.texasalliance.org; f. 2000 by merger of the North Texas Oil & Gas Asscn and the West Central Texas Oil & Gas Asscn; *c.* 3,000 mems; Chair. MARK METZLER; Pres. ALEX MILLS.

Texas Independent Producers and Royalty Owners Association (TIPRO): 919 Congress Ave, Suite 1000, Austin, TX 78701; tel. (512) 477-4452; fax (512) 476-8070; e-mail jnoble@tipro.org; internet www.tipro.org; f. 1946; *c.* 2,400 mems; independent oil and gas producers; royalty owners; Pres. WALTER G. TAD MAYFIELD; Exec. Vice-Pres. ADAM P. HAYNES.

Western States Petroleum Association (WSPA): see Industrial and Employers' Organizations—Petroleum and Fuel.

WATER

STATISTICS

Water Withdrawals, by Water Use and by State, 2000

(millions of gallons per day, unless otherwise indicated; fresh water only)

	Public supply	Irrigation	Industrial	Thermoelectric	Total*†
Alabama	834	43	833	8,190	9,990
Alaska	80	1	8	34	161
Arizona	1,080	5,400	20	100	6,720
Arkansas	421	7,910	134	2,180	10,900
California	6,120	30,500	188	352	38,400
Colorado	899	11,400	120	138	12,600
Connecticut	424	30	11	187	708
Delaware	95	44	59	366	582
District of Columbia	—	0	—	10	10
Florida	2,440	4,290	291	658	8,140
Georgia	1,250	1,140	622	3,250	6,410
Hawaii	250	364	15	—	640
Idaho	244	17,100	56	—	19,500
Illinois	1,760	154	391	11,300	13,700
Indiana	670	101	2,400	6,700	10,100
Iowa	383	22	237	2,540	3,360
Kansas	416	3,710	53	2,260	6,610
Kentucky	525	29	317	3,260	4,160
Louisiana	753	1,020	2,680	5,610	10,400
Maine	102	6	247	113	504
Maryland	824	42	66	379	1,430
Massachusetts	739	126	37	108	1,050
Michigan	1,140	201	698	7,710	10,000
Minnesota	500	227	154	2,270	3,870
Mississippi	359	1,410	242	362	2,810
Missouri	872	1,430	63	5,640	8,230
Montana	149	7,950	61	110	8,290
Nebraska	330	8,790	38	2,820	12,200
Nevada	629	2,110	10	37	2,810
New Hampshire	97	5	45	236	447
New Jersey	1,050	140	132	650	2,170
New Mexico	296	2,860	11	56	3,260
New York	2,570	36	297	4,040	7,080
North Carolina	945	287	293	7,850	9,730
North Dakota	64	145	18	902	1,140
Ohio	1,470	32	807	8,590	11,100
Oklahoma	675	718	26	146	1,760
Oregon	566	6,080	195	15	6,930
Pennsylvania	1,460	14	1,190	6,980	9,950
Rhode Island	119	3	4	2	138
South Carolina	566	267	565	5,710	7,170
South Dakota	93	373	5	5	528
Tennessee	890	22	842	9,040	10,800
Texas	4,230	8,630	1,450	9,820	24,800
Utah	638	3,860	43	62	4,760
Vermont	60	4	7	355	447
Virginia	720	26	470	3,850	5,200
Washington	1,020	3,040	577	519	5,270
West Virginia	190	0	968	3,950	5,150
Wisconsin	623	196	447	6,090	7,590
Wyoming	107	4,500	6	243	4,940
Total*	42,700	137,000	18,400	136,000	345,000

* Totals are rounded to three significant figures and may not be equal to the sum of component parts as a result.

† Also includes data for domestic, commercial, livestock and mining withdrawals.

Note: 'Withdrawal' signifies water physically withdrawn from a source. A dash represents zero, while 0 represents a quantity greater than zero but less than 500,000 gallons.

Source: US Geological Survey.

ORGANIZATIONS AND CO-ORDINATING BODIES

American Water Resources Association (AWRA): 4 West Federal St, POB 1626, Middleburg, VA 20118-1626; tel. (540) 687-8390; fax (540) 687-8395; e-mail info@awra.org; internet www.awra.org; f. 1964; 3,000 mems; Pres. JANE ROWAN; Pres.-elect JERRY SEHLKE.

American Water Works Association: 6666 West Quincy Ave, Denver, CO 80235-3098; tel. (303) 794-7711; fax (303) 347-0804; e-mail custsvc@awwa.org; internet www.awwa.org; f. 1881; 57,000 mems; Pres. MICHAEL J. LEONARD; Exec. Dir GARY J. ZIMMERMAN.

American Water Works Association Research Foundation (AwwaRF): 6666 West Quincy Ave, Denver, CO 80235-3098; tel. (303) 347-6100; fax (303) 730-0851; e-mail info@awwarf.org; internet www.awwarf.org; f. 1966; Chair. DAVID RAGER.

Association of Metropolitan Water Agencies: 1620 I St, NW, Suite 500, Washington, DC 20006; tel. (202) 331-2820; fax (202) 785-1845; e-mail vandehei@amwa.net; internet www.amwa.net; f. 1981; 63 mems; Pres. BRIAN RAMALEY; Exec. Dir DIANE VANDE HEI.

Association of State and Interstate Water Pollution Control Administrators (ASIWPCA): 1221 Connecticut Ave, NW, 2nd Floor, Washington, DC 20036; tel. (202) 756-0600; fax (202) 756-0605; e-mail egilinsky@deg.virginia.gov; internet www.asiwpca.org; f. 1961; co-ordinates state, interstate and federal policy; Pres. ELLEN GILINSKY.

Association of State Drinking Water Administrators (ASDWA): 1025 Connecticut Ave, NW, Suite 903, Washington, DC 20036; tel. (202) 812-9505; e-mail info@asdwa.org; internet www.asdwa.org; f. 1984; Pres. LANCE NEILSEN; Exec. Dir JAMES TAFT.

Eastern Snow Conference (ESC): POB 339, Monmouth, ME 04259; e-mail djcowing@aol.com; internet www.easternsnow.org; joint Canadian-US org., researches uses of snow and ice; Sec.-Treas MILES ECCLESTONE (Canada), DERRILL COWLING (USA).

Groundwater Management Districts Association (GMDA): POB 905, Colby, KS 67701-0905; tel. (913) 462-3915; fax (913) 462-2693; e-mail dean@ymd.org; internet www.gmdausa.org; f. 1974; a unit of the NWRA; provides forum for exchange of information; Pres. DEAN PENNINGTON; Sec.-Treas. WAYNE BOSSERT.

International Boundary and Water Commission, US Section (IBWC): 4171 North Mesa, Suite C-100, El Paso, TX 79902-1441; tel. (915) 832-4157; internet www.ibwc.state.gov; f. 1889; manages boundary and water issues between the USA and Mexico; Commr (US Section) (vacant).

Interstate Council on Water Policy (ICWP): 51 Monroe St, Suite PE-08A, Rockville, MD 20850; tel. (703) 622-6660; fax (703) 243-7383; e-mail icwp2005@yahoo.com; internet www.icwp.org; f. 1959; fmrly Interstate Conference on Water Policy; officials with responsibility for matters concerning water quantity and quality; 41 mems; Exec. Dir PETER EVANS.

National Association of Water Companies: 1725 K St, NW, Suite 200, Washington, DC 20006; tel. (202) 833-8383; fax (202) 331-7442; e-mail peter@nawc.com; internet www.nawc.org; f. 1895; privately and commercially owned water cos; 161 mems; Pres. DIAN C. TAYLOR; Exec. Dir PETER L. COOK.

National Ground Water Association (NGWA): 601 Dempsey Rd, Westville, OH 43081-8978; tel. (614) 898-7791; fax (614) 898-7786; e-mail ngwa@ngwa.org; internet www.ngwa.org; f. 1948; fmrly National Water Well Asscn; professional education and industry promotion; 14,000 mems world-wide; Exec. Dir KEVIN B. MCCRAY.

National Rural Water Association: 2915 South 13th St, Duncan, OK 73533; tel. (580) 252-0629; fax (580) 255-4476; e-mail info@nrwa.org; internet www.nrwa.org; Pres. RODNEY TART; Exec. Man. ROB JOHNSON.

National Water Resources Association (NWRA): 3800 North Fairfax Dr., Suite 4, Arlington, VA 22203; tel. (703) 524-1544; fax (703) 524-1548; e-mail nwra@nwra.org; internet www.nwra.org; f. 1932; 5,000 mems; Pres. W. E. WEST, Jr.

National Waterways Conference, Inc (NWC): 4650 Washington Blvd, POB 608, Arlington, VA 22201; tel. (703) 243-4090; fax (866) 371-1390; e-mail amy@waterways.org; internet www.waterways.org; f. 1960; advocates use of waterways; Pres. AMY W. LARSON.

New England Interstate Water Pollution Control Commission (NEIWPCC): Boott Mills South, 116 John St, Lowell, MA 01852; tel. (978) 323-7929; fax (978) 323-7919; e-mail mail@neiwpcc.org; internet www.neiwpcc.org; f. 1947; covers Connecticut, Maine, Massachusetts, New Hampshire, New York, Rhode Island and Vermont; Chair. ALICIA GOOD.

Office of Water: Environmental Protection Agency, 1200 Pennsylvania Ave, NW, Washington, DC 20460; e-mail ow-general@epa.gov; internet www.epa.gov/water; implements federal water-related legislation; Asst. Admin. BENJAMIN H. GRUMBLES.

Soil and Water Conservation Society (SWCS): 945 Southwest Ankeny Rd, Ankeny, IA 50023-9723; tel. (515) 289-2331; fax (515) 289-1227; e-mail swcs@swcs.org; internet www.swcs.org; f. 1943; promotes sustainable management of natural resources; publs Journal of Soil and Water Conservation; over 5,000 mems world-wide; Pres. PEGGIE JAMES; Exec. Dir (vacant).

Tennessee Valley Authority: see Federal Executive—Independent Agencies.

United States Society on Dams (USSD): 1616 17th St, Suite 483, Denver, CO 80202; tel. (303) 628-5430; fax (303) 628-5431; e-mail stephens@ussdams.org; internet www.ussdams.org; f. 1928; mem. of the Int. Comm. on Large Dams; 1,200 mems; Pres. KENNETH STEELE; Exec. Dir LARRY D. STEPHENS.

Universities Council on Water Resources (UCOWR): 1000 Faner Dr., Rm 4543, Southern Illinois University, Carbondale, IL 62901-4526; tel. (618) 536-7571; fax (618) 453-2671; e-mail ucowr@siu.edu; internet www.ucowr.siu.edu; f. 1964; 90 mem. universities; Pres. JOHN C. TRACY.

US Committee on Irrigation and Drainage (USCID): 1616 17th St, Suite 483, Denver, CO 80202; tel. (303) 628-5430; fax (303) 628-5431; e-mail stephens@uscid.org; internet www.uscid.org; f. 1952; mem. of the Int. Comm. on Irrigation and Drainage; 700 mems; Pres. MARK SVENDSEN; Sec. JAMES E. AYARS.

Water Environment Federation (WEF): 601 Wythe St, Alexandria, VA, 22314-1994; tel. (703) 684-2400; fax (703) 684-2492; e-mail csc@wef.org; internet www.wef.org; f. 1928; technical and educational org; 81 mem. asscns world-wide; Pres. ADAM J. ZABINSKI.

Water Quality Association (WQA): 4151 Naperville Rd, Lisle, IL 60532-1088; tel. (630) 505-0160; fax (630) 505-9637; e-mail info@wqa.org; internet www.wqa.org; f. 1974; int. trade asscn representing individuals or firms involved in the manufacture or distribution of water treatment equipment and services; 2,400 mems; Exec. Dir PETER J. CENSKY.

Water Quality Research Foundation (WQRF): 4151 Naperville Rd, Lisle, IL 60532-3696; tel. (630) 505-0160; fax (630) 505-9637; e-mail info@wqa.org; internet www.wqa.org; f. 1950; education and research; fmrly Water Quality Research Council; 2,800 mems; Exec. Sec. JOSEPH F. HARRISON.

Western Snow Conference (WSC): POB 810, Soda Springs, CA 95728; tel. (530) 426-0318; e-mail ron.abramovich@is.usda.gov; internet www.westernsnowconference.org; f. 1939; researches the use of snow as source of water for irrigation and hydroelectric power; 900 mems; Chair., North Continental Cttee RON ABRAMOVICH.

Western States Water Council (WSWC): 942 East North Union Ave, Suite A-201, Midvale, UT 84047-1764; tel. (801) 561-5300; fax (801) 255-9642; e-mail credding@wswc.state.ut.us; internet www.westgov.org/wswc; f. 1965; co-ordinates water policy in 18 states; Exec. Dir CRAIG BELL.

MAJOR WATER COMPANIES

American States Water Co: 630 East Foothill Blvd, San Dimas, CA 91773; tel. (909) 394-3600; fax (909) 394-1382; e-mail customerservice@aswater.com; internet www.aswater.com; *c.* 267,000 customers in California and Arizona; Pres. and CEO FLOYD E. WICKS; Chair. LLOYD E. ROSS.

American Water: 1025 Laurel Oak Rd, POB 1770, Voorhees, NJ 08043-3508; tel. (856) 346-8200; fax (856) 346-8360; e-mail aw.investorrelations@amwater.com; internet www.amwater.com; f. 1886; became part of RWE Group (Germany) in 2003; water supply, sewerage systems, management services; 7,000 employees; 15.6m. customers; Pres. and CEO DONALD L. CORRELL.

Aqua America, Inc: 762 West Lancaster Ave, Bryn Mawr, PA 19010; tel. (610) 525-1400; internet www.aquaamerica.com; 1,600 employees; *c.* 2.8m. customers in 13 states; Chair., Pres. and CEO NICHOLAS DEBENEDICTIS.

California Water Service Group (Cal Water): 1720 North First St, San Jose, CA 95112-4598; tel. (408) 367-8200; internet www.calwatergroup.com; f. 1997 as holding co; 5 subsidiary cos operating in 4 states: California Water Service Co (f. 1926); Washington Water Service Co (f. 1999); New Mexico Water Service Co (f. 2000); Hawaii Water Service Co (f. 2003); and CWS Utility Services; over 470,000 customers; Chair. ROBERT W. FOY; Pres. and CEO PETER C. NELSON.

Southwest Water Company: 1 Wilshire Bldg, 624 South Grand Ave, Suite 2900, Los Angeles, CA 90017; tel. (213) 929-1800; fax (213) 929-1888; e-mail swwc@swwc.com; internet www.southwestwater.com; over 2m. customers in 10 states; Chair. and CEO MARK A. SWATEK.

United Water: 200 Old Hook Rd, Harrington Park, NJ 07640; tel. (201) 767-9300; e-mail lisa.boyd-carlino@unitedwater.com; internet www.unitedwater.com; f. 1869; wholly owned subsidiary of Suez Group (France); 7m. customers in 18 states; COO BOB IACULLO.

Veolia Water North America: 14950 Heathrow Forest Pkwy, Suite 200, Houston, TX 77032; tel. (281) 449-1500; e-mail general.information@veoliawaterna.com; internet www.veoliawaterna.com; wholly owned subsidiary of Veolia Environnement; 80m. customers; Pres. and CEO J. JOSEPH BURGESS.

TRANSPORT

CO-ORDINATING BODIES AND TRANSPORT ASSOCIATIONS

Advanced Transit Association (ATRA): e-mail membership@advancedtransit.org; internet www.advancedtransit.org; f. 1976; 250 mems; Chair. JERAL POSKEY; Pres. BOB DUNNING.

Amalgamated Transit Union: see Industry—Trade Unions.

American Moving and Storage Association: 1611 Duke St, Alexandria, VA 22314; tel. (703) 683-7410; fax (703) 683-7527; e-mail info@moving.org; internet www.promover.org; f. 1936; incorporates Household Goods Carriers' Bureau; companies transporting household goods, office equipment and high-value products; 3,200 mems; Pres. and CEO LINDA BAUER DARR.

American Public Transportation Association (APTA): see Industry—Industrial and Employers' Organizations.

American Society of Transportation and Logistics: 1331 H St, Suite 500, Washington, DC 20005; tel. (202) 580-7270; fax (202) 962-3939; e-mail info@astl.org; internet www.astl.org; f. 1946; over 1,000 mems; Chair. MICHAEL A. REGAN; Exec. Dir LAURIE DENHAM.

National Industrial Transportation League: 1700 North Moore St, Suite 1900, Arlington, VA 22209-1904; tel. (703) 524-5011; fax (703) 524-5017; e-mail info@nitl.org; internet www.nitl.org; f. 1907; 1,400 mems; Chair. CURT WARFEL; Vice-Chair. MARK MALESKI.

American Traffic Safety Services Association: 15 Riverside Pkwy, Suite 100, Fredericksburg, VA 22406-1022; tel. (540) 368-1701; fax (540) 368-1717; e-mail peterspeer@filtrona.com; internet www.atssa.com; f. 1969; over 1,600 mems; Chair. HENRY ROSS.

Association for Commuter Transportation: 1444 I St, NW, Suite 700, Washington, DC 20005; tel. (202) 712–9030; e-mail info@actweb.org; internet www.actweb.org; f. 1976; 770 mems; Pres. JON MARTZ; Exec. Dir MARK WRIGHT.

Bureau of Explosives: 55500 DOT Rd, Pueblo, CO 81001; tel. (719) 584-1749; fax (719) 585-1895; e-mail boe@aar.com; internet boe.aar.com; f. 1907; established by the Asscn of American Railroads to assist all carriers, manufacturers and producers operating under the US Dept of Transportation's hazardous materials regulations; 189 mems; Field Operations Dir ARMAND CICCARELLI.

Center for Transportation Research (CTR): University of Texas at Austin, 3208 Red River, Suite 200, Austin, TX 78705; tel. (512) 232-3100; fax (512) 232-3151; e-mail ctrlib@uts.cc.utexas.edu; internet www.utexas.edu/research/ctr; f. 1963 as Center for Highway Research; 750 mems; Dir Dr RANDY B. MACHEMEHL.

Council on the Safe Transportation of Hazardous Articles (COSTHA): 7803 Hill House Court, Fairfax Station, VA 22039; tel. (703) 451-4031; fax (703) 451-4207; e-mail mail@costha.com; internet www.costha.com; f. 1972; federation of shipper trade asscns, traffic conferences and associated cos; 194 mems; Admin. LARA MEHR CURRIE; Pres. WILLIAM DUFF.

Federal Transit Administration: East Bldg, 1200 New Jersey Ave, SE, Washington, DC 20590; tel. (202) 366-4043; e-mail fta.adaassistance@dot.gov; internet www.fta.dot.gov; Admin. JAMES S. SIMPSON.

National Business Travel Association: 110 North Royal St, 4th Floor, Alexandria, VA 22314; tel. (703) 684-0836; fax (703) 684-0263; e-mail info@nbta.org; internet www.nbta.org; f. 1968; corporate travel managers concerned with promoting the interests of the business traveller; 4,000 mems; Exec. Dir and COO BILL CONNORS; Pres. and CEO KEVIN MAGUIRE.

National Defense Transportation Association: 50 South Pickett St, Suite 220, Alexandria, VA 22304-7296; tel. (703) 751-5011; fax (703) 823-8761; e-mail info@ndtahq.com; internet www.ndtahq.com; f. 1944; military, govt and commercial transportation professionals; 8,000 mems, 200 corporate mems; Chair. and CEO RAYMOND P. EBELING.

National Freight Transportation Association: POB 1321, Exton, PA 19341; tel. (610) 363-7747; fax (610) 363-2971; e-mail nfta2000@aol.com; internet www.nftahq.org; f. 1905; 400 mems; Pres. DAVID GARIN; Exec. Dir G. P. TURNER.

National Highway Traffic Safety Administration (NHTSA): see Government—Selected Federal Agencies.

National Shippers Strategic Transportation Council (NASSTRAC): 9382 Oak Ave, Waconia, MN 55387; tel. (952) 442-8850; fax (952) 442-3941; e-mail brian2008@nasstrac.org; internet www.nasstrac.org; f. 1952; protects the interests of cos making small shipments by rail, motor or air; 300 mems; Chair. GAIL RUTKOWSKI; Pres. ERIC MORLEY.

National Transportation Safety Board: 490 L'Enfant Plaza, SW, Washington, DC 20594; tel. (202) 314-6000; internet www.ntsb.gov; f. 1967; seeks to ensure that all types of transportation in the USA are conducted safely; carries out studies and accident investigations; Chair. MARK V. ROSENKER (acting).

SAFE Association: POB 130, Creswell, OR 97426; tel. (541) 895-3012; fax (541) 895-3014; e-mail safe@peak.org; internet www.safeassociation.com; f. 1956; designers, engineers, manufacturers and users of safety and survival equipment; 10 regional groups; Pres. Dr WILLIAM B. ALBERY.

Surface Transportation Board: Mercury Bldg, 1925 K St, NW, Washington, DC 20423-0001; tel. (202) 245-0245; fax (202) 565-9016; internet www.stb.dot.gov; f. 1995 to succeed Interstate Commerce Commission; exercises regulatory authority over domestic surface common carriers; jurisdiction extends over rail, inland waterways and motorized traffic; Chair. CHARLES D. NOTTINGHAM.

Transport Workers' Union of America: see Industry—Trade Unions.

Transportation Clubs International: POB 2223, Ocean Shores, WA 98569; tel. (877) 858-8627; e-mail dtam@transportationclubsinternational.com; internet www.transportationclubsinternational.com; f. 1921; personnel in the traffic and transportation fields; more than 70 affiliated clubs, cos and individuals in the USA, Canada and Mexico; Chair. DENNIS TAM; Pres. MACK LEONARD.

Transportation Communications International Union (TCU): see Industry—Trade Unions.

Transportation Security Administration (TSA): 601 South 12th St, Arlington, VA 22202-4220; tel. (866) 289-9673; e-mail tsa-contactcenter@dhs.gov; internet www.tsa.gov; f. 2001 to ensure the security of the country's transport system against possible terrorist attacks; 50,000 employees; Admin. KIP HAWLEY.

United Transportation Union: see Industry—Trade Unions.

RAILWAYS

Summary

(traffic on class I railroads only, unless otherwise indicated)

	2003	2004	2005
Length of railroad ('000 miles)*	117	123	121
Freight services:			
revenue tons carried (million)	2,240	2,398	2,448
revenue ton-miles ('000 million)	1,551	1,663	1,696
freight revenue ($ million)	35,413	39,131	44,457
Passenger services:†			
revenue passengers carried ('000)	24,595	25,215	25,076
revenue passenger-miles (million)	5,680	5,511	5,381
passenger revenue ($ million)	1,421.1	1,432.6	1,461.7

* Length of cleared railroad line (excludes yard tracks, sidings and parallel lines). Includes estimate for class II and III railroads.
† AMTRAK passenger traffic only.
Source: Association of American Railroads, Washington, DC.

Directory

REGULATORY BODY

Federal Railroad Administration: Dept of Transportation, 1200 New Jersey Ave, SE, Washington, DC 20005; tel. (202) 493-6000; fax (202) 493-6013; e-mail webmaster@fra.dot.gov; internet www.fra.dot.gov; f. 1966; part of the Dept of Transportation; formulates federal railway policies and administers and enforces safety regulations; Admin. JOSEPH H. BOARDMAN.

PRINCIPAL RAILWAYS

Alaska Railroad Corpn: 327 West Ship Creek Ave, Anchorage, AK 99510; tel. (907) 265-2695; fax (907) 265-2312; e-mail thompsont@akrr.com; internet www.akrr.com; f. 1912; independent corpn owned by the State of Alaska; year-round freight service and summer passenger service; operates 845 km of track; Pres. and CEO PATRICK GAMBLE.

Amtrak (National Railroad Passenger Corpn): 60 Massachusetts Ave, NE, Washington, DC 20002; tel. (202) 906-3860; fax (202) 906-3306; internet www.amtrak.com; f. 1970; govt-funded private corpn operating inter-city passenger services over 33,796 track-km in 46 states; Chair. DONNA MCLEAN; Pres. and CEO ALEXANDER KUMMANT.

BNSF Railway: 2650 Lou Menk Dr., Fort Worth, TX 76131-2830; tel. (913) 551-4479; fax (913) 551-4285; e-mail steven.forsberg@bnsf.com; internet www.bnsf.com; fmrly Burlington Northern Santa Fe Corpn; freight services; 51,498 track-km; Pres., Chair. and CEO MATTHEW K. ROSE.

Consolidated Rail Corpn (Conrail): 2001 Market St, Philadelphia, PA 19103; tel. (215) 209-2000; e-mail info@conrail.com; internet www.conrail.com; f. 1976 by fed. govt merger of six bankrupt freight carriers; jtly owned by CSX (42%) and Norfolk Southern (58%); switching and terminal railroad operating in three locations: Northern New Jersey, Southern New Jersey/Philadelphia, and Detroit, MI; Pres. and COO RONALD L. BATORY.

CSX Transportation, Inc (Rail Transport): 500 Water St, Jacksonville, FL 32202; tel. (904) 359-3100; internet www.csx.com; f. 1980 by merger; operates 34,371 km of track (2005); Pres. and CEO MICHAEL J. WARD.

Florida East Coast Railway Co (FEC): 7411 Fullerton St, Suite 300, Jacksonville, FL 32256; tel. (904) 538-6128; fax (904) 256-0458; e-mail trballas@feci.com; internet www.fecrwy.com; f. 1895; 565 track-km; Chair. ADOLFO HENRIQUES; Pres. JOHN GILES.

Kansas City Southern Railway Co: 427 West 12th St, Kansas City, MO 64105; POB 219335, Kansas City, MO 64121-9335; tel. (816) 983-1303; fax (816) 983-1418; internet www.kcsi.com; 3,226 track-km; Chair. and CEO MICHAEL R. HAVERTY; Pres. and COO DAVID L. STARLING.

Long Island Rail Road Co: Jamaica Station, Jamaica, NY 11435-4380; tel. (718) 558-7400; internet www.mta.info/lirr; f. 1834; operates 3,291 km of track (Dec. 2007); operated by the Metropolitan Transportation Authority—State of New York; Chair. H. DALE HEMMERDINGER (acting); Exec. Dir and CEO ELLIOT G. SANDER.

Norfolk Southern Corpn: NS Tower, 3 Commercial Pl., Norfolk, VA 23510; tel. (757) 629-2600; fax (757) 664-5117; e-mail contactus@nscorp.com; internet www.nscorp.com; f. 1988; operates 37,600 miles of track (2008); Pres., Chair. and CEO CHARLES W. MOORMAN.

Pan Am Railways: 1700 Iron Horse Park, North Billerica, MA 01862; tel. (978) 663-1130; e-mail customerservice@panamrailways.com; internet www.guilfordrail.com; frmly Guilford Rail System; name changed as above in 2006; Pres. DAVID FINK.

Railroad Development Corpn (RDC): 381 Mansfield Ave, Suite 500, Pittsburgh, PA 15220; tel. (412) 928-0777; fax (412) 928-7715; e-mail rdc@rrdc.com; internet www.rrdc.com; f. 1987; 11,498 track-km in the USA and world-wide (2007); Chair. HENRY POSNER, III; Pres. ROBERT A. PIETRANDREA.

Iowa Interstate Railroad (IAIS): 5900 Sixth St, SW, Cedar Rapids, IA 52404; tel. (319) 298-5400; fax (319) 298-5457; e-mail rrwolfe@iaisrr.com; internet www.iaisrr.com; f. 1984; 1,005 track-km in Nebraska, Iowa and Illinois; Pres. and CEO DENNIS H. MILLER.

Union Pacific Railroad Co: 1400 Douglas St, Omaha, NE 68179; tel. (402) 544-5000; fax (402) 350-7362; internet www.uprr.com; f. 1897; division of Union Pacific Corpn; operates 52,143 km of track in 23 states; Pres. and CEO JAMES R. YOUNG.

ASSOCIATIONS

American Association of Private Railroad Car Owners: 630 Constitution Ave, NE, Suite B, Washington, DC 20002; tel. (202) 547-5696; fax (202) 547-5623; e-mail execdirector@aaprco.com; internet www.aaprco.com; Exec. Dir DIANE ELLIOTT.

American Association of Railroad Superintendents: POB 200, La Fox, IL 60147; tel. (331) 643-3369; fax (630) 762-0755; e-mail aars@railroadsuperintendents.org; internet www.railroadsuperintendents.org; f. 1881; 500 mems; Pres. and COO RON BATORY.

American Railway Development Association (ARDA): POB 44369, Eden Prairie, MN 55344-4369; tel. (952) 828-9750; fax (952) 828-9751; e-mail gil@amraildev.com; internet www.amraildev.com; f. 1906; environmental, marketing, real-estate and industrial development officers of railroads; 210 mems; Pres. ROGER BENNETT; Exec. Dir BILL KRUPINSKI.

American Railway Engineering and Maintenance of Way Association (AREMA): 10003 Derekwood Lane, Suite 210, Lanham, MD 20706; tel. (301) 459-3200; fax (301) 459-8077; e-mail chemely@arema.org; internet www.arema.org; f. 1997 by merger of three engineering support asscns—the American Railway Bridge and Building Asscn, the American Railway Engineering Asscn and the Roadmasters and Maintenance of Way Asscn, in addition to functions of the Communications and Signal Division of the Asscn of American Railroads; 6,900 mems; Pres. and Chair. LARRY L. ETHERTON; Exec. Dir and CEO Dr CHARLES H. EMELY.

American Short Line and Regional Railroad Association: 50 F St, NW, Suite 7020, Washington, DC 20001; tel. (202) 628-4500; fax (202) 628-6430; e-mail aslrra@aslrra.org; internet www.aslrra.org; f. 1913; 418 mems; operates and maintains 29% of US rail mileage; Pres. and Treas. RICHARD F. TIMMONS.

American Train Dispatchers' Associations: 1370 Ontario St, Suite 1040, Cleveland, OH 44113; tel. (216) 241-2770; fax (216) 241-6286; e-mail atdamccann@aol.com; internet atdd.homestead.com/atddpg1.html; f. 1917; 3,000 mems; Pres. F. L. MCCANN.

Association of American Railroads: 50 F St, NW, Washington, DC 20001-1564; tel. (202) 639-2100; fax (202) 639-2286; e-mail preilly@aar.org; internet www.aar.org; f. 1934; membership represents virtually all major railroads in the USA, Canada and Mexico, as well as rail industry products and services; oversees 173,000 miles of track; Pres. and CEO EDWARD R. HAMBERGER.

Brotherhood of Locomotive Engineers and Trainmen (BLET): Standard Bldg, 1370 Ontario St, Mezzanine, Cleveland, OH 44114-1702; tel. (216) 241-2630; e-mail execstaff@ble-t.org; internet www.ble.org; f. 2004 by merger of the Brotherhood of Locomotive Engineers and the International Brotherhood of Teamsters; 59,000 mems; Pres. ED RODZWICZ.

Brotherhood of Maintenance of Way Employees: see Industry—Trade Unions.

Brotherhood of Railroad Signalmen: 917 Shenandoah Shores Rd, Front Royal, VA 22630-6418; tel. (540) 622-6522; fax (540) 622-6532; e-mail wdp@brs.org; internet www.brs.org; f. 1901; 9,500 mems; Int. Pres. W. DAN PICKETT.

High Speed Ground Transportation Association (HSGTA): 1001 G St, NW, Suite 400, Washington, DC 20001; tel. (202) 464-0530; fax (202) 638-3516; e-mail info@hsgta.com; internet peyser.com/hsgta; lobbies for legislation and federal funding for high-speed trains; Dir of Operations MICHAEL E. RIVERA.

National Association of Railroad Passengers: 900 Second St, NE, Suite 308, Washington, DC 20002-3557; tel. (202) 408-8362; fax (202) 408-8287; e-mail narp@narprail.org; internet www.narprail.org; f. 1967; promotes public awareness of rail passenger service; 23,000 mems; Exec. Dir ROSS B. CAPON.

National Association of Railroad Trial Counsel (NARTC): 1430 East Missouri, Suite B200, Phoenix, AR 85014; tel. (602) 265-2700; fax (602) 265-2705; e-mail info@nartc.org; internet www.nartc.org; f. 1955; 1,200 mems; Exec. Dir MICHELLE MILLS-THORPE.

National Association of Railway Business Women: 2720 Mayfield Rd, Cleveland Heights, OH 44106; tel. (216) 321-0971; e-mail narbwinfo@narbw.org; internet www.narbw.org; f. 1921; 900 mems; Nat. Pres. BARBARA BARTHLE.

National Railroad Construction and Maintenance Association (NRC): 500 New Jersey Ave, NW, Suite 400, Washington, DC 20001; tel. (202) 715-2920; fax (202) 318-0867; e-mail info@nrcma.org; internet www.nrcma.org; f. 1972; manufacturing, supply and service firms; 574 mems; Chair. MANNY RAMIREZ; Pres. CHUCK BAKER.

National Railway Labor Conference (NRLC): 1901 L St, NW, Suite 500, Washington, DC 20036; tel. (202) 862-7200; fax (202) 862-7230; e-mail gevans@rrnrlc.org; internet www.nrlc.ws; f. 1963; management collective bargaining agency for the railroad freight industry; 40 mems; Chair. ROBERT F. ALLEN.

New Hampshire Railroad Revitalization Association: POB 193, Weare, NH 03281-0193; tel. (603) 471-1242; fax (603) 471-1243; e-mail info@nhrra.org; internet www.nhrra.org; Pres. PETER J. GRIFFIN.

North American Rail Shippers Association (NARS): 2115 Portsmouth Dr., Richardson, TX 75082-4839; tel. (972) 690-4740; fax (972) 644-8208; e-mail nars@railshippers.com; internet www.railshippers.com; Pres. DIANE EL-HAKIM; Exec. Dir E. LEO MOUNTJOY.

Railway Engineering-Maintenance Suppliers Association: 417 West Broad St, Suite 203, Falls Church, VA 22046; tel. (703) 241-8514; fax (703) 241-8589; e-mail contact@remsa.org; internet www.remsa.org; f. 1965; distributors and manufacturers of track supplies; 226 mems; Exec. Dir JUDI MEYERHOEFFER.

Railway Supply Institute (RSI): 50 F St, NW, Suite 7030, Washington, DC 20001; tel. (202) 347-4664; fax (202) 347-0047; e-mail rpi@railwaysupply.org; internet www.rsiweb.org; f. 1908; trade asscn of the railway equipment and supply asscn; brs in Washington, DC and Chicago, IL; 216 mems; Exec. Dir HOWARD E. TONN (Chicago).

American Railway Car Institute: e-mail rpi@rpi.org; internet www.rsiweb.org/committees/com_arci.aspx; f. 1915; cttee of the RSI since 1994; 22 mems; Chair. MARTIN GRAHAM.

Railway Systems Suppliers, Inc: 9306 New LaGrange Rd, Suite 100, Louisville, KY 40242; tel. (502) 327-7774; fax (502) 327-0541; e-mail rssi@rssi.org; internet www.rssi.org; f. 1966; 240 mems; trade asscn for suppliers of signalling and communications products to the rail industry; Exec. Dir DONALD REMALEY.

Railway Tie Association: 115 Commerce Dr., Suite C, Fayetteville, GA 30214; tel. (770) 460-5553; fax (770) 460-5573; e-mail ties@rta.org; internet www.rta.org; f. 1919; promotes the use of wooden railway sleepers (crossties); Pres. JANET SEAMAN.

States for Passenger Rail Coalition: c/o WisDOT, Railroads and Harbors Section, POB 7914, Madison, WI 53707; tel. (608) 266-9498; e-mail sec.exec@dot.state.wi.us; internet www.s4prc.org; f. 2000; an alliance of 27 state depts of transportation that supports intercity passenger rail initiatives and advocates for federal funding; Chair. FRANK J. BUSALACCHI.

ROADS

Public Road Length, 2006

(miles by functional system)

	Area		Function				
	Urban	Rural	Interstate	Arterial/Other freeway	Collector	Local	**Total roads**
Alabama	21,846	74,675	908	9,269	20,530	65,814	96,521
Alaska	2,370	12,417	1,081	1,516	2,829	9,361	14,787
Arizona	22,560	37,816	1,169	5,887	8,121	45,199	60,376
Arkansas	11,272	87,733	655	6,978	20,325	71,047	99,005
California	86,565	83,725	2,460	28,500	31,992	107,338	170,290
Colorado	19,066	68,955	954	9,243	16,253	61,571	88,021
Connecticut	15,081	6,168	346	2,995	3,200	14,708	21,249
Delaware	2,920	3,259	41	668	1,052	4,418	6,179
District of Columbia	1,500	—	13	286	156	1,045	1,500
Florida	81,789	40,206	1,471	13,438	14,287	92,799	121,995
Georgia	37,325	80,874	1,244	14,127	22,651	80,177	118,199
Hawaii	2,290	2,040	55	787	829	2,659	4,330
Idaho	4,755	42,350	612	4,041	10,311	32,141	47,105
Illinois	40,403	98,594	2,169	14,589	21,724	100,515	138,997
Indiana*	21,780	74,470	1,169	8,100	22,684	64,297	96,250
Iowa	11,197	102,887	781	9,710	31,548	72,045	114,084
Kansas	12,790	127,591	874	9,706	33,524	96,277	140,381
Kentucky	12,325	65,906	762	5,931	16,084	55,454	78,231
Louisiana	15,932	44,993	903	5,587	10,048	44,387	60,925
Maine	2,972	19,811	367	2,193	5,985	14,238	22,783
Maryland	17,099	14,000	481	4,077	5,044	21,497	31,099
Massachusetts	27,977	7,961	573	6,488	4,826	24,051	35,938
Michigan	35,619	86,103	1,241	14,916	24,503	81,062	121,722
Minnesota	16,756	115,553	913	13,653	29,759	87,984	132,309
Mississippi	10,681	63,727	685	7,500	15,488	50,735	74,408
Missouri†	19,244	107,961	1,181	10,538	24,903	90,583	127,205
Montana	2,973	70,175	1,192	6,037	16,221	49,698	73,148
Nebraska	6,191	87,188	482	8,097	20,730	64,070	93,379
Nevada	7,143	26,560	571	3,150	4,994	24,988	33,703
New Hampshire	4,733	10,914	225	1,590	2,754	11,078	15,647
New Jersey	31,252	7,309	431	6,164	4,150	27,816	38,561
New Mexico	7,996	55,800	1,000	5,106	8,511	49,179	63,796
New York	47,744	65,873	1,697	14,612	20,664	76,644	113,617
North Carolina	32,310	71,190	1,082	9,960	17,467	74,991	103,500
North Dakota	1,870	84,969	571	5,912	11,778	68,578	86,839
Ohio	44,594	80,513	1,574	11,399	22,589	89,545	125,107
Oklahoma	15,640	97,445	933	8,386	25,260	78,506	113,085
Oregon	12,698	51,660	728	7,077	17,614	38,939	64,358
Pennsylvania	44,923	76,369	1,758	13,819	19,791	85,924	121,292
Rhode Island	5,261	1,267	71	918	884	4,655	6,528
South Carolina	16,444	49,798	843	7,276	15,081	43,042	66,242
South Dakota	2,828	81,401	679	6,401	19,127	58,022	84,229
Tennessee	21,639	69,777	1,104	9,195	17,851	63,266	91,416
Texas	83,683	221,587	3,233	30,069	63,477	208,491	305,270
Utah	10,610	33,159	936	3,477	7,737	31,619	43,769
Vermont	1,421	12,985	320	1,322	3,131	9,633	14,406
Virginia	21,700	50,631	1,117	8,556	14,090	48,568	72,331
Washington	22,469	60,787	764	8,024	16,680	57,788	83,256
West Virginia	4,514	32,540	555	3,330	8,730	24,439	37,054
Wisconsin	21,998	92,487	743	12,683	21,677	79,382	114,485
Wyoming	2,618	25,216	913	3,593	11,147	12,181	27,834
Total	1,029,366	2,987,375	46,630	406,876	790,791	2,772,444	4,016,741

* Excludes 788 miles of Federal agency owned roads.

† Includes 274 miles of miscoded non-interstate functional system length or rural/urban categorization or both.

Source: Federal Highway Administration, US Department of Transportation.

Motor-Vehicle Registrations by State, 2006

(Note: Figures represent registrations covering publicly and privately owned vehicles.)

	Motor vehicles				
	Automobiles	Buses	Trucks	**Total**	Motorcycles
Alabama	1,795,596	9,082	2,825,636	4,630,314	104,075
Alaska	242,487	2,706	429,901	675,094	24,122
Arizona	2,189,979	4,961	1,987,392	4,182,332	114,443
Arkansas	958,640	8,201	1,027,414	1,994,255	58,694
California	19,835,554	56,814	13,289,690	33,182,058	726,095
Colorado*	858,967	5,829	943,027	1,807,823	117,159
Connecticut†	1,999,809	10,492	1,041,651	3,051,952	64,959
Delaware	432,509	2,167	378,512	813,188	22,788
District of Columbia	168,916	2,889	47,300	219,105	1,367
Florida	7,425,148	48,929	8,899,488	16,373,565	588,962
Georgia	4,141,179	21,343	4,123,932	8,286,454	142,276
Hawaii	538,581	5,671	464,288	1,008,540	31,317
Idaho	541,487	3,767	729,861	1,275,115	50,514
Illinois	5,947,468	18,036	3,910,742	9,876,246	293,078
Indiana*	2,694,901	31,974	2,228,559	4,955,434	147,544
Iowa	1,744,519	8,429	1,593,003	3,345,951	161,133
Kansas	872,878	3,918	1,512,396	2,389,192	72,078
Kentucky	1,969,142	14,249	1,574,731	3,558,122	58,959
Louisiana	1,950,372	22,102	1,900,270	3,872,744	61,128
Maine	581,797	3,399	486,680	1,071,876	45,488
Maryland	2,656,597	12,155	1,819,645	4,488,397	72,625
Massachusetts	3,310,725	11,207	2,063,283	5,385,215	143,853
Michigan	4,765,547	26,248	3,362,440	8,154,235	248,002
Minnesota	2,512,491	17,610	2,174,813	4,704,914	215,664
Mississippi	1,118,200	9,521	869,860	1,997,581	27,553
Missouri	2,715,297	11,485	2,230,390	4,957,172	85,466
Montana	447,446	2,503	616,613	1,066,562	85,874
Nebraska	832,511	6,995	893,627	1,733,133	36,966
Nevada	679,828	1,923	684,806	1,366,557	56,973
New Hampshire†	585,455	1,873	472,635	1,059,963	70,778
New Jersey†	3,692,966	23,827	2,241,195	5,957,988	163,636
New Mexico	699,312	3,552	877,956	1,580,820	43,495
New York†	8,528,457	70,015	2,685,424	11,283,896	203,145
North Carolina	3,659,926	33,720	2,607,790	6,301,436	110,637
North Dakota	345,502	2,587	364,080	712,169	25,353
Ohio	6,438,988	44,484	4,345,371	10,828,843	332,355
Oklahoma	1,606,517	18,634	1,576,680	3,201,831	94,289
Oregon	1,427,597	14,822	1,538,960	2,981,379	84,224
Pennsylvania†	5,842,819	38,029	4,013,315	9,894,163	330,947
Rhode Island†	508,389	1,726	295,433	805,548	31,131
South Carolina	1,964,994	18,078	1,470,771	3,453,843	87,774
South Dakota	375,760	2,644	465,580	843,984	53,481
Tennessee	2,878,136	19,979	2,193,213	5,091,328	134,134
Texas	8,805,316	90,173	8,642,899	17,538,388	355,878
Utah	1,079,455	1,308	1,155,325	2,236,088	50,896
Vermont	309,972	1,745	275,951	587,668	24,543
Virginia	4,031,355	18,264	2,586,357	6,635,976	81,172
Washington	3,087,818	11,665	2,590,014	5,689,497	194,263
West Virginia	734,599	2,794	703,706	1,441,099	40,730
Wisconsin	2,639,984	14,347	2,317,130	4,971,461	271,151
Wyoming	228,057	3,088	414,047	645,192	33,791
Total	135,399,945	821,959	107,943,782	244,165,686	6,678,958

* 2005 data.

† Data exclude farm trucks, registered at a nominal fee and restricted to use in the vicinity of the owner's farm: Connecticut 16,744; New Hampshire 9,556; New Jersey 8,734; New York 23,077; Pennsylvania 25,094; and Rhode Island 1,626.

Source: Federal Highway Administration, US Department of Transportation.

Directory

REGULATORY BODY

Federal Highway Administration (FHWA): 1200 New Jersey Ave, SE, Washington, DC 20590; tel. (202) 366-0604; fax (202) 366-3244; internet www.fhwa.dot.gov; part of the Dept of Transportation; implements federal highway policy and promotes road safety; Admin. THOMAS J. MADISON, Jr.

PRINCIPAL COMPANIES

Arrow Stage Lines, Inc: 720 East Norfolk Ave, Norfolk, NE 68701; tel. (402) 371-3850; fax (402) 371-3267; e-mail steve@arrowstagelines.com; internet www.arrowstagelines.com; f. 1928; intercity and rural highway passenger transportation; Chair. DOYLE BUSSKOHL; Pres. STEVE BUSSKOHL.

Badger Coaches, Inc: 5501 Femrite Dr., Madison, WI 53718; tel. (608) 255-1511; e-mail info@badgerbus.com; internet www.badgerbus.com; f. 1920; intercity highway and passenger charter transportation; Pres. and Treas. ROBERT S. MEIER.

Coach USA, Inc: 1 Riverway, Suite 500, Houston, TX 77056-1921; tel. (713) 888-0104; fax (713) 888-0257; internet www.coachusa.com; owned by Stagecoach Group plc (United Kingdom); owns and operated 20 coach companies across the USA; CEO BRIAN SOUTER.

Decatur Transit, Inc: 500 Market St, NW, POB 1784, Decatur, AL 35602; tel. (256) 353-9601; fax (256) 353-1777; e-mail info@decaturtransit.com; internet www.decaturtransit.com; f. 1931; truck transportation, truck and car rental and leasing, marine cargo handling; Pres. and CEO T. E. DOBBS.

Greyhound Lines, Inc: POB 660362, Dallas, TX 75266-0362; tel. (214) 849-8966; e-mail ifsr@greyhound.com; internet www.greyhound.com; f. 1914; intercity bus transportation and package delivery; Pres. and CEO DAVE LEACH.

Texas, New Mexico and Oklahoma Coaches, Inc (TNM&O): 1313 13th St, POB 1800, Lubbock, TX 79408; tel. (806) 687-4500;

internet www.tnmo.com; serves south-west USA; Man JACK W. HAUGSLAND.

Trailways: 3554 Chain Bridge Rd, Suite 301, Fairfax, VA 22030; tel. (703) 691-3052; fax (703) 691-9047; e-mail bustrails@trailways.com; internet www.trailways.com; country-wide network of bus and train routes; Pres. and CEO GALE ELLSWORTH.

Valley Transit Co (VTC): POB 530010, Harlingen, TX 78553-0010; tel. (956) 423-4710; fax (956) 423-4888; e-mail info@valleytransitcompany.com; internet www.valleytransitcompany.com; wholly owned subsidiary of Greyhound Lines, Inc; serves the south-central Texas and north-Mexico border.

Lakeland Bus Lines, Inc: 425 East Blackwell St, Dover, NJ 07801-0898; tel. (973) 366-0600; fax (973) 366-3145; e-mail lblinfo@lakelandbus.com; internet www.lakelandbus.com; f. 1952; interstate bus line; charter and tour services to 48 states and Canada; Pres. MAUREEN LEO; Vice-Pres. DON MAZZARISI.

Martz Group: 239 Old River Rd, Wilkes Barre, PA 18702; tel. (570) 821-3838; fax (570) 821–3835; e-mail info@martzgroup.com; internet www.martzgroup.com; f. 1908; interstate bus routes; charter and tour services; Chair. FRANK M. HENRY; CEO CRAIG SMITH.

Peter Pan Bus Lines, Inc: POB 1776, Springfield, MA 01102-1776; tel. (800) 843-9999; e-mail info@peterpanbus.com; internet www.peterpanbus.com; f. 1933; intercity bus line, charter buses; Pres. PETER A. PICKNELLY.

Southeastern Stages, Inc: 260 University Ave, SW, Atlanta, GA 30315-2125; tel. (404) 591-2750; fax (404) 591-2745; e-mail charters@southeasternstages.com; internet www.southeasternstages.com; f. 1933; operates regular scheduled services from Atlanta, GA, via Augusta, GA, to Columbia, SC, Charleston, SC, and Fayetteville, NC; provides charter and tour services throughout the USA and Canada; Pres. MICHAEL DIXON.

ASSOCIATIONS

American Association of Motor Vehicle Administrators (AAMVA): 4301 Wilson Blvd, Suite 400, Arlington, VA 22203; tel. (703) 522-4200; fax (703) 908-2851; e-mail inquiries@aamva.org; internet www.aamva.org; f. 1933; Pres. and CEO NEIL D. SCHUSTER.

American Association of State Highway and Transportation Officials: 444 North Capitol St, NW, Suite 249, Washington, DC 20001; tel. (202) 624-5800; fax (202) 624-5806; e-mail info@aashto.org; internet www.transportation.org; f. 1914; public officials in state agencies responsible for highways and transportation; 76 mems; Pres. PETE RAHN; Exec. Dir JOHN HORSLEY.

American Bus Association: 700 13th St, NW, Suite 575, Washington, DC 20005-5923; tel. (202) 842-1645; fax (202) 842-0850; e-mail abainfo@buses.org; internet www.buses.org; f. 1926; 3,300 mems; Chair. DOUGLAS ANDERSON; Pres. and CEO PETER J. PANTUSO.

American Highway Users' Alliance: 1101 14th St, NW, Suite 750, Washington, DC 20005; tel. (202) 857-1200; fax (202) 857-1220; e-mail info@highways.org; internet www.highways.org; f. 1932; non-profit org. promoting safe highways; 400 mems; Pres. and CEO GREGORY COHEN.

American Road and Transportation Builders' Association: ARTBA Bldg, 1219 28th St, NW, Washington, DC 20007-3389; tel. (202) 289-4434; e-mail sbarrett@artba.org; internet www.artba.org; f. 1902; over 5,000 mems; Chair., Pres. and CEO LEO VECELLIO, JR.

American Trucking Associations (ATA): 950 North Glebe Rd, Suite 210, Arlington, VA 22203-4181; tel. (703) 838-1700; fax (703) 838-1994; e-mail media@trucking.org; internet www.truckline.com; f. 1933; 37,000 mems; Chair. RAY KUNTZ; Pres. and CEO BILL GRAVES.

Arkansas Trucking Association: 1401 West Capitol, Suite 185, Little Rock, AR 72201; POB 3476, AR 72203; tel. (501) 372-3462; fax (501) 376-1810; e-mail getinfo@arkansastrucking.com; internet www.arkansastrucking.com; f. 1932; Pres. LANE KIDD; Chair. GREGORY P. CARMAN.

Association of Asphalt Paving Technologists (AAPT): 4711 Clark Ave, Suite G, White Bear Lake, MN 55110-3268; tel. (651) 293-9188; fax (651) 293-9193; e-mail aapt@qwest.net; internet www.asphalttechnology.org; f. 1924; over 800 mems world-wide; Pres. R. MICHAEL ANDERSON.

Association of Professional Truck Drivers of America (APTDA): 16476 Chesterfield Airport Rd, Chesterfield, MO 64017; tel. (888) 972-7832; fax (888) 972-7831; e-mail aptda@tasinsurance.com; internet www.aptda.com; provides insurance; Dir of Admin. PAULA BRENNAN.

Buses International Association: POB 9337, Spokane, WA 99209; tel. (509) 328-2494; e-mail billluke@ztc.net; f. 1981; Exec. Dir WILLIAM A. LUKE.

Intermodal Association of North America (IANA): 11785 Beltsville Dr., Suite 1100, Calverton, MD 20705; tel. (301) 982-3400; fax (301) 982-4815; e-mail iana@intermodal.org; internet www.intermodal.org; f. 1991; promotes the benefits of intermodal freight transportation; Pres. and CEO JOANNE (JONI) F. CASEY.

International Bridge, Tunnel and Turnpike Association (IBTTA): 1146 19th St, NW, Washington, DC 20036-3725; tel. (202) 659-4620; fax (202) 659-0500; e-mail sbuse@ibtta.org; internet www.ibtta.org; f. 1932; cos and public agencies operating toll facilities; 280 mems; Pres. SUSAN BUSE; Exec. Dir PATRICK D. JONES.

International Road Federation: 500 Montgomery St, 5th Floor, Alexandria, VA 22314; tel. (703) 535-1001; fax (703) 535-1007; e-mail info@irfnews.org; internet www.irfnet.org; f. 1948; automotive, oil, rubber and construction firms; Chair. PETER J. BOYD; Dir-Gen. and CEO C. PATRICK SANKEY.

Maine Motor Transport Association (MMTA): 142 Whitten Rd, POB 857, Augusta, ME 04332-0857; tel. (207) 623-4128; fax (207) 623-4096; e-mail daleh@mmta.com; internet www.mmta.com; promotes the motor transportation industry in Maine and elsewhere; Pres. and CEO DALE E. HANINGTON.

Michigan Trucking Association: 1131 Centennial Way, Lansing, MI 48917; tel. (517) 321-1951; fax (517) 321-0884; e-mail info@mitrucking.org; internet www.mitrucking.org; f. 1934; Exec. Dir WALTER G. HEINRITZI.

Mid-West Truckers Association: 2727 North Dirksen Pkwy, Springfield, IL 62702; tel. (217) 525-0310; fax (217) 525-0342; e-mail info@mid-westtruckers.com; internet www.mid-westtruckers.com; f. 1961; 2,700 mem. cos; Exec. Vice-Pres. DONALD H. SCHAEFER.

Middlewest Motor Freight Bureau: 4218 Roanoke Rd, Suite 200, Kansas City, MO 64111-4735; tel. (816) 931-4333; fax (816) 931–4339; e-mail info@middlewest.com; internet www.middlewest.com; fmrly Distributors and LTL Carriers Asscn; Pres. and CEO GLEN MICHALSON.

Minnesota Transport Services Association (MTSA): 840 Hampden Ave, Suite 207, St Paul, MN 55114; tel. (651) 646-4075; fax (651) 641-0764; e-mail maryann@mtsa.org; internet www.mtsa.org; f. 1936; represents Minnesota's small to mid-sized motor carriers, household goods movers and private carrier industry; Exec. Dir HOWARD MARKUS.

Minnesota Trucking Association (MTA): 2277 Hwy 36 West, Suite 302, Roseville, MN 55113; tel. (651) 646-7351; fax (651) 641-8995; e-mail mta@mntruck.org; internet www.mntruck.org; f. 1932; over 700 mems; Pres. JOHN HAUSLADEN; Chair. JACK SHAWN.

Montana Motor Carriers Association: 501 North Sanders, Suite 201, Helena, MT 59601; tel. (406) 442-6600; fax (406) 443-4281; e-mail mmca@mttrucking.org; internet www.mttrucking.org; f. 1939; over 200 mem. cos; Exec. Dir MIKE WILSON.

National Asphalt Pavement Association (NAPA): NAPA Bldg, 5100 Forbes Blvd, Lanham, MD 20706; tel. (301) 731-4748; fax (301) 731-4621; e-mail macott@hotmix.org; internet www.hotmix.org; f. 1955; producers of asphalt for paving roads; over 1,100 mems; Pres. MIKE ACOTT.

National Association of Independent Truckers, Inc (NAIT): 11020 North-West Ambassador Dr., Suite 500, Kansas City, MO 64153; tel. (816) 891-7997; fax (816) 891-0000; internet www.naitusa.com; f. 1981; over 30,000 mems; CEO CHERYL WOMACK.

National Association of Women Highway Safety Leaders (NAWHSL): 2743 North Albany, Chicago, IL 60647; tel. (773) 278-8476; fax (773) 278-7135; e-mail judikeippel@aol.com; internet www.nawhsl.org; f. 1967; promotes road safety and police enforcement; Pres. DEBRA H. GARVIN; Exec. Dir JUDI KEIPPEL.

National Motor Freight Traffic Association (NMFTA): 1001 North Fairfax, Suite 600, Alexandria, VA 22314; tel. (703) 838-1810; fax (703) 683-6296; e-mail customerservice@nmfta.org; internet www.nmfta.org; f. 1956; 940 mem cos; Chair. LARRY KERR.

National Private Truck Council (NPTC): 950 North Glebe Rd, Suite 530, Arlington, VA 22203-4183; tel. (703) 683-1300; fax (703) 683-1217; e-mail info@nptc.org; internet www.nptc.org; f. 1939; Pres. and CEO GARY F. PETTY.

NATSO, Inc (National Asscn of Truck Stop Operators, Inc): 1737 King St, Suite 200, Alexandria, VA 22314; tel. (703) 549-2100; fax (703) 684-4525; e-mail mlong@natso.com; internet www.natso.com; f. 1960; represents over 1,020 travel plazas and truckstops nation-wide, owned by more than 257 cos; Chair. DAN ALSAKER; Pres. and CEO LISA J. MULLINGS.

Nevada Motor Transport Association: 2215 Green Vista Dr., Suite 304, Sparks, NV 89431; tel. (775) 673-6111; fax (775) 673-1700; e-mail pje@nmta.com; internet www.nmta.com; f. 1932; CEO PAUL J. ENOS; Pres. DAVID L. IPSON.

North American Transportation Management Institute (NATMI): 2460 West 26th Ave, Suite 17C, Denver, CO 80211; tel. (303) 952-4013; fax (775) 370-4055; e-mail info@natmi.org; internet www.natmi.org; f. 1945; fmrly National Committee for Motor Fleet

Supervisor Training; bus, automobile, insurance and safety orgs; Exec. Dir JEFF ARNOLD.

Ohio Trucking Association: 50 West Broad St, Suite 1111, Columbus, OH 43215; tel. (614) 221-5375; fax (614) 221-3717; e-mail info@ohiotruckingassn.org; internet www.ohiotruckingassn.org; f. 1918; over 1,100 mems; Chair. JOHN N. HOFSTETTER; Pres. LARRY A. DAVIS.

Oregon Trucking Associations: 4005 South-East Naef Rd, Portland, OR 97267; tel. (503) 513-0005; fax (503) 513-0008; e-mail ortruck@ortrucking.org; internet www.ortrucking.org; f. 1951; 1,000 mems; Pres. BOB RUSSELL.

Owner/Operator Independent Drivers' Association of America (OOIDA): 1 North-West OOIDA Dr., Grain Valley, MO 64029; tel. (816) 229-5791; e-mail ooida@ooida.com; internet www.ooida.com; f. 1973; 160,972 mems; Pres. JIM JOHNSTON.

Pennsylvania Motor Truck Association (PMTA): 910 Linda Lane, Camp Hill, PA 17011; tel. (717) 761-7122; fax (717) 761-8434; e-mail jrunk@pmta.org; internet www.pmta.org; f. 1928; Pres. and CEO JAMES RUNK; Chair. PETER COSTELLO.

Professional Truck Driver Institute, Inc: 555 East Braddock Rd, Alexandria, VA 22314; tel. (703) 647-7015; fax (703) 836-6610; e-mail ptdi@truckload.org; internet www.ptdi.org; f. 1986; trade asscns, manufacturers and suppliers to the trucking industry; Chair. TERRY BURNETT; Pres. CHRIS BURRUSS.

Taxicab, Limousine & Paratransit Association: 3200 Tower Oaks Blvd, Suite 220, Rockville, MD 20852; tel. (301) 984-5700; fax (301) 984-5703; e-mail info@tlpa.org; internet www.tlpa.org; f. 1917; 1,100 mem. cos; Pres. LARRY SLAGLE; Pres.-elect ELLIS HOUSTON; CEO ALFRED LAGASSE.

Tennessee Trucking Association: 4531 Trousdale Dr., Nashville, TN 37204; tel. (615) 777-2882; fax (615) 777-2024; e-mail dhuneryager@tntrucking.org; internet www.tntrucking.org; over 500 mem cos; Pres. and CEO DAVE HUNERYAGER.

Texas Motor Transportation Association (TMTA): 700 East 11th St, Austin, TX 78701-2673; tel. (512) 478-2541; fax (512) 474-6494; e-mail info@tmta.com; internet www.tmta.com; f. 1932; Pres. and CEO JOHN ESPARZA.

Trucking Industry Defense Association (TIDA): 915 Main St, Suite 505, Evansville, IN 47708; tel. (847) 647-7226; fax (847) 647-8940; e-mail terrir@tida.org; internet www.tida.org; f. 1993; over 1,200 mems; Pres. JAMES DILL.

Truckload Carriers Association: 555 East Braddock Rd, Alexandria, VA 22314; tel. (703) 838-1950; fax (703) 836-6610; e-mail tca@truckload.org; internet www.truckload.org; f. 1939; 1,000 mems; Chair. RAY HAIGHT.

United Highway Carriers Association (UHCA): 1817 South Fresno Ave, Stockton, CA 95206; tel. (800) 483-8343; fax (800) 669-2699; e-mail info@uhca.com; internet www.uhca.com; over 700 mem cos.

United Motorcoach Association: 113 South West St, 4th Floor, Alexandria, VA 22314-2824; tel. (703) 838-2929; fax (703) 838-2950; e-mail info@uma.org; internet www.uma.org; f. 1971 as the United Bus Owners of America; name changed as above in 1996; over 875 mem cos; Chair. GODFREY LEBRON; Pres. and CEO VICTOR S. PARRA.

Wisconsin Motor Carriers Association: 562 Grand Canyon Dr., Madison, WI 53719; POB 44849, Madison, WI 53744-4849; tel. (608) 833-8200; fax (608) 833-2875; e-mail thowells@witruck.org; internet www.witruck.org; Pres. TOM HOWELLS; Chair. TOM VANDENBERG.

INLAND WATERWAYS

Freight Carried

(million short tons)

	2004	2005	2006
Lake waterways	103.5	96.2	96.9
Coastal waterways	220.6	213.7	201.8
Internal waterways*	626.2	624.0	627.6
Total (incl. others)†	1,047.1	1,028.9	1,023.5

* Internal refers to freight moved solely within US boundaries, excluding traffic on the Great Lakes system. Figures also exclude waterway improvement materials and fish.

† Totals include intra-port and intra-territorial traffic.

Source: Waterborne Commerce Statistics Center, US Army Corps of Engineers.

Directory

St Lawrence Seaway Development Corpn: US Dept of Transportation, 400 Seventh St, SW, Suite 5424, Washington, DC 20590; tel. (202) 366-0091; fax (202) 366-7147; e-mail tim.downey@sls.dot.gov; internet www.seaway.dot.gov; responsible for the operations and maintenance of sections of the St Lawrence Seaway within the territorial limits of the USA; Admin. COLLISTER JOHNSON, Jr.

PRINCIPAL COMPANIES

Allied Marine Industries, Inc: POB 717, Norfolk, VA 23501; tel. (800) 446-8241; river and canal transportation, towing and tugboat service and marine cargo handling; Gen. Man. BRUCE LAW.

Alter Barge Line, Inc: 2117 State St, Bettendorf, IA 52722; tel. (563) 344-5100; fax (563) 344-5102; internet www.alterbarge.com; f. 1960; river transportation except on St Lawrence Seaway, intracoastal freight transportation; Pres. LARRY DAILY; CEO JEFF GOLDSTEIN.

American Commercial Lines, Inc: 1701 East Market St, Jeffersonville, IN 47130; tel. (812) 288-0100; e-mail aclinfo@aclines.com; internet www.aclines.com; f. 1915; operates barge services along c. 24,000 km of the Mississippi and Ohio rivers and tributaries to the Gulf Intracoastal Waterway; fleet of 3,375 barges and 120 towboats; Pres. and CEO MICHAEL P. RYAN.

American Steamship Co: 500 Essjay Rd, Williamsville, NY 14221; tel. (716) 635-0222; fax (716) 635-0220; e-mail ascinfo@gatx.com; internet www.americansteamship.com; f. 1907; 18 vessels; Pres. and CEO JEROME K. WELSCH, Jr.

Bernert Barge Lines, Inc: 421 High St, Suite 108, Oregon City, OR 97045; tel. (503) 656-8288; fax (503) 657-3922; internet business.gorge.net/digitaldesigner/bbl; river barge transportation; 14 barges and 4 tugboats; Pres. KEN BERNERT.

Circle Line Sightseeing Yachts: Pier 83, West 42nd St at the Hudson River, New York, NY 10036-1095; tel. (212) 563-3200; fax (212) 631-0569; e-mail info@circleline42.com; internet www.circleline42.com; f. 1945; cruise services on the Hudson River between New York City and Poughkeepsie; Chair. KARL G. ANDREN; Pres. and CEO ROBERT MAHER.

Crounse Corpn: 2626 Broadway, Paducah, KY 42001-3177; tel. (502) 444-9611; internet www.crounse.com; f. 1948; river transportation; serves the Ohio, Tennessee, Kanawha, Monongahela, Allegheny, Green, Big Sandy, Licking, Cumberland, Tenn-Tom and Mid-Mississippi Rivers; 860 barges and 27 towboats; Chair. GEORGE P. CROUNSE.

Foret Enterprises, Inc: 15201 East Freeway, Suite 109, Channelview, TX 77530; tel. (281) 452-9940; fax (281) 452-9941; e-mail davidf@foretinc.com; internet www.foretinc.com; logistical consultancy to the river freight industry; Pres., Marine Services Capt. DAVID A. FORET, Jr.

Great Lakes Dredge & Dock Corpn: 2122 York Rd, Oak Brook, IL 60523; tel. (630) 574-3000; fax (630) 574-2909; internet www.gldd.com; f. 1890; dredging, marine construction and reclamation; operates tugboats, drillboats, carfloats, barges and dredges; 180 vessels; Pres. and CEO DOUGLAS B. MACKIE.

Great Lakes Fleet, Inc: 212 South 37th St, W, Suite 200, Duluth, MN 55802–2819; tel. (218) 723-2406; fax (218) 723-2408; e-mail gregg.ruhl@cn.ca; internet www.cn.ca/specialized/great_lakes/en_KFGreatLakes.shtml; acquired by Canadian National Railway Co (CN) in 2004; frmly United States Steel Great Lakes Fleet; 8 vessels; Dir GREGG RUHL.

Ingram Barge Co: 4400 Harding Rd, Nashville, TN 37205-2290; tel. (615) 298-8200; fax (615) 298-8213; e-mail craig.philip@ingrambarge.com; internet www.ingrambarge.com; f. 1946; 100 vessels and *c.* 4,000 barges; Group CEO and Chair. ORRIN H. INGRAM; Pres. and CEO CRAIG E. PHILIP.

Interlake Steamship Co: 4199 Kinross Lakes Pkwy, Richfield, OH 44268-9372; tel. (330) 659-1400; fax (330) 659-1445; e-mail personnel@interlake-steamship.com; internet www.interlakesteamship.com; f. 1913; 10 vessels; Pres. JAMES R. BARKER.

James Marine, Inc: 4540 Clarks River Rd, Paducah, KY 42003; tel. (270) 898-7392; e-mail ronnie@jamesmarine.com; internet www.jamesmarine.com; f. 1986; Man. C. RONALD JAMES.

Patton-Tully Transportation LLC: 1242 North Second St, Memphis, TN 38107; tel. (901) 576-1400; e-mail jack@pattontully.com; internet www.pattontully.com; f. 1906; subsidiary of Anderson Tully Co; engineers specializing in river transport infrastructure; Vice-Pres. of Operations WILLARD BARGERY.

Warrior and Gulf Navigation Co: 50 Viaduct Rd, Chickasaw, AL 36671; tel. (251) 452-6000; fax (251) 452-6021; internet www.tstarinc.com/wgn; river and canal freight transportation; subsidiary of Transtar, Inc; operates 24 towboats and 260 covered barges; Pres. JOHN C. PRANAITIS.

ASSOCIATIONS

American Waterways Operators: 801 North Quincy St, Suite 200, Arlington, VA 22203; tel. (703) 841-9300; fax (703) 841-0389; internet www.americanwaterways.com; f. 1944; over 400 mems; Pres. THOMAS A. ALLEGRETTI.

Dredging Contractors of America (DCA): 503 D St, NW, Suite 150, Washington, DC 20001; tel. (202) 737-2674; fax (202) 737-2677; e-mail dan@dredgeamerica.com; internet www.dredgingcontractors.org; 19 mems and two assoc. mems; Pres. DAN MCDOUGAL; Exec. Dir JIM RAUSCH.

Estuarine Research Federation: POB 510, Port Republic, MD 20676; tel. (410) 326-7467; fax (410) 326-7466; e-mail jbarth@erf.org; internet www.erf.org; f. 1971; promotes research and education on estuarine and coastal waters; *c.* 1,650 mems and 1,000 affiliate mems; Pres. ROBERT W. H. HOWARTH; Exec. Dir JOY BARTHOLOMEW.

Inland River Ports and Terminals: 316 Board of Trade Pl., New Orleans, LA 70130; tel. (504) 585-0715; fax (504) 525-8197; e-mail admin@irpt.net; internet www.irpt.net; f. 1974; 214 mems; Chair. RANDY RICHARDSON; Pres. JERRY SAILORS.

Lake Carriers' Association: 20325 Center Ridge Rd, Suite 720, Rocky River, OH 44116; tel. (440) 333-4444; fax (440) 333-9993; e-mail info@lcaships.com; internet www.lcaships.com; f. 1892; 18 mem. cos; Pres. JAMES H. I. WEAKLEY.

National Waterways Conference, Inc: 4650 Washington Blvd, Suite 608, Arlington, VA 22201; tel. (703) 243-4090; fax (866) 371-1390; e-mail info@waterways.org; internet www.waterways.org; f. 1960; 200 mems; Chair. GARY LAGRANGE; Pres. AMY W. LARSON.

OCEAN SHIPPING

Statistics

MERCHANT FLEET
(registered at 31 December)

	2004	2006	2007
Number of vessels	6,472	6,498	6,486
Total displacement ('000 grt)	11,058.4	11,217.6	11,411.3

Source: Lloyd's Register-Fairplay, *World Fleet Statistics*.

TRAFFIC AT PRINCIPAL US PORTS
(vessels equal to or exceeding 1,000 gross registered tons, 2007)

	All vessels		Container vessels	
Port	Calls	Capacity ('000 dwt)	Calls	Capacity ('000 dwt)
Los Angeles/Long Beach, CA	5,492	335,898	3,058	169,562
New York and New Jersey	4,968	232,426	2,549	127,359
San Francisco, CA	3,945	212,966	2,046	115,246
Virginia Ports, VA	2,775	137,548	1,940	91,138
Savannah, GA	2,615	121,811	1,807	93,739
Charleston, SC	2,160	96,571	1,589	76,622
Seattle, WA	1,042	59,936	666	39,485
Miami, FL	927	31,184	563	26,078
Houston, TX	6,195	267,045	818	34,090
Tacoma, WA	1,241	62,621	621	33,262
Total US ports (incl. others)*	63,804	3,295,980	19,863	947,862

* Including Puerto Rico.

Note: Figures include transshipments.

Source: Bureau of Transportation Statistics, US Department of Transportation.

INTERNATIONAL MARITIME CONTAINER TRAFFIC
(million TEUs)

	2005	2006	2007
Imports	17.4	18.6	18.5
Exports	8.7	9.0	10.5

Source: Bureau of Transportation Statistics, US Department of Transportation.

Directory

REGULATORY BODIES

Federal Maritime Commission: 800 North Capitol St, NW, Washington, DC 20573; tel. (202) 523-5725; fax (202) 523-0014; e-mail secretary@fmc.gov; internet www.fmc.gov; f. 1961; to regulate the waterborne foreign commerce of the USA; comprises 5 Commrs; Chair. (vacant).

Maritime Administration: 1200 New Jersey Ave, SE, Washington, DC 20590; tel. (202) 366-5807; e-mail pao.marad@dot.gov; internet www.marad.dot.gov; concerned with promoting the US Merchant Marine; also administers subsidy programmes to ship operators; Administrator SEAN T. CONNAUGHTON.

United States Coast Guard: 2100 Second St, SW, Washington, DC 20593; tel. (202) 267-1587; internet www.uscg.mil; Commandant Adm. THAD W. ALLEN.

PRINCIPAL PORTS

The three largest ports in the USA, in terms of traffic handled, are the Port of South Louisiana, handling 225m. short tons in 2006, Houston (more than 222m. tons in 2006) and New York/New Jersey (158m. tons in 2006). Many other large ports serve each coast, 31 of them handling between 25m. and 85m. tons of traffic in 2006. The deepening of channels and locks on the St Lawrence–Great Lakes Waterway, allowing the passage of large ocean-going vessels, has increased the importance of the Great Lakes ports, of which the largest, Duluth-Superior, handled nearly 47.0m. tons in 2006. At 31 December 2007 6,486 vessels, with a total displacement of 11,411,335 grt, were registered in the USA.

PRINCIPAL COMPANIES

AET (American Eagle Tankers): 1900 West Loop South, Suite 920, Houston, TX 77027; tel. (832) 615-2000; fax (713) 622-2256; internet www.eagletankers.com; f. 1994; 68 vessels; wholly owned subsidiary of Malaysian International Shipping Corpn; Pres. and CEO AMIR HAMZAH BIN AZIZAN.

AHL Shipping Co: 219 E. Houston St, Suite 300 San Antonio, TX 78205; tel. (210) 228-2700; fax (210) 228-9102; e-mail ships@ahlsc.com; internet www.ahlsc.com; f. 1985; 4 vessels.

Alaska Tanker Co: Parkside Bldg, Suite A400, 15400 North West Greenbrier Pkwy, Beaverton, OR 97006; tel. (503) 207-0046; fax (503) 207-0055; e-mail helpdesk@aktanker.com; internet www.aktanker.com; f. 1999; CEO ANIL MATHUR.

American Overseas Marine: 100 Newport Ave Extension, North Quincy, MA 02171-1734; tel. (617) 786-8300; e-mail rbooth@gdamsea.com; internet www.gdamsea.com; f. 1984; ship operating segment of General Dynamics Marine Systems; 14 vessels; Pres. THOMAS W. MERRELL.

American President Lines Ltd (APL): 1111 Broadway, Oakland, CA 94607-5500; tel. (510) 272-8000; e-mail paul_barrett@nol.com.sg; internet www.apl.com; f. 1938; serves east and west coasts of North America, Mexico, Caribbean Basin, Middle East and Far East; wholly owned subsidiary of Neptune Orient Lines (Singapore); 100 vessels; CEO ENG AIK MENG.

Bouchard Transportation Co: 58 South Service Rd, Suite 150, Melville, NY 11747; tel. (631) 390-4900; fax (631) 390-4905; e-mail dispatcher@bouchardtransport.com; internet www.bouchardtransport.com; f. 1918; barge and tug transportation; Pres. and CEO MORTON S. BOUCHARD, III.

Chevron Shipping Co: 6001 Bollinger Canyon Rd, San Ramon, CA 94583-5177; tel. (925) 842-1000; e-mail comment@chevron.com; internet www.chevron.com; f. 1895; subsidiary of Chevron Corpn; world-wide tanker sevices; regional offices in Houston, London and Singapore; 39 tankers; Chair. and CEO DAVID J. O'REILLY.

Clipper Americas, Inc: Destec Tower, Suite 500, 2500 City West Blvd, Houston, TX 77042; tel. (713) 953-2200; fax (713) 953-2201; e-mail dae@clipper-group.com; internet www.clipper-group.com; f. 1972; international bulk shipper; 250 vessels; Chair. and CEO TORBEN G. JENSEN.

Colonial Marine Industries, Inc: Hamilton House, 26 East Bryan St, POB 9981, Savannah, GA 31412; tel. (912) 233-7000; fax (912) 232-8216; e-mail colonial@colonialmarine.com; internet www.colonialmarine.com; 5 vessels; Exec. Vice-Pres. RICHARD C. WIGGER.

Coscol Marine Corpn: 9 Greenway Plaza, Houston, TX 77046; tel. (713) 877-3370; fax (713) 877-3433; e-mail edward.knutsen@coastalcorp.com; subsidiary of the Coastal Corpn; 4 tankers; Pres. EDWARD W. KNUTSEN.

Crowley Maritime Corpn: 555 12th St, Suite 2130, Oakland, CA 94607; tel. (510) 251-7500; fax (510) 251-7510; internet www.crowley.com; f. 1892; 280 vessels; Pres., Chair, and CEO THOMAS B. CROWLEY, Jr.

Energy Transportation Group, Inc: 654 Madison Ave, New York, NY 10022; tel. (212) 813-9360; fax (212) 813-6390; e-mail info@etgglobal.com; internet www.etgglobal.com; 8 vessels; Chair. and CEO KIMBALL C. CHEN; Pres. and COO ALEX W. EVANS.

Horizon Lines: 4064 Colony Rd, Suite 200, Charlotte, NC; tel. (704) 973-7000; e-mail jstory@horizonlines.com; internet www.horizon-lines.com; f. 2001 as Horizon Services Group following restructuring of CSX Lines; 21 containerships; Chair., Pres. and CEO CHARLES G. RAYMOND.

International Shipholding Corpn: 11 North Water St, Suite 18290, Mobile, AL 36602; tel. (251) 243-9100; e-mail iscir@intship.com; internet www.intship.com; 28 vessels; Chair. and CEO NIELS M. JOHNSEN; Pres. ERIK L. JOHNSEN.

Central Gulf Lines, Inc: 11 North Water St, Suite 18290, Mobile, AL 36602; tel. (251) 243-9228; e-mail wildkm@intship.com; internet www.intship.com/cgl.htm; Vice-Pres. KEVIN M. WILD.

Waterman Steamship Corpn: 1 Whitehall St, New York, NY 10004; tel. (212) 747-8550; fax (212) 747-8588; e-mail waterman@intship.com; internet www.waterman-steamship.com; f. 1919; owned by International Shipholding Corpn; services between the USA and the Middle East..

Matson Navigation Co: 555 12th St, Suite 700, Oakland, CA 94607; tel. (510) 628-4000; e-mail general_info@matson.com; internet www.matson.com; f. 1901; container and other freight services between US west coast and Hawaii; container leasing world-wide; subsidiary of Alexander & Baldwin, Inc; 17 vessels; Chair. W. ALLEN DOANE; Pres. and CEO JAMES S. ANDRASICK.

Overseas Shipholding Group, Inc (OSG): 666 Third Ave, New York, NY 10017; tel. (212) 953-4100; fax (212) 578-1832; e-mail pslater@osg.com; internet www.osg.com; f. 1948; bulkshipper; 90 vessels; Pres. and CEO MORTEN ARNTZEN.

Reinauer Transportation Cos: 1983 Richmond Terrace, Staten Island, NY 10302; tel. (718) 816-8167; fax (718) 816-8922; e-mail info@reinauer.com; internet www.reinauer.com; f. 1923; 75 vessels.

Seabulk International, Inc: 2200 Eller Dr., POB 13038, Fort Lauderdale, FL 33316; tel. (954) 523-2200; fax (954) 524-9185; e-mail info.ftl@ckor.com; internet www.seabulkinternational.com; f. 1958; bulkshipping and towing; 155 vessels; Chair., Pres. and CEO CHARLES FABRIKANT.

Stolt-Nielsen Transportation Group, Inc: 800 Connecticut Ave, 4th Floor, East Norwalk, CT 06854; tel. (203) 838-7100; fax (203) 299-0067; internet www.stolt-nielsen.com; over 130 tankers; Chair. JACOB. STOLT-NIELSEN; CEO NIELS G. STOLT-NIELSEN.

United Maritime Group: 601 S Harbour Island Blvd, Suite 230, Tampa, FL 33602; tel. (813) 209-4200; internet www.unitedmaritimegroup.com; owns and runs the subsidiaries US United Ocean Services, US United Barge Line, US United Bulk Logistics and US United Bulk Terminal.

US Shipping Partners: 399 Thornall St, 8th Floor, Edison, NJ 08837; tel. (732) 635-1500; fax (732) 635-1918; internet www.usslp.com; 10 vessels; Pres. and CEO RONALD L. O'KELLEY.

ASSOCIATIONS

American Association of Port Authorities (AAPA): 1010 Duke St, Alexandria, VA 22314-3589; tel. (703) 684-5700; fax (703) 684-6321; e-mail info@aapa-ports.org; internet www.aapa-ports.org; f. 1912; 500 mems; Chair. KENNETH B. O'HOLLAREN.

American Bureau of Shipping: 16855 Northchase Dr., Houston, TX 77060; tel. (281) 877-5800; fax (281) 877-5803; e-mail abs-worldhq@eagle.org; internet www.eagle.org; f. 1862; 814 mems; Chair. ROBERT D. SOMMERVILLE; Pres. CHRISTOPHER WIERNICKI.

American Maritime Congress: Hall of the States, Suite G-50, 400 North Capitol St, NW, Washington, DC 20001; tel. (202) 347-8020; fax (202) 347-1550; internet www.americanmaritime.org; f. 1977 as Joint Maritime Congress; adopted current name 1989; mems represent major US-flag ship operating cos; Chair. DON KEEFE.

American Maritime Officers (AMO): 2 West Dixie Hwy, Dania Beach, FL 33004; tel. (954) 921-2221; fax (954) 926-5112; internet www.amo-union.org; f. 1949 as the Brotherhood of Marine Engineers; Pres. TOM BETHEL.

Boston Harbour Association (TBHA): 374 Congress St, Suite 609, Boston, MA 02210; tel. (617) 482-1722; fax (617) 482-9750; e-mail mail@tbha.org; internet www.tbha.org; f. 1973; 25 mems; Pres. RICHARD DIMINO; Exec. Dir VIVIEN LI.

Chamber of Shipping of America (CSA): 1730 M St, NW, Suite 407, Washington, DC 20036-4517; tel. (202) 775-4399; fax (202) 659-3795; e-mail omoore@knowships.org; internet www.knowships.org; frmly American Institute of Merchant Shipping; 31 mem. cos; Pres. and CEO JOSEPH J. COX.

Cruise Lines International Association (CLIA): 910 South East 17th St, Suite 400, Fort Lauderdale, FL 33316; tel. (754) 224-2200; fax (754) 224-2250; e-mail info@cruising.org; internet www.cruising.org; f. 1975; merged with International Council of Cruise Lines (ICCL) in 2006; trade asscn representing *c.* 16,000 travel agents and 24 mem. cruise lines; Pres. and CEO TERRY L. DALE.

Liberian Shipowners' Council: 99 Park Ave, Suite 1700, New York, NY 10016; tel. (212) 973-3896; fax (646) 317-3869; e-mail info@liberianshipowners.com; internet www.liberianshipowners.com; f. 1974; represents owners and operators of Liberian-flag ships; 82 mems; Gen. Sec. JOSEPH E. LUDWICZAK.

Marine Firemen's Union (MFOW&W): 240 Second St, San Francisco, CA 94105; tel. (415) 362-4592; fax (415) 348-8864; e-mail mfow_president@yahoo.com; internet www.mfoww.org; f. 1883; Pres. and Sec.-Treas. ANTHONY POPLAWSKI.

Maritime Association of the Port of New York/New Jersey: 17 Battery Pl., Suite 913, New York, NY 10004; tel. (212) 425-5704; fax (212) 635-9498; e-mail themaritimeassoc@erols.com; internet www.nymaritime.org; f. 1873; 450 mems; Exec. Dir EDWARD KELLY.

New York Shipping Association, Inc: 333 Thornall St, Suite 3A, Edison, NJ 08837; tel. (732) 452-7800; fax (732) 452-6315; e-mail bfedorko@nysanet.org; internet www.nysanet.org; f. 1932; advocates on behalf of marine cargo operators in the port of New York; 48 mems; Pres. FRANK M. MCDONOUGH.

North Atlantic Ports Association: 65 Rockland Ave, Portland, ME 04102; tel. and fax (207) 774-3600; e-mail director@northatlanticports.org; internet www.northatlanticports.org; f. 1949; cos with an interest in marine terminal facilities in the North Atlantic Range; 110 mems; Pres. CORINE E. BARBOUR; Sec.-Treas. THOMAS VALLEAU.

Offshore Marine Service Association (OMSA): 990 North Corporate Dr., Suite 210, Harahan, LA 70123; tel. (504) 734-7622; fax (504) 734-7134; e-mail kenwells@offshoremarine.org; internet www.offshoremarine.org; f. 1973; represents owners and operators of vessels serving offshore installations; 250 mem. cos; Pres. KEN WELLS.

Pacific Maritime Association: 555 Market St, San Francisco, CA 94105-2800; tel. (415) 576-3200; fax (415) 348-8392; internet www.pmanet.org; provides industrial relations services for the shipping industry; Pres. and CEO JIM C. MCKENNA.

Propeller Club of the United States: 3927 Old Lee Hwy, Suite 101A, Fairfax, VA 22030; tel. (703) 691-2777; fax (703) 691-4173; e-mail info@propellerclubhq.com; internet www.propellerclubhq.com; f. 1927; promotes the American Merchant Marine, and the development of Great Lakes, waterways and harbours; 13,000 mems; Int. Pres. ROCKY A. NIGRETTO.

Sailors' Union of the Pacific (SUP): 450 Harrison St, San Francisco, CA 94105; tel. (415) 777-3400; fax (415) 777-5088; internet www.sailors.org; f. 1885; publrs of monthly *West Coast Sailors* magazine; Pres. and Sec.-Treas. GUNNAR LUNDEBERG.

Seafarers International Union of North America: 5201 Auth Way, Camp Springs, MD 20746; tel. (301) 899-0675; fax (301) 899-7355; e-mail webmaster@seafarers.org; internet www.seafarers.org; f. 1938; Pres. MICHAEL SACCO; Exec. Vice-Pres. AUGUSTIN TELLEZ.

Society of Marine Port Engineers: 111 Broad St, POB 369, Eatontown, NJ 07724; tel. (732) 389-2009; fax (732) 389-2264; e-mail dmoore@smpe.org; internet www.smpe.org; f. 1946; Chair. SERGIO ANTONINI; Pres. MIKE FORD.

Steamship Association of Louisiana: 316 Board of Trade Pl., New Orleans, LA 70130; tel. (504) 522-9392; fax (504) 523-2140; e-mail steamship@sshipla.org; internet www.sshipla.org; f. 1912; steamship agents, owners and operators; Chair. PAUL CLANCEY; Gen. Man. SEAN M. DUFFY.

Transportation and Logistics Council, Inc: 120 Main St, Huntington, NY 11743; tel. (631) 549-8988; fax (631) 549-8962; e-mail tlc@transportlaw.com; internet www.tlcouncil.org; f. 1974 as the Shippers National Freight Claim Council, Inc; subsequently Transportation Consumer Protection Council, Inc; present name adopted 2005; represents claimants' interests in cases of loss, damage and overcharging; Chair. ROB STROUSE.

Transportation Institute: 5201 Auth Way, Camp Springs, MD 20746; tel. (301) 423-3335; e-mail info@trans-inst.org; internet www.trans-inst.org; f. 1967; US-flag shipping, towing and dredging companies concerned with research and education on transportation problems, particularly waterborne commerce; Chair. and Pres. JAMES L. HENRY.

CIVIL AVIATION

United States Air Carriers: Summary

(scheduled services, millions)

	2005		2006		2007	
	Domestic	International	Domestic	International	Domestic	International
Passengers enplaned	670.4	68.2	671.7	72.8	693.2	76.0
Revenue passenger miles	579,688	199,316	585,392	212,030	604,166	224,866
Passengers, revenue ton-miles flown	57,969	19,932	58,539	21,203	60,417	22,487
Cargo, ton-miles flown	13,354	14,682	13,274	16,008	13,221	16,304

Source: Air Transport Association of America.

Aircraft Departures, Enplaned Passengers and Freight by State

	Aircraft departures*	Enplaned passengers†	Freight (short tons)‡
Alabama	49,874	2,664,200	50,822
Alaska	72,516	4,696,137	837,455
Arizona	223,212	23,387,651	142,049
Arkansas	39,187	1,969,115	10,362
California	850,328	87,097,241	1,674,101
Colorado	233,812	24,845,029	145,825
Connecticut	47,479	3,452,667	90,056
Delaware	175	9,850	70,772
District of Columbia	176,519	20,827,931§	105,971
Florida	565,320	66,590,137	763,164
Georgia	441,386	42,611,075	311,446
Hawaii	168,075	16,555,584	298,686
Idaho	36,655	2,024,370	23,549
Illinois	517,833	47,030,377	569,233
Indiana	115,731	4,896,795	628,949
Iowa	44,221	1,606,576	71,157
Kansas	15,612	850,180	16,432
Kentucky	70,261	10,359,310	1,155,164
Louisiana	100,609	4,488,907	43,483
Maine	13,457	1,169,863	8,255
Maryland	102,192	10,371,742	61,654
Massachusetts	153,832	14,132,638	134,078
Michigan	311,078	20,160,826	134,201
Minnesota	249,694	17,391,693	158,178
Mississippi	29,225	1,251,931	7,097
Missouri	304,333	12,990,823	136,012
Montana	28,311	1,455,422	22,437
Nebraska	35,847	2,309,061	38,027
Nevada	195,286	24,774,406	79,745
New Hampshire	21,677	1,970,382	43,867
New Jersey	235,881	18,297,762	383,125
New Mexico	43,039	3,241,903	50,623
New York	395,086	42,621,183	415,398
North Carolina	254,950	21,587,620	169,685
North Dakota	15,076	668,670	11,575
Ohio	400,200	11,015,279	658,990
Oklahoma	61,512	3,453,886	38,887
Oregon	124,856	7,909,180	121,634

—continued	Aircraft departures*	Enplaned passengers†	Freight (short tons)‡
Pennsylvania	309,437	21,905,339	397,123
Rhode Island	31,876	2,604,910	9,059
South Carolina	54,343	3,138,696	178,776
South Dakota	21,613	649,159	24,933
Tennessee	213,265	11,569,563	2,094,688
Texas	963,557	69,899,601	743,058
Utah	90,379	10,412,863	84,496
Vermont	6,065	683,991	4,080
Virginia	60,118	3,823,501	59,043
Washington	231,144	16,956,692	230,831
West Virginia	10,299	356,839	2,464
Wisconsin	103,204	5,518,953	53,419
Wyoming	8,758	478,044	3,683
Total	8,851,395	752,154,089	13,570,797

* 2000 figures.
† 2007 figures, preliminary.
‡ 2005 figures.
§ Including Washington Dulles International and Ronald Reagan Washington National Airports, but excluding Baltimore/Washington International Thurgood Marshal Airport, which is located in Maryland.
Source: Bureau of Transportation Statistics, US Department of Transportation.

Directory

REGULATORY BODY

Federal Aviation Administration: 800 Independence Ave, SW, Washington, DC 20591; tel. (202) 366-4000; internet www.faa.gov; f. 1958; part of the Dept of Transportation; promotes safety in the air, regulates air commerce and assists in development of an effective national airport system; Administrator ROBERT A. STURGELL (acting).

PRINCIPAL SCHEDULED COMPANIES

Air Wisconsin Airlines Corpn (AWAC): W6390 Challenger Dr., Suite 203, Dutagamie Airport, Appleton, WI 54914-9120; tel. (920) 739-5123; fax (920) 749-4158; e-mail annette.daly@airwis.com; internet www.airwis.com; f. 1965; domestic flights to 69 cities in 26 states in the USA and Canada; Chair. RICHARD BARTLETT; Pres. and CEO JAMES P. RANKIN.

Alaska Airlines: 19300 International Blvd, POB 68900, Seattle, WA 98188; tel. (206) 433-3200; fax (206) 392-7750; e-mail reservations@alaskaair.com; internet www.alaskaair.com; f. 1932; scheduled passenger services to 70 destinations in the USA, Canada and Mexico; Pres., Chair. and CEO WILLIAM S. AYER.

Horizon Air: 19521 Pacific Hwy South, Seattle, WA 98188; tel. (206) 431-3647; e-mail support@horizonair.com; internet www.horizonair.com; f. 1981; scheduled cargo services; Pres. and CEO JEFFERY D. PINNEO.

American Airlines, Inc: POB 619612, Dallas/Fort Worth Airport, TX 75261-9612; tel. (817) 967-1234; fax (817) 962-4162; internet www.aa.com; f. 1934; coast-to-coast domestic routes and services to Canada, Hawaii, Mexico, the Caribbean, South America, Europe and the Far East; acquired Trans World Airlines in 2001; Pres., Chair. and CEO GERARD J. ARPEY.

Continental Airlines, Inc: POB 4607, Houston, TX 77210-4607; 1600 Smith St, Houston, TX 77002; tel. (713) 324-5152; fax (713) 324-2637; e-mail geninfo@coair.com; internet www.continental.com; f. 1934; serves 154 US destinations and 138 international destinations; Pres. JEFF SMISEK.

Delta Air Lines, Inc: 1030 Delta Blvd, POB 20706, Atlanta, GA 30320-6001; tel. (770) 715-2600; internet www.delta.com; f. 1928; domestic and international services to 295 destinations in 46 countries; announced an agreement to merge with Northwest Airlines in April 2008; CEO RICHARD ANDERSON.

FedEx Corpn: 942 South Shady Grove Rd, Memphis, TN 38120; tel. (901) 369-3600; e-mail smunoz@fedex.com; internet www.fedex.com; f. 1971; world's largest express transport co; serves over 220 countries; 670 aircraft; Pres., Chair. and CEO FREDERICK W. SMITH.

Hawaiian Airlines, Inc: 3375 Koapaka St, G-350, Honolulu, HI 96819; tel. (808) 835-3700; fax (808) 835-3690; internet www.hawaiianair.com; f. 1929 as Inter-Island Airways Ltd; inter-island, US mainland and South Pacific services; Pres. and CEO MARK B. DUNKERLEY.

Northwest Airlines, Inc: 2700 Lone Oak Parkway, Eagan, MN 55121-1534; tel. (612) 726-2111; fax (612) 726-0622; internet www.nwa.com; f. 1926; coast-to-coast domestic routes and services to Canada, Europe and the Far East; announced an agreement to merge with Delta Air Lines in April 2008; Chair. ROY BOSTOCK; Pres. and CEO DOUGLAS M. STEENLAND.

Piedmont Airlines, Inc: 5443 Airport Terminal Rd, Salisbury, MD 21804-1700; tel. (410) 742-2996; fax (410) 742-4478; internet www.piedmont-airlines.com; f. 1931; wholly owned subsidiary of US Airways Group, Inc; domestic and international services to 55 cities in the USA and Canada; Pres. and CEO STEPHEN R. FARROW.

Southwest Airlines: POB 36647, Dallas, TX 75235-1647; tel. (214) 792-4223; internet www.southwest.com; f. 1971; scheduled services to 64 cities in 32 states; Pres. COLLEEN BARRETT; Chair. and CEO GARY KELLY.

United Airlines Corpn: POB 66100, Chicago, IL 60666; tel. (847) 700-9838; fax (847) 700-4081; internet www.united.com; f. 1931; domestic and international services to over 200 destinations; Pres., Chair. and CEO GLENN F. TILTON, Jr.

US Airways, Inc: 4000 East Sky Harbor Blvd, Phoenix, AZ 85034; tel. (480) 693-0800; fax (480) 693-2300; internet www.usairways.com; f. 1939 as All-American Airways; merged with America West Airlines in 2005; scheduled passenger services to 237 destinations world-wide; Chair. and CEO DOUG PARKER; Pres. SCOTT KIRBY.

ASSOCIATIONS

Aerospace Industries Association of America, Inc (AIA): 1000 Wilson Blvd, Suite 1700, Arlington, VA 22209-3928; tel. (703) 358-1000; fax (703) 358-1012; e-mail membership@aia-aerospace.org; internet www.aia-aerospace.org; f. 1919; 104 mems and 175 assoc. mems; Pres. and CEO MARION C. BLAKEY.

Aircraft Electronic Association: 3570 NE Ralph Powell Rd, Lee's Summit, MO 64064; tel. (816) 347-8400; fax (816) 347-8405; e-mail info@aea.net; internet www.aea.net; over 1,300 mems; Pres. PAULA DERKS.

Aircraft Mechanics Fraternal Association (AMFA): 14001 E. Iliff Ave, Suite 217, Aurora, CO 80014; tel. (303) 752-2632; fax (303) 362-7736; e-mail admin@amfanatl.org; internet www.amfanatl.org; f. 1962; 13,532 mems; Nat. Dir STEVE MACFARLANE.

Aircraft Owners and Pilots Association (AOPA): 421 Aviation Way, Frederick, MD 21701; tel. (301) 695-2000; fax (301) 695-2375; e-mail aopahq@aopa.org; internet www.aopa.org; over 408,000 mems; Pres. PHIL BOYER.

Air Line Pilots Association (ALPA): 1625 Massachusetts Ave NW, Washington, DC 20036; tel. (703) 689-2270; internet www.alpa.org; f. 1931; represents 53,000 pilots at 37 airlines in USA and Canada; Pres. Capt. JOHN PRATER.

Air Traffic Control Association, Inc: 1101 King St, Suite 300, Alexandria, VA 22314; tel. (703) 299-2430; fax (703) 299-2437; e-mail info@atca.org; internet www.atca.org; f. 1956; 2,500 mems; Chair. NEIL PLANZER.

Air Transport Association of America, Inc: 1301 Pennsylvania Ave, NW, Suite 1100, Washington, DC 20004-1707; tel. (202) 626-4000; fax (202) 626-4181; e-mail ata@airlines.org; internet www.airlines.org; f. 1936; 18 US airlines mems, 3 non-US assoc. mems; Pres. and CEO JAMES C. MAY.

Airline Industrial Relations Conference: 1300 19th St, NW, Suite 750, Washington, DC 20036; tel. (202) 861-7550; fax (202) 861-7557; e-mail staff@aircon.org; internet www.aircon.org; f. 1971; 20 mems; Pres. DONALD W. MALINIAK.

Airport Ground Transportation Association: UMSL Center for Transportation Studies, 154 University Center, 8001 Natural Bridge Rd, St Louis, MO 63121-4499; tel. (314) 516-7271; fax (314) 516-7272;

e-mail admin@agtaweb.org; internet agtaweb.org; f. 1945; Pres. FAROUQ MASSOUD.

Airports Council International-North America (ACI-NA): 1775 K St, NW, Suite 500, Washington, DC 20006; tel. (202) 293-8500; fax (202) 331-1362; e-mail cshoemaker@aci-na.aero; internet www.aci-na.org; f. 1948; 213 mems, 546 assoc. mems in the USA and Canada; Chair. RANDALL H. WALKER; Pres. GREG PRINCIPATO.

American Association of Airport Executives (AAAE): 601 Madison St, Alexandria, VA 22314; tel. (703) 824-0500; fax (703) 820-1395; e-mail tyra.harpster@aaae.org; internet www.aaae.org; f. 1928; 4,000 mems; Pres. CHARLES M. BARCLAY.

American Helicopter Society (Vertical Flight Society): 217 North Washington St, Alexandria, VA 22314-2538; tel. (703) 684-6777; fax (703) 739-9279; e-mail staff@vtol.org; internet www.vtol.org; f. 1944; Pres. STEPHEN D. RAMSAY; Chair. JEFFREY PINO.

American Institute of Aeronautics and Astronautics (AIAA): 1801 Alexander Bell Dr., Suite 500, Reston, VA 20191-4344; tel. (703) 264-7500; fax (703) 264-7551; e-mail custserv@aiaa.org; internet www.aiaa.org; f. 1963; over 31,000 mems; Pres. GEORGE K. MUELLNER; Exec. Dir BOB DICKMAN.

Association of Flight Attendants-CWA (AFA): 501 Third St, NW, Washington, DC 20001; tel. (202) 434-1300; e-mail info@afacwa.org; internet www.afanet.org; 55,000 mems; Int. Pres. PATRICIA A. FRIEND.

Aviation Development Council (ADC): 141-07 20th Ave, Suite 404, Whitestone, NY 11357; tel. (718) 746-0212; fax (718) 746-1006; e-mail root@aviationdevelopmentcouncil.org; internet aviationdevelopmentcouncil.org; f. 1962; liaises between airlines and local communities; Dir WILLIAM HUISMAN.

Cargo Airline Association: 1220 19th St, NW, Washington, DC 20036; tel. (202) 293-1030; fax (202) 293-4377; e-mail info@cargoair.org; internet www.cargoair.org; f. 1948; 15 mems; Pres. STEPHEN A. ALTERMAN.

Council of Defense and Space Industry Associations (CODSIA): 1000 Wilson Blvd, Suite 1800, Arlington, VA 22209; tel. (703) 243-2020; fax (703) 243-8539; e-mail info@codsia.org; internet www.codsia.org; f. 1964; 10 mems.

Express Delivery and Logistics Association (XLA): 14 West Third St, Suite 200, Kansas City, MO 64105; tel. (816) 221-0254; fax (816) 472-7765; e-mail kristy@robstan.org; internet www.expressassociation.org; f. 1976 as Air Courier Conference of America; 300 mems; Exec. Dir KRISTY MCKIBBEN.

Flight Safety Foundation (FSF): 601 Madison St, Suite 300, Alexandria, VA 22314-1756; tel. (703) 739-6700; fax (703) 739-6708; internet www.flightsafety.org; f. 1947; 1,007 mems; Pres. and CEO WILLIAM R. VOSS.

General Aviation Manufacturers Association (GAMA): 1400 K St, NW, Suite 801, Washington, DC 20005; tel. (202) 393-1500; fax (202) 842-4063; e-mail sgoldstein@gama.aero; internet www.gama.aero; f. 1970; 56 mem. cos; Pres. PETER J. BUNCE, IV.

Helicopter Association International: 1635 Prince St, Alexandria, VA 22314; tel. (703) 683-4646; fax (703) 683-4745; internet www.rotor.com; f. 1948; publishes *ROTOR Magazine* (quarterly, circ. 20,000) and *The Helicopter Annual* (circ. 17,000); 2,683 mems; Chair. PATRICK CORR; Pres. MATTHEW S. ZUCARRO.

Helicopter Safety Advisory Conference: c/o Mark Fontenot, Bristow Group, Inc, 2000 West Sam Houston Pkwy S, Suite 1700, Houston, TX 77042; tel. (713) 267-7625; fax (713) 267-7620; e-mail mark.fontenot@bristowgroup.com; internet www.hsac.org; f. 1978; 115 mems; Chair. MARK FONTENOT.

International Air Cargo Association (TIACA): POB 661510, Miami, FL 33266-1510; tel. (786) 265-7011; fax (786) 265-7012; e-mail secgen@tiaca.org; internet www.tiaca.org; Chair. JACK BOISEN.

International Co-ordinating Council of Aerospace Industries Associations (ICCAIA): 1250 Eye St, NW, Washington, DC 20005; tel. (202) 371-8456; fax (202) 371-8471; e-mail info@iccaia.org; internet www.iccaia.org; f. 1987; official observer org. to the Int. Civil Aviation Organization (ICAO) representing manufacturers of civil aviation products; 5 mems; Chair. MARION C. BLAKEY.

International Council of Aircraft Owner and Pilot Associations (IAOPA): 421 Aviation Way, Frederick, MD 21701; tel. (301) 695-2220; fax (301) 695-2375; e-mail airmail@iaopa.org; internet www.iaopa.org; f. 1962; over 470,000 mems in 66 affiliate orgs; Pres. PHIL BOYER.

International Society of Women Airline Pilots: 2250E Tropicana Ave, Suite 19-395, Las Vegas, NV 89119-6594; e-mail isachairwoman@sbcglobal.net; internet www.iswap.org; f. 1978; 255 mems; Chair. ANN KIEFFER.

National Aeronautic Association of the USA (NAA): 1737 King St, Suite 220, Alexandria, VA 22314; tel. (703) 416-4888; fax (703) 416-4877; e-mail naa@naa.aero; internet www.naa.aero; f. 1905; 22 corporate mems and 14 affiliate mems; Pres. JONATHAN GAFFNEY.

National Air Carrier Association: 1000 Wilson Blvd, Suite 1700, Arlington, VA 22209; tel. (703) 358-8060; e-mail kbradley@naca.cc; internet www.naca.cc; f. 1962; 16 mems; Pres. TOM ZOELLER.

National Air Transportation Association: 4226 King St, Alexandria, VA 22302; tel. (703) 845-9000; fax (703) 845-8176; internet www.nata.aero; f. 1940; approx. 2,000 mems; Pres. JAMES. K. COYNE.

National Association of State Aviation Officials (NASAO): Washington National Airport Hangar 7, Suite 218, Washington, DC 20001; tel. (703) 417-1880; fax (703) 417-1885; e-mail henryo@nasao.org; internet www.nasao.org; f. 1931; represents aviation agency workers in all 50 states, Guam and Puerto Rico; Chair. TRAVIS VALLIN; Pres. and CEO HENRY M. OGRODZINSKI.

National Business Aviation Association, Inc: 1200 18th St, NW, Suite 400, Washington, DC 20036-2527; tel. (202) 783-9000; fax (202) 331-8364; e-mail info@nbaa.org; internet www.nbaa.org; f. 1947; 8,000 mems; Pres. and CEO ED BOLEN.

The Ninety Nines, Inc—International Organization of Women Pilots: 4300 Amelia Earhart Rd, Oklahoma City, OK 73159; tel. (405) 685-7969; fax (405) 685-7985; e-mail 99s@ninety-nines.org; internet www.ninety-nines.org; f. 1929; over 5,000 mems from 36 countries; Int. Pres. SUSAN LARSON.

Organization of Black Airline Pilots: 8630 Fenton St, Suite 126, Silver Spring, MD 20910; tel. (201) 568-8145; e-mail nationaloffice@obap.org; internet www.obap.org; f. 1976; over 2,500 mems; Chair. CHERYL CHEW; Pres. JAMES GORDON.

Professional Aviation Maintenance Association (PAMA): 400 Commonwealth Drive, Warrendale, PA 15096; tel. (724) 772-4092; fax (724) 772-4064; e-mail hq@pama.org; internet www.pama.org; f. 1972; 3,800 mems; Chair. CLARK GORDON.

Regional Airline Association: 2025 M St, NW, Suite 800, Washington, DC 20036-3309; tel. (202) 367-1170; fax (202) 367-2170; e-mail raa@raa.org; internet www.raa.org; f. 1975; 42 mems; Pres. RYAN BEDFORD.

Seaplane Pilots' Association: 3859 Laird Blvd, Suite C, Lakeland, FL 33811; tel. (863) 701-7979; fax (863) 701-7588; e-mail spa@seaplanes.org; internet www.seaplanes.org; f. 1972; 7,500 mems in the USA, Canada, Europe and Australia; Exec. Dir Dr JAMES MCMANUS.

United States Pilots' Association: 483 South Kirkwood Rd, Suite 10, St Louis, MO 63122; tel. (314) 849-8772; fax (309) 315-6323; e-mail jan@hoynacki.com; internet www.uspilots.org; f. 1981; 6,000 mems; Exec. Dir JAN HOYNACKI.

US Contract Tower Association (USCTA): 601 Madison St, Alexandria, VA 22314; tel. (703) 824-0500; fax (703) 820-1395; e-mail walt@ou.edu; internet www.contracttower.org; promotes aviation safety; Chair. WALTER B. STRONG.

Wings Club: POB 4464, New York, NY 10163; tel. (212) 867-1770; fax (212) 809-5435; e-mail wingsclub@aol.com; internet www.wingsclub.org; f. 1942; 900 mems; Pres. JOHN FEREN.

Wireless Airport Association (WAA): 601 Madison St, Alexandria, VA 22314; tel. (703) 820-1395; e-mail eryn.travis@airportnet.org; internet www.wirelessairport.org; f. 2001; asscn jtly formed by Int. Asscn of Airport Executives (IAAE), Air Transport Asscn (ATA) and Airports Council Int.-North America (ACI-NA, q.v.) to promote the use of wireless technology in airports; 166 airport mems, 36 airline mems and 853 assoc. mems; Exec. Dir CARTER MORRIS.

TELECOMMUNICATIONS

INTRODUCTION

The USA constitutes the world's biggest market for communications and broadcasting systems. In 2005 there were an estimated 594 telephone lines per 1,000 people. In 2006 there were 777 mobile cellular telephone subscribers per 1,000 people. In 2004 the US telecommunications industry generated revenues of US $291,123m., according to the US Census Bureau. The provision of telecommunications services was dominated by the Bell System, operated by AT&T (American Telegraph and Telephone Company) until 1982, when AT&T's role was modified following the settlement of an anti-trust suit. In that year AT&T made independent the 22 local Bell System operating companies in which it held more than a 50% stake. Two years later ownership of the local companies was transferred to seven new regional telephone companies. A number of mergers between those regional companies has since reduced their number to three. AT&T, Inc (see below) is now the largest local fixed-line operator in the USA, and is also the largest mobile cellular telephone network provider following its acquisition in 2006 of Cingular Wireless, which was formerly a joint-owned enterprise with the BellSouth Corpn (see below). Verizon Communications, Inc, and its wireless subsidiary, Verizon Wireless, follows close behind in both sectors. The long-distance telephone market was dominated by AT&T, Inc, Verizon and Sprint Nextel Corpn (which was formed by the merger of Sprint Corpn with Nextel Communications in December 2004). In November 2005 AT&T and SBC Communications merged to form AT&T, Inc and in January 2006 Verizon completed its acquisition of MCI, which had been formed in 2004 following the restructuring of WorldCom, Inc. In December 2006 AT&T, Inc merged with the BellSouth Corpn, while in 2008 Verizon announced a planned takeover of Alltel.

At the beginning of the 21st century the internet was a major method of communications in the USA. The internet existed from the late 1960s but was used only by the US military. It was not until the mid-1980s that it became more accessible to the general public. As the internet developed, it fragmented into networks owned and operated by different groups of people. In 2004 there were 664.5 internet hosts per 1,000 people, compared with 21.1 in 1995, while 630 in every 1,000 people in the USA had internet access.

By 2005 the use of internet telephony, especially for long-distance and international calls, was increasing dramatically. The so-called 'Voice over Internet Protocol' (VoIP) technology enables callers to communicate via headsets connected to computers. VoIP technology also allows for calls to be made from computers to fixed line or cellular telephones. Many of the larger US telephone service providers, including Verizon and AT&T, Inc, offered unlimited VoIP-enabled calls to the USA and selected other countries for a small monthly subscription fee. However, the sound quality of VoIP-enabled calls varied greatly, depending on hardware limitations and user demand, and call duration could be limited. There were also concerns over privacy. None the less, it was widely predicted by industry analysts that, as the technology and availability improved, internet telephony would come to dominate the long-distance and international telephony market. The acquisition in September 2005 of the internet telephony company Skype by the internet auction company eBay was valued at some US $2,600m. (with an additional $1,500m. in performance-dependent rewards), representing the largest investment to date in the market.

Regulatory Body

Telecommunications services are regulated within individual states by the state public utility commissions (see the chapter on The States, below). The Federal Communications Commission was established under the Communications Act of 1934 to regulate all interstate and international communications by radio, television, wire and cable, 'in the public interest'. Its responsibilities were extended under the Communications Satellite Act of 1962.

Federal Communications Commission (FCC): 445 12th St, SW, Washington, DC 20554; tel. (888) 225-5322; fax (202) 418-0232; e-mail fccinfo@fcc.gov; internet www.fcc.gov; f. 1934; Chair. Kevin J. Martin.

Use of Selected Telecommunications Technology, 2005–07

	2005	2006	2007
Telephones ('000 main lines in use)	175,160.9	167,459.9	163,170.8
Mobile cellular telephones ('000 subscribers)	213,000	241,800	255,396
Personal computers ('000 in use)	223,810.0*	n.a.	n.a.
Internet users ('000)	197,800	210,200	220,000
Broadband subscribers ('000)	48,089.8	60,522.0	65,616.4

* Estimate.

Source: International Telecommunication Union.

MAJOR TELECOMMUNICATIONS NETWORKS

Alltel Corpn (ALLTEL): Bldg 4, 3rd Floor, 1 Allied Dr., Little Rock, AR 72202-2099; tel. (501) 905-6078; e-mail dale.ingram@alltel.com; internet www.alltel.com; f. 1943 as Allied Telephone; current name adopted when merged with Mid-Continent in 1983; acquired by jt venture of TPG Capital and Goldman Sachs in May 2007; plans announced in June 2008 by Verizon Wireless, a jt venture of Verizon Communications and Vodafone Group PLC (United Kingdom), to acquire Alltel Corpn; mobile-only service operated from 2006; serves 13m. customers in 35 states; Pres. and CEO Scott Ford; c. 12m. subscribers.

AT&T, Inc (American Telegraph and Telephone): 175 East Houston St, San Antonio, TX 78205; tel. (212) 387-5400; fax (212) 226-4935; internet www.att.com; f. 1885; bought by SBC Communications in Jan. 2005, merger completed and present name adopted in Nov. 2005; merged with the BellSouth Corpn in Dec. 2006, and acquired full ownership of Cingular Wireless; 100m. customers; Chair. and CEO Randall L. Stephenson.

CenturyTel, Inc: 100 CenturyTel Dr., Monroe, LA 71203; tel. (318) 388-9000; fax (318) 340-5520; e-mail annmarie.sartor@centurytel.com; internet www.centurytel.com; f. 1930; operates 2.1m. access lines in 25 states; 600,000 internet customers; Chair. and CEO Glen F. Post, III; Pres. and COO Karen A. Puckett.

Comcast Corpn: 1500 Market St, Philadelphia, PA 19102; internet www.comcast.com; tel. (215) 286-7408; e-mail corporate_communications@comcast.com; f. 1963; acquired AT&T Broadband in 2002; acquired part of Adelphia Communications in 2006; 24.1m. cable subscribers in 39 states and the District of Columbia, 12.4m. internet customers, 3.5m. cable telephone subscribers; Chair. and CEO Brian L. Roberts; Exec. Vice Pres. David L. Cohen.

Frontier Communications: 3 High Ridge Park, Stamford, CT 06905-1390; tel. (203) 614-5600; fax (203) 614-4602; e-mail citizens@czn.com; internet www.czn.com; f. 1935; 3m. access lines in 24 states; fmrly Citizens Communications Co; acquisition of Commonwealth Telephone Enterprises completed in March 2007; Pres. and CEO Maggie Wilderotter; Exec. Vice-Pres. and COO Daniel McCarthy.

Qwest Communications International, Inc: 1801 California St, Denver, CO 80202; tel. (303) 992-1400; fax (303) 896-8515; e-mail qnews@qwest.com; internet www.qwest.com; telephone and internet provider to 21.8m. customers in the USA; acquired US West in 2000; Chair. and CEO Edward A. Mueller; Exec. Vice-Pres. of Operations Robert Tregemba.

SES Americom: 4 Research Way, Princeton, NJ 08540; tel. (609) 987-4000; fax (609) 987-4517; e-mail info.americom@ses-americom.com; internet www.ses-americom.com; f. 1975; fmrly GE Americom, part of SES Global following merger with SES Astra; 16 satellites covering North, Central, South America, the Caribbean, the People's Republic of China, North-East and South Asia; Pres. and CEO Robert Bednarek.

Sprint Nextel Corpn: 2001 Edmund Halley Dr., Reston, VA 20191; tel. (703) 433-4700; e-mail investor.relations@sprint.com; internet www.sprint.com; f. 2004 by merger of Sprint Corpn with Nextel Communications; digital cellular and wireless internet services; 52m. subscribers (2008); Chair. JAMES H. HANCE, Jr; CEO DANIEL R. HESSE.

Time Warner Cable: 290 Harbor Dr., Stamford, CT 06902; tel. (203) 328-3217; internet www.timewarnercable.com; f. 1989; jt purchase of Adelphia Communications Corpn with Comcast Corpn completed in 2006; 13.5m. customers in 33 states; Chair. DON LOGAN; Pres. and CEO JEFFREY L. BEWKES.

Verizon Communications: 140 West St, New York, NY 10007; tel. (800) 621-9900; internet www.verizon.com; f. 2000 by merger of Bell Atlantic Corpn and GTE Corpn; divisions include Verizon Business, fmrly MCI, Inc; 228,600 employees; Chair. and CEO IVAN G. SEIDENBERG; Pres. and COO DENNIS G. STRIGL.

Windstream Communications: 4001 Rodney Parham Rd, Little Rock, AR 72212; tel. (501) 748-5876; internet www.windstream.com; f. 2006 by merger of Alltel Corpn's fmr wireline business and VALOR Communications; around 3.2m. access lines in 16 states; 7,500 employees; Pres. and CEO JEFF R. GARDNER; Exec. Vice-Pres. BRENT WHITTINGTON.

Associations

COMPTEL: 900 17th St, NW, Suite 400, Washington, DC 20006; tel. (202) 296-6650; fax (202) 296-7585; e-mail mboles@comptel.org; internet www.comptel.org; f. 2005 by merger of CompTel/ASCENT and the Asscn for Local Telecommunications Services (ALTS); over 250 mem. cos; promotes competitiveness in long-distance telecommunications market; CEO JERRY JAMES (acting); Chair. J. SHERMAN HENDERSON, III.

CTIA—The Wireless Association: 1400 16th St, NW, Suite 600, Washington, DC 20036; tel. (202) 785-0081; fax (202) 785-0721; e-mail ctamayo@ctia.org; internet www.ctia.org; f. 1984; 277 mems; non-profit asscn representing cos from all sectors of wireless communications; Pres. and CEO STEVE LARGENT.

European Utilities Telecom Council (EUTC): 1901 Pennsylvania Ave, NW, 5th Floor, Washington, DC 20006; tel. (202) 872-0030; fax (202) 872-1331; e-mail admin@utc.org; internet www.eutc.org; f. 1948; non-profit asscn representing telecommunications and information interests of public utilities, natural gas pipelines and other infrastructure cos and their strategic business partners; Chair. MIGUEL ANGEL SÁNCHEZ FORNIÉ; Pres. and CEO WILLIAM R. MORONEY.

National Telecommunications Cooperative Association (NTCA): 4121 Wilson Blvd, Suite 1000, Arlington, VA 22203; tel. (703) 351-2000; fax (703) 351-2001; e-mail wmann@ntca.org; internet www.ntca.org; f. 1954; provides representation for small telecommunications cos and those operating in rural areas; 260 co-operative and 315 commercial co mems, 61 mem. asscns, 412 assoc. mems, 104 subsidiary mems, 10 int. mems; CEO MICHAEL E. BRUNNER.

United States Telecom Association (USTelecom): 607 14th St, NW, Suite 400, Washington, DC 20005; tel. (202) 326-7300; fax (202) 326-7333; e-mail pkrebs@ustelecom.org; internet www.ustelecom.org; Pres. and CEO WALTER B. MCCORMICK, Jr; Chair. RON B. MCCUE.

FINANCE

BANKING

Introduction

COMMERCIAL BANKING IN THE USA

The US banking system is the largest and, in many respects, the most comprehensive and sophisticated in the world. Banking has, however, been largely subject to state rather than federal jurisdiction, and this has created a structure very different from that in other advanced industrial countries. The Banking Act of 1933 prohibited out-of-state bank-holding companies from buying in-state banks. Federal anti-trust laws also limited mergers of banks within a state. These measures preserved the independence of a large number of banks. However, starting in the late 1970s and continuing through the 1980s, restrictions were relaxed on both state-wide and interstate branching. In June 1985 the US Supreme Court ruled that federal legislation prohibiting interstate banks did not preclude state governments from permitting regional interstate banking. Consequently, the influence of the traditionally dominant banks—the main banks in the industrial states of New York, North Carolina and Illinois—was increasingly challenged by the formation of several groupings of regional banks. The gradual removal of interstate branching restrictions culminated in the 1994 Riegle-Neal Interstate Banking and Branching Efficiency Act that allowed banks and bank-holding companies to establish branches in different states. Further changes to the regulatory framework was brought about by the 1999 Gramm-Leach-Bliley Financial Services Modernization Act that permitted greater horizontal and vertical integration among banks, securities firms and insurance companies. The Act aimed to increase competition and efficiency in the financial services industry and created a new type of financial services company, the financial holding company. In 2008 the banking industry came under severe strain following the sharp contraction in world-wide credit markets and the declared bankruptcy, in September, of the financial services firm Lehman Brothers. The Emergency Economic Stabilization Act of 2008, approved by Congress in October, provided some US $700,000m. of rescue aid to the US Treasury to redistribute in the markets. In the same month the Government subsequently announced that it would purchase equity stakes in nine of the largest financial institutions, at a cost of around $250,000m.

By 2006 eight banks had more than 1,000 branches in the USA. The number of commercial banks decreased from 12,329 in 1990 to 7,203 in mid-2008.Of these, small commercial banks with assets of less than US $1,000m. represented 93.1% of the total number and held 12.1% of total assets. In October 2003 the Bank of America announced the acquisition of FleetBoston Financial Corporation, creating the largest bank in the USA. In 2006 the restructured Bank of America operated 5,873 branch offices, and controlled total deposits of more than $937,052m. (or 14.6% of all domestic banking deposits in the USA). The merger in 2004 of JP Morgan Chase & Co and Bank One Corporation established the second largest bank in the USA, with 2,798 branches and total assets in December 2006 of $1,019,497m.

Although consolidation in the banking sector in the early 2000s substantially diminished the number of commercial banks, the number of bank branches and access to banking facilities continued to increase. There were, however, fewer credit unions and significantly fewer savings institutions in 2004 than in 1990, in terms of both banks and branches. The total number of savings institutions declined by more than one-third from 21,609 in 1990 to 13,691 in 2004. The possession of bank accounts and the use of banking facilities are perhaps more widespread among all regions and social groups in the USA than in any other country. This has influenced the formulation of monetary theory and policy, as bank credit has become a more important factor than currency supply in the regulation of the economy. The use of current accounts and credit cards is so common that many authorities claim that the USA can be regarded as effectively a cashless society.

Bank Holding Companies

Since 1956 bank holding companies, corporations that control one or more banks in the USA, have become significant elements in the banking system. These organizations control commercial banks which, at the end of 1989, held 93.4% of the total assets of insured commercial banks in the USA. The proportion of banks owned by holding companies increased from 62% in 1984 to 76% in 2000. In 2004 there were 5,151 bank-holding companies, of which some 12% had financial holding company status.

Expansion Overseas

From the mid-1960s, the leading banks rapidly expanded their overseas interests. At the end of 1960 there were only eight US banks operating foreign branches, mostly in Latin America and the Far East. By 1988 there were 147 US Federal Reserve System member banks operating 854 foreign branches. The main factors behind this expansion were the geographical limitations imposed by law at home; the rapid expansion of US business interests abroad; the faster economic growth of certain foreign markets; and finally the profitability of the 'Eurodollar' capital markets. The expansion in the overseas activities of US banks reached a high point in 1984. Subsequently declining levels of profitability in this area have resulted in the closure of some overseas offices, although the aggregate total of assets held has continued to rise.

In 1981 the Federal Reserve Board sanctioned the establishment of domestic International Banking Facilities, permitting commercial banks within the US (including US branches and agencies of foreign banks) to transact certain types of foreign deposit and loan business free of reserve requirements and, in most cases, state income tax liability.

Insuring Bodies

The Office of Thrift Supervision (OTS), established in 1989 as part of the Department of Treasury, is the primary regulator of all federally chartered and many state-chartered thrift institutions, which include savings banks, and savings and loan institutions. In 2007 a total of 826 institutions were supervised by the OTS. The Federal Deposit Insurance Corporation—FDIC, see Independent Agencies, in the Directory (Public Affairs)—was created in 1933 to provide insurance coverage for bank deposits. Under the Banking Act of 1935 the deposits of all banks which were members of the Federal Reserve System (see below) had to be insured by the FDIC. At 30 June 2008 there were 7,203 FDIC-insured commercial banks in the 50 states and the District of Columbia. At that time a total of 1,248 national savings institutions were insured by the FDIC.

The Federal Home Loan Bank Board was established in 1932 under the Federal Home Loan Bank Act to supervise and regulate the operations of savings and loan associations. The Board insured these associations through its subsidiary, the Federal Savings and Loan Insurance Corporation (FSLIC). In 1989 the FSLIC was abolished, and the Savings Association Insurance Fund (SAIF) was established under the Financial Institution and Reform Recovery and Enforcement Act. In March 2006 the SAIF merged with the Bank Insurance Fund to form the Deposit Insurance Fund.

The Federal Reserve System

(Board of Governors: 20th St and Constitution Ave, NW, Washington, DC 20551; tel. (202) 452-3000; fax (202) 452-3819; internet www.federalreserve.gov)

The Federal Reserve System was established on 23 December 1913, under the Federal Reserve Act of 1913, to provide the USA with a centralized banking system. The System comprises the Board of Governors, the 12 Federal Reserve Banks and their 25 branches, and the Federal Open Market Committee. The Federal Advisory Council, the Consumer Advisory Council and the Thrift Institutions Advisory Council are bodies which assist the Board of Governors in specific policy-making areas. All National Banks are required to be members of the Federal Reserve System. In 2004 some 2,200 commercial banks were members of the Federal Reserve System and held more than 55% of the nation's banking assets.

THE BOARD OF GOVERNORS

Policy affecting the nation's credit and monetary affairs is made by the Federal Reserve Board of Governors, whose seven members are appointed by the President of the USA, with the advice and consent of the Senate, to serve a 14-year term. The Board's chairman and vice-chairman, both of whom are appointed from among the members by the US President, serve renewable four-year terms. In addition to its policy-making responsibilities, the Board of Governors supervises the budgets and operations of the Federal Reserve Banks (see below).

Members (September 2008): BEN S. BERNANKE (Chair.), DONALD L. KOHN (Vice-Chair.), KEVIN M. WARSH, RANDALL S. KROSZNER, ELIZABETH A. DUKE.

FEDERAL RESERVE BANKS

The Reserve Banks were established by Congress as the operating arms of the nation's central banking system. They are empowered to issue Federal Reserve notes fully secured by the following assets, alone or in any combination: gold certificates; US government and agency securities; other eligible assets as described by statute; and Special Drawing Rights certificates. The Reserve Banks may discount paper for depository institutions and make properly secured advances to them. Many of the services performed by this network for depository institutions and for the government are similar to services performed by banks and thrift institutions for business customers and individuals. Reserve Banks hold the reserves of depository institutions and make loans to them. They move currency and coin into and out of circulation, and collect and process millions of cheques each day. They provide banking services for the Treasury, issue and redeem government securities, and act in other ways as fiscal agent for the US government. They also take part in the primary responsibility of the Federal Reserve System, the setting of monetary policy, through the Federal Market Open Committee (see below).

Each of the 12 Federal Reserve Banks has a board of directors consisting of nine members, three of whom (including the chairman and deputy chairman) are appointed by the Federal Reserve Board of Governors. The latter must also ratify the appointment of the president of each of the Reserve Banks.

Banks and Branches

Atlanta: 1000 Peachtree St, NE, Atlanta, GA 30309-4470; tel. (404) 498-8500; internet www.frbatlanta.org; Chair. V. LARKIN MARTIN; Pres. and CEO DENNIS P. LOCKHART; brs at Birmingham, AL 35283, Jacksonville, FL 32231, Miami, FL 33152, Nashville, TN 37203, and New Orleans, LA 70161.

Boston: 600 Atlantic Ave, Boston, MA 02210; tel. (617) 973-3000; e-mail Thomas.L.Lavelle@bos.frb.org; internet www.bos.frb.org; Chair. LISA M. LYNCH; Pres. and CEO ERIC S. ROSENGREN.

Chicago: 230 South LaSalle St, Chicago, IL 60604-1413; tel. (312) 322-5322; e-mail laura.labarbera@chi.frb.org; internet www.chicagofed.org; Chair. JOHN A. CANNING, Jr; Pres. and CEO CHARLES L. EVANS; br. at Detroit, MI 48207-1063.

Cleveland: 1455 East Sixth St, Cleveland, OH 44114; tel. (216) 579-2000; e-mail 4D.library@clev.frb.org; internet www.clevelandfed.org; Chair. TANNY B. CRANE; Pres. and CEO SANDRA PIANALTO; brs at Cincinnati, OH 45201 and Pittsburgh, PA 15230.

Dallas: 2200 North Pearl St, Dallas, TX 75201; tel. (214) 922-6000; e-mail info@dallasfed.org; internet www.dallasfed.org; Chair. JAMES T. HACKETT; Pres. and CEO RICHARD W. FISHER; brs at El Paso, TX 79901, Houston, TX 77019 and San Antonio, TX 78204.

Kansas City: 1 Memorial Dr., Kansas City, MO 64198-0001; tel. (816) 881-2000; internet www.kansascityfed.org; Chair. LU CÓRDOVA; Pres. and CEO THOMAS M. HOENIG; brs at Denver, CO 80202, Oklahoma City, OK 73102 and Omaha, NE 68102.

Minneapolis: 90 Hennepin Ave, Minneapolis, MN 55401; tel. (612) 204-5000; internet www.minneapolisfed.org; Chair. JAMES J. HYNES; Pres. GRAY H. STERN; br. at Helena, MT 59601.

New York: 33 Liberty St, New York, NY 10045; tel. (212) 720-5000; e-mail general.info@ny.frb.org; internet www.newyorkfed.org; Chair. STEPHEN FRIEDMAN; Pres. TIMOTHY F. GEITHNER; br. at Buffalo, NY 14202.

Philadelphia: 10 Independence Mall, Philadelphia, PA 19106-1574; tel. (218) 574-6000; internet www.philadelphiafed.org; Chair. WILLIAM F. HECHT; Pres. CHARLES I. PLOSSER.

Richmond: 701 East Byrd St, Richmond, VA 23219; tel. (804) 697-8000; internet www.richmondfed.org; Chair. THOMAS J. MACKELL, Jr; Pres. JEFFREY M. LACKER; brs at Baltimore, MD 21201 and Charlotte, NC 28202.

St Louis: 411 Locust St, St Louis, MO 63102; tel. (314) 444-8444; internet www.stlouisfed.org; Chair. IRL F. ENGELHARDT, Jr; Pres. and CEO JAMES B. BULLARD; brs at Little Rock, AR 72203, Louisville, KY 40202 and Memphis, TN 38101.

San Francisco: 101 Market St, San Francisco, CA 94105; tel. (415) 974-2000; internet www.frbsf.org; Chair. DAVID K. Y. TANG; Pres. and CEO JANET L. YELLEN; brs at Los Angeles, CA 90015, Portland, OR 97201, Salt Lake City, UT 84111 and Seattle, WA 98104.

ADVISORY COUNCILS

Federal Advisory Council

The Federal Advisory Council comprises one member from each Federal Reserve district, who is elected annually by the board of directors of the relevant Federal Reserve Bank. The Council meets with the Federal Reserve Board of Governors four times a year.

Consumer Advisory Council

The Consumer Advisory Council is a statutory body which comprises representatives of both consumers and creditors and advises the Federal Reserve Board of Governors on the implementation of consumer regulations and other consumer-related matters. Council meetings are held three times a year and are open to the public.

Thrift Institutions Advisory Council

The Thrift Institutions Advisory Council was created as a result of the Monetary Control Act of 1980 to provide advice on the special needs and problems of thrift institutions. The Council comprises representatives of mutual savings banks, savings and loan associations and credit unions.

PRINCIPAL MEANS OF MONETARY CONTROL

The Federal Reserve System has three main instruments at its disposal for the implementation of monetary policy. Firstly, reserve requirements applicable to all depository institutions are set by the Board of Governors. These determine the proportion of a bank's total funds that it may make available for loan. Secondly, the Board of Governors and the Federal Reserve Banks have joint responsibility for making adjustments to the discount rate—the interest rate at which depository institutions borrow funds from the Federal Reserve Banks. Thirdly, the cost and availability of money and credit may be regulated by what are known as 'open-market operations', which, through the purchase and sale of government bonds, can influence the availability of dollars to depository institutions. Open-market operations are regulated by the Federal Open Market Committee, which comprises the seven members of the Federal Reserve Board of Governors together with the president of the Federal Reserve Bank of New York and four other Reserve Bank presidents (the latter serving one-year terms on a rotation basis). The Committee sets annual objectives for growth in the supply of money and credit.

Comptroller of the Currency

Independence Sq., 250 E St, SW, Washington, DC 20219; tel. (202) 874-5000; e-mail Jesse.Stiller@occ.treas.gov; internet www.occ.treas.gov.

The Comptroller of the Currency has supervisory control over all federally chartered banks (see Federal Reserve System).

Comptroller: JOHN C. DUGAN.

Co-operative Bank

CoBank: 5500 South Quebec St, Greenwood Village, CO 80111; tel. (303) 740-4000; fax (303) 740-4366; e-mail webmaster@cobank.com; internet www.cobank.com; f. 1933; provides loan finance and domestic and international banking services for agricultural and farmer-owned co-operatives; cap. 1,791.4m.(Dec. 2007); Chair. EVERETT DOBRINSKI; Pres. and CEO ROBERT B. ENGEL.

Trade Bank

Export-Import Bank of the United States (Ex-Im Bank): 811 Vermont Ave, NW, Washington, DC 20571; tel. (202) 565-3946; fax (202) 565-3380; e-mail info@exim.gov; internet www.exim.gov; f. 1934; independent agency since 1945; cap. subscribed by the US Treasury; finances and facilitates US external trade, guarantees payment to US foreign traders and banks, extends credit to foreign governmental and private concerns; cap. 1,000.0m., res. −880.2m. (Sept. 2007); Chair. and Pres. JAMES H. (JIM) LAMBRIGHT.

Foreign Banks in the USA

(Banks are branches, unless otherwise indicated)

ABN AMRO, Inc (Netherlands): Park Ave Plaza, 55 East 52nd St, New York, NY 10055; tel. (212) 409-1000; fax (212) 980-9425; e-mail corporates.internet@nl.abnamro.com; internet www.corporates.abnamro.com/corporates/docs/country/unitedstates.jsp; part of ABN AMRO Bank NV; CEO JOHN K. NELSON.

AIB USA (Ireland): 405 Park Ave, New York, NY 10022; tel. (212) 339-8000; fax (212) 339-8008; internet www.aibusa.com; f. 1974; part of AIB Group; Mans JOHN CUSACK, DAVID KEATING.

Australia and New Zealand Banking Group Ltd: 1177 Ave of the Americas, New York, NY 10036; tel. (212) 801-9800; fax (212) 801-9859; internet www.anz.com/usa; f. 1968; Exec. Vice-Pres. R. SCOTT MCINNIS.

Banca CR Firenze SpA (Italy): 650 Fifth Ave, 16th Floor, New York, NY 10019-6108; tel. (212) 421-6010; fax (212) 759-6785; e-mail ppalli@crfnyc.comrep. office; Rep. GIOVANNI BERTACCA.

Banca Monte dei Paschi di Siena SpA (Italy): 55 East 59th St, New York, NY 10022-1112; tel. (212) 891-3600; fax (212) 891-3661; e-mail davide.nacci@banca.mps.it; Man. GENNARO MICCOLI.

Banco Bilbao Vizcaya Argentaria SA (BBVA) (Spain): 1345 Ave of the Americas, 45th Floor, New York, NY 10105; tel. (212) 728-1500; fax (212) 333-2906.

Banco Bradesco SA (Brazil): 450 Park Ave, 32nd and 33rd Floors, New York, NY 10022; tel. (212) 688-9855; fax (212) 754-4032; e-mail newyork@bradesco.com.br; Gen. Man. ROBERTO MEDEIROS PAULA.

Banco do Brasil SA: Rockfeller Center, 3rd Floor, 600 Fifth Ave, POB 4449, New York, NY 10020; tel. (212) 626-7000; fax (212) 626-7045; e-mail noviaiorque@bb.com.br; 2 rep. offices.

Banco de Crédito del Perú: 121 Alhambra Plaza, Suite 1200, Coral Gables, FL 33134; tel. (305) 448-0971; fax (305) 448-0981; e-mail gbenites@bcpmiami.com; Gen. Man. ALVARO CORREA.

Banco Español de Credito SA (Spain): 730 Fifth Ave, 7th Floor, New York, NY 10019; tel. (212) 835-5300; fax (212) 262-8410; Gen. Man. CARLOS SANTAMARIA.

Banco Espírito Santo SA (Portugal): 320 Park Ave, 29th Floor, New York, NY 10022; tel. (212) 702-3400; fax (212) 980-1777; Gen. Man. JOAQUIM GARNECHO.

Banco do Estado do Rio Grande do Sul SA (Brazil): 500 Fifth Ave,Suite 2310, New York, NY 10110; tel. (212) 827-0390; fax (212) 869-0844; e-mail banrisul@attmail.com.

Banco Industrial de Venezuela: 900 Third Ave, 14th Floor, New York, NY 10022; tel. (212) 688-2200; fax (212) 888–4921; 1 other br.

Banco Itaú SA (Brazil): 540 Madison Ave, 24th Floor, New York, NY 10022; tel. (212) 486-1280; fax (212) 888-9342; Gen. Man. MARCELO SANCHEZ.

Banco de la República Oriental del Uruguay: 1700 Broadway, Suite 3102, New York, NY 10019; tel. (212) 307-9600; fax (212) 307-6786; e-mail brouny@earthlink.net; internet www.brounybranch.com; Man. RENÉE GONZÁLEZ SILVA.

Banco de Sabadell SA (Spain): 701 Brickell Ave, 26th Floor, Suite 2650, Miami, FL 33131; tel. (305) 350-1200; fax (305) 350-1215; Gen. Man. MAURICI LLADÓ.

Banco Santander SA (Spain): 45 East 53rd St, 9th and 10th Floors, New York, NY 10022; tel. (212) 350-3500; fax (212) 350-3535; 1 rep. office.

Bangkok Bank Public Co Ltd (Thailand): 29 Broadway, 20th Floor, New York, NY 10006; tel. (212) 422-8200; fax (212) 422-0728; e-mail helpdesk.nyb@bbl.co.th; internet www.bangkokbank.com/newyork; Branch Man. Dr THAWEELAP RITTAPIROM.

Bank of Baroda (India): 1 Park Ave, New York, NY 10016; tel. (212) 578-4550; fax (212) 578-4565; e-mail barodanyk@aol.com; internet www.bankofbaroda-usa.com; f. 1979; CEO V. SESHADRI.

Bank of China (People's Republic of China): 410 Madison Ave, New York, NY 10017; tel. (212) 935-3101; fax (212) 593-1831; e-mail service_us@bank-of-china.com; internet www.bocusa.com; 2 other brs.

Bank of East Asia Ltd (Hong Kong): 202 Canal St, 2nd Floor, New York, NY 10013; tel. (212) 238-8208; fax (212) 219-3378; e-mail BEAUSAinfo@hkbea-us.com; internet www.hkbea-beausa; Pres. and CEO TANG PENG-WAH; 12 other brs.

Bank Hapoalim BM (Israel): 1177 Ave of the Americas, 14th Floor, New York, NY 10036; tel. (212) 782-2000; fax (212) 782-2222; Man. ZVI FUHRMAN; 3 other brs.

Bank of India: 277 Park Ave, New York, NY 10172-0083; tel. (212) 753-6100; fax (212) 319-6347; e-mail boiny@usa.com; internet www.boiusa.com; Chief Exec. S. RAMAN; 1 other br.

Bank Indonesia: 1 Liberty Plaza, 31st Floor, 165 Broadway, New York, NY 10006; tel. (212) 732-1958; rep. office.

Bank Leumi USA (Israel): 579 Fifth Ave, New York, NY 10017; tel. (800) 892-5430; fax (917) 542-2254; e-mail contactus@leumiusa.com; internet www.leumiusa.com; part of Bank Leumi le-Israel BM; Pres. and CEO UZI ROSEN; 3 other brs.

Bank of Montreal (Canada): 3 Times Sq., New York, NY 10036; tel. (212) 758-6300; fax (212) 702-1193; rep. office, 6 other brs.

Bank of Nova Scotia (Canada): 1 Liberty Plaza, 26th Floor, 165 Broadway, New York, NY 10006; tel. (212) 225-5000; fax (212) 225-5090; Man. Dir KEVIN RAY; 6 other brs.

Bank of Tokyo-Mitsubishi UFJ Ltd (Japan): 1251 Ave of the Americas, New York, NY 10020-1104; tel. (212) 782-4000; fax (212) 782-6414; e-mail sasai@us.mufg.jp; Gen. Man. SHIGERU ASAI; 11 other brs, 3 rep. offices.

Bank of Yokohama Ltd (Japan): 405 Park Ave, Suite 1101, New York, NY 10022; tel. (212) 750-0022; fax (212) 750-8008; Chief Rep. HARUMICHI OISHI; rep. office.

Barclays Bank PLC (United Kingdom): Tower 49, 12 East 49th St, New York, NY 10017; tel. (212) 415-5900; fax (212) 838-2225; 1 other br., 3 rep. offices.

Bayerische Hypo-und Vereinsbank AG (Germany): 150 East 42nd St, New York, NY 10017-4679; tel. (212) 672-6000; fax (212) 672-6026; e-mail newyorkbranch@unicreditgroup.eu; Man. MATTHEW DUNN.

Bayerische Landesbank (Germany): 560 Lexington Ave, New York, NY 10022; tel. (212) 310-9800; fax (212) 310-9822; Sr Exec. Vice-Pres. WILLFRIED FREUDENBURGER.

BNP Paribas SA (France): Equitable Tower, 787 Seventh Ave, New York, NY 10019; tel. (212) 841-2000; fax (212) 841-2146; internet www.usa.bnpparibas.com; 9 other brs.

Calyon (France): 1301 Ave of the Americas, New York, NY 10019; tel. (212) 261-7699; fax (212) 459-3166; 3 other brs, 1 rep. office.

Chiba Bank Ltd (Japan): 1133 Ave of the Americas, 15th Floor, New York, NY 10036; tel. (212) 354-7777; fax (212) 354-8575.

Chong Hing Bank Ltd (Hong Kong): International Bldg, 601 California St, San Francisco, CA 94108-2804; tel. (415) 433-6404; fax (415) 433-0686; Gen. Man. KI HONG CHAN.

Commerzbank AG (Germany): 2 World Financial Center, 33rd Floor, New York, NY 10281-1050; tel. (212) 266-7200; fax (212) 266-

7235; e-mail cbmailbox@cbkna.com; 3 other brs; Gen. Man. WERNER BÖNSCH.

Commonwealth Bank of Australia: 599 Lexington Ave, 17th Floor, New York, NY 10022; tel. (212) 848-9200; fax (212) 336-7725; Gen. Man. IAN M. PHILLIPS.

Crédit Industriel et Commercial (France): 520 Madison Ave, New York, NY 10022; tel. (212) 715-4400; fax (212) 715-4441; Gen. Man. SERGE BELLANGER.

Crédit Suisse (Switzerland): 11 Madison Ave, POB 103629, New York, NY 10010-3629; tel. (212) 325-2000; fax (212) 325-6665; internet www.credit-suisse.com/us; 26 other brs.

Deutsche Bank AG (Germany): 60 Wall St, New York, NY 10005-2858; tel. (212) 250-2500; fax (212) 469-4133; internet www.db.com/usa; CEO SETH WAUGH; 53 other brs, 1 rep. office.

DnB NOR Bank ASA (Norway): 200 Park Ave, 31st Floor, New York, NY 10166-0396; tel. (212) 681-3800; fax (212) 681-3900; Pres. TRULS NERGAARD.

Doha Bank Ltd (Qatar): 100 Wall St, 19th Floor, New York, NY 10005; tel. (212) 509-4030; fax (212) 509-4970; Chief Man. ANJUM NISAR.

Dresdner Bank AG (Germany): 1301 Ave of the Americas, New York, NY 10019; tel. (212) 895-5151; Gen. Mans HINRICH PEIPER, MUHAMMAD RAHMAN.

DZ Bank AG (Germany): 609 Fifth Ave, New York, NY 10017-1021; tel. (212) 745-1400; fax (212) 745-1405; e-mail new.york@dzbank.de; Gen. Man. ANDREAS NEUGEBAUER.

Fortis Bank NV/SA (Belgium): 520 Madison Ave, 3rd Floor, New York, NY 10022; tel. (212) 418-8700; fax (212) 418-6807; CEO WALDO ABBOT; 1 other br.

Gulf International Bank BSC (Bahrain): 330 Madison Ave, New York, NY 10017; tel. (212) 922-2300; fax (212) 922-2309; e-mail gregga.baxter@gibuk.com; Man. GREGGA BAXTER.

Habib Bank Ltd (Pakistan): 60 East 42nd St, Suite 535, 5th Floor, New York, NY 10165; tel. (212) 551-5000; fax (212) 599-6719; e-mail faiq.sadiq@hblusa.com; internet hblusa.com; Gen. Man. FAIQ SADIQ.

Hokuriku Bank Ltd (Japan): 780 Third Ave, 28th Floor, New York, NY 10017; tel. (212) 355-3883; fax (212) 355-3204; e-mail nyrep@hokugin.com; Rep. SHUICHI NAKAGAWA; rep. office.

Hong Kong and Shanghai Banking Corpn (HSBC) (Hong Kong): 452 Fifth Ave, 5th Floor, New York, NY 10018; tel. (212) 525-5000; fax (212) 525-6944; rep. office.

Intesa Sanpaolo SpA (Italy): 1 William St, New York, NY 10004; tel. (212) 607-3500; fax (212) 809-2124; e-mail gcorrias@intesasanpaolo.us; Gen. Man. GIANLUCA CORRIAS.

Iyo Bank Ltd (Japan): 780 Third Ave, 18th Floor, New York, NY 10017; tel. (212) 688-6031; fax (212) 688-6420; e-mail iyobkny@cs.com; Chief Rep. HISAJI SAKANAKA; rep. office.

Japan Bank for International Co-operation: 520 Madison Ave, 40th Floor, New York, NY 10022; tel. (212) 888-9500; fax (212) 888-9503; internet www.jbic-ny.org/en; 1 other br.

KASIKORNBANK Public Co Ltd (KBANK) (Thailand): 350 South Grand Ave, Suite 3050, Los Angeles, CA 90071; tel. (213) 680-9331; fax (213) 620-9362; e-mail kasikornbankla@aol.com; Gen. Man. PRASERTCHAO THUVANUTI.

Kaupthing New York Inc (Iceland): 230 Park Ave, Suite 1528, New York, NY 10169; tel. (212) 457-8700; fax (212) 457-8725; e-mail info@kaupthing.us; internet www.kaupthing.us; subsidiary of Kaupthing Bank hf; Man. Dir MAGNUS C. LEJDSTRÖM.

KBC Bank NV (Belgium): 1117 Ave of the Americas, New York, NY 10036; tel. (212) 541-0600; fax (212) 956-5580; Gen. Man. PATRICK DAEMS; 2 other brs.

Kookmin Bank (Republic of Korea): 565 Fifth Ave, 24th Floor, New York, NY 10017; tel. (212) 697-6100; fax (212) 697-1456; e-mail kbstarny@kmbny.com; Gen. Man. SANG-WON LEE.

Korea Development Bank (Republic of Korea): Mutual of America Life Insurance Bldg, 32nd Floor, 320 Park Ave, New York, NY 10022; tel. (212) 688-7686; fax (212) 421-5028; Gen. Man. SANG-WON LEE.

Krung Thai Bank Public Co Ltd (Thailand): Suite 3150, 707 Wilshire Blvd, Los Angeles, CA 90017; tel. (213) 488-9897; fax (213) 488-9899; e-mail ktbla@pacbell.net; Gen. Man. SOONTHORN PIPAKE.

Land Bank of Taiwan: 19F, 811 Wilshire Blvd, Los Angeles, CA 90017; tel. (213) 532-3789; fax (213) 532-3766; e-mail lb501@landbank.com.tw.

Land Bank of the Philippines: 619 East Chesnut St, Glendale, CA 91205; tel. (818) 240-0940; rep. office.

Landesbank Baden-Württemberg (Germany): West Bldg, 31st Floor, 280 Park Ave, New York, NY 10017; tel. (212) 584-1700; fax (212) 584-1799; e-mail lbbw@lbbwus.com; Gen. Man. ANDREAS OBEREM.

Landesbank Hessen-Thüringen Girozentrale (Germany): 420 Fifth Ave, New York, NY 10018; tel. (212) 703-5200; fax (212) 703-5256; Gen. Man. HANS-CHRISTIAN RITTER.

Lloyds TSB Bank PLC (United Kingdom): 1 Biscayne Tower, Suite 3200, 2 South Biscayne Blvd, Miami, FL 33131; tel. (305) 579-8900; fax (305) 371-8607; e-mail ccb@lloydstsb-usa.com; internet www.lloydstsb-usa.com; Exec. Vice-Pres. P. J. PHILLIPS; 1 other br.

Malayan Banking Berhad (Maybank) (Malaysia): 400 Park Ave, 9th Floor, New York, NY 10022; tel. (212) 303-1304; fax (212) 308-0109; e-mail fauzi@maybankusa.com; internet www.maybank2u.com.my/business/other_services/international_banking/worldwide_usa.shtml; Gen. Man. MOHD FAUZI ZULKIFLI.

MashreqBank PSC (UAE): 50 Broadway, Suite 1500, New York, NY 10004; tel. (212) 545–8200; fax (212) 545-0918; Gen. Man. MUHAMMAD GHAFOOR.

Mega International Commercial Bank Co Ltd (ICBC) (Taiwan): 65 Liberty St, New York, NY 10005; tel. (212) 608-4222; fax (212) 608-4943; e-mail nyicb@worldnet.att.net; Gen. Man. OWEN S. Y. HU; 1 agency; 3 other brs.

Mercantil CA Banco Universal (Venezuela): 11 East 51st St, New York, NY 10022-5903; tel. (212) 891-7400; fax (212) 891-7419; e-mail ljordan@bancomercantilny.com; Gen. Man. LOURDES JORDAN; agency.

Metropolitan Bank and Trust Co (Metrobank) (Philippines): 10 East 53rd St, New York, NY 10022; tel. (212) 832-0855; fax (212) 832-0993; e-mail customerservice@metrobankny.com; Gen. Man. ALFRED V. MADRID.

Mitsubishi UFJ Trust and Banking Corpn (Japan): 520 Madison Ave, 26th Floor, New York, NY 10022; internet (212) 838-7700; fax (212) 755-2349; Gen. Man. MAKOTO UENO.

Mizrahi Tefahot Bank Ltd (Israel): 800 Wilshire Blvd, Suite 1600, Los Angeles, CA 90017; tel. and fax (213) 362-2987; e-mail info@umtbusa.com; internet www.umtbusa.com; fmrly United Mizrahi Bank Ltd.

Mizuho Bank Ltd (Japan): 1251 Ave of the Americas, New York, NY 10020; tel. (212) 282-3000; fax (212) 282-4250; 2 other brs.

Mizuho Corporate Bank Ltd (Japan): 1251 Ave of the Americas, New York, NY 10020; tel. (212) 282-3000; fax (212) 282-4250; 3 other brs.

Nacional Financiera SNC (Mexico): 1615 L St, NW, Suite 310, Washington, DC 20036; tel. (202) 338-9010; fax (202) 338-9244; e-mail nafinusa@att.net; Exec. Rep. JESÚS RODRIGUEZ MONTERO; 1 other rep. office.

Nanyang Commercial Bank Ltd (Hong Kong): 50 California St, 31st Floor, San Francisco, CA 94111; tel. (415) 398-8866; fax (415) 398-0871; e-mail ncb@ncbusa.net; Mans KENNETH C. K. NG, SIMON CHAN.

National Australia Bank Ltd: 245 Park Ave, 28th Floor, New York, NY 10166-0001; tel. (212) 916-9500; fax (212) 983-1969; Exec. Vice-Pres. TOM HUNERSEN.

National Bank of Abu Dhabi (UAE): 1020 19th St, NW, Suite 500, Washington, DC 20036; tel. (202) 842-7900; fax (202) 842-7955; e-mail Nagy.Kolta@nbad.com; Exec. Vice-Pres. NAGY S. KOLTA.

National Bank of Canada: 65 East 55th St, 31st Floor, New York, NY 10022; tel. (212) 632-8585; fax (212) 632-8590; Man. LINA TOMAC; regional office.

National Bank of Egypt: 40 East 52nd St, New York, NY 10022; tel. (212) 326-8000; fax (212) 755-6944; internet www.nbeny.com; Gen. Mans HASSAN EISSA, NASSER EL KADY.

National Bank of Kuwait SAK: 299 Park Ave, New York, NY 10171; tel. (212) 303-9800; fax (212) 319-8269; e-mail info@nbkny.com; Gen. Man. MUHAMMAD KAMAL.

National Bank of Pakistan: 100 Wall St, 21st Floor, POB 500, New York, NY 10005; tel. (212) 344-8822; fax (212) 809-4720; e-mail nbprony@aol.com; internet www.nbpusa.com; Regional CEO M. RAFIQ BENGALI; Gen. Man. AHMER AZAM; 2 other brs, 1 rep. office.

National Westminster Bank PLC (NatWest Bank) (United Kingdom): 101 Park Ave, New York, NY 10178; tel. (212) 401-3200; 3 other brs.

Natixis (France): 1251 Ave of the Americas, New York, NY 10020; tel. (212) 872-5000; fax (212) 872-5045; e-mail jean-louis.galliot@natixis.us; 3 rep. offices.

Norddeutsche Landesbank Girozentrale (Germany): 1114 Ave of the Americas, New York, NY 10036; tel. (212) 398-7300; fax (212) 812-6860; e-mail maria.villani@nordlb.com; internet www.nordlbnewyork.com; Exec. Vice-Pres. THOMAS S. BÜRKLE.

Nordea Bank Finland PLC (Finland): 437 Madison Ave, New York, NY 10022; tel. (212) 318-9300; fax (212) 421-4420; e-mail general@nordeany.com; part of Nordea Bank AB (public) (Sweden).

Norinchukin Bank (Japan): 245 Park Ave, 21st Floor, New York, NY 10167-0104; tel. (212) 697-1717; fax (212) 697-5754; Gen. Man. NORITSUGU SATO.

Oversea-Chinese Banking Corpn Ltd (OCBC Bank) (Singapore): 801 South Figueroa St, Suite 970, Los Angeles, CA 90017; tel. (213) 624-1189; fax (213) 624-1386; e-mail charlesong@ocbc.com; Gen. Man. CHARLES ONG; agency; 1 other office.

Philippine National Bank: 30 Broad St, 36th Floor, New York, NY 10036; tel. (212) 790-9600; fax (212) 382-2238; e-mail pnbnyc@pnbnewyork.com; internet home.netcom.com/~pnbnyc; Sr Vice-Pres. and Gen. Man. ARMANDO M. MACALINO; 2 other brs.

Rabobank Nederland (Netherlands): 245 Park Ave, New York, NY 10167; tel. (212) 916-7800; fax (212) 818-0233; Man. COR BROEKHUYSE.

Raiffeisen Zentralbank Österreich AG (RZB—Austria) (Austria): 1133 Ave of the Americas, 16th Floor, New York, NY 10036; tel. (212) 593-7593; fax (212) 593-9870; internet www.rzbfinance.com; Rep. DIETER BEINTREXLER; rep. office.

Reserve Bank of Australia: 16th Floor, 505 Fifth Avenue, New York, NY 10017; tel. (212) 566-8466; fax (212) 566-8501; Chief Rep. JAMES WHITELAW; rep. office.

Riyad Bank (Saudi Arabia): Suite 4770, 700 Louisiana, Houston, TX 77002; tel. (713) 331-2001; fax (713) 331-2043; e-mail sheryle.diletto@riyadbank-americas.com; internet www.riyadbank-americas.com; f. 1990; agency.

Royal Bank of Canada: 1 Liberty Plaza, 3rd Floor, New York, NY 1006-1404; tel. (212) 428-6200; 1 other br.

Royal Bank of Scotland PLC (United Kingdom): 101 Park Ave, 10th Floor, New York, NY 10178; tel. (212) 401-3200; 11 other brs and 1 rep. office.

SG Private Banking (Suisse) SA (Switzerland): 701 Brickell Ave, Suite 1740, Miami, FL 33131; tel. (305) 379-3221; fax (305) 379-3696; rep. office.

Shanghai Commercial Bank Ltd (Hong Kong): 125 East 56th St, New York, NY 10022; tel. (212) 699-2800; fax (212) 299-2818; Man. TIMOTHY CHAN; 2 other brs.

Shinhan Bank (Republic of Korea): 800 Third Ave, 32nd Floor, New York, NY 10022; tel. (212) 371-8000; fax (212) 371-8875; Gen. Man. SUK-JIN KOH.

Shinkin Central Bank (Japan): 1251 Ave of the Americas, Suite 3820, New York, NY 10020; tel. (212) 642-4700; fax (212) 730-6000; e-mail scb@shinkinny.com; Gen. Man. KAZUHITO HARADA.

Shinsei Bank Ltd (Japan): 399 Park Ave, 27th Floor, New York, NY 10022; tel. (646) 840-9700; fax (212) 980-6423; Chief. Rep. SATOSHI SUZUKI; rep. office.

Shizuoka Bank Ltd (Japan): 801 South Figueroa St, Suite 800, Los Angeles, CA 90017; tel. (213) 622-3233; fax (213) 623-8674; agency in New York.

Shoko Chukin Bank (Japan): 666 Fifth Ave, New York, NY 10103; tel. (212) 581-2800; fax (212) 581-4850.

Skandinaviska Enskilda Banken AB (publ.) (Sweden): 245 Park Ave, 42nd Floor, New York, NY 10167; tel. (212) 907-4700; fax (212) 907-4762; Gen. Man. CHRISTIAN DAHLBERG.

Société Générale (France): 1221 Ave of the Americas, New York, NY 10020; tel. (212) 278-6000; fax (212) 278–5452; e-mail communications.us-corporate@sgcib.com; CEO, Americas DIONY LEBOT.

Standard Chartered Bank (United Kingdom): 1 Madison Ave, New York, NY 10010-3603; tel. (212) 667-0700; fax (212) 667-0380; e-mail elaine.chin@us.standardchartered.com; internet www.standardchartered.com/us; CEO DAVID F. STILEMAN; Regional Man. ELAINE CHIN.

State Bank of India: 460 Park Ave, New York, NY 10022; tel. (212) 521-3200; fax (212) 521-3360; e-mail ceo.nyb@statebank.com; internet www.statebank.com; Country Head PRADEEP KUMAR PANJA; 8 other brs, 1 rep. office.

Sumitomo Mitsui Banking Corpn (Japan): 277 Park Ave, New York, NY 10172; tel. (212) 224-4000; fax (212) 593-9522; Man. Dir and Gen. Man. TATSUO ABIRU; 2 other brs.

Sumitomo Trust and Banking Co Ltd (Japan): 527 Madison Ave, New York, NY 10022; tel. (212) 326-0600; fax (212) 644-3025; Gen. Man. JUNICHI SAYATO.

Svenska Handelsbanken AB (publ.) (Sweden): 875 Third Ave, 4th Floor, New York, NY 10022-7218; tel. (212) 326-5100; fax (212) 326-5196; e-mail stni03@handelsbanken.se; internet www.handelsbanken.us; Gen. Man. STEFAN NILSSON.

Taipei Fubon Commercial Bank Co Ltd (Taiwan): Suite 3300, 33rd Floor, 700 South Flower St, Los Angeles, CA 90017; tel. (213) 236-9151; fax (213) 236-9155; e-mail main@tpfbbkla.com; Gen. Man. ROBIN S. WU; agency in New York.

Taiwan Business Bank: 633 Fifth St West, Suite 2280, Los Angeles, CA 90071; tel. (213) 892-1260; fax (213) 892-1270.

Taiwan Co-operative Bank: 601 South Figueroa St, Suite 3500, Los Angeles, CA 90017; tel. (213) 489-5433; fax (213) 489-5195; e-mail fbcuser@pacbell.net; internet www.tcb-bank.com.tw/tcb/servicesloc/los_en.mht; 1 other br.

Toronto-Dominion Bank (Canada): 31 West 52nd St, 22nd Floor, New York, NY 10019-6101; tel. (212) 469-0560; fax (212) 262-1926; Man. DYLAN MACKENZIE; 2 other brs.

Türkiye Cumhuriyeti Ziraat Bankasi (Turkey): 475 Fifth Ave, 19th Floor, New York, NY 10017; tel. (212) 557-5612; fax (212) 490-8076; e-mail info@ziraatnewyork.com; internet www.ziraatnewyork.com; Man. ATILLA MERMER.

Türkiye Vakiflar Bankasi TAO (Turkey): 680 Fifth Ave, 23rd Floor, New York, NY 10019; tel. (212) 621-9400; fax (212) 707-8745; e-mail info@vakifbankusa.com; internet www.vakifbankusa.com; Gen. Man. YILDIRIM EROGLU.

UBS AG (Switzerland): 101 Park Ave, New York, NY 10178; tel. (212) 916-2000; fax (212) 916-2001.

Unibanco—União de Bancos Brasileiros, SA (Brazil): 65 East 55th St, 29th Floor, New York, NY 10022; tel. (212) 832-1700; fax (212) 754-4872; Gen. Man. WILLIAM BETHLEM; rep. office.

Unicard Banco Múltiplo SA (Brazil): 280 Park Ave, 38th Floor, New York, NY 10017; tel. (212) 972-7455; fax (212) 949-9158; rep. office in Miami, FL.

UniCredit Banca di Roma (Italy): 34 East 51st St, New York, NY 10022; tel. (212) 407-1600; fax (212) 407-1677; e-mail newyork@us.bdroma.com; Man. ALEXANDER VOLLER; 1 other br.

Unicredito Italiano SpA: 150 East 42nd St, New York, NY 10017; tel. (212) 546-9600; fax (212) 546-9675; e-mail newyorkbranch@unicreditgroup.eu; Chief Man. MAURIZIO BRENTEGANI.

United Bank Ltd (Pakistan): 80 Broad St, 24th Floor, New York, NY 10004-2209; tel. (212) 943-1275; fax (212) 968-0557; e-mail rauf@ublny.com; internet www.ubl.com.pk/ny; Gen. Man. M. A. RAUF.

United Bank for Africa PLC (Nigeria): 8th Floor, 1 Rockefeller Plaza, New York, NY 10022; tel. (212) 308-7222; fax (212) 688-0870.

United Overseas Bank Ltd (Singapore): UOB Bldg, 10th Floor, 592 Fifth Ave, New York, NY 10036; tel. (212) 382-0088; fax (212) 382-1881; e-mail UOB.NewYork@UOBgroup.com; Gen. Man. GEORGE LIM PHOON SENG; agency; other agency in Los Angeles, CA.

Vnesheconombank (Bank for Foreign Economic Affairs) (Russia): 400 Madison Ave, Suite 7B, New York, NY 10017; tel. (212) 421-8660; fax (212) 421-8677; e-mail vebusa@veb.ru; Man. ALEXANDER ALEKSEEVICH DANILOV; rep. office.

Westdeutsche ImmobilienBank AG (Germany): 1211 Ave of the Americas, 24th Floor, New York, NY 10036; tel. (212) 588-0065; fax (212) 588-0992; e-mail ny@westimmobank.com; Man. Dir ANDREW S. COOPER; rep. office.

WestLB AG (Germany): 1211 Ave of the Americas, New York, NY 10036; tel. (212) 852-6000; fax (212) 852-6300; e-mail ny@westimmobank.com; internet www.westlb.com.

Westpac Banking Corn (Australia): 575 Fifth Ave, 35th Floor, New York, NY 10017-2422; tel. (212) 551-1800; fax (212) 551-1999; Gen. Man. G. HETT.

Wing Lung Bank Ltd (Hong Kong): 201 East Valley Boulevard, Alhambra, CA 91801; tel. (626) 656–8118; internet www.winglungbankla.com.

Woori Bank (Republic of Korea): 245 Park Ave, 41st Floor, New York, NY 10167; tel. (212) 949-1900; fax (212) 490-7146; agency; 1 other agency in Los Angeles, CA.

Principal Commercial Banks

(br.(s) = branch(es); cap. = total capital and reserves; dep. = deposits; m. = million; amounts in US dollars)

ALABAMA

Compass Bank: 15 South 20th St, Birmingham, AL 35233; tel. (205) 933-3000; fax (205) 933-3996; e-mail feedback@compassbank.com; internet www.compassweb.com; cap. 1.0m., dep. 32,375.5m. (Dec. 2007); Chair. and CEO D. PAUL JONES.

First Commercial Bank NA: 800 Shades Creek Pkwy, Birmingham, AL 35209; tel. (205) 879-2800; fax (205) 868-6175; e-mail info@firstcommercialbank.com; internet www.firstcommercialbank.com; f. 1985; 100% owned by Synovus Financial Corpn (Columbus, OH); cap. 0.001m., dep. 1,636.7m. (Dec. 2007); Pres. and CEO NELSON BEAN.

Regions Bank: 417 North 20th St, POB 10247, Birmingham, AL 35202-0247; tel. (205) 326-7697; fax (205) 326-7779; internet www.regionsbank.com; f. 1928; cap. 0.1m., dep. 111,630.3m. (Dec. 2007); Pres. and CEO C. DOWD RITTER.

ALASKA

First National Bank Alaska: POB 100720, Anchorage, AK 99510; tel. (907) 276-6300; fax (907) 265-3528; e-mail customer.service@fnbalaska.com; internet www.fnbalaska.com; f. 1922; cap. 34.5m., dep. 1,841.8m. (Dec. 2006); Pres. and Chair. D. H. CUDDY; 29 brs.

ARIZONA

National Bank of Arizona: 6001 North 24th St, Phoenix, AZ 85016; tel. (602) 235-6000; internet www.nbarizona.com; f. 1984; 100% owned by Zions Bancorporation; total assets 5,270.0m., dep. 3,870.0m. (Dec. 2007); Chair. JOHN GISI; Pres. and CEO KEITH MAIO.

CALIFORNIA

Bank of the West: 180 Montgomery St, San Francisco, CA 94104; tel. (415) 765-4800; fax (415) 434-3470; internet www.bankofthewest.com; f. 1874; cap. 0.005m., dep. 51,869.7m. (Dec. 2007); Chair. and CEO DON J. MCGRATH; 663 brs.

California Bank and Trust: 11622 El Camino Real, Suite 200, San Diego, CA 92130; tel. (858) 793-7400; fax (858) 793-7438; e-mail info@calbanktrust.com; internet www.calbanktrust.com; f. 1998; cap. 3.2m., dep. 8,709.2m. (Dec. 2007); Chair. and CEO DAVID BLACKFORD.

City National Bank: 400 Roxbury Dr. North, Beverly Hills, CA 90210; tel. (310) 888-6000; fax (310) 888-6045; e-mail contact@cnb.com; internet www.cnb.com; f. 1954; cap. 90.0m., dep. 13,518.5m. (Dec. 2007); Chair. and CEO RUSSELL GOLDSMITH; Pres. CHRISTOPHER J. WARMUTH; 45 brs.

Union Bank of California NA: 400 California St, 1st Floor, San Francisco, CA 94104; tel. (415) 765-3434; fax (415) 765-3507; e-mail Investor.Relations@uboc.com; internet www.uboc.com; f. 1996; cap. 604.6m., dep. 35,067.0m. (Dec. 2002); Pres. and CEO MASAAKI TANAKA; 323 brs.

COLORADO

FirstBank: 12345 West Colfax Ave., Lakewood, CO 80215; tel. (303) 237-5000; e-mail banking@efirstbank.com; internet www.efirstbank.com; f. 1963; total assets 9,300.0m., dep. 7,900.0m. (Sep. 2007); Pres. RON TILTON; 126 brs.

CONNECTICUT

Citizens Bank, Connecticut: 237 Main St, Middletown, CT 06457; tel. (860) 638-4411; fax (860) 638-4444; e-mail intbank@citizensbank.com; internet www.citizensbank.com; f. 1996; a division of RBS Citizens NA since 2007; dep. 4,205.8m., total assets 4,617.0m. (Dec. 2006); Chair., Pres. and CEO RICHARD M. BARRY; 48 brs.

DELAWARE

Chase Bank USA NA: 200 White Clay Center Dr., 1st Floor, Newark, DE 19711; tel. (302) 758-2600; fax (302) 758-2603; internet www.chase.com; f. 1982 as Chase Manhattan Bank USA; present name adopted 2005; cap. 49.0m., dep. 52,254.9m. (Dec. 2007); Pres. MICHAEL J. BARRETT.

FLORIDA

Northern Trust NA: 700 Brickell Ave, Miami, FL 33131; tel. (305) 372-1000; fax (305) 789-1106; internet www.northerntrust.com; f. 1982; cap. 34.1m., dep. 9,608.5m. (Dec. 2007); Chair., Pres. and CEO WILLIAM L. MORRISON.

Ocean Bank: 780 Northwest 42nd Ave, Miami, POB 441140, FL 33126; tel. (305) 442-2660; fax (305) 444-8153; e-mail obmail@oceanbank.com; internet www.oceanbank.com; f. 1982; cap. 8.5m., dep. 4,912.0m. (Dec. 2007); Pres. and CEO JOSÉ A. CONCEPCIÓN; 23 brs.

GEORGIA

SunTrust Bank: 25 Park Pl., POB 4418, Atlanta, GA 30302; tel. (404) 588-7785; fax (404) 302-4782; internet www.suntrust.com; f. 1891; assumed all SunTrust Banks 2000; cap. 21.6m., dep. 147,282.57m. (Dec. 2007); Chair. and Pres. PHILLIP HUMANN.

HAWAII

Bank of Hawaii: 111 South King St, Honolulu, HI 96813; tel. (888) 643-3888; fax (808) 537-8440; e-mail info@boh.com; internet www.boh.com; f. 1897; cap. 14.9m., dep. 9,148.3m. (Dec. 2007); Chair., Pres. and CEO ALLAN R. LANDON.

First Hawaiian Bank: 999 Bishop St, Honolulu, HI 96813; tel. (808) 525-7000; fax (808) 525-8182; e-mail bfarias@fhb.com; internet www.fhb.com; f. 1858; cap. 16.2m., dep. 9,884.4m. (Dec. 2007); Chair. WALTER A. DODS, Jr; Pres. and CEO DONALD G. HORNER.

ILLINOIS

First Midwest Bank: 300 Park Blvd, Suite 400, Itasca, IL 60143; internet www.firstmidwest.com; cap. 40.0m., dep. 7,128.1m. (Dec. 2007); Chair. and CEO JOHN O'MEARA; 103 brs.

Harris National Association: 111 West Monroe St, 12th Floor, Chicago, IL 60603; tel. (312) 845-2028; fax (312) 845-2199; internet www.harrisbank.com; f. 1882 as N.W. Harris & Co; present name adopted 2005; cap. 155.1m., dep. 36,359.5m. (Dec. 2007); Dirs PASTORA SAN JUAN CAFFERTY, HAVEN E. COCKERHAM, ANTHONY (TONY) COMPER, SUSAN T. CONGALTON, WILLIAM A. DOWNE, DAVID A. GALLOWAY, WILBUR H. GANTZ, JAMES J. GLASSER, Dr LEO M. HENIKOFF, RICHARD M. JAFFEE, KAREN MAIDMENT, ALAN G. MCNALLY, FRANK T. TECHAR, RICHARD E. TERRY.

LaSalle Bank NA: 135 South LaSalle St, Chicago, IL 60603; tel. (312) 904-2000; fax (312) 904-2819; internet www.lasallebank.com; f. 1927; cap. 541.2m., dep. 58,252.9m. (Dec. 2007); Chair. JOOST C. L. KULPER; Pres. and CEO NORMAN R. BOBINS.

Northern Trust Co: 50 South LaSalle St, Chicago, IL 60675; tel. (312) 630-6000; fax (312) 444-5244; internet www.northerntrust.com; f. 1889; cap. 3.6m., dep. 51,765.6m. (Dec. 2007); Chair. and CEO WILLIAM A. OSBORN.

INDIANA

Ameriana Bancorp: 2118 Bundy Avenue, POB H, New Castle, IN 47362-1048; tel. (765) 529-2230; e-mail jerry.gassen@ameriana.com; internet www.ameriana.com; f. 1890; total assets 426.8m., deposits 314.7m. (Dec. 2007); Chair. MICHAEL E. KENT; Pres. and CEO JERRY GASSEN.

IOWA

United Bank of Iowa: 501 2nd St, Ida Grove, IA 51445-1384; tel. (712) 364-3393; e-mail info@unitedbk.com; internet www.unitedbk.com; f. 1932 as Ida County State Bank, present name adopted 1996; 100% owned by Ida Grove Bancshares, Inc.; cap 60.1m., deposits 487.6m. (June 2007); Chair.and CEO KENNETH L. VAN KEKERIX.

KANSAS

UMB Bank NA: 1010 Grand Ave, POB 419226, Kansas City, MO 64106; tel. (816) 860-7000; fax (816) 860-4858; internet www.umb.com; cap. 20.2m., dep. 7,467.0m. (Dec. 2007); Chair. and CEO J. MARINER KEMPER.

LOUISIANA

Whitney National Bank: 228 St Charles Ave, New Orleans, LA 70130; tel. (504) 586-7562; fax (504) 586-7412; e-mail lgarza@whitneybank.com; internet www.whitneybank.com; f. 1883; cap. 3,358.0m., dep. 9,624.6m. (Dec. 2007); Chair. and CEO JOHN C. HOPE, III; 130 brs.

MAINE

TD Bank NA: 2 Portland Square, Portland, ME 04101; tel. (207) 761-8762; e-mail jennifer.carlson@tdbanknorth.com; internet www.tdbanknorth.com; Chair. WILLIAM J. RYAN; Pres. and CEO BHARAT B. MASRANI.

MARYLAND

Provident Bank of Maryland: 114 East Lexington St, Baltimore, MD 21202-1725; tel. (410) 281-7000; fax (410) 277-2768; internet www.provbank.com; f. 1951; cap. 30.0m., dep. 5,675.6m. (Dec. 2007); Chair. and CEO PETER MARTIN.

MASSACHUSETTS

Citizens Bank, Massachusetts: 28 State St, Boston, MA 02109; tel. (617) 725-5500; fax (617) 725-5877; e-mail intbank@citizensbank.com; internet www.citizensbank.com; f. 1825; a division of RBS Citizens NA since 2007; dep. 30,403.2m., total assets 35,276.0m. (Dec. 2006); Chair., Pres. and CEO ROBERT E. SMYTH.

MICHIGAN

Citizens Bank: 328 South Saginaw St, Flint, MI 48502; tel. (313) 766-7500; fax (313) 768-6948; internet www.citizensonline.com; f. 1871; cap. 29.2m., dep. 11,265.41m. (Dec. 2007); Chair., Pres. and CEO WILLIAM R. HARTMAN.

Comerica Bank: Comerica Tower, Detroit Center, 500 Woodward Ave, Detroit, MI 48226; tel. (313) 222-3300; fax (313) 961-7349; e-mail info@comerica.com; internet www.comerica.com; f. 1849; cap. 378.5m., dep. 53,217.6m. (Dec. 2007); Chair., Pres. and CEO RALPH W. BABB, Jr.

Fifth Third Bank: 111 Lyon NW, Grand Rapids, MI 49503; tel. (616) 771-5000; fax (616) 774-1119; internet www.53.com; f. 1853; cap.

16.4m., dep. 46,150.0m. (Dec. 2007); Chair. George A. Schaefer, Jr; 361 brs.

LaSalle Bank Midwest NA: 2600 West Big Beaver Rd, POB 3703, Troy, MI 48007; tel. (248) 643-9600; fax (248) 637-2691; internet www.lasallebankmidwest.com; f. 1890; part of LaSalle Bank Corpn; cap. 84.9m., dep. 30,555.9m. (Dec. 2007); Pres. Scott Heitmann; 261 brs.

MINNESOTA

United Southwest Bank: 111 West Main St, Cottonwood, MN 56229-0288; tel. (507) 423-6285; fax (507) 423-6306; internet www.unitedswbank.com.

US Bank NA: 800 Nicollet Mall, Minneapolis, MN 55402; tel. (612) 303-0799; fax (612) 973-0838; e-mail international.banking@usbank.com; internet www.usbank.com; f. 1853; fmrly Firstar Bank NA, present name adopted in Aug. 2001; cap. 18.2m., dep. 194,839.3m. (Dec. 2007); Chair., CEO and Pres. Richard K. Davis; 2,498 brs.

MISSISSIPPI

Trustmark National Bank: 248 East Capitol St, POB 291, Jackson, MS 39201; tel. (601) 354-5863; fax (601) 949-2387; e-mail Trustmark@custhelp.com; internet www.trustmark.com; f. 1889; cap. 13.4m., dep. 7,686.8m. (Dec. 2007); Chair. and CEO Richard G. Hickson.

MISSOURI

Commerce Bank NA: 1000 Walnut St, POB 13686, Kansas City, MO 64106; tel. (816) 234-2000; fax (816) 234-2799; e-mail mymoney@commercebank.com; internet www.commercebank.com; f. 1865; cap. 10.2m., dep. 13,206.0m. (Dec. 2007); Chair. and CEO Jonathan M. Kemper.

MONTANA

First Interstate Bank of Montana NA: 2 Main St, POB 7130, Kalispell, MT 59904; tel. (406) 752-5001; internet www.firstinterstatebank.com; f. 1891; dep. 4,008.0m., total assets 5,091.2m. (Dec. 2007); Chair. Thomas W. Scott; Pres. and CEO Lyle R. Knight.

West One Bank: 222 West Idaho St, POB 7758, Kalispell, MT 59904-0758; tel. (406) 755-9781; fax (406) 755-9794; e-mail comment@westonebank.com; internet www.westonebank.com; Chair. Douglas K. Morton; Pres. Rod Leese.

NEBRASKA

First National Bank of Omaha: 1620 Dodge St, Omaha, NE 68102; tel. (402) 341-0500; fax (402) 633-3554; e-mail firstnational@fnni.com; internet www.firstnational.com; f. 1857; cap. 5.3m., dep. 7,935.6m. (Dec. 2007); Chair. Bruce R. Lauritzen; 31 brs.

NEVADA

Bank of Nevada: 2700 West Sahara Ave., Las Vegas, NV 89102; tel. (702) 248-4200, e-mail lharrison@bankofnevada.com; internet www.bankofnevada.com; owned by Western Alliance Bancorporation; Chair. Arthur Marshall; Pres. and CEO Bruce Hendricks.

NEW HAMPSHIRE

Citizens Bank, New Hampshire: 875 Elm St, Manchester, NH 03101; tel. (603) 634-7418; fax (603) 634-7481; e-mail intbank@citizensbank.com; internet www.citizensbank.com; f. 1853; a division of RBS Citizens NA since 2007; cap. 0.8m., dep. 9,250.3m. (Dec. 2006); Pres. Cathleen. Schmidt; 76 brs.

Laconia Savings Bank: 62 Pleasant St, Laconia, NH 03246; tel. (603) 542-3072; internet www.lsbdirect.com; f. 1831; dep. 694.8m., total assets 906.3m. (June 2008); Chair. Rodney N. Dyer; Pres. and CEO K. Mark Primeau.

NEW JERSEY

Provident Bank: POB 17, Jersey City, NJ 07306-9822; tel. (201) 915-5344; e-mail ken.wagner@providentnj.com; internet www.providentnj.com; dep. 4,224.8m., total assets 6,359.4m. (Dec. 2007); Chair. and CEO Paul M. Pantozzi; Pres. Christopher Martin.

NEW YORK

American Express Bank Ltd: American Express Tower, 23rd Floor, 200 Vesey St, New York, NY 10285-2300; tel. (212) 640-5000; fax (212) 693-1721; internet www.americanexpress.com; f. 1919; cap. 121.0m., res 612.0m., dep. 12,992.0m. (Dec. 2006); Chair. and CEO W. Richard Holmes.

Bank of New York Mellon: 1 Wall St, New York, NY 10286; tel. (212) 495-1784; fax (212) 495-1398; e-mail comments@bankofny.com; internet www.bankofny.com; f. 1784; re-named as above after merger of Bank of New York Co and Mellon Financial Corpn in 2007; cap. 1,135.3m., dep. 68,630.0m. (Dec. 2006); Chair. and CEO Robert P. Kelly; Pres. Gerald L. Hassell.

Bank of Tokyo–Mitsubishi UFJ Trust Co: 1251 Ave of the Americas, New York, NY 10020-1104; tel. (212) 782-4000; fax (212) 782-6415; internet www.btmna.com; f. 1955; cap. 132.9m., dep. 3,202.1m. (Dec. 2007); Chair. Naotaka Obata; Pres. and CEO Yukiharu Kiho.

Citibank NA: 399 Park Ave, New York, NY 10043; tel. (212) 559-1000; fax (212) 223-2681; internet www.citibank.com; f. 1812; cap. 751.0m., dep. 1,072,013.0m. (Dec. 2007); Chair., Pres. and CEO William R. Rhodes.

Deutsche Bank Trust Company Americas: 60 Wall St, New York, NY 10005; tel. (212) 250-2500; fax (212) 250-4429; internet www.deutsche-bank.com; f. 1903; fmrly Bankers' Trust Co, present name adopted April 2002; cap. 3,627.0m., dep. 23,509.0m. (Dec. 2006); Chair. and CEO Josef Ackerman; Pres. John A. Ross.

HSBC Bank USA NA: POB 2013, Buffalo, NY 14240; fax (716) 841-5391; internet www.banking.us.hsbc.com; f. 1999 following acquisition of Marine Midland Bank by Hongkong & Shanghai Banking Corpn; acquired Republic National Bank of New York in 2000; cap. 2.0m., dep. 164,636.3m. (Dec. 2007); Chair. Michael F. Geoghegan; Pres. and CEO Paul Lawrence.

JP Morgan Chase Bank National Asscn: 270 Park Ave, New York, NY 10017; tel. (212) 270-6000; fax (212) 682-3761; internet www.jpmorganchase.com; f. 1955; cap. 1,785.0m., dep. 1,125,220.0m. (Dec. 2007); merged with Bank One in 2004; Chair. and CEO James Dimon.

M&T Bank Corpn: 1 M & T Plaza, Buffalo, NY 14203-2399; tel. (716) 842-4200; fax (716) 842-5021; internet www.mtb.com; f. 1856; Manufacturers' and Traders' Trust Co; cap. 6,485m., dep. 41,266m. (Dec. 2007); Chair. and CEO Robert G. Wilmers; 736 brs.

Trustco Bank: 1 Sarnowski Dr., Glenville, NY 12302; tel. (518) 377-3311; fax (518) 381-3668; internet www.trustcobank.com; cap. 29.4m. (Dec. 2002), dep. 3,020.3m. (Dec. 2007); Pres. and CEO Robert A. McCormick.

NORTH CAROLINA

Bank of America NA: Bank of America Corporate Center, 100 North Tryon St, Charlotte, NC 28255; tel. (704) 386-5000; fax (704) 386-0981; internet www.bankamerica.com; f. 1904; cap. 2,878.9m., dep. 1,144,832.5m. (Dec. 2007); Chair. and CEO Kenneth D. Lewis.

Branch Banking and Trust Co: 200 West Second St, Winston-Salem, NC 27101; tel. (336) 733-2000; internet www.bbandt.com; f. 1872; cap. 26.4m., dep. 99,587.1m. (Dec. 2006); Chair. and CEO Kelly King.

Wachovia Bank NA: 301 South College St, Suite 4000, Charlotte, NC 28288-0013; tel. (704) 374-1246; internet www.wachovia.com; f. 1866; cap. 455.0m., dep. 544,178.0m. (Dec. 2007); Chair. and Acting CEO Lanty L. Smith.

OHIO

FirstMerit Bank NA: 3 Cascade Plaza, Akron, OH 44308; tel. (330) 996-6300; fax (330) 384-7008; e-mail customerservice@firstmerit.com; internet www.firstmerit.com; cap. 57.6m., dep. 9,199.9m. (Dec. 2007); Chair. and CEO Paul G. Greig.

Huntington National Bank: 41 South High St, Columbus, OH 43287; tel. (614) 480-4685; fax (614) 331-5900; e-mail international@huntington.com; internet www.huntington.com; f. 1866; cap. 40.0m., dep. 45,854.4m. (Dec. 2007); Chair. and CEO Thomas Hoaglin.

KeyBank NA: 127 Public Sq., Cleveland, OH 44114; tel. (216) 689-3000; fax (216) 689-3683; e-mail Investor_relations@keybank.com; internet www.key.com; f. 1849; cap. 50.0m., dep. 79,964.6m. (Dec. 2007); Chair. and CEO Henry L. Meyer, III.

National City Bank: 1900 East Ninth St, POB 94750, Cleveland, OH 44114-3484; tel. (216) 575-2000; fax (216) 575-9263; internet www.nationalcity.com; f. 1845; cap. 7.3m., dep. 118,055.2m. (Dec. 2007); Chair., Pres. and CEO Peter E. Raskind; c. 1,300 brs.

OKLAHOMA

Bank of Oklahoma NA: Bank of Oklahoma Tower, POB 2300, Tulsa, OK 74192; tel. (918) 588-6829; fax (918) 588-6026; internet www.bankofoklahoma.com; f. 1933; cap. 52.9m., dep. 13,089.6m. (Dec. 2007); Chair. George B. Kaiser; Pres. and CEO Stanley A. Lybarger; 56 brs.

OREGON

The Commerce Bank of Oregon: 1211 South West Fifth Ave, Suite 1250, Portland, OR 97204; tel. (503) 548-1000; fax (503) 548-1050; e-mail clientservice@tbcoregon.com; internet www.tcboregon.com; f. 2005; Pres. and CEO Michael V. Paul.

PENNSYLVANIA

Citizens Bank of Pennsylvania: 525 Willian Penn Pl., Pittsburgh, PA 15258; tel. (215) 553-3000; internet www.citizensbank.com; f. 2001; cap. 0.2m., dep. 34,640.3m. (Dec. 2007); Chair., Pres. and CEO Stephen D. Steinour; 411 brs.

PNC Bank, NA: 1 PNC Plaza, 249 Fifth Ave, Pittsburgh, PA 15222-2707; tel. (412) 762-2000; fax (412) 762-5022; internet www.pnc.com; f. 1959; cap. 740.1m., dep. 103,780.3m. (Dec. 2007); Chair., and CEO James E. Rohr; Pres. Joseph C. Guyaux; 854 brs.

Sovereign Bank: 1130 Berkshire Blvd, POB 37, Wyomissing, PA 19610; tel. (610) 320-8400; fax (610) 320-8448; e-mail investor@sovereignbank.com; internet www.sovereignbank.com; f. 1907; cap. 0.1m., res 9,287.0m., dep. 51,244.7m. (Dec. 2006); Pres., Chair. and CEO Joseph P. Campanelli; 664 brs.

RHODE ISLAND

Citizens Bank, Rhode Island: 1 Citizens Plaza, Providence, RI 02903; tel. (401) 454-2441; fax (401) 455-5859; e-mail intbank@citizensbank.com; internet www.citizensbank.com; f. 1996; cap. 1.0m., dep. 12,272.2m. (Dec. 2006); Chair., Pres. and CEO Joseph J. MarcAurele; 78 brs.

SOUTH CAROLINA

Carolina First Bank: 102 South Main St, POB 1029, Greenville, SC 29602; tel. (864) 255-7900; fax (864) 239-6401; e-mail customerassistance@carolinafirst.com; internet www.carolinafirst.com; cap. 7.9m., dep. 11,853.3m. (Dec. 2007); Chair. Mack I. Whittle, Jr; Pres. Maurice J. Spagnoletti.

SOUTH DAKOTA

Citibank (South Dakota) NA: 701 East 60th St, North, POB 6000, Sioux Falls, SD 57117; tel. (605) 331-2626; internet www.citibank.com; f. 1981; cap. 0.04m., dep. 4,768.1m. (Dec. 2005); Gen. Sec. David L. Zimbeck; Pres. Kendall E. Stork.

Wells Fargo Bank NA: 101 North Phillips Ave, Sioux Falls, SD 57117; tel. (605) 575-7300; fax (605) 575-4815; e-mail ipb@wellsfargo.com; internet www.wellsfargo.com; f. 1960 as Wells Fargo Bank American Trust Co; fmrly Norwest Bank South Dakota NA, present name adopted in 2004; cap. 520.0m., dep. 399,104.0m. (Dec. 2007); Pres. and CEO John G. Stumpf; 3,000 brs.

TENNESSEE

First Tennessee Bank NA: 165 Madison Ave, 9th Floor, POB 84, Memphis, TN 38101-0084; tel. (901) 523-4420; fax (901) 523-4438; internet www.firsttennessee.com; f. 1864; cap. 367.3m., dep. 31,333.5m. (Dec. 2007); Chair. Michael D. Rose; Pres. and CEO Bryan Jordan; 183 brs.

TEXAS

Frost National Bank: 100 West Houston St, POB 1600, San Antonio, TX 78296; tel. (210) 220-4011; e-mail frostbank@frostbank.com; internet www.frostbank.com; f. 1899; cap. 8.5m., dep. 11,704.5m. (Dec. 2007); Pres. Pat Frost; Chair. and CEO Richard W. Evans.

UTAH

Zions First National Bank: 1 South Main St, Salt Lake City, UT 84111; tel. (801) 974-8800; fax (801) 594-8172; internet www.zionsbank.com; f. 1873; cap. 15m., dep. 16,622.0m. (Dec. 2007); Pres. and CEO A. Scott Anderson.

VIRGINIA

Capital One National Association: 1680 Capital One Dr., McLean, VA 22102; tel. (504) 533–3333; e-mail mailus@solutions.hibernia.com; internet www.capitalone.com; f. 1933; name changed as above 2006; Capital One Financial Corpn; cap. 23.6m., dep. 75,446.7m.; Chair. E. R. Campbell; Pres. and CEO J. Herbert Boydstun.

Chevy Chase Bank, FSB: 7926 Jones Branch Dr., McLean, VA 22101; internet www.chevychasebank.com; f. 1955; total assets 15,106.6m. (Sep. 2007); Chair. and CEO B. Francis Saul, II.

WASHINGTON

Washington Trust Bank: POB 2127, Spokane, WA 99210-2127; tel. (509) 353–2265; fax (509) 358–3590; internet www.watrust.com; f. 1902; cap. 7.5m., dep. 3,358.3m.; Chair. and CEO Peter F. Stanton.

WEST VIRGINIA

United Bank, Inc: 514 Market St, Parkersburg, WV 26101-0000; tel. (304) 424-8800; internet www.unitedbank-wv.com; f. 1839; cap. 10.8m., dep. 3,922.9m. (Dec. 2007); Chair. and CEO Richard M. Adams.

WISCONSIN

Associated Bank NA: POB 19006, 200 North Adams St, Green Bay, WI 54307-9006; tel. (920) 433-3188; fax (920) 431-8016; internet www.associatedbank.com; cap. 0.2m., dep. 18,657.2m. (Dec. 2007); Pres. and CEO Paul S. Beideman.

M & I Marshall & Ilsley Bank: 770 North Water St, Milwaukee, WI 53202; tel. (414) 765-7700; fax (414) 270-5528; internet www.mibank.com; f. 1847; cap. 30.6m., dep. 46,284.8m. (Dec. 2007); Pres. and CEO Mark F. Furlong; Chair. Dennis J. Kuester.

Selected Savings Institutions

(dep. = deposits; m. = million; amounts in US dollars)

SAVINGS BANKS

Bank Mutual: Corporate Headquarters, 4949 West Brown Deer Rd, POB 245034, Milwaukee, WI 53224-9534; tel. (414) 354-1500; fax (414) 354-5450; e-mail customersvc@bankmutual.com; internet www.bankmutual.com; Chair., Pres. and CEO Michael T. Crowley, Jr.

Cambridge Savings Bank: 1374 Massachusetts Ave, POB 380206, Cambridge, MA 02238; tel. (617) 864-8700; e-mail info@cambridgesavings.com; internet www.cambridgesavings.com; f. 1834; Pres. and CEO Robert M. Wilson.

Dime Savings Bank of Williamsburgh: 209 Havemeyer St, Brooklyn, NY 11211; tel. (718) 782-6200; e-mail einfo@dimewill.com; internet www.dimewill.com; f. 1859; Chair. and CEO Vincent F. Palagiano; Pres. and COO Michael P. Devine.

Hudson City Savings Bank: 80 West Century Rd, Paramus, NJ 07652; tel. (201) 967-1900; fax (201) 986-0368; e-mail smunhall@hcsbnj.com; internet www.hcsbonline.com; f. 1868; dep. 15,153.4m. (2007); Chair., Pres. and CEO Ronald E. Hermance, Jr.

Sterling Savings Bank: 111 North Wall St, Spokane, WA 99201-0609; tel. (509) 354-8165; e-mail customer.service@sterlingsavings.com; internet www.sterlingsavingsbank.com; f. 1983; dep. 7,677.8m. (Dec 2007); Chair. and CEO Harold B. Gilkey.

Webster Bank: 145 Bank St, Webster Plaza, Waterbury, CT 06702; tel. (203) 578-2230; e-mail service@websterbank.com; internet www.websterbank.com; f. 1870; dep. 12,354.1m. (2007); Chair. and CEO James C. Smith.

SAVINGS AND LOAN ASSOCIATIONS

The Federal Deposit Insurance Corporation (see above), a government-sponsored body, was responsible for selling, acquiring or closing down bankrupt savings and loan associations. It succeeded the Resolution Trust Corporation in January 1996. The Resolution Trust Corporation, another government body, had been created in the 1980s following the failure of a number of savings and loan institutions in that decade.

Downey Savings and Loan Association, FA: 3501 Jamboree Rd, Newport Beach, CA 92658; tel. (949) 854-3100; internet www.downeysavings.com; f. 1957; Chair. Michael D. Bozarth; CEO Charles R. Rinehart.

Seneca Federal Savings and Loan Association: 35 Oswego St, Baldwinsville, New York, NY 13035; tel. (315) 638-0233; fax (315) 638-9871; e-mail sfederal@twcny.rr.com; internet www.senecafederal.com; f. 1928; Pres. Chris Demong.

Banking Associations

There is a state bankers' association in each state.

American Association of Bank Directors: National Capital Office, Suite P15, 4701 Sangamore Rd, Betheseda, MD 20816; tel. (301) 263-9841; fax (301) 229-2443; e-mail info@aabd.org; internet www.aabd.org; f. 1989; Pres. Keith Dalrymple; Exec. Dir David Baris.

American Bankers Association: 1120 Connecticut Ave, NW, Washington, DC 20036; tel. (202) 663-5000; fax (202) 828-4547; e-mail custserv@aba.com; internet www.aba.com; f. 1875; Pres. and CEO Edward (Ed) Yingling; Chair. Bradley E. Rock.

America's Community Bankers: 900 19th St, NW, Suite 400, Washington, DC 20006; tel. (202) 857-3100; fax (202) 296-8716; e-mail info@acbankers.org; internet www

.americascommunitybankers.com; f. 1992; 2,000 mems; Chair., MARK E. MACOMBER; Pres. and CEO DIANE CASEY-LANDRY.

Bank Administration Institute (BAI): 115 South LaSalle St, Suite 3300, Chicago, IL 60603-3801; tel. (312) 683-2464; fax (312) 683-2373; e-mail info@bai.org; internet www.bai.org; f. 1924; Chair. TIMOTHY P MOEN; Pres. and CEO DEBORAH L. BIANUCCI.

Bankers' Association for Finance and Trade: 1120 Connecticut Ave, NW, 5th Floor, Washington, DC 20036; tel. (202) 663-7575; fax (202) 663-5538; e-mail baft@aba.com; internet www.baft.org; affiliated to the American Bankers Asscn; Pres. CHARLES H. SILVERMAN.

Bond Club of New York: c/o Fahnestock & Co, Inc, 125 Broad St, 15th Floor, New York, NY 10004; e-mail jhill@bbandtcm.com; internet www.bondclubofnewyork.com; f. 1917; Sec. KATHLEEN WILSON.

Consumer Bankers Association: 1000 Wilson Blvd, Suite 2500, Arlington, VA 22209-3908; tel. (703) 276-1750; e-mail jbelew@cbanet.org; internet www.cbanet.org; f. 1919; 700 mems; Pres. JOE BELEW.

Financial and Security Products Association: Plaza Ladera, 5300 Sequoia Rd, NW, Suite 205, Albuquerque, NM 87120; tel. (505) 839-7958; fax (505) 839-0017; e-mail jv@fspa1.com; internet fspa1.com; f. 1973 as National Independent Bank Equipment and Systems Asscn; Chair. BILL MERCER; Pres. MICHAEL BODINE.

Financial Services Roundtable: 1001 Pennsylvania Ave, Washington, DC 20004; tel. (202) 289-4322; fax (202) 628-2507; e-mail info@fsround.org; internet www.fsround.org; f. 1993 by merger of the Asscn of Registered Bank Holding Cos and the Asscn of Reserve City Bankers to form the Bankers Roundtable; name changed as above in 2000; Chair. THOMAS A. RENYI; Pres. and CEO STEVE BARTLETT.

Financial Women International: 1027 West Roselawn Ave, Roseville, MN 55113; tel. (651) 487-7632; fax (651) 489-1322; e-mail info@fwi.org; internet www.fwi.org; f. 1921; fmrly the Nat. Asscn of Bank Women; 800 mems; Pres. REGINA BARR.

Independent Community Bankers of America: 1615 L St, NW, Suite 900, Washington, DC 20036; tel. (202) 659-8111; e-mail info@icba.org; internet www.icba.org; f. 1930; Pres. and CEO CAMDEN R. FINE; 5,000 banks.

Mortgage Bankers Association of America: 1919 Pennsylvania Ave, Washington, DC 20006; tel. (202) 557-2700; e-mail info@mbaa.org; internet mortgagebankers.org; f. 1914; Chair. KIERAN P. QUINN; Pres. and CEO JONATHAN L. KEMPNER; 2,700 mems.

National Association of Mortgage Brokers: 7900 Westpark Dr., Suite T309, McLean, VA 22102; tel. (703) 342-5900; fax (703) 342-5905; e-mail jotto@namb.org; internet www.namb.org; f. 1973; 25,000 mems; Pres. MARC S. SAVITT.

National Bankers Association: 1513 P St, Washington, DC 20005; tel. (202) 588-5432; fax (202) 588-5443; e-mail nahart@nationalbankers.org; internet www.nationalbankers.org; f. 1927; 160 mems; Pres. NORMA A. HART.

National Marine Bankers Association: 200 East Randolph Dr., Suite 5100, Chicago, IL 60601; tel. (312) 946-6260; e-mail bmcardle@nmma.org; internet www.marinebankers.org; f. 1980; 79 mems; Pres. JAMES COBURN.

Risk Management Association: 1801 Market St, Suite 300, Philadelphia, PA 19103-1628; tel. (215) 446-4000; fax (215) 446-4101; e-mail fwetzel@rmahq.org; internet www.rmahq.org; f. 1914; non-profit asscn; 2,850 mems; Chair. SONNY B. LYLES; Pres. and CEO KEVIN M. BLAKELY, II.

Urban Financial Services Coalition (UFSC): 1212 New York Ave, NW, Suite 950, Washington, DC 20005; tel. (202) 289-8335; fax (202) 842-0567; internet www.ufscnet.org; f. 1974 as National Asscn of Urban Bankers; named changed as above in 2001; 1,500 mems; Pres. DIANE EVANS.

FINANCIAL MARKETS

Principal Stock Exchanges

American Stock Exchange: 86 Trinity Pl., New York, NY 10006; tel. (212) 306-1000; fax (212) 306-1152; e-mail marketdataproducts@amex.com; internet www.amex.com; f. 1849; Chair. and CEO NEAL L. WOLKOFF; Pres. and COO PATRICIA RADO; mems: 661 regular, 160 associate, 203 option principal, 13 limited trading permit-holders.

Chicago Stock Exchange: 1 Financial Pl., 440 South LaSalle St, Chicago, IL 60605; tel. (312) 663-2222; e-mail info@chx.com; internet www.chx.com; f. 1882; Chair. MICHAEL H. KERR; CEO DAVID A. HERRON; 445 mems.

Nasdaq Stock Market Inc: 1 Liberty Plaza, 165 Broadway, New York, NY 10006; tel. (212) 401-8700; internet www.nasdaq.com; f. 1998 by the American Stock Exchange and the Nat. Asscn of Securities Dealers (NASD); world-wide electronic trading market; CEO ROBERT GREIFELD; Pres. MAGNUS BÖCKER.

National Stock Exchange SM (NSX): 440 South LaSalle St, Suite 2600, Chicago, IL 60605; tel. (312) 786-8803; fax (312) 939-7239; internet www.nsx.com; f. 1885; fmrly Cincinnati Stock Exchange, name changed as above in Nov. 2003; Chair. JAMES M. ANDERSON; CEO JOSEPH S. RIZZELLO.

New York Stock Exchange Euronext: 11 Wall St, New York, NY 10005; tel. (212) 656-3000; fax (212) 656-5646; e-mail mmedina@nyx.com; internet www.nyse.com; f. 1792; Chair. JAN MICHIEL HESSELS; CEO DUNCAN L. NIEDERAUER; 2,800 mems.

Philadelphia Stock Exchange (NASDAQ OMX PHLX): Stock Exchange Bldg, 1900 Market St, Philadelphia, PA 19103-3584; tel. (215) 496-5000; fax (215) 496-5460; e-mail info@phlx.com; internet www.phlx.com; f. 1790; acquired by NASDAQ OMX Group, Inc. 2008; Pres. THOMAS A. WITTMAN; CEO CHRISTOPHER R. CONCANNON; 505 mems.

SUPERVISORY BODY

Securities and Exchange Commission: Station Pl., 100 F St, NE, Washington, DC 20549; tel. (202) 942-8088; fax (202) 942-9646; e-mail help@sec.gov; internet www.sec.gov; f. 1935; Chair. CHRISTOPHER COX.

Trading Statistics, Selected Exchanges, 2007

	Shares sold (million)	Value of sales ($ million)
American	11,656	670,191
Nasdaq	543,611	15,320,133
New York (NYSE)	698,658	29,909,993

Source: World Federation of Exchanges.

Commodity Exchanges

CBOE Futures Exchange (CFE): 400 South LaSalle St, Chicago, IL 60605; tel. (312) 786-5600; e-mail lowenthal@cboe.com; internet cfe.cboe.com; f. 2003; subsidiary of Chicago Board Options Exchange (CBOE); Chair. WILLIAM BRODSKY.

CME Group: 20 South Wacker Dr., Chicago, IL 60606; tel. (312) 930-2316; e-mail info@cmegroup.com; internet www.cmegroup.com; f. 2007 following merger of Chicago Board of Trade and Chicago Mercantile Exchange; acquired New York Mercantile Exchange (NYMEX) 2008; Chair. TERRENCE A. DUFFY; CEO CRAIG S. DONOHUE; Pres. PHUPINDER GILL.

Fort Worth Grain Exchange: POB 4422, Fort Worth, TX 76164; tel. (817) 626-8213; fax (817) 626-1071; f. 1907; 36 mems; Exec. Vice-Pres. C. G. MATHEWS.

Galveston Cotton Exchange and Board of Trade: 2102 Mechanic St, Galveston, TX 77550; tel. (713) 765-5761; f. 1875; Sec. and Gen. Man. L. C. OLIVER.

Greenwood Cotton Exchange: POB 884, Greenwood, MS 38930; tel. (601) 455-4426; fax (601) 455-3158; f. 1927; 35 mems; Sec.-Treas. BILL HOLLAND.

ICE Futures US: World Financial Center, 13th Floor, 1 North End Ave, New York, NY 10282-1101; tel. (212) 748-4000; fax (212) 643-4537; e-mail ir@theice.com; internet www.theice.com; f. 2004; formerly the New York Board of Trade, created following merger agreed in 1998 between the Coffee, Sugar and Cocoa Exchange (CSCE—f.1979) and the New York Cotton Exchange (NYCE—f.1870); Chair and CEO JEFFREY C. SPRECHER; Pres. and COO CHARLES A. VICE.

Kansas City Board of Trade: Suite 303, 4800 Main St, Kansas City, MO 64112; tel. (816) 753-7500; fax (816) 753-3944; e-mail kcbt@kcbt.com; internet www.kcbt.com; f. 1856; 249 mems; Pres. and CEO JEFFREY C. BORCHARDT.

Lubbock Cotton Exchange: 1517 Texas Ave., Lubbock, TX 79401; tel. (806) 763-4646; fax (806) 763-8647; e-mail lcecotton@aol.com; internet www.lubbockcottonexchange.org; f. 1947; Pres. ANGIE GOODMAN.

Memphis Cotton Exchange: POB 3150, Memphis, TN 38173; tel. (901) 525-3361; fax (901) 525-3366; internet www.memphiscottonmuseum.org; f. 1873; 90 mems; Exec. Vice-Pres. RETA J. MARTIN.

Minneapolis Grain Exchange: 102 Grain Exchange Bldg, 400 South Fourth St, Minneapolis, MN 55415; tel. (612) 321-7101; e-mail mgex@mgex.com; internet www.mgex.com; f. 1881; 402 mems; Pres. and CEO MARK G. BAGAN; Chair. SCOTT A. CORDES.

New York Mercantile Exchange (NYMEX/COMEX): World Financial Center, 1 North End Ave, New York, NY 10282-1101; tel. (212) 299-2000; e-mail exchangeinformation@NYMEX.com.; internet www.nymex.com; f. 1872 as the Butter and Cheese Exchange of New York; name changed as above in 1882; merged with the Commodity Exchange in 1994 forming two divisions: NYMEX, on which energy, platinum and palladium trade; and COMEX, on which gold, silver, copper and aluminium trade; Chair. RICHARD SCHAEFFER; Pres. JAMES NEWSOME, Jr.

OneChicago: 141 West Jackson Blvd, Suite 2240, Chicago, IL 60604; tel. (312) 424-8500; fax (312) 424-8529; e-mail info@onechicago.com; internet www.onechicago.com; f. 2002; owned by CME, CBOT and CBOE; options and futures exchange; CEO DAVID G. DOWNEY.

Philadelphia Board of Trade (PBOT): 1900 Market St, Philadelphia, PA 19103-3584; tel. (215) 496-5017; fax (215) 496-5460; e-mail info@phlx.com; internet www.phlx.com/pbot; subsidiary of Philadelphia Stock Exchange (NASDAQ OMX PHLX); Pres. BEN CRAIG, Jr; Chair. MEYER S. FRUCHER.

Sioux City Grain Exchange: 518 Eighth St, Suite B, Sioux City, IA 51101; tel. (712) 258-6596; f. 1907; 22 mems; Treas. DOUGLAS PALMER.

INSURANCE

Principal Companies

Acacia Life Insurance Co: 7315 Wisconsin Ave, Bethesda, MD 20814-3202; tel. (301) 280-1000; fax (310) 280-1161; internet www.unificompanies.com; f. 1869; part of UNIFI Mutual Holding Co; life and health; Chair. and CEO HALUK ARITURK.

Allstate Corpn: 2775 Sanders Rd, Northbrook, IL 60062-6127; tel. (708) 402-5000; fax (708) 402-2351; e-mail directors@allstate.com; internet www.allstate.com; f. 1931; property and casualty, life, fire, indemnity; Pres. and CEO THOMAS J. WILSON.

American Family Insurance Group: 6000 American Pkwy, Madison, WI 53783-0001; tel. (608) 249-2111; internet www.amfam.com; f. 1927; life and annuities through subsidiary, American Family Life Insurance Co; property and casualty through eight other subsidiaries; Chair. and CEO DAVID R. ANDERSON; Pres. and COO JACK SALZWEDEL.

American Family Life Assurance Co of Columbus (AFLAC): 1932 Wynnton Rd, Columbus, GA 31999; tel. (706) 323-3431; internet news@aflac.com; internet www.aflac.com; f. 1955; life and health; Chair. and CEO DANIEL P. AMOS; Pres. KRISS CLONINGER, III.

American International Group, Inc (AIG): 70 Pine St, New York, NY 10270; tel. (212) 770-7000; fax (212) 943-1125; internet www.aig.com; life insurance through subsidiary, AIG Life Companies (US), in Wilmington, DE; property and casualty insurance through 14 subsidiaries throughout the USA; Chair.and CEO EDWARD M. LIDDY.

American National Insurance Co: 1 Moody Plaza, Galveston, TX 77550-7999; tel. (409) 763-4661; internet www.anico.com; f. 1905; operating in 50 states, the District of Columbia, Puerto Rico and American Samoa; life and health, annuities, property and casualty, credit insurance and pension plan services; Chair., Pres. and CEO ROBERT L. MOODY.

American United Life Insurance Co: 1 American Sq., POB 368, Indianapolis, IN 46206-0368; tel. (317) 285-1877; internet www.aul.com; f. 1877; part of OneAmerica Financial Partners, Inc; owned by American United Mutual Insurance Holding Company (AUMIHC); life and health, annuities; Pres. and CEO DAYTON H. MOLENDORP.

Americo Financial Life and Annuity Insurance Co: 300 West 11th St, Kansas City, MO 64105; tel. (816) 391-2000; e-mail contactamerico@americo.com; internet www.americo.com; f. 1909; owned by Americo, Inc; life and health, annuities; Chair. MICHAEL A. MERRIMAN; Pres. and CEO GARY L. MULLER.

Ameritas Life Insurance Corpn: 5900 O St, POB 81889, Lincoln, NE 68501-1889; fax (402) 467-7335; internet www.unificompanies.com; part of UNIFI Mutual Holding Co; life and health; Chair., Pres. and CEO JOANN M. MARTIN.

AmerUS Group: 699 Walnut St, Des Moines, IA 50309; tel. (515) 362-3600; fax (515) 557-2625; internet www.amerus.com; f. 1896; life and health, annuities; subsidiaries: AmerUS Annuity Group (Topeka, KS), AmerUS Life Insurance Co (Des Moines, IA), Bankers Life Insurance Co of New York (Woodbury, NY), Indianapolis Life Insurance Co (Indianapolis, IN); acquired by Aviva PLC in 2006; Chair., Pres. and CEO THOMAS C. GODLASKY.

Assurant: 1 Chase Manhattan Plaza, New York, NY 10005; tel. (212) 859-7000; internet www.assurant.com; life and health; Chair. JOHN MICHAEL PALMS; Pres. and CEO ROBERT B. POLLOCK.

Auto-Owners Insurance Group: 6101 Anacapri Blvd, Lansing, MI 48917; tel. (517) 323-1200; fax (517) 323-8796; internet www.auto-owners.com; f. 1916; property and casualty through Auto-Owners Insurance Co and four other subsidiaries; life through Auto-Owners Life Insurance Co; CEO R. L. LOOYENGA.

AXA-Equitable, Inc: 1290 Ave of the Americas, New York, NY; tel. (212) 554-1234; fax (212) 262-9019; internet www.axa-equitable.com; f. 1859; subsidiary of AXA Financial, Inc; life and health, annuities; Pres. and CEO CHRISTOPHER M. (KIP) CONDRON.

Baltimore Life Insurance Co: 10075 Red Run Blvd, Owings Mills, MD 21117-4871; tel. (410) 581-6600; fax (410) 581-6601; e-mail info@baltlife.com; internet www.baltlife.com; f. 1882; life and health; Chair., Pres. and CEO L. JOHN PEARSON.

W. R. Berkley Corpn: 475 Steamboat Rd, Greenwich, CT 06830; tel. (203) 629-3040; fax (203) 629-3073; e-mail khorvath@wrberkley.com; internet www.wrbc.com; f. 1967; property and casualty through subsidiaries, divided into five business sectors: regional, reinsurance, specialty, alternative markets and international; Chair. and CEO WILLIAM R. BERKLEY.

Berkshire Hathaway, Inc: 1440 Kiewit Plaza, Omaha, NE 68131; tel. (402) 346–1400; internet www.berkshirehathaway.com; general insurance through Berkshire Hathaway Group; life insurance through subsidiary, Medical Protective, in Fort Wayne, IN; Chair. and CEO WARREN E. BUFFETT.

Chubb Group of Insurance Companies: 15 Mountain View Rd, Warren, NJ 07059; tel. (908) 903-2000; fax (908) 903-2027; e-mail mschussel@chubb.com; internet www.chubb.com; part of Chubb Corpn; property and casualty, underwriting, reinsurance; Chair., Pres. and CEO JOHN D. FINNEGAN.

CIGNA Group Insurance: 2 Liberty Pl., 31st Floor, 1601 Chestnut St, Philadelphia, PA 19192; tel. (215) 761-4555; fax (215) 761-5588; internet www.cigna.com; f. 1982; part of CIGNA Corpn; life and health; Chair. and CEO H. EDWARD HANWAY.

CNA Insurance: 333 South Wabash, Chicago, IL 60604; tel. (312) 822-5000; e-mail cna_help@cna.com; internet www.cna.com; part of Loews Corpn; property and casualty; Chair. STEPHEN W. LILIENTHAL; Pres. and CEO JAMES R. LEWIS.

Combined Insurance Co of America (CICA): 1000 North Milwaukee Ave, Glenview, IL 60025; tel. (847) 953-2025; fax (847) 953-8030; internet www.combinedinsurance.com; f. 1949; life and health; operates as Combined Life Insurance Co of New York in NY; Chair. and CEO DOUGLAS R. WENDT.

Conseco, Inc: 11825 North Pennsylvania St, Carmel, IN 46032; tel. (317) 817-6100; internet www.conseco.com; f. 1979; life and health; subsidiaries: Conseco Life Insurance Co (IN), Conseco Insurance Co (IL), Conseco Variable Insurance Co (TX), Conseco Health Insurance Co (AZ), Conseco Senior Health Insurance Com (PA), Bankers Life & Casualty Co (Chicago, IL); Chair. R. GLENN HILLIARD; CEO C. JAMES PRIEUR.

Erie Insurance Group: 100 Erie Insurance Pl., Erie, PA 16530-0001; tel. (814) 870-2000; fax (814) 870-3126; e-mail mark.dombrowski@erieinsurance.com; internet www.erieinsurance.com; f. 1925; vehicle, home, commercial and life through network of independent agents; Pres. and CEO TERRENCE W. CAVANAUGH, Jr.

Farmers Insurance Group of Cos: 4680 Wilshire Blvd, Los Angeles, CA 90010-3807; tel. (213) 930-3200; fax (213) 932-3101;

internet www.farmers.com; f. 1928; part of Farmers Group, Inc; owned by Zurich Financial Services; vehicle, home and life; operates in 41 states; subsidiaries: Farmers Insurance Exchange, Truck Insurance Exchange, Fire Insurance Exchange, Farmers New World Life Insurance Co (Mercer Island, WA); acquired Foremost Insurance Co (MI) in 2000; CEO PAUL N. HOPKINS.

Fidelity National Financial (FNF): 601 Riverside Ave, Jacksonville, FL 32204; tel. (888) 934-3354; internet www.fnf.com; principal subsidiaries: Fidelity National Title Group and Fidelity National Property and Casualty Insurance Group; Chair WILLIAM P. FOLEY, II; CEO AL STINSON.

First American Corpn: 1 First American Way, Santa Ana, CA 92707; tel. (714) 800-3000; e-mail corporate.communications@firstam.com; internet www.firstam.com; f. 1889; Chair. and CEO PARKER S. KENNEDY.

Genworth Financial, Inc: 6620 West Broad St, Richmond, VA 23230; e-mail contactus@genworth.com; internet www.genworth.com; f. 1871 as The Life Insurance Co of Virginia; life, long-term care, annuities; Chair., Pres. and CEO MICHAEL D. FRAIZER.

The Guardian Life Insurance Co of America: 7 Hannover Sq., New York, NY 10004; tel. (212) 598-8000; fax (212) 353-7034; internet www.guardianlife.com; f. 1860; life and health through 12 subsidiaries and affiliates; Pres. and CEO DENNIS J. MANNING.

Hanover Insurance Group, Inc: 440 Lincoln St, Worcester, MA 01653-0002; tel. (508) 855-1000; fax (508) 853-6332; e-mail abanek@hanover.com; internet www.hanover.com; f. 1852; fmrly operated as Allmerica Financial Life Insurance and Annuity Co, name changed as above in 2005; property and casualty; operates as The Hanover Insurance Co, and as Citizens Insurance Co of America in MI; Chair. MICHAEL P. ANGELINI; Pres. and CEO FREDERICK H. EPPINGER.

Hartford Financial Services Group, Inc: Hartford Plaza, 690 Asylum Ave, Hartford, CT 06115; tel. (860) 547-5000; internet www.thehartford.com; f. 1810; vehicle, home, life, flood, property and casualty, group benefits, group reinsurance; Chair. and CEO RAMANI AYER; Pres. and COO THOMAS M. MARRA.

John Hancock Life Insurance Co: POB 111, Boston, MA 02117; tel. (617) 572-6000; fax (617) 572-4539; e-mail investor_relations@manulife.com; internet www.johnhancock.com; f. 1862; owned by Manulife (Canada); Pres. and CEO JOHN D. DESPREZ, III.

Kansas City Life Insurance Co: 3520 Broadway, Kansas City, MO 64141-6139; tel. (816) 753-7000; internet www.kclife.com; f. 1895; life and health; operates in 48 states and the District of Columbia; subsidiaries: Old American Insurance Co, Sunset Life Insurance Co of America; Chair., Pres. and CEO R. PHILIP BIXBY.

Liberty Mutual Group, Inc: 175 Berkeley St, Boston, MA 02116; tel. (617) 357-9500; fax (617) 350-7648; internet www.libertymutual.com; subsidiaries: Liberty Life Assurance Co of Boston, Liberty Mutual Insurance Co, Liberty Mutual Fire Insurance Co and Employers Insurance Co of Wasusau; Chair., Pres. and CEO EDMUND F. KELLY.

Lincoln National Life Insurance Co: 350 Church St, Hartford, CT 06103; tel. (877) 275-5462; e-mail personalservicecenter@lfg.com; internet www.lfg.com; f. 1905; part of Lincoln National Corpn; life and health; Chair. J. PATRICK BARRETT; Pres. and CEO DENNIS R. GLASS.

Massachusetts Mutual Life Insurance Co (MassMutual): 1295 State St, Springfield, MA 01111-0001; tel. (413) 788-8411; fax (413) 744-6005; internet www.massmutual.com; f. 1851; part of MassMutual Financial Group; mutual life and health; Chair., Pres. and CEO STUART H. REESE.

Metropolitan Life Insurance Co (MetLife): 1 Madison Ave, New York, NY 10010-3681; tel. (212) 578-2211; fax (212) 689-1980; internet www.metlife.com; f. 1863; life and health; Chair., Pres. and CEO C. ROBERT HENRIKSON.

Minnesota Life Insurance Co: 400 Robert St North, St Paul, MN 55101; tel. (651) 665-3500; fax (651) 665-4488; internet www.minnesotamutual.com; f. 1880; affiliated to Securian Financial Group, Inc; life and health; Chair., Pres. and CEO ROBERT L. SENKLER.

Mutual of Omaha Insurance Co: Mutual of Omaha Plaza, Omaha, NE 68175; tel. (402) 342-7600; internet mutualofomaha.com; f. 1909; life and health; operating in 50 states, the District of Columbia, the US Virgin Is, Puerto Rico and Guam; Chair. and CEO DANIEL P. NEARY; Pres. and COO JOHN A. STURGEON.

Nationwide Mutual Insurance Co: 1 Nationwide Plaza, Columbus, OH 43215-2220; tel. (614) 249-7111; e-mail casej6@nationwide.com; internet www.nationwide.com; f. 1925; property and casualty through 18 subsidiaries; life and retirement savings through 25 subsidiaries; also asset management and strategic investment; CEO JERRY JURGENSEN; Chair. and COO MARK THRESHER.

National Western Life Insurance Co: 850 East Anderson Lane, Austin, TX 78752-1602; tel. (512) 836-1010; fax (512) 719-8511; internet www.nationalwesternlife.com; f. 1956; life and health, annuities; Chair. and CEO ROBERT L. MOODY; Pres. and COO ROSS R. MOODY.

New York Life Insurance Co: 51 Madison Ave, New York, NY 10010-1603; tel. (212) 576-7000; fax (212) 576-6794; e-mail infonyl@e-mail.com; internet www.newyorklife.com; f. 1845; life and health; Chair. SEYMOUR (SY) STERNBERG; Pres. and CEO TED MATHAS.

The Northwestern Mutual Life Insurance Co: 720 East Wisconsin Ave, Milwaukee, WI 53202-4797; tel. (414) 271-1444; internet www.nmfn.com; f. 1857; mutual life and health; Pres. and CEO EDWARD J. ZORE.

One Beacon Insurance Group: 1 Beacon Lane, Canton, MA 02021; tel. (781 332-70006; e-mail info@onebeacon.com; internet www.onebeacon.com; f. 1861; property and casualty, specialty; Pres. and CEO T. MICHAEL MILLER; Chair. LOWNDES A. SMITH.

Pacific Life Insurance Co: 700 Newport Center Dr., Newport Beach, CA 92660-6397; tel. (949) 219-3011; fax (949) 219-7614; e-mail info@pacificlife.com; internet www.pacificlife.com; f. 1868; life, annuities and mutual funds; Chair., Pres. and CEO JAMES T. MORRIS; CFO KHANH T. TRAN.

Penn Mutual Life Insurance Co: 600 Dresher Rd, Horsham, PA 19044; tel. (215) 956-8000; fax (215) 956-7508; internet www.pennmutual.com; f. 1847; Chair., Pres. and CEO ROBERT E. CHAPPELL.

Phoenix Life Insurance Co: 1 American Row, POB 5056, Hartford, CT 06102-5056; tel. (860) 403-5000; e-mail webmaster@phoenixwm.com; internet www.phoenixwm.com; f. 1851; life and health, annuities; operating in all states, the District of Columbia, Puerto Rico, the US Virgin Is and Canada; Chair., Pres. and CEO DONA DAVIS YOUNG.

Pioneer Mutual Life Insurance Co: 101 North 10th St, Fargo, ND 58108; tel. (701) 297-5700; part of OneAmerica Financial Partners, Inc, owned by American United Mutual Insurance Holding Co (AUMIHC); life and health, annuities; Pres. and CEO DAYTON H. MOLENDORP.

Principal Financial Group, Inc: 711 High St, Des Moines, IA 50392; tel. (515) 247-5111; fax (515) 235–5491; internet www.principal.com; life and health; Chair. J. BARRY GRISWELL; Pres. and CEO LARRY D. ZIMPLEMAN.

The Progressive Group: 6300 Wilson Mills Rd, Mayfield Village, OH 44143; tel. (440) 461-5000; e-mail leah_knapp@progressive.com; internet www.progressive.com; f. 1937; part of The Progressive Corpn; Chair. PETER B. LEWIS; Pres. and CEO GLENN M. RENWICK.

Protective Life Insurance Co: 2801 Hwy 280 South, Birmingham, AL 35223-2488; tel. (205) 879-9230; fax (205) 268-1000; internet www.protective.com; f. 1907; part of Protective Life Insurance Corpn; life and health; Chair., Pres. and CEO JOHN D. JOHNS.

The Prudential Insurance Co of America: 751 Broad St, Newark, NJ 07102-3714; tel. (973) 802-6000; fax (973) 802-7277; e-mail investor.relations@prudential.com; internet www.prudential.com; f. 1875; life and health; Chair. and CEO JOHN R. STRANGFELD.

SAFECO Corpn: Safeco Plaza, 4333 Brooklyn Ave, NE, Seattle, WA 98185-0001; tel. (206) 545-5000; fax (206) 548-7117; internet www.safeco.com; f. 1929; part of Liberty Mutual Group since 2008; subsidiaries: SAFECO Property and Casualty Insurance Cos, SAFECO Surety; Pres. MICHAEL HUGHES.

Security Mutual Life Insurance Co of New York: 100 Court St, POB 1625, Binghamton, New York, NY 13902-1625; tel. (607) 723-3551; e-mail hpalmer@smlny.com; internet www.smlny.com; f. 1886; life and health, annuities; operating in all states; Chair., Pres. and CEO BRUCE W. BOYEA.

Standard Insurance Co: POB 711, Portland, OR 97207; tel. (503) 248-2700; fax (503) 321-7757; e-mail info@standard.com; internet www.standard.com; f. 1906; principal subsidiary of StanCorp Financial Group, Inc; disability, group diability, group life, group dental, annuities; Chair. and CEO ERIC E. PARSONS; Pres. and COO GREG NESS.

Standard Life Insurance Co of New York: POB 5031, White Plains, NY 10602; tel. (914) 989-4400; e-mail skulesa@standard.com; internet www.standard-ny.com; subsidiary of StanCorp Financial Group, Inc; group life, disability, dental; Chair., Pres. and CEO ERIC E. PARSONS; Asst Vice-Pres., Benefits STANLEY J. KULESA.

State Farm Insurance: 1 State Farm Plaza, Bloomington, IL 61710-0001; tel. (309) 766-2311; fax (309) 766-6169; internet www.statefarm.com; f. 1929; vehicle, fire, life and health insurance; Chair. and CEO EDWARD B. RUST, Jr.

State Life Insurance Co: 1 American Sq., POB 368, Indianapolis, IN 46206-0368; tel. (317) 681-5300; fax (317) 681-5492; f. 1894; part of OneAmerica Financial Partners, Inc, owned by American United Mutual Insurance Holding Company (AUMIHC); life and health, annuities; Chair. DAYTON H. MOLENDORP; Pres. RICHARD MERRILL.

Symetra Life Insurance Co: 777 108th Ave, NE, Suite 1200, Bellevue, WA 98004; tel. (425) 376-8284; e-mail communications@

symetra.com; internet www.symetra.com; fmrly SAFECO Life and Investments; name changed as above in 2004; life and health; Chair. DAVID T. FOY; Pres. and CEO RANDALL H. TALBOT.

Teachers Insurance and Annuity Association-College Retirement Equities Fund (TIAA-CREF): 730 Third Ave, New York, NY 10017-3206; internet www.tiaa-cref.org; mutual life and health; Pres. and CEO ROGER W. FERGUSON, Jr.

Thrivent Financial for Lutherans: 4321 North Ballard Rd, Appleton, WI 54919-0001; tel. (920) 734-5721; e-mail mail@thrivent.com; internet www.thrivent.com; life and health; Chair., Pres. and CEO BRUCE J. NICHOLSON.

Torchmark Corpn: 3700 South Stonebridge Dr., POB 8080, McKinney, TX 75070-8080; tel. (972) 569-4000; e-mail tmkir@torchmarkcorp.com; internet www.torchmarkcorp.com; life and health; principal subsidiaries: American Income Life Insurance Co (Waco, TX), First United American Life Insurance Co (Syracuse, NY), Globe Life And Accident Insurance Co (Oklahoma City, OK), Liberty National Life Insurance Co (Birmingham, AL), United American Insurance Co (McKinney, TX), United Investors Life Insurance Co (Birmingham, AL); Chair. and CEO MARK S. MCANDREW.

Transamerica Corpn: 1150 South Olive St, Los Angeles, CA 90015-2290; tel. (213) 741-7629; fax (213) 742-5280; internet www.transamerica.com; f. 1906; part of AEGON Insurance Group; life and health, annuities, reinsurance; subsidiaries: Transamerica Occidental Life Insurance Co, Transamerica Life Insurance Co, Transamerica Financial Life Insurance Co; Pres. RON WAGLEY; Chair. FRANK HERRINGER.

The Travelers Cos, Inc: 385 Washington St, Saint Paul, MN 55102; tel. (651) 310-7911; internet www.travelers.com; f. 2004 by merger of Travelers Property Casualty Corpn and the St Paul Cos; property and casualty insurance, surety products, risk management services; Chair., Pres. and CEO JAY FISHMAN.

Unigard Security Insurance Co: 15805 NE 24th St, Bellevue, WA 98008-2409; tel. (425) 641-4321; fax (425) 562-5256; internet www.unigard.com; f. 1901; parent cos: Winterthur Insurance Group, Credit Suisse Group; Pres. and CEO PETER CHRISTEN.

Union Central Life Insurance Co: 1876 Waycross Rd, POB 40888, Cincinnati, OH 45240; tel. (513) 595-2200; fax (513) 595-2559; internet www.unioncentral.com; f. 1867; part of UNIFI Mutual Holding Co; life and health; Chair. JOHN H. JACOBS.

Unitrin, Inc: 1 East Wacker Dr., Chicago, IL 60601; tel. (312) 661-4600; e-mail mediarelations@unitrin.com; internet www.unitrin.com; life and health through Unitrin Life & Health Insurance Group (five subsidiaries); property and casualty through Unitrin Property & Casualty Insurance Group (19 subsidiaries); two further subsidiaries and five affiliated cos; Chair. RICHARD C. VIE; Pres. and CEO DONALD G. SOUTHWELL.

UnumProvident Corpn: 1 Fountain Sq., Chattanooga, TN 37402; tel. (432) 294-1011; e-mail tawhite@unum.com; internet www.unumprovident.com; f. 1848; life and health; subsidiaries: Colonial Life Accident and Insurance Co, Paul Revere Life Insurance Co, Provident Life and Accident Insurance Co, Provident Life and Casualty Insurance Co, First Unum Insurance Co and Unum Life Insurance Co of America; Pres. and CEO THOMAS R. WATJEN.

USAA: 9800 Fredericksburg Rd, San Antonio, TX 78288; internet www.usaa.com; f. 1922; property and casualty through seven subsidiaries: United Service Automobile Asscn, USAA Casualty Insurance Co, USAA General Indemnity Co, Garrison Property and Casualty Insurance Co, USAA County Mutual Insurance Co, USAA Texas Lloyd's Co and USAA Ltd; life and annuities through two subsidiaries: USAA Life Insurance Co and USAA Life Insurance Company of New York (Highland Falls, NY); Pres. and CEO JOSUE (JOE) ROBLES, Jr.

Western & Southern Financial Group: 400 Broadway, Mail Station 90, Cincinnati, OH 45202; tel. (866) 832–7719; fax (513) 629-1220; internet www.westernsouthern.com; f. 1888; operating in 44 states; life and health; subsidiaries: Western & Southern Life Insurance Co, Western-Southern Life Assurance Co, Columbus Life Insurance Co, Integrity Life Insurance Co, Lafayette Life Insurance Co; Chair., Pres. and CEO JOHN F. BARRETT.

Zenith Insurance Co: 21255 Califa St, Woodland Hills, CA 91367; tel. (818) 713-1000; fax (818) 592-0480; e-mail dfreeman@thezenith.com; internet www.thezenith.com; specializes in workers' compensation; subsidiary: ZNAT Insurance Co; Chair. and Pres. STANLEY R. ZAX.

Insurance Organizations

American Bankers' Insurance Association (ABIA): 1120 Connecticut Ave, NW, Washington DC 20036; tel. (202) 663-5163; fax (202) 828-4546; e-mail vbarton@aba.com; internet www.aba.com/abia; Pres. and Chair. RICHARD L. SPICKARD.

American Council of Life Insurance (ACLI): 101 Constitution Ave, NW, Washington, DC 20001-2133; tel. (202) 624-2000; fax (202) 624-2319; e-mail Media@acli.com; internet www.acli.com; f. 1976; 400 mem. cos; Pres. and CEO FRANK KEATING, Jr.

American Institute of Marine Underwriters (AIMU): 14 Wall St, 21st Floor, New York, NY 10005-2145; tel. (212) 233-0550; fax (212) 227-5102; e-mail aimu@aimu.org; internet www.aimu.org; f. 1898; 105 mems; Chair. RICHARD J. DECKER; Pres. JAMES M. CRAIG.

American Insurance Association (AIA): 1130 Connecticut Ave, NW, Suite 1000, Washington, DC 20036; tel. (202) 828-7100; fax (202) 293-1219; e-mail info@aiadc.org; internet www.aiadc.org; f. 1964; 300 mems; Pres. MARC RACICOT.

America's Health Insurance Plans (AHIP): 601 Pennsylvania Ave, Suite 500, Washington, DC 20004; tel. (202) 778-3200; fax (202) 331-7487; e-mail ahip@ahip.org; internet www.ahip.org; Chair. GEORGE HALVORSON; 1,300 mems.

Casualty Actuarial Society: 4350 North Fairfax Dr., Suite 250, Arlington, VA 22203; tel. (703) 276-3100; fax (703) 276-3108; e-mail office@casact.org; internet www.casact.org; f. 1914; 4,400 mems; Pres. CHRISTOPHER S. CARLSON.

Insurance Information Institute (III): 110 William St, New York, NY 10038; tel. (212) 346-5500; e-mail members@iii.org; internet www.iii.org; Chair. KLAUS G. DORFI; Pres. ROBERT P. HARTWIG.

LIMRA International: 300 Day Hill Rd, Windsor, CT 06095; tel. (860) 688-3358; fax (860) 298-9555; e-mail customer.service@limra.com; internet www.limra.com; f. 1916; research and consultancy services for insurance cos; Chair. SUSAN D. WARING; Pres. and CEO ROBERT A. KERZNER; 850 mems.

LOMA (Life Office Management Association): 2300 Windy Ridge Pkwy, Suite 600, Atlanta, GA 30339-8443; tel. (770) 951-1770; fax (770) 984-6417; e-mail askloma@loma.org; internet www.loma.org; f. 1924; 1,200 mem. cos; Pres. ROBERT A. KERZNER.

National Association of Health Underwriters (NAHU): 2000 North 14th St, Suite 450, Arlington, VA 22201; tel. (703) 276-0220; fax (703) 841-7797; e-mail info@nahu.org; internet www.nahu.org; CEO JANET TRAUTWEIN.

National Association of Insurance and Financial Advisors (NAIFA): 2901 Telestar Ct, Falls Church, VA 22042-1205; tel. (703) 770-8100; e-mail communications@naifa.org; internet www.naifa.org; CEO JOHN J. HEALY; Pres. CLIFF F. WILSON.

National Association of Mutual Insurance Cos (NAMIC): 3601 Vincennes Rd, POB 68700, Indianapolis, IN 46268-0700; tel. (317) 875-5250; fax (317) 879-8408; e-mail service@namic.org; internet www.namic.org; f. 1895; 1,400 mems; Pres. and CEO CHARLES M. CHAMNESS.

Property Casualty Insurers Association (PCI): 2600 South River Rd, Des Plaines, IL 60018-3286; tel. (847) 297-7800; fax (847) 297-5064; e-mail pcinet@pciaa.net; internet www.pciaa.net; f. 2004; by merger of the Alliance of American Insurers and the National Asscn of Independent Insurers; Pres. DAVID A. SAMPSON.

Reinsurance Association of America: 1301 Pennsylvania Ave, NW, Suite 900, Washington, DC 20004; tel. (202) 638-3690; fax (202) 638-0936; e-mail infobox@reinsurance.org; internet www.reinsurance.org; f. 1969; 35 mems; Pres. FRANKLIN W. NUTTER.

TOURISM

STATISTICS

International Tourist Arrivals, Receipts and Departures

(Source: Office of Travel and Tourism Industries, International Trade Administration, US Department of Commerce.)

INTERNATIONAL TOURIST ARRIVALS*

	2005	2006	2007
Australia	581,773	603,275	669,536
Brazil	485,373	525,271	639,431
Canada	14,862,000†	15,992,242	17,761,000†
France	878,648	789,815	997,506
Germany	1,415,530	1,385,520	1,524,151
India	344,926	406,845	567,045
Italy	545,546	532,829	634,152
Japan	3,883,906	3,672,584	3,531,489
Korea, Republic	705,093	757,721	806,175
Mexico†	12,665,000	13,317,000	14,333,000
United Kingdom	4,344,957	4,176,211	4,497,858
Total (incl. others)	49,205,528	51,063,290	55,986,277

* List includes countries comprising 1% or more of total arrivals in any featured year.

† Rounded figure(s).

Tourism receipts ($ '000 million, incl. passenger transport): 102.8 in 2005; 107.8 in 2006; 122.3 in 2007.

INTERNATIONAL TOURIST DEPARTURES
('000 persons, excl. same-day visitors)

	2005	2006	2007
Bahamas	930	1,538	n.a.
Brazil	605	n.a.	687
Canada	14,391	13,855	13,371
China, People's Republic	1,295	1,327	1,374
France	2,217	2,231	2,217
Germany	1,670	1,688	1,936
Hong Kong	921	904	968
India	835	904	999
Ireland	691	844	749
Italy	2,044	2,201	2,373
Jamaica	1,353	1,688	1,530
Japan	1,497	1,538	1,718
Korea, Republic	662	633	687
Mexico	20,325	19,659	19,453
Netherlands	864	904	937
Spain	979	995	1,093
Switzerland	518	633	656
Taiwan	662	693	687
United Kingdom	3,829	3,286	3,123
Total (incl. others)	63,503	63,662	64,052

Note: Data were compiled on the basis of respondent sampling, and exclude destinations with fewer than 400 respondents. With the exception of Canada and Mexico, figures refer to air travel only.

Tourism expenditures ($ '000 million, incl. passenger transport): 95.1 in 2005; 99.6 in 2006; 104.7 in 2007.

NATIONAL ORGANIZATIONS

American Society of Travel Agents: 1101 King St, Alexandria, VA 22314; tel. (703) 739-2782; fax (703) 684-8319; e-mail askasta@asta.com; internet www.asta.org; f. 1931; Pres. and CEO CHERYL HUDAK; Exec. Vice-Pres. and COO WILLIAM A. MALONEY; over 20,000 mems.

Discover America Partnership: 1100 New York Ave, NW, Suite 450, Washington, DC 20005; tel. (202) 408-8422; fax (202) 408-1255; e-mail ckeefe@tia.org; internet www.poweroftravel.org; f. 2006 by leading private businesses to promote the USA's global image through travel; Exec. Dir GEOFF FREEMAN.

Office of Travel and Tourism Industries: International Trade Administration, US Department of Commerce, 14th and Constitution Ave, NW, Rm 1003, Washington, DC 20230; tel. (202) 482-0140; fax (202) 482-2887; e-mail tinet_info@ita.doc.gov; internet tinet.ita.doc.gov; f. 1996; fed. govt agency; collects and analyses data and develops US tourism policy; Dir HELEN MARANO; Dep. Asst Sec. for Services ANA GUEVARA.

Travel Industry Association of America: 1100 New York Ave, NW, Suite 450, Washington, DC 20005-3934; tel. (202) 408-8422; fax (202) 408-1225; internet www.tia.org; f. 1941; Pres. and CEO ROGER DOW; Chair. CAROLINE BETETA.

STATE TOURIST ATTRACTIONS AND ORGANIZATIONS

Alabama

Alabama has 23 state parks and five state park resorts, covering a total area of some 48,000 acres; four national forests: Talladega, William B. Bankhead, Conecuh and Tuskegee; and 23 state-managed fishing lakes. State parks and recreation areas were visited by 2,961,000 tourists in 2005, and the national park service areas received 790,039 recreation visits in 2006. The state's Gulf of Mexico beaches attract thousands of visitors; Point Clear, in particular, has been a well-known tourist destination since the early 19th century. Fishing is a popular activity in the state, and the Deep Sea Fishing Rodeo at Dauphin Island is a major attraction. Places of cultural and historical interest include the Tuskegee Institute National Historical Site, the Russell Cave National Monument, the First White House of the Confederacy at Montgomery, the Marshall Space and Rocket Center at Huntsville, the Natural History Museum and the Shakespeare Festival.

Alabama State Parks: 64 Union St North, Montgomery, AL 36130; tel. (334) 242-3486; fax (334) 242-2137; e-mail dcnr.commissioner@dcnr.alabama.gov; internet www.alapark.com; State Parks Dir MARK EASTERWOOD.

Bureau of Tourism and Travel: 401 Adams Ave, Suite 126, POB 4927, Montgomery, AL 36103-4297; tel. (334) 242-4169; fax (334) 242-4554; e-mail info@tourism.alabama.gov; internet www.800alabama.com; Dir LEE SENTELL.

Travel Council: 516 Oliver Rd, POB 210729, Montgomery, AL 36121; tel. (334) 271-0050; fax (334) 279-7798; e-mail jojo@alabamatravel.org; internet www.alabamatravel.org.

Alaska

Alaska has thousands of miles of scenic landscape, including over 3m. lakes and the 11 highest mountains in the USA. The national parks and wildlife enclosures cover more than 104m. acres. Denali National Park—the site of Mount McKinley—Glacier Bay National Park and Katmai National Park are among the principal tourist attractions. Alaska's state parks, which cover an area of over 3,353,000 acres, were visited by 4,678,000 visitors in 2005. National park service areas received 2,471,970 recreation visits in 2006. Within the parks there are alpine ski areas, numerous hiking trails and campsites. Cruise travel along the Gulf of Alaska is also becoming increasingly popular with visitors.

Alaska State Park Information: 550 West Seventh Ave, Suite 1260, Anchorage, AK 99501-3557; tel. (907) 269-8400; fax (907) 269-8901; e-mail pic@dnr.state.ak.us; internet www.dnr.state.ak.us.

Alaska Travel Industry Association: 2600 Cordova St, Suite 201, Anchorage, AK 99503; tel. (800) 327-9372; fax (800) 276-1042; e-mail info@AlaskaTIA.org; internet www.travelalaska.com.

Forest Service (Alaska Region): 709 West Ninth St, POB 21628, Juneau, AK 99802-1628; tel. (907) 586-8806; fax (907) 586-7892; internet www.fs.fed.us/r10.

National Park Service—Alaska Public Lands Information Centers: 605 West Fourth Ave, Suite 105, Anchorage, AK 99501; tel. (907) 271-2737; e-mail chris_smith@nps.gov; internet www.nps.gov/aplic.

Office of Tourism: Dept of Commerce, Community and Economic Development, State Office Bldg, 9th Floor, POB 110801, Juneau, AK 99811-0801; tel. (907) 465-2500.

Arizona

In 2005 Arizona's state parks and recreation areas were visited by 2,224,000 tourists, and national park service areas received a total of 10,543,205 recreation visits in 2006. The 25 national parks and monuments include Petrified Forest National Park, Saguaro National Monument, and Grand Canyon National Park. There are also 27 state parks, covering an area of more than 64,000 acres, and six national forests. The state's Navaho and Hopi historic sites, comprising Monument Valley and the Navaho National Monument are favourite destinations for sightseeing, while the reservations themselves offer good shopping facilities. Western towns such as Tucson and Tombstone attract visitors interested in the early days of the state. Water sports and fishing are popular recreations, with winter sports taking place in the mountain regions. Lake Havasu, the Colorado River and the Salt River lakes are among the principal tourist attractions.

National Park Service: 3115 North Third Ave, No. 101, Phoenix, AZ 85013; tel. (602) 640-5250.

Office of Tourism: 1110 West Washington, Suite 155, Phoenix, AZ 85007; tel. (602) 364-3701; fax (602) 240-5432; e-mail memmermann@azot.gov; internet www.arizonaguide.com; Dir Margie Emmermann.

State Parks: 1300 West Washington, Phoenix, AZ 85007; tel. (602) 542-4174; fax (602) 542-4188; internet azstateparks.com; Chair. William C. Scalzo.

Arkansas

In 2005 9,751,000 tourists visited Arkansas' 53,000 acres of state parks and recreation areas, while national park service areas received 2,556,666 recreation visits in 2006. Arkansas has six national park sites, 2.9m. acres of national forest lands and 13 major lakes. The Buffalo National River, the country's first national river park, is a major tourist attraction, as are the resorts of Hot Springs (in the Ouachita Mountains), Eureka Springs (in the Ozark Plateau) and Mammoth Springs, near the Missouri border, which offer spa and recreational facilities. The so-called Crater of Diamonds near Mursfreeboro also attracts visitors, who are permitted to keep any diamonds they find. Hunting is popular in the state, with the World Championship Duck Calling Contest, held in Stuttgart, a primary attraction for hunters.

Department of Parks and Tourism: 1 Capitol Mall, Little Rock, AR 72201; tel. (501) 682-7777; fax (501) 682-2523; e-mail communications@arkansas.com; internet www.arkansas.com; Dir Richard W. Davies.

California

California contains some of the largest and most well-known national parks in the USA, including the Redwood National Park, the Lassen Volcanic National Park, Yosemite National Park and Sequoia National Park. The 278 state parks cover an area of some 1.5m. acres and were visited by over 77,119,000 tourists in 2005, while national park service areas received 32,906,849 recreation visits in 2006. However, the San Francisco and Los Angeles metropolitan areas are the principal tourist destinations. The most popular attractions are the Golden Gate National Recreation Area, consisting of 68 sq m on both sides of the entrance to San Francisco Bay, the Disneyland amusement centre at Anaheim and Hollywood, where various tours connected with the film and television industries are offered.

California State Parks: Dept of Parks and Recreation, Communications Office, POB 942896, Sacramento, CA 94296; tel. (916) 654-6538; fax (916) 654-6374; e-mail info@parks.ca.gov; internet parks.ca.gov; Dir Ruth Coleman.

California Tourism: POB 1499, Sacramento, CA 95812-1499; tel. (916) 444-4429; fax (916) 322-3402; e-mail jjasper@visitcalifornia.com; internet www.visitcalifornia.com.

USDA Forest Service (Pacific Southwest Region): 1323 Club Dr., Vallejo, CA 94592; tel. (707) 562-8737; fax (707) 562-9130; e-mail wrwilliams@fs.fed.us; internet www.fs.fed.us/r5.

Colorado

Colorado has 10 national parks including Rocky Mountain, which comprises 265,828 acres in the Front Range, and Mesa Verde, which covers 52,122 acres in the south-west. The 41 state parks encompass an area of 410,000 acres and attracted an estimated 11,377,000 tourists in 2005, with national park service areas receiving 5,289,308 visits in 2006. The state is popular among skiers, with 28 ski areas, of which the most visited is the Vail resort centre, followed by the Keystone and Steamboat resorts. Colorado also offers 'white water' rafting opportunities. The US Air Force Academy, near Colorado Springs, is also a principal attraction for tourists. Sites of major historical interest in the state include the fossil beds at Dinosaur National Monument, Native American (Amerindian) cliff dwellings at Mesa Verde, the Black Canyon of the Gunnison and the Colorado National Monument.

Board of Tourism: 1625 Broadway, Suite 2700, Denver, CO 80202; tel. (303) 892-38850; fax (303) 892-3848; internet www.colorado.com.

Denver Metro Convention and Visitors Bureau: 1555 California St, Suite 300, Denver, CO 80202-4262; tel. (303) 892-1112; fax (303) 892-1636; e-mail visitorinfo@denver.org; internet www.denver.org; Pres. and CEO Richard Scharf.

National Park Service: POB 25287, Denver, CO 80255-0287; tel. (303) 236-4648; internet www.nps.gov/state/co.

State Parks: 1313 Sherman St, Suite 618, Denver, CO 80203; tel. (303) 866-3437; fax (303) 866-3206; e-mail parksinfo@state.co.us; internet parks.state.co.us; Chair. Dr Tom W. Ready.

USDA Forest Service (Rocky Mountain Region): 740 Simms St, POB 25127, Golden, CO 80401; tel. (303) 275-5367; e-mail dtomlin@fs.fed.us; internet www.fs.fed.us/r2; Regional Forester Rick Cables.

Connecticut

Connecticut's lakes and seashore recreation areas draw many tourists to the state. Among the attractions in these areas are the aquarium at the Mystic Seaport restoration and the Hammonasset beach. The most important aquatic event is the Harvard-Yale regatta, held each June on the Thames River in New London. There are numerous sporting facilities in the state, including golf courses, boat-launching sites and ski areas. The state also possesses one of the world's largest casinos, situated at Foxwoods Resort in Ledyard. The 117 state parks and recreation areas cover 204,000 acres and were visited by 6,235,000 tourists in 2005. The state's national park service area received 11,795 recreation visits in 2006. The numerous sites in the state associated with the heritage and freedom movement of African-American citizens are linked by the Freedom Trail, and the Mark Twain and Harriet Beecher Stowe Houses are also principal tourist attractions.

Connecticut Forest and Parks Association (CFPA): 16 Meriden Rd, Rockfall, CT 06481-2961; tel. (860) 346-2372; fax (860) 347-7463; e-mail info@ctwoodlands.org; internet www.ctwoodlands.org; f. 1895; Pres. David Platt; Exec. Dir Eric Hammerling.

Division of Tourism: Connecticut Commission on Culture and Tourism, 1 Constitution Plaza, Hartford, CT 06103; tel. (860) 256-2800; fax (860) 286-2811; e-mail ct.travelinfo@ct.gov; internet www.cultureandtourism.org; Exec. Dir Karen Senich.

Delaware

Delaware's 14 state parks and recreation areas cover 24,000 acres and attracted 4,557,000 tourists in 2005. The most notable among these parks are the Fenwick Island and Trapp Pond state parks. The principal tourist pastimes are fishing, clamming, crabbing and water sports, with Rehoboth Beach on the Atlantic Coast a famous and popular holiday destination, especially among federal officials and foreign diplomats. Delaware's annual festivities include Easter services and Delaware Day ceremonies, which commemorate the state's ratification of the Constitution.

Division of Fish and Wildlife: 89 Kings Hwy, POB 1401, Dover, DE 19901; tel. (302) 739-9910; e-mail dawn.webb@state.de.us; internet www.fw.delaware.gov; Dir PATRICK EMORY.

State Visitors Service: 630 State College Rd, Dover, DE 19901; tel. (800) 282-8667.

Tourism Office: 99 Kings Hwy, POB 1401, Dover, DE 19901; tel. (302) 739-4271; fax (302) 739-5749; internet www.visitdelaware.com.

District of Columbia

The District of Columbia is one of the world's chief tourist destinations. The federal capital offers an abundance of historical and cultural attractions, including the Washington Monument and the White House, the Supreme Court, the Library of Congress and the US Capitol buildings. Other leading attractions include the Smithsonian Air and Space Museum, the Museum of Natural History and the Museum of American History. National park service areas were visited by 32,867,947 tourists in 2006, with the National Capital parks, Rock Creek Park, the Vietnam Veterans' Memorial and the Lincoln Memorial attracting the greatest numbers of visitors.

Department of Parks and Recreation: 3149 16th St, NW, Washington, DC 20010; tel. (202) 673-7665; fax (202) 673-2087; e-mail dpr@dc.gov; internet www.dpr.dc.gov; Dir CLARK E. RAY.

Washington, DC, Convention and Tourism Corporation (WCTC): 901 Seventh St, NW, 4th Floor, Washington, DC 20001-3719; tel. (202) 789-7000; fax (202) 789-7037; e-mail francine .alexander@washington.org; internet www.washington.org; Pres. and CEO WILLIAM A. HANBURY.

Florida

Florida's beaches are an important asset to its tourism industry, attracting millions of visitors each year. Other major attractions are Walt Disney World (a large amusement park in Orlando), the Kennedy Space Center at Cape Canaveral and the St Augustine historic district. National park service areas received 7,983,175 recreation visits in 2006. Most popular were Gulf Islands National Seashore, near Pensacola, and Canaveral National Seashore. There are 159 state parks, covering a total area of over 696,000 acres; these attracted 18,202,000 tourists in 2005. The state also has 18 historical sites. Outdoor recreational activities for tourists include fishing and boating.

Bureau of Natural and Cultural Resources: 3900 Commonwealth Blvd, Mail Station 49, Tallahassee, FL 32399-3000; tel. (850) 245-2118; fax (850) 245-2128; internet www.dep.state.fl.us/parks/bncr; Bureau Chief KELLY LAYMAN.

Division of Forestry: 3125 Conner Blvd, Tallahassee, FL 32399-1650; tel. (850) 488-4274; fax (850) 488-0863; e-mail dof_support@doacs.state.fl.us; internet www.fl-dof.com; Dir JAMES R. KARELS.

Florida State Parks: Florida Division of Recreation and Parks, 3900 Commonwealth Blvd, Tallahassee, FL 32399; tel. (850) 245-2157; internet www.floridastateparks.org; Dir MIKE BULLOCK.

Georgia

Georgia has two national forests, six national parks and approximately 60 state parks and historic areas. The state parks and recreation areas cover an area of 84,000 acres and attracted 10,294,000 tourists in 2005, while recreation visits to national park service areas in 2006 numbered 6,462,784. Important tourist sites include Stone Mountain near Atlanta, the Okefenokee Swamp in southern Georgia and the Golden Isles. Hunting is a popular recreational activity in the state.

Department of Natural Resources: 2 Martin Luther King, Jr Dr., SE, Suite 1252, East Tower, Atlanta, GA 30334; tel. (404) 656-3500; fax (404) 656-0770; e-mail dnrboard@dnr.state.ga.us; internet www .gadnr.org; Commr NOEL HOLCOMB.

Division of Tourism: 75th St, Suite 1200, Atlanta, GA 30308; tel. (404) 962-4079; fax (404) 962-4093; e-mail jtatum@georgia.org; internet www.georgia.org/Business/Industries/Tourism.htm; Deputy Commr DAN ROWE.

Forestry Commission: Macon Office, 5645 Riggins Mill Rd, Dry Branch, GA 31020; tel. (478) 751-3500; fax (478) 751-3465; e-mail kodum@gfc.state.ga.us; internet www.gfc.state.ga.us; f. 1949; Dir ROBERT FARRIS, Jr.

USDA Forest Service (Southern Region): 1720 Peachtree Rd, NW, Atlanta, GA 30309; tel. (404) 347-4177; fax (404) 347-4821; e-mail rchaffin@fs.fed.us; internet www.fs.fed.us/r8.

Hawaii

Hawaii contains a wide range of recreational facilities, including seven national parks and historic sites, 69 state parks and 624 county parks. In 2004 state parks and recreation areas, which covered some 31,000 acres, were visited by an estimated 9,221,000 tourists. In 2006 national park service areas received 5,323,425 recreation visits. The national parks of Haleakale (on Maui) and Hawaii Volcanoes (on Hawaii) are among the major tourist attractions. The islands also offer opportunities for activities such as scuba diving, snorkelling, swimming, fishing and sailing. In addition, the state provides more than 80 golf courses and 1,600 recognized surfing sites.

Department of Business, Economic Development and Tourism: No. 1 Capitol District Bldg, 250 South Hotel St, POB 2539, Honolulu, HI 96813; tel. (808) 586-2423; fax (808) 587-2790; e-mail library@dbedt.hawaii.gov; internet www.hawaii.gov/dbedt; Dir THEODORE EM-PO LIU.

Hawaii Tourism Authority: Hawaii Convention Center, 1801 Kalakaua Ave, Honolulu, HI 96815; tel. (808) 973-2255; fax (808) 973-2253; e-mail info@hawaiitourismauthority.org; internet www .hawaiitourismauthority.org; Chair. KELVIN BLOOM.

Hawaii Visitors and Convention Bureau (HVCB): 2270 Kalakaua Ave, Suite 801, Honolulu, HI 96815; tel. (808) 924-0259; fax (808) 924-0291; e-mail info@hvcb.org; internet www.gohawaii.com; Dir GINA SALVADOR.

National Park Service: Pacific Islands Support Office, 300 Ala Moana Blvd, Box 50165, Honolulu, HI 96850-0053; tel. (808) 541-2693.

State Parks Division: Dept of Land and Natural Resources, Kalanimoku Bldg, 1151 Punchbowl St, Honolulu, HI 96813; tel. (808) 587-0300; fax (808) 587-0390; e-mail dlnr@hawaii.gov; internet www.hawaiistateparks.org; Admin. DAN QUINN.

Idaho

Idaho is popular for its wide variety of outdoor recreational facilities, offering such activities as skiing, hunting, camping, fishing and hiking. In 1996 1,222,193 hunting and fishing licences were issued. The state has 24 ski resorts, of which the largest is Sun Valley, a year-round resort in the Sawtooth Mountains. There are two national parks: the Craters of the Moon National Monument and the Nez Percé National Historical Park. Other tourist attractions include the Hell's Canyon and the Sawtooth national recreational areas. In 2003 state parks and recreation areas covered some 45,000 acres and were visited by 2,438,000 tourists. National park service areas received 435,806 recreation visits in 2006.

Division of Tourism Development: 700 West State St, POB 83720, Boise, ID 83720-0093; tel. (208) 334-2470; fax (208) 334-2631; e-mail info@tourism.idaho.gov; internet www.visitidaho.org; Dir CARL WILGUS.

State Parks and Recreation Department: POB 83720, Boise, ID 83720-0065; tel. (208) 514-2251; fax (208) 334-5232; e-mail jjohns@idpr.state.id.us; internet www.idahoparks.org; Dir ROBERT L. MEINEN.

Illinois

Illinois has 265 state parks, forests and recreation areas, which include the Lincoln Home National Historic Site in Springfield. State parks and recreation areas comprise some 481,000 acres and attracted an estimated 44,950,000 visitors in 2005, while in 2006 recreation visits to the national park service area totalled 388,887. In central Illinois the Abraham Lincoln Trail comprises various locations associated with the former statesman, and the Amish communities also attract visitors. The city of Chicago is a popular tourist destination, with one of the world's tallest buildings, the Sears Tower, one of its principal attractions. The city offers a wide range of cultural activities, including a number of renowned museums and art institutes, and is also a very popular shopping destination for tourists. In addition, the state offers opportunities for swimming, bicycling, hiking, riding, fishing, hunting and wildlife observation.

Bureau of Tourism: Dept of Commerce and Community Affairs, 100 Randolph St West, Suite 3-400, Chicago, IL 60601; tel. (312) 814-4732; fax (312) 814-6175; e-mail ceo.enjoyillinois@illinois.gov; internet www.enjoyillinois.com; Dir JACK LAVIN.

Department of Natural Resources: 1 Natural Resources Way, Springfield, IL 62702-1271; tel. (217) 782-6302; e-mail dnr .parksadmin@illinois.gov; internet www.dnr.state.il.us; Dir JOHN POHLMAN.

Indiana

Indiana's state parks and recreation areas, encompassing 178,000 acres, attracted 19,674,000 visitors in 2005, while its national park service areas received 2,190,492 recreation visits in 2006. The most notable state park is Brown County near Nashville. The state also contains 15 fish and wildlife refuges, which comprise 75,200 acres and include Pigeon River, near Howe, and Willow Slough at Morocco. Other natural attractions are the Indiana Dunes National Lakeshore on Lake Michigan, and Cataract Falls near Cloverdale. The reconstructed village of New Harmony, the Indianapolis Motor Speedway and Museum, and the George Rogers Clark National Historic Park, at Vincennes, are also popular with tourists. Hunting and fishing are favourite outdoor pastimes.

Division of State Parks and Reservoirs: Dept of Natural Resources, Govt Center South, 402 Washington St West, Indianapolis, IN 46204; tel. (317) 232-4124; fax (317) 232-8036; internet www.in.gov/dnr/parklake.

Indiana Office of Tourism Development: 1 North Capitol St, Suite 600, Indianapolis, IN 46204-2288; tel. (317) 232-8870; fax (317) 233-6887; internet www.in.gov/visitindiana/; Dir AMY VAUGHAN.

Iowa

Iowa has some 85,000 acres of lakes and reservoirs and 19,000 miles of fishing streams. These, together with the state's two main rivers, the Mississippi and the Missouri, provide excellent facilities for water sports, while the driftless bluffs of the Switzerland Range in the north-east are well suited to hiking and camping. The state's parks and recreation areas covered 68,000 acres in 2005 and attracted 13,580,000 visitors, while national park service areas received 225,179 recreation visits in 2006. Other major tourist attractions include the Effigy Mounds National Monument, near Marquette, the Amana colonies in east-central Iowa, Elk Horn's 'Danish Windmill' and the 'living history' farms in Des Moines. The State Capitol Building in Des Moines and the Herbert Hoover National Historic Site in West Branch also attract thousands of visitors each year.

Tourism Office: Dept of Economic Development, 200 Grand Ave East, Des Moines, IA 50309; tel. (515) 242-4700; fax (515) 242-4809; e-mail info@iowalifechanging.com; internet www.traveliowa.com; Man. NANCY LANDESS.

Kansas

Kansas has 22 state parks, 24 federal reservoirs, 48 state fishing lakes, over 100 campsites and more than 304,000 acres of public hunting and game management lands. The state parks and recreation areas covered 33,000 acres and were visited by 7,310,000 tourists in 2005. Recreation visits to national park service areas totalled 125,408 in 2006. The state contains two national historic sites, Fort Larned and Fort Scott (19th-century army bases on the old frontier), and also two frontier-town reproductions, Historic Wichita Cowtown and Old Front Street in Dodge City. The state capital, Topeka, is a popular tourist destination, with attractions such as the state historical museum and the Menninger Foundation.

Department of Wildlife and Parks: Office of the Secretary, 1020 South Kansas Ave, Suite 200, Topeka, KS 66612-1327; tel. (785) 296-2281; internet www.kdwp.state.ks.us; f. 1996; Sec. MIKE HAYDEN.

Travel and Tourism Development Division: 1000 South West Jackson St, Suite 100, Topeka, KS 66612-1354; tel. (785) 296-2009; fax (785) 296-6988; e-mail travtour@kansascommerce.com; internet www.travelks.com; f. 1982; part of Kansas Chamber of Commerce; Dir BECKY BLAKE.

Kentucky

Kentucky operates 52 parks, including 17 resort parks, and one interstate park. State parks and recreation areas covered an area of 58,000 acres and attracted 7,037,000 tourists in 2005, while national park service areas received 1,924,683 recreation visits in 2006. One of Kentucky's leading tourist attractions is Mammoth Cave National Park in the Pennyroyal region, containing a large network of underground passages. The national park system also comprises a re-creation of Abraham Lincoln's birthplace in Hodgenville, and Cumberland Gap National Historical Park.

Department of Parks: Capital Plaza Tower, 500 Mero St, Suite 1100, Frankfort, KY 40601-1974; tel. (502) 564-2172; fax (502) 564-9015; e-mail kentuckystateparks@ky.gov; internet parks.ky.gov.

Department of Tourism: Capital Plaza Tower, 22nd Floor, 500 Mero St, Frankfort, KY 40601-1968; tel. (502) 564-4930; e-mail cindy.briscoe@ky.gov; internet www.kentuckytourism.com; Commr RANDY FIVEASH.

Louisiana

The lively city of New Orleans is a principal tourist destination in the state and within the USA, offering renowned seafood restaurants, jazz clubs, the European-style French Quarter, the Superdome and Preservation Hall. The city's annual festivities attract many visitors, most notably for the Mardi Gras festival, which commences on the Wednesday before Shrove Tuesday. Other spectacles include the blessing of the shrimp fleet at the Louisiana Shrimp and Petroleum Festival on Labor Day weekend and the blessing of the cane fields during the Louisiana Sugar Cane Festival in September. The Jean Lafitte National Park is also a popular attraction. Altogether, Louisiana's state parks and recreation areas comprised 41,000 acres and attracted 1,598,000 visitors in 2005, while in 2006 recreation visits to national park service areas totalled 333,508.

Department of Culture, Recreation and Tourism: POB 94361, Baton Rouge, LA 70804-9361; tel. (225) 342-8115; fax (225) 342-3207; e-mail pjones@crt.state.la.us; internet www.crt.state.la.us; Sec. PAM BREAUX.

New Orleans Metropolitan Convention and Visitors Bureau: 2020 St Charles Ave, New Orleans, LA 70130; tel. (504) 566-5011; e-mail internet@neworleanscvb.com; internet www.neworleanscvb.com; Dir MARY BETH ROMIG.

Office of Tourism: POB 94291, Baton Rouge, LA 70804-9291; tel. (225) 342-8119; fax (225) 342-1051; e-mail louisiana@crt.state.la.us; internet www.louisianatravel.com.

Office of State Parks: Dept of Culture, Recreation and Tourism, POB 44426, Baton Rouge, LA 70804-4426; tel. (225) 342-8111; e-mail parks@crt.state.la.us; internet www.lastateparks.com.

Maine

Maine has 2,500 lakes and some 3,500 miles of coastline, with sandy beaches. Sailing, fishing and boating are the principal outdoor activities, while the Allagash Wilderness Waterway, in northern Maine, is popular for canoeing. In winter the state offers approximately 60 areas for cross-country skiing. Maine is also a favourite location for hunting. There are 29 state parks in Maine, including Acadia National Park, Bradbury Mountain State Park and Holbrook Island Sanctuary; 19 historic sites, including Eagle Island and Fort Knox, and over 450,000 acres of Public Reserved Lands. State parks and recreation areas comprise some 100,000 acres and were visited by an estimated 2,006,000 tourists in 2005. In 2006 the national park service area received 2,083,588 recreational visits.

Bureau of Parks and Lands: 22 State House Station, 18 Elkins Lane (AMHI Campus), Augusta, ME 04333-0022; tel. (207) 287-3821; fax (207) 287-8111; internet www.state.me.us/doc/parks.

Forest Service: Dept of Conservation, 22 State House Station, Augusta, ME 04333-0022; tel. (207) 289-2791; fax (207) 287-8422; e-mail alec.giffen@maine.gov; internet www.state.me.us/doc/mfs; Dir ALEC GIFFEN.

Maine Tourism Association: 327 Water St, Hallowell, ME 04347; tel. (207) 623-0363; fax (207) 623-0388; e-mail mtainfo@mainetourism.com; internet www.mainetourism.com; fmrly known as Maine Publicity Bureau, Inc.

Office of Tourism: 59 State House Station, 111 Sewall St, 3rd Floor, Augusta, ME 04333-0059; tel. (207) 287-5711; fax (207) 287-8070; e-mail info@visitmaine.com; internet www.visitmaine.com; Dir PATRICIA ELTMAN.

Maryland

Maryland has 47 state parks and six state forests, which, together with other recreation areas, cover an area of 137,000 acres. These areas received a total of 11,186,000 visitors in 2005, while recreational visits to national park service areas totalled 3,249,642 in 2006. Ocean City is the state's leading seaside resort, with many other resort towns located in Chesapeake Bay, the largest inland estuary in the USA and an extremely popular location for sailing and cruising. The state capital, Annapolis, receives many visitors, with the US Naval Academy and the State House, built in 1772, the principal attractions. The city of Baltimore is also a popular tourist destination, featuring the Edgar Allan Poe House, Fort McHenry and the Inner Harbor. Maryland has many historic sites associated with the Civil War, most notably, the Antietam National Battlefield. Hunting and horse-racing are also popular recreational activities in the state.

Office of Tourism Development: Dept of Business and Economic Development, 217 Redwood St East, 9th Floor, Baltimore, MD 21202-3316; tel. (410) 767-6278; fax (410) 333-6643; e-mail info@visitmaryland.org; internet visitmaryland.org.

Park Service: Maryland Dept of Natural Resources, Tawes State Office Bldg, 580 Taylor Ave, Annapolis, MD 21401; tel. (410) 260-

8367; e-mail customerservice@dnr.state.md.us; internet www.dnr.maryland.gov.

Massachusetts

Massachusetts is one of the most popular summer resort destinations in the USA, with its beaches and seashores attracting numerous visitors annually. A popular tourist destination is Barnstable County (Cape Cod—the Cape Cod National Seashore). Together with Nantucket and Martha's Vineyard, this area offers beaches, fishing and many villages to visit. The state capital of Boston also attracts millions of visitors each year, to sites such as Bunker Hill Monument, Faneuil Hall and Old North Church. The Berkshire Hills are the location of summer festivities, including the Berkshire Music Festival at Tanglewood. Nathaniel Hawthorne's House of Seven Gables is situated at Salem in Essex County, while Middlesex County and Bristol County also have many features of interest. Massachusetts has some 130 state-owned camping areas; state parks and recreation areas comprise 336,000 acres and attracted 33,162,000 visitors in 2005. In 2006 recreation visits to national park service areas totalled 9,813,899.

Boston National Historical Park Navy Yard Visitor Center: Charlestown Navy Yard, Boston, MA 02129; tel. (617) 242-5601; fax (617) 242-6006; internet www.nps.gov/bost.

Office of Travel and Tourism: 10 Park Plaza, Suite 4510, Boston, MA 02116; tel. (617) 973-8500; fax (617) 973-8525; e-mail vacationinfo@state.ma.us; internet www.massvacation.com.

Michigan

Michigan has thousands of inland lakes and streams, which provide many opportunities for swimming and other summer pastimes. The Metropolitan Beach on Lake St Clair, reputedly the largest artificial lake beach in the world, is the most well-known of these lakeside areas. Ice-fishing, skiing, autumn scenic tours and spring festivals attract visitors to the regions during the rest of the year, and camping is also becoming increasingly popular, with the federal Government operating extensive camping facilities. State parks and recreational areas, which comprised some 273,000 acres, received 23,057,000 visitors in 2005, with the Holland and Warren Dunes state parks on Lake Michigan among the most popular. Recreation visits to national park service areas in 2006 totalled 1,649,394.

Department of Natural Resources: Mason Bldg, 6th Floor, POB 30028, Lansing, MI 48909; tel. (517) 373-2329; fax (517) 335-4242; internet www.michigan.gov/dnr; Dir REBECCA A. HUMPHRIES.

Travel Michigan: 300 North Washington Sq., POB 30226, Lansing, MI 48909; tel. (517) 373-0670; fax (517) 373-0059; internet www.travel.michigan.org; Vice-Pres. GEORGE ZIMMERMANN.

Minnesota

Minnesota has diverse outdoor recreational facilities and a number of sites of cultural and historical interest. Among the principal attractions are Voyagers National Park, totalling 220,000 acres near the Canadian border, the Boundary Waters Canoe Area Wilderness and the Grand Portage National Monument, a former fur-trading centre in 'Arrowhead country'. The state's 300 miles of waterways are popular for boating, while winter sports, such as snowmobiling, ice-fishing, dog-sledding and cross-country skiing, also have a substantial following. The state operates 66 parks and four recreation areas (including extensive winter-sports areas), which cover some 220,000 acres and attracted an estimated 8,245,000 visitors in 2005. Recreation visits to national park service areas totalled 605,606 in 2006. Throughout Minnesota, and on the north shore of Lake Superior, an estimated 1,000 resorts provide a wide variety of amenities for visitors.

Division of Parks and Recreation: Dept of Natural Resources, 500 Lafayette Rd, St Paul, MN 55155-4040; tel. (651) 296-6157; fax (651) 297-1157; e-mail info@dnr.state.mn.us; internet www.mnstateparks.info; Dir COURTLAND NELSON.

Office of Tourism: Metro Sq. Blvd, Suite 100, 121 Seventh Pl. East, St Paul, MN 55101; tel. (651) 296-5029; fax (651) 296-7095; e-mail explore@state.mn.us; internet www.exploreminnesota.com.

Mississippi

Among Mississippi's most popular attractions are the state's *ante bellum* mansions and plantations, notably McRaven in Vicksburg, and the Delta and Pine Land Company plantation near Scott, which is one of the largest in the USA. Various historic sites associated with the Civil War also attract large numbers of visitors, as does the annual State Fair, held in Jackson during the second week in October. Mississippi's Tunica casino complex is the third largest such resort in the USA. The state's 36 fishing lakes and the Mississippi Gulf Coast offer outstanding fishing opportunities, and the Mississippi Beach area resorts provide opportunities for golfing, sailing and swimming. There are five national parks in the state, including Natchez Trace Parkway, Gulf Islands National Seashore, and Vicksburg National Military Park. National park service areas received 6,016,266 recreation visits in 2006. The 28 state parks and recreation areas cover an area of some 24,000 acres and attracted over 2,256,000 tourists in 2005. There are 1.5m. acres of national forest in the state, and hunting is a popular pastime.

Division of Parks and Recreation: Dept of Wildlife, Fisheries and Parks, 1505 Eastover Dr., Jackson, MS 39211-6374; tel. (601) 432-2400; internet home.mdwfp.com.

Division of Tourism Development: POB 849, Jackson, MS 39205; tel. (601) 432-2400; fax (601) 359-5757; e-mail tourdiv@mississippi.org; internet www.visitmississippi.org; Dir CRAIG MAY.

Missouri

Missouri's principal tourist attraction is the Gateway Arch in St Louis—the tallest man-made national monument in the USA. Kansas City also receives large numbers of visitors, with the Crown Center hotels and shopping plaza and the Truman Sport Complex among the main attractions. The boyhood home of the author, Mark Twain, is located in Hannibal, and the Harry Truman library and museum in Independence. Missouri contains over 80 historic sites and state parks, the largest and most-visited being the Lake of the Ozarks State Park, comprising 17,262 acres. The state parks and recreation areas cover 202,000 acres and were visited by 16,695,000 tourists in 2005, while recreation visits to national park service areas totalled 4,302,533 in 2006.

Department of Natural Resources: POB 176, Jefferson City, MO 65102; tel. (573) 751-3443; fax (573) 751-7627; e-mail contact@dnr.mo.gov; internet www.dnr.mo.gov; Dir DOYLE CHILDERS.

Division of Tourism: Dept of Economic Development, 301 High St West, POB 1055, Jefferson City, MO 65102; tel. (573) 751-4133; fax (573) 751-5160; e-mail tourism@ded.mo.gov; internet www.visitmo.com; Dir ROBERT SMITH (acting).

Montana

Montana's former gold-rush camps and ghost towns attract a number of visitors, and traditional Western rodeos and Native American celebrations are also popular. Historical sites include the Little Bighorn Battlefield, south-east of Billings, the Big Hole National Battlefield, near Wisdom, the Lewis and Clark Interpretive Center at Great Falls and the Custer Battlefield Monument. The most popular of the state's parks is Glacier National Park, which comprises 60 glaciers and 200 lakes and streams and covers an area of 1,013,572 acres. The state also contains Bighorn Canyon National Recreation Area and the northern part of Yellowstone Park. National park service areas received 3,897,415 recreation visits in 2006, while the state parks and recreation areas, totalling 55,000 acres, were visited by an estimated 5,671,000 tourists in 2005. The state also has many lakes and streams, on which boating and fishing are popular, and 11 renowned trout rivers.

Forestry Division: Dept of Natural Resources and Conservation, 2705 Spurgin Rd, Missoula, MT 59804; tel. (406) 542-4300; fax (406) 542-4217; e-mail dnrc_publicinfo@mt.gov; internet www.dnrc.mt.gov/forestry; State Forester and Admin. BOB HARRINGTON.

Parks Division: Dept of Fish, Wildlife and Parks, 1420 East Sixth Ave, POB 200701, Helena, MT 59620-0701; tel. (406) 444-2535; fax (406) 444-4952; internet www.fwp.state.mt.us; Dir JEFF HAGENER.

Travel Montana: Dept of Commerce, Montana Promotion Division, 301 South Park Ave, POB 200533, Helena, MT 59620-0501; tel. (406) 841-2870; fax (406) 841-2871; e-mail mt-webmaster@visitmt.com; internet www.visitmt.com.

USDA Forest Service (Northern Region): Federal Bldg, 200 East Bdwy, POB 7669, Missoula, MT 59807; tel. (406) 329-3511; fax (406) 329-3347; e-mail webmaster@fs.fed.us; internet www.fs.fed.us/r1.

Nebraska

Nebraska has six state parks, nine state historical parks, 12 federal areas and 55 recreational areas, of which the most frequented are Pawnee State Recreation Area and Fremont State Recreation Area. Among the most popular of the state parks are Fort Robinson and Arbor Lodge state parks. In total, state parks and recreation areas cover some 135,000 acres and were visited by 9,998,000 tourists in 2005. Recreation visits to national park service areas totalled 225,937 in 2006. Outdoor activities, including fishing, swimming and sightseeing, are popular tourist pastimes.

Division of Travel and Tourism: Dept of Economic Development, 301 Centennial Mall South, POB 98907, Lincoln, NE 68509-8907; tel. (402) 471-3796; fax (402) 471-3026; e-mail tourism@visitnebraska.org; internet www.visitnebraska.org; Dir CHRISTIAN HORNBAKER.

Game and Parks Commission: 2200 33rd St North, Lincoln, NE 68503; tel. (402) 471-0641; e-mail webmaster@ngpc.ne.gov; internet www.ngpc.state.ne.us.

Nevada

Nevada's primary attraction for tourists is the gambling industry, with visitors drawn by the casinos and resort facilities of Reno and Las Vegas. Outside the cities, the state's mining ghost towns are also popular tourist destinations. Nevada's parks and recreation areas include Cathedral Gorge National Park, Echo Canyon State Recreation Area, Lake Pyramid, Lake Mead National Recreation Area and Lehman Caves National Monument. State parks and recreation areas encompass an area of some 133,000 acres and attracted 3,178,000 visitors in 2005, while recreation visits to national park service areas totalled 5,911,839 in 2006.

Division of State Parks: 901 South Stewart St, 5th Floor, Suite 5005, Carson City, NV 89701-5248; tel. (775) 684-2770; fax (775) 684-2777; e-mail stparks@parks.nv.gov; internet www.parks.nv.gov.

Tourism Commission: 401 North Carson St, Carson City, NV 89701; tel. (775) 687-4322; fax (702) 687-6779; e-mail ncot@travelnevada.com; internet www.travelnevada.com; Chair. BRIAN K. KROLICKI.

New Hampshire

New Hampshire has a wide variety of outdoor facilities, including 33 alpine ski areas, 10 public golf courses and an estimated 85 trailer parks and camps. Of particular interest to visitors is Mount Washington, the highest peak in New England, which features a cog railway and many trails. Other attractions include Lake Winnipesaukee, the White Mountain National Forest and Strawberry Bank, a restored village in Portsmouth. In 2006 recreation visits to the national park service area totalled 25,858, while state parks and recreation areas, which cover an area of some 232,000 acres, were visited by 5,472,000 tourists in 2003.

Vacation Travel Promotion Office: Division of Travel and Tourism Development, 172 Pembroke Rd, POB 1856, Concord, NH 03302-1856; tel. (603) 271-2665; fax (603) 271-6870; e-mail travel@dred.state.nh.us; internet www.visitnh.gov.

New Jersey

The Jersey shores have been a popular summer vacation destination from the beginning of the 19th century, with a number of resorts catering to tourists. Atlantic City, previously the principal resort of the area, experienced a revival in the late 20th century owing to the development of a number of casino hotels. The state has five ski areas, three national wildlife refuges, 140 private and public golf courses and numerous amusement parks, including Six Flags Great Adventure in central Jersey. The Delaware Gap and Gateway National Recreation Areas are popular locations for boating and camping, while the state's inland lakes offer opportunities for fishing. State parks and recreation areas, which include the Monmouth and Washington Crossing Battlefield parks, cover some 397,000 acres in total and attracted 15,791,000 visitors in 2005. Recreation visits to national park service areas totalled 5,708,286 in 2006.

Division of Travel and Tourism: POB 460, Trenton, NJ 08625; tel. (609) 777-0885; internet www.state.nj.us/travel; Exec. Dir NANCY BYRNE.

Greater Atlantic City Tourism Council: POB 1656, Atlantic City, NJ 08404; tel. (609) 343-4882; fax (609) 652-5439; e-mail info@actourism.org; internet www.actourism.org; Chair. SUSAN ADELIZZI-SCHMIDT.

New Mexico

New Mexico has three national parks, 27,840 acres of designated wilderness reserves and nine national monuments, including the Carlsbad Caverns National Monument and the Fort Union National Monument. Native American relics and ruins are found at Aztec Ruins, Bandelier, El Morro, Gila Cliff Dwellings and Salinas, and visitors are also attracted to the pueblos, to experience native culture and to visit the gambling areas. In 1997 it was proposed to designate the old pioneer trail, Route 66, a National Heritage Highway, and to name the US portion of the El Camino Real de Tierra Adento, the oldest European road in the USA, a National Historic Trail. Many visitors were also attracted to the Roswell site (the location of an alleged unidentified flying object—UFO—crash) and to other 'UFO encounter' sites in the state. State parks and recreation areas comprise some 93,000 acres and attracted 4,157,000 visitors in 2005, while national park service areas received 1,620,457 recreation visits in 2006.

State Park Division: 1220 South St Francis Dr., POB 1147, Santa Fe, NM 87504-1147; tel. (505) 476-3355; fax (505) 476-3361; e-mail nmparks@state.nm.us; internet www.emnrd.state.nm.us/PRD/index.htm; Dir DAVID J. SIMON.

Tourism Department: Lamy Bldg, Rm 751, 491 Old Santa Fe Trail, Santa Fe, NM 87502; tel. (505) 827-7400; fax (505) 827-7402; e-mail enchantment@newmexico.org; internet www.newmexico.org; Sec. MICHAEL CERLETTI.

USDA Forest Service (Southwestern Region): 333 Bdwy SE, Albuquerque, NM 87102; tel. (505) 842-3292; fax (505) 842-3800; e-mail r3_webmaster@fs.fed.us; internet www.fs.fed.us/r3.

New York

New York City is the principal tourist destination of the state. The Statue of Liberty, the Empire State and United Nations Buildings, the Rockefeller Center, Bronx Zoo and Chinatown are just a few of the city's diverse attractions. Long Island, with its beaches and race-tracks, is second to the city in popularity. Other tourist areas include: the Hudson Valley, site of the US Military Academy at West Point; Albany, containing the Empire State Plaza and Fenimore House; Saratoga Springs; and the region of the Adirondacks. Among the state's scenic attractions are the resorts of the Catskills, the Finger Lakes region, featuring Taughannock Falls, and Niagara Falls to the west. State parks and recreation areas encompass an area of some 1,367,000 acres and received an estimated 56,405,000 visitors in 2005. In 2006 15,154,997 people paid recreational visits to New York's national park service areas.

Division of Tourism: 30 South Pearl St, Main Concourse, Suite 110, Albany, NY 12245; tel. (518) 474-4116; e-mail iloveny@empire.state.ny.us; internet www.iloveny.com.

State Office of Parks, Recreation and Historic Preservation: 20th Floor, Agency Bldg 1, Empire State Plaza, Albany, NY 12238; tel. (518) 474-0456; internet www.nysparks.state.ny.us; Commr CAROL ASH.

North Carolina

North Carolina has both outdoor recreational facilities, such as golf courses, mountain parks and coastal beaches, and sites of particular historical interest. Attractions include the Revolutionary War battle-grounds at Guildford Courthouse and Moore's Creek, the Fort Raleigh National Historic Site, and the Wright Brothers National Memorial at Kitty Hawk. The casino at the Qualla Boundary Reservation is also visited by approximately 5m. visitors per year. There are nine national parks in North Carolina, and in 2006 there were 20,091,486 recreational visitors to national park service areas. State parks and recreation areas cover an area of 187,000 acres and were visited by 12,674,000 tourists in 2005.

Department of Environment and Natural Resources: Archdale Bldg, 512 North Salisbury St, 1601 Mail Service Center, Raleigh, NC 27699-1601; tel. (919) 733-4984; fax (919) 715-3060; internet www.enr.state.nc.us; Sec. WILLIAM G. ROSS, Jr.

Division of Tourism and Film: North Carolina Dept of Commerce, 301 North Wilmington St, Raleigh, NC 27601; tel. (919) 733-8372; fax (919) 715-3097; internet www.visitnc.com.

North Dakota

North Dakota's recreational facilities include 19 state parks, four national parks, more than 100 golf courses, five downhill-ski resorts, 63 wildlife refuges and more than 150 fishing waters. State parks and recreation areas comprise some 18,000 acres and were visited by an estimated 948,000 tourists in 2005. In 2006 472,986 people made recreational visits to national park service areas. The Theodore Roosevelt National Park in the Badlands is a favourite destination. The parks are popular for hunting, fishing, canoeing, riding and snowmobiling. The state also has a number of historic sites, such as those located along the Lewis and Clark National Historic Trail, and the Fort Union Trading Post. The International Peace Garden, through which the international border with Canada runs, commemorates friendly US-Canadian relations.

Tourism Division: Century Center, 1600 East Century Ave, Suite 2, POB 2057, Bismarck, ND 58502-2057; tel. (701) 328-2525; fax (701) 328-4878; e-mail tourism@nd.gov; internet www.ndtourism.com; Dir SARA OTTE COLEMAN.

Ohio

Ohio's tourist attractions range from the beaches and parks around Lake Erie to the ski resorts in the eastern Allegheny region, and to numerous memorials and sites of historical interest. Among several memorials to US presidents are the William Henry Harrison Memorial at North Bend, Ulysses S. Grant's birthplace at Point Pleasant and the William McKinley memorial at Canton. Other notable tourist areas include Mound City Group National Monument near Chillicothe, which contains prehistoric burial mounds, and Perry's Victory and International Peace Memorial on South Bass Island. Ohio's 71 state parks and recreation areas cover some 1,745,000 acres and received 50,166,000 visitors in 2005. Alum Creek, East Harbour and Kelleys Island are among the most popular. There were 2,704,686 recreational visits to Ohio's national park service areas in 2006.

Division of Travel and Tourism: Dept of Development, Vern Riffe Center, 77 South High St, POB 1001, Columbus, OH 43216-1001; tel. (614) 466-3636; fax (614) 644-5167; e-mail tbrown@odod.state.oh.us; internet www.discoverohio.com; Dir BOB TAFT.

Experience Columbus: 277 West Nationwide Blvd., Suite 125, Columbus, OH 43215; tel. (614) 221-6623; fax (614) 221-5618; e-mail visitorinfo@experiencecolumbus.com; internet www.experiencecolumbus.com; Pres. and CEO PAUL D. ASTLEFORD.

Oklahoma

Oklahoma has 35 state parks, 22 state recreation areas and 140,696 acres of national wildlife reserves, including Optima, Salt Plains and the Wichita Mountains. State parks and recreation areas, comprising 72,000 acres, were visited by 13,282,000 tourists in 2005. Oklahoma has one national park, Chickasaw National Recreation Area, which centres on the man-made Lake Arbuckle. Cultural attractions of the state include the American Indian Hall of Fame at Anadarko, the T. B. Ferguson Home in Watonga and several museums. In 2006 1,358,201 recreational visits were made to Oklahoma's national park service areas.

Department of Tourism and Recreation: 120 North Robinson St, 6th Floor, Oklahoma City, OK 73102; tel. (405) 230-8400; e-mail information@travelok.com; internet www.oklatourism.gov; Exec. Dir HARDY WATKINS.

Oklahoma City Convention and Visitors Bureau: 189 West Sheridan, Oklahoma City, OK 73102; tel. (405) 297-8912; fax (405) 297-8888; e-mail okccvb@okccvb.org; internet www.okccvb.org; Pres. MIKE CARRIER.

Oregon

Oregon's natural resources are a primary attraction for visitors, with unspoiled coasts, numerous parks and the Rogue River, which offers opportunities for fishing. The National Park Service operates the one national park, Crater Lake, as well as three other areas: John Day Fossil Beds National Monument, Oregon Caves National Monument and Fort Clatsop National Memorial. The state park systems are among the most extensive in the USA, comprising around 225 parks and recreation areas, which encompass some 97,000 acres. State parks and recreation areas received 42,420,000 visitors in 2005, while in 2006 there were 806,344 recreational visits to national park service areas.

Department of Fish and Wildlife: 3406 Cherry Ave, NE, Salem, OR 97303-4924; tel. (503) 947-6000; e-mail odfw.info@state.or.us; internet www.dfw.state.or.us; Dir ROY ELICKER.

Parks and Recreation Department: North Mall Office Bldg, 725 Summer St, NE, Suite C, Salem, OR 97301; tel. (503) 986-0707; fax (503) 986-0794; e-mail park.info@state.or.us; internet www.oregon.gov/OPRD; Dir TIM WOOD.

Tourism Commission: 670 Hawthorne Ave, SE, Suite 240, Salem, OR 97301; tel. (503) 378-8850; fax (503) 378-4574; e-mail info@traveloregon.com; internet www.traveloregon.com; CEO TODD DAVIDSON.

USDA Forest Service (Pacific Northwest Region): 333 South West First Ave, POB 3623, Portland, OR 97208-3623; tel. (503) 808-2468; e-mail gsaunders@fs.fed.us; internet www.fs.fed.us/r6; Regional Forester LINDA GOODMAN.

Pennsylvania

Among the state's leading attractions are its many historical sites, including: the Independence National Historical Park in Philadelphia, which contains the Liberty Bell, Independence Hall and the US Mint; the Valley Forge National Historical Park; the Gettysburg National Military Park, which marks the site of the famous Civil War battle; and Gettysburg town, where the home of President Dwight D. Eisenhower is located. Hershey, home of the chocolate manufacturers, is another favourite tourist destination. Popular outdoor pursuits in the state include camping, hunting, boating, fishing and, in the east of the state, skiing and other winter sports. The Delaware Water Gap National Recreation Area, shared with New Jersey, is a popular destination for these activities, and the Pocono Mountains Region also attracts many visitors. In 2006 national park service areas received 8,842,235 recreational visitors. State parks, forests and recreational areas covered 291,000 acres and attracted 36,263,000 visitors in 2005.

Bureau of State Parks: Dept of Conservation and Natural Resources, Rachel Carson State Office Bldg, 400 Market St, POB 8767, Harrisburg, PA 17105-8767; tel. (717) 787-2869; e-mail ra-askdcnr@state.pa.us; internet www.dcnr.state.pa.us/stateparks.

Department of Conservation and Natural Resources: Rachel Carson State Office Bldg, 7th Floor, POB 8767, 400 Market St, Harrisburg, PA 17105-8767; tel. (717) 787-2869; fax (717) 772-9106; e-mail ra-askdcnr@state.pa.us; internet www.dcnr.state.pa.us; Sec. MICHAEL DIBERARDINIS.

Tourism Office: c/o Dept of Community and Economic Development, Commonwealth Keystone Bldg, 4th Floor, 400 North St, Harrisburg, PA 17120-0225; tel. (717) 787-5453; fax (717) 787-0687; e-mail feedback@experiencepa.com; internet www.visitpa.com.

Rhode Island

Among Rhode Island's principal tourist attractions are the historic mansions of Newport and Providence, and the earliest synagogue (at Touro Synagogue National Historic Site) and Baptist church in the USA. There are around 40 other museums and historic sites in the state. Rhode Island's state parks and recreation areas cover only 9,000 acres, but attracted 5,853,000 visitors in 2005. Block Island is a favourite holiday resort, and water sports, particularly yachting, are popular. In 2006 52,671 recreational visits were made to the state's national park service area.

Division of Tourism: 315 Iron Horse Way, Suite 101, Providence, RI 02903; tel. (401) 278-9100; fax (401) 273-8270; e-mail visitrhodeisland@riedc.com; internet www.visitrhodeisland.com.

South Carolina

The tourism industry of South Carolina is concentrated on Charleston and the Myrtle Beach and Hilton Head Island resorts, situated on the Atlantic coast. Charleston is famous for its many historic buildings, including several *ante bellum* mansions. At the entrance to the harbour is the Fort Sumter National Monument, marking the place where the Civil War began. The area also has several botanic gardens. In the north of the state the Cowpens National Battlefield Site and the King's Mountain National Military Park attract many visitors. There are several areas of national forest, and the foothills of the Blue Ridge Mountains offer hiking opportunities. South Carolina has 40 state parks, which, along with recreation areas, cover 81,000 acres. In 2004 these areas attracted 6,707,000 visitors, while in 2006 there were 1,383,500 recreational visits to national park service areas.

Department of Parks, Recreation and Tourism: 1205 Pendleton St, Suite 110, Columbia, SC 29201; tel. (803) 734-1700; fax (803) 734-1409; e-mail generalinfo@scprt.com; internet www.discoversouthcarolina.com; Dir CHAD PROSSER.

Forestry Commission: 5500 Broad River Rd, Columbia, SC 29212; tel. (803) 896-8800; fax (803) 798-8097; e-mail scfc@forestry.state.sc.us; internet www.state.sc.us/forest; State Forester ROBERT C. SCHOWALTER.

South Dakota

Many of South Dakota's tourist attractions lie towards the western border of the state. A large area is covered by the Black Hills National Forest, which is popular with hikers and skiers. Wind Cave National Park, Jewel Cave National Monument and Mount Rushmore National Memorial (where the heads of US presidents George Washington, Thomas Jefferson, Abraham Lincoln and Theodore Roosevelt are carved in the mountainside) are all within or adjacent to the forest boundaries. A little further is the Crazy Horse Monument, where the head of a Native American (Amerindian) hero is in the process of being carved into the mountain. To the east of the Black Hills forest is the Badlands National Park, a desolate area rich in fossil deposits. The Wounded Knee Massacre Site, commemorating the last major conflict between Indian and US troops, is situated to the south of the Badlands. Rodeos and ranch visits are popular among visitors to the state. State parks and recreation areas covered 103,000 acres and attracted 7,399,000 visitors in 2005. In 2006 national park service areas attracted 3,703,047 recreational visits.

Black Hills National Forest: USDA Forest Service, Supervisor's Office, 1019 North 5th St, Custer, SD 57730; tel. (605) 673-9200; e-mail r2_blackhills_webinfo@fs.fed.us; internet www.fs.fed.us/r2/blackhills.

Department of Tourism and State Development: Office of Tourism, Capitol Lake Plaza, 711 East Wells Ave, c/o 500 East Capitol Ave, Pierre, SD 57501-5070; tel. (605) 773-3301; fax (605) 773-3256; e-mail sdinfo@state.sd.us; internet www.travelsd.com; Dir BILIE JO WARRA.

Tennessee

The state's parks and recreation areas cover 141,000 acres and attracted 29,038,000 visitors in 2005. Areas designated as parts of the national park system are located near the state's borders and are all shared with other states. The Great Smoky Mountains National Park, which covers 520,000 acres and received over 9m. recreational visits in 1996, is shared with North Carolina, and the Big South Fork National River and Recreation Area and the Land of the Lakes Recreation Area are shared with Kentucky. The Natchez Trace Parkway, which received approximately 13m. recreational visits in 1996, starts in the centre of Tennessee and stretches south into Alabama and Mississippi. National park service areas in the state attracted 7,758,199 recreational visitors in 2006. Tennessee has many lakes, broad rivers and mountain streams, and fishing is a popular outdoor pursuit. The capital, Nashville, is also a famous centre for country-and-western music, housing the Grand Ole Opry, while Gracelands mansion, the home of Elvis Presley, the late popular singer, is located in Memphis.

Department of Tourist Development: 312 Rosa L. Parks Ave, 25th Floor, Nashville, TN 37243; tel. (615) 741-2159; fax (615) 741-7225; e-mail tourdev@tn.gov; internet www.tourism.state.tn.us; Commr SUSAN WHITAKER.

State Parks Bureau: c/o Dept of Environment and Conservation, 401 Church St, 1st Floor, Nashville, TN 37243-0435; tel. (615) 532-0104; fax (615) 532-0120; e-mail ask.tnstateparks@state.tn.us; internet www.state.tn.us/environment/parks.

Texas

The tourism industry of Texas is among the largest of any state in the USA. There are numerous scenic and historical attractions throughout the state. In the west are two national parks, Big Bend (covering 801,163 acres) and the Guadalupe Mountains; four large national forest areas are found in eastern Texas. Historical attractions include the sites of the Alamo and San Jacinto battles. Many beaches and wildlife refuges are located along the Gulf of Mexico coast. State parks and recreation areas cover 589,000 acres, and in 2005 attracted 10,189,000 visitors. Fishing (an estimated 3m. Texans participate in fishing each year), game hunting, hiking, bicycling and watersports are popular outdoor pursuits; rodeos are also numerous and popular, as are visits to ranches. In 2006 5,488,711 recreational visits were made to Texan national park service areas. The principal Texan cities are themselves important tourist attractions, particularly Dallas, San Antonio, Houston and Fort Worth.

National Forests and Grasslands in Texas: USDA Forest Service, 415 South First St, Suite 110, Lufkin, TX 75901; tel. (936) 639-8501; fax (936) 639-8588; e-mail mailroom_r8_texas@fs.fed.us; internet www.fs.fed.us/r8/texas; Forest Supervisor FRED SALINAS.

Texas Tourism: POB 141009, Austin, TX 78714-1009; tel. (512) 936-0101; fax (512) 936-0450; e-mail TRV-LIT@dot.state.tx.us; internet www.traveltex.com.

Utah

All or part of five national parks, Arches, Bryce Canyon, Canyonlands, Capitol Reef and Zion (which receives approximately 2m. visitors annually), are within the boundaries of Utah. In addition, the Glen Canyon and Flaming Gorge national recreation areas (the former covering 1.2m. acres), six national monuments (including the Dinosaur National Monument) and the Golden Spike National Historical Site are located in the state. Utah's state parks and recreation areas cover 150,000 acres and attracted 4,552,000 visitors in 2005, while the national park service areas received 7,840,356 recreational visits in 2006. Much of the centre of the state is covered by national forest areas. In the north-west are the Great Salt Lake and the Great Salt Lake Desert. Salt Lake City is the world centre of the Church of Jesus Christ of Latter-day Saints (the Mormons), and the Mormon Temple and Tabernacle attract many visitors.

Travel Council: Council Hall, Capitol Hill, Salt Lake City, UT 84114-1396; tel. (801) 538-1317; fax (801) 538-1399; e-mail dmwilliams@utah.gov; internet www.utah.com.

USDA Forest Service (Intermountain Region): Federal Bldg, 324 25th St, Ogden, UT 84401; tel. (801) 625-5306; fax (801) 625-5127; e-mail jodyrose@fs.fed.us; internet www.fs.fed.us/r4; Regional Forester HARV FORSGREN.

Vermont

Vermont's summer and winter outdoor pursuits are concentrated in the Green Mountains region, which stretches across the length of the state. Much of this region is part of the Green Mountain National Forest Area. There are over 50 skiing regions in Vermont, which is perhaps best known for its winter-sports attractions. However, almost two-thirds of the state's tourism income is received during the summer months, when hiking, bicycling and watersports are popular, especially along the 200-mile coastline of Lake Champlain. Vermont's state parks and recreation areas covered 69,000 acres and attracted 690,000 visitors in 2005, while the national park service area received 22,484 recreational visits in 2006. Just outside Bennington, in south-west Vermont, the Bennington Battle Monument, commemorating a victory over the British in 1777, and the Bennington Museum attract a number of visitors.

Agency of Natural Resources: Center Bldg, 103 South Main St, Waterbury, VT 05671-0301; tel. (802) 241-3600; fax (802) 244-1102; e-mail canute.dalmasse@state.vt.us; internet www.anr.state.vt.us; Sec. GEORGE CROMBIE.

Department of Tourism and Marketing: National Life Bldg, 6th Floor, Drawer 20, Montpelier, VT 05620-0501; tel. (802) 828-3237; e-mail info@vermontvacation.com; internet www.vermontvacation.com.

Virginia

Virginia is particularly rich in historical sites from both the settlement and Civil War periods. Jamestown was the first permanent British (English) settlement, and Yorktown the scene of the British surrender to George Washington. Manassas National Battlefield Park is the site of the Battle of Bull Run, and the Appomattox Court House National Historical Park marks the site of the Confederate states' surrender in 1865. There are also many buildings associated with famous Americans (and, particularly, with Virginian-born Presidents) of the 18th and 19th centuries. The spectacular Skyline Drive, a continuation of the Blue Ridge Parkway, passes through the Shenandoah National Park in the west of the state, affording views of the Appalachian Mountain ranges. Virginia has an expansive system of 34 state parks, six historic sites and 45 natural areas, which offer hiking trails and other facilities. In 2004 there were 7,319,000 visitors to the state parks and recreation areas, which covered 66,000 acres. Virginia's national park service areas received 22,944,011 recreational visits in 2006.

Tourism Corporation: 19th Floor, 901 East Byrd St, Richmond, VA 23219-4048; tel. (804) 786-2051; fax (804) 786-1919; e-mail vainfo@helloinc.com; internet www.virginia.org; Pres. and CEO ALISA L. BAILEY.

Washington

The dramatic and varied scenic beauty of Washington is the state's main tourist attraction. The Olympic National Park covers 922,000 acres. Both this park and the Mount Rainier National Park contain glacier systems, with Mount Rainier's the largest among the 48 conterminous states. The third national park, North Cascades, and much of the remainder of the state is covered by national forest areas. Mount St Helens National Volcanic Monument was established in 1982, and covers approximately 110,000 acres of an area devastated by a volcanic eruption two years earlier. Hunting, particularly of deer, elk and game birds, is a popular outdoor pursuit, and there are several skiing areas in the Cascade Range of mountains. The islands of Puget Sound and the beaches on the Pacific coast are also popular tourist destinations. San Juan Island and the Klondike Gold Rush are national historical parks, and Fort Vancouver and the Whitman Mission national historic sites. The Seattle Center, comprising the Opera House, Pacific Science Center and Space Needle Tower, is a more modern attraction. The state parks and recreation areas, covering 106,000 acres, received 40,026,000 visitors in 2005. In 2006 recreational visits to the state's national park service areas totalled 6,518,791.

State Parks and Recreation Commission: 7150 Cleanwater Lane, POB 42650, Olympia, WA 98504-2650; tel. (360) 902-8844; e-mail infocent@parks.wa.gov; internet www.parks.wa.gov; Dir REX DERR.

Washington State Tourism: 128 10th Ave SW, POB 42525, Olympia, WA 98504-2525; tel. (360) 725-5052; fax (360) 753-4470; e-mail tourism@cted.wa.gov; internet www.experiencewashington.com.

West Virginia

West Virginia's 34 state parks, four wildlife management areas, two 'rail trails' and nine state forests cover some 177,000 acres and attracted 7,406,000 visitors in 2005. In 2006 recreation visits to the seven national park service areas totalled 1,737,487. The New River Gorge National River area, in the south of the state, and the rugged forested areas in the east of the state are some of the prominent scenic assets, and mountain-biking, rock-climbing and 'white water' rafting are popular activities in these areas. West Virginia also has several spa, spring and mountain ski resorts. The state has a number of historic sites associated with the Civil War, and forms a part of the interstate Civil War Discovery Trail. Harper's Ferry National Historical Park marks the site of John Brown's raid on the US Armory in 1859, and is among the principal tourist attractions, together with a number of historic buildings in nearby Charles Town.

Division of Tourism: 90 MacCorkle Ave, SW, South Charleston, WV 25303; tel. (304) 558-2200; fax (304) 558-2956; e-mail hengle@wvtourism.com; internet www.wvtourism.com; Commr BETTY CARVER.

Wisconsin

Wisconsin has more than 15,000 glacial lakes and 40,000 kms of rivers and streams within its boundaries, offering opportunities for fishing, swimming, sailing, canoeing, pleasure-boating and water-sports of all kinds. The areas of the state testifying to the effects of glaciation are protected in the Ice Age National Scientific Reserve. Other areas, such as the Apostle Islands National Lakeshore (on Lake Superior) and the St Croix and Lower St Croix National Scenic Riverways are major attractions. In total, there are 55 state parks and 10 state forests, which, along with recreation areas, covered 135,000 acres and received a total of 14,964,000 visitors in 2005. National park service areas received 442,472 recreation visits in 2006. There are over 5,000 campsites in the state, and fishing, deer and small game hunting are popular outdoor pursuits. There are many museums, historical sites and art galleries in Wisconsin, among the most interesting of which are the buildings of the renowned architect Frank Lloyd Wright. The state has more than 2,000 fairs and festivals every year, including the Great Circus Parade, the world's largest aviation and music festivals, and lumberjack championships.

Department of Tourism: POB 8690, Madison, WI 53708-8690; tel. (608) 266-7621; fax (608) 266-3403; e-mail mdelaney@travelwisconsin.com; internet www.agency.travelwisconsin.com; Sec. KELLI A. TRUMBLE.

USDA Forest Service (Eastern Region): 626 Wisconsin Ave East, Milwaukee, WI 53202; tel. (414) 297-3600; fax (414) 297-3808; e-mail rmoore@fs.fed.us; internet www.fs.fed.us/r9; Regional Forester RANDY MOORE.

Wyoming

Wyoming has two national parks: Yellowstone (the largest national park in the USA, at 2.2m. acres, which is shared with Idaho and Montana) and Grand Teton. Both have large lakes, while Yellowstone is renowned for its 3,000 geysers and hot springs. These two parks received 3,966,813 and 4,049,451 visitors, respectively, in 1996. There are also 12 state parks, which covered 121,000 acres and received 2,114,000 visitors in 2005. There were 5,322,531 recreational visits to national park service areas in 2006. Wildlife is a major attraction: the state is noted for its population of elk (particularly in the National Elk Refuge) and grizzly bear (in the Yellowstone National Park). Many kinds of game (mammal, birds and fish) are hunted, trapped and fished. The Devil's Tower and Fossil Butte national monuments are also found in the state, as is the Fort Laramie national historic site. There are various reminders of Wyoming's 'Wild West' heritage, including rodeos and the Buffalo Bill Historical Center in Cody.

Wyoming Travel and Tourism: I-25 at College Dr., Cheyenne, WY 82002; tel. (307) 777-7777; fax (307) 777-2877; internet www.wyomingtourism.org; Dir DIANE SHOBER.

PRINCIPAL NATIONAL PARKS

Acadia National Park: POB 177, Eagle Lake Rd, Bar Harbor, ME 04609; tel. (207) 288-3338; fax (207) 288-8813; e-mail acadia_information@nps.gov; internet www.nps.gov/acad; Supt SHERIDAN STEELE.

Arches National Park: POB 907, Moab, UT 84532-0907; tel. (435) 719-2299; fax (435) 719-2305; e-mail archinfo@nps.gov; internet www.nps.gov/arch; Supt LAURA JOSS.

Badlands National Park: 25216 Ben Reifel Rd, POB 6, Interior, SD 57750; tel. (605) 433-5361; fax (605) 433-5404; e-mail badl_information@nps.gov; internet www.nps.gov/badl; Supt Dr PAIGE BAKER.

Big Bend National Park: POB 129, TX 79834; tel. (432) 477-2251; fax (432) 477-1175; e-mail bibe_info@nps.gov; internet www.nps.gov/bibe; Supt WILLIAM WELLMAN.

Biscayne National Park: 9700 SW 328th St, Homestead, FL 33033-5634; tel. (305) 230-7275; fax (305) 230-1190; e-mail bisc_information@nps.gov; internet www.nps.gov/bisc; Supt MARK LEWIS.

Black Canyon of the Gunnison National Park: Park Headquarters, 102 Elk Creek, Gunnison, CO 81230; tel. (970) 641-2337; fax (970) 641-3127; e-mail cure_info@nps.gov; internet www.nps.gov/blca; Supt CONNIE RUDD.

Bryce Canyon National Park: POB 640201, Bryce Canyon, UT 84764-0201; tel. (435) 834-5322; fax (435) 834-4102; e-mail brca_reception_area@nps.gov; internet www.nps.gov/brca; Supt EDDIE LOPEZ.

Canyonlands National Park: 2282 SW Resource Blvd, Moab, UT 84532; tel. (435) 719-2100; fax (435) 719-2300; e-mail canyinfo@nps.gov; internet www.nps.gov/cany; Supt KATE CANNON.

Capitol Reef National Park: HC 70, POB 15, Torrey, UT 84775; tel. (435) 425-3791; fax (435) 425-3026; e-mail care_interpretation@nps.gov; internet www.nps.gov/care; Supt AL HENDRICKS.

Carlsbad Caverns National Park: 3225 National Parks Hwy, Carlsbad, NM 88220; tel. (505) 785-2232; fax (505) 785-2133; e-mail cave_park_information@nps.gov; internet www.nps.gov/cave; Supt JOHN BENJAMIN.

Channel Islands National Park: 1901 Spinnaker Dr., Ventura, CA 93001-4354; tel. (805) 658-5700; fax (805) 658-5799; e-mail chis_interpretation@nps.gov; internet www.nps.gov/chis; Supt RUSSELL GALIPEAU.

Congaree National Park: 100 National Park Rd, Hopkins, SC 29061-9118; tel. (803) 776-4396; fax (803) 783-4241; e-mail cosw_information@nps.gov; internet www.nps.gov/cosw; Supt TRACY SWARTOUT.

Crater Lake National Park: POB 7, Crater Lake, OR 97604; tel. (541) 594-3000; fax (541) 594-3010; e-mail crla_information_requests@nps.gov; internet www.nps.gov/crla; Supt CRAIG ACKERMAN.

Cuyahoga Valley National Park: 15610 Vaughn Rd, Brecksville, OH 44141; tel. (216) 524-1497; fax (440) 546-5989; e-mail cuva_info@nps.gov; internet www.nps.gov/cuva; Supt JOHN P. DEBO, Jr.

Death Valley National Park: POB 579, Death Valley, CA 92328; tel. (760) 786-3200; fax (760) 786-3283; e-mail deva_superintendent@nps.gov; internet www.nps.gov/deva; Supt J. T. REYNOLDS.

Denali National Park and Preserve: POB 9, AK 99755-0009; tel. (907) 683-2294; fax (907) 683-9612; e-mail denali_info@nps.gov; internet www.nps.gov/dena; Supt PAUL ANDERSON.

Dry Tortugas National Park: POB 6208, Key West, FL 33041; tel. (305) 242-7700; fax (305) 242-7711; e-mail drto_information@nps.gov; internet www.nps.gov/drto; Supt DAN KIMBALL.

Everglades National Park: 40001 State Rd, 9336 Homestead, FL 33034-6733; tel. (305) 242-7700; fax (305) 242-7711; e-mail ever_information@nps.gov; internet www.nps.gov/ever; Supt DAN KIMBALL.

Gates of the Arctic National Park and Preserve: Bettles Ranger Station, POB 30, Bettles, AK 99726; tel. (907) 692-5494; fax (907) 692-5400; e-mail gaar_visitor_information@nps.gov; internet www.nps.gov/gaar; Supt GREG DUDGEON.

Glacier Bay National Park and Preserve: 1 Park Rd, POB 140, Gustavus, AK 99826; tel. (907) 697-2230; fax (907) 697-2654; e-mail glba_administration@nps.gov; internet www.nps.gov/glba; Supt CHERRY PAYNE.

Glacier National Park: POB 128, West Glacier, MT 59936-0128; tel. (406) 888-7800; fax (406) 888-7808; e-mail glac_information@nps.gov; internet www.nps.gov/glac; f. 1910; Supt CHAS CARTWRIGHT.

Grand Canyon National Park: POB 129, Grand Canyon, AZ 86023; tel. (928) 638-7888; fax (928) 638-7797; e-mail grca_information@nps.gov; internet www.nps.gov/grca; Supt STEPHEN MARTIN.

Grand Teton National Park: POB 170, Moose, WY 83012-0170; tel. (307) 739-3300; fax (307) 739-3438; e-mail grte_info@nps.gov; internet www.nps.gov/grte; Supt Mary Gibson-Scott.

Great Basin National Park: 100 Great Basin National Park, Baker, NV 89311; tel. (775) 234-7331; fax (775) 234-7269; e-mail grba_interpretation@nps.gov; internet www.nps.gov/grba; Supt Andrew J. Ferguson.

Great Smoky Mountain National Park: 107 Park Headquarters Rd, Gatlinburg, TN 37738; tel. (865) 436-1200; fax (865) 436-1220; e-mail grsm_smokies_information@nps.gov; internet www.nps.gov/grsm; Supt Dale Ditmanson.

Guadalupe Mountains National Park: 400 Pine Canyon Rd, Salt Flat, TX 79847-9400; tel. (915) 828-3251; fax (915) 828-3269; e-mail gumo_superintendent@nps.gov; internet www.nps.gov/gumo; Supt John Lujan.

Haleakalā National Park: POB 369, Makawao, Maui, HI 96768; tel. (808) 572-4400; fax (808) 572-1304; e-mail hale_interpretation@nps.gov; internet www.nps.gov/hale; Supt Marylin Parris.

Hawaii Volcanoes National Park: POB 52, HI 96718-0052; tel. (808) 985-6000; fax (808) 985-6004; e-mail havo_interpretation@nps.gov; internet www.nps.gov/havo; Supt Cindy Orlando.

Hot Springs National Park: 101 Reserve St, Hot Springs, AR 71901; tel. (501) 620-6715; fax (501) 624-3458; e-mail hosp_interpretation@nps.gov; internet www.nps.gov/hosp; Supt Josie Fernandez.

Isle Royale National Park: 800 East Lakeshore Dr., Houghton, MI 49931-1896; tel. (906) 482-0984; fax (906) 482-8753; e-mail isro_parkinfo@nps.gov; internet www.nps.gov/isro; Supt Phyllis Green.

Joshua Tree National Park: 74485 National Park Dr., Twentynine Palms, CA 92277-3597; tel. (760) 367-5500; fax (760) 367-6392; e-mail jotr_info@nps.gov; internet www.nps.gov/jotr; Supt Curt Sauer.

Katmai National Park and Preserve: 1 King Salmon Mall, POB 7, King Salmon, AK 99613; tel. (907) 246-3305; fax (907) 246-2116; e-mail katm_visitor_information@nps.gov; internet www.nps.gov/katm; Supt Ralph Moore.

Kenai Fjords National Park: POB 1727, Seward, AK 99664-1727; tel. (907) 224-7500; fax (907) 224-7505; e-mail kefj_superintendent@nps.gov; internet www.nps.gov/kefj; Supt Jeff Mow.

Kobuk Valley National Park: POB 1029, Kotzebue, AK 99752; tel. (907) 442-3890; fax (907) 442-8316; e-mail wear_webmail@nps.gov; internet www.nps.gov/kova; Supt George Helfrich.

Lake Clark National Park and Preserve: 240 West 5th Avenue, Suite 236, Anchorage, AK 99501; tel. (907) 644-3626; fax (907) 644-3810; e-mail lacl_visitor_information@nps.gov; internet www.nps.gov/lacl; Supt Joel Hard.

Lassen Volcanic National Park: POB 100, Mineral, CA 96063; tel. (530) 595-4480; fax (530) 595-3262; e-mail lavo_information@nps.gov; internet www.nps.gov/lavo; Supt Darlene Koontz.

Mammoth Cave National Park: POB 7, 1 Mammoth Cave Parkway, Mammoth Cave, KY 42259-0007; tel. (270) 758-2180; fax (270) 758-9297; e-mail maca_information@nps.gov; internet www.nps.gov/maca; Supt Patrick H. Reed.

Mesa Verde National Park: POB 8, CO 81330-0008; tel. (970) 529-4465; fax (970) 529-4637; e-mail meve_general_information@nps.gov; internet www.nps.gov/meve; Supt Larry Wiese.

Mount Rainier National Park: 55210 238th Ave East, Ashford, WA 98304; tel. (360) 569-2211; fax (360) 569-2170; e-mail morainfo@nps.gov; internet www.nps.gov/mora; Supt David Uberuaga.

North Cascades National Park: 810 State Route 20, Sedro-Woolley, WA 98284-1239; tel. (360) 854-7200; fax (360) 856-1934; e-mail noca_interpretation@nps.gov; internet www.nps.gov/noca; Supt Chip Jenkins.

Olympic National Park: 600 East Park Ave, Port Angeles, WA 98362-6798; tel. (360) 565-3130; fax (360) 565-3015; e-mail olym_visitor_center@nps.gov; internet www.nps.gov/olym; Supt Karen Gustin.

Petrified Forest National Park: 1 Park Rd, POB 2217, AZ 86028-2217; tel. (928) 524-6228; fax (928) 524-3567; e-mail pefo_superintendent@nps.gov; internet www.nps.gov/pefo; Supt Cliff Spencer.

Redwood National and State Parks: 1111 Second St, Crescent City, CA 95531; tel. (707) 464-6101; fax (707) 464-1812; e-mail redw_information@nps.gov; internet www.nps.gov/redw; Supt Steve W. Chaney.

Rocky Mountain National Park: 1000 Hwy 36, Estes Park, CO 80517-8397; tel. (970) 586-1206; fax (970) 586-1256; e-mail romo_information@nps.gov; internet www.nps.gov/romo; Supt Vaughn Baker.

Saguaro National Park: 3693 South Old Spanish Trail, Tucson, AZ 85730-5601; tel. (520) 733-5100; fax (520) 733-5183; e-mail sagu_information@nps.gov; internet www.nps.gov/sagu; Supt Sarah Craighead.

Sequoia and Kings Canyon National Parks: 47050 Generals Hwy, Three Rivers, CA 93271-9700; tel. (559) 565-3341; fax (559) 565-3730; e-mail seki_interpretation@nps.gov; internet www.nps.gov/seki; Supt Craig Axtell.

Shenandoah National Park: 3655 US Hwy 211 East, Luray, VA 22835-9036; tel. (540) 999-3500; fax (540) 999-3601; e-mail shen_superintendent@nps.gov; internet www.nps.gov/shen; Supt Martha Bogle.

Theodore Roosevelt National Park: POB 7, Medora, ND 58645-0007; tel. (701) 623-4466; fax (701) 623-4840; e-mail thro_interpretation@nps.gov; internet www.nps.gov/thro; Supt Valerie Naylor.

Virgin Islands National Park: 1300 Cruz Bay Creek, St John, VI 00830; tel. (340) 776-6201; fax (340) 775-9592; e-mail viis_superintendent@nps.gov; internet www.nps.gov/viis; Supt Mark Hardgrove.

Voyageurs National Park: 3131 Hwy 53 South, International Falls, MN 56649-8904; tel. (218) 283-6600; fax (218) 285-7407; e-mail voya_superintendent@nps.gov; internet www.nps.gov/voya; f. 1975; Supt Mike Ward.

Wind Cave National Park: 26611 Hwy 385, Hot Springs, SD 57747-9430; tel. (605) 745-4600; fax (605) 745-4207; e-mail wica_interpretation@nps.gov; internet www.nps.gov/wica; Supt Vidal Davila.

Wrangell-St Elias National Park and Preserve: Mile 106.8 Richardson Hwy, POB 439, Copper Center, AK 99573-0439; tel. (907) 822-5234; fax (907) 822-7216; e-mail wrst_interpretation@nps.gov; internet www.nps.gov/wrst; Supt Meg Jensen.

Yellowstone National Park: POB 168, Yellowstone, WY 82190-0168; tel. (307) 344-7381; fax (307) 344-2014; e-mail yell_visitor_services@nps.gov; internet www.nps.gov/yell; Supt Suzanne Lewis.

Yosemite National Park: POB 577, Yosemite National Park, CA 95389; tel. (209) 372-0200; fax (209) 372-0220; e-mail yose_web_manager@nps.gov; internet www.nps.gov/yose; Supt Michael Tollefson.

Zion National Park: SR 9, Springdale, UT 84767-1099; tel. (435) 772-3256; fax (435) 772-3426; e-mail zion_park_information@nps.gov; internet www.nps.gov/zion; Supt Jock Whitworth.

EXTERNAL TRADE

Principal Commodities

(Note: The customs territory of the USA includes Puerto Rico and the US Virgin Islands. Figures exclude trade with other US possessions.)

(Source: Office of Trade and Industry Information—OTII, Manufacturing and Services, International Trade Administration, US Department of Commerce.)

IMPORTS C.I.F.
(distribution by SITC, $ million)

	2005	2006	2007
Food and live animals	51,440.9	56,102.0	60,879.2
Mineral fuels, lubricants, etc.	286,375.5	333,486.3	360,910.2
Petroleum, petroleum products, etc.	244,407.2	294,361.7	322,876.2
Chemicals and related products	128,386.6	142,899.5	155,358.6
Basic manufactures	190,744.2	222,989.1	227,224.7
Machinery and transport equipment	649,912.6	709,833.7	738,714.8
General industrial machinery, equipment and parts	52,351.8	59,677.0	63,938.8
Office machines and automatic data-processing machines	98,595.8	106,487.9	101,785.9
Telecommunications and sound equipment	104,125.7	115,294.5	129,802.5
Other electrical machinery, apparatus, etc.	99,132.6	109,742.7	113,622.6
Motor vehicles	196,070.3	211,708.3	210,650.4
Miscellaneous manufactured articles	259,753.7	276,409.7	293,818.7
Clothing and accessories (excl. footwear)	76,380.4	79,149.8	81,187.7
Total (incl. others)	1,670,940.4	1,855,119.3	1,953,698.8

EXPORTS F.O.B.
(distribution by SITC, $ million)

	2005	2006	2007
Food and live animals	48,292.5	54,259.8	68,250.4
Crude materials (inedible) except fuels	41,192.0	50,149.3	62,432.3
Mineral fuels, lubricants, etc.	26,382.7	34,881.1	41,957.0
Chemicals and related products	123,188.2	138,667.4	158,189.8
Basic manufactures	89,179.1	103,480.7	112,545.6
Machinery and transport equipment	433,665.7	494,452.5	536,409.3
Power-generating machinery and equipment	43,700.5	46,638.8	53,082.2
Machinery specialized for particular industries	35,360.8	40,029.5	51,399.9
General industrial machinery, equipment and parts	41,503.1	47,086.5	51,877.8
Office machines and automatic data-processing machines	46,882.4	49,143.8	46,192.1
Telecommunication equipment, parts and accessories	30,536.1	34,562.0	38,584.9
Other electrical machinery, apparatus, etc.	94,711.5	106,756.3	104,793.7
Motor vehicles	80,026.2	89,347.2	102,812.1
Transport equipment	53,872.5	71,998.7	81,670.0
Miscellaneous manufactured articles	103,808.5	115,968.2	127,064.2
Professional, scientific and controlling instruments, etc.	38,649.6	43,805.7	47,606.3
Total (incl. others)	904,379.8	1,037,143.0	1,162,708.3

Principal Trading Partners

(Note: The customs territory of the USA includes Puerto Rico and the US Virgin Islands. Figures exclude trade with other US possessions.)

(Source: Office of Trade and Industry Information—OTII, Manufacturing and Services, International Trade Administration, US Department of Commerce.)

IMPORTS C.I.F.
($ million)

	2005	2006	2007
Brazil	24,436.6	26,388.5	25,636.0
Canada	287,870.2	303,416.3	313,110.9
China, People's Republic	243,462.3	287,772.8	321,507.8
France (incl. Monaco)	33,847.4	37,148.6	41,589.0
Germany	84,812.5	89,072.8	94,364.5
India	18,807.5	21,826.3	24,024.4
Ireland	28,621.0	28,640.0	30,346.5
Israel	16,875.2	19,149.9	20,812.0
Italy	31,008.2	32,652.2	35,041.8
Japan	138,091.2	148,091.2	145,463.6
Korea, Republic	43,779.5	45,829.6	47,566.3
Malaysia	33,703.2	36,532.5	32,790.0
Mexico	170,197.9	198,258.6	210,799.0
Nigeria	24,188.3	27,916.4	32,770.2
Russia	15,278.6	19,783.5	19,360.2
Saudi Arabia	27,227.7	31,688.9	35,626.4
Taiwan	34,838.0	38,214.8	38,301.9
Thailand	19,892.4	22,471.5	22,752.9
United Kingdom	51,063.4	53,437.1	56,892.9
Venezuela	33,964.7	37,165.0	39,896.7
Total (incl. others)	1,670,940.4	1,855,119.3	1,953,698.8

EXPORTS F.O.B.
($ million)

	2005	2006	2007
Australia	15,770.9	17,781.8	19,205.1
Belgium	18,604.6	21,347.2	25,291.9
Brazil	15,345.5	19,227.5	24,628.4
Canada	211,420.5	230,256.8	248,437.2
China, People's Republic	41,836.5	55,224.2	65,238.3
France (incl. Monaco)	22,402.2	24,217.2	27,407.1
Germany	31,149.2	41,319.5	49,652.0
Hong Kong	16,322.6	17,778.6	20,120.5
India	7,958.0	10,091.1	17,592.5
Israel	9,731.9	10,964.4	13,018.9
Italy	11,512.2	12,566.7	14,141.3
Japan	55,409.6	59,649.2	62,665.0
Korea, Republic	27,670.4	32,455.5	34,703.0
Malaysia	10,450.9	12,550.1	11,679.8
Mexico	120,048.9	134,167.1	136,541.3
Netherlands	26,495.6	31,101.8	32,986.0
Singapore	20,646.4	24,683.2	26,284.5
Switzerland	10,740.1	14,376.0	17,039.6
Taiwan	22,049.6	23,023.3	26,358.5
United Arab Emirates	8,476.6	11,921.4	11,609.4
United Kingdom	38,628.7	45,393.0	50,296.2
Total (incl. others)	904,379.8	1,037,143.0	1,162,708.3

External Trade Organizations

American Association of Exporters and Importers (AAEI): 1050 17th St, NW, Suite 810, Washington, DC 20036; tel. (202) 857-8009; fax (202) 857-7843; e-mail hq@aaei.org; internet www.aaei.org; f. 1921; 1,200 mems; Pres. and CEO HALLOCK (HALL) NORTHCOTT; Chair. TIMOTHY VAN OOST.

American Cotton Shippers Association (ACSA): 88 Union Ave, Suite 1204, Memphis, TN 38103; tel. (901) 525-2272; fax (901) 527-8303; e-mail vboone@acsa-cotton.org; internet www.acsa-cotton.org; f. 1924; Pres. LITTLETON B. CAROTHERS, II; Exec. Vice-Pres. NEAL P. GILLEN.

American Hardwood Export Council (AHEC): 1111 19th St, NW, Suite 800, Washington, DC 20036; tel. (202) 463-2720; fax (202) 463-2787; e-mail michael_snow@afandpa.org; internet www.ahec.org; f. 1989; 114 mems; Exec. Dir MICHAEL SNOW.

American Importers Association, Inc (AIA): 214 Seventh St, North Safety Harbor, FL 34695; tel. (727) 726-0900; fax (727) 726-0119; e-mail information@americanimporters.org; internet www.americanimporters.org.

American International Automobile Dealers Association (AIADA): 211 North Union St, Suite 300, Alexandria, VA 22314; tel. (703) 519-7800; fax (703) 519-7810; e-mail goaiada@aiada.org; internet www.aiada.org; f. 1970; non-profit trade asscn dedicated to the representation of the USA's international nameplate automobile dealers; 11,000 mems; Chair. JOHN H. HAWKINS; Pres. CODY LUSK.

American League for Exports and Security Assistance (ALESA): 2175 K St, NW, Suite 200, Washington, DC 20037; tel. (202) 213-3747; internet www.alesa.org; f. 1976; Exec. Vice-Pres. TOBY ROTH.

Association of Women in International Trade: 1707 L St, NW, Suite 570, Washington, DC 20036; tel. (202) 293-2948; internet www

.wiit.org; f. 1987; 288 mems; Pres. SUSAN SCHMIDT; Pres.-elect TONYA KEMP.

Auto International Association: 7101 Wisconsin Ave, Suite 1300, Bethesda, MD 20814; tel. (301) 654-6664; fax (301) 654-3299; e-mail international@aftermarket.org; internet www.aiaglobal.org; f. 1983; importers and distributors of parts for imported vehicles; 320 mems; Chair. of Bd ANTHONY PERTICARI; Exec. Dir LEE KADRICH.

Business Council for International Understanding (BCIU): 1212 Ave of the Americas, 10th Floor, New York, NY 10036; tel. (212) 490-0460; fax (212) 697-8526; e-mail p-tichansky@bciu.org; internet www.bciu.org; f. 1959; supports business–government relations; Dir LAURA CANSICIO; Pres. and CEO PETER J. TICHANSKY.

CalChamber Council for International Trade: California Chamber of Commerce, 1215 K St, Suite 1400, POB 1736, Sacramento, CA 95814; tel. (916) 444-6670; fax (916) 325-1272; internet www.ccalchamber.com; f. 2007 by merger of California Council for International Trade and the California Chamber of Commerce International Trade Cttee; 16,000 mems; Pres. and CEO ALLAN ZAREMBERG.

Coal Exporters' Association (CEA): National Mining Asscn, 101 Constitution Ave, NW, Suite 500 East, Washington, DC 20001; tel. (202) 463-2600; fax (202) 463-2666; e-mail craulston@nma.org; f. 1945; 25 mems; affiliated to the National Mining Asscn; Pres. and CEO KRAIG R. NAASZ.

Consumers for World Trade (CWT): 1707 L St, NW, Suite 570, Washington, DC 20036; tel. (202) 293-2944; fax (202) 293-0495; internet www.cwt.org; Pres. MAUREEN SMITH.

Council of the Americas: 680 Park Ave, New York, NY 10021; tel. (212) 249-8950; fax (212) 249-1880; e-mail inforequest@as-coa.org; internet coa.counciloftheamericas.org; f. 1965; over 200 corporate mems involved in business with Latin America; Chair. WILLIAM R. RHODES; Pres. and CEO SUSAN L. SEGAL.

Environmental Export Council: 1300 Pennsylvania Ave, NW, Suite 200, Washington, DC 20004-3016; tel. (202) 312-2903; fax (202) 312-2925; e-mail dooleya@ctc.com; Exec. Dir JOHN F. MIZROCH.

Federation of International Trade Associations: 11654 Plaza America Dr., Suite 120, Reston, VA 20191; tel. (703) 621-1900; fax (703) 620-4922; e-mail info@fita.org; internet www.fita.org; f. 1984; over 450,000 mem. asscns; Chair. NELSON T. JOYNER.

Finance, Credit & International Business: 8840 Columbia 100 Pkwy, Columbia, MD 21045-2158; tel. (410) 423-1840; fax (410) 423-1845; e-mail fcib_info@fcibglobal.com; internet www.fcibglobal.com; f. 1919; over 1,000 int. mem. cos; Pres. RUSSELL D'SOUZA.

Food Export Association of the Midwest USA: 309 West Washington St, Suite 600, Chicago, IL 60606; tel. (312) 334-9200; fax (312) 334-9230; e-mail info@foodexport.org; internet www.foodexport.org; f. 1969 as Mid-America International Agri-Trade Council (MIATCO); adopted present name in 2006; a private, non-profit asscn that offers services to help cos from the midwestern region of the USA to promote their food and agricultural products in foreign markets; 12 mid-western mem. states; Exec. Dir TIM HAMILTON.

Food Export USA—Northeast: 1 Penn Center, 1617 JFK Blvd, Suite 420, Philadelphia, PA 19103; tel. (215) 829-9111; fax (215) 829-9777; e-mail info@foodexport.org; internet www.foodexportusa.org; f. 1973; represents 10 northeastern states; Exec. Dir TIM HAMILTON.

Global Offset and Countertrade Association (GOCA): 818 Connecticut Ave, NW, 12th Floor, Washington, DC 20006; tel. (202) 887-9011; fax (202) 872-8324; e-mail goca@globaloffset.org; internet www.globaloffset.org; f. 1986; fmrly known as American Countertrade Asscn, present name adopted in 2005; over 100 mem. cos world-wide; Chair. and CEO NEIL K. RUTTER.

International Food and Agricultural Trade Policy Council: 1616 P St, NW, Suite 100, Washington, DC, 20036; tel. (202) 328-5056; fax (202) 328-5133; e-mail agritrade@agritrade.org; internet www.agritrade.org; f. 1987; 41 mems; Chief Exec. CHARLOTTE HEBEBRAND; Chair. PIET BUKMAN.

International Trade Club of Chicago: 134 North LaSalle St, Suite 1300, Chicago, IL 60602; tel. (312) 368-9197; fax (312) 553-1470; e-mail execdir@itcc.org; internet www.itcc.org; f. 1919; promotes US export trade; 500 mems; Pres. SIDNEY SALVADORI.

Massachusetts Export Center: State Transportation Bldg, 10 Park Plaza, Suite 4510, Boston, MA 02116; tel. (617) 973-8664; fax (617) 973-8681; e-mail paula.murphy@state.ma.us; internet www.mass.gov/export; f. 1994; Dir PAULA MURPHY.

Meat Importers' Council of America (MICA): 1901 Fort Myer Dr., POB 1110, Arlington, VA 22209; tel. (703) 522-1910; fax (703) 524-6039; internet www.micausa.org; f. 1962; 200 mems (1999); Chair. DAVID R. RIND.

Music Distributors Association (MDA): 1026 Northwood Dr., Effingham, IL 62401; tel. and fax (217) 347-6699; e-mail geobev@consolidated.net; internet www.musicdistributors.org; f. 1939; 85 mems; Exec. Dir GLENDA PLUMMER.

National Association of Foreign-Trade Zones (NAFTZ): 1001 Connecticut Ave, NW, Suite 350, Washington, DC 20036; tel. (202) 331-1950; fax (202) 331-1994; e-mail info@naftz.org; internet www.naftz.org; f. 1973; 2,524 mems (2004); Pres. WILLARD M. BERRY; Chair. BRANDI HANBACK.

National Council on International Trade Development (NCITD): 1707 L St, NW, Suite 570, Washington, DC 20036; tel. (202) 872-9280; fax (202) 293-0495; e-mail registrar@ncitd.org; internet www.ncitd.org; f. 1967; 38 mems.

National Foreign Trade Council (NFTC): 1625 K St, NW, Suite 200, Washington, DC 20006; tel. (202) 887-0278; fax (202) 452-8160; e-mail nftcinformation@nftc.org; internet www.nftc.org; f. 1914; over 300 mem. cos; Pres. WILLIAM A. REINSCH.

NEXCO: POB 3949, Grand Central Station, New York, NY 10163-3949; tel. (877) 291-4901; fax (646) 349-9628; e-mail director@nexco.org; internet www.nexco.org; f. 1965; organizes seminars; 100 mems; Pres. BARNEY LEHRER; Exec. Dir GERRI CRISTANTIELLO.

North American Association for Exports to Eastern Europe (NAAFETEE): Englewood, FL 34295-0198; tel. (941) 697-7362; fax (941) 697-7364; e-mail naafetee@cyberstreet.com; internet www.ijs.com/naafetee; f. 1992.

North American Export Grain Association: 1250 I St, NW, Suite 1003, Washington, DC 20005; tel. (202) 682-4030; fax (202) 682-4033; e-mail info@naega.org; internet www.naega.org; f. 1912; 32 mems; Pres. and CEO GARY C. MARTIN.

North American Shippers Association (NASA): 1600 St Georges Ave, POB 249, Rahway, NJ 07065; tel. (732) 680-4535; fax (732) 388-6580; e-mail j.barrett@jfhillebrand.com; internet www.nasaships.com; f. 1987; Pres. ERIC WHITMAN.

Northwest Fruit Exporters: 105 South 18th St, Suite 227, Yakima, WA 98901-2149; tel. (509) 576-8004; fax (509) 576-3646; e-mail nfe@goodfruit.com; 106 mems; Man. JAMES R. ARCHER.

Pacific Lumber Exporters' Association (PLEA): 5857 Carman Dr., Lake Oswego, OR 97035; tel. (503) 270-5411; fax (503) 270-5401; e-mail info@lumber-exporters.org; internet www.lumber-exporters.org; f. 1923; 115 mems; Pres. MICHAEL PARR.

Small Business Exporters Association (SBEA): 1156 15th St, NW, Suite 1100, Washington, DC 20005; tel. (202) 659-9320; internet www.sbea.org; f. 1990; 150,000 mems; Pres. JAMES MORRISON.

Softwood Export Council (SEC): 520 South West Sixth Ave, Suite 810, Portland, OR 97204-1514; tel. (503) 248-0406; fax (503) 248-0399; e-mail info@softwood.org; internet www.softwood.org; 18 mems; 4 supporting mems; Pres. CRAIG LARSEN.

Southern United States Trade Association (SUSTA): 2 Canal St, Suite 2515, New Orleans, LA 70130; tel. (504) 568-5986; fax (504) 568-6010; e-mail susta@susta.org; internet www.susta.org; f. 1973; a non-profit agricultural export trade development asscn comprising the Depts of Agriculture of the 15 southern states and the Commonwealth of Puerto Rico; Exec. Dir JERRY HINGLE.

Speciality Crop Trade Council: 710 Striker Ave, Sacramento, CA 95834; tel. (916) 561-5900; fax (916) 561-5906; e-mail richn@dfaofca.com; internet www.cdfea.org; f. 1918 as California Dried Fruit Export Asscn; 93 mems; 14 associate mems; Pres. and CEO MERLE JACOBS.

Trade Compliance Center (TCC): US Dept of Commerce, 14th St and Constitution Ave, NW, Washington, DC 20230; tel. (202) 482-1191; fax (202) 482-6097; e-mail tcc@mail.doc.gov; internet tcc.export.gov; resolves trade-barrier issues for cos exporting from the USA.

United States Agricultural Export Development Council (USAEDC): 8233 Old Courthouse Rd, Suite 200, Vienna, VA 22182; tel. (703) 556-9290; fax (703) 790-0845; e-mail adurbin@usaedc.org; internet www.usaedc.org; f. 1954; non-governmental trade asscn; c. 80 mems; Chair. THOMAS M. COOK; Sec.-Treas. JOHN TOASPERN.

United States Council for International Business (USCIB): 1212 Ave of the Americas, New York, NY 10036; tel. (212) 354-4480; fax (212) 575-0327; e-mail info@uscib.org; internet www.uscib.org; f. 1945; over 300 mems; Chair. WILLIAM G. PARRETT; Pres. and CEO PETER M. ROBINSON.

United States Meat Export Federation (USMEF): 1050 17th St, Suite 2200, Denver, CO 80265; tel. (303) 623-6328; fax (303) 623-0297; e-mail info@usmef.org; internet www.usmef.org; f. 1976; 213 mem. orgs; Pres. and CEO PHILIP M. SENG.

US Dairy Export Council: 2101 Wilson Blvd, Suite 400, Arlington, VA 22201-3061; tel. (703) 528-3049; fax (703) 528-3705; e-mail info@usdec.org; internet www.usdec.org; f. 1995; 86 mems; Pres. TOM SUBER.

US Grains Council: 1400 K St, NW, Suite 1200, Washington, DC 20005; tel. (202) 789-0789; fax (202) 898-0522; e-mail grains@grains

.org; internet www.grains.org; f. 1960; develops export markets for cereals and related products; over 100 mem. orgs; Pres. and CEO KENNETH HOBBIE.

US International Trade Commission: see Government—Independent Agencies.

US Livestock Genetics Export, Inc (USLGE): 413 North Brdwy, Suite C, Salem, IL 62881; tel. (618) 548-9154; fax (618) 548-9709; e-mail uslge@uslge.org; internet www.uslge.org.

USA Poultry & Egg Export Council (USAPEEC): 2300 West Park Place Blvd, Suite 100, Stone Mountain, GA 30087; tel. (770) 413-0006; fax (770) 413-0007; e-mail usapeec@usapeec.org; internet www.usapeec.org; f. 1984; a non-profit, industry-sponsored trade org. dedicated to increasing exports of US poultry and egg food products in all foreign markets; Pres. JAMES H. SUMNER.

Washington Council on International Trade (WCIT): World Trade Center Bldg, 2200 Alaskan Way, Suite 430, Seattle, WA 98121-1678; tel. (206) 443-3826; fax (206) 443-3828; e-mail wcitinfo@wcit.org; internet www.wcit.org; Pres. KATHLEEN CONNORS.

Westconn International Trade Association, Inc: PMB Suite 14, 1002 Hope St, Stamford, CT 06902; tel. (973) 578-2177; fax (973) 690-3498; e-mail webmaster@westconn.org; internet www.westconn.org; f. 1972; Pres. PATRICIA HANTIN.

Western US Agricultural Trade Association (WUSATA): 4601 North East 77th Ave, Suite 120, Vancouver, WA 98662-6730; tel. (360) 693-3373; fax (360) 693-3464; e-mail andy@wusata.org; internet www.wusata.org; f. 1980; a non-profit trade asscn comprised of 13 state-funded agricultural promotion agencies; Exec. Dir ANDY ANDERSON.

World Trade Center of New Orleans: 2 Canal St, Suite 2900, New Orleans, LA 70130; tel. (504) 529-1601; fax (504) 529-1691; e-mail wtc-info@wtcno.org; internet www.wtcno.org; f. 1985 by merger of International House and International Trade Mart; promotes international trade for Louisiana; 1,900 mems; Man. Dir EUGENE J. SCHREIBER.

Foreign Chambers of Commerce in the USA

American Australian Association: 50 Broadway, Suite 2003, New York, NY 10004; tel. (212) 338-6860; fax (212) 338-6864; e-mail information@aaanyc.org; internet www.americanaustralian.org; f. 1948; 800 mems; Chair. MALCOLM BINKS; Pres. FRANCES M. CASSIDY.

American-Danish Business Council (ADBC): Embassy of Denmark, 3200 Whitehaven St, NW, Washington, DC 20008; tel. (202) 464-4190; fax (202) 328-1470; e-mail info@usadk.org; internet www.usadk.org; Co-Chairs FRIIS ARNE PETERSEN, ROBERT TRICE; Exec. Sec. ULRIK EVERSBUSCH.

American Egyptian Cooperation Foundation: 235 East 40th St, Suite 22A, New York, NY 10016; tel. (212) 867-2323; fax (212) 697-0465; e-mail aecf32@verizon.net; internet www.americanegyptiancoop.org; f. 1987; Pres. and CEO A. F. ZAKI.

American-Mideast Business Associates: 1137 South Green St, Tuckerton, NJ 08087-2428; tel. (609) 296-4783; f. 1951; Pres. I. F. YUSIF.

American-Southern Africa Chamber of Trade and Industry: 1080 Park Ave, Suite 4W, New York, NY 10128; tel. (212) 410-6560; f. 1966; 40 mems; Dir-Gen. ROBERT JOHN.

Argentine-American Chamber of Commerce (AACC): 630 Fifth Ave, 25th Floor, Rockefeller Center, New York, NY 10111; tel. (212) 698-2238; fax (212) 698-2239; e-mail argentinechamber@argentinechamber.org; internet www.argentinechamber.org; f. 1919; Pres. ALAN STOGA; Exec. Dir CLAUDIA SCHAEFER-FARRE.

Arizona-Mexican Chamber of Commerce: 4644 North 38th Dr., POB 626, Phoenix, AZ 85001-0626; tel. and fax (602) 252-6448; f. 1967; Pres. HECTOR LEDESMA.

Association of American-Israel Chambers of Commerce (AAICC): internet www.israeltrade.org

America-Israel Chamber of Commerce (Central Atlantic Region) (AICC): 200 South Broad St, Suite 700, Philadelphia, PA 19102-3869; tel. (215) 790-3722; fax (215) 790-3600; e-mail aicc@greaterphilachamber.com; internet www.americaisraelchamber.com; f. 1987; Exec. Dir DEBBIE BUCHWALD; Pres. DAVID GITLIN.

America-Israel Chamber of Commerce Chicago (AICC): 247 South State St, Suite 1325, Chicago, IL 60604; tel. (312) 641-2937; fax (312) 641-2941; e-mail info@americaisrael.org; internet www.americaisrael.org; Exec. Dir MICHAEL SCHMITT; Pres. ROBERT M. BERGER.

America-Israel Chamber of Commerce (Florida): 5011 S. State Rd 7, Suite 106, Davie, FL 33314; tel. (954) 725-2788; fax (954) 241-6846; e-mail info@israeltrade.org; internet www.floridaisraelchamber.org; f. 1993; Chair. KEITH WASSERSTROM; Exec. Dir LINDA CHASE.

American-Israel Chamber of Commerce and Industry, Inc (AICCI): 3 New York Plaza, 10th Floor, New York, NY 10004; tel. (212) 232-8440; fax (212) 646-3366; e-mail info@aicci.org; internet www.aicci.org; f. 1953; 22 mems; Chair. MAX BRANDSDORFER; Co-Pres JACOB M. KATZ, STEVEN G. TEPPER.

American-Israel Chamber of Commerce and Industry of Minnesota (AICCMN): 13100 Wayzata Blvd, Suite 130, Minneapolis, MN 55305; tel. (612) 701-8153; fax (952) 593-8668; e-mail info@aiccmn.org; internet www.aiccmn.org; f. 1980; Pres. DANIEL LIEBERMAN.

American-Israel Chamber of Commerce—Southeast Region (AICCSE): 1150 Lake Hearn Dr., Suite 130, Atlanta, GA 30342; tel. (404) 843-9426; fax (404) 843-1416; e-mail aiccse@aiccse.org; internet www.aiccse.org; f. 1992; 450 mems; Chair. ANDRE SCHNABL; Pres. TOM GLASER.

California-Israel Chamber of Commerce (CICC): 20883 Stevens Creek Blvd, Cupertino, CA 95014; tel. (408) 343-0917; fax (408) 343-1197; e-mail info@ca-israelchamber.org; internet www.ca-israelchamber.org; c. 5,000 mem. cos; Exec. Dir SHULY GALILI; Pres. ZVI ALON.

Maryland Israel Development Center (MIDC): 217 East Redwood St, Suite 1217, Baltimore, MD 21202; tel. (410) 767-0681; fax (410) 333-4302; e-mail info@marylandisrael.org; internet www.marylandisrael.org; f. 1992; Chair. HANAN SIBEL; Exec. Dir BARRY BOGAGE.

Ohio-Israel Chamber of Commerce: POB 39007, Cleveland, OH 44139-9998; tel. (216) 965-4474; fax (216) 248-4888; e-mail ohioisraelchamber@ameritech.net; internet www.ohioisraelchamber.com; f. 1996; Pres. HOWARD GUDELL.

Virginia Israel Advisory Board (VIAB): 8300 Boone Blvd, Suite 450, Vienna, VA 22182-2633; tel. (703) 288-1414; fax (877) 586-6833; e-mail robbins@viab.org; internet www.viab.org; Exec. Dir RALPH ROBBINS.

Association of Portuguese-American Chambers of Commerce (APACC):

Portuguese Chamber of Commerce of California: 84 West Santa Clara St, San Jose, CA 95113-1815; tel. (408) 288-7655; fax (408) 288-6182; e-mail maria.obrien@pccofca.org; internet www.portuguesechamber.com; Pres. HERBERTO SILVA.

Portugal-US Chamber of Commerce: 590 Fifth Ave, 3rd Floor, New York, NY 10036; tel. (212) 354-4627; fax (212) 575-4737; e-mail info@portugal-us.com; internet www.portugal-us.com; f. 1979; Exec. Dir THOMAS E. DIERSEN.

Australian Trade Commission: Embassy of Australia, 1601 Massachusetts Ave, NW, Washington, DC 20036; tel. (202) 797-3038; fax (202) 797-3300; e-mail info@austrade.gov.au; internet www.austrade.gov.au/usa; offices in Atlanta, Austin, California, Charlotte, Chicago, Colorado Springs, Fresno, Hawaii, Kansas City, Las Vegas, Los Angeles, Miami, New Orleans, New York, Phoenix, San Diego, San Francisco, Seattle and Washington, DC; Commr ALISON MCGUIGAN LEWIS.

Belgian-American Chamber of Commerce (BACC): c/o Consulate-General of Belgium, 1065 Ave of the Americas, 22nd Floor, New York, NY 10018; tel. (212) 340-6271; fax (212) 340-6270; e-mail info@belcham.org; internet www.belcham.org; f. 1918; chapters in Atlanta and Brussels, Belgium; Pres. JEAN-PIERRE PAULET.

Brazil-United States Business Council: 1615 H St, NW, Washington, DC 20062; tel. (202) 463-5485; fax (202) 463-3126; e-mail host@brazilcouncil.org; internet www.brazilcouncil.org; f. 1976; Chair. TOM CATANIA; Exec. Vice-Pres. ADREAN ROTHKOPF.

Brazilian-American Chamber of Commerce, Inc: 509 Madison Ave, Suite 304, New York, NY 10022; tel. (212) 751-4691; fax (212) 751-7692; e-mail info@brazilcham.com; internet www.brazilcham.com; f. 1969; c. 500 mems; Pres. Emeritus VICENTE J. BONNARD; Pres. RICHARD S. ALDRICH, Jr.

Brazilian-American Chamber of Commerce of Florida: POB 310038, Miami, FL 33231-0038; tel. (305) 579-9030; fax (305) 579-9756; e-mail baccf@brazilchamber.org; internet www.brazilchamber.org; f. 1981; over 300 mems; Pres. JOSE SAMPOL; Exec. Vice-Pres. CLAUDIO CURY.

Brazilian-American Chamber of Commerce of Georgia (BACC-GA): POB 93411, Atlanta, GA 30377; tel. (404) 880-1551; e-mail info@bacc-ga.com; internet www.bacc-ga.com; f. 1996; c. 100 mems; Pres. LUCIA JENNINGS; Chair. NATHAN FORRESTER.

British-American Business Council (BABC): 52 Vanderbilt Ave, 20th Floor, New York, NY 10017; tel. (212) 661-5660; fax (212) 661-1886; e-mail info@babinc.org; internet www.babc.org; 25 chapters, incl. those listed below; 3,000 mem. cos; Pres. STUART BAGSHAW; Chair. DAVID BIRCH.

British-American Business Association (BABA): POB 16482, Washington, DC 20041; tel. (202) 293-0010; fax (202) 296-3332; e-mail info@babawashington.org; internet www.babawashington.org; f. 1987; over 200 mems; Pres. MICHAEL FERGUSON; Exec. Dir PATRICIA A. KARHUSE.

British-American Business Council: 235 Montgomery, Suite 907, San Francisco, CA 94104; tel. (415) 296-8645; fax (415) 296-9649; e-mail info@babcsf.org; internet www.babcsf.org; f. 1954; fmrly British-American Chamber of Commerce (Northern California); Pres. STUART KEIRLE; Vice-Pres. KATHLEEN KIMURA.

British-American Business Council (Los Angeles): 11766 Wilshire Blvd, Suite 1230, Los Angeles, CA 90025-6557; tel. (310) 312-1962; fax (310) 312-1914; e-mail mindy@babcla.org; internet www.babcla.org; f. 1958; Pres. CATHERINE TOBER; Exec. Dir MINDY GAIL.

BritishAmerican Business (BABi): 52 Vanderbilt Ave, 20th Floor, New York, NY 10017; tel. (212) 661-5660; fax (212) 661-1886; e-mail babinc@babinc.org; internet www.babinc.org; f. 1920; over 700 mem. cos; Exec. Dir WENDY MENDENHALL; Chair. DANIEL S. GLASER.

British Trade and Investment Office: Consulate-General of the United Kingdom, 845 Third Ave, 11th Floor, New York, NY 10022; tel. (212) 745-0495; fax (212) 754-0456; e-mail uktiny@fco.gov.uk; internet www.britainusa.com/ny; Dir-Gen. Sir ALAN COLLINS.

Chinese Chamber of Commerce of Hawaii: 42 North King St, Suite 202, Honolulu, HI 96817; tel. (808) 533-3181; fax (808) 533-3184; e-mail info@chinesechamber.com; internet www.chinesechamber.com; f. 1911; 400 mems; Pres. TED C. T. LI; Pres.-elect DENNIS J. HWANG.

Chinese Chamber of Commerce of Los Angeles: 977 North Broadway, Ground Floor, Suite E, Los Angeles, CA 90012; tel. (213) 617-0396; fax (213) 617-2128; e-mail info@lachinesechamber.org; internet www.lachinesechamber.org; f. 1955; Pres. CHESTER CHONG.

Colombian-American Association: 30 Vesey St, Suite 506, New York, NY 10007; tel. (212) 233-7776; fax (212) 233-7779; e-mail andean@nyct.net; internet www.colombianamerican.org; f. 1927; 105 mems (2003); Chair. ROBERT A. GRAY; Pres. CHRISTIAN MURRLE.

Colombian American Chamber of Commerce: 250 Catalonia Ave, Suite 407, Coral Gables, FL 33134; tel. (305) 446-2542; fax (305) 446-2038; e-mail info@colombiachamber.com; internet www.colombiachamber.com; Pres. RICARDO TRIBIN.

Croatian-American Chamber of Commerce, Inc (CACC): 50–52 49th St, Woodside, NY 11377; tel. (718) 937-4040; fax (718) 392-6262; e-mail info@croamchamber.org; internet croamchamber.org; f. 1998; Pres. DOMAGOJ KERO; Sec. SANJA FLORICIĆ-BOGOVIĆ.

Cyprus Trade Centre: 13 East 40th St, New York, NY 10016; tel. (212) 213-9100; fax (212) 213-2918; e-mail ctcny@cyprustradeny.com; internet www.cyprustradeny.org; Trade Commr ARISTOS CONSTANTINE.

Czech-North American Chamber of Commerce (Chicago Chapter) (CNACC): c/o Linda Flores, CzechTrade Chicago, Merchandise Mart, Suite 938, Chicago, IL 60654; tel. (312) 644-1790; fax (312) 527 5544; e-mail linda.flores@czechtrade.cz; f. 1998; affiliated to the Canada-Czech Republic Chamber of Commerce; Chair. THOMAS J. BATA; Pres. PETR G. CHADRABA.

Danish-American Chamber of Commerce (DACC): 1 Dag Hammerskjöld Plaza, 885 Second Ave, 18th Floor, New York, NY 10017; tel. (212) 705-4945; fax (212) 754-1904; e-mail daccny@daccny.com; internet www.daccny.com; f. 1980; c. 200 mems; Exec. Dir NARGIS MCGUINNESS.

Ecuadorean American Association, Inc (EAA): 30 Vesey St, Suite 506, New York, NY 10007; tel. (212) 233-7776; fax (212) 233-7779; e-mail info@andean-us.com; internet www.ecuadoreanamerican.org; f. 1932; Pres. JUANA CAICEDO-SELINGER.

European-American Business Council (EABC): 1919 18th Street, NW, Suite 220, Washington, DC 20005; tel. (202) 828-9104; fax (202) 828-9106; e-mail katie@eabc.org; internet www.eabc.org; f. 1990; Pres. and CEO MICHAEL C. MAIBACH.

European-American Chamber of Commerce, San Francisco (EACC): POB 537, San Francisco, CA 94104; tel. (415) 425-0985; e-mail info@eaccsf.org; internet www.eaccsf.org; Pres. HANS J. J. NIEBERGALL.

Federation of Indian Chambers of Commerce and Industry, USA (FICCI): 1050 17th St, NW, Suite 600, Washington, DC 20036; tel. (202) 776-7181; fax (202) 331-8703; e-mail ficciusa@ficci.com; internet www.ficci.com; Asst Sec.-Gen. RANJANA KHANNA.

Finnish-American Chamber of Commerce (FACC): Consulate-General of Finland, 866 United Nations Plaza, Suite 250, New York, NY 10017; tel. (212) 821-0225; fax (212) 750-4418; e-mail neal.beaton@hklaw.com; internet www.facc-ny.com; f. 1948; one Finnish and eight US chapters; 515 mems in USA and Finland; Pres. NEAL BEATON.

French-American Chamber of Commerce in the United States, Inc (FACC): 122 East 42nd St, Suite 2015, New York, NY 10168; tel. (212) 867-0123; fax (212) 867-9050; e-mail info@faccnyc.org; internet www.faccnyc.org; f. 1896; 23 chapters; over 550 mems; Man. Dir MARTIN BISCHOFF.

German-American Chambers of Commerce (GACC): internet www.ahk-usa.com; see individual chambers below:.

German-American Chamber of Commerce of the Midwest, Inc (Chicago) (GACCoM): 401 North Michigan Ave, Suite 3330, Chicago, IL 60611-4212; tel. (312) 644-2662; fax (312) 664-0738; e-mail info@gaccom.org; internet www.gaccom.org; over 700 mems; Pres. and CEO SIMONE POHL.

German-American Chamber of Commerce New York, Inc (GACC): 75 Broad St, 21st Floor, New York, NY 10004; tel. (212) 974-8830; fax (212) 974-8867; e-mail info@gaccny.com; internet www.gaccny.com; f. 1947; 2,100 mems; brs in Philadelphia and San Francisco; Pres. and CEO SIMONE POHL.

German-American Chambers of Commerce of the Southern United States, Inc (GACC South): 530 Means St, Suite 120, Atlanta, GA 30318; tel. (404) 586-6800; fax (404) 586-6820; e-mail info@gaccsouth.com; internet www.gaccsouth.com; over 650 mems; Pres. and CEO KRISTIAN WOLF.

Guatemala-US Trade Association: 300 Sevilla Ave, Suite 210A, Coral Gables, FL 33134; tel. (305) 443-0343; fax (305) 443-0699.

Hellenic-American Chamber of Commerce: Atlantic Bank Bldg, 960 Ave of the Americas, Suite 1008, New York, NY 10001; tel. (212) 629-6380; fax (212) 564-9281; e-mail HellenicChamber-NYC@att.net; internet www.hellenicamerican.cc; f. 1947; 1,853 mems; Pres. JOHN C. STRATAKIS.

Hong Kong Trade Development Council, New York Office: 219 East 46th St, New York, NY 10017; tel. (212) 838-8688; fax (212) 838-8941; e-mail new.york.office@tdc.org.hk; internet info.hktdc.com; f. 1966; Regional Dir STEPHEN WONG; Dir, New York LOUIS HO.

Hungarian-American Chamber of Commerce of New England: 111 Huntington Ave, 26th Floor, Boston, MA 02199; tel. and fax (508) 347-2742; e-mail slengyel@ziprealty.com; internet www.hungarianamericanchamber.com; f. 1994; Pres. SOPHIA LENGYEL.

Innovation Norway: Royal Norwegian Embassy, 2720 34th St, NW, Washington, DC 20008; tel. (202) 333-6000; fax (202) 337-0870; e-mail washington@innovationnorway.no; internet www.innovationnorway.no; f. 1945 as Norwegian Trade Council; name changed to above in 2004; brs in Boston, Houston, New York and San Francisco; Dir KRISTIN DAHLE.

Ireland Chamber of Commerce in the USA, Inc (ICCUSA): 556 Central Ave, New Providence, NJ 07974; tel. (908) 286-1300; fax (908) 286-1200; e-mail larryh@iccusa.org; internet www.iccusa.org; f. 1988; 6 chapters; Pres. and CEO MAURICE A. BUCKLEY.

Italy-American Chamber of Commerce: 730 Fifth Ave, Suite 600, New York, NY 10019; tel. (212) 459-0044; fax (212) 459-0090; e-mail info@italchamber.org; internet www.italchamber.org; f. 1887; 1,150 mems (2003); Pres. ALBERTO COMINI; Sec.-Gen. FRANCO DE ANGELIS.

Italian Trade Commission: 33 East 67th St, New York, NY 10021-5949; tel. (212) 980-1500; fax (212) 758-1050; e-mail newyork@newyork.ice.it; internet www.italtrade.com/countries/americas/usa/newyork.htm; Trade Commr and Exec. Dir ANIELLO MUSELLA.

Japan External Trade Organization (JETRO): internet www.jetro.org; selected chapters listed below, also chapters in Atlanta, Houston, Los Angeles and San Francisco.

JETRO Chicago: 1 East Wacker Dr., Suite 600, Chicago, IL 60601; tel. (312) 832-6000; fax (312) 832-6066; internet www.jetro.org; Chief Exec. Dir MUNEO TAKASHI.

JETRO New York: McGraw Hill Bldg, 1221 Ave of the Americas, 42nd Floor, New York, NY 10020; tel. (212) 997-0400; fax (212) 997-0464; e-mail jetrony@jetro.go.jp; internet www.jetro.org; f. 1958; Pres. MASAHIKO HOSOKAWA.

Japanese Chamber of Commerce and Industry of Chicago (JCCC): 541 North Fairbanks Court, Chicago, IL 60611; tel. (312) 245-8344; fax (312) 245-8355; e-mail jccc@jccc-chi.org; internet www.jccc-chi.org; f. 1966; over 350 corporate mems; Pres. TOSHIYUKI SAKAI.

Japanese Chamber of Commerce and Industry of New York, Inc (JCCI): 145 West 57th St, New York, NY 10019-2288; tel. (212) 246-8001; fax (212) 246-8002; e-mail info@jcciny.org; internet www.jcciny.org; f. 1932; 340 mems (2006); Pres. and CEO YASUNORI YOKOTE.

Japanese Chamber of Commerce of Southern California (JCCSC): 224 South San Pedro St, Suite 504, Los Angeles, CA 90012; tel. (213) 626-3067; fax (213) 626-3070; e-mail office@jccsc.com; internet www.jccsc.com; f. 1951; 205 mems (2006); Pres. TATSUHIKO WAKAO.

Korea Society: 950 Third Ave, 8th Floor, New York, NY 10022; tel. (212) 759-7525; fax (212) 759-7530; e-mail peter.ny@koreasociety.org; internet www.koreasociety.org; f. 1962; 130 mems (2003); Pres. EVANS J. R. REVERE; Vice-Pres. and Exec. Dir FREDERICK F. CARRIERE.

Korea Trade Center (KOTRA): 460 Park Ave, Suite 402, New York, NY 10022; tel. (212) 826-0900; fax (212) 888-4930; e-mail kotrany@hotmail.com; internet english.kotra.or.kr; f. 1962; brs in Chicago, Dallas, Detroit, Los Angeles, Miami, San Francisco and Washington, DC; Pres. JAE-RYANG WOO.

Korean Chamber of Commerce and Industry in the USA, Inc (KOCHAM): 460 Park Ave, Suite 410, New York, NY 10022; tel. (212) 644-0140; fax (212) 644-9106; e-mail webmaster@kocham.org; internet www.kocham.org; f. 1992; over 300 mem. cos; Chair. YEUN-HO SUK.

Korean International Trade Association (KITA): 460 Park Ave, Suite 2200, New York, NY 10022; tel. (212) 421-8804 ext. 26; fax (212) 223-38270; e-mail inquiry@kita.net; internet global.kita.net; f. 1967 in New York; br. in Washington, DC; Chair. and CEO HEE-BEOM LEE.

Lithuanian Business Council (LBC): Lithuanian Consulate, 211 East Ontario St, Suite 1500, Chicago, IL 60611; e-mail aldas.gubaras@lbchicago.org; internet www.lbchicago.org; f. 1999; Pres. ANTANAS GRINA.

Luxembourg American Chamber of Commerce (LACC): 17 Beekman Pl., New York, NY 10022; tel. (212) 888-6701; fax (212) 935-5896; e-mail info@luxembourgbusiness.org; internet www.luxembourgbusiness.org; f. 1991; Dir TONI DUDSAK.

Mexican American Business Chamber (MABC): 5522 New Peachtree Rd, Suite 129, Chamblee, GA 30341; tel. (770) 441-7581; fax (770) 441-7909; e-mail info@mexicanchamber.org; internet www.mexicanchamber.org; Chair. RUDY BESERRA.

National US-Arab Chamber of Commerce (NUSACC): 1023 15th St, NW, Suite 400, Washington, DC 20005; tel. (202) 289-5920; fax (202) 289-5939; e-mail info@nusacc.org; internet www.nusacc.org; brs in Houston, New York and Los Angeles; Pres. and CEO DAVID HAMOD.

Netherlands Chamber of Commerce in the United States (NLCOC): 267 Fifth Ave, Suite 301, New York, NY 10016; tel. (212) 265-6460; fax (212) 265-6402; e-mail newyork@nlcoc.com; internet www.netherlands.org; f. 1903; c. 500 mem. cos; Man. Dir KERSEN J. DE JONG.

North American-Chilean Chamber of Commerce, Inc: 30 Vesey St, Suite 506, New York, NY 10007; tel. (212) 233-7776; fax (212) 233-7779; f. 1934; Exec. Dir DAVID SPENCER.

Norwegian-American Chamber of Commerce, Inc (NACC): 655 Third Ave, Suite 1810, New York, NY 10017; tel. (212) 421-1655; fax (212) 838-0374; e-mail shipping@ntcny.org; internet www.naccusa.org; f. 1915; chapters in Chicago, Houston, Los Angeles, Miami, Minneapolis, Seattle and Washington, DC; Pres. LAWRENCE RUTKOWSKI; Exec. Vice-Pres. BLAINE COLLINS.

Peruvian-American Chamber of Commerce: 8181 NW 14 St, Suite 250, Miami, FL 33126; tel. (305) 477-5483; fax (305) 436-1953; e-mail jvalderrama@perusachamber.com; internet www.peruvianchamber.org; over 300 mems and assocs (2006); Pres. ORLANDO LOLI.

Polish-American Chamber of Commerce of the Southeast United States (PACC): Bank of America Tower, 600 Peachtree St, Suite 4100, ICO/Hunton & Williams, Atlanta, GA 30303; tel. (404) 724-4500; fax (404) 633-9936; e-mail contact@csicorp-usa.com; internet www.pacc-south.com; Pres. WITOLD ZABINSKI.

Portuguese Trade Commission: 590 Fifth Ave, 3rd Floor, New York, NY 10036; tel. (212) 354-4610; fax (212) 575-4737; e-mail webmaster@portugal.org; internet www.portugal.org; Dir EDUARDO SOUTO MOURA.

Puerto Rican Chamber of Commerce of Illinois (PRCCI): 2622 West Division St, Chicago, IL 60622; tel. (773) 486-1331; fax (773) 486-1340; e-mail information@prcci.com; internet www.prcci.com; f. 1963; Pres. XAVIER NOGUERAS; Vice-Pres. EDUARDO PADRO.

Representative of German Industry and Trade: 1776 I St, NW, Suite 1000, Washington, DC 20006; tel. (202) 659-4777; fax (202) 659-4779; e-mail info@rgit-usa.com; internet www.rgit-usa.com; represents the Federation of German Industries and the Asscn of German Chambers of Industry and Commerce; Pres. BERNHARD WELSCHKE.

Spain-United States Chamber of Commerce: 350 Fifth Ave, Empire State Bldg, Suite 2600, New York, NY 10118; tel. (212) 967-2170; fax (212) 564-1415; e-mail info@spainuscc.org; internet www.spainuscc.org; f. 1959; 423 mems (2007); Exec. Dir BISILA BOKOKO; Chair. MARIO DÍAZ-CRUZ, III.

Swedish-American Chambers of Commerce (USA), Inc: 1403 King St, Alexandria, VA 22314; tel. (703) 836-6560; fax (703) 836-6561; e-mail info@sacc-usa.org; internet www.sacc-usa.org; f. 1906; comprises 19 regional chambers; over 2,300 mems in the USA and Sweden; Pres. GUNILLA GIRARDO.

Swedish Trade Council: 150 North Michigan Ave, Suite 1950, Chicago, IL 60601; tel. (312) 781-6222; fax (312) 276-8606; e-mail usa@swedishtrade.se; internet www.swedishtrade.com/usa; f. 1949; offices in Chicago, Los Angeles and New York; Trade Commr STEFAN BERGSTRÖM.

Swiss-American Chamber of Commerce (New York Chapter): 500 Fifth Ave, Rm 1800, New York, NY 10110; tel. (212) 246-7789; fax (212) 246-1366; e-mail newyork@amcham.ch; internet www.amcham.ch/chamber/m_ny_chapter.asp; chapters in Los Angeles, San Francisco, Florida, Georgia and North Carolina; Chair. JAMES E. ODELL.

Trade Commission of Denmark in Atlanta (Danish Trade Council): 1 Piedmont Center, 3565 Piedmont Rd, Suite 400, Atlanta, GA 30305; tel. (404) 588-1588; fax (678) 904-9714; e-mail atlhkt@um.dk; internet www.dtcatlanta.um.dk; Trade Commr JAN SAUER.

United States-Angola Chamber of Commerce: 1100 17th St, NW, Suite 1100A, Washington, DC 20036; tel. (202) 223-0540; fax (202) 223-0551; e-mail contactus@us-angola.org; internet www.us-angola.org; f. 1991; over 90 mem. cos; Exec. Dir MARIA DA CRUZ; Chair. SIMEON MOATS.

United States-Japan Business Council (USJBC): 2000 L St, NW, Suite 515, Washington, DC 20036; tel. (202) 728-0068; fax (202) 728-0073; internet www.usjbc.org; 70 mems; Chair. JEFFREY KINDLER.

United States-Mexico Chamber of Commerce (USMCOC): 1300 Pennsylvania Ave, NW, Suite G-0003, Washington, DC 20004-3021; tel. (202) 312-1520; fax (202) 312-1530; e-mail news-hq@usmcoc.org; internet www.usmcoc.org; f. 1973; 13,000 mems; Pres. and CEO ALBERT C. ZAPANTA; 7 chapters in the USA, incl.:

California Pacific Chapter (USMCOCCA): 2450 Colorado Ave, Suite 400E, Santa Monica, CA 90404; tel. (310) 586-7901; fax (310) 586-7800; e-mail info@usmcocca.org; internet www.usmcocca.org; f. 1980; Pres. LETVIA ARZA-GODERICH; Exec. Dir MARLEN MARROQUÍN GATI.

Northeast Chapter (USMCOCNE): 1540 Broadway, Suite 1400, New York, NY, 10036-4086; tel. (212) 471-4704; fax (212) 471-4701; e-mail northeast@usmcocne.org; internet www.usmcocne.org; Pres. EDUARDO RAMOS-GÓMEZ; Exec. Dir ALEJANDRO RAMOS.

US-ASEAN Business Council: 1101 17th St, NW, Suite 411, Washington, DC 20036; tel. (202) 289-1911; fax (202) 289-0519; e-mail mail@usasean.org; internet www.us-asean.org; f. 1978 as US-ASEAN Trade Council; 108 mems (2007); Chair. (vacant); Pres. MATTHEW DALEY.

US-Austrian Chamber of Commerce: 165 West 46th St, New York, NY 10036; tel. (212) 819-0117; fax (212) 819-0345; e-mail memberservices@usatchamber.com; internet www.usatchamber.com; f. 1949; 200 mems (2003); Pres. JOHANNES P. HOFER.

US-Cuba Trade and Economic Council, Inc: 30 Rockefeller Plaza, New York, NY 10112-0002; tel. (212) 246-1444; fax (212) 246-2345; e-mail council@cubatrade.org; internet www.cubatrade.org; f. 1994.

US Federation of Philippine American Chambers of Commerce, Inc (FPACC): 2887 College Ave No. 1, Box 106, Berkeley, CA 94705; tel. (510) 664-9952; fax (510) 841-5008; e-mail president@fpacc.com; internet www.fpacc.com; f. 1997; 42 chapters; over 5,000 mem. cos; Pres. YOLANDA ORTEGA STERN.

Filipino-American Chamber of Commerce of San Diego County: POB 87202, San Diego, CA 92138; tel. (619) 733-4156; e-mail info@faccsd.com; internet www.faccsd.com; f. 1985; Pres. MYRNA REYES.

Philippine American Chamber of Commerce of Arizona: Century 21 Arizona Foothills, 17235 North 75th Ave, Suite D-120, Glendale, AZ 85308; tel. (602) 549-1011; e-mail info@paccaz.com; internet www.paccaz.com; Pres. ETHEL LUZARIO.

US-Russia Business Council (USRBC): 1110 Vermont Ave, NW, Suite 350, Washington, DC 20005; tel. (202) 739-9180; fax (202) 659-5920; e-mail info@usrbc.org; internet www.usrbc.org; f. 1993; 300 mem. cos; Pres. and CEO EDWARD S. VERONA.

US-Saudi Arabian Business Council (USSABC): 8081 Wolftrap Rd, Suite 300, Vienna, VA 22182; tel. (703) 962-9300; fax (703) 204-0332; e-mail ussaudi@us-sabc.org; internet www.us-sabc.org; f. 1993; Co-Chairs Sheikh ABDULAZIZ AL-QURAISHI, PETER J. ROBERTSON; Pres. and Man. Dir EDWARD BURTON.

DIRECTORY ON SOCIETY

BROADCASTING

INTRODUCTION

The USA constitutes the world's biggest market for communications and broadcasting systems. In 2004 radio sets were in use in 99% of homes and in 2007 there were an estimated 311m. television receivers in use. There were 6,635 cable systems in operation in the same year, serving an estimated 64.9m. basic cable subscribers. In 2008 78.7% of households with television receivers used video cassette recorders.

Radio and Television

In 2004 there were 10,987 licensed commercial AM and FM radio stations operating in the USA. In 2004 the average US household had 8.0 radio sets in use.

In 2007 commercial television stations numbered 1,364; there were 357 public television stations, operated by 176 licensees, in the same year. The average US household had 2.8 television sets in use in January 2007. The USA has the highest ratio of radio and television receivers per head of population of any country in the world.

President Bill Clinton signed into law the Telecommunications Act in February 1996. The Act lifted restrictions and allowed companies to own more than 12 television stations and 20 AM band and 20 FM band radio stations. It required that all new television sets be fitted with a so-called 'v-chip', which would permit parents to block out programmes they considered unsuitable viewing for their children. It also abolished rate caps for cable companies with the exception of restrictions on charges for basic services.

Regulatory Bodies

Telecommunications services are regulated within individual states by the state public utility commissions (see chapter on the States of the Union and the District of Columbia, below). The Federal Communications Commission (FCC) was established under the Communications Act of 1934 to regulate all interstate and international communications by radio, television, wire and cable, 'in the public interest'. Its responsibilities were extended under the Communications Satellite Act of 1962. In October 2004 the FCC announced plans to end analogue broadcasting by the end of 2006, on the basis that 85% of US viewers would have converted to digital television sets by that time. Legislation was subsequently passed by Congress in February 2006 extending the transitional period to 17 February 2009, when all analogue broadcasting would cease.

Federal Communications Commission (FCC): 445 12th St, SW, Washington, DC 20554; tel. (202) 418-0200; fax (202) 418-0232; e-mail fccinfo@fcc.gov; internet www.fcc.gov; f. 1934; regulates inter-state and foreign communications by radio, television, wire and cable; Chair. Kevin J. Martin.

Television Usage in Households, 2005–07

('000, as at 1 January)

	2005	2006	2007
Television sets in use . . .	287,000	301,380	310,840
Households with a television .	109,600	110,200	111,400
Households with more than one television	86,620	89,470	91,900

2008: Households with a television 112,800; Households with more than one television 93,010.
Households with cable television: 74,430 in 2003; 73,860 in 2004; 73,930 in 2005.

Source: Television Bureau of Advertising, New York.

RADIO AND TELEVISION

Radio

DOMESTIC NETWORKS

ABC Radio Networks (American Broadcasting Company Radio Networks): 13725 Montfort Dr., Dallas, TX 75240; tel. (972) 991-9200; fax (214) 991-1071; e-mail omar.thompson@citcomm.com; internet www.abcradionetworks.com; f. 1944; fmrly wholly owned subsidiary of The Walt Disney Company; ABC Radio Business, as a spin-off concern of The Walt Disney Co, merged a wholly owned subsidiary of Citadel Broadcasting Corpn in June 2007; 4,500 affiliated radio stations broadcasting five full service line networks; Pres. James Robinson.

American Urban Radio Networks (AURN): 432 Park Ave, South, 14th Floor, New York, NY 10016; tel. (212) 883-2100; fax (212) 297-2571; e-mail jay@aurn.com; internet www.aurnol.com; serves over 300 stations; sole African-American-owned network radio co in the USA; Pres. E. J. (Jay) Williams.

CBS RADIO: CBS RADIO, 1515 Broadway, New York, NY 10036; tel. (212) 846-3939; internet www.cbsradio.com; f. 1928; fmrly Infinity Broadcasting; renamed as CBS Radio; division of CBS Corpn; owns CBS Radio Network serving more than 1,500 radio stations; operates 144 radio stations; Pres. and CEO Dan Mason.

Clear Channel Radio: 200 East Basse Rd, San Antonio, TX 78209; tel. (210) 822-2828; e-mail lisacdollinger@clearchannel.com; internet www.clearchannel.com/radio; c. 1,000 radio stations; Pres. and Chief Financial Officer Randall Mays; CEO Mark Mays.

CNN Radio Network: Turner Broadcasting, 1 CNN Center, NW, Atlanta, Georgia 30303-2762; tel. (404) 827-1700; fax (404) 827-1906; e-mail jerry.demink@turner.com; internet www.cnnradio.com; f. 1982; serves 2,000 stations world-wide; subsidiary of Time Warner; Vice Pres., News Services Jerry DeMink.

Educational Broadcasting Corporation (EBC): c/o Thirteen/WNET, 450 West 33rd St, New York, NY 10001; tel. (212) 560-1313; fax (212) 560-1314; e-mail programming@thirteen.org; internet www.thirteen.org; licensee of public broadcasters Thirteen/WNET, and WLIW New York; Pres. Neal Shapiro; CEO William F. Baker.

Moody Broadcasting Network (MBN): 820 North LaSalle Blvd, Chicago, IL 60610; tel. and fax (312) 329-4433; e-mail mbn@moody.edu; internet www.mbn.org; f. 1982; ministry of the Moody Bible Institute; owns and operates 35 radio stations nationally, serving 400 radio affiliates; has over 740 satellite-fed outlets; Vice-Pres. Wayne Pederson.

National Public Radio (NPR): 635 Massachusetts Ave, NW, Washington, DC 20001; tel. (202) 513-2300; fax (202) 513-3329; e-mail achristopher@npr.org; internet www.npr.org; f. 1970; private non-profit corpn providing programmes and support facilities to over 800 mem. stations nation-wide; also operates a global programme distribution service by radio, cable and satellite; Chair. Antoine W. van Agtmael; Pres. Kevin Klose.

Premiere Radio Networks, Inc: 15260 Ventura Blvd, 5th Floor, Sherman Oaks, CA 91403; tel. (818) 377-5300; fax (818) 377-5333; e-mail aforester@premiereradio.com; internet www.premrad.com; f. 1987; subsidiary of Clear Channel Communications; provides 90 radio programmes and services to more than 4,600 radio affiliations; Pres. Charlie Rahilly.

Public Radio International: 100 North Sixth St, Suite 900A, Minneapolis, MN 55403; tel. (612) 338-5000; fax (612) 330-9222;

internet www.pri.org; f. 1983 as American Public Radio; present name adopted 1994; serves almost 800 public radio stations via satellite; Pres. and CEO ALISA MILLER.

United Stations Radio Network (USRN): 1065 Ave of the Americas, 3rd Floor, New York, NY 10018; tel. (212) 869-1111; fax (212) 869-1115; internet www.unitedstations.com; fmrly Unistar Radio Network, merged with Westwood One in 1993; United Stations Radio Network created separately in 1994; provides services to over 600 stations; Chair. and CEO NICHOLAS J. VERBITSKY; Pres. and COO JAMES M. HIGGINS.

Univision Radio: Citigate Sard Verbinnen, 630 Third Ave, New York, NY 10017; tel. (212) 687-8080; e-mail publicrelations@univision.net; internet www.univision.com; completed acquisition of Hispanic Broadcasting Co in 2003; Spanish language broadcasting; owns and/or programmes 70 radio stations nation-wide and 5 in Puerto Rico; CEO JOE UVA; Pres. and COO RAY RODRIGUEZ.

USA Radio Network, Inc: 2290 Springlake Rd, Suite 107, Dallas, TX 75234; tel. (972) 484-3900; fax (972) 243-3489; e-mail mark@usaradio.com; internet www.usaradio.com; news and information programmes carried by 1,100 affiliates; also broadcasts on short-wave and to US Armed Forces Radio; Pres. MARK MADDOUX.

Wall Street Journal Radio Network/Dow Jones Radio Network: 1155 Ave of the Americas, 8th Floor, New York, NY 10036; tel. (212) 659-1908; fax (212) 659-1208; e-mail patrice.sikora@dowjones.com; internet www.wsjradio.com; over 250 affiliates; Exec. Dir NANCY ABRAMSON; Man. Editor PATRICE SIKORA.

Westwood One Inc: 40 West 57th St, 5th Floor, New York, NY 10019; tel. (212) 641-2000; e-mail david_hillman@westwoodone.com; internet www.westwoodone.com; f. 1934; managed by CBS Radio, Inc, fmrly Infinity Broadcasting Corpn; subsidiary of Viacom, Inc; largest domestic outsource provider of traffic reporting services, broadcasting to 7,700 radio stations; produces and distributes national news, sports, talk, music and special event programmes, in addition to local news, sports, weather and other information programming; operates BLAISE, CBS, CNN Max, Navigator, NBC, NeXt, Source Max and WONE radio networks; Pres. and CEO TOM BEUSSE.

EXTERNAL RADIO SERVICES

American Forces Radio and Television Service/American Forces Network (AFRTS/AFN): Defense Media Center (DMC), AFN Broadcast Center, 23755 Z St, Riverside, CA 92518; tel. (951) 413-2319; fax (951) 413-2227; e-mail larry.sichter@dodmedia.osd.mil; internet www.myafn.net; f. 1942; operated by Dept of Defense; provides encrypted US radio and TV programming in English exclusively to US military and Dept of Defense civilian personnel in 177 countries, US territories and aboard US Navy ships; Exec. Dir JEFFREY WHITE (DMC); Dir MELVIN RUSSELL (AFRTS).

RFE/RL (Radio Free Europe/Radio Liberty): 1201 Connecticut Ave, NW, Suite 1100, Washington, DC 20036; tel. (202) 457-6900; fax (202) 457-6992; e-mail jensend@rferl.org; internet www.rferl.org; f. 1950; private, non-profit corpn financed by the federal Govt; broadcasts from Prague, Czech Republic, to Eastern and South-Eastern Europe, Russia, the Caucasus, the Middle East, Central and South-West Asia; c. 1,000 hours weekly in 28 languages; Chair. JAMES K. GLASSMAN; Pres. JEFFREY GEDMIN.

Voice of America: 330 Independence Ave, SW, Washington, DC 20237; tel. (202) 203-4959; fax (202) 203-4960; e-mail askvoa@voanews.com; internet www.voanews.com; f. 1942; govt-funded; broadcasts c. 1,000 hours weekly in 45 languages to all areas of the world via radio, television and the internet; Dir DANFORTH W. AUSTIN.

Television

NETWORKS

ABC, Inc (American Broadcasting Co, Inc): 500 South Buena Vista St, Burbank, CA 91521-4551; tel. (818) 460-7477; e-mail netaudr@abc.com; internet abc.go.com; f. 1953; subsidiary of the Walt Disney Co since 1996; 10 owned and 226 affiliated stations; production through Touchstone Television and Disney television content distribution through Buena Vista Television; Pres., ABC-owned Television Stations WALTER C. LISS; Pres., Disney-ABC TV Group ANNE SWEENEY.

American Public Television: 55 Summer St, Boston, MA 02110; tel. (617) 338-4455; fax (617) 338-5369; e-mail info@aptonline.org; internet www.aptonline.org; Pres. and CEO CYNTHIA FENNEMAN.

C-SPAN (Cable-Satellite Public Affairs Network): 400 North Capitol St, Suite 650, Washington, DC 20001; tel. (202) 737-3220; e-mail viewer@c-span.org; internet www.c-span.org; private, non-profit public service; earns its operating revenues through licence fees paid by cable and satellite systems offering the network to their customers; Chair. and CEO BRIAN LAMB; Co-Pres SUSAN SWAIN, ROBERT KENNEDY.

CBS Television Network (Columbia Broadcasting System Television Network): 51 West 52nd St, New York, NY 10019-6188; tel. (212) 975-4321; internet www.cbs.com; f. 1928; subsidiary of CBS Corpn; serves more than 200 affiliated stations; parent CBS Corpn subsidiary, CBS Television Stations Group, operates 39 stations, incl. 21 CBS, 11 The CW, 3 MyNetworkTV and 4 independents; CBS Corpn Pres. and CEO LESLIE MOONVES; Chair. SUMNER REDSTONE.

CNN (Cable News Network): 1 CNN Center, POB 105366, Atlanta, GA 30348; tel. (404) 827-1700; fax (404) 827-1099; e-mail public.information@turner.com; internet www.cnn.com; subsidiary of Time Warner; Pres. JONATHAN KLEIN; Pres., CNN News Group JIM WALTON.

FOX Broadcasting Co: 10201 West Pico Blvd, Los Angeles, CA 90035; tel. (310) 369-3553; e-mail scott.grogin@fox.com; internet www.fox.com; f. 1986; subsidiary of News Corpn; more than 900 cable affiliations; Pres. KEVIN REILLY; Chair. PETER LIGUORI.

NBC Universal Television Stations: 30 Rockefeller Plaza, New York, NY 10112; tel. (212) 664-4444; fax (212) 664-5830; internet www.nbcuni.com; f. 1926; subsidiary of NBC Universal; 27 owned and over 200 affiliated stations; Pres. and CEO, NBC Universal JEFF ZUCKER.

PBS (Public Broadcasting Service): 2100 Crystal Dr, Arlington, VA 22202; tel. (703) 739-5000; fax (703) 739-0775; e-mail viewer@pbs.org; internet www.pbs.org; f. 1969; non-profit-making; financed by private subscriptions and federal govt funds; owned and operated by the 355 public US television stations; Pres. and CEO PAULA KERGER; COO WAYNE GODWIN.

Time Warner Cable, Inc (TWC): 290 Harbor Dr., Stamford, CT 06902-6732; tel. (203) 364-8203; fax (203) 328-0690; internet www.timewarnercable.com; cable television system serving c. 14.7m. subscribers in 33 states; acquired part of Adelphia Communications in 2005; 84% owned by Time Warner; Pres. and CEO GLENN A. BRITT; Chair. DON LOGAN.

Univision Network: 9405 North West 41st St, Miami, FL 33178-2301; tel. (305) 471-3900; fax (305) 471-4065; internet www.univision.com; subsidiary of Univision Communications, Inc; acquired by Broadcasting Media Partners Inc, group of private equity investors, in March 2007; Spanish-language television network; Pres. JOE UVA.

BROADCASTING ASSOCIATIONS

Associated Press (Broadcast Services): AP Broadcast News Center, 1100 13th St, Suite 700, Washington, DC 20005; tel. (202) 736-1108; fax (202) 736-1107; e-mail info@ap.org; internet www.apbroadcast.com; f. 1848; co-operative owned by and serving 1,700 daily newspapers, and more than 1,000 media web sites and 4,500 television and radio stations; 8,500 mems in 121 countries; 50 state groups; Pres. ED QUINN; Deputy Dir and Man. Editor BRAD KALBFELD, III.

Association of Public Television Stations (APTS): 2100 Crystal Dr., Suite 700, Arlington, VA 22202; tel. (202) 654-4200; fax (202) 654-4236; e-mail jeffrey@apts.org; internet www.apts.org; f. 1980 as Asscn of America's Public Television Stations; 146 mems; Pres. and CEO MARK ERSTLING (acting).

Broadcasting Board of Governors (BBG): 330 Independence Ave, SW, Washington, DC 20237; tel. (202) 203-4400; fax (202) 203-4585; e-mail publicaffairs@bbg.gov; internet www.bbg.gov; f. 1999; independent, autonomous entity responsible for all US govt and govt-sponsored, non-military international broadcasting; Exec. Dir JEFFREY N. TRIMBLE.

Corporation for Public Broadcasting (CPB): 401 Ninth St, NW, Washington, DC 20004-2129; tel. (202) 879-9600; fax (202) 879-9700; e-mail press@cpb.org; internet www.cpb.org; f. 1967; a non-profit, non-governmental agency; aims to promote and finance more than 1,000 non-commercial radio and television stations; Chair. CHRIS BOSKIN; Pres. and CEO PATRICIA DE STACY HARRISON.

National Association of Broadcasters (NAB): 1771 N St, NW, Washington, DC 20036; tel. (202) 429-5300; fax (202) 429-4199; e-mail nab@nab.org; internet www.nab.org; f. 1922; trade asscn of radio and TV stations and networks; 8,300 mems; Chair. JOHN L. (JACK) SANDER; Pres. and CEO DAVID K. REHR.

National Cable and Telecommunications Association (NCTA): 25 Massachusetts Ave, NW, Suite 100, Washington, DC 20001-1413; tel. (202) 222-2300; e-mail webmaster@ncta.com; internet www.ncta.com; f. 1952 as Nat. Cable Television Asscn; represents cable operators for over 90% of customers and over 200 cable program networks; internet and digital telephone service provider; c. 3,100 mems; Pres. and CEO KYLE MCSLARROW.

THE PRESS

INTRODUCTION

The USA publishes more newspapers and periodicals than any other country. Most dailies place a greater emphasis on local news because of the strong interest in local and regional affairs and the decentralized structure of many government services. These factors, together with the challenges of distribution in such a large country, are responsible for the lack of national newspapers. According to the Newspaper Association of America (NAA), an estimated 48.4% of the adult population read a daily newspaper in 2007.

In 1982 the first national general interest newspaper, *USA Today*, with editorial headquarters near Washington, DC, was introduced by Gannett. An international edition was launched in 1984. Most influential and highly respected among other newspapers with a national readership are *The Wall Street Journal* (the financial and news daily with editions in New York City, California, Illinois and Texas, as well as European and Asian editions), *The New York Times* (which introduced a national edition in 1980), *Los Angeles Times* and *The Washington Post*. In 2008, according to the Audit Bureau of Circulations, 53 daily newspapers had circulations of more than 250,000 copies. Among the largest of daily newspapers in 2008, in order of largest reported daily circulation, were *USA Today* (2,284,219), *The Wall Street Journal* (2,069,463), *The New York Times* (1,476,400), *Los Angeles Times* (1,101,981), *Chicago Tribune* (898,703), *The Washington Post* (890,163), *New York Daily News* (704,157), *New York Post* (702,488), *Houston Chronicle* (632,797) and *The Philadelphia Inquirer* (630,665).

According to the NAA, in 2007 there were 1,422 daily newspapers, with a total circulation of some 50,742,000 copies per day. The Sunday edition is an important and distinctive feature of US newspaper publishing; many Sunday newspapers run to over 300 pages. In 2007 there were 907 Sunday newspapers, with a total circulation of about 51,246,000. In 2005 6,659 weekly papers, with a total circulation of 49,541,617, were published.

A total of 13,846 periodicals were published in the USA in 2001. In 2002 10 magazines achieved a total average paid circulation of more than 4m. copies: in order, these were *Reader's Digest*, *TV Guide*, *Better Homes and Gardens*, *National Geographic Magazine*, *Good Housekeeping*, *Family Circle*, *Woman's Day*, *My Generation* (now *AARP The Magazine*), *Time* and *Ladies' Home Journal*.

The famous tradition of press freedom in the USA is ensured by the First Amendment to the Constitution, which declares that 'Congress shall make no law... abridging the freedom of speech or of the Press...', and confirmed in the legislations of many states, which prohibit any kind of legal restriction on the dissemination of news.

Legislation affecting the press is both state and federal. A source of controversy between the press and the courts has been the threat of the encroachment by judicial decrees on the area of courtroom and criminal trial coverage. In 1972 the Supreme Court ruled that journalists were not entitled to refuse to give evidence before grand juries on information received confidentially. Since then the frequent issuing of subpoenas to journalists and the imprisonment of several reporters for refusing to disclose sources has led to many 'shield' bills being presented to Congress and state legislatures urging immunity for journalists from both federal and state jurisdiction.

STATISTICS

Daily and Sunday Newspapers by State

SUMMARY

	Daily		Sunday	
	Number (as at 1 February 2006)	Net paid circulation ('000, as at 30 September 2006)*	Number (as at 1 February 2006)	Net paid circulation ('000, as at 30 September 2006)*
Alabama	25	604	21	673
Alaska	7	103	5	114
Arizona	16	721	11	822
Arkansas	28	453	16	523
California	86	5,177	57	5,297
Colorado	30	950	16	1,089
Connecticut	17	630	13	708
Delaware	2	128	2	156
District of Columbia	3	1,017	2	972
Florida	40	3,020	37	3,637
Georgia	35	966	30	1,214
Hawaii	6	266	6	294
Idaho	12	210	8	227
Illinois	66	2,125	32	2,337
Indiana	67	1,235	25	1,180
Iowa	37	576	13	613
Kansas	41	384	13	336
Kentucky	24	583	14	586
Louisiana	24	682	18	748
Maine	7	218	4	182
Maryland	11	465	8	607
Massachusetts	32	1,350	16	1,291
Michigan	48	1,563	27	1,769
Minnesota	25	825	15	1,058
Mississippi	23	350	19	351
Missouri	42	888	21	1,074
Montana	11	184	7	185
Nebraska	16	388	6	372
Nevada	8	292	4	316
New Hampshire	11	205	8	206
New Jersey	18	1,186	15	1,458
New Mexico	17	266	12	275
New York	60	6,832	38	5,026
North Carolina	47	1,232	39	1,362
North Dakota	10	150	7	157

—*continued*	Daily: Number (as at 1 February 2006)	Daily: Net paid circulation ('000, as at 30 September 2006)*	Sunday: Number (as at 1 February 2006)	Sunday: Net paid circulation ('000, as at 30 September 2006)*
Ohio	84	2,155	41	2,379
Oklahoma	39	571	31	701
Oregon	19	630	12	658
Pennsylvania	80	2,526	43	2,953
Rhode Island	6	196	3	238
South Carolina	16	586	14	678
South Dakota	11	150	4	130
Tennessee	26	819	19	966
Texas	82	2,644	77	3,339
Utah	6	332	6	367
Vermont	8	107	3	81
Virginia	23	3,146	17	929
Washington	22	952	16	1,084
West Virginia	20	373	14	385
Wisconsin	34	827	17	1,001
Wyoming	9	88	5	73
Total	1,437	52,329	907	53,175

* Circulation figures based on the principal community served by a newspaper, which is not necessarily the same location as the publisher's office.
Source: *2008 Editor & Publisher International Year Book* (copyright).

NATIONAL NEWSPAPER GROUPS

In the late 20th century, particularly, increased production costs subjected the industry to considerable economic pressure, resulting in mergers and takeovers, a great decline in competition between dailies in the same city, and the appearance of inter-city dailies catering for two or more adjoining centres. A consequence of these trends was the steady growth of newspaper groups or chains.

The following are among the principal daily newspaper groups:

Advance Publications, Inc: 950 Fingerboard Rd, Staten Island; tel. (212) 286-2860; fax (718) 981-1456; internet www.advance.net; Chair. Samuel I. (Si) Newhouse, Jr; Pres. Donald E. Newhouse; interests in cable television and internet news websites; owns Condé Nast Publications, Parade Publications, Fairchild Publications and American City Business Journals, among others.

American Community Newspapers: 14875 Landmark Blvd, Suite 110, Dallas, TX 75254; tel. (972) 628-4080; fax (972) 801-3496; e-mail gcarr@acnpapers.com; internet www.americancommunitynewspapers.com; CEO Gene M. Carr; 100 publs, incl. the Sun Newspapers group, and four speciality publs; combined circ. c. 1.4m.

Block Communications, Inc (BCI): 6450 Monroe St, Sylvania, OH 43560; tel. (419) 724-6212; e-mail info@blockcommunications.com; internet www.blockcommunications.com; f. 1900; Chair. William Block, Jr; Man. Dir Allan Block; 2 daily newspapers, *The Pittsburgh Post-Gazette* and *The Toledo Blade*; also owns 2 cable cos, 5 television stations and a telephone co; interests in security, cable construction and advertising.

Cox Newspapers, Inc: 6205 Peachtree Dunwoody Rd, Atlanta, GA 30328; tel. (678) 645-0000; e-mail christopher.caneles@coxinc.com; internet www.coxnews.com; f. 1898; Pres. Sandy Schwartz; 17 daily newspapers, incl. *The Atlanta Journal-Constitution*, and 26 weekly newspapers; combined weekday circ. 1.2m., combined Sun. circ. 1.6m.

Dow Jones & Co Inc: 1 World Financial Center, 200 Liberty St, New York, NY 10281; tel. (212) 416-2000; fax (212) 416-3478; internet www.dowjones.com; f. 1882; acquired by News Corporation in December 2007; CEO Les Hinton; publs incl. *The Wall Street Journal*, the weekly financial magazine *Barron's* and the monthly *Far Eastern Economic Review*; also incl. the community newspaper subsidiary.

Ottaway Newspapers, Inc (ONI): POB 401, Campbell Hall, NY 10916; tel. (845) 294-8181; e-mail dwaterman@ottaway.com; internet www.ottaway.com; f. 1936; merged with Dow Jones in 1970; Pres. and CEO Andrew Langhoff; 8 daily, and 15 weekly newspapers; over 20 other publs; daily print circ. 282,000, Sun. circ. 316,000 (Oct 2008).

Freedom Communications, Inc: 17666 Fitch, Irvine, CA 92614-6022; tel. (949) 253-2300; fax (949) 474-7675; e-mail info@link.freedom.com; internet www.freedom.com; Chair. Thomas W. Bassett; CEO Scott N. Flanders; 33 daily newspapers, incl. *The Orange County Register*, and 77 weekly publs; combined weekday circ. c. 1m.; owns 8 television stations.

Gannett Co Inc: 7950 Jones Branch Dr., McLean, VA 22107; tel. (703) 854-6000; fax (703) 854-2046; e-mail gcishare@gannett.com; internet www.gannett.com; f. 1906; Chair., Pres. and CEO Craig A. Dubow; 85 daily newspapers incl. *USA Today, Detroit Free Press* and *The Arizona Republic*, c. 900 non-daily publs; combined weekday circ. 7.2m. (of which c. 2.3m. *USA Today*); owns 23 television stations broadcasting to 20m. households; owns and operates Newsquest Media Group (United Kingdom).

Hearst Corpn: Hearst Tower, 12th Floor, 300 West 57th St, New York, NY 10019; tel. (212) 649-4190; fax (212) 649-2108; e-mail hearstnewspapers@hearst.com; internet www.hearstcorp.com; acquired Prime Time, Inc (publr, San Antonio region) in late 2006; Chair. George R. Hearst, Jr; Vice-Chair. and CEO Frank A. Bennack, Jr; 16 daily newspapers, incl. the *Houston Chronicle* and *San Francisco Chronicle*, and 7 weekly newspapers; 18 monthly magazines incl. *Good Housekeeping*, *Cosmopolitan*, *O, The Oprah Magazine* and *Redbook*; owns or operates 26 television stations broadcasting to 18% of the US market; interests in radio broadcasting, cable networks, interactive media and business information publishing.

Lee Enterprises: 201 North Harrison St, Davenport, IA 52801-1939; tel. (563) 383-2100; e-mail information@lee.net; internet www.lee.net; f. 1890; Chair., Pres. and CEO Mary E. Junck; 49 daily newspapers (jt interest in further 4 dailies) and more than 300 weekly newspapers and speciality publs; combined weekday circ. 1.6m., combined Sunday circ. 1.9m.; interests in publishing and purchasing and distribution of raw materials.

The McClatchy Co: 2100 Q St, Sacramento, CA 95816-6899; tel. (916) 321-1855; fax (916) 321-1869; e-mail contact@mcclatchy.com; internet www.mcclatchy.com; acquired Knight Ridder in 2006; established 10 foreign news bureaux in that year; sold largest daily *Star Tribune* to Avista Capital Partners (New York) in early 2007; Chair., Pres. and CEO Gary B. Pruitt; 31 daily newspapers, incl. the *Miami Herald*, and community newspapers.

Media General, Inc: 333 East Franklin St, Richmond, VA 23219; tel. (804) 649-6000; e-mail etucker@mediageneral.com; internet www.mediageneral.com; Chair. J. Stewart Bryan, III; Pres. and CEO Marshall N. Morton; 25 daily newspapers, incl. *The Tampa Tribune*, and c. 150 weekly newspapers and other publs; holds a 20% interest in *The Denver Post*; owns 20 network-affiliated television stations.

MediaNews Group: 101 Colfax Ave, Suite 1100, Denver, CO 80202; tel. (303) 954-6360; fax (303) 954-6320; e-mail contact@medianewsgroup.com; internet www.medianewsgroup.com; Vice-Chair. and CEO William Dean Singleton; Pres. Joseph J. Lodovic, IV; 54 daily newspapers incl. *The Denver Post* (under a jt operating agreement with *The Rocky Mountain News*, publ. by E. W. Scripps); combined weekday circ. 2.4m., combined Sun. circ. 2.7m.; owns a television station in Anchorage, AK and radio stations in Texas.

New York Times Co: 620 Eighth Ave, New York, NY 10018; tel. (212) 556-1234; internet www.nytco.com; Chair. Arthur Sulzber-

GER, Jr; Pres. and CEO JANET L. ROBINSON; 18 daily newspapers incl. *The New York Times*, *The International Herald Tribune* and *The Boston Globe*; owns one radio station and c. 50 internet websites; sold Broadcast Media Group to Oak Hill Capital Partners in May 2007.

E. W. Scripps Co: 312 Walnut St, 2800 Scripps Center, Cincinnati, OH 45202; POB 5380, Cincinnati, OH 45201; tel. (513) 977-3000; fax (513) 977-3721; e-mail corpcomm@scripps.com; internet www.scripps.com; Pres. and CEO KENNETH W. LOWE; Exec. Vice-Pres. and COO RICHARD A. BOEHNE; 21 daily newspapers, incl. *The Rocky Mountain News* (under a jt operating agreement with *The Denver Post*, publ. by MediaNews), and 8 community newspapers; owns the Scripps Howard News Service syndicate, 10 television stations, and 6 cable and satellite programming networks.

Tribune Publishing: 435 North Michigan Ave, Chicago, IL 60611; tel. (312) 222-9100; fax (312) 222-4760; e-mail corp.info@tribune.com; internet www.tribune.com; f. 1847; subsidiary of Tribune Co; merged with the Times Mirror Co in 2000; Tribune Co acquired by private investor in Dec. 2007; Chair., Pres. and CEO SAMUEL ZELL; 8 daily newspapers incl. the *Chicago Tribune*, the *Los Angeles Times*, the *Baltimore Sun* and the Spanish-language newspaper *Hoy*; over 130 other publs; combined weekday circ. 2.3m., combined Sun. circ. 3.4m; operates 20 television stations.

PRINCIPAL DAILY AND SUNDAY NEWSPAPERS

(Mon. = Monday; Thurs. = Thursday; Fri. = Friday; Sat. = Saturday; Sun. = Sunday; Publr = Publisher; papers are published seven days a week (Monday to Sunday) unless otherwise indicated; average net circulation figures as at March 2008, unless otherwise stated.)

Alabama

Anniston Star: 4305 McClellan Blvd, Anniston, POB 189, AL 36202; tel. (205) 236-1551; fax (205) 241-1991; e-mail kkirk@annistonstar.com; internet www.annistonstar.com; f. 1883; Mon. to Sat. evening, Sun. morning; Chair. and Publr H. BRANDT AYERS; Exec. Editor BOB DAVIS; circ. Mon. to Fri. 24,518, Sat. 23,429, Sun. 25,050.

Birmingham News: 2201 Fourth Ave North, POB 2553, Birmingham, AL 35203; tel. (205) 325-4444; fax (205) 325-3278; internet www.bhamnews.com; f. 1888; Publr VICTOR H. HANSON, III; Editor THOMAS SCARRITT; circ. Mon. to Fri. 140,438, Sat. 140,747, Sun. 170,151.

Decatur Daily: 201 First Ave, SE, POB 2213, Decatur, AL 35609; tel. (256) 353-4612; fax (256) 340-2366; e-mail webmaster@decaturdaily.com; internet decaturdaily.com; f. 1912; morning; Publr BARRETT C. SHELTON, Jr; Exec. Editor TOM WRIGHT; circ. Mon. to Sat. 20,770, Sun. 22,961.

Huntsville Times: 2317 South Memorial Parkway, Huntsville, AL 35801-5623; tel. (256) 532-4000; fax (256) 532-4213; e-mail kevin.wendt@htimes.com; internet www.htimes.com; f. 1910; Publr BOB LUDWIG; Editor KEVIN WENDT; circ. Mon. to Fri. 53,194, Sat. 50,981, Sun. 71,786.

Montgomery Advertiser: 425 Molton St, Montgomery, AL 36104; tel. (334) 262-1611; fax (334) 261-1521; e-mail editor@montgomeryadvertiser.com; internet www.montgomeryadvertiser.com; f. 1829 as The Planter's Gazette; Publr SCOTT M. BROWN; Exec. Editor WANDA S. LLOYD; circ. Mon. to Fri. 45,060, Sat. 43,556, Sun. 50,983.

Press-Register: 304 Government St, POB 2488, Mobile, AL 36652-2488; tel. (251) 219-5454; fax (334) 434-8662; e-mail cindy@al.com; internet www.press-register.com; f. 1813; CEO CINDY MARTIN; Editor-in-Chief KEN BOOTH; circ. Mon. to Fri. 99,433, Sat. 90,724, Sun 112,761.

Times Daily: POB 797, Florence, AL 35631; tel. (205) 766-3434; fax (205) 740-4717; e-mail stephen.schmidt@timesdaily.com; internet www.timesdaily.com; f. 1869; publ. by New York Times Co; morning; Publr STEPHEN A. SCHMIDT; Exec. Editor T. WAYNE MITCHELL; circ. Mon. to Fri. 29,200, Sat. 27,500, Sun. 29,843.

Tuscaloosa News: 315 28th Ave, POB 20587, Tuscaloosa, Alabama 35401; tel. (205) 345-0505; fax (205) 349-0802; e-mail ben.windham@tuscaloosanews.com; internet www.tuscaloosanews.com; f. 1818; morning; Publr TIM THOMPSON; Exec. Editor DOUG RAY; circ. Mon. to Fri. 32,789, Sat. 32,336, Sun. 34,606.

Alaska

Anchorage Daily News: POB 149001, Anchorage, AK 99514-9001; tel. (907) 257-4305; fax (907) 257-4544; e-mail newsroom@adn.com; internet www.adn.com; f. 1946; Pres. and Publr PATRICK DOYLE; Senior Vice-Pres. and Editor PAT DOUGHERTY; circ. Mon. to Fri. 62,893, Sat. 61,733, Sun. 69,893.

Ketchikan Daily News: 501 Dock St, POB 7900, Ketchikan, AK 99901; tel. (907) 225-3157; fax (907) 225-1096; e-mail news@ketchikandailynews.com; internet www.ketchikandailynews.com; division of Pioneer Printing, Inc; Publrs LEW WILLIAMS, III, TENA WILLIAMS; Man. Editor TERRY MILLER.

Arizona

Arizona Daily Star: 4850 South Park Ave, POB 26807, Tucson, AZ 85726-6807; tel. (520) 573-4215; fax (520) 573-4200; e-mail jhumenik@azstarnet.com; internet www.azstarnet.com; f. 1877; Publr and Editor JOHN M. HUMENIK; Exec. Editor BOBBIE JO BUEL-CARTER; circ. Mon. to Fri. 113,373, Sat. 104,584, Sun. 164,033.

Arizona Republic: 200 East Van Buren St, Phoenix, AZ 85004; tel. (602) 444-8000; fax (800) 699-0732; e-mail comments@azcentral.com; internet www.azcentral.com/arizonarepublic; f. 1890; Vice-Pres. and Exec. Editor RANDY LOVELY; circ. Mon. to Fri. 413,332, Sat. 422,466, Sun. 515,523.

East Valley Tribune: 120 West First Ave, POB 1547, Mesa, AZ 85210; tel. (480) 898-6500; fax (480) 898-6463; internet www.eastvalleytribune.com; f. 1890; morning; CEO and Publr TERRY HORNE; Exec. Editor JIM RIPLEY; circ. Mon. to Fri. 71,153, Sat. 64,635, Sun. 71,153.

Tucson Citizen: 4850 South Park Ave, Tucson, AZ 85714-1637; tel. (520) 573-4561; fax (520) 573-4569; e-mail citizen@tucsoncitizen.com; internet www.tucsoncitizen.com; f. 1870; Publr and Editor JENNIFER BOICE (acting); circ. Mon. to Fri. 23,756, Sat. 21,856.

Arkansas

Democrat-Gazette: 121 East Capitol Ave, POB 2221, Little Rock, AR 72203; tel. (501) 378-3400; fax (501) 372-4765; e-mail ffellone@arkansasonline.com; internet www2.arkansasonline.com; f. 1819; morning; Publr WALTER E. HUSSMAN, Jr; Exec. Editor GRIFFIN SMITH; circ. Mon. to Fri. 182,212, Sat. 179,749, Sun. 274,494.

Jonesboro Sun: 518 Carson, POB 1249, Jonesboro, AR 72401; tel. (501) 935-5525; fax (501) 935-5823; e-mail dmosesso@jonesborosun.com; internet www.jonesborosun.com; f. 1903; publ. by Paxton Media Group; morning; Publr DAVID MOSESSO; Editor ROY OCKERT, Jr; circ. Mon. to Sat. 19,830, Sun. 22,564.

Pine Bluff Commercial: 300 Beech St, POB 6469, Pine Bluff, AR 71611-6469; tel. (501) 534-3400; fax (501) 534-0113; e-mail pbcnews@pbcommercial.com; internet www.pbcommercial.com; f. 1881; publ. by Stephens Media Group; morning; Editor and Publr MICHAEL HENGEL.

Southwest Times Record: 3600 Wheeler Ave, POB 1359, Fort Smith, AR 72901; tel. (479) 785-7700; e-mail jhansen@swtimes.com; internet www.swtimes.com; f. 1882; Mon. to Fri. all day, Sat. and Sun. morning; Publr GENE KINCY; Exec. Editor BYRON L. TATE; circ. Mon. to Fri. 40,231, Sat. 36,398, Sun. 43,384.

California

Argus: 3850 Decoto Rd, Fremont, CA 94555; tel. (510) 353-7027; fax (510) 353-7072; e-mail swaterhouse@bayareanewsgroup.com; internet www.insidebayarea.com/argus; f. 1960; morning; Publr J. ALLAN MEATH; Editor STEVE WATERHOUSE; circ. Mon. to Fri. 26,749, Sat. 25,062, Sun. 25,173 (Dec. 2007).

Bakersfield Californian: 1707 Eye St, Bakersfield, CA 93301; tel. (805) 395-7500; fax (805) 395-7519; internet www.bakersfield.com; f. 1866; Publr and Chair. VIRGINIA F. MOORHOUSE; Exec. Editor MIKE JENNER; circ. Mon. to Fri. 59,433, Sat. 60,719, Sun. 68,825.

Californian: The Salinas Californian, 123 West Alisal St, Salinas, CA 93901; tel. (408) 424-2221; fax (408) 754-4286; internet www.californianonline.com; f. 1871; Mon. to Sat. morning; Publr TIM DOWD; Exec. Editor SCOTT FAUST; circ. Mon. to Fri. 15,740, Sat. 17,042.

Daily Breeze: Copley Los Angeles Newspapers, 5215 Torrance Blvd, Torrance, CA 90503; tel. (310) 540-5511; fax (310) 540-6272; e-mail newsroom@dailybreeze.com; internet www.dailybreeze.com; f. 1894; Mon. to Sat. evening, Sun. morning; Publr MARK FICCARA;

Exec. Editor PHILIP SANFIELD; circ. Mon. to Fri. 65,590, Sat. 67,184, Sun. 66,318.

Daily Californian: POB 1949, Berkeley, CA 94701-0949; tel. (510) 548-8300; fax (510) 849-2803; e-mail dailycalifornian@dailycal.org; internet www.dailycal.org; f. 1892; publ. by Independent Berkeley Students Publishing Co, Inc; independent, student-run; Mon. to Fri. during academic year; 2 a week during summer; Pres. and Editor-in-Chief BRYAN THOMAS; circ. Tuesday to Sat. 24,277, Sun. 25,784 (2007).

Daily News: 21221 Oxnard St, Woodland Hills, POB 4200, CA 91365; tel. (818) 713-3000; fax (818) 713-0058; e-mail feedback@dailynews.com; internet www.dailynews.com; f. 1911; publ. by Los Angeles Newspaper Group; morning; Publr EDWARD R. MOSS; Editor CAROLINA GARCIA; circ. Mon. to Fri. 137,344, Sat. 136,361, Sun. 145,164.

Daily Review: 116 West Winton Ave, Hayward, CA 94544; tel. (510) 783-6111; fax (510) 293-2499; e-mail custserv@bayareanewsgroup.com; internet www.insidebayarea.com/dailyreview; f. 1891; morning; Publr J. ALLAN MEATH; Editor KIM SANTOS (acting); circ. Mon. to Fri. 30,704, Sat. 28,467, Sun. 29,276.

The Desert Sun: 750 North Gene Autry Trail, Palm Springs, CA 92262; tel. (760) 322-8889; fax (760) 778-4654; e-mail jamie.price@thedesertsun.com; internet www.thedesertsun.com; f. 1927; morning; Publr RICHARD A. RAMHOFF; Editor (vacant); circ. Mon. to Fri. 53,091, Sat. 57,054, Sun. 57,383.

Enterprise-Record: 400 East Park Ave, Chico, CA 95928; tel. (530) 891-1234; fax (530) 342-3617; e-mail dlittle@chicoer.com; internet www.chicoer.com; f. 1853; Mon. to Fri. evening, Sat. and Sun. morning; Publr WOLF ROSENBERG; Editor DAVID LITTLE; circ. Mon. to Fri. 29,113, Sat. 26,484, Sun. 31,300.

Fresno Bee: 1626 E St, Fresno, CA 93786; tel. (559) 441-6111; fax (559) 441-6499; e-mail blumbye@fresnobee.com; internet www.fresnobee.com; f. 1922; Publr and Pres. RAY STEELE, Jr; Exec. Editor BETSY LUMBYE; circ. Mon. to Fri. 150,344, Sat. 144,056, Sun. 171,039.

Herald: Monterey County Herald, 8 Upper Ragsdale, POB 271, Monterey, CA 93942; tel. (831) 372-3311; fax (831) 648-1126; e-mail jlivernois@montereyherald.com; internet www.montereyherald.com; f. 1922; morning; Pres. and Publr GARY OMERNICK; Exec. Editor JOE LIVERNOIS; circ. Mon. to Fri. 28,933, Sat. 29,367, Sun. 30,803.

Hollywood Reporter: 5055 Wilshire Blvd, Suite 600, Los Angeles, CA 90036-4396; tel. (323) 525-2000; fax (323) 525-2377; e-mail jason.berkowitz@nielsen.com; internet www.hollywoodreporter.com; f. 1932; Mon. to Fri. morning; Publr ERIC MIKA; Editor ELIZABETH GUIDER; circ. Mon. to Fri. 20,964.

Inland Valley Daily Bulletin: 2041 East Fourth St, POB 4000, Ontario, CA 91764; tel. (909) 987-6397; fax (909) 948-9038; e-mail steve.lambert@inlandnewspapers.com; internet www.dailybulletin.com; f. 1885; morning; Pres. and Publr DAVE KUTA; Editor STEVE LAMBERT; circ. Mon. to Fri. 53,903, Sat. 54,934, Sun. 59,027.

Investor's Business Daily: 12655 Beatrice St, Los Angeles, CA 90066; tel. (310) 448-6700; fax (310) 577-7301; e-mail ibdnews@investors.com; internet www.investors.com; f. 1984; morning; Publr W. SCOTT O'NEILL; Editor-in-Chief WESLEY F. MANN; circ. Mon. to Fri. 161,421.

La Opinión: 700 South Flower St, Suite 3000, Los Angeles, CA 90017; tel. (213) 896-2000; e-mail editor@laopinion.com; internet www.impre.com/laopinion; f. 1926; owned by ImpreMedia LLC; morning; Spanish; CEO and Publr MÓNICA LOZANO; Exec. Editor PEDRO ROJAS; circ. Mon. to Fri. 114,892, Sat. 93,844, Sun. 56,027.

Los Angeles Times: 202 West First St, Los Angeles, CA 90012; tel. (213) 237-5000; fax (213) 237-7679; e-mail nancy.sullivan@latimes.com; internet www.latimes.com; f. 1881; Publr and CEO EDDY W. HARTENSTEIN; Editor RUSS STANTON; circ. Mon. to Fri. 773,884, Sat. 860,722, Sun. 1,101,981.

Marin Independent Journal: 150 Alameda del Prado, POB 6150, Novato, CA 94948-6150; tel. (415) 883-8600; fax (415) 883-5458; e-mail shenry@marinij.com; internet www.marinij.com; f. 1861; Mon. to Sat. evening, Sun. morning; Pres. and Publr MARIO VAN DONGEN; Exec. Editor DOUG BUNNELL; circ. Mon. to Fri. 31,909, Sat. 28,759, Sun. 33,910.

Merced Sun-Star: 3033 North G St, POB 739, Merced, CA 95341-0739; tel. (209) 722-1511; fax (209) 384-2226; e-mail hvanderveen@mercedsun-star.com; internet www.mercedsunstar.com; f. 1869; Mon. to Sat. morning; Publr HANK VANDERVEEN; Exec. Editor MIKE THARP; circ. Mon. to Fri. 15,015, Sat. 19,585.

Modesto Bee: 1325 H St, POB 3928, Modesto, CA 95352; tel. (209) 578-2000; fax (209) 578-2207; e-mail mrandazzo@modbee.com; internet www.modbee.com; f. 1884; Publr MARGARET RANDAZZO; Vice-Pres. and Editor MARK VASCHÉ; circ. Mon. to Fri. 78,001, Sat. 83,576, Sun. 81,952.

Napa Valley Register: 1615 Second St, POB 150, Napa, CA 94559; tel. (707) 226-3711; fax (707) 224-3963; e-mail bspeth@napanews.com; internet www.napavalleyregister.com; f. 1863; Mon. to Fri. evening, Sat. and Sun. morning; Publr BRENDA SPETH; Editor BILL KISLIUK; circ. Mon. to Fri. 16,263, Sat. 15,871, Sun. 16,993.

Oakland Tribune: 401 13th St, Alameda, CA 94612; tel. (510) 208-6300; fax (510) 208-6477; e-mail mreynolds@bayareanewsgroup.com; internet www.oaklandtribune.com; f. 1874; Editor PETE WEVURKSI; circ. Mon. to Fri. 96,535, Sat. 84,916, Sun. 91,343.

Orange Coast Daily Pilot: 299B East 17th St, Costa Mesa, CA 92627; tel. (714) 966-4600; fax (949) 631-6594; e-mail dailypilot@latimes.com; internet www.dailypilot.com; f. 1923; morning; Publr THOMAS H. JOHNSON; Man. Editor BRADY RHOADES.

Orange County Register: 625 North Grand Ave, POB 11626, Santa Ana, CA 92701-4347; tel. (877) 627-7009; fax (714) 796-3681; e-mail customerservice@ocregister.com; internet www.ocregister.com; Pres. and Publr TERRY HORNE; Editor KEN BRUSIC; circ. Mon. to Fri. 250,724, Sat. 275,919, Sun. 311,982.

Press Democrat: 427 Mendocino Ave, POB 569, Santa Rosa, CA 95402; tel. (707) 546-2020; fax (707) 521-5330; e-mail catherine.barratt@pressdemocrat.com; internet www.pressdemocrat.com; f. 1857; Publr BRUCE W. KYSE; Exec. Editor CATHERINE BARNETT; circ. Mon. to Fri. 78,022, Sat. 77,887, Sun. 78,505.

Press Enterprise: 3450 14th St, POB 792, Riverside, CA 92501; tel. (951) 368-9403; fax (951) 368-9022; e-mail mdevarenne@pe.com; internet www.pe.com; f. 1878; publ. by Belo Corpn; morning; Publr RONALD R. REDFERN; Editor MARIA DE VARENNE; circ. Mon. to Fri. 164,189, Sat. 163,089, Sun. 172,730.

Press-Telegram: 300 Oceangate, Long Beach, CA 90844-0001; tel. (562) 435-1161; fax (562) 437-7892; e-mail rich.archbold@presstelegram.com; internet www.presstelegram.com; Publr MARK FICARRA; Exec. Editor RICH ARCHBOLD; circ. Mon. to Fri. 85,595, Sat. 83,772, Sun. 85,191.

Sacramento Bee: 2100 Q St, POB 15779, Sacramento, CA 95826; tel. (916) 321-1000; fax (916) 321-1100; e-mail cdell@sacbee.com; internet www.sacbee.com; f. 1857; Pres. and Publr CHERYL DELL; Snr Vice-Pres. and Editor MELANIE SILL; circ. Mon. to Fri. 268,755, Sat. 276,776, Sun. 307,480.

San Bernardino County Sun: 4030 North Georgia Blvd, San Bernardino, CA 92407; tel. (909) 889-9666; fax (909) 381-8741; e-mail nancy.kay@sbsun.com; internet www.sbsun.com; f. 1894; part of Los Angeles Media Group; Publr FRED HAMILTON; Editor STEVE LAMBERT; circ. Mon. to Fri. 54,315, Sat. 52,580, Sun. 54,315.

San Diego Union-Tribune: 350 Camino de la Reina, San Diego, CA 92108; tel. (619) 299-3131; fax (619) 293-1896; e-mail letters@uniontrib.com; internet www.signonsandiego.com; f. 1868; Publr DAVID COPLEY; Sr Editor BILL OSBORNE; circ. Mon. to Fri. 288,669, Sat. 327,694, Sun. 355,537.

San Francisco Chronicle: 901 Mission St, San Francisco, CA 94103; tel. (415) 777-1111; fax (415) 896-1107; e-mail letters@sfchronicle.com; internet www.sfgate.com; f. 1865; subsidiary of Hearst Communications; Publr and Pres. FRANK J. VEGA; Exec. Vice-Pres. and Editor PHILIP BRONSTEIN; circ. Mon. to Fri. 370,345, Sat. 386,113, Sun. 424,603.

San Francisco Examiner: 450 Mission, San Francisco, CA 94105; tel. (415) 359-2600; fax (415) 359-2766; e-mail sfeditor@examiner.com; internet www.sfexaminer.com; f. 1887; Publr JOHN WILCOX; Exec. Editor JAMES PIMENTEL; circ. Mon. to Fri. 70,000, Sat. 90,000.

San Gabriel Valley Daily Tribune: 1210 North Azusa Canyon Rd, West Covina, CA 91790; tel. (626) 962-8811; e-mail letters.tribune@sgvn.com; internet www.sgvtribune.com; morning; Publr RON WOOD; Snr Editor FRANK PINE; circ. Mon. to Fri. 40,812, Sat. 39,434, Sun. 41,550.

San Jose Mercury News: 750 Ridder Park Dr., San Jose, CA 95190-0001; tel. (408) 920-5000; fax (408) 288-8060; e-mail jfensterwald@mercurynews.com; internet www.mercurynews.com; f. 1851; owned by MediaNews Group; Pres. and Publr MAC TULLY; Man. Editor DAVE SATTERFIELD; circ. Mon. to Fri. 234,772, Sat. 203,203, Sun. 251,851.

San Mateo County Times: 477 Ninth Ave, San Mateo, CA 94402; tel. (650) 348-4321; fax (650) 348-4446; e-mail grabinowitz@bayareanewsgroup.com; internet www.insidebayarea.com/sanmateocountytimes; f. 1889; morning; Exec. Editor GLENN RABINOWITZ; circ. Mon. to Fri. 25,982, Sat. 22,627, Sun. 28,788.

Santa Barbara News-Press: 715 Anacapa St, POB 1359, Santa Barbara, CA 93102; tel. (805) 564-5200; fax (805) 966-6258; e-mail voices@newspress.com; internet www.newspress.com; f. 1855; morning; Co-Publrs WENDY MCCAW, ARTHUR VON WIESENBERGER; Assoc. Editor SCOTT STEEPLETON; circ. Mon. to Fri. 35,061, Sat. 33,569, Sun. 35,195.

Santa Cruz Sentinel: 1800 Green Hills Rd, Suite 210, Scotts Valley, CA 95066; tel. (831) 423-4242; e-mail dmiller@santacruzsentinel.com; internet www.santacruzsentinel.com; f. 1856; morning; Publr MARIO VAN DONGEN; Editor DON MILLER; circ. Mon. to Fri. 23,290, Sat. 23,276, Sun. 23,168.

Stockton Record: 530 East Market St, POB 900, Stockton, CA 95201; tel. (209) 943-6568; fax (209) 547-8186; e-mail newsroom@recordnet.com; internet www.recordnet.com; f. 1895; publ. by Ottaway Newspapers, Inc; Publr ROGER COOVER; Editor MIKE KLOCKE; circ. Mon. to Fri. 57,486, Sat. 55,578, Sun. 62,585.

Times-Standard: 930 Sixth St, Eureka, CA 95501; tel. (707) 441-0500; fax (707) 445-0501; e-mail scolby@times-standard.com; internet www.times-standard.com; f. 1854; Mon. to Sat. evening, Sun. morning; owned by MediaNews Group; Publr DAVE KUTA; Man. Editor KIMBERLEY WEAR; circ. Mon. to Fri. 19,397, Sat. 17,980, Sun. 20,963.

The Tribune: 3825 South Higuera St, POB 112, San Luis Obispo, CA 93406; tel. (805) 781-7800; fax (805) 595-1184; e-mail tweber@thetribunenews.com; internet www.sanluisobispo.com; f. 1869; Mon. to Fri. evening, Sat. morning; Pres. and Publr BRUCE RAY; Exec. Editor SANDRA DUERR; circ. Mon. to Fri. 35,885, Sat. 37,329, Sun. 41,794.

Ventura County Star: POB 6006, Camarillo, CA 93011; tel. (805) 437-0000; fax (805) 482-6167; e-mail feedback@venturacountystar.com; internet www.venturacountystar.com; f. 1925; morning; Pres. and Publr GEORGE H. COGSWELL, III; Editor JOE HOWRY; circ. Mon. to Fri. 86,276, Sat. 85,642, Sun. 94,708.

Colorado

Coloradoan: 1300 Riverside Ave, Fort Collins, CO 80524; tel. (970) 493-6397; e-mail lauriepaben@coloradoan.com; internet www.coloradoan.com; f. 1873; morning; Publr and Pres. CHRISTINE CHIN; Exec. Editor ROBERT MOORE; circ. Mon. to Fri. 26,312, Sat. 25,638, Sun. 30,020.

Daily Camera: 1048 Pearl St, POB 591, Boulder, CO 80306; tel. (303) 442-1202; fax (303) 449-9358; e-mail kaufmank@dailycamera.com; internet www.dailycamera.com; f. 1891; morning; Publr ALBERT J. MANZI; Editor KEVIN KAUFMAN; circ. Mon. to Fri. 28,994, Sat. 30,059, Sun. 33,124.

Daily Sentinel: POB 668, Grand Junction, CO 81502; tel. (970) 242-5050; fax (970) 241-6860; e-mail alex.taylor@gjsentinel.com; internet www.gjsentinel.com; f. 1893; Mon. to Sat. evening, Sun. morning; Publr ALEX TAYLOR; Man. Editor LAURENA MAYNE DAVIS; circ. Mon. to Fri. 31,349, Sat. 30,785, Sun. 33,294.

Denver Post: 101 West Colfax Ave, Denver, CO 80202; tel. (303) 954-1010; fax (303) 820-1369; e-mail gmoore@denverpost.com; internet www.denverpost.com; f. 1892; Publr WILLIAM DEAN SINGLETON; Editor GREGORY MOORE; circ. Mon. to Fri. 225,193, Sun. 600,026.

The Gazette: 30 South Prospect, Colorado Springs, CO 80903; tel. (719) 632-5511; fax (719) 636-0202; e-mail liz.cobb@gazette.com; internet www.gazette.com; f. 1872; Pres. and Publr (vacant); Editor JEFF THOMAS; circ. Mon. to Fri. 93,859, Sat. 98,461, Sun. 109,603.

Greeley Tribune: c/o The Greeley Publishing Co, POB 1690, Greeley, CO 80632; tel. (970) 352-0211; e-mail web@greeleytrib.com; internet www.greeleytrib.com; f. 1870; Mon. to Sat. evening, Sun. morning; Publr BART SMITH; Man. Editor KELLY ANN TRACER; circ. Mon. to Thurs, Sat. 27,000, Fri. 34,000, Sun. 33,000 (2007).

Pueblo Chieftain: Star-Journal Publishing Co, 825 West Sixth St, POB 4040, Pueblo, CO 81003; tel. (719) 544-3520; fax (719) 546-3235; e-mail shenson@chieftain.com; internet www.chieftain.com; f. 1872; Publr and Editor ROBERT H. RAWLINGS; circ. Mon. to Fri. 49,169, Sat. 47,109, Sun. 50,243.

Rocky Mountain News: 101 West Colfax Ave, Suite 500, Denver, CO 80202; tel. (303) 954-5000; fax (303) 954-2841; e-mail metro@rockymountainnews.com; internet www.rockymountainnews.com; f. 1859; Publr, Pres. and Editor JOHN TEMPLE; circ. Mon. to Fri. 253,834, Sat. 550,088.

Connecticut

Advocate: POB 9307, Stamford, CT 06904; tel. (203) 964-2200; fax (203) 964-2345; e-mail letters.advocate@scni.com; internet www.stamfordadvocate.com; f. 1829; Mon. to Fri. all day, Sat. and Sun. morning; Publr JOHN M. DUNSTER; Editor TERRI VANECH; circ. Mon. to Fri. 23,088, Sat. 21,269, Sun. 24,086.

Connecticut Post: 410 State St, Bridgeport, CT 06604-4501; tel. (203) 333-0161; fax (203) 366-8158; e-mail edit@ctpost.com; internet www.connpost.com; f. 1883; Pres. and Publr ROBERT H. LASKA; Editor TOM BADEN; circ. Mon. to Fri. 76,014, Sat. 58,627, Sun. 85,032.

The Day: 47 Eugene O'Neill Dr., POB 1231, New London, CT 06320-1231; tel. (860) 442-2200; fax (860) 442-5599; internet www.theday.com; f. 1881; morning; Publr and Editor GARY FARRUGIA; Exec. Editor TIMOTHY DWEYER; circ. Mon. to Fri. 34,730, Sat. 34,672, Sun. 40,670.

Hartford Courant: 285 Broad St, Hartford, CT 06115; tel. (860) 241-6200; fax (860) 520-3176; e-mail nmeyer@courant.com; internet www.courant.com; f. 1764; Publr and CEO STEPHEN D. CARVER; Editor CLIFFORD TEUTSCH; circ. Mon. to Fri. 168,158, Sat. 151,938, Sun. 237,933.

Herald: 1 Herald Sq., New Britain, CT 06050; tel. (860) 225-4601; fax (860) 225-2611; e-mail nbnews@ctcentral.com; internet www.newbritainherald.com; f. 1880; Mon. to Sat. evening; Publr ED GUNDERSON; Exec. Editor MARK LEVY; circ. Mon. to Sat. 9,646, Sun. 20,096.

The Hour: 346 Main Ave, POB 790, Norwalk, CT 06852-0790; tel. (203) 846-3281; fax (203) 840-1802; e-mail dbertoli@thehour.com; internet www.thehour.com; f. 1871; Mon. to Sun. morning; Publr and COO CHET VALIANTE; Editor DONNA BERTOLI; circ. Mon. to Sat. 14,814, Sun. 15,200.

Journal Inquirer: 306 Progress Dr., POB 510, Manchester, CT 06045; tel. (860) 646-0500; fax (860) 646-9867; e-mail news@journalinquirer.com; internet www.journalinquirer.com; f. 1968; Mon. to Sat. morning; Publr ELIZABETH S. ELLIS; Man. Editor CHRIS POWELL; circ. Mon. to Fri. 37,475, Sat. 40,581.

New Haven Register: 40 Sargent Dr., New Haven, CT 06511; tel. (203) 789-5200; fax (203) 865-7894; e-mail mbrackenbury@nhregister.com; internet www.nhregister.com; f. 1812; Publr EDWARD CONTRA; Editor JACK KRAMER; circ. Mon. to Fri. 72,613, Sat. 58,289, Sun. 80,279.

News-Times: 333 Main St, Danbury, CT 06810; tel. (203) 744-5100; fax (203) 792-8730; e-mail acummings@newstimes.com; internet www.newstimes.com; f. 1883; morning; Publr DAVID R. DEAR, Jr; Editor ART CUMMINGS; circ. Mon. to Fri. 27,909, Sat. 27,646, Sun. 31,152.

Norwich Bulletin: 66 Franklin St, Norwich, CT 06360; tel. (203) 887-9211; fax (203) 887-9666; internet www.norwichbulletin.com; f. 1791; morning; Pres. and Publr ELLEN LIND; Exec. Editor JAMES KONRAD; circ. Mon. to Fri. 22,121, Sat. 21,251, Sun. 25,164.

Record Journal: 11 Crown St, Meriden, CT 06450; tel. (203) 235-1661; fax (203) 639-0210; e-mail newsroom@record-journal.com; internet www.erecordjournal.com; f. 1867; morning; Publr ELIOT C. WHITE; Man. Editor RALPH TOMASELLI; circ. Mon. to Sat. 30,752, Sun. 30,960 (2005).

Waterbury Republican-American: American-Republican, Inc, 389 Meadow St, POB 2090, Waterbury, CT 06722-2090; tel. (203) 574-3636; fax (203) 596-9277; e-mail ghanisek@rep-am.com; internet www.rep-am.com; f. 1844; morning; Publr WILLIAM J. PAPE, II; Exec. Editor JONATHAN F. KELLOGG; circ. Mon. to Fri. 50,903, Sat. 48,142, Sun. 57,385.

Delaware

Delaware State News: 110 Galaxy Dr., POB 737, Dover, DE 19903; tel. (302) 674-3600; fax (302) 741-8261; e-mail newsroom@newszap.com; internet www2.newszap.com/dsn; f. 1901; morning; Publr TAMRA BRITTINGHAM; Man. Editor ANDREW WEST; circ. Mon. to Sat. 23,000, Sun. 33,000 (2007).

News Journal: POB 15505, Wilmington, DE 19850; tel. (302) 324-2500; fax (302) 856-3919; e-mail newsroom@newsjournal.com; internet www.delawareonline.com; f. 1871; Publr CURTIS W. RIDDLE; Exec. Editor DAVID LEDFORD; circ. Mon. to Fri. 110,171, Sat. 102,698, Sun. 125,244.

District of Columbia

Washington Post: 1150 15th St, NW, Washington, DC 20071; tel. (202) 334-6000; fax (202) 334-5693; internet www.washingtonpost.com; f. 1877; Chair. BOISFEUILLET JONES; Publr KATHARINE WEYMOUTH; Exec. Editor LEONARD DOWNIE, Jr; Man. Editor PHILIP BENNETT; circ. Mon. to Fri. 673,180, Sat. 612,905, Sun. 890,163.

Washington Times: 3600 New York Ave, NE, Washington, DC 20002-1947; tel. (202) 636-3000; fax (202) 832-2982; internet www.washingtontimes.com; f. 1982; Editor-in-Chief WESLEY PRUDEN; Man. Editor FRANCIS B. COOMBS, Jr; circ. Mon. to Fri. 93,763, Sat. 76,701, Sun. 37,680.

Florida

Bradenton Herald: 102 Manatee Ave West, POB 921, Bradenton, FL 34206; tel. (941) 748-0411; e-mail bturner@bradenton.com; internet www.bradenton.com; f. 1926; morning; Publr and Pres. BOB TURNER; Exec. Editor JOAN KRAUTER; circ. Mon. to Fri. 48,618, Sat. 45,203, Sun. 54,210.

Daytona Beach News-Journal: 901 Sixth St, Daytona Beach, FL 32117; tel. (386) 252-1511; internet www.news-journalonline.com; f. 1904; morning; Publr, CEO and Pres. GEORGIA M. KANEY; Editor DON LINDLEY; circ. Mon. to Fri. 99,627, Sat. 103,909, Sun. 116,700.

Diario Las Américas: 2900 NW 39th St, Miami, FL 33142; tel. (305) 633-3341; fax (305) 635-7668; internet www.diariolasamericas.com; f. 1953; Spanish; Publr and Editor HORACIO AGUIRRE; circ. Mon. to Sat. 66,000, Sun. 70,000 (2007).

Florida Times-Union: 1 Riverside Ave, Jacksonville, FL 32202; POB 1949, Jacksonville, FL 322311; tel. (904) 359-4111; fax (904) 359-4478; e-mail rich.ray@jacksonville.com; internet jacksonville.com; f. 1864; Publr JIM CURROW; Exec. Editor RICH RAY; circ. Mon. to Fri. 144,391, Sat. 159,969, Sun. 201,352.

Florida Today: Cape Publs, Inc, POB 419000, Melbourne, FL 32941-9000; tel. (321) 242-3500; fax (321) 242-6601; internet www.floridatoday.com; f. 1966; morning; Publr and Pres. MARK MIKOLAJCZYK; Exec. Editor BOB STOVER; circ. Mon. to Fri. 79,499, Sat. 78,077, Sun. 93,604.

Fort Pierce Tribune: 600 Edwards Rd, Fort Pierce, FL 34982; tel. (772) 461-2050; fax (407) 467-1953; internet www.tcpalm.com; f. 1903; publ. by E. W. Scripps Co; part of the Treasure Coast News group of publs; morning; Publr THOMAS E. WEBER, Jr; Editor MARK TOMASIK; circ. Mon. to Sat. 24,944, Sun. 29,165 (2007).

Gainesville Sun: 2700 South West 13th St, Gainesville, FL 32608-2015; tel. (352) 374-5001; fax (352) 338-3128; e-mail osteenj@gvillesun.com; internet www.gainesvillesun.com; f. 1875; morning; Publr JAMES E. DOUGHTON; Exec. Editor JIM OSTEEN; circ. Mon. to Fri. 44,658, Sat. 44,250, Sun. 49,179.

Ledger: POB 408, Lakeland, FL 33802; tel. (863) 802-7000; fax (863) 802-7850; e-mail skip.perez@theledger.com; internet www.theledger.com; f. 1924; morning; Publr JEROME FERSON; Exec. Editor SKIP PEREZ; circ. Mon. to Fri. 65,948, Sat. 65,750, Sun. 83,860.

Leesburg Daily Commercial: 212 East Main St, POB 490007, Leesburg, FL 32749-0007; tel. (352) 365-8200; fax (904) 365-1951; e-mail news@dailycommercial.com; internet www.dailycommercial.com; f. 1875; Mon. to Sat. evening, Sun. morning; Publr RON WALLACE; Man. Editor DAN FIELDS; circ. Mon. to Fri. 25,294, Sat. 23,821, Sun. 25,019 (2006).

Miami Herald: 1 Herald Plaza, Miami, FL 33132-1693; tel. (305) 350-2111; fax (305) 376-5287; e-mail dwilson@miamiherald.com; internet www.miamiherald.com; f. 1910; Publr and Pres. DAVID LANDSBERG; Exec. Editor ANDERS GYLLENHAAL; circ. Mon. to Fri. 240,223, Sat. 261,156, Sun. 311,245.

Naples Daily News: 1075 Central Ave, Naples, FL 34102; tel. (239) 262-3161; fax (239) 435-3451; e-mail editor@naplesnews.com; internet www.naplesnews.com; f. 1923; morning; Interim Publr and Vice-Pres. Advertising CHRIS DOYLE; Editor PHIL LEWIS; circ. Mon. to Fri. 66,272, Sat. 65,056, Sun. 74,553.

News Herald: 501 West 11th St, Panama City, FL 32401; tel. (850) 747-5000; fax (850) 747-5097; e-mail news@pcnh.com; internet www.newsherald.com; f. 1937; morning; Publr KAREN HANES; Exec. Editor PHIL LUCAS; circ. Mon. to Fri. 30,829, Sat. 30,590, Sun. 34,574.

News-Press: 2442 Dr Martin Luther King Jr Blvd, Fort Myers, FL 33901-3987; tel. (941) 335-0200; fax (941) 335-0265; e-mail response@news-press.com; internet www.news-press.com; f. 1884; morning; Publr CAROL HUDLER; Sr Man. Editor CINDY MCCURRY-ROSS; circ. Mon. to Fri. 92,340, Sat. 92,362, Sun. 111,516.

Northwest Florida Daily News: 200 Racetrack Rd, Fort Walton Beach, FL 32547; tel. (850) 863-1111; fax (850) 862-5230; e-mail customerservice@nwfdailynews.com; internet www.nwfdailynews.com; f. 1946; morning; Publr TOM CONNER; Editor PATRICK RICE; circ. Mon. to Fri. 35,775, Sat. 35,762, Sun. 41,528.

Ocala Star-Banner: POB 490, Ocala, FL 34478; tel. (352) 867-4010; e-mail allen.parsons@starbanner.com; internet www.ocala.com; f. 1866; morning; Publr ALLEN PARSONS; Man. Editor TOM MCNIFF; circ. Mon. to Fri. 45,424, Sat. 46,994, Sun. 50,185.

Orlando Sentinel: 633 North Orange Ave, Orlando, FL 32801; tel. (407) 420-5000; fax (407) 420-5350; e-mail editor@orlandosentinel.com; internet www.orlandosentinel.com; f. 1876; morning; Publr HOWARD GREENBERG (acting); Editor CHARLOTTE HALL; circ. Mon. to Fri. 227,593, Sat. 226,375, Sun. 303,399.

Palm Beach Post: 2751 South Dixie Hwy, West Palm Beach, FL 33405; tel. (561) 820-4100; fax (561) 820-4407; internet www.palmbeachpost.com; f. 1916; Publr DOUG FRANKLIN; Man. Editor BILL ROSE; Editor JOHN BARTOSEK; circ. Mon. to Fri. 164,474, Sat. 163,087, Sun. 195,608.

Pensacola News Journal: 101 East Romana St, Pensacola, FL 32502; POB 12710, Pensacola, FL 32591; tel. (850) 435-8600; fax (850) 435-8633; e-mail news@pnj.com; internet www.pnj.com; f. 1889; Publr KEVIN DOYLE; Exec. Editor RICHARD A. SCHNEIDER; circ. Mon. to Fri. 57,089, Sat. 55,330, Sun. 68,962.

Sarasota Herald-Tribune: 1741 Main St, Sarasota, FL 34236; tel. (941) 953-7755; fax (941) 957-5276; internet www.heraldtribune.com; f. 1925; Publr DIANE MCFARLIN; Exec. Editor MIKE CONNELLY; circ. Mon. to Fri. 114,904, Sat. 110,747, Sun. 125,644.

St Petersburg Times: 490 First Ave South, POB 1121, St Petersburg, FL 33701; tel. (727) 893-8111; fax (727) 893-8675; e-mail local@sptimes.com; internet www.tampabay.com; f. 1884; division of Poynter Institute for Media Studies; Chair., Editor and CEO PAUL TASH; circ. Mon. to Fri. 316,007, Sat. 329,646, Sun. 432,779.

Stuart News: 1939 South Federal Hwy, POB 9009, Stuart, FL 34995-9009; tel. (772) 287-1550; fax (772) 221-4126; e-mail feedback@tcpalm.com; internet www.tcpalm.com; f. 1913; publ. by E. W Scripps Co; part of Treasure Coast News group of publs; morning; Editor THOMAS E. WEBER, Jr; circ. Mon. to Sat. 30,885, Sun. 37,498 (2006).

Sun-Sentinel: 200 East Las Olas Blvd, Fort Lauderdale, FL 33301-2293; tel. (954) 356-4000; fax (954) 356-4559; internet www.sun-sentinel.com; f. 1960; Publr HOWARD GREENBERG; Editor JEFF GLICK; circ. Mon. to Fri. 218,286, Sat. 226,375, Sun. 303,399.

Tallahassee Democrat: 277 North Magnolia Dr., POB 990, Tallahassee, FL 32302-0990; tel. (850) 599-2100; fax (850) 599-2295; e-mail jhmckenzie@tallahassee.com; internet www.tallahassee.com; f. 1905; acquired by Gannett in August 2005; morning; Pres. and Publr PATRICK DORSEY; Exec. Editor BOB GABORDI; circ. Mon. to Fri. 49,939, Sat. 51,767, Sun. 61,827.

Tampa Tribune: 200 Parker St, Tampa, FL 33606; POB 191, Tampa, FL 33601; tel. (813) 259-8225; fax (813) 254-4952; e-mail lomoto@tbo.com; internet www.tbo.com; f. 1893; morning; Publr and Pres. DENISE E. PALMER; Editor JANET COATS; circ. Mon. to Fri. 220,522, Sat. 220,109.

Vero Beach Press-Journal: POB 1268, Vero Beach, FL 32961-1268; tel. (407) 562-2315; fax (407) 562-6517; internet www.tcpalm.com; f. 1919; publ. by E. W. Scripps Co; part of Treasure Coast News group of publs; morning; Publr THOMAS E. WEBER; Man. Editor MARK A. TOMASIK.

Georgia

Albany Herald: POB 48, Albany, GA 31702-0048; tel. (229) 888-9300; fax (229) 888-9394; e-mail kim.peel@albanyherald.com; internet www.albanyherald.com; f. 1891; morning; Publr MICHAEL J. GEBHART; Exec. Editor JIM HENDRICKS; circ. Mon. to Sat. 33,000, Sun. 39,000 (2007).

Atlanta Journal-Constitution: 72 Marietta St, POB 4689, Atlanta, GA 30302-4689; tel. (404) 526-5151; fax (404) 526-5746; e-mail insideajc@ajc.com; internet www.ajc.com; f. 1950; Sun. morning; Publr JOHN MELLOT; Editor JULIA WALLACE; circ. Mon. to Fri. 326,907, Sat. 329,765, Sun. 497,149.

Augusta Chronicle: 725 Broad St, POB 1928, Augusta, GA 30903-1928; tel. (706) 724-0851; fax (706) 722-5746; internet chronicle.augusta.com; f. 1785; Morris Communications Co, LLC; Publr. WILLIAM S. MORRIS, III; Pres. DONALD W. BAILEY; circ. Mon. to Fri. 73,561, Sat. 72,650, Sun. 92,418.

Columbus Ledger-Enquirer: 17 West 12th St, Columbus, GA 31901; tel. (706) 571-8565; fax (706) 576-6290; e-mail mmcallister@ledger-enquirer.com; internet www.ledger-enquirer.com; f. 1828; morning; Publr VALERIE CANEPA; Exec. Editor BEN HOLDEN; circ. Mon. to Fri. 42,830, Sat. 42,875, Sun. 51,434.

Macon Telegraph: 120 Broadway, Macon, GA 31201; POB 4167, Macon, GA 31208; tel. (478) 744-4200; fax (478) 744-4663; e-mail letters@macontel.com; internet www.macon.com; f. 1826; Publr GEORGE MCCANLESS; Exec. Editor SHERRIE MARSHALL; circ. Mon. to Fri. 56,510, Sat. 54,075, Sun. 70,438.

Marietta Daily Journal: 580 Fairground St, POB 449, Marietta, GA 30061; tel. (770) 428-9411; fax (770) 422-9533; e-mail mdjnews@mdjonline.com; internet www.mdjonline.com; f. 1867; morning; Publr OTIS A. BRUMBY, Jr; Man. Editor BILLY MITCHELL; circ. Mon. to Sat. 17,218, Sun. 17,284.

Times: 345 Green St, POB 838, Gainesville, GA 30503; tel. (770) 532-1234; fax (404) 532-0457; e-mail lromero@gainesvilletimes.com; internet www.gainesvilletimes.com; f. 1947; Mon. to Sat. evening, Sun. morning; Publr DENNIS STOCKTON; Editor MITCH CLARKE.

Hawaii

Honolulu Advertiser: The News Bldg, 605 Kapi'olani Blvd, POB 3110, Honolulu, HI 96802; tel. (808) 525-8090; fax (808) 535-8037; e-mail hawaii@honoluluadvertiser.com; internet www.honoluluadvertiser.com; f. 1856; Pres. and Publr LEE P. WEBBER; Editor MARK PLATTE; circ. Mon. to Fri. 140,331, Sat. 149,069, Sun. 150,276.

Honolulu Star-Bulletin: Restaurant Row, 7 Waterfront Plaza, Suite 210, 500 Ala Moana, Honolulu, HI 96813; tel. (808) 529-4747; fax (808) 529-4750; e-mail mrovner@starbulletin.com; internet www.starbulletin.com; f. 1882; Pres. DENNIS FRANCIS; Editor FRANK BRIDGEWATER; circ. c. 66,000 (2003).

Idaho

Idaho Statesman: 1200 North Curtis Rd, POB 40, Boise, ID 83707; tel. (208) 377-6200; fax (208) 377-6449; e-mail vgowler@idahostatesman.com; internet www.idahostatesman.com; f. 1864; Publr MI-AI PARRISH; Editor and Vice-Pres. VICKI S. GOWLER; circ. Mon. to Fri. 61,927, Sat. 66,222, Sun. 81,939.

Lewiston Tribune: 505 C St, POB 957, Lewiston, ID 83501; tel. (208) 743-9411; fax (208) 746-1185; e-mail wh@lmtribune.com; internet www.lmtribune.com; f. 1892; morning; Publr and Editor A. L. (BUTCH) ALFORD, Jr; Man. Editor PAUL EMERSON.

Post-Register: 333 Northgate Mile, POB 1800, Idaho Falls, ID 83401; tel. (208) 522-1800; fax (208) 529-9683; e-mail mmckenzie@postregister.com; internet www.idahonews.com; f. 1880; Mon. to Fri. evening, Sun. morning; Publr and Editor ROGER PLOTHOW; Exec. Editor DEAN MILLER; circ. Mon. to Fri. 26,542, Sat. 23,668, Sun. 26,290 (2006).

Illinois

Beacon-News: 495 N. Commons Drive, Aurora, IL 60504; tel. (630) 978-8880; fax (630) 978-8509; e-mail beaconviewpoint@scn1.com; internet www.suburbanchicagonews.com/beaconnews; f. 1846; part of Sun-Times News Group; Mon. to Sun. morning; Publr RICK NAGEL; Man. Editor DENISE CROSBY; circ. Mon. to Fri. 27,238, Sat. 26,294, Sun. 28,467.

Belleville News-Democrat: 120 South Illinois St, POB 427, Belleville, IL 62220; tel. (618) 239-2451; fax (618) 235-0556; e-mail newsroom@bnd.com; internet www.bnd.com; f. 1855; morning; Publr JAY TEBBE; Editor JEFFRY COUCH; circ. Mon. to Fri. 51,974, Sat. 54,820, Sun. 63,113.

Chicago Defender: 200 South Michigan Ave, Suite 1700, Chicago, IL 60604; tel. (312) 225-2400; fax (312) 225-9231; e-mail lgibson@chicagodefender.com; internet www.chicagodefender.com; f. 1956; Mon. to Thurs., Sat. morning; Publr. HIRAM JACKSON; Exec. Editor LOU RANSOM.

Chicago Sun-Times: 350 N. Orleans St, 10th Floor, Chicago, IL 60654; tel. (312) 321-3000; fax (312) 321-3084; e-mail letters@suntimes.com; internet www.suntimes.com; f. 1948; Publr CYRUS J. FREIDHEIM, Jr; Editor-in-Chief MICHAEL COOKE; circ. Mon. to Fri. 312,274, Sat. 225,383, Sun. 247,469.

Chicago Tribune: 435 North Michigan Ave, Chicago, IL 60611-4041; tel. (312) 222-3232; fax (312) 222-4674; internet www.chicagotribune.com; f. 1847; publ. by Chicago Tribune Co; two sister newspapers: *RedEye* and *Hoy Chicago*; Publr, Pres. and CEO SCOTT C. SMITH; Editor GERALD KERN; circ. Mon. to Fri. 566,827, Sat 473,849, Sun. 940,620.

Courier News: 300 Lake St, POB 531, Elgin, IL 60120; tel. (847) 888-7800; fax (847) 888-7836; e-mail mbailey@scn1.com; internet www.suburbanchicagonews.com/couriernews; f. 1874 as Elgin Courier News; part of Sun-Times News Group; Mon. to Fri. evening, Sat. and Sun. morning; Publr. ROBERT WALL; Man. Editor MIKE BAILEY; circ. Mon. to Fri. 11,263, Sat. 11,196, Sun. 11,638.

Daily Dispatch: 1720 Fifth Ave, Moline, IL 61265; tel. (309) 764-4344; fax (309) 797-0321; e-mail feedback@qconline.com; internet www.qconline.com; f. 1878; Mon. to Fri. evening, Sat. and Sun. morning; Publr and Editor GERALD J. TAYLOR; circ. Mon. to Fri. 31,752, Sat. 31,640, Sun. 33,595 (2007).

Daily Herald: POB 280, Arlington Heights, IL 60006; tel. (847) 427-4300; fax (847) 427-4608; e-mail jbaumann@dailyherald.com; internet www.dailyherald.com; f. 1872; owned by Paddock Publications Inc; Publr and Chair. DANIEL E. BAUMANN; Senior Vice-Pres. Editor JOHN LAMPINEN; circ. Mon. to Fri. 143,152, Sat. 134,585, Sun. 141,091.

Daily Journal: 8 Dearborn Sq., Kankakee, IL 60901; tel. (815) 937-3300; e-mail mfrey@daily-journal.com; internet www.daily-journal.com; f. 1884; Mon. to Fri. evening, Sun. morning; Publr and Editor JEAN ALICE SMALL; Man. Editor SUZY SCHULTZ.

Herald-News: 300 Caterpillar Dr., Joliet, IL 60436; tel. (815) 729-6161; fax (815) 729-6131; e-mail dmonaghan@sn1.com; internet www.suburbanchicagonews.com/heraldnews; f. 1839; part of Sun-Times News Group; Mon. to Sat. evening, Sun. morning; Publr LARRY RANDA; Man. Editor DAVE MONAGHAN; circ. Mon. to Fri. 38,520, Sat. 37,706, Sun. 41,750.

Hoy: 435 North Michigan Ave, 22nd Floor, Chicago, IL 60611; tel. (312) 527-8400; e-mail aescalona@tribune.com; internet www.hoyinternet.com; f. 2003; in Spanish, distributed free; also published in New York and Los Angeles; Tribune Publishing; Acting Publr JAVIER ADALPE; Gen. Man. JOHN TRAINOR.

Journal Star: 1 News Plaza, Peoria, IL 61643; tel. (309) 686-3000; fax (309) 686-3296; e-mail kmauser@pjstar.com; internet www.pjstar.com; f. 1855; Publr KEN MAUSER; Man. Editor JOHN PLEVKA; circ. Mon. to Fri. 65,320, Sat. 70,255, Sun. 80,394.

News-Gazette: 15 Main St, POB 677, Champaign, IL 61820; tel. (217) 351-5252; fax (217) 351-5374; e-mail foreman@news-gazette.com; internet www.news-gazette.com; f. 1852; Mon. to Fri. evening, Sat. and Sun. morning; Publr JOHN R. FOREMAN; Exec. Editor JOHN BECK; circ. Mon. to Fri. 42,302, Sat. 41,257, Sun. 45,030.

Pantagraph: 301 West Washington St, POB 2907, Bloomington, IL 61702-2907; tel. (309) 829-9000; fax (309) 829-9104; e-mail bwinterland@pantagraph.com; internet www.pantagraph.com; f. 1837; Publr RICHARD JOHNSTON; Man. Editor JULIE GERKE; circ. Mon. to Fri. 47,764, Sat. 43,704, Sun. 50,081.

Quincy Herald Whig: 130 South Fifth St, Quincy, IL 62301; tel. (217) 223-5100; fax (217) 223-9757; e-mail jhutmacher@whig.com; internet www.whig.com; f. 1835; Mon. to Sat. evening, Sun. morning; Gen. Man. DON COOPER; Exec. Editor MIKE HILFRINK; circ. Mon. to Fri. 19,996, Sat. 22,055, Sun. 23,939.

Rockford Register Star: 99 East State St, Rockford, IL 61104; tel. (815) 987-1200; fax (815) 987-1365; internet www.e-rockford.com; f. 1888; acquired by GateHouse Media from Gannett Co in 2007; Publr SCOTT BOWERS; Gen. Man. TOM LASLEY; circ. Mon. to Fri. 55,913, Sat. 54,416, Sun. 69,693.

Southern Illinoisan: 710 North Illinois Ave, POB 2108, Carbondale, IL 62902; tel. (618) 351-5000; fax (618) 529-3774; e-mail dennis.derossett@thesouthern.com; internet www.thesouthern.com; f. 1877; morning; Publr DENNIS DEROSSETT; Editor GARY METRO; circ. Mon. to Fri. 27,413, Sat. 27,755, Sun. 36,975.

State Journal-Register: 1 Copley Plaza, POB 219, Springfield, IL 62705-0219; tel. (217) 788-1300; fax (217) 788-1551; e-mail sjr@sj-r.com; internet www.sj-r.com; f. 1831; Publr SCOTT BOWERS; Exec. Editor JON BROADBOOKS; circ. Mon. to Fri. 49,839, Sat. 49,108, Sun. 58,272.

Telegraph: 111 East Bdwy, POB 278, Alton, IL 62002; tel. (618) 463-2551; fax (618) 463-2578; e-mail publisher@thetelegraph.com; internet www.thetelegraph.com; f. 1836; Mon. to Fri. evening, Sat. and Sun. morning; Publr JIM SHRADER; Exec. Editor DAN BRANNAN; circ. Mon. to Fri. 26,060, Sat. 23,354, Sun. 26,041 (2007).

Indiana

Evansville Courier and Press: 300 Walnut St, POB 268, Evansville, IN 47713; tel. (812) 424-7711; fax (812) 422-8196; e-mail courierpress@evansville.net; internet www.courierpress.com; f. 1845; Publr and Pres. JACK PATE; Man. Editor LINDA NEGRO; circ. Mon. to Fri. 68,220, Sat. 65,597, Sun. 86,201.

Herald-Bulletin: 1133 Jackson St, Anderson, IN 46016; tel. (765) 622-1212; e-mail judi.litsey@heraldbulletin.com; internet www.theheraldbulletin.com; f. 1868; morning; Publr HENRY BIRD; circ. Mon. to Sat. 21,810, Sun. 23,370.

Herald-Times: 1900 South Walnut St, POB 909, Bloomington, IN 47402; tel. (812) 332-4401; fax (812) 331-4285; e-mail mmaloney@heraldt.com; internet www.heraldtimesonline.com; f. 1877; morning; Publr E. MAYER MALONEY, Jr; Editor ROBERT ZALTSBERG; circ. Mon. to Fri. 27,103, Sat. 29,354.

Indianapolis Star: POB 145, Indianapolis, IN 46206-0145; tel. (317) 444-8005; fax (317) 633-1038; internet www.indystar.com; Publr and Pres. MICHAEL G. KANE; Editor DENNIS R. RYERSON; circ. Mon. to Fri. 255,303, Sat. 217,991, Sun. 324,349.

Journal and Courier: Federated Publications, Inc, 217 North Sixth St, Lafayette, IN 47901; tel. (765) 423-5511; fax (765) 742-5633; internet www.jconline.com; f. 1829; morning; Publr and Pres. GARY SUISMAN; Exec. Editor JULIE DOLL; circ. Mon. to Fri. 34,545, Sat. 34,276, Sun. 40,448.

Journal-Gazette: 600 West Main St, Fort Wayne, IN 46802; tel. (260) 461-8831; fax (219) 461-8648; e-mail pbeber@jg.net; internet www.journalgazette.net; f. 1863; publ. by Fort Wayne Newspapers; Publr JULIE INSKEEP; Editor CRAIG KLUGMAN; circ. Mon. to Fri. 64,304, Sat. 86,020, Sun. 111,485.

Kokomo Tribune: 300 North Union St, POB 9014, Kokomo, IN 46901; tel. (765) 459-3121; e-mail jeff.kovaleski@kokomotribune.com; internet www.kokomotribune.com; f. 1850; Mon. to Sat. evening, Sun. morning; Publr ROBYN MCCLOSKEY; Man. Editor JEFF KOVALESKI; circ. Mon. to Sat. 20,587, Sun. 20,570.

News-Sentinel: 600 West Main St, POB 100, Fort Wayne, IN 46802; tel. (260) 461-8324; fax (260) 461-8817; e-mail nsnews@news-sentinel.com; internet www.news-sentinel.com; f. 1833; publ. by Fort Wayne Newspapers; Publr MICHAEL J. CHRISTMAN; Editor LEO MORRIS; circ. Mon. to Fri. 24,196, Sat. 24,053.

Post-Tribune: 1433 East 83rd Ave, Merrillville, IN 46410; tel. (219) 648-3100; fax (219) 648-3249; internet www.post-trib.com; f. 1907; Publr MURDOCH DAVIS; Exec. Editor PAULETTE HADDIX; circ. Mon. to Fri. 60,325, Sat. 57,120, Sun. 61,118.

South Bend Tribune: 225 West Colfax Ave, South Bend, IN 46626; tel. (574) 235-6161; fax (574) 236-1765; e-mail sfunk@sbtinfo.com; internet www.southbendtribune.com; f. 1872; Publr and Editor DAVID C. RAY; circ. Mon. to Fri. 66,886, Sat. 76,046, Sun. 89,802.

The Star Press: POB 2408, Muncie, IN 47307-0408; tel. (317) 213-5701; fax (765) 213-5937; e-mail gwilliams@muncie.gannett.com; internet www.thestarpress.com; f. 1889; morning; Publr JULI METZGER; Exec. Editor GENE WILLIAMS; circ. Mon. to Fri. 31,312, Sat. 29,421, Sun. 32,589.

The Times: 601 45th Ave, Munster, IN 46321; tel. (219) 933-3223; fax (219) 933-9249; e-mail dasher@nwitimes.com; internet www.thetimesonline.com; f. 1906; morning; Publr BILL MASTERSON, Jr; Exec. Editor WILLIAM NANGLE; circ. Mon. to Fri. 85,195, Sat. 82,481, Sun. 92,347.

Tribune-Star: 222 South Seventh St, Terre Haute, IN 47807; tel. (812) 231-4219; fax (812) 321-4234; e-mail susan.duncan@tribstar.com; internet www.tribstar.com; f. 1903; morning; Publr JEREMIAH TURNER; Editor MAX JONES; circ. Mon. to Fri. 25,579, Sat. 24,569, Sun. 28,986 (2007).

Iowa

Cedar Rapids Gazette: 500 Third Ave, SE, Cedar Rapids, IA 52401; tel. (319) 398-8211; fax (319) 398-5846; e-mail steve.buttry@gazcomm.com; internet www.gazetteonline.com; f. 1883; Publr DAVE STOREY; Man. Editor DAN GEISER; circ. Mon. to Fri. 57,945, Sat. 65,373, Sun. 71,521.

Des Moines Register: 715 Locust St, POB 957, Des Moines, IA 50306-0957; tel. (515) 284-8000; fax (515) 268-2504; e-mail letters@dmreg.com; internet www.dmregister.com; f. 1849; Pres. and Publr LAURA HOLLINGSWORTH; Editor CAROLYN WASHBURN; circ. Mon. to Fri. 138,519, Sat. 138,585, Sun. 222,122.

Quad-City Times: 500 East Third St, POB 3828, Davenport, IA 52801; tel. (563) 383-2200; fax (563) 383-2223; internet www.qctimes.com; f. 1855; division of Lee Enterprises, Inc.; Publr JULIE BECHTEL; Editor STEVE THOMAS; circ. Mon. to Fri. 51,890, Sat. 54,968, Sun. 67,753.

Sioux City Journal: 515 Pavonia St, Sioux City, IA 51102; tel. (712) 293-4250; fax (712) 279-5059; internet www.siouxcityjournal.com; f. 1864; subsidiary of Lee Enterprises, Inc.; Publr RON PETERSON; Editor MITCH PUGH; circ. Mon. to Fri. 41,096, Sat. 40,235, Sun. 42,354.

Telegraph Herald: 801 Bluff St, POB 688, Dubuque, IA 52004-0688; tel. (563) 588-5611; fax (563) 588-5739; e-mail jnormandin@wcinet.com; internet www.thonline.com; f. 1836; Publr JIM NORMANDIN; Exec. Editor BRIAN COOPER; circ. Mon. to Fri. 28,207, Sat. 27,594, Sun. 33,506.

Waterloo Courier: 501 Commercial St, POB 540, Waterloo, IA 50704; tel. (319) 291-1400; fax (319) 291-2069; e-mail barb.anderson@wcfcourier.com; internet www.wcfcourier.com; f. 1858; Mon. to Fri. evening; Sun. morning; Publr DAVID A. BRATON; Editor NANCY NEWHOFF; circ. Mon. to Fri. 41,142, Sat. 36,967, Sun. 50,322.

Kansas

Hutchinson News: 300 West Second St, POB 190, Hutchinson, KS 67504-0190; tel. (620) 694-5700; fax (620) 662-4186; e-mail jmont@hutchnews.com; internet www.hutchnews.com; f. 1872; morning; Publr and Editor JOHN MONTGOMERY; circ. Mon. to Fri. 31,019, Sat. 30,114, Sun. 34,073.

Topeka Capital-Journal: 616 SE Jefferson St, Topeka, KS 66607; tel. (785) 295-1111; fax (785) 295-1230; e-mail pete.goering@cjonline.com; internet www.cjonline.com; f. 1879; Publr MARK NUSBAUM; Exec. Editor PETE GOERING; circ. Mon. to Fri. 44,864, Sat. 45,238, Sun. 53,180.

Wichita Eagle: 825 East Douglas Ave, POB 820, Wichita, KS 67201; tel. (316) 268-6000; fax (316) 268-6438; e-mail wenews@wichitaeagle.com; internet www.kansas.com; f. 1872; Publr LOU HELDMAN; Editor SHERRY CHISENHALL, Jr; circ. Mon. to Fri. 82,912, Sat. 94,486, Sun. 130,333.

Kentucky

Courier-Journal: 525 West Broadway, Louisville, KY 40201-7431; POB 740031, Louisville, KY 40201; tel. (502) 582-4011; fax (502) 582-4200; e-mail publisher@courier-journal.com; internet www.courier-journal.com; f. 1868; Publr and Pres. ARNOLD GARSON; Editor BENNIE L. IVORY; circ. Mon. to Fri. 215,328, Sat. 197,516, Sun. 258,778.

Lexington Herald-Leader: 100 Midland Ave, Lexington, KY 40508-1999; tel. (859) 231-3221; e-mail laustin@herald-leader.com; internet www.kentucky.com; f. 1860; Pres. and Publr TIM KELLY; Editor LINDA AUSTIN; circ. Mon. to Fri. 109,624, Sat. 109,495, Sun. 135,250.

Messenger-Inquirer: POB 1480, Owensboro, KY 42302-1480; tel. (270) 926-0123; fax (502) 685-3446; e-mail jjordan@messenger-inquirer.com; internet www.messenger-inquirer.com; f. 1875; morning; Publr BOB MORRIS; News Editor JACQUELINE JORDAN; circ. Mon. to Fri. 27,276, Sat. 27,045, Sun. 29,621.

Sun: 408 Kentucky Ave, POB 2300, Paducah, KY 42002-2300; tel. (270) 575-8600; fax (270) 575-8780; e-mail dconover@paducahsun.com; internet www.paducahsun.com; f. 1871; morning; Publr JIM PAXTON; Man. Editor DUKE CONOVER; circ. Mon. to Fri. 24,768, Sat. 23,455, Sun. 26,833.

Louisiana

Advertiser: 231 Jefferson St, POB 5310, Lafayette, LA 70502; tel. (337) 289-6300; fax (318) 237-8940; e-mail publisher@theadvertiser.com; internet www.theadvertiser.com; f. 1865; morning; Pres. and Publr LESLIE HURST; Exec. Editor DENISE RICHTER; circ. Mon. to Fri. 40,496 (2008), Sat. 45,754 (2008), Sun. 52,638 (2007).

Advocate: POB 588, Baton Rouge, LA 70821-0588; tel. (225) 383-1111; fax (225) 388-0371; internet www.2theadvocate.com; f. 1904; morning; Publr DOUGLAS L. MANSHIP; Man. Editor MILFORD FRYER; circ. Mon. to Fri. 97,912, Sat. 101,085, Sun. 121,677.

Alexandria Daily Town Talk: POB 7558, Alexandria, LA 71306; tel. (318) 487-6397; fax (318) 487-6315; internet www.thetowntalk.com; f. 1883; morning; Publr and Pres. ED HUMPHREY; Exec. Editor PAUL V. CARTY; circ. Mon. to Fri. 30,858, Sat. 29,763, Sun. 34,382.

American Press: 4900 Hwy 90 East, POB 2893, Lake Charles, LA 70602-2893; tel. (337) 494-4061; fax (337) 494-4070; e-mail news@americanpress.com; internet www.americanpress.com; f. 1896; morning; Publr TOM SHEARMAN; Editor BRETT DOWNER; circ. Mon. to Fri. 36,270, Sat. 35,775, Sun. 39,825.

News-Star: 411 North Fourth St, POB 1502, Monroe, LA 71210; tel. (318) 322-5161; e-mail dpetty@thenewsstar.com; internet www.thenewsstar.com; f. 1892; morning; Publr DAVID D. PETTY; Editor KATHY SPURLOCK; circ. Mon. to Fri. 33,239, Sat. 31,295, Sun. 37,003.

The Times: 222 Luke St, POB 30222, Shreveport, LA 71130; tel. (318) 459-3200; e-mail pzanmill@gannett.com; internet www.shreveporttimes.com; f. 1872; Publr PETE ZANMILLER; Exec. Editor ALAN ENGLISH; circ. Mon. to Fri. 52,267, Sat. 50,635, Sun. 62,753.

Times-Picayune: 3800 Howard Ave, New Orleans, LA 70125-1429; tel. (504) 826-3279; fax (504) 826-3700; e-mail pkovacs@timespicayune.com; internet www.nola.com/t-p; f. 1880; Publr ASHTON PHELPS, Jr; Editor JON DONLEY; circ. Mon. to Fri. 179,834, Sat. 176,709, Sun. 199,647.

Maine

Bangor Daily News: 491 Main St, POB 1329, Bangor, ME 04401; tel. (207) 990-8000; fax (207) 941-9476; e-mail bdnnews@bangordailynews.net; internet www.bangornews.com; f. 1834; Publr RICHARD J. WARREN; Exec. Editor A. MARK WOODWARD; circ. Mon. to Fri. 55,627, Sat. and Sun. 63,299.

Maine Sunday Telegram: 390 Congress St, POB 1460, Portland, ME 04104; tel. (207) 822-4076; fax (207) 879-1042; e-mail info@mainetoday.com; internet www.mainetoday.com; f. 1887; Publr CHARLES COCHRANE; Man. Editor JEANNINE GUTTMAN; circ. 99,116.

Portland Press Herald: 390 Congress St, POB 1460, Portland, ME 04101-5009; tel. (207) 791-6650; fax (207) 791-6931; e-mail herald@portland.com; internet pressherald.mainetoday.com; f. 1862; Publr CHARLES COCHRANE; Editor and Vice-Pres. JEANNINE A. GUTTMAN; circ. Mon. to Fri. 64,938, Sat. 62,284.

Sun: Lewiston Sun-Journal/Sunday Sun-Journal, 104 Park St, Lewiston, ME 04240; POB 4400, Lewiston, Maine 04243-4400; tel. (207) 784-5411; fax (207) 784-5955; internet www.sunjournal.com; f. 1893; morning; Publr JAMES R. COSTELLO, Sr; Exec. Editor REX E. RHOADES.

Maryland

Baltimore Sun: 501 North Calvert St, POB 1377, Baltimore, MD 21278; tel. (410) 332-6000; fax (410) 752-6049; e-mail publiceditor@baltsun.com; internet www.baltimoresun.com; f. 1837; Publr, Pres. and CEO TIMOTHY E. RYAN; Editor and Sr Vice-Pres. TIM FRANKLIN; circ. Mon. to Fri. 232,360, Sat. 210,901, Sun. 372,970.

The Capital: 2000 Capital Dr., POB 911, Annapolis, MD 21404; tel. (410) 268-5000; fax (410) 268-4643; e-mail lharing@capitalgazette.com; internet www.hometownannapolis.com; f. 1884; Mon. to Sat. evening, Sun. morning; Publr and Editor TOM MARQUARDT; Man.

Editor Loretta Haring; circ. Mon. to Fri. 42,825, Sat. 43,320, Sun. 44,776.

Massachusetts

Berkshire Eagle: 75 South Church St, POB 1171, Pittsfield, MA 01202; tel. (413) 447-7311; fax (413) 499-3419; e-mail letters@berkshireeagle.com; internet www.berkshireeagle.com; f. 1789; morning; Publr and CEO Andrew Mick; Exec. Editor Tim Farkas; circ. Mon. to Fri. 26,427, Sat. 26,991, Sun. 29,838.

Boston Globe: 135 Morrissey Blvd, POB 55819, Boston, MA 02205-5819; tel. (617) 929-2000; fax (617) 929-3192; e-mail letters@globe.com; internet bostonglobe.com; f. 1872; Publr Steve Ainsley; Editor Martin D. Baron; circ. Mon. to Fri. 350,605, Sat. 330,547, Sun. 525,959.

Boston Herald: 1 Herald Sq., Boston, MA 02118; tel. (617) 426-3000; fax (617) 426-1896; e-mail letterstotheeditor@bostonherald.com; internet www.bostonherald.com; f. 1825; Publr Patrick Purcell; Man. Editor Kevin Convey; circ. Mon. to Fri. 182,350, Sat. 143,282, Sun. 105,629.

Cape Cod Times: 319 Main St, Hyannis, MA 02601; tel. (508) 775-1200; fax (508) 771-3292; e-mail pmeyer@capecodonline.com; internet www.capecodonline.com; f. 1936; morning; Publr Peter Meyer; Editor-in-Chief Paul Pronovost; circ. Mon. to Fri. 43,709, Sat. 41,729, Sun. 47,482.

Christian Science Monitor: 1 Norway St, Boston, MA 02115-3195; tel. (617) 450-7929; internet www.csmonitor.com; f. 1908; publ. by The First Church of Christ, Scientist; Editor John Yemma; circ. Mon. to Fri. 56,083.

Eagle-Tribune: Eagle Tribune Publishing Co, 100 Turnpike St, North Andover, MA 01845; tel. (978) 946-2000; fax (978) 685-1588; e-mail agetler@eagletribune.com; internet www.eagletribune.com; f. 1867; acquired by Community Newspaper Holdings, Inc in 2004; morning; Publr Al Getler; Editor Al White; circ. Mon. to Fri. 46,059, Sat. 45,249, Sun. 47,060.

The Enterprise: 60 Main St, POB 1450, Brockton, MA 02303-1450; tel. (508) 427-4054; fax (508) 427-4027; e-mail newsrooom@enterprisenews.com; internet www.enterprisenews.com; f. 1880; mem. of the South of Boston Media Group; Mon. to Fri. evening and Sun. morning; Editor Chaz Dowaliby; circ. Mon. to Fri. 30,405, Sun. 34,932.

Herald News: 207 Pocasset St, Fall River, MA 02722; tel. (508) 676-8211; fax (508) 676-2566; e-mail editor@heraldnews.com; internet www.heraldnews.com; f. 1872; Mon. to Sat. evening, Sun. morning; Publr Sean Burke; News Editor Scott Dolan; circ. Mon. to Sat. 19,309, Sun. 19,849.

Lowell Sun: 491 Dutton St, Lowell, MA 01853; tel. (978) 458-7100; fax (978) 970-4600; e-mail moneil@lowellsun.com; internet www.lowellsun.com; f. 1878; Mon. to Fri. evening, Sat. and Sun. morning; Publr and Pres. Mark O'Neil; Editor James Campanini; circ. Mon. to Fri. 44,439, Sat. 40,205, Sun. 50,245.

MetroWest Daily News: 33 New York Ave, Framingham, MA 01701, tel. (508) 626-4412; fax (508) 626-4400; e-mail mctrowcst@cnc.com; internet www.metrowestdailynews.com; f. 1897; Mon. to Sat. evening, Sun. morning; Publr Kirk Davis; Editor Richard Lodge; circ. Mon. to Fri. 22,613, Sat. 20,704, Sun. 27,308.

Patriot Ledger: 400 Crown Colony Dr., POB 699159, Quincy, MA 02269-9159; tel. (617) 786-7200; fax (617) 786-7393; e-mail delivery@ledger.com; internet www.patriotledger.com; f. 1837; mem. of the South of Boston Media Group; Mon. to Fri. evening, weekend; Publr Kirk A. Davis; Editor Chazy Dowaliby; circ. Mon. to Fri. 51,105, Sat. and Sun. 60,953.

The Republican: 1860 Main St, Springfield, MA 01101; tel. (413) 788-1000; fax (413) 788-1301; e-mail csimison@repub.com; internet www.repub.com; f. 1824; fmrly Sunday Republican, merged with Union-News in 2003; Publr and CEO Larry A. McDermott; Exec. Editor Wayne E. Phaneuf; circ. Mon. to Fri. 83,897, Sat. 74,880, Sun. 119,021.

Sentinel and Enterprise: 808 Main St, POB 730, Fitchburg, MA 01420; tel. (978) 343-6911; fax (978) 342-1158; e-mail rthurman@sentinelandenterprise.com; internet www.sentinelandenterprise.com; f. 1838; Mon. to Sat. evening, Sun. morning; Publr Rick Thurman; Editor Jeff McMenemy; circ. Mon. to Sat. 15,319, Sun. 17,854.

Standard-Times: 25 Elm St, New Bedford, MA 02740; tel. (508) 979-4440; e-mail newsroom@s-t.com; internet www.southcoasttoday.com; f. 1850; Mon. to Fri. evening, Sat. and Sun. morning; Publr William Kennedy; Editor Bob Unger; circ. Mon. to Fri. 30,306, Sat. 28,157, Sun. 30,549.

Worcester Telegram & Gazette: 20 Franklin St, POB 15012, Worcester, MA 01615-0012; tel. (508) 793-9100; fax (508) 793-9313; e-mail kparent@telegram.com; internet www.telegram.com; f. 1866; Publr Bruce Gaultney; Editor Harry T. Whitin; circ. Mon. to Fri. 81,437, Sat. 87,586.

Michigan

Ann Arbor News: 339 East Liberty St, Suite 210, Ann Arbor, MI 48104; tel. (734) 997-7090; fax (734) 994-6879; internet www.annarbornews.com; f. 1835; Mon. to Sat. evening, Sun. morning; Publr Laurel Champion; Editor Ed Petykiewicz; circ. Mon. to Fri. 47,058, Sat. 47,439, Sun. 57,057.

Daily Tribune: 210 East Third St, Royal Oak, MI 48067; tel. (248) 541-3000; fax (248) 541-7093; e-mail jeff.payne@dailytribune.com; internet www.dailytribune.com; f. 1902; Mon. to Fri. evening, Sun. morning; Publr Jeffrey Parra; Editor Jeff Payne; circ. Mon. to Fri. 9,396, Sun. 10,339.

Detroit Free Press: 615 West Lafayette Blvd, Detroit, MI 48226; tel. (313) 222-6400; fax (313) 222-5981; internet www.freep.com; f. 1831; subsidiary of the Gannett Corpn, Inc.; Mon. to Fri. morning, Sat. and Sun.; Publr David Hunke; Vice Pres. and Editor Paul Anger; circ. Mon. to Fri. 308,944, Sat. 288,231, Sun. 606,374.

The Detroit News: 615 West Lafayette Blvd, Detroit, MI 48226-3197; tel. (313) 222-2300; fax (313) 222-2335; e-mail jon.wolman@detnews.com; internet www.detnews.com; f. 1873; Publr and Editor Jonathan Wolman; circ. Mon. to Fri. 188,171, Sat. 172,357.

Enquirer: 155 West Van Buren St, Battle Creek, MI 49015; tel. (800) 333-4139; fax (616) 964-0299; e-mail tszafran@battlecr.gannett.com; internet www.battlecreekenquirer.com; f. 1900; Mon. to Sat. evening, Sun. morning; Publr and Pres. Tim Dowd; Exec. Editor Michael McCullough; circ. Mon. to Sat. 20,854, Sun. 26,983.

Flint Journal: 200 East First St, Flint, MI 48502-1925; tel. (810) 766-6100; fax (810) 767-7518; e-mail fj@flintjournal.com; internet www.mlive.com/flintjournal; f. 1876; Mon. to Fri. evening, Sat. and Sun. morning; Publr David C. Sharp; Editor Tony Dearing; circ. Mon. to Fri. 76,288, Sat. 76,109, Sun. 91,017.

Grand Rapids Press: 155 Michigan St, NW, Grand Rapids, MI 49503-2302; tel. (616) 222-5818; e-mail dgaydou@grpress.com; internet www.mslive.com/grpress; f. 1890; Publr Dan Gaydou; Editor Michael S. Lloyd; circ. Mon. to Fri. 128,930, Sat. 155,480, Sun. 177,026.

Herald Palladium: 3450 Hollywood Rd, POB 128, St Joseph, MI 49085; tel. (269) 429-2400; fax (616) 429-8344; internet www.heraldpalladium.com; f. 1919; Mon. to Fri. evening, Sat. and Sun. morning; Publr David Holgate; Man. Editor Dave Brown; circ. Mon. to Sat. 20,905, Sun. 22,470.

Jackson Citizen Patriot: 214 South Jackson St, Jackson, MI 49201; tel. (517) 787-2300; fax (517) 789-1249; e-mail questions@citpat.com; internet www.mslive.com/citpat; f. 1837; Mon. to Fri. evening, Sat. and Sun. morning; Publr Sandy Petykiewicz; Editor Eileen Lehnert; circ. Mon. to Fri. 30,825, Sat. 30,196, Sun. 34,812.

Kalamazoo Gazette: 401 South Burdick St, Kalamazoo, MI 49007; tel. (269) 345-3511; fax (269) 345-0583; e-mail jstephanak@kalamazoogazette.com; internet www.mlive.com/kgazette; f. 1883; Publr James Stephanak; Editor Rebecca Pierce; circ. Mon. to Fri. 49,127, Sat. 58,499, Sun. 22,470.

Lansing State Journal: 120 East Lenawee St, Lansing, MI 48919-0001; tel. (517) 377-1000; fax (517) 377-1298; e-mail publisher@lsj.com; internet www.lansingstatejournal.com; f. 1855; Pres. and Publr Brian Priester; Exec. Editor Michael Hirten; circ. Mon. to Fri. 58,948, Sat. 62,539, Sun. 76,887.

Macomb Daily: 100 Macomb Daily Dr., Mount Clemens, MI 48043; tel. (586) 469-4510; fax (313) 469-2892; internet www.macombdaily.com; f. 1860; Mon. to Fri. evening, Sun. morning; Publr Jeffrey Parra; Exec. Editor Richard Kelley; circ. Mon. to Fri. 48,741, Sat. 41,260, Sun. 59,863.

Monroe Evening News: Monroe Publishing Co, 20 West First St, Monroe, MI 48161; tel. (734) 242-1100; fax (734) 242-3175; e-mail lonnie@monroenews.com; internet www.monroenews.com; f. 1825; Mon. to Sat. evening, Sun. morning; Publr Lonnie Peppler-Moyer; Editor Deborah Saul; circ. Mon. to Sat. 19,877, Sun. 22,853.

Muskegon Chronicle: 981 Third St, POB 59, Muskegon, MI 49443-0059; tel. (231) 722-3161; fax (231) 722-2552; e-mail pkeep@muskegonchronicle.com; internet www.mlive.com/chronicle; f. 1857; Mon. to Fri. evening, Sat. and Sun. morning; Publr and Editor D. Paul Keep; circ. Mon. to Fri. 41,114, Sat. 42,094, Sun. 45,583.

Oakland Press: 48 West Huron St, POB 436009, Pontiac, MI 48343; tel. (248) 332-8181; fax (248) 332-8294; e-mail glenn.gilbert@oakpress.com; internet www.theoaklandpress.com; f. 1843; Publr and Pres. Kevin Haezebroeck; Exec. Editor Glenn Gilbert; circ. Mon. to Fri. 66,422, Sat. 66,525, Sun. 76,937.

Saginaw News: 203 South Washington Ave, Saginaw, MI 48607; tel. (989) 776-9764; e-mail pchaffee@thesaginawnews.com; internet www.mlive.com/saginawnews; f. 1859; Mon. to Fri. evening, Sat. and

Sun. morning; Publr and Editor PAUL CHAFFEE; circ. Mon. to Fri. 39,143, Sat. 39,738, Sun. 48,839.

Times: 311 Fifth St, Bay City, MI 48708-5853; tel. (989) 894-9613; fax (517) 895-5910; e-mail gweiss@bc-times.com; internet www.mlive.com/bctimes; f. 1873; Mon. to Fri. evening, Sat. and Sun. morning; Publr C. KEVIN DYKEMA; Editor JOHN P. HINER; circ. Mon. to Fri. 30,183, Sat. 31,480, Sun. 38,715.

Times Herald: 911 Military St, Port Huron, MI 48061-5009; tel. (810) 985-7171; fax (313) 984-4230; e-mail editor@thetimesherald.com; internet www.thetimesherald.com; f. 1910; Mon. to Sat. evening, Sun. morning; Publr TIM DOWD; Exec. Editor JEANIE RUDDICK; circ. Mon. to Fri. 25,386, Sat. 26,926, Sun. 34,174.

Minnesota

Duluth News Tribune: 424 West First St, Duluth, MN 55802; tel. (218) 723-5281; fax (218) 720-4120; e-mail news@duluthnews.com; internet www.duluthnewstribune.com; f. 1869; morning; Publr STEVEN MCLISTER; Exec. Editor ROB KARWATH; circ. Mon. to Fri. 40,305, Sat. 40,082, Sun. 62,468 (2007).

Post-Bulletin: 18 First Ave, SE, POB 6118, Rochester, MN 55903-6118; tel. (507) 285-7600; fax (507) 285-7666; e-mail rchapman@postbulletin.com; internet www.postbulletin.com; f. 1859; Mon. to Sat. evening; Publr RANDY CHAPMAN; Man. Editor JAY PATRICK FURST; circ. Mon. to Fri. 44,012, Sat. 47,165 (2006).

Star Tribune: 425 Portland Ave South, Minneapolis, MN 55488; tel. (612) 673-4000; fax (612) 673-4359; e-mail readerrep@startribune.com; internet www.startribune.com; f. 1920; Publr CHRIS HARTE; Editor and Sr Vice-Pres. NANCY BARNES; circ. Mon. to Fri. 322,362, Sat. 350,392, Sun. 534,750.

St Paul Pioneer Press: 345 Cedar St, St Paul, MN 55101; tel. (651) 222-1111; fax (651) 228-5500; e-mail infodesk@pioneerpress.com; internet www.twincities.com; f. 1849; Publr GUY L. GILMORE; Snr Editor THOM FLADUNG; circ. Mon. to Fri. 191,768, Sat. 190,864, Sun. 252,055.

Mississippi

Clarion-Ledger: 201 South Congress St, Jackson, MS 39201; tel. (601) 961-7000; fax (601) 961-7211; e-mail publisher@clarionledger.com; internet www.clarionledger.com; f. 1954; Publr and Pres. LARRY WHITAKER; Exec. Editor RONNIE AGNEW; circ. Mon. to Fri. 82,695, Sat. 82,709, Sun. 95,180.

Hattiesburg American: 825 North Main St, Hattiesburg, MS 39401; tel. (601) 582-4321; e-mail shaik@hattiesburgamerican.com; internet www.hattiesburgamerican.com; f. 1917; Mon. to Sat. evening, Sun. morning; Publr SKIPPY HAIK; Exec. Editor KATHLEEN WILLIAMS; circ. Mon. to Sat. 17,462, Sun. 20,970.

Meridian Star: 814 22nd Ave, Meridian, MS 39302; tel. (601) 693-1551; fax (601) 485-1275; e-mail sgillespie@themeridianstar.com; internet www.meridianstar.com; f. 1879; Mon. to Sat. evening, Sun. morning; Publr CRYSTAL DUPRE; Editor FREDIE CARMICHAEL; circ. Mon. to Sat. 13,964, Sun. 14,911.

Northeast Mississippi Daily Journal: Journal Publishing Co, 1655 South Green, POB 909, Tupelo, MS 38802-0909; tel. (601) 842-2611; fax (601) 842-2233; e-mail mike.tonos@djournal.com; internet www.djournal.com; f. 1870; morning; Publr, Chair. and CEO WILLIAM L. CREWS; Editor LLOYD GRAY; circ. Mon. to Fri. 36,929, Sat. 35,441, Sun. 36,809.

Sun Herald: Gulf Publishing Co, Inc, 205 DeBuys Rd, POB 4567, Biloxi, MS 39535-4567; tel. (228) 896-2390; e-mail tiner@sunherald.com; internet www.sunherald.com; f. 1884; morning; Publr RICKY MATHEWS; Exec. Editor STAN TINER; circ. Mon. to Fri. 44,613, Sat. 43,139, Sun. 48,757.

Missouri

Globe: 117 East Fourth St, POB 7, Joplin, MO 64802-0007; tel. (417) 623-3480; fax (417) 623-8450; e-mail cstark@joplinglobe.com; internet www.joplinglobeonline.com; f. 1896; morning; Publr DAN CHIODO; Editor CAROL STARK; circ. Mon. to Fri. 30,680, Sat. 28,027, Sun. 35,989 (2007).

Kansas City Star: 1729 Grand Blvd, Kansas City, MO 64108; tel. (816) 234-4741; fax (816) 234-4467; e-mail mfannin@kcstar.com; internet www.kansascity.com; f. 1880; Publr MARK ZIEMAN; Editor MIKE FANNIN; circ. Mon. to Fri. 252,785, Sat. 255,889, Sun. 345,332.

News-Leader: 651 Boonville Ave, Springfield, MO 65806; tel. (417) 836-1100; fax (417) 837-1381; e-mail rbates@news-leader.com; internet www.news-leader.com; f. 1933; morning; Publr THOMAS A. BOOKSTAVER; Exec. Editor DON WYATT; circ. Mon. to Fri. 58,576, Sat. 58,716, Sun. 83,104.

St Joseph News-Press: 825 Edmond St, St Joseph, MO 65401; tel. (816) 271-8500; fax (816) 271-8692; e-mail lsawyer@npgco.com; internet stjoenews.net; f. 1845; morning; Publr and Editor DAVID R. BRADLEY, Jr; Exec. Editor DENNIS ELLSWORTH; circ. Mon. to Fri. 33,546, Sat. 32,090, Sun. 35,784.

St Louis Post-Dispatch: 900 North Tucker Blvd, St Louis, MO 63101; tel. (314) 657-3300; fax (314) 340-3050; e-mail generalmanager@stltoday.com; internet www.stltoday.com; f. 1878; Pres. and Publr KEVIN MOWBRAY; Editor ARNIE ROBBINS; circ. Mon. to Fri. 255,057, Sat. 253,947, Sun. 414,564.

Montana

Billings Gazette: POB 36300, Billings, MT 59107; tel. (406) 657-1200; fax (406) 657-1208; e-mail mgulledge@billingsgazette.com; internet billingsgazette.net; f. 1885; Publr MIKE GULLEDGE; Editor STEVE PROSINSKI; circ. Mon. to Fri. 45,530, Sat. 46,062, Sun. 50,940.

Great Falls Tribune: 205 River Dr. South, Great Falls, MT 59405; tel. (406) 791-1444; fax (406) 791-1431; e-mail tribpublisher@sofast.net; internet www.greatfallstribune.com; f. 1884; morning; Publr JIM STRAUSS; Man. Editors DAN HOLLOW, GARY MOSEMAN; circ. Mon. to Fri. 30,631, Sat. 30,129, Sun. 33,066.

Missoulian: 500 South Higgins, POB 8029, Missoula, MT 59807; tel. (406) 523-5200; fax (406) 523-5221; e-mail sdevlin@missoulian.com; internet www.missoulian.com; f. 1873; morning; Publr STACEY MUELLER; Editor SHERRY DEVLIN; circ. Mon. to Fri. 27,955, Sat. 28,596, Sun. 32,480.

Nebraska

Lincoln Journal Star: Journal Star Printing Co, 926 P St, POB 81609, Lincoln, NE 68508; tel. (402) 475-4200; fax (402) 473-7291; e-mail jmaherk@journalstar.com; internet journalstar.com; f. 1867; morning; Publr JOHN F. MAHER; Editor MICHAEL NELSON; circ. Mon. to Fri. 78,350, Sat. 69,345, Sun. 82,266.

Omaha World-Herald: 1334 Douglas St, Omaha, NE 68102-1122; tel. (402) 444-1000; fax (402) 345-0183; e-mail mike.reilly@owh.com; internet www.omaha.com; f. 1885; CEO and Publr JOHN GOTTSCHALK; Exec. Editor MIKE REILLY; circ. Mon. to Fri. 178,545, Sat. 168,427, Sun. 219,795.

Nevada

Las Vegas Review-Journal: 1111 West Bonanza Rd, POB 70, Las Vegas, NV 89125; tel. (702) 383-0211; fax (702) 383-4676; e-mail afleming@reviewjournal.com; internet www.reviewjournal.com; f. 1908; Publr SHERMAN R. FREDERICK; Editor THOMAS MITCHELL; circ. Mon. to Fri. 174,341, Sat. 171,181, Sun. 199,602.

Las Vegas Sun: 2275 Corporate Circle Dr., Suite 300, Henderson, NV 89074; tel. (702) 385-3111; fax (702) 383-7264; internet www.lasvegassun.com; f. 1950; Mon. to Fri. evening; Publr BARBARA GREENSPUN; Pres. and Editor BRIAN GREENSPUN.

Reno Gazette-Journal: POB 22000, Reno, NV 89520-2000; tel. (775) 788-6200; fax (775) 788-6458; e-mail rgjfeedback@rgj.com; internet www.rgj.com; f. 1870; Publr TED POWER; Exec. Editor BERYL LOVE; circ. Mon. to Fri. 57,423, Sat. 55,565, Sun. 66,465.

New Hampshire

New Hampshire Union Leader, New Hampshire Sunday News: Union Leader Corpn, 100 William Loeb Dr., POB 9555, Manchester, NH 03108-9555; tel. (603) 668-4321; fax (603) 668-0382; e-mail publisher@unionleader.com; internet www.unionleader.com; f. 1863 (New Hampshire Union Leader); f. 1946 (New Hampshire Sunday News); Pres. and Publr JOSEPH W. MCQUAID; Editorial Vice-Pres. CHARLES PERKINS, III; circ. Mon. to Fri. 51,782, Sat. 49,900, Sun. 67,226.

New Jersey

Asbury Park Press: 3601 Hwy 66, POB 1550, Neptune, NJ 07754-1550; tel. (732) 922-6000; fax (732) 918-4818; e-mail garys@app.com; internet www.app.com; f. 1879; Publr and Pres. THOMAS M. DONOVAN; Exec. Editor HOLLIS TOWNES; circ. Mon. to Fri. 140,882, Sat. 143,071, Sun. 184,095.

Burlington County Times: 4284 Route 130 North, Willingboro, NJ 08046; tel. (609) 871-8000; fax (609) 877-2706; internet www.phillyburbs.com/bct; f. 1958; Mon. to Fri. evening, Sat. and Sun. morning; Publr STANLEY M. ELLIS; Exec. Editor RONALD L. MARTIN; circ. Mon. to Fri. 32,784, Sat. 33,028, Sun. 36,948.

Courier-News: 1201 Route 22 West, Bridgewater, NJ 08807-0600; tel. (908) 722-8800; fax (908) 707-3252; e-mail couriernews@c-n.com; internet www.mycentraljersey.com; f. 1884; Publr and Pres. WILLIAM C. HIDLAY; Man. Editor CHARLES PAOLINO; circ. Mon. to Fri. 31,370, Sat. 26,867, Sun. 30,940.

Courier-Post: 301 Cuthbert Blvd, POB 5300, Cherry Hill, NJ 08034; tel. (856) 663-3600; fax (856) 663-2831; e-mail thearon@courierpostonline.com; internet www.courierpostonline.com; f. 1875; Pres. and Publr WALT T. LAFFERTY; Exec. Editor EVERETT J. MITCHELL, II; circ. Mon. to Fri. 66,617, Sat. 70,461, Sun. 78,706.

Daily Record: 800 Jefferson Rd, POB 217, Parsippany, NJ 07054; tel. (973) 428-6200; fax (973) 428-6666; e-mail joec@gannett.com; internet www.dailyrecord.com; f. 1900; morning; Publr JOSEPH L. CAVONE; Exec. Editor JAMES A. FLACHSENHAAR; circ. Mon. to Fri. 33,405, Sat. 32,411, Sun. 36,296.

Home News Tribune: 35 Kennedy Blvd, East Brunswick, NJ 08816; tel. (732) 246-5500; fax (732) 565-7208; e-mail hntmetro@thnt.com; internet www.mycentraljersey.com; f. 1879; Publr and Pres. WILLIAM C. HIDLAY; Exec. Editor CHARLES PAOLINO; circ. Mon. to Fri. 49,076, Sat. 46,414, Sun. 54,170.

Jersey Journal: 30 Journal Sq., Jersey City, NJ 07306; tel. (201) 653-1000; fax (201) 217-2455; e-mail jjletters@jjournal.com; internet www.thejerseyjournal.com; f. 1867; Publr KENDRICK ROSS; Editor JUDITH A. LOCORRIERE; circ. Mon. to Fri. 24,940, Sat. 24,934.

The Press of Atlantic City: 11 Devins Lane, Pleasantville, NJ 08232; tel. (609) 272-7266; fax (609) 272-7059; e-mail pmerkoski@pressofac.com; internet www.pressofatlanticcity.com; f. 1895; morning; Publr KEITH L. DAWN; Exec. Editor PAUL A. MERKOSKI; circ. Mon. to Fri. 66,822, Sat. 71,708, Sun. 78,797.

The Record: 150 River St, Hackensack, NJ 07601-7172; tel. (201) 646-4000; fax (201) 646-4135; e-mail scandale@northjersey.com; internet www.northjersey.com; f. 1895; Chair. MALCOLM A. BORG; Editor and Vice-Pres. FRANK SCANDALE; circ. Mon. to Fri. 163,329, Sat. 165,916, Sun. 195,525.

Star-Ledger: 1 Star-Ledger Plaza, Newark, NJ 07102; tel. (973) 392-4121; e-mail jdennan@starledger.com; internet www.nj.com/starledger; f. 1917; Publr GEORGE ARWADY; Editor JIM WILLSE; circ. Mon. to Fri. 345,130, Sat. 281,901, Sun. 500,382.

The Times: 500 Perry St, POB 847, Trenton, NJ 08605; tel. (609) 989-5454; fax (609) 394-2819; e-mail letters@njtimes.com; internet www.nj.com/times; f. 1882; Publr RICHARD BILOTTI; Exec. Editor BRIAN S. MALONE; circ. Mon. to Fri. 54,745, Sat. 51,943, Sun. 56,449.

Trentonian: 600 Perry St, Trenton, NJ 08602; tel. (609) 989-7800; fax (609) 393-6072; e-mail editor@trentonian.com; internet www.trentonian.com; f. 1946; Publr WILLIAM T. (BILL) MURRAY; Editor AARON NOBEL; circ. Mon. to Fri. 39,449, Sat. 32,613, Sun. 26,496.

New Mexico

Albuquerque Journal: Albuquerque Publishing Co, 7777 Jefferson St NE, Albuquerque, NM 87109; tel. (505) 823-3800; e-mail jangel@abqjournal.com; internet www.abqjournal.com; f. 1880; Publr T. H. LANG; Editor KENT WALZ; circ. Mon. to Fri. 102,902, Sat. 107,887, Sun. 137,623.

New Mexican: 202 East Marcy St, POB 2048, Santa Fe, NM 87504-2048; tel. (505) 983-3303; fax (505) 984-1785; e-mail rdean@sfnewmexican.com; internet www.santafenewmexican.com; f. 1849; morning; Publr and Editor ROBIN M. MARTIN; Man. Editor ROB DEAN; circ. Mon. to Fri. 25,450, Sat. 25,106, Sun. 26,080 (2007).

New York

Albany Times Union: Times Union, News Plaza, POB 15000, Albany, NY 12212; tel. (518) 454-5694; fax (518) 454-5628; e-mail ghearst@timesunion.com; internet www.timesunion.com; f. 1856; Publr MARK E. ALDAM; Exec. Editor REX SMITH; circ. Mon. to Fri. 89,256, Sat. 78,535, Sun. 141,064.

Buffalo News: 1 News Plaza, POB 100, Buffalo, NY 14240; tel. (716) 856-5555; fax (716) 856-5150; internet www.buffalonews.com; f. 1880; Publr STANFORD LIPSEY; Editor MARGARET M. SULLIVAN; circ. Mon. to Fri. 178,365, Sat. 181,570, Sun. 260,445.

Daily Gazette: 2345 Maxon Rd, Schenectady, NY 12308; POB 1090, Schenectady, NY 12301-1090; tel. (518) 374-4141; fax (518) 395-3089; e-mail gazette@dailygazette.com; internet www.dailygazette.com; f. 1894; Publr and Editor JOHN E. N. HUME, III; circ. Mon. to Fri. 47,277, Sat. 46,807, Sun. 46,356.

Democrat and Chronicle: 55 Exchange Blvd, Rochester, NY 14614-2001; tel. (585) 258-2220; fax (585) 258-3027; e-mail azoibi@gannett.com; internet www.democratandchronicle.com; f. 1833; Publr ALI M. ZOIBI; Editor KAREN MAGNUSON; circ. Mon. to Fri. 145,913, Sat. 163,585, Sun. 199,533.

Newsday: 235 Pinelawn Rd, Melville, NY 11747; tel. (631) 843-2000; fax (516) 843-2953; e-mail editor@newsday.com; internet www.newsday.com; f. 1940; Publr TIMOTHY P. KNIGHT; Editor JOHN MANCINI; circ. Mon. to Fri. 379,613, Sat. 339,389, Sun. 441,728.

Observer Dispatch: 221 Oriskany Plaza, Utica, NY 13501; tel. (315) 792-5000; internet www.uticaod.com; f. 1817; morning; Publr DONNA M. DONOVAN; Exec. Editor JOSEPH KIETA; circ. Mon. to Fri. 39,293, Sat. 39,197, Sun. 46,103.

Post-Standard: Clinton Sq., POB 4915, Syracuse, NY 13221; tel. (315) 470-0011; fax (315) 470-3081; e-mail mconnor@syracuse.com; internet post-standard.com; f. 1829; Editor and Publr STEPHEN A. ROGERS; Exec. Editor MICHAEL J. CONNOR; circ. Mon. to Fri. 110,061, Sat. 107,508, Sun. 158,529.

Post-Star: Lawrence and Cooper Sts, Glens Falls, NY 12801; tel. (518) 792-3131; e-mail tingley@poststar.com; internet www.poststar.com; f. 1904; morning; Publr (vacant); Man. Editor KEN TINGLEY; circ. Mon. to Fri. 30,265, Sat. 30,102, Sun. 32,977.

Poughkeepsie Journal: POB 1231, Poughkeepsie, NY 12602; tel. (845) 454-2000; fax (845) 437-4921; e-mail rsutherl@poughkeepsie.gannett.com; internet www.poughkeepsiejournal.com; f. 1785; morning; Publr BARRY ROTHFELD; Exec. Editor STUART SHINSKE; circ. Mon. to Fri. 37,265, Sat. 35,060, Sun. 43,661.

Press & Sun-Bulletin: 4421 Vestal Parkway East, Vestal, NY 13850; tel. (607) 798-1234; fax (607) 352-2645; internet www.pressconnects.com; f. 1985; Publr SHERMAN M. BODNER; Exec. Editor CALVIN STOVALL; circ. Mon. to Fri. 48,306 Sat. 47,564, Sun. 60,482.

Record: 501 Broadway, Troy, NY 12181; tel. (518) 270-1200; fax (518) 270-1202; e-mail newsroom@troyrecord.com; internet www.troyrecord.com; f. 1896; morning; Publr MICHAEL F. O'SULLIVAN, Sr; Editor LISA ROBERT LEWIS; circ. Mon. to Sat. 13,755, Sun. 15,001.

Star-Gazette: 201 Baldwin St, POB 285, Elmira, NY 14902; tel. (607) 734-5151; fax (607) 733-4408; e-mail lowilson@stargazette.com; internet www.stargazette.com; f. 1829; morning; Publr MONTE I. TRAMMER; Man. Editor LOIS WILSON, Jr; circ. Mon. to Fri. 23,995, Sat. 23,059, Sun. 31,521.

Times Herald-Record ('The Record'): 40 Mulberry St, POB 2046, Middletown, NY 10940; tel. (914) 341-1100; fax (914) 343-2170; e-mail dosenenko@th-record.com; internet www.recordonline.com; f. 1956; Publr JOE VANDERHOOF; Exec. Editor DEREK OSENENKO; circ. Mon. to Fri. 75,745, Sat. 71,429, Sun. 81,794.

Watertown Daily Times: 113-115 West Main St, POB 140, Watertown, WI 53094-0140; tel. (920) 261-5161; e-mail jimc@wdtimes.com; internet www.wdtimes.com; f. 1861; Mon. to Fri. evening, Sat. and Sun. morning; Publr JAMES CLIFFORD; Man. Editor TOM SCHULTZ; circ. Mon. to Fri. 26,375, Sat. 26,733, Sun. 29,329.

NEW YORK CITY

El Diario/La Prensa: 1 Metrotech Center, 18th Floor, Brooklyn, NY 11201; tel. (212) 807-4600; fax (212) 807-4617; e-mail editor@eldiariony.com; internet www.impre.com/eldiariony; f. 1913; Mon. to Fri. morning; Spanish; Publr ROSSANA ROSADO; Editor-in-Chief ALBERTO VOURVOULIAS-BUSH; circ. Mon. to Fri. 53,856, Sat. 44,973, Sun. 37,168.

New York Daily News: 450 West 33rd St, New York, NY 10001; tel. (212) 210-2100; fax (212) 682-4953; internet www.nydailynews.com; f. 1919; Publr MORTIMER B. ZUCKERMAN; circ. Mon. to Fri. 703,137, Sat. 473,019, Sun. 704,157.

New York Post: 1211 Ave of the Americas, New York, NY 10036-8790; tel. (212) 930-8000; fax (212) 930-8540; e-mail aaquilina@nypost.com; internet www.nypost.com; f. 1801; Publr RUPERT MURDOCH; Editor-in-Chief COL ALLAN; circ. Mon. to Fri. 702,488, Sat. 433,956, Sun. 401,315.

New York Sun: 105 Chambers St, 2nd Floor, New York, NY 10007; tel. (212) 406-2000; fax (212) 571-9836; e-mail inquiries@nysun.com; internet www.nysun.com; f. 2002; Publr RONALD WEINTRAUB; Editor and Pres. SETH LIPSKY; circ. Mon. to Fri. 132,199 (2006).

New York Times: 620 Eighth Ave, New York, NY 10018; tel. (212) 556-1234; e-mail public@nytimes.com; internet www.nytimes.com; f. 1851; Chair. and Publr ARTHUR OCHS SULZBERGER, Jr; Pres. and Gen. Man. SCOTT H. HEEKIN-CANEDY; Exec. Editor BILL KELLER; circ. Mon. to Fri. 1,077,256, Sat. 994,044, Sun. 1,476,400.

Staten Island Advance: 950 Fingerboard Rd, Staten Island, New York, NY 10305; tel. (718) 981-1234; fax (718) 981-5679; e-mail silverstein@siadvance.com; internet www.statenislandadvance.com; f. 1886; Mon. to Sat. evening, Sun. morning; Publr CAROLINE DIAMOND HARRISON; Editor BRIAN J. LALINE; circ. Mon. to Fri. 56,875, Sat. 52,736, Sun. 69,311.

The Wall Street Journal: 200 Liberty St, New York, NY 10281; tel. (212) 416-2000; internet www.wsj.com; f. 1889; publ. by Dow Jones & Co Inc; morning; Chair. M. PETER MCPHERSON; CEO LES HINTON; Man. Editor ROBERT THOMSON; circ. Mon. to Fri. 2,062,312, Sat. 1,968,413.

North Carolina

Charlotte Observer: 600 South Tryon St, POB 32188-28232, Charlotte, NC 28202-1842; tel. (704) 358-5000; fax (704) 358-5036; e-mail charlottefeedback@charlotteobserver.com; internet www.charlotte.com; f. 1886; Publr and Pres. ANN CAULKINS; Editor RICK THAMES; circ. Mon. to Fri. 210,616, Sat. 228,117, Sun. 264,170.

Citizen-Times: 14 Ohenry Ave, POB 2090, Asheville, NC 28802; tel. (828) 232-5934; fax (828) 251-0585; e-mail pfernandez@citizen-times.com; internet www.citizen-times.com; f. 1870; morning; Publr and Pres RANDY HAMMER; Exec. Editor PHIL FERNANDEZ; circ. Mon. to Fri. 50,160, Sat. 44,436, Sun. 55,991.

Enterprise: 210 Church Ave, POB 1009, High Point, NC 27261; tel. (336) 888-3500; fax (336) 88-3367; e-mail mstarn@hpe.com; internet www.hpe.southernheadlines.com; f. 1885; morning; Publr MIKE STARN; Editor THOMAS L. BLOUNT; circ. Mon. to Sat. 19,483, Sun. 22,467.

Fayetteville Observer-Times: Fayetteville Publishing Co, 458 Whitfield St, POB 849, Fayetteville, NC 28302; tel. (910) 323-4848; fax (919) 486-3531; e-mail cbwell@fayobserver.com; internet www.fayobserver.com; f. 1816; morning; Publr CHARLES BROADWELL; Exec. Editor BRIAN TOLLEY; circ. Mon. to Fri. 61,875, Sat. 61,033, Sun. 65,595.

Gaston Gazette: 1893 Remount Rd, Gastonia, NC 28054; tel. (704) 869-1700; fax (704) 867-5751; e-mail gastongazette@link.freedom.com; internet www.gastongazette.com; f. 1880; morning; Publr JENNIE LAMBERT; Editor HUNTER BRETZIUS; circ. Mon. to Fri. 30,103, Sat. 27,017, Sun. 30,567.

Greensboro News and Record: 200 East Market St, POB 20848, Greensboro, NC 27420-0848; tel. (336) 373-7000; fax (336) 373-7067; e-mail jrobinson@news-record.com; internet www.news-record.com; f. 1905; Publr and Pres. ROBIN SAUL; Exec. Editor JOHN ROBINSON; circ. Mon. to Fri. 84,339, Sat. 82,522, Sun. 101,409.

Herald-Sun: Durham Herald Co, 2828 Pickett Rd, POB 2092, Durham, NC 27705; tel. (919) 419-6500; fax (919) 419-6837; e-mail bashley@heraldsun.com; internet www.heraldsun.com; f. 1889; morning; Publr RICK BEAN; Editor ROBERT ASHLEY; circ. Mon. to Fri. 32,845, Sat. 27,340, Sun. 32,711.

News and Observer: 215 South McDowell St, POB 191, Raleigh, NC 27602; tel. (919) 829-4500; fax (919) 829-4872; internet www.news-observer.com; f. 1872; Publr ORAGE QUARLES, III; Exec. Editor JOHN DRESCHER; circ. Mon. to Fri. 176,083, Sat. 170,527, Sun. 211,245.

Star-News: POB 840, Wilmington, NC 28402; tel. (919) 343-2000; fax (919) 343-2229; e-mail robyn.tomlin@starnewsonline.com; internet www.starnewsonline.com; f. 1867; morning; Publr ROBERT J. GRUBER; Exec. Editor ROBYN TOMLIN; circ. Mon. to Fri. 47,620, Sat. 47,352, Sun. 53,746.

Times-News: 707 South Main St, POB 481, Burlington, NC 27215; tel. (336) 227-0131; fax (336) 228-1889; internet www.thetimesnews.com; f. 1887; Mon. to Fri. evening, Sat. and Sun. morning; Publr STEVE BUCKLEY; Man. Editor JAY ASHLEY; circ. Mon. to Fri. 16,949, Sat. 16,473, Sun. 17,173.

Winston-Salem Journal: 418 North Marshall St, POB 3159, Winston-Salem, NC 27102-3159; tel. (336) 727-7211; fax (336) 727-4071; e-mail mhall@journalnow.com; internet www.wsjournal.com; Publr and Pres. MICHAEL MILLER; Exec. Editor CARL CROTHERS; circ. Mon. to Fri. 81,930, Sat. 85,915, Sun. 92,360.

North Dakota

Bismarck Tribune: POB 5516, Bismarck, ND 58506; tel. (701) 223-2500; fax (701) 223-2063; e-mail john.irby@bismarcktribune.com; internet www.bismarcktribune.com; f. 1873; morning; Publr BRIAN KROSHUS; Editor JOHN IRBY; circ. Mon. to Fri. 27,051, Sat. 26,544, Sun. 30,321.

The Forum: 101 Fifth St North, Box 2020, Fargo, ND 58107; tel. (701) 235-7311; fax (701) 241-5406; internet www.in-forum.com; f. 1878; Publr WILLIAM C. MARCIL; Editor MATT VON PINNON; circ. Mon. to Fri. 48,303, Sat. 54,023, Sun. 58,277.

Grand Forks Herald: 375 North Second Ave, POB 6008, Grand Forks, ND 58206-6008; tel. (701) 780-1100; fax (701) 780-1189; e-mail aanderson@gfherald.com; internet www.grandforksherald.com; f. 1879; morning; Publr and Editor MIKE JACOBS; Man. Editor KEVIN GRINDE; circ. Mon. to Fri. 27,650, Sat. 28,379, Sun. 28,755.

Minot Daily News: POB 1150, Minot, ND 58702; tel. (701) 857-1900; fax (701) 852-3570; e-mail news@minotdailynews.com; internet www.minotdailynews.com; f. 1884; morning; Publr BART LEATH; Editor BRYAN L. OBENCHAIN; circ. Mon. to Sat. 18,972, Sun. 19,441.

Ohio

Akron Beacon Journal: 44 East Exchange St, POB 640, Akron, OH 44308; tel. (330) 996-3000; fax (330) 996-3033; internet www.ohio.com; f. 1839; Publr ANDREA MATHEWSON; Editor BRUCE WINGES; circ. Mon. to Fri. 122,373, Sat. 147,325, Sun. 157,713.

Canton Repository: 500 Market Ave South, Canton, OH 44711-2112; tel. (330) 580-8300; fax (330) 454-5610; e-mail newsroom@cantonrep.com; internet www.cantonrep.com; f. 1815; Publr KEVIN KAMPMAN; Editor JEFF GAUGER; circ. Mon. to Fri. 65,789, Sat. 67,236, Sun. 78,066.

Chronicle-Telegram: 225 East Ave, POB 4010, Elyria, OH 44036; tel. (216) 329-7000; fax (216) 329-7282; e-mail ctnews@chroniclet.com; internet www.chroniclet.com; f. 1829; Mon. to Sat. evening, Sun. morning; Publr A. COOPER HUDNUTT; Editor-in-Chief ANDREW YOUNG; circ. Mon. to Fri. 25,698, Sat. 23,507, Sun. 24,963.

Cincinnati Enquirer: 312 Elm St, Cincinnati, OH 45202; tel. (513) 768-8000; fax (513) 768-8340; e-mail mperry@enquirer.com; internet www.cincinnati.com; f. 1841; Publr and Pres. MARGARET E. BUCHANAN; Editor TOM CALLINAN; circ. Mon. to Fri. 212,369, Sat. 212,019, Sun. 279,825.

Cleveland Plain Dealer: 1801 Superior Ave East, Cleveland, OH 44114-2198; tel. (216) 999-4800; fax (216) 999-6354; e-mail tegger@plaind.com; internet www.plaindealer.com; f. 1842; Pres. and Publr TERRENCE C. Z. EGGER; Editor SUSAN GOLDBERG; circ. Mon. to Fri. 330,280, Sat. 310,320, Sun. 428,090.

Columbus Dispatch: 34 South Third St, Columbus, OH 43215; tel. (614) 461-5000; fax (614) 461-7580; e-mail letters@dispatch.com; internet www.dispatch.com; f. 1871; Pres. MICHAEL FIORILE; Editor BEN MARRISON; circ. Mon. to Fri. 199,524, Sat. 257,776, Sun. 334,422.

Dayton Daily News: 1611 South Main St, Dayton, OH 45409; tel. (937) 222-5700; fax (937) 225-2489; e-mail kriley@coxohio.com; internet www.daytondailynews.com; Publr MICHAEL JOSEPH; Editor KEVIN RILEY; circ. Mon. to Fri. 160,690, Sat. 108,477, Sun. 157,833.

The Journal: 1657 Broadway, Lorain, OH 44052; tel. (216) 245-6901; fax (216) 245-5637; e-mail tskoch@morningjournal.com; internet www.morningjournal.com; f. 1879; morning; Publr JEFF SUDBROOK; Editor TOM SKOCH; circ. Mon. to Fri. 25,334, Sat. 24,559, Sun. 27,248.

Lima News: 3515 Elida Rd, POB 690, Lima, OH 45802-0690; tel. (419) 223-1010; fax (419) 229-0426; e-mail info@limanews.com; internet www.limanews.com; f. 1884; morning; Acting Publr JAMES SHINE; Man. Editor DIANE PACETTI; circ. Mon. to Fri. 32,860, Sat. 32,829, Sun. 40,092.

News-Herald: 7085 Mentor Ave, Willoughby, OH 44094; tel. (440) 951-0000; fax (440) 951-0917; e-mail lkessel@news-herald.com; internet www.news-herald.com; f. 1880; Mon. to Sat. evening, Sun. morning; Publr STEVE ROSZCZYK; Exec. Editor TRICIA AMBROSE; circ. Mon. to Fri. 36,948, Sat. 37,383, Sun. 44,322.

News-Journal: 70 West Fourth St, Mansfield, OH 44903; tel. (419) 522-3311; fax (419) 521-7415; e-mail tbrennan@nncogannett.com; internet www.mansfieldnewsjournal.com; f. 1930; Mon. to Sat. evening, Sun. morning; Publr TOM BRENNAN; Man. Editor CARL HUNNELL; circ. Mon. to Fri. 28,272, Sat. 26,723, Sun. 35,000.

Springfield News-Sun: Springfield Newspapers, Inc, 202 North Limestone St, Springfield, OH 45503; tel. (513) 328-0300; fax (513) 328-0221; internet www.springfieldnewssun.com; f. 1817; morning; Publr KEVIN RILEY; Editor KARLA GARRETT HARSHAW; circ. Mon. to Fri. 24,684, Sat. 23,502, Sun. 31,038.

Toledo Blade: 541 North Superior St, Toledo, OH 43660-1000; tel. (419) 724-6000; fax (419) 245-6191; e-mail luannsharp@theblade.com; internet www.toledoblade.com; f. 1835; Co-Publrs JOHN ROBINSON BLOCK, DIANA E. BLOCK; Exec. Editor RON ROYHAB; circ. Mon. to Fri. 119,901, Sat. 116,342, Sun. 147,141.

Tribune Chronicle: 240 Franklin St, SE, Warren, OH 44782; tel. (330) 841-1600; fax (330) 841-1721; e-mail lenblose@tribtoday.com; internet www.tribunetoday.com; f. 1812; Mon. to Sat. evening, Sun. morning; Publr CHARLES JARVIS; Editor FRANK ROBINSON; circ. Mon. to Fri. 29,364, Sat. 30,789, Sun. 34,236.

The Vindicator: 107 Vindicator Sq., POB 780, Youngstown, OH 44501-0780; tel. (330) 747-1471; fax (330) 747-6712; e-mail bjagnow@vindy.com; internet www.vindy.com; Publr BETTY H. BROWN JAGNOW; Gen. Man. MARK BROWN; circ. Mon. to Fri. 56,412, Sat. 59,082, Sun. 75,257.

Oklahoma

Daily Oklahoman: 9000 North Broadway, POB 25125, Oklahoma City, OK 73125; tel. (405) 475-3311; fax (405) 475-3183; internet www.newsok.com; f. 1894; Publr DAVID THOMPSON; Exec. Editor SUE HALE; circ. Mon. to Fri. 210,771, Sat. 183,122, Sun. 262,150.

Tulsa World: 315 South Boulder Ave, POB 1770, Tulsa, OK 74103; tel. (918) 581-8300; fax (918) 581-8353; e-mail letters@tulsaworld.com; internet www.tulsaworld.com; f. 1906; Publr ROBERT E. LORTON, III; Exec. Editor JOE WORLEY; circ. Mon. to Fri. 112,968, Sat. 125,200, Sun. 160,052.

Oregon

The Oregonian: 1320 SW Broadway, Portland, OR 97201-3469; tel. (503) 221-8150; fax (503) 294-4193; e-mail s.rowe@news.oregonian.com; internet www.oregonian.com; f. 1850; Publr. FRED A. STICKEL; Editor SANDY ROWE; circ. Mon. to Fri. 304,399, Sat. 280,930, Sun. 361,988.

The Register-Guard: POB 10188, Eugene, OR 97440-2188; tel. (541) 485-1234; fax (541) 683-7631; e-mail tbaker@guardnet.com; internet www.registerguard.com; f. 1867; Publr and Editor TONY BAKER; circ. Mon. to Fri. 67,400, Sat. 72,278, Sun. 70,193.

Statesman Journal: 280 Church St, NE, POB 13009, Salem, OR 97309-3009; tel. (503) 399-6611; fax (503) 399-6706; e-mail newsroom@statesmanjournal.com; internet www.statesmanjournal.com; f. 1851; Publr and Pres. STEVE SILBERMAN; Exec. Editor BILL CHURCH; circ. Mon. to Fri. 47,131, Sat. 47,481, Sun. 53,101.

Pennsylvania

Altoona Mirror: 301 Cayuga Ave, Altoona, PA 16602; tel. (814) 946-7411; fax (814) 946-7547; e-mail news@altoonamirror.com; internet www.altoonamirror.com; f. 1874; Mon. to Fri. evening, Sat. and Sun. morning; Publr EDWARD KRUGER; Man. Editor NEIL RUDEL; circ. Mon. to Fri. 31,658, Sat. 32,810, Sun. 37,658.

Beaver County Times: 400 Fair Ave, Beaver, PA 15009; tel. (724) 775-3200; fax (724) 775-4180; e-mail kbriscoe@timesonline.com; internet www.timesonline.com; f. 1946; owned by Beaver Newspapers, Inc (Calkins Media); Mon. to Fri. evening, Sun. morning; Publr ALAN BUNCHER; Exec. Editor KEITH BRISCOE; circ. Mon. to Fri. 38,466, Sat. 38,987, Sun. 44,994.

Bucks County Courier Times: 8400 Route 13, Levittown, PA 19057-5198; tel. (215) 949-4000; fax (215) 949-4114; e-mail pwalker@phillyburbs.com; internet www.phillyburbs.com; f. 1910; owned by Calkins Media Inc; Publr DALE LARSON; Exec. Editor PATRICIA S. WALKER; circ. Mon. to Fri. 60,233, Sat. 55,673, Sun. 63,571.

Butler Eagle: POB 271, Butler, PA 16003-0271; tel. (412) 282-8000; fax (412) 282-1280; e-mail letters@butlereagle.com; internet www.butlereagle.com; f. 1869; Mon. to Fri. evening, Sun. morning; Publr VERNON L. WISE, Jr; Editor JOHN LAING WISE, Jr; circ. Mon. to Fri. 27,423, Sun. 30,153.

Citizens' Voice: 75 North Washington St, Wilkes-Barre, PA 18711; tel. (570) 821-2000; fax (570) 821-2249; internet www.citizensvoice.com; f. 1978; Mon. to Sat. morning; Publr SCOTT LYNETT; Man. Editor LARRY HOLEVA; circ. Mon. to Fri. 32,890, Sat. 31,520 (2006).

Daily Local News: Daily Local News Co, 250 North Bradford Ave, West Chester, PA 19382; tel. (610) 696-1775; fax (610) 430-1180; e-mail news@dailylocal.com; internet www.dailylocal.com; f. 1872; morning; Publr RANDALL P. NOTTER; Man. Editor E. WILLIAM MARCH; circ. Mon. to Fri. 25,686, Sat. 21,768, Sun. 24,795.

Daily Times: 500 Mildred Ave, Primos, PA 19018; tel. (215) 622-8800; fax (215) 622-8887; e-mail editor@delcotimes.com; internet www.delcotimes.com; f. 1876; morning; Publr PHILIP E. HERON; Man. Editor LINDA DEMEGLIO; circ. Mon. to Fri. 42,879, Sat. 35,985, Sun. 37,889.

Erie Times-News: 205 West 12th and Sassafras Sts, Erie, PA 16534; tel. (814) 870-1600; fax (814) 570-1615; internet www.goerie.com; f. 1888; Mon. to Fri. evening; Publr ROSANNE CHEESEMAN; Exec. Editor RICK SAYERS; circ. Mon. to Fri. 55,397, Sat. 53,801, Sun. 75,746.

Express-Times: 30 North Fourth St, POB 0391, Easton, PA 18044-0391; tel. (215) 258-7171; fax (215) 258-2100; e-mail mtill@express-times.com; internet www.lehighvalleylive.com/expresstimes; f. 1855; morning; Pres. and Publr MARTIN K. TILL; Man. Editor JIM DEEGAN; circ. Mon. to Fri. 44,561, Sat. 40,116, Sun. 44,323.

Intelligencer: 333 North Broad St, POB 858, Doylestown, PA 18901-0858; tel. (215) 345-3000; fax (215) 345-3150; e-mail dgilmartin@phillyburbs.com; internet www.phillyburbs.com; f. 1804; morning; Exec. Editor LANNY MORGNANESI; circ. Mon. to Fri. 40,015, Sat. 39,848, Sun. 45,278.

Intelligencer Journal: Lancaster Newspapers, Inc, 8 West King St, POB 1328, Lancaster, PA 17603; tel. (717) 291-8811; fax (717) 291-8653; e-mail intell@lnpnews.com; internet lancasteronline.com/lol_pages/paper/intell; f. 1794; Mon. to Sat. morning; Editor RAY SHAW; circ. Mon. to Fri. 46,357, Sat. 48,547.

Lancaster New Era: Lancaster Newspapers, Inc, 8 West King St, Lancaster, PA 17603; tel. (717) 291-8733; fax (717) 399-6506; e-mail pmekeel@lnpnews.com; internet lancasteronline.com/lol_pages/paper/newera; f. 1877; Mon. to Sat. evening; Editor ERNIE SCHREIBER; circ. Mon. to Fri. 40,068, Sat. 41,028.

The Morning Call: 101 North Sixth St, POB 1260, Allentown, PA 18105; tel. (610) 820-6553; fax (610) 820-6693; e-mail marie.herb@mcall.com; internet www.mcall.com; Publr TIMOTHY R. KENNEDY; Editor ARDITH HILLIARD; circ. Mon. to Fri. 108,797, Sat. 113,178, Sun. 140,789.

Observer-Reporter: Observer Publishing Co, 122 South Main St, Washington, PA 15301; tel. (412) 222-2200; fax (412) 222-3982; internet www.observer-reporter.com; f. 1808; morning; Publrs THOMAS NORTHROP; Editor A. PARKER BURROUGHS; circ. Mon. to Fri. 31,755, Sat. 31,400, Sun. 34,388.

The Patriot-News: 812 Market St, Harrisburg, PA 17101; tel. (717) 255-8100; fax (717) 257-4726; e-mail lcarlson@patriot-news.com; internet www.patriot-news.com; f. 1854; daily (except Sat.) morning; Publr and Editor JOHN A. KIRKPATRICK; Exec. Editor DAVID NEWHOUSE; circ. Mon. to Fri. 95,588, Sat. 91,577, Sun. 140,217.

Philadelphia Daily News: 400 North Broad St, POB 7788, Philadelphia, PA 19130; tel. (215) 854-5900; fax (215) 854-5910; e-mail dailynews.opinion@phillynews.com; internet www.philly.com; f. 1925; Publr MARK J. FRISBY; Man. Editor MICHAEL DAYS; circ. Mon. to Fri. 107,269, Sat. 70,066.

Philadelphia Inquirer: 400 North Broad St, POB 8623, Philadelphia, PA 19101; tel. (215) 854-2000; fax (215) 854-4974; e-mail mleary@phillynews.com; internet www.philly.com/inquirer; f. 1829; Publr BRIAN TIERNEY; Editor WILLIAM K. MARIMOW; circ. Mon. to Fri. 334,150, Sat. 328,117, Sun. 630,665.

Pittsburg Post-Gazette: 34 Blvd of the Allies, Pittsburgh, PA 15222; tel. (412) 263-1100; fax (412) 391-8452; e-mail ssmith@post-gazette.com; internet www.post-gazette.com; f. 1786; Publrs WILLIAM BLOCK, Jr, JOHN ROBINSON BLOCK; Exec. Editor DAVID M. SHRIBMAN, Jr; circ. Mon. to Fri. 214,374, Sat. 198,096, Sun. 331,053.

Reading Eagle: 345 Penn St, POB 582, Reading, PA 19603-0582; tel. (215) 371-5000; fax (215) 371-5194; e-mail hdeitz@readingeagle.com; internet www.readingeagle.com; f. 1868; Mon. to Fri. evening, Sun. morning; Publr WILLIAM S. FLIPPIN; Man. Editor DAVID S. MOWERY; circ. Mon. to Fri. 59,262, Sat. 62,414, Sun. 79,787.

Scranton Times-Tribune: 149 Penn Ave, POB 3311, Scranton, PA 18505; tel. (570) 348-9100; fax (570) 348-9145; e-mail letters@timesshamrock.com; internet www.scrantontimes.com; f. 2005 following merger of Scranton Times (f. 1870) with Scranton Tribune (f. 1891); owned by Times-Shamrock Communications Group; Mon. to Sat. evening, Sun. morning; Publrs EDWARD J. LYNETT, Jr, GEORGE V. LYNETT, WILLIAM R. LYNETT; Man. Editor EDWIN E. ROGERS; circ. Mon. to Fri. 53,325, Sun. 71,030 (2007).

Sunday News: Lancaster Newspapers, Inc, 8 West King St, POB 1328, Lancaster, PA 17608; tel. (717) 291-8811; fax (717) 399-6506; e-mail madams@lnpnews.com; internet www.lancasteronline.com/lol_pages/paper/sundaynews; f. 1923; Editor MARV ADAMS; circ. 100,060 (2007).

Times Herald: POB 591, Norristown, PA 19404; tel. (215) 272-2500; fax (215) 272-1935; e-mail shuskey@timesherald.com; internet www.timesherald.com; f. 1799; Publr SHELLEY MEENAN; Editor STAN HUSKEY; circ. Mon. to Sat. 13,823, Sun. 24,225.

Tribune-Democrat: 425 Locust St, POB 340, Johnstown, PA 15907-0340; tel. (814) 532-5050; fax (814) 539-1409; e-mail cminemyer@tribdem.com; internet www.tribune-democrat.com; f. 1853; morning; Publr ROBIN QUILLON; Editor CHIP MINEMYER; circ. Mon. to Fri. 37,673, Sat. 37,857, Sun. 41,430.

Tribune-Review: 622 Cabin Hill Dr., Greensburg, PA 15601; tel. (724) 834-1151; fax (724) 838-5170; internet www.pittsburghlive.com/x/pittsburghtrib; f. 1886; morning; Publr RICHARD M. SCAIFE; Editor FRANK CRAIG; circ. Mon. to Fri. 150,911, Sat. 159,613, Sun. 192,423.

York Daily Record: 1891 Loucks Rd, York, PA 17408; tel. (717) 771-2000; fax (717) 771-2009; e-mail dmandl@ydr.com; internet www.inyork.com/ydr; f. 1796; Mon. to Sat. morning; Publr FRED UFFELMAN; Man. Editor JAMES MCCLURE; circ. Mon. to Fri. 47,753, Sat. 67,044.

York Dispatch: 205 North George St, York, PA 17401; tel. (717) 854-1575; fax (717) 843-2958; internet yorkdispatch.inyork.com; f. 1876; Mon. to Fri. evening; Editor LORI GOODLIN; circ. Mon. to Fri. 31,694.

Rhode Island

Call: 75 Main St, POB A, Woonsocket, RI 02895; tel. (401) 762-3000; fax (401) 765-2834; e-mail publisher@woonsocketcall.com; internet www.woonsocketcall.com; f. 1892; Mon. to Sat. evening, Sun. morning; Publr BARRY M. MECHANIC; Man. Editor DAN TRAFFORD; circ. Mon. to Sat. 10,732, Sun. 15,319 (2006).

Providence Journal: 75 Fountain St, Providence, RI 02902-0050; tel. (401) 277-7000; fax (401) 277-7346; e-mail sareson@projo.com; internet www.projo.com; f. 1829; publ. by Belo Corpn; Publr HOWARD G. SUTTON; Exec. Editor JOEL P. RAWSON; circ. Mon. to Fri. 139,055, Sat. 177,824, Sun. 192,849.

Times: 23 Exchange St, Pawtucket, RI 02862; tel. (401) 722-9292; fax (401) 727-9252; e-mail editor@pawtuckettimes.com; internet www.pawtuckettimes.com; f. 1885; Mon. to Sat. morning; Publr BARRY M. MECHANIC; circ. 8,960 (2006).

South Carolina

Anderson Independent-Mail: 1000 Williamston Rd, POB 2507, Anderson, SC 29622; tel. (803) 224-4321; fax (803) 260-1250; e-mail hughesb@independentmail.com; internet www.independentmail.com; f. 1899; morning; Publr BUTCH HUGHES; Editor DONALD KAUSLER, Jr; circ. Mon. to Fri. 36,374, Sat. 35,487, Sun. 41,048 (2006).

Greenville News: 305 South Main St, POB 1688, Greenville, SC 29601-2605; tel. (864) 298-4100; fax (864) 298-4805; e-mail letters@greenvillenews.com; internet www.greenvilleonline.com; f. 1874; Publr STEVEN BRANDT; Editor JOHN S. PITTMAN; circ. Mon. to Fri. 81,010, Sat. 77,529, Sun. 108,568.

Herald: 132–36 West Main St, POB 29731, Rock Hill, SC 29730; tel. (803) 329-4000; fax (803) 329-4021; e-mail dabels@heraldonline.com; internet www.heraldonline.com; f. 1871; morning; Publr DEBBIE ABELS; Editor PAUL OSMUNDON; circ. Mon. to Fri. 30,848, Sat. 29,303, Sun. 31,568.

Herald Journal: POB 1657, Herald Sq., Spartanburg, SC 29304; tel. (803) 582-4511; fax (803) 594-6350; e-mail david.roberts@shj.com; internet www.goupstate.com; f. 1844; morning; Publr DAVID O. ROBERTS; Exec. Editor CARL E. BECK, Jr; circ. Mon. to Fri. 42,380, Sat. 42,012, Sun. 50,956.

Morning News: 310 South Dargan St, POB 100528, Florence, SC 29501-0528; tel. (803) 317-6397; fax (803) 317-7292; e-mail kginfreda@florencenews.com; internet www.scnow.com/scp/community/morning_news; f. 1923; morning; Publr MARK LASKOWSKI; News Editor KIMBERLEY GINFRIDA; circ. Mon. to Fri. 31,237, Sat. 30,387, Sun. 33,600.

The Post and Courier: 134 Columbus St, Charleston, SC 29403-4800; tel. (843) 577-7111; fax (843) 937-5579; e-mail publiceditor@postandcourier.com; internet www.charleston.net; f. 1803; Publr LARRY W. TARLETON, Jr; Exec. Editor BILL HAWKINS; circ. Mon. to Fri. 100,400, Sat. 94,716, Sun. 110,289.

The State: 1401 Shop Rd, POB 1333, Columbia, SC 29202; tel. (803) 771-8380; fax (803) 771-8430; e-mail stateeditor@thestate.com; internet www.thestate.com; f. 1891; Publr HENRY HAITZ, III; Exec. Editor MARK LETT; circ. Mon. to Fri. 101,010, Sat. 106,822, Sun. 128,564.

Sun-News: 914 Frontage Rd East, POB 406, Myrtle Beach, SC 29577; tel. (803) 626-8555; fax (803) 626-0356; e-mail toconnor@thesunnews.com; internet www.myrtlebeachonline.com; f. 1936; morning; Publr P. J. BROWNING; Exec. Editor TRISHA O'CONNOR; circ. Mon. to Fri. 49,889, Sat. 49,550, Sun. 61,238.

South Dakota

Argus Leader: 200 South Minnesota Ave, POB 5034, Sioux Falls, SD 57117-5034; tel. (605) 331-2200; fax (605) 331-2294; e-mail jzimmerm@argusleader.com; internet www.argusleader.com; f. 1881; Publr RANDELL BECK; Exec. Editor MARICARROL KUETER; circ. Mon. to Fri. 48,960, Sat. 45,210, Sun. 65,709.

Rapid City Journal: 507 Main St, POB 450, Rapid City, SD 57709; tel. (605) 394-8300; fax (605) 394-8446; internet www.rapidcityjournal.com; f. 1878; morning; Publr BRAD SLATER; Editor MIKEL LEFORT; circ. Mon. to Fri. 29,437, Sat. 31,820, Sun. 33,782.

Tennessee

Chattanooga Times-Free Press: 400 East 11th St, Chattanooga, TN 37403; tel. (423) 756-6900; fax (423) 757-6383; e-mail tgriscom@timesfreepress.com; internet www.timesfreepress.com; f. 1888; Publr and Exec. Editor TOM GRISCOM; circ. Mon. to Fri. 71,716, Sat. 83,272, Sun. 95,039.

The Commercial Appeal: 495 Union Ave, Memphis, TN 38103; tel. (901) 529-2211; fax (901) 529-2522; internet www.commercialappeal.com; f. 1841; Pres. and Publr JOSEPH PEPE; Editor CHRIS PECK; circ. Mon. to Sat. 149,165, Sun. 190,828.

Kingsport Times-News: 701 Lynn Garden Dr., POB 479, Kingsport, TN 37662; tel. (423) 246-8121; fax (423) 392-1392; e-mail publisher@timesnews.net; internet www.timesnews.net; f. 1920; Mon. to Fri. all day, Sat. and Sun. morning; Publr KEITH D. WILSON; Man. Editor EDWARD T. COMO; circ. Mon. to Fri. 44,096, Sat. 41,577, Sun. 44,480.

Knoxville News-Sentinel: 2332 News Sentinel Dr., Knoxville, TN 37921-5731; tel. (865) 523-3131; fax (865) 342-8650; internet www.knoxnews.com; f. 1886; Publr BRUCE HARTMANN; Editor JACK MCELROY; circ. Mon. to Fri. 117,262, Sat. 124,493, Sun. 147.939.

The Tennessean: 1100 Broadway St, Nashville, TN 37203; tel. (615) 259-8800; fax (615) 259-8093; e-mail publisher@tennessean.com; internet www.tennessean.com; f. 1812; Publr ELLEN LEIFELD; Editor MARK SILVERMAN; circ. Mon. to Fri. 161,131, Sat. 168,881, Sun. 219,044.

Texas

Austin American-Statesman: 305 South Congress Ave, Austin TX 78704; POB 670, Austin, TX 78767; tel. (512) 445-3500; fax (512) 445-3679; internet www.statesman.com; f. 1871; Publr MICHAEL VIVIO; Editor FRED ZIPP; circ. Mon. to Fri. 170, 209, Sat. 167,278, Sun. 206,505.

Beaumont Enterprise: 380 Main St, POB 3071, Beaumont, TX 77701-2331; tel. (409) 833-3311; fax (409) 838-2857; e-mail tkelly@hearstnp.com; internet www.beaumontenterprise.com; f. 1880; Publr JOHN E. NEWHOUSE, II; Editor TIM KELLY; circ. Mon. to Fri. 45,684, Sat. 44,720, Sun. 51,342.

Corpus Christi Caller-Times: 820 North Lower Broadway, POB 9136, Corpus Christi, TX 78469; tel. (361) 884-2011; fax (361) 886-3732; internet www.caller.com; f. 1883; Publr PATRICK J. BIRMINGHAM; Editor LIBBY AVERYT; circ. Mon. to Fri. 53,368, Sat. 57,135, Sun. 73,746.

Dallas Morning News: 508 Young St, Dallas, TX 75202; tel. (214) 977-8222; fax (214) 977-8319; internet www.dallasnews.com; f. 1885; publ. by Belo Corpn; Publr JAMES M. MORONEY, III; Editor ROBERT W. MONG, Jr; circ. Mon. to Fri. 368,313, Sat. 362,834, Sun. 520,215.

El Paso Times: Times Plaza, El Paso, TX 79901-1470; tel. (915) 546-6104; fax (915) 546-6415; internet www.elpasotimes.com; f. 1881; Publr RAY M. STAFFORD; Editor (vacant); circ. Mon. to Fri. 72,027, Sat. 70,809, Sun. 82,927.

Fort Worth Star-Telegram: 400 West 7th St, Fort Worth, TX 76102; tel. (817) 390-7400; fax (817) 390-7789; e-mail newsroom@star-telegram.com; internet www.star-telegram.com; f. 1909; Publr GARY WORTEL; Exec. Editor JIM WITT; circ. Mon. to Fri. 207,045, Sat. 209,384, Sun. 289,974.

Globe News: 900 South Harrison St, Amarillo, TX 79101; tel. (806) 376-4488; internet www.amarillo.com; f. 2001; Publr LESTER T. SIMPSON; circ. 44,764, Sat. 43,484, Sun. 53,773.

Houston Chronicle: 801 Texas Ave, Houston, TX 77002; tel. (713) 362-7171; fax (713) 362-3575; e-mail online@chron.com; internet www.chron.com; f. 1901; Publr JACK SWEENEY; Editor JEFF COHEN; circ. Mon. to Fri. 494,131, Sat. 482,152, Sun. 632,797.

Lubbock Avalanche-Journal: 710 Ave J, POB 491, Lubbock, TX 79401-1808; tel. (806) 762-8844; fax (806) 744-9603; e-mail terry.greenberg@lubbockonline.com; internet www.lubbockonline.com; f. 1900; Publr STEPHEN A. BEASLEY; Editor TERRY GREENBERG; circ. Mon. to Fri. 49,094, Sat. 47,068, Sun. 55,484.

Reporter-News: 101 Cypress St, Abilene, TX 79601; tel. (915) 673-4271; fax (915) 673-1901; internet www.reporter-news.com; f. 1881; morning; Publr KIM NUSSBAUM; Editor BARTON CROMEENS; circ. Mon. to Fri. 29,108, Sat. 32,202, Sun. 39,716.

San Antonio Express-News: 301 Ave E, San Antonio, TX 78205; tel. (210) 250-3000; fax (210) 250-3105; e-mail rrivard@express-news.net; internet www.mysanantonio.com; f. 1864; Publr THOMAS A. STEPHENSON; Editor ROBERT RIVARD; circ. Mon. to Fri. 225,447, Sat. 220,575, Sun. 315,959.

Standard Times: Harte-Hanks Communications, Inc, 34 West Harris Ave, San Angelo, TX 76903; tel. (915) 659-8200; fax (915) 658-7341; e-mail raguilar@standardtimes.com; internet www.gosanangelo.com; f. 1884; morning; Publr and Pres. ROBERT AGUILAR; Editor TIM ARCHULETA; circ. Mon. to Sat. 24,919, Sun. 28,578.

Texarkana Gazette: 315 Pine St, Texarkana, TX 75501; tel. (903) 794-3311; fax (903) 792-7183; e-mail clerk@texarkanagazette.com; internet www.texarkanagazette.com; f. 1875; morning; Publr MAURICE (BUDDY) KING; Man. Editor LES MINOR; circ. Mon. to Fri. 30,073, Sat. 32,513, Sun. 32,904 (2007).

Times Record News: Times Publishing Co, Inc, 1301 Lamar St, POB 120, Wichita Falls, TX 76307; tel. (817) 767-8341; fax (817) 767-1741; e-mail watsond@timesrecordnews.com; internet www.timesrecordnews.com; f. 1907; morning; Publr DARRELL COLEMAN;

Editor DEANNA WATSON; circ. Mon. to Fri. 28,888, Sat. 28,107, Sun. 31,196.

Tyler Morning Telegraph: 410 West Erwin St, POB 2030, Tyler, TX 75710; tel. (903) 597-8111; fax (903) 595-0335; e-mail ajg@tylerpaper.com; internet www.tylerpaper.com; f. 1877; Mon. to Sat. morning; Pres. and Publr NELSON CLYDE, IV; Exec. Editor JIM GIAMETTA; circ. Mon. to Fri. 35,598, Sat. 36,854, Sun. 40,701.

Victoria Advocate: 311 East Constitution St, Victoria, TX 77901; tel. (361) 575-1451; fax (361) 574-1225; e-mail feedback@vicad.com; internet www.victoriaadvocate.com; f. 1846; morning; Publr JOHN M. ROBERTS; Editor CHRIS COBLER; circ. Mon. to Fri. 33,549, Sat. 32,322, Sun. 34,604.

Waco Tribune-Herald: POB 2588, Waco, TX 76702; tel. (254) 757-5757; fax (254) 756-0302; e-mail csanchez@wacotrib.com; internet www.wacotrib.com; f. 1981; morning; Publr BELINDA GAUDET; Editor CARLOS SANCHEZ; circ. Mon. to Fri. 36,708, Sat. 37,122, Sun. 42,919.

Utah

Deseret Morning News: 30 East 100 South, POB 1257, Salt Lake City, UT 84110; tel. (801) 236-6000; fax (801) 237-2121; e-mail rhall@desnews.com; internet www.deseretnews.com; f. 1850; Publr JIM M. WALL; Editor JOSEPH A. CANNON; circ. Mon. to Fri. 73,817, Sat. 74,126, Sun. 75,022.

Salt Lake Tribune: 90 South 400 West, Suite 700, Salt Lake City, UT 84101; tel. (801) 237-8782; fax (801) 257-8525; e-mail fitz@sltrib.com; internet www.sltrib.com; f. 1871; Man. Editor TIM FITZPATRICK; circ. Mon. to Fri. 121,699, Sat. 116,912, Sun. 143,296.

Standard-Examiner: 332 Standard Way, POB 12790, Ogden, UT 84412-2790; tel. (801) 625-4200; fax (801) 625-4508; e-mail ahowell@standard.net; internet www.standard.net; f. 1888; Publr LEE CARTER; Exec. Editor ANDY HOWELL; circ. Mon. to Fri. 61,696, Sat. 60,496, Sun. 64,439.

Vermont

Burlington Free Press: 191 College St, POB 10, Burlington, VT 05402-0010; tel. (802) 863-3441; fax (802) 660-1802; e-mail bhart@bfp.burlingtonfreepress.com; internet www.burlingtonfreepress.com; f. 1827; Publr BRAD ROBERTSON; Exec. Editor MIKE TOWNSEND; circ. Mon. to Fri. 41,901, Sat. 39,248, Sun. 47,566.

Virginia

Daily Press: 7505 Warwick Blvd, Newport News, VA 23607; tel. (757) 247-4600; fax (757) 245-8618; e-mail mccormick@aol.com; internet www.dailypress.com; f. 1896; Publr DIGBY A. SOLOMON; Editor ERNEST C. GATES; circ. Mon. to Fri. 81,241, Sat. 89,114, Sun. 103,308.

Daily Progress: 685 West Rio Rd, POB 9030, Charlottesville, VA 22906; tel. (804) 978-7200; fax (804) 978-2985; internet www.dailyprogress.com; f. 1892; morning; Publr LAWRENCE MCCONNELL; Man. Editor MCGREGOR MCCANCE; circ. Mon. to Fri. 28,697, Sat. 28,240, Sun. 31,508.

The Free Lance-Star: 616 Amelia St, Fredericksburg, VA 22401; tel. (540) 374-5000; fax (540) 374-5449; e-mail newsroom@fredericksburg.com; internet www.fredericksburg.com; f. 1885; daily; Publr JOSIAH P. ROWE, III; Editor EDWARD JONES; circ. Mon. to Fri. 47,288, Sat. 49,227, Sun. 51,234.

Herald-Courier: 320 Morrison Blvd, Bristol, VA 24201; tel. (276) 669-2181; fax (276) 669-3696; e-mail tfoster@bristolnews.com; internet www.tricities.com; f. 1870; Mon. to Fri. all day, Sat. and Sun. morning; Publr CARL ESPOSITO; Editor J. TODD FOSTER; circ. Mon. to Fri. 39,333, Sat. 38,747, Sun. 41,318.

News and Advance: 101 Wyndale Dr., POB 10129, Lynchburg, VA 24506; tel. (804) 385-5555; fax (804) 385-5538; e-mail tjamerson@newsadvance.com; internet www.newsadvance.com; f. 1866; Mon. to Fri. all day, Sat. and Sun. morning; Publr TERRY JAMERSON; Man. Editor JOE STINNETT; circ. Mon. to Fri. 36,826, Sat. 36,035, Sun. 42,231.

Richmond Times-Dispatch: 300 East Franklin St, POB 85333, Richmond, VA 23219; tel. (804) 649-6000; e-mail letters@timesdispatch.com; internet www.timesdispatch.com; f. 1850; Publr THOMAS A. SILVESTRI; Exec. Editor GLENN PROCTOR; circ. Mon. to Fri. 186,441, Sat. 184,175, Sun. 214,971.

Roanoke Times: 201 West Campbell Ave, POB 2491, Roanoke, VA 24010-2491; tel. (540) 981-3340; fax (540) 981-3346; internet www.roanoke.com; Publr DEBBIE MEADE; Editor CAROLE TARRANT; circ. Mon. to Fri. 88,927, Sat. 88,822, Sun. 100,120.

USA Today: 7950 Jones Branch Dr., McLean, VA 22108-0605; tel. (703) 276-3400; internet www.usatoday.com; f. 1982; Pres. and Publr CRAIG A. MOON; Editor KENNETH PAULSON; circ. Mon. to Fri. 2,284,219.

Virginian-Pilot: 150 West Brambleton Ave, POB 449, Norfolk, VA 23501-0449; tel. (757) 446-2000; fax (757) 446-2051; e-mail letters@pilotonline.com; internet thevirginianpilot.com; f. 1876; Publr BRUCE BRADLEY; Man. Editor MARIA CARILLO; circ. Mon. to Fri. 175,005, Sat. 183,434, Sun. 200,012.

Washington

Columbian: 415 West 6th St, Vancouver, WA 98660; tel. (206) 694-3391; fax (206) 699-6029; e-mail newsroom@columbian.com; internet www.columbian.com; Mon. to Fri. evening, Sun. morning; Publr SCOTT CAMPBELL; Editor LOU BRANCACCIO; circ. Mon. to Fri. 44,623, Sat. 41,125, Sun. 50,277.

The Herald: 1213 California St, Everett, WA 98201; POB 930, Everett, WA 98206; tel. (425) 339-3435; fax (425) 339-3049; e-mail funk@herald.net; internet www.heraldnet.com; f. 1891; Publr ALLEN B. FUNK; Exec. Editor NEAL PATTISON; circ. Mon. to Fri. 50,272, Sat. 47,987, Sun. 53,946.

Kitsap Sun: 545 Fifth St, Bremerton, WA 98310; tel. (206) 377-3711; e-mail sware@kitsapsun.com; internet www.kitsapsun.com; f. 1935; Mon. to Fri. evening, Sat. and Sun. morning; Publr MIKE LEVI; Editor SCOTT WARE; circ. Mon. to Fri. 28,792, Sat. 30,057, Sun. 31,730.

News Tribune: 1950 South State St, POB 11000, Tacoma, WA 98411; tel. (253) 597-8742; fax (253) 597-8451; e-mail karen.peterson@thenewstribune.com; internet www.thenewstribune.com; f. 1883; Pres. and Publr DAVID A. ZEECK; Exec. Editor KAREN PETERSON; circ. Mon. to Fri. 111,778, Sat. 107,286, Sun. 125,955.

Seattle Post-Intelligencer: 101 Elliott Ave West, POB 1909, Seattle, WA 98111-1909; tel. (206) 448-8000; fax (206) 448-8165; e-mail editpage@seattlepi.com; internet seattlepi.nwsource.com; f. 1863; Publr and Editor ROGER OGLESBY; Man. Editor DAVID MCCUMBER; circ. Mon. to Fri. 129,563, Sat. 112,739.

Seattle Times: 1120 John St, POB 70, Seattle, WA 98111-0070; tel. (206) 464-2111; fax (206) 464-2261; e-mail pfoote@seattletimes.com; internet seattletimes.nwsource.com; f. 1896; Publr FRANK A. BLETHEN; Exec. Editor DAVID BOARDMAN; circ. Mon. to Fri. 220,863, Sat. 196,377.

Spokesman-Review: 999 West Riverside, POB 2160, Spokane, WA 99210; tel. (509) 459-5000; fax (509) 459-3815; e-mail editor@spokesman.com; internet www.spokesman.com; f. 1883; Publr WILLIAM STACEY COWLES; Editor (vacant); circ. Mon. to Fri. 89,779, Sat. 101,310, Sun. 113,081.

Tri-City Herald: 107 North Cascade St, Kennewick, WA 99336; tel. (509) 582-1500; fax (509) 582-1453; e-mail rfriday@tri-cityherald.com; internet www.tri-cityherald.com; f. 1947; morning; Publr RUFUS FRIDAY; Exec. Editor KEN ROBERTSON; circ. Mon. to Fri. 40,830, Sat. 39,720, Sun. 42,646.

West Virginia

Charleston Daily Mail: 1001 Virginia St East, Charleston, WV 25301-2835; tel. (304) 348-5140; fax (304) 348-4847; e-mail dmnews@dailymail.com; internet www.dailymail.com; f. 1973; evening; Publr and Editor NANYA FRIEND; Man. Editor BOB KELLY; circ. Mon. to Fri. 21,723.

Wisconsin

Green Bay Press-Gazette: 435 East Walnut St, POB 23430, Green Bay, WI 54305-3430; tel. (920) 435-4411; fax (920) 431-8499; e-mail jdye@greenbaypressgazette.com; internet www.greenbaypressgazette.com; f. 1915; bought by Gannett Co in 1980; Publr WILLIAM T. NUSBAUM; Exec. Editor JOHN DYE; circ. Mon. to Fri. 53,600, Sat. 61,853, Sun. 16,894.

Milwaukee Journal Sentinel: 333 West State St, POB 371, Milwaukee, WI 53201; tel. (414) 224-2919; fax (414) 224-2047; e-mail gstanley@journalsentinel.com; internet www.jsonline.com; f. 1837; Publr ELIZABETH 'BETSY' BRENNER; Editor MARTIN KAISER; circ. Mon. to Fri. 217,755, Sat. 208,586, Sun. 384,539.

Post-Crescent: 306 West Washington St, POB 59, Appleton, WI 54911; tel. (920) 733-4411; fax (920) 733-1983; e-mail gmagno@postcrescent.com; internet www.postcrescent.com; f. 1920; Mon. to

Sat evening, Sun. morning; Publr GENIA LOVETT; Exec. Editor DAN FLANNERY; circ. Mon. to Fri. 51,509, Sat. 57,923, Sun. 67,070.

Wisconsin State Journal: 1901 Fish Hatchery Rd, POB 8058, Madison, WI 53713; tel. (608) 252-6100; fax (608) 252-6119; e-mail wsjcity@madison.com; internet www.madison.com/wsj; f. 1839; Publr WILLIAM K. JOHNSTON; Snr Editor DAVID DOMBROWSKI; circ. Mon. to Fri. 87,930, Sat. 92,260, Sun. 138,276.

Wyoming

Star-Tribune: 170 Star Lane, POB 80, Casper, WY 82602; tel. (307) 266-0500; fax (307) 266-0568; e-mail nathan.bekke@trib.com; internet www.trib.com; f. 1891; Publr NATHAN BEKKE; Editor CHAD BALDWIN; circ. Mon. to Fri. 28,312, Sat. 28,216, Sun. 29,860.

SELECTED PERIODICALS

AARP The Magazine: 601 E St, NW, Washington, DC 20049; tel. (202) 434-2560; e-mail aarpmagazine@aarp.org; internet www.aarpmagazine.org; f. 1958 following merger of *My Generation* and *Modern Maturity*; publ. of the American Asscn of Retired Persons; 6 a year; general interest for the over-50s; Group Publr, Vice-Pres. and Publr JIM FISHMAN; Editor-in-Chief HUGH DELAHANTY; Editor NANCY GRAHAM (acting); circ. 23,893,285; AARP also publishes *AARP Bulletin* (11 a year, circ. 24,248,164) and *AARP Segunda Juventud* (quarterly, in Spanish and English).

Allure: 4 Times Sq., New York, NY 10036; tel. (212) 286-2860; fax (212) 286-4654; internet www.allure.com; f. 1991; publ. by Condé Nast Publs Inc; monthly; women's fashion and wellbeing; Vice-Pres. and Publr AGNES CHAPSKI; Editor-in-Chief LINDA WELLS; circ. 1,091,147.

The American Legion Magazine: 700 North Pennsylvania St, POB 1055, Indianapolis, IN 46206-1055; tel. (317) 630-1298; fax (317) 630-1223; e-mail magazine@legion.org; internet www.legion.org; f. 1919; publ. of The American Legion; monthly; Editor JEFF STOFFER; circ. 2,515,624.

American Rifleman: NRA Publications, 11250 Waples Mill Rd, Fairfax, VA 22030; tel. (703) 267-1329; e-mail publications@nrahq.org; internet www.nrapublications.org; f. 1885; official journal of the Nat. Rifle Asscn; monthly; Editor-in-Chief MARK A. KEEFE, IV; circ. 1,394,573.

American Teacher: 555 New Jersey Ave, NW, Washington, DC 20001-2079; tel. (202) 879-4400; fax (202) 783-2014; e-mail mailbox@aft.org; internet www.aft.org; f. 1916; 8 a year; Editor ROGER GLASS; circ. 800,000.

Architectural Digest: Condé Nast Publications Inc, 6300 Wilshire Blvd, Los Angeles, CA 90048; tel. (213) 965-3700; fax (213) 965-4975; internet www.architecturaldigest.com; f. 1920; monthly; Vice-Pres. and Publr GIULIO CAPUA; Editor-in-Chief PAIGE RENSE; circ. 850,502.

Arthritis Today: 1330 West Peachtree St, NW, Suite 100, Atlanta, GA 30309; tel. (404) 965-7635; e-mail atmail@arthritis.org; internet www.arthritis.org/resources/arthritistoday; f. 1987; publ. by the Arthritis Foundation; 6 a year; health and lifestyle magazine for sufferers of arthritis; Publr CINDY MCDANIEL; Editor-in-Chief MARCY O'KOON MOSS; circ. 721,367.

Barron's: 200 Liberty St, 9th Floor, New York, NY 10281; tel. (212) 416-2000; e-mail editors@barrons.com; internet www.barrons.com; f. 1921; publ. by Dow Jones & Co, Inc; Dow Jones & Co, Inc acquired by News Corpn in 2008; weekly; business and finance; Pres. and Editor EDWIN A. FINN, Jr; circ. 308,116.

Better Homes and Gardens: 1716 Locust St, Des Moines, IA 50309-3023; tel. (515) 284-3000; fax (515) 284-3684; internet www.bhg.com; f. 1922; monthly; Vice-Pres. and Publr JAMES T. CARR; Editor-in-Chief GAYLE BUTLER; Exec. Editor KITTY MORGAN; circ. 7,651,178.

Bon Appétit: 6300 Wilshire Blvd, 10th Floor, Los Angeles, CA 90048; tel. (323) 965-3600; fax (323) 930-2369; internet www.bonappetit.com; f. 1955; monthly; Vice-Pres. and Publr PAUL JOWDY; Editor-in-Chief BARBARA FAIRCHILD; circ. 1,371,495.

Boys' Life: 1325 West Walnut Hill Lane, POB 152079, Irving, TX 75015-2079; tel. (972) 580-2263; fax (972) 580-2079; e-mail boyslifemagazine@netbsa.org; internet www.boyslife.org; f. 1911; publ. by Boy Scouts of America; monthly; Publr J. WARREN YOUNG; Editor J. D. OWEN; circ. 1,183,133.

BusinessWeek: 1221 Ave of the Americas, 43rd Floor, New York, NY 10120; tel. (212) 512-2511; e-mail lou_tosto@businessweek.com; internet www.businessweek.com; f. 1929; publ. by BusinessWeek Group, a subsidiary of The McGraw-Hill Cos, Inc; weekly; business, finance and technology; Editor-in-Chief STEPHEN J. ADLER; circ. 925,226.

Car and Driver: 1585 Eisenhower Pl., Ann Arbor, MI 48108; tel. (734) 971-3600; fax (734) 971-9188; e-mail editors@caranddriver.com; internet www.caranddriver.com; f. 1956; publ. by Hachette Filipacchi Media US, Inc; Publr ROBERT G. HOUGHTLIN, III; Editor-in-Chief CSABA CSERE; circ. 1,303,077.

Catholic Digest: 1 Montauk Ave, Suite 200, New London, CT 06320-4967; tel. (800) 321-0411; fax (860) 572-0788; e-mail connors@catholicdigest.com; internet www.catholicdigest.com; f. 1936; monthly; Publr KATHLEEN STAUFFER; Editor DAN CONNORS; circ. 283,548.

Condé Nast Traveler: 4 Times Sq., 14th Floor, New York, NY 10036-6561; tel. (212) 286-2860; fax (212) 286-2094; e-mail beth_lusko@condenast.com; internet www.concierge.com/cntraveler; f. 1954; monthly; Publr LISA HENRIQUES HUGHES; Editor-in-Chief KLARA GLOWCZEWSKA; circ. 820,217.

Congressional Digest: Congressional Digest Corpn, POB 240, Boyds, MD 20841-0240; tel. (301) 634-3113; fax (240) 599-7679; e-mail info@congressionaldigest.com; internet www.congressionaldigest.com; f. 1921; monthly; Publr PAGE B. ROBINSON THOMAS.

Consumer Reports: 101 Truman Ave, Yonkers, NY 10703-1057; tel. (914) 378-2000; fax (914) 378-2900; e-mail pressroom@consumer.org; internet www.consumerreports.org; f. 1936; monthly; Editor-in-Chief KIM KLEMAN; Man. Editor ROBERT TIERNAN; circ. 4,000,000.

Consumers Digest: Consumers Digest Communications, 520 Lake Cook Rd, Suite 500, Deerfield, IL 60015; tel. (847) 607-3000; e-mail postmaster@consumersdigest.com; internet www.consumersdigest.com; f. 1959; 6 a year; Publr RANDY WEBER; circ. 1,200,000.

Cosmopolitan: 300 West 57th St, New York, NY 10019-3299; tel. (212) 649-3570; e-mail cosmo@hearst.com; internet www.cosmopolitan.com; f. 1886; monthly; women's interest; Publr DONNA KALAJIAN LAGANI; Editor-in-Chief KATE WHITE; circ. 2,937,861.

Country Home: 1716 Locust St, Des Moines, IA 50309; tel. (515) 284-2015; e-mail countryhome@meredith.com; internet www.countryhome.com; f. 1979; publ. by Meredith Corpn; 10 a year; lifestyle; Publr ANTHONY IMPERATO; Editor-in-Chief CAROL SHEEHAN; circ. 1,271,782.

Country Living: 300 West 57th St, New York, NY 10019-3788; tel. (212) 649-3500; e-mail countryliving@hearst.com; internet www.countryliving.com; f. 1978; monthly; Publr STEVEN GRUNE; Editor-in-Chief NANCY MERNIT SORIANO; circ. 1,625,836.

Discover: 90 Fifth Ave, New York, NY 10011; tel. (212) 624-4800; fax (212) 624-4813; e-mail bhostetter@discover.com; internet www.discovermagazine.com; f. 1980; publ. by Discover Media LLC; science and technology; Publr WILLIAM C. HOSTETTER; Exec. Editor COREY S. POWELL; circ 717,122.

Domino: 4 Times Sq., 8th Floor, New York, NY 10036; tel. (212) 286-2860; internet www.dominomag.com; f. 2005; publ. by Condé Nast Publs Inc; monthly; home improvement and decoration; Vice-Pres. and Publr BETH FUCHS BRENNER; Editor-in-Chief DEBORAH NEEDLEMAN; circ. 1,115,390.

Ebony: Johnson Publishing, 820 South Michigan Ave, Chicago, IL 60605-2191; tel. (312) 322-9200; fax (312) 322-0039; internet www.ebonyjet.com/ebony; f. 1945; monthly; African-American general interest; Publr KENARD GIBBS; Editorial Dir BRYAN MONROE; circ. 1,450,416.

Elks Magazine: 2750 North Lakeview Ave, Chicago, IL 60614-1889; tel. (773) 755-4740; fax (773) 755-4792; e-mail elksmag@elks.org; internet www.elks.org/elksmag; f. 1922; 10 a year; publ. by the Benevolent and Protective Order of Elks of the United States of America; Editor CHERYL T. STACHURA; circ. 980,000.

Elle: 1633 Broadway, 44th Floor, New York, NY 10019; tel. (212) 767-5800; fax (212) 767-5980; internet www.elle.com; f. 1985; publ. by Hachette Filipacchi Media US, Inc; monthly; women's fashion; Sr Vice-Pres. and Group Publishing Dir CAROL SMITH; Editor-in-Chief ROBERTA MYERS; circ. 1,082,278.

Endless Vacation: 360 Lexington Ave, 19th Floor, New York, NY 10017; tel. (212) 481-3452; fax (212) 213-1287; e-mail barbara.peck@endlessvacation.com; internet www.endlessvacation.com; f. 1975; publ. by Resort Condominiums Int.; 5 a year; Publr HEMEN DALAL; Editor BARBARA PECK; circ. 1,814,218.

Entertainment Weekly: 1675 Broadway, 30th Floor, New York, NY 10019; tel. (212) 522-5600; fax (212) 522-4482; e-mail letters@ew

.com; internet www.ew.com; f. 1990; Publr SCOTT DONATON; Man. Editor RICK TETZELI; circ. 1,813,411.

ESPN The Magazine: 19 East 34th St, New York, NY 10016; tel. (212) 515-1000; fax (212) 515-1275; e-mail ms_support@espn.go.com; internet espn.go.com/magazine; f. 1998; fortnightly; subsidiary of Walt Disney DIS; men's sports and lifestyle; Editor-in-Chief GARY HOENIG; circ. 2,047,969.

ESPN RISE Magazine: SchoolSports, Inc, 971 Commonwealth Ave, Boston, MA 02215-1305; tel. (617) 779-9000; fax (617) 779-9100; e-mail feedback@risemag.com; internet www.risemag.com; f. 1997 as *SchoolSports Magazine*; acquired by ESPN in 2007; 9 a year; 25 regional edns distributed to c. 6,500 schools; sports and teenage active lifestyle; Editor-in-Chief JONATHAN SEGAL; circ. 912,506.

Esquire: 300 West 57th St, New York, NY 10019-3797; tel. (212) 649-4020; fax (212) 649-4303; e-mail esquire@hearst.com; internet www.esquire.com; f. 1933; monthly; Vice-Pres. and Publr KEVIN O'MALLEY; Editor-in-Chief DAVID GRANGER; circ. 726,358.

Essence: 135 West 50th St, 4th Floor, New York, NY 10020; tel. (212) 642-0600; fax (212) 921-5173; e-mail info@essence.com; internet www.essence.com; f. 1970; monthly; African-American general interest; Editor-in-Chief ANGELA BURT-MURRAY; circ. 1,051,130.

Family Circle: 375 Lexington Ave, 9th Floor, New York, NY 10017-5514; tel. (212) 499-2000; fax (212) 499-6740; e-mail support@familycircle.com; internet www.familycircle.com; f. 1932; publ. by Meredith Corpn; every 3 weeks; Editor-in-Chief LINDA FEARS; circ. 3,896,088.

FamilyFun: 244 Main St, Northampton, MA 01060; tel. (212) 633-4485; e-mail ellen.antoville@disney.com; internet familyfun.go.com; f. 1991; publ. by Disney Publishing Worldwide; monthly; general interest for families with young children; Editor ANN HALLOCK; circ. 1,834,166.

Family Handyman (Home Service Publications): 2915 Commers Dr., Suite 700, Eagan, MN 55121; tel. (651) 454-9200; fax (651) 994-2250; e-mail fheditor@readersdigest.com; internet www.rd.com/familyhandyman; f. 1951; publ. by Reader's Digest Asscn, Inc; 10 a year; Editor-in-Chief KEN COLLIER; circ. 1,162,273.

Fast Company: 7 World Trade Center, New York, NY 10007-2195; tel. (212) 389-5300; fax (212) 389-5496; e-mail loop@fastcompany.com; internet www.fastcompany.com; f. 1995; monthly; acquired by Mansueto Ventures LLC in 2005; global business practice; Publr HAROLD BOLLING; Editor-in-Chief ROBERT SAFIAN; circ. 742,316.

Field & Stream: 2 Park Ave, New York, NY 10016-5601; tel. (212) 779-5000; fax (212) 779-5114; e-mail fsletters@time4.com; internet www.fieldandstream.com; f. 1895; publ. by Bonnier Corpn; 11 a year; Publr ERIC ZINCZENKO; Editor ANTHONY LICATA; circ. 1,530,786.

Fitness: 375 Lexington Ave, New York, NY 10017; tel. (212) 499-2000; internet www.fitnessmagazine.com; f. 1992; acquired by Meredith Corpn in 2005; women's health and fitness; Publr LEE SLATTERY; Editor-in-Chief BETTY WONG; circ. 1,574,067.

Food & Wine: 1120 Ave of the Americas, New York, NY 10036; tel. (212) 382-5600; fax (212) 382-5879; e-mail christina.r.grdovic@aexp.com; internet www.foodandwine.com; f. 1978; publ. by American Express Publishing Corpn; monthly; Publr CHRISTINA R. GRDOVIC; Editor-in-Chief DANA COWIN; circ. 958,348.

Forbes: 60 Fifth Ave, New York, NY 10011-8802; tel. (212) 620-2200; fax (212) 620-1875; e-mail readers@forbes.com; internet www.forbes.com; f. 1917; fortnightly; Pres. and Editor-in-Chief STEVE FORBES; Publr RICHARD KARLGAARD; Editor WILLIAM BALDWIN; circ. 926,899.

Fortune: 1271 Ave of the Americas, New York, NY 10020; tel. (212) 522-1212; fax (212) 522-0810; e-mail letters@fortune.com; internet www.fortune.com; f. 1930; Man. Editor ANDREW SERWER; circ. 866,859.

Game Informer: 724 North First St, 4th Floor, Minneapolis, MN 55401; tel. (612) 486-6100; fax (612) 486-6101; e-mail andy@gameinformer.com; internet www.gameinformer.com; f. 1991; owned by Sunrise Publs; monthly; computer gaming; Publr CATHY PRESTON; Editor-in-Chief ANDY MCNAMARA; circ. 3,498,935.

Glamour: 4 Times Sq., 16th Floor, New York, NY 10036; tel. (212) 286-2860; fax (212) 286-8336; e-mail letters@glamour.com; internet us.glamour.com; f. 1939; publ. by Condé Nast Publs Inc; monthly; Publr WILLIAM WACKERMANN; Editor-in-Chief CYNTHIA LEIVE; circ. 2,354,973.

Golf Digest: 20 Westport Rd, POB 850, Wilton, CT 06897; tel. (800) 438-0491; fax (203) 761-5135; e-mail editor@golfdigest.com; internet www.golfdigest.com; f. 1950; publ. by Condé Nast Publs Inc; monthly; Vice-Pres. and Publr THOMAS J. BAIR; Editor-in-Chief JERRY TARDE; circ. 1,647,048.

Golf Magazine: 2 Park Ave, New York, NY 10016-5601; tel. (212) 779-5000; fax (212) 779-5588; e-mail golfletters@golfonline.com; internet www.golfonline.com; f. 1959; publ. by Time Inc; monthly; Publr CHARLIE KAMMERER; Editor DAVID CLARKE; circ. 1,411,237.

Good Housekeeping: 300 West 57th St, New York, NY 10019-5288; tel. (212) 649-2000; fax (212) 265-3307; e-mail ghkletters@hearst.com; internet www.goodhousekeeping.com; f. 1885; monthly; Publr PATRICIA HAEGELE; Editor-in-Chief ROSEMARY ELLIS; circ. 4,668,818.

Gourmet: 4 Times Sq., 9th Floor, New York, NY 10036; tel. (212) 286-8050; fax (212) 286-2932; internet www.epicurious.com/gourmet; f. 1941; sister publ. of *Bon Appétit*, under parent publ. *Epicurious*; owned by CondéNet, online affiliate of Condé Nast Publs Inc; monthly; Vice-Pres. and Publr NANCY BERGER CARDONE; Editor RUTH REICHL; circ. 983,836.

GQ: 4 Times Sq., New York, NY 10036; tel. (212) 286-6410; fax (212) 286-7969; internet us.gq.com; f. 1957; publ. by Condé Nast Publs Inc; monthly; men's lifestyle; Vice-Pres. and Publr PETER HUNSINGER; Editor-in-Chief JIM NELSON; circ. 915,173.

Guideposts: 39 Seminary Hill Rd, Carmel, NY 10512; tel. (212) 929-1300; fax (212) 929-9574; e-mail gpeditors@guideposts.org; internet www.guidepostsmag.com; f. 1945; monthly; other publs incl. *Positive Thinking Magazine* (10 a year, circ. 335,000), *Angels on Earth* (6 a year, circ. 600,000) and *Guideposts Sweet 16* (6 a year); personal and spiritual development; Publr JANINE SCOLPINO; Editor-in-Chief EDWARD GRINNAN; circ. 2,213,354.

HANDY: 12301 Whitewater Dr., Minnetonka, MN 55343; tel. (952) 988-7294; fax (952) 988-7486; e-mail lokrend@namginc.com; internet www.handymanclub.com; f. 1993; publ. by North American Media Group Inc; official publ. of the Handyman Club of America; 6 a year; home improvement; Publr TOM SWEENEY; Editor LARRY OKREND; circ. 874,097.

Harper's Bazaar: 300 West 57th St, New York, NY 10019-3799; tel. (212) 903-5000; fax (212) 262-7101; e-mail bazaar@hearst.com; internet www.harpersbazaar.com; monthly; Publr VALERIE SALEMBIER; Editor-in-Chief GLENDA BAILEY; circ. 716,850.

Health: 2100 Lakeshore Dr., Birmingham, AL 35209; tel. (205) 445-6476; fax (205) 445-5123; e-mail health@timeinc.com; internet www.health.com; f. 1987; publ. by Southern Progress Corpn, a subsidiary of Time Inc; 10 a year; women's health and wellbeing; Publr and Vice-Pres. RENEE TULENKO; Editor-in-Chief ELLEN KUNES; circ. 1,383,173.

Highlights for Children: 803 Church St, Honesdale, PA 18431; tel. (570) 253-1080; fax (570) 253-0179; internet www.highlights.com; f. 1946; monthly; Editor-in-Chief CHRISTINE FRENCH CLARK; circ. 1,800,000 (2007).

Home: 1633 Broadway, 44th Floor, New York, NY 10019; tel. (212) 767-5518; e-mail homeeditor@hfnm.com; internet www.homemag.com; f. 1981; publ. by Hachette Filipacchi Media US Inc; 10 a year; home improvement and decoration; Vice-Pres. and Publr JOHN H. GRANT; Vice-Pres. and Editor-in-Chief DONNA SAPOLIN; circ. 828,630.

Hot Rod Magazine: 6420 Wilshire Blvd, Los Angeles, CA 90048-5515; tel. (332) 782-2000; fax (323) 782-2223; e-mail hotrod@primedia.com; internet www.hotrod.com; f. 1948; monthly; Sr Vice-Pres. and Group Publr DOUG EVANS; Editor-in-Chief DAVID FREIBURGER; circ. 675,535.

House Beautiful: 300 West 57th St, 24th Floor, New York, NY 10019-5970; tel. (212) 903-5206; internet www.housebeautiful.com; f. 1896; monthly; Publr KATE KELLY SMITH; Editor-in-Chief STEPHEN DRUCKER; circ. 844,258.

Inc.: 7 World Trade Center, New York, NY 10007-2195; tel. (212) 389-5300; fax (212) 389-5393; e-mail mail@inc.com; internet www.inc.com; f. 1987; acquired by Mansueto Ventures LLC in 2005; monthly; small business resources and advice; Publr JOHN TEBEAU; Editor-in-Chief JANE BERENTSON; circ. 724,110.

In Style: 1271 Ave of the Americas, New York, NY 10020; tel. (212) 522-1212; internet www.instyle.com; f. 1994; publ. by Time Inc; celebrity, women's lifestyle and fashion; Man. Editor CHARLA LAWHON; circ. 1,827,644.

In Touch Weekly: 270 Sylvan Ave, Englewood Cliffs, NJ 07632; tel. (201) 569-6699; fax (201) 569-3584; e-mail contactintouch@intouchweekly.com; internet www.intouchweekly.com; f. 2002; publ. by Bauer Publishing USA; weekly; celebrity and entertainment; Publr MARK OLTARSH; Editor-in-Chief RICHARD SPENCER; circ. 955,719.

Jet: Johnson Publishing, 820 South Michigan Ave, Chicago, IL 60605-2191; tel. (312) 322-9200; fax (312) 322-0951; internet www.ebonyjet.com; f. 1951; weekly; African-American general interest; Man. Editor MALCOLM R. WEST; circ. 929,538.

Junior Scholastic: 557 Broadway, New York, NY 10012; tel. (212) 343-6100; fax (212) 343-6333; e-mail junior@scholastic.com; f. 1937; 18 a year; Editor LEE BAIER; circ. 615,000.

Kiplinger's Personal Finance: 1729 H St, NW, Washington, DC 20006-3904; tel. (202) 887-6400; fax (202) 331-8637; e-mail magazine@kiplinger.com; internet www.kiplinger.com; f. 1947; monthly; Editor FRED FRAILEY; circ. 831,306.

Ladies' Home Journal: 125 Park Ave, New York, NY 10017-5599; tel. (212) 557-6600; fax (212) 455-1010; e-mail lhj@meredith.com; internet www.lhj.com; f. 1883; monthly; Publr JULIE PINKWATER; Editor-in-Chief SALLY LEE; circ. 3,844,222.

The Lion: 300 22nd St, Oak Brook, IL 60523-8842; tel. (630) 571-5466; fax (630) 571-1685; e-mail magazine@lionsclubs.org; f. 1918; 11 a year; business and professional; Editor ROBERT KLEINFELDER; circ. 403,473.

Lucky: 4 Times Sq., 6th Floor, New York, NY 10036; tel. (212) 286-2860; fax (212) 286-4986; internet www.luckymag.com; f. 2000; publ. by Condé Nast Publs Inc; monthly; fashion and shopping; Vice-Pres. and Publr GINA SANDERS; Editor-in-Chief KIM FRANCE; circ. 1,156,306.

Marie Claire: 1790 Broadway, 3rd Floor, New York, NY 10019; tel. (212) 649-5000; fax (212) 501-5050; e-mail marieclairepromo@hearst.com; internet www.marieclaire.com; f. 1994; monthly; Publr SUSAN D. PLAGEMANN; Editor-in-Chief JOANNA COLES; circ. 979,529.

Martha Stewart Living: 11 West 42nd St, 25th Floor, New York, NY 10036; tel. (212) 827-8000; fax (212) 827-8204; e-mail mstewart@marthastewart.com; internet www.marthastewart.com; f. 1991; publ. by Martha Stewart Living Omnimedia, Inc; monthly; lifestyle and general interest; Group Publr SALLY PRESTON; Editor-in-Chief MICHAEL BOODRO; circ. 2,037,630; other publs incl. *Everyday Food* (f. 2003, circ. 982,589).

Maxim: 1040 Ave of the Americas, New York, NY 10018; tel. (212) 302-2626; fax (212) 302-2631; e-mail editors@maximmag.com; internet www.maximonline.com; f. 1997; publ. by Alpha Media Group; monthly; men's lifestyle and general interest; Editorial Dir JAMES KAMINSKY; circ. 2,535,884.

MediZine Healthy Living: 500 Fifth Ave, Suite 1900, New York, NY 10110; tel. (212) 695-2223; fax (212) 695-2936; e-mail requestinfo@medizine.com; internet www.medizine.com; f. 1994; quarterly; health and wellbeing; other publs incl. *Remedy* (f. 1995, circ. 2,400,000); *Diabetes Focus* (f. 2003, circ. 1,500,000); Editorial Dir DIANE UMANSKY; circ. 3,650,000.

Men's Fitness: 1 Park Ave, 10th Floor, New York, NY 10016; tel. (212) 545-4800; fax (212) 685-9644; e-mail jkimmel@amilink.com; internet www.mensfitness.com; f. 1985; publ. by AMI/Weider Publs; 10 a year; men's health, fitness and lifestyle; Publr MARC RICHARDS; Editor-in-Chief ROY S. JOHNSON; circ. 716,626.

Men's Health: 733 Third Ave, 15th Floor, New York, NY 10017; tel. (212) 573-0555; e-mail jon.hammond@rodale.com; internet www.menshealth.com; f. 1988; men's health and general interest; 10 a year; publ. by Rodale Inc; Vice-Pres. and Publr JACK ESSIG; Editor-in-Chief DAVID ZINCZENKO; circ. 1,816,671.

Men's Journal: 1290 Ave of the Americas, New York, NY 10104-0298; tel. (212) 484-1616; fax (212) 484-3429; e-mail eric.bizzak@mensjournal.com; internet www.mensjournal.com; f. 1992; publ. by Wenner Media, Inc; monthly; men's general interest and active lifestyle; Publr WILL SCHENCK; Editor BRAD WIENERS; circ. 710,255.

Metropolitan Home: 1633 Broadway, 44th Floor, New York, NY 10019-6741; tel. (212) 767-5522; fax (212) 767-5636; e-mail metletters@hfnm.com; internet www.methome.com; f. 1981; publ. by Hachette Filipacchi Media US Inc; 10 a year; interior design and architecture; Publr DEBORAH BURNS; Editor-in-Chief DONNA WARNER; circ. 563,417.

Midwest Living: 1716 Locust St, Des Moines, IA 50309; tel. (515) 284-3000; fax (515) 284-2700; e-mail brian.kightlinger@meredith.com; internet www.midwestliving.com; f. 1987; publ. by Meredith Corpn; 6 a year; lifestyle with focus on US Midwest; Publr BRIAN KIGHTLINGER; Editor-in-Chief GREG PHILBY; circ. 955,750.

Money: Time & Life Bldg, Rockefeller Center, New York, NY 10020; tel. (212) 522-1210; fax (212) 522-0970; e-mail managing_editor@moneymail.com; internet money.cnn.com; f. 1972; monthly; Publr JOHN DONNELLY; Man. Editor ERIC SCHURENBERG; circ. 1,956,109.

More: 125 Park Ave, New York, NY 10017-5529; tel. (212) 557-6600; fax (212) 455-1244; internet www.more.com; f. 1998; publ. by Meredith Corpn; 10 a year; women's lifestyle; Publr BRENDA SAGET DARLING; Editor-in-Chief LESLEY JANE SEYMOUR; circ. 1,266,980.

Motor Trend: 6420 Wilshire Blvd, Los Angeles, CA 90048-5515; tel. (323) 782-2220; internet www.motortrend.com; f. 1949; publ. by Primedia, Inc; monthly; Publr IRA GABRIEL; Editor-in-Chief ANGUS MACKENZIE; circ. 1,112,574.

National Enquirer: 600 South East Coast Ave, Lantana, FL 33462-0001; tel. (561) 586-1111; fax (561) 540-1010; e-mail letters@nationalenquirer.com; internet www.nationalenquirer.com; f. 1926; publ. by American Media Inc; weekly; Publr DAVID JACKSON; Editor DAVID PEREL; circ. 956,095.

National Geographic Magazine: 1145 17th St, NW, Washington, DC 20036; tel. (212) 610-5500; fax (202) 775-6141; e-mail ngm@nationalgeographic.com; internet ngm.nationalgeographic.com; f. 1888; monthly; Pres. and CEO JOHN FAHEY; Editor-in-Chief CHRIS JOHNS; circ. 5,061,047.

National News: American Legion Auxiliary, 777 North Meridian St, 3rd Floor, Indianapolis, IN 46260; tel. (317) 569-4500; fax (317) 569-4502; e-mail nnpr@legion-aux.org; internet www.legion-aux.org; publ. of the American Legion Auxiliary (ALA); quarterly; Editor STEPHANIE L. HOLLOWAY; circ. 754,932 (June 2007).

The New Yorker: 4 Times Sq., New York, NY 10036-7448; tel. (212) 286-5400; fax (212) 286-4168; e-mail themail@newyorker.com; internet www.newyorker.com; f. 1925; weekly; Publr DREW SCHUTTE; Editor DAVID REMNICK; circ. 1,043,931.

Newsweek: Newsweek Bldg, 251 West 57th St, New York, NY 10019-1894; tel. (212) 445-4000; fax (212) 445-5068; e-mail editors@newsweek.com; internet www.newsweek.com; f. 1933; weekly; Publr PATRICK HAGERTY; Editor JOHN MEACHAM; circ. 2,737,450.

Nick Jr. Family Magazine: 1515 Broadway, 32nd Floor, New York, NY 10036; tel. (212) 654-6198; fax (212) 846-1907; e-mail nickjreditors@nick.com; internet www.nickjr.com; f. 1999; subsidiary of Viacom Int. Inc; monthly; parenting; Editor-in-Chief FREDDI GREENBERG; circ. 431,136.

North American Hunter: 12301 Whitewater Dr., Minnetonka, MN 55343; tel. (320) 846-6090; fax (320) 846-6092; e-mail rsundberg@namginc.com; internet www.huntingclub.com; f. 1979; publ. by North American Media Group Inc; 8 a year; official publ. of the North American Hunting Club; hunting and conservation; Publr RICH SUNDBERG; Editor GORDY KRAHN; circ. 767,892.

O, The Oprah Magazine: 300 West 57th St, New York, NY 10019-5915; tel. (212) 903-5366; fax (212) 903-5388; e-mail omail@hearst.com; internet www.oprah.com/omagazine; f. 2001; monthly; Vice-Pres. and Publr JILL SEELIG; Editor-in-Chief SUSAN K. REED; circ. 2,394,303.

Organic Gardening: 400 South 10th St, Emmaus, PA 18098; tel. (610) 967-7711; fax (610) 967-8963; e-mail og@rodale.com; internet www.organicgardening.com; f. 1942; publ. by Rodale, Inc; 6 a year; Publr CHRIS LAMBIASE; Editor-in-Chief SCOTT MEYER; circ. 247,194.

Outdoor Life: 2 Park Ave, 10th Floor, New York, NY 10016-5601; tel. (212) 779-5316; fax (212) 779-5118; e-mail amanda.mcnally@bonniercorp.com; internet www.outdoorlife.com; f. 1898; publ. by Bonnier Corpn; 10 a year; Editor-in-Chief TODD W. SMITH; Exec. Editor JOHN SNOW; circ. 949,183.

Outside: 400 Market St, Santa Fe, NM 87501; tel. (505) 989-7100; fax (505) 989-4700; e-mail letters@outsidemag.com; internet outside.away.com; f. 1976 as Mariah; publ. by Mariah Media Inc; monthly; adventure travel and outdoor recreation; Chair. and Editor-in-Chief LAWRENCE J. BURKE; Vice-Pres. and Publr SCOTT PARMELEE; circ. 694,244.

Parenting: 2 Park Ave, New York, NY 10016; tel. (212) 779-5000; internet www.parenting.com; f. 1987; publ. by Bonnier Corpn; monthly; other publs. incl. *Babytalk* (f. 1935, circ. 2,000,000); Editor-in-Chief SUSAN KANE; Publr GREG SCHUMANN; circ. 2,013,268.

Parents' Magazine: 375 Lexington Ave, 10th Floor, New York, NY 10017-5514; tel. (212) 878-8700; fax (212) 986-2656; e-mail support@parents.com; internet www.parents.com; f. 1926; monthly; Publr DIANE NEWMAN; Editor-in-Chief DANA POINTS; circ. 2,086,768.

PC Magazine: 28 East 28th St, New York, NY 10016; tel. (212) 503-5100; fax (212) 503-5000; e-mail stephanie_chang@ziffdavis.com; internet www.pcmag.com; f. 1981; publ. by Ziff Davis Media Inc; fortnightly; personal computer industry; Editor-in-Chief LANCE ULANOFF; circ. 645,886.

PC World: PC World Communications, 501 Second St, San Francisco, CA 94107; tel. (415) 243-0500; fax (415) 442-1891; e-mail pcwletters@pcworld.com; internet www.pcworld.com; f. 1982; publ. by PC World Communications, Inc, a subsidiary of International Data Group; monthly; computer technology; Snr Vice-Pres. and Publr MICHAEL CARROLL; Editor ED ALBRO; circ. 618,520.

People: Time and Life Bldg, 28th Floor, Rockefeller Center, 1271 Ave of the Americas, New York, NY 10020; tel. (212) 522-3347; fax (212) 522-0883; e-mail editor@people.com; internet www.people.com; f. 1974; publ. by Time Inc; weekly; celebrity and entertainment; Group Pres. PAUL CAINE; Man. Editor LARRY HACKETT; circ. 3,803,217.

Playboy: 680 North Lake Shore Dr., Chicago, IL 60611-4402; tel. (312) 751-8000; fax (312) 751-2818; e-mail edit@playboy.com; internet www.playboy.com/magazine-toc.html; f. 1953; monthly; men's interest; Publr LOUIS MOHN; Editor-in-Chief HUGH M. HEFNER; circ. 2,700,653.

Popular Mechanics: 300 West 57th St, New York, NY 10019-5899; tel. (212) 649-2000; e-mail popularmechanics@hearst.com; internet www.popularmechanics.com; f. 1902; monthly; Publr WILLIAM CONGDON; Editor-in-Chief JAMES B. MEIGS; circ. 1,239,827.

Popular Science: 2 Park Ave, 9th Floor, New York, NY 10016; tel. (212) 779-5000; fax (212) 779-5108; e-mail letters@popsci.com; internet www.popsci.com; f. 1872; publ. by Bonnier Corpn; monthly; Publr GREGG R. HANO; Editor MARK JANNOT; circ. 1,350,562.

Prevention: 400 South 10th St, Emmaus, PA 18098; tel. (610) 967-8045; fax (610) 967-9198; e-mail prevention@rodale.com; internet www.prevention.com; f. 1950; monthly; Vice-Pres. and Editor-in-Chief LIZ VACCARIELLO; circ. 3,331,080.

Progressive Farmer: Lakeshore Park Plaza, 2204 Lakeshore Dr., Birmingham, AL 35209; tel. (205) 414-4700; fax (205) 414-4705; e-mail jodle@progressivefarmer.com; internet www.progressivefarmer.com; f. 1886; monthly; Publr ADRIAN BLAKE; Editor JACK ODLE; circ. 675,000.

Reader's Digest: Reader's Digest Rd, Pleasantville, NY 10570-7000; tel. (914) 238-1000; fax (914) 238-4559; internet www.rd.com; f. 1922; monthly; Editor-in-Chief PEGGY NORTHROP; circ. 8,445,916.

Real Simple: Time and Life Bldg, 1271 Ave of the Americas, Suite 41–46B, New York, NY 10020; tel. (212) 522-1212; fax (212) 467-1396; internet www.realsimple.com; f. 2000; publ. by Time Inc; monthly, plus two special issues; women's lifestyle and general interest; Publr KEVIN WHITE; Man. Editor KRISTIN VAN OGTROP; circ. 2,026,466.

Redbook: 224 West 57th St, 6th Floor, New York, NY 10019-3796; tel. (212) 649-3450; fax (212) 581-8114; e-mail redbook@hearst.com; internet www.redbookmag.com; f. 1903; monthly; Vice-Pres. and Publr MARY E. MORGAN; Editor-in-Chief STACY MORRISON; circ. 2,227,957.

Road & Track: 1499 Monrovia Ave, Newport Beach, CA 92663-2752; tel. (949) 720-5300; fax (949) 631-2757; e-mail rtletters@hfmus.com; internet www.roadandtrack.com; f. 1947; monthly; Publr JOHN C. DRISCOLL, Jr; Editor-in-Chief MATT DELORENZO; circ. 703,056.

Rolling Stone: 1290 Ave of the Americas, 2nd Floor, New York, NY 10104-0298; tel. (212) 484-1616; fax (212) 484-3429; e-mail feedback@rollingstone.com; internet www.rollingstone.com; f. 1967; fortnightly; Publr JANN S. WENNER; Man. Editor WILL DANA; circ. 1,453,385.

Scholastic Parent & Child: 557 Broadway, New York, NY 10012; tel. (212) 343-6100; e-mail news@scholastic.com; internet teacher.scholastic.com/products/classmags/parent_child.htm; f. 1995; publ. by Scholastic Inc; 8 a year; Publr RISA CRANDALL; Editor-in-Chief STEPHANIE IZAREK; circ. 1,347,780.

Scientific American: 415 Madison Ave, New York, NY 10017-1179; tel. (212) 451-8200; fax (212) 754-1138; e-mail editors@sciam.com; internet www.sciam.com; f. 1845; monthly; Vice-Pres. and Publr BRUCE BRANDFON; Exec. Editor MARIETTE DICHRISTINA; circ. 637,794.

Scouting Magazine: 1325 West Walnut Hill Lane, POB 152079, Irving, TX 75015-2079; tel. (972) 580-2000; fax (972) 580-2079; e-mail scole@netbsa.org; internet www.scoutingmagazine.org; f. 1913; publ. by Boy Scouts of America; 6 a year; Publr J. WARREN YOUNG; Editor-in-Chief J. D. OWEN; Man. Editor SCOTT DANIELS; circ. 1,020,594.

SELF Magazine: 4 Times Sq., 5th Floor, New York, NY 10036; tel. (212) 286-2860; fax (212) 286-6174; e-mail comments@self.com; internet www.self.com; f. 1979; publ. by Condé Nast Publs Inc; monthly; Vice-Pres. and Publr KIMBERLY ANDERSON KELLEHER; Editor-in-Chief LUCY DANZIGER; circ. 1,495,033.

Seventeen: 300 West 57th St, New York, NY 10019-1798; tel. (212) 649-2000; e-mail mail@seventeen.com; internet www.seventeen.com; f. 1944; publ. by Hearst Corpn; monthly; Publr JAYNE JAMISON; Editor-in-Chief ANN SHOKET; circ. 2,024,147.

Shape: 1 Park Ave, 10th Floor, New York, NY 10016; tel. (212) 545-4800; fax (212) 252-1131; internet www.shape.com; f. 1981; publ. by American Media, Inc; women's health and fitness; Publr SABINE FELDMANN; Editor-in-Chief VALERIE LATONA; circ. 1,703,421.

Sierra: 85 Second St, 2nd Floor, San Francisco, CA 94105; tel. (415) 977-5572; fax (415) 977-5794; e-mail sierra.mail@sierraclub.org; internet www.sierraclub.org/sierra; f. 1893; official publ. of the Sierra Club; 6 a year; nature and ecology; Editor-in-Chief BOB SIPCHEN; circ. 612,221.

SmartMoney: 1755 Broadway, 2nd Floor, New York, NY 10019; tel. (212) 765-7323; e-mail editors@smartmoney.com; internet www.smartmoney.com; f. 1992; jt venture of Dow Jones & Co, Inc and Hearst Corpn; Publr BILL SHAW; Editor-in-Chief JONATHAN DAHL; circ. 826,822.

Smithsonian Magazine: 420 Lexington Ave, Suite 2335, New York, NY 10170; tel. (212) 916-1300; fax (212) 986-4259; e-mail bianchik@si.edu; internet www.smithsonianmag.com; f. 1970; monthly; Publr KERRY BIANCHI; Editor CAREY WINFREY; circ. 2,035,769.

Southern Living: 2100 Lakeshore Dr., Birmingham, AL 35209-6721; tel. (205) 877-6000; fax (205) 445-7523; internet www.southernliving.com; f. 1966; monthly; Vice-Pres. and Editor-in-Chief ELEANOR GRIFFIN; circ. 2,802,444.

Sporting News: 475 Park Ave South, 27th Floor, New York, NY 10016; tel. (646) 424-2227; fax (646) 424-2232; e-mail ebaker@sportingnews.com; internet www.sportingnews.com; f. 1886; acquired by American City Business Journals, Inc in 2006; weekly; Publr ED BAKER; Editor JOHN D. RAWLINGS; circ. 715,521.

Sports Illustrated: 1271 Ave of the Americas, 33rd Floor, New York, NY 10020-1339; tel. (212) 522-1212; fax (212) 522-0475; internet sportsillustrated.cnn.com; f. 1954; weekly; Editor TERRY MCDONNELL; circ. 3,260,964.

Star: 1 Park Ave, 3rd Floor, New York, NY 10016; tel. (212) 743-6523; fax (212) 532-0940; e-mail djackson@starmagazine.com; internet www.starmagazine.com; f. 1974; weekly; Vice-Pres. and Publr DAVID JACKSON; Editor-in-Chief CANDACE TRUNZO; circ. 1,320,963.

Sunset Magazine: 80 Willow Rd, Menlo Park, CA 94025-3691; tel. (650) 321-3600; fax (650) 327-5737; internet www.sunset.com; f. 1898; monthly; travel, home, garden, food and drink; Snr Vice-Pres. and Publr KEVIN LYNCH; Editor-in-Chief KATIE TAMONY; circ. 1,233,742.

TENNIS: 79 Madison Ave, 8th Floor, New York, NY 10016; tel. (212) 636-2700; fax (212) 636-2720; e-mail jwilliams@tennismagazine.com; internet www.tennis.com; f. 1965; acquired by Miller Publishing Group LLC in 1997; 10 a year; tennis, travel and lifestyle; Publr JEFF WILLIAMS; Editor-in-Chief JAMES MARTIN; circ. 604,177.

This Old House: 135 West 50th St, 10th Floor, New York, NY 10020; tel. (212) 522-9465; fax (212) 522-9435; e-mail toh_letters@thisoldhouse.com; internet www.thisoldhouse.com; f. 1995; publ. by Time Inc; 10 a year; home improvement; Editor J. SCOTT OMELIANUK; circ. 969,333.

Time: Time and Life Bldg, Rockefeller Center, 1271 Ave of the Americas, New York, NY 10020-1393; tel. (212) 522-1212; fax (212) 522-0023; e-mail letters@time.com; internet www.time.com; f. 1923; weekly; Pres. and Publr EDWARD R. MCCARRICK; Man. Editor RICHARD STENGEL; circ. 3,389,166.

Traditional Home: 125 Park Ave, New York, NY 10017; tel. (212) 557-6600; fax (212) 551-6914; e-mail traditionalhome@meredith.com; internet www.traditionalhome.com; f. 1978; publ. by Meredith Corpn; 8 a year; Publr DEBRA BRANDT; Editor-in-Chief ANN OMVIG MAINE; circ. 972,928.

Travel & Leisure: 1120 Ave of the Americas, 10th Floor, New York, NY 10036-6770; tel. (212) 382-5600; fax (212) 768-1568; e-mail tlquery@amexpub.com; internet www.travelandleisure.com; f. 1971; monthly; Editor-in-Chief NANCY NOVOGROD; circ. 975,505.

TV Guide: 11 West 42nd St, New York, NY 10036; tel. (212) 852-7500; fax (212) 852-7323; internet www.tvguide.com; f. 1953; weekly; Snr Vice-Pres. and Publr PETE HAEFFNER; Editor-in-Chief DEBRA BIRNBAUM; circ. 3,274,187.

US Weekly: 1290 Ave of the Americas, 2nd Floor, New York, NY 10104-0298; tel. (212) 484-1616; fax (212) 484-4242; e-mail letters@usmagazine.com; internet www.usmagazine.com; f. 1977; weekly; Publr VICTORIA LASDON ROSE; Editor-in-Chief JANICE MIN; circ. 1,905,014.

US News & World Report: 1050 Thomas Jefferson St, NW, Washington, DC 20007–3837; tel. (202) 955-2000; fax (202) 955-2685; e-mail letters@usnews.com; internet www.usnews.com; f. 1933; weekly; Publr KERRY F. DYER; Chair. and Editor-in-Chief MORTIMER B. ZUCKERMAN; Editor BRIAN KELLY; circ. 1,828,293.

Vanity Fair: 4 Times Sq., 7th Floor, New York, NY 10036; tel. (212) 286-2860; fax (212) 286-7036; e-mail vfmail@vf.com; internet www.vanityfair.com; f. 1983; publ. by Condé Nast Publs Inc; monthly; Publr EDWARD MENICHESCHI; Editor-in-Chief GRAYDON CARTER; circ. 1,144,001.

VFW Magazine: 406 West 34th St, Kansas City, MO 64111-2736; tel. (816) 756-3390; fax (816) 968-1169; e-mail info@vfw.org; internet www.vfw.org; f. 1912; 11 a year; Editor RICHARD K. KOLB; circ. 1,546,196.

VIA: 150 Van Ness Ave, San Francisco, CA 94102-5208; tel. (415) 565-2451; fax (415) 863-4726; e-mail viamail@csaa.com; internet www.viamagazine.com; f. 1917; publ. by the California State Automobile Asscn; 6 a year; motoring; Editor BRUCE ANDERSON; circ. 2,836,029.

VIBE: 215 Lexington Ave, New York, NY 10016; tel. (212) 448-7300; fax (212) 448-7400; internet www.vibe.com; f. 1993; acquired by Keith Glen Media from VIBE/Spin Ventures in 2006; monthly; urban music and culture; also publ. *VIBE Vixen* (quarterly, circ. 340,000); Publr LEN BURNETT; Editor-in-Chief DANYEL SMITH; circ. 863,283.

Vogue: 4 Times Sq., 12th Floor, New York, NY 10036; tel. (212) 286-2810; fax (212) 286-8593; e-mail voguemail@aol.com; internet www.style.com/vogue; f. 1892; monthly; also publ. *Men's Vogue* (10 a year, circ. 368,898) and *Teen Vogue* (10 a year, circ. 1,017,125); Snr Vice-Pres. and Publishing Dir THOMAS A. FLORIO; Editor ANNA WINTOUR; circ. 1,224,131.

Weight Watchers Magazine: 747 Third Ave, 24th Floor, New York, NY 10017; tel. (212) 370-0644; fax (212) 687-4398; f. 1968; monthly; Publr ANDREW AMILL; Editor KATE GREER; circ. 1,309,931.

WHERE: c/o Morris Visitor Publications, 699 Broad St, Suite 500, Augusta, GA 30901; tel. (800) 680-4035; internet wheretraveler.com; f. 1936; monthly; int. visitor information; 23 regional edns; Group Publr PETER BLACKWELL; Editorial Dir MARQ DE VILLIERS; circ. 1,120,373.

Woman's Day: 1633 Broadway, 42nd Floor, New York, NY 10019; tel. (212) 767-6418; e-mail womansday@hfmus.com; internet www.womansday.com; f. 1931; owned by Hachette Filipacchi; 17 a year; women's general interest; Vice-Pres. and Publr CARLOS LAMADRID; Editor-in-Chief JANE CHESNUTT; circ. 3,876,483.

Woman's World: Bauer Publishing, 270 Sylvan Ave, Englewood Cliffs, NJ 07632; tel. (201) 569-6699; fax (201) 569-5303; e-mail gregslattery@baueradsales.com; f. 1981; publ. by Bauer Publishing USA; weekly; women's general interest; other publs incl. *First* (circ. 1,377,895, *J-14* (circ. 440,857) and *Life & Style Weekly* (circ. 528,294); Publr GREG SLATTERY; Editor-in-Chief STEPHANIE SAIBLE; circ. 1,387,414.

Working Mother: 60 East 42nd St, 27th Floor, New York, NY 10165-0001; tel. (212) 351-6400; fax (212) 351-6483; e-mail editors@workingmother.com; internet www.workingmother.com; f. 1978; publ. by Working Mother Media, Inc; lifestyle magazine with focus on working mothers; Pres. and Publr JOAN SHERIDAN LABARGE; Editor-in-Chief SUZANNE RISS; circ. 831,150.

NEWS AGENCIES

US News and Features Syndicates

Artists and Writers Syndicate: POB 60688, Washington, DC 20039-0688; tel. (202) 882-8882; fax (202) 829-9283; e-mail srcmarjorie@aol.com; Pres. and Exec. Editor PHILIP STEITZ; Man. Editor MARJORIE STEITZ.

Associated Press (AP): 450 West 33rd St, New York, NY 10001; tel. (212) 621-1500; fax (212) 621-1679; e-mail info@ap.org; internet www.ap.org; f. 1848; Pres. and CEO TOM CURLEY; c. 1,700 newspaper mems in the USA, 6,000 broadcast mems and over 8,500 subscribers abroad.

Black Press International: 2054 National Press Bldg, Washington, DC 20045; tel. (202) 547-4125; fax (202) 547-1992; e-mail busxchng@his.com; internet www.blackpressinternational.com; Pres. WILLIAM REED.

Bloomberg News: 731 Lexington Ave, New York, NY 10022; tel. (212) 318-2000; fax (212) 893-5999; internet www.bloomberg.com; f. 1981; Editor-in-Chief MATTHEW WINKLER.

Business Wire: 44 Montgomery St, Suite 3900, San Francisco, CA 94104; tel. (415) 986-4422; fax (415) 788-5335; internet www.businesswire.com; Chair. LORRY I. LOKEY; Pres. and CEO CATHY BARON TAMRAZ.

City News Service, Inc: 11400 West Olympic Blvd, Suite 780, Los Angeles, CA 90064; tel. (310) 481-0401; fax (310) 481-0416; e-mail info@socalnews.com; internet www.socalnews.com; regional news agency covering four counties in Southern California; Pres. DOUGLAS FAIGIN.

Congressional Quarterly, Inc: 1255 22nd St, NW, Washington, DC 20037; tel. (202) 419-8500; fax (202) 463-4549; e-mail customerservice@cq.com; internet www.cq.com; f. 1984; Pres. and Editor-in-Chief ROBERT W. MERRY; Publr and Snr Vice-Pres. KEITH WHITE.

Creators News Service: 123 Camino de la Reina, Suite S202, POB 120190, San Diego, CA 92108; tel. (619) 293-1818; internet www.creators.com; f. 1955 as Copley News Service; acquired by Creators Syndicate in 2008.

Creators Syndicate: 5777 West Century Blvd, Suite 700, Los Angeles, CA 90045; tel. (310) 337-7003; fax (310) 337-7625; e-mail info@creators.com; internet www.creators.com; f. 1987; Pres. RICHARD S. NEWCOMBE.

Dow Jones Newswires: Harborside Financial Center, 600 Plaza II, Jersey City, NJ 07311-3992; tel. (201) 938-5400; fax (201) 938-5600; e-mail newswires@dowjones.com; internet www.djnewswires.com; parent co, Dow Jones & Company, acquired by News Corpn in 2008; Snr Vice-Pres. and Man. Editor NEAL LIPSCHUTZ.

Falls Church News-Press: 929 West Broad St, Suite 200, Falls Church, VA 22046; tel. (703) 532-3267; fax (703) 532-3396; e-mail fcnp@fcnp.com; internet www.fcnp.com; Owner and Editor-in-Chief NICHOLAS F. BENTON.

Gannett Co, Inc: 7950 Jones Branch Dr., McLean, VA 22107; tel. (703) 854-6000; fax (703) 854-2001; e-mail gcishare@gannett.com; internet www.gannett.com; Chair., Pres. and CEO CRAIG A. DUBOW.

Hearst News Service: 700 12th St, NW, Suite 1000, Washington, DC 20005; tel. (202) 263-6400; fax (202) 263-6441; internet www.hearst.com; Bureau Chief CHARLES J. LEWIS.

Hispanic Link News Service: 1420 N St, NW, Washington, DC 20005; tel. (202) 234-0280; fax (202) 234-4090; e-mail editor@hispaniclink.org; internet www.hispaniclink.org; f. 1980; Publr CHARLES A. ERICKSEN.

Jewish Telegraphic Agency, Inc (JTA): 330 Seventh Ave, 17th Floor, New York, NY 10001; tel. (212) 643-1890; fax (212) 643-8498; e-mail info@jta.org; internet www.jta.org; f. 1917; world-wide coverage of Jewish news; offices in Washington, DC, and Jerusalem, Israel; Pres. DANIEL J. KRIFCHER; Exec. Editor and Publr MARK J. JOFFE.

King Features Syndicate, Inc: 300 West 57th St, 15th Floor, New York, NY 10019-5238; tel. (212) 969-7550; internet www.kingfeatures.com; division of Hearst Corpn; Pres. T. R. SHEPARD, III; Vice-Pres. and Gen. Man. KEITH MCCLOAT.

Los Angeles Times/Washington Post News Service: 1150 15th St, NW, Washington, DC 20071-0070; tel. (202) 334-6173; fax (202) 334-5096; e-mail latwp@newsservice.com; internet www.newsservice.com; Pres. and Editorial Dir AL LEEDS.

National News Bureau: POB 43039, Philadelphia, PA 19129; tel. (215) 849-9016; fax (215) 893-5394; internet www.nationalnewsbureau.com; Publr and Editor-in-Chief HARRY JAY KATZ.

New York Times News Service: 620 Eighth Ave, 9th Floor, New York, NY 10018; tel. (212) 556-1927; fax (212) 556-3535; e-mail nytns@nytimes.com; internet www.nytsyn.com/newsservice.html; Exec. Editor LAURENCE M. PAUL.

New York Times Syndicate: 500 Seventh Av, 8th Floor, New York, NY 10018; tel. (212) 556-8738; fax (212) 921-2003; e-mail nytsf@nytimes.com; internet www.nytsyn.com; Man. Editor MICHAEL ORICCHIO.

Newhouse News Service: 1101 Connecticut Ave, NW, Suite 300, Washington, DC 20036; tel. (202) 383-7800; fax (202) 383-7820; internet www.newhousenews.com; Bureau Chief LINDA FIBICH.

Newspaper Enterprise Association, Inc: 200 Madison Ave, New York, NY 10166; tel. (212) 293-8500; fax (212) 293-8600; internet www.unitedfeatures.com/ufsapp/nea.do; division of United Media; Pres. and CEO DOUGLAS R. STERN.

NewsUSA, Inc: 2841 Hartland Rd, Suite 301, Falls Church, VA 22043; tel. (703) 462-2041; fax (703) 734-6314; e-mail office@newsusa.com; internet www.newsusa.com; Pres. and CEO RICK SMITH.

Ottaway News Service: 97 Route 416, Campbell Hall, NY 10916; tel. (845) 294-8181; fax (845) 294-1659; internet www.ottaway.com; a subsidiary of Dow Jones & Co; Chair. and CEO ANDREW LANGHOFF.

Platt's: 2 Penn Plaza, 25th Floor, New York, NY 10121–2298; tel. (212) 904-3070; fax (212) 438-3078; e-mail support@platts.com; internet www.platts.com; f. 1984; information on energy and metals industries; owned by The McGraw-Hill Companies; Pres. VICTORIA CHU PAO.

Press Associates Inc: 1000 Vermont Ave, NW, Suite 101, Washington, DC 20005; tel. (202) 898-4825; fax (202) 898-9004; e-mail unionnews@hotmail.com; f. 1955; weekly news and analysis for trade unions, the media and govt groups; Editor MARK GRUENBERG.

Religion News Service: 1101 Connecticut Ave, NW, Suite 350, Washington, DC 20036; tel. (202) 463-8777; fax (202) 463-0033; e-mail info@religionnews.com; internet www.religionnews.com; Editor KEVIN ECKSTROM.

Scripps-Howard News Service: 1090 Vermont Ave, NW, Suite 1000, Washington, DC 20005; tel. (202) 408-1484; fax (202) 408-2062; e-mail copelandp@snhs.com; internet www.shns.com; Editor and Gen. Man. PETER COPELAND.

Stephens Washington News Bureau: 666 11th St, NW, Suite 535, Washington, DC 20001; tel. (202) 783-1760; fax (202) 783-1955; e-mail stetreault@nationalpress.com; internet www.stephensdc.com; Bureau Chief STEVE TETREAULT.

Thomson Reuters: 3 Times Sq., New York, NY 10036; tel. (646) 223-4000; e-mail editor.reuters@reuters.com; internet www.reuters.com; f. 2008 by merger of Reuters Group and Thomson Corpn (Canada); CEO TOM GLOCER.

Tribune Media Services, Inc: 435 North Michigan Ave, Suite 1500, Chicago, IL 60611; tel. (312) 222-4444; fax (312) 222-2581;

e-mail mfioritto@tribune.com; internet www.tms.tribune.com; Pres. and CEO DAVID D. WILLIAMS.

United Feature Syndicate, Inc: 200 Madison Ave, New York, NY 10016; tel. (212) 293-8500; fax (212) 293-8720; internet www.unitedfeatures.com; Pres. and CEO DOUGLAS R. STERN; Snr Vice-Pres. and Gen. Man. LISA KLEM WILSON.

United Media (UM): 200 Madison Ave, 4th Floor, New York, NY 10016; tel. (212) 293-8500; fax (212) 293-8505; e-mail pdixon@unitedmedia.com; internet www.unitedmedialicensing.com; f. 1978; licensing and syndication of news features; Pres. and CEO DOUGLAS R. STERN.

United Press International (UPI): 1133 19th St, NW, Washington, DC 20036; tel. (202) 898-8000; fax (202) 898-8048; e-mail editorforms@upi.com; internet www.upi.com; f. 1907; Chair. and Pres. CHUNG HWAN KWAK; serves c. 1,000 newspaper clients worldwide.

Washington Post Writers Group: 1150 15th St, NW, Washington, DC 20071; tel. (202) 334-6375; fax (202) 334-5669; e-mail writersgrp@washpost.com; internet www.postwritersgroup.com; Editorial Dir and Gen. Man. ALAN SHEARER; Man. Editor JAMES S. HILL.

Principal Foreign Bureaux

CANADA

Canadian Press (Washington, DC): National Press Bldg, 529 14th St, NW, Suite 1128, Washington, DC 20045; tel. (202) 638-3367; fax (202) 638-3369; internet www.thecanadianpress.com; Bureau Chief LEE-ANNE GOODMAN.

Kipling News Service (Washington, DC): 12611 Farnell Dr., Silver Spring, MD 20906; tel. (301) 929-0760; fax (301) 949-8519; Canadian and US Affairs Bureau Chief BOGDAN KIPLING.

CHINA, PEOPLE'S REPUBLIC

Xinhua (New China) News Agency (New York): 405 East 42nd St, New York, NY 10017; tel. (718) 335-8388; fax (718) 335-8778; Bureau Dir JIYONG DUAN.

Xinhua (New China) News Agency (Washington, DC): National Press Bldg, 529 14th St, NW, Suite 1145, Washington, DC 20045; tel. (202) 661-8181; fax (202) 661-8182; Bureau Dir GE XIANGWEN.

CHINA (TAIWAN)

Central News Agency (CNA) (Washington, DC): National Press Bldg, Suite 1173, 592 14th St, NW, Washington, DC 20045; tel. (202) 628-2738; fax (202) 637-6788; e-mail cnausa@aol.com; Bureau Chief JORGE LIU; also offices in New York, San Francisco and Los Angeles.

CZECH REPUBLIC

Česká tisková kancelář (ČTK) (New York): 21–24 East 19th Street, Brooklyn, New York, NY 11229; tel. (212) 753-0017; fax (718) 459-5315; Bureau Chief VLASTIMIL MILY.

EGYPT

Middle East News Agency (New York): United Nations Bldg, Rm 301, New York, NY 10017; tel. (212) 963-7131; fax (212) 583-9890; Bureau Chief AHMED MORSI.

FRANCE

Agence France-Presse (AFP) (New York): 747 Third Ave, 35th Floor, New York, NY 10017; tel. (212) 755-1750; fax (212) 755-1928; e-mail afp-us@afp.com; internet www.afp.com; Correspondent MATHIEU DEMESTER.

Agence France-Presse (AFP) (Washington, DC): Southern Railway Bldg, 1500 K St, NW, Suite 600, Washington, DC 20005; tel. (202) 289-0700; fax (202) 414-0525; internet www.afp.com; Bureau Chief PIERRE TAILLEFER; also offices in Chicago, Los Angeles, Miami, San Francisco and the United Nations building (New York).

GERMANY

Deutsche Presse-Agentur (dpa) (New York): United Nations Bldg, Rm 352, 405 East 42nd St, New York, NY 10017; tel. (212) 319-6626; fax (212) 753-6168; internet www.dpa.de.

Deutsche Presse-Agentur (dpa) (Washington, DC): National Press Bldg, Suite 969, 592 14th St, Washington, DC 20045; tel. (202) 662-1220; fax (202) 662-1270; e-mail dpausa@dpa.com; internet www.dpa.de; Bureau Chief FRANK FUHRIG; also offices in Fort Worth, Los Angeles, Miami, San Francisco and Seattle.

HUNGARY

Magyar Távirati Iroda (MTI) (Washington, DC): 8515 Farrell Dr., Chevy Chase, MD 20815; tel. (301) 565-2221; fax (301) 589-6907; e-mail karpmti@aol.com; internet www.mti.hu; Correspondent JÁNOS KÁRPÁTI.

INDIA

Press Trust of India (Washington, DC): 4450 South Park Ave, Suite 1719, Chevy Chase, MD 20815-3646; tel. (301) 951-8657; e-mail tparasuram@aol.com; internet www.ptinews.com; Correspondent T. V. PARASURAM.

ITALY

Agenzia Nationale Stampa Associata (ANSA) (New York): 866 United Nations Plaza, Suite 476, New York, NY 10017; tel. (212) 319-6802; fax (212) 644-8798; internet www.ansa.it; Bureau Chief ALESSANDRA BALDINI.

Agenzia Nationale Stampa Associata (ANSA) (Washington, DC): National Press Bldg, 529 14th St, NW, Suite 1285, Washington, DC 20045; tel. (202) 628-3317; fax (202) 638-1792; e-mail ansa.washington@ansa.it; internet www.ansa.it; also office in Miami.

Inter Press Service: United Nations Bldg, Rm S-485, New York, NY 10017; tel. (212) 963-6156; fax (212) 888-6099; e-mail ipsun@aol.com; internet www.ipsnews.net; Regional Dir, North America THALIF DEEN.

JAPAN

Jiji Tsushin (Jiji Press Ltd) (Washington, DC): National Press Bldg, Suite 550, 529 14th St, Washington, DC 20045; tel. (202) 783-4330; fax (202) 783-6093; e-mail jijipressdc@nationalpress.com; internet www.jiji.com; Bureau Chief KENSUKE KARUBE.

Kyodo Tsushin (Kyodo News) (New York): 747 Third Ave, Suite 1803, New York, NY 10017; tel. (212) 603-6600; fax (212) 307-6623; e-mail kyodony@aol.com; Bureau Chief MITSUO SAKURAI.

Kyodo Tsushin (Kyodo News) (Washington, DC): National Press Bldg, Suite 400, 592 14th St, Washington, DC 20045; tel. (202) 347-5767; fax (202) 393-2342; e-mail wtn@kyododc.com; internet www.kyodo.co.jp; Bureau Chief HIROKI SUGITA.

MEXICO

Notimex (New York): United Nations Bldg, Rm C-322, New York, NY 10017; tel. (212) 371-1289; fax (212) 754-0296; e-mail usantx@aol.com; internet www.notimex.com.mx.

Notimex (Washington, DC): 425 National Press Bldg, 592 14th St, Washington, DC 20045; tel. (202) 347-5227; fax (202) 347-5126; internet www.notimex.com.mx; Bureau Chief JOSÉ LÓPEZ ZAMORANO.

RUSSIA

ITAR—TASS (Information Telegraphic Agency of Russia—Telegraphic Agency of the Sovereign Countries) (New York): 50 Rockefeller Plaza, Suite 501, New York, NY 10020-1696; tel. (212) 245-4250; fax (212) 245-4258; e-mail itar@aol.com; internet www.itar-tass.com; Bureau Chief ALEKSEI S. BEREZHKOV.

ITAR—TASS (Information Telegraphic Agency of Russia—Telegraphic Agency of the Sovereign Countries) (Washington, DC): National Press Bldg, Suite 1004, 592 14th St, Washington, DC 20045; tel. (202) 662-7080; fax (202) 393-6495; e-mail washtass@aol.com; Bureau Chief ANDREI SITOV.

SPAIN

Agencia EFE (Houston): 11757 Katy Freeway, Suite 975, Houston, TX 77079; tel. (281) 759-2225; fax (281) 759-2220; e-mail mbenito@efeamerica.com; internet www.efe.com; Delegate MARCELINO BENITO.

Agencia EFE (Miami): 5959 Blue Lagoon Dr., Suite 102, Miami, FL 33126; tel. (305) 262-7575; fax (305) 442-2728; e-mail ecsanchez@efeamerica.com; internet www.efe.com; Delegate EMILIO C. SÁNCHEZ.

Agencia EFE (New York): 25 West 43rd St, Suite 1114, New York, NY 10036; tel. (212) 867-5757; fax (212) 867-9074; e-mail efenyc@efeamerica.com; internet www.efe.es; Delegate ELENA MORENO.

Agencia EFE (Washington, DC): National Press Bldg, Suite 1252, 592 14th St, Washington, DC 20045; tel. (202) 745-7692; fax (202) 393-4119; e-mail azpiazum@efeamerica.com; internet www.efe.com; Bureau Chief MARÍA LUISA AZPIAZU.

UNITED KINGDOM

Reuters (Boston): 53 State St, 14th Floor, Boston, MA 02109; tel. (617) 367-4100; fax (617) 248-9563.

Reuters (Chicago): Board of Trade Bldg, Suite 1860, 141 West Jackson Blvd, Chicago, IL 60604; tel. (312) 408-8500.

Reuters (Dallas): Dallas, TX 75201; tel. (972) 661-2645.

Reuters (Houston): Houston, TX 77046; tel. (713) 751-1900.

Reuters (Kansas City): 4800 Main St, Kansas City, MO 64112; tel. (816) 561-4766.

Reuters (Los Angeles): 445 South Figueroa St, Suite 2000, Los Angeles, CA 90071; tel. (213) 680-4800; fax (213) 624-8782; Bureau Chief KEVIN KROLICKI.

Reuters (Miami): Brickell Bay Tower, Suite 1601, 1001 South Bayshore Dr., Miami, FL 33131; tel. (305) 374-5013.

Reuters (Minneapolis): Piper Jaffray Tower, Suite 2920, 222 South Ninth St, Minneapolis, MN 55402; tel. (612) 339-5940.

Reuters (New York): The Reuters Bldg, 3 Times Sq., Fourth Floor, New York, NY 10036; tel. (646) 223-4000; fax (646) 223-6615; internet www.reuters.com.

Reuters (San Francisco): San Francisco, CA 94108; tel. (415) 677-2500.

Reuters (Washington, DC): 1333 H St, NW, Suite 400, Washington, DC 20005; tel. (202) 898-8366; fax (202) 898-8383; e-mail rob .doherty@reuters.com; Bureau Chief ROBERT DOHERTY.

NATIONAL PRESS ASSOCIATIONS

American Business Media: 675 Third Ave, Suite 415, New York, NY 10017-5704; tel. (212) 661-6360; fax (212) 370-0736; e-mail info@ abmmail.com; internet www.americanbusinessmedia.com; f. 1906; Pres. and CEO GORDON T. HUGHES, II; 350 mem. cos, 124 assoc. mems.

American Press Institute, Inc (API): 11690 Sunrise Valley Dr., Reston, VA 20191-1498; tel. (703) 620-3611; fax (703) 620-5814; e-mail info@americanpressinstitute.org; internet americanpressinstitute.org; f. 1946; Chair. MARK G. CONTRERAS; Pres. and Exec. Dir DREW B. DAVIS.

American Society of Business Publication Editors (ASBPE): 214 North Hale St, Wheaton, IL 60187; tel. (630) 510-4588; fax (630) 510-4501; e-mail info@asbpe.org; internet www.asbpe.org; f. 1964; Pres. STEVEN ROLL; Exec. Dir JANET SVAZAS.

American Society of Magazine Editors (ASME): 810 Seventh Ave, 24th Floor, New York, NY 100192; tel. (212) 872-3700; fax (212) 906-0128; e-mail asme@magazine.org; internet asme.magazine.org; Chief Exec. SID HOLT; Exec. Dir MARLENE KAHAN; 850 mems.

American Society of Media Photographers Inc: 150 North Second St, Philadelphia, PA 19106; tel. (215) 451-2767; fax (215) 451-0880; e-mail webmaster@asmp.org; internet www.asmp.org; f. 1944; Pres. JUDY HERRMANN; Exec. Dir EUGENE MOPSIK; 5,000 mems.

American Society of Newspaper Editors: 11690B Sunrise Valley Dr., Reston, VA 20191-1409; tel. (703) 453-1122; fax (703) 453-1133; e-mail asne@asne.org; internet www.asne.org; f. 1922; Pres. CHARLOTTE HALL; Exec. Dir SCOTT BOSLEY; 1,000 mems.

Associated Press Broadcast Services: 1825 K St, NW, Suite 800, Washington, DC 20006; tel. (202) 955-7212; fax (202) 955-7347; e-mail info@ap.org; internet www.apbroadcast.com; f. 1941; Dir JAMES R. WILLIAMS, III; 8,500 subscribers.

Associated Press Managing Editors: 450 West 33rd St, New York, NY 10001; tel. (212) 621-1838; fax (212) 506-6102; e-mail apme@ap.org; internet www.apme.com; f. 1933; Pres. BOBBIE JO BUEL; Exec. Dir MARK MITTELSTADT; 1,000 mems.

Association of Free Community Papers: 200 Union Blvd, Suite 205, Lakewood, CO 80228; tel. (877) 203-2327; fax (781) 459-7770; e-mail afcp@afcp.org; internet www.afcp.org; f. 1950; 3,000 mems; Exec. Dir CRAIG MCMULLIN.

Audit Bureau of Circulations (ABC): 900 North Meacham Rd, Schaumburg, IL 60173-4968; tel. (847) 605-0909; fax (847) 605-0483; e-mail kammi.altig@accessabc.com; internet www.accessabc.com; f. 1914; Chair. DONALD J. MICELI; Pres. and Man. Dir MICHAEL J. LAVERY; over 4,000 mems.

City and Regional Magazine Association: 1970 East Grand Ave, Suite 330, El Segundo, CA 90245; tel. (310) 364-0193; fax (310) 364-0196; e-mail administrator@list.citymag.org; internet www.citymag .org; f. 1978; Pres. RANDY HANO; Exec. Dir C. JAMES DOWDEN; 50 mems.

Council of Literary Magazines and Presses (CLMP): 154 Christopher St, Suite 3C, New York, NY 10014-9110; tel. (212) 741-9110; fax (212) 741-9112; e-mail info@clmp.org; internet www .clmp.org; f. 1967; provides services to non-commercial US literary magazines and presses; Exec. Dir JEFFREY LEPENDORF; 347 mems.

Hollywood Foreign Press Association (HFPA): 646 North Robertson Blvd, West Hollywood, CA 90069; tel. (310) 657-1731; fax (310) 657-5576; tel. info@hfpa.org; internet www.hfpa.org; f. 1943; Pres. JORGE CAMARA; Man. Dir CHANTAL DINNAGE; 83 mems.

International Motor Press Association: 4 Park St, Harrington Park, NJ 07640; tel. (201) 750-3533; fax (201) 750-2010; e-mail info@ impa.org; internet www.impa.org; f. 1962; Pres. FRED CHIECO; 500 mems.

International Newspaper Marketing Association: 10300 North Central Expressway, Suite 467, Dallas, TX 75231; tel. (214) 373-9111; fax (214) 373-9112; e-mail inma@inma.org; internet www.inma .org; f. 1930; Exec. Dir EARL J. WILKINSON; 1,200 mems.

International Society of Weekly Newspaper Editors: Institute of International Studies, Missouri Southern State University, 3950 East Newman Rd, Joplin, MO 64801-1595; tel. (417) 625-9736; fax (417) 659-4445; e-mail stebbins-c@mssu.edu; internet www.iswne .org; f. 1954; Pres. DON BROD; Exec. Dir Dr CHAD STEBBINS; 249 mems.

Investigative Reporters and Editors: 138 Neff Annex, Missouri School of Journalism, Columbia, MO 65211; tel. (573) 882-2042; fax (573) 882-5431; e-mail info@ire.org; internet www.ire.org; f. 1975; Pres. CHERYL PHILLIPS; Exec. Dir MARK HORVIT (acting); 4,200 mems.

Magazine Publishers of America (MPA): 810 Seventh Ave, 24th Floor, New York, NY 100192; tel. (212) 872-3700; fax (212) 888-4217; e-mail mpa@magazine.org; internet www.magazine.org; f. 1919; Pres. and CEO NINA B. LINK; 200 mem. cos and 90 assoc. mems.

National American Legion Press Association: POB 334, West Seneca, NY 14224-0334; tel. (716) 675-0560; internet www.nalpa .org; f. 1923; Pres. DOLLY ZITUR; Exec. Dir MICHAEL P. DUGGAN; more than 1,000 mems.

National Newspaper Association: 134 Neff Annex, POB 7540, Columbia, MO 65205-7540; tel. (573) 882-5800; fax (573) 884-5490; e-mail info@nna.org; internet www.nna.org; f. 1885 as National Editorial Association; present name adopted 1964; Pres. JOHN W. STEVENSON; Exec. Dir BRIAN STEFFENS; over 2,700 mems.

National Press Club: National Press Bldg, Suite 1386, 529 14th St, NW, Washington, DC 20045; tel. (202) 662-7500; fax (202) 662-7569; e-mail president@press.org; internet www.press.org; f. 1908; Pres. SYLVIA SMITH; 4,600 mems.

National Press Photographers' Association: 3200 Croasdaile Dr., Suite 306, Durham, NC 27705; tel. (919) 383-7246; fax (919) 383-7261; e-mail info@nppa.org; internet www.nppa.org; f. 1946; Pres. BOB CAREY; Exec. Dir JIM STRAIGHT; 10,000 mems.

Newspaper Association of America: 4401 Wilson Blvd, Suite 900, Arlington, VA 22203-1867; tel. (571) 366-1000; fax (571) 366-1195; internet www.naa.org; f. 1992; Chair. BO JONES; Pres. and CEO GARY B. PRUITT; more than 2,000 mems in USA and Canada accounting for over 87% of US daily newspaper circulation.

The Newspaper Guild: 501 Third St, NW, Washington, DC 20001-2797; tel. (202) 434-7177; fax (202) 434-1472; e-mail guild@ cwa-union.org; internet www.newsguild.org; f. 1933; journalists' org., organ of the Communications Workers of America trade union; Pres. BERNARD J. LUNZER; over 34,000 mems in the USA, Puerto Rico and Canada.

Overseas Press Club of America: 40 West 45th St, New York, NY 10036; tel. (212) 626-9220; fax (212) 626-9210; e-mail sonya@ opcofamerica.org; internet www.opcofamerica.org; f. 1939; Pres. ALAN DODDS FRANK; Exec. Dir SONYA FRY; 600 mems.

Periodical & Book Association of America Inc: 481 Eighth Ave, Suite 826, New York, NY 10001; tel. (212) 563-6502; fax (212) 563-4098; e-mail lscott@pbaa.net; internet www.pbaa.net; Pres. RICHARD ALLEGER; Exec. Dir LISA W. SCOTT; 110 mems.

Publishers' Information Bureau: 810 Seventh Ave, New York, NY 10019; tel. (212) 872-3722; fax (212) 753-2768; e-mail pib@ magazine.org; internet www.magazine.org/pib; f. 1945; part of Magazine Publishers of America; tracks advertising carried by consumer magazines; 250 mem. publications; Pres. WAYNE EADIE.

Suburban Newspapers of America: 116 Cass St, Traverse City, MI 49684; tel. (888) 486-2466; fax (231) 932-2985; e-mail sna@ suburban-news.org; internet www.suburban-news.org; f. 1971; Pres. NANCY LANE; Exec. Dir SUSAN KAROL; over 2,400 mem. daily and weekly newspapers in the USA and Canada.

PUBLISHING

DIRECTORY

Publishers

Abbeville Press, Inc: 137 Varick St, New York, NY 10013; tel. (212) 366-5585; fax (212) 366-6966; e-mail abbeville@abbeville.com; internet www.abbeville.com; f. 1977; fine arts and illustrated books; Pres. and Publr ROBERT E. ABRAMS.

ABC-CLIO: 130 Cremona Dr., Santa Barbara, CA 93117; tel. (805) 968-1911; fax (805) 685-9685; e-mail library@abc-clio.com; internet www.abc-clio.com; f. 1953; history, social sciences, humanities and reference; CEO RONALD BOEHM.

Abingdon Press: 201 Eighth Ave South, POB 801, Nashville, TN 37202-0801; tel. (615) 749-6290; fax (615) 749-6512; e-mail publicity@abingdonpress.com; internet www.abingdonpress.com; an imprint of The United Methodist Publishing House (f. 1789); religious; Vice-Pres. TAMMY GAINES.

Harry N. Abrams, Inc (HNA): 115 West 18th St, New York, NY 10011; tel. (212) 206-7715; fax (212) 519-1210; internet www.hnabooks.com; f. 1949; acquired by Times Mirror Co in 1966; imprints incl. Abrams Books (art, photography, design, architecture), Stewart, Tabori & Chang (f. 1981, cooking, design, gardening, crafts, pets, health, sports, and popular culture) and Amulet Books (f. 2004, youth fiction and non-fiction); owned by Groupe de la Martinière, France; Pres. and CEO MICHAEL JACOBS.

AFB Press: 11 Penn Plaza, Suite 300, New York, NY 10001; tel. (212) 502-7651; fax (212) 502-7774; e-mail press@afb.net; internet www.afb.org/store; publishing arm of the American Foundation for the Blind; books, journals, videos, and electronic materials on visual impairment for professionals, researchers and blind or visually impaired individuals and their families; Pres. and CEO CARL R. AUGUSTO; Dir and Editor-in-Chief NATALIE HILZEN.

Alfred Publishing Co, Inc: POB 10003, Van Nuys, CA 91410-0003; tel. (818) 892-2492; fax (818) 891-4875; e-mail customerservice@alfred.com; internet www.alfred.com; f. 1922; educational music, methods and texts; Pres. MORTY MANUS; CEO STEVEN MANUS.

Andrews McMeel Publishing: c/o Simon & Schuster, Inc, 100 Front St, Riverside, NJ 08075; tel. (816) 932-6700; fax (816) 932-6706; e-mail licensing@amuniversal.com; internet www.andrewsmcmeel.com; f. 1970; humour, general trade; Pres. and CEO HUGH T. ANDREWS.

Ashgate Publishing Co: 101 Cherry St, Suite 420, Burlington, VT 05401-4405; tel. (802) 865-7641; fax (802) 865-7847; e-mail bdecoff@ashgate.com; internet www.ashgate.com; f. 1979; professional, scholarly and reference; Pres. BARBARA J. CHURCH.

Aspen Publishers, Inc: 76 Ninth Ave, 7th Floor, New York, NY 10011; tel. (212) 771-0600; fax (212) 771-0885; internet www.aspenpublishers.com; f. 1959; owned by Wolters Kluwer; reference, health, business and professional textbooks; Exec. Vice-Pres. and Group Publr RICHARD H. KRAVITZ.

Augsburg Fortress, Publishers: 100 South Fifth St, POB 1209, Minneapolis, MN 55440; tel. (612) 330-3300; fax (612) 330-3455; e-mail info@augsburgfortress.org; internet www.augsburgfortress.org; f. 1890; publishing arm of the Evangelical Lutheran Church in America; religious (evangelical Lutheran) non-fiction; Pres. and CEO BETH LEWIS.

August House Inc, Publishers: 3500 Piedmont Rd, NE Suite 310, Atlanta, GA 30305; tel. (404) 442-4420; fax (404) 442-4435; e-mail ahinfo@augusthouse.com; internet www.augusthouse.com; f. 1979; Southern regional, history, humour and folklore; CEO STEVE FLOYD.

B&H Publishing Group: 127 Ninth Ave North, Nashville, TN 37234-0143; tel. (615) 251-5614; fax (615) 251-2701; e-mail miriam.evans@bhpublishinggroup.com; internet www.bhpublishinggroup.com; f. 1891; fmrly Broadman & Holman Publrs; present name adopted in 2006; religious (Protestant), fiction, non-fiction, reference and juvenile; Pres. KENNETH H. STEPHENS; Publr DAVID SHEPHERD.

Baker Publishing Group: 6030 East Fulton Rd, Ada, MI 49301; tel. (616) 676-9185; fax (616) 676-9573; e-mail media@bakerbooks.com; internet www.bakerpublishinggroup.com; f. 1939; imprints incl. Brazos Press (Protestant and evangelical, Roman Catholic and Eastern Orthodox), Chosen Books (f. 1971, evangelical and charismatic Christian non-fiction), and Revell (Christian fiction and non-fiction); Pres. DWIGHT BAKER.

Bantam Dell Publishing Group, Inc: 1745 Broadway, New York, NY 10019; tel. (212) 782-9000; fax (212) 302-7985; e-mail bdpublicity@randomhouse.com; internet www.randomhouse.com/bantamdell; f. 1945; division of Random House, Inc; general fiction and non-fiction; Pres. IRWYN APPLEBAUM.

Barnes and Noble Books: 122 5th Ave, 2nd Floor, New York, NY 10011; tel. (800) 422-7717; fax (212) 352-3660; e-mail customerservice@bn.com; internet www.barnesandnoble.com; f. 1873; division of Rowman & Littlefield Publrs, Inc; educational and general; Chair. LEONARD RIGGIO; CEO STEPHEN RIGGIO.

Barron's Educational Series, Inc: 250 Wireless Blvd, Hauppauge, NY 11788; tel. (631) 434-3311; fax (631) 434-3723; e-mail fbrown@barronseduc.com; internet www.barronseduc.com; f. 1945; general non-fiction, educational and juvenile; Chair. and CEO MANUEL H. BARRON; Pres. and Publr ELLEN SIBLEY.

Beacon Press: 25 Beacon St, Boston, MA 02108; tel. (617) 742-2110; fax (617) 723-3097; e-mail lriviere@beacon.org; internet www.beacon.org; f. 1854; dept of the Unitarian Universalist Asscn; world affairs, religion and general non-fiction; Dir HELENE ATWAN.

Beekman Books, Inc: 300 Old All Angels Hill Rd, Wappingers Falls, NY 12590; tel. (845) 297-2690; fax (845) 297-1002; e-mail manager@beekmanbooks.com; internet www.beekmanbooks.com; f. 1972 as Beekman Publrs, Inc; health and wellbeing, music, business, juvenile and Welsh; Pres. MICHAEL S. ARTHUR.

Bethany House Publishers: 11400 Hampshire Ave, S, Minneapolis MN 55438; Baker Book House, POB 6287, Grand Rapids, MI 49516; tel. (952) 829-2500; fax (952) 829-2503; e-mail media@bakerbooks.com; internet www.bethanyhouse.com; f. 1956; division of Baker Publishing Group; Christian fiction, living and devotional books; Publr GARY L. JOHNSON.

Birkhäuser Boston: 675 Massachusetts Ave, 12th Floor, Cambridge, MA 02139; tel. (617) 876-2333; fax (212) 876-1272; e-mail service@birkhauser.com; internet www.birkhauser.com; f. 1979; scientific and technical, architecture and design; Exec. Editor ANN KOSTANT.

Blackwell Publising Inc: 350 Main St, Malden, MA 02148; tel. (781) 388-8200; fax (781) 388-8210; e-mail customerservices@blackwellpublishing.com; internet www.blackwellpublishing.com; f. 1970; acquired by John Wiley and Sons, Inc in 2007; academic, medical and scientific, professional society publications; CEO RENÉ OLIVERI; Pres. GORDON TIBBITS, III.

Thomas Bouregy and Co, Inc (Avalon Books): 160 Madison Ave, New York, NY 10016; tel. (212) 598-0222; fax (212) 979-1862; e-mail avalon@avalonbooks.com; internet www.avalonbooks.com; f. 1950; romantic fiction, mysteries and westerns; Pres. WILHELM MICKELSEN.

R. R. Bowker LLC: 630 Central Ave, New Providence, NJ 07974; tel. (888) 269-5372; fax (888) 286-1090; e-mail info@bowker.com; internet www.bowker.com; f. 1872; reference and bibliography; Pres. and CEO ANNIE CALLANAN.

Branden Books, Inc: POB 812094, Wellesley, MA 02482; tel. (781) 734-2046; fax (781) 790-1056; internet www.branden.com; f. 1909; art, music, classics, fiction and non-fiction; Pres. ROBERT CASO; Editor and Treas. ADOLPH CASO.

George Braziller, Inc: 171 Madison Ave, New York, NY 10016; tel. (212) 889-0909; fax (212) 689-5405; e-mail info@georgebraziller.com; internet www.georgebraziller.com; f. 1955; art, fiction and non-fiction; Publr GEORGE BRAZILLER.

Brookings Institution Press: 1775 Massachusetts Ave, NW, Washington, DC 20036-2103; tel. (202) 797-6000; fax (202) 536-3623; e-mail bibooks@brookings.edu; internet www.brookings.edu; f. 1927; economics, govt, foreign policy; Dir ROBERT L. FAHERTY.

Cambridge University Press: 32 Ave of the Americas, New York, NY 10013-2473; tel. (212) 924-3900; fax (212) 691-3239; e-mail information@cup.org; internet www.cambridge.org/us; scholarly; CEO STEPHEN BOURNE; Pres. RICHARD ZIEMACKI.

Catholic University of America Press: 620 Michigan Ave, NE, Washington, DC 20064; tel. (202) 319-5052; fax (202) 319-4985; e-mail cua-press@cua.edu; internet cuapress.cua.edu; f. 1939; scholarly; Dir DAVID J. MCGONAGLE.

Caxton Press: 312 Main St, Caldwell, ID 83605; tel. (208) 647-6465; fax (208) 459-7450; e-mail sgipson@caxtonpress.com; internet www.caxtonpress.com; f. 1903; Western Americana; Vice-Pres. and Publr SCOTT GIPSON.

CCH, Inc: 2700 Lake Cook Rd, Riverwoods, IL 60015; tel. (847) 267-7000; fax (847) 224-8299; e-mail mediahelp@cch.com; internet www.cch.com; tax and business law; f. 1913; a division of Wolters Kluwer; Pres. MIKE SABBATIS.

Cengage Learning: POB 6904, Florence, KY 41022-6904; tel. (800) 354-9706; fax (800) 487-8488; e-mail esales@cengage.com; internet www.cengage.com; f. 1945; frmly Thomson Learning; imprints incl. Brooks/Cole (f. 1966, maths, statistics, and the sciences), Duxbury (statistics), South-Western (f. 1906, business and economics) and Wadsworth (f. 1956, social sciences and humanities), Heinle (languages) and Schirmer (music); Pres. and CEO RONALD G. DUNN.

Chelsea House Publishers: 132 West 31st St, 17th Floor, New York, NY 10001; tel. (800) 322-8755; fax (800) 678-3633; e-mail custserv@factsonfile.com; internet www.chelseahouse.com; f. 1966; acquired by Facts on File in 2005; youth non-fiction; Pres. and CEO ROBERT LARONGA.

Chicago Review Press, Inc: 814 North Franklin St, Chicago, IL 60610; tel. (312) 337-0747; fax (312) 337-5110; e-mail frontdesk@chicagoreviewpress.com; internet www.chicagoreviewpress.com; f. 1973; imprints incl. A Capella (music and film), Lawrence Hill Books (African-American and left-wing non-fiction) and Zephyr Press (educational and teaching); Man. Editor ALLISON FELUS; Publr CYNTHIA SHERRY.

The Child's World, Inc: 1980 Lookout Dr., Mankato, MN 56003; tel. (507) 385-1044; fax (507) 385-1026; e-mail sales@childsworld.com; internet www.childsworld.com; f. 1968; childhood education; Editorial Dir E. RUSSELL PRIMM, III.

Cliffs Notes, Inc: 111 River St, Hoboken, NJ 07030-5774; tel. (201) 748-6000; fax (201) 748-6088; e-mail pressctr@wiley.com; internet www.cliffs.com; f. 1957; study and teaching aids, language study, photo humour; division of John Wiley and Sons, Inc; CEO JOHN KILCULLEN.

Columbia University Press: 61 West 62nd St, New York, NY 10023; tel. (212) 459-0600; fax (212) 459-3678; e-mail cup_publicity@columbia.edu; internet www.columbia.edu/cu/cup; f. 1893; trade, educational, scientific and reference; Pres. and Dir JAMES D. JORDAN.

Concordia Publishing House (CPH): 3558 South Jefferson Ave, St Louis, MO 63118-3968; tel. (800) 325-3040; fax (800) 490-9889; e-mail order@cph.org; internet www.cph.org; f. 1869; publishing arm of the Lutheran Church-Missouri Synod; religious (Lutheran) children's books, devotionals and curriculum music; Pres. and CEO BRUCE G. KINTZ.

The Conference Board, Inc: 845 Third Ave, New York, NY 10022; tel. (212) 759-0900; fax (212) 980-7014; e-mail info@conference-board.org; internet www.conference-board.org; f. 1916; studies in management practices, economics and public affairs; Chair. and CEO NIALL FITZGERALD; Pres. GAIL FOSLER; CEO JONATHAN SPECTOR.

David C. Cook: 4050 Lee Vance View, Colorado Springs, CO 80918; tel. (719) 536-0100; fax (719) 536-3269; internet www.davidccook.com; f. 1875; religion (Christian); Pres. and CEO CRIS DOORNBOS.

Cornell University Press: Sage House, 512 East State St, POB 250, Ithaca, NY 14850; tel. (607) 257-2338; fax (607) 277-2374; e-mail cupressinfo@cornell.edu; internet www.cornellpress.cornell.edu; f. 1869; scholarly, non-fiction; Dir JOHN G. ACKERMAN.

Council of State Governments: 2760 Research Park Dr., POB 11910, Lexington, KY 40578-1910; tel. (859) 244-8000; fax (859) 244-8001; e-mail press@csg.org; internet www.csg.org; f. 1933; reference publs on state govt and regional topics; CEO and Exec. Dir DAN SPRAGUE.

CQ Press: 2300 N St, NW, Suite 800, Washington, DC 20037; tel. (202) 729-1800; fax (202) 729-1418; e-mail lwallace@cqpress.com; internet www.cqpress.com; f. 1945; fmrly Congressional Quarterly Books; division of SAGE Publications; business, education and govt; directories; Pres. and Publr JOHN A. JENKINS.

Creative Co: 123 South Broad St, POB 227, Mankato, MN 56001; tel. (507) 388-6273; fax (507) 388-2746; f. 1932; juvenile; Pres. TOM PETERSON.

Crossroad Publishing Co: 16 Penn Plaza, Suite 1550, New York, NY 10001; tel. (212) 868-1801; fax (212) 868-2171; e-mail ask@crossroadpublishing.com; internet cpcbooks.com; f. 1980; part of Herder & Herder family; religion (Roman Catholic), philosophy, psychology, literature, history, biography and reference; Pres. GWENDOLIN HERDER.

Crown Publishing Group: 1745 Broadway, New York, NY 10019; tel. (212) 940-2537; fax (212) 940-7381; e-mail crownpublicity@randomhouse.com; internet www.randomhouse.com/crown; division of Random House, Inc; imprints incl. Clarkson Potter (f. 1959, cookery and lifestyle) and Crown (f. 1933, general fiction and non-fiction); Pres. and Publr JENNY FROST.

Da Capo Press: 11 Cambridge Center, Cambridge, MA 02142; tel. (617) 252-5200; fax (617) 252-5285; e-mail custserve@lrp.com; internet www.dacapopress.com; f. 1975; division of Perseus Books Group since 1999; history, biography, music, film, art, photography, sports and humour; Pres. and CEO JACK MCKEOWN.

F. A. Davis Co: 1915 Arch St, Philadelphia, PA 19103; tel. (215) 568-2270; fax (215) 568-5065; e-mail info@fadavis.com; internet www.fadavis.com; f. 1879; medical, nursing and allied health textbooks; Pres. ROBERT H. CRAVEN, Jr.

DAW Books, Inc: 375 Hudson St, New York, NY 10014-3658; tel. (212) 366-2096; fax (212) 366-2090; e-mail daw@us.penguingroup.com; internet www.dawbooks.com; f. 1971; science fiction and fantasy; Publrs ELIZABETH R. WOLLHEIM, SHEILA E. GILBERT.

Delmar Cengage Learning: POB 6904, Florence, KY 41022-6904; tel. (800) 354-9706; fax (800) 487-8488; e-mail esales@cengage.com; internet www.delmarlearning.com; f. 1945; division of Cengage Learning; textbooks, technology, health care, mathematics and vocational studies, travel; Pres. MANUEL GUZMAN (acting).

DK Publishing, Inc: 375 Hudson St, New York, NY 10014; tel. (212) 213-4800; fax (212) 213-4828; e-mail publicity@dk.com; internet us.dk.com; f. 1974 as Dorling Kindersley; division of Penguin Group; illustrated and children's reference books; CEO JOHN SARGENT.

Dorchester Publishing Co, Inc: 200 Madison Ave, Suite 2000, New York, NY 10016; tel. (212) 725-8811; fax (212) 532-1054; e-mail customerservice@dorchpub.com; internet www.dorchesterpub.com; f. 1971; imprints include Leisure Books, Love Spell, Making It and Smooch; mass-market, fiction and non-fiction, reprints; Pres. and Publr JOHN PREBICH.

Doubleday Broadway: 1745 Broadway, New York, NY 10019; tel. (212) 782-9000; fax (212) 302-7985; e-mail ddaypub@randomhouse.com; internet doubleday.com; f. 1897; division of Random House, Inc; imprints include Spiegel & Grau, Broadway, Nan A. Talese and Flying Dolphin Press; general fiction and non-fiction, religion and finance; Pres. and Publr STEPHEN RUBIN.

Dover Publications, Inc: 31 East Second St, Mineola, NY 11501; tel. (516) 294-6953; fax (516) 742-5049; internet www.doverpublications.com; f. 1941; trade, reprints, scientific, classics, language, arts and crafts; Pres. PAUL NEGRI.

The Dramatic Publishing Co: 311 Washington St, Woodstock, IL 60098-3308; tel. (815) 338-7170; fax (815) 338-8981; e-mail plays@dramaticpublishing.com; internet www.dramaticpublishing.com; f. 1885; plays; Pres. CHRISTOPHER T. SERGEL.

Dufour Editions, Inc: POB 7, Chester Springs, PA 19425-0007; tel. (610) 458-5005; fax (610) 458-7103; e-mail info@dufoureditions.com; internet www.dufoureditions.com; f. 1949; literature, political science, humanities, music and history; Pres. CHRISTOPHER MAY.

Duke University Press: POB 90660, Duke University, Durham, NC 27708-0660; tel. (888) 651-0122; fax (888) 651-0124; e-mail bpublicity@dukeupress.edu; internet www.dukeupress.edu; f. 1921; scholarly; Editor-in-Chief KEN WISSOKER.

Duquesne University Press: 600 Forbes Ave, Pittsburgh, PA 15282; tel. (412) 396-6610; fax (412) 396-5984; e-mail wadsworth@duq.edu; internet www.dupress.duq.edu; f. 1927; scholarly; Dir SUSAN WADSWORTH-BOOTH; Production Editor KATHY MEYER.

Ediciones Universal: 3090 South West Eighth St, Miami, FL 33135; tel. (305) 642-3234; fax (305) 642-7978; e-mail ediciones@ediciones.com; internet www.ediciones.com; f. 1965; Spanish language fiction and non-fiction; Man. JUAN MANUEL SALVAT.

Wm B. Eerdmans Publishing Co: 2140 Oak Industrial Dr., NE, Grand Rapids, MI 49503; tel. (616) 459-4591; fax (616) 459-6540; e-mail info@eerdmans.com; internet www.eerdmans.com; f. 1911; social concerns, regional history, religion, scholarly and juvenile; Pres. WILLIAM B. EERDMANS, Jr.

Elsevier: 11830 Westline Industrial Dr., St Louis, MO 63146; tel. (314) 453-7010; fax (314) 453-7095; e-mail usbkinfo@elsevier.com; internet www.elsevier.com; f. 1962; division of Reed Elsevier Group PLC; health sciences imprints incl. Butterworth-Heinemann (f. 1975, technology, medicine and management), Churchill Livingstone (f. 1972, medicine), Hanley & Belfus (f. 1984, medical textbooks and reference materials), Mosby (f. 1906, textbooks and reference materials on medicine, nursing, allied health and veterinary medicine), and W. B. Saunders Co (f. 1888, medicine); science and technology imprints incl. Academic Press (science, technology and business), Architectural Press (architecture), Focal Press (media technology), and Morgan Kaufmann (f. 1984, computing); CEO ERIK ENGSTROM.

Encyclopaedia Britannica, Inc: 331 North LaSalle Street, Chicago, IL 60610; tel. (800) 621-3900; fax (800) 344-9624; e-mail international@eb.com; internet www.eb.com; f. 1768; encyclopaedias, atlases, dictionaries; CEO JORGE CAUZ.

Facts On File Inc: 132 West 31st St, 17th Floor, New York, NY 10001; tel. (212) 896-4269; fax (917) 339-0323; e-mail lkatz@factsonfile.com; internet www.factsonfile.com; f. 1941; acquired by Veronis Suhler Stevenson in 2005; imprints incl. Ferguson Publishing (f. 1907, children's reference); non-fiction, reference and electronic databases; Publr MARK MCDONNELL.

Fairleigh Dickinson University Press: The Gatehouse, M-GH2-01, 285 Madison Ave, Madison, NJ 07940; tel. (973) 443-8564; fax (973) 443-8364; e-mail fdupress@fdu.edu; internet www.fdu.edu/fdupress; f. 1967; scholarly; Dir HARRY KEYISHIAN.

Farrar, Straus and Giroux, Inc (FSG): 19 Union Sq. West, New York, NY 10003; tel. (212) 741-6900; fax (212) 633-9385; internet www.fsgbooks.com; e-mail fsg.publicity@fsgbooks.com; f. 1946; acquired by Holtzbrinck Publrs, LLC in 1994; imprints incl. Hill and Wang (f. 1956), Faber and Faber, Inc, and North Point Press; literature, international fiction, history, current affairs and science; Chair. ROGER W. STRAUS; Pres. JONATHAN GALASSI.

Fodor's Travel Publications: 1745 Broadway, 15th Floor, New York, NY 10019; tel. (212) 572-8784; fax (212) 572-2248; e-mail lpalmer@fodors.com; internet www.fodors.com; division of Random House, Inc; travel guides; Exec. Dir LAUREN PALMER.

Fordham University Press: University Box L, Bronx, NY 10458-5172; tel. (718) 817-4795; fax (718) 817-4785; e-mail bkaobrien@fordham.edu; internet www.fordhampress.com; f. 1907; scholarly; Editorial Dir HELEN TARTAR.

W. H. Freeman & Co, Publishers: 41 Madison Ave, 37th Floor, New York, NY 10010; tel. (212) 576-9400; fax (212) 689-2383; e-mail international@whfreeman.com; internet www.whfreeman.com; f. 1946; part of Holtzbrinck Publrs, LLC; textbooks; Pres. ELIZABETH WIDDICOMBE.

Samuel French, Inc: 45 West 25th St, New York, NY 10010; tel. (212) 206-8990; fax (212) 206-1429; e-mail info@samuelfrench.com; internet www.samuelfrench.com; f. 1830; plays; Man. Dir CHARLES R. VAN NOSTRAND.

Gale Cengage Learning: 27500 Drake Rd, Farmington Hills, MI 48331-3535; tel. (248) 669-4253; fax (248) 669-8064; e-mail galeord@gale.com; internet gale.cengage.com; f. 1954; division of Cengage Learning; reference; Pres. GORDON T. MACOMBER.

Genealogical Publishing Co: 3600 Clipper Mill Rd, Suite 260, Baltimore, MD 21211; tel. (410) 837-8271; fax (410) 752-8492; e-mail info@genealogical.com; internet www.genealogical.com; f. 1959; genealogy, immigration studies, heraldry and local history; Editor-in-Chief MICHAEL TEPPER.

Glencoe/McGraw-Hill: 148 Princeton-Hightstown Rd, Hightstown, NJ 08520-1450; tel. (609) 426-5793; fax (609) 426-7917; internet www.glencoe.com; f. 1971; division of McGraw-Hill Education; textbooks and educational materials; Pres. STEVEN E. MCCLUNG.

Gospel Light: 1957 Eastman Ave, Ventura, CA 93003; tel. (805) 644-9721; fax (805) 677-6818; e-mail michellebasich@gospellight.com; internet www.gospellight.com; f. 1963; incl. the imprint Regal (f. 1965, non-denominational Christian and adult); religious (non-denominational Christian), educational and juvenile; Chair. and Pres. WILLIAM T. GREIG, III.

Warren H. Green, Inc: 8356 Olive Blvd, St Louis, MO 63132; tel. (314) 991-8758; fax (314) 997-1788; e-mail editorial@whgreen.com; internet www.whgreen.com; f. 1966; imprints incl. Epoch Press (f. 1986, subsidy publishing, internet www.epoch-press.net); medical, science, technology and philosophy; Pres. LUCY KNAPP; Vice-Pres. PAULINE MUELLER.

Greenwood Publishing Group, Inc: 88 Post Rd West, POB 5007, Westport, CT 06881; tel. (203) 226-3571; fax (203) 222-1502; e-mail webmaster@greenwood.com; internet www.greenwood.com; f. 1967; division of Reed Elsevier Group PLC, comprises Greenwood Press (reference), Heinemann (f. 1978, educational, teaching, professional development), Praeger Publrs (f. 1949, academic and general-interest non-fiction) and Libraries Unlimited (educational and reference); business reference and non-fiction; Pres. WAYNE SMITH.

Grove/Atlantic, Inc: 841 Broadway, New York, NY 10003-4793; tel. (212) 614-7850; fax (212) 614-7886; e-mail info@groveatlantic.com; internet www.groveatlantic.com; f. 1993 by merger of Grove Press and Atlantic Monthly Press (f. 1917); fiction, non-fiction, biography, history, social science, poetry; Pres. MORGAN ENTREKIN.

Walter de Gruyter, Inc: 545 Eighth Ave, Suite 16SW, New York, NY 10018; tel. (212) 564-9223; fax (212) 564-9224; e-mail info@degruyterny.com; internet www.degruyter.com; f. 1971; scholarly and scientific books, journals, databases, CD-ROM, e-books; 3 imprints: Mouton de Gruyter, K. G. Saur, Max Niemeyer Verlag; Dir, North America PETER NUESSER.

Hachette Book Group USA: 237 Park Ave, New York, NY 10017; tel. (212) 522-8700; fax (212) 522-2067; e-mail customer.service@hbgusa.com; internet www.hachettebookgroupusa.com; f. 2006 following acquisition of Time Warner Book Group by Hachette Livre, France; divisions incl. Little, Brown and Co (f. 1837, fiction and non-fiction) and Grand Central Publishing (f. 1970 as Warner Books, paperbacks, reprints, business, fiction and non-fiction); Chair. and CEO DAVID YOUNG.

Hammond World Atlas Corpn: American Map-Langenscheidt Publishing Group, 15 Tyger River Dr., Duncan, SC 29334; tel. (864) 486-8289; fax (864) 486-0214; e-mail customerservice@americanmap.com; internet www.hammondmap.com; f. 1900; division of American Map-Langenscheidt Publishing Group; maps, atlases, cartography; Chair. and CEO STUART DOLGINS.

Harcourt Inc: 6277 Sea Harbor Dr., Orlando, FL 32887; tel. (407) 345-2000; fax (407) 352-3445; internet www.harcourt.com; f. 1919; division of Reed Elsevier Group PLC; fiction, textbooks, general; Pres. and CEO JAMES LEVY.

HarperCollins Publishers: 10 East 53rd St, New York, NY 10022; tel. (212) 207-7000; fax (212) 207-7759; internet www.harpercollins.com; f. 1817; subsidiary of News Corpn; imprints incl. Avon (f. 1941, romantic fiction), Collins (general reference), Rayo (Latino culture) and William Morrow (f. 1926, fiction and non-fiction); fiction, non-fiction, religious, children's, medical, general; Pres. and CEO BRIAN MURRAY.

Harvard University Press: 79 Garden St, Cambridge, MA 02138; tel. (617) 495-2600; fax (401) 531-2801; e-mail contact_hup@harvard.edu; internet www.hup.harvard.edu; f. 1913; classics, fine arts, philosophy, science, medicine, law, literature, political science, religion, history and govt; Dir WILLIAM P. SISLER.

Hastings House/Daytrips Publishers: POB 908, Winter Park, FL 32790-0908; tel. (407) 339-3600; fax (407) 339-5900; e-mail hastings_daytrips@earthlink.net; internet www.hastingshousebooks.com; f. 1936; travel; Publr PETER LEERS.

Haworth Press, Inc: 10 Alice St, Binghamton, NY 13904-1580; tel. (607) 722-5857; fax (607) 771-0012; e-mail getinfo@haworthpress.com; internet www.haworthpress.com; f. 1978; part of Taylor & Francis Group; technical, social and behavioural sciences; Pres. and Publr BILL COHEN.

William S. Hein & Co, Inc: 1285 Main St, Buffalo, NY 14209; tel. (716) 882-2600; fax (716) 883-8100; e-mail mail@wshein.com; internet www.wshein.com; f. 1962; legal; Pres. KEVIN M. MARMION.

Herald Press: 616 Walnut Ave, Scottdale, PA 15683; tel. (724) 887-8500; fax (724) 887-3111; e-mail patricia@mph.net; internet www.heraldpress.com; f. 1908; owned by the Mennonite Church USA and Mennonite Church Canada; religious (Anabaptist); Dir LEVI MILLER.

Hippocrene Books, Inc: 171 Madison Ave, New York, NY 10016; tel. (718) 454-2366; fax (718) 228-6355; e-mail info@hippocrenebooks.com; internet www.hippocrenebooks.com; f. 1970; history, food, travel, foreign-language dictionaries and study guides, Judaica, militaria; Pres. and Editorial Dir GEORGE BLAGOWIDOW.

Holiday House, Inc: 425 Madison Ave, New York, NY 10017; tel. (212) 688-0085; fax (212) 421-6134; e-mail info@holidayhouse.com; internet www.holidayhouse.com; f. 1935; juvenile; Pres. JOHN H. BRIGGS, Jr.

Holmes & Meier Publishers, Inc: POB 943, Teaneck, NJ 07666; tel. (201) 833-2270; fax (201) 833-2272; e-mail info@holmesandmeier.com; internet www.holmesandmeier.com; f. 1969; imprints incl. Africana Publishing Co (f. 1969); history, political science, area studies, Africana, Judaica, foreign literature in translation, college texts and scholarly; Publr MIRIAM H. HOLMES.

Henry Holt and Co: 175 Fifth Ave, New York, NY 10010; tel. (646) 307-5095; fax (212) 633-0748; e-mail publicity@hholt.com; internet www.henryholt.com; f. 1866; acquired by Holtzbrinck Publrs, LLC in 1985; imprints incl. Metropolitan Books (f. 1995, fiction and non-fiction) and Times Books (f. 2001, science, business and current affairs); Pres. and Publr JOHN STERLING.

Holt, Rinehart & Winston, Inc: 10801 North MoPac Expressway, Bldg 3, Austin, TX 78759; tel. (512) 721-7000; e-mail holtinfo@hrw.com; internet www.hrw.com; f. 1866; division of Harcourt, Inc; school textbooks; Pres. JUDY FOWLER.

Hoover Institution Press: 434 Galvez Mall, Stanford University, Stanford, CA 94305-6010; tel. (650) 723-1754; fax (650) 723-1687; e-mail horaney@hoover.stanford.edu; internet www.hoover.org; f. 1962; scholarly; Assoc. Dir JEFFREY BLISS.

Houghton Mifflin Co: 222 Berkeley St, Boston, MA 02116; tel. (617) 351-5000; fax (617) 351-3604; e-mail trade_generalinterest@hmco.com; internet www.hmco.com; f. 1832; owned by Houghton Mifflin Riverdeep PLC, Ireland; general and educational; Chair. and CEO ANTHONY LUCKI; Pres. and COO GERALD HUGHES.

Indiana University Press: 601 North Morton St, Bloomington, IN 47404-3797; tel. (812) 855-8817; fax (812) 855-7931; e-mail iupress@indiana.edu; internet www.iupress.indiana.edu; f. 1950; trade and scholarly non-fiction; Dir JANET RABINOWITCH.

International Universities Press, Inc: 59 Boston Post Rd, Madison, CT 06443; tel. (203) 245-4000; fax (203) 245-0775; e-mail info@iup.com; internet www.iup.com; f. 1943; publrs of PsychoSocial Press; psychology, psychiatry, medicine, social sciences and journals; Exec. Vice-Pres. Dr MARGARET EMERY.

Islamic Books/Tahrike Tarsile Qur'ān, Inc: POB 731115, Elmhurst, NY 11373-0115; tel. (718) 446-6472; fax (718) 446-4370; e-mail read@koranusa.org; internet www.koranusa.org; f. 1978; Koran and Islamic religious texts; Pres. AUN ALI KHALFAN.

Jewish Publication Society: 2100 Arch St, 2nd Floor, Philadelphia, PA 19103; tel. (215) 832-0608; fax (215) 568-2017; e-mail jewishbook@jewishpub.org; internet www.jewishpub.org; f. 1888; Judaica; CEO and Editor-in-Chief Dr Ellen Frankel.

Johns Hopkins University Press: 2715 North Charles St, Baltimore, MD 21218-4319; tel. (410) 516-6900; fax (410) 516-6998; e-mail rr@press.jhu.edu; internet www.press.jhu.edu; f. 1878; social and physical sciences, humanities, health sciences, economics, literary criticism, history; Dir Kathleen Keane.

Jossey-Bass: 989 Market St, San Francisco, CA 94103-1741; tel. (415) 433-1740; fax (415) 433-0499; e-mail custserv@wiley.com; internet www.josseybass.com; f. 1966; acquired by John Wiley & Sons, Inc in 1999; business, education, religion and spirituality, parenting, health, conflict resolution and relationships; Vice-Pres. and Publr Cedric Crocker.

Kendall/Hunt Publishing Co: 4050 Westmark Dr., POB 1840, Dubuque, IA 52004-1840; tel. (563) 589-1000; fax (563) 589-1046; e-mail orders@kendallhunt.com; internet www.kendallhunt.com; f. 1944; business and educational; CEO Mark Falb.

Kensington Publishing Corpn: 850 Third Ave, New York, NY 10022; tel. (800) 221-2647; e-mail publicity@kensingtonbooks.com; internet www.kensingtonbooks.com; f. 1975; mass-market, fiction and non-fiction; imprints include Zebra (romance, westerns, horror and humour), Pinnacle (thrillers etc.), Citadel (non-fiction), Aphrodisia (f. 2006, erotica), Dafina (African American writing) and Holloway House Classics (African American fiction and non-fiction); Pres. Stephen Zacharius.

Knopf Publishing Group: 1745 Broadway, New York, NY 10019; tel. (212) 751-2600; fax (212) 572-2390; e-mail knopfwebmaster@randomhouse.com; internet www.randomhouse.com/knopf; f. 1915; division of Random House, Inc; imprints incl. Alfred A. Knopf, Inc (f. 1915, fiction, non-fiction, textbooks, general literature, poetry and cookery), Pantheon Books, Inc (fiction, non-fiction, history, philosophy, art and illustrated edns), Schocken Books (f. 1945, Judaica, biography, cookery and fiction), and Vintage Books (f. 1954, paperbacks); Pres. and Editor-in-Chief Sonny Mehta.

Krieger Publishing Co: 1725 Krieger Dr., Malabar, FL 32950; tel. (321) 724-9542; fax (321) 951-3671; e-mail info@krieger-pubishing.com; internet www.krieger-publishing.com; f. 1970; space technology, adult education, history and natural sciences; Pres. Donald E. Krieger.

KTAV Publishing House, Inc: 930 Newark Ave, 4th Floor, Jersey City, NJ 07306; tel. (201) 963-9524; fax (201) 963-0102; e-mail adam@ktav.com; internet www.ktav.com; f. 1924; Jewish literature, juvenile, textbooks; Pres. Sol Scharfstein.

Peter Lang Publishing, Inc: 29 Broadway, 18th Floor, New York, NY 10006; tel. (212) 647-7706; fax (212) 647-7707; e-mail customerservice@plang.com; internet www.peterlangusa.com; f. 1982; monographs in humanities and social sciences; Sr Editor Dr Heidi Burns.

Lerner Publishing Group: 1251 Washington Ave, N, Minneapolis, MN 55401-1036; tel. (612) 332-3344; fax (612) 332-7615; e-mail info@lernerbooks.com; internet www.lernerbooks.com; f. 1959; imprints incl. Carolrhoda Books, Inc (f. 1969); juvenile, fiction and non-fiction; Pres. Harry J. Lerner.

LexisNexis Matthew Bender and Co, Inc: 744 Broad St, Newark, NJ 07102; tel. (973) 820-2000; e-mail corpcomm@lexisnexis.com; internet bender.lexisnexis.com; f. 1887; division of Reed Elsevier; legal, accountancy, insurance and banking texts, and electronic databases; CEO Andy Prozes.

Loyola Press: 3441 North Ashland Ave, Chicago, IL 60657; tel. (773) 281-1818; fax (773) 281-0885; e-mail lane@loyolapress.com; internet www.loyolapress.org; f. 1912; owned by the Society of Jesus, Chicago Province; religious (Roman Catholic) education and language, religious trade and arts; Pres. George A. Lane.

McCutchan Publishing Corpn: 3220 Blume Dr., Suite 197, Richmond, CA 94806; tel. (510) 758-5510; fax (510) 758-6078; e-mail mccutchanpublish@sbcglobal.net; internet www.mccutchanpublishing.com; professional and college textbooks; Pres. and Publr Nancy Runyon.

McGraw-Hill Companies, Inc: POB 182604, Columbus, OH 43272; tel. (877) 833-5524; fax (614) 759-3749; e-mail customer.service@mcgraw-hill.com; internet www.mcgraw-hill.com; f. 1888; information texts and services for business, industry, govt and the general public; Chair. and CEO Harold McGraw, III.

Meredith Corpn: 1716 Locust St, Des Moines, IA 50309-3023; tel. (515) 284-3000; fax (515) 284-2700; e-mail art.slusark@meredith.com; internet www.meredith.com; f. 1902; trade; Pres. and COO Stephen M. Lacy.

Merriam-Webster Inc: 47 Federal St, POB 281, Springfield, MA 01102; tel. (413) 734-3134; fax (413) 731-5979; e-mail jwithgott@merriam-webster.com; internet www.merriam-webster.com; f. 1831; subsidiary of Encyclopaedia Britannica, Inc; dictionaries, reference; Pres. and Publr John M. Morse.

Michigan State University Press: Manly Miles Bldg, Suite 25, 1405 South Harrison Rd, East Lansing, MI 48823-5245; tel. (517) 355-9543; fax (517) 432-2611; e-mail msupress@msu.edu; internet msupress.msu.edu; f. 1947; scholarly; Dir Gabriel Dotto.

The MIT Press: 55 Hayward St, Cambridge, MA 02142; tel. (617) 253-5646; fax (617) 258-6779; internet mitpress.mit.edu; f. 1932; computer sciences, architecture, design, linguistics, economics, philosophy, general science, neuroscience, cognitive science and engineering; Dir Ellen W. Faran.

Moody Publishers: 820 North LaSalle Blvd, Chicago, IL 60610; tel. (312) 329-2101; fax (312) 329-4157; e-mail pressinfo@moody.edu; internet www.moodypublishers.org; f. 1894; publishing division of Moody Bible Institute (f. 1886); religious; Vice-Pres., Publications Greg Thornton.

National Academy Press (NAP): 500 Fifth St, NW, POB 285, Washington, DC 20055; tel. (202) 334-3180; fax (202) 334-2793; e-mail bkline@nas.edu; internet www.nap.edu; f. 1863; division of Nat. Academy of Sciences; scientific and technical reports, abstracts, bibliographies, catalogues; Dir Barbara Kline Pope.

National Learning Corpn: 212 Michael Dr., Syosset, NY 11791; tel. (516) 921-8888; fax (516) 921-8743; e-mail info@passbooks.com; internet www.passbooks.com; f. 1967; professional and vocational study guides; Pres. Michael P. Rudman.

Thomas Nelson, Inc: POB 141000, Nashville, TN 37214; tel. (615) 889-9000; fax (615) 391-5225; e-mail dambrose@thomasnelson.com; internet www.thomasnelson.com; f. 1961; religious (Roman Catholic), juvenile and trade; Pres. and CEO Michael S. Hyatt.

New Directions Publishing Corpn: 80 Eighth Ave, New York, NY 10011; tel. (212) 255-0230; fax (212) 255-0231; e-mail editorial@ndbooks.com; internet www.ndpublishing.com; f. 1936; modern literature, poetry and criticism; Pres. and Publr Peggy L. Fox.

New York University Press: 838 Broadway, 3rd Floor, New York, NY 10003-4812; tel. (212) 998-2575; fax (212) 995-3833; e-mail information@nyupress.org; internet www.nyupress.org; f. 1916; scholarly and non-fiction; Dir Steve Maikowski.

Northwestern University Press: 629 Noyes St, Evanston, IL 60208; tel. (847) 491-2046; fax (847) 491-8150; e-mail nupress@northwestern.edu; internet www.nupress.northwestern.edu; f. 1958; scholarly and trade; Dir Donna Shear.

W. W. Norton & Co Inc: 500 Fifth Ave, New York, NY 10110; tel. (212) 354-5500; fax (212) 869-0856; e-mail srothbard@wwnorton.com; internet www.wwnorton.com; f. 1924; college textbooks, paperbacks, fiction and non-fiction; CEO Stephen King; Pres. Drake McFeely.

The Ohio State University Press: 180 Pressey Hall, 1070 Carmack Rd, Columbus, OH 43210-1002; tel. (614) 292-6930; fax (614) 292-2065; e-mail info@osupress.org; internet www.ohiostatepress.org; f. 1957; scholarly; Dir Malcolm Litchfield.

Ohio University Press: 19 Circle Dr., The Ridges, Athens, OH 45701; tel. (740) 593-1154; fax (740) 593-4536; e-mail cunningh@ohio.edu; internet www.ohiou.edu/oupress; f. 1964; scholarly and regional studies; Dir David Sanders.

Omnigraphics, Inc: POB 31-1640, Detroit, MI 48231; tel. (313) 961-1340; fax (313) 961-1383; e-mail info@omnigraphics.com; internet www.omnigraphics.com; f. 1985; reference; Publr Peter E. Ruffner.

Open Court Publishing Co: 70 East Lake St, Suite 300, Chicago, IL 60601; tel. (312) 701-1720; fax (312) 701-1728; e-mail opencourt@caruspub.com; internet www.opencourtbooks.com; f. 1887; philosophy and general non-fiction; Pres. and Publr Andre Carus.

Orbis Books: Walsh Bldg, POB 308, Maryknoll, NY 10545-0308; tel. (914) 941-7590; fax (914) 945-0670; e-mail orbisbooks@maryknoll.org; internet www.orbisbooks.com; f. 1970; theology, religion and social concerns; Publr Robert Ellsberg.

Oxford University Press Inc: 198 Madison Ave, New York, NY 10016; tel. (212) 726-6000; fax (212) 726-6446; e-mail custserv.us@oup.com; internet www.oup.com/us; f. 1896; non-fiction, trade, religious, reference, college textbooks, medical and music; Pres. Tim Barton.

Paladin Press: Gunbarrel Tech Center, 7077 Winchester Circle, Boulder, CO 80301; tel. (303) 443-7250; fax (303) 442-8741; e-mail service@paladin-press.com; internet www.paladin-press.com; f. 1970; imprints incl. Sycamore Island Books and Flying Machines Press; military science and history; Chair. and Pres. Peder C. Lund.

Palgrave Macmillan: 175 Fifth Ave, New York, NY 10010; tel. (888) 330-8477; fax (800) 672-2054; e-mail customerservice@vhpsva.com; internet www.palgrave-usa.com; part of Holtzbrinck Publrs, LLC; academic and scholarly; Pres. Garrett Kiely.

Paragon House: 1925 Oakcrest Ave, Suite 7, St Paul, MN 55113-2619; tel. (651) 644-3087; fax (651) 644-0997; e-mail paragon@paragonhouse.com; internet www.paragonhouse.com; f. 1982; general trade non-fiction, university texts and reference; Exec. Dir Gordon L. Anderson.

Paulist Press: 997 Macarthur Blvd, Mahwah, NJ 07430-2096; tel. (201) 825-7300; fax (800) 836-3161; e-mail info@paulistpress.com; internet www.paulistpress.com; f. 1881 as The Columbus Press; religious (Roman Catholic), philosophical and social; Pres. and Publr LAWRENCE BOADT.

Pearson Education: 1 Lake St, Upper Saddle River, NJ 07458; tel. (201) 922-0579; e-mail communications@pearsoned.com; internet www.pearsoned.com; imprints incl. Addison-Wesley, Allyn & Bacon, FT Prentice Hall, Scotts Foreman, Benjamins Cummings and Longman; educational; CEO JOHN FALLON.

Penguin Group (USA) Inc: 375 Hudson St, New York, NY 10014; tel. (212) 366-2000; fax (212) 366-2666; internet us.penguingroup.com; f. 1996 by merger between Penguin Books USA and the Putnam Berkley Group; imprints incl. Ace Books (f. 1953, science fiction), Avery (f. 1976, health, self-help, diet, and fitness), Alpha (f. 1991, general reference) Berkley (f. 1955, mass-market and trade paperback), Dutton (f. 1852, fiction and non-fiction), Gotham (f. 2001, non-fiction), Putnam (f. 1838, fiction and non-fiction), HP Books (automotive, photography, gardening, health and child care), Hudson Street Press (f. 2003, hardcover non-fiction), Jeremy P. Tarcher (f. 1976, non-fiction), NAL (f. 1948, paperback fiction), Penguin (f. 1936, paperback), Plume (f. 1970, paperback), Portfolio (f. 2001, business), Riverhead (f. 1994, fiction), Sentinel (f. 2003, conservative), and Viking (f. 1925, fiction and non-fiction); CEO DAVID SHANKS; Pres. SUSAN PETERSEN KENNEDY.

Pennsylvania State University Press: University Support Bldg I, Suite C, 820 North University Dr., University Park, PA 16802; tel. (814) 865-1327; fax (814) 863-1408; e-mail info@psupress.org; internet www.psupress.org; f. 1956; scholarly non-fiction; Dir SANFORD G. 'SANDY' THATCHER.

Perseus Books Group: 387 Park Ave South, 12th Floor, New York, NY 10016; tel. (212) 340-8100; internet www.perseusbooks.com; imprints include Basic Books (scholarly), Westview Press (q.v.), Da Capo Press (q.v.), Running Press (science, history, children's, food and wine, lifestyle, gift books), Vanguard Press (fiction), Avalon Travel, Nation Books (politics, current issues, history, popular science), Seal Press (women's interest), PublicAffairs (politics, history, biography); Pres. and CEO DAVID STEINBERGER.

Picador: 175 Fifth Ave, New York, NY 10010; tel. (646) 307-5629; fax (212) 253-9627; e-mail publicity@picadorusa.com; internet www.picadorusa.com; f. 1995; imprint of MacMillan; part of Holtzbrinck Publrs, LLC; fiction and non-fiction in paperback; Publr FRANCES COADY.

Presbyterian Publishing Corpn (PPC): 100 Witherspoon St, Louisville, KY 40202-1396; tel. (502) 569-5081; fax (502) 569-5113; e-mail publicity@wjkbooks.com; internet www.ppcbooks.com; f. 1938; publishing arm of the Presbyterian Church (USA); imprints incl. Geneva Press (religious trade) and Westminster John Knox Press (f. 1938, non-denominational Christian, modern religious and scholarly); Pres. and Publr DAVIS PERKINS.

Princeton University Press: 41 William St, Princeton, NJ 08540; tel. (609) 258-4900; fax (609) 258-6305; e-mail webmaster@press.princeton.edu; internet press.princeton.edu; f. 1905; scholarly; Dir PETER J. DOUGHERTY; Editor-in-Chief BRIGITTA VAN RHEINBERG.

Psychology Press: 270 Madison Ave, New York, NY 10016; tel. (212) 216-7800; fax (212) 563-2269; internet www.psypress.com; part of the Taylor & Francis Group; textbooks, monographs and professional books.

Quite Specific Media Group Ltd: 7373 Pyramid Pl., Hollywood, CA 90046; tel. (323) 851-5797; fax (323) 851-5798; e-mail info@quitespecificmedia.com; internet www.quitespecificmedia.com; f. 1967; costume, design, fashion and performing arts; Publr RALPH PINE.

Rand McNally: 8255 North Central Park Ave, Skokie, IL 60076; tel. (800) 934-3479; fax (847) 329-6361; e-mail kconkey@reynoldsgroup.com; internet www.randmcnally.com; f. 1856; maps, atlases, travel guides and educational; Pres. and CEO ROBERT APATOFF.

Random House Publishing Group: 1745 Broadway, New York, NY 10019; tel. (212) 782-9000; fax (212) 572-8026; internet www.randomhouse.com; f. 2003 by merger of the Random House Trade Group and Ballantine Books Group; imprints incl. Random House Inc (f. 1925, originals, reprints, paperbacks, juvenile, series, textbooks), Ballantine Books (f. 1952, hardcover, trade and mass-market paperback), Del Rey (f. 1977, science fiction and fantasy), Modern Library (f. 1925, non-fiction and history), One World (f. 1991, multicultural), Presidio Press (military history), and Villard (f. 1983, general fiction and non-fiction); Chair. and CEO MARKUS DOHLE.

Reader's Digest Association: Reader's Digest Rd, Pleasantville, NY 10570-7000; tel. (914) 238-1000; fax (914) 238-4559; internet www.rd.com; reference and non-fiction; Pres. and CEO MARY BERNER.

Review & Herald Publishing Asscn: 55 West Oak Ridge Dr., Hagerstown, MD 21740; tel. (301) 393-3000; e-mail info@rhpa.org; internet www.rhpa.org; f. 1855; religion (Seventh-day Adventists), health care; Pres. ROBERT S. SMITH.

Lynne Rienner Publishers, Inc: 1800 30th St, Suite 314, Boulder, CO 80301; tel. (303) 444-6684; fax (303) 444-0824; e-mail questions@rienner.com; internet www.rienner.com; f. 1984; scholarly; Pres. LYNNE RIENNER.

Riverside Publishing Co: 3800 Golf Rd, Suite 100, Rolling Meadows, IL 60008; tel. (630) 467-7000; fax (630) 467-7192; e-mail rpcwebmaster@hmco.com; internet www.riversidepublishing.com; f. 1979; division of Houghton Mifflin Co; educational; Pres. RICHARD SWARTZ.

Rizzoli International Publications: 300 Park Ave South, New York, NY 10010-5399; tel. (212) 387-3400; fax (212) 387-3535; e-mail tkayiatos@rizzoliusa.com; internet www.rizzoliusa.com; f. 1975; division of RCS Media Group (Italy); fine arts, performing arts, architecture; Pres. and CEO MARCO AUSENDA; Vice-Pres. and Publr CHARLES MIERS.

Routledge: 270 Madison Ave, New York, NY 10016-0602; tel. (212) 216-7800; fax (212) 563-2269; e-mail info@taylorandfrancis.com; internet www.routledge-ny.com; f. 1977; imprint of Taylor & Francis Group (q.v.); scholarly, professional, trade, humanities, social sciences.

Rowman & Littlefield Publishing Group, Inc: 4501 Forbes Blvd, Suite 200, Lanham, MD 20706; tel. (301) 459-3366; fax (301) 429-5748; e-mail custserv@rowman.com; internet www.rowmanlittlefield.com; f. 1949; imprints incl. Jason Aronson, Inc (f. 1965, psychotherapy), Bridge Works (f. 1992, trade fiction), Cooper Square Press (f. 1961, general interest trade), Ivan R. Dee (f. 1988 history, politics, biography, literature, philosophy and theatre), Derrydale Press (f. 1927, sports and outdoor pursuits), M. Evans and Co (f. 1960, adult fiction and non-fiction), Madison Books, Inc (f. 1985, general interest trade), Roberts Rinehart (f. 1983, history, literature, culture and politics of Ireland, the American West, natural history and national parks), Rowman & Littlefield (f. 1949, academic and trade), Sheed & Ward (f. 1926, religious—Roman Catholic), and Taylor Trade Publishing (fiction and non-fiction, Americana); Publr JONATHAN SISK.

Rutgers University Press: 100 Joyce Kilmer Ave, Piscataway, NJ 08854; tel. (732) 445-7762; fax (732) 445-7039; e-mail jwi@rutgers.edu; internet rutgerspress.rutgers.edu; f. 1936; trade, scholarly and regional; Dir MARLIE WASSERMAN.

William H. Sadlier Inc: 9 Pine St, New York, NY 10005; tel. (212) 227-2120; fax (212) 267-8696; e-mail wsd@sadlier.com; internet www.sadlier.com; f. 1832; textbooks; Pres. WILLIAM SADLIER DINGER.

Sage Publications, Inc: 2455 Teller Rd, Thousand Oaks, CA 91320; tel. (805) 499-4721; e-mail info@sagepub.com; internet www.sagepub.com; f. 1964; professional, reference, social and behavioural sciences; Publr and Chair. SARA MILLER MCCUNE; Pres. and CEO BLAISE R. SIMQU.

SAMS Technical Publishing, LLC: 9850 East 30th St, Indianapolis, IN 46229; tel. (317) 396-9850; fax (800) 552-3910; e-mail webmaster@samswebsite.com; internet www.samswebsite.com; f. 1946; part of AGS Capital, Inc; textbooks, scientific and technical; CEO ALAN SYMONS; Pres. SCOTT WEAVER.

St Martin's Press Inc: 175 Fifth Ave, New York, NY 10010; tel. (212) 674-5151; fax (212) 420-9314; e-mail webmaster@stmartins.com; internet www.stmartins.com; f. 1952; part of Holtzbrinck Publrs, LLC; general, scholarly, college textbooks, trade, mass-market and scholarly; Pres. JOHN SARGENT.

Santillana USA Publishing Co, Inc: 2105 North-West 86th Ave, Doral, FL 33122; tel. (305) 591-9522; fax (310) 591-7164; e-mail customer.service@santillanausa.com; internet www.santillanausa.com; f. 1972; subsidiary of Grupo Editorial Santillana (Spain); textbooks; foreign language materials; Pres. and CEO MIGUEL A. TAPIA.

Scarecrow Press, Inc: 4501 Forbes Blvd, Suite 200, Lanham, MD 20706; tel. (301) 459-3366; fax (301) 429-5748; e-mail custserv@rowman.com; internet www.scarecrowpress.com; f. 1950; subsidiary of Rowman & Littlefield, Inc; music, film, theatre, reference, textbooks, library and information science; Publr and Editorial Dir EDWARD KURDYLA.

Scholastic Library Publishing: 90 Sherman Turnpike, Danbury, CT 06816; tel. (203) 797-3500; fax (203) 797-3720; e-mail news@scholastic.com; internet librarypublishing.scholastic.com; fmrly Grolier Publishing, Inc; division of Scholastic, Inc; imprints incl. Children's Press (f. 1945, educational), Franklin Watts (f. 1942, youth non-fiction) and Grolier (f. 1895, juvenile and youth reference); children's periodicals, textbooks, educational materials; Chair., Pres. and CEO M. RICHARD ROBINSON.

Simon & Schuster, Inc: 1230 Ave of the Americas, New York, NY 10020; tel. (212) 698-7000; fax (212) 698-7007; internet www.simonsays.com; f. 1924; part of the CBS Group; trade, juvenile, reference, educational, business and professional; imprints include

Aladdin Paperbacks (juvenile fiction), Free Press (politics, history, religion, business, fiction), Howard Books (f. 1969, religion, gift books), Pocket Books (f. 1939, fiction), and Scribner (f. 1846, fiction); Pres. and CEO CAROLYN REIDY.

Slavica Publishers: Indiana University, 2611 East 10th St, Bloomington, IN 47408; tel. (812) 856-4186; fax (812) 856-4187; e-mail slavica@indiana.edu; internet www.slavica.com; f. 1966; division of Indiana University; textbooks, scholarly, Russian and Eastern European languages and culture; Publr GEORGE H. FOWLER.

Peter Smith Publisher, Inc: 5 Lexington Ave, Magnolia, MA 01930; tel. (978) 525-3562; fax (978) 525-3674; reprints; Pres. MARY ANN LASH.

Southern Illinois University Press: 1915 University Press Dr., Carbondale, IL 62901-4323; 1915 University Press Dr., SIUC Mail Code 6806, Carbondale, IL 62902-6806; tel. (618) 453-2281; fax (618) 453-1221; e-mail ladkins@siu.edu; internet www.siu.edu/~siupress; f. 1953; scholarly non-fiction; Dir ARTHUR M. (LAIN) ADKINS.

Springer: 233 Spring St, New York, NY 10013; tel. (212) 460-1500; fax (212) 460-1575; e-mail service-ny@springer.com; internet www.springer.com; f. 1964; part of Springer Science+Business Media; scientific, technical and medical; CEO DERK HAANK.

SRA/McGraw-Hill: 220 East Danieldale Rd, Desoto, TX 75115-2490; tel. (312) 984-7000; internet www.sraonline.com; f. 1938 as Science Research Associates (SRA); division of McGraw-Hill Education; educational and instructional material; Vice-Pres. T. J. KARLE.

Stackpole Books: 5067 Ritter Rd, Mechanicsburg, PA 17055; tel. (717) 796-0411; fax (717) 796-0412; e-mail jbender@stackpolebooks.com; internet www.stackpolebooks.com; f. 1930; nature, outdoor sports, crafts and hobbies, militaria, history and Pennsylvania; Pres. M. DAVID DETWEILER.

Stanford University Press: 1450 Page Mill Rd, Palo Alto, CA 94304; tel. (650) 723-9434; fax (650) 725-3457; e-mail info@www.sup.org; internet www.sup.org; f. 1925; Dir GEOFFREY BURN.

State University of New York Press: 194 Washington Ave, Suite 305, Albany, NY 12210-2384; tel. (518) 472-5000; fax (518) 472-5038; e-mail info@sunypress.edu; internet www.sunypress.edu; f. 1966; scholarly and general interest; Exec. Dir GARY DUNHAM.

Sterling Publishing Co, Inc: 387 Park Ave South, New York, NY 10016; tel. (212) 532-7160; fax (212) 213-2495; e-mail publicity@sterlingpub.com; internet www.sterlingpub.com; f. 1949; subsidiary of Barnes and Noble, Inc; imprints incl. Lark Books and Hearst; non-fiction and illustrated; Chair. BURTON H. HOBSON.

Syracuse University Press: Suite 110, 621 Skytop Rd, Syracuse, NY 13244-5290; tel. (315) 443-5534; fax (315) 443-5545; e-mail supress@syr.edu; internet www.syracuseuniversitypress.syr.edu; f. 1943; scholarly; Dir ALICE RANDAL PFEIFFER.

Taplinger Publishing Co Inc: POB 175, Marlboro, NJ 07746; tel. (305) 256-7880; fax (305) 256-7816; e-mail taplingerpub@yahoo.com; f. 1955; general fiction and non-fiction; Pres. LOUIS STRICK.

Taylor & Francis Group: 270 Madison Ave, New York, NY 10016; tel. (212) 216-7800; fax (212) 564-7854; e-mail info@taylorandfrancis.com; internet www.taylorandfrancis.com; f. 1972; division of Informa PLC; imprints incl. CRC Press (f. 1913, reference, science, engineering and medicine), Garland Science Publishing (f. 1969, molecular biology, immunology and protein science textbooks), Routledge (q.v.), and Taylor & Francis Books (f. 1972, academic, science and reference); Pres. EMMETT DAGES.

Charles C Thomas, Publisher: 2600 South First St, Springfield, IL 62794-9265; tel. (217) 789-8980; fax (217) 789-9130; e-mail books@ccthomas.com; internet www.ccthomas.com; f. 1927; textbooks and reference on education, medicine, psychology and criminology; Pres. MICHAEL P. THOMAS.

Thomson RIA: 395 Hudson St, New York, NY 10019; tel. (212) 367-6300; fax (212) 971-5025; internet ria.thomson.com; f. 1935 as Research Institute of America; division of Thomson Reuters Corpn; imprints incl. Warren, Gorham & Lamont, Inc (f. 1846); law, business, engineering, taxation, finance; Chair., Pres. and CEO RUSSELL WHITE.

Transaction Publishers: Rutgers University, 35 Berrue Circle, Piscataway, NJ 08854-8042; tel. (732) 445-2280; fax (732) 445-3138; e-mail trans@transactionpub.com; internet www.transactionpub.com; f. 1962; social sciences, textbooks, reference; Chair. IRVING L. HOROWITZ; Pres. MARY E. CURTIS.

Tuttle Publishing: Airport Business Park, 364 Innovation Dr., North Clarendon, VT 05759-9436; tel. (802) 773-8930; fax (802) 773-6993; e-mail info@tuttlepublishing.com; internet peripluspublishinggroup.com/tuttle; f. 1948; part of the Periplus Publishing Group; the Far East, particularly Japan, languages, art, crafts, martial arts, culture, juvenile, cookery; Publishing Dir EDWARD WALTERS.

United Nations Publications: United Nations Plaza, Room DC2-0853, New York, NY 10017; tel. (212) 963-8302; fax (212) 963-3489; e-mail publications@un.org; internet unp.un.org; f. 1946; world and national economies, international trade, social questions, human rights and international law; Chief of Section CHRISTOPHER WOODTHORPE.

University of Alabama Press: POB 870380, Tuscaloosa, AL 35487; tel. (205) 348-5180; fax (205) 348-9201; e-mail sgriffit@uapress.ua.edu; internet www.uapress.ua.edu; f. 1945; scholarly; Dir DANIEL J. J. ROSS.

University of Alaska Press: POB 756240, Fairbanks, AK 99775-6240; tel. (907) 474-5831; fax (907) 474-5502; e-mail fypress@uaf.edu; internet www.uaf.edu/uapress; f. 1967; scholarly regional non-fiction, history, anthropology of the circumpolar north; Chair. of Editorial Bd PATRICIA H. PARTNOW.

University of Arizona Press: 355 South Euclid Ave, Suite 103, Tucson, AZ 85719; tel. (520) 621-1441; fax (520) 621-8899; e-mail uapress@uapress.arizona.edu; internet www.uapress.arizona.edu; f. 1959; scholarly, popular, regional and non-fiction; Dir CHRISTINE SZUTER.

University of Arkansas Press: McIlroy House, 105 N McIlroy Ave, Fayetteville, AR 72701; tel. (479) 575-3246; fax (479) 575-6044; e-mail cmoss@uark.edu; internet www.uapress.com; f. 1980; humanities, literature, regional studies, natural history, Middle Eastern studies, poetry, civil rights studies and American history; Dir LARRY MALLEY.

University of California Press: 2120 Berkeley Way, Berkeley, CA 94704-1012; tel. (510) 642-4247; fax (510) 643-7127; e-mail askucp@ucpress.edu; internet www.ucpress.edu; f. 1893; academic and scholarly; Dir LYNNE WITHEY.

University of Chicago Press: 1427 East 60th St, Chicago, IL 60637; tel. (773) 702-7700; fax (773) 702-9756; e-mail publicity@press.uchicago.edu; internet www.press.uchicago.edu; f. 1891; scholarly and general; Dir PAULA BARKER DUFFY.

University of Georgia Press: 330 Research Dr., Athens, GA 30602-4901; tel. (706) 369-6148; fax (706) 369-6131; e-mail books@ugapress.uga.edu; internet www.ugapress.org; f. 1938; academic, scholarly, poetry, fiction, non-fiction and literary trade; Dir NICOLE MITCHELL.

University of Hawaii Press: 2840 Kolowalu St, Honolulu, HI 96822; tel. (808) 956-8255; fax (808) 988-6052; e-mail uhpbooks@hawaii.edu; internet www.uhpress.hawaii.edu; f. 1947; Asian, Pacific and Hawaiian studies; Dir WILLIAM H. HAMILTON.

University of Illinois Press: 1325 South Oak St, Champaign, IL 61820; tel. (217) 333-0950; fax (217) 244-8082; e-mail uipress@uillinois.edu; internet www.press.uillinois.edu; f. 1918; scholarly and trade; Dir WILLIS REGIER.

University of Massachusetts Press: POB 429, Amherst, MA 01004-0429; tel. (413) 545-2217; fax (413) 545-1226; e-mail info@umpress.umass.edu; internet www.umass.edu/umpress; f. 1963; scholarly; Dir BRUCE G. WILCOX.

University of Michigan Press: 839 Greene St, Ann Arbor, MI 48104-3209; tel. (734) 764-4388; fax (734) 615-1540; e-mail dshafer@umich.edu; internet www.press.umich.edu; f. 1930; academic, textbooks and paperbacks; Dir PHILIP POCHODA.

University of Minnesota Press: 111 Third Ave South, Suite 290, Minneapolis, MN 55401-5250; tel. (612) 627-1970; fax (612) 627-1980; e-mail ump@umn.edu; internet www.upress.umn.edu; f. 1925; scholarly and general; Dir DOUGLAS M. ARMATO.

University of Missouri Press: 2910 LeMone Blvd, Columbia, MO 65201; tel. (573) 882-7641; fax (573) 884-4498; e-mail upress@umsystem.edu; internet press.umsystem.edu; f. 1958; scholarly; Dir BEVERLY JARRETT.

University of Nebraska Press: 1111 Lincoln Mall, Lincoln, NE 68588-0630; tel. (402) 472-3581; fax (402) 472-6214; e-mail pressmail@unl.edu; internet www.nebraskapress.unl.edu; f. 1941; scholarly and general; Dir LADETTE RANDOLPH.

University of New Mexico Press: 1312 Basehart SE, Suite 200s, Albuquerque, NM 87106; tel. (505) 277-2346; fax (505) 277-7141; e-mail unmpress@unm.edu; internet www.unmpress.com; f. 1929; scholarly and regional studies; Dir LUTHER WILSON.

University of North Carolina Press: 116 South Boundary St, Chapel Hill, NC 27514-3808; tel. (919) 966-3561; fax (919) 966-3829; e-mail uncpress@unc.edu; internet www.uncpress.unc.edu; f. 1922; biography, regional and scholarly; Dir KATE D. TORREY.

University of Notre Dame Press: 310 Flanner Hall, Notre Dame, IN 46556; tel. (574) 631-6346; fax (574) 631-8148; e-mail undpress.1@nd.edu; internet www.undpress.nd.edu; f. 1949; humanities and social sciences; Dir BARBARA J. HANRAHAN.

University of Oklahoma Press: 2800 Venture Dr., Norman, OK 73069-8216; tel. (405) 325-2000; fax (405) 325-4000; internet www.oupress.com; f. 1928; scholarly; Editor-in-Chief CHARLES E. RANKIN; Dir B. BYRON PRICE.

University of Pennsylvania Press: 3905 Spruce St, Philadelphia, PA 19104-4112; tel. (215) 898-6261; fax (215) 898-0404; e-mail custserv@pobox.upenn.edu; internet www.upenn.edu/pennpress; f. 1890; scholarly; Dir Eric Halpern.

University of Pittsburgh Press: Eureka Bldg, 3400 Forbes Ave, 5th Floor, Pittsburgh, PA 15260; tel. (412) 383-2456; fax (412) 383-2466; e-mail press@pitt.edu; internet www.upress.pitt.edu; f. 1936; scholarly; Dir Cynthia Miller.

University Press of America, Inc: 4501 Forbes Blvd, Suite 200, Lanham, MD 20706; tel. (301) 459-3366; fax (301) 429-5749; internet www.univpress.com; f. 1975; scholarly; Vice-Pres. and Dir Judith Rothman.

University Press of Florida: 15 North West 15th St, Gainesville, FL 32611-2079; tel. (352) 392-1351; fax (352) 392-7302; internet www.upf.com; f. 1945; general, scholarly, regional; Dir Meredith Morris-Babb.

University Press of Kansas: 2502 Westbrooke Circle, Lawrence, KS 66045; tel. (785) 864-4155; fax (785) 864-4586; e-mail upress@ku.edu; internet www.kansaspress.ku.edu; f. 1946; scholarly; Dir Fred M. Woodward.

University Press of Kentucky: 663 South Limestone St, Lexington, KY 40508-4008; tel. (606) 257-8400; fax (606) 323-1873; internet www.kentuckypress.com; f. 1943; non-fiction, scholarly and regional; Dir Stephen M. Wrinn.

University Press of Mississippi: 3825 Ridgewood Rd, Jackson, MS 39211; tel. (601) 432-6205; fax (601) 432-6217; e-mail press@ihl.state.ms.us; internet www.upress.state.ms.us; f. 1970; scholarly, non-fiction and regional; Dir Leila Salisbury.

University Press of New England: 1 Court St, Lebanon, NH 03766; tel. (603) 448-1533; fax (603) 448-7006; e-mail upneweb@dartmouth.edu; internet www.upne.com; f. 1970; scholarly; Dir Michael P. Burton.

University of South Carolina Press: 1600 Hampton St, 5th Floor, Columbia, SC 29208; tel. (803) 777-5243; fax (800) 868-0740; e-mail lfogle@gwm.sc.edu; internet www.sc.edu/uscpress; scholarly and regional studies; Dir Curtis L. Clark.

University of Tennessee Press: Conference Center Bldg, 600 Henley St, Suite 110, Knoxville, TN 37996-4108; tel. (865) 974-3321; fax (865) 974-3724; e-mail custserv@utk.edu; internet www.utpress.org; f. 1940; scholarly, regional, and literary fiction; Dir Jennifer M. Siler.

University of Texas Press: POB 7819, Austin, TX 78713-7819; tel. (512) 471-7233; fax (512) 232-7178; e-mail utpress@uts.cc.utexas.edu; internet www.utexas.edu/utpress; f. 1950; general, scholarly non-fiction; Dir Joanna Hitchcock.

University of Utah Press: 1795 East South Campus Dr., 101, Salt Lake City, UT 84112-9402; tel. (801) 585-9786; fax (801) 581-3365; e-mail peter.delafosse@utah.edu; internet www.uofupress.com; f. 1949; scholarly, regional and Middle East studies; Dir Joe Herring.

University of Virginia Press: POB 400318, Charlottesville, VA 229034-4318; tel. (434) 924-3468; fax (434) 982-2655; e-mail lrb6c@virginia.edu; internet www.upress.virginia.edu; f. 1963; scholarly, literary criticism, women's studies, political science and African studies; Chair. Gustavo Pellón; Dir Penelope J. Kaiserlian.

University of Washington Press: POB 50096, Seattle, WA 98145-5096; tel. (206) 543-4050; fax (206) 543-3932; e-mail hfscustserv@press.jhu.edu; internet www.washington.edu/uwpress; f. 1920; general, scholarly, non-fiction and reprints; Dir Pat Soden.

University of Wisconsin Press: 1930 Monroe St, 3rd Floor, Madison, WI 53711-2059; tel. (608) 263-1110; fax (608) 263-1120; e-mail uwiscpress@uwpress.wisc.edu; internet www.wisc.edu/wisconsinpress; f. 1936; scholarly and trade; Interim Dir Sheila Leary.

Vanderbilt University Press: POB 1813, Nashville, TN 37235; tel. (615) 322-3585; fax (615) 343-8823; e-mail vupress@vanderbilt.edu; internet www.vanderbiltuniversitypress.com; f. 1940; scholarly and trade; Dir Michael Ames.

Walch Publishing: 40 Walch Dr., Portland, ME 04103-1286; tel. (207) 772-2846; fax (207) 772-3105; e-mail customer_service@walch.com; internet www.walch.com; f. 1927; fmrly J. Weston Walch Publr; educational; Chair. Peter S. Walch; Pres. Al Noyes.

Walker & Co: 175 Fifth Ave, New York, NY 10010; tel. (212) 727-8300; fax (212) 727-0984; e-mail mbaran@walkerbooks.com; internet www.walkerbooks.com; f. 1959; division of Bloomsbury USA; distributed by MacMillan; history, science and juvenile; Pres. and Publr George L. Gibson.

Wayne State University Press: 4809 Woodward Ave, Detroit, MI 48201; tel. (313) 577-6120; fax (313) 577-6131; e-mail jane.hoehner@wayne.edu; internet wsupress.wayne.edu; f. 1941; scholarly; Dir Jane Hoehner.

Weigl Educational Publishers: 350 Fifth Ave, Suite 3304, PMB 6G, New York, NY 10118-0069; tel. (866) 649-3445; fax (866) 449-3445; e-mail linda@weigl.com; internet www.weigl.com; f. 1979; educational; social studies, science, languages, arts, biography and physical education; Publr Linda A. Weigl.

West: 610 Opperman Dr., POB 64526, St Paul, MN 55123; tel. (612) 687-7000; fax (612) 687-5461; e-mail west_lawschool@thomson.com; internet west.thomson.com; f. 1876; fmrly West Publishing Co; division of Thomson Reuters Corpn; imprints incl. Foundation Press (f. 1931, law teaching materials and casebooks), Gilbert (f. 1953, law study aids) and West Law School (textbooks and study aids); Pres. and CEO Peter Warwick.

Westview Press: 2465 Central Ave, Boulder, CO 80301; tel. and fax (720) 406-7336; e-mail westview.press@perseusbooks.com; internet www.perseusbooksgroup.com/westview; social sciences, humanities and science textbooks; f. 1975; part of the Perseus Books Group; Publr Marcus Boggs.

John Wiley and Sons, Inc: 111 River St, Hoboken, NJ 07030-5774; tel. (201) 748-6000; fax (201) 748-6088; e-mail info@wiley.com; internet www.wiley.com; f. 1807; higher education, scientific, technical, medical, professional and trade; Chair. Peter B. Wiley; Pres. and CEO William J. Pesce.

H. W. Wilson Co: 950 University Ave, Bronx, NY 10452; tel. (718) 588-8400; fax (718) 590-1617; e-mail esutter@hwwilson.com; internet www.hwwilson.com; f. 1898; reference and indices; Pres. and CEO Harold Regan.

Wolters Kluwer Health: 161 West Washington St, Suite 1100, Conshohocken, PA 19428; tel. (610) 234-4511; e-mail robert.dekker@wolterskluwer.com; internet www.wkhealth.com; division of Wolters Kluwer; medical and scientific reference; imprints, incl. Lippincott, Williams & Wilkins (f. 1792, dentistry, science, human and veterinary medicine); Pres. and CEO Jeffery McCaulley.

World Book, Inc: 233 North Michigan, Suite 2000, Chicago, IL 60601; tel. (312) 729-5800; fax (312) 729-5600; e-mail sub.questions@worldbookonline.com; internet www.worldbook.com; f. 1917; reference; Editorial Admin. Janet T. Peterson.

Yale University Press: POB 209040, New Haven, CT 06520-9040; tel. (203) 432-0960; fax (203) 432-0948; e-mail ivan.lett@yale.edu; internet yalepress.yale.edu/yup; f. 1908; scholarly; Dir John Donatich.

Zondervan Publishing House: 5300 Patterson Ave SE, Grand Rapids, MI 49530; tel. (616) 698-6900; fax (616) 698-3235; e-mail zprod@zondervan.com; internet www.zondervan.com; f. 1931; religious (Protestant); Pres. and CEO Moe Girkins.

GOVERNMENT PUBLISHING HOUSE

Government Printing Office: 732 North Capitol St, NW, Washington, DC 20401; tel. (202) 512-0000; fax (202) 512-2104; e-mail contactcenter@gpo.gov; internet www.gpo.gov; Public Printer and CEO Robert C. Tapella.

Publishers' Organizations and Associations

American Book Producers' Association: 611 Broadway, Suite 611, New York, NY 10012; tel. (212) 645-2368; fax (212) 802-2893; e-mail office@abpaonline.org; internet www.abpaonline.org; f. 1980; 55 mems; Pres. Dan Tucker.

American Booksellers' Association (ABA): 200 White Plains Rd, Tarrytown, NY 10591; tel. (914) 591-2665; fax (914) 591-2724; e-mail avin@bookweb.org; internet www.bookweb.org; f. 1900; 2,500 mems; Pres. Gayle Shanks; CEO Avin Mark Domnitz.

American Business Media: 675 Third Ave, Suite 400, New York, NY 10017-5704; tel. (212) 661-6360; fax (212) 370-0736; e-mail info@abmmail.com; internet www.americanbusinessmedia.com; f. 1906; c. 350 mems; Pres. and CEO Gordon T. Hughes, II.

American Society of Composers, Authors and Publishers (ASCAP): ASCAP Bldg, 1 Lincoln Plaza, New York, NY 10023; tel. (212) 621-6000; fax (212) 724-9064; internet www.ascap.com; f. 1914; over 330,000 mems; Pres. and Chair. Marilyn Bergham.

Association of American Publishers, Inc (AAP): 71 Fifth Ave, New York, NY 10003-3004; tel. (212) 255-0200; fax (212) 255-7007; e-mail amyg@publishers.org; internet www.publishers.org; f. 1970; 300 mems; Chair. Richard Sarnoff; Pres. and CEO Patricia S. Schroeder.

Association of American University Presses, Inc: 71 West 23rd St, New York, NY 10010; tel. (212) 989-1010; fax (212) 989-0275; e-mail info@aaupnet.org; internet www.aaupnet.org; f. 1937; 125 mems; Exec. Dir Peter J. Givler.

Black Americans in Publishing, Inc (BAIP): POB 6275, FDR Station, New York, NY 10150; tel. (212) 772-5951; e-mail president@

baip.org; internet www.baip.org; f. 1979 as Black Women in Publishing; Pres. LYNETTE VELASCO.

Book Industry Study Group, Inc (BISG): 370 Lexington Ave, Suite 900, New York, NY 10017; tel. (646) 336-7141; fax (646) 336-6214; e-mail info@bisg.org; internet www.bisg.org; f. 1976; 200 mem. cos; Exec. Dir JAN NATHAN.

Book Manufacturers' Institute, Inc: 2 Armand Beach Dr., Suite 1B, Palm Coast, FL 32137; tel. (386) 986-4552; fax (386) 986-4553; e-mail info@bmibook.com; internet www.bmibook.org; f. 1933; 90 mems; Exec. Vice-Pres. BRUCE W. SMITH.

Catholic Book Publishers' Association, Inc: 8404 Jamesport Dr., Rockford, IL 61108; tel. (815) 332-3245; fax (815) 332-3476; e-mail info@cbpa.org; internet www.cbpa.org; f. 1987; 235 mems; Pres. JILL KURTZ.

The Children's Book Council, Inc: 12 West 37th St, 2nd Floor, New York, NY 10018-7480; tel. (212) 966-1990; fax (212) 966-2073; internet www.cbcbooks.org; f. 1945; 75 mems; Chair. SUZANNE MURPHY.

Church Music Publishers' Association: POB 158992, Nashville, TN 37215; tel. (615) 791-0273; fax (615) 790-8847; internet www.cmpamusic.org; f. 1925; 46 mems; Pres. JERRY WEIMER.

Copyright Society of the USA: 352 Seventh Ave, Suite 739, New York, NY, 10001; tel. (212) 345-6401; fax (212) 354-2847; e-mail amy@csusa.org; internet www.csusa.org; f. 1953; promotes study of copyright law and related rights in traditional and new media; 850 mems; Pres. KAREN FRANK.

Evangelical Christian Publishers' Association (ECPA): 9633 South 48th St, Suite 140, Phoenix, AZ 85044; tel. (480) 966-3998; fax (480) 996-1944; e-mail info@ecpa.org; internet www.ecpa.org; f. 1974; 272 corporate mems; Pres. and CEO MARK KUYPER.

Florida Publishers Association, Inc: POB 430, Highland City, FL 33846-0430; tel. and fax (836) 647-5951; e-mail fpabooks@aol.com; internet www.flbookpub.org; f. 1983; fmrly Nat. Asscn of Independent Publrs; 150 mems; Exec. Dir BETSY WRIGHT-LAMPE.

Independent Book Publishers' Association (IBPA): 627 Aviation Way, Manhattan Beach, CA 90266; tel. (310) 372-2732; fax (310) 374-3342; e-mail info@ibpa-online.org; internet www.ibpa-online.org; f. 1983 as Publishers' Marketing Asscn; over 4,000 mem. publrs; Pres. FLORRIE BINFORD KICHLER; Exec. Dir TERRY NATHAN.

Independent Publishers Group: 814 North Franklin St, Chicago, IL 60610; tel. (312) 337-0747; fax (312) 337-5985; e-mail frontdesk@ipgbook.com; internet www.ipgbook.com; f. 1971; Pres. MARK SUCHOMEL; CEO CURT MATTHEWS.

Music Publishers' Association of the US: 243 5th Ave, Suite 236, New York, NY 10016; tel. (212) 327-4044; e-mail admin@mpa.org; internet www.mpa.org; f. 1895; 600 mems; Pres. LAUREN KEISER.

National Association of Publishers' Representatives: 1901 N Roselle Road, Suite 920, Schaumburg, IL 60195; tel. (847) 885-7400; fax (847) 885-8393; e-mail napr@napronline.org; internet napronline.org; f. 1950; over 250 mems; Exec. Dir ARMAND VILLIGER.

Protestant Church-Owned Publishers' Association (PCPA): 2850 Kalamazoo Ave SE, Grand Rapids, MI 49560; tel. (616) 224-0831; e-mail mulder@pcpaonline.org; internet www.pcpanews.org; f. 1951; 41 mems; Asscn Dir GARY MULDER.

Publishers' Advertising and Marketing Association (PAMA): c/o D. Nudo, 530 E 86th St, New York, NY 10028; tel. (917) 690-6897; e-mail president@pama-ny.org; internet www.pama-ny.org; f. 1921; 300 mems; Pres. DAVID NUDO.

Publishers' Publicity Association (PPA): c/o Random House Children's, 1745 Broadway, New York, NY 10019; tel. (212) 762-8626; fax (212) 782-9004; e-mail jhaut@randomhouse.com; internet www.publisherspublicity.org; f. 1963; 250 mems; Pres. JUDITH HAUT.

Society for Scholarly Publishing: 10200 West 44th Ave, Suite 304, Wheat Ridge, CO 80033-2840; tel. (303) 422-3914; fax (303) 422-8894; e-mail info@sspnet.org; internet www.sspnet.org; f. 1978; 1,000 mems; Pres. OCTOBER IVINS.

Women in Scholarly Publishing: Rutgers University Press, 100 Joyce Kilmer Rd, Livingston Campus, Piscataway, NJ 08854-8099; tel. (732) 445-7762; fax (732) 445-7039; internet www.womeninscholarlypublishing.org; f. 1979; 300 mems; Pres. MARIA COUGHLIN.

Women's National Book Association: c/o Susannah Greenberg Public Relations, POB 237, FDR Station, New York, NY 10150-0231; tel. and fax (212) 208-4629; e-mail publicity@bookbuzz.com; internet www.wnba-books.org; f. 1917; 1,000 mems; Pres. JOAN GELFAND.

Yellow Pages Association (YPA): 400 Connell Dr., Suite 1100, Berkeley Heights, NJ 07922-2747; tel. (908) 286-2380; fax (908) 286-0620; e-mail neg.norton@ypassociation.org; internet www.ypassociation.org; f. 1988 as Yellow Pages Publrs Asscn by merger of the Asscn of North American Directory Publrs (f. 1898) and the Nat. Yellow Pages Service Asscn (f. 1975); Chair. DAVID SWANSON; Pres. NEG NORTON.

HEALTH AND WELFARE

INTRODUCTION

In the 21st century US health and welfare programmes were dependent upon a mixture of federal and state government funds, private-sector finance and philanthropy. The Social Security Administration operated three principal programmes: Retirement, Survivors' and Disability Insurance, which included the Medicare programme; Supplemental Security Income; and Aid to Families with Dependent Children.

Federal government involvement in health care took the form of Medicare. This was a national health insurance programme for social-security beneficiaries over the age of 65 years and disabled people under 65 who were entitled to social-security disability benefits for at least two years. The programme also covered certain insured workers with end-stage kidney disease, and their dependants. Medicare had two components: hospital insurance and a voluntary supplementary medical insurance, financed in part by monthly premiums paid by the beneficiary upon reaching 65 years. The programme was financed largely by federally purchased private insurance. Those unable to qualify for Medicare could be eligible for Medicaid, which was a state-administered programme supported partly by the federal Government. Medicaid aimed to provide adequate medical care for the old, blind, disabled and members of families with dependent children where one parent was unemployed, absent or incapacitated. Although there were broad national guidelines as to the form of the programme, eligibility, payment to medical staff and organization varied from state to state. Individuals were encouraged, through tax incentives, to purchase private health insurance or to join a Health Maintenance Organization (HMO). Provision of health insurance by employers for employees was mandatory. Upon acceptance by an HMO, the individual paid a premium and was then entitled to receive both necessary medical attention and preventive care, thus avoiding the fee-for-service method of private medical insurance. In a further effort to control the costs of health care, the federal Government introduced Diagnosis Related Groups (DRGs) under the Medicare scheme, whereby fees payable by the federal Government for Medicare patients were dependent upon the diagnosis. DRGs operated as a national system of price regulation. In November 2003 Congress enacted legislation extending Medicare benefits to cover the cost of most prescription drugs; several measures included within the new legislation attracted much criticism (for further details, see In A Complicated State: Health and Welfare Policy in the USA, in Essays on US Economic and Social Affairs).

HMO membership rose by 45.2% between 1990 and 2000. At 1 January 2006 some 23.8% of US citizens were enrolled in HMOs. In 1998 85% of all employees in employer-sponsored health plans belonged to some form of managed care, compared with 29% in 1988. In 2006 some 59.7% of the total population was covered by employment-based health insurance, compared with 59.5% in 2005. In 2006 some 43.2m. people in the USA (equivalent to 14.5% of the total population) were enrolled in the Medicare programme. In that year 38.3m. people (equivalent to 12.9% of the total population) were enrolled in the Medicaid programme. The number of people with health insurance increased by 2.5m. in 2006, to 249.8m. (equivalent to some 84.2% of the population). However, an estimated 47.0m. were without health insurance coverage in that year, up from 46.6m. people in 2005, with the percentage of those uninsured increasing to 15.8% of the total population. Of all children, 11.7% (some 8.7m.) were uninsured in 2006, while 19.3% of children in poverty were uninsured. The highest rates of uninsurance among any racial group or minority were found among Hispanic people in the USA, 34.1% (or 15.3m.) of whom were without any form of health insurance in 2006.

In some areas, private companies and state and local governments, acting on behalf of their dependent populations, used the Preferred Provider Organization as a means of reducing the cost of health care. Under this system companies and governments made contracts with certain providers of health care to provide care at a lower cost than normal. The main disadvantage to this system was that programme members could receive health care from stipulated providers only. Those who were turned away by the above systems—the destitute and uninsured—either received charitable care or were paid for by the surplus from fee-paying patients. The 'Oregon Basic Health Plan' was devised in the early 1990s, with the objective that all employers should provide universal health care coverage for employees and their dependants at least equal to that provided under the Medicaid programme; and to provide cover for more of the state's poor for fewer treatments, rather than a more limited Medicaid population for more treatments. Consequently, some medical procedures were not covered, and concerns were raised that political factors could deny the necessary treatment to marginalized groups, such as drug addicts or those suffering from HIV or AIDS. The Plan was given approval for a five-year trial period by President Bill Clinton's Administration in 1993. In June 2001 the Senate approved the Patients' Bill of Rights, extending new rights to citizens in managed health care plans, whether through private insurance or an HMO, as well as federal employees and Medicare recipients (those without insurance would not be covered). The Bill made emergency medical care, access to specialists and necessary prescription drugs more readily available, and enabled patients to challenge decisions by insurers and HMOs, and to sue them where decisions led to injury or death. A new premium plan for Medicare, which entered into effect in January 2006, involved the introduction of surcharges for higher-income beneficiaries.

Retirement, Survivors' and Disability Insurance, or 'Social Security', was an insurance programme administered by the federal Government under the provisions of the Social Security Act of 1935. It aimed to provide retirement income for elderly persons, benefit for insured workers under 65 years of age with a prolonged disability and for the workers' dependants, survivor benefit for the dependants of deceased insured workers, and medical care for the elderly (see above). Survivors' and disability benefits were payable to spouses and children of insured workers at one or more levels. Full benefits were normally payable to a surviving spouse at the age of 65 years, with reduced benefits available from the age of 60. Benefits were payable to surviving children until they reached the age of 18 years, or, if still in full-time education, until the age of 19; surviving children disabled before the age of 22 years could also receive benefits. Under certain circumstances disabled widows or widowers were eligible for benefits from the age of 50 years. To qualify, a certain percentage of a person's wage must have been contributed to social security for a specified amount of time, the cost shared equally between the employee and employer. Self-employed persons also contributed. A worker could become eligible for full benefit at the age of 65 years, or later, depending on the year of birth. Reduced benefit was payable from the age of 62 years.

The Supplemental Security Income programme was established in 1972, whereby a minimum income was paid monthly to those with limited resources who were over 65 years of age, blind or disabled. The programme was administered by the federal Government and financed by general funds from the Treasury rather than by social security payments. Entitlement was based on income and assets. States supplemented the federal payment for persons adversely affected by the transition from former public assistance programmes, and could elect to supplement payments to all recipients.

Aid to Families with Dependent Children was set up under the Social Security Act of 1935 with the aim of providing basic support for children living with one parent or relative. It was administered by the states with federal assistance and worked according to national government regulations. In 1997 the broadly similar Temporary Assistance for Needy Families (TANF), administered by the Department of Health and Human Services, replaced this scheme.

In 1996 welfare legislation was introduced that permitted each state to set its own welfare rules and to decide how funds were allocated. Some basic criteria, however, had to be met: within two years of claiming welfare at least one-half of adult recipients must have jobs and, over the course of a lifetime, a person may only claim welfare for a maximum of five years. The food-stamp programme remained under the control of the federal Government.

Unemployment compensation programmes were state-administered and varied from state to state, in terms of both the length of time for which a person was eligible to receive benefit and the amount paid. Common to the various state unemployment-insurance programmes, however, was the entitlement of workers to receive benefit related to past earnings provided that they: (a) worked for a specified period in employment covered by the scheme (about 97% of workers were covered); (b) were registered for work at a public employment office and were able and willing to work; and (c) did not wantonly bring about their own state of unemployment. Benefits, in most states, were payable for 26 weeks. In times of high unemployment the benefit could be payable over an extended period under a federal-state programme. Unemployment insurance was funded from a federal unemployment tax levied on the taxable payrolls of employers.

Workers' compensation, for employment-related injuries and deaths, was provided by all states and usually related to the worker's salary. Federal employees, longshoremen and harbour workers, and private employees in the District of Columbia were covered by federal law. The federal Government also provided compensation for coal miners disabled by pneumoconiosis, their survivors and dependants.

National government assistance and private philanthropy were brought together by a federal agency, ACTION. This agency was established in 1971 to co-ordinate various social service agencies, among them being VISTA, or Volunteers in Service to America. In 1993 the National Service Trust Act combined ACTION with the Commission on National and Community Service and the White House Office of National Service to form a single entity, the Corporation for National and Community Service (CNS). VISTA was absorbed into AmeriCorps and administered by the CNS.

SELECTED STATISTICS

Health

NATIONAL HEALTH EXPENDITURE, BY TYPE
($ '000 million)

	2004	2005	2006
Total private expenditures	1,014.8	1,076.6	1,135.2
Health services and supplies	946.9	1,003.1	1,054.1
Out-of-pocket payments	234.9	247.1	256.5
Insurance premiums*	645.8	685.6	723.4
Other	66.2	70.4	74.1
Medical research	3.4	3.7	4.0
Medical facilities construction	64.5	69.8	77.1
Total public expenditures	837.5	896.8	970.3
Health services and supplies	783.7	840.6	912.1
Medicare†	309.3	338.0	401.3
Public assistance medical payments‡	297.3	319.0	317.0
Other	181.1	183.6	193.8
Medical research	35.4	36.9	37.8
Medical facilities construction	18.4	19.3	20.4
Total expenditures	1,852.3	1,973.3	2,105.5

* Covers insurance benefits and amount retained by insurance companies for expense, additions to reserves, and profits (net cost of insurance).
† Represents expenditures for hospital care and public health activities and administrative cost from federal hospital and medical insurance trust funds under old-age, survivors', disability and health insurance programmes.
‡ Payments made directly to the suppliers of medical aid (primarily Medicaid).
Source: US Centers for Medicare & Medicaid Services.

NATIONAL HEALTH EXPENDITURES, BY OBJECT
($ '000 million)

	2004	2005	2006
Spent by:			
Consumers	880.7	932.7	980.0
Government	837.5	896.8	970.3
Other	134.1	143.9	155.3
Spent for:			
Health services and supplies	1,730.6	1,843.6	1,966.2
Personal health care expenses	1,547.7	1,653.7	1,762.0
Hospital care	564.4	605.5	648.2
Physicians' services	393.6	422.6	447.6
Dentists' services	81.5	86.6	91.5
Other professional services*	52.4	56.2	58.9
Home health care	42.7	47.9	52.7
Prescription drugs	188.8	199.7	216.7
Other non-durable medical products	33.1	34.4	35.6
Durable medical equipment	22.8	23.2	23.7
Nursing home care	115.2	120.7	124.9
Other personal health care	53.2	56.8	62.2
Net cost of insurance and administration†	129.0	133.6	145.4
Government public-health activities	53.9	56.3	58.7
Medical research	38.8	40.6	41.8
Medical facilities construction	83.0	89.1	97.6
Total	1,852.3	1,973.3	2,105.5

* Includes services of registered and practical nurses in private duty, podiatrists, optometrists, physical therapists, clinical psychologists, chiropractors, naturopaths and Christian Science practitioners.
† Includes administrative expenses of federally financed health programmes.
Source: US Centers for Medicare & Medicaid Services.

MEDICAL PROFESSIONALS BY STATE
(as at 31 December of year stated)*

	Physicians (2004)		Dentists (1999)		Nurses (2004)†	
	Total	Per 100,000 resident population	Total	Per 100,000 resident population	Total	Per 100,000 resident population
Alabama	9,627	213	1,903	43.5	36,538	806
Alaska	1,463	222	451	72.7	6,777	1,034
Arizona	11,955	222	2,275	47.6	39,136	681
Arkansas	5,577	208	1,076	42.2	20,115	731
California	92,907	259	22,636	68.3	211,640	590
Colorado	11,871	258	2,790	68.8	34,654	753
Connecticut	12,761	363	2,611	79.6	32,718	934
Delaware	2,061	248	352	46.7	8,633	1,040
District of Columbia	4,423	248	751	144.7	11,583	2,093
Florida	42,665	245	8,034	53.2	132,758	763
Georgia	19,589	220	3,546	45.5	66,512	753
Hawaii	3,912	310	1,004	84.7	9,335	739
Idaho	2,351	169	656	52.4	8,753	628
Illinois	34,514	272	8,173	67.4	113,779	895
Indiana	13,283	213	2,850	48.0	54,624	876
Iowa	5,518	187	1,557	54.3	32,664	1,106
Kansas	6,021	220	1,343	50.6	24,869	909
Kentucky	9,523	230	2,214	55.9	37,631	908
Louisiana	11,898	264	2,109	48.2	35,369	783
Maine	3,512	267	600	47.9	15,077	1,145
Maryland	22,863	411	3,955	76.5	47,124	848
Massachusetts	28,827	450	5,017	81.2	75,398	1,175
Michigan	24,287	240	5,892	59.7	84,967	840
Minnesota	14,303	281	2,918	61.1	51,914	1,018
Mississippi	5,251	181	1,098	39.7	24,009	827
Missouri	13,790	239	2,691	49.2	57,365	997
Montana	2,047	221	491	55.6	7,914	854
Nebraska	4,181	239	1,092	65.5	18,532	1,061
Nevada	4,333	186	710	39.2	14,095	604
New Hampshire	3,372	260	691	57.5	16,670	1,283
New Jersey	26,580	306	6,544	80.4	72,980	839
New Mexico	4,563	240	784	45.1	13,570	713
New York	74,924	389	15,130	83.1	174,208	906
North Carolina	21,609	253	3,297	43.1	76,761	899
North Dakota	1,539	242	306	48.3	7,484	1,180
Ohio	29,833	261	6,106	54.2	112,806	984
Oklahoma	6,031	171	1,658	49.4	24,433	694
Oregon	9,429	263	2,236	67.4	30,850	858
Pennsylvania	36,381	294	8,068	67.3	127,013	1,024
Rhode Island	3,786	351	590	59.5	11,368	1,052
South Carolina	9,646	230	1,765	45.4	30,711	732
South Dakota	1,687	219	361	49.2	9,278	1,204
Tennessee	15,357	261	2,919	53.2	54,338	921
Texas	47,617	212	9,654	48.2	145,336	646
Utah	5,061	209	1,356	63.7	15,778	660
Vermont	2,249	362	357	60.1	6,444	1,037
Virginia	20,183	270	3,994	58.1	56,726	760
Washington	16,443	265	3,750	65.3	48,121	780
West Virginia	4,150	229	835	46.2	16,042	884
Wisconsin	14,005	254	3,084	58.7	51,679	938
Wyoming	949	188	272	56.7	4,079	805
Total USA‡	780,662	266	164,664	60.4	2,421,458	825

* Excludes doctors of osteopathy, federally employed persons, and physicians with addresses unknown.
† Registered nurse population in March. Based on a sample survey of 35,636 registered nurses.
‡ Totals may differ from the sum of state totals owing to incomplete data on permanent residence and rounding.
Sources: Bureau of the Census estimates, US Department of Commerce, American Medical Association, *Physician Characteristics and Distribution in the US* (copyright); American Dental Association, Survey Center, *1999 Distribution of Dentists in the United States by Region and State* and Population Estimates Program, Population Division, US Census Bureau, Washington, DC; www.census.gov/population/estimates/state/st-99–1.txt (copyright); Bureau of Health Professions, *The Registered Nurse Population*.

Welfare

TOTAL SUPPLEMENTAL SECURITY INCOME (SSI) PROGRAM PAYMENTS
($ million)

	1980	1990	2000	2004	2005	2006
Federal SSI	5,866	12,894	27,290	31,887	33,058	34,736
Old age	1,860	2,521	3,598	3,774	3,837	3,953
Blindness	132	238	312	327	331	326
Other disability	3,875	10,134	23,380	27,785	28,891	30,457
Federally administered state supplement	1,848	3,239	3,381	4,179	4,178	4,153
Old age	757	1,038	943	1,133	1,128	1,163
Blindness	54	91	74	85	84	83
Other disability	1,037	2,111	2,365	2,960	2,966	2,907
Total	7,715	16,133	30,672	36,065	37,236	38,889

Source: Social Security Administration, *SSI Annual Statistical Report, 2006*.

SOCIAL SECURITY (OASDI) PAYMENT STATUS
(August 2008)

Benefit type	Number of beneficiaries ('000)	Total benefit for month ($ million)*	Average monthly amount ($)
Retired workers and their family members	35,011	36,400	1,040.5
Retired workers	32,113	34,900	1,086.1
Wives and husbands	2,399	1,300	534.3
Children	499	300	539.4
Survivors of deceased workers	6,418	6,000	928.6
Children	1,851	1,300	705.6
Widowed mothers and fathers	162	100	787.6
Aged widows and widowers	4,174	4,400	1,048.4
Disabled widows and widowers	229	100	645.8
Parents of deceased workers	2	1	923.7
Disabled workers and their family members	9,068	7,800	863.8
Disabled workers	7,272	7,300	1,004.1
Wives and husbands	151	40	267.7
Children	1,645	500	298.3
Total†	50,497	50,200	994.5

* Calculations based on number of beneficiaries and average monthly income; figures are rounded.
† Figures include special age-72 beneficiaries, but exclude entitled non-applicants.
Source: Social Security Administration.

HEALTH AND WELFARE AGENCIES AND ORGANIZATIONS

Agency for Healthcare Research and Quality: 540 Gaither Rd, Suite 2000, Rockville, MD 20850; tel. (301) 427-1364; fax (301) 427-1875; internet www.ahrq.gov; f. 1989 as the Agency for Health Care Policy and Research; present name adopted in 1999; established to improve the quality, safety and efficiency of health care for all US citizens; Dir Carolyn Clancy.

Agency for Toxic Substances and Disease Registry: 1825 Century Blvd, Atlanta, GA 30345; tel. (404) 562-1788; fax (404) 562-1790; e-mail vbrandon@cdc.gov; internet www.atsdr.cdc.gov; Dir Howard Frumkin.

America's Health Insurance Plans (AHIP): 601 Pennsylvania Ave, NW, South Bldg, Suite 500, Washington, DC 20004; tel. (202) 778-3200; fax (202) 331-7487; e-mail ahip@ahip.org; internet www.ahip.org; f. 1956; fmrly known as Health Insurance Asscn of America; name changed as above following merger with American Asscn of Health Plans; c. 1,300 mems; Pres. and CEO Karen Ignagni.

AmeriCorps*VISTA: Corpn for National and Community Service (CNS), 1201 New York Ave, NW, Washington, DC 20525; tel. (202) 606-5000; fax (202) 606-3472; e-mail questions@americorps.org; internet www.americorps.org/vista; f. 1964 as VISTA (Volunteers in Service to America), adopted current name in 1993; nine regional groups; assistance programme administered by CNS (fmrly ACTION); CEO David Eisner.

Centers for Disease Control and Prevention (CDC): Office of Public Health and Science, 1600 Clifton Rd, NE, Atlanta, GA 30333; tel. (404) 639-3311; e-mail cdcinfo@cdc.gov; internet www.cdc.gov; f. 1946; Dir Dr Julie L. Gerberding.

CDC National Center for Health Statistics: 3311 Toledo Rd, Hyattsville, MD 20782; tel. (800) 232-4636; e-mail nchsquery@cdc.gov; internet www.cdc.gov/nchs; fed. Govt's principal health statistics agency; collates and analyses data on health, illness and disability, and the use of health services; Dir Edward Sondik.

Centers for Medicare and Medicaid Services (CMS): 7500 Security Blvd, Baltimore, MD 21244-1850; tel. (410) 786-3000; internet www.cms.hhs.gov; fmrly the Health Care Financing Administration; oversees the Medicare, Medicaid and State Children's Health Insurance programmes; Admin. Kerry N. Weems (acting).

Corporation for National and Community Service (CNS): 1201 New York Ave, NW, Washington, DC 20525; tel. (202) 606-5000; fax (202) 606-3472; e-mail info@cns.gov; internet www.nationalservice.org; f. 1993; fmrly ACTION; CEO David Eisner.

Department of Health and Human Services: 200 Independence Ave, SW, Washington, DC 20201; tel. (202) 619-0257; internet www.os.dhhs.gov; f. 1980; Sec. Michael O. Leavitt.

Employee Benefits Security Administration: US Dept of Labor, 200 Constitution Ave, NW, Washington, DC 20210; tel. (202) 693-8300; fax (202) 219-5526; internet www.dol.gov/ebsa; fmrly the Pension and Welfare Benefits Administration; Asst Sec. Bradford P. Campbell.

Health Resources and Services Administration: US Dept of Health and Human Services, Parklawn Bldg, 5600 Fishers Lane, Rockville, MD 20857; tel. (301) 443-3376; e-mail comments@hrsa.gov; internet www.hrsa.gov; Admin. Elizabeth M. Duke.

Office of Community Services (OCS): c/o Administration for Children and Families, 370 L'Enfant Promenade, SW, Washington, DC 20201; tel. (202) 401-9215; fax (202) 205-9688; e-mail mwerner@acf.hhs.gov; internet www.acf.hhs.gov/programs/ocs; administers Community Services grant programmes; Dir Josephine B. Robinson.

Office of Human Resources: Social Security Administration, Windsor Park Bldg, 6401 Security Blvd, Baltimore, MD 21235; tel. (410) 965-8904; fax (410) 966-9973; e-mail press.office@ssa.gov; internet www.ssa.gov; Deputy Commr REGINALD F. WELLS.

Office of Public Health and Science: US Dept of Health and Human Services, Humphrey Bldg, Rm 716G, 200 Independence Ave, SW, Washington, DC 20201; tel. (202) 690-7694; fax (202) 205-4747; e-mail lbeauch@opophs.dhhs.gov; internet www.hhs.gov/ophs/; Asst Sec. for Health Dr JOXEL GARCIA.

Office of the Surgeon-General: Parklawn Bldg, 5600 Fishers Lane, Rm 18-66, Rockville, MD 20857; tel. (301) 443-4000; fax (301) 443-3574; internet www.surgeongeneral.gov; Surgeon-Gen. Rear Adm. STEVEN K. GALSON (acting).

Pension Benefit Guaranty Corporation: 1200 K St, NW, Washington, DC 20005-4026; tel. (202) 326-4343; fax (202) 326-4344; e-mail askogc@pbgc.gov; internet www.pbgc.gov; f. 1974; govt corpn; guarantees basic pension benefits in covered private plans if they terminate with insufficient assets; Dir CHARLES E. F. MILLARD.

Sexuality Information and Education Council of the United States: 90 John St, Suite 704, New York, NY 10038; tel. (212) 819-9770; fax (212) 819-9776; e-mail siecus@siecus.org; internet www.siecus.org; Pres. and CEO JOSEPH DINORCIA, Jr.

Social Security Administration: Office of Public Enquiries, Windsor Park Bldg, 6401 Security Blvd, Baltimore, MD 21235; tel. (401) 965-8882; fax (401) 966-1463; internet www.ssa.gov; Commr MICHAEL J. ASTRUE.

Substance Abuse and Mental Health Services Administration: US Dept of Health and Human Services, 1 Choke Cherry Rd, Rockville, MD 20857; tel. (240) 276-2000; fax (240) 276-2010; e-mail info@samhsa.gov; internet www.samhsa.gov; Admin. Dr TERRY CLINE.

Unemployment Insurance Service: Employment and Training Administration, US Dept of Labor, 200 Constitution Ave, Rm S-4231, NW, Washington, DC 20210; tel. (202) 693-2700; e-mail etapagemaster@dol.gov; internet www.doleta.gov; Asst Sec. for Employment and Training (vacant).

EDUCATION

INTRODUCTION

In the early 21st century public schools were funded and controlled by local, state or federal government, and public education was free in every state from elementary school to high school. The individual states had their own systems of public education and differed in the ways in which they regulated their private schools. Each school was administered by a local school district. Although the districts levied taxes to fund schools, state governments provided additional support in order to overcome inequality of financial resources. In 2002/03 the federal Government provided an estimated 8.4% of funding for public schools, while state governments provided 49.0%, and local government and other sources provided 42.7%. Estimated spending by the federal Government on education totalled US $89,300m. in 2008/09. The period for which education is compulsory varies between the states, but most states require attendance between the ages of seven and 16 years. Projected figures for the 2007/08 academic year estimated that there were 34.6m. pupils enrolled in public elementary schools (Kindergarten–grade 8, or 'K–8') and 15.0m. in public secondary schools (grades 9–12). Private schools, many of which were traditionally affiliated with the Roman Catholic Church, enrolled 4.8m. at elementary level and 1.4m. at secondary level.

In the 2005/06 academic year there were 4,276 degree-granting universities and colleges, with a total of 1,290,426 teachers, while total enrolment in 2007/08 reached about 18.0m. students, of whom 13.5m. attended public institutions and 4.5m. private institutions. Almost all states provided guaranteed loans to state residents who wished to attend institutions of higher education in the USA. The larger states also offered assistance programmes for students in low-income groups. The US Department of Education and various federal agencies offered grants and loans, as did many private organizations. The Department of Education allocated an estimated US $95,000m. of the 2009 budget towards new student grants and loans. In 1999 the federal Government provided 10.8% of funding for public institutions of higher education, while the states provided 35.8%. Other sources, including tuition, fees and auxiliary enterprises, provided the remaining 53.4%. In 2003/04 the federal Government provided an estimated $20.9m. of funding for higher education programmes and an estimated $2.9m. of funding for research programmes at universities and related institutions. State and local government expenditure on education was $727,967m. in the 2005/06 financial year.

STATISTICS

Enrolment: Summary

('000, as at fall)

	2003	2004*	2005*	2006†	2007†
Pre-kindergarten to Grade 8:					
Public	34,202	34,178	34,205	34,387	34,592
Private	4,788	4,773	4,736	4,779	4,784
Grades 9 to 12:					
Public	14,338	14,617	14,909	14,983	15,018
Private	1,311	1,360	1,376	1,375	1,368
Colleges:					
Public	12,859	12,980	13,022	13,252	13,457
Private	4,053	4,292	4,466	4,420	4,501

* Private elementary and secondary school data are projected.

† Projected figures.

Source: National Center for Education Statistics, US Department of Education, *Digest of Education Statistics*, annual.

Teachers: Summary

('000, as at fall)

	2002	2003	2004	2005
Elementary and secondary (including kindergarten and junior high)*	3,476	3,490	3,537	3,588
Public	3,034	3,049	3,090	3,137
Private	442†	441	447‡	451‡
Higher Education	1,156†	1,175	1,237†	1,290†
Public	795†	793	819‡	841
Private	361†	382	418‡	449

* Including teachers in local public school systems and in most private schools.
† Estimate.
‡ Projection.

2006 ('000 teachers at fall, projections): Elementary and secondary 3,637 (Public 3,177, Private 460).
2007 ('000 teachers at fall, projections): Elementary and secondary 3,679 (Public 3,213, Private 466).
Source: National Center for Education Statistics, US Department of Education, *Digest of Education Statistics*, annual.

Public Elementary and Secondary Education by State, 2005/06

	Schools	Pupils	Teachers
Alabama	1,585	741,758	57,757
Alaska	502	133,288	7,912
Arizona	2,078	1,094,454	51,376
Arkansas	1,138	474,206	32,997
California	9,650	6,437,202	309,128*
Colorado	1,707	779,826	45,841
Connecticut	1,111	575,059	39,687
Delaware	222	120,937	7,998
District of Columbia	229	76,876	5,481*
Florida	3,723	2,675,024	158,962
Georgia	2,389	1,598,461	108,535
Hawaii	285	182,818	11,226
Idaho	706	261,982	14,521
Illinois	4,401	2,111,706	133,857
Indiana	1,977	1,035,074	60,592
Iowa	1,512	483,482	35,181
Kansas	1,407	467,285	33,608
Kentucky	1,409	679,878	42,413
Louisiana	1,390	654,526	44,660
Maine	679	195,498	16,684
Maryland	1,430	860,020	56,685
Massachusetts	1,879	971,909	73,596
Michigan	4,090	1,741,845	99,838
Minnesota	2,644	839,243	51,107
Mississippi	1,051	494,954	31,433
Missouri	2,361	917,705	67,076
Montana	840	145,416	10,369
Nebraska	1,225	286,646	21,359
—continued			
Nevada	557	412,395	21,744
New Hampshire	480	205,767	15,536
New Jersey	2,474	1,395,602	112,673
New Mexico	854	326,758	22,021
New York	4,669	2,815,581	218,989
North Carolina	2,347	1,416,436	95,664
North Dakota	539	98,283	8,003
Ohio	4,007	1,839,683	117,982
Oklahoma	1,788	634,739	41,833
Oregon	1,260	552,194	28,256
Pennsylvania	3,250	1,830,684	122,397
Rhode Island	338	153,422	14,299*
South Carolina	1,152	701,544	48,212
South Dakota	725	122,012	9,129
Tennessee	1,700	953,928	59,596
Texas	8,517	4,525,394	302,425
Utah	956	508,430	22,993*
Vermont	392	96,638	8,851
Virginia	2,079	1,214,472	96,158
Washington	2,269	1,031,985	53,508
West Virginia	784	280,866	19,940
Wisconsin	2,246	875,174	60,127
Wyoming	379	84,409	6,706
Total	97,382	49,113,474	3,136,921*

* Includes imputation for underreporting.

Source: National Center for Education Statistics, US Department of Education, *Digest of Education Statistics*, annual.

RELIGION

STATISTICS

Christian Church, Jewish and Muslim Adherents, by State

	Christian Church adherents, 2000			
	Number ('000)	As % of population	Jewish adherents, 2004 ('000)*	Muslim adherents, 2000 ('000)*
Alabama	2,418	54.4	9	8
Alaska	210	33.6	3	1
Arizona	1,946	37.9	106	12
Arkansas	1,516	56.7	2	2
California	14,328	42.3	1,194	260
Colorado	1,604	37.3	79	15
Connecticut	1,828	53.7	112	30
Delaware	299	38.2	14	4
District of Columbia	331	57.8	28	n.a.
Florida	5,904	57.8	653	32
Georgia	3,528	36.9	127	39
Hawaii	431	35.6	7	1
Idaho	624	48.3	1	—
Illinois	6,457	52.0	279	125
Indiana	2,578	42.4	17	11
Iowa	1,698	58.0	6	5
Kansas	1,307	48.6	18	3
Kentucky	2,141	53.0	11	5
Louisiana	2,599	58.2	16	13
Maine	450	35.3	10	1
Maryland	2,012	38.0	235	53
Massachusetts	3,725	58.7	275	41
Michigan	3,970	39.9	88	81
Minnesota	2,974	60.5	47	12
Mississippi	1,549	54.5	1	4
Missouri	2,813	50.3	59	19
Montana	401	44.4	1	1
Nebraska	995	58.2	7	3
Nevada	604	30.2	70	2
New Hampshire	571	46.2	10	4
New Jersey	4,262	50.7	480	121
New Mexico	1,041	57.2	11	3
New York	9,569	50.4	1,618	224
North Carolina	3,598	44.7	26	20
North Dakota	468	72.9	—	1
Ohio	4,912	43.3	145	41
Oklahoma	2,079	60.3	5	6
Oregon	1,029	30.1	32	5
Pennsylvania	6,751	55.0	285	71
Rhode Island	646	61.7	19	2
South Carolina	1,874	46.7	11	58
South Dakota	510	67.6	—	—
Tennessee	2,867	50.4	19	18
Texas	11,316	54.3	131	115
Utah	1,659	74.3	4	4
Vermont	230	37.8	6	—
Virginia	2,807	39.7	98	51
Washington	1,872	31.8	43	16
West Virginia	646	35.7	2	2
Wisconsin	3,198	59.6	28	8
Wyoming	229	46.4	—	—
Total†	133,377	47.4	6,452	1,559‡

* Estimates.
† Includes data for outlying areas.
‡ Including unallocated data.

Sources: US Census Bureau, *Statistical Abstract of the United States*; American Religion Data Archive; *American Jewish Year Book* (copyright; permission granted by the American Jewish Committee).

Religious Bodies

(figures refer to 2005, unless otherwise indicated)*

	Members ('000)	Churches, etc.
Roman Catholic Church	69,135	18,992
Southern Baptist Convention	16,270	43,669
United Methodist Church[1]	8,075	34,660
Jewish[1]	6,452	n.a.
Church of Jesus Christ of Latter-day Saints	5,691	12,753
Church of God in Christ[2]	5,500	15,300
National Baptist Convention, USA[1]	5,000	9,000
Evangelical Lutheran Church in America	4,851	10,549
National Baptist Convention of America[3]	3,500	n.a.
Presbyterian Church, USA	3,099	10,960
Assemblies of God	2,831	12,298
Lutheran Church—Missouri Synod	2,441	6,144
African Methodist Episcopal Church[4]	2,500	4,174
National Missionary Baptist Convention of America[5]	2,500	n.a.
Progressive National Baptist Convention[6]	2,500	2,000
Episcopal Church[1]	2,248	7,200
Churches of Christ	1,639	15,000
Muslim/Islamic[7]	1,559	1,209
Greek Orthodox Archdiocese of America	1,500	566
Pentecostal Assemblies of the World[8]	1,500	1,750
African Methodist Episcopal Zion Church	1,440	3,260
American Baptist Churches, USA	1,397	5,740
United Church of Christ	1,224	5,567
Baptist Bible Fellowship International[9]	1,200	4,500
Christian Churches and Churches of Christ[10]	1,072	5,579
Orthodox Church in America[1]	1,064	737
Jehovah's Witnesses	1,046	12,384
Church of God (Cleveland, TN)	1,013	6,587
Seventh-day Adventist Church	965	4,750
Christian Methodist Episcopal Church	850	3,320
Christian Church (Disciples of Christ), USA and Canada[1]	786	3,691

* Membership refers to those who are full communicants or confirmed members plus other members baptized, non-confirmed or non-communicant. Definitions of membership differ from denomination to denomination.

[1] 2004.
[2] 1991.
[3] 2000.
[4] 1999.
[5] 1992.
[6] 1995.
[7] 2000.
[8] 1998.
[9] 1997.
[10] 1988.

Sources: US Census Bureau, *Statistical Abstract of the United States*; American Religion Data Archive.

DIRECTORY

Principal Denominations

BAHÁ'Í FAITH

At mid-2000 there were an estimated 753,000 adherents of the Bahá'í faith in the USA.

National Spiritual Assembly of Bahá'ís of the United States: External Affairs Office, 1320 19th St, NW, Suite 701, Washington, DC 20036-1610; tel. (202) 833-8990; fax (202) 833-8988; e-mail bahai-info@usbnc.org; internet www.bahai.us; f. 1844 in Persia (Iran); Chair. Jacqueline Left Hand Bull Delahunt; Sec.-Gen. Kenneth E. Bowers.

BUDDHISM

At mid-2000 there were an estimated 2.5m. Buddhists in the USA.

Association of American Buddhists: 301 West 45th St, New York, NY 10036; tel. (212) 489-1075; e-mail iwanttoknow@buddhismonline.us; internet www.buddhismonline.us; f. 1980; 15 regional groups; Pres. Ven. Dr Kevin R. O'Neil.

Buddhist Churches of America: 1710 Octavia St, San Francisco, CA 94109-4341; tel. (415) 776-5600; fax (415) 771-6293; e-mail bcahq@pacbell.net; internet buddhistchurchesofamerica.org; f. 1899; Hongwanji-ha Jodo Shinshu denomination; c. 230,000 mems; Presiding Bishop Socho Koshin Ogui; Exec. Dir Henry Shibata.

CHRISTIANITY

Adventist Churches

Advent Christian Church: POB 690848, Charlotte, NC 28227; tel. (704) 545-6161; fax (704) 573-0712; e-mail execdirect@acgc.us; internet www.adventchristian.org; f. 1864; 302 churches; 25,702 mems; Exec. Dir Rev. Ronald Thomas.

Anglican Communion

The Episcopal Church in the USA: 815 Second Ave, New York, NY 10017-4564; tel. (212) 716-6000; fax (212) 697-5892; e-mail pboffice@episcopalchurch.org; internet www.ecusa.anglican.org; f. 1607; mem. of the Worldwide Anglican Communion and World Council of Churches; 7,200 parishes and missions; 2.4m. mems (2008); Presiding Bishop Most Rev. Katharine Jefferts Schori; Exec. Officer and Sec. Rev. Dr Gregory S. Straub.

Baptist Churches

In 1998 there were an estimated 33.1m. adherents in 15 bodies, of which the following have the greatest number of members:

American Baptist Association: 4605 North State Line Ave, Texarkana, TX 75503-2928; tel. (903) 792-2783; fax (903) 792-8128; e-mail bssc@abaptist.org; internet www.abaptist.org; f. 1905; 1,867 churches; 280,973 mems (2000); Pres. Dr Neal Clark.

American Baptist Churches in the USA: POB 851, Valley Forge, PA 19482-0851; 588 North Gulph Rd, King of Prussia, PA 19406; tel. (610) 768-2000; fax (610) 768-2275; e-mail cathy.brubaker@abc-usa.org; internet www.abc-usa.org; f. 1907; mem. of the World Council of Churches; 5,800 churches (2008); 1.5m. mems (2008); Pres. Rev. Mary Armacost Hulst; Gen. Sec. Rev. Dr A. Roy Medley.

Baptist General Conference: 2002 South Arlington Heights Rd, Arlington Heights, IL 60005; tel. (847) 228-0200; fax (847) 228-5376; e-mail ckolb@baptistgeneral.org; internet www.convergeww.org; f. 1879; 913 churches; 145,436 mems (2003); Pres. Jerry Sheveland.

Baptist Missionary Association of America: 9219 Sibley Hole Rd, POB 30910, Little Rock, AR 72260; tel. (501) 455-4977; fax (501) 455-3636; e-mail bmaam@bmaam.com; internet www.bmaam.com; f. 1950; fmrly North American Baptist Asscn; 1,384 churches; 234,110 mems (2008); Exec. Dir Grady Higgs.

Conservative Baptist Association of America: 3686 Stagecoach Rd, Unit F, Longmont, CO 80504-5660; tel. (720) 283-3030; fax (303) 772-5690; e-mail info@cbamerica.org; internet www.cbamerica.org; f. 1947; 1,200 churches; 200,000 mems; Nat. Exec. Dir Rev. Stephen LeBar.

General Association of Regular Baptist Churches: 1300 North Meacham Rd, Schaumburg, IL 60173-4806; tel. (888) 588-1600; fax (847) 843-3757; internet www.garbc.org; 1,330 churches; 245,636 mems (2000); Nat. Rep. Rev. John Greening.

National Association of Free Will Baptists: 5233 Mount View Rd, Antioch, TN 37013-2306; POB 5002, Antioch, TN 37011-5002; tel. (615) 731-6812; fax (615) 731-0771; e-mail exoff@nafwb.org; internet www.nafwb.org; f. 1727; 2,425 churches; 198,924 mems (2006); Moderator Tim York.

National Baptist Convention, USA: 1700 Baptist World Center Dr., Nashville, TN 37207; tel. (615) 228-6292; fax (615) 262-3917; e-mail president@nationalbaptist.com; internet www.nationalbaptist.com; f. 1880; mem. of the World Council of Churches;

2,500 churches; 7.5m. mems; Pres. Dr. William J. Shaw; Gen. Sec. Rev. Roscoe Cooper.

National Primitive Baptist Convention, USA, Inc: POB 7451, Tallahassee, FL 32314; tel. (850) 421-6163; e-mail natlpbconv@aol.com; internet natlprimbaptconv.org; f. 1907; 547 congregations; 66,452 mems (2000); Gen. Pres. Ernest Ferrell.

North American Baptist Conference: 1 South 210 Summit Ave, Oakbrook Terrace, IL 60181; tel. (630) 495-2000; fax (630) 495-3301; e-mail serve@nabconf.org; internet www.nabconference.org; more than 400 churches; more than 74,000 mems; Exec. Dir Dr Robert McClelland.

Progressive National Baptist Convention, Inc: 601 50th St, NE, Washington, DC 20019; tel. (202) 396-0558; fax (202) 398-4998; internet www.pnbc.org; f. 1961; mem. of the World Council of Churches; c. 2,000 churches; 2.5m. mems; Pres. Rev. Dr T. DeWitt Smith, Jr; Gen. Sec. Dr Tyrone S. Pitts.

Southern Baptist Convention: 901 Commerce St, Nashville, TN 37203-3629; tel. (615) 244-2355; fax (615) 742-8919; e-mail cpmissions@sbc.net; internet www.sbc.net; f. 1845; 42,972 churches; 16.4m. mems (2003); Pres. Exec. Cttee Dr Morris H. Chapman.

Brethren Churches

Brethren in Christ Church: 431 Grantham Rd, POB A, Grantham, PA 17027-0290; tel. (717) 697-2634; fax (717) 796-4781; e-mail bic@bic-church.org; internet www.bic-church.org; f. 1788; 275 churches; 26,088 mems; Moderator Warren L. Hoffman; Gen. Sec. Don McNiven.

Christian Congregation, Inc: 804 West Hemlock St, La Follette, TN 37766; tel. (615) 562-8511; e-mail revalnas@aol.com; internet www.netministries.org/see/churches.exe/ch10619; f. 1887; 1,438 churches; 118,209 mems; Gen. Supt Rev. Ora W. Eads; Administrator Alan Panek.

Christian Methodist Episcopal Church: 4466 Elvis Presley Blvd, POB 161545, Memphis, TN 38116; tel. (901) 345-0580; e-mail WHGraves@aol.com; internet www.c-m-e.org; f. 1870; mem. of the Churches Uniting in Christ and World Council of Churches; 3,300 churches; 850,000 mems (2002); Sr Bishop William H. Graves.

The Christian and Missionary Alliance: 8595 Explorer Dr., Colorado Springs, CO 80920; POB 35000, Colorado Springs, CO 80935-3500; tel. (719) 599-5999; e-mail webmaster@cmalliance.org; internet www.cmalliance.org; f. 1887; 2,004 churches; 425,000 mems; Pres. Dr Gary M. Benedict.

Church of the Brethren: 1451 Dundee Ave, Elgin, IL 60120; tel. (847) 742-5100; fax (847) 742-6103; e-mail cobweb@brethren.org; internet www.brethren.org; f. 1708; fmrly German Baptist Brethren; mem. of the World Council of Churches; 1,074 congregations; 171,281 mems (2000); Gen. Sec. Stanley J. Noffsinger.

Churches of Christ in Christian Union (CCCU): 1426 Lancaster Pike, 10 Circleville, OH 43113; tel. (740) 474-8856; fax (740) 477-7766; e-mail info@cccuhq.org; internet www.cccuhq.org; f. 1909; 216 churches; 10,104 mems; Gen. Supt Dr Tom Hermiz.

Fellowship of Grace Brethren Churches: POB 384, Winona Lake, IN 46590; tel. (219) 269-1269; fax (219) 269-1709; e-mail editor4@fgbc.org; internet www.fgbc.org; f. 1708; more than 260 churches; 30,371 mems; Moderator Tom McIntosh; Co-ordinator Rev. Thomas Avey.

Lutheran Churches

In 1998 there were an estimated 8.3m. adherents in 10 bodies, of which the following have the greatest number of members:

Association of Free Lutheran Congregations: 3110 East Medicine Lake Blvd, Plymouth, MN 55441; tel. (763) 545-5631; fax (763) 545-0079; e-mail president@aflc.org; internet www.aflc.org; f. 1962; 268 churches; 32,098 mems (2000); Pres. Rev. Eldon K. Nelson.

Evangelical Lutheran Church in America: 8765 West Higgins Rd, Chicago, IL 60631; tel. (773) 380-2700; fax (773) 380-1465; e-mail info@elca.org; internet www.elca.org; f. 1988; mem. of the World Council of Churches; 10,448 churches; 4.7m. mems (2007); Leader Bishop Rev. Mark Stephen Hanson; Sec. David D. Swartling.

Lutheran Church—Missouri Synod: 1333 South Kirkwood Rd, St Louis, MO 63122-7295; tel. (314) 965-9000; fax (314) 996-1016; e-mail infocenter@lcms.org; internet www.lcms.org; f. 1847; 6,150 churches; 2.5m. mems (2007); Pres. Dr Gerald B. Kieschnick; Sec. Dr Raymond Hartwig.

Wisconsin Evangelical Lutheran Synod (WELS): 2929 North Mayfair Rd, Milwaukee, WI 53222; tel. (414) 256-3888; fax (414) 256-3899; e-mail mark.schroeder@sab.wels.net; internet www.wels.net; f. 1850; over 1,200 churches; over 400,000 mems; Pres. Rev. Mark Schroeder.

Methodist Churches

In 1998 there were an estimated 13.4m. adherents in eight bodies, of which the following have the greatest number of members:

African Methodist Episcopal Church: 500 Eighth Ave South, Nashville, TN 37203; tel. (615) 254-0911; fax (615) 254-0912; e-mail cio@ame-church.com; internet www.ame-church.com; f. 1816; mem. of the Churches Uniting in Christ and World Council of Churches; 4,174 churches; 2.5m. mems (1999); Sr Bishop John Bryant; Gen. Sec. Dr Clement W. Fugh.

African Methodist Episcopal Zion Church: 3225 Sugar Creek Rd, POB 32843, Charlotte, NC 28269; tel. (704) 599-4630; e-mail admin@amez.org; internet www.amez.org; f. 1796; mem. of the Churches Uniting in Christ; 3,236 churches; 1.4m. mems (2003); Gen.-Sec. Rev. Dr W. Robert Johnson, III.

Free Methodist Church of North America: 770 North Highschool Rd, POB 535002, Indianapolis, IN 46253-5002; tel. (317) 244-3660; fax (317) 244-1247; e-mail info@freemethodistchurch.org; internet www.freemethodistchurch.org; c. 1,100 churches; 72,455 mems (2008); Lead Bishop David Kendall, Bishops Matthew Thomas, David Roller.

United Methodist Church: POB 320, Nashville, TN 37202; e-mail umc@umcom.org; internet www.umc.org; f. 1968; mem. of the Churches Uniting in Christ and World Council of Churches; 34,892 churches; 8.2m. mems (2003); President of Council of Bishops Bishop Janice Riggle Huie; Exec. Sec. Ernest S. Lyght.

Orthodox Churches

At mid-2000 there were an estimated 5.8m. adherents in 12 bodies, of which the following have the greatest number of members:

Antiochian Orthodox Christian Archdiocese of North America (Greek Orthodox Patriarchate of Antioch and all the East): POB 3258, Englewood, NJ 07631-3798; tel. (201) 871-1355; fax (201) 871-7954; e-mail editor@antiochian.org; internet www.antiochian.org; f. 1895; mem. of the World Council of Churches; 210 churches; 82,374 mems (2000); Primate Metropolitan Philip (Saliba); Auxiliaries Bishop Antoun (Khouri), Bishop Basil (Essey), Bishop Joseph (Zehlaoui), Bishop Alexander (Mufarrij), Bishop Mark (Maymon), Bishop Thomas (Joseph).

Armenian Apostolic Church of America: *Eastern Prelacy:* 138 East 39th St, New York, NY 10016; tel. (212) 689-7810; fax (212) 689-7168; e-mail email@armenianprelacy.org; internet www.armenianprelacy.org; *Western Prelacy:* 6252 Honolulu Ave, Suite 100, La Crescenta, CA 91214; tel. (818) 248-7737; fax (818) 248-7745; e-mail prelacy@aol.com; f. 1887; mem. of the World Council of Churches; 38 churches; 23,200 mems (2000); Prelate (Eastern Prelacy) Archbishop Oshagan Choloyan; Prelate (Western Prelacy) Archbishop Moushegh Mardirosian.

Armenian Church of America: *Eastern Diocese*, 630 Second Ave, New York, NY 10016; tel. (212) 686-0710; fax (212) 686-0245; e-mail primate@armenianchurch.net; internet www.armenianchurch.net; *Western Diocese*, 3325 North Glenoaks Blvd, Burbank, CA 91504; tel. (818) 558-7474; fax (818) 558-6333; e-mail info@armenianchurchwd.com; internet www.armenianchurchwd.com; f. 1889; mem. of the World Council of Churches; 89 churches; 45,800 mems (2000); Primate (Eastern Diocese) Archbishop Khajag Barsamian; Primate (Western Diocese) Archbishop Hovnan Derderian.

Coptic Orthodox Church: 427 West Side Ave, Jersey City, NJ 08816-3848; tel. (201) 333-0004; fax (201) 333-0502; internet www.copticchurch.net; mem. of the World Council of Churches; over 100 churches; 180,000 mems; Archpriest Fr Abraam D. Sleman.

Greek Orthodox Archdiocese of America: 8–10 East 79th St, New York, NY 10021-0191; tel. (212) 570-3500; fax (212) 774-0251; e-mail archdiocese@goarch.org; internet www.goarch.org; f. 1921 as Greek Orthodox Archdiocese of North and South America; mem. of the World Council of Churches; 540 churches; 1.5m. mems (2008); Primate Archbishop Dimitrios; Chancellor Bishop Savas (of Troas).

Orthodox Church in America: POB 675, Syosset, NY 11791; tel. (516) 922-0550; fax (516) 922-0954; e-mail info@oca.org; internet www.oca.org; f. 1794; fmrly Russian Orthodox Greek Catholic Church of North America; mem. of the World Council of Churches; 456 churches; 115,000 mems (2000); Primate Metropolitan Herman; Chancellor Archpriest Alexander Garklavs.

Romanian Orthodox Episcopate of America: POB 309, Grass Lake, MI 49240-0309; tel. (517) 522-4800; fax (517) 522-5907; e-mail doancea@roea.org; internet www.roea.org; f. 1929; mem. of the World Council of Churches; 57 churches; 23,800 mems (2000); Ruling Archbishop Most Rev. Dr Nathaniel Popp; Chancellor Rev. Archdeacon David Oancea.

Serbian Orthodox Church in North and South America: St Sava Monastery, 32377 N. Milwaukee Ave, POB 519, Libertyville, IL 60048; tel. (847) 367-0698; e-mail metrochris@hotmail.com; internet www.serborth.org; mem. of the World Council of Churches; 120

churches; 300,000 mems (2007); Presiding Bishop of Episcopal Council His Eminence CHRISTOPHER KOVACEVICH.

Syrian (Syriac) Orthodox Church of Antioch, Archdiocese for the Eastern USA: 260 Elm Ave, Teaneck, NJ 07666; tel. (201) 801-0660; fax (201) 801-0603; e-mail info@syrianorthodoxchurch.org; internet www.syrianorthodoxchurch.org; f. 1995; mem. of the World Council of Churches; 31 churches; 32,500 mems (2003); Prelate Archbishop MOR CYRIL APHREM KARIM; Gen. Sec. Very Rev. CHOREPISCOPUS JOHN MENO.

Ukrainian Orthodox Church of the USA: POB 495, South Bound Brook, NJ 08880; tel. (732) 356-0090; fax (732) 356-9437; e-mail consistory@verizon.net; internet www.uocofusa.org; f. 1919; 106 churches; 30,000 mems (2000); Metropolitan CONSTANTINE.

The Albanian, Bulgarian, Macedonian and Russian Orthodox Churches are also represented.

Pentecostal Churches

Assemblies of God: 1445 North Boonville Ave, Springfield, MO 65802-1894; tel. (417) 862-5554; fax (417) 863-6614; e-mail asstsup@ag.org; internet www.ag.org; f. 1914; 2.8m. mems in 12,311 churches in USA (2006); Gen. Supt GEORGE O. WOOD; Gen. Sec. JOHN M. PALMER.

Bible Way Church of Our Lord Jesus Christ World-Wide, Inc: 261 Rochester Ave, Brooklyn, NY 11213; tel. (718) 774-0401; e-mail bwc@biblewaychurch.org; internet www.biblewaychurch.org; f. 1957; 350 churches; *c.* 300,000 mems; Presiding Archbishop HUIE L. ROGERS.

Church of God (Cleveland, Tennesee): 2490 Keith St, POB 2430, Cleveland, TN 37320-2430; tel. (423) 472-3361; fax (423) 478-7066; e-mail gocog@churchofgod.org; internet www.churchofgod.org; f. 1886; 6,623 churches; 961,000 mems (2003); Gen. Overseer Dr RAYMOND F. CULPEPPER.

Foursquare Church: 1910 Sunset Blvd West, Suite 200, POB 26902, Los Angeles, CA 90026-0176; tel. (213) 989-4220; fax (213) 989-4590; e-mail nco@foursquare.org; internet www.foursquare.org; f. 1923; fmrly Intl Church of the Foursquare Gospel; mem. of the Pentecostal/Charismatic Churches of North America (PCCNA); 1,834 churches; 269,349 mems; Pres. Dr JACK W. HAYFORD.

International Pentecostal Holiness Church: 7300 North-West 39th Expressway, POB 12609, Bethany, OK 73008; tel. (405) 787-7110; fax (405) 789-3957; e-mail info@iphc.org; internet arc.iphc.org; f. 1911 by merger of the Holiness Church of North Carolina and Fire-Baptized Holiness Church; 1,843 congregations; 241,828 mems (2000); Presiding Bishop JAMES D. LEGGETT.

Open Bible Churches: 2020 Bell Ave, Des Moines, IA 50315; tel. (515) 288-6761; fax (515) 288-2510; e-mail info@openbible.org; internet www.openbible.org; f. 1935 by merger of the Bible Standard Conference and Open Bible Evangelistic Asscn; present name adopted in 1996; 357 churches; 35,700 mems; Pres. JEFF FARMER; Sec.-Treas. TERI BEYER.

Pentecostal/Charismatic Churches of North America: c/o Church of God in Christ, 1027 West Tennyson Rd, Hayward, CA 94544; tel. (510) 783-9377; fax (510) 783-8673; e-mail PastorJWM@aol.com; internet www.pccna.org; f. 1994; Chairs Bishop JERRY MACKLIN, Dr WILLIAM MORROW.

Pentecostal Church of God: 4901 Pennsylvania, POB 850, Joplin, MO 84802; tel. (417) 624-7050; fax (417) 624-7102; e-mail pcg@pcg.org; internet www.pcg.org; f. 1919; 1,170 churches; 90,000 mems; Gen. Bishop CHARLES SCOTT; Gen. Sec. WAYMON C. MING, Jr.

Pentecostal Free Will Baptist Church, Inc: POB 1568, Dunn, NC 28335; tel. (910) 892-4161; fax (910) 892-6876; e-mail paulah@intrstar.net; internet www.pfwb.org; f. 1959; 150 churches; 28,000 mems; Gen. Supt Rev. PRESTON HEATH.

United Pentecostal Church International: 8855 Dunn Rd, Hazelwood, MO 63042-2211; tel. (314) 837-7300; fax (314) 837-7304; e-mail info@upci.org; internet www.upci.org; f. 1945 by merger of the Pentecostal Church, Inc, and Pentecostal Assemblies of Jesus Christ; 4,358 churches (USA and Canada); c. 600,000 mems; Gen. Supt Rev. KENNETH N. HANEY; Gen. Sec. JERRY JONES.

Presbyterian Churches

In 1998 there were an estimated 4.1m. adherents in nine bodies, of which the following have the greatest number of members:

Associate Reformed Presbyterian Church: 1 Cleveland St, Suite 110, Greenville, SC 29601-3646; tel. (864) 232-8297; fax (864) 271-3729; e-mail pbell@arpsynod.org; internet www.arpchurch.org; f. 1782 as the Associate Reformed Synod; publrs of *ARP Magazine*; 10 Presbyteries in the USA; 282 congregations; 34,988 mems (2007); Moderator GORDON QUERY; Principal Clerk RONALD BEARD.

Cumberland Presbyterian Church: 8207 Traditional Place, Cordova, TN 38016; tel. (901) 276-4572; fax (901) 272-3913; e-mail emg@cumberland.org; internet www.cumberland.org; f. 1810; 759 churches; 81,464 mems; Dir. of Ministries EDITH M. GHOLSON; Stated Clerk ROBERT D. RUSH.

Evangelical Presbyterian Church: 17197 North Laurel Park Dr., Suite 567, Livonia, MI 48152; tel. (734) 742-2020; fax (734) 742-2033; e-mail epchurch@epc.org; internet www.epc.org; f. 1981; 207 churches; 78,000 mems; Moderator Rev. WILLIAM VOGLER.

Orthodox Presbyterian Church: 607 North Easton Rd, Bldg E, Box P, Willow Grove, PA 19090-0920; tel. (215) 830-0900; fax (215) 830-0350; e-mail duff.1@opc.org; internet www.opc.org; f. 1936; 263 churches; 57 missions; 28,780 mems (2007); Moderator Rev. ALLAN D. STRANGE; Stated Clerk Rev. DONALD J. DUFF.

Presbyterian Church in America: 1700 North Brown Rd, Lawrenceville, GA 30043-8143; tel. (678) 825-1000; fax (678) 825-1001; e-mail ac@pcanet.org; internet www.pcanet.org; f. 1973; 1,600 churches; 300,000 mems; Moderator E. J. NUSBAUM; Stated Clerk Dr L. ROY TAYLOR.

Presbyterian Church (USA): 100 Witherspoon St, Louisville, KY 40202-1396; tel. (502) 569-5000; fax (502) 569-8005; e-mail presbytel@pcusa.org; internet www.pcusa.org; f. 1983; mem. of the Churches Uniting in Christ and World Council of Churches; 11,100 churches; 2.4m. mems (2007); Stated Clerk GRADYE PARSONS; Moderator BRUCE REYES-CHOW; Exec. Dir LINDA VALENTINE.

Reformed Presbyterian Church of North America: 7408 Penn Ave, Pittsburgh, PA 15208; tel. (412) 731-1177; fax (412) 731-8861; e-mail rptrustees@aol.com; internet reformedpresbyterian.org; f. 1871; 89 churches; 6,105 mems; Moderator JAMES PENNINGTON; Stated Clerk JAMES MCFARLAND.

The Roman Catholic Church

In 2006 there were 194 dioceses, including 33 archdioceses, with some 66.6m. mems, equivalent to 22% of the population.

United States Conference of Catholic Bishops: 3211 Fourth St, NE, Washington, DC 20017-1194; tel. (202) 541-3000; fax (202) 541-3322; internet www.usccb.org; f. 2001 by merger of the Nat. Conference of Catholic Bishops (f. 1966) and US Catholic Conference (f. 1966); Pres. Cardinal FRANCIS GEORGE (Archbishop of Chicago); Gen. Sec. Mgr DAVID MALLOY.

Archbishops

Anchorage: ROGER L. SCHWIETZ.

Atlanta: WILTON D. GREGORY.

Baltimore: EDWIN F. O'BRIEN.

Boston: SÉAN PATRICK O'MALLEY.

Chicago: Cardinal FRANCIS E. GEORGE.

Cincinnati: DANIEL E. PILARCZYK.

Denver: CHARLES J. CHAPUT.

Detroit: Cardinal ADAM J. MAIDA.

Dubuque: JEROME G. HANUS.

Galveston-Houston: Cardinal DANIEL N. DINARDO.

Hartford: HENRY J. MANSELL.

Indianapolis: DANIEL M. BUECHLEIN.

Kansas City in Kansas: JOSEPH F. NAUMAN.

Los Angeles: Cardinal ROGER M. MAHONY.

Louisville: JOSEPH E. KURTZ.

Miami: JOHN C. FAVALORA.

Milwaukee: TIMOTHY M. DOLAN.

Mobile: OSCAR H. LIPSCOMB.

Newark: JOHN JOSEPH MYERS.

New Orleans: ALFRED C. HUGHES.

New York: Cardinal EDWARD MICHAEL EGAN.

Oklahoma City: EUSEBIUS J. BELTRAN.

Omaha: ELDEN F. CURTISS.

Philadelphia: Cardinal JUSTIN F. RIGALI, STEFAN SOROKA (Ukrainian, Byzantine Rite).

Pittsburgh: BASIL MYRON SCHOTT.

Portland in Oregon: JOHN G. VLAZNY.

Saint Louis: RAYMOND L. BURKE.

Saint Paul and Minneapolis: HARRY J. FLYNN.

San Antonio: JOSÉ H. GÓMEZ.

San Francisco: GEORGE H. NIEDERAUER.

Santa Fe: MICHAEL J. SHEEHAN.

Seattle: ALEXANDER J. BRUNETT.

Washington: DONALD W. WUERL.

Other Christian Churches

Christian Church (Disciples of Christ) in the USA and Canada: 130 East Washington St, POB 1986, Indianapolis, IN 46206-1986; tel. (317) 635-3100; fax (317) 635-3700; e-mail news@cm.disciples.org; internet www.disciples.org; f. 1804; 3,754 congregations (2008); 691,160 mems (2008); mem. of the Churches Uniting in Christ and World Council of Churches; Gen. Minister and Pres. Rev. Dr SHARON E. WATKINS.

Christian Reformed Church in North America: 2850 Kalamazoo Ave, SE, Grand Rapids, MI 49560; tel. (616) 224-0832; fax (616) 224-5895; e-mail crcna@crcna.org; internet www.crcna.org; f. 1857; Calvinist; 1,023 churches; 270,500 mems (USA and Canada); Exec. Dir Rev. GERARD L. DYKSTRA.

Church of Christ: POB 472, Independence, MO 64051; tel. (816) 833-3995; fax (816) 833-0210; e-mail cofctl@sbcglobal; internet www.churchofchrist-tl.org; f. 1830; Sec. Council of Apostles Gen. Church Rep. WILLIAM A. SHELDON.

Church of Christ, Scientist: 210 Massachusetts Ave, Boston, MA 02115; tel. (617) 450-2000; fax (617) 450-3554; e-mail info@churchofchristscientist.org; internet www.tfccs.com; f. 1879; 2,400 congregations world-wide; Pres. MARK SWINNEY; Man. PHILIP G. DAVIS.

Church of God Ministries: POB 2420, Anderson, IN 46018-2420; tel. (765) 642-0256; fax (765) 642-5652; e-mail drepass@chog.org; internet www.chog.org; f. 1881; 2,248 churches; 242,905 mems (2008); Gen. Dir Dr RONALD V. DUNCAN.

Church of God in Christ: Mason Temple, 939 Mason St, Memphis, TN 38126; e-mail laity@cogic.org; internet www.cogic.org; f. 1907; 15,300 churches; 5,500,000 mems (1991); Presiding Bishop CHARLES EDWARD BLAKE.

Church of God of Prophecy: 3720 Keith St, POB 2910, Cleveland, TN 37320-2910; tel. (423) 559-5100; internet www.cogop.org; f. 1923; 1,858 congregations; 91,106 mems (2000); Gen. Observer Bishop RANDALL E. HOWARD.

Church of Jesus Christ of Latter-day Saints (Mormon): 47 East South Temple St, Salt Lake City, UT 84150-0001; tel. (801) 240-1000; fax (801) 240-2033; internet www.lds.org; f. 1830; 12,112 wards and brs (congregations) in USA; 5.5m. mems in USA (2003); Pres. THOMAS S. MONSON.

Church of the Nazarene: 6401 The Paseo, Kansas City, MO 64131; tel. (816) 333-7000; fax (816) 361-4983; e-mail gensec@nazarene.org; internet www.nazarene.org; f. 1908; 18,690 churches; 1.6m. mems (2006); Gen. Sec. DAVID P. WILSON.

Church of the United Brethren in Christ, USA: 302 Lake St, Huntington, IN 46750; tel. (260) 356-2312; e-mail steve@ub.org; internet www.ub.org; f. 1767; 215 churches; 25,000 mems (2005); Chair. Bishop RON RAMSEY.

Churches of God, General Conference: 700 East Melrose, POB 926, Findlay, OH 45839; tel. (419) 424-1961; fax (419) 424-3433; e-mail director@cggc.org; internet www.cggc.org; f. 1825; 336 churches; 32,208 mems; Exec. Dir ED ROSENBERRY.

Community of Christ: 1001 West Walnut, Independence, MO 64050-3562; tel. (816) 833-1000, fax (816) 521-3095; e-mail contact@cofchrist.org; internet www.cofchrist.org; f. 1830; 892 churches; 250,000 mems (2007); fmrly Reorganized Church of Jesus Christ of Latter-day Saints; present name adopted in 2001; Pres. STEPHEN M. VEAZEY.

Conservative Congregational Christian Conference: 8941 Highway 5, Lake Elmo, MN 55042-8900; tel. (651) 739-1474; fax (651) 739-0750; e-mail dmjohnson@ccccusa.com; internet www.ccccusa.com; f. 1949; 284 congregations; 41,772 mems (2008); Conference Minister Rev. Dr STEPHEN A. GAMMON.

Evangelical Covenant Church: 5101 North Francisco Ave, Chicago, IL 60625; tel. (773) 784-3000; fax (773) 784-4366; e-mail president@covchurch.org; internet www.covchurch.org; f. 1885; 671 churches; 102,342 mems; Pres. GARY WALTER.

Evangelical Free Church of America (EFCA): 901 East 78th St, Minneapolis, MN 55420; tel. (952) 853-8441; fax (953) 853-8488; e-mail adminfin@efca.org; internet www.efca.org; f. 1950 by merger of the Swedish Evangelical Free Church and Norwegian-Danish Evangelical Free Church Asscn; asscn of 1,278 autonomous churches; 356,205 mems (2006); Pres. Dr WILLIAM J. HAMEL.

Evangelical Friends International: 5350 Broadmoor Circus, NW, Canton, OH 44709; tel. (330) 493-1660; fax (330) 493-0852; e-mail efcer@aol.com; internet www.evangelicalfriends.org; f. 1965; Quaker; c. 300 churches; 41,000 mems; Dirs Dr RON STANSELL, JOHN P. WILLIAMS (North America).

Friends General Conference: 2B, 1216 Arch St, Philadelphia, PA 19107; tel. (215) 561-1700; fax (215) 561-0759; e-mail friends@fgcquaker.org; internet www.fgcquaker.org; f. 1900; Quaker; mem. of the World Council of Churches; 505 churches; 32,977 mems; Gen. Sec. BRUCE BIRCHARD.

Friends United Meeting: 101 Quaker Hill Dr., Richmond, IN 47374-1980; tel. (765) 962-7573; fax (765) 966-1293; e-mail info@fum.org; internet www.fum.org; f. 1902; Quaker; mem. of the World Council of Churches; 44,000 mems (USA and Canada); Gen. Sec. SYLVIA GRAVES.

Independent Fundamental Churches of America: 3520 Fairlanes Ave, POB 810, Grandville, MI 49468-0810; tel. (800) 347-1840; fax (616) 531-1814; e-mail office@ifca.org; internet www.ifca.org; f. 1930; 1000 churches across the USA; 62,000 mems; Pres. JERRY SMITH; Exec. Dir Rev. LES LOFQUIST.

Jehovah's Witnesses: 25 Columbia Heights, Brooklyn, NY 11201-2483; tel. (718) 560-5000; internet www.watchtower.org; f. 1879; 12,494 congregations; 1.1m. mems (2007); Pres. DAN ADAMS.

Mariavite Old Catholic Church—Province of North America: 2803 10th St, Wyandotte, MI 48192-4994; tel. and fax (734) 281-3082; e-mail mariaviteocc@hotmail.com; f. 1930; 158 churches; 357,100 mems; Prime Bishop Most Rev. Archbishop Dr ROBERT R. J. M. ZABOROWSKI.

Mennonite Church USA: 1601 West Beardsley Ave, Elkhart, IN 46515; tel. (574) 294-7523; fax (574) 293-1892; e-mail elkhart@mennoniteusa.org; internet www.mennoniteusa.org; f. 1690; 939 churches; 109,000 mems (2008); Exec. Dir JIM SCHRAG.

Missionary Church: 3811 Vanguard Dr., POB 9127, Fort Wayne, IN 46809-3304; tel. (260) 747-2027; fax (260) 747-5331; e-mail mcdenomusa@aol.com; internet www.mcusa.org; present name adopted in 1969; Trinitarian; mem. of the Nat. Asscn of Evangelicals; over 400 congregations; 49,528 mems; Pres. Rev. Dr BILL HOSSLER.

Moravian Church in America (United Fratrum): *Northern Province:* 1021 Center St, POB 1245, Bethlehem, PA 18016; tel. (610) 867-7566; fax (610) 866-9223; e-mail pubs@mcnp.org; internet www.mcnp.org; *Southern Province:* 459 South Church St, Winston-Salem, NC 27101; tel. (336) 725-5811; fax (336) 723-1029; e-mail bwm@mcsp.org; internet www.mcsp.org; f. 1740; mem. of the World Council of Churches; 96 churches; Pres. DAVID L. WICKMANN; f. 1740; 58 churches; Pres. Rev. Dr WAYNE BURKETTE.

National Association of Congregational Christian Churches (NACCC): 8473 South Howell Ave, POB 288, Oak Creek, WI 53154; tel. (414) 764-1620; fax (414) 764-0319; e-mail naccc@naccc.org; internet www.naccc.org; f. 1955; 426 churches; 84,380 mems (2000); Exec. Sec. Rev. Dr THOMAS M. RICHARD.

Polish National Catholic Church of America: 1006 Pittston Ave, Scranton, PA 18505; tel. (570) 346-9131; fax (570) 346-2188; e-mail pncccenter@comcast.net; internet www.pncc.org; f. 1897; mem. of the World Council of Churches; 25,000 mems (2006); Prime Bishop Most Rev. ROBERT M. NEMKOVICH.

Reformed Church in America: 475 Riverside Dr., New York, NY 10115-0001; tel. (212) 870-3071; fax (212) 870-2499; e-mail questions@rca.org; internet www.rca.org; f. 1628; Calvinist; mem. of the World Council of Churches; 935 churches; 329,437 mems; Gen. Sec. Rev. WESLEY GRANBERG-MICHAELSON.

Salvation Army: 615 Slaters Lane, POB 269, Alexandria, VA 22313; e-mail webmaster@usn.salvationarmy.org; internet www.salvationarmyusa.org; f. 1880; 1,286 churches; 422,543 mems; Nat. Commdr Commr ISRAEL L. GAITHER; Nat. Pres. of Women's Ministries Commr EVA D. GAITHER.

Seventh-day Adventists: 12501 Old Columbia Pike, Silver Spring, MD 20904-6600; tel. (301) 680-6400; fax (301) 680-6464; e-mail roscoe.howard@nad.adventist.org; internet www.nadadventist.org; f. 1863; 5,026 churches; c. 1m. mems (USA and Canada); Pres. H. DON SCHNEIDER; Sec. ROSCOE J. HOWARD, III.

United Church of Christ: 700 Prospect Ave, Cleveland, OH 44115; tel. (216) 736-2100; fax (216) 736-2103; e-mail guessb@ucc.org; internet www.ucc.org; f. 1957; mem. of the Churches Uniting in Christ and World Council of Churches; 5,633 churches; 1.2m. mems; Gen. Minister and Pres. Rev. JOHN H. THOMAS.

Universal Fellowship of Metropolitan Community Churches: POB 1374, Abilene, TX 79604; tel. (310) 360-8640; fax (325) 690-6328; e-mail info@mccchurch.org; internet www.mccchurch.com; f. 1968; 300 groups; 43,000 mems; Moderator Rev. Elder NANCY WILSON.

US Conference of Mennonite Brethren Churches: POB 220, Hillsboro, KS 67063-0220; tel. (316) 558-8688; fax (316) 744-7472; e-mail offices@usmb.org; internet www.usmb.org; f. 1954; 200 churches; 35,500 mems (2008); Exec. Dir ED BOSCHMANN.

Vineyard, USA: POB 2089, Stafford, TX 77497; tel. (281) 313-8463; fax (281) 313-8464; e-mail info@vineyardusa.org; internet www.vineyardusa.org; f. 1974; 594 congregations; 121,741 mems (2007); Nat. Dir BERT WAGGONER.

Wesleyan Church: POB 50434, Indianapolis, IN 46250; tel. (317) 774-7900; e-mail information@wesleyan.org; internet www.wesleyan.org; f. 1968; 1,723 churches; 136,717 mems; Gen. Sec. Dr RONALD D. KELLY; Gen. Supts Rev. Dr CARLSTON CHRISTIE, Rev. Dr THOMAS E. ARMIGER, Rev. Dr JO ANNE LYON.

Interdenominational Organizations

American Bible Society: 1865 Broadway, New York, NY 10023-9980; tel. (212) 408-1200; fax (212) 408-1512; e-mail info@americanbible.org; internet www.americanbible.org; f. 1816; 500,000 mems; Exec. Vice-Pres Dr LAMAR VEST, Jr, SIMON BARNES.

Churches Uniting in Christ (CUIC): 475 East Lockwood, Webster Groves, MO 63119; tel. (314) 252-3161; fax (314) 252-3162; e-mail cuic@eden.edu; internet www.cuicinfo.org; f. 2002 as successor to the Consultation on Church Union; 10 mem. churches; Pres. Rev. Dr SUZANNE WEBB; Sec. ABRAHAM WRIGHT.

National Association of Evangelicals: POB 23269, Washington, DC 20026; tel. (202) 789-1011; fax (202) 842-0392; e-mail govaffairs@nae.net; internet www.nae.net; f. 1942; 4m. mems; voluntary asscn of individuals, denominations, churches, universities, colleges and orgs; represents 43,000 churches from 50 denominations; Pres. LEITH ANDERSON.

National Council of the Churches of Christ in the USA: 475 Riverside Dr., Suite 880, New York, NY 10115; tel. (212) 870-2252; fax (212) 870-2030; e-mail info@ncccusa.org; internet www.councilofchurches.org; f. 1950; mem. of the World Council of Churches; ecumenical org. of 35 Protestant and Orthodox denominations representing 45m. mems; Gen. Sec. Rev. Dr MICHAEL KINNAMON (acting).

International Council of Community Churches: 21116 Washington Parkway, Frankfort IL 60423; tel. (815) 464-5690; fax (815) 464-5692; e-mail leroy.mccreary@sbcglobal.net; internet www.icccusa.com; f. 1950; mem. of the Churches Uniting in Christ, World Council of Churches, National Council of Community Churches, and Christian Churches Together; Exec. Dir Rev. MICHAEL LIVINGSTON.

US Conference for the World Council of Churches: 475 Riverside Dr., Rm 1370, New York, NY 10115; tel. (212) 870-2533; fax (212) 870-2528; internet www.wcc-usa.org; f. 1948; 34 Protestant and Orthodox mem. churches in the USA; Program Exec. DEBORAH DEWINTER.

HINDUISM

At mid-2000 there were an estimated 1.0m. Hindus in the USA.

Ramakrishna-Vivekananda Center: 17 East 94th St, New York, NY 10128; tel. (212) 534-9445; fax (212) 828-1618; e-mail rvcnewyork@worldnet.att.net; internet www.ramakrishna.org; f. 1933; teachings based on the system of Vedanta; Minister and Spiritual Leader SWAMI YUKTATMANANDA; Dir BARRY ZELIKOVSKY.

ISLAM

At mid-2000 there were an estimated 4.1m. Muslims in the USA, of whom some 40% were African-American.

Council of Masajid of United States (CMUS): 45 Lilac St, Edison, NJ 08817; tel. (732) 985-3304; fax (732) 572-0486; e-mail dawud10@optonline.net; f. 1978; educational agency representing 650 local groups; Pres. DAWUD ASSAD.

Islamic Center of America: 19500 Ford Rd, Dearborn, MI 48228; tel. (313) 593-0000; fax (313) 582-0988; e-mail info@icofa.com; internet www.icofa.com; Leader Imam HASSAN AL-QAZWINI.

Islamic Center of New York: 1711 Third Ave, New York, NY 10029-7303; tel. (212) 722-5234; fax (212) 722-5936; internet www.icnyu.org; f. 1966; Dir KHALID LATIF.

Islamic Mission of America: 143 State St, Brooklyn, NY 11201; tel. (718) 875-6607; f. 1948; maintains an educational and training institute; 15,000 mems; Chair. MOHAMED KABBAJ; Dir Hajj D. A. HAROON.

JUDAISM

In 2004 there were an estimated 6.5m. Jews in the USA.

Agudath Israel of America: 42 Broadway, 14th Floor, New York, NY 1004; tel. (212) 797-9000; fax (212) 533-5335; internet www.ou.org/network/agudah/aboutagudah.htm; f. 1921; 100,000 mems; Exec. Dir (vacant).

American Council for Judaism: POB 2836, Ponte Vedra Beach, FL 32004-2836; tel. (904) 280-3131; e-mail acjsln@aol.com; internet www.acjna.org; f. 1943; Pres. STEPHEN L. NAMAN.

American Jewish Committee: POB 705, New York, NY 10150; tel. (212) 751-4000; fax (212) 891-1450; e-mail pr@ajc.org; internet www.ajc.org; f. 1906; 45,000 mems; Pres. RICHARD SIDEMAN; Exec. Dir DAVID A. HARRIS.

American Jewish Congress: 825 Third Ave, New York, NY 10022; tel. (212) 879-4500; fax (212) 758-1633; e-mail contact@ajcongress.org; internet www.ajcongress.org; f. 1918; 50,000 mems; Chair. JACK ROSEN; Exec. Dir NEIL B. GOLDSTEIN.

American Zionist Movement: 633 Third Ave, New York, NY 10017; tel. (212) 318-6100; e-mail info@azm.org; internet www.azm.org; f. 1939; 20 mem. orgs; Chair. MARLENE E. POST; Pres. WILLIAM D. HESS; Nat. Exec. Dir KAREN J. RUBINSTEIN.

Central Conference of American Rabbis: 355 Lexington Ave, New York, NY 10017; tel. (212) 972-3636; fax (212) 692-0819; e-mail info@ccarnet.org; internet www.ccarnet.org; f. 1889; organized rabbinate of Reform Judaism; 1,840 mems; Pres. PETER S. KNOBEL.

The Rabbinical Assembly: 3080 Broadway, New York, NY 10027-4650; tel. (212) 280-6000; fax (212) 749-9166; e-mail info@rabbinicalassembly.org; internet www.rabbinicalassembly.org; f. 1901; 1,550 mems; Pres. Rabbi ALVIN K. BERKUN; Exec. Vice-Pres. Rabbi JOEL H. MEYERS.

Union of Orthodox Jewish Congregations of America: 11 Broadway, New York, NY 10004; tel. (212) 563-4000; fax (212) 564-9058; e-mail info@ou.org; internet www.ou.org; f. 1898; 1,000 affiliated congregations representing c. 1.0m. mems; Chair. HARVEY BLITZ; Pres. STEVEN J. SAVITSKY.

Union for Reform Judaism: 633 Third Ave, New York, NY 10017-6778; tel. (212) 650-4000; fax (212) 650-4169; e-mail urj@urj.org; internet urj.org; f. 1873 as the Union of American Hebrew Congregations; present name adopted 2003; more than 900 affiliated congregations representing c. 1.5m. mems; Pres. Rabbi ERIC H. YOFFIE; Sr Vice-Pres. Rabbi DANIEL FREELANDER.

United Synagogue of Conservative Judaism: 820 Second Ave, New York, NY 10017-4504; tel. (212) 533-7800; e-mail info@uscj.org; internet www.uscj.org; f. 1913; c. 700 affiliated congregations in North America representing c. 1.5m. mems; Pres. Dr RAYMOND GOLDSTEIN; Exec. Vice-Pres. Rabbi JEROME EPSTEIN.

SIKHISM

At mid-2000 there were an estimated 234,000 Sikhs in the USA.

Sikh Study Circle: 1821 South Hairston Rd, St Mountain, GA 30088; tel. (770) 808-6320; e-mail sikhatlanta@gmail.com; internet www.sikh-atlanta.org; f. 1989; conducts services, disseminates information about Sikh religion and culture; Pres. HARMINDERJIT SINGH SAINI.

OTHER RELIGIONS AND CULTS

Ananda Marga: 97–38 42nd Ave, 1F, Corona, NY 11368; tel. (718) 898-1603; fax (718) 898-1604; e-mail north-america@anandamarga.org; internet www.anandamarga.org; f. 1955; 50 state groups, 100 local groups; Pres. JAMES F. KAESER.

Church of Scientology International: 6331 Hollywood Blvd, Suite 1200, Los Angeles, CA 90028; tel. (213) 960-3500; fax (323) 960-3508; e-mail info@scientology.net; internet www.scientology.org; f. 1954; 10m. mems world-wide; applied religious philosophy; Pres. Rev. HEBER JENTZSCH.

Self-Realization Fellowship: 3880 San Rafael Ave, Dept 9W, Los Angeles, CA 90065-3928; tel. (323) 225-2471; internet www.yogananda-srf.org; f. 1920; Pres. Sri DAYA MATA.

Unitarian Universalist Association: 25 Beacon St, Boston, MA 02108; tel. (617) 742-2100; fax (617) 367-3237; e-mail info@uua.org; internet www.uua.org; f. 1961; *c.* 1,000 congregations; 182,698 (2000); Pres. Rev. WILLIAM G. SINKFORD; Moderator GINI COURTER.

THE STATES

THE STATES OF THE UNION AND THE DISTRICT OF COLUMBIA

Alabama

Gross Area: 135,293 sq km (52,237 sq miles).

Resident Population (1 July 2007, estimate): 4,627,851.

State Capital: Montgomery.

Principal Cities (1 July 2006, estimate): Birmingham 229,424; Montgomery (capital) 201,998; Mobile 192,830; Huntsville 168,132.

LOCATION, TOPOGRAPHY AND CLIMATE

The State of Alabama (nicknamed 'The Heart of Dixie') lies in the South; it is bordered by Tennessee to the north, Georgia to the east, Florida to the south-east and Mississippi to the west. In the south-west Alabama has a short coastline on the Gulf of Mexico. The southern half of the state is a low-lying coastal plain across which the 'Black Belt', a band of rich, chalky soil, stretches. The land rises towards the north, with Alabama's highest elevation, Cheaha Mountain, in the north-east, at 734 m (2,407 ft). The Tennessee River crosses the north of the state, and the Alabama and Tombigbee Rivers flow through the southern plain, joining to form the Mobile, which runs down into the Gulf of Mexico. The climate is subtropical in the south, with long, hot summers, mild winters and high rainfall. Towards the north of the state the climate is temperate, with occasional snow in winter.

HISTORICAL BACKGROUND

The Creek, Cherokee, Chickasaw, Alabama and Choctaw peoples inhabited the region when Spanish explorers arrived in the early 16th century. The French established the first permanent settlement, Fort Louis de la Mobile, in 1702. In 1763 the region was ceded to the British Crown under the terms of the Treaty of Paris, but Spanish forces gained control of the Mobile Bay area in 1780, which then remained under Spanish rule until US troops seized it in 1813. The Louisiana Purchase of 1803 had brought most of modern Alabama under US control. In 1814 Gen. Andrew Jackson's victory at Horseshoe Bend weakened the presence of the native tribes. In 1817 the region was granted territorial status and Alabama was admitted to the Union as the 22nd state on 14 December 1819. The state played an important role in the Civil War, owing to the power of its pro-slavery plantation owners. In 1861 Alabama seceded from the Union and Jefferson Davis was inaugurated as President of the Confederation at Montgomery. Confederacy troops suffered a major naval defeat in Mobile Bay in 1864. In the 1950s and 1960s Alabama featured prominently in civil rights demonstrations, with Dr Martin Luther King, Jr, leading a march from Selma to Montgomery in 1965.

ECONOMY

Alabama's principal economic activities are manufacturing, mining and quarrying, agriculture, wholesale and retail trade and finance, insurance and real estate. Gross domestic product by state in 2007 was US $165,796m., and the state's per-head average income was $32,401; 16.9% of the population were below the poverty line in 2007, the sixth highest rate of any state. The civilian labour force totalled 2,197,700 in mid–2008, while the unemployment rate was 5.5% (121,200 persons). Union membership accounted for 9.5% of all workers in 2007, with a total of 10.6% of employees covered by union agreements.

Farmland covered 26.3% of Alabama's total land area in 2005. Cropland accounted for 41.9% of total farmland in 2002; some 2.7% of cropland was under irrigation. There were 43,000 farms in 2007, with an average farm size of 200 acres (81 ha); farmland covered 8.6m. acres in that year. In 2007 19% of farm income was generated by crop sales and 81% by livestock and livestock products. The state's leading agricultural commodities in that year were broilers, cattle and calves, greenhouse and nursery products and chicken eggs. In 2007 Alabama was ranked fourth among all states for broiler production (after Georgia, Arkansas and North Carolina) and tenth for eggs. There were some 23m. acres of forestland in 2002. In 2004 Alabama was the nation's seventh most important timber-producing state, with softwoods accounting for 90% of production. The value of the state's commercial fish landings totalled US $49m. in 2006. Alabama is the USA's second leading producer of catfish, behind Mississippi, and its fourth largest producer of shrimp.

In 2007 the value of non-fuel mineral production in Alabama was an estimated US $1,340m., with the state ranked 16th in the nation. Cement, crushed stone, lime and construction sand and gravel were among the leading minerals produced which together in 2005 accounted for 94% of the state's non-fuel mineral production value. Alabama was the third leading producer of kaolin in 2005 and was also ranked third for lime, common clay and iron oxide pigments and fourth for bentonite and masonry cement. No metals are mined in Alabama. The state has valuable coal, petroleum and natural gas deposits; it was ranked 15th for coal production in 2007 and 11th for natural gas in 2005.

In 2003 the state's principal manufactured goods included food and paper products, chemicals, metals, textiles and clothing, and computer, electronic and transportation equipment. The state ranked 19th in the USA in terms of its value of shipments in 2006. Total manufacturing shipments in 2006 stood at US $101,862m., of which 40% was added during manufacture.

The combined assets of Alabama's commercial banks were US $233,300m. at the end of 2006, the 15th highest across the states. Domestic travel expenditures were $5,969m. in Alabama in 2004. Total general expenditures by the state government in 2006 were $21,047m., while general revenue totalled $20,306m., of which $6,977m. was from the federal Government and $8,530m. was derived from taxes. In 2006 Alabama received $6,565m. in federal aid.

CONSTITUTION AND GOVERNMENT

The current Constitution of Alabama is the state's sixth and became effective on 28 November 1901. Constitutional amendments proposed by the Legislature have to be approved by a three-fifths' majority vote in each house, and must then be ratified by a simple majority of state voters. The Governor is elected separately from the Lieutenant-Governor to serve a four-year term of office, and may serve no more than two terms consecutively. The cabinet consists of 27 members who are appointed by the Governor and meet at least twice a month. The Legislature consists of 35 senators and 105 representatives, and both chambers are elected every four years. Regular legislative sessions are held annually and are limited to 30 legislative days. A bill becomes law once it has been passed by a majority of a quorum of both houses and has been signed by the Governor. The Governor has 10 days to consider a bill, after which it becomes law unless vetoed. A gubernatorial veto may be overridden by a majority vote of the elected members in each house. Most enacted bills become effective immediately. The Republican incumbent, Bob Riley, was victorious in the 2006 gubernatorial election, receiving 58% of the vote. In the 2008 presidential election the Republicans secured some 60% of the votes cast in the state. Alabama has 67 administrative counties.

Elected Executive Branch Officials

Governor (2007–13): BOB RILEY (Rep.).

Lieutenant-Governor: JIM FOLSOM, Jr (Dem.).

Secretary of State: BETH CHAPMAN (Rep.).

Attorney-General: TROY KING (Rep.).

Treasurer: KAY IVEY (Rep.).

Auditor: SAMANTHA SHAW (Rep.).

Commissioner of Agriculture and Industries: RON SPARKS (Dem.).

Selected Government Addresses

Office of the Governor: State Capitol, Rm N-104, 600 Dexter Ave, Montgomery, AL 36130; tel. (334) 242-7100; fax (334) 353-0004; internet www.governor.alabama.gov.

Office of the Lieutenant-Governor: Alabama State House, 11 South Union St, Suite 725, Montgomery, AL 36130; tel. (334) 242-7900; fax (334) 242-4661; internet www.ltgov.alabama.gov.

Office of the Secretary of State: POB 5616, Montgomery, AL 36130 5616; tel. (334) 242-7200; fax (334) 242-4993; e-mail tamara .cofield@sos.alabama.gov; internet www.sos.state.al.us.

Office of the Attorney-General: Alabama State House, 11 South Union St, 3rd Floor, Montgomery, AL 36130; tel. (334) 242-7300; fax (334) 242-7458; internet www.ago.state.al.us.

Office of the Treasurer: State Capitol, 600 Dexter Ave, Rm S-106, Montgomery, AL 36104; tel. (334) 242-7500; fax (334) 242-7592; e-mail alatreas@treasury.alabama.gov; internet www.treasury.alabama.gov.

Office of the Auditor: State Capitol, Rm S-101, 600 Dexter Ave, Montgomery, AL 36130; tel. (334) 242-7010; fax (334) 242-7650; e-mail demea.mercer@auditor.alabama.gov; internet www.auditor.state.al.us.

Department of Agriculture and Industries: Richard Beard Bldg, 1445 Federal Dr., Montgomery, AL 36107-1100; tel. (334) 240-7100; fax (334) 240-7190; e-mail ron.sparks@agi.alabama.gov; internet www.agi.state.al.us.

Bureau of Tourism and Travel: 401 Adams Ave, Suite 126, POB 4927, Montgomery, AL 36103-4927; tel. (334) 242-4169; fax (334) 353-4554; e-mail info@tourism.alabama.gov; internet www.alabama.travel; Dir LEE SENTELL.

Department of Corrections: 301 South Ripley St, POB 301501, Montgomery, AL 36130-1501; tel. (334) 353-3883; fax (334) 242-9399; e-mail pio@doc.alabama.gov; internet www.doc.alabama.gov; Commr RICHARD F. ALLEN.

Department of Economic and Community Affairs: 410 Adams Ave, POB 5690, Montgomery, AL 36103-5690; tel. (334) 242-5100; fax (334) 242-5099; internet www.adeca.alabama.gov; Dir BILL JOHNSON.

Department of Education: Gordon Persons Office Bldg, 50 North Ripley St, POB 302101, Montgomery, AL 36104-2101; tel. (334) 242-9700; fax (334) 242-9708; e-mail jmorton@alsde.edu; internet www.alsde.edu/html/home.asp; Supt Dr JOSEPH B. MORTON.

Department of Environmental Management: 1400 Coliseum Blvd, POB 301463, Montgomery, AL 36130-1463; tel. (334) 271-7700; fax (334) 271-7950; e-mail permitsmail@adem.state.al.us; internet www.adem.state.al.us; Dir TREY GLENN, III.

Department of Finance: State Capitol, 600 Dexter Ave, Suite N-105, Montgomery, AL 36130; tel. (334) 242-7160; fax (334) 353-3300; e-mail donna.newman@finance.alabama.gov; internet www.finance.alabama.gov; Dir JAMES A. MAIN.

Department of Insurance: 201 Monroe St, Suite 1700, POB 303351, Montgomery, AL 36130-3351; tel. (334) 269-3550; fax (334) 241-4192; e-mail insdept@insurance.alabama.gov; internet www.aldoi.gov; Commr WALTER A. BELL.

Department of Labor: RSA Union, 6th floor, 100 North Union St, POB 303500, Montgomery, AL 36130-3500; tel. (334) 242-3460; fax (334) 240-3417; e-mail renae.easterly@alalabor.alabama.gov; internet www.alalabor.state.al.us; Commr JIM BENNETT.

Department of Public Health: RSA Tower, 201 Monroe St, POB 303017, Montgomery, AL 36130-3017; tel. (334) 206-5300; fax (334) 206-2008; e-mail donwilliamson@adph.state.al.us; internet www.adph.org; State Health Officer Dr DONALD E. WILLIAMSON.

Department of Revenue: Gordon Persons Office Bldg, 50 North Ripley St, Montgomery, AL 36132; tel. (334) 242-1170; fax (334) 242-0550; internet www.ador.alabama.gov; Commr TIM RUSSELL.

Department of Transportation: 1409 Coliseum Blvd, Montgomery, AL 36110; tel. (334) 242-6358; fax (334) 262-2677; e-mail aldotinfo@dot.state.al.us; internet www.dot.state.al.us; Dir DUNCAN (JOE) MCINNES.

Military Department: 1720 Congressman W. L. Dickinson Dr., Montgomery, AL 36109-2602; tel. (334) 271-7200; fax (334) 2131-7511; internet www.alguard.state.al.us; Adj.-Gen. Maj.-Gen. ABNER C. BLALOCK.

Public Service Commission: RSA Union, 100 North Union St, Suite 850, POB 304260, Montgomery, AL 36130-4260; tel. (334) 242-5218; fax (334) 242-0509; e-mail angier.johnson@psc.alabama.gov; internet www.psc.state.al.us; Pres. JIM SULLIVAN.

Legislature

(August 2008)

Senate

Dem. 22; Rep. 13; Total 35

President and Presiding Officer: Lt-Gov. JIM FOLSOM, Jr (Dem.).

President Pro Tempore: HINTON MITCHEM (Dem.).

Secretary: CHARLES MCDOWELL LEE.

House of Representatives

Dem. 62; Rep. 43; Total 105

Speaker: SETH HAMMETT (Dem.).

Speaker Pro Tempore: DEMETRIUS NEWTON (Dem.).

Clerk: GREG PAPPAS.

Alaska

Gross Area: 1,717,854 sq km (663,267 sq miles).

Resident Population (1 July 2007, estimate): 683,478.

State Capital: Juneau (population 30,737 at 1 July 2006, estimate).

Principal City (population at 1 July 2006, estimate): Anchorage 278,700.

LOCATION, TOPOGRAPHY AND CLIMATE

The State of Alaska, situated to the extreme north-west of the North American continent, is the largest state in the Union, covering 16% of the total US land area. It is nicknamed 'The Last Frontier'. The borders of the state are formed by the Beaufort Sea to the north, Canada (the Yukon Territory and British Columbia) to the east, the Pacific Ocean to the south, and the Bering Sea to the west. Alaska's mainland is surrounded by numerous islands, including the volcanic Aleutian Islands (of which the western ones are Russian), sweeping south-west from the Alaska Peninsula, and the Alexander Archipelago, extending along the narrow strip of coast in the south-east. The interior of the state is mountainous, and contains the USA's 17 highest peaks, five of which mark the border with Canada. The two principal mountain ranges are the Brooks Range, within the Arctic Circle, and the Alaska Range in the south, which includes Mount McKinley, the highest point in North America at 6,194 m (20,320 ft). The main lowland area is in the centre of the state, where the Yukon River runs westwards from Canada towards the Bering Sea. There are many lakes, the largest of which is Iliamna Lake at about 2,600 sq km (1,000 sq miles). Northern Alaska has a 'tundra' climate, with a permanently frozen subsoil, while in the central lowlands the winters are long and harsh but the short summers may be hot. Towards the south-east of the state the climate becomes milder. Heavy rainfall occurs across the south and also in the west.

HISTORICAL BACKGROUND

The Tlingit-Haida people and tribes of the Athabascan family were among the earliest inhabitants of Alaska, followed *c.* 2000 BC by the Aleut and Inuit peoples from Siberia. As a result of exploration by Russian groups, in 1741 Europeans started arriving in Alaska to exploit the hunting skills of the Aleuts for the fur trade; their first permanent settlement was established on Kodiak Island in 1784. The fur trade was monopolized by the Russian-American Co, but its success wavered in the first half of the 19th century and, in 1867, the US Secretary of State, William H. Seward, persuaded the Russians to part with their American territory for US $7.2m. Gold was discovered at Juneau in 1880, after which Alaska's population expanded rapidly; the Organic Act of 1884 granted it a government and courts. The region was granted territorial status in 1912. By 1915 the gold-rush had subsided and fishing had become the primary industry. In 1957 petroleum was discovered on the Kenai Peninsula and further discoveries led to the building of the Trans-Alaska Pipeline System (TAPS), completed in 1977. Alaska became the 49th state of the USA on 3 January 1959. The discovery of significant hydrocarbons reserves in the 1960s helped ambitious economic development plans in the new state. The impediment of extensive aboriginal (Aleut and Inuit—Eskimo) land claims was resolved by the Alaska Native Claims Settlement Act in 1971. Thereafter, the dominant controversy in Alaska was over the environment, with attention focusing on the potential exploitation of the fossil-fuel reserves of the Arctic National Wildlife Reserve. In June 2002 construction work began on a controversial missile defence system for the USA, based at Fort Greely in the middle of the state.

ECONOMY

Gross domestic product by state in 2007 was US $44,517m., making Alaska the sixth smallest state economy in the USA. Government expenditure, services, trade and contract construction are the leading contributors to Alaska's economy, while the principal industries are energy products, tourism, mining, forestry and fishing and food-processing. In 2007 the state had an average per-head income of $39,934; just 8.9% of the population were registered as living below the poverty line in that year. The civilian labour force totalled some 369,200 in mid-2008, with 6.1% unemployed (22,400 persons). In 2007 23.8% of the work-force belonged to a trade union, while 24.7% of its workers were covered by union agreements. In both measures the state ranked second highest nationally.

Alaska has a negligible amount of commercial agriculture: there were 900,000 acres (0.2% of total land area) in farms in 2007, with cropland accounting for 100,000 acres in 2002. In 2007 there were 660 farms, with an average size of 1,364 acres. Alaska's farm income was the lowest among the 50 states in 2007, with 21% of the total derived from livestock products and 79% from crops. Greenhouse and nursery products, hay, potatoes and cattle and calves dominated what cultivation there was. Alaska's forestland totalled 126.9m. acres in 2002. Its fish catch, the highest of any state, was valued at US $1,342m. in 2006: pollock, cod, halibut and salmon are the principal species caught in terms of value, with Alaska accounting for 97% of the USA's total landings of Pacific salmon in 2007 (at an estimated value of $348m.). There have been tensions in the past between the USA and Canada over the implementation of measures designed to prevent over-fishing.

In 2007 the value of non-fuel mineral production in Alaska was US $3,430m.; ranking as the fifth most important producer of all the states in the nation. Metallic minerals consistently account for more than 90% of the state's total output, with zinc, gold, lead and silver the leading metals in that year. Copper was also produced, in addition to construction sand and gravel and crushed stone. Alaska was the USA's leading producer of zinc and silver in 2007, and its second most important producer of lead and gold in that year. The state produced 1.32m. short tons of coal in 2007, and is the nation's second largest producer of crude petroleum after Texas, and the seventh largest producer of natural gas. Over 90% of Alaska's petroleum output originates from fields in the extreme north of the state (by far the largest of which is Prudhoe Bay) and is transported southwards, via the TAPS, to the ice-free port of Valdez.

Alaska ranked 49th in the USA in terms of the value of its manufacturing shipments in 2006. Its most important industries are food-processing (especially seafood), printing, petroleum-refining, mining and the manufacture of lumber and wood products. Anchorage is the leading manufacturing centre. The total value of Alaska's manufacturing shipments in 2006 was US $7,082m.; 23% of value was added during manufacture.

Alaska's still relatively unspoilt scenery gives it great tourism potential. Sport fishing, sport hunting and 'eco-tourism' attract tourists to the state's vast forests, parks and recreation areas. Domestic travel expenditures totalled just US $1,470m. in 2004, the third lowest total of any state.

Total general expenditures by the state government were US $8,599m. in 2006, while total general revenue amounted to $8,920m. Transfers from the federal Government stood at $2,152m. and taxes contributed $2,484m. The state budget was largely supported by petroleum revenues, which enabled general state expenditure per head to reach $12,912 in 2004, compared with an average of $6,481 across the USA. In 2006 Alaska received a total of $2,425m. in federal aid.

CONSTITUTION AND GOVERNMENT

Alaska's only Constitution was adopted in 1956 and became effective on 3 January 1959. A constitutional amendment proposed by the Legislature requires a vote by three-fifths of the elected members of each house, and ratification by a majority of state voters. The Governor and Lieutenant-Governor are elected jointly to serve four-year terms, neither being allowed to serve more than two consecutive terms. The Governor may not stand for re-election for four years after completion of a second consecutive term. There are 20 senators and 40 representatives in the Legislature, serving terms of four and two years, respectively. Alternate halves of the Senate are re-elected every two years. Regular legislative sessions commence in January each year and last for no longer than 120 calendar days. A bill becomes law when it has been approved by both houses of the Legislature and has been signed by the Governor. During session the Governor has 15 days in which to consider a bill, after which it becomes law unless vetoed. After session a bill becomes law unless vetoed within 20 days of being presented to the Governor. The Governor's veto may usually be overridden by a two-thirds' vote of the elected representatives in each house. Legislation becomes effective 90 days after enactment. In 2006 Sarah Palin, the Republican candidate, was elected Governor of Alaska with 48% of the votes cast. In the presidential election of November 2008, the Republicans secured an estimated 62% of the votes cast. Alaska has 16 boroughs and 11 geographical census areas, instead of administrative counties.

Elected Executive Branch Officials

Governor (2007–11): Sarah Palin (Rep.).

Lieutenant-Governor: Sean R. Parnell (Rep.).

Selected Government Addresses

Office of the Governor: State Capitol Bldg, 120 Fourth St, POB 110001, Juneau, AK 99811-0001; tel. (907) 465-3500; fax (907) 463-3532; internet gov.state.ak.us.

Office of the Lieutenant-Governor: State Capitol Bldg, 120 Fourth St, 3rd Floor, POB 110015, Juneau, AK 99811-0015; tel. (907) 465-3520; fax (907) 465-5400; internet ltgov.alaska.gov.

Department of Administration: State Office Bldg, 10th Floor, POB 110200, Juneau, AK 99811-0200; tel. (907) 465-2200; fax (907) 465-2135; internet www.state.ak.us/admin; Commr Annette Kreitzer.

Department of Commerce, Community and Economic Development: State Office Bldg, 9th Floor, POB 110800, Juneau, AK 99811-0800; tel. (907) 465-2500; e-mail questions@alaska.gov; internet www.dced.state.ak.us; Commr Emil Notti.

Department of Corrections: 802 3rd St, Douglas, AK 99824; tel. (907) 465-4652; fax (907) 269-7340; e-mail marc_antrim@correct.state.ak.us; internet www.correct.state.ak.us; Commr Joe Schmidt.

Department of Education and Early Development: 801 West 10th St, Suite 200, POB 110500, Juneau, AK 99811-0500; tel. (907) 465-2800; fax (907) 465-4156; e-mail eed.webmaster@alaska.gov; internet www.eed.state.ak.us; Commr Larry LeDoux.

Department of Environmental Conservation: 410 Willoughby Ave, Suite 303, POB 111800, Juneau, AK 99811-1800; tel. (907) 465-5066; fax (907) 465-5070; e-mail dec.commissioner@alaska.gov; internet www.dec.state.ak.us; Commr Larry Hartig.

Department of Fish and Game: 1255 West Eighth St, POB 115526, Juneau, AK 99811-5526; tel. (907) 465-4100; fax (907) 465-2332; e-mail dfg.commissioner@alaska.govs; internet www.adfg.state.ak.us; Commr Denby S. Lloyd.

Department of Health and Social Services: 350 Main St, Rm 404, POB 110601, Juneau, AK 99811-0601; tel. (907) 465-3030; fax (907) 465-3068; e-mail william.hogan@alaska.gov; internet www.hss.state.ak.us; Commr William (Bill) Hogan.

Department of Labor and Workforce Development: 1111 West Eighth St, POB 111149, Juneau, AK 99811-1149; tel. (907) 465-2700; fax (907) 465-2784; e-mail commissioner.labor@alaska.gov; internet www.labor.state.ak.us; Commr Click Bishop.

Department of Military and Veterans Affairs: Camp Denali, POB 5800, Fort Richardson, AK 99505-5800; tel. (907) 428-6003; fax (907) 428-6019; e-mail mike_haller@ak-prepared.com; internet www.ak-prepared.com/dmva; Adj.-Gen. and Commr Maj.-Gen. Craig E. Campbell.

Department of Natural Resources: 400 Willoughby Ave, Suite 500, POB 111000, Juneau, AK 99811–1000; tel. (907) 465-2400; fax (907) 465-3886; e-mail sero@alaska.gov; internet www.dnr.state.ak.us; Commr Tom Irwin.

Department of Public Safety: 5700 East Tudor Rd, Anchorage, AK 99507; tel. (907) 269-5086; fax (907) 338-4543; e-mail megan.peters@alaska.gov; internet www.dps.state.ak.us; Commr John D. Glass (acting).

Department of Revenue: State Office Bldg, 333 West Willoughby Ave, 11th Floor, POB 110400, Juneau, AK 99811-0400; tel. (907) 465-2300; fax (907) 465-2389; e-mail patrick_galvin@revenue.state.ak.us; internet www.revenue.state.ak.us; Commr Patrick S. Galvin.

Department of Transportation and Public Facilities: 3132 Channel Dr., POB 112500, Juneau, AK 99811-2500; tel. (907) 465-3900; fax (907) 586-8365; e-mail dot.commissioner@alaska.gov; internet www.dot.state.ak.us; Commr Leo von Scheben.

Office of the Attorney-General and Department of Law: 450 Diamond Courthouse, POB 110300, Juneau, AK 99811-0300; tel. (907) 465-2133; fax (907) 465-2075; e-mail attorney.general@alaska.gov; internet www.law.state.ak.us; Attorney-Gen. Talis J. Colberg.

Legislature
(August 2008)

Senate

Rep. 11; Dem. 9; Total 20

President: Lyda Green (Rep.).

Secretary: Kirsten Waid.

House of Representatives

Rep. 23; Dem. 17; Total 40

Speaker: John Harris (Rep.).

Chief Clerk: Suzi Lowell.

Arizona

Gross Area: 295,294 sq km (113,998 sq miles).

Resident Population (1 July 2007, estimate): 6,338,755.

State Capital: Phoenix.

Principal Cities (population at 1 July 2006, estimate): Phoenix (capital) 1,512,986; Tucson 518,956; Mesa 447,541; Glendale 246,531; Chandler 240,595; Scottsdale 231,127; Gilbert 191,517; Tempe 169,712; Peoria 142,024.

LOCATION, TOPOGRAPHY AND CLIMATE

The State of Arizona (nicknamed 'The Grand Canyon State') lies in the south-west of the USA and is bordered by Utah to the north, New Mexico to the east and California and Nevada to the west. In the south there is an international border with Mexico. In the north of Arizona is the Colorado Plateau, a high, arid region, rising to the state's highest point, Humphreys Peak (3,860 m—12,663 ft). A rocky escarpment—the Mogollon Rim—divides the plateau from the Sonoran Desert to the south, and a high central region of forest-covered ranges stretches from the north-west to the south-east. The Colorado River cuts through the northern plateau, flowing through the one-mile-deep Grand Canyon to form most of the state's western boundary. The Little Colorado River likewise runs across the Plateau. Some fertile land in the south has been created by the irrigation of the Gila and Salt river valleys, although the south-west remains characterized by desert and barren, mountainous areas, while the south-east has only sparse vegetation. Arizona's climate is hot and very sunny. The central region has the highest rainfall in the state (which otherwise receives an extremely low level of precipitation) and has heavy snowfall in winter.

HISTORICAL BACKGROUND

The area now known as Arizona was inhabited by the Anasazi, Mogollan and Hohokam civilizations from c. 300 BC to AD 1300. They were succeeded by the Pueblo peoples, with the Apache and Navaho tribes arriving in the 15th century. The Spanish Franciscan monk Marcos de Niza entered the area in 1539 and the Spanish explorer Francisco Vásquez de Coronado arrived in 1540. Missionaries and silver-prospectors followed the explorers and a military outpost was established at Tubac in 1752. In 1821 much of the region was annexed by Mexico. After the Mexican War (1846–48) most of Arizona was ceded to the USA as part of the territory of New Mexico, and the Gadsden Purchase of 1853 added the southern strip. Arizona was established as a territory in 1863, during the Civil War. With the discovery of gold, silver and copper in the 1870s–90s, settlers began to arrive in the region in large numbers. The agricultural potential of the territory was increased by the Salt River Project, established in 1917, the first of many major irrigation projects in Arizona. Arizona became the 48th state of the Union on 14 February 1912. Previous to this date, 14 of the 17 federally appointed governors had been Republicans, but statehood coincided with a period of dominance by the Democratic Party, which lasted until the 1950s. In June–July 2002 major forest fires destroyed over 400,000 acres of forest in the state; some 30,000 people were evacuated and many homes were destroyed.

ECONOMY

Arizona's principal economic activities include manufacturing, construction, tourism, mining, agriculture and wholesale and retail trade. Gross domestic product by state was US $247,028m. in 2007 and in that year the state's per-head income averaged $32,900, while 14.2% of the population were estimated to be living below the poverty line in that year. The civilian labour force totalled 3,100,000 in mid-2008, of which 168,200 (5.4%) were unemployed. In 2007 8.8% of all employees were union members, while 9.7% were covered by union agreements.

Cropland covered 1.3m. acres (0.5m. ha) in 2002. In 2007 the average size of the state's 10,000 farms was 2,600 acres—the second largest in the USA, after Wyoming. Farmland accounted for an estimated 26.0m. acres in the same year. In 2007 54% of farm income was derived from crops and 46% from livestock and livestock products. Irrigation schemes were in operation throughout the state, with approximately 70.4% of total cropland under irrigation in 2002. In May of that year 14 of Arizona's counties were designated 'disaster areas', following severe drought. The principal agricultural products in 2007 were dairy products, cattle and calves, lettuce and hay. In that year Arizona was the USA's second largest producer of lettuces after California, and was ranked third for all vegetables (behind California and Florida). Forestland covers some 19.4m. acres and lumbering is the most important economic activity in the north of the state. Softwoods account for the whole of the state's timber production.

In 2007 the value of Arizona's non-fuel mineral production was, at US $7,380m., the highest in the USA, accounting for 10.9% of the nation's total. The state ranks first for copper, with 62% of total US production in 2004, and was also the leading state for molybdenum, ranking second for gemstones and pumice/pumicite. It was ranked third for perlite and construction sand and gravel, seventh for silver and 10th for gold. Copper accounted for 64% of the state's total mineral production in 2004. Arizona produced just under 8.0m. short tons of coal in 2007.

Manufacturing is among the state's foremost economic activities, with abundant supplies of land, electricity and labour. The principal manufacturing sectors include food, chemicals, fabricated metals and computer, electronic and transportation equipment. In 2006 the total value of Arizona's manufacturing shipments was US $50,007m., of which 54% was added during manufacture. The state ranked 31st in the USA in terms of the value of its shipments in that year.

Tourism and travel is an important industry for Arizona in terms of receipts; in 2004 domestic travel expenditures totalled US $9,974m. While the majority of visitors were US citizens, Arizona also attracted significant numbers of tourists from Mexico.

Direct general expenditures by the state government in 2006 reached US $25,731m., with total general revenue at $23,155m. Federal transfers stood at $7,607m., while revenue from taxes totalled $11,890m. Arizona received $8,190m. in federal aid in 2006.

CONSTITUTION AND GOVERNMENT

Arizona's only Constitution was adopted in 1911 and became effective on 14 February 1912. An amendment to the Constitution proposed by the Legislature must be passed by a two-thirds' majority in each house; approval by a majority of state voters is then required to ratify the amendment. The Governor is elected to serve a four-year term, with the Secretary of State succeeding to the office of Governor in the event of a vacancy or incapacity. Arizona is the only state to elect a Mine Inspector. There are 30 senators and 60 representatives in the state Legislature, both houses being re-elected together every two years. Regular legislative sessions commence annually in January and there is no statutory limit to their length. Bills must be passed by both houses and signed by the Governor to become law. During session the Governor has five days in which to consider a bill, after which it becomes law unless vetoed. After adjournment of the session a bill becomes law unless vetoed by the Governor within 10 days. The Governor's veto may be overridden by a two-thirds' vote from the elected members of each house. Legislation becomes effective 90 days after adjournment of the session. In the 2006 gubernatorial election the Democratic incumbent, Janet Napolitano, was re-elected with 63% of the votes cast. Over 1.9m. people voted in the 2008 presidential election, when an estimated 54% of the votes cast were for the Republican candidate, Arizona Senator John McCain. Arizona has 15 administrative counties.

Elected Executive Branch Officials

Governor (2007–11): JANET NAPOLITANO (Dem.).

Secretary of State: JAN BREWER (Rep.).

Attorney-General: TERRY GODDARD (Dem.).

Treasurer: DEAN MARTIN (Rep.).

Superintendent of Public Instruction: TOM HORNE (Rep.).

Mine Inspector: JOE HART (Rep.).

Selected Government Addresses

Office of the Governor: Capitol Executive Tower, West Wing, 9th Floor, 1700 West Washington St, Phoenix, AZ 85007; tel. (602) 542-4331; fax (602) 542-1381; internet www.governor.state.az.us.

Office of the Secretary of State: Capitol Executive Tower, West Wing, 7th Floor, 1700 West Washington St, Phoenix, AZ 85007-2888; tel. (602) 542-4285; fax (602) 542-1575; internet azsos.gov.

Office of the Attorney-General: 1275 West Washington St, Phoenix, AZ 85007; tel. (602) 542-5025; fax (602) 542-4085; e-mail aginfo@azag.gov; internet www.azag.gov.

Office of the Treasurer: Capitol Executive Tower, West Wing, 1st Floor, 1700 West Washington St, Phoenix, AZ 85007; tel. (602) 604-7800; fax (602) 542-7176; e-mail info@aztreasury.gov; internet www.aztreasury.gov.

Department of Education: 1535 West Jefferson St, Phoenix, AZ 85007; tel. (602) 542-5393; fax (602) 542-5440; internet www.azed.gov; headed by the Supt of Public Instruction.

Office of the Mine Inspector: 1700 West Washington St, 4th Floor, Phoenix, AZ 85007; tel. (602) 542-5971; fax (602) 542-5335; internet www.asmi.state.az.us; headed by the Mine Inspector.

Department of Agriculture: 1688 West Adams St, Phoenix, AZ 85007; tel. (602) 542-4373; fax (602) 542-0111; internet www.azda.gov; Dir DONALD BUTLER.

Department of Commerce: Executive Tower, Suite 600, 1700 West Washington St, Phoenix, AZ 85007; tel. (602) 771-1100; e-mail arizonadepartmentofcommerce@azcommerce.com; internet www.azcommerce.com; Dir JAN LESHER.

Department of Corrections: 1601 West Jefferson St, Phoenix, AZ 85007; tel. (602) 542-5886; fax (602) 542-3965; e-mail paccess@azcorrections.gov; internet www.azcorrections.gov; Dir DORA B. SCHRIRO.

Department of Economic Security: 1717 West Jefferson St, 050Z-1, Rm 119, Phoenix, AZ 85007; tel. (602) 542-4296; fax (602) 542-8457; e-mail fvender@azdes.gov; internet www.azdes.gov; Dir TRACY WAREING.

Department of Emergency and Military Affairs: 5636 East McDowell Rd, Phoenix, AZ 85008-3495; tel. (602) 267-2710; fax (602) 267-2715; internet www.azdema.gov; Adj.-Gen. Maj.-Gen. DAVID P. RATACZAK.

Department of Environmental Quality: 1110 West Washington St, Phoenix, AZ 85007; tel. (602) 771-2300; fax (602) 771-2270; internet www.azdeq.gov; Dir STEPHEN A. OWENS.

Department of Health Services: 150 North 18th Ave, Phoenix, AZ 85007; tel. (602) 542-1000; fax (602) 542-0883; e-mail webmaster@azdhs.gov; internet www.azdhs.gov; Dir JANUARY CONTRERAS (acting).

Department of Insurance: 2910 North 44th St, Suite 210, Phoenix, AZ 85018-7269; tel. (602) 364-3100; e-mail info@id.state.az.us; internet www.id.state.az.us; Dir CHRISTINA URIAS.

Department of Land: 1616 West Adams St, Phoenix, AZ 85007; tel. (602) 542-4631; fax (602) 542-2590; e-mail inquiry@land.state.az.us; internet www.land.state.az.us; Commr MARK WINKLEMAN.

Department of Mines and Mineral Resources: 1502 West Washington St, Phoenix, AZ 85007; tel. (602) 771-1600; fax (602) 771-1616; e-mail madan.singh@mines.az.gov; internet www.admmr.state.az.us; Dir Dr MADAN M. SINGH.

Department of Public Safety: 2102 West Encanto Blvd, POB 6638, Phoenix, AZ 85005-6638; tel. (602) 223-2000; fax (602) 223-2917; e-mail pio@azdps.gov; internet www.azdps.gov; Dir ROGER VANDERPOOL.

Department of Revenue: 1600 West Monroe St, Phoenix, AZ 85007-2650; tel. (602) 716-6090; fax (602) 542-4772; internet www.azdor.gov; Dir GALE GARRIOTT.

Department of Transportation: 206 South 17th Ave, Phoenix, AZ 85007; tel. (602) 712-7355; e-mail info@azdot.gov; internet www.azdot.gov; Dir VICTOR MENDEZ.

Office of Tourism: 1110 West Washington St, Suite 155, Phoenix, AZ 85007; tel. (602) 364-3700; fax (602) 364-3701; e-mail memmermann@azot.gov; internet www.azot.com; Dir MARGIE EMMERMANN.

Legislature
(August 2008)

Senate

Rep. 17; Dem. 13; Total 30

President: TIM BEE (Rep.).

President Pro Tempore: ROBERT BLENDU (Rep.).

Secretary: CHARMION BILLINGTON.

House of Representatives

Rep. 33; Dem. 27; Total 60

Speaker: JAMES P. (JIM) WEIERS (Rep.).

Speaker Pro Tempore: BOB ROBSON (Rep.).

Clerk: NORMAN MOORE.

Arkansas

Gross Area: 137,732 sq km (53,179 sq miles).

Resident Population (1 July 2007, estimate): 2,834,797.

State Capital, Principal City: Little Rock (estimated population 184,422 at 1 July 2006).

LOCATION, TOPOGRAPHY AND CLIMATE

The State of Arkansas (nicknamed 'The Natural State') lies in the south of the USA. Its borders are formed by Missouri to the north, Tennessee and Mississippi to the east, Louisiana to the south and Texas and Oklahoma to the west. The south-east is low-lying and fertile and forms part of both the Gulf Coastal Plain and the Mississippi Alluvial Plain. The Mississippi River, which forms the eastern boundary of Arkansas, is fed by numerous rivers running across the state from the forested uplands in the north-west, where the Arkansas River divides the Ozark Plateau from the Ouachita Mountains. The highest point in the state is Magazine Mountain, at 839 m (2,753 ft). Arkansas has a temperate climate.

HISTORICAL BACKGROUND

When the Spanish arrived in Arkansas in 1541, Native American (Amerindian) tribes occupying the area included Quapaw, Caddo, Osage, Choctaw and Cherokee. The first white settlement was established by the French in 1686 at Arkansas Post. Arkansas, as part of Louisiana, came under Spanish control in 1762, was returned to the French in 1800, and was transferred to the USA by the Louisiana Purchase of 1803. In 1819 Arkansas became a territory, joining the Union as the 25th state on 15 June 1836. During the Civil War Arkansas was on the side of the Confederacy. It was at the forefront of national politics in 1957 when President Dwight Eisenhower sent troops to enforce a federal court order to integrate the Central High School at Little Rock, which had maintained segregation on the orders of the Democratic Governor, Orval E. Faubus. Faubus served six terms as Governor until 1966, when Winthrop Rockefeller became the first Republican Governor since post-Civil War Reconstruction. The Democratic Governor of Arkansas, William (Bill) Clinton, was elected to the presidency in 1992 and again in 1996.

ECONOMY

Gross domestic product by state was US $95,371m. in 2007. Manufacturing, wholesale and retail trade, agriculture and mining are the principal economic activities in Arkansas. The state had an average per-head income of $30,100 in 2007, the fourth lowest in the country. In that year 17.9% of the population (the fourth highest proportion among the states) were living below the poverty threshold. In mid-2008 Arkansas's civilian labour force numbered 1,397,600, while its unemployment rate was 4.9% (68,200 people). Of those employed in 2007, 5.4% were unionized, with 6.5% covered by union agreements.

In 2002 cropland covered 9.6m. acres (3.9m. ha). Some 43.3% of total cropland was irrigated. There were 46,500 farms in 2007, with an average size of 308 acres, while total land in farms was estimated at 14.3m. acres. Crops supplied 43% of farm marketings in 2007, while livestock and livestock products contributed 57%. Principal commodities produced in that year, in order of marketing receipts, were broilers, rice, soybeans, and cotton. The state ranked second for its broiler production (after Georgia) in 2007. Arkansas was the USA's largest producer of rice in 2007, and it also ranked third for production of cotton (behind Texas and California) and seventh for chicken eggs in that year. The state was the fourth largest producer of turkeys in 2007. Soybeans are also an important cash crop. Forestland covered 18.8m. acres in 2002. Almost all of this was commercial timberland—the state ranked third in lumber production in 2004 with a total of 2,990m. board feet, 81% of which was softwood production. Fish (especially catfish and minnow) farming is also an important agricultural activity. Arkansas ranked third for catfish production in 2005, behind Mississippi and Alabama.

In 2007 Arkansas's non-fuel mineral production was valued at US $913m., with the state ranked 26th in the USA. In 2007 Arkansas ranked first in the nation for bromine production (Michigan was the only other US producer). The state was also the sole producer of silica. Other important minerals included crushed stone, portland cement, construction sand and gravel, lime, tripoli (ranked third) and gemstones and gypsum (ranked fifth). The state possesses the USA's only diamond field and also produces crude petroleum, coal (for production of which it ranked 26th among the states) and natural gas.

In terms of its value of shipments, Arkansas ranked 27th in the nation in 2006. Manufacturing activity is dominated (in terms of value added) by food, paper, fabricated and primary metal products and electronic equipment. The total value of manufacturing shipments in 2006 was US $60,674m., of which 45% was added during manufacture.

Domestic travel expenditures totalled US $4,281m. in 2004. Total general expenditures by the state government amounted to $14,370m. in 2006. Total general revenue was $13,701m., of which $4,267m. was from federal government and $7,016m. was derived from taxes. Arkansas received $4,335m. in federal aid in 2006.

CONSTITUTION AND GOVERNMENT

The current Constitution of Arkansas is the state's fifth and became effective on 30 October 1874. Amendments to the Constitution, which are proposed by the General Assembly (the state legislature), must be approved by the majority of elected members in each house and then ratified by a majority of voters. The Governor and Lieutenant-Governor are elected separately to serve four-year terms. There are 35 senators and 100 representatives in the General Assembly, serving terms of four and two years, respectively. Alternate halves of the Senate are elected every two years. Regular legislative sessions take place biennially in odd-numbered years beginning in January, and last for 60 days; sessions may be extended beyond this limit with the approval of two-thirds of the members of both houses. After a bill has been approved by both houses of the General Assembly, it has to be considered by the Governor. During session the Governor has five days to consider a bill, after which it becomes law unless vetoed. After session a bill becomes law if not vetoed within 20 days. A gubernatorial veto may be overridden by majority votes by the elected members in each house. Enacted legislation becomes effective 90 days after adjournment of the session. In 2006 the Democratic candidate, Mike Beebe, won the gubernatorial election with 55% of the vote. The Republicans were successful in the 2008 presidential election, when they secured some 59% of the votes cast in the state. Arkansas has 75 administrative counties.

Elected Executive Branch Officials

Governor (2007–13): MIKE BEEBE (Dem.).

Lieutenant-Governor: BILL HALTER (Dem.).

Secretary of State: CHARLIE DANIELS (Dem.).

Attorney-General: DUSTIN MCDANIEL (Dem.).

Treasurer: MARTHA SHOFFNER (Dem.).

Auditor: JIM WOOD (Dem.).

Commissioner of State Lands: MARK WILCOX (Dem.).

Selected Government Addresses

Office of the Governor: State Capitol Bldg, Rm 250, Little Rock, AR 72201; tel. (501) 682-2345; fax (501) 682-1382; internet www.governor.arkansas.gov.

Office of the Lieutenant-Governor: State Capitol Bldg, Suite 270, Little Rock, AR 72201-1061; tel. (501) 682-2144; fax (501) 682-2894; internet ltgovernor.arkansas.gov.

Office of the Secretary of State: State Capitol Bldg, Rm 256, Little Rock, AR 72201; tel. (501) 682-1010; fax (501) 682-3510; e-mail general_info@sos.arkansas.gov; internet www.sosweb.state.ar.us.

Office of the Attorney-General: 323 Center St, Suite 200, Little Rock, AR 72201; tel. (501) 682-2007; fax (501) 682-8084; e-mail oag@ag.state.ar.us; internet www.ag.state.ar.us.

Office of the Treasurer: State Capitol Bldg, Rm 220, Little Rock, AR 72201; tel. (501) 682-5888; fax (501) 682-3820; internet www.state.ar.us/treasury.

Office of the Auditor: 1401 West Capitol Ave, Suite 325, Little Rock, AR 72201-1096; tel. (501) 682-6030; fax (501) 682-2521; e-mail info@auditorjimwood.org; internet www.auditorjimwood.org.

Office of the Commissioner of State Lands: State Capitol Bldg, Rm 109, Little Rock, AR 72201; tel. (501) 324-9222; fax (501) 324-9421; e-mail land@cosl.org; internet www.cosl.org.

Department of Correction: POB 8707, Pine Bluff, AR 71611-8707; tel. (870) 267-6999; fax (870) 267-6258; e-mail adc.webmaster@arkansas.gov; internet www.adc.arkansas.gov; Dir LARRY B. NORRIS.

Department of Economic Development: 1 Capitol Mall, Rm 4C300, Little Rock, AR 72201; tel. (501) 682-1121; fax (501) 682-7394; e-mail info@arkansasedc.com; internet www.arkansasedc.com; Exec. Dir MARIA HALEY.

Department of Education: Arch Ford Education Bldg, 4 Capitol Mall, Little Rock, AR 72201; tel. (501) 682-4475; e-mail ade.communications@arkansas.gov; internet arkansased.org; Commr Dr T. KENNETH JAMES.

Department of Finance and Administration: DFA Bldg, Suite 401, 1509 West 7th St, POB 3278, Little Rock, AR 72203-3278; tel. (501) 682-2242; fax (501) 682-1029; e-mail richard.weiss@dfa.state.ar.us; internet www.state.ar.us/dfa; Dir RICHARD WEISS.

Department of Health: 4815 West Markham St, Little Rock, AR 72205; tel. (501) 661-2000; fax (501) 671-1450; internet www.healthyarkansas.com; Dir Dr PAUL HALVERSON.

Department of Highways and Transportation: 10324 Interstate 30, POB 2261, Little Rock, AR 72203-2261; tel. (501) 569-2000; fax (501) 569-2400; e-mail info@arkansashighways.com; internet www.arkansashighways.com; Dir DAN FLOWERS.

Department of Insurance: 1200 West Third St, Little Rock, AR 72201-1904; tel. (501) 371-2600; fax (501) 371-2618; e-mail sandy.currington@arkansas.gov; internet insurance.arkansas.gov; Commr JULIE BENAFIELD BOWMAN.

Department of Labor: 10421 West Markham St, Little Rock, AR 72205; tel. (501) 682-4500; fax (501) 682-4535; e-mail asklabor@arkansas.gov; internet www.state.ar.us/labor; Dir JAMES L. SALKELD.

Department of the Military: Camp Robinson, North Little Rock, AR 72199-9600; tel. (501) 212-5001; fax (501) 212-5009; e-mail christopher.heathscott@ar.ngb.army.mil; internet www.arguard.org; Adj.-Gen. Maj.-Gen. WILLIAM D. WOFFORD.

Department of Parks and Tourism: 1 Capitol Mall, Room 4A-900, Little Rock, AR 72201; tel. (501) 682-7777; fax (501) 682-1364; e-mail info@arkansas.com; internet www.arkansas.com; Exec. Dir RICHARD W. DAVIES.

Department of State Police: 1 State Police Plaza Dr., Little Rock, AR 72209; tel. (501) 618-8000; fax (501) 618-8222; e-mail info@asp.state.ar.us; internet www.asp.state.ar.us; Dir Col WINFORD E. PHILLIPS.

Development Finance Authority: 423 Main St, Suite 500, POB 8023, Little Rock, AR 72203-8023; tel. (501) 682-5900; fax (501) 682-5939; e-mail drose@adfa.state.ar.us; internet www.state.ar.us/adfa; Pres. MAC DODSON.

State Bank Department: Sedgwick Center, 400 Hardin Rd, Suite 100, AR 72211-3502; tel. (501) 324-9019; fax (501) 324-9028; e-mail asbd@banking.state.ar.us; internet www.arkansas.gov/bank; Commr CANDACE A. FRANKS.

General Assembly
(August 2008)

Senate

Dem. 27; Rep. 8; Total 35

President: Lt-Gov. BILL HALTER (Dem.).

President Pro Tempore: JACK CRITCHER (Dem.).

Secretary: ANN CORNWELL.

House of Representatives

Dem. 75; Rep. 25; Total 100

Speaker: BENNY C. PETRUS (Dem.).

Speaker Pro Tempore: SCOTT SULLIVAN (Dem.).

Chief Clerk: JO RENSHAW.

California

Gross Area: 423,970 sq km (163,696 sq miles).

Resident Population (1 July 2007, estimate): 36,553,215.

State Capital: Sacramento.

Principal Cities: (estimated population at 1 July 2006)

Los Angeles	3,849,378	Oxnard	184,463
San Diego	1,256,951	Moreno Valley	183,571
San Jose	929,936	Ontario	173,351
San Francisco	744,041	Rancho Cucamonga	170,714
Long Beach	472,494	Santa Clarita	168,008
Fresno	466,714	Garden Grove	166,296
Sacramento (capital)	453,781	Oceanside	165,803
Oakland	397,067	Fontana	170,099
Santa Ana	340,024	Santa Rosa	154,212
Anaheim	334,425	Pomona	154,271
Bakersfield	308,392	Corona	150,253
Riverside	293,761	Salinas	145,032
Stockton	290,141	Pasadena	144,133
Chula Vista	212,756	Torrance	142,350
Modesto	205,721	Lancaster	140,804
Fremont	201,691	Hayward	140,606
Glendale	199,463	Palmdale	138,790
San Bernardino	198,985	Orange	135,070
Huntington Beach	194,436	Escondido	133,510
Irvine	193,956	Fullerton	132,918

LOCATION, TOPOGRAPHY AND CLIMATE

The State of California (nicknamed 'The Golden State') lies in the west of the USA, on the Pacific Ocean. It is bordered by Oregon to the north and Nevada and Arizona to the east. There is an international border with Mexico in the south. The Sierra Nevada mountain range runs parallel to the coast, in the east of the state, with the Mojave Desert beyond. The highest and lowest points of the 48 conterminous states of the USA occur in this area, within a relatively short distance of each other: Mount Whitney in the Sierra Nevada range has an elevation of 4,418 m (14,494 ft), and Death Valley in the Mojave Desert is 86 m (282 ft) below sea level. The Central Valley, enclosed to the east by the Sierra Nevada and to the west by the Coast Ranges, is drained in the north by the Sacramento River and in the south by the San Joaquin River. Both rivers flow into the Pacific Ocean at San Francisco Bay, the only point at which the Coast Ranges are broken. There are two groups of islands off the coast of California: the Santa Barbara Islands and the Farallon Islands. The Salton Sea, in the extreme south of the state, and Lake Tahoe, on the border with Nevada, are among the USA's largest natural lakes. The climate in California is varied, but generally summers are long, hot and dry, and winters are mild and wet. Temperatures are colder in high regions.

HISTORICAL BACKGROUND

When the first European explorers arrived in the 16th century California was inhabited by more than 100 Native American (Amerindian) tribes. The first permanent settlement, a Spanish mission at San Diego, was founded in 1769, and in 1822 the area came under Mexican control. US traders and settlers arrived in the 19th century and in 1846 revolted against Mexican rule; in 1848, at the end of the Mexican War, California was ceded to the USA under the Treaty of Guadalupe-Hidalgo. In the same year gold was discovered along the America River and the gold rush, which lasted into the 1870s, began, leading to a rapid expansion of the population. On 9 September 1850 California was admitted to the Union as the 31st state and, under the Compromise of 1850, slavery was abolished. The transcontinental railway was completed in 1869, further augmenting the number of new settlers. A major earthquake in 1906 virtually demolished the city of San Francisco, but did nothing to deter the influx of settlers; by 1963 California had the highest population of any state in the USA.

ECONOMY

California leads the USA in many areas of economic activity and has a larger economy, in terms of gross state product, than any other state and most countries of the world. In 2007 gross domestic product by state totalled US $1,812,968m. Agriculture, entertainment (in particular, the film industry), manufacturing, services, trade and tourism are the principal industries, and California also possesses the largest aerospace industry in the USA. In 2007 the state had an average per-head income of $41,580, eighth highest in the nation, while 12.4% of the population were living below the poverty line. The civilian labour force numbered 18,555,300 in mid-2008 and unemployment affected 1,411,900 workers (7.6%) the fourth highest rate among the states. Of the total number of employees in 2007, 16.7% were union members and 17.8% were covered by union agreements.

Land in farms accounted for 26.3% of the state's total land area in 2005. In 2007 farmland covered 26.2m. acres (10.6m. ha), when the average size of farms was 349 acres (141 ha) and there were an estimated 75,000 farms. In 2007 71% of California's total farm receipts came from crops and 29% from livestock and livestock products. Principal commodities farmed were dairy products, greenhouse and nursery products, grapes (used for the manufacture of wine, raisins, table grapes and processing), lettuce and almonds. For all of these, California ranks first among the states; it is the only producer of almonds. In 2006 California was also the most important US producer of milk, and led production of fruits and nuts, hay, onions, strawberries, tomatoes and vegetables in 2007. The state ranked second in the production of cotton, oranges and rice, behind Texas, Florida and Arkansas, respectively, in that year. Some 72.3% of total cropland was under irrigation in 2002 and agriculture continued to consume a very high proportion of the state's water supplies. Forestland covered 40.2m. acres in 2002, accounting for more than 5% of the nation's total forestland—a proportion surpassed only by Alaska. The state was ranked fifth for lumber production in 2004, with the wood-products industry important to the state economy. Commercial fishing is well established: in 2006 California's catch was valued at US $130m. Salmon, swordfish and tuna are the principal species fished. The state was the USA's second most important supplier of salmon in 2004 (behind Alaska) and its third leading producer of trout (behind Idaho and North Carolina).

With a value of US $4,390m. in 2007, California was the third highest-ranked producer of non-fuel minerals. Industrial minerals account for more than 95% of total production in the state, with the rest mostly gold, silver and iron ore production. Leading industrial minerals were construction sand and gravel and portland cement (for both of which California consistently ranks first nation-wide), boron minerals and diatomite, for which it also ranked first in 2007, and crushed stone. California remains the only producer of boron among the states. In 2004 it was ranked second for masonry cement and soda ash, third for feldspar, and fourth for pumice and natural gemstones. Its relative importance for gold production increased in 2004 from sixth to fifth overall. The state was also the third largest producer of petroleum in the nation in 2005, and ranked ninth for the output of natural gas in that year.

California dominates the USA in terms of manufacturing production, which is centred in the metropolitan areas surrounding San Francisco and Los Angeles. The total value of shipments in 2006 was US $466,573m., of which 51% was added during manufacture. The state ranked second in the USA in terms of value of shipments in that year. Principal manufactured products include food, apparel, paper, chemicals, plastics and rubber, computers and electronic equipment. Silicon Valley is the name given to the concentration of high-technology industries on the San Francisco peninsula. The main manufacture of the Valley is semi-conductor chips. The petroleum and coal and printing and publishing industries are also significant.

California's banking industry has continued to thrive. Total assets of commercial banks stood at US $573,800m. in 2006, ranking the state fourth nation-wide. The Pacific Stock Exchange is situated in San Francisco.

Tourism, both domestic and international, is a major industry in California. Domestic travel expenditures were US $65,700m. in 2004, with the state ranked first in terms of tourism receipts.

Total general expenditures by the state government in 2006 were US $225,317m. Total general revenue was $188,444m., with federal government revenue contributing $48,287m. and taxes $111,347m. California received $46,033m. in federal aid in 2006.

CONSTITUTION AND GOVERNMENT

California's current Constitution is its second and became effective on 4 July 1879. A constitutional amendment proposed by the bicameral Legislature has to be approved by two-thirds of the members of both houses and then ratified by a majority of voters. The Governor and Lieutenant-Governor are elected separately for terms of four years, and limited to two terms in office. There are 40 senators and 80 assembly members in the Legislature, serving terms of four and two years, respectively. Alternate halves of the Senate are elected every two years. Term limits, enacted by referendum, limit senators to two terms in office and assembly members to three terms. Regular sessions of the Legislature begin in the January following an election and last until November of the following year. Bills may be introduced by either house; they are then referred to committees and read three times before each house. Before being presented to the Governor, bills must be approved by an absolute majority in each house; a bill becomes law unless vetoed by the Governor within 12 days. A gubernatorial veto may be overridden by a two-thirds' vote of the elected members of each house. Legislation usually becomes effective in the January following enactment, providing a 90-day period has elapsed. In the November 2002 gubernatorial election the Democratic incumbent, Gray Davis, was re-elected with a 47% share of the votes cast. However, on 7 October 2003, owing to serious concerns over his management of the economy, Davis was recalled as Governor. He was succeeded as Governor by Republican candidate and film actor Arnold Schwarzenegger. (According to state law, a Governor must contest a recall vote if demanded by a number of signatories equivalent to 12% of participants in the last gubernatorial election.) Schwarzenegger, one of 135 candidates, received 50.5% of the final vote (his closest rival, Lieutenant-Governor Cruz Bustamante, won 32.8% of the ballot). He was re-elected in 2006, securing 56% of the vote. In the 2008 presidential election, in which some 10m. people voted, the Democrats retained the largest share of the vote, with some 61%. California is divided into 58 administrative counties.

Elected Executive Branch Officials

Governor (2007–11): ARNOLD SCHWARZENEGGER (Rep.).

Lieutenant-Governor: JOHN GARAMENDI (Dem.).

Secretary of State: DEBRA BOWEN (Dem.).

Attorney-General: EDMUND G. (JERRY) BROWN, Jr (Dem.).

Treasurer: BILL LOCKYER (Dem.).

Controller: JOHN CHIANG (Dem.).

Insurance Commissioner: STEVE POIZNER (Rep.).

Superintendent of Public Instruction: JACK O'CONNELL (Dem.).

Selected Government Addresses

Office of the Governor: State Capitol, 1st Floor, Sacramento, CA 95814; tel. (916) 445-2841; fax (916) 588-3160; e-mail www.govmail.ca.gov; internet gov.ca.gov.

Office of the Lieutenant-Governor: State Capitol, Rm 1114, Sacramento, CA 95814; tel. (916) 445-8994; fax (916) 323-4998; internet www.ltg.ca.gov.

Office of the Secretary of State: 1500 11th St, Sacramento, CA 95814; tel. (916) 653-6814; fax (916) 653-4795; internet www.sos.ca.gov.

Office of the Attorney-General: 1300 First St, Suite 1101, POB 944255, Sacramento, CA 94244-2550; tel. (916) 322-3360; fax (916) 323-5341; internet ag.ca.gov.

Office of the Treasurer: 915 Capitol Mall, Suite C-15, POB 942809, Sacramento, CA 94209-0001; tel. (916) 653-2995; fax (916) 653-3125; internet www.treasurer.ca.gov.

Office of the Controller: 300 Capitol Mall, 18th Floor, POB 942850, Sacramento, CA 94250-5872; tel. (916) 445-2636; fax (916) 322-4404; internet www.sco.ca.gov.

Department of Insurance: 300 Capitol Mall, Suite 1700, Sacramento, CA 95814; tel. (916) 492-3500; fax (916) 445-5280; internet www.insurance.ca.gov; headed by the Insurance Commr.

Department of Education: 1430 North St, Sacramento, CA 95814-5901; tel. (916) 319-0800; fax (916) 319-0100; internet www.cde.ca.gov; headed by the Supt of Public Instruction.

Business, Transportation and Housing Agency: 980 Ninth St, Suite 2450, Sacramento, CA 95814-2719; tel. (916) 323-5400; fax (916) 323-5440; internet www.bth.ca.gov; Sec. DALE E. BONNER.

California Energy Commission: 1516 Ninth St, MS-29, Sacramento, CA 95814-5512; tel. and fax (916) 654-4287; e-mail mediaoffice@energy.state.ca.us; internet www.energy.ca.gov; Exec. Dir MELISSA JONES.

California Highway Patrol: 815 S St, POB 942898, Sacramento, CA 942898-0001; tel. and fax (916) 657-7261; e-mail webmaster@chp.ca.gov; internet www.chp.ca.gov; Commr J. A. FARROW.

Department of Corrections: 1515 S St, POB 942883, Sacramento, CA 94283-0001; tel. (916) 445-7682; fax (916) 323-2877; e-mail secretary@cdcr.ca.gov; internet www.cdcr.ca.gov; Sec. MATTHEW CATE.

Department of Employment Development: 800 Capitol Mall, MIC 83, Sacramento, CA 95814; tel. (916) 654-8210; fax (916) 657-5294; internet www.edd.ca.gov; Dir PATRICK W. HENNING.

Department of Finance: 915 L St, Sacramento, CA 95814; tel. (916) 445-3878; internet www.dof.ca.gov; Dir MICHAEL C. GENEST.

Department of Food and Agriculture: 1220 N St, Sacramento, CA 95814-5607; tel. (916) 654-0462; fax (916) 657-4240; e-mail cdfapublicaffairs@cdfa.ca.gov; internet www.cdfa.ca.gov; Sec. A. G. KAWAMURA.

Department of Transportation: 1120 N St, POB 942873, Sacramento, CA 94273-0001; tel. (916) 654-5266; fax (916) 653-3291; internet www.dot.ca.gov; Dir WILL KEMPTON.

Environmental Protection Agency: 1001 I St, POB 2815, Sacramento, CA 95812-2815; tel. (916) 323-2514; e-mail cepacomm@calepa.ca.gov; internet www.calepa.ca.gov; Sec. LINDA S. ADAMS.

Health and Human Services Agency: 1600 Ninth St, Rm 460, Sacramento, CA 95814-6404; tel. (916) 654-3454; fax (916) 654-3343; internet www.chhs.ca.gov; Sec. KIM BELSHÉ.

Lands Commission: 100 Howe Ave, Suite 100 South, Sacramento, CA 95825-8202; tel. (916) 574-1900; fax (916) 574-1810; e-mail thayerp@slc.ca.gov; internet www.slc.ca.gov; Exec. Officer PAUL D. THAYER.

National Guard: 9800 Goethe Rd, Sacramento, CA 95827; tel. (916) 854-3500; fax (916) 854-3671; e-mail generalinfo@ca.ngb.army.mil; internet www.calguard.ca.gov; Adj.-Gen. Maj.-Gen. WILLIAM H. WADE, II.

Public Utilities Commission: 505 Van Ness Ave, San Francisco, CA 94102-3298; tel. (415) 703-2782; fax (415) 703-1758; internet www.cpuc.ca.gov; Pres. MICHAEL R. PEEVEY.

Resources Agency: 1416 Ninth St, Suite 1311, Sacramento, CA 95814; tel. (916) 653-5656; fax (916) 653-8102; e-mail secretary@resources.ca.gov; internet resources.ca.gov; Sec. MIKE CHRISMAN.

Legislature
(August 2008)

Senate

Dem. 25; Rep. 15; Total 40

President: Lt-Gov. JOHN GARAMENDI (Dem.).

President Pro Tempore: DON PERATA (Dem.).

Secretary: GREG SCHMIDT.

Assembly

Dem. 48; Rep. 32; Total 80

Speaker: KAREN BASS (Dem.).

Speaker Pro Tempore: SALLY J. LIEBER (Dem.).

Chief Clerk: E. DOTSON WILSON.

Colorado

Gross Area: 269,601 sq km (104,094 sq miles).

Resident Population: (1 July 2007, estimate) 4,861,515.

State Capital: Denver.

Principal Cities: (estimated population at 1 July 2006)
Denver (capital) 566,974; Colorado Springs 372,437; Aurora 303,582; Lakewood 140,024; Fort Collins 129,467; Thornton 109,155; Westminster 105,753; Arvada 104,830; Pueblo 103,730.

LOCATION, TOPOGRAPHY AND CLIMATE

The state of Colorado (nicknamed 'The Centennial State') is in the west of the USA and is bordered by Wyoming to the north, Nebraska to the north-east and Kansas to the east. In the south-east corner of the state a relatively narrow strip of Oklahoma separates Colorado from Texas, while New Mexico lies to the south and Utah to the west. In the east about one-third of the state consists of high plateau, part of the western Great Plains, which rises towards the foothills of the Rocky Mountains in the centre of the state. The east and west slopes of the Rockies are separated by the Continental Divide, the range of mountain peaks that bisects the continent and traverses western Colorado from north to south. Colorado has the largest number of peaks over 14,000 ft of any state in the USA, the highest point being Mount Elbert at 4,399 m (14,433 ft). It is also the state with the highest mean elevation, at 6,800 ft. To the west of the mountains is mesa country—flat tableland with deep ravines and gorges. Six major rivers flow through Colorado: the Colorado, South Platte, North Platte, Rio Grande, Arkansas and Republican. Colorado has a highland continental climate, with wide seasonal (and daily) temperature variations—dry and sunny in summer, with cold, snowy winters in the high mountains.

HISTORICAL BACKGROUND

The earliest inhabitants of Colorado were the Anasazi, who settled around the Mesa Verde area; later Ute, Commanchero, Cheyenne, Arapaho and Kiowa peoples lived in the region. French explorers and Spanish gold prospectors arrived in the 18th century and the area passed from Spanish to French sovereignty. The USA acquired eastern Colorado in the Louisiana Purchase of 1803 and the rest of the state was taken from Mexico under the Treaty of Guadalupe Hidalgo in 1848. After the Mexican War US immigrants arrived in the area and the first permanent settlement was established at San Luis. Gold discoveries during the second half of the 19th century led to the founding of many mining towns, including Denver and Boulder, and a large increase in the population of European descent. Colorado fought for the Union during the Civil War. The 1860s saw a period of warfare against the native Indians, beginning with the so-called Sand Creek Massacre of 1864, in which more than 200 Cheyenne and Arapaho were killed, and ending with two severe Indian defeats, at Beecher Island (1868) and Summit Spring (1869). All the remaining Native American (Amerindian) population was later removed to Oklahoma. In 1861 the region was granted territorial status and Colorado entered the Union as the 38th state on 1 August 1876.

ECONOMY

Gross domestic product by state was US $236,324m. in 2007. Colorado's principal economic activities are manufacturing, construction, agriculture, wholesale and retail trade, services, finance, insurance and real estate, government and tourism. It also has an important mining industry. In 2007 per-head income in the state averaged $41,019, while 12.0% of the population were living below the poverty line in 2007. The state's civilian labour force numbered 2,792,300 in mid-2008, with an unemployment rate of 5.2% (144,600 persons). Of the total number of employees in 2007 some 8.7% were union members, with 9.2% covered by union agreements.

Cropland covered 11.5m. acres (4.7m. ha) in 2002. There were 30.7m. acres of farmland in 2007, when the state's 31,000 farms recorded an average size of 990 acres. Some 18.9% of cropland was irrigated in 2002. Livestock and livestock products provided 68% of farm marketings in 2007, with crops providing 32%. The principal agricultural products in that year were cattle and calves, dairy products, wheat and corn. In 2007 Colorado ranked third in production of lettuces among the states, and was fourth in production of cattle and calves in 2006. Forestland covered 21.6m. acres of the state in 2002, representing around 3% of total US timberland. However, there is relatively little commercial forestry activity. In 2004 135m. board feet of lumber were produced.

Colorado's non-fuel mineral production was valued at US $1,940m. in 2007, with the state ranked 11th in the USA. The majority of total state production consists of industrial minerals, especially construction sand and gravel, portland cement and crushed stone. Molybdenum, gold, silver and soda ash were also produced, with Colorado ranked second in production of molybdenum concentrates in 2004, third for soda ash and fourth for gold. The state's only zinc and lead mine closed in January 1999. The state is also an important producer of petroleum, natural gas (it was the USA's sixth largest producer in 2005) and coal (ranking seventh nationally in 2007).

Colorado is the location for much of the manufacturing activity of the Rocky Mountain states. The principal manufactured products are food and related products, chemicals, fabricated metals, machinery, computers and electrical goods, scientific instruments and transportation equipment. The total value of manufacturing shipments in 2006 was US $40,430m., of which 52% was added during manufacture. The state ranked 34th in the USA in terms of its value of shipments in that year.

Tourism is very important to the state: in 2004 domestic travel expenditures amounted to US $9,965m. Much of the tourist expenditure occurs in the winter months, owing to the popularity of the state for skiing.

Total general expenditures by the state government in 2006 were US $20,151m. Total general revenue was $17,493m., of which $4,657m. was from federal Government and $8,522m. from taxes. Colorado received a total of $4,751m. in federal aid in 2006.

CONSTITUTION AND GOVERNMENT

Colorado's only Constitution became effective on 1 August 1876. The Constitution may be amended if a proposal by the General Assembly, the bicameral state legislature, is passed by a two-thirds' vote in both houses, followed by approval by a majority of voters. The Governor and Lieutenant-Governor are elected together to serve a four-year term and may not serve more than two consecutive terms. There are 35 senators and 65 representatives in the General Assembly, serving terms of four and two years, respectively. Alternate halves of the Senate are re-elected every second year. Regular legislative sessions are held annually, beginning in January, and are limited to 120 days in even-numbered years. A bill may become law when it has been passed by a majority vote in each house and signed by the Governor. During session the Governor has 10 calendar days in which to consider a bill, after which it becomes law unless vetoed. Following the adjournment of the General Assembly a bill becomes law unless vetoed by the Governor within 30 calendar days. The Governor's veto may be overridden by a two-thirds' vote by elected legislators. Legislation becomes effective immediately, unless a date is specified. In the 2006 gubernatorial election the Democratic candidate, Bill Ritter, was elected with 56% of the votes cast. The Democrats were also successful in the presidential election of 2008, when they secured over 1m. votes for an estimated share of 53%, compared with an estimated 45% for the Republicans. Colorado has 64 administrative counties.

Elected Executive Branch Officials

Governor (2007–11): BILL RITTER (Dem.).

Lieutenant-Governor: BARBARA O'BRIEN (Rep.).

Secretary of State: MIKE COFFMAN (Rep.).

Attorney-General: JOHN SUTHERS (Rep.).

Treasurer: CARY KENNEDY (Dem.).

Selected Government Addresses

Office of the Governor: 136 State Capitol Bldg, Denver, CO 80203-1792; tel. (303) 866-2471; fax (303) 866-2003; internet www.colorado.gov/governor.

Office of the Lieutenant-Governor: 130 State Capitol Bldg, Denver, CO 80203-1792; tel. (303) 866-2087; fax (303) 866-5469; e-mail ltgovernor.obrien@state.co.us; internet www.colorado.gov/ltgovernor.

Office of the Secretary of State: 1700 Broadway, Denver, CO 80290; tel. (303) 894-2200; fax (303) 869-4860; e-mail administration@sos.state.co.us; internet www.sos.state.co.us.

Office of the Attorney-General: 1525 Sherman St, 7th Floor, Denver, CO 80203; tel. (303) 866-4500; fax (303) 866-5691; e-mail attorney.general@state.co.us; internet www.ago.state.co.us/.

Office of the Treasurer: 140 State Capitol Bldg, Denver, CO 80203; tel. (303) 866-2441; fax (303) 866-2123; e-mail treasurer.kennedy@state.co.us; internet www.colorado.gov/treasury.

Department of Agriculture: 700 Kipling St, Suite 4000, Lakewood, CO 80215-8000; tel. (303) 239-4100; fax (303) 239-4125; internet www.ag.state.co.us; Commr JOHN R. STULP.

Department of Corrections: 2862 South Circle Dr., Colorado Springs, CO 80906-4195; tel. (719) 579-9580; fax (719) 226-4755; e-mail pio@doc.state.co.us; internet www.doc.state.co.us; Exec. Dir ARISTEDES ZAVARAS.

Department of Education: 201 East Colfax Ave, Denver, CO 80203-1799; tel. (303) 866-6600; fax (303) 830-0793; e-mail commissioner@cde.state.co.us; internet www.cde.state.co.us; Commr DWIGHT D. JONES.

Department of Labor and Employment: 633 17th St, Suite 201, Denver, CO 80202-3660; tel. (303) 318-8000; fax (303) 318-8070; e-mail donald.j.mares@state.co.us; internet www.coworkforce.com; Exec. Dir DONALD J. MARES.

Department of Military and Veterans' Affairs: 6848 South Revere Pkwy, Centennial, CO 80112-6703; tel. (720) 250-1500; e-mail janelle.darnell@dmva.state.co.us; internet www.dmva.state.co.us; Adj.-Gen. Maj.-Gen. H. MICHAEL EDWARDS.

Department of Natural Resources: 1313 Sherman St, Rm 718, Denver, CO 80203; tel. (303) 866-3311; fax (303) 866-2115; e-mail feedback.dnr@state.co.us; internet dnr.state.co.us; Exec. Dir HARRIS SHERMAN.

Department of Public Health and the Environment: 4300 Cherry Creek Dr. South, Denver, CO 80246-1530; tel. (303) 692-2000; e-mail cdphe.information@state.co.us; internet www.cdphe.state.co.us; Exec. Dir JAMES B. MARTIN.

Department of Public Safety: 700 Kipling St, Suite 1000, Denver, CO 80215; tel. (303) 239-4400; fax (303) 239-4670; e-mail public.safety@cdps.state.co.us; internet www.cdpsweb.state.co.us; Exec. Dir PETER A. WEIR.

Department of Revenue: 1375 Sherman St, Rm 409, Denver, CO 80261; tel. (303) 866-3091; fax (303) 866-2400; e-mail edo@spike.dor.state.co.us; internet www.revenue.state.co.us; Exec. Dir ROXY HUBER.

Department of Transportation: 4201 East Arkansas Ave, Denver, CO 80222; tel. (303) 757-9011; fax (303) 757-9717; internet www.dot.state.co.us; Exec. Dir RUSSELL GEORGE.

Office of Economic Development and International Trade: 1625 Broadway, Suite 2700, Denver, CO 80202; tel. (303) 892-3840; fax (303) 892-3848; e-mail don.elliman@state.co.us; internet www.colorado.gov/cs/Satellite/OEDIT/OEDIT/1162927366334; Dir DON ELLIMAN.

General Assembly

(August 2008)

Senate

Dem. 20; Rep. 15; Total 35

President: PETER C. GROFF (Dem.).

President Pro Tempore: ABEL J. TAPIA (Dem.).

Secretary: KAREN GOLDMAN.

House of Representatives

Dem. 40; Rep. 25; Total 65

Speaker: ANDREW ROMANOFF (Dem.).

Speaker Pro Tempore: CHERI JAHN (Dem.).

Chief Clerk: MARILYN EDDINS.

Connecticut

Gross Area: 14,357 sq km (5,543 sq miles).

Resident Population (1 July 2007, estimate): 3,502,309.

State Capital: Hartford.

Principal Cities (estimated population at 1 July 2006): Bridgeport 137,912; New Haven 124,001; Hartford (capital) 124,512; Stamford 119,261; Waterbury 107,251.

LOCATION, TOPOGRAPHY AND CLIMATE

Connecticut (nicknamed 'The Constitution State') is one of the six states comprising New England and is bordered by Massachusetts to the north, Rhode Island to the east and New York to the west. The waters of Long Island Sound lie to the south. In the centre of Connecticut are lowlands formed by the river valleys of the Quinnipiac and Connecticut Rivers. The latter bisects the state from north to south and is the longest river in New England. The Eastern and Western Highlands lie to either side of the central lowlands, with the land gradually rising from the coastal plain to the north of the state, where the highest elevations are to be found. Connecticut's highest mountain is Mount Frissell, at 725 m (2,380 ft). The coast consists of gravel and sand beaches and rocky peninsulas. The climate is generally temperate.

HISTORICAL BACKGROUND

The first European settlers to arrive in Connecticut were the Dutch, who built a fort on the site of Hartford in 1633. The Dutch were shortly followed by the English, who established settlements at Windsor (1633), Wethersfield (1634) and Hartford (1636). In 1639 the three communities formed the Connecticut Colony, which received royal recognition in 1662, and, in 1665, was joined by the colony of New Haven (established in 1638). Most of the region's Algonquian-speaking Indian inhabitants were killed by European-spread diseases or during King Philip's War (1675–76). Connecticut operated almost as an autonomous republic during the colonial period and was an American patriot stronghold during the Revolution, the War of American Independence against British rule. Connecticut joined the Union as the fifth state on 9 January 1788. During the Civil War the state sent 55,000 men to fight for the Union.

ECONOMY

In 2007 gross domestic product by state totalled US $216,266m. Manufacturing, particularly defence-related, is the mainstay of the economy, while wholesale and retail trade, finance, insurance, real estate and services are other important industries. Connecticut residents enjoyed the second highest average per-head income in the country in 2007, behind that of the District of Columbia, at $54,984. It was estimated that just 7.9% of the population were living below the poverty line in that year—the second lowest figure among the states. Connecticut's civilian labour force totalled 1,929,300 in mid-2008, when the state's unemployment rate was 6.1% (affecting 117,900 persons). Trade-union membership was held by 15.6% of employees in 2007, although 16.6% were covered by union agreements.

Cropland and grassland pasture covered just 170,000 acres (68,800 ha) in 2002. The average size of the state's 4,200 farms in 2007 was also relatively low, at 86 acres; total land in farms amounted to 360,000 acres in that year. Around 6% of total cropland was irrigated in 2002. Crops made up 64% of farm marketings in 2007 and livestock and livestock products 36%, with the principal commodities in terms of marketing receipts being greenhouse and nursery products, dairy products, chicken eggs and aquaculture products. Forestland covered some 52% of the state's land area in 2002, and there is some lumber production. Connecticut's commercial fisheries achieved a catch valued at US $36.9m. in 2006. In 2004 the state was the fourth largest producer of scallops.

As in other states of New England, mining is very limited. Connecticut has no significant fuel resources, and non-fuel mining production is dominated by stone, sand and gravel. Some common clay and gemstones are also produced. The value of non-fuel mineral production was estimated at US $181m. in 2007.

Connecticut ranked 30th in the USA in 2006 in terms of its value of manufacturing shipments. Total shipments were valued at US $51,871m. in that year, of which 62% was added during manufacture. The state is a leading manufacturer of aircraft engines, submarine parts, helicopters and small firearms. Computer, electronic and electric equipment, medical and scientific instruments and pharmaceuticals are also significant.

Financial services are an important industry, with many insurance companies headquartered in Hartford. Tourism has also grown in importance, with domestic travel expenditures of US $7,132m. in 2004.

Total general expenditures by the state government in Connecticut amounted to US $20,675m. in 2006; general revenue in that year was $19,460m., of which $4,161m. was from federal government and $12,132m. derived from taxes. In 2006 Connecticut received $5,017m. in federal aid.

CONSTITUTION AND GOVERNMENT

Connecticut's current Constitution is its fourth and became effective on 30 December 1965. An amendment to the Constitution, proposed by the General Assembly, requires either a vote by three-quarters of the members of each house at one session, or a majority vote in each house in two sessions. After being passed by the General Assembly, the amendment must be ratified by a majority of the voters in the state. The Governor is elected jointly with the Lieutenant-Governor for a period of four years. The General Assembly has 36 senators and 151 representatives, with both houses serving two-year terms. Regular sessions are held annually, beginning in January or February. Once a bill has been approved by both houses, it is passed to the Governor for signing. After presentation to the Governor a bill will automatically become law unless vetoed within five days during legislative sessions, or within 15 days outside session. A gubernatorial veto may be overridden by a vote of two-thirds of the elected legislators in each house. Bills become effective on 1 October following enactment. Republican John Rowland was re-elected to a third term in the 2002 gubernatorial election, with 56% of the votes cast. Rowland resigned from office in June 2004, amid investigations of corruption, and was replaced as Governor in July by Lieutenant-Governor M. Jodi Rell. Rell subsequently won the gubernatorial election of 2006, securing 63% of the votes cast. In the 2008 presidential election some 60% of voters supported the Democrats.

Elected Executive Branch Officials

Governor (2007–11): M. JODI RELL (Rep.).

Lieutenant-Governor: MICHAEL FEDELE (Dem.).

Secretary of State: SUSAN BYSIEWICZ (Dem.).

Attorney-General: RICHARD BLUMENTHAL (Dem.).

Treasurer: DENISE L. NAPPIER (Dem.).

Comptroller: NANCY WYMAN (Dem.).

Selected Government Addresses

Office of the Governor: State Capitol, 210 Capitol Ave, Hartford, CT 06106; tel. (860) 566-4840; fax (860) 524-7397; e-mail governor.rell@ct.gov; internet www.ct.gov/governorrell.

Office of the Lieutenant-Governor: State Capitol, Rm 304, 210 Capitol Ave, Hartford, CT 06106; tel. (860) 524-7384; fax (860) 524-7304; e-mail ltgovernor.fedele@ct.gov; internet www.ct.gov/ltgovmfedele.

Office of the Secretary of State: State Capitol, Suite 104, 210 Capitol Ave, POB 150470, Hartford, CT 06115-0470; tel. (860) 509-6200; fax (860) 509-6209; e-mail valeriano.ramos@po.state.ct.us; internet www.sots.ct.gov.

Office of the Attorney-General: 55 Elm St, Hartford, CT 06106; tel. (860) 808-5318; fax (860) 808-5387; e-mail attorney.general@po.state.ct.us; internet www.ct.gov/ag.

Office of the Treasurer: 55 Elm St, Hartford, CT 06106; tel. (860) 702-3125; fax (860) 566-8820; e-mail state.treasurer@po.state.ct.us; internet www.state.ct.us/ott.

Office of the Comptroller: 55 Elm St, Hartford, CT 06106; tel. (860) 702-3300; fax (860) 702-3319; e-mail comptroller.wyman@po.state.ct.us; internet www.osc.state.ct.us.

Department of Agriculture: 165 Capitol Ave, Hartford, CT 06106; tel. (860) 713-2500; fax (860) 713-2514; e-mail ctdeptag@ct.gov; internet www.ct.gov/doag; Commr F. PHILIP PRELLI.

Department of Banking: 260 Constitution Plaza, Hartford, CT 06103-1800; tel. (860) 240-8299; fax (860) 240-8178; e-mail howard.pitkin@ct.gov; internet www.ct.gov/dob; Commr HOWARD F. PITKIN.

Department of Correction: 24 Wolcott Hill Rd, Wethersfield, CT 06109; tel. (860) 692-7780; fax (860) 692-7783; e-mail doc.pio@po.state.ct.us; internet www.ct.gov/doc; Commr THERESA C. LANTZ.

Department of Economic and Community Development: 505 Hudson St, Hartford, CT 06106-7106; tel. (860) 270-8000; fax (860) 721-7650; e-mail decd@po.state.ct.us; internet www.ct.gov/ecd; Commr JOAN MCDONALD.

Department of Education: State Office Bldg, 165 Capitol Ave, Hartford, CT 06106-1630; tel. (860) 713-6543; fax (860) 713-7001; e-mail ctsde.netservices@ct.gov; internet www.state.ct.us/sde; Commr Dr MARK K. MCQUILLAN.

Department of Environmental Protection: 79 Elm St, Hartford, CT 06106-5127; tel. (860) 424-3000; fax (860) 424-4053; e-mail dep.webmaster@ct.gov; internet www.ct.gov/dep; Commr GINA MCCARTHY.

Department of Insurance: 153 Market St, POB 816, Hartford, CT 06103-0816; tel. (860) 297-3800; fax (860) 566-7410; e-mail ctinsdept.administration@ct.gov; internet www.ct.gov/cid; Commr THOMAS R. SULLIVAN.

Department of Labor: 200 Folly Brook Blvd, Wethersfield, CT 06109; tel. (860) 263-6000; fax (860) 263-6536; e-mail dol.webhelp@ct.gov; internet www.ctdol.state.ct.us; Commr PATRICIA H. MAYFIELD.

Department of Public Health: 410–474 Capitol Ave, POB 340308, Hartford, CT 06134-0308; tel. (860) 509-8000; fax (860) 509-7286; e-mail webmaster.dph@ct.gov; internet www.ct.gov/dph; Commr J. ROBERT GALVIN.

Department of Public Safety: 1111 Country Club Rd, Middletown, CT 06457; tel. (860) 685-8190; fax (860) 685-8354; e-mail dps.feedback@po.state.ct.us; internet www.ct.gov/dps; Commr JOHN A. DENAHER, III.

Department of Public Utility Control: 10 Franklin Sq., New Britain, CT 06051; tel. (860) 827-1553; fax (860) 827-2613; e-mail dpuc.information@po.state.ct.us; internet www.ct.gov/dpuc; Chair. DONALD W. DOWNES.

Department of Revenue Services: 25 Sigourney St, Suite 2, Hartford, CT 06106-5032; tel. (860) 297-5962; fax (860) 297-5698; e-mail drs@po.state.ct.us; internet www.ct.gov/drs; Commr PAM LAW.

Department of Social Services: 25 Sigourney St, Hartford, CT 06106-5033; tel. (860) 424-5024; fax (860) 424-4960; e-mail pgr.dss@ct.gov; internet www.ct.gov/dss; Commr MICHAEL P. STARKOWSKI.

Department of Transportation: 2800 Berlin Turnpike, POB 317546, Newington, CT 06131-7546; tel. (860) 594-2000; e-mail judd.everhart@po.state.ct.us; internet www.ct.gov/dot; Commr JOSEPH F. MARIE.

Military Department: National Guard Armory, 360 Broad St, Hartford, CT 06105; tel. (860) 524-4991; fax (860) 548-3247; e-mail thaddeus.martin@ct.ngb.army.mil; internet www.ct.gov/mil; Adj.-Gen. Maj.-Gen. THADDEUS MARTIN.

General Assembly
(August 2008)

Senate

Dem. 23; Rep. 13; Total 36

President: Lt-Gov. MICHAEL FEDELE (Dem.).

President Pro Tempore: DONALD E. WILLIAMS, Jr (Dem.).

Chief Clerk: THOMAS P. SHERIDAN.

House of Representatives

Dem. 107; Rep. 44; Total 151

Speaker: JAMES A. AMANN (Dem.).

Chief Clerk: GAREY E. COLEMAN.

Delaware

Gross Area: 6,448 sq km (2,490 sq miles).

Resident Population (1 July 2007, estimate): 864,764.

State Capital: Dover (population 34,735 at 1 July 2006, estimate).

Principal City: Wilmington (population 72,826 at 1 July 2006, estimate).

LOCATION, TOPOGRAPHY AND CLIMATE

The State of Delaware (nicknamed 'The First State') lies on the east coast of the USA and is bordered by Pennsylvania to the north, the Delaware River (beyond which lies New Jersey), Delaware Bay and the Atlantic Ocean to the east and Maryland to the south and west. Most of the state lies within the Atlantic Coastal Plain. The rolling hills of the Piedmont Plateau in the north of the state slope down towards low-lying fertile plains and marshes in the east, with sandy beaches and dunes along the coast. Delaware's many rivers include the Christina, Appoquinimink, Leipsic and Nantichoke; there are also numerous fresh-water lakes. The state's mean elevation is 18 m (60 ft), the lowest in the USA. The climate is temperate and humid.

HISTORICAL BACKGROUND

When Henry Hudson, an English navigator in the pay of the Dutch West India Co, sailed up Delaware Bay in 1603, the region now known as Delaware was inhabited by Indians, including the Leni-Lanape (Delaware), Nautichoke and Assateague tribes. The first white settlement, Swanendael (present-day Lewes), was established in 1631 but was destroyed by Indians in the following year. Delaware was subsequently colonized by the Swedes and, again, the Dutch before coming under English (British) rule and being granted to William Penn by the Duke of York (later King James II) in 1682. Delaware was granted an elected assembly in 1704, but remained under Pennsylvania until the Revolution in 1776. On 7 December 1787 Delaware became the first state to ratify the federal Constitution. The state was on the side of the Union during the Civil War, although it had not abolished slavery and blacks were not enfranchised until 1890.

ECONOMY

Gross domestic product by state was US $60,118m. in 2007. Delaware's principal economic activities include chemicals production, agriculture, finance, tourism, transportation equipment production, automobile assembly and food-processing. In 2007 the state had an average per-head income of $40,058; 10.5% of the population were estimated to be living below the poverty threshold in that year. Delaware's civilian labour force numbered 452,000 in mid-2008. Unemployment in that year was 4.5% (20,600 persons). In 2007 12.0% of those employed were members of trade unions, with 12.8% covered by union agreements.

In 2002 cropland and grassland pasture covered some 463,700 acres (187,700 ha) of the state. The average size of the state's 2,200 farms in 2007 was 234 acres; farmland accounted for 515,000 acres in that year. Some 79% of farm sales were of livestock and livestock products in 2007, with crops accounting for the remaining 21%. The principal agricultural products were broilers, corn, soybeans and greenhouse and nursery products. Delaware was the USA's seventh largest producer of broilers in 2007. Forestland covers approximately 383,000 acres of the state, with almost all of this being commercial timberland. Fishing was traditionally important to the state, but the value of the catch by 2006 was only US $5.7m.

Delaware has the smallest output of minerals of any state. In 2007 the value of non-fuel mineral production was US $33.8m. Principal contributors to this total were construction sand and gravel and magnesium compounds, with the latter used in the manufacture of chemical and pharmaceutical products. Gemstones are mined in the state by hobbyists. The state has no known fossil-fuel resources.

Delaware ranked 36th in the nation in terms of its value of shipments in 2006. Chemicals and allied products are by far the state's most important manufactures, with the chemical company DuPont, based in Wilmington, one of the largest industrial corporations in the USA. Other important manufactures include food and kindred products, rubber and plastic products, scientific instruments and paper products. In 2006 the total value of Delaware's manufacturing shipments was US $24,424m., of which some 32% was added during manufacture.

Travel and tourism is one of the state's most important industries; nevertheless, at US $1,181m. in 2004, domestic travel expenditures were the lowest of all the states.

Total general expenditures by the Delaware state government in 2006 were US $6,520m. General revenue totalled $5,955m., of which $1,177m. was from federal government and $2,861m. was derived from taxes. In 2006 Delaware received $1,194m. in federal aid.

CONSTITUTION AND GOVERNMENT

Delaware's current Constitution is its fourth and became effective on 10 June 1897. Constitutional amendments proposed by the General Assembly have to be approved by two-thirds of the elected members of each house in two successive sessions, with an election in between. Delaware is the only state where a constitutional amendment need not be ratified by the electorate. The Governor is elected separately from the Lieutenant-Governor to serve a four-year term, and may hold office no more than twice. There are 21 senators and 41 representatives in the state General Assembly, serving four- and two-year terms, respectively. Elections for alternate halves of the Senate are held every two years. Regular legislative sessions are held annually, lasting from January to June. A bill becomes law when it has been passed by both houses of the General Assembly and has been signed by the Governor. During session a bill also becomes law unless vetoed within 10 days of presentation to the Governor. Outside session a bill dies if it remains unsigned for 30 days after adjournment of the legislature. A gubernatorial veto may be overridden by three-fifths of the elected members of each house. Enacted legislation becomes effective immediately. The Democratic candidate, Jack Markell, was elected in the 2008 gubernatorial election with 67.5% of the votes cast. The Democrats secured an estimated 61% of the votes cast in the presidential election held concurrently. Delaware has three administrative counties.

Elected Executive Branch Officials

Governor (2005–09): RUTH ANN MINNER (Dem.).

Governor-elect (2009–13): JACK MARKELL (Dem.).

Lieutenant-Governor: JOHN C. CARNEY, Jr (Dem.).

Attorney-General: JOSEPH R. BIDEN, III (Dem.).

Treasurer: JACK MARKELL (Dem.).

Auditor: R. THOMAS WAGNER, Jr (Rep.).

Insurance Commissioner: MATT DENN (Dem.).

Selected Government Addresses

Office of the Governor: Tatnall Bldg, 2nd Floor, 150 William Penn St, Dover, DE 19901; tel. (302) 744-4101; fax (302) 739-2775; e-mail governor.minner@state.de.us; internet www.governor.delaware.gov.

Office of the Lieutenant-Governor: Tatnall Bldg, 3rd Floor, 150 William Penn St, Dover, DE 19901; tel. (302) 744-4333; fax (302) 739-6965; e-mail ltgov@state.de.us; internet www.ltgov.delaware.gov.

Office of the Attorney-General: 102 West Water St, Dover, DE 19904; tel. (302) 739-7641; fax (302) 739-7652; e-mail attorney.general@state.de.us; internet www.attorneygeneral.delaware.gov.

Office of the Treasurer: 820 Silver Lake Blvd, Suite 100, Dover, DE 19904; tel. (302) 672-6700; fax (302) 739-5635; e-mail statetreasurer@state.de.us; internet www.treasurer.delaware.gov.

Office of the Auditor: Townsend Bldg, Suite 1, 401 Federal St, Dover, DE 19901; tel. (302) 739-4241; fax (302) 739-6707; e-mail r.thomas.wagner@state.de.us; internet www.auditor.delaware.gov.

Department of Insurance: Rodney Bldg, 841 Silver Lake Blvd, Dover, DE 19904-1507; tel. (302) 674-7300; e-mail matthew.denn@state.de.us; internet www.delawareinsurance.gov; headed by the Insurance Commr.

Department of Agriculture: 2320 South DuPont Hwy, Dover, DE 19901; tel. (302) 698-4500; fax (302) 697-6287; internet www.dda.delaware.gov; Sec. MICHAEL T. SCUSE.

Department of Correction: Central Administration Bldg, 245 McKee Rd, Dover, DE 19901; tel. (302) 739-5601; fax (302) 739-8220; e-mail doc.commissioner@state.de.us; internet www.doc.delaware.gov; Commr CARL C. DANBERG, Jr.

Department of Education: John G. Townsend Bldg, 401 Federal St, Suite 2, Dover, DE 19901-3639; tel. (302) 735-4000; fax (302) 739-4654; e-mail dedoe@doe.k12.de.us; internet www.doe.k12.de.us; Sec. VALERIE A. WOODRUFF.

Department of Finance: Thomas Collins Bldg, 3rd Floor, 540 South DuPont Hwy, Dover, DE 19901; tel. (302) 744-1100; fax (302) 744-1109; e-mail tom.cook@state.de.us; internet www.finance.delaware.gov; Sec. RICHARD S. CORDREY.

Department of Health and Social Services: 1901 North DuPont Hwy, Main Bldg, New Castle, DE 19720; tel. (302) 255-9040; fax (302) 255-4429; e-mail dhssinfo@state.de.us; internet www.dhss.delaware.gov/dhss; Sec. VINCENT P. MECONI.

Department of Labor: 4425 North Market St, 4th Floor, Wilmington, DE 19802; tel. (302) 761-8000; fax (302) 761-6621; e-mail dlabor@state.de.us; internet www.delawareworks.com; Sec. THOMAS B. SHARP.

Department of Natural Resources and Environmental Control: 89 Kings Hwy, POB 1401, Dover, DE 19901; tel. (302) 739-9900; fax (302) 739-6242; e-mail michael.globetti@state.de.us; Sec. JOHN A. HUGHES.

Department of Safety and Homeland Security: Safety and Homeland Security Bldg, 303 Transportation Circle, POB 818, Dover, DE 19903; tel. (302) 744-2680; fax (302) 739-4874; internet dshs.delaware.gov; Sec. DAVID B. MITCHELL.

Department of State: 401 Federal St, Suite 3, Dover, DE 19901; tel. (302) 739-4111; fax (302) 739-3811; e-mail dosdoc_web@state.de.us; internet sos.delaware.gov; Sec. of State HARRIET N. SMITH WINDSOR.

Department of Technology and Information: William Penn Bldg, 801 Silver Lake Blvd, Dover, DE 19904; tel. (302) 739-9500; fax (302) 739-1442; e-mail thomas.jarrett@state.de.us; internet www.dti.delaware.gov; Sec. THOMAS M. JARRETT.

Department of Transportation: 800 Bay Rd, POB 778, Dover, DE 19903-0778; tel. (302) 760-2000; fax (302) 739-2895; e-mail dotpr@state.de.us; internet www.deldot.gov; Sec. CAROLANN WICKS.

Economic Development Office: 99 King's Hwy, Dover, DE 19901-7305; tel. (302) 739-4271; fax (302) 739-5749; e-mail judy.cherry@state.de.us; internet www.dedo.delaware.gov; Dir JUDY MCKINNEY-CHERRY.

National Guard: First Regiment Rd, Wilmington, DE 19808-2191; tel. (302) 326-7000; fax (302) 325-3399; e-mail frank.vavala@de.ngb.army.mil; internet www.delawarenationalguard.com; Adj.-Gen. Maj.-Gen. FRANCIS D. VAVALA.

General Assembly
(August 2008)

Senate

Dem. 13; Rep. 8; Total 21

President: Lt-Gov. JOHN C. CARNEY, Jr (Dem.).

President Pro Tempore: THURMAN ADAMS (Dem.).

Secretary: BERNARD J. BRADY.

House of Representatives

Rep. 22; Dem. 19; Total 41

Speaker: TERRY R. SPENCE (Rep.).

Chief Clerk: JOANN M. HEDRICK.

District of Columbia

Gross Area: 177 sq km (68 sq miles).

Resident Population (1 July 2007, estimate): 588,292.

LOCATION, TOPOGRAPHY AND CLIMATE

The District of Columbia lies in north-eastern USA and is bordered by Maryland to the north-west, east and south, and by the Virginia bank of the Potomac River to the south-west. The district is situated within the Atlantic Coastal Plain and is mainly low-lying, with marshes surrounding the Potomac River and reclaimed land flanking the Anacostia River in the south-east. Rock Creek flows from the north-west plateau into the Potomac River. The highest area of the District is the north, where there are rolling hills. The District of Columbia has a temperate climate, with hot, humid summers and mild winters.

HISTORICAL BACKGROUND

Algonquian peoples inhabited the region now called the District of Columbia until they were driven out in the early 18th century. The land, part of the Maryland colony, was covered in plantations. In 1791 President George Washington chose the site for the federal government and Pierre L'Enfant, a French engineer and architect, was appointed to design the city, a task completed by Andrew Ellicott and Benjamin Banneker. The District became the nation's capital on 1 December 1800 and, in 1802, it was granted a federally appointed mayor and an elected council. Residents of the District of Columbia were barred from voting in national elections, and from electing their own officials, until the 23rd Amendment to the Constitution was passed in 1961. This permitted them to vote for the President and Vice-President. In 1970 legislation was passed allowing the District one congressional delegate to the House of Representatives, who could only vote in committee. In 1993 the delegate was given full voting rights. Congress granted the District an elected Mayor and Council to administer a certain measure of 'home rule' from 1974. However, impending financial crises and allegations of administrative mismanagement prompted the federal government to suspend the powers of the elected officials in August 1997. Extra powers and authority were given to a Control Board. Following the appointment of the District's former CFO, Anthony Williams, to the position of Mayor in November 1998, some powers were returned. The Control Board ceased operations at the end of September 2000, when full powers were restored to the District government. On 11 September 2001, in the most serious terrorist attack in the USA's history, a hijacked passenger plane was crashed into the Pentagon (the headquarters of the federal Department of Defense), causing significant damage and killing hundreds of people.

ECONOMY

Economic activity in the District of Columbia is centred on government, which employed over 33% of the local work-force in 2007. The District has no agricultural, forestry, fishing or mineral industry; printing and publishing is the major manufacturing activity, with the services and tourism industries also relatively important.

Gross domestic product by state totalled US $93,819m. in 2007. The District's per-head income averaged $61,397 in 2007, the highest of any of the 50 states. However, 16.4% of the population were estimated to be living below the poverty threshold in that year, one of the highest proportions in the country. The District's civilian labour force numbered 340,400 in mid-2008, with unemployment affecting 7.2% of the work-force (24,500 persons), the sixth highest rate (alongside Ohio) nation-wide. Union membership was held by 10.3% of workers in 2007, while union agreements covered 13.6% of all employees.

The total value of the District's manufacturing shipments was US $273m. in 2006—the lowest in the USA. However, 63% of this total was added during manufacture. The print and food sectors were of most significance.

Tourism is an important industry in the District; domestic travel expenditures totalled US $4,776m. in 2004.

The District regained its powers of home rule in late 2001 after fulfilling a number of conditions, including producing four consecutive balanced budgets. Total expenditures by the District government in 2006 were US $10,091m., with total revenue at $9,171m. Federal grants to the District amounted to $3,060m. in 2006.

CONSTITUTION AND GOVERNMENT

The government of the District of Columbia operates according to the Charter of 1974, which allows residents to elect a Mayor and City Council. The Council has 13 members, of whom the chairman or chairwoman and four other members are elected at-large, the remaining members being elected from the District's eight wards. Of those members elected at-large, there may not be more than three affiliated to the same political party. Members are elected to serve a four-year term of office, with one-half of both the ward and at-large members being elected every two years. The Mayor, chief executive officer of the District, is also elected to hold office for four years. A bill becomes law when it has been passed by a majority of the Council present at two readings and has been signed by the Mayor, who has 10 days to consider it. The Mayor's veto may be overridden by two-thirds of those members of the Council who are present. Under the federal Constitution, all legislation enacted by the District of Columbia is subject to a mandatory period of review by the US Congress. A bill becomes law after 30 days (60 days in the case of criminal legislation), unless vetoed by the President. Congress may also pass laws on any matter affecting the District.

In 1982 a constitution was drafted and it was proposed that the district should become the state of New Columbia. The draft constitution was approved by the district electorate. An amendment to the federal Constitution giving the District of Columbia full voting representation in Congress had been approved by Congress in 1978, but failed to become law after having been ratified by only 16 out of the requisite 38 states before the statutory deadline was reached in August 1985. In 1993 the delegate of the District of Columbia to the House of Representatives was granted extra voting rights. The city is traditionally a stronghold of support for the Democratic Party. Adrian M. Fenty was elected mayor in November 2006, securing

57% of the vote. In the 2008 presidential election the Democrats won some 93% of the votes cast.

Elected Executive Branch Official

Mayor (2007–11): ADRIAN M. FENTY (Dem.).

Selected Administration Addresses

Executive Office of the Mayor: John A. Wilson Bldg, Suite 316, 1350 Pennsylvania Ave, NW, Washington, DC 20004; tel. (202) 727-2980; fax (202) 727-1977; e-mail carrie.brooks@dc.gov; internet www.dc.gov.

Department of Corrections: 1923 Vermont Ave, NW, Rm 207N, Washington, DC 20001; tel. (202) 673-7316; fax (202) 671-2043; internet doc.dc.gov; Dir DEVON BROWN.

Department of Health: 825 North Capitol St, NE, Washington, DC 20002; tel. (202) 442-5955; fax (202) 442-4795; e-mail doh@dc.gov; internet doh.dc.gov; Dir Dr PIERRE VIGILANCE.

Department of Insurance, Securities and Banking: 810 First St, NE, Suite 701, Washington, DC 20002; tel. (202) 727-8000; fax (202) 535-1196; e-mail disb@dc.gov; internet disb.dc.gov; Commr THOMAS E. HAMPTON.

Department of Public Works: Franklin D. Reeves Municipal Center, 6th Floor, 2000 14th St, NW, Washington, DC 20009; tel. (202) 673-6833; fax (202) 671-0642; e-mail dpw@dc.gov; internet dpw.dc.gov; Dir WILLIAM O. HOWLAND, Jr.

District of Columbia Public Schools: 825 North Capitol St, NE, Suite 9076, Washington, DC 20002; tel. (202) 442-5885; fax (202) 724-5198; internet www.k12.dc.us; Chancellor MICHELLE A. RHEE.

District Department of the Environment: 51 N St, NE, 6th Floor, Washington, DC 20002; tel. (202) 535-2600; fax (202) 535-2881; e-mail ddoe@dc.gov; internet ddoe.dc.gov; Dir GEORGE S. HAWKINS.

Metropolitan Police Department: 300 Indiana Ave, NW, Washington, DC 20001; tel. (202) 727-4218; fax (202) 727-9524; e-mail mpd@dc.gov; internet mpdc.dc.gov; Chief CATHY L. LANIER.

Office of the Auditor: 717 14th St, NW, Suite 900, Washington, DC 20005; tel. (202) 727-3600; fax (202) 724-8814; e-mail odca@dc.gov; internet www.dcauditor.org; Auditor DEBORAH K. NICHOLS.

Public Service Commission: 1333 H St, NW, Suite 200, West Tower, Washington, DC 20005; tel. (202) 626-5100; fax (202) 393-1389; internet www.dcpsc.org; ind. agency; Chair. AGNES ALEXANDER YATES.

City Council
(August 2008)

Members

Dem. 11; Rep. 1; Ind. 1; Total 13

Chairperson: VINCENT C. GRAY (Dem.).

Chairperson Pro Tempore: JACK EVANS (Dem.).

Secretary: CYNTHIA BROCK-SMITH.

Florida

Gross Area: 170,314 sq km (65,783 sq miles).

Resident Population (1 July 2007, estimate): 18,251,243.

State Capital: Tallahassee.

Principal Cities (population at 1 July 2006, estimate): Jacksonville 794,555; Miami 404,048; Tampa 332,888; St Petersburg 248,098; Hialeah 217,141; Orlando 220,186; Fort Lauderdale 185,804; Tallahassee (capital) 159,012; Cape Coral 151,389; Pembroke Pines 150,064; Hollywood 145,794; Port St. Lucie 143,868; Coral Springs 129,805; Gainesville 108,655; Miramar 108,072; Clearwater 107,742; Pompano Beach 104,402.

LOCATION, TOPOGRAPHY AND CLIMATE

The State of Florida (nicknamed 'The Sunshine State') is situated at the south-eastern extremity of the USA and is bordered by Alabama and Georgia to the north. It abuts into the sea, with the Atlantic Ocean to the east, the Straits of Florida to the south (separating it from the Bahamas and Cuba) and the Gulf of Mexico to the west. Curving south-west from the tip of Florida into the Gulf of Mexico is the archipelago of 'Ten Thousand Islands', the most southerly of which, Key West, is also the southern-most point of the 48 conterminous states of the USA. Large areas of the Florida peninsula are covered in marshes. In the south and south-east is the Everglades, a large sawgrass swamp with occasional mounds where cypress and mahogany are found; to the west and north of the Everglades is Big Cypress Swamp. Inlets and bays characterize the west coast, while sand-banks lie along the east coast. The centre of the peninsula is gently undulating and scattered with lakes. In south-central Florida is Lake Okeechobee, one of the largest lakes situated entirely within the USA, with an area of about 1,800 sq km (700 sq miles). The state has numerous caves, springs and rivers. The principal rivers are the St Johns, flowing into the Atlantic at Jacksonville; the Suwannee, flowing south from Georgia into the Gulf of Mexico; and the Apalachicola, also running south into the Gulf of Mexico. Florida has a humid, mild and sunny climate, tropical in the extreme south and subtropical in the north.

HISTORICAL BACKGROUND

When Juan Ponce de Léon claimed Florida for Spain in 1513, the land was inhabited by numerous Native American (Amerindian) tribes, among them the Apalachee, Timucua and Tocobaga peoples. Their numbers were greatly reduced by European-spread diseases or in battles against the settlers. France established a colony, Fort Caroline, on the St Johns River in 1564, and Spain, after defeating the French settlers, founded St Augustine one year later. This was the first permanent European settlement in the territory of the modern USA, and remains today. Florida came under British rule in 1763, but was returned to the Spanish in 1783. In 1818 Gen. Andrew Jackson led a US invasion; the region was ceded to the USA one year later and granted territorial status in 1821. The Second Seminole War of 1835–42 finally defeated the Seminole peoples who had moved into northern Florida at the end of the previous century. Most of them were removed to Oklahoma. On 3 March 1845 Florida joined the Union as the 27th state, but seceded in 1861 and was part of the Confederation in the Civil War. Florida was readmitted to the Union in 1868. In 1961 the rocket carrying the first American to enter space was launched from Cape Canaveral (now Cape Kennedy), which was also the launch site of subsequent manned space missions.

ECONOMY

Manufacturing, construction, agriculture, wholesale and retail trade, finance, insurance and real estate, services and tourism are the principal economic activities in Florida. Gross domestic product by state totalled US $734,519m. in 2007, making Florida the USA's fourth largest economy, while the state had an average per-head income of $38,316. In that year 12.1% of the population were estimated to be living below the poverty line. Florida's civilian work-force numbered 9,433,600 in mid-2008, with an unemployment rate of 6.5% (637,200 workers). Of those employed in 2007, 5.9% were union members, while union agreements covered 7.3%.

In 2002 cropland covered 3.7m. acres (1.5m. ha). The average size of the state's 40,000 farms in 2007 was 250 acres. Some 46% of total cropland was under irrigation in 2002. Crop sales in 2007 provided 81% of total farm marketings, and sales of livestock and livestock products provided 19%. Florida's principal agricultural commodities in that year were greenhouse and nursery products, oranges (of which it was the foremost producer nationally), tomatoes and dairy products. Livestock production included milk, cattle and broilers. Florida produced more than 79% of the USA's citrus production in 2004 and accounts for more than one-half of its total sugar-cane production. The state was also a significant producer of greenhouse and nursery products, leading production of tangerines, grapefruits and fresh tomatoes in 2006 (ahead of California for all three crops); it ranked second, behind California, for production of strawberries and tomatoes in 2007. Forestland covered around 16.3m. acres of Florida's land area in 2002, representing some 2% of the USA's total timber resources. However, the state's lumbering industry is relatively modest. Fishing, however, is an important commercial activity: Florida's catch in 2006 was valued at US $192m., the sixth largest catch nationally. The state ranked first in 2007 for spiny lobster (accounting for 85% of the USA's total landings), and was ranked third in 2005 for crabs (behind Oregon and Maryland). In 2004 Florida's aquaculture sales, mostly of tropical fish, totalled $95m.

The value of Florida's non-fuel mineral production in 2007 was US $3,190m., the sixth highest in the USA, with the state accounting for almost 5% of the US total. The principal minerals produced in that year were crushed stone, phosphate rock, portland and masonry cement and sand and gravel. Florida was the sole US producer of rutile concentrates and staurolite in 2004. It ranked first for phosphate rock production in 2007 (when, together with North Carolina, it contributed 85% of total US output), and was also the leading producer of peat, zirconium concentrates and titanium mineral concentrates. It ranked third for magnesium compounds and crushed stone and fourth for cement. There is also some crude petroleum and natural gas production in the state.

Much of Florida's manufacturing activity is centred on the processing of agricultural and other raw materials found in the state; the cities of Miami, Tampa, St Petersburg, Fort Lauderdale and Orlando all have important industrial bases. Major sectors include food and kindred products, printing and publishing, computers, and other electrical and transportation equipment. In 2006 the total value of

Florida's manufacturing shipments was US $97,848m., with 52% of this being added during manufacture. The state ranked 20th in the nation in terms of its value of shipments.

Florida is a major tourism centre with many attractions; domestic travel expenditures amounted to US $46,672m. in 2004, and the state ranked second (after California) in terms of receipts.

Total general expenditures by the state government in 2006 were US $76,142m.; general revenue totalled $66,561m., of which $19,709m. was supplied by the federal Government and $37,202m. was derived from taxes. Federal aid totalled $19,115m. in 2006.

CONSTITUTION AND GOVERNMENT

The current Constitution of Florida is the state's sixth and became effective on 7 January 1969. An amendment to the Constitution introduced by the Legislature requires approval by three-fifths of the elected members of each house, followed by a majority of voters. The Governor and Lieutenant-Governor are elected jointly to serve terms of four years, the Governor serving no more than two consecutive terms. Cabinet members, six in total, are elected to specified offices and meet every two weeks. There are 40 senators and 120 representatives in the Legislature, elected for four- and two-year terms, respectively. Alternate halves of the Senate are re-elected every two years. Regular sessions of the Legislature take place annually in February and last for no longer than 60 calendar days. A bill becomes law when it has been passed by a majority of elected members present in both houses of the Legislature and has been signed by the Governor. During session the Governor has seven calendar days in which to consider a bill, after which it becomes law unless vetoed. After session a bill becomes law unless vetoed within 15 calendar days. A gubernatorial veto may be overridden by a vote of two-thirds of the elected members in each house. Enacted legislation becomes effective 60 days after adjournment of the session. In the November 2006 gubernatorial election the Republican candidate, Charlie Crist, secured the most votes (56%). In the 2008 presidential election the Democrats secured an estimated 51% of the vote. Florida has 67 administrative counties.

Elected Executive Branch Officials

Governor (2007–11): CHARLIE CRIST (Rep.).

Lieutenant-Governor: JEFFREY D. KOTTKAMP (Rep.).

Attorney-General: BILL MCCOLLUM (Rep.).

Chief Financial Officer: ALEX SINK (Dem.).

Commissioner of Agriculture: CHARLES H. BRONSON (Rep.).

Selected Government Addresses

Office of the Governor: The Capitol, 400 South Monroe St, Tallahassee, FL 32399-0001; tel. (850) 488-7176; fax (850) 487-0801; e-mail charlie.crist@myflorida.com; internet www.flgov.com.

Office of the Lieutenant-Governor: The Capitol, 400 South Monroe St, PL-05, Tallahassee, FL 32399-0001; tel. (850) 488-4711; fax (850) 921-6114; e-mail jeff.kottkamp@myflorida.com; internet www.flgov.com/meet_lt_gov.

Office of the Attorney-General: The Capitol, 400 South Monroe St, PL-01, Tallahassee, FL 32399-1050; tel. (850) 414-3300; fax (850) 410-1630; e-mail ag.mccollum@myfloridalegal.com; internet myfloridalegal.com.

Department of Agriculture and Consumer Services: The Capitol, 400 South Monroe St, Tallahassee, FL 32399-0800; tel. (850) 488-3022; fax (850) 488-1806; e-mail commissioner@doacs.state.fl.us; internet www.doacs.state.fl.us; headed by the Commr of Agriculture.

Department of Corrections: 2601 Blair Stone Rd, Tallahassee, FL 32399-2500; tel. (850) 488-5021; fax (850) 488-4534; e-mail publicaffairs@mail.dc.state.fl.us; internet www.dc.state.fl.us; Sec. WALTER A. MCNEIL.

Department of Education: Turlington Bldg, Suite 1514, 325 West Gaines St, Tallahassee, FL 32399; tel. (850) 245-0505; fax (850) 245-9667; e-mail commissioner@fldoe.org; internet www.fldoe.org; Commr Dr ERIC J. SMITH.

Department of Environmental Protection: 3900 Commonwealth Blvd, MS-49, Tallahassee, FL 32399; tel. (850) 245-2118; fax (850) 245-2128; e-mail bonnie.hazleton@dep.state.fl.us; internet www.dep.state.fl.us; Sec. MICHAEL W. SOLE.

Department of Financial Services: 200 East Gaines St, Tallahassee, FL 32399-0300; tel. (850) 413-3100; fax (850) 413-4993; e-mail cfo@myfloridacfo.com; internet www.fldfs.com; headed by the Chief Financial Officer.

Department of Health: 2585 Merchants Row Blvd, Tallahassee, FL 32399; tel. (850) 245-4444; fax (850) 487-3729; e-mail health@doh.state.fl.us; internet www.doh.state.fl.us; State Surgeon General Dr ANA M. VIAMONTE ROS.

Department of Law Enforcement: 2331 Phillips Rd, POB 1489, Tallahassee, FL 32302-1489; tel. (850) 410-7000; e-mail info@fdle.state.fl.us; internet www.fdle.state.fl.us; Commr GERALD M. BAILEY.

Department of Military Affairs: St Francis Barracks, 82 Marine St, St Augustine, FL 32084; tel. (850) 823-0364; fax (850) 823-0112; internet www.dma.state.fl.us; Adj.-Gen. Maj.-Gen. DOUGLAS BURNETT.

Department of Revenue: 104 Carlton Bldg, 5050 West Tennessee St, Tallahassee, FL 32399-0100; tel. (850) 488-5050; e-mail emaildor@dor.state.fl.us; internet dor.myflorida.com/dor; Exec. Dir LISA ECHEVERRI.

Department of Transportation: 605 Suwannee St, MS-59, Tallahassee, FL 32399-0450; tel. (850) 414-5205; fax (850) 414-5201; e-mail fdot@dot.state.fl.us; internet www.dot.state.fl.us; Sec. STEPHANIE C. KOPELOUSOS.

Office of the Auditor-General: Claude Denson Pepper Bldg, 111 West Madison St, Tallahassee, FL 32399-1450; tel. (850) 488-5534; fax (850) 488-6975; e-mail flaudgen@aud.state.fl.us; internet www.state.fl.us/audgen; Auditor-Gen. DAVID W. MARTIN.

Public Service Commission: 2540 Shumard Oak Blvd, Tallahassee, FL 32399-0850; tel. (850) 413-6100; fax (850) 413-6861; e-mail contact@psc.state.fl.us; internet www.floridapsc.com; Chair. MATTHEW M. CARTER, II.

Legislature
(August 2008)

Senate

Rep. 26; Dem. 14; Total 40

President: KEN PRUITT (Rep.).

President Pro Tempore: LISA CARLTON (Rep.).

Secretary: FAYE W. BLANTON.

House of Representatives

Rep. 77; Dem. 42; 1 vacancy; Total 120

Speaker: MARCO RUBIO (Rep.).

Speaker Pro Tempore: MARSHA (MARTY) BOWEN (Rep.).

Chief Clerk: WILLIAM S. (BO) PITTMAN, III.

Georgia

Gross Area: 153,952 sq km (59,463 sq miles).

Resident Population (1 July 2007, estimate): 9,544,750.

State Capital: Atlanta.

Principal Cities (population at 1 July 2006, estimate): Atlanta (capital) 486,411; Augusta–Richmond County 189,366; Columbus 185,702; Savannah 127,889; Athens–Clarke County 111,580.

LOCATION, TOPOGRAPHY AND CLIMATE

The State of Georgia (nicknamed 'The Empire State of the South') is bordered by Tennessee and North Carolina to the north, South Carolina to the north-east, Florida to the south and Alabama to the west. In the east of the state there is an Atlantic coastline, off which lie the Sea Islands, of which the largest are Tybee, Ossabaw, St Catherines, Sapelo, St Simons, Sea Island, Jekyll and Cumberland. The south of the state consists of flat, coastal plains with marshy areas along the coast, and the Okefenokee Swamp in the south-east. A ridge of sandy hills marks the beginning of the Piedmont Plateau, which occupies central Georgia. The Blue Ridge Mountains reach into the north, and the state's highest point is Brasstown Bald, at 1,458 m (4,784 ft). Georgia's main rivers are the Savannah, which forms part of the border with South Carolina; the Chattahoochee, flowing across the state before forming the southern half of the Alabama boundary; the Ocmulgee and Oconee, joining to create the Altamaha, which flows east into the Atlantic; the Flint, which meets with the Chattahoochee to form the Apalachicola; and the Suwannee, which rises in the Okefenokee Swamp and runs into Florida. Georgia has hot summers and mild winters. Temperatures are cooler in the mountainous north and the east central region is drier.

HISTORICAL BACKGROUND

Before the Spanish established missions on the Sea Islands of St Simons and Jekyll, around 1566, the region now known as Georgia was inhabited by Creek and Cherokee peoples. In 1742 Gen. James Oglethorpe defeated the Spanish at the Battle of Bloody Marsh and, from 1754 to 1782, Georgia was a British colony. On 2 January 1788 Georgia became the fourth state to ratify the Constitution of the USA. Ceding its western lands to Alabama and Mississippi, the state took on its present form in 1802. The Cherokee people were removed to Oklahoma Territory in 1832–38 on a march known as the 'Trail of

Tears', because of the large numbers who died along the route. In 1861 the powerful interests of the cotton-plantation owners, who relied on black slave labour, caused Georgia to secede from the Union. The state was invaded by Union forces under Gen. William Sherman in 1864 and Atlanta was taken. Georgia was readmitted to the Union in 1870. In 1996 Atlanta was the host city for the 26th Games of the Olympiad (Olympic Summer Games) of the modern era.

ECONOMY

Georgia's principal economic activities are manufacturing, retail and wholesale trade and services. Agriculture, which dominated the economy before the Second World War, lost much of its importance in the post-war period. Gross domestic product by state was US $396,504m. in 2007, still the 10th largest economy in the USA. The state had an average per-head income of $33,416 in that year, while 14.3% of the population were thought to be living below the poverty threshold. Georgia's civilian labour force numbered 4,963,700 in mid-2008 and the unemployment rate was 6.3% (311,800 persons). Of the total number of employees in 2007, just 4.4% were union members (the fourth lowest figure among the states) and 5.4% were covered by union agreements.

Farmland accounted for 28% of Georgia's land area in 2005, with cropland accounting for 4.7m. acres in 2002. In 2002 18% of total cropland was irrigated. The average farm size in 2007 was 211 acres, when there were 47,500 farms and farmland covered 10m. acres. In 2007 some 36% of the value of farm marketings was derived from crops and 64% from livestock and livestock products. The most important agricultural products in that year were broilers, cotton, chicken eggs and greenhouse and nursery products. Georgia was the USA's leading producer of broilers in 2007, and continued to rank first in peanut production; it was placed third for chicken eggs (behind Iowa and Ohio) and also ranked fourth among the states for cotton production. Of Georgia's total land area, 64% is forested. The timber industry is important and productive: in 2004 Georgia produced the USA's fourth largest amount of lumber, of which 87% was softwood, predominantly pine. Commercial fishing is well established, with a catch value of US $11.5m. in 2006, but its contribution to the economy is small.

Georgia was ranked 10th among the states in the production of non-fuel minerals in 2007. In that year its non-fuel mineral production was valued at US $2,110m. The state's principal non-fuel mineral products are kaolin and other clays (of which it is by far the leading producer, accounting for almost one-quarter of the nation's production in 2005) and crushed stone. Portland cement and construction sand and gravel are also important, and Georgia is the nation's leading producer of crude iron oxide pigments. The state's only recoverable fossil-fuel resources are small amounts of coal.

Georgia's most important manufacturing industries are food and kindred products, pulp and paper products, chemicals and electrical and transportation equipment. Reflecting the state's history as a cotton-growing state, textiles and apparel are also significant. The state's most famous manufacture is Coca-Cola: the soft-drinks manufacturer Coca-Cola Co is based in Atlanta. The total value of Georgia's manufacturing shipments in 2006 was US $140,892m., of which 44% was added during manufacture. Georgia ranked 13th among the states, in terms of the value of shipments, in that year.

Banking is an important industry in the state, as is travel and tourism. Georgia's commercial banks had a combined asset base of US $284,800m. at the end of 2006, placing it 11th in importance in the USA in this regard, while domestic travel expenditures were $15,390m. in 2004, with the state ranked ninth.

Total general expenditures by the state government in 2006 were US $34,945m. General revenue totalled $32,353m., of which $10,336m. was provided by the federal Government and $17,034m. was derived from taxes. Federal aid of $9,278m. was received in 2006.

CONSTITUTION AND GOVERNMENT

The current Constitution of Georgia, the state's 10th, was adopted in 1982 and became effective on 1 July 1983. Constitutional amendments proposed by the General Assembly must be approved by two-thirds of each house and must then be ratified by a majority of state voters. The Governor and Lieutenant-Governor are elected separately, the Governor being elected to serve a four-year term and serving no more than two terms consecutively. Georgia has no formal cabinet system. There are 56 senators and 180 representatives in the state General Assembly and both houses are re-elected every two years. Regular sessions of the General Assembly are held annually, beginning in January and lasting for 40 legislative days. A bill becomes law when it has been passed by both houses and signed by the Governor. During session the Governor must either sign or veto a bill within six calendar days of receipt; otherwise, it automatically becomes law. After session a bill becomes law unless vetoed within 40 days from adjournment of the session. A gubernatorial veto may be overridden by a vote by two-thirds of the legislators in each house. Enacted legislation generally becomes effective in the following July. In 2006 the Republican incumbent, Sonny Perdue, won some 58% of the votes cast in the gubernatorial election. In the 2008 presidential election the Republicans gained the largest share of the votes cast, with an estimated 52%. Georgia has 159 administrative counties.

Elected Executive Branch Officials

Governor (2007–11): GEORGE (SONNY) PERDUE (Rep.).

Lieutenant-Governor: CASEY CAGLE (Rep.).

Secretary of State: KAREN HANDEL (Dem.).

Attorney-General: THURBERT E. BAKER (Dem.).

Insurance and Safety Fire Commissioner: JOHN W. OXENDINE (Dem.).

Superintendent of Schools: KATHY COX (Rep.).

Commissioner of Agriculture: THOMAS T. IRVIN (Dem.).

Commissioner of Labor: MICHAEL L. THURMOND (Dem.).

Selected Government Addresses

Office of the Governor: 211 State Capitol, Atlanta, GA 30334; tel. (404) 656-1776; fax (404) 657-7332; internet www.gov.state.ga.us.

Office of the Lieutenant-Governor: 240 State Capitol, Atlanta, GA 30334; tel. (404) 656-5030; fax (404) 656-6739; internet ltgov.georgia.gov.

Office of the Secretary of State: 214 State Capitol, Atlanta, GA 30334; tel. (404) 656-2881; fax (404) 656-0513; internet www.sos.state.ga.us.

Office of the Attorney-General: 40 Capitol Sq., SW, Atlanta, GA 30334; tel. (404) 656-3300; fax (404) 657-8733; internet law.ga.gov.

Office of the Insurance and Safety Fire Commissioner: 2 Martin Luther King Jr Dr., SE, Suite 704, West Tower, Atlanta, GA 30334; tel. (404) 656-2070; fax (404) 657-8542; e-mail safetyed@oci.go.gov; internet www.gainsurance.org.

Department of Education: 2066 Twin Towers East, 205 Jesse Hill Jr Drive SE, Atlanta, GA 30334; tel. (404) 656-2800; fax (404) 651-8737; e-mail state.superintendent@doe.k12.ga.us; internet public.doe.k12.ga.us; headed by the Supt of Schools.

Department of Agriculture: Agriculture Bldg, 19 Martin Luther King Jr Dr., SW, Atlanta, GA 30334; tel. (404) 656-3645; e-mail tirvin@agr.state.ga.us; internet agr.georgia.gov; headed by the Commr of Agriculture.

Department of Labor: 148 Andrew Young International Blvd, NE, Atlanta, GA 30303-1751; tel. (404) 232-7300; fax (404) 463-0904; internet www.dol.state.ga.us; headed by the Commr of Labor.

Department of Banking and Finance: 2990 Brandywine Rd, Suite 200, Atlanta, GA 30341-5565; tel. (770) 986-1633; fax (770) 986-1654; e-mail robertb@dbf.state.ga.us; internet www.gadbf.org; Commr ROBERT BRASWELL.

Department of Community Health: 2 Peachtree St, NW, 40th Floor, Atlanta, GA 30303; tel. (404) 656-4507; fax (404) 651-6880; internet dch.georgia.gov; Commr Dr RHONDA MEDOWS.

Department of Corrections: 2 Martin Luther King Jr Dr., SE, Rm 854, East Tower, Atlanta, GA 30334; tel. (404) 656-9772; fax (404) 651-6434; e-mail info@dcor.state.ga.us; internet www.dcor.state.ga.us; Commr JAMES E. DONALD.

Department of Defense: POB 17965, Atlanta, GA 30316-0965; tel. (678) 569-6060; internet www.dod.state.ga.us; Adj.-Gen. Maj.-Gen. WILLIAM T. NESBITT.

Department of Economic Development: 75 Fifth St, NW, Suite 1200, Atlanta, GA 30308; tel. (404) 962-4000; fax (404) 962-4001; internet www.georgia.org; Commr KENNETH C. STEWART.

Department of Natural Resources: 2 Martin Luther King Jr Dr., SE, Suite 1252, East Tower, Atlanta, GA 30334; tel. (404) 656-3500; fax (404) 656-0770; internet www.gadnr.org; Commr NOEL HOLCOMB.

Department of Public Safety: 959 East Confederate Ave, SE, POB 1456, Atlanta, GA 30371-1456; tel. (404) 624-7000; e-mail gadpsweb@gsp.net; internet www.dps.georgia.gov; Commr Col BILL HITCHENS.

Department of Revenue: 1800 Century Center Blvd, NE, Atlanta, GA 30345-3205; tel. (404) 417-4477; fax (404) 417-4327; e-mail charles.willey@dor.ga.gov; internet www.dor.ga.gov; Commr BART L. GRAHAM.

Department of Transportation: 1 Georgia Center, 600 West Peachtree, NW, Atlanta, GA 30308; tel. (404) 631-1000; fax (404) 631-1844; e-mail webmaster@dot.state.ga.us; internet www.dot.state.ga.us; Commr GENA ABRAHAM.

Public Service Commission: 244 Washington St, SW, Atlanta, GA 30334; tel. (404) 656-4501; fax (404) 656-2341; e-mail gapsc@psc.state.ga.us; internet www.psc.state.ga.us; Chair. CHUCK EATON.

General Assembly
(August 2008)

Senate

Rep. 34; Dem. 22; Total 56

President: Lt-Gov. CASEY CAGLE (Rep.).

President Pro Tempore: ERIC JOHNSON (Rep.).

Secretary: BOB EWING.

House of Representatives

Rep. 107; Dem. 73; Total 180

Speaker: GLENN RICHARDSON (Rep.).

Speaker Pro Tempore: MARK BURKHALTER (Rep.).

Clerk: ROBERT E. RIVERS, Jr.

Hawaii

Gross Area: 28,313 sq km (10,935 sq miles).

Resident Population (1 July 2007, estimate): 1,283,388.

State Capital, Principal City: Honolulu (population 377,357 at 1 July 2006, estimate).

LOCATION, TOPOGRAPHY AND CLIMATE

The State of Hawaii (nicknamed 'The Aloha State') consists of an archipelago of 132 islands stretching for 2,451 km (1,523 miles) from Kure Island to Hawaii Island, and lying about 3,900 km (2,400 miles) south-west of San Francisco (California) in the northern Pacific Ocean. The eight major islands, extending roughly north-west to south-east, are Niihau, Kauai, Oahu, Molokai, Lanai, Maui, Kahoolawe and Hawaii. Hawaii is the largest island, at 10,451 sq km (4,035 sq miles). The islands, mountainous and mostly fertile, were formed by volcanic eruptions. Mauna Loa, on Hawaii Island, is still an active volcano. The state's highest peak is Mauna Kea (4,205 m—13,796 ft), also on the island of Hawaii. Hawaii's climate is tropical, tempered by strong, cool winds. Rainfall varies greatly, with the islands' interiors and high mountain slopes mainly dry, and the north-eastern slope of the islands receiving heavy precipitation.

HISTORICAL BACKGROUND

When the British navigator Capt. James Cook reached the islands of Hawaii in 1778, they were inhabited by Polynesians, who had arrived from other Pacific islands in AD 500–1000. By 1810 Hawaii was united under King Kamehameha I (born in 1758 and died in 1819). During the reign of Kamehameha III (1824–54) Honolulu became the kingdom's capital and sugar plantations began to dominate the economy, many of them run by former US missionaries. The Chinese, who arrived in the 1850s, were the first of many groups of immigrants who came to work on the plantations. An increasing US presence on the islands and a weakening of the Kamehameha dynasty led to a bloodless revolution in 1893, when the last monarch, Queen Liliuokalani, was deposed (she renounced her claim to the throne in 1895), and Hawaii declared a republic, with Sanford B. Dole as president. Hawaii was annexed by the USA in 1898, and Dole became its first territorial governor in 1900. The Japanese attack on the US Pacific fleet at Pearl Harbor in 1941 brought the USA into the Second World War. Hawaii became the 50th state of the Union on 21 August 1959.

ECONOMY

The economy of Hawaii is heavily dependent on tourism, national defence programmes and agriculture. Manufacturing is a relatively unimportant contributor to the state's income. Gross domestic product by state was US $61,532m. in 2007 and Hawaiians' average per-head income was measured at $39,060 in the same year. In 2007 8.0% of the state population were considered to be living below the poverty line, the third lowest figure in the country. The civilian labour force numbered 672,200 in mid-2008, of which 4.2% were unemployed (28,400 persons). In 2007 23.4% of those employed belonged to a trade union, while 24.2% were covered by union agreements—these proportions were the third highest in the nation.

Farmland covered some 1.3m. acres (526,000 ha) in 2007, with some 28% of total cropland irrigated. The average size of the 5,500 farms in 2007 was 236 acres. In that year some 86% of total farm income was derived from crops and 14% from livestock and livestock products. The dominant agricultural products in 2007 were greenhouse and nursery products, sugar-cane, coffee and cattle and calves (the most important livestock commodity). Hawaii is the sole focus of commercial pineapple and macadamia nut production in the USA, while the state also ranks third for sugar-cane output, behind Florida and Louisiana. Approximately 25% of Hawaii is forested, with most forestland located on the island of Hawaii. Commercial forestry is, however, limited. Fishing is an expanding economic force, with a catch value of some US $66.8m. in 2006.

Hawaii has no known fossil-fuel resources. Its non-fuel mineral production was valued at US $150m. in 2007. Stone is quarried to produce crushed stone, and sand and gravel is extracted for use by the construction industry. Gemstones are also mined. The Oahu portland cement manufacturing plant was closed in 2001.

Hawaii ranked 49th in the nation in 2006 in terms of its value of shipments. Its principal manufacturing sectors include food and kindred products, apparel, fabricated metal products and stone, clay and glass products. The canning and preserving of locally produced fruit and vegetables provides a major source of employment, as does the manufacture of sugar and confectionery products. The value of Hawaii's manufacturing shipments totalled US $7,301m. in 2006, with 28% of value added during manufacture.

Domestic travel expenditures totalled US $8,032m. in 2004, and travel and tourism generated a large proportion of the state's jobs. While most tourists were US citizens, a substantial number of visitors came from Japan.

Total general expenditures by the state government in 2005 were US $8,405m.; general revenue totalled $8,552m., of which $1,833m. was from federal Government and $4,919m. came from taxes. In 2006 Hawaii received $1,858m. in federal aid.

CONSTITUTION AND GOVERNMENT

As a US state, Hawaii has had one Constitution, which was adopted in 1950 and became effective on 21 August 1959. Constitutional amendments proposed by the Legislature must be passed by either two-thirds of the elected members of each house at one session, or a majority of each house in two sessions. Amendments must then be ratified by a majority of voters. The Governor and Lieutenant-Governor are jointly elected to serve four-year terms and may serve no more than two terms consecutively. The Legislature consists of 25 senators and 51 representatives, serving terms of four and two years, respectively. Alternate halves of the Senate are re-elected every two years. Regular sessions of the Legislature take place annually, beginning in January and lasting no longer than 60 days. A bill becomes law when it has been approved by both houses of the Legislature and signed by the Governor. The Governor has 10 days in which to consider a bill, during session, after which it automatically becomes law unless vetoed. Outside session a bill becomes law unless vetoed within 45 days of adjournment. The Governor's veto may be overridden by a two-thirds' vote of the elected members of the Legislature. Enacted legislation becomes effective immediately. The Republican incumbent, Linda Lingle, was re-elected to the governorship in 2006, with 62% of the votes cast. The Democrats secured some 72% of the votes cast in the presidential election of 2008. There are four counties in Hawaii (Kalawao, sometimes referred to as the fifth county, is wholly under the authority of the state Department of Health).

Elected Executive Branch Officials

Governor (2007–11): LINDA LINGLE (Rep.).

Lieutenant-Governor: JAMES R. (DUKE) AIONA, Jr (Rep.).

Selected Government Addresses

Office of the Governor: State Capitol, Rm 415, Honolulu, HI 96813; tel. (808) 586-0034; fax (808) 586-0006; e-mail governor.lingle@hawaii.gov; internet www.hawaii.gov/gov.

Office of the Lieutenant-Governor: State Capitol, 5th Floor, Honolulu, HI 96813; tel. (808) 586-0255; fax (808) 586-0231; e-mail ltgov@hawaii.gov; internet www.hawaii.gov/ltgov.

Department of Agriculture: 1428 South King St, Honolulu, HI 96814; tel. (808) 973-9560; fax (808) 973-9613; e-mail hdoa.info@hawaii.gov; internet www.hawaiiag.gov/hdoa; Chair. SANDRA LEE KUNIMOTO.

Department of the Attorney-General: Auhau Bldg, 425 Queen St, Honolulu, HI 96813; tel. (808) 586-1500; fax (808) 586-1239; e-mail hawaiiag@hawaii.gov; internet www.hawaii.gov/ag; Attorney-Gen. MARK J. BENNETT.

Department of Budget and Finance: No. 1 Capitol District Bldg, 250 South Hotel St, POB 150, Honolulu, HI 96810; tel. (808) 586-1518; fax (808) 586-1976; e-mail hi.budgetandfinance@hawaii.gov; internet www.hawaii.gov/budget; incorporates Public Utilities Commission; Dir GEORGINA K. KAWAMURA.

Department of Business, Economic Development and Tourism: No. 1 Capitol District Bldg, 250 South Hotel St, Honolulu, HI 96813; tel. (808) 586-2423; fax (808) 587-2790; e-mail library@dbedt.hawaii.gov; internet www.hawaii.gov/dbedt; Dir THEODORE E. LIU.

Department of Commerce and Consumer Affairs: King Kalakaua Bldg, 335 Merchant St, Honolulu, HI 96813; tel. (808) 586-2850; fax (808) 586-2856; e-mail dcca@dcca.hawaii.gov; internet www.hawaii.gov/dcca; Dir LAWRENCE REIFURTH.

Department of Defense: 3949 Diamond Head Rd, Honolulu, HI 96816-4495; tel. (808) 672-1201; fax (808) 733-4238; e-mail jeff.hickman@us.army.mil; internet www.dod.state.hi.us; Adj.-Gen. Maj.-Gen. ROBERT G. F. LEE.

Department of Education: Queen Liliuokalani Bldg, 1390 Miller St, POB 2360, Honolulu, HI 96804; tel. (808) 586-3230; fax (808) 586-3234; e-mail doe_info@notes.k12.hi.us; internet doe.k12.hi.us; Supt PATRICIA HAMAMOTO.

Department of Health: Kinau Bldg, 1250 Punchbowl St, Honolulu, HI 96813; tel. (808) 586-4400; fax (808) 586-4444; e-mail janice.okubo@doh.hawaii.gov; internet www.hawaii.gov/health; Dir Dr CHIYOME LEINAALA FUKINO.

Department of Human Resources Development: Kamehameha Bldg, Suite 1400, 235 South Beretania St, Honolulu, Hawaii 96813; tel. (808) 587-1100; fax (808) 587-1106; internet www.hawaii.gov/hrd; Dir MARIE C. LADERTA.

Department of Human Services: Queen Liliuokalani Bldg, 1390 Miller St, Rm 209, Honolulu, HI 96813; tel. (808) 586-4997; fax (808) 586-4890; e-mail dhs@dhs.hawaii.gov; internet www.hawaii.gov/dhs; Dir LILLIAN B. KOLLER.

Department of Labor and Industrial Relations: Princess Ruth Keelikolani Bldg, 830 Punchbowl St, Honolulu, HI 96813; tel. (808) 586-8842; fax (808) 586-9099; e-mail dlir.director@hawaii.gov; internet www.hawaii.gov/labor; Dir DARWIN CHING.

Department of Land and Natural Resources: Kalanimoku Bldg, 1151 Punchbowl St, Honolulu, HI 96813; tel. (808) 587-0400; fax (808) 587-0390; e-mail dlnr@hawaii.gov; internet www.hawaii.gov/dlnr; Chair. LAURA H. THIELEN.

Department of Taxation: POB 259, Honolulu, HI 96809-0259; tel. (808) 587-4242; fax (808) 587-1488; e-mail tax.webmaster@hawaii.gov; internet www.hawaii.gov/tax; Dir KURT KAWAFUCHI.

Department of Transportation: Aliiaimoku Bldg, 869 Punchbowl St, Honolulu, HI 96813; tel. (808) 587-2150; fax (808) 587-2167; e-mail dotpao@hawaii.gov; internet www.hawaii.gov/dot; Dir BRENNON MORIOKA.

Legislature
(August 2008)

Senate

Dem. 21; Rep. 4; Total 25

President: COLLEEN HANABUSA (Dem.).

Vice-President: DONNA MERCADO KIM (Dem.).

Chief Clerk: CAROL TANIGUCHI.

House of Representatives

Dem. 44; Rep. 7; Total 51

Speaker: CALVIN K. Y. SAY (Dem.).

Vice-Speaker: PONO CHONG (Dem.).

Chief Clerk: PATRICIA MAU-SHIMIZU.

Idaho

Gross Area: 216,456 sq km (83,574 sq miles).

Resident Population (1 July 2007, estimate): 1,499,402.

State Capital, Principal City: Boise City (population 198,638 at 1 July 2006, estimate).

LOCATION, TOPOGRAPHY AND CLIMATE

The State of Idaho (nicknamed 'The Gem State') lies in the west of the USA and is bordered by Montana to the north-east, Wyoming to the east, Utah and Nevada to the south and Oregon and Washington to the west. To the north there is also a short border with the Canadian province of British Columbia. The northern two-thirds of Idaho are mountainous; the largest ranges are Bitterroot, Clearwater, Salmon River, Sawtooth, Lost River and Lemhi. Borah Peak in the Lost River Range is the state's highest elevation, at 3,859 m (12,662 ft). At the southern end of the main mountain region, the Snake River (one of the longest in the USA, with a length of 1,671 km—1,038 miles) curves across the state from east to west. The river then bends northwards to form part of Idaho's western boundary, passing through Hell's Canyon, which, at 7,900 ft, is the deepest gorge in North America. South of the Snake River Plain the land is arid and hilly, except in the state's south-eastern extremity, where there is a greener and more mountainous area. In the far north of the state is Lake Pend Oreille, covering 383 sq km (148 sq miles). The climate in Idaho varies according to altitude, with hot, dry summers in the south of the state and cold, snowy winters in the mountains. Eastern Idaho has a continental climate, with greater extremes of temperature.

HISTORICAL BACKGROUND

In 1805, when Meriwether Lewis and William Clark explored the region, Idaho was inhabited by the Shoshone, Northern Paiute, Salishan and Shapwailutan peoples. Fur traders set up posts in the area in 1809–34. Idaho officially became part of the USA in 1846, but the first permanent settlement was not established until Mormons founded Franklin in 1860. In the same year gold was discovered in northern Idaho, bringing large numbers of speculators to the region. Idaho Territory was organized in 1863 and Boise became the capital in the following year. The occupation of the land by increasing numbers of white settlers led to battles with the native tribes in the 1870s, which culminated in the capture and surrender of Chief Joseph of the Nez Percé in 1877. A second influx of speculators arrived in the 1880s, when large deposits of silver and lead were discovered. Idaho became the 43rd state to join the Union on 3 July 1890.

ECONOMY

Agriculture, lumber, mining, manufacturing, electronics and tourism are Idaho's principal industries. Gross domestic product by state was US $51,149m. in 2007 and per-head income in the state averaged $31,703 in the same year. In 2007 12.1% of the state population were thought to be living below the poverty threshold. The civilian labour force totalled 763,000 in mid-2008, with unemployment standing at 27,700 people (3.6%), ranking as the fifth lowest rate (alongside Nebraska and Utah) in the USA. Of the total number of employees in 2007, 5.3% were members of unions, the sixth lowest proportion nationally, while 6.4% were covered by union agreements.

In 2007 farmland covered 11.7m. acres (4.7m. ha). The average farm size in that year was 478 acres and there were 24,500 farms. There is a great need for irrigation in the state: some 46% of total cropland was irrigated in 2002. Crops provided 42% of the value of farm marketings in 2007, with livestock and livestock products contributing the remaining 58%. The principal agricultural commodities in that year were dairy products, cattle and calves, potatoes, hay and wheat. In 2007 Idaho was the USA's largest potato producer; it was ranked third for sugar beet production (behind Minnesota and North Dakota) and hay, and fifth for dairy products. Forestland covers approximately 41% of the state's area, and the timber industry is well established, with production composed entirely of softwoods. Idaho was the USA's leading producer of trout in 2004.

Idaho's mining industry is restricted to non-fuel minerals. Principal minerals in 2007 were molybdenum concentrates (for which the state ranked fourth in 2004), construction sand and gravel, phosphate rock and lead (ranked third in 2007) and silver. Idaho was also ranked fifth for pumice and pumicite and eighth for gemstones in 2007. The state produces over 70 types of precious and semi-precious stones, earning itself the nickname 'The Gem State'. In 2007 the value of Idaho's total mineral production was US $817m., with the state ranked 28th.

Manufacturing activity in the state is concentrated in the areas of processed food, lumber and wood products, primary and fabricated metals, electronic and computer equipment, industrial machinery and chemicals. Idaho's manufacturing shipments were valued at US $14,904m. in 2006, of which 47% was added during manufacture. The state ranked 41st in terms of its value of shipments in that year.

Domestic travel expenditures generated US $2,404m. in 2004; the state was ranked 41st among the states in terms of these expenditures.

Total general expenditures by the state government in 2006 were US $6,353m. General revenue totalled $5,979m., of which $1,823m. was provided by the federal Government and $3,143m. was derived from taxes. Federal aid totalled $1,829m. in 2006.

CONSTITUTION AND GOVERNMENT

Idaho's only Constitution was adopted in 1889 and became effective on 3 July 1890. An amendment to the Constitution proposed by the Legislature has to be passed by two-thirds of the elected members of each house, followed by a majority of voters. The Governor and Lieutenant-Governor are elected separately to serve four-year terms and there is no limit to the number of terms they may serve. The Legislature has 35 senators and 70 representatives, all serving two-year terms. Regular sessions of the Legislature take place annually, starting in January. A bill becomes law when it has been passed by both houses and signed by the Governor. During session the Governor has five days in which to consider a bill, after which it becomes law unless vetoed. After session a bill becomes law unless vetoed within 10 days after adjournment. A vote by two-thirds of the elected legislators in each house is required to override the Governor's veto. Legislation generally becomes effective in the July following enactment. In 2006 the Republican candidate, C. L. 'Butch' Otter, was elected to the governorship, securing 52% of the votes cast. In the 2008 presidential election the Republicans secured an estimated 62% of the votes cast. There are 44 administrative counties in Idaho.

Elected Executive Branch Officials

Governor (2007–11): C. L. (BUTCH) OTTER (Rep.).

Lieutenant-Governor: JAMES E. RISCH (Rep.).

Secretary of State: BEN YSURSA (Rep.).

Attorney-General: LAWRENCE G. WASDEN (Rep.).

Treasurer: RON G. CRANE (Rep.).

Controller: DONNA M. JONES (Rep.).

Superintendent of Public Instruction: TOM LUNA (Rep.).

Selected Government Addresses

Office of the Governor: State Capitol Bldg, 2nd Floor, 700 West Jefferson St, POB 83720, Boise, ID 83720-0034; tel. (208) 334-2100; fax (208) 334-2175; e-mail governor@gov.state.id.us; internet gov.idaho.gov.

Office of the Lieutenant-Governor: State Capitol Bldg, Rm 225, 700 West Jefferson St, Boise, ID 83720-0057; tel. (208) 334-2200; fax (208) 334-3259; e-mail ehodson@lgo.idaho.gov; internet lgo.idaho.gov.

Office of the Secretary of State: 304 North 8th St, POB 83720, Boise, ID 83720-0080; tel. (208) 334-2300; fax (208) 334-2282; e-mail sosinfo@sos.idaho.gov; internet www.idsos.state.id.us.

Office of the Attorney-General: 700 West State St, POB 83720, Boise, ID 83720-0010; tel. (208) 334-2400; fax (208) 854-8071; internet www2.state.id.us/ag.

Office of the Treasurer: 304 North 8th St, Rm 208, POB 83720, Boise, ID 83720-0091; tel. (208) 334-3200; fax (208) 332-2960; internet www.sto.idaho.gov.

Office of the Controller: 700 West State St, POB 83720, Boise, ID 83720-0011; tel. (208) 334-3100; fax (208) 334-2671; e-mail bhoaglun@sco.idaho.gov; internet www.sco.idaho.gov.

Department of Agriculture: 2270 Old Penitentiary Rd, POB 790, Boise, ID 83701-0790; tel. (208) 332-8500; fax (208) 334-2170; e-mail info@agri.idaho.gov; internet www.agri.idaho.gov; Dir CELIA R. GOULD.

Department of Commerce: 700 West State St, Boise, ID 83720; tel. (208) 334-2470; fax (208) 334-6300; e-mail webmaster@commerce.idaho.gov; internet commerce.idaho.gov; Dir DONALD A. DIETRICH.

Department of Correction: 1299 North Orchard St, Suite 110, Boise, ID 83706; tel. (208) 658-2000; e-mail inquire@idoc.idaho.gov; internet www.idoc.idaho.gov; Dir BRENT REINKE.

Department of Education: 650 West State St, POB 83720, Boise, ID 83720-0027; tel. (208) 332-6800; fax (208) 334-2228; e-mail mrmcgrath@sde.idaho.gov; internet www.sde.idaho.gov; headed by the Supt of Public Instruction.

Department of Finance: 800 Park Blvd, Suite 200, Boise, ID 83712; tel. (208) 332-8000; fax (208) 332-8097; e-mail finance@finance.idaho.gov; internet finance.idaho.gov; Dir GAVIN M. GEE.

Department of Health and Welfare: 450 West State St, POB 83720, Boise, ID 83720-0036; tel. (208) 334-5500; fax (208) 334-6558; e-mail apsportal@idhw.state.id.us; internet www.healthandwelfare.idaho.gov; Dir RICHARD ARMSTRONG.

Department of Insurance: 700 West State St, POB 83720, Boise, ID 83720-0043; tel. (208) 334-4250; fax (208) 334-4398; internet www.doi.idaho.gov; Dir BILL DEAL.

Department of Labor: 317 West Main St, Boise, ID 83735; tel. (208) 332-3570; fax (208) 334-6300; e-mail www@labor.idaho.gov; internet labor.idaho.gov; Dir ROGER B. MADSEN.

Department of Lands: 300 North 6th St, Suite 103, POB 83720, Boise, ID 83720-0050; tel. (208) 334-0200; fax (208) 334-3698; e-mail gbacon@idl.idaho.gov; internet www.idl.idaho.gov; Dir GEORGE BACON.

Department of Transportation: 3311 West State St, POB 7129, Boise, ID 83707-1129; tel. (208) 334-8000; fax (208) 334-3858; internet www.itd.idaho.gov; Dir PAMELA LOWE.

Department of Water Resources: 322 East Front St, POB 83720, Boise, ID 83720-0098; tel. (208) 287-4800; fax (208) 287-6700; e-mail idwrinfo@idwr.idaho.gov; internet www.idwr.idaho.gov; Dir DAVID R. TUTHILL, Jr.

Military Division: Joint Force Headquarters, 3882 West Ellsworth St, Bldg 440, Boise, ID 83705; tel. (208) 272-3553; fax (208) 272-3560; e-mail alex.shaffer@us.army.mil; internet www.idahoarmyguard.org; Adj.-Gen. Maj.-Gen. LAWRENCE F. LAFRENZ.

Public Utilities Commission: 472 West Washington St, POB 83720, Boise, ID 83720-0074; tel. (208) 334-0300; fax (208) 334-3762; e-mail glene.fadness@puc.idaho.gov; internet www.puc.state.id.us; Pres. PAUL KJELLANDER.

Tax Commission: 800 Park Blvd, Plaza IV, POB 36, Boise, ID 83722-0410; tel. (208) 334-7660; fax (208) 334-7660; e-mail taxrep@tax.idaho.gov; internet tax.idaho.gov; Chair. ROYCE CHIGBROW.

Legislature
(August 2008)

Senate

Rep. 28; Dem. 7; Total 35

President: Lt-Gov. JAMES E. RISCH (Rep.).

President Pro Tempore: ROBERT L. GEDDES (Rep.).

Secretary: JEANNINE WOOD.

House of Representatives

Rep. 51; Dem. 19; Total 70

Speaker: LAWRENCE DENNEY (Rep.).

Chief Clerk: BONNIE ALEXANDER.

Illinois

Gross Area: 150,007 sq km (57,918 sq miles).

Resident Population (1 July 2007, estimate): 12,852,548.

State Capital: Springfield.

Principal Cities (population at 1 July 2006, estimate): Chicago 2,833,321; Aurora 170,617; Rockford 155,138; Naperville 142,901; Joliet 142,702; Springfield (capital) 116,482; Peoria 113,107.

LOCATION, TOPOGRAPHY AND CLIMATE

The State of Illinois (nicknamed 'The Prairie State') lies in the Midwest region of the USA, bordered by Wisconsin to the north, Indiana to the east, Kentucky to the south-east and Missouri and Iowa to the west. In the north-east the state has a shoreline with Lake Michigan. The state lies within the Central Plains and is mainly flat; however, the land becomes hilly in the north-west, towards the Driftless Area of Wisconsin, and in the south, where it rises towards the Ozark Plateau. The Mississippi River forms Illinois' western border and the Ohio and Wabash its southern and eastern boundaries, respectively. The Illinois River traverses the state from north-east to south-west before flowing into the Mississippi River at Grafton, just north of the confluence of the Mississippi and Missouri. Illinois's climate is generally temperate, with hot, wet summers and cold, snowy winters.

HISTORICAL BACKGROUND

Algonquian peoples inhabited Illinois when the first Europeans explored the region in the 17th century. The first permanent European settlements were established by the French near what is now St Louis in 1699 and at Kaskaskia in 1703. The area was ceded to the United Kingdom in 1763, but in 1778 the rebel colonist general, George Rogers Clark, took Kaskaskia. Granted territorial status in 1809, Illinois was admitted to the Union as the 21st state on 3 December 1818 and Springfield became the capital in 1839. Until the 19th century Illinois was only sparsely populated by white settlers, but the defeat of the local American Indians in the Black Hawk War of 1832 made land available in the south and many farmers from Kentucky moved into the region. Illinois remained divided over the slavery issue until 1856, when slavery was abolished. The state fought for the Union during the Civil War.

ECONOMY

The principal economic activities in Illinois are manufacturing, construction, services, finance, insurance, real estate, wholesale and retail trade, travel, health care and agriculture. Gross domestic product by state totalled US $609,570m. in 2007, the fifth highest in the USA. In that year average per-head income in the state totalled $40,919, while 11.9% of the population were estimated to be living below the poverty line. The civilian labour force numbered 6,850,600 in mid-2008, with unemployment affecting more than 505,700 workers, or 7.4% of the work-force. In 2007 union membership applied to 14.5% of the total number of employees, while 15.2% were covered by union agreements.

Farmland covered 27.3m. acres, or 76.3% of Illinois' land area, in 2007. The average size of the 72,500 farms in that year was 377 acres. Just 1.6% of total cropland was irrigated in 2002. In 2007 crops accounted for 82% of farm income, and livestock and livestock products for 18%. Illinois ranked seventh among the states in terms of farm marketings in that year. Its most valuable agricultural commodities were corn (maize), soybeans, hogs, and cattle and calves. In 2007 it was ranked second for the production of corn and soybeans (after Iowa) and fifth for hog production. Forestland covers some 4.3m. acres (about 12% of the total land area) and is concentrated in the south and west of the state.

Coal is widely mined in Illinois; the state produced 32.4m. short tons of coal in 2007, when it was the USA's ninth largest producer.

Crude petroleum and a small amount of natural gas are also produced. Non-fuel mineral production was valued at US $1,220m. in 2007, the 20th highest among the states. This was derived entirely from production of industrial minerals; no metals have been produced in Illinois since 1996. The leading minerals in 2007 were crushed stone, portland cement, sand and gravel and lime. The state was ranked first in production of industrial sand and gravel and sixth for crushed stone; production of fuller's earth, tripoli (diatomite) and peat was also important.

Manufacturing activity is centred on Chicago, but occurs throughout the state and is well diversified. Illinois ranked fourth in the USA in 2006 in terms of the value of shipments. The major industry groups are food and kindred products, print products, chemicals, plastics, computer, electric and electronic equipment, primary and fabricated metals, machinery and transportation equipment. The state ranked fifth in the nation for the manufacture of raw steel in 2000. Illinois's manufacturing shipments were valued at US $242,525m. in 2006, with 44% of this value added during manufacture.

Chicago became established as the financial centre of the Midwest states at the time of the Civil War, but has recently lost out to Ohio in this regard. At the end of 2006 the combined assets of commercial banks totalled US $381,000m., with Illinois ranked ninth in the country. The state is also an extremely important insurance centre, with the Midwest Stock Exchange in Chicago second only to that of New York in size.

Chicago is a significant convention centre and a major tourist attraction. Domestic travel expenditures amounted to US $23,010m. (the sixth highest in the nation) in 2004.

Total general expenditures by the state government in 2006 were US $55,768m. Total general revenue in that year was $49,271m., of which $12,849m. was provided by the federal Government and $28,129m. came from taxes. Illinois received $14,689m. in federal aid in 2006.

CONSTITUTION AND GOVERNMENT

Illinois' current Constitution, its fourth, was adopted in 1970 and became effective on 1 July 1971. A constitutional amendment proposed by the General Assembly needs to be approved by three-fifths of the elected members of each house and then ratified by either the majority of those voting in an election or three-fifths of the electorate voting specifically on the amendment. The Governor and Lieutenant-Governor are elected jointly, both serving four-year terms of office. There is no limit to the number of terms that may be served. The General Assembly has 59 senators and 118 representatives, the latter serving two-year terms. The entire Senate is re-elected every 10 years, senators being elected for two four-year terms and one two-year term within each 10-year period. Regular sessions of the General Assembly begin in January and there are no statutory limitations on their length. A bill becomes law when it has been passed by the General Assembly and signed by the Governor. The Governor is allowed 60 days to consider a bill, after which it becomes law if not acted upon. A gubernatorial veto may be overridden by a two-thirds' majority of each house. In 2006 Rod Blagojevich, the Democratic incumbent, received 50% of the votes cast in the gubernatorial election. In the 2008 presidential election the Democratic candidate, Illinois Senator Barack Obama, gained the largest share of the votes cast, taking some 62%. Illinois has 102 administrative counties.

Elected Executive Branch Officials

Governor (2007–11): Rod R. Blagojevich (Dem.).

Lieutenant-Governor: Pat Quinn (Dem.).

Secretary of State: Jesse White (Dem.).

Attorney-General: Lisa Madigan (Dem.).

Treasurer: Alexi Giannoulias (Dem.).

Comptroller: Daniel W. Hynes (Dem.).

Selected Government Addresses

Office of the Governor: 207 State House, Springfield, IL 62706; tel. (217) 782-0244; fax (217) 524-4049; internet www.illinois.gov/gov.

Office of the Lieutenant-Governor: 214 State House, Springfield, IL 62706; tel. (217) 782-7884; fax (217) 524-6262; internet www.standingupforillinois.org.

Office of the Secretary of State: 213 State House, Springfield, IL 62756; tel. (217) 782-5763; fax (217) 785-0358; e-mail jessewhite@ilsos.net; internet www.sos.state.il.us.

Office of the Attorney-General: 500 South 2nd St, Springfield, IL 62706; tel. (217) 782-1090; fax (217) 782-7046; internet www.illinoisattorneygeneral.gov.

Office of the Treasurer: 219 Statehouse, Springfield, IL 62706; tel. (217) 782-2211; fax (217) 785-2777; e-mail webmaster@treasurer.state.il.us; internet www.treasurer.il.gov.

Office of the Comptroller: 201 State House, Springfield, IL 62706-0001; tel. (217) 782-6000; fax (217) 782-7561; internet www.ioc.state.il.us.

Department of Agriculture: State Fairgrounds, POB 19281, Springfield, IL 62794-9281; tel. (217) 782-2172; fax (217) 785-4505; e-mail agr.pio@illinois.gov; internet www.agr.state.il.us; Dir Tom Jennings (acting).

Department of Commerce and Economic Opportunity: 620 East Adams St, Springfield, IL 62701; tel. (217) 782-7500; fax (217) 524-1627; internet www.commerce.state.il.us/dceo; Dir Jack Lavin.

Department of Corrections: 1301 Concordia Ct, POB 19277, Springfield, IL 62794-9277; tel. (217) 522-2200; fax (217) 522-8719; e-mail info@doc.illinois.gov; internet www.idoc.state.il.us; Dir Roger E. Walker, Jr.

Department of Financial and Professional Regulation, Division of Insurance: 320 West Washington St, 4th Floor, Springfield, IL 62767-0001; tel. (217) 782-4515; fax (217) 782-5020; e-mail director@ins.state.il.us; internet www.idfpr.com/doi/default2.asp; Dir Michael T. McRaith.

Department of Labor: 1 West Old State Capitol Plaza, Rm 300, Springfield, IL 62701; tel. (217) 782-6206; fax (217) 782-0598; e-mail pio.dol@illinois.gov; internet www.state.il.us/agency/idol; Dir Catherine Shannon.

Department of Military Affairs: 1301 North MacArthur Blvd, Springfield, IL 62702-2399; tel. (217) 761-3569; fax (217) 761-3527; e-mail ngilstaffpao@ng.army.mil; internet www.il.ngb.army.mil; Adj.-Gen. Maj.-Gen. William L. Enyart.

Department of Natural Resources: 1 Natural Resources Way, Springfield, IL 62702-1271; tel. (217) 782-6302; internet www.dnr.state.il.us; Dir Sam Flood (acting).

Department of Public Health: 535 West Jefferson St, 5th Floor, Springfield, IL 62761; tel. (217) 782–4977; fax (217) 782-3987; e-mail dph.mailus@illinois.gov; internet www.idph.state.il.us; Dir Dr Damon T. Arnold.

Department of Revenue: Willard Ice Bldg, 101 West Jefferson St, Springfield, IL 62702; tel. (217) 785-3336; fax (217) 782-6337; internet www.revenue.state.il.com; Dir Brian Hamer.

Department of Transportation: 2300 South Dirksen Pkwy, Springfield, IL 62764; tel. (217) 782-7820; fax (217) 782-6121; internet www.dot.il.gov; Sec. Milton R. Sees.

Environmental Protection Agency: 1021 North Grand Ave East, POB 19276, Springfield, IL 62794-9276; tel. (217) 782-3397; fax (217) 782-9039; e-mail dennis.mcmurray@illinois.gov; internet www.epa.state.il.us; Dir Douglas P. Scott.

State Board of Education: 100 North First St, Springfield, IL 62777-0001; tel. (217) 782-4321; fax (217) 524-8585; internet www.isbe.state.il.us; State Supt of Schools Dr Christopher Koch.

State Police: 801 South 7th St, POB 19461, Springfield, IL 62794-9461; tel. (217) 782-6637; fax (217) 524-4661; e-mail askisp@isp.state.il.us; internet www.isp.state.il.us; Dir Larry G. Trent.

General Assembly

(August 2008)

Senate

Dem. 37; Rep. 22; Total 59

President: Emil Jones, Jr (Dem.).

Secretary: Deborah Shipley.

House of Representatives

Dem. 67; Rep. 51; Total 118

Speaker: Michael J. Madigan (Dem.).

Chief Clerk: Mark Mahoney.

Indiana

Gross Area: 94,328 sq km (36,420 sq miles).

Resident Population (1 July 2007, estimate): 6,345,289.

State Capital: Indianapolis.

Principal Cities (population at 1 July 2006, estimate): Indianapolis (capital) 785,597; Fort Wayne 248,637; Evansville 115,738; South Bend 104,905.

LOCATION, TOPOGRAPHY AND CLIMATE

The State of Indiana (nicknamed 'The Hoosier State') is in the Midwest region of the USA, with Michigan to its north, Ohio to the east, Kentucky to the south and Illinois to the west. In the north-west there is a lacustrine coast on Lake Michigan. Undulating land in the north of the state gives way to rougher hill-country in the south.

The most fertile region of Indiana is in the north-central area, which has numerous lakes and streams. Indiana's major rivers are the Wabash, flowing across the state from north-east to the west and turning south to form the southern half of the boundary with Illinois, and the Ohio, forming the boundary with Kentucky. The climate is humid and continental.

HISTORICAL BACKGROUND

When the French explorers Jacques Marquette and Robert Cavelier, Sieur de la Salle, arrived in Indiana in the 1670s, the region was inhabited by the Miami, Potawatomi, Kickapoo, Piankashaw, Shawnee and Wea American Indians. In the early 18th century white settlements were established at Fort Miami (now Fort Wayne), Kekionga, Fort Ouiatanon and Vincennes. Indiana was part of the territory ceded by France to the United Kingdom in 1763. The first US settlement was Clarksville, established in 1784. Indiana was granted territorial status in 1800 and assumed its present boundaries on joining the Union as the 19th state on 11 December 1816. Indianapolis became the capital in 1825. The state fought for the Union during the Civil War, although there was initially some sympathy with the Southern cause.

ECONOMY

Manufacturing, wholesale and retail trade, finance, agriculture, public utilities, transportation and services are the main contributors to the economy of Indiana. Gross domestic product by state was US $246,439m. in 2007, while per-head income in the state totalled $33,152. In that year 12.3% of the population were considered to be living below the poverty threshold. The civilian labour force numbered 3,281,100 in mid-2008, with unemployment affecting 201,100 workers (6.1%). Of the total number of workers in 2007, 12.0% were union members and 12.9% were covered by union agreements. A particularly high proportion of those employed in manufacturing are unionized.

Farmland covered 15m. acres, or some 65% of Indiana's land area, in 2007. The average farm size in 2007 was 255 acres and there were 58,800 farms. In that year 67% of the value of farm sales was derived from crops and 33% from livestock and livestock products. Indiana's principal agricultural products (in terms of value) in 2007 were corn, soybeans, hogs and dairy products. The state ranked fourth overall in the production of soybeans in 2007, fifth for corn and sixth for hogs. It was sixth among the states for tomatoes in 2007. Chicken eggs, cattle and calves and turkeys were also important contributors to livestock income. Indiana is the USA's leading producer of ducks, with over 30% of the total annual US production. Indiana's forestland base has risen by approximately 430,000 acres since 1917. Some 19% of the land is covered by around 4.5m acres of forest. Hardwoods account for 99% of the state's modest timber production.

Indiana's non-fuel mineral production was valued at US $997m. in 2007, with the state ranked 22nd in this respect. It was second only to Wisconsin in the production of dimension stone nationally in 2007, and among the most significant producers of masonry cement and peat; Indiana also ranked seventh for production of gypsum in that year. Crushed stone, portland cement, sand and gravel and lime were other important minerals. The state is also an important producer of coal (ranking eighth in the USA, with an output of 34.0m. short tons in 2007), and produces some petroleum and natural gas.

While much manufacturing activity is centred around Indianapolis, the city of Gary and the nearby region is an important steel-making centre for the nation. Indiana continued to lead the states in production of raw steel in 2007, with around 24% of total US output, and was ranked third for production of aluminium in 2003. In terms of its value of shipments, Indiana ranked seventh in the nation in 2006. Its manufacturing shipments were valued at US $207,504m. in that year; of this, 43% was added during manufacture. The principal industrial sectors include transportation equipment and motor vehicles, primary metal industries, industrial machinery and equipment, chemical products, and electric and electronic equipment. With Indianapolis the junction of several interstate highways, the state is the base for many US trucking lines.

In 2004 domestic travel expenditures amounted to US $7,143m.; the state was ranked 26th in the nation.

Total general expenditures by the state government amounted to US $26,959m. in 2006; general revenue in that year came to $29,604m., with $7,059m. of this from federal Government and $13,626m. derived from taxes. Indiana received $6,990m. in federal aid in 2006.

CONSTITUTION AND GOVERNMENT

The current Constitution of Indiana is the state's second and became effective on 1 November 1851. Constitutional amendments proposed by the General Assembly have to be approved by a majority of the elected members in each house in two successive sessions, and then ratified by a majority of state voters. The Governor and Lieutenant-Governor of Indiana are elected jointly to serve a term of four years, the Governor serving no more than two terms consecutively. Indiana has no formal cabinet system. The state General Assembly has 50 senators and 100 representatives, elected to serve four- and two-year terms, respectively. Alternate halves of the Senate are re-elected every two years. Regular legislative sessions take place annually, beginning in January. Sessions may last no longer than 61 legislative days in odd-numbered years and 30 days in even-numbered years. A bill becomes law (except in an emergency) after it has been approved by both houses of the General Assembly, has been signed by the Governor and has been published and circulated to all counties. The Governor is allowed seven days to consider a bill, after which it becomes law unless vetoed. A gubernatorial veto may be overridden by a majority of the elected legislators in each house. In the 2008 gubernatorial election the Republican incumbent, Mitch Daniels, was re-elected with some 58% of the vote. In the concurrent presidential election the Democrats secured a very narrow majority, winning just under 50% of the votes cast in the state. Indiana has 92 administrative counties.

Elected Executive Branch Officials

Governor (2009–13): MITCHELL (MITCH) E. DANIELS (Rep.).

Lieutenant-Governor: BECKY SKILLMAN (Rep.).

Secretary of State: TODD ROKITA (Rep.).

Attorney-General: STEVE CARTER (Rep.).

Treasurer: RICHARD MOURDOCK (Rep.).

Auditor: TIM BERRY (Rep.).

Superintendent of Public Instruction: Dr SUELLEN K. REED (Rep.).

Selected Government Addresses

Office of the Governor: 206 State House, 200 West Washington St, Indianapolis, IN 46204-2797; tel. (317) 232-4567; fax (317) 232-3443; e-mail jjankowski@gov.in.gov; internet www.in.gov/gov.

Office of the Lieutenant-Governor: 333 State House, 200 West Washington St, Indianapolis, IN 46204-2797; tel. (317) 234-4258; fax (317) 232-4788; e-mail cdenault@lg.in.gov; internet www.in.gov/lgov.

Office of the Secretary of State: 201 State House, 200 West Washington St, Indianapolis, IN 46204; tel. (317) 232-6531; fax (317) 233-3283; e-mail jgavin@sos.in.gov; internet www.in.gov/sos.

Office of the Attorney-General: Indiana Government Center South, 302 West Washington St, Indianapolis, IN 46204; tel. (317) 232-6201; fax (317) 232-7979; e-mail constituent@atg.in.gov; internet www.in.gov/attorneygeneral.

Office of the Treasurer: 242 State House, 200 West Washington St, Indianapolis, IN 46204; tel. (317) 232-6386; fax (317) 233-1780; e-mail tosstaff@tos.state.in.us; internet www.in.gov/tos.

Office of the Auditor: 240 State House, 200 West Washington St, Indianapolis, IN 46204-2793; tel. (317) 232-3300; fax (317) 233-2794; e-mail comments@auditor.in.gov; internet www.in.gov/auditor.

Department of Education: 229 State House, 200 West Washington St, Indianapolis, IN 46204-2798; tel. (317) 232-6665; fax (317) 232-8004; e-mail sreed@doe.in.gov; internet www.doe.state.in.us; headed by the Supt of Public Instruction.

Budget Agency: 212 State House, 200 West Washington St, Indianapolis, IN 46204; tel. (317) 232-5610; fax (317) 233-3323; e-mail budgetagency@sba.state.in.us; internet www.in.gov/sba; Dir CHRISTOPHER A. RUHL.

Department of Correction: Indiana Government Center South, Rm E334, 302 West Washington St, Indianapolis, IN 46204; tel. (317) 232-5780; fax (317) 232-6798; e-mail dsgarrison@doc.in.gov; internet www.in.gov/indcorrection; Commr EDWIN G. BUSS.

Department of Environmental Management: Indiana Government Center North, 100 North Senate Ave, Mail Code 50-01, Indianapolis, IN 46204-2251; tel. (317) 232-8603; fax (317) 233-6647; internet www.in.gov/idem; Commr THOMAS W. EASTERLY.

Department of Health: 2 North Meridian St, Indianapolis, IN 46204; tel. (317) 233-1325; internet www.in.gov/isdh; Commr Dr JUDITH A. MONROE.

Department of Insurance: 311 West Washington St, Suite 300, Indianapolis, IN 46204-2787; tel. (317) 232-3520; e-mail doi@doi.state.in.us; internet www.in.gov/idoi; Commr JIM ATTERHOLT.

Department of Labor: Indiana Government Center South, Rm W195, 402 West Washington St, Indianapolis, IN 46204; tel. (317) 232-2655; fax (317) 233-3790; e-mail commissioner@dol.in.gov; internet www.in.gov/labor; Commr LORI A. TORRES.

Department of Natural Resources: Indiana Government Center South, Rm W160, 402 West Washington St, Indianapolis, IN 46204; tel. (317) 232-4200; fax (317) 233-6811; internet www.in.gov/dnr; Dir ROBERT E. CARTER, Jr.

Department of Revenue: Indiana Government Center North, Rm N248, 100 North Senate Ave, Indianapolis, IN 46204; tel. (317) 234-3793; e-mail smcfarland@dor.in.gov; internet www.in.gov/dor; Commr JOHN ECKART.

Department of Transportation: Indiana Government Center North, Rm 755, 100 North Senate Ave, Indianapolis, IN 46204; tel. (317) 232-5533; fax (317) 233-1481; e-mail indot@indot.in.gov; internet www.in.gov/dot; Commr KARL B. BROWNING.

Economic Development Corporation (IEDC): 1 North Capitol Ave, Suite 700, Indianapolis, IN 46204; tel. (317) 232-8992; fax (317) 233-5123; e-mail nfeltman@iedc.in.gov; internet www.in.gov/doc; Sec. of Commerce and IEDC Pres. NATHAN J. FELTMAN.

State Police Department: Indiana Government Center North, Rm N340, 100 North Senate Ave, Indianapolis, IN 46204-2259; tel. (317) 232-8241; fax (317) 232-0652; internet www.in.gov/isp; Supt Dr PAUL E. WHITESELL.

Utility Regulatory Commission: National City Center, Suite 1500E, 101 West Washington St, Indianapolis, IN 46204; tel. (317) 232-2701; fax (317) 232-6758; e-mail info@urc.state.in.us; internet www.in.gov/iurc; Chair. DAVID LOTT HARDY.

General Assembly
(August 2008)

Senate

Rep. 33; Dem. 17; Total 50

President: Lt-Gov. BECKY SKILLMAN (Rep.).

President Pro Tempore: DAVID LONG (Rep.).

Principal Secretary: (vacant).

House of Representatives

Dem. 51; Rep. 49; Total 100

Speaker: B. PATRICK BAUER (Dem.).

Principal Clerk: M. CLINT MCKAY.

Iowa

Gross Area: 145,754 sq km (56,276 sq miles).

Resident Population (1 July 2007, estimate): 2,988,046.

State Capital: Des Moines.

Principal Cities (population at 1 July 2006, estimate): Des Moines (capital) 193,886; Cedar Rapids 124,417.

LOCATION, TOPOGRAPHY AND CLIMATE

The State of Iowa (nicknamed 'The Hawkeye State') lies in the Midwest region of the USA and is bordered by Minnesota to the north, Wisconsin and Illinois to the east, Missouri to the south and Nebraska and South Dakota to the west. Iowa's intensely cultivated rolling plain gradually rises in altitude from the south-east to the north-west. The land is drained by two major rivers: the Mississippi, which forms the eastern boundary of the state, and the Missouri, which provides the southern two-thirds of the western boundary. Numerous tributaries running across Iowa flow into these two rivers. The state has a humid, continental climate.

HISTORICAL BACKGROUND

Among the native American Indians occupying Iowa when the Frenchmen Louis Joliet and Jacques Marquette travelled through the region in 1673 were the Illinois, Sioux and Iowa tribes. Before the USA took control of Iowa under the Louisiana Purchase of 1803, the only person to have exploited the land was a French Canadian, Julien Dubuque, who had opened a lead mine in 1788. After the Black Hawk War of 1832 Indian land became increasingly available to white settlers, who poured into the region to take advantage of the fertile prairie. Granted territorial status in 1838, Iowa joined the Union on 28 December 1846 as the 29th state, and Des Moines became the capital in 1857. Iowa was fiercely anti-slavery and fought on the side of the Union during the Civil War.

ECONOMY

Iowa is one of the USA's most important agricultural states. Its manufacturing activity is focused on the processing of farm products and the manufacture of agricultural equipment. Other main components of its gross domestic product by state of US $129,026m. in 2007 were finance, insurance and services. In the same year the state had an average per-head income of $34,796; it was estimated that 11.0% of the population were living below the poverty line in that year. The civilian labour force numbered 1,698,300 in mid-2008 with an unemployment rate of 3.8% of the work-force (65,200 persons). Of those employed in 2007, 10.5% were members of a trade union, although 13.1% were covered by union agreements.

Farmland covered some 31.6m. acres, or 88.1% of Iowa's total land area, in 2005. There were 88,400 farms in 2007, when land in farms accounted for 31.5m. acres and the average farm occupied 356 acres. The state had the third highest farming income of any state, behind California and Texas, in 2007, at US $19,037m. Of this total, 46% came from crops and 54% from livestock and livestock products. Iowa's most important products in 2007, in terms of marketing receipts, were corn, hogs, soybeans and cattle and calves. Wheat is grown towards the south of the state, and poultry-farming is also important. The state ranked first in the USA for production of chicken eggs in 2007. It was also the leading producer of hogs, corn and soybeans in that year. Approximately 6% of Iowa is forested—the lumber industry is relatively insignificant.

The state's non-fuel mineral production was valued at US $674m. in 2007, ranking 32nd in the USA. The leading minerals were crushed stone, portland cement, construction sand and gravel, crude gypsum and lime. Iowa was ranked second in production of crude gypsum in 2007. No metals are mined in the state.

Iowa's initial manufacturing activity was in the areas of food-processing and the manufacture of agricultural equipment. These industries have remained prominent, joined by the manufacture of chemicals and allied products (including agricultural chemicals), electronic and other electric equipment, household furniture and automobile accessories. Metal production is also significant, using raw materials obtained from outside the state. In terms of value of shipments, the state ranked 22nd in the USA in 2006. The total value of Iowa's manufacturing shipments in that year was US $91,484m.; of this, 45% was added during manufacture.

Tourism is not a major contributor to state income; domestic travel expenditures in 2004 amounted to just US $5,014m.

Total general expenditures by the state government were US $14,942m. in 2006; general revenue totalled $13,434m. The federal Government provided revenue of $4,089m. and taxes contributed $6,119m. Iowa received a total of $3,651m. in federal aid in 2006.

CONSTITUTION AND GOVERNMENT

Iowa's Constitution, its second, became effective on 3 September 1857. An amendment to the Constitution proposed by the General Assembly has to be approved by a majority of the elected members of each house and then ratified by a majority of state voters. The Governor is elected separately from the Lieutenant-Governor, to serve a four-year term of office, and there is no limit to the number of terms he or she may serve. There is no formal cabinet system. The General Assembly consists of 50 senators and 100 representatives, serving four- and two-year terms, respectively. Alternate halves of the Senate are re-elected every two years. The General Assembly convenes annually in January and there is no limit to the number of days a session may last. A bill must be approved by a simple majority of the elected members of each house before being presented to the Governor. During session the Governor is allowed three days to consider a bill, after which it becomes law unless vetoed. Outside session a bill becomes law unless vetoed within 30 days from the adjournment of the session. A gubernatorial veto may be overridden by a two-thirds' vote in each house of the General Assembly. Legislation generally becomes effective on 1 July following enactment. The Democratic candidate, Chester 'Chet' Culver, won the gubernatorial election in 2006, with 54% of the votes cast. In the presidential election in 2008 the Democrats secured an estimated 54% of the votes. There are 99 administrative counties in Iowa.

Elected Executive Branch Officials

Governor (2007–11): CHESTER (CHET) CULVER (Dem.).

Lieutenant-Governor: PATTY JUDGE (Dem.).

Secretary of State: MICHAEL A. MAURO (Dem.).

Attorney-General: TOM MILLER (Dem.).

Treasurer: MICHAEL L. FITZGERALD (Dem.).

Auditor: DAVID A. VAUDT (Rep.).

Secretary of Agriculture: BILL NORTHEY (Rep.).

Selected Government Addresses

Office of the Governor: State Capitol, 1007 East Grand Ave, Des Moines, IA 50319; tel. (515) 281-5211; fax (515) 281-6611; internet www.governor.iowa.gov.

Office of the Lieutenant-Governor: State Capitol, 1007 East Grand Ave, Des Moines, IA 50319; tel. (515) 281-5211; fax (515) 281-6611; internet www.governor.iowa.gov.

Office of the Secretary of State: State Capitol, Rm 105, 1007 East Grand Ave, Des Moines, IA 50319; tel. (515) 281-5204; fax (515) 242-5952; e-mail sos@sos.state.ia.us; internet www.sos.state.ia.us.

Office of the Attorney-General: Hoover Bldg, 1305 East Walnut St, Des Moines, IA 50319; tel. (515) 281-5164; fax (515) 281-4209; e-mail webteam@ag.state.ia.us; internet www.state.ia.us/government/ag.

Office of the Treasurer: State Capitol, 1007 East Grand Ave, Des Moines, IA 50319; tel. (515) 281-5368; fax (515) 281-7562; e-mail treasurer@iowa.gov; internet www.treasurer.state.ia.us.

Office of the Auditor: State Capitol, Rm 111, 1007 East Grand Ave, POB 333, Des Moines, IA 50302-0333; tel. (515) 281-5834; fax (515) 242-6134; e-mail info@auditor.state.ia.us; internet auditor.iowa.gov.

Department of Agriculture and Land Stewardship: Henry A. Wallace Bldg, 502 East 9th St, Des Moines, IA 50319; tel. (515) 281-5321; fax (515) 281-6236; e-mail agri@idals.state.ia.us; internet www.agriculture.state.ia.us; headed by the Sec. of Agriculture.

Department of Commerce: 200 East Grand Ave, Suite 300, Des Moines, IA 50309-1827; tel. (515) 281-4014; fax (515) 281-4862; e-mail walding@iowaabd.com; internet www.state.ia.us/government/com; Dir THOMAS B. GRONSTAL.

Department of Corrections: 510 East 12th St, Des Moines, IA 50319; tel. (515) 725-5701; e-mail doc.information@doc.state.ia.us; internet www.doc.state.ia.us; Dir JOHN R. BALDWIN.

Department of Economic Development: 200 East Grand Ave, Des Moines, IA 50309; tel. (515) 242-4700; fax (515) 242-4809; e-mail info@iowalifechanging.com; internet www.iowalifechanging.com; Dir MIKE TRAMONTINA.

Department of Education: Grimes Bldg, 400 East 14th St, Des Moines, IA 50319-0146; tel. (515) 281-5295; fax (515) 281-4122; e-mail elaine.watkins-miller@iowa.gov; internet www.state.ia.us/educate; Dir JUDY JEFFREY.

Department of Management: State Capitol, Des Moines, IA 50319; tel. (515) 281-3322; e-mail charles.krogmeier@iowa.gov; internet www.dom.state.ia.us; Dir CHARLES KROGMEIER.

Department of Natural Resources: Henry A. Wallace Bldg, 502 East Ninth St, Des Moines, IA 50319-0034; tel. (515) 281-5918; fax (515) 281-8895; e-mail kevin.baskins@dnr.iowa.gov; internet www.iowadnr.com; Dir RICHARD LEOPOLD.

Department of Public Defense: Joint Forces Headquarters, Iowa National Guard, 7105 North West 70th Ave, Johnston, IA 50131-1824; tel. (515) 252-4582; fax (515) 252-4656; e-mail paoia@ng.army.mil; internet www.iowanationalguard.com; Adj.-Gen. Maj.-Gen. RON DARDIS.

Department of Public Health: Lucas Bldg, 321 East 12th St, Des Moines, IA 50319-0075; tel. (515) 281-7689; internet www.idph.state.ia.us; Dir TOM NEWTON.

Department of Public Safety: 215 East 7th St, Des Moines, IA 50319; tel. (515) 725-6182; fax (515) 242-6136; e-mail dpsinfo@dps.state.ia.us; internet www.dps.state.ia.us; Commr EUGENE T. MEYER.

Department of Revenue: Hoover Bldg, 4th Floor, 1305 East Walnut St, POB 10460, Des Moines, IA 50306-0460; tel. (515) 281-3204; fax (515) 242-6487; e-mail idr@iowa.gov; internet www.state.ia.us/tax; Dir MARK R. SCHULING.

Department of Transportation: 800 Lincoln Way, Ames, IA 50010; tel. (515) 239-1101; fax (515) 239-1639; internet www.dot.state.ia.us; Dir NANCY J. RICHARDSON.

General Assembly
(August 2008)

Senate

Dem. 30; Rep. 20; Total 50

President: JOHN P. (JACK) KIBBIE (Dem.).

President Pro Tempore: JEFF DANIELSON (Dem.).

Secretary: MICHAEL E. MARSHALL.

House of Representatives

Dem. 53; Rep. 47; Total 100

Speaker: PAT MURPHY (Dem.).

Speaker Pro Tempore: POLLY BUKTA (Dem.).

Chief Clerk: MARK BRANDSGARD.

Kansas

Gross Area: 213,111 sq km (82,314 sq miles).

Resident Population (1 July 2007, estimate): 2,775,997.

State Capital: Topeka.

Principal Cities (population at 1 July 2006, estimate): Wichita 357,698; Overland Park 166,722; Kansas City 143,801; Topeka (capital) 122,113; Olathe 114,662.

LOCATION, TOPOGRAPHY AND CLIMATE

The State of Kansas (nicknamed 'The Sunflower State') is in the Midwest region of the USA, bordered by Nebraska to the north, Missouri to the east, Oklahoma to the south and Colorado to the west. The western part of Kansas lies in the eastern extremity of the Great Plains and is the highest region of the state, reaching 1,231 m (4,039 ft) at Mount Sunflower. The Smoky Hills and the Central Plains occupy the centre of the state. The land slopes down from the arid country near the Colorado border towards the east, where the Osage Plains, Flint Hills and Arkansas River Lowlands are found. The major rivers of Kansas are: the Missouri, which forms the state's north-eastern boundary; the Arkansas, curving across the state from Colorado to Oklahoma; and the Kansas and its tributaries, traversing the state to join the Missouri at Kansas City in the east. Kansas has a temperate but continental climate, with great annual and seasonal variations. High winds and tornadoes frequently sweep across the state.

HISTORICAL BACKGROUND

The first European explorer to enter Kansas was Francisco Coronado, a Spaniard, in 1541. At this time the region was inhabited by the Wichita, Pawnee, Kansa and Osage peoples, who were later joined by the Cheyenne, Arapaho, Comanche and Kiowa tribes. France and Spain claimed the area in the 18th century, but, in 1803, the French sold it to the USA as part of the Louisiana Purchase. Large numbers of Native American peoples were removed to the state after 1830. Kansas was granted territorial status in 1854 and a dispute as to whether it would become a free or a slave state ensued. Several violent incidents related to this dispute supplied the nickname 'Bleeding Kansas'. Kansas eventually entered the Union as a free state on 29 January 1861, becoming the 34th state to accede. Kansas fought on the side of the Union in the Civil War. Prohibition of alcoholic beverages was in force between 1880 and 1948.

ECONOMY

Principal economic activities in Kansas include agriculture, manufacturing, finance, insurance and real estate and services. In 2007 the gross domestic product by state totalled US $117,305m. Kansans had an average per-head income of $36,483 in that year, when it was estimated that 11.2% of the population were living below the poverty line. The civilian labour force totalled 1,517,900 in mid-2008, with unemployment affecting 74,900 workers, or 4.9% of the labour force. Of the total number of employees in 2007, 7.0% were union members and union agreements covered 8.7%.

Farmland covered 47.2m. acres (19.1m. ha) in 2007. This represented 89.9% of Kansas' land area, the second highest proportion of any state (behind Nebraska). In 2007 there were 63,800 farms, with an average size of 740 acres. In 2002 9% of total cropland was under irrigation. The state's farm income was the sixth highest in the country in 2007, with 61% derived from sales of livestock and livestock products and 39% from crops. The principal farm products in that year were cattle and calves, wheat, corn and soybeans. The state ranked second, behind North Dakota, in the production of wheat in 2007. It was third in the production of cattle and calves in 2007 (behind Texas and Nebraska). Approximately 3% of Kansas is forested.

The value of non-fuel mineral production in Kansas in 2007 was US $967m., with the state ranked 24th in the nation. Leading minerals were portland cement, grade-A helium (for which the state was ranked first in 2007), crushed stone and salt (ranked fifth). No metals were mined in the state. Kansas was the USA's ninth largest natural-gas and crude petroleum producer in 2005 and also produced a tiny amount of coal.

Manufacturing industry is concentrated in and around the Kansas City metropolitan area, Topeka and Wichita. Reflecting the economy's agricultural base, food and kindred products are among the leading industries, which also include chemicals, plastics, transportation equipment and machinery. The state's total manufacturing shipments were valued at US $68,258m. in 2006, with 37% added during manufacture. Kansas ranked 25th among the states in terms of its value of shipments in that year.

Tourism does not play a great part in the economy of the state; in 2004 domestic travel expenditures amounted to US $4,172m.

Total general expenditures by the state government in 2006 were US $12,553m., while general revenue totalled $11,449m. In that year the federal government contribution was $3,229m. and taxes contributed $6,275m. Kansas received $3,242m. in federal aid in 2006.

CONSTITUTION AND GOVERNMENT

Kansas's only Constitution was adopted in 1859 and became effective on 29 January 1861. Constitutional amendments proposed by the Legislature have to be approved by two-thirds of the elected members of each house and then ratified by a majority of state voters. The Governor and Lieutenant-Governor are elected jointly to serve a four-year term; neither office may be held for more than two terms consecutively. There are 40 senators and 125 representatives in the state Legislature, serving terms of four and two years, respectively. Regular sessions of the Legislature are held annually, beginning in January. In even-numbered years sessions are limited in length to 90 calendar days; in odd-numbered years no limit applies. After approval by a majority of the elected members in each house, a bill is presented to the Governor for consideration; it becomes law when signed or, if it remains unsigned, after a 10-day consideration period. A two-thirds' vote is required from each house to override a gubernatorial veto. Enacted legislation becomes effective upon publication. In 2006 the Democratic incumbent, Kathleen Sebelius, was re-elected Governor with 58% of the vote. However, in the 2008 presidential election, in which over 1.2m. people voted, the Republicans secured the largest share of the votes cast in the state, with an estimated 57%. There are 105 administrative counties in Kansas.

Elected Executive Branch Officials

Governor (2007–11): KATHLEEN SEBELIUS (Dem.).

Lieutenant-Governor: MARK PARKINSON (Dem.).

Secretary of State: RON THORNBURGH (Rep.).

Attorney-General: STEPHEN N. SIX (Dem.).

Treasurer: LYNN JENKINS (Rep.).

Commissioner of Insurance: SANDY PRAEGER (Rep.).

Selected Government Addresses

Office of the Governor: State Capitol, Suite 212–S, 300 SW 10th Ave, Topeka, KS 66612-1590; tel. (785) 296-3232; fax (785) 368-8788; internet www.governor.ks.gov.

Office of the Lieutenant-Governor: State Capitol, Room 231–North, 300 SW 10th Ave, Topeka, KS 66612-1590; tel. (785) 296-2213; fax (785) 296-5669; e-mail lt.governor@gov.state.ks.us; internet www.governor.ks.gov/ltgov.

Office of the Secretary of State: Memorial Hall, 1st Floor, 120 SW 10th Ave, Topeka, KS 66612-1594; tel. (785) 296-4564; fax (785) 296-4570; e-mail ron_thornburgh@kssos.org; internet www.kssos.org.

Office of the Attorney-General: Memorial Hall, 2nd Floor, 120 SW 10th Ave, Topeka, KS 66612-1597; tel. (785) 296-2215; fax (785) 296-6296; e-mail general@ksag.org; internet www.ksag.org.

Office of the Treasurer: 201 Landon State Office Bldg, Rm 201N, 900 SW Jackson St, Topeka, KS 66612-1235; tel. (785) 296-3171; fax (785) 296-7950; e-mail lynn@treasurer.state.ks.us; internet www.treasurer.state.ks.us.

Department of Insurance: 420 SW Ninth St, Topeka, KS 66612-1678; tel. (785) 296-3071; fax (785) 296-2283; e-mail commissioner@ksinsurance.org; internet www.ksinsurance.org; headed by Commr of Insurance.

Department of the Adjutant-General: 2800 SW Topeka Blvd, Topeka, KS 66611-1287; tel. (785) 274-1000; fax (785) 274-1616; e-mail sharon.watson3@us.army.mil; internet www.kansas.gov/ksadjutantgeneral; Adj.-Gen. Maj.-Gen. TOD M. BUNTING.

Department of Agriculture: 109 SW Ninth St, 4th Floor, Topeka, KS 66612-1280; tel. (785) 296-3556; fax (785) 296-8389; e-mail ksag@kda.ks.gov; internet www.ksda.gov; Sec. ADRIAN J. POLANSKY.

Department of Commerce: 1000 SW Jackson St, Suite 100, Topeka, KS 66612-1354; tel. (785) 296-3481; fax (785) 296-5055; e-mail jmonaco@kansascommerce.com; internet www.kansascommerce.com; Sec. DAVID D. KERR.

Department of Corrections: Landon State Office Bldg, 4th Floor, 900 SW Jackson St, Topeka, KS 66612-1284; tel. (785) 296-3317; fax (785) 296-0014; e-mail kdocpub@doc.ks.gov; internet docnet.dc.state.ks.us; Sec. ROGER WERHOLTZ.

Department of Health and Environment: Curtis State Office Bldg, 100 SW Jackson St, Topeka, KS 66012-1290; tel. (785) 296-1500; fax (785) 368-6368; e-mail info@kdhe.state.ks.us; internet www.kdheks.gov; Sec. RODERICK L. BREMBY.

Department of Revenue: Docking State Office Bldg, 915 SW Harrison St, Rm 155, Topeka, KS 66625-1588; tel. (785) 296-3909; fax (785) 291-3614; e-mail joan_wagnon@kdor.state.ks.us; internet www.ksrevenue.org; Sec. JOAN WAGNON.

Department of Social and Rehabilitation Services: Docking State Office Bldg, 915 SW Harrison St, Rm 603N, Topeka, KS 66612-1570; tel. (785) 296-3959; fax (785) 296-2173; internet www.srskansas.org; Sec. DON JORDAN.

Department of Transportation: Dwight D. Eisenhower State Office Bldg, 700 SW Harrison St, Topeka, KS 66612-1568; tel. (785) 296-3566; fax (785) 296-0287; e-mail publicinfo@ksdot.org; Sec. DEB MILLER.

Development Finance Authority: 555 South Kansas Ave, Suite 202, Topeka, KS 66603; tel. (785) 357-4445; fax (785) 357-4478; e-mail sweatherford@kdfa.org; internet www.kdfa.org; Pres. STEVE WEATHERFORD.

Division of the Highway Patrol: 122 SW Seventh St, Topeka, KS 66603-3847; tel. (785) 296-6800; fax (785) 296-5956; e-mail info@khp.state.ks.us; internet www.kansashighwaypatrol.org; Supt Col TERRY MAPLE.

State Board of Education: Department of Education, 120 SE 10th Ave, Topeka, KS 66612-1182; tel. (785) 296-3201; fax (785) 296-7933; internet www.ksde.org; Commr ALEXA POSNY.

Legislature

(August 2008)

Senate

Rep. 30; Dem. 10; Total 40

President: STEPHEN MORRIS (Rep.).

Vice-President: JOHN VRATIL (Rep.).

Secretary: PAT SAVILLE.

House of Representatives

Rep. 78; Dem. 47; Total 125

Speaker: MELVIN NEUFELD (Rep.).

Speaker Pro Tempore: DONALD DAHL (Rep.).

Chief Clerk: JANET E. JONES.

Kentucky

Gross Area: 104,665 sq km (40,411 sq miles).

Resident Population (1 July 2007, estimate): 4,241,474.

State Capital: Frankfort (population 27,077 at 1 July 2006, estimate).

Principal Cities (population at 1 July 2005): Louisville 556,429; Lexington-Fayette 268,080.

LOCATION, TOPOGRAPHY AND CLIMATE

The Commonwealth of Kentucky (nicknamed 'The Bluegrass State') lies in the South region of the USA. Its northern boundary is marked by the Ohio River and is bordered by Illinois, Indiana and Ohio; the north-eastern boundary is formed by the Big Sandy River, dividing Kentucky from West Virginia; the south-east shares a border with Virginia; and the south and west are bordered, respectively, by Tennessee and by Missouri (across the Mississippi River). The south-east of Kentucky is dominated by the Appalachian Mountains, rising to 1,263 m (4,145 ft) at Black Mountain. The Cumberland Plateau, at the edge of the mountains, slopes down towards the Lexington Plain in the north—'Bluegrass' country—and the hilly terrain of the Pennyroyal in the south-centre of the state. The limestone Pennyroyal region contains some of the world's largest caves, the most famous of which is Mammoth Cave. The extreme south-western part of the state lies in the low coastal plain of the Mississippi River. In addition to those forming its boundaries, Kentucky's rivers include the Kentucky, Green, Tradewater, Licking and Cumberland. Kentucky has a temperate and humid climate, with colder winters in the mountainous south-east.

HISTORICAL BACKGROUND

Kentucky was used as a hunting ground by the Shawnee, Delaware, Wyandot and Cherokee Indians when Thomas Walker and Christopher Gist first explored the region in 1750 and 1751. The first permanent white settlement was established by James Harrod, a Virginian, at Harrodsville (now Harrodsburg) in 1774. In 1776 Kentucky became a county of Virginia. During the second half of the 18th century the area became the main route for migration into the Mississippi Valley and new settlements sprang up, particularly in the 'Bluegrass' region. Kentucky entered the Union as the 15th state on 1 June 1792. Kentucky was divided over the slavery issue prior to the Civil War and, initially, declared itself neutral before opting for the Union side in 1861. Both Union and Confederate leaders, Abraham Lincoln and Jefferson Davis, were native Kentuckians.

ECONOMY

The most important sectors of Kentucky's economy are manufacturing, finance, insurance and real estate, retail trade and other service industries. Gross domestic product by state was US $154,184m. in 2007, with average per-head income at $30,787, the sixth lowest rate in the country. In that year 17.3% of the population were thought to be living below the poverty threshold, the fifth highest figure nationally. The civilian labour force totalled 2,065,000 in mid-2008 and the unemployment rate was 6.8% (139,900 persons), with the state ranked 15th nationally in this regard. In 2007 9.1% of workers belonged to a trade union, although 11.1% were covered by union agreements.

In 2007 farmland covered some 13.7m. acres (5.5m. ha). There were 83,000 farms in that year and the average farm size was low, at 165 acres. In 2007 livestock and livestock products accounted for 67% of farm income, while crop sales provided 33%. Kentucky's most important agricultural products, in terms of value, were horses and mules, broilers, cattle and calves and corn; soybeans and tobacco were also significant commodities. In 2007 Kentucky was the USA's largest producer of horses and mules, and ranked second only to North Carolina in tobacco production. Forestland covered 12.7m. acres of the state in 2003.

Kentucky is the USA's third most significant producer of coal, with an output of 115.3m. short tons in 2007. Crude petroleum and natural gas are also produced in the state. The value of Kentucky's non-fuel mineral production was US $913m. in 2007, ranked 25th in the nation. Crushed stone was the leading mineral, accounting for almost 55% of total state production in 2005, followed by lime (for which the state was ranked second in the nation in 2007) and portland cement. Construction sand and gravel, ball clays and gemstones are also produced. No metals have been mined in the state since 1990, although exploration is now under way.

Kentucky is a leading producer of American whisky and also a major supplier of the nation's motor vehicles. In 2006 the state ranked 14th in terms of value of shipments, with a total of US $112,695m., of which 38% was added during manufacture. Food and allied products, chemicals, machinery and transportation equipment are among the state's principal manufactured goods. Primary aluminium and raw steel are processed in Kentucky from materials obtained from other states and from abroad. The state was the USA's leading centre of primary aluminium production in 2005.

Domestic travel expenditures amounted to US $5,868m. in 2004. Total general expenditures by the state government in 2006 amounted to $21,992m., while general revenue totalled $20,061m., including federal contributions of $6,354m. and taxes of $9,953m. In 2006 the state received $5,828m. in federal aid.

CONSTITUTION AND GOVERNMENT

Kentucky's Constitution is the state's fourth and became effective on 28 September 1891. Amendments to the Constitution proposed by the General Assembly must be approved by three-fifths of the elected members of each house, and must then be ratified by a majority of state voters. The Governor and Lieutenant-Governor are elected jointly to serve four-year terms and may serve for two consecutive periods. There are 38 senators and 100 representatives in the state General Assembly, elected for four- and two-year terms, respectively. Alternate halves of the Senate are re-elected every two years. Regular legislative sessions, which start in January, may last no longer than 60 legislative days in even-numbered years and 30 days in odd-numbered years. A bill becomes law when it has been approved by a majority of the General Assembly equal to at least two-fifths of the membership of each house, and has been signed by the Governor. The Governor has 10 days in which to consider a bill, after which it becomes law unless vetoed. A gubernatorial veto may be overridden by a majority vote by the elected members of each house. Enacted legislation becomes effective 90 days after adjournment of the legislative session. The Republican candidate, Ernie Fletcher, was elected in the gubernatorial election in 2003, with 55% of the votes cast, but failed to win a further term in office in an election on 6 November 2007. Instead, Democratic challenger Steve Beshear secured the governorship. In the presidential election of 2008, the Republicans again triumphed over the Democrats, with some 58% of the votes cast. Kentucky has 120 administrative counties.

Elected Executive Branch Officials

Governor (2008–12): Steve Beshear (Dem.).

Lieutenant-Governor: Dr Daniel Mongiardo (Dem.).

Secretary of State: Trey Grayson (Rep.).

Attorney-General: Jack Conway (Dem.).

Treasurer: Todd Hollenbach (Dem.).

Auditor: Crit Luallan (Dem.).

Commissioner of Agriculture: Richie Farmer (Rep.).

Selected Government Addresses

Office of the Governor: 700 Capitol Ave, Suite 100, Frankfort, KY 40601; tel. (502) 564-2611; fax (502) 564-2517; e-mail governor@mail.state.ky.us; internet governor.ky.gov.

Office of the Lieutenant-Governor: 700 Capitol Ave, Suite 142, Frankfort, KY 40601; tel. (502) 564-2611; fax (502) 564-2849; internet ltgovernor.ky.gov.

Office of the Secretary of State: 700 Capitol Ave, Suite 152, Frankfort, KY 40601; tel. (502) 564-3490; fax (502) 564-5687; internet www.sos.ky.gov.

Office of the Attorney-General: 700 Capitol Ave, Suite 118, Frankfort, KY 40601-3449; tel. (502) 696-5300; fax (502) 564-2894; e-mail attorney.general@ag.ky.gov; internet ag.ky.gov.

Office of the Treasurer: 1050 US Hwy 127 South, Suite 100, Frankfort, KY 40601; tel. (502) 564-4722; fax (502) 564-6545; e-mail treasury.web@ky.gov; internet www.kytreasury.com.

Office of the Auditor: 105 Sea Hero Rd, Suite 2, Frankfort, KY 40601; tel. (502) 573-0050; fax (502) 573-0067; e-mail crit.luallen@auditor.ky.gov; internet www.auditor.ky.gov.

Department of Agriculture: 32 Fountain Place, Frankfort, KY 40601; tel. (502) 564-4696; fax (502) 564-2133; e-mail ag.web@ky.gov; internet www.kyagr.com; headed by the Commr of Agriculture.

Department of Corrections: Health Services Bldg, 275 East Main St, POB 2400, Frankfort, KY 40602-2400; tel. (502) 564-4726; fax (502) 564-5037; internet corrections.ky.gov; Commr LaDonna H. Thompson.

Department of Military Affairs: 100 Minuteman Parkway, Frankfort, KY 40601-6168; tel. (502) 607-1738; e-mail steven.bullard@ky.ngb.army.mil; internet www.military.ky.gov; Adj.-Gen. Maj.-Gen. Edward W. Tonini.

Department of Revenue: 501 High St, Frankfort, KY 40620; tel. (502) 564-4581; fax (502) 564-3875; internet revenue.ky.gov; Commr Tom Miller.

Department of Travel: Capital Plaza Tower, 22nd Floor, 500 Mero St, Frankfort, KY 40601; tel. (502) 564-4930; e-mail mike.cooper@ky.gov; internet travel.ky.gov; Commr Mike Cooper.

Economic Development Cabinet: Old Capitol Annex, 300 West Broadway, Frankfort, KY 40601; tel. (502) 564-7140; fax (502) 564-3256; e-mail econdev@ky.gov; internet www.thinkkentucky.com; Sec. Larry Hayes (acting).

Education Cabinet: Capitol Plaza Tower, 500 Mero St, 3rd Floor, Frankfort, KY 40601; tel. (502) 564-0372; fax (502) 564-5959; e-mail helen.mountjoy@ky.gov; internet educationcabinet.ky.gov; Sec. Helen W. Mountjoy.

Energy and Environment Cabinet: Capitol Plaza Tower, 500 Mero St, 5th Floor, Frankfort, KY 40601; tel. (502) 564-5525; fax (502) 564-3354; e-mail cynthia.schafer@ky.gov; internet www.eppc.ky.gov; Sec. Dr Len Peters.

Finance and Administration Cabinet: Capitol Annex, Rm 383, Frankfort, KY 40601; tel. (502) 564-4240; fax (502) 564-6785; e-mail finance.cabinet@ky.gov; internet finance.ky.gov; Sec. Jonathan Miller.

Health and Family Services Cabinet: 275 East Main St, Suite 5W-A, Frankfort, KY 40621; tel. (502) 564-7042; fax (502) 564-7091; e-mail vikki.franklin@ky.gov; internet chs.ky.gov; Sec. Janie Miller.

Labor Cabinet: 1047 US Hwy 127 South, Suite 4, Frankfort, KY 40601; tel. (502) 564-3070; fax (502) 564-5387; e-mail susan.long@ky.gov; internet www.labor.ky.gov; Commr J. R. Gray.

Public Protection Cabinet: Capital Plaza Tower, 5th Floor, 500 Mero St, Frankfort, KY 40601; tel. (502) 564-3350; internet www.ppc.ky.gov; Sec. Robert Vance.

Public Service Commission: 211 Sower Blvd, POB 615, Frankfort, KY 40602-0615; tel. (502) 564-3940; fax (502) 564-3460; e-mail psc.info@ky.gov; internet www.psc.ky.gov; Chair. David L. Armstrong.

State Police Department: 919 Versailles Rd, Frankfort, KY 40601; tel. (502) 695-6300; fax (502) 564-6615; e-mail kspmedia@ky.gov; internet www.kentuckystatepolice.org; Commr Rodney Brewer.

Transportation Cabinet: 200 Mero St, Frankfort, KY 40622; tel. (502) 564-4890; fax (502) 564-9540; e-mail kytc.comments@ky.gov; internet transportation.ky.gov; Sec. Joe Prather.

General Assembly

(August 2008)

Senate

Rep. 22; Dem. 14; Ind. 1; 1 vacancy; Total 38

President: David L. Williams (Rep.).

President Pro Tempore: Katie Kratz Stine (Rep.).

Clerk: Donna Holiday.

House of Representatives

Dem. 63; Rep. 36; 1 vacancy; Total 100

Speaker: Jody Richards (Dem.).

Speaker Pro Tempore: Larry Clark (Dem.).

Chief Clerk: Jean Burgin.

Louisiana

Gross Area: 134,275 sq km (51,863 sq miles).

Resident Population (1 July 2007, estimate): 4,293,204.

State Capital: Baton Rouge.

Principal Cities (population at 1 July 2006, estimate): New Orleans 223,388; Baton Rouge (capital) 229,553; Shreveport 200,199; Lafayette 114,214.

LOCATION, TOPOGRAPHY AND CLIMATE

The State of Louisiana (nicknamed 'The Pelican State') is in the South region of the USA and is bordered by Arkansas to the north, Mississippi to the east and Texas to the west. The Gulf of Mexico lies to the south. The state lies entirely within the area known as the Gulf Coastal Plain. In the south-east of Louisiana is the Mississippi Delta, which features Lake Pontchartrain, a coastal lagoon covering 1,619 sq km (625 sq miles). The region of coastal lowlands stretching west from the Delta consists of flood plains, bayous and marshes. Off the coast are numerous islands. Louisiana's main rivers are: the Mississippi, forming the northern half of the border with the state of the same name; the Red, flowing across the state from north-west to east to join the Mississippi; the Pearl, which provides the southern part of the boundary with Mississippi; and the Sabine, which flows out of the Toledo Bend Reservoir, on the border with Texas. The Atchafalaya branches off from the Mississippi and channels about 25% of its outflow to the Gulf of Mexico. The land gradually rises towards the north of the state, where there are rolling hills to the east and west of central alluvial plains. Louisiana has a subtropical climate.

HISTORICAL BACKGROUND

Among the Native American Indians inhabiting Louisiana when Spanish explorers arrived in the region in the 16th century were the Caddo, Atakapa, Muskogean, Natchez and Tunican-speaking tribes. Robert Cavelier, Sieur de la Salle, claimed the entire Mississippi valley for Louis XIV of France in 1682, but the French did not succeed in building Natichitoches, their first permanent settlement in Louisiana, until 1714. New Orleans was established in 1718. The descendants of early French and Spanish settlers in Louisiana were known as Creoles, while the descendants of Canary Islanders brought to the region by a Spanish governor in 1770 were known as Islenos. In 1755 about 4,000 Acadians, French settlers in Nova Scotia (now part of Canada), were moved by the British to Louisiana—they settled near Bayou Teche and their descendants became known as Cajuns. In 1762 Louisiana passed from French to Spanish control; it was then returned to France in 1800, before being sold to the USA in 1803—thus doubling the size of US territory—for the sum of US $15m. In 1804 the area south of 33°N was separated and named the Territory of Orleans. Along with the west of what was then Florida, this region entered the Union as Louisiana, the 18th state, on 30 April 1812. In 1814–15, at the end of the War of 1812, the army of Gen. Andrew Jackson inflicted a major defeat on the British, who were attempting to capture New Orleans. Owing to the economic and political power of the pro-slavery plantation owners, Louisiana fought for the Confederacy during the Civil War. On 28 August 2005 the city of New Orleans was subject to catastrophic damage after Hurricane Katrina struck southern Louisiana, breaking levees in the city. Some 150,000 properties were destroyed or damaged in America's worst ever natural disaster. Large numbers of the population lost their homes and although a city-wide mandatory evacuation was ordered, at least 1,577 people died in the disaster. On 1 September 2008 Louisiana—still recovering from the devastation wrought by Hurricane Katrina, and with crucial defences only partially rebuilt—again suffered the impact of hurricanes tracking from the Caribbean when Hurricane Gustav made landfall on the state's Atlantic coast. Following the severe domestic and international criticism of the state and federal governments' response to New Orleans' plight, extensive improvements to disaster preparedness had been implemented in the interim, and—while 34 of the state's 64 parishes were declared disaster areas, experiencing widespread flooding and power outages—unofficial reports attributed 43 deaths to the hurricane, state-wide.

ECONOMY

Louisiana's principal economic activities are manufacturing, tourism, government, construction, wholesale and retail trade, and mining (particularly petroleum and gas extraction). Gross domestic product by state totalled US $216,146m. in 2007, with average per-head income at $35,770 in that year. In 2007 18.6% of the population were estimated to be living below the poverty line—the second highest level in the USA. The civilian labour force totalled 2,050,900 in mid-2008 and the unemployment rate was 4.4% (91,200 persons). In 2007 5.6% of those employed belonged to a trade union, although 6.5% were covered by union agreements.

In 2007 farmland covered 7.8m. acres (3.2m. ha). The average farm in that year occupied an area of 291 acres and there were 26,800 farms. Some 18.3% of total cropland was irrigated in 2002; 65% of farm marketings were derived from sales of crops in 2007, with 35% coming from livestock and livestock products. The principal commodities produced in that year, in order of marketing receipts, were sugar-cane, corn (maize), cotton and rice. Louisiana was the third most important producer of rice in 2007, after Arkansas and California. Forestland covers some 42% of the state; in 2004 Louisiana ranked 12th overall for lumber production, with softwoods accounting for 86% of total production. The value of Louisiana's commercial fish catch in 2006 was US $255.3m. Louisiana led all other states in 2006 for crab landings, accounting for 32% of the US total; it ranked second among the Atlantic Gulf states for shrimp in 2007 and fourth nationwide for catfish in 2005.

In 2007 the value of Louisiana's non-fuel mineral production was US $385m., with the state ranked 38th. The state's leading minerals in that year were sand and gravel, salt (for which it was ranked first in the USA in 2004), crushed stone and common clays. Production of construction sand and gravel increased significantly after 1999, following the opening of a new mine. While production of natural gas and petroleum declined from the 1970s, the state still ranked fourth nationally for petroleum and fifth for natural gas in 2005. Louisiana produced 3.2m. short tons of coal in 2007

From the early 20th century the petrochemicals industry played a leading role in the state's economy. Louisiana ranked ninth among the states in 2006 in terms of its value of shipments. Principal manufactured goods include chemicals and allied products, petroleum and coal products, transportation equipment, electronic equipment, lumber, paper and food and kindred products. The total value of Louisiana's manufacturing shipments in 2006 was US $183,498m., of which 42% was added during manufacture.

In 2004 domestic travel expenditures totalled US $9,539m. Total general expenditures by the state government in 2006 amounted to $24,221m.; general revenue totalled $22,926m., of which $9,026m. was contributed by the federal Government and $9,651m. was derived from taxes. Louisiana received $9,014m. from the federal Government in the form of aid in 2006.

CONSTITUTION AND GOVERNMENT

The current Constitution of Louisiana is the state's 11th and became effective on 1 January 1975. Constitutional amendments proposed by the Legislature must be approved by two-thirds of the elected members of each house, and then ratified by a majority of state voters. The Governor is elected separately from the Lieutenant-Governor to serve a term of four years, and may serve no more than two terms consecutively. Louisiana is the only state to elect an elections commissioner. The Legislature consists of 39 senators and 105 representatives, all members being re-elected every four years. Regular sessions of the Legislature take place annually, beginning in April and lasting for no longer than 60 days in odd-numbered years and 30 days in even-numbered years. A bill becomes law after having been approved by both houses of the Legislature and signed by the Governor. During session the Governor is allowed 10 days in which to consider a bill, after which it becomes law unless vetoed. Outside session, the consideration period is 20 days from adjournment. A two-thirds' vote by the elected members of each house is required to override a gubernatorial veto. Enacted legislation becomes effective 60 days after adjournment of the Legislature. In the gubernatorial election of 20 October 2007 Republican candidate Bobby Jindal defeated two Democratic rivals to secure the governorship. Jindal attracted an estimated 54% of the votes cast, enough to avoid a second round ballot. In the presidential election of 2008 the Republicans secured some 59% of the votes cast, with nearly 2m. people voting. Louisiana is divided into 64 parishes for administrative purposes.

Elected Executive Branch Officials

Governor (2008–12): Bobby Jindal (Rep.).

Lieutenant-Governor: Mitch Landrieu (Dem.).

Secretary of State: Jay Dardenne (Rep.).

Attorney-General: James D. (Buddy) Caldwell, Jr (Dem.).

Treasurer: John Neely Kennedy (Dem.).

Commissioner of Agriculture and Forestry: Michael G. Strain (Rep.).

Commissioner of Insurance: James J. Donelon.

Selected Government Addresses

Office of the Governor: State Capitol, POB 94004, Baton Rouge, LA 70804-9004; tel. (225) 342-7015; fax (225) 342-7099; e-mail timmy.teepell@la.gov; internet www.gov.louisiana.gov.

Office of the Lieutenant-Governor: Capitol Annex Bldg, 1051 North Third Street, POB 44243, Baton Rouge, LA 70804-4243; tel. (225) 342-7009; fax (225) 342-1949; internet www.crt.state.la.us/ltgovernor.

Office of the Secretary of State: POB 94125, Baton Rouge, LA 70804-9125; tel. (225) 922-2880; fax (225) 922-2003; e-mail admin@sos.louisiana.gov; internet www.sos.louisiana.gov.

Office of the Attorney-General: Livingston Bldg, 300 Capitol Dr., POB 94005, Baton Rouge, LA 70804; tel. (225) 326-6705; fax (225) 326-6793; e-mail admininfo@ag.state.la.us; internet www.ag.state.la.us.

Office of the Treasurer: State Capitol, 3rd Floor, POB 44154, Baton Rouge, LA 70804; tel. (225) 342-0010; fax (225) 342-0046; internet www.treasury.state.la.us.

Department of Agriculture and Forestry: POB 631, Baton Rouge, LA 70821-0631; tel. (225) 922-1234; fax (225) 922-1253; e-mail info@ldaf.state.la.us; internet www.ldaf.state.la.us.

Department of Corrections: 504 Mayflower St, POB 94304, Baton Rouge, LA 70804-9304; tel. (225) 342-6740; fax (225) 342-3095; internet www.corrections.state.la.us; Sec. JAMES M. LEBLANC.

Department of Culture, Recreation and Tourism: POB 94361, Baton Rouge, LA 70804-9361; tel. (225) 342-8115; fax (225) 342-3207; e-mail secretary@crt.state.la.us; internet www.crt.state.la.us; Sec. ANGÈLE DAVIS.

Department of Education: Claiborne Bldg, 1201 North Third St, POB 94064, Baton Rouge, LA 70804-9064; tel. (225) 342-3600; fax (225) 342-7316; e-mail paulpastorek@la.gov; internet www.doe.state.la.us; Supt PAUL G. PASTOREK.

Department of Environmental Quality: Galvez Bldg, 602 North Fifth St, POB 4301, Baton Rouge, LA 70821-4301; tel. (225) 219-3953; fax (225) 219-3971; e-mail deq-wwwofficeofthesecretarycontact@la.gov; internet www.deq.louisiana.gov; Sec. HAROLD LEGGETT.

Department of Health and Hospitals: 628 North Fourth Street, POB 629, Baton Rouge, LA 70821-0629; tel. (225) 342-9500; fax (225) 342-5568; e-mail webadmin@dhh.la.gov; internet www.dhh.louisiana.gov; Sec. ALAN LEVINE.

Department of Insurance: Poydras Bldg, 1702 North Third St, POB 94214, Baton Rouge, LA 70802; tel. (225) 342-5900; fax (225) 342-8622; e-mail public@ldi.state.la.us; internet www.ldi.louisiana.gov; headed by the Commr of Insurance.

Department of Natural Resources: LaSalle Bldg, 617 North Third St, POB 94396, Baton Rouge, LA 70804-9396; tel. (225) 342-2710; fax (225) 342-5861; e-mail info@dnr.state.la.us; internet dnr.louisiana.gov; Sec. SCOTT ANGELLE.

Department of Public Safety: 8001 Independence Blvd, Baton Rouge, LA 70806-6411; tel. (225) 925-6226; fax (225) 925-4019; e-mail webmaster@dps.state.la.us; internet www.dps.louisiana.gov; Sec. RICHARD L. STALDER.

Department of Revenue: 617 North Third St, POB 201, Baton Rouge, LA 70821-0201; tel. (225) 219-2448; internet www.revenue.louisiana.gov; Sec. CYNTHIA BRIDGES.

Department of Transportation and Development: 1201 Capitol Access Rd, POB 94245, Baton Rouge, LA 70804-9245; tel. (225) 379-1200; fax (225) 379-1851; e-mail marklambert@dotd.la.gov; internet www.dotd.louisiana.gov; Sec. JOHNNY B. BRADBERRY.

Louisiana Economic Development Department: 1051 North Third Street, POB 94185, Baton Rouge, LA 70804-9185; tel. (225) 342-3000; fax (225) 342-9095; e-mail lisa.bryant@la.gov; internet www.lded.state.la.us; Sec. STEPHEN MORET.

Military Department: Jackson Barracks, New Orleans, LA 70146-0330; tel. (225) 278-8211; fax (225) 278-6554; e-mail bennett.landreneau@la.ngb.army.mil; internet www.la.ngb.army.mil; Adj.-Gen. Maj.-Gen. BENNETT C. LANDRENEAU.

Public Service Commission: Galvez Bldg, 12th Floor, 602 North Fifth St, POB 91154, Baton Rouge, LA 70821-9154; tel. (225) 342-4404; fax (225) 342-2831; e-mail joahn@lpsc.org; internet www.lpsc.org; Exec. Sec. LAWRENCE C. ST BLANC.

Workforce Commission: 1001 North 23rd St, POB 94094, Baton Rouge, LA 70804-9094; tel. (225) 342-3111; fax (225) 342-3778; e-mail os@ldol.state.la.us; internet www.laworks.net; Sec. JOHN WARNER SMITH.

Legislature

(August 2008)

Senate

Dem. 23; Rep. 16; Total 39

President: JOEL T. CHAISSON, II (Dem.).

President Pro Tempore: SHARON WESTON BROOME (Dem.).

Secretary: GLENN KOEPP.

House of Representatives

Dem. 53; Rep. 50; Ind. 2; Total 105

Speaker: JAMES W. (JIM) TUCKER (Rep.).

Speaker Pro Tempore: KAREN CARTER PETERSON (Dem.).

Clerk: ALFRED W. SPEER.

Maine

Gross Area: 91,653 sq km (35,401 sq miles).

Resident Population (1 July 2007, estimate): 1,317,207.

State Capital: Augusta (population 18,626 at 1 July 2005).

Principal City: Portland (population 63,011 at 1 July 2006, estimate).

LOCATION, TOPOGRAPHY AND CLIMATE

The State of Maine (nicknamed 'The Pine Tree State') is in the Northeast region of the USA. It is one of the six states of New England and is the most easterly state in the Union. Maine is bordered to the north-west, north and east by the Canadian provinces of Québec and New Brunswick, to the south and south-east by the Atlantic Ocean and to the south-west by New Hampshire. In the west and centre of Maine is the high land of the Longfellow Mountains, the northernmost range of the Appalachian chain, reaching 1,606 m (5,268 ft) at Mount Katahdin. North of the mountains is a region of high plateau. The land is low-lying around the river basins of the St John River in the north, the Penobscot River in the east and the Androscoggin, Kennebec and Saco Rivers in the south. The state has numerous rivers and over 2,000 lakes, of which the largest is Moosehead Lake, at 303 sq km (117 sq miles). The coast has sandy beaches in the south-west, becoming more rocky towards the north-east with deep inlets and jagged promontories. There are hundreds of offshore islands. The climate is dry in the north with cool summers and cold winters. The northern interior of the state has heavy snow in winter. Temperatures are more moderate in the coastal region.

HISTORICAL BACKGROUND

When Giovanni da Verrazano, a Florentine explorer in the service of France, visited Maine in 1524 (the first recorded visit of a European), the region was inhabited by Algonquian peoples. Maine lands were granted to Sir Ferdinando Gorges by the Council of New England (which he dominated) in 1622. The first permanent European settlements were established on the Saco River in 1623 and at York in 1624. The region came under the jurisdiction of Massachusetts in 1659, following the death of Gorges. The first naval skirmish of the Revolution occurred in 1775, when the Americans captured a British vessel in Machias Bay. Maine, the 23rd state, was admitted to the Union as a free state on 15 March 1820 (under the Missouri Compromise). In 1851 Maine became the first state to introduce a prohibition law, which was later adopted as part of its Constitution, and was not repealed until 1934.

ECONOMY

The most important elements of Maine's economy are manufacturing (particularly paper-making), agriculture, wholesale and retail trade, services and finance, insurance and real estate. Forestry and fishing are also significant sources of income. In 2007 gross domestic product by state totalled US $48,108m. and per-head income averaged $33,962. The percentage of the population estimated to be living below the poverty line in 2007 stood at 12.0%. The civilian labour force totalled 730,600 in mid-2008, with an unemployment rate of 5.1% (37,500 persons). In 2007 11.7% of those employed belonged to a trade union, although 13.8% were covered by union agreements.

Farmland covered 1.4m. acres (550,372 ha) in 2007 (representing just 6.0% of land area, the lowest proportion of any state other than Alaska). There were 7,100 farms in 2007, with the average farm covering an area of 192 acres. In 2002 around 3.6% of total cropland was irrigated. In 2007 50% of farm marketings were derived from livestock and livestock products and 50% from crops. Maine's most important agricultural commodities in that year, in order of value, were dairy products, potatoes, wild blueberries and chicken eggs. In 2007 the five–six week blueberry season yielded a field crop that contributed US $83m. to the state economy. Forestland covered 17.7m. acres of the state in 2003, representing the second highest proportion of forested land (78.1%) of any state, behind New Hampshire. The state ranked 17th in the USA for lumber production in 2004, with softwoods accounting for 86% of total lumber production.

Fishing is also important to Maine's economy; the state had a catch valued at some $362m. in 2006.

Non-fuel mineral production in Maine was valued at just US $156m. in 2007, with the state ranking 44th in the country. Leading minerals were portland cement, construction sand and gravel, crushed stone and dimension stone. Sand, gravel and crushed stone together accounted for almost 63% of Maine's mineral production in 2005.

Until the end of the 19th century shipbuilding and lumber dominated Maine's manufacturing economy. Later, the paper and allied products, transportation equipment (including ship- and boat-building and repairing), food and computer equipment industries grew in importance. In 2006 the state ranked 40th in the USA in terms of its value of shipments; total shipments were US $15,231m., with 51% added during manufacture.

Travel and tourism are important to Maine, and the sector is a major employer in the state. In 2004 domestic travel expenditures totalled US $2,085m.

In 2006 total general expenditures by the state government were US $7,855m.; general revenue totalled $7,574m., of which $2,573m. was provided by the federal Government and $3,599m. was derived from taxes. Maine received $2,455m. in federal aid in 2006.

CONSTITUTION AND GOVERNMENT

Maine's only Constitution was adopted in 1819 and became effective on 15 March 1820. An amendment to the Constitution proposed by the Legislature has to be approved by two-thirds of the elected members of both houses and then ratified by a majority of voters. The Governor is the state's only elected executive branch official. He or she is elected to serve a term of four years and may serve no more than two terms consecutively. There is no Lieutenant-Governor, and the President of the Senate succeeds in the absence of the Governor. The Legislature consists of 35 senators and 151 representatives, both houses being re-elected every two years. The House also has two non-voting members, representing the Penobscot Nation and the Passamaquoddy tribes. Limits on the number of terms senators may serve are being gradually introduced. After the 2000 legislative election Democrats and Republicans were equally balanced in the Senate. A power-sharing arrangement was introduced, under which the President and President Pro Tempore, along with some other Senate staff, exchanged roles in December 2001. The first of two regular sessions of the legislative term begins in the December following an election and lasts for a maximum of 100 days. The second session (restricted to budgetary legislation) is limited to 50 days. A bill becomes law when it has been approved by the Legislature and signed by the Governor. During session the Governor is allowed 10 days in which to consider a bill, after which it becomes law unless vetoed. Bills vetoed after adjournment must be returned to the Legislature for reconsideration within the first three days of the next session. A gubernatorial veto may be overridden by a vote of two-thirds of the elected members of each house. Enacted legislation becomes effective 90 days after adjournment of the session. In 2006 John E. Baldacci, the Democratic Governor, was re-elected with 38% of the vote. In the 2008 presidential election the Democrats secured some 58% of the vote. For administrative purposes, Maine is divided into 16 counties.

Elected Executive Branch Official

Governor (2007–11): JOHN E. BALDACCI (Dem.).

Selected Government Addresses

Office of the Governor: 1 State House Station, Augusta, ME 04333-0001; tel. (207) 287-3531; fax (207) 287-1034; e-mail governor@maine.gov; internet www.maine.gov/governor.

Bureau of Insurance: 34 State House Station, Augusta, ME 04333-0034; tel. (207) 624-8475; fax (207) 624-8599; internet www.state.me.us/pfr/ins/ins_index.htm; Supt ERIC A. CIOPPA (acting).

Department of Administrative and Financial Services: Burton M. Cross Bldg, 3rd Floor, 78 State House Station, Augusta, ME 04333-0078; tel. (207) 624-7800; fax (207) 624-7804; internet www.maine.gov/dafs; Commr RYAN LOW.

Department of Agriculture: Deering Bldg, 28 State House Station, Augusta, ME 04333-0028; tel. (207) 287-3419; fax (207) 287-7548; e-mail agriculture.commissioner@maine.gov; internet www.maine.gov/agriculture; Commr SETH H. (BRAD) BRADSTREET, III.

Department of the Attorney-General: Burton M. Cross Bldg, 6th Floor, 6 State House Station, Augusta, ME 04333; tel. (207) 626-8800; fax (207) 287-3145; internet www.maine.gov/ag; Attorney-Gen. G. STEVEN ROWE.

Department of Corrections: Tyson Bldg, 3rd Floor, Tyson Dr., 111 State House Station, Augusta, ME 04333-0111; tel. (207) 287-2711; fax (207) 287-4370; e-mail marty.magnusson@state.me.us; internet www.maine.gov/corrections; Commr MARTIN A. MAGNUSSON.

Department of Defense, Veterans and Emergency Management: Camp Keyes, Augusta, ME 04333; tel. (207) 626-4271; fax (207) 287-4509; e-mail john.libby@me.ngb.army.mil; internet www.maine.gov/va/defense/dvs.htm; Commr and Adj.-Gen. Maj.-Gen. JOHN W. (BILL) LIBBY.

Department of Economic and Community Development: Burton M. Cross Bldg, 111 Sewall St, 3rd Floor, 59 State House Station, Augusta, ME 04333-0059; tel. (207) 624-9800; fax (207) 287-8461; e-mail biz.growth@maine.gov; internet www.econdevmaine.com; Commr JOHN RICHARDSON.

Department of Education: 23 State House Station, Augusta, ME 04333-0023; tel. (207) 624-6600; fax (207) 624-6700; e-mail susan.gendron@maine.gov; internet www.maine.gov/education; Commr SUSAN A. GENDRON.

Department of Environmental Protection: 17 State House Station, Augusta, ME 04333-0017; tel. (207) 287-7688; fax (207) 287-2814; e-mail david.p.littell@maine.gov; internet www.maine.gov/dep; Commr DAVID P. LITTELL.

Department of Health and Human Services: 221 State St, Augusta, ME 04333-0011; tel. (207) 287-3707; fax (207) 287-3005; internet www.maine.gov/dhhs/index.shtml; Commr DORA ANNE MILLS.

Department of Labor: 54 State House Station, Augusta, ME 04333; tel. (207) 623-7900; e-mail mdol@maine.gov; internet www.maine.gov/labor; Commr LAURA A. FORTMAN.

Department of Public Safety: 45 Commerce Dr., Suite 1, 104 State House Station, Augusta, ME 04333-0104; tel. (207) 626-3800; fax (207) 287-3042; e-mail anne.h.jordan@maine.gov; internet www.maine.gov/dps; Commr ANNE H. JORDAN.

Department of Transportation: Transportation Bldg, Child St, 16 State House Station, Augusta, ME 04333-0016; tel. (207) 624-3000; fax (207) 624-3001; e-mail exec.mainedot@maine.gov; internet www.maine.gov/mdot; Commr DAVID A. COLE.

Office of the Secretary of State: 148 State House Station, Augusta, ME 04333; tel. (207) 626-8400; fax (207) 287-8598; e-mail sos.office@maine.gov; internet www.maine.gov/sos; Sec. of State MATTHEW DUNLAP.

Office of the Treasurer: Burton M. Cross Office Bldg, 3rd Floor, 39 State House Station, 111 Sewall St, Augusta, ME 04333-0039; tel. (207) 624-7477; fax (207) 287-2367; e-mail state.treasurer@maine.gov; internet www.maine.gov/treasurer; Treasurer DAVID G. LEMOINE.

Public Utilities Commission: 242 State St, 18 State House Station, Augusta, ME 04333-0018; tel. (207) 287-3831; fax (207) 287-1039; e-mail maine.puc@maine.gov; internet www.maine.gov/mpuc; Chair. SHARON M. REISHUS.

State Police: 42 State House Station, 45 Commerce Dr., Augusta, ME 04333-0042; tel. (207) 624-7200; fax (207) 287-3042; e-mail stephen.mccausland@maine.gov; internet www.maine.gov/dps/msp; Chief Col PATRICK J. FLEMING.

Legislature
(August 2008)

Senate

Dem. 18; Rep. 17; Total 35

President: Lt-Gov. BETH EDMONDS (Dem.).

Secretary: JOY J. O'BRIEN.

House of Representatives

Dem. 90; Rep. 59; Ind. 2; Total 151

Speaker: GLENN A. CUMMINGS (Dem.).

Clerk: MILLICENT M. MCFARLAND.

Maryland

Gross Area: 32,134 sq km (12,412 sq miles).

Resident Population (1 July 2007, estimate): 5,618,344.

State Capital: Annapolis (population 36,408 at 1 July 2006, estimate).

Principal City: Baltimore (population 631,366 at 1 July 2006, estimate).

LOCATION, TOPOGRAPHY AND CLIMATE

The State of Maryland (nicknamed 'The Old Line State' and 'The Free State') is in the South region of the USA and is bordered by Pennsylvania to the north, Delaware to the east, the Atlantic Ocean to the south-east, Virginia to the south and west, the District of Columbia to the west, and West Virginia to the north-west. The

Potomac River forms the western and north-western boundary and flows out into Chesapeake Bay, which divides Maryland from north to south, extending 314 km (195 miles) inland from the Atlantic Ocean. The Susquehanna River flows into the Bay in the north. West of the Atlantic Coastal Plain surrounding Chesapeake Bay is the Piedmont Plateau, an area of undulating hills rising towards the Appalachian mountain chain in the far north-west of the state, with a peak of 1,024 m (3,360 ft) at Backbone Mountain. Maryland has hot summers and mild winters in the coastal region and around Chesapeake Bay, with cooler temperatures in the western uplands.

HISTORICAL BACKGROUND

Maryland was inhabited by Algonquian-speaking peoples when European explorers entered the Chesapeake region in the 16th century. Capt. John Smith, an Englishman, explored and charted the region in 1608. George Calvert, Baron of Baltimore, a Roman Catholic, was granted land north of the Potomac River by King Charles I of England and Scotland in the 1620s, and his descendants had extensive governmental powers over the region until the American Revolution. Maryland joined the Union as the seventh state on 28th April 1788. The state was officially Unionist during the Civil War, but many of its landowners relied on slave labour for their tobacco plantations and there was considerable sympathy with the South. A major military confrontation, the Battle of Antietam, a Unionist victory, took place in the state in 1862. By 1864 the government of Maryland was fully behind the Union and the state's new Constitution included the abolition of slavery.

ECONOMY

The principal contributors to Maryland's gross domestic product by state of US $268,685m. in 2007 were services, tourism, information technology, biotechnology and manufacturing. Per-head income averaged $46,646 in 2007, the seventh highest in the country, while 8.3% of the population were estimated to be living below the poverty line in that year, the fourth lowest level in the USA. The civilian labour force numbered 3,082,100 in mid-2008 and the unemployment rate was 4.5% (140,000 persons). In 2007 12.9% of those employed were members of a trade union, although 14.5% were covered by union agreements.

Farmland covered 2.0m. acres (823,535 ha) in 2007. There were some 12,000 farms in that year, with the average farm covering an area of 170 acres. Irrigated land accounted for 5.4% of total cropland in 2002. In 2007 sales of livestock and livestock products constituted 58% of farm income, with crops providing 42%. Maryland's principal agricultural commodities, in terms of value, were broilers, greenhouse and nursery products, dairy products and corn. Tobacco is a long-established crop, but is gradually declining in significance. Forestland covers 2.6m. acres (some 32%) of the state. Maryland's fish catch was valued at US $54m. in 2006.

Maryland's most important non-fuel mineral products in 2007 were crushed stone, portland and masonry cement, construction sand and gravel and dimension stone. With an estimated value of US $725m., the state ranked 29th in the nation for the value of its non-fuel mineral production in 2007. Coal (all bituminous), Maryland's only exploited fossil-fuel resource, is mined along the border with Pennsylvania, with an estimated 2.3m. short tons produced in 2007.

Baltimore, originally an important centre for the production of machinery and steel, and, later, for motor vehicles, has maintained its importance for manufacturing. Principal manufactured goods in the state include food and allied products, print products, computers and electrical and transportation equipment. The state ranked 32nd in the country in terms of its value of shipments in 2006. The total value of the state's manufacturing shipments in that year was US $42,126m., with 54% added during manufacture.

In 2004 domestic travel expenditures amounted to US $9,734m. Total general expenditures by the state government were $28,966m. in 2006; general revenue totalled $26,270m., with $6,738m. provided by the federal Government and $14,625m. derived from taxes. In 2006 Maryland received $7,006m. in federal aid.

CONSTITUTION AND GOVERNMENT

Maryland has had four constitutions. The current Constitution became effective on 5 October 1867. Amendments to the Constitution proposed by the General Assembly must be approved by three-fifths of the members of each house, and must then be ratified by a majority of state voters. The Governor is elected with the Lieutenant-Governor to serve a four-year term and, after two consecutive terms, is not eligible to stand for office again until a period of four years has elapsed. There are 47 senators and 141 delegates in the General Assembly, both houses serving terms of four years. Regular sessions are held annually, starting in January and lasting for no longer than 90 calendar days. A bill becomes law after being approved by a majority in both houses and signed by the Governor. The Governor is allowed six days to consider a bill during session, after which it becomes law unless vetoed. After session a bill becomes law unless vetoed within 30 days of being presented to the Governor. A three-fifths' vote is required to override a gubernatorial veto. Enacted legislation becomes effective on the following 1 June unless another date is specified. In the 2006 gubernatorial election the Democrat candidate, Martin O'Malley, was elected, with 53% of the votes cast. In the 2008 presidential election the Democrats secured some 61% of the votes cast. Maryland is divided into 24 counties for administrative purposes.

Elected Executive Branch Officials

Governor (2007–11): MARTIN O'MALLEY (Dem.).

Lieutenant-Governor: ANTHONY G. BROWN (Dem.).

Attorney-General: DOUGLAS F. GANSLER, Jr (Dem.).

Comptroller of the Treasury: PETER FRANCHOT (Dem.).

Selected Government Addresses

Office of the Governor: State House, 100 State Circle, Annapolis, MD 21401-1925; tel. (410) 974-3901; fax (410) 974-3275; internet www.gov.state.md.us.

Office of the Lieutenant-Governor: State House, 100 State Circle, Annapolis, MD 21401-1925; tel. (410) 974-3901; fax (410) 974-5882; e-mail ltgovernor@gov.state.md.us; internet www.gov.state.md.us/ltgovernor/index.asp.

Office of the Attorney-General: 200 St Paul Pl., Baltimore, MD 21202; tel. (410) 576-6300; fax (410) 576-6404; e-mail oag@oag.state.md.us; internet www.oag.state.md.us.

Office of the Comptroller of the Treasury: Goldstein Treasury Bldg, 80 Calvert St, Annapolis, MD 21401; tel. (410) 260-7801; fax (410) 974-3808; e-mail pfranchot@comp.state.md.us; internet www.comp.state.md.us.

Department of Agriculture: Wayne A. Cawley Jr Bldg, 50 Harry S Truman Pkwy, Annapolis, MD 21401; tel. (410) 841-5700; fax (410) 841-5914; e-mail richarrl@mda.state.md.us; internet www.mda.state.md.us; Sec. ROGER L. RICHARDSON.

Department of the Budget and Management: 45 Calvert St, 1st Floor, Annapolis, MD 21401; tel. (410) 260-7041; fax (410) 974-2585; e-mail marylandgov@dbm.state.md.us; internet www.dbm.state.md.us; Sec. T. ELOISE FOSTER.

Department of Business and Economic Development: 217 East Redwood St, 9th Floor, Baltimore, MD 21202-3316; tel. (410) 767-6300; fax (410) 333-8628; e-mail communications@choosemaryland.org; internet www.choosemaryland.org; Sec. DAVID EDGERLEY.

Department of Education: 200 West Baltimore St, Baltimore, MD 21201; tel. (410) 767-0600; fax (410) 333-6033; e-mail ngrasmick@msde.state.md.us; internet marylandpublicschools.org/msde; Supt Dr NANCY S. GRASMICK.

Department of the Environment: 1800 Washington Blvd, Baltimore, MD 21230; tel. (410) 537-3000; fax (410) 631-3888; e-mail webmaster@mde.state.md.us; internet www.mde.state.md.us; Sec. SHARI T. WILSON.

Department of Health and Mental Hygiene: 201 West Preston St, Suite 500, Baltimore, MD 21201; tel. (410) 767-6500; fax (410) 767-6489; e-mail constituentservices@dhmh.state.md.us; internet www.dhmh.state.md.us; Sec. JOHN M. COLMERS.

Department of Labor, Licensing and Regulation: 500 North Calvert St, Rm 401, Baltimore, MD 21201; tel. (410) 230-6001; fax (410) 333-0853; e-mail pio@dllr.state.md.us; internet www.dllr.state.md.us; Sec. THOMAS E. PEREZ.

Department of Natural Resources: Tawes State Office Bldg, 580 Taylor Ave, Annapolis, MD 21401; tel. (410) 260-8100; fax (410) 260-8111; e-mail customerservice@dnr.state.md.us; internet www.dnr.state.md.us; Sec. JOHN R. GRIFFIN.

Department of Planning: 301 West Preston St, Suite 1101, Baltimore, MD 21201-2305; tel. (410) 767-4500; fax (410) 767-4480; internet www.mdp.state.md.us; Sec. RICHARD EBERHART HALL.

Department of Public Safety and Correctional Services: 300 East Joppa Rd, Suite 1000, Towson, MD 21286-3020; tel. (410) 339-5000; fax (410) 339-4240; internet www.dpscs.state.md.us; Sec. GARY D. MAYNARD.

Department of Transportation: 7201 Corporate Center Dr., Hanover, MD 21076; tel. (410) 865-1000; fax (410) 865-1334; e-mail ksaab@mdot.state.md.us; internet www.mdot.state.md.us; Sec. JOHN D. PORCARI.

Military Department: Fifth Regiment Armory, 29th Division St, Baltimore, MD 21201-2288; tel. (410) 576-6097; fax (410) 576-6079; e-mail remarks@mdmildep.org; internet www.mdmildep.org; Adj.-Gen. Brig.-Gen. JAMES A. ADKINS.

Office of the Secretary of State: 16 Francis St, Annapolis, MD 21401; tel. (410) 974-5521; fax (410) 974-5190; e-mail mdsos@sos.state.md.us; internet www.sos.state.md.us; Sec. of State JOHN P. MCDONOUGH.

Office of the State Treasurer: Goldstein Treasury Bldg, 80 Calvert St, Annapolis, MD 21401; tel. (410) 260-7533; fax (410) 974-3530; internet www.treasurer.state.md.us; State Treas. NANCY K. KOPP.

Public Service Commission: William Donald Schaefer Tower, 16th Floor, 6 St Paul St, Baltimore, MD 21202; tel. (410) 767-8000; fax (410) 333-6495; internet www.psc.state.md.us; Chair. DOUGLAS R. M. NAZARIAN.

State Police: 1201 Reistertown Rd, Pikesville, MD 21208; tel. (410) 653-4200; internet www.mdsp.org; Sec. Col TERRENCE B. SHERIDAN.

General Assembly
(August 2008)

Senate

Dem. 33; Rep. 14; Total 47

President: THOMAS V. (MIKE) MILLER, Jr (Dem.).

President Pro Tempore: NATHANIEL J. MCFADDEN (Dem.).

Secretary: WILLIAM B. C. ADDISON, Jr.

House of Delegates

Dem. 104; Rep. 37; Total 141

Speaker: MICHAEL ERIN BUSCH (Dem.).

Speaker Pro Tempore: ADRIENNE A. JONES (Dem.).

Chief Clerk: MARY MONAHAN.

Massachusetts

Gross Area: 27,337 sq km (10,559 sq miles).

Resident Population (1 July 2007, estimate): 6,449,755.

State Capital: Boston.

Principal Cities (population at 1 July 2006, estimate): Boston (capital) 590,763; Worcester 175,454; Springfield 151,176; Lowell 103,229; Cambridge 101,365.

LOCATION, TOPOGRAPHY AND CLIMATE

The Commonwealth of Massachusetts (nicknamed 'The Bay State' or 'The Old Colony'), one of the six states of New England, lies in the Northeast region of the USA, with Vermont and New Hampshire to the north, the Atlantic Ocean to the east and south-east, Rhode Island and Connecticut to the south-west, and New York to the west. Eastern Massachusetts is a region of coastal lowlands. South of hook-shaped Cape Cod are Massachusetts' largest islands, Martha's Vineyard and Nantucket Island. The coast is rocky, and higher in the north than the south, rising towards the interior eastern uplands, where there are forest-covered hills. Massachusetts' main rivers are: the Merrimack, in the north-east; the Taunton, flowing into Mount Hope Bay in the south; and the Connecticut, running southward through west-central Massachusetts. West of the Connecticut River Valley are the Berkshire Hills and the Taconic Mountains, part of the Appalachian chain, with the state's highest point at Mount Greylock, 1,064 m (3,491 ft). The climate in Massachusetts is temperate, with cold, dry winters and cool summers in the west of the state.

HISTORICAL BACKGROUND

The main Indian tribes inhabiting the Massachusetts area in the early 17th century were the Nauset, Massachuset, Wampanoag, Nipmuc and Pocumtuc. The first permanent European settlement was established at Plymouth, in 1620, by a group of English (British) Puritans, known as the Pilgrim Fathers, who arrived in the *Mayflower*. In 1630 a larger group of Puritans settled the Massachusetts Bay Colony in Salem. The two separate colonies were united under a royal charter in 1692. Strict trade regulations imposed by the colonial power in the 1760s were unpopular, and the offloading of tea cargoes into Boston harbour in 1773 to prevent the United Kingdom from benefiting from their taxation (an incident famed as the 'Boston Tea Party') marked explicit resistance to British rule. The Battle of Bunker Hill and the British evacuation of Boston in 1775 were also major developments in the American Revolution. On 6 February 1788 Massachusetts became the sixth state to join the Union. The state was a Unionist stronghold during the Civil War, and 'Yankee' Republicans dominated state politics from the 1850s until 1928, when the Democrats began to emerge as the leading party.

ECONOMY

The principal economic activities in Massachusetts include services, manufacturing and wholesale and retail trade. In 2007 gross domestic product by state totalled US $351,514m. and the state's average per-head income was $49,142, the fourth highest level nationally. In that year 9.9% of the population were thought to be living below the poverty line. The civilian labour force totalled 3,473,900 in mid-2008, with an unemployment rate of 5.2% (179,000 persons). In 2007 13.2% of those employed belonged to a trade union and 14.0% were covered by union agreements.

Farmland covered just 520,000 acres (210,400 ha) in 2007. There were 6,100 farms in that year, with the average farm covering an area of just 85 acres. Some 11% of total cropland was under irrigation in 2002. In 2007 78% of farm marketings were derived from crop sales and 22% from sales of livestock and livestock products. Greenhouse and nursery products, cranberries, dairy products and sweetcorn were the principal commodities by value in that year. Forestland covers approximately 46% of the state, but forestry is a relatively minor industry. In 2003 the value of Massachusetts' fish catch was the second highest in the country at US $326m. However, while still a significant producer (total landings in 2006 were valued at $437m.), the fishing industry has become relatively less important to the state economy in recent years.

Massachusetts produces no fossil fuels. Its non-fuel mineral output was valued at US $433m. in 2007, ranking it 37th among the states, with crushed stone, construction sand and gravel, dimension stone, lime and common clays being its major minerals.

Massachusetts was the first major industrial state in the USA and remains a regional manufacturing centre, particularly of high-technology goods. In 2006 it ranked 24th in terms of value of shipments. Principal manufactured goods include chemicals, print products, fabricated metals, machinery and computer equipment. The total value of Massachusetts' manufacturing shipments was US $84,219m. in 2006, with 58% added during manufacture. In the late 1990s the state caused strains in the USA's international relations by legislating to ban government purchases from companies carrying out business in Myanmar (Burma), in protest at alleged human rights violations. Sanctions legislation was also passed against the People's Republic of China and Nigeria. The legislation was subsequently deemed unconstitutional by the federal courts.

By the mid-19th century Boston had become an important banking centre; banking continues to be a principal sector of the state's economy, although the rise of the banking sector in other states has led Massachusetts to drop down the ranking order (14th among the states at the end of 2006). The Boston Stock Exchange was founded in 1846.

In 2004 domestic travel expenditures totalled US $10,975m. and Massachusetts ranked 15th in terms of money spent. Massachusetts' beaches (especially Cape Cod) represent a major tourist attraction.

In 2006 total general expenditures by the state government amounted to US $39,880m., while general revenue totalled $36,522m., of which $8,431m. was provided by the federal Government and $19,395m. was derived from taxes. Massachusetts received $10,438m. in federal aid in 2006.

CONSTITUTION AND GOVERNMENT

Massachusetts' only Constitution became effective on 25 October 1780. Constitutional amendments proposed by the General Court (the state legislature) must be approved by a majority of the elected members of each house at two successive sessions and must then be ratified by a majority of state voters. The Governor and Lieutenant-Governor are elected jointly to serve a four-year term and there is no limit to the number of times a Governor may hold office. Elections for the 40 senators and 160 representatives in the General Court are held every two years. Regular sessions are called annually in January and there is no statutory limit to the number of days a session may last. A bill must be approved by a majority of members in both houses before being presented to the Governor. During session the Governor is allowed 10 days to consider a bill, after which it becomes law unless vetoed. After session a bill dies unless it is signed or vetoed within 10 days of being presented to the Governor. A gubernatorial veto may be overridden by a two-thirds' vote of the members present in each house. Legislation becomes effective 90 days after enactment. A Democrat, Deval L. Patrick, was elected to the governorship in 2006, with 56% of the vote. In the 2008 presidential election the Democrats secured some 62% of the state vote, with over 3m. people voting. There are seven counties and seven geographical census areas in Massachusetts.

Elected Executive Branch Officials

Governor (2007–11): DEVAL L. PATRICK (Dem.).

Lieutenant-Governor: TIMOTHY P. MURRAY (Dem.).

Secretary of the Commonwealth: WILLIAM FRANCIS GALVIN (Dem.).

Attorney-General: MARTHA COAKLEY (Dem.).

Treasurer and Receiver-General: TIMOTHY P. CAHILL (Dem.).

Auditor: A. JOSEPH DENUCCI (Dem.).

Selected Government Addresses

Office of the Governor: State House, Rm 360, Boston, MA 02133; tel. (617) 725-4005; fax (617) 727-9725; internet www.mass.gov/gov.

Office of the Lieutenant-Governor: State House, Rm 360, Boston, MA 02133; tel. (617) 725-4005; fax (617) 727-9725; internet www.mass.gov/gov.

Office of the Secretary of the Commonwealth: 1 Ashburton Pl., Rm 1611, Boston, MA 02108-1512; tel. (617) 727-7030; fax (617) 742-4528; e-mail cis@sec.state.ma.us; internet www.sec.state.ma.us.

Office of the Attorney-General: 1 Ashburton Pl., Rm 2010, Boston, MA 02108-1698; tel. (617) 727-2200; e-mail ago@state.ma.us; internet www.ago.state.ma.us.

Office of the Treasurer and Receiver-General: State House, Rm 227, Boston, MA 02133; tel. (617) 367-6900; fax (617) 248-0372; e-mail webmaster@tre.state.ma.us; internet www.mass.gov/treasury.

Office of the Auditor: State House, Rm 230, Boston, MA 02133; tel. (617) 727-2075; fax (617) 727-2383; e-mail auditor@sao.state.ma.us; internet www.mass.gov/sao.

Department of Agricultural Resources: 251 Causeway St, Suite 500, Boston, MA 02114-2152; tel. (617) 626-1700; fax (617) 626-1850; e-mail doug.petersen@state.ma.us; internet www.mass.gov/agr; Commr DOUGLAS W. PETERSEN.

Department of Correction: 50 Maple St, Suite 3, Milford, MA 01757; tel. (508) 422-3300; fax (508) 422-3386; internet www.mass.gov/doc; Commr HAROLD W. CLARKE.

Department of Elementary and Secondary Education: 350 Main St, Malden, MA 02148-5023; tel. (781) 388-3000; fax (781) 388-3770; internet www.doe.mass.edu; Commr MITCHELL D. CHESTER.

Department of Environmental Protection: 1 Winter St, Boston, MA 02108-4746; tel. (617) 292-5500; fax (617) 556-1049; internet www.mass.gov/dep; Commr LAURIE BURT.

Department of Housing and Economic Development: 100 Cambridge St, Boston, MA 02114; tel. (617) 573-1100; fax (617) 573-1120; e-mail dhcdweb@hotmail.com; internet www.mass.gov/dhcd; Sec. DANIEL O'CONNELL.

Department of Labor: 1 Ashburton Pl., Rm 2112, Boston, MA 02108; tel. (617) 626-7100; e-mail dol@dia.state.ma.us; internet www.mass.gov/dol; Dir GEORGE NOEL.

Department of Public Health: 250 Washington St, 6th Floor, Boston, MA 02108-4619; tel. (617) 210-5000; internet www.mass.gov/dph; Commr JOHN AUERBACH, Jr.

Department of Public Utilities: 1 South Station, Boston, MA 02110; tel. (617) 305-3500; fax (617) 345-9101; e-mail dpu.administration.state.ma.us; Chair. PAUL J. HIBBARD.

Department of Revenue: 100 Cambridge St, Boston, MA 02114; tel. (617) 626-2201; internet www.dor.state.ma.us; Commr NAVJEET BAL.

Department of State Police: 470 Worcester Rd, Framingham, MA 01702; tel. (508) 820-2300; fax (617) 727-6874; internet www.mass.gov/msp; Supt Col MARK F. DELANEY.

Department of Telecommunications and Cable: 2 South Station, 4th Floor, Boston, MA 02110; tel. (617) 305-3580; fax (617) 478-2590; internet www.mass.gov/dtc; Commr SHARON E. GILLETT.

Executive Office of Administration and Finance: State House, Rm 373, Boston, MA 02133; tel. (617) 727-2040; fax (617) 727-2779; e-mail contactanf@state.ma.us; internet www.mass.gov/eoaf; Sec. LESLIE A. KIRWAN.

Executive Office of Housing and Economic Development: 1 Ashburton Pl., Rm 2101, Boston, MA 02108; tel. (617) 788-3610; fax (617) 788-3605; internet www.mass.gov/econ; Sec. DANIEL O'CONNELL.

Executive Office of Public Safety and Security: 1 Ashburton Pl., Suite 2133, Boston, MA 02108; tel. (617) 727-7775; fax (617) 727-4764; e-mail eopsinfo@state.ma.us; internet www.mass.gov/dps; Sec. KEVIN M. BURKE.

Executive Office of Transportation: 10 Park Plaza, Suite 3170, Boston, MA 02116; tel. (617) 973-7000; fax (617) 973-8031; e-mail feedback.eot@eot.state.ma.us; internet www.eot.state.ma.us; Sec. BERNARD COHEN.

MassDevelopment: 160 Federal St, Boston, MA 02110; tel. (617) 451-2477; fax (617) 451-3429; internet www.massdevelopment.com; Pres. and CEO ROBERT L. CULVER.

National Guard: 50 Maple St, Milford, MA 01757; tel. (508) 233-6561; e-mail ma-pao@ng.army.mil; internet www.mass.gov/guard; Adj.-Gen. Maj.-Gen. JOSEPH C. CARTER.

General Court
(August 2008)

Senate

Dem. 35; Rep. 5; Total 40

President: THERESE MURRAY (Dem.).

Clerk: WILLIAM F. WELCH.

House of Representatives

Dem. 141; Rep. 19; Total 160

Speaker: SALVATORE F. DIMASI (Dem.).

Clerk: STEVEN T. JAMES.

Michigan

Gross Area: 250,465 sq km (96,705 sq miles).

Resident Population (1 July 2007, estimate): 10,071,822.

State Capital: Lansing.

Principal Towns and Cities (population at 1 July 2006, estimate): Detroit 871,121; Grand Rapids 193,083; Warren 135,589; Sterling Heights 127,991; Flint 117,068; Lansing (capital) 114,276; Ann Arbor 113,206.

LOCATION, TOPOGRAPHY AND CLIMATE

The state of Michigan (nicknamed 'The Wolverine State') is in the Midwest region of the USA and consists of two peninsulas. The Upper Peninsula is bordered to the west by Wisconsin and to the north and east by the Canadian province of Ontario, with the boundary passing through St Mary's River and Lake Superior. Lake Huron lies to the east and Lake Michigan to the south, separated by the Straits of Mackinac, across which lies the lower Peninsula, stretching southwards towards Ohio in the south-east and Indiana in the south-west. The Lower Peninsula is bordered to the north by Lake Michigan and Lake Huron (an international border); to the east by Ontario, with the boundary passing through Lake Huron, the St Clair River, Lake St Clair and the Detroit River; to the south-east by Lake Erie, sharing a shoreline with Ontario and Ohio; and to the west by Lake Michigan. Michigan is mainly flat, with areas of higher land in the west of both peninsulas. In the east of the Lower Peninsula is low, rolling land, while the east of the Upper Peninsula is marshy, with hills along the shore of Lake Michigan and sandstone ridges on that of Lake Superior. In addition to its Great Lakes waters, Michigan has thousands of smaller lakes and ponds. Michigan's climate is temperate, with well-defined seasons. Temperatures are colder in the Upper Peninsula.

HISTORICAL BACKGROUND

When European settlement of what is now the state of Michigan began in the early 17th century, the region was inhabited by Algonquian-speaking Winnebago and Huron Native Americans (Amerindians). Fur-trading and missionary posts were established by the French at Sault Sainte Marie in 1668 and St Ignace in 1671. In 1701 a permanent settlement was created on the site of present-day Detroit. After the defeat of the French in the French and Indian War (1754–63, known in Europe as the Seven-Years War), Michigan came under British authority. The region did not come under US sovereignty until 1796. After being captured by the British during the War of 1812, Michigan was finally returned to the USA under the Treaty of Ghent in 1814. Given territorial status in 1805, Michigan entered the Union as the 26th state on 26 January 1837. The state was controlled by the Democratic Party until the 1850s, when the slavery issue brought the Republicans to power as the proponents of anti-slavery; Michigan fought for the Union during the Civil War. Republicans continued to dominate the government until the 1930s.

ECONOMY

The principal elements in Michigan's economy are manufacturing (particularly motor vehicles), services, tourism, agriculture and mining. In 2007 gross domestic product by state was US $381,963m., while average per-head income stood at $34,342. Some 14.0% of the population were estimated to be living below the poverty line in that year. The civilian labour force numbered 5,045,500 in mid-2008, and the unemployment rate was 9.1% (equivalent to 460,900 persons and the highest rate nationally). In 2007 19.5% of those employed—the fifth highest proportion in the USA—were members of a trade union. The state also occupied fifth position nationally in terms of the proportion of workers covered by union agreements, with 20.6%.

In 2007 10.0m. acres (4.0m. ha) of Michigan's land area consisted of cropland and grassland pasture; there were 52,800 farms in that year, with the average farm covering an area of 189 acres. Irrigated land accounted for 6% of total cropland in 2002. In 2007 some 59% of farm income was generated by crop sales and 41% by livestock and livestock products. The state's leading agricultural commodities in that year (in order of value) were dairy products, corn, greenhouse and nursery products, and soybeans. Michigan was ranked third overall for apple production (behind Washington and New York states) and fourth for sugar beets in 2007. Forestland covered 19.3m. acres of the state in 2003, with almost all of this being commercial timberland. Michigan was the USA's leading lumber-producing state in the latter part of the 19th century; while production declined during the 20th century, the lumber industry remained the principal economic activity in the western part of the Upper Peninsula. Hardwoods accounted for 50% of lumber produced in 2004. Michigan's commercial fisheries landed catch with a total value of US $6.0m. in 2006.

Michigan ranked 12th in 2007 in terms of the value of its non-fuel mineral production, which totalled US $1,910m. The state's leading mineral was iron ore (for which it was ranked first among the states in 2007 and, together with Minnesota, accounted for 95% of total US iron shipments), followed by portland cement, construction sand and gravel (ranked ninth), crushed stone and salt. In 2004 the state ranked first in production of magnesium compounds, second in bromine, peat and iron oxide pigments, third in potash and fourth in portland cement. Lime and common clays were also significant minerals. The state produces some crude petroleum and natural gas, for the latter of which it ranked 12th in the nation in 2005.

The development of the motor-vehicle industry in the early 20th century helped the state to become one of the world's principal manufacturing areas. Among the states, Michigan ranked sixth in its value of shipments in 2006, with a total of US $215,504m. (41% added during manufacture). In addition to transportation equipment (mainly motor vehicles and equipment), principal manufactured goods in the state include industrial machinery and equipment, primary and fabricated metal products, food and kindred products, and chemicals and allied products. The state ranked third in the manufacture of raw steel in 2003, with 7% of total US output. Detroit is the principal manufacturing centre.

Michigan was an important banking centre from the 1840s but its importance has declined in recent years. Tourism also played an important role in the state's economy from the 19th century. In 2004 domestic travel expenditures amounted to US $12,751m., and the state ranked 13th in terms of money spent.

In 2006 total general expenditures by the state government were US $51,408m.; general revenue totalled $46,001m., of which $12,329m. was from federal Government and $23,715m. was derived from taxes. Michigan received $11,645m. in federal aid in 2006.

CONSTITUTION AND GOVERNMENT

Michigan's Constitution, the state's fourth, was adopted in 1963 and became effective on 1 January 1964. An amendment to the Constitution proposed by the Legislature has to be passed by a two-thirds' vote in each house in two successive sessions, and must then be ratified by a majority of state voters. The Governor and Lieutenant-Governor are jointly elected to serve a four-year term, and there is no limit to the number of times they may hold office. There are 38 senators and 110 representatives in the Legislature, serving terms of four and two years, respectively. Regular sessions are held annually, starting in January; there is no statutory limit to their length. A bill must be passed by both houses of the Legislature and signed by the Governor to become law. The Governor is allowed 10 days to consider a bill during session, after which it becomes law unless vetoed. After session a bill dies unless signed within 10 days of the session's adjournment. A two-thirds' vote by each house is required to pass bills over the Governor's veto. Enacted legislation becomes effective 90 days after adjournment of the session. In the 2006 gubernatorial election the Democratic candidate, Jennifer Granholm, was re-elected with 56% of the votes cast. In the presidential election in 2008 the Democrats secured an estimated 57% of the votes cast, with nearly 5m. people voting. There are 83 administrative counties in Michigan.

Elected Executive Branch Officials

Governor (2007–11): JENNIFER M. GRANHOLM (Dem.).

Lieutenant-Governor: JOHN D. CHERRY, Jr (Dem.).

Secretary of State: TERRI LYNN LAND (Rep.).

Attorney-General: MIKE COX (Rep.).

Selected Government Addresses

Office of the Governor: Olds Plaza, POB 30013, Lansing, MI 48909; tel. (517) 373-3400; fax (517) 335-6863; e-mail governor@michigan.gov; internet www.michigan.gov/gov.

Office of the Lieutenant-Governor: POB 30013, Lansing, MI 48909; tel. (517) 373-6800; fax (517) 241-3956; e-mail ltgov@michigan.gov; internet www.michigan.gov/ltgov.

Department of the Secretary of State: Lansing, MI 48918; tel. (517) 373-2510; fax (517) 335-4329; e-mail soswebmaster@michigan.gov; internet www.michigan.gov/sos.

Office of the Attorney-General: G. Mennen Williams Bldg, 7th Floor, 525 West Ottawa St, POB 30212, Lansing, MI 48909; tel. (517) 373-1110; fax (517) 373-3042; e-mail miag@michigan.gov; internet www.michigan.gov/ag.

Department of Agriculture: POB 30017, Lansing, MI 48909; tel. (517) 373-1104; fax (517) 373-9146; e-mail mda-info@michigan.gov; internet www.michigan.gov/mda; Dir DONALD KOIVISTO.

Department of Community Health: Capitol View Bldg, 201 Townsend St, Lansing, MI 48913; tel. (517) 373-3740; e-mail norris@michigan.gov; internet www.michigan.gov/mdch; Dir JANET OLSZEWSKI.

Department of Corrections: 206 East Michigan Ave, Grandview Plaza, POB 30003, Lansing, MI 48909; tel. (517) 335-1426; e-mail correctionsinfo@michigan.gov; internet www.michigan.gov/corrections; Dir PATRICIA L. CARUSO.

Department of Education: Hannah Bldg, 608 West Allegan St, POB 30008, Lansing, MI 48909; tel. (517) 373-3324; fax (517) 335-4575; e-mail mdeweb@michigan.gov; internet www.michigan.gov/mde; Supt MICHAEL P. FLANAGAN.

Department of Environmental Quality: POB 30473, Lansing, MI 48909-7973; tel. (517) 373-7917; fax (517) 241-7401; e-mail deq-officeofcommunication@michigan.gov; internet www.michigan.gov/deq; Dir STEVEN E. CHESTER.

Department of Labor and Economic Growth: 611 West Ottawa St, 4th Floor, Lansing, MI 48933; tel. (517) 373-9280; fax (517) 241-1580; e-mail mediainfo@michigan.gov; internet www.michigan.gov/cis; Dir KEITH W. COOLEY.

Department of Management and Budget: Lewis Cass Bldg, 320 South Walnut St, POB 30026, Lansing, MI 48909; tel. (517) 373-1004; fax (517) 373-7268; internet www.michigan.gov/dmb; Dir LISA WEBB SHARPE.

Department of Military and Veterans' Affairs: Michigan Army and Air National Guard Joint Public Affairs Office, 3411 Martin Luther King Jr Blvd, Lansing, MI 48906; tel. (517) 481-8140; e-mail paocmn@michigan.gov; internet www.michigan.gov/dmva; Adj.-Gen. Maj.-Gen. THOMAS G. CUTLER.

Department of Natural Resources: Mason Bldg, 6th Floor, POB 30028, Lansing, MI 48909; tel. (517) 373-2329; fax (517) 335-1880; internet www.michigan.gov/dnr; Dir REBECCA A. HUMPHRIES.

Department of Transportation: 425 West Ottawa St, POB 30050, Lansing, MI 48909; tel. (517) 373-2090; fax (517) 373-0167; e-mail mdotdirector@michigan.gov; internet www.michigan.gov/mdot; Dir KIRK T. STEUDLE.

Department of the Treasury: 430 West Allegan St, Lansing, MI 48922; tel. (517) 373-3223; fax (517) 373-4968; e-mail mistatetreasurer@michigan.gov; internet www.michigan.gov/treasury; Treas. ROBERT J. KLEINE.

Economic Development Corporation: 300 North Washington Sq., Lansing, MI 48913; tel. (517) 373-9808; e-mail medcservices@michigan.org; internet www.themedc.org; Pres. and CEO JAMES C. EPOLITO.

Public Service Commission: 6545 Mercantile Way, Suite 7, POB 30221, Lansing, MI 48909; tel. (517) 241-6180; fax (517) 241-6181; e-mail mpsc_commissioners@michigan.gov; internet www.michigan.gov/mpsc; Chair. ORJIAKOR N. ISIOGU.

State Police Department: 714 South Harrison Rd, East Lansing, MI 48823; tel. (517) 332-2521; internet www.michigan.gov/msp; Dir Lt-Col PETER C. MUNOZ.

Legislature
(August 2008)

Senate

Rep. 21; Dem. 17; Total 38

President: Lt-Gov. JOHN D. CHERRY, Jr (Dem.).

President Pro Tempore: RANDY RICHARDVILLE (Rep.).

Secretary: CAROL MOREY VIVENTI.

House of Representatives

Dem. 58; Rep. 52; Total 110

Speaker: ANDY DILLON (Dem.).

Speaker Pro Tempore: MICHAEL SAK (Dem.).

Clerk: RICHARD J. BROWN.

Minnesota

Gross Area: 225,182 sq km (86,943 sq miles).

Resident Population (1 July 2007, estimate): 5,197,621.

State Capital: St Paul.

Principal Towns and Cities (population at 1 July 2006): Minneapolis 372,833; St Paul (capital) 273,535.

LOCATION, TOPOGRAPHY AND CLIMATE

The state of Minnesota (nicknamed 'The North Star State') is in the Midwest region of the USA and is bordered by the Canadian provinces of Manitoba and Ontario to the north, Lake Superior and Wisconsin to the east, Iowa to the south, and South Dakota and North Dakota to the west. Minnesota lies at the edge of the Central Plains region and the land is mainly flat. However, in the south-east there are undulating hills and in the north-east lie the rugged, forested Mesabi and Vermilion Ranges. The state is characterized by its large number of lakes and rivers, including: Lake of the Woods at 3,846 sq km (1,485 sq miles) and Rainy Lake at 894 sq km (345 sq miles) in the north (both shared with Canada); Lower and Upper Red Lake, at 1,168 sq km (451 sq miles); Mille Lacs, at 536 sq km (207 sq miles); and Leech Lake, at 456 sq km (176 sq miles). The Mississippi River runs south from its source at Lake Itasca in the north-west and forms the state's south-eastern boundary. Other major rivers in Minnesota are the St Croix, forming part of the eastern boundary with Wisconsin; the Red River of the North, flowing north into Canada and forming the north-western boundary with North Dakota; and the Minnesota River, running across the south of the state into the Mississippi River. Minnesota has a continental climate, with cold winters and warm summers.

HISTORICAL BACKGROUND

When the French began to explore Minnesota in the 1650s the region was inhabited by Dakota, Ojibwa and Sioux peoples. In 1679 Daniel Greysolon claimed the area for France. The region east of the Mississippi came under British rule in 1763, following the French and Indian War (Seven-Years War) and became US land after the American Revolution. The remainder of the land was acquired from the French under the Louisiana Purchase of 1803. Minnesota was granted territorial status in 1849 and, on 11 May 1858, became the 32nd state to join the Union. In 1837, following a series of treaties, the USA bought Native American lands in the state. The Sioux people revolted—after their defeat at the Battle of Woods Lake in 1862, they were driven from the state. Minnesota fought on the side of the Union during the Civil War and remained politically dominated by the anti-slavery Republican Party until the early 20th century. It was then challenged by the Democrats and others, including the Non-Partisan League and the associated Farmer-Labor Party, which later merged with the Democratic Party.

ECONOMY

Manufacturing, agribusiness, forest products, finance, insurance and real estate, wholesale and retail trade, tourism and services are the principal components of Minnesota's economy. Gross domestic product by state totalled US $254,970m. in 2007, when average per-head income was $40,969. In 2007 just 9.5% of the population were estimated to be living below the poverty threshold. The civilian labour force totalled 2,975,600 in mid-2008, with an unemployment rate of 5.6% (166,500 persons). In 2007 16.3% of all employees were union members and 17.0% were covered by union agreements.

Farmland covered 27.4m. acres (11.1m. ha) in 2007. There were 79,000 farms in that year, with the average farm covering an area of 347 acres. Just 2% of total cropland was irrigated in 2002. In 2007 55% of farm marketings (which were the fifth highest in the USA) were derived from sales of crops and 45% from livestock and livestock products. Minnesota's principal agricultural commodities were corn, soybeans, hogs and dairy products. The state was ranked first in 2007 for production of sugar beets. In the same year it ranked first for turkeys and third for soybean and hog production. Some 30% of Minnesota's land area is covered by forest, and there is some lumbering activity.

In 2007 Minnesota ranked eighth in the USA in terms of the value of its non-fuel mineral output, which totalled US $2,550m. Iron ore is the state's leading mineral, and Minnesota was ranked second (behind Michigan) nation-wide in 2007 for production of this mineral. Sand and gravel, crushed stone and dimension stone were also important, while the state was ranked third for peat production, its only known fossil-fuel resource.

Canning and meatpacking became important industries in the early 20th century, and food processing remains a leading industrial activity in Minnesota. Much of the state's manufacturing activity is concentrated in the Minneapolis-St Paul area. In 2006 Minnesota ranked 18th in the USA in terms of the value of its shipments. The principal industrial sectors are food and allied products, print products, fabricated metals, machinery, computers and transportation equipment. The total value of Minnesota's manufacturing shipments in 2006 was US $101,945m., with 48% added during manufacture.

Domestic travel expenditures totalled US $8,494m. in 2004. In 2006 total general expenditures by the state government amounted to $30,989m. General revenue totalled $27,691m., of which $6,479m. was provided by the federal Government and $17,331m. came from taxes. A total of $6,441m. in federal aid was received in 2006.

CONSTITUTION AND GOVERNMENT

Minnesota's only Constitution was adopted in 1857 and became effective on 11 May 1858. Amendments to the Constitution proposed by the Legislature have to be approved by a majority of elected members in each house and then ratified by a majority of voters in the following election. The Governor and Lieutenant-Governor are elected jointly to serve a four-year term of office. There are 67 senators and 134 representatives in the Legislature, serving terms of four and two years, respectively. In the first term of a new decade Senate members serve for two years. In Minnesota there is legal provision for regular sessions of the Legislature to be held in January in odd-numbered years only, but, in practice, sessions are also held in even-numbered years. Regular sessions may last no longer than 120 days. Before being presented to the Governor a bill must be passed by both houses of the Legislature. During session a bill becomes law unless vetoed within three days of presentation to the Governor. Outside session the Governor is allowed 14 days to consider a bill, after which it dies unless signed. A gubernatorial veto may be overridden by a two-thirds' vote by the elected members of each house. Enacted legislation becomes effective on 1 August following, except for fiscal legislation, which becomes effective immediately. In 2006 Tim Pawlenty, the Republican candidate, was re-elected to the governorship by a narrow margin, securing 47% of the votes cast. In the presidential election of 2008, the candidate for the Democratic Farmer Labor Party (DFL), the official name for Minnesota's Democratic Party, gained 54% of the votes cast, compared with 44% for the Republican Party. Minnesota has 87 administrative counties.

Elected Executive Branch Officials

Governor (2007–11): TIM PAWLENTY (Rep.).

Lieutenant-Governor: CAROL MOLNAU (Rep.).

Secretary of State: MARK RITCHIE (DFL).

Attorney-General: LORI SWANSON (DFL).

Auditor: REBECCA OTTO (DFL).

Selected Government Addresses

Office of the Governor: 130 State Capitol, 75 Rev. Dr Martin Luther King Jr Blvd, St Paul, MN 55155; tel. (651) 296-3391; fax (651) 296-2089; e-mail tim.pawlenty@state.mn.us; internet www.governor.state.mn.us.

Office of the Lieutenant-Governor: 130 State Capitol, 75 Rev. Dr Martin Luther King Jr Blvd, St Paul, MN 55155; tel. (651) 296-3391; fax (651) 296-2089; internet www.governor.state.mn.us.

Office of the Secretary of State: 180 State Office Bldg, 100 Rev. Dr Martin Luther King Jr Blvd, St Paul, MN 55155-1299; tel. (651) 215-1440; fax (651) 296-9073; e-mail secretary.state@state.mn.us; internet www.sos.state.mn.us.

Office of the Attorney-General: 1400 Bremer Tower, 445 Minnesota St, St Paul, MN 55101; tel. (651) 296-3353; fax (651) 297-4193; e-mail attorney.general@state.mn.us; internet www.ag.state.mn.us.

Office of the Auditor: 525 Park St, Suite 500, St Paul, MN 55103; tel. (651) 296-2551; fax (651) 296-4755; e-mail state.auditor@state.mn.us; internet www.osa.state.mn.us.

Department of Agriculture: 625 Robert St North, St Paul, MN 55155-2538; tel. (651) 201-6015; fax (651) 201-6118; e-mail mda.info@state.mn.us; internet www.mda.state.mn.us; Commr GENE L. HUGOSON.

Department of Commerce: 85 Seventh Place East, Suite 500, St Paul, MN 55101; tel. (651) 296-4026; fax (651) 297-1959; e-mail general.commerce@state.mn.us; internet www.commerce.state.mn.us; Commr GLENN WILSON, Jr.

Department of Corrections: 1450 Energy Park Dr., Suite 200, St Paul, MN 55108-5219; tel. (651) 361-7200; fax (651) 642-0223; e-mail shari.burt@state.mn.us; internet www.corr.state.mn.us; Commr JOAN FABIAN.

Department of Education: 1500 Hwy 36 West, Roseville, MN 55113-4266; tel. (651) 582-8200; internet www.education.state.mn.us; Commr ALICE SEAGREN.

Department of Employment and Economic Development: First National Bank Bldg, 332 Minnesota St, Suite E200, St Paul, MN 55101-1351; tel. (651) 259-7114; fax (651) 296-0994; e-mail deed.customerservice@state.mn.us; internet www.deed.state.mn.us; Commr DAN MCELROY.

Department of Finance and Employee Relations: 400 Centennial Office Bldg, 658 Cedar St, St Paul, MN 55155-1603; tel. (651) 259-3637; fax (651) 296-8685; e-mail employ.relations@state.mn.us; internet www.finance.state.mn.us; Commr TOM HANSON.

Department of Health: POB 64975, St Paul, MN 55164-0975; tel. (651) 201-5000; internet www.health.state.mn.us; Commr Dr SANNE MAGNAN.

Department of Labor and Industry: 443 Lafayette Rd North, St Paul, MN 55155-4307; tel. (651) 284-5005; fax (651) 284-5721; internet www.doli.state.mn.us; Commr STEVE SVIGGUM.

Department of Military Affairs: Veterans Service Bldg, 20 West 12th St, St Paul, MN 55155-2098; tel. (651) 296-4666; fax (651) 282-4541; e-mail public.affairs@mn.ngb.army.mil; internet www.dma.state.mn.us; Adj.-Gen. Maj.-Gen. LARRY W. SHELLITO.

Department of Natural Resources: 500 Lafayette Rd, St Paul, MN 55155-4040; tel. (651) 296-6157; fax (651) 296-4799; e-mail info@dnr.state.mn.us; internet www.dnr.state.mn.us; Commr MARK HOLSTEN.

Department of Public Safety: Town Sq. Bldg, 444 Cedar St, St Paul, MN 55101; tel. (651) 201-7000; e-mail dps.webmaster@state.mn.us; internet www.dps.state.mn.us; Commr MICHAEL CAMPION.

Department of Transportation: 395 John Ireland Blvd, St Paul, MN 55155; tel. (651) 296-3000; fax (651) 297-3160; e-mail info@dot.state.mn.us; internet www.dot.state.mn.us; Commr THOMAS K. SOREL.

Public Utilities Commission: 121 Seventh Pl. East, Suite 350, St Paul, MN 55101-2147; tel. (651) 296-7124; fax (651) 297-7073; e-mail consumer.puc@state.mn.us; internet www.puc.state.mn.us; Chair. Dr DAVID C. BOYD.

Legislature
(August 2008)

Senate

DFL 45; Rep. 22; Total 67

President: JAMES P. METZEN (DFL).

President Pro Tempore: DENNIS R. FREDERICKSON (Rep.).

Secretary: PATRICK E. FLAHAVEN.

House of Representatives

DFL 85; Rep. 49; Total 134

Speaker: MARGARET ANDERSON KELLIHER (DFL).

Chief Clerk: AL MATHIOWETZ.

Mississippi

Gross Area: 125,443 sq km (48,452 sq miles).

Resident Population (1 July 2007, estimate): 2,918,785.

State Capital, Principal City: Jackson (population 176,614 at 1 July 2006).

LOCATION, TOPOGRAPHY AND CLIMATE

The State of Mississippi (nicknamed 'The Magnolia State') lies in the South region of the USA and is bordered by Tennessee to the north, Alabama to the east, Louisiana to the south-west and Arkansas to the west. In the south-east there is a coastline on the Gulf of Mexico. The Mississippi River forms the western boundary of the state. To the east of this river is the Mississippi Alluvial Plain, or Delta, a broad band of flat, fertile land, which becomes narrower towards the south. The rest of the state lies within the Gulf Coastal Plain, rising towards the highest region in the north-eastern corner and including the Red Clay Hills of east-central Mississippi and the Piney Woods of the south. Sandy beaches extend along the coast. Numerous oxbow lakes, which were once part of the Mississippi River, lie along the state's western boundary. The other principal rivers of the state are the Pearl, flowing south into the Gulf of Mexico, and the Big Black and Yazoo Rivers, flowing south-west into the Mississippi. Mississippi has long, humid summers and short winters. Winters are mild in the south, which has a subtropical climate.

HISTORICAL BACKGROUND

Choctaw, Chickasaw and Natchez peoples inhabited the area when Hernando de Soto, a Spaniard, explored the region in 1540. In 1682 Robert La Salle traced the Mississippi River from Illinois and claimed the entire valley for France. The first permanent French settlement was established at Biloxi Bay in 1699 and Mississippi was incorporated into French Louisiana territory. Passing frequently between French, Spanish and British rule from the 1760s onwards, the region came under US control in 1795. In 1798 the Territory of Mississippi, comprising the whole of Alabama and Mississippi, was formed, and administered by the USA. Treaties made with native peoples in 1820 and 1832 made available fertile land in the north of the state, leading to the establishment of cotton plantations in the area and the introduction of black slave labour. Mississippi was a leading Confederate state in the Civil War, but its territory was the scene of three major Unionist victories, at Corinth and Iuka in 1862 and at Vicksburg in 1863. The state was readmitted to the Union in 1870.

ECONOMY

Mississippi's economy is dominated by manufacturing, wholesale and retail trade, finance, insurance and real estate and services. Until the Second World War the economy was principally dependent on the cotton industry. Gross domestic product by state was US $88,546m. in 2007. In terms of per-head income, which averaged just $28,527, Mississippi ranked as the poorest state in the Union in 2007. Unsurprisingly, more than one-fifth—some 20.6%—of the population were living below the poverty threshold in that year—the highest proportion in the nation. The civilian labour force totalled 1,355,500 in mid-2008 and the unemployment rate was 8.6%, the second highest in the USA (after Michigan), affecting 116,600 persons. Rates of union membership, previously among the lowest in the country, have risen slightly in recent years. In 2007 6.7% of employees belonged to a trade union and 8.9% were covered by union agreements.

Farmland covered 11.0m. acres (4.5m. ha) in 2007. There were 41,700 farms in that year, with the average farm covering an area of 264 acres. In 2002 some 20.2% of total cropland was irrigated. In 2007 63% of farm income was derived from sales of livestock and livestock products and 37% from crops. Mississippi's leading agricultural products in that year were broilers, cotton, soybeans and corn. The state ranked fifth nationally for broilers and cotton production in 2007. It was also the lead producer of aquaculture products among the states in that year (ahead of Louisiana and Arkansas), and a significant producer of rice, for which it ranked fourth overall. Forestland covers 18.6m. acres, equivalent to 48% of the state's land area; in 2004 the state ranked sixth in the USA in timber production with an output of 2,740m. board feet, of which 82% was softwood. Fish landings in 2006 were valued at US $22m.

Mississippi's non-fuel mineral production was valued at US $257m. in 2007, placing it 39th among the states. Construction sand and gravel was the state's leading mineral product by value in that year, while crushed stone, clays (fuller's earth, ball clay and bentonite) and portland cement were also important. Mississippi is the USA's second leading producer of bentonite and ranked third in 2005 for ball clay and fuller's earth. The state is a significant producer of natural gas and also produces some coal and crude petroleum.

In 2006 Mississippi ranked 28th in the nation in terms of its value of shipments. The state's most important industries include electronic equipment, food and kindred products, apparel, furniture, lumber and wood products and transportation equipment. In 2006 manufacturing shipments amounted to US $56,300m., of which 37% of value was added in manufacture.

In 2004 domestic travel expenditures amounted to US $5,697m. Total general expenditures by the state government in 2005 were $14,705m.; general revenue was $14,604m., of which the federal Government provided $6,855m. and taxes $5,990m. Mississippi received $7,183m. in federal aid in 2006.

CONSTITUTION AND GOVERNMENT

Mississippi's current Constitution, its fourth, became effective on 1 November 1890. Amendments to the Constitution introduced by the Legislature must be approved by two-thirds of the elected members of each house and then ratified by a majority of state voters. The Governor, elected separately from the Lieutenant-Governor, serves a four-year term and may serve no more than two successive terms. Mississippi has no formal cabinet system. The Legislature comprises 52 senators and 122 representatives, both houses serving four-year terms. Regular sessions are held annually in January and the first session of a legislative term is limited to 125 days. Thereafter, sessions have a 90-day limit. A bill must be approved by both houses of the Legislature before being presented to the Governor, who has five days to consider it, after which it becomes law unless vetoed. After session a bill becomes law unless vetoed within 15 days of being presented to the Governor. The

Governor's veto may be overridden by a two-thirds' vote by the elected members of each house. Legislation becomes effective 60 days after enactment. The gubernatorial election of 2003 was won by the Republican candidate, Haley Barbour. Barbour secured a further term in office in the 2007 election. In the 2008 presidential election just over 1.2m. people voted, with the Republicans securing an estimated 56% of the votes cast. Mississippi is divided into 82 administrative counties.

Elected Executive Branch Officials

Governor (2008–12): HALEY R. BARBOUR (Rep.).

Lieutenant-Governor: PHIL BRYANT (Rep.).

Secretary of State: DELBERT HOSEMANN (Rep.).

Attorney-General: JIM HOOD (Dem.).

Treasurer: TATE REEVES (Rep.).

Auditor: STACEY PICKERING (Rep.).

Commissioner of Agriculture: Dr LESTER SPELL, Jr (Rep.).

Commissioner of Insurance: MIKE CHANEY (Rep.).

Selected Government Addresses

Office of the Governor: POB 139, Jackson, MS 39205-0139; tel. (601) 359-3150; fax (601) 359-3741; internet www.governor.state.ms.us.

Office of the Lieutenant-Governor: New Capitol Bldg, 3rd Floor, POB 1018, Jackson, MS 39215-1018; tel. (601) 359-3200; fax (601) 359-4054; internet www.ltgovbryant.com.

Office of the Secretary of State: 401 Mississippi St, POB 136, Jackson, MS 39205-0136; tel. (601) 359-1350; fax (601) 359-1499; internet www.sos.state.ms.us.

Office of the Attorney-General: Walter Sillers Bldg, Suite 1200, 550 High St, POB 220, Jackson, MS 39205-0220; tel. (601) 359-3680; internet www.ago.state.ms.us.

Office of the Treasurer: POB 138, Jackson, MS 39205-0138; tel. (601) 359-3600; fax (601) 359-2001; internet www.treasury.state.ms.us.

Office of the Auditor: Woolfolk Bldg, 501 North West St, Suite 801, Jackson, MS 39201; tel. (601) 576-2800; fax (601) 364-2687; e-mail auditor@osa.state.ms.us; internet www.osa.state.ms.us.

Department of Agriculture and Commerce: 121 North Jefferson St, POB 1609, Jackson, MS 39215; tel. (601) 359-1100; fax (601) 354-6290; internet www.mdac.state.ms.us; headed by the Commr of Agriculture.

Department of Corrections: 723 North President St, Jackson, MS 39202; tel. (601) 359-5600; fax (601) 359-5738; e-mail cepps@mdoc.state.ms.us; internet www.mdoc.state.ms.us; Commr CHRISTOPHER B. EPPS.

Department of Education: Central High School, POB 771, 359 North West St, Jackson, MS 39205; tel. (601) 359-3513; fax (601) 359-2566; e-mail webhelp@mde.k12.ms.us; internet www.mde.k12.ms.us; Supt Dr HANK M. BOUNDS.

Department of Environmental Quality: POB 2261, Jackson, MS 39225; tel. (601) 961-5171; fax (601) 961-5660; internet www.deq.state.ms.us; Exec. Dir TRUDY D. FISHER.

Department of Finance and Administration: Woolfolk Bldg, Suite 1301, 501 North West St, POB 267, Jackson, MS 39201; tel. (601) 359-3402; fax (601) 359-2405; e-mail webmaster@dfa.state.ms.us; internet www.dfa.state.ms.us; Exec. Dir Col J. K. STRINGER, Jr.

Department of Health: 570 East Woodrow Wilson Dr., POB 1700, Jackson, MS 39215-1700; tel. (601) 576-7400; fax (601) 576-7517; internet www.msdh.state.ms.us; State Health Officer Dr F. ED THOMPSON.

Department of Public Safety: POB 958, Jackson, MS 39205; tel. (601) 987-1212; fax (601) 987-1498; e-mail fphillips@mdps.state.ms.us; internet www.dps.state.ms.us; Commr STEPHEN B. SIMPSON.

Department of Transportation: 401 North West St, POB 1850, Jackson, MS 39215-1850; tel. (601) 359-7001; fax (601) 359-7050; e-mail comments@mdot.state.ms.us; internet www.gomdot.com; Exec. Dir LARRY L. (BUTCH) BROWN, Jr.

Development Authority: 501 North West St, POB 849, Jackson, MS 39205; tel. (601) 359-3449; fax (601) 359-2832; e-mail gswoope@mississippi.org; internet www.mississippi.org; Exec. Dir. GRAY SWOOPE.

Insurance Department: Woolfolk Bldg, 501 North West St, Suite 1001, POB 79, Jackson, MS 39205; tel. (601) 359-3569; fax (601) 359-1077; e-mail commissioner@mid.state.ms.us; internet www.mid.state.ms.us; headed by the Commr of Insurance.

National Guard: POB 5027, Jackson, MS 39296-5027; tel. (601) 973-6232; fax (601) 973-6251; internet www.ngms.state.ms.us; Adj.-Gen. Maj.-Gen. WILLIAM L. FREEMAN, Jr.

Public Service Commission: Woolfolk Bldg, 501 North West St, Jackson, MS 39201; tel. (601) 961-5430; fax (601) 961-5824; internet www.psc.state.ms.us; Chair. LEONARD BENTZ.

Tax Commission: 1577 Springridge Rd, Raymond, MS 39154-9602; POB 1033, Jackson, MS 39215-1033; tel. (601) 923-7000; fax (601) 923-7318; internet www.mstc.state.ms.us; Chair. and Commr of Revenue JOSEPH L. BLOUNT.

Legislature
(August 2008)

Senate

Dem. 27; Rep. 25; Total 52

President: Lt-Gov. PHIL BRYANT (Rep.).

President Pro Tempore: BILLY HEWES, III (Rep.).

Secretary: JOHN GILBERT.

House of Representatives

Dem. 75; Rep. 47; Total 122

Speaker: WILLIAM J. MCCOY (Dem.).

Speaker Pro Tempore: J. P. COMPRETTA (Dem.).

Clerk: ED PERRY.

Missouri

Gross Area: 180,546 sq km (69,709 sq miles).

Resident Population (1 July 2007, estimate): 5,878,415.

State Capital: Jefferson City (population 39,274 at 1 July 2006).

Principal Cities (population at 1 July 2006, estimate): Kansas City 447,306; St Louis 347,181; Springfield 150,797; Independence 109,400.

LOCATION, TOPOGRAPHY AND CLIMATE

The State of Missouri (nicknamed 'The Show Me State') is in the Midwest region of the USA and is bordered by Iowa to the north, Illinois, Kentucky and Tennessee to the east (across the Mississippi River), Arkansas to the south and Oklahoma, Kansas and Nebraska to the west. The Missouri River forms the western boundaries with Nebraska and part of Kansas and then flows eastwards across the state to join the Mississippi, which denotes the eastern boundary; these two rivers are the longest in the USA. North of the Missouri is a region of undulating hills and fertile plains known as the Dissected Till Plains. South of the Missouri, stretching into Arkansas, is the Ozark Plateau, the highest area of the state. In the west of the state are the low hills and prairies of the Osage Plains and in the south-eastern corner the fertile lowlands of the Mississippi Alluvial Plain. Other principal rivers include the White and the Osage. Missouri has a continental climate, with the south-east region receiving the heaviest precipitation.

HISTORICAL BACKGROUND

When French explorers, Jacques Marquette and Louis Joliet, travelled down the Mississippi River in 1673, Missouri's main inhabitants were Algonquian and Siouan peoples. The first settlement was established by French hunters and miners *c.* 1735 at Ste Geneviève, and the French continued to dominate the settlement of Missouri during the 18th century, despite a period of Spanish rule in 1763–1800. The USA acquired the region as part of the Louisiana Purchase of 1803 and Missouri Territory was established in 1812. Under Spanish rule many slave-owning farmers had settled in the region; Missouri became the 24th state to enter the Union, on 10 August 1821, as a slave-holding state under the so-called Missouri Compromise. Despite substantial support for the Confederate cause, Missouri was officially on the side of the Union during the Civil War. The Battle of Westport in 1864, in which Confederate forces were defeated, was one of the many confrontations that took place in the state. In 1865 Missouri became the first slave state to free all black slaves. After Reconstruction, when the Radical Republicans threatened to disenfranchise all Confederacy sympathizers, there was a general move towards the Democratic Party, which remained in power into the 20th century.

ECONOMY

Manufacturing, agriculture, tourism and the aerospace industries are most important to Missouri's economy. In 2007 gross domestic product by state totalled US $229,470m. and per-head income averaged $33,984 in the same year. In 2007 13.0% of the state population were recorded as living below the poverty threshold. The civilian labour force totalled 3,061,300 in mid-2008, with an unemployment rate of 6.5% (199,800 persons). In 2007 10.7% of those employed were members of trade unions and 11.9% were covered by union agreements.

In 2007 farmland covered 30.0m. acres (12.1m. ha). There were 104,500 farms in 2007, the second highest total of any state except Texas, while the average farm covered an area of 287 acres. In 2002 some 5.4% of total cropland was irrigated. In 2007 50% of farm income was derived from sales of livestock and livestock products and 50% from crops. The principal agricultural commodities in that year were soybeans, cattle and calves, corn and hogs. The state was ranked third for turkey production in 2007, behind Minnesota and North Carolina. Forestland covers some 31% of Missouri's land area; there is some commercial lumber production, with hardwood predominating.

Missouri's non-fuel mineral production was valued at US $2,210m. in 2007, with the state ranked ninth in this regard. Crushed stone was the state's leading mineral, followed by portland cement, lead and lime (for which the state was ranked first and third, respectively, in the USA in 2007), and zinc (ranked second). Missouri was the leading producer of fireclay in 2004, and was ranked second for production of fuller's earth in the same year. There is a little coal production.

The leading manufacturing centres of Missouri are the St Louis and Kansas City areas. The principal industrial sectors are transportation equipment (mainly motor vehicles and aeroplanes), food and kindred products, chemicals, fabricated metals, machinery and computer equipment. Missouri is also an important centre for the leather and leather products industry. The total value of Missouri's manufacturing shipments in 2006 was US $103,909m., with 43% added during manufacture. The state ranked 17th in the USA in terms of its value of shipments.

In 2004 domestic travel expenditures totalled US $9,465m. Total general expenditures by the state government in 2006 amounted to $24,335m. General revenue was $22,373., of which $7,773m. was contributed by the federal Government and $10,180m. was derived from taxes. Missouri received $7,374m. in federal aid in 2006.

CONSTITUTION AND GOVERNMENT

The current Constitution of Missouri is the state's fourth and became effective on 30 March 1945. Constitutional amendments proposed by the General Assembly have to be passed by a majority of elected members in each house and then ratified by a majority of state voters. The Governor (elected separately from the Lieutenant-Governor) and the Treasurer may serve no more than two terms of office, each term lasting for four years. There are 34 senators and 163 representatives in the General Assembly, serving terms of four and two years, respectively. Limits exist on the number of terms members of the legislature may serve. Alternate halves of the Senate are re-elected every two years. Regular legislative sessions are held annually, beginning in January and ending no later than 30 May. To become law, a bill requires the approval of both houses of the General Assembly and must be signed by the Governor. If, after a 15-day consideration period, the Governor has neither signed nor vetoed the bill, the legislators may present it to the Secretary of State of Missouri for enactment. A bill presented to the Governor after session becomes law unless vetoed within 45 days. A gubernatorial veto may be overridden by a vote by two-thirds of the elected members of each house. Enacted legislation becomes effective 90 days after adjournment of the session, except for legislation authorizing the expenditure of state funds, which becomes effective at the beginning of the state fiscal year on 1 July. In the gubernatorial election of 2008 the Democrats regained power, with their candidate, Jay Nixon, obtaining some 58% of the vote. In the presidential elections of that year the Republicans gained an estimated 49.5% of the votes cast, compared with 49.3% for the Democrats. There are 115 administrative counties in Missouri.

Elected Executive Branch Officials

Governor (2005–09): MATT BLUNT (Rep.).

Governor-elect (2009–13): JEREMIAH W. (JAY) NIXON (Dem.).

Lieutenant-Governor: PETER KINDER (Rep.).

Secretary of State: ROBIN CARNAHAN (Dem.).

Attorney-General: JEREMIAH W. (JAY) NIXON (Dem.).

Treasurer: SARAH STEELMAN (Rep.).

Auditor: SUSAN MONTEE (Dem.).

Selected Government Addresses

Office of the Governor: State Capitol Bldg, Rm 216, POB 720, Jefferson City, MO 65102-0720; tel. (573) 751-3222; fax (573) 751-1495; internet www.gov.mo.gov.

Office of the Lieutenant-Governor: State Capitol Bldg, Rm 224, Jefferson City, MO 65101; tel. (573) 751-4727; fax (573) 751-9422; e-mail ltgovinfo@ltgov.mo.gov; internet www.ltgov.mo.gov.

Office of the Secretary of State: State Capitol Bldg, Rm 208, Jefferson City, MO 65101; tel. (573) 751-4936; fax (573) 526-4903; e-mail sosmain@sos.mo.us; internet www.sos.mo.gov.

Office of the Attorney-General: Supreme Court Bldg, 207 West High St, POB 899, Jefferson City, MO 65102; tel. (573) 751-3321; fax (573) 751-0774; e-mail ag@ago.mo.gov; internet www.ago.mo.gov.

Office of the Treasurer: POB 210, Jefferson City, MO 65102; tel. (573) 751-2411; fax (573) 751-0343; internet www.treasurer.missouri.gov.

Office of the Auditor: 301 West High St, Office 880, POB 869, Jefferson City, MO 65102; tel. (573) 751-4213; fax (573) 751-7984; e-mail moaudit@auditor.mo.gov; internet www.auditor.mo.gov.

Department of Agriculture: 1616 Missouri Blvd, POB 630, Jefferson City, MO 65102; tel. (573) 751-3359; fax (573) 751-1784; e-mail aginfo@mda.mo.gov; internet www.mda.mo.gov; Dir DON STEEN.

Department of Corrections: 2729 Plaza Dr., POB 236, Jefferson City, MO 65102; tel. (573) 751-2389; fax (573) 751-4099; e-mail mocorxns@doc.mo.gov; internet www.doc.missouri.gov; Dir LARRY CRAWFORD.

Department of Economic Development: 301 West High St, POB 1157, Jefferson City, MO 65102-1157; tel. (573) 751-4962; fax (573) 526-7700; e-mail ecodev@ded.mo.gov; internet www.ded.mo.gov; Dir GREGORY A. STEINHOFF.

Department of Elementary and Secondary Education: 205 Jefferson St, POB 480, Jefferson City, MO 65102-0480; tel. (573) 751-4212; fax (573) 751-8613; e-mail pubinfo@dese.mo.gov; internet dese.mo.gov; Commr D. KENT KING.

Department of Health and Senior Services: Wildwood Dr., POB 570, Jefferson City, MO 65102; tel. (573) 751-6400; fax (573) 751-6010; e-mail info@dhss.mo.gov; internet www.dhss.mo.gov; Dir JANE DRUMMOND.

Department of Insurance, Financial Institutions, and Professional Registration: 301 West High St, Room 530, POB 690, Jefferson City, MO 65102-0690; tel. (573) 751-4126; fax (573) 751-1165; e-mail askmdi@mail.state.mo.us; internet difp.mo.gov; Dir LINDA BOHRER (acting).

Department of Labor and Industrial Relations: 421 East Dunklin St, POB 504, Jefferson City, MO 65102-0504; tel. (573) 751-9691; fax (573) 751-4135; e-mail diroffice@dolir.mo.gov; internet www.dolir.mo.gov; Dir TODD SMITH.

Department of Natural Resources: POB 176, Jefferson City, MO 65102; tel. (573) 751-3443; fax (573) 751-7627; e-mail contact@dnr.mo.gov; internet www.dnr.mo.gov; Dir DOYLE CHILDERS.

Department of Public Safety: Harry S. Truman State Office Bldg, Rm 870, 301 West High St, POB 749, Jefferson City, MO 65102; tel. (573) 751-4905; fax (573) 751-5399; e-mail dpsinfo@dps.state.mo.us; internet dps.mo.gov; Dir MARK S. JAMES.

Department of Revenue: Harry S Truman State Office Bldg, 301 West High St, Jefferson City, MO 65101; tel. (573) 751-4450; fax (573) 751-7150; e-mail dormail@dor.mo.gov; internet dor.mo.gov; Dir OMAR DAVIS.

Department of Transportation: 105 West Capitol Ave, POB 270, Jefferson City, MO 65102-0270; tel. (573) 751-2551; fax (573) 751-6555; internet www.modot.mo.gov; Dir PETE RAHN.

National Guard: 2302 Militia Dr., Jefferson, MO 65101; internet www.moguard.com; Adj.-Gen. Maj.-Gen. KING E. SIDWELL.

Public Service Commission: Governor Office Bldg, 200 Madison St, POB 360, Jefferson City, MO 65102-0360; tel. (573) 751-3234; fax (573) 751-1847; e-mail pscinfo@psc.mo.gov; internet www.psc.missouri.gov; Chair. JEFF DAVIS.

General Assembly
(August 2008)

Senate

Rep. 20; Dem. 14; Total 34

President: Lt-Gov. PETER KINDER (Rep.).

President Pro Tempore: MICHAEL GIBBONS (Rep.).

Secretary: TERRY L. SPIELER.

House of Representatives

Rep. 92; Dem. 71; Total 163

Speaker: ROD JETTON (Rep.).

Speaker Pro Tempore: BRYAN PRATT (Rep.).

Chief Clerk: D. ADAM CRUMBLISS.

Montana

Gross Area: 380,850 sq km (147,103 sq miles).

Resident Population (1 July 2007, estimate): 957,861.

State Capital: Helena (population 27,885 at 1 July 2006, estimate).

Principal Cities (population at 1 July 2006, estimate): Billings 100,148; Missoula 64,081; Great Falls 56,215.

LOCATION, TOPOGRAPHY AND CLIMATE

The State of Montana (nicknamed 'The Treasure State') is in the West region of the USA and is bordered by the Canadian provinces of British Columbia, Alberta and Saskatchewan to the north; North Dakota and South Dakota to the east; Wyoming to the south; and Idaho to the south-west and west. The Rocky Mountains extend along the west of the state, the crest of the Bitterroot Range forming part of the border with Idaho. The Continental Divide passes through Montana, from the Lewis Range in the north-west to the Bitterroot Range in the south-west. The high, undulating land of the northern Great Plains forms the central and eastern regions of the state. The highest elevation in Montana is Granite Peak, at 3,901 m (12,799 ft), near the Wyoming border. The state's main rivers are the Missouri, which has its source in the south-west and flows north and then east across Montana; and the Yellowstone, flowing from the south-east to join the Missouri in North Dakota. Montana has a continental climate, with heavy snow in the west.

HISTORICAL BACKGROUND

Sioux, Blackfoot, Arapaho and Cheyenne American Indians were among those occupying Montana at the beginning of the 19th century. In 1803 most of Montana became part of the USA under the Louisiana Purchase from France; an expedition led by Meriwether Lewis and William Clark in 1804–06 explored the rest of Montana and it became US land. Fur traders were the main settlers until gold was discovered near present-day Drummond in 1858, after which many miners moved into the region. Another influx occurred in 1880, with the discovery of copper at Butte. It was not until the Indians had been subdued and removed onto reserves that farmers, particularly cattle and sheep ranchers, began to move into the area. One of the most famous Indian victories took place in Montana: the Battle of the Little Big Horn (1876), where Col George Custer and all 266 men of a unit from the Seventh US Cavalry regiment were killed by Sioux and Cheyenne Indians led by Chiefs Sitting Bull, Crazy Horse and Gall. The Native American tribes were fully defeated soon afterwards. Granted territorial status in 1864, Montana became the 41st state of the Union on 8 November 1889. At the turn of the century the state was troubled by the civil unrest of the so-called War of the Copper Kings, fought over control of the rich mineral resources of Butte.

ECONOMY

Montana's main industries are mining, agriculture, lumber and tourism. It has the fifth smallest economy of any state. In 2007 gross domestic product by state totalled US $34,253m. and the state's per-head income averaged $33,145. It was estimated that 14.1% of the population were living below the poverty threshold in 2007. The civilian labour force was 514,900 in mid-2008, with an unemployment rate of 3.5% (18,100 persons), the fourth lowest level nationwide. In 2007 13.5% of those employed belonged to a trade union, although 15.6% were covered by union agreements.

In 2007 farmland covered some 60.0m. acres (24.3m. ha). There were 28,300 farms in that year, with an average area of 2,120 acres, the fourth largest in the country. In 2002 8.5% of total cropland was under irrigation. In 2007 52% of farm income was derived from crops and 48% from sales of livestock and livestock products. Cattle and calves, wheat, barley and hay were Montana's most valuable agricultural products in that year. Montana had 23.3m. acres of forest-land in 2003; its lumber production is entirely made up of softwood.

In 2007 Montana's non-fuel mineral production was valued at US $1,290m., ranked 18th among the states. The leading products in that year were copper, molybdenum concentrates, palladium, platinum and gold. It also remained a significant producer of zinc (for which it was ranked third among the states) and gemstones (ranked seventh) in 2007. Montana continued to be the only notable producer of primary palladium and platinum in the USA (negligible quantities were produced by Texas and Utah as byproducts of copper refining); it was ranked fifth for copper and also led production of talc in 2007. The state was placed fifth nationally for production of molybdenum concentrates, silver and lead, and third for bentonite, in 2004. Metallic minerals, which also include gold (for which Montana ranked eighth) and silver, accounted for almost 71% of the total value in the same year. In 2002 the state was ranked first in the USA for the size of its known coal reserves (although these were mainly of sub-bituminous quality), but it ranked only fifth for coal production in 2007, with production of 43m. short tons of coal. Petroleum and natural gas are also extracted in the state.

Montana ranked 47th in the USA in terms of its value of shipments in 2006. Its principal manufactured goods include food and kindred products, wood and paper products, primary metals, petroleum and coal products, and machinery. In 2006 the total value of Montana's manufacturing shipments was US $9,555m., of which 36% was added during manufacture.

In 2004 domestic travel expenditures amounted to US $2,184m. Total general expenditures by the state government were $5,195m. in 2006; general revenue amounted to $4,935m., with $1,819m. being provided by the federal Government and $2,126m. derived from taxes. In 2006 Montana received $1,755m. in federal aid.

CONSTITUTION AND GOVERNMENT

Montana's Constitution, the state's second, was adopted in 1972 and became effective on 1 July 1973. Amendments to the Constitution proposed by the Legislature have to be passed by a two-thirds vote in both houses and ratified by a majority of state voters. The Governor and Lieutenant-Governor, elected jointly, serve a four-year term and may serve no more than two terms. The Legislature consists of 50 senators and 100 representatives. Following each decennial reapportionment of seats, lots are drawn for one-half of the senators to serve an initial two-year term, after which they are elected for four-year terms; representatives serve two-year terms. Regular sessions of the Legislature are held biennially in odd-numbered years. They begin in January and may last no longer than 90 days. A bill becomes law when it has been passed by a simple majority in both houses and signed by the Governor. During session the Governor has 10 days to consider a bill, after which it becomes law unless vetoed. After session a bill becomes law unless vetoed within 25 days. A gubernatorial veto may be overridden by two-thirds of the members present in each house. Legislation becomes effective on 1 October following enactment, except for fiscal legislation, which becomes effective on 1 July. In the 2008 gubernatorial election the incumbent Democratic Governor, Brian Schweitzer, was re-elected with 65% of the votes cast. In the presidential election of the same year the Republicans secured just over 50% of the votes cast. For administrative purposes, Montana is divided into 56 counties.

Elected Executive Branch Officials

Governor (2009–13): BRIAN SCHWEITZER (Dem.).

Lieutenant-Governor: JOHN BOHLINGER (Dem.).

Secretary of State: BRAD JOHNSON (Rep.).

Attorney-General: MIKE MCGRATH (Rep.).

Auditor: JOHN MORRISON (Dem.).

Superintendent of Public Instruction: LINDA MCCULLOCH (Dem.).

Public Service Commissioner: BOB RANEY (Dem.).

Selected Government Addresses

Office of the Governor: State Capitol Bldg, POB 200801, Helena, MT 59620-0801; tel. (406) 444-3111; fax (406) 444-5529; internet governor.mt.gov.

Office of the Lieutenant-Governor: State Capitol Bldg, POB 200801, Helena, MT 59620-1901; tel. (406) 444-3111; fax (406) 444-4648; internet governor.mt.gov/ltgov.

Office of the Secretary of State: POB 202801, Helena, MT 59620-2801; tel. (406) 444-2034; fax (406) 444-3976; e-mail sos@mt.gov; internet sos.mt.us.

Office of the Attorney-General: Department of Justice, POB 201401, Helena, MT 59620-1401; tel. (406) 444-2026; fax (406) 444-3549; e-mail contactdoj@.mt.gov; internet doj.mt.gov.

Office of the Auditor: 840 Helena Ave, Helena, MT 59601; tel. (406) 444-2040; fax (406) 444-3497; e-mail stateauditor@mt.gov; internet sao.mt.gov.

Office of Public Instruction: POB 202501, Helena, MT 59620-2501; tel. (406) 444-3095; fax (406) 444-9299; e-mail opisupt@mt.gov; internet www.opi.mt.gov; State Supt LINDA MCCULLOCH.

Department of Agriculture: 303 North Roberts St, POB 200201, Helena, MT 59620-0201; tel. (406) 444-3144; fax (406) 444-5409; e-mail agr@mt.gov; internet www.agr.mt.gov; Dir RON DE YONG.

Department of Commerce: 301 South Park Ave, POB 200501, Helena, MT 59620-0501; tel. (406) 841-2700; fax (406) 841-2701; internet commerce.mt.gov; Dir ANTHONY J. PREITE.

Department of Corrections: 1539 11th Ave, POB 201301, Helena, MT 59620-1301; tel. (406) 444-3930; fax (406) 444-4920; internet www.cor.state.mt.us; Dir MIKE FERRITER.

Department of Labor and Industry: Walt Sullivan Bldg, 1327 Lockey Ave, POB 1728, Helena, MT 59624-1728; tel. (406) 444-2840;

fax (406) 444-1394; e-mail dliquestions@mt.gov; internet dli.mt.gov; Commr KEITH KELLY.

Department of Military Affairs: 1956 Mt Majo St, POB 4789, Fort Harrison, MT 59636-4789; tel. (406) 324-3000; fax (406) 841-3335; e-mail krevious@mt.gov; internet www.state.mt.us/dma; Adj.-Gen. Maj-Gen. RANDALL D. MOSLEY.

Department of Natural Resources and Conservation: 1625 11th Ave, POB 201601, Helena, MT 59620-1601; tel. (406) 444-2074; fax (406) 444-2684; e-mail dnrc_publicinfo@mt.gov; internet www.dnrc.mt.gov; Dir MARY SEXTON.

Department of Public Health and Human Services: 111 North Sanders St, Rm 301, POB 4210, Helena, MT 59604-4210; tel. (406) 444-5622; fax (406) 444-1970; internet www.dphhs.mt.gov; Dir JOAN MILES.

Department of Revenue: Sam W. Mitchell Bldg, 3rd Floor, 125 North Roberts St, POB 5805, Helena, MT 59604-5805; tel. (406) 444-6900; fax (406) 444-3696; internet mt.gov/revenue; Dir DAN BUCKS.

Department of Transportation: 2701 Prospect Ave, POB 201001, Helena, MT 59620-1001; tel. (406) 444-6201; fax (406) 444-7643; internet www.mdt.mt.gov; Dir JIM LYNCH.

Highway Patrol Division: 2550 Prospect Ave, POB 201419, Helena, MT 59620-1419; tel. (406) 444-3780; fax (406) 444-4169; e-mail mhphqcontact@mt.gov; internet doj.mt.gov/enforcement/highwaypatrol; Chief Admin. PAUL K. GRIMSTAD.

Public Service Commission: Vista Bldg, 1701 Prospect Ave, POB 202601, Helena, MT 59620-2601; tel. (406) 444-6199; fax (406) 444-7618; e-mail gjergeson@mt.gov; internet www.psc.state.mt.us; Chair. GREG JERGESON.

Legislature

(August 2008)

Senate

Dem. 26; Rep. 24; Total 50

President: MIKE COONEY (Dem.).

President Pro Tempore: DAN HARRINGTON (Dem.).

Secretary: JOHN MUDD.

House of Representatives

Rep. 50; Dem. 49; Constitution Party 1; Total 100

Speaker: SCOTT SALES (Rep.).

Speaker Pro Tempore: DEBBY BARRETT (Rep.).

Chief Clerk: MARILYN MILLER.

Nebraska

Gross Area: 200,358 sq km (77,358 sq miles).

Resident Population (1 July 2007, estimate): 1,768,331.

State Capital: Lincoln.

Principal Cities (population at 1 July 2006, estimate): Omaha 419,545; Lincoln (capital) 241,167.

LOCATION, TOPOGRAPHY AND CLIMATE

The State of Nebraska (nicknamed 'The Cornhusker State') is in the Midwest region of the USA, bordered by South Dakota to the north, Iowa and Missouri to the east, Kansas to the south, Colorado to the south-west and Wyoming to the west. The land in Nebraska slopes down from table-land in the west at the edge of the Rocky Mountains to prairie in the central region, part of the Great Plains. The alluvial lowlands of the Missouri valley are found in the east. The north-central area is a region of grass-covered sand-dunes and small lakes. The state's main rivers are the Missouri, forming part of the northern border with South Dakota and the entire eastern boundary; and the Platte and the Niobrara, which both flow from west to east to join the Missouri. Nebraska has a continental, semi-arid climate with greatly variable temperatures. Precipitation is heaviest in the east.

HISTORICAL BACKGROUND

When French and Spanish fur traders travelled through the region in the 18th century Nebraska was occupied by the Pawnee, Ponca, Omaha, Sioux and Oto peoples. The land became US territory through the Louisiana Purchase of 1803, and Bellevue, established in 1823, was the first permanent European settlement. Although the Indian Intercourse Act of 1834 forbade white settlement, thousands of people crossed Nebraska in the mid-19th century on their way westwards to Oregon and California. Many settled in the region and military forts were established in the 1840s to protect them from Indian attack. The 1862 Homestead Act offered further Plains land to settlers for free. Continuing conflicts with the settlers in the following two decades eventually forced the Native American peoples onto reservations. Granted territorial status in 1854, Nebraska became the 37th state to join the Union on 1 March 1867.

ECONOMY

Nebraska's economy, including its manufacturing and services sectors, is highly dependent on agriculture. Gross domestic product by state totalled US $80,093m. in 2007, while 11.2% of the population were thought to be living below the poverty line. Per-head income averaged $36,189 in that year. The civilian labour force stood at 1,010,900 in mid-2008, and the unemployment rate was 3.6% (36,000 persons)—the fifth lowest rate (together with Idaho and Utah) in the USA. In 2007 7.8% of all employees were union members and 9.7% were covered by union agreements.

Farmland covered 45.6m. acres (18.5m. ha) in 2007. There were 47,300 farms in that year, with the average farm covering an area of 964 acres. Some 7.5m. acres of farmland were under irrigation in 2002. Nebraska's farm income was the fourth highest among the states in 2007, with 57% of this generated by sales of livestock and livestock products and 43% by crop sales. The principal agricultural products were cattle and calves, corn, soybeans and hogs. In 2007 Nebraska was ranked second for cattle and calf production (behind Texas), third for corn, and fifth for soybeans and seventh for hogs and sugar beets. Wheat, hay, sorghum, oats, potatoes and barley were subsidiary crops, while sheep and lambs, chickens, turkeys, eggs, wool and honey were also produced. Forestland covers just 2% of Nebraska's land area.

In 2007 Nebraska's non-fuel mineral production was valued at just US $214m. (for which it ranked 41st in the country). The leading minerals were portland cement, construction sand and gravel, crushed stone and lime. Petroleum and natural gas were also extracted.

Omaha is a leading location for manufacturing establishments and employment in the state. Nebraska's principal manufactured goods are processed foods, industrial machinery (mostly farm and garden machinery), electrical equipment and printing and publishing products. In 2006 the total value of Nebraska's manufacturing shipments was US $40,632m., of which 38% was added during manufacture. The state ranked 33rd in the USA in terms of its value of shipments.

Travel and tourism is an important generator of out-of-state revenue. In 2004 domestic travel expenditures totalled US $2,982m.

In 2006 total general expenditures by the state government were US $7,702m. Total general revenue was $8,045m., of which $2,417m. was derived from the federal Government and $3,961m. from taxes. In 2006 Nebraska received $2,240m. in federal aid.

CONSTITUTION AND GOVERNMENT

Nebraska's current Constitution is the state's second and became effective on 12 October 1875. Constitutional amendments proposed by the unicameral Legislature must be approved by a three-fifths vote from the elected members and ratified by a majority of state voters. The majority vote must amount to at least 35% of the votes cast at the election. The Governor is elected jointly with the Lieutenant-Governor to serve a four-year term and, after two consecutive terms, is not eligible to hold the office of Governor again until a four-year period has elapsed. The Legislature consists of 49 senators who are elected to serve four-year terms of office, alternate halves being elected every two years. After serving for two consecutive terms, senators must wait four years before standing for membership of the legislature again. Regular sessions of the Legislature are held annually in January and are limited in length to 60 days in even-numbered years and 90 days in odd-numbered years. A bill becomes law when it has been passed by a majority in the Legislature and has been signed by the Governor; it also becomes law automatically if it remains neither signed nor vetoed five days after having been presented to the Governor. A gubernatorial veto may be overridden by a three-fifths vote by the elected members of the Legislature. Legislation becomes effective three months after adjournment. In the 2002 gubernatorial election the Republican incumbent, Mike Johanns, won 69% of the votes cast. Following Johanns' appointment to the Federal Cabinet in 2005, Dave Heineman, hitherto Lieutenant-Governor, took over as Governor. He was re-elected in 2006, receiving 70% of the votes cast. In the presidential election in 2008 the Republicans secured 57% of the votes cast. There are 93 administrative counties in Nebraska.

Elected Executive Branch Officials

Governor (2007–11): DAVE HEINEMAN (Rep.).

Lieutenant-Governor: RICHARD J. SHEEHY (Rep.).

Secretary of State: JOHN A. GALE (Rep.).

Attorney-General: JON BRUNING (Rep.).

Treasurer: RON ROSS (Rep.).

Auditor of Public Accounts: MIKE FOLEY (Rep.).

Selected Government Addresses

Office of the Governor: State Capitol, POB 94848, Lincoln, NE 68509-4848; tel. (402) 471-2244; fax (402) 471-6031; internet www.governor.nebraska.gov.

Office of the Lieutenant-Governor: State Capitol, Rm 2315, POB 94863, Lincoln, NE 68509-4863; tel. (402) 471-2256; fax (402) 471-6031; e-mail ltgov.ne.gov; internet www.ltgov.ne.gov.

Office of the Secretary of State: State Capitol, Rm 2300, POB 94608, Lincoln, NE 68509-4608; tel. (402) 471-2554; fax (402) 471-3237; e-mail receptionist@sos.ne.gov; internet www.sos.ne.gov.

Office of the Attorney-General: State Capitol, 2nd Floor, Rm 2115, Lincoln, NE 68509; tel. (402) 471-2682; fax (402) 471-3297; internet www.ago.ne.gov.

Office of the Treasurer: State Capitol, Rm 2003, POB 94788, Lincoln, NE 68509-4788; tel. (402) 471-2455; fax (402) 471-4390; e-mail info@treasurer.org; internet www.treasurer.state.ne.us.

Office of the Auditor of Public Accounts: State Capitol, Rm 2303, POB 98917, Lincoln, NE 68509-8917; tel. (402) 471-2111; fax (402) 471-3301; e-mail mike.foley@apa.ne.gov; internet www.auditors.state.ne.us.

Department of Agriculture: 301 Centennial Mall South, 4th Floor, POB 94947, Lincoln, NE 68509-4947; tel. (402) 471-2341; fax (402) 471-6876; e-mail agr.webmaster@nebraska.gov; internet www.agr.state.ne.us; Dir GREG IBACH.

Department of Banking and Finance: Commerce Court, Suite 400, 1230 O St, POB 95006, Lincoln, NE 68509-5006; tel. (402) 471-2171; fax (402) 471-3062; internet www.ndbf.org; Dir JOHN MUNN.

Department of Correctional Services: Folsom and West Prospector Pl., POB 94661, Lincoln, NE 68509-4661; tel. (402) 471-2654; fax (402) 479-5623; internet www.corrections.state.ne.us; Dir ROBERT P. HOUSTON.

Department of Economic Development: 301 Centennial Mall South, POB 94666, Lincoln, NE 68509-4666; tel. (402) 471-3111; fax (402) 471-3778; e-mail richard.baier@nebraska.gov; internet www.neded.org; Dir RICHARD BAIER.

Department of Education: 301 Centennial Mall South, POB 94987, Lincoln, NE 68509-4987; tel. (402) 471-2295; fax (402) 471-0117; internet www.nde.state.ne.us; Interim Commr Dr MARGE HAROUFF.

Department of Environmental Quality: The Atrium, Suite 400, 1200 N St, POB 98922, Lincoln, NE 68509-8922; tel. (402) 471-2186; fax (402) 471-2909; e-mail ndeq.moreinfo@nebraska.gov; internet www.deq.state.ne.us; Dir MIKE LINDER.

Department of Insurance: Terminal Bldg, Suite 400, 941 O St, Lincoln, NE 68508-3639; tel. (402) 471-2201; fax (402) 471-4610; e-mail pjasa@doi.state.ne.us; internet www.doi.ne.gov; Dir ANN M. FROHMAN.

Department of Labor: 550 South 16th St, POB 94600, Lincoln, NE 68509-4600; tel. (402) 471-2600; fax (402) 471-9867; e-mail ndol.lmi_ne@nebraska.gov; internet www.dol.state.ne.us; Commr FERNANDO (BUTCH) LECUONA, III.

Department of Natural Resources: 301 Centennial Mall South, Lincoln, NE 68509-4676; tel. (402) 471-2363; fax (402) 471-2900; e-mail awoods-rogers@dnr.ne.gov; internet www.dnr.ne.gov; Dir BRIAN P. DUNNIGAN (acting).

Department of Revenue: 301 Centennial Mall South, POB 94818, Lincoln, NE 68509-4818; tel. (402) 471-5729; fax (402) 471-5608; internet www.revenue.ne.gov; Tax Commr DOUGLAS EWALD.

Department of Roads: 1500 Nebraska Hwy 2, POB 94759, Lincoln, NE 68509-4759; tel. (402) 471-4567; fax (402) 479-4325; e-mail john.craig@nebraska.gov; internet www.nebraskatransportation.org; Dir JOHN CRAIG.

Military Department: 1300 Military Rd, Lincoln, NE 68508-1090; tel. (402) 309-7210; fax (402) 309-7147; internet www.neguard.com/nmd; Adj.-Gen. Brig.-Gen. TIMOTHY J. KADAVY.

Public Service Commission: The Atrium, Suite 300, 1200 N St, Lincoln, NE 68508; tel. (402) 471-3101; fax (402) 471-0254; e-mail anne.boyle@psc.ne.gov; internet www.psc.state.ne.us; Chair. ANNE C. BOYLE.

State Patrol: 1600 Nebraska Hwy 2, POB 94907, Lincoln, NE 68509-4907; tel. (402) 471-4545; internet www.nsp.state.ne.us; Supt Col BRYAN TUMA.

Legislature (August 2008)

Nebraska's legislature is unicameral and comprises 49 members elected on a non-partisan basis, all of whom go by the title of senator.

President of the Legislature: Lt-Gov. RICHARD J. SHEEHY.

Speaker of the Legislature: MIKE FLOOD.

Chair. of Executive Board: L. PATRICK ENGEL.

Clerk of the Legislature: PATRICK J. O'DONNELL.

Nevada

Gross Area: 286,367 sq km (110,567 sq miles).

Resident Population (1 July 2007, estimate): 2,565,382.

State Capital: Carson City (population 55,289 at 1 July 2006, estimate).

Principal Cities (population at 1 July 2006, estimate): Las Vegas 552,539; Henderson 240,614; Reno 210,255; North Las Vegas 197,567.

LOCATION, TOPOGRAPHY AND CLIMATE

The State of Nevada (nicknamed 'The Silver State') is in the West region of the USA and is bordered by Oregon and Idaho to the north, Utah to the east, Arizona to the south-east and California to the south and west. Nevada lies largely in the Great Basin, a high region of short, rugged ranges and arid basins stretching in a north-south direction. Ranges include the Ruby, Egan, Snake, Schell Creek, Hot Creek, Monitor, Toiyabe and Carson. The state's highest elevation is Boundary Peak in the White Mountains near the border with California, at 4,006 m (13,143 ft). Nevada's rivers frequently dry up, and many flow into saline marshes or lakes: these include the Humboldt, the state's longest river, which flows south-west into Humboldt Sink. The Colorado River forms Nevada's extreme south-eastern boundary. Among the state's lakes are Pyramid Lake at 487 sq km (188 sq miles), Lake Tahoe, shared with California, and Lake Mead, created by the Hoover Dam on the Colorado and shared with Arizona. Nevada is the driest state in the USA, with a semi-arid and arid climate, although there is heavy snow in the mountains. Temperatures vary greatly from day to day, but generally winters are very cold in the north and summers are extremely hot in the south.

HISTORICAL BACKGROUND

When Francisco Garcés, a Spanish priest, entered Nevada in 1776, the region was inhabited by the Southern Paiute, Northern Paiute, Shoshoni and Washo peoples. Hudson's Bay Co trappers explored the northern and central regions in 1825. The area was acquired by the USA in 1848, at the end of the Mexican War, and the first permanent European settlement was established at Mormon Station (later Genoa) one year later. Carson City was founded in 1858. In 1859 the discovery of the Comstock Lode, a substantial silver and gold deposit, attracted large numbers of settlers to the area. Nevada Territory was created in 1861 and, on 31 October 1864, Nevada became the 36th state to join the Union. Further discoveries of gold and silver deposits in the early 20th century supported the mining industry after Comstock Lode was exhausted. In 1931 gambling was legalized, rapidly becoming the economic mainstay of the state, and particularly of the cities of Las Vegas and Reno. The first atomic bomb was successfully tested in Nevada in 1953; subsequent US and British nuclear-explosion testing was carried out underground in the state.

ECONOMY

Tourism and gambling revenues are the principal contributors to Nevada's economy, with mining also of significant economic importance. Manufacturing, retailing, warehousing and the road freight transport industries also play an important role, and employment in the state and local governments is considerable. In 2007 gross domestic product by state was US $127,213m. and the state's average per-head income was $39,649. It was estimated that in that year 10.7% of the population were living below the poverty line. The civilian labour force stood at 1,407,400 in mid-2008, with an unemployment rate of 6.7% (94,700 persons). In 2007 15.4% of all employees were union members and 17.7% were covered by union agreements.

Farmland covered 6.3m. acres (2.6m. ha) in 2007. There were 3,000 farms in that year, with an average farm size of 2,100 acres (the fifth largest average size in the USA). Irrigation is used throughout the state, with 57% of total cropland irrigated in 2002. In 2007 61% of farm income was derived from sales of livestock and livestock products and 39% from crops. The principal commodities produced in that year were cattle and calves, hay, dairy products and onions. Some 14% of the state is covered by forest.

In 2007 Nevada ranked second in the USA in terms of the value of its non-fuel mineral production. With total state production of US $5,210m., Nevada accounted for 7.7% of overall US production. Nevada is the leading state for gold and the second leading state (behind Alaska) for silver mining, producing approximately 80% of total US gold in 2007 and 24% of total US silver output in 2003. Construction sand and gravel, lime and crushed stone were also significant mineral products.

Nevada ranked 43rd in the USA in terms of value of manufacturing shipments in 2006. The state's industrial activity is small but diversified. The principal manufacturing sectors are food and kindred products, non-metallic minerals, print products, plastics, primary and fabricated metals and computers and electrical equipment. The total value of Nevada's manufacturing shipments in 2006 was US $12,845m., of which 58% was added during manufacture.

Tourism is of primary importance to Nevada's economy. In 2004 domestic travel expenditures were US $26,250m., with the state ranked fifth in terms of money spent. Casino revenues represent a large share of the total income from tourism, and the hotel, gaming and recreation industries dominate Nevada's service sector, providing more than one-half of the service-related jobs in the state. The financial sector has also developed in recent years, with the state's commercial banks reporting total assets of $1,416,000m. at the end of 2006—Nevada was ranked third in this respect, after North Carolina and Ohio.

Total general expenditures by the state government in 2006 amounted to US $10,342m. General revenue totalled $9,461m., with $1,827m. being provided by the federal Government and $6,153m. derived from taxes. Nevada received $2,792m. in federal aid in 2006.

CONSTITUTION AND GOVERNMENT

Nevada's only Constitution became effective on 31 October 1864. Amendments to the Constitution proposed by the Legislature must be approved by a majority of elected members in each house in two successive sessions and ratified by a majority of state voters. The Governor, elected separately from the Lieutenant-Governor, serves a four-year term and may serve no more than two terms consecutively. Nevada has no formal cabinet system. There are 21 senators and 42 representatives in the Legislature, serving terms of four and two years, respectively; alternate halves of the Senate are re-elected every two years. Limits to the number of terms that may be served are to be introduced from 2010. Regular sessions of the Legislature take place biennially in February in odd-numbered years, and may last no longer than 120 calendar days. A bill becomes law when it has been passed by the Legislature and signed by the Governor. During session the Governor has five days to consider a bill, after which it becomes law unless vetoed. Outside session the consideration period is 10 days from adjournment of the Legislature. A gubernatorial veto may be overridden by a two-thirds' vote in each house. Enacted legislation becomes effective on 1 October following, or on a specified date. In the gubernatorial election of 2006 the Republican candidate, James A. Gibbons, received 48% of the votes cast. The Democrats secured the largest share of the votes cast (some 55%) in the 2008 presidential election. Nevada is divided into 17 administrative counties.

Elected Executive Branch Officials

Governor (2007–11): JAMES A. GIBBONS (Rep.).

Lieutenant-Governor: BRIAN KROLICKI (Rep.).

Secretary of State: ROSS MILLER (Dem.).

Attorney-General: CATHERINE CORTEZ MASTO (Dem.).

Treasurer: KATE MARSHALL (Dem.).

Controller: KIM WALLIN (Dem.).

Selected Government Addresses

Office of the Governor: Capitol Bldg, 101 North Carson St, Carson City, NV 89701; tel. (775) 684-5670; fax (775) 684-5683; internet gov.state.nv.us.

Office of the Lieutenant-Governor: Capitol Bldg, 101 North Carson St, Suite 2, Carson City, NV 89701; tel. (775) 684-7111; fax (775) 684-7110; e-mail ltgov@ltgov.nv.gov; internet ltgov.nv.gov.

Office of the Secretary of State: Capitol Bldg, 101 North Carson St, Suite 3, Carson City, NV 89701-4786; tel. (775) 684-5708; fax (775) 687-5724; e-mail sosmail@govmail.state.nv.us; internet sos.state.nv.us.

Office of the Attorney-General: 100 North Carson St, Carson City, NV 89701-4717; tel. (775) 684-1100; fax (775) 684-1108; e-mail aginfo@ag.state.nv.us; internet ag.state.nv.us.

Office of the Treasurer: Capitol Bldg, 101 North Carson St, Suite 4, Carson City, NV 89701; tel. (775) 684-5600; fax (775) 684-5623; e-mail statetreasurer@nevadatreasurer.gov; internet nevadatreasurer.gov.

Office of the Controller: Capitol Bldg, 101 North Carson St, Suite 5, Carson City, NV 89701-4786; tel. (775) 684-5750; fax (775) 684-5695; e-mail kwallin@govmail.state.nv.us; internet controller.nv.gov.

Department of Agriculture: 350 Capitol Hill, Reno, NV 89502; tel. (775) 688-1180; fax (775) 688-1178; e-mail ndoa@agri.state.nv.us; internet agri.state.nv.us; Dir TONY LESPERANCE.

Department of Business and Industry: 555 East Washington Ave, Suite 4900, Las Vegas, NV 89701; tel. (702) 486-2750; fax (702) 486-2758; e-mail biinfo@dbi.state.nv.us; internet business.nv.gov; Dir MENDY K. ELLIOTT.

Department of Conservation and Natural Resources: 901 South Stewart St, Suite 5001, Carson City, NV 89701; tel. (775) 684-2700; fax (775) 6847-2715; e-mail abiaggi@dcnr.nv.gov; internet dcnr.nv.gov; Dir ALLEN BIAGGI.

Department of Corrections: POB 7011, Carson City, NV 89702; tel. (775) 887-3285; fax (775) 687-6715; internet www.doc.nv.gov; Dir HOWARD SKOLNIK.

Department of Education: 700 East Fifth St, Carson City, NV 89701-5096; tel. (775) 687-9200; fax (775) 687-9101; e-mail krheault@doe.nv.gov; internet www.doe.nv.gov; Supt KEITH W. RHEAULT.

Department of Public Safety: 555 Wright Way, Carson City, NV 89711-0900; tel. (775) 684-4808; fax (775) 684-4809; internet dps.nv.gov; Dir JERRY HAFEN.

Department of Taxation: 1550 College Pkwy, Carson City, NV 89706; tel. (775) 684-2000; fax (775) 684-2020; e-mail dicianno@tax.state.nv.us; internet www.tax.state.nv.us; Exec. Dir DINO DICIANNO.

Department of Transportation: 1263 South Stewart St, Carson City, NV 89712; tel. (775) 888-7000; fax (775) 888-7115; e-mail info@dot.state.nv.us; internet www.nevadadot.com; Dir SUSAN MARTINOVICH.

Division of Environmental Protection: 901 South Stewart St, Suite 4001, Carson City, NV 89701-5249; tel. (775) 687-4670; fax (775) 687-5856; e-mail ldrozdof@ndep.nv.gov; internet ndep.nv.gov; Admin. LEO M. DROZDOFF.

Economic Development Commission: 108 East Proctor St, Carson City, NV 89701; tel. (775) 687-4325; fax (775) 687-4450; e-mail mskaggs@bizopp.state.nv.us; internet www.expand2nevada.com; Exec. Dir MICHAEL E. SKAGGS.

Health Division: 4150 Technology Way, Suite 300, Carson City, NV 89706; tel. (775) 684-4200; fax (775) 684-4211; e-mail jflamm@health.nv.gov; internet health2k.state.nv.us; Health Officer Dr MARY GUINAN (acting).

Labor Commission: 555 East Washington Ave, Suite 4100, Las Vegas, NV 89101-1050; tel. (702) 486-2650; fax (702) 486-2660; e-mail mail1@laborcommissioner.com; internet www.laborcommissioner.com; Commr MICHAEL TANCHEK.

National Guard: 2460 Fairview Dr., Carson City, NV 89701; tel. (775) 887-7252; fax (775) 887-7246; e-mail cindy.kirkland@nv.ngb.army.mil; internet www.nv.ngb.army.mil; Adj.-Gen. Maj.-Gen. CINDY KIRKLAND.

Public Utilities Commission: 1150 East William St, Carson City, NV 89701-3109; tel. (775) 684-6101; fax (775) 684-6110; e-mail mquintero@puc.state.nv.us; internet pucweb1.state.nv.us; Chair. JO ANN P. KELLY.

Legislature
(August 2008)

Senate

Rep. 11, Dem. 10, Total 21

President: Lt-Gov. BRIAN KROLICKI (Rep.).

President Pro Tempore: MARK E. AMODEI (Rep.).

Secretary: CLAIRE J. CLIFT.

Assembly

Dem. 27; Rep. 15; Total 42

Speaker: BARBARA BUCKLEY (Dem.).

Speaker Pro-Tempore: BERNIE ANDERSON (Dem.).

Chief Clerk: SUSAN FURLONG REIL.

New Hampshire

Gross Area: 24,219 sq km (9,355 sq miles).

Resident Population (1 July 2007, estimate): 1,315,828.

State Capital: Concord (population 42,378 at 1 July 2006, estimate).

Principal City: Manchester (population 109,497 at 1 July 2006, estimate).

LOCATION, TOPOGRAPHY AND CLIMATE

The State of New Hampshire (nicknamed 'The Granite State') is in the Northeast region of the USA and is one of the six states that constitute New England. It is bordered by Maine to the east, Massachusetts to the south and Vermont to the west. The state tapers northwards to an international border with Canada, beyond which, to the north and north-west, lies the province of Québec. In the south-east there is a coastline along the Atlantic Ocean. New Hampshire is mainly rocky, hilly and tree-covered. In the south and west are the New England Uplands, a region with numerous lakes, of which the largest is Lake Winnipesaukee (181 sq km—70 sq miles). In the north are the White Mountains (part of the Appalachian chain), including Mount Washington at 1,917 m (6,288 ft). Lowlands characterize the coastal region in the south-east. Three of the nine rocky Isles of Shoals, in the Atlantic, belong to New Hampshire. The state's main rivers are the Connecticut, which forms the border with Vermont; the Merrimack, forming part of the border with Massachusetts; the Salmon Falls and Piscataqua Rivers, forming part of the border with Maine; and the Androscoggin in the north-east. The climate is temperate and changeable, with severe, snowy winters in the mountains and cool summers inland. Temperatures are warmer on the coast.

HISTORICAL BACKGROUND

Algonquian-speaking peoples inhabited what is now New Hampshire when the Dutch, French and English explored the coast in the 17th century. First to penetrate the region were Martin Pring of the Netherlands in 1603, Samuel de Champlain of France in 1604 and Capt. John Smith of England in 1614. The British claim prevailed, and New Hampshire was a province of Massachusetts from 1643 to 1680, when it became a separate colony, although its boundary with Massachusetts remained under dispute until 1740. In 1776 New Hampshire became the first of the 13 rebel colonies to establish a government independent of the United Kingdom. On 21 June 1788 it became the ninth state to join the Union. Concord became the state capital in 1808. New Hampshire fought with the Unionist forces during the Civil War, but was too far north to witness any fighting within its boundaries.

ECONOMY

The economy of New Hampshire is dominated by manufacturing, with services and finance, insurance and real estate other important elements. Gross domestic product by state totalled US $57,341m. in 2007, with per-head income, at an average of $41,444 in that year. In 2007 it was estimated that just 7.1% of the population—the smallest proportion among all the states—were living below the poverty threshold. The civilian labour force totalled 757,100 in mid-2008, while the unemployment rate stood at 3.8% (28,400 persons). In 2007 9.7% of those employed belonged to a trade union, while 11.2% were covered by union agreements.

Farmland covered just 450,000 acres (7.8% of the state's total land area) in 2007. There were 3,400 farms in that year, with the average farm covering an area of 132 acres. In 2002 1.7% of total cropland was under irrigation. New Hampshire's farm income, at US $184m., was one of the lowest in the USA in 2007 (only exceeding those of Rhode Island and Alaska); in that year crops accounted for 57% of farm marketings and livestock and livestock products for 43%. The state's principal commodities in 2007, in order of marketing receipts, were greenhouse and nursery products, dairy products, apples and cattle and calves. Approximately 81% of New Hampshire is forested, the highest proportion of any state. There is a little commercial fishing activity; in 2006 the catch was valued at US $19m.

Mining plays a minor role in the state's economy. The state's non-fuel mineral production was estimated at just US $115m. in 2007, and mainly comprised construction sand and gravel and crushed and dimension stone, with some gemstone mining. The state's moniker was derived from its granite quarries.

Shipbuilding, formerly New Hampshire's principal industry, was superseded during the 19th century by textiles. Other industries expanded in the 20th century. The state ranked 38th in the USA in terms of the value of its shipments in 2006. Principal manufactured goods included industrial machinery and equipment, electronic and other electric equipment, fabricated metal products, plastics and rubber, paper products and computers. In 2006 the total value of manufacturing shipments was US $16,992m., of which some 54% was added during manufacture.

In 2004 domestic travel expenditures totalled US $2,860m. Total general expenditures by the state government in 2006 were $5,988m.; general revenue was $5,186m., with $1,522m. provided by the federal Government and $2,080m. derived from taxes. New Hampshire received $1,579m. in federal aid in 2006.

CONSTITUTION AND GOVERNMENT

New Hampshire's Constitution, its second, became effective on 2 June 1784. An amendment to the Constitution proposed by the General Court, the state legislature, has to be approved by three-fifths of the elected members of each house and ratified by a majority of state voters. The Governor, New Hampshire's only elected executive branch official, holds office for two years and is succeeded in his or her absence by the President of the Senate. There is no formal cabinet system in New Hampshire, but there is a five-member Executive Council (The Governor's Council), which is elected to serve as the executive branch of government. The General Court has 24 senators and 400 representatives, who are re-elected every two years. Regular legislative sessions are held annually in January and may last no longer than 45 legislative days. To become law a bill must be passed by a majority of the General Court and signed by the Governor. During session a bill also becomes law unless vetoed within five days of presentation to the Governor; after session a bill dies unless signed within five days of presentation. A gubernatorial veto may be overridden by two-thirds of the elected members of each house. Legislation becomes effective 60 days after enactment. The Democratic incumbent, John Lynch, was re-elected to the governorship in 2008 with 70% of the votes cast. In the concurrent presidential election the Democrats secured some 54% of the votes cast. There are 10 counties in New Hampshire.

Elected Executive Branch Official

Governor (2009–11): JOHN LYNCH (Dem.).

Executive Council: RAYMOND S. BURTON (Rep.), JOHN D. SHEA (Dem.), BEVERLY A. HOLLINGWORTH (Dem.), RAYMOND J. WIECZOREK (Rep.), DEBORA PIGNATELLI (Dem.).

Selected Government Addresses

Office of the Governor: State House, 25 Capitol St, Concord, NH 03301; tel. (603) 271-2121; fax (603) 271-7680; internet www.governor.nh.gov.

Executive Council Office: State House, Rm 207, 107 North Main St, Concord, NH 03301-4951; tel. (603) 271-3632; fax (603) 271-3633; e-mail gcweb@nh.gov; internet www.nh.gov/council.

Business Finance Authority: 2 Pillsbury St, Suite 201, Concord, NH 03301; tel. (603) 415-0190; fax (603) 415-0194; e-mail brendap@nhbfa.com; internet www.nhbfa.com; Chair. EDWARD F. CARON.

Department of Agriculture, Markets and Food: State House Annex, 25 Capitol St, 2nd Floor, POB 2042, Concord, NH 03302-2042; tel. (603) 271-3551; fax (603) 271-1109; e-mail lmerrill@agr.state.nh.us; internet www.nh.gov/agric; Commr LORRAINE STUART MERRILL.

Department of Corrections: State Office Park South, 105 Pleasant St, POB 1806, Concord, NH 03302-1806; tel. (603) 271-5600; fax (603) 271-5643; e-mail info@nhdoc.state.nh.us; internet www.nh.gov/nhdoc; Commr WILLIAM L. WRENN.

Department of Education: 101 Pleasant St, Concord, NH 03301-3860; tel. (603) 271-3494; fax (603) 271-1953; e-mail meghan.henley@ed.state.nh.us; internet www.ed.state.nh.us/education; Commr Dr LYONEL B. TRACY.

Department of Environmental Services: 29 Hazen Dr., POB 95, Concord, NH 03302-0095; tel. (603) 271-4974; fax (603) 271-2867; e-mail pip@des.state.nh.us; internet www.des.state.nh.us; Commr THOMAS S. BURACK.

Department of Health and Human Services: 129 Pleasant St, Concord, NH 03301-3857; tel. (603) 271-4331; fax (603) 271-4912; internet www.dhhs.state.nh.us; Commr NICHOLAS A. TOUMPAS.

Department of Insurance: 21 South Fruit St, Suite 14, Concord, NH 03301; tel. (603) 271-2261; fax (603) 271-1406; e-mail requests@ins.nh.gov; internet www.nh.gov/insurance; Commr ROGER A. SEVIGNY.

Department of Labor: 95 Pleasant St, Concord, NH 03301; tel. (603) 271-3176; fax (603) 271-6149; internet www.labor.state.nh.us; Commr GEORGE N. COPADIS.

Department of Resources and Economic Development: 172 Pembroke Rd, POB 1856, Concord, NH 03302-1856; tel. (603) 271-2411; fax (603) 271-2629; e-mail sboucher@dred.state.nh.us; internet www.dred.state.nh.us; Commr GEORGE BALD.

Department of Revenue Administration: 45 Chenell Dr., POB 457, Concord, NH 03302-0457; tel. (603) 271-2318; fax (603) 271-6121; internet www.nh.gov/revenue; Commr G. PHILIP BLATSOS.

Department of State: State House, Rm 204, 107 North Main St, Concord, NH 03301-3242; tel. (603) 271-3242; fax (603) 271-6316; e-mail elections@sos.state.nh.us; internet www.sos.nh.gov; Sec. of State WILLIAM M. GARDNER.

Department of Transportation: John O. Morton Bldg, 7 Hazen Dr., POB 483, Concord, NH 03302-0483; tel. (603) 271-3734; fax (603) 271-3914; internet www.nh.gov/dot; Commr GEORGE N. CAMPBELL, Jr.

Office of the Adjutant-General: 4 Pembroke Rd, Concord, NH 03301-5652; tel. (603) 225-1200; fax (603) 225-1341; e-mail peter.fortier1@ng.army.mil; internet www.nh.gov/adjgeneral; Adj.-Gen. Maj.-Gen. KENNETH R. CLARK.

Office of the Attorney-General: Dept of Justice, 33 Capitol St, Concord, NH 03301; tel. (603) 271-3658; fax (603) 271-2110; internet doj.nh.gov; Attorney-Gen. KELLY A. AYOTTE.

Office of the Treasurer: 25 Capitol St, Rm 121, Concord, NH 03301; tel. (603) 271-2621; fax (603) 271-3922; e-mail treasury@treasury.state.nh.us; internet www.nh.gov/treasury; Treas. CATHERINE A. PROVENCHER.

Public Utilities Commission: 21 South Fruit St, Suite 10, Concord, NH 03301-2429; tel. (603) 271-2431; fax (603) 271-3878; e-mail puc@puc.nh.gov; internet www.puc.state.nh.us; Chair. THOMAS B. GETZ.

General Court
(August 2008)

Senate

Dem. 14; Rep. 10; Total 24

President: SYLVIA LARSEN (Dem.).

President Pro-Tempore: MAGGIE HASSAN (Dem.).

Clerk: TAMMY L. WRIGHT.

House of Representatives

Dem. 236; Rep. 159; Ind. 1; 4 vacancies; Total 400

Speaker: TERIE NORELLI (Dem.).

Clerk: KAREN O. WADSWORTH.

New Jersey

Gross Area: 22,590 sq km (8,725 sq miles).

Resident Population (1 July 2007, estimate): 8,685,920.

State Capital: Trenton (population 83,923 at 1 July 2006).

Principal Cities (population at 1 July 2005): Newark 281,402; Jersey City 241,789; Paterson 148,708; Elizabeth 126,179.

LOCATION, TOPOGRAPHY AND CLIMATE

The State of New Jersey (nicknamed 'The Garden State') is in the Northeast region of the USA and is bordered by New York to the north, the Hudson River, New York Bay and the Atlantic Ocean to the east, Delaware Bay and Delaware to the south, and Pennsylvania to the west. The southern two-thirds of New Jersey lie in the Atlantic Coastal Plain, with sandy beaches, many barrier islands and narrow peninsulas, swamps and an area of pines and marshes known as the Pine Barrens. To the north and east is a region of gently rolling plains interrupted by the high traprock ridges of the Watchungs, Sourlands and Pallisades. Towards the west is a highland region, including the Ramapo Mountains, part of the Appalachian system, and many lakes. The state's highest elevations are in the Kittatinny Mountains in the north-west. New Jersey's main rivers are the Delaware, forming the western boundary with Pennsylvania, the Raritan, Passaic and Hackensack. New Jersey has a temperate climate, with warm, humid summers and cold winters.

HISTORICAL BACKGROUND

When Giovanni da Verrazano, a Florentine (Italian) navigator, sailed into Newark Bay in 1524 leading a French expedition, the region now known as New Jersey was inhabited by the Leni-Lanape (or Delaware) Indians. In 1609 Henry Hudson claimed the area for the Dutch and called it New Netherland. After being taken by the English in 1664, it was divided into two provinces until 1702, when the entire region came under the government of New York. New Jersey did not have its own government until 1738, when Lewis Morris became its first governor. Loyalties were divided between the colonial British authorities and the rebel cause during the American Revolution; many major battles were fought on New Jersey soil during the war, including the Battle of Trenton (1776) and the Battle of Monmouth (1778). On 18 December 1787 New Jersey became the third state to ratify the US Constitution. Although strong sympathies towards the South existed, mainly owing to economic links, New Jersey sent troops to fight on the Unionist side during the Civil War.

ECONOMY

Finance, insurance, real estate and services are the state's principal economic activities, with manufacturing and wholesale and retail trade also important. Gross domestic product by state totalled US $465,484m. in 2007, the eighth largest in the USA. The state's average per-head income amounted to $49,238 in 2007, the third highest in the USA. In that year, 8.6% of the population were estimated to be living below the poverty line—the fifth lowest proportion in the country. The civilian labour force totalled 4,582,200 in mid-2008, with an unemployment rate of 5.8% (268,000 persons). In 2007 19.2% of those employed were union members, while 20.6% were covered by union agreements—the sixth highest proportion among the states.

Farmland covered some 790,000 acres (319,700 ha) of New Jersey's land area in 2007. There were 9,800 farms in that year, and the average farm covered an area of just 81 acres—the smallest in the country apart from Rhode Island. In 2002 18% of total cropland was irrigated; 81% of farm income in 2007 was derived from crop sales and 19% from livestock and livestock products. The most valuable agricultural commodities in that year were greenhouse and nursery products, horses and mules, blueberries and peaches. New Jersey was the USA's second leading producer of horses and mules in 2007, behind Kentucky, and also ranked fourth for lettuce production. Forestland covered 2.1m. acres of the state in 2003, but the modest lumber industry is of little economic importance. New Jersey has a significant commercial fish catch, valued at US $136m. in 2006. The state ranked first in the nation for surf clam production and second for sea scallop production, behind Massachusetts, in 2007; together with Massachusetts it also accounted for 92% of US landings of Atlantic mackerel in that year.

New Jersey's non-fuel mineral production was valued at US $582m. in 2007. Leading minerals were crushed stone and sand and gravel. The state was the sole producer of greensand marl in 2006. Peat is the only fuel produced in the state.

From the early 19th century New Jersey was an important manufacturing centre of the USA, and in 2006 still ranked 15th in the nation in terms of its value of shipments. Chemicals and allied products, food products, electrical equipment, computers, and printing and publishing products were among the principal manufactures. The total value of manufacturing shipments in 2006 was US $107,349m., with 48% added during manufacture.

The city of Newark is the financial centre of New Jersey. For many years the state ranked among the nation's leaders in banking activity, but it has been overshadowed considerably in this respect by the burgeoning financial activities of other states. The tourism industry is of significant economic importance, with domestic travel expenditures of US $15,733m. in 2004, when the state ranked eighth in terms of spending. The gambling industry of Atlantic City accounts for a large share of the total income from tourism.

Total general expenditures by the state government amounted to US $54,073m. in 2006. General revenue totalled $46,446m., of which $10,828m. was provided by the federal Government and $26,266m. was derived from taxes. New Jersey received $11,117m. in federal aid in 2006.

CONSTITUTION AND GOVERNMENT

The current Constitution of New Jersey is the state's third and became effective on 1 January 1948. Constitutional amendments proposed by the Legislature have to be approved by either three-fifths of the elected members of each house at one session, or a majority of elected members at two successive sessions; they must then be ratified by a majority of state voters. The Governor is the state's sole elected executive branch official: he or she is elected to serve a regular term of four years and may serve no more than two terms consecutively; as there is no lieutenant-governor, the Governor is succeeded by the President of the Senate in the event of his or her resignation, incapacity or death. The Legislature consists of 40 senators and 80 representatives, re-elected every four and two years, respectively. In the first term of a new decade Senate members serve for two years. Regular legislative sessions take place annually, starting in January, and there is no statutory limit to their length. A bill becomes law once it has been passed by the Legislature and signed by the Governor, who has 45 days in which to sign or veto a bill. A gubernatorial veto may be overridden by a two-thirds' vote of the elected members in each house. Legislation becomes effective on 4 July following enactment, unless another date is specified. Former US Senator Jon Corzine, a Democrat, was elected to the New Jersey governorship in November 2005, with 55% of the votes cast. In the presidential election of 2008 the Democrats secured an estimated 57% of the votes cast, with some 3.7m. voting. There are 21 counties in New Jersey.

Elected Executive Branch Official

Governor (2006–10): JON S. CORZINE (Dem.).

Selected Government Addresses

Office of the Governor: State House, POB 001, Trenton, NJ 08625; tel. (609) 292-6000; fax (609) 292-5212; internet www.state.nj.us/governor.

Department of Agriculture: John Fitch Plaza, POB 330, Trenton, NJ 08625-0330; tel. (609) 292-3976; e-mail charles.kuperus@ag.state.nj.us; internet www.state.nj.us/agriculture; Sec. CHARLES M. KUPERUS.

Department of Banking and Insurance: 20 West State St, POB 325, Trenton, NJ 08625-0325; tel. (609) 292-7272; e-mail commissioner@dobi.state.nj.us; internet www.state.nj.us/dobi; Commr STEVEN M. GOLDMAN.

Department of Corrections: Whittlesey Rd, POB 863, Trenton, NJ 08625; tel. (609) 292-4036; fax (609) 292-9083; internet www.state.nj.us/corrections; Commr GEORGE W. HAYMAN.

Department of Education: Judge Robert L. Carter Bldg, 100 River View Plaza, POB 500, Trenton, NJ 08625-0500; tel. (609) 292-4450; fax (609) 777-4099; internet www.state.nj.us/education; Commr LUCILLE E. DAVY.

Department of Environmental Protection: 401 East State St, 7th Floor, East Wing, POB 402, Trenton, NJ 08625-0402; tel. (609) 292-2885; fax (609) 292-7695; internet www.state.nj.us/dep; Commr LISA P. JACKSON.

Department of Health and Senior Services: John Fitch Plaza, POB 360, Trenton, NJ 08625-0360; tel. (609) 292-7837; fax (609) 292-0053; internet www.state.nj.us/health; Commr HEATHER HOWARD.

Department of Labor and Workforce Development: John Fitch Plaza, POB 110, Trenton, NJ 08625-0110; tel. (609) 777-3200; fax (609) 633-9271; e-mail constituent.relations@dol.state.nj.us; internet lwd.state.nj.us/labor; Commr DAVID J. SOCOLOW.

Department of Law and Public Safety: Hughes Justice Complex, POB 080, Trenton, NJ 08625-0080; tel. (609) 292-4925; fax (609) 292-3508; internet www.state.nj.us/lps; Attorney-Gen. ANNE MILGRAM.

Department of Military and Veterans' Affairs: 101 Eggert Crossing Rd, Lawrenceville, NJ 08648; POB 340, Trenton, NJ 08625-0340; tel. (609) 530-6957; fax (609) 530-7097; e-mail glenn.rieth@njdmava.state.nj.us; internet www.state.nj.us/military; Adj.-Gen. Maj.-Gen. GLENN K. RIETH.

Department of State: 125 West State St, POB 300, Trenton, NJ 08625-0300; tel. (609) 984-1900; fax (609) 292-7665; internet www.state.nj.us/state; Sec. of State NINA MITCHELL WELLS.

Department of Transportation: David J. Goldberg Transportation Complex, 1035 Pkwy Ave, POB 600, Trenton, NJ 08625-0600; tel. (609) 530-3536; fax (609) 530-3894; internet www.state.nj.us/transportation; Commr KRIS KOLLURI.

Division of State Police: POB 7068, West Trenton, NJ 08628; tel. (609) 882-2000; fax (609) 882-6920; internet www.njsp.org; Supt Col RICK FUENTES.

New Jersey Commerce, Economic Growth and Tourism Commission: 20 West State St, POB 820, Trenton, NJ 08625-0820; tel. (609) 777-0885; fax (609) 777-4097; internet www.state.nj.us/commerce; Exec. Dir KEVIN DRENNAN.

Office of the Treasurer: State House, 1st Floor, POB 002, Trenton, NJ 08625-0002; tel. (609) 633-2826; internet www.state.nj.us/treasury; Treas. DAVID ROUSSEAU.

Legislature
(August 2008)

Senate

Dem. 23; Rep. 17; Total 40

President: RICHARD J. CODEY (Dem.).

President Pro Tempore: SHIRLEY K. TURNER (Dem.).

Secretary: ELLEN M. DAVENPORT.

General Assembly

Dem. 48; Rep. 32; Total 80

Speaker: JOSEPH J. ROBERTS, Jr (Dem.).

Speaker Pro Tempore: WILFREDO CARABALLO (Dem.).

Clerk: DANA M. BURLEY.

New Mexico

Gross Area: 314,939 sq km (121,598 sq miles).

Resident Population (1 July 2007, estimate): 1,969,915.

State Capital: Santa Fe (population 72,056 at 1 July 2006, estimate).

Principal City: Albuquerque (population 504,949 at 1 July 2006, estimate).

LOCATION, TOPOGRAPHY AND CLIMATE

The State of New Mexico (nicknamed 'The Land of Enchantment') lies in the West region of the USA and is bordered by Arizona to the west, Colorado to the north, Oklahoma to the north-east and Texas to the east and south-east. There is an international border with Mexico in the south-west. The east of the state lies in the western extremity of the Great Plains. The southern Rocky Mountains comprise the north-central part of New Mexico and include the state's highest elevation, Wheeler Peak, at 4,011 m (13,161 ft), in the Sangre de Cristo Mountains. Towards the north-west of the state lie the Colorado Plateau and the Chuska Mountains and across the south of New Mexico are the ranges of San Mateo, Caballo, San Andres, Sacramento and Guadalupe. The main rivers of New Mexico are the Rio Grande, which bisects the state as it flows south from Colorado; the San Juan, curving across the north-west corner; the Pecos, running south into Texas; and the Canadian, flowing across the north-east into Texas. The Continental Divide runs from north-central to south-western New Mexico. The state has a semi-arid climate, the hottest temperatures being in the south. There is heavy snowfall in the northern mountains.

HISTORICAL BACKGROUND

The earliest inhabitants of the area now known as New Mexico were Mogollon and Anasazi peoples. They were followed by the Pueblo tribes and, in the 15th century, by the Navaho and Apache peoples. The first major European expedition to the area was led by the Spanish explorer, Francisco Vásquez de Coronado, in 1540, and in 1598 the first permanent European settlement was established at San Juan Pueblo. Santa Fe became the capital in 1610. In 1680 the Pueblo peoples revolted, driving the Spanish into Texas, but by 1692 Spanish rule was re-established. New Mexico came under Mexican rule in 1821, with Mexico's independence from Spain. In 1846, during the Mexican War, a US general, Stephen Kearney, captured Santa Fe; two years later the region was officially ceded to the USA under the Treaty of Guadalupe-Hidalgo. Land disputes between new settlers, Spanish inhabitants and Native Americans, in addition to the Civil War and the Lincoln County War of 1878–81 (waged between cattlemen and merchants), delayed New Mexico's entry into the Union until 6 January 1912, when it became the 47th state to accede. In 1945 the first atomic bomb was exploded at Alamogordo.

ECONOMY

The principal industries of New Mexico are government, services and trade. Until the 1940s agriculture dominated the economy, with mining, manufacturing and tourism subsequently gaining in importance. Gross domestic product by state was US $76,178m. in 2007 and the state's per-head income averaged $30,604, the fifth lowest among the states. It was estimated that 18.1% of the population were living below the poverty line in 2007—the third highest proportion in the country. The civilian labour force stood at 967,200 in mid-2008 and the unemployment rate was 4.6% (44,800 persons). In 2007 7.7% of all those employed belonged to a trade union, while union agreements covered 11.4%.

Farmland covered 45.0m. acres (18.2m. ha) in 2007. There were 17,500 farms in that year, with an average farm size of 2,500 acres—the third largest in the USA, after Wyoming and Arizona. Water resources are scarce in the state, and approximately 25% of total cropland was under irrigation in 2002. In 2007 sales of livestock and livestock products accounted for 77% of farm income, with the remaining 23% derived from crop sales. New Mexico's principal agricultural commodities in that year were dairy products, cattle and calves, hay and pecans. The state had 16.7m. acres of forestland in 2003, and there is a small amount of lumbering activity, all concerned with the production of softwoods.

New Mexico ranked 15th among the states for non-fuel mineral production in 2007, valued at US $1,520m. Leading minerals included copper (for which the state was ranked third in 2007), potash (ranked second) and zeolites, construction sand and gravel, molybdenum concentrates and portland cement. New Mexico was also the lead producer of perlite in 2007; it was ranked first for production of zeolites in 2003. Salt, pumice (for which the state ranked third in 2007), iron ore and mica are also produced. New Mexico was the country's third most important producer of natural gas, by volume, in 2005 behind Texas and Oklahoma. The state also produces significant amounts of petroleum, ranking sixth in the nation in 2005. In 2007 it registered an output of 24.5m. short tons of coal, thereby ranking 12th in the USA.

The total value of New Mexico's manufacturing shipments in 2006 was US $16,477m., of which 55% was added during manufacture. The state ranked 39th among the states in terms of value of shipments in that year. The most important manufacturing sectors were food products, non-metallic mineral products, printing and publishing products, computers and electrical equipment. The majority of New Mexico's industry is located in the Albuquerque area.

Actively encouraged by the state government, tourism has become a major economic activity. In 2004 domestic travel expenditures amounted to US $4,348m.

Total general expenditures by the state government in 2006 were US $13,399m. Total general revenue was $12,117m., of which $3,750m. was provided by the federal Government and $5,111m.

was derived from taxes. In 2006 New Mexico received $4,070m. in federal aid.

CONSTITUTION AND GOVERNMENT

New Mexico's only Constitution was adopted in 1911 and became effective on 6 January 1912. Most constitutional amendments proposed by the Legislature have to be approved by a majority of elected members in each house, before being ratified by a majority of state voters. The Governor, elected with the Lieutenant-Governor, serves a four-year term of office, and, after serving two consecutive terms, must wait four years before being eligible to stand for election again. There are 42 senators and 70 representatives in the Legislature, serving terms of four and two years, respectively. Regular legislative sessions take place annually in January and may last no longer than 60 calendar days in odd-numbered years and 30 days in even-numbered years. A bill becomes law when it has been passed by the Legislature and signed by the Governor. During session a bill also becomes law unless vetoed within three days of presentation to the Governor. Outside session a bill dies unless signed by the Governor within 20 days after adjournment. A gubernatorial veto may be overridden by a two-thirds' vote from the elected members present in each house. Enacted legislation becomes effective 90 days after the adjournment of the Legislature, except for fiscal legislation, which becomes effective immediately. In the 2006 gubernatorial election the Democratic incumbent, Bill Richardson, was elected with 68% of the votes cast. In the 2008 presidential election the Democrats obtained some 57% of the votes cast in the state. New Mexico has 33 administrative counties.

Elected Executive Branch Officials

Governor (2007–11): BILL RICHARDSON (Dem.).

Lieutenant-Governor: DIANE D. DENISH (Dem.).

Secretary of State: MARY HERRERA (Dem.).

Attorney-General: GARY KING (Rep.).

Treasurer: JAMES B. LEWIS (Dem.).

Auditor: HECTOR H. BALDERAS (Dem.).

Commissioner of Public Lands: PATRICK H. LYONS (Rep.).

Selected Government Addresses

Office of the Governor: State Capitol Bldg, 4th Floor, Rm 400, 490 Old Santa Fe Trail, Santa Fe, NM 87501; tel. (505) 476-2200; internet www.governor.state.nm.us.

Office of the Lieutenant-Governor: State Capitol Bldg, Suite 417, Santa Fe, NM 87501; tel. (505) 476-2250; fax (505) 476-2257; internet www.ltgovernor.state.nm.us.

Office of the Secretary of State: 325 Don Gaspar, Suite 300, Santa Fe, NM 87503; tel. (505) 827-3600; fax (505) 827-8081; e-mail marye.herrera@state.nm.us; internet www.sos.state.nm.us.

Office of the Attorney-General: Villagra Bldg, 408 Galisteo St, POB 1508, Santa Fe, NM 87504-1508; tel. (505) 827-6000; fax (505) 827-5826; internet www.nmag.gov.

Office of the Treasurer: Bldg K, 2019 Galisteo St, POB 608, Santa Fe, NM 87504-0608; tel. (505) 955-1120; fax (505) 955-1195; e-mail vickie.brown@state.nm.us; internet www.stonm.org.

Office of the Auditor: 2113 Warner Circle, Santa Fe, NM 87505-5499; tel. (505) 476-3800; fax (505) 827-3512; internet www.saonm.org.

State Land Office: State Land Office Bldg, 310 Old Santa Fe Trail, POB 1148, Santa Fe, NM 87504-1148; tel. (505) 827-5760; fax (505) 827-5766; e-mail plyons@slo.state.nm.us; internet www.nmstatelands.org; headed by the Commr of Public Lands.

Department of Agriculture: MSC 3189, POB 30005, Las Cruces, NM 88003-8005; tel. (575) 646-3007; fax (575) 646-8120; e-mail nmagsec@nmda.nmsu.edu; internet nmdaweb.nmsu.edu; Dir Dr I. MILEY GONZALEZ.

Department of Corrections: 4337 NM 14, Santa Fe, NM 87508; tel. (505) 827-8709; fax (505) 827-8220; e-mail tia.bland@state.nm.us; internet corrections.state.nm.us; Sec. JOE R. WILLIAMS.

Department of Economic Development: Joseph M. Montoya Bldg, Suite 1060, 1100 St Francis Dr., Santa Fe, NM 87505; tel. (505) 827-0300; fax (505) 827-0328; e-mail edd.info@state.nm.us; internet www.edd.state.nm.us; Sec. FRED MONDRAGÓN.

Department of Education: Jerry Apodaca Education Bldg, 300 Don Gaspar St, Santa Fe, NM 87501-2786; tel. (505) 827-5800; fax (505) 827-6696; e-mail askcommunityrelations@state.mn.us; internet www.ped.state.nm.us; Supt VERONICA GARCÍA.

Department of Energy, Minerals and Natural Resources: 1220 South St Francis Dr., POB 6429, Santa Fe, NM 87505; tel. (505) 476-3200; fax (505) 476-3220; e-mail sandra.haug@state.nm.us; internet www.emnrd.state.nm.us; Sec. JOANNA PRUKOP.

Department of the Environment: 1190 St Francis Dr., Suite N4050, POB 26110, Santa Fe, NM 87502-0110; tel. (505) 827-2855; fax (505) 827-2836; e-mail ron_curry@nmenv.state.nm.us; internet www.nmenv.state.nm.us; Sec. RON CURRY.

Department of Health: 1190 South St Francis Dr., POB 26110, Santa Fe, NM 87502-6110; tel. (505) 827-2613; fax (505) 827-2530; e-mail comments@doh.state.nm.us; internet www.health.state.nm.us; Sec. Dr ALFREDO VIGIL.

Department of Public Safety: 4491 Cerrillos Rd, POB 1628, Santa Fe, NM 87504-1628; tel. (505) 827-3370; fax (505) 827-3434; e-mail peter.olson@state.nm.us; internet www.dps.nm.org; Sec. JOHN DENKO.

Department of Taxation and Revenue: 1100 South St Francis Dr., POB 630, Santa Fe, NM 87504-0630; tel. (505) 827-0341; fax (505) 827-0331; e-mail poffice@state.nm.us; internet www.tax.state.nm.us; Sec. RICK HOMANS.

Department of Transportation: 1120 Cerrillos Rd, POB 1149, Santa Fe, NM 87504-1149; tel. (505) 827-5100; fax (505) 827-5469; internet www.nmshtd.state.nm.us; Sec. RHONDA G. FAUGHT.

Department of Workforce Solutions: 401 Broadway NE, Albuquerque, POB 1928, NM 87103; tel. (505) 841-8409; fax (505) 841-8491; e-mail infodol@state.nm.us; internet www.dws.state.nm.us; Sec. BETTY SPARROW DORIS.

National Guard: 47 Bataan Blvd, Rm 201, Santa Fe, NM 87505; tel. (505) 474-1200; fax (505) 474-1355; e-mail kenny.montoya@nm.ngb.army.mil; internet www.nm.ngb.army.mil; Adj.-Gen. Maj.-Gen. KENNY MONTOYA.

Public Regulation Commission: 1120 Paseo de Peralta, POB 1269, Santa Fe, NM 87501; tel. (505) 827-4084; fax (505) 827-4068; e-mail leroy.aragon@state.nm.us; internet www.nmprc.state.nm.us; Chair. JASON A. MARKS.

Legislature
(August 2008)

Senate

Dem. 24; Rep. 18; Total 42

President: Lt-Gov. DIANE D. DENISH (Dem.).

President Pro Tempore: TIMOTHY Z. JENNINGS (Dem.).

Chief Clerk: LENORE NARANJO.

House of Representatives

Dem. 42; Rep. 28; Total 70

Speaker: BEN LUJAN (Dem.).

Chief Clerk: STEVEN R. ARIAS.

New York

Gross Area: 141,080 sq km (54,492 sq miles).

Resident Population (1 July 2007, estimate): 19,297,729.

State Capital: Albany (population 93,963 at 1 July 2006, estimate).

Principal Cities (population at 1 July 2006, estimate): New York 8,214,426; Buffalo 279,059; Rochester 208,123; Yonkers 197,852; Syracuse 140,658.

LOCATION, TOPOGRAPHY AND CLIMATE

The State of New York (nicknamed 'The Empire State') is in the Northeast region of the USA and is bordered by Vermont, Massachusetts and Connecticut to the east, New Jersey to the south and Pennsylvania to the south-west. In the south-east Long Island extends into the Atlantic Ocean. Between Pennsylvania and Vermont, the entire length of New York's north-western boundary is formed by the international frontier with Canada (provinces of Ontario and Québec), much of it bisecting Lakes Erie and Ontario. Extensive highland areas cover much of the state. The Adirondack Mountains in the north-east contain New York's highest elevations, including Mount Marcy, at 1,629 m (5,344 ft). In the south of the state are the Catskill Mountains and the Kittatinny Mountain Ridge, both belonging to the Appalachian Highlands stretching across southern New York. The Great Lakes Plain and the coastal area of Long Island are the state's main lowland regions. New York's major rivers are the Hudson, flowing from the north-east to New York Bay in the south, the Mohawk, flowing west from east-central New York to join the Hudson, and the St Lawrence, forming the boundary with Ontario in the north. Other rivers include: the Oswego, Black and Geneseo, flowing into Lake Ontario; the Poultney, forming part of the eastern boundary; and the Delaware, forming part of the southern boundary. The state's most outstanding natural feature is Niagara Falls, on the Niagara River (the boundary with Canada, between Lakes Erie and

Ontario). Apart from the Great Lakes, there are numerous lakes in New York, including the 11 long, narrow Finger Lakes in the south. New York has a humid, continental climate. The south-east is the warmest region, and the Great Lakes Plain area experiences some of the heaviest snowfall in the USA.

HISTORICAL BACKGROUND

The main Native American (Amerindian) tribes inhabiting New York when the Florentine (Italian) navigator, Giovanni da Verrazano, sailed into New York harbour in 1524 in the pay of the King of France, belonged to the Iroquois language group. In 1609 Henry Hudson sailed up the Hudson River almost as far as present-day Albany and claimed the region for the Netherlands. New Amsterdam was founded in 1626. In 1664 the British forced the Dutch to surrender the colony and both it and New Amsterdam were renamed New York, in honour of the king's brother. Many battles were fought on New York soil during the American Revolution, including what was probably the turning point of the war, when the British were defeated at Saratoga in 1777. On 26 July 1788 New York became the 11th state to ratify the US Constitution. In New York City, which served as the US capital between 1785 and 1790, George Washington was inaugurated as the first President of the USA on 30 April 1789. In 1825 the Erie Canal between Albany and Buffalo was opened and New York became a primary trade route as well as the nation's commercial and financial centre. On 11 September 2001 New York City bore the brunt of the worst terrorist attack in the USA's history. Hijacked passenger planes were crashed into the twin towers of the World Trade Center (417 m and 415 m high, respectively). The towers subsequently collapsed. The death toll was estimated to be almost 3,000 and many businesses were destroyed.

ECONOMY

Finance, insurance and real estate, services, wholesale and retail trade and manufacturing are among New York's principal economic activities. Mining and agriculture are of local importance, but less essential to the overall economy. It is the third largest state economy behind California and Texas, with a gross domestic product by state of US $1,103,0244m. in 2007. Per-head income in that year averaged $46,664, the sixth highest in the country. In the same year, however, it was estimated that 13.7% of the population were living below the poverty line. The civilian labour force totalled 9,753,200 in mid-2008, with an unemployment rate of 5.3% (521,200 persons). In 2007 New York state had the most highly unionized work-force in the USA, with 25.2% of those employed belonging to a union and 26.3% covered by trade union agreements.

Farmland covered 7.5m. acres (3.0m. ha) in 2007. There were 34,200 farms in that year, with the average farm covering an area of 219 acres. In 2002 1.4% of total cropland was irrigated. In 2007 livestock and livestock products accounted for 61% of farm income and crops for the remaining 39%. By value, the leading agricultural commodities in that year were dairy products, greenhouse and nursery products, apples and corn. In addition to corn (for grain and silage), field crops produced included hay, potatoes and wheat. New York ranked second in apple production among the states in 2007 (behind Washington), and was third for dairy products and fourth for grapes. Some 53% of the state was covered by forest in 2003. There is some fishing activity, with a catch valued at US $58m. in 2006. New York state is the country's leading producer of anchovies.

In 2007 New York's non-fuel mineral production was valued at US $1,330m., with the state ranked 17th. Leading minerals in 2007 included crushed stone, portland cement, sand and gravel, salt (for which the state was ranked third in 2004) and wollastonite (of which it remained the sole producer). Together, these commodities accounted for 98% of the state's total non-fuel mineral production in 2004. Estimated reserves of petroleum and natural gas in New York are relatively small, but there is some production of both.

Until the 1970s New York led the nation in industrial production of many kinds; however, by 2006 its manufacturing shipments (totalling US $162,412m.) were only the tenth highest in the country. In that year 57% of the total value of shipments was added during manufacture. The state's principal manufactured goods include printing and publishing goods, scientific instruments, chemicals and allied products, electrical equipment, clothing, pharmaceuticals, automotive and aircraft components, industrial machinery and equipment and food products.

Banking is of major economic importance to New York. At the end of 2005 the state's commercial banks held assets of US $1,198,700m., with the state ranked third in the country behind Ohio and North Carolina. Previous to the rise in importance of those two states, New York City was by some distance the USA's primary banking centre. By the end of 2006, however, the value of the state's commercial banks' assets had almost halved (to $523,500), demoting it to sixth rank overall. Nonetheless, New York remains an important base for life insurance and the centre of US securities trading. It is the site of the nation's two foremost securities markets, the New York Stock Exchange and the American Stock Exchange.

New York state, with its two main attractions of New York City and Long Island, is a major tourist centre. Domestic travel expenditures amounted to US $30,458m. in 2004, when the state ranked fourth in terms of money spent. Tourist numbers fell by 14% in 2001 following the terrorist attacks of September, but have recovered in subsequent years, to reach an estimated 41m. in 2005.

In 2006 total general expenditures by the state government amounted to US $142,853m., while general revenue totalled $123,561m. Revenue transfers from the federal Government amounted to $39,168m., while taxes contributed $57,403m. New York received $41,863m. in federal aid in 2006.

CONSTITUTION AND GOVERNMENT

New York's Constitution, its fourth, was adopted in 1894 and became effective on 1 January 1895. An amendment to the Constitution proposed by the Legislature needs to be passed by a majority of the elected members in each house in two successive sessions before being ratified by a majority of state voters. The Governor and Lieutenant-Governor are elected jointly to serve a four-year term. There are 62 senators and 150 representatives in the New York Legislature, both houses being re-elected every two years. Regular sessions take place annually, starting in January; there is no statutory limit to their length. A bill becomes enacted when it has been approved by both houses of the Legislature and signed by the Governor. During session the Governor has 10 days to consider a bill, after which it becomes law unless vetoed. Outside session a bill dies if it remains unsigned for 30 days after adjournment of the Legislature. A two-thirds' vote by the elected members of each house is required to override a gubernatorial veto. Legislation becomes effective 20 days after enactment. The Democratic candidate, Eliot Spitzer, was successful in the gubernatorial election of 2006, winning 69% of the votes cast. However, he resigned in early 2008 following a prostitution scandal and was succeeded by Democrat David Paterson. In the presidential election of 2008 the Democrats secured the largest share of the votes cast (an estimated 62%). New York state has 58 administrative counties.

Elected Executive Branch Officials

Governor (2008–11): DAVID A. PATERSON (Dem.).

Lieutenant-Governor: DEAN G. SKELOS (acting) (Rep.).

Attorney-General: ANDREW M. CUOMO (Dem.).

Comptroller: THOMAS P. DINAPOLI (Dem.).

Selected Government Addresses

Office of the Governor: State Capitol, Albany, NY 12224; tel. (518) 474-8390; fax (518) 474-3767; internet www.state.ny.us/governor.

Office of the Lieutenant-Governor: State Capitol, Rm 326, Albany, NY 12224-0341; tel. (518) 486-4001; fax (518) 486-4710; internet www.state.ny.us/governor/ltgov.

Office of the Attorney-General: State Capitol, Albany, NY 12224-0341; tel. (518) 474-5481; internet www.oag.state.ny.us.

Office of the Comptroller: 110 State St, Albany, NY 12236; tel. (518) 474-4044; fax (518) 473-8940; e-mail contactus@osc.state.ny.us; internet www.osc.state.ny.us.

Department of Agriculture and Markets: 10B Airline Dr., Albany, NY 12235; tel. (518) 457-3880; e-mail info@agmkt.state.ny.us; internet www.agmkt.state.ny.us; Commr PATRICK HOOKER.

Department of Correctional Services: State Campus, Bldg 2, 1220 Washington Ave, Albany, NY 12226-2050; tel. (518) 457-8126; fax (518) 457-7070; internet www.docs.state.ny.us; Commr BRIAN FISCHER.

Department of Education: Education Bldg, 89 Washington Ave, Albany, NY 12234; tel. (518) 474-3852; fax (518) 473-2827; internet www.nysed.gov; Commr RICHARD P. MILLS.

Department of Environmental Conservation: 625 Broadway, Albany, NY 12233-1011; tel. (518) 402-9401; fax (518) 402-9016; e-mail dpaeweb@qw.dec.state.ny.us; internet www.dec.ny.gov; Commr PETE GRANNIS.

Department of Health: Corning Tower, Empire State Plaza, Albany, NY 12237; tel. (518) 474-2011; fax (518) 474-4471; e-mail dohweb@health.state.ny.us; internet www.health.state.ny.us; Commr Dr RICHARD F. DAINES.

Department of Insurance: 1 Commerce Plaza, Albany, NY 12257; tel. (518) 474-4567; internet www.ins.state.ny.us; Supt ERIC R. DINALLO.

Department of Labor: State Campus, Building 12, 1220 Washington Ave, Albany, NY 12240-0003; tel. (518) 457-9000; fax (518) 485-6297; e-mail nysdol@labor.state.ny.us; internet www.labor.state.ny.us; Commr M. PATRICIA SMITH.

Department of State: 1 Commerce Plaza, 99 Washington Avet, Albany, NY 12231-0001; tel. (518) 474-4752; fax (518) 474-4597; internet www.dos.state.ny.us; Sec. of State LORRAINE CORTÉS-VÁZQUEZ.

Department of Taxation and Finance: State Campus, Bldg 9, 1220 Washington Ave, Albany, NY 12227; tel. (518) 457-4242; fax (518) 457-7427; internet www.tax.state.ny.us; Commr ROBERT MEGNA.

Department of Transportation: 50 Wolf Rd, 6th Floor, Albany, NY 12232; tel. (518) 457-6195; fax (518) 457-6506; e-mail jpost@dot.state.ny.us; internet www.nysdot.gov; Commr ASTRID C. GLYNN.

Division of Military and Naval Affairs: 330 Old Niskayuna Rd, Latham, NY 12110-3514; tel. (518) 786-4786; fax (518) 786-4649; e-mail dmnawm@ny.ngb.army.mil; internet www.dmna.state.ny.us; Adj.-Gen. Maj.-Gen. JOSEPH J. TALUTO.

Division of Tourism: 30 South Pearl St, Albany, NY 12245; tel. (518) 292-5361; fax (518) 292-5802; internet www.iloveny.com.

Empire State Development: 30 South Pearl St, Albany, NY 12245; tel. (518) 474-4116; fax (518) 486-7416; e-mail esd@empire.state.ny.us; internet www.empire.state.ny.us; Co-Chair. ROBERT G. WILMERS, KENNETH SCHOETZ (acting).

Public Service Commission: Agency Bldg 3, Empire State Plaza, Albany, NY 12223-1350; tel. (518) 474-7080; fax (518) 474-0421; e-mail web_questions@dps.state.ny.us; internet www.dps.state.ny.us; Chair. GARRY A. BROWN.

State Police Division: State Campus, Bldg 22, 1220 Washington Ave, Albany, NY 12226-2252; tel. (518) 457-6721; fax (518) 457-3207; e-mail pio@troopers.state.ny.us; internet www.troopers.state.ny.us; Supt HARRY J. CORBITT.

Legislature
(August 2008)

Senate

Rep. 32; Dem. 30; Total 62

President Pro Tempore: DEAN G. SKELOS (Rep.).

Secretary: STEVEN M. BOGGESS.

Assembly

Dem. 108; Rep. 42; Total 150

Speaker: SHELDON SILVER (Dem.).

Speaker Pro Tempore: AURELIA GREENE (Dem.).

Clerk: KAREN MCCANN (acting).

North Carolina

Gross Area: 139,397 sq km (53,842 sq miles).

Resident Population (1 July 2007, estimate): 9,061,032.

State Capital: Raleigh.

Principal Cities (population at 1 July 2006): Charlotte 630,478; Raleigh (capital) 356,321; Greensboro 236,865; Durham 209,009; Winston-Salem 196,990; Fayetteville 168,033; Cary 112,414.

LOCATION, TOPOGRAPHY AND CLIMATE

The State of North Carolina (nicknamed 'The Tar Heel State') is in the South of the USA and is bordered by Virginia to the north, South Carolina to the south and Tennessee to the west. In the east a chain of narrow offshore islands of shifting sandbanks, called the Outer Banks, runs parallel to the Atlantic coastline. In the west are the highest ranges of the Appalachian system, principally the Great Smoky and Blue Ridge Mountains; separating these two ranges are the Black Mountains, with the state's highest elevation, Mount Mitchell, at 2,037 m (6,684 ft). To the east is the rolling land of the Piedmont Plateau, which stretches for 200 miles (320 km) across the centre of the state, descending gradually until a sudden drop occurs along a line between the Roanoke Rapids and Rockingham. The east of the state lies in the Atlantic Coastal Plain, with swampy regions on the coast and higher fertile land towards the interior. The New River and the Watauga, French Broad, Little Tennessee and Hiwassee Rivers flow westward from the mountains towards the Mississippi and, east of the Blue Ridge, the Chowan, Roanoke, Tar, Neuse and Cape Fear are among the rivers flowing towards the coast. North Carolina's climate is humid and subtropical, with long, hot summers and short, mild winters. Temperatures are cooler in the mountain region.

HISTORICAL BACKGROUND

When Europeans explored the region in the 16th century, North Carolina was inhabited by Algonquian, Siouan and Iroquoian peoples. One of the first Europeans to arrive in the region was the Florentine (Italian) navigator, Giovanni da Verrazano, in 1524, in the employ of the French. In 1585–87 two English attempts to colonize Roanoke Island, organized by Sir Walter Raleigh, failed; the first settlers returned to England, the second group, now known as the 'Lost Colony', disappeared. Permanent settlers arrived from Virginia in about 1660. Charles I of England and Scotland claimed all the land from 30°N to 60°N for the British Crown in 1629, and in 1663 Charles II divided the territory known as Carolina between eight proprietors. The proprietors' attempts to collect royal taxes from the settlers led to the Culpepper Rebellion of 1677. In 1691 Carolina was divided and in 1729 North Carolina became a royal colony. In 1776 North Carolina's provincial congress voted for independence from the United Kingdom, the first colonial congress to do so. North Carolina ratified the US Constitution on 21 November 1789, when it joined the Union as the 12th state. North Carolina was the last of the Southern states to secede from the Union in 1861, but provided more troops to the Confederacy than any other state. In 1865 the last major Confederate army surrendered to Gen. William T. Sherman at Bennet House near Hillsborough. North Carolina was readmitted to the Union in 1868.

ECONOMY

North Carolina's economy was dominated by agriculture (particularly tobacco production) until the acceleration of industrialization in the late 19th century. Manufacturing then expanded to replace agriculture as the most important contributor to the economy, although agriculture remained a principal industry. Finance, insurance and real estate, tourism and services are also important components of the gross domestic product by state, which totalled US $399,446m. in 2007. It was estimated that 14.3% of the population were living below the poverty line in that year, when the state's per-head income averaged $33,663. The civilian labour force numbered 4,664,800 in mid-2008, and the unemployment rate was 6.9%, affecting 320,000 persons. In 2007 only 3.0% of the work-force was unionized, while union agreements covered just 3.9%—the lowest rates in the USA.

Farmland accounted for 25.5% (equivalent to 8.8m. acres, or 3.6m. ha) of North Carolina's land area in 2007. There were 48,000 farms in that year, with the average farm covering 183 acres. Sales of livestock and livestock products accounted for 66% of farm income in 2007 and crop sales for 34%. The leading agricultural products in that year were broilers, hogs, greenhouse and nursery products and tobacco. Turkeys, chicken eggs, corn, soybeans, conifers (Christmas trees) and peanuts were also significant. North Carolina was ranked first for tobacco in 2007, second for production of hogs (after Iowa) and turkeys (after Minnesota), third for strawberries and broilers and fifth for greenhouse and nursery products. North Carolina has 19.3m. acres of forestland, concentrated along the coast and beyond the Blue Ridge: in 2004 it was the USA's eighth largest timber producer. There is a small but well-established commercial fishing industry, with a catch worth US $70m. in 2006. North Carolina was the country's second leading producer of trout in 2004 (behind Idaho).

North Carolina's non-fuel mineral production was valued at US $986m. in 2007, in which respect it ranked 23rd nation-wide. The state's leading mineral products in that year were crushed stone, phosphate rock, sand and gravel, and common clays. North Carolina was ranked first in the USA in 2007 for feldspar and mica, and second for phosphate rock; it was the USA's lead producer of common clays, olivine and pyrophyllite in 2004. Peat was also a significant product. Reserves of coal are negligible.

A leading industrial state, North Carolina ranked eighth in 2006 in terms of the value of its shipments, which totalled US $200,822m., with 53% added during manufacture. The state's major manufacturing sectors include electrical and electronic goods, machinery, food and kindred products, textile mill products, chemical products, computers and transportation equipment.

North Carolina's financial sector has expanded dramatically in recent years. At the end of 2005 the combined assets of the state's commercial banks had risen to US $1,707,800m., putting the state in first place nationally. In 2004 domestic travel expenditures amounted to $13,253m. and the state ranked 11th in terms of money spent.

Total general expenditures by the state government in 2006 were US $41,108m. General revenue totalled $38,884m., with $12,183m. provided by the federal Government and $20,603m. derived from taxes. Federal aid to North Carolina totalled $11,455m. in 2006.

CONSTITUTION AND GOVERNMENT

The current constitution of North Carolina, the state's third, was adopted in 1970 and became effective on 1 July 1971. Constitutional amendments proposed by the General Assembly require a vote by three-fifths of the elected members of each house and ratification by a majority of state voters. The Governor is elected with the Lieutenant-Governor to serve a four-year term and may serve no more than two consecutive terms. Cabinet members, 10 in total, are appointed by the Governor and meet monthly. The cabinet acts as an advisory body, while a council of state, provided for in the Constitution and made up of elective administrative officials, makes policy decisions. The General Assembly consists of 50 senators and 120 representatives, both houses being re-elected every two years. There is statutory provision for regular legislative sessions to be held in odd-numbered years, starting in January, but in practice sessions are also held in even-numbered years; there is no statutory limit to their length. A bill becomes law when it has been passed by each house of the General Assembly at three readings, and signed by the Governor. The Governor has 10 days in which to sign or veto a bill (30 days outside of session); if no action is taken, the bill becomes law. A gubernatorial veto may be overruled by a vote by three-fifths of the members of each house. Enacted legislation becomes effective 30 days after adjournment of the session. In the 2008 gubernatorial election the Democratic candidate, Lieutenant-Governor Bev Perdue, was elected with 50% of the votes. In the presidential election in the same year, the Democrats won a very close victory, securing just under 50% of the votes cast. There are 100 administrative counties in North Carolina.

Elected Executive Branch Officials

Governor (2005–09): MICHAEL F. EASLEY (Dem.).

Governor-elect (2009–13): BEVERLY (BEV) PERDUE (Dem.).

Lieutenant-Governor: BEVERLY (BEV) PERDUE (Dem.).

Secretary of State: ELAINE F. MARSHALL (Dem.).

Attorney-General: ROY A. COOPER, III (Dem.).

Treasurer: RICHARD H. MOORE (Dem.).

State Auditor: LESLIE MERRITT (Rep.).

Superintendent of Public Instruction: JUNE ST. CLAIR ATKINSON (Dem.).

Commissioner of Agriculture: STEVE TROXLER (Rep.).

Commissioner of Insurance: JAMES (JIM) E. LONG (Dem.).

Commissioner of Labor: CHERIE K. BERRY (Rep.).

Selected Government Addresses

Office of the Governor: 116 West Jones St, 20301 Mail Service Center, Raleigh, NC 27699-0301; tel. (919) 733-4240; fax (919) 733-2120; e-mail governor.office@ncmail.net; internet www.governor.state.nc.us.

Office of the Lieutenant-Governor: 310 North Blount St, 20401 Mail Service Center, Raleigh, NC 27699-0401; tel. (919) 733-7350; fax (919) 733-6595; e-mail ltgovernor@ncmail.net; internet www.ltgov.state.nc.us.

Office of the Secretary of State: Old Revenue Bldg, 2 South Salisbury St, POB 29622, Raleigh, NC 27626-0622; tel. (919) 807-2000; e-mail webhelp@sosnc.com; internet www.secstate.state.nc.us.

Office of the Attorney-General: Old Education Bldg, 114 West Edenton St, 9001 Mail Service Center, Raleigh, NC 27699-9001; tel. (919) 716-6400; fax (919) 716-6750; internet www.ncdoj.com.

Office of the Treasurer: Albemarle Bldg, 325 North Salisbury St, Raleigh, NC 27603-1385; tel. (919) 508-5176; fax (919) 508-5167; internet www.nctreasurer.com/dsthome.

Office of the Auditor: Old Revenue Bldg, 2 South Salisbury St, 20601 Mail Service Center, Raleigh, NC 27699-0601; tel. (919) 807-7500; fax (919) 807-7647; e-mail chris_mears@ncauditor.net; internet www.ncauditor.net.

Department of Agriculture and Consumer Services: 2 West Edenton St, 1001 Mail Service Center, Raleigh, NC 27699-1001; tel. (919) 733-7125; fax (919) 733-1141; internet www.ncagr.com; headed by the Commr of Agriculture.

Department of Insurance: Dobbs Bldg, 430 North Salisbury St, POB 2638, Raleigh, NC 27611; tel. (919) 733-3058; fax (919) 733-6495; e-mail kmilam@ncdoi.net; internet www.ncdoi.com; headed by the Commr of Insurance.

Department of Labor: 4 West Edenton St, 1101 Mail Service Center, Raleigh, NC 27699-1101; tel. (919) 733-7166; fax (919) 733-6197; e-mail neal.obriant@nclabor.com; internet www.nclabor.com; headed by the Commr of Labour.

Department of Commerce: 301 North Wilmington St, 4th Floor, 4301 Mail Service Center, Raleigh, NC 27699-4301; tel. (919) 733-4151; fax (919) 733-8356; internet www.nccommerce.com; Sec. JIM FAIN.

Department of Correction: 214 West Jones St, Rm 103, 4201 Mail Service Center, Raleigh, NC 27699-4201; tel. (919) 716-3700; fax (919) 716-3794; e-mail info@doc.state.nc.us; internet www.doc.state.nc.us; Sec. THEODIS BECK.

Department of Environment and Natural Resources: Archdale Bldg, 512 North Salisbury St, 1601 Mail Service Center, Raleigh, NC 27699-1601; tel. (919) 733-4984; fax (919) 715-3060; e-mail diana.kees@ncmail.net; internet www.enr.state.nc.us; Sec. WILLIAM G. ROSS, Jr.

Department of Health and Human Services: Adams Bldg, Dix Campus, 101 Blair Dr., 2001 Mail Service Center, Raleigh, NC 27699-2001; tel. (919) 733-9190; fax (919) 733-9903; internet www.dhhs.state.nc.us; Sec. DEMPSEY BENTON.

Department of Public Instruction: 301 North Wilmington St, Raleigh, NC 27601; tel. (919) 807-3430; fax (919) 807-3445; e-mail information@dpi.state.nc.us; internet www.ncpublicschools.org/organization; headed by the Supt of Public Instruction.

Department of Revenue: 501 North Wilmington St, POB 25000, Raleigh, NC 27640-0640; tel. (919) 733-5327; internet www.dor.state.nc.us; Sec. REGINALD S. HINTON.

Department of Transportation: 1 South Wilmington St, 1503 Mail Service Center, Raleigh, NC 27699-1503; tel. (919) 733-2522; fax (919) 733-9980; internet www.ncdot.org; Sec. LYNDO TIPPETT.

Division of the Highway Patrol: Dept of Crime Control and Public Safety, 512 North Salisbury St, 4701 Mail Service Center, Raleigh, NC 27699-4701; tel. (919) 733-2126; fax (919) 733-8477; internet www.nccrimecontrol.org; Sec. of Crime Control and Public Safety BRYAN E. BEATTY.

National Guard: Claude T. Bowers Military Center, 4105 Reedy Creek Rd, Raleigh, NC 27607-6410; tel. (919) 664-6242; fax (919) 664-6500; e-mail pao@nc.ngb.army.mil; internet www.nc.ngb.army.mil; Adj.-Gen. Maj.-Gen. WILLIAM E. INGRAM, Jr.

General Assembly

(August 2008)

Senate

Dem. 31; Rep. 19; Total 50

President: Lt-Gov. BEVERLY PERDUE (Dem.).

President Pro Tempore: MARC BASNIGHT (Dem.).

Principal Clerk: JANET PRUITT.

House of Representatives

Dem. 68; Rep. 52; Total 120

Speaker: JOE HACKNEY (Dem.).

Speaker Pro Tempore: WILLIAM L. WAINWRIGHT (Dem.).

Principal Clerk: DENISE G. WEEKS.

North Dakota

Gross Area: 183,123 sq km (70,704 sq miles).

Resident Population (1 July 2007, estimate): 639,715.

State Capital: Bismarck (population 58,333 at 1 July 2006).

Principal City: Fargo (population 90,056 at 1 July 2005).

LOCATION, TOPOGRAPHY AND CLIMATE

The State of North Dakota (nicknamed 'The Peace Garden State') lies in the Midwest region of the USA and is bordered by the Canadian provinces of Saskatchewan and Manitoba to the north, Minnesota to the east, South Dakota to the south and Montana to the west. The eastern boundary is formed by the Red River of the North as it flows towards Canada. The land rises from the flat Red River Valley towards the Drift Prairie, which covers most of the eastern half of the state. The Missouri River flows into the state from the north-west, then loops south-east into South Dakota. Inside the river's curve the Missouri Plateau forms the highest area of the state, rising to White Butte at 1,069 m (3,506 ft). The Plateau is divided from the Drift Prairie by the Missouri Escarpment. North Dakota has a continental climate, with short, hot summers and very cold winters. Precipitation is low, particularly in the west.

HISTORICAL BACKGROUND

Native Americans inhabiting North Dakota at the beginning of the 18th century included the Hidatsa, Arikara, Mandan and Ojibwa peoples. The French fur trader, Pierre Gaultier de Varennes, Sieur de la Vérendrye, was one of the first Europeans to explore the region in 1738, followed later by the British. The USA acquired about one-half of the area in the Louisiana Purchase from the French (1803) and the Corps of Discovery expedition, under Meriwether Lewis and William Clark, wintered at Fort Mandan in 1804–05. US ownership of the rest of North Dakota was confirmed by agreement with the United Kingdom in 1818. The

American Fur Co established a post at Fort Union in 1829 and the first permanent community was established at Pembina in 1812. Missouri River steamboats reached the area in 1832 and the Northern Pacific Railroad, completed as far as Fargo in 1872, brought many new settlers, with the native Indian peoples confined to reservations. On 2 November 1889 North Dakota joined the Union as the 39th state. The Republican Party held power in the state government for 58 of the years between 1889 and 1960, with the Non-Partisan League holding the governorship between 1916 and 1921. The state was the first to hold a national presidential primary, in 1912. In early 1997 severe flooding along the Red River, combined with fires in the city of Grand Forks, resulted in the state being declared a disaster area. Troops were dispatched to assist with the evacuation of 50,000 people from the city.

ECONOMY

Agriculture, mining, manufacturing, telecommunications, energy production, food processing and tourism are the principal industries in North Dakota. Its economy is the second smallest (larger only than Vermont) of all the states in the Union. In 2007 gross domestic product by state totalled US $27,725m., while the state's per-head income averaged $35,955. It was estimated that, in that year, 12.1% of the population were living below the poverty line. The total civilian labour force in mid-2008 numbered 383,100, with an unemployment rate which, at 3.2% (12,400 persons), was the third lowest in the country. In 2007 6.4% of those employed were union members and 7.6% were covered by union agreements.

In 2007 farmland covered 39.4m. acres (15.9m. ha). There were 30,100 farms in 2007, with an average farm occupying an area of 1,309 acres. In 2002 just 0.8% of total cropland was irrigated; 83% of farm income came from crop sales in 2007 and the remaining 17% from livestock and livestock products. The state's principal agricultural products were wheat, soybeans, cattle and calves, and corn. In 2007 North Dakota ranked first in the USA for wheat (ahead of Kansas) and second for sugar beets (behind Minnesota). The state was also a significant producer of potatoes, barley, sunflowers, oats, flaxseed, pinto beans and other dry edible beans. In 2002 some 21% of the state's population was employed in agriculture, or related businesses. Forestland covers just 1.5% of the state's land area, and forestry products contribute little to the economy.

The value of North Dakota's non-fuel mineral production totalled US $56m. in 2007, the third lowest in the USA. Construction sand and gravel accounted for around 75% of total state production in 2004, with lime, common clays, crushed stone and industrial sand and gravel also significant. There are large known recoverable reserves of coal (all lignite, and all suitable for surface mining), and production totalled 29.6m. short tons in 2007, ranking the state 10th in the country for coal output. Petroleum production in the state was the eight highest in the USA in 2005, and natural gas is also produced.

By value of shipments, North Dakota ranked 46th in the USA in 2006. The most important manufacturing industries were those relating to farm equipment, processed foods, fabricated metals and high-technology electronics. The total value of the state's manufacturing shipments in 2006 was US $9,789m., of which 40% was added during manufacture.

Tourism is important to North Dakota's economy; however, on a national level, the state ranked lower than any other (with the exception of Delaware) in terms of domestic travel expenditures in 2004, when such receipts totalled just US $1,340m.

Total general expenditures by the state government in 2006 amounted to US $3,633m.; general revenue totalled $3,667m., of which $1,188m. was provided by the federal Government and $1,622m. was derived from taxes. North Dakota received $1,274m. in federal aid in 2006.

CONSTITUTION AND GOVERNMENT

North Dakota's only Constitution became effective on 1 October 1889. Amendments to the Constitution proposed by the Legislative Assembly have to be approved by a majority of the elected members of each house followed by a majority of state voters. The Governor and Lieutenant-Governor are elected jointly to serve a four-year term and there is no limit to the number of times they may hold office. There is no formal cabinet system in the state. The Legislative Assembly currently has 47 senators and 94 representatives. One-half of the members of the House of Representatives are elected to four-year terms and one-half to two-year terms. Alternate halves of the Senate are re-elected every two years, for terms of four years. Regular sessions of the Legislative Assembly are held biennially, starting in January and lasting no longer than 80 days. A bill becomes law when it has been passed by the Legislative Assembly and signed by the Governor. During session the Governor has three days to consider a bill, after which it becomes law unless vetoed. Outside session a bill becomes law unless vetoed within 15 days from adjournment. A gubernatorial veto may be overridden by a two-thirds vote from the elected members in each house. Enacted appropriation bills become effective on 1 July, while all other bills not specifying a date become effective on 1 August. In 2008 the Republican incumbent, John Hoeven, gained 75% of the total votes in the gubernatorial election. In the presidential election of the same year the Republicans again secured the largest share of the votes cast, with 53%. North Dakota has 53 counties.

Elected Executive Branch Officials

Governor (2009–13): JOHN HOEVEN (Rep.).

Lieutenant-Governor: JACK DALRYMPLE (Rep.).

Secretary of State: ALVIN A. (AL) JAEGER (Rep.).

Attorney-General: WAYNE STENEHJEM (Rep.).

Treasurer: KELLY L. SCHMIDT (Rep.).

Auditor: ROBERT R. (BOB) PETERSON (Rep.).

Superintendent of Public Instruction: Dr WAYNE G. SANSTEAD (Ind.).

Commissioner of Agriculture: ROGER JOHNSON (Dem.).

Commissioner of Insurance: ADAM HAMM (Rep.).

Tax Commissioner: CORY FONG (Rep.).

Public Service Commissioners: SUSAN E. WEFALD (Rep.), KEVIN CRAMER (Rep.), TONY CLARK (Rep.).

Selected Government Addresses

Office of the Governor: State Capitol, Dept 101, 600 East Blvd Ave, Bismarck, ND 58505-0001; tel. (701) 328-2200; fax (701) 328-2205; e-mail governor@nd.gov; internet www.governor.nd.gov.

Office of the Lieutenant-Governor: State Capitol, Dept 101, 600 East Blvd Ave, Bismarck, ND 58505-0001; tel. (701) 328-2200; fax (701) 328-2205; e-mail governor@nd.gov; internet governor.state.nd.us/dalrymple.

Office of the Secretary of State: State Capitol, 1st Floor, Dept 108, 600 East Blvd Ave, Bismarck, ND 58505-0500; tel. (701) 328-2900; fax (701) 328-2992; e-mail sos@nd.gov; internet www.nd.gov/sos.

Office of the Attorney-General: State Capitol, Dept 125, 600 East Blvd Ave, Bismarck, ND 58505; tel. (701) 328-2210; fax (701) 328-3535; e-mail ndag@nd.gov; internet www.ag.state.nd.us.

Office of the Treasurer: State Capitol, 3rd Floor, Dept 120, 600 East Blvd Ave, Bismarck, ND 58505-0660; tel. (701) 328-2643; fax (701) 328-3002; e-mail treasurer@nd.gov; internet www.nd.gov/ndtreas.

Office of the Auditor: State Capitol, 3rd Floor, 600 East Blvd Ave, Bismarck, ND 58505-0060; tel. (701) 328-2241; fax (701) 328-3000; e-mail ndsao@nd.gov; internet www.nd.gov/auditor.

Department of Public Instruction: State Capitol, Dept 201, 600 East Blvd Ave, Bismarck, ND 58505-0440; tel. (701) 328-2260; fax (701) 328-2461; e-mail info@nd.gov; internet www.dpi.state.nd.us; headed by the Supt of Public Instruction.

Department of Agriculture: State Capitol, 600 East Blvd Ave, Dept 602, Bismarck, ND 58505-0020; tel. (701) 328-2231; fax (701) 328-4567; e-mail ndda@nd.gov; internet www.agdepartment.com; headed by the Commr of Agriculture.

Department of Insurance: State Capitol, 5th Floor, 600 East Blvd Ave, Bismarck, ND 58505-0320; tel. (701) 328-2440; fax (701) 328-4880; e-mail insurance@nd.gov; internet www.nd.gov/ndins; headed by the Commr of Insurance.

Office of the Tax Commissioner: State Capitol, Dept 127, 600 East Blvd Ave, Bismarck, ND 58505-0599; tel. (701) 328-2770; fax (701) 328-3700; e-mail taxinfo@nd.gov; internet www.nd.gov/tax.

Department of Commerce: Century Center, 1600 East Century Ave, Suite 2, POB 2057, Bismarck, ND 58503; tel. (701) 328-5300; fax (701) 328-5320; e-mail commerce@nd.gov; internet www.ndcommerce.com; Commr SHANE GOETTLE.

Department of Corrections and Rehabilitation: 3100 Railroad Ave, Bismarck, ND 58501; tel. (701) 328-6390; fax (701) 328-6651; e-mail docr@nd.gov; internet www.nd.gov/docr; Dir LEANN K. BERTSCH.

Department of Health: State Capitol, 600 East Blvd Ave, Bismarck, ND 58505-0200; tel. (701) 328-2372; fax (701) 328-4727; e-mail tdwelle@nd.gov; internet www.ndhealth.gov; State Health Officer Dr TERRY DWELLE.

Department of Labor: State Capitol, Dept 406, 600 East Blvd Ave, Bismarck, ND 58505-0340; tel. (701) 328-2660; fax (701) 328-2031; e-mail labor@nd.gov; internet www.nd.gov/labor; Commr LISA FAIR MCEVERS.

Department of Land: 1707 North Ninth St, POB 5523, Bismarck, ND 58506-5523; tel. (701) 328-2800; fax (701) 328-3650; e-mail gpreszle@nd.gov; internet www.land.nd.gov; Commr GARY PRESZLER.

Department of Transportation: 608 East Blvd Ave, Bismarck, ND 58505-0700; tel. (701) 328-2500; fax (701) 328-4545; e-mail dot@nd.gov; internet www.dot.nd.gov; Dir FRANCIS G. ZIEGLER.

Highway Patrol: State Capitol, Judicial Wing, Dept 504, 600 East Blvd Ave, Bismarck, ND 58505-0240; tel. (701) 328-2455; fax (701) 328-1717; e-mail ndhpinfo@nd.gov; internet www.nd.gov/ndhp; Supt Col MARK NELSON.

Office of Management and Budget: State Capitol, 4th Floor, Dept 110, 600 East Blvd Ave, Bismarck, ND 58505-0400; tel. (701) 328-2680; fax (701) 328-3230; e-mail omb@nd.gov; internet www.nd.gov/omb; Dir PAM SHARP.

Office of the Military: Joint Force Headquarters, North Dakota National Guard, 4200 East Divide Ave, POB 5511, Bismarck, ND 58506-5511; tel. (701) 224-5100; fax (701) 333-3180; e-mail jfhqhhd@ng.army.mil; internet www.guard.bismarck.nd.us; Adj.-Gen. Maj.-Gen. DAVID SPRYNCZYNATYK.

Public Service Commission: State Capitol, Dept 408, 600 East Blvd Ave, Bismarck, ND 58505-0480; tel. (701) 328-2400; fax (701) 328-2410; e-mail ndpsc@nd.gov; internet www.psc.state.nd.us; Pres. SUSAN E. WEFALD.

Legislative Assembly
(August 2008)

Senate

Rep. 26; Dem. 21; Total 47

President: Lt-Gov. JACK DALRYMPLE (Rep.).

President Pro Tempore: JUDY LEE (Rep.).

Secretary: WILLIAM R. HORTON.

House of Representatives

Rep. 61; Dem. 33; Total 94

Speaker: JEFF DELZER (Rep.).

Chief Clerk: BUELL REICH.

Ohio

Gross Area: 116,103 sq km (44,828 sq miles).

Resident Population (1 July 2007, estimate): 11,466,917.

State Capital: Columbus.

Principal Cities (population at 1 July 2006): Columbus (capital) 733,203; Cleveland 444,313; Cincinnati 332,252; Toledo 298,446; Akron 209,704; Dayton 156,771.

LOCATION, TOPOGRAPHY AND CLIMATE

The State of Ohio (nicknamed 'The Buckeye State') is in the Midwest region of the USA and is bordered by Pennsylvania to the east, West Virginia to the south-east, Kentucky to the south, Indiana to the west and Michigan to the north-west. Lake Erie lies to the north of the state, with Canada (Ontario) beyond. In the east of the state are the rugged foothills of the Allegheny Mountains. The Allegheny Plateau gradually descends as it reaches westwards towards the Central Plains. Immediately south of Lake Erie is a flat, marshy area. A low ridge stretches from the middle of the border with Indiana to the north-east: the Maumee, Portage, Sandusky, Vermilion, Cuyahoga and Grand Rivers drain from it into Lake Erie. The rolling hills of the south decline towards the Ohio River, which forms the state's southern boundary. Among the rivers flowing into the Ohio from south of the low ridge are the Miami, Little Miami, Scioto, Raccoon, Hocking and Muskingum. Ohio has a humid, temperate climate, with cold winters.

HISTORICAL BACKGROUND

When European exploration of Ohio began in the 17th century, the region was sparsely inhabited by Wyandot, Leni-Lanape (Delaware), Miami and Shawnee peoples. Robert Cavelier, Sieur de la Salle, visited the region in 1669 and France claimed the area in 1682. A separate British claim to the region led to the French and Indian War (known in Europe as the Seven-Years War), ending in French defeat in 1763. American colonists seized the territory during the struggle for independence, and the United Kingdom formally ceded it to the USA in 1783. The first permanent settlement was established at Marietta in 1788. The increasing presence of white settlers caused conflicts with the native tribes, culminating in the Battle of Fallen Timbers in 1794 and the surrender of Indian land in southern Ohio. On 1 March 1803 Ohio became the 17th state to join the Union. During the War of 1812 a British fleet was defeated by Commodore Oliver Hazard Perry at Put In Bay on Lake Erie—thereafter, the Great Lakes were demilitarized. There was considerable sympathy with the cause of the Confederacy in Ohio before the Civil War, but the state eventually fought for the Union, providing 320,000 volunteers.

ECONOMY

Ohio's principal economic activities are manufacturing, services, agriculture and wholesale and retail trade. Gross domestic product by state was US $466,309m. in 2007, the seventh highest in the USA, and per-head income averaged $34,509. It was estimated that 13.1% of the population were living below the poverty line in that year. The civilian labour force totalled 6,087,100 in mid-2008 and the unemployment rate was the sixth highest in the nation (alongside that of the District of Columbia), at 7.2% (438,800 persons). Of the total number of employees in 2007, 14.1% were union members, while union agreements covered 15.4%.

Agriculture makes a significant contribution to the state's economy. Farmland covered 14.2m. acres (5.7m. ha) in 2007. There were 75,700 farms in that year, with the average farm covering 188 acres. In 2002 only 0.3% of total cropland was irrigated. Some 62% of farm income was generated by crop sales in 2004 and 38% by livestock and livestock products. The principal agricultural commodities produced in that year were soybeans, corn, dairy products, and greenhouse and nursery products. Ohio ranked second for chicken egg production, third for tomatoes, and sixth for greenhouse and nursery products, soybeans and corn in 2007. It was also a leading producer of apples and hogs. Forestland comprised 27% of the state's land area in 2003.

In 2007 Ohio's non-fuel mineral production was valued at US $1,240m., with the state ranked 19th. The leading products in that year were crushed stone, construction sand and gravel, salt, lime and portland cement. Ohio is also an important producer of clays. Natural gas and petroleum are also extracted in significant quantities, as is coal, with production of 22.6m. short tons in 2007.

In the late 19th century Ohio led the nation in the production of machine tools, and became the second most important steel-producing state, a ranking it retains today, with a contribution of around 15% of US output. The state was later among the leaders in the establishment of an automobile industry. Its principal manufactures now include transportation equipment (principally motor vehicles and equipment), industrial machinery and equipment, computers, food products and primary and fabricated metal products. The total value of shipments for Ohio in 2006 was US $283,939m., of which 44% was added during manufacture. The state ranked third (after Texas and California) in terms of its value of shipments.

Ohio's commercial banking sector ranked second in the USA, after North Carolina, at the end of 2006, with total commercial bank assets in the state reaching US $1,874,700m. In 2004 domestic travel expenditures amounted to $13,171m. and Ohio ranked 12th in the USA in this respect. Total general expenditures by the state government in 2006 amounted to $64,929m. and total general revenue was $51,249m., of which $16,120m. was provided by the federal Government and $24,536. was derived from taxes. Ohio received $14,275m. in federal aid in 2006.

CONSTITUTION AND GOVERNMENT

Ohio's Constitution, the state's second, became effective on 1 September 1851. An amendment to the Constitution proposed by the General Assembly has to be approved by three-fifths of the elected members of each house and ratified by a majority of state voters. The Governor, elected with the Lieutenant-Governor, serves a four-year term of office and may serve no more than two terms consecutively. The 33 senators and 99 representatives in the General Assembly are re-elected every four and two years, respectively, with alternate halves of the Senate being re-elected every two years. Senators are restricted to two consecutive terms in office, and representatives to four consecutive terms. Regular sessions are held annually, starting in January, and there is no statutory limit to the number of days they may last. Bills require the approval of both houses of the General Assembly before being presented to the Governor for signing. During session the Governor has 10 days to consider a bill, after which it becomes law unless vetoed. Outside session a bill becomes law unless vetoed within 10 days from adjournment. A gubernatorial veto may be overridden by three-fifths of the elected members in each house. Enacted legislation becomes effective 90 days after being filed with the Secretary of State of Ohio. In the gubernatorial election of 2006 the Democrat candidate, Ted Strickland, was successful, winning 60% of the vote. In the 2008 presidential election the Democrats narrowly secured victory, with an estimated 51% of the votes cast. Ohio has 88 administrative counties.

Elected Executive Branch Officials

Governor (2007–11): TED STRICKLAND (Dem.).

Lieutenant-Governor: LEE FISHER (Dem.).

Secretary of State: JENNIFER BRUNNER (Dem.).

Attorney-General: NANCY H. ROGERS (interim) (Dem.).

Treasurer: RICHARD CORDRAY (Dem.).

Auditor: MARY TAYLOR (Rep.).

Selected Government Addresses

Office of the Governor: Riffe Center, 30th Floor, 77 South High St, Columbus, OH 43215-6108; tel. (614) 466-3555; fax (614) 466-9354; internet governor.ohio.gov.

Office of the Lieutenant-Governor: Riffe Center, 30th Floor, 77 South High St, Columbus, OH 43215-6108; tel. (614) 466-3379; fax (614) 644-0745; e-mail lt.governor@governor.ohio.gov.

Office of the Secretary of State: 180 East Broad St, 16th Floor, Columbus, OH 43215; tel. (614) 466-2655; fax (614) 466-2892; internet www.sos.state.oh.us.

Office of the Attorney-General: State Office Tower, 17th Floor, 30 East Broad St, Columbus, OH 43215-3428; tel. (614) 466-4320; fax (614) 466-5087; internet www.ag.state.oh.us.

Office of the Treasurer: State Office Tower, 30 East Broad St, 9th Floor, Columbus, OH 43266-0421; tel. (614) 466-2160; fax (614) 644-7313; e-mail treasurer@tos.ohio.gov; internet www.ohiotreasurer.org.

Office of the Auditor: 88 East Broad St, 5th Floor, POB 1140, Columbus, OH 43216-1140; tel. (614) 466-4514; fax (614) 466-4490; internet www.auditor.state.oh.us.

Department of Agriculture: 8995 East Main St, Reynoldsburg, OH 43068-3399; tel. (614) 728-6200; fax (614) 466-6124; e-mail communications@mail.agri.state.oh.us; internet www.ohioagriculture.gov; Dir ROBERT J. BOGGS.

Department of Commerce: 77 South High St, 23rd Floor, Columbus, OH 43215-6123; tel. (614) 466-3636; fax (614) 644-8292; e-mail directorsoffice@com.state.oh.us; internet com.state.oh.us; Dir KIMBERLY A. ZURZ.

Department of Development: 77 South High St, POB 1001, Columbus, OH 43216-1001; tel. (614) 466-2609; fax (614) 466-5167; internet www.odod.state.oh.us; Dir Lt-Gov. LEE FISHER.

Department of Education: 25 South Front St, 7th Floor, Columbus, OH 43215-4183; tel. (614) 466-7578; fax (614) 644-0599; e-mail contact.center@ode.state.oh.us; internet www.ode.state.oh.us; Supt of Public Instruction Dr SUSAN TAVE ZELMAN.

Department of Health: 246 North High St, POB 118, Columbus, OH 43266-0118; tel. (614) 466-3543; fax (614) 644-8526; e-mail opa@odh.ohio.gov; internet www.odh.ohio.gov; Dir Dr ALVIN D. JACKSON.

Department of Insurance: 50 West Town St, 3rd Floor, Suite 300, Columbus, OH 43215; tel. (614) 644-2658; fax (614) 644-3743; internet www.ohioinsurance.gov; Dir MARY JO HUDSON.

Department of Natural Resources: 2045 Morse Rd, Columbus, OH 43229-6693; tel. (614) 265-6811; internet www.dnr.state.oh.us; Dir SEAN D. LOGAN.

Department of Rehabilitation and Correction: 770 West Broad St, Columbus, OH 43222; tel. (614) 752-1159; fax (614) 752-1085; e-mail drc.publicinfo@odrc.state.oh.us; internet www.drc.ohio.gov; Dir TERRY J. COLLINS.

Department of Taxation: 30 East Broad St, 22nd Floor, Columbus, OH 43215; tel. (614) 466-2166; fax (614) 466-6401; internet www.tax.ohio.gov; Commr RICHARD A. LEVIN.

Department of Transportation: 1980 West Broad St, Columbus, OH 43223; tel. (614) 466-2335; fax (614) 644-8662; internet www.dot.state.oh.us; Dir JAMES G. BEASLEY.

Environmental Protection Agency: 50 West Town St, Suite 700, POB 1049, Columbus, OH 43216-1049; tel. (614) 644-2160; fax (614) 644-2737; internet www.epa.state.oh.us; Dir CHRIS KORLESKI.

Highway Patrol Division: 1970 West Broad St, POB 182074, Columbus, OH 43223; tel. (614) 466-2990; fax (614) 752-6409; internet statepatrol.ohio.gov; Supt Col RICHARD H. COLLINS.

National Guard: 2825 West Dublin Granville Rd, Columbus, OH 43235-2789; tel. (614) 336-7000; fax (614) 889-7074; e-mail pao.oh@oh.ngb.army.mil; internet www.ohionationalguard.com; Adj.-Gen. Maj.-Gen. GREGORY L. WAYT.

Public Utilities Commission: 180 East Broad St, Columbus, OH 43215-3793; tel. (614) 466-3292; fax (614) 752-8351; internet www.puco.ohio.gov; Chair. ALAN R. SCHRIBER.

General Assembly
(August 2008)

Senate

Rep. 21; Dem. 12; Total 33

President: BILL HARRIS (Rep.).

President Pro Tempore: JEFF JACOBSON (Rep.).

Clerk: VINCENT L. KEERAN.

House of Representatives

Rep. 53; Dem. 46; Total 99

Speaker: JON A. HUSTED (Rep.).

Speaker Pro Tempore: KEVIN DE WINE (Rep.).

Clerk: LAURA P. CLEMENS.

Oklahoma

Gross Area: 181,048 sq km (69,903 sq miles).

Resident Population (1 July 2007, estimate): 3,617,316.

State Capital: Oklahoma City.

Principal Cities (population at 1 July 2006, estimate): Oklahoma City (capital) 537,734; Tulsa 382,872; Norman 102,827.

LOCATION, TOPOGRAPHY AND CLIMATE

The State of Oklahoma (nicknamed 'The Sooner State') is in the South region of the USA, with Colorado and Kansas to the north, Missouri and Arkansas to the east, Texas to the south and south-west, and New Mexico to the west. The high Great Plains occupy Western Oklahoma, giving way to prairie towards the centre of the state. In the South are the Wichita and Arbuckle ranges and in the east the Ouachita and Boston Mountains, the latter forming part of the Ozark Plateau. The south-east tip of Oklahoma lies in the Gulf Coastal Plain. The state's highest elevation is Black Mesa at 1,516 m (4,973 ft) in the north-west corner, near the Colorado and New Mexico borders. The state's major rivers are the Arkansas, looping across the north-east, the Red, forming the southern boundary, and the Canadian and Cimarron, which run from the west and north-west, respectively, to join the Arkansas. Oklahoma has a temperate climate, with hot summers and cold winters. The south and east are humid and the western zones dry.

HISTORICAL BACKGROUND

Oklahoma was only sparsely populated by Native Americans (Indians) when Spanish explorers arrived in the 16th century, among them Hernando de Soto and Francisco Vásquez de Coronado. French traders visited the region in the 16th and 17th centuries and it was claimed for France. Most of Oklahoma became part of the USA through the Louisiana Purchase in 1803 and was established as Indian Territory, without territorial government. After the forced removal of Native Americans from the eastern USA between 1828 and 1846, the region became home to the 'Five Civilized Tribes'—the Cherokee, Chickasaw, Choctaw, Creek and Seminole peoples. During the Civil War, these tribes, some of which were slave-owners, fought for the Confederacy and, in 1866, much of their western land was confiscated in retaliation. Native unrest culminated in the tribes' defeat by Col George Custer and the Seventh Cavalry regiment at the Battle of Washita in 1868. As native land became available for farming, and as the state's coal, lead, zinc and petroleum resources began to be exploited, large numbers of settlers arrived in western Oklahoma. This region was granted territorial status in 1890, with the eastern Indian Territory remaining separate until 1906. Oklahoma became the 46th state to join the Union on 16 November 1907. A prolonged drought in the mid-1930s, accompanied by dust storms, exacerbated the effects of the Great Depression on the state's farmers. Thousands were financially ruined and left Oklahoma. In April 1995 a bomb exploded outside the Oklahoma City federal building, causing great damage and killing 168 people. In June 1997 a US citizen, Timothy McVeigh, was convicted of the attack; he was executed in June 2001.

ECONOMY

Oklahoma's principal economic activities are services, manufacturing, agriculture, mineral extraction, energy production and finance, insurance and real estate. In 2007 gross domestic product by state was US $139,323m. and average per-head income stood at $34,910. It was estimated that 15.9% of the population, the 10th highest proportion in the country, were living below the poverty threshold in that year. The civilian labour force totalled 1,754,200 in mid-2008, while the unemployment rate was the seventh lowest among the states, standing at 4.0% (70,500 persons). Of the total number of employees, 7.1% were union members in 2007, while union agreements covered 8.5%.

Farmland covered 33.7m. acres (13.8m. ha) in 2007. There were 82,500 farms in that year, with an average farm covering an area of 408 acres. In 2002 3.2% of total cropland was irrigated; in 2007 77% of farm income was generated by sales of livestock and livestock products and 23% by crops. The state's main agricultural products were cattle and calves, hogs, broilers and wheat. Oklahoma was ranked sixth for cattle and calves and seventh for wheat production in 2007. Some 17% of the state was covered by forest in 2002.

Oklahoma's non-fuel mineral production was valued at US $678m. in 2007, with the state ranked 31st nation-wide. Leading minerals were crushed stone (accounting for one-third of the state's total non-fuel mineral production), portland cement, sand and gravel (for production of which Oklahoma ranked seventh nationally) and crude iodine. Lime, helium, gemstones and ammonia (fixed nitrogen) were also produced. Oklahoma is the only state to produce iodine. It was ranked first for gypsum and fourth for feldspar in 2007; production of tripoli (diatomite) was the second greatest, nationwide, in 2004. No metals are mined in the state. Oklahoma was the second most important producer of natural gas (behind Texas), and the fifth most important producer of crude petroleum, in 2005. A small amount of coal was also extracted.

Oklahoma's manufacturing industry was initially based on the processing of agricultural products and petroleum, but became increasingly diversified. In terms of value of shipments, the state ranked 29th in the nation in 2006. The leading manufacturing product groups were machinery and equipment, food products, chemicals, plastics and rubber, fabricated metal products and transportation equipment. The total value of Oklahoma's manufacturing shipments in 2006 was US $55,791., of which 43% was added during manufacture.

Domestic travel expenditures amounted to US $4,456m. in 2004. Total general expenditures by the state government in 2006 were $16,882m.; total general revenue amounted to $16,266m., of which $5,045m. was provided by the federal Government and $7,817m. was derived from taxes. Federal aid to the state totalled $5,092m. in 2006.

CONSTITUTION AND GOVERNMENT

Oklahoma's only Constitution became effective on 16 November 1907. Constitutional amendments proposed by the Legislature have to be approved by a majority of the elected members of each house and then ratified by a majority of state voters. The Governor, elected separately from the Lieutenant-Governor, holds office for four years before re-election and may serve no more than two terms consecutively. There are 48 senators and 101 representatives in the Legislature, serving terms of four and two years, respectively; alternate halves of the Senate are re-elected every two years. Regular legislative sessions take place annually, starting in February and lasting until no later than the end of May. A bill becomes law when it has been passed by the Legislature and signed by the Governor. During session a bill also becomes law if it is not vetoed and remains unsigned five days after being presented to the Governor. After session a bill dies unless signed within 15 days from adjournment of the Legislature. A gubernatorial veto may be overridden by a two-thirds' vote from the elected members of each house. Enacted legislation becomes effective 90 days after adjournment. In the 2006 gubernatorial election the Democratic candidate, Brad Henry, was re-elected with 66% of the votes cast. In the presidential election in 2008 over 1.4m. people voted, with the Republicans gaining 66% of the total votes. Oklahoma has 77 administrative counties.

Elected Executive Branch Officials

Governor (2007–11): BRAD HENRY (Dem.).

Lieutenant-Governor: JARI ASKINS (Dem.).

Attorney-General: W. A. DREW EDMONDSON (Dem.).

Treasurer: SCOTT MEACHAM (Dem.).

Auditor and Inspector: STEVE BURRAGE (Dem.).

Superintendent of Public Instruction: SANDY GARRETT (Dem.).

Labor Commissioner: LLOYD L. FIELDS (Dem.).

Insurance Commissioner: KIM HOLLAND (Dem.).

Selected Government Addresses

Office of the Governor: 212 State Capitol, 2300 North Lincoln Blvd, Oklahoma City, OK 73105; tel. (405) 521-2342; fax (405) 521-3353; internet www.gov.ok.gov.

Office of the Lieutenant-Governor: 211 State Capitol, 2300 North Lincoln Blvd, Oklahoma City, OK 73105; tel. (405) 521-2161; fax (405) 525-2702; internet www.ok.gov/ltgovernor.

Office of the Attorney-General: 313 Northeast 21st St, Oklahoma City, OK 73105; tel. (405) 521-3921; fax (405) 521-4534; internet www.oag.state.ok.us.

Office of the Treasurer: 217 State Capitol, 2300 North Lincoln Blvd, Oklahoma City, OK 73105; tel. (405) 521-3191; fax (405) 521-4994; e-mail carrie.bowen@treasurer.ok.gov; internet www.treasurer.state.ok.us.

Office of the Auditor and Inspector: 100 State Capitol, 2300 North Lincoln Blvd, Oklahoma City, OK 73105; tel. (405) 521-3495; fax (405) 521-3426; e-mail twatkins@sai.ok.gov; internet www.sai.state.ok.us.

Department of Education: 2500 North Lincoln Blvd, Oklahoma City, OK 73105-4599; tel. (405) 521-3301; fax (405) 521-6205; e-mail sandy_garrett@.sde.state.ok.us; internet www.sde.state.ok.us; headed by the Supt of Public Instruction.

Department of Labor: 4001 North Lincoln Blvd, Oklahoma City, OK 73105; tel. (405) 528-1500; fax (405) 528-5751; e-mail mbarnes@oklaosf.state.ok.us; internet www.ok.gov/odol; headed by the Labor Commr.

Department of Insurance: 2401 NW 23rd St, Suite 28, POB 53408, Oklahoma City, OK 73152-3408; tel. (405) 521-2828; fax (405) 521-6635; e-mail lancethomas@insurance.state.ok.us; internet www.ok.gov/oid; headed by the Insurance Commr.

Department of Agriculture, Food and Forestry: 2800 North Lincoln Blvd, POB 528804, Oklahoma City, OK 73152; tel. (405) 521-3864; fax (405) 522-4912; e-mail terry.peach@oda.state.ok.us; internet www.oda.state.ok.us; Commr. TERRY L. PEACH.

Department of Commerce: 900 North Stiles Ave, POB 26980, Oklahoma City, OK 73126-0980; tel. (405) 815-6552; e-mail info@okcommerce.gov; internet www.okcommerce.gov; Exec. Dir NATALIE SHIRLEY.

Department of Corrections: 3400 Martin Luther King Ave, POB 11400, Oklahoma City, OK 73136-0400; tel. (405) 425-2500; fax (405) 425-2578; e-mail director@doc.state.ok.us; internet www.doc.state.ok.us; Dir JUSTIN JONES.

Department of Environmental Quality: 707 North Robinson St, POB 1677, Oklahoma City, OK 73101-1677; tel. (405) 702-1000; fax (405) 702-1001; e-mail oseinfo3@environment.ok.gov; internet www.deq.state.ok.us; Sec. J. D. STRONG.

Department of Health: 1000 NE 10th St, Oklahoma City, OK 73117-1299; tel. (405) 271-5600; fax (405) 271-3431; e-mail webmaster@health.ok.gov; internet www.health.state.ok.us; Commr Dr JAMES MICHAEL (MIKE) CRUTCHER.

Department of Public Safety: 3600 North Martin Luther King Ave, POB 11415, Oklahoma City, OK 73136-0415; tel. (405) 425-2424; e-mail comment@dps.state.ok.us; internet www.dps.state.ok.us; Commr KEVIN WARD.

Department of Transportation: 200 North East 21st St, Oklahoma City, OK 73105-3204; tel. (405) 521-6000; fax (405) 521-6528; e-mail odotinfo@odot.org; internet www.okladot.state.ok.us; Sec. PHIL TOMLINSON.

Land Office (School Land Trust): Paragon Bldg, 5801 Broadway, Suite 200, POB 26910, Oklahoma City, OK 73126-0910; tel. (405) 604-8100; fax (405) 604-8199; e-mail clifton.scott@clo.state.ok.us; internet www.clo.state.ok.us; Sec. CLIFTON H. SCOTT.

Military Department: 3501 Military Circle, Oklahoma City, OK 73111-4398; tel. (405) 228-5212; fax (405) 606-7274; e-mail henry.scully@us.army.mil; internet www.okguard.org; Adj.-Gen. Maj.-Gen. HARRY M. WYATT, III.

Office of the Secretary of State: 101 State Capitol, 2300 North Lincoln Blvd, Oklahoma City, OK 73105-4897; tel. (405) 521-3912; fax (405) 521-3771; internet www.sos.state.ok.us; Sec. of State M. SUSAN SAVAGE.

Office of State Finance: 122 State Capitol, 2300 North Lincoln Blvd, Oklahoma City, OK 73105-4801; tel. (405) 521-2444; fax (405) 521-2871; internet www.ok.gov.osf; Dir TONY HUTCHISON.

Tax Commission: 2501 North Lincoln Blvd, Oklahoma City, OK 73194; tel. (405) 521-3637; fax (405) 521-2035; e-mail otcmaster@tax.ok.gov; internet www.tax.ok.gov; Chair. THOMAS KEMP, Jr.

Legislature
(August 2008)

Senate

Dem. 24; Rep. 24; Total 48

President: Lt-Gov. JARI ASKINS (Dem.).

President Pro Tempore: MIKE MORGAN (Dem.).

Chief of Staff: TOM WALLS.

House of Representatives

Rep. 57; Dem. 44; Total 101

Speaker: CHRIS BENGE (Rep.).

Speaker Pro Tempore: GUS BLACKWELL (Rep.).

Chief Clerk: JOEL KINTSEL.

Oregon

Gross Area: 254,819 sq km (98,424 sq miles).

Resident Population (1 July 2007, estimate): 3,747,455.

State Capital: Salem.

Principal Cities (population at 1 July 2006, estimate): Portland 537,081; Salem (capital) 152,239; Eugene 146,356.

LOCATION, TOPOGRAPHY AND CLIMATE

The State of Oregon (nicknamed 'The Beaver State') lies in the West region of the USA and is bordered by Washington to the north, Idaho to the east, Nevada to the south-east and California to the south-west. The Pacific Ocean lies to the west. The sandy beaches and promontories of the Pacific coast rise to the Coast Range and Cascade Mountains, the latter containing Oregon's highest point, Mount Hood, a dormant volcano, at 3,424 m (11,235 ft). Between the two ranges are fertile valleys, the largest being that of the Willamette River in the north. East of the Cascades is an arid plateau consisting of undulating hills in the north, rising towards the Wallowa and Blue Mountains in the north-west of the state. In the south-east is the Great Basin, a bare, dry region. Oregon's main rivers are: the Columbia, the fourth largest river in the USA in terms of outflow, forming the western two-thirds of the northern border; the Willamette, draining into the Columbia; and the Snake, forming the northern half of the eastern border and flowing through Hell's Canyon, one of the deepest gorges in North America. The state's largest lake is Upper Klamath Lake, covering 229 sq km (142 sq miles). Crater Lake, formed after the eruption of Mount Mazama, is the deepest lake in the USA, at 589 m (1,932 ft). Oregon's climate is generally temperate; there is heavy precipitation in the west, while the east is dry, with greater extremes of temperature.

HISTORICAL BACKGROUND

Among the peoples inhabiting Oregon before the arrival of Europeans were the Bannock, Klamath, Nez Percé and Shoshone tribes. Various European voyagers made sightings of the Oregon coast in the 16th–18th centuries, but the first to sail up the Columbia River (named after his ship) was Robert Gray, a citizen of the newly independent USA, in 1792. The Meriwether Lewis and William Clark Expedition reached the mouth of the Columbia River in 1805, and in 1811 a fur-trading post was established at Astoria. The United Kingdom, which claimed the region, and the USA agreed to joint occupation in 1818. The first large influx of settlers occurred in the early 1840s; these people formed a provisional government in 1843, which remained intact until Oregon became a territory in 1849, three years after the British had accepted the Canadian boundary along the 49th parallel (49°N). In 1859 Oregon was reduced to its present size, and became the 33rd state on 14 February of that year. The state remained isolated until the completion of the transcontinental railway in 1883.

ECONOMY

Manufacturing, service industries and tourism are Oregon's main economic activities. Gross domestic product by state was US $158,233m. in 2007 and average per-head income stood at $35,027. In the same year it was estimated that 12.9% of the population were living below the poverty line. The total civilian labour force numbered 1,971,700 in mid-2008, while the unemployment rate was 5.7% (113,000 persons). In 2007 14.3% of those employed belonged to a trade union, although 15.4% were covered by union agreements.

Farmland covered 17.0m. acres (6.9m. ha) in 2007; there were 38,300 farms in that year, with the average farm occupying 444 acres. In 2002 26% of total cropland was irrigated. In 2007 76% of farm income came from crops and 24% from livestock and livestock products. In terms of value, the leading agricultural commodities in that year were greenhouse and nursery products, cattle and calves, dairy products and wheat. Other products of importance included hay, ryegrass, potatoes, pears and hazelnuts. The state was ranked third overall in 2007 for grape production (behind California and Washington), fourth for strawberries and greenhouse and nursery products and fifth for onions. Approximately 47% of Oregon was forested in 2004. Although the industry is declining, Oregon was still the largest lumber producer in that year, with production of 7,081m. board feet. Softwoods regularly account for 97%–98% of total state production. There is some commercial fishing activity, with a value of US $108m. in 2006; the most valuable species fished is crab, in which Oregon traditionally led the nation but in which it was superseded by Washington in 2007; in addition it ranked fourth for Pacific salmon in 2007.

In 2007 Oregon's non-fuel mineral production was valued at US $505m., with the state ranked 36th in this respect. Construction sand and gravel and crushed stone together accounted for more than 68% of total state production in 2003. The state was ranked second for gemstone production in 2007, third for diatomite and fourth for pumice and pumicite. It also produced crude perlite (for which it ranked second in 2004), talc and lime.

Oregon ranked 26th in the USA in 2006 in terms of the value of shipments. The lumber and wood products industry dominated the state's manufacturing activity, with electronics and technology products, scientific instruments, machinery and food and kindred products also significant. In 2006 the total value of manufacturing shipments in Oregon was US $65,536m., of which 60% was added during manufacture.

Oregon's rugged coast and extensive system of national and state parks make it a major US tourism attraction; in 2004 domestic travel expenditures amounted to US $5,835m.

Total general expenditures by the state government in 2006 amounted to US $20,071m.; general revenue was $16,495m., with intergovernmental revenue from the federal Government totalling $4,611m. and taxes providing $7,590m. In 2006 Oregon received $4,821m. in federal aid.

CONSTITUTION AND GOVERNMENT

Oregon's only Constitution became effective on 14 February 1859. Amendments to the Constitution proposed by the Legislative Assembly require the approval of a majority of elected members of both houses and ratification by a majority of state voters. The Governor, elected to serve a four-year term of office, may serve no more than two terms consecutively and is succeeded in his or her absence by the Secretary of State. Oregon has no formal cabinet system. The 30 senators and 60 representatives in the Legislative Assembly are re-elected every four and two years, respectively, alternate halves of the Senate being re-elected every two years. Regular legislative sessions are held biennially, starting in January, and have no statutory limit to their length. A bill becomes law when it has been passed by a majority in the Legislative Assembly and signed by the Governor. During session the Governor has five days in which to consider a bill, after which it becomes law unless vetoed. After session a bill becomes law unless vetoed within 30 days from adjournment. A gubernatorial veto may be overridden by a two-thirds' vote of those present in each house. Enacted bills become effective on 1 January following. The Democratic candidate, Ted Kulongoski, was re-elected in the 2006 gubernatorial election, with 54% of the votes cast. In the presidential election in 2008 the Democrats defeated the Republicans with some 57% of the votes cast. Oregon has 36 administrative counties.

Elected Executive Branch Officials

Governor (2007–11): THEODORE R. (TED) KULONGOSKI (Dem.).

Secretary of State: BILL BRADBURY (Dem.).

Attorney-General: HARDY MYERS (Dem.).

Treasurer: RANDALL EDWARDS (Dem.).

Superintendent of Public Instruction: SUSAN CASTILLO (Dem.).

Commissioner of Labor and Industries: BRADLEY P. AVAKIAN (Dem.).

Selected Government Addresses

Office of the Governor: State Capitol, Rm 160, 900 Court St, NE, Salem, OR 97301-4047; tel. (503) 378-4582; fax (503) 378-6827; internet www.oregon.gov/gov.

Office of the Secretary of State: State Capitol, Rm 136, 900 Court St, NE, Salem, OR 97310-0722; tel. (503) 986-1523; fax (503) 986-1616; e-mail oregon.sos@state.or.us; internet www.sos.state.or.us.

Office of the Attorney-General: 1162 Court St, NE, Salem, OR 97301-4096; tel. (503) 378-4400; fax (503) 378-4017; e-mail jan.margosian@state.or.us; internet www.doj.state.or.us.

Office of the Treasurer: 350 Winter St, NE, Suite 100, Salem, OR 97301-3896; tel. (503) 378-4329; fax (503) 373-7051; e-mail oregon.treasurer@state.or.us; internet www.ost.state.or.us.

Bureau of Labor and Industries: 800 Oregon St, NE, Suite 1045, Portland, OR 97232; tel. (971) 673-0761; fax (971) 673-0762; e-mail boli.mail@state.or.us; internet www.oregon.gov/boli; headed by Commr of Labor and Industries.

Department of Agriculture: 635 Capitol St, NE, Salem, OR 97301-2532; tel. (503) 986-4550; fax (503) 986-4747; e-mail info@oda.state.or.us; internet www.oregon.gov/oda; Dir KATY COBA.

Department of Consumer and Business Services: 350 Winter St, NE, POB 14480, Salem, OR 97309-0405; tel. (503) 378-4100; fax (503) 378-6444; e-mail dcbs.info@state.or.us; internet www.oregon.gov/dcbs; Dir CORY STREISINGER.

Department of Corrections: 2575 Center St, NE, Salem, OR 97301-4667; tel. (503) 945-0920; fax (503) 373-1173; e-mail doc.info@doc.state.or.us; internet www.oregon.gov/doc; Dir MAX WILLIAMS.

Department of Education: 255 Capitol St, NE, Salem, OR 97310-0203; tel. (503) 947-5600; fax (503) 378-5156; e-mail ode.frontdesk@state.or.us; internet www.oregon.gov/ode; headed by the Supt of Public Instruction.

Department of Economic and Community Development: 775 Summer St, NE, Salem, OR 97301-1280; tel. (503) 986-0123; fax (503) 581-5115; e-mail oedd.info@state.or.us; internet www.oregon.gov/ecdd; Dir TIM MCCABE.

Department of Environmental Quality: 811 Sixth Ave, SW, Portland, OR 97204-1390; tel. (503) 229-5696; fax (503) 229-6124; e-mail deq.info@deq.state.or.us; internet www.deq.state.or.us; Dir DICK PEDERSEN.

Department of Human Services: 500 Summer St, NE, Suite E15, Salem, OR 97301-1097; tel. (503) 945-5944; fax (503) 378-2897; e-mail dhs.info@state.or.us; internet www.oregon.gov/dhs; Dir BRUCE GOLDBERG.

Department of Military: AGDD - Rm 237, POB 14350, Salem, OR 97309-5047; tel. (503) 584-3985; fax (503) 584-3987; e-mail agdd@mil.state.or.us; internet www.oregon.gov/omd; Adj.-Gen. Maj.-Gen. RAYMOND F. REES.

Department of Revenue: 955 Center St, NE, Salem, OR 97301; tel. (503) 378-4988; fax (503) 945-8738; e-mail questions.dor@state.or.us; internet www.oregon.gov/dor; Dir ELIZABETH S. HARCHENKO.

Department of State Police: 255 Capitol St, NE, 4th Floor, Salem, OR 97310; tel. (503) 378-3720; fax (503) 378-8282; e-mail ask.osp@state.or.us; internet egov.oregon.gov/osp; Supt TIMOTHY MCLAIN.

Department of Transportation: 355 Capitol St, NE, Salem, OR 97301-3871; tel. (503) 986-3455; fax (503) 986-3432; internet www.oregon.gov/odot; Dir MATTHEW L. GARRETT.

Public Utility Commission: 550 Capitol St, NE, Suite 215, POB 2148, Salem, OR 97308-2148; tel. (503) 378-8962; fax (503) 378-5505; e-mail puc.commission@state.or.us; internet www.oregon.gov/puc; Chair. LEE BEYER.

Legislative Assembly
(August 2008)

Senate

Dem. 18; Rep. 11; Ind. 1; Total 30

President: PETER COURTNEY (Dem.).

President Pro Tempore: MARGARET CARTER (Dem.).

Secretary: JUDY HALL.

House of Representatives

Dem. 31; Rep. 29; Total 60

Speaker: JEFF MERKLEY (Dem.).

Speaker Pro Tempore: DIANE ROSENBAUM (Dem.).

Chief Clerk: RAMONA KENADY.

Pennsylvania

Gross Area: 119,291 sq km (46,058 sq miles).

Resident Population (1 July 2007, estimate): 12,432,792.

State Capital: Harrisburg (population 47,164 at 1 July 2006, estimate).

Principal Cities (population at 1 July 2005): Philadelphia 1,448,394; Pittsburgh 312,819; Allentown 107,294; Erie 102,036.

LOCATION, TOPOGRAPHY AND CLIMATE

The Commonwealth of Pennsylvania (nicknamed 'The Keystone State') is in the Northeast region of the USA and is bordered by Lake Erie (beyond which lies Ontario—Canada) and New York to the north, New Jersey to the east, Delaware, Maryland and West Virginia to the south, and West Virginia and Ohio to the west. From the Delaware River, which forms the eastern border of the state, the land slopes up to the rolling hills of the Piedmont Plateau in the south-east and the high Pocono Plateau in the north-east. West of the Great Valley, curving from north-east to south, are the ridges of the Allegheny Mountains, part of the Appalachian system. To the west and north is the Allegheny High Plateau, with Mount Davis in the south-west, at 979 m (3,213 ft), the state's highest peak. In the north-west tip the land slopes down to form a narrow lowland region around Lake Erie. Much of Pennsylvania is drained by the Susquehanna River, which flows through the Appalachians and down into Chesapeake Bay. The west is drained by the Allegheny and Monongahela Rivers, which join to form the Ohio. South-eastern Pennsylvania has long, warm summers and mild winters, while the high Appalachian region has short, cool summers and harsh winters. Around Lake Erie summers are long and there is heavy snowfall in winter.

HISTORICAL BACKGROUND

Pennsylvania was inhabited by Leni-Lanape (Delaware), Nantichoke, Shawnee and Iroquoian-speaking peoples when Cornelis Jacobssen, a Dutchman (probably the first European to arrive in the region), entered Delaware Bay in 1614. Swedes began farming along the Delaware River in 1638, and the region was known as New Sweden until the Dutch took the land in 1655, surrendering it to the British in 1664. In 1781 the British monarch Charles II granted the region to William Penn in payment for his father's services in the war against the Dutch. Penn, a Quaker (Society of Friends), secured peace from Indian wars for the new colony by concluding a treaty with the Native American tribes in 1683. British taxation of the American colonies and the Proclamation of 1763, which aimed to prevent settlement west of the Allegheny Mountains, infuriated Pennsylvanians. In 1774 Philadelphia became the meeting place for the Continental Congress and, in 1776, the Declaration of Independence was proclaimed from Independence Hall. Philadelphia served as the US capital from 1778 to 1783 and, again, from 1790 to 1800. On 12 December 1780 Pennsylvania became the second state to join the Union by ratifying the Federal Constitution. The state fought for the Union during the Civil War: the Battle of Gettysburg, fought on Pennsylvanian soil in 1863, was a turning point in the fortunes of the Union. A disaster was narrowly averted at Three Mile Island in 1979, when a nuclear reactor malfunctioned.

ECONOMY

Manufacturing, services, finance, insurance, real estate, tourism and wholesale and retail trade are major contributors to Pennsylvania's economy. In 2007 gross domestic product by state totalled US $531,110m., the sixth highest in the country, and the state's per-head income averaged $38,740 in that year. It was estimated that 11.6% of the population were living below the poverty threshold in 2007. In mid-2008 the civilian labour force totalled 6,480,800, with an unemployment rate of 5.4% (353,000 persons). In 2007 15.1% of those employed were members of a trade union, while 16.6% were covered by union agreements.

In 2007 farmland covered some 7.7m. acres (3.1m. ha). There were 58,000 farms in that year, with an average size of 132 acres. Of total farm income in 2007, 67% was generated by sales of livestock and livestock products and 32% by crops. Dairy products, cattle and calves, mushrooms and corn were the most valuable agricultural commodities in that year. Other important sources of farm income were greenhouse and nursery products, chicken eggs, broilers, hogs, hay, soybeans and turkeys. The state was ranked fourth for production of dairy produce in 2007; it also ranked fifth for apples, chicken eggs and strawberries, and sixth for grapes, in that year. There are 17m. acres of forestland in Pennsylvania, covering around 57% of the land area, but lumber production is no longer a major industry in the state.

Non-fuel mineral production in Pennsylvania was estimated at US $1,760m. in 2007, with the state ranked 13th, accounting for some 3% of total national production. Pennsylvania is a leading producer of crushed stone, portland cement, and construction sand and gravel. Lime and masonry cement are also produced. It is also a major producer of coal, ranked fourth, with production of 65m. short tons in 2007. Natural gas and a small amount of petroleum are also produced.

Pennsylvania remains a major manufacturing centre, although the contribution of this sector to the overall US economy declined in the 20th century. In terms of value of shipments, the state ranked fifth in the USA in 2006. Leading industries include food and kindred products, chemicals and allied products (the bulk of which comprise pharmaceutical drugs), industrial machinery and equipment, computer software, paper and plastics. Primary metal industries (principally blast-furnace and basic steel products) and fabricated metal products are also important to the state. The town of Bethlehem is home to one of the largest steel-makers in the USA, and the state was the fourth largest manufacturer of raw steel in 2003, using materials from other sources. In 2006 the total value of Pennsylvania's manufacturing shipments was US $231,725m., of which 49% was added during manufacture.

Pennsylvania is a prominent centre for both banking and insurance; total assets of the state's commercial banks stood at US $415,200m. at the end of 2006, the eighth highest in the nation. The Philadelphia Stock Exchange is the country's oldest and was for many years its most significant. Tourism is very important to the state economy; domestic travel expenditures totalled $16,175m. in 2004, when the state ranked seventh nation-wide in terms of money spent.

Total general expenditures by the state government in 2006 were US $64,917m.; general revenue totalled $55,419m., of which $15,100m. was provided by the federal government and $29,051m. was derived from taxes. The federal Government gave $17,963m. to the state in aid in 2006.

CONSTITUTION AND GOVERNMENT

Pennsylvania's Constitution, the state's fifth, became effective in 1968. An amendment to the Constitution proposed by the General Assembly has to be approved by a majority of the elected members in each house in two successive sessions and ratified by a majority of state voters. The Governor and Lieutenant-Governor are jointly elected to serve a four-year term of office; neither office may be held for more than two consecutive terms. The 50 senators and 203 representatives in the General Assembly are re-elected every four and two years, respectively, alternate halves of the Senate being re-elected every two years. Regular legislative sessions are held biennially, starting in January, and there is no statutory limit to their duration. To become law a bill must be passed by the General Assembly and signed by the Governor. During session the Governor is allowed 10 days to consider a bill, after which it becomes law unless vetoed. Outside session a bill becomes law unless vetoed within 30 days from adjournment. The Governor's veto can be overridden by a two-thirds' vote from the elected members of each house. Legislation generally becomes effective immediately upon enactment. In 2006 a Democrat, Edward Rendell, was re-elected to the governorship with 56% of the votes cast. In the presidential election in 2008 the Democrats secured an estimated 55% of the votes cast, with over 5.7m. people voting. There are 67 administrative counties in Pennsylvania.

Elected Executive Branch Officials

Governor (2007–11): Edward G. Rendell (Dem.).

Lieutenant-Governor: Catherine Baker Knoll (Dem.).

Attorney-General: Tom Corbett (Rep.).

Treasurer: Robin L.P. Wiessmann (Dem.).

Auditor-General: Jack Wagner (Dem.).

Selected Government Addresses

Office of the Governor: Main Capitol Bldg, Rm 225, Harrisburg, PA 17120; tel. (717) 787-2500; fax (717) 772-8284; internet www.governor.state.pa.us.

Office of the Lieutenant-Governor: Main Capitol Bldg, Rm 200, Harrisburg, PA 17120-0002; tel. (717) 787-3300; fax (717) 783-0150; e-mail lieutenant-governor@state.pa.us; internet www.ltgovernor.state.pa.us.

Office of the Attorney-General: Strawberry Sq., 16th Floor, Harrisburg, PA 17120; tel. (717) 787-3391; fax (717) 787-8242; internet www.attorneygeneral.gov.

Office of the Treasurer: Finance Bldg, Rm 129, Harrisburg, PA 17120-0018; tel. (717) 787-2465; fax (717) 787-8242; internet www.patreasury.org.

Office of the Auditor-General: Finance Bldg, Rm 229, Harrisburg, PA 17120-0018; tel. (717) 787-2543; fax (717) 783-4407; e-mail auditorgen@auditorgen.state.pa.us; internet www.auditorgen.state.pa.us.

Department of Agriculture: 2301 North Cameron St, Harrisburg, PA 17110-9408; tel. (717) 787-4737; fax (717) 772-2780; internet www.agriculture.state.pa.us; Sec. Dennis Wolff.

Department of Community and Economic Development: Keystone Bldg, 4th Floor, 400 North St, Harrisburg, PA 17120-0225; tel. (717) 783-3840; fax (717) 234-4560; e-mail readysetsucceed@newpa.com; internet www.newpa.com; Sec. Dennis Yablonsky.

Department of Conservation and Natural Resources: Rachel Carson State Office Bldg, 7th Floor, 400 Market St, POB 8767, Harrisburg, PA 17105-8767; tel. (717) 787-2869; fax (717) 772-9106; e-mail ra-askdcnr@state.pa.us; internet www.dcnr.state.pa.us; Sec. Michael DiBerardinis.

Department of Corrections: 2520 Lisburn Rd, POB 598, Camp Hill, PA 17001-0598; tel. (717) 975-4859; fax (717) 703-3621; e-mail ra-cenpressoffice@state.pa.us; internet www.cor.state.pa.us; Commr Dr Jeffrey A. Beard.

Department of Education: 333 Market St, Harrisburg, PA 17126; tel. (717) 783-6788; fax (717) 783-4517; e-mail 00sec@psupen.psu.edu; internet www.pde.state.pa.us; Sec. Dr Gerald L. Zahorchak.

Department of Environmental Protection: Rachel Carson State Office Bldg, 16th Floor, POB 2063, Harrisburg, PA 17105-2063; tel. (717) 783-2300; fax (717) 783-8926; e-mail ra-epcontactus@state.pa.us; internet www.depweb.state.pa.us; Sec. Joseph R. Powers (acting).

Department of Health: Health and Welfare Bldg, Seventh and Forster Sts, POB 90, Harrisburg, PA 17120; tel. (717) 787-6436; fax (717) 772-6959; e-mail webmaster@health.state.pa.us; internet www.dsf.health.state.pa.us; Sec. Calvin B. Johnson.

Department of Insurance: 1326 Strawberry Sq., Harrisburg, PA 17120; tel. (717) 787-2317; fax (717) 787-8585; e-mail ra-in-consumerliaison@state.pa.us; internet www.ins.state.pa.us; Commr Joel Ario.

Department of Labor and Industry: Seventh and Forster Sts, Rm 1700, Harrisburg, PA 17120; tel. (717) 787-5279; fax (717) 787-8826; e-mail ra-li-oit-webteam@state.pa.us; internet www.dli.state.pa.us; Sec. Sandi Vito (acting).

Department of Military and Veterans' Affairs: Bldg S-O-47, Fisher Ave, Fort Indiantown Gap, Annville, PA 17003-5002; tel. (717) 861-8500; fax (717) 861-8481; e-mail ra-dmva_webmaster@state.pa.us; internet www.milvet.state.pa.us; Adj.-Gen. Maj.-Gen. Jessica L. Wright.

Department of Revenue: Strawberry Sq., Fourth and Walnut Sts Lobby, Harrisburg, PA 17128-0101; tel. (717) 783-1405; fax (717) 783-4447; internet www.revenue.state.pa.us; Sec. Thomas W. Wolf.

Department of State: 302 North Office Bldg, Harrisburg, PA 17120; tel. (717) 787-6458; fax (717) 787-1734; e-mail st-press@state.pa.us; internet www.dos.state.pa.us; Sec. of the Commonwealth Pedro A. Cortés.

Department of Transportation: Keystone Bldg, 400 North St, Harrisburg, PA 17120; tel. (717) 787-2838; fax (717) 787-1738; internet www.dot.state.pa.us; Sec. Allen D. Biehler.

Public Utility Commission: Keystone Bldg, 400 North St, POB 3265, Harrisburg, PA 17105-3265; tel. (717) 783-9504; fax (717) 787-4193; internet www.puc.state.pa.us; Chair. James H. Cawley.

State Police: 1800 Elmerton Ave, Harrisburg, PA 17110-9758; tel. (717) 783-5558; fax (717) 787-2948; e-mail ra-webadmin@state.pa.us; internet www.psp.state.pa.us; Commr Col Jeffrey Miller.

General Assembly
(August 2008)

Senate

Rep. 29; Dem. 21; Total 50

President: Lt-Gov. Catherine Baker Knoll (Rep.).

President Pro Tempore: Joseph B. Scarnati, III (Rep.).

Chief Clerk: W. Russell Faber.

House of Representatives

Dem. 102; Rep. 101; Total 203

Speaker: Dennis M. O'Brien (Rep.).

Chief Clerk: Roger Nick.

Rhode Island

Gross Area: 4,002 sq km (1,546 sq miles).

Resident Population (1 July 2007, estimate): 1,0757,832.

State Capital, Principal City: Providence (population 175,255 at 1 July 2006, estimate).

LOCATION, TOPOGRAPHY AND CLIMATE

The State of Rhode Island and Providence Plantations (nicknamed 'Little Rhody' and 'The Ocean State'), is the smallest of the 50 states. One of the six states comprising New England, it lies in the Northeast region of the USA and is bordered by Massachusetts to the north and east, the Atlantic Ocean to the south, and Connecticut to the west. Block Island, the largest of the 38 offshore islands, is 14 km (9 miles) south-west of Point Judith; Narragansett Bay, extending inland for 48 km (30 miles), contains three of the largest islands of the state: Rhode Island itself (also known as Aquidneck), Prudence and Conanicut. In the state's southern and eastern coastal region there are sandy beaches, marshes and lagoons. Towards the interior the land rises, and western Rhode Island state lies within the New England Uplands—rugged, forest-covered hills scattered with lakes. The state's main rivers are the Blackstone, which flows from northeastern Rhode Island into Providence River, and the Pawtucket, flowing into Block Island Sound. Rhode Island's climate is humid with short summers and cold winters.

HISTORICAL BACKGROUND

The main indigenous Indian tribes inhabiting Rhode Island in the 16th century were the Narragansett and Wampanoag. The first permanent European settlement in Rhode Island was established by the United Kingdom at Providence in 1636, followed by Portsmouth (1638), Newport (1639) and Warwick (1642). In 1644 these settlements were united as a single colony, the Providence Plantations. Increasing settlement caused Indian unrest, resulting in King Philip's War (1675–76), in which the Indians were defeated.

In 1776 Rhode Island declared itself independent from Britain. On 29 May 1790 the region became the last of the 13 original states to accede to the Union. Despite the increasing development of industry during the 19th century, political power remained in the hands of the landowners until a new constitution was drawn up in 1843. The state was, thereafter, dominated by the Republican Party until the 1930s, when the Democrats became the major political force.

ECONOMY

The principal economic activities in Rhode Island are manufacturing and services, with lesser contributions made by construction, agriculture, mining, forestry, fishing, real estate and wholesale and retail trade. In 2007 gross domestic product by state stood at US $46,900m. and income averaged $39,712 per head. In the same year it was estimated that 12.0% of the population were living below the poverty line. The civilian labour force totalled 580,700 in mid-2008, while the unemployment rate was the third highest nationwide, standing at 8.1% (47,300 persons). In 2007 15.0% of those employed belonged to a trade union, with 15.8% covered by union agreements.

In 2007 farmland covered 60,000 acres (24,000 ha). There were just 850 farms in that year, with an average farm covering an area of 71 acres, the smallest average in the country. In 2002 17% of total cropland was irrigated, while in 2007 84% of farm income came from crop sales and 16% was generated by livestock and livestock products. Total farm income, at US $69.8m., was the smallest of any state except Alaska. In terms of value, the leading agricultural products in 2007 were greenhouse and nursery products, dairy products, sweet corn, dairy products and potatoes. Apples are also significant. Approximately 39% of the land area of Rhode Island was covered by forest in 2003, with most forestland suitable for use as commercial timberland. Commercial fishing also contributes to the state's economy; the value of Rhode Island's catch of fish in 2006 was $99m. Lobster fishing is important; the state ranked fourth in the nation in 2004 in this regard.

In 2007 Rhode Island's non-fuel mineral production was valued at just US $44.4m., the lowest value of any state other than Delaware. The state's principal minerals, in terms of value, were sand and gravel and crushed stone. Gemstones are also mined.

Rhode Island ranked 42nd among the states in terms of the value of its shipments in 2006. Leading manufactures include machinery, fabricated metal products, fashion jewellery products and computer and electrical equipment. The total value of manufacturing shipments in 2006 was US $14,175m., of which 55% was added during manufacture.

Domestic travel expenditures in Rhode Island amounted to $1,510m. in 2004, with the state ranked 47th in this respect. Total general expenditures by the state government in 2006 amounted to $6,956m., while general revenue totalled $6,194m., of which $2,028m. was provided by the federal Government and $2,742m. was derived from taxes. Rhode Island received $2,007m. in federal aid in 2006.

CONSTITUTION AND GOVERNMENT

Rhode Island's current Constitution is its second; it was adopted in 1843 and rewritten in 1986. Constitutional amendments proposed by the General Assembly must be passed by a majority of elected members in both houses and ratified by a majority of voters. The Governor, elected separately from the Lieutenant-Governor, serves a four-year term and there is no statutory limit to the number of terms of office he or she may serve. There is no formal cabinet system in Rhode Island. The state General Assembly has 38 senators and 75 representatives, who are re-elected every two years. From 2003 Senate members elected one of their own number to serve as President, replacing the Lieutenant-Governor in this role. Regular legislative sessions take place annually, starting in January and generally lasting until May or June. A bill becomes law when it has been passed by the General Assembly and signed by the Governor. During session a bill also becomes law if it remains unsigned six days after being presented to the Governor for consideration. Outside session a bill becomes law unless vetoed within 10 days after adjournment of the General Assembly. A three-fifths' vote by all members present in each house is required to override a gubernatorial veto. Enacted legislation becomes effective on the following 1 July. The Republican candidate, Donald L. Carcieri, was re-elected in 2006, with 51% of the votes. In the presidential election of 2008 the Democrats secured some 63% of the votes cast. Rhode Island consists of five counties.

Elected Executive Branch Officials

Governor (2007–11): DONALD L. CARCIERI (Rep.).

Lieutenant-Governor: ELIZABETH H. ROBERTS (Dem.).

Secretary of State: A. RALPH MOLLIS (Dem.).

Attorney-General: PATRICK C. LYNCH (Dem.).

General Treasurer: FRANK CAPRIO (Dem.).

Selected Government Addresses

Office of the Governor: State House, Rm 115, Providence, RI 02903-1196; tel. (401) 222-2080; fax (401) 222-8096; internet www.governor.ri.gov.

Office of the Lieutenant-Governor: State House, Rm 116, Providence, RI 02903; tel. (401) 222-2371; fax (401) 222-2012; e-mail ijeng@ltgov.state.ri.us; internet www.ltgov.ri.gov.

Office of the Secretary of State: State House, Rm 217, Providence, RI 02903; tel. (401) 222-2357; fax (401) 222-1356; e-mail comments@sec.state.ri.us; internet www.state.ri.us.

Office of the Attorney-General: 150 South Main St, Providence, RI 02903; tel. (401) 274-4400; fax (401) 222-2725; e-mail mhealey@riag.state.ri.us; internet www.riag.ri.gov.

Office of the General Treasurer: State House, Rm 102, Providence, RI 02903; tel. (401) 222-2397; fax (401) 222-6140; e-mail generaltreasurer@treasury.state.ri.us; internet www.treasury.ri.us.

Department of Corrections: John O. Pastore Government Center, 40 Howard Ave, Cranston, RI 02920; tel. (401) 462-1000; fax (401) 464-2630; e-mail director@doc.ri.gov; internet www.doc.ri.gov; Dir ASHBEL T. WALL, II.

Department of Elementary and Secondary Education: 255 Westminster St, Providence, RI 02903; tel. (401) 222-4600; fax (401) 227-6178; e-mail maureen.dandrea@ride.ro.gov; internet www.ridoe.net; Commr PETER MCWALTERS.

Department of Environmental Management: 235 Promenade St, Providence, RI 02908-5767; tel. (401) 222-6800; fax (401) 222-6802; e-mail rayna.santoro@dem.ri.gov; internet www.dem.ri.gov; Dir Dr W. MICHAEL SULLIVAN.

Department of Health: 3 Capitol Hill, Providence, RI 02908; tel. (401) 222-5960; fax (401) 222-6548; e-mail andrea.bagnell-degos@health.ri.gov; internet www.health.ri.gov; Dir Dr DAVID R. GIFFORD.

Department of Labor and Training: Center General Complex, 1511 Pontiac Ave, Cranston, RI 02920; tel. (401) 462-8000; e-mail mmadonna@dlt.ri.gov; internet www.dlt.ri.gov; Dir SANDRA M. POWELL.

Department of Transportation: 2 Capitol Hill, Providence, RI 02903; tel. (401) 222-2481; fax (401) 222-6038; e-mail franseg@dot.ri.gov; internet www.dot.state.ri.us; Dir MICHAEL P. LEWIS.

Economic Development Corporation: 315 Iron Horse Way, Suite 101, Providence, RI 02908; tel. (401) 278-9100; fax (401) 273-8270; e-mail info@riedc.com; internet www.riedc.com; Exec. Dir SAUL KAPLAN.

Office of the Adjutant-General: 645 New London Ave, Cranston, RI 02920-3097; tel. (401) 275-4100; fax (401) 275-4338; internet www.riguard.com; Adj.-Gen. Maj.-Gen. ROBERT T. BRAY.

Office of the Auditor-General: 86 Weybosset St, Providence, RI 02903-2800; tel. (401) 222-2435; fax (401) 222-2111; e-mail ag@oag.ri.gov; internet www.oag.ri.gov; Auditor-Gen. ERNEST A. ALMONTE.

Public Utilities Commission: 89 Jefferson Blvd, Warwick, RI 02888; tel. (401) 941-4500; fax (401) 941-8827; e-mail mary.kent@ripuc.org; internet www.ripuc.ri.gov; Chair. ELIA GERMANI.

State Police: 311 Danielson Pike, Scituate, RI 02857-1907; tel. (401) 444-1000; fax (401) 444-1105; internet www.risp.state.ri.us; Supt Col BRENDAN P. DOHERTY.

General Assembly
(August 2008)

Senate

Dem. 32; Rep. 5; 1 vacancy; Total 38

President: JOSEPH A. MONTALBANO (Dem.).

President Pro Tempore: JOHN C. REVENS, Jr (Dem.).

Clerk: RAYMOND T. HOYAS, Jr.

House of Representatives

Dem. 61; Rep. 13; Ind. 1; Total 75

Speaker: WILLIAM J. MURPHY (Dem.).

Recording Clerk: LOUIS D'ANTUONO.

South Carolina

Gross Area: 82,902 sq km (32,021 sq miles).

Resident Population (1 July 2007, estimate): 4,407,709

State Capital: Columbia.

Principal Cities (population at 1 July 2006, estimate): Columbia (capital) 119,961; Charleston 107,845.

LOCATION, TOPOGRAPHY AND CLIMATE

The State of South Carolina (nicknamed 'The Palmetto State') is in the South region of the USA and is flanked by North Carolina to the north and Georgia to the south-west. The Atlantic Ocean lies to the south-east. Along the coastline of the state are marshes and numerous islands. The low-lying Atlantic Coastal Plain extends inland for about 160 km (100 miles), with the land rising very gradually towards the undulating Piedmont Plateau in the north-west. In the north-west corner are the Blue Ridge Mountains, part of the Appalachian system, with Sassafras Mountain, at 1,085 m (3,560 ft), the state's highest point. South Carolina's principal rivers are the Pee Dee, flowing from the north-east into Winyah Bay; the Santee, running through the centre of the state; and the Savannah, forming the boundary with Georgia. The state's climate is humid and subtropical.

HISTORICAL BACKGROUND

When the Spanish and French attempted to found settlements in the 16th century, the region was inhabited by the Cherokee, Catawba, Yamasee and Muskogan peoples. The first permanent European settlement was established by the British at Albemarle Point in 1670, moving to the present site of Charleston in 1680. The colonists seized control of government in 1775. The British took Charleston in 1780, but were defeated at King's Mountain in the same year and at Cowpens and Eutaw Springs in 1781. South Carolina became the eighth state to ratify the US Constitution on 23 May 1788. In 1861, when South Carolina became the first state to secede from the Union, more than one-half of the state's population consisted of black slaves. The Civil War's first battle took place at Fort Sumter, Charleston harbour, in that year, when Confederate troops forced the surrender of US troops. South Carolina was readmitted to the Union in 1868.

ECONOMY

Until the end of the Second World War South Carolina's economy was largely dependent upon agriculture and the textile industry. Subsequently, there was greater diversification, with tourism and manufacturing increasing in significance. In 2007 gross domestic product by state totalled US $152,830m. and average per-head income was $31,048, the seventh lowest in the Union. In that year 15.0% of the population were thought to be living below the poverty threshold. The civilian labour force totalled 2,197,400 in mid-2008, while the state's unemployment rate was seven highest in the nation at 7.1% (155,500 persons). In 2007 just 4.1% of employees were union members and 5.9% were covered by union agreements—the third lowest rate of unionization of any state in the USA, after North Carolina and Virginia.

Farmland covered 4.9m. acres (2m. ha) in 2007. In that year there were 24,700 farms, with an average farm covering 196 acres. In 2002 4% of total cropland was irrigated. Livestock and livestock product marketings accounted for 61% of farm income in 2007, with crops making up the remaining 39%. South Carolina's principal farm products in that year were broilers, greenhouse and nursery products, turkeys and cattle and calves. The state also produces cotton (the major crop of the state in the 19th century and the basis of the important textile-mill industry), eggs, milk, soybeans and other field crops. It was ranked fifth for raw tobacco production and eighth for turkeys in 2007. South Carolina had 12.5m. acres of forestland in 2003, covering 61% of the state's land area. Fish landings were valued at US $17.0m. in 2006.

South Carolina's non-fuel mineral production was valued at US $565m. in 2007, with the state ranked 34th in the nation. Leading minerals in that year were cement, crushed stone, and sand and gravel. In 2007 the state was ranked first of the two states that produced vermiculite and fourth for mica production; it was placed second for production of fireclay and third for kaolin and masonry cement in 2003). Gold production ceased in 1999. Altogether, production of cement (masonry and portland), crushed stone and construction sand and gravel accounted for 91% of the state's non-fuel mineral production in 2003.

In terms of its value of shipments, the state ranked 23rd in the nation in 2006. South Carolina's most important manufactures include chemicals and allied products, textile mill products, paper products and industrial machinery and equipment. The total value of manufacturing shipments was US $90,419m. in 2006, of which 42% was added during manufacture.

In 2004 domestic travel expenditures amounted to US $7,764m. Total general expenditures by the state government in 2006 were $23,431m. General revenue totalled $19,436m., of which $6,463m. was provided by the federal Government and $7,760m. was derived from taxes. South Carolina received $5,851m. in federal aid in 2006.

CONSTITUTION AND GOVERNMENT

South Carolina's Constitution, the state's seventh, became effective on 1 January 1896. Amendments to the Constitution proposed by the General Assembly have to be approved by two-thirds of the elected members of each house, and then by a majority of voters, before being returned for consideration at a second session where the approval of a majority of members of each house is required. The Governor is elected separately from the Lieutenant-Governor to serve a four-year term and may serve no more than two terms consecutively. South Carolina is the only state to elect its Adjutant-General. There is no formal cabinet system. The General Assembly has 46 senators and 124 representatives, re-elected every four and two years, respectively. Regular legislative sessions are held annually, starting in January and not extending beyond the first Thursday in June. A bill becomes law after it has been approved by the General Assembly and signed by the Governor. During session the Governor has five days to consider a bill, after which it becomes law unless vetoed. A gubernatorial veto may be overridden by a two-thirds' vote from the members present in both houses. Legislation becomes effective on a date specified in the act itself. In 2006 the Republican candidate, Mark Sanford, was re-elected as Governor with 55% of the vote. In the presidential election of 2008 some 1.9m. people voted. The Republicans secured the largest share of the votes cast, with an estimated 54% of the total. South Carolina has 46 administrative counties.

Elected Executive Branch Officials

Governor (2007–11): MARSHALL C. (MARK) SANFORD (Rep.).

Lieutenant-Governor: R. ANDRÉ BAUER (Rep.).

Secretary of State: MARK HAMMOND (Rep.).

Attorney-General: HENRY MCMASTER (Rep.).

Treasurer: CONVERSE A. CHELLIS, III (Rep.).

Comptroller-General: RICHARD ECKSTROM (Rep.).

Superintendent of Education: JIM REX (Dem.).

Commissioner of Agriculture: HUGH E. WEATHERS (Rep.).

Adjutant-General: Maj.-Gen. STANHOPE S. SPEARS (Rep.).

Selected Government Addresses

Office of the Governor: State House, POB 12267, Columbia, SC 29211; tel. (803) 734-2100; fax (803) 734-5167; internet www.scgovernor.com.

Office of the Lieutenant-Governor: State House, 1st Floor, POB 142, Columbia, SC 29202; tel. (803) 734-2080; fax (803) 734-2082; e-mail ltgov@scsenate.org; internet ltgov.sc.gov.

Office of the Secretary of State: Edgar Brown Bldg, Suite 525, 1205 Pendleton St, POB 11350, Columbia, SC 29211; tel. (803) 734-2157; fax (803) 734-1661; internet www.scsos.com.

Office of the Attorney-General: Rembert C. Dennis Bldg, 1000 Assembly St, Rm 519, POB 11549, Columbia, SC 29211; tel. (803) 734-3970; fax (803) 734-4323; e-mail info@scattorneygeneral.org; internet www.scattorneygeneral.org.

Office of the Treasurer: Wade Hampton Office Bldg, 1200 Senate St, POB 11778, Columbia, SC 29211; tel. (803) 734-2101; fax (803) 734-2690; e-mail treasurer@sto.state.sc.us; internet treasurer.sc.gov.

Office of the Comptroller-General: Wade Hampton Office Bldg, Suite 305, 1200 Senate St, Columbia, SC 29201; tel. (803) 734-2121; fax (803) 734-2064; e-mail cgoffice@cg.sc.gov; internet www.cg.sc.gov.

Department of Agriculture: Wade Hampton Office Bldg, 5th Floor, 1200 Senate St, POB 11280, Columbia, SC 29211; tel. (803) 734-2210; fax (803) 734-2192; internet agriculture.sc.gov; headed by Commr of Agriculture.

Department of Education: Rutledge Bldg, 10th Floor, 1429 Senate St, Columbia, SC 29201; tel. (803) 734-8500; fax (803) 734-3389; e-mail info@ed.sc.gov; internet ed.sc.gov; headed by Supt of Education.

Office of the Adjutant-General: 1 National Guard Rd, Columbia, SC 29201-4766; tel. (803) 806-4200; fax (803) 806-4468; e-mail brookspj@tag.scmd.state.sc.us; internet www.scguard.com.

Budget and Control Board: Wade Hampton Office Bldg, Suite 612, POB 12444, Columbia, SC 29211; tel. (803) 734-2320; fax (803) 734-2117; e-mail msponho@ped.state.sc.us; internet www.bcb.sc.gov; Exec. Dir FRANK FUSCO.

Department of Commerce: 1201 Main St, Suite 1600, Columbia, SC 29201-3200; tel. (803) 737-0400; fax (803) 737-0418; internet www.sccommerce.com; Sec. JOE E. TAYLOR, Jr.

Department of Corrections: 4444 Broad River Rd, POB 21787, Columbia, SC 29221-1787; tel. (803) 896-8500; fax (803) 896-1220; e-mail corrections.info@doc.state.sc.us; internet www.doc.sc.gov; Dir JON OZMINT.

Department of Health and Environmental Control: 2600 Bull St, Columbia, SC 29201; tel. (803) 898-3432; fax (803) 734-4777; e-mail info@dhec.sc.gov; internet www.scdhec.net; Commr C. EARL HUNTER.

Department of Insurance: Capitol Center, 1201 Main St, Suite 1000, POB 100105, Columbia, SC 29202; tel. (803) 737-6160; fax (803) 737-6205; e-mail info@doi.sc.gov; internet www.doi.sc.gov; Dir SCOTT RICHARDSON.

Department of Labor, Licensing and Regulation: Synergy Business Park, Kingstree Bldg, 110 Centerview Dr., POB 11329, Columbia, SC 29211; tel. (803) 896-4390; e-mail contactllr@llr.sc.gov; internet www.llr.state.sc.us; Dir ADRIENNE RIGGINS YOUMANS.

Department of Natural Resources: Rembert C. Dennis Bldg, 1000 Assembly St, Columbia, SC 29201; tel. (803) 734-4007; fax (803) 734-9809; internet www.dnr.sc.gov; Dir JOHN E. FRAMPTON.

Department of Public Safety: 10311 Wilson Blvd, POB 1993, Blythewood, SC 29016; tel. (803) 896-8713; internet www.scdps.org; Dir MARK A. KEEL.

Department of Transportation: 955 Park St, POB 191, Columbia, SC 29202-0191; tel. (803) 737-2314; fax (803) 737-1719; e-mail contact@scdot.org; internet www.scdot.org; Sec. H. B. 'BUCK' LIMEHOUSE, Jr.

Office of the State Auditor: 1401 Main St, Suite 1200, Columbia, SC 29201; tel. (803) 253-4160; fax (803) 343-0723; e-mail stateauditor@osa.state.sc.us; internet osa.sc.gov; Auditor RICHARD H. GILBERT, Jr (interim).

Public Service Commission: 101 Executive Center Dr., Suite 100, Columbia, SC 29210; tel. (803) 896-5100; e-mail contact@psc.sc.gov; internet www.psc.sc.gov; Chair. ELIZABETH B. (LIB) FLEMING.

General Assembly
(August 2008)

Senate

Rep. 27; Dem. 19; Total 46

President: Lt-Gov. R. ANDRÉ BAUER (Rep.).

President Pro Tempore: GLENN F. MCCONNELL (Rep.).

Clerk: JEFFREY S. GOSSETT.

House of Representatives

Rep. 72; Dem. 51; 1 vacancy; Total 124

Speaker: ROBERT W. HARRELL, Jr (Rep.).

Speaker Pro Tempore: W. DOUGLAS SMITH (Rep.).

Clerk: CHARLES F. REID.

South Dakota

Gross Area: 199,744 sq km (77,121 sq miles).

Resident Population (1 July 2007, estimate): 796,214.

State Capital: Pierre (population 14,052 at 1 July 2005).

Principal City: Sioux Falls (population 142,396 at 1 July 2006, estimate).

LOCATION, TOPOGRAPHY AND CLIMATE

The State of South Dakota (nicknamed 'The Coyote State' and 'The Mount Rushmore State') is in the Midwest region of the USA and is bordered by North Dakota to the north, Minnesota and Iowa to the east, Nebraska to the south and Wyoming and Montana to the west. The Missouri River bisects the state from north to south. To the west of the river is the Missouri Plateau, part of the Great Plains, comprising the Black Hills in the south-west and the High Plains in the south. North-west of the High Plains is the Badlands, a bare region with fossil deposits and eroded gullies. South Dakota's highest point is Harney Peak, at 2,207 m (7,242 ft), in the Black Hills. Tributaries of the Missouri flowing through the state include the Grand, Moreau, Cheyenne, Bad and White in the west, and the James, Vermilion and Big Sioux in the east. South Dakota has a continental climate, with hot summers, cold winters, low precipitation and high winds.

HISTORICAL BACKGROUND

When the first Europeans arrived in South Dakota, the region was inhabited by the Hidatsa, Mandan and Arikara tribes. The region was explored in 1742–43 and claimed for France. In 1803 the USA acquired the area in the Louisiana Purchase and the expedition of Meriwether Lewis and William Clark passed through the region in 1804–06. Fur traders and missionaries remained the only European inhabitants of the area until 1874, when the discovery of gold in the Black Hills brought large numbers of prospectors. Dakota Territory (including Wyoming, Montana and North and South Dakota) was formed in 1861 and South Dakota became the 40th state to join the Union on 2 November 1889. The state included nine American Indian (Amerindian) reservations, but made more land available for white settlement. Wars against the Indians culminated in 1890 with the massacre of hundreds of Sioux at Wounded Knee. In 1973 200 Native Americans occupied Wounded Knee for 70 days as a protest against the removal of their land in the Black Hills.

ECONOMY

South Dakota's principal economic activities are agriculture, tourism, manufacturing, services and wholesale and retail trade. In 2007 gross domestic product by state totalled US $33,934m., making it the fourth smallest state economy, and average per-head income was $35,664. In that year 13.1% of the population were registered as living below the poverty line. The civilian labour force totalled 454,700 in mid-2008, while the unemployment rate was 2.8% (12,900 persons), the lowest among all the states. In 2007 6.5% of the work-force held union membership, while 7.7% were covered by union agreements.

Farmland covered 43.7m. acres (18m. ha) in 2007. In that year there were 31,300 farms, with an average farm size of 1,396 acres. In 2002 some 2% of land was irrigated. In 2007 crop sales accounted for 53% of farm marketings, while livestock and livestock products generated the remaining 47%. The principal agricultural commodities produced in that year were cattle and calves, corn, soybeans and wheat. South Dakota ranked fifth in the nation in 2007 for production of wheat, seventh for cattle and calves and eighth for soybeans. Just 3% of the state is covered by forestland.

Non-fuel mineral production in the state was valued at US $227m. in 2007, with the state ranked 40th in this regard nationally. The state's leading minerals were portland cement, construction sand and gravel, crushed stone, granite dimension stone and lime. Fossil-fuel resources in South Dakota are negligible.

South Dakota ranked 44th in 2006 in terms of the value of its shipments. The most important manufacturing industry groups include food-processing, plastics, machinery and computer equipment. Lumber and wood products and printing and publishing, although unimportant on a national scale, also make a significant contribution to state income. In 2006 the total value of the state's manufacturing shipments was US $11,206m., with 48% added during manufacture.

Since 2003 the South Dakotan banking sector has expanded rapidly to become the seventh largest of any state. Total assets of commercial banks were measured at US $499,000m. at the end of 2006.

In 2004 domestic travel expenditures amounted to US $1,663m., one of the lowest levels in the USA. Total general expenditures by the state government in 2006 were $3,465m. and total general revenue amounted to $3,220m., of which $1,236m. was provided by the federal Government and $1,189m. was derived from taxes. In 2006 South Dakota received $1,422m. in federal aid.

CONSTITUTION AND GOVERNMENT

South Dakota's only Constitution became effective on 2 November 1889. An amendment to the Constitution has to be approved by a majority of elected members in each house of the Legislature and ratified by a majority of state voters. The Governor and Lieutenant-Governor are elected jointly to serve a four-year term of office, neither serving more than two consecutive terms. There are 35 senators and 70 representatives in the Legislature, all of whom are re-elected every two years. Regular legislative sessions are held annually, starting in January, and are limited in length to 40 days in odd-numbered years and 35 days in even-numbered years. A bill becomes law when it has been passed by the Legislature and signed by the Governor. During session it also becomes law if it remains unsigned five days after being presented to the Governor. Outside session a bill becomes law unless vetoed within 15 days after adjournment of the Legislature. A gubernatorial veto may be overridden by a two-thirds' vote of the elected members in each house. Enacted legislation becomes effective no sooner than 90 days after adjournment of the session, usually on 1 July. In the 2006 gubernatorial election the Republican candidate, Mike Rounds, was re-elected with some 62% of the votes cast. In the 2008 presidential election the Republicans secured 53% of the votes cast. There are 66 administrative counties in South Dakota.

Elected Executive Branch Officials

Governor (2007–11): MIKE ROUNDS (Rep.).
Lieutenant-Governor: DENNIS DAUGAARD (Rep.).
Secretary of State: CHRIS NELSON (Rep.).
Attorney-General: LARRY LONG (Rep.).
Treasurer: VERNON L. LARSON (Dem.).
Auditor: RICH SATTGAST (Rep.).
Commissioner of School and Public Lands: JARROD JOHNSON (Rep.).

Selected Government Addresses

Office of the Governor: State Capitol, 500 East Capitol Ave, Pierre, SD 57501; tel. (605) 773-3212; fax (605) 773-5844; internet www.state.sd.us/governor.

Office of the Lieutenant-Governor: State Capitol, 500 East Capitol Ave, Pierre, SD 57501; tel. (605) 773-3661; fax (605) 773-4711; e-mail dennis.daugaard@state.sd.us; internet www.state.sd.us/lt.gov.

Office of the Secretary of State: State Capitol, Suite 204, 500 East Capitol Ave, Pierre, SD 57501-5070; tel. (605) 773-3537; fax (605) 773-6580; e-mail sdsos@state.sd.us; internet www.sdsos.gov.

Office of the Attorney-General: 1302 East Hwy 14, Suite 1, Pierre, SD 57501-8501; tel. (605) 773-3215; fax (605) 773-4106; e-mail atghelp@state.sd.us; internet www.state.sd.us/attorney.

Office of the Treasurer: State Capitol, Suite 212, 500 East Capitol Ave, Pierre, SD 57501-5070; tel. (605) 773-3378; fax (605) 773-3115; e-mail vern.larson@state.sd.us; internet www.sdtreasurer.com.

Office of the Auditor: State Capitol, 2nd Floor, 500 East Capitol Ave, Pierre, SD 57501-5070; tel. (605) 773-3341; fax (605) 773-5929; internet www.sdauditor.gov.

School and Public Lands Office: State Capitol, 500 East Capitol Ave, Pierre, SD 57501-5070; tel. (605) 773-3303; fax (605) 773-5520; internet www.sdpubliclands.com; headed by Commr of Schools and Public Lands.

Bureau of Finance and Management: State Capitol, 500 East Capitol Ave, Pierre, SD 57501; tel. (605) 773-3411; fax (605) 773-4711; e-mail bfminfo@state.sd.us; internet www.state.sd.us/bfm; Commr JASON DILGES.

Department of Agriculture: Foss Bldg, 523 East Capitol Ave, Pierre, SD 57501-3182; tel. (605) 773-5436; fax (605) 773-3481; e-mail agmail@state.sd.us; internet www.state.sd.us/doa; Sec. WILLIAM EVEN.

Department of Corrections: Solem Public Safety Center, 3200 East Hwy 34, c/o 500 East Capitol Ave, Pierre, SD 57501; tel. (605) 773-3478; fax (605) 773-3194; internet doc.sd.gov; Sec. TIM REISCH.

Department of Education: 700 Governors Dr., Pierre, SD 57501-2291; tel. (605) 773-3134; fax (605) 773-6139; e-mail rick.melmer@state.sd.us; internet www.doe.sd.gov; Sec. Dr RICK MELMER.

Department of Environment and Natural Resources: Joe Foss Bldg, 523 East Capitol Ave, Pierre, SD 57501; tel. (605) 773-3151; fax (605) 773 6035; e-mail denrinternet@state.sd.us; internet www.state.sd.us/denr/denr.html; Sec. STEVEN M. PIRNER.

Department of Health: 600 East Capitol Ave, Pierre, SD 57501-2536; tel. (605) 773-3361; fax (605) 773-5683; e-mail doh.info@state.sd.us; internet doh.sd.gov; Sec. DONEEN HOLLINGSWORTH.

Department of Labor: 700 Governors Dr., Pierre, SD 57501-2291; tel. (605) 773-3101; fax (605) 773-6184; e-mail dawn.dovre@state.sd.us; internet www.state.sd.us/dol; Sec. PAMELA S. ROBERTS.

Department of Military and Veterans' Affairs: Soldiers and Sailors Memorial Bldg, 425 East Capitol Ave, Pierre, SD 57501-5070; tel. (605) 773-3269; fax (605) 773-5380; e-mail andy.gerlach@state.sd.us; internet mva.sd.gov; Adj.-Gen. Maj.-Gen. STEVEN R. DOOHEN.

Department of Revenue and Regulation: 445 East Capitol Ave, Pierre, SD 57501; tel. (605) 773-3311; fax (605) 773-6729; e-mail feedback@state.sd.us; internet www.state.sd.us/drr2/revenue.html; Sec. PAUL KINSMAN.

Department of Transportation: Becker-Hansen Bldg, 700 East Broadway Ave, Pierre, SD 57501; tel. (605) 773-3265; fax (605) 773-3921; e-mail shirleen.fuggitt@state.sd.us; internet www.sddot.com; Sec. DARIN BERGQUIST.

Public Utilities Commission: State Capitol, 1st Floor, 500 East Capitol Ave, Pierre, SD 57501-5070; tel. (605) 733-3201; fax (605) 773-3809; e-mail dustin.johnson@state.sd.us; internet puc.sd.gov; Chair. GARY HANSON.

Legislature
(August 2008)

Senate

Rep. 20; Dem. 15; Total 35

President: Lt-Gov. DENNIS DAUGAARD (Rep.).
President Pro Tempore: BOB GRAY (Rep.).
Secretary: TRUDY EVENSTAD.

House of Representatives

Rep. 50; Dem. 20; Total 70
Speaker: THOMAS J. DEADRICK (Rep.).
Speaker Pro Tempore: TIM RAVE (Rep.).
Chief Clerk: KAREN GERDES.

Tennessee

Gross Area: 109,158 sq km (42,146 sq miles).
Resident Population (1 July 2007, estimate): 6,156,719.
State Capital: Nashville.
Principal Cities (population at 1 July 2006, estimate): Memphis 670,902; Nashville (capital) 552,120; Knoxville 182,337; Chattanooga 155,190; Clarksville 113,175.

LOCATION, TOPOGRAPHY AND CLIMATE

The State of Tennessee (nicknamed 'The Volunteer State') lies in the South region of the USA and is bordered by Kentucky and Virginia to the north, North Carolina to the east, Georgia, Alabama and Mississippi to the south, and Arkansas and Missouri to the west. Western Tennessee lies in the Gulf Coastal Plain and has fertile land sloping down towards the low-lying Mississippi Flood Plains. In the centre of the state is the rolling land of the Central Basin, encircled by the Highland Rim. The Cumberland Plateau covers much of east-central Tennessee and includes the Cumberland Mountains in the north. The Unaka Mountains, in the extreme east of the state, are part of the Appalachian system. The state's highest point is Clingman's Dome in the Great Smoky Mountains, at 2,025 m (6,643 ft). Tennessee's main rivers are the Mississippi, which forms the western border; the Tennessee, which flows southwards through the Great Valley, separating the Cumberland Plateau from the Unaka Mountains, into Alabama and then back into Tennessee on its way northwards to Kentucky; and the Cumberland, which enters from Kentucky, and then curves across northern Tennessee before flowing back into Kentucky. Tennessee's climate is generally temperate, with warm summers and mild winters. Summers are humid in the west and winters are severe in the mountainous east.

HISTORICAL BACKGROUND

Creek, Yuchi, Cherokee, Chickasaw and Shawnee Native Americans (Amerindians) inhabited the region now known as Tennessee when Hernando de Soto, a Spaniard, explored the area in 1540. In 1790 the region was given territorial status by the newly independent USA, as the Southwest Territory, and on 1 June 1796 it was admitted to the Union as the 16th state. The state opted for the Confederacy in 1861 and was a major theatre of battle during the Civil War. Fort Donelson and Fort Henry were taken by the Union in 1862, while in 1863 Confederate troops routed Union forces in the Battle of Chickamauga. In 1864 a Confederate General, John Hood, received a crushing defeat at Nashville. An important development of the 20th century was the creation of the Tennessee Valley Authority in 1933, which, through building dams and generating electricity, sought to make the state attractive to industry. In 1968 the civil rights leader Dr Martin Luther King, Jr, was assassinated in the city of Memphis.

ECONOMY

Manufacturing, wholesale and retail trade, services and finance, insurance and real estate are the most important components of Tennessee's gross state product, while agriculture and tourism are also valuable economic activities. In 2007 gross domestic product by state totalled US $243,869m., while the state's average per-head income was measured at $33,373. It was estimated that 15.9% of the population were living below the poverty line at that time. The civilian labour force numbered 3,081,100 in mid-2008, and the unemployment rate was 7.0% (214,200 persons). In 2007 some 5.3% of those employed belonged to a trade union, while 6.4% were covered by union agreements—among some of the lowest rates nationally.

Farmland covered 11.4m. acres (4.6m. ha) in 2007. There were 79,000 farms in that year, with the average farm covering an area of 144 acres. In 2002 0.8% of total cropland was irrigated. Some 49% of farm income was generated by crops in 2007, with livestock and livestock products accounting for 51%. The principal agricultural commodities, in terms of value, were cattle and calves, broilers, cotton and greenhouse and nursery products. Also important were corn, dairy products, soybeans, tobacco, hay, hogs, wheat, tomatoes and chicken eggs. The state was ranked third for raw tobacco production in 2007. Forestland covered around 14.4m. acres of the state in 2003 (some 53% of the total land area), with the majority being commercial timberland. Timber-based manufacturing (including lumber and wood products, furniture and fixtures, and paper and allied products) is important to the state economy.

In 2007 Tennessee's non-fuel mineral production was valued at US $842m., with the state ranked 27th in this respect. Crushed stone is an important mineral, accounting for over half of total state production, while the state was ranked first for gemstones in 2007. Of the two states producing cadmium in 2007, Tennessee led production. The state ranked third for zinc in 2003, although facility closures since then have significantly reduced output. Portland cement and construction sand and gravel production were also significant. Tennessee is a minor coal producing state and also ranked eighth in the nation in the production of primary aluminium in 2003.

In terms of its value of shipments, the state ranked 12th in the USA in 2006. Principal manufactures include chemicals and allied products, transportation equipment, food and kindred products, and rubber and plastic products. Other important manufacturing groups are fabricated metal products, industrial machinery and equipment, printing and publishing and lumber products. In 2006 the total value of Tennessee's manufacturing shipments was US $141,286m., of which some 44% was added during manufacture.

Domestic travel expenditures amounted to US $11,164m. in 2004, when Tennessee ranked 14th in the USA in terms of money spent. Total general expenditures by the state government in 2006 amounted to $23,968m.; general revenue totalled $23,644m., with federal Government contributing $8,024m. and taxes providing $10,650m. Tennessee received $8,169m. in federal aid in 2006.

CONSTITUTION AND GOVERNMENT

The current Constitution of Tennessee is the state's third and became effective on 23 February 1870. Constitutional amendments proposed by the General Assembly have to be approved first by a majority and then by two-thirds of the members elected to both houses, followed by ratification by a majority of all those voting for the Governor at election. The Governor of Tennessee (the only elected executive branch official) serves a four-year term of office and may serve no more than two terms consecutively. The Speaker of the Senate, who has the statutory title of Lieutenant-Governor, succeeds in the absence of the Governor. The 33 senators and 99 representatives in the state General Assembly are elected to serve four- and two-year terms, respectively, with alternate halves of the Senate being re-elected every two years. Statutory provision is made for regular sessions to be held in odd-numbered years only, beginning in January, but in practice sessions are also held in even-numbered years. Regular sessions are limited in length to 90 days. A bill becomes law when it has been read and passed three times in each house and has been signed by the Governor; during session it also becomes law unless vetoed within 10 days of presentation to the Governor. After session a bill becomes law unless vetoed within 10 days from adjournment of the General Assembly. A majority vote by the elected members in each house is required to override a gubernatorial veto. Legislation becomes effective 40 days after enactment. The Democratic candidate, Phil Bredesen, was re-elected in the gubernatorial election of 2006, with 69% of the votes cast. The Republicans secured 57% of the votes cast in the presidential election in 2008. There are 95 administrative counties in Tennessee.

Elected Executive Branch Official

Governor (2007–11): PHIL BREDESEN (Dem.).

Selected Government Addresses

Office of the Governor: State Capitol Bldg, Nashville, TN 37243-0001; tel. (615) 741-2001; fax (615) 532-9711; e-mail phil.bredesen@state.tn.us; internet www.tennesseeanytime.org/governor.

Department of Agriculture: Ellington Agriculture Center, POB 40627, Melrose Station, Nashville, TN 37204; tel. (615) 857-5103; fax (615) 857-5333; e-mail tn.agriculture@state.tn.us; internet state.tn.us/agriculture; Commr KEN GIVENS.

Department of Commerce and Insurance: Davy Crockett Tower, 500 James Robertson Pkwy, Nashville, TN 37243-0565; tel. (615) 741-2241; fax (615) 532-8079; e-mail christopher.garrett@state.tn.us; internet state.tn.us/commerce; Commr LESLIE A. NEWMAN.

Department of Correction: Rachel Jackson Bldg, 6th Floor, 320 Sixth Ave North, Nashville, TN 37243-0465; tel. (615) 741-1000; fax (615) 532-8281; e-mail tdoc.webmaster@state.tn.us; internet www.state.tn.us/correction; Commr GEORGE LITTLE.

Department of Economic and Community Development: 312 Rosa L. Parks Ave, 11th Floor, Nashville, TN 37243; tel. (615) 741-1888; fax (615) 741-7306; e-mail matt.kisber@state.tn.us; internet state.tn.us/ecd; Commr MATTHEW KISBER.

Department of Education: Andrew Johnson Tower, 6th Floor, 710 James Robertson Pkwy, Nashville, TN 37243-0375; tel. (615) 741-2731; fax (615) 741-6236; e-mail education.comments@state.tn.us; internet state.tn.us/education; Commr Dr TIMOTHY K. WEBB.

Department of the Environment and Conservation: Life and Casualty Annex, 1st Floor, 401 Church St, Nashville, TN 37243; tel. (615) 532-0109; fax (615) 532-0120; e-mail ask.tdec@state.tn.us; internet state.tn.us/environment; Commr JIM FYKE.

Department of Finance and Administration: State Capitol, Nashville, TN 37243-0285; tel. (615) 741-2401; fax (615) 741-9872; e-mail lola.potter@state.tn.us; internet state.tn.us/finance; Commr DAVE GOETZ.

Department of Health: Cordell Hull Bldg, 3rd Floor, 425 Fifth Ave North, Nashville, TN 37247; tel. (615) 741-3111; fax (615) 741-2491; e-mail tn.health@state.tn.us; internet health.state.tn.us; Commr SUSAN R. COOPER.

Department of Labor and Workforce Development: 220 French Landing Dr., Nashville, TN 37248-0655; tel. (615) 741-6642; fax (615) 741-5078; e-mail james.neeley@tn.gov; internet state.tn.us/labor-wfd; Commr JAMES NEELEY.

Department of the Military: Houston Barracks, 3041 Sidco Dr., POB 41502, Nashville, TN 37204-1502; tel. (615) 313-3001; fax (615) 313-3100; internet www.tnmilitary.org; Adj.-Gen. Maj.-Gen. GUS L. HARGETT, Jr.

Department of Revenue: Andrew Jackson Bldg, Rm 1200, 500 Deaderick St, Nashville, TN 37242-1099; tel. (615) 741-2461; e-mail sophie.moery@state.tn.us; internet state.tn.us/revenue; Commr REAGAN FARR.

Department of Safety: 1150 Foster Ave, Nashville, TN 37243; tel. (615) 251-5166; e-mail email.safety@state.tn.us; internet state.tn.us/safety; Commr DAVID MITCHELL.

Department of Transportation: James K. Polk Bldg, Suite 700, 505 Deaderick St, Nashville, TN 37243-0349; tel. (615) 741-2848; fax (615) 741-2508; e-mail tdot.comments@state.tn.us; internet www.tdot.state.tn.us; Commr GERALD F. NICELY.

Office of the Attorney-General: POB 20207, Nashville, TN 37202-0207; tel. (615) 741-3491; internet www.attorneygeneral.state.tn.us; Attorney-Gen. ROBERT E. COOPER, Jr.

Office of the Comptroller: State Capitol, 1st Floor, Nashville, TN 37243; tel. (615) 741-2501; fax (615) 741-7328; e-mail comptroller.web@state.tn.us; internet www.comptroller.state.tn.us; Comptroller JOHN G. MORGAN.

Office of the Secretary of State: William R. Snodgrass Tower, 8th Floor, 312 Eighth Ave North, Nashville, TN 37243; tel. (615) 741-2819; e-mail sos.information@state.tn.us; internet state.tn.us/sos; Sec. of State RILEY C. DARNELL.

Office of the Treasurer: State Capitol, 1st Floor, Nashville, TN 37243; tel. (615) 741-2956; fax (615) 532-8725; e-mail treasury.webmaster@state.tn.us; internet www.treasury.state.tn.us; Treas. DALE SIMS.

Tennessee Regulatory Authority: 460 James Robertson Pkwy, Nashville, TN 37243-0505; tel. (615) 741-84648; internet state.tn.us/tra; Chair. TRE HARGETT.

General Assembly
(August 2008)

Senate

Rep. 16; Dem. 16; Ind. 1; Total 33

Speaker: Lt-Gov. RON RAMSEY (Rep.).

Speaker Pro Tempore: ROSALIND KURITA (Rep.).

Chief Clerk: RUSSELL HUMPHREY.

House of Representatives

Dem. 53; Rep. 46; Total 99

Speaker: JAMES O. NAIFEH (Dem.).

Speaker Pro Tempore: LOIS M. DEBERRY (Dem.).

Chief Clerk: BURNEY DURHAM.

Texas

Gross Area: 695,676 sq km (268,705 sq miles).

Resident Population (1 July 2007, estimate): 23,904,380.

State Capital: Austin.

Principal Towns and Cities: (population at 1 July 2006, estimate)

Houston	2,144,491	Garland	217,963
San Antonio	1,296,682	Laredo	215,484
Dallas	1,232,940	Lubbock	212,169
Austin (capital)	709,893	Irving	196,084
Fort Worth	653,320	Amarillo	185,525
El Paso	609,415	Brownsville	172,437
Arlington	367,197	Grand Prairie	153,812
Corpus Christi	285,267	Pasadena	144,793
Plano	255,009	Mesquite	131,447

LOCATION, TOPOGRAPHY AND CLIMATE

The State of Texas (nicknamed 'The Lone Star State') lies in the South region of the USA and is the largest of the conterminous states of the USA. It is bordered by New Mexico to the north-west, Oklahoma to the north, Arkansas to the north-east and Louisiana to the east. The Gulf of Mexico lies to the south-east, while the Mexican states of Tamaulipas, Nuevo León, Coahuila and Chihuahua lie beyond the international border (the Rio Grande) in the south-west. Between the Pecos and Rio Grande rivers in the west of Texas is the mountainous trans-Pecos region, including the highest point in Texas, Guadalupe Peak, at 2,667 m (8,751 ft), near the New Mexico border. The Great Plains extend into the north from Edward's Plateau in west-central Texas, separated from the North Central Plains by Cap Rock Escarpment. The North Central Plains largely consist of rolling prairie, but also include the Burnet-Llano Basin and Hill Country. Dividing the North Central Plains from the eastern Coastal and southern Rio Grande Plains is the Balcones Escarpment, which stretches across central Texas. The Gulf Coastal Plain in the east consists of the north-eastern Piney Woods, the flat Post Oak Belt and the undulating prairie of the Blackland Belt towards central Texas. The state's main rivers include: the Rio Grande, forming the south-western boundary with Mexico; the Colorado (which is to be distinguished from the longer river of the same name that flows through the western USA), traversing central Texas on its way to the Gulf of Mexico; the Red, forming part of the northern border; the Canadian, flowing from New Mexico to Oklahoma through the north; and the Sabine, forming part of the eastern boundary. Texas has an extremely varied climate, owing to its size. Generally, the Gulf Coast region has a maritime climate with heavy precipitation in the north-east; the interior of the state has a continental climate, semi-arid in the trans-Pecos region.

HISTORICAL BACKGROUND

Native Americans belonging to the Coahuiltecan, Karankawa, Tonkawa, Caddo and Jumano tribes inhabited Texas when the Spanish explorer, Alonso Alvarez de Piñeda, entered the region in 1519. Cabeza de Vaca and Coronado visited the interior in 1541. The Spanish established the first settlement at Ysleta in 1682. The construction of Fort St Louis by the French in 1685 spurred the Spanish into setting up mission-forts in the area, including San Antonio de Bexar in 1718, near present-day San Antonio. After Mexico, of which Texas was a part, became independent from Spain in 1821, the region began to be settled by the USA and, by 1835, those of US origin outnumbered Mexicans by four to one. The Mexican presidency of Antonio López de Santa Anna provoked revolt in Texas from 1835 and resulted in eventual Mexican defeat at San Jacinto in 1836. Independence was proclaimed the same year and the region existed as an independent republic for 10 years with Sam Houston as president. Controversy over Texas's slave-owning status delayed its admission to the Union until 29 December 1845, when it became the 28th state to accede. This annexation led to the USA's Mexican War of 1846–48. Texas fought for the Confederacy during the Civil War; the last battle of that conflict was fought in Texas at Palmito Ranch, near Brownsville, in 1865. Important developments in the early 20th century included the growth of the cattle and petroleum industries. President John F. Kennedy was assassinated in the city of Dallas in 1963. The Republican Governor of Texas from 1995, George W. Bush, was elected to the presidency in 2000 and re-elected in 2004.

ECONOMY

From the 1970s the economy of Texas has relied largely upon the state's petroleum and natural-gas resources. Other important contributors to the gross product include manufacturing, mining, services, wholesale and retail trade and agriculture. The aerospace and high technology sectors have grown in importance in recent years. Gross domestic product by state totalled US $1,141,965m. in 2007—only California enjoyed a higher level.

In 2007 the state's average per-head income was US $37,006. However, it was estimated that 16.3% of the state population were living below the poverty threshold, giving Texas the ninth highest poverty rate among all the states. The civilian labour force totalled 11,809,200 in mid-2008, while the unemployment rate was 5.0% (594,000 persons). Of the total number of employees in 2007, 4.7% were union members and 5.7% were covered by union agreements. Texas is the fifth least-unionized state in the USA.

In 2007 farmland covered 129.5m. acres (52.4m. ha). There were 229,000 farms in that year, with the average farm covering an area of 566 acres. Irrigation is essential in parts of the state; in 2002 12% of total cropland was irrigated. In 2007 60% of farm income was derived from livestock and livestock products and 40% from crops. Texas ranked second, after California, in terms of total farm income: its leading commodities were cattle and calves, cotton, greenhouse and nursery products and dairy products, but many other products were also cultivated. In 2007 Texas led the nation in the production of livestock products (specifically cattle and calves) and cotton and was ranked second for hay (after California) and third for greenhouse and nursery products, onions and oranges. Texas was also a significant producer of eggs and milk.

Forestland covered 17.1m. acres of the state in 2003—some 10% of the total land area. Repeated infestations by pine bark beetle and a high incidence of forest fires caused massive destruction of the state's forests in the 1970s and 1980s. Production of timber (mostly softwoods) remains an important economic activity. Texas's commercial fish catch reached a value of US $197m. in 2006.

Texas is a major mineral-producing state, with non-fuel mineral production valued at US $2,900m. in 2007, putting the state in seventh place nation-wide. The leading minerals in that year were portland cement (for which the state ranked second in the USA in 2007), crushed stone (ranked first), sand and gravel (ranked second), lime (ranked seventh) and salt (ranked second in 2007). Together, these minerals accounted for some 93% of total state production in 2003. In terms of metals, the state produces copper, primary aluminium and raw steel. It is also a significant producer of grade-A helium, clay, gypsum, talc, zeolites and sulphur, and was one of only two states producing sodium sulphate in 2007. Texas is the nation's largest producer of natural gas and crude petroleum, providing 28% of national natural gas output and 21% of oil output in 2005, in volume terms. It ranked sixth for coal production in 2007, with output of an estimated 42.0m. short tons.

Texas ranked first in the USA in 2006 in terms of value of shipments. Leading manufacturing sectors include chemicals and allied products, petroleum and coal, food and kindred products, industrial machinery and equipment, plastics, fabricated metal products, computers and transportation equipment. The total value of Texas' manufacturing shipments in 2006 was US $527,622m., of which 37% was added during manufacture.

Texas is an important domestic and international tourism centre. In 2004 domestic travel expenditures amounted to US $33,818m., and the state ranked third nationally in terms of money spent.

Total general expenditures by the state government in 2006 were US $85,514m. General revenue totalled $83,471m., of which $27,814m. was provided by the federal Government and $36,592m. was derived from taxes. Texas received $29,327m. in federal aid in 2006.

CONSTITUTION AND GOVERNMENT

The current Constitution of Texas, the state's fifth, became effective on 15 February 1876. A constitutional amendment proposed by the bicameral Legislature requires the approval of two-thirds of the elected members of each house, followed by ratification by a majority of state voters. The Governor is elected separately from the Lieutenant-Governor and serves a four-year term of office. There is no formal cabinet system. The Legislature has 31 senators and 150 representatives, elected to serve terms of four and two years, respectively; alternate halves of the Senate are re-elected every two years. Regular sessions of the Legislature are held every two years, beginning in January in odd-numbered years, and are limited in length to 140 days. A bill becomes law once it has been approved by a majority of the elected members present in each house (which must be equal to at least two-thirds of the entire membership of each house) and has either been signed by the Governor or, during session, left unsigned 10 days after being presented to the Governor. Outside session a bill becomes law if it remains unsigned for 20 days from adjournment of the session. A gubernatorial veto can be overridden by two-thirds of the elected members present in each house. Enacted legislation becomes effective 90 days after the Legislature's adjournment. In the gubernatorial election of 2006 the Republican Governor, Rick Perry, was re-elected, although securing just 39% of votes cast. In the 2008 presidential election the Republicans again collected the majority vote in the state with 56% of the total votes cast. Texas has 254 administrative counties.

Elected Executive Branch Officials

Governor (2007–11): RICK PERRY (Rep.).

Lieutenant-Governor: DAVID DEWHURST (Rep.).

Attorney-General: GREG ABBOTT (Rep.).

Comptroller of Public Accounts: SUSAN COMBS (Rep.).

Commissioner of General Land Office: JERRY PATTERSON (Rep.).

Selected Government Addresses

Office of the Governor: State Capitol, POB 12428, Austin, TX 78711-2428; tel. (512) 463-2000; fax (512) 463-1849; internet www.governor.state.tx.us.

Office of the Lieutenant-Governor: State Capitol, POB 12068, Austin, TX 78711-2068; tel. (512) 463-0001; fax (512) 463-0677; internet www.ltgov.state.tx.us.

Office of the Attorney-General: 300 West 15th St, POB 12548, Austin, TX 78711-2548; tel. (512) 463-2007; e-mail public.information@oag.state.tx.us; internet www.oag.state.tx.us.

Office of the Comptroller of Public Accounts: Lyndon B. Johnson Bldg, 111 East 17th St, POB 13528, Austin, TX 78711-3528; tel. (512) 463-4000; fax (512) 475-0352; e-mail comptroller.help@cpa.state.tx.us; internet www.window.state.tx.us.

General Land Office: 1700 North Congress Ave, Suite 935, Austin, TX 78701-1495; tel. (512) 463-5001; fax (512) 475-1558; e-mail jerry.patterson@glo.state.tx.us; internet www.glo.state.tx.us; headed by the Commr of the General Land Office.

Commission on Environmental Quality: 12100 Park 35 Circle, POB 13087, Austin, TX 78711-3087; tel. (512) 239-3900; fax (512) 239-3939; e-mail ac@tceq.state.tx.us; internet www.tceq.state.tx.us; Exec. Dir MARK R. VICKERY.

Department of the Adjutant-General: 2200 West 35th St, POB 5218, Austin, TX 78763-5218; tel. (512) 782-5001; fax (512) 782-5578; e-mail paotx@tx.ngb.army.mil; internet www.agd.state.tx.us; Adj.-Gen. Maj.-Gen. CHARLES G. RODRIGUEZ, III.

Department of Agriculture: Stephen F. Austin Bldg, 11th Floor, 1700 North Congress Ave, POB 12847, Austin, TX 78711-2847; tel. (512) 463-7476; e-mail pub.info@agr.state.tx.us; internet www.agr.state.tx.us; Commr TODD STAPLES.

Department of Criminal Justice: Price Daniel Bldg, 5th Floor, 209 West 14th St, POB 13084, Austin, TX 78711-3084; tel. (512) 463-9988; e-mail questions@tdcj.state.tx.us; internet www.tdcj.state.tx.us; Exec. Dir BRAD LIVINGSTON.

Department of Insurance: 333 Guadalupe St, POB 149104, Austin, TX 78714-9104; tel. (512) 463-6169; fax (512) 475-2005; e-mail pio@tdi.state.tx.us; internet www.tdi.state.tx.us; Commr MIKE GEESLIN.

Department of Public Safety: 5805 North Lamar Blvd, POB 4087, Austin, TX 78773-0001; tel. (512) 424-2000; fax (512) 483-5708; e-mail pio@txdps.state.tx.us; internet www.txdps.state.tx.us; Dir Col THOMAS A. DAVIS, Jr.

Department of State Health Services: 1100 West 49th St, Austin, TX 78756-3199; tel. (512) 458-7111; e-mail @web.masterdshs.state.tx.us; internet www.dshs.state.tx.us; Commr Dr DAVID L. LAKEY.

Department of Transportation: 125 East 11th St, Austin, TX 78701-2483; tel. (512) 305-9500; fax (512) 463-0283; internet www.dot.state.tx.us; Exec. Dir AMADEO SAENZ, Jr.

Education Agency: William Travis Bldg, 1701 North Congress Ave, Austin, TX 78701; tel. (512) 463-9734; fax (512) 463-9838; internet www.tea.state.tx.us; Commr ROBERT SCOTT.

Finance Commission: 2601 North Lamar Blvd, Austin, TX 78705-4294; tel. (512) 936-7640; fax (512) 936-7610; e-mail finance.commission@occc.state.tx.us; internet www.fc.state.tx.us; Exec. Dir LESLIE L. PETTIJOHN.

Office of the Auditor: Robert E. Johnson Sr Bldg, 1501 North Congress Ave, POB 12067, Austin, TX 78711-2067; tel. (512) 936-9500; fax (512) 936-9400; e-mail auditor@sao.state.tx.us; internet www.sao.state.tx.us; State Auditor JOHN KEEL.

Office of the Secretary of State: State Capitol, Suite 1E.8, POB 12887, Austin, TX 78711-2887; tel. (512) 463-9981; fax (512) 475-2761; e-mail secretary@sos.state.tx.us; internet www.sos.state.tx.us; Sec. of State ESPERANZA (HOPE) ANDRADE.

Public Utility Commission: 1701 North Congress Ave, POB 13326, Austin, TX 78711-3326; tel. (512) 936-7000; fax (512) 936-7003; e-mail customer@puc.state.tx.us; internet www.puc.state.tx.us; Chair. BARRY T. SMITHERMAN.

Legislature
(August 2008)

Senate

Rep. 20; Dem. 11; Total 31

President: Lt-Gov. DAVID DEWHURST (Rep.).

President Pro Tempore: MARIO GALLEGOS, Jr (Dem.).

Secretary: PATSY SPAW.

House of Representatives

Rep. 79; Dem. 71; Total 150

Speaker: TOM CRADDICK (Rep.).

Speaker Pro Tempore: SYLVESTER TURNER (Dem.).

Chief Clerk: ROBERT HANEY.

Utah

Gross Area: 219,902 sq km (84,904 sq miles).

Resident Population (1 July 2007, estimate): 2,645,330.

State Capital: Salt Lake City.

Principal Cities: (population at 1 July 2006, estimate) Salt Lake City (capital) 178,858; Provo 113,984; West Valley City 119,841.

LOCATION, TOPOGRAPHY AND CLIMATE

The State of Utah (nicknamed 'The Beehive State') is in the West region of the USA, bordered by Idaho and Wyoming to the north, Colorado to the east, Arizona to the south and Nevada to the west. In the south and east of Utah is the Colorado plateau, cut by numerous canyons, including the Glen Canyon, which is formed by the Colorado River. To the north are the Rocky Mountain ranges of Uinta and Wasatch: King's Peak, at 4,123 m (13,528 ft), is the state's highest point, and is found near the Wyoming border in the Uintas. Western Utah is dominated by the Great Basin. In the north-west the Great Salt Lake and the Great Salt Lake Desert are the remains of a prehistoric sea. The area of the Great Salt Lake varies greatly with weather cycles—it averages a length of 70 miles and a width of 30 miles. The largest body of fresh water in the state is Utah Lake (363 sq km—140 sq miles). Utah's principal rivers are the Colorado; the Green, which flows from the north into the Colorado; and the Sevier, running through central and southern Utah. Utah's climate is generally arid, with the highest temperatures occurring in the south-west. The eastern, mountainous region is cooler, with greater precipitation.

HISTORICAL BACKGROUND

The Ute, Goshute, Southern Paiute and Navaho peoples inhabited the region when the first Spanish and Mexican traders arrived in the mid-18th century. Fur traders from the USA followed. The arrival of the Mormons (Church of Jesus Christ of Latter-day Saints) and their leader, Brigham Young, in the Great Basin area in 1847 was the beginning of permanent settlement. The region was formally annexed to the USA as a result of the Treaty of Guadalupe-Hidalgo in 1848, and was granted territorial status in 1850. From the 1850s Utah's non-Mormon population increased as miners came to the region to extract ore deposits in the south-west. The Walker War of 1853–54 and the Black Hawk War of 1865–68 resulted in the removal of the majority of the native peoples of Utah to reservations. Utah's entry into the Union was delayed by a long period of controversy over the practice of polygamy, with the Mormons, who dominated the political scene, defending the practice. Polygamy was renounced in 1890 and on 4 January 1896 Utah joined the Union as the 45th state. The 19th Winter Olympics were held in Salt Lake City in February 2002.

ECONOMY

Manufacturing, services, government, utilities, transportation and wholesale and retail trade are significant industries in Utah. The high technology, aerospace and mining industries also make important contributions to the state economy. In 2007 gross domestic product by state totalled US $105,658m. and the state's per-head income averaged $30,090—the third lowest in the USA. In 2007 9.7% of the population were thought to be living below the poverty line. The civilian labour force totalled 1,395,700 in mid-2008 and the unemployment rate was 3.6% (50,300 persons), the fifth lowest level (alongside Idaho and Nebraska) among the states. In 2007 5.8% of those employed were union members, the seventh lowest percentage of any state in the USA, and union agreements covered 6.8%.

Farmland covered 11.6m. acres (4.8m. ha) in 2007. In that year there were 15,000 farms, with the average farm covering an area of 773 acres. In 2002 37.7% of total cropland was irrigated. Some 71% of farm income was generated by sales of livestock and livestock products in 2007, and 29% by crop sales. The principal agricultural commodities were dairy products, cattle and calves, hay and hogs. Greenhouse and nursery products, chicken eggs, sheep and lambs, corn, barley and cherries were also important. Some 29% of Utah was forested in 2003, and there is some lumbering activity (all softwoods).

Utah's non-fuel mineral production was valued at US $3,940m. in 2007, with the state ranked fourth nation-wide. Metals accounted for almost 60% of the state's total in 2003, with copper—for which the state was ranked second nation-wide in 2007—the principal mineral. Utah was the only state to produce magnesium metal and beryllium concentrates. In addition to copper, it ranked third for potash, and fourth for phosphate rock in that year; the state ranked third for gold and molybdenum concentrates and fourth for silver in 2003. Portland cement, salt, construction sand and gravel and lime were also important. Some petroleum and natural gas are produced (Utah ranked 10th for natural gas production among the states in 2005), while coal output reached 24.3m. short tons in 2007 (ranking the state 13th).

Utah ranked 35th in the USA in 2006 in terms of its value of manufacturing shipments. Leading manufactures included transportation equipment, primary and fabricated metals, food and kindred products, petroleum products, machinery and electrical equipment and computers. Utah has become a leader in the high technology sector. In 2006 the total value of Utah's manufacturing shipments was US $36,440m., with 46% added during manufacture.

Domestic travel expenditures amounted to US $4,030m. in 2004. Total general expenditures by the state government in 2006 were $12,045m.; general revenue totalled $11,789m., of which $3,157m. was provided by the federal Government and $5,462m. was derived from taxes. Utah received $2,774m. in federal aid in 2006.

CONSTITUTION AND GOVERNMENT

Utah's only state Constitution became effective on 4 January 1896. Amendments to the Constitution proposed by the Legislature must be passed by two-thirds of the elected members of each house and ratified by a majority of state voters. The Governor and Lieutenant-Governor are jointly elected to serve a four-year term and there is no limit to the number of times they may hold office. The 29 senators and 75 representatives in the Legislature are re-elected every four and two years, respectively, alternate halves of the Senate being re-elected every two years. Regular legislative sessions are held annually in January and are limited in length to 45 days. A bill becomes law when it has been passed by the Legislature and signed by the Governor. During session the Governor has 10 days in which to consider a bill, after which it becomes law unless vetoed. Outside session a bill becomes law unless vetoed within 20 days from adjournment of the Legislature. A gubernatorial veto may be overridden by a two-thirds' vote of the elected members of each house. Enacted legislation becomes effective 60 days after adjournment. In the gubernatorial election of 2008 the Republican incumbent, Jon Huntsman, secured 78% of votes cast. In the presidential election of the same year an estimated 63% of the votes cast were for the Republicans. There are 29 administrative counties in Utah.

Elected Executive Branch Officials

Governor (2009–13): JON HUNTSMAN, Jr (Rep.).

Lieutenant-Governor: GARY R. HERBERT (Rep.).

Attorney-General: MARK SHURTLEFF (Rep.).

Treasurer: EDWARD T. ALTER (Rep.).

Auditor: AUSTON G. JOHNSON (Rep.).

Selected Government Addresses

Office of the Governor: State Capitol Complex, East Office Bldg, Suite E220, Salt Lake City, UT 84114-2220; tel. (801) 538-1000; fax (801) 538-1528; internet www.utah.gov/governor.

Office of the Lieutenant-Governor: State Capitol Complex, 350 North State St, Suite 220, POB 142220, Salt Lake City, UT 84114-2220; tel. (801) 538-1041; fax (801) 538-1133; e-mail gherbert@utah.gov; internet lt.utah.gov.

Office of the Attorney-General: State Capitol Complex, 350 North State, Suite 320, POB 142320, Salt Lake City, UT 84114-2320; tel. (801) 538-9600; fax (801) 538-1121; e-mail uag@utah.gov; internet attorneygeneral.utah.gov.

Office of the Treasurer: State Capitol Complex, East Office Bldg, Suite 180, 350 North State St, POB 142315, Salt Lake City, UT 84114-2315; tel. (801) 538-1042; fax (801) 538-1465; e-mail kimoliver@utah.gov; internet www.treasurer.state.ut.us.

Office of the Auditor: 211 State Capitol Complex, East Office Bldg, Suite E310, POB 142310, Salt Lake City, UT 84114-2310; tel. (801) 538-1025; fax (801) 538-1383; e-mail austonjohnson@utah.gov; internet www.sao.state.ut.us.

Department of Agriculture and Food: 350 North Redwood Rd, POB 146500, Salt Lake City, UT 84114-6500; tel. (801) 538-7100; fax (801) 538-7126; e-mail udaf-information@utah.gov; internet ag.utah.gov; Commr LEONARD BLACKHAM.

Department of Commerce: Heber Wells Bldg, 160 East 300 South, POB 146701, Salt Lake City, UT 84114-6701; tel. (801) 530-66461; fax (801) 530-6446; internet www.commerce.utah.gov; Exec. Dir FRANCINE A. GIANI.

Department of Community and Culture: 324 South State St, Suite 500, Salt Lake City, UT 84111; tel. (801) 538-8700; fax (801) 538-8888; e-mail palmer@utah.gov; internet community.utah.gov; Exec. Dir PALMER DEPAULIS.

Department of Corrections: 14717 South Minuteman Dr., Draper, UT 84020; tel. (801) 545-5500; fax (801) 545-5670; e-mail corrections@utah.gov; internet www.corrections.utah.gov; Exec. Dir TOM PATTERSON.

Department of Environmental Quality: 168 North 1950 West St, POB 144810, Salt Lake City, UT 84114-4810; tel. (801) 536-4402; fax (801) 536-0061; e-mail deqinfo@utah.gov; internet www.deq.utah.gov; Exec. Dir RICK SPROTT.

Department of Health: Cannon Health Bldg, 4th Floor, POB 141000, Salt Lake City, UT 84114-1000; tel. (801) 538-6111; fax (801) 538-6306; e-mail thudachko@utah.gov; internet health.utah.gov; Dir Dr DAVID N. SUNDWALL.

Department of Insurance: State Office Bldg, Rm 3110, Salt Lake City, UT 84114-6901; tel. (801) 538-3800; fax (801) 538-3829; e-mail administration.uid@utah.gov; internet insurance.utah.gov; Commr D. KENT MICHIE.

Department of Public Safety: 4501 South 2700 West St, 1st Floor, POB 141775, Salt Lake City, UT 84114-1775; tel. (801) 965-4461; fax (801) 965-4756; e-mail dpspiohelp@utah.gov; internet publicsafety.utah.gov; Commr SCOTT T. DUNCAN.

Department of Transportation: 4501 South 2700 West St, POB 141200, Salt Lake City, UT 84114-1200; tel. (801) 965-4000; fax (801) 965-4391; e-mail srwebmail@utah.gov; internet www.udot.utah.gov; Exec. Dir JOHN NJORD.

Governor's Office of Economic Development: 324 South State St, Suite 500, Salt Lake City, UT 84111; tel. (801) 538-8700; fax (801) 538-8888; e-mail jpperry@utah.gov; e-mail goed.utah.gov; internet goed.utah.gov; Exec. Dir JASON PERRY.

National Guard: 12953 South Minuteman Dr., Draper, UT 84020-1776; tel. (801) 523-4400; fax (801) 523-4677; e-mail hank.mcintire@ut.ngb.army.mil; internet www.ut.ngb.army.mil; Adj.-Gen. Maj.-Gen. BRIAN L. TARBET.

Office of Education: 250 East 500 South St, POB 144200, Salt Lake City, UT 84114-4200; tel. (801) 538-7500; fax (801) 538-7521; e-mail lorraine.austin@schools.utah.gov; internet www.schools.utah.gov; Supt of Public Instruction PATTI HARRINGTON.

Public Service Commission: Heber M. Wells Bldg, 4th Floor, 160 East 300 South St, Salt Lake City, UT 84111; tel. (801) 530-6716; fax (801) 530-6796; internet www.psc.state.ut.us/; Chair. TED BOYER.

Tax Commission: 210 North 1950 West, Salt Lake City, UT 84134; tel. (801) 297-2200; fax (801) 297-7699; e-mail taxmaster@utah.gov; internet www.tax.utah.gov; Chair. PAM HENDRICKSON.

Legislature
(August 2008)

Senate

Rep. 21; Dem. 8; Total 29

President: JOHN L. VALENTINE (Rep.).

Secretary: ANNETTE B. MOORE.

House of Representatives

Rep. 55; Dem. 20; Total 75

Speaker: GREG CURTIS (Rep.).

Chief Clerk: SANDY D. TENNEY.

Vermont

Gross Area: 24,903 sq km (9,615 sq miles).

Resident Population (1 July 2007, estimate): 621,254.

State Capital: Montpelier (population 8,003 at 1 July 2005).

Principal City: Burlington (population 38,358 at 1 July 2006, estimate).

LOCATION, TOPOGRAPHY AND CLIMATE

The State of Vermont (nicknamed 'The Green Mountain State') is in the Northeast region of the USA and is one of the six states constituting New England. It is bordered by the Canadian province of Québec to the north, New Hampshire to the east, Massachusetts to the south and New York to the west. Dominating Vermont are the forest-covered Green Mountains, which extend from Canada to Massachusetts. The state's highest point is Mount Mansfield, at 1,339 m (4,393 ft), in the Green Mountains. In the south-west and reaching into New York are the lower Taconic Mountains. Lying to the west of the Green Mountains in the north of the state are the narrow Valley of Vermont, through which the Poultney River flows, and the broad Champlain Valley, alongside Lake Champlain. East of the Green Mountains in the north is the Vermont Piedmont. The eastern border of the state is formed by the Connecticut River. Vermont has a temperate climate, with heavy precipitation and severe winters in the mountains.

HISTORICAL BACKGROUND

When Samuel de Champlain explored Vermont in 1609 the region was inhabited by Algonquian-speaking native Indians. Although explored by the French, the first permanent settlement established by Europeans was Fort Dummer, built by the British, in 1724, near present-day Brattleboro. Disputes over land ownership between New Hampshire and New York caused problems for settlers who, in 1770, led by Ethan Allen, organized themselves into a force called the Green Mountain Boys. In 1775 Allen's men captured Fort Ticonderago from the British, and in 1777 Vermont troops won a victory for the rebel colonists at Bennington. Vermont was admitted to the Union as the 14th state on 4 March 1791, after New York's claims had been settled. In 1864, during the Civil War, Confederates crossed the Canadian border to raid Vermont banks.

ECONOMY

Vermont's principal economic activities are manufacturing, wholesale and retail trade, finance, insurance and real estate, tourism and agriculture. It has the smallest economy of any state in the USA, with gross domestic product by state at US $24,543m. in 2007; personal income averaged $37,446 per head in the same year. Some 10.1% of the population were thought to be living below the poverty line in that year. The civilian labour force totalled 358,100 in mid-2008 and the unemployment rate was 4.5% (16,300 persons). In 2007 10.4% of those employed belonged to a trade union, although 12.2% were covered by union agreements.

In 2007 farmland covered 1.2m. acres (493,716 ha). There were 6,200 farms in that year, with the average farm covering 1978 acres. Farm marketings were among the lowest in the country. In 2007 86% of farm income was generated by sales of livestock and livestock products and 14% by crop marketings. The main sources of income were dairy products, cattle and calves, greenhouse and nursery products and hay. Forestland covered some 75% of Vermont's land area in 2003 (representing the third highest proportion of forestland in the USA); much of it is used as commercial timberland. The state is the largest producer of maple syrup in the USA, yielding about 31% of total US output in 2007.

In 2007 Vermont's non-fuel mineral production was estimated at US $93m. Leading minerals are construction sand and gravel, dimension stone (for production of which the state ranked fourth in 2007), crushed stone, construction sand and gravel, talc (ranked fourth) and gemstones.

Vermont ranked 45th in the USA in terms of its value of shipments in 2006. Leading manufacturing sectors include electronic equipment, fabricated metal products, print and paper products and machinery. In 2006 the total value of Vermont's manufacturing shipments was US $10,712m., of which 48% was added during manufacture.

Tourism is a major industry in Vermont, owing, in part, to the state's facilities for skiing. In 2004 domestic travel expenditures amounted to US $1,446m., with the state ranked third from bottom in terms of expenditures.

Total general expenditures by the state government in 2006 amounted to US $4,648m.; general revenue totalled $4,459m., of which $1,288m. was provided by the federal Government and $2,407m. came from taxes. Federal aid to Vermont totalled $1,294m. in 2006.

CONSTITUTION AND GOVERNMENT

Vermont's Constitution, the state's third, became effective on 9 July 1793. Constitutional amendments proposed by the General Assembly must be considered at two sessions: a two-thirds' vote by the elected members of the Senate and a majority vote by the House of Representatives is required at the first session, while a majority vote by both houses is needed at the second. Amendments must then be ratified by a majority of state voters. The Governor is elected separately from the Lieutenant-Governor and serves a two-year term. The General Assembly comprises 30 senators and 150 representatives and both houses are re-elected every two years. Legal provision is made for regular sessions of the General Assembly to be held in odd-numbered years only, but in practice sessions are also held in even-numbered years. Regular sessions convene in January. A bill becomes law when it has been passed by a majority in each house and signed by the Governor. During session the Governor has five days to consider a bill, after which it becomes law unless vetoed. Outside session a bill dies if it remains unsigned for three days from the adjournment of the General Assembly. A vote by two-thirds of the members present in each house is required to override a gubernatorial veto. Legislation becomes effective on 1 July following enactment. The Republican incumbent, Jim Douglas, was elected to a fourth term as Governor in 2008, obtaining 54% of votes cast. In the presidential election of that year the Democrats secured 67% of the vote. Vermont has 14 administrative counties.

Elected Executive Branch Officials

Governor (2009–11): JAMES H. (JIM) DOUGLAS (Rep.).

Lieutenant-Governor: BRIAN E. DUBIE (Rep.).

Secretary of State: DEBORAH L. MARKOWITZ (Dem.).

Attorney-General: WILLIAM H. SORRELL (Dem.).

Treasurer: JEB SPAULDING (Dem.).

State Auditor: THOMAS M. SALMON (Dem.).

Selected Government Addresses

Office of the Governor: Pavilion Office Bldg, 109 State St, Montpelier, VT 05609-0101; tel. (802) 828-3333; fax (802) 828-3339; internet governor.vermont.gov.

Office of the Lieutenant-Governor: State House, 115 State St, Montpelier, VT 05633-5401; tel. (802) 828-2226; fax (802) 828-3198; internet ltgov.vermont.gov.

Office of the Secretary of State: Redstone Bldg, 26 Terrace St, Drawer 09, Montpelier, VT 05609-1101; tel. (802) 828-2363; fax (802) 828-2496; e-mail dmarko@sec.state.vt.us; internet www.sec.state.vt.us.

Office of the Attorney-General: Pavilion Office Bldg, 109 State St, Montpelier, VT 05609-1001; tel. (802) 828-3171; fax (802) 828-2154; e-mail atginfo@atg.state.vt.us; internet www.atg.state.vt.us.

Office of the Treasurer: Pavilion Office Bldg, 109 State St, 4th Floor, Montpelier, VT 05633-6200; tel. (802) 828-2301; fax (802) 828-2772; e-mail treasurers.office@state.vt.us; internet www.vermonttreasurer.gov.

Office of the Auditor: 132 State St, Montpelier, VT 05633-5101; tel. (802) 828-2281; fax (802) 828-2198; e-mail auditor@state.vt.us; internet auditor.vermont.gov.

Agency of Agriculture, Food and Markets: 116 State St, Drawer 20, Montpelier, VT 05620-2901; tel. (802) 828-2430; fax (802) 828-3831; e-mail roger.allbee@state.vt.us; internet www.vermontagriculture.com; Sec. ROGER ALLBEE.

Agency of Commerce and Community Development: National Life Bldg, North Drawer 20, Montpelier, VT 05620-0501; tel. (802) 828-3211; fax (802) 828-3383; e-mail kevin.dorn@state.vt.us; internet www.dca.state.vt.us; Sec. KEVIN DORN.

Agency of Natural Resources: Center Bldg, 103 South Main St, Waterbury, VT 05671-0301; tel. (802) 241-3600; fax (802) 244-1102; e-mail george.crombie@state.vt.us; internet www.anr.state.vt.us; Sec. GEORGE CROMBIE.

Agency of Transportation: 1 National Life Dr., Drawer 33, Montpelier, VT 05633-5001; tel. (802) 828-2657; fax (802) 828-3522; e-mail david.dill@state.vt.us; internet www.aot.state.vt.us; Sec. DAVID DILL.

Department of Corrections: 103 South Main St, Waterbury, VT 05671-1101; tel. (802) 241-2276; fax (802) 241-2565; e-mail robert.hofmann@ahs.state.vt.us; internet doc.vermont.gov; Commr ROBERT HOFMANN.

Department of Economic Development: National Life Bldg, Drawer 20, Montpelier, VT 05620-0501; tel. (802) 828-3080; fax (802) 828-3258; e-mail info@thinkvermont.com; internet www.thinkvermont.com; Commr MIKE QUINN.

Department of Education: State Office Bldg, 120 State St, Montpelier, VT 05620-2501; tel. (802) 828-3135; fax (802) 828-3140; e-mail doe-edinfo@state.vt.us; internet www.state.vt.us/educ; Commr BILL TALBOTT (acting).

Department of Finance and Management: Pavilion Office Bldg, 109 State St, Montpelier, VT 05609-0401; tel. (802) 828-2376; e-mail jim.reardon@state.vt.us; internet finance.state.vt.us; Commr JAMES REARDON.

Department of Health: 108 Cherry St, POB 70, Burlington, VT 05402-0070; tel. (802) 863-7200; fax (802) 865-7754; internet healthvermont.gov; Commr Dr WENDY DAVIS.

Department of Labor: 5 Green Mountain Dr., POB 488, Montpelier, VT 05601-0488; tel. (802) 828-4000; fax (802) 828-4022; e-mail pat.moulton.powden@state.vt.us; internet www.labor.vermont.gov; Commr Patricia Moulton Powden.

Department of Public Service: 112 State St, Drawer 20, Montpelier, VT 05620-2601; tel. (802) 828-2811; fax (802) 828-2342; e-mail vtdps@state.vt.us; internet publicservice.vermont.gov; Commr David O'Brien.

Department of Taxes: 133 State St, POB 429, Montpelier, VT 05601-4229; tel. (802) 828-2505; fax (802) 828-2701; e-mail vttaxdept@state.vt.us; internet www.state.vt.us/tax; Commr Tom Pelham.

National Guard: 789 Vermont National Guard Rd, Colchester, VT 05446-3099; tel. (802) 338-3246; fax (802) 655-3247; internet www.vtguard.com; Adj.-Gen. Maj.-Gen. Michael Dubie.

State Police: State Office Complex, 103 South Main St, Waterbury, VT 05671-2101; tel. (802) 244-7345; internet www.vtsp.org; Dir Col James W. Baker.

General Assembly
(August 2008)

Senate

Dem. 23; Rep. 7; Total 30

President: Lt-Gov. Brian Dubie (Rep.).

President Pro Tempore: Peter Shumlin (Dem.).

Secretary: David A. Gibson.

House of Representatives

Dem. 93; Rep. 49; Vermont Progressive Party 6; Ind. 2; Total 150

Speaker: Gaye Symington (Dem.).

Clerk: Donald G. Milne.

Virginia

Gross Area: 110,792 sq km (42,793 sq miles).

Resident Population (1 July 2007, estimate): 7,712,091.

State Capital: Richmond.

Principal Cities (population at 1 July 2006, estimate): Virginia Beach 435,619; Norfolk 229,112; Chesapeake 220,560; Arlington 195,965 (1 July 2005, estimate); Richmond (capital) 192,913; Newport News 178,281; Hampton 145,017; Alexandria 136,974; Portsmouth 101,377.

LOCATION, TOPOGRAPHY AND CLIMATE

The Commonwealth of Virginia (nicknamed 'Old Dominion') is in the South region of the USA and is bordered by West Virginia to the north-west, Maryland and the District of Columbia to the north-east, North Carolina to the south, Tennessee to the south-west and Kentucky to the west. The Atlantic Ocean provides an eastern border. In south-eastern Virginia the Tidewater, a low-lying plain cut by the James, York, Rappahanock and Potomac Rivers, gradually slopes up towards the fertile, rolling hills of the Piedmont Plateau. The Piedmont covers much of the centre of Virginia, broadening out towards the south. Parallel with the West Virginia and Kentucky borders are the Blue Ridge and Allegheny Mountains (parts of the Appalachian system), divided by the Shenandoah Valley of Virginia. Mount Rogers, the state's highest point at 1,746 m (5,729 ft), is in the Blue Ridge Mountains, near the border with North Carolina. Virginia has a mild, humid climate. Temperatures are cooler in the mountainous west.

HISTORICAL BACKGROUND

When the first Europeans arrived in Virginia (named for the English queen, Elizabeth I), the region was mainly inhabited by Algonquian-speaking Indians. The first permanent British settlement in America was established at Jamestown in 1607 by the Virginia Co. In 1619 the colonists formed their first representative assembly. Virginia became a royal colony in 1624. Resistance to British rule led the colony to declare independence—the first to do so—in 1775. Playing a major part in the American Revolution, Virginia was the scene of the surrender of the British General, Charles Cornwallis, to George Washington in 1781. On 25 June 1788 Virginia became the 10th state to join the Union. The state was divided over the slavery issue, but in 1861 seceded from the Union, with Richmond becoming the capital of the Confederacy. This step led to the western third of Virginia establishing itself as West Virginia, with the latter being admitted to the Union in 1863. Virginia was the main scene of battle during the Civil War, with victories by the Confederate General, Robert E. Lee, at Bull Run (1861), Fredericksburg (1862) and Chancellorsville (1864); Lee eventually surrendered at Appomattox in 1865.

ECONOMY

Government, services, manufacturing, finance, insurance and real estate and wholesale and retail trade are important components of Virginia's gross state product. The service sector, particularly business and professional services and activities related to communications and information management, is the largest employer. Government is also a major employer, partly owing to the number of military bases in the state, and partly because many state residents work for federal government offices in Washington, DC. Gross domestic product by state totalled US $382,964m. in 2007, while the state's average per-head income was $41,561 in that year. It was estimated that 9.9% of the population were living below the poverty line. The civilian labour force stood at 4,214,200 in mid-2008, while the unemployment rate was relatively low, in a national context, at 4.5% (123,600 workers). In 2007 just 3.7% of those employed were trade-union members and 4.8% were covered by union agreements—the third lowest level, in both respects, in the country.

Farmland covered 8.5m. acres (3.4m. ha) in 2007. There were 47,100 farms in that year, with the average farm occupying 181 acres. In 2002 2.3% of total cropland was irrigated. Some 70% of farm income came from sales of livestock and livestock products in 2007, and 30% from crops. The main agricultural commodities in that year were broilers, cattle and calves, dairy products and turkeys. Other important crops were greenhouse and nursery products, soybeans, corn, chicken eggs, tobacco and tomatoes. Hogs and sheep were also a significant source of income. It also ranked fourth for tomatoes and for tobacco production in 2007. Virginia had 16.1m. acres of forestland in 2003, with some commercial forestland in every county. There is also commercial fishing in the state, with a catch value of US $109m. in 2006.

Virginia's non-fuel mineral production was valued at US $1,100m. in 2007, with the state ranked 21st in this respect. Crushed stone accounts for around 59% of state production. Construction sand and gravel, portland cement, lime and zirconium were other important minerals, while titanium, feldspar and vermiculite were also produced. The state has reserves of bituminous coal and natural gas and produced 25.3m. short tons of coal in 2007, ranking 11th among coal-producing states.

Virginia ranked 21st among the states in 2006 in terms of its value of shipments. The principal manufacturing sectors are food and allied products, print products, chemicals, computers and electrical equipment, textiles and transportation equipment. The manufacture of tobacco products (cigarettes and the processes of tobacco stemming and redrying) is also a major industry. The total value of Virginia's manufacturing shipments in 2006 was US $93,671m., of which 54% was added during manufacture.

Tourism makes a significant contribution to Virginia's economy, with domestic travel expenditures amounting to US $15,041m. in 2004. The state ranked 10th in the USA in that year in terms of expenditures.

Total general expenditures by the state government in 2006 amounted to US $34,776m.; general revenue totalled $32,619m., of which $6,196m. was provided by the federal Government and $17,192m. was derived from taxes. Virginia received $6,997m. in federal aid in 2006.

CONSTITUTION AND GOVERNMENT

Virginia's current Constitution, its sixth, became effective on 1 July 1971. An amendment to the Constitution proposed by the General Assembly must be passed by a majority of the elected members of each house at two consecutive sessions, and then ratified by a majority of state voters. The Governor, elected separately from the Lieutenant-Governor, serves a four-year term and may not serve consecutive terms. There are 40 senators and 100 representatives in the General Assembly, serving terms of four and two years, respectively. Regular legislative sessions take place annually, starting in January, and are limited in length to 60 days in odd-numbered years and 30 days in even-numbered years. To become law, a bill must be approved by the General Assembly and signed by the Governor. During session a bill becomes law if it remains neither signed nor vetoed seven days after being presented to the Governor for consideration. Outside session, if the Governor fails to sign a bill within 30 days after adjournment of the General Assembly, the bill becomes law. A gubernatorial veto may be overridden by a two-thirds' vote of members present in each house (which must be at least a majority of the elected members). Legislation usually becomes effective on 1 July following enactment. Tim Kaine, a Democratic candidate, won the gubernatorial election in November 2005, with 52% of the votes cast. In the presidential election of 2008 the Democrats won some 52% of the votes, with over 3.6m. people voting. There are 96 administrative counties and 40 independent cities in Virginia.

Elected Executive Branch Officials

Governor (2006–10): Timothy M. Kaine (Dem.).

Lieutenant-Governor: William T. Bolling (Rep.).

Attorney-General: Robert F. McDonnell (Rep.).

Selected Government Addresses

Office of the Governor: State Capitol, Patrick Henry Bldg, 3rd Floor, 1111 East Broad St, Richmond, VA 23219; tel. (804) 786-2211; fax (804) 371-6351; internet www.governor.virginia.gov.

Office of the Lieutenant-Governor: 102 Governor St, POB 1195, Richmond, VA 23218; POB 1195, Richmond, VA 23218; tel. (804) 786-2078; fax (804) 786-7514; e-mail ltgov@ltgov.virginia.gov; internet www.ltgov.virginia.gov.

Office of the Attorney-General: 900 East Main St, 6th Floor, Richmond, VA 23219; tel. (804) 786-2071; fax (804) 786-1991; e-mail tucker.martin@oag.state.va.us; internet www.oag.state.va.us.

Department of Agriculture and Consumer Services: 102 Governor St, Richmond, VA 23219; tel. (804) 786-2373; fax (804) 371-6097; e-mail webmaster.vdacs@vdacs.virginia.gov; internet www.vdacs.state.va.us; Commr Todd P. Haymore.

Department of Corrections: 6900 Atmore Dr., POB 26963, Richmond, VA 23261-6963; tel. (804) 674-3000; fax (804) 674-3536; e-mail docmail@vadoc.virginia.gov; internet www.vadoc.virginia.gov; Dir Gene M. Johnson.

Department of Education: James Monroe Bldg, 101 North 14th St, 25th Floor, POB 2120, Richmond, VA 23218; tel. (804) 225-2403; e-mail policy@doe.virginia.gov; internet www.doe.virginia.gov; Supt of Public Instruction Dr Billy K. Cannaday, Jr.

Department of Environmental Quality: 629 East Main St, POB 1105, Richmond, VA 23218; tel. (804) 698-4000; fax (804) 698-4500; e-mail wphayden@deq.virginia.gov; internet www.deq.virginia.gov; Dir David K. Paylor.

Department of Health: 109 Governor St, POB 2448, Richmond, VA 23218-2448; tel. (804) 864-7002; fax (804) 864-7022; e-mail rosanne.kolesar@vdh.virginia.gov; internet www.vdh.state.va.us; Commr Dr Karen Remley.

Department of Labor and Industry: Powers-Taylor Bldg, 13 South 13th St, Richmond, VA 23219-4101; tel. (804) 371-2327; fax (804) 371-6524; e-mail webmaster@doli.virginia.gov; internet www.doli.virginia.gov; Commr C. Ray Davenport.

Department of Planning and Budget: 1111 East Broad St, Rm 5040, Richmond, VA 23219-3418; tel. (804) 786-7455; fax (804) 225-3291; internet www.dpb.virginia.gov; Dir Richard D. Brown.

Department of State Police: 7700 Midlothian Turnpike, POB 27472, Richmond, VA 23261-7472; tel. (804) 674-2000; fax (804) 674-2267; e-mail supt@vsp.virginia.gov; internet www.vsp.state.va.us; Supt Col W. Steven Flaherty.

Department of Transportation: 1401 East Broad St, Richmond, VA 23219; tel. (804) 786-2801; fax (804) 786-2940; e-mail vdotinfo@vdot.virginia.gov; internet www.virginiadot.org; Commr David S. Ekern, Sr.

Department of the Treasury: Monroe Bldg, 3rd Floor, 101 North 14th St, Richmond, VA 23219; tel. (804) 225-2142; fax (804) 225-3187; e-mail robert.young@trs.virginia.gov; internet www.trs.virginia.gov; Treasurer J. Braxton Powell.

Economic Development Partnership: 901 East Byrd St, POB 798, Richmond, VA 23218-0798; tel. and fax (804) 545-5600; e-mail rrichardson@yesvirginia.org; internet www.yesvirginia.org; Exec. Dir Jeffrey M. Anderson.

National Guard: 202 North Ninth St, 4th Floor, Richmond, VA 23219; tel. (804) 786-4400; fax (804) 371-0073; internet vko.va.ngb.army.mil/virginiaguard; Adj.-Gen. Maj.-Gen. Robert B. Newman, Jr.

Secretariat of the Commonwealth: 1111 East Broad St, 4th Floor, POB 2454, Richmond, VA 23218; tel. (804) 786-2441; fax (804) 371-0017; internet www.commonwealth.virginia.gov; Sec. Katherine K. Hanley.

General Assembly

(August 2008)

Senate

Dem. 21; Rep. 19; Total 40

President: Lt-Gov. William T. Bolling (Rep.).

President Pro Tempore: Charles J. Colgan (Dem.).

Clerk: Susan Clarke Schaar.

House of Delegates

Rep. 53; Dem. 45; Ind. 2; Total 100

Speaker: William J. Howell (Rep.).

Clerk: Bruce F. Jamerson.

Washington

Gross Area: 184,672 sq km (71,329 sq miles).

Resident Population (1 July 2007, estimate): 6,468,424.

State Capital: Olympia (population 44,645 at 1 July 2006, estimate).

Principal Cities (population at 1 July 2006, estimate): Seattle 582,454; Spokane 198,081; Tacoma 196,532; Vancouver 158,855; Bellevue 118,186.

LOCATION, TOPOGRAPHY AND CLIMATE

The State of Washington (nicknamed 'The Evergreen State') is in the West region of the USA and is bordered by the Canadian province of British Columbia to the north, Idaho to the east, Oregon to the south and the Pacific Ocean to the west. In the west of the state are the northernmost mountains of the Coast Ranges, consisting of the Olympic Mountains in the north-west Olympic Peninsula and the Willapa Hills in the south-west. Cutting 130 km (80 miles) southward into the state between the Coast Ranges and the higher Cascade Range is Puget Sound. The Cascades include the highest mountains in the state—all volcanic: Mount Baker, Glacier Peak, Mount Rainier (the highest point in Washington at 4,392 m—14,410 ft), Mount St Helens (which erupted destructively in 1980) and Mount Adams. The two lowland areas of the state are the Western Corridor, formed by Puget Sound, and the Columbia Plateau, east of the Cascades. In north-eastern Washington are the Okanogan Highlands, and in the south-east are the Palouse Hills and Blue Mountains. The main rivers are the Columbia, flowing south-west from Canada to become part of the state's southern boundary, and the Snake, curving across south-eastern Washington from Idaho and joining the Columbia. The Cascades divide Washington into two climatic regions: mild weather with heavy precipitation predominates in the west, while in the east there are seasonal extremes of temperature and low rainfall.

HISTORICAL BACKGROUND

When the Spanish explored the region in the 18th century Washington was inhabited by American Indians of the Nootkin, Salishan and Shahaptian language groups. The first documented exploration of the coast was by Juan Pérez in 1774. In 1792 US Capt. Robert Gray discovered the mouth of the Columbia River. The Meriwether Lewis and William Clark Expedition of 1804–06 excited the interest of fur trappers, and in 1836 the first missionaries established a settlement at Waiilatpu, near present-day Walla Walla. In 1848 Oregon Territory, which included Washington, was organized; Washington (including part of Idaho) became a separate territory in 1853. The discovery of gold in the Walla Walla region and the completion of the Northern Pacific Railroad in 1883 increased the flow of settlers to the area and, on 11 November 1889, Washington became the 42nd state to join the Union. In 1919 Washington was the scene of the first general strike in the USA. The eruption of Mount St Helens caused widespread destruction in 1980.

ECONOMY

Washington's principal economic activities are wholesale and retail trade, manufacturing (particularly lumber, computer software and aerospace products—Boeing is the state's leading company), services, agriculture and tourism. Gross domestic product by state totalled US $311,270m. in 2007, while per-head income in the state averaged $41,062. It was estimated that in that year 11.4% of the population were living below the poverty threshold. The civilian labour force stood at 3,486,500 in mid-2008, and the unemployment rate was 5.4% (187,900 persons). In 2007 20.2% of the state's labour force were members of a trade union and 21.4% were covered by union agreements, representing the fourth highest level of unionization in the country.

Farmland covered 15.1m. acres (6.1m. ha) in 2007. There were 33,000 farms in that year and the average farm covered 458 acres. In 2002 some 20.8% of total cropland was irrigated. In 2007 crop sales accounted for 71% of farm marketings, and livestock and livestock products for 29%. Washington's principal agricultural commodities by value in that year were apples, dairy products, wheat and cattle and calves. The state was ranked second in 2007 for grapes and onions, in both cases after California, and second for potatoes, after

Idaho; it ranked third for wheat and fifth for hay in the same year. Washington was the USA's leading apple producer. Greenhouse products, other fruit, hops and chicken eggs also contributed to farm income.

Washington had some 21.8m. acres of forestland in 2003; it was ranked second for lumber production in 2004, after Oregon. Almost all the lumber produced was softwoods. In 2006 the state's fish catch had a value of US $234m., fifth largest in the nation. It is surpassed in the volume and value of its salmon production only by Alaska.

Washington's non-fuel mineral production was valued at US $680m. in 2007, with the state ranked 30th in the nation. Construction sand and gravel, crushed stone, zinc (for production of which the state ranked fourth in 2007), portland cement and lime were the leading minerals. Other minerals of importance to the state economy included olivine (of which Washington was the sole producer in 2007) and diatomite (ranked fourth). The state produced 2.6m. short tons of coal in 2006.

The state ranked 16th in terms of the value of its shipments in 2006. Its principal manufactured goods include aerospace products, food and kindred products, lumber and wood products, machinery, chemicals and transportation equipment. Production of aluminium in the state decreased significantly from 2001, owing to the closure of most of its primary plants following a sharp increase in energy costs. In 2006 the total value of Washington's manufacturing shipments was US $105,658m., of which 46% was added during manufacture.

Tourism is important to the state; domestic travel expenditures totalled US $8,594m. in 2004. In 2006 total general expenditures by the state government amounted to $33,915m.; general revenue totalled $29,284m., with transfers from the federal Government amounting to $7,438m. and taxes contributing $16,411m. Washington received $7,375m. in federal aid in 2006.

CONSTITUTION AND GOVERNMENT

Washington's only Constitution became effective on 11 November 1889. Amendments to the Constitution proposed by the Legislature have to be approved by two-thirds of the elected members of each house and ratified by a majority of state voters. The Governor, elected separately from the Lieutenant-Governor, serves a four-year term and there is no limit on the number of times he or she may hold office. There are 49 senators and 98 representatives in the Legislature, elected to serve terms of four and two years, respectively; alternate halves of the Senate are re-elected every two years. Regular sessions are held annually, starting in January, and last no longer than 105 days in odd-numbered years and 60 days in even-numbered years. A bill becomes law once it has been passed by a majority of the elected members in each house and signed by the Governor. During session the Governor is allowed five days to consider a bill, after which it becomes law unless vetoed. After session a bill becomes law unless vetoed within 20 days of being presented to the Governor. A two-thirds' vote of members present in each house is required to override a gubernatorial veto. Enacted legislation becomes effective 90 days after adjournment of the session. In the gubernatorial election of 2008 the Democratic incumbent, Christine Gregoire, obtained some 54% of the votes cast. In the same year the Democrats secured an estimated 58% of the votes cast in the presidential election. Washington has 39 administrative counties.

Elected Executive Branch Officials

Governor (2009–13): CHRISTINE O. GREGOIRE (Dem.).

Lieutenant-Governor: BRAD OWEN (Dem.).

Secretary of State: SAM REED (Rep.).

Attorney-General: ROB MCKENNA (Rep.).

Treasurer: MICHAEL J. MURPHY (Dem.).

Auditor: BRIAN SONNTAG (Dem.).

Superintendent of Public Instruction: Dr TERRY BERGESON (Ind.).

Insurance Commissioner: MIKE KREIDLER (Dem.).

Commissioner of Public Lands: DOUG SUTHERLAND (Rep.).

Selected Government Addresses

Office of the Governor: Legislative Bldg, 2nd Floor, POB 40002, Olympia, WA 98504-0002; tel. (360) 902-4111; fax (360) 753-4110; internet www.governor.wa.gov.

Office of the Lieutenant-Governor: Legislative Bldg, Rm 220, 416 Sid Snyder Ave, SW, POB 40400, Olympia, WA 98504-0400; tel. (360) 786-7700; fax (360) 786-7749; e-mail ltgov@leg.wa.gov; internet www.ltgov.wa.gov.

Office of the Secretary of State: 520 Union Ave, SE, POB 40220, Olympia, WA 98504-0220; tel. (360) 902-4151; fax (360) 586-5629; e-mail sreed@secstate.wa.gov; internet www.secstate.wa.gov.

Office of the Attorney-General: 1125 Washington St, SE, POB 40100, Olympia, WA 98504-0100; tel. (360) 753-6200; fax (360) 586-7671; internet www.atg.wa.gov.

Office of the Treasurer: Legislative Bldg, POB 40200, Olympia, WA 98504-0200; tel. (360) 902-9000; fax (360) 902-9044; e-mail watreas@tre.wa.gov; internet www.wa.gov/tre.

Office of the State Auditor: Insurance Bldg, Suite 200, POB 40021, Olympia, WA 98504-0021; tel. (360) 902-0370; fax (360) 753-0646; internet www.sao.wa.gov.

Office of the Superintendent of Public Instruction: Old Capitol Bldg, 600 South Washington St, POB 47200, Olympia, WA 98504-7200; tel. (360) 725-6000; fax (360) 753-6712; internet www.k12.wa.us.

Office of the Insurance Commissioner: 5000 Capitol Blvd, Tumwater, WA 98501; POB 40256, WA 98504-0256; tel. (360) 725-7080; fax (360) 586-2018; e-mail askmike@oic.wa.gov; internet www.insurance.wa.gov.

Office of the Commissioner of Public Lands: Department of Natural Resources, 1111 Washington St, SE, POB 47001, Olympia, WA 98504-7001; tel. (360) 902-1004; fax (360) 902-1775; e-mail cpl@dnr.wa.gov; internet www.dnr.wa.gov.

Department of Agriculture: Natural Resources Bldg, 2nd Floor, 1111 Washington St, SE, POB 42560, Olympia, WA 98504-2560; tel. (360) 902-1800; fax (360) 902-2092; e-mail slaney@agr.wa.gov; internet agr.wa.gov; Dir VALORIA H. LOVELAND.

Department of Community, Trade and Economic Development: Ali Raad Bldg, 128 10th Ave, SW, POB 42525, Olympia, WA 98504-2525; tel. (360) 725-4000; fax (360) 586-8440; internet www.cted.wa.gov; Dir JULI WILKERSON.

Department of Corrections: 7345 Linderson Way, SW, Tumwater, WA 98501-6504; POB 41100, Olympia, WA 98504-1100; tel. (360) 753-8213; e-mail doccorrespondence@doc1.wa.gov; internet www.doc.wa.gov; Sec. ELDON VAIL.

Department of Ecology: 300 Desmond Dr., SE, Lacey, WA 98503; POB 47600, Olympia, WA 98504-7600; tel. (360) 407-6000; fax (360) 407-6989; e-mail jaym461@ecy.wa.gov; internet www.ecy.wa.gov; Dir JAY MANNING.

Department of Health: 101 Israel Rd, SE, POB 47890, Olympia, WA 98504-7890; tel. (360) 236-4030; fax (360) 586-7424; e-mail information@doh.wa.gov; internet www.doh.wa.gov; Sec. MARY SELECKY.

Department of Labor and Industries: 7273 Linderson Way, SW, Tumwater, WA 98501-5414; POB 4400, Olympia, WA 98504-4000; tel. (360) 902-5800; fax (360) 902-5798; e-mail piet235@lni.wa.gov; internet www.lni.wa.gov; Dir JUDY SCHURKE.

Department of Revenue: Gen. Admin. Bldg, POB 47450, Olympia, WA 98504-7450; tel. (360) 705-6705; internet dor.wa.gov; Dir CINDI L. HOLMSTROM.

Department of Transportation: Transportation Bldg, 310 Maple Park Ave, SE, POB 47300, Olympia, WA 98504-7300; tel. (360) 705-7000; fax (360) 705-6800; e-mail hammonp@wsdot.wa.gov; internet www.wsdot.wa.gov; Sec. PAULA J. HAMMOND.

Military Department: Bldg 1, Camp Murray, Tacoma, WA 98430-5000; tel. (360) 512-8000; fax (360) 512-8497; e-mail wamil@mil.wa.gov; internet www.mil.wa.gov; Adj.-Gen. Maj.-Gen. TIMOTHY J. LOWENBERG.

Office of Financial Management: Insurance Bldg, Rm 300, POB 43113, Olympia, WA 98504-3113; tel. (360) 902-0555; fax (360) 664-2832; e-mail information@ofm.wa.gov; internet www.ofm.wa.gov; Dir VICTOR A. MOORE.

State Patrol: Gen. Admin. Bldg, POB 42600, Olympia, WA 98504-2600; tel. (360) 596-4000; fax (360) 664-0663; e-mail questions@wsp.wa.gov; internet www.wsp.wa.gov; Chief JOHN R. BATISTE.

Legislature
(August 2008)

Senate

Dem. 32; Rep. 17; Total 49

President: Lt-Gov. BRAD OWEN (Dem.).

President Pro Tempore: ROSA FRANKLIN (Dem.).

Secretary: TOM HOEMANN.

House of Representatives

Dem. 63; Rep. 35; Total 98

Speaker: FRANK CHOPP (Dem.).

Speaker Pro Tempore: JEFF MORRIS (Dem.).

Chief Clerk: BARBARA BAKER.

West Virginia

Gross Area: 62,759 sq km (24,231 sq miles).

Resident Population (1 July 2007, estimate): 1,812,035.

State Capital: Charleston.

Principal Cities (population at 1 July 2006, estimate): Charleston (capital) 50,846; Huntington 49,007.

LOCATION, TOPOGRAPHY AND CLIMATE

The State of West Virginia (nicknamed 'The Mountain State') is in the South region of the USA and is bordered by Ohio to the north-west, Pennsylvania and Maryland to the north-east, Virginia to the south-east and Kentucky to the south-west. The east of Virginia lies in the Ridge and Valley region of the Appalachian Highlands. Much of the south-eastern border runs parallel with the Allegheny Mountains, which include West Virginia's highest point, Spruce Knob, at 1,482 m (4,863 ft). The land drops abruptly at the Allegheny Front, giving way to the rugged Allegheny Plateau, which covers the rest of the state. Flowing through the Allegheny Plateau and into the Ohio River, which forms the boundary with the state of the same name, are the Big Sandy, Guyandotte, Kanawha, Little Kanawha and Monongahela Rivers. The main river in the east of the state is the Potomac, forming the border with Maryland. West Virginia has hot, humid summers and cool winters.

HISTORICAL BACKGROUND

Iroquois, Cherokee, Shawnee, Tuscarora and Leni-Lanape (Delaware) Indians inhabited the region now called West Virginia when the French and English explored the Ohio Valley in the 17th century. West Virginia was part of Virginia when the latter joined the Union in 1788. By the early 19th century farmers and industrialists in West Virginia considered themselves unrepresented in the state legislature, which was dominated by the slaveholding plantation-owners of the east. When Virginia joined the Confederacy in 1861 West Virginia refused to secede from the Union. It established the Reorganized Government at Wheeling and became the 35th state to join the Union on 20 June 1863.

ECONOMY

Extractive industries, manufacturing, services, agriculture and tourism are West Virginia's most important economic activities. Gross domestic product by state stood at US $57,711m. in 2007, while the state's per-head income averaged $29,293, the second lowest in the nation. In that year, some 16.9% of the population were believed to be living below the poverty threshold, the sixth highest percentage (alongside Alabama) among the states. The civilian labour force in mid-2008 totalled 820,500, while the unemployment rate was 4.2% (34,300 persons). In that year 13.3% of those employed were trade-union members, although 14.7% were covered by union agreements.

Farmland covered 3.6m. acres (1.5m. ha) in 2007. There were 21,400 farms in that year, with an average farm occupying 168 acres. In 2007 83% of farm marketings were generated by livestock and livestock products and 17% were derived from crops. The state's principal farm commodities in 2007, in terms of value, were broilers, cattle and calves, turkeys and dairy products. Chicken eggs, hay, corn for grain and silage, apples, soybeans, peaches and sheep and lambs also contributed to farm income. Forestland covered 78.1% of the state's land area in 2003 (the second highest proportion in the country behind New Hampshire, and equal with Maine), with almost all the timber being hardwood.

In 2007 West Virginia's non-fuel mineral production was valued at US $207m. Crushed stone was the major mineral produced, followed by portland and masonry cement, lime and industrial sand and gravel. Together, these minerals accounted for around 98% of the state's total output in 2003. West Virginia ranked second (after Wyoming) in the production of bituminous coal in 2007, with an output of 153.5m. short tons. Natural gas and petroleum are also major mineral commodities.

In terms of its value of shipments, West Virginia ranked 37th in the USA in 2006. The state's principal manufactured goods include chemicals, primary and fabricated metal products, and stone, clay and glass products. In 2006 the total value of West Virginia's manufacturing shipments was US $23,919m., of which 44% was added during manufacture.

In 2004 domestic travel expenditures amounted to US $1,966m. Total general expenditures by the state government in 2006 were $9,791m.; general revenue totalled $10,262m., of which $3,157m. was provided by the federal Government and $4,558m. came from taxes. Federal aid to West Virginia totalled $3,353m. in 2006.

CONSTITUTION AND GOVERNMENT

West Virginia's current Constitution, the state's second, became effective on 9 April 1872. Constitutional amendments proposed by the Legislature must be approved by a two-thirds vote by the elected members of each house and ratified by a majority of state voters. The Governor, succeeded in his or her absence by the President of the Senate, is elected to serve a four-year term of office and may serve no more than two terms successively. The Legislature has 34 senators and 100 delegates, serving terms of four and two years, respectively; alternate halves of the Senate are re-elected every two years. Regular sessions of the Legislature are held annually in January to March and may last no longer than 60 days. A bill becomes law when it has been passed by the Legislature and signed by the Governor. During session the Governor is allowed five days to consider a bill, after which it becomes law unless vetoed. Outside session a bill becomes law unless vetoed within 15 days from adjournment of the legislature, or within five days for appropriation bills. A gubernatorial veto may be overridden by a vote by a majority of the elected members of both houses, except where the veto is applied to an appropriation bill, in which case a two-thirds' vote is required. Legislation becomes effective 90 days after enactment. The Democratic incumbent, Joe Manchin, III, won the gubernatorial election in 2008, with 70% of the votes. However, in the presidential election of the same year the Republicans secured the largest proportion of the votes cast (some 57%). There are 55 administrative counties in West Virginia.

Elected Executive Branch Officials

Governor (2009–13): JOE MANCHIN, III (Dem.).

Secretary of State: BETTY IRELAND (Rep.).

Attorney-General: DARRELL V. MCGRAW, Jr (Dem.).

Treasurer: JOHN D. PERDUE (Dem.).

Auditor: GLEN B. GAINER, III (Dem.).

Commissioner of Agriculture: GUS R. DOUGLASS (Dem.).

Selected Government Addresses

Office of the Governor: State Capitol Bldg, 1900 Kanawha Blvd East, Charleston, WV 25305; tel. (304) 558-2000; fax (304) 558-1558; e-mail governor@wvgov.org; internet www.wvgov.org.

Office of the Secretary of State: State Capitol Complex, Bldg 1, Suite 157K, 1900 Kanawha Blvd East, Charleston, WV 25305-0770; tel. (304) 558-6000; fax (304) 558-0900; e-mail wvsos@wvsos.com; internet www.wvsos.com.

Office of the Attorney-General: State Capitol Complex, Bldg 1, Rm E-26, 1900 Kanawha Blvd East, Charleston, WV 25305; tel. (304) 558-2021; fax (304) 558-0140; e-mail consumer@wvago.gov; internet www.wvago.gov.

Office of the Treasurer: State Capitol Complex, Bldg 1, Suite E-145, 1900 Kanawha Blvd East, Charleston, WV 25305; tel. (304) 558-5000; fax (304) 346-6602; e-mail webadmin@wvsto.com; internet www.wvsto.gov.

Office of the Auditor: State Capitol Complex, Bldg 1, Rm W-100, 1900 Kanawha Blvd East, Charleston, WV 25305; tel. (304) 558-2251; fax (304) 558-5200; e-mail glen.gainer@wvsao.gov; internet www.wvsao.gov.

Department of Agriculture: Rm E-28, 1900 Kanawha Blvd East, Charleston, WV 25305-0170; tel. (304) 558-3200; fax (304) 558-2203; e-mail douglass@ag.state.wv.us; internet www.wvagriculture.org; headed by the Commr of Agriculture.

Department of Commerce: State Capitol Complex, Bldg 6, Rm 525, 1900 Kanawha Blvd East, Charleston, WV 25305-0311; tel. (304) 558-2234; internet www.boc.state.wv.us; Sec. KELLEY GOES.

Department of Education: State Capitol Complex, Bldg 6, Rm 262, 1900 Kanawha Blvd East, Charleston, WV 25305-0330; tel. (304) 558-2699; fax (304) 558-0882; e-mail dvermill@access.k12.wv.us; internet wvde.state.wv.us; State Supt of Schools Dr STEVEN L. PAINE.

Department of Environmental Protection: 601 57th St, Charleston, WV 25304; tel. (304) 926-0440; fax (304) 926-0446; internet www.wvdep.org; Sec. RANDY C. HUFFMAN.

Department of Health and Human Resources: State Capitol Complex, Bldg 3, Rm 206, 1900 Kanawha Blvd East, Charleston, WV 25305; tel. (304) 558-7899; fax (304) 558-7075; internet www.wvdhhr.org; Sec. MARTHA YEAGER WALKER.

Department of Military Affairs and Public Safety: State Capitol Complex, Bldg 1, Rm W-400, 1900 Kanawha Blvd East, Charleston, WV 25305-0155; tel. (304) 558-2930; fax (304) 341-6466; e-mail james.w.spears@wv.gov; internet www.wvs.state.wv.us/dmaps; Sec. JAMES W. SPEARS.

Department of Revenue: State Capitol Complex, Bldg 1, Rm W-300, 1900 Kanawha Blvd East, POB 963, Charleston, WV 25324-0963; tel. (304) 558-0211; fax (304) 558-2324; internet www.wvrevenue.gov; Sec. VIRGIL T. HELTON.

Department of Transportation: State Capitol Complex, Bldg 5, 1900 Kanawha Blvd East, Charleston, WV 25305; tel. (304) 558-0444; fax (304) 558-1004; e-mail dot.secretary@v.gov; internet www.wvdot.com; Sec. PAUL A. MATTOX, Jr.

Development Office: State Capitol Complex, Bldg 6, Rm 553, 1900 Kanawha Blvd East, Charleston, WV 25305-0311; tel. (304) 558-2234; fax (304) 558-0449; e-mail kgoes@commercewv.org; internet www.wvdo.org; Exec. Dir and Sec. of Commerce KELLEY GOES.

Division of Natural Resources: State Capitol Complex, Bldg 3, Rm 669, 1900 Kanawha Blvd East, Charleston, WV 25305-0060; tel. (304) 558-2754; fax (304) 558-2768; internet www.wvdnr.gov; Dir FRANK JEZIORO.

Public Service Commission: 201 Brooks St, POB 812, Charleston, WV 25323; tel. (304) 340-0300; fax (304) 340-0325; e-mail webmaster@psc.state.wv.us; internet www.psc.state.wv.us; Chair. MICHAEL A. ALBERT.

State Police: 725 Jefferson Rd South, Charleston, WV 25309-1698; tel. (304) 746-2100; fax (304) 746-2106; e-mail troopers@wvstatepolice.com; internet www.wvstatepolice.com; Supt Col DAVID L. LEMMON.

Legislature

(August 2008)

Senate

Dem. 23; Rep. 11; Total 34

President: Lt-Gov. EARL RAY TOMBLIN (Dem.).

President Pro Tempore: WILLIAM R. SHARPE, Jr (Dem.).

Clerk: DARRELL E. HOLMES.

House of Delegates

Dem. 72; Rep. 28; Total 100

Speaker: RICHARD THOMPSON (Dem.).

Speaker Pro Tempore: RON FRAGALE (Dem.).

Clerk: GREGORY M. GRAY.

Wisconsin

Gross Area: 169,643 sq km (65,499 sq miles).

Resident Population (1 July 2007, estimate): 5,601,640.

State Capital: Madison.

Principal Cities (population at 1 July 2006, estimate): Milwaukee 573,358; Madison (capital) 223,389; Green Bay 100,353.

LOCATION, TOPOGRAPHY AND CLIMATE

The State of Wisconsin (nicknamed 'The Badger State') is in the Midwest region of the USA and is bordered by the state of Michigan to the north-east, Illinois to the south and Iowa and Minnesota to the west. Lake Superior lies to the north-west and Lake Michigan to the east. The Apostle Islands, in Lake Superior, and Washington Island, in Lake Michigan, belong to Wisconsin. In the north of the state, below Lake Superior, are the forest-covered hills of the Superior Upland—the highest region of the state. Craggy, unglaciated hills known as the Driftless Area cover the south-west of Wisconsin. The centre of the state consists of a broad, sandy plain, occasionally broken by buttes. Lowland prairie occupies the south-east and east of Wisconsin, around Lake Michigan and Green Bay. The state has large areas of fresh water, with over 8,000 lakes; the largest inland lake is Lake Winnebago in the east, covering 557 sq km (215 sq miles). The Mississippi River and its tributary, the St Croix, form most of the western boundary and the Wisconsin River flows from south to south-west. Other rivers include the Chippewa, Black, Fox, Wolf and Menominee. Wisconsin has a continental climate, with warm summers and severe winters.

HISTORICAL BACKGROUND

When the first French explorers arrived in Wisconsin in the 17th century, the region was inhabited by the Ojibwa, Winnebago, Sauk, Fox, Potawatomi and Kickapoo tribes. The American manifestation of Europe's Seven-Years War, the French and Indian War of 1754–63, ended French dominance of the region when it became part of Québec (now part of Canada) under British rule. Wisconsin was ceded to the USA in 1783, but the British were not ousted until after the War of 1812. Territorial status was not granted until 1836. In 1816 the US government established a fort on Wisconsin's border with Iowa. Native Americans in the area rebelled against the loss of their tribal lands in the Black Hawk War of 1832, but a series of treaties from 1829–48 effectively withdrew their right to ownership of the land. On 29 May 1848 Wisconsin joined the Union as the 30th state. The state supported the abolition of slavery and fought for the Union during the Civil War. Wisconsin became the first state to pass old-age pension and unemployment compensation acts, in 1925 and 1932, respectively.

ECONOMY

Wisconsin's most important economic activities are manufacturing, services, trade, government, tourism and agriculture—in particular, dairy farming. Gross domestic product by state totalled US $232,293m. in 2007, while the state's average per-head income was $36,241. In that year 10.8% of the state population were thought to be living below the poverty threshold. The civilian labour force numbered 3,116,600 in mid-2008, while the unemployment rate was 4.8% (148,300 persons). Of the total number of employees in 2007, 14.3% were members of a trade union and 15.4% were covered by union agreements.

In 2007 farmland covered 15.2m. acres (6.2m. ha). There were 76,000 farms in that year, with the average farm occupying an area of 200 acres. In 2002 3.5% of total cropland was irrigated. Livestock and livestock products accounted for 70% of farm marketings in 2007 (which were the eighth highest in the country) and crop sales for 30%. The principal commodities produced were dairy products, corn, cattle and calves, and soybeans. Wisconsin was ranked second for dairy products in 2007 (after California), and third for potatoes. Wisconsin is also the leading mink-producing state (ahead of Utah), with 914,100 pelts (equivalent to 32% of total US production) produced in 2007. Forestland covered approximately 38% of the state's land area in 2003; hardwoods accounted for 81% of the lumber produced in that year. Wisconsin's commercial fisheries had a total catch value of US $3m. in 2006.

Mining does not contribute greatly to Wisconsin's economy. In 2007 the value of the state's non-fuel mineral production was estimated at US $552m. The major minerals produced are construction sand and gravel and crushed stone, with lime, industrial sand and gravel (for which the state was ranked fourth in 2007), dimension stone (ranked second), silica stone, gemstones and peat also contributing to the total. Wisconsin was ranked fifth for peat production in 2003. There are no known major fuel resources in the state.

In terms of the value of its shipments, Wisconsin ranked 11th among the states in 2006. The state's principal industrial sectors are paper and allied products, food and kindred products, electrical equipment and fabricated metal products. The total value of Wisconsin's manufacturing shipments in 2006 was US $154,050m., of which 47% was added during manufacture.

Wisconsin has a thriving tourism industry, with domestic travel expenditures amounting to US $7,581m. in 2004. Total general expenditures by the state government in 2006 were $30,125m., while general revenue totalled $25,708m., of which $6,488m. was provided by the federal Government and $13,795m. was derived from taxes. Federal aid to Wisconsin totalled $6,240m. in 2004.

CONSTITUTION AND GOVERNMENT

Wisconsin's only Constitution became effective on 29 May 1848. An amendment to the Constitution proposed by the Legislature must be approved by a majority of the elected members of each house in two consecutive sessions and ratified by a majority of voters. The Governor, elected with the Lieutenant-Governor, serves a four-year term; there is no limit on the number of terms he or she may serve. The 33 senators and 99 representatives in the Legislature serve four- and two-year terms, respectively, alternate halves of the Senate being re-elected every two years. Regular legislative sessions are held annually, beginning in January, and there is no statutory limit to their duration. A bill becomes law after being passed by both houses and signed by the Governor. During session the Governor has six days to consider a bill, after which it becomes law unless vetoed. Outside session a bill dies if it remains unsigned for six days after being presented to the Governor. A two-thirds' vote by the members present in each house is required to override a gubernatorial veto. Enacted legislation becomes effective the day after publication. In the 2006 gubernatorial election the Democratic incumbent, Jim Doyle, was re-elected, with 53% of the vote. In the 2008 presidential election the Democrats obtained some 56% of the votes cast. Wisconsin has 72 administrative counties.

Elected Executive Branch Officials

Governor (2007–11): JAMES E. (JIM) DOYLE (Dem.).

Lieutenant-Governor: BARBARA C. LAWTON (Dem.).

Secretary of State: DOUGLAS LAFOLLETTE (Dem.).

Attorney-General: JOHN B. VAN HOLLEN (Rep.).

Treasurer: DAWN MARIE SASS (Dem.).

Superintendent of Public Instruction: ELIZABETH BURMASTER (Dem.).

Selected Government Addresses

Office of the Governor: 115 East State Capitol, Madison, WI 53702; tel. (608) 266-1212; fax (608) 267-8983; internet www.wisgov.state.wi.us.

Office of the Lieutenant-Governor: 19 East State Capitol, POB 2043, Madison, WI 53702; tel. (608) 266-3516; fax (608) 267-3571; e-mail ltgov@wisconsin.gov; internet www.ltgov.wisconsin.gov.

Office of the Secretary of State: 30 West Mifflin St, 10th Floor, POB 7848, Madison, WI 53707-7848; tel. (608) 266-8888; fax (608) 266-3159; e-mail statesec@sos.state.wi.us; internet www.sos.state.wi.us.

Office of the Attorney-General: Dept of Justice, POB 7857, Madison, WI 53707-7857; tel. (608) 266-1221; fax (608) 267-2779; e-mail webmaster@doj.state.wi.us; internet www.doj.state.wi.us.

Office of the Treasurer: 1 South Pinckney St, Suite 550, POB 7871, Madison, WI 53707-7871; tel. (608) 266-1714; fax (608) 266-2647; e-mail treasury@ost.state.wi.us; internet www.ost.state.wi.us.

Department of Public Instruction: 125 South Webster St, POB 7841, Madison, WI 53707-7841; tel. (608) 266-3390; fax (608) 267-1052; e-mail webadmin@dpi.wi.gov; internet www.dpi.wi.gov; headed by Supt of Public Instruction.

Department of Agriculture, Trade and Consumer Protection: POB 8911, Madison, WI 53708-8911; tel. (608) 224-5012; fax (608) 224-5045; e-mail rod.nilsestuen@wisconsin.gov; internet www.datcp.state.wi.us; Sec. ROD NILSESTUEN.

Department of Commerce: 201 West Washington Ave, POB 7970, Madison, WI 53717-7970; tel. (608) 266-1018; fax (608) 264-6154; e-mail eaaron.oliver@wisconsin.gov; internet www.commerce.state.wi.us; Sec. DICK J. LEINENKUGEL.

Department of Corrections: 3099 East Washington Ave, POB 7925, Madison, WI 53707-7925; tel. (608) 240-5000; fax (608) 240-3300; e-mail docweb@doc.state.wi.us; internet www.wi-doc.com; Sec. RICK RAEMISCH.

Department of Health and Family Services: 1 West Wilson St, Madison, WI 53703; tel. (608) 266-1865; fax (608) 266-7882; e-mail webmaster@dhfs.state.wi.us; internet dhfs.wisconsin.gov; Sec. KAREN TIMBERLAKE.

Department of Military Affairs: 2400 Wright St, PO Box 8111, Madison, WI 53708-8111; tel. (608) 242-3050; fax (608) 242-3051; e-mail tim.donovan@us.army.mil; internet dma.wi.gov; Adj.-Gen. Col DONALD DUNBAR.

Department of Natural Resources: 101 South Webster St, POB 7921, Madison, WI 53707-7921; tel. (608) 266-2621; fax (608) 261-4380; internet dnr.wi.gov; Sec. MATTHEW J. FRANK.

Department of Revenue: 2135 Rimrock Rd, POB 8933, Madison, WI 53708-8933; tel. (608) 266-6466; fax (608) 266-5718; e-mail dorsecretary@revenue.wi.gov; internet www.dor.state.wi.us; Sec. ROGER M. ERVIN.

Department of Transportation: 4802 Sheboygan Ave, POB 7910, Madison, WI 53707-7910; tel. (608) 266-3581; fax (608) 266-9912; e-mail sec.exec@dot.state.wi.us; internet www.dot.wisconsin.gov; Sec. FRANK BUSALACCHI.

Department of Workforce Development: 201 East Washington Ave, GEF-1, Rm A400, POB 7946, Madison, WI 53707-7946; tel. (608) 266-3131; fax (608) 266-1784; e-mail howard.cosgrove@dwd.state.wi.us; internet www.dwd.state.wi.us; Sec. ROBERTA GASSMAN.

Housing and Economic Development Authority: 201 West Washington Ave, Suite 700, POB 1728, Madison, WI 53701-1728; tel. (608) 266-7884; fax (608) 267-1099; e-mail info@wheda.com; internet www.wheda.com; Exec. Dir ANTONIO RILEY.

Insurance Commission: 125 South Webster St, Madison, WI 53703-3474; tel. (608) 266-3585; fax (608) 266-9935; e-mail ociinformation@wisconsin.gov; internet oci.wi.gov; Commr SEAN DILWEG.

Public Service Commission: 610 North Whitney Way, POB 7854, Madison, WI 53707-7854; tel. (608) 266-5481; fax (608) 266-3957; e-mail sandra.paske@psc.state.wi.us; internet psc.wi.gov; Chair. ERIC CALLISTO.

Legislature
(August 2008)

Senate

Dem. 17; Rep. 14; 2 vacancies; Total 33

President: FRED RISSER (Dem.).

President Pro Tempore: TIM CARPENTER (Dem.).

Chief Clerk: ROBERT J. MARCHANT.

Assembly

Rep. 52; Dem. 47; Total 99

Speaker: MICHAEL HUEBSCH (Rep.).

Speaker Pro Tempore: MARK GOTTLIEB (Rep.).

Chief Clerk: PATRICK E. FULLER.

Wyoming

Gross Area: 253,349 sq km (97,818 sq miles).

Resident Population (1 July 2007, estimate): 522,830.

State Capital: Cheyenne.

Principal Cities (population at 1 July 2006, estimate): Cheyenne (capital) 55,314; Casper 52,089.

LOCATION, TOPOGRAPHY AND CLIMATE

The State of Wyoming (nicknamed 'The Equality State') is in the West of the USA and is bordered by Montana to the north, South Dakota and Nebraska to the east, Colorado and Utah to the south and Utah, Idaho and Montana to the west. Much of the eastern half of Wyoming belongs to the flat Great Plains. The land rises to the Black Hills in the north-east corner, the Big Horn Mountains in the north and the Laramie and Medicine Bow Mountains in the south. In the south-west of Wyoming is the flat Wyoming Basin, an extension of the Great Plains that divide the Southern and Middle Rocky Mountains, the latter occupying the north-west of the state. Gannett Peak in the Rocky Mountains is Wyoming's highest point, at 4,207 m (13,804 ft). The Continental Divide runs in a north-west-south direction through the state. Except for the North Platte, which curves across the south-east from Colorado to Nebraska, all Wyoming's principal rivers—the Yellowstone, Powder, Big Horn, Green, Snake, Belle Fourche, Cheyenne, Bear and Niobrara—have their sources within the state's boundaries. The state's largest lake is Yellowstone, at 347 sq km (134 sq miles). Wyoming has a continental, semi-arid climate.

HISTORICAL BACKGROUND

Soshone, Sioux, Cheyenne, Oglala and Arapaho tribes lived in Wyoming when the first French-Canadian traders, including François and Louis-Joseph Vérendrye, arrived in the area in the 18th century. John Colter, a US fur trader, was the first to traverse the north-west of the region in 1807–08 and more trappers and traders followed in the 1820s. With the discovery of gold in California in 1848, thousands of people began to cross Wyoming on the Oregon Trail and supply towns were established along the route. The arrival of the Union Pacific Railroad in 1867 encouraged settlement in the region and in 1868 Wyoming was given territorial status. In 1869 the territorial legislature became the first in the USA to grant suffrage to women. Wyoming became the 44th state of the Union on 10 July 1890. Conflicts between large land owners and small ranches in the area resulted in the Johnson County Cattle War in 1892, when federal troops were called in to restore order.

ECONOMY

Agriculture, mining and the tourism and recreation industries are the chief bases of economic activity in Wyoming. In 2007 gross domestic product by state was US $31,514m.—the third lowest level in the USA after Vermont and North Dakota. Average per-head income by state was the fifth highest nationally—$47,038—in 2007, when it was estimated that 8.7% of the state population were living below the poverty line. The civilian labour force numbered 296,800 in mid-2008 when the state demonstrated the second lowest rate of unemployment nation—wide, at 3.0% (8,900 persons). In 2007 7.09% of those employed belonged to a trade union, while union agreements covered 9.4%.

Farmland covered 34.4m. acres (13.9m. ha) in 2007. There were 8,800 farms in that year, with an average size of 3,909 acres, the largest average farm size in the USA. In 2002 some 32.1% of total cropland was irrigated. Sales of livestock and livestock products made up 83% of farm income in 2007, with crops accounting for the remaining 17%. Cattle and calves, hay, hogs and sheep and lambs were the most important agricultural commodities in that year. Sugar beets, dairy products, wheat, barley, dry beans, greenhouse and nursery products and honey also contributed to farm income. Approximately 18% of Wyoming was forested in 2003, and there is some lumbering activity, all concerned with softwood production.

The value of Wyoming's non-fuel mineral production was US $1,670m. in 2007, with the state ranked 14th in the USA in this respect. Leading minerals were soda ash (an inorganic chemical) and bentonite, for both of which the state was ranked first nationwide, and grade-A helium (for which Wyoming ranked second). Construction sand and gravel and portland cement were also important. The state was the foremost bituminous-coal producer in 2007, with output of 453.6m. short tons; in 2005 it ranked fourth for natural gas production and seventh for crude oil.

Wyoming ranked 48th of the US states, in terms of the value of its shipments, in 2006. Manufacturing does not make a major contribution to the state economy. The leading manufacturing sectors include chemicals, lumber and wood products, printing and publishing, machinery and food and kindred products. The state's manufacturing shipments were valued at US $7,598m. in 2006, of which 45% was added during manufacture.

In 2004 domestic travel expenditures amounted to US $1,842m., and Wyoming ranked 45th among the states in terms of money spent. Total general expenditures by the state government in 2006 were $4,011m. General revenue totalled $4,897m., of which $1,956m. was provided by the federal Government and $2,122m. was derived from taxes. Wyoming received $1,998m. in federal aid in 2006.

CONSTITUTION AND GOVERNMENT

Wyoming's only Constitution became effective on 10 July 1890. Amendments to the Constitution proposed by the Legislature must be approved by a two-thirds' vote of the elected members of each house, and ratified by a majority of voters in an election. The Governor is elected to serve a four-year term of office and is succeeded in his or her absence by the Secretary of State. The Legislature has 30 senators and 60 representatives, who are elected to serve terms of four and two years respectively; alternate halves of the Senate are elected every two years. Regular legislative sessions are held annually: in odd-numbered years the session starts in January and lasts for no longer than 40 days; in even-numbered years the session starts in February and lasts for a maximum of 20 days. A bill becomes law when it has been passed by the Legislature and signed by the Governor. During session it may also become law if it remains unsigned for three days after presentation to the Governor. Outside session the Governor has 15 days from the adjournment of the session to consider a bill, after which it becomes law unless vetoed. A gubernatorial veto may be overridden by a vote by two-thirds of the elected members of each house. Enacted legislation becomes effective immediately. In 2006 the Democratic incumbent, Dave Freudenthal, won a comfortable victory in the gubernatorial election with 70% of the vote. In the 2008 presidential election the Republicans secured 65% of votes cast. There are 23 administrative counties in Wyoming.

Elected Executive Branch Officials

Governor (2007–11): Dr DAVID D. (DAVE) FREUDENTHAL (Dem.).

Secretary of State: MAX MAXFIELD (Rep.).

Treasurer: JOSEPH B. MEYER (Rep.).

Auditor: RITA C. MEYER (Rep.).

Superintendent of Public Instruction: Dr JAMES M. MCBRIDE (Rep.).

Selected Government Addresses

Office of the Governor: State Capitol, 200 West 24th St, Cheyenne, WY 82002-0010; tel. (307) 777-7434; fax (307) 632-3909; e-mail governor@state.wy.us; internet governor.wy.gov.

Office of the Secretary of State: State Capitol, 200 West 24th St, Cheyenne, WY 82002; tel. (307) 777-7378; fax (307) 777-6217; e-mail secofstate@state.wy.us; internet soswy.state.wy.us.

Office of the Treasurer: State Capitol, 200 West 24th St, Cheyenne, WY 82002; tel. (307) 777-7408; fax (307) 777-5411; e-mail treasurer@state.wy.us; internet treasurer.state.wy.us.

Office of the Auditor: State Capitol, Rm 114, 200 West 24th St, Cheyenne, WY 82002; tel. (307) 777-7831; fax (307) 777-6983; e-mail cteter1@state.wy.us; internet sao.state.wy.us.

Department of Education: Hathaway Bldg, 2nd Floor, 2300 Capitol Ave, Cheyenne, WY 82002-0050; tel. (307) 777-7690; fax (307) 777-6234; e-mail supt@educ.state.wy.us; internet www.k12.wy.us; headed by Supt of Public Instruction.

Department of Agriculture: 2219 Carey Ave, Cheyenne, WY 82002-0100; tel. (307) 777-7321; fax (307) 777-6593; e-mail jetche@state.wy.us; internet wyagric.state.wy.us; Dir JOHN ETCHEPARE.

Department of Corrections: 700 West 21st St, Cheyenne, WY 82002-3427; tel. (307) 777-7208; fax (307) 777-7479; internet doc.state.wy.us; Dir ROBERT O. LAMPERT.

Department of Environmental Quality: Herschler Bldg, 122 West 25th St, Cheyenne, WY 82002; tel. (307) 777-7937; fax (307) 777-7682; e-mail deqwyo@state.wy.us; internet deq.state.wy.us; Dir JOHN V. CORRA.

Department of Health: Hathaway Bldg, Rm 401, 2300 Capitol Ave, Cheyenne, WY 82002; tel. (307) 777-7656; fax (307) 777-7439; e-mail wdh@state.wy.us; internet wdh.state.wy.us; Dir Dr BRENT SHERARD.

Department of Insurance: 106 East 6th Ave, Cheyenne, WY 82002; tel. (307) 777-7401; fax (307) 777-2446; e-mail wyinsdep@state.wy.us; internet insurance.state.wy.us; Commr KEN VINES.

Department of Revenue: Herschler Bldg, 2nd Floor West, 122 West 25th St, Cheyenne, WY 82002-0110; tel. (307) 777-7961; fax (307) 777-7722; e-mail directorofrevenue@wy.gov; internet revenue.state.wy.us; Dir EDMUND J. SCHMIDT.

Department of Transportation: 5300 Bishop Blvd, Cheyenne, WY 82009-3340; tel. (307) 777-4375; fax (307) 777-4289; internet dot.state.wy.us; Dir JOHN COX.

Military Department: 5500 Bishop Blvd, Cheyenne, WY 82009-3320; tel. (307) 772-5253; fax (307) 772-5132; e-mail deidre.forster@us.army.mil; internet www.wy.ngb.army.mil; Adj.-Gen. Maj.-Gen. EDWARD L. WRIGHT, Jr.

Office of the Attorney-General: State Capitol, Rm 123, 200 West 24th St, Cheyenne, WY 82002; tel. (307) 777-7841; fax (307) 777-6869; e-mail agwebmaster@state.wy.us; internet attorneygeneral.state.wy.us; Attorney-Gen. BRUCE A. SALZBURG.

Office of State Lands and Investments: Herschler Bldg, 3rd Floor West, 122 West 25th St, Cheyenne, WY 82002; tel. (307) 777-7331; fax (307) 777-5400; e-mail slfmail@state.wy.us; internet slf-web.state.wy.us; Dir LYNNE BOOMGAARDEN.

Public Service Commission: Hansen Bldg, Suite 300, 2515 Warren Ave, Cheyenne, WY 82002; tel. (307) 777-7427; fax (307) 777-5700; e-mail wyoming_psc@state.wy.us; internet psc.state.wy.us; Chair. KATHLEEN A. (CINDY) LEWIS.

Wyoming Business Council: 214 West 15th St, Cheyenne, WY 82002-0240; tel. (307) 777-2800; fax (307) 777-2838; e-mail info@wyomingbusiness.org; internet www.wyomingbusiness.org; CEO ROBERT JENSEN.

Legislature

(August 2008)

Senate

Rep. 23; Dem. 7; Total 30

President: JOHN SCHIFFER (Rep.).

Vice-President: JIM ANDERSON (Rep.).

Chief Clerk: LIV C. HANES.

House of Representatives

Rep. 43; Dem. 17; Total 60

Speaker: ROY COHEE (Rep.).

Speaker Pro Tempore: TOM LUBNAU (Rep.).

Chief Clerk: PAUL S. GALEOTOS.

Part Three

CANADA

INTRODUCTION

CANADA: A CHRONOLOGY SINCE COLONIZATION

982–1016: Norse explorers from Greenland are thought to have explored and established temporary settlements on the eastern coast of present-day Canada.

1497–98: Giovanni Caboto (John Cabot) explored the coast between Labrador and Chesapeake Bay (now in the USA).

1522: Temporary settlements established by European fishermen on Newfoundland.

1534: Jacques Cartier sailed up the St Lawrence River to the sites of present-day Québec City and Montréal (Québec).

1583: The island of Newfoundland claimed for the English Crown.

1603: Samuel de Champlain became the first governor of Canada, claiming Newfoundland, New France and Acadia for France. In the next two years French settlements were founded on the St Croix River and at Port Royal (later Annapolis Royal).

1608: Québec City founded; it subsequently became the administrative centre of New France.

1610: Henry Hudson discovered what became known as Hudson's Bay.

1615–16: William Baffin explored Canada's northern coastline.

1621: Acadia granted to a Scottish nobleman by the English Crown and named Nova Scotia.

1629: English forces occupied Québec City.

1632: Control of New France and Acadia yielded to the French by King Charles I of England and of Scotland.

1642: The city of Montréal founded.

1663: New France became a French royal colony.

1670: The Hudson's Bay Company received its trading monopoly charter from the English (British) monarch, together with control of territory on and to the west of Hudson Bay.

1713: The Peace of Utrecht, which followed a series of Franco–British conflicts, awarded control over Newfoundland, mainland Acadia and the islands of Saint Pierre and Miquelon to the United Kingdom.

1754–63: The French and Indian War (part of what is known in Europe as the Seven-Years War) between France and the United Kingdom; it was concluded by the Treaty of Paris which secured for the United Kingdom control over all formerly French-claimed lands in North America, except for Saint Pierre and Miquelon, which were restored to France.

1755: Many of the French settlers in Acadia began to be forcibly deported.

1758: British North America's first elected legislative assembly met at Halifax, Nova Scotia.

1763: Having gained sovereignty throughout present-day Canada, the British Crown determined the boundaries of Québec and established a new government there; Cape Breton Island annexed to Nova Scotia for the first time, and Labrador united with Newfoundland.

1774: The Québec Act extended the colony's boundaries and guaranteed subjects religious and linguistic freedom.

1776: The North West Company founded by traders in Montréal.

1778: The British navigator, Capt. James Cook, landed in Nootka Sound on the British Columbia coast.

1784: New Brunswick separated from Nova Scotia.

1786: St John's Island separated from Nova Scotia.

1791: The Constitutional Act established representative government in Canada; the colony was divided into Upper Canada (later Ontario) and Lower Canada (Québec), each with its own system of government.

1799: St John's Island renamed Prince Edward Island.

1802: Saint Pierre and Miquelon, taken by the British in 1793 during the war with revolutionary France, were returned under the Treaty of Amiens.

1812–14: In the so-called War of 1812 the USA failed to drive the British out of North America, but the demilitarization of the Great Lakes was later agreed.

1815–18: The Métis (Canadians of mixed French-(North American) Indian ancestry) rebelled in the Red River area.

1816: With the conclusion of the French-British wars, Saint Pierre and Miquelon finally restored to French control.

1821: The Hudson's Bay and North West Companies merged under the name of the former.

1825: The boundaries of present-day Alaska set by the treaty between the British and Russian Empires.

1837: The Rebellions of 1837, in Montréal and Toronto (now Ontario), sought a wider measure of self-government for francophone Canadians.

1840: The Act of Union united Upper and Lower Canada, renaming them Canada West and Canada East, respectively.

1842: The Canadian border with the USA (Maine and present-day Minnesota) fixed by the Webster-Ashburton Treaty.

1846: The western US–Canadian boundary fixed at the 49th parallel (49°N), with the United Kingdom securing control over Vancouver Island.

1848: The joint 'reform ministry'—the first real cabinet—was formed in Canada.

1855: Newfoundland gained full colonial status and its own government.

1858: Full colonial status awarded to British Columbia, following the commencement of a 'gold rush' in the Fraser and Thompson valleys.

1864: A conference in Charlottetown, Prince Edward Island, discussed unification of the Maritime colonies; Canada obtained permission to attend. The Québec Conference, held less than six weeks later, drafted an agreement for the confederation of all the British North American colonies.

1866: Vancouver Island united with British Columbia.

1867: The British North America Act (later known as the first Constitution Act) formed the Dominion of Canada, consisting of the provinces of New Brunswick, Nova Scotia, Ontario and Québec; John Alexander MacDonald, a Conservative, took office as the first federal Prime Minister and the first Parliament convened at Ottawa.

1869: Jacques Riel led the Métis in the Northwest Rebellion. Rupert's Land and other north-western territories sold to Canada by the Hudson's Bay Company.

1870: Land purchased from the Hudson's Bay Company formally constituted as the province of Manitoba (which entered the Dominion) and the Northwest Territories.

1871: British Columbia entered the Dominion.

1873: Establishment of the North West Mounted Police (later the Royal Canadian Mounted Police). Prince Edward Island entered the Dominion. The Liberals, under Alexander Mackenzie, won the general election, but were displaced by the Conservatives in 1878.

1880: An Imperial Order-in-Council formally annexed all British possessions in North America, except Newfoundland but including the Arctic islands, to Canada.

1885: The Canadian Pacific railway completed in British Columbia. The Métis rebelled in Saskatchewan, again led by Jacques Riel.

1896: Discovery of gold at Bonanza Creek in the Klondike (present-day Yukon Territory). The Liberal Party provided the federal Government (until 1911).

1898: Yukon Territory separated from the Northwest Territories.

1903: The border of British Columbia with Alaska (a US possession since 1867) fixed by tribunal. A Norwegian expedition completed the first navigation of the Northwest Passage.

1905: The Northwest Territories Act established new boundaries in the region and created the provinces of Alberta and Saskatchewan, which joined the Dominion.

1909: The Boundary Waters Treaty established the International Joint Commission to settle disputes between the USA and Canada.

1914: Canada supported the United Kingdom, when it declared war on Germany, and entered the First World War.

1917: General conscription introduced, provoking riots in Québec City in the following year.

1919: Canada joined the League of Nations as an independent member.

1921: The Liberals' leader, W. L. Mackenzie King, became Prime Minister for the first time. (Apart from a few months in 1926, he held office until 1930.)

1927: The Newfoundland–Québec border on Labrador was determined.

1931: The Statute of Westminster guaranteed British recognition of the autonomy and equal status of each of the Dominions of the Commonwealth.

1933: Owing to a fiscal crisis, Newfoundland, which had achieved dominion status after the First World War, reverted to being a British crown colony.

1935: A Liberal victory in the general election returned Mackenzie King to the federal premiership (until 1948—the Liberals were to retain power until 1957).

1939: Canada issued a separate declaration of war on Germany and entered the Second World War.

1945: Canada joined the United Nations.

1947: The Canadian Citizenship Act was passed.

1949: The second British North America or Constitution Act enabled the Canadian Parliament to enact constitutional amendments in matters affecting the federal Government; the system of appeals to the Judicial Committee of the Privy Council (based in the United Kingdom) was abolished in full. Newfoundland joined the Dominion of Canada.

1952: Vincent Massey became Canada's first Canadian Governor-General.

1957: Lester B. Pearson, the Secretary of State for External Affairs, was awarded the Nobel Peace Prize. The Liberal Prime Minister (since 1948), Louis St-Laurent, however, led his party to a defeat in the general election and John Diefenbaker formed a Progressive Conservative (PC) administration.

1958: The North American Defense Organization (NORAD) was founded.

1959: The St Lawrence Seaway was opened to sea-going vessels.

1960: The Canadian Bill of Rights gained royal assent.

1962: Official opening of the Trans-Canada Highway.

1963: Lester Pearson led the Liberals to victory in the general election. The Royal Commission on Bilingualism and Biculturalism was appointed.

1965: The 'maple leaf' flag became the official flag of Canada.

1968: Prime Minister Pearson resigned and was replaced by Pierre Trudeau; the latter led the Liberal Party to achieve the first overall majority in the House of Commons since 1962 (it also won the general elections of 1972 and 1974).

1979: Joe Clark formed a minority PC administration.

1980: Trudeau and the Liberals were returned to power in the general election. A referendum in Québec rejected proposals for 'sovereignty-association' by almost 60% of those voting.

1982: The Canada or Constitution Act ended the last formal vestiges of Canada's colonial status by empowering it to amend ('patriating') its own Constitution.

1984: Trudeau resigned and John Turner became Liberal leader and Prime Minister, but, following a general election, Brian Mulroney formed a PC federal administration (re-elected in 1988).

1987: The Meech Lake Accord finalized—it recognized Québec as a 'distinct society' within the Canadian federation and granted the provinces new powers, but it required ratification by the federal Parliament and all 10 provincial legislatures.

1989: The Free Trade Agreement between Canada and the USA came into effect.

1990: The Meech Lake Accord lapsed in June, the Newfoundland legislature having rescinded its earlier endorsement and Manitoba having maintained its opposition. In Québec there were armed confrontations between the civil authorities and militant aboriginal (Indian) groups.

1992: The Charlottetown Agreement, a new federal-provincial constitutional compact designed to reassure Québec, was rejected in a national referendum in October.

1993: The division of the Northwest Territories agreed, with an Inuit territory, Nunavut, projected to come into existence in 1999. In June Mulroney resigned as PC leader and was succeeded by Kim Campbell, who became Canada's first female Prime Minister. In October the PC was defeated in the general election, its representation being reduced to just two seats, and a Liberal Government under Jean Chrétien assumed office.

1994: The North American Free Trade Agreement (NAFTA) came into effect, combining Canada, Mexico and the USA into a free trade area.

1995: Canada's relations with the European Union were strained over fishing quotas in the north-west Atlantic, particularly following the impounding of a Spanish trawler. A referendum in Québec narrowly rejected the 'sovereignty' proposed by the ruling Parti Québécois (PQ, in power since the previous September).

1996: The Chief of Staff of the Armed Forces relinquished his post, following an inquiry into alleged attempts to suppress information concerning the maltreatment of a Somali citizen by Canadian peace-keeping troops in 1993.

1997: Canada and the USA failed to agree the annual quota for the fishing of Pacific salmon, resulting in some animosities. The Liberals narrowly retained power in the general election of 2 June.

1998: At the provincial legislative election in November in Québec, the Liberals gained 48 seats in the 125-seat legislature, compared with the PQ's 76 seats.

1999: On 1 April the Northwest Territories was divided and Nunavut joined the Federation of Canada as a separate territory. The long-standing disagreement with the USA over the demarcation of salmon-fishing rights off the Pacific coast was resolved in June.

2000: At the general election of 27 November the Liberals received 40.8% of the votes cast and won 172 of the 301 seats in the House of Commons. The Canadian Alliance (CA) secured 66 parliamentary seats, the Bloc Québécois obtained 38 seats, the New Democratic Party (NDP) 13 seats and the PC 12.

2001: In January Lucien Bouchard announced his resignation as Premier of Québec, as a member of the provincial legislature and as leader of the PQ. In December the Province of Newfoundland was officially renamed the Province of Newfoundland and Labrador.

2002: In March Ernie Eves succeeded Michael Harris as Premier of Ontario. In August Chrétien announced that he would stand down as Prime Minister in February 2004 and hand over the leadership to another member of the Liberal Party. Dennis Fentie succeeded Pat Duncan as Premier of the Yukon Territory in November.

2003: In April the World Health Organization declared that travel to Toronto was unadvisable as a result of an outbreak of Severe Acute Respiratory Syndrome (SARS). Chrétien retired as Prime Minister in December; he was succeeded by Paul Martin. Also in December the federal branches of the PC and the CA merged to become the Conservative Party.

2004: At the general election in late June the Liberal Party won 135 of the 308 seats in the newly enlarged House of Commons; although lacking a majority, the Liberals formed a minority Government and Martin was returned as Prime Minister. The Conservatives secured a further term in office in Alberta, following a provincial election in November.

2005: In May the Government survived a vote of 'no confidence' by one vote. In June the House of Commons approved legislation legalizing same-sex marriages. The decision prompted the resignation of minister of state Joe Comuzzi from the Federal Ministry. The legislation was approved by the Senate in July. In late September Michaëlle Jean was sworn in as Governor-General. In November a Commission of Inquiry into the alleged misappropriation of campaign funds in Québec in 1997–2001 found that the Liberal Party had illegally obtained election funds. Prime Minister Martin and the current Liberal Government were exonerated, although Martin pledged to hold a general election within 30 days of the publication of the final part of the Commission of Inquiry's report; however, in late November the Government was defeated in a parliamentary vote of 'no confidence' and Parliament was dissolved.

2006: At a general election on 23 January the Liberals were defeated, winning only 103 of the 308 seats in the House of Commons, while the Conservative Party won 124 seats. Lacking a majority, the Conservatives formed a minority Government and party leader Stephen J. Harper was sworn in as Prime Minister in early February. In Nova Scotia the Conservatives were re-elected with reduced representation at a provincial election in June. The Liberals won a provincial election in New Brunswick in September, while the Yukon Party was returned to power in Yukon in October. In November legislation recognizing Québec as a 'nation within a united Canada' was approved by a very large majority in the House of Commons. Although a largely symbolic gesture, the development prompted Minister of Intergovernmental Affairs, Michael D. Chong, to resign from the Cabinet in protest at what he described as 'ethnic nationalism'. In December Ralph Klein, the country's longest serving provincial Premier, retired from the post in Alberta and was succeeded by Ed Stelmach. Also in December Stéphane Dion was elected to the leadership of the Liberal Party, following the resignation of Paul Martin in February.

2007: In early January Prime Minister Stephen Harper effected a reallocation of cabinet portfolios. The appointment of John Baird, former President of the Treasury Board, as Minister of the Environment, was seen by some observers as an attempt by Harper to highlight his Government's environmental policies. A provincial election in Québec in March resulted in a loss of seats for the Liberal Party and led to the re-elected Premier, Jean Charest, presiding over a minority government. Further provincial elections in May resulted in the re-election of the ruling NDP administration in Manitoba and a Liberal victory over the governing PCP in Prince Edward Island. In October the incumbent administrations were re-elected in Ontario and Newfoundland and Labrador. Finally, in November Brad Wall became Premier of Saskatchewan, after his Saskatchewan Party won a majority in the provincial election.

2008: At a provincial election in Alberta in March the PC was returned to power with an increased majority. The Federal Minister of Foreign Affairs, Maxime Bernier, resigned in May after it emerged that he had left classified documents at the home of a former girlfriend. The resignation prompted a cabinet reorganization, in which David Emerson assumed the foreign affairs portfolio. Michael Fortier succeeded Emerson as Minister of International Trade and Christian Paradis became Minister of Public Works and Government Services. In September Prime Minister Harper called an early general election for 14 October, hoping to achieve a majority in the House of Commons for his Conservative Party. However, according to preliminary results, the Conservatives only succeeded in increasing their representation by 16 seats, to 143 seats, falling short of the 155 seats needed for a majority. The Liberal Party won 76 legislative seats. Harper failed to increase support for his party in Québec, where voters elected 50 members of the Bloc Québécois to Parliament. The NDP secured 37 seats and independent candidates were elected to the final two seats. Dion was criticized for the Liberal Party's relatively poor performance in the election, which was in part attributed to his unpopular proposals for a tax on carbon dioxide emissions. He subsequently announced his decision to resign from the party leadership.

PRIME MINISTERS OF CANADA

July 1867–November 1873: Sir John A. MacDonald (Conservative).

November 1873–October 1878: Alexander Mackenzie (Liberal).

October 1878–June 1891: Sir John A. MacDonald (Conservative).

June 1891–November 1892: Sir John J. C. Abbott (Conservative).

December 1892–December 1894: Sir John S. D. Thompson (Conservative).

December 1894–April 1896: Sir Mackenzie Bowell (Conservative).

May 1896–July 1896: Sir Charles Tupper (Conservative).

July 1896–October 1911: Sir Wilfred Laurier (Liberal).

October 1911–October 1917: Sir Robert L. Borden (Conservative).

October 1917–July 1920: Sir Robert L. Borden (Unionist).

July 1920–December 1921: Arthur Meighen (Unionist).

December 1921–June 1926: W. L. Mackenzie King (Liberal).

June 1926–September 1926: Arthur Meighen (Conservative).

September 1926–August 1930: W. L. Mackenzie King (Liberal).

August 1930–October 1935: R. B. Bennett (Conservative).

October 1935–November 1948: W. L. Mackenzie King (Liberal).

November 1948–June 1957: Louis St-Laurent (Liberal).

June 1957–April 1963: John G. Diefenbaker (Progressive Conservative).

April 1963–April 1968: Lester B. Pearson (Liberal).

April 1968–June 1979: Pierre Elliott Trudeau (Liberal).

June 1979–March 1980: Joe Clark (Progressive Conservative).

March 1980–June 1984: Pierre Elliott Trudeau (Liberal).

June 1984–September 1984: John N. Turner (Liberal).

September 1984–June 1993: M. Brian Mulroney (Progressive Conservative).

June 1993–November 1993: Kim Campbell (Progressive Conservative).

November 1993–December 2003: Jean Chrétien (Liberal).

December 2003–February 2006: Paul Martin (Liberal).

February 2006–: Stephen J. Harper (Conservative).

AREA AND POPULATION

(Source: Statistics Canada, Ottawa, ON K1A 0T6.)

Area, Population and Density

(Note: Totals may not be equal to the sum of components, owing to rounding. Figures for area predate 2006 census.)

SUMMARY

Area (sq km)	
Land	9,093,507*
Inland water	891,163
Total	9,984,670†
Population (census results)	
1851	2,436,297
1901	5,371,315
1951‡	14,009,429
1991§	27,296,860
1996§	28,846,761
2001§	30,007,094
at 16 May 2006	
Males‖	15,475,970
Females‖	16,136,925
Total	31,612,897
Population (postcensal estimate, at 1 July)	
2007	32,976,026
Density (per sq km) at 1 July 2007	3.3

* Land area was reported as 9,012,112 sq km at 2001 census, and 9,017,699 sq km according to preliminary figures for 2006 census.

† 3,855,102 sq miles.

‡ Newfoundland included for the first time. Excluding Newfoundland, the total would have been 13,648,013.

§ Excluding census data for one or more incompletely enumerated Indian reserves or Indian settlements and excluding adjustment for underenumeration.

‖ Figures are rounded to the nearest 5 persons.

PROVINCES AND TERRITORIES
(official estimates at 1 July 2007)

	Area (sq km)				
	Land	Inland water	Total	Population	Density (per sq km, land area only)
Alberta	642,317	19,531	661,848	3,473,984	5.4
British Columbia	925,186	19,549	944,735	4,380,256	6.8
Manitoba	553,556	94,241	647,797	1,186,679	2.1
New Brunswick	71,450	1,458	72,908	749,782	10.5
Newfoundland and Labrador	373,872	31,340	405,212	506,275	1.4
Northwest Territories	1,183,085	163,021	1,346,106	42,637	0.04
Nova Scotia	53,338	1,946	55,284	934,147	17.5
Nunavut	1,936,113	157,077	2,093,190	31,113	0.02
Ontario	917,741	158,654	1,076,395	12,803,861	14.0
Prince Edward Island	5,660	—	5,660	138,627	24.5
Québec	1,365,128	176,928	1,542,056	7,700,807	5.6
Saskatchewan	591,670	59,366	651,036	996,869	1.7
Yukon Territory	474,391	8,052	482,443	30,989	0.07
Total	9,093,507	891,163	9,984,670	32,976,026	3.6

Note: According to preliminary results of 2006 census, revised total land area was 9,017,699 sq km.

Population by Province or Territory and Selected Ethnic Origins

(Note: Census figures exclude data for one or more incompletely enumerated Indian reserves or Indian settlements.)

SUMMARY
(respondents to census of 16 May 2006; rounded figures)

	Single origins	Multiple origins*	Total respondents
Alberta	1,526,430	1,729,925	3,256,355
British Columbia	2,131,295	1,943,095	4,074,385
Manitoba	566,005	567,510	1,133,515
New Brunswick	388,220	331,425	719,650
Newfoundland and Labrador	347,230	153,380	500,610
Northwest Territories	25,110	15,950	41,055
Nova Scotia	442,030	461,055	903,090
Nunavut	24,815	4,515	29,325
Ontario	6,854,340	5,174,555	12,028,895
Prince Edward Island	61,805	72,395	134,205
Québec	5,511,560	1,924,340	7,435,905
Saskatchewan	427,700	526,150	953,850
Yukon Territory	13,045	17,145	30,195
Total	18,319,580	12,921,445	31,241,030

* Includes persons who reported more than one origin.

SINGLE ORIGINS
(respondents to census of 16 May 2006)

	British*	French†	Other European	Chinese	Other Asian, Arab and African	Central and South American‡	Aboriginal peoples§	Other North American‖	Total (incl. others)
Alberta	268,825	43,330	456,715	110,900	235,935	25,735	89,340	293,720	1,526,430
British Columbia	400,620	35,230	461,245	377,550	465,690	22,180	90,970	271,160	2,131,295
Manitoba	75,145	20,815	202,340	12,480	67,250	7,715	96,790	83,370	566,005
New Brunswick	85,025	52,320	12,410	2,155	5,910	810	10,415	219,120	388,220
Newfoundland and Labrador	145,735	3,765	3,595	1,165	3,025	395	12,395	177,125	347,230
Northwest Territories	2,770	485	1,835	280	1,455	115	15,020	3,125	25,110
Nova Scotia	146,070	25,835	35,650	3,655	16,210	1,215	11,670	201,695	442,030
Nunavut	1,130	220	300	55	185	35	22,185	705	24,815
Ontario	1,174,720	184,240	1,907,515	543,320	1,416,395	313,955	98,775	1,213,795	6,854,340
Prince Edward Island	26,330	5,455	2,830	200	920	150	660	25,260	61,805
Québec	155,900	871,040	479,030	74,945	368,725	157,270	90,420	3,313,985	5,511,560
Saskatchewan	63,310	13,550	160,750	8,410	15,690	2,235	87,940	75,675	427,700
Yukon Territory	2,745	635	2,435	245	510	70	3,835	2,545	13,045
Total single origins	2,548,330	1,256,905	3,726,655	1,135,370	2,597,905	531,900	630,425	5,881,285	18,319,580

* Includes the single origins of English, Irish, Scottish, Welsh, British not included elsewhere and Other British.
† Includes the single origins of French and Acadian.
‡ Includes the Caribbean.
§ Includes the single origins of Inuit, Métis and North American Indians.
‖ Includes those classifying themselves as single origin Canadians.

Population by Age

SUMMARY
(census of 16 May 2006, preliminary)

	Male	Female	Total	%
0–4	864,600	825,940	1,690,540	5.3
5–9	926,855	882,520	1,809,375	5.7
10–14	1,065,860	1,014,060	2,079,925	6.6
15–19	1,095,285	1,045,205	2,140,490	6.8
20–24	1,047,950	1,032,435	2,080,385	6.6
25–29	975,945	1,009,635	1,985,580	6.3
30–34	987,720	1,032,515	2,020,230	6.4
35–39	1,083,495	1,124,780	2,208,270	7.0
40–44	1,285,535	1,324,925	2,610,455	8.3
45–49	1,290,125	1,330,470	2,620,600	8.3
50–54	1,158,970	1,198,330	2,357,300	7.5
55–59	1,026,395	1,058,230	2,084,620	6.6
60–64	780,135	809,730	1,589,870	5.0
65–69	593,810	640,770	1,234,575	3.9
70–74	493,460	560,320	1,053,785	3.3
75–79	386,485	493,095	879,575	2.8
80–84	251,420	395,285	646,705	2.0
85–89	114,585	228,095	342,685	1.1
90 and over	47,345	130,585	177,925	0.6
Total	15,475,970	16,136,930	31,612,895	100.0

Note: Figures are rounded to the nearest 5 persons: totals may not be equal to the sum of component parts, owing to rounding to the nearest 5 persons.

PROVINCES AND TERRITORIES
('000 persons, official estimates at 1 July 2007)

	Under 14 years	15–64 years	65 years and over	Total
Alberta	648.1	2,463.9	361.9	3,474.0
British Columbia	689.5	3,072.9	617.8	4,380.3
Manitoba	227.8	798.1	160.8	1,186.7
New Brunswick	115.5	525.7	108.6	749.8
Newfoundland and Labrador	76.6	359.1	70.6	506.3
Northwest Territories	10.1	30.4	2.2	42.6
Nova Scotia	144.7	651.1	138.4	934.1
Nunavut	10.3	19.8	1.0	31.1
Ontario	2,240.7	8,877.4	1,685.7	12,803.9
Prince Edward Island	23.5	95.1	20.1	138.6
Québec	1,230.9	5,364.3	1,105.5	7,700.8
Saskatchewan	190.0	658.6	148.3	996.9
Yukon	5.4	23.2	2.4	31.0
Total	5,613.0	22,939.6	4,423.4	32,976.0

Census Metropolitan Areas

(census of 16 May 2006)

Toronto	5,113,149	Victoria	330,088
Montréal	3,635,571	Windsor	323,342
Vancouver	2,116,581	Saskatoon	233,923
Ottawa-Gatineau	1,130,761	Regina	194,971
Calgary	1,079,310	Sherbrooke	186,952
Edmonton	1,034,945	St John's (NL)	181,113
Québec	715,515	Barrie	177,061
Winnipeg	694,668	Kelowna	162,276
Hamilton	692,911	Abbotsford	159,020
London	457,720	Greater Sudbury/Grand Sudbury	158,258
Kitchener	451,235	Kingston	152,358
St Catharines-Niagara	390,317	Saguenay	151,643
Halifax	372,858	Trois-Rivières	141,529
Oshawa	330,594	Guelph	127,009

Principal Incorporated Cities and Towns

(census of 16 May 2006)

Toronto	2,503,281	Halifax	372,679	Richmond	174,461	Abbotsford	123,864
Montréal	1,620,693	Laval	368,709	Oakville	165,613	Cambridge	120,371
Calgary	988,193	London	352,395	Burlington	164,415	Kingston	117,207
Ottawa	812,129	Markham	261,573	Richmond Hill	162,704	Guelph	114,943
Edmonton	730,372	Gatineau	242,124	Greater Sudbury/ Grand Sudbury	157,857	Coquitlam	114,565
Mississauga	668,549	Vaughan	238,866	Sherbrooke	147,427	Whitby	111,184
Winnipeg	633,451	Longueuil	229,330	Saguenay	143,692	Thunder Bay	109,140
Vancouver	578,041	Windsor	216,473	Oshawa	141,590	Saanich	108,265
Hamilton	504,559	Kitchener	204,668	St Catharines	131,989	Chatham-Kent	108,177
Québec	491,142	Burnaby	202,799	Lévis	130,006	Kelowna	106,707
Brampton	433,806	Saskatoon	202,340	Barrie	128,430	Cape Breton	102,250
Surrey	394,976	Regina	179,246	Trois-Rivières	126,323	St John's (NL)	100,646

Immigrant Arrivals

	2005	2006	2007
Europe	40,950	37,948	39,008
France	5,430	4,917	5,528
Germany	2,635	3,029	2,554
Greece	145	138	189
Italy	344	421	425
Netherlands	929	892	630
Poland	1,206	1,191	1,157
Portugal	291	405	399
United Kingdom	6,109	6,856	8,485
Asia	159,968	149,523	133,383
Hong Kong	448	459	364
India	33,148	30,758	26,065
Philippines	17,525	17,711	19,068
Viet Nam	1,821	3,123	2,548
Australasia	1,507	1,349	1,495
North and Central America	20,187	21,829	23,453
USA	9,262	10,944	10,450
Caribbean (West Indies)	6,905	6,740	7,958
South America	13,720	13,431	12,898
Africa	25,535	27,172	26,092
Total (incl. others)	262,239	251,652	236,762

Source: Statistics Canada, adapted from CANSIM II Table 051-0006, September 2008.

ESSAYS

ESSAYS ON PUBLIC AFFAIRS

RECENT POLITICAL HISTORY OF CANADA

Prof. CLAUDE DENIS

INTRODUCTION

For almost three years after the general election of January 2006 Prime Minister Stephen J. Harper clung to power before challenging opposition parties to defeat his minority Government in the House of Commons. A weak opposition, however, repeatedly refused to take the initiative, creating the longest election watch in living Canadian memory. Finally, after 32 months, in early September 2008 Harper called for a general election to be held on 14 October, hoping that voters would trust him at last with a majority mandate. This was not to be. Harper's Conservative Party increased its seat count but remained short of a majority, while the Liberal Party remained as the official opposition thanks to its worst performance since confederation in 1867. Days later Stéphane Dion, the Liberal leader, called on his party to select a new head within the next few months. Thus, uncertainty strengthened its claim to be the decade's keyword of Canadian politics.

There have been three federal elections since 2005, four in the last eight years. The country's currency strengthened well above parity with the US dollar at the end of 2007 for the first time in several decades, after falling as low as US $0.63 in the 1990s; towards the end of 2008 it dropped below $0.80 again. During the ongoing world-wide financial crisis that began in 2007, the Canadian banking system has been rated the best in the world by the World Economic Forum, but the country's manufacturing sector is suffering badly, as are the natural resource industries that fed the currency's rise and overall economic growth over the past several years.

Canada stands to suffer, like most countries, from the US-driven financial crisis, which increased in severity in the second half of 2008. However, its own financial system has remained strong and, seemingly, relatively insulated from the ripple effects that have crippled banks, their clients and their investors the world over. Recognizing that Canadian banks and brokerages are feeling pressure despite their basic soundness, the Bank of Canada and the federal Department of Finance have acted, on their own and in concert with their international counterparts, to strengthen credit markets. Interest rates have been reduced, C $25,000m. worth of healthy mortgages have been purchased by the Government in order to increase the banks' ability to extend new loans, and extra liquidities have been made available. Nevertheless, the slowing global economy is already affecting the Canadian economy in other ways, as the country's high levels of exports of natural resources are falling sharply, leading to severe drops in value on the Toronto Stock Exchange and a precipitous decline in the country's currency. For their part, the manufacturing and forestry industries had already been badly damaged by the high Canadian dollar.

Ontario, which was the main driver of the country's economy throughout the 20th century, is on the verge of becoming a 'have-not' province, meaning that its per-head income is poised to fall below the Canadian average. Despite this, in October 2007 Ontarians re-elected a majority Liberal Government, the first such consecutive win for the Liberals in 70 years. Québec nationalism, long seen as a threat to the country's very existence and a particular evil to the western Conservatives, has been celebrated in the House of Commons in the form of a resolution—introduced in November 2006 by Stephen Harper, a western Conservative—recognizing Québec as a nation. In November 2007 voters in Saskatchewan elected the populist Saskatchewan Party in place of the social-democratic Government. In addition, Canada's northern frontier is melting, not only the Arctic Ocean but also the permafrost upon which communities are literally built. However, in March 2008 Alberta's electorate, as was expected, elected another Conservative provincial Government, now headed by Ed Stelmach, who had been a long-serving member of former Premier Ralph Klein's Cabinet.

THE HARPER AGENDA AND THE PEOPLE'S DOUBTS

Stephen Harper's decision to hold an election in 2008 was risky, but not reckless. In published opinion polls, his Conservative Party almost never obtained the support of 40% of the electorate, which was needed to secure a parliamentary majority. However, the main opposition parties were even weaker and showed no signs of improving. Harper decided to run a classic incumbent's campaign, offering little to voters other than the promise of a steady and tested leadership. He went so far as to wait until the last week of the campaign before releasing his party's electoral platform. The Liberal Party, for its part, ran its campaign on a bold environmental platform, the 'Green Shift', which was closely associated with the party's leader and which hinged on establishing a carbon tax, the revenues of which would allow both a reduction in income tax and support for the development of a green economy. In so doing, the Liberals overlooked the fact—or Dion did not want to acknowledge—that opposition parties do not generally *win* elections in Canada; rather, governments *lose* them with the aid of the opposition offensive against them. The Bloc Québécois (BQ), which controlled three-quarters of Québec's 75 seats, was on the defensive, and fearful of losing a large number of seats to the Conservatives.

Early in the five-week campaign the results of opinion polls were favourable towards Harper, but in the days before the campaign was launched the Government had announced a C $45m. reduction in funding for the arts. Although the amount was relatively small, the arts community reacted with outrage and launched a protest movement that gradually became a source of vexation for Harper, especially in Québec. The BQ seized on this opportunity to remind the residents of Québec that the Conservatives could not be trusted and had little respect for the arts. Harper subsequently compounded the problem by making a proposal that adolescents as young as 14 should be sentenced to life in prison when convicted of serious crimes such as rape and murder. As the prevailing attitude in Québec regarding youth crime was to focus on rehabilitation, this harshly punitive approach was denounced to great effect by Gilles Duceppe, the leader of the BQ, with the result that the gains that had been confidently predicted for the Conservatives in Québec evaporated. Harper's oddly passive performance in both the French- and English-language televised debates, and his slowness in responding to the rapidly unfolding global financial crisis, confirmed that the Conservatives would remain shy of their parliamentary majority. Their reputation was also damaged by a listeriosis outbreak in mid-2008 in several parts of the country that led to the deaths of at least 14 people: government agencies were apparently slow to react to the crisis and the Conservatives were vulnerable to claims that they wanted to deregulate and privatize food-safety inspection, leading to fears that this would further endanger the populace. Conversely, the disastrously unconvincing Liberal campaign and poor perception of the party's leader among the electorate provided a realistic opportunity for the Conservatives to increase their plurality. The New Democratic Party (NDP), which was led for the third time in an election campaign by Jack Layton, marginally increased its percentage of the vote, but benefited greatly from the Liberal collapse and vote-splitting: 38 of the NDP's candidates were elected to Parliament.

The 2008 electoral campaign heralded the arrival of the Green Party as a truly significant player on Canada's political scene. Elizabeth May, its dynamic—if controversial—leader, was a credible presence on the campaign trail, her role boosted by her friend Stéphane Dion's major focus on the environment. Ultimately, no Green candidates were elected, but the party secured a respectable and unprecedented 6.8% of total votes cast. Once again, however, the environment failed to be the major election issue that environmentalists had counted on for years as the financial crisis became an increasingly pressing issue in the final two weeks before voting day. It is not entirely surprising, therefore, that Canada displayed little evidence of its commitment to the Kyoto Protocol: greenhouse gas emissions increased by 25% between 1990 and 2005, and no meaningful plan to reverse the trend has been put forward. Harper's talk of Canada as an 'energy superpower', on the strength of massive growth in the exploitation of bituminous sands in Alberta, certainly did not signal moves towards more climate-friendly practice.

Perhaps sensing that the election campaign lacked a significant purpose, a substantial number of registered voters did not take part in the ballot, leading to the lowest recorded turnout in a general election, of 59.1%. Frustration was the first sentiment expressed by many Canadians on the following morning. Despite election spending totalling some C $300m., Canadians were presented with very little change other than the prospect of a new leader for the Liberal Party in the first half of 2009. The new Harper Government was expected to have little manoeuvring space around the opposition, and all parties were likely to be wary of the implications of confidence votes in the House of Commons: holding another election soon would certainly incur the wrath of an electorate that is little impressed with its political class. In the same vein, the Government will be closely scrutinized for its economic management in a time of financial chaos and looming recession.

Canadians first elected a very conservative minority federal Government in January 2006, while showing no signs of wanting to revoke social programmes or legislation that allowed same-sex couples to marry, for example, and retaining a poor view of the Administration of President George W. Bush in the USA. By October the new Government had already acted decisively on many fronts to implement right-wing policies that would set the country on a course significantly different from that pursued by its several predecessors—if it managed to hold on to power or to obtain an improbable majority after the next general election. Although the previous Government, under Prime Minister Paul Martin, also lacked a parliamentary majority and collapsed after 18 months, it had been on the same broad course that Canadians have come to expect from their Government over the past two decades: moderately progressive on social issues, free-trading and close to the USA economically, multilateralist and orientated to peace operations in foreign policy and, since the mid-1990s, wedded to balancing the federal budget. In contrast, while maintaining a free-trading orientation, Harper's Conservatives would veer towards a market- and family-centred approach in social policy; a reduction in the federal Government's role in many areas by returning responsibilities to the provinces; the adoption of a strict law-and-order approach in criminal justice; and, on the international scene, an affirmation of a close alignment with Israel and the development of Canada as a war-making power. Although Harper worked hard to portray his party as modern and moderate, the uncomfortable fact remained that many members of his team did not thoroughly conform to this image. In particular, Harper himself, several of his cabinet ministers and as many as 70 of his Members of Parliament were evangelical Christians, many of them connected to some of the most conservative Christian organizations in the USA and Canada. Such connections were bound to raise questions regarding the Government's relationship with Canada's political mainstream, particularly in areas such as the rights of homosexuals, the strengthening of the country's day-care system and even on the issue of support for Israel.

Despite the narrowness of the Conservatives' electoral victory in 2006, Harper quickly established a bold style and agenda of government, both very much at odds with the outgoing administration. Harper himself became the nearly exclusive spokesperson for the Government, feeding the perception that he was excessively controlling and in doing so he proved to be remarkably non-communicative. The Government announced a narrowly focused agenda of five priorities, most of which could produce quick results in anticipation of an early election: accountability, health care, crime fighting, tax reductions and child care. In its first few months in office the new Government introduced an ambitious Federal Accountability Act; cancelled a federal-provincial agreement on child day care and replaced it with a financial incentive for parents and private care operators; and eliminated the registry of long guns created by the Liberals in the early 1990s. Furthermore, the Government also extended the Canadian military's mission in Afghanistan by two years while increasing the armed forces' financing, and agreed to an expansion of the North American Defense Organization (NORAD), about which the Liberals had been unsure; in a stealthy way, this confirmed Canada's quiet and somewhat indirect participation in the Bush Administration's anti-missile shield. The Conservatives' first truly remarkable move, however, was a negotiated settlement of Canada's decades-long conflict with the USA on the trade of softwood lumber (timber). While the settlement was controversial because of significant concessions made to the US Government, the agreement dramatized Harper's drive to get things done.

On a track parallel to these features of Conservative governance, the Government was much focused on improving its electoral prospects in preparation for the next ballot. The 2006 win was made possible by some improvement in Conservative popularity in Québec at the expense of both the BQ and the Liberals: three-quarters of the increase in the Conservative vote was, surprisingly, in Québec, where the Liberals lost six seats and the BQ lost four. In other parts of the country, small percentage changes and many closely fought three-way races benefited Harper's party and the NDP, while costing the Liberals most of their lost seats. But the Conservatives remained shut out of the country's largest cities, Toronto, Montreal and Vancouver. Drawing the conclusions from these voting patterns, the Conservatives calculated that their future majority depended on making further gains in Québec, by displacing the BQ, and overcoming the recalcitrance of Toronto-area voters. A sustained effort to woo the Québécois and assuage urban Ontarians ensued.

With most of the agenda embodied in the five electoral priorities dispatched in its first nine months in office, the Harper Government found itself with not much to do in the following two years other than managing crises, some of its own making, while waiting for unco-operative opinion polls to improve. Nevertheless, one major commitment, a key component of the strategy to appeal to the Québécois, remained to be settled: reducing the fiscal imbalance. There was much pressure on the second Harper budget, announced in March 2007, to deliver on this count, especially considering that, should the Government lose the vote of confidence implicit in the finance measure, the defeated budget would become the Conservative electoral platform. In the event, the budget was adopted and transferred thousands of millions of dollars in funding to the provinces in several policy areas, thereby attending to the fiscal imbalance; it cut a variety of taxes, in keeping with the Conservative aversion to taxation; and it funded environmental programmes in an attempt to address one of the Government's key weaknesses—its credibility on dealing with climate change. On this front, it did not help that Harper was widely seen, both in Canada and internationally, as playing a rather destructive role at the UN Climate Change Conference held in Bali, Indonesia in December.

The 2007 budget also changed the equalization formula, through which the federal Government transferred money from richer to poorer provinces. A seemingly technical issue, this change involved the inclusion of provincial petroleum revenues in the formula; this had the effect of reducing the amounts that could be received by otherwise 'have-not' provinces such as Nova Scotia, Saskatchewan and Newfoundland and Labrador, while benefiting other 'have-not' provinces—notably Québec. Having promised federal-provincial harmony, the Harper Government thus triggered a major crisis that was to prove costly to the Conservatives in the electoral battle to come: Danny Williams, the popular Conservative Premier of Newfoundland and Labrador, felt betrayed and launched a major political offensive against Harper. The campaign was effective, as Harper's party lost all of its seats in the province in the general election of October 2008. Harper's Minister of Finance, James Flaherty, also angered many investors and pensioners by bringing to an end the growth of 'income trusts', a way of structuring corporate ownership that had allowed an increasing number of large companies to shield their (and their shareholders') income from taxes. While this latter move caused consternation in key constituencies of the Conservative Party, it had become increasingly unavoidable, as income trusts were costing the federal Government's coffers thousands of millions of dollars.

The absence of a parliamentary majority left the Harper Government with few domestic policies to implement, helping international issues to continue to dominate much of the political calendar: climate change and Canada's role in the North Atlantic Treaty Organization (NATO) mission in Afghanistan proved especially troublesome for the Government. The ministers whom Harper initially appointed to deal with these issues, Rona Ambrose at Environment Canada and Gordon O'Connor at the Department of National Defence, did not prove up to the task and were eventually moved to less demanding departments. However, major weaknesses remained in the Cabinet, as was illustrated dramatically in 2008 by the travails of Maxime Bernier as Minister of Foreign Affairs, a post to which he was transferred from Industry Canada in the same cabinet reshuffle. Bernier's partner, Julie Couillard, apparently used her cabinet access to lobby on behalf of a real estate firm that was more or less employing her. As this information gradually emerged in the media, it was revealed that Bernier had left confidential NATO briefing documents at the house of Couillard, a potentially serious compromise of national security. At a time when Harper had hoped to be driving successfully toward an election campaign, the Government's credibility was seriously damaged.

A strong majority of Canadians had long held a positive view of the Kyoto Protocol, a fact that the Harper Government was slow to recognize and take seriously. No Canadian election, it must be admitted, was ever fought and lost on the environment as an issue, and the Conservatives were probably counting on that trend continuing. However, concern over climate change attained such levels by the mid-2000s that old truths about the electoral weakness of environmental issues might have become obsolete. The Conservative Government first promoted a 'Green Plan' focusing on air pollution rather than on climate change, with an outlook on the latter close to that of the Bush Administration in the USA. With a strong electoral base and many of its intellectual roots in petroleum-producing Alberta, Harper's party was strongly averse to the logic of the Kyoto Protocol and to its demands for reducing carbon emissions. Accordingly, throughout 2007 the Government sought to mollify public opinion, first with the appointment of a new environment minister, John Beard, who used stronger rhetoric recognizing the reality of climate change and the necessity to fight it, and with the introduction of a number of carbon-reducing measures in the 2007 budget. Nevertheless, Harper continued to oppose the Kyoto process, tracking the positions of the USA and Australia, and applying to join these two 'Kyoto resisters' in the Asia-Pacific Partnership on Clean Development and Climate.

Like its predecessor, the final budget of the first Harper Government, in early 2008, was thought to provide the opposition a golden opportunity to trigger an election. Now that the value of the Canadian dollar was higher than its US counterpart, and Canadian manufacturing and resource-exporting industries were suffering accordingly, the budget's key plank was a support package for forestry and manufacturing. With no legislative programme left to implement, the Government was operating reactively and the worsening economic situation was putting it on the defensive. However, if the Government seemed weak, the opposition was even weaker. The BQ, which had reliably taken three-quarters of Québec's seats in all elections since the early 1990s, was badly affected by the crisis of the Parti Québécois (PQ) on the provincial stage and by its own leader's abortive part in it (see below). Also, and of more widespread importance, the Liberal Party was not faring well under its new leader, Stéphane Dion, and remained extremely vulnerable financially, as several of the 2006 leadership candidates (including Dion) had difficulty in reimbursing their campaign debts, thereby limiting the party's ability to build its 'war chest'. For the longest time, then, the Liberals and, to a lesser extent, the BQ denounced the Government in the most severe terms while stopping short of calling for a general election to be held.

FROM CHRÉTIEN TO HARPER: QUEBEC AND THE SPONSORSHIP SCANDAL

That Harper even gained a first chance to govern owes much to a governance crisis that Canada inherited from Jean Chrétien's premiership (1993–2003), and that ruined the long-term prospects for Chrétien's Liberal successor and short-lived Prime Minister Paul Martin (2003–06). Although the crisis was exacerbated to some extent by political miscalculations on the part of Martin's incoming administration, seeds of trouble had been planted long ago by Chrétien, who just managed to retire before having to account for them. Martin was indeed humbled in June 2004, in a rare summer election that produced the country's first minority Government in 25 years, and then beaten in early 2006.

As Chrétien was about to retire after four decades in politics and one decade—with three electoral majorities, in 1993, 1997 and 2000—in the office of Prime Minister, he was leading a popular Government and had just made the major decision to ratify the Kyoto Protocol on climate change and to refuse to involve Canada in the US-led invasion and occupation of Iraq. Moreover, Martin, Chrétien's enormously successful and popular Minister of Finance, was the successor that most of the Liberal Party of Canada and much of the country had been waiting for, it seemed, for almost as long as Chrétien had been in power—which did not keep Chrétien himself from enjoying high approval ratings throughout his tenure. Taking into consideration all these factors and the fact that the opposition was divided between two conservative parties, a social-democratic party and a Québec nationalist party, Martin seemed unbeatable. As Canada was nearing an election expected in early 2004, the prospect of more Liberal years focused the minds of the country's two conservative parties on the necessity for them to unite. After earlier failures, the Progressive Conservative Party (PC) and the Canadian Alliance merged in December 2003, to form the Conservative Party of Canada. This was the first of many political surprises that the country was about to see.

Chrétien had become Prime Minister only one year after the 1992 rejection, by referendum, of the constitutional settlement proposed in the Charlottetown Agreement, which would have, among several other things, allowed some recognition of Québec's distinct status within Canada and recognized an 'inherent right to self-government' for the country's aboriginal peoples. This followed a decade of constitutional turmoil, starting with Québec's first sovereignty referendum in 1980 (60% voted 'no') and Prime Minister Trudeau's 1982 patriation of the Constitution, which included the adoption of a Charter of Rights and Freedoms, over Québec's objection. A first attempt to overcome this objection, negotiated at Meech Lake by Prime Minister Brian Mulroney (1984–92), failed to be ratified by all provinces, which led to a second—and final—attempt at Charlottetown. After that failure most Canadians wanted nothing more to do with grand schemes for reforming the country; they were looking for a Government that would merely run it, and Chrétien seemed just the right man.

Other than in dealing with chronic budget deficits (see below), Chrétien's approach as Prime Minister was characterized by a lack of intervention. Despite its popularity with many Canadians, Chrétien's policy of doing nothing on most fronts, including the high politics of the Constitution, was bound to lead to trouble. After Charlottetown, Québec's constitutional demands remained unfulfilled, and the Québécois had grown quite disillusioned with other Canadians' unwillingness to recognize the mostly francophone province as a 'distinct society'. Moreover, with Québec politics evenly split between the federalist Liberal Party and the pro-sovereignty PQ, it was only a matter of time before the PQ returned to power and launched another referendum. The re-elected PQ did indeed hold a referendum in 1995 and almost won it, thanks in part to the mostly disengaged campaign of Chrétien's federal Government: with a record 93% participation rate, 49.4% of voters answered 'yes' to the question of whether they wanted sovereignty, followed by negotiation of an economic association with Canada.

The Chrétien Government reacted to the referendum outcome with uncharacteristic energy and with a paradoxical attitude to the rules of the political game and even to the rule of law. This is when Prime Minister Chrétien recruited Stéphane Dion, a rare and outspoken Trudeau federalist among Québec's intellectuals, to take on the sovereigntists. As Minister of Intergovernmental Affairs, Dion first proved remarkably successful at setting new, strict rules for an eventual Québec 'secession'. The first step involved obtaining a Supreme Court of Canada opinion that denied Québec any legal right to declare its independence unilaterally, although the Court also affirmed the Canadian Government's obligation to negotiate with Québec if the sovereigntists won outright in a referendum with a clear question. However, the Court did not define what question or margin of victory would count as 'clear'. The Chrétien Government, with Dion as its pointman, took the opportunity to offer such definitions unilaterally in its so-called Clarity Act, establishing benchmarks that most observers considered unattainable by sovereigntists. The PQ and the BQ (the sovereigntist party created in the late 1980s to contest elections to the federal Parliament) were unable to counter these moves and found themselves gravely weakened as Chrétien approached 10 years in power.

Not content with its punitive—and successful—strategy of confining the sovereigntists, the federal Government launched a semi-covert campaign to win the support of the Québécois. It did so, in part, with a few relatively minor legislative moves such as a statement by the House of Commons recognizing Québec as a 'distinct society'. More significantly, however, it launched a vast public relations offensive with the aim of increasing the Canadian Government's visibility in Québec, through the sponsoring of numerous cultural events in exchange for the display of Canadian flags and 'wordmarks' (logos). However, the key feature of this branding operation would only become visible later: the sponsorship programme circumvented the rules and processes of Canadian public administration and spending, in order to provide hidden financing to the Liberal Party by funnelling many millions of dollars to Liberal-friendly advertising and communications firms, which then channelled much of the money illegally to the party and retained a commission.

This operation, costing some C $250m. between 1997 and 2002, was uncovered gradually through a series of audits that culminated in the devastating report of the Auditor General of Canada. The report portrayed a rogue unit within the Department of Public Works and Government Services, with direct access to, and political cover from, the Minister's office and the Office of the Prime Minister, awarding contracts, approving payments and transferring money from one agency to another, all in highly irregular ways. In proroguing Parliament ahead of schedule in November 2003 and then retiring promptly, Chrétien kept Auditor General Sheila Fraser from submitting her report to the House of Commons before his departure. As Paul Martin assumed the duties of Prime Minister in December 2003 and planned to hold a general election in early 2004, he felt compelled to recall Parliament (in February) in order to complete some business left unfinished as a result of Chrétien's hasty prorogation. This allowed the release of the Auditor General's report, to which Martin reacted by acknowledging the gravity of what had happened and by trying to distance himself and his Government from his predecessor, an awkward move given his own prominent role in the Chrétien Cabinet. He took immediate corrective measures in the administration of government, postponed the election (eventually until late June) and appointed an independent Commission of Inquiry, headed by Justice John Gomery of the Superior Court of Québec.

Canadians were outraged by the sponsorship scandal and, when the election was finally held on 28 June 2004, the electorate reduced the Liberals to a minority Government. Most importantly perhaps, Québécois voters were so incensed that they gave the BQ very strong support, with 49% of the popular vote there (12% nation-wide) and 54 of the 75 seats in the province. The Gomery Commission began public hearings in September, beginning to reveal—or confirm—unheard-of levels of political corruption, seemingly all the way up to former Prime Minister Chrétien himself. In the poisoned atmosphere of the scandal, the opposition parties tried but failed to defeat the Martin Government over its proposed budget in early 2005. They then decided that their best chance of defeating the Liberals was immediately after the Gomery Commission's 'factual report', due in November (to be followed by a series of recommendations in February 2006). The factual report was not particularly critical of Martin himself, but massively damning of the Liberal Party. The Liberals were still doing relatively well in the opinion polls, so the Government did not try very hard to win the motion of no confidence brought in mid-November. Parliament was dissolved and a general election was set for 23 January 2006. Stephen Harper was finally presented with his best chance.

WELFARE STATE STRAINS AND THE FISCAL IMBALANCE

In keeping with an often and loudly expressed love for the country, Chrétien saw nothing particularly wrong with Canada, except for the state of its public finances. Although the previous PC Government of Brian Mulroney had gone some way towards narrowing the gap between the federal Government's financial commitments and its ability to raise revenue—notably through the introduction of an extremely unpopular value-added federal sales tax, known as the goods and services tax—it had not managed significantly to reduce the actual budget deficit. Eliminating the deficit through government 'restructuring' became Chrétien's defining mission, responsibility for which he handed to Martin. Chrétien may have calculated that this thankless task would damage his rival's popularity, but a strong economy through the mid- and late 1990s and Martin's skill at budget-making not only erased what had seemed intractable deficits, but also made the Minister of Finance increasingly popular. As Martin never stopped manoeuvring and angling for the post of Prime Minister, his relationship with Chrétien deteriorated to the point where he resigned from the Cabinet in June 2002, just as Chrétien was ready to dismiss him.

Martin then became Prime Minister at a time when Canada had just undergone a decade of shrinking government programmes and agencies as part of a neo-liberal reinvention of the role of government in society. As a result, the country found itself with a number of challenges that the welfare state had sought to mitigate—from child poverty that had been growing from the early 1990s, rather than shrinking as the Chrétien Government had promised, to the severely understaffed and underfinanced public health care system. While the federal Government succeeded in eliminating its budget deficits, to the point that it could reliably count on large budgetary surpluses year after year, provincial and municipal administrations struggled with deteriorating programmes and services. At the same time as Canada avoided a severe recession for almost 15 years, Canadians were increasingly concerned that essential services on which they had grown accustomed to count were weakening.

To a considerable extent, Martin's fiscal virtuosity as Minister of Finance in the 1990s had been illusory, as he severely and unilaterally reduced federal financial transfers to the provincial governments, which were implementing important 'shared cost' programmes in health care, education and social services. As the health of the federal treasury improved dramatically, provincial finances came under unprecedented pressure: provincial budget cuts resulted in a weakening of programmes, which, over a decade, crippled social services, threatened the viability of the country's cherished public health care system and made municipalities the ultimate recipients of devolved responsibilities and reduced financial resources. Despite such desperate measures, few provinces were able to balance their books securely, as they called for an end to the 'fiscal imbalance' between themselves and the federal Government—the imbalance being defined as the provinces having more responsibilities than fiscal resources and the federal Government having more resources than responsibilities.

By the time Martin finally became Prime Minister, in December 2003, his main promises were: to resolve the problems in the health care system 'for a generation', while keeping it public; to establish a pan-Canadian day care system; and to support municipalities in their infrastructure expenses. Only some Canadians saw the irony in this set of promises from the very man most responsible, along with Chrétien, for establishing the regime of governmental under-investment. Martin had an early chance, in August 2004, to deliver on the health care promise, when he and the provincial Premiers negotiated an agreement on much more federal funding of the health system over the following 10 years, in exchange for an acceptance by the provinces of pan-Canadian standards and improved accountability. Although much remained uncertain about the agreement's ability to bring health commitments under control and put the system on a stable footing, it went much further than anything Chrétien had ever attempted. This was a Martin accomplishment that Harper could not easily rescind, nor might he want to, as it could be inserted into his strategy for reducing the fiscal imbalance. Another agreement, negotiated a little later by Martin, was not so fortunate: the so-called Kelowna Accord with the representatives of aboriginal peoples and the provincial Premiers, which was similarly ambitious and aimed to transfer significant administrative responsibilities to aboriginal organizations, essentially lost most of its funding in the Conservatives' first budget.

The Martin Government also developed a series of ad hoc agreements with individual provinces addressing their various grievances—from a commitment to Newfoundland and Labrador allowing that province a greater fiscal share, temporarily, of its offshore petroleum production, to a rebalancing of Ontario's fiscal contribution to the country's system of equalization of revenues for poorer provinces. Finally, having to placate the left-leaning NDP, the Martin Government presented a budget in 2005 that planned considerable investment in municipal infrastructures, in environmental measures intended to make a contribution to Canada's Kyoto targets and in a pan-Canadian day-care system for pre-school children. However, Martin was never able to implement the measures, and the soon-elected Harper Government moved in directions quite different from those indicated in that budget.

Martin resigned as Liberal leader immediately after the 2006 election, and the party began a protracted leadership race, won in December of that year by Stéphane Dion to general surprise. A former political science professor from Québec, Dion had held the Canadian unity and the environment portfolios successively in previous Liberal ministries. Seen as an uncompromising federalist in the tradition of former Prime Minister Pierre Elliot Trudeau (1968–79 and 1980–84), Dion had little appeal to Québec's francophone majority. Running on an almost single-mindedly 'green' policy platform, he had been expected to score far behind the two front-runners, whose party support, it turned out, peaked in the region of 35%, allowing Dion to emerge as a rather fragile compromise winner.

SOLIDARITY AND DIFFERENCE: NATIONALISM, RIGHTS AND MULTICULTURALISM

The turmoil around the sponsorship scandal stemmed from the long-standing fault line between the Canadian and Québécois national movements. The 'brand Canada' sponsorship programme and its illegal financing of the Liberal Party was the latest in a chain of constitutional crises. It had seemed, under Prime Minister Chrétien, that the only way for Canadian politics to avoid the existential crisis of Québec's place in Canada was to avoid the subject altogether—while still flying the flag. However, the fallout of the sponsorship scandal brought about a reconciliatory development that few if any observers would have expected: the quasi-unanimous recognition in the House of Commons that Québec constitutes a nation within Canada.

With the Québécois badly alienated from the Liberal Party after the scandal, Harper's Conservatives saw an opportunity to make gains among them through a series of decentralizing commitments consistent with their own outlook and congenial to Québec's nationalist political culture. In parallel, the candidates for Martin's Liberal succession understood that Québec was a key battleground. Michael Ignatieff, the former academic and public intellectual, had recently returned to Canada from years abroad to begin a career in politics and seek the Liberal crown. Little burdened by his party's and the country's accumulated taboos regarding Québec, and supremely confident in his analytical powers, he called for the recognition of Québec's nationhood. Received with pleasure in Québec and with horror elsewhere (contributing to Ignatieff's eventual failure to win the Liberal leadership), the proposal encouraged the BQ to introduce a motion to the same effect in the House of Commons. The BQ fully expected that the motion would be voted down, thus embarrassing all federalist parties in Québec. However, Prime Minister Harper, in perhaps his boldest move yet, reacted by introducing his own motion, which also recognized the Québécois as a nation, but added 'in a united Canada'. The Bloc and the Liberals were now embarrassed into voting with the Government, with the NDP generally content to comply. The long-term effect of this extraordinary development of November 2006 remained difficult to evaluate, but it seemed certain to change the terms of the debate, and the positioning of the players, on the question of Québec's place in Canada.

While this old time-bomb was somehow defused, at least for the present, the ongoing multiculturalist debate on cultural and religious pluralism took new turns, largely in the context of the growing Muslim presence in Canada, but also in the tense aftermath of the terrorist attacks on US cities on 11 September 2001 and the 2005 London bombings in the United Kingdom. The extent to which religious beliefs should be accommodated in the public sphere replaced the Québec question, for the moment, as the big challenge to Canadian identity. What launched the controversy was a 2005 proposal in Ontario to allow *Shari'a*-based arbitration in family and commercial matters—if all parties consented, under the authority of the Canadian Charter of Rights and Freedoms. This proposal followed the lead of Judaic arbitration, an established practice for many years in Ontario. In the face of vehement opposition, the Government of Ontario withdrew the proposal, and eliminated Judaic arbitration on the grounds that the same regime should apply to all. This controversy was followed by broadly publicized incidents in which young girls wearing the *hijab* (the Islamic headscarf) were forbidden from participating in football (soccer) and martial arts competitions, and then by the bizarre adoption of a 'life code' by the town council of Hérouxville, a small Québec community with no Muslim presence, which barred not only the *hijab* and the *niqab* (veil), but also such practices (obviously unheard of in Canada) as the stoning of women. Other incidents involved an orthodox Jewish community in Montréal, rather than Muslims. The growing malaise, fuelled by a right-wing nationalist leader Mario Dumont (see below), prompted the Premier of Québec, Jean Charest, to create a commission of inquiry on 'reasonable accommodation'. The inquiry was co-chaired by the internationally recognized philosopher Charles Taylor and the historian Gérard Bouchard.

The Consultation Commission on Accommodation Practices Related to Cultural Differences (CCPARDC) attracted a large amount of interest in Québec and broad media coverage in the rest of the country. At public audiences in all regions of Québec, but especially outside Montréal (where most immigrants and cultural minorities are established), a remarkable reticence was expressed toward the expression of religious pluralism in the public space, echoing similar debates in countries such as the United Kingdom, the Netherlands and France. Across Québec the commissioners heard much testimony that could only be described as uninformed and intolerant, counterbalanced mostly in Montréal by submissions that showed far greater familiarity with and acceptance of mutual accommodation by majorities and minorities. Unsurprisingly, the commissioners' report, which was presented to the Government of Québec in May 2008, paid far greater heed to the accommodating outlooks than to the others. The report concluded that there was no crisis of cultural accommodation in Québec, but rather that there was the perception of a crisis much fuelled by sensationalist media (and, it suggested more discreetly, by opportunistic politicians).

The outright hostility to accommodation that was expressed at the CCPARDC sat in rather awkward relation to the Canadian Charter of Rights and Freedoms, which was understood as protecting the religious expression of all Canadians in their relations with public institutions—although much of the opposition to 'reasonable accommodation' of Islam derived from the governing importance of gender equality, a key component of Charter culture. Twenty-five years after its adoption the Charter had indeed become a keystone of Canadian politics and identity. In the same process, the Supreme Court of Canada had acquired a prestige that few other institutions could match; in August 2004 Prime Minister Martin had made the nine-member Court perhaps the most gender-balanced high court in the world, by adding two new female justices to the two female incumbents. A culture of rights quickly developed after the Charter took effect in 1982, and a series of fundamental court decisions affirmed the equality of women and men and the rights of official-language and religious minorities, while at the same time the courts bolstered economically dominant interests and curtailed labour rights.

Most contentiously, the courts interpreted the Charter as outlawing discrimination on the basis of sexual orientation; consequently, they invalidated the Canadian law that defined marriage as the union of a man and a woman. In mid-2003 same-sex marriage became legal in parts of Canada, and the federal Government had to begin planning for a revised, non-discriminatory marriage law to introduce that provision across the country. However, strong opposition emerged, which led the Government to refer its draft legislation to the Supreme Court, asking the justices to provide an opinion as to whether same-sex marriage was consistent with the Charter. The Supreme Court, unsurprisingly, answered 'yes' and the proposed law was therefore moved through Parliament, becoming law in June 2005, in the midst of passionate debate and with opinion polls showing Canadians to be divided on the issue. Canada became the third country (after Belgium and the Netherlands) in the world to recognize same-sex marriage.

Another fundamental court-related change in Canada's political culture concerned the rights of aboriginal peoples, which were being affirmed through Section 35 of the Constitution Act 1982 and through three decades of jurisprudence. For more than a century it had been a policy objective as well as an intellectual assumption that 'the Indians' were on the path to assimilation and that, for their own good, the process should be expedited. As a result, indigenous peoples were unrepresented politically. The Supreme Court of Canada began changing this assumption in a 1973 decision (the so-called Calder case), by confirming the long-standing indigenous claim that they had collective rights. By the 1980s this transformation had begun registering in the body politic, such that Canadians gradually became convinced that some accommodation and recognition of indigenous rights were necessary. However, progress remained slow, as tensions erupted periodically in various regions of the country; one of the most recent, lasting through much of 2004 and the first half of 2005, being a sequel to the 'Oka Crisis' of 1990, with the Mohawk community of Kanesatake racked by internal divisions that were at least in part an outcome of the previous crisis. In 2006 another crisis erupted in Caledonia, Ontario, where the Six Nations community erected barricades to prevent a new housing development from being built on land that it claimed as its own. Meanwhile, in September 2007, at the UN General Assembly, the Harper Government voted against the proposed UN Treaty on the Rights of Indigenous Peoples, arguing that various clauses of the treaty were in conflict with Canadian law; this stance flowed from and hardened the Martin Government's earlier resistance to the treaty.

INTERNATIONAL AFFAIRS: SECURITY AND THE ALL-IMPORTANT RELATIONSHIP WITH THE USA

When the Conservatives formed a Government following the January 2006 general election, the tension between Canada and the USA over Canada's refusal to participate in the war in Iraq had already eased somewhat. It was, however, replaced by difficulties ranging from the Canadian Government's announcement that it would not participate in the US missile shield and would defend the sovereignty of Canadian airspace, to US reluctance to comply with a North American Free Trade Agreement (NAFTA) arbitration panel decision on lumber trade that favoured Canada. Another irritant was the continuing controversy regarding the effect on human rights of the 'war on terror' launched after the 2001 terrorist attacks in the USA.

In 2003 Maher Arar, a Syrian-born Canadian citizen, returned to Canada after 10 months in a Syrian prison, where he had reportedly been tortured, after his deportation from a US border post in September 2002. Arar had been in transit at a New York airport, on his way back to Canada after a holiday in Tunisia, when he was detained and deported by the US authorities, which were acting on information from Canadian security services supposedly linking him to terrorists. A media campaign led by his wife, Monia Mazigh, to pressure the Canadian Government into obtaining Arar's release from Syria, first led to his return to Canada, and then to a commission of inquiry into the role of Canadian agencies in his ordeal. The commission, headed by Justice Dennis O'Connor of the Ontario Court of Appeal, found, first, that there was no credible evidence linking Arar to terrorism. Second, it found that Canadian security agencies, abetted at various points by complaisant media, had exercised considerable influence over Arar's detention in the USA, his imprisonment and torture in Syria (the practice of 'extraordinary rendition'), and the blackening of his reputation in Canada even after his return. Another commission, headed by retired Supreme Court Justice Frank Iacobucci, was later established to investigate the role of Canadian agencies in similar ordeals undergone in Syria by three other Canadians of Arab origins. Iacobucci found, in October 2008, that Canadian officials bore 'indirect responsibility' for the imprisonment and torture of these men.

The Anti-terrorism Act, adopted after the terrorist attacks in September 2001 and similar to the so-called 'Patriot Act' (Uniting and Strengthening America by Providing the Appropriate Tools Required to Intercept and Obstruct Terrorism—PATRIOT—Act of 2001) in the USA, came under intense scrutiny and criticism from its very inception. However, several of its more controversial clauses allowing such things as preventive detention and warrantless searches duly expired in 2007. In September 2008 the Act's first criminal conviction was obtained, when a young man from Toronto (who was a minor at the time of the offence) was found to have been involved with a group of up to 20 men who had been seeking to commit terrorist acts in Toronto and the parliament building in Ottawa. Another terrorism trial was under way in Ottawa in 2008: the suspect had apparent links to a group based in London, the United Kingdom, which had planned to attack targets such as shopping malls in that country (several members of this group were convicted on terrorism-related charges in London in 2007).

As a whole range of Bush Administration policies continued to arouse widespread disapproval in Canada, opinion polls indicated for the first time that Canadians held an increasingly unfavourable view of the USA in general, and not just of the Bush Administration. This fall in Canadian esteem of Americans was, according to at least one reputable poll, the most severe among traditional allies of the USA. Prime Minister Harper lost no time in attempting to improve that most important of relationships for Canada. Although many Canadians had reservations about the Conservatives' closeness to the USA, Harper's efforts seemed to have been successful, at least initially, as public opinion in Canada in mid- to late 2006 softened towards the USA (although not towards the Bush Administration). If this shift continued, it would represent quite a change in a relationship that had been deteriorating for several years. The Chrétien-Bush relationship had not prospered from the early days of the Bush presidency, and it worsened in the months preceding the invasion of Iraq in 2003. Indeed, it was difficult to find many moments in the recent history of the two countries when relations had been so strained.

The long border between Canada and the USA had been, famously, undefended. Since the 1989 Canada-United States Free Trade Agreement, it had also been increasingly open, and border crossings of people and merchandise had risen substantially over two decades. However, the terrorist attacks of September 2001 caused the US Government to rethink its sense of the border, leading quickly to its 'securitization'. Vastly increased numbers of border guards, helicopters, even modified Predator drones, now patrol this extensive area. Canadians entering the USA and Americans returning to their country by air now need a passport to cross the border. The same restriction was due to come into force for road and train crossings by mid-2009. For Canada, which depends heavily on trade with the USA (and for border states that depend to a large extent on business with Canada), this outlook is deeply problematic. Canadian business and government leaders immediately sought to counteract it with all manner of proposals, ranging from a 'smart border' to a shared security perimeter. After years of pressure, the US Government finally agreed in late 2007 to accept 'enhanced' drivers' licences at land border posts, rather than the much more burdensome passport.

In most respects, Canada remained close to its neighbour, although the appropriate degree of closeness was always a much debated issue among Canadians. Indeed, the two countries' political culture and social values seemed to drift apart at the same time that they became more closely integrated economically. At the beginning of the 21st century there was a high level of US ownership of Canadian firms and enterprises. Moreover, the USA accounted for more than 70% of Canada's imports and nearly 85% of its exports, although rapid growth in the People's Republic of China and India significantly reduced these numbers from 2005 onwards. In the same competitive vein, there were several attempts by US and Chinese companies from around this time—many successful and some not—to take over a number of key Canadian corporations, notably in the mining and steel sectors. In mid-2007, for instance, the last major Canadian-owned steel maker, Stelco, was purchased by US Steel. Due to the fact that foreign purchases of Canadian assets became so widespread—and considering most Chinese corporations were state-owned—finance minister Flaherty announced national security screening for such purchasing attempts.

After Chrétien's retirement, Martin identified a clear need to make a visible effort to improve relations with the USA, and he let it be known that he would seek to undo the damage supposedly done by Chrétien. Nevertheless, in early 2005 Martin announced, to widespread surprise, that Canada would not participate in the missile shield, because of his Government's opposition to the 'weaponization' of space. This was badly received by the US Administration, as Martin's earlier signals had suggested the opposite. His much-publicized attempt to reinvigorate the bilateral relationship was failing. Nevertheless, in 2004 Martin's Government had quietly agreed to allow NORAD installations in Canada to be integrated into the anti-missile shield warning system. This amounted, in effect, to Canadian participation, and it was all that the USA really needed from Canada, other than, perhaps, symbolic support. Martin's practical 'yes' followed by a symbolic 'no' was a repetition of the Chrétien Government's practice around the Iraq war: while announcing that it would not participate, it had provided military assets—for the most part outside the Iraqi theatre of operations, such as in the Persian (Arabian) Gulf and in Afghanistan—that released some US assets for deployment in the Iraq campaign. In both cases a majority of Canadians were pleased that the Government was refusing the US request to participate, not noticing that, operationally, Canada was following at least part of the US lead.

In the post-11 September 2001 context, the Martin Government committed to a significant reinvestment in the armed forces for the first time in a generation, both through budgetary appropriations and a large-scale reorganization. The Harper Government moved further in this direction, with more defence funding and an outlook more comfortable with the assertion of 'hard power'. Indeed, from 1999 to 2006 Canada was the Americas' top purchaser of US military hardware direct from the US Government (that is, excluding purchases from the manufacturers themselves). The Liberal Government had agreed early to participate in the establishment of a new, post-Taliban regime in Afghanistan, moving in 2005 to an increasing military presence in the country's troubled south. The situation in that region deteriorated significantly after early 2006 (with heavy Leopard tank units having to be sent to Qandahar in late 2006) and the Harper Government experienced more pressure to make its case for Canada's continuing presence there. From this perspective, the Government appeared set to be increasingly defined as a 'war government'. However, with public opinion steadfastly opposed to Canada's military role and under pressure from opposition parties, the Government was initially compelled to promise an end to Canada's role in Afghanistan by February 2009, independent of the situation on the ground. A rising number of casualties (98 Canadians killed, including one diplomat, as of September 2008) and numerous pessimistic reports of Taliban strength only increased the pressure on the Government to keep that promise, despite its own apparent preference to extend the mission. In early 2008, however, the Government obtained a two-year extension of Canada's presence in Afghanistan from Parliament. The overall cost of the mission was later estimated by the Parliamentary Budget Officer to be as high as C $18,000m.

The heavy involvement in Afghanistan and the reinvestment in defence contrasted with Canadian practice in the 1990s, when Canada's contribution to international affairs declined from what had been significant participation in numerous multilateral initiatives, notably UN peace-keeping missions. None the less, Canada took the lead in developing and promoting what eventually became the 1997 international convention against anti-personnel mines or landmines. Also, the growing adoption by the international community of a 'human security' norm, in combination with states' collective responsibility to protect civilian populations across borders, was in part an outcome of Canadian diplomacy from the 1990s. The UN's 2005 world summit adopted a version of this norm that was decried by some as toothless, and praised by others as a valuable first step. In addition, in 1990 the Canadian Government had played an important part in persuading the USA to operate through the UN in taking action against Iraq after the latter's invasion of Kuwait, and Canada also continued—although to an increasingly limited degree—to contribute to peace-keeping forces in politically unstable locations, notably in Bosnia and Herzegovina from the mid-1990s and, from 1999, in the autonomous Serbian province of Kosovo and Metohija (Serbia was then part of the Federal Republic of Yugoslavia). Similarly, Canada contributed forces in late 2001 to the US-led international coalition in Afghanistan. From mid-2002, however, when it became clear that the US Administration was intent on invading Iraq with or without the authority of the UN, the relationship deteriorated rapidly, as Canada refused to join the USA in taking unilateral action and reaffirmed its commitment to multilateralism and the UN.

An emerging security area for Canada, and a source of tension not only with the USA but also with the European Union (EU) and Russia, was the high Arctic. As the polar ice cap melted, the Northwest Passage from one side of the North American continent to the other became navigable in mid-2007, for the first time in many centuries, and then again in 2008—years earlier than what most scientific models of climate warming had expected—giving added urgency to Canadian claims to sovereignty over vast Arctic regions, including the fabled sea route. In addition to the huge economic impact of trans-Arctic commercial shipping within two decades and of the extraction of newly available mineral resources, such as petroleum and natural gas, the disappearance of the ice would mean profound changes to the way of life of the Inuit people and serious risks to the region's fragile environment. Canadian state capacity in this area was severely lacking, a situation at least somewhat recognized by the Martin Government in early 2005 as it announced a 'northern strategy', much of which remained to be defined, and subsequently by the Harper Government's 'Arctic strategy' one year later. In 2007 the Government announced the construction of several mid-sized, ice-hardened ships that would patrol the newly navigable Arctic. Along with these ships, which were due to enter service in the mid-2010s, the armed forces were set to increase their northern capacity, jointly to enforce Canadian sovereignty in this area of frantically growing international competition.

QUÉBÉCOIS POLITICS

From 1960 all Québec Governments but one were able to count on being re-elected at the end of their first term and then on losing to the main opposition party at the end of their second term. This would merely be a case of well-ordered 'alternance' if one of the parties involved in this exchange were not promoting Québec's accession to the status of a sovereign state. However, from 1976, when the PQ first formed the Government, under the leadership of its founder, René Lévesque, this is just what happened. Furthermore, near the end of its first term, in 1980, the PQ held a referendum in which the Québécois were asked if they wanted their Government to negotiate 'sovereignty-association' with the rest of Canada: 60% answered 'no'. In 1995, in the middle of another first term, the PQ tried again, asking this time if the Québécois wanted to become sovereign and then attempt to negotiate an economic association with the rest of Canada: 49% said 'yes'.

As had happened in 1981, when it was re-elected after losing a referendum, the PQ was re-elected in 1998, under the leadership of Lucien Bouchard. However, Bouchard soon left politics, to be replaced by the long-serving PQ minister Bernard Landry. In April 2003 the pattern reasserted itself, as the PQ lost power to the Liberal Party, led by Jean Charest, a former minister in Brian Mulroney's federal Government. The morning after the election Charest claimed to be the strongest federalist ever to have been Québec's Premier. It took little time, however, for Charest to adopt a more Québec-centrist tone with the federal Government, as the logic of Canadian federalism pushed him to assert the prerogatives of his Government in the face of the federal administration's fiscal resources and often centralizing projects.

While the PQ presented itself as a centrist, generally social-democratic party, the Liberals promised to reduce the role of the State in the lives of the Québécois, in a process of implementing neo-liberal policies of deregulation, privatization and budget cuts. The Charest Liberals had campaigned on the theme of 'We are ready' (to take power), but their first months in office revealed a Government that was unprepared and clumsy, even as it tried to push through radical changes to the province's social pact. The new Government quickly became extraordinarily unpopular. It consequently softened its rhetoric—with less talk of 're-engineering'—but took longer before it effectively moderated its policies. Most of the Charest Government's second year provided something of a respite, although it remained unpopular. In early 2005 it stumbled into a large conflict with college and university students over a severe downgrading of scholarships, and was forced to compromise after the students staged a weeks-long strike. The Government also found it exceedingly difficult to negotiate a collective agreement with its civil servants.

While remarkably unpopular, the Charest Government was fortunate to be facing a PQ that expended much energy trying to find its proper stance as the official opposition. To make matters worse for the PQ as an effective opposition, Landry resigned as party leader in mid-2005, after a confidence vote within his party that left him unexpectedly weakened. In the ensuing leadership race, the popular federal-level BQ leader, Gilles Duceppe, could have won, but he chose instead to remain BQ leader in the national Parliament. PQ members instead chose André Boisclair, a popular young former cabinet minister under Landry, to be their new leader. Somewhat to the right of Landry and of the party's centre, Boisclair—who was openly homosexual—had to admit during the campaign that he had used the illegal drug cocaine in his days as a cabinet minister. This did not appear to weaken his initial appeal within the PQ, but the Liberal Party seemed to think that this damaged him enough that its chances had improved. This assessment turned out to be prescient, as Boisclair's leadership weakened with every passing month, crashing in a March 2007 provincial election held amid growing concerns about the 'reasonable accommodation' of religious minorities fuelled by the right-wing nationalist Mario Dumont, the leader of heretofore third-placed Action Démocratique du Québec (ADQ).

With Charest's Liberals still unpopular, but remaining in first place, and Boisclair failing badly, support for Dumont's ADQ surged, and the election produced the first minority Government in Québec in over a century (still under Charest). The PQ dropped to third place for the first time in 35 years, and the ADQ formed an extremely inexperienced official opposition. Boisclair was soon replaced as the head of the PQ by veteran former cabinet minister Pauline Marois. As many expected, the ADQ proved to be an extremely weak official opposition. A much more controlled performance by the governing Liberals and the decision by Marois's PQ put the sovereignty option in abeyance and realigned Québec's political map much to the disadvantage of the ADQ. By the end of 2008 Dumont's party seemed close to becoming irrelevant, the Charest Government was more popular than ever, and the PQ, while not performing very well, was firmly back in its position as the main alternative to the Liberals.

CONCLUSION

As happened in many countries, the effects of the attacks on the USA of 11 September 2001 destabilized established political patterns in Canada. Defence and security issues and expenditures acquired an importance unprecedented in several decades, the country's safety and respect for human rights came into question and the relationship with the USA suffered. In addition, the only major domestic crisis of the Chrétien years, the outcome of Québec's 1995 sovereignty referendum, saw the federal Government launch into what became the sponsorship scandal and the quasi-destruction of Canada's natural governing party, the Liberals. Although public finances and the economy performed well until 2007, compared with other advanced capitalist countries, the slowly deteriorating public services were far from having fully recovered from the set-backs experienced in the second half of the 1990s. Furthermore, the continuing dependence on US economic dynamism remained the most important determinant of Canada's economic success. On this count, the US financial crisis, recession and resurgent currency towards the end of 2008 were extremely worrying for the Canadian economy, despite the country's strong banking system. The recognition of indigenous rights and the country's performance in fighting global climate change remained weak, while the recognition of Québécois nationhood may or may not amount to a promising development. To sum up, the challenges faced by the new crop of political leaders were considerable.

FROM INTERNATIONALISM TO REGIONALISM: THE EVOLUTION OF CANADIAN FOREIGN POLICY IN THE POST-COLD WAR PERIOD

ATHANASIOS HRISTOULAS

INTRODUCTION

Since the end of the Cold War, Canadian foreign policy decision makers have been struggling to define a direction for the country in terms of its external affairs. Cold War 'internationalism' was replaced in the 1990s by a more up-to-date version, which introduced 'human security' as a guiding principle in foreign policy. The events of 11 September 2001 resulted in a further foreign policy review, with yet another foreign policy orientation, this time much more focused on the North American region. This essay seeks to outline the evolution of Canadian foreign policy, particularly since the end of the Cold War. However, first, a number of constants or invariants in Canadian foreign policy will be outlined. These invariants serve as critical elements in the understanding of Canadian foreign policy because they transcend time. They are, in other words, important in whatever historical period Canada finds itself.

GEOGRAPHY

According to Kim Richard Nossal, one of the most important invariants is Canada's geographic location. For the first eight decades after confederation in 1867, Canada was physically removed from the centre of great power rivalry. This meant that Canada was essentially isolated from the planet's major problems. It meant, according to Nossal, that until the end of the Second World War (1939–45) Canada was never confronted by real security threats. The USA had attacked Canada twice: in the war of 1812 and during the American Civil War (1861–65), but for most of the 19th century the relationship between Canada and the USA was peaceful.

However, with the emergence of the Cold War after 1945, Canada's geostrategic position shifted dramatically. For all intents and purposes, Canada occupied 'the most vital airspace in the world'. This reduced Canada's leverage or independence in foreign policy. Given the Cold War situation, Canada always had to be seen as the good neighbour of the USA and this dramatically weakened Canada's ability to act independently. With the end of the Cold War, Canada's strategic importance once again declined. This was probably an important advantage for Canada and the making of its foreign policy. Canadian decision makers found themselves much more free to pursue their own agenda, which did not necessarily have to reflect the interests of the USA at all times.

However, strategic location aside, demographically, culturally, economically, and ideologically, the USA is the most important focus for Canadian foreign policy. For want of a better phrase, 'Canadians look south'. Cross-border linkages, be they economic, social or cultural, are much better defined than trans-Canada linkages. A Montrealer is much more likely to identify with a New Yorker that with someone from Vancouver.

ECONOMIC STRUCTURE

Nossal also argued that Canada was—and continues to be—extremely dependent on foreign trade for its well-being. Almost one-third of the country's gross domestic product is generated by exports. The necessity of marketing the surplus in Canadian commodities was always the principal concern of Canadian foreign policy. This meant that, historically, foreign relations were essentially trade relations. Moreover, over the course of the 20th century, Canada's trade became progressively unbalanced and concentrated in one market—that of the USA. In the late 1930s only 25% of Canadian exports went to the USA, whereas 40% went to the United Kingdom. By the mid-1950s 60% went to the USA and 9% to the United Kingdom; by 1985 the US percentage had risen to 75%. Two decades later, by the mid-2000s, close to 90% of Canada's exports went to the USA. So, not only did Canada become dependent on foreign trade for its prosperity, but also increasingly dependent on a single market to sustain that prosperity. The implications of this economic imperative was that, in general, the political and security interests of Canada would hinge on trade.

The first priority for a country like Canada, which is so dependent on the stability and predictability of the international economy, is the stability of the international economic system. This feature of Canada explains why, historically, Canada has been so concerned with the maintenance of global peace and, especially, the avoidance of systemic war—instability is not good for business. Beyond the obvious economic benefits, Canada's interest in signing a free trade agreement with the USA in 1987 (that became the North American Free Trade Agreement—NAFTA—on the inclusion of Mexico in 1994) can be explained by the USA's historical behaviour. The USA is a country whose legislature likes to punish other countries for having foreign policies that conflict with its own. An important way to punish is economic sanctions. Moreover, the USA has gone through important phases of protectionism. The signing of NAFTA provided an institutional guarantee of market access to the USA for Canada, circumventing political conditions within the USA that often motivate punitive trade practices. NAFTA for Canada, therefore, was not viewed as a limitation on sovereignty or freedom of action in international relations, but rather was a way to free Canada and allow it to pursue more independent foreign policies. Indeed, much of the impetus for the Canadian-US free trade agreement negotiated by the Brian Mulroney Government (1984–93) in 1986 and 1987 came from a Canadian fear of what the US Congress might do in the future.

A final important consequence of Canada's economic sensitivity and vulnerability was that virtually all foreign policy issues became linked to Canadian-US relations. Decisions tended to be based on a calculation of the degree to which the issue and the options being discussed would impinge on the relationship with the USA. Policies on such diverse issues as human rights violations by the Government of the People's Republic of China, the acquisition of aircraft for Air Canada, relations with Cuba or, even, the Canadian position on the use of air strikes against the Serbs in the former Yugoslavia, tended to be filtered through the Canadian-US lens.

On multiple occasions Canadian policy was determined by a Canadian assessment that a divergent policy would not be worth the damage that such a divergence would likely cause to Canadian-US relations. An excellent example of how economic interests are intimately linked with other global issues was the occasion of the US bombing of Libya in April 1986. Despite criticisms in Canada's House of Commons, from both Liberals and Conservatives, the Mulroney Government came out fully in support of US policy. The reason for this was simple. In the week that US President Ronald Reagan authorized the strike against Libya, the finance committee of the US Senate was considering whether to approve the start of Canadian-US free trade negotiations. This case shows that Canada feels self-imposed pressure on many issues, rather than the USA sending some kind of outright threat against Canada and its interests.

However, there were times where the Government thought a matter important enough to diverge from US policy. John Diefenbaker (Prime Minister, 1957–63) criticized the USA during the Cuban missile crisis, Pierre Elliot Trudeau (1968–79 and 1980–84) was famous for consistently criticizing US policy, and even Jean Chrétien (1993–2003) criticized US policy with regards to the UN. Yet such examples are rare indeed.

CANADIAN DEPENDENCE ON THE USA

The previous discussion suggests that, for all intents and purposes, Canada is a dependency of the USA, borrowing a term more commonly used during the 1960s and 1970s. This point of view is based on Canada being dependent economically on the USA, as well as being locked into a series of military alliances with its southern neighbour that, in theory, seriously limit Canada's ability to act independently.

However, there are important reasons why Canada should not be viewed as a 'dependent' state—notably, the conscious attempt on the part of US policy makers to maintain good relations with Canada throughout the 20th century and into the 2000s. In other words, US behaviour south of its border did not repeat itself northwards.

First, there is a long tradition of bilateral co-operation between Canada and the USA in matters of security. Beginning with the Second World War, Canada and the USA worked together to assure the defence of North America. In 1940, for example, Prime Minister William Lyon Mackenzie King (1921–26, 1926–30, 1935–48) and US President Franklin D. Roosevelt signed the Ogdensburg Agreement, which institutionalized security co-operation in the event of an attack against the North American continent. The most important bilateral defence treaty between the USA and Canada is the North American Aerospace Defence Command (NORAD). Created in 1957, the NORAD Center is located in the US state of Colorado and is jointly manned by US and Canadian forces. The Center provides early warning of missile and air attack. More importantly, NORAD defends North American air sovereignty and is also responsible for providing air defence in the event of an attack.

Second—with some notable exceptions, such as the war in Iraq—Canada truly is a good ally of the USA. There is a convergence of ideology, economic systems and culture, a friendship that dates back multiple generations. Americans often do not consider Canadians as foreigners. Indeed, after the terrorist attacks of 11 September 2001 Canadians travelling into the USA from a third country could use the US nationals queue through the immigration procedures. Moreover, Canada is the only country in the world that is exempt from the US visitor system, which fingerprints and photographs all foreign nationals and was implemented in the USA after the 2001 terrorist attacks on New York and Washington, DC. In many ways, the US-Canadian relationship is often likened to one of a big brother and a little brother.

Canada participated actively in multilateral security institutions to try to balance the influence of the USA. This included not only an extremely active participation in the UN and its peace-keeping operations, but the North Atlantic Treaty Organization (NATO) as well. Indeed, in the early years of the Cold War Canada's NATO contingent accounted for approximately 45% of the Canadian defence budget.

CANADA AS A MIDDLE AND MORAL POWER

Canadian decision makers commonly prefer to present the country as a 'middle power'. After the Second World War the country's decision makers wanted to project an image of Canada's place in the world or the international system that was consistent with the country's contribution to the war effort. Canadian decision-makers believed that Canada's role was important enough to warrant calling it what Canadians refer to as a middle power. According to the Canadian definition, a middle power is a country with a small population that lacks colonial possessions. This means that the country is not a great power; however, such a country's natural wealth and human capacity implies that it is not a minor power either. According to this logic, Canada stands somewhere in between—in 1945 the term 'middle power' was adopted by the Government to describe Canada's rank.

Middle power does not only denote a relative ranking. For Canadian decision makers, middle power also implies a particular style of foreign policy. Being a middle power means a specific or special type of diplomacy—which can be called 'middlepowermanship'. The term implies that the principle role of middle power is to help maintain systemic peace.

Therefore, during the Cold War—but in the post-Cold War period as well—Canada was eager to participate in institutionalized methods for resolving disputes and conflicts. It is precisely this middlepowermanship that resulted in Canada's significant and ongoing role in UN peace-keeping operations. In sum, middlepowermanship means an activist mediatory foreign policy, which emphasizes institutional linkages, and with the maintenance of regional and global stability and peace as its objective. Although by the 2000s Canadian decision makers no longer openly used this term, much of what the Governments of Chrétien, Paul Martin (2003–06) and Stephen Harper (2006–) did was very much in the tradition of Canadian middlepowermanship.

The concept of a national role of middlepowermanship was put into operation with a policy of internationalism. The policy embraces as its main goal the avoidance of conflict. It seeks to achieve that end by political, social and economic engagement of the international system. Internationalism accepts the argument that peace is indivisible. In other words, internationalists hold that the fate of any one state and the peace of the international system as a whole are interconnected. The outbreak of war or hostilities in a distant part of the globe has a very high potential for plunging the whole international system into conflict.

The solution is four-fold. First, each state has a responsibility for playing a constructive part in the management of conflict. Second, multilateralism is seen as critical for defusing the clash of interests that can lead to war. Third, a commitment to international institutions is necessary, because institutions promote multilateralism. Fourth, the state must give concrete support to international institutions.

Canada's internationalism during the Cold War meant that the country participated actively in international institutions, especially the UN. Indeed, it is important to note that a former Canadian Prime Minister, Lester B. Pearson (1963–68), invented peace-keeping in the context of the 1956 Middle East crisis. The goal here was to avoid, or at least manage, situations that might lead to a confrontation between the USA and the USSR.

With the end of the Cold War, internationalism changed as well. The focus was no longer on managing disputes between states, but to deal with new threats, such as failed, fragmented statehood, especially in Africa. However, apart from that shift, strong continuities exist. The Chrétien, Martin and Harper approach to foreign policy remained fully multilateralist, with Canada continuing to support, participate in and contribute to a wide range of international institutions.

A third perspective paints Canada as a 'moral power'. This morality, which can be referred to as the human security agenda, is broadly defined as 'safety for people from both violent and non-violent threats'. It is a condition or state of being that is characterized 'by freedom from pervasive threats to people's rights, their safety, or even their lives'. More precisely, Canadian foreign policy decision makers see human security as an alternative way of seeing the world, in other words, 'taking people as its point of reference, rather than focusing exclusively on the security of territory or governments'.

The role of Canada here is to serve as a model political and economic system for other, less developed states in the international system. Canadian decision-makers argue that the country's democratic institutions, its excellent human rights record and its ability to integrate peoples and cultures from different parts of the world make the country an example for others to follow. As others, and I, have argued in different contexts, this makes Canada a post-national state.

Post-nationalism places emphasis on the idea that the international system changed dramatically after the end of the Cold War and that the classic definitions of national and international security (defence of the territory and sovereignty of the state) are less than useful constructs upon which to base policy. States need to redefine these concepts in order to take into account less traditional threats, such as human rights violations, the global environment, international organized crime and corruption, just to name a few.

Second, in order to resolve these new security threats, states need to co-operate, not to compete. State competition in the area of new security is not only considered outdated in the post-Cold War world, but also dangerous. Third, this co-operation might require a pooling of resources—what is often referred to as collective security. In turn, to make collective security function properly, states must be more flexible in their definitions of sovereignty. This post-nationalist foreign policy orientation was presented in the 1995 Canadian foreign policy review, which placed emphasis on three priorities: the promotion of prosperity and employment; the protection of Canada's security within a stable global framework; and the projection of Canadian values and culture.

UNDERSTANDING HUMAN SECURITY

A number of complementary explanations can be employed to understand the motivations and interest Canada has in the human security agenda. The first explanation places emphasis on the fact that civil society groups and public opinion within Canada agree with the policy. Partly correct, this perspective suggests that the human security agenda buys votes. A second perspective argues that human security gives Canada international prestige and serves as an important tool to distinguish the country from its more powerful cousin to the south, the USA. A more practical, third perspective suggests that human security directly affects Canada's economic interests. This politico-economic approach links human security to Canada's global trade policy. To understand this final, and extremely practical, explanation for human security one needs to look at Canada's historic relations with the Europeans.

The common perception of Canadian-European relations is that they are essentially peaceful and mutually prosperous. Canada and Europe enjoy a common history and culture, and Canada maintains strong political ties with the United Kingdom and France. Canada was the first American nation to participate in the First World War (1914–18) and, later, in the Second World War, was instrumental in liberating large parts of Western Europe, alongside the United Kingdom and the USA. During the Cold War Canada maintained a large military contingent in Europe under the auspices of NATO and, with the end of the Cold War, Canada still maintained its presence in Europe by participating in collective security operations throughout the region.

However, despite the strength of the political, cultural and security linkages between Canada and the Europeans, the same is not true of trade. The value of Canadian exports to Europe was minuscule when compared to the value of total European Union (EU) imports to Canada (2% in 2007), and was expected to get even smaller. The most obvious answer to why this occurred was that Canada was too small economically to be of interest to the Europeans.

Canadian governments throughout the 20th century implicitly recognized this fact, which is why they emphasized the cultural and common historical linkages to continental Europe and the United Kingdom. In essence, the argument for why the Europeans should pay attention to the Canadians is that, in some important ways, Canada is European.

Given this perspective, the end of the Cold War was not the best event so far as European-Canadian relations were concerned, for three particular reasons. First, Canada would continue to lose its small market share in the EU of the 15 pre-2004 members, as Western Europe becomes increasingly autonomous and self-sustaining with the inclusion of the Eastern European states. Second, Canada would lose its market share in Eastern Europe, which would no longer be able to maintain autonomous trade relations with Canada within an enlarged EU. Third, Canada was in a weak bargaining position in comparison to the Europeans; a larger EU would make that problem even worse.

Given EU expansion geographically, as well as in functions and roles, Canada was likely to place much more attention on Latin America in the future. However, given that many Latin American states had a long way to go in terms of democratization, economic partnerships with these countries would be questioned at a domestic level. In other words, Canadian public opinion will not easily accept economic linkages with countries that experience high levels of corruption or that systematically violate human rights. In that sense, human security serves an important public opinion purpose within Canada: it demonstrates that Canadian foreign policy is not only trade policy and that, therefore, Canada will make future economic co-operation with Latin America conditional on how successful these countries are in modernizing their political and social systems.

A related explanation for the emphasis on human security in Latin America stems from the Canadian belief that, in order to establish a successful economic relationship with a country, that country must be a political success as well. Pressure on issues such as human rights, electoral reform, social justice and the emphasis on collective security themes (such as peace-keeping and peace-making) were considered necessary in order to assist Latin American countries in achieving political stability. Ultimately, this political success would assure economic success, which in turn would directly benefit Canadians. Indeed, Prime Minister Chrétien emphasized this thinking in 2000, when Vicente Fox, Mexico's President-elect, suggested that a priority for his new Government would be the eradication of poverty. Chrétien's response was that this would be good for Canada, because Mexicans would now be able to buy Canadian products.

APPLYING HUMAN SECURITY: THE AMERICAS AND THE OAS

From the mid-1990s Canada pushed the human security agenda within the context of the Organization of American States (OAS). After joining the organization officially in January 1990, Canada saw itself as taking a leading role, pushing forward consensus on issues such as landmines, institutional renewal, human rights and illegal drugs. According to statements by the Department of Foreign Affairs and International Trade (DFAIT), Canadian human security priorities include eight specific areas.

The first priority identified by DFAIT for the General Assembly of the OAS was promoting the concept of human security itself. DFAIT statements repeatedly explained the importance of the concept, arguing that globalization and the changing nature of the international system necessitated a redefinition of our understanding of security. The second priority area for the OAS General Assembly from the Canadian perspective was the illicit trade in drugs. However, rather than framing the issue as a challenge to legal systems and state sovereignty, Canada attempted to bring the states of the region to look at the issue in the light of human security.

The third and fourth priority policy issues for Canada at the OAS were landmines and firearms. Largely owing to Canadian initiatives, the organization signed agreements to eliminate landmines in the hemisphere in the long term, and to control the manufacturing and trafficking of firearms. The Canadian Government argued that each of these issues had an obvious human security aspect, although other states in the region again associated the two areas with questions of national sovereignty and of traditional security.

Human rights and the promotion of democracy constituted the fifth and sixth priority areas for Canada in the OAS from the 1990s. These two issues demonstrated the truly radical nature of Canada's redefinition of security, for human rights violations and non-democratic systems could be included under the heading of violent and non-violent threats. The seventh area to reflect the influence of the human security paradigm was Canada's drive to strengthen civil society throughout the Americas. The influence of civil society in the Canadian foreign policy process was largely responsible for the human security agenda, and now Canada seemed to want to bring about similar social and policy structures throughout the region.

Canada's more specific goals in its hemispheric relations in the 21st century also concerned the question of the economic future of the region, in particular, of free trading relations throughout the Americas. In this second area Canada again saw itself as pursuing a leadership role. It was undeniable that the Canadian Government wanted to project an image of leadership; the DFAIT website cites Canada's active interest and role in the Americas as resulting in the country emerging as a leader in the region. Of course, 'leadership' would appear to be a difficult term to apply to Canada, as most people immediately identify the concept with power. Canada clearly lacked the power to force its views on other states, be they within or outside the region. Thus, analysts of Canadian foreign policy, and indeed DFAIT itself, historically see Canada as a 'moral' and intellectual power, one that leads both by example and through finding workable and acceptable solutions to common problems.

While Canadian negotiators did not talk explicitly about the issue of human security with reference to the Free Trade Area of the Americas, the two were inextricably connected when the nations of the hemisphere came together for the Summit of the Americas in Québec City in 2001; it must be remembered that the Summit of the Americas is as much a political as an economic forum. In 2007 it remained unclear how the Canadian Government would link, or distinguish between, its two main goals in the hemisphere. What was clear was that, after the growing protests against globalization and global capitalism witnessed since the 1990s, Canadian non-governmental organizations and civil society would not welcome DFAIT signing a free trade agreement with those nations in the region with suspect human rights and democratic records.

This societal pressure on DFAIT ensured that Canada would attempt to secure agreement on both human security and free trade. As suggested earlier, the Canadian Government perceived no tension between the two areas: for DFAIT, human security was closely tied to the long-term prosperity of individuals throughout the region, as well as to Canada as a country. The interdependence of human security, stability and economic growth was endemic to the world vision of the Canadian Government.

11 SEPTEMBER 2001: ITS IMPACT ON CANADIAN FOREIGN POLICY AND THE 2005 FOREIGN POLICY REVIEW.

The terrorist attacks in the USA on 11 September 2001 served as a wake-up call to Canadian decision makers. The events of that day also resulted in a new foreign policy review, the second since the end of the Cold War, which was released in 2005. The document recognized that when the USA worries about security, so must its closest trading partners. More importantly, for the purposes of this essay, it reorientated Canadian foreign policy once again in the post-Cold War period. Irrespective of internationalism and middlepowermanship, Canadian decision makers decided that, given national interests and limited material resources, the future of the nation's foreign policy must focus on North America.

In the hours following the terrorist attacks, the USA shut down its borders with Canada, essentially imposing an embargo on the North American continent in the name of national security. Border crossings into the USA that ordinarily delay travellers and commerce for only a few moments were converted into vast parking lots spanning kilometres and lasting up to 15 hours. Canadian leaders understandably panicked, not because of the terrorist attacks per se, but rather because of the impact that the terrorist attacks had had and would continue to have on their relations with the USA. The business of bilateral relations would no longer be the same.

The post-September 2001 continental security discussions were designed to achieve two interrelated goals. The first, of course, was to free the North American continent of terrorists and terrorist organizations and to make sure that terrorists operating in Canada were captured and/or not allowed to enter the USA. To achieve this first anti-terrorist objective, a number of proposals were suggested, including, but not limited to: further co-operation with the USA in information- and intelligence-gathering; the transfer of technology; the harmonization of immigration policy; jointly manned US-Canadian border points; and the (possible) interoperability of military and public security forces.

The second objective of continental and border security—one that was much more important to Canada—was the free flow of legitimate goods and of legitimate business and leisure travel. Here policy makers and analysts alike were examining how mechanisms such as pre-clearance fast border lanes and North American travel identity cards could make travel more efficient in a world of 'just-in-time' commercial and industrial delivery. Why did the USA worry about Canada? US public opinion and policy makers alike saw the country as a hotbed for terrorist activity. Although exaggerated, because none of the terrorists entered from Canada, this perception might not be all that far from the truth. Canada was primarily a 'venue of opportunity' to support, plan or mount attacks elsewhere. This was mainly because of the country's flexible immigration and refugee laws, which allowed terrorists and terrorist organizations to operate within the country with relative ease. It was estimated by Canadian sources (Canadian Security Intelligence Service—CSIS) that there were at least 50 terrorist groups operating in the country, primarily in the areas of fund-raising and the planning and execution of terrorist activities elsewhere.

In response to these fears, Canada signed a border agreement with the USA in late 2001. The agreement outlined bilateral mechanisms with regards to border infrastructure, in order to secure the flow of goods and people. The agreement also placed special emphasis on the twin principles of co-ordination and information-sharing as critical components of a secure common border. Progress on the agreement was no less spectacular, with almost all of the 32 measures fully implemented by 2007.

One of the more significant parts of the 'smart' border agreement implemented what were referred to as Integrated Border Enforcement Team (IBET) programmes along 23 border points. This binational partnership enabled the five core law enforcement partners to share information and work together daily with other local, state and provincial enforcement agencies on issues relating to national security, organized crime and other criminality crossing the Canada-US border between ports of entry. The IBET partner agencies from Canada and the USA were the Royal Canadian Mounted Police (RCMP), the Canadian Border Services Agency (CBSA), US Customs and Border Protection, the US Bureau of Immigration and Customs Enforcement and the US Coast Guard.

Canada also put into place four Integrated National Security Enforcement Teams (INSETs) in major Canadian urban centres—Toronto, Montréal, Vancouver and Ottawa. The INSETs increased the capacity for the collection, sharing and analysis of intelligence among different Canadian security agencies with respect to targets that were a threat to national security. The INSETs were made up of representatives of the RCMP, the CBSA, Citizenship and Immigration Canada, CSIS and provincial and municipal police services.

With respect to legislation, Canada introduced Bill C-11, which limited access to appeals on the part of rejected refugee claimants and, at the same time, made it easier to deport individuals whose specific requests for asylum had been rejected. With respect to terrorist activities specifically, the Liberal Government introduced Bill C-36, which provided for additional resources and police powers to identify and punish terrorists and terrorist support groups. More specifically, the legislation made it illegal to raise funds on behalf of terrorists, allowed the Government to seize assets of terrorist organizations and expanded police authority to pursue suspected terrorists.

By 2007 the Government had spent approximately C $7,700m. in order to enhance its security and defence capacity. This included: $1,200m. for the Department of National Defence; $1,600m. for the hiring of more intelligence officers, better co-ordination between different security agencies, better coastal surveillance and measures to control terrorist financing; $1,000m. to enhance measures against illegal migration; $2,200m. for airport security; and $1,200m. for border infrastructure.

Equally important was the meeting between Prime Minister Martin, US President George W. Bush and Mexican President Fox in Waco, Texas (USA), in March 2005, which resulted in the signing of the Security and Prosperity Partnership (SPP). The SPP describes itself as a partnership intended 'to increase security and enhance prosperity' in the three countries by means of greater co-operation and information-sharing. Through the formation of trilateral cabinet-level working groups, the agreement charged the three countries with:

planning for and timetabling the securing of North America; ensuring that legitimate travellers and cargo could efficiently cross the shared borders; enhancing the competitive position of North American industries in the global marketplace; and providing greater economic opportunities for each of the three societies, while maintaining high standards of health and safety. It was clear then that the events of 11 September 2001 had had a dramatic impact on Canadian policy, in both domestic and international affairs. Indeed, this SPP would now serve as the guiding principle of Canadian foreign policy and, thus, signalled an important shift for Canada, away from global affairs to more regional ones, which included not only the USA, but Mexico as well.

There were essentially three reasons why trilateral security co-operation in the North American context was necessary. The first was economic in nature: the increasing levels of trade between the three states created a situation where security co-operation was inevitable. As early as the mid-1990s it became evident that border controls had somehow to be modified or 'updated' in some very profound manner, in order to be able to handle the dramatically increasing level of commercial traffic. The process of reforming border procedures, therefore, pre-dated 11 September 2001 by almost six years. The logic in favour of border reform was simple and often employed by those in the business community. The argument was that the best solution was to strengthen border control along the perimeter of North America, in order to convert the sub-regional borders into 'zones of confidence'. Within a context of 'just-in-time' production schedules, every hour lost at a border inspection translated into important financial losses for transnational firms.

The second argument in favour of security co-operation relations rested on the three states essentially being exposed to the same threats. Without a doubt the USA was the central target of these common threats, but both Canada and Mexico were directly involved for three central reasons. First, another terrorist attack on the USA would have a direct impact on both Canada and Mexico, as had occurred in September 2001, when the USA essentially imposed a trade embargo on itself by shutting down its borders with both other neighbouring countries. Thus, US security concerns were of prime interest to Canada and Mexico, because both countries' economic prosperity depended directly on how 'safe' US policymakers felt.

The third factor justifying a trilateral approach to North American security was the multifaceted nature of the terrorist threat. The ways in which terrorism could manifest itself were many: they could target transportation routes, such as border crossings, railway lines, gas pipelines, maritime ports, containers, etc., as well as visible and public objects, such as critical infrastructure and symbolic monuments. What might prove to be even more alarming were the weapons that might be employed in the future. No one was willing to rule out the possible use of biological, chemical and maybe even nuclear terrorist attacks against the North American continent.

WHY A NEW 'NEW' FOREIGN POLICY REVIEW?

In 2003 DFAIT announced to the Canadian nation that it would be conducting a review of foreign policy that would involve a wide range of actors in society and a broadly-based public debate. The need for such a review had been clear to many students of Canadian foreign policy for several years, but by 2003 it had become widely accepted that changing global realities required a shift in Canadian priorities and methods. What is more, a potentially damaging rift had emerged between Canada and the USA over the issue of disarming Iraq.

For a country like Canada, which has limited ambitions in the international system and is more shaped by, than a shaper of, the international structure, frequent review is a necessary element in maintaining an effective foreign policy. During the 50 years of the Cold War such frequent review was not urgently needed as the system was relatively stable, the distribution of power relatively unchanged and the priorities for Canada comparatively fixed. However, in the aftermath of the Cold War and with the emergence of a new polarity in the system, Canada was forced to re-evaluate its foreign policy objectives in line with the changing realities of international relations.

By the beginning of the 21st century a number of commentators were urging a re-evaluation of the 1995 policy statement, arguing that it was vague and outdated. For some there was a feeling that, given obvious limitations in terms of resources and power, Canada must determine its goals in the system with great care and apply resources in such a way that foreign policy achieves maximum return on the investment.

Denis Stairs, for example, while questioning the logic of the human security perspective, argued that its promotion to the guiding paradigm of Canadian foreign policy meant that the agenda for Canada's foreign relations, if taken seriously, would require expenditures well beyond anything Canada (or any other contributing state) has been prepared to contemplate thus far. In its place, he advocated the Government be more conservative in defining foreign policy goals, insisting that Canada's international rhetoric should exceed neither its resources (what he called 'grasp') nor what Canadians really want ('aspirations').

David Dewitt similarly argued that Canada needed to define carefully what its intentions and goals were in the international system. Noting that Canada was in the process of moving from being a marginal actor at the centre to being a central actor at the margins, Dewitt questioned the wisdom of replacing traditional definitions of security with the more general idea of human security. Instead, while accepting that Canada's security was threatened directly and indirectly by a number of non-traditional issues, Dewitt urged a rethink of the guiding principles of Canada's international security policy.

AN ALTERED INTERNATIONAL REALITY: THE CHANGING GLOBAL CONTEXT SINCE THE 1995 REVIEW

Though the end of the Cold War was clearly the defining event of the late 20th century, the full implications of the unravelling of the bipolar order had not become clear until beyond the middle of the 1990s. Thus, when DFAIT carried out a foreign policy review in 1995, it was operating on the basis of a perception of the post-Cold War world that was later shown to be rather less than accurate. Certainly, the opening of the system meant a reordering of the international agenda, and the rise of prosperity as an equal partner to security in the goals of states. It was true that the end of the Cold War meant that the prospect of armed conflict between the great powers had receded further into the background than previously.

Furthermore, new threats had emerged and there was a need to redefine the traditional conceptions of security. However, the Canadian redefinition of security to embrace its individual, human dimensions was shown, by recent events in the international system, to have missed a large and pressing part of the reality of international security. The end of the Cold War did not just mean the end of bipolarity and of the existence of two superpowers in the system. Instead, it saw the emergence of a complex rearrangement of the structure, in which a number of medium and great powers existed alongside what had come to be known as the 'hyperpower'. The term originated with the French foreign minister of the late 1990s, Hubert Vedrine, lamenting the unparalleled and unchallenged position of the USA in the post-Cold War world, which had become a state so far ahead of all the others that it possessed the capability to go it alone.

As Nossal showed, the term 'hyperpower', however, should be used to refer not only to the capacity of the USA, but also to its willingness to pursue its own interests at the expense of other states. In this sense, Nossal argued, the country should be seen as a 'hyper-active' power. Nossal's paper not only showed the potency of the hyperpower, but also its willingness both to spoil multilateral efforts and to act unilaterally if the consent of other states for its actions was not forthcoming. The presence of a single state that was so far ahead of the rest of the world in its military and economic capacities, and that had a political system that allowed it to adjust to the changing realities of the international system, both economic and political, meant a fundamental shift in the structure of that system, and posed a serious challenge to both rivals and allies alike.

THE OPTIONS FOR CANADA

It might be useful to look at three possible scenarios for future directions in Canadian foreign and security policy in the near term. By examining these three alternative futures, some light might be shed on the potential costs and benefits of either a conservative or a more radical review of Canada's role in the world.

'Status quo': in the first scenario Canada continues as it has been, working closely with the USA on some issues, striking out in a different direction on others. In this scenario Canada would continue to stress the importance of Canadian values, emphasize human security over more traditional conceptions, and to look to the UN to authorize international security missions. Pursuing objectives unpopular in the US capital of Washington, DC, such as the ban on anti-personnel landmines, would help to distinguish Canadian foreign and security policy. Canada would continue to adopt an ambiguous public attitude to the USA and would decide on support or opposition to US international actions based on the perceived merits of each case.

'Further integration': in this scenario Canada would seek to align its foreign and security policy more directly with that of the USA (and Mexico). While not rejecting the perspective of human security, Canada would move towards performing a niche role in pursuing joint objectives in international security with the USA. At times this would mean military action, focusing on specialized activities in which Canada held the capabilities to succeed. At other times it would mean using Canadian expertise to assist in areas such as non-proliferation and the fight against terrorist-financing. The most significant implication of this scenario was that it would refocus Canadian foreign policy on the North American region. The International Policy Statement, released in April 2005, seemed to bring Canadian foreign policy closer to this scenario.

The 2005 document argued that, first, countries faced a new 'cluster of threats', ranging from global terrorism through environmental degradation to disease. Second, that there existed a 'new global distribution of power', whereby the USA surpassed all potential rivals by a wide and ever increasing margin. Third, the 'global marketplace' was evolving: 'First, ideas have become the engine of productivity and the currency of global success. Innovation determines the wealth of nations and their capacity to provide a high quality of life for their citizens. Second, today's business models are driven not by geography, but by investment decisions and information technology.'

The foreign policy review dedicated an entire section to the future role of Canada within the context of North America. The section, entitled 'Revitalizing our North American Partnership', signalled a shifting emphasis away from a global approach to foreign policy, to a more regionally based one. The section privileged the role of the Canadian-US relationship, describing it as 'the bedrock of that partnership' and 'built upon more than two centuries of close economic, security and personal ties. Over several generations, Canadians and Americans have intermingled through migration, cross-border work and travel, and the exchange of ideas. Our joint achievements—the world's largest bilateral trading relationship and the world's longest unmilitarized border—are the envy of the world.' In sum, the International Policy Statement reorientation served as a continuation—even a reinforcement—of the SPP agreement signed by Canada the previous month.

The election of Stephen Harper as Prime Minister further moved Canadian foreign policy closer to that of the USA, and to a focus on regional rather than global issues. The Harper Government took it upon itself to repair the damaged Canada-US relationship caused by personality and policy differences between Jean Chrétien and George Bush. For example, the Chrétien Administration did not support the invasion of Iraq, thereby breaking ranks with its traditional allies. Although inter-agency co-operation between Canada and the USA increased after the events of 11 September 2001, it was abundantly clear that relations remained strained between the leaders of the two countries. By comparison, under Harper, Canada embraced the bilateral and North American relationship, favouring it over all others. One clear example of this emphasis on the USA was Canada's active participation in the conflict in Afghanistan. Since coming to power Harper has more than doubled the Canadian deployment in Afghanistan to almost 2,500 combat troops. By Canadian standards, the country's new Conservative Government paid dearly for this Canadian 'surge' with over 100 combat deaths.

'Going it alone': in this third scenario Canada would embark on a revolutionary rethink of its relations with the USA, and would attempt to maintain its vital economic relationship while aligning itself more closely with nations that were looking to the UN to play a more active role in international affairs and to ways of constraining the US hyperpower. Military actions would be relegated to a second tier, while the pursuit of human security would colour all Canadian foreign relations and international activities. NATO commitments would be all but forgotten and Canada would seek to increase its international credibility through an emphasis on foreign aid and a commitment to international law.

It was clear that the third scenario existed here only as a 'straw man', designed to demonstrate the dangers for Canada in irritating US sensibilities. Although some elements, such as an effective withdrawal from NATO were within the realms of reality, a stubborn insistence on UN authorization and international law would clearly be highly damaging to the bilateral relationship in the face of continuing US unilateralism. What is more, the risk of signalling to the USA that Canada was not pulling its weight in terms of military commitments was that the US Government would no longer look to Canada as a reliable partner, but rather as an irrelevant sideshow.

Obviously the first and second scenarios fit more closely to current realities and to the history of Canada's relations with the USA. The first option was attractive because it involved the least amount of change and the least expense in both financial and political terms. However, it was unclear whether or not the USA would be content to give the same political and economic benefits to a similarly ambiguous northern neighbour in the future. The unwillingness of Canada to support the USA in Iraq led the US Government to express its disappointment with Canada. In the long run this was unlikely to be translated into real costs for Canada and, in the short term, most of the US anger was being directed towards the French and, to a lesser extent, Germany and Russia. However, continued recalcitrance on the part of Canada in what the USA sees as a friend's duties would only tempt fate.

The second option, however, would be vigorously resisted by vocal sections of the Canadian public and would threaten the legitimacy of Canada's claim to have an independent foreign and security policy. None the less, there has already been a small move towards such an option with the suggestion of inter-operability for the Canadian armed forces with their US counterparts. One cannot help but feel that Canada's decision not to participate in the invasion of Iraq at the least delayed the achievement of this goal and at the worst damaged Canada's image with the US military, while the United Kingdom and Australia gained valuable loyalty points and experience. A strong impetus from the Canadian Government towards the harmonization of the Canadian and US forces would help to overcome these difficulties, as would employing Canadian expertise in areas such as non-proliferation. Indeed, pursuing alternative, non-military contributions to the US 'war on terror' and the proliferation of weapons of mass destruction would help enormously in offsetting the greatly weakened position of the Canadian military.

The best option for Canadian interests, if not for Canadian values, lies somewhere in between the first two scenarios. The 2005 foreign policy review pointed to a closer alignment with US foreign policy, while at the same time trying to persuade the USA to seek multilateral solutions. If Canada truly wanted to have influence on the future of US foreign policy, it must accept that there is a world of difference between the triumphant superpower of 1991 and the wounded hyperpower of 2007.

GLOBAL WARMING: UNEXPECTED OPPORTUNITY?

The first half of 2008 saw very little change in Canada's foreign policy activity. The constant prospect of an election within the context of a minority Harper Government implied that Canadian decision makers were spending much more time focusing on domestic rather than foreign policy. There was, however, one notable exception.

In 2008 the realization of global warming's likely impact on Canada became a major factor in the country's foreign and defence policy. The Arctic ice sheet, as many scientists had warned for years, shrank to an unprecedented extent, thus opening up a new naval trade route from the east to the west. Most importantly, this east–west trade link was significantly shorter than the one offered by the Panama Canal, which may mean that the Arctic passage will eventually become the preferred route of cost- and time-conscious shippers throughout the world. Equally important is the speculation by geologists that the area might hold significant reserves of oil and natural gas. The Arctic is said to hold 13% of the world's undiscovered oil and 30% of its undiscovered natural gas.

It is easy to see, therefore, how no fewer than five countries could become embroiled in a dispute over territory that only a few years ago was solely inhabited by Inuit and polar bears. Canada, Russia, the USA, Denmark (because of Greenland) and even Norway have directly become involved in the dispute over who owns the Arctic. The problem concerns overlapping claims, with the Canadians and the Russians disputing the largest part of the Arctic. In 2007 it led the Russian navy to plant a Russian flag in the disputed waters. It also led Canada to increase its military presence in the region. The Canadian Defense department has decided to build a military base in the region and deploy as many as eight combat ice breakers to patrol the region.

The net effect of this dispute has been to focus Canadian foreign policy further into one region: that of North America.

CONCLUSION

Canadian foreign policy went through a number of evolutionary stages, particularly after the end of the Cold War. A Cold War policy of internationalism, which focused on the avoidance of great power conflict, gave way to human security and morality in the foreign policy of the 1990s. In many ways a pursuance of internationalism (the 'new' policy enshrined in the 1995 review) continued to urge an international foreign policy, but with a focus on new kinds of non-traditional threats. In 2001 the US terrorist attacks made Canadian decision makers rethink the country's foreign policy direction: as stated in 2005, Canada would now place more emphasis on what was going on closer to home. Given Canada's limited resources, the brewing territorial dispute over who has sovereign rights over the Arctic will only reinforce this tendency.

FORGING A NEW RELATIONSHIP: ABORIGINAL PEOPLES IN CANADA

GEOFFREY MERCER

Aboriginal peoples' sense of injustice at their treatment in Canada generated wide-ranging demands for change. These encompassed the affirmation of Aboriginal rights, including self-government and entitlement to an historic land base, reassertion of the unique relations with the federal Government and the elimination of enduring social and economic inequalities. Aboriginal peoples similarly sought recognition and renewal of their distinctive identities and cultures—as (North American) Indians or First Nations, Inuit (previously called Eskimos) and Métis (descendants of Indian and Euro-Canadian unions). Hopes of building a new relationship with other Canadians based on mutual understanding and respect depended on achieving a satisfactory resolution of these issues.

HISTORICAL BACKGROUND

Throughout the 19th century Aboriginal peoples were commonly perceived as an obstacle to national development and in need of 'protection', religious conversion or 'civilization' prior to their eventual assimilation. The Euro-Canadian expansion westward generated extensive treaty activity, except in British Columbia and the Far North, throughout the second half of the 19th and early 20th century. A central aim was to 'extinguish' Aboriginal land title and segregate Indians on reserves. The repressive colonial regime resulted in significant and enduring harm to Aboriginal peoples' land bases and natural resources, economic and social institutions, traditional cultures and ways of life. Equally dramatically, contact with Europeans led to a drastic reduction in the Aboriginal population through disease and violence.

The British North America Act of 1867 authorized federal Government jurisdiction over Indians and the lands reserved for them. The 1876 Indian Act consolidated and extended existing legislation, with control vested in a separate federal Indian department. A 'status' (or 'registered') Indian was defined as a member of a band, who was eligible to live on a reserve, with some also entitled to 'treaty benefits'. They were regarded as wards or dependants of the federal Government and band (First Nation) governments exercised only limited powers. Additionally, a policy of 'enfranchisement' was promoted, whereby Indians were granted full citizenship in return for relinquishing their registered status. In contrast, non-status Indians and Métis were excluded from Indian Act and treaty rights, and viewed primarily as a provincial responsibility. The Indian nations and Métis bore the brunt of white colonialism and cultural domination. The Inuit avoided their full impact until the early 20th century, and it was not until 1939 that the Supreme Court ruled that they were subject to federal jurisdiction.

The general direction of Canadian policy continued on its colonial course into the 1960s, when there was a groundswell of Aboriginal action to resolve historic grievances and reassert their distinct status as 'nations within' Canada. Initially, the federal Government outlined a programme for full-blown assimilation in its 1969 White Paper, including proposals to extinguish the unique federal Government-First Nations relationship. Aboriginal peoples united in rejecting this option. They stressed that their economic and social conditions were equivalent to those experienced by people living in a poor, developing country, despite living in one of the richest countries in the world. There were high profile campaigns at the UN, and cross-national Aboriginal organizations, such as the Inuit Circumpolar Conference, were established to advance their common interests. Protests were bolstered by the increasing preoccupation of the federal Government with the prospect of massive economic (resource) development in areas occupied by Aboriginal peoples, notably in the Canadian North (above latitude 60°N), which comprised 40% of the country's landmass. This combination of Aboriginal resistance and international focus on their plight proved a powerful incentive for governments to re-evaluate their policies.

DEMOGRAPHIC TRENDS

One indicator of the increasing confidence and vitality of the Aboriginal population has been its growth through the second half of the 20th century, with a remarkable rise in the number reporting an Aboriginal identity, from 165,000 in 1951 to 720,000 in 1991. The equivalent question in the 2001 Census—'Do you consider yourself an Aboriginal person, that is, North American Indian, Métis or Inuit?'—estimated the Aboriginal population at 976,305, or 3.3% of the Canadian population. This comprised 608,850 North American Indian (62%), 292,305 Métis (30%) and 45,075 Inuit (5%), while 30,080 opted for a multi-group or 'other' identity (3%). Yet a different question on ancestry—'To which ethnic or cultural group(s) did your ancestors belong?'—produced 1m. people claiming sole or part Aboriginal origins in 1991, and 1,319,890, or 4.4% of all Canadians, in the 2001 Census. In 2006 Aboriginal numbers (based on identity) rose to 1,172,785 or 3.8% of all Canadians. This population was much younger, with a median age of 27 years, compared with 40 years for all Canadians. In 2006 four-fifths of Aboriginal people lived in Ontario and the four Western Provinces; yet their proportion of all inhabitants within individual provinces and territories ranged from 85% in Nunavut, 50% in the Northwest Territories, 25% in the Yukon, 16% in Manitoba, 15% in Saskatchewan, 6% in Alberta, 5% in British Columbia and less in each of the other provinces. Almost four-fifths of Métis lived in a provincial belt from Ontario to British Columbia, while nearly one-half of all Inuit were located in Nunavut, 22% in Québec, and 9% in Newfoundland and Labrador.

Data collected by the Department of Indian Affairs and Northern Development (DIAND) identified a corresponding rise in the registered Indian population, from 317,000 in 1980, through 490,000 in 1990, to 763,555 in 2006. This included a sudden surge following amendments to the Indian Act in 1985 that allowed over 170,000 individuals (between 1985 and 1999) to 'regain' their registered entitlement (such as Indian women who had married non-status men). In 2005 22% of registered Indians lived in Ontario, with 13%–16% in each of the Prairie Provinces and British Columbia. There were 615 registered Indian bands distributed across 2,889 reserves and settlements. Many were small, with over 60% of reserves having fewer than 500 residents, and only 6% with more than 2,000 inhabitants. The proportion of status Indians living 'on-reserve' declined from 80% in the mid-1970s to 56% in 2006, although it is predicted to rise back to 75% by 2021. Conversely, the Aboriginal population living in urban areas, comprising status as well as non-status Indians and Métis, expanded appreciably, to around 70% of all those reporting an Aboriginal identity. Another notable population movement involved a large-scale relocation of the Inuit within the Canadian North in the 1960s and 1970s to newly constructed permanent settlements with an average total of 500 residents.

ECONOMIC AND SOCIAL CONDITIONS

A destructive legacy of the colonial relationship has been the extreme disparities in economic and social conditions between the Aboriginal and non-Aboriginal population. Traditional subsistence economies and lifestyles were undermined, but few of the Aboriginal population obtained secure, well-paid jobs in the wage labour economy. Unemployment levels from the 1990s were more than twice that of the non-Aboriginal population, with some of the highest rates among registered Indians living on reserves. According to the 2001 Census, overall Aboriginal average income was only 64% of the total Canadian figure, and fell to 49% for the on-reserve population. Again, poverty rates and dependence on income assistance were much higher, with two-fifths of registered Indians and four-fifths of Aboriginal households headed by a single female, living at or below the poverty line, compared with around 15% nationally.

This pattern of economic inequalities was replicated across a diverse group of social indicators. Aboriginal mortality and morbidity rates stayed much higher even as the registered Indian life expectancy climbed from 60.9 to 70.4 between 1980 and 2001, and the gap between registered Indians and all Canadians fell from 11 to 6.4 years (6.6 for females and 6.1 for males) over the same period. On-reserve infant mortality declined from 82 to 7.2 deaths per 1,000 live births between 1955 and 2001. The Aboriginal population also exhibited much higher rates of chronic illness (notably tuberculosis and diabetes) and impairment (physical and mental), together with a faster rise in new cases of HIV/AIDS, particularly among younger people. There were ominous levels of alcoholism and drug abuse, while youth suicide rates were six times the national average. Aboriginal peoples had a higher involvement with the criminal justice system, whether as offenders or victims, and were over eight times more likely to receive a prison sentence. Families were also beset by high levels of sexual abuse and violence, and the number of children placed in care was 10 times the national average. This pattern of social malaise, disadvantage and discrimination was reinforced by a breakdown in traditional community support networks.

The wretched historical failings of the segregated, residential school system belatedly attracted policy attention from the 1970s. This led to slow improvements in Aboriginal educational performance, ranging from the proportion graduating from high school, enrolling in post-secondary education or studying at a university, but standards remained much below national rates. The percentage of First Nations youth on reserves completing high school rose from 31% to 66% between 1991 and 2006, but remained far below the 85% rate in the country as a whole, as did post-secondary performance (of those in the 25–64 age group, 8% have a university degree, compared with 23% of the non-Aboriginal population, with the gap increasing over the decade since the mid-1990s). Another concern was the parlous state of reserve housing, with an acknowledged shortage of suitable and affordable units and ample evidence of overcrowding. In 2004/05 28% of dwellings were rated as inadequate (i.e. requiring minor or major renovations or replacement), which was four times the national rate. For the Aboriginal population living in urban areas there were similar problems over accommodation, plus high levels of homelessness. More positively, since the 1990s the percentage of reserve dwellings with adequate water supply grew from 86% to 98% by the late 2000s, and those with acceptable sewerage disposal from 80% to 96%, but extensive upgrading was required to ensure a regular supply of clean, safe drinking water and waste-water facilities. Other important aspects of the reserve infrastructure, such as the quality of roads, were widely characterized as 'poor'.

Over recent decades there has been increased investment in a broad spectrum of social and economic programmes. Another target is the enhancement of Aboriginal cultures and languages, fuelled by concerns illustrated by the decline among Inuit reporting Inuktitut as their mother tongue from 73% in 1981 to 53% in 2001, and a fall in its regular use at home from 66% to 43% over the same period. A noteworthy success was the establishment of the Aboriginal Peoples Television Network in 1999, giving control of its own broadcasting and media language across the country. Yet a stark divide still separates the everyday experiences of Aboriginal communities from those of other Canadians. This accumulation of socio-economic exclusion and threats to their cultures contributes to a 'heritage of dependency, powerlessness and distrust' and represents a primary test of federal Government policies.

ABORIGINAL RIGHTS AND LAND CLAIMS

It was not until the 1970s that the largely dismissive stance taken in Canadian courts towards Aboriginal treaty claims and rights showed signs of weakening. The landmark case that exposed divisions within the Supreme Court was Calder (1973): three judges followed the orthodoxy that English common law upheld Aboriginal title to land, but that it had been extinguished by pre-Confederation enactment; three judges reached the more 'radical' conclusion that the title had never been extinguished; while the seventh dismissed the case on a technicality. This breach in legal opinion widened with subsequent decisions, such as Baker Lake (1980) and Guérin (1984), which decreed that rights need not be site-specific or linked to Aboriginal title (that is, exclusive use and occupancy) and could only be extinguished with explicit Aboriginal consent. The new 1982 Constitution Act added a fresh stimulus to change by its inclusion of clauses that 'recognized and affirmed' Aboriginal and treaty rights, and specified the Métis along with the Inuit and Indian peoples within its definition of 'Aboriginal'.

Generally, the legal path to affirming Aboriginal rights and land claims was uncertain, slow and expensive. Nevertheless, in 1990 the Canadian Supreme Court ruled in the Sparrow judgment that Aboriginal peoples enjoyed 'constitutional protection against provincial legislative power', while a series of decisions confirmed the special status and rights of Aboriginal peoples, for example, with respect to traditional hunting and harvesting activities. There were also reversals, with the denial of the Delgamuukw claim by the British Columbia Supreme Court in 1991 generating most alarm. Yet its national counterpart overturned this judgment in 1997, ruling that Aboriginal title to land existed as a communal right, protected under the 1982 Constitution Act, at least where exclusive occupation of lands could be established when non-Aboriginal sovereignty was declared in 1846.

A further key outcome of the Calder decision in 1973 was the conversion of the federal Government to the value of making 'modern treaties'. Two main types of claims were identified: 'comprehensive' (based on Aboriginal title to lands and natural resources not addressed by treaty or other legal means) and 'specific' (stemming from undischarged treaty obligations). The potential of the comprehensive claims process was highlighted after the Cree of James Bay in Québec won a court decision to stop a massive hydroelectricity project that threatened their traditional lands and way of life. In the resulting negotiations, large-scale economic development was linked with a settlement of local Aboriginal peoples' rights to land (including sub-surface) rights, substantial financial payments, enlarged self-government powers and participation in decisions on land, wildlife and water management. The talks culminated in the 1975 James Bay and Northern Québec Agreement (JBNQA) with the Cree and Inuit of northern (mainland) Québec. It was extended to incorporate the Naskapi of north-eastern Québec in 1978, and followed by an agreement signed with the Inuvialuit of the western Arctic in 1984. In 1986 the comprehensive route was revised to permit more flexibility in land tenure arrangements, and settlements no longer required the surrender of Aboriginal title.

The JBNQA provided valuable new opportunities for Aboriginal peoples to manage their own economic development and sustain Aboriginal communities and their ways of life. Compensation funding was paid into the Cree Regional Authority and the Makivik Corporation (for the Inuit). These funded a range of economic and social programmes, including minerals, forestry, fisheries and agriculture (Nunavik Arctic Foods), airlines (Air Inuit and First Air), shipping, construction, manufacturing and service companies. Besides these, a system of co-operatives was set up, providing retail stores, crafts, services and hotels in the Northwest Territories and Québec that became the main local employers after the Government. Federal programmes to generate Aboriginal employment and business activity and to make local communities self-reliant were also expanded. However, the James Bay project was interrupted by protests and litigation at its harmful effects on Aboriginal lands and peoples. This led to negotiations between Québec and the Cree about Canada's obligations under the JBNQA that validated Cree interests, particularly in natural resources and the environment, and contained a new basis for economic and community governance and development. An agreement was finally reached with the federal Government in 2007 that allowed work on the hydroelectric projects to resume.

Another dramatic outcome of the modern treaty-making process was the acceptance, in a plebiscite in 1982, of the principle of dividing the Northwest Territories with the aim of granting Inuit claims to their traditional lands in the central and eastern sections. Ensuing negotiations produced an accord on the status and boundaries of the new Inuit territory in 1992. Nunavut (Inuktitut for 'Our Land') finally came into existence in April 1999, with powers and institutions akin to those of a territorial government. It covered 2.2m. sq km (nearly one-fifth of the Canadian landmass), with a population of only 26,745 in 2001 (85% of whom were Inuit). Of this total, slightly more than 5,200 people lived in the capital, Iqaluit, with most of the remainder distributed across 28 smaller communities. This led to a highly decentralized form of administration, with some government departments located outside the capital. The Nunavut agreement comprised a substantial cash settlement of C $1,140m. over 14 years, land management and wildlife hunting rights and self-government. All the same, Nunavut faced considerable problems in generating better employment opportunities and income levels, as well as improvements in the education and training of local Inuit, both to staff local businesses and the new Government. In 2005 there was a settlement of Labrador Inuit land claims to disputed offshore areas of Québec and of Labrador, as well as northern Labrador land and resource rights. Furthermore, the Dene and Métis in the western Northwest Territories concluded a comprehensive land claim and self-government agreement in the Northwest Territories with the Tlicho (formerly Dogrib) First Nation. This included the largest bloc of First Nation-owned land in Canada. The federal Government also devolved more 'provincial responsibilities' to the northern territorial governments.

In British Columbia there was a long-standing political and judicial rejection of Aboriginal title and the treaty-making process. An alternative 'made in BC' approach was agreed, with the provincial Government involved as a full participant, but substantive progress proved elusive and the British Columbia Treaty Commission was set up in 1991 to advance negotiations, along with a committee to advise on treaty-related issues including fisheries, forestry, lands, governance and the environment. An important factor in persuading the provincial Government of the need for change was the calculation that the province would lose C $1,000m. of investment and 1,500 jobs per year in the mining and forestry sectors if treaty settlements were not finalized. Yet negotiated agreements faced many barriers, including the lack of suitable Crown land to transfer. In 2002 the British Columbia Court of Appeal corroborated the duty of the Crown (federal and provincial governments) to 'engage, consult and accommodate' First Nations where their rights, title and interests are affected by developments, such as of natural resources, on their traditional lands, in an action brought by the Haida and Taku River Tlingit First Nations—a conclusion reiterated by the Supreme Court of Canada in 2004.

Even so, the first comprehensive claim settlement in the province was negotiated outside the 'made in BC' process with the Nisga'a Indian Band, whose action triggered the 1973 Calder judgment. Their claim was formally entered in 1976, but it was not until 1999 that the final agreement was ratified, and one year later endorsed in the Nisga'a Final Agreement Act. This was the first 'modern treaty' to specify a First Nation's Aboriginal rights as guaranteed in the 1982 Constitution Act. It comprised a land settlement of almost 2,000 sq km, a cash component of C $190m., institution of Nisga'a self-government and ownership of surface and sub-surface treaty rights such as resource (fisheries and wildlife) harvesting (with some co-management), culture and heritage. The Nisga'a also took over existing 'reserve lands' under the Indian Act. Moreover, the Treaty could only be amended with the consent of all three Governments.

In 2004 a new British Columbia Liberal administration proclaimed its commitment to forging 'new relations' with First Nations, but it was 2007 before the first two 'made in BC' agreements were ratified, with another four negotiations on final agreements still under way in 2008, and 36 sets of negotiations at the 'agreement in principle' stage. Legislation approving the first 'urban treaty', with the Tsawwassen First Nation in British Columbia, was passed in the federal legislature in 2008. It included a land settlement, financial package, and rights to traditional hunting and fishing for food and social and ceremonial purposes. It stipulated a transition period after which the Indian Act would no longer apply to Tsawwassen First Nation land and members, to be replaced by a new constitution, including procedures for the involvement of non-members resident on Tsawwassen lands. As a way of promoting participation, interim deals were sanctioned that offered 'partial' options, such as the establishment of Aboriginal-controlled school and health boards, and cost-shared 'treaty-related measures', where, for example, likely settlement lands were acquired or protected, and funding was made available for linked schemes covering economic development, land management, work-related education and training. Extra legal support for the Aboriginal position was contained in the British Columbia Supreme Court declaration in 2007 on an action brought by the Tsilhqot'in Nation that the federal Government alone exercised the legal authority of the Crown and, hence, the provincial Government's land use and forestry activities 'unjustifiably infringed' on Aboriginal rights. Moreover, in 2008 the Canadian Supreme Court dismissed arguments that the federal Aboriginal Fisheries Strategy was unconstitutional and 'race-based' by disallowing non-Aboriginal commercial fishing.

Policy action on Métis land claims was heavily constrained by court decisions that, during the historic treaty-making period of 1870–1930, the Métis had declined the offer of Indian treaty status in favour of taking negotiable land scrip. This over-rode contrary provisions in the Manitoba Act 1870 that conferred the right to land on the 'mixed-blood' populations of Red River. The necessary breakthrough had to await the 2003 Powley decision, when the Supreme Court affirmed that a Métis community in Ontario possessed an Aboriginal right to harvest moose for subsistence purposes. This triggered intergovernmental discussions with the Métis about the wider implementation of such rights in other localities across Canada.

The main alternative path in treaty negotiations covered 'specific' claims. These related to unfulfilled treaty obligations and the federal administration of Aboriginal lands and assets. In 1991 an Indian Specific Claims Commission (ISCC) was established to investigate previously rejected cases. By mid-2003 251 claims had been settled, at a cost of C $1,250m., but a large backlog of cases remained, with over 650 specific claims still under negotiation or assessment. Typical outcomes involved financial payments from federal and provincial governments, but land entitlement agreements were concluded as well, notably in Alberta and Saskatchewan. The process attracted enormous criticism from Aboriginal groups, which argued that the federal Government was defendant, judge and arbiter; and from non-Aboriginal communities and provincial governments, which disputed the return of land and resources to First Nations. The Specific Claims Resolution Act 2003 was passed in an effort to speed up the negotiation process, with separate bodies for supporting negotiations and settling disputes, involving potential cash compensation to a maximum of $10m.

The new Progressive Conservative federal Government introduced the Specific Claims Tribunal Act passed in 2008. This established an independent body with dedicated funding and powers to make binding decisions on claims rejected by the Government or those where negotiations had broken down, with new deadlines for dealing with claims. The new tribunal replaced the ISCC. Since 1973 1,308 specific claims had been submitted: 765 were outstanding, with 300 settled through negotiation and 243 by other means, from an administrative remedy through to closure of the file. A First Nation might still opt to pursue a court action, with 74 such cases currently under consideration.

ACHIEVING SELF-GOVERNMENT

The pursuit of self-government constituted a key demand in the struggle for Aboriginal-led solutions to community healing and regeneration. The land settlement treaties of the 1970s and 1980s generated a huge stimulus to Aboriginal demands. Decisively, the JBNQA in 1975 provided for a Kativik Regional Government for the Inuit in the northern villages of Québec and a similar arrangement was concluded with the Cree-Naskapi (of Québec) in 1984. Outside these comprehensive claims agreements, the Sechelt Indian Band on Vancouver Island gained municipal status authority under provincial legislation in 1986. The general pace of change was slow, although in 1994 the Supreme Court of Canada recognized the inherent Aboriginal right to self-government. A conspicuous advance was realized with the self-government package contained in the 2000 Nisga'a Act. The governing body exercised various levels of law-making authority, assuming primary responsibilities in fields such as administration, culture and language, whereas in other areas, such as the Criminal Code, federal and provincial laws retained precedence. In addition, Nisga'a laws had priority if they met or exceeded federal or provincial standards, for example, in child and family support services. The Nisga'a Government was also entitled to set up police, correctional and court services on its lands. Another crucial aim was sustained economic development, and the treaty identified a range of opportunities for the Nisga'a in prominent sectors such as fisheries and forestry. The funding for self-government formed part of an agreement negotiated every five years between the three Governments. The Nisga'a Government must contribute to the costs of its programmes and services, through, for example, income and sales taxes, or its own revenues, while the Treaty eliminated Indian Act tax exemptions. These arrangements could only be changed if Canada, British Columbia and the Nisga'a all agreed.

Another important self-government initiative involved the Inuit living in northern Québec. A political accord in 1999 between the federal and provincial Governments and the Nunavik (Inuit) Party outlined a new form of public government covering a region of some 500,000 sq km, within the province, rather than a separate territory. Of the 11,000 permanent residents, 90% were Inuit. It was based on the JBNQA agreement, amalgamating existing institutions in a new authority, with powers that went beyond the municipal level, including its own elected legislative assembly, and executive and judicial branches, plus greater involvement in developing natural resources and the sponsorship of Inuit culture and language. While the Inuit chose self-determination through public forms of government (i.e. open to all Inuit and non-Inuit permanent residents), they retained the option of exercising their inherent right to self-government in the future. An agreement-in-principle was also signed in late 2007 to establish a Nunavik government, and legislation introduced to generate long-term economic and social development.

Another crucial step towards self-government occurred in 1983 with the publication of the Penner Report by a House of Commons committee, which recommended that Indian communities should devise forms of band government to replace the limited structures available under the Indian Act. Whereas the Indian Act restricted band-council powers to areas such as traffic, water supply and community health, bilateral agreements offered a new way forward. In 1985 DIAND formalized this approach by establishing a self-government office to facilitate negotiations for upgrading community government, even if the exact form varied according to local circumstances, traditions and aspirations. The proportion of DIAND programme expenditures administered by Aboriginal groups expanded from under 40% in the 1979/80 financial year to an average of 85% throughout the late 1990s. A linked scheme envisaged the closure of DIAND's regional offices with First Nations taking over its responsibilities for service delivery.

Subsequent instances of the expanding opportunities included the partial devolution of Aboriginal health services and a growth in the number of band-run schools from 64 in 1976/77 to 496 in 2002/03. Yet Aboriginal peoples criticized the level of federal support as inadequate and too symptomatic of a 'band aid' attitude. There has been ample evidence from across the provinces and territories that individual schools with a small population base that lack adequate and appropriate resources and support produce disappointing pupil educational outcomes. Fresh attempts to generate tangible progress concentrated on building an integrated Aboriginal school system: for example, an innovative agreement was concluded between Nova Scotia and the Mi'kmaq First Nation, which cemented Aboriginal control while incorporating considerable input from the provincial ministry of education. In a parallel initiative, federal legislation was passed substantiating First Nations' jurisdiction over education in British Columbia, effective from November 2007.

Off-Reserve Governance

According to the 2001 Census, almost one-half of the Aboriginal (identity) population lived in urban areas. Their experience of social exclusion and loss of a traditional culture and way of life have been widely noted, although in some areas, such as western Canada, the urban Aboriginal population is a well established and distinctive community. More generally, overlapping identities raised highly contentious cross-jurisdictional and citizenship issues and uncertainty about the entitlements of the different groups within the urban Aboriginal population. These constituted a major challenge when devising appropriate governance solutions. Among the 40% of status Indians living off-reserve, many claimed that their rights and services had been denied, with non-status Indians and Métis people arguing that both federal and provincial governments ignored them. Where services and programmes were offered, these were criticized as inadequate and delivered in culturally inappropriate ways. Hence, the mounting calls for off-reserve governance, to ensure Aboriginal control of service organization and delivery to reflect their values, identities and priorities.

A number of options were identified for enhancing Aboriginal influence over local institutions and processes. These included guaranteed representation on school and health boards, or permanent Aboriginal affairs committees in local councils or agencies. More flexibility was offered to First Nations in the use of housing funds. What had to be resolved was whether the focus was on Aboriginal people as a whole, or on specific communities. The absorption of all Aboriginal peoples into one heterogeneous constituency overlooked the sometimes significant different circumstances and interests within the Aboriginal population, evident also in the competing policy diagnoses and solutions identified by the Congress of Aboriginal Peoples (CAP), representing off-reserve Indians and Métis people, compared with the Assembly of First Nations. It argued strongly for repeal of the 'archaic' Indian Act, with its dated imposition of 'Indian-ness' and resulting marked contrasts across Aboriginal peoples in their entitlement to programmes and services, from post-secondary education to non-insured health benefits. Similar criticism underpinned CAP demands for repeal of Section 67 of the Canadian Human Rights Act, because it allowed on-reserve government to avoid democratic scrutiny and representation.

With respect to the Métis, the federal Government confirmed its willingness to include, with provincial agreement, ratification of agreements under Section 35 of the Constitution Act. Self-government might take a number of forms, including a public government, devolution of programmes and services, or the development of specific institutions to supply services. Still, the initiative has been left largely with provincial governments. Of those with a land base, a group of eight Alberta Métis Settlements made the most notable progress. The provincial Government introduced legislation in the late 1980s that granted land ownership rights and new forms of local self-government. This 'made in Alberta' solution represented a move towards more Métis control, with slightly enhanced revenue sources, but left unresolved how far Métis laws and services should apply to individuals living off their land base.

The basic local government structure set out in the Métis Settlements Act of 1990 identified the basic institutions and how these would carry out their legislative and executive functions and resolve disputes. This constituted a marked change from previous arrangements, where all power was vested in the Minister. Moreover, unlike non-Aboriginal local governments, the local council/settlement cannot make by-laws without local community consent. A Métis Settlements General Council acted to choose individual settlement actions, manage land interests, resource development and consolidated funds. The Settlements considered themselves within provincial jurisdiction, except in respect of their Aboriginal rights, such as hunting, fishing and gathering.

The pace of negotiating self-government agreements between DIAND and First Nations, Inuit and Métis communities across Canada was slow, and ranged from multiple to single jurisdictions (such as education or child welfare), or as part of broader comprehensive land claims. None the less, self-government negotiations were criticized because too often they resulted in a form of local government with only a modest devolution of administrative responsibility for services and without a secure funding basis.

CONSTITUTIONAL REFORM AND THE ABORIGINAL AGENDA

Since the 1970s wider discussions on constitutional reform in Canada have influenced the formulation and reception of Aboriginal peoples' political demands, such as Québec's claim for recognition of its distinct status. Likewise, new possibilities for challenging the Indian Act emerged after the passage of the Constitution Act 1982 and the Canadian Charter of Rights and Freedoms. A series of first ministers' conferences (comprising federal and provincial premiers and representatives from the main Aboriginal peoples' organizations) during the 1980s endeavoured, but failed, to agree the details of Aboriginal and treaty rights, including self-governance. In 1990 there was a graphic illustration of the potential for unresolved conflicts to degenerate into violence. A dispute over land claimed by the Mohawks from Kanesatake in the nearby town of Oka, in Québec, escalated into an armed confrontation with the provincial police, who were aided by the Canadian military. Within a couple of months the federal Government proclaimed its 'Aboriginal Agenda', described as a 'wide-sweeping commitment to change', and in 1991 set up the Royal Commission on Aboriginal Peoples (RCAP) to identify ways of renewing and enhancing contacts between Aboriginal peoples and the rest of Canada.

The RCAP report, entitled *People to People, Nation to Nation*, appeared in late 1996. It explored various answers to the basic question: what are the foundations of a fair and honourable relationship between the Aboriginal and non-Aboriginal people of Canada? Its own conclusions reiterated the basic tenets of Aboriginal thinking that 'Aboriginal peoples are nations' and, despite all the attempts to displace and assimilate them, they have remained 'proudly different'. The overall goal was not independence from Canada, but acceptance of their status as 'nations within'. The report urged a wholly new framework in Aboriginal-state interaction that affirmed Aboriginal rights and nationhood, secured a proper material base for self-government and gave Aboriginal peoples a strong presence within federal governing institutions, including a representative body.

The RCAP report outlined proposals for a 'comprehensive strategy over 20 years to restore social, economic and political health to Aboriginal peoples and rebuild their relationship with all Canadians'. The proposals encompassed respect for: 'the reality of societal and cultural difference; the right to self-government; the nature of "Aboriginal nationhood"; and the requirement for adequate land, resources and self-reliant Aboriginal economies'. It was understood that the meaningful exercise of self-government depended on bands or communities being of a sufficient size, with a secure land and resource base, to allow sustained economic growth and self-determination. About 60–80 'nations' were recognized by the commissioners, including the Algonquin, the Blood, the Innu, the Mi'kmaq, the Ojibwa, the Red River Métis, with some such as the Cree and the Inuit organized territorially. More generally, the report emphasized the importance of developing a radical strategy to replace the Indian Act, backed by appropriate funding to implement the federal Government's responsibilities in creating and overturning deeply entrenched injustices. It sought new ways to settle outstanding land and resource claims, as a prerequisite for 'cultural renewal, economic self-reliance and self-determination'.

The federal Government delivered its formal response, *Gathering Strength*, in 1998. Ministers acknowledged past mistakes and injustices and set long-term objectives centred on reconciliation, recognition of Aboriginal rights and ways of life, and enhancing the well-being of Aboriginal communities. The policy emphasis was on redoubling efforts to negotiate agreements on Aboriginal rights and land claims, sponsor Aboriginal self-government and improve life chances across the whole Aboriginal population. However, some of the most radical changes recommended by the RCAP, including the creation of a 'fourth level' of Aboriginal government, were rejected or substantially diluted. This was reinforced by the changing discourse at both federal and provincial levels around Aboriginal issues, with an emphasis on renewal and establishing a 'new relationship' between Aboriginal peoples and the rest of Canada. In practice, many of the subsequent policy initiatives were in the pipeline before the RCAP report appeared; but a new urgency was attached to breaking the vicious circle of poverty, transfer dependency and low investment that had devastated many Aboriginal communities. This was manifested in the inception of larger and better-resourced programmes, such as the launch of the Urban Aboriginal Strategy in 1998 (since expanded and extended to 2007), with funding available initially for projects to reduce Aboriginal deprivation in 12 cities across Canada. Immediate targets included a range of social and economic problems such as crime, ill health, drug use, unemployment and poor education. Closure was sought on the horrors of residential schooling, spurred by rising litigation from survivors of the residential school system since 1988. Even so, it was not until 2006 that the new federal Conservative Government announced an out-of-court dispute resolution system, supported by at least C $1,900m. in funding, which offered 'advanced payments' for an estimated 80,000 former pupils (now aged 65 years or older) at listed Indian Residential Schools. Individuals were entitled to an immediate $8,000 payment, with higher sums (of up to $430,000 where loss of income was demonstrated) for victims of serious sexual or physical abuse. Moreover, in June 2008 the Prime Minister publicly apologized for the 'lasting and damaging impact' of the residential school policy on Aboriginal peoples.

The federal Government sought to speed up the integration of Aboriginal entrepreneurs and businesses into the national, market-driven economy, while allowing that most Aboriginal communities had an insufficient population and land base, and little infrastructural capacity, to generate and sustain economic growth. Legislative action included the First Nations Land Management Act of 1999. This extended an earlier (1996) scheme beyond the original 14 First Nations signatories to encourage reserve land development hitherto constrained by the Indian Act (with just over 100 First Nations involved by 2003). It promised an important boost to opportunities for economic expansion, including Aboriginal authority over reserve resources, such as petroleum and gas, within a context of sound environmental management and protection. Aboriginal groups frequently complained about the lack of appreciation of the significance of considering the environmental impact of resource development schemes, although the Yukon Environmental and Socio-economic Assessment Act (implemented in late 2004) was an exception. The Aboriginal goal of appropriate and sustainable economic development similarly emphasized social and cultural priorities.

The First Nations Fiscal and Statistical Management Act (2005) further dismantled the restrictions imposed by the Indian Act, by outlining a new fiscal association, including an innovative 'way of combining public and private enterprise support' with the 'practical tools' for sustained development. Participating First Nations were able to generate a more secure financial basis for community renewal, including access to private sources of capital currently only available to recognized governments. Specific options ranged over local (property) taxation, transfers from other government levels, treaty settlements and borrowing at preferred rates to boost community infrastructure, such as roads, water supply and sanitation. In return, the federal Government imposed 'higher standards' of financial management, statistical information and, crucially, accountability. Two other pieces of legislation in 2005—the First Nations Oil and Gas Moneys Management Act and the First Nations Commercial and Industrial Development Act—reinforced the opportunities for Aboriginal control over economic development on reserve lands. A broader aim was First Nations' involvement in some of the country's major economic projects, such as James Bay Hydro and Voisey's Bay Nickel Development, or the Alaska and Mackenzie Valley Natural Gas Pipeline schemes, as well as the exploitation of new diamond mines in the Northwest Territories and Nunavut. The federal budget in 2008 outlined a reformed framework for Aboriginal economic development, with more attention to 'joined-up' government, supplemented by value-for-money audits.

More contentiously, in June 2002 the federal Government had introduced First Nations Governance (FNG) legislation. The limitations of the 'antiquated' Indian Act were admitted, with a Supreme Court decision (Corbière) in 1999 upholding the voting rights of band members living off-reserve. The Government took this as a justification to 'modernize' First Nations governance and instil more openness and accountability. It attached particular importance to the separation of political and administrative functions, accountability (political and financial) and governance structures and processes (notably leadership selection and voting rights). The primary objective was to allow First Nations to choose between a 'default' option of self-governance, perhaps with changes to specific provisions, and a wholly 'band-designed' system that harmonized with distinctive traditions and circumstances. First Nations opposition centred on the perceived reimposition of colonial values about what constituted 'good government'. This forced the withdrawal of the FNG bill, but reform of First Nation governance resurfaced in 2007, with the federal Government again seeking to extend the Canada Human Rights Act to band arrangements. This refocused debates on the proper balance between individual and collective Aboriginal and treaty rights, and distinctive legal traditions.

Plans to devolve more responsibilities to Aboriginal communities were constrained by a highly complex intergovernmental political context, with jurisdictional disputes over statutory and fiduciary obligations, and occasionally by diverse aspirations within the Aboriginal population. Moreover, the 'rising tide' of litigation, which increased from 99 cases in 1986/87 to more than 1,200 cases in 2002/03, alarmed both federal and provincial governments. These spanned: treaty rights and obligations; Aboriginal rights and entitlements; the fiduciary relationship between First Nations and the federal Government; protection of rights of Aboriginal women; and day-to-day operations covered by the Indian Act. There was heightened criticism of the legal process as too costly, time-consuming, adversarial, narrow in remit and uncertain in implementation. The federal Government emphasized the merits of negotiations to settle Aboriginal grievances. For their part, Aboriginal peoples argued that the principle of community self-government backed by adequate funding did not have widespread acceptance.

With continuing slow progress in achieving earlier programme goals, a 10-year plan was launched in 2005 to raise the standard of living of Aboriginal peoples to the national level, with specific targets in education, health, housing and economic development, along with a comprehensive Northern Strategy.

REVIEW

The experience of Aboriginal peoples since Confederation has been one of continuing discrimination, dependency and cultural corrosion. Throughout, Aboriginal societies and cultures have demonstrated extraordinary resilience, adaptability and, over recent decades, restored vitality and a political determination to overturn past wrongs. At the same time there has been intense debate among the main Aboriginal constituencies about the desired character and scope of change, reflecting the often significant variation in their histories and opportunities for development. For its part, the federal Government has been converted lately by arguments that the costs of failing to respond to legitimate grievances were both politically and economically unacceptable. Yet attempts to build a new relationship between Canada and its Aboriginal peoples have proven far from straightforward—as indicated by the Canadian Government's refusal (like its counterparts in Australia, New Zealand and the USA) to sign the UN Declaration on the Rights of Indigenous Peoples in 2007, fearing that it might be used to reopen historic treaties and contemporary agreements, and supply Aboriginal peoples with a veto even on policies affecting all Canadians.

Since the 1970s the federal agenda has encompassed moves to recognize Aboriginal rights, to negotiate land claims, to enhance Aboriginal self-government, to eliminate social and economic inequalities and to advance the renewal of Aboriginal communities and ways of life, including for those living in urban areas. While acknowledging the important improvements in the lives of Aboriginal peoples, substantial suspicion remained that assimilation had not been entirely removed from the political agenda, and that there was insufficient understanding of the radical policy shift required to satisfy the central demands of the 'nations within'.

SELECT BIBLIOGRAPHY

Boldt, M. *Surviving as Indians*. Toronto, ON, University of Toronto Press, 1993.

Cairns, A. C. *Citizens Plus: Aboriginal Peoples and the Canadian State*. Vancouver, BC, University of British Columbia Press, 2000.

Hylton, J. (Ed.). *Aboriginal Self-Government in Canada: Current Trends and Issues*. Saskatoon, SK, Purich Publishing, 1999.

Newhouse, D., and Peters, E. (Eds). *Not Strangers in These Parts*. Ottawa, ON, Minister of Supply and Services Canada, 2003.

Ponting, R. J. (Ed.). *First Nations in Canada: Perspectives on Opportunity, Empowerment and Self-Determination*. Toronto, ON, McGraw-Hill Ryerson, 1997.

Royal Commission on Aboriginal Peoples. *Report of the Royal Commission on Aboriginal Peoples*, Vols 1–5. Ottawa, ON, Minister of Supply and Services Canada, 1996.

Woolford. A. *Between Justice and Certainty: Treaty Making in British Columbia*. Vancouver, BC, University of British Columbia Press, 2005.

CANADA: THE COURTS AND THE CHARTER

Prof. DAVID ROBERTSON

THE STRUCTURE OF THE COURT SYSTEM

As Canada, like the USA, is a federal state, it inevitably has a more complicated legal structure than a unitary state such as the United Kingdom. Canadian provinces have legislative power to make laws that apply only within their own borders, and over areas where the federal Government in Ottawa cannot act. To a limited extent, court decisions inside the provinces can also make a common law, which will not be the same in detail as elsewhere in the country. Canada is also a multicultural society, with Québec being not only linguistically, but also legally, different from the rest of the country, a fact to which both the structures and doctrines of Canadian law have had to adapt. Québec applies a civil code ultimately derived from French civil law. In this context, 'civil' includes criminal law—the contrast is with Anglo-American 'common law'. Federal criminal law, where it exists, is superior to provincial criminal law. In the USA, of course, the majority of criminal law is not federal, but this local predominance is not found in Canada. The USA has a similar example, in that Louisiana is also a 'civil law' jurisdiction. However, Québec's role is of far greater importance in the Canadian legal system than that of Louisiana in the USA's system. There is, for example, an unbroken, yet unofficial, rule that at least three of Canada's Supreme Court justices will come from the Québec system—no one would ever argue for special treatment at that level for Louisiana.

Further complexity is added to Canada's legal culture and institutions by the problems of the territories, and by Canada's attempts to respect the traditions and needs of its indigenous peoples. This has led, *inter alia*, to partially different court structures, such as the unified Nunavut Court of Justice, and even to practices such as the 'sentencing circles' pioneered for these peoples and defined by the Native Law Centre of Canada as:

> 'a method of dealing with members of the community that have broken the law. A sentencing circle is conducted after the individual has been in the present Western justice system and found guilty, or if the accused has accepted guilt and is willing to assume their responsibility. This sentencing method encourages the offender and the community to accept responsibility and acknowledges the harm that they have done to society and to their victims. A sentencing circle's aim is to shift the process of sentencing from punishment to rehabilitation and responsibility. It provides a new alternative for courts to incarceration. The sentencing circle proves an opportunity to start the healing process for both the offender and the victim. The offender is presented with the impact of their actions in front of respected community members, elders, peers, family, the victim and their family, stimulating an opportunity for real change.'

For these reasons Canada can seem at times to have an inordinately complex judicial structure—the official government website and many other texts, for example, describe it as having a four-tier structure. Furthermore, a bewildering variety of names are used to label essentially similar courts in different provinces. (Although this is also true of the USA, the stronger position of states compared with that of provinces makes it more meaningful.)

In practice, much of the complexity arises, as it does throughout Canadian politics, from the country's highly 'moderated' federalism. In addition, Canada is one of the most liberal of all judicial regimes, and this has led to a high level of experimentation, adding further layers of apparent complexity to what is, in fact, a functional and largely unified system. However, Canada's federalism is moderate, and the unifying processes and themes are more powerful than the divergent ones. The courts generally fall into three categories: lower courts, entirely run and appointed by the provincial governments; provincial superior courts; and Federal Courts. Only in the lowest level of courts, the provincial lower courts, which try the simpler criminal and civil cases, are judges appointed by the provincial government, and even there they are all appointed in much the same way from province to province. At this lowest level there are frequently a host of specialized courts. This may also be the case at the superior level, where specialized branches deal only with certain matters such as family law or small claims. In many cases remnants of legal terminology from the United Kingdom add to the apparent confusion. For example, the Ontario Superior Court of Justice has a 'Divisional Court' (hearing judicial reviews of administrative tribunals) whose decisions have greater binding authority than those from the main Ontario Superior Court. Thus, the Supreme Court is not necessarily the highest court in its respective province or territory.

As far as federal involvement is concerned, the contrast with the USA is immediate. In the USA the vast majority of courts are state courts, and the federal Government has no role to play in appointing state court judges. Furthermore, a very wide range of methods exist among the states for making these appointments, with elections being held for a very large proportion of all state judgeships. Although it varies from state to state, the ablest of judges can have careers of great significance, indeed, in some cases, of national significance, without ever holding a federal appointment. For example, the New York State Court of Appeals has often been a leader in legal thought, influencing the US Supreme Court itself. No equivalent exists in Canada. There the provincial superior courts (the most common title) exercise jurisdiction over the more serious criminal and the financially more important civil cases as courts of first instance, as well as serving an appellate function to the lower provincial courts. Yet the judges on these courts are appointed by the federal Government, as are the judges on the provincial appeal courts, the apex of the provincial system. The only 'local' aspect of their appointment is that the judges must be qualified to practise law in the province in question. The provinces have jurisdiction over the constitution, organization and maintenance of these courts, but without the right of appointment. To any American the idea that someone holding a position of such power as, say, the Chief Justiceship of the California Supreme Court should be appointed, not elected, and appointed from Washington, DC, at that, would be unthinkable.

As well as the 'mixed' provincial/federal courts, there exist the purely federal courts below the Supreme Court. These are best viewed as another category of courts, rather than an extra level. The Federal Court of Canada, which has both a trial court and an appeal division, exists to deal with cases arising directly, and solely, from certain federal statute laws believed to require a high degree of national uniformity in their application, such as cases arising under the Competition Act and most intellectual property law. The argument is that the economy is a national phenomenon, and provincial variance cannot be allowed. For similar reasons only the Federal Court can hear citizenship cases; this court and its appeal branch deal exclusively with cases involving 'Crown Corporations' or federal government departments, and only it can review decisions of federal boards, commissions and tribunals. As such, the Federal Court is essentially parallel to the highest provincial courts, and comes closer to replicating the role of the Federal District and Circuit courts in the USA, though the analogy is far from exact. For one thing the Federal Court is entirely based in Ottawa, although its judges do travel to hear cases elsewhere in the country, and no effort is made to match local loyalties or knowledge to where a case originates. Above all these courts, and entitled to hear appeals from any of them (after a case has ascended through the relevant hierarchy of courts), is the Supreme Court of Canada. Common to all federal systems is the problem of legal coherence. If courts in different provinces can make decisions on similar legal issues without having to pay any attention to their equivalent courts in other provinces, legal rules end up being highly localized. One primary function of the Supreme Court is to avoid this. Thus, when deciding whether or not to hear an appeal, the Supreme Court takes special care to decide cases where conflicting opinions have been issued by two or more provincial supreme courts. One provincial court is not obliged to respect the ideas of a neighbour, but both must follow the precedents of the federal Supreme Court.

THE SUPREME COURT AND THE CONSTITUTION

It should be said that this apparent dominance of the federal Government in appointing the judiciary is less problematic in Canada than it might be elsewhere. There has never been as intense a sense of 'states' rights', and dislike of federal control in Canada as has often been the case in the USA. Moreover, appointments still retain a highly local nature because there is no national élite of lawyers centred round the federal capital. The leading lawyers in Canada originate from the provincial metropolises, and unlike the USA, where, for example, New York and Washington, DC, monopolize the huge law firms, Canada has many centres where legal careers can be pursued with equal reward and status. The federal Government may appoint, for instance, the Chief Justice of the Ontario Court of Appeal, but it will have no choice but to appoint a person whose home, connections and distinction come from Toronto. Only with regard to the Supreme Court can it be claimed that there exists a national judicial élite. One thing that differentiates the Canadian Supreme Court from most similar courts is the fact that not all of its members have had much, if any, judicial experience. Leading lawyers are often appointed directly from practice, or after only a brief period serving on a provincial court of appeal, as are legal academics. Typically, these are people who possess a national (and often an international) reputation, but they frequently lack the lengthy experience of sitting on routine appeals typical of most US appointments. A glance at the career of a recent, not atypical, Supreme Court judge shows how much the route taken by the Court's members differs from the usual route to senior judicial posts in the USA or the United Kingdom, as well as how far removed they are from any narrow provincial basis. Justice Michel Bastarache, who served from 1997 to 2008, was a member of the bar in three provinces, worked for both the federal and the New Brunswick civil services, had a successful business career in the insurance industry, had been a professor at two different law schools, and practised law in New Brunswick and Ottawa. He was also completely bilingual, and had published a textbook on French law as well as one on language rights. Yet his first ever judicial appointment was to the New Brunswick Court of Appeal in 1995, and only two years later he was appointed to the Supreme Court of Canada. The Court also almost certainly has the best record for gender equality of any major court in the advanced democratic world (currently four of the nine justices are women, including the current Chief Justice, who was the first female to hold that position). In September 2008 Justice Bastarache's seat in the Supreme Court was filled by another man from the same region, Nova Scotia Court of Appeal Justice Thomas Cromwell, some attempt at regional balance being viewed as important. Cromwell was also fully bilingual, another vital balance issue in the Court. Appointments to the Supreme Court lie entirely in the Prime Minister's hands, although increasingly there have been attempts to make the process of nomination more transparent through the establishment of advisory committees.There is a possible consequence of this appointment style; Canadian Supreme Court decisions are often more adventurous, and even 'radical', in the eyes of the legal fraternity. This will be discussed later. The Court is, like the US Supreme Court and the Australian High Court, both a general purpose final appeal court, and the country's constitutional court, in contrast to most of Europe and Latin America, where these two roles are separated. The Canadian Supreme Court can, and does, settle the law on any and all issues. Indeed, it has the unusual role of being able to accept references on any matter at all if the federal Government, or a provincial government, chooses to ask its advice. As one distinguished commentator remarked, 'in theory a Canadian government can ask the Supreme Court what time it is, and they will have to tell them.' Such advisory opinions are, however, very rare. Yet despite being rare, they can be vital for the Government. The Canadian Government can effectively pre-test potentially controversial legislation by asking the Supreme Court for an advisory opinion on the core issues of the proposed legislation. In this way it insulates itself from future legal challenges. A good example is the Civil Marriage Act of 2005, which legalized same-sex marriages. Though this went through the House of Commons easily, it was far less uniformly popular in the country as a whole. However, the Government had taken the precaution of sending the main questions to the Supreme Court in *Reference re Same-Sex Marriage*, 2004 SCC 79. The fact that the Supreme Court ruled that the federal Government had the power to pass this Act, and that it did not breach the Charter of Rights and Freedoms, not only made passage through the Commons easier, but has precluded any future challenge. This tool has been used at crucial times in Canadian history, with particular effect, for example, on the question of possible secession by Québec, and at its most vital, on the whole question of the validity of the Constitution itself in 1982.

Most importantly, the Supreme Court has the power of judicial review—it can rule that a federal or provincial statute is unconstitutional and therefore invalid. Such review is inevitable in any federal state, because where a constitution restricts what laws can be passed by a specific level of government, there is always the problem of one level 'trespassing' on the rights of another, requiring some third party to act as a referee. For most of its history since its creation in 1875, the Supreme Court's judicial review powers were limited to issues such as striking down federal laws passed in areas that should be the sole interest of the provinces, and vice versa. Otherwise, it acted as an ordinary second level of appeal in civil and criminal cases, attempting mainly to produce as much uniformity as possible while respecting parliamentary supremacy, including the supremacy, within their own ambits, of provincial parliaments. This was clearly in keeping with the original intention of those who drafted Canada's first Constitution, the British North America Act of 1867 (BNA). The BNA expressly insisted that Canada have a form of government 'similar in principle to that of the United Kingdom'. As such, the federal Parliament could pass any law it wanted to, with no court interference based on natural or constitutional law, providing, in this case, that the specific terms of the BNA were complied with. The BNA did, in fact, protect certain rights—largely religious rights for the Protestant and Roman Catholic churches arising from the need to keep peace between Québec and other provinces—but there was minimal interference with federal legislation. Equally important, at least for Québec, was the protection of minority language rights. Nor was the Canadian Supreme Court actually supreme at this stage, as a limited right of appeal existed from its decisions to the Judicial Committee of the Privy Council in the United Kingdom; this right was common to all of the United Kingdom's Dominions. Along with Australia and other British dependencies, Canada subsequently abrogated this right, but not until 1949. The result was that, though not an insignificant body as far as ordinary law went, the Canadian Supreme Court was, until relatively recently, of no great political importance. One earlier initiative by the federal Government might have increased its power when, in 1960, the Government of John Diefenbaker (1957–63) approved a federal statute known as The Canadian Bill of Rights. This was a short but fairly typical list of basic political and social rights which could, had the court wished, have granted it the ability to question the validity of legislation. It contained what was termed a 'notwithstanding clause', which a government could invoke to prevent the court striking down an act it thought was vital, but this was used only in exceptional and rare circumstances, mainly for extreme law and order issues dealing with national security in the face of political extremism. In truth, the judges of the day were themselves so convinced of the value of parliamentary supremacy that they had no desire or inclination to use whatever powers they might have been awarded to expand the role of the court. In this they were typical of judges throughout the English common law world of the time. Only in the USA was there a spirit of judicial activism characterized by the radical direction taken by the Supreme Court under Earl Warren (1953–69).

From the early 1970s Canadians became increasingly dissatisfied with the anomalous situation that the country's Constitution was merely an act of a foreign legislature. The move to 'patriate' the Constitution and to give Canada its own full legitimacy began in 1971 under Prime Minister Pierre Trudeau (1968–79 and 1980–84), who managed to secure general agreement from most of the provinces for the development of a purely Canadian Constitution with a written and entrenched Bill of Rights. This was formalized in what became known as the Victoria Charter. The Victoria Charter, however, did not meet the objections of either Alberta or, less surprisingly, French-speaking Québec, and this movement came to nothing. When he was returned to the federal premiership in 1980 Trudeau originally threatened that the Canadian Government would unilaterally petition the United Kingdom for patriation of the Constitution. The Supreme Court itself was involved at this stage to rule on the legality of any such process, although its decisions were anything but firm and clear. The Court has always been conscious that it must tread warily where highly 'political' decisions are involved. This showed, for example, when it was asked to rule on the legality of a potential unilateral declaration of independence by Québec. Although the Court ruled that such an action would be unconstitutional, it also insisted that the other provinces and territories of Canada had a strong obligation to negotiate in good faith to satisfy Québec's aspiration. The political deadlock was broken by a new agreement concluded by all the provincial premiers, with the exception of René Lévesque of Québec, who demanded even further protection of that province's language rights. The resulting agreement was the 'Vancouver Consensus formula', which laid down rules for further constitutional change. This, coupled with a newly drafted Charter of Rights and Freedoms, was the basis on which the United Kingdom agreed to repatriate the Constitution by passing the Canada Act of the United Kingdom in 1982.

The new Constitution and its Charter came into operation on 17 April 1982, and the Supreme Court began very rapidly to become a major influencing factor in Canadian politics. The new Charter, unlike the 1960 Bill of Rights, was entrenched and could not simply be abolished by a new act of parliament; it was lengthy and detailed, and contained nothing as powerful as the 'notwithstanding clause'. Just one example may serve at this stage to demonstrate how far the Supreme Court can, when it wishes, involve itself in serious policy-making in Canada. On 9 June 2005 the Supreme Court, by seven votes to two, issued its opinion on *Chaoulli v. Québec*. This opinion struck down a vital and long-standing Québec provincial law forbidding anyone to buy or sell private medical insurance. This ban on private medical insurance had long been regarded by the Québec Government as a critical component of its overall medical provisions, as it effectively made it impossible to practise private medicine in the province and thus prevented any dilution of the state-funded health scheme. Very similar provisions exist in other provinces, and it was believed that it would only be a matter of time before they too were struck down, potentially forcing a major reorganization of Canadian health services. It ought to be added that all the judges in the Québec courts who heard the case on its way to the Supreme Court sided with the Québec Government, and that both of the Supreme Court dissenters (Justices Binnie and LeBel) were Québec appointees. The argument for *Chaoulli* came straight from the Charter, which guarantees the right to life, and the Court held that the queues for some medical treatment in the Québec system were so long that patients were forced to take risks they would not have to face if they were allowed to buy insurance and therefore could afford private medical treatment. This case demonstrated perfectly why the Charter is vitally important in Canadian life, and how it has made the Supreme Court such a powerful body.

The Supreme Court's influence is helped by the fact that it has almost complete control of its docket, that is, it can choose which appeals to hear. There are between 500 and 650 requests for appeals filed each year, only 20 to 30 of which are 'as of right', which the Court is obliged to hear, nearly all of these being in criminal law. The hearing of hundreds of appeals by the Supreme Court every year would be impossible, and, in fact, the Court has passed judgment in an average annual of only 82 cases over the last decade. This figure is itself misleading, because a number of cases are so simple that the Court is able to pronounce its decision immediately after the hearing. If one considers instead only 'reserved' judgments, where the Court takes time privately to debate in depth and produces reasoned opinions, the figure falls to an average of 65 cases per year, slightly lower than the typical figure for the US Supreme Court. Of these, approximately one-quarter are split cases where the justices cannot agree on the law—a much lower dissent rate than in the USA, but notably higher than for most comparable courts internationally. Such dissent rates are a typical sign of a court that avoids making decisions on highly political matters and that presides over a highly pluralistic society. Many of these cases arise from Canadian human rights law. This does not mean, however, that the Canadian Supreme Court can never be united on cases of major political importance. For example, in May 2008 the Court issued a unanimous opinion, without even reserving it, that represented a major criticism of the Canadian Government. The case was *Canada v. Khadr* in which the Supreme Court forced the disclosure to the last remaining Canadian prisoner held in the US special prison at Guantánamo Bay in Cuba of the records of his interrogation by US and Canadian intelligence officers. The Canadian Government had claimed that 'international comity' required them to accept the US Administration's views that such sensitive material should not be released. In response, the Supreme Court said, tersely:

> 'K is entitled to disclosure from the appellants of the records of the interviews, and of information given to US authorities as a direct consequence of conducting the interviews. The principles of international law and comity of nations, which normally require that Canadian officials operating abroad comply with local law and which might otherwise preclude application of the *Charter* to Canadian officials acting abroad, do not extend to participation in processes that violate Canada's binding international human rights obligations. The process in place at Guantánamo Bay at the time Canadian officials interviewed K and passed on the fruits of the interviews to US officials has been found by the US Supreme Court, with the benefit of a full factual record, to violate US domestic law and international human rights obligations to which Canada subscribes. The comity concerns that would normally justify deference to foreign law do not apply in this case. Consequently, the *Charter* applies.'

THE SUPREME COURT AND THE CHARTER OF RIGHTS AND FREEDOMS

It could hardly be expected that such a powerful court would escape criticism from those whose power may have waned in consequence of its rise, especially the provincial governments. Provincial interest has focused on attempting to dilute the power of the Prime Minister to make appointments to the Supreme Court. Québec has twice been joined by other provinces (at the Meech Lake Accord of 1987 and the Charlottetown Accord of 1992) in an attempt to ensure that the federal Government appoint only from a list of names submitted by the provinces. Equal hostility has come from the federal Parliament at times. More interesting, perhaps, has been the considerable doubt expressed by legal academics regarding the legitimacy of the Court's 'judicial activism'. Whether the Court has, in truth, been especially active in the sense of enforcing restrictions on government action that in some sense go beyond those which are purely legally necessary is far too complex a debate to take up here, but most non-Canadian observers would be unlikely to rank the Canadian Supreme Court as one of the most active. More likely it is that the sheer breadth of the Charter itself requires the Court, willingly or not, to pronounce on a far wider range of issues than Canadian political culture was prepared for. As a former Chief Justice stated, 'our decisions hit harder because they hit wider'.

There is no doubt that Canadian legal and political culture has moved in a direction some saw as being similar to that of the USA, in that it has become much more of a 'rights culture', and less of a culture with a high level of deference to parliamentary supremacy. However, this is not so much a shift towards a US style as part of a world-wide development towards a judicially supported insistence on rights. The United Kingdom, the home of parliamentary supremacy, joined this shift with its 1998 Human Rights Act, although it may be significant that when the Act was drafted the British Government deliberately rejected the Canadian Charter as a model in favour of the much weaker New Zealand Bill of Rights Act. It is certainly not appropriate to see the Canadian Supreme Court as a unified activist body determined to force its view on an unwilling society, because, as we have noted, it is far from unanimous. The activism, if that is the right word, of the Supreme Court varies greatly over time as different groups of judges come and go, but it is probably true that governments have had increasing difficulties dealing with the Court. This is, in part, a matter of its maturity—it has now been in existence for more than 20 years—so that a generation of judges, who have experienced the Charter for much of their professional life, are coming to appointable times in their careers and see recourse to the Charter as a much less unusual activity than did the earlier generations. Certainly, the Supreme Court judges during its earlier years were highly conscious of the need to move slowly and carefully. This slowness, however, also meant that some of the important issues in Canadian society were not handled very positively by the Court. In particular the Court has an ambivalent record on trade union rights, and Canada remains a country where organized labour has an important political voice.

The power of judicial precedent is such that no sensible judge on a newly empowered court will make many bold decisions in case those decisions set the court almost irrevocably along a mistaken track. This can be easily seen in some of the earlier decisions where the Supreme Court quite deliberately reduced its own potential power. The most important of these was a famous decision, *Retail, Wholesale and Department Store Union v. Dolphin Delivery Ltd* in 1986, only four years after the Charter came into effect. It concerned an apparently obscure, but in actual fact vital, question of constitutional law. Did the Constitution only refer to relations between the Government and the individual, or did individuals have constitutional rights against each other? If the latter answer was given, as it had been in Germany and South Africa, there would have been virtually no area of social life in which the Supreme Court could not intervene, citing constitutional rights and duties. However, if the former answer was given, the range of the Court's power would be much restricted. It would have been possible for the Canadian Supreme Court to come to either conclusion as the Charter was sufficiently imprecise on the matter. The Court unanimously and unhesitatingly gave the first answer, forswearing for itself the greater and wider powers. However, no legal doctrine can last for ever, and certainly not if courts, like the Canadian Supreme Court, are aware of the need for the law to keep up with social developments. Thus over the last few years it has appeared that the Court is edging nearer to altering, if not actually overturning, its ruling in *Dolphin Delivery*. As this is probably the most widely criticized decision it has ever made, critics might argue that it has taken the Supreme Court far too long to reach its present stage. The right to life cases mentioned earlier are another example of change. Ten years ago it would have been clear that the Court would never accept the legal enforceability of 'positive rights', but several less notable cases in recent years have already indicated a possible change in direction, and one which is likely to go much further.

Even given this caution, there are vitally important areas where the Supreme Court has already had to start changing direction. Again, one example may serve; it is in an area of special concern for the whole issue of judicial versus parliamentary power, and also makes it possible to consider the question of the possible 'Americanization' of Canadian constitutional politics. It is not true that the Charter contains no equivalent to the old 'notwithstanding clause' contained within the Bill of Rights. Section 33 of the Charter provides a modified version, which covers only some of the rights in the Charter, and even then only allows legislation to impose on them for a maximum of five years, although it has never been invoked. Far more important is the 'limitations' clause found in all modern constitutions, with the exception of the US Constitution. Some version of this clause almost always appears in modern constitutions. It is impossible to claim that any right is so vital and absolute that it can never, under any circumstances, be restricted. Instead, Section 1 of the Canadian Charter states that the rights covered in the Charter are guaranteed subject to 'reasonable limits' that can be 'demonstrably justified in a free and democratic society'. Section 1 does, however, allow the courts to decide for themselves whether, all things considered, the Government is entitled to limit a right in some specific way and context.

In 1986 the Supreme Court set up a test of how to decide if an infringement on rights was thus democratically justifiable. In the criminal law case *Regina v. Oakes* the Court decided that there were two aspects: the Government had to demonstrate that its aim in the legislation was sufficiently important in general to justify the rights limitation; and it had to show that the law was 'proportional', a word that appears in legal argument in most countries with a written constitution. To be proportional, the act had to be 'rationally connected' to the avowed purpose, it must be the least the Government could do to achieve its aims, and the overall benefit had to be greater than the overall costs to individuals who had their rights infringed. For example, is the freedom of speech guarantee enough to prevent a school teacher being punished under criminal law for overtly and explicitly teaching racist and anti-Semitic doctrines in class? In the case in question (*Regina v. Keegstra*, 1990), the Supreme Court agreed that the part of the criminal code used was in breach of both the right to freedom of speech and the right to be presumed innocent in a criminal trial. But it also found that both breaches of the Constitution were justified. It was not a unanimous decision, however, and many believed that the dissenting judges made the better arguments.

That test may appear fairly neutral, but in recent years some members of the Supreme Court, and many human rights activists, have argued that the way it has operated has tended to be far too lenient to the Government. As a result, there have been a series of cases in the last 10 years where members of the Court, not always in the majority, have made great efforts to strengthen its powers and further to restrict the Government. However, the sheer weight of it being an early decision, and the ever present judicial preference for legal certainty, has made any reformist argument very difficult. The result is that currently there is a considerable lack of certainty as to when the Government will be allowed to take advantage of the limitations clause. Perhaps what is most important here is simply to realize that if a constitution does charge a court with so politically delicate a job as deciding whether a human right should give way to a government's ideas on the grounds that the policy is 'demonstrably justified in a free and democratic society', it is simply inevitable that the court will become instantly deeply involved in making substantive political choices. This is what has happened to the Canadian Supreme Court. In the 25 years since the patriation of the Constitution, the Court has been drawn inexorably into details of Canadian politics in a way many feared from the beginning. During the original political debates there had been gloomy warnings of what was called 'Lochnerization', after the famous US Supreme Court case *Lochner v. New York* in 1905, which is regarded as the beginnings of the US courts obstructing politicians' right to make policy unfettered by anything but election results.

THE CHARTER RIGHTS

The Charter of Rights and Freedoms is usually considered to protect six groups of rights: fundamental freedoms (Section 2); democratic rights (Sections 3–5); mobility rights (Section 6); legal rights (Sections 7–14); equality rights (Section 15); and language rights (Sections 16–22).

Sections 3 and 6 are specific to the Canadian situation, aimed at protecting the compromises and agreements which, over time, have maintained a united nation in Canada despite both its formal federalism and its deeply entrenched biculturalism. They ensure that any Canadian citizen can live and work anywhere, and will have his/her linguistic heritage protected wherever he/she is. (That is, as long as that language is either English or French; increasingly there have been complaints by recent immigrants to whom neither is a mother tongue about granting such privileged status to the two languages. The courts have not yet been persuaded of their case.) These rights, incidentally, are not subject to the 'notwithstanding clause' as they can never legally be abrogated. The other rights are typical of those found in any modern bill of rights, with no more than local alterations in wording. Fundamental rights, protected in Section 2, are the rights to freedom of conscience and religion, and freedom of thought, belief, opinion and expression. This last includes freedom of the press and other media. The more political rights of peaceful assembly and freedom of association are included in this section, along with the right to run for elected office. The democratic rights section includes both individual rights, such as the right to vote and to stand for parliament, and more structural constitutional requirements, including that the term of a parliament has a maximum duration of five years between elections, and that it must meet at least once in each year.

Legal rights are the procedural rights needed to ensure justice and fairness in the legal system. They apply not only to citizens, but to 'legal individuals' such as corporations, and cover aliens as well as Canadians, which is not always the case even in liberal societies. They are spelled out in unusual detail in the Charter, which is elsewhere often rather vague. (For a full list of legal rights please refer to the Constitution Act 1982, in Part Three, Directory.)

The equality rights guaranteed in Section 15 have formed a major part of the Supreme Court's case load over the years, including many of its most contentious decisions. The problems of amending its earlier position on the limitations clause, mentioned above, have been central to rights claims under this section. The detailed listing might appear harmless enough. Section 15 (1) is where the trouble arises, because it spells out some of the things that will constitute illegal discrimination. 'Every individual is equal before and under the law and has the right to the equal protection and equal benefit of the law without discrimination and, in particular, without discrimination based on race, national or ethnic origin, colour, religion, sex, age or mental or physical disability.' The judges, in their judicial formulation, have extended this to mean 'or on any ground that is analogous'. It was thus entirely predictable that this section would cause problems—indeed it was expected to, and was deliberately delayed so that it did not come into force until three years after the Constitution and the Charter had been introduced. There are two main sources of problems, one of which has already been touched upon. Even outright discrimination on grounds of ethnic origin could be justified under the limitations analysis. However, how would one demonstrate that any such legal discrimination was democratically justified, necessary, proportional and so on? The second source of difficulty is the additional seven words of the judicial formulation: 'or on any ground that is analogous'. Every law discriminates. That is how policy is applied, giving to some and taking from others, granting privileges to some and leaving others without assistance. Over time cultures have come to understand that some ways of distinguishing between people are simply not acceptable, even if it might be considered convenient to do so. That has, nevertheless, been a slow process of social consensus-building. Now the Canadian Supreme Court is empowered to add to the list overnight, on the basis of its own thinking; it need only rule that one characteristic that differentiates between people is 'analogous' to one of the forbidden characteristics in the list. Almost immediately after the Charter came into effect, pressure groups campaigned to seek to draw the Court's attention to these analogies.

One of the earliest such cases (*Regina v. Big M Drug Mart Ltd*, 1985) involved alleged discrimination on religious grounds when a series of laws, which forced shops to close on Sundays, were held to be in breach of the ban on religious discrimination. Treating Sunday as special was seen to be discriminatory because not all religions shared that day as one of worship. If the state deemed it to be special, it was giving unacceptable prominence to one among many religions. Many other criteria have been challenged as discriminatory, including sexual orientation, marital status, and even age in compulsory retirement policies. The court has had to work out for itself a rationale for when a discrimination is 'analogous' to those listed, and has done so by creating a social philosophy of how Canadian life should be. Typical statements of this philosophy are: 'the promotion of equality entails the promotion of a society in which all are secure in the knowledge that they are recognized at law as human beings equally deserving of concern, respect and consideration.' This comes from the first of the major discrimination cases which had to consider 'analogous' criteria, *Andrews v. Law Society of British Columbia*, in 1989. Andrews had been refused entry to the legal profession because he was not a Canadian national, which was not a category explicitly included in the Charter list.

A current judicial definition is: 'a person or group of persons has been discriminated against when members of that group have been made to feel, by virtue of the impugned legislative distinction, that they are less capable, or less worthy of recognition or value as human beings or as members of Canadian society, equally deserving of concern, respect, and consideration.' These are the core elements of a definition of 'discrimination'. This definition was taken from the 1995 case, *Egan v. Canada*, which involved sexual orientation.

In other areas the Court has also had to create a philosophy to assist with the otherwise arbitrary process of defining the meaning of words in the Charter, or the application of a state power. Canada may not be the country with the most 'activist' of Supreme Courts, but if it is not at the top, it is very close to that position. What makes it so remarkable is that 25 years ago, before the introduction of the Charter, it would have been thought to have one of the most passive and state-respecting court systems among Western democracies. It needs also to be said that the Canadian governments, both federal and provincial, have been more accepting of court policy than in many jurisdictions. Often, cases that go against the government in question are not appealed, with the government preferring to adapt its policy. Indeed, government departments regularly have compliance units attached in an attempt to pre-check legislation before the Court can intervene. Another measure of its success may be that Canadian judgments are very widely cited nowadays in other countries. The very active South African Constitutional Court makes extensive use of Canadian decisions in trying to craft a law under its own new Constitution, and it has also been cited in new Central and Eastern European democracies with their own powerful courts, most notably in Hungary.

SELECT BIBLIOGRAPHY (PUBLIC AFFAIRS)

Domestic Politics

Adamoski, R., Chunn, D. E., and Menzies, R. (Eds). *Contesting Canadian Citizenship: Historical Readings*. Peterborough, ON, Broadview Press, 2002.

Archer, K., Young, L., and Schwartz, M. (Eds). *Regionalism and Party Politics in Canada*. Toronto, ON, Oxford University Press, 2000.

Bakvis, H., and Skogstad, G. (Eds). *Canadian Federalism*. Toronto, ON, Oxford University Press, 2001.

Balthazar, L., and Hero, Jr, A. O. *Le Québec dans l'espace américain*. Montréal, QC, Québec Amérique, 1999.

Beiner, R., and Norman, W. *Canadian Political Philosophy: Contemporary Reflections*. Toronto, ON, Oxford University Press, 2000.

Bickerton, J., and Gagnon, A. G. *Canadian Politics*, 4th edn. Toronto, ON, Broadview Press, 2004.

Bickerton, J., Gagnon, A. G., and Smith, P. J. *Ties That Bind*. Toronto, ON, University of Toronto Press, 1999.

Blais, A., Gidengil, E., Nevitte, N., and Johnson, R. *The Challenge of Direct Democracy: The 1992 Canadian Referendum*. Montréal, QC, and Kingston, ON, McGill-Queen's University Press, 1996.

Blake, R. B. (Ed.). *Transforming the Nation: Canada and Brian Mulroney*. Montréal, QC, and Kingston, ON, McGill-Queen's University Press, 2007.

Boyd, D. R. *Unnatural Law: Rethinking Canadian Environmental Law and Policy*. Vancouver, BC, University of British Columbia Press, 2003.

Bratt, D. *Readings in Canadian Foreign Policy: Classic Debates and New Ideas*. New York, Oxford University Press, 2006.

Brodie, J., and Trimble, L. (Eds). *Reinventing Canada: Politics of the 21st Century*. Toronto, ON, Prentice Hall, 2003.

Brooks, S. *Canadian Democracy*, 5th edn. New York, Oxford University Press, 2006.

Brownsley, K., and Howlett, M. (Eds). *The Provincial State: Politics in Canada's Provinces and Territories*. Toronto, ON, Broadview Press, 2000.

Cairns, A. C. *Citizens Plus: Aboriginal Peoples and the Canadian State*. Vancouver, BC, University of British Columbia Press, 2001.

Carment, D., Stack, J. F., and Harvey F. P. (Eds). *The International Politics of Québec Secession*. New York, Praeger Publrs, 2001.

Carty, R. K. *Politics is Local: National Politics at the Grassroots*. New York, Oxford University Press, 2005.

Carty, R. K., Cross W., and Young, L. *Rebuilding Canadian Party Politics*. Vancouver, BC, University of British Columbia Press, 2000.

Christian, W., and Campbell, C. *Political Parties and Ideologies in Canada: Liberals, Conservatives, Socialists, Nationalists*, 4th edn. Scarborough, ON, McGraw-Hill Ryerson, 1995.

Coates, K. *The Marshall Decision and Native Rights*. Montréal, QC, and Kingston, ON, McGill-Queen's University Press, 2000.

Cormier, J. *The Canadianization Movement: Emergence, Survival and Success*. Toronto, ON, University of Toronto Press, 2004.

Courchene, T., and Telmar, C. *From Heartland to North American Region State*. Toronto, ON, University of Toronto Press, 1998.

Cowen, D. *Military Workfare: The Soldier and Social Citizenship in Canada*. Toronto, ON, University of Toronto Press, 2008.

Cross, W. (Ed.). *Political Parties, Representation and Democracy in 21st Century Canada*. Toronto, ON, Oxford University Press, 2001.

Dion, S. *Straight Talk: On Canadian Unity*. Montréal, QC, and Kingston, ON, McGill-Queen's University Press, 1999.

Dornan, C., and Pammett, J. H. *The Canadian General Election of 2000*. Toronto, ON, Dundurn Press, 2001.

Dutil, P. *Searching for Leadership: Secretaries to Cabinet in Canada*. Toronto, ON, University of Toronto Press, 2008.

Fraser, G. *René Lévesque and the Parti Québécois in Power*. Montréal, QC, and Kingston, ON, McGill-Queen's University Press, 2001.

Frizzell, A., and Pammett, J. H. (Eds). *The Canadian General Election of 1993*. Ottawa, ON, Carleton University Press, 1994.

The Canadian General Election of 1997. Toronto, ON, Dundurn Press, 1998.

Fudge, D., and Brewin, J. *Collective Bargaining in Canada: Human Rights or Canadian Illusion*. Peterborough, ON, Fernwood Books Ltd, 2005.

Gaffield, C., and Gould, K. L. (Eds). *The Canadian Distinctiveness into the XXIst Century*. Ottawa, ON, University of Ottawa Press, 2003.

Gagnon, A. G. (Ed.). *Quebec: State and Society*. Scarborough, ON, Nelson, 1993.

Gibbins, R. *Conflict and Unity: An Introduction to Canadian Political Life*. Scarborough, ON, Nelson, 1994.

Goldring, L., and Krishnamurti, S. (Eds). *Organizing the Transnational: Politics and Social Change*. Vancouver, BC, University of British Columbia Press, 2007.

Goldsworthy, J. *Interpreting Constitutions: A Comparative Study*. New York, Oxford University Press, 2006.

Good, D. A. *The Politics of Public Money: Spenders, Guardians, Priority Setters, and Financial Watchdogs Inside the Canadian Government*. Toronto, ON, University of Toronto Press, 2007.

Greene, I. *The Courts (The Canadian Democratic Audit)*. Vancouver, BC, University of British Columbia Press, 2007.

Hallowell, G. (Ed.). *Oxford Companion To Canadian History*, 2nd edn. Oxford, Oxford University Press, 2005.

Hazell, S. *Canada vs the Environment: Federal Environmental Assessment 1984–1998*. Toronto, ON, Canadian Environmental Defence Fund, 1999.

Helliwell, J. *How Much do National Borders Matter?* Washington, DC, Brookings Institution Press, 1998.

Hesketh, B., and Hackett, C. *Canada: Confederation to Present*. Edmonton, AB, University of Alberta-Chinook Multimedia (CD-Rom with web access), 2003.

Howe, P., and Russell, P. H. (Eds). *Judicial Power and Canadian Democracy*. Montréal, QC, and Kingston, ON, McGill-Queen's University Press, 2001.

Hunter, J. 'The New North: A Revamped Arctic Begins Building for the Next Generation', in *Macleans*, 3 August 1998, pp. 14–19.

Hylton, J. (Ed.). *Aboriginal Self-Government in Canada: Current Trends and Issues*. Saskatoon, SK, Purich Publishing, 1999.

Jackson, R. J., and Jackson, D. *Politics in Canada: Culture, Institutions, Behaviour and Public Policy*, 5th edn. Scarborough, ON, Prentice-Hall Allyn and Bacon Canada, 2001.

Jacob, J. W. *Canadian Charter of Rights and Freedoms: Democracy for the People and for Each Person*. Victoria, BC, Trafford Publishing, 2007.

James, C. (Ed.). *Possibilities and Limitations: Multicultural Policies and Programs in Canada*. Peterborough, ON, Fernwood Books Ltd, 2005.

James, M. *Misrecognized Materialists: Social Movements in Canadian Constitutional Politics*. Vancouver, BC, University of British Columbia Press, 2006.

Johnson, W. *A Canadian Myth: Quebec—Between Canada and the Illusion of Utopia*. Montréal, QC, and Toronto, ON, Rupert Davies Publishing, 1994.

Kelly, J. B. *Governing with the Charter*. Vancouver, BC, University of British Columbia Press, 2006.

Lazar, H. *The State of the Federation, 2000–1*. Chapel Hill, NC, Duke University Press, 2002.

Lindsay, K. M., and Smith, D. W. *Review of Environmental Assessment Processes*. Edmonton, AB, Northern Resources Research Centre and the Canadian Circumpolar Institute Press, Occasional Publication No. 50, 2001.

McAllister, M. L. *Governing Ourselves? The Politics of Canadian Communities*. Vancouver, BC, University of British Columbia Press, 2004.

MacDonald, I. *From Bourassa to Bourassa*. Montréal, QC, and Kingston, ON, McGill-Queen's University Press, 2002.

McGillivray, B. *Geography of British Columbia: People and Landscapes in Transition*. Vancouver, BC, University of British Columbia Press, 2000.

McMenemy, J. *The Language of Canadian Politics: A Guide to Important Terms and Concepts*. West Waterloo, ON, Wilfrid Laurier University Press, 1995.

Mackey, E. *The House of Difference. Cultural Politics and National Identity in Canada*. Toronto, ON, University of Toronto, 2002.

Macklem, P. *Indigenous Difference and the Constitution of Canada*. Toronto, ON, University of Toronto Press, 2001.

Maclure, J. *Quebec Identity: The Challenge of Pluralism*. Montréal, QC, and Kingston, ON, McGill-Queen's University Press, 2000.

Malcomson, P., and Myers, R. *The Canadian Regime: An Introduction to Parliamentary Government in Canada*. Peterborough, ON, Broadview Press, 2005.

Mancuso, M., Price, R., and Wagenburg, R. *Leaders and Leadership in Canada*. Toronto, ON, Oxford University Press, 1994.

Marsh, James H. (Ed.) *The Canadian Encyclopaedia*. 3 vols. Edmonton, AB, Hurtig Publrs, 1885.

Martin, R. I. *The Most Dangerous Branch: How the Supreme Court of Canada Has Undermined Our Law and Our Democracy*. Montréal, QC, and Kingston, ON, McGill-Queen's University Press, 2005.

Mouritsen, P., and Jorgensen, K. E. (Eds). *Constituting Communities: Political Solutions to Cultural Differences*. New York, Palgrave Macmillan, 2008.

Muirhead, B. *Dancing Around the Elephant: Creating a Prosperous Canada in an Era of American Dominance, 1957–1973*. Toronto, ON, University of Toronto Press, 2005.

Mutimer, D. (Ed.) *Canadian Annual Review of Politics and Public Affairs*. Toronto, ON, University of Toronto Press, 2005.

Naiman, J. *How Societies Work: Class, Power and Change in a Canadian Context*. Peterborough, ON, Fernwood Press, 2008.

Ornstein, M., and Stevenson, H. M. *Politics and Ideology in Canada: Elite and Public Opinion in the Transformation of a Welfare State*. Montréal, QC, and Kingston, ON, McGill-Queen's University Press, 2003.

Peach, I. (Ed.). *Constructing Tomorrow's Federalism: New Perspectives on Canadian Governance*. Winnipeg, MB, University of Manitoba Press, 2007.

Pound, R. (Ed.). *The Fitzhenry & Whiteside Book of Canadian Facts and Dates*. Markham, ON, Fitzhenry & Whiteside, 2004.

Rocher, F., and Smith, M. (Eds). *New Trends in Canadian Federalism*, 2nd edn. Peterborough, ON, Broadview Press, 2003.

Samson, C. *A Way of Life That Does Not Exist: Canada and the Extinguishment of the Innu*. London and New York, Verso, 2003.

Samuels, H. R. (Ed.). *Prime Ministers of Canada*. Toronto, ON, Agora Cosmopolitan, 2002.

Progressive Compendium on Canadian Social and Political Issues: v. 1. Toronto, ON, Agora Cosmopolitan, 2005.

Savoie, D. J. *Governing from the Centre: The Concentration of Power in Canadian Politics*. Toronto, ON, University of Toronto Press, 1999.

Schouls, T. *Shifting Boundaries: Aboriginal Identity, Pluralist Theory, and the Politics of Self-Government*. Vancouver, BC, University of British Columbia Press, 2003.

Seymour, M. (Ed.). *The Fate of the Nation State*. Montréal, QC, and Kingston, ON, McGill-Queen's University Press, 2004.

Simpson, J. *Faultlines: Struggling for a Canadian Vision*. Toronto, ON, HarperCollins, 1993.

Slowey, G. *Navigating Neoliberalism: Self-Determination and the Mikisew Cree First Nation*. Vancouver, BC, University of British Columbia Press, 2008.

Smith, D. E. *The Canadian Senate in Bicameral Perspective*. Toronto, ON, University of Toronto Press, 2003.

Statistics Canada. *Canada Yearbook 2006*. Ottawa, ON, Statistics Canada, 2006.

Stevenson, G. *Unfulfilled Union. Canadian Federalism and National Unity*, 4th edn. Montréal, QC, and Kingston, ON, McGill-Queen's University Press, 2004.

Story, D. (Ed.) *The Diefenbaker Legacy: Canadian Politics Law and Society Since 1957 (Canadian Plains Proceedings, 30)*. Regina, SK, Canadian Plains Research Center, 1998.

Thorburn, H. G. (Ed.). *Party Politics in Canada*, 8th edn. Scarborough, ON, Prentice-Hall Canada, 2001.

Trent, J. E., Young, R., and Lachapelle, G. (Eds). *Québec-Canada: What is the Path Ahead?* Ottawa, ON, University of Ottawa Press, 1997.

Vaughan, F. *The Canadian Federalist Experiment: From Defiant Monarchy to Reluctant Republic*. Montréal, QC, and Kingston, ON, McGill-Queen's University Press, 2004.

Waiser, W. *Saskatchewan: A New History*. Calgary, AB, Fifth House Ltd, 2005.

White, P. *Canadian Politics for Dummies*. Toronto, ON, John Wiley & Sons, 2004.

Wiseman, N. *In Search of Canadian Political Culture*. Vancouver, BC, University of British Columbia Press, 2007

Young, R. A. *The Secession of Québec and the Future of Canada*. Montréal, QC, and Kingston, ON, McGill-Queen's University Press, 1995.

The International Role of Canada

Appel Molat, M., and Osler Hampson, F. (Eds). *Canada Among Nations 2000*. Oxford, Oxford University Press, 2000.

Banting, K., Hoberg, G., and Simeon, R. (Eds). *Degrees of Freedom: Canada and the United States in a Changing World*, Montréal, QC, and Kingston, ON, McGill-Queen's University Press, 1997.

Brawley, M. R. *The Politics of Globalization: Gaining Perspective, Assessing Consequences*. Peterborough, ON, Broadview Press, 2003.

Cameron, M. A., and Tomlin, B. W. *The Making of NAFTA*. Ithaca, NY, Cornell University Press, 2000.

Campbell, B., and Finn, E. (Eds) *Living with Uncle: Canada-US Relations in an Age of Empire*. Toronto, ON, James Lorimer and Co Ltd, 2006.

Canadian International Council (CIC). *Behind the Headlines*, series. Toronto, ON, CIC.

Canada in World Affairs, Vols 1–14. Toronto, ON, CIIA.

Chapnick, A. *The Middle Power Project: Canada and the Founding of the United Nations*. Vancouver, BC, University of British Columbia Press, 2005.

Clarkson, S. *Uncle Sam and Us: Globalization, Neoconservatism, and the Canadian State*. Toronto, ON, University of Toronto Press, 2002.

Cohen, A. *While Canada Slept: How We Lost Our Place in the World*. Toronto, ON, McClelland & Stewart, 2003.

Cooper, A. E., and Hayes, G. (Eds). *Worthwhile Initiatives? Canadian Mission-Oriented Diplomacy*. Toronto, ON, Irwin, 2001.

Donaghy, G. *Tolerant Allies. Canada and the United States 1963–1968*. Montréal, QC, and Kingston, ON, McGill-Queen's University Press, 2003.

Donaghy, G., and Roy, P. E. (Eds). *Contradictory Impulses: Canada and Japan in the Twentieth Century*. Vancouver, BC, University of British Columbia Press, 2008.

Doran, C. F. *Why Canadian Unity Matters and Why Americans Care: Democratic Pluralism at Risk*. Toronto, ON, University of Toronto Press, 2001.

Ek, C., Fergusson, I. F., and Nunez-Neto, Blas. *Canada-US Relations in Focus*. Hauppauge, NY, Nova Science Publishers, 2008.

Foreign Affairs and International Trade Canada. *Human Security: Safety for People in a Changing World*. Ottawa, ON, April 1999.

Gammer, N. *From Peacekeeping to Peacemaking: Canada's Response to the Yugoslav Crisis*. Montréal, QC, and Kingston, ON, McGill-Queen's University Press, 2000.

Hamilton, D. *Inside Canadian Intelligence: Exposing the New Realities of Espionage and International Terrorism*. Toronto, ON, Dundurn Press, 2007.

Hampson, F. O., Hart, M., and Rudner, M. (Eds). *Canada Among Nations: A Big League Player?* Toronto, ON, Oxford University Press, 1999.

Harris, R. G. (Ed.). *North American Linkages: Opportunities and Challenges for Canada*. Calgary, AB, University of Calgary Press, 2003.

Hillmer, N., and Molot, M. A. *Canada Among Nations 2002*. Toronto, ON, Oxford University Press, 2002.

Holloway, S. K. *Canadian Foreign Policy: Defining the National Interest*. Peterborough, ON, Broadview Press, 2006.

Institute for Research on Public Policy. *At the Global Crossroads, the Sylvia Ostry Foundation Lectures*. Montréal, QC, and Kingston, ON, McGill-Queen's University Press, 2004.

Jockel, J. T., and Sokolsky, J. 'Lloyd Axworthy's Legacy: Human Security and the Rescue of Canadian Defence Policy', in *International Journal*, pp. 1–18, Toronto, ON, Winter 2000–01.

Konrad, V. 'Borderlines and Borderlands', in Randall, S. J., and Konrad, H. W. (Eds). *NAFTA In Transition*. Calgary, AB, University of Calgary Press, 1996.

Kreinin, M. E. (Ed.). *Building a Partnership: The Canada-United States Free Trade Agreement*. Ann Arbor, MI, Anniversary Conference of the Canada-United States Free Trade Agreement, University of Michigan Press, 2000.

McKenna, P. *Canada and the OAS*. Montréal, QC, and Kingston, ON, McGill-Queen's University Press, 1995.

National Defence (Canada). *Shaping the Future of Canadian Defence: A Strategy for 2020*. Ottawa, ON, June 1999.

Neman, J. *Women, Politics and Public Policy: The Political Struggles of Canadian Women*. New York, Oxford University Press, 2006.

Nossal, K. R. *The Politics of Canadian Foreign Policy*, 3rd edn. Scarborough, ON, Prentice-Hall Canada, 1997.

Smith, G., and Wolfish, D. (Eds). *Who is Afraid of the State? Canada in a World of Multiple Centres of Power*. Toronto, ON, University of Toronto Press, 2001.

Stevens, K. *Border Diplomacy: The Caroline and McLeod Affairs in Anglo-American-Canadian Relations, 1837–1842*. Tuscaloosa, AL, University of Alabama Press, 2005.

Thomas, D. M. *Canada and the United States: Differences that Count*, 2nd edn. Peterborough, ON, Broadview Press, 2000.

Thompson, J. H., and Randall, S. J. *Canada and the United States: Ambivalent Allies*. Atlanta, GA, University of Georgia Press, 2002.

Trovato, F. *Canada's Population in a Global Context*. Toronto, ON, Oxford University Press, 2008.

Welsh, J. *At Home in the World: Canada's Vision for the 21st Century*. Toronto, ON, HarperCollins, 2004.

Zhao, J., Drew, D., and Murray, T. S. *Brain Drain and Brain Gain: The Migration of Knowledge Workers From and To Canada*. Catalogue No. 81-003, Ottawa, ON, Statistics Canada, 2000.

ESSAYS ON CANADIAN ECONOMIC AND SOCIAL AFFAIRS

OVERVIEW OF THE CANADIAN ECONOMY

SANDY MARKWICK

LAND AND PEOPLE

Covering a land area of 9.1m. sq km, Canada is the world's second largest country, after Russia. Its limits extend from the Atlantic island of Newfoundland in the east to the Pacific coast of British Columbia in the west and from the border with the USA in the south to the Arctic Circle in the north. Extreme cold throughout much of the year makes much of the vast landscapes of northern Canada inhospitable to human settlement. Given Canada's land area, an estimated population of 33.2m. in July 2008 represents a population density of approximately 3.6 people per sq km of land, one of the lowest in the world. However, this is misleading, as Canadians are overwhelmingly concentrated along a strip of southern Canada within 300 km of the US border. Canada's population is very urbanized, with 80% living in towns of 10,000 inhabitants or more. Six greater metropolitan areas had populations of more than 1m. in mid-2008, with Toronto (Ontario, 5.5m.), Montréal (Québec, 3.7m.) and Vancouver (British Columbia, 2.3m.) the largest.

Population growth slowed to an average annual rate of less than 1.0% for the five-year period between the 1996 and 2001 censuses. This compares with average annual growth of 2.0% in 1941–96 and 4.3% in the first half of the 20th century. Historically low population growth rates continued between the 2001 and 2006 censuses, averaging just over 1.0% per year, although the long-term decline in population growth abated. Low population growth is consistent with trends in other advanced industrialized nations. A lower birth rate resulting from a trend for smaller families is a principal cause for slower population growth in recent decades. Two-thirds of population growth in 2001–06 stemmed from net immigration, averaging 140,000 per year since 1971. The most heavily populated of Canada's 10 provinces and three territories is Ontario, home to Toronto and the federal capital, Ottawa, and a focus for much of Canada's industrial development. Ontario accounted for 38.8% of the total population in mid-2008. The next most populous provinces were Québec, with 23.4% of the total, and British Columbia, with 13.3%. Alberta, the fourth largest province in terms of population, recorded the fastest population growth rate in 1999–2005, averaging 1.6% annually for the period.

The ethnic origin of Canadians has changed significantly in the post-war period. While Canadians tracing their ancestry from the British Isles and France continued to be the largest groups, immigrants from elsewhere in Europe, particularly southern and eastern Europe, as well as the West Indies, the Indian subcontinent and South-East Asia, have ensured that modern Canada is highly multicultural. In mid-2008 some 1.2m. people identified themselves as aboriginal, representing 3.6% of the total Canadian population.

NATURAL RESOURCES

Canada has abundant natural resources of economic significance. Around 46% of the total area of Canada is forested, ensuring large-scale logging and paper industries. Rich reserves of oil and gas are concentrated in Alberta, while Canada is a leading supplier of coal as well as numerous non-fuel minerals. Canada's large Atlantic and Pacific coastlines present significant opportunities for fishing. The non-forested land, particularly the vast prairies of Alberta, supports a range of cattle and agriculture. Areas of outstanding natural beauty such as the Rocky Mountains in western Canada and the country's vast network of freshwater lakes, which make up 8.9% of Canada's total area, support an important tourism industry. The Great Lakes, spanning the border with the USA, provide an important route for industrial shipping as well as recreational transport, linking directly to the Atlantic via the St Lawrence River.

ECONOMIC STRUCTURE

Canada's wealth in natural resources has been historically important to the development of the economy. Primary economic activities (i.e. agriculture, hunting, forestry, fishing, mining and petroleum and gas extraction) continue to account for a significant proportion of export earnings, contributing 33.5% of the total in 2007, and in some provinces they are the principal source of income. However, modern Canada saw the economy shift towards a high level of diversification, in which primary economic activities represented just 7.0% of gross domestic product (GDP) in 2007, employing 4.0% of the work-force. By contrast, the services sector, including utilities and public administration, contributed 71.7% of GDP in 2007 and employed 77.1% of the work-force. Manufacturing and construction combined accounted for 21.4% of GDP and employed 18.8% of the work-force.

GDP AND GROWTH

GDP in 2007 was C $1,535,646m., at current prices, making Canada the smallest economy within the Group of Seven (G7) leading industrialized nations. GDP per head was C $46,254, above average for the economies comprising the Organisation for Economic Co-operation and Development (OECD). Within the G7, Canada's GDP per head on a purchasing power parity basis, taking into account local prices, ranked second in 2007, behind the USA.

In 2003 outbreaks of Severe Acute Respiratory Syndrome (SARS) and bovine spongiform encephalopathy (BSE) had a negative effect on tourism and beef exports and restricted GDP growth to 1.9%. Despite an improvement in 2004, with an increase in GDP of 3.1%, growth remained slower than that experienced in the preceding five-year period, 1998–2002, when the economy grew by an average of 4.0% per year, partly owing to the strength of the Canadian dollar. Real GDP rose by 2.7% in 2007, a lower rate of growth than in the previous year, when output increased by 3.1%. The economy grew rapidly, by a seasonally adjusted annual rate of 2.5%, in the second quarter of 2008, but was expected to slow thereafter, reflecting the global financial crisis and stagnation in the US economy.

The Canadian economy maintained relatively consistent growth after emerging from recession in 1991 and has outperformed several other G7 countries in recent years. The strong performance, particularly in the second half of the 1990s, stemmed largely from increased demand for Canadian exports, fuelled by a Canadian-US Free Trade Agreement (CUFTA), which was introduced in January 1989. The CUFTA was expanded into the North American Free Trade Agreement (NAFTA) when Mexico joined in January 1994. The contribution of exports to GDP increased from 25% in 1990 to a high of 42% in 2001 (and amounted to 30.2% in 2007). Another source of GDP growth during this period was investment, particularly associated with the stock market 'bubble' in information technology and telecommunications stocks. This came to an abrupt halt in Canada in 2000, as it did elsewhere. Investment picked up again in 2003, focusing on less speculative businesses with a greater emphasis on profitability. Meanwhile, consumer spending and housing were significant drivers of GDP growth, underpinned by tax cuts and historically low interest rates. The unemployment rate, at 6.0% of the labour force in 2007, was the lowest rate for decades; although it exceeded the 5.6% average for OECD countries, it was lower than the 7.4% average for the European Union (EU) member states. In August 2008 the unemployment rate in Canada was 6.1%.

INFLATION

Since a recession in 1990–91, the Bank of Canada has maintained a firm discipline in managing inflationary pressures in the economy. The federal Government set the Bank of Canada an inflation target range of 1%–3% in 1993. Inflation was insignificant from the early 1990s until pressures increased after 2000, principally because of higher energy prices. Annual inflation reached 3.3% in January 2003. Inflation was reduced subsequently (the average rate for 2003 was 2.8%), owing to the Bank of Canada's policy of higher interest rates, as well as lower growth in 2003. The strength of the currency relative to the US dollar kept inflation down thereafter, with the rate falling to an average of 1.8% in 2004. However, higher energy prices in the second half of 2005 caused renewed inflationary pressures, resulting in a rise in the rate to an average of 2.2% in that year. A cut in value-added taxes helped limit the growth in the Consumer Price Index (CPI) to 2.0% in 2006. The inflation rate continued at this level into the first half of 2007. However, underlying inflationary trends stemming from a tight labour market and high levels of consumption were reflected in the Core CPI, which ignores value-added taxes, as well as the most volatile products, and is used by the Bank of Canada to measure inflation for the purpose of monetary policy. Consumer prices rose by 3.4% during the year to mid-2008.

THE PROVINCES

The structures of provincial economies vary significantly, ensuring that economic trends are far from uniformly experienced across Canada. The largest provincial economy was Ontario, which contributed 38.0% of Canadian GDP in 2007, compared with 19.5% contributed by Québec, the next largest provincial economy. Manufacturing is concentrated in Ontario and Québec, which benefited most from US demand following the CUFTA (later NAFTA) and economic expansion in the USA in the 1990s. These provinces were also adversely affected by the US slowdown in 2001. Growth rates in 2007 were below the national average, at 2.1% in Ontario and 2.4% in Québec, largely because of the strength of the Canadian dollar vis-à-vis the US dollar, which damaged exports. British Columbia contributed 12.4% of national GDP in 2007. Here, principal industries are forestry, energy and mining and related industries. In common with other provinces where primary exports are key to growth, British Columbia's economy was adversely affected by the economic crisis in Asia in 1997–98. A depressed forestry industry was offset by oil and gas investment, leading to growth of 3.1% in 2007, following growth of 3.3% and 4.5% in 2006 and 2005, respectively.

The Prairie provinces of Manitoba, Saskatchewan and Alberta accounted for a combined 23.5% of Canada's GDP in 2007. Cattle and grain are key industries in the Prairies, along with oil and gas, mining and hydroelectricity. Alberta was Canada's fastest growing province during the 1990s, but output slowed following severe drought in 2001–02. In 2005 Alberta was again the fastest growing provincial economy, recording growth of 5.3%, and even stronger growth, of 6.6%, in 2006, largely owing to improved commodity prices. The rate of growth declined to 3.3% in 2007, partly owing to a fall in demand on the part of the USA for exports and to the global 'credit crunch', which undermined housing construction. A fiscal surplus, of C $4,600m., in Alberta in 2007/08, while larger than expected, was significantly smaller than the average annual surplus of C $8,600m. recorded during the previous two years and reflected the slowdown in the economy and lower tax revenues. The large budgetary surpluses resulting from the royalties from high energy prices provoked discord and debate around the issue of federalism. Calls from elsewhere in Canada for the federal Government to force Alberta to share its windfall with the rest of the country (which intensified as high oil prices increased inflationary pressures) were fiercely resisted by the province. Saskatchewan's economy grew by 2.8% in 2007, owing to strong commodity prices following a contraction in growth of 0.4% in 2006, stemming from lower production volumes of uranium, potash and wheat, which are key to the province. This decline followed average annual growth of 3.7% in the period 2003–05, supported by earnings from grain, oil and gas exports. Manitoba's GDP rose marginally from 3.2% in 2006 to 3.3% in 2007. The performance of industries, related to a housing boom, fuelled growth and offset a weak agricultural sector. The four Maritime provinces have Atlantic coastlines: New Brunswick; Prince Edward Island; Nova Scotia; and Newfoundland and Labrador. Together, they contributed 6.1% of national GDP in 2007. Oil and gas development and other large infrastructure projects have boosted these economies and reduced their reliance on fishing. Newfoundland and Labrador led Canadian provinces in terms of economic growth in 2007, registering an expansion of 9.1%, largely as a result of the new Voisey's Bay nickel mine and the Terra Nova offshore oilfield becoming fully operational. Growth of 3.3% in 2006 represented a marked recovery following growth of only 0.2% in the previous year and a contraction in output of 1.7% in 2004, which was partly owing to production problems at the Terra Nova oilfield, as well as industrial unrest among mining and public sector employees. This followed two years of impressive growth, of 5.8% in 2003 and 15.6% in 2002, stemming from the development of Terra Nova and another oilfield, Hibernia. New Brunswick's growth of 1.6% in 2007 was down from 3.0% in 2006, under pressure from the strength of the Canadian dollar and lower demand from the USA and despite being supported by the construction of the Canaport Liquid Natural Gas terminal in Saint John and the refurbishment of the Point Lepreau nuclear power plant. Nova Scotia also recorded growth of 1.6% in 2007, compared with 0.9% in 2006. Prince Edward Island is Canada's smallest province and is heavily reliant on tourism and agriculture, particularly potato production. Prince Edward Island experienced growth of 2.0% in 2007, compared with 2.6% in 2006.

SOCIAL INDICATORS

The Canadian work-force is highly educated. Some 55% of the population over 15 years of age undergo at least some post-secondary education, with some 44% receiving a diploma or university degree. Within the G7, Canada spends a relatively high proportion of public money on education. Health care is the largest recipient of public funding, which is largely administered at provincial level. All Canadians are entitled to a minimum standard of publicly funded health care, which includes access to a general practitioner and emergency hospital services. Beyond this, services vary between provinces in terms of emphasis on research, primary care and the role of the private sector. Conditions attached to federal transfers to health care budgets, as well as their size, are a major source of political dispute between the federal and provincial governments. Across all indicators of social welfare, Canada displays the characteristics expected of a member of the G7. Average life expectancy in 2005 was 79 years at birth. In 2005 the rate of infant mortality was 5.4 per 1,000 live births. The most significant regional variations in social welfare reflect higher rates of poverty in aboriginal communities. Infant mortality was 11.0 per 1,000 live births in Yukon Territory in 2004 and 10.0 in Nunavut Territory in 2005.

FINANCIAL SERVICES

The financial services sector, including finance, insurance and real estate, made the largest contribution to Canada's GDP in 2007, of C $301,107m., at current prices, or 19.6% of the total. The financial services sector employed some 1,040,500 people in 2006, or 6.3% of all employed Canadians.

The Bank of Canada is independent of the Government and is responsible for those functions normally associated with a central bank, including setting interest rates and managing foreign exchange reserves, public funds and debt. The Office of the Superintendent of Financial Institutions oversees the financial stability of the banking sector, pension funds and other regulated financial institutions.

Canada's financial sector is dominated by six commercial banks: Royal Bank of Canada; Bank of Montréal; Canadian

Imperial Bank of Commerce; Toronto-Dominion Bank; Bank of Nova Scotia (Scotiabank); and National Bank of Canada. Together, these six institutions own more than 90% of Canada's banking assets, of which mortgage loans are the most important. Deregulation from the late 1980s led to consolidation in financial services, as banks increasingly expanded their range of services, either through developing internal capabilities or through acquisition, to include brokerage, mutual funds and insurance. Meanwhile, a number of life insurance companies demutualized their ownership structure, allowing them to raise finance through share issues. Consolidation resulted in three large insurers offering diversified financial services: Manufacturers Life Insurance Co (Manulife Financial), Sun Life Financial Canada and Great-West Life Assurance Co.

In the interests of competition, governments blocked merger proposals in the late 1990s. The prospect of mergers in the financial sector remained a highly charged political issue in the face of commercial pressures for further consolidation. Competition from foreign banking institutions prompted banks to seek greater clarity from the Government over rules for alliances or mergers. A Bank of Canada study suggested that greater consolidation in the banking sector could add efficiencies while not necessarily undermining competition. There were expectations that the Government would relax its rules to allow further mergers. Following restructuring in 1999, the Toronto Stock Exchange (TSX) is the only exchange trading senior stocks. Prior to 1999 exchanges in Vancouver, Alberta and Montréal played a supporting role, contributing approximately 20% of the value of total traded equity. A subsidiary of the TSX, the TSX Venture Exchange is a junior market for mining, energy and technology stocks formerly traded in Vancouver and Alberta. Derivatives are traded in Montréal and commodities on the Winnipeg Commodities Exchange in Manitoba. Canadian stock indexes are weighted towards companies based on natural resources. Canadian equities have followed a pattern familiar to stock markets in the USA and Western Europe. Gains in the late 1990s, partially disrupted by the Asian financial crisis of 1997–98, reached a peak in 2000, based on speculation around technology stocks. The end of the high-technology 'bubble' saw 40% of value disappear in a 12-month period. Recovery followed in 2003–04, based on high commodity prices and low interest rates, although in 2005 the financial markets were affected by volatile commodity prices and uncertainty surrounding interest rate and exchange rate forecasts.

MANUFACTURING AND CONSTRUCTION

Manufacturing output amounted to C $231,744m. in 2007, at current prices, representing 15.1% of GDP. Manufacturing accounted for an average of 16.8% of total annual GDP between 2001 and 2006. Manufacturing GDP contracted in 2007 (by 1.0%) for the second year in succession (0.9% in 2006) following slow growth in 2005. Manufacturing is highly integrated with US production, and a considerable proportion of Canadian output is exported south to the USA. The sector is vulnerable to diminished demand from US importers. In 2003 manufacturing was adversely affected by the strength of the Canadian dollar, particularly against the US dollar. In 2001 a contraction in manufacturing output of 4.7% was a result of recession in the USA in that year.

The most important manufacturing sub-sectors were transportation equipment, which accounted for 18.9% of sectoral GDP in 2007, followed by primary and fabricated metal products (14.1%), food (10.3%), chemicals (8.6%) and machinery (7.8%). The contribution to manufacturing GDP of these sub-sectors was largely stable in the previous five years. The introduction of free trade with the USA in the 1990s boosted exports of Canadian manufactured products. In 2003 over 70% of manufactured goods were exported, compared with just 25% in the 1980s. However, increasing integration of production and trade with the USA has made Canadian producers vulnerable to the performance of the US economy and to fluctuations in exchange rates.

Manufactured goods accounted for 63.5% of all exports in 2007. The main sub-categories were industrial goods and materials, led by metals and alloys, and chemicals, plastics and fertilizers, which together earned C $104,421m. in that year; machinery and equipment, which earned C $93,428m.; and automotive products, which earned export revenues of C $77,304m. The manufacturing sector was a significant importer as well as exporter, leading to trade deficits in machinery and consumer goods and an overall deficit in the manufacturing sector of C $42,670m. in 2007.

Output from the construction sector was C $96,464m. in 2007, in current prices; growth of 3.8% was recorded in the sector in that year. This followed growth of 7.2% in 2006 and consistent annual growth averaging 4.8% in 2001–05. The share of GDP contributed by the construction sector was 6.3% in 2007. The share during 2003–05 averaged 5.7% annually. Construction activity has been fuelled by a boom in residential housing, with the value of building permits reaching a record C $66,300m. in 2006, up 9.0% over the 2005 value, following annual increases of 9.3% and 9.4% in the previous two years. Ontario accounted for 36% of the total value of all building permits in Canada in July 2008. This was followed by Quebec, with 20.6%, Alberta, with 17.7% and British Columbia, with 13.4%. The share of the work-force employed in the construction industry rose to 6.7% in 2007, up from 6.5% in 2006 and 6.3% in 2005. Some 2m. people were engaged in manufacturing in 2007, a slight decline compared with the preceding year. Manufacturing's share of the total work-force was 12.1% in 2007, a steady decline from 14.9% in 2002.

AGRICULTURE

The agricultural sector, including forestry, hunting and fishing, was fundamental to the economic development of Canada. Furs and timber were the principal economic activity of the first settlers through into the late 19th century. Wheat emerged as a staple crop from 1890 and fuelled a rapid expansion of the Canadian economy for decades. After Canada developed into an advanced industrial nation, the relative importance of agriculture to the economy declined. Primary production in the agricultural sector accounted for 2.2% of GDP in 2007. The sector's annual share of GDP averaged 2.4% between 1999 and 2005. Employment in agriculture (excluding forestry and fishing) declined from some 15% in 1960 to 2.0% in 2007. The smaller number of workers in agriculture is also a reflection of advances in technology and production methods, which has seen a trend towards consolidation of family-operated farms into fewer, larger units. The number of farms declined by 10.7% between 1996 and 2001, to 246,923, and Canada's farm population declined by 14.6% in the same period. The number of farms fell by a further 7.1% between 2001 and 2006, to 229,373m.

GDP in the agricultural sector was C $33,972m., at current prices, in 2007. Agricultural GDP declined by 2.8% in that year and by 1.6% in 2006, following average annual growth of 6.5% between 2003 and 2005. In 1999–2002 output declined by an average of 0.2% per year. In 2007 45.0% of farm receipts came from animal products, 44.9% from crops and the remainder in the form of government assistance grants. The Government protects farmers from fluctuating earnings through several collective marketing schemes.

Of the animal products, the most important was beef, with output valued at C $6,292m. in 2007, slightly down from production recorded the previous year. Growth in beef output had been restored in 2005 after severe recession in 2003, when sectoral decline measured 33.1%, from a value of C $7,654m. in 2002, and a further small decrease of 0.9% in 2004. The decline resulted from the discovery of BSE (so-called 'mad cow' disease) in a herd in Alberta, the province that hosts 40% of Canadian cattle. The disease led to a ban on live cattle exports to the USA. Ranchers in Alberta were particularly badly affected; farm incomes in the province declined by 72% in 2003, a situation exacerbated by rising costs of fuel, seed and fertilizer. The ban on cattle exports to the USA was lifted in July 2005 following the decision of a US court. After beef, the most important animal product category was dairy, with output valued at C $5,197m. in 2007, compared with C $4,831m. in 2005. Agricultural land along the St Lawrence River from Ontario, through Québec and into the Maritimes is the principal area for dairy production. Pork and poultry followed, in terms of value, among animal products, with output in 2007 valued at C $3,328m. and C $2,069m., respectively.

Canada is the world's second largest crop exporter. Wheat is the most important crop, with export revenue amounting to C $4,637m. in 2007, a significant increase from the C $2,704m. earned in 2005. The wheat crop, grown in the Prairies, averaged annual export earnings of C $3,357m. in 2000–04. In terms of output, wheat, at C $4,212m. in 2007, was followed by rapeseed, or canola, at C $3,413m. Other important produce included soybeans, corn and a range of vegetables and fruit grown in British Columbia and a small area in south-western Ontario. Principal vegetables were sweetcorn, peas and beans, while blueberries, apples, grapes and strawberries were the most important fruits produced. Canada's climate means that corn and barley production are modest.

Restrictions on fishing in Atlantic areas, imposed in 1992 following years of overfishing by foreign as well as domestic fleets, had a devastating effect on Canada's Atlantic fishing industry. Most restrictions remain in place, as stocks have been slow to recover. In response, the industry shifted to shellfish and fish farming. Farmed fish account for around one-quarter of all production in the sub-sector. The total value of commercial sea fish landings in 2007 was C $1,888m., of which 7.5% was shellfish, including lobster, shrimp, crab and scallop. The 2007 landings value represented a 1.7% increase compared with 2006, although it was down considerably from the C $2,077m. value of total sea landings recorded in 2005. Exports in 2006 earned revenues of C $4,092m., a decline of 5.1% from 2005. Canada registered a trade surplus of C $8,874m. in agricultural and fishing products (excluding forestry) in 2007.

Canada is home to an estimated 10% of the world's temperate and boreal forests, most of which are productive, and is the largest exporter of timber products. About one-third of logging takes place in British Columbia. Canada earned C $29,263m. from exports of forestry products in 2007. Exports to the USA account for about 55% of total forestry exports. A trade dispute led the USA to impose duties on Canadian softwood imports in 2002, which threatened the industry. Canada won a ruling under NAFTA ordering the USA to remove the duties on Canadian softwood and refund more than US $4,000m. already collected. However, the USA refused to comply and subsequently received support from the World Trade Organization. In September 2006 the two sides signed a seven-year agreement on softwood lumber, which took effect from October. The USA agreed to cancel the duties and refund revenue collected since 2002 in return for new export taxes to be imposed on Canadian producers if lumber prices fell below predetermined levels.

Exports from the combined agriculture, forestry and fishing sector earned Canada C $63,633m. in 2007, leading to a trade surplus in the sector of C $35,142m. The sectoral surplus averaged an annual C $44,452m. in the preceding six years.

EXTRACTIVE INDUSTRIES: MINING, OIL AND GAS

The GDP for the combined mining and oil and gas extraction sector in 2007 was C $73,711m., at current prices; the sector's GDP increased by 2.0% in that year, matching the growth of the previous year. The sector contributed 4.8% of total GDP in 2007; its share of GDP averaged 3.8% per year in 1999–2005. Canada's mining, oil and gas industry is concentrated in Alberta, where 74% of businesses in the sector are located.

Canada's oil reserves of 178,600m. barrels in 2008 are the second largest in the world after Saudi Arabia. These reserves include an estimated 174,100m. barrels located in vast tar sands deposits, similar to bitumen, in northern Alberta. Until the technological advances of the 1980s, exploitation of the tar sands was not considered economically viable. The remaining reserves are located in oilfields in western Canada and off shore in the Atlantic.

Exploitation of the tar sands increased total output significantly and was forecast to account for most growth in the future. Production was increased further with the development of the Hibernia and Terra Nova oilfields in the Atlantic, off the coast of Newfoundland, which began operations in 1997 and 2002, respectively. Canada produced 158.9m. cu m of crude oil in 2007, 3.6% more than in the previous year. Canada ranked seventh in the world as an oil producer in 2006. Canada earned 27.1% more from exports of crude petroleum in 2006 (C $38,574m.) compared with 2005, when, in turn, a 19.0% increase over 2004 was recorded.

Alberta is also the main producer of natural gas, representing more than two-thirds of total output. British Columbia and Saskatchewan are the next most important contributors. Development of the Sable Island gas field off the coast of Nova Scotia, which began production in 1999, brought on stream a new source of natural gas, as will, it is expected, newly discovered reserves in the Northwest Territories. Output increased by some 70% in the 1990s. In 2007 Canada produced 165.3m. cu m of natural gas, a moderate decline from a peak in 2001. Canada is the third largest producer of natural gas in the world, after the USA and Russia. Proven reserves stood at an estimated 1,600,000m. cu m in 2007, but as yet undiscovered reserves are expected to increase that figure many times over. Canadian exports of natural gas earned C $28,378m. in 2007, a 2.1% increase over the previous year, but still below record earnings in 2005. Since that year average prices for natural gas have been lower, as has demand from the USA.

Canada extracts and processes more than 60 different minerals. It is one of the world's largest producers of potash, uranium, nickel, zinc and asbestos. Canada is also a major source of copper, cadmium, aluminium, salt, gold, diamonds and cobalt. Canada exported 25.4m. metric tons of coal in 2006, 40.3% of the total output of 62.9m. tons. During 1999–2005 exports averaged 31.9m. tons per year, or 46.9% of the average total output of 68.0m. tons. The western provinces of British Columbia, Alberta and Saskatchewan accounted for almost all coal production in 2007. Coal reserves amounted to 6,578m. tons at the end of 2007. Along with forestry products, energy products were a major contributor to Canada's trade surplus. Exports of all energy products earned C $91,647m. in 2007, ensuring a trade surplus in the sector of C $55,078m.

UTILITIES

The utilities sector comprises the treatment, generation or distribution of electricity, water and gas (the extraction of natural gas is considered separately, along with mining and oil production). The utilities sector recorded output of C $39,107m. in 2007, at current prices, stable at 2.5% of total GDP (the average annual share for 1998–2005 was 2.8%). The utilities sector employed only 0.8% of the work-force in 2007. Canada's installed capacity of electricity is 120 GW. Approximately 60% of Canada's electricity production is derived from hydroelectric power, reflecting its vast network of lakes and rivers. Canada generates 15.8% of its electricity production from 18 nuclear power reactors currently in operation, 16 of which are in Ontario (some 45% of the province's electricity is nuclear-generated). Of the remaining two, one is located in Québec, generating 3% of the province's electricity, and the other is in New Brunswick, accounting for some 30% of its electrical power. The remainder of the country's electricity requirements are met by coal, oil and gas, and renewable sources.

The principal producers and distributors of electricity are state utilities, owned and controlled by the provincial governments. These utilities generated some 90% of the total 537,500m. kWh generated in 2006, distributed via an electricity grid integrated with the grid in the USA; in 2004 6.6% of electricity output was exported to the USA. The average annual output for the 2001–05 period was 574,392m. kWh. A minority share of electricity production, amounting to 8.1% in 2003, is generated by large private-sector industrial units in mining, aluminium smelting and pulp and paper manufacturing for their own use.

TRANSPORT AND COMMUNICATIONS

The GDP of the transport sector was C $70,640m. in 2007, at current prices, representing 4.6% of total GDP. Output increased by 1.6% in that year, following an increase of

2.7% in 2006. The transport sector employed 4.9% of the work-force in 2007. The Canadian road network comprises 1.4m. km of urban or rural roads and highways. This includes the 7,821-km Trans-Canada Highway, the world's longest, which stretches from Victoria (British Columbia) to St John's (Newfoundland). Annual sales of new vehicles rose by 2.2% in 2006, with 1.67m. sold, following sales growth of 3.5% in 2005. A peak in 2002, of 1.73m. new vehicles sold, followed seven years of growth in sales. There were 27.6m. vehicles registered in 2007. The rail network in 2007 was composed of 72,131 km of track and was one of the world's largest, although it contracted after 1975, when it had 96,633 km of track. There are two principal private sector operators who own and manage the rail tracks: Canadian National Railway (CN), which operates 47% of the total track, and Canadian Pacific Railway (CPR), which operates 27%. In addition, there are several smaller operators who have bought track. Mergers and acquisitions of US rail companies were part of the shifting focus of CN transcontinental trade. The state passenger rail service, VIA Rail, operates using CN and CPR tracks. The St Lawrence Seaway connects the Atlantic Ocean with the western edge of the Great Lakes, a passage of 3,769 km. The Seaway was built by the USA and Canada from the St Lawrence River and opened in 1959. In 2006 freight totalling 37.4m. gross registered metric tons was carried on the Welland Canal section of the Seaway, with a further 35.6m. tons carried on the Montréal–Lake Ontario section. Shipping using the Great Lakes has increased as trade between the USA and Canada has been fuelled by free trade.

There are 15 major ports in Canada. Vancouver is the principal port, handling 15% of passenger traffic and about 46% of freight. Other important ports are: Saint John (New Brunswick), which specializes in oil imports; Sept-Iles (Québec), serving an iron-ore terminal; Montréal; Québec City (Québec); and Halifax (Nova Scotia).

Despite increased competition from low-cost carriers, air transport remains dominated by the privatized former national carrier, Air Canada, which, along with an affiliate airline, Jazz, accounts for about 65% of the domestic market. Despite difficult trading conditions for airlines in 2008, stemming from high fuel prices and global economic insecurity, the main domestic rival, WestJet, based in Calgary (Alberta), had aggressive plans to increase its 35% market share. Air Transat is Air Canada's main Canadian competition on international routes. Air Canada was privatized in 1989. The 1990s were a difficult period for the profitable operation of the airline, which faced competition from the other national carrier, Canadian Airlines. In 1999 the Government permitted the takeover by Air Canada of Canadian Airlines. Air Canada continued to struggle under the burden of debt, labour costs and a downturn in demand in 2003, following the terrorist attacks of 11 September 2001 in the USA and an outbreak of SARS. Air Canada filed for protection from creditors in April 2003 to allow restructuring. Toronto's Lester B. Pearson International Airport is Canada's busiest, with 31m. passengers using it in 2006, followed by Vancouver and Montréal.

Fixed-line telephony penetration, while remaining high, declined by 4.7% between 2000 and 2006, to 55.3 lines per 100 inhabitants, mainly reflecting increased usage of mobile cellular telephones. There were 21.5m. mobile telephone users in 2008. Mobile telephone services are concentrated in larger urban areas and in areas with greater transport links. The three largest wireless providers in 2008 were Rogers Communications Inc, Bell Canada and TELUS.

Internet penetration is high in Canada, with 84.3% of the population regularly accessing it. In terms of high-speed internet penetration, Canada ranks among the world's top 10 countries. Consumer and business-orientated e-commerce has increased rapidly in recent years. The internet is an important sales channel, accounting for sales valued at C $62,700m. in 2007, 27% more than in 2006. The state-owned Canadian Broadcasting Corporation is the dominant broadcaster, although services have expanded rapidly via cable and satellite platforms. Most newspapers are regional or city-focused.

FOREIGN TRADE AND BALANCE OF PAYMENTS

Canada's small population and domestic market relative to other large advanced economies ensured that foreign trade was highly significant in its economic development. In earlier stages of development primary products and raw materials, particularly furs, timber and wheat, dominated exports. Natural resource commodities were no longer the principal source of export revenue, as Canada developed its industrial base. In terms of trade balance, the largest surpluses are in product areas having benefited from value-added processing, but reflect Canada's wealth of natural resources. Primary resources still generate the largest surpluses. Exports contributed 34.7% of GDP in 2007, compared with 36.0% in 2006 and an average annual of 41.3% in 1999–2004. Approximately 30% of employment is dependent on exports.

The strength of the Canadian dollar vis-à-vis the US dollar adversely affected exports after 2000. Nominal export earnings were restored in 2005. Total exports of goods and services in 2007 earned C $532,118m., up 1.8% from the previous year. Exports of industrial goods and materials recorded the strongest growth in 2007 and 2006 (averaging increases of 11.4% each year). Agriculture and fishing registered the next highest growth in export earnings in 2007, up 10.1%, followed by energy, with growth of 5.6%. Exports in other sectors stagnated or declined. In terms of absolute value of exports, industrial goods and materials, machinery and equipment and energy products were the most important sectors. Exports of automotive products were one of the principal beneficiaries of free trade with the USA, which encouraged the integration of industrial manufacturing in North America. In the 1990s exports of automotive products increased three-fold, peaking at C $97,886m. in 2000. Revenues from exports of automotive products declined by 6.1% in 2007, following a decline averaging 4.6% over the previous two years, largely as a result of the appreciation of the Canadian dollar. Canada recorded a trade surplus of C $48,046m. in 2007. The total cost of imports was C $415,006m. The main contributors to the overall surplus were energy and forestry products, with surpluses of C $55,078.4m. and C $26,268.2m., respectively. The overall trade surplus, in terms of Canadian dollars, was 2.9% smaller than in 2006, as an increase in total exports (2.6%) outpaced the rise in imports (2.1%). Industrial goods and materials showed the largest sectoral trade surplus increase in 2007, more than doubling to C $19,289m. Surplus increases were also registered by the agricultural and energy sectors. Other sectors saw trade surpluses decrease or deficits widen. Canada's trade surplus averaged an annual C $58,279.5m. in the five years from 2002–06. Over this period exports averaged C $429,210m. annually and imports C $370,930m.

Canada's main trading partner is the USA, the destination of 76.9% of exports and source of 65.0% of imports in 2007. From the late 1970s Canada registered a merchandise trade surplus with the USA, as it continued to sell it primary commodities while increasing its exports of manufactured goods. The trade surplus with the USA was C $86,342m. in 2007, down from a record high of C $108,454m. in 2005. Trading between Canada and the USA was given a major boost by the CUFTA (later NAFTA), which phased out most tariffs on trade between the two countries over a 10-year period. Bilateral trade between Canada and the USA amounted to C $625,847m. in 2007. The People's Republic of China overtook Canada as the largest exporter to the USA during July 2005. However, growth in Chinese exports to the USA, largely a result of US companies taking advantage of lower labour costs, was not generally at the expense of Canadian exports. Canadian industrial manufacturing remains a deeply integrated contribution to cross-border industrial production. Trade between Canada and Mexico is small, but expanded significantly in the wake of NAFTA. After the USA, Canada's principal trading partner is China, with which it ran an increasing trade deficit of approximately C $30,000m. in 2007, in part owing to the appreciation of the Canadian dollar vis-à-vis the US-dollar-pegged Chinese renminbi.

Canada's trade surplus contributed to a current account surplus of C $13,607m. in 2007, equivalent to 0.9% of GDP, despite deficits in services and investment income. In 2007 Canada earned C $67,280m. from trade in services and spent

C $86,468m., to record a C $19,188m. deficit. A services deficit is traditional, largely as a result of the flow of tourism revenues and payment for transport and commercial services to the USA, but the deficits from 2003 (C $11,521m.) were considerably above an average annual services deficit of C $6,631m. recorded between 1999 and 2002. The deficit increases in the services account since 2003 reflect increased net outflows in tourism and commercial services spending. Tourism spending in Canada increased by an estimated 2.6% in 2007, despite a 1.6% decline in visits. The number of visits fell after 1999, when there were 49.1m. Tourism benefits from proximity to the USA. The strong Canadian dollar discouraged visitors, particularly from the USA, from where 74.4% of tourist visits came in 2007 (down from 91.1% in 2002). The United Kingdom, Japan, France and Germany are other main sources of tourists. Tourists are attracted principally by Canada's abundant natural resources, and winter sports are a particularly popular tourist activity. Canadians spent C $26,663m. outside Canada in 2007 on 25.1m. visits, 70.6% of which were to the USA. The deficit on the international travel account amounted to C $10,029m. in 2007. A deficit in investment income is also common, reflecting a large stock of foreign investment. The deficit amounted to C $14,194m. in 2007, up 6.1% during the year following a 47% reduction of the deficit in 2006 compared with 2005, and lower still than the average annual of C $31,935m. recorded during 1999–2003. The improved investment balances in 2004–06 were partly a result of improved public finances reducing the debt interest burden to investors.

The investment, services and merchandises balances all contributed to a smaller current account surplus in 2007, down 32.7% compared with the previous year. Current account surpluses are a relatively recent phenomenon. Public sector deficits ensured the current account was in deficit from the 1970s, reaching a peak of C $28,100m. in 1993, until 1999, when a surplus of C $2,570m. was recorded. The surplus averaged C $22,760m. per year in the four-year period 2000–03. The shift to current account surpluses was primarily a result of the improved merchandise trade balance, fuelled by free trade with the USA. The stock of foreign direct investment (FDI) in Canada stood at C $500,851m. at the end of 2007, up from C $437,801m. in 2006. The energy and minerals sector was the destination of 59.4% of net FDI in Canada in 2006. The next largest shares went to services and retailing (6.0%), machinery and transportation equipment (5.9%) and the finance and insurance sector (4.5%). The USA was the origin of 65.1% of the total FDI stock in Canada in 2006. The United Kingdom, France, the Netherlands and Japan largely accounted for the remainder. Inflows of investment into Canada remained static, at C $8,200m., in 2004, following a marked decline in 2003 from approximately C $28,000m. in 2002. The stock of Canadian direct investment abroad declined to C $514,540m. in 2007 from C $529,969m. in 2006, following four years of growth averaging 8.1% per year. Assets in the USA accounted for 43.6% of Canadian FDI in 2004, up from a 41.3% share in 2003. The main destinations after the USA were the United Kingdom, Barbados and Ireland. In 2003 finance and insurance accounted for 42.2% of Canadian FDI abroad, with energy and minerals taking the next largest share, at 22.0%.

GOVERNMENT FINANCE

The principal levels of government in terms of tax-raising powers and delivery of services are the federal and provincial governments. Municipal government and the territories raise property taxes. Only the federal Government can raise income through import duties and taxes on non-residents, while only the provinces can raise property taxes, royalties on natural resources and taxes on gaming and alcohol. The federal Government raised C $250,782m. in general revenue in 2007/08, compared with C $276,776m. raised by all 10 provinces and three territories combined. The provinces and territories received an additional C $61,035m. in transfers from other levels of government. The balance of public revenues shifted towards the provinces following the introduction of a Tax Reduction Plan in 2000, which was to be phased in over five years. The Plan involved C $100,000m. of federal tax cuts, focusing on personal income tax, while increasing cash transfers to the provinces.

From a consolidated perspective across all federal, provincial, territorial and local government, a total of C $590,718m. was raised in taxes, medical insurance premiums, social security contributions, sales and investments in the fiscal year ending March 2008. The largest contributor to overall state revenues was income tax, at 45.3%. Total revenue in 2007/08 was 5.3% more than that raised in 2006/07; income tax revenues were the main source of the increase. The federal Government registered a general budget surplus of C $13,761m. in the fiscal year ending March 2008, after spending C $242,814m. This was the 11th consecutive year in which the federal Government had registered a fiscal surplus, allowing it to pay off some of its debt burden. The largest proportion of federal spending, 37.0%, was on social services, followed by protection of persons and property (11.8%), general purpose transfers (11.3%), health (10.6%) and debt charges (8.4%). The provincial and territorial governments combined ran a fiscal surplus in 2004/05 for the first time since 2000, largely as a consequence of high oil prices helping Alberta register a surplus. The general surplus amounted to C $6,366m. in 2007/08. New social security responsibilities devolved to the provinces have complicated efforts to balance budgets at provincial level, particularly in the aftermath of federal cuts in unemployment benefits in the late 1990s. In 2007/08 health was the recipient of 33.6% of general provincial and territorial spending, the largest share, followed by education (20.0%) and social services (16.8%). There were 3.2m. Canadians employed in the public sector in 2007, 50.8% of whom were employed at the provincial level, including health, education, social services and publicly funded business, and 34.1% and 15.1% at municipal and federal levels respectively.

Substantial federal and provincial budget deficits registered from 1970 until the mid-1990s led to a consolidated public debt of C $832,000m. in 1996, equivalent to 103% of GDP. Greater fiscal discipline from the mid-1990s resulted in federal budget surpluses from 1998. Debt repayments reduced the federal debt-to-GDP ratio from 70.9% in 1996, the second highest debt burden within the G7, to an estimated 33.1% in 2007. The consolidated public debt amounted to C $776,603m. in 2006.

FEDERAL ENERGY POLICY IN CANADA

KEITH BROWNSEY

INTRODUCTION

After three years in office, the outlines of an energy strategy of the Conservative Government of Prime Minister Stephen J. Harper have emerged. While building on the work of previous governments, the Harper policy is based on market solutions and a respect for provincial ownership of natural resources. While Harper and the Minister of Natural Resources, Gary Lunn, continue to describe Canada as an energy superpower, they have abandoned any attempt by the federal Government to implement a national strategy for energy resources. Instead, the Conservative Government has stated that it will respect provincial jurisdiction over natural resources, including petroleum, natural gas, coal and other sources of energy (with the exception of uranium), and that market mechanisms are the most appropriate methods of producing and distributing energy resources.

Aside from complaints about rising petrol prices, Conservative energy policy has received little coverage in Canada. The media has focused on the Government's claims that Canada is a 'clean energy superpower'. In July 2006, at a meeting of the Canada-United Kingdom Chamber of Commerce, Prime Minister Harper stated that Canada ranks 'third and seventh in global gas and oil production, respectively. We generate more hydroelectric power than any other country on Earth. And we are the world's largest supplier of uranium.' The Conservative Government is enthusiastic about the potential of the western Canadian oil sands, describing them as the second largest oil deposit in the world. The Prime Minister, moreover, has claimed that Canada is the only non-OPEC (Organization of the Petroleum Exporting Countries) country with growing oil deliverability. Both Harper and Lunn have stated that Canada is 'a stable, reliable producer in a volatile, unpredictable world', and that the Canadian Government believes 'in the free exchange of energy products based on competitive market principles, not self-serving monopolistic political strategies'. As a result of its energy wealth and government policy, Canada has become the key to North American energy security.

Prime Minister Harper has sought to distinguish his Government's energy policies from those of his two Liberal predecessors, Jean Chrétien (1993–2003) and Paul Martin (2003–06). Harper has made it clear that his Government would never use energy as a weapon in economic and political disputes with the USA or with any other country, with the possible exception of the People's Republic of China. Harper's profession of faith in free-market mechanisms and his belief that natural resources are under the jurisdiction of the provinces signalled an end to the energy and environmental policies of the preceding Liberal Governments. Canada's efforts to sell energy would no longer be based on commitments to the 1997 Kyoto Protocol, to the United Nations' Framework Convention on Climate Change, or to a policy of sustainable development. Instead, Canada's energy policy is now based on free-market principles and a respect for the constitutional division of powers.

The recent changes in Canadian energy policy reflect the ideology of the new Government in the context of a federal political system. The transition from the Chrétien/Martin energy policy has been one of degree rather than direction. While the Liberals had promoted Canada as a reliable and secure source of energy to the USA, they had also signed and ratified the Kyoto Protocol and had implemented a policy of sustainable development. Furthermore, efforts to open new markets for Canadian energy in the Asia-Pacific region, especially in China, had reinforced the Liberal Government's image of opposition to the US Administration of George W. Bush (2001).

Since coming to office in January 2006, the Harper Government has given Canadian energy policy a coherence it lacked under the Liberals. For example, the Conservative Government's first Minister of the Environment, Rona Ambrose, from the oil-rich province of Alberta, announced the Government's intention to replace the Kyoto Protocol with a Canadian-devised clean air strategy. This removed the threat of massive costs being incurred through requirements to reduce 'greenhouse' gas emissions from the production of both conventional and non-conventional oil. The Conservatives have helped to expand markets for Canadian energy, although these efforts appeared to be directed towards the USA rather than towards new buyers in Asia and elsewhere. In addition, the federal Government has been forced to defend several attempts by US legislators and other officials to restrict imports of Canadian energy because of environmental concerns. While the Conservatives may not have significantly altered Canadian energy policy thus far, the changes they have implemented reflect their opposition to several of the previous Liberal governments' key environmental commitments and their own ideological inclinations toward a free market and federal disengagement from areas of provincial responsibility.

CANADA'S ENERGY SUPPLY

The vast majority of Canada's energy supply comes from hydroelectricity, nuclear power, fossil-fuel-generated electricity, oil, natural gas and coal. This list does not include several less efficient sources of energy, such as wood, animal parts and crop residues, which are still in use, but account for an increasingly small portion of total energy production. In addition, new, environmentally friendly sources, such as wind and solar power, provide a small portion of overall energy needs. In 2007, according to the National Energy Board, Canada produced an estimated 599.7 terawatts (TW) of electricity from various sources: 60.3% from hydroelectricity (361.8 TW hours—TWh), 23.6% (141.6 TWh) from thermal electricity production—burning coal, natural gas and oil—and 15.4% (92.8 TWh) from nuclear power[1]. In 2007 Canadian crude petroleum production (including both conventional and non-conventional crude) was estimated at 2.6m. barrels per day (b/d). Coal production reached an estimated 63.0m. metric tons in 2006, while marketable natural gas production was 17,000m. cu ft per day (ft ^{3}/d) in 2007.[2]

Alberta accounted for 80% of Canada's total natural gas production in 2006, followed by British Columbia at 16% and Saskatchewan at 4%. The remaining gas-producing provinces and territories, namely Nova Scotia, Ontario, the Northwest Territories, and Yukon, produced 2% of the total. The National Energy Board (NEB) estimated marketable gas reserves at 58,100,000m. cu ft at the end of 2006. Reserve additions were 7,000,000m. cu ft in 2006 and replaced 116% of annual production. In 2007 gross natural gas exports from Canada reached 10,400m. ft^3/d, while imports of gas totalled 1,300m. cu ft. In the same year crude oil production reached 404,000 cu m per day (m ^{3}/d) or 2.56m. b/d.[3] Atlantic offshore production of conventional crude was 368,617 b/d in 2007, while the western sedimentary basin produced 1,018,458 b/d. Between 2002 and 2006 additions to established reserves of conventional light and heavy crude replaced 92% of production.

Production of non-conventional crude oil in the oil sands of Western Canada reached 1,199,485 b/d or approximately 46.3% of Canada's total crude production in 2007.[4] The NEB estimated that remaining Canadian conventional crude oil and bitumen reserves stood at 205,100m. barrels in 2006. Conventional crude reserves estimates declined by 8% from 2006, while reserves in the oilsands declined by 3%, from 178,870m. barrels to 173,426m. barrels.

The largest coal deposits in Canada are located in British Columbia, Alberta and Saskatchewan. Domestic coal production totalled an estimated 63.0m. metric tons in 2006. In 2005 Canada imported 23.6m. tons of coal and exported 28.0m. tons. The largest coal-producing (and coal-consuming) province is Alberta, with output of 32m. tons in 2005, closely followed by British Columbia at 24m. tons and Saskatchewan at 10.4m tons. Most of the coal produced in Canada is used for the domestic generation of electricity. For example, in 2005 almost all of Alberta's total consumption of coal, 26m. tons, was used to generate electricity. Canada has 8,000m. tons of proven coal reserves.[5]

Beginning in the mid-1990s, electricity markets throughout North America began a process of restructuring and deregulation. Because electricity generation, transmission and distribution mainly fall under provincial jurisdiction, there has been a diversity of policies across Canada. The NEB, which has authority over interprovincial and international transmission, believed that deregulation would enhance competition, improve market efficiency and offer greater choice of services and suppliers. The goal of deregulation was, therefore, to separate the functions of provincially owned or controlled electric utilities—generation, transmission and distribution—to lower price and increase supply. Alberta and Ontario have gone the furthest in deregulation while British Columbia, Saskatchewan, New Brunswick, Nova Scotia and Québec have established wholesale markets and limited retail access.[6]

The incentive for the restructuring came from the USA. Under the authority of the Energy Policy Act 1992, the US Federal Energy Regulatory Commission established a series of regional competitive wholesale electricity markets. These new regulations also mandated that any utility selling into the US market had to provide open access transmission services as a condition of receiving transmission access from transmission-owning public utilities in the USA.[7] With large publicly owned electric utilities with excess capacity, British Columbia and Québec immediately opened their transmission lines. Alberta, with no spare capacity and private ownership of electric utilities, engaged in a deregulation process in the hopes of increasing electricity generation and the eventual sale of excess supply to the USA. The result in Alberta has been a dramatic increase in consumer prices and marginal increases in supply. Overall, electricity deregulation has not met expectations. In those provinces where it has occurred consumer prices have risen while supply has not noticeably increased.

REGULATIONS, LAWS, CONSTITUTIONS AND TREATIES

Under sections 92, 92(a), and 109 of the 1867 Constitution Act, provincial governments were given control over natural resources. However, this was not always the reality in some provinces. The introduction of the Dominion Lands Act in 1872 provided the legal framework for federal control of natural resources in the Northwest Territories, a vast tract of territory in western and northern Canada governed by the Hudson Bay Company, but transferred to the Dominion of Canada in 1870. After the provinces of Alberta and Saskatchewan were created in 1905 out of the Northwest Territories[8], the federal Government retained control over natural resources. Jurisdiction was transferred to the Prairie provinces by the Natural Resources Transfer Agreement in 1930. Under Canada's constitutional arrangements the provinces—but not the northern territories of the Yukon, the present Northwest Territories and Nunavut—have authority over most sources of energy, with the exception of nuclear energy. The 1867 Constitution Act, however, assigned the federal Government jurisdiction over interprovincial and international trade as well as other economic powers. The federal Government has used its authority to play a significant role in the Canadian energy sector. Through its regulatory arm, the NEB, it oversees international and interprovincial energy flows. The best known example of federal involvement in the energy sector was the 1980 National Energy Program (NEP). Federal acts that directly affect the energy sector include the National Energy Board Act, the Canada Labour Code, the Canada Oil and Gas Operations Act, the Canada Petroleum Resources Act, the Canadian Environmental Assessment Act, the Energy Administration Act, the Mackenzie Valley Resource Management Act, the Northern Pipeline Act, and the Species at Risk Act. Within each of these pieces of legislation there are various regulations and procedures for environmental protection, worker safety and public consultation. For example, under the Canada Oil and Gas Operations Act there are eight sets of regulations dealing with issues such as drilling, spillages and debris. Furthermore, several of the Acts affecting energy production have guidelines and guidance notes to explain the regulations.[9]

Federal energy policy focuses on five areas: resource management on frontier lands; uranium and nuclear power; interprovincial and international trade and commerce; transboundary environmental impacts; and policies of national interest, including economic development, energy security and science and technology. These areas deal mainly with interprovincial and international movements of energy and with projects that extend beyond provincial boundaries. As a result, the federal Government, through Natural Resources Canada, has enacted policies to regulate international and interprovincial trade, pipelines and electricity transmission. Furthermore, the federal Government has broad taxing and spending powers which have allowed it to have a significant role in energy development.

Federal energy policy is also framed by domestic and international treaty arrangements. International treaties include the North American Free Trade Agreement (NAFTA) between Canada, the USA, and Mexico and the Canadian-US Clean Air Agreement, which limits emissions of sulphur dioxide and nitrous oxide—the components of acid rain. Offshore revenue agreements form key parts of Canadian energy policy. Foreign domestic policies have also had an impact on Canadian energy. The most important are the USA's National Energy Policy of May 2001, the August 2005 Energy Policy Act, the Energy Independence and Security Act 2007, and the rules and regulations of the US Securities and Exchange Commission and the Federal Energy Regulatory Commission. All of these pieces of legislation, policy and regulation have a direct impact on Canadian energy policy.

THE HISTORY OF CANADIAN ENERGY POLICY

There is no simple characterization of the history of federal energy policy in Canada. The federal Government has, at times, neglected the energy sector while, at others, it has made it the centre of its economic strategy. After years of protesting at their semi-colonial status, the Prairie provinces of Alberta, Manitoba and Saskatchewan were given control over their natural resources in 1930.[10] During the Second World War the federal Government used its declaratory power under the peace, order and good government provisions of section 91 of the 1867 Constitution Act to take control of almost all energy production in Canada. After 1945 energy returned to provincial jurisdiction, although the federal Government retained control over uranium production and nuclear power. The key federal department at this time was Energy, Mines and Resources. Its focus was on the development of Canada's vast energy reserves in the north and the regulation of electric transmission and oil and gas pipelines. In the 1950s energy debate centred on the construction of interprovincial oil and gas pipelines and electricity transmission lines. The famous 1956 pipeline parliamentary debate concerned federal subsidies and the route of a transcontinental line to bring western natural gas to central and eastern Canada. The National Oil Policy of 1960 was a federal response to demands by the western petroleum-producing provinces to open markets for its crude oil and natural gas in central Canada.

It was not until the 1973 'oil shock' (when international petroleum prices rose sharply) that the federal Government took an active role in the area of energy policy. The price of a barrel of crude oil increased suddenly from approximately US $3 per barrel of West Texas Intermediate (WTI—the US 'marker' crude) to over $12 per barrel of WTI. The federal Government was mystified at the sudden shortages and price 'spike'.[11] In 1974 the Government in Ottawa, feeling it needed greater involvement in the oil and gas sector, and inspired by Canadian nationalists, created a state-owned oil company, Petro-Canada. Petro-Canada, or PetroCan, was resented by both 'oilpatch veterans' and the governments in the producing provinces. The resulting federal–provincial conflict created a lack of coherence in energy policy. Instead of working towards maximization of revenues and recovery and a coherent set of environmental regulations, the two levels of government were in a continuous conflict over the direction and control of the oil and gas industry.[12]

A second 'oil shock' came with the 1979 Iranian Revolution. Following the seizure of 63 hostages at the US embassy in

Tehran in November of that year, the USA imposed economic sanctions, froze Iranian assets in the United States and prohibited the import of Iranian oil into the country. In response, the Iranian revolutionaries simply suspended oil exports to the west. Oil and gas prices increased dramatically from just under US $20 per barrel to $40. There was also the expectation that petroleum prices would increase further.

The federal Government responded to the increase in oil prices with the introduction in 1980 of the NEP, which offered incentives for drilling in Canadian lands, increased export taxes on oil and gas and introduced a variety of 'off-oil' measures, in an effort to conserve domestic oil and gas reserves while decreasing dependence on foreign energy supplies. As well as wanting to alleviate the shock of the 1979–80 increases in the cost of oil and natural gas by keeping prices below world levels, the federal Government wished to increase its share of revenues from the petroleum industry, to continue to promote the 'Canadianization' of the industry and to have a national voice in energy affairs. Although a number of domestic companies benefited from federal initiatives, the NEP was strongly resented by the petroleum industry and by the Alberta, British Columbia, and Saskatchewan provincial governments. After a series of negotiations between the producing provinces and Ottawa, an agreement was reached concerning pricing and taxation. Furthermore, the provinces were able to secure an amendment to the existing constitutional division of powers, which strengthened provincial control over natural resources. Nevertheless, the 1982 constitutional amendments and negotiations with the federal Government maintained the basic structure of the NEP.

The Conservative Government of Brian Mulroney was elected in September 1984 partly on the promise of ending the NEP. With the signing of the Western and Atlantic Accords in early 1985, direct federal involvement in the energy sector—except for nuclear power—came to an end. The Canadian-US Free Trade Agreement (CUFTA) of 1989 guaranteed US companies and consumers national treatment and proportional access to Canadian energy sources. The effort to 'Canadianize' the industry was replaced by a policy of continental integration. Market forces would dictate the price and supply of energy while the federal Government would concern itself with environmental and competition regulation.

The election of the Liberal Government of Jean Chrétien in 1993 did little to change Canadian energy policy. Although the Liberals were committed to environmental and energy sustainability, they ratified NAFTA with the USA and Mexico. NAFTA came into force in January 1994 and extended the energy provisions of the 1989 CUFTA. Chapter 6 of NAFTA commits the USA, Mexico and Canada to free trade in energy and basic petrochemicals. This goal is to be achieved through sustained liberalization. Any form of quantitative restriction is prohibited, as are minimum and maximum export requirements and price requirements. Although there are exemptions for Mexico's state-owned oil and gas industry, no party to NAFTA 'may adopt or maintain any duty, tax or other charge on the export of any energy or basic petrochemical good' to the other signatories. Moreover, if restrictions on energy exports are enacted, this will not reduce the proportion of total export shipments. In other words, proportional access to Canada's energy supplies are guaranteed under NAFTA.[13]

THE NEW NEP AND THE KYOTO PROTOCOL

In May 2001 the Bush Administration in the USA released its National Energy Policy report. Written by the National Energy Policy Development Group (NEPDG) and chaired by Dick Cheney, the US Vice-President and former Chief Executive Officer of Halliburton (one of the world's largest oil and gas service companies), the report called for secure supplies of oil and gas and electricity for the USA through such mechanisms as enhanced recovery, increasing domestic supplies and global alliances. The NEPDG report recognized Canada's deregulated energy sector as the USA's largest energy trading partner and leading supplier of natural gas, oil and electricity. According to the report, in 2000 Canada supplied 14% of US energy needs through an integrated network of pipelines and electricity lines. Canadian energy supplies, especially natural gas and oil, were not described as a foreign source of energy, but as part of the US domestic supply. US recognition of Canada's importance as a source of energy was seen as part of the evolution of an integrated North American energy sector.

The federal Government's enthusiasm for the USA's National Energy Policy was, however, contradictory. The Liberal Chrétien Government (and its successor under Paul Martin) committed Canada to a policy of sustainable development. All relevant government departments incorporated this concept into their policies. The Sustainable Development Strategy was tabled in Parliament in 1997, but it was not until the release of Natural Resources Canada's *Energy in Canada 2000* that the concept was incorporated into energy policy. The sustainability framework had three main objectives. The first was to develop a competitive and innovative energy sector. This was to be achieved through the promotion of the long-term development of Canadian energy resources, the wise use of energy resources and maximization of economic opportunities. The second feature of the sustainability framework was to encourage environmental stewardship by mitigating the environmental impact of energy development and transportation through the integration of environmental objectives into all policies and programmes. Finally, the sustainability framework was to establish secure access to energy resources by ensuring that current and future generations of Canadians had sufficient competitively priced energy. This was to be achieved by making efficient use of existing resources.

Within this framework four domains were the focus of energy policy: rapidly developing energy markets; the environmental impact of energy development and use; nuclear power; and frontier lands oil and gas exploration and development. The federal Government recognized that the conventional energy supply of hydrocarbons and electricity was evolving to meet the demands of the North American market. Natural Resources Canada began to question the need for economic regulation as well as the appropriate roles for federal and provincial governments. Open access to the US market necessitated new regulatory approaches. By 2006 Canadian natural gas production, for example, was integrated into a North American market, which, according to the natural resources ministry, would lead to a lessening of the regulatory role for the federal Government.

Canada signed the Kyoto Protocol on 11 December 1997. In doing so, Canada committed itself to reducing greenhouse gas emissions to 6% below 1990 levels by 2012. Although adherence to the Kyoto agreement was the centrepiece of Liberal energy and environmental policies, the Chrétien Government failed to ratify it or to set out a policy framework for its implementation. It was not until Paul Martin succeeded Chrétien as Prime Minister in late 2003 that Canadians began to get a clearer picture of how the federal Government would meet its Kyoto commitments. The Kyoto Protocol was ratified by the Canadian Government on 16 February 2005. In the 2005 budget the Martin administration specified six policy instruments to meet its Kyoto goals. The first was the introduction of a C $1,000m. Clean Fund to encourage the most cost-effective projects to reduce greenhouse gases while promoting the development of a market for emissions trading. Second, the federal Government committed itself to increasing wind-power production and quadrupled the number of homes eligible for grants to reduce heating and cooling costs. Third, several tax measures were introduced, including incentives for investment in efficient and renewable energy generation equipment. Fourth, the Government allocated $300m. for a Green Municipal Fund and $5,000m. over five years from the federal gasoline tax to support sustainable infrastructure. Fifth was the creation of a Sustainable Energy Science and Technology Strategy. Finally, the federal Government pledged to pursue agreements with large final emitters and vehicle manufacturers to establish greenhouse gas reductions. It was hoped that these policies would create a clean energy future and increase the efficiency, sustainability and competitiveness of the Canadian economy.

Another piece of legislation that would have a significant impact on Canadian energy policy was the US Energy Policy Act. Approved by the US Congress in August 2005, this legislation included a section directed towards the implementation of mandatory electric reliability standards, as well as provisions to secure safe and reliable sources of energy. While not mentioned explicitly in the Act, it was widely assumed that Canada would be the source of much of the energy needed. The new legislation also gave the US Federal Energy Regulatory Commission the task of establishing and overseeing an independent Electric Reliability Organization (ERO), which would create and enforce mandatory standards for the transmission of electricity. Because of the interconnectedness of the North American electricity grid, the ERO would have a direct impact on the Canadian electricity industry. In response to the US initiative, in late 2005 the North American Electric Reliability Council began consultations with the NEB and provincial regulators to discuss how Canada's interests could best be represented on the ERO.[14]

While the Martin Government attempted to bring coherence to its energy strategy, it lacked the ability to implement it. Key personnel changes at the highest political and administrative levels impeded its ability to put an energy policy in place. The Deputy Minister of Natural Resources retired in early 2005 and was not replaced for more than four months. Furthermore, the Minister of Natural Resources, John Efford, was forced to resign because of ill health. He was replaced in late 2005 by the Minister of National Revenue, John McCallum, a Toronto area deputy with little knowledge of the energy sector. The failure to appoint the senior civil servant, as well as the absence of the minister in the department responsible for the administration's key energy and environmental policy, reinforced the Martin Government's image as dithering over the energy issue.

The Martin Government signalled a change in Canada's relationship with the USA. Although the Liberals had set closer relations with the USA as one of their priorities, disputes over a US tariff on Canada's softwood lumber exports as well as a number of other trade and security issues with the Bush Administration had forced them to re-evaluate their thinking. Part of this shift was to send the new energy minister, McCallum, to China, in an effort to secure new markets and investment for Canada's unconventional oil and natural gas. However, with its close ties to the USA, many in the energy sector were worried about offending their US customers. Canada supplied more than twice as much oil and natural gas to the USA as Saudi Arabia and Mexico combined. Furthermore, the Americans had made it clear that they were anxious to construct two Arctic pipelines for natural gas, one down the Mackenzie River Valley and the other from the North Slope of Alaska down the Alaska Highway. In both the May 2001 Energy Policy statement and the August 2005 Energy Policy Act, the USA recognized Canada as a secure and strategic source of oil and gas and electricity. The attempt to expand China's role in Canada's energy sector was seen by the Bush Administration and its Canadian allies in the energy sector as counter to US strategic interests in the North Pacific.

In December 2007 the US Congress passed, and President Bush signed, new energy legislation. While very similar to its 2005 predecessor, the Energy Independence and Security Act was designed to reduce US dependence on foreign petroleum and to increase domestic supplies through renewable energy initiatives and other programmes. Section 526 of the Act, however, has caused some consternation for Canadian energy producers and policy makers. That section of the bill, entitled Procurement and Acquisition of Alternative Fuels, stated that no 'federal agency shall enter into a contract for procurement of an alternative or synthetic fuel, including a fuel produced from nonconventional petroleum sources, for any mobility-related use, other than for research or testing, unless the contract specifies that the lifecycle greenhouse gas emissions associated with the production and combustion of the fuel supplied under the contract must, on an ongoing basis, be less than or equal to such emissions from the equivalent conventional fuel produced from conventional petroleum sources'. While this provision in the legislation appears to exclude Canadian oilsands from the US market—the production of unconventional oil from bitumen produces amounts of greenhouse gases far in excess of that found in conventional oil production—both industry and government officials have been given assurances that Canadian oil from the oilsands will not be excluded. In June 2008 another threat to the Canadian oil and gas industry appeared in the form of a resolution of the US Conference of Mayors, which called for guidelines 'to track the life-cycle impact of different fossil fuels'. Member cities were also urged 'to stop using unconventional sources of energy' when their production caused excessive carbon emissions. Furthermore, the resolution stated that 'the production of tarsands oil from Canada emits approximately three times the carbon dioxide pollution per barrel as does conventional oil production and significantly damages Canada's Boreal forest ecosystem'.[15]

THE NEW CONSERVATIVES

On 23 January 2006 Canadians elected a minority Conservative Government. Led by Harper, a one-time member of Parliament for the right-wing populist Reform Party and a past President of the National Citizens' Coalition, a right-wing lobby group, the Conservatives campaigned on a platform of accountability and transparency in government. However, the Conservatives were denied a majority government: Harper won only 124 seats in the 308-member House of Commons and this was, at best, a precarious minority.

Even though the Conservatives faced a very fractious and divided Parliament, they had several advantages. First, the country had been through two general election campaigns in 18 months; there was no desire among voters or the major parties to have another election in the near future. Second, the Liberals, in official opposition, were divided and without a leader. Paul Martin's resignation following the election set in place a lengthy and divisive leadership race with no clear frontrunner. Consumed by the search for a new leader and with lingering animosity between the Chrétien and Martin factions, the Liberals were in no position to bring down the Government. The other two parties in the House, the New Democratic Party and the Bloc Québecois, faced a variety of issues and were not inclined to defeat the new Government. Third, the Conservatives had campaigned with a simple five-point agenda, which won them praise in the media and with voters.

Although the new Harper Government managed its five-point agenda through the House of Commons, it was vague on a number of other issues, including energy. It was understood that the Conservatives were opposed to the Kyoto Protocol and any federal intrusion into areas of provincial jurisdiction, including oil and gas and other energy sources. Beyond this it was unclear what direction—if any—the new Government would take in energy policy. The first Conservative budget, presented in 2006, for example, contained no explicit mention of energy. There was only a promise to reduce carbon and other emissions by providing C $1,300m. for public transit infrastructure and a tax credit for bus passes. No mention was made of Canada's Kyoto commitments or any other energy initiative.

The new Minister of Natural Resources, Gary Lunn, a lawyer from southern Vancouver Island with experience in the resource sector, has had little to say publicly about energy. However, an outline of Conservative policy has emerged. While in opposition the Conservatives had been opposed to the Kyoto Protocol for several reasons. First, many in the Conservative caucus, including the Prime Minister, expressed scepticism that global warming was occurring and, if it was, believed that human beings were not responsible for it. Second, the Government argued that the rejection by the Bush Administration of the Kyoto Protocol made any effort by Canada to reduce greenhouse gas emissions economically unfeasible. Meeting its Kyoto commitments would put Canada at a comparative economic disadvantage with its largest trading partner. Moreover, the oil and gas producing provinces—with the exception of British Columbia—of Newfoundland and Labrador, Saskatchewan, and Alberta believed that they would suffer a disproportionate burden of the costs of reducing greenhouse gases if the Protocol were to be implemented. These provincial governments were concerned that the added costs of greenhouse gas reduction would price non-conventional and offshore reserves out of the North American and world markets and thereby reduce provincial revenues. Thousands of millions of dollars in planned investment could be lost and the future economic prosperity of the provinces might be threatened. In western producing provinces the Kyoto Protocol has been compared to the widely unpopular 1980 NEP.

In September 2006 Lunn announced that the Government would put in place a 'made in Canada' plan for reducing greenhouse gases and ensuring clean air, water, land and energy. As part of the as yet unannounced environmental plan, Lunn put an end to 15 climate change-related programmes. Among these were a project designed to assess the regulatory and economic issues related to the interprovincial electricity trade, a study of the feasibility of carbon sequestration to help offset greenhouse gas emissions, and the one-ton challenge, the former Liberal Government's high profile advertising campaign to encourage Canadians to reduce their greenhouse gas emissions.

In April 2007 the new Minister of the Environment, John Baird, announced mandatory targets to reduce greenhouse gas emissions and air pollution. The goal was to reduce greenhouse gas emissions by 150m. metric tons per year by 2020 as well as to impose fuel efficiency standards on cars and light trucks beginning with the 2011 model year.[16] The new policy was, however, vague. It lacked any enforcement mechanism and did not provide a framework in which the stated goals could be achieved. The details of the new environmental policies were released in March 2008 in a document entitled *Turning the Corner*. The aim of the document was to strengthen the regulatory framework of April 2007. The Harper Government required all oilsands upgraders that come into operation after 2012 to meet new standards on carbon capture by 2018; all coal-fired electric generation plants that come into operation after 2012 were required to meet the same emission standards by 2018; and the new policy established a clean electricity task force to work with industry and the provinces to meet an additional 25m. tons reduction in greenhouse gases by 2020. The new regulatory framework was criticized as ineffective. Its detractors claimed that the Conservative Government had abandoned any effort immediately to meet its Kyoto commitments and had, instead, produced a plan that would reduce greenhouse gas emissions in the future. The Conservatives' approach to air quality issues closely followed the US and Australian models, which have done little to reduce greenhouse gases.[17]

While the Conservative Government had the support of the oil and gas industry and large segments of the electricity generating sector, the provinces of Alberta and Saskatchewan also supported the new federal energy and environmental initiatives. With economies dependent on the oil and gas industry, the two provincial governments feared an economic slowdown if restrictions were placed on carbon dioxide emissions. On the other hand, several provinces strongly opposed any attempt to dilute Canada's international commitments to reducing greenhouse gases. Manitoba and Québec—both with large hydroelectric capacities—supported Kyoto and have, along with Ontario and British Columbia, joined the Western Climate Initiative, a group of eight western states that have agreed to substantial reductions in greenhouse gas emissions. Additionally, the province of British Columbia introduced a comprehensive greenhouse gas reduction policy on 1 July 2008, as well as the first carbon tax in Canada and a number of incentives to reduce dependence on fossil fuels. The government of Québec announced that it would proceed with the implementation of the Kyoto Protocol without the support of the federal Government. The climate change programmes of both British Columbia and Québec produced political problems and opportunities for the Harper Government. The negative reaction to British Columbia's carbon tax allowed the Conservatives to attack the federal Liberal Party's carbon tax proposals in the national elections of October 2008. The Liberals lost four seats in these elections in that province, while the Conservatives gained five. In Québec the Conservatives failed to expand on their existing 10 seats, due, in part, to the Harper Government's failure to act more forcefully on the question of climate change.

Furthermore, the federal equalization programme has become an issue in the debate over energy policy in Canada. Equalization was a constitutionally entrenched programme designed 'to ensure that provincial governments have sufficient revenues to provide reasonably comparable services at reasonably comparable levels of taxation'. The federal Government gives those provinces that are not able to raise sufficient revenue additional transfers. The complicated formula for calculating equalization payments is based on a five-province average that excludes the wealthiest and poorest provinces. With thousands of millions of dollars in surplus oil and gas revenues, the province of Alberta has opposed efforts made by the other provinces and the national Government to include energy and resource revenues in the equalization formula. Although equalization is a federal programme, the Alberta government has vowed to fight 'tooth and nail' against any attempt to tap into the province's enormous energy wealth. This debate is a reflection of regional division within the Canadian federation caused by enormous oil and gas windfalls of the past several years.

The outline of Conservative energy strategy was articulated at a North American heads of government summit in Cancún, Mexico, in late March 2006. Prime Minister Harper, US President Bush and Mexican President Vicente Fox emphasized the importance of collaborating on energy technologies and facilitating energy markets in order to enhance security. This message of increased North American co-operation was reiterated in a meeting of energy ministers in Washington, DC, in early May. Canadian natural resources minister Lunn stated that Canada, the USA and Mexico were 'committed to working together to improve our understanding of the distinct energy capacities of our nations, and to sharing our expertise in key areas such as energy technology'.[18]

The Conservative Government's commitment to a free market was evident in the July 2006 speech Harper gave to a meeting of the Canada-United Kingdom Chamber of Commerce, in which the Prime Minister stated that investors 'have recognized Canada's emergence as a global energy powerhouse—the emerging "energy superpower" our government intends to build.' He also reminded his audience that Canada has the second largest oil reserves in the world—the oilsands. These enormous reserves are exceeded only by Saudi Arabia. Canadian production was expected to reach 4m. b/d by 2015, two-thirds of which will be from the oilsands. He made it clear that Canada was 'a stable, reliable, producer in a volatile, unpredictable world.' Canada's energy policy, he stated, was based on the idea of the free exchange of 'products based on competitive market principles, not self-serving monopolistic political strategies'.[19]

The Prime Minister and the Minister of Natural Resources now seldom refer to Canada as an emerging energy superpower, a clean energy superpower, or an energy superpower. They do, however, continue to speak of the importance of energy to the Canadian and North American economies. In a speech made at the Newfoundland and Labrador Oil and Gas Industries Association Annual Conference in June 2008 Lunn outlined what he described as Canada's unique situation. Canada, he stated, is the world's second largest generator of hydroelectricity, the world's numberone producer of uranium, and contains immense petroleum resources, which include 14% of the global oil reserves as well a vast stores of natural gas. Every region, Lunn claimed, has 'a role to play in our reaching this goal of becoming an energy superpower'.[20]

CONCLUSION

Since coming to power in early 2006, the Conservative Government of Stephen Harper has not made any major changes to Canadian energy policy. As with its Liberal predecessors, the Harper Government was committed to selling Canadian energy resources on regional markets. Nevertheless, there has been a change in emphasis. For example, the Conservatives have announced an alternative climate change strategy to the Kyoto protocol as well as a 'made in Canada' clean air strategy. Furthermore, the Conservatives have abandoned Liberal attempts to diversify Canadian energy markets. While the Liberal governments of the 1990s and first decade of the 2000s made an effort to lessen dependence on the USA, the new Conservative administration has embraced the idea to the exclusion of alternatives. This was evident in the cooling of relations between Canada and China, as well as in Harper's criticism of Russian energy policies. Conservative energy policy reflected the broader ideological orientation of the party. The Government is committed to closer North American economic and political integration as well as to a decentralized State. Its free-market ideology fitted in with the Bush Administration's emphasis on meeting increased demand with increased supply. Representatives of Barack Obama, the Democratic candidate for the US presidency, have stated that, should he be elected, they will implement a new strategy to reduce greenhouse gases in order to mitigate the effects of global warming. Furthermore, several states, as well as the US Conference of Mayors, have proposed restrictions on Canadian oil imports that would prohibit the importation of oil that exceeds the carbon emissions from conventional supplies. Canadian producers are concerned that this prohibition will affect exports to the USA. As a result, Canadian diplomats and trade officials have lobbied the US Government to exclude Canadian oil exports from any future import restrictions.

There were three identifiable trends in Canadian energy policy under the Conservative Government. The first was the abandonment of the Kyoto Protocol. While the Conservatives have not officially ended Canada's commitments (mainly for political reasons) to Kyoto, they have made evident their dislike of the agreement and proposed alternatives. The second shift in Canadian energy policy was a move towards North American energy integration and away from efforts to diversify Canada's energy customers. The federal Government has not acted on Russian proposals to distribute liquified natural gas in North America and has actively discouraged Chinese plans to invest in the oilsands of western Canada. This change of direction in Canada's foreign and energy policy was based as much on ideology as on market considerations, despite rhetoric about free markets. While the Canadian Government has shifted its focus away from global energy markets, it has emphasized North American energy integration and Canada's role as a stable and secure source of energy in the region. There has been an emphasis on the North American Energy Working Group, a forum for co-operation on energy issues ranging from regulatory co-operation to the oil sands. The Working Group was responsible for implementing the commitments made under the Security and Prosperity Partnership of North America. Third, the Minister of Natural Resources has made numerous statements about the need to streamline the regulatory process in order to bring new supplies of energy to market. He has also emphasized a need for innovative, green technologies. However, there has been no effort on his part positively to act on these issues.

Prime Minister Harper's declaration that Canada is now an 'energy superpower' may be an exaggeration. In the USA, the incoming administration, as well as various city and state governments, pose a potential threat to Canadian oil and other energy exports. For its part, the Canadian Government has emphasized the importance of access to the USA. Canada's vast energy resources—from uranium to hydroelectricity—have an increasingly important role to play in North American and global energy markets. The question remains, however, whether an ideologically committed right-wing Government could shape an energy policy that would be able to adapt to a complex and changing energy environment.

FOOTNOTES

[1] National Energy Board. Canadian Energy Overview 2007. Calgary, AB, National Energy Board, 2008.

[2] Canadian Association of Petroleum Producers Oil and Natural Gas Production, 2008.

[3] Ibid.

[4] Ibid.

[5] Coal Association of Canada, *Coal Economics*. Calgary, AB, Coal Association of Canada.

[6] National Energy Board. *Annual Report to Parliament 2004*. Calgary, AB, National Energy Board, 2005, pp. 23–27.

[7] Doern, G. B., and Gattinger, M. *Power Switch: Energy Regulatory Governance in the Twenty-First Century*. Toronto, ON, University of Toronto Press, 2003, pp. 71–91.

[8] Breen, D. H. *Alberta's Petroleum Industry and the Conservation Board*. Edmonton, AB, University of Alberta Press and the Energy Resources Conservation Board, 1993.

[9] National Energy Board. *Annual Report to Parliament 2004*. Calgary, AB, National Energy Board, 2005.

[10] Whitaker, R. *The Government Party. Organizing and Financing the Liberal Party of Canada, 1930–58*. Toronto, ON, University of Toronto Press, 1977, pp. 12–13.

[11] Foster, P. *The Blue-Eyed Sheiks: The Canadian Oil Establishment*. Toronto, ON, Collins, 1979, p. 51.

[12] Fossum, J. E. *Oil, the State, and Federalism: The Rise and Demise of Petro-Canada as a Statist Impulse*. Toronto, ON, University of Toronto Press, 1997, p. 10.

[13] Supply and Services Canada. *Canada, North American Free Trade Agreement*. Ottawa, ON, 1993, chapter 6.

[14] National Energy Board. *Annual Report to Parliament 2005*. Calgary, AB, National Energy Board, 2006, p. 29.

[15] DeSouza, M. 'U.S. Mayors Take Aim at Oil Sands Sector'. *National Post*, 24 June 2008, FP5.

[16] Environment Canada. 'Canada's New Government Announces Mandatory Industrial Targets to Tackle Climate Change and Reduce Air Pollution'. News release, 26 April 2007.

[17] *Canada: Turning the Corner. Regulatory Framework for Industrial Greenhouse Gas Emissions*. Ottawa, ON, Environment Canada, 2008.

[18] Natural Resources Canada. 'Natural Resources Minister Lunn Meets with U.S. and Mexican Counterparts to Discuss North American Energy'. Media release, 4 May 2006.

[19] Harper, S. 'We Intend to Build "Energy Superpower"'. *Financial Post*, 29 July 2006.

[20] Lunn, The Hon. Gary. Transcript of Speech. Newfoundland and Labrador Oil and Gas Industries Association 2008 Annual Conference, St. John's Newfoundland, 2008.

CANADIAN MANUFACTURING AND CONSTRUCTION

SANDY MARKWICK

The importance of manufacturing to the Canadian economy is characteristic of advanced industrial nations. Accounting for 15.2% of gross domestic product (GDP) in 2007, manufacturing was a more significant contributor to Canadian output than primary activities (agriculture, forestry, fisheries and minerals), but its share of GDP was eclipsed by the services sector, including utilities, financial services, public administration, transportation and trade, which accounted for 72% of economic activity. The contribution to GDP from manufacturing in the other economies of the group of seven (G7) leading Western industrialized countries in 2001 ranged between 14% and 21%. The construction sector accounted for 6.0% of Canadian GDP in 2007.

Given the dominance of trade with the USA, Canada adopted the North American Industrial Classification System (NAICS) to analyse economic activity by sector and sub-sector. NAICS defined manufacturing as comprising those activities that create new products, finished or semi-processed, out of inputs involving some chemical or physical transformation, including assembly. Some exceptions to the broad definition were construction, post-harvest agricultural processing and product assembly carried out by retailers.

Between 1991 and 2001 Canada was the only G7 country to increase the relative importance of its manufacturing sector, helped by the signing of the North American Free Trade Agreement (NAFTA—which came into effect in 1994) with the USA and Mexico and by the historically low Canadian dollar during this period.

THE ECONOMIC IMPACT OF MANUFACTURING

Canadian manufacturing was highly integrated with US industrial production, and a considerable proportion of manufactured goods was exported south as links in North American supply chains. The sector was vulnerable to diminished demand from US importers, which in the 2000s stemmed from uncertainties in the US economy and from the strength of the Canadian dollar, particularly against its US counterpart. From 2002 the Canadian dollar appreciated against its US counterpart by 38%; in September 2007 the Canadian dollar surpassed the US dollar in value for the first time since 1976. Manufacturing GDP in 2007 amounted to C $233,418m. in current prices, representing a 0.9% contraction in output during the year. Manufacturing sales were static.

The most important manufacturing sub-sectors in terms of output and sales were transportation equipment, chemical products, food, wood products, fabricated metals, primary metals, machinery and paper.

Modest growth in manufacturing in 2007 followed recent years of similarly modest or negative growth: up 1.3% in 2006, 0.9% in 2005 and 2.0% in 2004, and down by 0.4% in 2003. In 2001 a contraction in manufacturing output of 4.7% was a result of recession in the USA in that year. In part a reflection of recent stagnation, the manufacturing sector's contribution to GDP had fallen since 1997, when it accounted for 17.4% of total output in the economy.

In terms of manufacturing sales, the worst performing sub-sector in 2007 was wood products, down by C $5,496.6m. or 18% during the year. Another poor performer, in terms of the value of sales, was transportation equipment, down $2,724.9m. (7.5%). Sales were also slightly down during the year in the paper, printing materials, plastics and rubber, beverage and tobacco products, chemicals, computer and electronics sub-sectors. The best performing sub-sectors in terms of sales were petroleum and coal products, up $5,205.3m. during 2007 (an 8.5% increase) and food, up $2,132.4m. (3.0%). More modest increases in sales were posted by sub-sectors including non-metallic minerals, primary and fabricated metals, machinery and electrical equipment.

Sales are an important indicator of manufacturing activity and are a function of the price of goods as well as the volume. However, by including the gross value of goods sold, these figures ignore the costs of inputs—of raw materials, semi-processed materials and machinery—that are required in manufacturing. The GDP reflects the added value gained as a result of the manufacturing process and is a better reflection of the overall contribution of industrial sectors to the economy as a whole. In 2003 manufacturing employees added C $107,300m. of value, on average, across the sector.

In addition to the direct impact of manufacturing activity on the economy in terms of contribution to GDP and employment, there is a large indirect impact of manufacturing activity on the rest of the economy. Manufacturing was the largest economic multiplier of all sectors in the Canadian economy. Each C $1.00 of output generated $3.05 of economic activity associated with the primary and intermediate inputs required and with the services attached to manufactured products.

EMPLOYMENT

Stagnation in overall manufacturing output was reflected in the size of the work-force employed. In 2007 there were 2.04m. workers employed in Canadian manufacturing, 12.1% of the labour force and the lowest share of the total work-force in decades. Close to a net 250,000 manufacturing jobs were lost in 2002–07, with 265,000 fewer jobs in the industrial heartland of Ontario and Québec offset by a gain of 18,400 in the rest of Canada. Manufacturing employment of 2.3m. in 2002 comprised 15.8% of the total work-force, up marginally from 15.6% in 1992. Manufacturing led the recovery and a decade of growth after the 1990–91 recession. Some 500,000 jobs were created during the 1990s at a compound annual growth rate (CAGR) of 2.0%, compared with 1.9% for the economy as a whole. Small and medium-sized enterprises (SMEs) accounted for the bulk of manufacturing businesses in Canada. Establishments employing fewer than 50 employees represented 84% of firms, while just 3% employed 200 people or more. SMEs generated just 10% of manufacturing output, compared with 62% from larger businesses.

PRODUCTIVITY

Improvements in productivity, as well as stagnation in the sector and commensurate market uncertainties, were also behind the fall in manufacturing jobs from 2002. Using the measure of real GDP per hour, labour productivity in the manufacturing sector increased in 1997–2002 from C $37.60 to $39.90, representing a CAGR of 1.2%. During this period the manufacturing sector measured higher growth than the economy as a whole, where productivity grew from $29.57 to $32.28. Labour productivity in the manufacturing sector increased strongly in 2004 and 2005, by 3.5% and 5.7%, respectively. Employment of 'production workers' engaged in core manufacturing activities, relative to 'non-production workers' carrying out auxiliary activities, increased from 75% to 81% between 1992 and 2001.

Output per employee fell in 2006 across all manufacturing sub-sectors, following two years of growth. Falling output lowered capacity utilization. Manufacturing operations had a capacity utilization rate of 76.7% in mid-2008, slightly below the economy as a whole (78.9%). Utilization rates in manufacturing declined from 83.3% in July 2006. The highest uses of industrial capacity were in primary metals (91.7%) and computers and electronics (87.8%), while the lowest were found in plastics and rubbers (63.9%) and wood products (65.0%).

Higher costs squeezed profits in the manufacturing sector. During 2000–04 the average selling price of manufactured goods fell 2.5%, while wage rates rose by 17.4%, raw materials by 45.4%, payroll taxes and benefits by 26.4%, electricity by 54.2% and industrial fuel by 138.5%.

INVESTMENT

Increased labour productivity after 2004 stemmed partly from increased capital investment in manufacturing—on construction, machinery and equipment. Manufacturing investment was up 6.7% in 2005 and an estimated 3.4% in 2006. A strong Canadian dollar encouraged capital investment by making imports cheaper. The increases followed a dip in investment levels in 2001–04 and, before that, only modest levels of investment since the early 1990s (with some exceptions, notably an investment 'boom' in 2000). Capital investment in manufacturing grew by a CAGR of 3.0% between 1992 and 2001, slower than all industries combined over the same period. Consequently, the manufacturing sector's share of total capital investment in the Canadian economy declined from 14% in 1992 to 11% in 2002. The relatively low investment growth rate in manufacturing during this period led to the share of capital stock associated with manufacturing declining from 12.9% to 11.5% over the same time. The share of capital investment spent on machinery and equipment stock fell from 33.3% to 24.7%.

Offsetting a relatively low level of capital investment was a relatively high level of investment in research and development compared with other industries. An estimated 70% of total research and development was spent by manufacturing companies, with information and communication technologies (ICT) manufacturing companies leading the way. Using a ratio of research and development expenditure to sectoral GDP, manufacturing was by some distance the sector with most investment in research and development of any in the Canadian economy, at 3.6% in 2007 compared with an average of 1.1% for the economy as a whole.

FOREIGN TRADE

In 2006 manufactured goods made up 70.4% of Canada's merchandise exports. This represented a slight decline on recent years, from 77.0% in 2001, largely owing to lower demand from the USA and sharp rises in international petroleum prices, which had increased the share of export revenues stemming from energy products. Total manufacturing export revenues grew marginally (by 0.5%) in 2007, to C $317,270m. Manufacturing export growth slowed after 2003, but this followed a period of rapid expansion at a CAGR of 9.3% from $125,000m. to $305,000m. between 1992 and 2002. During this period the manufacturing sector became increasingly focused on export markets, with the ratio of manufacturing shipments for export increasing from 45% to 56%.

The US market eclipsed all others in importance as a destination for Canada's manufacturing exports. In 2007 79.1% of sectoral exports were shipped to the USA. Economic slowdown in the USA reduced its share of Canadian exports from 84.3% in 2005 and 87.7% in 2002. The second most important export market for Canadian manufacturing in 2007 was the United Kingdom, the destination for 2.7% of the value of sector exports, followed by the People's Republic of China, Japan and Mexico. In 2006 the United Kingdom had displaced Japan, which had been the most important export market after the USA during 2002–05.

The introduction of free trade with the USA in the 1990s (notably following the US-Canadian Free Trade Agreement of 1988) boosted Canadian manufactured exports. However, increasing integration of production and trade with the USA made Canadian exports vulnerable to the performance of the US economy and to fluctuations in exchange rates.

The main sub-categories of manufacturing exports were: industrial goods and materials, led by chemicals, plastics and fertilizers, and metals and alloys, which earned C $104,300m. in 2007; machinery and equipment, which earned $95,500m.; and automotive products, which earned export revenues of $77,500m.

Despite significant manufacturing export revenues, Canada ran a manufacturing trade deficit. The value of sectoral imports in 2007 was C $349,649m. leading to a deficit of $32,379m. The deficit in that year was double the deficit in 2005. During 1992–2002 imports grew at a CAGR of 9.1%, which, although slower than export growth, led to wider manufacturing trade deficits in absolute terms, such was the scale of import costs compared with export revenues.

As well as being the main destination for Canada's manufacturing exports, the USA was also the principal source of manufacturing imports. Of total manufacturing imports in 2007, 56.0% came from the USA, 11.0% from the People's Republic of China, 4.9% from Mexico, 4.4% from Japan and 3.2% from Germany. The US share of imports had declined from 64.3% in 2002. The largest growth as a source of imports was China, which more than doubled the value of imports since 2002, when its share of total manufacturing imports was 5.0%. Canada ran a manufacturing deficit with China amounting to C $30,625m. in 2007, up from $12,515m. in 2002. Canada was in manufacturing trade deficit with its NAFTA partner, Mexico, valued at $11,522m. in 2007. Canada registered other significant deficits in its manufacturing trade account with Japan ($9,984m.) and Germany ($8,442m.).

Canada registered a manufacturing trade surplus of C $54,999m. with the USA in 2007, down 13.7% during the year. The next largest trade surpluses resulted from trade with Norway ($3,038m. in 2006) and the United Kingdom ($1,790m.). Apart from the USA, the United Kingdom and Russia (surplus of $528m. in 2007), Canada ran manufacturing trade deficits with all its G8 (i.e., G7 plus Russia) partners.

Manufactures represented 86.0% of all imports of goods in 2007. Canada ran trade surpluses in resource-based manufacturing industries where Canada had natural advantages, including primary metals (a C $17,535m. surplus in 2007), paper manufacturing ($13,665m.) and wood ($9,917m.). The largest deficit was in computers and electronics, the net cost to Canada being $21,713m., the bulk of which was owed to the People's Republic of China. Other principal deficits were in machinery ($12,132m.), chemicals ($7,819m.) and fabricated metals ($5,829m.). The most dramatic change in the sectoral trade balance was the deficit in transportation equipment, amounting to $6,281m. in 2007, from a surplus of $9,136m. in 2004. The change stemmed from declining demand in the USA, down to $76,942m. in 2007, compared with $95,728m. in 2002.

REGIONAL DIVERSITY

Canada's national manufacturing profile obscured significant variation between Canada's 10 provinces and three territories. Canada's manufacturing heartland, its traditional industrial base, has historically been in Ontario and Québec.

However, from the turn of the 21st century there was a small, but notable, shift away from Ontario and Québec towards the resource-based manufacturing industries located in the western provinces. Manufacturing shipments from Ontario and Québec fell by 3.6% between 2000 and 2005, while those from the four Western provinces of British Columbia, Alberta, Saskatchewan and Manitoba increased from 18.5% of total shipments to 20.6%. The Atlantic provinces increased their share from 4.0% to 4.8%.

Ontario

In 2007 Ontario accounted for 37.3% of Canada's manufacturing GDP and 48.0% of the value of manufacturing sales. Ontario accounted for almost one-half of Canada's manufacturing jobs (46.5% in 2007) and 39.8% of manufacturing operations. There were 950,600 manufacturing jobs in Ontario in 2007, representing 14.4% of the province's total work-force across all sectors. Manufacturing contributed 18.3% of Ontario's GDP in 2007, down from 19.1% in 2006 and 23.4% in 2000.

As the province with the most industrial activity in Canada, Ontario reflected the stagnation of the sector at national level. The performance of manufacturing in Ontario in 2006 was worse relative to the manufacturing sector nation-wide, because the province was more integrated into US manufacturing operations than was the case elsewhere. As such, Ontario was particularly vulnerable to a downturn in demand from the USA. Manufacturing output in Ontario contracted by 2.2% in 2007, following a fall of 3.9% in 2006. Manufacturing's contribution to provincial GDP had fallen from a 20.7% share in 2003. Recession in the provincial manufacturing sector continued into 2008.

The value of total manufacturing sales in Ontario fell by 1.5% in 2007, following a decline of 4.0% in 2006. Much of the decline in the value of manufacturing sales was accounted for by the performance of the transportation equipment sub-sector, revenues of which had declined by 3.4% to C $93,265.8m., in addition to the 9.3% decrease a year earlier. This sub-sector dominated manufacturing in Ontario, accounting for 23.7% of provincial manufacturing GDP and 32.0% of shipments in 2007. The correlation between the performance of total manufacturing shipments and transportation equipment shipments was close over the five-year period from 2002 to 2006, when the value of manufacturing shipments fell at an average annual rate of 0.9%. The decline was overwhelmingly the result of a commensurate fall in transportation equipment shipments.

Vehicles and vehicle parts dominated the transportation equipment sector. Automobile-related sub-sectors alone represented 21.0% of provincial manufacturing GDP in 2006. Heavily dependent on exports to the USA, demand was undermined by high energy costs and the appreciation of the Canadian dollar, as well as by fears of a recession in the USA, which affected consumer confidence. GDP in the Ontario automobile industry fell by 3.0% in 2007 and by 3.9% in 2006.

Other principal manufacturing sectors in Ontario were: the combined primary and fabricated metal products sectors, which contributed 13.9% of sectoral GDP in 2006; followed by food, beverage and tobacco products (11.3%); chemical and petroleum products (10.1%); and electrical and electronic products (9.6%).

The 2006 fall in output within the vehicles and vehicle parts sector was the largest in absolute terms in Ontario, representing C $1,004m. This was followed by combined primary and fabricated metals, which was down $694m. (5.6%), and paper and printing, which was down $548m. (9.0%). Two other troubled sub-sectors, plastics and rubber products and textiles, clothing and leather, saw output fall by 11.6% and 6.1%, respectively, in 2006. The best-performing manufacturing sector in Ontario in 2006 was transportation equipment, excluding the automobile industry. This sub-sector grew by 13.2%.

The Ontario Government sought to address the problems facing manufacturing in central Canada with strategic initiatives and investment. For example, the Ontario Automotive Investment Strategy (OAIS) leveraged C $7,000m. of investments in highly skilled jobs in the car industry. Meanwhile, the Advanced Manufacturing Investment Strategy (AMIS), another provincial government initiative, was launched in 2005 to provide interest-free loans to support investments in technology and innovation.

In all of the most important sub-sectors of manufacturing, Ontario had the largest share of establishments in operation. For example, 47.8% of Canada's machinery manufacturing establishments were based in Ontario, 47.7% of Canada's computer and electronics sub-sector was based in the province, while in paper, plastics and rubber the figures were 47.7%, 45.7% and 45.6%, respectively. Even where Ontario had among its lowest share of manufacturing establishments, such as wood (27%) and food (31%), there were more firms in operation than in any other province.

Québec

Manufacturing accounted for 19.4% of Québec's total GDP in 2006, making it Canada's most manufacturing-intensive province. Manufacturing GDP in Québec in 2006 was estimated at C $54,753m., or 23.4% of national manufacturing output. Manufacturing sales were valued at $148,260m., or 24.4% of the national total in 2007, consistent with a steady share in recent years. There were 543,800 workers employed in manufacturing in Québec in 2007, 26.6% of jobs in the sector across Canada as a whole and 14.1% of the province's entire workforce across all sectors.

Québec's manufacturing sales grew by 1.1% in 2007, outperforming the national average. The most important contributors in terms of sales performance were fabricated metals (up 11.6%), food (6.0%), primary metals (5.2%), petroleum and coal products (3.0%) and transportation equipment (2.0%). These increases were offset by declining sales in wood products (down by 10.1%), computer and electronics (down 7.6%), plastics and rubber products (4.5%) and chemicals (4.0%). Contraction in these sectors in Québec largely reflected the national trend.

The largest contributor to Québec's GDP among manufacturing sub-sectors was transportation equipment, output of which was valued at C $6,752m. in 2005, or 11.7% of the province's total manufacturing output. This was closely followed by primary metals, which contributed 10.5% of Québec's manufacturing GDP. Within the transportation equipment sector, aircraft and aircraft engines were particularly important. In 2007 13% of Québec's manufacturing exports were related to the province's aerospace and aeronautics industries. The province ranked sixth behind the USA, the United Kingdom, France, Germany and Japan in terms of aerospace production, with leading companies operational including Bombardier, Pratt & Whitney and CAE. Aircraft and parts exports from Québec were the province's fastest growing exports in 1988–2006.

Western Provinces

In the Western provinces (British Columbia, Alberta, Saskatchewan and Manitoba) manufacturing sales stagnated in 2007. Strong demand for natural resources led to increases in international prices, particularly for petroleum, which increased the value of resource-based manufacturing shipments. The Western provinces were rich in natural resources and industrial activity was relatively resource-based compared with Ontario and Québec.

The four provinces of the west combined accounted for 22.2% of nationwide manufacturing sales, compared with 18.0% in 2002. There were 433,600 people employed in manufacturing in the Western provinces, equivalent to 21.2% of total manufacturing workers across all of Canada.

Alberta was the principal focus of manufacturing in the west. Shipments from Alberta were valued at C $65,592.5m. in 2007, a 1.9% increase over the previous year, following faster growth in the two previous years of 7.1% and 14.9%. Alberta accounted for 10.8% of national manufacturing shipments, compared with 8.0% in 2002. The most important sub-sectors, in terms of value of sales, were petroleum products (at $15,065m. in 2007) and chemicals ($12,441m.).

Manufacturing GDP in Alberta contributed an estimated 9.6% to the provincial economy during the late 1990s and early 2000s. During this period the chemical products sub-sector was the most important, followed by food manufacturing. In 2006 manufacturing GDP was valued at C $17,760m., 7.4% of total provincial GDP. Between 1990 and 2003 manufacturing in Alberta grew 4.1% faster than the provincial economy generally.

British Columbia was the next most important manufacturing province in the west after Alberta. British Columbia accounted for 7.1% of nationwide manufacturing shipments in 2007, a share that had been stable since 2002. Shipments grew by 1.9% in 2007, following a 3.1% increase in 2006.

Manufacturing GDP in British Columbia amounted to C $16,400m. in 2006, equivalent to 11.0% of provincial GDP and an estimated 7.2% of nationwide manufacturing GDP. Manufacturing GDP grew by 2.9% in 2006.

In 2007 the largest sub-sector in British Columbia was wood products manufacturing, which earned revenues of C $7,993m. in 2007, down 24.4% during the year, the largest decline of any sub-sector. A fall in lumber (timber) prices undermined the value of British Columbia's manufacturing shipments. In 2004 wood-based products manufacturing had seen shipments grow by 6.6%, above the national average of 4.2%. British Columbia was the source of close to 50% of all Canada's wood products exports. Primary and fabricated metals output increased 16.6% in 2006, making it the best performing sub-sector.

The contributions of the Prairie provinces of Manitoba and Saskatchewan to national manufacturing output in 2006 were 2.4% and 1.8%, respectively, although the trend in both cases was towards an increasing share, up from 2.1% and 1.3%, respectively, in 2002.

Manitoba's manufacturing sales increased by 2.7% in 2007, following an increase of 8.3% in 2006. The most important sub-sector in Manitoba in terms of the value of manufacturing shipments was food, accounting for 22.3% of all sectoral shipments in the province, followed by primary metals, with a 19.0% share. The dominance of food manufacturing industries reflected Manitoba's important agricultural sector, including 7.7m. ha (19m. acres) of land used for crops or livestock, supplying 15% of Canada's total agricultural production. In transport equipment manufacturing, bus and coach building was the predominant activity. This sector was dominated by two large firms, Motor Coach Industries and New Flyer Industries, supplying the North American market. This sub-sector increased sales by 16.4% in 2007 despite uncertainties in the USA and an unfavourable exchange rate for exports south.

Saskatchewan's manufacturing sales increased by 3.6% in 2007, to C $10,435.8m., following annual growth rates of 4.4% in 2006 and 5.4% in 2005. The main contributor to growth was the machinery sector which earned revenues of $1,006.6m. in 2007, $214.5m. (27.1%) more than the previous year. The next major contributors to growth in sales were chemicals, which earned $172.6m. (18.6%) more in 2007 than in 2006, and food, which was up $117.7m. (5.1%). Growth in these sectors was offset by falls in sales of wood products, down $228.3m. (43.7%) and paper down $100.4m. (38.9% down). Food manufacturing was by some distance the most important manufacturing sub-sector in absolute terms, accounting for 23.3% of sectoral revenues in the province in 2007. The importance of food manufacturing, as with Manitoba, reflected the importance of agriculture to Saskatchewan.

Atlantic Provinces

The combined manufacturing revenues of the four Atlantic provinces of Prince Edward Island, New Brunswick, Nova Scotia and Newfoundland and Labrador amounted to C $32,239.5m. in 2007, just 5.3% of the nationwide total in 2007. Manufacturing sales from the Atlantic provinces increased by 6.5% in 2007, with sales from Newfoundland and Labrador rising by 20.7% with the other Atlantic provinces posting more modest increases. In the previous year sectoral sales in Nova Scotia and New Brunswick declined, following the completion of major infrastructure projects. Food manufacturing was the most important sub-sector in all four provinces except New Brunswick, where paper products shipments were of greatest value. Food product sales averaged 18.3% of all manufacturing sales across the Atlantic provinces. The Atlantic provinces' share of Canada's total manufacturing employees was 5.0% (102,245) in 2007.

The combined manufacturing sales in the territories of Yukon, Nunavut and Northwest Territories were C $82m., just 0.01% of the total across Canada. There were fewer than 2,000 people across all three territories employed in manufacturing.

MANUFACTURING SUB-SECTORS

Transportation Equipment

The most significant NAICS sub-sector was transportation equipment, which accounted for 19% of sectoral GDP and 19.1% of manufacturing shipments in 2007. Output of the transportation equipment sub-sector amounted to C $26,934m. in 2006, down 1.5% compared with 2005, while sales were valued at $116,15.5m. in 2007, a 2.3% decline during the year. There were 217,255 employees in the transportation equipment sector in 2007, down from 231,268 in 2003, though there was little change in the sectoral share of the manufacturing work-force.

Recession in the transportation equipment industry stemmed largely from uncertainties in the US economy and currency appreciation. More than any other sub-sector, transportation equipment was integrated into wider North American production processes dominated by the USA. As the largest contributor to manufacturing GDP in Canada, the performance of the transportation equipment sector had a significant effect on the performance of the manufacturing sector in general.

Transportation equipment was the most significant export product category, representing 26.7% of total manufacturing exports in 2007 and 18.8% of total exports across all goods producing sectors. Exports in the sub-sector were valued at C $84,600m. in 2007, down 3.9% during the year and substantially down from the $101,585m. in export revenues earned during 2002. In that year transportation equipment exports had contributed 33.3% of all manufacturing export earnings. Transportation equipment accounted for the largest fall in export earnings in absolute terms ($3,413m.) of all manufacturing sectors in 2007 and $4,867m. in 2006. The decline stemmed almost exclusively from lower demand in the USA, where 90.9% of exports were sent in 2007. Exports to the USA in 2007 declined by 4.4%, to $76,942m. After the USA, Mexico was the principal destination for Canada's transportation equipment products, encouraged by NAFTA. Canada sent $1,225m. worth of transportation equipment to Mexico in 2007, an increase of 11.0% during the year, on the back of rapid growth in the previous three years.

In 2007 some 83.3% of all transportation exports from Canada originated from Ontario, followed by 13.2% from Québec. In 2005 some 40.5% of all establishments working in transportation equipment manufacturing were located in Ontario, while 20.7% were in Québec and 17.6% in British Columbia.

The transportation equipment sub-sector is broken down further into motor vehicle and parts manufacturing, aerospace, railway rolling stock and shipbuilding. Three-quarters of output in the transportation sector stemmed from car manufacturing-related activities, including vehicle, body and parts manufacturing. After automobiles, aerospace manufacturing was the most important activity within transportation equipment, representing 17.5% of national transportation equipment manufacturing. The aerospace industries were concentrated in Québec.

Sluggish investment in Canadian manufacturing was felt in the transportation equipment sector. Capital investment fell by a CAGR of 1.0% between 1994 and 2003.

Chemical Products

Chemical products manufacturing was the second largest sub-sector in Canadian manufacturing, accounting for GDP of C $19,841m., 8.5% of national manufacturing output, and sales valued at $49,124.4m., equivalent to 8.1% of the national total in 2007. Chemical products growth was static in 2007 while the value of sales declined by 2.0%.

The most important activities within chemical products manufacturing were pharmaceuticals, accounting for 27.7% of chemicals GDP in 2006, and basic chemicals, including petrochemicals and industrial gas, which made up 23.9% of total chemicals GDP in the same year.

Ontario's chemicals sales revenues represented 45% of the national total in 2007 and were valued at C $22,114.6m., down 2.5% during the year. The next most import provinces in terms of chemical products manufacturing were Alberta, with sales of $12,441.4m. in 2007, slightly down in the year, and Québec, with shipments of $10,747.9m., a decrease of 4.0%.

Chemicals were one of the better performing sub-sectors in terms of exports in 2007, increasing by 11.8%, to C $32,335m. Chemicals exports accounted for 10.2% of all manufacturing exports, up from 8.5% in 2005. Three-quarters of chemical products exports went to the USA in 2007. The People's Republic of China was the next most important recipient, with 5.0% of chemicals exports. Ontario supplied 54.2% of exports, followed by Alberta supplying 22.4% and Québec 13.3% of the total. In the narrower petrochemicals sector, Alberta and Ontario between them accounted for about 85% of Canada's total exports.

Despite the significance of chemicals to the economy, the sub-sector employed relatively few people, just 4.7% of the manufacturing work-force in 2003. Capacity utilization rates within the chemicals industry were slightly above average in 2007, at 84.3%.

Food Manufacturing

Manufactured food products represented 12.2% of all Canada's manufacturing shipments and 8.1% of sectoral GDP in 2007. Modest growth in 2006 of 1.9% in output and 3.0% in sales helped offset manufacturing decline in other sectors. Output valued at C $356m. more than in 2006 was the largest increase in GDP among manufacturing sub-sectors, in absolute terms, after fabricated metals.

Exports revenues increased by 2.2%, to C $17,460m., in 2007. Food contributed a stable 5.5% of manufacturing export earnings in 2007. The share of food exports destined for the USA was 67.8% in 2007, with Japan the next largest destination, taking 7.9% of Canada's food exports. Exports were hurt by the strength of the Canadian dollar in comparison with the US dollar, but some diversification of export markets was helping to reduce dependence on the USA. Ontario accounted for 34.5% of food exports, followed by Québec (17.3%), Alberta (15.6%) and British Columbia (7.2%).

Within the manufactured foods sub-sector, the most important activities were meat product manufacturing (contributing 21.3% of sub-sector GDP in 2006), followed by bakeries (15.0%), dairy (13.3%) and fruit and vegetable preserving (13.3%). Some 13.0% of the permanently employed manufacturing work-force was employed in the food products sub-sector in 2007.

Wood Products

With output of C $14,707m. in 2007, wood products was a significant sub-sector within Canadian manufacturing, a result of Canada's abundant forests and lumber resources. In 2007 the sub-sectoral GDP represented 6.3% of total manufacturing GDP in Canada, and sales were 4.1% of the total. Wood products declined in 2007, by 10.5% in terms of GDP and by 18.0% in terms of shipments in 2007, largely as a result of a significant slowdown in the US housing market and continued Canadian currency appreciation.

Wood products experienced the fastest decline (22.9%) among all other manufacturing exports in 2007 and 2006 (14.1%), and the second largest decline in absolute earnings (C $3,870m.). Exports were valued at $13,015m. in 2007 and represented 4.1% of the total earned from manufacturing, compared with 6.3% in 2005. The great bulk of wood exports (82.1% in 2007) was shipped to the USA. Japan was the second most important destination, taking 6.8% of Canada's manufactured wood products exports. British Columbia was the source of 50.7% of Canadian wood products exports, followed by Québec (21.4%) and Ontario (13.5%).

Wood industry activity was evenly spread between British Columbia, Ontario and Québec; 77% of firms were located in these three provinces. Wood manufacturing employed 6.8% of manufacturing employees and had a higher proportion of production workers involved in core activities to administration workers (86% in 2003) compared with manufacturing as a whole (78%). Labour productivity in wood products increased at an average annual rate of 7.1% between 1997 and 2002, compared with the Canadian economy generally, which increased at an average annual rate of 2.3% during the same period.

Fabricated Metals

The fabricated metals sub-sector includes: hand tools; screws, nuts and bolts; springs and wire; boilers and containers; and other hardware. GDP in 2007 was C $18,142m., up 4.1% in the year. The sub-sector's share of manufacturing GDP was stable at 7.8%, while it contributed 6.0% of the value of manufacturing sales in Canada. There were 178,760 employees working in fabricated metals in 2007, down from 197,663 in 2003. Despite the decline in absolute employment, the sub-sector's share of manufacturing jobs increased from 9.5% in 2003 to 10.0% in 2007.

Exports of fabricated metals earned Canada C $9,276m. in 2007, a 0.8% increase compared with 2006, and accounted for 2.9% of total manufacturing export revenues. An overwhelming share of fabricated metals exports (83.3%) went to the USA in 2007. The United Kingdom, the People's Republic of China and Mexico had 1.3%, 1.2% and 1.1% shares of exports, respectively, in 2007. Ontario was the main source of sectoral exports, accounting for 58.9%, followed by Québec (22.0%) and Alberta (9.3%).

Primary Metals

Considered separately from fabricated metals, primary metals includes steel, aluminium (aluminum) and other non-ferrous metal manufacturing. The sub-sector stagnated in 2007, with output of C $14,999.7m. The share in overall manufacturing GDP held by primary metals manufacturing was stable at 6.4%, while it accounted for 8.7% of all Canada's manufacturing shipments in 2007.

There were 78,802 Canadians working in the primary metals sub-sector in 2007, representing 4.4% of total manufacturing workers across Canada, although this figure was 7.7% fewer than in 2003. Despite the decline the share of the manufacturing work-force was stable during this period. An increase in the proportion of employees classed as production workers, undertaking core activities, helped improve productivity by 5.2% per year between 1997 and 2002, compared with a 2.3% increase in the Canadian economy as a whole.

Primary metals was the best performing manufacturing sector in Canada in terms of exports in 2007 and 2006. Export revenues amounted to C $38,910m. in 2007, up 19.0% during the year following 28.7% growth in 2006. Primary metals exports increased their contribution to manufacturing sector export earnings from 8.1% in 2005 to 12.3% in 2007. The USA was the destination for 65.7% of primary metals exports. While the USA continued to dominate the export markets, demand in 2006–07 was more spread across other destinations than in the past, in particular the United Kingdom, Norway, the Netherlands and the People's Republic of China.

Ontario was the most important province in terms of the primary metals sub-sector. It was the location of 43.9% of primary metals manufacturing establishments (with 28.9% in Québec, the second most important) and it was the largest provincial source of exports with 46.2%, compared with 34.6% supplied by Québec. Manitoba, Alberta and British Columbia supplied 6.3%, 5.9% and 5.2%, respectively.

Machinery

Machinery, including equipment for agriculture, construction, mining, industry, commercial and service industries, heating and refrigeration, metal-working and power transmission, accounted for C $17,100m. of GDP in 2007, up 1.5% compared with the previous year. The sector's share of total Canadian manufacturing output was 7.3% in 2006, and its share of manufacturing sales in 2007 was 5.3%.

The machinery sector employed 139,714 people in 2007, or 7.8% of the total manufacturing work-force, a 1.9% increase in numbers compared with 2003.

Total machinery exports were valued at C $25,713m. in 2007, of which $17,985m., or 69.9%, were sent to the USA. The United Kingdom, Germany and the People's Republic of China each received 2.0% of Canadian machinery exports. Ontario was the origin of 56.2% of Canadian machinery exports, followed by Québec with 19.2%, Alberta with 12.0% and British Columbia with 6.2%. Revenues from machinery exports increased 5.0% during the year, taking the sub-sector's share of total manufacturing exports up from 7.8% to 8.1%.

Paper

The paper sub-sector includes paper and pulp mills as well as paper products manufacturing. This sector saw output decline by 4.7% in 2007, to C $13,007m. The contribution towards Canada's manufacturing sector output as a whole from paper was 5.6%, down from 6.7% in 2005. In 1997 the paper sub-sector's share of manufacturing output was 7.6%. The value of sales were also down in 2007, by 2.7% to $30,250m.

Paper sector exports declined too in 2007, down 3.7%, to C $19,873m. Export earnings from paper contributed 6.3% of manufacturing export earnings in 2007, down from 6.8% in 2005. The USA was the destination for 68.4% of paper products exports, with the People's Republic of China the next most important market, taking 7.3% of paper exports.

Québec dominated other provinces in terms of paper exports, accounting for 33.3% of Canada's exports in the sector, followed by British Columbia with 25.4% and Ontario with 20.2%. Québec dominated the pulp, paper and paperboard mills sector, while Ontario was the most important province for paper products manufacturing, including paper bags, paperboard containers and stationery. The paper sub-sector employed 79,380 people in 2007, 4.4% of the permanently employed manufacturing work-force, down from 96,994 in 2003, representing 5.0% of manufacturing workers.

Others

Of the remaining manufacturing sub-sectors, the most significant in terms of GDP were: computers and electronics; plastics and rubber products; non-metallic mineral products; printing and related support activities; furniture and related products; beverages and tobacco; and electrical equipment and appliance components.

The fastest growing sector in 2006, at 3.8%, was miscellaneous manufacturing, including medical equipment. The worst performers in 2007 were clothing, down 11.2%, and textile products, which declined by 4.7%. Among the less significant sub-sectors, clothing was also the worst performer in terms of absolute contribution to manufacturing output (down C $263m.) and experienced the greatest decline in export revenues (down 16.7%), followed by the textile mills sector (down 6.8%).

CONSTRUCTION

Output from the construction sector was C $96,746m. in 2007, at current prices. Growth of 7.9% was recorded in the sector in that year. This followed growth of 7.2% in 2006 and consistent annual growth averaging 4.8% in 2001–05. The share of GDP contributed by the construction sector was 6.3% in 2007. The share in the four-year period 2003–06 averaged 5.8% annually. The share of the work-force employed in the construction industry fell to 5.6% in 2007, up from 4.8% in.

The value of building permits reached a record C $74,378m. in 2007, up 12.3% over the 2006 value. Growth in 2007 followed annual increases averaging 9.2% in the previous three years. The bulk of the value of building permits in Canada (61.2%) was for residential construction. The remainder, covering non-residential construction, the commercial sector, including hotels, office buildings, shopping malls and warehouses, was the most important. The commercial sector had a 58.8% share of non-residential building permits in 2007, an increase of 18.4% from 2003. Investment in the commercial sector amounted to a 61.7% share of total non-residential construction investment in the second quarter of 2008, compared with

24.5% for public sector institutions, including health facilities, and 13.8% for industrial construction.

There were signs that the buoyancy in the construction sector of recent years was not being sustained into 2007 and 2008, particularly in the residential sector. There were 228,343 housing starts in 2007, just 0.4% more than in 2006, with the value of residential building permits up 10.9%. By mid-2008 the value of residential building permits had declined by a further 5.7%.

Volatility in global financial markets, tightening credit and fears of a recession in the USA were offset by Canada's relatively low exposure to high-risk 'sub-prime' mortgages, which were not widespread in the Canadian housing market, making up around 3% of the total, compared with more than 10% in the USA. Strong commodities and investment underpinned the housing market, particularly in western Canada, as well as Toronto (Ontario). The Bank of Canada raised interest rates in July 2007 for the first time in a year in an attempt to combat price inflation. The tightening of credit and the volatility in financial markets were expected to reduce demand for mortgages, but it was hoped that the strength of the Canadian economy would ensure a gradual softening of the housing boom rather than a crash.

Permits for non-residential construction reached record levels in 2007, increasing in value by 14.4%, to C $28,832.3m. Investment in non-residential construction increased 8.9% during the year up to mid-2008, stemming principally from the commercial sector, which grew 10.4% during this period. The value of non-residential permits increased 17.4% in the year to mid-July 2008.

A construction boom from 2002 led to labour shortages, which, in turn, increased wage appreciation and reduced productivity as firms hired less-skilled workers. These factors limited the growth of the construction industry in 2007.

Ontario accounted for 35.9% of the total value of all building permits in Canada in 2007. Alberta followed with 21.1% of the total value, Québec with 17.4% and British Columbia with 16.9%.

Construction activity from the mid-2000s was fuelled by the commodity-led economies of the Western provinces. While Ontario accounted for the largest share of any single province in terms of building permits, its share had declined from 47.1% in 2002. The Winter Olympic Games, due to be held in Vancouver (British Columbia) in 2010, fuelled a local boom in construction activity. In 2006 the growth in the value of permits in Canada, excluding British Columbia and Alberta, was just 1%. The value of permits increased by 13.4% in Alberta in 2007 and by 8.7% in British Columbia.

There were 48,336 housing starts in Alberta in 2007, marginally less than in 2006, the first annual decline following successive years of growth. Housing starts in Alberta increased at an average annual rate of 6.6% from 2002–06 and by 19.9% in 2006. This compared with growth at the national level of 0.4% in 2007 and an average annual rate of 2.7% from 2002–06. Housing starts were up 7.6% in British Columbia in 2007 and by an average annual rate of 17.1% from 2002–06. In contrast, Ontario had seen a decline in housing starts of 6.8% in 2006, and 7.2% in 2007. Quebec's housing starts rose slightly, by 1.4% in 2007, following 6.0% decline in 2006. In terms of the type of residential construction, there was a slight trend in 2002–06 towards apartment buildings and constructions with multiple dwellings and away from single-detached homes.

Alberta saw 14.3% growth across all non-residential construction in the year to July 2008, down from 43.4% a year earlier. Investment in commercial projects was particularly strong. Non-residential construction investment declined by 5.9% in British Columbia in this period, including rapid decline in industrial and institutional construction with slow growth in the commercial sector. Non-residential construction investment increased in Ontario by 8.9% and by 11.9% in Québec.

Expenditure on construction totalled C $208,146m. in 2007, the largest portion of which came from the housing sector, which accounted for $88,459m., or 42.5% of the total. The mining, petroleum and gas extraction industry supplied the next highest share (19.9%) of the construction sector, followed by public administration (10.9%) and utilities (7.1%). Manufacturing was the source of just 1.1% of spending on construction projects.

Ontario led the way among Canada's provinces in terms of capital expenditure on construction projects, with C $59,520m. spent in 2007 and $61,884m. earmarked for 2008. The 2007 figure was 28.6% of the nationwide total, closely followed by Alberta with 26.8%. Québec accounted for 17.3% of capital expenditure on construction projects and British Columbia 15.1%. Alberta was the location for 67.2% of all construction spending on mining, petroleum and gas extraction. Alberta also had the second highest number of large construction establishments, with 36 employing more than 500 (Ontario had 50), reflecting the large projects associated with the extractive industries. In 2007 Alberta had 52 major construction projects under way, valued at a total of $148,832m., primarily to develop the province's huge oil-sands deposits.

SUMMARY

The manufacturing sector in Canada was particularly vulnerable to the risk of economic slowdown in the USA. During periods of economic growth in the USA, Canada could exploit its natural advantage of close proximity to the largest consumer market in the world to send exports south. Furthermore, Canada's most significant manufacturing industries, such as automotives, were integrated into US production processes and, consequently, a large proportion of output was destined for export to the USA. At the same time the overwhelming dominance of the USA as an export market left Canadian manufacturers exposed during periods of stagnation. Slower growth in the USA from the mid-2000s, along with fears that a so-called credit 'squeeze' in that country could trigger a recession, saw demand from the USA decline and reduced Canadian manufacturing output. Demand was dampened further by the appreciation of the Canadian dollar. The effects of reduced demand from the USA and the high prices for Canadian commodities led to a modest westward shift in manufacturing activity, away from the main industrial provinces of Ontario and Québec, and away from relatively capital-intensive industry to resource-based manufacturing. There were some concerns that such industries were overly reliant on volatile commodity prices and involved a lower value of processing than high-technology industries or manufacturing, where there was a great degree of processing of intermediate inputs. These issues underlined the challenge for Canadian manufacturing—to increase productivity and investment and to diversify trading partners away from a reliance on the USA.

SERVICE INDUSTRIES IN CANADA

ALAN HALLSWORTH

INTRODUCTION

In terms of overall employment growth, services drive the Canadian economy, although the importance of the energy sector is often raised by factors such as high prices for that industry's products. In real terms, the gross domestic product (GDP) of the service sector was projected to reach C $865,700m. (2002 dollars) in 2008, equivalent to 70.2% of Canada's total industrial GDP; the sector had seen an average annual increase of 3.1% between 2000 and 2005. By 2007 the service sector accounted for over three-quarters of all employment—some 12,873,500 jobs. In contrast, the goods-producing sector employed just 3,993,000 workers. This expansion may be related to the fact that the World Bank rankings in 2007 placed Canada as the best place to start a business. The expansion of the service sector was also linked to a widening difference in wages between the highest- and lowest-paid workers. At the start of the 21st century the top 20% of earners in Canada were, broadly speaking, 500% better off than the poorest 20%. It is probable that in the 25-year period leading up to 2005, the lowest-paid workers actually experienced a reduction in wages in real terms. Statistics from the Canadian Council on Social Development show that the percentage of persons on low incomes or in poverty rose from 15.3% in 1990 to 16.2% in 1999. Such individuals were dependent on the public spending that was under attack throughout the 1990s, as debt reduction imperatives took hold of government policy. Such trends are difficult to divorce from a report released by Statistics Canada in September 2008 indicating that more Canadians were delaying their retirement: for example, the proportion of men aged between 65 and 69 years still working had risen from 17% in 1997 to at least 25%. Until the mid-1990s employment growth was strongest in the youth and female markets, especially in the part-time sector. However, the recession of the early 1990s affected all employment sectors, and even female employment declined slightly. In the mid-1990s employment prospects for under-skilled young people also began to attract increasing concern. In the decade to 1993 the average earnings of young men and women—by no means all of them in services, of course—fell by over 20%. After the 1990s recession women's employment rates continued to rise, but female participation rates in the 25–44-year-old age group remained at least 10 percentage points below those of men between 2002 and 2006; the gap was even wider for the 45 years and older category. In addition, the ratio of women's earnings to men's decreased from 72.4% in 1995 to 69.9% in 2004. Poverty trends into the last decade of the 20th century showed slight improvements in the situation of the elderly, while younger, poorer families were falling behind. Work-place stress increased from the 1980s, as did the number of low-paid individuals involuntarily working over 50 hours per week. The bulk of these were in the service sector, although not exclusively so. Any improvements in labour productivity in Canada tended to be achieved by shedding jobs rather than by innovative technological investments. This may have been connected to fears of a 'brain-drain' to the USA, with its higher salaries, and so diversification into technology became a national preoccupation for Canadians. The attractions of the USA were, in part, offset from 2000 by federal funding for university research posts.

Consideration of service sector employment is complicated by the division of constitutional power between the federal and provincial tiers of government. As in most developed economies, employment in, and the direct provision of services by, various levels of government was an essential element of the Canadian economy in the late 20th and early 21st centuries. In 2007 government employment at all levels (federal, provincial and local) accounted for 18% of the labour force (3.2m. workers), although this was below the peak of 23% reached in 1992. Within this public sector work-force, 46.7% of jobs were in provincial government, 32.3% in local government, 12.0% in federal government and 9.0% in government business enterprises. Underlying all the trends in services, as in other sectors, was the long-term policy of 'balanced budget' government, a trend that also characterized the provincial situation.

TRANSPORT, COMMUNICATIONS AND UTILITIES

Canada has been described as 'a triumph of transportation over geography' and by 2000 the World Economic Forum's report on global competitiveness had already placed Canada first among the Group of Seven (G7) leading Western industrialized countries for its transport infrastructure. This was largely a legacy of past government investment in infrastructure by way of substantial transport subsidies, which helped transfer high-quality produce to markets. The Department of Transport was created in 1936 from the Department of Railways and Canals, the Marine Department and the section of the Department of National Defence dealing with civil aviation. Much later, the transport sector experienced deregulatory pressures, with a National Transportation Act introduced in January 1988. In 1992 the Royal Commission on Passenger Transportation advocated a market-driven, subsidy-free system and particularly emphasized the cost inefficiencies of ferry and rail transport. The Canada Transportation Act of May 1996 promised further deregulation—much of the deregulatory pressure in the 1980s and 1990s fell upon the railways. By 2007 federal policy had begun to reflect increased concerns about the environmental impact of transportation: the Clean Air Regulatory Agenda set out the Government's plan for regulating emissions from various sources, while several initiatives were organized under the Government's C $100m. ecoTRANSPORT Strategy. These included programmes aimed at reducing emissions from urban passenger transportation, lessening the environmental and health effects of freight transport, and increasing incentives for the purchase of fuel-efficient vehicles.

Transportation forms a significant part of the Canadian economy: in 2007 the sector employed 822,800 people, commercial transportation contributed 4.0% of GDP, and government spending on transport equated to 0.9% of GDP. Canada's transport system carries over C $1,000,000m. worth of goods each year, and the sector experienced an average annual growth of 6.1% in 1992–2002. Personal expenditure on transport constitutes the largest part of transportation-related demand, standing at 8.5% of GDP in 2007, having experienced average annual growth of 5.2% between 2001 and 2006.

In 2007 Canada had 1,042,300 km of two-lane equivalent public roads, 75% of the total length of which was located in Ontario, Québec, Alberta and Saskatchewan. The large federal transportation budget was one of the principal targets of the important 1994 federal spending review (featuring privatization policies) undertaken by the Liberal Government under Jean Chrétien. As a result, patterns of investment, subsidy and privatization policy became especially volatile in this sector and changed with great regularity. Federal spending on transportation increased by 20% between 2001 and 2002, for example. Nevertheless, it is possible to note that total government expenditures on transportation, including transfers, held steady, at around C $17,000m., in 1996–2000, at which point they began to register year-on-year increases—reaching $24,800m. in the 2006/07 fiscal year. Nevertheless, total federal transport expenses amounted to just 14.5% of consolidated government transport spending in 2006/07. That year all levels of government spent $17,600m. on roads, $3,700m. on public transit services and $2,500m. on air, marine and rail transportation combined.

Railways

Railways in Canada traditionally found it difficult to attract financing, because of the distances involved and the generally low volumes of traffic, with millions of dollars lost annually on passenger operations. Nevertheless, the rail industry generated revenues of C $10,400m. in 2006, which represented a 25%

increase on the 2003 figure. In 2008 Canada's railways were operating an average of 775 passenger and freight trains a day. Passenger revenues were just a fraction of what was obtained from the freight sector, which moved 353.8m. revenue metric-ton kilometres in 2006. That said, with competition from road haulage, some 30,000 km of track had been lost since 1970—some abandoned, some transferred to short-line (feeder) carriers. Indeed, some 10,500 km of track was discontinued between 1990 and 2007, although this contraction had mostly abated by the end of this period. Statistics show that employment in the rail industry fell from 47,600 in 1996 to 34,150 in 2006. Management of passenger services (excluding commuter services) was consolidated with the creation of a crown corporation, VIA Rail Canada Inc, in 1978. By 1995 the scaled-down VIA Rail's operating revenues were only $175m., while subsidies amounted to $295m. With the recovery of federal finances by 2000, plans were made to invest almost $400m. in VIA Rail, then still a crown corporation. However, the direct federal subsidy for VIA Rail declined to $169m. in 2005/06, below the 1999 figure of $170m, although its revenues had increased consistently since 1996. VIA Rail dominates the inter-city rail passenger sector, registering approximately 90% of total passenger revenues in 2006. Elsewhere, changes to passenger services meant that the famous rail crossing of the Rocky Mountains was sold separately as a tourist service. At a more local level, some cities invested in rail-based light, rapid-transit systems, as well as in commuter underground services. The major-city rail passenger trade increased as commuter distances lengthened and there was a 50% rise in numbers between the mid-1990s and the mid-2000s, with 58.6m. passengers being handled in 2006. This increase may be linked to the necessity for two incomes to support mortgages on homes, which were increasingly built at great distance from employment centres. It is worth noting, however, that by 2007 urban transit accounted for just 2.1% of personal expenditure on transport.

The principal freight companies were Canadian National (CN) and Canadian Pacific Railway (CPR), together defined as the Class 1 carriers. They accounted for 74.8% of the rail network in 2007, equivalent to 89.5% of industry revenues and approximately 35,000 track km. They registered a combined operating profit of C $2,500m. in 2006, a 48.5% increase from two years previously, thanks to significantly increased revenues. As track was transferred to other users, the percentage of track that was federally regulated steadily fell and amounted to less than 80% (equivalent to 39,000 track miles) in 2002. In November 1995 CN was finally fully privatized and announced a restructuring, to place its routes between Toronto (Ontario) and Québec—as well as some of its US lines—in a separate business. By 2001 CN had merged with Illinois Central Railroad of the USA and added Wisconsin Central—further emphasizing the significance of infrastructure integration following the implementation of the North American Free Trade Agreement (NAFTA). As the decade progressed, both CN and CPR continued to expand their operations in the USA: in 2007 CN announced plans to buy the Elgin, Joliet and Eastern Railroad in Chicago, Illinois, while CPR was completing its purchase of the Dakota, Minnesota and Eastern Railroad in Wyoming. After acquiring Algoma Central Railway in 2003, in July 2004 CN took control of British Columbia Rail in a public-private partnership, which involved the transfer of some 2,300 km of track. These moves, alongside CPR's alliance with three US railway companies—CSX Transportation Inc, the Union Pacific Railroad Co and the Norfolk Southern Corpn—exemplified the reorientation of north–south rail connections. In the Prairie provinces, however, maintaining branch lines with access to the main network remained the key issue.

The changes at CN and CPR dominated the rail sector from the 1990s, but other trends were also significant. The 1996 Transportation Act led to an explosion in the number of short-line railways: 37 new short lines were created in 1996–2000; short-line revenues increased by more than 400% in 1995–2001; and employment in the sector rose by 263% in 1990–2003. However, the sector subsequently plateaued, with Transport Canada reporting that only a few more short lines had been created in the 21st century (in 2006 short-line revenues stood at C $425m., 4.1% of industry revenues). Broadly, this increase meant that the Class 1 carriers possessed a smaller proportion of the total track network, but still collected the dominant proportion of rail revenues—93% of industry revenues between 1990 and 2005 (including VIA Rail). Furthermore, a total of 29,900 km of line was rationalized after 1990. In other developments, many cities relocated their rail terminus to the periphery of the city, leaving a route that could be developed into the city centre and freeing substantial inner-city land. Thus, from the mid-1990s negotiations took place to sell former rail lands in larger centres—this was especially prominent in Toronto. Hopes to attract the 2008 Olympic Games (eventually awarded to the Chinese capital, Beijing) could not easily be divorced from optimistic plans for further regeneration of former railroad lands on the waterfront. The CN Tower and Skydome projects were an earlier part of this land redevelopment.

Shipping

The marine sector plays a significant role in the Canadian economy: in 2006 Canada's international marine trade was worth C $143,700m. (nearly one-half of Canada's total international trade, by value) and Canada's ports handled 478m. metric tons of cargo. Canada has access to two major shipping oceans and, in the St Lawrence Seaway, the world's longest inland waterway, which serves 15 major international ports and carries most of Canada's domestic marine traffic. Since October 1998 the waterway has been managed by the St Lawrence Seaway Management Corporation, a not-for-profit organization that has a 20-year management contract with the federal Government. In 2007 the combined traffic of the Seaway amounted to 43.0m. metric tons, which was close to the mean annual figure for the decade. Iron ore and grain remained the two main commodities transported (11.9m. tons and 10.4m. tons, respectively). Surveys suggest that the Seaway saves North American shippers approximately US $2,700m. annually.

Generally, tonnage was dominated by Vancouver (British Columbia), with bulk commodities, especially coal and timber, the principal products transported. Provincial trade figures for British Columbia tended to be distorted by its crucial export role for all western bulk commodities. Montréal (Québec), the other major city with a vital port function, was an alternative, eastern outlet for traffic that was not focused on the Pacific Rim or on Japan. This city's trade was of a quite different nature from that of commodity-dominated Vancouver, handling a much higher proportion of container trade. The Great Lakes system itself was used to move substantial quantities of cargo, especially coal, iron ore and grain. In 2006 the five largest ports by tons of cargo handled were Vancouver, Saint John (New Brunswick), Montréal, Québec and Sept-Îles (Québec), which accounted for 176.4m. metric tons between them. Notably, Sept-Îles registered a 28.0% increase in tonnage between 2004 and 2005. The more general picture showed that in 2004 Atlantic ports represented 30.4% of international shipping tonnage handled in Canada, closely followed by the Pacific region (30.3%), the St Lawrence region (24.3%) and the Great Lakes region (15.0%). Note, of course, that commodities dominate figures presented by tonnage rather than value.

The Canadian shipping sector overall was subject to the Canada Marine Act (CMA) of June 1996, implementing the National Marine Policy of 1995 (which came into force in 1998). This created a national ports system of independently managed port authorities—the total number of these rose to 19 in 2001, when the Port of Hamilton Authority was established. They include former Canada Ports Corporation's major divisional ports as well as former harbour commissions. In the mid-1990s there was a general commercialization or 'offloading' of ferries and pilotage (in that more minor ports were to be transferred to local control). By 2007, of the 549 public ports and port facilities controlled by Transport Canada before the National Marine Policy came into effect, 472 had been transferred, deproclaimed or demolished. Marine Liability and Canada Shipping Acts were signed in 2001. The Canada Shipping Act administers personal safety and environmental protection in the Canadian shipping sector, and streamlined the number of regulations from more than 50 to 24 in 2007. The

2003 review of the operations of the CMA since 1998 recommended a number of benefits for the Canada Port Authorities, including increased federal help for the authorities' infrastructure building. It also recommended greater stringency in punishing ships that violated the CMA and that the federal Government should aid provincial authorities in taking over public ports. In 2008 the federal Government allowed certain port authorities to obtain private financing for development work, modified borrowing regulations, and made it possible for two Canada Port Authorities to amalgamate.

Air Transport

Perhaps fortuitously, as with the electricity and telecommunications industries, Canada retained a stronger regulatory hand on air transport than most of its Organisation for Economic Co-operation and Development partners. Air transport is almost uniquely vunerable to fuel price fluctuations and, owing to a sharp rise in prices, 2008 joined 2001 as a very difficult year for the sector. However, as in many other countries, the terrorist attacks on the USA of September 2001 led to significant changes that effectively transformed the sector.

Prior to 2001 air had accounted for only 2.4% of government spending on transport, 63% lower than 1998 levels. The challenges faced by Canadian airlines after 11 September 2001 reversed this decline, and led the Government to be more proactive in funding and defending the domestically owned air sector. For example, the Government paid the industry almost C $100m. in compensation between October 2001 and May 2002, announced an $80m. short-term relief package in 2003 and reduced its Air Travellers' Security Charge by 40% in the latter year. The Canadian Air Transport Security Authority was established in 2002, and received $400m. of funding by the following year. As confirmed below, in the section dealing with Government Finances, this turnaround in subsidies was only possible as debt came under control; transport had been an early victim of the Liberals' budget pruning. However, the airlines were always subject to government controls: federal law requires that the air industry be at least 75% owned and de facto controlled by Canadians; while in 2000 Bills C-26 and C-23 attempted to enhance competition and prevent bullying tactics in the marketplace. In 2006 a range of legislative proposals aimed to modernize corporate governance, increase accountability for airport authorities, improve transparency in advertising and enable the confidential reporting of regulatory infractions. These proposals built on 2003 bills that had died mid-way through the legislative process; the intent of the new bills was in accordance with the stated Conservative focus on fiscal transparency and accountability.

By 2001, following the merger of the two main companies in Canadian aviation (see below), alternative carriers had begun to develop more markets—usually based on the city-to-city rather than the 'hub' model. Much of this change was confounded by the events of September 2001, which had an enormous impact on air traffic levels: the number of passengers carried declined from 60m. in 2000 to 54.0m. in 2002 and 53.9m. in 2003. Generally, 2001 was a traumatic year for air companies: Air Canada (which had just undergone a disruptive merger with former rival Canadian Airlines) reported a total loss of C $1,300m., Canada 3000 ceased operation and Air Transat (the second largest airline in terms of revenues) restructured its operations. By the mid-2000s it was clear that there had been a substantial recovery in passenger numbers: 2004 saw a return to the 60m. passenger level last registered in 2000; this was then surpassed by the record 63m. and 68m. passengers transported in 2005 and 2006, respectively. Growth in passenger numbers had slowed to 3% by 2007, however. In 2005 Canada and the United Kingdom signed an 'open skies' agreement, to take effect from September 2006. This would assist the activities of those carriers—numbering at least 12 at the time—operating between Canada and the United Kingdom and with passenger payloads exceeding 2m. Following this, in November 2005 Canada and the USA further liberalized their 1995 Air Transport Agreement, in order to bring it into line with the US 'open skies' system. The new agreement mainly concerned increased price flexibility and access to third countries from the USA. These developments paved the way for the announcement, in November 2006, of a new international air policy that recommended the negotiation of 'open skies' agreements, when in Canada's interests. The first agreements under this policy, with Croatia and Serbia, were signed in late 2006; a year later Canada opened negotiations on an 'open skies' agreement with the European Union (19 of whose 27 members had existing air pacts with Canada). As a consequence, by the end of 2007 Canada was subject to 79 international bilateral air transportation agreements.

Air Canada took a major step towards economic recovery in August 2004, when unions and the group's creditors approved a restructuring plan (involving thousands of job losses and decreased wages) and, on 30 September, it withdrew from bankruptcy protection. In May 2005 ACE Aviation Holdings Inc (Air Canada's parent company) reported reduced losses, despite escalating fuel prices. In the three months to 31 March 2005 the airline had lost C $77m., which was significantly less than the $303m. lost one year earlier; by the fourth quarter of 2008 it had moved to a profit of $35m. The consolidated Air Canada remains by far the largest Canadian airline, serving 99 destinations with $10,600m. in revenues in 2006/07 and a fleet of 207 aircraft. Indeed, 2007 saw the landmark event of a new Air Canada Boeing 777 landing at London's Heathrow airport in the United Kingdom—a sign of growing reinvestment. Furthermore, Air Canada's sister company, Jazz, served 64 other destinations with its fleet of smaller aircraft. Nevertheless, WestJet, based in Calgary, Alberta, has continued to grow, becoming Canada's second largest airline, serving 46 cities with 70 aircraft, 6,700 employees and 2007 revenues of just $2,150m., up from $863m. in 2003. Notably, WestJet experienced growth in total passenger kilometres flown of 19.9% during 2007. Significantly, WestJet was the only domestic air carrier not to end 2001 financially weakened, reporting a profit of $37m. In contrast, the budget airline Jetsgo, which held 7%–10% of the domestic market, collapsed in 2005, with major losses. The collapse of charter airline Canada 3000 in 2001 left a market opportunity that led to something of a resurgence in non-scheduled (charter) traffic for those seeking transatlantic services. Before the rapid escalation in fuel prices in 2008, this had seemingly reinforced prospects for groups such as Air Transat, Zoom, and the now merged MyTravel and Thomas Cook airlines, which all regularly serviced Canadian destinations from the United Kingdom.

Passenger traffic rebounded strongly in 2006, as the number of enplaned and deplaned passengers exceeded 100m., but it was not to last. Toronto remained in possession of the busiest airport, symbolized by a C $4,400m. improvement programme in 2006 and the 2007 opening of an inter-terminal rapid-transit system. Toronto was followed by Vancouver International Airport, Montréal's Pierre Elliot Trudeau (formerly Dorval) International Airport and Calgary International Airport. The busiest air route remained Toronto–Montréal, with 4,679 daily seats in 2007, followed by Toronto–Vancouver, with 3,777. Notably, WestJet held 46% of market share of the fourth most popular route, Calgary–Vancouver, against Air Canada's 53%. A key issue in 2005–06 was airport rentals paid to the federal Government. Between the implementation of airport devolution in 1992 and 2005, airports in the National Airport System had paid a combined and cumulative total of C $2,500m. in rental tax to the federal Government. For example, the leading airport (Toronto's Lester B. Pearson) was scheduled to increase its annual payments further, from $132m. in 2005 to $150m. by 2012, by which time it would be paying two-thirds of all rents collected at Canadian airports. Airport authorities claimed that these charges were unjustified and harmed the competitiveness of Canadian airports. In January 2006 a new rent system was implemented, which aimed to address inequities in payments and to provide nearly $8,000m. in rent relief to airport authorities over the course of their leases. The new charging formula was based on airport gross revenues and brought the system into line with other rent formulas employed by the Government of Canada. Nevertheless, the issue remained controversial, with some industry representatives concerned that the new system did not provide sufficient relief for the country's busiest airports. In 2008 Canada had 10 major international airports and around 300 smaller regional or local airports, all of which were affected by the fuel crisis of that year, which, in late August, led to the collapse of Zoom. In the immediate aftermath it was claimed that Zoom had debts of between $50m. and $120m., and that up to 60,000 passengers might in some way be affected. Air Canada was reported to be responding to fuel supply difficulties by importing its own fuel via Québec.

Pipelines

As of 2003 Canada had 23,500 km of pipelines capable of transporting crude and refined petroleum, and 75,000 km capable of transporting liquid petroleum gas. In the same year Canadian pipelines transported over 10m. cu m of liquid hydrocarbons each month and accounted for one-third of Canada's trade with the USA. In 2007 the USA's annual energy imports from Canada amounted to some C $1,000m., and 85% of the oil and gas produced in Canada went to the USA (amounting to an average of 2.7m. barrels of oil and 10,300m. cu ft of natural gas every day). Much of the pipeline network covered inhospitable terrain, with predictable operating difficulties, such as those experienced in 2006 by BP with its Prudhoe Bay Alaskan operations in the USA. Canadian pipeline transportation registered a GDP of $5,600m. in 2006 (in chained 2002 dollars).

With substantial valuable resources situated in remote and inhospitable regions, it was natural that pipeline transport would be an important issue in Canada. Many pipeline projects across areas that were inhospitable and ecologically fragile, as well as of significance to native peoples, generated intense public debate from the late 20th century. The national energy market was largely deregulated in 1985, but the deregulation of pipelines remained under federal control, although 'common carrier' legislation provided for open access. This separation of production and transmission/delivery made ownership and control of pipelines a lively area. For example, in November 2002 EnCana, Canada's largest petroleum and gas producer, decided to sell two of its major pipelines—the Express Pipeline System and the Cold Lake Pipeline System—for a combined total of C $1,600m. Pipeline projects are hugely expensive and their viability subject to the vagaries of the value of the resource that they are transporting. Oil-sand explorations, for example, are viable only when petroleum prices are high. In 2007 the continued high petroleum prices led to increased interest in the oil sands of Alberta; in February of that year Imperial Oil gained permission for its Kearl oil-sands project, which could produce 300,000 barrels per day by 2018. In 2006 402m. metric tons of oil sands were mined, producing 29,100 megalitres of synthetic crude petroleum. Another issue for pipeline projects is the need to negotiate with the local communities over rights of way through their lands. Such obstacles explained the fact that, although established pipelines might be profitable, construction was usually a long and costly enterprise. A case in point was the long-gestating project to run a pipeline through the Mackenzie Valley: a regulatory application was submitted in 2004, although by 2007 it was clear that regulatory and fiscal issues meant gas would not move before 2014. In December 2007 proponents of the project submitted a $16,200m. financial plan to the Minister of Industry; nevertheless, by mid-2008 the Joint Review Panel established by the Government in 2004 to evaluate the environmental and socio-economic impact of the project had not made a judgment on the case.

Roads

In the mid-2000s expenditure on roads accounted for about three-quarters of all government spending on transport. In 2006/07 government spending at all levels on roads amounted to C $17,600m. In July 1962 the Trans-Canada Highway system had been formally completed, although additional improvements took a further eight years and brought the total cost to some $1,000m. This system, including ferry links, created a 4,860-mile (7,821-km) national route, with its extremities at Victoria, in British Columbia, and St John's, in Newfoundland. Until 1997 a significant missing element was the lack of a fixed link to Prince Edward Island. This was resolved in June of that year when the ferry service was superseded by the 12.9-km long, 60-m high Confederation Bridge—the fourth longest water span in the world. The four-year project was financed through private sector bonds. The inauguration of the national coast-to-coast highway system had symbolized a major movement away from the rail transport of commodities; in the 1930s railways took some 85% of Canada's freight revenue, but as early as 1985 trucking (road freight transportation) accounted for a 50% share of revenue. Until 2001 the Canadian–US trans-border trucking trade had shown a decade of year-on-year growth. Increased security following the September 2001 terrorist attacks on the USA led to longer queues at border crossings, and the so-called 'smart border declaration' between Canada and the USA was signed in December of that year. Rapid growth in road transportation services had been experienced in the 1990s, with the development of fast courier or messenger services offering same-day or next-day delivery. Overall, the road network was approximately 1.4m. km in length, and a heavy maintenance burden was imposed by harsh Canadian winters. Innovations attempted included a high-occupancy vehicle lane on Highway 403, which Ontario claimed in 2006 was saving 15–20 minutes of commuter time. This was in the context of growing congestion; the Liberal Government had spent $838m. on transit schemes, plus $670m. on the extension of the Toronto subway to York. In comparison, highway improvements cost $992m. in 2004/05 and $1,200m. in 2005/06. An investment of $1,700m. in Ontario's highway system in the province's 2007 budget was followed by a new $400m. Municipal Roads and Bridges Fund in 2008.

In 2007 there were a total of 20.6m. registered road motor vehicles in Canada, and an average of 1.63m. new motor vehicles were sold annually between 2001 and 2005. Average annual vehicle use was 16,000 km in 2006. In terms of volume, passenger bus carriers were dominated by school bus services, although urban transit operations accounted for a far greater share of operating revenues. Public transport remained well supported in Canadian cities during the 1980s and 1990s, through bus routes, subway (metro) lines and commuter trains. The bus industry increased its revenues from C $5,400m. in 1995 to $9,600m. in 2006, and by that year 1,660m. passengers were using inter-city and urban transit bus services. Buses, subway trains and commuter trains were all well represented in Toronto's transport system, and both Toronto and Montréal had integrated the subway into subterranean shopping galleries. By 2006 Canada had a total of 67 urban transit systems, lower than the 1990 and 1980 figures (77 and 73, respectively), but a substantial increase from the 34 recorded in 1960. By 2005 some 20m. people were being provided with a transit service over 2,600 fixed routes that utilized buses, trolley coaches and light rail vehicles. In 2006 urban transit operators reported revenues of $6,620m., and passenger numbers of 1,710m.—the highest figure in two decades. Government contributions comprised 57% of these revenues; from 1996 to 2004 urban transit systems' operating revenues grew at an average annual rate of 5.1%, to reach $2,440m., increasing further, to $2,615m., in 2005. Commuter rail systems and motor-buses came to command a greater share of the operations at the expense of older forms of light-rail transport and of trolley-buses. Overall, Canadians were far more likely than their US counterparts to travel to work by public transport. The municipal authorities had responsibility for the construction and repair of highways, roads, streets and bridges. Maintenance costs increased with the pressures of truck growth; in 2005 it was reported that 18-wheel trucks were the fastest growing class of vehicle, with 11% more trucks over the previous three years. In winter, heavy snowfall presented extra problems and motorized sleds or 'snowmobiles' were in frequent use off the roads. This latter sector was an early contributor to the growth of Québec's Bombardier transportation manufacturing group. The later activities of Bombardier—which in 2007 announced 10 additional aircraft sales to Mesa Air Group of the USA—accounted for Canada's current rivalry with Brazil as a producer of short-haul/regional jet aircraft. In policy terms, key changes were the 2001 amendments to the Motor Vehicle Transport Act, which related mostly to safety issues. In 2006 the federal Government indicated that it would regulate the fuel consumption of road motor vehicles, starting in 2011. These regulations would build on the automobile industry's 2005 voluntary commitment to reduce greenhouse gases by 5.3m. metric tons by 2010 through improved fuel consumption.

Telecommunications

Canada is recognized as one of the most internet-friendly countries in the world, a status aided by low internet access costs. The World Economic Forum's Global Information Technology Report ranked Canada 10th, sixth, 11th and 13th in its global technology index in 2005, 2006, 2007 and 2008, respectively. One study ranked Canada as the best country in the world for 'e-government' for six years in a row (2000 to 2005). Statistics Canada noted that the public sector was 'wired' for internet communications to an unusually high degree compared with other countries—by 2007 93.2% of public sector enterprises had a website. Canada had the highest proportion of internet users in the world and was quick to take up high-speed internet access—85% of firms used broadband services in 2006, compared with 48% in 2001, and it appeared that uptake was reaching saturation point. Nevertheless, Canada lagged behind the USA in long-term computer investment and in e-commerce. Despite this, business-to-business (B2B) trade in Canada grew significantly in the late 1990s. By 2007 41% of Canadian companies had a website, compared with one-quarter in 2000. The value of sales over the internet increased to C $49,900m. in 2006, a 40% increase on the previous year; private sales comprised 93.2% of this total. It is worth noting, however, that by 2007 only 8% of private sector enterprises sold goods or services over the internet.

A general indication of internet usage was that by 2007 73% of individuals over 16 years of age had accessed the internet from some location or another in the preceding 12 months, although the figure was significantly lower for the over-65s. Internet usage is also associated with personal communications. Although Canadian young people used the internet more heavily than their US peers, they were still spending proportionately less on internet-ordered goods and services. It also appeared that by 2007 Alberta and British Columbia showed the highest levels of internet use, and that Newfoundland and Labrador and New Brunswick recorded the lowest. Internet usage is naturally highest where the population is generally younger and wealthier and, of course, work-places are a good source of internet access. A Canadian social trends report for 2002 noted that the use of the internet for government communications carried implications for social exclusion. The report stressed the age- and income-related biases in internet access. Indeed, in 2007 84% of individuals who had undergone some form of post-secondary education had internet access, compared with 58% for those who had not.

Despite the size of the country, the trans Canada telephone system was highly consolidated, the major holding company being Bell Canada Enterprises (BCE). The system had incorporated both publicly and privately owned carriers by the 1990s. The most significant change at that time was the entry of US firms such as Sprint Corpn and the American Telegraph and Telephone Co (AT&T) into the telephone market, as BCE lost its monopoly on long-distance telephone calls. BCE was, however, still Canada's largest telecommunications provider in 2007, with approximately 12m. fixed telephone lines and operating revenues of C $17,900m. However, the number of fixed lines had been dropping as increasing numbers of customers moved to wireless and other new technologies: the Canadian wireless industry had a market penetration of approximately 60% in 2007. By the end of 2006 BCE had 5.8m. wireless subscribers (up 7.9% on the previous year); supported 2.5m. high-speed internet users (a 12.2% increase); and supplied video content to 1.8m. customers. Nevertheless, Rogers Wireless remained the largest Canadian wireless provider, with almost 6.8m. voice and data subscribers by the end of 2006. While wireless telecommunications operators enjoyed an operating profit margin that increased by 26.2% in 2005, the profits of traditional wire-line operators fell by 12%, to $4,000m. Such changes indicated the importance of diversification, a policy that BCE pursued in its 2000 purchase of both the CTV television channel and Toronto's *Globe and Mail* newspaper (for many years Canada's only national newspaper) into Bell Globemedia, Inc. In late 2005, however, BCE reduced its stake in Bell Globemedia from 68.5% to 20.0%, before reducing its stake further, to 15.0%, in 2007—at which point the company was renamed CTVglobemedia and BCE considered it a discontinued operation. Moreover, in mid-2007 BCE was acquired, after significant counter-bidding, by a private equity consortium in which a significant presence was the Ontario Teachers' Pension Plan. Precise figures are always difficult to establish, but the all-cash transaction was valued at $51,700m. by BCE.

Telecommunications had long been significant in Canada—the size of the country had encouraged the rapid development of satellite technology and Canada was the third country, after the USA and the USSR, to put a satellite into orbit. By 2005 telecommunications services revenues had reached C $34,500m., driven by high-speed internet and wireless technologies. However, that year the sector became embroiled in controversy, following a ruling by the Canadian Radio-Television and Telecommunications Commission (CRTC) that traditional telephone and modern internet services were both serving the same purpose and should face similar regulation. The touchstone was Voice over Internet Protocol (VoIP) systems, which do not require a telephone line and hence brought internet, cable and traditional telephone companies into competition. The ruling required that the established telephone companies (with 98% control over the traditional telephone system) sign up to CRTC regulation in the VoIP sector. The ruling was clearly of greater benefit to new entrants to the market, since it prevented market leaders from pricing VoIP systems below cost in order to discourage competition. The ruling was received with dismay by the larger telephone companies, and the controversy continued.

The information and communications technology (ICT) sector contributed 5.9% of Canadian GDP in 2006 and employed 590,000 workers. The sector experienced an average annual growth rate of 8% between 1997 and 2005. Gross expenditure on research and development by ICT business enterprises amounted to C $14,850m. in 2006 (1.03% of GDP), but this only represented 38.6% of total ICT research and development spending. The satellite owner and operator Telesat Canada developed several orbiting satellites, and a number of television companies used 'satellite relay' signals. Remote northern locations could be integrated into the system via satellite-linked terminals linked to urban telecommunications networks. There was also progress in the area of fibre optics, with Saskatchewan Telecommunications initiating a project to create the longest fibre-optics system in the world. The federal Government made funds available to encourage innovation (including $240m. for Canada Research Chairs, a programme sponsoring research posts in universities, boosted by a further $113m. in 2008) and had set the target of being among the top five countries in research and development by 2010; at that point Canada had the 13th highest gross domestic expenditure on research and development, when measured as a proportion of GDP. The federal Government budgeted $9,200m. for science and technology spending in 2006/07 and published a new science and technology strategy, 'Mobilizing Science and Technology to Canada's Advantage', in May 2007. This strategy focused on nurturing a strong private commitment to science and technology, strengthening Canada's knowledge base and attracting talent in the field; it also included a $583m. award for research grants for 10,000 scientists.

Canada developed high-technology 'clusters' of research and manufacturing businesses—for example, high-tech and information services were concentrated in the main metropolitan areas of Toronto, Vancouver, Montréal, Ottawa-Hull, Edmonton (Alberta), Québec City and Calgary, which provided approximately one-half of this service sector. However, such developments were affected by economic contraction from 2001 (led by the 'dotcom' and telecommunications sectors in 2000). The collapse in stock market enthusiasm for internet-related and telecommunications activities caused the disappearance of many new companies, but also encouraged the investor-led pressure for mergers, acquisitions and disposals, which continued as 'telecoms' became less distinguishable from media generally (see below). This had the effect of reducing corporate research and development spending (for example, Nortel Networks cut such funding by 20% between 2002 and 2003), although expenditure had begun to rise slowly again by 2005. However, the talismanic BlackBerry, by Canada-based Research in Motion, continued to expand into new markets, with the People's Republic of China finally opening access in 2007.

The Canada Foundation for Innovation aimed to strengthen the research infrastructures of universities, hospitals and non-profit foundations. By 2008 the fund had awarded over C $3,800m. to nearly 5,800 projects at 128 research institutions, using a 40% contribution formula.

Utilities

Public utilities cover the production and distribution of electricity, gas, water and, often, telecommunications services—in particular, telephones. In Canada the electricity industry was long dominated by provincial crown corporations, the most important being Hydro Québec and Ontario Hydro, while gas supply was controlled privately. Use of 'Hydro' can be confusing—hydroelectricity per se was only a part of the generating system. That said, Québec in particular depended heavily on this 'clean' technology and, at the Robert-Bourassa power station, had the largest underground system in the world.

It is received wisdom that the high ratio of assets to revenue determined that electricity was best provided publicly; however, it must be noted that private electricity utilities did exist in the 1990s and, indeed, in Alberta they dominated the market. Whether publicly or privately owned, however, electricity utilities were all provincially regulated, except in the case of nuclear power generation, which was a federal responsibility. Utilities accounted for an estimated 90% of total energy production in the early 1990s, with heavy industries in major plant locations generating the remainder for their own use (for more detail and further developments, see the essay on Canadian Manufacturing and Construction). By 2006 the nuclear generation debate centred on whether the main technology of the future would be domestic CANDU reactors (which use pressurized heavy water, or deuterium oxide—the acronym comprises Canada, deuterium and uranium) or those supplied from foreign sources. Ontario, for example, had 20 CANDU reactors, but only five were in service in 2006. Atomic Energy of Canada Ltd (AECL) formed a 2006 consortium with SNC-Lavalin, GE Canada, Hitachi Canada and Babcock & Wilcox further to promote the CANDU technology. By 2008 it was being reported that the future of AECL was dependent on the success of its bid to build at least two of the two–four nuclear reactors proposed for Ontario. Should the bid fail, there were indications that the federal Government would sell AECL, a subsidized crown corporation. As so often occurs, the outcome of the deal was surrounded by the complexities of the relationship between a provincial contracting Government and a federally owned service provider, which raised questions regarding, for example, responsibility for cost over-runs.

Some provinces saw utilities as a possible way to offload debt, although Hydro Québec remained firmly in government hands and provided a good revenue stream to the provincial coffers—not least from selling power across the US border. The organization's large hydroelectric capacity provided a constant, predictable energy flow. However, future large-scale hydroelectric projects in Québec would face opposition on many fronts: environmental and land rights being prominent. Conversely, if the company failed to increase its base power generation capacity by the early 2010s, it would be exporting less and less electricity, as internal demands continued to grow. Other complications arose from long-standing, inter-province, fixed-price deals, which were entirely out of line with current prices.

In Ontario, by 2008 neither the generation facilities nor the main provincial distribution grid had been sold or privatized, although they had become independent, provincially owned companies, with the distribution portion being split from the group under the Ontario Power Generation umbrella. Ontario was not far from a 'crisis' situation vis-à-vis the availability of home-grown power, as the province's nuclear plants were ageing and needed to be refurbished or replaced. There was also the necessity of addressing the growing demand for power—the obverse of the 1990s downturn-induced power supply crisis. In 2006 the provincial Government of Ontario issued a directive that limited the nuclear power capacity of Ontario to 14,000 MW, while simultaneously urging that coal-fired power generation be replaced by cleaner methods within the earliest practical time frame. As of 2007 Ontario had four major sources of power: hydroelectric (with a capacity of around 7,000 MW); nuclear (installed capacity of 12,600 MW); coal (600 MW); and petroleum/gas (2,000 MW). In 2006 the Toronto-based Trillium Energy Corpn announced that it was seeking government approval for plans to build more than 140 wind turbines in Lake Ontario. The project would be the largest wind farm in North America, with a total capacity of 710 MW. As of 2006 the Ontario Power Authority had signed contracts for a total of 1,300 MW of wind-generated power. Finally, in a sign of the possible future development of Ontario's energy production, in 2007 the Ontario Power Authority signed 145 contracts for the construction of solar power systems with a total output of 250 MW (enough to power nearly 90,000 homes).

At the federal level, the 2005 budget offered C $3,000m. of funding for research into environmentally friendly energy production. This included $1,000m. for an innovative Clean Fund to tackle greenhouse gas emissions, $200m. to stimulate the use of wind power and nearly $100m. to encourage the uptake of other sources of renewable energy. This focus on renewable energy and climate change was followed up in the 2006 government budget, which provided $4,500m. for environmental initiatives, including $2,000m. over seven years to support the production of renewable fuels and $1,500m. for the Canada ecoTrust for Clean Air and Climate Change.

RETAILING AND WHOLESALING

Retailing

The 'Americanization' of, or growing US influence over, Canadian retailing was a prominent feature from the late 20th century. Many famous Canadian retail names, such as Eaton's Department Stores, were declared bankrupt. That said, retail is a constantly changing field, well covered by definitive reports from the Centre for the Study of Commercial Activity in Canada (CSCA) at Ryerson University, Toronto. In 2003 the CSCA noted that 'in recent years Canada has lost major retail chains such as Kmart and Eaton's, while gaining new ones like the Gap and Home Depot'. Incidentally, the reports began to use the North American Industrial Classification System, a sign of yet closer economic integration and accounting standards with the USA. The trend towards market polarization—particularly for department store type merchandise—underpinned these changes. The consumer 'middle market' seemed to split into those willing and able to shop for more expensive designer goods and those generally driven to seek the lowest price. The latter market proved especially attractive to the US-owned Wal-Mart and to other price-focused retailers, with their Canadian operations showing good sales performances in the late 1990s and beyond: Wal-Mart had 309 Canadian stores by 2008, a growing proportion of which were so-called 'supercenters'. The retail trade was also subject to the merger and acquisition pressures evidenced elsewhere, such as the 2001 merger of Indigo and Chapters in the book trade. Predictably, the health of the retail trade tends to mirror trends in the wider economy, and it can be used as a barometer of the economy in general and of consumer confidence in particular. By 2007 total Canadian retail trade turnover had reached C $412,000m., at current prices. In terms of provinces, in 2007 Ontario accounted for the largest share of the retail market (35.4%), followed by Québec (22.0%), Alberta (14.8%) and British Columbia (13.7%). These shares had not changed greatly since 1995, although Alberta's retail sector had grown (driven by the 'oil boom' economy), overtaking British Columbia's in 2006.

Overall, in competing for the consumer dollar, retailing was in constant competition with the attractions of financial investment and other commercial services and, thus, it did not necessarily benefit whenever the economy recovered from recession. Structurally, there was substantial market concentration in the late 20th century, with 'retail chains' (nationwide chains of retail stores) or 'multiple' traders dominating in the department store, grocery, variety and general merchandizing sectors. Although Québec retained a higher percentage of independent retailers (possibly reflecting a different distribution system for alcohol), these retailers suffered from declining demand and from the arrival of a significant number of new rivals throughout the 1990s.

Large shopping centres predominated in the retail system of the post-Second World War period—copying the US trend—and were for many years seen as the driving force of retail growth. Groups such as Cadillac Fairview and (through-cross-holdings) Olympia & York became synonymous with large urban and suburban developments. In 1995 there were 1,558 of these centres, with over 300m. sq ft (27.87m. sq m) of floor area (about one-third of the grand total area), containing more than one-half of all the chain stores. Developers of these centres still regarded department stores as the essential focus for any proposed scheme. However, the trend in the mid-1990s was to seek to incorporate many more of the smaller specialists in what had become a highly segmented market. Commercial pressures forced frequent redevelopments or refurbishments, and there was a tendency for larger stores to be reduced in size in order to free up more space for smaller store units. The largest regional centres and so-called 'mega malls' commonly dominated suburban shopping facilities, as metropolitan growth accelerated into previously undeveloped areas with little existing infrastructure. This led to the development of extremely large free-standing shopping centres or malls, such as the West Edmonton Mall in Alberta, which was expanded to an alleged total area of more than 5m. sq ft, making it the world's largest shopping centre. More conservative estimates calculated the size of the mall to be 3.8m. sq ft, still by far the largest of the 19 Canadian malls that had an area in excess of 1m. sq ft. (The West Edmonton Mall has since been surpassed in size by developments in China, such as the South China Mall.) A reluctance to invest in new mall developments resulted in a return to city centre redevelopments, the best-known being the Toronto Eaton Centre, built at a cost of C $265m. and with a gross leasable area of 2.6m. sq ft. The lack of prime sites in the 1990s, which obliged developers to target unfeasibly small settlements for new mall investments, coupled with new market competition, probably contributed to the restructuring of the long-established Eaton's chain in 1997, and to its later bankruptcy problems. Following this bankruptcy, the eponymous store disappeared from the north end of the Toronto Eaton Centre, an area which was further remodelled with new large retail units, parking and the new Ted Rogers Business School building for Ryerson University. Larger, and more established, developments in Toronto and Montréal had underground pedestrian links that were integrated with their respective rail subway systems. The post-NAFTA US invasion was much more dominated by low-cost, free-standing units or sheds. These housed giant, 'category-killer' stores, specializing in one highly focused sector. The lower land and construction costs for such retailers, and a heavy focus on price, led many more established Canadian chains into trading losses by 2002. Agglomeration of several such outlets in approximately the same location (a major freeway intersection, for example) gives rise to what is termed a 'power centre', with a market 'pull' sometimes approaching that of a shopping mall. Naturally, the build costs are far lower than those of a mall, thus aiding profitability.

The nature of the shopping mall market itself changed. As noted, developments that could be legitimately defined as regional shopping centres or malls had all but ceased by 1990. Not a single enclosed shopping mall was built in Ontario from approximately that date until the opening of the Vaughan Mills centre in the mid-2000s. That said, the Mills format did not feature traditional department stores, and the key attraction was the Pro-Bass sports and outdoor activities outlet, measuring 130,000 sq ft. By 2006 the Mills Corpn had sold its interests in the Vaughan mall to Ivanhoe-Cambridge in order to finance debts, and the following year the company itself was bought by the USA-based Simon Property group, resulting in the rebranding of all the former Mills malls. Vaughan typified the sprawl that now characterized the retail structure of the Greater Toronto area, most notably at the intersection of Highway 400 and Highway 7. Each quadrant of this major intersection was filled with retail 'big-box' sheds, including Wal-Mart and its Sam's format, IKEA, Costco and scores of other single outlets. Nearer the city centre, similar styles of outlets were now found at Eglinton and Warden. The established mall developers had become more concerned with the proper management of existing cornerstone assets. The Real Estate Investment Trusts (REITs) were more conservative retail players, but not immune from the wider changes. As noted, the consumer dollar was increasingly being spent in large retail sheds, predominantly owned by US corporations, and these, too, generated substantial property profits. In early 2005 FirstPro Shopping Centres sold big-box malls worth C $1,200m. to Calloway Real Estate Investment Trust. In September 2008 Canadian Real Estate Investment Trust announced that it had acquired eight stores from Canadian Tire Corpn, indicating market support for the big-box format. Meanwhile, The Great Atlantic & Pacific Tea Co (owner of the familiar Dominion format) was offered for sale in early 2005 for close to $1,800m. Competition laws were said to have made a bid by rival Loblaws (George Weston group) unlikely, and Metro Inc was the eventual purchaser. In August 2008 it was reported that Metro would brand all its stores as Metro. This announcement coincided with an increase in Metro's sales growth in the third quarter of 2008, to $3,370m. This process of consolidation left Canada with a very concentrated retail market and, as Loblaws sought to compete with Wal-Mart, it announced in 2007 a reduction of one-fifth of its roughly 5,000 head office jobs. This might have been inspired by the reality that Wal-Mart traditionally had a very lean and low-profile head office presence. A gradual leaching away of spending from traditional centres gave rise to fears that Canada might finally follow the USA down the road of deserted city centres. While Montréal, Toronto and Vancouver—all key immigrant destinations—remained robust, there was a 'hollowing out' of downtown areas in cities such as Edmonton and Winnipeg (Manitoba). As trade moved to sheds, of course, it further undermined the department stores that traditionally anchored shopping malls. The REITs were, therefore, not immune to the wider trends in retail shopping patterns.

More individualistic and often open-air city centre redevelopments exploited the trend towards leisure, heritage or 'festival' marketing. Unique historical locations, such as the Old Port in Montréal, the Byward Market in Ottawa and Gastown in Vancouver, were thereby exploited for retail opportunities as early as the 1970s. These developments also inevitably featured as tourist destinations (see below). It was suggested that more marginal inner-city retail locations might benefit from evolving into 'speciality' retail markets. It should also be noted that Toronto pioneered the concept of business improvement districts, and thriving ethnic retail areas, such as Greektown on the Danforth, profited as a result, strengthening the resistance to out-of-town developments.

The structure of the food store sector was profoundly affected from the late 1980s onwards by the development of 'superstores' or 'mega-markets' approaching the size of such stores in the United Kingdom or in France. Indeed, in 2005 Loblaws announced a move to prioritize these larger formats, after their success in areas such as Alberta. This move to large, free-standing food outlets generated a great deal of competition between the principal grocery chains, all of which began either to develop superstores or to react to their presence in some other way. Probably the most potent of the new competitive forces were the new arrivals from the USA. It was not clear if NAFTA had an effect in this aggressive movement of several US chains into Canada during the 1990s. Foremost among these chains was Wal-Mart, which obtained market entry by buying Woolco operations in Canada. As with Wal-Mart's early US operations, Woolco was dominantly a non-food retailer. As more of the Wal-Mart business in the USA came to encompass food sales, so newer Wal-Mart proposals in Canada included food sales. A more measured but, nevertheless, powerful market entry was made by warehouse membership clubs such as Price Costco. Market concentration was also evident in the 1990s, with a small number of Canadian chains controlling more than one-half of the market until the influx of US companies towards the end of the decade. From that point, big-box, US-owned corporations such as Home Depot became market-dominant. By 2006 94 major corporations accounted for 78.2% of all retail sales; the top three, with sales worth over

C $10,000m. (Weston, Wal-Mart and Sobeys), controlled 25% of all retail sales. Looking at the market share of the leading four chains (Wal-Mart, Costco, Hudson's Bay Co and Sears), the most concentrated sector was general merchandise, at 94.4%; in 2006 Hudson's Bay, a totemic name in Canadian business history and the sole Canadian operation among the top four, was itself sold to US-based interests. Wal-Mart courted controversy by closing a Québec store (Jonquière) in 2005. Allegations that this closure was a response to pro-trade union activities at the store led to a legal challenge, which reached the Canadian Supreme Court in 2008.

There was a growing trend towards franchising, particularly in fast food outlets originating in the USA. The most symbolic domestic fast food operation, Tim Horton's doughnut chain, eventually became embroiled in merger/demerger activity with US interests. By August 2008 Tim Horton's was registering sales of over C $510m. Franchising was also an increasing factor in the convenience store sector, albeit at a slower rate than for the fast food sector. Non-store-based selling was also well established in Canada: T. Eaton Co had introduced the first mail-order sales system in 1884. As in most other developed countries, the internet was growing as a source of goods and services. Indeed, online sales by private firms rose by 25% between 2006 and 2007, to $58,200m., although e-commerce only accounted for just under 2% of the total retail market. In 2005 43% of internet users said that they used the internet to order personal goods or services and 57% said that they 'window-shopped' online. Figures from 2005 showed that travel arrangements accounted for 36.4% of electronic orders by individuals, followed by books, magazines and online newspapers (35.4%) and clothing, jewellery and accessories (24.8%). The B2B implications of e-commerce were the most promising and consumer goods were far behind other sectors (such as the computer industry itself or the motor vehicle industry, with its 'just-in-time' delivery systems). Indeed, 62% of total online sales in 2007 were B2B. Business use of the internet to purchase goods varied greatly according to industry; in 2007 it was utilized by 74.0% of the information and cultural sector, but by only 31.3% of the accommodation and food sector. An adjunct to the pressures on retailers was the appeal, in 2008, to find ways of reducing the fees imposed by credit card issuers.

Wholesaling

Towards the end of the 20th century manufacturers and retailers reduced the scope of the wholesale 'middleman', although wholesale sales grew steadily in the first years of the 21st century, increasing from C $374,200m. in 2000 to $517,800m. in 2007. The wholesale industry was the fastest growing of all the major industrial sectors between 2001 and 2006, and employed just under 760,000 workers in 2007 (4.5% of total employment). In 2006 the sector achieved its best performance in seven years (measured in constant dollars), driven by the western provinces: between 2002 and 2005 wholesale sales in British Columbia, Manitoba, Saskatchewan and Alberta grew at an average annual rate of 9.1%. Alberta's performance was particularly noticeable: the province registered annual double-digit increases in sales between 2004 and 2006, although growth actually dipped below the national average in 2007. Notably, sales in Saskatchewan rose by 19.3% between 2006 and 2007, the highest rate of growth since the statistical series began in 1993. In contrast, the growth of Ontario's wholesale trade was limited by the poor performance of the automotive sector in 2005, although the province's performance picked up in 2006. Hitherto, pressure on wholesalers had come from manufacturers undertaking direct selling to the public or to a large retailer, and from the retailers sometimes having their own distribution networks. Indeed, this latter phenomenon was revolutionized in the 1990s by increased sophistication in retail logistics. Wal-Mart, for example, developed its own satellite-co-ordinated retail replenishment system. The general weakness of wholesale trade relative to retailers should not detract from its significance; it served export trades as well as retailers. However, the spatial and employment implications of wholesaling, an activity that was most prevalent in the major urban areas, were neither as complex nor as significant for society at large as those of retailing.

MEDIA

The Press

By 2008 the important distinction between content and delivery was fundamental to understanding change in the media as a whole, but especially in press and television broadcasting. Some organizations, such as the Canadian Broadcasting Corporation (CBC—see below) were declared to be content-providers, dedicated to producing news and programming. Other operators saw themselves as deliverers or disseminators of the products of others, or as technology providers to both. This question of positioning and control underpinned much contemporary change.

There was an early trend towards concentration of newspaper ownership after 1913, when 138 newspaper titles were in circulation. The increasing importance first of radio and then of television, with the ensuing competition for advertising revenue, soon precipitated a number of mergers and takeovers. (The advertising factor was crucial, as advertising space generated far more income than newspaper sales.) In time, the Toronto-based *Globe and Mail*, which published regional editions and obtained its second greatest circulation in Alberta, came closest of all to the concept of a 'national daily'. Its status was only later challenged by the *National Post*, started with the express intent of providing national coverage (see below). Although there remained a relatively high number of titles by the end of the 1990s, further market concentration during the decade meant that they were owned by a handful of media groups. Problems in the sector as a whole were experienced from the late 1980s onwards, when advertising revenues again began to decline, a problem that resurfaced in 2000–01. This left a very concentrated, monopolistic newspaper market, which had parallels in the magazine trade, where the Maclean-Hunter group predominated.

Other trends in the newspaper sector in the 1990s included a rise in the number of 'small city' dailies and the increasing use of new technology. There was an increase in the number of free, community-based newspapers; these too tended to be published by the major conglomerates. There were also a few minority language newspapers, serving local Chinese, Italian or other communities. Toronto, Montréal and Vancouver accounted for the majority of the daily newspaper circulation. Concentration, in information terms, was compounded by the fact that the newspaper owners also controlled the leading news agency, the Canadian Press. Most chains diversified into videotext, screen-print technology and online services. As a testimony to the enduring popularity of newspapers, it was estimated that they remained the most important recipients of advertising revenue in 1997—still well ahead of television. This was partly due to newspapers' penetration into higher income markets.

Substantial restructuring of the sector took place in 2000, with the sale of major parts of Conrad Black's Hollinger holdings in Canada. With 59 dailies and 300 community papers, Southam/Hollinger had a substantial press portfolio to dispose of as it contemplated moves into other delivery systems. By November 2000 CanWest, the owners of which were the Asper family of Global Television Network, had agreed a C $3,500m. deal to secure some 150 titles, including 13 major city dailies, 50% of the *National Post* (subject to some editorial constraints), a range of magazines and the portal Canada.com. This trade further stressed the schism between the provision of content and the ownership of delivery media. The Competition Bureau, for example, felt that newspapers, internet businesses and television were not in the same markets for retail advertising. Hence, it could see no conflict-of-interest or monopoly problems, although some cross-holding divestitures were occasionally demanded within particular diversified groups. There was also a feeling in some quarters that Hollinger was under actual pressure to offload titles. Whether or not this was true, the deal proved again that timing is all. By the time that the effects of the September 2001 terrorist attacks on the USA and the stock market falls of 2002 were factored in, the deal looked good for the vendor. As Nick Baxter-Moore, Associate Professor at Brock University, St Catharines, Ontario, has shown, a side agenda was an ongoing debate over the way that the takeover also appeared to bring a change in editorial perspectives (allegedly away from the Toronto-based norm). The economics of the deal were studied again in July 2002 when CanWest, in turn, sold 12 titles in Atlantic Canada and Saskatchewan, for a reported $255m., to Québec-based Transcontinental. At the time CanWest was reported to be $3,900m. in debt—a large part of it owing to the earlier Hollinger purchases. Inevitably, discussion of the CanWest deal became intertwined with the fate of all of Conrad Black's titles as a result of corporate governance issues. In July 2007 Black was found guilty by US courts in Chicago, Illinois, of a series of corporate governance malpractices, but was cleared of more serious charges of racketeering. The full implications of these convictions were unlikely to be clear for some time. That said, even by November 2005 the once-dominant Hollinger no longer owned any Canadian titles, as opposed to 26 in 1999 and 10 earlier in 2005—indeed, it was the disbursement of monies from the dispersals that, in part, occupied the courts. After Quebecor/Sun Media purchased Osprey Media in 2007, it became the largest newspaper owner, with 37 titles, followed by CanWest's 13, although CanWest remained the leader in terms of circulation (with 27% of total paid Canadian circulation). In 2007 the Canadian Thomson Corpn (owners of a 40% stake in the *Globe and Mail*) agreed a $48,700m. merger offer with the British news agency Reuters. Despite increasing choices in media, the total number of weekly readers in the top 17 markets grew steadily from 11.3m. in 1998 to 11.8m. in 2006. This included 8m. readers in the major markets of Toronto, Montréal, Ottawa, Calgary and Vancouver. Canada had some 100 general interest daily papers, with a total daily newspaper paid circulation of 31.1m. copies per week, which meant that every day one in five Canadians bought a daily newspaper. It is perhaps interesting to note that broadsheet dailies account for three-quarters of copies sold. The *Toronto Star* boasted the largest individual circulation, with a week-day circulation of 436,700 copies in 2007. This was significantly above the two titles with claim to 'national' status, the *Globe and Mail* (322,800) and Conrad Black's original initiative the *National Post* (203,800). Indeed, the regional bias of Canadian newspapers remained significant: of a newspaper's advertising content, local or retail advertising accounted for 53%, classified 28% and national or general 19%. A recent development in the newspaper sector was the rise of free newspapers: by 2006 five ownership groups published approximately 30 free dailies in Canada, with an estimated daily average circulation of 1.3m. It is suggested that such free newspapers might be successful in attracting a new, younger readership.

Radio and Television

The publicly owned CBC, established in 1936, provides a national radio and television broadcasting service in English and French. By 2006/07 its annual operating revenues were C $1,630m. and it had a well-established online presence. There were also several broadcasting organizations that received provincial funding. The principal private networks included the CTV Television Network (owned by CTVglobemedia), Global Television Network and TVA Réseau de Télévision (a French-language network). In 2005 Canadians had access to 467 English-language television services, 106 French-language services and 86 third-language services. In 2007 operating revenues in the television broadcasting sector reached $6,200m. and sales of airtime for Canadian broadcasters reached $3,300m., although growth appeared to be slowing.

From its introduction into Canada in the early 1950s, television broadcasting was increasingly influenced by developments in cable-transmission technology. Cable television, which offered improved reception, was already taken by some 74% of Canadian homes by 1991/92. Following a number of federal–provincial jurisdictional disputes during the 1970s, the CRTC liberalized its position in the 1980s and cable services were expanded. As in the USA, services were targeted at specific sub-sectors of the community rather than at specific geographical areas. Satellite technology and the development of fibre-optics both helped to enhance the capacity for wide spatial coverage to selected audiences. With many Canadians living close to the border with the USA (the Great Lakes-St Lawrence Lowlands area, for example, had more than one-half of the total Canadian population), cable television also brought good-quality reception of the main US channels to a majority of Canadian homes. In 2007 the dominant cable operators in Canada were Shaw in western Canada and Rogers in the east. Shaw had revenues of C $2,500m. in 2006 (an 11% increase on the previous year) and 2.2m. cable television customers (approximately 28% of the Canadian cable television market). Rogers Cable and Telecom had 2.3m. cable subscribers (approximately 30% of the market) and total revenues of $3,600m. in 2007. In that year the CRTC approved Rogers' acquisition of five CITY-TV stations from CTVglobemedia. Both Rogers and Shaw had high penetration levels, providing services to around 70% of homes covered. Both had also expanded to provide broadband, wireless and standard internet access. In addition, as noted above, VoIP technology formed an increasingly important part of cable companies' strategies. Such diversification was particularly important in helping Shaw to rebuff the challenge of Albertan telecommunications company TELUS, the growth of which had been posing a threat to the dominant provider since 2001. The market for which such companies compete is indeed vast: by 2005 99% of Canada's 12.6m. households owned a television set, while 63.7% owned two or more. In that year the average Canadian watched 25.1 hours of television per week. Nevertheless, cable television subscriptions declined in the early years of the 21st century, owing to the growing popularity of direct-to-home satellite services, which had attracted 2.2m. subscribers and a 23.4% market share by 2004. It appeared that the cable companies had halted this decline by that year, since their subscriber numbers climbed slightly in 2005 as well, to stand at 7.6m. Another noticeable trend has been the growth in pay and speciality television revenues, which rose to $2,700m. in 2007. This represented the strongest growth of all the television sectors, and there were signs that the revenues of speciality digital channels would soon overtake those generated by conventional television.

TOURISM AND RECREATION

By the mid-2000s the most prominent new tourist opportunity for Canada was the award of the 2010 Winter Olympics, to be hosted by several locations in British Columbia. Moreover, in 2005 the Canadian Tourism Commission, recognizing the rising importance of urban tourists to a dominantly urban country, announced that it would shelve its traditional focus on 'Mounties, mountains and moose'. The World Tourism Organization ranked Canada as the 10th most popular travel market, holding 2.5% of the total international travel market. Canada's tourism industry was a major contributor to the domestic economy (total tourism GDP reached C $28,600m. in 2007—2.3% of Canada's GDP). In 2007 tourism spending in Canada reached $70,800m., a 6.1% increase on the previous year. The sector employed 653,000 workers in 2007 and involved, directly or indirectly, many different government departments and agencies. However, looking more widely, a vital element of trade imbalances in Canada was the vastly greater amount spent by Canadians travelling abroad than by visitors coming to Canada: the deficit reached $5,800m. in 2005, as fewer US residents visited Canada while, at the same time, an increasing number of Canadians travelled to the USA. Driven by higher travel spending abroad, the deficit then surged to $7,200m. in 2006 and to a record $10,300m. in 2007, 68.9% of which was related to travel between the USA and Canada. Indeed, visitors from the USA constituted by far the largest group of foreign tourists, accounting for 25.7m. of the 30.4m. non-resident travellers entering Canada in 2007. Underpinning these trends, it became impossible to ignore the fact that some provinces were suffering quite badly. For example, in the summer of 2008 23 out of 30 major tourist destinations reported poorer year-on-year figures. Adding a high-valued Canadian currency to the mix, Ontario had begun to experience year-on-year falls in visitors from the USA. Whereas some 30m. US tourists visited in 1999, by 2006 the total had dropped to just 17.4m. While the USA was by far the most popular destination for Canadians, who made 17.8m. overnight visits there in 2007, overseas tourism was increasingly popular, accounting for more than 6m. overnight visits in that year. Mexico and the United Kingdom were the most popular destinations. Nevertheless, internal domestic tourism generated 77% of Canada's tourism income in 2007 (up from 66% in the late 1990s), and Canadians made an estimated 207m. trips within their country. For the smaller provinces, tourism was a crucial source of income and it represented the greatest single source of employment for Prince Edward Island. A large part of the tourism deficit was due to the number of short trips made by Canadians to the USA, often associated with cross-border shopping.

US citizens generally viewed Canada as a safe tourist destination, from a terrorist perspective at least, and after 2001 there was a trend for US and Canadian tourists to confine their tourism mainly to the North American continent. Despite this, the number of overnight trips by US residents to Canada fell significantly in the 21st century, from 16.2m. in 2002 to 13.4m. in 2007. Furthermore, a downward trend in overseas visitors to Canada had been established, steadily decreasing from 4.64m. visitors in 2000 to 3.91m. by 2003. The industry then staged a recovery, with tourism expenditure increasing each quarter between the third quarter of 2003 and the fourth quarter of 2005; this generated overall growth of 11%. Tourism GDP, employment and foreign and domestic demand all increased steadily after the trough of 2003. Indeed, by 2007 the number of non-US visitors was at its highest level since 1997.

Provinces naturally showed a great deal of variability in their capacity to appeal to tourists. For example, 2007 figures showed that Ontario attracted 42.4% of overnight trips, British Columbia 24.1%, Québec 15.0%, Alberta 8.9%, the Maritime provinces 5.2%, and Manitoba and Saskatchewan together 2.7%. The major cities, led by Toronto (where 15.9m. visitor nights were spent by Canadians alone in 2004), were favoured visitor destinations, but they also marketed themselves as event destinations (with, for example, Calgary holding the 1988 Winter Olympics and Edmonton, the Albertan capital, hosting the World Athletics Championships in 2001).

The National Parks system (dating from 1885) also remained popular, particularly given the importance of outdoor activities to Canada's strong domestic leisure market. The largest park, at 17,472 sq miles (44,802 sq km) in extent, was Wood Buffalo, designated a World Heritage site by UNESCO. Wood Buffalo straddles the border between northern Alberta and the Northwest Territories. More popular with tourists, however, was Banff, the first National Park to be created and home to popular destinations such as the town of Banff itself and nearby Lake Louise and Moraine Lake. This park was created west of Calgary, on the eastern slope of the Rocky Mountains; it covers 2,564 sq miles (6,641 sq km) and attracted 3.2m. visitors in 2005, generating over C $700m. in direct tourism revenues. Alberta's Jasper National Park, north of Banff, received nearly 2m. visitors in 2005.

BANKING AND FINANCE

The financial sector as a whole was an increasingly major part of the Canadian economy, representing over 6% of the country's GDP and employing some 600,000 people. Although Canada's first chartered bank was set up in Montréal in 1817, by 2004 all the leading Canadian financial concerns had their headquarters in Toronto (also the principal cheque-clearing centre for the country); nevertheless, some important organizations were still based in Montréal. Canada's 72 banks manage C $2,500,000m. in assets and the market capitalization of the leading six Canadian domestic banks stood at $198,900m. in 2005. In that year three Canadian banks featured in the global top five for shareholder returns. Canadian banking in 2005 was highly profitable, providing an average return on equity of 17.3%, although the market capitalization of Bank of Nova Scotia (the leader in shareholder returns) was barely 15% of that of Citibank in the USA.

The Canadian financial sector was historically seen as a 'four-pillar' structure, comprising first and foremost the 'Big Six' national chartered banks (Royal Bank of Canada, Canadian Imperial Bank of Commerce—CIBC, Bank of Montréal, Bank of Nova Scotia—Scotiabank, Toronto-Dominion Bank and National Bank of Canada). The other three pillars were trust companies, insurance companies and securities dealers. This situation prevailed until 1987, when the federal regulatory system was overhauled and the financial sector was deregulated. The pre-existing structure broadly resulted from the implementation of regulatory procedures that actively separated out the four functions, but from the early 1980s it was increasingly outdated, and the boundaries between the sectors became less distinct. Powerful conglomerates came to combine the operations of trust, insurance and mutual fund (unit trust) companies to give a scope far wider than that of the banks. It was clear that the system in general was influenced by the recession of 1981–82, when companies seeking loans from the financial sector were subject to vastly increased interest charges on loans, to the further detriment of their (already reduced) general trading performance. In addition, problems arose where banks had been involved in substantial lending to resource groups acquiring rival concerns on the assumption that petroleum prices would remain high.

Resultant moves away from straightforward loans from banks increased pressure for change in the financial sector, while the banks themselves responded by increasing the difference between borrowing and lending rates in order to maintain profits. High inflation in the 1970s worked in favour of banks, which could offer short-term loans, and against the trust companies, which were restricted to longer-term lending. Later, the trust companies constituted the banks' greatest trading competitors, as they moved quickly into the area of deposit and cheque accounts and credit cards. These factors, combined with a traditionally restrictive attitude to foreign competition in general, naturally led to pressures for liberalization. Examples of restrictions included limitations placed on individual holdings in chartered banks and restrictions on the scale of operations by foreign banks. These restrictions were eased in 1980 to allow foreign banks to own subsidiaries (known as Schedule B banks), which numbered 24 by 2007. One effect of prevailing restrictions was a virtually closed securities dealing market. This, functioning for a small domestic population, resulted in relatively high commissions, and was possibly one of the factors that led to the concentration of the securities market—a characteristic shared with chartered banks. Much deregulatory attention inevitably focused on securities trading, where again the federal–provincial dichotomy existed. Provincially, securities trading dominantly concerned Ontario, where trading firms had to be registered with the Ontario Securities Commission and registration was not open to non-residents of Ontario. This restriction on the principal securities trading forum for the country, the world's fourth largest equity market, was a target for revision of regulatory procedures. The Toronto Stock Exchange became the main centre of activity, and by 1995 it was already capitalized at US $332,500m. By 31 December 2003 the total market capitalization of its 3,600 issuers was nearly US $889,000m., and the bourse achieved a record US $1,100,000m. traded value in 2005. As with all major exchanges, private equity inputs—and corporate governance issues—were to the fore by 2007. In respect of the latter, a survey that year indicated that 23% of smaller venture operations on the Toronto Stock Exchange did not have appropriate corporate governance disclosure.

In the 1980s the Canadian banking system became subject to a series of disruptive influences, one of which was the 'Little Bang' regulatory reform of June 1987. The 'Little Bang' was perceived as a measured response to the financial deregulation following the United Kingdom's 'Big Bang' of 1986. Japanese, US and European interests quickly applied for the registration of subsidiaries with the Ontario Securities Commission, although the maximum proportion of foreign shareholding in full-service securities dealers was limited to 50% until mid-1988. For the initial foreign moves into the Canadian market, which needed approval from the federal Minister of Finance, companies from countries where Canada had equal trading rights, such as the United Kingdom, were favoured. Québec, where conglomerate chains had begun to appear prior to deregulation, was quick to follow the deregulation trend. Life insurance companies 'demutualized' and acquired both trust companies and estate agencies. Transparently, the crossing of traditional operating boundaries posed problems for the regulatory authorities.

Owing to the national scope of the property market, the loans to this sector, as in the United Kingdom and the USA, were considerable. For example, Olympia & York (O&Y), arguably the world's largest property company, was a principal consumer of credit in the late 1980s, as it pursued a policy of expansion. The economic recession of this period then left the company unable to service its debts and its trading was compromised in many of its centres of operation. (After extensive restructuring O&Y Properties—and its related income trust—came to the market in 2005 to receive bids for a property portfolio valued at around C $2,000m.) The same deregulation that had presaged endless growth led to merger and consolidation and, often, to a release of surplus office space, with negative effects on the property sector. Finally, a trend towards the creation of merchant banks became evident in the financial sector during the 1990s, as did the inevitable process of mergers between banks and trust companies. In 1999 federal regulators permitted foreign banks to operate full-service branches rather than function via subsidiaries.

New technology proved especially important to the Canadian banking industry; in 2006 alone Canada's six largest banks collectively spent C $4,400m. on technology. Canadians became the highest per-head users of debit card services (88.2 transactions per head in 2005) and automatic banking machines (ABMs—of which 16,424 were owned by banks in 2007). By 2007 the Canadian credit market was one of the most competitive in the world; the country had 64.1m. VISA and Mastercard credit cards in circulation, making transactions worth $224,000m. Per-head credit card transactions were almost double those of the United Kingdom, for instance. A 2006 survey found that 27% of customers banked primarily over the internet (up from 8% in 2000), while 45% of respondents had used online banking during the past year. These technological developments altered the way that Canadians banked: a 2006 Strategic Counsel survey found that the use of ABMs—more commonly known as ATMs or automated teller machines—was the main method of banking for 33% of customers, with 29% conducting their transactions in person and 27% over the internet. Although Canadians had the world's best access to ABMs, the introduction of usage fees meant that transactions at bank-owned ABMs fell in the 2000s, as customers took advantage of free 'cash back' services. It is noteworthy that, despite NAFTA, foreign banks still had to form subsidiaries in order to open branches in Canada. By 2007 there were 22 Schedule I domestic banks, 24 subsidiaries of foreign banks and 26 foreign bank branches. As of 2006 five Canadian banks ranked among the world's 100 leading banks, judged by asset size: the Royal Bank of Canada was placed 40th, with assets of $557,100m.; Toronto-Dominion Bank 47th ($407,800m.); Scotiabank 49th ($393,400m.); Bank of Montréal 56th ($324,600m.); and CIBC 58th ($315,500m.). While banking still accounted for over 55% of the financial sector's total assets, other areas had grown in significance. For example, mutual funds were the fastest growing segment of the financial services sector during the 1990s, with assets increasing from $25,000m. in December 1990 to $439,000m. by 2003. Such companies held $700,000m. of assets as of July 2007—approximately one-fifth of the financial services sector—and enjoyed growth in assets of $90,300m. in 2006. By that time there were approximately 70 fund management companies, employing 70,000 people. The share of domestic equity in mutual fund assets fell from 35% in December 2005 to 27% in July 2007 (the same as 2001 levels). The removal of restrictions in 2005 meant that investors could allocate as much as 100% of their registered portfolios into mutual funds. The proportion of foreign bank subsidiaries and full-service branches increased from 5.7% of the deposit-taking sector in 1997 to 7.9% in 2004. The securities industry grew significantly during the 1990s and into the 21st century: in 2007 it generated record revenues of $17,000m., 37% of which were derived from commissions from trading. However, Canada remained the only member of the International Organization of Securities Commissions that lacked a national security regulator, which meant that there were 13 different securities regulators accountable to 13 different governments. It has been estimated that Canada loses $10,000m. in economic output each year as a consequence of this fragmentation. The creation of a single securities regulator was outlined by the federal Government in its 2007 paper 'Creating a Canadian Advantage in Global Capital Markets', which had four strands: enhancing regulatory efficiency; strengthening market integrity; creating better opportunity for businesses and investors; and improving investor information. In February 2007 the Canadian Securities Administrators published the National Instrument 31-103 'Registration Requirements', which proposed the harmonizing, streamlining and modernizing of registration requirements across the 13 Canadian jurisdictions. Furthermore, in February 2008 the Canadian Expert Panel on Securities Regulation was created to advise the federal Government on the harmonization of securities regulation and to draft a 'model' securities act by the end of that year.

Consolidation was a feature of the Canadian financial services sector as a whole. For example, the total number of credit unions and caisses populaires declined from 2,700 in 1990 to 1,100 by 2005. By 2007 there were only 479 credit unions and caisses populaires affiliated to the Credit Union Central of Canada, although combined assets had risen by 43% since 2002. Mergers in the banking sector caused the most controversy. For example, in 2000 Toronto-Dominion carried out a successful C $8,000m. takeover of Canada Trust, a move that involved the potential closure of branches in overlapping catchment areas. This reignited the issue of branch closures, which had been central to earlier plans by the four largest banks to pair off—CIBC with Toronto-Dominion and the Royal Bank with the Bank of Montréal. Between them they controlled assets of $730,000m., leaving the next largest bank, Scotiabank, standing aloof. There were clear advantages in further concentrating an already concentrated market, not least in terms of the potentially lucrative property portfolio rationalization. Reaction to the proposals was mixed and a moratorium was declared, with the then Minister of Finance eventually making a statement on the framework for reform in June 1999. Central to discussion was the Bank Act, the last enacted in 1997, which was the principal legislative measure, with the Office of the Superintendent of Financial Institutions the principal federal agent. A key feature of the 1997 Act was that no single shareholder could hold more than 10% of any bank. The 1999 statement indicated that this would rise to 20% of voting and 30% of non-voting shares. In June 2002 legislation on merger regulation proposals (known as Bill C-8) finally received royal assent in Parliament. Revised ownership rules included allowing single investors to own up to 20% of any class of voting (30% non-voting) shares in a widely held bank. This permitted joint ventures and strategic alliances, although 'big bank' merger trends had by this time cooled. Should they resurface, any such process would be reviewed by three agencies, including the Competition Bureau. Nevertheless, the trend towards demutualization in other sectors meant that more conglomerates could be created. A further key aspect was the creation of the office of the Financial Consumer Agency of Canada, with a customer protection remit. The issue of mergers was revived later in 2002, when the Bank of Montréal and Scotiabank were reported to have approached Canadian Prime Minister Jean Chrétien with a merger proposal. This led the Minister of Finance, John Manley, to ask parliamentary banking committees to consider the issue of bank mergers, and they recommended that mergers be allowed under certain conditions. However, in 2003 Manley put any such mergers on hold until June 2004, requesting more time to consider the factors. The June 2004 federal election (which returned the Liberal Government as a minority) created a further delay, as did the financial scandal that dogged the Government until May 2005. In July the Minister of Finance, Ralph E. Goodale, started talks with opposition parties with the aim of producing a policy paper, but progress was interrupted by another general election and the formation of a new, minority, Conservative Government in early 2006. In September 2008 the Prime Minister, Stephen Harper, called a general election for October, just as recessionary conditions began to bite in the USA. Indeed, Canada itself had reported a shrinking trade surplus in June, and on 9 September the Toronto Stock Exchange's main index fell 488 points, losing nearly 4% of its value. Interestingly, given the problems being experienced by US banks, the Canadian Minister of Finance, Jim Flaherty, continued to indicate that bank mergers were not a priority for the Harper administration, despite continuing appeals for a relaxation in policy from leading banks.

Despite the controversy regarding bank mergers, in practical terms the rise of private equity was the prominent trend in the financial services sector by the mid-2000s. Echoing earlier, Trudeau-era concerns, there were anxieties in Canada (as in the United Kingdom, for instance) over the volume of enterprises being sold abroad. The Harper Government felt compelled to note that Canadian interests bought almost 500 foreign firms, worth C $111,000m., in 2006. Some sources indicated that 2002–06 saw 455 Canadian enterprises, worth US $137,000m., sold abroad. Such sales seemed to increase in 2006–07, with almost 600 foreign takeovers taking place in that period, worth a combined US $156,000m. Talismanic companies sold included the Molson brewing concern (which went to Coors of the USA for C $18,000m.), while in the computer sector the USA's AMD acquired ATI for US $5,400m. Notably, in 2007 Canada's Alcan rejected a hostile takeover bid from Alcoa Inc (which would have created the world largest aluminium producer), before accepting a US $38,100m. offer from Anglo-Australian Rio Tinto.

SUMMARY

The post-Second World War expansion of the service sector in Canada reflected a range of important developments. As agriculture, in particular, became mechanized and showed great labour productivity gains, the service sector increasingly became the home of mass labour. It was evident, too, that Canada showed the typical producer services and consumer services distinctions evident elsewhere. That is, services dedicated to serving other businesses (e.g. accountancy or advertising) as distinct from services dedicated to serving people directly (e.g. retailing or hairdressing). From the late 1990s job-shedding through computerization and other pressures had an effect, as in the case of the internet threatening counter services such as banking or travel agents. Indeed, from 2002 online real estate (property) sales began to show actual growth. That said, labour productivity in 2008 fell for three successive quarters: the worst performance since 1990. Such trends were ongoing in Canada, as elsewhere, and it was clear that the full long-term effects would only emerge completely as the 2000s progressed.

CANADIAN DOMESTIC AND EXTERNAL TRADE

ALAN HALLSWORTH

INTRODUCTION: CONTEMPORARY TRADING ISSUES

Canada's trading fortunes have been influenced by many longstanding factors: proximity to the USA and US attitudes towards trade or protectionism; constitutional separation of powers; exchange rates; and the global macroeconomy—latterly including the rise of the People's Republic of China. To that list could be added, as of July 2008, the apparent breakdown, in Geneva, Switzerland, of the Doha round of World Trade Organization (WTO) talks: a possible spur to future bilateral trade agreements. Few other countries have faced major debates on both domestic and external trade; yet Canada merits this debate for two reasons. First, the sheer size of a country spanning several time zones and climate regions leads to differences in local norms and standards, including the French language factor in Québec. Second, and more importantly, the British North America Act of 1867 devolved many meaningful powers to the provinces. The provinces then developed at different speeds and in subtly different directions. Such is the continued importance of the federal/provincial power dichotomy that provincial trading issues—and their associated income streams—first need to be considered. As a result of their rights under the British North America Act, the provinces and territories showed marked differences in policy with respect to external trade. Commodity and merchandise trade tended to dominate and, historically, Alberta was a supporter of liberalizing trade with the USA, not least because of its role in exporting fuels, notably natural gas and crude petroleum. Whereas such commodities comprised 19.8% of Canada's total goods exports in 2007, they represented 69.8% of the goods export trade from Alberta. British Columbia's wood products industries tended to lead to trade disputes with the USA over softwood lumber, although 2006 saw the signing of the seven-year US-Canadian Softwood Lumber Agreement (SLA), which was intended to create a stable trade environment for Canadian producers and returned to them more than US $4,400m. of duties collected by the USA since 2002. However, the signing of the SLA did not put an end to the disputes. In February 2007 the USA claimed that Canada was in breach of the SLA; after formal and informal consultations failed to resolve the matter, the USA lodged a request for arbitration. It seemed likely that lumber would continue to prove a difficult issue for quite some time. Until the issue of currency convergence combined with the 2007–08 energy crisis, Canadian relations with the USA were markedly more cordial when it came to the car industry: in 2006 Ontario, with 2.62m. vehicles, was at last outproducing US manufacturers based in Michigan, who produced 2.48m. By 2008, however, General Motors (GM) mooted the closure of its pick-up truck plant in Oshawa, Ontario, with the potential loss of over 2,000 jobs.

Even so, personal motor vehicles remained Ontario's principal merchandise export with its exports of motor vehicles and parts worth over C $68,900m. in 2006 (at current prices), from a total of C $199,660m., although this was noticeably down from the C $75,950m. recorded in 2004. The automobile trade contributed strongly to the fact that 86.4% of Ontario's foreign export trade was with the USA. Indeed, in 2007 Ontario accounted for 44.9% of all Canadian merchandise exports. By 1997 the USA received over 80% of Québec's exports, where the great commercial success story was Bombardier, the diversified transportation group. Bombardier continued to attract large contracts: in late 2006 it negotiated a US $2,230m. deal to supply 172 modernized commuter trains to France and 2008 saw further sales of its regional DASH aircraft to European and other airlines.

Québec symbolizes some of the key cross-border trade issues. Some 40 US states have Canada as their primary trading partner and, increasingly, Canadian provinces and US states are establishing cross-border structures to promote trade and investment. For example, in 1983 Québec arranged the sale of over 100,000m. kWh of electricity by Hydro-Québec to the New York Power Authority and the New York Power Pool. This relationship was highlighted some years later when much of the north-east seaboard of the USA suffered a major power blackout. Agreements between the government of Québec and the Cree and Inuit people of Northern Québec were made in order to generate an additional 12,000 MW of hydroelectricity. The US region of New England purchases some 20% of Québec's production and is likely to remain a key buyer. It is also noteworthy that some First Nation lands straddle the international border and the transfer of such products as tobacco within those areas has been known to generate debate.

In the Maritime provinces, Newfoundland and Labrador earned C $5,000m. in exports in 2006. Mineral fuels and oil dominated its exports, accounting for 48.7% of the total, a significant rise on previous years. Prince Edward Island exported merchandise goods with a value of $838m. in 2006, a 25.6% increase on the figures for 2004. Prince Edward Island's export trade was dominated by fish and vegetables, while 7.8% of the total, by value, came from machinery. In a wider context, leading businesses profited from being part of a North American economy, with the North American Free

Trade Agreement (NAFTA) having encouraged the 'continentalization' of manufacturing, for instance; notably in the automobile industry and new technologies.

THE INTERPROVINCIAL TRADE BARRIERS DEBATE

The fact that Canada quickly developed an interprovincial distinctiveness soon gave rise to the view that there must be an economic drag from interprovincial trade barriers. Not only was this brought into focus by the reduced US and Mexican barriers post-NAFTA, but such international liberalization was often used to illustrate the apparent problem. The interprovincial trade issue is more interesting than it may seem at first sight. While NAFTA does not facilitate the free movement of labour that the European Union (EU) permits, there are cognate issues. Canada's strong pro-immigration policy can be locally—that is, provincially—mediated. Accordingly, there may be concerns that, once in one province of Canada, individuals with lower qualifications than locals may enter across interprovincial borders. More conventionally, local standards may have arisen with little regard to how such standards are enforced in other provinces: most concerns tended to focus on the movement, or sale, of physical products. Again, as in the EU, there may be pressures in favour of local sourcing of, for example, fresh foodstuffs for schools. However, EU rules forbid preferences that discriminate against non-local suppliers; such preferences may yet persist in Canada and the USA. NAFTA brought into stark relief the fact that, apparently, it might be easier to transport goods into the USA than across Canada. Note that most provinces sit along the single US border, while moving beyond the adjacent province involves two border crossings. Accordingly provincial, territorial, and federal governments took steps to eliminate barriers to trade and in 1994 the provincial, territorial and federal Governments signed the Agreement on Internal Trade (AIT), which took effect on July 1 1995. The objective of the AIT was for the three levels of government to work together to reduce and eliminate barriers to the free movement of persons, goods, services and investments within Canada, and to establish an open, efficient and stable domestic market. Changes included the establishment of an Internal Trade Secretariat, which was to oversee, support and report on the progress of the implementation of the AIT. Implementation of the Agreement was slowed by several factors including an alleged lack of political will, a complex dispute resolution process, and poor level of resources allocated to the AIT. The Council of the Federation was initiated by provincial and territorial leaders at their annual meeting in July 2003 and the Council became an official body in December. The mandate of the Council of the Federation was to strengthen provincial and territorial collaboration by initially focusing on areas of common interest such as health, internal trade and fiscal imbalances (see below).

Predictably, many pro-market liberal organizations had long viewed any barriers as an extra cost on business in a range of areas: different regulatory standards between jurisdictions, labour mobility barriers, and, as noted, local preferences in government procurement. Predictably, many supporters of local standards such as labour standards, consumer protection measures, environmental regulations, and taxes noted that some of the most cited barriers were in fact related to clear social, health and moral issues. These parallel the British experience: British tobacco and alcohol duties are generally higher than those in nearby parts of Europe from which such goods may now freely be imported by individuals. The most common Canadian parallel is the fact that, traditionally, sale of alcohol was made through provincial liquor boards rather than via supermarket sales as happens in the United Kingdom. In some provinces, however, domestic wine producers do not have to sell through provincial liquor boards, while out-of-province wines may have to. Ontario, as both a wine producing and importing province, has been urged to equalize trade mark-up and improve wine distribution opportunities.

Trade liberalizers also pushed for a national accreditation system for engineering companies and engineering and inspection standards. They wished jurisdictions to unify national standards for training of employees and licensing, regulations and code interpretation, and also to allow all provincially or federally registered and incorporated companies to operate freely in all jurisdictions. Professionals registered in one province (engineers, teachers, some health care professionals, geologists, architects, etc.) should be able to work within all jurisdictions without further registration requirements. Many proposals seem very reasonable but can soon become politically charged. Like some Australian states, British Columbia has a publicly funded motor insurance scheme. For out-of-province drivers, however, additional costs may be incurred since the Insurance Corporation of British Columbia programme is mandatory. At one level, objections can be focused on the extra costs, at another, on the very notion of public involvement in insurance itself. Other objections have been raised to specific provincial statutes such as provincial law number 17 for the province of Ontario. Out-of-province businesses have complained this may make it impossible to get contracts from the province of Ontario and its municipalities. A particular instance is trucking where each province has its own rules and regulations with respect to motor vehicle weights and dimensions. For example, the length of a closed van, the number of axles on the ground and the weight that the trailer can carry often varies between jurisdictions. Frequently this can depend upon the normal severity of winter weather and the perceived damage that high axle-weight trucks may cause. To liberalizers this is a further market distortion since carriers must load to the lowest common denominator to ensure that the load is not overweight in any province through which the load must travel.

Another contentious issue that harked back to the British North America Act was the extra paperwork flowing from a lack of harmonization of provincial sales taxes. Less affluent provinces raised income from higher provincial sales taxes while resource-rich Alberta generally had low or zero sales taxes. Referring back to NAFTA, mention is often made of research conducted for the 1985 Macdonald Commission which concluded that interprovincial barriers cost no more than 0.05% of gross domestic product (GDP) and were not sufficiently a barrier to warrant major reform. Conceivably, the pro-NAFTA lobby wished to stress the importance of transnational trade barriers of the day. Latterly, these figures have come to be used to stress that interprovincial barriers are not a serious matter. Pulling interprovincial trade back to the forefront, however, was the Trade, Investment and Labour Mobility Agreement (TILMA) of April 2006, signed by the Governments of British Columbia and Alberta and which was to come into effect in April 2007. With encouragement from business lobbies, other provincial governments considered joining the agreement. The federal Government of Stephen Harper endorsed TILMA and identified reduced 'barriers to internal trade and labour mobility' as one of its economic policy objectives. As above, much of the proposal seems entirely reasonable: it prohibits public sector activities, other than those specifically exempted, that 'restrict or impair' trade, investment or labour mobility. However, it also goes on to empower businesses to sue governments for alleged violations. The enforcement mechanism is, in effect, a parallel to NAFTA's Chapter 11. Critics argue that fear of damaging and costly claims will pressure jurisdictions to abandon social programmes that could attract litigation. This would weaken existing provincial regulations that were intended to serve a wider public interest. It seems likely, at the least, that any new regulations or standards will be scrutinized by critics.

Reports by groups such as the Canadian Chambers of Commerce and the Conference Board of Canada have been critical of alleged barriers to interprovincial trade, mobility and investment. In 2006, for example, the latter group highlighted Québec's prohibition of margarine that is coloured like butter and Ontario's restriction on vegetable-oil-based substitutes for dairy products. Since some see these as less than significant problems, they argue that while international trade barriers are quite low, interprovincial barriers are even lower. Trade among provinces suggests that they are more than 10 times more likely to trade goods between themselves than internationally. Obviously this was subject to substantial variation but gross interprovincial trade has grown much faster than Canada's gross international trade. Sources suggest that interprovincial trade grew by 25% from 2000 to 2005, but international imports grew by only 9% in that period. Others claim that, at root, a federal system exists to facilitate democratically elected provincial governments in enacting different policies in response to different local conditions.

HISTORICAL DEVELOPMENT OF TRADE

Historically, most governmental finances were once largely raised by customs duties and excise taxes on trade, and so it is first useful to review Canada's trading history. Canada was founded on trade: from the establishment of the Hudson's Bay Company in 1670 through to the 21st century, at which point foreign trade regularly accounted for about 30% of the country's gross national income. Few other countries exceed this proportion, the United Kingdom being a notable exception. In terms of trading partners, the USA, the United Kingdom, Japan and, latterly, China all enjoyed strong trading links. To focus on key periods, in the 1920s the sheer volume of automobile trade across the 49th parallel (to the USA) decreased the United Kingdom's share of Canadian exports from 50% to just 27%. The dire effects on Canada of the recession of the 1930s were alleviated when long-serving Prime Minister Mackenzie King (1921–26, 1926–30 and 1935–48) agreed to reduce Canadian tariffs on 88 US goods in exchange for reciprocity on 60 Canadian items. Accordingly, the late 1930s were the prime years in which Canada strengthened its cross-border relationship with the USA.

In the period following the Second World War, Canada's external trade came to be dominated overwhelmingly by the USA. The USA received 65% of Canadian exports in 1950, with the United Kingdom at barely 15%. A few faltering attempts were made to revive 'imperial preference' deals between Canada and the United Kingdom, but these came to nothing. John Diefenbaker, Prime Minister in 1957–63, made overtures to the United Kingdom in the 1950s, but in so doing merely highlighted the difficulties of special relationships when Canada was already subject to globalization pressures. Interested in reducing dependence on the USA, Diefenbaker proposed that Canada increase its imports from the United Kingdom. However, this could no longer be done by preferential trading, as it would now infringe the General Agreement on Tariffs and Trade (GATT). As a trading nation, Canada was a strong supporter of GATT (now the WTO). In this context, it is still important, decades later, to study the economic policies of Liberal Governments led by Prime Minister Pierre Trudeau (1968–79 and 1980–84), for they have left an abiding legacy for contemporary fiscal policy. Trudeau was concerned about the dominance of foreign-owned companies and the successes and failures of his attempts to redress the balance can be seen in widely fluctuating trade and investment trends. By the end of 1970 non-residents, predominantly Americans, controlled over 30% of the capital employed in industry in Canada (excluding finance). In 1973, in the face of foreign ownership concerns, the Foreign Investment Review Agency (FIRA) was established. FIRA examined every application for production that originated from abroad and it was entitled to add some requirement for 'Canadian content'. Then, in October 1980, Trudeau introduced his ill-fated National Energy Policy (NEP), which was designed to repatriate some of the most profitable resource sectors of the 1970s. At that very same time, resource values decreased to a very low level but, conversely, following the rapprochement of the US and British administrations under President Ronald Reagan and Prime Minister Margaret Thatcher, respectively, the cost of the money borrowed to buy them increased dramatically. By the 1984 elections those factors had turned voters' attention from economic nationalism to the legacy of public debt and to inflation—a preoccupation that was to endure into the next century. Bonds, mainly government debt, also increased as a proportion of total external liabilities. While until the early 1970s the USA had accounted for 80% of total foreign ownership of bonds, this had fallen to under 30% by 1989. Japan in particular became important, but other countries participated too. Foreign direct investment (FDI) also came increasingly from Japan, the EU, and 'other' sources. By 1991 the USA's share of total stocks of foreign investment in Canada had fallen from its 1980 level of nearly 80% to under 45%. There was also increased accumulation of overseas assets by Canadians. Portfolio investment became more important, while by the mid-1980s Canadian FDI showed a sharp increase to Europe, notably the United Kingdom, France and the Netherlands. Such trends were in stark contrast to earlier years.

Elected to power in September 1984, the Progressive Conservative Party (PC), led by Brian Mulroney, totally reversed Trudeau's policies and expedited investment reversals, leading to a position that by 2001 almost 90% of Canadian merchandise exports were sold to the USA. Mulroney initiated the Atlantic Accord of 1985 on energy-pricing and taxation and the more significant Western Accord (between the federal Government and the governments of Alberta, British Columbia and Saskatchewan) later that year. It also negotiated trade agreements with the USA: bilateral trade negotiations formally began in June 1986. These led to the Canadian-US Free Trade Agreement of 1989 (CUFTA) and then to NAFTA. CUFTA was signed in draft form in January 1988 and came into effect in January 1989. The section on trade in goods demanded that tariffs be phased out over a 10-year period. Speculation remains that Canadian negotiators were convinced that this would remain a purely bilateral and uniquely advantageous arrangement. However, it was not long after CUFTA that NAFTA (which added Mexico to the trading area) superseded it. After its implementation on 1 January 1994—for a period of 15 years—Canada's merchandise trade with the USA continued to rise, as did the more modest merchandise trade with Mexico, worth C $20,400m. by 2006 (a three-fold increase over 1993). Those who favoured free trade in the 1980s listed expected benefits but may have minimized the associated costs. There was wide public exposure to reports predicting an almost 10% gain in aggregate Canadian welfare, a 28% rise in real wages, and an almost 30% increase in labour productivity alongside a 100% increase in the volume of bilateral Canada-US trade. Further predictions included a doubling of average output per firm in the manufacturing sector.

Others may have remembered that in 1971, as part of its abandonment of the Bretton Woods Exchange Rate system, the USA under President Richard Nixon brought in sweeping and unilateral import tax surcharges of the sort that the USA currently abhors when proposed by other states. Canada retained a perpetual fear of US protectionism, countervailing duties, anti-dumping measures and escape clause actions and so on. Critics of NAFTA worried that impacts of closer economic integration would affect wages, income distribution, and social programmes—often characterized as downward harmonization. Supporters admitted making a 'leap of faith' outlined by the Macdonald Commission itself, but suggested that there would be a long-term increase to real GDP of about 3% and long-term productivity growth in reaction to greater exposure to a more dynamic US economy. Overall growth would compensate for jobs lost in inefficient sectors. Both sides seemed unmindful of a newly changed world of borderless capital, privatization, deregulation, and so on. In fact supporters and detractors both seemed to imagine a sort of steady state where, oblivious to world trends, the US and Canadian economies would somehow harmonize. The CUFTA was, of course, negotiated in ignorance of it being so quickly superseded by NAFTA. Hopes were for higher wages in better jobs that supported Canada's social programmes. More realistically, those programmes were at risk in a new world in which they could be undercut by trade deals themselves once social support came to be seen as a business cost or a competitive distortion. It is notable that one possible destination of the 2008 pick-up truck jobs lost from Oshawa would be Mexico.

In fact, trade flows grew rapidly post-CUFTA: exports rose from 25.7% of GDP in 1989 to 45.5% in 2000, while in the same period imports reached 40.3% in 2000. However, this was not efficient restructuring of industries but the Reagan boom driven by a high-value dollar that was making imports cheaper. Logically, business turned to the USA—as it would have done in any case—and away from the domestic Canadian market. After the demise of FIRA, the USA began to return to takeovers of Canadian firms, a trend returned to in recent years. That said, larger Canadian firms also began to invest in the USA, thus increasing aggregate cross-border flows. Canadian banking was already more concentrated than US banking, which may have helped. Nevertheless, efficient Canadian firms moved into the US market but efficient US firms stayed home and served Canada from across the border: unpicking the presumed economic gains. Canada responded, as ever, with dollar devaluations to retain competitiveness. Equally, US insistence on local content was behind the pulling-in of Canadian (and Japanese, etc.) industries. Canada itself will not achieve a more sophisticated industrial economy given its low levels of investment in research and development. Such investment as does happen is driven by a tiny handful of leading industrial companies, or by government subsidy.

Canadian and US living standards have not converged as expected and, indeed, within Canada the poor have fallen further behind, as they have in the USA. Meanwhile, real wages have lagged behind productivity, and corporate profitability has increased: such growth, some argue, has come at the expense of quality of life. So, Canada still spends significantly more on social programmes and public services than the USA, but the difference has been reducing and Canada even spends relatively less than its neighbour on public education. Indeed, paralleling the early 1980s as well as the early 1970s, the macroeconomy of the early 1990s did Canada few favours. Labour market deterioration flowed from high interest rates and fiscal tightening, all happening as the US and Canadian economies converged, often with hints of currency convergence.

THE AUTO PACT OF 1965

Much may be understood about Canada's modern bilateral trade relations with the USA by considering the so-called Auto Pact, a much earlier trade deal. While Canada and the USA established several important bilateral, proactive agreements in the 20th century, the 1965 Auto Pact (the Automotive Products Agreement) was the most significant single-issue deal. Arguably CUFTA was, in essence, just a replacement for the Auto Pact. Trade in cars and car parts, largely 'managed' between the different parts of the US-owned North American car industry was, by this point, one of Canada's most important areas of cross-border (and thus technically export) trade—even though it was really Michigan-Ontario trade. Canada was running a visible goods surplus with the USA, which was seen as too precious to jeopardize through tariffs or protectionism. Indeed, Canada's goods trade surplus with the USA stood at C $108,454m. in 2005 (a record high), although the figure fell to $96,074m. in 2006. In the 1990s the importance of the USA to Canadian exports increased, peaking in 2000; while total exports continued to rise, the volume of goods and services moving to the USA declined thereafter. In 2007 the US share of Canada's total exports of goods and services fell below 80% for the first time since 1995 (while goods exports to the EU increased by over 20% the same year). Imports from the USA showed a similar pattern: at their 2000 peak, they represented 72% of total Canadian imports; by 2006 this figure was 57%. By 2006 83% of Canada's merchandise exports went to NAFTA countries. There have been calls for Canada to diversify its trade portfolio since although Canada's bilateral trade surplus with the USA broke the $100,000m. barrier in 2005, at the same time Canada's goods deficit with the rest of the world widened to $43,900m.; indeed, Canada's merchandise deficit with developing countries reached $63,649m. in 2006. Critics pointed out that Canada had only secured one bilateral trade agreement in 2001–06, with Costa Rica. The new Conservative Government placed greater emphasis on securing bilateral trade agreements with major economic players such as China. Consequently, in 2007 Canada concluded its first free trade deal since its agreement with Costa Rica in 2001. The agreement was with Iceland, Liechtenstein, Norway and Switzerland, members of the European Free Trade Association (but not of the EU), which received $3,100m. in goods from Canada in 2006. Furthermore, the collapse of the WTO talks in 2008 led to plans for Canada to aggressively pursue further bilateral trade deals. Canada remained one of the six designated strategic partners of the EU, along with the USA, China, Japan, Russia and India.

CONTEMPORARY EXTERNAL TRADE

Mirroring federal finances, Canada's trade balance moved from deficits to surpluses throughout the 1990s, since exports grew faster than imports. Although exports of goods and services as a share of GDP fell from 43.5% in 2001 to 31.9% in 2006, this was the second highest level registered in the Group of Eight (G8) leading industrialized countries. From the turn of the millennium, total exports have fallen faster than imports and so the overall trade surplus has declined. Nevertheless, this goods surplus remained strongly positive, at C $30,200m. in 2007, thanks to the continuing healthy trade balance with the USA. In that year exports of Canadian goods and services totalled $532,700m. In contrast, Canada's services account has persistently registered a deficit, despite the fact that in the 1990s services exports outpaced the growth in goods exports. The deficit in services with the USA widened in 2006, to $10,700m., up from $9,400m. in 2005; the deficit with non-US countries increased even more rapidly, registering a 49.0% rise on 2005 levels. These increases were mainly due to higher transportation and other costs incurred by Canadians travelling abroad. Overall, the total services deficit stood at a record $19,400m. in 2007. As ever, the USA remained the largest partner in Canadian trade, with exports to the EU, the second largest, standing at approximately 10% of exports to the USA. Exports of goods and services to the EU increased by 17.6% in 2007, to $52,800m., while imports stood at $57,800m., resulting in a considerably smaller trade deficit. As a rough generalization, then, Canada runs a visible trade surplus selling basic commodities to the USA, plus Japan and other parts of the Far East, and in doing so makes sufficient profit to run a deficit importing finished goods and services from its other trading partners and particularly from growing exporters such as China.

In the wider sphere, rising commodity prices mean that Canadian exports of resource-based commodities are taking a greater share of the economic pie. There is demand from China for commodities and the closer Canada-US exchange rate impacts upon Canadian exports of non-resource-based manufactured goods. Finally, both Canada and the USA have increased imports from China; Canada has done so at the expense of the USA. This latest trading phase developed only at the new millennium and showed that while trade linkages with the USA remained of greatest importance, they have become slightly less dominant. The pronounced trends of the 1990s have been reversed. Exports to the USA fell sharply in 2003, and although they recovered in the next two years values have subsequently tailed off again. The proportion of Canadian merchandise exports destined for the US market declined from 87.1% of the total in 2002 to 78.9% in 2007. One factor in this is the diminished international influence of the USA as a trading power. In contrast to the 1990s, the relatively sluggish performance of the US economy has been reflected in a reduced share of world imports. Compounding this for Canada has been the intense competition it has faced in that market, above all from China, and a sharply reduced share of imports. The appreciation of the Canadian dollar has been a handicap to exporters, and is likely to have influenced GM's Oshawa decision. In 2007 Canada was overtaken by China as the principal importer to the USA: China supplied 16.5% of US imports of goods, Canada 16%, with Mexico at 10.8%. Importers into Canada have also become more diverse: by 2007 the USA still led at over 50%, but Japan's share was falling with major gains dominated by China.

The USA has maintained its prominent place as an investor in Canada, accounting in 2007 for 57% of the total stock of investment, barely less than in 2000. Europe, especially the United Kingdom, has become an absolutely and relatively larger supplier of funds, while Japan and the 'Rest of the World' have become progressively less important. Canadian continentalism does not extend deeply into the Americas and while economic links with Mexico, starting from a low base, have grown rapidly since the formation of NAFTA, beyond Mexico connections for the most part remain weak.

Mexico, Central and Southern America and the Caribbean

Trudeau was the first Canadian Premier to see Latin America as a priority region: his so-called Third Option. Mexico, Central and Southern America and the Caribbean, however, have long posed complex problems. Most countries once relied on customs and excise for tax-raising and some countries in these regions have been slow to move towards corporate and personal taxation. This is one reason why some have 'tax haven' status. Certainly, Canadian financial investment outflows showed the Caribbean countries to be particularly prominent. Barbados, Bermuda and the Cayman Islands have proved the main attraction for Canadian investors, accounting together for 12% of Canada's global FDI holdings in 2006. With the recent take-over of Trinidad and Tobago's RBTT by the Royal Bank of Canada, Canadians now control the English-speaking Caribbean's three largest banks, with C $42,000m. in assets.

More significantly, there has been constant conflict between Latin American and Canadian (and US) views on what constitutes free trade. Especially for the USA, there has been an overlay—focused on Cuba—of anti-communism. A Latin American tradition of mercantilist or protectionist policies to build regional integration sits uneasily with neo-liberalism. The long-standing rejection by Latin America of free trade, and a general refusal to join GATT, may even at some times have pushed Canada further towards the USA. It was as recently as at the end of the 1990s that Latin America finally embraced the principles of free trade and investment. Other problems, however, showed a common bond: the foreign debt crisis affected both Mexico and Canada. Both, like the Latin American countries, faced drastic economic changes and structural adjustments towards privatizations, downsized government bureaucracy, neo-liberalism and anti-inflation policies. CUFTA and NAFTA brought closer ties with Mexico but also issues surrounding Brazil and Chile. Canada became a full member of the Organization of American States (OAS) in 1990, which was a strong multilateralist move. Conversely, President Bill Clinton's signing of the controversial anti-Cuba Helms-Burton Law in 1996 began to highlight Canadian–US differences over Cuba. Canada went on to host the Summit of the Americas in Québec City, and has since tried several strategies to move closer to Latin America. Slow progress both on negotiations of the Free Trade Agreement of the Americas and the WTO undermined the usual Canadian multilateralist strategy. Such reversals may be a future spur to bilateral negotiations. These include: free trade agreements with Chile (1997), Costa Rica (2002) Peru (2007) and Colombia (2008). As part of the negotiation of the trade agreement with Peru, the Canadian Government donated some C $1.1m. to implement trade and democracy initiatives.

Government policy is not the only engagement with Latin America: there have been private sector-led conflicts such as between Canadian mining companies and foreign Governments. The Canadian Government was periodically forced to mediate in conflicts over environmental and employment rights issues. In July 2007 Prime Minister Harper announced that one of the three priorities of his foreign policy would be the Americas, yet this came at a time when some (notably Nicaragua) foresaw the demise of the OAS. Statistically, Canadian balance of trade figures for Latin America show that its imports are three times higher than its exports. Mexico, its main trade partner in Latin America, represents 55% of its Latin American imports and 43% of exports. Exports to Mexico expanded at over 10% per annum in the 1990s and have continued to grow. Yet, according to Canadian statistics, exports to Mexico still represent only 1.1% of world-wide exports (although this fact masks so-called managed trade). It is likely that official figures overstated exports to the USA and understated the eventual export destination, namely Mexico. Mexican figures suggested Canada had possibly a further C $4,000m. in real trade in 2006, so the true total may be closer to 2% of Canadian exports. Imports from Mexico have proved still more dynamic, growing faster than exports, and from a larger base, and in 2007 Mexico displaced Japan to rank third as a source of Canadian imports. However, for the most part Mexico was as far as investment went. Mexico in the 1990s simply displaced other non-US western hemisphere suppliers, the total imports from which failed to keep pace with the overall expansion of Canadian imports. Only in the past decade has there been some relative recovery. When it comes to exports Latin America has also proved a disappointing market. Despite expansion to Mexico, total sales to Latin America and the Caribbean were lower in 2002 than they had been six years earlier, having been badly affected by the financial crises of 2001–02 that hit the major South American economies of Brazil and Argentina. Despite some revival, sales to the region, excluding Mexico, were less than in 2002, and well below the levels of a decade ago. Nor has continentalism had much bearing on investment linkages beyond the USA. Latin America has never been a major source of funds into Canada, although it has been more important as an outlet, as the Caribbean example suggests.

FEDERAL-PROVINCIAL TRENDS IN HISTORICAL PERSPECTIVE

Following the Second World War, provincial and municipal expenditures drove the expansion in government spending, stressing their degree of autonomy from the federal level. In 1951 federal expenditures per head were higher than provincial per head expenditures, with levels of C $236 and $100, respectively. However, by 1975 federal expenditures per head were $571, compared with $771 for other levels of government, partly because the health, education and pensions sectors came increasingly to dominate public expenditures, and much of this growth was provincially regulated. Taken as a whole, total government spending as a percentage of GDP rose from 34.7% in 1970 to 45.1% in 1988 and to 50.2% by 1994. The change in the fiscal regime as a result of the 1990s focus on debt repayment is indicated by the fact that in the period 1992–2002 total government programme spending as a share of GDP was reduced by 9.9%. This decrease in programme spending was the dominant factor in turning around the Government's finances: in 1992 the federal Government had been running a debt of $42,000m.; in 2001/02 it recorded a surplus of $8,900m., increasing to $11,104m. in 2006/07.

When considering these figures, it is important to remember that federal spending is only one part of the full equation. In 1999/2000 federal spending was C $169,800m.; provincial and territorial spending $196,400m.; and local government expenditure $74,200m. By 2003/04 federal spending was $201,713m.; provincial and territorial spending $234,575m.; and local government expenditure $91,633m. Thus, between 1999/2000 and 2003/04, when measured as a share of GDP, federal programme spending fell from 15.7% to 11.6%, and provincial-territorial spending from 19.1% to 15.6%. This decline was then checked by spending increases introduced by the final budget of the Government of Jean Chrétien, which meant the federal programme spending as a proportion of GDP increased to 13.7% by 2004/05, a figure that the Harper administration lowered to 12.8% the following year, mainly through targeting programme cuts. In 2007/08 federal spending stood at $237,021m., provincial and territorial expenditure was $298,592m., and the local government outlay was $112,166m.

Central to an understanding of how and why Canadian provinces developed differently are what have been characterized as the 'homogenizing' functions of government spending. Unlike the expenditure on communications, such expenditures only developed in the later decades of the 20th century, initiated by the Rowell-Sirois studies prior to 1940. Essentially, such expenditures led to 'horse-trading' between the federal and provincial levels of government. The structurally weaker Maritime provinces were generally the prime beneficiaries of this spending and it was argued that transfer payments could reduce inter-urban income disparities by some 25%. Government spending was further complicated by the question of equalization payments (below). Analysis of government spending in Canada was thus rarely straightforward.

Equalization Payments

Equalization payments started out as financial transfers from the richer provinces to the poorer provinces on social-equity grounds: with the aim of 'levelling out' living standards across Canada. This was, in effect, yet another unintended consequence of the 1867 British North America Act, which awarded control of potentially priceless undiscovered natural resources to the province in which they lay. In 1982, under Pierre Trudeau, the equalization programme was enshrined in the Constitution Act. Funds that had been raised by federal taxation could be disbursed by a provincial government or allocated to provinces for specific spending sectors. The constant rivalry between jurisdictions meant that all tiers of government liked their fiscal input to projects to be well advertised. Overall, locally raised revenues would be lowest in the poorer provinces and highest in the richer ones. If the federal Government transferred less to a province, a province would have to spend more of its own revenue. For this reason, Alberta, rich in resources (especially petroleum), tended to be at the head of provincial expenditure lists. Any federal Government concerned about debt burdens would seek to devolve as much as possible of the responsibility for spending. The strongest manifestation of this occurred in the mid-1990s, when Chrétien's Liberal Government aimed to reduce transfers from the equivalent of 5% of GDP in 1995/96 to 4% in 1998/99. In some sectors the interprovincial disparities in support that formed the basis of equalization payments were to be evened out over time.

The extent of equalization payments could be considerable—the programme transferred an annual average of some C $10,000m. to provinces between 1999/2000 and 2003/04—yet the practice itself remained largely uncontested. The programme was renewed for the period 2004–09, with more than $50,000m. allocated in payments. This renewal incorporated alterations to the equalization formula, including the use of a three-year moving average to determine payments. This developed in response to a series of large fluctuations in payments over the period 1999–2004. However, in October 2004 the Liberal administration announced fundamental changes to the equalization system. The new framework involved a considerable increase in payments (from $8,800m. in 2003/04 to $10,900m. in 2005/06), with planned annual growth of 3.5% and a guarantee that payments would not fall below $10,000m. In addition, the programme would be subject to an independent review by a panel of experts. The resulting expert panel, with a chair from oil-rich Alberta, produced recommendations that formed the basis for reforms put forward in the Harper administration's 2007 budget. These included the controversial decision that 50% of natural resource revenues would be excluded when determining each province's fiscal capacity. Furthermore, the introduction of a fiscal capacity cap ensured that transfers could not raise a receiving province's fiscal capacity above that of a non-receiving province. To increase stability and improve planning, payments were henceforth to be based on a three-year weighted moving average of provincial fiscal capacity, delayed by two years, and would no longer be subject to revision during the financial year.

For 2008/09 the leading recipient provinces were Québec (C $8,000m.), Manitoba ($2,100m.), New Brunswick ($1,600m.), Nova Scotia ($1,500m.), and Prince Edward Island ($300m.). On a per head basis, the main recipients were the smaller provinces, such as Prince Edward Island, New Brunswick and Newfoundland and Labrador. These payments were intended to ensure that every province had access to revenues equivalent to at least $6,200 per resident in order to fund public services. Overall, federal major transfers accounted for approximately one-quarter of provincial and territorial revenues. Predictably, Ontario and Alberta were the key contributors, the latter providing by far the largest equalization contribution of all the provinces. In 2006 Ontario claimed to have identified a $23,000m. payments gap and noted that its contribution to the equalization system was $4,900m., compared with $3,700m. in 2003; by 2008, Ontario was warning that the manufacturing downturn could soon turn it into a recipient province. The federal Government operates a similar funding scheme for Nunavut Territory, Northwest Territories and Yukon Territory, called Territorial Formula Financing (TFF). This gives official recognition to the higher costs of providing services in the harsher climates of the north. In 2006/07 total TFF transfers amounted to $2,300m., of which $944m. went to Nunavut, $805m. to the Northwest Territories, and $564m. to Yukon.

There were other means of transferring federal funds to the provinces and Established Programs Financing was the most significant of these. Under the Expenditure Control Plan, payment levels remained at 1989 levels until the mid-1990s. The federal share of post-secondary education costs thus decreased from around one-half to one-third, adding an estimated 5% of total expenditure to the provincial budgets. Federal involvement in sectors such as education was resurgent in the 2000s, by which time federal debt-reduction programmes had shown benefits and finance had become available again.

Increased investment also affected the Canada Health and Social Transfer (CHST) system, which played a major role in provincial funding from its inception in 1996. Indeed, payments under CHST in the late 1990s were set at almost three times the equalization payments. Subsequently, CHST increased to stand at C $35,300m. in 2002/03 (in comparison with equalization payments of $10,300m.). After 1 April 2004 CHST was split into the Canada Health Transfer (CHT) and the Canada Social Transfer (CST). CHT cash transfers were fixed until 2013/14, while tax transfers increased in line with economic growth. For 2007/08 CHT amounted to $34,600m., comprising $21,300m. in cash transfers and $13,300m. in tax transfers. CHT relates to one particular area of policy, i.e. health, where federal and provincial concerns might conflict. Political considerations might also have prompted the 2007 budget's commitment to equal per head support under CST and CHT. CST is a federal block transfer to provinces and territories in support of post-secondary education, social assistance and social services, including early childhood development. The 2007 budget also included a major expansion in funding for CST in order further to support secondary education and social programmes. CST was legislated to last until 2013, and an initial investment of $700m. in 2007/08 was to be followed by an automatic annual increase of 3%, amounting to $16,000m. over seven years. Bringing all these payment sectors together, major federal transfers for 2007/08 reached $67,100m.: $34,600m. from CHT; $17,600m. from CST; $12,700m. from equalization payments; and $2,200m. from TFF. This was considerably higher than in previous years (it represented a 40.7% increase on the 2003/04 total of $47,700m.), which demonstrated the scope of the 2004 framework review. It should be noted that transfers increased by an average of 8.7% annually between 2000/01 and 2005/06, compared with an average growth in federal revenues of 2.6%.

THE SPENDING DOWNSHIFT

In the 1990s trading strengths linked to an improving fiscal position made it politically expedient for a proportion of Canada's net public debt to be transferred ('downshifted') from the federal level to the provinces. Many provinces followed the lead of the federal Liberal Government and introduced measures to reduce debt. Most of these were labelled Balanced Budget Acts, and adopters included Québec (1996) and Ontario (1999). New Brunswick had such legislation as early as 1993, but set the commencement date for 1996. Saskatchewan legislated in 1995, as did Manitoba. Nova Scotia and British Columbia were slower to act, with amendments coming into force for their 2002/03 budgets.

A combination of these initiatives and the favourable economic conditions of the late 1990s meant that by 2000/01 eight provinces (and two territories) had budgetary surpluses. In smaller provinces that were still in deficit, such as Newfoundland and Labrador and Prince Edward Island, those deficits were far lower than in most previous years. However, by 2004/05 only five provinces were registering a surplus or balanced budget, with eight recording deficits. Furthermore, the remaining surpluses were considerably lower than in 2000/01: although Alberta posted a surplus of C $4,018m., the next largest, New Brunswick's, was just $43m. Ontario showed an alarming slide, from a surplus of $117m. in 2002/03 to a deficit of $5,621m. one year later. Nevertheless, provincial finances improved considerably from this point: the combined provincial-territorial budgetary balance moved from an overall deficit of $7,337m. in 2003/04 to consolidated surpluses of $7,604m., $7,753m. and $7,957m. in 2004/05, 2005/06 and 2006/07, respectively. This improvement reflected both national economic performance and provincial budgetary improvements, such as Alberta's increasing economic power and the reduction in Ontario's shortfalls, from around $5,500m. to $918m. in 2006/07. In British Columbia the economy had been struggling at the start of the 21st century, registering large deficits and experiencing spiralling debt. Indeed, in 2001/02–2003/04 the province posted a series of massive deficits, including one of $2,680m. in 2002/03, with the result that by 2004 each taxpayer was supporting $7,789 of debt. This led to new measures that saw the province reduce its deficit from $2,660m. in 2002/03 to $960m. in 2003/04. By 2005/06 British Columbia registered a surplus of $984m., and had turned its attention to reducing the $37,000m. of outstanding debt (which had cost the province $8,500m. in service payments in 2000–05). This surplus increased to $1,593m. in 2006/07, driven by provincial growth of 3.6% in 2006, and went towards tax cuts and a housing strategy in the province's 2007 budget.

Québec, too, had its debt and deficit situations under control by 2000, having succeeded in transforming its budget deficit into two consecutive years of surpluses. This, as was the case in other provinces, required spending reductions equal to about 4% of GDP per year. However, as elsewhere, the difficult economic conditions from 2001 turned the surplus into a C $528m. deficit; as in British Columbia, this deficit initiated new efforts to balance the budget. While a reduced deficit of $1,007m. was achieved in 2006/07, concerns remained over whether such improvement can be sustained. Furthermore, the province's accounting practices were criticized by its Auditor-General, who estimated in 2006 that the province's accumulated budget deficit stood at $5,300m., despite the fact that the government stated that it had a surplus of $192m. There were additional concerns about the fiscal health of the province's health and social services network.

In the early 1990s debt interest charges actually ranked with social security, health and education as the foremost areas of expenditure. With the transport sector largely privatized by the early 2000s, these remained the key spending sectors. Inevitably, the precise annual balance depends on the state of the economy and its consequences for tax revenues or welfare payments. For example, in 2006/07, of consolidated government expenditure of C $572,658m., social services accounted for 30.1%, health 18.7%, education 15.3% and interest charges 8.1% (a substantial reduction from the 2001 figure of 12.9%).

The present situation could be summarized thus: the provinces had benefited from generally favourable economic conditions from the late 1990s through into 2001, thereby easing their accumulated debt problem. The reduced costs of servicing debt had increased their reluctance to run deficits in the future. However, harsher economic conditions led to reduced surpluses (as in Alberta), a return to debt (as in Québec) or even greater deficit (as in British Columbia). Newfoundland and Labrador, Nova Scotia, Ontario and the three territories all posted increased deficits, while Prince Edward Island, Québec, Alberta and British Columbia improved their accounts. New Brunswick, Manitoba and Saskatchewan, meanwhile, experienced no significant change. This variation further reinforces the fact that while provinces are subjected to a wider set of economic circumstances, their individual microeconomic characteristics are also extremely significant. Figures for 2006/07 revealed that net debt for all provinces and territories had stabilized at roughly 20% of GDP, significantly reduced from the 28.7% recorded in 1999/2000. Ontario's 2006/07 deficit left its net debt equal to 19.7% of GDP, a significant improvement on the 25.3% registered in 2003/04.

TRADING WITH THE USA: COMPLEXITY AND CO-OPERATION

A new level of complexity was added to the North American trade situation following the 2001 World Trade Center attacks, with the border security measures adding complication and potential delay to commerce. For example, Québec's Premier and the Governor of New York State extended co-operation between them and made the Lacolle, Québec–Champlain, New York, border crossing and the Autoroute 15 (Québec) and US I-87 highways key foci of action. For example, Québec pledged US $48m. to improve the Québec side of the Lacolle–Champlain border crossing, which is used by some 45% of truck traffic between Québec and the USA. Nor would Québec be unmindful that in the decade of the 1990s there was an increase of over 300% in crossborder trade. Arguably, the burden of tighter border security measures falls disproportionately on Canadian partners. While downsizing government on both sides of the 49th parallel has involved withdrawals in areas such as social services, there has been increased government activity (and spending) on, in particular, homeland security.

The development of a new US national security agenda, led by the Department of Homeland Security, had wide-ranging implications for Canadian trade. As noted in respect of Québec, the US decision to temporarily ban trans-border shipments, plus suggestions that Canada was a haven for terrorists, accelerated the coupling of security issues with Canada's hard-won status as a major site for US investment. Many hoped that if Canada responded favourably to Washington's heightened defence, security, and other concerns, then the administration of George W. Bush would reward Canada with economic and trade security. In fact, this came to involve Mexico and led to a Task Force on the Future of North America covering, *inter alia*, enhancing security and deepening economic integration not least via harmonizing regulatory policy.

A further complicating factor is the fact that almost any tax, subsidy, or regulation—indeed practically any government law—may conflict with Canada's international trade commitments. Canadian cultural policies, some argue, have been under pressure from at least as far back as 1984, when US media representatives outlined obstacles they encountered when exporting products and services, and cited Canada as a problem. Subsequently there has been ongoing pressure to limit Canadian cultural policies, with both CUFTA and NAFTA used as tools. A cultural exemption in CUFTA and NAFTA seems not to have assisted Canadian content rules whilst restrictions on foreign ownership have been lifted and support measures removed. New trade deals seem structured to give protection to private foreign investors (almost inevitably US ones) while simultaneously limiting the ability of governments to pursue policies in the public interest, including health care. As apparent proof of this proposition, NAFTA's Chapter 11 has led to numerous investor rights lawsuits against member states, millions of dollars in damages, overturned laws, and abandoned policy initiatives. Other concerns include the possibility that, for example, foreign private involvement in public health care, once entrenched, may be impossible to reverse even if public sentiment were to turn against it.

Naturally, co-operating with the USA is not always the zero sum game suggested above. Under NAFTA Canada, the USA and Mexico made an environmental side agreement that established the North American Commission for Environmental Cooperation to investigate continent-wide environmental issues. It successfully reported on instances of toxic pollution, and so on and maintains an independent watchdog role. A growing area of interest is possible access to Canadian fresh water resources. A further possibility is that any fully integrated North American electricity market could result in prices being set by the USA. Under NAFTA, the USA has shown increased investment in Canadian energy markets, notably for natural gas. Indeed, Canada has become the leading foreign supplier of oil and gas to the USA. Some ultimately predict an EU-like common market possibly even extending to common immigration rules. While this may lead also to pressures for a common defence strategy, Canada has maintained its non-nuclear status and then-Premier Paul Martin opted out of the US-led missile defence plans from February 2005.

TRADE AND THE PUBLIC DEBT TURNAROUND

The centrality of the twin economic themes of trade and debt make it plausible to conclude by considering the two in tandem. The net ratio of public debt to GDP fell to 49.1% in 2002, from its peak of 70.9% in 1995/96, leaving foreign debt in a more advantageous position, pro rata, than that of the USA for the first time on record. Furthermore, the previous five years' debt repayments had run concurrently with the highest government surpluses (relative to size of economy) of all members of the Group of Seven (G7) industrialized economies. In 2002 Canada recorded a surplus equivalent to 0.6% of GDP, compared with an average deficit of 3.7% in the G7 countries. Remarkably, between 1997 and 2004 Canada was ranked first in the G7 in terms of average real GDP per head growth. These achievements built upon the announcement by Moody's Investors Service in May 2002 that it was restoring Canada's 'Triple-A' credit rating, which was withdrawn in 1995.

It was indicative of Canada's new-found economic resilience owing to debt reduction that, despite outbreaks of Severe Acute Respiratory Syndrome (SARS) and bovine spongiform encephalopathy (BSE) in 2003, the federal Government still recorded a surplus (albeit of only C $2,126m.) in 2003/04, and was the only G8 Government to do so. The new Liberal administration of former Minister of Finance Martin, which took office in mid-2004, continued to benefit from this fiscal discipline: Canada's total government sector debt burden declined to just 31% of GDP. By 2005/06 debt charges equated to 8.2 cents for every dollar of government revenue, compared with a high of 17.6 cents in 1995/96. Canada's provincial, territorial and local governments produced a combined surplus of $6,404m. in 2004/05, although this remained significantly below the surplus of $28,600m. recorded in 2000/01. It must be noted that the Liberals' success over debt was linked to the long period of economic expansion in the second half of the 1990s, dubbed the 'Clinton boom'. This was particularly strong in the USA, but was offset in Canada by the endemic burden of debt repayments. Greater financial security had been achieved by reducing programme spending and through economic growth—the 'virtuous cycle' of higher tax revenues and falling welfare payments (as unemployment declined from 11.4% of the total labour force in 1994 to an average of 7.2% in 2000–05, before reaching a 30-year low of 6.3% in 2006). Yet Canada really only mastered its financial situation as the millennium turned: GDP per head had increased to $44,333 by 2006, and 10 balanced budgets were presented in succession from 1997 to 2006. Indeed, the period 1996–2000 saw GDP growth averaging 4.8% per year, although this slowed to 2.5% between 2001 and 2005. Nevertheless, this 'virtuous cycle' was already unwinding by the early years of the 21st century, and IMF predictions of a global economic rebound were dented by the ongoing conflict in Iraq from 2003. There was a significant rise in US unemployment, while in Canada the issue of public debt, as ever, was not confined to the national (federal) tier of government. As noted, Canada had more than one tier of government with statutory powers to raise taxes, and this in itself created some internal tensions.

By 2007 there were indications that growth was being hampered by weakening US demand, a slowing housing market and an appreciating Canadian dollar. Despite these issues, Canada still registered real GDP growth of 2.8% in 2006, and the country continued to reduce its debt burden, which stood at 35.1% of GDP for the 2005/06 financial year and was predicted to dip below the 33.3% level in the following year. Canadian budgetary policy in the 21st century was, essentially, haunted by the recession of the early 1980s and the attendant decline in real production and in the value of petroleum-based resources. Many budget deficits at that time were greatly exacerbated by high interest rates. For example, interest payments quadrupled in 1976–82, and the interest rate at one point reached 21%. Interest payments alone were responsible for 30% of the increased budget deficit between 1981 and 1985. By 1985, after the first year of the PC Government of Brian Mulroney (Prime Minister in 1984–93), borrowing was well above the average for countries belonging to the Organisation for Economic Co-operation and Development. Early efforts by the Mulroney administration to reduce the deficit went some way towards the targets set, although predicted revenue declined as the energy sector failed to realize expected profits.

The financial turning point was 1997, when the Canada Foundation for Innovation (CFI) was established, an important move given increasing international concern over Canada's low level of research innovation relative to other comparable nations. The implication was that the severe spending reductions of preceding years had at last begun to produce the capacity to address underlying economic problems. In 2003/04 the Government felt sufficiently confident to assign C $1,700m. to research and innovation. Another major supra-budgetary spending structure was established in 2004, with the '10-Year Plan to Strengthen Health Care', which involved every level of government and was supported by $41,300m. of federal funding. The Government was anxious that markets should be well aware of its targets and its probity, while the internal political agenda reflected concerns about the part-time nature of many jobs and the international trend to 'jobless growth'. This policy of stressing prudence and openness with the financial markets was a crucial feature of the economic success of the late 1990s. By announcing inflation targets, and regularly bettering them, the federal Government signalled its intention that the economic future should be free from severe shocks and unexpected developments. The broad strategy, once federal surpluses were achieved, was to have a five-year programme under which budgets must be in surplus. Subject to contingency reserves, the Government made it clear that one-half of any surplus would be dedicated to debt reduction, and the remainder split between tax cuts and programme spending. This intention was modified in the 2003 budget, which saw no active attempt to pay off the national debt, which stood at $500,100m. (41.1% of GDP) in October 2004.

That budget attempted to reduce the debt-to-GDP ratio by increasing GDP, with programme spending taking an increased proportion of the surplus. Five-year 'benchmarking' tended to reduce the significance of individual budgets, with economic statements and clear messages about deficit reduction assuming more importance. The system took off once the federal Government began to post regular surpluses after 1997. For example, the massive C $18,100m. federal surplus in 2000/01 allowed the increases in spending of the 2003 budget. It is important to note that the 2005 budget maintained the $3,000m. Contingency Reserve, providing some assurance that balanced budget targets would be met. If the Reserve was not needed, it could be used to reduce the federal debt. In this way, the Liberal Government could maintain a focus on debt-repayment, but also guard against the caprices of an uncertain global economy.

The 2004 budget set a new objective of reducing the federal debt-to-GDP ratio to 25% within 10 years, and projected that programme expenses would rise in line with economic growth. Following the 2003 budget's programme reviews, the Office of the Comptroller-General was re-established, with the aim of strengthening the auditing process. The budget also consolidated the 2003 First Ministers' Accord on Health Care Renewal, providing a further C $2,000m. in funding. The budget also responded to the health crises of 2003 by establishing a new Canada Public Health Agency, which was to be principally responsible for disease-control and public health emergency response. The 2005 budget brought a restructuring of the Equalization and Territorial Formula Financing system: this provided a funding increase, spread over 10 years, representing $33,400m. over and above the annual amounts estimated in the previous year's budget. This exemplified the 2005 budget's focus on supporting diversity in Canadian society. These goals were reflected in the budget's global outlook, which announced major new targets for debt relief and aid in the developing world. Initiatives to increase support for African development efforts were first flagged by Chrétien at the G8 summit in Kananaskis, Canada, in 2002, rather than at the 2005 meeting held in Gleneagles, United Kingdom, as is often supposed. Despite this array of proactive government programmes, the 2005 budget also included a number of politically expedient tax-relief elements: the lower income tax threshold was raised to $10,000 and the corporate surtax was eliminated. In contrast to its predecessor's global perspective, the first budget of the new Conservative Government, in 2006, concentrated mainly on domestic issues, such as taxes and fiscal accountability. There was a strong commitment to agriculture, offering an additional $2,000m. in spending over two years including a one-off investment of $1,000m. to aid farmers in planning effectively for income stabilization. The budget also introduced a Universal Child Care Benefit (worth $3,700m. over two years) that would provide families with $100 per month for each child under six years of age. Both these programmes illustrated the Harper administration's decision to introduce a two-year planning horizon for budgetary initiatives. The following year's budget focused on the environment and debt reduction, but also committed $16,000m. over seven years to improve Canada's infrastructure, much of which was to be allocated to reflect the priorities of municipalities and provinces. As of 2008 the Harper Government—still a minority administration—continued to pursue liberalizing agendas.

CONTINUITY AND CHANGE: INCOME SECURITY, WELFARE, HEALTH AND EDUCATION IN CANADA

GEOFFREY MERCER

During the 1950s and 1960s the introduction of a wide range of innovative social programmes signalled the arrival of the Canadian welfare state. This attracted broad public and political support of a better life for all Canadians, although its growth was constrained by federal–provincial disputes over the proper roles and involvement of the different levels of government in administering social and welfare policy and programmes. In the late 1970s and the 1980s mounting economic problems, nationally and internationally, including those resulting from the globalization and restructuring of Western economies, prompted a critical scrutiny of the costs and benefits of state expenditure in general and of the role of social policy in particular. A neo-liberal, monetarist attack on 'excessive' and 'inappropriate' state expenditure and lack of market competition gained political support, with governments rethinking the balance of their welfare state strategy. This essay reviews the general trajectory of social (security) policy in Canada, with discussion of its key components—income security, social assistance (welfare), health and education—against the background of federal–provincial conflicts, and changing economic and political conditions.

GENERAL CONTEXTS AND TRENDS

Crucially for the development of the Canadian welfare state, the British North America Act of 1867 assigned jurisdiction over the range of social policy to the provinces. At that time, and extending into the early decades of the 20th century, local funding and administration was the norm for programmes in these policy areas. Nevertheless, worsening economic and social conditions between the First and Second World Wars, coupled with moves towards government intervention in Europe and in the USA, acted as the catalyst for rethinking the aims and character of social policy. Hitherto, a central constraint on the growth of social security programmes was disagreement about how to accommodate provincial responsibility for service delivery with federal control of the main sources of revenue and taxation. Shared-cost arrangements between the two levels of government offered one possibility for establishing a federal presence, and led to the Old Age Pension Act of 1927. Amendment of the British North America Act was another option to permit federal responsibility in social policy. This resulted in legislation to introduce unemployment insurance (UI) in 1940 and family allowances in 1944.

After the Second World War, despite evident public support for social reform, intergovernmental disputes inhibited wider federal policy involvement. There were a few exceptions in the 1950s, such as income security programmes for older and unemployed people, but it was not until the 1960s that the central pillars of the contemporary welfare state were constructed. These spanned hospital and medical insurance, consolidation and expansion of provincial social welfare assistance in the Canada Assistance Plan (CAP), the Canada and Québec Pension Plans (CPP/QPP), a compulsory contributory social insurance programme providing protection against loss of earnings because of retirement, disability or death, and the Guaranteed Income Supplement (GIS) for older people with little or no income beyond the public pension (Old Age Security—OAS). This trend continued into the 1970s, with the expansion of UI and family allowances and the launching of a Spouse's Allowance (SPA) for senior citizens and a refundable Child Tax Credit. The rationale was to establish a 'safety net' for those lacking basic social and economic support across the life course.

These programmes typically combined federal grants or cost-sharing arrangements, including some financial redistribution in favour of the poorer regions, with provincial jurisdiction over programme delivery and administration. The federal interest was mostly linked to the promotion of broad national 'standards', while allowing variation in provincial and territorial practice—such as types of welfare services, eligibility criteria and scales of benefits. In comparison with the USA, the emphasis was on 'universal' (or 'demogrant') programmes, with benefits paid automatically to all those in a specified group, as happened (at least initially) with old-age pensions, family allowances, health and elementary-secondary education. Nevertheless, as the example of income security for older people illustrated, competing 'layers' or 'logics' have underpinned programme development: the original means-tested Old Age Pension was widened into the universal OAS in 1961, while the CPP/QPP conformed to a contributory, social insurance approach, and the GIS, introduced a year later in 1966, targeted low-income seniors to counter their social exclusion.

However, deteriorating economic conditions in the 1970s, with rising government debt, inflation and unemployment, triggered attempts to control growing federal and provincial expenditure. Unease about federal lack of regulation over the funding of social welfare programmes underpinned the passage of the Established Programmes Financing (EPF) Act of 1977. This replaced the existing system of cost-sharing for health and post-secondary education favoured by the provinces with a complex formula consisting of block grants and tax points. The growth in EPF funding was set at the rate of increase in gross national income and provincial population rather than actual provincial expenditure. CAP was a particular federal concern because it required 50:50 cost-sharing of provincial welfare programmes and social services and the federal Government stressed that programme development should depend on larger provincial contributions.

In the mid-1980s a new federal Progressive Conservative (PC) Government adopted a more monetarist approach, emulating trends in the USA and the United Kingdom. The general aim was a drastic reduction in the public debt, with the retrenchment of the welfare state a primary target. Universal/demogrant principles yielded ground to a policy philosophy based on social insurance against risk, with this contributory approach reinforced by means-testing for benefit eligibility and the targeting of individuals deemed in greatest need. Complementary initiatives attacked the perceived upsurge of a 'benefits culture'—characterized by welfare dependency and a low work ethic—promoting instead investment in human capital to build work-based skills and experience. There was also a greater resort to the tax system to achieve social policy aims. Additionally, governments sought ways to give an enhanced role in social programmes to the private and voluntary sectors—a trend encouraged when a balanced budget became a legal requirement in several provinces.

Financial pressure on the provinces built up when the federal Government unilaterally restricted cash and tax transfers, with limits placed on the indexing of health and post-secondary education funding under EPF. Its 1990 budget imposed a 'cap on CAP' with a 5% ceiling on annual rises to the richer provinces of Ontario, Alberta and British Columbia, without achieving the intended redistribution of resources to advantage the 'poorer' provinces. In 1993 the incoming Liberal administration charted a similar monetarist course and immediately set about reducing the federal deficit, which stood at C $42,000m. (equivalent to 5.9% of gross domestic product—GDP). Moreover, it instigated a fundamental policy change by replacing EPF and CAP with the Canada Health and Social Transfer (CHST) block grant. In its first two years of operation (1996–98) $7,000m. was cut from what would have been transferred to the provinces under EPF. CHST also eliminated the commitment to fund one-half of all provincial and territorial social assistance and social service expenditures under CAP. This provoked intense provincial criticism of a 'fiscal imbalance' and, in the 1999 budget, the federal Government announced a one-off cash transfer for health care of $3,500m., and $2,500m. to cover both health and post-secondary education up to 2004, along with substantially increased funding, covering health care, post-secondary education and early childhood.

Parallel attempts to inject a more positive aspect into the federal–provincial relationship and to modernize social policies, led to every jurisdiction (except Québec) signing the Social Union Framework Agreement in 1999. Its policy aims included residency-based barriers to welfare entitlements and to inter-provincial labour mobility, as well as specific initiatives in such areas as early childhood, health and Aboriginal peoples. Campaigns multiplied among a diverse range of disadvantaged social groups—women, one-parent families, disabled people, Aboriginal peoples, and new immigrants—and raised fundamental questions of social equity and differential access to social programme benefits. Critics charged that the role of the welfare state in delivering a safety net was flawed in practice, and was both insufficient and uneven in its realization across the provinces and territories.

Quite remarkably among the Group of Seven (G7) industrialized countries, the Canadian federal Government recorded a budgetary surplus every year from 1998, in large part leaving the provinces to confront rising demand and costs of social policy programmes. This guaranteed that criticism of federal responsibility for the 'fiscal imbalance' was a perennial rallying call among the provincial and territorial governments. The continuing intergovernmental disagreements finally resulted in changes being implemented in the CHST, with increased funding, and the separation of health from other social transfers in 2004. In addition, the new PC Government in its 2007 budget identified further health funding streams and introduced changes to the equalization formula to restore 'fiscal balance in Canada' and to benefit the less prosperous provinces. The likely impact of these changes was contested: some commentators calculated that the amendments to equalization would favour the resource-rich provinces (such as Alberta), while changes in transfer financing would be to the advantage of the higher-income provinces (such as Ontario). Nevertheless, with the provinces seeking their own balanced budgets in 2006–08, the pressure to contain social policy expenditure remained intense. As yet, the effects have been less dramatic or far-reaching than the critics of monetarist policies anticipated or than the exponents of neo-liberalism wished.

INCOME SECURITY/MAINTENANCE

A central goal of social policy has been to support those unable to meet their financial needs through the labour market. Income security programmes seek to maintain the income of individuals or families experiencing a loss of earnings (due to work injury, unemployment or retirement) or to provide income assistance to low-wage workers (through earnings supplements, tax credits and a minimum wage). In the 1960s three programmes dominated overall expenditure: universal family allowances, universal old age security, and UI. While originally envisaged as a safety net for a relatively small proportion of the population, the number of income security recipients grew substantially in the early 1980s and the early 1990s, reaching a high point of 10.7% of Canadians in 1994, before falling to less than 6% since 2002. Hence, in the 1980s and 1990s funding trends mirrored the general increase in social programme expenditure. Across all levels of government it climbed steadily as a proportion of total spending, from 19.4% in 1980/81 to 26.7% in 1993/94, levelling out thereafter, with a shift to a social insurance focus in pensions and UI, and greater targeting of social assistance, which increased to one-half of all income security expenditure at the end of the 20th century. As a proportion of GDP, income security spending expanded from 8.2% in 1980/81 to a high of 11.9% in 1992/93, before declining to less than 9% in the early 2000s. Throughout this period provincial and municipal expenditures (in constant 2002 dollars) remained below one-third of total income security spending.

In respect of senior benefits—OAS, GIS and SPA—the main upward trend in expenditure was on OAS, while GIS evened out and SPA spending decreased. In the 1980s the PC Government reduced old-age benefits by a series of income-tax-related measures affecting higher-income pensioners. Despite these modifications, OAS (which accounted for 77% of the cost of 'elderly benefits' in 1998) remained a basically 'universal' package to all those aged 65 years and over. Then, at the end of the 1990s, the Liberal Government strengthened the emphasis on 'vertical equity', whereby benefits were generally maintained for seniors with an income below C $20,000, whereas those in middle- and upper-income groups received smaller or no payments. Further targeting of average–low income pensioners and the upgrading of GIS benefits has persisted in federal budgets. While the system of flat-rate benefits and means-tested supplements meant that the retirement income system was relatively more supportive of low-income earners, critics charged that the level of benefits was not particularly generous in international terms.

Demographic and social trends, such as the growing numbers of women in paid employment and a doubling of the population aged 65 years and over to 3.9m. between 1971 and 2001, exerted a direct impact on eligibility for retirement income benefits. OAS and GIS are funded by taxpayers and their costs escalated in the first decade of the 2000s. In contrast, CPP/QPP income includes both individual contributions and interest paid on accumulated reserves. When CPP/QPP expenditure began to grow faster than income in the 1980s, there were fears of a jump in premiums for both employers and employees, but a federal-provincial agreement in 1997 introduced stabilizing measures, including a 10% cap on contributions. There was also greater endorsement of private retirement savings schemes.

Family allowances and child benefits attracted particular government attention throughout the second half of the 20th century. Initially directed at middle- and low-income families, cost-cutting initiatives introduced in the late 1980s resulted in a partial indexation of child-benefit rates and subsequently a diminution of the 'universality' of family allowances through a 5% 'claw back' beyond a basic income threshold. The integrated Child Tax Benefit (CTB) implemented in 1993 similarly targeted those families with the lowest incomes. Furthermore, a federal-provincial review of child benefits proposed measures to reduce child poverty that resulted in the launching of the National Child Benefit/Supplement (NCB) in 1998. This social investment approach was allied to an integrated, means-tested child benefit that offered a further incentive to women to undertake paid employment. With full indexation and higher income thresholds, 12.4% of children were living in 'low income' households in 2003, compared with 18.6% in 1996. In 2006 the newly elected federal PC Government introduced further support with a new Universal Child Care Benefit and a Child Disability Benefit, and announced the reintroduction of the Child Tax Credit in 2007, without targeting low-income households.

UI has been a major focus of government intervention over recent decades. During the 1950s, 1960s and 1970s UI coverage and rates were increased, particularly in the early 1970s. The expansion of UI coverage pushed UI as a proportion of total income security expenditure up from 10% to 20% over this period. UI expenditure grew sharply with unemployment spreading in the early 1980s and early 1990s, but it subsequently fell as unemployment declined from 11.4% to 6.8% between 1993 and 2000. Thereafter, the unemployment rate moved upwards, reaching 7.5% in 2003, before diminishing steadily to 6.0% in mid-2007. Governments frequently fine-tuned the UI eligibility criteria, such as the qualifying period and duration of benefits. UI coverage expanded from 42% at its inception to 88% in 1972, while benefit levels also improved. However, reforms in the late 1980s and 1990s led to cut-backs. The neo-liberal objective of reducing state expenditure highlighted the importance of eradicating a culture of 'welfare dependency' and producing a more flexible work-force. UI was directly in the firing line—criticized as contradictory to the work ethic, a disincentive to returning to work, and a constraint on the movement of workers to parts of the country with relatively greater job opportunities. Moreover, in 1985 a new 'Jobs Strategy' diverted CAP funding from welfare benefit payments to more 'active' labour market support measures. These concentrated on programmes that encouraged unemployed people to acquire new skills and undertake work-related training.

In 1996, with unemployment increasing, the Liberal Government renamed UI Employment Insurance (EI) and introduced stricter qualifying criteria. These were set at 420–700 hours, depending on the regional unemployment rate, while the 'maximum insurable earnings' were reduced from C $815 to $750 per week, and repeat users were further penalized. These changes had a disproportionate impact on groups already over-represented among part-time and low-income workers, such as women, disabled people and recent immigrants. Coverage plummeted to 43% in 1997, leading to a substantial decline in the percentage of unemployed people receiving EI benefits, while rates were set at 55% of wages up to a maximum of $413 per month. This forced many to turn to social assistance for support, notwithstanding an expanding surplus in the EI account. Most recently, with reform of the major income replacement schemes attracting intense political interest, the federal Government and the majority of provincial governments concluded Labour Market Partnership Agreements to assist individuals not eligible for EI into paid employment. Earnings supplements, such as the minimum wage and the Working Income Tax Benefit (introduced in the 2007 federal budget), were designed to 'make work pay' and sponsor movement off welfare into the labour market, as well as to help some low-paid workers, but the qualifying criteria were typically strict.

Social assistance or 'welfare' was an increasingly prominent item within provincial and municipal expenditure. Following the EPF changes in 1977, CAP was the only major scheme that shared costs equally between the federal and provincial governments. Each province identified its own programmes designed to meet the basic necessities of people 'in need'. Although originally envisaged as providing a safety net or short-term emergency assistance to unemployed households lacking any other sources of income, by the mid-1990s it reached more than 13% of the adult working-age population. Recipients spanned the long-term unemployed, single parents and those moved out of long-stay institutions. Funding was available for programmes aimed at basic subsistence requirements, as well as selected social services, such as day care, homemaker and home support, rehabilitation and residential care, independent living programmes for disabled people, and approved work-activity projects. Attempts to control provincial welfare expenditure in the early 1990s led to a combination of expenditure reductions, including the removal of indexation and more restrictive eligibility criteria. This trend was reinforced because CHST, which replaced CAP in 1996, weakened welfare support for those 'in need', and provinces turned increasingly to 'workfare' schemes to move people off social assistance and into employment. Nevertheless, in different provinces research indicated that social assistance programmes, such as Ontario Works and the Ontario Disability Support Programme, provided inadequate support for poorer Canadians, with low benefit rates exacerbated by complex eligibility rules.

While general economic conditions affected changes in income security policies, a range of demographic, social and political factors also played an important role. The retreat from universality and benefit decreases was more evident in some areas (UI) compared to others (CPP/QPP), while both coverage and rates for CTB/NCB in 1998 were extended. However, there was a concerted push to weaken demogrants and needs-tested programmes by distributing benefits through the income tax system (as with CTB/NCB). In addition, a continued federal budgetary surplus, emulated in 2004 by the governments of Ontario, British Columbia and Alberta, meant that these provinces no longer qualified for federal 'equalization' payments to boost social programmes. There was further uncertainty about the impact of the newly separated Canada Social Transfer programme and whether governments would reverse recent drastic cut-backs in social programmes.

The impact of income security programmes in redistributing income was patchy. Income inequalities which widened in the 1990s, briefly abated, but have since grown again. Market income (employment, investments, private pensions and other non-public sources) demonstrated the greatest disparities, with families in the highest quintile 14.6 times better off than families in the bottom quintile. This differential fell to 4.9 after the inclusion of after-tax income and income security benefits. According to 2001 census figures, Canadian society had become more polarized over the preceding 30 years, with the income of the richest 10% rising much faster than that of the bottom 10%. As the then Prime Minister, Jean Chrétien, acknowledged, 'there are still too many (female) single-parent families, too many visible minorities, too many recent immigrants, too many Aboriginal Canadians living in poverty'. The Canadian welfare state safety net was increasingly described as 'tangled', with mounting demand for income security assistance, and criticism that benefits did not keep up with increases in the cost of living. Indeed, the distribution of government transfers to the least well-off has fallen slightly since its peak of 63% in 1981.

HEALTH

The first steps towards a publicly funded health insurance were taken in Saskatchewan, with four such provincial schemes established by 1950. The federal Government then paved the way for a putative national system by creating two voluntary cost-shared programmes—for in-patient services under the Hospital Insurance and Diagnostic Services Act of 1957, and an extension of this coverage in 1966, under the Medical Care Act. The resulting system of Medicare comprised an interlocking series of provincial insurance plans that guaranteed prepaid health care. Federal funding was contingent on the provincial health plan satisfying the following five principles for Canada's national health care system: administration on a non-profit basis; comprehensive coverage of insured services; universal population coverage; reasonable access to services; and inter-provincial portability of benefits. Other funding sources varied across provincial plans and spanned payroll taxes, general revenues and individual or family premiums. Medical care was privately delivered with physicians reimbursed on a fee-for-service basis, with the scale of fees determined by negotiation with the provincial medical association. All plans absorbed basic medical (hospital and physician) costs, with most other services paid for privately, although some provincial plans provided, for example, partial coverage of prescription medicines and dental care; community care was generally excluded.

Throughout the last quarter of the 20th century expenditure on health services was a significant and growing item in federal and provincial government budgets. In 1975 total health care spending amounted to 7% of GDP and this moved upwards unevenly to plateau at an average annual of just over 10% between 2002 and 2007. Annual growth in health expenditure per head slowed to around 0.8% under the fiscal restraint of the early 1990s, before accelerating again to an average of over 4% per year from 1996–2007, with health service costs rising faster than inflation. These trends were very similar to other G7 countries. In addition, health spending was an expanding budgetary item at all levels of government, with the provincial average escalating from 32% of total budgetary expenditure to 39% over the last decade. The major concern was that federal transfer funding was not keeping pace. Again, EPF transfers were conditional on provincial adherence to the underlying principles of Medicare, and tensions erupted in the early 1980s over federal claims that the practice of 'extra-billing' (physicians seeking payment above set rates) and the imposition of user charges were eroding Medicare standards. This led to the Canada Health Act of 1984, which consolidated earlier legislation and reaffirmed the commitment to a universal prepaid health insurance system run according to nationally agreed criteria. It also introduced financial penalties against any province allowing extra-billing and user charges.

Such concerns fuelled a continuing series of provincial and national inquiries and commissions throughout the 1990s. The diagnoses often overlapped. A key concern was the importance of controlling health spending while achieving a more explicit and equitable allocation of resources and access to services. In 2007 the four largest areas of expenditure were hospitals (28%), drugs (17%), physicians (13%) and other professionals (11%). As originally formulated, Medicare reimbursed hospital and physician services and later reforms focused on ways to control increased expenditure in these areas (such as reducing the number of hospital beds and revising the fee-for-service system of physician remuneration). The escalating demands on the health care system also led to shortages and rationing, with selected services removed from fee schedules, controls on the use of expensive drugs and waiting lists instituted for some non-elective procedures. All provinces experienced difficulties in the recruitment, retention and distribution of health service staff, leading to various initiatives to extend the roles of nurses, midwives and allied health professionals. Another policy trend was to greater devolution of responsibility in health service organization to regional authorities, in an attempt to instil more local accountability. Again, pressure (from insurance companies, the medical profession and some provincial governments) to allow more scope for private health care continued unabated. The share of health expenditures paid for by supplementary private insurance and individual patients peaked at just over 30% in 2002, leading to claims of 'creeping privatization'.

Another issue was whether health policy was interpreted too narrowly and failed to address the full range of causes of ill health and entrenched social divisions. This included arguments for the redirection of health interventions to encompass environmental, housing and workplace conditions, and recommendations for greater collaboration between, for example, social services, education and housing departments in developing an inter-sectoral policy approach. These calls were reinforced by evidence of continuing social inequalities in mortality and morbidity, across socio-economic groups, by gender and ethnicity, as well as between Aboriginal and non-Aboriginal Canadians. While most health policies stressed individual responsibility and the promotion of 'healthy lifestyles' rather than structural solutions, neither option received significant levels of government funding. Similarly, there was little movement towards a comprehensive health approach that widened Medicare coverage to community services, home care, dental care and 'medically necessary' drugs.

Nevertheless, the general public remained solidly supportive of the achievements of Medicare and regarded it as a symbol of Canadian values. There was a consensus among federal politicians that radical retreat from its stated principles was tantamount to political 'suicide', although governments consistently sought ways to ensure that health care policies demonstrated greater cost effectiveness. Intergovernmental wrangling over the shortfall in federal transfer funding following the move to CHST led to the federal Government substantially enlarging health care funding in 1999. Even so, there was a wide gulf between provincial claims that this represented a contribution of 14 cents to every dollar of health expenditure, and federal calculations that 40 cents was the correct figure. There was a general consensus that further substantial growth in health expenditures was required over the next decade because of the demands of an ageing population, more expensive health care technology and heightened patient/public expectations. Several provincial governments contemplated radical policy delivery changes. For example, Alberta prepared legislation allowing a more prominent role for private medicine, although it eventually bowed to public criticism and instead tightened provisions against extra-billing and queue jumping.

With political divisions becoming ever sharper, in 2001 the federal Government decided to establish a national inquiry, led by Roy Romanow, former Premier of Saskatchewan, to explore and make recommendations on future directions in Canada's public health care system. The final report appeared in October 2002 and a First Ministers' Health Accord, reinforced by the federal budget, in February 2003, confirmed a strategy for 'remodelling not demolishing' Medicare. Romanow argued that health spending was not out of control, but that federal transfers had declined significantly and provinces were deferring investment in staff and the physical infrastructure. Despite significant increases in federal health transfers introduced in 2000, he urged more stable and predictable funding arrangements, and the division of CHST with a dedicated (cash) Canada Health Transfer and built-in escalator. In response, the federal Government agreed to address the so-called 'Romanow gap' between what he recommended and what was actually transferred to the provinces. The federal budget for 2003 allocated C $34,800m. additional funding over the next five years, without returning to historic health funding levels. Action included an increase in the annual base for cash contributions and an escalator to ensure more predictable funding. Furthermore, the newly separated Health Transfer funding was directed at various priorities, such as improvements to home care, remote/rural services, primary health care, diagnostic services, catastrophic (very expensive) drugs coverage, and medical equipment. Additionally, First Ministers accepted the need for more spending on research; action on waiting lists; a new patient information system; a comprehensive human resources strategy; and recognition of minority group needs, with support for a partnership with aboriginal peoples. However, the provinces failed to persuade the federal Government to assume responsibility for the funding of public prescription drug or dental plans.

Romanow argued for a national health care system, rather than 14 separate (and uneven) systems. To this end, he advocated a Canadian Health Covenant (setting out the responsibilities and entitlements of governments, providers and citizens); modernization of the Canada Health Act (expanding the definition of 'comprehensiveness' to include priority diagnostic and home care services, clarifying the meaning of 'portability' and adding a new principle of 'accountability'); and the creation of a Health Council of Canada, a public forum that was designed to create a collaborative dialogue, with governments held to account for the performance of health services. There were also proposals to formulate 'aspirational' national health goals to enhance programme transparency and accountability, amid considerable political and public debate about identifying ways to promote efficiency and effectiveness in health care services.

Notwithstanding the time and resources expended on the Romanow Report, familiar unresolved issues around funding soon resurfaced to generate further intergovernmental conflict. The Alberta Government again championed greater privatization and revisions to the Canada Health Act and the reassignment of tax points to the provinces, in order to allow them more control over Medicare and its funding. In Québec, discussion of the contribution that private health practitioners, organizations and insurance might make to a predominantly publicly funded and controlled health care system gained new momentum following the Supreme Court ruling in June 2005 that the provincial ban on private insurance for services covered by Medicare violated the Québec Charter of Rights (although similar legislation existed in other provinces). This interpretation was justified on the grounds that the provincial Government had been unable to reduce significantly patient waiting times. A provincial task force was set up to investigate possible options. The task force published a report in February 2008 which resurrected arguments about whether Medicare was in need of basic reform by calling for a cap on provincial health spending through the partial privatization of health services, the encouragement of private insurance, an end to the public monopoly over hospital management, more health clinics and an increase in the provincial sales tax with the proceeds ring-fenced for health care. Recent proposals by the governments in Alberta and British Columbia for a new balance between public and private medicine suggest that Medicare has returned to centre-stage in political debates.

Notwithstanding its critics, Medicare has been recognized internationally as an efficient and effective health care system because of its capacity to control health care spending while delivering a quality service with one of the highest life expectancies and lowest infant mortality rates in the world. In contrast, as a proportion of GDP, the USA spent three times more on private health care than Canada. Overall, the publicly funded, universally accessible health care system provided a national rallying point, in direct contrast to its US counterpart.

EDUCATION

As with health policy, federal involvement in education stemmed primarily from the lack of funding resources at the provincial level and was conditional on intergovernmental agreement. There has been no federal department of education, although Ottawa was not averse to using funding as a policy lever, with universal, free elementary and secondary schooling established across the country. Instead, the Council of Ministers of Education (CMEC), which was created in 1967 as a forum for provincial and territorial ministers of education, has acted as the national voice on education. Despite some important differences between provinces in the organization, delivery and assessment of education, there has been less intergovernmental conflict over recent decades compared with the arguments surrounding health care.

Education is another major item of public expenditure, accounting for some 16.2% of total spending in 2006/07 (compared with 19.8% on health and 25.5% on income security and social assistance). The expansion of the educational budget from the 1960s was related to economic growth, demographic change, with an expanding under-25 age-group, and increased participation across the elementary, secondary and post-secondary sectors. The provinces contributed most of the funding, followed by federal direct and indirect grants and transfers, local taxation, fees and other sources. Overall (public and private) educational expenditure held steady as a proportion of GDP into the 1990s. It was higher than the average for Organisation for Economic Co-operation and Development (OECD) countries, although in 2005, with spending on education falling slightly, to 6.1% of GDP, Canada ranked marginally below the OECD average.

The major post-1945 expansion in post-secondary education was facilitated by federal grants for student aid, technical and vocational (re)training and universities (1951–67), plus transfers for post-secondary education under the EPF Act of 1977. However, the upward movement of federal transfers for education was trimmed during the 1980s and into the 1990s. Changing fiscal policies largely accounted for a 7% decline in per-head funding and a 3% drop in overall education expenditures between 1994 and 2001. The replacement of EPF by CHST further reduced post-secondary funding and led to a large hike in university tuition fees—with a significant upsurge in student debt and a stalling of enrolment. This sparked a modest addition to federal financial backing covering student loans, tax incentives to encourage parental support, an augmented scholarship programme and expansion in research council budgets. The transfer of additional CHST payments announced in the 1999 and 2000 federal budgets delivered a significant growth in funding, although critics argued that this did not compensate for earlier reductions.

The provinces, with federal government support, invested heavily in education as a means of achieving economic success, and for reasons of broader nation building. There was a significant extension of educational participation in elementary and secondary school attendance, completion of secondary school, and of recruitment to the post-secondary (college and university) sector. By 2003 the secondary school completion rate had risen to 74% (78% for girls and 70% for boys), while the proportion of 25–29-year-olds with less than high school education fell from 20% to 13% between the early 1990s and 2004. Moreover, during the same period the percentage of university graduates climbed from 17% to 26%, and by 2003 43% of adults aged 25–64 years had a college or university qualification, compared with the OECD average of 23%. Many upgraded their qualifications, with 1.4m. aged 25 years and over enrolled in education programmes. From the 1980s Canada consistently achieved a place in the top ranks of international league tables. It was second only to the USA in average years of formal schooling, while in 2003 a higher percentage of the Canadian population had a college or university-level qualification than in any other OECD country. In 2006 an international study of 15-year-olds found that Canada had one of the highest ratings in the world—spanning language, science and mathematics. Even so, the same study revealed that 42% of 15-year-olds were classified as lacking the literacy skills to meet some basic everyday requirements.

Although not as significant as in most European countries, socio-economic inequalities in performance have persisted: in the mid-1990s 34% from the lowest income quartile had not completed secondary school, compared with 23% from the highest income quartile, while in 2004 young Canadians from high-income families were more than twice as likely as their peers from low-income families to attend university. Continuing disparities, despite progress overall, characterized the educational attainments of aboriginal Canadians, particularly those living on reserves. In 2001 almost one-half of the Aboriginal population failed to graduate from secondary school, compared with 31% for Canadians as a whole, and only 2% of the Aboriginal population aged 20–24 years had a university degree, compared with 11% in the total population. However, the proportion completing secondary school and those graduating from post-secondary education was rising, with increased federal funding of loans and scholarships to undertake post-secondary courses. In addition, the participation and attainment of female students improved markedly from the 1980s. Women now constituted a clear majority of university students and were making inroads into traditional male strongholds, such as engineering, management and business studies.

The direction of educational policy (its organization, delivery and assessment) shifted significantly from the 1960s, with notable similarities and distinctive features between provinces. Across Canada there was also extensive discussion and wide-ranging reforms of the elementary and secondary school curriculum and teaching methods (becoming more learner-centred and 'progressive'). This paralleled continuing debates about the respective roles of provincial ministries of education compared to elected school boards, trustees and parents. Since the 1990s there has been a degree of decentralization, but overall the number of school boards has been halved and provincial control remains undiminished. For example, New Brunswick abolished school boards in 1996, allowing limited input from parent groups, before a subsequent Conservative Government reinvented school boards in the guise of District Education Councils in 2001. Similarly, Alberta opted for parental school councils. For its part, the Government of British Columbia recently decentralized powers to school boards with some revenue-raising options, but crucially, as with other provincial and territorial governments, retained control of educational funding with significant constraints placed on local autonomy.

In Ontario the Conservative Government elected in 1995 introduced a more performance-based funding formula and reforms to school governance and organizational structures inspired by the goal of enhanced management of resources and better 'value for money'. In 2002 school boards that refused to pass a balanced budget were taken over. The focus on educational practice led to a series of policy initiatives designed to raise pupil attainment, particularly in numeracy and literacy, with new, standardized performance testing of children throughout the province, more emphasis on school accountability, pupil/student and school/college achievement and review, and assessment of the quality of teaching. These initiatives emphasized inter-school comparison and ranking on provincial educational targets. Additionally, Ontario reduced the length of the secondary school curriculum by one year so that its students left at the end of grade 12. In contrast, post-secondary education in Québec begins with CEGEP (collèges d'enseignement général et professionnel) after graduation from grade 11. Students then took a pre-university programme of two or three years or a vocational/professional alternative.

Secondary schools attracted considerable criticism for not doing enough to prepare children for the rapidly changing economy and society. Diversity in the curriculum of the upper secondary years was encouraged to facilitate the transfer into work or post-secondary education. Various schemes were instituted to promote school discipline. These overlapped with changes in school governance, with particular weight attached to devolving some decision-making to schools and/or parents, and generating partnerships across the main educational stakeholders. These initiatives favoured an approach by which more information was provided to the consumer/user in the educational market place. However, the polarization of views around education and schooling, including the unpredictability of funding, produced a two-week teachers' strike in 1997, conflicts with school boards including school closures, legal actions and a series of contentious administrative regulations and legislation. A new provincial Government in Ontario reiterated the idea of 'partnership' between key interest groups to find ways to enhance publicly funded education. It prioritized the pre-school and primary years, achieving smaller class sizes and improving basic educational skills, with the aim of reducing significantly the numbers leaving school without graduating. It also announced a programme to upgrade school buildings and teacher certification.

Religious (Roman Catholic and Protestant) and linguistic (French and English) divisions have historically been significant features of Canadian educational policy, while the residential school system was central to attempts at assimilating Aboriginal peoples. However, with the changing ethnic composition of Canada's population, this religious dimension to educational systems has mostly been dismantled, except in Alberta, Saskatchewan, Ontario and the Northwest Territories. There were moves in the 1980s and 1990s to widen community involvement and to stress culturally appropriate curricula and programmes, including specific initiatives to support Aboriginal languages and teachers. While some public funding of legally established Christian (Roman Catholic and Protestant) schools continued, a question mark remained over its extension to other-faith religious schools. Instead, over recent years, there has been a growth in private, faith-based schools (e.g. Christian, Hindu, Jewish, Muslim and Sikh), sometimes with conditional public monies. In Québec a constitutional amendment was required to overturn the confessional school system established at Confederation, to be replaced by linguistic (French or English) school boards, although fluency in French was vigorously promoted. Nationally, the federal enthusiasm for bilingualism facilitated the growth of French and some English immersion programmes (where pupils were taught in their 'second' language). These flourished in the late 1970s and 1980s, although their numbers have stalled over the last decade, with around only 8% of non-francophone primary and secondary school pupils enrolled in such programmes.

Private education generally has grown in recent years. By the start of the 21st century the proportion of children attending private schools had increased to 8%, including 17% of the secondary school population in Québec, with an even higher proportion in urban centres. This expansion included a growth in enrolment in élite, preparatory and alternative (faith-based) schools over the last decade. The share of private funding of education climbed from 8% in the early 1980s to almost 12% by the early years of the 21st century, despite the fact that not all provinces/territories give financial assistance to private schools. The transition from public to private sources of funding was further evident at the post-secondary level, and many provinces allowed, if not encouraged, private degree-granting colleges and universities.

Although past OECD reports have argued that Canada's education policies lacked a 'national conception of the country's interests', this criticism seems misplaced given the recent direction of educational policy, and the country's impressive international performance rankings in educational attainment tables.

REVIEW

The post-Second World War expansion of the Canadian welfare state has been noteworthy both in terms of the quantity and character of social policy initiatives. Innovative developments in the nature of federal-provincial relations were crucial in determining the development of social programmes, with the resolution of funding and control proving the crucial factor. There was a broad majority among Canadians and their governments agreeing the basic merits of publicly funded income security, social welfare, health and education programmes, although specific details often proved contentious. Social policy contributed not only directly to social and economic life, but as regards education and particularly health care, became an expression of Canada's distinctive identity (values and institutions) within North America.

A striking feature of the period from the mid-1980s was the advent of a major 'neo-liberal' challenge to the post-1945 welfare state. This generated a re-evaluation of the objectives, direction and outcomes of state intervention in social policy, with a drastic retrenchment of social programmes. The responses encompassed a shift in the balance from universalism to means-testing, greater restrictions on eligibility and reductions in benefit rates, attacks on welfare dependency and disincentives to work, heightened recognition of private and voluntary sector involvement and solutions, and greater emphasis on measuring performance/outcomes and achieving 'value for money'. There were exceptions—such as NCB, introduced along with extra financial support for early childhood services—while recent federal budgets have offered the prospect of modest expansion.

Some commentators have identified a shift from the federally dominated 'co-operative federalism' of the 1960s and 1970s to 'framework federalism' since the 1990s, with more emphasis on negotiation between levels of government to conclude agreements in areas where the federal purse strings are crucial or in instances of shared jurisdiction. However, this has produced considerable contrasts in policy outcomes between provinces, albeit within broad national objectives and principles. Overall, reports of the demise of the federal role in social security and the beginning of a new era in social policy at the beginning of the 21st century proved exaggerated, with insufficient evidence of either significantly enhanced provincial control or an increased 'balkanization' and sharpening of provincial differences in social programmes.

SELECT BIBLIOGRAPHY

Battle, K., Mendelson, M. and Torjman, S. *Towards a New Architecture for Canada's Adult Benefits*. Ottawa, ON, Canadian Institute of Social Policy, 2006.

Boychuck, G. *The Canadian Social Model: The Logics of Policy Development*. Ottawa, ON, Canadian Policy Research networks, 2004.

Canadian Education Association. *Public Education In Canada: Facts, Trends and Attitudes*. Toronto, ON, Canadian Education Association, 2007.

Moscovitch, A. and Albert, J. (Eds). *The Benevolent Welfare State: The Growth of Welfare in Canada*. Toronto, ON, Garamond Press, 1987.

Rice, J. J. and Prince, M. J. *Changing Politics of Canadian Social Policy*. Toronto, ON, University of Toronto Press, 2000.

Romanow, R. J. (Commissioner). *Building on Values: The Future of Health Care in Canada*. Ottawa, ON, Government of Canada, 2002.

SELECT BIBLIOGRAPHY (ECONOMIC AFFAIRS)

Acheson, K., and Maude, C. *Much Ado About Culture: North American Trade Disputes*. Ann Arbor, MI, University of Michigan Press, 1999.

Alberta Statistical Review. Edmonton, AB, Government of Alberta, quarterly.

Anderson, R. B. *Economic Development among the Aboriginal Peoples in Canada: The Hope for the Future*. North York, ON, Captus Press Inc, 1999.

Andrew, C., Armstrong, P., and Lapierre, A. (Eds). *World Class Cities: Can Canada Play?* Ottawa, ON, University of Ottawa Press, 1999.

Angel, D. P. 'Inter-firm Collaboration and Technology Development Partnerships Within US Manufacturing Industries', in *Regional Studies*, Vol. 36, No. 4, pp. 333–44. Abingdon, Oxon, Taylor & Francis, June 2002.

Atkinson, K., and McDonald, A. T. (Eds). *Sustainability in Environmental Management in Canada*. Leeds, Canadian Studies Workshop, May 1997, Centre for Canadian Studies, University of Leeds, 2000.

Bacher, J. *Petrotyranny*. Toronto, ON, The Dundurn Group, 2000.

Banting, K., Sharpe, A., and St-Hilaire, F. (Eds). *The Review of Economic Performance and Social Progress: Towards a Social Understanding of Productivity*. Montréal, QC, and Kingston, ON, McGill-Queen's University Press, 2002.

Black, E., and Silver, J. *Building a Better World: An Introduction to Trade Unionism in Canada*. Peterborough, ON, Fernwood Publishing Co, 2008.

Bone, R. M. *The Geography of the Canadian North: Issues and Challenges*. Toronto, ON, Oxford University Press, 1992.

The Regional Geography of Canada. Don Mills, ON, Oxford University Press Canada, 2000.

British Journal of Canadian Studies (various issues). London, British Association for Canadian Studies, 2 a year.

Britton, J. N. H. 'Regional Implications of North American Integration: A Canadian Perspective on High Technology Manufacturing', in *Regional Studies*, Vol. 36, No. 4, pp. 359–74. Abingdon, Oxon, Taylor & Francis, June 2002.

(Ed.). *Canada and the Global Economy: The Geography of Structural and Technological Change*. Montréal, QC, and Kingston, ON, McGill-Queen's University Press, 1996.

Brownsey, K., and Howlett, M. (Eds). *The Provincial State in Canada: Politics in the Provinces and Territories*. Peterborough, ON, Broadview Press, 2001.

Buzzelli, M. 'What Explains Firm Transience in House-building?: A Regional Analysis of Ontario, Canada, 1991 and 1996'. *Regional Studies*, Vol. 39, No. 6, pp. 699–712. Abingdon, Oxon, Taylor & Francis, 2005.

Calvert, J., and Fraser, S. *Liquid Gold: Energy Privatization in British Columbia*. Peterborough, ON, Fernwood Publishing Co, 2008.

Canadian Economics Association. *Canadian Journal of Economics*. Oxford, Blackwells, quarterly.

Carree, M. A. 'Does Unemployment Affect the Number of Establishments? A Regional Analysis for US States', in *Regional Studies*, Vol. 36, No. 4, pp. 389–98. Abingdon, Oxon, Taylor & Francis, June 2002.

Centre for the Study of Commercial Activity in Canada (CSCA). *Commercial Activity in Canada: 2006*. Toronto, ON, Ryerson University, 2005.

Chambers, E. J., and Smith, P. H. (Eds). *NAFTA in the New Millennium*. Edmonton, AB, University of Alberta Press (with the Center for US-Mexican Studies, University of California, San Diego), 2004.

Clement, W. (Ed.). *Understanding Canada: Building on the New Canadian Political Economy*. Montréal, QC, and Kingston, ON, McGill-Queen's University Press, 1997.

The Conference Board of Canada. *Lost Over the Atlantic?: The Canada–EU Trade and Investment Relationship*. Report, The Canada Project, Ottawa, ON, June 2006.

Canada's Hub Cities: A Driving Force of the National Economy. Report, Economic Performance and Trends, The Canada Project, Ottawa, ON, July 2006.

Courchene, T., and Neave, E. *Reforming the Canadian Financial Sector: Canada in Global Perspective*. Montréal, QC, and Kingston, ON, McGill-Queen's University Press, 2001.

Crow, J. W. *Making Money: An Insider's Perspective on Finance, Politics, and Canada's Central Bank*. New York, NY, John Wiley & Sons, 2003.

Department of Finance. *Quarterly Economic Review* (various). Ottawa, ON, Canadian Government Publishing Centre.

Diochon, M. C. *Entrepreneurship and Community Economic Development*. Montréal, QC, and Kingston, ON, McGill-Queen's University Press, 2004.

Doloreux, D. 'Regional Innovation Systems in Canada: A Comparative Study', in *Regional Studies*, Vol. 38, No. 5, pp. 481–94. Abingdon, Oxon, Taylor & Francis, July 2004.

Dwivedi, O. P., Kyba, P., Stoett, P., and Tiessen, R. *Sustainable Development and Canada: National and International Perspectives*. Peterborough, ON, Broadview Press, 2001.

Economic Council of Canada. *Annual Review*. Ottawa, ON, Canadian Government Publishing Centre.

Epp, R., and Whitson, D. *Writing off the Rural West: Globalisation, Governments, and the Transformation of Rural Community*. Edmonton, AB, University of Alberta Press, 2001.

Fortin, S., Noel, A., and St-Hilaire, F. (Eds). *Forging the Canadian Social Union: SUFA and Beyond*. Montréal, QC, and Kingston, ON, McGill-Queen's University Press, 2003.

Froschauer, K. *White Gold: Hydroelectric Power in Canada*. Vancouver, BC, University of British Columbia Press, 1999.

Fuji Johnston, G. *Deliberative Democracy for the Future: The Case of Nuclear Waste Management in Canada*. Toronto, ON, Toronto University Press, 2008.

Gault, F. (Ed.). *Understanding Innovation in Canadian Industry*. Montréal, QC, and Kingston, ON, McGill-Queen's University Press, 2004.

Globerman, S., and Storer, P. *The Impact of 9/11 on Canada-US Trade*. Toronto, ON, University of Toronto Press, 2008.

Grady, P., and Sharpe, A. (Eds). *The State of Economics in Canada—Festschrift in Honour of David Slater*. Waterloo, ON, Wilfred Laurier University Press, 2001.

Harding, J. *Canada's Deadly Secret: Saskatchewan Uranium and the Global Nuclear System*. Peterborough, Fernwood Publishing Co, 2008.

Hart, M. *A Trading Nation: Canadian Trade from Colonialism to Globalization*. Vancouver, BC, University of British Columbia Press, 2002.

Hayter, R. *Flexible Crossroads: The Restructuring of British Columbia's Forest Economy*. Vancouver, BC, University of British Columbia Press, 2000.

Hessing, M., Howlett, M., and Summerville, T. *Canadian Natural Resource and Environmental Policy: Political Economy and Public Policy*, 2nd edn. Vancouver, BC, University of British Columbia Press, 2006.

Hodge, G., and Robinson, I. M. *Planning Canadian Regions*. Vancouver, BC, University of British Columbia Press, 2001.

Holbrook, J. A., and Wolfe, D. A. (Eds). *Innovation, Institutions and Territory: Regional Innovation Systems in Canada*. Montréal, QC, and Kingston, ON, McGill-Queen's University Press, 2001.

Knowledge, Clusters and Regional Innovation: Economic Development in Canada. Montréal, QC, and Kingston, ON, McGill-Queen's University Press, 2002.

Innis, H. A., and Ray, A. J. *The Fur Trade in Canada: An Introduction to Canadian Economic History*, 2nd edn. Toronto, ON, University of Toronto Press, 1999.

Institute for Competitiveness and Prosperity, Task Force on Competitiveness. Various *Annual Reports* and *Working Papers*, Toronto, ON, 2002–07.

Realizing Canada's Prosperity Potential. Presented at the Annual Meeting of the World Economic Forum, Davos, Switzerland. Toronto, ON, January 2005.

Time on the Job: Intensity and Ontario's Prosperity Gap. Working Paper 9, Toronto, ON, September 2006.

Ismael, S. *Child Poverty and the Canadian Welfare State: From Entitlement to Charity*. Edmonton, AB, University of Alberta Press, 2007.

Jackson, T., and Curry, J. 'Regional Development and Land Use Planning in Rural British Columbia: Peace in the Woods?', in *Regional Studies*, Vol. 36, No. 4, pp. 439–43. Abingdon, Oxon, Taylor & Francis, June 2002.

Karabegovic, A., Clemens, J., and Veldhuis, N. 'Measuring Labour Markets in Canada and the United States', in *Critical Issues Bulletin*. Vancouver, BC, The Fraser Institute Canada, 2003.

Karabegovic, A., McMahon, F., and Samida, D. *Economic Freedom of North America: 2004 Annual Report*. Vancouver, BC, The Fraser

Institute Canada and Washington, DC, the National Center for Policy Analysis of the United States of America, 2004.

Kunin, R. (Ed.). *Prospering Together: The Economic Impact of the Aboriginal Title Settlements in BC*, 2nd edn. Vancouver, BC, The Laurier Institution, 2001.

Lazar, H. *Canadian Fiscal Arrangements: What Works, What Might Work Better*. Montréal, QC, and Kingston, ON, McGill-Queen's University Press, 2005.

Lee, E., and Perl, A. *The Integrity Gap: Canada's Environmental Policy and Institutions*. Vancouver, BC, University of British Columbia Press, 2003.

Levitt, K. *Silent Surrender: The Multinational Corporation in Canada*. Montréal, QC, and Kingston, ON, McGill-Queen's University Press, 2002.

Lewis, T. *In the Long Run We're All Dead: the Canadian Turn to Fiscal Restraint*. Vancouver, BC, University of British Columbia Press, 2003.

Lindsay, K. M., and Smith, D. W. *A Review of Environmental Assessment Processes*. Edmonton, AB, Canadian Circumpolar Institute (CCI) Press, 2001.

Lucas, R, and Tepperman, L. *Minetown, Milltown, Railtown: Life in Canadian Communities of Single Industry*. Toronto, ON, Oxford University Press Canada, 2008.

McBride, S. *Paradigm Shift: Globalization and the Canadian State*. 2nd edn. Peterborough, ON, Fernwood Books Ltd, 2005.

McCann, L. D., and Dunn, A. (Eds). *Heartland and Hinterland: A Regional Geography of Canada*, 3rd edn. Scarborough, ON, Prentice Hall, 1998.

MacDonald, L. *The Bombardier Story: Planes, Trains, and Snowmobiles*. Etobicoke, ON, John Wiley & Sons Canada, 2001.

Nortel Networks: How Innovation and Vision Created a Network Giant. Etobicoke, ON, John Wiley & Sons Canada, 2000.

McGillivray, B. *Geography of British Columbia: People and Landscapes in Transition*. Vancouver, BC, University of British Columbia Press, 2000.

McHughen, A. *Biotechnology and Food for Canadians*. Vancouver, BC, and New York, NY, The Fraser Institute and The American Council on Science and Health, 2002.

MacLachlan, I. *Kill and Chill: Restructuring Canada's Beef Commodity Chain*. Toronto, ON, University of Toronto Press, 2001.

McNiven, C., and Puderer, H. *Delineation of Canada's North: An Examination of the North-South Relationship in Canada*. Geography Division—Statistics Canada, January 2000, Geography Working Paper Series No. 2000–03, Ottawa, ON.

McPherson, R. *New Owners—Minerals and Inuit Land Claims on Their Own Land*. Calgary, AB, University of Calgary Press (with the Arctic Institute of North America), 2003.

Marchildon, G. P. (Ed.). *Agriculture at the Border: Canada-US Trade Relations in the Global Food Regime*. Regina, SK, Canadian Plains Research Center, 2000.

Mitchell, B. *Resource and Environmental Management*. Harlow, Essex, Pearson, 2002.

Mussio, L. B. *Telecom Nation: Telecommunications, Computers, and Governments in Canada*. Montréal, QC, and Kingston, ON, McGill-Queen's University Press, 2001.

Nelles, H. V. *The Politics of Development: Forests, Mines, and Hydro-Electric Power in Ontario, 1849–1941*. Montréal, QC, and Kingston, ON, McGill-Queen's University Press, 2003.

New, W. H. *Borderlands: How We Talk about Canada*. Vancouver, BC, University of British Columbia Press, 1998.

Nicholls, C. C. *Mergers, Acquisitions, and Other Changes of Corporate Control* (Essentials of Canadian Law Series). Toronto, ON, Irwin Law Inc, 2007.

Norrie, K., and Owram, D. *A History of the Canadian Economy*, 3rd edn. Scarborough, ON, Thomson Nelson, 2002.

O'Brien, R. *Solidarity First: Canadian Workers and Social Cohesion*. Vancouver, BC, University of British Columbia Press, 2008.

OECD Economic Surveys. *Canada*. Paris, OECD, annual.

Porter, M., and Strange, W. C. *Geography, Industrial Organization and Agglomeration Economies*. Review of Economics and Statistics, 2003.

Pugh, T., and McLaughlin, D. (Eds). *Our Board Our Business: Why Farmers Support the Canadian Wheat Board*. Peterborough, ON, Fernwood Publishing Co, 2008.

Resnick, P. *The Politics of Resentment: British Columbia Regionalism and Canadian Unity*. Vancouver/Toronto, BC/ON, University of British Columbia Press, 2000.

Reynolds, M. B., and Nelson, J. K. (Eds). *Canadian Imports and Trade Issues*. Hauppauge, NY, Nova Science Publishers, 2008.

Rideout, V. *Continentalizing Canadian Telecommunications: The Politics of Regulatory Reform*. Montréal, QC, and Kingston, ON, McGill-Queen's University Press, 2004.

Ritchie, G. *Wrestling with the Elephant: The Inside Story of Canada-US Trade Wars*. Toronto, ON, MacFarlane, Walter & Ross, 1997.

Robert, M. *Negotiating Nafta: Explaining the Outcome in Culture, Textiles, Autos, and Pharmaceuticals*. Toronto, ON, University of Toronto Press, 2000.

Royle, S. 'Bridging the Gap: Prince Edward Island and the Confederation Bridge', in *British Journal of Canadian Studies*, Vol. 14, No. 2, pp. 242–54. Edinburgh, 1999.

Schmitz, A., and Furtan, H. *The Canadian Wheat Board: Marketing in the New Millennium*. Regina, SK, Canadian Plains Research Center, 2000.

Sharp, P. F. *The Agrarian Revolt in Western Canada*. Regina, SK, University of Regina, Canadian Plains Research Center, 1997.

Sharpe, A., St-Hilaire, F., and Banting, K. (Eds). *The Review of Economic Performance and Social Progress: Towards a Social Understanding of Productivity*. Montreal, QC, The Institute for Research on Public Policy, 2002.

Shavinina, L. V. (Ed.). *Silicon Valley North: A High Tech Cluster of Innovation and Entrepreneurship*. Amsterdam, Elsevier Press, 2004.

Simmons, J., in Stelter, G., and Artibise, A. (Eds). *Power and Place*. Vancouver, BC, University of British Columbia Press, 1986.

Skogstad, G. *Internationalization and Canadian Agriculture: Policy and Governing Paradigms*. Toronto, ON, University of Toronto Press, 2008.

Statistics Canada. *Canada Handbook*. Ottawa, ON, Canadian Government Publishing Centre, 2001.

Human Activity and the Environment 2000. Ottawa, ON, Canadian Government Publishing Centre, 2000.

Taylor, G. D. *The Rise of Canadian Business*. Toronto, ON, Oxford University Press, 2008.

Wagner, R. G., and Colombo, S. J. (Eds). *Regenerating the Canadian Forest: Principles and Practice for Ontario*. Markham, ON, Fitzhenry & Whiteside, 2001.

Wallace, I. A. *Geography of the Canadian Economy*. Don Mills, ON, Oxford University Press Canada, 2002.

Wesson, T. (Ed.). *Canada and the New World Economic Order: Strategic Briefings for Canadian Enterprise*, 2nd edn. North York, ON, Captus Press Inc, 2001.

Wolfe, D. *Clusters Old and New: The Transition to a Knowledge Economy in Canada's Regions*. Kingston, ON, Queen's School of Policy Studies, Queen's University, 2003.

Wolfe, D. A., and Gertler, M. S. *Clusters from the Inside and Out: Local Dynamics and Global Linkages*. Toronto, ON, Centre for International Studies, University of Toronto, May 2004.

Wonders, W. C. *Canada's Changing North*, revised edn. Montréal, QC, and Kingston, ON, McGill-Queen's University Press, 2003.

Zhang, D. *The Softwood Lumber War: Politics, Economics, and the Long US-Canadian Trade Dispute*. Baltimore, MD, Johns Hopkins University Press, 2008.

SELECT BIBLIOGRAPHY (SOCIAL AFFAIRS)

Abu-Laban, Y. *Gendering the Nation-State: Canadian and Comparative Perspectives*. Vancouver, BC, University of British Columbia Press, 2008.

Adams, M. *Sex in the Snow: Canadian Social Values at the End of the Millennium*. Toronto. ON, Penguin Books Canada, 1997.

'Canadians are Nothing Like Americans', in *The Walrus*, pp. 63–71, April/May, 2004.

Andrew, C., and Rogers, S. (Eds). *Women and the Canadian State*. Montréal, QC, and Kingston, ON, McGill-Queen's University Press, 1996.

Angus, I. *Border Within: National Identity, Cultural Plurality, and Wilderness*. Montréal, QC, and Kingston, ON, McGill-Queen's University Press, 1997.

Annual Report on the Operation of the Canadian Multiculturalism Act 1999–2000. Ministry of Public Works and Government Services Canada 2001, Catalogue No. C–95-1/2000.

Auditor-General of Canada. *Report of the Commissioner of the Environment and Sustainable Development*. Ottawa, ON, Environment Canada, 1998.

Bannerji, H. *The Dark Side of the Nation: Essays on Multiculturalism, Nationalism and Gender*. Toronto, ON, Canadian Scholars' Press Inc, 2000.

Banting, K., Sharpe, A., and St-Hilaire, F. (Eds). *The Review of Economic Performance and Social Progress. The Longest Decade: Canada in the 1990s*. Montréal, QC, and Ottawa, ON, The Institute for Research on Public Policy and Centre for the Study of Living Standards, 2001.

Battle, K. *Relentless Incrementalism: Deconstruction and Reconstruction in Canadian Income Security Policy*. Ottawa, ON, Canadian Institute of Social Policy, 2001.

Battle, K., Mendelson, M., and Torjman, S. *Towards a New Architecture for Canada's Adult Benefits*. Ottawa, ON, Canadian Institute of Social Policy, 2006.

Baxter-Moore, N. 'Making a Noise in this World: New Sounds from Canada's First Peoples', in *The London Journal of Canadian Studies*, Vol. 16, pp. 22–47, 2000/01.

Beaman, L. G., and Beyer, P. (Eds). *Religion and Diversity in Canada*. Boston, MA, Brill, 2008.

Beare, M. E. (Ed.). *Honoring Social Justice*. Toronto, ON, Toronto University Press, 2008.

Berkes, F. *Sacred Ecology: Traditional Ecological Knowledge and Resource Management*. Taylor & Francis Inc, Philadelphia, PA, and London, 1999.

Biles, J., Burstein, M., Frideres, J. S. (Eds). *Immigration and Integration in Canada in the Twenty-first Century*. Kingston, ON, Queen's University Press, 2008.

Blake R. B., and Keshen, J. A. (Eds). *Social Fabric or Patchwork Quilt: The Development of Social Policy in Canada*. Peterborough, ON, Broadview Press, 2006.

Bothwell, R. *Canada and Québec: One Country, Two Histories*. Vancouver, BC, University of British Columbia Press, 1996.

Bramadat, P. A., and Seljak, D. (Eds). *Christianity and Ethnicity in Canada*. Toronto, ON, Toronto University Press, 2008.

Breton, R. *Ethnic Relations in Canada: Institutional Dynamics*. Montréal, QC, and Kingston, ON, McGill-Queen's University Press, 2005.

Recent Social Trends in Canada, 1960–2000 (Comparative Charting of Social Change). Montréal, QC, and Kingston, ON, McGill-Queen's University Press, 2005.

Brune, N. and Sweeney, A. *History of Canada Online*. Waterloo, ON, Northern Blue Publishing, 2005. Available at canadachannel.ca

Buckner, P., and Francis, R. D. (Eds) *Canada and the British World: Culture, Migration, and Identity*. Vancouver, BC, University of British Columbia Press, 2006.

Bumsted, J. *Canada's Diverse Peoples: A Reference Sourcebook*. Santa Barbara, CA, ABC–Clio, 2003.

A History of the Canadian Peoples, 3rd edn. New York, Oxford University Press, 2007.

Cameron, E. (Ed.). *Canadian Culture: An Introductory Reader*. Toronto, ON, Canadian Scholars' Press Inc, 2003.

Campeau, G., and Howard, R. *From UI to EI: Waging War on the Welfare State*. Vancouver, BC, University of British Columbia Press, 2005.

Canada 2005: Draft Interim Report on Global Challenges and Opportunities. Assistant Deputy Ministers' Sub-Committee for Global Challenges and Opportunities, Ottawa, ON, February 1997.

Canadian Historical Review (various issues). Toronto, ON, University of Toronto Press, quarterly.

Cavell, R. (Ed.). *Love, Hate, and Fear in Canada's Cold War*. Toronto, ON, University of Toronto Press, 2004.

Chappell, N., and Penning, M. *Health and Health Care in Canada: A Sociological View*. Toronto, ON, Oxford University Press, 2008.

Chodkiewicz, J.-L., and Wiest R. (Eds). *Globalization and Community: Canadian Perspectives*. Winnipeg, MB, University of Manitoba Press, 2006.

Chunn, D. E., Boyd, S. B., and Lessard, H. (Eds). *Reaction and Resistance: Feminism, Law, and Social Change*. Vancouver, BC, University of British Columbia Press, 2008.

Citizenship and Immigration Canada. *Annual Reports and Immigration Statistics*. Ottawa, ON, CIC, 1995–.

Clement, W., and Vosko, L. F. (Ed.) *Changing Canada: Political Economy as Transformation*. Montréal, QC, and Kingston, ON, McGill-Queen's University Press, 2003.

Commission on the Future of Health Care in Canada. *Building on Values: The Future of Health Care in Canada*. Ottawa, ON, Government of Canada, 2002.

Conrad, M.. and Finkel, A. *Nation and Society: Readings in Post-Confederation Canadian History*. Toronto, ON, Pearson Longman, 2004.

Cooper, A. F., and Rowlands, D. (Eds). *Canada Among Nations, 2006: Minorities and Priorities*. Montréal, QC, and Kingston, ON, McGill-Queen's University Press, 2006.

Corbo, C. *Art, éducation et société postindustrielle*. Sillery, QC, Editions du Septentrion, 2006.

Cormier, J. *The Canadianization Movement: Emergence, Survival, and Success*. Toronto, ON, University of Toronto Press, 2004.

Council for Canadian Unity. *Portraits of Canada 2000: An Analysis of the results of CRIC's (Centre for Research and Information on Canada) national tracking poll*. Ottawa, ON, 27 November 2000.

Curtis, B. *The Politics of Population: State Formation, Statistics, and the Census of Canada, 1840–1875*. Toronto, ON, University of Toronto Press, 2002.

Doern, G. B., Pal, L., and Tomlin, B. (Eds). *Border Crossings: The Internationalization of Canadian Public Policy*. Toronto, ON, Oxford University Press, 1996.

Edwardson, R. *Canadian Content: Culture and the Quest for Nationhood*. Toronto, ON, University of Toronto Press, 2008.

Frideres, J. S. 'Revelation and Revolution: Fault Lines in Aboriginal-White Relations', in Kalbach, M., and Kalbach, W. (Eds), Perspectives on Ethnicity in Canada. Toronto, ON, Harcourt Canada, 2000.

Gertler, M. S. *Clusters from Inside Out: Local Dynamics and Global Linkages*. Toronto, ON, Centre for International Studies, University of Toronto, 2004.

Gleason, M. *Rethinking Canada: The Promise of Women's History*, 5th edn. New York, Oxford University Press, 2006.

Glenday, D., and Duffy, A. (Eds). *Canadian Society: Meeting the Challenges of the 21st Century*. Don Mills, ON, Oxford University Press, 2001.

Goldring, L., and Krishnamurti, S. (Eds). *Organizing the Transnational: Labour, Politics, and Social Change*. Vancouver, BC, University of British Columbia Press, 2008.

Haig-Brown, C., and Nock, D. A. (Eds). *With Good Intentions: Euro-Canadian and Aboriginal Relations in Colonial Canada*. Vancouver, BC, University of British Columbia Press, 2006.

Hammond Callaghan, M., and Hayday, M. (Eds). *Mobilizations, Protests & Engagements: Canadian Perspectives on Social Movements*. Peterborough, ON, Fernwood Press, 2008.

Hankivsky, O. *Social Policy and the Ethic of Care*. Vancouver, BC, University of British Columbia Press, 2005.

Hedican, E. J. *Applied Anthropology in Canada: Understanding Aboriginal Issues*. Toronto, ON, University of Toronto Press, 2008.

Hier, S. P., and Bolaria, B. S. *Identity and Belonging: Rethinking Race and Ethnicity in Canadian Society*. Toronto, ON, Canadian Scholars' Press Inc, 2006.

Hiller, H. (Ed.) *Urban Canada: Sociological Perspectives*. Toronto, ON, Oxford University Press, 2005.

Hunt, G., and Rayside, D. (Eds). *Equity, Diversity, and Canadian Labour*. Toronto, ON, University of Toronto Press, 2007.

Hurtig, M. *The Vanishing Country: Is It Too Late to Save Canada?* New York, Vintage, 2002.

Igartua, J. E. *The Other Quiet Revolution: National Identities in English Canada, 1945–71*. Vancouver, BC, University of British Columbia Press, August 2006.

Jackson, A. *Work and Labour in Canada: Critical Issues*. Toronto, ON, CSPI Books, 2005.

Jones, G. A. (Ed.). *Higher Education in Canada. Different Systems, Different Perspectives*. New York and London, Garland Science Publishing, 1997.

Kalbach, M., and Kalbach, W. E. (Eds). *Perspectives on Ethnicity in Canada*. Toronto, ON, Harcourt Canada, 2000.

Kalbach, W. E. 'Ethnic Diversity: Canada's Changing Cultural Mosaic', in Kalbach, M., and Kalbach, W. E. (Eds), *Perspectives on Ethnicity in Canada*. Toronto, ON, Harcourt Canada, 2000.

Kay, F. M., and Johnston, R. *Social Capital, Diversity and the Welfare State*. Vancouver, BC, University of British Columbia Press, 2006.

Keohane, K. *Symptoms of Canada: An Essay on the Canadian Identity*. Toronto, ON, University of Toronto Press, 1997.

Knowles, V. *Strangers at our Gates: Canadian Immigration and Immigration Policy, 1540–2007*, revised edn. Toronto, ON, Dundurn Press, 2007.

Lackenbauer, P. W. *Battle Grounds: The Canadian Military and Aboriginal Lands*. Vancouver, BC, University of British Columbia Press, 2006.

Larocque, S. *Gay Marriage: The Story of a Canadian Social Revolution*. Toronto, ON, James Lorimer and Co Ltd, 2006.

Larrivée, P. *Linguistic Conflict and Language Laws: Understanding the Quebec Question*. New York, Palgrave Macmillan, 2003.

Lazar, H., and Telford, H. (Eds). *Canada: The State of the Federation 2000/01—Canadian Political Culture(s) in Transition*. Waterloo, ON, Wilfred Laurier University Press, 2001.

Lee, E., and Perl, D. *The Integrity Gap: Canada's Environmental Policy and Institutions*. Vancouver, BC, University of British Columbia Press, 2004.

Li, P. *Destination Canada: Immigration Debates and Issues*. Toronto, ON, Oxford University Press, 2003.

Lightman, E. *Social Policy in Canada*. Toronto, ON, Oxford University Press, 2003.

McIntosh, T. *Federalism, Democracy and Labour Market Policy in Canada*. Kingston, ON, Queen's University Institute of Intergovernmental Research, 2001.

MacKenzie, C. *Pro-family Politics and Fringe Parties in Canada*. Vancouver, BC, University of British Columbia Press, 2005.

McRoberts, K. (Ed.-in-Chief). *Aboriginal Peoples and Canada*. Ottawa, ON, International Council for Canadian Studies, 1996.

Misconceiving Canada: The Struggle for National Unity. Toronto, ON, Oxford University Press, 1997.

Mann, S. *The Dream of a Nation: A Social and Intellectual History of Québec*. Montréal, QC, and Kingston, ON, McGill-Queen's University Press, 2002.

Matthews, B. *Buddhism in Canada*. Abingdon, Oxon, Taylor and Francis Group, 2006.

Milloy, J. S. *A National Crime: The Canadian Government and the Residential School System, 1879–1986*. Winnipeg, MB, University of Manitoba Press, 2006.

Moogk, P. *La Nouvelle France*. Ann Arbor, MI, Michigan State University Press, 2000.

Moscovitch, A., and Albert, J. (Eds). *The Benevolent Welfare State: The Growth of Welfare in Canada*. Toronto, ON, Garamond Press, 1987.

Nadasdy, P. *Hunters and Bureaucrats: Power, Knowledge and Aboriginal State Relations in the South West Yukon*. Vancouver, BC, University of British Columbia Press, 2003.

Nagle, P. 'The Aboriginal Issue in British Columbia', in *Opinion Canada*, Vol. 1, No. 28, 14 October 1999. Available at www.ccu-cuc.ca.

Nelson, S. *Canada's Changing Society, 1984–The Present (How Canada Became Canada)*. Broomall, PA, Mason Crest Publrs, 2005.

de Nevers, E. *L'Avenir du peuple canadien-français*. Montréal, QC, Les Editions du Boréal, 2006.

Newell, D., and Ommer, R. (Eds). *Fishing Places, Fishing People: Traditions and Issues in Canadian Small-Scale Fisheries*. Toronto, ON, University of Toronto Press, 2001.

Neysmith, S. M., Bezanson, K., and O'Connell, A. *Telling Tales: Living the Effects of Public Policy*. Peterborough, ON, Fernwood Books Ltd, 2005.

Nixdorf, D. *Squandering Billions: Health Care in Canada*. Surrey, BC, Hancock House Publrs, 2005.

Oakes, J., Riewe, R., Kinew, K., and Molony, E. (Eds). *Sacred Lands: Aboriginal World Views, Claims, and Conflicts*. Edmonton, AB, Canadian Circumpolar Institute (CCI) Press, 1998.

Pierce, J. T., and Dale, A. *Communities, Development, and Sustainability across Canada*. Vancouver, BC, University of British Columbia Press, 1999.

Prince, M., and Abele, F. 'Completing Confederation: Aboriginal-Canada Relations', in *Opinion Canada*, Vol. 2, No. 18, 11 May 2000. Available at www.ccu-cuc.ca.

Ralston Saul, J. *Fair Country: Telling Truths About Canada*. Toronto, ON, Penguin Canada, 2008.

Reisman, D., Glazer, N., and Denney, R. *The Lonely Crowd: A Study of the Changing American Character*. New Haven, CT, Yale University Press, 2001.

Rice, J. J., and Prince, M. J. *Changing Politics of Canadian Social Policy*. Toronto, ON, University of Toronto Press, 2000.

Richmond, T., and Saloojee, A. (Eds). *Social Inclusion: Canadian Perspectives*. Peterborough, ON, Fernwood Books Ltd, 2005.

Romanow, R. J. *Building on Values: The Future of Health Care in Canada*. Ottawa, ON, Government of Canada, 2002.

Royal Commission on Aboriginal Peoples. *Final Report* (Vols I–V). Ottawa, ON, Queen's Printer, 1996.

Sarra, J. (Ed.). *Corporate Governance in Global Capital Markets*. Vancouver, BC, University of British Columbia Press, 2003.

Simpson, J. *Star-Spangled Canadians*. Toronto, ON, Harper Collins, 2000.

Statistics Canada. 2001 *Census of Canada*. Ottawa, ON, Canadian Government Publishing Centre. Available at www.statcan.ca.

Canadian Social Trends. Ottawa, ON, quarterly.

Stern, P. R. *Historical Dictionary of the Inuit*. Historical Dictionaries of Peoples and Cultures No. 2. Lanham, MD, Scarecrow Press, 2004.

Taras, D., Bakardjieva, M., and Pannekoek, F. (Eds). *How Canadians Communicate II: Media, Globalization, and Identity*. Calgary, AB, University of Calgary Press, 2007.

Tepperman, L., and Curtis, J. *Social Problems: A Canadian Perspective*. Toronto, ON, Oxford University Press, 2003.

Thatcher, R. W. *Fighting Firewater Fictions: Moving Beyond the Disease Model of Alcoholism in First Nations*. Toronto, ON, University of Toronto Press, 2004.

Thornton, M., and Todd, R. (Eds). *Aboriginal People and Other Canadians: Shaping New Relationships* (International Canadian Studies Series). Ottawa, ON, University of Ottawa Press, 2001.

Tierney, S. *Multiculturalism and the Canadian Constitution*. Vancouver, BC, University of British Columbia Press, 2008.

Troper, H., and Weinfeld, M. (Eds). *Ethnicity, Politics and Public Policy: Case Studies in Canadian Diversity*. Toronto, ON, University of Toronto Press, 1999.

Wardaugh, R. (Ed.). *Toward Defining the Prairies: Region, Culture and History*. Winnipeg, MB, University of Manitoba Press, 2006.

Warner, T. *Never Going Back: A History of Queer Activism in Canada*. Toronto, ON, University of Toronto Press, 2002.

Westhues, A. (Ed.) *Canadian Social Policy: Issues and Perspectives*, 4th edn. Waterloo, ON, Wilfred Laurier University Press, 2007.

White, L. A., Simeon, R., Vipond, R. C., and Wallner, J. *The Comparative Turn in Canadian Political Science*. Vancouver, BC, University of British Columbia Press, 2008.

Whitehead, P. C., and Hayes, M. J. (Eds). *The Insanity of Alcohol: Social Problems in Canadian First Nations Communities*. Toronto, ON, Canadian Scholars' Press Inc, 2000.

Zawilski, V. *Social Inequality in Canada*. New York, Oxford University Press, January 2005.

DIRECTORY

DIRECTORY ON PUBLIC AFFAIRS

GOVERNMENT

THE CONSTITUTION ACT 1982

The Constitution Act was enacted as Schedule B to the Canada Act (United Kingdom) 1982. It entered into force on 17 April 1982.

The Canada Act of the United Kingdom, enacted on 29 March 1982, reads as follows:

1. The Constitution Act 1982 set out in Schedule B to this Act is hereby enacted for and shall have the force of law in Canada and shall come into force as provided in that Act.

2. No Act of Parliament of the United Kingdom passed after the Constitution Act 1982 comes into force shall extend to Canada as part of its law.

3. So far as it is not contained in Schedule B, the French version of this Act is set out in Schedule A to this Act and has the same authority in Canada as the English version thereof.

4. This Act may be cited as the Canada Act 1982.

The Constitution Act 1982 is detailed below.

Part I. Canadian Charter of Rights and Freedoms

Whereas Canada is founded upon principles that recognize the supremacy of God and the rule of law:

GUARANTEE OF RIGHTS AND FREEDOMS

1. The Canadian Charter of Rights and Freedoms guarantees the rights and freedoms set out in it subject only to such reasonable limits prescribed by law as can be demonstrably justified in a free and democratic society.

FUNDAMENTAL FREEDOMS

2. Everyone has the following fundamental freedoms:

(a) freedom of conscience and religion;

(b) freedom of thought, belief, opinion and expression, including freedom of the press and other media of communication;

(c) freedom of peaceful assembly; and

(d) freedom of association.

DEMOCRATIC RIGHTS

3. Every citizen of Canada has the right to vote in an election of members of the House of Commons or of a legislative assembly and to be qualified for membership therein.

4. (1) No House of Commons and no legislative assembly shall continue for longer than five years from the date fixed for the return of the writs of a general election of its members.

(2) In time of real or apprehended war, invasion or insurrection, a House of Commons may be continued by Parliament and a legislative assembly may be continued by the legislature beyond five years if such continuation is not opposed by the votes of more than one-third of the members of the House of Commons or the legislative assembly, as the case may be.

5. There shall be a sitting of Parliament and of each legislature at least once every twelve months.

MOBILITY RIGHTS

6. (1) Every citizen of Canada has the right to enter, remain in and leave Canada.

(2) Every citizen of Canada and every person who has the status of a permanent resident of Canada has the right

(a) to move to and take up residence in any province; and

(b) to pursue the gaining of a livelihood in any province.

(3) The rights specified in subsection (2) are subject to

(a) any laws or practices of general application in force in a province other than those that discriminate among persons primarily on the basis of province of present or previous residence; and

(b) any laws providing for reasonable residency requirements as a qualification for the receipt of publicly-provided social services.

(4) Subsections (2) and (3) do not preclude any law, program or activity that has as its object the amelioration in a province of conditions of individuals in that province who are socially or economically disadvantaged if the rate of employment in that province is below the rate of employment in Canada.

LEGAL RIGHTS

7. Everyone has the right to life, liberty and security of the person and the right not to be deprived thereof except in accordance with the principles of fundamental justice.

8. Everyone has the right to be secure against unreasonable search or seizure.

9. Everyone has the right not to be arbitrarily detained or imprisoned.

10. Everyone has the right on arrest or detention

(a) to be informed promptly of the reasons therefore;

(b) to retain and instruct counsel without delay and to be informed of that right; and

(c) to have the validity of the detention determined by way of *habeas corpus* and to be released if the detention is not lawful.

11. Any person charged with an offence has the right

(a) to be informed without unreasonable delay of the specific offence;

(b) to be tried within a reasonable time;

(c) not to be compelled to be a witness in proceedings against that person in respect of the offence;

(d) to be presumed innocent until proven guilty according to law in a fair and public hearing by an independent and impartial tribunal;

(e) not to be denied reasonable bail without just cause;

(f) except in the case of an offence under military law tried before a military tribunal, to the benefit of trial by jury where the maximum punishment for the offence is imprisonment for five years or a more severe punishment;

(g) not to be found guilty on account of any act or omission unless, at the time of the act or omission, it constituted an offence under Canadian or international law or was criminal according to the general principles of law recognized by the community of nations;

(h) if finally acquitted of the offence, not to be tried for it again and, if finally found guilty and punished for the offence, not to be tried or punished for it again; and

(i) if found guilty of the offence and if the punishment for the offence has been varied between the time of commission and the time of sentencing, to the benefit of the lesser punishment.

12. Everyone has the right not to be subjected to any cruel and unusual treatment or punishment.

13. A witness who testifies in any proceedings has the right not to have any incriminating evidence so given used to incriminate that witness in any other proceedings, except in a prosecution for perjury or for the giving of contradictory evidence.

14. A party or witness in any proceedings who does not understand or speak the language in which the proceedings are conducted or who is deaf has the right to the assistance of an interpreter.

EQUALITY RIGHTS

15. (1) Every individual is equal before and under the law and has the right to the equal protection and equal benefit of the law without discrimination and, in particular, without discrimination based on race, national or ethnic origin, colour, religion, sex, age or mental or physical disability (or on any grounds that is analogous).

(2) Subsection (1) does not preclude any law, program or activity that has as its object the amelioration of conditions of disadvantaged individuals or groups including those that are disadvantaged

because of race, national or ethnic origin, colour, religion, sex, age or mental or physical disability.

OFFICIAL LANGUAGES OF CANADA

16. (1) English and French are the official languages of Canada and have equality of status and equal rights and privileges as to their use in all institutions of the Parliament and Government of Canada.

(2) English and French are the official languages of New Brunswick and have equality of status and equal rights and privileges as to their use in all institutions of the legislature and Government of New Brunswick.

(3) Nothing in this Charter limits the authority of Parliament or a legislature to advance the equality of status or use of English and French.

17. (1) Everyone has the right to use English or French in any debates and other proceedings of Parliament.

(2) Everyone has the right to use English or French in any debates and other proceedings of the legislature of New Brunswick.

18. (1) The statutes, records and journals of Parliament shall be printed and published in English and French and both language versions are equally authoritative.

(2) The statutes, records and journals of the legislature of New Brunswick shall be printed and published in English and French and both language versions are equally authoritative.

19. (1) Either English or French may be used by any person in, or in any pleading in or process issuing from, any court established by Parliament.

(2) Either English or French may be used by any person in, or in any pleading in or process issuing from, any court of New Brunswick.

20. (1) Any member of the public in Canada has the right to communicate with, and to receive available services from, any head or central office of an institution of the Parliament or Government of Canada in English or French, and has the same right with respect to any other office of any such institution where

(a) there is a significant demand for communications with and services from that office in such language; or

(b) due to the nature of the office, it is reasonable that communications with and services from that office be available in both English and French.

(2) Any member of the public in New Brunswick has the right to communicate with, and to receive available services from, any office of an institution of the legislature or Government of New Brunswick in English or French.

21. Nothing in sections 16 to 20 abrogates or derogates from any right, privilege or obligation with respect to the English and French languages, or either of them, that exists or is continued by virtue of any other provision of the Constitution of Canada.

22. Nothing in sections 16 to 20 abrogates or derogates from any legal or customary right or privilege acquired or enjoyed either before or after the coming into force of this Charter with respect to any language that is not English or French.

MINORITY LANGUAGE EDUCATIONAL RIGHTS

23. (1) Citizens of Canada

(a) whose first language learned and still understood is that of the English or French linguistic minority population of the province in which they reside, or

(b) who have received their primary school instruction in Canada in English or French and reside in a province where the language in which they received that instruction is the language of the English or French linguistic minority population of the province, have the right to have their children receive primary and secondary school instruction in that language in that province.

(2) Citizens of Canada of whom any child has received or is receiving primary or secondary school instruction in English or French in Canada, have the right to have all their children receive primary and secondary school instruction in the same language.

(3) The right of citizens of Canada under subsections (1) and (2) to have their children receive primary and secondary school instruction in the language of the English or French linguistic minority population of a province

(a) applies wherever in the province the number of children of citizens who have such a right is sufficient to warrant the provision to them out of public funds of minority language instruction; and

(b) includes, where the number of those children so warrants, the right to have them receive that instruction in minority language educational facilities provided out of public funds.

ENFORCEMENT

24. (1) Anyone whose rights or freedoms, as guaranteed by this Charter, have been infringed or denied may apply to a court of competent jurisdiction to obtain such remedy as the court considers appropriate and just in the circumstances.

(2) Where, in proceedings under subsection (1), a court concludes that evidence was obtained in a manner that infringed or denied any rights or freedoms guaranteed by this Charter, the evidence shall be excluded if it is established that, having regard to all the circumstances, the admission of it in the proceedings would bring the administration of justice into disrepute.

GENERAL

25. The guarantee of this Charter of certain rights and freedoms shall not be construed so as to abrogate or derogate from any aboriginal treaty or other rights or freedoms that pertain to the aboriginal peoples of Canada including

(a) any rights or freedoms that have been recognized by the Royal Proclamation of October 7, 1763; and

(b) any rights or freedoms that may be acquired by the aboriginal peoples of Canada by way of land claims settlement.

26. The guarantee in this Charter of certain rights and freedoms shall not be construed as denying the existence of any other rights or freedoms that exist in Canada.

27. This Charter shall be interpreted in a manner consistent with the preservation and enhancement of the multicultural heritage of Canadians.

28. Notwithstanding anything in this Charter, the rights and freedoms referred to in it are guaranteed equally to male and female persons.

29. Nothing in this Charter abrogates or derogates from any rights or privileges guaranteed by or under the Constitution of Canada in respect of denominational, separate or dissentient schools.

30. A reference in this Charter to a province or to the legislative assembly or legislature of a province shall be deemed to include a reference to the Yukon Territory and the Northwest Territories, or the appropriate legislative authority thereof, as the case may be.

31. Nothing in this Charter extends the legislative powers of any body or authority.

APPLICATION OF CHARTER

32. (1) This Charter applies

(a) to the Parliament and Government of Canada in respect of all matters within the authority of Parliament including all matters relating to the Yukon Territory and Northwest Territories; and

(b) to the legislature and government of each province in respect of all matters within the authority of the legislature of each province.

(2) Notwithstanding subsection (1), section 15 shall not have effect until three years after this section comes into force.

33. (1) Parliament or the legislature of a province may expressly declare in an Act of Parliament or of the legislature, as the case may be, that the Act or a provision thereof shall operate notwithstanding a provision included in section 2 or sections 7 to 15 of this Charter.

(2) An Act or a provision of an Act in respect of which a declaration made under this section is in effect shall have such operation as it would have but for the provision of this Charter referred to in the declaration.

(3) A declaration made under subsection (1) shall cease to have effect five years after it comes into force or on such earlier date as may be specified in the declaration.

(4) Parliament or the legislature of a province may re-enact a declaration made under subsection (1).

(5) Subsection (3) applies in respect of a re-enactment made under subsection (4).

CITATION

34. This Part may be cited as the Canadian Charter of Rights and Freedoms.

Part II. Rights of the Aboriginal Peoples of Canada

35. (1) The existing aboriginal and treaty rights of the aboriginal peoples of Canada are hereby recognized and affirmed.

(2) In this Act, 'aboriginal peoples of Canada' includes the Indian, Inuit and Métis peoples of Canada.

Part III. Equalization and Regional Disparities

36. (1) Without altering the legislative authority of Parliament or of the provincial legislatures, or the rights of any of them with respect to the exercise of their legislative authority, Parliament and the legislatures, together with the Government of Canada and the provincial governments, are committed to

(a) promoting equal opportunities for the well-being of Canadians;

(b) furthering economic development to reduce disparity in opportunities; and

(c) providing essential public services of reasonable quality to all Canadians.

(2) Parliament and the Government of Canada are committed to the principle of making equalization payments to ensure that provincial governments have sufficient revenues to provide reasonably comparable levels of public services at reasonably comparable levels of taxation.

Part IV. Constitutional Conference

37. (1) A constitutional conference composed of the Prime Minister of Canada and the first ministers of the provinces shall be convened by the Prime Minister of Canada within one year after this Part comes into force.

(2) The conference convened under subsection (1) shall have included in its agenda an item respecting constitutional matters that directly affect the aboriginal peoples of Canada, including the identification and definition of the rights of those peoples to be included in the Constitution of Canada, and the Prime Minister of Canada shall invite representatives of those peoples to participate in the discussions on that item.

(3) The Prime Minister of Canada shall invite elected representatives of the governments of the Yukon Territory and the Northwest Territories to participate in the discussions on any item on the agenda of the conference convened under subsection (1) that, in the opinion of the Prime Minister, directly affects the Yukon Territory and the Northwest Territories.

Part V. Procedure for Amending the Constitution of Canada

38. (1) An amendment to the Constitution of Canada may be made by proclamation issued by the Governor-General under the Great Seal of Canada where so authorized by

(a) resolutions of the Senate and House of Commons, and

(b) resolutions of the legislative assemblies of at least two-thirds of the provinces that have, in the aggregate, according to the then latest general census, at least fifty per cent of the population of all the provinces.

(2) An amendment made under subsection (1) that derogates from the legislative powers, the proprietary rights or any other rights or privileges of the legislature or government of a province shall require a resolution supported by a majority of the members of each of the Senate, the House of Commons and the legislative assemblies required under subsection (1).

(3) An amendment referred to in subsection (2) shall not have effect in a province the legislative assembly of which has expressed its dissent thereto by resolution supported by a majority of its members prior to the issue of the proclamation to which the amendment relates unless that legislative assembly, subsequently, by resolution supported by a majority of its members, revokes its dissent and authorizes the amendment.

(4) A resolution of dissent made for the purposes of subsection (3) may be revoked at any time before or after the issue of the proclamation to which it relates.

39. (1) A proclamation shall not be issued under subsection 38 (1) before the expiration of one year from the adoption of the resolution initiating the amendment procedure thereunder, unless the legislative assembly of each province has previously adopted a resolution of assent or dissent.

(2) A proclamation shall not be issued under subsection 38 (1) after the expiration of three years from the adoption of the resolution initiating the amendment procedure thereunder.

40. Where an amendment is made under subsection 38 (1) that transfers provincial legislative powers relating to education or other cultural matters from provincial legislatures to Parliament, Canada shall provide reasonable compensation to any province to which the amendment does not apply.

41. An amendment to the Constitution of Canada in relation to the following matters may be made by proclamation issued by the Governor-General under the Great Seal of Canada only where authorized by resolutions of the Senate and House of Commons and of the legislative assembly of each province:

(a) the office of the Queen, the Governor-General and the Lieutenant-Governor of a province;

(b) the right of a province to a number of members in the House of Commons not less than the number of Senators by which the province is entitled to be represented at the time this Part comes into force;

(c) subject to section 43, the use of the English or the French language;

(d) the composition of the Supreme Court of Canada; and

(e) an amendment to this Part.

42. (1) An amendment to the Constitution of Canada in relation to the following matters may be made only in accordance with subsection 38 (1):

(a) the principle of proportionate representation of the provinces in the House of Commons prescribed by the Constitution of Canada;

(b) the powers of the Senate and the method of selecting Senators;

(c) the number of members by which a province is entitled to be represented in the Senate and the residence qualifications of Senators;

(d) subject to paragraph 41 (d), the Supreme Court of Canada;

(e) the extension of existing provinces into the territories; and

(f) notwithstanding any other law or practice, the establishment of new provinces.

(2) Subsections 38 (2) to (4) do not apply in respect of amendments in relation to matters referred to in subsection (1).

43. An amendment to the Constitution of Canada in relation to any provision that applies to one or more, but not all, provinces, including

(a) any alteration to boundaries between provinces, and

(b) any amendment to any provision that relates to the use of the English or the French language within a province, may be made by proclamation issued by the Governor-General under the Great Seal of Canada only where so authorized by resolution of the Senate and the House of Commons and of the legislative assembly of each province to which the amendment applies.

44. Subject to sections 41 and 42, Parliament may exclusively make laws amending the Constitution of Canada in relation to the executive Government of Canada or the Senate and House of Commons.

45. Subject to section 41, the legislature of each province may exclusively make laws amending the constitution of the province.

46. (1) The procedures for amendment under sections 38, 41, 42 and 43 may be initiated either by the Senate or the House of Commons or by the legislative assembly of a province.

(2) A resolution of assent made for the purposes of this Part may be revoked at any time before the issue of a proclamation authorized by it.

47. (1) An amendment to the Constitution of Canada made by proclamation under section 38, 41, 42 or 43 may be made without a resolution of the Senate authorizing the issue of the proclamation if, within one hundred and eighty days after the adoption by the House of Commons of a resolution authorizing its issue, the Senate has not adopted such a resolution and if, at any time after the expiration of that period, the House of Commons again adopts the resolution.

(2) Any period when Parliament is prorogued or dissolved shall not be counted in computing the one hundred and eighty day period referred to in subsection (1).

48. The Queen's Privy Council for Canada shall advise the Governor-General to issue a proclamation under this Part forthwith on the adoption of the resolutions required for an amendment made by proclamation under this Part.

49. A constitutional conference composed of the Prime Minister of Canada and the first ministers of the provinces shall be convened by the Prime Minister of Canada within fifteen years after this Part comes into force to review the provisions of this Part.

Part VI. Amendment to the Constitution Act, 1867

50. The Constitution Act, 1867 (formerly named the British North America Act, 1867) is amended by adding thereto, immediately after section 92 thereof, the following heading and section:

NON-RENEWABLE NATURAL RESOURCES, FORESTRY RESOURCES AND ELECTRICAL ENERGY

92A. (1) In each province, the legislature may exclusively make laws in relation to

(a) exploration for non-renewable natural resources in the province;

(b) development, conservation and management of non-renewable natural resources and forestry resources in the province, including laws in relation to the rate of primary production therefrom; and

(c) development, conservation and management of sites and facilities in the province for the generation and production of electrical energy.

(2) In each province, the legislature may make laws in relation to the export from the province to another part of Canada of the primary production from non-renewable natural resources and forestry resources in the province and the production from facilities in the province for the generation of electrical energy, but such laws may not authorize or provide for discrimination in prices or in supplies exported to another part of Canada.

(3) Nothing in subsection (2) derogates from the authority of Parliament to enact laws in relation to the matters referred to in that subsection and, where such a law of a Parliament and a law of a province conflict, the law of Parliament prevails to the extent of the conflict.

(4) In each province, the legislature may make laws in relation to the raising of money by any mode or system of taxation in respect of

(a) non-renewable natural resources and forestry resources in the province and the primary production therefrom, and

(b) sites and facilities in the province for the generation of electrical energy and the production therefrom, whether or not such production is exported in whole or in part from the province, but such laws may not authorize or provide for taxation that differentiates between production exported to another part of Canada and production not exported from the province.

(5) The expression 'primary production' has the meaning assigned by the Sixth Schedule.

(6) Nothing in subsections (1) to (5) derogates from any powers or rights that a legislature or government of a province had immediately before the coming into force of this section.

51. The said Act is further amended by adding thereto the following Schedule:

The Sixth Schedule

PRIMARY PRODUCTION FROM NON-RENEWABLE NATURAL RESOURCES AND FORESTRY RESOURCES

1. For the purposes of section 92A of this Act,

(a) production from a non-renewable natural resource is primary production therefrom if

(i) it is in the form in which it exists upon its recovery or severance from its natural state, or

(ii) it is a product resulting from processing or refining the resource, and is not a manufactured product or a product resulting from refining crude oil, refining upgraded heavy crude oil, refining gases or liquids derived from coal or refining a synthetic equivalent of crude oil; and

(b) production from a forestry resource is primary production therefrom if it consists of sawlogs, poles, lumber, wood chips, sawdust or any other primary wood product, or wood pulp, and is not a product manufactured from wood.

Part VII. General

52. (1) The Constitution of Canada is the supreme law of Canada, and any law that is inconsistent with the provisions of the Constitution is, to the extent of the inconsistency, of no force or effect.

(2) The Constitution of Canada includes

(a) the Canada Act 1982, including this Act;

(b) the Acts and orders referred to in this schedule; and

(c) any amendment to any Act or order referred to in paragraph (a) or (b).

(3) Amendments to the Constitution of Canada shall be made only in accordance with the authority contained in the Constitution of Canada.

53. (1) The enactments referred to in Column I of the schedule are hereby repealed or amended to the extent indicated in Column II thereof and, unless repealed, shall continue as law in Canada under the names set out in Column III thereof.

(2) Every enactment, except the Canada Act 1982, that refers to an enactment referred to in the schedule by the name in Column I thereof is hereby amended by substituting for that name the corresponding name in Column III thereof, and any British North America Act not referred to in the schedule may be cited as the Constitution Act followed by the year and number, if any, of its enactment.

54. Part IV is repealed on the day that is one year after this Part comes into force and this section may be repealed and this Act renumbered, consequentially upon the repeal of Part IV and this section, by proclamation issued by the Governor-General under the Great Seal of Canada.

55. A French version of the portions of the Constitution of Canada referred to in the schedule shall be prepared by the Minister of Justice of Canada as expeditiously as possible and, when any portion thereof sufficient to warrant action being taken has been so prepared, it shall be put forward for enactment by proclamation issued by the Governor-General under the Great Seal of Canada pursuant to the procedure then applicable to an amendment of the same provisions of the Constitution of Canada.

56. Where any portion of the Constitution of Canada has been or is enacted in English and French or where a French version of any portion of the Constitution is enacted pursuant to section 55, the English and French versions of that portion of the Constitution are equally authoritative.

57. The English and French versions of this Act are equally authoritative.

58. Subject to section 59, this Act shall come into force on a day to be fixed by proclamation issued by the Queen or the Governor-General under the Great Seal of Canada.

59. (1) Paragraph 23 (1)(a) shall come into force in respect of Québec on a day to be fixed by proclamation issued by the Queen or the Governor-General under the Great Seal of Canada.

(2) A proclamation under subsection (1) shall be issued only where authorized by the legislative assembly or Government of Québec.

(3) This section may be repealed on the day paragraph 23 (1)(a) comes into force in respect of Québec and this Act amended and renumbered, consequentially upon the repeal of this section, by proclamation issued by the Queen or the Governor-General under the Great Seal of Canada.

60. This Act may be cited as the Constitution Act, 1982, and the Constitution Acts 1867 to 1975 (No 2) and this Act may be cited together as the Constitution Acts, 1867 to 1982.

GOVERNMENT OF CANADA

Head of State and Governor-General

Head of State: HM Queen ELIZABETH II (succeeded to the throne 6 February 1952).

Governor-General: MICHAËLLE JEAN (took office on 27 September 2005).

Federal Ministry

(October 2008)

Prime Minister: STEPHEN J. HARPER.

Leader of the Government in the House of Commons: JAY D. HILL.

Minister of Foreign Affairs: LAWRENCE CANNON.

Minister of Labour: RONA AMBROSE.

Minister of Veterans' Affairs: GREGORY F. THOMPSON.

Leader of the Government in the Senate and Minister of State (Seniors): MARJORY LEBRETON.

Minister of Citizenship, Immigration and Multiculturalism: JASON KENNEY.

Minister of Agriculture and Agri-Food and Minister for the Canadian Wheat Board: GERRY RITZ.

Minister of Natural Resources: LISA RAITT.

Minister of Fisheries and Oceans: GAIL SHEA.

Minister of Public Safety: PETER VAN LOAN.

Minister of National Revenue and Minister of State (Agriculture): JEAN-PIERRE BLACKBURN.

Minister of Justice and Attorney-General of Canada: ROBERT D. NICHOLSON.

Minister of the Environment: JIM PRENTICE.

President of the Queen's Privy Council for Canada, Minister of Intergovernmental Affairs and Minister for La Francophonie: JOSÉE VERNER.

Minister of Human Resources and Skills Development: DIANE FINLEY.

Minister of National Defence and Minister of the Atlantic Gateway: PETER G. MACKAY.

Minister of Canadian Heritage and Official Languages: JAMES MOORE.

Minister of Indian Affairs and Northern Development and Federal Interlocutor for Métis and Non-Status Indians: CHARLES (CHUCK) STRAHL.

President of the Treasury Board: VIC TOEWS.

Minister of Industry: TONY CLEMENT.

Minister of Transport, Infrastructure and Communities: JOHN BAIRD.

Minister of Health: LEONA AGLUKKAQ.

Minister of Finance: JAMES M. (JIM) FLAHERTY.

Minister of International Co-operation: BEVERLEY J. ODA.

Minister of International Trade and Minister for the Asia-Pacific Gateway: STOCKWELL DAY.

Minister of Public Works and Government Services: CHRISTIAN PARADIS.

Minister of State and Chief Government Whip: GORDON O'CONNOR.

Minister of State (Atlantic Canada Opportunities Agency): KEITH ASHFIELD.

Minister of State (Small Business and Tourism): DIANE ABLONCZY.

Minister of State (Sport): GARY LUNN.

Minister of State (Status of Women): HELENA GUERGIS.

Minister of State (Economic Development Agency of Canada for the Regions of Quebec): DENIS LEBEL.

Minister of State (Transport): ROB MERRIFIELD.

Minister of State (Western Economic Diversification): LYNNE YELICH.

Minister of State (Democratic Reform): STEVEN J. FLETCHER.

Minister of State (Science and Technology): GARY GOODYEAR.

Minister of State of Foreign Affairs (Americas): PETER KENT.

Ministries

Office of the Prime Minister: Langevin Block, 80 Wellington St, Ottawa, ON K1A 0A2; tel. (613) 941-6888; fax (613) 941-6900; e-mail pm@pm.gc.ca; internet www.pm.gc.ca.

Agriculture and Agri-Food Canada: Sir John Carling Bldg, 930 Carling Ave, Ottawa, ON K1A 0C7; tel. (613) 759-1000; fax (613) 759-7977; e-mail info@agr.gc.ca; internet www.agr.gc.ca.

Atlantic Canada Opportunities Agency (ACOA): Blue Cross Centre, 3rd Floor, 644 Main St, POB 6051, Moncton, NB E1C 9J8; tel. (506) 851-2271; fax (506) 851-7403; internet www.acoa-apeca.gc.ca.

Canada Economic Development for the Regions of Québec: Tour de la Bourse 800, Sq. Victoria, bureau 3800, CP 247, Montréal, QC H4Z 1E8; tel. (514) 283-6412; fax (514) 283-3302; internet www.dec-ced.gc.ca.

Canada Revenue Agency: Office of the Minister of National Revenue, 7th Floor, 555 McKenzie Ave, Ottawa, ON K1A 0L5; tel. (613) 952-9184; internet www.cra-arc.gc.ca.

Canadian Heritage: 15 rue Eddy, Gatineau, QC K1A 0M5; tel. (819) 997-0055; fax (819) 953-5382; internet www.pch.gc.ca.

Citizenship and Immigration Canada: Jean Edmonds Towers, 21st Floor, 365 Laurier Ave West, Ottawa, ON K1A 1L1; tel. (613) 954-1064; fax (613) 957-2688; e-mail minister@cic.gc.ca; internet www.cic.gc.ca.

Department of Finance Canada: East Tower, 19th Floor, 140 O'Connor St, Ottawa, ON K1A 0G5; tel. (613) 992-1573; fax (613) 996-0518; e-mail consltcomm@fin.gc.ca; internet www.fin.gc.ca.

Department of Justice Canada: East Memorial Bldg, 284 Wellington St, Ottawa, ON K1A 0H8; tel. (613) 957-4222; fax (613) 954-0811; e-mail webadmin@justice.gc.ca; internet www.canada.justice.gc.ca.

Department of National Defence: National Defence Headquarters, Maj.-Gen. George R. Pearkes Bldg, 15 NT, 101 Colonel By Dr., Ottawa, ON K1A 0K2; tel. (613) 995-2534; fax (613)992-4739; e-mail information@forces.gc.ca; internet www.forces.gc.ca.

Environment Canada: 70 rue Crémazie, Gatineau, QC K1A 0H3; tel. (819) 997-2800; fax (819) 994-1412; e-mail enviroinfo@ec.gc.ca; internet www.ec.gc.ca.

Fisheries and Oceans Canada: Centennial Towers, 13th Floor, 200 Kent St, Station 13228, Ottawa, ON K1A 0E6; tel. (613) 993-0999; fax (613) 990-1866; e-mail info@dfo-mpo.gc.ca; internet www.dfo-mpo.gc.ca.

Foreign Affairs and International Trade Canada: Lester B. Pearson Bldg, 125 Sussex Dr., Ottawa, ON K1A 0G2; tel. (613) 944-4000; fax (613) 996-9709; e-mail enqserv@dfait-maeci.gc.ca; internet www.international.gc.ca.

Health Canada: Brooke Claxton Bldg, Tunney's Pasture, Ottawa, ON K1A 0K9; tel. (613) 957-2991; fax (613) 952-1154; e-mail info@hc-sc.gc.ca; internet www.hc-sc.gc.ca.

Human Resources and Social Development Canada: Phase IV, 140 promenade du Portage, Gatineau, QC K1A 0J9; tel. (819) 994-6313; fax (819) 953-7260; internet www.hrsdc.gc.ca; manages the Labour Program.

Indian and Northern Affairs Canada: Terrasses de la Chaudière, 10 Wellington, North Tower, Gatineau, ON K1A 0H4; tel. (819) 997-0811; fax (866) 817-3977; e-mail infopubs@ainc-inac.gc.ca; internet www.ainc-inac.gc.ca.

Industry Canada: C. D. Howe Bldg, 11th Floor, East Tower, 235 Queen St, Ottawa, ON K1A 0H5; tel. (613) 954-5031; fax (613) 954-2340; e-mail info@ic.gc.ca; internet www.ic.gc.ca.

Natural Resources Canada: 580 Booth St, Ottawa, ON K1A 0E4; tel. (613) 995-0947; fax (613) 996-9094; e-mail questions@nrcan.gc.ca; internet www.nrcan-rncan.gc.ca.

Public Safety Canada: 269 Laurier Ave West, Ottawa, ON K1A 0P8; tel. (613) 944-4875; fax (613) 954-5186; e-mail communications@ps-sp.gc.ca; internet www.ps-sp.gc.ca.

Public Works and Government Services Canada: 102 Corporate Communications, 16A1, Portage III, Gatineau, QC K1A 0S5; tel. (819) 956-3115; fax (819) 956-9062; e-mail questions@pwgsc.gc.ca; internet www.pwgsc.gc.ca.

Status of Women Canada: McDonald Bldg, 10th Floor, 123 Slater St, Ottawa, ON K1P 1H9; tel. (613) 995-7835; fax (613) 957-3359; e-mail communications@swc-cfc.gc.ca; internet www.swc-cfc.gc.ca.

Transport, Infrastructure and Communities Canada: Tower C, 29th Floor, pl. de Ville, 330 Sparks St, Ottawa, ON K1A 0N5; tel. (613) 990-2309; fax (613) 954-4731; e-mail webfeedback@tc.gc.ca; internet www.tc.gc.ca.

Treasury Board: Corporate Communications, l'Esplanade Laurier, 10th Floor, West Tower, 300 Laurier Ave West, Ottawa, ON K1A 0R5; tel. (613) 957-2400; fax (613) 998-9071; e-mail info@tbs-sct.gc.ca; internet www.tbs-sct.gc.ca.

Veterans Affairs Canada: 161 Grafton St, POB 7700, Charlottetown, PE C1A 8M9; tel. (613) 996-2242; fax (902) 566-8508; e-mail information@vac-acc.gc.ca; internet www.vac-acc.gc.ca.

Western Economic Diversification Canada: Canada Pl., 9700 Jasper Ave, Suite 1500, Edmonton, AB T5J 4H7; tel. (780) 495-4164; fax (403) 495-4557; e-mail donna.kinley@wd-deo.gc.ca; internet www.wd.gc.ca.

Selected Federal Government Agencies and Boards

Atomic Energy of Canada Ltd (AECL): 2251 Speakman Dr., Mississauga, ON L5K 1B2; tel. (905) 823-9040; fax (905) 823-7565; e-mail info@aecl.ca; internet www.aecl.ca; f. 1952; involved in the devt, design, engineering and construction of Canadian nuclear power plants; provides services to nuclear utilities world-wide in support of CANDU (Canadian deuterium uranium) products; designer of CANDU reactor technology; Pres. and CEO HUGH MACDIARMID; Chair. GLENNA CARR.

Canada Council for the Arts: 350 Albert St, POB 1047, Ottawa, ON K1P 5V8; tel. (613) 566-4414; fax (613) 566-4390; e-mail info@canadacouncil.ca; internet www.canadacouncil.ca; f. 1957; promotes and fosters the arts in Canada; Chair. JOSEPH L. ROTMAN; Dir ROBERT SIRMAN.

Canada Industrial Relations Board: C. D. Howe Bldg, 4th Floor West, 240 Sparks St, Ottawa, ON K1A 0X8; tel. (613) 947-5440; fax (613) 995-9493; e-mail info@cirb-ccri.gc.ca; internet www.cirb-ccri.gc.ca; Chair. ELIZABETH MACPHERSON.

Canadian Dairy Commission: Bldg 55, NCC Driveway, Central Experimental Farm, 960 Carling Ave, Ottawa, ON K1A 0Z2; tel. (613) 792-2000; fax (613) 792-2009; e-mail cdc-ccl@agr.gc.ca; internet www.cdc.ca; f. 1966; administers national dairy policy; Chair. RANDY WILLIAMSON; CEO JOHN CORE; Commr GILLES MARTIN.

Canadian Forest Service (CFS): 580 Booth St, 8th Floor, Ottawa, ON K1A 0E4; tel. (613) 947-7341; fax (613) 947-7397; internet cfs.nrcan.gc.ca; promotes sustainable devt and competitiveness of Canada's forest sector; Asst Deputy Minister JAMES FARRELL.

Canadian Grain Commission: 303 Main St, Suite 600, Winnipeg, MB R3C 3G8; tel. (204) 983-2770; fax (204) 983-2751; e-mail contact@grainscanada.gc.ca; internet www.grainscanada.gc.ca; f. 1912; regulates grain handling in Canada and establishes and maintains quality standards for Canadian grains through its Grain Research Laboratory; Chief Commr ELWIN HERMANSON (acting); COO GORDON MILES.

Canadian Human Rights Commission: 344 Slater St, 8th Floor, Ottawa, ON K1A 1E1; tel. (613) 995-1151; fax (613) 996-9661; internet www.chrc-ccdp.ca; f. 1977; Chief Commr JENNIFER LYNCH.

Canadian International Development Agency: pl. du Centre, 200 promenade du Portage, Gatineau, QC K1A 0G4; tel. (819) 997-5006; fax (819) 953-6088; e-mail info@acdi-cida.gc.ca; internet www.acdi-cida.gc.ca; administers approx. 80% of Canada's international devt assistance program; Pres. MARGARET BIGGS.

Canadian Transportation Agency (CTA): Ottawa, ON K1A 0N9; tel. (819) 994-0775; fax (819) 997-6727; e-mail info@otc-cta.gc.ca; internet www.cta.gc.ca; f. 1996 to replace the Nat. Transportation Agency; oversees the economic regulation of transport under federal jurisdiction; Chair. and CEO GEOFFREY C. HARE.

Canadian Wheat Board: 423 Main St, POB 816, Station Main, Winnipeg, MB R3C 2P5; tel. (204) 983-0239; fax (204) 983-3841; e-mail questions@cwb.ca; internet www.cwb.ca; sole marketing agency for western Canadian wheat and barley exports and for domestic sales of grains for human consumption; Chair. LARRY HILL; CEO IAN WHITE.

Correctional Service of Canada: 340 Laurier Ave West, Ottawa, ON K1A 0P9; tel. (613) 992-5891; fax (613) 943-1630; internet www.csc-scc.gc.ca; responsible for the treatment and rehabilitation of offenders; Commr DON HEAD.

Elections Canada: Jackson Bldg, 257 Slater St, Ottawa, ON K1A 0M6; tel. (613) 993-2975; fax (613) 954-8584; e-mail info@elections.ca; internet www.elections.ca; f. 1920; independent; Chief Electoral Officer MARC MAYRAND.

Export Development Canada: 151 O'Connor St, Ottawa, ON K1A 1K3; tel. (613) 598-2500; fax (613) 237-2690; internet www.edc-see.ca; f. 1944; provides trade finance and risk management services to Canadian exporters and investors; Pres. and CEO ERIC SIEGEL.

Farm Credit Canada: 1800 Hamilton St, POB 4320, Regina, SK S4P 4L3; tel. (306) 780-8100; fax (306) 780-5456; e-mail csc@fcc-fac.ca; internet www.fcc-fac.ca; f. 1959; Chair. GILL O. SHAW; Pres. and CEO GREG STEWART.

Immigration and Refugee Board (IRB): Canada Bldg, 12th Floor, Minto Pl., 344 Slater St, Ottawa, ON K1A 0K1; tel. (613) 995-6486; fax (613) 943-1550; e-mail info@irb-cisr.gc.ca; internet www.irb-cisr.gc.ca; Chair. BRIAN GOODMAN; Exec. Dir SIMON COAKELEY.

International Boundary Commission (Canadian Section): 615 Booth St, Suite 575, Ottawa, ON K1A 0E9; tel. (613) 992-1294; fax (613) 947-1337; e-mail aarsenea@nrcan.gc.ca; internet www.internationalboundarycommission.org; has jurisdiction over regulation and maintenance of the Canada-USA boundary; Commr (Canadian Section) PETER SULLIVAN.

National Energy Board: 444 Seventh Ave, SW, Calgary, AB T2P 0X8; tel. (403) 292-4800; fax (403) 292-5503; e-mail info@neb-one.gc.ca; internet www.neb-one.gc.ca; f. 1959; federal regulatory agency; Chair. and CEO GAÉTAN CARON; Sec. CLAUDINE DUTIL-BERRY.

National Farm Products Council: Canada Bldg, 10th Floor, 344 Slater St, Ottawa, ON K1R 7Y3; tel. (613) 995-6752; fax (613) 995-2097; e-mail nfpcweb@agr.gc.ca; internet www.nfpc-cnpa.gc.ca; f. 1972; advises the Minister of Agriculture on the establishment and operation of national agricultural marketing agencies; Chair. BILL SMIRLE.

National Film Board of Canada (NFBC): POB 6100, Station Centre-ville, Montréal, QC H3C 3H5; tel. (514) 283-9000; fax (514) 283-7564; internet www.nfb.ca; f. 1939; initiates and promotes the production and distribution of films in the national interest; Film Commr and Chair. TOM PERLMUTTER.

National Research Council Canada: Bldg M58, 1200 Montréal Rd, Ottawa, ON K1A 0R6; tel. (613) 993-9101; fax (613) 952-9907; e-mail info@nrc-cnrc.gc.ca; internet www.nrc.ca; f. 1916; carries out research and devt in life sciences, physical sciences, engineering, information technology, technology and industry support; Pres. Dr PIERRE COULOMBE; Sec.-Gen. Dr CARL CARON (acting).

Natural Resources Canada (NRCan): 580 Booth St, Ottawa, ON K1A 0E8; tel. (613) 995-0947; fax (613) 992-1405; e-mail questions@nrcan.gc.ca; internet www.nrcan.gc.ca; f. 1995 by merger of Energy, Mines and Resources with Forestry Canada; co-ordinates, promotes and recommends national policies concerning energy, mines, minerals and other renewable and non-renewable resources; responsible for the activities of the Northern Pipeline Agency since 2004; Assoc. Deputy Minister SERGE DUPONT.

Natural Sciences and Engineering Research Council (NSERC) (Science and Engineering Research Canada): Constitution Sq., 350 Albert St, Ottawa, ON K1A 1H5; tel. (613) 995-4273; fax (613) 992-5337; e-mail chantal.chauvet@nserc.ca; internet www.nserc.gc.ca; f. 1978; promotes investment in science and technology research; Pres. Dr SUZANNE FORTIER; Sec. BARBARA CONWAY.

Office of the Auditor General of Canada: 240 Sparks St, Ottawa, ON K1A 0G6; tel. (613) 995-3708; fax (613) 957-0474; e-mail communications@oag-bvg.gc.ca; internet www.oag-bvg.gc.ca; Auditor Gen. SHEILA FRASER.

Office of the Commissioner of Official Languages: 344 Slater St, 3rd Floor, Ottawa, ON K1A 0T8; tel. (613) 996-6368; fax (613) 993-5082; e-mail message@ocol-clo.gc.ca; internet www.ocol-clo.gc.ca; ensures respect for English and French as the official languages of Canada in federal institutions; Commr GRAHAM FRASER.

Office of the Privacy Commissioner: Tower B, 3rd Floor, 112 Kent St, pl. de Ville, Ottawa, ON K1A 1H3; tel. (613) 995-8210; fax (613) 947-6850; e-mail cmckay@privcom.gc.ca; internet www.privcom.gc.ca; investigates complaints from individuals who allege their privacy has been violated, oversees federal govt compliance with the Privacy Act (for the public sector) and the Personal Information and Protection and Electronic Documents Act (for the private sector); Privacy Commr JENNIFER STODDART.

Prairie Farm Rehabilitation Administration (PFRA): FCC Tower, 1800 Hamilton St, Suite 408, Regina, SK S4P 4L2; tel. (306) 780-5070; fax (306) 780-5018; e-mail info@agr.gc.ca; internet www.agr.gc.ca/pfra; f. 1935; division of Agriculture and Agri-Food Canada; devt of viable agricultural industry and sustainable rural economy in the Prairie provinces of Alberta, Manitoba and Saskatchewan, and the Peace River region of British Columbia; Dir-Gen. HARLEY OLSEN.

Privy Council Office: 85 Sparks St, Rm 1000, Ottawa, ON K1A 0A3; tel. (613) 957-5153; fax (613) 957-5043; e-mail info@pco-bcp.gc.ca; internet www.pco-bcp.gc.ca; provides public support to the Prime Minister, ministers within the Prime Minister's portfolio and the Cabinet; responsible for federal-provincial relations since 1993; Clerk of the Privy Council and Sec. to the Cabinet KEVIN G. LYNCH.

Public Service Commission: 300 Laurier Ave West, 19th Floor, Ottawa, ON K1A 0M7; tel. (613) 992-9562; fax (613) 992-9352; e-mail infocom@psc-cfp.gc.ca; internet www.psc-cfp.gc.ca; independent agency to safeguard integrity of public service staffing system and a non-partisan public service; Pres. MARIA BARRADOS; Commrs MANON VENNAT, DAVID ZUSSMAN.

Royal Canadian Mint: 320 Sussex Dr., Ottawa, ON K1A 0G8; tel. (613) 993-8990; fax (613) 998-4130; e-mail info@mint.ca; internet www.mint.ca; f. 1969; Pres. and CEO IAN BENNETT.

Royal Canadian Mounted Police (RCMP): Headquarters Bldg, 1200 Vanier Pkwy, Ottawa, ON K1A 0R2; tel. (613) 993-7267; fax (613) 993-0260; internet www.rcmp-grc.gc.ca; f. 1873 as North-West Mounted Police, present name adopted in 1920; Commr WILLIAM J. S. ELLIOTT.

St Lawrence Seaway Management Corpn: 202 Pitt St, Cornwall, ON K6J 3P7; tel. (613) 932-5170; fax (613) 932-7286; e-mail marketing@seaway.ca; internet www.greatlakes-seaway.com; f. 1998; responsible for management of the St Lawrence Seaway (f. 1959) allowing ocean-going vessels to enter the Great Lakes of North America; operated jtly with the USA; 43.0m. metric tons of freight in 2007; Chair. GUY C. VÉRONNEAU; Pres. and CEO RICHARD CORFE.

Standards Council of Canada: 270 Albert St, Suite 200, Ottawa, ON K1P 6N7; tel. (613) 238-3222; fax (613) 569-7808; e-mail info@scc.ca; internet www.scc.ca; promotes voluntary standardization in specific fields for products and other goods not expressly provided for by law; Exec. Dir (vacant).

Statistics Canada: 100 Tunney's Pasture Driveway, Ottawa, ON K1A 0T6; tel. (613) 951-8116; fax (613) 951-0581; e-mail infostats@statcan.ca; internet www.statcan.ca; national statistical agency; Chief Statistician of Canada MUNIR A. SHEIKH.

Transportation Safety Board of Canada: 200 promenade du Portage, 4th Floor, Pl. du Centre, Gatineau, QC K1A 1K8; tel. (819) 994-3741; fax (819) 997-2239; e-mail communications@tsb.gc.ca; internet www.tsb.gc.ca; f. 1990; independent body; Chair. WENDY A. TADROS; Exec. Dir GERARD MCDONALD.

Treasury Board of Canada: West Tower, 10th Floor, l'Esplanade Laurier, 300 Laurier Ave West, ON K1A 0R5; tel. (613) 957-2400; fax (613) 998-9071; e-mail info@tbs-sct.gc.ca; internet www.tbs-sct.gc.ca; Pres. VIC TOEWS; Sec. WAYNE G. WOUTERS.

VIA Rail Canada Inc: Station A, POB 8116, Montréal, QC H3C 3N3; tel. (514) 871-6000; fax (514) 871-6104; e-mail customer_relations@viarail.ca; internet www.viarail.ca; f. 1978; federal govt corpn; proposed transfer to private sector postponed Oct. 2007; operates passenger services over rail routes covering 13,822 km of track throughout Canada; Chair. DONALD A. WRIGHT; Pres. and CEO PAUL CÔTÉ.

FEDERAL LEGISLATURE (PARLIAMENT)

Senate

(October 2008)

Senators are appointed by the Governor-General on the recommendation of the Prime Minister of Canada. Senators hold their positions until they attain the age of 75 years.

Speaker of the Senate: NOËL A. KINSELLA (C).

Clerk of the Senate and Clerk of the Parliaments: PAUL C. BÉLISLE.

Party Standings

	Conservative	Liberal	Progressive Conservative	Independent New Democratic Party*	Independent	Vacant	Total
Alberta	1	4	1	—	—	—	6
British Columbia	1	2	—	—	—	3	6
Manitoba	2	3	—	—	1	—	6
New Brunswick	1	7	—	—	—	2	10
Newfoundland and Labrador	1	4	—	—	—	1	6
Northwest Territories	—	1	—	—	—	—	1
Nova Scotia	2	5	—	—	—	3	10
Nunavut Territory	—	1	—	—	—	—	1
Ontario	7	11	2	—	2	2	24
Prince Edward Island	—	3	—	—	—	1	4
Québec	3	15	—	—	2	4	24
Saskatchewan	3	2	—	1	—	—	6
Yukon Territory	—	—	—	—	—	1	1
Total	21	58	3	1	5	17	105

* The senator is an Independent member of the New Democratic Party.

MEMBERS
(with political party and year of appointment)

Alberta

Thomas B. Banks	Lib.	2000
Bert Brown	C	2007
Joyce Fairbairn	Lib.	1984
Elaine McCoy	PC	2005
Grant Mitchell	Lib.	2005
Claudette Tardif	Lib.	2005

British Columbia

Larry W. Campbell	Lib.	2005
Mobina S. B. Jaffer	Lib.	2001
Gerry St Germain	C	1993
(3 vacancies)		

Manitoba

Sharon Carstairs	Lib.	1994
Maria Chaput	Lib.	2002
Janis G. Johnson	C	1990
Mira Spivak	Ind.	1986
Terrance R. Stratton	C	1993
Rod. A. A. Zimmer	Lib.	2005

New Brunswick

John G. Bryden	Lib.	1994
Eymard G. Corbin	Lib.	1984
Joseph A. Day	Lib.	2001
Noël A. Kinsella	C	1990
Rose-Marie Losier-Cool	Lib.	1995
Sandra M. Lovelace Nicholas	Lib.	2005
Pierrette Ringuette	Lib.	2002
Fernand J. Robichaud	Lib.	1997
(2 vacancies)		

Newfoundland and Labrador

George S. Baker	Lib.	2002
Ethel M. Cochrane	C	1986
Joan Cook	Lib.	1998
George Furey	Lib.	1999
William Rompkey	Lib.	1995
(1 vacancy)		

Northwest Territories

Nick G. Sibbetson	Lib.	1999

Nova Scotia

Gerald J. Comeau	C	1990
Jane M. Cordy	Lib.	2000
James S. Cowan	Lib.	2005
Terry M. Mercer	Lib.	2003
Wilfred P. Moore	Lib.	1996
Donald H. Oliver	C	1990
Gerard A. (Jigger) Phalen	Lib.	2001
(3 vacancies)		

Nunavut Territory

Willie Adams	Lib.	1977

Ontario

Norman K. Atkins	PC	1986
Anne C. Cools	Ind.	1984
Consiglio Di Nino	C	1990
Arthur C. Eggleton	Lib.	2005
John T. Eyton	C	1990
Jerahmiel S. (Jerry) Grafstein	Lib.	1984
Mac Harb	Lib.	2003
Colin Kenny	Lib.	1984
Wilbert J. Keon	C	1990
Marjory LeBreton	C	1993
Francis W. Mahlovich	Lib.	1998
Michael A. Meighen	C	1990
Lorna A. Milne	Lib.	1995
Jim Munson	Lib.	2003
Lowell Murray	PC	1979
P. Michael Pitfield	Ind.	1982
Marie-Paule Poulin (Charette)	Lib.	1995
Vivienne Poy	Lib.	1998
Nancy Ruth	C	2005
Hugh Segal	C	2005
David P. Smith	Lib.	2002
Peter A. Stollery	Lib.	1981
(2 vacancies)		

Prince Edward Island

Catherine S. Callbeck	Lib.	1997
Percy Downe	Lib.	2003
Elizabeth (Libbe) Hubley	Lib.	2001
(1 vacancy)		

Québec

W. David Angus	C	1993
Lise Bacon	Lib.	1994
Michel Biron	Lib.	2001
Andrée P. Champagne	C	2005
Roméo Dallaire	Lib.	2005
Dennis Dawson	Lib.	2005
Pierre De Bané	Lib.	1984
Francis Fox	Lib.	2005
Joan Fraser	Lib.	1998
Yoine Goldstein	Lib.	2005
Céline Hervieux-Payette	Lib.	1995
Serge Joyal	Lib.	1997
Jean Lapointe	Lib.	2001
Raymond Lavigne	Lib.	2002
Paul J. Massicotte	Lib.	2003
Pierre Claude Nolin	C	1993
Lucie Pépin	Lib.	1997
Marcel Prud'homme	Ind.	1993
Jean-Claude Rivest	Ind.	1993
Charlie Watt	Lib.	1984
(4 vacancies)		

Saskatchewan

Raynell Andreychuk	C	1993
Lillian Eva Dyck	Ind. NDP	2005
Leonard J. Gustafson	C	1993
Pana Merchant	Lib.	2002
Robert W. Peterson	Lib.	2005
David Tkachuk	C	1993

Yukon Territory

(1 vacancy)

House of Commons

(October 2008)

Speaker: Peter A. S. Milliken (Lib.).

Leader of the Government: Peter Van Loan (C).

Official Opposition House Leader: Ralph E. Goodale (Lib.).

Party Standings (provisional)

	Conservative	Liberal	Bloc Québécois	New Democratic Party	Independent	Total
Alberta	27	—	—	1	—	28
British Columbia	22	5	—	9	—	36
Manitoba	9	1	—	4	—	14
New Brunswick	6	3	—	1	—	10
Newfoundland and Labrador	—	6	—	1	—	7
Northwest Territories	—	—	—	1	—	1
Nova Scotia	3	5	—	2	1	11
Nunavut Territory	1	1	—	—	—	1
Ontario	51	38	—	17	—	106
Prince Edward Island	1	3	—	—	—	4
Québec	10	13	50	1	1	75
Saskatchewan	13	1	—	—	—	14
Yukon Territory	—	1	—	—	—	1
Total	143	76	50	37	2	308

MEMBERS

(with political party)

Alberta

Diane Ablonczy	C
Rona Ambrose	C
Rob Anders	C
Leon E. Benoit	C
Blaine Calkins	C
Rick Casson	C
Earl Dreeshen	C
Linda Duncan	NDP
Peter Goldring	C
Stephen J. Harper	C
Laurie Hawn	C
Brian Jean	C
Jason Kenney	C
Mike Lake	C
Ted Menzies	C
Rob Merrifield	C
Deepak Obhrai	C
LaVar Payne	C
Jim Prentice	C
James Rajotte	C
Brent Rathgeber	C

Blake Richards	C
Lee Richardson	C
Devinder Shory	C
Kevin Sorenson	C
Brian Storseth	C
Tim Uppal	C
Chris Warkentin	C

British Columbia

Jim Abbott	C
Alex Atamanenko	NDP
Dawn Black	NDP
Dona Cadman	C
Ronald Cannan	C
Jean Crowder	NDP
Nathan Cullen	NDP
John M. Cummins	C
Don Davies	NDP
Elizabeth (Libby) Davies	NDP
Stockwell B. Day	C
Sukh Dhaliwal	Lib.
Ujjal Dosanjh	Lib.
John M. Duncan	C
Edward Fast	C
Hedy Fry	Lib.
Nina Grewal	C
Richard M. (Dick) Harris	C
Russ Hiebert	C
Jay D. Hill	C
Peter Julian	NDP
Randy Kamp	C
Gary Lunn	C
James D. Lunney	C
Keith P. Martin	Lib.
Colin Mayes	C
Cathy McLeod	C
James Moore	C
Joyce Murray	Lib.
Denise Savoie	NDP
Andrew Saxton	C
Bill Siksay	NDP
Charles (Chuck) Strahl	C
Mark Warawa	C
John Weston	C
Alice Wong	C

Manitoba

Niki Ashton	NDP
James Bezan	C
Rod Bruinooge	C
Steven J. Fletcher	C
Shelly Glover	C
Candice Hoeppner	C
Jim Maloway	NDP
Inky Mark	C
Pat Martin	NDP
Anita Neville	Lib.
Joy A. Smith	C
Vic Toews	C
Mervin C. Tweed	C
Judy Wasylycia-Leis	NDP

New Brunswick

Michael Allen	C
Keith Ashfield	C
Jean-Claude D'Amours	Lib.
Yvon Godin	NDP
Dominic LeBlanc	Lib.
Rob Moore	C
Brian Murphy	Lib.
Tilly O'Neill-Gordon	C
Gregory F. Thompson	C
Rodney Weston	C

Newfoundland and Labrador

Scott Andrews	Lib.
Gerry Byrne	Lib.
Siobhan Coady	Lib.
Judy Foote	Lib.
Jack Harris	NDP
Todd N. Russell	Lib.
Scott Simms	Lib.

Northwest Territories

Dennis Bevington	NDP

Nova Scotia

Scott Brison	Lib.
William D. (Bill) Casey	Ind.
Rodger Cuzner	Lib.
Mark Eyking	Lib.
Gerald Keddy	C
Greg Kerr	C
Megan Leslie	NDP
Peter G. MacKay	C
Geoffrey P. (Geoff) Regan	Lib.
Michael J. Savage	Lib.
Peter A. Stoffer	NDP

Nunavut Territory

Leona Aglukkaq	C

Ontario

Harold G. Albrecht	C
Malcolm Allen	NDP
Dean Allison	C
Charles J. (Charlie) Angus	NDP
Navdeep S. Bains	Lib.
John Baird	C
Mauril Bélanger	Lib.
Carolyn Bennett	Lib.
Maurizio Bevilacqua	Lib.
Peter Braid	C
Gord Brown	C
Lois Brown	C
Patrick W. Brown	C
Paul Calandra	C
John Cannis	Lib.
Colin Carrie	C
Chris Charlton	NDP
Michael D. Chong	C
Olivia Chow	NDP
David Christopherson	NDP
Tony Clement	C
Joseph J. (Joe) Comartin	NDP
Bonnie Crombie	Lib
Patricia Davidson	C
Bob Dechert	C
Dean Del Mastro	C
Barry Devolin	C
Paul Dewar	NDP
Ruby Dhalla	Lib.
Ken Dryden	Lib.
Kirsty Duncan	Lib.
Richard Dykstra	C
Diane Finley	C
James M. (Jim) Flaherty	C
Royal Galipeau	C
Cheryl Gallant	C
Gary Goodyear	C
Claude Gravelle	NDP
Albina Guarnieri	Lib.
Helena Guergis	C
Martha Hall Findlay	Lib.
Ed Holder	C
Mark Holland	Lib.
Carol Hughes	NDP
Bruce Hyer	NDP
Michael Ignatieff	Lib.
Andrew Kania	Lib.
Jim Karygiannis	Lib.
Gerard Kennedy	Lib.
Peter Kent	C
Daryl Kramp	C
Guy Lauzon	C
Jack Layton	NDP
Derek V. Lee	Lib.
Pierre Lemieux	C
Ben Lobb	C
Dave MacKenzie	C
Gurbax S. Malhi	Lib.
Wayne Marston	NDP
Tony Martin	NDP
Brian Masse	NDP
Irene Mathyssen	NDP
John McCallum	Lib.
Phil McColeman	C
David J. McGuinty	Lib.
John N. McKay	Lib.
Dan McTeague	Lib.
Larry Miller	C
Peter A. S. Milliken	Lib.
Maria Minna	Lib.
Robert D. Nicholson	C
Rick Norlock	C
Gordon O'Connor	C
Beverley J. (Bev) Oda	C
Rob Oliphant	Lib.

Glen Pearson	Lib.
Pierre Poilievre	C
Joe Preston	C
Robert K. (Bob) Rae	Lib.
John Rafferty	NDP
Lisa Raitt	C
Yasmin Ratansi	Lib.
Scott Reid	C
Greg Rickford	C
Anthony Rota	Lib.
Gary Schellenberger	C
Judy Sgro	Lib.
Beverly T. Shipley	C
Mario Silva	Lib.
Michelle Simson	Lib.
Ronald B. Stanton	C
David Sweet	C
Paul J. M. Szabo	Lib.
Glenn Thibeault	NDP
David A. Tilson	C
Alan Tonks	Lib.
Frank Valeriote	Lib.
David Van Kesteren	C
Peter Van Loan	C
Giuseppe (Joseph) Volpe	Lib.
Michael L. (Mike) Wallace	C
Jeffrey D. Watson	C
Bryon Wilfert	Lib.
Stephen Woodworth	C
Borys Wrzesnewskyj	Lib.
Terence H. Young	C

Prince Edward Island

Arnold W. (Wayne) Easter	Lib.
Lawrence A. MacAulay	Lib.
Shawn Murphy	Lib.
Gail A. Shea	C

Québec

Guy André	BQ
André Arthur	Ind.
Gérard Asselin	BQ
Claude Bachand	BQ
Josée Beaudin	BQ
André Bellavance	BQ
Maxime Bernier	C
Bernard Bigras	BQ
Jean-Pierre Blackburn	C
Raynald Blais	BQ
Steven Blaney	C
France Bonsant	BQ
Robert Bouchard	BQ
Sylvie Boucher	C
Diane Bourgeois	BQ
Paule Brunelle	BQ
Lawrence Cannon	C
Serge Cardin	BQ
Robert Carrier	BQ
Denis Coderre	Lib.
Irwin Cotler	Lib.
Paul Crête	BQ
Claude DeBellefeuille	BQ
Nicole Demers	BQ
Johanne Deschamps	BQ
Luc Desnoyers	BQ
Stéphane Dion	Lib.
Jean Dorion	BQ
Gilles Duceppe	BQ
Nicolas Dufour	BQ
Meili Faille	BQ
Raymonde Folco	Lib.
Carole Freeman	BQ
Christiane Gagnon	BQ
Marc Garneau	Lib.
Roger Gaudet	BQ
Jacques Gourde	C
Monique Guay	BQ
Claude Guimond	BQ
Michel Guimond	BQ
Marlene Jennings	Lib.
Jean-Yves Laforest	BQ
Mario Laframboise	BQ
Francine Lalonde	BQ
Carole Lavallée	BQ
Denis Lebel	C
Marc Lemay	BQ
Yves Lessard	BQ
Yvon Lévesque	BQ
Marcel Lussier	BQ
Luc Malo	BQ
Réal Ménard	BQ
Serge Ménard	BQ
Maria Mourani	BQ
Thomas J. Mulcair	NDP
Richard Nadeau	BQ
Christian Ouellet	BQ
Massimo Pacetti	Lib.
Pascal-Pierre Paillé	BQ
Pierre A. Paquette	BQ
Christian Paradis	C
Bernard Patry	Lib.
Daniel Petit	C
Louis Plamondon	BQ
Roger Pomerleau	BQ
Marcel Proulx	Lib.
Pablo Rodriguez	Lib.
Jean-Yves Roy	BQ
Francis Scarpaleggia	Lib.
Thierry St-Cyr	BQ
Ève-Mary Thaï Thi Lac	BQ
Justin Trudeau	Lib.
Josée Verner	C
Vincent Robert	BQ
Lise Zarac	Lib.

Saskatchewan

David L. Anderson	C
Kelly Block	C
Ray Boughen	C
Garry W. Breitkreuz	C
Rob Clarke	C
Ralph E. Goodale	Lib.
Randy Hoback	C
Ed Komarnicki	C
Tom Lukiwski	C
Gerry Ritz	C
Andrew Scheer	C
Bradley Trost	C
Maurice Vellacott	C
Lynne Yelich	C

Yukon Territory

Larry Bagnell	Lib.

GOVERNMENT FINANCES

(Note: Totals may differ from sums of component parts, owing to rounding.)

(Source: Statistics Canada.)

Federal Budget

(C $ million; estimated data for year ending 31 March)

REVENUE

	2005/06	2006/07	2007/08
Own source revenue	224,051	230,439	250,073
Income taxes	144,634	152,967	167,183
Consumption taxes	48,829	45,016	49,107
Other taxes	786	1,636	1,386
Contributions to social insurance plans	17,245	17,347	17,170
Sales of goods and services	5,740	5,811	6,151
Investment income	6,318	7,297	8,602
Other revenue from own sources	499	365	474
General purpose transfers	604	715	642
Specific purpose transfers	91	68	68
Total revenue	224,746	231,222	250,782

EXPENDITURE

	2005/06	2006/07	2007/08
General government services	8,891	9,011	8,831
Protection of persons and property	25,485	27,308	28,628
Transportation and communications	3,096	3,668	2,784
Health	21,823	22,898	25,805
Social services	65,211	67,822	73,401
Education	5,385	6,659	5,576
Resource conservation and industrial development	9,815	9,688	11,011
Environment	1,738	2,166	3,781
Recreation and culture	4,169	4,305	4,438
Labour, employment and immigration	1,976	2,102	2,172
Housing	2,119	3,502	2,018
Foreign affairs and international assistance	5,586	6,502	5,944
Regional planning and development	256	260	554
Research establishments	3,222	3,390	3,608
General purpose transfers	24,328	22,463	27,412
Debt charges	32,076	32,045	31,031
Other expenditures	31	63	27
Total expenditure	215,205	223,852	237,021

Provincial and Territorial Government Finances—Summary

(C $ million; year ending 31 March 2008)

REVENUE

	Transfers from other levels of government	Revenue from own sources				
		Taxes*	Social insurance contributions	Sales of goods and services	Return on investment	**Gross** (incl. others)
Alberta	3,125	19,330	2,092†	609	14,340	39,582
British Columbia	5,816	22,524	2,849‡	840	4,822	36,980
Manitoba	3,620	6,252	202	202	1,067	11,448
New Brunswick	2,525	3,609	163	170	647	7,128
Newfoundland and Labrador	2,705	2,669	165	172	753	6,471
Northwest Territories	1,063	302	35	36	34	1,472
Nova Scotia	3,342	4,353	242§	336	296	8,575
Nunavut Territory	1,134	58	0	38	5	1,237
Ontario	16,166	73,990	3,383	2,555	3,311	99,523
Prince Edward Island	533	679	28	80	45	1,365
Québec	14,612	51,500	4,404‖	2,369	6,630	79,783
Saskatchewan	1,878	5,895	247	402	2,040	10,486
Yukon Territory	751	95	10	20	30	906
Total	57,270	191,256	13,820	7,829	34,020	304,966

* Includes income, consumption, property and other taxes.
† Includes health insurance premiums of C $1,007m.
‡ Includes health insurance premiums of C $1,550m.
§ Includes health insurance premiums of C $18m.
‖ Includes health insurance premiums of C $849m.

EXPENDITURE
(by major category)

	A	B	C	D	E	F	G	H	**Gross** (incl. others)
Alberta	711	1,019	2,765	11,290	4,596	8,888	1,856	561	34,661
British Columbia	876	1,466	1,863	12,680	5,794	7,711	1,851	2,470	36,137
Manitoba	194	463	530	3,835	1,802	1,974	527	1,260	11,280
New Brunswick	143	218	886	2,378	847	1,582	247	905	7,580
Newfoundland and Labrador	183	343	501	1,913	757	1,247	269	557	6,123
Northwest Territories	125	108	143	273	131	251	127	15	1,468
Nova Scotia	80	426	363	3,052	980	1,763	276	1,014	8,410
Nunavut Territory	141	81	37	281	100	247	58	34	1,266
Ontario	1,583	3,916	4,778	38,323	16,487	19,599	2,911	9,283	100,216
Prince Edward Island	62	45	121	421	124	274	130	128	1,390
Québec	1,622	2,510	3,582	22,492	16,298	14,321	3,484	10,792	79,392
Saskatchewan	181	549	538	3,384	1,205	1,729	647	810	9,777
Yukon Territory	88	79	134	133	114	140	80	3	892
Total	5,989	11,223	16,241	100,455	49,235	59,726	12,463	27,832	298,592

Note: A = General government services; B = Protection of persons and property; C = Transport and communications; D = Health; E = Social services; F = Education; G = Resource conservation and industrial development; H = Debt charges.

POLITICAL ORGANIZATIONS

Action Démocratique du Québec: 740 rue Sainte-Maurice, bureau 108, Montréal, QC H3C 1L5; tel. (514) 270-4413; fax (514) 270-4469; e-mail adq@adq.qc.ca; internet www.adq.qc.ca; f. 1994; provincial nationalist; Leader MARIO DUMONT; Pres. TOM PENTEFOUNTAS.

Bloc Québécois: 3730 Cremazie Est, bureau 307, Montréal, QC H2A 1B4; tel. (514) 526-3000; fax (514) 526-2868; internet www.blocquebecois.org; f. 1990 by group of seven Progressive Conservative MPs representing Québec constituencies in federal Parliament; seeks negotiated sovereignty for Québec; Leader GILLES DUCEPPE.

Canadian Action Party: 916 West Broadway Ave, Suite 385, Vancouver, BC V5Z 1K7; tel. (604) 708-3372; fax (604) 872-1504; e-mail info@canadianactionparty.ca; internet www.canadianactionparty.ca; f. 1997; Leader CONNIE FOGAL.

Christian Heritage Party of Canada: POB 4958, Station E, Ottawa, ON K1S 5J1; tel. (819) 281-6686; fax (819) 281-7174; e-mail nationaloffice@chp.ca; internet www.chp.ca; f. 1986; Pres. LARRY SPENCER (acting); Leader RONALD O. GRAY.

Communist Party of Canada: 290A Danforth Ave, Toronto, ON M4K 1N6; tel. (416) 469-2446; fax (416) 469-4063; e-mail info@cpc-pcc.ca; internet www.communist-party.ca; f. 1921; Leader MIGUEL FIGUEROA.

Conservative Party of Canada: 130 Albert St, Suite 1204, Ottawa, ON K1P 5G4; tel. (613) 755-2000; fax (613) 755-2001; internet www.conservative.ca; f. 2003 by merger of federal brs of Canadian Alliance and Progressive Conservative Party of Canada; Leader STEPHEN J. HARPER.

Green Party of Canada: 204–396 Cooper St, Ottawa, ON K2P 2H7; tel. (613) 562-4916; fax (613) 482-4632; e-mail info@greenparty.ca; internet www.greenparty.ca; f. 1983; environmentalist; Leader ELIZABETH MAY; Chair. JOE FOSTER.

Liberal Party of Canada: 81 Metcalfe St, Suite 400, Ottawa, ON K1P 6M8; tel. (613) 237-0740; fax (613) 235-7208; e-mail info@liberal.ca; internet www.liberal.ca; Leader STÉPHANE DION; Pres. DOUGLAS FERGUSON.

Libertarian Party of Canada: 10125 109 St, Suite 405, Edmonton, AB T5J 3P1; tel. (416) 629-0764; fax (416) 286-0345; e-mail info@libertarian.ca; internet www.libertarian.ca; f. 1974; supports the extension of individual freedoms; Leader DENNIS YOUNG; Pres. ALAN MERCER.

Marijuana Party: 3865 rue Bélanger, Suite 23, Montréal, QC H1X 1B4; tel. (514) 223-8517; e-mail info@marijuanaparty.ca; internet www.marijuanaparty.ca; f. 2000; revolutionary; campaigns for the legalization of marijuana; Leader BLAIR T. LONGLEY.

Marxist-Leninist Party of Canada: 1867 Amherst St, Montréal, QC H2L 3L7; tel. and fax (514) 522-1373; e-mail info@mlpc.ca; internet www.mlpc.ca; f. 1970; publs The Marxist-Leninist Daily (English and French); Nat. Leader SANDRA L. SMITH.

New Democratic Party of Canada: 279 Laurier Ave West, Suite 300, Ottawa, ON K1P 5J9; tel. (613) 236-3613; fax (613) 230-9950; internet www.ndp.ca; f. 1961; social democratic; Leader JACK LAYTON; Pres. ANNE MCGRATH.

Parti Québécois: 1200 ave Papineau, bureau 150, Montréal, QC H2K 4R5; tel. (514) 526-0020; fax (514) 526-0272; e-mail info@pq.org; internet www.pq.org; f. 1968; social democratic; seeks political sovereignty for Québec; Leader PAULINE MAROIS; Pres. MONIQUE RICHARD; 100,000 mems (2007).

Progressive Canadian Party: 264 Queen's Quay West, POB 708, Toronto, ON M5J 1B5; tel. (905) 853-8949; fax (416) 408-1051; e-mail info@pcparty.org; internet www.progressivecanadian.ca; f. 2004; Leader SINCLAIR M. STEVENS; Pres. DORIAN BAXTER.

Saskatchewan Party: 324 McDonald St, Regina, SK S4N 6P6; tel. (306) 359-1638; fax (306) 359-9832; e-mail info@saskparty.com; internet www.saskparty.com; f. 1997; provincial; Leader BRAD WALL.

Socialist Party of Canada: POB 4280, Victoria, BC V8X 3X8; e-mail spc@iname.com; internet www.worldsocialism.org/canada; f. 1905; publ. journal, *Imagine*, on a sporadic basis; Gen. Sec. JOHN AYERS; Treas. WILLIAM JOHNSON.

Yukon Party: 211 Elliott St, POB 31113, Whitehorse, YT Y1A 5P7; tel. (867) 668-6505; e-mail info@yukonparty.ca; internet www.yukonparty.ca; provincial; Leader DENNIS FENTIE; Pres. DAN MACDONALD.

DIPLOMATIC REPRESENTATION

OVERSEAS REPRESENTATION IN CANADA

Embassies and Consulates-General

AFGHANISTAN

Embassy: 240 Argyle Ave, Ottawa, ON K2P 1B9; tel. (613) 563-4223; fax (613) 563-4962; e-mail contact@afghanemb-canada.net; internet www.afghanemb-canada.net; Ambassador OMAR SAMAD.

Consulate-General, Toronto: 477 Richmond St West, Suite 901, Toronto, ON M5V 3E7; tel. (416) 385-1033; fax (416) 385-3810; e-mail infoconsulate@cgoa.ca; internet www.cgoa.ca; Consul-Gen. HABIBULLAH QADERI.

ALBANIA

Embassy: 130 Albert St, Suite 302, Ottawa, ON K1P 5G4; tel. (613) 236-3053; fax (613) 236-0804; e-mail embassy.ottawa@mfa.gov.al; Ambassador BESNIK KONÇI.

ALGERIA

Embassy: 500 Wilbrod St, Ottawa, ON K1N 6N2; tel. (613) 789-8505; fax (613) 789-1406; e-mail info@embassyalgeria.ca; internet www.ambalgott.com; Ambassador SMAIL BENAMARA.

Consulate-General, Montréal: 3415 Saint-Urban, Montréal, QC H2X 2N2; tel. (514) 846-0442; fax (514) 846-8127; e-mail consalgmtl@consulatdz.ca; internet www.consulatalgeriemontreal.com; Consul-Gen. ABDELGHANI AMARA.

ANGOLA

Embassy: 189 Laurier Ave, Ottawa, ON K1N 6P1; tel. (613) 234-1152; fax (613) 234-1179; e-mail info@embangola-can.org; internet www.embangola-can.org; Ambassador MIGUEL MARIA N'ZAU PUNA.

ANTIGUA AND BARBUDA

(See entry for Eastern Caribbean States.)

ARGENTINA

Embassy: 81 Metcalfe Street, Suite 700 Ottawa, ON K1P 6K7; tel. (613) 236-2351; fax (613) 235-2659; e-mail embargentina@argentina-canada.net; internet www.argentina-canada.net; Ambassador ARTURO G. BOTHAMLEY.

Consulate-General, Montréal: 2000 rue Peel, Suite 600, Montréal, QC H3A 2W5; tel. (514) 842-6582; fax (514) 842-5797; e-mail info@consargenmtl.com; internet www.consargenmtl.com; Consul-Gen. JORGE BENITO RIABOI.

Consulate-General, Toronto: 5001 Yonge St, 2nd Floor, Suite 201, Toronto, ON M2N 6P6; tel. (416) 955-9075; fax (416) 955-0868; e-mail consarg@ca.inter.net; internet www.consargtoro.ca; Consul-Gen. JULIO MILLER.

ARMENIA

Embassy: 7 Delaware Ave, Ottawa, ON K2P 0Z2; tel. (613) 234-3710; fax (613) 234-3444; e-mail armcanadaembassy@mfa.am; internet www.armembassycanada.ca; Chargé d'affaires a.i. ARMAN AKOPIAN.

AUSTRALIA

High Commission: 50 O'Connor St, 7th Floor, Suite 710, Ottawa, ON K1P 6L2; tel. (613) 236-0841; fax (613) 236-4376; internet www.canada.embassy.gov.au; High Commr JUSTIN BROWN.

Consulate-General, Toronto: 175 Bloor St East, South Tower, Suite 1100, Toronto, ON M4W 3R8; tel. (416) 323-1155; fax (416) 323-3910; Consul-Gen. STEFAN TROFIMOVS.

AUSTRIA

Embassy: 445 Wilbrod St, Ottawa, ON K1N 6M7; tel. (613) 789-1444; fax (613) 789-3431; e-mail ottawa-ob@bmeia.gv.at; internet www.austro.org; Ambassador OTTO DITZ.

AZERBAIJAN

Embassy: 275 Slater St, Suite 904, Ottawa, ON K1P 5H9; tel. (613) 288-0497; fax (613) 230-8089; e-mail azerbaijan@azembassy.ca; internet www.azembassy.ca; Chargé d'affaires a.i. FARID SHAFIYEV.

BAHAMAS

High Commission: 50 O'Connor St, Suite 1313, Ottawa, ON K1P 6L2; tel. (613) 232-1724; fax (613) 232-0097; e-mail ottawamission@bahighco.com; High Commr MICHAEL DOUGLAS SMITH.

BANGLADESH

High Commission: 275 Bank St, Suite 302, Ottawa, ON K2P 2L6; tel. (613) 236-0138; fax (613) 567-3213; e-mail bangla@rogers.com; internet www.bdhc.org; High Commr A. M. YAKUB ALI (acting).

BARBADOS

High Commission: 55 Metcalfe St, Suite 470, Ottawa, ON K1P 6L5; tel. (613) 236-9517; fax (613) 230-4362; e-mail ottawa@foreign.gov.bb; internet www.foreign.gov.bb; High Commr GLYNE SAMUEL MURRAY.

Consulate-General, Toronto: 105 Adelaide St West, Suite 1010, Toronto, ON M5H 1P9; tel. (416) 214-9805; fax (416) 214-9815; e-mail barbados@interlog.org; Consul-Gen. LEROY H. MCCLEAN.

BELARUS

Embassy: 130 Albert St, Suite 600, Ottawa, ON K1P 5G4; tel. (613) 233-9994; fax (613) 233-8500; e-mail belamb@igs.net; Chargé d'affaires a.i. PAVEL MIHAJLOVICH PUSTOVOY.

BELGIUM

Embassy: 360 Albert St, Suite 820, Ottawa, ON K1P 1B7; tel. (613) 236-7267; fax (613) 236-7882; e-mail ottawa@diplobel.org; internet www.diplomatie.be/ottawa; Ambassador JEAN L. A. LINT.

Consulate-General, Montréal: 999 blvd de Maisonneuve ouest, Suite 1600, Montréal, QC H3A 3L4; tel. (514) 849-7394; fax (514) 844-3170; e-mail montreal@diplobel.fed.be; internet www.diplomatie.be/montreal; Consul-Gen. GODELIEVE VAN DEN BERGH.

BENIN

Embassy: 58 Glebe Ave, Ottawa, ON K1S 2C3; tel. (613) 233-4429; fax (613) 233-8952; e-mail ambaben@benin.ca; internet www.benin.ca; Ambassador HONORÉ THÉODORE AHIMAKIN.

BOLIVIA

Embassy: 130 Albert St, Suite 416, Ottawa, ON K1P 5G4; tel. (613) 236-5730; fax (613) 236-8237; e-mail bolivianembassy@bellnet.ca; Ambassador EDGAR TORREZ-MOSQUEIRA.

BOSNIA AND HERZEGOVINA

Embassy: 130 Albert St, Suite 805, Ottawa, ON K1P 5G4; tel. (613) 236-0028; fax (613) 236-1139; e-mail embassyofbih@bellnet.ca; internet www.bhembassy.ca; Ambassador MILENKO MIŠIĆ.

BRAZIL

Embassy: 450 Wilbrod St, Ottawa, ON K1N 6M8; tel. (613) 237-1090; fax (613) 237-6144; e-mail mailbox@brasembottawa.org; internet www.brasembottawa.org; Ambassador PAULO CORDEIRO DE ANDRADE PINTO.

Consulate-General, Montréal: 1 Westmount Sq., Suite 1700, Montréal, QC H3Z 2P9; tel. (514) 499-0968; fax (514) 499-3963; e-mail geral@consbrasmontreal.org; internet www.consbrasmontreal.org; Consul-Gen. WASHINGTON LUIS PEREIRA DE SOUSA NETO.

Consulate-General, Toronto: 77 Bloor St West, Suite 1109, Toronto, ON M5S 1M2; tel. (416) 992-2503; fax (416) 922-1832; e-mail info@consbrastoronto.org; internet www.consbrastoronto.org; Consul-Gen. AMERICO DYOTT FONTENELLE.

BRUNEI

High Commission: 395 Laurier Ave East, Ottawa, ON K1N 6R4; tel. (613) 234-5656; fax (613) 234-4397; e-mail bhco@bellnet.ca; High Commr RAKIAH Haji ABDUL LAMIT.

BULGARIA

Embassy: 325 Stewart St, Ottawa, ON K1N 6K5; tel. (613) 789-3215; fax (613) 789-3524; e-mail bgemb@storm.ca; internet www.mfa.bg/ottawa; Ambassador EVGUENI S. STOYTCHEV.

Consulate-General, Toronto: 65 Overlea Blvd, Suite 230, Toronto, ON M4H 1P1; tel. (416) 696-2420; fax (416) 696-8019; e-mail bulcontor@primus.ca; internet www.mfa.bg/toronto; Consul-Gen. GUENKA S. BELEVA.

BURKINA FASO

Embassy: 48 Range Rd, Ottawa, ON K1N 8J4; tel. (613) 238-4796; fax (613) 238-3812; e-mail burkina.faso@sympatico.ca; internet www.burkinafaso.ca; Ambassador JULIETTE BONKOUNGOU-YAMEOGO.

BURUNDI

Embassy: 325 Dalhousie St, Suite 815, Ottawa, ON K1N 7G2; tel. (613) 789-0414; fax (613) 789-9537; e-mail ambabucanada@infonet.ca; Ambassador APPOLONIE SIMBIZI.

CAMEROON

High Commission: 170 Clemow Ave, Ottawa, ON K1S 2B4; tel. (613) 236-1522; fax (613) 236-3885; e-mail cameroun@rogers.com; High Commr SOLOMON AZOH-MBI ANU'A-GHEYLE.

CHILE

Embassy: 50 O'Connor St, Suite 1413, Ottawa, ON K1P 6L2; tel. (613) 235-4402; fax (613) 235-1176; e-mail echileca@chile.ca; internet www.chile.ca; Ambassador EUGENIO LUIS ORTEGA RIQUELME.

Consulate-General, Montréal: 1010 Sherbrooke St West, Suite 710, Montréal, QC H3A 2R7; tel. (514) 499-0405; fax (514) 499-8914; e-mail consulado@chilemtl.ca; internet www.chilemtl.ca; Consul-Gen. PATRICIO VICTORIANO.

Consulate-General, Toronto: 2 Bloor St West, Suite 1801, Toronto, ON M4W 3E2; tel. (416) 924-0106; fax (416) 924-2627; e-mail consulate@congechiletoronto.com; internet www.congechiletoronto.com; Consul-Gen. RICARDO E. PLAZA DUCO.

Consulate-General, Vancouver: 1610-1185 West Georgia St, Suite 1250, Vancouver, BC V6E 4E6; tel. (604) 681-9162; fax (604) 687-0624; e-mail consulado@chilevancouver.com; internet www.chilevancouver.ca; Consul-Gen. MARÍA ELIANA CUEVAS BERNALES.

CHINA, PEOPLE'S REPUBLIC

Embassy: 515 St Patrick St, Ottawa, ON K1N 5H3; tel. (613) 789-3434; fax (613) 789-1911; e-mail chinaemb_ca@mfa.gov.cn; internet www.chinaembassycanada.org; Ambassador LAN LIJUN.

Consulate-General, Calgary: 1011 Sixth Ave South West, Suite 100, Calgary, AB T2P 0W1; tel. (403) 264-3322; fax (403) 264-6656; e-mail chinaconsul_cal_ca@mfa.gov.cn; internet calgary.china-consulate.org; Consul-Gen. SONG XIZHU.

Consulate-General, Toronto: 240 St George St, Toronto, ON M5R 2P4; tel. (416) 964-7260; fax (416) 324-6468; e-mail china_consultor_ca@mfa.gov; internet toronto.chineseconsulate.org; Consul-Gen. ZHU TAOYING.

Consulate-General, Vancouver: 3380 Granville St, Vancouver, BC V6H 3K3; tel. (604) 734-7492; fax (604) 737-0154; internet vancouver.china-consulate.org; Consul-Gen. YANG QIANG.

COLOMBIA

Embassy: 360 Albert St, Suite 1002, Ottawa, ON K1R 7X7; tel. (613) 230-3760; fax (613) 230-4416; e-mail embajada@embajadacolombia.ca; internet www.embajadacolombia.ca; Ambassador JAIME GIRÓN DUARTE.

Consulate-General, Montréal: 1010 Sherbrooke St West, Suite 920, Montréal, QC H3A 2R7; tel. (514) 849-4852; fax (514) 849-4324; e-mail concolmt@videotron.ca; Consul-Gen. MARTA LUCÍA PIÑEROS DE CAMACHO.

Consulate-General, Toronto: 1 Dundas St West, Suite 2108, Toronto, ON M5G 1Z3; tel. (416) 977-0098; fax (416) 977-1025; e-mail info@consuladocolombia.com; Consul-Gen. ANA CATALINA DEL LLANO RESTREPO.

CONGO, DEMOCRATIC REPUBLIC

Embassy: 18 Range Rd, Ottawa, ON K1N 8J3; tel. (613) 230-6391; fax (613) 230-1945; e-mail info@ambassadesrdcongo.org; Chargé d'affaires a.i. LOUISE NZANGA RAMAZANI.

COSTA RICA

Embassy: 325 Dalhousie St, Suite 407, Ottawa, ON K1N 7G2; tel. (613) 562-2855; fax (613) 562-2582; e-mail embcrica@costaricaembassy.com; internet www.costaricaembassy.com; Ambassador EMILIA MARÍA ALVAREZ NAVARRO.

CÔTE D'IVOIRE

Embassy: 9 Marlborough Ave, Ottawa, ON K1N 8E6; tel. (613) 236-9919; fax (613) 563-8287; e-mail embaci@ican.net; Ambassador LOUIS LEON BOGUY BONY.

CROATIA

Embassy: 229 Chapel St, Ottawa, ON K1N 7Y6; tel. (613) 562-7820; fax (613) 562-7821; e-mail croemb.ottawa@mvpei.hr; internet ca.mfa.hr; Ambassador VESELA MRĐEN KORAĆ.

Consulate-General, Toronto: 918 Dundas St East, Suite 302, Mississauga, ON L4Y 2B3; tel. (905) 277-9051; fax (905) 277-5432; e-mail croconsulate.miss@mvpei.hr; Consul-Gen. BRANKA PAZIN (acting).

CUBA

Embassy: 388 Main St, Ottawa, ON K1S 1E3; tel. (613) 563-0141; fax (613) 563-0068; e-mail cuba@embacubacanada.net; internet www.embacubacanada.net; Ambassador ERNESTO A. SENTÍ DARIAS.

Consulate-General, Montréal: 4542 Décarie blvd, Montréal, QC H3X 2H5; tel. (514) 843-8897; fax (514) 845-1063; e-mail consulgralcuba@bellnet.ca; Consul-Gen. SERGIO VÉLEZ CAMHI.

Consulate-General, Toronto: 5353 Dundas St West, Kipling Sq., Suite 401, Toronto, ON M9B 6H8; tel. (416) 234-8181; fax (416) 234-2754; e-mail cubaconsul@caspar.net; Consul-Gen. LAUREANO CARDOSO.

CYPRUS

Consulate-General, Toronto: 365 Bloor St East, Suite 1010, Toronto, ON M4W 3L4; tel. (416) 944-0998; fax (416) 944-9149; e-mail consulcy@rogers.com; Consul-Gen. PENELOPE EROTOKRITOU.

CZECH REPUBLIC

Embassy: 251 Cooper St, Ottawa, ON K2P 0G2; tel. (613) 562-3875; fax (613) 562-3878; e-mail ottawa@embassy.mzv.cz; internet www.mzv.cz/ottawa; Ambassador PAVEL VOŠALÍK.

Consulate-General, Montréal: 1305 Pine Ave West, Montréal, QC H3G 1B2; tel. (514) 849-4495; fax (514) 844-1894; e-mail montreal@embassy.mzv.cz; internet www.mfa.cz/montreal; Consul-Gen. VIERA JARESOVA.

DENMARK

Embassy: 47 Clarence St, Suite 450, Ottawa, ON K1N 9K1; tel. (613) 562-1811; fax (613) 562-1812; e-mail ottamb@um.dk; internet www.ambottawa.um.dk; Ambassador POUL ERIK DAM KRISTENSEN.

DOMINICA

(See entry for Eastern Caribbean States.)

DOMINICAN REPUBLIC

Embassy: 130 Albert St, Suite 418, Ottawa, ON K1P 5G4; tel. (613) 569-9893; fax (613) 569-8673; e-mail info@drembassy.org; internet www.drembassy.org; Ambassador LUIS ARIAS NUÑEZ.

Consulate-General, Montréal: 1470 Peel St, Tower A, Suite 263, Montréal, QC H3A 1T1; tel. (514) 284-5455; fax (514) 284-5511; e-mail gpichardo@sympatico.ca; Consul-Gen. RAQUEL JOSEFINA JACOBO DE CABRAL.

Consulate-General, Toronto: 2 Adelaide St West, Suite 301, Toronto, ON M5H 1L6; tel. (416) 369-0403; fax (416) 369-1685; Consul-Gen. GUILLERMO J. ESTRELLA GABRIEL.

EASTERN CARIBBEAN STATES

High Commission: 130 Albert St, Suite 700, Ottawa, ON K1P 5G4; tel. (613) 236-8952; fax (613) 236-3042; e-mail echcc@travel-net.com; internet www.oecs.org/ottawa; High Commr BRENDON CALVERT BROWNE; covers Antigua and Barbuda, Dominica, Grenada, Saint Christopher and Nevis, Saint Lucia, Saint Vincent and the Grenadines and the United Kingdom Overseas Territory of Montserrat.

Consulate-General of Antigua and Barbuda, Toronto: 60 St Clair Ave East, Suite 601, Toronto, ON M4T 1N5; tel. (416) 961-3143; fax (416) 961-7218; e-mail info@antigua-barbuda-ca.com; Consul-Gen. MADELINE BLACKMAN.

Consulate-General of Saint Lucia, Toronto: 65 Overlea Blvd, Toronto, ON M4H 1P1; tel. (416) 203-8400; fax (416) 203-8486; e-mail sluconca@ionsys.com; Consul-Gen. EGBERT LIONEL.

Consulate-General of Saint Vincent and the Grenadines, Toronto: 333 Wilson Ave, Suite 601, Toronto, ON M3H 1T2; tel.

(416) 398-4277; fax (416) 398-4199; e-mail consulategeneral@rogers .com; Consul-Gen. STEVE O. PHILLIPS.

ECUADOR

Embassy: 50 O'Connor St, Suite 316, Ottawa, ON K1P 6L2; tel. (613) 563-8206; fax (613) 235-5776; e-mail mecuacan@rogers.com; internet www.vivecuador.com; Chargé d'affaires a.i. OSCAR FELIPE IZQUIERDO ARBOLEDA.

Consulate-General, Montréal: 2055 Peel St, Suite 501, Montréal, QC H3A 1V4; tel. (514) 874-4071; fax (514) 874-9078; e-mail consecuador-montreal@iq.ca; internet www.consecuador-quebec .org; Consul-Gen. VERÓNICA AUGUSTA BUSTAMANTE PONCE.

EGYPT

Embassy: 454 Laurier Ave East, Ottawa, ON K1N 6R3; tel. (613) 234-4931; fax (613) 234-4398; e-mail egyptemb@sympatico.ca; internet www.mfa.gov.eg; Ambassador SHAMEL NASSER.

Consulate-General, Montréal: 1000 rue de la Gauchetière Ouest, Suite 3320, Montréal, QC H3B 4W5; tel. (514) 866-8455; fax (514) 866-0835; Consul-Gen. WAFAA MUHAMMADD EL-HADIDY.

EL SALVADOR

Embassy: 209 Kent St, Ottawa, ON K2P 1Z8; tel. (613) 238-2939; fax (613) 238-6940; e-mail embajada@elsalvador-ca.org; Ambassador RAFAEL ANGEL ALFARO PINEDA.

Consulate-General, Montréal: 2055 Peel St, Suite 840, Montréal, QC H3A 1V4; tel. (514) 861-6515; (514) 861-6513; e-mail consuladoelsalvador@gc.aira.com; Consul-Gen. VERONICA PATRICIA PICHINTE CHACON.

Consulate-General, Toronto: 151 Bloor St West, Suite 320, Toronto, ON M5S 1S4; tel. (416) 975-0812; fax (416) 975-0283; e-mail amurra@rree.gob.sv; Consul-Gen. ANA HAYDEE MURRA SACA.

Consulate-General, Vancouver: 938 Howe St, Suite 411, Vancouver, BC V6Z 1N9; tel. (604) 732-8142; fax (604) 696-0038; e-mail romeza@axion.net; Consul-Gen. ROSA ELENA MORENO MALDONADO.

ERITREA

Embassy: 75 Albert St, Suite 610, Ottawa, ON K1P 5E7; tel. (613) 234-3989; fax (613) 234-6213; Ambassador AHFEROM BERHANE GHEBREMEDHIN.

ESTONIA

Embassy: 260 Dalhousie St, Suite 210, Ottawa, ON K1N 7E4; tel. (613) 789-4222; fax (613) 789-9555; e-mail embassy.ottawa@mfa.ee; internet www.estemb.ca; Ambassador VÄINO REINART.

ETHIOPIA

Embassy: 151 Slater St, Suite 210, Ottawa, ON K1P 5H3; tel. (613) 235-6637; fax (613) 235-4638; e-mail info.ethio@ethiopianembassy .net; internet www.ottawa.ethiopianembassy.net; Ambassador GETACHEW HAMUSSA HAILEMARIAM.

FINLAND

Embassy: 55 Metcalfe St, Suite 850, Ottawa, ON K1P 6L5; tel. (613) 288-2233; fax (613) 288-2244; e-mail embassy@finland.ca; internet www.finland.ca; Ambassador RISTO PIIPPONEN.

FRANCE

Embassy: 42 Sussex Dr., Ottawa, ON K1M 2C9; tel. (613) 789-1795; fax (613) 562-3735; e-mail politique@ambafrance-ca.org; internet www.ambafrance-ca.org; Ambassador FRANÇOIS MARIE DELATTRE.

Consulate-General, Moncton: 777 Main St, Suite 800, Moncton, NB E1C 1E9; tel. (506) 857-4191; fax (506) 858-8169; e-mail info@consulfrance-moncton.org; internet www.consulfrance-moncton .org; Consul-Gen. GILLES COURREGELONGUE.

Consulate-General, Montréal: 1501 McGill College, Bureau 1000, Montréal, QC H4A 3M8; tel. (514) 878-4385; fax (514) 878-3981; e-mail info@consulfrance-montreal.org; internet www .consulfrance-montreal.org; Consul-Gen. PIERRE ROBION.

Consulate-General, Québec: Kent House, 25 rue St-Louis, Québec, QC G1R 3Y8; tel. (418) 266-2500; fax (418) 266-2515; e-mail info@consulfrance-quebec.org; internet www.consulfrance-quebec .org; Consul-Gen. FRANÇOIS SIMON R. M. ALABRUNE.

Consulate-General, Toronto: 2 Bloor St East, Suite 2200, Toronto, ON M4W 1A8; tel. (416) 847-1900; fax (416) 847-1901; e-mail info@consulfrance-toronto.org; internet www.consulfrance-toronto .org; Consul-Gen. PHILIPPE P. P. DELACROIX.

Consulate-General, Vancouver: 1130 West Pender St, Suite 1100, Vancouver, BC V6E 4A4; tel. (604) 681-4345; fax (604) 681-4287; e-mail info@consulfrance-vancouver.org; internet www .consulfrance-vancouver.org; Consul-Gen. LUC BERNARD J. SEROT ALMERAS.

GABON

Embassy: 4 Range Rd, Ottawa, ON K1N 8J3; tel. (613) 232-5301; fax (613) 232-6916; e-mail ambgabon@sprint.ca; Ambassador ANDRE WILLIAM ANGUILE.

GERMANY

Embassy: 1 Waverley St, Ottawa, ON K2P 0T8; tel. (613) 232-1101; fax (613) 594-9330; e-mail germanembassyottawa@on.aibn.com; internet www.ottawa.diplo.de; Ambassador MATTHIAS MARTIN A. HÖPFNER.

Consulate-General, Montréal: 1250 blvd René-Lévesque ouest 4315, Montréal, QC H3B 4W8; tel. (514) 931-2277; fax (514) 931-7239; e-mail mail@montr.diplo.de; internet www.montreal.diplo.de; Consul-Gen. JÖRG METGER.

Consulate-General, Toronto: 77 Bloor St West, Suite 1703, Toronto, ON M5S 1M2; tel. (416) 925-2813; fax (416) 925-2818; e-mail info@toronto.diplo.de; internet www.toronto.diplo.de; Consul-Gen. HOLGER RAASCH.

Consulate-General, Vancouver: World Trade Centre, Suite 704, 999 Canada Pl., Vancouver, BC V6C 3E1; tel. (604) 684-8377; fax (604) 684-8334; e-mail germanconsulatevancouver@telus.net; Consul-Gen. KLAUS ACHENBACH.

GHANA

High Commission: 153 Gilmour St, Ottawa, ON K2P 0N8; tel. (613) 236-0871; fax (613) 236-0874; e-mail ghanacom@ghc-ca.com; internet www.ghc-ca.com; High Commr Dr MARGARET IVY AMOAKOHENE.

Consulate-General, Toronto: 4665 Yonge St, Units 205 and 206, North York, ON M2N 0B4; tel. (416) 848-1015; fax (416) 848-1017; e-mail ghanaconsulate@rogers.com; Consul-Gen. KWABENA ASARE.

GREECE

Embassy: 76–80 MacLaren St, Ottawa, ON K2P 0K6; tel. (613) 238-6271; fax (613) 238-5676; e-mail embassy@greekembassy.ca; internet www.greekembassy.ca; Ambassador NIKOLAOS MATSIS.

Consulate-General, Montréal: 1170 pl. du Frère André, 3e étage, Montréal, QC H3B 3C6; tel. (514) 875-2119; fax (514) 875-8781; e-mail info@grconsulatemtl.net; internet www.grconsulatemtl.net; Consul-Gen. MARIA KARNOUTSOU.

Consulate-General, Toronto: 365 Bloor St East, Suite 1800, Toronto, ON M4W 3L4; tel. (416) 515-0133; fax (416) 515-0209; e-mail toronto.consulate@greekembassy.ca; internet grconsulate .com; Consul-Gen. EFTHYMIOS EFTHYMIADES.

GRENADA

(See entry for Eastern Caribbean States.)

GUATEMALA

Embassy: 130 Albert St, Suite 1010, Ottawa, ON K1P 5G4; tel. (613) 233-7237; fax (613) 233-0135; e-mail embassy1@embaguate-canada .com; internet www.embaguate-canada.com; Ambassador GEORGES DE LA ROCHE PLIHAL.

GUINEA

Embassy: 483 Wilbrod St, Ottawa, ON K1N 6N1; tel. (613) 789-8444; fax (613) 789-7560; e-mail ambassadedeguinee@bellnet.ca; Chargé d'affaires a.i. KABA HAWA DIAKITE.

GUYANA

High Commission: Burnside Bldg, 151 Slater St, Suite 309, Ottawa, ON K1P 5H3; tel. (613) 235-7249; fax (613) 235-1447; e-mail guyanahcott@rogers.com; High Commr RAJNARINE SINGH.

HAITI

Embassy: 130 Albert St, Suite 1500, Ottawa, ON K1P 5G4; tel. (613) 238-1628; fax (613) 238-2986; e-mail bohio@sympatico.ca; Chargé d'affaires a.i. MARIE NATHALIE MENOS-GISSEL.

HOLY SEE

Apostolic Nunciature: 724 Manor Ave, Rockcliffe Park, Ottawa, ON K1M 0E3; tel. (613) 746-4914; fax (613) 746-4786; e-mail nuntius@rogers.com; Nuncio Most Rev. LUIGI VENTURA (Titular Archbishop of Equilio).

HONDURAS

Embassy: 151 Slater St, Suite 805, Ottawa, ON K1P 5H3; tel. (613) 233-8900; fax (613) 232-0193; e-mail embhonca@embassyhonduras.ca; internet www.embassyhonduras.ca; Ambassador DELIA BEATRIZ VALLE MARICHAL.

HUNGARY

Embassy: 299 Waverley St, Ottawa, ON K2P 0V9; tel. (613) 230-2717; fax (613) 230-7560; e-mail mission.ott@kum.hu; internet www.mfa.gov.hu/emb/ottawa; Ambassador Dr PAL VASTAGH.

Consulate-General, Toronto: 425 Bloor St East, Suite 501, Toronto, ON M4W 3R5; tel. (416) 923-8981; fax (416) 923-2732; Consul-Gen. SANDOR GYORGY BEER.

ICELAND

Embassy: 360 Albert St, 7th Floor, Suite 710, Ottawa, ON K1R 7X7; tel. (613) 482-1944; fax (613) 482-1945; e-mail icemb.ottawa@utn.stjr.is; internet www.iceland.org/ca; Ambassador SIGRÍDUR ANNA THÓRDARDÓTTIR.

Consulate-General, Winnipeg: 1 Wellington Cres., Suite 100, Winnipeg, MB R3M 3Z2; tel. (204) 284-1535; fax (204) 284-1539; e-mail icecon.winnipeg@utn.stjr.is; internet www.iceland.org/ca/win; Consul-Gen. ATLI ASMUNDSSON.

INDIA

High Commission: 10 Springfield Rd, Ottawa, ON K1M 1C9; tel. (613) 744-3751; fax (613) 744-0913; e-mail hicomind@hciottawa.ca; internet www.hciottawa.ca; High Commr RAJAMANI LAKSHMI NARAYAN.

Consulate-General, Toronto: 365 Bloor St East, 7th Floor, Toronto, ON M4W 3L4; tel. (416) 960-0751; fax (416) 960-9812; e-mail cgindia@cgitoronto.ca; internet www.cgitoronto.ca; Consul-Gen. SATISH CHAND MEHTA.

Consulate-General, Vancouver: 325 Howe St, 2nd Floor, Vancouver, BC V6C 1Z7; tel. (604) 662-8811; fax (604) 682-2471; e-mail indiacg@telus.net; internet www.cgivancouver.com; Consul-Gen. ASHOK KUMAR.

INDONESIA

Embassy: 55 Parkdale Ave, Ottawa, ON K1Y 1E5; tel. (613) 724-1100; fax (613) 724-1105; e-mail info@indonesia-ottawa.org; internet www.indonesia-ottawa.org; Ambassador DJOKO HARDONO.

Consulate-General, Toronto: 129 Jarvis St, Toronto, ON M5C 2H6; tel. (416) 360-4020; fax (416) 360-4295; e-mail info@indonesiatoronto.org; internet www.indonesiatoronto.org; Consul-Gen. BAMBANG CAHYO GUNAWAN.

Consulate-General, Vancouver: 1630 Alberni St, Vancouver, BC V6G 1A6; tel. (604) 682-8855; fax (604) 662-8396; e-mail congen@indonesiavancouver.org; internet www.indonesiavancouver.org; Consul-Gen. BUNYAN SAPTOMO.

IRAN

Embassy: 245 Metcalfe St, Ottawa, ON K2P 2K2; tel. (613) 235-4726; fax (613) 232-5712; e-mail iranemb@salamiran.org; internet www.salamiran.org; Chargé d'affaires a.i. BAHRAM GHASEMI.

IRAQ

Embassy: 215 McLeod St, Ottawa, ON K2P 0Z8; tel. (613) 236-9177; fax (613) 236-9641; e-mail media@iraqembassy.ca; internet www.iraqembassy.ca; Ambassador HOWAR M. ZIAD.

IRELAND

Embassy: 130 Albert St, Ottawa, ON K1P 5G4; tel. (613) 233-6281; fax (613) 233-5835; e-mail embassyofireland@rogers.com; Ambassador DECLAN MICHAEL KELLY.

ISRAEL

Embassy: 50 O'Connor St, Suite 1005, Ottawa, ON K1P 6L2; tel. (613) 567-6450; fax (613) 567-9878; e-mail info@ottawa.mfa.gov.il; internet www.embassyofisrael.ca; Ambassador MIRIAM ZIV.

Consulate-General, Montréal: 1155 blvd René-Lévesque ouest, Suite 2620, Montréal, QC H3B 4S5; tel. (514) 940-8500; fax (514) 940 8555; e-mail fpress@montreal.mfa.gov.il; internet montreal.mfa.gov.il; Consul-Gen. YORAM ELRON.

Consulate-General, Toronto: 180 Bloor St West, Suite 700, Toronto, ON M5S 2V6; tel. (416) 640-8500; fax (416) 640-8555; e-mail cgsec@toronto.mfa.gov.il; internet toronto.mfa.gov.il; Consul-Gen. AMIR R. GISSIN.

ITALY

Embassy: 275 Slater St, 21st Floor, Ottawa, ON K1P 5H9; tel. (613) 232-2401; fax (613) 233-1484; e-mail ambasciata.ottawa@esteri.it; internet www.ambottawa.esteri.it; Ambassador GABRIELE SARDO.

Consulate-General, Montréal: 3489 Drummond St, 2nd Floor, Montréal, QC H3G 1X6; tel. (514) 849-8351; fax (514) 499-9471; e-mail consolato.montreal@esteri.it; internet www.consmontreal.esteri.it; Consul-Gen. FRANCESCO PAOLO VENIER.

Consulate-General, Toronto: 136 Beverley St, Toronto, ON M5T 1Y5; tel. (416) 977-1566; fax (416) 977-1119; e-mail archivio.toronto@esteri.it; internet www.constoronto.esteri.it; Consul-Gen. GIANNI BARDINI.

Consulate-General, Vancouver: 510 West Hastings St, Suite 1100, Vancouver, BC V6B 1L8; tel. (604) 684-7288; fax (604) 685-4263; e-mail consolato.vancouver@esteri.it; internet www.consvancouver.esteri.it; Consul-Gen. UBERTO VANNI D'ARCHIRAFI.

JAMAICA

High Commission: 275 Slater St, Suite 800, Ottawa, ON K1P 5H9; tel. (613) 233-9311; fax (613) 233-0611; e-mail hc@jhcottawa.ca; Ambassador RUBY VIOLET EVADNE COYE.

Consulate-General, Toronto: 303 Eglinton Ave East, Toronto, ON M4P 1L3; tel. (416) 598-3008; fax (416) 598-4928; e-mail congentoronto@on.aibn.com; Consul-Gen. ANNE MARIE BONNER.

JAPAN

Embassy: 255 Sussex Dr., Ottawa, ON K1N 9E6; tel. (613) 241-8541; fax (613) 241-7415; e-mail infocul@embjapan.ca; internet www.ca.emb-japan.go.jp; Ambassador TSUNEO NISHIDA.

Consulate-General, Calgary: Trans Canada Tower, 23rd Floor, 450 First St, South West, Calgary, AB T2P 5H1; tel. (403) 294-0782; fax (403) 294-1645; e-mail infocul@conjapan.ab.ca; internet www.calgary.ca.emb-japan.go.jp; Consul-Gen. YASUO MINEMURA.

Consulate-General, Montréal: 600 rue de la Gauchetière ouest, Suite 2120, Montréal, QC H3B 4L8; tel. (514) 866-3429; fax (514) 395-6000; internet www.montreal.ca.emb-japan.go.jp; Consul-Gen. ATSUSHI NISHIOKA.

Consulate-General, Toronto: Royal Trust Tower, Suite 3300, Toronto-Dominion Centre, 77 King St, POB 10, Toronto, ON M5K 1A1; tel. (416) 363-7038; fax (416) 367-9392; e-mail access@japancg-toronto.org; internet www.japancg-toronto.org; Consul-Gen. KOICHI KAWAKAMI.

Consulate-General, Vancouver: 1177 West Hastings St, Suite 800, Vancouver, BC V6E 2K9; tel. (604) 684-5868; fax (604) 684-6939; e-mail consul@consuljpnvan.com; internet www.vancouver.ca.emb-japan.go.jp; Consul-Gen. SEIICHI OTSUKA.

JORDAN

Embassy: 100 Bronson Ave, Suite 701, Ottawa, ON K1R 6G8; tel. (613) 238-8090; fax (613) 232-3341; e-mail ottawa@fm.gov.jo; internet www.embassyofjordan.ca; Ambassador NABIL ALI MUHAMMAD BARTO.

KENYA

High Commission: 415 Laurier Ave East, Ottawa, ON K1N 6R4; tel. (613) 563-1773; fax (613) 233-6599; e-mail info@kenyahighcommission.ca; internet www.kenyahighcommission.ca; High Commr Prof. JUDITH M. BAHEMUKA.

KOREA, REPUBLIC

Embassy: 150 Boteler St, Ottawa, ON K1N 5A6; tel. (613) 244-5010; fax (613) 244-5043; e-mail web@mofat.go.kr; internet www.koreanembassy.ca; Ambassador SOO DONG KIM.

Consulate-General, Montréal: 1 pl. Ville-Marie, Suite 2015, Montréal, QC H3B 2C4; tel. (514) 845-2555; fax (514) 845-1119; e-mail korean@koreanconsulate.qc.ca; internet www.koreanconsulate.qc.ca; Consul-Gen. GIL-SOU SHIN.

Consulate-General, Toronto: 555 Avenue Rd, Toronto, ON M4V 2J7; tel. (416) 920-3809; fax (416) 924-7305; e-mail toronto@mofat.go.kr; internet www.koreanconsulate.on.ca; Consul-Gen. JI-IN HONG.

Consulate-General, Vancouver: 1090 West Georgia St, 16th Floor, Suite 1600, Vancouver, BC V6E 3V7; tel. (604) 681-9581; fax (604) 681-4864; e-mail web@mofat.go.kr; internet can-vancouver.mofat.go.kr; Consul-Gen. TONG MO SUH.

KUWAIT

Embassy: 333 Sussex Dr., Ottawa, ON K1N 1J9; tel. (613) 780-9999; fax (613) 780-9905; e-mail info@embassyofkuwait.com; internet www.embassyofkuwait.ca; Ambassador MUSAED RASHED A. AL-HAROUN.

LATVIA

Embassy: 350 Sparks St, Suite 1200, Ottawa, ON K1R 7S8; tel. (613) 238-6014; fax (613) 238-7044; e-mail embassy.canada@mfa.gov.lv; internet www.am.gov.lv/ottawa; Ambassador MARĢERS KRAMS.

LEBANON

Embassy: 640 Lyon St, Ottawa, ON K1S 3Z5; tel. (613) 236-5825; fax (613) 232-1609; e-mail info@lebanonembassy.ca; internet www.lebanonembassy.ca; Ambassador MASSOUD MAALOUF.

Consulate-General, Montréal: 40 chemin Côte Ste-Catherine, Outremont, Montréal, QC H2V 2A2; tel. (514) 276-2638; fax (514) 276-0090; e-mail consuliban@qc.aira.com; internet www.consulibanmontreal.org; Consul-Gen. KHALIL EL-HABRE.

LESOTHO

High Commission: 130 Albert St, Suite 1820, Ottawa, ON K1P 5G4; tel. (613) 234-0770; fax (613) 234-5665; e-mail lesotho.ottawa@bellnet.ca; internet www.lesothocanada.gov.ls; High Commr MOTŠEOA PHILADEL SENYANE.

LIBYA

People's Bureau: 81 Metcalfe St, Suite 1000, Ottawa, ON K1P 6K7; tel. (613) 230-0919; fax (613) 230-0683; e-mail info@libya-canada.org; internet www.libya-canada.org; Ambassador AHMED ALI JARRUD.

LIECHTENSTEIN

(See entry for Switzerland.)

LITHUANIA

Embassy: 130 Albert St, Suite 204, Ottawa, ON K1P 5G4; tel. (613) 567-5458; fax (613) 567-5315; e-mail litemb@storm.ca; internet www.lithuanianembassy.ca; Ambassador GINTĖ BERNADETA DAMUŠIS.

MACEDONIA, FORMER YUGOSLAV REPUBLIC

Embassy: 130 Albert St, Suite 1006, Ottawa, ON K1P 5G4; tel. (613) 234-3882; fax (613) 233-1852; e-mail ottawa@mfa.gov.mk; internet www3.sympatico.ca/emb.macedonia.ottawa; Ambassador SAŠKO NASEV.

Consulate-General, Toronto: 90 Eglinton Ave East, Suite 210, Toronto, ON M4P 2Y3; tel. (416) 322-2196; fax (416) 322-2412; Consul-Gen. MARTIN TRENEVSKI.

MADAGASCAR

Embassy: 3 Raymond St, Ottawa, ON K1R 1A3; tel. (613) 567-0505; fax (613) 567-2882; e-mail ambamadcanada@bellnet.ca; internet www.madagascar-embassy.ca; Ambassador SIMON CONSTANT HORACE.

MALAYSIA

High Commission: 60 Boteler St, Ottawa, ON K1N 8Y7; tel. (613) 241 5182; fax (613) 241-5214; e-mail malottawa@kln.gov.my; internet www.kln.gov.my/perwakilan/ottawa; High Commr HATIMI ABBAS (acting).

Consulate-General, Vancouver: 1805–111 West Georgia St, Vancouver, BC V6E 4M3; tel. (604) 685-9550; fax (604) 685-9520; e-mail cgenmly@axionet.com; internet www.kln.gov.my/perwakilan/vancouver; Consul-Gen. MOHAMMED HASSAN BIN BAL.

MALI

Embassy: 50 Goulburn Ave, Ottawa, ON K1N 8C8; tel. (613) 232-1501; fax (613) 232-7429; e-mail ambassadedumali@rogers.com; internet www.ambamalicanada.org; Ambassador MAMADOU BANDIOUGOU DIAWARA.

MEXICO

Embassy: 45 O'Connor St, Suite 1000, Ottawa, ON K1P 1A4; tel. (613) 233-8988; fax (613) 235-9123; e-mail info@embamexcan.com; internet www.sre.gob.mx/canada; Ambassador EMILIO RAFAEL JOSÉ GOICOECHEA LUNA.

Consulate-General, Montréal: 2055 Peel St, Suite 1000, Montréal, QC H3A 1V4; tel. (514) 288-2502; fax (514) 288-8287; e-mail comexmt@consulmex.qc.ca; internet www.sre.gob.mx/montreal; Consul-Gen. EDGARDO FLORES RIVAS.

Consulate-General, Toronto: Commerce Ct West, 199 Bay St, Suite 4440, POB 266, Toronto, ON M5L 1E9; tel. (416) 368-2875; fax (416) 368-8343; e-mail consulad@interlog.com; internet www.consulmex.com; Consul-Gen. CARLOS PUJALTE PINEIRO.

Consulate-General, Vancouver: 1177 West Hastings St, Suite 710, Vancouver, BC V6E 2K3; tel. (604) 684-3547; fax (604) 684-2485; e-mail mexico@direct.ca; internet www.consulmexvan.com; Consul-Gen. ANGEL VILLALOBOS RODRÍGUEZ.

MONGOLIA

Embassy: 151 Slater St, Suite 503, Ottawa, ON K1P 5H3; tel. (613) 569-3830; fax (613) 569-3916; e-mail mail@mongolembassy.org; internet www.mongolembassy.org; Ambassador Dr DUGERJAV GOTOV.

MONTSERRAT

(See entry for Eastern Caribbean States.)

MOROCCO

Embassy: 38 Range Rd, Ottawa, ON K1N 8J4; tel. (613) 236-7391; fax (613) 236-6164; e-mail sifamaot@bellnet.ca; internet www.ambamaroc.ca; Ambassador MUHAMMAD TANGI.

Consulate-General, Montréal: 2192 René Lévesque Blvd West, Montréal, QC H3H 1R6; tel. (514) 288-8750; fax (514) 288-4859; e-mail consumam@videotron.net; Consul-Gen. SOURIYA OTMANI.

MYANMAR

Embassy: 85 Range Rd, Suite 902–903, Ottawa, ON K1N 8J6; tel. (613) 232-9990; fax (613) 232-6999; e-mail meott@magma.ca; Chargé d'affaires a.i. U MAUNG MAUNG.

NETHERLANDS

Embassy: 350 Albert St, Suite 2020, Ottawa, ON K1R 1A4; tel. (877) 388-2443; fax (613) 237-6471; e-mail nlgovott@netcom.ca; internet www.netherlandsembassy.ca; Ambassador WIM J. P. GEERTS.

Consulate-General, Montréal: 1002 Sherbrooke St West, Suite 2201, Montréal, QC H3A 3L6; tel. (877) 388-2443; fax (514) 849-8260; e-mail nlgovmon@qc.aibn.com; internet www.cgmontreal.org; Consul-Gen. HANS GLAUBITZ.

Consulate-General, Toronto: 1 Dundas St West, Suite 2106, POB 2, Toronto, ON M5G 1Z3; tel. (416) 598-2520; fax (416) 598-8064; e-mail tor@minbuza.nl; internet www.dutchconsulate.toronto.on.ca; Consul-Gen. JOHANNES SYTZE KRAMER.

Consulate-General, Vancouver: 3 Bentall Centre, Suite 883, 595 Burrard St, Vancouver, POB 49068, BC V7X 1C4; tel. (604) 684-6448; fax (604) 684-3549; e-mail info@netherlandsconsulatevancouver.ca; internet www.mfa.nl/van; Consul-Gen. HENRI HUBERT DRIESSER.

NEW ZEALAND

High Commission: Clarica Centre, 99 Bank St, Suite 727, Ottawa, ON K1P 6G3; tel. (613) 238-5991; fax (613) 238-5707; e-mail info@nzhcottawa.org; internet www.nzembassy.com/canada; High Commr KATHLEEN (KATE) J. LACKEY.

Consulate-General, Vancouver: 888 Dunsmuir St, Suite 1200, Vancouver, BC V6C 3K4; tel. (604) 684-7388; fax (604) 684-7333; e-mail anne.chappaz@nzte.govt.nz; Consul-Gen. and Trade Commr ANNE BELINDA CHAPPAZ.

NIGER

Embassy: 38 Blackburn Ave, Ottawa, ON K1N 8A3; tel. (613) 232-4291; fax (613) 230-9808; e-mail ambanigeracanada@rogers.com; internet www.ambanigeracanada.ca; Ambassador NANA AICHA MOUCTARI FOUMAKOYE.

NIGERIA

High Commission: 295 Metcalfe St, Ottawa, ON K2P 1R9; tel. (613) 236-0521; fax (613) 236-0529; e-mail chancery@nigeriahcottawa; internet www.nigeriahcottawa.com; High Commr Prof. IYORWUESE HAGHER.

NORWAY

Embassy: 150 Metcalfe St, Suite 1300, Ottawa, ON K2P 1P1; tel. (613) 238-6571; fax (613) 238-2765; e-mail emb.ottawa@mfa.no; internet www.emb-norway.ca; Ambassador TOR BERNTIN NÆSS.

PAKISTAN

High Commission: 10 Range Rd, Ottawa, ON K1N 8J3; tel. (613) 238-7881; fax (613) 238-7296; e-mail parepottawa@rogers.com; internet www.pakmission.ca; High Commr MUSA JAVED CHOHAN.

Consulate-General, Montréal: 3421 Peel St, Montréal, QC H3A 1W7; tel. (514) 845-2297; fax (514) 845-1354; e-mail parepmontreal@bellnet.ca; internet www.pakmission.ca; Consul-Gen. SAIF ULLAH CHATTHA.

Consulate-General, Toronto: 1120 Finch Ave West, Suite 202, Toronto, ON M3J 3H7; tel. (416) 250-1255; fax (416) 250-1321; e-mail pareptoronto@rogers.com; internet www.pakmission.ca; Consul-Gen. Tassaduq Hussain.

PANAMA

Embassy: 130 Albert St, Suite 300, Ottawa, ON K1P 5G4; tel. (613) 236-7177; fax (613) 236-5775; e-mail embassyofpanama@gmail.com; Ambassador Romy Vásquez de González.

Consulate-General, Montréal: 1425 René Lévesque Blvd West, Suite 504, Montréal, QC H3G 1T7; tel. (514) 874-1929; fax (514) 874-1947; internet www.consulateofpanama.org; Consul-Gen. Isaac García Sitton.

Consulate-General, Toronto: 2788 Bathurst St, Suite 211, 2nd Floor, Toronto, ON M6B 3A3; tel. (416) 651-2350; fax (416) 651-3141; e-mail conpantor@look.ca; Consul-Gen. Gilberto A. Boyd Díaz.

Consulate-General, Vancouver: 1112 West Pender St, Suite 407, Vancouver, BC V6E 2S1; tel. (604) 682-6128; fax (604) 682-0528; Consul-Gen. Eduardo Arango Arias.

PAPUA NEW GUINEA

Papua New Guinea: 130 Albert St, Suite 300, Ottawa, ON K1A 5G4; fax (613) 236-5775; e-mail info@pngembassy.org; internet www.pngembassy.org; High Commr Evan J. Paki.

PARAGUAY

Embassy: 151 Slater St, Suite 501, Ottawa, ON K1P 5H3; tel. (613) 567-1283; fax (613) 567-1679; e-mail consularsection@embassyofparaguay.ca; internet www.embassyofparaguay.ca; Ambassador Juan Esteban O. Aguirre Martínez.

PERU

Embassy: 130 Albert St, Suite 1901, Ottawa, ON K1P 5G4; tel. (613) 238-1777; fax (613) 232-3062; e-mail emperuca@bellnet.ca; internet www.embassyofperu.ca; Ambassador Jorge Juan Castañeda Méndez.

Consulate-General, Montréal: 550 Sherbrooke St West, Tour Ouest, Suite 970, Montréal, QC H3A 1B9; tel. (514) 844-5123; fax (514) 843-8425; e-mail perou@videotron.net; internet www.consuladoperumontreal.com; Consul-Gen. Lucía Trindade de Buitron.

Consulate-General, Toronto: 10 St Mary St, Suite 301, Toronto, ON M4Y 1P9; tel. (416) 963-9696; fax (416) 963-9074; e-mail info@conperutoronto.com; internet www.conperutoronto.com; Consul-Gen. Gabriel García Pike.

Consulate-General, Vancouver: 505 Burrard St, Suite 260, Vancouver, BC V7X 1M6; tel. (604) 662-8880; fax (604) 662-3564; e-mail infovan@consuladoperu.ca; internet www.consuladoperu.ca/vancouver; Consul-Gen. Carlos M. Román Heredia.

PHILIPPINES

Embassy: 130 Albert St, Suite 606, Ottawa, ON K1P 5G4; tel. (613) 233-1121; fax (613) 233-4165; e-mail ambassador@philippineembassy.ca; internet philippineembassy.ca; Ambassador José S. Brillantes.

Consulate-General, Toronto: 161 Eglinton Ave East, Toronto, ON M4P 1J5; tel. (416) 922-7181; fax (416) 922-2638; e-mail torontopc@philcongen-toronto.com; tel. www.philcongen-toronto.com; Consul-Gen. Alejandro Mosquera.

Consulate-General, Vancouver: 700 West Pender St, Suite 1405, Vancouver, BC V6C 1G8; tel. (604) 685-7645; fax (604) 685-9945; e-mail phyvr@telus.net; internet vancouverpcg.net; Consul-Gen. Ruth Morales Prado.

POLAND

Embassy: 443 Daly Ave, Ottawa, ON K1N 6H3; tel. (613) 789-0468; fax (613) 789-1218; e-mail ottawa@ottawa.polemb.net; internet www.ottawa.polemb.net; Ambassador Piotr Ogrodzinski.

Consulate-General, Montréal: 1500 Pine Ave West, Montréal, QC H3G 1B4; tel. (514) 937-9481; fax (514) 937-7271; e-mail montreal@montreal.polemb.net; internet www.montreal.polemb.net; Consul-Gen. Włodzimierz Zdunowski.

Consulate-General, Toronto: 2603 Lakeshore Blvd West, Toronto, ON M8V 1G5; tel. (416) 252-5471; fax (416) 252-0509; e-mail toronto@toronto.polemb.net; internet www.torontokg.polemb.net; Consul-Gen. Piotr Konowrocki.

Consulate-General, Vancouver: 1177 West Hastings St, Suite 1600, Vancouver, BC V6E 2K3; tel. (604) 688-3530; fax (604) 688-3537; e-mail vancouver@vancouver.polemb.net; internet www.vancouverkg.polemb.net; Consul-Gen. Maciej Krych.

PORTUGAL

Embassy: 645 Island Park Dr., Ottawa, ON K1Y 0B8; tel. (613) 729-0883; fax (613) 729-4236; e-mail embportugal@embportugal-ottawa.org; internet www.embportugal-ottawa.org; Ambassador João Pedro da Silveira Carvalho.

Consulate-General, Montréal: 2020 University St, Suite 2425, Montréal, QC H3A 2A5; tel. (514) 499-0359; fax (514) 499-0366; e-mail mail@cgmrl.dgaccp.pt; Consul-Gen. Carlos M. Folhadela de Macedo Oliveira.

Consulate-General, Toronto: 438 University Ave, 14th Floor, Suite 1400, Toronto, ON M5G 2K8; tel. (416) 217-0966; fax (416) 217-0973; e-mail mail@toronto.dgacp.pt; Consul-Gen. Maria Amélia Maio de Paiva.

Consulate-General, Vancouver: 925 West Georgia St, Suite 920, Vancouver, BC V6C 3L2; tel. (604) 688-6514; fax (604) 685-7042; e-mail mail@cnvan.dgaccp.pt; Consul-Gen. Joao Luis Laranjeira de Abreu.

ROMANIA

Embassy: 655 Rideau St, Ottawa, ON K1N 6A3; tel. (613) 789-3709; fax (613) 789-4365; e-mail romania@romanian-embassy.com; internet ottawa.mae.ro; Ambassador Elena Stefoi.

Consulate-General, Montréal: 1010 rue Sherbrooke Ouest, Bureau 610, Etage 6, Montréal, QC H3A 2R7; tel. (514) 876-1792; fax (514) 876-1797; e-mail romanian.consulate@bellnet.ca; internet montreal.mae.ro; Consul-Gen. Ion-Bogdan Bucur.

Consulate-General, Toronto: 555 Richmond St West, Unit 1108, POB 210, Toronto, ON M5V 3B1; tel. (416) 585-5802; fax (416) 585-4798; e-mail cgrt@romaniacanada.com; internet toronto.mae.ro; Consul-Gen. Valentin Naumescu.

RUSSIA

Embassy: 285 Charlotte St, Ottawa, ON K1N 8L5; tel. (613) 235-4341; fax (613) 236-6342; e-mail rusemb@rogers.com; internet www.rusembcanada.mid.ru; Ambassador Georgii Mamedov.

Consulate-General, Montréal: 3655 Museum Ave, Montréal, QC H3G 2E1; tel. (514) 843-5901; fax (514) 842-2012; e-mail consulat_mtl@bellnet.ca; internet www.montreal.mid.ru; Consul-Gen. Igor Golubovskiy.

Consulate-General, Toronto: 175 Bloor St East, South Tower, Suite 801, Toronto, ON M4W 3R8; tel. (416) 962-9911; fax (416) 962-6611; e-mail rusconsul@bellnet.ca; internet www.toronto.mid.ru; Consul-Gen. Andrey Veklenko.

RWANDA

Rwanda: 121 Sherwood Drive, Ottawa, ON K1Y 3V1; tel. (613) 569-5420; fax (613) 569-5421; e-mail generalinfo@ambarwaottawa.ca; internet www.ambarwaottawa.ca; Ambassador Edda Mukabagwiza.

SAINT CHRISTOPHER AND NEVIS

(See entry for Eastern Caribbean States.)

SAINT LUCIA

(See entry for Eastern Caribbean States.)

SAINT VINCENT AND THE GRENADINES

(See entry for Eastern Caribbean States.)

SAUDI ARABIA

Embassy: 201 Sussex Dr., Ottawa, ON K1N 1K6; tel. (613) 237-4100; fax (613) 237-0567; Ambassador Dr Abdulaziz H. al-Sowayegh.

SENEGAL

Embassy: 57 Marlborough Ave, Ottawa, ON K1N 8E8; tel. (613) 238-6392; fax (613) 238-2695; e-mail ambassn@sympatico.ca; Ambassador Issakha Mbacke.

SERBIA

Embassy: 17 Blackburn Ave, Ottawa, ON K1N 8A2; tel. (613) 233-6289; fax (613) 233-7850; e-mail diplomat@serbianembassy.ca; internet www.serbianembassy.ca; Ambassador Dušan Batakovic.

Consulate-General, Toronto: 377 Spadina Rd, Toronto, ON M5P 2V7; tel. (416) 483-1080; fax (416) 483-1847; e-mail info@gktoronto.com; internet www.gktoronto.com; Consul-Gen. Dragan Grkovic.

SLOVAKIA

Embassy: 50 Rideau Terrace, Ottawa, ON K1M 2A1; tel. (613) 749-4442; fax (613) 749-4989; e-mail ottawa@slovakembassy.ca; internet www.ottawa.mfa.sk; Ambassador Stanislav Opiela.

SLOVENIA

Embassy: 150 Metcalfe St, Suite 2200, Ottawa, ON K2P 1P1; tel. (613) 565-5781; fax (613) 565-5783; e-mail vot@gov.si; internet ottawa.embassy.si/en; Ambassador TOMAZ KUNSTELJ.

SOUTH AFRICA

High Commission: 15 Sussex Dr., Ottawa, ON K1M 1M8; tel. (613) 744-0330; fax (613) 741-1639; e-mail rsafrica@southafrica-canada.ca; internet www.southafrica-canada.ca; High Commr ABRAHAM SOKAYA NKOMO.

Consulate-General, Toronto: 110 Sheppard Ave East, Suite 600, Toronto, ON M2N 6Y8; tel. (416) 944-8825; fax (416) 944-0925; e-mail njemlan@foreign.gov.za; Consul-Gen. MANLEY BARNARD.

SPAIN

Embassy: 74 Stanley Ave, Ottawa, ON K1M 1P4; tel. (613) 747-2252; fax (613) 744-1224; e-mail emb.ottawa@mae.es; internet www.mae.es/embajadas/ottawa; Ambassador MARIANO ALONSO-BURÓN Y ABERASTURI.

Consulate-General, Montréal: 1 Westmount Sq., Suite 1456, Montréal, QC H3Z 2P9; tel. (514) 935-5235; fax (514) 935-4655; e-mail conspmontreal@mail.mae.es; Consul-Gen. CARLOS DÍAZ VALCARCEL.

Consulate-General, Toronto: 2 Bloor St East, Suite 1201, Toronto, ON M4W 1A8; tel. (416) 977-1661; fax (416) 593-4949; Consul-Gen. JULIO FERNÁNDEZ TORREJÓN.

SRI LANKA

High Commission: 333 Laurier Ave West, Suite 1204, Ottawa, ON K1P 1C1; tel. (613) 233-8449; fax (613) 238-8448; e-mail slhcit@rogers.com; internet www.srilankahcottawa.org; High Commr AKURANAGE WEERASINGHE PATHIRAJA (acting).

Consulate-General, Toronto: 40 St Claire Ave West, Suite 405, Toronto, ON M4V 1M2; tel. (416) 323-9133; fax (416) 323-3205; e-mail srilanka@bellnet.ca; Consul-Gen. BANDULA PARAKUM JAYASEKARA.

SUDAN

Embassy: 354 Stewart St, Ottawa, ON K1N 6K8; tel. (613) 235-4000; fax (613) 235-6880; e-mail sudanembassy-canada@rogers.com; internet www.sudanembassy.ca; Ambassador Dr FAIZA HASSAN TAHA ARMOUSA.

SWEDEN

Embassy: 377 Dalhousie St, Ottawa, ON K1N 9N8; tel. (613) 244-8200; fax (613) 241-2277; e-mail sweden.ottawa@foreign.ministry.se; internet www.swedishembassy.ca; Ambassador INGRID M. IREMARK.

SWITZERLAND

(also responsible for the interests of Liechtenstein)

Embassy: 5 Marlborough Ave, Ottawa, ON K1N 8E6; tel. (613) 235 1837; fax (613) 563-1394; e-mail ott.vertretung@eda.admin.ch; internet www.eda.admin.ch/canada; Ambassador WERNER BAUMANN.

Consulate-General, Montréal: 1572 Dr Penfield Ave, Montréal, QC H3G 1C4; tel. (514) 932-7181; fax (514) 932-9028; e-mail mon.vertretung@eda.admin.ch; Consul-Gen. CLAUDE DUVOISIN.

Consulate-General, Toronto: 154 University Ave, Suite 601, Toronto, ON M5H 3Y9; tel. (416) 593-5371; fax (416) 593-5083; e-mail tor.vertretung@eda.admin.ch; Consul-Gen. BRUNO RYFF.

Consulate-General, Vancouver: World Trade Centre, Suite 790-999 Canada Pl., Vancouver, BC V6C 3E1; tel. (604) 684-2231; fax (604) 684-2806; e-mail van.vertretung@eda.admin.ch; Consul-Gen. WALTER DEPLAZES.

SYRIA

Embassy: 151 Slater St, Suite 1000, Ottawa, ON K1P 5H3; tel. (613) 569-5556; fax (613) 569-3800; e-mail info@syrianembassy.ca; internet www.syrianembassy.ca; Ambassador JAMIL SAKR.

TANZANIA

High Commission: 50 Range Rd, Ottawa, ON K1N 8J4; tel. (613) 232-1509; fax (613) 232-5184; e-mail contact@tzrepottawa.ca; internet www.tzrepottawa.ca; High Commr PETER ALLAN KALLAGHE.

THAILAND

Embassy: 180 Island Park Dr., Ottawa, ON K1Y 0A2; tel. (613) 722-4444; fax (613) 722-6624; e-mail thaiott@magma.ca; internet www.thaiembottawa.org; Ambassador SNANCHART DEVAHASTIN.

Consulate-General, Vancouver: 1040 Burrard St, Vancouver, BC V6E 3Z3; tel. (604) 687-1143; fax (604) 687-4434; e-mail info@thaicongenvancouver.org; Consul-Gen. KOSIT CHATPAIBOON.

TOGO

Embassy: 12 Range Rd, Ottawa, ON K1N 8J3; tel. (613) 238-5916; fax (613) 235-6425; e-mail ambatogoca@hotmail.com; Ambassador BAWOUMONDOM AMELETE.

TRINIDAD AND TOBAGO

High Commission: 200 First Ave, 3rd Level, Ottawa, ON K1S 2G6; tel. (613) 232-2418; fax (613) 232-4349; e-mail ottawa@ttmissions.com; internet www.ttmissions.com; High Commr CAMILLE ROBINSON–REGIS.

Consulate-General, Toronto: 2005 Sheppard Ave East, Suite 303, Toronto, ON M2J 5B4; tel. (416) 495-9442; fax (416) 495-6934; e-mail information@ttconsulatetoronto.com; internet www.ttconsulatetoronto.com; Consul-Gen. MICHAEL G. LASHLEY.

TUNISIA

Embassy: 515 O'Connor St, Ottawa, ON K1S 3P8; tel. (613) 237-0330; fax (613) 237-7939; e-mail atottawa@comnet.ca; Ambassador MOULDI SAKRI.

TURKEY

Embassy: 197 Wurtemburg St, Ottawa, ON K1N 8L9; tel. (613) 789-4044; fax (613) 789-3442; e-mail turkishottawa@mfa.gov.tr; internet www.turkishembassy.com; Ambassador RAFET AKGÜNAY.

UGANDA

High Commission: 231 Cobourg St, Ottawa, ON K1N 8J2; tel. (613) 789-7797; fax (613) 789-8909; e-mail uhc@ugandahighcommission.com; internet www.ugandahighcommission.com; High Commr GEORGE M. ABOLA.

UKRAINE

Embassy: 310 Somerset St West, Ottawa, ON K2P 0J9; tel. (613) 230-2961; fax (613) 230-2400; e-mail emb_ca@ukremb.ca; internet www.ukremb.ca; Ambassador Dr IHOR OSTASH.

Consulate-General, Toronto: 2120 Bloor St West, Toronto, ON M6S 1M8; tel. (416) 763-3114; fax (416) 763-2323; e-mail tem-ukraine@sympatico.ca; internet ukrconsulate.com; Consul-Gen. OLEKSANDR DANYLEIKO.

UNITED ARAB EMIRATES

Embassy: 125 Boteler St, Ottawa, ON K1N 0A4; tel. (613) 565-7272; fax (613) 565-8007; e-mail safara@uae-embassy.com; internet www.uae-embassy.com; Ambassador HASSAN MUHAMMAD OBAID AL-SUWAIDI.

UNITED KINGDOM

High Commission: 80 Elgin St, Ottawa, ON K1P 5K7; tel. (613) 237-1530; fax (613) 237-7980; e-mail generalenquiries@britainincanada.org; internet www.britainincanada.org; Ambassador ANTHONY JOYCE CARY.

Consulate-General, Montréal: 1000 rue de la Gauchetière ouest, Suite 4200, Montréal, QC H3B 4W5; tel. (514) 866-5863; fax (514) 866-0202; e-mail bcgmtl@bellnet.ca; Consul-Gen. ANNE JARRETT.

Consulate-General, Toronto: 777 Bay St, Suite 2800, College Park, Toronto, ON M5G 2G2; tel. (416) 593-1290; fax (416) 593-1229; e-mail toronto@britainincanada.org; Consul-Gen. NICHOLAS ARMOUR.

Consulate-General, Vancouver: 1111 Melville St, Suite 800, Vancouver, BC V6E 3V6; tel. (604) 683-4421; fax (604) 681-0693; e-mail vancouver@britainincanada.org; Consul-Gen. ALEXANDER BUDDEN.

USA

Embassy: 490 Sussex Dr., Ottawa, ON K1N 1G8; tel. (613) 238-5335; fax (613) 688-3082; e-mail web1@ottawa.usembassy.gov; internet ottawa.usembassy.gov; Ambassador DAVID HORTON WILKINS.

Consulate-General, Calgary: 615 Macleod Trail, South East, Suite 1050, Calgary, AB T2G 4T8; tel. (403) 266-8962; fax (403) 264-6630; internet calgary.usconsulate.gov; Consul-Gen. THOMAS HUFFAKER.

Consulate-General, Halifax: Purdy's Wharf Tower II, Suite 904, 1969 Upper Water St, Halifax, NS B3J 3R7; tel. (902) 429-2480; fax (902) 423-6861; internet halifax.usconsulate.gov; Consul-Gen. HAROLD FOSTER.

Consulate-General, Montréal: 1155 St Alexandre St, Montréal, QC H2Z 1Z2; tel. (514) 398-9695; fax (514) 398-0973; e-mail usconsulatemtl@state.gov; internet montreal.usconsulate.gov; Consul-Gen. LEE MCCLENNY.

Consulate-General, Québec: 2 pl. Terasse Dufferin, POB 939, Québec, QC G1R 4T9; tel. (418) 692-2095; fax (418) 692-4640; internet quebec.usconsulate.gov; Consul-Gen. DAVID FETTER.

Consulate-General, Toronto: 360 University Ave, Toronto, ON M5G 1S4; tel. (416) 595-1700; fax (416) 595-1090; internet toronto.usconsulate.gov; Consul-Gen. JOHN NAY.

Consulate-General, Winnipeg: 201 Portage Ave, Suite 860, Winnipeg, MB R3B 3K6; tel. (204) 940-1800; fax (204) 940-1809; internet winnipeg.usconsulate.gov; Consul-Gen. MARY SPEER.

Consulate-General, Vancouver: 1095 West Pender St, 21st Floor, Vancouver, BC V6E 2M6; tel. (604) 685-4311; fax (604) 685-5285; internet vancouver.usconsulate.gov; Consul-Gen. PHILLIP CHICOLA.

URUGUAY

Embassy: 130 Albert St, Suite 1905, Ottawa, ON K1P 5G4; tel. (613) 234-2727; fax (613) 233-4670; e-mail embassy@embassyofuruguay.ca; internet embassyofuruguay.ca; Ambassador Dr ALVARO MARCELO MOERZINGER PAGANI.

VENEZUELA

Embassy: 32 Range Rd, Ottawa, ON K1N 8J4; tel. (613) 235-5151; fax (613) 235-3205; e-mail info.canada@misionvenezuela.org; internet www.misionvenezuela.org; Chargé d'affaires a.i. JOSÉ ANTONIO RODRÍGUEZ DE LA SIERRA.

Consulate-General, Montréal: 2055 Peel St, Suite 400, Montréal, QC H3A 1V4; tel. (514) 842-3417; fax (514) 287-7101; e-mail informacion@consulvenemontreal.org; internet www.consulvenemontreal.org; Chargé d'affaires ELIO RAFAEL VITRIAGO ABREU.

Consulate-General, Toronto: 365 Bloor St East, Suite 1904, Toronto, ON M4W 3L4; tel. (416) 960-6070; fax (416) 960-6077; e-mail info@consulventoronto.com; internet www.consulventoronto.com; Dep. Consul-Gen. MIRNA QUERO DE PENA.

VIET NAM

Embassy: 470 Wilbrod St, Ottawa, ON K1N 6M8; tel. (613) 236-0772; fax (613) 236-2704; e-mail vietem@istar.ca; internet www.vietnamembassy-canada.ca; Ambassador NGUYEN DUC HUNG.

YEMEN

Embassy: 54 Chamberlain Ave, Ottawa, ON K1S 1V9; tel. (613) 729-6627; fax (613) 729-8915; e-mail info@yemenincanada.ca; internet www.yemenincanada.ca; Ambassador Dr ABDULLAH ABDULWALI NASHER.

ZAMBIA

High Commission: 151 Slater St, Suite 205, Ottawa, ON K1P 5H3; tel. (613) 232-4400; fax (613) 232-4410; e-mail info@zambiahighcommission.ca; internet www.zambiahighcommission.ca; High Commr DAVID CLIFFORD SAVIYE.

ZIMBABWE

High Commission: 332 Somerset St West, Ottawa, ON K2P 0J9; tel. (613) 237-4388; fax (613) 563-8269; e-mail zimembassy@bellnet.ca; internet www.zimbabweembassy.ca; High Commr FLORENCE ZANO CHIDEYA.

Note: The ambassador to the USA or to the UN (each based in the USA—see The USA, Directory on Public Affairs) is also accredited as ambassador or, in the case of Commonwealth countries, high commissioner to Canada for the following countries: Azerbaijan, Belize, Bhutan, Botswana, Cambodia, Cape Verde, the Central African Republic, Chad, the Comoros, the Republic of the Congo, Cyprus, Djibouti, Equatorial Guinea, Eritrea, Estonia, Fiji, The Gambia, Georgia, Guinea-Bissau, Kazakhstan, Democratic People's Republic of Korea, Kyrgyzstan, Laos, Luxembourg, Malta, Marshall Islands, Mauritius, Moldova, Mozambique, Namibia, Nepal, Nicaragua, Oman, Papua New Guinea, Qatar, Rwanda, Samoa, São Tomé and Príncipe, Seychelles, Sierra Leone, Singapore, Solomon Islands, Suriname, Swaziland, Tonga, Turkmenistan, Uzbekistan and Zambia.

CANADIAN REPRESENTATION ABROAD

Embassies and High Commissions

(All diplomatic offices listed below are embassies or high commissions, unless otherwise indicated.)

Afghanistan: House 256, St 15, Wazir Akbar Khan, POB 2052, Kabul; tel. (799) 742800; fax (799) 742805; e-mail info.afghanistan@international.gc.ca; internet www.afghanistan.gc.ca; Ambassador RON HOFFMANN.

Albania: see Italy.

Algeria: BP 48, 18 rue Mustapha Khalef, Ben Aknoun, 16035 Algiers; tel. (70) 08-30-00; fax (70) 08-30-70; e-mail alger@international.gc.ca; internet www.international.gc.ca/world/embassies/algeria; Ambassador PATRICK PARISOT.

Andorra: see Spain.

Angola: see Zimbabwe.

Antigua and Barbuda: see Barbados.

Argentina: Tagle 2828, C1425EEH Buenos Aires; tel. (11) 4808-1000; fax (11) 4808-1111; e-mail bairs-webmail@international.gc.ca; internet www.buenosaires.gc.ca; Ambassador TIM MARTIN; also covers Paraguay.

Armenia: see Russia.

Australia: Commonwealth Ave, Canberra, ACT 2600; tel. (2) 6270-4000; fax (2) 6270-4081; e-mail cnbra@international.gc.ca; internet www.australia.gc.ca; High Commr MICHAEL LEIR; also covers the Marshall Islands, the Federated States of Micronesia, Nauru, Palau, Papua New Guinea, Solomon Islands and Vanuatu.

Austria: Laurenzerberg 2, 1010 Vienna; tel. (1) 531-38-3000; fax (1) 531-38-3321; e-mail vienn@international.gc.ca; internet geo.international.gc.ca/canada-europa/austria; Ambassador MARIE GERVAIS-VIDRICAIRE.

Azerbaijan: see Turkey.

Bahamas: see Jamaica.

Bahrain: see Saudi Arabia.

Bangladesh: House 16A, Rd 48, Gulshan Model Town, POB 569, Dhaka 1212; tel. (2) 988-7091; fax (2) 882-3043; e-mail dhaka@international.gc.ca; internet www.bangladesh.gc.ca; High Commr ROBERT MCDOUGALL.

Barbados: Bishop's Court Hill, POB 404, St Michael, Bridgetown; tel. 429-3550; fax 429-3780; e-mail bdgtn@international.gc.ca; internet geo.international.gc.ca/latin-america/barbados; High Commr DAVID MARSHALL; also covers Antigua and Barbuda, Dominica, Grenada, Saint Christopher and Nevis, Saint Lucia, Saint Vincent and the Grenadines, the United Kingdom Overseas Territories of Anguilla, the British Virgin Islands and Montserrat, and the French Overseas Departments of Guadeloupe and Martinique.

Belarus: see Poland.

Belgium: 2 ave de Tervuren, 1040 Brussels; tel. (2) 741-06-11; fax (2) 741-06-43; e-mail bru@international.gc.ca; internet www.ambassade-canada.be; Ambassador LOUIS DE LORIMIER; also covers Luxembourg.

Belize: see Guatemala.

Benin: see Côte d'Ivoire.

Bhutan: see India.

Bolivia: see Peru.

Bosnia and Herzegovina: 71000 Sarajevo, 4 Grbavicka; tel. (33) 222033; fax (33) 222044; e-mail sjevo@international.gc.ca; internet www.dfait-maeci.gc.ca/canada-europa/bosnia-herzegovina; Ambassador DAVID HUTCHINGS.

Botswana: see Zimbabwe.

Brazil: Setor de Embaixadas Sul, Avda das Naçoes, Suite 803, Lote 16, 70410-900, Brasília, DF; tel. (61) 33424-5400; fax (61) 33424-5490; e-mail brsla@international.gc.ca; internet www.canadainternational.gc.ca/brazil; Ambassador PAUL HUNT.

Brunei: 1 Jalan McArthur, 5th Floor, Bandar Seri Begawan BS 8711; tel. (2) 220043; fax (2) 220040; e-mail bsbgn@international.gc.ca; internet www.dfait-maeci.gc.ca/brunei; High Commr LÉOPOLD BATTEL.

Bulgaria: see Romania.

Burkina Faso: 316 Ave Professeur Joseph Ki-Zerbo, 01 BP 548, Ouagadougou 01; tel. 50-31-18-94; fax 50-31-19-00; e-mail ouaga@

international.gc.ca; internet www.dfait-maeci.gc.ca/burkina_faso; Ambassador JULES SAVARIA.

Burundi: see Kenya.

Cambodia: Villa 9, R. V. Senei Vinnavaut Oum, Sangkat Chartaumuk, Khan Daun Penh, Phnom-Penh; tel. (23) 213470; fax (23) 211389; e-mail pnmpn@international.gc.ca; internet geo.international.gc.ca/asia/cambodia; Chargé d'affaires a.i. MICHAEL RYMEK.

Cameroon: Immeuble Stamatiades, pl. de l'Hôtel de Ville, BP 572, Yaoundé; tel. 2223-2311; fax 2222-1090; e-mail yunde@international.gc.ca; internet www.dfait-maeci.gc.ca/world/embassies/cameroon; High Commr M. JEAN PIERRE LAVOIE; also covers the Central African Republic, Chad, Equatorial Guinea, Gabon and São Tomé and Príncipe.

Cape Verde: see Senegal.

Central African Republic: see Cameroon.

Chad: see Cameroon.

Chile: Casilla 139, Correo 10, Santiago; tel. (2) 652-3800; fax (2) 652-3912; e-mail stago@international.gc.ca; internet geo.international.gc.ca/latin-america/chile; Ambassador NORBERT KALISCH.

China, People's Republic: 19 Dong Zhi Men Wai Dajie, Chao Yang Qu, Beijing 100600; tel. (10) 51394000; fax (10) 51394435; e-mail beijing@international.gc.ca; internet www.beijing.gc.ca; Ambassador ROBERT WRIGHT; also covers Mongolia.

Colombia: Carrera 7, No 115-33, 14°, Bogotá, DC; tel. (1) 657-9800; fax (1) 657-9912; e-mail bgota@international.gc.ca; internet geo.international.gc.ca/latin-america/colombia; Ambassador MATTHEW LEVIN.

Comoros: see Tanzania.

Congo, Democratic Republic: 17, ave Pumbu, Commune de la gombe, BP 8341, Kinshasa 1; tel. (89) 8950310; fax (99) 9975403; e-mail kinshasa@international.gc.ca; internet www.dfait-maeci.gc.ca/world/embassies/drc; Ambassador SIGRID JOHNSON.

Costa Rica: Oficentro Ejecutivo La Sabana, Edif. 5, 3°, detrás de la Contracoría, Centro Colón, Apdo 351, 1007 San José; tel. 2242-4400; fax 2242-4410; e-mail sjcra@international.gc.ca; internet geo.international.gc.ca/latin-america/sanjose; Ambassador NEIL REEDER; also covers Honduras and Nicaragua.

Côte d'Ivoire: Immeuble Trade Centre, 23 ave Noguès, BP 4104, Le Plateau, Abidjan 01; tel. 20-30-07-00; fax 20-30-07-20; e-mail abdjn@international.gc.ca; internet www.dfait-maeci.gc.ca/abidjan; Ambassador MARIE-ISABELLE MASSIP; also covers Benin, Niger, Liberia and Sierra Leone.

Croatia: 10000 Zagreb, Prilaz Gjure Dezelica; tel. (1) 4881200; fax (1) 4881230; e-mail zagrb@international.gc.ca; internet geo.international.gc.ca/canada-europa/croatia; Ambassador THOMAS MARR.

Cuba: Calle 30, No 518, esq. Avda 7, Miramar, Havana; tel. (7) 204-2516; fax (7) 204-2044; e-mail havan@international.gc.ca; internet www.havana.gc.ca; Ambassador JEAN-PIERRE JUNEAU.

Cyprus: see Syria.

Czech Republic: Muchova 6, 160 00 Prague 6; tel. (2) 72101800; fax (2) 72101894; e-mail prgue@international.gc.ca; internet www.canada.cz; Ambassador MICHAEL CALCOTT; also covers Slovakia.

Denmark: Kr. Bernikowsgade 1, 1105 Copenhagen K; tel. 33-48-32-00; fax 33-48-32-20; e-mail copen@international.gc.ca; internet www.denmark.gc.ca; Ambassador PETER LUNDY.

Djibouti: see Ethiopia.

Dominica: see Barbados.

Dominican Republic: Capitan Eugenio de Marchena No 39, La Esperilla, POB 2054, Santo Domingo, DN; tel. 685-1136; fax 682-2691; e-mail sdmgo@international.gc.ca; internet www.santodomingo.gc.ca; Ambassador PATRICIA FORTIER.

Ecuador: Edif. Josueth González, 4°, Avda 6 de Diciembre 28-16 y Paul Rivet, Apdo 17-11-65-12, Quito; tel. (2) 2455-499; fax (2) 2277-672; e-mail quito@international.gc.ca; internet www.ecuador.gc.ca; Ambassador CHRISTIAN LAPOINTE.

Egypt: POB 1667, 26 Kamel El Shenawy, Cairo; tel. (2) 7918700; fax (2) 7918860; e-mail cairo@international.gc.ca; internet www.dfait-maeci.gc.ca/cairo; Ambassador FERRY DE KERAKHOVE.

El Salvador: Centro Financiero Gigante, 63 Avda Sur y Alameda Roosevelt, San Salvador; tel. 2279-4655; fax 2279-0765; e-mail ssal@international.gc.ca; internet www.sansalvador.gc.ca; Ambassador CLAIRE POULIN.

Equatorial Guinea: see Cameroon.

Eritrea: see Kenya.

Estonia (Embassy Office): Toom Kooli 13, 15168 Tallinn; tel. 627-3311; fax 627-3312; e-mail tallinn@canada.ee; internet www.dfait-maeci.gc.ca/canada-europa/baltics; Ambassador R. SCOTT HEATHERINGTON (resident in Latvia).

Ethiopia: POB 1130, Addis Ababa; tel. (11) 3713022; fax (11) 3713033; e-mail addis@international.gc.ca; internet www.dfait-maeci.gc.ca/world/embassies/ethiopia; Ambassador YVES BOULANGER; also covers Djibouti.

Fiji: see New Zealand.

Finland: Pohjoisesplanadi 25 B, POB 779, 00101 Helsinki; tel. (9) 228530; fax (9) 601060; e-mail hsnki@international.gc.ca; internet www.canada.fi; Ambassador SCOTT FRASER.

France: 35–37 ave Montaigne, 75008 Paris; tel. 1-44-43-29-00; fax 1-44-43-29-99; e-mail paris@international.gc.ca; internet www.amb-canada.fr; Ambassador MARC LORTIE; also covers Monaco and the French Overseas Collectivity of French Polynesia.

Gabon: see Cameroon.

The Gambia: see Senegal.

Georgia: see Turkey.

Germany: Leipziger Platz 17, 10117 Berlin; tel. (30) 203120; fax (30) 20312590; e-mail brlin@international.gc.ca; internet www.dfait-maeci.gc.ca/canada-europa/germany; Ambassador PETER BOEHM.

Ghana: 42 Independence Ave, Sankara Interchange, POB 1639, Accra; tel. (21) 211521; fax (21) 211523; e-mail accra@international.gc.ca; internet www.dfait-maeci.gc.ca/accra; High Commr DARREN SCHEMMER; also covers Togo.

Greece: Odos Ioannou Gennadiou 4, 115 21 Athens; tel. (1) 7273400; fax (1) 7273460; e-mail athns@international.gc.ca; internet geo.international.gc.ca/canada-europa/greece; Ambassador RENATA WIELGOSZ.

Grenada: see Barbados.

Guatemala: 13 Calle 8-44, Zona 10, Edyma Plaza, Apdo 400, Guatemala City; tel. (2) 363-4348; fax (2) 365-1210; e-mail gtmla@international.gc.ca; internet geo.international.gc.ca/latin-america/guatemala; Ambassador KENNETH M. COOK; also covers Belize.

Guinea: see Senegal.

Guinea-Bissau: see Senegal.

Guyana: High and Young Sts, POB 10880, Georgetown; tel. 227-2081; fax 225-8380; e-mail grgtn@international.gc.ca; internet www.guyana.gc.ca; High Commr CHARLES COURT; also covers Suriname.

Haiti: Route de Delmas entre Delmas 71 et 75, BP 826, Port-au-Prince; tel. 2249-9000; fax 2249-9920; e-mail prnce@international.gc.ca; internet www.port-au-prince.gc.ca; Ambassador GILLES RIVARD.

Holy See: Via della Conciliazione 4D, 00193 Rome, Italy; tel. (06) 68307316; fax (06) 68806283; e-mail vatcn@international.gc.ca; internet geo.international.gc.ca/canada-europa/holysee; Ambassador ANNE LEAHY.

Honduras: see Costa Rica.

Hungary: 1027 Budapest, Ganz u. 12-14; tel. (1) 392-3360; fax (1) 392-3390; e-mail bpest@international.gc.ca; internet www.canadaeuropa.gc.ca/hungary; Ambassador PIERRE GUIMOND; also covers Slovenia.

Iceland: Túngata 14, 101 Reykjavík; tel. 5756500; fax 5756501; e-mail rkjvk@international.gc.ca; internet www.canada.is; Ambassador ANNA BLAUVELDT.

India: 7–8 Shantipath, Chanakyapuri, POB 5207, New Delhi 110021; tel. (11) 41782000; fax (11) 41782020; e-mail delhi@international.gc.ca; internet www.india.gc.ca; High Commr JOSEPH CARON; also covers Bhutan and Nepal.

Indonesia: POB 8324/JKS.MP, Jakarta 12083; tel. (21) 25507800; fax (21) 25507811; e-mail jkrta@international.gc.ca; internet www.jakarta.gc.ca; Ambassador JOHN T. HOLMES; also covers Timor-Leste.

Iran: POB 11155-4647, 57 Shahid Sarafraz St, Ostad Motahari Ave, Tehran 15868; tel. (21) 81520000; fax (21) 81523900; e-mail teran@international.gc.ca; internet www.iran.gc.ca; Chargé d'affaires a.i. JAMES J. CARRICK.

Iraq: see Jordan.

Ireland: 7–8 Wilton Terrace, Dublin 2; tel. (1) 2344000; fax (1) 2344001; e-mail dubln@international.gc.ca; internet www.canada.ie; Ambassador PATRICK G. BINNS.

Israel: POB 9442, 3–5 Nirim St, Tel-Aviv 67060; tel. 3-6363300; fax 3-6363380; e-mail taviv@international.gc.ca; internet www.dfait-maeci.gc.ca/telaviv; Ambassador JOHN ALLEN.

Italy: Via Salaria 243, 00199 Rome; tel. (06) 854441; fax (06) 854443947; e-mail rome@international.gc.ca; internet www.canada.it; Ambassador ALEXANDER HIMELFARB; also covers Albania, Malta and San Marino.

Jamaica: 3 West Kings House Rd, POB 1500, Kingston 10; tel. 926-1500; fax 511-3494; e-mail kngtn@international.gc.ca; internet www.jamaica.gc.ca; High Commr DENIS KINGSLEY; also covers the Bahamas, and the United Kingdom Overseas Territories of the Cayman Islands and the Turks and Caicos Islands.

Japan: 7-3-38, Akasaka Minato-ku, Tokyo 107-8503; tel. (3) 5412-6200; fax (3) 5412-6247; e-mail tokyo@international.gc.ca; internet www.canadanet.or.jp; Ambassador JONATHAN T. FRIED; also covers the US External Territory of Guam.

Jordan: POB 815403, Amman 11180; tel. (6) 5203300; fax (6) 5203396; e-mail amman@international.gc.ca; internet www.amman.gc.ca; Ambassador MARGARET HUBER; also covers Iraq.

Kazakhstan: 34 Karasai Batyr St, Almaty 050010; tel. (727) 250-11-51; fax (727) 258-24-93; e-mail almat@international.gc.ca; internet geo.international.gc.ca/canada-europa/kazakhstan; Ambassador MARGARET SKOK; also covers Kyrgyzstan and Tajikistan.

Kenya: Limuru Rd, POB 1013, 00621 Gigiri, Nairobi; tel. (20) 3663000; fax (20) 3663900; e-mail nrobi@international.gc.ca; internet www.nairobi.gc.ca; High Commr ROSS HYNES; also covers Burundi, Eritrea, Rwanda Somalia, Uganda and the French Overseas Department of Réunion.

Kiribati: see New Zealand.

Korea, Republic: 16-1 Jeong-dong, Jung-gu, POB 6299, Seoul 100; tel. (2) 3783-6000; fax (2) 3783-6239; e-mail seoul@international.gc.ca; internet www.korea.gc.ca; Ambassador TED LIPMAN.

Kuwait: POB 25281, Safat 13113; tel. 2563025; fax 2560173; e-mail kwait@international.gc.ca; internet www.dfait-maeci.gc.ca/kuwait; Ambassador DENIS THIBAULT; also covers Qatar.

Kyrgyzstan: see Kazakhstan.

Laos: see Thailand.

Latvia: 20–22 Baznicas St, 6th Floor, Rīga 1010; tel. 781-3945; fax 781-3960; e-mail riga@international.gc.ca; internet www.latvia.gc.ca; Ambassador R. SCOTT HEATHERINGTON.

Lebanon: POB 60163, 1e étage, Immeuble Coolrite, Autostrade Jal ed-Dib 43, Beirut; tel. (4) 713900; fax (4) 710595; e-mail berut.webmaster@international.gc.ca; internet www.dfait-maeci.gc.ca/beirut; Ambassador LOUIS DE LORIMIER.

Lesotho: see South Africa.

Liberia: see Côte d'Ivoire.

Libya: Al-Fateh Tower Post Office, POB 93392, Tripoli; tel. (21) 3351633; fax (21) 3351630; e-mail trpli@international.gc.ca; internet www.dfait-maeci.gc.ca/libya/menu-en.asp; Ambassador HAIG SARAFIAN.

Liechtenstein: see Switzerland.

Lithuania (Embassy Office): Business Center 2000, Jogailos St 4, 7th floor, Vilnius 01116; tel. (5) 249-0950; fax (5) 249-7865; e-mail vilnius@canada.lt; internet www.dfait-maeci.gc.ca/canada-europa/baltics; Ambassador R. SCOTT HEATHERINGTON (resident in Latvia).

Luxembourg: see Belgium.

Macedonia, former Yugoslav republic: see Serbia.

Madagascar: see Tanzania.

Malawi: see Zambia.

Malaysia: Menara Tan & Tan, 17th Floor, 207 Jalan Tun razak, 50400 Kuala Lumpur; POB 10990, 50732 Kuala Lumpur; tel. (3) 27183333; fax (3) 27183399; e-mail klmpr@international.gc.ca; internet www.dfait-maeci.gc.ca/kualalumpur; High Commr DAVID COLLINS.

Maldives: see Sri Lanka.

Mali: Immeuble Séméga, Route de Koulikoro, BP 198, Hippodrome, Bamako; tel. 221-22-36; fax 221-43-62; e-mail bmako@international.gc.ca; internet www.bamako.gc.ca; Ambassador ISABELLE ROY.

Malta: see Italy.

Marshall Islands: see Australia.

Mauritania: see Morocco.

Mauritius: see South Africa.

Mexico: Calle Schiller 529, Col. Polanco, 11560 México, DF; tel. (55) 5724-7900; fax (55) 5724-7980; e-mail mxico@international.gc.ca; internet www.canada.org.mx; Ambassador GUILLERMO E. RISHCHYNSKI.

Micronesia, Federated States: see Australia.

Moldova: see Romania.

Monaco: see France.

Mongolia: see the People's Republic of China.

Morocco: 13 bis rue Jaâfar as-Sadik, BP 709, Rabat-Agdal; tel. (3) 7687400; fax (3) 7687430; e-mail rabat@international.gc.ca; Ambassador MICHÈLE LÉVESQUE; also covers Mauritania.

Mozambique (High Commission Office): Avda Kenneth Kaunda, No. 1138, POB 1578, Maputo; tel. 21492623; fax 21492667; e-mail mputo@international.gc.ca; High Commr PHILIP BAKER (resident in Zimbabwe).

Myanmar: see Thailand.

Namibia: see South Africa.

Nauru: see Australia.

Nepal: see India.

Netherlands: Sophialaan 7, POB 30820, 2500 GV The Hague; tel. (70) 3111600; fax (70) 3111620; e-mail info@canada.nl; internet www.canada.nl; Ambassador JAMES CORNELIUS WALL.

New Zealand: 125 The Terrace, Level 11, Wellington; tel. (4) 473-9577; fax (4) 471-2082; e-mail wlgtn@international.gc.ca; internet www.wellington.gc.ca; High Commr PENNY B. REEDIE; also covers Fiji, Kiribati, Samoa, Tonga, Tuvalu and the French Overseas Collectivities of French Polynesia and the Wallis and Futuna Islands.

Nicaragua (Embassy Office): Costado Oriental de la Casa Nasareth, Calle El Noval, Managua; tel. (2) 68-0433; fax (2) 68-0437; e-mail mngua@international.gc.ca; internet geo.international.gc.ca/latin-america/sanjose/embassy/mngua-en.aspx; Ambassador NEIL REEDER (resident in Costa Rica).

Niger (Embassy Office): blvd Mali Béro, BP 362, Niamey; tel. 75-36-86; fax 75-31-07; e-mail niamy@international.gc.ca; Ambassador MICHÈLE LÉVESQUE (resident in Côte d'Ivoire).

Nigeria: 15 Bobo St, Maitama, Abuja; tel. (9) 4139910; fax (9) 4139932; e-mail abuja@international.gc.ca; internet www.dfait-maeci.gc.ca/nigeria; High Commr CAROLINE CHRÉTIEN.

Norway: Wergelandsveien 7, 0244 Oslo; tel. 22-99-53-00; fax 22-99-53-01; e-mail oslo@international.gc.ca; internet www.canada.no; Ambassador JILLIAN STIRK.

Oman: see Saudi Arabia.

Pakistan: Diplomatic Enclave, Sector G-5, POB 1042, Islamabad; tel. (51) 2086000; fax (51) 2086900; e-mail isbad@international.gc.ca; internet www.dfait-maeci.gc.ca/islamabad; High Commr RANDOLPH MANK.

Panama: Calle 53E, Marbella, World Trade Centre, Galería Comercial, Apdo 0832-2446, Panamá; tel. 264-9731; fax 263-8083; e-mail panam@international.gc.ca; internet www.panama.gc.ca; Ambassador JOSÉ HERRÁN-LIMA.

Papua New Guinea: see Australia.

Paraguay: see Argentina.

Peru: Calle Bolognesi 228, Miraflores, Lima 18; tel. (1) 3193200; fax (1) 4464912; e-mail lima@international.gc.ca; internet www.dfait-maeci.gc.ca/peru; Ambassador GENEVIÈVE DES RIVIÈRES; also covers Bolivia.

Philippines: Tower 2, Levels 6–8, RCBC Plaza, 6819 Ayala Ave, POB 2098, 1200 Makati City, Manila; tel. (2) 8579000; fax (2) 8431082; e-mail manil@international.gc.ca; internet www.dfait-maeci.gc.ca/manila; Ambassador ROBERT DESJARDINS.

Poland: ul. Jana Matejki 1/5, 00-481 Warsaw; tel. (22) 5843100; fax (22) 5843190; e-mail wsaw@international.gc.ca; internet geo.international.gc.ca/canada-europa/poland; Ambassador DAVID PRESTON; also covers Belarus.

Portugal: Avda da Liberdade 198-200, 3rd Floor, 1269-121 Lisbon; tel. (21) 3164600; fax (21) 3164693; e-mail lsbon@international.gc.ca; internet www.portugal.gc.ca; Ambassador ANNE-MARIE BOURCIER.

Qatar: see Kuwait.

Romania: 011411 Bucharest, 1–3 Str. Tuberozelor; tel. (1) 3075000; fax (1) 3075010; e-mail bucst@international.gc.ca; internet geo.international.gc.ca/canada-europa/romania; Ambassador MARTA MOSZCZENSKA; also covers Bulgaria, Cyprus and Moldova.

Russia: 119002 Moscow, Starokonyushennyi per. 23; tel. (495) 925-60-00; fax (495) 925-60-25; e-mail mosco@international.gc.ca; internet www.dfait-maeci.gc.ca/missions/russia-russie; Ambassador RALPH JAMES LYSYSHYN; also covers Armenia and Uzbekistan.

Rwanda (Embassy Office): rue Akagera, BP 1177, Kigali; tel. 573210; fax 572719; e-mail kgali@international.gc.ca; Ambassador ROSS HYNES (resident in Kenya).

Saint Christopher and Nevis: see Barbados.

Saint Lucia: see Barbados.

Saint Vincent and the Grenadines: see Barbados.

Samoa: see New Zealand.

San Marino: see Italy.

São Tomé and Príncipe: see Cameroon.

Saudi Arabia: POB 94321, Riyadh 11693; tel. (1) 488-2288; (1) 488-1997; e-mail ryadh@international.gc.ca; internet www.saudiarabia.gc.ca; Ambassador RONALD DAVIDSON; also covers Bahrain, Oman and Yemen.

Senegal: Rue Galliéni–Amadou Cissé Dia, BP 3373, Dakar; tel. 33-889-4700; fax 33-889-4720; e-mail dakar@international.gc.ca; internet www.dfait-maeci.gc.ca/dakar; Ambassador JEAN-PIERRE BOLDUC; also covers Cape Verde, The Gambia, Guinea and Guinea-Bissau.

Serbia: 11000 Belgrade, Kneza Miloša 75; tel. (11) 3063000; fax (11) 3063042; e-mail bgrad@international.gc.ca; internet www.serbia.gc.ca; Ambassador ROBERT MCDOUGALL; also covers the former Yugoslav republic of Macedonia.

Seychelles: see Tanzania.

Sierra Leone: see Côte d'Ivoire.

Singapore: 1 George Street, 11-01, Singapore 049145; tel. 68545900; fax 68545930; e-mail spore@international.gc.ca; internet www.international.gc.ca/singapore; High Commr DAVID SEVIGNY.

Slovakia: see Czech Republic.

Slovenia: see Hungary.

Solomon Islands: see Australia.

Somalia: see Kenya.

South Africa: Private Bag X13, Hatfield, Pretoria 0028; tel. (12) 4223000; fax (12) 4223052; e-mail pret@international.gc.ca; internet www.dfait-maeci.gc.ca/southafrica; High Commr RUTH F. ARCHIBALD; also covers Lesotho, Mauritius, Namibia and Swaziland.

Spain: Edif. Goya, Calle Núñez de Balboa 35, 28001 Madrid; tel. (91) 4233250; fax (91) 4233251; e-mail mdrid@international.gc.ca; internet www.canada-es.org; Ambassador MALCOLM MCKECHNIE; also covers Andorra.

Sri Lanka: 6 Gregory's Rd, Cinnamon Gardens, POB 1006, Colombo 7; tel. (11) 5226232; fax (11) 5226296; e-mail clmbo@international.gc.ca; High Commr ANGELA BOGDAN; also covers Maldives.

Suriname: see Guyana.

Swaziland: see South Africa.

Sweden: Tegelbacken 4, 7th Floor, POB 16129, 103 23 Stockholm; tel. (8) 453-30-00; fax (8) 453-30-16; e-mail stkhm@international.gc.ca; internet www.stockholm.gc.ca; Ambassador ALEXANDRA VOLKOFF.

Switzerland: Kirchenfeldstrasse 88, 3005 Berne; tel. 313573200; fax 313573210; e-mail bern@international.gc.ca; internet www.canada-ambassade.ch; Ambassador ROBERT COLLETTE; also covers Liechtenstein.

Syria: POB 3394, Damascus; tel. (11) 6116692; fax (11) 6114000; e-mail dmcus@dfait-maeci.gc.ca; internet damascus.gc.ca; Ambassador (vacant); also covers Cyprus.

Tajikistan: see Kazakhstan.

Tanzania: 38 Mirambo St and Garden Ave, POB 1022, Dar es Salaam; tel. (22) 2163300; fax (22) 2116897; e-mail dslam@international.gc.ca; internet www.daressalaam.gc.ca; High Commr JANET SIDDAL; also covers the Comoros, Madagascar and Seychelles.

Thailand: Abdulrahim Bldg, 15th Floor, 990 Thanon Rama IV, Bangrak, Bangkok 10500; tel. (2) 636-0540; fax (2) 636-0566; e-mail bngkk@international.gc.ca; internet www.thailand.gc.ca; Ambassador DAVID SPROULE; also covers Laos and Myanmar.

Timor-Leste: see Indonesia.

Togo: see Ghana.

Tonga: see New Zealand.

Trinidad and Tobago: Maple House, 3–3A Sweet Briar Rd, St Clair, POB 1246, Port of Spain; tel. 622-6232; fax 628-2576; e-mail pspan@international.gc.ca; internet www.portofspain.gc.ca; High Commr HOWARD STRAUSS.

Tunisia: 3 rue du Senégal, pl. d'Afrique, BP 31, Belvédère 1002, Tunis; tel. (71) 104-000; fax (71) 104-190; e-mail tunis@international.gc.ca; internet tunis.gc.ca; Ambassador BRUNO PICARD.

Turkey: Cinnah Cad. 58, Cankaya 06690, Ankara; tel. (312) 4092700; fax (312) 4092811; e-mail ankra@international.gc.ca; internet geo.international.gc.ca/canada-europa/turkey; Ambassador MARK BAILEY; also covers Azerbaijan, Georgia and Turkmenistan.

Turkmenistan: see Turkey.

Tuvalu: see New Zealand.

Uganda: see Kenya.

Ukraine: Kiev 01901, POB 200, vul. Yaroslaviv val 31; tel. (44) 590-31-00; fax (44) 590-31-34; e-mail kyiv@international.gc.ca; internet www.kyiv.gc.ca; Ambassador G. DANIEL CARON.

United Arab Emirates: Abu Dhabi Trade Towers, West Tower, 9th and 10th Floors, POB 6970, Abu Dhabi; tel. (2) 6940300; fax (2) 6940399; e-mail abdbi@international.gc.ca; internet www.uae.gc.ca; Ambassador SARA HRADECKY.

United Kingdom: Canada House, Trafalgar Sq., London SW1Y 5BJ; tel. (20) 7258-6421; fax (20) 7258-6476; e-mail ldn@international.gc.ca; internet www.london.gc.ca; High Commr JAMES R. WRIGHT.

USA: 501 Pennsylvania Ave, NW, Washington, DC 20001; tel. (202) 682-1740; fax (202) 682-7619; e-mail webmaster@canadianembassy.org; internet www.washington.gc.ca; Ambassador MICHAEL WILSON; also covers the United Kingdom Overseas Territory of Bermuda.

Uruguay: 749 Plaza Independencia, Suite 102, Montevideo 11100; tel. (2) 9022030; fax (2) 9022029; e-mail mvdeo@international.gc.ca; internet www.montevideo.gc.ca; Ambassador ALAIN LATULIPPE.

Uzbekistan: see Russia.

Vanuatu: see Australia.

Venezuela: Avda Francisco de Miranda con Avda Altamira Sur, Caracas 1060A; tel. (2) 600-3000; fax (2) 261-8741; e-mail crcas@international.gc.ca; internet www.caracas.gc.ca; Ambassador PERRY CALDERWOOD; also covers the Netherlands Dependencies of Aruba and the Netherlands Antilles.

Viet Nam: 31 Hung Vuong St, Hanoi; tel. (4) 3734-5000; fax (4) 3734-5049; e-mail hanoi@international.gc.ca; internet www.hanoi.gc.ca; Ambassador DEANNA HORTON.

Yemen: see Saudi Arabia.

Zambia: Plot 5199, United Nations Ave, POB 31313, 10101 Lusaka; tel. (1) 250833; fax (1) 254176; e-mail lsaka@international.gc.ca; internet www.lusaka.gc.ca; High Commr PIERRE-PAUL PERRON (acting); also covers Malawi.

Zimbabwe: 45 Baines Ave, POB 1430, Harare; tel. (4) 252181; fax (4) 252186; e-mail hrare-cs@international.gc.ca; internet www.harare.gc.ca; Ambassador BARBARA RICHARDSON; also covers Angola and Botswana.

JUDICIAL SYSTEMS OF CANADA

INTRODUCTION

Common law is in force in Canada, with the exception of the province of Québec, where *le droit civil* (based on the Code Napoléon) prevails in private law. The right to pass legislation on the various aspects of civil law is shared between the federal Parliament and the provincial and territorial legislatures. Provinces and territories have jurisdiction over contract, property and tort laws, while the federal Parliament has jurisdiction over banking, bankruptcy and insolvency, and patents and copyrights. Jurisdiction is shared on corporation and tax laws.

The criminal-law system of Canada has its origins in the Constitution Act of 1867 (formerly known as the British North America Act) and subsequent amendments, such as the Criminal Code of Canada (1893). Provincial attorney-generals have responsibility for criminal prosecutions within their province that fall under the terms of the Criminal Code. The Attorney-General of Canada has responsibility for proceedings under federal statutes other than the Criminal Code. All criminal proceedings in the Northwest Territories and Yukon Territory come under the jurisdiction of the Attorney-General of Canada.

According to the Constitution Act, the administration of justice in the provinces, including the Constitution, maintenance and organization of provincial courts, in both civil and criminal departments, rests with the provincial government.

THE FEDERAL JUDICIAL SYSTEM

Supreme Court of Canada

(Supreme Court Bldg, 301 Wellington St, Ottawa, ON K1A 0J1; tel. (613) 995-4330; fax (613) 996-3063; e-mail reception@scc-csc.gc.ca; internet www.scc-csc.gc.ca)

The Supreme Court of Canada was established in 1875 by the Supreme and Exchequer Court Act and is now governed by the Supreme Court Act of 1985. It is the ultimate court of appeal in both civil and criminal cases throughout Canada. The judgment of the Court is final and conclusive. The Supreme Court is also required to advise on questions referred to it by the Governor in Council. Questions concerning the interpretation of the Constitution Act, the constitutionality or interpretation of any federal or provincial law, the powers of Parliament or of the provincial legislatures or of both levels of government, among other matters, may be referred by the federal Government to the Supreme Court for consideration.

In civil cases, appeals may be brought from any final judgment of the highest court of last resort in a province. The Supreme Court will grant permission to appeal if it believes that a question of public importance that transcends the immediate concerns of the parties to the litigation is involved. In criminal cases, the Court will hear appeals as of right, concerning indictable offences where an acquittal has been set aside or where there has been dissent on a point of law in a provincial court of appeal. Appeals are also heard from the appeal division of the Federal Court of Appeal. The Supreme Court may, in addition, hear appeals on questions of law concerning both summary conviction and all other indictable offences if permission to appeal is first granted by the Court.

There are nine Supreme Court judges, including the Chief Justice of Canada, and at least five judges are required to be present for a case to be heard (although it is normal for the full Court to sit in most instances). The judges are appointed by the Governor in Council and hold office until reaching the age of 75 years. Judges may only be removed from office by the Governor-General on address of the federal Senate and House of Commons.

Chief Justice of Canada: BEVERLEY MCLACHLIN.

Puisne Judges: WILLIAM I. CORNEIL BINNIE, LOUIS LEBEL, MARIE DESCHAMPS, MORRIS J. FISH, ROSALIE SIBERMAN ABELLA, LOUISE CHARRON, MARSHALL ROTHSTEIN.

Federal Court of Appeal

(Supreme Court Bldg, Kent and Wellington Sts, Ottawa, ON K1A 0H9; tel. (613) 996-6795; fax (613) 952-7226; e-mail reception@cas-satj.gc.ca; internet www.fca-caf.gc.ca)

The Federal Court of Appeal became a separate court in July 2003 following amendments to the Federal Courts Act. It was formerly a division of the Federal Court that was established in 1971 under section 101 of the Constitution Act of 1867, and that replaced the Exchequer Court of Canada, which had existed since 1875.

The Federal Court of Appeal comprises a chief justice and 12 judges (appointed by the Governor in Council) and has jurisdiction over appeals from the Federal Court and from the Tax Court of Canada. It has a determination on references made by federal tribunals, boards and commissions, or by the Attorney-General of Canada, and also on judicial review over the decisions of federal tribunals, boards and commissions as listed in section 28 of the Federal Courts Act.

Chief Justice: JOHN D. RICHARD.

Court of Appeal Judges: ALICE DESJARDINS, ROBERT DÉCARY, ALLEN M. LINDEN, GILLES LÉTOURNEAU, MARC NOËL, MARC NADON, J. EDGAR SEXTON, JOHN MAXWELL EVANS, KAREN SHARLOW, J. D. DENIS PELLETIER, C. MICHAEL RYER, JOHANNE TRUDEL, PIERRE BLAIS.

Federal Court

(Supreme Court Bldg, Kent and Wellington Sts, Ottawa, ON K1A 0H9; tel. (613) 947-3177; fax (613) 952-7226; e-mail reception@fct-cf.gc.ca; internet www.fct-cf.gc.ca)

The Federal Court became a separate court in July 2003 following amendments to the Federal Courts Act. It was formerly the Trial Division of the Federal Court of Canada, which had existed since 1971. The Federal Court is composed of 32 judges and a chief justice who are appointed by the Governor in Council. It has jurisdiction in claims against the Crown, claims by the Crown, miscellaneous cases involving the Crown and its officers and servants, relief (including judicial review) against federal boards, commissions and other tribunals, jurisdiction over interprovincial and federal–provincial disputes, income tax and estate tax appeals, industrial or intellectual property matters, maritime and admiralty matters, citizenship appeals, aeronautics and interprovincial works and undertakings. The Court has residuary jurisdiction for relief if there is no other Canadian court that has such jurisdiction, and jurisdiction in specific matters conferred by federal statutes.

Chief Justice: ALLAN LUTFY.

Trial Division Judges: YVON PINARD, SANDRA J. SIMPSON, DANIÈLE TREMBLAY-LAMER, DOUGLAS R. CAMPBELL, FRANÇOIS LEMIEUX, JOHN A. O'KEEFE, ELIZABETH HENEGHAN, DOLORES HANSEN, ELEANOR R. DAWSON, EDMOND P. BLANCHARD, MICHAEL A. KELEN, MICHEL BEAUDRY, LUC MARTINEAU, CAROLYN LAYDEN-STEVENSON, SIMON NOËL, JUDITH A. SNIDER, JAMES RUSSELL, JOHANNE GAUTHIER, JAMES O'REILLY, SEAN J. HARRINGTON, RICHARD MOSLEY, MICHEL M. J. SHORE, MICHAEL L. PHELAN, ANNE L. MACTAVISH, YVES DE MONTIGNY, ROGER T. HUGHES, ROBERT L. BARNES, LEONARD S. MANDAMIN, RUSSEL W. ZINN.

Court Martial Appeal Court of Canada

(Thomas D'Arcy McGee Bldg, 90 Sparks St, Ottawa, ON K1A 0H9; tel. (613) 995-5063; fax. (613) 941-9454; e-mail reception@cas-satj.gc.ca; internet www.cmac-cacm.ca)

Chief Justice: EDMOND P. BLANCHARD.

Tax Court of Canada

(200 Kent St, Ottawa, ON K1A 0M1; tel. (613) 992-0901; fax (613) 957-9034; email web@tcc-cci.gc.ca; internet www.tcc-cci.gc.ca)

The Tax Court of Canada has jurisdiction over appeals concerning the Income Tax Act, the Canada Pension Plan, the Old Age Security Act, the Petroleum and Gas Revenue Tax Act, the Employment Insurance Act and Part IX of the Excise Tax Act for the Goods and Services Tax. The Court also has jurisdiction to hear and determine appeals on matters arising under the War Veterans Allowance Act and the Merchant Navy and Civilian War-related Benefits Act. Hearings may be held in major centres throughout the country for income tax appeals and in smaller communities for appeals relating to unemployment insurance. The Federal Court of Canada may hear appeals of Tax Court decisions.

Chief Justice: GERALD J. RIP.

Associate Chief Justice: EUGENE ROSSITER.

Judges: LOUISE LAMARRE PROULX, THEODORE E. MARGESON, PIERRE ARCHAMBAULT, CAMERON HUGH MCARTHUR, LUCIE LAMARRE, ALAIN TARDIF, ERIC A. BOWIE, JOE E. HERSHFIELD, DIANE CAMPBELL, CAMPBELL J. MILLER, FRANÇOIS. M. ANGERS, LESLIE M. LITTLE, BRENT PARIS, JUDITH WOODS, GEORGETTE ANNE SHERIDAN, PAUL BÉDARD, RÉAL FAVREAU, EUGENE ROSSITER, WYMAN W. WEBB, GASTON JORRÉ, PATRICK J. BOYLE, VALERIE MILLER, ROBERT JAMES HOGAN.

LOCAL OFFICES

British Columbia

Vancouver: Pacific Centre, 3rd Floor, 701 West Georgia St, Vancouver, BC V7Y 1B6; tel. (604) 666-7987; fax (604) 666-7967.

Ontario

London: 231 Dundas St, 3rd Floor, London, ON N6A 1H1; tel. (519) 645-4203; fax (519) 675-3391.

Toronto: 180 Queen St West, Suite 200, Toronto, ON M5V 3L6; tel. (416) 973-9181; fax (416) 973-5944.

Québec

Montréal: 30 McGill St, Montréal, QC H2Y 3Z7; tel. (514) 283-9912; fax (514) 496-1996.

Courts Administration Service

(Supreme Court Bldg, Kent and Wellington Sts, Ottawa, ON K1A 0H9; e-mail reception@cas-satj.gc.ca; internet www.cas-satj.gc.ca)

The Courts Administration Service (CAS) was established in July 2003 as a result of the consolidation of the former registries of the Federal Court of Canada and of the Tax Court of Canada under the 2002 Courts Administration Service Act. The CAS provides administrative services to the Federal Court of Appeal, the Federal Court, the Court Martial Appeal Court of Canada and the Tax Court of Canada. The service aims to increase financial transparency and to ensure judicial independence.

Chief Administrator: R. P. GUENETTE.

LOCAL OFFICES

Alberta

Calgary: 635 Eighth Ave, SW, 3rd Floor, POB 14, Calgary, AB T2P 3M3; tel. (403) 292-5920; fax (403) 292-5329.

Edmonton: Scotia Pl., Tower 1, Suite 530, 10060 Jasper Ave, POB 51, Edmonton, AB T5J 3R8; tel. (403) 495-4651; fax (403) 495-4681.

British Columbia

Vancouver: Pacific Centre, 701 Georgia St West, POB 10065, Vancouver, BC V7Y 1B6; tel. (604) 666-3232; fax (604) 666-8181; e-mail gail.maciver@cas-satj.gc.ca; Regional Dir GAIL MACIVER.

Manitoba

Winnipeg: 363 Broadway, 4th Floor, Winnipeg, MB R3C 3N9; tel. (204) 983-2509; fax (204) 983-7636.

New Brunswick

Fredericton: Westmorland Pl., 82 Westmorland St, Suite 100, Fredericton, NB E3B 3L3; tel. (506) 452-3016; fax (506) 452-3584; District Admin. WILLA DOYLE.

Saint John: Provincial Bldg, 4th Floor, Rm 413, 110 Charlotte St, Saint John, NB E2L 2J4; tel. (506) 636-4990; fax (506) 658-3070.

Newfoundland and Labrador

St John's: Court House, 309 Duckworth St, POB 937, St John's, NL A1C 5M3; tel. (709) 772-2884; fax (709) 772-6351.

Northwest Territories

Yellowknife: Court House, 4905 49th St, POB 1320, Yellowknife, NT X1A 2L9; tel. (867) 873-2044; fax (867) 873-0291.

Nova Scotia

Halifax: 1801 Hollis St, 17th Floor, Suite 1720, Halifax, NS B3J 3N4; tel. (902) 426-3282; fax (902) 426-5514; District Admin. FRANÇOIS PILON.

Ontario

Toronto: 180 Queen St West, Suite 200, Toronto, ON M5V 3L6; tel. (416) 973-3356; fax (416) 973-2154; Regional Dir IMTIAZ RAJAB.

Prince Edward Island

Charlottetown: Sir Louis Henry Davies Law Courts, 42 Water St, POB 2000, Charlottetown, PE C1A 8B9; tel. (902) 368-0179; fax (902) 368-0266.

Québec

Montréal: 30 McGill St, Montréal, QC H2Y 3Z7; tel. (514) 283-4820; fax (514) 283-6004; Regional Dir MARIE-CHRISTINE HAUBERT.

Québec: Palais de Justice, Rms 500A and 500E, 300 blvd Jean-Lesage, Québec, QC G1K 8K6; tel. (418) 648-4920; fax (418) 648-4051.

Saskatchewan

Regina: Court House, 2425 Victoria Ave, Regina, SK S4P 3V7; tel. (306) 780-5268; fax (306) 787-7217.

Saskatoon: Court House, 520 Spadina Cres. East, Saskatoon, SK S7K 2H6; tel. (306) 975-4509; fax (306) 975-4818.

Yukon Territory

Whitehorse: Andrew A. Phillipsen Law Centre, 2134 Second Ave, Whitehorse, YT Y1A 5H6; POB 2703, Whitehorse, YT Y1A 2C6; tel. (867) 667-5441; fax (867) 393-6212.

Pension Appeals Board

(381 Kent St, Suite 327, POB 8567, Ottawa, ON K1G 3H9; tel. (613) 995-0612; fax (613) 995-6834; email info@pab-cap.gc.ca; internet www.pab-cap.gc.ca)

The Pension Appeals Board is responsible for hearing appeals arising from the decisions of the review tribunals under the Canada Pension Plan. Appeals are heard in all provinces and territories and the findings of the board are sent to all parties connected with the appeal.

Chairman: ROBERT C. DESMARAIS.

Vice-Chairman: DOUGLAS J. A. RUTHERFORD.

Office of the Commissioner for Federal Judicial Affairs

(99 Metcalfe St, 8th Floor, Ottawa, ON K1A 1E3; tel. (613) 995-5140; fax (613) 995-5615; e-mail info@fja.gc.ca; internet www.fja.gc.ca)

The Office of the Commissioner for Federal Affairs is responsible for administrative matters relating to the Federal Court of Canada, the Tax Court of Canada, the Canadian Judicial Council and all federally appointed judges, with the exception of those of the Supreme Court of Canada.

Commissioner: CLAUDE PROVENCHER.

Deputy Commissioner: MARC A. GIROUX.

PROVINCIAL AND TERRITORIAL JUDICIAL SYSTEMS

The Provincial Court System—General Introduction

Provincial courts are constituted under provincial legislation; while their names may vary from province to province, their structures are generally similar. There are three levels of provincial courts.

The highest level of court in a province is the Superior or Supreme Court, which hears serious criminal and civil cases and has the authority to grant divorces. The Superior Court may be a single court with a Trial Division and an Appellate Division, or it may consist of two separate courts—the Court of Queen's Bench and the Court of Appeal. The Appellate Division or the Court of Appeal may also hear appeals in both civil and criminal cases from all the trial courts in the province. Judges are appointed by the federal Government and are compulsorily retired at the age of 75 years.

All provinces, with the exception of Québec, have an intermediate level of courts, called County or District Courts. These possess immediate jurisdiction, dealing with criminal cases (apart from the most serious) and cases beyond the jurisdiction of the Small Claims Court. Judges are appointed by the federal Government; the compulsory age of retirement is 70 years.

Finally, each province has inferior courts which, with some variations, consist of the Juvenile Court, the Family Court, the Provincial Court (Criminal Division) and the Small Claims Court. These cover minor civil and criminal matters and settle the majority of such cases. Judges are appointed by the provincial governments and are compulsorily retired in accordance with the statutes that established the respective courts—usually at the age of 70 years.

Alberta

Alberta's Provincial Court (the lowest level of courts) includes the Family and Youth Division, the Civil Division, the Traffic Division and the Criminal Division. There are 11 judicial districts, with headquarters at Calgary, Drumheller/Hanna, Edmonton, Fort McMurray, Grande Prairie, Lethbridge/Macleod, Medicine Hat, Peace River, Red Deer, St Paul and Wetaskiwin. The highest level of courts comprises the Court of Appeal and the Court of Queen's Bench.

COURT OF APPEAL

Chief Justice of Alberta: CATHERINE A. FRASER (Edmonton).

Calgary: Court of Appeal of Alberta, TransCanada Pipelines Tower, 2600, 450 First St, SW, Calgary, AB T2P 5H1; tel. (403) 297-2206; fax (403) 297-5294; internet www.albertacourts.ab.ca; Justices of Appeal C. M. CONRAD, E. A. MCFADYEN, C. D. HUNT, M. S. PAPERNY, C. D. O'BRIEN, P. W. L. MARTIN, P. A. ROWBOTHAM.

Edmonton: Law Courts Bldg, 1A Sir Winston Churchill Sq. South, Edmonton, AB T5J 0R2; tel. (780) 422-2416; fax (78) 422-4127; Justices of Appeal J. E. L. CÔTÉ, E. I. PICARD, R. L. BERGER, P. T. COSTIGAN, K. G. RITTER, J. WATSON, F. F. SLATTER.

COURT OF QUEEN'S BENCH

Chief Justice: ALLAN H. J. WACHOWICH (Edmonton).

Associate Chief Justice: N. C. WITTMANN (Calgary).

Calgary: Courts Centre, 601 Fifth St, SW, Calgary, AB T2P 5P7; tel. (403) 297-7538; fax (403) 297-8617; Justices A. B. SULATYCKY, A. M.

Lutz, D. B. Mason, B. L. Rawlins, R. M. Cairns, J. D. Rooke, T. F. McMahon, S. M. Bensler, D. G. Hart, L. D. Wilkins, C. A. Kent, P. J. McIntyre, C. S. Philips, P. M. Clark, S. J. LoVecchio, W. P. Sullivan, C. L. Kenny, G. C. Hawco, C. S. Brooker, B. E. C. Romaine, R. E. Nation, A. G. Park, B. E. Mahoney, E. A. Hughes, M. C. Erb, K. M. Horner, S. L. Martin, A. D. Macleod, J. D. B. McDonald, K. M. Eidsvik, E. C. Wilson, J. Strekaf.

Edmonton: Law Courts Bldg, 1A Sir Winston Churchill Sq. South, Edmonton, AB T5J 0R2; tel. (780) 422-2492; fax (780) 422-9742; Justices J. B. Veit, E. P. MacCallum, E. A. Marshall, M. B. Bielby, P. L. J. Smith, J. L. Lewis, D. Lee, M. T. Moreau, R. P. Marceau, R. P. Belzil, M. A. Binder, S. M. Sanderman, D. A. Sulyma, B. R. Burrows, G. A. Verville, L. D. Acton, T. D. Clackson, A. B. Moen, S. J. Greckol, E. F. Macklin, V. O. Ouellette, D. C. Read, S. D. Hillier, J. E. Topolniski, A. W. Germain, J. M. Ross, J. J. Gill, D. R. G. Thomas, R. A. Graesser, D. L. Shelley, K. G. Nielsen, M. G. Crighton, D. J. Manderscheid, K. D. Yamauchi.

Lethbridge: Courthouse, 320 Fourth St South, Lethbridge, AB T1J 1Z8; tel. (403) 381-5196; fax (403) 381-5128; Justices W. V. Hembroff, J. H. Langston, D. K. Miller.

Red Deer: Courthouse, 4909 48th Ave, Red Deer, AB T4N 3T5; tel. (403) 340-5220; fax (403) 340-7984; Justices J. L. Foster, D. A. Sirrs, K. L. Sisson.

PROVINCIAL COURT

There are 21 provincial court districts and 111 judges.

Chief Provincial Court Judge: A. G. Vickery.

Deputy Chief Judge: A. H. Lefever.

Assistant Chief Judges: D. R. Pahl, M. R. Bast, E. W. Peterson, J. R. McIntosh, J. K. Wheatley, R. J. Wilkins.

British Columbia

British Columbia's highest provincial court is the Court of Appeal, followed by the Supreme Court. There are 17 Court of Appeal judges and 102 judges in the Supreme Court, who sit in eight judicial districts. The Governor-General in Council appoints all provincial judges.

COURT OF APPEAL

Chief Justice of British Columbia: Lance Sidney George Finch.

Vancouver: Law Courts, 800 Smithe St, Vancouver, BC V6Z 2E1; tel. (604) 660-2468; fax (604) 660-1951; e-mail jjordan@courts.gov.bc.ca; internet www.courts.gov.bc.ca; Justices of Appeal M. Anne Rowles, Jo-Ann E. Prowse, Catherine Anne Ryan, Ian T. Donald, Mary V. Newbury, Carol Mahood Huddart, John E. Hall, Kenneth C. Mackenzie, Mary E. Saunders, Richard T. A. Low, Risa E. Levine, Kenneth J. Smith, P. D. Lowry, Pamela A. Kirkpatrick, Edward Chiasson, S. David Frankel, David Franklin Tysoe, Robert J. Bauman, Daphne M. Smith, Kathryn E. Neilson, Harvey M. Groberman.

SUPREME COURT

Chief Justice: Donald Ian Brenner.

Associate Chief Justice: Patrick Donald Dohm.

Vancouver: Law Courts, 800 Smithe St, Vancouver, BC V6Z 2E1; Justices Marion J. Allan, Wendy G. Baker, Sandra K. Ballance, Elizabeth A. Bennett, Mary Ellen Boyd, Brenda Brown, Bruce Butler, Grant D. Burnyeat, Bruce I. Cohen, Frank W. Cole, Austin F. Cullen, Victor R. Curtis, Jane Dardi, Barry M. Davies, Gail Dickson, Janice R. Dillon, William Ehrcke, Lauri Ann Fenlon, Nicole J. Garson, Laura B. Gerow, Kirsti M. Gill, Richard Goepel, Christopher Grauer, Susan Griffin, Victoria Gray, Joel R. Groves, Christopher Hinkson, Heather J. Holmes, Ronald R. Holmes, Mary A. Humphries, Stephen F. Kelleher, M. Marvyn Koenigsberg, Peter D. Leask, Linda A. Loo, Anne Mackenzie, Donna J. Martinson, David M. Masuhara, Nancy Morrison, Elliott M. Myers, Paul Pearlman, Ian H. Pitfield, Bruce M. Preston, Bryan F. Ralph, Eric Rice, Selwyn R. Romilly, Carol J. Ross, Loryl D. Russell, Deborah Satanove, John Savage, William Scarth, Duncan W. Shaw, Jon S. Sigurdson, Arne H. Silverman, Janet A. Sinclair Prowse, Harry A. Slade, William Smart, C. Lynn Smith, Nathan H. Smith, Allan M. Stewart, Sunni S. Stromberg-Stein, Paul Walker, Terrance P. Warren, Catherine A. Wedge, L. Paul Williamson, Randall S. K. Wong.

Chilliwack: 46085 Yale Rd, Chilliwack, BC V2P 2L8; Justices William G. E. Grist, Brian M. Joyce.

Cranbrook: Court House, 102 11th Ave South, Cranbrook, BC V1C 2P3; Justice Thomas J. Melnick.

Kamloops: Court House, 223-455 Columbia St, Kamloops, BC V2C 6K4; Justices Richard M. L. Blair, Ian. C. Meiklem, Robert E. Powers.

Kelowna: Court House, 1355 Water St, Kelowna, BC V1Y 9R3; tel. (250) 470-6900; fax (250) 470-6768; Justices G. M. Barrow, Alison J. Beames, T. Richard Brooke, P. J. Rogers.

Nanaimo: Court House, 35 Front St, Nanaimo, BC V9R 5J1; Justices D. A. Halfyard, S. James Shabbits, A. Fraser Wilson.

Nelson: Court House, 320 Ward St, Nelson, BC V1L 1S6; Justice T. Mark McEwan.

New Westminster: Court House, Begbie Sq., New Westminster, BC V3M 1C9; Justices Elizabeth A. Arnold-Bailey, Lance W. Bernard, David J. Brine, Neill Brown, Catherine J. Bruce, Robert Crawford, Barbara Fisher, Geoffrey R. J. Gaul, J. Miriam Gropper, Ian B. Josephson, Kathleen M. Ker, Ronald A. McKinnon, John D. Truscott, James W. Williams.

Prince George: Court House, 250 George St, Prince George, BC V2L 5S2; Justices Eric G. Chamberlist, Ian C. Meiklem, W. Glen Parrett.

Prince Rupert: Court House, 100 Market Pl., Prince Rupert, BC V8J 1B8; Justice D. A. Halfyard.

Victoria: Law Courts, 850 Burdett Ave, Victoria, BC V8W 1B4; Justices J. Keith. Bracken, Jacqueline L. Dorgan, Robert Johnston, Malcolm D. Macaulay, Robert W. Metzger, David H. Vickers, R. Dean Wilson.

PROVINCIAL COURT

The provincial court system comprises 97 locations and 151 judges.

Chief Judge of the Provincial Court: Hugh Campbell Stansfield.

Vancouver: Pacific Centre, Suite 602, 700 West Georgia St, POB 10287, Vancouver, BC V7Y 1E8; tel. (604) 660-2864; fax (604) 660-1108; e-mail info@provincialcourt.bc.ca; internet www.provincialcourt.bc.ca; Assoc. Chief Judges Brian M. Neal, Jim Threlfall.

Manitoba

Manitoba has 15 administrative and judicial centres, situated in Beausejour, Brandon, Dauphin, Flin Flon, Killarney, Minnedosa, Morden, Portage la Prairie, Russell, Selkirk, Steinbach, Swan River, The Pas, Thompson and Virden. These handle Court of Queen's Bench and provincial court matters. The superior courts are the Court of Appeal and the Court of Queen's Bench.

COURT OF APPEAL

Chief Justice of Manitoba: Richard J. Scott.

Winnipeg: Law Courts Bldg, Suite 100E, 408 York Ave, Winnipeg, MB R3C 0P9; tel. (204) 945-2647; fax (204) 948-2072; internet www.manitobacourts.mb.ca; Judges of Appeal Michel A. Monnin, Freda M. Steel, Barbara M. Hamilton, Martin H. Freedman, Richard J. F. Chartier, Alan D. MacInnes.

COURT OF QUEEN'S BENCH

Chief Justice: Marc M. Monnin.

Associate Chief Justice: Jeffrey J. Oliphant.

Associate Chief Justice (Family Division): Gerald W. Mercier.

Winnipeg: Law Courts Bldg, 408 York Ave, Winnipeg, MB R3C 0P9; tel. (204) 945-0344; fax (204) 945-2369; Judges Robert Carr, Gil R. Goodman, Kenneth R. Hanssen, Daniel P. Kennedy, Robyn M. Diamond, A. L. Clearwater, Leá A. Duval, Holly C. Beard, Nathan Nurgitz, Kris Stefanson, Perry Schulman, Sylvia Guertin-Riley, Brenda L. Keyser, Deborah J. McCawley, Donald M. Little, Morris Kaufman, Laurie P. Allen, Douglas D. Yard, Donald P. Bryk, Frank Aquila, Robert B. Doyle, C. Murray Sinclair, Joan G. McKelvey, John Scurfield, Colleen Suche, Marilyn E. Goldberg, Shawn D. Greenberg, Karen I. Simonsen, Marianne Rivoalen, Lori T. Spivak, A. Lori Douglas, A. Catherine Everett, Michael A. Thomson, Glenn D. Joyal, Douglas N. Abra.

Brandon: Courthouse, 1104 Princess Ave, Brandon, MB R7A 0P9; tel. (204) 726-6240; fax (204) 726-6574; Judges Rodney H. Mykle, John A. Menzies, Robet G. Cummings.

Dauphin: 114 River Ave West, Dauphin, MB R7N 0J7; tel. (204) 622-2087; fax (204) 622-2099; Judge Brian Midwinter.

PROVINCIAL COURT

There are six provincial court districts and 34 judges.

Chief Judge: Raymond E. Wyant.

Associate Chief Judges: Mary Kate Harvie, Murray Thompson.

Winnipeg: Law Courts Bldg, 408 York Ave, Winnipeg, MB R3C 0P9; tel. (204) 945-3454; fax (204) 945-7130.

New Brunswick

New Brunswick comprises eight judicial districts, with headquarters at Bathurst, Campbellton, Edmundston, Fredericton, Miramichi, Moncton, Saint John and Woodstock. The highest courts are the Court of Appeal and the Court of Queen's Bench, which is divided into a Trial Division and a Family Division. In 1979 the former district courts were amalgamated with the Court of Queen's Bench.

COURT OF APPEAL

Chief Justice of New Brunswick: J. Ernest Drapeau.

Fredericton: Justice Bldg, 427 Queen St, Rm 202, POB 6000, Fredericton, NB E3B 5H1; tel. (506) 453-2452; fax (506) 453-7921; internet www.gnb.ca/cour; Judges Wallace S. Turnbull, Margaret E. L. Larlee, Joseph Z. Daigle, Alexandre Deschênes, Joseph T. Robertson, J. C. Marc Richard.

COURT OF QUEEN'S BENCH

Chief Justice: David D. Smith (Moncton).

Fredericton: Justice Bldg, 427 Queen St, POB 6000, Fredericton, NB E3B 5H1; divided into Trial Division and Family Division; Judges Robert J. Higgins (Saint John), Guy W. Boisvert (Bathurst), Jacques A. Sirois (Moncton), Raymond J. Guérette (Campbellton), Paul S. Creaghan (Moncton), Alfred R. Landry (Moncton), David H. Russell (Fredericton), Hugh H. McLellan (Saint John), Roger Savoie (Moncton), Thomas W. Riordon (Miramichi), Roger McIntyre (Bathurst), Myrna F. Athey (Fredericton), Judy L. Clendening (Fredericton), Gladys J. Young (Campbellton), Zoël R. Dionne (Moncton), Bradley V. Green (Saint John), Jean-Paul Ouellette (Miramichi), David S. Smith (Moncton), George S. Rideout (Moncton), Paulette C. Garnett (Fredericton), Peter S. Glennie (Saint John), Brigitte M. Robichaud (Moncton), Réginald Léger (Bathurst), Lucie A. LaVigne (Edmundston), Anne D. Wooder (Fredericton), Colette M. d'Entremont (Moncton), Robert L. Tuck (Saint John), William T. Grant (Saint John), Stephen J. McNally (Moncton and Miramichi), Thomas E. Cyr (Edmundston), Michel A. Robichaud (Bathurst), Barbara L. Baird (Saint John), Raymond T. French (Woodstock).

PROVINCIAL COURT

There are 14 courts and 24 judges, two judges sitting on a per diem basis and three supernumerary judges in the provincial court system.

Chief Judge: R. Leslie Jackson.

Associate Chief Judge: Pierre W. Arseneault.

Newfoundland and Labrador

The Provincial Court of Newfoundland and Labrador includes a Juvenile Court and a Traffic Court. There are judicial centres situated at Clarenville, Corner Brook, Gander, Goose Bay, Grand Bank, Grand Falls, Harbour Grace, Placentia, St John's, Stephenville and Wabush. The Supreme Court is divided into a Court of Appeal, a Unified Family Court and a Trial Division.

SUPREME COURT

(Court House, 287 Duckworth St, POB 937, St John's, NL A1C 5M3; tel. (709) 729-0066; fax (709) 729-7909; internet www.court.nl.ca/supreme)

Court of Appeal

Chief Justice of Newfoundland and Labrador: Clyde K. Wells.

Judges: Margaret A. Cameron, Denis M. Roberts, Malcolm H. Rowe, B. Gale Welsh, Keith J. Mercer, Leo Barry.

Trial Division

Chief Justice: J. Derek Green.

Judges: Raymond J. Halley, David L. Russell, Mary E. Noonan, Seamus B. O'Regan, Abe Schwartz, David B. Orsborn, Maureen Dunn, James P. Adams, J. Douglas Cook, Wayne G. Dymond, Alphonse E. Faour, Robert A. Fowler, Kendra J. Goulding, Robert M. Hall, Garrett A. Handrigan, Richard D. LeBlanc, Alan C. Seaborn, Carl R. Thompson, William N. Goodridge, Michael F. Harrington, Gillian D. Butler, Deborah E. Fry, Lois R. Hoegg, Raymond P. Whalen.

PROVINCIAL COURT

The provincial court system comprises a total of 11 courts and 23 judges.

St John's

Atlantic Pl., 215 Water St, POB 68, St John's, NL A1C 6C9; tel. (709) 729-1004; fax (709) 729-2161; internet www.court.nl.ca/provincial.

Chief Judge: Milton R. Reid.

Judges: Joseph A. Woodrow, David Peddle, Robert T. Smith, Randolph J. Whiffen, Robert B. Hyslop, Gregory O. Brown, Kymil Howe, David Power, David Orr, Gloria Harding, William English, Wayne Gorman, Patrick J. B. Kennedy, Colin J. Flynn, Harold Porter, Timothy Chalker, Lynn Spracklin, Catherine Allen-Westby, Bruce Short, John Joy, Wynn Anne Trahey.

Northwest Territories

The Northwest Territories has a Territorial Court, which includes a Criminal Division, Small Claims Division, Juvenile Division and Family and Citizenship Division. The judiciary consists of one Supreme Court judge, four territorial judges, 15 judicial officers and 52 justices of the peace. Both judges and justices of the peace are appointed by the Territories' Commissioner. Court sessions are held in Yellowknife and on court circuits throughout the Territories. The superior courts of the Territories are the Court of Appeal and the Supreme Court. The Court of Appeal comprises the judges of the Court of Appeal of Alberta, one judge of the Court of Appeal of Saskatchewan and the judges and ex officio judge of the Supreme Court of the Northwest Territories.

COURT OF APPEAL

Chief Justice: Catherine A. Fraser (Edmonton, Alberta).

Judges: J. E. Côté, J. E. Richard, J. Z. Vertes, C. M. Conrad, E. A. McFadyen, E. Picard, C. Hunt, V. A. Schuler, R. L. Berger, B. A. Browne, R. G. Kilpatrick, P. T. Costigan, M. S. Paperny, K. G. Ritter, R. S. Veale, E. Johnson, L. F. Gower, C. O'Brien, P. W. L. Martin, L. A. M. Charbonneau, J. Watson, F. F. Slatter, P. A. Rowbotham, Donald M. Cooper.

Yellowknife: Courthouse, 4903 49th St, POB 550, Yellowknife, NT X1A 2N4; tel. (867) 920-8760; internet www.nwtcourts.ca.

SUPREME COURT

Judges of the Supreme Court: John Z. Vertes (Sr Judge), J. Edward Richard, Virginia A. Schuler, Louise A. M. Charbonneau, Donald M. Cooper.

Ex officio Judges: B. A. Browne (Iqaluit, NU), R. G. Kilpatrick (Iqaluit, NU), R. S. Veale (Whitehorse, YT), E. Johnson (Iqaluit, NU).

Yellowknife: Courthouse, 4903 49th St, POB 1320, Yellowknife, NT X1A 2N4.

There are 45 deputy judges from the Superior Courts of Alberta, British Columbia, Manitoba, Newfoundland and Labrador, Nova Scotia, Ontario, Québec, Saskatchewan and the Yukon Territory.

TERRITORIAL COURT

Chief Judge: Brian A. Bruser.

Judges: Bernadette E. Schmaltz, Robert D. Gorin.

Nova Scotia

Nova Scotia has seven county court districts. The provincial Supreme Court consists of a Trial Division and a Family Division. Its judges are appointed by the provincial cabinet.

Chief Justice of Nova Scotia: Michael MacDonald.

COURT OF APPEAL

Chief Justice: Michael MacDonald.

Justices: Nancy J. Bateman, Thomas A. Cromwell, Joel E. Fichaud, M. Jill Hamilton, Linda L. Oland, Elizabeth A. Roscoe, Jamie W. S. Saunders.

Halifax: 1815 Upper Water St, Halifax, NS B3J 1S7; tel. (902) 424-6937; fax (902) 424-0646; e-mail piccolj@gov.ns.ca; internet www.courts.ns.ca.

SUPREME COURT

Chief Justice: Joseph Phillip Kennedy.

Associate Chief Justice: Deborah K. Smith.

Associate Chief Justice (Family Division): Robert F. Ferguson.

Trial Division

Justices: Duncan R. Beveridge, Allan P. Boudreau, Felix A. Cacchione, Kevin Coady, C. Richard Coughlan, John M. Davison, Patrick J. Duncan, Frank C. Edwards, Walter R. E. Goodfellow, Charles E. Haliburton, Suzanne M. Hood, Arthur J. LeBlanc,

A. David MacAdam, Simon J. MacDonald, Douglas L. MacLellan, Glen G. McDougall, Gerald R. P. Moir, John D. Murphy, Arthur W. D. Pickup, M. Heather Robertson, J. Edward (Ted) Scanlan, N. M. (Nick) Scaravelli, Margaret Stewart, Gregory M. Warner, Robert W. Wright.

Halifax: 1815 Upper Water St, Halifax, NS B3J 1S7; tel. (902) 424-4900; fax (902) 424-0524; e-mail boucheam@gov.ns.ca.

Family Division

Justices: Douglas C. Campbell, Leslie J. Dellapinna, Theresa M. Forgeron, Deborah Gass, Moira C. Legere-Sers, Mona Lynch, Beryl A. MacDonald, M. Claire MacLellan, Lawrence I. O'Neil, R. James Williams, Darryl W. Wilson.

Halifax: 3380 Devonshire Ave, POB 8988, Halifax, NS B3K 5M6; tel. (902) 424-3990; fax (902) 424-0562; internet www.courts.ns.ca.

PROVINCIAL COURT

There are 12 courts and 25 judges in the provincial court system.

Chief Judge: Patrick Curran.

Associate Chief Judge: R. Brian Gibson.

Judges: Jean-Louis Batiot, Barbara Beach, Carole A. Beaton, Fiona Inglis Buchan, James H. Burrill, Jamie S. Campbell, Marc C. Chisholm, Anne E. Crawford, Anne S. Derrick, William Digby, John D. Embree, Laurel J. Halfpenny MacQuarrie, Claudine MacDonald, Clyde F. MacDonald, D. William MacDonald, John G. MacDougall, Alanna Murphy, Robert M. Prince, G. Hughes Randall, A. Peter Ross, David J. Ryan, Michael B. Sherar, Robert A. Stroud, Alan T. Tufts, Castor H. Williams, Pamela S. Williams, Brian D. Williston.

Nunavut Territory

Following the division of Northwest Territory in 1999, the Nunavut Court of Justice assumed the powers and functions formerly exercised by the Northwest Territories judicial system, with the exception of the territorial Court of Appeal. The Court of Appeal comprises the superior court judges of Northwest Territory, Nunavut Territory and Yukon Territory, and judges of the Courts of Appeal of Alberta and Saskatchewan. The Nunavut Court of Justice is a single level court, which hears any type of case, including civil, family and criminal disputes, in both adult and youth courts. The Nunavut Court of Justice provides court services to approximately 85% of the communities across the Territory, through a travelling circuit court. There are some 80 justices of the peace in the territorial communities.

COURT OF APPEAL

Chief Justice: Catherine A. Fraser (Edmonton, Alberta).

Judges: H. C. B. Maddison, J. D. Bracco, C. F. Tallis, M. M. Hetherington, A. B. Sulatycky, H. L. Irving, R. L. Berger, J. E. Côté, J. E. Richard, J. Z. Vertes, C. D. Hunt, A. H. Russell, V. A. Schuler, B. Browne, R. Kilpatrick, R. Foisy, N. Wittmann.

COURT OF JUSTICE

(Nunavut Justice Centre, Bldg 510, POB 297, Iqaluit, NU X0A 0H0; tel. (867) 975-6100; fax (867) 975-6168; email courtlibrary@gov.nu.ca; internet www.nucj.ca)

Judges of the Court of Justice: B. A. Browne, R. G. Kilpatrick, E. D. Johnson.

Ontario

The Superior Court of Justice consists of the High Court of Justice, the District Court, the Surrogate Court, the Divisional Court and the Small Claims Court. The Ontario Court of Justice consists of the Provincial Offences Court, the Criminal Division and the Family Division. The Unified Family Court has overall jurisdiction in family law cases. The province is divided into eight judicial districts. The Supreme Court consists of the Court of Appeal.

SUPREME COURT

(Osgoode Hall, 130 Queen St West, Toronto, ON M5H 2N5; internet www.ontariocourts.on.ca)

Court of Appeal

Chief Justice of Ontario: Warren K. Winkler.

Associate Chief Justice of Ontario: Dennis R. O'Connor.

Justices: Robert P. Armstrong, Robert A. Blair, Stephen Borins, Eleanore A. Cronk, David H. Doherty, Gloria J. Epstein, Kathryn N. Feldman, Eileen E. Gillese, Stephen T. Goudge, Russell G. Juriansz, Harry S. Laforme, Susan E. Lang, John I. Laskin, Jean L. MacFarland, James C. MacPherson, Michael J. Moldaver, Marc Rosenberg, Paul S. Rouleau, Robert J. Sharpe, Janet M. Simmons, John D. Watt, Karen M. Weiler.

SUPERIOR COURT OF JUSTICE

Chief Justice: Heather Forster Smith.

Associate Chief Justice: J. Douglas Cunningham.

Senior Judge (Family Court): Justice Mary J. Hatton.

ONTARIO COURT OF JUSTICE

Chief Justice: Annemarie E. Bonkalo.

Associate Chief Justice: Peter D. Griffiths.

Courts Administration: 720 Bay St, Toronto, ON M5G 2K1.

Prince Edward Island

Prince Edward Island comprises three judicial counties, with headquarters at Georgetown, Charlottetown and Summerside. The Supreme Court consists of two branches: an Appeal Division and a Trial Division.

SUPREME COURT

(Sir Louis Henry Davies Law Courts Bldg, 42 Water St, POB 2000, Charlottetown, PE C1A 7N8; tel. (902) 368-4000; email island@gov.pe.ca; internet www.gov.pe.ca/courts)

Chief Justice of Prince Edward Island: David H. Jenkins.

Appeal Division

Chief Justice: David H. Jenkins.

Justices: John A. McQuaid, Michele M. Murphy.

Trial Division

Chief Justice: Jacqueline R. Matheson.

Justices: Gordon L. Campbell, Wayne D. Cheverie, Benjamin B. Taylor, John K. Mitchell.

PROVINCIAL COURT

Chief Provincial Court Judge: John R. A. Douglas.

Judges: Nancy K. Orr, Jeffrey E. Lantz.

Charlottetown: Law Courts Bldg, POB 2290, Charlottetown, PE C1A 1A4.

Summerside: Law Courts Bldg, POB 2020, Summerside, PE C1N 4M1.

Québec

Québec's court system differs from the court hierarchy of other provinces, in that it has no District Courts but a greater number of inferior courts. These have four components: the Court of Québec, which has Civil, Criminal and Youth divisions; the Municipal Court; the Small Claims Court; and the Court of Justices of the Peace, which issues warrants and enforces municipal by-laws. The highest courts in the province are the Court of Appeal and the Superior Court.

COUR D'APPEL/COURT OF APPEAL

Chief Justice of Québec: J. J. Michel Robert.

Judges: Marc Beauregard, Paul-Arthur Gendreau, Jean-Louis Baudouin, André Brossard, Jacques Delisle, Louise Otis, Jacques Chamberland, Joseph R. Nuss, André Forget, France Thibault, Louis Rochette, François Pelletier, Benoît Morin, André Rochon, Pierre J. Dalphond, Pierrette Rayle, Yves-Marie Morissette, Allan R. Hilton, François Doyon, Julie Dutil, Marie-France Bich, Paul Vézina, Lorne Giroux, Jacques Dufresne, Lise Côté, Nicole Duval Hesler.

Montréal: Édif. Ernest-Cormier, 100 rue Notre-Dame est, Montréal, QC H2Y 4B6; tel. (514) 393-2022; fax (514) 864-7270; e-mail courdappel@justice.gouv.gc.ca; internet www.tribunaux.qc.ca/mjq_en/c-appel/index-ca.html.

Québec: 300 blvd Jean-Lesage, bureau 4.27, Québec, QC G1K 8K6; tel. (418) 649-3401; fax (418) 646-6961.

COUR SUPÉRIEURE/SUPERIOR COURT

The Superior Court system comprises 13 courts and 144 judges.

Chief Justice: François Rolland.

Deputy Chief Justice: Robert Pidgeon.

Montréal: 100 rue Notre-Dame est, Montréal, QC H2Y 4B6; tel. (514) 393-2022; fax (514) 864-7270.

Québec: 300 blvd Jean-Lesage, Québec, QC G1K 8K6; tel. (418) 649-3400.

COUR DU QUÉBEC/COURT OF QUÉBEC

The Court of Québec operates in two regional sections and comprises 270 judges.

Chief Justice: GUY GAGNON.

Senior Associate Chief Justice: RENÉ DE LA SABLONNIÈRE (Québec).

Associate Chief Justices: GILLES CHAREST, PAULE GAUMOND, MICHEL SIMARD, MAURICE GALARNEAU.

Saskatchewan

The province of Saskatchewan has 15 judicial centres, located at Assiniboia, Battleford, Estevan, Humboldt, Kerrobert, Melfort, Melville, Moose Jaw, Prince Albert, Regina, Saskatoon, Swift Current, Weyburn, Wynyard and Yorkton. The superior courts in the province are the Court of Appeal and the Court of Queen's Bench.

COURT OF APPEAL

Chief Justice of Saskatchewan: JOHN KLEBUC.

Regina: Courthouse, 2425 Victoria Ave, Regina, SK S4P 3V7; e-mail mrodie@sasklawcourts.ca; internet www.sasklawcourts.ca; Judges S. J. CAMERON, W. J. VANCISE, M. A. GERWING, N. M. SHERSTOBITOFF, J. G. LANE, G. R. JACKSON, R. G. RICHARDS, G. A. SMITH, D. C. HUNTER, Y. G. K. WILKINSON.

COURT OF QUEEN'S BENCH

Chief Justice: R. D. LAING (Saskatoon).

Battleford: Courthouse, 291 23rd St West, POB 340, Battleford, SK S0M 0E0; tel. (306) 446-7670; fax (306) 446-7737; Judge D. B. KONKIN.

Estevan: Courthouse, 1016 Fourth St, Estevan, SK S4A 0W5; tel. (306) 637-4527; fax (306) 637-4536; Judge G. A. J. CHICOINE.

Humboldt: Courthouse, POB 490, 805 Eighth Ave, Humboldt, SK S0K 2A0; tel. (306) 682-6730; fax (306) 682-3536.

Melfort: Courthouse, POB 6500, 409 Main St, Melfort, SK S0E 1A0; tel. (306) 752-6265; fax (306) 752-6264.

Moose Jaw: Courthouse, 64 Ominica St West, Moose Jaw, SK S6H 1W9; tel. (306) 694-3602; fax (306) 694-3056; Judge L. B. MACDONALD.

Prince Albert: Courthouse, 1800 Central Ave, Prince Albert, SK S6V 4W7; tel. (306) 953-3200; fax (306) 953-3210; Judges R. D. MAHER, A. R. ROTHERY.

Regina: Courthouse, 2425 Victoria Ave, Regina, SK S4P 3V7; tel. (306) 787-5377; fax (306) 787-7217; Judges D. P. BALL, R. L. BARCLAY, C. L. DAWSON, W. F. GEREIN, E. J. GUNN, F. J. KOVACH, G. M. KRAUS, L. A. KYLE, E. C. MALONE, D. E. W. MCINTYRE, I. D. MCLELLAN, J. E. MCMURTRY, R. K. OTTENBREIT, N. S. SANDORMIRSKY, E. A. SCHEIBEL, P. A. WHITMORE, D. L. WILSON, C. R. WIMMER, T. C. ZARZECZNY.

Saskatoon: 520 Spadina Cres. East, Saskatoon, SK S7K 2H6; tel. (306) 933-5135; fax (306) 975-4818; Judges M. D. ACTON, G. N. ALLBRIGHT, G. M. CURRIE, M. L. DOVELL, G. D. DUFOUR, P. FOLEY, N. G. GABRIELSON, I. GOLDENBERG, P. HRABINSKY, J. D. KOCH, R. C. MILLS, M. D. POPESCUL, J. A. RYAN-FROSLIE, R. S. SMITH, M. E. R. WRIGHT.

Swift Current: Courthouse, 121 Lorne St West, Swift Current, SK S9H 0J4; tel. (306) 778-8400; fax (306) 778-8581; Judge M. J. HERAUF.

Weyburn: Courthouse, 301 Prairie Ave, Weyburn, SK S4H 0L4; tel. (306) 848-2361; fax (306) 848-2540.

Wynyard: Courthouse, POB 369, 410 Ave C East, Wynyard, SK S0A 4T0; tel. (306) 554-5520; fax (306) 554-5531.

Yorkton: Courthouse, 29 Darlington St East, Yorkton, SK S3N 0C2; tel. (306) 786-1515; fax (306) 786-1521; Judge J. L. PRITCHARD.

PROVINCIAL COURT

Saskatchewan's provincial court system comprises 13 courts and 46 judges.

Chief Judge: C. A. SNELL.

Regina: Provincial Court of Saskatchewan, 1815 Smith St, Regina, SK S4P 3V7; tel. (306) 787-5250; fax (306) 787-7037.

Yukon Territory

The superior courts of the Yukon Territory are the Court of Appeal and the Supreme Court. The Court of Appeal is composed of two judges from the Yukon Supreme Court, two from the Supreme Court of the Northwest Territories and 22 from the British Columbia Court of Appeal. The Supreme Court consists of two resident justices, six justices from the Northwest Territories and Nunavut, and a number of deputy judges. Justices for both Courts are appointed by the federal Government. The Territorial Court of Yukon consists of one chief judge and two puisne judges. There are permanent courtrooms at Whitehorse, Watson Lake and Dawson and regular court circuits at other locations.

COURT OF APPEAL

Chief Justice: LANCE S. G. FINCH (British Columbia).

Judges: T. DONALD, W. A. ESSON, H. A. HOLLINRAKE, J. D. LAMBERT, J. PROWSE, M. A. ROWLES, C. A. RYAN, M. F. SOUTHIN, M. V. NEWBURY, C. M. HUDDART, T. R. BRAIDWOOD, J. E. HALL, K. C. MACKENZIE, M. E. SAUNDERS, R. T. A. LOW, R. E. LEVINE, K. J. SMITH, A. D. THACKRAY; (all of Vancouver, BC).

Whitehorse: Court Registry, Law Courts, 2134 Second Ave, Ground Floor, Whitehorse, YT Y1A 5H6; tel. (867) 667-3429; fax (867) 393-6212; e-mail courtservices@gov.yk.ca; internet www.yukoncourts.ca/courts/appeal.html.

SUPREME COURT

Chief Justice: RONALD S. VEALE.

Judge of the Supreme Court: L. F. GOWER HUDSON (Whitehorse).

The Supreme Court has 42 deputy judges from the superior courts of British Columbia, Alberta, Québec, Saskatchewan, Ontario and Manitoba.

TERRITORIAL COURT

Chief Judge: KAREN RUDDY.

Whitehorse: Law Courts, 2134 Second Ave, Whitehorse, YT Y1A 5H6; tel. (867) 667-5441; fax (867) 393-6212; Judges MICHAEL COZENS, JOHN FAULKNER.

DIRECTORY ON THE ECONOMY

NATIONAL ECONOMIC INDICATORS

Currency and Exchange Rates

MONETARY UNITS

100 cents = 1 Canadian dollar (C $).

DENOMINATIONS

Coins: 1, 5, 10, 25 and 50 cents; 1 and 2 dollars.

Notes: 5, 10, 20, 50 and 100 dollars.

INTERNATIONAL VALUE OF THE DOLLAR

Average Exchange Rates
(units of foreign currency equivalent to C $1)

	2005	2006	2007
Euro area (euro)	0.6627	0.7024	0.6807
Japan (yen)	90.62	102.53	109.64
United Kingdom (pound sterling)	0.4532	0.4788	0.4654
USA (dollar)	0.8253	0.8818	0.9304

Source: Bank of Canada.

FOREIGN CURRENCY EQUIVALENTS
(29 August 2008)

Euro Area: C $100 = €64.16; €1 = C $1.5586.

Japan: C $1 = ¥102.29; ¥1,000 = C $9.776.

United Kingdom: C $100 = £51.74; £1 sterling = C $1.9329.

USA: C $100 = US $94.11; US $1 = C $1.0626.

Source: Bank of Canada.

INTERNATIONAL RESERVES
(US $ million at 31 December)

	2005	2006	2007
Gold (national valuation)	56	69	91
IMF special drawing rights	897	963	1,016
Reserve position in IMF	1,401	833	661
Foreign exchange	30,664	33,198	39,314
Total	33,018	35,063	41,082

Source: IMF, *International Financial Statistics*.

MONEY SUPPLY
(C $ '000 million at 31 December)

	2005	2006	2007
Currency outside banks	41.22	43.87	44.74
Demand deposits at deposit money banks	375.32	409.60	342.97
Total money	416.54	453.47	387.71

Source: IMF, *International Financial Statistics*.

Cost of Living

(Consumer Price Index; base: 2002 = 100)

	2005	2006	2007
Food	106.4	108.9	111.8
Housing	109.2	113.1	116.9
Household expenses and furnishings	101.7	102.2	103.2
Clothing and footwear	97.6	95.8	95.7
Transport	112.0	115.2	117.1
Health and personal care	104.6	105.9	107.3
Recreation, education and reading	100.8	100.6	101.8
Tobacco and alcohol	119.1	121.7	125.5
All items	107.0	109.1	111.5

Source: Statistics Canada.

National Accounts

NATIONAL INCOME AND PRODUCT
(C $ million at current prices)

	2005	2006	2007
Compensation of employees	695,093	743,313	788,357
Net operating surplus and mixed income	346,611	361,757	384,030
Domestic factor incomes	1,041,704	1,105,070	1,172,387
Consumption of fixed capital	175,961	185,206	195,229
Gross domestic product at factor cost	1,217,665	1,290,276	1,367,616
Indirect taxes, less subsidies	155,467	160,840	167,349
Statistical discrepancy	–506	–626	681
GDP at market prices	1,372,626	1,450,490	1,535,646

Source: Statistics Canada.

Gross national income (C $ '000 million at current prices): 1,344.21 in 2005; 1,422.19 in 2006; 1,511.65 in 2007 (Source: IMF, *International Financial Statistics*).

Gross national disposable income (C $ '000 million at current prices): 1,343.99 in 2005; 1,422.35 in 2006; 1,511.33 in 2007 (Source: IMF, *International Financial Statistics*).

EXPENDITURE ON THE GROSS DOMESTIC PRODUCT
(C $ million at current prices)

	2005	2006	2007
Government final consumption expenditure	260,197	278,922	296,472
Private final consumption expenditure	759,239	803,260	852,770
Increase in stocks	9,357	8,052	9,821
Gross fixed capital formation	292,271	323,981	347,401
Total domestic expenditure	1,321,064	1,414,215	1,506,464
Exports of goods and services	518,909	522,698	532,118
Less Imports of goods and services	467,852	487,048	502,255
Statistical discrepancy	505	625	–681
GDP at market prices	1,372,626	1,450,490	1,535,646

Source: Statistics Canada.

GROSS DOMESTIC PRODUCT BY ECONOMIC ACTIVITY
(C $ million at chained 2002 prices)

	2005	2006	2007
Agriculture, hunting, forestry and fishing	28,437	27,847	27,077
Mining, petroleum and gas extraction	56,044	57,174	58,342
Utilities	30,550	30,128	31,169
Construction	68,527	74,087	76,884
Manufacturing	188,478	186,631	184,712
Wholesale trade	63,879	68,383	71,334
Retail trade	65,132	69,015	72,915
Transportation and warehousing	53,802	55,501	56,377
Finance, insurance, real estate and leasing	221,951	230,362	240,054
Professional, scientific and technical services	53,793	55,377	57,296
Administration and support, waste management and remediation services	28,756	30,524	31,666
Educational services	55,008	56,221	57,571
Health care and social assistance	72,784	74,780	76,753
Information and cultural industries	41,848	43,147	44,202
Arts, entertainment and recreation	10,940	11,410	11,713
Accommodation and food services	26,418	27,365	27,681
Public administration	65,309	66,758	67,973
Other services	29,346	30,072	30,904
Statistical discrepancy	–978	–877	–674
GDP at basic prices	1,160,024	1,193,905	1,223,949

Source: Statistics Canada.

Balance of Payments

(US $ million)

	2005	2006	2007
Exports of goods f.o.b.	373,254	401,786	434,049
Imports of goods f.o.b.	–320,575	–356,641	–388,211
Trade balance	52,679	45,146	45,838
Exports of services	55,313	59,332	63,152
Imports of services	–65,333	–72,649	–81,254
Balance on goods and services	42,659	31,829	27,736
Other income received	39,860	54,344	59,601
Other income paid	–58,397	–64,760	–74,332
Balance on goods, services and income	24,121	21,413	13,006
Current transfers received	6,754	8,517	8,957
Current transfers paid	–7,467	–9,133	–9,148
Current balance	23,408	20,797	12,815
Capital account (net)	4,889	3,702	3,981
Direct investment abroad	–33,584	–45,391	–49,478
Direct investment from abroad	29,142	69,068	110,369
Portfolio investment assets	–44,072	–69,405	–40,180
Portfolio investment liabilities	7,933	28,675	–34,593
Other investment assets	–16,567	–30,375	–55,629
Other investment liabilities	26,997	28,212	53,555
Net errors and omissions	3,189	–4,458	3,064
Overall balance	1,335	826	3,906

Source: IMF, *International Financial Statistics*.

Economically Active Population

(Source: Statistics Canada.)

SUMMARY
(annual averages, '000 persons aged 15 years and over)*

	2005	2006	2007
Agriculture	343.7	346.4	337.2
Forestry, fishing, mining, petroleum and gas	306.4	330.1	339.3
Utilities	125.3	122.0	138.0
Construction	1,019.5	1,069.7	1,133.5
Manufacturing	2,207.4	2,117.7	2,044.9
Trade	2,574.6	2,633.5	2,682.4
Transportation and warehousing	793.6	802.2	822.8
Finance, insurance, real estate and leasing	987.8	1,040.5	1,060.4
Professional, scientific and technical services	1,050.0	1,089.9	1,136.9
Business, building and other support services†	654.4	690.0	702.1
Educational services	1,106.1	1,158.4	1,183.2
Health care and social assistance	1,734.6	1,785.5	1,846.1
Information, culture and recreation	735.1	745.0	782.0
Accommodation and food services	1,004.5	1,015.0	1,069.4
Public administration	833.1	837.4	864.6
Other services	693.4	701.0	723.5
Total employed	16,169.7	16,484.3	16,866.4
Unemployed	1,172.8	1,108.4	1,079.4
Total labour force	17,342.6	17,592.8	17,945.8
Males	9,243.7	9,335.4	9,492.8
Females	8,098.8	8,257.3	8,453.0

* Figures exclude military personnel, inmates of institutions, residents of the Yukon, Northwest and Nunavut Territories, and Indian Reserves.
† Formerly management of companies, administrative and other support services.

LABOUR FORCE BY PROVINCE
(annual averages, '000 persons, 2007)

	Employed		Unemployed		Labour force		
	Males	Females	Males	Females	Males	Females	**Total**
Alberta	1,075.4	884.1	37.2	33.9	1,112.6	918.0	2,030.6
British Columbia	1,210.9	1,055.4	50.6	49.4	1,261.5	1,104.9	2,366.4
Manitoba	318.7	277.8	15.0	12.4	333.7	290.2	623.9
New Brunswick	186.3	176.6	17.9	11.7	204.2	188.2	392.4
Newfoundland and Labrador	111.8	105.3	19.6	14.5	131.4	119.8	251.2
Nova Scotia	226.7	220.9	23.2	15.8	249.9	236.8	486.7
Ontario	3,437.2	3,156.6	250.1	199.7	3,687.3	3,356.2	7,043.5
Prince Edward Island	34.8	34.5	4.4	3.5	39.2	38.1	77.3
Québec	2,017.4	1,834.3	173.7	124.7	2,191.1	1,959.0	4,150.1
Saskatchewan	269.9	231.9	12.0	10.0	281.9	241.9	523.8
Total*	8,888.9	7,977.5	603.9	475.5	9,492.8	8,453.0	17,945.8

* Residents of the Yukon, Nunavut and Northwest Territories, those living on Indian Reserves, full-time Armed Forces members and inmates of Institutions are excluded from the survey.

AGRICULTURE, FORESTRY, FISHING AND TRAPPING

Farmland Use

(Source: Statistics Canada.)

SUMMARY
(census results, excl. Northwest, Nunavut and Yukon Territories, hectares)

	1996	2001	2006
Improved pasture	4,349,136	4,804,496	5,694,387
Land in crops	34,918,733	36,395,150	35,912,247
Summer fallow	6,260,725	4,680,398	3,505,573
All other land	22,526,362	21,622,402	22,474,532
Total area of farms	68,054,956	67,502,446	67,586,739

PROVINCES AND TERRITORIES
(2006 census, excl. Northwest, Nunavut and Yukon Territories, '000 hectares)

	Tame or seeded pasture	Under crops	Summer fallow	Other land	**Total farm area** (incl. other)
Alberta	2,484	9,622	906	1,554	21,095
British Columbia	246	586	26	478	2,835
Manitoba	498	4,701	127	844	7,719
New Brunswick	17	152	0	200	395
Newfoundland and Labrador	2	9	0	14	36
Nova Scotia	23	117	1	230	403
Ontario	303	3,661	12	960	5,386
Prince Edward Island	11	171	0	56	251
Québec	147	1,933	4	1,219	3,463
Saskatchewan	1,962	14,960	2,429	1,476	26,003

Production of Principal Crops

(Source: Statistics Canada.)

SUMMARY
('000 metric tons, estimates)

	2005	2006	2007
Wheat	25,748.1	25,265.4	20,054.0
Oats	3,282.7	3,852.2	4,696.3
Barley	11,677.6	9,573.1	10,983.9
Rye	330.4	382.9	233.0
Mixed grains	316.4	346.5	262.6
Corn for grain	9,332.2	8,989.8	11,648.7
Buckwheat	4.6	7.4	2.3
Peas, dry	2,993.6	2,519.9	2,934.8
Beans, dry	307.6	372.4	276.7
Flaxseed	990.6	988.8	633.5
Soybeans	3,155.6	3,465.5	2,695.7
Mustard seed	183.8	108.2	114.3
Rapeseed (canola)	9,483.3	9,000.3	8,750.7
Sunflower seed	84.4	157.3	124.8
Sugar beets	607.8	870.9	762.0
Tame hay	29,576.0	29,999.8	30,244.6
Fodder corn	7,380.9	9,680.6	8,136.6

Source: Statistics Canada, CANSIM II Table 001-00101, September 2008.

PROVINCES
('000 metric tons, 2007)

	Wheat	Oats	Barley	Rye	Corn for grain	Peas, dry
Alberta	6,076	627	5,114	37	23	528
British Columbia	49	55	58	—	—	—
Manitoba	3,211	1,205	1,195	54	494	98
New Brunswick	5	24	45	—	19	—
Newfoundland and Labrador	—	—	—	—	—	—
Nova Scotia	5	5	7	—	28	—
Ontario	1,442	88	218	43	6,985	—
Prince Edward Island	33	12	94	—	—	—
Québec	174	280	308	—	4,100	—
Saskatchewan	9,058	2,401	3,945	99	—	2,310

PROVINCES—CONTINUED

	Flaxseed	Soybeans	Rapeseed (canola)	Sugar beets	Tame hay	Fodder corn
Alberta	16	—	2,994	762	9,276	839
British Columbia	—	—	48	—	1,579	408
Manitoba	105	212	1,715	—	3,538	817
New Brunswick	—	—	—	—	381	58
Newfoundland and Labrador	—	—	—	—	27	—
Nova Scotia	—	—	—	—	376	73
Ontario	—	2,000	28	—	5,216	3,992
Prince Edward Island	—	11	—	—	376	73
Québec	—	472	19	—	4,040	1,880
Saskatchewan	512	—	3,949	—	5,511	—

Source: Statistics Canada, CANSIM II Table 001-00101, September 2008.

Livestock and Poultry on Farms

(Source: Statistics Canada.)

SUMMARY
('000 head, mostly at 1 July, estimates)

	2005	2006	2007
Milch cows*	1,025.1	1,000.4	979.1
Beef cows	5,436.2	5,164.6	5,112.6
Sheep†	630.1	615.4	583.9
Pigs	15,195.0	15,065.0	14,690.0
Chicks‡	673,552	663,869	691,507
Turkeys‡	20,602	21,823	22,863

* All females that have calved, raised mainly for milk purposes.
† Aged one year or older.
‡ Placement of chicks and turkey poults for production, annual total.
Source: Statistics Canada, CANSIM II Tables 003-0032, 003-0031, 003-0004, 003-0021, September 2008.

PROVINCES
(estimates, '000 head, mostly at 1 July 2007)

	Cattle	Pigs	Sheep and lambs	Chicks	Turkeys
Alberta	6,470	1,970	205	62,832	2,018
British Columbia	805	129	58	105,723	2,796
Manitoba	1,540	2,965	70	33,989	2,057
New Brunswick	87	99	8	13,074	458
Newfoundland and Labrador	13	2	4	18,074	31
Nova Scotia	102	88	27	23,815	616
Ontario	1,956	3,887	305	220,657	9,065
Prince Edward Island	88	111	4	2,446	34
Québec	1,395	4,120	295	180,469	4,879
Saskatchewan	3,430	1,320	120	30,430	908

Source: Statistics Canada, CANSIM II Tables 003-0032, 003-0031, 003-0004, 003-0021, September 2008.

Livestock Products

(Source: Statistics Canada.)

SUMMARY
(metric tons, unless otherwise indicated)

	2005	2006	2007
Beef and veal ('000 lb)	3,675,694	3,491,311	n.a.
Mutton and lamb ('000 lb)	84,996	91,944	n.a.
Pork ('000 lb)	4,638,875	4,628,624	n.a.
Poultry	1,155,493	1,160,904	1,199,054
Milk ('000 litres)	7,579,128	7,435,149	7,593,403
Creamery butter*	83,519	75,412	78,642
Cheddar cheese	131,808	139,326	144,937
Ice-cream mix ('000 litres)	172,699	171,295	160,137
Eggs ('000 dozen)	577,217	580,258	577,443

* Excluding Newfoundland and Labrador.

Source: Statistics Canada, CANSIM II Tables 003-0037, 003-00181, 003-0010, 003-00111, 003-00091, 003-00201, September 2008.

LIVESTOCK AND POULTRY PRODUCTION BY PROVINCE*
(2007)

	Egg production			Total volume of milk sold ('000 litres)	Poultry production ('000)	
	Number of layers ('000)	Eggs per 100 layers (average)	Net production of eggs ('000 dozen)		Chickens	Fowl
Alberta	2,317	23,968	46,278	633,679	54,696	402
British Columbia	3,179	24,363	64,543	632,342	99,183	2,370
Manitoba	2,980	28,675	71,208	298,485	29,343	180
New Brunswick	771	25,028	16,084	133,773	18,236	216
Newfoundland and Labrador	349	30,576	8,885	58,560	n.a.	n.a.
Nova Scotia	744	30,299	18,793	172,984	22,262	93
Ontario	9,416	28,980	227,397	2,494,631	197,205	8,776
Prince Edward Island	129	30,554	3,277	100,832	n.a.	n.a.
Québec	4,804	25,366	101,547	2,846,696	165,088	4,727
Saskatchewan	1,130	20,634	19,431	221,418	25,521	137
Total	25,819	26,838	577,443	7,593,400	n.a.	n.a.

* Data for Territories not available.

Source: Statistics Canada, adapted from CANSIM II Tables 003-00201, 003-00111, September 2008.

Forestry

HARVESTED FOREST LAND BY PROVINCE OR TERRITORY
(hectares)

	2006		2007	
	Total harvested	Clearcut	Total harvested	Clearcut
Alberta*	81,709	79,706	81,754	79,751
British Columbia*	197,599	193,846	197,599	193,846
Manitoba*	13,648	13,648	13,648	13,648
New Brunswick*	92,697	68,801	92,626	68,758
Newfoundland and Labrador*	17,280	17,265	16,999	16,977
Northwest Territories*†	141	141	141	141
Nova Scotia*	43,682	41,302	43,682	41,302
Ontario	211,874	198,998	170,248*	160,010*
Prince Edward Island*	2,195	2,165	2,110	2,082
Québec	321,078	297,713	311,124*	296,827*
Saskatchewan*	29,183	29,158	29,150	29,150
Yukon Territory*	12	12	12	12
Total	1,011,098	942,755	959,093	902,504

* Estimate(s).

† Includes Nunavut Territory, constituted as a separate Territory in 1999.

Source: National Forestry Database Program.

ROUNDWOOD REMOVALS—SUMMARY
(merchantable volume, '000 cu m, estimates)

	2002	2003	2004	2005	2006
Logs and bolts	164,388	146,850	173,107	172,478	157,865
Pulpwood	25,557	27,902	28,583	23,442	22,903
Other industrial roundwood	3,298	3,315	3,583	4,326	4,438
Total industrial roundwood	193,243	178,066	205,272	200,246	185,206
Fuelwood and firewood	2,885	2,843	2,789	3,045	2,997
Total	196,128	180,909	208,062	203,321*	188,236*

* Including an estimated 30,000 cu m of New Brunswick removals not allocated by type.

Source: National Forestry Database Program.

ROUNDWOOD REMOVALS—PROVINCES AND TERRITORIES
(net merchantable volume, '000 cu m, estimates)

	2002	2003	2004	2005	2006
Alberta	24,661	24,220	23,494*	27,535	25,266†
British Columbia	77,864	65,358	86,998	86,880	88,060
Manitoba	2,106	2,106*	2,106*	2,498	2,511*
New Brunswick	9,989	10,788	11,004	9,968	9,971*
Newfoundland and Labrador*	2,561	2,289	2,327	2,400	2,050
Northwest Territories	30	26	26	24*	24*
Nova Scotia	6,066	6,085	6,889	6,249	5,209
Ontario	26,327*	24,347*	25,147*	23,371*	25,927
Prince Edward Island*	635	650	657	569	602
Québec	41,525*	40,102	43,269	38,461	33,084*
Saskatchewan	4,309	4,898	6,103	5,330	3,502
Yukon Territory	42	32	26	24	19

* Estimate(s).

† Provisional.

Source: National Forestry Database Program.

LUMBER PRODUCTION—SUMMARY
('000 cubic metres, dry)

	2004	2005	2006
Coniferous	82,773.8	81,172.0	79,228.3
Broadleaved	1,815.8	1,717.1	1,641.9
Total	84,589.6	82,889.1	80,870.2

Source: Statistics Canada, adapted from CANSIM II Table 303-00092, September 2008.

LUMBER PRODUCTION—PROVINCES
('000 cubic metres, dry, 2007)

	C*	B†	**Total**
Alberta	7,569.1	14.2	7,583.3
British Columbia	36,677.3	—	36,677.3
Manitoba	n.a.	—	n.a.
New Brunswick	3,207.1	141.7	3,348.8
Newfoundland and Labrador	n.a.	n.a.	n.a.
Nova Scotia	1,222.2	2.3	1,224.5
Ontario	7,301.2	452.3	7,753.5
Prince Edward Island	n.a.	n.a.	n.a.
Québec	13,797.7	790.4	14,588.1
Saskatchewan	n.a.	n.a.	n.a.

* Coniferous.

† Broadleaved.

Source: Statistics Canada, adapted from CANSIM II Table 303-00092, September 2008.

Fishing

(Source: Department of Fisheries and Oceans.)

MARINE LANDINGS—SUMMARY
(metric tons, live weight, preliminary)

	2005	2006	2007
Cod	26,156	27,307	26,593
Herring	163,263	159,849	166,965
Mackerel	55,282	53,714	52,012
Clams/quahaugs	26,216	26,003	21,494
Scallop*	57,151	63,272	65,054
Lobster	50,721	53,368	43,474
Shrimp	167,386	178,507	185,974
Queen Crab	95,347	89,382	90,273
Atlantic total (incl. others)	823,848	823,709	801,617
Hake	104,189	96,198	66,668
Salmon	27,190	23,709	19,951
Pacific total (incl. others)†	248,440	211,497	171,011
Canada total (incl. others)	1,072,288	1,035,206	972,628

* Includes meat with roe.
† British Columbia data only; includes quantities of tuna caught by Canadian fishermen in international waters and landed in Canada, and hake sold to foreign vessels under joint venture arrangements.

Note: Figures exclude landings of aquatic plants ('000 metric tons): 2 in 2005; nil in 2006; 11,498 in 2007. Also excluded are landings of lumpfish roe ('000 metric tons): 1,334 in 2005; 1,135 in 2006; 453 in 2007, and miscellaneous other landings ('000 metric tons): 23,021 in 2005; 41,053 in 2006; 2,343 in 2007.

All LANDINGS—PROVINCES AND TERRITORIES
(marine and inland fish and other marine products, 2006, preliminary)

	Quantity (metric tons)	Landed value (C $ '000)
Alberta	1,457	1,748
British Columbia	211,816	324,327
Manitoba	11,632	23,818
New Brunswick	111,829	153,267
Newfoundland and Labrador	374,067	468,730
Northwest Territories	614	610
Nova Scotia	284,271	656,694
Ontario	13,737	36,430
Prince Edward Island	37,873	136,502
Québec	59,545	119,086
Saskatchewan	2,788	2,843
Total	1,109,627	1,924,056

Trapping

(Source: Statistics Canada.)

PELT PRODUCTION—PROVINCES AND TERRITORIES
('000 pelts)

	2002	2003	2004	2005
Alberta	148.1	148.8	n.a.*	168.3
British Columbia	n.a.*	n.a.*	n.a.*	209.8
Manitoba	115.5	124.4	127.9	138.1
New Brunswick	n.a.*	n.a.*	68.3	67.9
Newfoundland†	n.a.*	n.a.*	25.2	74.4
Northwest Territories	31.8	23.5	42.7	24.0
Nova Scotia	487.2	764.2	806.2	800.4
Nunavut Territory	11.0	12.3	6.6	12.0
Ontario	526.2	538.7	556.2	492.3
Prince Edward Island	48.6	40.6	41.5	34.1
Québec	242.6	261.7	252.4	276.7
Saskatchewan	85.7	84.8	62.6	67.7
Yukon Territory	8.3	4.0	3.5	5.8
Total‡	2,036.1	2,387.0	2,392.5	2,371.6

* Figure undisclosed owing to confidentiality restrictions.
† Newfoundland and Labrador from December 2001.
‡ Includes undisclosed provincial and territorial data.

Value of pelts (C $ '000): 103,673.7 in 2003; 109,975.1 in 2004; 128,038.4 in 2005.
Source: Statistics Canada, mostly CANSIM II Table 003-0013, October 2007.

Selected Agricultural, Forestry, Fisheries and Fur Trade Organizations

Agricultural Groups Concerned about Resources and the Environment (AGCare): 100 Stone Rd West, Suite 106, Guelph, ON N1G 5LG; tel. (519) 837-1326; fax (519) 837-3209; e-mail agcare@agcare.org; internet www.agcare.org; f. 1987; provides research on environmental issues; Chair. RICHARD BLYLEVEN; 17 mem. orgs.

Agricultural Institute of Canada (AIC): 280 Albert St, Suite 900, Ottawa, ON K1P 5G8; tel. (613) 232-9459; fax (613) 594-5190; e-mail office@aic.ca; internet www.aic.ca; f. 1920; Pres GRAHAM GILCHRIST; CEO MYLES FROSST; 22 provincial mem. institutes.

Agriculture Producers' Association of New Brunswick/Association des producteurs agricoles du Nouveau Brunswick (APANB): 303–259 Brunswick St, Suite 303, Fredericton, NB E3B 1G8; tel. (506) 452-8101; fax (506) 452-1085; e-mail alliance@fermenbfarm.ca; internet www.fermenbfarm.ca; Pres. ROBERT ENGLISH; CEO CHARLINE CORMIER.

Agricultural Producers' Association of Saskatchewan (APAS): 2400 College Ave, Suite 100, Regina, SK S4P 1C8; tel. (306) 789-7774; fax (306) 789-7779; e-mail info@apas.ca; internet www.apas.ca; Pres. GLENN BLAKELY; Gen. Man. SHELLEY DIRK.

Alberta Association of Agricultural Societies (AAAS): J. G. O'Donoghue Bldg, Rm 200, 7000 113th St, Edmonton, AB T6H 5T6; tel. (780) 427-2174; fax (780) 422-7755; e-mail aaas@

albertaagsocieties.ca; internet www.albertaagsocieties.ca; f. 1947; Pres. MIKE SIDORYK; Exec. Dir SHARON JENSEN; 294 mems.

Alberta Canola Producers' Commission (ACPC): 14315 118th Ave, Suite 170, Edmonton, AB T5L 4S6; tel. (780) 454-0844; fax (780) 451-6933; e-mail web@canola.ab.ca; internet www.canola.ab.ca; f. 1989; Chair. KEVIN AUCH; Gen. Man. WARD TOMA; 24,000 mems (2003).

Alberta Farm Animal Care Association (AFAC): Cambrian POB 75028, Calgary, AB T2K 6J8; tel. (403) 932-8050; fax (403) 932-8052; e-mail info@afac.ab.ca; internet www.afac.ab.ca; f. 1993; Chair. DAVID HYINK; Man. SUSAN CHURCH.

Alberta Milk: 1303 91 St South West, Edmonton, AB T6X 1H1; tel. (780) 453-5942; fax (780) 455-2196; e-mail cthrall@albertamilk.com; internet www.albertamilk.com; f. 2002 by merger of Dairy Nutrition Council of Alberta and Alberta Dairy Control Bd; Gen. Man. MIKE SOUTHWOOD; 714 mems.

Animal Nutrition Association of Canada/Association de nutrition animale du Canada (ANAC): 109 Murray St, Suite 2, Ottawa, ON K1N 5M5; tel. (613) 241-6421; fax (613) 241-7970; e-mail info@anac-acac.ca; internet www.anac-anac.ca; Chair. JIM LINAKER; Exec. Dir GRAHAM COOPER; 180 mems (2007).

Association of Seafood Producers: Baine Johnston Centre, Suite 302, Fort William Pl., St John's, NL A1C 1K4; tel. (709) 726-3730; fax (709) 726-3731; e-mail info@seafoodproducers.org; internet www.seafoodproducers.org; Chair. HERB M. CLARKE; Exec. Dir E. DEREK BUTLER.

British Columbia Agricultural Council (BCAC): 1473 Water St, Kelowna, BC V1Y 1J6; tel. (250) 763-9790; fax (250) 763-9722; e-mail bcac@bcac.bc.ca; internet www.bcac.bc.ca; f. 1997; Chair. DICK KLEIN GELTINK; Exec. Dir STEVE THOMSON.

British Columbia Dairy Foundation (BCDF): 3236 Beta Ave, Burnaby, BC V5G 4K4; tel. (604) 294-3775; fax (604) 294-8199; e-mail contactus@bcdf.ca; internet www.bcdairyfoundation.ca; f. 1974; Pres. GAY HAHN; Exec. Dir ROBIN SMITH.

British Columbia Fruit Growers' Association (BCFGA): 1473 Water St, POB 160, Kelowna, BC V1Y 1J6; tel. (250) 762-5226; fax (250) 861-9089; e-mail info@bcfga.com; internet www.bcfga.com; f. 1889; Pres. JOE SARDINHA.

The British Columbia Seafood Alliance: 1200 West 73rd Ave, Suite 1100, Vancouver, BC V6P 6G5; tel. (604) 377-9213; fax (604) 683-4510; e-mail cburridge@smartt.com; internet bcseafoodalliance.com; f. 1999; Exec. Dir CHRISTINA BURRIDGE; 18 mem. asscns.

Canada Beef Export Federation (Canada Beef): 6715 Eighth St, NE, Suite 235, Calgary, AB T2E 7H7; tel. (403) 274-0005; fax (403) 274-7275; e-mail canada@cbef.com; internet www.cbef.com; f. 1989; Chair. BEN THORLAKSON; Pres. TED HANEY.

Canada Grains Council: 220 Portage Ave, Suite 1215, Winnipeg, MB R3C 0A5; tel. (204) 925-2130; fax (204) 925-2132; e-mail office@canadagrainscouncil.ca; internet www.canadagrainscouncil.ca; f. 1969; Chair. RICHARD WANSBUTTER; 34 mems.

Canada Mink Breeders' Association: 65 Skyway Ave, Suite B, Toronto, ON M9W 6C7; tel. (416) 675-9400; fax (416) 675-9401; e-mail cmba@ica.net; internet canadamink.ca; Man. Dir GARY HAZLEWOOD; 250 mems.

Canadian Cattlemen's Association (CCA): 6715 Eighth St, NE, Suite 310, Calgary, AB T2E 7H7; tel. (403) 275-8558; fax (403) 274-5686; e-mail feedback@cattle.ca; internet www.cattle.ca; f. 1932; Pres. HUGH LYNCH-STAUNTON; eight mem. orgs.

Canadian Christmas Tree Growers' Association/Association canadienne des producteurs d'arbres de Noël (CCTGA/ACPAN): c/o Lewis Downey, 120 King St, Waterville, QC J0B 3H0; tel. and fax (819) 837-1146; e-mail hellewdowney@yahoo.ca; internet www.christmastree.net; Pres. LARRY DOWNEY; Exec. Dir LEWIS DOWNEY; six provincial asscn mems.

Canadian Co-operative Wool Growers Ltd (CCWG): 142 Franktown Rd, Carleton Pl., POB 130, Ottawa, ON K7C 3P3; tel. (613) 257-2714; fax (613) 257-8896; e-mail ccwghq@wool.ca; internet www.wool.ca; f. 1918; Pres. JOHN BALDERSON; Gen. Man. ERIC BJERGSO.

Canadian Dairy Commission/Commission canadienne du lait (CDC/CCL): Bldg 55, NCC Driveway, Central Experimental Farm, 960 Carling Ave, Ottawa, ON K1A 0Z2; tel. (613) 792-2000; fax (613) 792-2009; e-mail cdc-ccl@agr.gc.ca; internet www.cdc-ccl.gc.ca; f. 1966; Chair RANDY WILLIAMSON; CEO JOHN CORE; Commr GILLES MARTIN.

Canadian Farm Business Management Council/Conseil canadien de la gestion d'entreprise agricole (CFBMC/CCGEA): 250 City Centre Ave, Suite 300, Ottawa, ON K1R 6K7; tel. (613) 237-9060; fax (613) 237-9330; e-mail council@cfbmc.com; internet www.farmcentre.com; Chair. DONALD DAIGLE; Exec. Dir WENDELL JOYCE.

Canadian Federation of Agriculture/Fédération Canadienne de l'agriculture (CFA/FCA): 75 Albert St, Suite 1101, Ottawa, ON K1P 5E7; tel. (613) 236-3633; fax (613) 236-5749; e-mail info@cfafca.ca; internet www.cfa-fca.ca; f. 1935; Exec. Dir BRIGID RIVOIRE; 21 mems.

Canadian Forestry Association/Association forestière canadienne (CFA/AFC): 1027 Pembroke St East, Suite 200, Pembroke, ON K8A 3M4; tel. (613) 732-2917; fax (613) 732-3386; e-mail manager@canadianforestry.com; internet www.canadianforestry.com; f. 1900; Chair. BARRY WAITO; Gen. Man. DAVE LEMKAY; 6,000 mems.

Canadian Honey Council (CHC): 234-5149 Country Hills Blvd NW, Suite 236, Calgary, AB T3A 5K8; tel. (403) 208-7141; fax (403) 547-4317; e-mail chc-ccm@honeycouncil.ca; internet www.honeycouncil.ca; f. 1940; Pres. ED NOWEK; CEO HEATHER CLAY; 11 mem. asscns.

Canadian Horticultural Council: 9 Corvus Ct, Ottawa, ON K2E 7Z4; tel. (613) 226-4880; fax (613) 226-4497; e-mail question@hortcouncil.ca; internet www.hortcouncil.ca; f. 1922; Pres. LARRY BUBA; Exec. Vice-Pres. ANNE FOWLIE.

Canadian Institute of Forestry/Institut forestier du Canada (CIF/IFC): c/o Canadian Ecology Centre, POB 430, 6905 Highway 17 West, Mattawa, ON P0H 1V0; tel. (705) 744-1715; fax (705) 744-1716; e-mail admin@cif-ifc.org; internet www.cif-ifc.org; f. 1908; Pres. FRED PINTO; Exec. Dir JOHN PINEAU; 2,000 individual mems (2007).

Canadian Lumbermen's Association/Association canadienne de l'industrie du bois (CLA/ACIB): 30 Concourse Gate, Suite 200, Ottawa, ON K2E 7V7; tel. (613) 233-6205; fax (613) 233-1929; e-mail info@cla-ca.ca; internet www.canadianlumbermen.com; f. 1907; Pres. and Exec. Dir JEAN-FRANÇOIS HOUDE; Chair. JEAN-PAUL LUPIEN; 206 mems.

Canadian Meat Council/Conseil des viandes du Canada (CMC/CVC): 955 Green Valley Cres., Suite 305, Ottawa, ON K2C 3V4; tel. (613) 729-3911; fax (613) 729-4997; e-mail info@cmc-cvc.com; internet www.cmc-cvc.com; f. 1919; Pres. BRIAN NILSSON; Exec. Dir JAMES M. LAWS; 45 regular and 60 assoc. mems.

Canadian Nursery Landscape Association/Association canadienne des pépiniéristes et des paysagistes: 7856 Fifth Line South, RR 4, Stn Main, Milton, ON L9T 2X8; tel. (905) 875-1399; fax (905) 875-1840; e-mail info@canadanursery.com; internet www.canadanursery.com; f. 1922 as the Eastern Canada Nurserymen's Asscn; present name adopted in 1999; Pres. MICHAEL MURRAY; Exec. Dir VICTOR SANTACRUZ; 3,200 mems.

Canadian Organic Growers (COG): 323 Chapel St, Ottawa, ON K1N 7Z2; tel. (613) 216-0741; fax (613) 236-0743; e-mail office@cog.ca; internet www.cog.ca; f. 1975; Pres. ARNOLD TAYLOR; Exec. Dir LAURA TELFORD.

Canadian Pork Council/Conseil canadien du porc (CPC/CCP): 75 Albert St, Suite 1101, Ottawa, ON K1P 5E7; tel. (613) 236-9239; fax (613) 236-6658; e-mail info@cpc-ccp.com; internet www.cpc-ccp.com; Pres. JURGEN PREUGSCHAS; nine mems.

Canadian Poultry and Egg Processors' Council/Conseil canadien des transformateurs d'oeufs et de volailles (CPEPC/CCTOV): 1545 Carling Ave, Suite 400, Ottawa, ON K1Z 8P9; tel. (613) 724-6605; fax (613) 724-4577; e-mail robinhorel@cpepc.ca; internet www.cpepc.ca; f. 1951; Chair. PAUL BORG; Pres. and CEO ROBIN HOREL; 170 mems, 60 assoc. mems.

Canadian Produce Marketing Association (CPMA): 162 Cleopatra Dr., Ottawa, ON K2G 5X2; tel. (613) 226-4187; fax (613) 226-2984; e-mail question@cpma.ca; internet www.cpma.ca; Chair. LARRY MCINTOSH; Pres. DANNY DEMPSTER; Exec. Vice-Pres. RON LEMAIRE; over 600 mems.

Canadian Seed Growers' Association: 240 Catherine St, Suite 202, POB 8455, Ottawa, ON K1G 3T1; tel. (613) 236-0497; fax (613) 563-7855; e-mail seeds@seedgrowers.ca; internet www.seedgrowers.ca; f. 1904; Pres. ED LEFSRUD; Exec. Dir DALE ADOLPHE; 4,500 mems.

Canadian Sheep Breeders' Association/La société canadienne des eleveurs de moutons (CSBA/SCEM): 1489 Route 560, Deerville, NB E7K 1W7; fax (506) 328-8165; e-mail office@sheepbreeders.ca; internet www.sheepbreeders.ca; Pres. MICHAEL RIEBERGER; Vice-Pres. DANIEL DION; over 1,000 mems.

Canadian Society of Agronomy (CSA): POB 637, Pinawa, MB R0E 1L0; tel. (204) 753-2747; fax (204) 753-8478; e-mail sheppards@ecomatters.com; internet www.agronomycanada.com; f. 1954; Pres. TOM BRUULSEMA; Exec. Dir STEVE SHEPPARD; c. 300 mems.

Canadian Wheat Board: see Government—Selected Federal Government Agencies and Boards.

Canadian Wood Council (CWC/CCB): 99 Bank St, Suite 400, Ottawa, ON K1P 6B9; tel. (613) 747-5544; fax (613) 747-6264; e-mail webmaster@cwc.ca; internet www.cwc.ca; f. 1959; Pres. PAULINE ROCHEFORT; Chair. YVES LAFLAMME; 14 mem. asscns.

Canola Council of Canada: 167 Lombard Ave, Suite 400, Winnipeg, MB R3B 0T6; tel. (204) 982-2100; fax (204) 942-1841; e-mail admin@canola-council.org; internet www.canola-council.org; Chair. STEWART GILROY; Pres. JOANN BUTH.

Chicken Farmers of Canada/Les producteurs de poulet du Canada (CFC/PPC): 350 Sparks St, Suite 1007, Ottawa, ON K1R 7S8; tel. (613) 241-2800; fax (613) 241-5999; e-mail cfc@chicken.ca; internet www.chicken.ca; f. 1978; Chair. DAVID FULLER; 2,800 mems.

Conseil de l'industrie laitière du Québec inc/Québec Dairy Council: 8585 blvd St-Laurent, bureau 310, Montréal, QC H2P 2M9; tel. (514) 381-5331; fax (514) 381-6677; e-mail info@cilq.ca; internet www.cilq.ca; f. 1963; Pres. PIERRE M. NADEAU.

Council of Forest Industries (COFI): I Business Bldg, Suite 1501, 700 West Pender St, Pender Pl., Vancouver, BC V6C 1G8; tel. (604) 684-0211; fax (604) 687-4930; e-mail info@cofi.org; internet www.cofi.org; f. 1960; Pres. and CEO JOHN ALLAN; Chair. BLAIR MAYES; 51 mems.

Dairy Farmers of Canada/Producteurs laitiers du Canada (DFC/PLC): 21 Florence St, Ottawa, ON K2P 0W6; tel. (613) 236-9997; fax (613) 236-0905; internet www.dairygoodness.ca; f. 1934; Dir-Gen. RICHARD DOYLE; 12 mems.

Dairy Farmers of Manitoba (DFM): 36 Scurfield Blvd, POB 724, Station Main, Winnipeg, MB R3C 2K3; tel. (204) 488-6455; fax (204) 488-4772; e-mail general@milk.mb.ca; internet www.milk.mb.ca; f. 1974; Chair. DAVID WEINS; Gen. Man. BRENT ACHTEMICHUK; nine mems.

Dairy Farmers of Nova Scotia (DFNS): 4060 Hwy 236, Suite 100, Truro, NS B2N 5A9; tel. (902) 893-6455; fax (902) 897-9768; e-mail hboyd@dfns.ca; internet www.dfns.ca; f. 2001 by merger of the Nova Scotia Dairy Comm. and the Nova Scotia Milk Producers' Asscn; Chair. BARRON BLOIS; Gen. Man. BRIAN CAMERON; over 295 mems.

Dairy Farmers of Ontario (DFO): 6780 Campobello Rd, Mississauga, ON L5N 2L8; tel. (905) 821-8970; fax (905) 821-3160; e-mail questions@milk.org; internet www.milk.org; f. 1995; Chair. BRUCE SAUNDERS; Gen. Man. and CEO PETER GOULD.

Farm Animal Council Saskatchewan, Inc (FACS): 502 45th St West, Saskatoon, SK S7L 6H2; tel. (306) 249-3227; fax (306) 244-4497; e-mail facs@sasktel.net; internet www.facs.sk.ca; f. 1992; Exec. Dir ADELE BUETTNER.

Fisheries Council of Canada: 170 Laurier Ave West, Suite 900, Ottawa, ON K1P 5V5; tel. (613) 727-7450; fax (613) 727-7453; e-mail info@fisheriescouncil.org; internet www.fisheriescouncil.ca; f. 1915; Pres. PATRICK MCGUINNESS; six mem. asscns, over 110 mem. cos.

Flax Council of Canada: 167 Lombard Ave, Suite 465, Winnipeg, MB R3B 0T6; tel. (204) 982-2115; fax (204) 982-2128; e-mail flax@flaxcouncil.ca; internet www.flaxcouncil.ca; f. 1986; Pres. BARRY HALL; Chair. ERIC FRIDFINNSON.

Forest Products Association of Canada/Association des produits forestiers du Canada (FPAC/APFC): 99 Bank St, Suite 410, Ottawa, ON KIP 6B9; tel. (613) 563-1441; fax (613) 563-4720; e-mail ottawa@fpac.ca; internet www.fpac.ca; f. 1913; fmrly the Canadian Pulp and Paper Asscn; Pres. and CEO AVRIM LAZAR; 20 mem. cos.

Fur Council of Canada/Conseil canadien de la fourrure (FCC/CCF): 1435 rue St Alexandre, Suite 1270, Montréal, QC H3A 2G4; tel. (514) 844-1945; fax (514) 844-8593; e-mail info@furcouncil.com; internet www.furcouncil.com; f. 1964; Pres. PAULA LISHMAN.

Fur Institute of Canada/Institut de la fourrure du Canada (FIC/IFC): 331 Cooper St, Suite 701, Ottawa, ON K2P 0G5; tel. (613) 231-7099; fax (613) 231-7940; e-mail info@fur.ca; internet www.fur.ca; f. 1983; Chair. BRUCE WILLIAMS; Exec. Dir ROB CAHILL.

Furriers Guild of Canada: 4174 Dundas St West, Suite 211, Toronto, ON M8X 1X3; tel. (416) 234-9494; fax (416) 234-2244; e-mail furriersguildca@ica.net; Exec. Dir LYNDA JAGROS-MAY.

Manitoba Association of Agricultural Societies: 1129 Queens Ave, Brandon, MB R7A 1L9; tel. (204) 726-6195; fax (204) 726-6260; e-mail egauer@gov.mb.ca; internet www.gov.mb.ca/agriculture/organizations/agsocieties; Pres. DORIS FLETCHER.

Manitoba Farm Animal Council (MFAC): 36 Scurfield Blvd, POB 723, Winnipeg, MB R3Y 1N9; tel. (204) 487-4031; fax (204) 489-0547; e-mail info@mbfac.ca; internet www.mbfac.ca; f. 1990; Chair. GARY TOLTON; Exec. Dir SHANYN SILINSKI.

Mushrooms Canada: 7660 Mill Rd, Suite 4, Guelph, ON N1H 6J1; tel. (519) 829-4125; fax (519) 837-0729; e-mail cmga@sentex.net; internet www.mushrooms.ca; f. 1955; Exec. Vice-Pres. WILLIAM STEVENS.

National Farmers Union (NFU): 2717 Wentz Ave, Saskatoon, SK S7K 4B6; tel. (306) 652-9465; fax (306) 664-6226; e-mail nfu@nfu.ca; internet www.nfu.ca; f. 1969; Pres. STEWART WELLS; 10,000 mems.

Nova Scotia Federation of Agriculture (NSFA): Covington Pl., 2nd Floor, 332 Willow St, Truro, NS B2N 5A5; tel. (902) 893-2293; fax (902) 893-7063; e-mail info@nsfa-fane.ca; internet www.nsfa-fane.ca; f. 1895; Pres. WILLY VERSTEEG; CEO LAURENCE NASON; 1,800 individual mems, 13 federated mems, 20 group mems.

Nova Scotia Fruit Growers' Association (NSFGA): Kentville Agricultural Centre, 32 Main St, Kentville, NS B4N 1J5; tel. (902) 678-1093; fax (902) 678-1567; internet www.nsapples.com/intrnsfg.htm; f. 1863; Pres. GEORGE LEMMON; Exec. Dir DELA ERITH.

Ontario Agri-Business Association (OABA): 160 Research Lane, Suite 104, Guelph, ON N1G 5B2; tel. (519) 822-3004; fax (519) 822-8862; e-mail info@oaba.on.ca; internet www.oaba.on.ca; f. 1965; name changed as above in 1999; Pres. GWEN PADDOCK; CEO DAVE BUTTENHAM.

Ontario Dairy Council (ODC): 6533 Mississauga Rd, Unit D, Mississauga, ON L5N 1A6; tel. (905) 542-3620; fax (905) 542-3624; e-mail info@ontariodairies.ca; internet www.ontariodairies.ca; f. 1971; Pres. TOM KANE; Chair. YVES LEROUX; 43 mems, 46 assoc. mems (2005).

Ontario Farm Animal Council (OFAC): Ontario AgriCentre, 100 Stone Rd, Suite 106, Guelph, ON N1G 5L3; tel. (519) 837-1326; fax (519) 837-3209; e-mail info@ofac.org; internet www.ofac.org; f. 1988; Chair. JOHN MAASKANT; Exec. Dir CRYSTAL MACKAY.

Ontario Federation of Agriculture (OFA): Ontario AgriCentre, 100 Stone Rd, Suite 206, Guelph, Ontario, ON N1G 5L3; tel. (519) 821-8883; fax (519) 821-8810; e-mail inquiries@ofa.on.ca; internet www.ofa.on.ca; f. 1937; Pres. and Chair. GERI KAMENZ; Gen. Man. NEIL CURRIE; 38,000 individual mems, 30 mem. orgs.

Ontario Forest Industries Association: 20 Toronto St West, Suite 950, Toronto, ON M5C 2B8; tel. (416) 368-6188; fax (416) 368-5445; e-mail info@ofia.com; internet www.ofia.com; f. 1943; Pres. and CEO JAMIE LIM; 20 mem. cos, 10 affiliate mems.

Ontario Fruit and Vegetable Growers' Association: 355 Elmira Rd North, Unit 105, Guelph, ON N1K 1S5; tel. (519) 763-6160; fax (519) 763-6604; e-mail artsmith@ofvga.org; internet www.ofvga.org; Chair. BRENDA LAMMENS; CEO ART SMITH; 28 mem. orgs representing more than 7,500 individual mems.

Ontario Lumber Manufacturers' Association (OLMA): 65 Queen St West, Suite 210, Toronto, ON M5H 2M5; tel. (416) 367-9717; fax (416) 367-3415; e-mail info@olma.ca; internet www.olma.ca; f. 1967; Pres. DAVID G. MILTON.

Organic Agriculture Centre of Canada/Centre d'agriculture biologique du Canada (OACC/CABC): Nova Scotia Agricultural College, POB 550, Truro, NS B2N 5E3; tel. (902) 893-7256; fax (902) 896-7095; e-mail oacc@nsac.ca; internet www.oacc.info; f. 2001; Dir Dr RALPH C. MARTIN.

Prince Edward Island Federation of Agriculture: 420 University Ave, Charlottetown, PEI C1A 7Z5; tel. (902) 368-7289; fax (902) 368-7204; e-mail miken@peifa.ca; internet www.peifa.ca; f. 1941; Pres. JOHN COLWILL; Exec. Dir MIKE NABUURS.

Québec Farmers' Association: 555 Blvd, Roland-Therrien, Suite 255, Longueuil, QC J4H 4E7; tel. (450) 679-0540; fax (450) 463-5291; e-mail qfa@upa.qc.ca; internet www.quebecfarmers.org; f. 1957; affiliated to the Union des Producteurs Agricoles; Pres. GIB DRURY; Exec. Dir IVAN HALE.

Society of Ontario Nut Growers (SONG): RR 3, Niagara-on-the-Lake, ON L0S 1J0; tel. (905) 934-6887; internet www.songonline.ca; f. 1972; Treas. ERNIE GRIMO; 300 mems.

Union des producteurs agricoles: 555 blvd Roland-Therrien, bureau 100, Longueuil, QC J4H 3Y9; tel. (450) 679-0530; fax (450) 679-5436; e-mail upa@upa.qc.ca; internet www.upa.qc.ca; f. 1924; Pres. CHRISTIAN LACASSE; 44,000 mems.

Viterra: CanWest Global Pl., 201 Portage Ave, POB 6600, Winnipeg, MB R3C 3A7; tel. (204) 944-5411; fax (204) 944-5454; e-mail susan.cline@viterra.ca; internet www.viterra.ca; f. 2007 by merger of Agricore United and Saskatchewan Wheat Pool; Chair. THOMAS BIRKS; Pres. and CEO MAYO SCHMIDT.

Western Barley Growers' Association: Agriculture Centre, 97 East Lake Ramp, NE, Airdrie, AB T4A 0C3; tel. (403) 912-3998; fax (403) 948-2069; e-mail wbga@wbga.org; internet www.wbga.org; f. 1977; Pres. JEFF NIELSEN.

Western Canadian Wheat Growers Association (WCWGA): 502 45th St West, 2nd Floor, Saskatoon, SK S7L 6H2; tel. (306) 586-5866; fax (306) 244-4497; e-mail info@wheatgrowers.ca; internet www.wheatgrowers.ca; f. 1970; Chair. MIKE BAST; Pres. CHERILYN JOLLY-NAGEL; 395 mems (2005).

MINING

Mineral Fuels

(Source: Statistics Canada.)

SUMMARY

	2003		2004		2005	
	Quantity	Value (C $ million)	Quantity	Value (C $ million)	Quantity	Value (C $ million)
Coal ('000 metric tons)	62,125	1,492.2	65,997	1,596.5	65,317	2,328.5
Natural gas (marketable, million cu m)	166,457	37,044.6	167,503	38,103.9	170,740	51,101.9
Natural gas by-products ('000 cu m)	29,440	5,702.6	30,062	6,260.9	30,254	7,942.0
Crude petroleum and equivalent ('000 cu m)	144,813	33,610.5	149,160	40,640.0	146,208	49,159.8

PROVINCES AND TERRITORIES
(2005 unless otherwise indicated)

	Coal ('000 metric tons)*	Crude petroleum and equivalent ('000 cu m)	Natural gas (million cu m)	Natural gas by-products ('000 cu m†)
Alberta	31,250	98,879	131,798	27,968
British Columbia	21,131	2,461	26,938	1,766
Manitoba	—	812	—	—
New Brunswick	108	—	—	—
Newfoundland and Labrador (incl. offshore)	—	17,678	—	—
Nova Scotia (incl. offshore)	0	742	3,946	407
Northwest Territories	—	1,174	411	—
Ontario	—	139	255	—
Saskatchewan	10,441	24,324‡	7,243	115
Yukon Territory	—	—	151	—
Total	62,929	146,208	170,740	30,256

* 2006.
† Includes estimates for ethane before solvent flood.
‡ Excludes volume of upgraded crude petroleum.

Metals

(Source: Natural Resources Canada, Minerals and Mining Statistics Division.)

SUMMARY
(shipments, metric tons, metal content unless otherwise indicated)

	2005		2006		2007*	
	Quantity	Value (C $ million)	Quantity	Value (C $ million)	Quantity	Value (C $ million)
Cobalt	2,391	102.0	2,899	124.8	3,211	223.2
Copper	577,304	2,572.5	586,489	4,470.2	577,255	4,533.2
Gold (kg)	119,549	2,071.8	103,513	2,280.9	100,157	2,376.9
Iron ore ('000 metric tons, gross weight)	30,387	2,339.5	33,543	2,530.3	33,158	2,512.1
Lead	72,828	86.1	79,171	115.7	68,735	199.4
Molybdenum†	7,667	n.a.	7,117	n.a.	6,812	n.a.
Nickel	192,855	3,510.3	224,565	6,165.9	245,146	9,902.2
Niobium (columbium)†	3,710	n.a.	4,177	n.a.	4,313	n.a.
Platinum group (kg)	22,709	405.4	23,170	498.2	23,042	542.8
Silver	1,063	304.0	970	409.2	831	380.6
Tungsten	484	8.2	2,500	64.5	2,700	71.9
Uranium	12,597	1,131.6	9,781	1,430.6	9,098	2,522.7
Zinc	618,844	1,035.9	601,481	2,182.8	584,682	2,087.9

* Provisional.

† Figures relating to the value of molybdenum production are undisclosed owing to confidentiality restrictions. In 2001 8,556 metric tons of molybdenum were produced, valued at C $73.8m. Historical data on the value of niobium production were unavailable.

PROVINCES AND TERRITORIES
(2007, provisional figures)

	Copper (metric tons)	Gold (kg)	Iron ore ('000 metric tons)	Lead (metric tons)	Nickel (metric tons)	Silver (metric tons)	Uranium (metric tons)	Zinc (metric tons)
Alberta	—	53	—	—	—	—	—	—
British Columbia	252,177	12,101	75	2,562	—	261	—	30,355
Manitoba	55,517	3,738	—	—	33,617	40	—	105,602
New Brunswick	8,906	230	—	66,173	—	191	—	244,251
Newfoundland and Labrador	60,680	268	18,436	—	72,881	18	—	15,678
Northwest Territories	—	—	—	—	—	—	—	—
Nova Scotia	—	—	—	—	—	—	—	—
Nunavut Territory	—	—	—	—	—	—	—	—
Ontario	178,673	53,034	—	—	114,026	133	—	84,019
Québec	21,303	27,354	14,647	—	24,622	187	—	104,777
Saskatchewan	—	1,391	—	—	—	—	9,098	—
Yukon Territory	—	1,988	—	—	—	—	—	—
Total	577,255	100,157	33,158	68,735	245,146	831	9,098	584,682

Non-Metallic Minerals

(Source: Natural Resources Canada, Minerals and Mining Statistics Division.)

SUMMARY
(shipments, '000 metric tons unless otherwise indicated)

	2005		2006		2007*	
	Quantity	Value (C $ million)	Quantity	Value (C $ million)	Quantity	Value (C $ million)
Asbestos†	n.a.	n.a.	n.a.	n.a.	n.a.	n.a.
Diamonds ('000 carats)	12,314	1,762.1	13,278	1,282.1	17,008	1,444.7
Gypsum‡	8,570	113.9	9,036	127.0	7,638	112.1
Nepheline syenite	745	63.3	734	60.7	765	67.0
Peat	1,304	219.1	1,217	219.7	1,187	237.0
Potash§	10,140	2,437.5	8,518	2,240.7	11,426	3,142.0
Quartz‡	1,807	59.7	2,146	67,495	2,263	78.4
Salt	13,463	432.0	14,460	460.7	11,818	426.6
Sand and gravel‡	243,440	1,180.3	238,515	1,275.7	234,658	1,316.5
Soapstone, talc, pyrophyllite	70	26.2	72	24.2	67	23.5
Stone‡	141,275	1,215.0	153,897	1,372.9	145,825	1,333.1
Sulphur (in smelter gas)	653	36.0	676	34.3	632	25.9
Sulphur (elemental)	7,757	234.2	7,762	126.4	7,603	180.8

* Provisional figures.
† Figures undisclosed owing to confidentiality restrictions.
‡ Excludes shipments to Canadian cement, lime and clay plants.
§ Excludes shipments to Canadian potassium sulphate plants.

PROVINCES AND TERRITORIES
('000 metric tons, 2007 unless otherwise indicated, provisional)

	Asbestos*	Diamonds ('000 carats)	Gypsum†	Peat	Salt	Sand and gravel†	Stone†
Alberta	—	—	—	184	283	50,248	1,702
British Columbia	—	—	n.a.‡	n.a.‡	—	33,541	11,693
Manitoba	—	—	n.a.‡	111	n.a.‡	11,903	5,444
New Brunswick	—	—	—	432	n.a.‡	3,055	5,560
Newfoundland and Labrador	—	—	—	—	—	2,237	5,094
Northwest Territories	—	16,638	—	—	—	567	499
Nova Scotia	—	—	6,455	n.a.‡	—	3,930	10,790
Nunavut	—	370	—	—	—	—	—
Ontario	—	—	n.a.‡	—	7,618	99,646	61,822
Prince Edward Island	—	—	—	n.a.‡	—	149	—
Québec	242	—	—	355	n.a.‡	18,814	43,221
Saskatchewan	—	—	—	n.a.‡	1,170	9,371	—
Yukon Territory	—	—	—	—	—	1,196	—
Total§	242	17,008	7,638	1,187	11,818	234,658	145,825

* 2002 figures; more recent figures are unavailable owing to confidentiality restrictions.
† Excludes shipments to Canadian cement, lime and clay plants.
‡ Figure undisclosed owing to confidentiality restrictions.
§ Including, in some cases, undisclosed provincial data.

Selected Mining Organizations

Association for Mineral Exploration British Columbia (AME BC): 889 West Pender St, Suite 800, Vancouver, BC V6C 3B2; tel. (604) 689-5271; fax (604) 681-2363; e-mail info@amebc.ca; internet www.amebc.ca; f. 1912; Chair. ROBERT STEVENS; Pres. and CEO DAN M. JEPSEN; over 4,000 individual mems, 100 corporate mems.

Association minière du Québec/Québec Mining Association Inc: Tour Belle Cour, Suite 2620, 2600 blvd Laurier, Sainte-Foy, QC G1V 4M6; tel. (418) 657-2016; fax (418) 657-2154; e-mail mines@amq-inc.com; internet www.amq-inc.com; Chair. SERGE VÉZINA; Pres. DAN TOLGYESI; 28 mems, four assoc. mems.

Canada-Newfoundland Offshore Petroleum Board: 140 Water St, TD Pl., 5th Floor, St John's, NL A1C 6H6; tel. (709) 778-1400; e-mail information@cnopb.nl.ca; internet www.cnlopb.nl.ca; Chair. and CEO MAX RUELOKKE.

Canada-Nova Scotia Offshore Petroleum Board: TD Centre, 6th Floor, 1791 Barrington St, Halifax, NS B3J 3K9; tel. (902) 422-5588; fax (902) 422-1799; e-mail postmaster@cnsopb.ns.ca; internet www.cnsopb.ns.ca; independent agency of the Govts of Canada and Nova Scotia; Chair. and Acting CEO DIANA LEE DALTON.

Canadian Association of Mining Equipment and Services for Export (CAMESE): 345 Renfrew Dr., Suite 101, Markham, ON L3R 9S9; tel. (905) 513-0046; fax (905) 513-1834; e-mail minesupply@camese.org; internet www.camese.org; Man. Dir JON BAIRD.

Canadian Association of Petroleum Producers (CAPP): 350 Seventh Ave, SW, Suite 2100, Calgary, AB T2P 3N9; tel. (403) 267-1100; fax (403) 261-4622; e-mail communication@capp.ca; internet www.capp.ca; f. 1952; represents the upstream petroleum and natural gas industry; Chair. GERARD PROTTI; Pres. DAVID COLLYER; 150 mems, 125 assoc. mems.

Canadian Gas Association: see Energy—Petroleum and Gas.

Canadian Institute of Mining, Metallurgy and Petroleum: 3400 blvd de Maisonneuve ouest, Suite 855, Montréal, QC H3Z 3B8; tel. (514) 939-2710; fax (514) 939-2714; e-mail cim@cim.org; internet www.cim.org; f. 1898; Pres. and CEO JAMES K. GOWANS; Exec. Dir JEAN VAVREK.

Canadian Mining Contractors Association: 1088 Staghorn Court, Mississauga, ON L5C 3R2; tel. (905) 279-0104; fax (905) 279-1646; Pres. BRUCE CAMPBELL.

Canadian Mining Industry Research Organization (CAMIRO): 935 Ramsey Lake Rd, Sudbury, ON P3E 2C6; tel. (705) 673-6595; fax (705) 671-6606; e-mail info@camiro.org; internet www.camiro.org; includes three divisions operating as separate entities: exploration, mining and metallurgical processing; Man. Dir CHARLES B. GRAHAM.

Coal Association of Canada: 205 Ninth Ave, SE, Suite 150, Calgary, AB T2G 0R3; tel. (403) 262-1544; fax (403) 265-7604; e-mail info@coal.ca; internet www.coal.ca; f. 1973; Chair. GEORGE WHITE; Pres. and CEO ALLEN WRIGHT; 50 mem. cos.

Mining Association of British Columbia (MABC): 9th Floor, 808 West Hastings St, Suite 900, Vancouver, BC V6C 2X4; tel. (604) 681-4321; fax (604) 681-5305; e-mail mabcinfo@mining.bc.ca; internet www.mining.bc.ca; f. 1901; Pres. and CEO PIERRE GRATTON; 48 mem. cos.

Mining Association of Canada (MAC): 350 Sparks St, Suite 1105, Ottawa, ON K1R 7S8; tel. (613) 233-9391; fax (613) 233-8897; e-mail info@mining.ca; internet www.mining.ca; f. 1935; Chair. JAMES GOWANS; Pres. and CEO GORDON R. PEELING; 29 mems, 41 assoc. mems.

Mining Association of Manitoba Inc (MAMI): 305 Broadway Ave, Suite 700, Winnipeg, MB R3C 3J7; tel. (204) 989-1890; fax (204) 989-1899; e-mail dmarkham@mines.ca; internet www.mines.ca; Exec. Vice-Pres. ED HUEBERT.

Mining Association of Nova Scotia: POB 2171, 4548 RR 3, Windsor, NS B0N 2T0; tel. (902) 406-7625; fax (902) 406-7626; e-mail info@tmans.com; internet www.tmans.ca; Pres. PETER ORAM; Exec. Dir MICHELLE LANDREVILLE.

Mining Society of Nova Scotia: 88 Leeside Dr., Sydney, NS B1R 1S6; tel. and fax (902) 567-2147; e-mail msns@cim.org; f. 1892; Pres. FENTON ISENOR; Sec.-Treas. GEORGE SIGUT.

New Brunswick Mining Association: 236 St George St, Suite 104, Moncton, NB E1C 1W1; tel. (506) 857-3056; fax (506) 857-3059; e-mail dplante@nbnet.nb.ca; Exec. Dir DAVID R. PLANTE.

Newfoundland and Labrador Chamber of Mineral Resources: Prince Charles Bldg, 120 Torbay Rd, Suite W280, St John's, NL A1A 2G8; tel. (709) 722-9542; fax (709) 722-8588; e-mail director@nlcmr.ca; internet www.nlcmr.ca; Chair. TIMOTHY FROUDE; Exec. Dir GERRY O'CONNELL.

Northwest Territories and Nunavut Chamber of Mines: POB 2818, Yellowknife, NT X1A 2R1; tel. (867) 873-5281; fax (867) 920-2145; e-mail nwtmines@ssimicro.com; internet www.miningnorth.com; f. 1967 as Northwest Territories Chamber of Mines; present name adopted in 2000; Pres. LOUIS COVELLO; Gen. Man. MIKE VAYDIK; 600 mems.

Ontario Mining Association: 5775 Yonge St, Suite 520, North York, ON M2M 4J1; tel. (416) 364-9301; fax (416) 364-5986; internet www.oma.on.ca; f. 1920; Pres. CHRIS HODGSON; 55 mems.

Petroleum Services Association of Canada: 800 Sixth Ave, SW, Suite 1150, Calgary, AB T2P 3G3; tel. (403) 264-4195; fax (403) 263-7174; e-mail info@psac.ca; internet www.psac.ca; Chair. FRANK TIRPAK; Pres. and CEO ROGER SOUCY; over 260 mems.

Prospectors and Developers Association of Canada (PDAC): 135 King St East, Toronto, ON M5C 1G6; tel. (416) 362-1969; fax (416) 362-0101; e-mail info@pdac.ca; internet www.pdac.ca; f. 1932; Pres. JON BAIRD; Exec. Dir ANTHONY J. ANDREWS; 5,300 individual mems, c. 700 corporate mems.

Saskatchewan Mining Association: 2002 Victoria Ave, Suite 1740, Regina, SK S4P 0R7; tel. (306) 757-9505; fax (306) 569-1085; e-mail saskmining@sasktel.net; internet www.saskmining.ca; Pres. BRUCE LAMBERT; Exec. Dir PAMELA SCHWANN; 31 mems.

Yukon Chamber of Mines: 3151B Third Ave, Whitehorse, YT Y1A 1G1; tel. (867) 667-2090; fax (867) 668-7127; e-mail info@ycmines.ca; internet www.ycmines.ca; f. 1947; Pres. CARL SCHULZE; Exec. Officer SCOTT KENT; 500 mems.

INDUSTRY

Manufacturing Production

(Source: Statistics Canada.)

SUMMARY OF SHIPMENTS
(C $ million)

	2005	2006	2007
Food industries	67,594.8	71,721.2	73,853.6
Beverage and tobacco products industries	12,646.2	11,318.7	10,859.1
Textile mills	3,319.6	2,539.6	2,231.4
Textile product mills	2,578.5	2,473.1	2,465.9
Clothing industries	5,289.6	4,981.0	4,325.4
Leather and allied products industries	516.2	464.0	510.4
Wood industries	34,092.3	30,497.8	25,001.2
Paper and allied products industries	32,499.4	31,097.8	30,249.7
Printing, publishing and allied industries	11,866.5	10,989.3	10,612.6
Refined petroleum and coal products industries	57,029.9	61,487.2	66,692.5
Chemical and chemical products industries	49,614.8	50,119.8	49,124.4
Plastics and rubber products industries	26,825.4	27,620.6	25,937.3
Non-metallic mineral products industries	12,727.3	14,113.2	14,473.3
Primary metal industries	43,029.4	50,829.2	52,987.9
Fabricated metal products industries	34,276.4	34,754.9	36,647.6
Machinery industries	30,167.9	31,056.0	32,288.5
Computer and electronic products industries	19,762.4	19,541.2	18,968.1
Electrical equipment, appliance and component industries	9,899.8	10,475.6	10,679.3
Transportation equipment industries	124,785.8	118,776.4	116,051.5
Furniture and fixture industries	13,342.9	13,397.9	13,762.7
Other manufacturing industries	8,484.6	9,125.7	9,621.7
Total (incl. others)	600,349.6	607,380.3	607,343.9

PROVINCES AND TERRITORIES
(value of shipments, C $ million)

	2005	2006	2007
Alberta	60,439.1	64,381.8	65,592.5
British Columbia	42,983.8	44,943.9	42,929.5
Manitoba	13,702.3	14,854.2	16,111.3
New Brunswick	15,248.1	14,835.7	15,679.6
Newfoundland and Labrador	2,781.9	4,356.4	5,257.6
Northwest Territories	90.8	64.2	45.8
Nova Scotia	10,017.9	9,655.0	9,873.7
Nunavut Territory	6.3	7.0	6.5
Ontario	304,036.9	296,105.2	291,692.9
Prince Edward Island	1,276.8	1,412.7	1,428.6
Québec	140,084.5	146,657.0	148,260.3
Saskatchewan	9,656.1	10,080.5	10,435.8
Yukon Territory	24.9	26.7	29.7

Construction

VALUE OF CONSTRUCTION WORK PURCHASED
(C $ million)

	2003	2004	2005
Total building construction	88,978.8	100,009.1	105,053.7
Total residential building construction	61,607.5	70,060.2	73,574.9
Single-detached houses	20,949.5	23,288.2	23,350.8
Semi-detached houses	1,687.1	1,801.7	1,789.9
Apartments and row houses	8,036.3	10,054.0	11,394.2
Other residential buildings	30,934.6	34,916.3	37,040.0
Total non-residential building construction	27,371.3	29,948.9	31,478.9
Industrial building construction	4,024.9	3,952.7	3,841.7
Plants for manufacturing, processing and assembling goods	1,905.9	1,662.5	1,570.2
Commercial building construction	14,303.3	16,890.0	17,458.2
Office buildings	4,135.3	4,278.7	5,315.2
Shopping centres, plazas, malls, stores	3,947.7	5,837.7	5,490.2
Indoor recreational buildings	938.1	1,660.3	1,551.4
Institutional building construction	9,043.0	9,106.2	10,178.9
Schools, colleges, universities and other educational buildings	4,237.1	4,347.4	4,715.1
Hospitals, health centres, clinics, other health care	2,003.2	2,073.1	2,730.2
Nursing homes, homes for the aged	1,692.7	1,301.0	1,192.6
Penitentiaries, detention centres and courthouses	171.4	211.3	247.9
Total engineering construction	47,784.6	54,116.1	66,911.0
Marine engineering construction	201.8	286.6	365.1
Transportation engineering construction	8,299.7	8,770.4	10,811.1
Waterworks engineering construction	1,756.1	2,188.9	2,575.7
Sewage engineering construction	1,888.1	2,092.8	2,246.3
Electric power engineering construction	6,159.3	6,141.3	6,302.2
Communication engineering construction	1,993.3	1,983.8	2,193.9
Oil and gas engineering construction	23,831.0	27,996.1	36,998.5
Mining engineering construction	1,907.1	2,943.9	3,760.5
Other engineering construction	1,748.2	1,712.3	1,657.8
Total capital expenditures on construction	136,763.3	154,125.1	171,964.8

Source: Statistics Canada, CANSIM II Table 029-0039, September 2008.

Chambers of Commerce

NATIONAL AND REGIONAL ORGANIZATIONS

Atlantic Provinces Chambers of Commerce: 236 St George St, Suite 21, Moncton, NB E1C 1W1; tel. (506) 857-3980; fax (506) 859-6131; e-mail info@apcc.ca; internet www.apcc.ca; f. 1896; Chair. JONATHAN DANIELS.

The Canadian Chamber of Commerce: 360 Albert St, Suite 420, Ottawa, ON K1R 7X7; tel. (613) 238-4000; fax (613) 238-7643; e-mail bzeiler-kligman@chamber.ca; internet www.chamber.ca; f. 1925; part of the Int. Chamber of Commerce, and of the Business and Industry Advisory Cttee to the Organisation for Economic Co-operation and Development (OECD); Chair. JOHN PELLER; Pres. and CEO PERRIN BEATTY; 170,000 mems.

Northwest Territories Chamber of Commerce (NWT Chamber of Commerce): 13 50th Ave, Suite 4910, Yellowknife, NT X1A 3S5; tel. (867) 920-9505; fax (867) 873-4174; e-mail admin@nwtchamber.com; internet www.nwtchamber.com; f. 1973; board of directors comprises representatives from each regional chamber within the Northwest Territories; Pres. DON YAMKOWY; Exec. Dir ROBIN WOTHERSPOON; 865 mems.

ORGANIZATIONS BY PROVINCE AND TERRITORY

Alberta

Alberta Chambers of Commerce: 102A 10025 Ave, Suite 1808, Edmonton, AB T5J 2Z2; tel. (780) 425-4180; fax (780) 429-1061; e-mail pbrace@abchamber.ca; internet www.abchamber.ca; Chair. JACK GRANT; Pres. and CEO KEN KOBLY; 127 mems.

Calgary Chamber of Commerce: 100 Sixth Ave, SW Calgary, AB T2P 0P5; tel. (403) 750-0400; fax (403) 266-3413; e-mail chinfo@calgarychamber.com; internet www.calgarychamber.com; Chair. BRIAN HAHN; Pres. and CEO HEATHER DOUGLAS.

Edmonton Chamber of Commerce: 9990 Jasper Ave, Suite 700, Edmonton, AB T5J 1P7; tel. (780) 426-4620; fax (780) 424-7946; e-mail info@edmontonchamber.com; internet www.edmontonchamber.com; f. 1889; Chair. PATRICK LAFORGE; Pres. and CEO MARTIN SALLOUM; c. 3,700 mems.

British Columbia

British Columbia Chamber of Commerce: 750 West Pender St, Suite 1201, Vancouver, BC V6C 2T8; tel. (604) 683-0700; fax (604) 683-0416; e-mail bccc@bcchamber.org; internet www.bcchamber.org; f. 1951; Chair. JUSTIN RIGSBY; Pres. JOHN WINTER.

Greater Victoria Chamber of Commerce: 852 Fort St, Suite 100, Victoria, BC V8W 1H8; tel. (250) 383-7191; fax (250) 385-3552; e-mail chamber@gvcc.org; internet www.victoriachamber.ca; Chair. MARGARET LUCAS; CEO BRUCE CARTER.

Vancouver Board of Trade: World Trade Centre, 999 Canada Pl., Suite 400, Vancouver, BC V6C 3E1; tel. (604) 681-2111; fax (604) 681-0437; e-mail contactus@boardoftrade.com; internet www.boardoftrade.com; f. 1887; Chair. DON RIX; Man. Dir DARCY REZAC.

Manitoba

Brandon Chamber of Commerce: 1043 Rosser Ave, Brandon, MB R7A 0L5; tel. (204) 571-5340; fax (204) 571-5347; e-mail info@brandonchamber.ca; internet www.brandonchamber.ca; f. 1883; Pres. RON CUMMING; Gen. Man. NATHAN PETO; over 1,000 mems.

Manitoba Chambers of Commerce: 227 Portage Ave, Winnipeg, MB R3B 2A6; tel. (204) 948-0100; fax (204) 948-0110; e-mail mbchamber@mbchamber.com; internet www.mbchamber.mb.ca; Chair. KEN WILK; Pres. GRAHAM S. STARMER.

Winnipeg Chamber of Commerce: Int. Business Centre, 259 Portage Ave, Suite 100, Winnipeg, MB R3B 2A9; tel. (204) 944-8484; fax (204) 944-8492; e-mail info@winnipeg-chamber.com; internet www.winnipeg-chamber.com; Chair. KENNETH JONES; Pres. and CEO DAVE ANGUS.

New Brunswick

Saint John Board of Trade: 40 King St, POB 6037, Saint John, NB E2L 4R5; tel. (506) 634-8111; fax (506) 632-2008; e-mail igilman@sjboardoftrade.com; internet www.sjboardoftrade.com; Chair. MICHAEL BARRY; Pres. IMELDA GILMAN.

Newfoundland and Labrador

St John's Board of Trade: Bd of Trade Bldg, 66 Kenmount Rd, Suite 301, POB 5127, St John's, NL A1C 5V5; tel. (709) 726-2961; fax

(709) 726-2003; e-mail info@bot.nf.ca; internet www.bot.nf.ca; f. 1971; Pres. DONNA STONE; CEO NANCY HEALEY.

Northwest Territories

Fort Simpson Chamber of Commerce: POB 244, Fort Simpson, NT X0E 0N0; tel. (867) 695-2456; fax (867) 695-2001; e-mail duffy1@cancom.net; Pres. ANDREW GAULE; Dir DUNCAN CANZIN.

Yellowknife Chamber of Commerce: 4910 50th Ave, 3/F, NWT Commerce Place, Yellowknife, NT X1A 3S5; tel. (867) 920-4944; fax (867) 920-4640; e-mail generalmanager@ykchamber.com; internet www.ykchamber.com; f. 1973; Pres. JIM EIRIKSON; Exec. Dir MARINO CASEBEER.

Nova Scotia

Halifax Chamber of Commerce: 656 Windmill Rd, Suite 200, Dartmouth, NS B3B 1B8; tel. (902) 468-7111; fax (902) 468-7333; e-mail info@halifaxchamber.com; internet www.halifaxchamber.com; Chair. KIM WEST; Pres. VALERIE PAYN.

Truro and District Chamber of Commerce: 605 Prince St, POB 54, Truro, NS B2N 1G2; tel. (902) 895-6328; fax (902) 897-6641; e-mail tim@trurochamber.com; internet www.trurochamber.com; Pres. TED JORDAN; Exec. Dir TIM TUCKER.

Nunavut Territory

Kugluktuk Chamber of Commerce: POB 227, Kugluktuk, Nunavut, NU X0E 0E0; tel. (867) 982-3232; fax (867) 982-3229; Pres. RANDY MULDER.

Ontario

Greater Kingston Chamber of Commerce: 67 Brock St, Kingston, ON K7L 1R8; tel. (613) 548-4453; fax (613) 548-4743; e-mail info@kingstonchamber.on.ca; internet www.kingstonchamber.on.ca; f. 1841; Pres. MARK LEWIS; Gen. Man. BOB SCOTT.

Greater Sudbury Chamber of Commerce: 40 Elm St, Suite 1, Sudbury, ON P3C 1S8; tel. (705) 673-7133; fax (705) 673-2944; e-mail cofc@sudburychamber.ca; internet www.sudburychamber.ca; Chair. BRIAN R. GATIEN; Pres. and CEO DEBBI NICHOLSON.

Hamilton Chamber of Commerce: 555 Bay St North, ON L8L 1H1; tel. (905) 522-1151; fax (905) 522-1154; e-mail hdcc@hamiltonchamber.on.ca; internet www.hamiltonchamber.on.ca; Pres. TYLER MACLEOD; CEO JOHN DOLBEC.

London Chamber of Commerce: 238 Pall Mall St, POB 3295, London, ON N6A 5P6; tel. (519) 432-7551; fax (519) 432-8063; e-mail info@londonchamber.com; internet www.chamber.london.on.ca; Pres. JACK SMIT; CEO and Gen. Man. GERRY MACARTNEY.

Ontario Chamber of Commerce: 180 Dundas St West, Suite 505, Toronto, ON M5G 1Z8; tel. (416) 482-5222; fax (416) 482-5879; e-mail info@occ.on.ca; internet www.occ.on.ca; Pres. and CEO LEN CRISPINO; Chair. SHAYNE SMITH.

Ottawa Chamber of Commerce: 1701 Woodward Dr., Suite LL-20, Ottawa, ON K2C 0R4; tel. (613) 236-3631; fax (613) 236-7498; e-mail info@ottawachamber.ca; internet www.ottawachamber.ca; f. 1857 as the Ottawa Bd of Trade; Chair. RICHARD CLAYMAN; Pres. GAIL LOGAN.

Toronto Board of Trade: 1 First Canadian Pl., POB 60, Toronto, ON M5X 1C1; tel. (416) 366-6811; fax (416) 366-8406; e-mail info@bot.com; internet www.bot.com; f. 1845; Chair. PAUL MASSARA; Pres. and CEO CAROL WILDING.

Prince Edward Island

Greater Summerside Chamber of Commerce: 263 Harbour Dr., Suite 10, Summerside, PE C1N 5P1; tel. (902) 436-9651; fax (902) 436-8320; e-mail info@chamber.summerside.ca; internet www.chamber.summerside.ca; Pres. GARTH DOIRON; Gen. Man. JOHN J. MACDONALD.

Québec

Chambre de commerce de Lévis: 4950 blvd de la Rive-Sud, bureau 206, Lévis, QC G6V 4Z6; tel. (418) 837-3411; fax (418) 837-8497; e-mail cclevis@cclevis.ca; internet www.cclevis.ca; Pres. MARIO LÉVESQUE; Dir-Gen. SYLVIE GIRARD.

Chambre de commerce du Montréal métropolitain: 380 St-Antoine ouest, bureau 6000, Montréal, QC H2Y 3X7; tel. (514) 871-4000; fax (514) 871-1255; e-mail info@ccmm.qc.ca; internet www.ccmm.qc.ca; Chair. HÉLÈNE DESMARAIS; Pres. and CEO ISABELLE HUDON.

Chambre de commerce de l'ouest-de-l'île de Montréal: 207 pl. Frontenac, Pointe-Claire, QC H9R 4Z7; tel. (514) 697-4228; fax (514) 697-2562; e-mail info@ccoim.ca; internet www.ccoim.ca; Pres. J. DAVID PECHO; Exec. Dir ANDRÉE BÉLANGER.

Chambre de commerce du Québec: 555 blvd René Lévesque ouest, 19e étage, Montréal, QC H2Z 1B1; tel. (514) 844-9571; fax (514) 844-0226; e-mail info@fccq.ca; internet www.fccq.ca; Chair. RICHARD CÔTÉ; Pres. and Dir-Gen. FRANÇOISE BERTRAND.

Chambre de commerce et d'industrie de l'est de l'île de Montréal: 5790 ave Pierre-de-Coubertin, bureau 201, Montréal, QC H1N 1R4; tel. (514) 354-5378; fax (514) 354-5340; e-mail info@ccieim.qc.ca; internet www.ccieim.qc.ca; Pres. DANIEL MARCOUX; Pres. of Bd of Dirs MICHEL TOURANGEAU.

Chambre de commerce et d'industrie du Québec métropolitain: 17 rue St-Louis, Québec, QC G1R 3Y8; tel. (418) 692-3853; fax (418) 694-2286; e-mail info@ccquebec.ca; internet www.ccquebec.ca; Chair. DANIEL A. DENIS; Pres. CHRISTIAN GOULET.

Saskatchewan

Prince Albert and District Chamber of Commerce: City Hall, 3rd Floor, 1084 Central Ave, Prince Albert, SK S6V 7P3; tel. (306) 764-6222; fax (306) 922-4727; e-mail admin.pachamber@sasktel.net; internet www.princealbertchamber.com; Chair. ALLAN HOPKINS; CEO LYN BROWN.

Regina Chamber of Commerce: 2145 Albert St, Regina, SK S4P 2V1; tel. (306) 757-4658; fax (306) 757-4668; e-mail info@reginachamber.com; internet www.reginachamber.com; CEO JOHN HOPKINS; Pres. FRED TITANICH.

Saskatchewan Chamber of Commerce: Chateau Tower, 1920 Broad St, Suite 1630, Regina, SK S4P 3V2; tel. (306) 352-2671; fax (306) 781-7084; e-mail info@saskchamber.com; internet www.saskchamber.com; Pres. DALE LEMKE; CEO STEVE MCLELLAN.

Yukon Territory

Whitehorse Chamber of Commerce: T. C. Richards Bldg, 302 Steele St, Suite 101, Whitehorse, YT Y1A 2C5; tel. (867) 667-7545; fax (867) 667-4507; e-mail business@whitehorsechamber.com; internet www.whitehorsechamber.com; f. 1948; Chair. ANDRE ROOTHMAN; Pres. RICK KARP.

Yukon Chamber of Commerce: 307 Jarvis St, Suite 101, Whitehorse, YT Y1A 2H3; tel. (867) 667-2000; fax (867) 667-2001; e-mail president@yukonchamber.com; internet www.yukonchamber.com; Chair. ROB MCINTYRE; Pres. and CEO J. D. AUSTIN.

Industrial and Employers' Organizations

AGRICULTURE AND HORTICULTURE

(See Selected Agricultural, Forestry, Fisheries and Fur Trade Organizations)

BUILDING AND CONSTRUCTION

Canadian Construction Association: 75 Albert St, Suite 400, Ottawa, ON K1P 5E7; tel. (613) 236-9455; fax (613) 236-9526; e-mail cca@cca-acc.com; internet www.cca-acc.com; f. 1918; Pres. MICHAEL ATKINSON; over 20,000 mems.

Canadian Institute of Steel Construction: 201 Consumers Rd, Suite 300, Willowdale, ON M2J 4G8; tel. (416) 491-4552; fax (416) 491-6461; e-mail info@cisc-icca.ca; internet www.cisc-icca.ca; f. 1930; Chair. DON OBOROWSKY; Pres. MIKE GILMOR; 245 mems.

Canadian Paint and Coatings Association: 170 Laurier Ave West, Suite 1200, Ottawa, ON K1P 5V5; tel. (613) 231-3604; fax (613) 231-4908; e-mail cpca@cdnpaint.org; internet www.cdnpaint.org; f. 1913; Chair. JIM QUICK; 70 mems.

Canadian Precast/Prestressed Concrete Institute (CPCI): 196 Bronson Ave, Suite 100, Ottawa, ON K1R 6H4; tel. (613) 232-2619; fax (613) 232-5139; e-mail info@cpci.ca; internet www.cpci.ca; Pres. JOHN R. FOWLER; 26 active, 36 assoc., 12 supporting and 100 professional and student mems.

Ontario Painting Contractors Association: 211 Consumers Rd, Suite 305, Willowdale, ON M2J 4G8; tel. (416) 498-1897; fax (416) 498-6757; e-mail info@ontpca.org; internet www.ontpca.org; f. 1967; Pres. GILBERT SATOV; Exec. Dir ANDREW SEFTON; 100 mems.

CHEMICALS

Canadian Chemical Producers' Association: 350 Sparks St, Suite 805, Ottawa, ON K1R 7S8; tel. (613) 237-6215; fax (613) 237-4061; e-mail glaurin@ccpa.ca; internet www.ccpa.ca; f. 1962; Chair. PAUL TIMMONS; Pres. and CEO RICHARD PATON; 70 mems.

Chemical Institute of Canada: 130 Slater St, Suite 550, Ottawa, ON K1P 6E2; tel. (613) 232-6252; fax (613) 232-5862; e-mail info@cheminst.ca; internet www.cheminst.ca; f. 1945; Chair. MURRAY GRAY; Exec. Dir ROLAND ANDERSSON; 5,800 mems, 1,300 student mems.

CLOTHING AND TEXTILES

Apparel Quebec/Vêtement Québec (Institut des manufacturiers du vêtement du Québec—IMVQ): 555 rue Chabanel ouest, bureau 801, Montréal, QC H2N 2H8; tel. (514) 382-3846; fax (514) 383-1689; e-mail info@vetementquebec.com; internet www.apparelquebec.com; Exec. Dir AGAR GRINBERG.

Canadian Apparel Federation: 124 O'Connor St, Suite 504, Ottawa, ON K1P 5M9; tel. (613) 231-3220; fax (613) 231-2305; e-mail info@apparel.ca; internet www.apparel.ca; f. 1977; Exec. Dir BOB KIRKE.

Canadian Carpet Institute: 1064 Cadboro Rd, Ottawa, ON K1J 8E1; tel. (819) 684-8444; fax (819) 684-5444; e-mail info@canadiancarpet.org; internet www.canadiancarpet.org; f. 1963; Pres. ALEXANDRE LACROIX; Exec. Dir JEAN-CLAUDE CARISSE; four regular mems, six assoc. mems, one affiliated mem.

Canadian Textiles Institute: 222 Somerset St West, Suite 500, Ottawa, ON K2P 2G3; tel. (613) 232-7195; fax (613) 232-8722; e-mail cti@textiles.ca; internet www.textiles.ca; f. 1935; Chair. HARVEY L. PENNER; Pres. ELIZABETH SIWICKI; 60 mems.

Textile Federation of Canada: c/o CTT, 3000 rue Boullé, St-Hyacinthe, QC J2S 1H9; tel. (450) 778-1870; fax (450) 778-9016; e-mail groupetextile@videotron.ca; Exec. Sec. STEPHEN LARAMEE; 1,250 mems.

ELECTRICAL AND ENERGY

(see Energy—Associations)

ENGINEERING AND MACHINERY

Association of Consulting Engineers of Canada: 130 Albert St, Suite 616, Ottawa, ON K1P 5G4; tel. (613) 236-0569; fax (613) 236-6193; e-mail info@acec.ca; internet www.acec.ca; f. 1925; Chair. CHRIS NEWCOMB; Pres. and COO JEFF MORRISON; 11 mem. orgs.

Canadian Council of Technicians and Technologists: 1101 Prince of Wales Dr., Suite 295, Ottawa, ON K2C 3W7; tel. (613) 238-8123; fax (613) 238-8822; e-mail ccttadm@cctt.ca; internet www.cctt.ca; Pres. STEPHEN GOULD; Exec. Dir YAROSLAW ZAJAC; over 49,000 mems.

Canadian Machine Tool Distributors' Association: POB 262, Minden, ON K0M 2K0; tel. (705) 286-6921; fax (705) 286-6905; e-mail info@cmtda.com; internet www.cmtda.com; Pres. BRIAN DONNELLY; Exec. Dir JAMES BURROWS.

Engineers Canada: 180 Elgin St, Suite 1100, Ottawa, ON K2P 2K3; tel. (613) 232-2474; fax (613) 230-5759; e-mail info@engineerscanada.ca; internet www.engineerscanada.ca; f. 1936 as the Canadian Council of Professional Engineers; Pres. RICHARD FLETCHER; CEO CHANTAL GUAY.

Municipal Engineers' Association: 6355 Kennedy Rd, Unit 2, Mississauga, ON L5T 2L5; tel. (905) 795-2555; fax (905) 795-2660; e-mail info@municipalengineers.on.ca; internet www.municipalengineers.on.ca; f. 1974; Pres. JOHN F. HAMMER; Exec. Dir P. JEFFREY SEATON.

FISHERIES

(See Selected Agricultural, Forestry, Fisheries and Fur Trade Organizations)

FOOD AND BEVERAGES

(See also Selected Agricultural, Forestry, Fisheries and Fur Trade Organizations)

Association des détaillants en alimentation du Québec (ADA): 300 rue Léo-Pariseau, bureau 1100, Montréal, QC H2X 4C1; tel. (514) 982-0104; fax (514) 849-3021; e-mail info@adaq.qc.ca; internet www.adaq.qc.ca; f. 1955; Pres. ANNICK GAZAILLE.

Baking Association of Canada: 7895 Tranmere Dr., Mississauga, ON L5S 1V9; tel. (905) 405-0288; fax (905) 405-0993; e-mail info@baking.ca; internet www.baking.ca; f. 1947; Pres. and CEO PAUL HETHERINGTON; 1,400 institutional mems, 200 assoc. mems.

Brewers Association of Canada/L'Association des brasseurs du Canada: 100 Queen St, Suite 650, Ottawa, ON K1P 1J9; tel. (613) 232-9601; fax (613) 232-2283; e-mail info@brewers.ca; internet www.brewers.ca; f. 1943; Chair. BRUCE MCCUBBIN; Pres. and CEO IAN FARIS; 15 mems.

Canadian Association of Sales and Marketing Agencies/Association canadienne des agences en vente et marketing (CASMA/ACAVM): 885 Don Mills Rd, Suite 301, Toronto, ON M3C 1V9; tel. (416) 385-2322; fax (416) 510-8043; e-mail btordoff@casmaonline.ca; internet www.casmaonline.ca; f. 1942; fmrly the Canadian Food Brokers Asscn; mem. of the Asscn of Sales and Marketing Cos Int. (USA); Pres. KEITH BRAY; 70 mems, 60 assoc. mems.

Canadian Council of Grocery Distributors: 6455 Jean-Talon East, Suite 402, St-Léonard, QC H1S 3E8; tel. (514) 982-0267; fax (514) 982-0659; internet www.ccgd.ca; f. 1919; Chair. BILL SEXSMITH; Pres. and CEO NICK JENNERY; 69 institutional mems, 115 assoc. mems.

Canadian National Millers' Association: 408 Queen St, Ottawa, ON K1R 5A7; tel. (613) 238-2293; fax (613) 235-5866; e-mail gharrison@canadianmillers.ca; internet www.canadianmillers.ca; f. 1920; Pres. GORDON HARRISON; 17 mems.

Confectionery Manufacturers Association of Canada/L'Association canadienne des fabricants confiseries (CMAC): 885 Don Mills Rd, Suite 301, Don Mills, ON M3C 1V9; tel. (416) 510-8034; fax (416) 510-8044; e-mail info@cmaconline.ca; internet www.confectioncanada.com; f. 1919; Pres. JOHN ROWSOME; 70 mems.

Food and Consumer Products of Canada: 885 Don Mills Rd, Suite 301, Don Mills, ON M3C 1V9; tel. (416) 510-8024; fax (416) 510-8043; e-mail info@fcpc.ca; internet www.fcpc.ca; Chair. ALLAN COSMAN; Pres. and CEO NANCY CROITORU; 150 corporate mems.

Food Processors of Canada: 350 Sparks St, Suite 605, Ottawa, ON K1R 7S8; tel. (613) 722-1000; fax (613) 722-1404; e-mail fpc@foodprocessors.ca; internet www.foodprocessors.ca; f. 1989; fmrly Food Institute of Canada; Pres. CHRISTOPHER KYTE; 200 mems.

Refreshments Canada: 885 Don Mills Rd, Suite 301, Toronto, ON M3C 1V9; tel. (416) 362-2424; fax (416) 362-3229; e-mail info@refreshments.ca; internet www.refreshments.ca; f. 1942 as Canadian Bottlers of Carbonated Beverages; present name adopted in 2001; Pres JUSTIN SHERWOOD; Dir, Research and Policy ANTHONY VAN HEYNINGEN; 20 mems.

FORESTRY AND LUMBER

(See also Selected Agricultural, Forestry, Fisheries and Fur Trade Organizations)

Canadian Hardwood Plywood and Veneer Association: 47 rue de Richelieu, Chambly, QC J3L 2C3; tel. and fax (514) 733-2777; e-mail michel.tremblay2@bellnet.ca; internet www.chpva.ca; f. 1997; Pres. GAÉTAN LAUZON; Exec. Vice-Pres. MICHEL G. TREMBLAY; 62 mem. cos.

HOTELS AND CATERING

(See also Tourism—National Organizations)

Canadian Restaurant and Foodservices Association: 316 Bloor St West, Toronto, ON M5S 1W5; tel. (416) 923-8416; fax (416) 923-1450; e-mail info@crfa.ca; internet www.crfa.ca; f. 1944; Chair. MICHAEL ARONOVICI; Pres. DOUGLAS NEEDHAM; 14,000 mems.

Hotel and Restaurant Suppliers Association, Inc/Association des fournisseurs d'hôtels et restaurants, inc: 9300 Henri Bourassa Blvd West, Suite 230, St-Laurent, QC H4S 1L5; tel. (514) 334-5161; fax (514) 334-1279; e-mail info@afhr.com; internet www.afhr.com; f. 1936; Pres. and CEO VICTOR FRANCOEUR; Gen. Man. RICHARD MAINVILLE.

MINING

(See Selected Mining Organizations)

PHARMACEUTICAL

Canada's Research-Based Pharmaceuticals/Les compagnies de recherche pharmaceutique du Canada (Rx&D): 55 Metcalfe St, Suite 1220, Ottawa, ON K1P 6L5; tel. (613) 236-0455; fax (613) 236-6756; e-mail info@canadapharma.org; internet www.canadapharma.org; f. 1914 as Pharmaceutical Mfrs Asscn of Canada; Chair. RONNIE MILLER; Pres. RUSSELL WILLIAMS; c. 50 mems.

Canadian Generic Pharmaceutical Association (CGPA): 4120 Yonge St, Suite 409, Toronto, ON M2P 2B8; tel. (416) 223-2333; fax (416) 223-2425; e-mail info@canadiangenerics.ca; internet www.canadiangenerics.ca; fmrly Canadian Drug Mfrs' Asscn; Pres. JIM KEON; Chair. JACK KAY; 18 mems.

RETAILING

Retail Alberta: 208 111 Ave, Suite 14907, Edmonton, AB T5M 2P6; tel. (780) 453-1192; fax (780) 488-9965; e-mail info@retailalberta.ca; internet www.retailalberta.ca; f. 1896; Chair. BETTY LITTLE; CEO SIBÉAL MCCOURT-BINCOLETTO; 1,800 mem. cos.

Retail Council of Canada: 1255 Bay St, Suite 800, Toronto, ON M5R 2A9; tel. (416) 922-6678; fax (416) 922-8011; e-mail mbeazley@retailcouncil.org; internet www.retailcouncil.org; f. 1963; Chair. KEVIN LAYDEN; Pres. and CEO DIANE J. BRISEBOIS; c. 9,000 mems.

TOBACCO

Canadian Tobacco Manufacturers' Council: 99 Bank St, Suite 701, Ottawa, ON K1P 6B9; tel. (613) 238-2799; fax (613) 238-4463; f. 1963; Pres. JOHN BARNETT.

TRANSPORT

(See Transport section)

MISCELLANEOUS

Canadian Consumer Specialty Products Association: 130 Albert St, Suite 800, Ottawa, ON K1P 5G4; tel. (613) 232-6616; fax (613) 233-6350; e-mail assoc@ccspa.org; internet www.ccspa.org; f. 1958; Pres. SHANNON COOMBS; more than 40 mem. cos.

Canadian Printing Industries Association: 151 Slater St, Suite 1110, Ottawa, ON K1P 5H3; tel. (613) 236-7208; fax (613) 236-8169; e-mail info@cpia-aci.ca; internet www.cpia-aci.ca; Chair. SEAN MURRAY; Pres. BOB ELLIOT; 789 mems.

Trade Unions

In January 2007 there were 4,480,020 union members in Canada, representing 25.5% of the civilian labour force. Of these, 28.1% belonged to international unions. Unions affiliated to the Canadian Labour Congress represented 63.5% of total union membership in 2007.

Canadian Labour Congress: 2841 Riverside Dr., Ottawa, ON K1V 8X7; tel. (613) 521-3400; fax (613) 521-4655; e-mail hyussuff@clc-ctc.ca; internet www.canadianlabour.ca; f. 1956; Pres. KENNETH V. GEORGETTI; Sec.-Treas. HASSAN YUSSUFF; 3.2m. mems (2007).

Affiliated unions with more than 15,000 members:

Amalgamated Transit Union: 61 International Blvd, Suite 210, Rexdale, ON M9W 6K4; tel. (416) 679-8846; fax (416) 679-9195; e-mail director@atucanada.ca; internet www.atucanada.ca; Dir ROBIN WEST; 25,000 mems (2007).

American Federation of Musicians of the United States and Canada: 75 The Donway West, Suite 1010, Don Mills, ON M3C 2E9; tel. (416) 391-5161; fax (416) 391-5165; e-mail afmcan@afm.org; internet www.afm.org; Vice-Pres. in Canada BILL SKOLNIK; 15,000 mems (2006).

British Columbia Nurses' Union: 4060 Regent St, Burnaby, BC V5C 6P5; tel. (604) 433-2268; fax (604) 433-7945; e-mail dmcpherson@bcnu.org; internet www.bcnu.org; Pres. DEBRA MCPHERSON; 26,000 mems (2007).

Canadian Union of Postal Workers: 337 Bank St, Ottawa, ON K2P 1Y3; tel. (613) 236-7238; fax (613) 563-7861; e-mail feedback@cupw-sttp.org; internet www.cupw.ca; f. 1965; Nat. Pres. DENIS LEMELIN; 54,000 mems (2007).

Canadian Union of Public Employees (CUPE): 1375 St Laurent, Ottawa, ON K1G 0Z7; tel. (613) 237-1590; fax (613) 237-5508; e-mail cupemail@cupe.ca; internet www.cupe.ca; Nat. Pres. PAUL MOIST; 550,000 mems (2006).

Communications, Energy and Paperworkers Union of Canada/Syndicat canadien des communications, de l'energie et du papier (CEP): 301 Laurier Ave West, Ottawa, ON K1P 6M6; tel. (613) 230-5200; fax (613) 230-5801; e-mail info@cep.ca; internet www.cep.ca; Pres. DAVE COLES; 150,000 mems (2006).

International Association of Fire Fighters: 350 Sparks St, Suite 403, Ottawa, ON K1R 7S8; tel. (613) 567-8988; fax (613) 567-8986; e-mail jlee@iaff.org; internet www.iaff.org; Asst to the Gen. Pres. JIM LEE; 20,000 mems (2008).

International Association of Machinists and Aerospace Workers: 15 Gervais Dr., Suite 707, North York, ON M3C 1Y8; tel. (416) 386-1789; fax (416) 386-0210; e-mail info@iamaw.ca; internet www.iamaw.ca; Gen. Vice-Pres. in Canada DAVE L. RITCHIE; c. 47,000 mems (2007).

International Brotherhood of Electrical Workers: 1450 Meyerside Dr., Suite 300, Mississauga, ON L5T 2N5; tel. (905) 564-5441; fax (905) 564-8114; e-mail ivpd_01@ibew.org; internet www.ibew1st.org; Int. Vice-Pres. PHILLIP FLEMING; 54,780 mems (2005).

International Union of Operating Engineers: 4333 Ledger Ave., Burnaby, BC V5G 3T3; tel. (604) 291-8831; fax (604) 473-5235; e-mail gkroeker@iuoe115.com; internet www.iuoe.org; Vice-Pres. and Business Man., Local 115 GARY KROEKER; 36,000 mems (2005).

IWA Canada (Industrial Wood and Allied Workers of Canada): 1285 Pender St, Suite 500, Vancouver, BC V6E 4B2; tel. (604) 683-1117; fax (604) 688-6416; internet www.iwa.ca; f. 1937; Pres. D. C. HAGGARD; 42,500 mems (2005).

Labourers' International Union of North America: 44 Hughson St South, Hamilton, ON L8N 2A7; tel. (905) 522-7177; fax (905) 522-9310; e-mail joseph@liuna.ca; internet www.liuna.ca; Canadian Dir and Vice-Pres. JOSEPH S. MANCINELLI; 72,500 mems (2005).

National Automobile, Aerospace Transportation and General Workers Union of Canada (CAW–Canada): 205 Placer Court, North York, Willowdale, ON M2H 3H9; tel. (416) 497-4110; fax (416) 495-6552; e-mail caw@caw.ca; internet www.caw.ca; f. 1985; Nat. Pres. KEN LEWENZA; 250,000 mems (2006).

National Union of Public and General Employees: 15 Auriga Dr., Nepean, ON K2E 1B7; tel. (613) 228-9800; fax (613) 228-9801; e-mail national@nupge.ca; internet www.nupge.ca; Nat. Pres. JAMES CLANCY; 340,000 mems (2007).

Office and Professional Employees' International Union: 1200 ave Papineau, bureau 250, Montréal, QC H2K 4S6; tel. (514) 522-6511; fax (514) 522-9000; internet www.opeiu.org/canadian.html; Pres. MICHEL LAJEUNESSE; 35,000 mems (2005).

Ontario English Catholic Teachers' Association: 65 St Clair Ave East, Suite 400, Toronto, ON M4T 2Y8; tel. (416) 925-2493; fax (416) 925-7764; e-mail a.oconnor@oecta.on.ca; internet www.oecta.on.ca; Pres. ELAINE MAC NEIL; 36,000 mems (2007).

Ontario Secondary School Teachers' Federation: 60 Mobile Dr., Toronto, ON M4A 2P3; tel. (416) 751-8300; fax (416) 751-3394; internet www.osstf.on.ca; f. 1919; Pres. KEN CORAN; 60,000 mems (2008).

Public Service Alliance of Canada: 233 Gilmour St, Ottawa, ON K2P 0P1; tel. (613) 560-4200; fax (613) 567-0385; e-mail nat-pres@psac-afpc.com; internet www.psac-afpc.com; f. 1966; Nat. Pres. JOHN GORDON; 186,000 mems (2008).

Service Employees International Union: 2180 Steeles Ave., Suite 305, West Concord, ON L4K 2Z5; tel. (905) 695-1203; fax (905) 695-1209; e-mail stewarts@seiu.ca; internet www.seiu.ca; Int. Canadian Vice-Pres. SHARLEEN STEWART; Nat. Rep. BOB LAURIE; 95,000 mems (2006).

Teamsters Canada: 2540 Daniel-Johnson, bureau 804, Laval, QC H7T 2S3; tel. (450) 682-5521; fax (450) 681-2244; internet www.teamsters-canada.org; Canadian Pres. ROBERT BOUVIER; 121,500 mems (2006).

UNITE-HERE: 460 Richmond St West, 2nd Floor, Toronto, ON M5V 1Y1; tel. (416) 510-0887; fax (416) 510-0891; e-mail info@unitehere.ca; internet www.unitehere.ca; f. 1995 by merger of Union of Needletrades, Industrial and Textile Employees and Hotel Employees and Restaurant Employees Union; Dirs ALEXANDRA DAGG, NICK WORHAUG; 50,000 mems (2006).

United Association of Journeymen and Apprentices of the Plumbing and Pipe Fitting Industry of the United States and Canada: 225 Metcalfe St, Suite 600, Ottawa, ON K2P 1P9; tel. (613) 565-1100; fax (613) 565-1200; e-mail uacanada@on.aibn.com; internet www.uacanada.ca; Dir of Canadian Affairs JOHN TELFORD; 39,600 mems (2005).

United Brotherhood of Carpenters and Joiners of America (UBC): 5500 Canotek Rd, Suite 104, Ottawa, ON K1J 1K6; tel. (613) 741-2603; fax (613) 741-4421; e-mail gorc@on.aibn.com; internet www.carpenters.org; Gen. Exec. Bd Mem. JAMES E. SMITH; 53,000 mems (2005).

United Food and Commercial Workers Canada: 61 International Blvd, Suite 300, Rexdale, ON M9W 6K4; tel. (416) 675-1104; fax (416) 675-6919; e-mail ufcw@ufcw.ca; internet www.ufcw.ca; f. 1979; National Pres. WAYNE HANLEY; 240,000 mems (2000).

United Steel, Paper and Forestry, Rubber, Manufacturing, Energy, Allied Industrial and Service Workers International Union (United Steelworkers): 234 Eglinton Ave East, 8th Floor, Toronto, ON M4P 1K7; tel. (416) 487-1571; fax (416) 482-5548; e-mail usw@usw.ca; internet www.usw.ca; f. 1943; Nat. Dir for Canada KEN NEUMANN; 280,000 mems (2007).

OTHER CENTRAL CONGRESSES

Centrale des syndicats démocratiques: 801 4e rue, bureau 300, Québec, QC G1J 2T7; tel. (418) 529-2956; fax (418) 529-6323; e-mail info@csd.qc.ca; internet www.csd.qc.ca; f. 1972; Pres. FRANÇOIS VAUDREUIL; Sec. JEAN-CLAUDE DUFRESNE; 60,000 mems (2004).

Centrale des syndicats du Québec: 9405 rue Sherbrooke est, Montréal, QC H1L 6P3; tel. (514) 356-8888; fax (514) 356-9999; internet www.csq.qc.net; f. 1974; name changed as above in 2000; Pres. RÉJEAN PARENT; 13 affiliated federations, 230 affiliated unions, more than 155,000 mems.

Affiliated union with more than 15,000 mems:

Fédération des syndicats de l'enseignment: 320 rue St-Joseph est, bureau 100, Québec, QC G1K 9E7; tel. (418) 649-8888; fax (418) 649-1914; internet www.fse.qc.net; Pres. JOHANNE FORTIER; 80,000 mems (2006).

Confederation of Canadian Unions: Station B, POB 1117, Ottawa, ON K1P 5R2; tel. (416) 736-5109; fax (416) 736-5519; e-mail ccucsc@ca.inter.net; f. 1969; Pres. JANE GRANT.

Confédération des syndicats nationaux: 1601 ave de Lorimier, Montréal, QC H2K 4M5; tel. (514) 598-2121; fax (514) 598-2052; e-mail csncommunications@csn.qc.ca; internet www.csn.qc.ca; f. 1921; Pres. CLAUDETTE CARBONNEAU; nine federated unions.

Federated unions with more than 15,000 members:

Fédération du commerce inc: 1601 ave de Lorimier, Montréal, QC H2K 4M5; tel. (514) 598-2181; fax (514) 598-2304; e-mail ann.potvin@csn.qc.ca; internet www.fc.csn.qc.ca; Pres. JEAN LORTIE; 38,000 mems (2005).

Fédération des employées et employés de services publics inc: 1601 ave de Lorimier, Montréal, QC H2K 4M5; tel. (514) 598-2231; fax (514) 598-2398; e-mail feesp.courrier@csn.qc.ca; internet www.feesp.csn.qc.ca; Pres. GINETTE GUÉRIN; 46,368 mems (2006).

Fédération de la métallurgie: 2100 blvd de Maisonneuve est, bureau 204, Montréal, QC H2K 4S1; tel. (514) 529-4937; fax (514) 529-4935; e-mail metallurgie.executif@qc.aira.com; internet www.metallurgiecsn.ca; Pres. ALAIN LAMPRON; 21,500 mems (2005).

Fédération nationale des enseignantes et des enseignants du Québec (FNEEQ): 1601 ave de Lorimier, Montréal, QC H2K 4M5; tel. (514) 598-2241; fax (514) 598-2190; e-mail ronald.cameron@csn.qc.ca; internet www.fneeq.qc.ca; f. 1969; Pres. RONALD CAMERON; 23,500 mems (2006).

Fédération de la santé et des services sociaux: 1601 ave de Lorimier, Montréal, QC H2K 4M5; tel. (514) 598-2210; fax (514) 598-2223; e-mail fsss@fsss.qc.ca; internet www.fsss.qc.ca; Pres. FRANCINE LEVESQUE; 113,385 mems (2006).

The American Federation of Labor and Congress of Industrial Organizations (AFL-CIO), with headquarters in Washington, DC, USA, represented 2.0% of the total union membership in Canada in 2005.

Affiliated union with more than 15,000 members:

International Association of Bridge, Structural and Ornamental Iron Workers: 46 County Rd, Suite 4069, RR 3, Maidstone, ON N0R 1K0; tel. (519) 737-7110; fax (519) 737-7113; e-mail mdugallu700@kelcom.igs.net; internet www.ironworkerslocal700.com; Pres. WAYNE MCDONALD; 15,300 mems (2005).

PRINCIPAL UNAFFILIATED UNIONS

Alberta Teachers' Association: 11010 142nd St, NW, Edmonton, AB T5N 2R1; tel. (780) 447-9400; fax (780) 455-6481; e-mail postmaster@ata.ab.ca; internet www.teachers.ab.ca; Pres. FRANK BRUSEKER; Exec. Sec. GORDON R. THOMAS; 39,300 mems (2006).

British Columbia Teachers' Federation: 550 West Sixth Ave, Suite 100, Vancouver, BC V5Z 4P2; tel. (604) 871-2283; fax (604) 871-2294; e-mail ilanzinger@bctf.ca; internet bctf.ca; f. 1917; Pres. IRENE LANZINGER; 41,000 mems (2007).

Canadian Telecommunications Employees' Association (CTEA): 1010 de La Gauchetière ouest (pl. du Canada), Suite 360, Montréal, QC H3B 2N2; tel. (514) 861-9963; fax (514) 861-5985; internet www.acet-ctea.com; f. 1943; Pres. BRENDA KNIGHT; 12,000 mems (2007).

Christian Labour Association of Canada (CLAC): 2335 Argentia Rd, Mississauga, ON L5N 5N3; tel. (905) 812-2855; fax (905) 812-5556; e-mail headoffice@clac.ca; internet www.clac.ca; Exec. Dir DICK HEINEN; 43,000 mems (2007).

Elementary Teachers' Federation of Ontario: 480 University Ave, Suite 1000, Toronto, ON M5G 1V2; tel. (416) 962-3836; fax (416) 642-2424; internet www.etfo.on.ca; f. 1998; Pres. DAVID CLEGG; 70,000 mems (2007).

Fédération interprofessionnelle de la santé du Québec: 2050 rue de Bleury, 4e étage, Montréal, QC H3A 2J5; tel. (514) 987-1141; fax (514) 987-7273; e-mail info@fiqsante.qc.ca; internet www.fiqsante.qc.ca; f. 1987; fmrly Fédération des infirmières et d'infirmiers du Québec; Pres. LINA BONAMIE; 56,500 mems (2006).

Ontario Nurses' Association: 85 Grenville St, Suite 400, Toronto, ON M5S 3A2; tel. (416) 964-8833; fax (416) 964-8864; e-mail onamail@ona.org; internet www.ona.org; Pres. LINDA HASLAM-STROUD; 53,000 mems (2007).

Ontario Public Service Employees Union: 100 Lesmill Rd, North York, ON M3B 3P8; tel. (416) 443-8888; fax (416) 443-9670; e-mail wthomas@opseu.org; internet www.opseu.org; f. 1911; Pres. WARREN (SMOKEY) THOMAS; c. 100,000 mems (2006).

Professional Employees' Association: 1001 Wharf St, Suite 201, Victoria, BC V8W 1T6; tel. (250) 385-8791; fax (250) 385-6629; e-mail jjensen@pea.org; internet www.pea.org; f. 1974; Pres. KATHRYN DANCHUK; Sec.-Treas. JOHN FOXGORD; 2,500 mems.

Professional Institute of the Public Service of Canada: 250 Tremblay Rd, Ottawa, ON K1G 3J8; tel. (613) 228-6310; fax (613) 228-9048; e-mail michele@pipsc.ca; internet www.pipsc.ca; Pres. MICHÈLE DEMERS; 50,000 mems (2007).

Syndicat de la fonction publique Québec: 5100 blvd des Gradins, Québec, QC G2J 1N4; tel. (418) 623-2424; fax (418) 623-6109; e-mail communication@sfpq.qc.ca; internet www.sfpq.qc.ca; Gen. Pres. MICHEL SAWYER; 37,000 mems (2007).

Union of Canadian Transportation Employees (UCTE): 233 Gilmour St, Suite 702, Ottawa, ON K2P 0P2; tel. (613) 238-4003; fax (613) 236-0379; e-mail ucte_webmaster@psac.com; internet www.ucte.com; Pres. MICHAEL WING; 7,500 mems (2007).

United Nurses of Alberta: 10611 98th Ave, Suite 900, Edmonton, AB T5K 2P7; tel. (780) 425-1025; fax (780) 426-2093; e-mail provincialoffice@una.ab.ca; internet www.una.ab.ca; f. 1977; Pres. HEATHER SMITH; 19,280 mems (2005).

ENERGY

INTRODUCTION

In 2007 Canada's total electric energy production was an estimated 602,765m. kWh. In 2005 the industrial sector consumed 37.9% of total secondary energy consumed, while the transportation and residential sectors consumed 29.5% and 16.5%, respectively. The largest exporters of electricity were Québec, Ontario, British Columbia, New Brunswick and Manitoba. In 2007 energy products as a whole accounted for 19.8% of Canada's total exports and 8.8% of imports.

Legislative authority for the generation, transmission and distribution of electricity rests with the provinces, although the federal Government controls the production of nuclear energy (through the Canadian Nuclear Safety Commission) and the regulation of international and inter-provincial energy trade (with the advice of the National Energy Board).

Canada's two major energy sources are natural gas and petroleum. These commodities accounted for 37.8% and 37.5% of total energy production, respectively, in 2006. Approximately 75% of Canada's natural gas and petroleum was produced in Alberta in that year. In 2007 Canada ranked third for world production of natural gas, with total production in that year amounting to 183,700m. cu m. Hydroelectric power is a major source of energy in Canada and accounted for 60.5% (364,504m. kWh) of the total electricity generated in 2007. In that year thermal power accounted for 24.8% (149,604m. kWh) and nuclear power 14.7% (88,657m. kWh) of the country's total electricity production. Most hydroelectric energy is produced by Québec, and the largest hydro stations are in Newfoundland and Labrador, Québec and British Columbia.

Canada's largest conventional thermal stations are found in Ontario, Alberta and New Brunswick. Coal is the primary source of Ontario's thermal energy production. Ontario Power Generation (formerly Ontario Hydro), Canada's largest public utility, owns 16 of Canada's 18 operational nuclear reactors, six of which are leased to Bruce Power.

Energy efficiency has helped to minimize growth in energy consumption. Efficiency improved by some 16% in 1990–2005, which translated into savings of C $20,100m. in 2005. Improved efficiency in that year also helped to avoid an estimated 64.0m. metric tons of greenhouse gas emissions.

STATISTICS

Electric Energy Production by Fuel Type

(million kWh)

	2003	2004	2005	2006	2007
Hydro	332,888	335,089	358,605	351,084	364,504
Thermal:					
steam	139,798	127,338	128,914	118,197	124,233
internal combustion	937	996	950	938	1,004
combustion turbines	19,944	22,598	21,948	22,460	24,367
Nuclear	70,653	85,270	86,830	92,419	88,657
Total	564,218	571,291	597,247	585,098	602,765

Source: Statistics Canada, CANSIM II Table 127-0001, September 2008.

Fuels Used to Generate Electricity

(million kWh, 2006)

	Thermal					
	Coal	Natural gas	Fuel oil	Total (incl. others)	Hydro	Nuclear
Alberta	46,592	11,402	125	61,399	2,709	—
British Columbia	—	3,833	65	7,611	54,247	—
Manitoba	352	34	23	503	33,976	—
New Brunswick	3,513	2,054	3,923	10,108	3,730	4,367
Newfoundland and Labrador	—	279	789	1,058	41,710	—
Nova Scotia and Prince Edward Island	7,054	300	2,777	10,312	1,185	—
Ontario	28,494	8,766	66	38,389	36,178	83,457
Québec	—	633	351	1,379	173,010	4,595
Saskatchewan	11,620	3,355	33	15,061	4,604	—
Yukon, Northwest Territories and Nunavut	—	110	460	570	607	—
Total*	97,625	30,766	8,613	146,390	351,934	92,419

* May not be equal to the sum of regional totals owing to rounding and discrepancies in regional reporting.

Source: Statistics Canada, *Energy Supply and Demand in Canada*.

Nuclear Generating Stations in Canada

NUCLEAR POWER STATIONS IN OPERATION
(September 2008)

Reactor	Province	Rated net capacity (MW)
Bruce 3	Ontario	750
Bruce 4	Ontario	750
Bruce 5	Ontario	822
Bruce 6	Ontario	822
Bruce 7	Ontario	806
Bruce 8	Ontario	795
Darlington 1	Ontario	878
Darlington 2	Ontario	878
Darlington 3	Ontario	878
Darlington 4	Ontario	878
Gentilly 2	Québec	635
Pickering 1	Ontario	515
Pickering 4	Ontario	515
Pickering 5	Ontario	516
Pickering 6	Ontario	516
Pickering 7	Ontario	516
Pickering 8	Ontario	516
Point Lepreau	New Brunswick	635

Source: International Atomic Energy Agency.

DIRECTORY

Regulatory and Co-ordinating Authorities

Alberta Utilities Commission: Fifth Avenue Pl., 4th Floor, 425 First St, SW, Calgary, AB T2P 3L8; tel. (403) 592-8845; fax (403) 592-4406; e-mail info@auc.ab.ca; internet www.auc.ab.ca; f. 2008 after realignment of Alberta Energy and Utilities Bd into two separate bodies; regulates Alberta's electric, gas, and water utilities; Chair. WILLIE GRIEVE; CEO BOB HEGGIE.

Alternative Energy Division, British Columbia Ministry of Energy and Mines: 1810 Blanshard St, 4th Floor, Victoria, BC V8W 9N1; tel. (250) 952-0819; fax (250) 952-0657; e-mail paul.wieringa@gov.bc.ca; internet www.em.gov.bc.ca/alternativeenergy; Dir PAUL WIERINGA.

British Columbia Utilities Commission: 900 Howe St, 6th Floor, Box 250, Vancouver, BC V6Z 2N3; tel. (604) 660-4700; fax (604) 660-1102; e-mail commission.secretary@bcuc.com; internet www.bcuc.com; Chair. LEONARD F. KELSEY.

Canada/Newfoundland Offshore Petroleum Board: TD Pl., 5th Floor, 140 Water St, St John's, NL A1C 6H6; tel. (709) 778-1400; fax (709) 778-1473; e-mail information@cnlopb.nl.ca; internet www.cnlopb.nl.ca; Chair. and CEO MAX RUELOKKE.

Canadian Nuclear Safety Commission: 280 Slater St, POB 1046, Station B, Ottawa, ON K1P 5S9; tel. (613) 995-5894; fax (613) 995-5086; e-mail info@cnsc-ccsn.gc.ca; internet www.nuclearsafety.gc.ca; f. 1946; Pres. and CEO MICHAEL BINDER; Sec. MARC LEBLANC.

Energy and Minerals Unit, Prince Edward Island Department of the Environment, Energy and Forestry: Shaw Bldg, 5th Floor, POB 2000, Charlottetown, PE C1A 7N8; tel. (902) 894-0289; fax (902) 368-4242; e-mail dwmacquarrie@gov.pe.ca; internet www.gov.pe.ca/development/eam-info/index.php3; Dir WAYNE MACQUARRIE.

Energy Branch, Newfoundland and Labrador Department of Natural Resources: POB 8700, St John's, NL A1B 4J6; tel. (709) 729-2349; fax (709) 729-2871; e-mail ptobin@gov.nl.ca; internet www.nr.gov.nl.ca/mines&en/aboutus/energy; Assoc. Dep. Minister PIERRE TOBIN (acting).

Energy Branch, Yukon Department of Energy, Mines and Resources: 211 Main St, Suite 400, POB 2703, Whitehorse, YK Y1A 2C6; tel. (867) 667-5015; fax (867) 667-8601; e-mail energy@gov.yk.ca; internet www.emr.gov.yk.ca; Dep. Minister ANGUS ROBERTSON.

Energy Resources Conservation Board: 640 Fifth Ave, SW, Calgary, AB T2P 3G4; tel. (403) 297-8311; fax (403) 297-7336; e-mail inquiries@ercb.ca; internet www.ercb.ca; f. 2008 after realignment of Alberta Energy and Utilities Bd into two separate bodies; regulates Alberta's oil and gas industries; Chair. DAN MCFADYEN.

Manitoba Public Utilities Board: 330 Portage Ave, Suite 400, Winnipeg, MB R3C 0C4; tel. (204) 945-2638; fax (204) 945-2643; e-mail publicutilities@gov.mb.ca; internet www.pub.gov.mb.ca; Chair. GRAHAM F. J. LANE.

Mineral Resources Branch, Nova Scotia Department of Natural Resources: Founders Sq., 3rd Floor, 1701 Hollis St, Halifax, NS B3J 3M8; POB 698, Halifax, NS B3J 2T9; tel. (902) 424-2035; fax (902) 424-7735; e-mail hsswinde@gov.ns.ca; internet www.gov.ns.ca/natr/meb; Exec. Dir SCOTT SWINDEN.

Mineral Resources Division, Manitoba Industry, Economic Development and Mines: 1395 Ellice Ave, Suite 360, Winnipeg, MB R3G 3P2; tel. (204) 945-4317; fax (204) 945-1406; e-mail john.fox@gov.mb.ca; internet www.gov.mb.ca/iedm/mrd/index.html; Asst Dep. Minister JOHN FOX.

Minerals, Policy and Planning Division, New Brunswick Department of Natural Resources: Hugh John Flemming Forestry Centre, 1350 Regent St, Fredericton, NB E3C 2G6; POB 6000, Fredericton, NB E3B 5H1; tel. (506) 453-2207; fax (506) 444-5839; e-mail cecil.freeman@gnb.ca; internet www.gnb.ca/0078/index-e.asp; Asst Dep. Minister CECIL FREEMAN.

Mining, Oil and Gas Division, Northwest Territories Department of Industry, Tourism and Investment: Scotia Centre, 5102 50th Ave, 9th Floor, POB 1320, Yellowknife, NT X1A 2L9; tel. (867) 920-3222; fax (867) 873-0254; e-mail christy_campbell@gov.nt.ca; internet www.iti.gov.nt.ca/miningoilgas; Dir DEB ARCHIBALD.

National Energy Board: 444 Seventh Ave, SW, Calgary, AB T2P 0X8; tel. (403) 292-4800; fax (403) 292-5503; e-mail info@neb-one.gc.ca; internet www.neb-one.gc.ca; f. 1959; federal regulatory agency; Chair. and CEO GAÉTAN CARON; Sec. CLAUDINE DUTIL-BERRY.

New Brunswick Energy and Utilities Board: 15 Market Sq., Suite 1400, POB 5001, Saint John, NB E2L 4Y9; tel. (506) 658-2504; fax (506) 643-7300; e-mail rgorman@pub.nb.ca; internet www.pub.nb.ca; Chair. RAYMOND GORMAN; Sec. LORRAINE R. LÉGÈRE.

Newfoundland and Labrador Board of Commissioners of Public Utilities: POB 21040, St John's, NL A1A 5B2; tel. (709) 726-8600; fax (709) 726-9604; e-mail ito@pub.nl.ca; internet www.pub.nf.ca; Chair. and CEO ANDY WELLS.

Northern Pipeline Agency Canada: c/o Jean Boulais, NRCan ATIP Secretariat, 11th Floor, 580 Booth St, Ottawa, ON K1A 0E4; tel. (613) 995-1305; fax (613) 995-0693; govt body established under the Northern Pipeline Act (1985), to oversee construction of Alaska Natural Gas Transportation System; transferred to administration of Natural Resources Canada in 2004; Commr CASSIE J. DOYLE; Asst Commr and Comptroller PHILIP JENNINGS (acting).

Nova Scotia Utility and Review Board: POB 1692, Postal Unit M, Halifax, NS B3J 3S3; tel. (902) 424-4448; fax (902) 424-3919; e-mail uarb.board@gov.ns.ca; internet www.nsuarb.ca; Chair. PETER W. GURNHAM.

Oil and Gas Division, British Columbia Ministry of Energy, Mines and Petroleum Resources: Station Provincial Govt, 5th Floor, 1810 Blanshard St, POB 9323, Victoria, BC V8W 9N3; tel. (250) 952-0115; fax (250) 952-0922; e-mail gordon.goodman@gov.bc.ca; internet www.em.gov.bc.ca/subwebs/oilandgas; Asst Dep. Minister GORDON GOODMAN.

Ontario Energy Board: 2300 Yonge St, 27th Floor, POB 2319, Toronto, ON M4P 1E4; tel. (416) 481-1967; fax (416) 440-7656; e-mail webmaster@oeb.gov.on.ca; internet www.oeb.gov.on.ca; Chair. HOWARD I. WETSTON.

Petroleum Branch, Manitoba Industry, Economic Development and Mines: 227 King St West, Virden, MB R0M 2C0; tel. (204) 748-4260; fax (204) 748-2208; e-mail christine.winter@gov.mb.ca; internet www.gov.mb.ca/iedm/petroleum; Dir KEITH LOWDON.

Prince Edward Island Regulatory and Appeals Commission: 134 Kent St, Suite 501, POB 577, Charlottetown, PE C1A 7L1; tel. (902) 892-3501; fax (902) 566-4076; e-mail info@irac.pe.ca; internet www.irac.pe.ca; f. 1991 as Public Utilities Commission; regulatory and appeal body for energy, utilities, etc.; Chair. and CEO MAURICE (MOE) RODGERSON; Vice-Chair. BRIAN J. MCKENNA.

Major Producers and Distributors

AltaGas Income Trust: 355 Fourth Ave, SW, Suite 1700, Calgary, AB T2P 0J1; tel. (403) 691-7575; fax (403) 691-7576; e-mail feedback@altagas.ca; internet www.altagas.ca; processes and distributes natural gas and liquefied natural gas; provides retail energy services to commercial, industrial and institutional users; Chair. and CEO DAVID W. CORNHILL; Pres. and COO RICHARD M. ALEXANDER.

ATCO Ltd: 909 11th Ave, SW, Suite 1600, Calgary, AB T2R 1N6; tel. (403) 292-7500; fax (403) 292-7532; e-mail info@atco.com; internet www.atco.ca; conventional thermal and hydro power, and gas; operates ATCO Electric and ATCO Gas cos; Chair. RONALD D. SOUTHERN; Pres. and CEO NANCY C. SOUTHERN.

BC Hydro: 9611 Southpoint Dr., Burnaby, BC V3N 4X8; tel. (604) 224-9376; e-mail bob@bchydro.bc.ca; internet www.bchydro.com; serves 1.5m. customers in British Columbia; Chair. MOSSADIQ UMEDALY; Pres. and CEO BOB ELTON.

Boralex, Inc: 36 Lajeunesse St, Kingsey Falls, QC J0A 1B0; tel. (819) 363-5860; fax (819) 363-5866; e-mail patricia.lemaire@boralex.com; internet www.boralex.com; private producer of 'green' and renewable energy; Chair. BERNARD LEMAIRE; Pres. and CEO PATRICK LEMAIRE.

Bruce Power: POB 3000, Tiverton, ON N0G 2T0; tel. (519) 361-2673; e-mail info@brucepower.com; internet www.brucepower.com; six nuclear reactors in operation; Chair. BERNARD MICHEL; Pres. and CEO DUNCAN HAWTHORNE.

Canadian Hydro Developers, Inc: 1324 17th Ave, SW, Suite 500, Calgary, AB T2T 5S8; tel. (403) 269-9379; fax (403) 244-7388; e-mail canhydro@canhydro.com; internet www.canhydro.com; produces energy from renewable sources; Pres. and COO J. ROSS KEATING; CEO JOHN D. KEATING.

Emera: Barrington Tower, Scotia Sq., 1894 Barrington St, Halifax, NS B3J 2A8; tel. (902) 450-0507; fax (902) 428-6112; e-mail sasha.irving@emera.com; internet www.emera.com; Pres. and CEO CHRIS HUSKILSON; Chair. DEREK OLAND.

Nova Scotia Power Inc: POB 910, Halifax, NS B3J 2W5; tel. (902) 428-6230; fax (902) 428-6110; internet www.nspower.ca; fmrly Crown Corpn of Nova Scotia; privatized in 1992; distributes power to over 460,000 customers; utility subsidiary of Emera; Pres. and CEO ROB BENNETT.

EnCana Corpn: 855 Second St, SW, Suite 1800, POB 2850, Calgary, AB T2P 2S5; tel. (403) 645-2000; fax (403) 645-3400; e-mail media.relations@encana.com; internet www.encana.com; f. 2002 by merger of Alberta Energy Co Ltd and PanCanadian Energy Corpn; Pres. and CEO RANDY ERESMAN; Chair. DAVID P. O'BRIEN.

EPCOR Utilities: 10065 Jasper Ave, 18th Floor, Edmonton, AB T5J 3B1; tel. (780) 412-3414; fax (780) 412-4295; e-mail corpafrs@epcor.ca; internet www.epcor.ca; provides water, gas and power to 1.6m. customers; Pres. and CEO DONALD J. LOWRY; Chair. HUGH J. BOLTON.

EPCOR Power L.P.: 10065 Jasper Ave, Edmonton, AB T5J 3B1; tel. (780) 412-4297; fax (780) 412-3808; e-mail investorinquiries@epcorpowerlp.ca; internet www.epcorpowerlp.ca; f. 1997 under the name TransCanada Power L.P.; name changed as above in 2005 following acquisition by Epcor Utilities; Chair. DONALD J. LOWRY; Pres. BRIAN T. VAASJO.

Fortis, Inc: Fortis Bldg, 139 Water St, Suite 1201, POB 8837, St John's, NL A1B 3T2; tel. (709) 737-2800; fax (709) 737-5307; e-mail investorrelations@fortisinc.com; internet www.fortisinc.com; Pres. and CEO H. STANLEY MARSHALL; Chair. GEOFFREY F. HYLAND.

FortisAlberta: 320 17th Ave, SW, Calgary, AB T2S 2V1; tel. (403) 514-4000; fax (403) 514-4001; internet www.fortisalberta.com; f. 1987, fmrly Aquila Networks Canada (Alberta), present name adopted in 2004; distribution in Alberta; Chair GREGORY E. CONN; Pres. and CEO KARL W. SMITH.

FortisBC: 1975 Springfield Rd, Suite 100, Kelowna, BC V1Y 7V7; tel. (250) 469-8000; fax (866) 335-6295; e-mail fortisbc@fortisbc.com; internet www.fortisbc.com; f. 1897 as West Kootenay Power and Light Co, present name adopted in 2004; electricity generation, transmission and distribution in British Columbia; Pres. and CEO JOHN C. WALKER.

FortisOntario: POB 1218, 1130 Bertie St, Fort Erie, ON L2A 5Y2; tel. (905) 871-0330; fax (905) 871-8676; e-mail general@fortisontario.com; internet www.fortisontario.com; f. 1892 as Canadian Niagara Power Co Ltd; hydroelectric generation, transmission and distribution in Ontario; Pres. and CEO BILL DALEY.

Newfoundland Power: 55 Kenmount Rd, POB 8910, St John's, NL A1B 3P6; tel. (709) 737-2802; fax (709) 737-2903; e-mail icsmail@newfoundlandpower.com; internet www.newfoundlandpower.com; f. 1966 as Newfoundland Light & Power Co Ltd; operates 23 hydroelectric generating plants, three diesel plants and three gas turbine facilities; maintains over 10,000 km of transmission and distribution lines; Pres. and CEO EARL LUDLOW.

Terasen Gas: 16705 Fraser Hwy, Surrey, BC V4N 0E8; tel. (604) 576-7000; fax (604) 576-7122; e-mail mediarelations@terasengas.com; internet www.terasengas.com; acquired by Fortis, Inc from Kinder Morgan, Inc in May 2007; distributes gas to approx. 900,000 customers; Pres. RANDALL J. JESPERSEN.

Hydro One Inc: 483 Bay St, North Tower, 15th Floor, Toronto, ON M5G 2P5; tel. (416) 345-5000; fax (416) 506-2526; e-mail media.relations@hydroone.com; internet www.hydroone.com; transmission and distribution to 1.3m. customers in Ontario; Chair. JAMES ARNETT; Pres. and CEO LAURA FORMUSA.

Hydro-Québec: 75 blvd René-Lévesque ouest, Montréal, QC H2Z 1A4; tel. (514) 289-2211; fax (514) 289-3691; e-mail cote.flavie@hydro.qc.ca; internet www.hydro.qc.ca; f. 1944; govt-owned supplier to 3.8m. customer accounts in Québec; sold its largest international interest, HQI Transelec Chile SA, in 2006; Chair. MICHAEL L. TURCOTTE; Pres. and CEO THIERRY VANDAL.

Manitoba Hydro: 820 Taylor Ave, POB 815, Winnipeg, MB R3C 2P4; tel. (204) 474-3311; fax (204) 475-9044; e-mail publicaffairs@hydro.mb.ca; internet www.hydro.mb.ca; Pres. and CEO ROBERT B. BRENNAN.

Maxim Power Corporation: 715 Fifth Ave, SW, Suite 1210, Calgary, AB T2P 2X6; tel. (403) 263-3021; fax (403) 263-9125; e-mail maxim@maximpowercorp.com; internet www.maximpowercorp.com; Chair. BRUCE CHERNOFF; Pres. and CEO JOHN BOBENIC.

New Brunswick Power Corporation (NB Power): 515 King St, POB 2010, Fredericton, NB E3B 5G4; tel. (506) 458-4444; fax (506) 458-4000; e-mail questions@nbpower.com; internet www.nbpower.com; conventional thermal and nuclear power; Pres. and CEO DAVID D. HAY.

Newfoundland and Labrador Hydro: Hydro Pl., 500 Columbus Dr., POB 12400, St John's, NL A1B 4K7; tel. (709) 737-1859; fax (709) 737-1816; e-mail hydro@nlh.nl.ca; internet www.nlh.nl.ca; publicly owned electricity wholesaler; Pres. and CEO ED MARTIN; Chair. JOHN OTTENHEIMER.

Northwest Territories Power Corporation: 4 Capital Dr., Hay River, NT X0E 1G2; tel. (867) 874-5200; fax (867) 874-5229; e-mail info@ntpc.com; internet www.ntpc.com; f. 1988; Chair. LEW VOYTILLA; Pres. and CEO LEON COURNEYA.

Ontario Power Generation, Inc (OPG): 700 University Ave, Suite 1900, Toronto, ON M5G 1X6; tel. (416) 592-2555; fax (416) 971-3691; e-mail webmaster@opg.com; internet www.opg.com; f. 1907 as Ontario Hydro, renamed as above in 1999; Canada's largest utility and main nuclear power producer; generating capacity of 22,000 MW; crown corpn; Chair. JAKE EPP; Pres. and CEO JAMES HANKINSON.

Prince Edward Island Energy Corporation: Jones Bldg, 11 Kent St, 4th Floor, POB 2000, Charlottetown, PE C1A 7N8; tel. (902) 894-0289; fax (902) 894-0290; e-mail dwmacquarrie@gov.pe.ca; internet www.gov.pe.ca/development/ec-info; CEO WAYNE MACQUARRIE.

SaskEnergy, Inc: 1777 Victoria Ave, Regina, SK S4P 4K5; tel. (306) 777-9225; fax (306) 352-4438; internet www.saskenergy.com; responsible for Transgas Ltd; distributes power to over 327,000 customers; Chair. ROBERT PLETCH; Pres. and CEO DOUG KELLN.

SaskPower: 2025 Victoria Ave, Regina, SK S4P 0S1; tel. (306) 566-2121; fax (306) 566-3306; internet www.saskpower.com; f. 1930; conventional thermal, and alternative power; distributes power to over 439,000 customers; Chair. JOE TEAL; Pres. and CEO PATRICIA YOUZWA.

SOQUIP Energie: 1195 Lavigerie Ave, Suite 400, Sainte-Foy, QC G1V 4N3; tel. (418) 651-9543; fax (418) 651-2292; e-mail soquip@soquip.com; internet www.soquip.com; wholly owned by Société générale de financement du Québec; Chair., Pres. and Gen. Man. PIERRE SHEDLEUR.

Toronto Hydro Corporation: 14 Carlton St, 8th Floor, Toronto, ON M5B 1K5; tel. (416) 542-3000; fax (416) 542-3452; e-mail investorrelations@torontohydro.com; internet www.torontohydro.com; Chair. CLARE R. COPELAND; Pres. and CEO DAVID O'BRIEN.

TransAlta Corporation: 110 12th Ave, SW, POB 1900, Station M, Calgary, AB T2P 2M1; tel. (403) 267-7110; fax (403) 267-2590; e-mail michael_lawrence@transalta.com; internet www.transalta.com; Chair DONNA SOBLE KAUFMAN; Pres. and CEO STEPHEN G. SNYDER.

Associations

Association of Major Power Consumers in Ontario (AMPCO): Sterling Tower, Suite 1702, 372 Bay St, Toronto, ON M5H 2W9; tel. (416) 260-0280; fax (416) 260-0442; e-mail info@ampco.org; internet www.ampco.org; f. 1975; Chair. JOHN LEMAY; Pres. ADAM WHITE; 50 mems.

Association of Power Producers of Ontario (APPrO): 25 Adelaide St East, Suite 1602, Toronto, ON M5C 3A1; POB 1084, Station F, Toronto, ON M4Y 2T7; tel. (416) 322-6549; fax (416) 481-5785; e-mail appro@appro.org; internet www.appro.org; fmrly Independent Power Producers' Society of Ontario; non-profit org.; Pres. DAVID BUTTERS; more than 100 mem. orgs.

British Columbia Electrical Association: 3989 Henning Dr., Suite 224, Burnaby, BC V5C 6N5; tel. (604) 291-7708; fax (604) 291-7795; e-mail bcea@bcea.bc.ca; internet www.bcea.bc.ca; Exec. Dir BARBETTE CEJALVO; over 160 mems.

Canadian Coalition for Nuclear Responsibility: CP 236, Snowdon Station, Montréal, QC H3X 3T4; tel. and fax (514) 489-5118; e-mail ccnr@web.net; internet www.ccnr.org; f. 1975; non-profit org. with registered charitable status; Pres. Dr GORDON EDWARDS.

Canadian Electrical Contractors' Association (CECA): 170 Attwell Dr., Suite 460, Toronto, ON M9W 5Z5; tel. (416) 675-3226; fax (416) 675-7736; e-mail ceca@ceca.org; internet www.ceca.org; f. 1955; Pres. RICK BRODHURST.

Corporation des maîtres électriciens du Québec/Corporation of Master Electricians of Québec (CMEQ): blvd Décarie, bureau 5925, Montréal, QC H3W 3C9; tel. (514) 738-2184; fax (514) 738-2192; e-mail webmestre@cmeq.org; internet www.cmeq.org; f. 1950; Pres. MICHEL BERGERON.

Electrical Contractors' Association of Alberta (ECCA): 11235 120 St, Edmonton, AB T5G 2X9; tel. (780) 451-2412; fax (780) 455-9815; e-mail ecaa@ecaa.ab.ca; internet www.ecaa.ab.ca; f. 1962; Exec. Dir SHERI MCLEAN; Pres. TODD MCKAY; over 400 mems.

Electrical Contractors' Association of British Columbia (ECABC): 3989 Henning Dr., Suite 201, Burnaby, BC V5C 6N5; tel. (604) 294-4123; fax (604) 294-4120; e-mail eca@eca.bc.ca; internet www.eca.bc.ca; f. 1952; Exec. Dir DEBORAH CAHILL.

Electrical Contractors' Association of New Brunswick, Inc: 850 Prospect St West, POB 322, Fredericton, NB E3B 4Y9; tel. (506) 452-7627; fax (506) 452-1786; e-mail dwe@eca.nb.ca; internet www.eca.nb.ca; Exec. Dir DAVID ELLIS.

Electrical Contractors' Association of Ontario: 170 Attwell Dr., Suite 460, Toronto, ON M9W 5Z5; tel. (416) 675-3226; fax (416) 675-7736; e-mail ecao@ecao.org; internet www.ecao.org; f. 1948; Exec. Vice-Pres. ERYL M. ROBERTS.

Electrical Contractors' Association of Saskatchewan: 1939 Elphinstone St, Regina, SK S4T 3N3; tel. (306) 525-0171; fax (306) 347-8595; e-mail michaelf@scaonline.ca; internet www.ecas.ca; Exec. Dir MICHAEL FOUGERE.

Canadian Electricity Association, Inc: 350 Sparks St, Suite 907, Ottawa, ON K1R 7S8; tel. (613) 230-9263; fax (613) 230-9326; e-mail info@canelect.ca; internet www.canelect.ca; f. 1891; Pres. and CEO PIERRE GUIMOND.

Canadian Fluid Power Association: 2175 Sheppard Ave East, Suite 310, Toronto, ON M2J 1W8; tel. (416) 499-1416; fax (416) 491-1670; e-mail carolyne@taylorenterprises.com; internet cfpa.ca; f. 1976; Chair. JOHN BACHMANN; 80 mems.

Canadian Nuclear Association: 130 Albert St, Suite 1610, Ottawa, ON K1P 5G4; tel. (613) 237-4262; fax (613) 237-0989; e-mail fosterm@cna.ca; internet www.cna.ca; f. 1960; Chair. PIERRE CHARLEBOIS; Pres. and CEO MURRAY ELSTON; 82 mems.

Canadian Nuclear Society: 480 University Ave, Suite 200, Toronto, ON M5G 1V2; tel. (416) 977-7620; fax (416) 977-8131; e-mail cns-snc@on.aibn.com; internet www.cns-snc.ca; f. 1979; Pres. JIM HARVIE.

Canadian Renewable Fuels Association: 350 Sparks Street, Suite 1005, Ottawa, ON K1R 7S8; tel. (613) 594–5528; fax (613) 594–3076; e-mail j.fijalkowska@greenfuels.org; internet www.greenfuels.org; f. 1994; promotes the use of biofuels for automotive transportation; Pres. GORDON QUAIATTINI.

Canadian Solar Industries Association (CanSIA): 2378 Holly Lane, Suite 208, Ottawa, ON K1V 7P1; tel. (613) 736-9077; fax (613) 736-8938; e-mail info@cansia.ca; internet www.cansia.ca; works to enhance the professionalism of cos, foster domestic and international markets, and promote the use of renewable energies; Pres. DAVE EGLES; Exec. Dir ELIZABETH A. MCDONALD; 170 mems.

Canadian Wind Energy Association, Inc: 170 Laurier Ave West, Suite 810, Ottawa, ON K1P 5V5; tel. (613) 234-8716; fax (613) 234-5642; e-mail info@canwea.ca; internet www.canwea.ca; f. 1984; Pres. ROBERT HORNUNG.

Coal Association of Canada: 205 Ninth Ave, SE, Suite 150, Calgary, AB T2G 0R3; tel. (403) 262-1544; fax (403) 265-7604; e-mail info@coal.ca; internet www.coal.ca; Pres. and CEO ALLEN WRIGHT; Chair. GEORGE WHITE.

Electrical Power Systems Construction Association (EPSCA): 700 University Ave, Suite H19, Toronto, ON M5G 1X6; tel. (416) 592-2098; fax (416) 592-4520; e-mail labourreladm@opg.com; internet www.epsca.ca; Pres. JOHN D. MURPHY.

Electrical Utilities Safety Association of Ontario: 5110 Creekbank Rd, Suite 400, Mississauga, ON L4W 0A1; tel. (905) 625-0100; fax (905) 625-8998; e-mail info@eusa.on.ca; internet www.eusa.on.ca; f. 1915; Pres., CEO and Sec.-Treas. TED VANDEVIS.

Electricity Distributors Association: 3700 Steeles Ave West, Suite 1100, Vaughan, ON L4L 8K8; tel. (905) 265-5300; fax (905) 265-5301; e-mail email@eda-on.ca; internet www.eda-on.ca; fmrly Municipal Electric Asscn; Pres. and CEO CHARLIE C. MACALUSO.

Energy Council of Canada (EEC): 350 Sparks St, Suite 608, Ottawa, ON K1R 7S8; tel. (613) 232-8239; fax (613) 232-1079; e-mail brigitte.dignard@energy.ca; internet www.energy.ca; f. 1924; Canadian Mem. Cttee of the World Energy Council; non-profit org.; Pres. CARMEN DYBWAD; over 100 mems.

Manitoba Electrical League: 1780 Wellington Ave, Suite 104, Winnipeg, MB R3H 1B3; tel. (204) 783-4125; fax (204) 783-4216; e-mail office@meleague.net; internet www.meleague.net; Pres. LEONA HERZOG.

Ontario Electrical League: 5800 Explorer Dr., Suite 200, Mississauga, ON L4W 5K9; tel. (905) 238-1382; fax (905) 238-1420; e-mail league@oel.org; internet www.oel.org; f. 1966; Pres. MARY INGRAM-HAIGH; over 2,500 mems.

Ontario Energy Association (OEA): 77 Bloor St West, Suite 1104, Toronto, ON M5S 1M2; tel. (416) 961-2339; fax (416) 961-1173; e-mail oea@energyontario.ca; internet www.energyontario.ca; Pres. and CEO SHANE T. POSPISIL; Chair. JEFF ROSENTHAL.

Organization of CANDU Industries (OCI): 1 Yonge St, Suite 1801, Toronto, ON M5W 1W7; tel. (416) 363-7845; fax (416) 369-0515; e-mail neil.alexander@oci-aic.org; internet www.oci-aic.org; represents CANDU (Canadian deuterium uranium) industries; Pres. NEIL ALEXANDER; 86 mems.

Planetary Association for Clean Energy, Inc: 100 Bronson Ave, Suite 1001, Ottawa, ON K1R 6G8; tel. (613) 236-6265; fax (613) 235-5876; e-mail pacenet@canada.com; internet pacenet.homestead.com; f. 1975; international collaborative network of scientists; facilitates and oversees implementation of clean technologies (electricity, water, agriculture, bldgs) and clean-up of wastes, incl. nuclear and toxic; Pres. Dr ANDREW MICHROWSKI.

Society of Energy Professionals: 425 Bloor St East, Suite 300, Toronto, ON M4W 3R4; tel. (416) 979-2709; fax (416) 979-5794; e-mail society@society.on.ca; internet www.thesociety.ca; Pres. RODNEY SHEPPARD; 6,000 mems.

Solar Energy Society of Canada, Inc (SESCI): McLaughlin Hall, Suite 406, Queen's University, Kingston, ON K7L 3N6; tel. (613) 533-2657; fax (613) 533-6550; e-mail info@sesci.ca; internet www.sesci.ca; f. 1974; non-profit org. with registered charitable status; promotes increased use of solar and other renewable energies in Canada; Pres. FRÉDÉRIC POUYOT.

PETROLEUM AND GAS

Canadian Association of Drilling Engineers: 540 Fifth Ave, SW, Suite 800, Calgary, AB T2P 0M2; tel. (403) 264-4311; fax (403) 263-3796; e-mail cris@terradrill.ca; internet www.cade.ca; Pres. DAVID WHITE; 575 mems.

Canadian Association of Oilwell Drilling Contractors (CAODC): 540 Fifth Ave, SW, Suite 800, Calgary, AB T2P 0M2; tel. (403) 264-4311; fax (403) 263-3796; e-mail info@caodc.ca; internet www.caodc.ca; Pres. DON HERRING; 134 assoc. mems.

Canadian Association of Petroleum Landmen (CAPL): 500 Fifth Ave, SW, Suite 350, Calgary, AB T2P 3L5; tel. (403) 237-6635; fax (403) 263-1620; e-mail dgrieve@landman.ca; internet www.capl.ca; Pres. ROBERT J. TELFORD; 1,500 mems.

Canadian Association of Petroleum Producers (CAPP): 350 Seventh Ave, SW, Suite 2100, Calgary, AB T2P 3N9; tel. (403) 267-1100; fax (403) 261-4622; e-mail communication@capp.ca; internet www.capp.ca; f. 1952; represents the upstream petroleum and natural gas industry; Chair. GERARD PROTTI; Pres. DAVID COLLYER; 150 mems, 125 assoc. mems.

Canadian Energy Pipeline Association: Bow Valley Square II, 205 Fifth Ave, SW, Suite 1860, Calgary, AB T2P 2V7; tel. (403) 221-8777; fax (403) 221-8760; e-mail info@cepa.com; internet www.cepa.com; Chair. MURRAY BIRCH; Pres. BRENDA KENNY.

Canadian Gas Association (CGA): 350 Sparks St, Suite 809, Ottawa, ON K1R 7S8; tel. (613) 748-0057; fax (613) 748-9078; e-mail info@cga.ca; internet www.cga.ca; f. 1907; represents the natural gas delivery industry; Chair. JULIE DILL; Pres. and CEO MICHAEL CLELAND; 200 corporate mems.

Canadian Society of Petroleum Geologists (CSPG): 640 Eighth Ave, SW, Suite 600, Calgary, AB T2P 1G7; tel. (403) 264-5610; fax (403) 264-5898; e-mail reception@cspg.org; internet www.cspg.org; f. 1927; Pres. GRAEME BLOY; 3,300 mems.

Gas Processing Association of Canada (GPAC): 900 Sixth Ave, SW, Suite 505, Calgary, AB T2P 3K2; tel. (403) 705-0223; fax (403) 263-6886; e-mail info@gpacanada.ca; internet www.gpacanada.com; f. 2005, following the merger of Canadian Gas Processors' Asscn and Canadian Gas Processors' Suppliers' Asscn; Pres. RICHARD BOSOMWORTH.

Industrial Gas Users Association: 99 Metcalfe St, Suite 1201, Ottawa, ON K1P 6L7; tel. (613) 236-8021; fax (613) 230-9531; e-mail igua@magma.ca; internet www.igua.ca; f. 1973; Pres. MURRAY A. NEWTON; 43 mem. cos.

Offshore/Onshore Technologies Association of Nova Scotia: 1718 Argyle St, Suite 400, Halifax, NS B3J 3N6; tel. (902) 425-4774; fax (902) 422-2332; e-mail otans@otans.com; internet www.otans.com; f. 1982; Chair. MARK HEALEY; Man. Dir PAUL MCEACHERN; over 400 mem. orgs.

Ontario Petroleum Institute, Inc: 555 Southdale Rd East, Suite 104, London, ON N6E 1A2; tel. (519) 680-1620; fax (519) 680-1621; e-mail jvanoverberghe@ontpet.com; internet www.ontpet.com; f. 1963; Exec. Dir JOE VAN OVERBERGHE; 400 mems.

Petroleum Joint Venture Association (PJVA): POB 6173, Station D, Calgary, AB T2P 2C8; tel. (403) 244-4487; fax (403) 244-2340; e-mail pjva@pjva.ca; internet www.pjva.ca; incorporated in 1985; Pres. CHARLENE CAUFIELD.

Petroleum Services Association of Canada: 800 Sixth Ave, SW, Suite 1150, Calgary, AB T2P 3G3; tel. (403) 264-4195; fax (403) 263-7174; e-mail info@psac.ca; internet www.psac.ca; Chair. FRANK TIRPAK; Pres. and CEO ROGER SOUCY; over 260 mems.

Petroleum Society, Canadian Institute of Mining, Metallurgy and Petroleum: 500 Fifth Ave, SW, Suite 425, Calgary, AB T2P 3L5; tel. (403) 237-5112; fax (403) 262-4792; e-mail nancyh@petsoc.org; internet www.petsoc.org; Chair. ULIANA ROMANOVA.

Propane Gas Association of Canada Inc: 717 Seventh Ave, Suite 800, Calgary, AB T2P 0Z3; tel. (403) 543-6500; fax (403) 543-6508; e-mail info@propanegas.ca; internet www.propanegas.ca; Chair. DAN MCPHEE; Pres. ANN MARIE HANN; 274 mems.

Research Organizations

Alberta Research Council: 250 Karl Clark Rd, Edmonton, AB T6N 1E4; tel. (780) 450-5111; fax (780) 450-5333; e-mail referral@arc.ab.ca; internet www.arc.ab.ca; Pres. and CEO JOHN R. MCDOUGALL.

Atomic Energy of Canada Ltd: see Government—Selected Federal Government Agencies and Boards.

Canadian Energy Research Institute: 3512 33rd St, NW, Suite 150, Calgary, AB T2L 2A6; tel. (403) 282-1231; fax (403) 284-4181; e-mail ceri@ceri.ca; internet www.ceri.ca; f. 1975; Pres. and CEO MARWAN MASRI; over 100 mems.

Canadian Institute of Energy: 987 Devon Road, North Vancouver, BC V7R 1V8; tel. (604) 290-0880; fax (604) 922-2002; e-mail info@cienergy.org; internet www.cienergy.org; Chair. PENNY COCHRANE; 150 mems.

Centre québécois de valorisation des biotechnologies (CQVB): 2875 blvd Laurier, bureau 620, Québec, QC G1V 2M2; tel. (418) 657-3853; fax (418) 657-7934; e-mail cqvb@cqvb.qc.ca; internet www.cqvb.qc.ca; Chair. PAUL BEAULIEU; Pres. and Exec. Dir JEAN-MAURICE PLOURDE.

Energy Probe Research Foundation: 225 Brunswick Ave, Toronto, ON M5S 2M6; tel. (416) 964-9223; fax (416) 964-8239; e-mail webadmin@eprf.ca; internet www.eprf.ca; Chair. GAIL REGAN; Pres. PATRICIA ADAMS.

Wood Energy Technology Transfer: 296 Jarvis St, Unit 7, Toronto, ON M5B 2C5; tel. (416) 968-7718; fax (416) 968-6818; e-mail wett@funnel.ca; internet www.wettinc.ca; Pres. PATRICK CORMIER; Exec. Dir ANTHONY LAYCOCK.

WATER

ORGANIZATIONS AND CO-ORDINATING BODIES

Alberta Water and Wastewater Operators Association (AWWOA): 11810 Kingsway Ave, Edmonton, AB T5G 0X5; tel. (780) 454-7745; fax (780) 454-7748; e-mail awwoa@telus.net; internet www.awwoa.ab.ca; f. 1976; Exec. Dir DEL MORRISON.

Association des enterprises spécialisées en eau du Québec (AESEQ): 5930 blvd Louis-Hippolyte Lafontaine, Anjou, QC H1M 1S7; tel. (514) 353-9960; fax (514) 352-5259; e-mail contact@aeseq.com; internet www.aeseq.com; f. 1964 as Asscn des puisatiers du Québec (APQ); Pres. FRÉDÉRIC AYOTTE; Dir-Gen. DANIEL SCHANCK.

Atlantic Canada Water Works Association (ACWWA) (New Brunswick, Newfoundland, Nova Scotia, Prince Edward Island): POB 41002, Dartmouth, NS B2Y 4P7; tel. (902) 434-6002; fax (902) 435-7796; e-mail acwwa@hfx.andara.com; internet acwwa.ca; subsidiary of American Water Works Asscn; Chair. MARK BUTLER; Dir SANDY ROBERTSON; 29 mems.

British Columbia Water and Waste Association (BCWWA) (British Columbia and Yukon): 8678 Greenhall Ave, Suite 221, Burnaby, BC V5J 3M4; tel. (604) 433-4389; fax (604) 433-9859; e-mail bcwwa@bcwwa.org; internet www.bcwwa.org; f. 1973; subsidiary of American Water Works Asscn; Pres. MIKE NOLAN; CEO DAISY FOSTER (acting); 3,700 mems.

Canadian Association on Water Quality/Association canadienne sur la qualité de l'eau (CAWQ/ACQE): POB 5050, Burlington, ON L7R 4A6; tel. (905) 336-6291; fax (905) 336-4877; internet www.cawq.ca; f. 1967; Pres. Dr RON DROSTE.

Canadian Ground Water Association (CGWA): 1600 Bedford Hwy, Suite 100-409, Bedford, NS B4A 1E8; tel. (902) 845-1885; fax (902) 845-1886; e-mail info@cgwa.org; internet www.cgwa.org; Pres. FRANCIS GALE.

Affiliated associations include the following::

British Columbia Ground Water Association (BCGWA): 197 A St, Suite 1708, Langley, BC V2Z 1K2; tel. and fax (604) 530-8934; e-mail secretary@bcgwa.org; internet www.bcgwa.org; Pres. REMI ALLARD; 167 mems.

Manitoba Water Well Association: POB 1648, Winnipeg, MB R3C 2Z6; tel. and fax (204) 667-6643; e-mail mwwa@shaw.ca; internet www.mwwa.ca; Pres. ERIC HENSTRIDGE.

New Brunswick Ground Water Association Inc: POB 7016, Sussex Corner, NB E4E 5M3; tel. (506) 433-6767; fax (506) 432-6888; e-mail nbgwa@nb.sympatico.ca; internet www.nbgwa.ca; Pres. ROGER ROY; Exec. Dir BILL KYTE.

Newfoundland/Labrador Ground Water Association: POB 160, Doyles, NL A0N 1J0; tel. (709) 955-2561; fax (709) 955-3402; e-mail gwater@nf.sympatico.ca; Contact FRANCES GALE.

Nova Scotia Ground Water Association (NSGWA): 644 Portland St, Suite 417, Dartmouth, NS B2W 2M3; tel. (902) 434-7354; fax (902) 435-0089; e-mail nsgwa@ns.aliantzinc.ca; internet www.nsgwa.ca; Pres. PAUL VERGE.

Ontario Ground Water Association (OGWA): 48 Front St East, Strathroy, ON N7G 1Y6; tel. (519) 245-7914; fax (519) 245-7916; e-mail ogwa@ogwa.ca; internet www.ogwa.ca; f. 1952; Pres. CRAIG STAINTON; Exec. Dir EARL MORWOOD.

Prince Edward Island Ground Water Association: POB 857, RR 2, Cornwall, PE C0A 1H0; tel. and fax (902) 675-2360; Rep. E. WATSON MACDONALD.

Saskatchewan Ground Water Association: POB 9434, Saskatoon, SK S7K 7E9; tel. (306) 244-7551; fax (306) 343-0001; Exec. Sec. KATHLEEN WATSON.

Canadian Water Network/Réseau canadien de l'eau (CWN/RCE): 200 University Ave West, Waterloo, ON N2L 3G1; tel. (519) 888-4567; fax (519) 883-7574; e-mail info@cwn-rce.ca; internet www.cwn-rce.ca; f. 2001; research and development of water management projects; Chair. WILLIAM BORLAND; Exec. Dir BERNADETTE CONANT.

Canadian Water Quality Association (CWQA): 295 The West Mall, Suite 330, Toronto, ON M9C 4Z4; tel. (416) 695-3068; fax (416) 695-2945; e-mail k.wong@cwqa.com; internet www.cwqa.com; f. 1967; Pres. MYRON LUPAL; Exec. Dir KEVIN WONG.

Canadian Water Resources Association/Association canadienne des ressources hydriques (CWRA/ACRH): 280 Albert St, Suite 900, Ottawa, ON K1P 5G8; tel. (613) 237-9363; fax (613) 594-5190; e-mail fjross@telusplanet.net; internet www.cwra.org; f. 1947; Pres. SONYA MEEK; Exec. Dir F. A. (RICK) ROSS.

Canadian Water and Wastewater Association/Association canadienne des eaux potables et usées (CWWA/ACEPU): 1010 Polytek St, Suite 11, Ottawa, ON K1J 9H9; tel. (613) 747-0524; fax (613) 747-0523; e-mail admin@cwwa.ca; internet www.cwwa.ca; f. 1986; Exec. Dir T. DUNCAN ELLISON.

International Joint Commission/Commission mixte internationale (Canadian Section): 234 Laurier Ave West, 22nd Floor, Ottawa, ON K1P 6K6; tel. (613) 947-1420; fax (613) 993-5583; e-mail beckhoffb@ottawa.ijc.org; internet www.ijc.org; prevents and resolves disputes between the USA and Canada under the 1909 Boundary Waters Treaty; Chair. HERB GRAY; Commrs PIERRE TRÉPANIER, JACK P. BLANEY.

Manitoba Water Stewardship: 200 Saulteaux Cres., POB 11, Winnipeg, MB R3J 3W3; tel. (204) 945-6398; fax (204) 948-2684; e-mail wsd@gov.mb.ca; internet www.gov.mb.ca/waterstewardship; Minister of Water Stewardship CHRISTINE MELNICK.

Manitoba Water and Wastewater Association (MWWA): POB 1600, Portage la Prairie, MB R1N 3P1; tel. (204) 239-6868; fax (204) 239-6872; e-mail mwwa@mts.net; internet www.mwwa.net; Exec. Dir IVA LAST; Chair. TREVOR RICHARDSON.

Maritime Provinces Water and Wastewater Association (MPWWA): POB 41001, Dartmouth, NS B2Y 4P7; tel. (902) 434-8874; fax (506) 357-6038; e-mail mpwwa@eastlink.ca; internet www.mpwwa.ca; f. 1979; Chair. JODY COMEAU; Sec. DAN HARVEY.

National Water Research Institute/Institut national de recherche sur les eaux (NWRI/INRE): Environment Canada, 867 Lakeshore Rd, POB 5050, Burlington, ON L7R 4A6; tel. (905) 336-4625; internet (905) 336-6444; e-mail nwriscience.liaison@ec.gc.ca; internet www.nwri.ca; f. 1999; Dir-Gen. of Water, Science and Technology Dr J. H. CAREY.

Northern Territories Water and Waste Association (NTWWA): 4817 49th St, Suite 201, Yellowknife, NT X1A 3S7; tel. (867) 873-4325; fax (867) 669-2167; e-mail info@ntwwa.com; internet www.ntwwa.com; Pres. SEAN AUSTMAN KUNKEL.

Ontario Water Works Association (OWWA): 1092 Islington Ave, Suite 210, Toronto, ON M8Z 4R0; tel. (416) 231-1555; fax (416) 231-1556; e-mail waterinfo@owwa.ca; internet www.owwa.com; f. 1916; subsidiary of American Water Works Asscn; Pres. TOM MOULTON; Exec. Dir BILL BALFOUR; over 1,100 mems.

RESEAU environnement: 911 rue Jean-Talon Est, bureau 220, Montréal, QC H2R 1V5; tel. (514) 270-7110; fax (514) 270-7154; e-mail info@reseau-environnement.com; internet www.reseau-environnement.com; subsidiary of American Water Works Asscn; fmrly Asscn québécoise des techniques de l'eau; Pres. ANN LAJOIE; Sec.-Treas. JACQUES BOURBONNAIS; 1,900 mems.

Saskatchewan Water and Wastewater Association (SWWA): 46 Windfield Rd, Regina, SK S4V 0E7; tel. (306) 761-1278; fax (306) 761-1279; e-mail swwa.office@sasktel.net; internet www.swwa.sk.ca; Pres. RICK HANSON.

Société québécoise d'assainissement des eaux/Water Treatment Corporation (SQAE): 800 rue du Victoria, bureau 2.45, Tour de la Bourse, CP 83, Montréal, QC H4Z 1B7; tel. (514) 873-3335; fax (514) 873-8257; e-mail michel.gagnon@mamr.gouv.qc.ca; f. 1980; Pres. and Dir-Gen. MARC PINSONNAULT.

Water Environment Association of Ontario (WEAO): POB 176, Milton, ON L9T 4N9; tel. (416) 410-6933; fax (416) 410-1626; e-mail julie.vincent@weao.org; internet www.weao.org; f. 1971; promotes water environment industry; Pres. GEORGE LAI; Exec. Dir CATHERINE JEFFERSON.

Water Management Division, Prince Edward Island Department of the Environment and Energy: Jones Bldg, 4th and 5th Floors, 11 Kent St, POB 2000, Charlottetown, PE C1A 7N8; tel. (902) 368-5028; fax (902) 368-5830; e-mail sjmoore@gov.pe.ca; internet www.gov.pe.ca/enveng/wm-info; Dir JIM YOUNG.

Water Management Operations, Alberta Environment (WMO): Provincial Bldg, 2nd Floor, 200 Fifth Ave South, Lethbridge, AB T1J 4L1; tel. (403) 382-4247; fax (403) 381-5969; e-mail tannis.natte@gov.ab.ca; internet www3.gov.ab.ca/env/water/wmo; Dir DENIS MAGOWAN.

Water Resources Branch, Ontario, Ministry of Environment and Energy: 135 St Clair Ave West, 1st Floor, Toronto, ON M4V 1P5; tel. (416) 325-4000; fax (416) 314-7337; e-mail picemail.moe@ontario.ca; internet www.ene.gov.on.ca/en/water/index.php; Dir Dr JAMES ASHMAN.

Water Resources Management Division, Newfoundland and Labrador Department of Environment and Conservation: Confederation Bldg, West Block, 4th Floor, POB 8700, St John's, NL A1B 4J6; tel. (709) 729-2563; fax (709) 729-0320; e-mail water@gov.nl.ca; internet www.env.gov.nl.ca/env/Env/water_resources.asp; f. 1949; Dir MARTIN GOEBEL.

Water Resources Section, Yukon Department of the Environment: POB 2703, Whitehorse, YT Y1A 2C6; tel. (867) 667-3171; fax (867) 667-3195; e-mail hillery.blower@gov.yk.ca; internet environmentyukon.gov.yk.ca.

Water Stewardship Division, British Columbia Ministry of Environment: POB 9339, Station Provincial Govt, Victoria, BC V8W 9M1; tel. (604) 582-5200; fax (250) 953-3414; e-mail sarah.andrews@gov.bc.ca; internet www.env.gov.bc.ca/wsd; Minister of Environment and Minister Responsible for Water Stewardship and Sustainable Communities BARRY PENNER.

Water and Wastewater Management Section, New Brunswick Department of the Environment: Marysville Pl., 20 McGloin St, POB 6000, Fredericton, NB E3B 5H1; tel. (506) 453-2690; fax (506) 453-2390; e-mail mike.wesson@gnb.ca; internet www.gnb.ca/0009/index-e.asp.

Western Canada Water and Wastewater Association (WCWWA) (Alberta, Saskatchewan, Manitoba): POB 1708, 126 Third Ave West, Cochrane, Alberta T4C 1B6; tel. (403) 709–0064; fax (403) 709–0068; e-mail member@wcwwa.ca; internet www.wcwwa.ca; f. 1948; Pres. WILLIAM A. (BILL) HEYWOOD; Exec. Dir AUDREY ARISMAN; c. 4,000 mems.

Western Canada Section, American Water Works Association (WCS AWWA) (Alberta, Saskatchewan, Manitoba): 301 14th St, Suite 203, NW, Calgary, AB T2N 2A1; tel. (877) 283-2003; fax (877) 283-2007; e-mail aarisman@wcwwa.ca; internet www.wcsawwa.net; subsidiary of American Water Works Asscn; Chair. RYAN JOHNSON; Exec. Dir AUDREY ARISMAN.

MAJOR WATER COMPANIES

Epcor Water Services Inc: 10065 Jasper Ave, Edmonton, AB T5J 3B1; tel. (780) 412-4000; e-mail water@epcor.ca; internet www.epcor.ca; provides water for 50 communities across western Canada; Vice-Pres. and Gen. Man. STEPHEN STANLEY.

Manitoba Water Services Board: 2022 Currie Blvd, POB 22080, Brandon, MB R7A 6Y9; tel. (204) 726-6076; fax (204) 726-6290; e-mail mwsb@gov.mb.ca; internet www.gov.mb.ca/tgs/mwsb.

Northwest Territories Water Board: CJCD Bldg, 2nd Floor, 49 St, Suite 5114, POB 1326, Yellowknife, NT X1A 2N9; tel. (867) 765-0106; fax (867) 765-0114; e-mail info@nwtwb.com; internet www.nwtwb.com; Chair. EDDIE DILLON.

Nunavut Water Board: POB 119, Gjoa Haven, NU X0B 1J0; tel. (867) 360-6338; fax (867) 360-6369; e-mail exec@nunavutwaterboard.org; internet www.nunavutwaterboard.org; Chair. THOMAS KABLOONA (acting); Exec. Dir DIONNE FILIATRAULT.

Ontario Clean Water Agency/Agence ontarienne des eaux (OCWA): 1 Yonge St, Suite 1700, Toronto, ON M5E 1E5; tel. (416) 314-5600; e-mail ocwa@ocwa.com; internet www.ocwa.com; f. 1993; Chair. JOHN BURKE; Pres. and CEO DANTE PONTONE.

Saskwater: 111 Fairford St East, 2nd Floor, Suite 200, Moose Jaw, SK S6H 1C8; tel. (306) 694-3098; fax (306) 694-3207; e-mail comm@saskwater.com; internet www.saskwater.com; Chair. GLEN RITTINGER; Pres. STUART KRAMER.

Toronto Water: e-mail askwater@toronto.ca; internet www.toronto.ca/water; Gen. Man. LOU DI GIRONIMO.

Yukon Water Board: 419 Range Rd, Suite 106, Whitehorse, YT Y1A 3V1; tel. (867) 456-3980; fax (867) 456-3890; e-mail ywb@yukonwaterboard.ca; internet www.yukonwaterboard.ca; Chair. BRUCE WILLIS.

TRANSPORT

CO-ORDINATING BODIES AND TRANSPORT ASSOCIATIONS

Association québécoise du transport et des routes: 1255 rue University, bureau 200, Montréal, QC H3B 3B2; tel. (514) 523-6444; fax (514) 523-2666; e-mail info@aqtr.qc.ca; internet www.aqtr.qc.ca; f. 1964; Pres. DANIEL TOUTANT; Dir-Gen. DOMINIQUE LACOSTE.

Canadian Industrial Transportation Association: 580 Terry Fox Dr., Suite 405, Ottawa, ON K2L 4C2; tel. (613) 599-3283; fax (613) 599-1295; e-mail info@cita-acti.ca; internet www.cita-acti.ca; f. 1916; Chair. ROBERT BRYSON; Pres. ROBERT BALLANTYNE; 120 mem. cos.

Canadian Institute of Traffic and Transportation: 10 King St East, Suite 400, Toronto, ON M5C 1C3; tel. (416) 363-5696; fax (416) 363-5698; e-mail info@citt.ca; internet www.citt.ca; f. 1958; 800 mems; Chair. PATRICK K. BOHAN; Pres. CATHERINE VIGLAS.

Canadian Transportation Agency (CTA): see Government—Selected Federal Government Agencies and Boards.

Canadian Transportation Research Forum: POB 23033, Woodstock, ON N4T 1R9; tel. (519) 421-9701; fax (519) 421-9319; e-mail cawoudsma@ctrf.ca; internet www.ctrf.ca; f. 1965; Pres. DARRYL ANDERSON.

Canadian Urban Transit Association: 55 York St, Suite 1401, Toronto, ON M5J 1R7; tel. (416) 365-9800; fax (416) 365-1295; e-mail shuell@cutaactu.ca; internet www.cutaactu.ca; f. 1904 as the Canadian Street Railway Asscn; mems include: 120 transit systems; 15 govt agencies; 50 affiliates; and 250 business mems; Chair. STEVE NEW; Pres. and CEO MICHAEL ROSCHLAU.

Transport Canada: see Government of Canada—Ministries.

Transport 2000 Canada: 211 Bronson Ave, Suite 303, Ottawa, ON K1R 6H5; tel. (613) 594-3290; fax (613) 594-3271; e-mail t2000@transport2000.ca; internet www.transport2000.ca; f. 1976; nat. federation of consumers of public transportation engaged in research, education and advocacy; Pres. DAVID JEANES; Nat. Office Man. BERT TITCOMB.

Transportation Association of Canada: 2323 St Laurent Blvd, Ottawa, ON K1G 4K6; tel. (613) 736-1350; fax (613) 736-1395; e-mail secretariat@tac-atc.ca; internet www.tac-atc.ca; Pres. JOHN LAW; Exec. Dir MICHEL GRAVEL; 550 mem. orgs.

Transportation Health and Safety Association of Ontario: 555 Dixon Rd, Suite 101, Etobicoke, ON M9W 1H8; tel. (416) 242-4771; fax (416) 242-4714; e-mail info@thsao.mail.net; internet www.thsao.on.ca; Pres. and CEO MICHAEL J. BURKE.

RAILWAYS

Length of Main-line Track Operated by Area

(km)

	2004	2005	2006
Alberta	7,284	7,184	6,888
British Columbia	6,920	6,965	6,869
Manitoba	5,238	5,229	5,235
New Brunswick	1,139	1,139	1,139
Newfoundland and Labrador	459	634	459
Northwest Territories*	122	122	121
Nova Scotia	758	758	758
Ontario	11,949	11,817	11,792
Québec	6,134	6,134	6,071
Saskatchewan	9,164	8,911	8,911
Total†	64,411	63,782	64,438

* Includes Nunavut Territory, constituted as a separate Territory in 1999.

† Totals also include VIA running rights, commuter and freight running rights and routes operating through USA.

Source: Railway Association Canada, *Railway Trends*.

Railway Rolling Stock in Service

	2004	2005	2006
Locomotives	3,234	3,253	3,271
Freight cars	99,141	101,606	99,946
Passenger cars	465	538	537

Source: Railway Association Canada, *Railway Trends*.

Summary of Operations

(Note: Includes only the short line and regional railways formerly part of the Canadian National or Canadian Pacific Railway networks.)

	2004	2005	2006
Operating revenues (C $ million)	8,823	9,940	10,613
Operating expenses (C $ million)	7,119	7,776	8,211
Revenue (freight) (C $ million)	7,931	8,794	9,430
Revenue (passenger) (C $ million)*†	386	576	622
Freight transportation ('000 metric tons)	306,563	311,590	307,897
Number of passengers ('000)*	4,181	4,322	4,320
Freight revenue ton-km ('000)	343,232	352,912	355,831
Passenger-km ('000)*	1,439	1,479	1,458

* Intercity trains only.

† Excluding government funding.

Source: Railway Association Canada, *Railway Trends*.

Directory

The Canadian Pacific Railway Ltd (CPR) and CN (Canadian National Railways) companies own or control over 90% of all railway mileage in Canada. Passenger services are operated over CP and CN tracks by the crown corporation VIA Rail Canada, Inc.

PRINCIPAL RAILWAY COMPANIES

BNSF Railway: 963 Lindsay St, Winnipeg, MB R3N 1X6; tel. (204) 453-4415; fax (204) 477-0046; e-mail vicc@bnsf.com; internet www.bnsf.com; f. 1996 as Burlington Northern Santa Fe Railway; name changed as above 2005; subsidiary of Burlington Northern Santa Fe Corpn, Fort Worth, TX, USA; Chair., Pres. and CEO MATTHEW K. ROSE.

Canada and Gulf Terminal Railway/Chemin de fer de la matapédia et du golfe (CFMG): 206 ave Hébert, CP 122, Mont-Joli, QC G5H 3L3; tel. (418) 775-0005; fax (418) 775-5050; e-mail jocelyn.ouellet@cfqc.com; 356 km (221 miles) of track; owned by the Société des Chemins de Fer de Québec (Quebec Railway Corpn); merged with Chemin de Fer Baie des Chaleurs (CBC)—235 km (146 miles) of track—in 2002; Gen. Man. LUCIE RIOUX.

Canadian Pacific Railway Ltd (CPR): Gulf Canada Sq., 401 Ninth Ave, SW, Suite 500, Calgary, AB T2P 4Z4; tel. (403) 319-7000; e-mail ed_greenberg@cpr.ca; internet www.cpr.ca; f. 1881; 26,208 km (16,300 miles) of mainline track in Canada and the north-east and mid-west of the USA; Chair. JOHN E. CLEGHORN; Pres. and CEO FRED J. GREEN.

Carlton Trail Railway: 1545 5th Ave, Prince Albert, SK S6V 7Z5; tel. (306) 763-9475; fax 306) 763-9471; e-mail aglastetter@omnitrax.com; internet www.omnitrax.com/rail_ctr.aspx; 449 km (279 miles) of track in Saskatchewan; Gen. Man. ANDREW GLASTETTER.

Cartier Railway Co: 24 des Iles blvd, Rm 201, Port-Cartier, QC G5B 2H3; tel. (418) 766-2000; fax (418) 768-2428; e-mail communications@qcmines.com; 416 km (258 miles) of track; owned and operated by ArcelorMittal Mines Canada (fmrly Québec Cartier Mining Co); freight only; CEO GUY DUFRESNE.

CN Rail: 935 rue de la Gauchetière ouest, succursale A, CP 8100, Montréal, QC H3B 2M9; tel. (514) 399-4937; fax (514) 399-6910; e-mail contact@cn.ca; internet www.cn.ca; f. 1919; investor-owned; 32,500 km of track; Chair. DAVID G. A. MCLEAN; Pres. and CEO E. HUNTER HARRISON.

Algoma Central Railway/CN: 129 Bay St, POB 130, Sault Ste Marie, ON P6A 6Y2; tel. (705) 946-7300; fax (705) 541-2989; e-mail tourinfo@cn.ca; internet www.algomacentralrailway.com; f. 1899; owned by CN; day tour trains and regular passenger service on 476 km (296 miles) of track in Ontario.

CSX Transportation, Inc: 500 Water St, Jacksonville, FL 32202, USA; tel. (904) 359-3200; fax (313) 464-4893; internet www.csxt.com; f. 1980; 267 km (166 miles) of track in Canada; Chair., Pres. and CEO MICHAEL J. WARD.

Essex Terminal Railway: 1601 Lincoln Rd, POB 24025, Windsor, ON N8Y 4Y9; tel. (519) 973-8222; fax (519) 973-7234; e-mail etr@etr.ca; internet www.essexterminalrailway.com; f. 1902; freight railway; 35 km (22 miles) of track; Pres. BRIAN G. MCKEOWN.

Hudson Bay Railway: POB 2129, 728 Bignell Ave, The Pas, MB R9A 1L8; tel. (204) 627-2007; fax (204) 623-3095; e-mail aglastetter@omnitrax.com; internet www.omnitrax.com/rail_hbry.aspx; 1,303 km (810 miles) of track in northern Manitoba; Gen. Man. ANDREW GLASTETTER.

Norfolk Southern Corporation: c/o 3 Commercial Pl., Norfolk, VA 23510-9217, USA; tel. (757) 629-2600; e-mail fsbrown@nscorp.com; internet www.nscorp.com; 488 km (303 miles) of track in Canada; Chair., Pres. and CEO CHARLES W. MOORMAN.

Ontario Northland Transportation Commission: 555 Oak St East, North Bay, ON P1B 8L3; tel. (705) 472-4500; fax (705) 476-5598; e-mail info@ontc.on.ca; internet www.ontc.on.ca; agency of the Govt of Ontario; operates rail services over 1,120 km (696 miles) of track; Commr and Chair. TED HARGREAVES; Pres. and CEO STEVE CARMICHAEL.

RailAmerica, Inc: 7411 Fullerton Street, Suite 300, Jacksonville, FL 32256, USA; tel. (904) 538-6100; internet www.railamerica.com; f. 1986; operates railways in three Canadian provinces; CEO JOHN GILES; Pres. DONALD D. REDFEARN.

Cape Breton and Central Nova Scotia Railway: POB 2240, 121 King St, Stellarton, NS B0K 1S0; tel. (902) 752-3357; e-mail jim.ryan@railamerica.com; owned by RailAmerica; 383 km (238 miles) of track in Nova Scotia; Assistant Gen. Man. JIM RYAN.

Goderich–Exeter Railway: 101 Shakespeare St, 2nd Floor, Stratford, ON N5A 3W5; tel. (519) 271-4441; fax (519) 271-1337; e-mail douglas.mackenzie@railamerica.com; Gen. Man. DOUGLAS MACKENZIE.

Ottawa Valley Railway: 445 Oak St East, North Bay, ON P1B 1A3; tel. (705) 472-6200; e-mail scott.campbell@railamerica.com; acquired by RailAmerica in 1999; 626 km (389 miles) of track in Québec and Ontario; Gen. Man. SCOTT CAMPBELL.

Southern Ontario Railway: 241 Stuart St West, POB 953, Hamilton, ON L8N 3P9; tel. (905) 777-1234; e-mail jan.polley@railamerica.com; Gen. Man. JAN POLLEY.

Roberval and Saguenay Railway: CP 1277, Jonquière (Arvida), QC G7S 4K8; tel. (418) 544-9634; e-mail marc.gratton@alcan.com; f. 1908; acquired by Alcan Aluminium Ltd in 1925; freight only; 160 km (99 miles) of track; Gen. Man. MARC GRATTON.

Southern Railway of British Columbia Ltd: 2102 River Dr., New Westminster, BC V3M 6S3; tel. (604) 521-1966; fax (604) 526-0914; internet www.sryraillink.com; freight only; 194 km (125 miles) of track; Pres. FRANK BUTZELAAR.

Southern Railway of Vancouver Island: 2102 River Dr., New Westminster, BC V3M 6S3; tel. (604) 521-1966; internet www.sryraillink.com/vancouver_isl_service.htm; 290 km (180 miles) of track; purchased by the Southern Railway of British Columbia in 2006; fmrly Esquimalt and Nanaimo (E&N) Railway Co Ltd; Gen. Man. DONALD S. MCGREGOR.

VIA Rail Canada, Inc: see Government—Selected Federal Government Agencies and Boards.

White Pass and Yukon Route: 1109 First Ave, Suite 4, Whitehorse, YK Y1A 5G4; tel. (907) 983-9816; fax (907) 983-2734; e-mail info@whitepass.net; internet www.whitepassrailroad.com; f. 1898; owned by the Tri-White Corpn; 177 km (110 miles) of track; Pres. GARY C. DANIELSON.

ASSOCIATIONS

Alberta Pioneer Railway Association: POB 70014 LRPO, Edmonton, AB T5C 3R6; tel. (780) 472-6229; fax (780) 968-0167; e-mail hdixon@incentre.net; internet www.railwaymuseum.ab.ca; f. 1968; Pres. HERB DIXON.

Association of Regional Railways of Canada: 68 Robertson Rd, Suite 105, Ottawa, ON K2H 8P5; tel. (613) 726-7111; fax (613) 726-7139; e-mail hick@arrc.ca; internet www.arrc.ca; f. 2001; Pres. BOB BALLANTYNE.

Canadian Railroad Historical Association: 110 rue St-Pierre, St-Constant, QC J5A 1G7; tel. (450) 638-1522; fax (450) 638-1563; e-mail info@exporail.org; internet www.exporail.org; f. 1932; Sec. DANIEL LAURENDEAU.

Railway Association of Canada: 99 Bank St, Suite 1401, Ottawa, ON K1P 6B9; tel. (613) 567-8591; fax (613) 567-6726; e-mail rac@railcan.ca; internet www.railcan.ca; f. 1917; Pres. and CEO CLIFF MACKAY; 60 mems.

West Coast Railway Association: POB 2790, Station Terminal, Vancouver, BC V6B 3X2; tel. (604) 524-1011; e-mail info@wcra.org; internet www.wcra.org; f. 1961; Exec. Dir DON EVANS; 600 mems.

ROADS

Length of Roads and Highways by Province or Territory

(Source: Transport Canada, *Transportation in Canada—2007 Annual Report.*)

EXTENT
('000 two-lane equivalent km, 2007)

	Paved roads	Unpaved roads	Total
Alberta	61.7	164.6	226.3
British Columbia	48.2	22.9	71.1
Manitoba	19.3	67.3	86.6
New Brunswick	19.5	12.0	31.5
Newfoundland and Labrador	10.6	8.6	19.3
Northwest Territories	0.9	3.6	4.5
Nova Scotia	18.1	9.0	27.1
Nunavut Territory	—	0.3	0.3
Ontario	119.8	71.1	191.0
Prince Edward Island	4.3	1.8	6.0
Québec	81.5	63.2	144.7
Saskatchewan	29.5	198.7	228.2
Yukon Territory	2.2	3.5	5.8
Total	415.6	626.7	1,042.3

Motor-Vehicle Registrations by Province or Territory

(Source: Statistics Canada.)

SUMMARY
(2007)

	Passenger cars and light trucks (less than 4,500 kilograms)	Heavy trucks (4,500 kilograms and over)	Buses	Motorcycles and mopeds	Other*
Alberta	2,453,491	201,840	14,138	81,695	1,104,708
British Columbia	2,499,237	133,122	9,351	47,810	378,963
Manitoba	643,580	28,296	3,808	10,891	237,155
New Brunswick	471,013	11,974	2,932	16,518	129,719
Newfoundland and Labrador	268,190	7,542	1,239	7,460	179,997
Northwest Territories	21,451	2,161	134	564	5,702
Nova Scotia	548,111	16,708	1,847	13,528	104,752
Nunavut Territory	3,095	368	19	45	1,030
Ontario	7,038,695	216,379	27,457	153,441	2,554,294
Prince Edward Island	77,873	4,271	92	2,165	12,630
Québec	4,464,896	97,905	17,478	180,836	2,114,531
Saskatchewan	683,507	65,521	3,760	6,759	149,492
Yukon Territory	25,815	3,177	324	718	11,289
Total†	19,198,960	789,272	82,583	522,433	6,984,302

* Includes trailers, off-road, construction and farm vehicles.
† May not be equal to the sum of the listed regions, owing to regional discrepancies in enumeration.

Directory

Provincial governments are responsible for roads within their boundaries. The federal Government is responsible for major roads in the Yukon Territory, the Northwest Territories and Nunavut Territory, and in national parks. In 2004 there were 1,408,800 km of roads (including 16,900 km of freeways and 200,400 km of highways).

The Trans-Canada Highway extends from St John's, Newfoundland and Labrador, to Victoria, British Columbia.

NATIONAL REGULATORY AGENCY

Canadian Transportation Agency (CTA): see Government—Selected Federal Government Agencies and Boards.

ASSOCIATIONS

Association des propriétaires d'autobus du Québec: 225 blvd Charest est, Suite 107, Québec, QC G1K 3G9; tel. (418) 522-7131; fax (418) 522-6455; e-mail apaq@apaq.qc.ca; internet www.apaq.qc.ca; f. 1926; Pres. PIERRE HÉLIE; Exec. Vice-Pres. ROMAIN GIRARD; 300 mem. cos.

Canadian Automobile Association: 1145 Hunt Club Rd, Suite 200, Ottawa, ON K1V 0Y3; tel. (613) 247-0117; fax (613) 247-0118; e-mail info@national.caa.ca; internet www.caa.ca; f. 1913; Pres. TIM SHEARMAN.

Canadian Bus Association: 451 Daly Ave, Ottawa, ON K1N 6H6; tel. (613) 238-1800; fax (613) 241-4936; e-mail sbeaudin@buscanada.com; internet www.buscanada.ca; Exec. Dir SHEILAGH BEAUDIN.

Canadian Council of Motor Transport Administrators: 2323 St Laurent Blvd, Ottawa, ON K1G 4J8; tel. (613) 736-1003; fax (613) 736-1395; e-mail ccmta-secretariat@ccmta.ca; internet www.ccmta.ca; mems comprised of federal, provincial and territorial transportation depts; Pres. SHERRY WOLF.

Canadian Motorcycle Association: 605 James St North, 4th Floor, POB 448, Hamilton, ON L8L 8C4; tel. (905) 522-5705; fax (905) 522-5716; e-mail registration@canmocycle.ca; internet www.canmocycle.ca; f. 1946; Exec. Officer MARILYN BASTEDO; c. 10,000 mems.

Canadian Trucking Alliance: 324 Somerset St West, Ottawa, ON K2P 0J9; tel. (613) 236-9426; fax (613) 563-2701; e-mail info@cantruck.ca; internet www.cantruck.com; f. 1937; Pres. and CEO DAVID BRADLEY; 4,500 mems

Alberta Motor Transport Association: 3660 Blackfoot Trail, SE, Calgary, AB T2G 4E6; tel. (403) 243-4161; fax (403) 243-4610; e-mail amtamsc@amta.ca; internet www.amta.ca; Pres. GREG SOKIL; Exec. Dir MAYNE ROOT; over 12,000 mems.

Association du camionnage du Québec Inc: 6450 rue Notre-Dame ouest, bureau 200, Montréal, QC H4C 1V4; tel. (514) 932-0377; fax (514) 932-1358; e-mail info@carrefour-acq.org; internet www.carrefour-acq.org; f. 1951; Pres. ERIC GIGNAC; CEO MARC CADIEUX; over 1,000 mems.

Atlantic Provinces Trucking Association: 725 Champlaln St, Suite 400, Dieppe, NB E1A 1P6; tel. (866) 855-2782; fax (506) 853-7424; e-mail apta@apta.ca; internet www.apta.ca; Exec. Dir PETER NELSON; c. 400 mems.

British Columbia Trucking Association: 20111, 93A Ave, Langley, BC V1M 4A9; tel. (604) 888-5319; fax (604) 888-2941; e-mail bcta@bctrucking.com; internet www.bctrucking.com; f. 1913; Chair. GREG ROGGE; Pres. and CEO PAUL LANDRY.

Manitoba Trucking Association: 25 Bunting St, Winnipeg, MB R2X 2P5; tel. (204) 632-6600; fax (204) 694-7134; e-mail info@trucking.mb.ca; internet www.trucking.mb.ca; f. 1932; Pres. EARL COLEMAN; Gen. Man. BOB DOLYNIUK.

Northwest Territories Motor Transport Association: POB 574, Yellowknife, NT X1A 2N4; tel. (403) 873-2831; fax (403) 255-2724; Pres. JOE AGREY.

Ontario Trucking Association: 555 Dixon Rd, Toronto, ON M9W 1H8; tel. (416) 249-7401; fax (416) 245-6152; e-mail info@ontruck.org; internet www.ontruck.org; f. 1926; Chair. MARK SEYMOUR; Pres. and CEO DAVID BRADLEY.

Saskatchewan Trucking Association: 1335 Wallace St, Regina, SK S4N 3Z5; tel. (306) 569-9696; fax (306) 569-1008; e-mail georgetta@sasktrucking.com; internet www.sasktrucking.com; f. 1937; Pres. DENIS PRUDHOMME; Exec. Dir AL ROSSEKER.

Canadian Vehicle Manufacturers' Association: 170 Attwell Dr., Suite 400, Toronto, ON M9W 5Z5; tel. (416) 364-9333; fax (416) 367-3221; e-mail info@cvma.ca; internet www.cvma.ca; f. 1926; Pres. MARK A. NANTAIS; four mems.

Dominion Automobile Association: POB 5817, London, ON N6A 4T3; tel. (519) 434-2185; fax (519) 439-9040; e-mail jmctaggart@daa.ca; internet www.daa.ca; f. 1948; Chair. and CEO MICHAEL MEAGHER; eight provincial offices.

Freight Carriers' Association of Canada: 427 Garrison Rd, Units 3 and 4, Fort Erie, ON L2A 6E6; tel. (800) 559-7421; fax (905) 994-0117; e-mail info@fca-natc.org; internet www.fca-natc.org; Pres. DAVID J. SIRGEY.

Ontario Good Roads Association: 6355 Kennedy Rd, Unit 2, Mississauga, ON L5T 2L5; tel. (905) 795-2555; fax (905) 795-2660; e-mail info@ogra.org; internet www.ogra.org; Pres. DAVID A. LECKIE; Exec. Dir JOSEPH W. TIERNAY; mems incl. 429 municipalities, 120 corpns and 25 First Nations.

Private Motor Truck Council of Canada: 1155 North Service Rd West, Suite 11, Oakville, ON L6M 3E3; tel. (905) 827-0587; fax (905) 827-8212; e-mail info@pmtc.ca; internet www.pmtc.ca; Pres. BRUCE J. RICHARDS.

Western Canada Motor Coach Association: POB 4520, Station C, Calgary, AB T2T 5N3; tel. (403) 244-4487; fax (403) 244-2340; Exec. Dir SIMONE HAMBLY.

INLAND WATERWAYS

Traffic

(St Lawrence Seaway, '000 gross registered metric tons)

	2005	2006	2007
Montréal–Lake Ontario	31,273	35,572	31,955
Welland Canal	34,150	37,420	34,935

Source: St Lawrence Seaway Management Corpn.

Directory

ST LAWRENCE RIVER AND GREAT LAKES SHIPPING

The St Lawrence River and the Great Lakes provide Canada and the USA with a system of inland waterways extending from the Atlantic Ocean to the western end of Lake Superior, a distance of 3,769 km (2,342 miles). There is a 10.7-m (35-foot) navigation channel from Montréal to the sea and an 8.25-m (27-foot) channel from Montréal to Lake Erie. The St Lawrence Seaway (see below), which was opened in 1959, was initiated partly to provide a deep waterway and partly to satisfy the increasing demand for electric power. Power development has been undertaken by the provinces of Québec and Ontario, and by New York State. In 2007 cargo traffic through the Seaway amounted to 43.0m. metric tons. The navigation facilities and conditions are within the jurisdiction of the federal Governments of the USA and Canada.

Selected Organizations

Algoma Central Corpn: 421 Bay St, POB 7000, Sault Ste Marie, ON P6A 5P6; tel. (705) 946-7200; internet www.algonet.com; f. 1899; transportation co moving bulk cargo by water; also has interests in commercial property devt; Chair. RADCLIFFE R. LATIMER; Pres. and CEO GREG D. WIGHT.

Canada Steamship Lines: 759 Victoria Sq., Montréal, QC H2Y 2K3; tel. (514) 982-3800; fax (514) 982-3802; e-mail ships@cslmtl.com; internet www.csl.ca/new; f. 1845; subsidiary of CSL Group Inc; 15 vessels; Pres. and CEO GERRY CARTER.

Great Lakes Pilotage Authority: 202 Pitt St, 2nd Floor, POB 95, Cornwall, ON K6H 5R9; tel. (613) 933-2991; fax (613) 932-3793; e-mail rlemire@glpa-apgl.com; internet www.glpa-apgl.com; f. 1972; provides pilotage services in Canadian waters of the St Lawrence River commencing at the northern entrance of St Lambert Lock, the Great Lakes area and the Port of Churchill, Manitoba; CEO ROBERT F. LEMIRE.

Laurentian Pilotage Authority: 555 René-Lévesque Blvd West, Suite 1501, Montréal, QC H2Z 1B1; tel. (514) 283-6320; fax (514) 496-2409; e-mail administration@apl.gc.ca; internet www.pilotagestlaurent.gc.ca; f. 1971; provides pilotage services in the province of Québec north of St Lambert Lock; CEO Capt. RÉJEAN LANTEIGNE.

St Lawrence Seaway Management Corpn: 202 Pitt St, Cornwall, ON K6J 3P7; tel. (613) 932-5170; fax (613) 932-7286; e-mail marketing@seaway.ca; internet www.greatlakes-seaway.com; f. 1998; responsible for management of the St Lawrence Seaway (f. 1959) allowing ocean-going vessels to enter the Great Lakes of North America; operated jtly with the USA; 43.0m. metric tons of freight in 2007; Chair. GUY C. VÉRONNEAU; Pres. and CEO RICHARD CORFE.

Upper Lakes Group Inc: 49 Jackes Ave, Toronto, ON M4T 1E2; tel. (416) 920-7610; fax (416) 922-6159; e-mail inquires@upperlakes.com; internet www.upperlakes.com; eight self-unloading bulk carriers and 13 conventional bulk carriers; capacity 545,000 dwt; Chair. and Dir J. D. LEITCH; Pres. and CEO PAT LODUCA.

Associations

Canadian Canal Society: 124 Welland Ave, POB 23016, Midtown Post Office, ON L2R 7P6; tel. (416) 682-0253; e-mail info@canadiancanalsociety.org; internet www.canadiancanalsociety.org; Pres. TOM WHITELAW; mems: 120 individuals and 12 govt agencies.

International Association of Great Lakes Ports: c/o Chamber of Maritime Commerce, 350 Sparks St, Suite 704A, Ottawa, ON K1R 7S8; tel. (613) 233-8779; fax (613) 233 3743; Sec.-Treas. GENEVIEVE HARRISON.

Lake Shippers' Clearance Association: 500-101 Syndicate Ave North, Thunder Bay, ON P7C 3V4; tel. (807) 623-8491; fax (807) 623-2676.

OCEAN SHIPPING

Summary of Operations

(Source: Statistics Canada, Transportation Division and *Shipping in Canada*.)

SUMMARY

	2002	2003	2004
Goods ('000 metric tons):			
loaded	174,270.2	191,424.0	196,101.9
unloaded	108,464.2	115,215.3	118,458.4
Vessels (number):			
arrived	24,466	25,098	23,895
departed	24,547	25,156	24,039

GOODS LOADED AND UNLOADED BY REGION—INTERNATIONAL CARGO
('000 metric tons)

	2002		2003		2004	
	Loaded	Unloaded	Loaded	Unloaded	Loaded	Unloaded
Pacific	70,403.6	10,945.9	74,881.5	11,647.2	82,253.1	13,132.2
St Lawrence	39,443.0	32,884.2	45,522.0	34,202.1	40,553.9	35,833.5
Atlantic	48,551.0	32,314.3	54,568.0	38,235.9	55,544.1	39,997.3
Great Lakes	15,872.6	32,319.8	16,415.2	31,228.3	17,750.7	29,495.4

GOODS LOADED AND UNLOADED BY REGION—DOMESTIC CARGO
('000 metric tons)

	2002		2003		2004	
	Loaded	Unloaded	Loaded	Unloaded	Loaded	Unloaded
Pacific	15,767.9	15,777.5	15,977.3	15,978.4	16,159.6	16,222.9
St Lawrence	11,648.0	12,120.9	11,799.7	13,989.6	12,321.3	14,270.3
Atlantic	21,635.1	19,312.2	26,950.4	24,124.0	25,249.0	22,577.7
Great Lakes	13,530.4	15,405.7	13,757.3	14,501.9	15,167.0	15,800.3

Directory

SELECTED COMPANIES

British Columbia Ferry Services Inc. (BC Ferries): 1112 Fort St, Victoria, BC V8V 4V2; tel. (250) 381-1401; fax (250) 381-5452; e-mail investor.relations@bcferries.com; internet www.bcferries.com; 36 passenger and car ferries; Chair. ELIZABETH HARRISON; Pres. and CEO DAVID HAHN.

Fednav Ltd: 1000 rue de la Gauchetière ouest, Montréal, QC H3B 4W5; tel. (514) 878-6500; fax (514) 878-6642; e-mail info@fednav.com; internet www.fednav.com; f. 1944; shipowners, operators, contractors, terminal operators; owned and chartered fleet of 85 vessels; Pres. LAURENCE PATHY.

Groupe Desgagnés Inc: 21 rue du Marché-Champlain, bureau 100, Québec, QC G1K 8Z8; tel. (418) 692-1000; fax (418) 692-6044; e-mail info@desgagnes.com; internet www.desgagnes.com; f. 1866; private co; 16 vessels; Chair. and CEO LOUIS-MARIE BEAULIEU.

Marine Atlantic Inc: 10 Fort William Pl., Suite 802, Baine Johnston Centre, St John's, NL A1C 1K4; tel. (709) 772-8957; fax (709) 772-8956; e-mail info@marine-atlantic.ca; internet www.marine-atlantic.ca; serves Atlantic coast of Canada; four vessels, incl. passenger, roll-on/roll-off and freight ferries; 405,336 passengers in 2006; Chair. ROB CROSBIE; Pres. and CEO WAYNE FOLLETT.

Pacific Pilotage Authority: 1130 West Pender St, Suite 1000, Vancouver, BC V6E 4A4; tel. (604) 666-6771; fax (604) 666-1647; e-mail info@ppa.gc.ca; internet www.ppa.gc.ca; operates pilotage services in Canadian waters in and around British Columbia; Chair. DAVID GARDINER; CEO KEVIN OBERMEYER.

Seaboard International Shipping Co Ltd: 20 Brooksbank Ave, North Vancouver, BC V7J 2B8; tel. (604) 980-1113; fax (604) 980-1951; e-mail melb@seaboardintl.com; internet www.seaboardintl.com; Australia, Japan, Europe and Puerto Rico; Pres. C. D. G. ROBERTS.

Teekay Corporation: 550 Burrard St, Suite 2000 Bentall 5, Vancouver, BC V6C 2K2; tel. (604) 683-3529; fax (604) 844-6600; internet www.teekay.com; f. 1973; Chair. C. SEAN DAY; Pres. and CEO BJORN MOLLER; 158 vessels.

ASSOCIATIONS

Association of Canadian Port Authorities (ACPA): 85 Albert St, Suite 1502, Ottawa, ON K1P 6A4; tel. (613) 232-2036; fax (613) 232-9554; e-mail leroux@acpa-ports.net; internet www.acpa-ports.net; f. 1958; Chair. SEAN HANRAHAN; Exec. Dir GARY LEROUX.

British Columbia Ferry and Marine Workers' Union: 1511 Stewart Ave, Nanaimo, BC V9S 4E3; tel. (250) 716-3454; fax (250) 716-3455; e-mail mailroom@bcfmwu.com; internet www.bcfmwu.com; Pres. JACKIE MILLER; Sec.-Treas. SID ALLINSON.

Canadian Ferry Operators' Association: Fraser River Transportation Co, POB 1078, Station Albion, Maple Ridge, BC V2W 1W1; tel. (604) 467-7298; fax (604) 463-5693; e-mail dave_miller@translink.bc.ca; internet www.cfoa.ca; Pres. and CEO DAVE MILLER; Exec. Dir ANTHONIE A. DE HOOG.

Canadian Marine Officers' Union (CMOU): 9670 rue Notre-Dame est, Montréal, QC H1L 3P8; tel. (514) 354-8321; fax (514) 354-8368; e-mail cmou@cogeco.net; internet www.cmou.ca; Pres. RICHARD VÉZINA; Sec.-Treas. HAROLD ANDERSON.

Canadian Shipowners Association (CSA): 350 Sparks St, Suite 705, Ottawa, ON K1R 7S8; tel. (613) 232-3539; fax (613) 232-6211; e-mail morrison@shipowners.ca; internet www.shipowners.ca; f. 1953; Pres. DONALD N. MORRISON; seven mem. cos.

Chamber of Maritime Commerce: 350 Sparks St, Suite 700, Ottawa, ON K1R 7S8; tel. (613) 233-8779; fax (613) 233-3743; e-mail info@cmc-ccm.com; internet www.cmc-ccm.com; Chair. GUY DUFRESNE; Pres. RAYMOND JOHNSTON.

Council of Marine Carriers: 1575 West Georgia St, Suite 200, Vancouver, BC V6G 2V3; tel. (604) 687-9677; fax (604) 687-1788; e-mail cmc@comc.cc; internet www.comc.cc; f. 1972; Chair. WAYNE CAMMELL; Pres. Capt. PHILLIP J. NELSON; 32 mems.

Interferry: 8-735 Moss St, Victoria, BC V8V 4N9; tel. (250) 592-9612; fax (250) 592-9613; e-mail len.roueche@interferry.com; internet www.interferry.com; f. 1976 as the International Marine Transit Asscn, adopted present name in 2001; represents the world-wide ferry industry; CEO LEN ROUECHE; 500 mems.

Shipbuilding Association of Canada: 222 Queen St, Ottawa, ON K1P 5V9; tel. (613) 232-7127; fax (613) 238-5519; e-mail pcairns@cfncon.com; internet www.shipbuilding.ca; f. 1995; Chair. ROLLIE WEBB; Pres. PETER CAIRNS; six mems, nine assoc. mems.

Shipping Federation of Canada: 300 rue du St-Sacrement, bureau 326, Montréal, QC H27 1X4; tel. (514) 849-2325; fax (514) 849-8774; e-mail info@shipfed.ca; internet www.shipfed.ca; f. 1903; Chair. DAVID CARDIN; Pres. MICHAEL H. BROAD; 71 mems.

CIVIL AVIATION

Summary of Operations

(Note: Major Canadian airlines.)

	2005	2006	2007
Passengers ('000)	32,091	33,439	35,568
Passenger-km	83,909,440	88,323,198	93,363,940
Goods carried (kilograms)	268,947	265,470	242,511
Goods ton-km	1,378,548	1,425,103	1,301,260

Source: Statistics Canada, CANSIM II Table 401-0001, September 2008.

Principal Airports

(Source: Statistics Canada.)

SUMMARY*

	Passengers ('000)		Flights		Cargo (metric tons)	
	1996	2006	1996	2006	1996	2006
Toronto (Lester B. Pearson International)	22,669	29,468	326,821	3465,706	336,654	322,729
Vancouver International	13,090	16,200	214,030	223,674	190,814	149,994
Montréal (Dorval International)	6,142	11,370	144,233	157,335	23,744	76,860
Calgary International	6,662	11,158	132,732	152,362	53,557	58,324
Edmonton International	2,897	5,288	57,382	82,317	13,156	6,638
Ottawa (MacDonald Cartier International)	2,763	3,541	70,342	62,941	4,890	8,330
Halifax International	2,462	3,290	70,203	52,732	17,926	20,473
Winnipeg International	2,830	3,590	66,937	73,554	12,113	16,087
Victoria International	879	1,344	32,809	32,133	852	231
Montréal (Mirabel International)	2,392	n.a.	18,394	n.a.	82,065	41,980

* Itinerant aircraft movements at airports with air traffic control towers.

Source: Statistics Canada, *Air Carrier Traffic at Canadian Airports*.

Directory

REGULATORY AUTHORITY

Transport Canada: See Government of Canada—Ministries.

PRINCIPAL SCHEDULED COMPANIES

Air Canada: Air Canada Centre, CP 14000, Dorval, Québec, QC H4Y 1H4; tel. (514) 422-5000; e-mail media.relations@aircanada.ca; internet www.aircanada.com; f. 1937; fmrly Trans-Canada Air Lines; subsidiary of ACE Aviation Holdings Inc.; acquired Canadian Airlines in Jan. 2001; operates services to 170 cities world-wide; Chair. DAVID I. RICHARDSON; Pres. and CEO MONTIE R. BREWER.

Air Canada Jazz: 310 Goudey Dr., Halifax International Airport, Enfield, NS B2T 1E4; tel. (902) 873-5000; fax (902) 873-2098; internet www.flyjazz.ca; f. 2002; operates regional air services; services 84 destinations in Canada and the USA; part-owned by Air Canada; Pres. and CEO JOSEPH D. RANDELL.

Air Creebec: 101 Seventh St, POB 430, Val d'Or, QC J9P 4P4; tel. (819) 825-8355; fax (819) 825-0208; e-mail lefebvrep@aircreebec.ca; internet www.aircreebec.ca; f. 1979; services to 17 destinations in Québec and Ontario; Pres. ALBERT W. DIAMOND.

Air Georgian: 2450 Derry Rd East, Shell Aerocentre, Mississauga, ON L5S 1B2; tel. (905) 676-1106; fax (905) 676-1151; e-mail pmulrooney@airalliance.ca; internet www.airgeorgian.ca; f. 1985; private charter and cargo services; operates some domestic scheduled services in partnership with Air Canada; Pres. PAUL MULROONEY; Gen. Man. LORI SHAW.

Air Inuit: 547 Meloche Ave, Dorval, QC H9P 2W2; tel. (514) 636-9445; fax (514) 636-8916; e-mail info@airinuit.com; internet www.airinuit.com; f. 1977; owned by the Makivic Corpn; operates services in Québec; Chair. GEORGE BERTHE.

Air Labrador: 15 Duffy Pl., POB 13485, Station A, St John's, NL A1B 4B8; tel. (709) 758-0002; fax (709) 753-7787; e-mail jbrett@airlabrador.com; internet www.airlabrador.com; f. 1948 as Newfoundland Airways; services 29 destinations in Québec and Newfoundland and Labrador; Chair. and CEO ROGER W. PIKE.

Air Mikisew: Airport Rd, Hangar 1, Fort McMurray, AB T9H 3G3; tel. (780) 743-8218; fax (780) 743-8225; e-mail gwdavis@airmikisew.com; internet www.airmikisew.com; f. 1961; fmrly Contact Air; Operations Man. GRAHAM DAVIS.

Air North: 150 Condor Rd, POB 4998, Whitehorse, YT Y1A 6E6; tel. (867) 668-2228; fax (867) 668-6224; e-mail office@flyairnorth.com; internet www.flyairnorth.com; f. 1977; Pres. JOSEPH T. SPARLING.

Air Tindi: POB 1693, Yellowknife, NT X1A 2P3; tel. (867) 669-8200; e-mail alex@airtindi.com; internet www.airtindi.com; f. 1988; scheduled and charter services in the Northwest Territories; Pres. ALEX ARYCHUK.

Air Transat: pl. du Parc, 300 rue Léo-Pariseau, bureau 600, Montréal, QC H2X 4C2; tel. (514) 987-1660; fax (514) 987-8089; e-mail communications@transat.com; internet www.transat.com; f. 1986; operates services throughout Canada and USA, also to Europe, the Caribbean, Mexico and South America; Chair., Pres. and CEO JEAN-MARC EUSTACHE.

Aklak Air: POB 1190, Inuvik, NT X0E 0T0; tel. (867) 777-3777; fax (867) 777-3388; e-mail info@aklakair.ca; internet www.aklakair.ca; f. 1977; Man. KEN DALTON.

Buffalo Airways: POB 2015, 108 Berry St, Yellowknife, NT X1A 2R3; tel. (867) 873-6112; fax (867) 873-8393; e-mail jmcbryan@buffaloairways.com; internet www.buffaloairways.com; f. 1970; passenger and cargo services; Pres. JOE MCBRYAN.

Canadian North: 5201 50th Ave, Suite 300, Yellowknife, NT X1A 3S9; tel. (867) 669-4000; fax (867) 669-4040; e-mail reception@canadiannorth.com; internet www.cdn-north.com; f. 1989; Pres. TRACY MEDVE.

Central Mountain Air: 6431 Airport Rd, POB 998, Smithers, BC V0J 2N0; tel. (250) 877-5000; fax (250) 847-3744; e-mail info@flycma.com; internet www.flycma.com; f. 1987; Pres. DOUGLAS MCCREA.

First Air: 20 Cope Dr., Kanata, ON K2M 2V8; tel. (613) 254-6200; fax (613) 254-6398; e-mail reservat@firstair.ca; internet www.firstair.ca; f. 1946; owned by Makivik Corpn; services to 25 destinations in Canada; Chair. PITA AATAMI; Pres. and CEO SCOTT BATEMAN (acting).

Porter Airlines: Toronto City Centre Airport, Toronto, ON M5V 1A1; tel. (416) 203-8100; fax (416) 203-8150; e-mail info@flyporter.com; internet www.flyporter.com; f. 2006; destinations include Halifax, Montréal, Mont Tremblant, Ottawa and Toronto; Chair. DONALD J. CARTY; Pres. and CEO ROBERT DELUCE.

Skyservice Airlines: 31 Fasken Dr., Etobicoke, ON M9W 1K6; tel. (416) 679-5700; fax (416) 679-5703; e-mail customer_service@skyservice.com; internet www.skyserviceairlines.com; f. 1986; Pres. and CEO RUSSELL L. PAYSON.

WestJet: 5055 11th St, NE, Calgary, AB T2E 8N4; tel. (888) 293-7853; fax (866) 477-6535; internet www.westjet.com; f. 1996; services destinations in Canada, the USA, Mexico and the Caribbean; Chair., Pres. and CEO SEAN DURFY.

ASSOCIATIONS

Aero Club of Canada: 1710 Hickey Rd, Apt 506, St John, NB E2J 3S6; tel. (506) 658-9059; e-mail aeroclub@nb.sympatico.ca; internet www.aeroclub.ca; Pres. MARY ANNE STEVENS.

Aerospace Industries Association of Canada: 60 Queen St, Suite 1200, Ottawa, ON K1P 5Y7; tel. (613) 232-4297; fax (613) 232-1142; e-mail info@aiac.ca; internet www.aiac.ca; Chair. JEAN PIERRE MORTREUX; Pres. and CEO CLAUDE LAJEUNESSE; 400 mems.

Air Line Pilots' Association, International (ALPA): 1625 Massachusetts Ave, NW, Washington, DC 20036, USA; tel. (703) 689-2270; internet www.alpa.org; f. 1931 by merger of Canadian Air Line Pilots' Asscn and Air Line Pilots' Asscn Int.; Pres. Capt. JOHN PRATER; 60,000 mems in the USA and Canada.

Air Transport Association of Canada (ATAC): 255 Albert St, Suite 1100, Ottawa, ON K1P 6A9; tel. (613) 233-7727; fax (613) 230-8648; e-mail atac@atac.ca; internet www.atac.ca; f. 1934 as the Commercial Air Transport and Mfrs' Asscn of Canada; present name adopted in 1962 following withdrawal of industrial mems; mems collectively account for more than 97% of national commercial air transport revenues; Chair. MIKE DOIRON; Pres. and CEO MICHAEL SKROBICA (acting).

Canadian Aeronautics and Space Institute: 350 Terry Fox Dr., Suite 104, Kanata, ON K2K 2W5; tel. (613) 591-8787; fax (613) 591-7291; e-mail casi@casi.ca; internet www.casi.ca; Pres. NASHED A. YOUSSEF; Exec. Dir GEOFF LANGUEDOC; six sections and three societies.

Canadian Airports Council (CAC): 350 Sparks St, Suite 706, Ottawa, ON K1R 7S8; tel. (613) 560-9302; fax (613) 560-6599; e-mail sharon.redden@cacaiports.ca; internet www.cacairports.ca; f. 1991; Chair. BARRY REMPEL; Pres. and CEO JIM FACETTE.

Canadian Air Traffic Control Association: 265 Carling Ave, Suite 304, Ottawa, ON KS1 2E1; tel. (613) 225-3553; fax (613) 225-8448; e-mail catca@catca.ca; internet www.catca.ca; Pres. GREG MYLES; 2,000 mems.

Canadian Business Aviation Association: 55 Metcalfe St, Suite 430, Ottawa, ON K1P 6L5; tel. (613) 236-5611; fax (613) 236-2361; e-mail info@cbaa.ca; internet www.cbaa.ca; f. 1962; business aviation, conventions and trade shows; Pres. and CEO SAM BARONE; Chair. DOUG WARE; 400 mem. cos.

Canadian Federal Pilots Association: 350 Sparks St, Suite 509, Ottawa, ON K1R 7S8; tel. (613) 230-5476; fax (613) 230-2668; e-mail cfpa@cfpa-apfc.ca; internet www.cfpa-apfc.ca; Chair. GREG HOLBROOK; Nat. Sec.-Treas. GREG MCCONNELL.

Canadian Owners' and Pilots' Association (COPA): 71 Bank St, 7th Floor, Ottawa, ON K1P 5N2; tel. (613) 236-4901; fax (613) 236-8646; e-mail copa@copanational.org; internet www.copanational.org; f. 1952; Pres. and CEO KEVIN PSUTKA; more than 15,000 mems.

International Air Transport Association (IATA): 800 pl. Victoria, POB 113, Montréal, QC H4Z 1M1; tel. (514) 874-0202; fax (514) 874-9632; e-mail corpcomms@iata.org; internet www.iata.org; f. 1945 as successor to the Int. Air Transport Asscn (f. 1919); Chair. CHOON SENG CHEW; Dir-Gen. and CEO GIOVANNI BISIGNANI; represents 260 world airlines.

International Business Aviation Council Ltd (IBAC): 999 rue University, Suite 1633, Montréal, QC H3C 5J9; tel. (514) 954-8054; fax (514) 954-6161; e-mail info@ibac.org; internet www.ibac.org; f. 1981; Chair. RUI THOMAZ DE AQUINO; Dir-Gen. DONALD D. SPRUSTON; 12 mem. asscns.

International Civil Aviation Organization (ICAO): 999 University St, Montréal, QC H3C 5H7; tel. (514) 954-8219; fax (514) 954-6077; e-mail icaohq@icao.int; internet www.icao.int; f. 1944; UN specialized agency responsible for setting int. standards, recommended practices and procedures covering the technical, economic and legal fields of int. civil aviation operations; Pres. of the Council ROBERTO KOBEH GONZÁLEZ; Sec.-Gen. Dr TAÏEB CHÉRIF; 188 mem. countries.

Ninety Nines (Organization of International Women Pilots): (International HQ) 4300 Amelia Earhart Rd, Oklahoma City, OK 73159, USA; tel. (405) 685-7969; fax (405) 685-7985; e-mail 99s@ninety-nines.org; internet www.ninety-nines.org; f. 1929; Pres. SUSAN LARSON; Sec. PAT THEBERGE; over 5,500 mems world-wide.

Northern Air Transport Association: POB 2457, Yellowknife, NT X1A 2P8; tel. (867) 920-2985; fax (867) 920-2983; e-mail nata-yzf@theedge.ca; internet www.nata-yzf.ca; Pres. STEPHEN NOURSE; Exec. Dir DON DOUGLAS.

TELECOMMUNICATIONS

INTRODUCTION

The federal regulatory body is the Canadian Radio-Television and Telecommunications Commission (CRTC—see below). The CRTC's main purpose, with regard to telecommunications services, was to regulate carriers on an interprovincial level and ensure that the rates charged for services were just and reasonable. Telecommunications within the provinces were the responsibility of provincial bodies. The federal Department of Communications was responsible for establishing national policy, most of which was formulated by the CRTC. Long-distance telephone services were deregulated in 1992. From January 1998 new competitors were allowed to compete in local telephone markets and telephone companies were allowed to provide cable television services.

Telephone companies, of which there were more than 100 in Canada, ranged from small rural co-operatives to large privately owned or government organizations. The largest regional company was Bell Canada Enterprises (BCE). Telecom Canada (previously the

Trans-Canada Telephone System), an association of telephone companies, co-ordinated facilities for long-distance services. International telecommunications were operated by Téléglobe Canada, previously a crown corporation, which was sold to private interests in 1988. Under the terms of an agreement with the World Trade Organization, Téléglobe's monopoly on long-distance international telecommunications ended in 1998.

Mobile radio and radio-paging services in Canada were provided by about 200 radio common carriers. The federal department Canadian Heritage issued licences to private users. The cellular radio system (mobile radio communications) was introduced on a national level in 1985. Cantel Cellular Radio Group and the telephone companies in each province were licensed to provide services.

Canada was the first country to establish a domestic communications satellite system with the launching of Anik A-1 in 1972. By 2007 there were 13 Anik satellites in orbit, with the latest, Anik F-3, launched in April of that year. The Canadian commercial satellite communications system is owned and operated by Telesat Canada, itself a subsidiary of BCE. Telesat transmits audio and video signals, used mainly by broadcasters, and voice and data signals. Telesat also operated four Nimiq satellites, which provided digital and high-definition services. A fifth Nimiq satellite was scheduled to be launched in 2009.

In 2007 there were some 18.2m. telephone lines in Canada, and an estimated 20.3m. mobile cellular telephone subscribers. In 2006 9.6m. households had home computers and 8.7m. households had access to the internet.

Regulatory Body

Telecommunications services in Canada are provided by both government (federal, provincial and municipal) and private organizations. Telecommunications carriers under federal jurisdiction and the broadcasting system (radio, television, cable television and pay television) are regulated by the Canadian Radio-Television and Telecommunications Commission (CRTC). The CRTC was created through the 1968 Broadcasting Act, which also established the Canadian Broadcasting Corporation (CBC). Programming policy is to use predominantly Canadian creative and other resources. Services are operated in both English and French.

Canadian Radio-Television and Telecommunications Commission (CRTC): Ottawa, ON K1A 0N2; tel. (819) 997-0313; fax (819) 994-0218; internet www.crtc.gc.ca; f. 1968; offices in Dartmouth, Winnipeg and Vancouver; Chair. KONRAD VON FINCKENSTEIN; Vice-Chair. (Broadcasting) MICHEL ARPIN; Vice-Chair. (Telecommunications) LEONARD KATZ; Sec.-Gen. ROBERT A. MORIN; regulates c. 3,300 radio, television and cable broadcasters and 78 telecommunications carriers.

Use of Selected Telecommunication Technologies

(Source: Statistics Canada, *Survey of Household Spending*.)

SUMMARY
('000 households)

	2004	2005	2006
Total households	12,343	12,587	12,756
Homes with a telephone	12,211	12,450	12,649
Homes with a cellular phone	7,266	8,079	8,638
Homes with a computer	8,476	9,059	9,618
Homes with internet	7,380	8,092	8,682

PROVINCES AND TERRITORIES
('000 households, 2006 unless otherwise indicated, estimates)

	Total households	Fixed line telephone	Mobile cellular telephone	Home computer	Internet
Alberta	1,281	1,277	1,033	1,068	979
British Columbia	1,708	1,694	1,246	1,364	1,266
Manitoba	450	443	271	313	273
New Brunswick	300	298	179	203	176
Newfoundland and Labrador	200	196	129	132	116
Northwest Territories*	14	14†	7†	10†	9†
Nova Scotia	380	375	251	270	241
Nunavut*	6	5†	n.a.‡	3†	2†
Ontario	4,737	4,704	3,385	3,708	3,411
Prince Edward Island	54	54	35	37	34
Québec	3,268	3,236	1,843	2,263	1,955
Saskatchewan	378	373	266	260	231
Yukon Territory*	12	11†	4†	8†	8†

* Estimates for territories were designed to represent approximately 90% of the population.
† 2005.
‡ Figure deemed too unreliable for publication.

MAJOR TELECOMMUNICATIONS NETWORKS

Bell Aliant Regional Communications Income Fund: 6 South, Maritime Centre, 1505 Barrington St, Halifax, NS B3J 2W3; tel. (902) 487-4609; fax (902) 425-0708; e-mail brenda.reid@aliant.ca; internet bell.aliant.ca; f. 2006 by merger of Aliant and Bell operations; partly owned by Bell Canada and BCE Inc; operates as Aliant in Atlantic Canada and as Bell in central Canada; world-wide communications and information technology solutions; Pres. and CEO STEPHEN WETMORE.

Bell Canada Enterprises Inc (BCE Inc): 1000 rue de la Gauchetière ouest, bureau 3700, Montréal, QC H3B 4Y7; tel. (514) 870-8777; fax (514) 870-4385; e-mail bcecomms@bce.ca; internet www.bce.ca; f. 1880; privatization sale to consortium, led by Ontario Teachers' Pension Plan Board, agreed in Sept. 2007; provides fixed-line and mobile telecommunications, satellite and internet services; Chair. RICHARD J. CURRIE; Pres. and CEO GEORGE COPE.

Bell Canada: POB 8716, Station A, Montréal, QC H3C 4R5; e-mail bell.direct@bell.ca; internet www.bell.ca; 80% owned by BCE Inc; holds a monopoly in most of Québec and Ontario; CEO GEORGE COPE.

Bell Mobility: 105 rue Hotel de Ville, 5e étage, Hull, QC J8X 4H7; e-mail mobility@bell.ca; internet www.bellmobility.ca; mobile telecommunications; Pres. WADE OOSTERMAN.

Bell West: 111 Fifth Ave, SW, Calgary, AB T2P 3Y6; tel. (403) 410-8600; e-mail customercare@bell.ca; internet www.bell.ca; 100% owned by Bell Canada; Pres. (Western Region) CHARLES BROWN.

Manitoba Telecom Services Inc (MTS): 333 Main St, POB 6666, Winnipeg, MB R3C 3V6; tel. (204) 225-5687; fax (204) 772-6391; e-mail corporate.communications@mtsallstream.com; internet www.mts.ca; full-service (wireline voice, data, wireless and television services) telecommunications co for Manitoba; national broadband fibre optic network of 24,300 km; Allstream (National) Division serves business customers nation-wide; Chair. THOMAS E. STEFANSON; CEO PIERRE BLOUIN.

Northwestel Inc: 301 Lambert St, POB 2727, Whitehorse, YT Y1A 4Y4; tel. (867) 668-5300; fax (867) 668-7079; internet www.nwtel.ca; f. 1979, bought by BCE Inc in 1988; provides fixed-line and mobile telecommunications services to 110,000 customers in Yukon Territory, Northwest Territories, Nunavut Territory and British Columbia; Chair. TERRY MOSEY; Pres. and CEO PAUL FLAHERTY.

Télébec: 555 ave Centrale, Val-d'Or, QC J9P 1P6; e-mail telebec@telebec.com; internet www.telebec.com; f. 1969; owned by Bell Nordiq Group Inc, subsidiary of BCE Inc; mobile telecommunications (Télébec Mobilité) and internet services (Télébec Internet).

Telesat Canada: 1601 Telesat Court, Ottawa, ON K1B 5P4; tel. (613) 748-0123; fax (613) 748-8712; e-mail info@telesat.ca; internet www.telesat.ca; f. 1969 by Act of Parliament; subsidiary of BCE Inc; owns eight satellites and operates a further seven on behalf of customers; carrier and distributor of more than 200 TV signals in North America; provides voice and data transmission services to telecommunication carriers in North and South America and wireless data business networks in Canada and the USA; Pres. and CEO DANIEL S. GOLDBERG.

Glentel: 8501 Commerce Ct, Burnaby, BC V5A 4N3; tel. (604) 415-6500; fax (604) 415-6565; internet www.glentel.com; f. 1963; wireless communications; Chair., Pres. and CEO THOMAS E. SKIDMORE.

Globalstar Canada Co: 115 Matheson Blvd West, Suite 100, Mississauga, ON L5R 3L1; tel. (905) 890-1377; fax (905) 890-2175; e-mail info@globalstar.ca; internet www.globalstar.ca; satellite voice and data communications; Chair. and CEO JAY MONROE.

Primus Telecommunications Canada Inc: 5343 Dundas St West, Suite 400, Etobicoke, ON M9B 6K5; tel. (416) 236-3636; fax (888) 865-1234; e-mail info@primustel.ca; internet www.primustel.ca; f. 1997; long-distance, international and internet services; Pres. and COO EDMUND (TED) CHISLETT.

Rogers Communications Inc: 333 Bloor St East, 9th Floor, Toronto, ON M4W 1G9; tel. (416) 935-8200; internet www.rogers.com; subsidiaries: Rogers Cable and Telecom provides fixed-line telephony, cable and internet services; Rogers Wireless Inc provides wireless and mobile cellular services; Chair. ALAN D. HORN; Pres. and CEO EDWARD S. ROGERS.

Fido: 333 Bloor St East, 10th Floor, Toronto, ON M4W 1G9; e-mail info.communications@fidomobile.ca; internet www.fido.ca; f. 1996; by Microcell Solutions Inc; subsidiary of Rogers Communications Inc since Nov. 2004; Vice-Pres. and Gen. Man. SYLVAIN ROY.

Saskatchewan Telecommunications International (SaskTel): 2121 Saskatchewan Dr., 12th Floor, Regina, SK S4P 3Y2; tel. (306) 777-4509; fax (306) 359-7475; internet www.sasktel.com; f. 1986; provides mobile, satellite and internet services for Saskatchewan; Chair. GRANT J. KOOK; Pres. and CEO ROBERT WATSON.

SaskTel Mobility: 446 Second Ave North, Saskatoon, SK S7K 1W8; internet www.sasktel.com.

Sierra Wireless, Inc: 13811 Wireless Way, Richmond, BC V6V 3A4; tel. (604) 231-1100; fax (604) 231-1109; e-mail smyers@sierrawireless.com; internet www.sierrawireless.com; f. 1993; Chair. CHARLES LEVINE; CEO JASON W. COHENOUR.

SR Telecom Inc: 8150 Trans-Canada Hwy, Montréal, QC H4S 1M5; tel. (514) 335-1210; fax (514) 334-7783; e-mail info@srtelecom.com; internet www.srtelecom.com; f. 1981; Chair. PAUL GRISWOLD; Pres. and CEO SERGE FORTIN.

TELUS: TELUS Corpn, TELUS Plaza South, 32nd Floor, 10020 100 St, Edmonton, AB T5J 0N5; tel. (780) 493-6197; e-mail jim.johannsson@telus.com; internet www.telus.com; f. 2001 following merger of TELUS Communications and BC Telecom; Chair. BRIAN A. CANFIELD; Pres. and CEO DARREN ENTWISTLE.

TELUS Mobility: 200 Consilium Pl., Suite 1600, Scarborough, ON M1H 3J3; internet www.telusmobility.com; mobile telecommunications; incorporates Clearnet, QuébecTel and TELUS Mobility West; Acting Pres. and CEO DARREN ENTWISTLE.

TELUS Québec: 9 rue Jules-A.-Brillant, CP 2070, Rimouski, QC G5L 7E4; tel. (514) 977-8766; e-mail stacey.masson@telus.com; internet www.telusquebec.com; fmrly QuébecTel; adopted current name following acquisition by TELUS corpn in 2001; telecommunications for Québec; Pres. KAREN RADFORD.

FINANCE

BANKING

Introduction

(br.(s) = branches; cap. = capital; res = reserves; dep. = deposits; m. = million; amounts in Canadian dollars)

The Bank of Canada Act of 1980 reorganized the structure of the Canadian banking system by creating two categories of banking institution. Schedule I banks are domestic chartered banks, in which the proportion of shares held by any one interest is restricted, while Schedule II banks are either subsidiaries of foreign banks or domestic banks under private or semi-private ownership.

Major revisions to the Bank Act, the federal Trust and Loans Companies Act, the federal Insurance Companies Act and the Co-operative Credit Associations Act came into force in June 1992. This legislation permits federal financial institutions, with some restrictions, to diversify into each other's markets through subsidiaries. By 1 January 1995, following ratification of the North American Free Trade Agreement (NAFTA) and the enactment of the World Trade Organization Implementation Act, the domestic asset limitations on foreign-owned Schedule II banks in the Canadian market were removed.

In the past, the Bank Act was generally reviewed once every 10 years. As a result of extensive revisions to the federal financial institutions legislation in 1992, a further review of the Bank Act was carried out in 1997. In addition, a Task Force on the Future of the Canadian Financial Services Sector was appointed by the federal Government in 1996 to review the legislative framework of the financial services sector. The report of the Task Force, published in September 1998, recommended the abolition of existing barriers preventing financial institutions from providing unified services in banking, insurance and motor vehicle leasing. It was also proposed that commercial banks and trust companies (see below) be permitted to market all classes of insurance through their branch networks by 2002. The Task Force expressed support for the entry of foreign banks into the commercial loans market, and for the adoption of new regulations for consumer protection. In 1999 the Government adopted legislation permitting foreign banks to establish operations in Canada without their being obliged to establish Canadian-incorporated subsidiaries. Foreign bank branches (known as Schedule III banks) are prohibited from accepting deposits of less than C $150,000. The Bank Act Reform, a series of extensive changes to federal financial institutions, finally entered into effect in October 2001. This provided for much greater flexibility of the financial services system, as recommended by the Task Force, and also included an increase in the maximum level of single ownership in large banks from 10% to 20%, while any one interest was henceforth permitted to control as much as 65% of a medium-sized bank; the minimum amount of capital required to apply for a bank licence was halved to $5m. In October 2008, according to the Office of the Superintendent of Financial Institutions, the banking industry included 21 domestic banks, 24 foreign bank subsidiaries and 23 full-service foreign bank branches. Although domestic banks continued to dominate the sector, foreign bank institutions increased their share of the financial services market to 8.4% in 2007 (compared with 5.7% in 1997). At July 2008 the combined assets of all banks (excluding foreign subsidiaries) totalled $2,702,354.4m.

The Bank of Canada

(234 Wellington St, Ottawa, ON K1A 0G9; tel. (613) 782-8111; fax (613) 782-8655; e-mail paffairs@bankofcanada.ca; internet www.bankofcanada.ca)

The Bank of Canada was established as the nation's central bank in 1934 by the Bank of Canada Act, revisions to which were made in 1936, 1938, 1954, 1967, 1980 and 1987. Its principal responsibility is the control of credit through monetary action in order to promote the economic and financial welfare of Canada. The Bank is managed by a Board of Directors, comprising the Governor (its chief executive officer), the Senior Deputy Governor and 10 part-time directors. The part-time directors are appointed by the Minister of Finance, with the approval of the Governor-in-Council, for three-year terms and they, in turn, appoint the Governor for seven-year terms. In addition, the Deputy Minister of Finance is a non-voting ex officio member of the Board. While the Bank of Canada may operate with a considerable amount of independence, it liaises closely with the federal Government, which has ultimate responsibility for monetary policy. Capital and reserves of the Bank of Canada totalled C $154.7m. at December 2007, with deposits at $2,981m.

Governor: MARK CARNEY.

CANADA DEPOSIT INSURANCE CORPN

(50 O'Connor St, 17th Floor, POB 2340, Station D, Ottawa, ON K1P 5W5; tel. (613) 996-2081; fax (613) 996-6095; e-mail info@cdic.ca; internet www.cdic.ca)

The Canada Deposit Insurance Corpn (CDIC) was established in 1967 by the Canada Deposit Insurance Corpn Act. The CDIC insures individual deposits against loss because of the insolvency of a member institution. Member institutions may be banks or trust and loan companies. The 2005 federal budget announced an increase in the level of deposit insurance coverage per depositor in each member institution from C $60,000 to $100,000 (effective from February). The CDIC's board comprises a chairperson (appointed by the Governor-in-Council), five ex officio directors (including the Governor of the Bank of Canada, the Deputy Minister of Finance, the Superintendent of Financial Institutions and a Deputy Superintendent of Financial Institutions) and five private sector members. Some 43 member institutions have failed since CDIC's creation. Following the increase in the deposit insurance coverage limit, the amount of insured deposits at the end of March 2007 stood at $455,000m., a 4.1% increase on the previous year's total.

Chair.: BRYAN P. DAVIES.

Pres. and CEO: GUY L. SAINT-PIERRE.

PRINCIPAL METHODS OF MONETARY CONTROL

The principal methods by which the Bank of Canada controls monetary supply are: (a) transferring, as fiscal agent of the federal Government, government deposits to the direct-clearing deposit-taking institutions, adding to their settlement balances and enabling them to make investments or reduce liabilities in the money market; (b) selling or purchasing government securities under an agreement to reverse the transaction on the subsequent day, thereby influencing the cost of overnight financing in the money market; (c) selling or purchasing government securities outright, thereby influencing the prevailing rates of interest at the corresponding terms to maturity; and (d) participating in the weekly tender of three-month government treasury bills. From February 1996 the Bank Rate was set at the upper limit of the Bank's operating band for the overnight financing rate.

Chartered Banks

The first Canadian commercial bank was founded in 1817. A further 34 banks were established over the next 50 years, and, following confederation in 1867, the Bank Act of 1871 gave the federal Government regulatory powers over banking operations throughout Canada. Canadian banks operate according to laws set out in the Bank Act and are chartered by the federal Parliament. While the number of banks diminished during the 20th century, the number of branches increased greatly. In 2003 there were nearly 9,000 bank branches in Canada. The sector is dominated by the six largest domestic banks—the Canadian Imperial Bank of Commerce, the Bank of Nova Scotia (Scotiabank), the Bank of Montréal, the National Bank of Canada, Toronto-Dominion Bank and the Royal Bank of Canada—which together account for some 90% of the total assets held by the banking industry. At October 2007 the combined assets of the six largest banks totalled C $2,224,772m. (compared with $1,385,569m. at October 2000).

Trust and loan companies, which were originally formed to provide mortgage finance and private customer loans, occupied an important place in the Canadian financial system, offering current account facilities and providing access to money transfer services.

Principal Commercial Banks

(Schedule I Banks)

Bank of Montréal: 129 rue St-Jacques, Montréal, QC H2Y 1L6; tel. (514) 877-1285; fax (514) 877-6922; internet www.bmo.com; f. 1817; cap. 5,607m., res –1,475m., dep. 232,050m. (Oct. 2007); Chair. DAVID A. GALLOWAY; Pres. and CEO WILLIAM DOWNE; 975 brs in Canada, 173 foreign brs.

Bank of Nova Scotia (Scotiabank): Scotia Plaza, 44 King St West, Toronto, ON M5H 1H1; tel. (416) 866-6161; fax (416) 866-3750; e-mail ann_derabbie@scotiacapital.com; internet www.scotiabank.com; f. 1832; acquired NBG Bank Canada (Greece) in Nov. 2005; cap. 5,201m., dep. 288,458m. (Oct. 2007); Chair. ARTHUR R. A. SCACE; Pres. and CEO RICHARD E. WAUGH; 1,272 brs in Canada, 143 foreign brs.

Canadian Imperial Bank of Commerce: Commerce Court, Toronto, ON M5L 1A2; tel. (416) 980-2211; fax (416) 368-8843; internet www.cibc.com; f. 1961 by merger of Canadian Bank of Commerce (f. 1867) and Imperial Bank of Canada (f. 1875); cap. 5,464., res –992m., dep. 231,672m. (Oct. 2007); Pres. and CEO GERALD T. MCCAUGHEY; 1,061 brs in Canada.

Canadian Western Bank: 10303 Jasper Ave, Suite 2300, Edmonton, AB T5J 3X6; tel. (780) 423-8888; fax (780) 423-8897; internet www.cwbankgroup.com; f. 1988 by merger of the Bank of Alberta and the Western and Pacific Bank of Canada; cap. 219.0m., res 3,750.0m., dep. 8,256.9m. (Oct. 2007); Chair. JACK C. DONALD; Pres. and CEO LARRY M. POLLOCK; 35 brs.

Laurentian Bank of Canada/Banque Laurentienne du Canada: Laurentian Bank Tower, 1981 ave Collège McGill, Montréal, QC H3A 3K3; tel. (514) 284-4500; fax (514) 284-3396; internet www.laurentianbank.com; f. 1846 as Montreal City and District Savings Bank; name changed as above 1987; cap. 466.4m., res 1.0m., dep. 13,878.7m. (Oct. 2007); Chair. DENIS DESAUTELS; Pres. and CEO REJEAN ROBITAILLE; 158 brs.

National Bank of Canada/Banque Nationale du Canada: 600 rue de la Gauchetière ouest, Montréal, QC H3B 4L2; tel. (514) 394-5000; fax (514) 394-8434; internet www.nbc.ca; f. 1859; cap. 1,975m., res –131m., dep. 70,798m. (Oct. 2007); Chair. LOUIS VACHON; Pres. and CEO RÉAL RAYMOND; 451 brs in Canada, 3 foreign brs.

Pacific and Western Bank of Canada: 140 Fullarton St, Suite 2002, London, ON N6A 5P2; tel. (519) 645-1919; fax (519) 645-2060; e-mail tellus@pwbank.com; internet www.pwbank.com; f. 1980 as Pacific and Western Trust Corpn; granted approval to become a Schedule I Bank in 2002 and name changed as above; subsidiary of Pacific and Western Credit Corpn; dep. 1,202m. (Oct. 2007); Pres. and CEO DAVID R. TAYLOR.

Royal Bank of Canada: 1 pl. Ville Marie, Montréal, QC H3C 3B5; tel. (514) 874-2110; fax (514) 974-4472; e-mail banks@rbc.com; internet www.rbc.com; f. 1869; bought RBTT Ltd in 2007; cap. 9,350m., res –3,078m., dep. 365,205m. (Oct. 2007); Chair DAVID P. O'BRIEN; CEO GORDON M. NIXON; 1,443 brs.

Toronto-Dominion Bank: Toronto-Dominion Centre, 55 King St West and Bay St, Toronto, ON M5K 1A2; tel. (416) 982-8222; fax (416) 982-5671; e-mail customer.service@td.com; internet www.td.com; f. 1955 by merger of the Bank of Toronto (f. 1855) and the Dominion Bank (f. 1869); acquired Commerce Bancorp Inc in 2007; cap.

7,002m., res –1,552m., dep. 276,393m. (Oct. 2007); Chair. JOHN M. THOMPSON; Pres. and CEO W. EDMUND CLARKE; 953 brs.

Savings Institutions with Provincial Charters

ATB Financial: ATB Pl., 2nd Floor, 9888 Jasper Ave, Edmonton, AB T5J 1P1; tel. (780) 495-0667; fax (780) 422-4998; e-mail apm@atb.com; internet www.atb.com; f. 1938 as Alberta Treasury Branches; name changed as above in 2002; assets 23,300m. (March 2008); Pres. and CEO DAVID MOWAT; 162 brs.

Desjardins Credit Union: 1615 Dundas St East, Whitby, ON L1N 2L1; tel. (905) 743-5790; fax (905) 743-6156; e-mail info@dcu.desjardins.com; internet www.desjardins.com/en/dcu; f. 1921, as Province of Ontario Savings Office; acquired by Desjardins Credit Union in 2003; total assets 144,000m. (Dec. 2007); Pres. and COO ALFRED PFEIFFER; Chair. PAUL E. GARFINKEL (acting); 29 brs.

Development Bank

Business Development Bank of Canada: 5 pl. Ville Marie, Suite 400, Montréal, QC H3B 5E7; tel. (514) 283-5904; fax (514) 283-2872; e-mail info-bdc@bdc.ca; internet www.bdc.ca; f. 1944; fed. govt corpn; auth. shareholders' equity 1,218.5m. (March 2004); Chair. JOHN A. MACNAUGHTON; Pres. and CEO JEAN-RENÉ HALDE; 94 brs.

Schedule II Banks

(incl. foreign banks in Canada)

Amex Bank of Canada (USA): 101 McNabb St, Markham, ON L3R 4H8; tel. (905) 474-8000; fax (905) 940-7702; internet www.americanexpress.com/canada; f. 1990; Chair., Pres. and CEO DENISE PICKETT.

Bank of China (Canada) (People's Republic of China): 396 Dundas St West, Toronto, ON M5T 1G8; tel. (416) 362-2991; fax (416) 362-3047; e-mail boccanada@ca.bocusa.com; internet www.boc.cn/cn/html/canada; f. 1992; cap. 65.2m., dep. 162.1m. (Dec. 2006); Pres. and CEO DASHU ZHU; Chair. ZAOHANG LI.

Bank of East Asia (Canada) (Hong Kong): Suite 102–103, East Asia Centre, 350 Hwy 7 East, Richmond Hill, ON L4B 3N2; tel. (905) 882-8182; fax (416) 882-5220; e-mail beacan@hkbea.ca; internet www.hkbea.ca; f. 1992; cap. 38m., dep. 462.4m. (Dec. 2007); Gen. Man. and CEO CEDRIC C. K. NG; 6 brs in Canada.

Bank of Tokyo-Mitsubishi UFJ (Canada) (Japan): Suite 1700, South Tower, Royal Bank Plaza, POB 42, Toronto, ON M5J 2J1; tel. (416) 865-0220; fax (416) 865-9511; f. Jan. 2006 through merger of Bank of Tokyo-Mitsubishi (Canada) (f. 1996) and UFJ Bank Canada (f. 2001); cap. 335.6m., res 0.1m., dep. 2,683.0m. (Oct. 2007); Pres. and CEO TAKASHI ANDO.

BNP Paribas (Canada) (France): BNP Tower, 1981 McGill College Ave, Montréal, QC H3A 2W8; tel. (514) 285-6000; fax (514) 285-6278; e-mail bnpp.canada@americas.bnpparibas.com; internet www.bnpparibas.ca; f. 2000 by merger of Banque Nationale de Paris Canada (f. 1961) into Paribas Bank of Canada (f. 1981); cap. 345.6m., res –2.3m., dep. 4,221.6m. (Dec. 2007); Chair. JACQUES H. WAHL; Pres. and CEO EDWARD SPEAL.

Caisse Centrale Desjardins: 1 Complexe Desjardins, South Tower, 40th Floor, Montréal, QC H5B 1B3; tel. (514) 281-7070; fax (514) 288-5153; internet www.desjardins.com; cap. 961m., res 8,321m., dep. 95,766m. (Dec. 2007); Pres. and CEO MONIQUE F. LEROUX; Gen. Man. BRUNO MORIN.

Citibank Canada (USA): Suite 1000, Citibank Pl., 123 Front St West, Toronto, ON M5J 2M3; tel. (416) 947-5500; fax (416) 947-5628; internet www.citibank.com/canada; f. 1981; subsidiary of Citibank NA (USA); cap. 258.0m., res 15.5m., dep. 6,632.0m. (Dec. 2006); Chair. and CEO KENNETH QUINN; 1 br.

CTC Bank (Canada) (Hong Kong): 1518 West Bdwy, Vancouver, BC V6J 1W8; tel. (604) 683-3882; fax (604) 683-3723; e-mail service@ctcbank.com; internet www.ctcbank.com; cap. 15m., dep. 163.7m. (Dec. 2007); Chair. STEVE CHOU, Jr; Pres. and CEO FRANK LIN.

Deutsche Bank (Canada) (Germany): 199 Bay St, Suite 4700, POB 196, Toronto, ON M5K 1E7; tel. (416) 682-8000; fax (416) 682–8383; internet www.db.com/canada; f. 1981; CEO, Americas SETH WAUGH; Principal Officer PAUL JURITZ.

Habib Canadian Bank: Suite 1B, 918 Dundas St East, Mississauga, ON L4Y 4H9; tel. (905) 276-5300; fax (905) 276-5400; e-mail habibcanadian@on.aibn.com; internet www.habibcanadian.com; f. 2001; cap. 15.0m., dep. 53.7m. (Dec. 2006); Chair. MUHAMMAD HABIB; Pres. and CEO MUSLIM HASSAN.

HSBC Bank Canada: 300–885 West Georgia St, Vancouver, BC V6C 3E9; tel. (604) 685-1000; fax (604) 641-1849; e-mail info@hsbc.ca; internet www.hsbc.ca; f. 1981 as Hongkong Bank of Canada; merged with Barclays Bank of Canada in 1996; subsidiary of HSBC Holdings plc (United Kingdom); cap. 1,575m., res. 211m., dep. 48,877m. (Dec. 2007); Chair. MICHAEL GEOGHEGAN; Pres. and CEO LINDSAY GORDON; c. 127 brs.

ING Bank of Canada: 111 Gordon Baker Rd, Suite 111, North York, Toronto, ON M2H 3R1; e-mail clientservices@ingdirect.ca; internet www.ingdirect.ca; f. 1997; Chair. ARKADI KUHLMANN; Pres. and CEO PETER R. ACETO.

International Commercial Bank of Cathay: North York Madison Centre, 4950 Yonge St, Suite 1002, Toronto, ON M2N 6K1; tel. (416) 947-2800; fax (416) 947-9964; e-mail megato@ipoline.com; f. 1982; subsidiary of Mega International Commercial Bank (Taiwan); Chair. SHUE SHENG WANG; Pres. and CEO CHEN CHANG CHIN; 3 brs.

Korea Exchange Bank of Canada (Republic of Korea): Madison Centre, Suite 1101, Madison Centre, 4950 Yonge St, Toronto, ON M2N 6K1; tel. (416) 222-5200; fax (416) 222-5822; e-mail keboc@interlog.com; internet www.kebcanada.com; f. 1981; cap. 33.4m., dep. 619.9m. (Dec. 2006); Pres. and Chair. JONG WOOK LEE.

Mizuho Corporate Bank (Canada) (Japan): Suite 1102, 100 Yonge St, POB 29, Toronto, ON M5C 2W1; tel. (416) 874-0222; fax (416) 367-3452; e-mail inquiries@mizuhocbus.com; f. 1982 following merger of Dai-Ichi Kangyo Bank and Industrial Bank of Japan; name changed as above in 2002; cap. 165.2m., dep. 1,398.3m. (Oct. 2006); Pres. TAKAHIKO UEDA; 1 br.

J. P. Morgan Chase Bank (USA): Royal Bank Plaza, South Tower, 200 Bay St, Suite 1800, Toronto, ON M5J 2J2; tel. (416) 981-9200; fax (416) 981-9133; Pres. ADAM HOWARD; Man. Dir ROBERT LEE.

Société Générale (Canada): 1501 ave Collège McGill, bureau 1800, Montréal, QC H3A 3M8; tel. (514) 841-6000; fax (514) 841-6250; e-mail christina.carvalho@sgcib.com; internet www.socgen.com; f. 1981; subsidiary of Société Générale SA (France); cap. 250.8m., res 30.0m., dep. 1,916.8m. (Dec. 2006); Chair. JEAN-JACQUES OGIER; Pres. and CEO EDOUARD-MALO HENRY; 3 brs.

State Bank of India (Canada): North Tower, Suite 1600, Royal Bank Plaza, 200 Bay St, POB 81, Toronto, ON M5J 2J2; tel. (416) 865-0414; fax (416) 865-1735; e-mail sbican@sbicanada.com; internet www.sbicanada.com; cap. 16.3m., res 5.9m., dep. 243.3m. (Dec. 2005); f. 1982; Chair. O. P. BHATT; Pres. S. VERMA; 5 brs.

Sumitomo Mitsui Banking Corpn of Canada (Japan): Toronto-Dominion Centre, Suite 1400, 222 Bay St, Toronto, ON M5K 1H6; tel. (416) 368-4766; fax (416) 367-3565; f. 2001 following merger of Sakura Bank and Sumitomo Bank of Canada; cap. 169.0m., dep. 1,701.5m. (Oct. 2007); Chair. TETSUYA KUBO; Pres. MINAMI AIDA.

UBS Bank (Canada): 154 University Ave, Toronto, ON M5H 3Z4; tel. (416) 343-1800; fax (416) 343-1900; internet www.ubs.com/canada; f. 1981; cap. 8.5m., res 124.7m., dep. 638.8m. (Dec. 2005); Chair. MARTIN LIECHTI; Pres. and CEO GRANT RASMUSSEN.

Principal Trust and Loan Companies

(m. = million; amounts in Canadian dollars)

Canada's first trust company was incorporated in 1872. Both provincially and federally incorporated companies may set up offices in any province upon registration in the province. Trust companies may manage property and investments, offer current account facilities, provide access to money transfer services, accept savings deposits and issue Guaranteed Investment Certificates. They may also provide mortgage finance and offer trustee, executor and financial agency services, and services to companies. In October 2008, according to the Office of the Superintendent of Financial Institutions, 48 trust companies and 19 loan companies, which were regulated under the federal Trust and Loan Companies Act, were operating in Canada.

AGF Trust Co: c/o AGF Management Ltd, Toronto-Dominion Bank Tower, 31st Floor, 66 Wellington St West, Toronto, ON M5K 1E9; tel. (866) 273-9971; fax (866) 713-1187; e-mail tiger@agf.com; internet www.agf.com; Pres. BLAKE C. GOLDRING.

Bank of Nova Scotia Trust Co: Scotia Plaza, 44 King St West, Toronto, ON M5H 1H1; tel. (416) 933-3000; fax (416) 933-3009; internet www.scotiabank.com; assets 878m. (Dec. 1999); Pres. RICHARD E. WAUGH.

Canadian Western Trust Corporation: 600–750 Cambie St, Vancouver, BC V6B 0A2; tel. (604) 685-2081; fax (604) 669–6069; e-mail informationservices@cwt.ca; internet www.cwt.ca/default2.htm; assets 285.0m. (Oct. 1999); Pres. and CEO LARRY M. POLLOCK.

CIBC Mellon: 320 Bay St, 4th Floor, POB 1, Toronto, ON M5H 4A6; tel. (416) 643-5000; e-mail generalinquiries@cibcmellon.com; internet www.cibcmellon.com; f. 1997; privately owned jt venture between CIBC and Mellon Financial; provides custody services (CIBC Mellon Global Securities Services Co) and trust services

(CIBC Mellon Trust Co); Pres. and CEO THOMAS C. MACMILLAN; Chair. RICHARD E. VENN.

CIBC Trust Corpn: Commerce Ct West, 199 Bay St, 56th Floor, Toronto, ON M5L 1A2; tel. (416) 861-7000; fax (416) 862-2272; internet www.cibc.com; Pres. and CEO GERALD T. MCCAUGHEY.

Citizens Trust Co: 815 West Hastings St, Suite 401, Vancouver, BC V6C 1B4; tel. (604) 708-7876; fax (604) 708-7882; e-mail service@citizensbank.ca; internet www.citizensbank.ca; Pres. and CEO JASON FARRIS.

Community Trust Co Ltd: 2271 Bloor St West, 3rd Floor, Toronto, ON M6S 1P1; tel. (416) 763-2291; fax (416) 763-2444; e-mail communitytrust@on.aibn.com; Exec. Vice-Pres. and Gen. Man. MICHAEL N. WYTIUK.

Concentra Trust: 333 Third Ave North, Saskatoon, SK S7K 2M2; tel. (800) 788-6311; fax (800) 575-4013; e-mail servicecentre@concentrafinancial.ca; internet www.concentrafinancial.ca; fmrly Co-operative Trust Co of Canada; name changed as above in Jan. 2005; wholly owned subsidiary of Concentra Financial; assets 3,600m. (Dec. 2007); CEO and Pres. MYRNA BENTLEY.

Effort Trust Co: 240 Main St East, Hamilton, ON L8N 1H5; tel. (905) 528-8956; fax (905) 528-8182; e-mail tweisz@efforttrust.ca; internet www.efforttrust.ca; f. 1978; Pres. THOMAS J. WEISZ; Vice-Pres. and Sec. GERALD ASA.

Fiducie Desjardins Inc/Desjardins Trust Inc: 1 Complexe Desjardins, CP 34, Montréal, QC H5B 1E4; tel. (514) 286-9441; fax (514) 286-3418; internet www.fiduciedesjardins.com; Pres. and CEO ALBAN D'AMOURS.

Home Trust Co: 145 King St West, Suite 1910, Toronto, ON M5H 1J8; tel. (416) 360-4663; fax (416) 360-0401; internet www.hometrust.ca; f. 1977 as Home Savings and Loan Corpn; above name adopted in 2000; Pres. and CEO GERALD M. SOLOWAY.

Household Trust Co: 3881 Steele's Ave East, Suite 300, Toronto, ON M2H 3S7; tel. (416) 443-3600; fax (416) 443-1428; Pres. TOM ARNDT.

Investors Group Trust Co Ltd: 1 Canada Centre, 447 Portage Ave, Winnipeg, MB R3C 3B6; tel. (204) 943-0361; fax (204) 956-7688; internet www.investorsgroup.com; Pres. and CEO MURRAY J. TAYLOR.

MCAN Mortgage Corporation: 200 King St West, Suite 400, Toronto, ON M5H 3T4; tel. (416) 598-2665; fax (416) 598-4142; e-mail mcanexecutive@mcanmortgage.com; internet www.mcanmortgage.com; f. 2000 as MCAP Inc, following merger of Mutual Trust Co Mortgage Investment Corpn (MTC MIC) and MCAP Financial Corpn; name changed as above Sept. 2006; Pres. and CEO BLAINE WELCH; 17 brs.

National Trust Co Ltd: 44 King St West, Toronto, ON M5H 1H1; tel. (416) 361-3611; fax (416) 361-4037; f. 1898; subsidiary of Scotiabank since 1997; Pres. and CEO RICHARD E. WAUGH.

Northern Trust Co, Canada: BCE Pl., 161 Bay St, Suite 4540, Toronto, ON M5J 2S1; tel. (416) 365-7161; fax (416) 365-9484; internet www.northerntrust.com; Pres. ROBERT J. BAILLIE.

Peace Hills Trust Co: Kensington Pl., 10th Floor, 10011 109th St, Edmonton, AB T5J 3S8; tel. (403) 421-1606; fax (403) 426-6568; e-mail pht@peacehills.com; internet www.peacehills.com; f. 1980; Pres. and COO GERALD T. KINSELLA; Chair. and CEO WARREN W. HANNAY.

Peoples Trust Co: 888 Dunsmuir St, 14th Floor, Vancouver, BC V6C 3K4; tel. (604) 683-2881; fax (604) 331-3469; e-mail people@peoplestrust.com; internet www.peoplestrust.com; Pres. and CEO FRANK A. RENOU.

ResMor Trust Co: 555 Fourth Ave, Suite 400, SW, Calgary, AB T2P 3E7; tel. (403) 539-4920; internet www.resmor.com; f. 1964 as Equisure Trust Co; acquired in 2003 by ResMor Capital Corpn; Pres. and CEO TRACIE TESSER.

Royal Trust Corporation of Canada: Royal Bank Plaza, 200 Bay St, Toronto, ON M5W 1P9; tel. (416) 974-1400; fax (416) 861-9658; f. 1899; subsidiary of Royal Bank of Canada; Chair. and CEO GEORGE LEWIS.

Standard Life Trust Co: 1245 rue Sherbrooke ouest, Montréal, QC H3G 1G3; tel. (514) 499-8855; fax (514) 499-4908; e-mail information@standardlife.ca; internet www.standardlife.ca; assets 40,500m. in Canada (Dec. 2005); Pres. and CEO JOSEPH IANNICELLI.

Sun Life Financial Trust Inc: 225 King St West, 5th Floor, Toronto, ON M5V 3C5; tel. (416) 943-6532; fax (416) 365-9401; internet www.sunlife.ca; Pres. RONALD W. OSBORNE.

TD Canada Trust: Toronto-Dominion Centre, 55 King St West, 12th Floor, POB 1, Toronto, ON M5K 1H6; tel. (416) 982-6744; fax (416) 944-5853; internet www.tdcanadatrust.com; Co-Chairs BERNIE DORVAL, TIM HOCKEY.

TD Mortgage Corpn: TD Centre, 55 King St West, 12th Floor, Toronto, ON M5K 1A2; tel. (416) 982-6744; fax (416) 944-5853; internet www.tdcanadatrust.com/cdic; Pres. W. EDMUND CLARK.

Trust La Laurentienne du Canada Inc/Laurentian Trust of Canada Inc: 425 blvd de Maisonneuve ouest, Suite 040, Montréal, QC H3A 3G5; tel. (514) 284-7000; fax (514) 284-3210; Dir-Gen. ALAIN FORTIN.

Western Pacific Trust Co: Suite 500, 1130 West Pender St, Vancouver, BC V6E 4A4; tel. (604) 683-0455; fax (604) 669-6978; internet www.westernpacifictrust.com; f. 1999; Pres., CEO and Chair. Dr ANTHONY LISCIO.

CREDIT UNIONS

Canadian credit unions and *caisses populaires* are consumer-owned financial institutions. They provide various savings and loan services, cheque and travellers' cheque facilities and financial advice. The Credit Union Central of Canada (formerly known as the Canadian Co-operative Credit Society) and the Mouvement des caisses Desjardins act as co-ordinating bodies for the credit unions and *caisses populaires,* respectively. The Mouvement des caisses Desjardins has consolidated the 11 regional federations of *caisses* and the Conféderation des caisses populaires et d'économie Desjardins du Québec to form the Féderation des caisses Desjardins du Québec. In June 2008, according to the Credit Union Central of Canada, the sector comprised 1,019 affiliated and non-affiliated credit unions and *caisses populaires* (a decline compared with the total of 2,700 credit unions and *caisses populaires* registered in 1990). Credit unions and *caisses populaires* reported combined membership of 10,871,540 Canadian citizens and combined assets of C $188,125m. at the end of June 2008.

Credit Union Central of Canada: 300 The East Mall, Suite 500, 5th Floor, Toronto, ON M9B 6B7; tel. (416) 232-1262; fax (416) 232-9196; e-mail inquiries@cucentral.com; internet www.cucentral.ca; f. 1953 as Canadian Co-operative Credit Soc.; Chair. GARTH MANNESS; Pres. and CEO DAVID PHILLIPS; 449 credit unions and associated *caisses populaires*, with total membership of 5,045,266 and combined assets of C $109,106m. in mid-2008.

BANKERS' ORGANIZATIONS

Canadian Bankers Association: Commerce Court West, Suite 3000, 199 Bay St, Box 348, Toronto, ON M5L 1G2; tel. (416) 362-6092; fax (416) 362-7705; e-mail inform@cba.ca; internet www.cba.ca; f. 1891; Chair. W. JAMES WESTLAKE; Pres. and CEO NANCY HUGHES ANTHONY; 51 mems.

Institute of Canadian Bankers: Tour Scotia, 1002 Sherbrooke St West, Suite 1000, Montréal, QC H3A 3M5; tel. (514) 282-9480; e-mail icb.info@csi.ca; internet www.icb.org; f. 1967; bought by CSI Global Education in 2007; provides financial training for the banking industry; Exec. Dir MARIE MULDOWNEY.

FINANCIAL MARKETS

Stock Exchanges

Bourse de Montréal/Montreal Exchange: Tour de la Bourse, CP 61, 800 sq. Victoria, Montréal, QC H4Z 1A9; tel. (514) 871-2424; fax (514) 871-3568; e-mail info@m-x.ca; internet www.m-x.ca; f. 1874; Chair. JEAN TURMEL; Pres. and CEO LUC BERTRAND; 91 approved participants.

Toronto Stock Exchange (TSX): The Exchange Tower, 130 King St West, Toronto, ON M5X 1J2; tel. (416) 947-4700; fax (416) 947-4662; e-mail info@tsx.com; internet www.tsx.com; f. 1861; volume of trade: 61,277m. shares (valued at some C $833,907m.) in 2004; Chair. WAYNE C. FOX; CEO THOMAS KLOET; 121 mems.

Commodity Exchange

ICE Futures Canada: 400 Commodity Exchange Tower, 360 Main St, Winnipeg, MB R3C 3Z4; tel. (204) 925-5000; fax (204) 943-5448; e-mail ICECanada@theice.com; internet www.theice.com/wce.jhtml; f. 1887 as Winnipeg Commodity Exchange, Inc; bought by IntercontinentalExchange in 2007 and name changed as above; Chair. JEFFREY C. SPRECHER; Pres. and COO BRAD VANNAN.

INSURANCE

Jurisdiction over life and health insurers is divided between federal and provincial governments. Federal supervision encompasses federally incorporated insurers and branches of foreign companies, which hold more than 90% of industry assets. The provinces generally regulate licensing and marketing, while the Office of the Superintendent of Financial Institutions conducts prudential reviews of the companies. The Canadian Life and Health Insurance Compensation Corpn ensures that member companies' policies are continued in the event of insolvency. In October 2008 some 306 insurance companies (including 93 life insurance companies) were authorized to operate in Canada under the Insurance Companies Act.

Principal Companies

AIG Life Insurance Co of Canada: 60 Yonge St, Toronto, ON M5E 1H5; tel. (416) 596-3900; fax (416) 596-4143; e-mail aiglifecainfo@aig.com; internet www.aiglife.ca; owned by American International Group (AIG) Inc; Pres. and CEO PETER C. MCCARTHY.

Assumption Life: Assumption Pl. Bldg, 770 Main St, POB 160, Moncton, NB E1C 8L1; tel. (506) 853-6040; e-mail comments@assumption.ca; internet www.assumption.ca; f. 1903; Chair. PHILIPPE DESROSIERS; Pres. and CEO DENIS LOSIER.

Aviva Canada Inc: 2206 Eglinton Ave East, Scarborough, ON M1L 4S8; tel. (416) 288-1800; e-mail glenn_cooper@avivacanada.com; internet www.avivacanada.com; f. 1906; fmrly known as CGU Group Canada Ltd following merger of General Accident, Commerical Union and Canadian General Insurance Group in 1999; present name adopted 2003; commercial and personal insurance; Pres. and CEO ROBIN L. SPENCER.

Blue Cross Life Insurance Co of Canada: 644 Main St, POB 220, Moncton, NB E1C 8L3; tel. (506) 853-1811; fax (506) 853-4646; e-mail cabcpwebmaster@pac.bluecross.ca; internet www.bluecross.ca; life, accident and illness; Pres. and CEO JIM K. GILLIGAN.

The CUMIS Group Ltd: 151 North Service Rd, POB 5065, Burlington, ON L7R 4C2; tel. (905) 632-1221; e-mail customer.service@cumis.com; internet www.cumis.com; owns Cumis General Insurance Co (f. 1980) and Cumis Life Insurance Co (f. 1977); Chair. RUSS FAST; Pres. and CEO KENNETH W. LALONDE.

Desjardins sécurité financière/Desjardins Financial Security: 200 rue des Commandeurs, Lévis, QC G6V 6R2; tel. (418) 838-7800; fax (418) 833-5985; e-mail info@desjardinssecuritefinanciere.com; internet www.dsf-dfs.com; fmrly Assurance-vie Desjardins-Laurentienne, merged with Imperial Life Assurance in 2001; Pres. and COO RICHARD FORTIER.

Dominion of Canada General Insurance Co: 165 University Ave, Toronto, ON M5H 3B9; tel. (416) 362-7231; fax (416) 362-9918; internet www.thedominion.ca; f. 1887; Chair. DUNCAN N. R. JACKMAN; Pres. and CEO GEORGE L. COOKE.

Empire Life Insurance Co: 259 King St East, Kingston, ON K7L 3A8; tel. (613) 548-1881; fax (613) 920-5868; e-mail buildingempires@empire.ca; internet www.empire.ca; f. 1923; Chair. DUNCAN N. R. JACKMAN; Pres. and CEO LESLIE (LES) C. HERR.

Equitable Life of Canada: 1 Westmount Rd North, POB 1603, Waterloo, ON N2J 4C7; tel. (519) 886-5110; fax (519) 886-5210; e-mail headoffice@equitable.ca; internet www.equitable.ca; f. 1920; Chair. DOUGLAS W. DODDS; Pres. and CEO RONALD E. BEETTAM.

Federation Insurance Co of Canada: 111 Westmount Road South, POB 2000, Waterloo, ON N2J 4S4; tel. (514) 875-5790; fax (514) 875-9769; f. 1947; Pres. and CEO NOEL WALPOLE.

GCAN Insurance Co: 181 University Ave, Suite 1000, Toronto, ON M5H 3M7; tel. (416) 682-5300; fax (416) 682-9213; e-mail head.office@gcan.ca; internet www.gcan.ca; f. 1955; Pres. and CEO DAVID HUEBEL.

Great-West Life Assurance Co: 100 Osborne St North, POB 6000, Winnipeg, MB R3C 3A5; tel. (204) 946-1190; fax (204) 946-7838; e-mail contactus@gwl.ca; internet www.greatwestlife.com; f. 1891; owns London Life Insurance Co and Canada Life Assurance Co; Pres. and CEO DAVID ALLEN LONEY; COO (Canada) DENIS J. DEVOS.

Industrial Alliance Pacific Life Insurance Co: 2165 Broadway West, POB 5900, Vancouver, BC V6B 5H6; tel. (604) 734-1667; fax (604) 734-8221; e-mail intouch@iaplife.com; internet www.iaplife.com; f. 2000; Pres. and CEO YVON CHAREST.

ING Insurance Company of Canada: 700 University Ave, Suite 1500-A, Toronto, ON M5G 0A1; tel. (416) 341-1464; fax (416) 941-5320; e-mail infoING@INGcanada.com; internet www.inginsurance.ca; CEO CHARLES BRINDAMOUR.

The Kings Mutual Insurance Co: POB 10, Berwick, NS B0P 1E0; tel. (902) 538-3187; fax (902) 538-7271; e-mail info@kingsmutual.ns.ca; internet www.kingsmutual.ns.ca; f. 1904; Chair. DAVID DAVIES.

Kingsway General Insurance Co: 7120 Hurontario St, Suite 700, Mississauga, ON L4W 5H8; tel. (905) 677-8889; fax (905) 677-5008; e-mail caxford@kingsway-general.com; internet www.kingsway-general.com; f. 1986; incorporates York Fire and Casualty Insurance Co; Pres. and CEO JOHN L. MCGLYNN.

Manufacturers Life Insurance Co (Manulife): 200 Bloor St East, Toronto, ON M4W 1E5; e-mail manulife_bank@manulife.com; internet www.manulife.ca; f. 1887; acquired Commercial Union Life Assurance Co of Canada in 2001; merged in 2004 with Maritime Life Assurance's holding co, John Hancock Financial Services, creating the Manulife Financial Group; Pres. and CEO DOMINIC D'ALESSANDRO.

Metropolitan Life Insurance Co: Constitution Sq., 360 Albert St, Suite 1750, Ottawa, ON K1R 7X7; tel. (613) 237-7171; fax (613) 237-7585; internet www.metlife.com; CEO C. ROBERT HENRIKSON.

Optimum General Inc: 425 blvd de Maisonneuve ouest, bureau 1500, Montréal, QC H3A 3G5; tel. (514) 288-8725; fax (514) 288-0760; e-mail rdube@opsa.qc.ca; internet www.optimum-general.com; f. 1969; fmrly the Société National d'Assurance Inc; operates Optimum West Insurance Co, Optimum Insurance Co Inc and Optimum Farm Insurance Inc; Chair. GILLES BLONDEAU; Pres. and CEO JEAN-CLAUDE PAGÉ.

Portage Mutual Insurance Co: 749 Saskatchewan Ave East, POB 340, Portage la Prairie, MB R1N 3B8; tel. (204) 857-3415; fax (204) 239-6655; e-mail info@portagemutual.com; internet www.portagemutual.com; f. 1884; Pres. and CEO RANDY L. CLARK.

RBC Insurance Co of Canada: West Tower, 6880 Financial Dr., Mississauga, ON L5N 7Y5; internet www.rbcinsurance.com; fmrly Westbury Life; bought Unum Provident Canada and the Canadian operation of Provident Life and Accident Insurance Co in 2004; Pres. and CEO STANLEY W. SEGGIE.

Royal & Sun Alliance Insurance Co of Canada: 10 Wellington St East, Toronto, ON M5E 1L5; tel. (416) 366-7511; fax (416) 367-9869; internet www.royalsunalliance.ca; f. 1851; Pres. and CEO ROWAN SAUNDERS.

Sovereign General Insurance Co: 140 Sovereign Centre, 6700 Macleod Trail, SE, Calgary, AB T2H 0L3; tel. (403) 298-4200; fax (403) 298-4217; internet www.sovereigngeneral.com; f. 1894; COO ROB WESSELING.

Sun Life Financial Canada: 227 King St South, POB 1601, Station Waterloo, ON N2J 4C5; tel. (416) 979-9966; fax (416) 585-9546; e-mail service@sunlife.com; internet www.sunlife.ca; f. 1871; merged with Clarica in 2007; Pres. DEAN CONNOR.

Transamerica Life Canada: 5000 Yonge St, Toronto, ON M2N 7J8; tel. (416) 883-5000; e-mail webmaster.canada@aegoncanada.ca; internet www.transamerica.ca; f. 1927; wholly owned by Aegon NV (Netherlands); Chair., Pres. and CEO PAUL READURN.

Unity Life of Canada: 100 Milverton Dr., Suite 400, Mississauga, ON L5R 4H1; tel. (905) 219-8000; fax (905) 219-8121; e-mail info@unitylife.ca; internet www.unitylife.ca; f. 1898; originally the Insurance Dept of Subsidiary High Court of the Ancient Order of Foresters, subsequently Toronto Mutual Life Insurance Co. until amalgamation with its subsidiary Western Life Assurance Co in 2002; Pres. and CEO ANTHONY W. POOLE.

Wawanesa Mutual Insurance Co: 191 Broadway, Winnipeg, MB R3C 3P1; tel. (204) 985-3923; fax (204) 942-7724; internet www.wawanesa.com; f. 1896; Pres. and CEO K. E. MCCREA.

Western Life Assurance Co: 717 Portage Ave, 4th Floor, Winnipeg, MB R3G 0M8; tel. (204) 784-6900; fax (204) 783-6913; e-mail info@westernlife.com; internet www.westernlifeassurance.net; f. 1851; fmrly Federated Life Insurance Company of Canada, present name adopted 2005; CEO BRUCE RATZLAFF.

Zurich Canada: 400 University Ave, Toronto, ON M5G 1S7; tel. (416) 586-3000; fax (416) 586-2525; internet www.zurichcanada.com; CEO ALISTER CAMPBELL.

Insurance Organizations

Advocis (Financial Advisors Association of Canada): 350 Bloor St East, 2nd Floor, Toronto, ON M4W 3W8; tel. (416) 444-5251; fax (416) 444-8031; e-mail info@advocis.ca; internet www.advocis.ca; f. 2002 by merger of the Canadian Asscn of Insurance and Financial Advisors and Canadian Asscn of Financial Planners; fmrly Life Underwriters Asscn of Canada (f. 1906); Chair. TERESA BLACK HUGHES; Pres and CEO STEVE HOWARD; c. 12,000 mems.

Assuris: 250 Yonge Street, Suite 3110, POB 23, Toronto, ON M5B 2L7; tel. (416) 359-2001; fax (416) 955-9688; e-mail info@assuris.ca; internet www.assuris.ca; fmrly Canadian Life and Health Insurance Compensation Corpn (CompCorp), name changed as above in Dec. 2005; total assets $122m. (Dec. 2006); Pres. and CEO GORDON M. DUNNING; 190 mems.

Canadian Association of Mutual Insurance Companies: 311 McArthur Ave, Suite 205, Ottawa, ON K1L 6P1; tel. (613) 789-6851; fax (613) 789-7665; e-mail nflafreniere@camic.ca; internet www.camic.ca; Chair. JOE DIETRICH; Pres. NORMAN LAFRENIÈRE; 99 mems.

Canadian Life and Health Insurance Association Inc: 1 Queen St East, Suite 1700, Toronto, ON M5C 2X9; tel. (416) 777-2221; fax (416) 777-1895; internet www.clhia.ca; f. 1894; Chair. PIERRE-YVES JULIEN; 74 mems.

Insurance Brokers Association of Canada: 155 University Ave, Suite 1230, Toronto, ON M5H 3B7; tel. (416) 367-1831; fax (416) 367-3687; e-mail ibac@ibac.ca; internet www.ibac.ca; f. 1921; Chair. DANNY CRAIG; Pres. PETER FREDERICKS; 11 mem. asscns.

Insurance Bureau of Canada: 777 Bay St, Suite 2400, POB 121, Toronto, ON M5G 2C8; tel. (416) 362-2031; fax (416) 361-5952; e-mail jgeuzebroek@ibc.ca; internet www.ibc.ca; f. 1964; Pres. and CEO MARK YAKABUSKI.

Insurance Institute of Canada: 18 King St East, 6th Floor, Toronto, ON M5C 1C4; tel. (416) 362-8586; fax (416) 362-4239; e-mail iicmail@insuranceinstitute.ca; internet www.insuranceinstitute.ca; f. 1952; Pres. PETER G. HOHMAN; 35,000 mems.

Chartered Insurance Professionals' Society (CIP Society): 18 King St East, 6th Floor, Toronto, ON M5C 1C4; tel. (416) 362-5130; fax (416) 362-4239; e-mail genmail@insuranceinstitute.ca; internet cip.iic-iac.org; a division of the Insurance Institute of Canada; represents c. 15,000 insurance professionals..

LOMA Canada: 1243 Islington Ave, Suite 505, Toronto, ON M8X 1Y9; tel. (416) 234-5661; fax (416) 233-5031; e-mail liic@loma.org; internet www.lomacanada.org/en; f. 1924; Life Insurance Institute of Canada renamed LOMA Canada June 2006, following 2002 merger with LOMA; Pres. and CEO THOMAS P. DONALDSON; Exec. Dir ROSS TURNEY; over 1,200 mem. cos in 84 countries.

TOURISM

STATISTICS

Visits and Expenditure

(2007)

	Number ('000)	Expenditure (C $ million)
Austria	138	98
China, People's Republic	258	455
Cuba	724	629
Dominican Republic	690	599
France	745	973
Germany	370	323
Hong Kong	177	209
Ireland	166	203
Italy	352	514
Mexico	1,019	1,084
Netherlands	258	210
Spain	187	246
Switzerland	148	107
United Kingdom	947	1,149
USA	17,759	11,545

Source: Statistics Canada.

Destination by Province of Overnight International Travellers

('000 overnight visits)

	2006		2007	
	USA	Other	USA	Other
Alberta	937.9	792.9	932.1	812.9
British Columbia	3,518.1	1,433.0	3,394.2	1,516.3
Manitoba	283.1	78.7	264.2	88.1
New Brunswick	367.2	58.8	357.9	60.3
Newfoundland and Labrador	49.1	23.2	49.3	23.8
Nova Scotia	373.5	142.6	332.6	148.3
Northwest Territories*	26.3	7.6	16.5	14.8
Prince Edward Island	154.2	33.4	131.7	34.8
Ontario	6,898.6	2,046.3	6,586.9	2,026.3
Québec	2,107.7	1,090.4	1,982.0	1,058.7
Saskatchewan	158.9	50.8	153.3	50.7
Yukon Territory	225.1	36.0	254.5	46.7

* Includes Nunavut.

Source: Statistics Canada.

National Parks

	Area (sq km)
Aulavik, NT	12,200.0
Auyuittuq, Baffin Island, NU	19,089.0
Banff, AB	6,641.0
Bruce Peninsula, ON	154.0
Cape Breton Highlands, NS	948.0
Elk Island, AB	194.0
Forillon, QC	240.4
Fundy, NB	205.9
Georgian Bay Islands, ON	25.6
Glacier, BC	1,349.3
Grasslands, SK	906.4
Gros Morne, NL	1,805.0
Gulf Islands, BC*	33.3
Gwaii Haanas, BC*	1,495.0
Ivvavik, YT	9,750.0
Jasper, AB	10,878.0
Kejimujik, NS	403.7
Kluane, YT*	22,061.0
Kootenay, BC	1,406.4
Kouchibouguac, NB	239.2
La Mauricie, QC	536.1
Mingan Archipelago, QC*	150.7
Mount Revelstoke, BC	259.7
Nahanni, NT*	4,766.0
Pacific Rim, BC*	510.8
Point Pelee, ON	15.2
Prince Albert, SK	3,874.3
Prince Edward Island, PE	27.0
Pukaskwa, ON	1,877.8
Quttinirpaaq, NU	37,775.0
Riding Mountain, MB	2,970.0
Sirmilik, NU	22,200.0
St Lawrence Islands, ON	8.3
Terra Nova, NL	396.7
Torngat Mountains, NL	9,700.0
Tuktut Nogait, NT	16,340.0
Ukkusiksalik, NU	20,558.0
Vuntut, YT	4,345.0
Wapusk, MB	11,475.0
Waterton Lakes, AB	505.0
Wood Buffalo, AB–NT	44,802.0
Yoho, BC	1,313.1
Total	274,430.9

* National Park Reserve: an area set aside as a national park, pending settlement of any outstanding aboriginal land claims.

NATIONAL ORGANIZATIONS

Association of Canadian Travel Agencies: 350 Sparks St, Suite 510, Ottawa, ON K1R 7S8; tel. (613) 237-3657; fax (613) 237-7052; e-mail actacan@acta.travel; internet www.acta.ca; f. 1977; Chair. JEAN COLLETTE; Vice-Chair. JACQUELINE JAMIESON; seven regional councils.

Association of Corporate Travel Executives Canada (ACTE Canada): POB 85020, Stittsville, ON K2S 1X6; tel. (613) 836-7652; fax (613) 836-0619; e-mail canada@acte.org; internet www.acte.org; merged with Canadian Business Travel Asscn in 2007; Regional Chair. ANNEMARIE REININGER.

Canadian Camping Association: 2494 Route 125 South, St. Donat, QC J0T 2C0; tel. (819) 424-2662; fax (819) 424-4145; e-mail info@ccamping.org; internet www.ccamping.org; Pres. LEIGHANA SHOCKEY; nine provincial asscns.

Canadian Institute of Travel Counsellors (CITC): 505 Consumers Rd, Suite 406, Toronto, ON M2J 4V8; tel. (416) 484-4450; fax (416) 484-4140; e-mail info@citc.ca; internet www.citc.ca; 3,000 mems; Pres. and COO STEVE GILLICK; 7 regional brs.

Canadian Tourism Commission: Four Bentall Centre, 1055 Dunsmuir St, Suite 1400, Box 49230, Vancouver, BC V5P 1L2; tel. (604) 638-8300; e-mail ctx_feedback@ctc-cct.ca; internet www.canadatourism.com; Chair. STEVE ALLAN; Pres. and CEO MICHELE McKENZIE.

Hostelling International—Canada: 205 Catherine St, Suite 400, Ottawa, ON K2P 1C3; tel. (613) 237-7884; fax (613) 237-7868; e-mail info@hihostels.ca; internet www.hihostels.ca; f. 1933; Nat. Exec. Dir JOËL MARIER.

Hotel Association of Canada: 130 Albert St, Suite 1206, Ottawa, ON K1P 5G4; tel. (613) 237-7149; fax (613) 238-8928; e-mail info@hotelassociation.ca; internet www.hotelassociation.ca; f. 1913; Pres. ANTHONY P. POLLARD; 10 provincial asscns; 28 corp. mems.

Parks Canada Agency: Jules Léger Bldg, 25 Eddy St, Gatineau, QC K1A 0M5; tel. (819) 994-3023; fax (819) 953-5523; e-mail information@pc.gc.ca; internet www.pc.gc.ca; CEO ALAN LATOURELLE.

Tourism Industry Association of Canada: 116 Lisgar St, Suite 600, Ottawa, ON K2P 0C2; tel. (613) 238-3883; fax (613) 238-3878; e-mail info@tiac.travel; internet www.tiac-aitc.ca; f. 1931; private-sector asscn, encourages travel to and within Canada; promotes devt of travel services and facilities; Chair. KEN LAMBERT; Pres. and CEO RANDY WILLIAMS.

PROVINCIAL AND TERRITORIAL TOURIST ATTRACTIONS AND ORGANIZATIONS

Alberta

Alberta has two very different principal tourism areas. The Rocky Mountains in the west of the province are rich in scenic and natural beauty, protected in the Banff and Jasper National Parks. Popular activities in these parks include winter and summer sports (particularly skiing and golf), walking and camping. In contrast, further east are the towns of Calgary and Edmonton, both with striking modern architecture as well as examples of their cattle-ranching and gold-rush heritage. Calgary has an annual 'Stampede' rodeo in July and its museums and galleries, zoo and prehistoric park attract visitors all year round. Edmonton hosts the 'Klondike Days' festival in July each year and the Canadian 'Finals Rodeo' in mid-November. West Edmonton Mall claims to be the world's largest shopping complex, with a variety of leisure facilities. The province has three other national parks: Waterton Lakes on the border with Montana (USA), a continuation of the US Glacier National Park; Elk Island in central Alberta, where large herds of buffalo, deer, elk and moose are found; and Wood Buffalo National Park, noted for wildlife such as bison and whooping crane, stretching across the northern border of the province into the Northwest Territories. The five national parks cover a total of 49,319 sq km. There are also 115 provincial parks (including wilderness areas and provincial recreation areas), covering 12,514 sq km. International overnight visitation to Alberta was estimated at 1,745,000 visits in 2007.

Alberta Country Vacations Association: POB 5245, High River, AL T1V 1M4; tel. (403) 217-5740; fax (403) 652-5907; e-mail info@albertacountryvacation.com; internet www.albertacountryvacation.com; Exec. Dir ROBERTA MACLEOD.

Alberta Economic Development: Tourism Development Branch, Commerce Pl., 6th Floor, 10155 102 St, Edmonton, AB T5J 4L6; tel. (780) 415-1319; fax (780) 422-1759; internet www.alberta-canada.com; Dir JANICE SCHROEDER.

Alberta Hotel and Lodging Association: Centre 104, Suite 401, 5241 Calgary Trail, Edmonton, AB T6H 5G8; tel. (780) 436-6112; fax (780) 436-5404; e-mail info@ahla.ca; internet www.ahla.ca; Chair. LINA VENCHIARUTTI; Pres. and CEO DAVE P. KAISER.

Alberta Sport, Recreation, Parks and Wildlife Foundation: 905 Standard Life Centre, 10405 Jasper Ave, Edmonton, AB T5J 4R7; tel. (780) 415-1167; fax (780) 415-0308; e-mail laurel.murphy@

gov.ab.ca; internet www.cd.gov.ab.ca/asrpwf; Chair. OREST KORBUTT; Sec. BILL WERRY; Gen. Man. LLOYD BENTZ.

Association of Canadian Travel Agencies—ACTA (Alberta): POB 50024, RPO Clareview, Edmonton, AB T5Y 2M9; tel. (780) 475-3483; fax (780) 475-3693; e-mail shelley.morris@mts.net; internet www.acta.ca; Regional Man. COLLEEN GANNON; Regional Chair. RICK YEARWOOD.

Canadian Institute of Travel Counsellors—CITC (Alberta): tel. (403) 777-0727; fax (403) 777-0709; e-mail lemairec@macewan.ca; internet www.citc.ca; 300 individual mems; Regional Chair. CARLA LEMAIRE.

Edmonton Economic Development Corporation (EEDC): World Trade Center, 3rd Floor, 9990 Jasper Ave, Edmonton, AB T5J 1P7; tel. (780) 424-9191; fax (780) 425-5283; e-mail info@edmonton.com; internet www.edmonton.com/eedc; Pres. and CEO RON GILBERTSON; Chair. ROBERT CARWELL.

Tourism Calgary: 200–238 11th Ave, SE, Calgary, AB T2G 0X8; tel. (403) 263-8510; fax (403) 262-3809; e-mail viquih@tourismcalgary.com; internet www.tourismcalgary.com; Chair. JULIEN DESCHUTTER; Pres. and CEO JOE FARDELL.

British Columbia

Tourism is British Columbia's second largest industry, after timber, with the southern half of the province attracting the greatest number of visitors. Skiing resorts are found throughout the southern area and there are hot springs resorts in the Rocky Mountains, where the glaciers and snowfields are also popular attractions. The tourism potential of the more remote north of the province remains largely undeveloped. The province has seven national parks, including Gwaii Haanas (South Moresby), comprising the ancient rainforest and coastline of the southern Queen Charlotte's Islands, and the Pacific Rim National Park, formed from parts of the western coastline of Vancouver Island and including fjords and beaches. Four further national parks—Mount Revelstoke, Glacier, Yoho and Kootenay—are located in the south-eastern part of the province, covering the Rocky Mountains and associated ranges. White-water rafting is a particularly popular activity in the mountain areas. Gulf Islands National Park, established in 2003, consists of 16 islands and numerous islets and reef areas in the Strait of Georgia, west of the province's principal city, Vancouver. Vancouver, in itself an attraction for tourists, is a modern, cosmopolitan city located in a setting of mountains, waterways and islands. The city has many museums, with the Science World and the Museum of Anthropology, featuring traditional native Canadian arts, particularly popular. The capital of British Columbia, Victoria, is situated on Vancouver Island and reached by ferry from Vancouver itself. Victoria offers many examples of Canada's history as a British colony and is noted for its traditional architecture, particularly the Parliament Buildings. British Columbia has 390 provincial parks, covering 53,800 sq km. National parks cover 4,900 sq km and national aboriginal reserves 3,410 sq km. Fishing is a popular recreational activity in the province. International overnight visitation to British Columbia was estimated at 4,910,500 visits in 2007.

Association of Canadian Travel Agencies—ACTA (British Columbia): 213-5760 Minoru Blvd, Richmond, BC V6X 2A9; tel. (604) 231-0544; fax (604) 231-6020; e-mail actabcyu@telus.net; internet www.acta.ca; Vice-Pres. DAVID MCCAIG; Regional Chair. JACQUELINE JAMIESON.

British Columbia Camping Association: c/o Sasamat Outdoor Centre, 3302 Senkler Rd, Belcarra, BC V3H 4S3; tel. (604) 931-6449; fax (604) 939-8522; e-mail info@bccamping.org; internet www.bccamping.org; Pres. SIMON ADAMS.

British Columbia Lodging and Campgrounds Association: 3003 St John's St, Suite 209, Port Moody, BC V3H 2C4; tel. (604) 945-7676; fax (604) 945-7606; e-mail info@bclca.com; internet www.bclca.com; Pres. CHRIS BOWER; Exec. Dir JOSS PENNY.

British Columbia and Yukon Hotels' Association: 948 Howe St, 2nd Floor, Vancouver, BC V6Z 1N9; tel. (604) 681-7164; fax (604) 681-7649; e-mail hotel@bcyha.com; internet www.bcyha.com; Pres. EARL WILDE; CEO JAMES CHASE.

Canadian Heritage (Pacific and Yukon Regional Office): 300 West Georgia St, 4th Floor, Vancouver, BC V6B 6C6; tel. (604) 666-0176; fax (604) 666-3508; e-mail wro-pch@pch.gc.ca; internet www.pch.gc.ca.

Canadian Institute of Travel Counsellors—CITC (British Columbia): tel. (604) 683-7400; fax (604) 683-2411; e-mail arlene.windward@silk.net; internet www.citc.ca; Regional Chair. ARLENE HENDERSON.

Council of Tourism Associations of British Columbia: 409 Granville St, Suite 1208, Vancouver, BC V6E 3L2; tel. (604) 685-5956; fax (604) 685-5915; e-mail info@cotabc.com; internet www.cotabc.com; Pres. and CEO STEPHEN REGAN.

Ministry of Environment: POB 9339, Victoria, BC V8W 9M1; tel. (250) 387-6121; fax (250) 387-5669; e-mail enquirybc@gov.bc.ca; internet www.gov.bc.ca/environment; Minister BARRY PENNER.

Ministry of Tourism, Culture and the Arts: Parliament Bldgs, Victoria, BC V8V 1X4; tel. (250) 953-4246; fax (250) 953-4250; e-mail enquirybc@gov.bc.ca; internet www.gov.bc.ca/tca; Minister BILL BENNETT.

Tourism British Colombia: 510 Burrard St, 12th Floor, Vancouver, BC V6C 3A8; tel. (604) 660-2861; e-mail bettina.giblin@tourismbc.com; internet www.tourismbc.com; Pres. and CEO ROD J. HARRIS.

Tourism Vancouver—Greater Vancouver Convention and Visitors Bureau: 200 Burrard St, Suite 210, Vancouver, BC V6C 3L6; tel. (604) 682-2222; fax (604) 682-1717; e-mail comments@tourismvancouver.com; internet www.tourismvancouver.com; Pres. and CEO RICK ANTONSON; Chair. GEOFFREY HOWES.

Manitoba

Manitoba's landscape is varied, ranging from the grain fields of the south, through forest and parkland region, to the treeless tundra of the north. With one-sixth of the total area of Manitoba covered in water, several of the province's principal tourist attractions are associated with this topographical feature. Swimming, fishing and boating are all popular activities, and can be pursued in many of Manitoba's 147 provincial parks (which cover 15,000 sq km). Lake Winnipeg also offers many beaches. The province has two national parks: Riding Mountain, a preserved wilderness area within the dominant prairie farmland, which has forests, lakes, streams and trails for hiking and horseriding; and Wapusk, in the north of the province, which protects an important polar bear habitat and is representative of the Hudson-James lowlands. International overnight visitation to Manitoba was estimated at 352,300 visits in 2007.

Association of Canadian Travel Agencies—ACTA (Manitoba): 700–177 Lombard Ave, Winnipeg, MB R3B 0W5; tel. (204) 831-0831; fax (204) 925-8000; e-mail actambsk@acta.travel; internet www.acta.ca; Regional Man. SHELLEY MORRIS; Regional Chair. PHILIP HOUDE.

Canadian Institute of Travel Counsellors—CITC (Manitoba): tel. (204) 947-8338; fax (204) 942-2871; e-mail rpenner@tpi.ca; internet www.citc.ca; Regional Chair. REBECCA PENNER.

Destination Winnipeg Inc: 300–259 Portage Ave, Winnipeg, MB R3B 2A9; tel. (204) 943-1970; fax (204) 942-4043; e-mail wpginfo@destinationwinnipeg.ca; internet www.destinationwinnipeg.ca; Pres. STUART DUNCAN.

Manitoba Country Vacations Association: Box 11, Lake Audy, MB R0J 0Z0; tel. and fax (204) 848-2265; fax 848-2088; internet www.countryvacations.mb.ca; Pres. JIM IRWIN.

Manitoba Culture, Heritage, Tourism and Sport: 118 Legislative Bldg, 450 Broadway Ave, Winnipeg, MB R3B 1N3; tel. (204) 945-3729; e-mail mincht@leg.gov.mb.ca; internet www.gov.mb.ca/chc.

Manitoba Hotel Association: 1534 Gamble Pl., Suite 200, Winnipeg, MB R3T 1N6; tel. (204) 942-0671; fax (204) 942-6719; e-mail pfagg@manitobahotelassociation.ca; internet www.manitobahotelassociation.mb.ca; Pres. and CEO JIM BAKER; Exec. Dir JERRY WEIR.

Manitoba Natural Resources, Parks and Natural Areas Branch: 200 Saulteaux Cres., POB 50, Winnipeg, MB 3RJ 3W3; tel. (204) 945-4362; fax (204) 945-0012; internet www.gov.mb.ca/natres/parks; Minister STAN STRUTHERS.

Travel Manitoba: 155 Carlton St, 10th Floor, Winnipeg, MB R3C 3H8; tel. (204) 945-3796; fax (204) 945-2302; internet www.travelmanitoba.com; Minister of Culture, Heritage and Tourism ERIC ROBINSON.

New Brunswick

New Brunswick's coastline is its principal tourist attraction. The highest rise of tidal water in the world has been recorded in the Bay of Fundy, the great volume of water advancing and retreating sculpting dramatic rock formations and leaving extensive beaches and mud flats, where many kinds of wildlife, especially whales and birds, can be observed. Fundy National Park is located at the east end of the Bay. New Brunswick's other national park, Kouchibouguac, preserves a system of lagoons, barrier beaches, sand dunes and salt marshes at the northern end of the Northumberland Strait. Inland attractions include the Saint John river valley, with several covered bridges and waterfalls, and the forest, hills and streams of the Restigouche Uplands. New Brunswick has 11 provincial parks and one international park: the Roosevelt Campobello International Park. International overnight visitation to the province was estimated at 418,200 visits in 2007.

Campground Owners' Association of New Brunswick: Ocean Surf Trailer Park, POB 5132, Shediac, NB E4P 8T8; tel. (506) 532-5480.

Department of Tourism and Parks New Brunswick: POB 12345, Campbellton, NB E3N 3T6; e-mail Danielle.McFarlane@gnb.ca; internet www.tourismnewbrunswick.ca; Dir DANIELLE MCFARLANE.

Farm Vacation Association, New Brunswick: c/o Shirley Reid, 116 Parkwood Dr., Woodstock, NB E7M 5G1; tel. (506) 325-2756; fax (506) 276-4292.

New Brunswick Bed and Breakfast Association: tel. (506) 488-8989; fax (506) 488-3038; e-mail islebb@nbnet.nb.ca; internet www.bbcanada.com/associations/newbrunswick.

Tourism Saint John: City Hall, 11th Floor, 15 Market Sq., POB 1971, Saint John, NB E2L 4L1; tel. (506) 658-2990; fax (506) 632-6118; e-mail visitsj@saintjohn.ca; internet www.tourismsaintjohn.com.

Tourism Industry Association of New Brunswick: POB 23001, Fredericton, NB E3B 7B3; tel. (506) 458-5646; fax (506) 459-3634; e-mail info@tianb.com; internet www.tianb.com; Pres. JOANNE BÉRUBÉ-GAGNÉ; Exec. Dir RÉAL ROBICHAUD.

Newfoundland and Labrador

Tourism in the province of Newfoundland and Labrador is concentrated on the Island of Newfoundland, the mainland area of Labrador to the north being largely undeveloped. The coastline of the island is rugged, with many fjords and bays; icebergs and ice floes occur frequently in the area, especially in late winter and early spring, and whale-watching is popular. Terra Nova National Park is on the east coast, at Bonavista Bay; Gros Morne National Park, on the west coast at Bonne Bay, comprises mountains, rock plateaux, lakes, forests and fjords. A national park reserve was sited in the Torngat Mountains on the Labrador peninsula, and was expected to attain National Park status in 2008. L'Anse-Aux-Meadows National Historic Site, at the northern tip of the island, marks the site of the 10th-century Viking settlement, and is, along with Gros Morne National Park, a UNESCO World Heritage Site. On the east coast, the town of St John's features historic buildings and holds a regatta every year, while Trinity Harbour, the site of North America's first European-style court of justice, also attracts visitors. There are 14 provincial parks, six Natural Scenic Attractions and 18 Wilderness and Ecological Reserves. Outdoor pursuits include bird-watching, fishing, hunting (principally for game mammals) and skiing. International overnight visitation to the province was estimated at 73,100 visits in 2007.

Department of Tourism, Culture and Recreation: Confederation Bldg, West Block, 2nd Floor, Prince Philip Dr., POB 8700, St John's, NL A1B 4J6; tel. (709) 729-0862; fax (709) 729-0870; e-mail tcrinfo@gov.nl.ca; internet www.tcr.gov.nl.ca/tcr; Minister CLYDE JACKMAN.

Hospitality Newfoundland and Labrador: ICON Bldg, 2nd Floor, 187 Kenmount Rd, St John's, NL A1B 3P9; tel. (709) 722-2000; fax (709) 722-8104; e-mail hnl@hnl.ca; internet www.hnl.ca; Pres. BRUCE SPARKES; Exec. Dir CAROL-ANN GILLIARD.

Newfoundland and Labrador Camping Association: POB 50846, St John's, NL A1B 4M2; tel. (709) 576-6198; fax (709) 576-8146; e-mail malcolmcturner@gmail.com.

St John's Department of Economic Development, Tourism and Culture: 348 Water St, POB 908, St John's, NL A1C 5M2; tel. (709) 576-8394; fax (709) 576-8300; e-mail business@stjohns.ca; internet www.stjohns.ca; f. 1888; Dir ELIZABETH LAWRENCE.

Northwest Territories

Tourism is developing steadily in the Northwest Territories, despite its remoteness from the major population centres of Canada and its severe weather and long winters. There is a limited road network in the Mackenzie Valley area, otherwise access is only possible by water and air. The Northwest Territories has four national parks, including Wood Buffalo, which has the largest known herd of free-roaming buffalo and is shared with the province of Alberta. Nahanni National Park, in the west, has high waterfalls, canyons, hot springs and opportunities for white-water canoeing or rafting; it is also a UNESCO World Heritage Site. Aulavik National Park is located on Banks Island, featuring river canyons and rugged landscape, while Tuktut Nogait National Park includes the Hornaday River and the Melville Hills east of Paulatuk. The native Canadian culture of the region attracts visitors, with native artwork and crafts particularly popular. International overnight visitation to the Northwest Territories was estimated at 31,300 visits in 2007.

Department of Industry, Tourism and Investment: POB 1320, Yellowknife, NT X1A 2L9; tel. (867) 669-2388; fax (867) 873-0306; e-mail info@iti.ca; internet www.iti.gov.nt.ca; Dir, Tourism and Parks GERRY LEPRIEUR.

Northwest Territories Tourism: 4916 47th St, 3rd Floor, POB 610, Yellowknife, NT X1A 2N5; tel. (867) 873-7200; fax (867) 873-4059; e-mail info@spectacularnwt.com; internet www.spectacularnwt.com; Exec. Dir DAVID GRINDLAY.

Nova Scotia

With its long coastline (7,400 km) along the south-eastern boundary of Canada, Nova Scotia was the location for some of the earliest European settlements, including the earliest agricultural settlement, Port-Royal (now Annapolis Royal). A replica of Port-Royal has been developed as a tourist attraction. There are several other historic sites and buildings preserved throughout the province, including the Fortress Louisbourg and the Halifax Citadel Fort. There are two national parks in Nova Scotia: Kejimkujik, south-west of Halifax, a wilderness area with lakes and rivers; and Cape Breton Highlands, which is located at the north of Cape Breton Island, with coastline on both sides of a rocky peninsula, and includes the northernmost part of the Cabot Trail Highway. The Highlands includes a golf course, and whale-watching is popular along the coastline. Nova Scotia's 122 provincial parks cover 218 sq km. The province has established 10 scenic travelways linking scenery and cultural attractions. The capital, Halifax, has the world's second largest natural harbour, the popular Maritime Museum of the Atlantic and the Historic Properties area. International overnight visitation to the province was estimated at 480,900 visits in 2007.

Association of Canadian Travel Agencies—ACTA (Atlantic): POB 21007, Quispamsis, NB E2E 4Z4; tel. (506) 847-4030; fax (506) 847-4048; e-mail actaatlantic@acta.ca; internet www.acta.ca; Regional Man. LORIE COHEN HACKETT; Regional Chair. ELLEN TUCKER.

Camping Association of Nova Scotia: POB 33039, Halifax, NS B3L 4T6; tel. (902) 425-5454; fax (902) 876-1076; e-mail info@campingns.ca; internet www.campingns.ca; f. 1941; Pres. HEATHER MACDONALD.

Department of Tourism, Culture and Heritage: World Trade Centre, 6th Floor, 1800 Argyle St, POB 456, Halifax, NS B3J 2R5; tel. (902) 424-5000; fax (902) 424-0129; e-mail tns@gov.ns.ca; internet www.gov.ns.ca/tch; Minister BILL DOOKS.

Halifax Visitor Services: POB 1749, Halifax, NS B3J 3A5; tel. (902) 490-4000; fax (902) 490-7117; e-mail visitorinfo@halifax.ca; internet www.halifax.ca/visitors; Man. MICHAEL RYAN.

Nova Scotia Bed and Breakfast Association: 1099 Marginal Rd, Suite 201, Halifax, NS B3H 4P7; tel. (902) 423-4480; fax (902) 422-0186; e-mail tians@tourism.ca; internet www.bbcanada.com/associations/novascotia; Pres. JAN WHEELER.

Nova Scotia Tourism: POB 456, Halifax, NS B3J 3N8; tel. (902) 490-5946; fax (902) 424-2668; e-mail explore@gov.ns.ca; internet www.novascotia.com.

Tourism Cape Breton: POB 1448, Sydney, NS B1P 6R7; tel. (902) 563-4636; fax (902) 564-5422; e-mail caroline@dcba.ca; internet www.cbisland.com; Chair. GORDON HEADING; Gen. Man. SANDRA MACDONALD.

Tourism Industry Association of Nova Scotia: 1099 Marginal Rd, Suite 201, Halifax, NS B3H 4P7; tel. (902) 423-4480; fax (902) 422-0184; e-mail information_central@tians.org; internet www.tians.org; Chair. DANNY MORTON; Pres. DARLENE GRANT FIANDER.

Nunavut Territory

The Inuit territory of Nunavut, formerly the eastern part of the Northwest Territories, was constituted in April 1999. There are four national parks in the province. Sirmilik National Park covers approximately 22,200 sq km in three areas: Oliver Sound and its surroundings; east Borden Peninsula; and the mountains and lowlands of Bylot Island. Auyuittuq National Park on Baffin Island comprises numerous fjords, glaciers and mountains. Quttinirpaaq (formerly Ellesmere Island) National Park is located in the northernmost part of Canada, separated from northern Greenland by the narrow Nares Strait. Within the park are many species of mammals, including musk ox and arctic hare; in general, wildlife watching is popular among visitors to the parks. Ukkusiksalik National Park, which was founded in 2003, surrounds Wager Bay, a 100-km long saltwater inlet on the north-east coast of Hudson Bay. Nunavut also contains several Inuit archaeological sites, parks, museums and interpretive centres. Non-resident visitation to the national parks sites in the province was estimated at 605 visits in 2001/02.

Department of Environment (including Parks): Box 1000, Station 1300, Iqaluit, NU X0A 0H0; tel. (867) 975-7700; fax (867) 975-7740; e-mail cwelsh@gov.nu.ca; internet www.gov.nu.ca/env; Minister OLAYUK AKESUK.

Nunavut Tourism: POB 1450, Iqaluit, NU X0A 0H0; tel. (867) 979-6551; fax (867) 979-1261; e-mail info@nunavuttourism.com; internet www.nunavuttourism.com; CEO MAUREEN BUNDGAARD.

Ontario

Ontario accounted for over one-third of all domestic tourist visits in Canada in 2004. In addition, 9,279,700 foreign tourists visited Ontario in the same year. The size of the province's area and population are in part responsible for this, but no less so than the attractions of great cities and natural beauty. Ontario is the province of the Great Lakes (parts of Lakes Ontario, Erie, Huron and Superior are within the province's boundaries). Niagara Falls, on the Niagara River linking Lakes Erie and Ontario, is one of the world's most famous tourist attractions. The province's five national parks (Bruce Peninsula, Georgian Bay Islands, Point Pelee, Pukaskwa and St Lawrence Islands) are all located on one or other of the Great Lakes. Ontario's 261 provincial parks (including the massive Algonquin Provincial Park, wilderness and recreation areas, nature reserves, and historical sites) cover a total area of 63,284 sq km, and offer opportunities for hiking, fishing, camping, skiing and various other outdoor pursuits. In contrast, Toronto is a modern cosmopolitan city, particularly favoured for its architecture, entertainment facilities and general cleanliness. Ottawa, on the border with the province of Québec, is the federal capital, and has a number of national museums and galleries. International overnight visitation to Ontario was estimated at 8,613,200 visits in 2007.

Association of Canadian Travel Agencies—ACTA (Ontario): 2560 Matheson Blvd East, Suite 328, Mississauga, ON L4W 4Y9; tel. (905) 282-9294; fax (905) 282-9826; e-mail hcraig-peddie@acta.travel; internet www.acta.ca; Regional Man. HEATHER CRAIG-PEDDIE; Regional Chair. MICHAEL FOSTER.

Canadian Institute of Travel Counsellors—CITC (Ontario Region): tel. (905) 474-8886; fax (905) 474-0840; e-mail warrenkathleen@hotmail.com; internet www.citc.ca; Regional Chair. KATHLEEN WARREN.

Federation of Ontario Bed and Breakfast Accommodation: 293 Park St South, Hamilton, ON L8P 3G5; tel. (519) 568-8878; e-mail info@fobba.com; internet www.fobba.com; f. 1987; Pres. ADDE WALKER.

Ministry of Tourism and Recreation: Hearst Block, 9th Floor, 900 Bay St, Toronto, ON M7A 2E1; tel. (416) 326-9326; fax (416) 326-9338; e-mail general_info@mtr.gov.on.ca; internet www.tourism.gov.on.ca; Minister MONIQUE SMITH.

Niagara Falls Tourism: 5400 Robinson St, Niagara Falls, ON L2G 2A6; tel. (905) 356-6061; fax (905) 356-5567; e-mail info@niagarafallstourism.com; internet www.niagarafallstourism.com; Exec. Dir ANNA PIERCE.

Ontario Accommodation Association: 347 Pido Rd, Unit 2, RR 6, Peterborough, ON K9J 6X7; tel. (705) 745-4982; fax (705) 745-4983; e-mail info@ontarioaccommodation.com; internet www.ontarioaccommodation.com; f. 1949; trade asscn; Pres. BRUCE M. GRAVEL.

Ontario Camping Association: 250 Merton St, Suite 301, Toronto, ON M4S 1B1; tel. (416) 485-0425; fax (416) 485-0422; e-mail info@ontariocamps.ca; internet www.ontariocamps.ca.

Ontario Restaurant, Hotel and Motel Association: 2600 Skymark Ave, Suite 8-201, Mississauga, ON L4W 5B2; tel. (905) 361-0268; fax (905) 361-0288; e-mail telenis@orhma.com; internet www.orhma.com; Pres. and CEO TONY ELENIS.

Ontario Parks: 300 Water St, 6th Floor, POB 7000, Peterborough, ON K9J 8M5; tel. (800) 667-1940; fax (705) 755-1701; internet www.ontarioparks.com; Man. Dir ADAIR IRELAND-SMITH.

Ontario Private Campground Association: 220 Royal Crest Ct, Unit 8, Markham, ON L3R 9Y2; tel. (905) 947-9500; fax (905) 947-9501; e-mail opca@campinginontario.ca; internet www.campgrounds.org; Exec. Dir BETH POTTER.

Ontario Snow Resorts Association: 125 Napier St, POB 575, Collingwood, ON L9Y 4E8; tel. (705) 443-5450; fax (705) 443-5460; e-mail osra@skiontario.on.ca; internet www.skiontario.on.ca; Exec. Dir BRUCE HAYNES.

Ontario Tourism Marketing Partnership Corpn: Hearst Block, 10th Floor, 900 Bay St, Toronto, ON M7A 2E1; fax (416) 314-7574; e-mail info@tourismpartners.com; internet www.tourismpartners.com; f. 1999; govt agency in partnership with Ontario tourism operators; Chair. WILLIAM M. DURON.

Resorts of Ontario: 29 Albert St North, Orillia, ON L3V 5J9; tel. (705) 325-9115; fax (705) 325-7999; e-mail escapes@resortsofontario.com; internet www.resorts-ontario.com; Man. Dir GRACE CERNIUK.

Tourism Industry Association of Ontario: 40 Holly St, Toronto, ON M4S 3C3; tel. (519) 856-0818; e-mail bill.allen@wragroup.ca; internet www.tiao.travel; f. 1996 as Tourism Federation of Ontario, name changed as above in March 2007; umbrella org. for the 28 not-for-profit asscns serving Ontario's tourism industry; Pres. BILL ALLEN.

Tourism Toronto: Queen's Quay Terminal, 207 Queen's Quay West, POB 126, Toronto, ON M5J 1A7; tel. (416) 203-2600; fax (416) 203-6753; e-mail toronto@torcvb.com; internet www.torontotourism.com; Pres. and CEO DAVID WHITAKER; Chair. CHARLES CUTTS.

Prince Edward Island

The tourism industry, although small by comparison with Canada's larger provinces, plays an important role in the economic life of Prince Edward Island, where it is the second largest industry. The island's coastline is 1,800 km long and there are many sandy beaches. Prince Edward Island National Park, which occupies the north-central part of the shoreline, is a principal tourist attraction, with sand dunes, red sandstone cliffs and fishing villages. The Confederation Trail has been developed for hikers and cyclists, while deep-sea fishing, kayaking, canoeing and golf are popular recreational activities. In winter the province offers opportunities for snowmobiling and skiing. The home of the author L. M. Montgomery is located in the National Park and the province has several other attractions associated with the author. There are 25 provincial parks, 11 of which offer camping facilities. A number of historic sites, such as Province House in Charlottetown, have been developed as tourist attractions. The Confederation Bridge, opened in 1997, links the province to New Brunswick and is the longest continuous marine span bridge in the world. International overnight visitation to the province was estimated at 166,500 visits in 2007.

Department of Tourism: Shaw Bldg, 3rd Floor North, 95 Rochford St, POB 2000, Charlottetown, PE C1A 7N8; tel. (902) 368-4444; fax (902) 368-5277; e-mail island@gov.pe.ca; internet www.tourismpei.com; Minister VALERIE E. DOCHERTY.

Tourism Charlottetown and the Prince Edward Island Convention Partnership: 91 Water St, POB 972, Charlottetown, PE C1A 4B3; fax (902) 892-5486; e-mail info@seasidesocial.com; internet www.seasidesocial.com; CEO KIM GREEN.

Tourism Industry Association of Prince Edward Island: 25 Queen St, 3rd Floor, POB 2050, Charlottetown, PE C1A 7N7; tel. (902) 566-5008; fax (902) 368-3605; e-mail tiapei@tiapei.pe.ca; internet www.tiapei.pe.ca; Pres. ADAM DOIRON; Exec. Dir DON CUDMORE.

Québec

Perhaps the most distinctive aspect of Québec is the predominance of French Canadians, dating from the French settlement of the area in the 17th century. There are three national parks within the province: Forillon, at the eastern tip of the Gaspé Peninsula, has rugged cliffs and is noted for its sea birds; the Mingan Archipelago, on the northern side of the St Lawrence River, is known for its sea birds as well as sea plants; La Mauricie, a hilly area between Montréal and Québec City, with woods and lakes, offers opportunities for fishing and skiing. In addition, the Sagueney-St Lawrence National Marine Park features a fjord and a large amount of wildlife. Fishing and hunting (of deer, caribou, moose and black bear) are very popular outdoor pursuits in Québec, with snowmobiling also increasing in popularity. Provincial and regional parks, of which there are 50 (including wilderness preserves, hunting and fishing preserves and salmon streams), cover a larger area than in any other province, at 71,000 sq km. The province's cities also attract large numbers of tourists. Montréal is the second-largest French-speaking city in the world, after Paris, with architecture both modern and, in Vieux Montréal, traditional. It is also popular among visitors for shopping and for its large casino, while the Olympic Park and stadium receive many visits. Québec City's architecture and cultural heritage have been affected remarkably little by modern business life and it has been designated a UNESCO World Heritage Treasure. Québec City has a number of museums, including the Musée du Québec and the Musée de la civilisation and hosts a jazz and blues festival in the summer. International overnight visitation to Québec was estimated at 3,040,700 visits in 2007.

Association des camps du Québec: 4545 ave Pierre-de-Coubertin, CP 1000, Succursale M, Montréal, QC H1V 3R2; tel. (514) 252-3113; fax (514) 252-1650; e-mail info@camps.qc.ca; internet www.camps.qc.ca; f. 1961; 125 mem. camps for children.

Association of Canadian Travel Agencies—ACTA (Québec): POB 599, St Lazare, QC J7T 2Z7; tel. (450) 455-9916; fax (450) 455-4677; e-mail pmartinet@acta.travel; internet www.acta.ca; Gen. Dir. PATRICK MARTINET; Regional Chair. MOUSCOU CÔTÉ.

Association des hôteliers du Québec/Hotel Association of Quebec: 425 blvd de Maisonneuve ouest, bureau 1004, Montréal, QC H3A 3G5; tel. (514) 448-6215; fax (514) 849-1157; e-mail info@

hoteliersquebec.org; internet www.hoteliersquebec.org; f. 1949; Gen. Man. DANIELLE CHAYER.

Camping Québec: 2001 de la Métropole St, Bureau 700, Longueuil, QC J4G 1S9; tel. (514) 651-7396; fax (514) 651-7397; e-mail atcq@campingquebec.com; internet www.campingquebec.com; Pres. MICHAEL HEALEY.

Canadian Institute of Travel Counsellors—CITC (Québec): tel. (514) 335-7655; fax (514) 335-7166; e-mail pmorrissette@vision2000.com; internet www.citc.ca; Regional Chair. FRANÇOIS PATRICE DÉNOMMÉE.

Fédération des agricotours du Québec: 4545 ave Pierre-de-Coubertin, CP 1000, Succursale M, Montréal, QC H1V 3R2; tel. (514) 252-3138; fax (514) 252-3173; e-mail www.agricotours.qc.ca; internet www.agricotours.qc.ca; Pres. PIERRE PILON.

Institut de tourisme et d'hôtellerie du Québec: 3535 rue St Denis, Montréal, QC H2X 3P1; tel. (514) 282-5120; fax (514) 873-9893; e-mail hotel@ithq.qc.ca; internet www.ithq.qc.ca; f. 1968; govt-owned training institute; Dir-Gen. LUCILLE DAOUST.

Ministry of Sustainable Development, Environment and Parks/Ministère du Développement durable, de l'environnement et des parcs: Edif. Marie-Guyart, 29e étage, 675 blvd René-Lévesque est, Québec, QC G1R 5V7; tel. (418) 521-3830; fax (418) 646 5974; e-mail info@mddep.gouv.qc.ca; internet www.mddep.gouv.qc.ca; Minister LINE BEAUCHAMP.

Ministry of Tourism/Tourisme Québec: 900 blvd René-Lévesque est, Bureau 400, Québec, QC G1R 2B5; tel. (418) 643-5959; fax (418) 646-8723; e-mail info@bonjourquebec.com; internet www.bonjourquebec.com; Minister RAYMOND BACHAND.

Office du tourisme de Québec: 399 rue de Saint-Joseph est, Québec, QC G1K 8E2; tel. (418) 641-6654; fax (418) 641-6578; e-mail pierre.labrie@quebecregion.com; internet www.quebecregion.com; Gen. Man. PIERRE LABRIE.

Tourisme Montréal: POB 979, Montréal, QC H3C 2W3; tel. (514) 873-2015; fax (514) 864-3838; e-mail info@tourisme.gouv.qc.ca; internet www.tourisme-montreal.org; Pres. and CEO CHARLES LAPOINTE.

Saskatchewan

Saskatchewan has many lakes and rivers and outdoor pursuits associated with these, particularly fishing, are popular. Camping, hiking and cross-country skiing are other attractions, which can be pursued in some of the 34 provincial parks (which cover a total area of 9,080 sq km). Visits to mineral spas are also popular among tourists. The province has two national parks: Grasslands, on the southern border with Montana (USA), preserves an area of original short-grass prairie; Prince Albert National Park, in central Saskatchewan, has glacial lakes and other glacial landmarks, in addition to forests and prairie grasslands. This park is particularly rich in wildlife, including elk, moose, caribou, wolves and beavers. The noted conservationist, Archibald Belaney ('Grey Owl'), had close associations with the park. The province contains many historical attractions, including Wanuskewin, a National Heritage Park comprising prehistoric sites, Teepee Village and the four Western Development museums. International overnight visitation to Saskatchewan was estimated at 204,000 visits in 2007.

Association of Canadian Travel Agencies—ACTA (Saskatchewan): 700-177 Lombard Ave, Winnipeg, MB R3B 0W5; tel. (204) 831-0831; fax (204) 925-8000; e-mail smmorris@mts.net; internet www.acta.ca; Regional Man. SHELLEY MORRIS; Regional Chair. SHARON KAENDO.

Canadian Institute of Travel Counsellors—CITC (Saskatchewan): POB 22012, Wildwood Mall, Saskatoon, SK S7H 5P1; tel. (306) 665-5577; fax (306) 653-1808; e-mail lmbray@shaw.ca; internet www.citc.ca; Regional Chair. LISA BRAY; 70 mem. orgs, 30 assoc. orgs, 20 student orgs.

Department of Culture, Youth and Recreation: 1919 Saskatchewan Dr., 4th Floor, Regina, SK S4P 3V7; tel. (306) 787-5729; fax (306) 798-0033; e-mail info@cyr.gov.sk.ca; internet www.cyr.gov.sk.ca; Minister SANDRA MORIN.

Saskatchewan Bed and Breakfast Association: Box 694, Lumsden, SK S0G 3C0; tel. (306) 731-2646; fax (306) 731-2768; e-mail bbsask@canada.com; internet www.bbsask.ca; Pres. ANNETTE DUBÉ; Exec. Dir BRYAN TUDOR.

Saskatchewan Hotel and Hospitality Association (SHHA): 2080 Broad St, Suite 302, Regina, SK S4P 1Y3; tel. (306) 522-1664; fax (306) 525-1944; e-mail lorane.has@sasktel.net; internet www.hotelsofsask.com; fmrly Hotels Asscn of Saskatchewan; Pres. and CEO TOM MULLIN.

Saskatchewan Outfitters Association: 3700 Second Ave West, Prince Albert, SK S6W 1A2; tel. (306) 763-5434; fax (306) 922-6044; e-mail soa@sasktel.net; internet www.soa.ca; Exec. Dir HAL STUPNIKOFF.

Saskatchewan Parks and Facilities: Environment and Resource Management, 3211 Albert St, Regina, SK S4S 5W6; tel. (306) 787-2846; fax (306) 787-7000; e-mail inquiry@serm.gov.sk.ca; internet www.se.gov.sk.ca; Minister JOHN NILSON.

Tourism Regina: Hwy 1 East, POB 3355, Regina, SK S4P 3H1; tel. (306) 789-5099; fax (306) 789-3171; e-mail info@tourismregina.com; internet www.tourismregina.com; Exec. Dir STEPHEN MCLELLAN.

Tourism Saskatchewan: 1922 Park St, Regina, SK S4N 7M4; tel. (306) 787-9600; fax (306) 787-0715; e-mail travel.info@sasktourism.com; internet www.sasktourism.com; Pres. and CEO Dr LYNDA HAVERSTOCK.

Tourism Saskatoon: 305 Idylwyld Dr. North, Suite 6, Saskatoon, SK S7L 0Z1; tel. (306) 242-1206; fax (306) 242-1955; e-mail info@tourismsaskatoon.com; internet www.tourismsaskatoon.com; Exec. Dir TODD BRANDT.

Yukon Territory

Tourism is vital to the economy of the Yukon Territory, because of the vulnerability of the other economic mainstay, mining, to international commodity market conditions. Mining itself, through the Klondike Gold Rush of the late 19th and early 20th centuries, created one of the territory's principal tourist attractions. Dawson City has many reconstructed buildings from the gold-rush period and the US and Canadian national parks services worked together to develop the Klondike Gold Rush International Historical Park. Much tourism trade is derived from visitors passing through the territory to or from Alaska (USA). The Yukon Territory has three national parks: Kluane, in the south-east corner bordering Alaska and British Columbia, is a largely glaciated area containing the highest point in Canada, Mount Logan (5,959 m); Vuntut and Ivvavik National Parks are located in the north of the territory and contain a large amount of protected wildlife, including caribou, grizzly, black and polar bears, and waterfowl. International overnight visitation to Yukon Territory was estimated at 301,200 visits in 2007.

Department of Tourism and Culture: Tourism and Culture Centre, 100 Hanson St, POB 2703, Whitehorse, YT Y1A 2C6; tel. (867) 667-5036; fax (867) 667-3546; internet www.tc.gov.yk.ca; Minister ELAINE TAYLOR.

Klondike Visitors' Association: POB 389C, Dawson City, YT Y0B 1G0; tel. (867) 993-5575; fax (867) 993-6415; e-mail kva@dawson.net; internet www.dawsoncity.ca; f. 1959; Contact D'ARCY BUTLER.

Parks Branch: POB 2703, Whitehorse, YT Y1A 2C6; tel. (867) 667-5648; fax (867) 393-6223; e-mail yukonparks@gov.yk.ca; internet www.environmentyukon.gov.yk.ca/parks/index.html.

Tourism Industry Association of the Yukon: 1109 First Ave, Suite 3, Whitehorse, YT Y1A 5G4; tel. (867) 668-3331; fax (867) 667-7379; e-mail tiayukon@klondiker.com; internet www.tiayukon.com; Chair. ROD TAYLOR.

Yukon Outfitters' Association: 302 Steele St, Whitehorse, YT Y1A 2C5; tel. 668-4118; fax 668-4120; e-mail info@yukonoutfitters.net; internet www.yukonoutfitters.net.

NATIONAL PARKS

Aulavik: POB 29, Sachs Harbour, NT X0E 0Z0; tel. (867) 690-3904; fax (867) 690-4808; e-mail inuvik.info@pc.gc.ca; internet www.pc.gc.ca/aulavik.

Auyuittuq: POB 353, Pangnirtung, NU X0A 0R0; tel. (867) 473-2500; fax (867) 473-8612; e-mail nunavut.info@pc.gc.ca; internet www.pc.gc.ca/auyuittuq; f. 1976.

Banff: POB 900, Banff, AB T1L IK2; tel. (403) 762-1550; fax (403) 762-3380; e-mail banff.vrc@ph.gc.ca; internet www.pc.gc.ca/banff; f. 1885.

Bruce Peninsula: POB 189, Tobermory, ON N0H 2R0; tel. (519) 596-2233; fax (519) 596-2298; e-mail bruce-fathomfive@pc.gc.ca; internet www.pc.gc.ca/bruce; f. 1987; Supt IVAN SMITH.

Cape Breton Highlands: Ingonish Beach, Cape Breton, NS B0C 1L0; tel. (902) 224-2306; fax (902) 285-2866; e-mail information@pc.gc.ca; internet www.pc.gc.ca/pn-np/ns/cbreton; f. 1936; Supt TIM REYNOLDS.

Elk Island: Site 4, RR 1, Fort Saskatchewan, AB T8L 2N7; tel. (780) 992-2950; fax (780) 992-2983; e-mail elk.island@pc.gc.ca; internet www.pc.gc.ca/elkisland; f. 1906; Supt MARILYN PECKETT.

Forillon: 122 Gaspé Blvd, Gaspé, QC G4X 1A9; tel. (418) 368-5505; fax (418) 368-6837; e-mail parkscanada-que@pc.gc.ca; internet www.pc.gc.ca/forillon; f. 1970; Dir STÉPHANE MARCHAND.

Fundy: POB 1001, Alma, NB E4H 1B4; tel. (506) 887-6000; fax (506) 887-6008; e-mail fundy.info@pc.gc.ca; internet www.pc.gc.ca/fundy; f. 1948.

Georgian Bay Islands: 901 Wye Valley Rd, POB 9, Midland, ON L4R 4K6; tel. (705) 526-9804; fax (705) 526-5939; e-mail info.gbi@pc.gc.ca; internet www.pc.gc.ca/georgianbay; f. 1929.

Glacier: POB 350, Revelstoke, BC V0E 2S0; tel. (250) 837-7500; fax (250) 837-7536; e-mail revglacier.reception@pc.gc.ca; internet www.pc.gc.ca/glacier; f. 1886.

Grasslands: Box 150, Val Marie, SK S0N 2T0; tel. (306) 298-2257; fax (306) 298-2042; e-mail grasslands.info@pc.gc.ca; internet www.pc.gc.ca/grasslands; f. 1988.

Gros Morne: POB 130, Rocky Harbour, NL A0K 4N0; tel. (709) 458-2417; fax (709) 458-2059; e-mail grosmorne.info@pc.gc.ca; internet www.pc.gc.ca/grosmorne; f. 1973.

Gulf Islands: 2220 Harbour Rd, Sidney, BC V8L 2P6; tel. (250) 654-4000; fax (250) 654-4014; e-mail gulf.islands@pc.gc.ca; internet www.pc.gc.ca/gulfislands; f. 2003.

Gwaii Haanas (National Park Reserve and Haida Heritage Site): POB 37, Queen Charlotte, BC V0T 1S0; tel. (250) 559-8818; fax (250) 559-8366; e-mail gwaii.haanas@pc.gc.ca; internet www.pc.gc.ca/gwaiihaanas; f. 1987 (fmrly South Moresby National Reserve).

Ivvavik: Western Arctic Field Unit, POB 1840, Inuvik, NT X0E 0T0; tel. (867) 777-8800; fax (867) 777-8820; e-mail inuvik.info@pc.gc.ca; internet www.pc.gc.ca/ivvavik; f. 1984 (fmrly Northern Yukon National Park).

Jasper: POB 10, Jasper, AB T0E 1E0; tel. (780) 852-6176; fax (780) 852-6152; e-mail pnj.jnp@pc.gc.ca; internet www.pc.gc.ca/jasper; f. 1907.

Kejimkujik: POB 236, Maitland Bridge, NS B0T 1B0; tel. (902) 682-2772; fax (902) 682-3367; e-mail kejimkujik.info@pc.gc.ca; internet www.pc.gc.ca/kejimkujik; f. 1969; Operational Supt H. S. DELONG.

Kluane: POB 5495, Haines Junction, YT Y0B 1L0; tel. (867) 634-7250; fax (867) 634-7208; e-mail kluane.info@pc.gc.ca; internet www.pc.gc.ca/kluane; f. 1972.

Kootenay: POB 220, Radium Hot Springs, BC V0A 1M0; tel. (250) 347-9505; fax (250) 347-9980; e-mail kootenay.info@pc.gc.ca; internet www.pc.gc.ca/kootenay; f. 1920.

Kouchibouguac: 186 Route 117, Kouchibouguac National Park, NB E4X 2P1; tel. (506) 876-2443; fax (506) 876-4802; e-mail kouch.info@pc.gc.ca; internet www.pc.gc.ca/kouchibouguac; f. 1969; Man., Visitor Services/Heritage Presentation MICHEL BUJOLD.

La Mauricie: 702 Fifth St, POB 160, Shawinigan, QC G9N 6T9; tel. (819) 538-3232; fax (819) 536-3661; e-mail parcscanada-que@pc.gc.ca; internet www.pc.gc.ca/mauricie; f. 1970.

Mingan Archipelago: 1340 de la Digue St, Havre-Saint-Pierre, QC G0G 1P0; tel. (418) 538-3331; fax (418) 538-3595; e-mail parcscanada-que@pc.gc.ca; internet www.pc.gc.ca/pn-np/qc/mingan; f. 1984; Dir PIERRE KAVANAGH.

Mount Revelstoke: POB 350, Revelstoke, BC V0E 2S0; tel. (250) 837-7500; fax (250) 837-7536; e-mail revglacier.reception@pc.gc.ca; internet www.pc.gc.ca/revelstoke; f. 1914.

Nahanni: POB 348, Fort Simpson, NT X0E 0N0; tel. (867) 695-3151; fax (867) 695-2446; e-mail nahanni.info@pc.gc.ca; internet www.pc.gc.ca/nahanni; f. 1972.

Pacific Rim: POB 280, 2185 Ocean Terrace Rd, Ucluelet, BC V0R 3A0; tel. (250) 726-3500; fax (250) 726-3520; e-mail pacrim.info@pc.gc.ca; internet www.pc.gc.ca/pacificrim; f. 1971; Supt KIM SEWARD-HANNAM.

Point Pelee: 407 Monarch Lane, RR 1, Leamington, ON N8H 3V4; tel. (519) 322-2365; fax (519) 322-1277; e-mail pelee.info@pc.gc.ca; internet www.pc.gc.ca/pointpelee; f. 1918; Supt MARIAN STRANAK.

Prince Albert: Northern Prairies Field Unit, POB 100, Waskesiu Lake, SK S0J 2Y0; tel. (306) 663-4522; e-mail panp.info@pc.gc.ca; internet www.pc.gc.ca/princealbert; f. 1927; Supt KEVIN VAN TIGHEM.

Prince Edward Island: 2 Palmers Lane, Charlottetown, PE C1A 5V6; tel. (902) 672-6350; fax (902) 672-6370; e-mail pnipe.peinp@pc.gc.ca; internet www.pc.gc.ca/pei; f. 1937.

Pukaskwa: POB 212, Heron Bay, ON P0T 1R0; tel. (807) 229-0801; fax (807) 229-2097; e-mail ont-pukaskwa@pc.gc.ca; internet www.pc.gc.ca/pukaskwa; f. 1983.

Quttinirpaaq (Ellesmere Island): POB 278, Iqaluit, NU X0A 0H0; tel. (867) 975-4673; fax (867) 975-4674; e-mail nunavut.info@pc.gc.ca; internet www.pc.gc.ca/quttinirpaaq; f. 1986.

Riding Mountain: Wasagaming, MB R0J 2H0; tel. (204) 848-7275; fax (204) 848-2596; e-mail rmnp.info@pc.gc.ca; internet www.pc.gc.ca/riding; f. 1933; Supt GREG FENTON.

Sirmilik: POB 300, Pond Inlet, NU X0A 0S0; tel. (867) 899-8092; fax (867) 899-8104; e-mail sirmilik.info@pc.gc.ca; internet www.pc.gc.ca/sirmilik.

St Lawrence Islands: 2 County Rd, Suite 5, RR3, Mallorytown, ON K0E 1R0; tel. (613) 923-5261; fax (613) 923-1021; e-mail ont-sli@pc.gc.ca; internet www.pc.gc.ca/sli; f. 1904.

Terra Nova: General Delivery, Glovertown, NL A0G 2L0; tel. (709) 533-2801; fax (709) 533-2706; e-mail info.tnnp@pc.gc.ca; internet www.pc.gc.ca/terranova; f. 1957.

Torngat Mountains (National Park Reserve): POB 471, Nain, NL A0P 1L0; tel. (709) 922-1290; fax (709) 922-1294; e-mail torngats.info@pc.gc.ca; internet www.pc.gc.ca/pn-np/nl/torngats; expected to attain national park status in 2008.

Tuktut Nogait: POB 91, Paulatuk, NT X0E 1N0; tel. (867) 580-3233; fax (867) 580-3234; e-mail inuvik.info@pc.gc.ca; internet www.pc.gc.ca/tuktutnogait.

Ukkusiksalik: POB 220, Repulse Bay, NU X0C 0H0; tel. (867) 462-4500; fax (867) 462-4095; e-mail ukkusiksalikinfo@pc.gc.ca; internet www.pc.gc.ca/pn-np/nu/ukkusiksalik; f. 2003.

Vuntut: General Delivery, Old Crow, YT Y0B 1N0; tel. (867) 667-3910; fax (867) 966-3432; e-mail brenda.frost-charlie@pc.gc.ca; internet www.pc.gc.ca/vuntut; Community Liaison Officer BRENDA FROST-CHARLIE.

Wapusk: POB 127, Churchill, MB R0B 0E0; tel. (204) 675-8863; fax (204) 675-2026; e-mail wapusk.np@pc.gc.ca; internet www.pc.gc.ca/wapusk; Supt CAM ELLIOTT.

Waterton Lakes: Waterton Park, POB 200, AB T0K 2M0; tel. (403) 859-2224; fax (403) 859-2650; e-mail waterton.info@pc.gc.ca; internet www.pc.gc.ca/waterton; f. 1885; Supt ROD BLAIR.

Wood Buffalo: POB 750, Fort Smith, NT X0E 0P0; tel. (867) 872-7900; fax (867) 872-3910; e-mail wbnp.info@pc.gc.ca; internet www.pc.gc.ca/buffalo; f. 1922; CEO ALAN LATOURELLE.

Yoho: POB 99, Field, BC V0A 1G0; tel. (250) 343-6783; fax (250) 343-6012; e-mail yoho.info@pc.gc.ca; internet www.pc.gc.ca/yoho; f. 1886.

EXTERNAL TRADE

Principal Commodities

(Source: Statistics Canada.)

IMPORTS F.O.B.
(C $ million)

	2005	2006	2007
Agricultural and fishing products	22,040.1	23,454.1	25,496.2
Fruits and vegetables	6,396.9	6,698.9	7,241.2
Other agricultural and fishing products	15,643.2	16,755.3	18,254.8
Energy products	33,668.8	34,628.4	36,568.9
Crude petroleum	21,581.9	22,562.0	23,670.5
Other energy products	12,086.9	12,066.4	12,898.4
Forestry products	3,134.0	3,083.9	2,995.0
Industrial goods and materials	78,578.4	84,015.6	85,132.3
Metals and metal ores	23,985.4	28,157.3	28,761.3
Chemicals and plastics	28,672.2	29,758.5	30,184.8
Other industrial goods and materials	25,920.8	26,099.8	26,186.2
Machinery and equipment	110,921.6	114,655.7	116,632.1
Industrial and agricultural machinery	29,714.4	31,759.8	31,555.7
Aircraft and other transportation equipment	14,951.3	14,783.3	16,581.5
Office machines and equipment	15,947.7	15,967.1	15,029.1
Other machinery and equipment	50,308.2	52,145.5	53,465.8
Automotive products	78,383.7	79,849.8	80,002.0
Passenger autos and chassis	23,478.8	25,146.4	26,274.2
Trucks and other motor vehicles	15,290.7	16,767.5	17,496.8
Motor vehicle parts	39,614.2	37,935.9	36,231.0
Other consumer goods	49,488.0	52,021.7	54,793.9
Apparel and footwear	9,432.3	10,048.7	10,591.2
Miscellaneous consumer goods	40,055.7	41,973.0	44,202.7
Special transactions trade	4,649.6	4,771.3	5,192.1
Unallocated adjustments	6,939.9	7,772.2	8,192.9
Total	387,804.0	404,252.6	415,005.7

EXPORTS F.O.B.
(C $ million)

	2005	2006	2007
Agricultural and fishing products	30,096.8	31,210.3	34,370.3
Wheat	2,697.2	3,609.2	4,637.4
Other agricultural and fishing products	27,399.6	27,601.1	29,732.9
Energy products	86,962.4	86,788.9	91,647.3
Crude petroleum	30,418.3	38,574.6	40,997.6
Natural gas	35,988.6	27,804.7	28,377.6
Other energy products	20,555.5	20,409.6	22,272.1
Forestry products	36,447.8	33,331.4	29,263.2
Lumber and sawmill products	18,788.1	16,158.6	12,613.3
Wood pulp and other wood products	5,830.4	6,141.6	6,685.0
Newsprint and other paper and paperboard products	11,829.3	11,031.2	9,964.9
Industrial goods and materials	83,963.6	93,905.5	104,420.9
Metals and metal ores	8,772.6	11,347.7	14,405.4
Chemicals, plastics and fertilizers	29,919.5	30,600.4	33,191.0
Metals and alloys	27,122.2	33,928.9	38,225.7
Other industrial goods and materials	18,149.3	18,028.5	18,598.8
Machinery and equipment	93,005.1	93,271.5	93,428.3
Industrial and agricultural machinery	19,941.3	20,549.7	22,329.3
Aircraft and other transportation equipment	19,794.7	20,159.8	20,897.4
Other machinery and equipment	53,269.1	52,562.0	50,201.6
Automotive products	87,994.5	82,298.3	77,304.4
Passenger autos and chassis	44,593.0	42,372.8	39,995.9
Trucks and other motor vehicles	16,168.6	14,966.5	13,021.1
Motor vehicle parts	27,232.9	25,959.0	24,287.4
Other consumer goods	17,147.7	17,810.5	18,736.7
Special transactions trade	8,288.2	8,732.4	8,175.9
Unallocated adjustments	6,243.6	6,383.6	5,704.4
Total	450,149.9	453,732.4	463,051.4

Principal Trading Partners

(Source: Statistics Canada.)

IMPORTS F.O.B.
(C $ million)

	2005	2006	2007
USA*	259,348.2	265,023.0	269,752.5
Japan	11,210.8	11,858.3	11,972.3
United Kingdom	9,061.2	9,549.2	9,894.3
Other European Union countries	29,457.0	32,529.8	32,402.9
Other OECD	24,304.5	23,673.3	25,034.2
Other countries	54,422.3	61,618.9	65,949.4
Total	387,804.0	404,252.6	415,005.7

EXPORTS F.O.B.
(C $ million)

	2005	2006	2007
USA*	368,414.7	361,440.4	356,094.2
Japan	10,168.2	10,279.2	9,989.2
United Kingdom	9,355.4	11,281.2	14,154.8
Other European Union countries	18,630.6	20,900.2	24,187.0
Other OECD	14,528.0	16,773.9	19,690.5
Other countries	29,052.9	33,057.6	38,935.8
Total	450,149.9	453,732.4	463,051.4

* Including Puerto Rico and US Virgin Is.

External Trade Organizations

Association for the Export of Canadian Books (AECB/AELC): 1 Nicholas St, Suite 504, Ottawa, ON K1N 7B7; tel. (613) 562-2324; fax (613) 562-2329; e-mail aecb@aecb.org; internet www.aecb.org; f. 1972; Chair. PHILIP CERCONE; Exec. Dir SUZANNE BOSSÉ.

Canada Beef Export Federation: 6715 Eighth St, NE, Suite 235, Calgary, AB T2E 7H7; tel. (403) 274-0005; fax (403) 274-7275; e-mail canada@cbef.com; internet www.cbef.com; f. 1989; Pres. TED HANEY; Chair. GIB DRURY.

Canadian Association of Fish Exporters: 1770 Woodward Dr., Suite 212, Ottawa, ON K2C 0P8; tel. (613) 228-9220; fax (613) 228-9223; f. 1978; Pres. Dr JANE BARNETT.

Canadian Association of Importers and Exporters (I. E. Canada): 160 Eglinton Ave East, Suite 300, Toronto, ON M4P 3B5; tel. (416) 595-5333; fax (416) 595-8226; e-mail info@iecanada.com; internet www.iecanada.com; f. 1932 as the Canadian Importers and Traders Asscn; name changed as above in 2000; Chair. ISABEL ALEXANDER; Pres. and CEO MARY ANDERSON; 650 mem. cos.

Canadian Association of Regulated Importers: 2525 St Laurent Blvd, Suite 203, Ottawa, ON K1H 8P5; tel. (613) 738-1729; fax (613) 733-9501; e-mail devalkc@magma.ca; internet www.cariimport.org; f. 1986; 67 mems; Chair. LUCKY BILKHU; Gen. Man. ROBERT G. DE VALK.

Canadian Fair Trade Association: 774 Blvd St Joseph, Suite 2, Gatineau, QC J8Y 4B9; tel. (819) 595-1424; fax (819) 595-4702; e-mail info@fair-trade.ca; internet www.fair-trade.ca; Pres. FRANCISCO LANZAS.

Canadian Federation of Trading House Associations: 15 pl. du Vésinet, Montréal, QC H2V 2L7; tel. (514) 844-3959; fax (514) 586-4007; e-mail info@caftha.ca; internet www.caftha.ca; f. 1996; Pres. EMMANUEL KAMPOURIS; Exec. Dir KARL MIVILLE-DE-CHÊNE; three mems.

Canadian Manufacturers and Exporters: 1 Nicholas St, Suite 1500, Ottawa, ON K1N 7B7; tel. (613) 238-8888; fax (613) 563-9218; e-mail janet.boden@cme-mec.ca; internet www.cme-mec.ca; f. 1871 as the Ontario Manufacturers' Asscn, later renamed the Canadian Manufacturers' Asscn; merged with the Canadian Exporters' Asscn in 1943 to form the Alliance of Manufacturers and Exporters Canada; present name adopted in 2000; Chair. DAVID T. FUNG; Pres. JAYSON MYERS; Gen. Man. JACK RADFORD; 3,500 mems.

Foreign Chambers of Commerce in Canada

Asia Pacific Foundation of Canada: 890 West Pender St, Suite 220, Vancouver, BC V6C 1J9; tel. (604) 684-5986; fax (604) 681-1370; e-mail info@asiapacific.ca; internet www.asiapacific.ca; f. 1984; Chair. JOHN H. MCARTHUR; Pres. and CEO WOO YUEN PAU.

Belgian-Canadian Business Association: 161 Bay St, 27th Floor, POB 508, Toronto, ON M5J 2S1; tel. (416) 572-2345; fax (416) 572-2201; e-mail pboutquin@belgium-canada.ca; internet www.belgium-canada.ca; f. 1979; Pres. BARRY WEIGHEL; Treas. ELLY DE WINNE.

British-Canadian Chamber of Trade and Commerce: POB 1358, Station K, Toronto, ON M4P 3J4; tel. (416) 502-0847; fax (416) 502-9319; e-mail central@bcctc.ca; internet www.bcctc.ca; f. 1951; Pres. DAVID KINGSLAND.

Canada-Arab Business Council: 357 Bay St, Suite 600, Toronto, ON M5H 2T7; tel. (416) 362-0050; fax (416) 362-7633; e-mail info@canada-arabbusiness.org; internet www.canada-arabbusiness.org; f. 1983; Chair. and CEO J. HUGH O'DONNELL; Dirs-Gen. RICHARD MANN, DAVID HUTTON; 87 mems.

Canada China Business Council: 100 Adelaide St West, Suite 407, Toronto, ON M5H 1S3; tel. (416) 954-3800; fax (416) 954-3806; e-mail ccbc@ccbc.com; internet www.ccbc.com; f. 1978; Chair. PETER KRUYT; Exec. Dir SARAH KUTULAKOS; 284 mems.

Canada-Czech Republic Chamber of Commerce and Czech-North American Chamber of Commerce: POB 163, Station A, Etobicoke, ON M9C 4V3; tel. (416) 559-2868; fax (289) 232-1352; e-mail admin@ccrcc.net; internet www.ccrcc.net; f. 1994; covers Canada, Mexico and the USA; Pres. MIROSLAV PRINC.

Canada Eurasia Energy and Industry Alliance (CEEIA): Guinness House, Suite 1400, 727 Seventh Ave, SW, Calgary, AB T2P OZ5; tel. (403) 218-4822; fax (403) 218-8727; f. 1995; Exec. Dir DENNIS GORESKY; 43 mems.

Canada-Finland Chamber of Commerce: c/o Finnish Credit Union, 191 Eglinton Ave East, Toronto, ON M4P 1K1; tel. (416) 486-1533; fax (416) 486-1592; e-mail info@canadafinlandcc.com; internet www.canadafinlandcc.com; f. 1971; Pres. TUULA KIVINEN.

Canada-India Business Council: 1 St Clair Ave East, Suite 1004, Toronto, ON M4T 2V7; tel. (416) 214-5947; fax (416) 214-9081; e-mail info@canada-indiabusiness.ca; internet www.canada-indiabusiness.ca; f. 1982; Chair. ROY MACLAREN; Pres. and Exec. Dir KAM RATHEE.

Canada-Japan Business Association (CJBA): 10303 Jasper Ave, Edmonton, AB T5J 3N6; tel. (780) 428-0501; fax (780) 429-2559; e-mail jcoombs@wittenlaw.com; Pres. JONATHAN COOMBS.

Canada-Korea Business Association: 2420 Dollarton Hwy, Vancouver, BC V7H 2Y1; tel. (604) 688-3768; fax (604) 688-9684; e-mail yena.h@ciscanada.net; internet www.ckba.org; f. 1972; Pres. ROBERT FAIRWEATHER; 100 mems.

Canada-Pakistan Business Council: 7825 Bayview Ave, Suite 1311, Thornhill, ON L3T 7N2; tel. (905) 763-8281; fax (905) 763-8104; e-mail cpbc@rogers.com; internet www.cpbc.info; f. 1981; Chair. DOUGLAS BARKER; Pres. ANWAR (ANDY) MERCHANT.

Canada Philippines Business Council: 116 Albert St, Suite 814, Ottawa, ON K1P 5G3; tel. (613) 566-7045; fax (613) 566-7086; e-mail asn@anatividad.ca; internet www.canphil.com; f. 1995; Pres. ALICIA NATIVIDAD; 100 mems.

Canada-Poland Chamber of Commerce: 77 Stoneham Rd, Toronto, ON M9C 4Y7; tel. (416) 621-2032; e-mail info@canada-poland.com; internet www.canada-poland.com; Pres. WOJCIECH SNIEGOWSKI.

Canada-Singapore Business Association: 349 West Georgia St, POB 3727, Vancouver, BC V6B 3Z1; tel. (604) 464-0019; fax (604) 464-0872; e-mail info@csba.ca; internet www.csba.ca; Chair. BRIAN M. COLE; Pres. BETTY JO TOCCOLI.

Canada-South Africa Chamber of Business: 55 Bloor St West, POB 19553, Toronto, ON M4W 3T9; tel. (416) 588-7749; fax (416) 588-7504; e-mail bshapiro@canadasachamber.com; internet www.canadasachamber.com; f. 1994; Chair. PETER SACKS; Pres. BRUCE SHAPIRO.

Canada-Sri Lanka Business Council: B3-220 Duncan Mill Rd, Lower level, Toronto, ON M3B 3J5; tel. (416) 445-3744; fax (416) 285-8494; e-mail cslbcbiz@rogers.com; internet www.cslbcbiz.com; f. 1990; Pres. LOUISE ROBERGE.

Canada-Taiwan Trade Association: 5687 Yew St, Suite 300, Vancouver, BC V6M 3Y2; tel. (604) 263-1021; fax (604) 263-2737; e-mail ctta@uniserve.com; f. 1988; Pres. GARTH EDGAR; 100 mems.

Canada-Tunisia Chamber of Commerce: 276 rue St-Jacques, bureau 806, Montréal, QC H2Y 1N3; tel. (514) 847-1281; fax (514) 849-4910; e-mail info@cccantun.ca; internet www.cccantun.ca; Pres. ABDELJELIL OUANÈS.

Canadian Council for the Americas: POB 1227, Oakville, ON L6J 5C7; tel. (416) 367-4313; fax (416) 364-3555; e-mail cflores@cogeco.ca; internet www.ccacanada.com; f. 1987; Chair. KENNETH FRANKEL; Dir-Gen. CRISTINA FLORES; 600 mems.

Canadian-German Chamber of Industry and Commerce: 480 University Ave, Suite 1500, Toronto, ON M5G 1V2; tel. (416) 598-3355; fax (416) 598-1840; e-mail info@germanchamber.ca; internet www.germanchamber.ca; additional offices in Montréal and Vancouver; Pres. and CEO THOMAS BECK; more than 600 mems.

Canadian-Lebanese Chamber of Commerce and Industry: 4915, rue de Salaberry, Bureau 107, Montréal, QC H4J 1H8; tel. (514) 495-8000; fax (514) 495-1109; e-mail ccicl@ccicl.ca; internet www.ccicl.ca; Pres. BACHIR AZZI.

Canadian Slovenian Chamber of Commerce: 747 Browns Line, Toronto, ON M8W 3V7; tel. (416) 251-8456; fax (416) 252-2092; e-mail info@cdnslocc.ca; internet www.cdnslocc.ca; f. 1990; Pres. JOSEPH CESTNIK.

Canadian Turkish Business Council: 701-165 University Ave, Toronto, ON M5H 3B8; tel. (416) 979-1875; fax (416) 979-0825; e-mail rsvp@ctbc.ca; internet www.ctbc.ca; f. 2002; Chair. RON DENOM; 15 mems.

Chamber of Commerce Ecuador-Canada: 55 Bonniewood Rd, Toronto, ON M1K 2L9; fax (416) 751-0833; e-mail info@ccec.on.ca; internet www.ccec.on.ca; f. 1993; Chair. CÉSAR TELLO; Pres. JUAN SANTOS.

Chambre de commerce, d'industrie et du tourisme Canada-Afrique de l'Ouest et du Centre: 455 Michel-Jasmin, Dorval, QC H9P 1C2; tel. (514) 422-8800; fax (514) 422-8888; Pres. M. ASSELIN.

Chambre de commerce française au Canada: 1819 blvd René-Lévesque ouest, bureau 202, Montréal, QC H3H 2P5; tel. (514) 281-1246; fax (514) 289-9594; e-mail accueil@ccfcmtl.ca; internet www.ccfcmtl.ca; f. 1886; Pres. MYRIAM PAIRAULT; 1,500 mems.

Danish-Canadian Chamber of Commerce: 2 Bloor St West, Suite 2120, Toronto, ON MW4 3E2; tel. (416) 923-1811; fax (416) 962-3668; e-mail info@dccc.ca; internet www.dccc.ca; f. 1992; Exec. Dir K. WESTERGAARD.

European Union Chamber of Commerce in Toronto (EUCOCIT): 350 First Canadian Pl., Toronto, ON M5X 1C1; tel. (416) 816-9154; fax (416) 435-3436; e-mail info@eucocit.com; internet www.eucocit.com; f. 1995; Pres. CHRISTIAN D. FRAYSSIGNES.

Hellenic-Canadian Board of Trade: 31 Adelaide St East, POB 801, Toronto, ON M4C 2K1; tel. (416) 410-4228; e-mail president@hcbt.com; internet www.hcbt.com; Pres. GEORGE MATHEACAKIS.

Hong Kong-Canada Business Association: Hong Kong Trade Centre, 2nd Floor, 9 Temperance St, Toronto, ON M5H 1Y6; tel. (416) 366-2642; fax (416) 366-1569; e-mail nationaled@hkcba.com; internet www.hkcba.com; f. 1984; Nat. Chair. LENORE GIBSON.

Hong Kong Trade Development Council: Hong Kong Trade Centre, 1st Floor, 9 Temperance St, Toronto, ON M5H 1Y6; tel. (416) 366-3594; fax (416) 366-1569; e-mail toronto.office@tdc.org.hk; internet www.hktdc.com; f. 1966; Dir ANDREW YUI.

Hungarian-Canadian Chamber of Commerce: POB 24, Westmount, Montréal, QC H3Z 2T1; tel. and fax (514) 932-5188; e-mail info@hungariancc.ca; internet www.hungariancc.ca; f. 1988; Pres. CLAUDE LEBLANC.

Indo-Canada Chamber of Commerce (ICCC): 45 Sheppard Ave East, Suite 900, Toronto, ON M2N 5W9; tel. (416) 224-0090; fax (416) 224-0089; e-mail iccc@iccc.org; internet www.iccc.org; f. 1977; Pres. ASHA LUTHRA.

Ireland-Canada Chamber of Commerce: 705 Bourget St, Suite 105, Montréal, QC H4C 2M6; tel. (514) 845-0973; fax (514) 845-0973; e-mail contact@icccmtl.com; internet www.icccmtl.com; Pres. PAUL LOFTUS.

Israel Economic Mission: 180 Bloor St West, Toronto, ON; tel. (416) 640-8540; fax (416) 640-8546; e-mail istrade@on.aibn.com; internet www.israeltrade.gov.il; Economic Consul JONATHAN LEVY.

Italian Chamber of Commerce in Canada: 550 rue Sherbrooke ouest, Suite 1150, Montréal, QC H3A 1B9; tel. (514) 844-4249; fax (514) 844-4875; e-mail info.montreal@italchamber.qc.ca; internet www.italchamber.qc.ca; additional office in Québec City; f. 1964; Exec. Dir DANIELLE VIRONE; 60,000 mems.

Japan-Canada Chamber of Commerce: c/o Pacific Western Brewing Company, 8535 Eastlake Dr., Burnaby, BC V5C 2K8; tel. (604) 803-0660; e-mail info@jc-coc.com; internet www.jc-coc.com; Pres. GARY MATSON.

Portugal Canada Chamber of Commerce and Industry: POB 145, Station Main, Edmonton, AB T5J 2G9; tel. (780) 476-9099; fax (780) 475-6757; e-mail aurelio@canada-portugal.com; internet www.canada-portugal.com; Chair. AURÉLIO FERNANDES.

Scandinavian-Canadian Business Association: POB 201, c/o Klaes Secher, Treasurer, Asger Pedersen Insurance, 3148 Kingston Rd, Scarborough, ON M1M 1P4; tel. (416) 264-3295; fax (416) 264-0776; Treas. KLAES SECHER.

Slovak Canadian Chamber of Commerce: 1B Richview Rd, Suite 1004, Toronto, ON M9A 4M6; tel. (416) 614-0385; fax (416) 607-6840; e-mail agglo@globalserve.ca; internet www.skccc.ca; Pres. PETER L. WEINWURM; Man. Dir PAUL DZACKO.

Swedish-Canadian Chamber of Commerce (SCCC): 2 Bloor St West, Suite 2120, Toronto, ON M4W 3E2; tel. (416) 925-8661; fax (416) 929-8639; e-mail mglindmark@sccc.ca; internet www.sccc.ca; Chair. DAVE THOMPSON; Exec. Dir MONIKA G. LINDMARK.

Swiss-Canadian Chamber of Commerce (Montréal) Inc: 1572 ave du Docteur Penfield, Montréal, QC H3G 1C4; tel. (514) 937-5822; fax (514) 693-1032; e-mail info@cccsmtl.com; internet www.cccsmtl.com; additional office in Ontario; Pres. JACQUES THEVENOZ.

DIRECTORY ON SOCIETY

BROADCASTING

INTRODUCTION

In Canada radio and television services are available to over 99% of the population. In 2006 8.3m. households had cable television (65.2% of households), while 3.1m. households (24.1% of households) had a satellite dish. In that year 12.6m. households (99.0% of households) had at least one colour television.

Many privately owned television and radio stations have affiliation agreements with the Canadian Broadcasting Corporation (CBC) and help to distribute the national services. The major private television networks with affiliates are CTV (which was acquired by Bell Globemedia Inc), TVOntario (which mostly serves the province of Ontario), TQS (which serves the province of Québec) and Global Television (which serves eight provinces), as well as the educational networks.

Radio

CBC operates four national networks broadcasting on AM and FM, two each in English and French. CBC's Northern Service provides both national network programming in English and French, and special local and short-wave programmes, some of which are broadcast in the languages of the native Indian and Inuit peoples. CBC also operates a number of satellite and internet radio networks. CBC radio service, which is virtually free of commercial advertising, is within reach of 99.5% of the population. Radio Canada International, CBC's overseas short-wave service, broadcasts daily in nine languages and distributes recorded programmes free for use worldwide. In December 2006 there were 1,238 over-the-air radio services authorized to broadcast in Canada, including 76 digital outlets.

Television

The CBC operates two national free-to-air television networks, one in English and one in French. CBC's Northern Service, created in 1958, provides both radio and television service to 98% of the 90,000 inhabitants of northern Québec, the Northwest Territories, Nunavut Territory and Yukon Territory. Almost 41% of these inhabitants are native Canadians, and programming is provided in Dene and Inuktitut languages as well as English and French. Broadcast time is also made available to native groups who produce their own programmes. CBC also provides speciality services, including the CBC Newsworld network and a digital channel (Country Canada). At March 2004 CBC television was carried on 1,387 outlets. CBC television is available to approximately 99% of the English- and French-speaking population.

Canadian Satellite Communication Inc (Cancom) of Toronto, Ontario, was licensed in April 1981 by the Canadian Radio-Television and Telecommunications Commission (CRTC) to carry on a multi-channel television and radio broadcasting operation via Anik satellite for the distribution of CTV, TVA and independent television and radio programmes (one AM and nine FM radio stations) to serve remote and under-served communities. Cancom, which was renamed Shaw Satellite Services (a subsidiary of Shaw Communications Inc) in 2006, also distributes the programme output of five US television networks, via Anik satellites. The CRTC licensed a second satellite broadcaster, Star Choice, in June 1998.

CanWest Global Communications Corpn owned Global Television Network, which operates 11 stations in eight provinces, broadcasting to some 94% of the English-speaking population. CanWest also owns three local stations, CH Hamilton, CH Vancouver Island and CH Montréal.

In March 2004 there were 663 licensed cable operators. There are five educational services: TVOntario in Ontario and Radio-Québec in Québec operate their own television stations and networks; Learning and Skills Television of Alberta provides educational programming in that province; the Saskatchewan Communications Network Corpn distributes educational programming in Saskatchewan; and the Open Learning Agency (OLA) provides child and adult education by television in British Columbia.

Regulatory Body

Telecommunications services in Canada are provided by both government (federal, provincial and municipal) and private organizations. Telecommunications carriers under federal jurisdiction and the broadcasting system (radio, television, cable television and pay television) are regulated by the CRTC. The CRTC was created through the 1968 Broadcasting Act, which also established the CBC. Programming policy is to use predominantly Canadian creative and other resources. Services are operated in both English and French. In 2002 the CRTC published a regulatory framework for guiding the transition to digital television, and in 2007 it announced its intention to cease analogue transmission by 31 August 2011. By the end of 2006 it was estimated that there were almost 5.8m. digital television subscribers in Canada.

Canadian Radio-Television and Telecommunications Commission (CRTC): Ottawa, ON K1A 0N2; tel. (819) 997-0313; fax (819) 994-0218; internet www.crtc.gc.ca; f. 1968; regional offices in Dartmouth, Winnipeg and Vancouver; Chair. KONRAD VON FINCKENSTEIN; Vice-Chair. (Broadcasting) MICHAEL ARPIN; Vice-Chair. (Telecommunications) LEONARD KATZ.

Television Usage in Households

(Source: Statistics Canada, *Survey of Household Spending*.)

SUMMARY
('000 households)

	2004	2005	2006
Total households	12,343	12,587	12,756
Homes with colour television	12,239	12,467	12,629
Homes with cable television	8,182	8,226	8,311
Homes with a satellite dish	2,712	2,848	3,080

PROVINCES AND TERRITORIES
('000 households, 2006 unless otherwise indicated, estimates)

	Total households	Colour television	Cable television	Satellite dish
Alberta	1,281	1,261	783	373
British Columbia	1,708	1,678	1,310	268
Manitoba	450	441	285	105
New Brunswick	300	298	173	99
Newfoundland and Labrador	200	199	133	56
Northwest Territories*†	14	14	7	6
Nova Scotia	380	378	231	106
Nunavut*†	6	6	4	1
Ontario	4,737	4,712	3,188	1,178
Prince Edward Island	54	54	29	20
Québec	3,268	3,233	1,974	745
Saskatchewan	378	375	205	130
Yukon Territory*†	12	12	6	4

* 2005.
† Estimates for territories were designed to represent approximately 90% of the population.

RADIO AND TELEVISION

Broadcasting Networks

Canadian Broadcasting Corporation/Société Radio Canada (CBC/SRC): POB 3220, Station C, Ottawa, ON K1Y 1E4; tel. (613) 288-6000; fax (613) 724-5707; e-mail liaison@cbc.ca; internet www.cbc.radio-canada.ca; f. 1936; financed mainly by public funds, with supplementary revenue from commercial advertising on CBC Television; eight national radio and television networks, numerous regional stations and affiliates, a digital television channel (Country Canada) and music network (Galaxie); services in French, English, and eight native Canadian languages, incl. Dene and Inuktitut; production facilities and broadcast transmitters in many locations throughout Canada; Pres. and CEO HUBERT T. LACROIX; Chair. TIMOTHY W. CASGRAIN.

French Networks: 1400 blvd René-Lévesque est, CP 6000, Montréal, QC H3C 3A8; tel. (514) 597-6000; e-mail auditoire@radio-canada.ca; internet www.cbc.radio-canada.ca; Exec. Vice-Pres. SYLVAIN LAFRANCE.

Radio Canada International: 1400 blvd René-Lévesque est, Montréal, QC H2L 2M2; tel. (514) 597-7500; fax 597-7760; e-mail info@rcinet.ca; internet www.rcinet.ca; f. 1945; operates short-wave, satellite and audio internet services; broadcasts in French, English, Spanish, Arabic, Russian, Ukrainian, Mandarin, Cantonese and Portuguese; Exec. Dir JEAN LARIN.

Aboriginal Peoples Television Network (APTN): 339 Portage Ave, 2nd Floor, Winnipeg, MB R3B 2C3; tel. (204) 947-9331; fax (204) 947-9307; e-mail info@aptn.ca; internet www.aptn.ca; f. 1999; fmrly Television Northern Canada—TVNC; broadcasts in English, French and a number of aboriginal languages; Chair. MIKE METATAWABIN; CEO JEAN LAROSE.

Astral Media Inc: Maison Astral, 2100 rue Ste-Catherine ouest, Suite 1000, Montréal, QC H3H 2T3; tel. (514) 939-5000; fax (514) 939-1515; e-mail info@astral.com; internet www.astralmedia.com; operates 20 television networks and 82 radio stations in eight Canadian provinces; acquired Standard Radio from Standard Broadcasting Corpn Ltd in 2007; Pres. and CEO IAN GREENBERG; Chair. ANDRÉ BUREAU.

Corus Entertainment Inc: 630 Third Ave, SW, Suite 501, Calgary, AB T2P 4L4; tel. (403) 444-4244; fax (403) 444-4242; e-mail investor.relations@corusent.com; internet www.corusent.com; f. 1999; operates 52 radio stations and 17 television channels, including 11 special interest television channels; Pres. and CEO JOHN M. CASSADAY.

W Network: 64 Jefferson Ave, Unit 18, Toronto, ON M6K 3H4; tel. (416) 534-1191; e-mail comments@wnetwork.com; internet www.wnetwork.com; f. 1995 as Women's Television Network; women's network; owned by Corus Entertainment Inc; Gen. Man. WENDY HERMAN.

CTV Television Network: 9 Channel Nine Court, POB 9, Station O, Scarborough, Toronto, ON M4A 2M9; tel. (416) 332-5000; fax (416) 299-2643; e-mail programming@ctv.ca; internet www.ctv.ca; 25 privately owned affiliated stations from coast to coast (including one satellite-to-cable service), with 247 rebroadcasters; covers 99% of English-speaking Canadian TV households; Pres. and CEO IVAN FECAN.

CTV British Columbia (CTV): 750 Burrard St, Suite 300, Vancouver, BC V6Z 1X5; tel. (604) 608-2868; fax (604) 608-2698; e-mail bccomments@ctv.ca; internet www.ctvbc.ca.

Global Television Network: 81 Barber Greene Rd, Don Mills, ON M3C 2A2; tel. (416) 446-5311; fax (416) 446-5447; e-mail globalnews.bc@globaltv.com; internet www.canada.com/globaltv; 11 stations in eight provinces; a subsidiary of CanWest Global Communications Corpn; Pres. GERRY NOBLE.

Golden West Broadcasting Ltd: 201–125 Centre Ave, POB 950, Altona, MB R0G 0B0; tel. (204) 324-6464; fax (204) 324-8918; internet www.goldenwestradio.com; operates eight radio stations; CEO ELMER HILDEBRAND.

Knowledge Network: 4355 Mathissi Pl., Burnaby, BC V5G 4S8; tel. (604) 431-3222; fax (604) 431-3387; e-mail knowline@ola.bc.ca; internet www.knowledgenetwork.ca; f. 1981; Pres. and CEO RUDY BUTTIGNOL; Chair. Dr RON BURNETT.

Rawlco Communications Ltd: 715 Saskatchewan Cres. West, Saskatoon, SK S7M 5V7; tel. (306) 934-2222; fax (306) 373-7587; internet www.rawlco.com; 10 radio stations; Pres. and CEO GORDON RAWLINSON.

Réseau des Appalaches: 327 rue Labbé, CP 69, Thetford Mines, QC G6G 5S3; tel. (418) 335-7533; fax (418) 335-9009; e-mail info@passionrock.com; internet www.passionrock.com; f. 1972; 2 stations; Pres. FRANÇOIS LABBÉ.

Réseau TVA: CP 170, succursale C, Montréal, QC H2L 4P6; tel. (514) 790-0461; fax (514) 598-6085; internet tva.canoe.com; f. 1960 as Corporation Télé-Métropole; runs the Canoë network; French-language network, with nine stations in Québec and 19 rebroadcasters serving 98% of the province and francophone communities in Ontario and New Brunswick; Pres. and CEO PIERRE DION.

RNC Media Inc: 171 rue Jean-Proulx, Gatineau, QC J8Z 1W5; tel. (819) 770-1040; fax (819) 770-0272; e-mail pbrosseau@rncmedia.ca; internet www.radionord.com; f. 1948 as radio Nord Communications Inc; 16 radio stations and five television stations; Pres. and CEO PIERRE R. BROSSEAU; Man. RAYNALD BRIÈRE.

Rogers Broadcasting Ltd (Rogers Media): 333 Bloor St East, 10th Floor, Toronto, ON M4W 1G9; tel. (416) 935-8200; fax (416) 935-8270; e-mail info@rogers.com; internet www.rogers.com; subsidiary of Rogers Communications Inc; 51 radio stations and eight television channels; Pres. RAEL MERSON.

Score Media Inc: 370 King St, Suite 435, Toronto ON M5V 1J9; tel. (416) 977-6787; fax (416) 977-7851; internet www.scoremedia.ca; fmrly Headline Media Group; present name adopted in 2005; special interest TV channels include The Score Television Network Ltd and PrideVision Inc; Chair. and CEO JOHN S. LEVY.

Shaw Communications Inc: 630 Third Ave, SW, Suite 900, Calgary, AB T2P 4L4; tel. (403) 750-4500; fax (403) 750-4501; internet www.shaw.ca; f. 1966 as Capital Cable Television Co Ltd, present name adopted in 1993; Exec. Chair. J. R. SHAW; CEO JIM SHAW.

Shaw Broadcast Services: 2055 Flavelle Blvd, Mississauga, ON L5K 1Z8; tel. (905) 403-2020; fax (905) 403-2022; e-mail gaston.dufour@sjrb.ca; internet www.shawbroadcast.com; fmrly Canadian Satellite Communications Inc (Cancom); present name adopted 2006; a division of Shaw Communications Inc; responsible for providing and managing the distribution of television channels to cable companies via satellite; also operates StarChoice, a Canadian direct broadcast satellite service; Gen. Man. GASTON DUFOUR.

Standard Broadcasting Corporation Ltd: 2 St Clair Ave West, 11th Floor, Toronto, ON M4V 1L6; tel. (416) 960-9911; fax (416) 323-6828; subsidiary, Standard Radio, bought by Astral Media Inc in 2007; Exec. Chair. ALLAN SLAIGHT; Pres. and CEO GARY SLAIGHT.

Taqramiut Nipingat Inc: 185 Dorval Ave, Suite 501, Dorval, QC H9S 5J9; tel. (514) 631-1394; fax (514) 631-6258; e-mail cgrenier@taqramiut.qc.ca; internet inuit.pail.ca/taqramiut-nipingat.htm; f. 1975; broadcasts programming in Inuktitut, French and English to Arctic regions of Québec (Nunavik); Pres. GEORGE KAKAYUK; Dir-Gen. CLAUDE GRENIER.

TQS Inc/Cogeco Radio-Télévision Inc: 612 rue St-Jacques, bureau 100, Montréal, QC H3C 5R1; tel. (514) 390-6035; fax (514) 390-6067; e-mail tvpublic@tqs.ca; internet www.tqs.ca; f. 1986 as Télévision Quatre Saisons; 60% owned by COGECO and 40% by CTVglobemedia; French-language; six television stations and one retransmitter in Québec; operates three French television stations in partnership with CTV Television; radio stations in Montréal, Québec City, Trois-Rivières and Sherbrooke; Pres. RENÉ GUIMOND.

TVOntario/TV Français Ontario: 2180 Yonge St, POB 200, Station Q, Toronto, ON M4T 2T1; tel. (416) 484-2600; fax (416) 484-6285; e-mail asktv@tvo.org; internet www.tvo.org; f. 1970; Chair. PETER O'BRIAN; CEO LISA DE WILDE.

Wawatay Native Communications Society: POB 1180, 16 Fifth Ave, Sioux Lookout, ON P8T 1B7; tel. (807) 737-2951; fax (807) 737-3224; e-mail webmaster@wawatay.on.ca; internet www.wawatay.on.ca; f. 1974; broadcasts programmes of interest to aboriginal peoples of Nishnawbe-Aski Nation (northern Ontario); CEO CHRISTINE CHISEL.

Broadcasting Associations

British Columbia Association of Broadcasters: c/o Okanagan Radio Ltd, 2419 Hwy 97 North, Kelowna, BC V1X 4J2; tel. (250) 868-4713; fax (250) 860-8856; e-mail mcdan@theq.fm; internet www.bcab.ca; Pres. DAN MCALLISTER.

Canadian Association of Broadcasters/L'Association canadienne des radiodiffuseurs: 700–745 O'Connor St, Ottawa, ON K1P 1A4; tel. (613) 233-4035; fax (613) 233-6961; e-mail cab@cab-acr.ca; internet www.cab-acr.ca; f. 1926; over 600 mem. broadcasting stations; Pres. and CEO GLENN O'FARRELL; Chair. (Board of Dirs) CHARLOTTE BELL; Chair., Radio Council PAUL SKI; Chair., Television Council RAEL MERSON.

North American Broadcasting Association (NABA): POB 500, Station A, Toronto, ON M5W 1E6; tel. (416) 598-9877; fax (416) 598-9774; e-mail info@nabanet.com; internet www.nabanet.com; f. 1972; fmrly North American National Broadcasters Asscn; represents broadcasters in Canada, Mexico and the USA; Pres. LEONARDO RAMOS.

Radio Advisory Board of Canada/Conseil consultatif canadien de la radio: 811–116 Albert St, Ottawa, ON K1P 5G3; tel. (613) 230-3261; fax (613) 728-3278; e-mail rabc.gm@on.aibn.com; internet www.rabc.ottawa.on.ca; 21 mem. asscns; Gen. Man. ROGER POIRIER.

Television Bureau of Canada: 160 Bloor St East, Suite 1005, Toronto, ON M4W 1B9; tel. (416) 923-8813; fax (416) 413-3879; e-mail tvb@tvb.ca; internet www.tvb.ca; f. 1962; 150 mems; Pres. and CEO THERESA TREUTLER.

Western Association of Broadcast Engineers (WABE): c/o CityTV Television, 180 West Second Ave, Vancouver, BC V5Y 3T9; tel. (604) 872-6163; fax (604) 876-4898; e-mail info@wabe.ca; internet www.wabe.ca; f. 1950; Pres. PETER GILLESPIE.

Women in Film and Television—Toronto: 110 Eglinton Ave East, Suite 601, Toronto, ON M4P 2Y1; tel. (416) 322-3430; fax (416) 322-3703; e-mail wift@wift.com; internet www.wift.com; Exec. Dir SADIA ZAMAN.

THE PRESS

INTRODUCTION

Traditionally the daily press in Canada was essentially local in coverage, influence and distribution. In October 1998 publication began of Canada's first national newspaper, the *National Post*. A national edition of the Toronto *Globe and Mail*, established in 1981, was also available coast to coast, as was (from 1988) a national edition of the *Financial Post*.

In 1981 a royal commission, appointed by the Government to investigate the effects of concentration of ownership in the newspaper industry, reported that the existing concentration constituted a threat to press freedom. It recommended that some groups should be compelled to sell some of their newspaper interests in areas where there was extreme ownership concentration. The Government subsequently continued to restrict cross-media ownership of newspapers, radio and television, and to prohibit non-media companies from owning daily newspapers.

Chain ownership has traditionally been predominant: at the beginning of 2000 63% of daily newspaper circulation was represented by two major groups, Hollinger Inc (42% of daily newspaper circulation) and Quebecor Media Inc (21%). However, in 2000 both Hollinger and the Thomson Corpn (11%) divested themselves of significant proportions of their newspaper interests, with control over the *Globe and Mail* being subsequently transferred to Bell Globemedia Inc, a joint venture between companies including Thomson and the telecommunications operator BCE Inc. In November 2000 CanWest Global Communications Corpn acquired 14 daily metropolitan newspapers, a number of community newspapers and a 50% interest in the *National Post*. (In 2001 CanWest acquired the remaining 50% interest in the *National Post*.) In the process, CanWest acquired Hollinger's Southam Inc division, while in 2006 Hollinger's remaining Canadian operations were sold to Glacier Ventures International Corpn (subsequently renamed Glacier Media Inc). In 2007 Quebecor Media Inc acquired Osprey Media Group Inc, thus creating Canada's largest newspaper publishing enterprise in terms of the number of titles produced. In that year Quebecor, including its subsidiary Sun Media Corpn, owned 37 daily newspapers (and controlled some 26% of total paid newspaper circulation), CanWest Publishing Inc owned 13 (with the greatest share of total circulation, at 27%), Transcontinental Inc 11 and Glacier Media nine.

In 2007 there were 99 daily newspapers, with a combined daily circulation of some 4.7m.; of these only four were independent. The Canadian Community Newspaper Association comprised 742 weekly and twice-weekly community newspapers, serving mainly the more remote areas of the country.

There were numerous periodicals for business, trade, professional, recreational and special interest readership, although periodical publishing, particularly, suffered from substantial competition from publications originating in the USA. In 2008 the principal industry association, Magazines Canada, comprised more than 300 consumer titles. Among periodicals, the only one that could be regarded as national in its readership and coverage was the weekly news magazine *Maclean's*.

PRINCIPAL NATIONAL NEWSPAPER GROUPS

CanWest Publishing Inc: 1450 Don Mills Road, Don Mills, ON M3B 2X7; tel. (416) 383-2300; fax (416) 442-2077; internet www.canwest.com; subsidiary of CanWest Global Communications Corpn; owns 11 English-language major metropolitan daily newspapers and 28 other newspapers in Canada; Pres. DENNIS SKULSKY.

Glacier Media Inc: 1970 Alberta St, Vancouver, BC V5Y 3X4; tel. (604) 872-8565; fax (604) 879-1483; internet www.glacierventures.com; f. 2000; fmrly Glacier Ventures International Corpn; owns nine daily newspapers; Chair. SAM GRIPPO; Pres. and CEO JONATHAN KENNEDY.

Quebecor Media Inc: 612 rue St-Jacques, Montréal, QC H3C 4M8; tel. (514) 954-0101; e-mail webmaster@quebecor.com; internet www.quebecor.com; f. 1965; acquired Osprey Media Group Inc in 2007; through its subsidiaries Sun Media Corpn and Osprey Media Group, publishes 37 English- and French-language dailies and over 180 community papers; television, cable, telecommunications and publishing interests in 17 countries; Pres. and CEO PIERRE KARL PÉLADEAU.

Sun Media Corpn: 333 King St East, Toronto, ON M5A 3X5; tel. (416) 947-2222; e-mail qi_info@quebecor.com; internet www.sunmedia.ca; f. 1965; Pres. and CEO PIERRE FRANCOEUR.

Torstar Corpn: 1 Yonge St, Toronto, ON M5E 1P9; tel. (416) 869-4010; fax (416) 869-4183; e-mail torstar@torstar.ca; internet www.torstar.com; f. 1958; incorporates the Star Media Group and Metroland Media Group; owns four daily newspapers (weekly circ. 4.5m.), 10 weekly publs, and 95 community newspapers; Chair. FRANK IACOBUCCI; Pres. and CEO J. ROBERT PRITCHARD.

Transcontinental Media: 1100 René-Lévesque Blvd ouest, 24th Floor, Montréal, QC H3B 4X9; tel. (514) 392-9000; fax (514) 954-4016; internet www.medias-transcontinental.com; f. 1978; publ. 11 dailies (daily circ. 250,000) and more than 125 weekly, fortnightly and monthly newspapers (circ. 2.4m.); Chair. ANDRÉ PRÉFONTAINE; Pres. NATALIE LARIVIÈRE.

PRINCIPAL DAILY AND SUNDAY NEWSPAPERS

Alberta

Calgary Herald: 215 16th St, SE, POB 2400, Station M, Calgary, AB T2P 0W8; tel. (403) 235-7232; fax (403) 235-7379; e-mail calgaryherald@reachcanada.com; internet www.canada.com/calgaryherald; f. 1883; Publr MALCOLM KIRK; Exec. Editor RON NEWELL; circ. Mon. to Sat. 123,793, Sun. 118,639.

Calgary Sun: 2615 12th St, NE, Calgary, AB T2E 7W9; tel. (403) 410-1010; fax (403) 250-4176; e-mail callet@calgarysun.com; internet www.calgarysun.com; f. 1980; Publr and CEO GORDON NORRIE; Editor-in-Chief JOSE RODRIGUEZ; circ. Mon. to Sat. 61,235, Sun. 84,190.

Daily Herald-Tribune: 10604 100th St, Postal Bag 3000, Grande Prairie, AB T8V 6V4; tel. (780) 532-1110; fax (780) 532-2120; e-mail frinne@bowesnet.com; internet www.dailyheraldtribune.com; f. 1913; evening; Publr KENT KEEBAUGH; Man. Editor JEFF MCCOSHEN; circ. 7,625.

Edmonton Journal: POB 2421, Edmonton, AB T5J 2S6; tel. (780) 429-5100; fax (780) 429-5536; e-mail letters@thejournal.canwest.com; internet www.canada.com/edmontonjournal; f. 1903; Publr JOHN J. MCDONALD; Editor-in-Chief ALLAN MAYER; circ. Mon. to Sat. 124,822, Sun. 122,810.

Edmonton Sun: 4990 92nd Ave, Suite 250, Edmonton, AB T6B 3A1; tel. (780) 468-0100; fax (780) 468-0128; e-mail mailbag@edmsun.com; internet www.edmontonsun.com; f. 1978; Publr and CEO DAVID BLACK; Editor-in-Chief GRAHAM DALZIEL; circ. Mon. to Sat. 68,342, Sun. 87,464.

Fort McMurray Today: 8550 Franklin Ave, Bag 4008, Fort McMurray, AB T9H 3G1; tel. (780) 743-8186; fax (780) 790-1006; e-mail editorial@fortmcmurraytoday.com; internet www.fortmcmurraytoday.com; evening; Publr TIM O'ROURKE; Man. Editor MICHAEL HALL; circ. Mon. to Fri. 3,761.

Lethbridge Herald: 504 Seventh St South, POB 670, Lethbridge, AB T1J 3Z7; tel. (403) 328-4411; fax (403) 328-4536; e-mail dsugimoto@lethbridgeherald.com; internet www.lethbridgeherald.com; f. 1907; evening and Sun.; Gen. Man. BOB CAREY; circ. Mon. to Sat. 18,138, Sun. 16,348.

Medicine Hat News: 3257 Dunmore Rd, SE, POB 10, Medicine Hat, AB T1A 7E6; tel. (403) 527-1101; fax (403) 527-1244; e-mail apoirier@medicinehatnews.com; internet www.medicinehatnews.com; f. 1887; evening; Publr MICHAEL J. HERTZ; Man. Editor ALAN POIRIER; circ. 13,001.

Red Deer Advocate: 2950 Bremner Ave, Bag 5200, Red Deer, AB T4N 5G3; tel. (403) 343-2400; fax (403) 341-6560; e-mail editorial@reddeeradvocate.com; internet www.reddeeradvocate.com; f. 1894; Publr FRED GORMAN; Man. Editor JOE MCLAUGHLIN; circ. Mon. to Sat. 17,229.

British Columbia

Alaska Highway News: 9916 98th St, Fort St John, BC V1J 3T8; tel. (250) 785-5631; fax (250) 785-3522; e-mail ahnews@awink.com; internet www.canada.com/fortstjohn; f. 1940; evening; Publr WILLIAM JULIAN; Man. Editor MIKE HEINTZMAN; circ. 3,790.

Alberni Valley Times: 4918 Napier St, POB 400, Port Alberni, BC V9Y 3H5; tel. and fax (250) 723-8171; fax (250) 723-0586; e-mail lpatterson@avtimes.net; internet www.canada.com/albernivalleytimes; Publr LINDA PATTERSON; Man. Editor CALE COWAN; circ. Mon. to Sat. 4,876.

Cranbrook Daily Townsman: 822 Cranbrook St North, Cranbrook, BC V1C 3R9; tel. (250) 426-5201; fax (250) 426-5003; e-mail editorial@dailytownsman.com; internet www.dailytownsman.com; evening; Publr STEEN JORGENSEN; Editor BARRY COULTER; circ. 3,521.

Daily Courier: 550 Doyle Ave, Kelowna, BC V1Y 7V1; tel. (250) 762-4445; fax (250) 762-3866; e-mail alison.yesilcimen@ok.bc.ca; internet www.kelownadailycourier.ca; f. 1904; morning; Publr ALISON YESILCIMEN; Man. Editor TOM WILSON; circ. Mon. to Sat. 16,298, Sun. 15,731.

Kamloops Daily News: 393 Seymour St, Kamloops, BC V2C 6P6; tel. (250) 372-2331; fax (250) 374-3884; e-mail kamloopsnews@telus.net; internet www.kamloopsnews.ca; f. 1930; evening; Publr DON HERRON; Editor MEL ROTHENBURGER; circ. 12,679.

Nanaimo Daily News: 2575 McCullough Rd, Nanaimo, BC V9S 5W5; tel. (250) 729-4200; fax (250) 729-4247; e-mail dnews@island.net; internet www.nanaimodailynews.com; f. 1874; evening; Publr CURT DUDDY; Man. Editor CALE COWAN; circ. 7,466.

Nelson Daily News: 266 Baker St, Nelson, BC V1L 4H3; tel. (250) 352-3552; fax (250) 352-2418; e-mail news@nelsondailynews.com; f. 1902; evening; Publr PETER HOWIE; Editor DREW EDWARDS; circ. 3,148.

Penticton Herald: 186 Nanaimo Ave West, Suite 101, Penticton, BC V2A 1N4; tel. (250) 492-4002; fax (250) 492-2403; e-mail editor@pentictonherald.ca; internet www.pentictonherald.ca; morning; Publr ALISON YESILCIMEN; Man. Editor S. PAUL VARGA; Gen. Man. ANDRÉ MARTIN; circ. Mon. to Fri. 7,885, Sat. 8,164, Sun. 7,353.

Prince George Citizen: 150 Brunswick St, POB 5700, Prince George, BC V2L 5K9; tel. (250) 562-2441; fax (250) 562-7453; e-mail news@princegeorgecitizen.com; internet www.princegeorgecitizen.com; f. 1916; morning; Publr DEL LAVERDURE; Man. Editor DAVE PAULSON; circ. 15,485.

The Province: 200 Granville St, Suite 1, Vancouver, BC V6C 3N3; tel. (604) 605-2000; fax (604) 605-2759; e-mail wmoriarty@theprovince.com; internet www.canada.com/theprovince; f. 1898; Publr DENNIS SKULSKY; Editor-in-Chief WAYNE MORIARTY; circ. Mon. to Fri. 141,164, Sun. 173,016.

Sing Tao Daily News (Eastern Canada Edition): 8508 Ash St, Vancouver, BC V6P 3M2; tel. (416) 596-8140; fax (416) 599-6688; e-mail vanadmin@singtao.ca; internet singtao.ca; f. 1978; Chinese; Editor PAUL TSANG; circ. Mon. to Sat. 15,000.

Times Colonist: 2621 Douglas St, Victoria, BC V8T 4M2; tel. (250) 380-5211; fax (250) 380-5353; e-mail lchodan@tc.canwest.com; internet www.canada.com/victoriatimescolonist; f. 1980 by merger; Publr BOB MCKENZIE; Editor-in-Chief LUCINDA CHODAN; circ. Mon. to Sat. 71,811, Sun. 71,761.

Trail Daily Times: 1163 Cedar Ave, Trail, BC V1R 4B8; tel. (250) 368-8551; fax (250) 368-8550; e-mail editor@trailtimes.ca; internet www.canada.com/cityguides/trail; evening; Publr BARB BLATCHFORD; Editor TRACY GILCHRIST; circ. 5,006.

The Vancouver Sun: 200 Granville St, Suite 1, Vancouver, BC V6C 3N3; tel. (604) 605-2000; fax (604) 605-2720; e-mail info@png.canwest.com; internet www.canada.com/vancouversun; f. 1886; Pres. and Publr KEVIN D. BENT; Editor-in-Chief PATRICIA GRAHAM; circ. Mon. to Fri. 165,144, Sat. 204,971.

World Journal (Vancouver): 2288 Clark Dr., Vancouver, BC V5N 3G8; tel. (604) 876-1338; fax (604) 876-9191; internet www.worldjournal.com; f. 1976; Chinese; Publr WILSON CHIEN; circ. 10,000.

Manitoba

Brandon Sun: 501 Rosser Ave, Brandon, MB R7A 0K4; tel. (204) 727-2451; fax (204) 725-0976; e-mail rsmith@brandonsun.com; internet www.brandonsun.com; f. 1882; evening and Sun.; Publr EWAN POW; Man. Editor JAMES O'CONNOR; circ. Mon. to Fri. 14,267, Sat. 17,478, Sun. 12,253.

Daily Graphic: 1941 Saskatchewan Ave West, POB 130, Portage La Prairie, MB R1N 3B4; tel. (204) 857-3427; fax (204) 239-1270; e-mail editor.dailygraphic@shawcable.com; internet www.portagedailygraphic.com; evening; Publr BARRY CLAYTON; Man. Editor CLARISE KLASSEN; circ. 2,615.

Winnipeg Free Press: 1355 Mountain Ave, Winnipeg, MB R2X 3B6; tel. (204) 697-7000; fax (204) 697-7375; e-mail bob.cox@freepress.mb.ca; internet www.winnipegfreepress.com; f. 1872; morning; Publr BOB COX; Editor MARGO GOODHAND; circ. Mon. to Fri. 120,984, Sat. 162,399, Sun. 118,667.

Winnipeg Sun: 1700 Church Ave, Winnipeg, MB R2X 3A2; tel. (204) 694-2022; fax (204) 697-0759; e-mail kevin.klein@sunmedia.ca; internet www.winnipegsun.com; f. 1980; Publr and CEO KEVIN KLEIN; Editor-in-Chief STEPHEN RIPLEY; circ. Mon. to Fri. 38,032, Sat. 36,707, Sun. 44,916.

New Brunswick

L'Acadie Nouvelle: 476 blvd St-Pierre ouest, CP 5536, Caraquet, NB E1W 1B7; tel. (506) 727-4444; fax (506) 727-7620; e-mail infos@acadienouvelle.com; internet www.acadienouvelle.com; f. 1984; Publr GILLES GAGNÉ; Editor BRUNO GODIN; circ. 20,152.

The Daily Gleaner: POB 3370, Fredericton, NB E3B 5A2; tel. (506) 452-6671; fax (506) 452-7405; e-mail news@dailygleaner.com; internet dailygleaner.canadaeast.com; f. 1881; morning; Publr ERIC LAWSON; Man. Editor PETER HAGGERT; circ. 23,094.

Telegraph–Journal: 210 Crown St, POB 2350, Saint John, NB E2L 3V8; tel. (506) 632-8888; fax (506) 648-2654; e-mail newsroom@nbpub.com; internet www.telegraphjournal.com; Publr JAMES C. IRVING; Man. Editor RON BARRY; circ. Mon. to Fri. 35,296, Sat. 38,066.

The Times and Transcript: 939 Main St, POB 1001, Moncton, NB E1C 8P3; tel. (506) 859-4905; fax (506) 859-4904; e-mail news@timestranscript.com; internet www.timestranscript.com; f. 1983; Mon. to Sat. evening, Sat. morning; Publr ERIC LAWSON; Man. Editor AL HOGAN; circ. Mon. to Fri. 37,115, Sat. 42,085.

Newfoundland and Labrador

Telegram: 430 Topsail Rd, St John's, NL A1E 4N1; tel. (709) 364-6300; fax (709) 364-9333; e-mail telegram@thetelegram.com; internet www.thetelegram.com; f. 1879; evening; Publr CHARLES STACEY; Exec. Editor KERRY HANN; circ. Mon. to Fri. 30,014, Sat. 47,189, Sun. 26,423.

Western Star: 106 West St, POB 460, Corner Brook, NL A2H 6E7; tel. (709) 634-4668; fax (709) 634-9824; e-mail tturner@thewesternstar.com; internet www.thewesternstar.com; f. 1900; Publr and Gen. Man. SHAWN WOODFORD; Man. Editor TROY TURNER; circ. Mon. to Sat. 7,448.

Northwest Territories

There are no daily or Sunday newspapers in the Northwest Territories. The following are the leading weekly newspapers:

Northern News Services: 5108 50th St, Yellowknife, NT X1A 2R1; tel. (867) 873-4031; fax (867) 873-8507; e-mail nnsl@nnsl.com; internet www.nnsl.com; f. 1945 as *News/North*; weekly; Publr JACK SIGVALDASON; Man. Editor BRUCE VALPY; circ. 11,000.

Slave River Journal: 207 McDougal Rd, POB 990, Fort Smith, NT X0E 0P0; tel. (867) 872-3000; fax (867) 872-2754; e-mail reception@auroranet.nt.ca; internet www.srj.ca; f. 1978; weekly; Publr and Man. Editor DON JAQUE; circ. 1,750.

Nova Scotia

Amherst Daily News: 147 South Albion St Town Sq., POB 280, Amherst, NS B4H 2X2; tel. (902) 661-5426; fax (902) 667-0419; e-mail bworks@amherstdaily.com; internet www.amherstdaily.com; f. 1893; Publr RICHARD RUSSELL; Man. Editor BRAD WORKS; circ. Mon. to Sat. 3,054.

Cape Breton Post: 255 George St, POB 1500, Sydney, NS B1P 6K6; tel. (902) 563-3843; fax (902) 562-7077; e-mail fjackson@cbpost.com; internet www.capebretonpost.com; f. 1901; Publr ANITA DELAZZER; Man. Editor FRED JACKSON; circ. Mon. to Sat. 25,151.

Chronicle–Herald: 1650 Argyle St, POB 610, Halifax, NS B3J 2T2; tel. (902) 426-2811; fax (902) 426-1158; e-mail reception@herald.ca; internet thechronicleherald.ca; f. 1875; Publr GRAHAM W. DENNIS; Man. Editor TERRY O'NEIL; circ. Mon. to Fri. 107,553, Sat. 114,141, Sun. 84,465.

The Evening News: 352 East River Rd, POB 159, New Glasgow, NS B2H 5E2; tel. (902) 752-3000; fax (902) 752-1945; e-mail news@ngnews.ca; internet www.ngnews.ca; f. 1910; evening; Publr RICHARD RUSSELL; Man. Editor DAVE GLENEN; circ. 8,258.

Truro Daily News: 6 Louise St, POB 220, Truro, NS B2N 5C3; tel. (902) 893-9405; fax (902) 893-0518; e-mail news@trurodaily.com; internet www.trurodaily.com; f. 1891; evening; Publr RICHARD RUSSELL; Man. Editor CARL FLEMING; circ. Mon. to Fri. 6,704, Sat. 7,754.

Nunavut Territory

There are no daily or Sunday newspapers in Nunavut Territory. The following is the leading weekly newspaper:

Nunatsiaq News: POB 8, Iqaluit, NU X0A 0H0; tel. (867) 979-5357; fax (867) 979-4763; e-mail editor@nunatsiaq.com; internet www.nunatsiaq.com; f. 1973; weekly; English and Inuktitut; Publr STEVEN ROBERTS; Editor JIM BELL; circ. 8,000.

Ontario

Barrie Examiner: 571 Bayfield St North, Barrie, ON L4M 4Z9; tel. (705) 726-6537; fax (705) 726-5414; internet www.thebarrieexaminer.com; f. 1864; evening; Publr MIKE POWER; Man. Editor MIKE BEAUDIN; circ. 7,990.

Beacon Herald: 16 Packham Rd, POB 430, Stratford, ON N5A 6T6; tel. (519) 271-2220; fax (519) 271-1026; e-mail jkastner@bowesnet.com; internet www.stratfordbeaconherald.com; f. 1854; evening; Publr and Sales Man. DAVE CARTER; Man. Editor JOHN KASTNER; circ. Mon. to Sat. 9,861.

Brockville Recorder and Times: 1600 California Ave, POB 10, Brockville, ON K6V 5T8; tel. (613) 342-4441; fax (613) 342-4456; e-mail wb.raison@recorder.ca; internet www.recorder.ca; f. 1821; evening; Publr BOB PEARCE; Editor BARRY RAISON; circ. 11,694.

Chatham Daily News: 45 Fourth St, POB 2007, Chatham, ON N7M 5M6; tel. (519) 354-2000; fax (519) 354-9489; e-mail bcorcoran@chathamdailynews.ca; internet www.chathamdailynews.ca; f. 1862; evening; Publr JIM BLAKE; Man. Editor BRUCE CORCORAN; circ. 12,691.

Chronicle–Journal: 75 Cumberland St South, Thunder Bay, ON P7B 1A3; tel. (807) 343-6200; fax (807) 345-9409; e-mail julio.gomes@chroniclejournal.com; internet www.chroniclejournal.com; Publr and Gen. Man. COLIN J. BRUCE; Man. Editor JULIO GOMEZ; circ. Mon. to Fri. 28,100, Sat. 29,685, Sun. 24,542.

Cobourg Daily Star: 99 King St West, POB 400, Cobourg, ON K9A 4L1; tel. (905) 372-0131; fax (905) 372-4966; internet www.northumberlandtoday.com; evening; Group Publr DON MACLEOD; Editorial Dir MANDY MARTIN; circ. 4,837.

Daily Observer: 186 Alexander St, Pembroke, ON K8A 4L9; tel. (613) 732-3691; fax (613) 732-2226; e-mail editor@thedailyobserver.ca; internet www.thedailyobserver.ca; f. 1855; evening; Publr STEVE GLOSTER; Man. Editor PETER LAPINSKIE; circ. 5,830.

The Daily Press: 187 Cedar South, Timmins, ON P4N 7G1; tel. (705) 268-5050; fax (705) 268-7373; internet www.timminspress.com; f. 1933; Publr and Gen. Man. BRUCE COWAN; Man. Editor TOM PERRY; circ. Mon. to Sat. 8,523.

Le Droit: 47 rue Clarence, bureau 222, CP 8860, succursale Terminus, Ottawa, ON K1G 3J9; tel. (613) 562-0111; fax (613) 562-6280; e-mail ledroit@ledroit.com; internet www.cyberpresse.ca; f. 1913; Publr JAQUES PRONOVOST; Man. Editor ANDRÉ LAROCQUE; circ. Mon. to Fri. 36,058, Sat. 39,829.

The Expositor: 53 Dalhousie St, POB 965, Brantford, ON N3T 5S8; tel. (519) 756-2020; fax (519) 756-4911; e-mail publisher@theexpositor.com; internet www.brantfordexpositor.ca; f. 1852; Publr MICHAEL PEARCE; Editor DAVE JUDD; circ. 21,006.

The Globe and Mail: 444 Front St West, Toronto, ON M5V 2S9; tel. (416) 585-5000; fax (416) 585-5085; e-mail newsroom@globeandmail.ca; internet www.globeandmail.com; f. 1844; Publr and CEO PHILLIP CRAWLEY; Editor-in-Chief EDWARD GREENSPON; circ. Mon. to Fri. 322,807, Sat. 410,285.

Guelph Mercury: 8–14 Macdonnell St, Guelph, ON N1H 6P7; tel. (519) 822-4310; fax (519) 767-1681; e-mail editor@guelphmercury.com; internet www.guelphmercury.com; f. 1854; evening; Group Publr DANA ROBBINS; Man. Editor PHIL ANDREWS; circ. 14,326.

Hamilton Spectator: 44 Frid St, Hamilton, ON L8N 3G3; tel. (905) 526-3333; fax (905) 526-0147; internet www.thespec.com; f. 1846; Publr DANA ROBBINS; Editor-in-Chief DAVID ESTOK; circ. Mon. to Fri. 106,530, Sat. 117,172.

Intelligencer: 45 Bridge St East, Belleville, ON K8N 5C7; tel. (613) 962-9171; fax (613) 962-9652; e-mail bglisky@intelligencer.ca; internet www.intelligencer.ca; f. 1870; evening; Publr MICHAEL A. POWER; Man. Editor BILL GLISKY; circ. 13,403.

The Kingston Whig-Standard: 6 Cataraqui St, POB 2300, Kingston, ON K7L 4Z7; tel. (613) 544-5000; fax (613) 530-4118; e-mail whiglocal@thewhig.com; internet www.thewhig.com; f. 1834; Publr RON LAURIN; circ. Mon. to Fri. 25,195, Sat. 30,582.

London Free Press: 369 York St, POB 2280, London, ON N6A 4G1; tel. (519) 679-6666; fax (519) 667-4503; e-mail letters@lfpress.com; internet www.lfpress.com; f. 1849; Publr and CEO SUSAN MUSZAK; Editor-in-Chief PAUL BERTON; circ. Mon. to Fri. 82,369, Sat. 97,766, Sun. 60,010.

Ming Pao Daily News: 1355 Huntingwood Dr., Scarborough, ON M1S 3J1; tel. (416) 321-0088; fax (416) 321-9663; e-mail newsdesk@mingpaoca.com; internet www.mingpaotor.com; Chinese; Editor-in-Chief RICHARD KWOK-KAI NG; circ. Mon. to Fri. 68,600, Sat. 97,000, Sun. 102,000.

National Post: 1450 Don Mills Rd, Suite 300, Don Mills, ON M3B 3R5; tel. (416) 383-2300; fax (416) 442-2212; e-mail queries@nationalpost.com; internet www.nationalpost.com; f. 1998; incorporates the *Financial Post* (f. 1907); national newspaper with printing centres in nine cities; owned by CanWest Global Communications Corpn; Publr GORDON FISHER; Editor-in-Chief DOUG KELLY; circ. Mon. to Fri. 203,781, Sat. 217,115.

Niagara Falls Review: 4801 Valley Way, POB 270, Niagara Falls, ON L2E 6T6; tel. (905) 358-5711; fax (905) 356-0785; e-mail pconradi@nfreview.com; internet www.niagarafallsreview.ca; f. 1879; morning; Publr DAVID A. BEATTIE; Man. Editor PETER CONRADI; circ. Mon. to Fri. 15,419, Sat. 17,433.

North Bay Nugget: 259 Worthington St, POB 570, North Bay, ON P1B 3B5; tel. (705) 472-3200; fax (705) 472-1438; e-mail news@nugget.ca; internet www.nugget.ca; f. 1909; evening; Publr DAN JOHNSON; Man. Editor JOHN SIZE; circ. Mon. to Fri. 14,595, Sat. 15,727.

Northern Daily News: 8 Duncan Ave, POB 1030, Kirkland Lake, ON P2N 3L4; tel. (705) 567-5321; fax (705) 567-6162; e-mail news@northernnews.ca; internet www.northernnews.ca; f. 1922; evening; Publr and Gen. Man. TIM CRESWELL; Man. Editor JOE O'GRADY; circ. 3,379.

Orillia Packet and Times: 31 Colborne St East, Orillia, ON L3V 1T4; tel. (705) 325-1355; fax (705) 325-4033; internet www.orilliapacket.com; f. 1926 by merger; evening; Publr TERRI-LYNN ROSE; Man. Editor MARK BISSET; circ. 6,972.

Ottawa Citizen: 1101 Baxter Rd, POB 5020, Ottawa, ON K2C 3M4; tel. (613) 829-9100; fax (613) 596-3664; e-mail sanderson@thecitizen.canwest.com; internet www.canada.com/ottawa/ottawacitizen; f. 1845; Publr and Gen. Man. JAMES ORBAN; Exec. Editor GRAHAM GREEN; circ. Mon. to Fri. 129,631, Sat. 139,615, Sun. 132,161.

Ottawa Sun: 6 Antares Dr., Phase 3, Ottawa, ON K1G 5H7; tel. (613) 739-7000; fax (613) 739-9383; e-mail rick.gibbons@ott.sunpub.com; internet www.ottawasun.com; Publr RICK GIBBONS; Editor-in-Chief MIKE THERIEN; circ. Mon. to Fri. 48,891, Sat. 41,523, Sun. 47,001.

Peterborough Examiner: 730 Kingsway, Peterborough, ON K9J 8L4; tel. (705) 745-4641; fax (705) 743-4581; internet www.thepeterboroughexaminer.com; f. 1847; evening; Publr and Gen. Man. DARREN MURPHY; Man. Editor ED N. ARNOLD; circ. Mon. to Thur. 19,549, Fri. 18,996, Sat. 20,272.

The Record: 160 King St East, Kitchener, ON N2G 4E5; tel. (519) 894-2231; fax (519) 894-3912; e-mail business@therecord.com; internet www.therecord.com; f. 1878; evening; Dir of Operations KEVIN BROOKS; Editor-in-Chief LYNN HADDRALL; circ. Mon. to Fri. 64,485, Sat. 71,963.

St Catharines Standard: 17 Queen St, St Catharines, ON L2R 5G5; tel. (905) 684-7251; fax (905) 684-6032; internet www.stcatharinesstandard.ca; f. 1891; evening; Publr PAUL MCCUAIG; Man. Editor ANDREA KRILUCK; circ. Mon. to Fri. 38,284, Sat. 30,078.

St Thomas Times–Journal: 16 Hincks St, St Thomas, ON N5R 5Z2; tel. (519) 631-2790; fax (519) 631-5653; e-mail news@stthomastimesjournal.com; internet www.stthomastimesjournal.com; f. 1882; evening; Publr BEV PONTON; Man. Editor ROSS PORTER; circ. 6,537.

Sarnia Observer: 140 Front St South, POB 3009, Sarnia, ON N7T 7M8; tel. (519) 344-3641; fax (519) 332-2951; e-mail rhilts@theobserver.ca; internet www.theobserver.ca; f. 1853; evening; Publr DARYL C. SMITH; Man. Editor ROD HILTS; circ. Mon. to Fri. 17,939, Sat. 20,731.

Sault Star: 145 Old Garden River Rd, POB 460, Sault Ste Marie, ON P6A 5M5; tel. (705) 759-3030; fax (705) 759-0102; internet www.saultstar.com; f. 1912; evening; Publr LOU A. MAULUCCI; Man. Editor JOHN HALUCHA; circ. 17,877.

Sentinel–Review: 16 Brock St, POB 1000, Woodstock, ON N4S 3B4; tel. (519) 537-2341; fax (519) 537-3049; e-mail sentinelreview@bowesnet.com; internet www.woodstocksentinelreview.com; f. 1886; evening; Publr PAT LOGAN; Man. Editor BILL SCRIVEN; circ. 7,097.

Simcoe Reformer: 50 Gilbertson Dr., POB 370, Simcoe, ON N3Y 4L2; tel. (519) 426-5710; fax (519) 426-9255; e-mail refedit@bowesnet.com; internet www.simcoereformer.ca; f. 1858; evening; Group Publr CAM MCKNIGHT; Man. Editor KIM NOVAK; circ. 7,434.

Sing Tao Daily News: 417 Dundas St West, Toronto, ON M5T 1G6; tel. (416) 596-8140; fax (416) 599-6688; e-mail editor_toronto@singtao.ca; internet www.singtao.ca; Chinese; Editor-in-Chief ROBERT LEUNG; circ. Mon. to Sun. 160,693.

Standard-Freeholder: 44 Pitt St, Cornwall, ON K6J 3P3; tel. (613) 933-3160; fax (613) 933-3664; e-mail news@standard-freeholder.com; internet www.standard-freeholder.com; Publr and Gen. Man. MILTON S. ELLIS; Editor JACK ROMANELLI; circ. 14,074.

Sudbury Star: 33 MacKenzie St, Sudbury, ON P3C 4Y1; tel. (705) 674-5271; fax (705) 674-6834; internet www.thesudburystar.com; f. 1909; evening; Publr DAVID KILGOUR; Man. Editor BRIAN MACLEOD; circ. Mon. to Thur. 18,632, Fri. 16,170, Sat. 17,812.

Sun Times: 290 Ninth St East, POB 200, Owen Sound, ON N4K 5P2; tel. (519) 376-2250; fax (519) 376-7190; internet www.owensoundsuntimes.com; f. 1853 as *The Times*; evening; Publr CHERYL A. MCMENEMY; Man. Editor MICHAEL DEN TANDT; circ. 15,680.

Toronto Star: 1 Yonge St, Toronto, ON M5E 1E6; tel. (416) 367-2000; fax (416) 869-4328; e-mail city@thestar.ca; internet www.thestar.com; f. 1892; Publr DON BABICK (Interim); Editor-in-Chief J. FRED KUNTZ; circ. Mon. to Fri. 436,694, Sat. 634,886, Sun. 442,265.

Toronto Sun: 333 King St East, Toronto, ON M5A 3X5; tel. (416) 947-2222; fax (416) 947-3228; internet www.torontosun.com; f. 1971; Publr and CEO KIN-MAN LEE; Editor-in-Chief GLENN GARNETT; circ. Mon. to Fri. 179,004, Sat. 151,583, Sun. 311,689.

Welland-Port Colborne Tribune: 228 East Main St, POB 278, Welland, ON L3B 5P5; tel. (905) 732-2411; fax (905) 732-3660; e-mail tribme@wellandtribune.ca; internet www.wellandtribune.ca; f. 1863; Publr MIKE WALSH; Man. Editor ANGUS SCOTT; circ. 13,051.

Windsor Star: 167 Ferry St, Windsor, ON N9A 4M5; tel. (519) 255-5743; fax (519) 255-5515; e-mail letters@thestar.canwest.com; internet www.canada.com/windsorstar; f. 1918; Editor JOHN COLEMAN; circ. Mon. to Fri. 66,644, Sat. 74,913.

World Journal (Toronto): 7755 Warden Ave, Unit 9, Markham ON L3R 0N3; tel. (416) 778-0888; fax (416) 778-1037; internet www.worldjournal.com; Chinese; Pres. DAVID TING; Editor-in-Chief PAUL CHANG; circ. 38,000.

Prince Edward Island

Guardian: 165 Prince St, POB 760, Charlottetown, PE C1A 4R7; tel. (902) 629-6000; fax (902) 566-3808; e-mail letters@theguardian.pe.ca; internet www.theguardian.pe.ca; f. 1887; Publr DON BRANDER; Man. Editor GARY MACDOUGALL; circ. Mon. to Sat. 20,540.

Journal–Pioneer: 316 Water St, POB 2480, Summerside, PE C1N 4K5; tel. (902) 436-2121; fax (902) 436-0784; e-mail newsroom@journalpioneer.com; internet www.journalpioneer.com; f. 1865; evening; Publr SANDY RUNDLE; Man. Editor MIKE TURNER; circ. 8,950.

Québec

Le Devoir: 2050 rue de Bleury, 9e étage, Montréal, QC H3A 3M9; tel. (514) 985-3333; fax (514) 985-3360; e-mail redaction@ledevoir.com; internet www.ledevoir.com; Publr BERNARD DESCÔTEAUX; Editor-in-Chief JEAN ROBERT SANSFAÇON; circ. Mon. to Fri. 27,490, Sat. 45,161.

The Gazette: 1010 rue Ste-Catherine ouest, Suite 200, Montréal, QC H3B 5L1; tel. (514) 987-2222; fax (514) 987-2270; e-mail letters@thegazette.canwest.com; internet www.canada.com/montrealgazette; f. 1778; English; Publr ALAN ALLNUTT; Editor-in-

Chief ANDREW PHILLIPS; circ. Mon. to Fri. 138,827, Sat. 150,078, Sun. 129,808.

Le Journal de Montréal: 4545 rue Frontenac, Montréal, QC H2H 2R7; tel. (514) 521-4545; fax (514) 525-4542; e-mail transmission@journalmtl.com; internet www.canoe.com/journaldemontreal; f. 1964; Publr and Editor LYNE ROBITAILLE; Editor-in-Chief DANY DOUCET; circ. Mon. to Fri. 267,404, Sat. 319,899, Sun. 264,733.

Le Journal de Québec: 450 ave Béchard, Vanier, QC G1M 2E9; tel. (418) 683-1573; fax (418) 683-1027; e-mail commentaires@jdeq.com; internet www.canoe.com/journaldequebec; f. 1967; Publr PIERRE FRANCOEUR; Chief Editor SERGE GOSSELIN; circ. Mon. to Fri. 103,220, Sat. 126,781, Sun. 106,412.

Le Nouvelliste: 1920 rue Bellefeuille, CP 668, Trois Rivières, QC G9A 3Y2; tel. (819) 376-2501; fax (819) 376-0946; e-mail information@lenouvelliste.qc.ca; internet www.cyberpresse.ca/le-nouvelliste; f. 1920; Pres. and Publr RAYMOND TARDIF; Editor-in-Chief STÉPHAN FRAPPIER; circ. Mon. to Fri. 43,626, Sat. 45,893.

La Presse: 7 rue St-Jacques, Montréal, QC H2Y 1K9; tel. (514) 285-7070; fax (514) 285-6930; e-mail nouvelles@lapresse.ca; internet www.cyberpresse.ca/actualites/regional/montreal; f. 1884; Pres. and Editor GUY CREVIER; circ. Mon. to Fri. 204,545, Sat. 277,624, Sun. 224,233.

Le Quotidien du Saguenay-Lac-St-Jean: 1051 blvd Talbot, Chicoutimi, QC G7H 5C1; tel. (418) 545-4474; fax (418) 690-8824; e-mail redaction@lequotidien.com; internet www.cyberpresse.ca/le-quotidien; f. 1973; Editor-in-Chief MICHEL SIMARD; circ. Mon. to Sat. 27,665, Sun. 36,816.

The Record: 1195 Galt St East, CP 1200, Sherbrooke, QC J1G 1Y7; tel. (819) 569-9525; fax (819) 821-3179; e-mail newsroom@sherbrookerecord.com; internet www.sherbrookerecord.com; f. 1897; Publr KENNETH L. WELLS; Editor ELEANOR BROWN; circ. 4,806.

Le Soleil: 410 blvd Charest est, CP 1547, succursale Terminus, Québec, QC G1K 7J6; tel. (418) 686-3394; fax (418) 686-3374; e-mail redaction@lesoleil.com; internet www.cyberpresse.ca/le-soleil; f. 1896; Publr CLAUDE GAGNON; Editor-in-Chief PIERRE-PAUL NOREAU; circ. Mon. to Fri. 79,136, Sat. 108,164, Sun. 83,969.

La Tribune: 1950 rue Roy, Sherbrooke, QC J1K 2X8; tel. (819) 564-5450; fax (819) 564-8098; e-mail redaction@latribune.qc.ca; internet www.cyberpresse.ca/la-tribune; f. 1910; Pres. and Publr LOUISE BOISVERT; Editor-in-Chief MAURICE CLOUTIER; circ. Mon. to Fri. 32,765, Sat. 38,599.

La Voix de L'Est: 76 rue Dufferin, Granby, QC J2G 9L4; tel. (450) 375-4555; fax (450) 777-4865; e-mail redaction@lavoixdelest.qc.ca; internet www.cyberpresse.ca/la-voix-de-lest; f. 1945; Pres. and Publr GUY GRANGER; circ. Mon. to Fri. 15,804, Sat. 18,438.

Saskatchewan

Daily Herald: 30 10th St East, Prince Albert, SK S6V 0Y5; tel. (306) 764-4276; fax (306) 763-3331; e-mail editorial@paherald.sk.ca; internet www.paherald.sk.ca; f. 1894; Publr IAN JENSEN; Man. Editor VERN FAULKNER; circ. Mon. to Sat. 7,096.

Leader–Post: 1964 Park St, POB 2020, Regina, SK S4P 3G4; tel. (306) 781-5211; fax (306) 781-5484; e-mail feedback@leaderpost.canwest.com; internet www.leaderpost.com; f. 1883; Publr GREG MCLEAN; Editor JANICE DOCKHAM; circ. Mon. to Fri. 51,066, Sat. 54,475.

StarPhoenix: 204 Fifth Ave North, Saskatoon, SK S7K 2P1; tel. (306) 657-6231; fax (306) 657-6437; e-mail spnews@sp.canwest.com; internet www.canada.com/saskatoon/starphoenix; f. 1902; Publr DALE BRIN; Editor STEVE GIBB; circ. Mon. to Fri. 54,885, Sat. 60,107.

Times–Herald: 44 Fairford St West, POB 3000, Moose Jaw, SK S6H 6E4; tel. (306) 692-6441; fax (306) 692-2101; e-mail editorial@mjtimes.sk.ca; internet www.mjtimes.sk.ca; f. 1889; evening; Publr and Gen. Man. ROB CLARK; Man. Editor LESLEY SHEPPARD; circ. 8,200.

Yukon Territory

Whitehorse Star: 2149 Second Ave, Whitehorse, Yukon, YT Y1A 1C5; tel. (867) 667-4481; fax (867) 668-7130; e-mail star@whitehorsestar.com; internet www.whitehorsestar.com; f. 1900; evening; Publr JACKIE PIERCE; Editor JIM BUTLER; circ. 2,393.

SELECTED PERIODICALS

Alberta

Canadian Journal of Sociology: Dept of Sociology, University of Alberta, Edmonton, AB T6G 2H4; tel. (780) 492-3297; fax (780) 492-7196; e-mail cjscopy@gpu.srv.ualberta.ca; internet www.cjsonline.ca; f. 1975; quarterly; Editor Dr KEVIN HAGGERTY.

Oilweek: Suite 300, 5735 Seventh St, NE, Calgary, AB T2E 8V3 133; tel. (403) 265-3700; fax (403) 265-3706; internet www.oilweek.com; monthly magazine; f. 1948; Publr AGNES ZALEWSKI; Man. Editor DARRELL STONEHOUSE; circ. 7,500.

Ukrainski Visti (Ukrainian News): 12227 107th Ave, Suite 1, Edmonton, AB T5M 1Y9; tel. (780) 488-3693; fax (780) 488-3859; e-mail ukrnews@compusmart.ab.ca; f. 1929; fortnightly; Ukrainian and English; Publr and Editor MARCO LEVYTSKY; circ. 3,274.

Western Catholic Reporter: 8421 101st Ave, Edmonton, AB T6A 0L1; tel. (403) 465-8030; fax (403) 465-8031; e-mail wcr@wcr.ab.ca; internet www.wcr.ab.ca; f. 1965; publ. by the Roman Catholic Archdiocese of Edmonton; weekly; Editor and Gen. Man. GLEN ARGAN; circ. 37,000.

Western Sportsman: 9644 54th Ave, Suite 202, Edmonton, AB T6E 5V1; tel. (780) 643-3961; fax (780) 643-3960; e-mail editor@westernsportsman.com; internet www.westernsportsman.com; f. 1968; 6 a year; Editor DAVE WEBB; circ. 20,086.

British Columbia

BCBusiness Magazine: 4180 Lougheed Hwy, 4th Floor, Burnaby, BC V5C 6A7; tel. (604) 299-7311; fax (604) 299-9188; e-mail ttjaden@canadawide.com; internet www.bcbusinessmagazine.com; f. 1972; monthly; Editor MATT O'GRADY; circ. 26,000.

BC Outdoors—Sport, Fishing and Outdoor Adventure: OP Publishing Ltd, 1080 Howe St, Suite 900, Vancouver, BC V6Z 2T1; tel. (604) 606-4644; fax (604) 687-1925; e-mail bcoutdoors@oppublishing.com; internet www.bcosportfishing.com; f. 1945; 6 a year; Publr MARK YELIC; Editor MIKE MITCHELL; circ. 37,000.

Canadian Aviator: OP Publishing Ltd, 200 West Esplanade, Suite 500, North Vancouver, BC V6Z 2T1; tel. (604) 998-3310; e-mail editor@canadianaviatormagazine.com; internet www.canadianaviatormagazine.com; f. 1990; 6 a year; Editor RUSS NILES; circ. 14,000.

Cottage: OP Publishing Ltd, 200 West Esplanade, Suite 500, North Vancouver, BC V6Z 2T1; tel. (604) 606-4644; fax (604) 687-1925; e-mail editor@cottagemagazine.com; internet www.cottagemagazine.com; f. 1992; 7 a year; Editor and Marketing Dir DESIREE DANIEL; circ. 8,895.

Journal of Commerce: 4299 Canada Way, Suite 101, North Burnaby, BC V5G 1H3; tel. (604) 433-8164; fax (604) 433-9549; e-mail jocinfo@reedbusiness.com; internet www.joconl.com; 2 a week; construction industry; Editor FRANK LILLQUIST; circ. 5,300.

Pacific Yachting: OP Publishing Ltd, 200 West Esplanade, Suite 500, North Vancouver, BC V6Z 2T1; tel. (604) 998-3310; fax (604) 998-3320; e-mail editor@pacificyachting.com; internet www.pacificyachting.com; f. 1968; monthly; Editor PETER A. ROBSON; circ. 17,069.

Vancouver Magazine: 2608 Granville St, Suite 560, Vancouver, BC V6H 3V3; tel. (604) 877-7732; fax (604) 877-4823; e-mail mail@vancouvermagazine.com; internet www.vancouvermagazine.com; f. 1967; 11 a year; Publr KIM PEACOCK; Editor-in-Chief GARY ROSS; circ. 60,000.

Western Living: 2608 Granville St, Suite 560, Vancouver, BC V6H 3V3; tel. (604) 877-7732; fax (604) 877-4838; e-mail wlmail@westernlivingmagazine.com; internet www.westernlivingmagazine.com; f. 1971; 10 a year; Editor JIM SUTHERLAND; circ. 192,350.

WestWorld BC: 4180 Lougheed Hwy, 4th Floor, Burnaby, BC V5C 6A7; tel. (604) 299-7311; fax (604) 299-9188; e-mail cwm@canadawide.com; internet www.canadawide.com/westworldbc_ad.htm; f. 1974; quarterly; travel and sport; Publr and Pres. PETER LEGGE; Editor ANNE ROSE; circ. 517,000.

Manitoba

The Beaver—Canada's History Magazine: 167 Lombard Ave, Suite 478, Winnipeg, MB R3B 0T6; tel. (204) 988-9300; fax (204) 988-9309; e-mail editors@historysociety.ca; internet www.beavermagazine.ca; f. 1920; 6 a year; Canadian history; Pres. and CEO DEBORAH MORRISON; Editor MARK REID; circ. 50,000.

Canadian Dimension: 2E Emma Goldman Centre, 91 Albert St, Winnipeg, MB R3B 1G5; tel. (204) 957-1519; fax (204) 943-4617; e-mail info@canadiandimension.com; internet www.canadiandimension.com; f. 1963; 6 a year; left-wing politics and culture; Publr and Co-ordinating Editor CY GONICK.

Cattlemen: 1666 Dublin Ave, Winnipeg, MB R3H 0H1; tel. (204) 944-5753; fax (204) 944-5416; e-mail gren@fbcpublishing.com; internet www.canadiancattlemen.ca; f. 1938; 13 a year; animal husbandry; Editor GREN WINSLOW; circ. 28,000.

Country Guide: 1666 Dublin Ave, Winnipeg, MB R3H 0H1; tel. (204) 944-5754; fax (204) 942-8463; e-mail tbutton@twinbanks.com; internet www.country-guide.ca; f. 1882; 10 a year; agriculture; Publr BOB WILCOX; Editor TOM BUTTON; circ. 43,000.

Grainews: 1666 Dublin Ave, Winnipeg, MB R3H 0H1; tel. (204) 954-1450; fax (204) 944-5416; e-mail jay@fbcpublishing.com; internet www.grainews.ca; f. 1975; 17 a year; grain and cattle farming; Editor JAY WHETTER; circ. 43,000.

Kayak, Canada's History Magazine for Kids: 167 Lombard Ave, Suite 478, Winnipeg, MB R3B 0T6; tel. (204) 988-9300; fax (204) 988-9309; e-mail editors@kayakmag.ca; internet kayakmag.ca; f. 2005; 6 a year; publ. by Canada's National History Society; Pres. and CEO DEBORAH MORRISON; Editor JILL FORAN; circ. 8,000.

The Manitoba Co-operator: 1666 Dublin Ave, Winnipeg, MB R3H 0H1; tel. (204) 944-5767; fax (204) 954-1422; e-mail daveb@fbcpublishing.com; internet www.manitobacooperator.ca; f. 1925; owned by Farm Business Communications, a subsidiary of Glacier Ventures International Corpn; weekly; for the farming community; Man. Editor DAVE BEDARD; Editor LAURA RANCE; circ. 13,800.

New Brunswick

Brunswick Business Journal: 178B Water St, Campellton, NB E3N 1B6; tel. (506) 7532-8237; internet nbbusinessjournal.canadaeast.com; f. 1984; monthly; Man. Editor NANCY COOK.

Newfoundland and Labrador

Atlantic Business Magazine: 251 Empire Ave, Suite 102, St John's, NL A1C 3H9; tel. (709) 726-9300; fax (709) 726-3013; e-mail dchafe@atlanticbusinessmagazine.com; internet www.atlanticbusinessmagazine.com; f. 1987; 6 a year; business; Publr HUBERT HUTTON; Editor DAWN CHAFE; circ. 29,060.

Northwest Territories

L'Aquilon: POB 1325, Yellowknife, NT X1A 2N9; tel. (867) 873-6603; fax (867) 873-2158; e-mail aquilon@internorth.com; internet www.aquilon.nt.ca; f. 1985; weekly; Editor ALAIN BESSETTE; circ. 1,000.

Hay River Hub: 8–4 Courtoreille St, Hay River, NT X0E 1G3; tel. (867) 874-6577; fax (867) 874-2679; e-mail editor@hayriverhub.com; internet www.hub.awna.com; f. 1973; weekly; Publr CHRIS BRODEUR; Man. Editor SEAN PERCY; circ. 3,000.

Inuvik Drum: POB 2820, Yellowknife, NT X1A 2R1; tel. (867) 777-4545; fax (867) 777-4412; e-mail inuvikdrum@nnsl.com; internet www.nnsl.com/inuvik; f. 1965; weekly; English; distributed in Inuvik, Aklavik, Fort McPherson, Tuktoyaktuk and Arctic Red River; Editor DEZ LOREEN; circ. 1,436.

Northern News Services: 5108 50th St, Yellowknife, NT X1A 2R1; tel. (867) 873-4031; fax (867) 873-8507; e-mail nnsl@nnsl.com; internet www.nnsl.com; f. 1945 as *News/North*; weekly; Publr JACK SIGVALDASON; Man. Editor BRUCE VALPY; circ. 11,000.

Slave River Journal: 207 McDougal Rd, POB 990, Fort Smith, NT X0E 0P0; tel. (867) 872-3000; fax (867) 872-2754; e-mail reception@auroranet.nt.ca; internet www.srj.ca; f. 1978; weekly; Publr and Man. Editor DON JAQUE; circ. 1,750.

Yellowknifer: POB 2820, Yellowknife, NT X1A 2R1; tel. (867) 873-4031; fax (867) 873-8507; e-mail nnsl@nnsl.com; internet www.nnsl.com; weekly; Publr JACK SIGVALDASON; Man. Editor BRUCE VALPY; circ. 6,200.

Nova Scotia

The Dalhousie Review: Dalhousie University, Halifax, NS B3H 4R2; tel. (902) 494-2541; fax (902) 494-3561; e-mail dalhousie.review@dal.ca; internet dalhousiereview.dal.ca; f. 1921; 3 a year; literary and general; Editor ANTHONY STEWART.

Progress: 1660 Hollis St, Penthouse, Suite 1201, Halifax, NS B3J 1V7; tel. (902) 494-0999; fax (902) 494-0997; e-mail news@progresscorp.com; internet www.progresscorp.com; f. 1993; 8 a year; regional business; Editor PAMELA SCOTT-CRACE; circ. 25,800.

Nunavut Territory

Kivalliq News: Rankin Inlet, NU; tel. (867) 645-3223; fax (867) 645-3225; e-mail kivalliqnews@nnsl.com; internet www.nnsl.com; f. 1994; weekly; owned by Northern News Services; English and Inuktitut; Publr JACK SIGVALDASON; Editor DARRELL GREER; circ. 1,400.

Nunatsiaq News: POB 8, Iqaluit, NU X0A 0H0; tel. (867) 979-5357; fax (867) 979-4763; e-mail editor@nunatsiaq.com; internet www.nunatsiaq.com; f. 1973; weekly; English and Inuktitut; Publr STEVEN ROBERTS; Editor JIM BELL; circ. 8,000.

Ontario

Anglican Journal: 80 Hayden St, Toronto, ON M4Y 3G2; tel. (416) 924-9192; fax (416) 921-4452; e-mail editor@national.anglican.ca; internet www.anglicanjournal.com; f. 1871; 10 a year; official publ. of the Anglican Church of Canada; Editor KEITH KNIGHT (acting); circ. 190,000.

Better Farming: 21400 Service Rd, Vankleek Hill, ON K0B 1R0; tel. (613) 678-2232; fax (613) 678-5993; e-mail admin@betterfarming.com; internet www.betterfarming.com; f. 1999; 10 a year; Publr PAUL NOLAN; Man. Editor ROBERT C. IRWIN; circ. 41,000.

Boat Guide: 447 Speers Rd, Suite 4, Oakville, ON L6K 357; tel. (905) 842-6591; fax (905) 842-6843; e-mail critchie@formulamediagroup.com; internet www.boatguidecanada.com; f. 1984; 2 a year; owned by Formula Media Group.

CAmagazine: The Canadian Institute of Chartered Accountants, 277 Wellington St West, Toronto, ON M5V 3H2; tel. (416) 977-3222; fax (416) 204-3409; e-mail christian.bellavance@cica.ca; internet www.camagazine.com; f. 1911; 10 a year; Editor-in-Chief CHRISTIAN BELLAVANCE; circ. 83,558 (68,198 in English; 15,360 in French).

Canada Gazette: Canada Gazette Directorate, Public Works and Govt Services Canada, 350 Albert St, Ottawa, ON K1A 0S5; tel. (613) 996-1268; fax (613) 991-3540; e-mail ncr.gazette@pwgsc.gc.ca; internet canadagazette.gc.ca; f. 1841; weekly; official newspaper of the Govt of Canada; English and French; Editor-in-Chief JOSÉE BOISVERT.

Canadian Architect: 12 Concorde Pl., Suite 800, Toronto, ON M3C 4J2; tel. (416) 510-6807; fax (416) 510-5140; e-mail editors@canadianarchitect.com; internet www.canadianarchitect.com; f. 1955; monthly; Publr TOM ARKELL; Editor IAN CHODIKOFF; circ. 14,000.

Canadian Art: 215 Spadina Ave, Suite 320, Toronto, ON M5T 2C7; tel. (416) 368-8854; fax (416) 368-6135; e-mail info@canadianart.ca; internet www.canadianart.ca; quarterly; Publr MELONY WARD; Editor RICHARD RHODES; circ. 21,000.

Canadian Bar Review/Revue du Barreau canadien: Canadian Bar Foundation, 500–865 Carling Ave, Ottawa, ON K1S 5S8; tel. (613) 237-2925; fax (613) 237-0185; e-mail review@cba.org; internet www.cba.org; f. 1923; quarterly, comprising 3 internet-publ. issues and 1 yearly consolidated vol.; Editor Prof. BETH BILSON; circ. 36,000.

Canadian Business: 1 Mount Pleasant Rd, 11th Floor, Toronto, ON M4Y 2Y5; tel. (416) 764-1200; fax (416) 764-1255; e-mail help@canadianbusiness.com; internet www.canadianbusiness.com; f. 1928; 24 a year; owned by Rogers Media; Publr DEBORAH ROSSER; Editor-in-Chief JOE CHIDLEY; circ. 88,278.

Canadian Chemical News: 130 Slater St, Suite 550, Ottawa, ON K1P 6E2; tel. (613) 232-6252; fax (613) 232-5862; e-mail info@accn.ca; internet www.accn.ca; f. 1949; 10 a year; Editor-in-Chief MICHELLE PIQUETTE; Chair. and Pres. JOE SCHWARCZ; circ. 6,500.

Canadian Electronics: CLB Media Inc, 240 Edward St, Aurora, ON L4G 3S9; tel. (905) 727-0077; fax (905) 727-0017; e-mail ce@clbmedia.ca; internet www.electronicsincanada.com; f. 1986; 7 a year; Publr ROGER HERITAGE; Editor TIM GOULDSON; circ. 22,000.

Canadian Geographic: 1155 Lola St, Suite 200, Ottawa, ON K1K 4C1; tel. (613) 745-4629; fax (613) 744-0947; e-mail editorial@canadiangeographic.ca; internet www.canadiangeographic.ca; f. 1930; 6 a year; publ. of the Royal Canadian Geographical Soc; Editor RICK BOYCHUK; circ. 218,342.

Canadian Home Workshop: 25 Sheppard Ave, West Toronto, ON M2N 6S7; tel. (416) 733-7600; fax (905) 475-9246; e-mail editorial@canadianhomeworkshop.com; internet www.canadianhomeworkshop.com; f. 1977; monthly; home improvement; Editorial Dir DOUGLAS THOMSON; Man. Editor JODI AVERY MACLEAN; circ. 125,015.

Canadian House & Home: 511 King St West, Suite 120, Toronto, ON M5V 2Z4; tel. (416) 593-0204; fax (416) 591-1630; e-mail chheditorial@hhmedia.com; internet www.canadianhouseandhome.com; f. 1982; 12 a year; Editor COBI LADNER; circ. 248,378.

Canadian Jewish News: 1500 Don Mills Rd, Suite 205, North York, ON M3B 3KY; tel. (416) 391-1836; fax (416) 391-0829; e-mail info@cjnews.com; internet www.cjnews.com; f. 1971; weekly; Gen. Man. GARY LAFORET; Editor MORDECHAI BEN-DAT; circ. 50,000.

Canadian Living: 25 Sheppard Ave West, Suite 100, North York, ON M2N 6S7; tel. (416) 733-7600; fax (416) 733-3398; e-mail letters@canadianliving.com; internet www.canadianliving.com; f. 1975; monthly; Editor-in-Chief SUSAN ANTONACCI; circ. 516,824.

Canadian Metalworking: 1 Mount Pleasant Rd, 7th Floor, Toronto, ON M4Y 2Y5; tel. (416) 764-1508; fax (416) 764-3937; e-mail dan.pelton@cmm.rogers.com; internet www.canadianmetalworking.com; f. 1905; 8 a year; Sr Publr LARRY BONIKOWSKY; Editor MARY SCIANNA; circ. 16,600.

Canadian Manager: Canadian Institute of Management, 250 Consumer Rd, Suite 301, Toronto, ON M2J 4V6; tel. (416) 493-0155; fax (416) 495-8723; e-mail office@cim.ca; internet www.cim.ca/nresources/canadianmanager.asp; f. 1942; quarterly; circ. 12,000.

Canadian Medical Association Journal: 1867 Alta Vista Dr., Ottawa, ON K1G 5W8; tel. (613) 731-8610; fax (613) 565-5471; e-mail pubs@cma.ca; internet www.cmaj.ca; f. 1911; 25 a year; Editor Dr PAUL HÉBERT; circ. 69,700.

Canadian Military Journal/Revue militaire canadienne: Canadian Defence Academy, POB 17000, Station Forces, Kingston, ON K7K 7B4; tel. (613) 541-6000; fax (613) 541-6866; e-mail cmj.rmc@forces.gc.ca; internet www.journal.dnd.ca; quarterly; Editor-in-Chief DAVID L. BASHOW.

Canadian Musician: 23 Hannover Dr., Suite 7, St Catharines, ON L2W 1A3; tel. (905) 641-3471; fax (905) 641-1648; e-mail mail@nor.com; internet www.canadianmusician.com; f. 1979; 6 a year; Editor JEFF MACKAY; circ. 27,000.

Canadian Nurse/L'infirmière canadienne: 50 Driveway, Ottawa, ON K2P 1E2; tel. (613) 237-2159; fax (613) 237-3520; e-mail editor@canadian-nurse.com; e-mail redaction@cna-aiic.ca; internet www.canadian-nurse.com; f. 1905 as journal of the Canadian Nurses' Asscn; publ. in separate French and English edns since 2000; 9 a year; Editor-in-Chief LUCILLE AUFFREY; Man. Editor LISA BRAZEAU; circ. 126,000.

Canadian Pharmacists Journal: 1785 Alta Vista Dr., Ottawa, ON K1G 3Y6; tel. (613) 523-7877; fax (613) 523-2332; e-mail cpj@pharmacists.ca; internet www.pharmacists.ca/content/hcp/resource_centre/cpj/cpj_contacts.cfm; f. 1868; fmrly *Canadian Pharmaceutical Journal*; 6 a year; Publr LEESA BRUCE; Editor-in-Chief ROSEMARY KILLEEN; circ. 15,000.

Canadian Poultry Magazine: 105 Donly Dr., South Simcoe, POB 530, ON N3Y 4N5; tel. (519) 836-4394; fax (519) 582-3412; e-mail knudds@annexweb.com; internet www.canadianpoultrymag.com; f. 1928; monthly; Publr MARILYN WHITE; Editor KIRSTY NUDDS; circ. 8,549.

The Canadian Sportsman: 25 Old Plank Rd, POB 129, Straffordville, ON N0J 1Y0; tel. (519) 866-5558; fax (519) 866-5596; e-mail dbriggs@canadiansportsman.ca; internet www.canadiansportsman.ca; f. 1870; 26 a year; harness racing; Publr GARY FOERSTER; Editor DAVE BRIGGS.

Canadian Theatre Review: University of Toronto Press, 5201 Dufferin St, Toronto, ON M3H 5T8; tel. (416) 667-7810; fax (416) 667-7881; e-mail preynen@uoguelph.ca; internet www.utpjournals.com/ctr; f. 1974; quarterly; Editor RIC KNOWLES; circ. 1,500.

Canadian Travel Press Weekly: 310 Dupont St, Toronto, ON M5R 1V9; tel. (416) 968-7252; fax (416) 968-2377; e-mail ctp@baxter.net; internet www.travelpress.com; 46 a year; Editor-in-Chief EDITH BAXTER; Man. Editor MIKE BAGINSKI; circ. 14,000.

Carguide/Le Magazine Carguide: 447 Speers Rd, Suite 4, Oakville, ON L6K 3S7; tel. (905) 842-6591; fax (905) 842-6843; e-mail formulamediagroup@cdsglobal.ca; internet www.carguidemagazine.com; f. 1971; 6 a year in English, quarterly in French; Publr J. SCOTT ROBINSON; Editor GRAHAM FLETCHER.

Chatelaine: 1 Mount Pleasant Rd, 8th Floor, Toronto, ON M4Y 2Y5; tel. (416) 764-1888; fax (416) 764-2413; internet www.chatelaine.com; f. 1928; publ. by Rogers Publishing Inc; monthly; women's journal; Publr KERRY MITCHELL; Editor-in-Chief MARYAM SANATI; circ. 615,559.

CMA Magazine: 1 Robert Speck Pkwy, Suite 1400, Mississauga, ON L4Z 3M3; tel. (905) 949-4200; fax (905) 949-0888; e-mail info@cma-canada.org; internet www.cma-canada.org; f. 1926; 10 a year; journal of the Society of Management Accountants of Canada; Publr R. DAVID FLETCHER; Editor ANDREA CIVICHINO; circ. 46,000.

ComputerWorld Canada: 55 Town Centre Ct, Suite 302, Scarborough, ON M1P 4X4; tel. (416) 290-0240; fax (416) 290-0238; e-mail general@itworldcanada.com; internet www.itworldcanada.com; f. 1984; 25 a year; Editor SHANE SCHICK; circ. 42,000.

Design Product News: CLB Media Inc, 240 Edward St, Aurora, ON L4G 3S9; tel. (905) 727-0077; fax (905) 727-0017; e-mail medwards@clbmedia.ca; internet www.dpncanada.com; f. 1973; 6 a year; mechanical design engineering; Publr NIGEL BISHOP; Editor MIKE EDWARDS; circ. 20,000.

Dogs in Canada: 89 Skyway Ave, Suite 200, Etobicoke, ON M9W 6R4; tel. (416) 798-9778; fax (416) 798-9671; e-mail info@dogsincanada.com; internet www.dogsincanada.com; f. 1889; monthly; for pedigree dog breeders; Publr ANN McDONAGH; Editor-in-Chief KELLY CALDWELL.

Flare: 1 Mount Pleasant Rd, 8th Floor, Toronto, ON M4Y 2Y5; tel. (416) 764-2863; fax (416) 764-2866; e-mail Raquel.Lowe@flare.rogers.com; internet www.teenflare.com; f. 1970; monthly; fashion, beauty and health; Publr ORIETTA MINATEL; circ. 157,156.

Foodservice and Hospitality: 23 Lesmil Rd, Suite 101, Don Mills, ON M3B 3P6; tel. (416) 447-0888; fax (416) 447-5333; e-mail rcaira@foodservice.ca; internet www.foodserviceworld.com; f. 1968; monthly; Editor and Publr ROSANNA CAIRA; circ. 25,130.

Hi-Rise: 95 Leeward Glenway, Unit 121, Don Mills, ON M3C 2Z6; tel. (416) 424-1393; fax (416) 467-8262; e-mail sec.valdunn@vif.com; internet www.geocities.com/athens/atrium/1620/hi-rise; f. 1980; 11 a year; city lifestyle; Editor and Publr VALERIE M. DUNN; circ. 50,000.

The Hockey News: Transcontinental Publishing, 25 Sheppard Ave West, Suite 100, North York, ON M2N 6S7; tel. (416) 340-8000; fax (416) 340-2786; e-mail editorial@thehockeynews.com; internet www.thehockeynews.com; f. 1947; 34 a year; Man. Editor JASON KAY; circ. 102,599.

Holstein Journal: 30 East Beaver Creek Rd, Suite 210, Richmond Hill, ON L4B 1J2; tel. (905) 886-4222; fax (905) 886-0037; e-mail subs@holsteinjournal.com; internet www.holsteinjournal.com; f. 1938; publ. by The Holstein Journal Group, Inc; monthly; news and information pertaining to Holstein dairy cattle; Publr G. PETER ENGLISH; Editor BONNIE E. COOPER; circ. 4,223.

Journal of the Canadian Dental Association: 1815 Alta Vista Dr., Ottawa, ON K1G 3Y6; tel. (613) 523-1770; fax (613) 523-7736; e-mail rgalipeau@cda-adc.ca; internet www.cda-adc.ca/jcda; f. 1935; 11 a year; Editor Dr JOHN P. O'KEEFE; circ. 20,000.

Kanadai Magyarsag (Hungarian-Canadians): 74 Advance Rd, Etobicoke, ON M8Z 2T7; tel. (416) 233-3131; fax (416) 233-5984; e-mail magyarsag@wellerpublishing.com; internet canadahun.com; weekly; Publr IRENE VOROSVARY; Editor and Man. CSABA GAAL; circ. 9,800.

Legion Magazine: 86 Aird Pl., Kanata, ON K2L 0A1; tel. (613) 591-0116; fax (613) 591-0146; e-mail editor@legionmagazine.com; internet www.legionmagazine.com; f. 1926; 6 a year; publ. for Canadian veterans and Legionnaires; Gen. Man. JENNIFER MORSE; circ. 290,512.

Maclean's: 1 Mount Pleasant Rd, 11th Floor, Toronto, ON M4Y 2Y5; tel. (416) 764-1339; fax (416) 764-1332; e-mail letters@macleans.ca; internet www.macleans.ca; f. 1905 as *The Business Magazine*; present name adopted in 1911; weekly; Publr and Editor-in-Chief KENNETH WHYTE; Editor MARK STEVENSON; circ. 368,000.

Metalworking Production and Purchasing: CLB Media Inc, 240 Edward St, Aurora, ON L4G 3S9; tel. (905) 727-0077; fax (905) 727-0017; e-mail jcook@clbmedia.ca; internet www.metalworkingcanada.com; f. 1974; 6 a year; Publr NIGEL BISHOP; Editor JERRY COOK; circ. 18,200.

The Milk Producer: 6780 Campobello Rd, Mississauga, ON L5N 2L8; tel. (905) 821-8970; fax (905) 821-3160; e-mail bdimmick@milk.org; internet www.milk.org/Corporate/pdf/PublicationsMilkProducer.pdf; f. 1925; monthly; publ. of the Dairy Farmers of Ontario; Editor BILL DIMMICK; circ. 10,500.

Municipal World: Box 399, Station Main, St Thomas, ON N5P 3V3; tel. (519) 633-0031; fax (519) 633-1001; e-mail mwadmin@municipalworld.com; internet www.municipalworld.com; f. 1891; monthly; Exec. Editor SUSAN M. GARDNER; circ. 7,500.

Nature Canada: 85 Albert St, Suite 900, Ottawa, ON K1P 6A4; tel. (613) 562-3447; fax (613) 562-3371; e-mail info@naturecanada.ca; internet www.naturecanada.ca; f. 1972; journal of Nature Canada, fmrly the Canadian Nature Federation; Pres. JULIE GELFAND.

Northern Miner: 12 Concorde Pl., Suite 800, Toronto, ON M3C 4J2; tel. (416) 442-2122; fax (416) 442-2191; e-mail northernminer2@northernminer.com; internet www.northernminer.com; f. 1915; owned by the Business Information Group; weekly; Publr DOUGLAS DONNELLY; Editor JOHN CUMMING; circ. 11,000.

Now: 189 Church St, Toronto, ON M5B 1Y7; tel. (416) 364-1300; fax (416) 364-1166; e-mail newmedia@nowtoronto.com; internet www.nowtoronto.com; f. 1981; weekly; young adult; Publr and Editor MICHAEL HOLLETT; CEO and Editor ALICE KLEIN; circ. 406,000.

Ontario Medical Review: 525 University Ave, Suite 200, Toronto, ON M5G 2K7; tel. (416) 599-2580; fax (416) 340-2232; e-mail jeff_henry@oma.org; internet www.oma.org; f. 1922; monthly; publ. of the Ontario Medical Asscn; Editor JEFF HENRY; Man. Editor ELIZABETH PETRUCELLI; circ. 24,000.

Oral Health: 12 Concorde Pl., Suite 800, Toronto, ON M3C 4J2; tel. (416) 510-6785; fax (416) 510-5140; e-mail cwilson@oralhealthjournal.com; internet www.oralhealthjournal.com; f. 1911; monthly; dentistry; Editorial Dir CATHERINE WILSON; circ. 19,232.

Photo Life: 185 St Paul St, Québec, QC G1K 3W2; tel. (800) 905-7468; fax (800) 664-2739; e-mail editor@photolife.com; internet www.photolife.com; f. 1976; 6 a year; Editor-in-Chief ANITA DAMMER; circ. 55,000.

Presbyterian Record: 50 Wynford Dr., Toronto, ON M3C 1J7; tel. (416) 441-1111; fax (416) 441-2825; e-mail record@presbyterianrecord.ca; internet www.presbyterianrecord.ca; f. 1876; 11 a year; Man. Editor ANDREW FAIZ; Editor DAVID HARRIS; circ. 40,000.

Purchasing B2B: 1 Mount Pleasant Rd, 7th Floor, Toronto, ON M4Y 2Y5; tel. (416) 764-1491; fax (416) 764-1740; e-mail tim.dimopoulos@pb2b.rogers.com; internet www.purchasingb2b.ca; 10 a year; Publr TIM DIMOPOULOS; Editor LISA WICHMANN.

Quill & Quire: 111 Queen St East, 3rd Floor, Toronto, ON M5C 1S2; tel. (416) 364-3333; fax (416) 595-5415; e-mail mstrimas@quillandquire.com; internet www.quillandquire.com; f. 1935; 10 a year; book publishing industry; Editor DEREK WEILER; circ. 5,000.

Style: 1106–60 Bloor St West, Toronto, ON M4W 3B8; tel. (416) 203-7900; fax (416) 703-6392; internet www.style.ca; f. 1888; monthly; fashion and clothing trade; owned by Rive Gauche Media; Pres. OLIVIER FELICIO; Editor BRYAN SOROKA; circ. 12,000.

Style at Home: 25 Sheppard Ave West, Suite 100, Toronto, ON M2N 6S7; tel. (416) 733-7600; fax (416) 218-3632; e-mail letters@styleathome.com; internet www.styleathome.com; f. 1997; 12 a year; Editor GAIL JOHNSTON HABS; circ. 231,023.

Sympatico Netlife: 25 Sheppard Ave West, Suite 100, North York, ON M2N 6S7; tel. (416) 733-7600; fax (416) 733-8272; e-mail giffen@sympatico.ca; internet www.ab.sympatico.ca/mags/netlife; 6 a year; computer technology; Man. Editor THERESA DILLON; Editor PETER GIFFEN; circ. 450,000.

Tėviškės Žiburiai (Lights of the Homeland): 2185 Stavebank Rd, Mississauga, ON L5C 1T3; tel. (905) 275-4672; fax (905) 290-9802; e-mail tevzib@pathcom.com; f. 1949; 49 a year; Lithuanian; publ. by the Lithuanian-Canadian Roman Catholic Cultural Society 'Žiburiai'; Editor-in-Chief Rev. Dr PRANAS GAIDA; circ. 3,000.

Time (Canada edn): 175 Bloor St East, Suite 602, North Tower, Toronto, ON M4W 3R8; tel. (416) 929-1115; fax (416) 929-0019; e-mail time_canada@timeinc.com; internet www.timecanada.com; f. 1943; weekly; Pres.-Editor GEORGE RUSSELL; circ. 234,018.

Toronto Life Magazine: 111 Queen St East, Suite 320, Toronto, ON M5C 1S2; tel. (416) 364-3333; fax (416) 861-1169; e-mail editorial@torontolife.com; internet www.torontolife.com; f. 1966; monthly; Publr MARINA GLOGOVAC; Editor SARAH FULFORD; circ. 92,269.

Tribute Magazine: 71 Barber Greene Rd, Don Mills, Toronto, ON M3C 2A2; tel. (416) 445-0544; fax (416) 445-2894; e-mail generalinfo@tribute.ca; internet www.tribute.ca; f. 1981; 9 a year; entertainment; Editor-in-Chief SANDRA I. STEWART; circ. 500,000.

TV Times: 1605 Main St West, Hamilton, ON L8S 1E6; tel. (289) 396-2070; fax (289) 396-2011; e-mail tvtimes@canwest.com; internet www.canada.com/entertainment/television/tvtimes.html; f. 1969; publ. by CanWest MediaWorks Publs Inc; weekly; 10 regional edns; Editor ERIC KOHANIK; circ. 1,941,000.

Wings: 105 Donly Dr., South Simcoe, ON N3Y 4N5; tel. (519) 428-3471; fax (519) 429-3094; e-mail dmccarthy@annexweb.com; internet www.wingsmagazine.com; f. 1957; 6 a year; corporate, commercial and military aviation; Publr TIM MUISE; Editor DREW MCCARTHY; circ. 6,850.

Québec

L'Actualité: 1200 ave McGill College, bureau 800, Montréal, QC H3B 4G7; tel. (514) 843-2564; fax (514) 843-2186; e-mail redaction@lactualite.rogers.com; internet www.lactualite.com; f. 1976; monthly; current affairs; Editor RÉAL GERMAIN; Editor-in-Chief CAROLE BEAULIEU; circ. 185,684.

Affaires Plus: 1100 blvd René-Lévesque ouest, 24e étage, Montréal, QC H3B 4X9; tel. (514) 392-9000; fax (514) 392-4726; e-mail daniel.germain@transcontinental.ca; internet www.affairesplus.com; f. 1978; monthly; Editor-in-Chief DANIEL GERMAIN; circ. 87,684.

Le Bulletin des Agriculteurs: 1200 ave McGill College, bureau 800, Montréal, QC H3B 4G7; tel. (514) 845-5141; fax (514) 843-2180; e-mail info@lebulletin.rogers.com; internet www.lebulletin.com; f. 1918; monthly; Editor-in-Chief YVON THÉRIEN; circ. 13,323.

Canadian Journal of Economics/Revue canadienne d'économique: Cireq, Université de Montréal, bureau C-6086, 3150 Jean Brillant, succursale centre-ville, Montréal, QC H3T 1N8; tel. (514) 343-2104; fax (514) 343-5831; e-mail cje@umontreal.ca; internet economics.ca/cje; f. 1968; quarterly; Man. Editor DAVID GREEN; circ. 3,000.

Canadian Public Policy/Analyse de Politiques: CIREQ, Université de Montréal, CP 6128, succursale Centre-ville Montréal, QC H3C 3J7; tel. (514) 343-2104; fax (514) 343-5831; e-mail cpp@umontreal.ca; internet economics.ca/cpp; quarterly; Man. Editor JAMES B. DAVIES; circ. 1,100.

Châtelaine: 1001 blvd de Maisonneuve ouest, bureau 800, Montréal, QC H3A 3E1; tel. (514) 843-2504; fax (514) 843-2185; internet redaction@chatelaine.rogers.com; internet www.chatelaine.qc.ca; f. 1960; monthly; circ. 202,744.

CIM Magazine: 3400 blvd de Maisonneuve ouest, bureau 855, Montréal, QC H3Z 3B8; tel. (514) 939-2710; fax (514) 939-2714; e-mail cim@cim.org; internet www.cim.org; monthly; fmrly *CIM Bulletin*; publ. by the Canadian Inst. of Mining, Metallurgy and Petroleum; Editor HEATHER EDNIE; circ. 10,460.

Il Cittadino Canadese: 5960 Jean-Talon est, bureau 209, Montréal, QC H1S 1M2; tel. (514) 253-2332; fax (514) 253-6574; e-mail journal@cittadinocanadese.com; internet www.cittadinocanadese.com; f. 1941; weekly; Italian; Editor BASILIO GIORDANO; circ. 38,500.

Commerce: 1100 blvd René-Lévesque ouest, 24e étage, Montréal, QC H3B 4X9; tel. (514) 392-9000; fax (514) 392-4726; e-mail commerce@transcontinental.ca; internet www.magazinecommerce.com; f. 1898; monthly; Editor-in-Chief DIANE BÉRARD; circ. 40,135.

Décormag: 1100 Blvd René-Lévesque, 24e étage, Montréal, QC H3B 4X9; tel. (514) 392-9000; e-mail redaction@decormag.com; internet www.decormag.com; f. 1973; 10 a year; home decorating; Editor MARIE-CHRISTINE TREMBLAY; circ. 84,160.

Harrowsmith Country Life: 3100 Concorde East Blvd, Suite 213, Laval, QC H7E 2B8; tel. (450) 665-0271; fax (450) 665-2974; e-mail info@harrowsmithcountrylife.ca; internet www.harrowsmithcountrylife.ca; f. 1976; 6 a year; Editor TOM CRUICKSHANK; circ. 126,862.

ICAO Journal: 999 rue Université, Montréal, QC H3C 5H7; tel. (514) 954-8219; e-mail icaohq@icao.int; fax (514) 954-6077; internet www.icao.int/icao/en/jr/jr.cfm; f. 1946; 9 a year; aviation; English, French and Spanish; publ. of International Civil Aviation Organization; Editor ERIC MACBURNIE; circ. 15,000.

Le Journal Industriel du Québec: 1200 ave McGill College, bureau 800, Montréal, QC H3B 4G7; tel. (450) 785-2590; fax (450) 785-2591; e-mail ygauthier@industriel.qc.ca; internet www.industriel.qc.ca; f. 1985; 8 a year; Publr YVAN GAUTHIER; Editor LUC BOILY; circ. 19,300.

Le Producteur de Lait Québecois: 555 blvd Roland-Thérrien, Longueuil, QC J4H 3Y9; tel. (450) 679-8483; fax (450) 670-4788; internet www.lait.org/zone3/producteur/index.asp; f. 1980; 10 a year; dairy farming; publ. by Fédération des producteurs de lait du Québec; Publr DANIEL BOULANGER; Editor-in-Chief JEAN VIGNEAULT; circ. 12,000.

Progrès-Dimanche: 1051 blvd Talbot, Chicoutimi, QC G7H 5C1; tel. (418) 545-4474; fax (418) 690-8805; e-mail msimard@lequotidien.com; f. 1964; weekly; Editor-in-Chief MICHEL SIMARD; circ. 45,000.

Québec Science: 4388 rue St-Denis, bureau 300, Montréal, QC H2J 2L1; tel. (514) 843-6888; fax (514) 843-4897; e-mail courrier@quebecscience.qc.ca; internet www.quebecscience.qc.ca; internet www.cybersciences.com; f. 1969; 10 a year; Editor-in-Chief RAYMOND LEMIEUX; circ. 32,000.

Reader's Digest: 1100 blvd Réné-Lévesque ouest, Montréal, QC H3B 5H5; tel. (514) 934-0751; fax (514) 940-3637; internet www.readersdigest.ca; f. 1948; monthly; English edn; Editor-in-Chief PETER STOCKLAND; circ. 948,019.

Rénovation Bricolage: 7 chemin Bates, Outremont, QC H2V 4V7; tel. (514) 848-7164; fax (514) 848-0309; e-mail renobrico@tva-publications.com; internet tva.canoe.ca/groupetva/filiales/tva_publications.html; f. 1976; 9 a year; Publr and Editor CLAUDE LECLERC; Editor-in-Chief VINCENT ROY; circ. 33,588.

Sélection du Reader's Digest: 1100 blvd Réne-Lévesque ouest, Montréal, QC H3B 5H5; tel. (514) 940-0751; fax (514) 940-7340; e-mail manon.sylvain@readersdigest.com; internet www.selection.ca; f. 1947; monthly; Editor ROBERT GOYETTE; circ. 249,843.

La Terre de Chez Nous: 555 blvd Roland-Therrien, Longueuil, QC J4H 3Y9; tel. (450) 679-8483; fax (450) 670-4788; e-mail laterre@laterre.ca; internet www.laterre.ca; f. 1929; weekly; agriculture and forestry; Editor-in-Chief MARC-ALAIN SOUCY; circ. 35,576.

Tidings, Canada's Food and Wine Magazine: 5165 Sherbrooke St West, Montréal, QC H4A 1T6; tel. (514) 481-5892; fax (514) 481-9699; e-mail editor@tidingsmag.com; internet www.tidingsmag.com; f. 1973; 8 a year; Editor-in-Chief ALDO PARISE; circ. 31,000.

TV Hebdo: 7 chemin Bates, Outremont, QC H2V 4V7; tel. (514) 848-7000; fax (514) 848-7070; e-mail tv@tvhebdo.com; internet www

.tvhebdo.com; f. 1960; weekly; Editor-in-Chief JEAN-LOUIS PODLESAK; circ. 119,215.

Saskatchewan

Saskatchewan FarmLife: 2206A Ave C. North, Saskatoon, SK S7L 6C3; tel. (306) 384-3276; fax (306) 668-6164; e-mail adsales@farmpressltd.com; circ. 60,000.

Western Producer: 2310 Millar Ave, POB 2500, Saskatoon, SK S7K 2C4; tel. (306) 665-9600; fax (306) 653-8750; e-mail newsroom@producer.com; internet www.producer.com; f. 1923; weekly; agriculture; Editor BARB GLEN; circ. 74,000.

Yukon Territory

Yukon News: 211 Wood St, Whitehorse, YT Y1A 2E4; tel. (867) 667-6285; fax (867) 668-3755; e-mail rmostyn@yukon-news.com; internet www.yukon-news.com; f. 1960; 3 a week; Editor RICHARD MOSTYN; circ. 8,000.

NEWS AGENCIES

The Canadian Press: 36 King St East, Toronto, ON M5C 2L9; tel. (416) 364-0321; fax (416) 364-0207; internet www.cp.org; f. 1917; national news co-operative; c. 100 mem. newspaper and 500 broadcast partners; Pres. ERIC MORRISON; Editor-in-Chief SCOTT WHITE.

Regional bureaux:

Atlantic (Halifax): 1888 Brunswick St, Suite 701, Halifax, NS B3J 3J8; tel. (902) 422-8496; fax (902) 425-2675; Bureau Chief KEVIN WARD.

British Columbia (Vancouver): 840 Howe St, Suite 250, Vancouver, BC V6Z 2L2; tel. (604) 687-1662; fax (604) 687-5040; Bureau Chief WENDY COX.

Ontario (Toronto): 36 King St East, Toronto, ON M5C 2L9; tel. (416) 364-0321; fax (416) 364-0207; e-mail lgoodman@cp.org; Bureau Chief WENDY MCCANN.

Ottawa: 165 Sparks St, Suite 800, Ottawa, ON K1P 5B9; tel. (613) 236-4122; fax (613) 238-4452; e-mail rrusso@cp.org; Bureau Chief ROB RUSSO.

Prairies (Edmonton): 10109 106th St, Suite 504, Edmonton, AB T5J 3L7; tel. (780) 428-6107; fax (780) 428-0663; e-mail kbell@cp.org; Bureau Chief HEATHER BOYD.

Québec (Montréal): 215 rue St-Jacques ouest, Suite 100, Montréal, QC H2Y 1M6; tel. (514) 849-3212; fax (514) 282-6915; Vice-Pres., French Services JEAN ROY; Bureau Chief DONALD MCKENZIE.

Principal Foreign Bureaux

CHINA, PEOPLE'S REPUBLIC

Xinhua (New China) News Agency (Ottawa): 2084 Lamira St, Ottawa, ON K1H 8P1; tel. (613) 738-7705; fax (613) 738-9268; e-mail hgy@xinhuanet.com; Bureau Chief HU GUANGYAO.

FRANCE

Agence France-Presse (Montréal): 180 blvd René-Lévesque est, Suite 200, Montréal, QC H2X 1N6; tel. (514) 288-2777; fax (514) 288-3506; e-mail afpcanada@afp.com; Bureau Chief HERVÉ GUILBAUD.

Agence France-Presse (Ottawa): National Press Bldg, 150 Wellington St, Suite 750, Ottawa, ON K1P 5A4; tel. (613) 232-2943; fax (613) 233-7673; Correspondent DAVID CHAN.

Agence France-Presse (Toronto): 34 King St East, Suite 550, Toronto, ON M5C 2X8; tel. (415) 361-0725; fax (415) 361-0762.

ITALY

Agenzia Nazionale Stampa Associata (ANSA): National Press Bldg, 150 Wellington St, Rm 703, Ottawa, ON K1P 5A4; tel. (613) 235-4248; fax (613) 235-2428; Rep. ELIO COPPOLA.

RUSSIA

Informatsionnoye Telegrafnoye Agentstvo Rossii—Telegrafnoye Agentstvo Suverennykh Stran (ITAR—TASS): 200 Rideau Terrace, Suite 1305, Ottawa, ON K1M 0Z3; tel. (613) 745-4310; fax (613) 745-5581; e-mail tasscnd@sympatico.ca; Bureau Chief IGOR BORISENKO.

UNITED KINGDOM

Reuters Canada Ltd (Calgary): 4 Ave SW, Suite 355, Calgary, AB T2P 0J1; tel. (403) 531-1620; fax (403) 262-5548.

Reuters Canada Ltd (Montréal): 800 Blvd René Levesque ouest, Suite 300, Montréal, QC H3B 1X9; tel. (514) 982-5600; fax (514) 844-2327; internet www.reuters.ca.

Reuters Canada Ltd (Ottawa): Booth Bldg, 165 Sparks St, Suite 400, Ottawa, ON K1P 5B9; tel. (613) 235-6745; fax (613) 235-5890; Bureau Chief RANDALL PALMER.

Reuters Canada Ltd (Québec): c/o Tribune de la Presse, 1055 rue Louis-Alexandre Taschereau, bureau 208, Québec, QC G1R 5J1; tel. (408) 648-6442; fax (408) 648-8234.

Reuters Canada Ltd (Toronto): Standard Life Centre, 121 King St West, Suite 2000, Toronto, ON M5H 3T9; tel. (416) 941-8000; fax (416) 941-9064; internet ca.reuters.com; Man. Dir (Reuters Canada) JOE DESARIO.

Reuters Canada Ltd (Vancouver): 625 Howe St, Suite 200, Vancouver, BC; tel. (604) 669-6033; fax (604) 681-0491.

Reuters Canada Ltd (Winnipeg): 240 Graham Ave, Suite 6, Winnipeg, MB; tel. (204) 947-3548; fax (204) 947-5167.

USA

Associated Press (Toronto): 36 King St East, Suite 301, Toronto, ON M5C 2L9; tel. (416) 368-1388; fax (416) 364-0207.

United Press International (UPI) (Ottawa): c/o Parliamentary Press Gallery, House of Commons, 350 North Centre Block, Ottawa, ON K1A 0A8; tel. (613) 992-4511.

United Press International (UPI) (Toronto): 144 Front St West, Suite 432, Toronto, ON M5J 2L7; tel. (416) 340-7276; fax (416) 340-7277.

NATIONAL PRESS ASSOCIATIONS

Canadian Association of Journalists/L'Association Canadienne des Journalistes (CAJ/ACJ): Algonquin College, 1385 Woodroffe Ave, B224, Ottawa, ON K2G 1V8; tel. (613) 526-8061; fax (613) 521-3904; e-mail caj@caj.ca; internet www.caj.ca; f. 1978; Exec. Dir JOHN DICKINS; Pres. MARY AGNES WELCH; Chair. SALEEM KHAN; over 1,500 mems.

Canadian Business Press: 4195 Dundas St West, Suite 346, Toronto, ON M8X 1Y4; tel. (416) 239-1022; fax (416) 239-1076; e-mail admin@cbp.ca; internet www.cbp.ca; f. 1920; Chair. ALEX PAPANOU; Pres. PHILIP J. BOYD; over 170 mems.

Canadian Community Newspapers Association: 890 Yonge St, Suite 200, Toronto, ON M4W 3P4; tel. (416) 482-1090; fax (416) 482-1908; e-mail info@ccna.ca; internet www.communitynews.ca; f. 1919; Chair. CAM MCKNIGHT; CEO JOHN HINDS; 7 regional asscns; more than 700 mems.

Canadian Newspaper Association/Association Canadienne des Journaux (CNA/ACJ): 890 Yonge St, Suite 200, Toronto, ON M4W 3P4; tel. (416) 923-3567; fax (416) 923-7206; e-mail info@cna-acj.ca; internet www.cna-acj.ca; f. 1996; Chair. ALAN ALLNUTT; Vice-Chair. NATALIE LARIVIÈRE.

Magazines Canada (The Magazine Asscn of Canada): 425 Adelaide St West, Suite 700, Toronto, ON M5V 3C1; tel. (416) 504-0274; fax (416) 504-0437; internet www.magazinescanada.ca; f. 1973 as the Canadian Magazine Publrs Asscn; present name adopted 2005; represents over 300 of the country's consumer titles; Chair. ROBERT GOYETTE; CEO MARK JAMISON.

PUBLISHING

PUBLISHERS

Addison-Wesley Canada Ltd: 26 Prince Andrew Pl., Toronto, ON M3C 2T8; tel. (416) 447-5101; fax (416) 443-0948; e-mail webinfo .pubcanada@pearsoned.com; internet vig.pearsoned.ca; division of Pearson Canada; f. 1916; mathematics, science, language, business and social sciences textbooks, trade, juvenile; CEO BILL BARKE.

Thomas Allen and Son Ltd: 390 Steelcase Rd East, Markham, ON L3R 1G2; tel. (905) 475-9126; fax (905) 475-4255; e-mail info@t-allen .com; internet www.thomas-allen.com; f. 1916; Pres. T. J. ALLEN.

Annick Press Ltd: 15 Patricia Ave, Toronto, ON M2M 1H9; tel. (416) 221-4802; fax (416) 221-8400; e-mail annickpress@annickpress .com; internet www.annickpress.com; f. 1975; children's; Dir RICK WILKS.

Arsenal Pulp Press Book Publishers Ltd: 341 Water St, Suite 200, Vancouver, BC V6B 1B8; tel. (604) 687-4233; fax (604) 687-4283; e-mail info@arsenalpulp.com; internet www.arsenalpulp.com; f. 1982; literary fiction and non-fiction, cultural studies, gay and lesbian; Publr BRIAN LAM.

Bayard Canada Books, Inc: 4475 rue Frontenac, Montréal, QC H2H 2S2; tel. (514) 278-3020; fax (514) 278-3030; e-mail sspino@ bayard-inc.com; internet www.bayardcanada.ca; owned by les Pères Augustins de l'Assomption; f. 1991; acquired Owl Communications in 1997, Novalis Publishing in 2000, Editions Banjo in 2004 and Maple Tree Press in 2008; religion, general interest, literature, children; English and French; Pres. SUZANNE SPINO.

Beauchemin: 7001 blvd St-Laurent, Laval, QC H2S 3E3; tel. (514) 273-1066; fax (514) 276-0324; internet www.cheneliere.ca; f. 1842; imprint of Chenelière Education; educational and general.

Black Rose Books: pl. du Parc, CP 1258, Montréal, QC H2W 2R3; tel. (514) 844-4076; fax (514) 849-1956; e-mail info@blackrosebooks .net; internet www.blackrosebooks.net; f. 1969; social studies, humanities; Pres. JACQUES ROUX.

Les Editions du Boréal: 4447 rue St-Denis, Montréal, QC H2J 2L2; tel. (514) 287-7401; fax (514) 287-7664; e-mail boreal@editionsboreal .qc.ca; internet www.editionsboreal.qc.ca; f. 1963; history, biography, fiction, politics, economics, educational, children's; Dir-Gen. PASCAL ASSATHIANY.

Borealis Press Ltd: 8 Mohawk Cres., Ottawa, ON K2H 7G6; tel. (613) 829-0150; fax (613) 829-7783; e-mail drt@borealispress.com; internet www.borealispress.com; f. 1972; Canadian fiction and non-fiction, drama, juvenile, poetry; Pres. FRANK TIERNEY.

Boston Mills Press: 132 Main St, Erin, ON N0B 1T0; tel. (519) 833-2407; fax (519) 833-2195; e-mail books@bostonmillspress.com; internet www.bostonmillspress.com; f. 1974; Canadian and US history and general non-fiction; Man. Editor NOEL HUDSON.

Breakwater Books: 100 Water St, POB 2188, St John's, NL A1C 6E6; tel. (709) 722-6680; fax (709) 753-0708; e-mail info@breakwater .nf.net; internet www.breakwaterbooks.com; f. 1973; fiction, non-fiction, children's, educational, folklore; Vice-Pres. REBECCA ROSE.

Broadview Press: 280 Perry St, Unit 5, POB 1243, Peterborough, ON K9J 7H5; tel. (705) 743-8990; fax (705) 743-8353; e-mail customerservice@broadviewpress.com; internet www .broadviewpress.com; f. 1985; English Studies and Philosophy; Pres. DON LEPAN.

Canada Law Book, Inc: 240 Edward St, Aurora, ON L4G 3S9; tel. (905) 841-6472; fax (905) 841-5085; e-mail w.moffatt@ canadalawbook.ca; internet www.canadalawbook.ca; f. 1855; law reports, law journals, legal textbooks, etc.; Pres. STUART MORRISON.

CCH Canadian Ltd: 90 Sheppard Ave East, Suite 300, Toronto, ON M2N 6X1; tel. (416) 224-2224; fax (416) 224-2243; e-mail service@cch .ca; internet www.cch.ca; f. 1946; owned by Wolters Kluwer nv (Netherlands); tax, legal, human resources, business and financial planning; Pres. and CEO IAN RHIND.

Les Editions CEC, Inc: 8101 blvd Métropolitain est, Anjou, Montréal, QC H1J 1J9; tel. (514) 351-6010; fax (514) 351-1845; e-mail ressourceshumaines@ceceditions.com; internet www .editionscec.com; f. 1956; textbooks; Pres. and Dir-Gen. CHRISTIAN JETTÉ.

Charlton Press: POB 820, Station Willowdale B, North York, ON M2K 2RI; tel. (416) 488-1418; fax (416) 488-4656; e-mail chpress@ charltonpress.com; internet www.charltonpress.com; f. 1963; Pres. WILLIAM K. CROSS.

Chenelière Education: 7001 blvd St-Laurent, Montréal, QC H2S 3E3; tel. (514) 273-1066; fax (514) 276-0324; e-mail chene@ dlcmcgrawhill.ca; internet www.cheneliere.ca; textbooks; Pres. JACQUES ROCHEFORT.

Coach House Books: 401 Huron St, Toronto, ON M5S 2G5; tel. (416) 979-2217; fax (416) 977-1158; internet www.chbooks.com; f. 1965; fiction, poetry, drama; Publr STAN BEVINGTON.

Copp Clark Professional: 1675 Sismet Rd, Unit 1, Mississauga, ON L4W 4K8; tel. (905) 238-2882; fax (905) 238-3413; e-mail info@ coppclark.com; internet www.coppclark.com; f. 1841; division of Pearson Canada Inc. (subsidiary of Pearson plc); data and publs relating to financial services sector; Publr and CEO RONALD MARR; Editorial Dir GRACE D'ALFONSO.

Crabtree Publishing Co, Ltd: 616 Welland Ave, St Catharines, ON L2M 5V6; tel. (905) 682-5221; fax (905) 682-7166; e-mail custserv@crabtreebooks.com; internet www.crabtreebooks.com; f. 1978; children's non-fiction; Pres. PETER A. CRABTREE; Gen. Man. JOHN SIEMENS.

Doubleday Canada Ltd: 105 Bond St, Toronto, ON M5B 1Y3; tel. (416) 977-7891; fax (416) 977-8707; internet doubleday.com; f. 1944; imprint of Random House of Canada Ltd; general, trade, textbooks, mass market; Pres. JOHN NEALE.

Douglas & McIntyre Ltd: 2323 Québec St, Suite 201, Vancouver, BC V5T 4S7; tel. (604) 254-7191; fax (604) 254-9099; e-mail dm@ douglas-mcintyre.com; internet www.dmpibooks.com; f. 1964; imprints incl. Greystone Books, New Society Publrs; general non-fiction, literary fiction; Pres. SCOTT MCINTYRE.

The Dundurn Group: 3 Church St, Suite 200, Toronto, ON M5E 1M2; tel. (416) 214-5544; fax (416) 214-5556; e-mail info@dundurn .com; internet www.dundurn.com; f. 1972; drama and performing arts, history, reference, fiction and non-fiction; Pres. KIRK HOWARD.

ECW Press: 2120 Queen St East, Suite 200, Toronto, ON M4E 1E2; tel. (416) 694-3348; fax (416) 698-9906; e-mail info@ecwpress.com; internet www.ecwpress.com; f. 1974; sports, biography, non-fiction; Co-Publr JACK DAVID; Man. Editor CRISSY BOYLAN.

H. B. Fenn and Co Ltd: 34 Nixon Rd, Bolton, ON L7E 1W2; tel. (905) 951-6600; fax (905) 951-6601; e-mail administrator@hbfenn.com; internet www.hbfenn.com; f. 1977; fiction and non-fiction; major shareholder in Key Porter Books; Pres. and CEO HAROLD FENN; Publr C. JORDAN FENN.

Editions Fides: 306 rue Saint-Zotique Est, Montréal QC H2S 1L6; tel. (514) 745-4290; fax (514) 745-4299; e-mail editions@fides.qc.ca; internet www.fides.qc.ca; f. 1937; juvenile, history, theology, textbooks and literature; Dir-Gen. MICHEL MAILLÉ.

Fifth House Publishers Ltd: 1511–1800 4th St, SW Calgary, AB T2S 2S5; tel. (403) 571-5241; fax (403) 571-5232; e-mail charlene@ fifthhousepublishers.ca; internet www.fifthhousepublishers.ca; f. 1982; imprint of Fitzhenry & Whiteside Ltd; native, literary and non-fiction; Publr. CHARLENE DOBMEIER.

Fitzhenry & Whiteside Ltd: 195 Allstate Pkwy, Markham, ON L3R 4T8; tel. (905) 477-9700; fax (905) 477-2834; e-mail godwit@ fitzhenry.ca; internet www.fitzhenry.ca; f. 1966; children's fiction and non-fiction, textbooks, trade, educational, poetry; Pres. SHARON FITZHENRY.

Groundwood Books Ltd: 110 Spadina Ave, Suite 801, Toronto ON M5V 2K4; tel. (416) 363-4343; fax (416) 363-1017; e-mail susanm@ groundwood-dm.com; internet www.groundwoodbooks.com; owned by House of Anansi Press Inc; f. 1978; children's books; incl. Spanish language imprint, Libros Tigrillo; Publr PATRICIA ALDANA.

Groupe Modulo: 233 ave Dunbar, bureau 300, Montréal, QC H3P 2H4; tel. (514) 738-9818; fax (514) 738-5838; e-mail claire.demers@ thomson.com; internet www.groupemodulo.com; f. 1975; division of Nelson Education; five imprints: Modulo Editeur, Modulo-Griffon, Griffon d'argile, Éditions Du Phare, Mondia Éditeurs, and Duval Éducation; educational; Dir-Gen. JEAN BOUCHARD.

Guérin Editeur Ltée: 4501 rue Drolet, Montréal, QC H2T 2G2; tel. (514) 842-3481; fax (514) 842-4923; e-mail france.larochelle@ guerin-editeur.qc.ca; internet www.guerin-editeur.qc.ca; f. 1970; professional and textbooks.

Harlequin Enterprises Ltd: 225 Duncan Mill Rd, Don Mills, ON M3B 3K9; tel. (416) 445-5860; fax (416) 445-8655; e-mail customer_ecare@harlequin.ca; internet www.eharlequin.com; f. 1949; fiction, paperbacks; imprints: Silhouette, MIRA Books, Red Dress Ink, LUNA Books, HQN Books, Steeple Hill Books, Steeple Hill Café, Kimani Press, Spice and Harlequin Ginger Blossom; Chair. and CEO DONNA M. HAYES.

HarperCollins Canada Ltd: 2 Bloor St East, Toronto, ON M4W 1A8; tel. (416) 975-9334; fax (416) 975-5223; internet www.harpercanada.com; f. 1989; trade, bibles, dictionaries, juvenile, paperbacks; Pres. and CEO DAVID KENT.

The Frederick Harris Music Co Ltd: Unit 1, 5865 McLaughlin Rd, Mississauga, ON L5R 1B8; tel. (905) 501-1595; fax (905) 501-0929; e-mail fhmc@frederickharrismusic.com; internet www.frederickharrismusic.com; f. 1904; Pres. and CEO RON KELLY.

Editions Héritage: 300 rue Arran, St-Lambert, QC J4R 1K5; tel. (514) 875-0327; fax (514) 672-1481; e-mail information@editionsheritage.com; f. 1968; history, biography, sport, juvenile; Pres. LUC PAYETTE.

Editions de l'Hexagone: 1010 rue de la Gauchetière est, Montréal, QC H2L 2N5; tel. (514) 523-1182; fax (514) 282-7530; e-mail vml@sogides.com; internet www.edhexagone.com; f. 1953; part of Quebecor Media Inc; literature; Editorial Dir JEAN-YVES SOUCY.

Les Editions de l'Homme: 955 rue Amherst, Montréal, QC H2L 3K4; tel. (514) 523-1182; fax (514) 597-0370; e-mail edhomme@sogides.com; internet www.edhomme.com; f. 1958; practical skills incl. cookery, general interest, biographies, popular psychology and novels; Pres. CELINE MASSICOTTE.

Institut de Recherches Psychologiques, Inc/Institute of Psychological Research, Inc: 34 rue Fleury ouest, Montréal, QC H3L 1S9; tel. (514) 382-3000; fax (514) 382-3007; e-mail info@i-p-r.ca; internet www.i-p-r.ca; f. 1964; educational and psychological; Adviser ROBERT CHEVRIER.

Key Porter Books: 6 Adelaide St East, 10th Floor, Toronto, ON M5C 1H6; tel. (416) 862-7777; fax (416) 862-2304; e-mail rob.howard@keyporter.com; internet www.keyporter.com; f. 1979; majority owned by H. B. Fenn and Co Ltd; general trade; Publr and Vice-Pres. JORDAN FENN.

Kids Can Press Ltd: 29 Birch Ave, Toronto, ON M4V 1E2; tel. (416) 925-5437; fax (416) 960-5437; e-mail customerservice@kidscan.com; internet www.kidscanpress.com; f. 1973; children's and young adults' books; Editor-in-Chief SHEILA BARRY.

Leméac Editeur: 4609 d'Iberville, 3e étage, Montréal, QC H2H 2L9; tel. (514) 525-5558; fax (514) 524-3145; e-mail lemeac@lemeac.com; f. 1957; literary, academic, theatre, general; Gen. Dir LISE P. BERGEVIN.

LexisNexis Canada Inc: 123 Commerce Valley Dr. East, Suite 700, Markham, ON L3T 7W8; tel. (905) 479-2665; fax (905) 479-2826; e-mail info@lexisnexis.ca; internet www.lexisnexis.ca; f. 1912; legal, professional; Pres. and CEO PATRICK J. COLLINS.

Lidec Inc: 4350 ave de l'Hôtel-de-Ville, Montréal, QC H2W 2H5; tel. (514) 843-5991; fax (514) 843-5252; e-mail lidec@lidec.qc.ca; internet www.lidec.qc.ca; f. 1965; educational, textbooks; Pres. MARC-AIMÉ GUÉRIN.

James Lorimer & Co Ltd: 317 Adelaide St West, Suite 1002, ON M5V 1P9; tel. (416) 362-4762; fax (416) 362-3939; e-mail jlorimer@lorimer.ca; internet www.formac.ca/lorimer; f. 1971; urban and labour studies, children's, general non-fiction; Publr CHRIS KEEN.

McClelland and Stewart Ltd: 75 Sherbourne St, 5th Floor, Toronto, ON M5A 2P9; tel. (416) 598-1114; fax (416) 598-7764; internet www.mcclelland.com; f. 1906; trade and illustrated; Pres. and Publr DOUG PEPPER; Chair. AVIE J. BENNETT.

McGill-Queen's University Press: 3430 rue McTavish, Montréal, QC H3A 1X9; tel. (514) 398-3750; fax (514) 398-4333; e-mail info@mcgill.ca; internet www.mqup.ca; f. 1960; scholarly and general interest; Exec. Dir PHILIP J. CERCONE.

McGraw-Hill Ryerson Ltd: 300 Water St, Whitby, ON L1N 9B6; tel. (905) 430-5000; fax (905) 430-5191; internet www.mcgrawhill.ca; f. 1944; general; three divisions: educational publishing, higher education and professional publishing; Exec. Dir ROBERT J. BAHASH.

Micromedia ProQuest: 20 Victoria St, Toronto, ON M5C 2N8; tel. (416) 362-5211; fax (416) 362-6161; e-mail info@micromedia.ca; internet www.micromedia.ca; f. 1972; part of Cambridge Information Group; reference, business, government; Dir of Sales MIKE BAIDA.

Mosaic Press: 1252 Speers Rd, Unit 1, Oakville, ON L6L 5N9; tel. and fax (905) 825-2130; e-mail info@mosaic-press.com; internet www.mosaic-press.com; f. 1975; literary, scholarly and cultural; Publr HOWARD ASTER.

Editions du Noroît: 4609 rue d'Iberville, Montréal, QC H2H 2L9; tel. (514) 727-0005; fax (514) 723-6660; e-mail lenoroit@lenoroit.com; internet www.lenoroit.com; f. 1971; poetry; Dir PAUL BÉLANGER.

Novalis: 4475 rue Frontenac, Montréal, QC H2H 2S2; tel. (514) 278-3020; fax (514) 278-0072; e-mail ralbert@novalis-inc.com; internet www.novalis.ca; f. 1935; juvenile and young adult, religious; Dir-Gen. RONALD ALBERT.

Oberon Press: 145 Spruce St, Suite 205, Ottawa, ON K1R 6P1; tel. and fax (613) 238-3275; e-mail oberon@sympatico.ca; internet www.oberonpress.ca; f. 1966; poetry, fiction and general non-fiction; Pres. MICHAEL MACKLEM.

Oolichan Books: POB 10, Lantzville, BC V0R 2H0; tel. and fax (250) 390-4839; e-mail oolichanbooks@telus.net; internet www.oolichan.com; f. 1974; poetry, fiction and non-fiction; Publr RON SMITH; Man. Editor HIRO BOGA.

OP Publishing Ltd: 200 West Esplanade, Suite 500, Vancouver, BC V7M 14A; tel. (604) 998-3310; fax (604) 998-3320; e-mail info@oppublishing.com; internet www.oppublishing.com; sports and outdoor activities; Pres. MARY MILLS; Publr MARK YELIC.

Oxford University Press Canada: 70 Wynford Dr., Don Mills, ON M3C 1J9; tel. (416) 441-2941; fax (416) 444-0427; e-mail webmaster.ca@oup.com; internet www.oupcanada.com; f. 1904; general, education, scholarly, Canadiana; Pres. DAVID STOVER.

Peace Research Institute—Dundas (PRI-D): 25 Dundana Ave, Dundas, ON L9H 4E5; tel. (905) 628-2356; fax (905) 628-1830; e-mail info@prid.on.ca; f. 1976; journals; Office Man. LINDA CARROLL.

Pearson Education Canada, Inc: 26 Prince Andrew Pl., Toronto, ON M3C 2T8; tel. (416) 447-5101; fax (416) 443-0948; e-mail webinfo.pubcanada@pearsoned.com; internet www.pearsoned.ca; educational; Pres. ALLAN REYNOLDS.

Penguin Group (Canada): 90 Eglinton Ave East, Suite 700, Toronto, ON M4P 2Y3; tel. (416) 925-2249; fax (416) 925-0068; e-mail info@penguin.ca; internet www.penguin.ca; f. 1974; division of Pearson; Pres. ED CARSON; Publr DAVID DAVIDAR.

Pippin Publishing Corpn: POB 242, Don Mills, ON M3C 2S2; tel. (416) 510-2918; fax (416) 510-3359; e-mail cynthia@pippinpub.com; internet www.pippinpub.com; f. 1995; educational and trade; Pres. JONATHAN LOVAT DICKSON.

Pontifical Institute of Mediaeval Studies: 59 Queen's Park Cres. East, Toronto, ON M5S 2C4; tel. (416) 926-7142; fax (416) 926-7292; e-mail barbara.north@utoronto.ca; internet www.pims.ca; f. 1939; scholarly publs concerning the Middle Ages; Pres. JAMES MCCONICA.

Les Presses de l'Université Laval: Pavillon Maurice-Pollack, bureau 3103, 2305 rue de l'Université, Québec, QC G1V 0A6; tel. (418) 656-2803; fax (418) 656-3305; e-mail presses@pul.ulaval.ca; internet www.pulaval.com; f. 1950; scholarly; Dir-Gen. DENIS DION.

Les Presses de l'Université de Montréal: 306 rue Saint-Zotique Est, Montréal, QC H2S 1L6; tel. (514) 343-6933; fax (514) 343-2232; e-mail pum@umontreal.ca; internet www.pum.umontreal.ca; f. 1962; scholarly and general; Dir-Gen. ANTOINE DEL BUSSO.

Les Presses de l'Université du Québec: Edif. le Delta I, 2875 blvd Laurier, Suite 450, Québec, QC G1V 2M2; tel. (418) 657-4399; fax (418) 657-2096; e-mail puq@puq.ca; internet www.puq.ca; f. 1969; scholarly and general; Dir-Gen. CÉLINE FOURNIER.

Random House of Canada Ltd: 1 Toronto St, Unit 300, Toronto, ON M5C 2V6; tel. (416) 364-4449; fax (416) 364-6863; internet www.randomhouse.ca; f. 1944; merged with Doubleday Canada Ltd in 1999; Chair. (vacant); Pres. and CEO BRAD MARTIN.

Editions du Renouveau Pédagogique, Inc: 5757 rue Cypihot, St-Laurent, QC H4S 1R3; tel. (514) 334-2690; fax (514) 334-4720; e-mail info@erpi.com; internet www.erpi.com; f. 1965; textbooks; Pres. NORMAND CLÉROUX.

Scholastic Canada Ltd: 175 Hillmont Rd, Markham, ON L6C 1Z7; tel. (905) 887-7323; fax (905) 887-3643; e-mail custserv@scholastic.ca; internet www.scholastic.ca; f. 1957; wholly owned subsidiary of Scholastic, Inc; imprints include North Winds Press, Éditions Scholastic; Co-Pres LINDA GOSNELL, IOLE LUCCHESE.

Self-Counsel Press Ltd: 1481 Charlotte Rd, North Vancouver, BC V7J 1H1; tel. (604) 986-3366; fax (604) 986-3947; e-mail service@self-counsel.com; internet www.self-counsel.com; f. 1971; reference, self-help, business, law; Pres. DIANA R. DOUGLAS.

Editions du Septentrion: 1300 ave Maguire, Sillery, QC G1T 1Z3; tel. (418) 688-3556; fax (418) 527-4978; e-mail sept@septentrion.qc.ca; internet www.septentrion.qc.ca; f. 1988; history, essays, general; Man. GILLES HERMAN.

Thistledown Press Ltd: 633 Main St, Saskatoon, SK S7H 0J8; tel. (306) 244-1722; fax (306) 244-1762; e-mail editorial@thistledownpress.com; internet www.thistledownpress.com; f. 1975; Canadian fiction, non-fiction and poetry; Publr ALLAN FORRIE.

Thomson Carswell: 1 Corporate Plaza, 2075 Kennedy Rd, Toronto, ON M1T 3V4; tel. (416) 609-8000; fax (416) 298-5094; e-mail carswell.customerrelations@thomson.com; internet www.carswell.com; f. 1864; fmrly Carswell-Thomson Professional Publishing Canada; legal, financial, business; Pres. and CEO DON VAN MEER.

Thomson Nelson: 1120 Birchmount Rd, Scarborough, ON M1K 5G4; tel. (416) 752-9448; fax (416) 752-8101; e-mail inquire@nelson.com; internet www.nelson.com; f. 1914; OMERS Capital Partners; retailing, consumer affairs, textbooks; Pres. GREG NORDAL.

Thompson Educational Publishing Inc: 20 Ripley Ave, Toronto, ON M6S 3N9; tel. (416) 766-2763; fax (416) 766-0398; e-mail publisher@thompsonbooks.com; internet www.thompsonbooks.com; f. 1989; textbooks; Pres. KEITH THOMPSON.

Turnstone Press Ltd: 100 Arthur St, Suite 607, Winnipeg, MB R3B 1H3; tel. (204) 947-1555; fax (204) 942-1555; internet www.turnstonepress.com; f. 1976; literary and regional; Man. Editor TODD BESANT.

University of Alberta Press (UAP): Ring House 2, Edmonton, AB T6G 2E1; tel. (780) 492-3662; fax (780) 492-0719; e-mail linda.cameron@ualberta.ca; internet www.uap.ualberta.ca; f. 1969; scholarly, general non-fiction; Dir LINDA D. CAMERON.

University of British Columbia Press (UBC Press): 2029 West Mall, Vancouver, BC V6T 1Z2; tel. (604) 822-5959; fax (604) 822-6083; e-mail info@ubcpress.ca; internet www.ubcpress.ca; f. 1971; law, politics, history, environmental studies, anthropology, Canadian studies, sociology, military history; Dir R. PETER MILROY.

University of Calgary Press: 2500 University Dr., NW, Calgary, AB T2N 1N4; tel. (403) 220-7578; fax (403) 282-0085; e-mail ucpress@ucalgary.ca; internet www.uofcpress.com; f. 1981; Dir Dr GEOFFERY SIMMINS (acting).

University of Manitoba Press: 301 St John's College, University of Manitoba, Winnipeg, MB R3T 2M5; tel. (204) 474-9495; fax (204) 474-7566; e-mail uofm_press@umanitoba.ca; internet www.umanitoba.ca/uofmpress; f. 1967; native, Arctic and Canadian history; Icelandic and Canadian literature; Dir DAVID CARR; Man. Editor GLENN BERGEN.

University of Ottawa Press/Les Presses de l'Université d'Ottawa: 542 King Edward, Ottawa, ON K1N 6N5; tel. (613) 562-5246; fax (613) 562-5247; e-mail press@uottawa.ca; internet www.uopress.uottawa.ca; f. 1936; university texts, scholarly and literary works in English and French; Man. Dir ERIC NELSON.

University of Toronto Press Inc: 10 St Mary St, Suite 700, Toronto, ON M4Y 2W8; tel. (416) 978-2239; fax (416) 978-4738; e-mail publishing@utpress.utoronto.ca; internet www.utppublishing.com; f. 1901; scholarly books and journals; Pres., Publr and CEO JOHN YATES.

Whitecap Books Ltd: 351 Lynn Ave, North Vancouver, BC V7J 2C4; tel. (604) 980-9852; fax (604) 980-8197; e-mail whitecap@whitecap.ca; internet www.whitecap.ca; f. 1977; culinary, outdoor guides; children's books under Walrus Books imprint; Pres. MICHAEL E. BURCH.

John Wiley and Sons Canada Ltd: 6045 Freemont Blvd, Mississauga, ON L5R 4J3; tel. (416) 236-4433; fax (416) 236-8743; e-mail canada@wiley.com; internet ca.wiley.com; f. 1968; general and trade; CEO WILLIAM J. PESCE.

Wilfrid Laurier University Press: Wilfrid Laurier University, 75 University Ave West, Waterloo, ON N2L 3C5; tel. (519) 884-0710; fax (519) 725-1399; e-mail press@wlu.ca; internet www.wlupress.wlu.ca; f. 1974; academic and scholarly; Dir BRIAN HENDERSON.

Worldwide Library: 225 Duncan Mill Rd, Don Mills, ON M3B 3K9; tel. (416) 445-5860; fax (416) 445-8655; e-mail dianne_moggy@harlequin.ca; division of Harlequin; f. 1982; mass-market fiction; Exec. Editor FEROZE MOHAMMED.

Government Publishing House

Government of Canada Publications: 350 Albert St, 5th Floor, Ottawa, ON K1A 0S5; tel. (613) 941-5995; fax (613) 954-5779; e-mail publications@pwgsc.gc.ca; internet publications.gc.ca; f. 1876; books and periodicals on numerous subjects, incl. agriculture, economics, environment, geology, history and sociology; Dir CHRISTINE LEDUC.

PUBLISHERS' ORGANIZATIONS AND ASSOCIATIONS

National Organizations and Associations

Association of Canadian Publishers: 174 Spadina, Suite 306, Toronto, ON M5T 2C2; tel. (416) 487-6116; fax (416) 487-8815; e-mail admin@canbook.org; internet www.publishers.ca; f. 1976; trade asscn of Canadian-owned English-language book publrs; represents Canadian publishing internationally; 125 mems; Exec. Dir CAROLYN WOOD.

Association of Canadian University Presses/Association des Presses Universitaires Canadiennes: 10 St Mary St, Suite 700, Toronto, ON M4Y 2W8; tel. (416) 978-2239 (ext. 237); fax (416) 978-4738; e-mail clarose@utpress.utoronto.ca; internet www.acup.ca; f. 1965; Pres. LINDA CAMERON.

Association for the Export of Canadian Books: see External Trade Organizations.

Association Nationale des Editeurs de Livres (ANEL): 2514 blvd Rosemont, Montréal, QC H1Y 1K4; tel. (514) 273-8130; fax (514) 273-9657; e-mail info@anel.qc.ca; internet www.anel.qc.ca; f. 1992; 125 mem. cos; Pres. GAÉTAN LÉVESQUE; Dir-Gen. PIERRE LE FRANÇOIS.

Book and Periodical Council (BPC): 192 Spadina Ave, Suite 107, Toronto, ON M5T 2C2; tel. (416) 975-9366; fax (416) 975-1839; e-mail info@thebpc.ca; internet www.bookandperiodicalcouncil.ca; f. 1975; 16 mem. orgs, 10 assoc. mem. orgs and six affiliate mem. orgs; Exec. Dir ANNE MCCLELLAND.

The Canadian Copyright Licensing Agency (Access Copyright): 1 Yonge St, Suite 1900, Toronto, ON M5E 1E5; tel. (416) 868-1620; fax (416) 868-1621; e-mail info@accesscopyright.ca; internet www.accesscopyright.ca; f. 1988; 35 mem. orgs; Co-Chairs MIKE O'REILLY, BILL ZERTER.

Canadian Publishers' Council: 250 Merton St, Suite 203, Toronto, ON M4S 1B1; tel. (416) 322-7011; fax (416) 322-6999; e-mail pubadmin@pubcouncil.ca; internet www.pubcouncil.ca; f. 1910; trade asscn of Canadian-owned publrs and Canadian-incorp. subsidiaries of British and US publrs; 24 mems; Pres. KEVIN HANSON.

Literary Press Group of Canada (LPG): 192 Spadina Ave, Suite 501, Toronto, ON M5T 2C2; tel. (416) 483-1321; fax (416) 483-2510; e-mail info@lpg.ca; internet www.lpg.ca; f. 1975; affiliated to the ACP; 51 mem. cos; Exec. Dir RONDA KELLINGTON.

Regional Organizations and Associations

Association of Book Publishers of British Columbia (ABPBC): 100 West Pender St, Suite 107, Vancouver, BC V6B 1R8; tel. (604) 684-0228; fax (604) 684-5788; e-mail admin@books.bc.ca; internet www.books.bc.ca; f. 1974; affiliated to the ACP; over 50 mem. cos; Exec. Dir MARGARET REYNOLDS.

Association of English-language Publishers of Quebec/Association des Editeurs de Langue Anglaise du Québec (AELAQ): 1200 Atwater Ave, Suite 3, Montréal, QC H3Z 1X4; tel. (514) 932-5633; fax (514) 932-5456; e-mail info@aelaq.org; internet www.aelaq.org; f. 1990; affiliated to the ACP; 17 mem. cos; Exec. Dir MARGARET GOLDIK.

Association of Manitoba Book Publishers (AMBP): 100 Arthur St, Suite 404, Winnipeg, MB R3B 1H3; tel. (204) 947-3335; fax (204) 956-4689; e-mail ambp@mts.net; internet www.bookpublishers.mb.ca; f. 1979; affiliated to the ACP; 19 mem. cos; Exec. Dir MICHELLE PETERS.

Atlantic Publishers Marketing Association (APMA): 1484 Carlton St, Halifax, NS B3H 3B7; tel. (902) 420-0711; fax (902) 423-4302; e-mail apma.admin@atlanticpublishers.ca; internet www.atlanticpublishers.ca; affiliated to the ACP; 30 mem. cos and orgs; Exec. Dir PEGGY WALT.

Book Publishers Association of Alberta (BPAA): 100th Ave, Suite 10523, Edmonton, AB T5J 0A8; tel. (780) 424-5060; fax (780) 424-7943; e-mail info@bookpublishers.ab.ca; internet www.bookpublishers.ab.ca; f. 1975; affiliated to the ACP; 35 mem. cos; Exec. Dir KATHERINE SHUTE.

Newfoundland and Labrador Publishers Association (NLPA): 100 Water St, St John's, NL A1C 6E6; e-mail nlpa.breakwater@thezone.net; internet www.netfx.ca/nlpa; 4 mem. cos; Exec. Dir MICHELLE CABLE-FOOTE.

Organization of Book Publishers of Ontario (OBPO): 20 Maud St, Suite 401, Toronto, ON M5V 2M5; tel. (416) 536-7584; fax (416) 536-7692; e-mail marganne@obpo.ca; internet www.ontariobooks.ca; f. 1990; 43 mem. orgs; Exec. Dir MARG ANNE MORRISON.

Saskatchewan Publishers Group (SPG): 2405 11th Ave, Regina, SK S4P 0K4; tel. (306) 780-9808; fax (306) 780-9810; e-mail spg@saskpublishers.sk.ca; internet www.saskpublishers.sk.ca; f. 1989; affiliated to the ACP; 35 mem. cos; Exec. Dir BRENDA NISKALA.

HEALTH AND WELFARE

INTRODUCTION

Health

Federal and provincial and territorial governments shared the responsibility for health care in Canada, although the provinces and territories were principally responsible for most health care services. The federal Government, through Health Canada, was responsible for setting and administering national standards for the health care system. It also assisted in the financing of provincial and territorial health care services through fiscal transfers and administered programmes which catered for the needs of specific groups, such as native peoples, those living on Indian reserves, military personnel, public employees and for specific groups of immigrants and refugees. Health Canada also monitored disease and aimed to protect the public from, among other dangers, hazardous food, drugs and environmental conditions. Under the Canada Assistance Plan (CAP) of 1966 (see below) the federal Government worked alongside the provincial governments to assist those in need by providing lower-cost health care and social services. The provincial and territorial governments were responsible for planning and managing their health care systems, as well as managing certain aspects of prescription care and public health. To this end, in September 2000 the federal Government announced the establishment of an C $800m. Primary Health Care Transition Fund (PHCTF) to help provincial and territorial governments to implement reform of their health care systems during 2000–06. In February 2007 a national conference was held at which representatives from the primary health care sector shared their experiences in developing and implementing primary health care renewal initiatives under the Fund. An evaluation of the PHCTF conducted in order to determine how effectively it met its objectives was completed in March 2008. Meanwhile, in September 2004 the Canadian Government introduced the 10-Year Plan to Strengthen Health Care, which, *inter alia*, aimed to ensure timely access to quality health care and to increase the supply of health care professionals in Canada. The cost of the Plan was put at $41,300m.

In 1996 the Government revised arrangements for transferring federal funds to the provinces and territories. Established Programs Financing (EPF), which covered health care and higher education, and the CAP, which covered social welfare services, were aggregated into a single grant, the Canada Health and Social Transfer (CHST). The new grant allowed the provinces greater freedom in the allocation of funding among various social programmes. Federal Government still controlled federal transfers, however, which caused tension with provincial governments. As a result, every jurisdiction (with the exception of Québec) signed the Social Union Framework Agreement (SUFA) in 1999, which was designed to encourage federal funding directed at social problems that spanned federal and provincial responsibilities. In April 2004 the CHST was restructured into two separate entities: the Canada Health Transfer (CHT), covering health services and receiving 62% of funding; and the Canada Social Transfer (CST), covering post-secondary education, social assistance and social services and receiving 38% of funding.

Health insurance plans were the responsibility of the individual provinces and territories. The Canada Health Act, which became effective on 1 April 1984, outlined the essential elements required from all provincial health insurance plans. Hospital insurance programmes included acute, general, chronic and convalescent hospital services. The Medical Care Act of 1966–67 provided for payments to be made by the federal Government to provinces operating medical-care insurance plans, given that the plans fulfilled certain obligations. As a result, at the beginning of the 21st century almost all persons were insured for essential medical services. The federal contribution to health care varied according to the average rate of growth in gross domestic product (GDP) and the population statistics. The provinces could choose how to finance their share of the cost of health care services. Alberta and British Columbia imposed premiums (with assistance for those in need and, in Alberta, for elderly persons), while the other provinces paid for the cost from general revenue. Apart from the statutory health care benefits provided through provincial health insurance plans, additional benefits were available at the discretion of the individual provincial governments; benefits might include the services of osteopaths, psychologists and dentists. Provincial and territorial health care provision extended to remote areas, which might have to be serviced by special facilities, such as flying ambulance services. Total health expenditure by federal, provincial and territorial governments was estimated at C $126,260m. in 2007/08, equivalent to 23.6% of total expenditure.

Social Security

The Constitution Act of 1867 (formerly known as the British North America Act) sets out the jurisdictional responsibilities of federal, provincial and municipal governments with regard to social security. The federal Government administered some programmes for the aged, families and other selected groups, and was involved in the funding of many provincial initiatives. Provincial and local governments operated direct services and a number of financial assistance programmes.

Income security programmes funded by the federal Government comprised: benefits for senior citizens; family allowances; Child Tax Credit; programmes for native peoples; programmes for veterans of the Canadian Forces; and training allowances. Senior citizens' benefits consisted of the Old Age Security Pension (OAS), providing monthly benefits to those over the age of 65 who met residence requirements; Guaranteed Income Supplement (GIS), for pensioners with little or no other income; and a Spouse's Allowance (SPA). Benefits and obligations were extended to same-sex common-law partners in 2000. The 1973 Family Allowances Act provided for benefit, linked to the cost of living, to be paid to Canadian families with dependants up to the age of 18. A Special Allowance was paid to dependent children in care. The Act allowed provincial governments to specify the amount to be awarded, but by 1991 only Québec and Alberta exercised this option. A supplement to the Family Allowance was provided in Québec. In 1998 National Child Benefit (NCB) was introduced, which merged federal and provincial schemes for enhanced eligibility and reduced disincentives to paid employment. Québec chose not to participate in the NCB programme, but adopted its own system of income support for children.

The federal department of Indian and Northern Affairs Canada maintained levels of assistance for native peoples, especially those living on reserves, and encouraged the involvement of native peoples in their own assistance programmes. A social-assistance programme provided for basic needs. Programmes for veterans of the Canadian Forces were administered, in the main, by Veterans Affairs Canada. Training allowances were paid by the federal Government to those taking part in the national training programme that aimed to encourage workers to upgrade their skills in answer to the demands of the labour market. The Canadian Jobs Strategy (CJS) programme, introduced in 1985, provided training and retraining programmes, and involved co-operation between the federal Government, the provinces, business, labour and community groups. The CJS was succeeded in 1991 by the Labour Force Development Strategy/ Employment Insurance Regime (see below).

In 1966 the Canada Assistance Plan (CAP) was set up to provide direct financial assistance for families and individuals in need. Responsibility was divided between the federal and provincial governments. Eligibility depended upon the needs and means of the applicant. The exact structure of the programme varied from province to province, but there were certain common elements to all programmes, such as the provision of food, shelter and fuel, homes for the elderly and accommodation for battered women and children.

The Unemployment Insurance Act of 1940 introduced Canada's first public income-insurance programme. From the early 1970s the programme applied to almost all paid workers and members of the armed forces. Those exempt included persons over 65 years and those who worked fewer than 15 hours per week and earned less than 20% of the maximum weekly insurable earnings. The programme was financed largely by employer and employee contributions, with federal government general revenue financing about 20% of the cost of the programme. In 1996 the Unemployment Insurance scheme was replaced with Employment Insurance (EI), in an attempt to reduce expenditure on benefits; the unemployed were encouraged to undertake work-related training, the maximum level of insurable earnings was reduced, and frequent or repeat users saw a reduction in their benefits.

Canada's main social insurance programmes were the Canada Pension Plan (CPP), which applied to all provinces and territories except Québec, and the Québec Pension Plan (QPP). Both plans were financed by equal contributions of 2.2% of contributory earnings from employee and employer. Self-employed persons paid the full 4.4%. (Under an amendment in 1998 CPP contribution rates were to rise to 9.9% by 2003, shared equally between employer and employee; similar reform was introduced in Québec that established a level of 9.9% until at least 2050.) The two plans differed in the details of eligibility and levels of benefit, but both provided the same range of benefits. Retirement pensions were available to those aged 60 years and over, although the full rate did not apply to those under 65 years of age. Persons over 65 years received increased benefit. Survivor benefit was available to the dependants of deceased contributors. Disability pensions were paid to those whose condition required them to stop working. Children's benefits were provided for dependent children of disability pensioners and children of a surviving spouse. Benefit applies until the age of 18, and was extended to the age of 25 if the child was still in full-time education. Death benefit was paid to the estate of a contributor who died before retirement and contributed to the CPP or QPP for at least three years.

The federal Government also provided funds for various social-support programmes which—unlike Unemployment Insurance, the CPP and the QPP—did not involve direct payments.

Provincial government boards administered workers' compensation programmes that provided financial benefits and medical and rehabilitative services to those injured at work. The programmes were funded entirely from employers' contributions. Public employees' compensation was funded by the federal Government.

Most provincial governments provided supplementary payments to recipients of both OAS and GIS benefits. Disabled people and low-income families might also receive additional benefit from provincial programmes.

SELECTED STATISTICS

Health

NATIONAL HEALTH EXPENDITURE, BY CATEGORY
(C $ million)

	2003	2004	2005	2006*	2007*
Hospitals	35,560.8	38,224.2	40,362.6	43,055.3	45,481.5
Other institutions	13,007.9	13,889.2	14,759.0	15,695.7	16,707.6
Physicians	16,256.6	17,296.9	18,536.1	19,845.3	21,529.9
Other professionals	13,177.3	14,180.6	15,208.4	16,220.1	17,256.7
Drugs (prescribed and non-prescribed)	20,204.3	21,851.7	23,340.4	25,101.0	26,895.8
Other expenditures	25,680.3	26,369.5	29,034.7	30,351.8	32,262.0
Total health expenditure	123,887.2	131,812.1	141,241.2	150,269.2	160,133.5

* Forecasts.

Source: Canadian Institute for Health Information.

NATIONAL HEALTH EXPENDITURE, BY PROVINCE AND TERRITORY
(C $ million)

	2005	2006*	2007*
Alberta	15,259.4	16,513.0	18,403.2
British Columbia	18,480.1	19,503.1	20,542.3
Manitoba	5,602.8	5,808.7	6,212.6
New Brunswick	3,311.5	3,558.7	3,802.7
Newfoundland and Labrador	2,234.6	2,368.0	2,550.9
Northwest Territories	320.0	322.2	334.9
Nova Scotia	4,029.8	4,298.0	4,540.2
Nunavut Territory	301.7	339.5	337.8
Ontario	56,630.7	60,194.4	63,813.3
Prince Edward Island	576.3	602.7	651.5
Québec	29,875.1	31,774.1	33,632.4
Saskatchewan	4,430.5	4,776.1	5,090.9
Yukon Territory	188.6	210.7	220.8
Total	141,241.2	150,269.2	160,133.5

* Forecasts.

Source: Canadian Institute for Health Information.

HEALTH PROFESSIONALS—SUMMARY

	2000	2001	2002	2003	2004
Physicians	64,454	65,226	66,289	66,583	68,171
Dentists	17,314	17,691	17,961	18,265	18,313
Nurses	232,566	231,512	230,957	241,342	246,575
Pharmacists	24,518	25,643	26,346	27,612	28,537
Optometrists	3,780	3,858*	3,893*	3,921	4,045

* Estimate.

Source: Canadian Institute for Health Information, *Health Personnel Trends in Canada, 1995–2004*.

HEALTH PROFESSIONALS—PROVINCES AND TERRITORIES
(per 100,000 population, 2006)

	Physicians	Dentists	Nurses	Pharmacists	Optometrists
Alberta	192	55	753	93	12
British Columbia	199	66	665	73	10
Manitoba	180	50	924	96	9
New Brunswick	177	39	1,026	87	14
Newfoundland and Labrador	200	32	1,084	109	8
Northwest Territories	n.a.	122	1,420*	53	—
Nova Scotia	219	55	941	84	10
Nunavut Territory	32	158	n.a.	55	n.a.
Ontario	174	62	708	73	12
Prince Edward Island	150	45	1,030	102	14
Québec	215	54	834	92	17
Saskatchewan	160	37	858	104	12
Yukon Territory	224	64	1,044	93	16
All Canada	191	58	772	83	13

* Includes Nunavut Territory.

Source: Canadian Institute for Health Information, *Health Indicators 2008*.

Social Welfare

SOCIAL SECURITY EXPENDITURES BY WELFARE PROGRAMME
(C $ '000)

	2000/01	2001/02	2002/03
Welfare programme expenditures	108,093,970	114,323,041	118,287,363
Child tax benefit	7,027,118	7,639,494	7,740,546
Old age security	18,833,059	19,756,217	20,464,192
Guaranteed income supplement	5,037,685	5,216,783	5,470,623
Spouse's allowance	387,771	392,372	399,211
Human resources investment programmes	575,232	632,418	775,067
Registered Indians:			
Social assistance	609,777	598,581	611,788
Social services	429,500	457,717	466,366
Veterans' benefits:			
War veterans' and civilian war allowances	34,125	31,444	28,044
Veterans' and civilians' disability allowances	1,245,347	1,336,242	1,473,118
Goods and services tax credit	2,890,687	2,983,507	2,426,593
Canada and Québec pension plans:			
Retirement benefits	17,758,452	18,788,811	19,832,002
Survivors' benefits	4,295,883	4,476,439	4,663,225
Disability pensions	3,053,353	3,164,152	3,330,019
Child benefits	464,070	466,237	477,030
Unemployment insurance:			
Regular benefits	7,238,921	8,464,005	8,874,819
Sickness benefits	590,709	645,767	702,374
Family benefits	1,231,798	2,116,471	2,776,233
Fishing benefits	250,597	286,680	312,708
Work-sharing benefits	9,818	46,632	25,438
Employment benefits and support	1,973,586	2,106,506	2,136,162
Workers' compensation	5,333,086	5,733,409	6,062,873
Employment assistance for persons with disabilities	378,318	378,318	378,318
Other welfare programmes:			
Provincial tax credit/rebate	4,626,341	4,501,968	4,570,987
Provincial welfare	20,178,457	20,552,751	20,552,751
Provincial and territorial child benefits	1,303,177	1,122,508	1,048,019
Net municipal welfare	2,337,104	2,427,611	2,688,856
Health expenditures	70,365,850	75,827,050	81,162,750
Education expenditures	57,578,000	58,121,000	58,121,000
Total social security expenditures	236,037,820	248,271,091	257,571,113

Source: Social Development Canada.

HEALTH AND WELFARE AGENCIES AND ORGANIZATIONS

Association des Auxiliaires Bénévoles des Etablissements de Santé du Québec (ABESQ): 505 blvd Maisonneuve ouest, bureau 400, Montréal, QC H3A 3C2; tel. (514) 282-4264; fax (514) 282-4289; e-mail louiseabesq@hotmail.com; f. 1952; Pres. PAULETTE SICARD; Sec. LOUISE TREMBLAY.

Association des Etablissements Privés Conventionnés Santé et Services Sociaux: 204 Notre-Dame ouest, bureau 200, Montréal, QC H2Y 1T3; tel. (514) 499-3630; fax (514) 873-7063; e-mail info@aepc.qc.ca; internet www.aepc.qc.ca; 66 mems; Exec. Vice-Pres. ANDRÉ CÔTÉ; Sec. MIREILLE MATHIEU.

Canadian Association of Healthcare Auxiliaries (CAHA): 17 York St, Suite 100, Ottawa, ON K1N 9J6; tel. (613) 236-9364; fax (613) 236-9350; e-mail caha.office@rogers.com; internet www.caha.freeservers.com; Pres. JOYCE NASH.

Canadian Association of Naturopathic Doctors: 1255 Sheppard Ave East, Toronto, ON M2K 1E2; tel. (416) 496-8633; fax (416)

496-8634; e-mail info@naturopathicassoc.ca; internet www.cand.ca; f. 1955; fmrly the Canadian Naturopathic Asscn; represents c. 1,500 naturopathic doctors and medical students; Chair. IVA LLOYD; Exec. Dir and Dir of Govt Relations SHAWN O'REILLY.

Canadian Council on Health Services Accreditation: 1730 St Laurent Blvd, Suite 100, Ottawa, ON K1G 5L1; tel. (613) 738-3800; fax (613) 738-7755; e-mail international@accreditation-canada.ca; internet www.accreditation-canada.ca; Pres. and CEO WENDY NICKLIN.

Association Québécoise d'Etablissements de Santé et de Services Sociaux (AQESSS): 505 blvd de Maisonneuve ouest, bureau 400, Montréal, QC H3A 3C2; tel. (514) 842-4861; fax (514) 282-4271; internet www.aqesss.qc.ca; 135 mem. institutions; Pres. ALEX G. POTTER.

Health Boards of Alberta (HBA): HBA Services, 900 109 St, Suite 9925, Edmonton, AB T5K 2J8; tel. (780) 426-8500; fax (780) 424-4309; e-mail mail@hbas.ca; internet www.hbas.ca; comprises nine regional health boards and the Alberta Cancer Board.

Health Employers Association of British Columbia (HEABC): 1333 West Broadway, Suite 200, Vancouver, BC V6H 4C6; tel. (604) 736-5909; fax (604) 736-2715; e-mail contact@heabc.bc.ca; internet www.heabc.bc.ca; represents c. 300 British Columbian health care employees; Chair ALICE DOWNING.

New Brunswick Healthcare Association (NBHA): 930 Prospect St, Fredericton, NB E3B 2T8; tel. (506) 451-0750; fax (506) 451-0760; e-mail nbha@nbhealthcare.com; internet www.nbhealthcare.com; f. 1961; fed. of eight regional health bodies; Chair. ADÉLARD CORMIER.

Newfoundland and Labrador Health Boards Association (NLHBA): Beothuck Bldg, 2nd Floor, 20 Crosbie Pl., St John's, NL A1B 3Y8; tel. (709) 364-7701; fax (709) 364-6460; e-mail nlhba@nlhba.nl.ca; internet www.nlhba.nl.ca; f. 1962 as the Newfoundland Hospital Asscn; provides services to four regional health authorities; Exec. Dir JOHN PEDDLE.

Nova Scotia Association of Health Organizations (NSAHO): Bedford Professional Centre, 2 Dartmouth Rd, Bedford, NS B4A 2K7; tel. (902) 832-8500; fax (902) 832-8505; internet www.nsaho.ns.ca; f. 1960; 97 mem. health and community services providers; Pres. and CEO MARY LEE.

Ontario Hospital Association (OHA): 200 Front St West, Suite 2800, Toronto, ON M5V 3L1; tel. (416) 205-1300; fax (416) 205-1301; e-mail info@oha.com; internet www.oha.com; f. 1924; represents 154 public hospitals; Chair. GARRY D. CARDIFF; Pres. and CEO HILARY SHORT.

Regional Health Authorities of Manitoba (RHAM): 155 Carlton St, Suite 1800, Winnipeg, MB R3C 4Y1; tel. (204) 926-7012; fax (204) 943-8014; e-mail mebbitt@rham.mb.ca; internet www.rham.mb.ca; f. 1998; comprises 11 mem. health authorities; Chair. CARMEL OLSON; CEO RANDY LOCK.

Saskatchewan Association of Health Organizations: 2002 Victoria Ave, Suite 600, Regina, SK S4P 0R7; tel. (306) 347-5500; fax (306) 525-1960; e-mail info@saho.org; internet www.saho.org; c. 150 mem. orgs; Chair. ALEX TAYLOR; Pres. and CEO SUSAN ANTOSH.

Canadian Healthcare Association: 17 York St, Suite 100, Ottawa, ON K1N 9J6; tel. (613) 241-8005; fax (613) 241-5055; e-mail info@cha.ca; internet www.cha.ca; incorporated the Canadian Asscn for Community Care in 2007; Pres. and CEO PAMELA C. FRALICK.

Canadian Institutes of Health Research: 160 Elgin St, 9th Floor, Address Locator 4809A, Ottawa, ON K1A 0W9; tel. (613) 941-2672; fax (613) 954-1800; e-mail info@cihr-irsc.gc.ca; internet www.cihr-irsc.gc.ca; f. 2000; incorporates: the Institute of Aboriginal Peoples' Health; Institute of Aging; Institute of Cancer Research; Institute of Circulatory and Respiratory Health; Institute of Gender and Health; Institute of Genetics; Institute of Health Services and Policy Research; Institute of Human Devt, Child and Youth Health; Institute of Infection and Immunity; Institute of Musculoskeletal Health and Arthritis; Institute of Neurosciences, Mental Health and Addiction; Institute of Nutrition, Metabolism and Diabetes; and Institute of Population and Public Health; Pres. ALAN BEAUDET.

Canadian Medical Association: 1867 Alta Vista Dr., Ottawa, ON K1G 5W8; fax (613) 236-8864; e-mail cmamsc@cma.ca; internet www.cma.ca; f. 1867; represents more than 65,000 physicians, medical residents and students; Chair. Dr MICHAEL GOLBEY; Pres. Dr ROBERT QUELLET.

Canadian Mental Health Association: Phenix Professional Bldg, Suite 303, 595 Montreal Rd, Ottawa, ON K1K 4L2; tel. (613) 745-7750; fax (613) 745-5522; e-mail info@cmha.ca; internet www.cmha.ca; f. 1918 as the Canadian Nat. Cttee for Mental Hygiene; CEO Dr TAYLOR ALEXANDER; Pres. GORDON MATHESON.

Canadian Public Health Association: 1565 Carling Ave, Suite 400, Ottawa, ON K1Z 8R1; tel. (613) 725-3769; fax (613) 725-9826; e-mail info@cpha.ca; internet www.cpha.ca; f. 1912; Chair. RON DE BURGER; CEO DEBRA LYNKOWSKI.

Catholic Health Association of Canada: 1247 Kilborn Pl., Ottawa, ON K1H 6K9; tel. (613) 731-7148; fax (613) 731-7797; e-mail info@chac.ca; internet www.chac.ca; f. 1939; fmrly the Catholic Hospital Asscn of Canada; present name adopted in 1976; seven provincial mem. asscns; advocates on behalf of, and supports, a Catholic governance model of health care facilities in Canada; Exec. Dir JAMES ROCHE (acting).

Consumer Health Organization of Canada (CHOC): 355 St Clair Ave West, Suite 1901, Toronto, ON M5P 1N5; tel. (416) 924-9800; fax (416) 924-6404; e-mail info@consumerhealth.org; internet www.consumerhealth.org; f. 1975; promotes holistic and alternative medicine; Pres. LIBBY GARDON.

Health Canada: Brooke Claxton Bldg, Tunney's Pasture, Ottawa, ON K1A 0K9; tel. (613) 957-2983; fax (613) 952-7747; e-mail info@hc-sc.gc.ca; internet www.hc-sc.gc.ca; incorporates: the First Nations and Inuit Health Branch (f. 1962 as the Medical Services Branch); Healthy Environments and Consumer Safety Branch; Health Policy Branch; Health Products and Food Branch; and the Office of the Chief Dental Officer (f. 2004); and Office of the Chief Scientist; Chief Dentist Dr PETER V. COONEY; Chief Scientist Dr PIERRE GERLIER-FOREST.

Public Health Agency of Canada: 130 Colonnade Rd, Address Locator 6501H, Ottawa, ON K1A 0K9; tel. (613) 941-4338; fax (613) 957-2991; e-mail phac_web_mail@phac-aspc.gc.ca; internet www.phac-aspc.gc.ca; Chief Public Health Officer Dr DAVID BUTLER-JONES.

EDUCATION

INTRODUCTION

Education in Canada was predominantly the responsibility of provincial and territorial governments. However, the federal Government had some involvement: through Indian and Northern Affairs Canada, it paid for the schooling of Indian students in federal, Indian-band-controlled or provincial schools. Governments of the Yukon Territory and the Northwest Territories and Nunavut Territory were responsible, alongside the Department of Indian and Northern Affairs, for Indian and Inuit education in their own territories. Through the Department of National Defence, the federal Government also administered and funded schools for the dependants of the Canadian armed forces serving overseas. The Constitution Act of 1867 (formerly known as the British North America Act) gave legislative power over education to the provincial and territorial governments, which were also in charge of the finance and administration of educational establishments, from elementary schools to universities.

Provincial and territorial government departments or ministries of education formed educational policy, which was embodied in School or Education Acts and University and College Acts. Ministries of education supervised standards of teaching and awarded teaching certificates; approved programmes of teaching, curricula and textbooks; provided financial assistance; and established guide-lines for members of school boards, principals and teachers. School boards were the local units of administration and were in charge of implementing policy in elementary schools (grades one to six or eight) and secondary schools (grades seven or nine to 12). On the level of higher education, some provinces had grants councils or commissions to which the provincial and territorial governments delegated responsibility for the planning and financing of post-secondary education. The individual regional governments varied as to whether the two levels of education (elementary-secondary and post-secondary) were the responsibility of one department or two.

All provinces and territories provided elementary and secondary public education, which was financed from regional revenue. A transition from public to private sources of funding was encouraged, especially at a post-secondary level, and Ontario brought forward proposals to establish private universities. Some provinces provided tax support for schools on a denominational basis. In 2007/08 total federal and provincial government expenditure on education totalled C $65,302m., equivalent to 12.2% of total expenditure.

Pre-school, or kindergarten, education for five-year-olds was publicly supported in most provinces, while some provinces also provided junior kindergartens for those aged four. Alberta's Early Childhood Services programme provided for the admittance of children aged three-and-a-half upwards. Private kindergartens were licensed by provincial departments of education or of social services. Elementary schools were for children between the ages of six and 11 or 13, while secondary, or 'high', schools for ages 12–14 to 18. Some provinces and territories provided a separate 'junior high' school for ages 12–14; 'senior high', therefore, catered for older children. While elementary schools provided a general education in a broad range of subjects, secondary schools had a compulsory 'core' curriculum around which students could select subjects. Most secondary schools offered academic, technical and business (or vocational) courses, to reflect different abilities. Some areas had separate specialist schools for technical and business-oriented courses. Québec's secondary education system was different in that French was the main language of instruction, and that after five years at secondary school students spent two or three years at a collège d'enseignement général et professionnel (CEGEP) from where they could go on to higher education. Private schools could operate provided they met certain criteria stipulated by the various provincial governments, and some provinces gave financial assistance; both enrolment and government funding in private institutions rose in the 1990s. In 2005/06 4,937,675 students were enrolled in elementary and secondary schools across Canada.

The provincial and territorial departments of education were responsible for providing education to those who were unable to reach schools owing to their distance from centres of population. This was made easier from the late 20th century through the use of advanced telecommunications. 'Distant education' could be funded from the general provincial education budget or from a separate budget. All provinces provided educational facilities for those with special needs, whether owing to physical or mental disability. The overall aim was to integrate such persons into the local educational system.

Vocational and technical education was partly financed by the federal Government. Federal government policy was directed towards providing a work-force armed with skills relevant to a modern industrial nation. Under the 1982 National Training Act a Skills Growth Fund was established to provide the provinces and territories with finances for training institutions and training facilities. The Canadian Occupational Projection system had the task of identifying areas of need in terms of skill shortages and, therefore, ensured that resources were targeted at the relevant training courses. The Canadian Jobs Strategy training programme, established in 1985, was a co-operative programme involving federal and provincial and territorial governments, business, labour and community groups.

Post-secondary education was available from a variety of institutions, including universities, community colleges, technical institutes, agriculture and art colleges and schools of nursing attached to hospitals. Community colleges varied from province to province, some emphasizing pre-university education, some specializing in courses that prepared students for a career. A unifying factor among community colleges was the availability of education to all people, regardless of their academic prowess. Specialized vocational schools and hospital schools of nursing were increasingly incorporated into the colleges. There were 84 university institutions in Canada in 2005/06. Graduation from high school, or, in the case of Québec, completion of a two-year programme at a CEGEP, was a prerequisite for university entrance. Each university could decide upon further entrance requirements. Universities charged fees but also received considerable financial support from the relevant provincial and territorial government departments. In 2005/06 an estimated 1,047,705 students were enrolled in post-secondary education.

STATISTICS

Educational Institutions

SUMMARY

	1997/98	1998/99	1999/2000
Elementary-secondary	15,566	15,637	15,595
Post-secondary	270	274	274*
Universities	75	75	75*
Colleges	195	199	199*
Total	15,836	15,911	15,869

* Estimate.

2003/04: Post-secondary (universities only) 81.
2004/05: Post-secondary (universities only) 83.
2005/06: Post-secondary (universities only) 84.

Source: Statistics Canada.

Teachers

SUMMARY*

	1997/98	1998/99	1999/2000
Elementary-secondary	296,901	300,261	302,977
Post-secondary	65,429	65,753	61,633
Universities	33,702	33,665	33,801
Colleges	31,727	32,088	27,832†
Total	362,330	366,014	364,610

* Full-time only. Includes all teaching and non-teaching academic staff (principals, vice-principals, department heads and subject supervisors).
† Preliminary figure.

2003/04: Elementary-secondary teachers 336,237; University teachers 37,203.
2004/05: Elementary-secondary teachers 355,169; University teachers 38,574.
2005/06: Elementary-secondary teachers 359,813; University teachers 39,615.

Source: Statistics Canada.

Enrolment

SUMMARY
('000, full-time only)

	1997/98	1998/99	1999/2000
Elementary-secondary*	5,386	5,370	5,397
Post-secondary	972	984	998†
Universities	573	580	591†
Colleges	399	404	407†
Total	6,358	6,354	6,395

* Includes Department of National Defence schools overseas.
† Estimate.

2003/04 ('000): Elementary-secondary 5,287; Universities 993.
2004/05 ('000): Elementary-secondary 4,976; Universities 1,018.
2005/06 ('000): Elementary-secondary 4,938; Universities 1,048.

Source: Statistics Canada.

Elementary and Secondary Education by Province or Territory

(2005/06 unless otherwise indicated)

	Expenditure (C $ million)*	Average expenditure per student (C $)	Teachers	Enrolment
Alberta	5,410.0	10,293	40,298	551,740
British Columbia	4,618.8	9,798	36,886	575,089
Manitoba	1,759.7	10,048	13,106	182,371
New Brunswick	n.a.†	9,193	7,510	114,820
Newfoundland and Labrador	723.1	8,665	7,230	76,827
Northwest Territories	76.4	14,647	n.a.	9,571
Nova Scotia	1,042.5	8,835	9,708	141,966
Nunavut	n.a.‡	13,509	n.a.	9,062
Ontario	18,370.2	9,882	137,889	2,118,544
Prince Edward Island	180.4	7,655	1,505	21,948
Québec	9,597.7	9,154	93,260	957,697
Saskatchewan	1,686.2	9,570	11,683	172,705
Yukon Territory	n.a.‡	18,533	738	5,335
Total	43,464.9§	9,704	359,813‖	4,937,675

* School board expenditure (year ending 31 December 2007).
† School boards of New Brunswick are administrated by provincial general government.
‡ School boards of Nunavut and Yukon are administrated by territorial general government.
§ Excluding New Brunswick, Nunavut and Yukon Territory.
‖ Excluding Northwest Territories and Nunavut.

Source: Statistics Canada.

Post-Secondary Education by Province or Territory

(2005/06 figures, unless otherwise indicated)

	Expenditure (C $ million)*	Teachers†	Enrolment†
Alberta	4,706.5	3,792	91,713
British Columbia	4,756.8	4,296	108,159
Manitoba	1,011.8	1,680	39,735
New Brunswick	480.3	1,212	25,014
Newfoundland and Labrador	581.5	867	18,333
Northwest Territories	38.8	n.a.	n.a.
Nova Scotia	1,153.8	2,160	43,308
Nunavut	29.7	n.a.	n.a.
Ontario	14,494.3	14,676	431,049
Prince Edward Island	170.1	222	3,783
Québec	7,337.4	9,186	265,995
Saskatchewan	1,038.1	1,524	20,622
Yukon Territory	n.a.	n.a.	n.a.
Total (incl. other)	35,823.4	39,615‡	1,047,705

* Universities and colleges expenditure (year ending 31 March 2008).
† Universities only.
‡ Total excluding Northwest Territories, Nunavut and Yukon Territory.

Source: Statistics Canada.

RELIGION

STATISTICS

Population by Religion and Sex*

(Note: Census of 2001, based on 20% sample data, figures rounded to the nearest five persons.)

(Source: Statistics Canada.)

	Male	Female	Total†
Roman Catholic	6,271,680	6,665,235	12,936,910
Latin Rite	6,200,855	6,592,270	12,793,125
Ukrainian Rite	61,665	64,535	126,200
Protestant	4,054,705	4,600,145	8,654,850
Adventist	28,100	34,780	62,875
Anglican	954,835	1,080,660	2,035,500
Baptist	341,750	387,725	729,475
Brethren in Christ	9,560	11,025	20,590
Christian and Missionary Alliance	31,500	34,785	66,280
Churches of Christ, Disciples	8,220	9,625	17,845
Church of the Nazarene	6,375	7,585	13,960
Hutterite	12,845	13,455	26,295
Jehovah's Witnesses	68,255	86,495	154,750
Latter-day Saints (Mormons)	49,170	55,575	104,750
Church of Latter-day Saints	47,770	54,035	101,805
Lutheran	287,920	318,670	606,590
Mennonite	93,905	97,560	191,465
Methodist bodies	49,440	57,105	106,545
Evangelical Missionary Church	31,005	35,700	66,705
Free Methodist	6,795	7,320	14,110
Pentecostal	169,895	199,580	369,480
Presbyterian	189,270	220,560	409,830
Reformed bodies	57,595	58,135	115,735
Canadian and American Reformed Church	7,605	7,750	15,355
Christian Reformed	37,740	38,930	76,670
Salvation Army	42,560	45,225	87,790
Unitarian	7,195	10,285	17,480
United Church	1,318,535	1,520,590	2,839,125
Wesleyan	5,390	6,235	11,630
Eastern Orthodox	240,800	238,820	479,620
Armenian Orthodox	5,310	5,640	10,955
Coptic Orthodox	5,245	5,040	10,280
Greek Orthodox	108,675	106,495	215,175
Russian Orthodox	7,020	8,590	15,610
Serbian Orthodox	10,635	9,885	20,525
Ukrainian Orthodox	15,650	17,070	32,720
Eastern non-Christian religions	916,715	906,415	1,823,135
Bahá'í	8,480	9,540	18,020
Buddhist	142,490	157,855	300,345
Hindu	150,070	147,125	297,200
Islam	303,565	276,075	579,640
Jewish	160,990	169,000	329,995
Sikh	141,115	137,295	278,410
Aboriginal spirituality	14,865	14,955	29,820
Pagan	7,825	13,255	21,085
No religious preference	2,674,220	2,225,870	4,900,095
No religion	2,610,665	2,185,660	4,796,325
Agnostic	10,690	7,125	17,810
Atheist	12,500	6,100	18,605
Other	39,100	26,145	65,245
Total	14,564,275	15,074,755	29,639,030

* Excludes census data for one or more incompletely enumerated Indian reserves or Indian settlements.

† May not be equal to the sum of component parts, owing to rounding.

Population by Selected Religion and Province or Territory

(Note: Census of 2001, based on 20% sample data, figures rounded to the nearest five persons.)

(Source: Statistics Canada.)

	Roman Catholic	Protestant	Christian Orthodox	Christian n.i.e.	Muslim	Jewish
Alberta	786,360	1,145,460	44,475	123,140	49,040	11,085
British Columbia	675,320	1,213,295	35,655	200,345	56,220	21,230
Manitoba	323,690	475,185	15,645	44,535	5,095	13,040
New Brunswick	386,050	263,075	635	8,120	1,275	670
Newfoundland and Labrador	187,440	303,195	365	2,480	630	140
Northwest Territories	16,990	11,610	130	915	180	25
Nova Scotia	328,700	438,150	3,580	10,105	3,545	2,120
Nunavut	6,215	17,785	20	835	30	—
Ontario	3,911,760	3,935,745	264,055	301,935	352,530	190,795
Prince Edward Island	63,265	57,080	245	3,205	195	55
Québec	5,939,715	335,590	100,375	56,750	108,620	89,915
Saskatchewan	305,390	449,195	14,280	27,070	2,230	865
Yukon Territory	6,015	9,485	150	1,010	60	35
Total	12,936,910	8,654,650	479,620	780,450	579,640	329,995

POPULATION BY SELECTED RELIGION AND PROVINCE OR TERRITORY—CONTINUED

	Buddhist	Hindu	Sikh	Eastern religions	Other religions	No religious affiliation
Alberta	33,410	15,965	23,470	3,335	10,560	694,840
British Columbia	85,540	31,500	135,310	9,970	16,205	1,388,300
Manitoba	5,745	3,835	5,485	795	4,780	205,865
New Brunswick	545	475	90	330	790	57,665
Newfoundland and Labrador	185	405	135	110	135	12,865
Northwest Territories	155	65	45	95	280	6,600
Nova Scotia	1,730	1,235	270	565	1,155	106,405
Nunavut	15	10	—	65	40	1,655
Ontario	128,320	217,555	104,785	17,780	18,985	1,841,290
Prince Edward Island	140	30	—	105	100	8,950
Québec	41,380	24,525	8,225	3,425	3,870	413,190
Saskatchewan	3,050	1,585	500	780	6,750	151,455
Yukon Territory	130	10	100	190	330	11,015
Total	300,345	297,200	278,410	37,550	63,975	4,900,090

DIRECTORY

Principal Denominations

BAHÁ'Í FAITH

Bahá'í Community of Canada: 7200 Leslie St, Thornhill, ON L3T 6L8; tel. (905) 889-8168; fax (905) 889-8184; e-mail info@ca.bahai.org; internet www.ca.bahai.org; f. 1902; 30,000 mems (2004); Sec.-Gen. Karen McKye.

BUDDHISM

According to census figures, there were some 300,345 Buddhists in Canada in 2001.

Buddhist Churches of Canada (Jodo Shinshu Buddhist Temples of Canada): 11786 Fentiman Pl., Richmond, BC V7E 6M6; tel. (604) 272-3330; fax (604) 272-6865; e-mail bccheadquarters@shaw.ca; internet www.bcc.ca; f. 1905; Bishop Orai Fujikawa.

CHRISTIANITY

About 75% of the population belong to the three main Christian churches: Roman Catholic, United and Anglican. Numerous other Christian denominations are represented.

Adventist Church

Seventh-day Adventist Church in Canada: 1148 King St East, Oshawa, ON L1H 1H8; tel. (905) 433-0011; fax (905) 433-0982; e-mail communications@sdacc.org; internet www.sdacc.org; 340 congregations, 57,770 mems (2008); f. 1901; Pres. Daniel Jackson; Sec. Cathy Anderson.

Anglican Communion

The Anglican Church of Canada (L'église anglicane du Canada) comprises 30 dioceses in four ecclesiastical provinces (each with a Metropolitan archbishop). The Church had more than 800,000 members in 30 dioceses in 2004.

General Synod of the Anglican Church of Canada: 80 Hayden St, Toronto, ON M4Y 3G2; tel. (416) 924-9192; fax (416) 968-7983; e-mail info@national.anglican.ca; internet www.anglican.ca; f. 1893; Gen. Sec. The Venerable Michael Pollesel.

Primate of the Anglican Church of Canada: Most Rev. Fred Hiltz.

Province of British Columbia and Yukon: Metropolitan Most Rev. Terrence O. Buckle (Archbishop of Yukon).

Province of Canada: Metropolitan Most Rev. Bruce A. Stavert (Archbishop of Québec) (until early 2009).

Province of Ontario: Metropolitan Most Rev. Caleb J. Lawrence (Archbishop of Moosonee).

Province of Rupert's Land: Metropolitan Most Rev. John Clarke (Bishop of Athabasca).

Baptist Churches

According to census figures, there were some 729,475 members of Baptist churches in Canada in 2001.

Alberta Baptist Association: 11525 23rd Ave, Edmonton, AB T6J 4T3; tel. (780) 438-8852; fax (780) 434-9170; e-mail aba@nab.ca; internet www.nab.ca; 62 congregations (2007); Regional Minister Rev. Bob Walther.

Canadian Baptist Ministries: 7185 Millcreek Dr., Mississauga, ON L5N 5R4; tel. (905) 821-3533; fax (905) 826-3441; e-mail communications@cbmin.org; internet www.cbmin.org; more than 1,000 churches; 250,000 mems (2008); Gen. Sec. Rev. Dr Gary Nelson.

Fellowship of Evangelical Baptist Churches in Canada: 351 Elizabeth St, Guelph, ON N1E 2X9; tel. (519) 821-4830; fax (519) 821-9829; e-mail administration@fellowship.ca; internet www.fellowship.ca; f. 1953; 503 churches; 60,434 mems (2004); Pres. Dr John E. Kaiser.

Brethren Churches

Canadian Conference of the Brethren in Christ Church: 2700 Bristol Circle, Oakville, ON L6H 6E1; tel. (905) 339-2335; fax (905) 337-2120; e-mail biccanada@bellnet.ca; internet www.canadianbic.ca; 3,304 mems; Bishop Brian J. Bell.

Christian and Missionary Alliance in Canada: 30 Carrier Dr., Suite 100, Toronto, ON M9W 5T7; tel. (416) 674-7878; fax (416) 674-0808; e-mail info@cmacan.org; internet www.cmacan.org; f. 1972; 428 churches; Chair. Rev. Dr T. V. Thomas.

United Brethren Church in Canada: 501 Whitelaw Rd, Guelph, ON N1H 6Y2; tel. (519) 836-0180; fax (519) 821-8385; e-mail ubcomm@golden.net; internet www.ubcanada.org; f. 1854; 12 churches; Bishop Brian K. Magnus.

Lutheran Churches

According to census figures, there were some 606,590 members of Lutheran churches in Canada in 2001.

Estonian Evangelical Lutheran Church Abroad: 383 Jarvis St, Toronto, ON M5B 2C7; tel. (416) 925-5465; fax (416) 925-5688; e-mail e.e.l.k.@eelk.ee; internet www.eelk.org; f. 1947; 11 churches; 5,089 mems; Archbishop Rev. Dr Andres Põder.

Evangelical Lutheran Church in Canada (ELCIC): 393 Portage Ave, Suite 302, Winnipeg, MB R3B 3H6; tel. (204) 984-9150; fax (204) 984-9185; e-mail tgallop@elcic.ca; internet www.elcic.ca; f. 1986 by merger of the fmr Evangelical Lutheran Church of Canada and Lutheran Church in America—Canada Section; 611 congregations; 162,100 mems (2008); Nat. Bishop Rev. Susan Johnson, Vice-Pres. Roger Kingsley.

Lutheran Church—Canada: 3074 Portage Ave, Winnipeg, MB R3K 0Y2; tel. (204) 895-3433; fax (204) 832-3018; e-mail info@lutheranchurch.ca; internet www.lutheranchurch.ca; f. 1988 by three Canadian congregations of the Lutheran Church—Missouri Synod; 329 congregations; 75,765 mems (2005); Pres. Rev. Robert Bugbee.

Lutheran Council in Canada: 393 Portage Ave, Suite 302, Winnipeg, MB R3B 3H6; tel. (204) 984-9150; fax (204) 984-9185; e-mail rschultz@elcic.ca; f. 1967; co-ordinating agency for Evangelical Lutheran Church in Canada and Lutheran Church—Canada; Pres. Bishop Raymond L. Schultz.

Mennonite Churches

According to census figures, there were some 191,465 members of Mennonite churches in Canada in 2001.

Canadian Conference of Mennonite Brethren Churches: 1310 Taylor Ave, Winnipeg, MB R3M 3Z6; tel. (204) 669-6575; fax (204) 654-1865; e-mail marilyn@bcmb.org; internet www.mbconf.ca; f. 1945; 246 congregations; 35,770 mems (2006); Moderator JASCHA BOGE; Exec. Dir DAVID WIEBE; Sec. MARILYN HIEBERT.

Evangelical Mennonite Conference: 440 Main St, POB 1268, Steinbach, R5G 1Z5; tel. (204) 326-6401; fax (204) 326-1613; e-mail emconf@mts.net; internet www.emconf.ca; f. 1812; 58 churches; 7,300 mems (2008); Gen. Sec. TIM DYCK.

Evangelical Mennonite Mission Conference: 755 St Anne's Rd, Box 52059, Niakwa Post Office, Winnipeg, MB R2M 5P9; tel. (204) 253-7929; fax (204) 256-7384; e-mail info@emmc.ca; internet www.emmc.ca; f. 1936; 37 congregations; 5,402 mems (2006); Moderator JAKE THIESSEN; Sec. GIN THIESSEN.

Hutterian Brethren: General Delivery, Decker, MB R0M 0K0; e-mail mark@hutterites.org; internet www.hutterites.org; 330 congregations; 10,000 mems (2006); Presiding Officer DARIUS STAHL.

Mennonite Central Committee—Canada: 134 Plaza Dr., Winnipeg, MB R3T 5K9; tel. (204) 261-6381; fax (204) 269-9875; e-mail canada@mennonitecc.ca; internet www.mcc.org/canada; f. 1963; 600 congregations; 120,000 mems; Exec. Dir ARIF KLASSEN.

Mennonite Church Canada: 600 Shaftesbury Blvd, Winnipeg, MB R3P 0M4; tel. (204) 888-6781; fax (204) 831-5675; e-mail office@mennonitechurch.ca; internet www.mennonitechurch.ca; f. 1902; 225 congregations; 33,000 mems (2006); Gen. Sec. ROBERT J. SUDERMAN; Exec. Sec. DAVE BERGEN.

Old Colony Mennonite Church—Ontario (Independent and Unaffiliated) (OCO): 30 Sutton Dr., Leamington, ON N8H 3V7; tel. (519) 326-8815; f. 1966; 9 congregations; 4,203 mems in Ontario (2003); Presiding Officer Bishop CORNELIUS ENNS.

Old and New Order Amish Church: c/o Heritage Historical Library, 52445 Glencolin Line, Aylmer, ON N5H 2R3; f. 1824; 30 congregations; 1,800 mems (2006).

Old Order Mennonite Church: c/o Riverdale Meeting House, 571320 Southgate Side Rd 57, Mount Forest, ON; 15 congregations; 3,000 mems (2000).

Reinland Mennonite Church: 350 Fourth St, POB 508, Winkler, MB R6W 1J8; tel. (204) 331-3309; f. 1958; 6 congregations; 1,045 mems; Rep. Bishop WILLIAM H. FRIESEN.

Methodist Churches

According to census figures, there were some 106,545 members of Methodist bodies in Canada in 2001.

African Methodist Episcopal Church (Canadian Conference): 135 Mountainash Rd, Brampton, ON L6R 1H8; tel. (416) 690-5169; fax (416) 690-5176; e-mail grantamechurch@yahoo.ca; internet www.fourthdistrictame.org; part of the Fourth Episcopal District of the AME Church, USA; Presiding Elder Rev. CORY MILLBEN.

British Methodist Episcopal Church of Canada: BME Christ Church St James, 1828 Eglinton Ave West, ON M6E 2H6; tel. (416) 534-3831; fax (416) 534-3367; e-mail info@bmechristchurch.org; internet bmechristchurch.org; f. 1856; assoc. mem. of the Canadian Council of Churches; Gen. Superintendent Rev. MAURICE HICKS.

Free Methodist Church in Canada: 4315 Village Centre Ct, Mississauga, ON L4Z 1S2; tel. (905) 848-2600; fax (905) 848-2603; e-mail ministrycentre@fmc-canada.org; internet www.fmc-canada.org; f. 1876; merged with the Holiness Movt in 1959; self-governing Gen. Conference since 1990; 148 churches; 12,000 mems (2004); Pres. Bishop KEITH A. ELFORD.

Wesleyan Church of Canada: (Atlantic District) 1830 Mountain Rd, Moncton, NB E1G 1A9; tel. (506) 383-8326; fax (506) 383-8333; e-mail office@atlanticdistrict.com; internet www.atlanticdistrict.com; (Central Canada District) 17 St Paul St, Belleville, ON K8N 1A4; tel. (613) 966-7527; fax (613) 968-6190; e-mail deh@on.aibn.com; f. 1889; 11,630 mems (2001); District Supts DAVID W. LEROY (Atlantic District), Rev. DONALD E. HODGINS (Central Canada District).

Orthodox Churches

According to census figures, there were some 479,620 members of Eastern Orthodox churches in Canada in 2001.

Belarusian Autocephalous Orthodox Church: 524 St Clarens Ave, Toronto, ON M6H 3W7; tel. (416) 530-1025; fax (416) 267-0798; e-mail serget@juno.com; internet www.belaoc.org; f. 1954; Chair. MICHAIL TOUPUNOV; Sec. IRYNA VARABIEY.

Greek Orthodox Metropolis of Toronto (Canada): 86 Overlea Blvd, Toronto, ON M4H 1C6; tel. (416) 429-5757; fax (416) 429-4588; e-mail metropolis@gocanada.org; internet www.gocanada.org; 215,175 mems (2001); Metropolitan Archbishop SOTIRIOS ATHANASSOULAS.

Orthodox Church in America—Archdiocese of Canada: 2801 Newman Rd, RR 5, POB 179, Spencerville, ON K0E 1X0; tel. (613) 925–5226; fax (613) 925-1521; e-mail vladyka@archdiocese.ca; internet www.archdiocese.ca; f. 1916; self-governing since 1970; 102 congregations (2007); fmrly Russian Orthodox Greek Catholic Church of America; Pres. Rt Rev. SERAPHIM (Bishop of Ottawa and Canada); Chancellor Rev. DENNIS PIHACH.

Patriarchal Parishes of the Russian Orthodox Church (Moscow Patriarchate) in Canada: 108 St, Suite 10812, Edmonton, AB T5E 1K9; tel. (780) 455-6314; internet www.orthodoxcanada.net; f. 1897; Admin. His Grace JOB (Bishop of Kashira).

Romanian Orthodox Church in America (Canadian Parishes): 6340 blvd Saint-Michel, Montréal, QC H1Y 2E7; tel. (514) 727-3527; e-mail romarch67@aol.com; internet www.romarch.org; f. 1902; Dean Very Rev. Fr GEORGE CHISCA.

Self-Ruled Antiochian Orthodox Christian Archdiocese of North America (Diocese of Ottawa, Eastern Canada and Upstate New York): Montreal Chancery, 10820 Laverdure, Montréal, QC H3L 2L9; tel. (514) 276-8533; fax (514) 276-6740; e-mail info@steliascathedral.com; internet www.antiochian.org/canam; Bishop Rt Rev. ALEXANDER (Bishop of Ottawa, Eastern Canada and Upstate New York).

Serbian Orthodox Church, Diocese of Canada: 7470 McNiven Rd, RR 3, Campbellville, ON L0P 1B0; tel. (905) 878-00043; fax (905) 878-1909; e-mail vladika@istocnik.com; internet www.istocnik.com; f. 1921 in North America; 20,525 mems (2001); Pres. Rt Rev. Bishop GEORGIJE DJOKIC.

Ukrainian Orthodox Church of Canada: 9 St John's Ave, Winnipeg, MB R2W 1G8; tel. (204) 586-3093; fax (204) 582-5241; e-mail consistory@uocc.ca; internet www.uocc.ca; f. 1918; 281 parishes; 32,720 mems (2001); Metropolitan of Winnipeg and of all Canada His Eminence JOHN; Presidium Chair. Fr BOHDAN HLADIO.

Other Eastern Churches

Diocese of the Armenian Church of Canada: 615 ave Stuart, Outremont, QC H2V 3H2; tel. (514) 276-9479; fax (514) 276-9960; e-mail adiocese@armenianchurch.ca; internet www.armenianchurch.ca; f. 1930; self-governing since 1983; 10,955 mems (2001); Canadian Primate Bishop BAGRAT GALSTANIAN.

Armenian Evangelical Church of Toronto: 2600 14th Ave, Markham, ON L3R 3X1; tel. (905) 305-8144; fax (905) 305-8125; e-mail church@aecot.org; f. 1960; Pastor Rev. SAMUEL ALBARIAN.

Coptic Orthodox Church in Canada: c/o St Mark's Coptic Orthodox Church, 41 Glendenning Ave, Scarborough, Toronto, ON M1W 3E2; tel. (416) 494-4449; fax (416) 494-4196; e-mail mail@coptorthodox.ca; internet www.stmark.toronto.on.coptorthodox.ca; f. 1964; 10,280 mems (2001); Leader Archpriest Father MARCOS A. MARCOS.

Polish National Catholic Church of America in Canada: 171 Dunn Ave, Toronto, ON M6K 2R8; tel. (416) 532-8249; fax (416) 532-4653; e-mail bpbigaj@pnccofcanada.com; internet www.pnccofcanada.com; f. 1967; the Eastern Seniorate comprises four parishes and the Western Seniorate comprises five; Very Rev. SYLVESTER BIGAJ (Bishop of the Canadian Diocese).

Pentecostal Churches

According to census figures, there were some 369,480 members of Pentecostal churches in Canada in 2001.

Apostolic Church in Canada: 220 Adelaide St North, London, ON N6B 3H4; tel. (519) 852-7755; e-mail nlt@apostolic.ca; internet www.apostolic.ca; f. 1927; 17 churches; 1,600 mems; Nat. Leader D. KARL THOMAS.

Apostolic Church of Pentecost of Canada: 2340 Pegasus Way, NE, Suite 119, Calgary, AB T2E 8M5; tel. (403) 273-5777; fax (403) 273-8102; e-mail acop@acop.ca; internet www.acop.ca; f. 1921; amalgamated with the Evangelical Churches of Pentecost in 1953; 153 churches; c. 20,000 mems; Pres. and Nat. Dir Rev. WESLEY E. MILLS.

Church of God of Prophecy in Canada: (Canada East) 5145 Tomken Rd, Mississauga, ON L4W 1P1; tel. (905) 625-1278; fax (903) 625-1316; e-mail info@cogop.ca; internet www.cogop.ca; (Canada West) POB 200443, Vernon, BC V1T 9L4; tel. (250) 260-6174; fax (250) 260-6194; e-mail wdoroshuk@aol.com; internet www.cogop.ca; f. 1903; 40 churches; 3,107 mems; Nat. Overseer Bishop LEVI CLARKE.

Foursquare Gospel Church of Canada: 2099 Lougheed Hwy, Port Coquitlam, BC V3B 1A8; tel. (604) 941-8414; fax (604) 941-8415; e-mail info@foursquare.ca; internet www.foursquare.ca; f. 1928 as the Kingsway Foursquare Church; 56 churches; 2,810 mems (1999); Pres. BARRY BUZZA.

General Conference of the Canadian Assemblies of God: 200–7695 Papineau Ave, Montréal, QC H2E 2H1; tel. (514) 279-1100; fax (514) 279-1131; e-mail info@caogonline.org; internet www.caogonline.org; f. 1912; fmrly Italian Pentecostal Church of Canada, and later Canadian Assemblies of God; Gen. Supt Rev. DAVID MORTELLITI.

Independent Assemblies of God International—Canada: 330 Victoria Ave, POB 653, Chatham ON N7M 5K8; tel. (519) 352-1743; fax (519) 351-6070; e-mail pmcphail@ciaccess.com; internet www.iaogcan.com; f. 1935; 440 churches; Gen. Sec. Rev. PAUL J. MCPHAIL.

Pentecostal Assemblies of Canada: 2450 Milltower Court, Mississauga, ON L5N 5Z6; tel. (905) 542-7400; fax (905) 542-7313; e-mail info@paoc.org; internet www.paoc.org; f. 1919; 1,103 congregations; 245,279 mems (2005); Gen. Supt Dr WILLIAM D. MORROW.

Pentecostal Assemblies of Newfoundland and Labrador: 57 Thorburn Rd, POB 8895, Station A, St John's, NL A1B 3T2; tel. (709) 753-6314; fax (709) 753-4945; f. 1911; 124 churches; 24,670 mems; Gen. Supt Rev. H. PAUL FOSTER.

Pentecostal Holiness Church of Canada: c/o Calvary Christian Church, 16293 104th Ave, Surrey, BC V4N 1Z7; tel. (604) 583-5551; fax (604) 583-6746; e-mail june@calvary.ca; internet www.phcc.ca; f. 1971; Bishop Dr GORDON MCDONALD.

Presbyterian Churches

According to census figures, there were some 409,830 members of Presbyterian churches in Canada in 2001.

Presbyterian Church in America (Canadian Section): 2581 East 45th St, Vancouver, BC V5R 3B9; e-mail info@faithvan.com; internet www.pcaac.org; tel. (604) 438-8755; f. 1982; divided into the two presbyteries of Eastern and Western Canada; 1,100 mems.

Presbyterian Church in Canada: 50 Wynford Dr., Toronto, ON M3C 1J7; tel. (416) 441-1111; fax (416) 441-2825; e-mail pccweb@presbycan.ca; internet www.presbyterian.ca; f. 1875; 997 congregations; 125,509 mems (2003); Moderator Rev. Dr J. HANS KOUWENBERG; Prin. Clerk Rev. STEPHEN KENDALL.

Reformed Churches

According to census figures, there were some 115,735 members of Reformed churches in Canada in 2001.

Reformed Church in America (Regional Synod of Canada): The Regional Synod of Canada, 201 Paradise Rd North, Hamilton, ON L8S 3T3; tel. (519) 622-1777; fax (519) 622-1993; e-mail blaidlaw@reformed-church.com; internet www.reformed-church.com; f. 1628 in North America; Regional Synod of Canada established in 1993; Pres. LAURIE HERON; Exec. Sec. JOHN KAPTEYN.

Christian Reformed Church in North America (Canadian Council): 3475 Mainway, POB 5070, Burlington, ON L7R 3Y8; tel. (905) 336-2920; fax (905) 336-8344; internet www.crcna.org; f. 1857; 246 congregations; 78,400 mems (2007); Dir in Canada Rev. BRUCE ADEMA.

Roman Catholic Church

For Catholics of the Latin rite, Canada comprises 18 archdioceses (including one directly responsible to the Holy See) and 45 dioceses. There are also one archdiocese and four dioceses of the Ukrainian rite. In addition, the Maronite, Melkite and Slovak rites are each represented by one diocese (all directly responsible to the Holy See). In 2006 the Roman Catholic Church had about 14.2m. adherents in Canada.

Canadian Conference of Catholic Bishops/Conférence des évêques catholiques du Canada: 2500 Don Reid Dr., Ottawa, ON K1H 2J2; tel. (613) 241-9461; fax (613) 241-9048; e-mail cecc@cccb.ca; internet www.cccb.ca; Pres. Most Rev. V. JAMES WEISGERBER (Archbishop of Winnipeg); Vice-Pres. Rt Rev. PIERRE MORISSETTE (Bishop of Baie-Comeau); Gen. Sec. MARIO PAQUETTE.

Latin Rite

Archbishop of Edmonton: Most Rev. RICHARD SMITH.

Archbishop of Gatineau: Most Rev. ROGER ÉBACHER.

Archbishop of Grouard-McLennan: Most Rev. GÉRARD PETTIPAS.

Archbishop of Halifax: Most Rev. ANTHONY MANCINI.

Archbishop of Keewatin-Le Pas: Most Rev. SYLVAIN LAVOIE.

Archbishop of Kingston: Most Rev. BRENDAN M. O'BRIEN.

Archbishop of Moncton: Most Rev. ANDRÉ RICHARD.

Archbishop of Montréal: Most Rev. Cardinal JEAN-CLAUDE TURCOTTE.

Archbishop of Ottawa: Most Rev. TERRENCE PRENDERGAST.

Archbishop of Québec: Cardinal MARC OUELLET.

Archbishop of Regina: Most Rev. DANIEL J. BOHAN.

Archbishop of Rimouski: Most Rev. PIERRE-ANDRÉ FOURNIER.

Archbishop of St Boniface: Most Rev. EMILIUS GOULET.

Archbishop of St John's, NL: Most Rev. MARTIN WILLIAM CURRIE.

Archbishop of Sherbrooke: Most Rev. ANDRÉ GAUMOND.

Archbishop of Toronto: Most Rev. THOMAS COLLINS.

Archbishop of Vancouver: Most Rev. RAYMOND ROUSSIN.

Archbishop of Winnipeg: Most Rev. V. JAMES WEISGERBER.

Ukrainian Rite

Ukrainian Catholic Archeparchy of Winnipeg (Metropolitan See of Canada): 233 Scotia St, Winnipeg, MB R2V 1V7; tel. (204) 338-7801; fax (204) 339-4006; e-mail chancery@archeparchy.ca; internet www.archeparchy.ca; 126,200 mems (2001); Archeparch-Metropolitan of Winnipeg Most Rev. LAWRENCE HUCULAK.

United Church of Canada

The United Church of Canada (l'Eglise Unie du Canada) was founded in 1925 with the union of Methodist, Congregational and 70% of Presbyterian churches in Canada. The Evangelical United Brethren of Canada joined in 1968. It is the largest Protestant denomination in Canada. At 31 December 2006 there were 3,405 congregations and 558,129 confirmed members. (According to census figures, in 2001 some 2.8m. people identified themselves as adherents of the United Church.)

Moderator: Rt Rev. DAVID GIULIANO.

General Secretary: NORA SANDERS, 3250 Bloor St West, Suite 300, Toronto, ON M8X 2Y4; tel. (416) 231-5931; fax (416) 231-3103; e-mail info@united-church.ca; internet www.united-church.ca.

Other Christian Churches

Associated Gospel Churches: 1500 Kerns Rd, Burlington, ON L7P 3A7; tel. (905) 634-8184; fax (905) 634-6283; e-mail admin@agcofcanada.com; internet www.agcofcanada.com; f. 1922; 21,000 mems; Pres. Rev. BILL FIETJE.

Bible Holiness Movement: POB 223, Station A, Vancouver, BC V6C 2M3; tel. (250) 492-3376; internet www.bible-holiness-movement.com; f. 1949; 83,938 mems world-wide; Bishop-Gen. WESLEY H. WAKEFIELD.

Canadian Unitarian Council: 018–1179A King St West, Toronto, ON, M6K 3C5; tel. (416) 489-4121; e-mail info@cuc.ca; internet www.cuc.ca; 5,100 mems (2006); Pres. JEAN PFLEIDERER.

Christadelphians in Canada: (British Columbia) 1396 McKenzie Ave, Victoria, BC, Canada V8P 2M3; tel. (250) 477-2112; e-mail info@victoriabiblestudy.com; internet www.victoriabiblestudy.com; (Nova Scotia) 1658 Bedford Hwy, POB 44023, Bedford, NS B4A 3X5; e-mail info@christadelphians.ns.ca; internet www.christadelphians.ns.ca; (Ontario) c/o the Bible Magazine, POB 514, Burford, ON N0E 1A0; tel. (519) 449-3446; fax (519) 449-3660; e-mail contact@biblemagazine.com; internet www.biblemagazine.com.

Christian Church (Disciples of Christ) in Canada: POB 1, Springfield, ON N0L 2J0; tel. (519) 269-9800; e-mail ccinca@execulink.com; internet www.disciplesofchrist.ca; f. 1830; 26 churches; 3,285 mems; Regional Minister Dr CATHY HUBBARD.

Christian Science: c/o First Church of Christ, Scientist, in Ottawa, 280 Gilmour St. Ottawa, ON Canada K2P 0P8; tel. (613) 233-1427; e-mail fccsott@magma.ca; internet www.christianscienceottawa.ca; f. 1899; c. 56 congregations in Canada, brs of First Church of Christ Scientist in Boston, MA, USA.

Church Army in Canada: 105 Mountain View Dr., Saint John, NB E2J 5B5; tel. (506) 642-2210; fax (506) 657-8217; e-mail info@churcharmy.com; internet www.churcharmy.com; f. 1929; Chair. PETER BLOOM; Dir Capt. BRUCE SMITH.

Church of God in Canada: POB 333, Station B, Toronto, ON M9W 5L3; tel. (416) 741-9222; fax (416) 741-3717; e-mail moderator@churchofgodincanada.com; internet www.churchofgodincanada.com; f. 1919; 11,000 mems; Nat. Moderator RALPH GLAGAU.

Church of Jesus Christ of Latter-day Saints (Mormon): 28 St South, Suite 2410, Lethbridge, AB T1K 2V9; tel. (403) 328-8552; f. 1832; 481 congregations; 166,505 mems in Canada (2004); Dir GORDON GEDLAMAN.

Church of the Nazarene—Canada: 20 Regan Rd, Unit 9, Brampton, ON L7A 1C3; tel. (905) 846-4220; fax (905) 846-1775; e-mail national@nazarene.ca; internet www.nazarene.ca; f. 1902; 13,960 mems (2001); Nat. Dir Rev. K. CLAIR MACMILLAN.

Community of Christ: (Canada East Mission) 390 Speedvale Ave East, Guelph, ON N1E 1N5; tel. (519) 822-4150; fax (519) 822-1236; internet www.communityofchrist.ca; (Canada West Mission) 6415 Ranchview Dr., NW, Calgary AB T3G 1B5; tel. (403) 239-8070; fax (403) 239-3542; e-mail info@communityofchrist.ca; internet www.communityofchrist.ca; f. 1830, reorg. 1860; 12,465 mems; Bishop of Canada Bishop JAMES A. POIRIER; Pres KEN BARROWS (East Mission), DARRELL BELROSE (West Mission).

Evangelical Alliance Mission of Canada, Inc: 2635 32nd St, SW, Calgary, AB T3E 2R8; tel. (403) 248-2344; fax (403) 207-6025; e-mail team@teamcanada.org; internet www.teamcanada.org; Regional Dirs CHARLES MCCORDIC (Eastern), R. PAUL (BUD) JACKSON (Western).

Evangelical Covenant Church of Canada: POB 34025, RPO Fort Richmond, Winnipeg, MB R3T 5T5; tel. (204) 269-3437; fax (204) 269-3584; e-mail messengr@escape.ca; internet www.canadacovenantchurch.org; f. 1904; 23 churches; 1,290 mems; Supt Rev. JEFF ANDERSON.

Evangelical Fellowship of Canada: 600 Alden Rd, Suite 300, Markham, ON L3R 0E7; MIP Box 3745, Markham, ON L3R 0Y4; tel. (905) 479-5885; fax (905) 479-4742; e-mail efc@efc-canada.com; internet www.evangelicalfellowship.ca; f. 1964; 40 denominations; 1,000 congregations; Chair. DAVID WELLS; Pres. BRUCE J. CLEMENGER.

Evangelical Free Church of Canada: POB 850 Langley Station LCD1, Langley, BC V3A 8S6; tel. (604) 513-2185; fax (604) 888-3108; e-mail efcc@twu.ca; internet www.efcc.ca; f. 1917; merged with the Fellowship of Gospel Churches in 1957; 147 churches; 24,054 mems; Pres. Dr RON J. UNRUH.

Evangelical Missionary Church of Canada: 130 Fergus Ave, Kitchener, ON N2A 2H2; tel. (877) 375-7600; fax (519) 894-0941; e-mail info@emcc.ca; internet www.emcc.ca; Moderator RANDY STEINWAND.

Independent Holiness Churches: 1564 John Quinn Rd, RR1, Greely, ON K4P 1J9; tel. (613) 821-2237; e-mail gs@holiness.ca; internet www.holiness.ca; f. 1960; 5 churches; Gen. Supt Rev. ROBERT VOTARY.

The New Church: General Church of the New Jerusalem in Canada: c/o The Calgary New Church, 248 Arbour Crest Dr., NW, Calgary, Alberta, T3G 4V3; tel. and fax (403) 374-0087; e-mail outreach@newchurch.org; internet www.newchurch.org; f. 1971; regional chapter of the Gen. Church of the New Jerusalem, PA, USA; Dir Rev. MICHAEL D. GLADISH.

New Apostolic Church—Canada: Administration Office, 319 Bridgeport Rd East, Waterloo, ON N2J 2K9; tel. (519) 884-2862; fax (519) 884-3438; e-mail info@naccanada.org; internet www.naccanada.org; Apostle Patriarch WILHELM LEBER.

OMF Canada: 5155 Spectrum Way, Bldg 21, Mississauga, ON L4W 5A1; tel. (905) 568-9971; fax (905) 568-9974; e-mail omfcanada@omf.ca; internet www.ca.omf.org; f. 1865; Nat. Dir RICHARD J. KONIECZNY.

Religious Society of Friends: 91A Fourth Ave, Ottawa, ON K1S 2L1; tel. (613) 235-8553; fax (613) 235-1753; e-mail cym-office@quaker.ca; internet www.quaker.ca; Clerk of Canadian Yearly Meeting DALE DEWAR.

Salvation Army in Canada: Canada and Bermuda Territorial Headquarters, 2 Overlea Blvd, Toronto, ON M4H 1P4; tel. (416) 425-2111; fax (416) 425-6157; e-mail andrew_burditt@can.salvationarmy.org; internet www.salvationarmy.ca; f. 1882; 320 churches; c. 53,000 mems; Commr WILLIAM FRANCIS; Chief Sec. Col GLEN SHEPHERD.

Stanley Park Community Church: 9 Dreger Ave, Kitchener, ON N2A 2A4; tel. (519) 893-8186; e-mail office@stanleyparkchurch.ca; internet www.stanleyparkchurch.ca; f. as the Berlin Mission Station; current name adopted in 2002; Senior Pastor JOHN PEARCE.

Swedenborgian Church (Church of the Good Shepherd): 116 Queen St North, Kitchener, ON N2H 2H7; tel. (519) 743-3845; e-mail secretary@churchofthegoodshepherd.ca; internet churchofthegoodshepherd.ca; Rev. JOHN MAINE.

Union of Spiritual Communities of Christ (Orthodox Doukhobors in Canada): POB 760, Grand Forks, BC V0H 1H0; tel. (250) 442-8252; fax (250) 442-3433; e-mail info@usccdoukhobors.org; internet www.usccdoukhobors.org; f. 1899 in Canada; Hon. Chair. JOHN J. VERIGIN.

Universal Fellowship of Metropolitan Community Churches: Headquarters Offices, POB 1374, Abilene, TX 79604, USA; tel. (310) 360-8640; fax (310) 362-8971; e-mail info@mccchurch.netmedia@mcctoronto.com; internet www.mccchurch.org; f. 1968; Regional Elders Rev. DIANE FISHER (Eastern Canada), Rev. JIM MITULSKI (Manitoba and Nunavut), Rev. LILLIE BROCK (Western Canada).

Watch Tower Bible and Tract Society of Canada (Jehovah's Witnesses): POB 4100, Halton Hills, Georgetown, ON L7G 4Y4; tel. (416) 873-4100; fax (416) 873-4554; f. 1918 in Canada; 154,750 mems (2001).

Interdenominational Organizations

Avant Ministries Canada: 2121 Henderson Hwy, Winnipeg, MB R2G 1P8; tel. (204) 338-7831; fax (204) 339-3321; internet www.avantministries.org; f. 1951; fmrly Gospel Missionary Union of Canada; Canadian Dir GRANT MORRISON.

Canadian Council of Christians and Jews (CCCJ): 4211 Yonge St, Box 17, Toronto, ON M2P 2A9; tel. (416) 597-9693; fax (416) 597-9775; e-mail info@cccj.ca; internet www.cccj.ca; f. 1947; founding partner of the Canadian Christian Jewish Consultation (f. 1977); Pres. AMANDA L. SHERRINGTON.

Canadian Council of Churches/Conseil canadien des églises: 47 Queen's Park Cres. East, Toronto, ON M5S 2C3; tel. (416) 972-9494; fax (416) 927-0405; e-mail admin@ccc-cce.ca; internet www.ccc-cce.ca; f. 1944; 21 mem. churches, one assoc. mem.; Pres. Rev. Dr JAMES CHRISTIE (United Church of Canada); Gen. Sec. Rev. Dr KAREN HAMILTON.

National Muslim-Christian Liaison Committee (NMCLC): c/o Asscn of Progressive Muslims of Canada Canadian Council on Muslim Women, 82 Delamere Ave, Toronto, ON M6N 1Z7; tel. (416) 394-7773; fax (416) 394-6230; e-mail barbara.siddiqui@tdsb.on.ca; internet interreligion.com/page16.html; f. 1991; incl. reps from 19 Muslim and Christian orgs or denominations; Co-Chair. BARBARA SIDDIQUI, JIM PAYTON.

ISLAM

According to census figures, there were some 579,640 Muslims in Canada in 2001.

Ahmadiyya Movement in Islam (Canada): 10610 Jane St, Maple, ON L6A 3A2; tel. (905) 303-4000; fax (905) 832-3220; e-mail info@ahmadiyya.ca; internet www.ahmadiyya.ca; f. 1965; Pres. LAL KHAN MALIK; Gen. Sec. Dr ASLAM DAUD.

Canadian Islamic Congress (CIC): 675 Queen St South, Suite 208, Kitchener, ON N2M 1A1; tel. (519) 746-1242; fax (519) 746-2929; e-mail np@canadianislamiccongress.com; internet www.canadianislamiccongress.com; f. 1998; Chair. and Nat. Pres. Dr MOHAMED I. ELMASRY; Nat. Exec. Dir Imam Dr ZIJAD DELIC.

Canadian Muslim Union (CMU): Toronto, ON; tel. (416) 558-4777; e-mail secretary@muslimunion.ca; internet www.muslimunion.ca; f. 2006 following split from the Muslim Canadian Congress; Sec.-Gen. EL-FAROUK KHAKI.

Canadian Society of Muslims: POB 143, Station P, Toronto, ON M5S 2S7; e-mail info@muslim-canada.org; internet muslim-canada.org; Pres. SYED MUMTAZ ALI.

Council of Muslim Communities of Canada (CMCC): 1521 Trinity Dr., Unit 16, Mississauga, ON L5T1P6; tel. and fax (416) 512-2106; f. 1971; umbrella org. representing c. 30 communities nationwide; Pres. HANNY HASSAN.

Council on American-Islamic Relations Canada (CAIR-CAN): POB 13219, Ottawa, ON K2K 1X4; tel. (613) 254-9704; fax (613) 254-9810; e-mail info@caircan.ca; internet www.caircan.ca; f. 1996; Chair. ABDUL-BASIT KHAN.

Muslim Association of Canada (MAC): 1568 Merivale Rd, Suite 332, Ottawa, ON K2G 5Y7; tel. (613) 321-5000; fax (613) 321-5001; e-mail mac@macnet.ca; internet www.macnet.ca; f. 1997; Chair. ISMAEL MUKHTAR; Dir and Pres. SHARAF SHARAFELDIN.

Muslim Canadian Congress (MCC): Toronto, ON; tel. (416) 473-2552; e-mail mcc@muslimcongress.ca; internet www.muslimcanadiancongress.org; f. 2002; Pres. FARZANA HASSAN; Sec.-Gen. AKBAR HUSSEIN.

Organization of North American Shi'a Itha-Asheri Muslim Communities (NASIMCO): 300 John St, POB 87629, Thornhill, ON L3T 7R3; tel. (905) 763-7512; fax (905) 763-7509; e-mail director@nasimco.org; internet www.nasimco.org; Pres. HUSSEIN WALJI; Sec. HABIB DHALLA.

JUDAISM

According to census figures, there were some 329,995 Jews in Canada in 2001.

Canadian Jewish Congress: 100 Sparks St, Suite 650, Ottawa, ON K1P 5B7; tel. (613) 233-8703; fax (613) 233-8748; e-mail canadianjewishcongress@cjc.ca; internet www.cjc.ca; f. 1919; 10 regional offices; CEO BERNIE M. FARBER; Co-Pres. Rabbi REUVEN BULKA, SYLVAIN ABITBOL.

United Synagogue of Conservative Judaism: 1000 Finch Ave West, Suite 508, Toronto, ON M3J 2V5; tel. (416) 667-1717; fax (416) 667-1818; e-mail canadian@uscj.org; internet www.uscj.org; Pres. Dr RAYMOND B. GOLDSTEIN.

URJ Canadian Council for Reform Judaism: 3845 Bathurst St, Suite 301, Toronto, ON M3H 3N2; tel. (416) 630-0375; fax (416) 630-5089; e-mail ccrj@urj.org; internet urj.org/ccrj; mem. of the Union for Reform Judaism; 26 congregations; Pres. ELLIOT JACOBSON; Exec. Dir Rabbi SHARON L. SOBEL.

SIKHISM

According to census figures, there were some 278,410 Sikhs in Canada in 2001.

Canadian Sikh Council (CSC): 4103 Sherbrooke St West, Montréal, QC H3Z1A7; tel. (416) 630-0375; fax (416) 630-5089; e-mail info@sikhcouncil.ca; internet www.sikhcouncil.ca; f. 2001; Dir Dr MANJIT SINGH.

World Sikh Organization of Canada (WSO Canada): 1183 Cecil Ave, Ottawa, ON K1H 7Z6; tel. (613) 521-1984; fax (613) 521-7454; e-mail wsopanth@gmail.com; internet worldsikh.org; f. 1984; Pres. GURPREET SINGH BAL; Exec. Dir ANNE LOWTHIAN.

ZOROASTRIANS

Federation of Zoroastrian Associations of North America in Canada (FEZANA): 955 Audley Rd South, Ajax, ON L1Z1N3; tel. (905) 619-9385; e-mail secretary@fezana.org; internet www.fezana.org; Sec. FIRUZI POONEVALLA.

THE PROVINCES AND TERRITORIES

THE PROVINCES AND TERRITORIES OF THE DOMINION

The British North America Act (Constitution Act) of 1867 was the basis of the federal and provincial systems of government. Under the Constitution Act of 1982 the last traces of British involvement in the constitutional order of Canada were removed, although formal representatives of the Crown remained. The monarch's representative in provincial government is the Lieutenant-Governor, who is appointed by the Governor-General of Canada on the advice of the federal Government and presides over a unicameral provincial legislature. The Legislative Assembly of each province is elected by the people for a maximum statutory term of five years. It is customary for the Lieutenant-Governor to appoint the leader of the majority party as provincial Premier. The Premier selects his or her cabinet from among the elected members of the Legislative Assembly, together forming the policy-making executive council. Nearly all cabinet members are portfolio-holding ministers. The size of the cabinet may range from 10 to 30 members.

Bills are generally introduced by the executive council, although private members' bills may be introduced. To become law a bill must receive two readings, a detailed review in committee stage and a third reading before being passed to the Lieutenant-Governor for formal assent.

Provincial governments have legislative power over all provincial matters, including public schooling, health, social services, roads and local government. The provinces have authority over natural resources, over which they also have power of taxation. Provincial taxation is otherwise limited to direct taxation. The federal Government's power to disallow a provincial statute within one year of its enactment was last used in 1943.

The system of government operating in each of the territories (as distinct from the provinces) is outlined, where relevant, below.

Alberta

Area: 661,848 sq km (258,534 sq miles).

Population (at 1 July 2007, estimate): 3,473,984.

Capital: Edmonton.

Principal Cities (population at census of 16 May 2006): Calgary 988,193; Edmonton (capital) 730,372.

LOCATION, TOPOGRAPHY AND CLIMATE

Alberta lies in the south-west of Canada and is the westernmost of the three Prairie provinces. It is bordered by Saskatchewan to the east, the Northwest Territories to the north and British Columbia to the west. The US state of Montana forms the southern boundary. The Rocky Mountains range marks the southern part of the boundary with British Columbia and includes Mount Columbia, Alberta's highest point, at 3,747 m (12,293 ft). The south of the province consists of dry prairie land, while in the north regions of poplar forests and open prairies merge into mixed forest. The greater part of southern Alberta drains through the South and North Saskatchewan Rivers into Hudson Bay; the Athabasca, Hay and Peace Rivers flow through northern Alberta, draining into the Great Slave Lake (Northwest Territories) and, ultimately, into the Arctic Ocean. Alberta's two principal lakes are Lake Claire (1,436 sq km) and Lesser Slave Lake (1,168 sq km); Lake Athabasca (7,936 sq km) is shared with Saskatchewan. The province has a cool, temperate climate. Winters are cold, although occasionally moderated by the warm, dry Chinook winds. Low precipitation habitually causes droughts, particularly in the south-west.

HISTORICAL BACKGROUND

In 1754 the British explorer, Anthony Henday of the Hudson's Bay Company (HBC), spent the winter near the site of present-day Edmonton. At that time American Indian tribes inhabiting the area now known as Alberta included the Blackfoot, Blood, Perigan, Gros Ventre and Sarcee. Fur-trading posts were established from 1778 along the Athabasca River, and the period until 1821 was dominated by rivalry between the HBC and the Montréal-based North West Fur Company. Following its absorption of the North West Fur Company in 1821, the HBC controlled the territory until 1869, when it was sold to the Government of the newly formed Dominion of Canada. The area lying between the Rocky Mountains and Manitoba was organized in 1870 as the Northwest Territories of Canada; the Northwest Territories Act of 1875 provided it with a Lieutenant-Governor and legislature. In 1877 the last major agreement between native tribes and the Canadian Government was signed with the Blackfoot, Sarcee and Stoney peoples. The Province of Alberta was created and admitted to the confederation on 1 September 1905.

ECONOMY

Alberta's leading industries are oil production, mining, agriculture (including ranching), tourism and other services, construction and manufacturing.

Median annual family income in Alberta was C $78,400 in 2006, the third highest among the provinces, and per-head median income stood at $31,400. The minimum hourly rate of pay for adult workers in the province was increased from $7.00 to $8.40 per hour in April 2008. Total civilian employment in 2007 was some 1,959,400 persons and the unemployment rate was measured at 3.5%, the lowest rate nation-wide.

Alberta had 52.1m. acres (21.1m. ha) of agricultural land in 2006, and the average size of a farm was 1,055 acres, the second largest area after Saskatchewan. There were 49,431 farms in that year, the second highest number in the country, after Ontario. Alberta is Canada's sole producer of sugar beets. It was the main producer of forage and seed grass, honey, hay and clover, and wool in 2007, and was second to Saskatchewan in barley, wheat (including durum wheat), canola (rapeseed), dry peas, mustard seed, chick-peas and lentil production. The province was the chief producer of cattle in 2007, with its hog, dairy and poultry farms also making a large contribution to farm income. Other commodities produced included potatoes, rye, flaxseed, floriculture products, oats, greenhouse and other vegetables, dry beans, forest products, eggs, sheep and lambs. Farm cash receipts in 2007 totalled C $8,730m., the second highest level in the country after Ontario.

Alberta produced 168,300 wildlife pelts in 2005, for a total of C $5.7m. Total forestland (harvested) was estimated to cover 81,684 ha in 2006; total lumber production in that year was an estimated 25.3m. cu m of roundwood, some 60% of which was softwood production. The province's lakes afford some limited commercial fishing activity; the value of freshwater fisheries production in 2006 was an estimated $1.7m., representing about 1,457 metric tons of fish.

Alberta is Canada's largest producer of coal, crude petroleum and natural gas—it possesses 80% of the nation's crude oil reserves and 90% of natural gas reserves. Crude oil production in 2007 was recorded at 525,000 barrels per day. In 2006 Alberta produced an estimated 32.3m. metric tons of coal (leading British Columbia and Saskatchewan). In 2007 it produced 13,200m. cu ft of natural gas per day. The province's metal production was negligible in 2007, with just an estimated 53 kg of gold being mined, but it was a world leader in its production of elemental sulphur and the second most important Canadian producer of sand and gravel, after Ontario. Peat, quartz, salt and stone are also produced. Total non-fuel mineral production was valued at C $1,580m. in 2006.

Alberta's manufacturing shipments had a total value of C $67,132m. in 2007, the third highest among the provinces and territories. The province's leading manufacturing industries are related to its raw materials, with refinery products, chemicals and food-processing being particularly significant. The aerospace and transportation equipment sectors are growing in importance.

Tourism is the fourth largest industry in Alberta, with hundreds of thousands of people visiting the Rocky Mountains. Tourist expenditure in 2004 amounted to C $4,960m., with Albertans themselves accounting for 73% of visits and overseas visitors for just 4% in the same year. Gross general expenditures by the provincial government were $34,661m. in 2007/08, with 32.6% spent on health, 25.6% on education and 13.3% on social services. Gross general revenue was $39,582m., with 7.9% provided by transfers from other levels of government and 48.8% derived from taxes.

GOVERNMENT

The Province of Alberta was admitted to the confederation on 1 September 1905, as a result of the Alberta Act of 20 July 1905. The provincial government consists of the Lieutenant-Governor, the Executive Council—comprising the cabinet and Premier—and an 83-member Legislative Assembly. Local government is organized through 13 cities, 109 towns, 174 villages, 37 municipal districts and 30 counties. In the 2004 provincial election the Progressive Conservative Party secured 62 seats in the Legislative Assembly. In December 2006 Premier Ralph Klein retired and was succeeded by Ed Stelmach. The Progressive Conservatives increased their representation in the legislature to 72 in the 2008 provincial election. In the 2008 federal general election an estimated 1,270,294 votes were polled in the province. The Conservative Party gained 27 provincial seats in the House of Commons, while the New Democratic Party won one seat.

Lieutenant-Governor: NORMAN L. KWONG.

Executive Council

Premier and President of the Executive Council: ED STELMACH.

Deputy Premier and Minister of International and Intergovernmental Relations: RON STEVENS.

Attorney-General and Minister of Justice: ALISON REDFORD.

President of Treasury Board: LLOYD SNELGROVE.

Minister of Aboriginal Relations: GENE ZWOZDESKY.

Minister of Advanced Education and Technology: DOUG HORNER.

Minister of Agriculture and Rural Development: GEORGE GROENEVELD.

Minister of Children and Youth Services: JANIS TARCHUK.

Minister of Culture and Community Spirit: LINDSAY BLACKETT.

Minister of Education: DAVID HANCOCK.

Minister of Employment and Immigration: HECTOR GOUDREAU.

Minister of Energy: MEL KNIGHT.

Minister of Environment: ROB RENNER.

Minister of Finance and Enterprise: IRIS EVANS.

Minister of Health and Wellness: RON LIEPERT.

Minister of Housing and Urban Affairs: YVONNE FRITZ.

Minister of Infrastructure: JACK HAYDEN.

Minister of Municipal Affairs: RAY DANYLUK.

Minister of Seniors and Community Supports: MARY ANNE JABLONSKI.

Minister Responsible for Service Alberta: HEATHER KLIMCHUK.

Minister of Sustainable Resource Development: TED MORTON.

Solicitor-General and Minister of Public Security: FRED LINDSAY.

Minister of Tourism, Parks and Recreation: CINDY ADY.

Minister of Transportation: LUKE OUELLETTE.

Selected Government Addresses

Office of the Lieutenant-Governor: Legislature Bldg, 3rd Floor, 10800 97th Ave, NW, Edmonton, AB T5K 2B6; tel. (780) 427-7243; fax (780) 422-5134; internet www.lieutenantgovernor.ab.ca.

Office of the Premier: Legislature Bldg, Rm 307, 10800 97th Ave, NW, Edmonton, AB T5K 2B7; tel. (780) 427-2251; fax (780) 427-1349; internet premier.alberta.ca.

Alberta Advanced Education and Technology: Phipps-McKinnon Bldg, 7th Floor, 10020 101A Ave, Edmonton, AB T5J 3G2; tel. (780) 422-5400; fax (780) 427-0821; e-mail aet.info@gov.ab.ca; internet www.advancededucation.gov.ab.ca.

Alberta Agriculture and Food: J. G. O'Donoghue Bldg, 3rd Floor, 7000 113th St, Edmonton, AB T6H 5T6; tel. (780) 742-7901; fax (780) 427-6035; e-mail duke@gov.ab.ca; internet www.agric.gov.ab.ca.

Alberta Children's Services: Sterling Pl., 12th Floor, 9940 106th St, Edmonton, AB T5K 2N2; tel. (780) 422-3004; fax (780) 422-3071; e-mail cs.communications@gov.ab.ca; internet www.child.gov.ab.ca.

Alberta Culture and Community Spirit: Standard Life Centre, 7th Floor, 10405 Jasper Ave, Edmonton, AB T5J 4R7; tel. (780) 427-2921; e-mail tprc.communications@gov.ab.ca; internet culture.alberta.ca.

Alberta Education: Commerce Pl., 7th Floor, 10155 102nd St, Edmonton, AB T5J 4L5; tel. (780) 427-7219; fax (780) 427-7733; e-mail comm.contact@learning.gov.ab.ca; internet education.alberta.ca.

Alberta Employment and Immigration: Labour Bldg, 10th Floor, 10808 99th Ave, Edmonton, AB T5K 0G5; tel. (780) 427-8305; fax (780) 422-9205; e-mail eii.communications@gov.ab.ca; internet employment.alberta.ca.

Alberta Energy: Petroleum Plaza, North Tower, 7th Floor, 9945 108th St, Edmonton, AB T5K 2G6; tel. (780) 427-7425; fax (780) 422-0698; internet www.energy.gov.ab.ca.

Alberta Environment: Petroleum Plaza, South Tower, 10th Floor, 9915 108th St, Edmonton, AB T5K 2G8; tel. (780) 427-6236; fax (780) 427-0923; e-mail env.infocent@gov.ab.ca; internet environment.alberta.ca.

Alberta Finance and Enterprise: Terrace Bldg, Rm 426, 9515 107th St, Edmonton, AB T5K 2C3; tel. (780) 427-3035; fax (780) 427-1147; internet www.finance.gov.ab.ca.

Alberta Gaming and Liquor Commission: 50 Corriveau Ave, St Albert, AB T8N 3T5; tel. (780) 447-8600; fax (780) 447-8950; e-mail aglc_feedback@aglc.gov.ab.ca; internet www.aglc.gov.ab.ca; Chair. of Bd MARGUERITE TRUSSLER.

Alberta Health and Wellness: Telus Plaza, North Tower, 23rd Floor, 10025 Jasper Ave, POB 1360, Station Main, Edmonton, AB T5J 2N3; tel. (780) 427-7164; fax (780) 427-1577; e-mail health.ahinform@gov.ab.ca; internet www.health.alberta.ca.

Alberta Infrastructure: Infrastructure Bldg, 6950 113th St, Edmonton, AB T6H 5V7; tel. (780) 415-0507; fax (780) 427-2187; e-mail infra.contact.us.m@gov.ab.ca; internet www.infrastructure.alberta.ca.

Alberta International, Intergovernmental and Aboriginal Relations: Commerce Pl., 13th Floor, 10155 102nd St, Edmonton, AB T5J 4G8; tel. (780) 427-644; fax (780) 423-6654; internet www.international.gov.ab.ca.

Alberta Justice: Bowker Bldg, 3rd Floor, 9833 109th St, Edmonton, AB T5K 2E8; tel. (780) 427-2745; fax (780) 427-6821; internet www.justice.gov.ab.ca.

Alberta Municipal Affairs and Housing: Commerce Pl., 18th Floor, 10155 102nd St, Edmonton, AB T5J 4L4; tel. (780) 427-2732; fax (780) 422-1419; e-mail minister.ma@gov.ab.ca; internet www.municipalaffairs.gov.ab.ca.

Alberta Seniors and Community Supports: POB 3100, Edmonton, AB T5J 4W3; tel. (780) 427-7876; fax (780) 422-5954; e-mail alberta.seniors@gov.ab.ca; internet www.seniors.gov.ab.ca.

Alberta Solicitor-General and Public Security: John E. Brownlee Bldg, 9th Floor, 10365 97th St, Edmonton, AB T5J 3W7; tel. (780) 427-3441; fax (780) 427-1903; e-mail andy.weiler@gov.ab.ca; internet www.solgps.alberta.ca.

Alberta Sustainable Resource Development: 9920 108th St, Main Floor, Edmonton, AB T5K 2M4; tel. (780) 944-0313; fax (780) 427-4407; e-mail srd.infocent@gov.ab.ca; internet www.srd.gov.ab.ca.

Alberta Tourism, Parks and Recreation: Standard Life Centre, 7th Floor, 10405 Jasper Ave, Edmonton, AB T5J 4R7; tel. (780) 427-6530; e-mail comdev.communications@gov.ab.ca; internet www.tprc.alberta.ca.

Alberta Transportation: Twin Atria Bldg, 2nd Floor, 4999 98th Ave, Edmonton, AB T6B 2X3; tel. (780) 427-2731; fax (780) 466-3166; e-mail trans.contact.us.m@gov.ab.ca; internet www.transportation.alberta.ca.

Service Alberta: Commerce Pl., 13th Floor, 10155 102nd St, Edmonton, AB T5J 4L4; tel. (780) 427-4088; fax (780) 427-4999; e-mail service.alberta@gov.ab.ca; internet www.servicealberta.gov.ab.ca.

Legislative Assembly
(September 2008)

Speaker: KEN KOWALSKI (PC).

Clerk: W. J. DAVID MCNEIL.

Election, 3 March 2008

	Seats at election
Progressive Conservative (PC)	72
Liberal	9
New Democratic Party	2
Total	83

British Columbia

Area: 944,735 sq km (369,037 sq miles).

Population (at 1 July 2007, estimate): 4,380,256.

Capital: Victoria (population at census of 16 May 2006, 78,057).

Principal Cities (population at census of 16 May 2006): Vancouver 578,041; Surrey 394,976; Burnaby 202,799; Richmond 174,461; Abbotsford 123,864; Coquitlam 114,565; Saanich 108,265; Kelowna 106,707; Delta 96,723.

LOCATION, TOPOGRAPHY AND CLIMATE

British Columbia is Canada's westernmost province (only Yukon Territory extends further west). It is bordered by Alberta to the east (the southern half of the boundary being marked by the Rocky Mountains), Yukon Territory and the Northwest Territories to the north and the Pacific Ocean to the west. The province is bordered to the north-west by the US state of Alaska and to the south by the US states of Washington, Idaho and Montana. The Cordilleran Region dominates the province, consisting of parallel mountain ranges running north–south, with an accompanying set of parallel valleys; plateaux occupy much of the centre of the province. The mountain ranges include the Rocky Mountains in the east (rising to Mount Robson at 3,954 m—12,972 ft) and the Coast Mountains in the west. The latter stretch the length of the province, starting from the St Elias Mountains in the north, around the border with Yukon Territory and Alaska, which include Mount Fairweather (British Columbia's highest peak at 4,663 m—15,298 ft), on the boundary with Alaska. Numerous islands lie off the coast, including the large Vancouver Island and the Queen Charlotte Islands group, separated from the mainland by the Strait of Georgia, Queen Charlotte Strait and Hecate Strait. The western boundary of the Rocky Mountains is formed by the Rocky Mountain Trench, extending 1,500 km (932 miles) from Montana to Yukon Territory. The headwaters of the Kootenay, Columbia, Fraser, Peace and Liard Rivers flow from the Trench. British Columbia has a variable climate, with mild, wet winters and dry summers in the south-east, and colder weather and moderate precipitation in the north.

HISTORICAL BACKGROUND

The Spanish explorer, Juan Pérez Hernández, sighted and claimed an area of the British Columbia coast for his country in 1774. Four years later the British navigator, Capt. James Cook, sailed into Nootka Sound on the west coast of present-day Vancouver Island. The Nootka Conventions of 1790–92 gave Spain and the United Kingdom equal trading rights in the area, while British claims to ownership strengthened with George Vancouver's charting of the coast. Exploration of the interior began at about this time and fur-trading posts were established under the control of the Hudson's Bay Company (HBC). The 1846 Oregon Treaty fixed the border between British and US territories in the west of the continent, along the 49th parallel (49°N), but excluded Vancouver Island. The latter was granted to the HBC in 1849, and a legislative assembly was established on the island in 1856. The discovery of gold along the Lower Fraser River the following year precipitated the rapid settlement of the surrounding area, and the mainland colony of British Columbia was established in 1858; in 1866 it was united with Vancouver Island. British Columbia joined the confederation on 20 July 1871, having first made the condition that the federal Government should construct a transcontinental railway to link it with eastern Canada. The Canadian Pacific Railway reached the south-western coast in 1885, built largely with the assistance of Chinese immigrant workers. The Alaska–British Columbia boundary was fixed by tribunal in 1903.

ECONOMY

Forestry, mining, tourism, agriculture and fishing, and manufacturing are the leading industries in British Columbia. Median family income in the province was C $62,600 in 2006, while median individual income measured $26,100 per inhabitant in that year. In November 2001 the minimum hourly rate of pay for adult workers was set at $8.00—the highest rate in the country after the Northwest Territories at that time but which, having remained at this level since, constituted one of the lowest rates nationally at mid-2008 (second only to New Brunswick, at $7.75 per hour). Total civilian employment in 2007 was 2,266,300 persons and the unemployment rate was 4.2%.

Farmland covered 7.0m. acres (2.8m. ha) in 2006, representing about 4% of the national total. The average farm size in 2006 was 353 acres and there were 19,844 farms. Total farm cash receipts amounted to C $2,399m. in 2007. The province's main agricultural commodities are floriculture and nursery products (for which the province ranked second in Canada in 2007), dairy products, poultry and cattle; calves, eggs, hogs and turkeys are also important livestock products, while important crops also include vegetables, berries and grapes (of which it is the leading Canadian producer), apples and other tree fruits and ginseng (for all of which the province ranked second in production value behind Ontario), canola (rapeseed) and hay and clover. Wildlife pelt production is another source of income, with 35,571 pelts (valued at $1.7m.) produced in 2005. British Columbia was also the third greatest producer of ranch-raised mink fur in 2006, after Nova Scotia and Ontario, with production standing at 194,700 pelts (valued at $9.4m.).

Harvested forestland covered some 197,599 ha in 2005 and the province produced an estimated 80.1m. cu m of roundwood in 2006—more than any other province. Of total production, 96% consisted of softwood. The value of the province's landed fish catch was C $314.3m. in 2005, with halibut, shrimp and salmon accounting for the majority of this. The province was Canada's leading producer of halibut, salmon, herring, redfish (ocean perch), hake, clams, sea urchin, dogfish and skate in 2005. British Columbia also ranked foremost among the provinces and territories for its aquaculture industry in that year, with total production valued at $337m. (representing 47% of the national total).

In terms of value, the province was Canada's leading producer of coal in 2006, leading Alberta (the leading producer by volume), with an estimated 23.1m. metric tons of coal mined at a value of C $2.1m. Natural gas and crude petroleum were also extracted; the province again ranked second to Alberta in natural gas production with 15% of the Canadian total in 2007, while natural gas discoveries during 2007 elevated known reserves in the territory to 483,000m. cu m (from 462,400m. cu m in 2006). Crude oil production in 2006 amounted to an estimated 28,805 barrels per day. British Columbia led the country in its production of copper (accounting for some 47% of Canada's total) in 2007, and was also the leading producer of silver. It was the only province producing molybdenum and was ranked second for lead (after New Brunswick), third for gold and cement production (after Ontario and Québec), and third for sand and gravel (behind Ontario and Alberta). Zinc, iron ore and stone were other important minerals. The value of the province's mineral production was estimated at $5,672m. in 2007, the third highest in the country after Ontario and Saskatchewan.

In 2007 manufacturing shipments were valued at C $42,930m., with the province ranked fourth in this respect. The main manufacturing industries are related to the province's forestry, agriculture and mining industries, with wood and related products, foods and beverages, primary metals, fabricated metal products and machinery the most important sectors. Other industries of importance include petroleum and coal products, chemicals, plastics and rubber products. Hi-tech industries, particularly in the telecommunications and aerospace sectors, are becoming more prominent.

The tourist trade plays a significant part in the economy of British Columbia. In 2005 overnight visitor revenues in the province were forecast at C $9,878m., of which British Columbians were predicted to account for $2,694m. and other Canadians $2,837m. Tourism from the countries of the Pacific Rim is important, and was expected to supply revenue of $1,046m. (9.1% of the 2005 total). Overnight visitors to the province were expected to total 23.0m. in 2005. Tourism employed some 120,400 people in British Columbia in 2006.

Gross general expenditures by the provincial government were C $36,137m. in 2007/08, with 35.1% spent on health, 21.3% on education and 16.0% on social services. Gross general revenue amounted to $36,980m.; 60.9% of this was revenue from taxation, and 15.7% contributions from other levels of government.

GOVERNMENT

British Columbia was admitted to the confederation on 20 July 1871 by the Imperial Order-in-Council of 16 May 1871. The government consists of: the Lieutenant-Governor; the Executive Council, comprising the Premier and cabinet; and the Legislative Assembly. In 1987 British Columbia was divided into eight 'development regions', each of which is represented by a minister of state in the cabinet. There are 79 members of the Legislative Assembly, elected to serve a maximum five-year term. Local government is directed through the province's 39 cities, 15 towns, 46 villages and 48 districts. In addition, there are regional districts, which provide services not only to those municipalities with which they overlap, but also to previously unorganized areas. In the 2001 provincial election the Liberal Party was elected to office, gaining 77 of the legislature's 79 seats. The Liberals were returned to power in the 2005 provincial election, but with a much smaller majority, gaining 46 seats. In the federal general election of 2008 an estimated 1,793,373 votes were cast in British Columbia. The Conservative Party won 22 of the province's 36 seats in the House of Commons, while the New Democratic Party won nine and the Liberal Party gained five seats.

Lieutenant-Governor: STEVEN L. POINT.

Executive Council

Premier and President of the Council: GORDON CAMPBELL.

Deputy Premier, Minister of Education and Minister Responsible for Early Learning and Literacy: SHIRLEY BOND.

Attorney-General and Minister responsible for Multiculturalism: WALLY OPPAL.

Minister of Aboriginal Relations and Reconciliation: MICHAEL DE JONG.

Minister of Advanced Education and Minister responsible for Labour Market Development: MURRAY COELL.

Minister of Agriculture and Lands: STAN HAGEN.

Minister of Children and Family Development: TOM CHRISTENSEN.

Minister of Community Development: BLAIR LEKSTROM.

Minister of Energy, Mines and Petroleum Resources: RICHARD NEUFELD.

Minister of Environment: BARRY PENNER.

Minister of Finance and Minister responsible for the Olympics: COLIN HANSEN.

Minister of Forests and Range: PAT BELL.

Minister of Health Services: GEORGE ABBOTT.

Minister of Healthy Living and Sport: MARY POLAK.

Minister of Housing and Social Development: RICH COLEMAN.

Minister of Labour and Citizens' Services: IAIN BLACK.

Minister of Public Safety and Solicitor-General: JOHN VAN DONGEN.

Minister of Small Business and Revenue and Minister responsible for Regulatory Reform: KEVIN KRUEGER.

Minister of Technology, Trade and Economic Development and Minister responsible for the Asia-Pacific Initiative: IDA CHONG.

Minister of Tourism, Culture and the Arts: BILL BENNETT.

Minister of Transportation and Infrastructure: KEVIN FALCON.

Minister of State for Childcare: LINDA A. REID.

Minister of State for Intergovernmental Relations: JOAN MCINTYRE.

Minister of State for Mining: GORDON HOGG.

Minister of State for ActNow BC: GORDON HOGG.

Selected Government Addresses

Office of the Lieutenant-Governor: Government House, 1401 Rockland Ave, Victoria, BC V8S 1V9; tel. (250) 387-2080; fax (250) 387-2078; e-mail ghinfo@gov.bc.ca; internet www.ltgov.bc.ca.

Office of the Premier: Parliament Bldgs, West Annex, Suite 156, POB 9041, Victoria, BC V8W 9E1; tel. (250) 387-1715; fax (250) 387-0087; e-mail premier@gov.bc.ca; internet www.gov.bc.ca/premier.

Ministry of Aboriginal Relations and Reconciliation: Parliament Bldgs, Rm 310, POB 9052, Station Provincial Government, Victoria, BC V8W 9E2; tel. (250) 953-4844; fax (250) 953-4856; e-mail mike.dejong.mla@leg.bc.ca; internet www.gov.bc.ca/arr.

Ministry of Advanced Education and Labour Market Development: Parliament Bldgs, Rm 247, POB 9059, Station Provincial Government, Victoria, BC V8W 9E2; tel. (250) 356-2771; fax (250) 356-3000; e-mail murray.coell.mla@leg.bc.ca; internet www.gov.bc.ca/aved.

Ministry of Agriculture and Lands: Parliament Bldgs, Rm 28, POB 9043, Station Provincial Government, Victoria, BC V8W 9E2; tel. (250) 387-1023; fax (250) 387-1522; e-mail stan.hagen.mla@leg.bc.ca; internet www.gov.bc.ca/al.

Ministry of the Attorney-General: Parliament Bldgs, Rm 243, POB 9044, Station Provincial Government, Victoria, BC V8W 9E2; tel. (250) 387-1866; fax (250) 387-6411; e-mail wally.oppal.mla@leg.bc.ca; internet www.gov.bc.ca/ag.

Ministry of Children and Family Development: Parliament Bldgs, Rm 347, POB 9057, Station Provincial Government, Victoria, BC V8W 9E2; tel. (250) 387-9699; fax (250) 387-9722; e-mail tom.christensen.mla@leg.bc.ca; internet www.gov.bc.ca/mcf.

Ministry of Community Development: Parliament Bldgs, Rm 133, POB 9056, Station Provincial Government, Victoria, BC V8W 9E2; tel. (250) 387-2283; fax (250) 387-4312; e-mail blair.lekstrom.mla@leg.bc.ca; internet www.gov.bc.ca/cserv.

Ministry of Education: Parliament Bldgs, Rm 248, POB 9045, Station Provincial Government, Victoria, BC V8W 9E2; tel. (250) 387-1977; fax (250) 387-3200; e-mail shirley.bond@leg.bc.ca; internet www.gov.bc.ca/bced.

Ministry of Energy, Mines and Petroleum Resources: Parliament Bldgs, Rm 134, POB 9060, Station Provincial Government, Victoria, BC V8W 9E2; tel. (250) 387-5896; fax (250) 356-2965; e-mail empr.minister@gov.bc.ca; internet www.gov.bc.ca/empr.

Ministry of Environment: Parliament Bldgs, Rm 112, POB 9047, Station Provincial Government, Victoria, BC V8W 9E2; tel. (250) 387-1187; fax (250) 387-1356; e-mail env.minister@gov.bc.ca; internet www.gov.bc.ca/env.

Ministry of Finance: Parliament Bldgs, Rm 153, POB 9048, Station Provincial Government, Victoria, BC V8W 9E2; tel. (250) 387-3751; fax (250) 387-5594; e-mail colin.hansen.mla@leg.bc.ca; internet www.gov.bc.ca/fin.

Ministry of Forests and Range: Parliament Bldgs, Rm 138, POB 9049, Station Provincial Government, Victoria, BC V8W 9E2; tel. (250) 387-6240; fax (250) 387-1040; e-mail sophia.proctor@gov.bc.ca; internet www.gov.bc.ca/for.

Ministry of Health Services: Parliament Bldgs, Rm 337, POB 9050, Station Provincial Government, Victoria, BC V8W 9E2; tel. (250) 953-3547; fax (250) 356-9587; e-mail hlth.health@gems1.gov.bc.ca; internet www.gov.bc.ca/health.

Ministry of Healthy Living and Sport: Parliament Bldgs, Rm 325, POB 9067, Station Provincial Government, Victoria, BC V8W 9E2; tel. (250) 387-3504; fax (250) 387-3420; e-mail feedback@gov.bc.ca; internet www.gov.bc.ca/hls.

Ministry of Housing and Social Development: Parliament Bldgs, Rm 128, POB 9933, Station Provincial Government, Victoria, BC V8W 9R2; tel. (250) 387-6489; fax (250) 356-7801; e-mail rich.coleman.mla@leg.bc.ca; internet www.gov.bc.ca/hsd.

Ministry of Labour and Citizens' Services: Parliament Bldgs, Rm 342, POB 9052, Station Provincial Government, Victoria, BC V8W 9E2; tel. (250) 356-6348; fax (250) 356-6595; e-mail enquirybc@gov.bc.ca; internet www.gov.bc.ca/lcs.

Ministry of Public Safety and Solicitor-General: Parliament Bldgs, Rm 236, POB 9053, Station Provincial Government, Victoria, BC V8W 9E2; tel. (250) 356-7717; fax (250) 356-8270; e-mail pssgwebfeedback@gov.bc.ca; internet www.gov.bc.ca/pssg.

Ministry of Small Business and Revenue: Parliament Bldgs, Rm 124, POB 9065, Station Provincial Government, Victoria, BC V8W 9E2; tel. (250) 356-6611; fax (250) 356-8294; e-mail msbroffice@gov.bc.ca; internet www.gov.bc.ca/sbr.

Ministry of Technology, Trade and Economic Development: Parliament Bldgs, Rm 323, POB 9046, Station Provincial Government, Victoria, BC V8W 9E2; tel. (250) 356-7411; fax (250) 356-6376; e-mail feedback.cse@gov.ba.ca; internet www.gov.bc.ca/ecdev.

Ministry of Tourism, Culture and the Arts: Parliament Bldgs, Rm 301, POB 9071, Station Provincial Government, Victoria, BC V8W 9E9; tel. (250) 953-4246; fax (250) 953-4250; e-mail tca.minister@gov.bc.ca; internet www.gov.bc.ca/tca.

Ministry of Transportation and Infrastructure: POB 9850, Station Provincial Government, Victoria, BC V8W 9T5; tel. (250) 387-3198; fax (250) 356-7706; e-mail tran.webmaster@gov.bc.ca; internet www.gov.bc.ca/tran.

Utilities Commission: 900 Howe St, 6th Floor, POB 250, Vancouver, BC V6Z 2N3; tel. (604) 660-4700; fax (604) 660-1102; e-mail commission.secretary@bcuc.com; internet www.bcuc.com; Chair. LEN KELSEY.

Legislative Assembly
(September 2008)

Speaker: BILL BARISOFF (Liberal).

Clerk: E. GEORGE MACMINN.

Election, 17 May 2005

	Seats at election	Seats at September 2008
Liberal	46	46
New Democratic Party (NDP)	33	32
Vacant	—	2
Total	79	79

Manitoba

Area: 647,797 sq km (253,046 sq miles).

Population (at 1 July 2007, estimate): 1,186,679.

Capital, Principal City: Winnipeg (population at census of 16 May 2006, 633,451).

LOCATION, TOPOGRAPHY AND CLIMATE

Manitoba is situated in southern central Canada and is the easternmost of the three Prairie provinces. Its borders are formed by Saskatchewan to the west, Nunavut to the north and Ontario to the east. The US states of North Dakota and Minnesota form the southern boundary. In the north-east the coastline of Hudson Bay marks the land boundary of the province. Manitoba is divided into four distinct geographic regions: the Lake Agassiz Lowland, the Western Upland, the Precambrian Upland and the Hudson Bay Lowland. The Lake Agassiz Lowland, in the south-central region of Manitoba, contains the province's three largest lakes: Winnipeg, Winnipegosis and Manitoba. The Western Upland lies in the south-western part of Manitoba and is formed by a series of low plateaux. The Precambrian Upland, consisting of rocky outcrop and numerous lakes, is utilized for hydroelectric generation. The Hudson Bay Lowland comprises the area surrounding the coastline of the Bay. The topography of the province varies from arable country in the south-west to wilderness in a section east of a line drawn from the south-east corner of the province to the border with Saskatchewan at Flin Flon. This area of wilderness constitutes two-thirds of the province and forms part of the Canadian Shield—a large band of Precambrian rocks running across the southern part of Canada. The province's principal rivers include the Nelson, which flows from Lake Winnipeg into Hudson Bay, the Saskatchewan, the Red, the Assiniboine and the Winnipeg. Manitoba has a continental climate, with very cold winters and moderately warm summers.

HISTORICAL BACKGROUND

The area occupied by present-day Manitoba was granted to the Hudson's Bay Company (HBC) on its establishment in 1670 by King Charles II of England and Scotland. The region formed part of the territory known as Rupert's Land. HBC employee Henry Kelsey and the La Vérendrye family from France explored lands to the south-west and west of Hudson Bay, respectively, during the late 17th and early 18th centuries. Fur-trading posts were supplemented by agricultural settlements from 1812. Conflicts arose over agricultural expansion into land claimed by the Métis (those of mixed French and Indian descent) in the Red River Valley area; in 1815–18 a major rebellion by the Métis took place. A second period of unrest and Métis rebellion occurred in 1869–70. In 1869 the Dominion of Canada purchased Rupert's Land from the HBC and in 1870 the area was divided into the Northwest Territories (including present-day Alberta and Saskatchewan) and the new Province of Manitoba, which entered the confederation on 15 July of the same year. The province's boundaries were confirmed in 1881. During the 1880s the development of the railways in North America opened the province to increased numbers of settlers and assisted in the economic development of the region. Winnipeg, the 'hub' or central point of the railway network, grew in importance as a transportation centre, until the Panama Canal opened up a cheap east–west sea cargo route in 1914. In 1919 there was a general strike in Winnipeg, the result of a localized economic depression, partly arising from the loss of this important east–west trade role.

ECONOMY

Manitoba's foremost employers are the community, business and personal services, trade and manufacturing, agricultural and food-processing sectors.

The province's median family income in 2006 was C $58,700, while median per-head income in that year stood at $25,100. Total civilian employment in 2007 was 596,500 persons, with an unemployment rate of 4.4%. The minimum hourly rate of pay for adult workers was raised from $7.60 to $8.50 in April 2008.

Farmland covered 19.1m. acres (7.7m. ha) of Manitoba's land area in 2006, accounting for 11% of the national total. The average size of a farm was 1,001 acres and there were 19,054 farms. Manitoba is one of Canada's leading agricultural provinces, ranking first in the production of sunflower seed, potatoes and chicks and poults from hatcheries in 2007. In that year the province also ranked second for oats, flaxseed, dry beans, rye and canary seed. Hogs, cattle, canola (rapeseed), wheat, barley, soybeans, dairy products, poultry and eggs are also significant to farm income. In 2007 farm receipts stood at C $4,313m.

The fur trade, Manitoba's oldest industry, continues to contribute to the provincial economy, although it is no longer a major source of income. In 2005 the province produced 97,177 wildlife pelts, with a total value of C $3.3m.; production of ranch-raised mink fur stood at 47,580 pelts in 2006, with a total value of $2.4m.

In 2002 about 57% of the land area was wooded, with harvested forestland covering 15m. ha; the area of forest harvested in 2005 totalled 14m. ha. In 2006 the merchantable roundwood volume was 2.5m. cu m, 70% of which was softwoods. Manitoba has some 57,000 sq km of rivers and lakes; the value of freshwater fisheries production was an estimated C $24m. in 2006, representing around 11,632 metric tons of fish. Pickerel, whitefish, sauger, pike, perch and mullet are the principal varieties of fish caught.

In 2006 crude petroleum production in Manitoba amounted to an estimated 18,977 barrels per day. Income in the extractive sector in 2007 was mainly derived from non-fuel minerals, namely zinc (for which the province was ranked second, after New Brunswick), nickel and cobalt (ranked third), copper and gold (ranked fourth). The province also produced significant quantities of sand and gravel, stone and silver and was the leading producer of selenium in 2007. It was the only province to produce tantalum and tellurium. The total value of non-fuel mineral production was estimated at C $2,493m. in 2007.

Manufacturing contributed about 13% to total provincial GDP in 2005. Food-processing is the largest industry, followed by transportation equipment. In 2007 Manitoba's manufacturing shipments were valued at C $16,111m., the fifth highest among the provinces and territories.

Gross general expenditures by the provincial government amounted to C $11,280m. in 2007/08, with 34.0% of this spent on health, 17.5% on education and 16.0% on social services. Gross general revenue totalled $11,448m., with 31.6% provided by other levels of government and 54.6% derived from taxes.

GOVERNMENT

The Province of Manitoba was admitted to the confederation on 15 July 1870 by the Manitoba Act of 1870 and the Imperial Order-in-Council of 23 June 1870. The formal head of the provincial government is the Lieutenant-Governor. Manitoba has a 16-member Executive Council comprising the Premier and the cabinet. The Legislative Assembly has 57 members. Local government is administered by the province's 105 rural municipalities, 35 towns, 39 villages and five cities. In the provincial election of May 2007 the New Democratic Party (NDP) secured a further term in office. In the federal general election of 2008 some 466,889 people voted in Manitoba. The Conservative Party gained nine seats in the House of Commons, while the New Democratic Party won four seats and the Liberal Party won one seat.

Lieutenant-Governor: JOHN HARVARD.

Executive Council

Premier, President of the Council and Minister of Federal-Provincial Relations: GARY DOER.

Deputy Premier and Minister of Agriculture, Food and Rural Initiatives, Minister responsible for Co-operative Development: ROSANN WOWCHUK.

Minister of Aboriginal and Northern Affairs: OSCAR LATHLIN.

Minister of Advanced Education and Literacy: DIANE MCGIFFORD.

Minister of Competitiveness, Training and Trade, of Manitoba Liquor Control Commission and of Manitoba Lotteries Corporation: ANDREW SWAN.

Minister of Conservation: STAN STRUTHERS.

Minister of Culture, Heritage, Tourism and Sport: ERIC ROBINSON.

Minister of Education, Citizenship and Youth: PETER BJORNSON.

Minister of Family Services and Housing and Minister responsible for Persons with Disabilities: GORD MACKINTOSH.

Minister of Finance and Minister responsible for French Language Services, for the Crown Corporations Public Review and Accountability Act, for the Civil Service and for Manitoba Hydro: GREGORY F. SELINGER.

Minister of Health: THERESA OSWALD.

Minister of Healthy Living: KERRI IRVIN-ROSS.

Minister of Infrastructure and Transportation: RON LEMIEUX.

Minister of Intergovernmental Affairs: STEVE ASHTON.

Minister of Justice and Attorney-General: DAVE CHOMIAK.

Minister of Labour and Immigration and Minister responsible for Multiculturalism and for the Status of Women: NANCY ALLAN.

Minister of Science, Technology, Energy and Mines: JIM RONDEAU.

Minister of Water Stewardship: CHRISTINE MELNICK.

Selected Government Addresses

Office of the Lieutenant-Governor: 235 Legislative Bldg, 450 Broadway Ave, Winnipeg, MB R3C 0V8; tel. (204) 945-2753; fax (204) 945-4329; e-mail ltgov@leg.gov.mb.ca; internet www.lg.gov.mb.ca.

Office of the Premier: 204 Legislative Bldg, 450 Broadway Ave, Winnipeg, MB R3C 0V8; tel. (204) 945-3714; fax (204) 949-1484;

e-mail premier@leg.gov.mb.ca; internet www.gov.mb.ca/minister/premier.

Manitoba Aboriginal and Northern Affairs: 344 Legislative Bldg, 450 Broadway Ave, Winnipeg, MB R3C 0V8; tel. (204) 945-3719; fax (204) 945-8374; e-mail anaweb@gov.mb.ca; internet www.gov.mb.ca/ana.

Manitoba Agriculture, Food and Rural Initiatives: 165 Legislative Bldg, 450 Broadway Ave, Winnipeg, MB R3C 0V8; tel. (204) 945-3722; fax (204) 945-3470; e-mail minagr@leg.gov.mb.ca; internet www.gov.mb.ca/agriculture.

Manitoba Competitiveness, Training and Trade: 358 Legislative Bldg, 450 Broadway Ave, Winnipeg, MB R3C 0V8; tel. (204) 945-0067; fax (204) 945-4882; e-mail minctt@leg.gov.mb.ca; internet www.gov.mb.ca/ctt.

Manitoba Conservation: 330 Legislative Bldg, 450 Broadway Ave, Winnipeg, MB R3C 0V8; tel. (204) 945-3730; fax (204) 945–3586; e-mail mincon@leg.gov.mb.ca; internet www.gov.mb.ca/conservation.

Manitoba Culture, Heritage, Tourism and Sport: 118 Legislative Bldg, 450 Broadway Ave, Winnipeg, MB R3C 0V8; tel. (204) 945-3729; fax (204) 945-5223; e-mail mincht@leg.gov.mb.ca; internet www.gov.mb.ca/chc.

Manitoba Education, Citizenship and Youth: 168 Legislative Bldg, 450 Broadway Ave, Winnipeg, MB R3C 0V8; tel. (204) 945-3720; fax (204) 945-1291; e-mail minedu@leg.gov.mb.ca; internet www.edu.gov.mb.ca.

Manitoba Family Services and Housing: 357 Legislative Bldg, 450 Broadway Ave, Winnipeg, MB R3C 0V8; tel. (204) 945-4173; fax (204) 945-5149; e-mail minfam@leg.gov.mb.ca; internet www.gov.mb.ca/fs.

Manitoba Finance: 103 Legislative Bldg, 450 Broadway Ave, Winnipeg, MB R3C 0V8; tel. (204) 945-3952; fax (204) 945-6057; e-mail minfin@leg.gov.mb.ca; internet www.gov.mb.ca/finance.

Manitoba Health: 302 Legislative Bldg, 450 Broadway Ave, Winnipeg, MB R3C 0V8; tel. (204) 945-3731; fax (204) 945-0441; e-mail minhlt@leg.gov.mb.ca; internet www.gov.mb.ca/health.

Manitoba Healthy Living: 310 Legislative Bldg, 450 Broadway Ave, Winnipeg, MB R3C 0V8; tel. (204) 945-1373; fax (204) 948-2703; e-mail minhliv@leg.gov.mb.ca; internet www.gov.mb.ca/healthyliving.

Manitoba Infrastructure and Transportation: 203 Legislative Bldg, 450 Broadway Ave, Winnipeg, MB R3C 0V8; tel. (204) 945-3723; fax (204) 945-7610; e-mail mininfratran@leg.gov.mb.ca; internet www.gov.mb.ca/mit.

Manitoba Intergovernmental Affairs: 301 Legislative Bldg, 450 Broadway Ave, Winnipeg, MB R3C 0V8; tel. (204) 945-3788; fax (204) 945-1383; e-mail minia@leg.gov.mb.ca; internet www.gov.mb.ca/ia.

Manitoba Justice: 104 Legislative Bldg, 405 Broadway Ave, Winnipeg, MB R3C 3L6; tel. (204) 945-3728; fax (204) 945-2517; e-mail minjus@leg.gov.mb.ca; internet www.gov.mb.ca/justice.

Manitoba Labour and Immigration: 317 Legislative Bldg, 450 Broadway Ave, Winnipeg, MB R3C 0V8; tel. (204) 945-4079; fax (204) 948-8312; e-mail minlab@leg.gov.mb.ca; internet www.gov.mb.ca/labour.

Manitoba Science, Technology, Energy and Mines: 333 Legislative Bldg, 450 Broadway Ave, Winnipeg, MB R3C 0V8; tel. (204) 945-5356; fax (204) 948-2692; e-mail minstem@leg.gov.mb.ca; internet www.gov.mb.ca/stem.

Manitoba Water Stewardship: Main Office, POB 11, 200 Saulteaux Crescent, Winnipeg, MB R3J 3W3; tel. (204) 945-6398; fax (204) 948-2684; e-mail wsd@gov.mb.ca; internet www.gov.mb.ca/waterstewardship.

Legislative Assembly
(September 2008)

Speaker: GEORGE HICKES (NDP).

Clerk: PATRICIA CHAYCHUK.

Election, 22 May 2007

	Seats at election
New Democratic Party (NDP)	36
Progressive Conservative (PC)	19
Liberal Party	2
Total	57

New Brunswick

Area: 72,908 sq km (28,480 sq miles).

Population (at 1 July 2007, estimate): 749,782.

Capital: Fredericton.

Principal Cities (population at census of 16 May 2006): Saint John 68,043; Moncton 64,128; Fredericton (capital) 50,535.

LOCATION, TOPOGRAPHY AND CLIMATE

New Brunswick, one of the three Maritime provinces, lies in the east of Canada, bordered by Québec to the north and north-west, Nova Scotia to the south-east and the US state of Maine to the west. The Bay of Fundy lies to the south and to the east is the Northumberland Strait (which separates New Brunswick from Prince Edward Island) and the Gulf of St Lawrence. The province is composed of uplands in the north and low, rolling hills in the central and eastern regions, while steep hills on the southern coast descend to tidal marshes and a low plain in the south-east. The southern region contains several lakes, including Grand Lake, which is over 30 km in length. New Brunswick has a continental climate, more extreme in the interior than on the coasts, where it is moderated by the proximity of the sea.

HISTORICAL BACKGROUND

Micmac communities inhabited the area of present-day New Brunswick for many years prior to French attempts at settlement on the Saint Croix River (which forms part of the border with Maine) and at Port Royal (Nova Scotia) in 1604–05. Following the French move to the Québec region from 1608, the Micmac remained in the St John valley, from which the French later launched raids against New England (now part of the USA) in the 1690s. In 1621 New Brunswick formed part of the area granted to a Scottish nobleman, Sir William Alexander, by King James I of England (James VI of Scotland); it was renamed Nova Scotia. Under the Peace of Utrecht in 1713, most of the area of Nova Scotia (known to the French as Acadia), including New Brunswick, was transferred to the British; almost all Acadians, who sympathized with the French, were deported from 1755, after which the land was occupied by immigrants, many from New England. Loyalist refugees settled on the north shore of the Bay of Fundy after the American Revolution and founded the city of Saint John. New Brunswick received separate colonial status from the rest of Nova Scotia in 1784, and was part of the new Canadian confederation at its inception on 1 July 1867. During the 1960s a series of legislative measures was passed in an attempt to rectify severe disparities between standards of living in the urban south of the province and those in the rural north.

ECONOMY

The main areas of employment in New Brunswick are community, business and personal services, trade, manufacturing, mining, and the forestry and fisheries industries.

Median family income was C $54,000 in 2006, with only Newfoundland and Labrador registering a lower level. In 2006 per-head median income was $22,900—again, one of the lowest levels in the country behind Newfoundland and Labrador. The minimum hourly wage for adult workers was increased from $7.25 to $7.75 in March 2008. In 2007 the unemployment rate was 7.5% and total civilian employment stood at 362,800.

Farmland covered 976,648 acres (395,228 ha) in 2006; the size of an average farm was 351 acres and there were 2,776 farms. Potatoes are the province's chief crop, followed by floriculture and nursery products. Dairy products are also a major source of farm revenue. Other important agricultural commodities include poultry, hogs, cattle, berries and grapes, eggs and maple products (for which the province ranked third behind Québec and Ontario in 2007). New Brunswick's farm receipts totalled C $444m. in 2007. Wildlife pelt production was valued at just over $1.1m. in 2005, while production of ranch-raised fur and mink generated almost $2.4m. in 2006.

New Brunswick had an estimated 111,290 ha of harvested forestland in 2006. In that year the province produced an estimated 10.0m. cu m of roundwood—of which 66% was softwoods. The value of the province's landed fish catch in 2006 was C $153m., representing 110,620m. tons. In 2005 some 40% of the fishing harvest's total value was accounted for by the lobster catch, and a further 40% by the crab harvest. New Brunswick was Canada's leading producer of alewife, eels and smelt in 2005. The province was a major contributor to Canada's aquaculture economy (second only to British Columbia), with a production value of $230.5m. in 2005, with farmed salmon contributing almost 98% of this total.

From the 1950s mining has been of major importance to the New Brunswick economy. In 2007 total non-fuel mineral production was valued at C $1,569m. Minerals produced included bismuth, zinc and peat (for all of which New Brunswick was ranked first in Canada), antimony, lead, silver and sulphur, in smelter gas (ranked second for all four mineral types), copper, gold, sand and gravel, and stone. Coal is also mined, with an estimated 136,078 metric tons produced in 2007 (placing the province fourth nationally in this regard). Canada's largest oil refinery is situated in Saint John.

Manufacturing activity in the province is based mainly around agriculture and forestry. The food and beverages industry is the leading manufacturing sector, followed by paper, pulp and allied products. The metals and transportation equipment industries are also significant, and the province is promoting growth in its information technology sector. Manufacturing shipments were valued at C $15,680m. in 2007, with the province ranked sixth in the country in this respect.

In 2004 tourism expenditures amounted to C $1,100m., while the sector provided 31,000 jobs. Gross general expenditures by the provincial government in 2007/08 were $7,580m., of which 31.4% was spent on health, 11.2% on social services and 20.9% on education. Gross general revenue amounted to $7,128m.; 35.4% came from other levels of government and 50.6% from taxes.

GOVERNMENT

The Province of New Brunswick was admitted to the confederation on 1 July 1867 by the British North America Act of the same year. The government of the province consists of: a Lieutenant-Governor; a Premier and cabinet, or Executive Council; and a Legislative Assembly of 55 members. The legislature is elected for a five-year term. New Brunswick's local government is directed through its six cities, 27 towns and 84 villages. There are also 282 unincorporated local service districts, which perform a similar function to municipal organizations. In the provincial election of 2006 the Liberal Party defeated the incumbent Progressive Conservative Party government, winning 29 of the Legislative Assembly's 55 seats. The Progressive Conservatives secured the remaining 26 seats. In the federal general election of 2008 some 368,035 people voted in New Brunswick. The Conservative Party won six seats in the House of Commons, while the Liberal Party won three seats and the New Democratic Party secured the remaining seat.

Lieutenant-Governor: HERMÉNÉGILDE CHIASSON.

Executive Council

Premier and President of the Council, Minister of Intergovernmental Affairs and Minister responsible for the Premier's Council on the Status of Disabled Persons and for the Office of Self-Sufficiency: SHAWN GRAHAM.

Attorney-General and Minister of Justice and Consumer Affairs: THOMAS J. BURKE.

Solicitor-General and Minister of Public Safety: JOHN FORAN.

Minister of Agriculture and Aquaculture: RONALD OUELLETTE.

Minister of Business New Brunswick: GREG BYRNE.

Minister of Education: KELLY LAMROCK.

Minister of Energy and of Supply and Services: JACK KEIR.

Minister of the Environment and Minister responsible for the Northern New Brunswick Initiative: ROLAND HACHÉ.

Minister of Finance and Minister responsible for the Regional Development Corporation: VICTOR BOUDREAU.

Minister of Fisheries: RICK DOUCET.

Minister of Health: MICHAEL MURPHY.

Minister of Local Government and Minister responsible for Community Non-Profit Organizations Secretariat: CARMEL ROBICHAUD.

Minister of Natural Resources: DONALD ARSENAULT.

Minister of the Office of Human Resources: WALLY STILES.

Minister of Post-secondary Education, Training and Labour and Minister responsible for Aboriginal Affairs Secretariat: EDWARD DOHERTY.

Minister of Social Development and Minister responsible for Advisory Council on the Status of Women: MARY SCHRYER.

Minister of Tourism and Parks: STAURT JAMIESON.

Minister of Transportation: DENIS LANDRY.

Minister of Wellness, Culture and Sport and Minister responsible for Francophonie: HÉDARD ALBERT.

Minister of State for Seniors and Housing: EUGENE MCGINLEY.

Selected Government Addresses

Office of the Lieutenant-Governor: Old Government House, 51 Woodstock Rd, POB 6000, Fredericton, NB E3B 5H1; tel. (506) 453-2505; fax (506) 444-5280; internet www.gnb.ca/lg/index.htm.

Office of the Premier: Centennial Bldg, 670 King St, POB 6000, Fredericton, NB E3B 5H1; tel. (506) 453-2144; fax (506) 453-7407; e-mail premier@gnb.ca; internet www.gnb.ca/0089/index-e.asp.

Business New Brunswick: Centennial Bldg, 670 King St, POB 6000, Fredericton, NB E3B 5H1; tel. (506) 444-5228; fax (506) 453-5428; e-mail ryan.donaghy@gnb.ca; internet www.gnb.ca/0398/index-e.asp.

Department of Agriculture and Aquaculture: Agricultural Research Station (Experimental Farm), 850 Lincoln Rd, POB 6000, Fredericton, NB E3B 5H1; tel. (506) 453-2666; e-mail alain.bryar@gnb.ca; internet www.gnb.ca/0027/index-e.asp.

Department of Education: Pl. 2000, 250 King St, POB 6000, Fredericton, NB E3B 5H1; tel. (506) 453-3678; fax (506) 453-3325; e-mail angelique.binet@gnb.ca; internet www.gnb.ca/0000/index-e.asp.

Department of Energy: Brunswick Sq., 1 Germain St, Suite M100, POB 5001, Saint John, NB E2L 4Y9; tel. (506) 658-3180; fax (506) 658-3191; e-mail bonnie.doyle@gnb.ca; internet www.gnb.ca/0085/index-e.asp.

Department of the Environment: Marysville Pl., 20 McGloin St, POB 6000, Fredericton, NB E3B 5H1; tel. (506) 453-2690; fax (506) 457-4991; e-mail jennifer.graham@gnb.ca; internet www.gnb.ca/0009/index-e.asp.

Department of Finance: Centennial Bldg, 670 King St, POB 6000, Fredericton, NB E3B 5H1; tel. (506) 453-2451; fax (506) 457-4989; e-mail marc.belliveau@gnb.ca; internet www.gnb.ca/0024/index-e.asp.

Department of Health: HSBC Pl., 520 King St, POB 5100, Fredericton, NB E3B 5G8; tel. (506) 457-4800; fax (506) 453-5243; e-mail hw_sme@gnb.ca; internet www.gnb.ca/0051/index-e.asp.

Department of Intergovernmental Affairs: Centennial Bldg, 2nd Floor, Rm 274, 670 King St, POB 6000, Fredericton, NB E3B 5H1; tel. (506) 444-5418; fax (506) 453-2995; e-mail iga@gnb.ca; internet www.gnb.ca/0056/index-e.asp.

Department of Justice and Consumer Affairs: Centennial Bldg, 670 King St, Rm 412, POB 6000, Fredericton, NB E3B 5H1; tel. (506) 462-5100; fax (506) 453-3651; e-mail justice.comments@gnb.ca; internet www.gnb.ca/0062/index-e.asp.

Department of Local Government: Marysville Pl., 20 McGloin St, POB 6000, Fredericton, NB E3B 5H1; tel. (506) 453-2690; e-mail daniel.lessard@gnb.ca; internet www.gnb.ca/0370/index-e.asp.

Department of Natural Resources: Hugh John Flemming Forestry Centre, 1350 Regent St, POB 6000, Fredericton, NB E3B 5H1; tel. (506) 453-2207; fax (506) 444-5839; e-mail dnrweb@gnb.ca; internet www.gnb.ca/0078/index-e.asp.

Department of Post-Secondary Education, Training and Labour: Chestnut Complex, 470 York St, POB 6000, Fredericton, NB E3B 5H1; tel. (506) 453-2597; fax (506) 453-3618; e-mail shawn.hearn@gnb.ca; internet www.gnb.ca/0105/index-e.asp.

Department of Public Safety: Argyle Pl., 364 Argyle St, POB 6000, Fredericton, NB E3B 5H1; tel. (506) 453-3992; fax (506) 453-7481; e-mail chrystiane.mallaley@gnb.ca; internet www.gnb.ca/0276/index-e.asp.

Department of Social Development: Sartain MacDonald Bldg, 551 King St, POB 6000, Fredericton, NB E3B 5H1; tel. (506) 453-2001; fax (506) 453-7478; e-mail mary.schryer@gnb.ca; internet www.gnb.ca/0017/index-e.asp.

Department of Supply and Services: Marysville Pl., 4th Floor, 20 McGloin St, POB 6000, Fredericton, NB E3B 5H1; tel. (506) 453-3742; fax (506) 444-4400; e-mail judy.cole@gnb.ca; internet www.gnb.ca/0099/index-e.asp.

Department of Transportation: Kings Pl., 440 King St, POB 6000, Fredericton, NB E3B 5H1; tel. (506) 453-3939; fax (506) 453-2900; e-mail tracey.burkhardt@gnb.ca; internet www.gnb.ca/0113/index-e.asp.

Department of Wellness, Culture and Sport: Pl. 2000, 4th Floor, POB 6000, Fredericton, NB E3B 5H1; tel. (506) 453-2909; fax (506) 453-6548; e-mail vicky.deschenes@gnb.ca; internet www.gnb.ca/0131/index-e.asp.

Office of the Attorney-General: Centennial Bldg, 670 King St, Rm 412, POB 6000, Fredericton, NB E3B 5H1; tel. (506) 453-3132; fax (506) 453-3651; e-mail valerie.kilfoil@gnb.ca; internet www.gnb.ca/0227/index-e.asp.

Office of the Auditor-General: HSBC Pl., 6th Floor, 520 King St, Fredericton, NB E3B 6G3; tel. (506) 453-2243; fax (506) 453-3067; e-mail mike.ferguson@gnb.ca; internet www.gnb.ca/oag-bvg/index.htm; Auditor-Gen. MIKE FERGUSON.

Office of Human Resources: Centennial Bldg, Rm 345, 670 King St, POB 6000, Fredericton, NB E3B 5H1; tel. (506) 453-2264; fax (506) 453-7195; e-mail sarah.ketcheson@gnb.ca; internet www.gnb.ca/0163/index-e.asp.

Regional Development Corporation: RDC Bldg, 836 Churchill Row, POB 428, Fredericton, NB E3B 5R4; tel. (506) 453-2277; fax (506) 453-7988; e-mail gisele.bordage@gnb.ca; internet www.gnb.ca/0096/index-e.asp; Pres. BILL LEVESQUE.

Legislative Assembly
(September 2008)

Speaker: Roy Boudreau (Liberal).

Clerk: Loredana Catalli Sonier.

Election, 18 September 2006

	Seats at election	Seats at September 2008
Liberal	29	32
Progressive Conservative (PC)	26	23
Total	55	55

Newfoundland and Labrador

Area: 405,212 sq km (158,286 sq miles).

Population (at 1 July 2007, estimate): 506,275.

Capital and Principal City: St John's (census metropolitan area population at 1 July 2006, estimated at 182,328).

LOCATION, TOPOGRAPHY AND CLIMATE

Newfoundland and Labrador, Canada's easternmost province, consists of the mainland territory of Labrador and the smaller Island of Newfoundland to its south. Labrador is bounded by the Atlantic Ocean and the Labrador Sea to the east and by Québec to the west and south; the Island of Newfoundland lies east of the Gulf of St Lawrence, separated from the mainland by the Strait of Belle Isle. To the south-west of the Island of Newfoundland are the French islands of Saint Pierre and Miquelon. The mainland is generally barren and rugged, dominated by the Torngat Mountains in the north and a vast, forested plateau in the interior. On the Island of Newfoundland the Long Range Mountains extend along the length of the west coast, reaching 815 m (2,674 ft) at their highest point at Gros Morne. The mountains are interspersed with valleys and several large bays, including the Bay of Islands and Bonne Bay. The interior of the island is an undulating plateau, drained by the Exploits, Gander, Humber and Terra Nova Rivers. The north-eastern coast is characterized by numerous bays, islands and fiords caused by glaciation. Temperatures are variable, but generally winters are very cold, with summers cool on the coast and warmer inland.

HISTORICAL BACKGROUND

Beothuk Indians inhabited the Island of Newfoundland at the time when Leif Ericsson and other Norse voyagers travelling from Greenland are thought to have visited the area. John Cabot (Giovanni Caboto—an Italian in the employ of the English Crown) charted the coast in 1497 and by the 16th century the rich fishing grounds around the island were being plied by fishermen from various European countries. In 1583 the island was claimed for England by Humphrey Gilbert, but permanent settlement did not begin until the end of the 17th century. French claims to the island were negated under the Peace of Utrecht in 1713, but France retained some fishing rights off the north shore. During the French and Indian War (1754–63, part of the European conflict known as the Seven-Years War, which started in 1756) the area was occupied again by French forces. The Treaty of Paris (1763) returned it to the United Kingdom, but awarded France the islands of Saint Pierre and Miquelon. Also in 1763, Labrador was annexed to Newfoundland. Full colonial status was awarded in 1855 and a government established. Representatives of Newfoundland attended the confederation conferences in 1864–67, but declined membership at that time. French fishing rights were curtailed in 1904. In the late 1920s and the 1930s Newfoundland was severely affected by economic depression and eventually resumed colonial status, despite having been a dominion in its own right. During the Second World War it assumed great strategic importance as a military base, and economic recovery was completed. Following two referendums and much debate, Newfoundland joined the Canadian confederation on 31 March 1949. In December 2001 the province was renamed Newfoundland and Labrador.

ECONOMY

The economy of Newfoundland and Labrador is largely based on fishing, mining, minerals-processing and manufacturing linked to fish and forest resources. In addition, community, business and personal services and trade are important employers. The development of offshore petroleum and natural gas reserves is likely to bring greater prosperity to the province.

In 2006 median family income stood at C $50,500, while per-head median income was recorded at $20,500. In both measures Newfoundland and Labrador ranked the lowest of all the provinces and territories. The minimum hourly wage rate for adult workers was raised from $7.50 to $8.00 in April 2008. The unemployment rate in 2007 was 13.6%, the highest percentage in the country, and total civilian employment stood at 217,100.

Farmland covered just 89,441 acres (36,195 ha) in 2006, with an average farm covering 161 acres. There were 558 farms in that year. Agricultural commodities produced by the province include dairy products, eggs, floriculture and nursery products, vegetables, potatoes, cattle and hogs. Farm receipts totalled just C $105m. in 2007, by some distance the lowest of any province. Wildlife pelt production totalled 22,730 pelts at a value of $1.1m. in 2005; the province produced 112,780 ranch-raised mink and fox pelts, valued at $5.3m., in 2006.

Forestland (harvested) covered an estimated 22,681 ha in 2006, and roundwood removals in the province totalled an estimated 2.1m. cu m in that year, of which 95% consisted of softwoods. Fishing is of major importance to the province's economy; the value of the landed fish catch was C $469m. in 2006—second only to Nova Scotia—representing 374,067 metric tons of fish caught. The aquaculture industry is increasing in importance—sales of aquaculture products and services were valued at $52m. in 2006.

Total non-fuel mineral production in Newfoundland and Labrador was valued at an estimated C $5,020m. in 2007. Minerals of significance to the provincial economy were iron ore (for which the province was ranked first in the nation), cobalt and nickel (ranking second for both of which), copper (ranked third), zinc, sand and gravel and silver. In 2006 the province produced an estimated 303,765 barrels per day of crude oil; it was ranked third for this commodity. In the mid- to late 1990s extensive exploration programmes revealed significant hydrocarbons reserves off the coast. Crude oil reserves were estimated at 1,606m. barrels in 2006, while natural gas reserves were put at some 9,300,000m. cu ft in 2002.

The principal manufacturing industries in Newfoundland and Labrador are fish-processing, the pulp and paper industries, the chemical and chemical products industries, boat production, food and beverages, and clothing. The total value of the province's manufacturing shipments in 2007 was C $5,258m., the ninth highest in the nation.

It was estimated that non-resident visitors to Newfoundland and Labrador in 2006 totalled 490,100 and generated C $357m. in receipts. Gross general revenue of the provincial government totalled $6,471m. in 2007/08, of which 41.8% came from transfers from other levels of government and 41.2% from taxes. Gross general expenditures were $6,123m., with 31.2% spent on health, 12.4% on social services and 20.4% on education.

GOVERNMENT

The Province of Newfoundland joined the confederation on 31 March 1949, as a result of the British North America Act (later the Newfoundland Act) of the same year. The provincial government has: a Lieutenant-Governor; an Executive Council, consisting of the Premier and his or her cabinet; and a 48-member House of Assembly, elected to serve a term of no more than five years. Local government is administered by the province's incorporated municipalities, which comprise three cities, 171 towns and 139 communities. There are also 175 'local service districts', which are quasi-municipal areas. In the provincial election of October 2007 the Progressive Conservatives were re-elected for a second term, increasing their majority by securing 43 of the 48 seats in the House of Assembly. In the federal general election of 2008 some 195,397 people voted in Newfoundland and Labrador. The Liberal Party won six seats in the House of Commons, while the New Democratic Party won the province's remaining seat.

Lieutenant-Governor: John Crosbie.

Executive Council

Premier, President of the Council and Minister of Business: Danny Williams.

Deputy Premier: (vacant).

Attorney-General and Minister of Justice: Jerome P. Kennedy.

Minister of Aboriginal Affairs: Patty Pottle.

Minister of Business: Paul Oram.

Minister of Education and Minister responsible for the Status of Women: Joan Burke.

Minister of Environment and Conservation: Charlene Johnson.

Minister of Finance, President of the Treasury Board and Minister responsible for the Public Service Secretariat: Thomas W. Marshall.

Minister of Government Services and Minister responsible for the Government Purchasing Agency: KEVIN O'BRIEN.

Minister of Health and Community Services: ROSS WISEMAN.

Minister of Human Resources, Labour and Employment, Acting Minister of Fisheries and Aquaculture and Minister responsible for Persons with Disabilities, for the Labour Relations Agency and for the Newfoundland Housing Corporation: SHAWN SKINNER.

Minister of Innovation, Trade and Rural Development and Minister responsible for the Rural Secretariat: TREVOR TAYLOR.

Minister of Intergovernmental Affairs and Minister responsible for the Volunteer and Non-Profit Sector: THOMAS J. HEDDERSON.

Minister of Labrador Affairs: JOHN HICKEY.

Minister of Municipal Affairs, Minister responsible for Emergency Preparedness and Registrar General: DAVE DENINE.

Minister of Natural Resources and Minister responsible for the Forestry and Agrifoods Agency: KATHY DUNDERDALE.

Minister of Tourism, Culture and Recreation: CLYDE JACKMAN.

Minister of Transportation and Works: DIANNE C. WHALEN.

Selected Government Addresses

Office of the Lieutenant-Governor: Government House, Military Rd, St John's, POB 5517, NL A1C 5W4; tel. (709) 729-4494; fax (709) 729-2234; e-mail governmenthouse@gov.nl.ca; internet www.mun.ca/govhouse.

Office of the Premier: Confederation Bldg, East Block, POB 8700, St John's, NL A1B 4J6; tel. (709) 729-3570; fax (709) 729-5875; e-mail premier@gov.nl.ca; internet www.premier.gov.nl.ca.

Department of Education: Confederation Bldg, West Block, 3rd Floor, 100 Prince Philip Dr., POB 8700, St John's, NL A1B 4J6; tel. (709) 729-5097; fax (709) 729-5896; e-mail education@gov.nl.ca; internet www.ed.gov.nl.ca.

Department of Environment and Conservation: Confederation Bldg, West Block, 4th Floor, POB 8700, St John's, NL A1B 4J6; tel. (709) 729-2664; fax (709) 729-6639; internet www.env.gov.nl.ca.

Department of Finance: Confederation Bldg, POB 8700, St John's, NL A1B 4J6; tel. (709) 729-2913; fax (709) 729-6944; e-mail finance@gov.nl.ca; internet www.fin.gov.nl.ca.

Department of Fisheries and Aquaculture: Petten Bldg, 30 Strawberry Marsh Rd, POB 8700, St John's, NL A1B 4J6; tel. (709) 729-3723; fax (709) 729-6082; e-mail fishaqwebmaster@gov.nl.ca; internet www.fishaq.gov.nl.ca.

Department of Government Services: Confederation Bldg, East Block, 10th Floor, POB 8700, St John's, NL A1B 4J6; tel. (709) 637-2389; fax (709) 637-2905; e-mail dlandrew@gov.nl.ca; internet www.gs.gov.nl.ca.

Department of Health and Community Services: Confederation Bldg, West Block, 1st Floor, POB 8700, St John's, NL A1B 4J6; tel. (709) 729-1377; fax (709) 729-5824; e-mail healthinfo@gov.nl.ca; internet www.health.gov.nl.ca.

Department of Human Resources, Labour and Employment: Confederation Bldg, POB 8700, St John's, NL A1B 4J6; tel. (709) 729-7888; e-mail hreweb@gov.nl.ca; internet www.hrle.gov.nl.ca.

Department of Innovation, Trade and Rural Development: Confederation Bldg, POB 8700, St John's, NL A1B 4J6; tel. (709) 729-7000; fax (709) 729-0654; e-mail itrd@gov.nl.ca; internet www.intrd.gov.nl.ca.

Department of Justice: Confederation Bldg, East Block, 4th Floor, POB 8700, St John's, NL A1B 4J6; tel. (709) 729-5942; fax (709) 729-2129; e-mail justice@gov.nl.ca; internet www.justice.gov.nl.ca.

Department of Labrador and Aboriginal Affairs: Confederation Bldg, West Block, 5th Floor, POB 8700, St John's, NL A1B 4J6; tel. (709) 729-4776; fax (709) 729-4900; e-mail laa@gov.nl.ca; internet www.laa.gov.nl.ca.

Department of Municipal and Provincial Affairs: Confederation Bldg, West Block, Main Floor, POB 8700, St John's, NL A1B 4J6; tel. (709) 729-3048; fax (709) 729-0943; e-mail mapainfo@gov.nl.ca; internet www.mpa.gov.nl.ca.

Department of Natural Resources: Natural Resources Bldg, 7th Floor, 50 Elizabeth Ave, POB 8700, St John's, NL A1B 4J6; tel. (709) 729-2920; fax (709) 729-0059; internet www.nr.gov.nl.ca.

Department of Tourism, Culture and Recreation: Confederation Bldg, West Block, 2nd Floor, POB 8700, St John's, NL A1B 4J6; tel. (709) 729-0862; fax (709) 729-0870; e-mail tcrinfo@gov.nl.ca; internet www.tcr.gov.nl.ca.

Department of Transportation and Works: Confederation Bldg, West Block, 6th Floor, POB 8700, St John's, NL A1B 4J6; tel. (709) 729-3679; fax (709) 729-4285; e-mail twminister@gov.nl.ca; internet www.tw.gov.nl.ca.

Intergovernmental Affairs Secretariat (Executive Council): Confederation Bldg, POB 8700, St John's, NL A1B 4J6; tel. (709) 729-3164; fax (709) 729-5038; e-mail iga@gov.nl.ca; internet www.exec.gov.nl.ca/exec/iga/iga-ovr.htm.

Public Service Commission: Sir Brian Dunfield Bldg, 3rd Floor, 2 Canada Dr., POB 8700, St John's, NL A1B 4J6; tel. (709) 729-5810; fax (709) 729-6234; internet www.psc.gov.nl.ca/psc; Chair. and CEO ED WALSH.

House of Assembly
(September 2008)

Speaker: ROGER FITZGERALD (PC).

Clerk: WILLIAM MACKENZIE.

Election, 9 October 2007

	Seats at election	Seats at September 2008
Progressive Conservative (PC)	43	44
Liberal	3	3
New Democratic Party (NDP)	1	1
Vacant	1	—
Total	48	48

Northwest Territories

Area: 1,346,106 sq km (525,823 sq miles).

Population (at 1 July 2007, estimate): 42,637.

Capital and Principal City: Yellowknife (population at census of 16 May 2006, 18,700).

LOCATION, TOPOGRAPHY AND CLIMATE

The Northwest Territories is the second largest of Canada's three territories. It lies north of the 60th parallel of latitude (60°N), stretching from the Arctic Ocean in the north to the Mackenzie Mountains in the west, with the borders of British Columbia, Alberta and Saskatchewan in the south and the border with Nunavut in the east. The creation of the territory of Nunavut in 1999 reduced the area of the Northwest Territories by approximately two-thirds. The Northwest Territories comprises two broad geographical regions: the taiga, a boreal forest belt that circles the subarctic zone, and the tundra, a rocky Arctic region. The Arctic Archipelago in the north is characterized by high mountain ranges, although the western islands are mainly low-lying. West of the Canadian Shield lies the Mackenzie Valley area, rising sharply in the west to the Cordillera mountain region, which contains peaks of over 2,700 m. The territory's main river, the Mackenzie (4,241 km—2,635 miles in length, the longest in Canada), traverses this area, draining into the Beaufort Sea. Two of Canada's largest lakes, Great Slave and Great Bear Lakes, are in the Northwest Territories, which also includes Bank Island in its territory. There are extreme variations in climate in the Mackenzie Valley area, where temperatures can be hot in summer, but very cold in winter. The climate of the Archipelago is moderate, with mild winters and short, cool summers.

HISTORICAL BACKGROUND

A wide variety of indigenous cultures existed in the area known as the Northwest Territories prior to European exploration, with the nomadic Inuit (Eskimos) inhabiting the area north of the Arctic Circle and the Chipewyan, Yellowknife, Slave, Dogrib, Hare, Nahanni and Kutchin American Indian peoples living in the subarctic region. Norse voyagers from Greenland settlements first visited the area circa 1000 and several European expeditions in the late 16th century sought unsuccessfully to locate the Northwest Passage. The area became the property of the Hudson's Bay Company (HBC) in 1670; an HBC employee, Samuel Hearne, made an overland trip from the bayside settlement of Churchill (now in Manitoba) to the Coppermine River in 1770–71. Alexander Mackenzie charted the length of the Mackenzie River in 1789 for the HBC's rival, the North West Fur Company, and fur-trading posts were later established along his route, remaining the principal settlements until the 1930s. The Northwest Territories was formally constituted on 15 July 1870 from the areas known as Rupert's Land and the North West Territory. Its area was subsequently reduced by the reorganization of the borders of Manitoba in 1881; the creation of the Yukon Territory in 1898; and the entry into the confederation of Alberta and Saskatchewan in 1905. The last discoveries of Arctic islands were made in 1913–18. Mineral exploration from the 1930s led to the development of the Mackenzie Valley, and radar and weather stations were established in the Arctic from the Second World War onwards. In 1953 the federal Department of Northern Affairs and Natural Resources (now the federal Department of Indian Affairs and Northern Development Canada) was created to aid the development of health, housing, educational and communications facilities in the territory. In September 1988 the federal Government formally transferred an area covering 673,000 sq km (259,845 sq miles) to indigenous ownership. Arrangements to divide the Northwest Territories into two self-governing units were approved by the Northwest Territories legislature in January 1987 and endorsed by a plebiscite among Northwest Territories residents in May 1992. The western area was to continue to be known as the Northwest Territories, with the eastern region forming a semi-autonomous area, to be named Nunavut Territory. On 1 April 1999 the Northwest Territories was formally divided.

ECONOMY

In 2006 median family income in the Northwest Territories was C $88,800, the highest level among the provinces and territories. Mean per-head income in 2006 measured $37,600, again the highest figure in the nation. The minimum hourly rate of pay for adult workers has been set at $8.25 since December 2003. The unemployment rate is subject to wide seasonal variations, exacerbated by the small size of the labour force. In August 2007 the rate stood at 6.1% (some 1,500 people). Economic activity centres around the region's natural resources, although fur-trapping, once the primary economic activity, is now of only minor significance. Agriculture is also of little value, as it is cheaper to import products from the south. Mining, fossil fuel production and refining, native arts and crafts, hunting and trapping, fishing and tourism are the major industries in the territory.

Forestland (harvested) covered an estimated 141 ha of the Northwest Territories in 2006. In that year an estimated 24,000 cu m of roundwood was produced, all of it softwood. Some commercial freshwater fishing occurs, mainly on Great Slave Lake. In 2006 the Northwest Territories recorded a catch of 614 metric tons of fish (live weight), valued at C $610,000, principally whitefish, yellow pickerel, inconnu, pike and trout. Hunting and fishing remain important at a local level, especially for those living in small, relatively isolated communities. In 2005 23,967 wildlife pelts were produced; the pelts of the highest value were those of the marten, lynx, beaver and muskrat. The total value of wildlife pelt production in that year was $1.4m.

In 2007 total non-fuel mineral production in the Northwest Territories was valued at C $1,493m. (which included sand and gravel production of Nunavut territory). Minerals produced included tungsten, sand and gravel, and stone. Gold mining in the territory ceased in 2003. Diamond output in the Northern Territories in 2007, which represented over 98% of Canada's total, was valued at an estimated $1,412m. The territory ranks highly among Canadian producers of both crude petroleum and natural gas, with output of 964,323 cu m and 270m. cu m, respectively, in 2007.

Total manufacturing shipments from the Northwest Territories were valued at C $45.8m. in 2007—the third lowest level in Canada, with only Yukon Territory and Nunavut recording lower figures. Art and crafts produced by native people are exported internationally and are an increasing source of income.

In 2002 some 44,000 people visited the Northwest Territories. Total foreign tourist expenditures in the territory were C $86.2m. in that same year. During the summer of 2006 (15 May to 15 September) alone there were 39,000 visitors to the Northwest Territories, generating receipts valued at $48.7m. There is a growing aurora borealis tourism market, which especially attracts Japanese tourists; while visitors for aurora viewings rose to 10,200 during the 2005/06 period, numbers had declined to an estimated 7,000 for 2006/07. 'Aurora spending' was estimated at $7.9m. in 2001.

Gross general expenditures by the territorial government totalled C $1,468m. in 2007/08, with 18.6% spent on health, 8.9% on social services and 17.1% spent on education. Gross general revenue amounted to $1,472m., of which 72.2% was derived from grants and 20.5% came from taxes.

GOVERNMENT

The Northwest Territories became part of the Dominion of Canada on 15 July 1870 by the Rupert's Land Act of 1868 and the Imperial Order-in-Council of 23 June 1870. The Northwest Territories Act of 1970 provided the present system of government. The government comprises: a Commissioner, appointed by the federal Government and under the direction of the federal Minister of Indian Affairs and Northern Development; an Executive Council of up to eight members including the government leader (redesignated premier in 1994), all of whom are nominated by the Legislative Assembly; and a 19-member Legislative Assembly (the numbers were reduced from 24 to 19 following the division of the Territories in 1999 and an amendment to electoral districts). Members of the Legislative Assembly are elected for four years and usually meet twice a year. The Assembly is not arranged along party lines. A majority of its members are of native descent. As in the provinces, the territorial government has authority over most territorial matters, except for those pertaining to non-renewable resources. Since the creation of Nunavut, local government in the Northwest Territories has been organized through one city, four towns, one village and 10 hamlets. Elections to the non-partisan provincial legislature were held on 1 October 2007. In the federal general election of 2008 some 13,677 votes were polled; the New Democratic Party retained control of the territories' seat in the House of Commons.

Commissioner: ANTHONY W. J. WHITFORD.

Deputy Commissioner: MARGARET M. THOM.

Cabinet

Premier, Minister of Aboriginal Affairs and Intergovernmental Relations and Minister responsible for the Executive and for the Northwest Territories Power Corporation: FLOYD K. ROLAND.

Deputy Premier, Minister of Finance and of the Environment and Natural Resources and Minister responsible for the Financial Management Board Secretariat: J. MICHAEL MILTENBERGER.

Minister of Education, Culture and Employment and of Justice: JACKSON LAFFERTY.

Minister of Health and Social Services and of Municipal and Community Affairs and Minister responsible for the Status of Women, for Persons with Disabilities, for the Homeless, for Seniors and for Youth: SANDY LEE.

Minister of Public Works and Services and of Transportation, and Minister responsible for the Northwest Territories Housing Corporation: MICHAEL MCLEOD.

Minister of Human Resources and of Industry, Tourism and Investment and Minister responsible for the Public Utilities Board and for Workers Safety and Compensation Commission: BOB MCLEOD.

Minister without portfolio and Member for Sahtu: NORMAN YAKELEYA.

Selected Government Addresses

Office of the Commissioner: 803 Northwest Tower, 5201 50th Ave, POB 1320, Yellowknife, NT X1A 2L9; tel. (867) 873-7400; fax (867) 873-0223; e-mail commissioner@gov.nt.ca; internet www.commissioner.gov.nt.ca.

Office of the Premier: Legislative Assembly, POB 1320, Yellowknife, NT X1A 2L9; tel. (867) 669-2311; fax (867) 873-0385; e-mail premier@gov.nt.ca; internet www.premier.gov.nt.ca.

Department of Aboriginal Affairs and Intergovernmental Relations: 4910 52nd St, POB 1320, Yellowknife, NT X1A 2L9; tel. (867) 873-7143; fax (867) 873-0233; e-mail ngan_trinh@gov.nt.ca; internet www.daair.gov.nt.ca.

Department of Education, Culture and Employment: Lahm Ridge Tower, 3rd Floor, 4501 50th Ave, POB 1320, Yellowknife, NT X1A 2L9; tel. (867) 669-2399; fax (867) 873-0274; e-mail morven_macpherson@gov.nt.ca; internet www.ece.gov.nt.ca.

Department of Environment and Natural Resources: Lahm Ridge Tower, 3rd Floor, 4501 50th Ave, POB 1320, Yellowknife, NT X1A 2L9; tel. (867) 873-7379; fax (867) 873-0114; e-mail judy_mclinton@gov.nt.ca; internet www.enr.gov.nt.ca.

Department of the Executive: Laing Bldg, 6th Floor, 5003 49th St, POB 1320, Yellowknife, NT X1A 2L9; tel. (867) 873-7897; fax (867) 873-0662; e-mail executive@gov.nt.ca; internet www.executive.gov.nt.ca.

Department of Finance: YK Center, 3rd Floor, 4922 48th St, POB 1320, Yellowknife, NT X1A 2L9; tel. (867) 669-2355; fax (867) 873-0169; e-mail michael_miltenberger@gov.nt.ca; internet www.fin.gov.nt.ca.

Department of Health and Social Services: Centre Square Tower, 8th Floor, 5022 49th St, POB 1320, Yellowknife, NT X1A 2L9; tel. (867) 669-2344; fax (867) 873-0481; e-mail gail_mccurdy@gov.nt.ca; internet www.hlthss.gov.nt.ca.

Department of Human Resources: Laing Bldg, 3rd Floor, 5003 49th St, POB 1320, Yellowknife, NT X1A 2L9; tel. (867) 920-8900; fax (867) 873-0282; e-mail hrhelpdesk@gov.nt.ca; internet www.hr.gov.nt.ca.

Department of Industry, Tourism and Investment: 5102 50th Ave, Suite 800, POB 1320, Yellowknife, NT X1A 2L9; tel. (867) 920-8696; fax (867) 873-0645; e-mail drew_williams@gov.nt.ca; internet www.iti.gov.nt.ca.

Department of Justice: Courthouse Bldg, 6th Floor, 4903 49th St, POB 1320, Yellowknife, NT X1A 2L9; tel. (867) 669-2399; fax (867)

873-0169; e-mail jackson_lafferty@gov.nt.ca; internet www.justice.gov.nt.ca.

Department of Municipal and Community Affairs: Northwest Tower, Suite 600, 5201 50th Ave, POB 1320, Yellowknife, NT X1A 2L9; tel. (867) 873-7118; fax (867) 873-0309; e-mail debbie_delancey@gov.nt.ca; internet www.maca.gov.nt.ca.

Department of Public Works and Services: Stuart Hodgson Bldg, 3rd Floor, 5009 49th St, POB 1320, Yellowknife, NT X1A 2L9; tel. (867) 873-7114; fax (867) 873-0226; e-mail mike_aumond@gov.nt.ca; internet www.pws.gov.nt.ca.

Department of Transportation: Lahm Ridge Tower, 2nd Floor, 4501 50th Ave, POB 1320, Yellowknife, NT X1A 2L9; tel. (867) 873-7712; fax (867) 873-0363; e-mail michael_mcleod@gov.nt.ca; internet www.dot.gov.nt.ca.

Northwest Territories Business Development and Investment Corporation: Northwest Tower, Suite 701, 5201 50th Ave, Yellowknife, NT X1A 3S9; tel. (867) 920-6455; fax (867) 765-0652; e-mail bdicinfo@gov.nt.ca; internet www.bdic.ca; CEO PAWAN CHUGH.

Public Utilities Board: 203 B 62 Woodland Dr., POB 4211, Hay River, NT X0E 1G1; tel. (867) 874-3944; fax (867) 874-3639; e-mail louise-ann_larocque@gov.nt.ca; internet www.nwtpublicutilitiesboard.ca.

Legislative Assembly
(September 2008)

Speaker: PAUL DELOREY.

Clerk: TIM MERCER.

The Legislative Assembly consists of 19 independent members without formal party affiliation.

Nova Scotia

Area: 55,284 sq km (21,595 sq miles).

Population (at 1 July 2007, estimate): 934,147.

Capital and Principal City: Halifax (population of metropolitan area at 1 July 2006, estimated at 383,281).

LOCATION, TOPOGRAPHY AND CLIMATE

Nova Scotia, one of the three Maritime provinces, is a peninsula lying in the extreme east of Canada, connected to New Brunswick by the Isthmus of Chignecto. It is bounded by Cabot Strait, the Gulf of St Lawrence and Northumberland Strait to the north, the Atlantic Ocean to the south and the Bay of Fundy to the west. The Strait of Canso divides Cape Breton Island from mainland Nova Scotia. Cape Breton Island is bisected by the Bras d'Or Lake (1,099 sq km), which stretches from north-east to south-west. The province's highest point is found on the Island—White Hill, at 538 m (1,765 ft). The province can be divided into four distinct regions: the rugged, granite coastline of the Atlantic shore; the fertile region of the Annapolis Valley; the Northumberland seashore; and the highlands of Cape Breton Island. Nova Scotia has a generally temperate climate, although fog is common, especially in the spring. The coastal areas are both milder and wetter than the inland regions, with frequent storms in winter.

HISTORICAL BACKGROUND

Algonquian-speaking Micmac peoples were inhabitants of Nova Scotia at the time of European settlement. It was claimed that John Cabot—Giovanni Caboto, an Italian working for the English Crown—landed on Cape Breton Island in 1497. Permanent settlement began with the establishment of Port Royal (now Annapolis Royal) by the French in 1605, in an area they named Acadia, comprising the present-day regions of Nova Scotia, New Brunswick and Prince Edward Island (known as Ile Saint-Jean). In 1621 Acadia was granted by King James I of England (James VI of Scotland) to a Scottish nobleman, Sir William Alexander, and renamed Nova Scotia; it was occupied by both French and English troops several times during the 17th and early 18th centuries. In 1713, under the Peace of Utrecht, Nova Scotia (which then included New Brunswick) was placed under British control and in 1755 French sympathizers began to be forcibly deported. Cape Breton Island (then named Ile Royale) and Prince Edward Island remained French until 1763, when they too were ceded to the United Kingdom under the Treaty of Paris. In 1744 French and native peoples invaded the region, but failed to take Annapolis Royal. The first popularly elected legislative assembly in British North America met at Halifax in 1758. In 1784 the colonies of New Brunswick and Cape Breton were separated from Nova Scotia; the future Prince Edward Island (by now renamed St John's Island) was separated permanently in 1786. Cape Breton Island was re-annexed to Nova Scotia in 1820. Following the American Revolution there was much Loyalist immigration from the USA into Nova Scotia. Despite considerable opposition from some sections of the community, the province entered the confederation on 1 July 1867. In 1917 two ships, one carrying explosives, collided in Halifax harbour; the resulting explosion killed 1,800 people and caused substantial damage to buildings in the area. Nova Scotia was at the forefront of the Maritime Rights movement of the 1920s, protesting against unfavourable freight rates and the protective tariff. Halifax was one of the most significant naval bases during the Second World War.

ECONOMY

Service industries are Nova Scotia's largest employer. The most important individual sectors are tourism, manufacturing, fishing, agriculture, mining, forestry and retail trade. Halifax is a major port. The development of the Sable oil and natural gas pipeline project, which will transport oil and gas to markets in New England, is expected to boost employment and income in the province.

In 2006 the province's median per-head personal income was C $23,900, while the median annual family income in that year was $56,400. Total civilian employment in 2007 comprised 447,600 people and the unemployment rate was measured at 8.0%. In May 2008 the minimum hourly rate of pay for experienced workers was set at $8.10.

Farmland covered 1m. acres (403,044 ha) of Nova Scotia's total land area in 2006, with the average farm measuring 262 acres. There were 3,795 farms in the province in that year. Farm receipts in 2007 were C $449m. The most significant components of the agricultural sector are dairy farming, poultry production, fur farming (in which it leads the nation), floriculture and nursery production, eggs, fruit (especially berries, grapes and apples), cattle, hogs, vegetables, Christmas trees (conifers) and forest products. The province ranked second after Québec for Christmas tree production in 2007. Nova Scotia's trapping industry produced 37,200 wildlife pelts (with a total value of $651,242) in 2005, while production of ranch-raised pelts (fox and mink) in 2006 reached 854,800 (valued at $49.3m.), accounting for 52% of total national production in that year. Forestland (harvested) covered an estimated 54,326 ha in 2006 and lumbering makes a significant contribution to the provincial economy: roundwood production amounted to 5.2m. cu m in that year, with the majority (88%) being softwoods. In 2006 the value of fish landings totalled $657m., the highest in Canada, with 284,271 metric tons caught (live weight). Production of aquaculture products in 2005 was $40.4m., with finfish (mostly salmon and steelhead) accounting for 73% of the total and shellfish making up the remaining 27%.

Nova Scotia's total non-fuel mineral production was valued at an estimated C $300m. in 2007. Traditionally, the province's most important mineral resource was coal, but mine closures since 2000 have reduced production to 355,500 metric tons in 2003. Crude petroleum was also produced, and in 2006 natural gas production reached 367m. cu ft per day (in which respect Nova Scotia ranked fourth nationally). Other minerals of importance were gypsum (with the province the only national producer of this mineral in 2007), sand and gravel, and stone.

The manufacturing industry in Nova Scotia is largely based on the province's agriculture, forestry and transportation sectors. In 2007 Nova Scotia's manufacturing shipments were valued at C $9,874m., with the province ranked eighth in this respect.

The tourism industry generated estimated receipts of C $1,330m. in 2007. The sector provided employment for an estimated 32,700 people in that year, directly and indirectly. Non-resident visitors to the province in 2007 totalled 2.14m. Some 54% of these were Atlantic Canadians and a further 33% came from other Canadian provinces.

Gross general expenditures by the provincial government totalled C $8,410m. in 2007/08, with 36.3% spent on health, 21.0% on education and 11.7% on social services. Gross general revenue was $8,575m., with transfers from other levels of government amounting to 39.0% of the total and revenue from taxes accounting for 50.8%.

GOVERNMENT

The Province of Nova Scotia was admitted to the confederation on 1 July 1867, on the foundation of the Dominion of Canada, by the British North America Act of the same year and the Imperial Order-in-Council of 22 May 1867. The provincial government comprises: the Lieutenant-Governor; the Executive Council, consisting of the Premier and the cabinet, chosen by the Premier; and the 52-member House of Assembly, which sits twice a year and is elected for five-year terms. Local government in Nova Scotia is administered through 18 counties, with three incorporated cities and 39 incorporated towns. In February 2006 Rodney J. MacDonald succeeded John Hamm as Premier after the latter retired. In the provincial election of June 2006 the Progressive Conservative Party won 23 seats in the 52-seat House of Assembly, two fewer than their previous tally, and again formed a minority government. The New Democrats won 20 seats, while the Liberals came third, with nine seats. In the 2008 federal general election an estimated 436,008 votes were polled in the province; the Liberal Party won five seats in the House of Commons. The Conservative Party held onto its three seats, while the New Democratic Party secured two seats. The remaining seat was won by an independent candidates.

Lieutenant-Governor: MAYANN E. FRANCIS.

Executive Council

Premier, President of the Executive Council and Minister of Intergovernmental Affairs: RODNEY J. MACDONALD.

Deputy Premier and Minister of Economic Development and of Gaelic Affairs: ANGUS MACISAAC.

Attorney-General and Minister of Justice: CECIL P. CLARKE.

Minister of Agriculture: BROOKE TAYLOR.

Minister of Community Services and of Communications Nova Scotia: JUDY STREATCH.

Minister of Education: KAREN CASEY.

Minister of Energy: RICHARD HURLBURT.

Minister of the Environment and of Labour and Workforce Development: MARK PARENT.

Minister of Finance and of Aboriginal Affairs: MICHAEL G. BAKER.

Minister of Fisheries and Aquaculture: RON CHISHOLM.

Minister of Health and of Acadian Affairs: CHRIS A. D'ENTREMONT.

Minister of Health Promotion and Protection, of African Nova Scotian Affairs and of Volunteerism: BARRY BARNET.

Minister of Human Resources, of the Public Service Commission and of Seniors, and Chair of the Senior Citizens' Secretariat: CAROLYN BOLIVAR-GETSON.

Minister of Immigration: LEN GOUCHER.

Minister of Natural Resources: DAVID M. MORSE.

Minister of Service Nova Scotia and Municipal Relations and Chair of the Treasury and Policy Board: JAMIE MUIR.

Minister of Tourism, Culture and Heritage: BILL DOOKS.

Selected Government Addresses

Office of the Lieutenant-Governor: Maritime Centre, 11th Floor, 1505 Barrington St, Suite 1140, Halifax, NS B3J 3K3; tel. (902) 424-7001; fax (902) 424-1790; e-mail lgoffice@gov.ns.ca; internet lt.gov.ns.ca.

Office of the Premier: 1 Government Pl., 7th Floor, 1700 Granville St, POB 726, Halifax, NS B3J 2T3; tel. (902) 424-6600; fax (902) 424-7648; e-mail premier@gov.ns.ca; internet www.gov.ns.ca/premier.

Department of Agriculture: 1741 Brunswick St, 3rd Floor, POB 2223, Halifax, NS B3J 3C4; tel. (902) 424-4560; fax (902) 424-4671; internet www.gov.ns.ca/agri.

Department of Community Services: Nelson Pl., 5675 Spring Garden Rd, POB 696, Halifax, NS B3J 2T7; tel. (902) 424-4304; fax (902) 424-3287; internet www.gov.ns.ca/coms.

Department of Education: 2021 Brunswick St, Suite 402, POB 578, Halifax, NS B3J 2S9; tel. (902) 424-5168; fax (902) 424-0511; internet ednet.ns.ca.

Department of Energy: Bank of Montreal Bldg, Suite 400, 5151 George St, Suite 400, POB 2664, Halifax, NS B3J 3P7; tel. (902) 424-4575; fax (902) 424-0528; e-mail mclaren@gov.ns.ca; internet www.gov.ns.ca/energy.

Department of the Environment: 5151 Terminal Rd, POB 442, Halifax, NS B3J 2T8; tel. (902) 424-3600; fax (902) 424-0503; e-mail messerv@gov.ns.ca; internet www.gov.ns.ca/nse.

Department of Finance: 1723 Hollis St, POB 187, Halifax, NS B3J 2N3; tel. (902) 424-5554; fax (902) 429-0635; e-mail financeweb@gov.ns.ca; internet www.gov.ns.ca/fina.

Department of Health: Joseph Howe Bldg, 4th Floor, 1690 Hollis St, POB 488, Halifax, NS B3J 2R8; tel. (902) 424-5818; fax (902) 424-0559; e-mail dohweb@gov.ns.ca; internet www.gov.ns.ca/health.

Department of Health Promotion and Protection: Summit Pl., 5th Floor, Lower Water St, PO Box 487, Halifax, NS B3J 2R7; tel. (902) 424-4807; fax (902) 424-4716; e-mail healthpromotion@gov.ns.ca; internet www.gov.ns.ca/hpp.

Department of Justice: 5151 Terminal Rd, POB 7, Halifax, NS B3J 2L6; tel. (902) 424-4030; fax (902) 424-0510; e-mail justweb@gov.ns.ca; internet www.gov.ns.ca/just.

Department of Labour and Workforce Development: 5151 Terminal Rd, POB 697, Halifax, NS B3J 2T8; tel. (902) 424-5301; fax (902) 424-0503; e-mail lwdweb@gov.ns.ca; internet www.gov.ns.ca/lwd.

Department of Natural Resources: Founders Sq., 3rd Floor, 1701 Hollis St, POB 698, Halifax, B3J 2T9; tel. (902) 424-5935; fax (902) 424-7735; e-mail dnrweb@gov.ns.ca; internet www.gov.ns.ca/natr.

Department of Tourism, Culture and Heritage: World Trade Centre, 6th Floor, 1800 Argyle St, POB 456, Halifax, NS B3J 2R5; tel. (902) 424-5000; fax (902) 424-0129; e-mail tns@gov.ns.ca; internet www.gov.ns.ca/dtc.

Department of Transportation and Infrastructure Renewal: Johnston Bldg, 1672 Granville St, POB 186, Halifax, NS B3J 2N2; tel. (902) 424-2297; fax (902) 424-0532; e-mail tpwpaff@gov.ns.ca; internet www.gov.ns.ca/tran.

Treasury and Policy Board: 1 Government Pl., 5th Floor, 1700 Granville St, POB 1617, Halifax, NS B3J 2Y3; tel. (902) 424-8910; fax (902) 424-7638; e-mail tpbenquiries@gov.ns.ca; internet www.gov.ns.ca/tpb.

Office of Aboriginal Affairs: Centennial Bldg, Suite 910, 1660 Hollis St, POB 1617, Halifax, NS B3J 2Y3; tel. (902) 424-7409; fax (902) 424-4225; e-mail oaa@gov.ns.ca; internet www.gov.ns.ca/abor.

Office of Acadian Affairs: Dennis Bldg, 7th Floor, 1740 Granville St, POB 682, Halifax, NS B3J 2T3; tel. (902) 424-0497; fax (902) 428-0124; internet www.gov.ns.ca/acadian.

Office of African Nova Scotian Affairs: 5670 Spring Garden Rd, Suite 604, POB 2691, Halifax, NS B3J 3B7; tel. (902) 424-5555; fax (902) 424-7189; internet www.gov.ns.ca/ansa.

Office of the Auditor-General: 1888 Brunswick St, Suite 302, Halifax, NS B3J 3J8; tel. (902) 424-5907; fax (902) 424-4350; e-mail lapoinjr@gov.ns.ca; internet www.gov.ns.ca/audg; Auditor-Gen. JACQUES R. LAPOINTE.

Office of Economic Development: Centennial Bldg, 1660 Hollis St, Suite 600, POB 2311, Halifax, NS B3J 3C8; tel. (902) 424-0377; fax (902) 424-7008; e-mail comm@gov.ns.ca; internet www.gov.ns.ca/econ.

Public Service Commission: 1 Government Pl., 4th Floor, 1700 Granville St, POB 943, Halifax, NS B3J 2V9; tel. (902) 424-7660; internet www.gov.ns.ca/psc.

Service Nova Scotia and Municipal Relations: Maritime Centre, 8th Floor South, 1505 Barrington St, Halifax, NS B3J 3K5; tel. (902) 424-5200; fax (902) 424-0720; e-mail askus@gov.ns.ca; internet www.gov.ns.ca/snsmr.

House of Assembly
(September 2008)

Speaker: ALFIE MACLEOD (PC).

Clerk: RODERICK K. MACARTHUR.

Election, 13 June 2006

	Seats at election	Seats at September 2008
Progressive Conservative (PC)	23	22
New Democratic Party (NDP)	20	20
Liberal	9	9
Independent	—	1
Total	52	52

Nunavut Territory

Area: 2,093,190 sq km (817,652 sq miles).

Population (at 1 July 2007, estimate): 31,113.

Capital: Iqaluit (population at census of 16 May 2006, 6,184).

LOCATION, TOPOGRAPHY AND CLIMATE

Nunavut is the largest of Canada's three territories. Formed from the central and eastern parts of the Northwest Territories in 1999, it lies north of the 60th parallel of latitude (60°N). Nunavut has borders with Manitoba to the south, Hudson Bay to the east and the Northwest Territories to the west and far north-west. The border with the Northwest Territories cuts through Victoria Island and smaller islands to the north. The territory includes Baker Lake and Baffin Island (where the capital, Iqaluit, is situated), as well as Quttinirpaaq (formerly Ellesmere Island), the most northerly part of Canada. Several islands in Hudson Bay are also included in the territory. The arctic mainland consists of barren Canadian Shield terrain, an undulating, rocky surface of low altitude intersected by rivers and lakes. There are large fiords on the eastern islands of the Arctic Archipelago. Mount Barbeau, which rises to 2,616 m (8,583 ft) on Quttinirpaaq, is the highest point. Summers can be hot in the arctic mainland, with winters very cold. The climate of the Archipelago is moderate, however, with mild winters and short, cool summers.

HISTORICAL BACKGROUND

Prior to European exploration, a wide variety of indigenous cultures existed in the area now known as Nunavut and the Northwest Territories. The nomadic Inuit (Eskimos) inhabited the area north of the Arctic Circle and the Chipewyan, Yellow-knife, Slave, Dogrib, Hare, Nahanni and Kutchin American Indian peoples lived in the subarctic region. Norse voyagers from Greenland settlements first visited the area circa 1000 and several European expeditions in the late 16th century sought unsuccessfully to locate the Northwest Passage. The area became the property of the Hudson's Bay Company (HBC) in 1670; an HBC employee, Samuel Hearne, made an overland trip from the bay-side settlement of Churchill (now in Manitoba) to the Coppermine River in 1770–71. Alexander Mackenzie charted the length of the Mackenzie River in 1789 for the HBC's rival, the North West Fur Company, and fur-trading posts were later established along his route, remaining the principal settlements until the 1930s. The Northwest Territories was formally constituted on 15 July 1870, from the areas known as Rupert's Land and the North West Territory. Its area was subsequently reduced by the reorganization of the borders of Manitoba in 1881, the creation of the Yukon Territory in 1898 and the entry into the confederation of Alberta and Saskatchewan in 1905. The last discoveries of Arctic islands were made in 1913–18.

In 1973 the Inuit Tapirisat of Canada (ITC) began a study of land use and occupancy to determine the extent of Inuit aboriginal title in the Northwest Territories. The study formed the basis for a proposal to divide the territories: the western area would continue to be known as the Northwest Territories, while the eastern region would form a semi-autonomous area, to be named Nunavut ('Our Land' in the Inuktitut language). Arrangements to divide the territories were approved by the Northwest Territories legislature in January 1987 and approved by a majority of territory voters in a plebiscite in May 1992. In November 1992 the Inuit of Nunavut ratified the Nunavut Land Claim Agreement (NLCA). This, together with the Nunavut Act, was adopted by the federal Parliament in 1993 and secured royal assent. Amendments were adopted in 1998. The Nunavut Act gave a guarantee of Inuit participation in the civil service at a level representative of the Inuit share of the population. The NLCA transferred control of some 356,000 sq km of the new territory (including mineral rights to 35,257 sq km) to the Inuit people. On 1 April 1999 the Northwest Territories was divided and Nunavut joined the Federation of Canada as a separate territory.

ECONOMY

Nunavut's economy is heavily dependent on the public sector. Other sectors of activity include fishing and hunting, manufacturing (arts and crafts and food-processing) and mining. The relative importance of the public sector to the economy is expected to decline as other business develops. The land-based (or subsistence) economy is equal in importance to the wage-based economy, and provides a large proportion of average household income, supplemented by transfers from the federal Government. Median family income in Nunavut was C $54,300 in 2006, the third lowest in Canada ahead of Newfoundland and Labrador and New Brunswick. In 2006 median per-head income totalled $24,800. The general minimum wage in the territory increased from $8.50 to $10.00 in September 2008, becoming the highest hourly rate of pay among the provinces and territories.

In 2001 an average of 9,760 people were employed in the territory, with 2,800 of these working for the government. There were around 500 people employed in the mining sector—the largest private sector employer—but 85% were non-residents. Some 2,500 people are believed to work full time in manufacturing and selling native arts and crafts. The unemployment rate in 1999 was estimated at 27.2%, with unemployment among the Inuit put at 35.8%. Unemployment among Inuits aged 15–24 years was estimated at 48.1%. These rates were by far the highest among the provinces and territories. Of the 12,635 people registered as comprising the Nunavut labour force in 2006, according to Census data for that year, 10,670 were employed; the unemployment rate for that year stood at 15.6% (with unemployment among the Inuit estimated at 20.1%)—although much reduced, still the highest rate nationally.

Nunavut produced an estimated 12,000 wildlife pelts in 2005. In 2007 total non-fuel mineral production in the territory was valued at an estimated C $32.4m. Nunavut is home to Canada's three largest gold exploration projects; two further gold-mining sites were scheduled to become operational by 2010. Diamonds and silver are also produced.

Nunavut has the smallest manufacturing sector of any Canadian province or territory. Manufacturing shipments in the territory were valued at just C $6.5m. in 2007.

Tourism, heavily promoted in the first year of the new territory's existence, contributed an estimated C $50m. to the territory's economy in 1999. There were around 18,000 visitors. Gross general revenue of the territorial government was $1,237m. in 2007/08, with transfers from the federal Government amounting to 91.7% of the total and taxes contributing 4.7%. Gross general expenditure was $1,266m.; 22.2% of the total was spent on health, 8.1% on social services and 20.0% on education. Under the Nunavut Land Claim Agreement (NCLA) of 1993, the Inuit were granted a settlement of $1,100m. from the federal Government, to be paid in equal instalments until 2007.

GOVERNMENT

Nunavut became part of the Federation of Canada on 1 April 1999, by the Nunavut Act of 1993. The Nunavut Land Claim Agreement (NCLA) of the same year established the Inuit's right to self-government and self-determination. The Inuit decided to establish a public government framework to represent all residents, including non-Inuit peoples. The territorial government comprises: a Commissioner, appointed by the federal Government; an Executive Council of eight members including the Premier, all of whom are nominated by the Legislative Assembly; and a 19-member Legislative Assembly. The Assembly is non-partisan and governs by consensus. There are three administrative regions, with 26 communities outside of the capital. An election to the Legislative Assembly was held on 27 October 2008, with a turn-out of 71%: 17 members were elected, while by-elections were due to be held in the remaining two constituencies. In the federal general election of 2008 an estimated 8,068 votes were polled in Nunavut. The Conservative Party won the territory's seat in the House of Commons.

Commissioner: Ann M. Hanson.

Executive Council

Premier, Minister of Justice and of Executive and Intergovernmental Affairs: Paul Okalik.

Deputy Premier and Minister of Community and Government Services and Minister responsible for the Status of Women: Levinia Brown.

Minister of Health and Social Services, Minister Responsible for the Status of Women: Leona Aglukkaq.

Government House Leader, Minister of Education and of Energy and Minister responsible for Nunavut Arctic College and for Homelessness and Immigration: Ed Picco.

Minister of the Environment: Olayuk Akesuk.

Minister of Economic Development and Transportation and Minister responsible for Nunavut Housing Corporation: Patterk Netser.

Minister of Finance and Administration and of Culture, Language, Elders and Youth: Louis Tapardjuk.

Minister of Human Resources and Minister responsible for the Workers' Compensation Board: Levi Barnabus.

Selected Government Addresses

Office of the Commissioner: Box 2379, Iqaluit, NU X0A 0H0; tel. (867) 975-5120; fax (867) 975-5123; e-mail mfortier@gov.nu.ca; internet www.gov.nu.ca/commissioner.

Office of the Premier: Box 1200, Iqaluit, NU X0A 0H0; tel. (867) 975-5050; fax (867) 975-5051; e-mail premier@gov.nu.ca; internet www.gov.nu.ca/english/premier.

Department of Community and Government Services: W. G. Brown Bldg, 4th Floor, Box 1000, Station 700, Iqaluit, NU X0A 0H0; tel. (867) 975-5400; fax (867) 975-5305; internet cgs.gov.nu.ca/en.

Department of Culture, Language, Elders and Youth: Box 1000, Station 800, Iqaluit, NU X0A 0H0; tel. (867) 975-5500; fax (867) 975-5504; e-mail dstenton1@gov.nu.ca; internet www.gov.nu.ca/cley.

Department of Economic Development and Transportation: Bldg 1104, Inuksugait Plaza, POB 1000, Station 1510, Iqaluit, NU X0A 0H0; tel. (867) 975-7800; fax (867) 975-7870; e-mail edt@gov.nu.ca; internet www.edt.gov.nu.ca.

Department of Education: Box 1000, Station 204, Iqaluit, NU X0A 0H0; tel. (867) 975-5600; fax (867) 975-5605; internet www.gov.nu.ca/education.

Department of Environment: Box 1000, Station 1300, Iqaluit, NU X0A 0H0; tel. (867) 975-7700; fax (867) 975-7740; e-mail environment@gov.nu.ca; internet www.gov.nu.ca/env.

Department of the Executive and Intergovernmental Affairs: Box 1000, Station 204, Iqaluit, NU X0A 0H0; tel. (867) 975-6000; fax (867) 975-6099; internet www.gov.nu.ca/eia.

Department of Finance: Box 1000, Station 330, Iqaluit, NU X0A 0H0; tel. (867) 975-5800; fax (867) 975-5805; internet www.gov.nu.ca/finance.

Department of Health and Social Services: Bldg 1107, 1st Floor, Sivummut, Box 1000, Station 1000, Iqaluit, NU X0A 0H0; tel. (867) 975-5702; fax (867) 975-5705; e-mail health@gov.nu.ca; internet www.gov.nu.ca/health.

Department of Human Resources: Trigram, Bldg 903, Box 1000, Station 400, Iqaluit, NU X0A 0H0; tel. (867) 975-6213; fax (867) 975-6216; e-mail gnhr@gov.nu.ca; internet www.gov.nu.ca/hr.

Department of Justice: Box 1000, Station 500, Iqaluit, NU X0A 0H0; tel. (867) 975-6170; fax (867) 975-6195; e-mail justice@gov.nu.ca; internet www.justice.gov.nu.ca.

Legislative Assembly
(September 2008)

Speaker: PETER KILABUK.

Clerk: JOHN QUIRKE.

The Legislative Assembly consists of 19 independent members without formal party affiliation. An election was held to the legislature on 27 October 2008 but, subsequently, two of the mandates stood vacant, pending the holding of by-elections.

Ontario

Area: 1,076,395 sq km (420,467 sq miles).

Population (at 1 July 2007, estimate): 12,803,861.

Capital: Toronto.

Principal Cities: (population at census of 16 May 2006)

Toronto	2,503,28	Kitchener	204,668
Ottawa	812,129	Burlington	164,415
Mississauga	668,549	Oshawa	141,590
Hamilton	504,559	St Catharines	131,989
Brampton	433,806	Cambridge	120,371
London	352,395	Kingston	117,207
Vaughan	238,866	Thunder Bay	109,140
Windsor	216,473	Chatham-Kent	108,177

LOCATION, TOPOGRAPHY AND CLIMATE

Ontario is situated in south-central Canada. It is bordered by Manitoba to the west, Hudson Bay to the north and north-east and Québec to the east. Its southern and south-eastern borders, with the USA (the states of New York, Pennsylvania, Ohio, Michigan and Minnesota), are marked by the St Lawrence River and by boundaries drawn through Lakes Ontario, Erie, Huron and Superior. There is also a land border in the south with the US state of Minnesota. Ontario extends further to the south than any other Canadian province, owing to its boundary along the Great Lakes. The province is composed of two geological areas, each with distinctive terrain. The Canadian Shield region comprises the eastern Ontario plain, with rolling hills and plains in the west descending into flat country in the extreme south-west. The southern lowlands region is characterized by glacial features, such as morainal hills, drumlins and numerous plains. The Great Lakes–St Lawrence forest region is an area of mixed forest, stretching eastwards and westwards of Lake Superior. Lakes (including the Great Lakes) and rivers comprise one-sixth of the province's total land area. Major rivers, in addition to the St Lawrence, include the Ottawa, Albany and Attawapiskat. The largest lake contained wholly within the province is Lake Nipigon, at 4,848 sq km. Climate within the province varies greatly according to differences in altitude, with upland areas distinctly cooler. Winters throughout the province are generally severe and stormy.

HISTORICAL BACKGROUND

Algonquian and Iroquoian peoples inhabited the area now known as Ontario when the French explorer, Samuel de Champlain, travelled along the Ottawa River in 1613–15. The Ontario region became an increasingly important link between French settlements in Québec and the Mississippi region. The British also began to settle in the area in the mid-18th century. The 1783 Treaty of Paris, which marked the end of the American Revolution, set the southern border of what is now Ontario. Up to 10,000 Loyalist immigrants are thought to have entered the area as a result of the Revolution; in 1812 it was estimated that as many as 80% of the settlers in southern Ontario were of US origin. The province of Upper Canada was created under the Constitutional Act of 1791, with its first capital at Newark (now Niagara-on-the-Lake). Following the Rebellions of 1837 in Montréal and Toronto, Upper Canada (Ontario) and Lower Canada (Québec) were united under the Act of Union in 1840 and renamed Canada West and Canada East, respectively. The first real cabinet was formed in 1848. Canada West and Canada East attended the Charlottetown Conference in 1864 and proposed the idea of a federation of all the British North American colonies; thus, Ontario became a member of the confederation on 1 July 1867. The federal capital was established at Ottawa, where the first Parliament was convened. The province's western boundary was not finally determined until 1912.

ECONOMY

Community, business and personal services (especially finance), trade, manufacturing, construction, tourism, agriculture and forestry are Ontario's leading economic sectors.

Ontario's median annual family income was C $66,600 in 2006. Median per-head income totalled $27,900 in that year. Total civilian employment numbered 6,593,800 in 2007 and the unemployment rate was 6.4%. The minimum hourly rate of pay for experienced workers rose to $8.75 in March 2008.

Farmland covered some 13.3m. acres (5.4m. ha) in 2006. There were 57,211 farms in that year, the largest number of any province or territory, and the average size of farms was 232 acres. Agriculture in the province is diverse. In 2005 Ontario was the leading province for the production of floriculture and nursery products, soybeans, vegetables, corn, tobacco (of which it was Canada's sole producer), canary seed, apples and other tree fruits, dry beans and ginseng. It was ranked second in that year for the production of berries and grapes (after British Columbia), hay and clover (after Alberta), strawberries, forest products and maple products (after Québec), while wheat, oats, barley, potato, calf and honey production are also significant. In terms of livestock products, in 2007 the province was ranked second for cattle production (after Alberta), hogs and dairy products (after Québec), and led the nation in the production of sheep and lambs. In that year the province also ranked second (after Nova Scotia) for fur farming. It was also the leading producer of eggs and of all types of poultry in 2007. Market receipts amounted to C $9,296m. in 2007, the highest farm income of any province and some 23.0% of the Canadian total.

In 2007 the province produced an estimated 227,200 wildlife pelts at a value of C $7.1m., more than any other province or territory, accounting for 24% of the national total. Harvested forestland covered 225,213 ha in 2005. In 2006 the province produced an estimated 25.9m. cu m of roundwoods. Lumber production was in the form of both soft- and hardwoods, with softwoods accounting for around 75% of the total. Fishing makes only a minor contribution to the economy.

Mining remains of major importance to the provincial economy. In 2007 Ontario's total non-fuel mineral production was valued at C $10,675m., the highest provincial total nation-wide. Small amounts of natural gas and crude oil are also produced. In 2007 Ontario was Canada's sole producer of platinum group metals, clay products, lime and nepheline syenite. It led Canada's other provinces in production of cobalt, gold, nickel, cement, quartz (silica), salt, sand and gravel, soapstone and talc, stone and sulphur (in smelter gas), among others. It ranked second to Québec in the production of cadmium and to British Columbia for copper. Barite, silver and zinc are also produced.

Ontario is Canada's foremost manufacturing province, helped by its proximity to major US markets. The province accounted for approximately one-half (48%) of the value of the nation's manufacturing shipments in 2007. Ontario's leading manufacturing sector is transportation equipment, followed by food products, chemicals, fabricated metal products, primary metals, machinery, plastics and rubber products, and petroleum and coal products. The total value of Ontario's manufacturing shipments in 2007 was C $291,693m.

Toronto is Canada's leading financial centre. All of the principal chartered banks are based in the city, as are Canada's largest stock exchanges. Tourism is an important source of revenue. In 2004 tourism expenditures in the province totalled C $17,081m. In 2006 Ontario accounted for 2.0m. overnight visits by overseas visitors; these visitors spent an estimated $2,519m. in that year. The province is also the major domestic tourist destination, attracting 30% of all intra-Canadian tourist spending in 2004.

Gross general expenditure by the provincial government amounted to C $100,216m. in 2007/08, with 38.2% of the total spent on health care, 19.6% on education and 16.5% spent on social services. Gross general revenue was $99,523m., of which 16.2% was derived from other levels of government and 74.3% from taxes.

GOVERNMENT

Ontario was admitted to the confederation on 1 July 1867 by the British North America Act of the same year, which founded the Dominion of Canada. The provincial government comprises: the Lieutenant-Governor; the Executive Council, consisting of the Premier and his or her chosen cabinet; and the Legislative Assembly, which has 103 members. Local government in southern Ontario is organized through 27 counties, one metropolitan municipality (encompassing five cities and one borough) and 10 regional municipalities. Northern Ontario, which is much less densely populated, has 10 districts and one district municipality. Following the provincial election of October 2007 the Liberal Party remained in power, having secured 71 seats in the legislature. Dalton McGuinty began a second term as Premier. In the 2008 federal general election an estimated 5,153,321 votes were polled in the province. The Conservative Party increased its representation in the House of Commons from 40 seats to 51 seats. The Liberal Party's standing was reduced to 38 seats, while the New Democratic Party secured 17 seats.

Lieutenant-Governor: DAVID C. ONLEY.

Executive Council

Premier and President of the Executive Council: DALTON MCGUINTY.

Deputy Premier and Minister of Energy and Infrastructure: GEORGE SMITHERMAN.

Attorney-General: CHRIS BENTLEY.

Chairman of the Cabinet, Minister without portfolio: GERRY PHILIPS.

Minister of Aboriginal Affairs and Government House Leader: MICHAEL BRYANT.

Minister of Agriculture, Food and Rural Affairs: LEONA DOMBROWSKY.

Minister of Children and Youth Services and Minister responsible for Women's Issues: DEB MATTHEWS.

Minister of Citizenship and Immigration: MICHAEL CHAN.

Minister of Community and Social Services and Minister responsible for Francophone Affairs: MADELEINE MEILLEUR.

Minister of Community Safety and Correctional Services: RICK BARTOLUCCI.

Minister of Culture and Minister responsible for Seniors: AILEEN CARROLL.

Minister of Economic Development and Trade: SANDRA PUPATELLO.

Minister of Education: KATHLEEN WYNNE.

Minister of the Environment: JOHN GERRETSEN.

Minister of Finance and Chairman of the Management Board of Cabinet: DWIGHT DUNCAN.

Minister of Government Services: TED MCMEEKIN.

Minister of Health Promotion: MARGARETT BEST.

Minister of Labour: BRAD DUGUID.

Minister of Municipal Affairs and Housing: JIM WATSON.

Minister of Natural Resources: DONNA CANSFIELD.

Minister of Northern Development and Mines: MICHAEL GRAVELLE.

Minister of Research and Innovation: JOHN WILKINSON.

Minister of Revenue: MONIQUE SMITH.

Minister of Small Business and Consumer Services: HARINDER TAKHAR.

Minister of Tourism: PETER FONSECA.

Minister of Training, Colleges and Universities: JOHN MILLOY.

Minister of Transportation: JIM BRADLEY.

Government Addresses

Office of the Lieutenant-Governor: Legislative Bldg, Rm 131, Queen's Park, Toronto, ON M7A 1A1; tel. (416) 325-7780; fax (416) 325-7787; e-mail ltgov@gov.on.ca; internet www.lt.gov.on.ca.

Office of the Premier: Legislative Bldg, Rm 281, Queen's Park, Toronto, ON M7A 1A1; tel. (416) 325-1941; fax (416) 325-3745; internet www.premier.gov.on.ca.

Ministry of Aboriginal Affairs: 720 Bay St, 4th Floor, Toronto, ON M5G 2K1; tel. (416) 326-4740; fax (416) 326-4017; e-mail michael.bryant@ontario.ca; internet www.nativeaffairs.jus.gov.on.ca/english/onas.htm.

Ministry of Agriculture, Food and Rural Affairs: 1 Stone Rd West, Guelph, ON N1G 4Y2; tel. (519) 826-3100; e-mail ag.info.omafra@ontario.ca; internet www.omafra.gov.on.ca.

Ministry of the Attorney-General: McMurtry-Scott Bldg, 720 Bay St, 11th Floor, Toronto, ON M5G 2K1; tel. (416) 326-2220; fax (416) 326-4007; e-mail sheamus.murphy@ontario.ca; internet www.attorneygeneral.jus.gov.on.ca.

Ministry of Children and Youth Services: 900 Bay St, M-1B114, Macdonald Block, Toronto, ON M7A 1N3; tel. (416) 212-7432; fax (416) 325-5191; e-mail laura.dougan@ontario.ca; internet www.children.gov.on.ca.

Ministry of Citizenship and Immigration: 400 University Ave, 6th Floor, Toronto, ON M7A 2R9; tel. (416) 327-2422; fax (416) 314-4965; e-mail info.mci@ontario.ca; internet www.citizenship.gov.on.ca.

Ministry of Community and Social Services: Hepburn Block, 6th Floor, 80 Grosvenor St, Toronto, ON M7A 1E9; tel. (416) 325-5666; fax (416) 325-3347; e-mail madeleine.meilleur@ontario.ca; internet www.css.gov.on.ca.

Ministry of Community Safety and Correctional Services: George Drew Bldg, 25 Grosvenor St, 18th Floor, Toronto, ON M7A 1Y6; tel. (416) 326-5000; fax (416) 325-6067; e-mail joanne.campea@ontario.ca; internet www.mcscs.jus.gov.on.ca.

Ministry of Culture: Mowat Block, 5th Floor, 900 Bay St, Toronto, ON M7A 1L2; tel. (416) 212-0644; fax (416) 325-1726; e-mail info.mcl@ontario.ca; internet www.culture.gov.on.ca.

Ministry of Economic Development and Trade: Hearst Block, 8th Floor, 900 Bay St, Toronto, ON M7A 2E1; tel. (416) 325-6666; fax (416) 325-6688; e-mail info@edt.gov.on.ca; internet www.ontario-canada.com.

Ministry of Education: 880 Bay St, 2nd Floor, Toronto, ON M7A 1N3; tel. (416) 325-2929; fax (416) 325-6348; e-mail thomas.teahen@ontario.ca; internet www.edu.gov.on.ca.

Ministry of Energy and Infrastructure: Hearst Block, 4th Floor, 900 Bay St, Toronto, ON M7A 2E1; tel. (416) 327-6758; fax (416) 327-0033; e-mail ron.planche2@ontario.ca; internet www.energy.gov.on.ca.

Ministry of the Environment: 135 St Clair Ave West, 1st Floor, Toronto, ON M4V 1P5; tel. (416) 325-4000; fax (416) 323-4264; e-mail picemail.moe@ontarion.ca; internet www.ene.gov.on.ca.

Ministry of Finance: 33 King St West, POB 627, Oshawa, ON L1H 8H5; tel. (416) 325-0400; fax (416) 325-0374; e-mail financecommunications.fin@ontario.ca; internet www.fin.gov.on.ca.

Ministry of Government Services: 250 Yonge St, 32nd Floor, Toronto, ON M5B 2N5; tel. (416) 326-8555; fax (416) 326-8665; internet www.gov.on.ca/mgs.

Ministry of Health and Long-Term Care: 900 Bay St, M-1B114 Macdonald Block, Toronto, ON M7A 1N3; tel. (416) 314-5518; fax (416) 314-8721; e-mail infoline.moh@ontario.ca; internet www.health.gov.on.ca.

Ministry of Health Promotion: 777 Bay St, 18th Floor, Toronto, ON M7A 1S5; tel. (416) 326-8475; fax (416) 326-4864; e-mail info@mhp.gov.on.ca; internet www.mhp.gov.on.ca.

Ministry of Labour: 400 University Ave, 14th Floor, Toronto, ON M7A 1T7; tel. (416) 326-7600; fax (416) 326-1449; e-mail susan.mcconnell@ontario.ca; internet www.labour.gov.on.ca.

Ministry of Municipal Affairs and Housing: 777 Bay St, 17th Floor, Toronto, ON M5G 2E5; tel. (416) 585-7041; fax (416) 585-6470; e-mail jim.watson@ontario.ca; internet www.mah.gov.on.ca.

Ministry of Natural Resources: Whitney Block, Rm 6630, 99 Wellesley St West, Toronto, ON M7A 1W3; tel. (416) 314-2301; fax (416) 325-5316; e-mail ivan.langrish@ontario.ca; internet www.mnr.gov.on.ca.

Ministry of Northern Development and Mines: Whitney Block, Rm 5630, 99 Wellesley St West, Toronto, ON M7A 1W3; tel. (416) 327-0633; fax (416) 327-0665; e-mail anne-marie.flanagan@ontario.ca; internet www.mndm.gov.on.ca.

Ministry of Public Infrastructure Renewal: Ministry of Energy and Infrastructure, Hearst Block, 4th Floor, 900 Bay St, Toronto, ON M7A 2E1; tel. (416) 325-0424; fax (416) 325-8440; e-mail info.pir@ontario.ca; internet www.pir.gov.on.ca.

Ministry of Tourism: Hearst Block, 9th Floor, 900 Bay St, Toronto, ON M7A 2E1; tel. (416) 326-9326; fax (416) 314-7854; e-mail general_info@mtr.gov.on.ca; internet www.tourism.gov.on.ca.

Ministry of Training, Colleges and Universities: 880 Bay St, 2nd Floor, Toronto, ON M7A 1N3; tel. (416) 325-2929; fax (416) 325-6348; e-mail annette.phillips@ontario.ca; internet www.edu.gov.on.ca/eng/tcu.

Ministry of Transportation: Ferguson Block, 3rd Floor, 77 Wellesley St West, Toronto, ON M7A 1Z8; tel. (416) 327-9200; fax (416) 327-9185; internet www.mto.gov.on.ca.

Office of Francophone Affairs: 777 Bay St, 6th Floor, Toronto, ON M7A 2J4; tel. (416) 325-4949; fax (416) 325-4980; e-mail ofa@ontario.ca; internet www.ofa.gov.on.ca.

Legislative Assembly

(September 2008)

Speaker: STEVE PETERS.

Clerk: DEBORAH DELLER.

Election, 10 October 2007

	Seats at election	Seats at September 2008
Liberal	71	71
Progressive Conservative (PC)	26	25
New Democratic Party (NDP)	10	10
Independent	—	1
Total	107	107

Prince Edward Island

Area: 5,660 sq km (2,185 sq miles).

Population (at 1 July 2007): 138,627.

Capital, Principal City: Charlottetown (population at census of 16 May 2006, 32,174).

LOCATION, TOPOGRAPHY AND CLIMATE

Prince Edward Island, one of the three Maritime provinces, is situated in the Gulf of St Lawrence, in the east of the country. It is Canada's smallest province. Across the Northumberland Strait to the east and south is Nova Scotia, with New Brunswick to the south-west. To the north are the Iles de la Madeleine, part of the province of Québec. The land surface of the island is level in the west, rising to gentle hills in the central and eastern regions. The deep red soil that characterizes the island is interspersed with outcrops of sedimentary rock. Tidal inlets indent the coastline, while sandbanks lie along the northern shore. Prince Edward Island has a temperate climate, with long, mild winters and cool summers.

HISTORICAL BACKGROUND

The Micmac peoples inhabited present-day Prince Edward Island for many generations before the French explorer, Jacques Cartier, landed in 1534. French settlement of the island (which was named Ile Saint-Jean and was a dependency of Ile Royale—Cape Breton Island, now part of Nova Scotia) commenced in the 1720s. The island was ceded to the British under the Treaty of Paris in 1763 and renamed St John's Island. It remained part of Nova Scotia until 1769, when it was given a separate government; it was then restored to Nova Scotia in 1784, but separated once again in 1786. In 1799 the island was renamed Prince Edward Island, in honour of King George III's fourth son (later Duke of Kent and father of Queen Victoria). Questions of land ownership caused political problems for the island until confederation. The Charlottetown Conference was held on the island in 1864, originally to discuss a union of the Maritime colonies; Prince Edward Islanders declined to join the larger confederation at its inception in 1867. Financial difficulties and other pressures, however, persuaded them to enter the Dominion of Canada on 1 July 1873.

ECONOMY

Prince Edward Island's economy strengthened during the later decades of the 20th century, but the province remains heavily reliant upon federal government assistance. The island's dependence on agriculture, its lack of mineral resources and the cost of transportation make it one of the poorer provinces. Agriculture, tourism and light manufacturing are the major contributors to the provincial economy. In 2006 median annual family income was C $56,100, while median per-head income averaged of $23,800, the third lowest in the country. Total civilian employment was approximately 69,300 persons in 2007 and the minimum hourly rate of pay for experienced workers was set at $8.0 in October 2008. The unemployment rate in 2007 was 10.3%—the second highest level among the provinces after Newfoundland and Labrador.

Farmland covered 619,897 acres (250,859 ha) in 2006. The average size of a farm was 366 acres and there were 1,700 farms. Prince Edward Island is an important producer of potatoes, second only to Manitoba in 2007 in terms of production. Other crops grown include barley, wheat, vegetables, floricultural and nursery products, forest products, strawberries, berries and grapes, oats, and hay and clover. Dairying, cattle, hogs and eggs are also significant to the island's farming industry. Farm receipts totalled C $364m. in 2007.

In 2006 forestland (harvested) covered an estimated 2,195 ha. Little of this was commercially valuable: only an estimated 602,000 cu m of merchantable timber, of which 61% was softwoods, was produced in 2006. Fishing, however, is a major employer. In 2006 output of aquaculture products totalled 20,147 metric tons, with the province ranked first for shellfish production, accounting for well over half of national production in terms of volume. In 2006 the total value of the fishing catch was C $137m. (37,873 tons live weight). In 2005 the province produced 5,400 wildlife pelts, while fur production in 2007 generated $5.3m.

Total non-fuel mineral production was valued at an estimated C $4.1m. in 2007, the lowest level among the provinces and territories. Sand and gravel were the only minerals of significance.

Prince Edward Island's manufacturing industry relies upon its farm and fishing products, with food-processing the leading sector. Other important industry groups are transportation equipment, chemicals and chemical products and the printing, publishing and allied industries. Various government schemes are attempting to attract more diverse industries to the island, with particular emphasis on the high-technology sector. Manufacturing shipments were valued at C $1,429m. in 2007, with only the Northwest Territories, Yukon Territory and Nunavut Territory registering lower levels.

Tourism plays an important role in the provincial economy, and the province's beaches are popular for water sports. Total visitors to the island (including business travellers) were estimated at 998,866 in 2004 and their expenditure was estimated at C $291.7m.

Gross general expenditure by the provincial government totalled C $1,390m. in 2007/08, with 30.3% spent on health care, 19.7% on education and 8.9% on social services. Gross general revenue was $1,365m. in that year, with 39.0% provided by transfers from other levels of government and 49.7% derived from taxes.

GOVERNMENT

The Province of Prince Edward Island was admitted to the confederation on 1 July 1873 by the Imperial Order-in-Council of 26 June 1873. The provincial government consists of: the Lieutenant-Governor; the Premier and cabinet, who together form the Executive Council; and a Legislative Assembly of 27 members. Local government is administered by 75 incorporated municipalities, in which there are two cities, seven towns and 66 communities. In the provincial election of May 2007 the Liberal Party gained 23 out of the total of 27 seats. The Liberal Party won three of the province's four seats in the House of Commons in the 2008 federal general election, while the remaining seat was won by the Conservative Party.

Lieutenant-Governor: BARBARA A. HAGERMAN.

Executive Council

Premier, President of the Executive Council and Minister for Intergovernmental Affairs: ROBERT GHIZ.

Attorney-General and Minister of Education and Early Childhood Development: L. GERARD GREENAN.

Provincial Treasurer: WESLEY J. SHERIDAN.

Minister of Agriculture: NEIL J. LECLAIR.

Minister of Communities, Cultural Affairs and Labour: CAROLYN I. BERTRAM.

Minister of Environment, Energy and Forestry: GEORGE T. WEBSTER.

Minister of Fisheries, Aquaculture and Rural Development: ALLAN V. CAMPBELL.

Minister of Health and of Social Services and Seniors: DOUG W. CURRIE.

Minister of Innovation and Advanced Learning: RICHARD E. BROWN.

Minister of Tourism: VALERIE E. DOCHERTY.

Minister of Transportation and Public Works: RON W. MCKINLEY.

Selected Government Addresses

Office of the Lieutenant-Governor: Government House, POB 846, Charlottetown, PE C1A 7L9; tel. (902) 368-5480; fax (902) 368-5481; e-mail island@gov.pe.ca; internet www.gov.pe.ca/lg.

Office of the Premier: Shaw Bldg, 5th Floor South, 95 Rochford St, POB 2000, Charlottetown, PE C1A 7N8; tel. (902) 368-4400; fax (902) 368-4416; e-mail rwjghiz@gov.pe.ca; internet www.gov.pe.ca/premier.

Department of Agriculture: Jones Bldg, 5th Floor, 11 Kent St, POB 2000, Charlottetown, PE C1A 7N8; tel. (902) 368-4880; fax (902) 368-4857; e-mail njleclair@gov.pe.ca; internet www.gov.pe.ca/af.

Department of Communities, Cultural Affairs and Labour: Shaw Bldg, 4th Floor, 95 Rochford St, POB 2000, Charlottetown, PE C1A 7N8; tel. (902) 368-5250; fax (902) 368-4121; e-mail cibertram@gov.pe.ca; internet www.gov.pe.ca/cca.

Department of Education and Early Childhood Development: Sullivan Bldg, 2nd Floor, 16 Fitzroy St, POB 2000, Charlottetown, PE C1A 7N8; tel. (902) 368-4600; fax (902) 368-4663; e-mail glgreenan@gov.pe.ca; internet www.gov.pe.ca/educ.

Department of the Environment, Energy and Forestry: Jones Bldg, 4th and 5th Floors, 11 Kent St, POB 2000, Charlottetown, PE C1A 7N8; tel. (902) 368-5000; fax (902) 368-5830; e-mail gtwebster@gov.pe.ca; internet www.gov.pe.ca/envengfor.

Department of Fisheries and Aquaculture: Jones Bldg, 5th Floor, 11 Kent St, POB 2000, Charlottetown, PE C1A 7N8; tel. (902) 368-6330; fax (902) 368-5542; e-mail avcampbell@gov.pe.ca; internet www.gov.pe.ca/fa/faweb.

Department of Health: 16 Garfield St, 1st Floor, POB 2000, Charlottetown, PE C1A 7N8; tel. (902) 368-6130; fax (902) 368-6136; e-mail mxflanagan-leclair@gov.pe.ca; internet www.gov.pe.ca/health.

Department of Innovation and Advanced Learning: Shaw Bldg, 5th Floor, 105 Rochford St, POB 2000, Charlottetown, PE C1A 7N8; tel. (902) 368-4240; fax (902) 368-4242; e-mail rebrown@gov.pe.ca; internet www.gov.pe.ca/ial.

Department of the Provincial Treasury: Shaw Bldg, 2nd Floor South, 95 Rochford St, POB 2000, Charlottetown, PE C1A 7N8; tel. (902) 368-4050; fax (902) 368-6575; e-mail wjsheridan@gov.pe.ca; internet www.gov.pe.ca/pt.

Department of Social Services and Seniors: Jones Bldg, 2nd Floor, 11 Kent St, POB 2000, Charlottetown, PE C1A 7N8; tel. (902) 368-4930; fax (902) 368-4974; e-mail dwcurrie@gov.pe.ca; internet www.gov.pe.ca/sss.

Department of Tourism: POB 2000, Charlottetown, PE C1A 7N8; tel. (902) 368-4801; fax (902) 368-5277; e-mail vedocherty@gov.pe.ca; internet www.gov.pe.ca/visitorsguide.

Department of Transportation and Public Works: Jones Bldg, 2nd and 3rd Floors, 11 Kent St, POB 2000, Charlottetown, PE C1A 7N8; tel. (902) 368-5100; fax (902) 368-5395; e-mail asgsprague@gov.pe.ca; internet www.gov.pe.ca/tpwpei.

Office of the Attorney-General: Shaw Bldg North, 4th Floor, 105 Rochford St, POB 2000, Charlottetown, PE C1A 7N8; tel. (902) 368-5152; fax (902) 368-4910; e-mail madover@edu.pe.ca; internet www.gov.pe.ca/oag.

Office of Intergovernmental Affairs: Shaw Bldg North, 5th Floor, 105 Rochford St, POB 2000, Charlottetown, PE C1A 7N8; tel. (902) 368-4502; fax (902) 368-6118.

Legislative Assembly
(September 2008)

Speaker: KATHLEEN CASEY (Liberal).

Clerk: CHARLES MACKAY.

Election, 28 May 2007

	Seats at election	Seats at September 2008
Liberal	23	24
Progressive Conservative	4	3
Total	27	27

Québec

Area: 1,542,056 sq km (602,366 sq miles).

Population (at 1 July 2007, estimate): 7,700,807.

Capital: Québec.

Principal Cities: (population at census of 16 May 2006)

Montréal	1,620,693	Sherbrooke	147,427
Québec	491,142	Saguenay	143,692
Longueuil	229,330	Lévis	130,006
Laval	368,709	Trois-Rivières	126,323
Gatineau	242,124		

LOCATION, TOPOGRAPHY AND CLIMATE

In terms of its area, Québec is the largest province in Canada. It is bounded to the west by Hudson Bay and to the north-east by the Hudson Strait, while Labrador (part of Newfoundland and Labrador) forms the northern border. The province is bordered to the south by the US states of Maine, New Hampshire, Vermont and New York. The Gulf of St Lawrence and the province of New Brunswick lie to the south-east; to the south-west is Ontario, across the Ottawa River. Major islands of the province include the Ile d'Anticosti, in the mouth of the St Lawrence River, and the Iles de la Madeleine, north of Prince Edward Island and Nova Scotia. Québec is divided into three distinct geological regions. The Canadian Shield, a huge plateau divided by numerous lakes and rivers, covers the greater part of the province to the north. The St Lawrence River valley and lowlands to the south is a fertile area, formed by a series of broad terraces that decline towards the river. The third section, the Appalachian foothills south of the St Lawrence River, forms part of the Appalachian Mountains range, stretching from Newfoundland Island to Alabama (USA) and intersected by arable plateaux and plains. Québec's most important waterway is the St Lawrence River, which flows for over 3,600 km through the Great Lakes before reaching the Atlantic Ocean, and is among the world's greatest rivers. The highest point is Mount Iberville, in the Torngat Mountains in northern Québec, rising to 1,652 m (5,420 ft)—the highest point in mainland Canada east of the Rocky Mountains. The climate in Québec is severe, with extreme temperatures and long winters, although the south of the province around Montréal and Québec City receives pleasant summers.

HISTORICAL BACKGROUND

The present-day province of Québec was the site of Canada's first permanent European settlement: Samuel de Champlain established what was to become Québec City on the site of an Iroquois village in 1608. The colony of New France grew slowly, as the frequency of wars with the British increased; calm was briefly restored by the Peace of Utrecht in 1713 (whereby France lost much of its claimed territory in Canada), but conflict resumed, and the cities of Québec and Montréal were occupied in 1759 and 1760, respectively, by British forces. The Treaty of Paris (1763), which ended the French and Indian War (Seven-Years War), also ended French claims to the area. The United Kingdom Parliament passed the Québec Act in 1774 and attempted to recreate the boundaries of New France. The Constitutional Act of 1791 divided the British and French majority populations of the area then known as Canada into the colonies of Upper and Lower Canada, respectively. Following the Rebellions of 1837 in Montréal and Toronto, the two colonies were reunited under the 1840 Act of Union, with English as the official language. In 1848 the French language regained its official status. The federal structure of confederation was accepted as a means of increasing control over language, religion and civil law, and Québec became a separate province at confederation on 1 July 1867. During the First World War the province experienced civil unrest owing to the introduction of conscription. The reforms of the 'Quiet Revolution' in the 1960s transformed Québec into a modern society, but also marked the resurgence of separatist feeling in the francophone population. In 1980 a referendum on 'sovereignty-association' was held, but the electorate rejected the proposal. However, debate about the status of the province within Canada continued, prompting a federal-provincial conference to propose that Québec be recognized as a 'distinct society' within the confederation. This Meech Lake Accord failed to be endorsed, and lapsed in 1990. The subsequent Charlottetown Agreement was rejected by the national electorate in 1992, emphasizing Québec's sense of isolation. A provincial referendum in 1995 narrowly favoured the status quo. In 1998 the federal Supreme Court ruled that Québec could not separate unilaterally. The federal Government remains strongly opposed to independence for the province, and in 1999 introduced strict new measures governing any future referendums on the issue.

ECONOMY

Québec's economic activities are comparatively diverse. The main sectors, in terms of the numbers of people employed, are community, business and personal services, and trade. The province is highly industrialized.

In 2006 median family income in Québec was C $59,000 and median per-head income averaged $24,900. The minimum hourly wage rate for adult workers was set at $8.50 from May 2008. In 2007 total civilian employment comprised about 3,851,700 persons, and the unemployment rate was 7.2%.

Farmland in Québec covered 8.6m. acres (3.5m. hectares) in 2006, when an average farm measured 279 acres. There were 30,675 farms in that year. In 2007 farm market receipts totalled C $6,751m., or 16.7% of the Canadian total. Québec was Canada's leading producer of dairy products and hogs in 2007 and was ranked second for poultry, eggs, sheep and lambs (after Ontario), and also for calves. The province was ranked second for soybean and corn production in 2007, again after Ontario. It was the leading producer of forest products, Christmas trees (conifers), strawberries and maple syrup, accounting for 86% of the national total of maple products in that year.

In 2005 the province was the largest producer of wildlife pelts in Canada, with total production of 230,600 pelts reaping a value of C $8.7m. By 2007, however, the total value of fur production had declined to $2.8m., with the province ranked fourth nation-wide in this regard. Forestland (harvested) was estimated to cover 316,377 ha in 2006 and the merchantable roundwood harvest in that year amounted to an estimated 33.1m. cu m, mostly softwoods (74%), the second highest provincial total behind British Columbia.

Fishing makes a moderate contribution to Québec's economy. The province's fish catch (sea and freshwater) was valued at $119.1m. in 2007, which equalled 59,545 metric tons. Aquaculture, principally of trout and mussels, contributed $12.2m. in 2006.

In 2007 Québec's non-fuel mineral production was valued at an estimated C $5,516m. The province ranked first for production of cadmium in that year; second for gold, iron ore, selenium, cement, peat, quartz (silica), and stone; and third for antimony, silver, zinc and sulphur (in smelter gas). Cobalt, copper, nickel and sand and gravel were also produced.

Québec's leading manufacturing sectors are primary metal industries, food-processing, transportation equipment, petroleum and coal products, paper and allied products, chemicals and chemical products, wood industries, fabricated metal products and plastic and rubber electronic products. Sectors growing in importance include aeronautics, pharmaceuticals and telecommunications equipment. Manufacturing shipments were valued at C $148,260m. in 2007, with only Ontario registering a higher level.

Tourism is an important source of revenue for the province. In 2006 26.2m. tourists visited Québec, and expenditures on tourism totalled C $10,070m.

Gross general revenue of the provincial government amounted to C $79,783m. in 2007/08, with 18.3% provided by transfers from other levels of government and 64.6% contributed by taxes. Gross general expenditures totalled $79,392m., with 28.3% spent on health, 20.5% on social services and 18.0% on education.

GOVERNMENT

Québec was one of the four provinces united in the confederation of the Dominion of Canada on 1 July 1867 by the British North America Act. The provincial government has: a Lieutenant-Governor; a Conseil Exécutif or Conseil des Ministres (Executive Council), consisting of the Premier Ministre (Premier) and his or her ministers; and the Assemblée Nationale (National Assembly), which has 125 members. One-third of Québec is organized municipally, while the remainder is governed directly by the provincial government. The province is divided into 17 administrative regions; these in turn include 96 regional county municipalities, three urban communities and 1,398 municipalities, following a municipal reorganization in 2000. At the provincial election in March 2007 the Liberal Party was elected by a narrow margin, having won 48 of the seats in the Assemblée Nationale. The Action Démocratique du Québec party secured 41 seats. In the 2008 federal general election some 3,620,362 votes were polled. The Bloc Québécois won 50 of the province's 75 seats in the House of Commons, while the Liberal Party secured 13 seats, the Conservatives 10 seats and the New Democratic Party one seat. An independent candidate won the remaining seat.

Lieutenant-Governor: PIERRE DUCHESNE.

Executive Council

Premier: JEAN CHAREST.

Deputy Premier, Minister of Municipal Affairs and Regions: NATHALIE NORMANDEAU.

Minister of Agriculture, Fisheries and Food: LAURENT LESSARD.

Minister responsible for Canadian Intergovernmental Affairs and Aboriginal Affairs: BENOÎT PELLETIER.

Minister of Culture, Communications and the Status of Women: CHRISTINE ST-PIERRE.

Minister of Economic Development, Innovation and Export Trade and of Tourism: RAYMOND BACHAND.

Minister of Education, Recreation and Sports and of Families: MICHELLE COURCHESNE.

Minister of Employment and Social Solidarity: SAM HAMAD.

Minister of Finance and of Government Services, Chair of the Treasury Board: MONIQUE JÉRÔME-FORGET.

Minister of Health and Social Services: YVES BOLDUC.

Minister of Immigration and Cultural Communities: YOLANDE JAMES.

Minister of International Relations, Minister responsible for la Francophonie: MONIQUE GAGNON-TREMBLAY.

Minister of Justice and of Public Security: JACQUES DUPUIS.

Minister of Labour: DAVID WHISSELL.

Minister of Natural Resources and Wildlife: CLAUDE BÉCHARD.

Minister of Revenue, Government House Leader: JEAN-MARC FOURNIER.

Minister responsible for Seniors: MARGUERITE BLAIS.

Minister of Sustainable Development, Environment and Parks: LINE BEAUCHAMP.

Minister of Transport: JULIE BOULET.

Government Addresses

Office of the Lieutenant-Governor: Edif. André-Laurendeau, 1050 rue des Parlementaires, Québec, QC G1A 1A1; tel. (418) 643-5385; fax (418) 644-4677; e-mail lieut-gouv@mce.gouv.qc.ca; internet www.lieutenant-gouverneur.qc.ca.

Office of the Premier: Edif. Honoré-Mercier, 3e étage, 835 blvd René-Lévesque est, Québec, QC G1A 1B4; tel. (418) 643-5321; fax (418) 643-3924; internet www.premier.gouv.qc.ca.

Ministry of Agriculture, Fisheries and Food: 200 chemin Ste-Foy, 12e étage, Québec, QC G1R 4X6; tel. (418) 380-2525; fax (418) 380-2184; e-mail ministre.mapaq@mapaq.gouv.qc.ca; internet www.mapaq.gouv.qc.ca.

Ministry of Culture, Communications and the Status of Women: 225 Grande Allée est, Bloc A, 1er étage, Québec, QC G1R 5G5; tel. (418) 380-2310; fax (418) 380-2311; e-mail ministre@mcccf.gouv.qc.ca; internet www.mcccf.gouv.qc.ca.

Ministry of Economic Development, Innovation and Export Trade: 710 pl. D'Youville, 6e étage, Québec, QC G1R 4Y4; tel. (418) 691-5650; fax (418) 643-8553; e-mail ministre@mdeie.gouv.qc.ca; internet www.mdeie.gouv.qc.ca.

Ministry of Education, Recreation and Sports: Edif. Marie-Guyart, 28e étage, 1035 rue de la Chevrotière, Québec, QC G1R 5A5; tel. (418) 643-7095; fax (418) 646-6561; e-mail ministre@mels.gouv.qc.ca; internet www.mels.gouv.qc.ca.

Ministry of Employment and Social Solidarity: 425 rue Saint-Amable, rez-de-chaussée 175, Québec, QC G1R 4Z1; tel. (418) 643-4721; e-mail ministre@mess.gouv.qc.ca; internet www.mess.gouv.qc.ca.

Ministry of the Executive Council: Edif. H, Bureau RC.01, 875 Grande Allée est, Québec, QC G1R 4Y8; tel. (418) 646-3021; fax (418) 528-9242; internet www.mce.gouv.qc.ca.

Ministry of the Family and Seniors: 425 rue St-Amable, rez-de-chaussée, Québec, QC G1R 4Z1; tel. (418) 643-4721; fax (418) 646-7769; e-mail m.blais@aines.gouv.qc.ca; internet www.mfa.gouv.qc.ca.

Ministry of Finance: Edif. Gérard-D.-Levesque, 1er étage, 12 rue St-Louis, Québec, QC G1R 5L3; tel. (418) 528-9323; fax (418) 646-1631; e-mail info@finances.gouv.qc.ca; internet www.finances.gouv.qc.ca.

Ministry of Government Services: Edif. H–875, Grande Allée est, 4e étage, section 500, Québec, QC G1R 5R8; tel. (418) 643-8383; fax (418) 528-6153; e-mail communication@msg.gouv.qc.ca; internet www.msg.gouv.qc.ca.

Ministry of Health and Social Services: Edif. Catherine-de-Longpré, 16e étage, 1075 chemin Ste-Foy, Québec, QC G1S 2M1; tel. (418) 644-4545; fax (418) 266-4574; e-mail info@msss.gouv.qc.ca; internet www.msss.gouv.qc.ca.

Ministry of Immigration and Cultural Communities: Edif. Gérald-Godin, 4e étage, 360 rue McGill, Montréal, QC H29 2E9; tel. (514) 873-9940; fax (514) 864-2899; e-mail cabinet@micc.gouv.qc.ca; internet www.micc.gouv.qc.ca.

Ministry of International Relations: Edif. Hector-Fabre, 525 blvd René-Lévesque est, Québec, QC G1R 5R9; tel. (418) 649-2300; fax (418) 649-2656; e-mail communications@mri.gouv.qc.ca; internet www.mri.gouv.qc.ca.

Ministry of Justice: Edif. Louis-Philippe-Pigeon, 6e étage, 1200 route de l'Eglise, Québec, QC G1V 4M1; tel. (418) 643-5140; fax (418) 646-4449; e-mail informations@justice.gouv.qc.ca; internet www.justice.gouv.qc.ca.

Ministry of Labour: 200 chemin Ste-Foy, 6e étage, Québec, QC G1R 5S1; tel. (418) 643-4817; fax (418) 528-0559; e-mail service_clientele@travail.gouv.qc.ca; internet www.travail.gouv.qc.ca.

Ministry of Municipal Affairs and Regions: Aile Chauveau, 3e étage, 10 rue Pierre-Olivier-Chauveau, Québec, QC G1R 4J3; tel. (418) 691-2019; fax (418) 643-7385; e-mail communications@mamr.gouv.qc.ca; internet www.mamr.gouv.qc.ca.

Ministry of Natural Resources and Wildlife: 880 chemin Ste-Foy, rez-de-chaussée 120-C, QC G1S 4X4; tel. (418) 627-8600; fax (418) 644-6513; e-mail service.clientele@mrnf.gouv.qc.ca; internet www.mrn.gouv.qc.ca.

Ministry of Public Security: Tour des Laurentides, 5e étage, 2525 blvd Laurier, Québec, QC G1V 2L2; tel. (418) 644-2112; fax (418) 646-6168; e-mail ministre@msp.gouv.qc.ca; internet www.msp.gouv.qc.ca.

Ministry of Revenue: 3800 rue de Marly, secteur 6-2-5, Québec, QC G1X 4A5; tel. (418) 659-6299; fax (418) 646-7379; e-mail cabinet@revenu.gouv.qc.ca; internet www.revenu.gouv.qc.ca.

Ministry of Sustainable Development, Environment and Parks: Edif. Marie-Guyart, 29e étage, 675 blvd René-Lévesque est, Québec, QC G1R 5V7; tel. (418) 521-3830; fax (418) 646-5974; e-mail info@mddep.gouv.qc.ca; internet www.mddep.gouv.qc.ca.

Ministry of Tourism (Tourisme Québec): 900 blvd René-Lévesque est, Bureau 400, Québec, QC G1R 2B5; tel. (514) 873-2015; fax (514) 864-3838; e-mail info@bonjourquebec.com; internet www.bonjourquebec.com.

Ministry of Transportation: 700 blvd René-Lévesque est, 27e étage, Québec, QC G1R 5H1; tel. (418) 643-6980; fax (418) 643-1269; e-mail communications@mtq.gouv.qc.ca; internet www.mtq.gouv.qc.ca.

Treasury Board Secretariat: Edif. J, 4e étage, 875 Grande Allée est, Québec, QC G1R 5R8; tel. (418) 643-5926; fax (418) 643-7824; e-mail communication@sct.gouv.qc.ca; internet www.tresor.gouv.qc.ca.

Assemblée Nationale/National Assembly
(September 2008)

President: (vacant).

Secretary-General: François Côté.

Election, 26 March 2007

	Seats at election	Seats at September 2008
Liberal	48	47
Action Démocratique du Québec	41	41
Parti Québécois (PQ)	36	36
Vacant	—	1
Total	125	125

Saskatchewan

Area: 651,036 sq km (254,311 sq miles).

Population (at 1 July 2007, estimate): 996,869.

Capital: Regina.

Principal Cities (population at census of 16 May 2006): Saskatoon 202,340; Regina (capital) 179,246.

LOCATION, TOPOGRAPHY AND CLIMATE

Saskatchewan is in western-central Canada, bordered to the east and west, respectively, by the other two Prairie provinces of Manitoba and Alberta. To the north is the Northwest Territories and to the south the US states of Montana and North Dakota. The Canadian Shield, which characterizes the northern third of the province, is a region of rocky outcrops and lakes. To the south lie the prairie lowlands, a fertile, grain-producing area. On the western and south-western boundaries another prairie region is characterized by undulating plains of a higher altitude. The Cypress Hills in the extreme south-west rise to 1,468 m (4,816 ft). About 12% of the province is accounted for by fresh water, including several large lake systems. The Qu'Appelle and Saskatchewan Rivers eventually drain into Hudson Bay, by way of Lake Winnipeg (Manitoba). The outflow of the Churchill River is also into Hudson Bay, by way of Churchill Lake and the Southern Indian Lake (Manitoba). Lake Athabasca (7,936 sq km), which is shared with Alberta, feeds into the Mackenzie River by way of the Great Slave Lake (both in the Northwest Territories), and eventually flows to the Beaufort Sea. Saskatchewan has a continental climate, dry and warm in summer, with long, cold winters.

HISTORICAL BACKGROUND

Athapaskan-, Algonquian- and Siouan-speaking Indians were present in the area now known as Saskatchewan at the time of the first explorations in the late 17th century. Henry Kelsey of the Hudson's Bay Company (HBC) was the first voyager to penetrate the plains south of the Saskatchewan River. Fur-trading was the overriding preoccupation of the first European settlers. Following the purchase of Rupert's Land from the HBC by the newly created Dominion of Canada in 1869 there was much immigration, while the relative presence of the native Indian population dropped sharply. Saskatchewan was the site of an important rebellion by the Métis (people of mixed French and Indian descent) in 1885. The province entered the confederation on 1 September 1905, after which the southern arable lands were settled quickly. Despite the maintenance of crown lands until 1930, the province became a major agricultural power.

ECONOMY

The largest share of non-agricultural employment in Saskatchewan is taken by mining, services-related industries and manufacturing.

Median family income in the province was C $60,500 in 2006, and per-head median income measured $25,200. In 2007 civilian employment totalled 501,800 persons, with the unemployment rate standing at 4.2%. The minimum hourly wage rate was raised to $8.60 in May 2008.

Some 37m. acres (15m. ha) of the province were used for cropland in 2006, and the average size of a farm was 1,451 acres (the largest average size in the nation). In that year there were 44,329 farms. Market receipts totalled C $7,606m. in 2007. The province was Canada's leading producer of canola (rapeseed), wheat, dry peas, barley, lentils, oats, flaxseed, mustard seed, canary seed and chickpeas in 2007 and was ranked second for honey and forage and grass seed production (after Alberta) and for sunflower seeds (after Manitoba). It was also ranked first in terms of calf production in 2007. Cattle, hogs, dairy produce, poultry, floriculture and nursery products, hay and clover, potatoes and eggs also contribute to farm income. Wildlife pelt production is another important source of income: an estimated 67,600 wildlife pelts were produced in 2005, while fur production in 2007 generated $2.4m.

Saskatchewan's harvested forestland covered 41,825 ha. in 2005, and roundwood removals (both soft- and hardwoods, with the latter accounting for 62%) totalled an estimated 3.5m. cu m in 2006. Trout is the only aquaculture product of any significance, contributing C $4.6m. to the economy in 2002. There is also some freshwater fishing: total commercial landings in 2006 were valued at $2.8m., representing 2,788 metric tons of fish (live weight).

Saskatchewan is a major petroleum-producing province, second only to Alberta, with 428,117 barrels per day of crude oil produced in 2006. Natural gas is also extracted (926m. cu ft per day in 2006, ranking the province third overall) as well as coal (11.3m. metric tons in 2006). Total non-fuel mineral production in 2007 was valued at an estimated C $5,832m. (Saskatchewan was the second greatest contributor to total national non-fuel mineral production in that year). The province's principal non-fuel mineral is uranium (of which it is the only significant Canadian producer, and the largest producer internationally—Saskatchewan was estimated to account for approximately 30% of annual world uranium production). Other minerals produced include gold, selenium, silver, and salt (for which it ranks second to Ontario), elemental sulphur, and sand and gravel.

Saskatchewan has an expanding manufacturing sector. Food industries, based on the province's agricultural output, dominate the manufacturing sector. Other important sectors are chemicals and chemical products, wood industries, machinery, fabricated metal products, paper and allied products and transportation equipment. Total manufacturing shipments were valued at C $10,081m. in 2007, in which year the province ranked seventh in Canada.

The province's tourism industry has burgeoned in recent years to become one of the largest employment sectors; it was estimated that over 53,000 people (equivalent to approximately 10% of the labour force) worked in roles supported, directly or indirectly, by tourism in 2006. It was estimated that there were 8.2m. visits to and within Saskatchewan in that year, with spending by all travellers generating over C $1,440m. The provincial government significantly increased expenditure on the tourism sector for the 2008/09 fiscal year (to $16m.) in an effort to enhance Saskatchewan's industrial competitiveness.

Gross general expenditures by the provincial government were C $9,777m. in 2007/08, of which 34.6% was spent on health, 12.3% on social services and 17.7% on education. Gross general revenue amounted to $10,486m., with 17.9% provided by other levels of government and 56.2% derived from taxes.

GOVERNMENT

The Province of Saskatchewan was created on 1 September 1905 as a result of the Saskatchewan Act of 20 July 1905. The provincial government consists of: a Lieutenant-Governor; an Executive Council, comprising the Premier and his or her chosen cabinet; and a Legislative Assembly of 58 members. Local government in the province is organized through 13 cities, 146 towns, 325 villages, 25 northern municipalities and 298 rural municipalities. Following the 1999 provincial general election the New Democratic Party (NDP) formed a coalition government. On 5 November 2003 the NDP was re-elected, but in the provincial election held on 7 November 2007 the Saskatchewan Party secured a victory, winning 38 seats in the legislature while the NDP won the remaining 20 seats. In the federal general election of 2008 some 418,842 votes were cast. The Conservative Party won 13 of the province's 14 seats in the House of Commons, with the Liberal Party securing the remaining seat.

Lieutenant-Governor: Dr Gordon L. Barnhart.

Executive Council

Premier and President of the Council: Brad Wall.

Deputy Premier and Minister of Education: KEN KRAWETZ.

Attorney-General, Minister of Justice: DON MORGAN.

Minister of Advanced Education, Employment and Labour: ROB NORRIS.

Minister of Agriculture: BOB BJORNERUD.

Minister of Corrections, Public Safety and Policing: DARRYL HICKIE.

Minister of Crown Corporations: KEN CHEVELDAYOFF.

Minister of Energy and Resources: BILL BOYD.

Minister of Enterprise and Innovation: LYLE STEWART.

Minister of Environment: NANCY HEPPNER.

Minister of Finance, Government House Leader: ROD GANTEFOER.

Minister of First Nations and Métis Relations: JUNE DRAUDE.

Minister of Government Services: DAN D'AUTREMONT.

Minister of Health: DON MCMORRIS.

Minister of Highways and Infrastructure, Provincial Secretary: WAYME ELHARD.

Minister of Municipal Affairs: BILL HUTCHINSON.

Minister of Social Services: DONNA HARPAUER.

Minister of Tourism, Parks, Culture and Sport: CHRISTINE TELL.

Selected Government Addresses

Office of the Lieutenant-Governor: Government House, 4607 Dewdney Ave, Regina, SK S4P 1B7; tel. (306) 787-4070; fax (306) 787-7716; e-mail lgo@ltgov.sk.ca; internet www.ltgov.sk.ca.

Office of the Premier: 226 Legislative Bldg, Regina, SK S4S 0B3; tel. (306) 787-9433; fax (306) 787-0885; e-mail premier@gov.sk.ca; internet www.gov.sk.ca/govinfo/premier.

Crown Investments Corporation of Saskatchewan: 2400 College Ave, Suite 400, Regina, SK S4P 1C8; tel. (306) 787-6851; fax (306) 787-8125; internet www.cicorp.sk.ca.

Ministry of Advanced Education, Employment and Labour: 1945 Hamilton St, Regina, SK S4P 2C8; tel. (306) 787-7071; fax (306) 798-0975; e-mail aeeinquiry@gov.sk.ca; internet www.aeel.gov.sk.ca.

Ministry of Agriculture (Saskatchewan Agriculture): 3085 Albert St, Regina, SK S4S 0B1; tel. (306) 787-5140; e-mail aginfo@gov.sk.ca; internet www.agriculture.gov.sk.ca.

Ministry of Corrections, Public Safety and Policing: 1874 Scarth St., 10th Floor, Regina, SK S4P 4B3; tel. (306) 787-7872; fax (306) 787-5331; e-mail minister.cpsp@gov.sk.ca; internet www.cpsp.gov.sk.ca.

Ministry of Education: 2220 College Ave, Regina, SK S4P 4V9; tel. (306) 787-6030; fax (306) 787-2045; e-mail learninginquiry@sasked.gov.sk.ca; internet www.education.gov.sk.ca.

Ministry of Energy and Resources: Legislative Bldg, Rm 361, 2405 Legislative Dr., Regina, SK S4S 0B3; tel. (306) 787-9124; fax (306) 787-0395; e-mail minister.er@gov.sk.ca; internet www.er.gov.sk.ca.

Ministry of Enterprise and Innovation: 3085 Albert St, Suite 200, Regina, SK S4S 0B1; tel. (306) 787-2225; fax (306) 798-0629; internet www.ei.gov.sk.ca.

Ministry of Environment: 3211 Albert St, 2nd Floor, Regina, SK S4S 5W6; tel. (306) 787-2584; fax (306) 787-9544; e-mail inquiry@serm.gov.sk.ca; internet www.environment.gov.sk.ca.

Ministry of Finance: 2350 Albert St, Regina, SK S4P 4A6; tel. (306) 787-6768; fax (306) 787-6055; e-mail minister.fin@gov.sk.ca; internet www.finance.gov.sk.ca.

Ministry of First Nations and Métis Relations: 1855 Victoria Ave, Suite 210, Regina, SK S4P 3T2; tel. (306) 787-6250; fax (306) 787-5832; e-mail minister.fnmr@gov.sk.ca; internet www.fnmr.gov.sk.ca.

Ministry of Government Services: 1920 Rose St, Regina, SK S4P 0A9; tel. (306) 787-6911; fax (306) 787-1061; e-mail minister.gs@gov.sk.ca; internet www.gs.gov.sk.ca.

Ministry of Health: 3475 Albert St, Regina, SK S4S 6X6; tel. (306) 787-7345; fax (306) 787-0237; e-mail minister.he@gov.sk.ca; internet www.health.gov.sk.ca.

Ministry of Highways and Infrastructure: Victoria Tower, 1855 Victoria Ave, Regina, SK S4P 3T2; tel. (306) 787-4800; fax (306) 787-1736; e-mail minister.hi@gov.sk.ca; internet www.highways.gov.sk.ca.

Ministry of Justice, Office of the Attorney-General: 1874 Scarth St, Regina, SK S4P 3V7; tel. (306) 787-8971; fax (306) 787-1232; e-mail minister.ju@gov.sk.ca; internet www.justice.gov.sk.ca.

Ministry of Municipal Affairs: 1855 Victoria Ave, Regina, SK S4P 3T2; tel. (306) 787-2635; fax (306) 787-0399; e-mail minister.ma@gov.sk.ca; internet www.municipal.gov.sk.ca.

Ministry of Social Services: 1920 Broad St, Regina, SK S4P 3V6; tel. (306) 787-3700; fax (306) 787-0656; e-mail minister.ss@gov.sk.ca; internet www.socialservices.gov.sk.ca.

Ministry of Tourism, Parks, Culture and Sport: 1919 Saskatchewan Dr., 4th Floor, Regina, SK S4P 4H2; tel. (306) 787-5729; fax (306) 798-0033; e-mail minister.tpcs@gov.sk.ca; internet www.tpcs.gov.sk.ca.

Office of the Provincial Secretary: Legislative Bldg, Rm 204, 2405 Legislative Dr., Regina, SK S4S 0B3; tel. (306) 787-6447; fax (306) 787-1736; e-mail minister.hi@gov.sk.ca; internet www.ops.gov.sk.ca.

Public Service Commission: 2100 Broad St, 5th Floor, Regina, SK S4P 1Y5; tel. (306) 787-7146; fax (306) 787-7558; e-mail webmaster@psc.gov.sk.ca; internet www.psc.gov.sk.ca; Chair. CLARE ISMAN.

Legislative Assembly
(September 2008)

Speaker: DON TOTH (Saskatchewan Party).

Clerk: GREGORY A. PUTZ.

Election, 7 November 2007

	Seats at election	Seats at September 2008
New Democratic Party (NDP)	38	38
Saskatchewan Party	20	20
Total	58	58

Yukon Territory

Area: 482,443 sq km (188,454 sq miles).

Population (at 1 July 2007, estimate): 30,989.

Capital, Principal City: Whitehorse (population at census of 16 May 2006, 20,461).

LOCATION, TOPOGRAPHY AND CLIMATE

Yukon Territory lies in the extreme north-west of Canada, bordered by the US state of Alaska to the west, the Northwest Territories to the east, the Beaufort Sea and Mackenzie Bay to the north and British Columbia to the south. A large part of the territory consists of plateaux, divided by mountain ranges and valleys that stretch westwards into Alaska. The central Yukon Plateau, dissected by numerous valleys, is separated from the Porcupine Plateau by the Ogilvie Mountains on the north. Its eastern boundary is marked by the Selwyn and Mackenzie mountain ranges. In the south-west lie the St Elias and Coast Mountains, including Mount Logan, which, at 5,951 m (19,524 ft), is the highest point in Canada and the second highest peak in North America after Mount McKinley (Alaska). The northernmost part of the territory is occupied by a continuation from Alaska of the Arctic Coastal Plain. The greater part of the territory is drained by the Yukon River (3,185 km—1,979 miles), which flows into the Bering Sea at Kwiguk in Alaska. Yukon has a continental climate, with very cold winters and warm summers.

HISTORICAL BACKGROUND

The indigenous inhabitants of the Yukon Territory are all Athapaskan-speaking and, at the time of the first European explorations, included Nahanni in the east and groups such as the Teslin, Tutchone and Tagish in the south and west. Fur-trading was the first motive for exploration, but gold prospectors from British Columbia began to cross into the area from the late 19th century. The most famous gold rush in history began on a tributary of the Klondike River in 1896. The Yukon Territory, formerly part of the Northwest Territories, was created on 13 June 1898, with its capital at Dawson. Whitehorse, the seat of government since 1953, grew in importance during the Second World War, when it became a transportation and services hub. The decline of the gold-mining industry commenced as early as 1906, but further mineral developments throughout the territory have helped to maintain its fragile economy.

ECONOMY

Government is the main employer in Yukon Territory, accounting for almost one-quarter of the labour force (in addition to the territorial government, the federal Government's regional administration headquarters are located in Whitehorse). Service industries, transportation and utilities are also important sectors for employment, while the tourism industry is the largest private sector employer. The labour force stood at 17,300 persons in July 2007; the average unemployment rate was 5.2%. Average family income was C $76,000 in 2006, while per-head median income stood at $33,900 in that year, the second highest level in Canada after Northwest Territories. The minimum hourly wage for adult workers increased to $8.58 in April 2008.

Farming and fishing are practised only on a small scale in Yukon, and products are mainly sold to local markets. Improved transportation means that farmers have difficulty competing with cheaper imported goods. It is thought that there is considerable potential for further agricultural development in the territory.

Total harvested forestland was estimated to cover just 12 ha of the territory's land area in 2006, with roundwood removals in that year totalling 19,000 cu m of softwoods. Furs, although still produced, are no longer of great importance to the economy, with only around 5,800 wildlife pelts produced in 2005; fur production in the territory generated $428,810 in 2006, with marten and lynx pelts accounting for the greatest proportion of that value (88%).

Mineral exploration activity has continued to support the economy. Total non-fuel mineral production in 2007 was valued at an estimated C $53.2m. Gold, silver, and sand and gravel are the principal minerals produced. Yukon also produced an estimated 103m. cu m of natural gas in 2007.

There is potential for development in Yukon's renewable resources and manufacturing sectors. Manufacturing shipments totalled C $29.7m. in 2007, the second lowest level, after Nunavut Territory, of all the provinces and territories. Tourism provides the territory with a significant source of income. There were an estimated 324,284 visitors to the territory in 2005, of which 71% were from the USA and 20% from other Canadian provinces. The territorial government is hoping to boost tourist numbers by promoting adventure, cultural and environmental tourism.

Gross general expenditures by the territorial government in 2007/08 were C $892m., with 14.9% spent on health, 15.7% on education and 12.8% on social services. Gross general revenue amounted to $906m., with 10.4% provided by taxes and 82.9% derived from transfers from other levels of government.

GOVERNMENT

Yukon Territory was created as a separate territory on 13 June 1898 by the Yukon Territory Act. The system of government is based on this Act, which provides for a federally appointed Commissioner and a Legislative Assembly. The commissioner's role is similar to that of a provincial lieutenant-governor, except that he or she is responsible to the federal Government through the federal Minister of Indian Affairs and Northern Development. The Executive Council consists of a cabinet of elected members of the Legislative Assembly, headed by the Premier. The 18 members of the Legislative Assembly are elected to serve for four years. After the establishment of the territory the federal Government retained control over certain sectors, including non-renewable natural resources and forestry. Initially, there was only a gradual transfer of jurisdiction. In October 2001, however, a new Yukon Act was introduced into the federal parliament. This outlined a legal framework (in effect, a constitution) for the territory, formally recognized the prevailing system of government and provided for the transfer of responsibility for all land and resource management to the territorial government from 1 April 2003. Local government is administered by Yukon Territory's one city, three towns, four villages, three hamlets and 13 settlements. Administration of a few unorganized communities is carried out by the territorial government. The Yukon Party won a second term in office in the territorial election in October 2006, winning 10 of the legislature's 18 seats. In the federal general election of 2008 the Liberal Party secured the territory's seat in the House of Commons. Some 14,511 people participated in the ballot.

Commissioner: GERALDINE VAN BIBBER.

Executive Council

Premier, Minister of the Executive Council Office, Minister of Finance: DENNIS FENTIE.

Deputy Premier, Minister of Tourism and Culture and of Environment: ELAINE TAYLOR.

Minister of Community Services and of Highways and Public Works: ARCHIE LANG.

Minister of Economic Development: JIM KENYON.

Minister of Education and Minister responsible for the Public Service Commission: PATRICK ROUBLE.

Minister of Energy, Mines and Resources: BRAD CATHERS.

Minister of Health and Social Services: GLENN HART.

Minister of Justice: MARIAN HORNE.

Selected Government Addresses

Office of the Commissioner: Closeleigh Manor Bldg, 1098 First Ave, POB 2703, Whitehorse, YK Y1A 0C1; tel. (867) 667-5121; fax (867) 393-6201; e-mail commissioner@gov.yk.ca; internet www.gov.yk.ca/commissioner.

Office of the Premier: Administration Bldg, 2071 Second Ave, POB 2703, Whitehorse, YT Y1A 1B2; tel. (867) 667-8660; fax (867) 393-6252; e-mail premier@gov.yk.ca; internet www.yukonpremier.ca.

Department of Community Services: POB 2703, Whitehorse, YT Y1A 2C6; tel. (867) 667-5811; fax (867) 393-6295; e-mail inquiry@gov.yk.ca; internet www.community.gov.yk.ca.

Department of Economic Development: 212 Main St, Suite 209, Whitehorse, YT Y1A 2A9; tel. (867) 456-3914; fax (867) 393-6412; e-mail economics@gov.yk.ca; internet www.economicdevelopment.gov.yk.ca.

Department of Education: POB 2703, Whitehorse, YT Y1A 2C6; tel. (867) 667-5141; fax (867) 393-6254; e-mail contact.education@gov.yk.ca; internet www.education.gov.yk.ca.

Department of Energy, Mines and Resources: POB 2703, Whitehorse, YT Y1A 2C6; tel. (867) 667-3130; fax (867) 667-8601; e-mail emr@gov.yk.ca; internet www.emr.gov.yk.ca.

Department of the Environment: 10 Burns Rd, POB 2703, Whitehorse, YT Y1A 2C6; tel. (867) 667-5652; fax (867) 393-6213; e-mail environmentyukon@gov.yk.ca; internet www.environmentyukon.gov.yk.ca.

Department of Finance: Administration Bldg, 3rd Floor, 2071 Second Ave, POB 2703, Whitehorse, YT Y1A 2C6; tel. (867) 667-5343; fax (867) 393-6217; e-mail fininfo@gov.yk.ca; internet www.finance.gov.yk.ca.

Department of Health and Social Services: 307 Black St, POB 2703, Whitehorse, YT Y1A 2C6; tel. (867) 667-3673; fax (867) 667-3096; e-mail hss@gov.yk.ca; internet www.hss.gov.yk.ca.

Department of Highways and Public Works: POB 2703, Whitehorse, YT Y1A 2C6; tel. (867) 393-7193; fax (867) 393-6218; e-mail hpw-info@gov.yk.ca; internet www.hpw.gov.yk.ca.

Department of Justice: Andrew A. Philipsen Law Centre, 2130 Second Ave, POB 2703, Whitehorse, YT Y1A 2C6; tel. (867) 667-3033; fax (867) 667-5790; e-mail jus.msb@gov.yk.ca; internet www.justice.gov.yk.ca.

Department of Tourism and Culture: 100 Hanson St, Whitehorse, YT Y1A 2C6; tel. (867) 667-5036; fax (867) 667-3546; internet www.tc.gov.yk.ca.

Executive Council Office: Administration Bldg, 2071 Second Ave, POB 2703, Whitehorse, YT Y1A 2C6; tel. (867) 667-5393; fax (867) 393-6214; e-mail ecoinfo@gov.yk.ca; internet www.eco.gov.yk.ca.

Public Service Commission: POB 2703, Whitehorse, YT Y1A 2C6; tel. (867) 667-5252; fax (867) 667-6705; e-mail pscwebsite@gov.yk.ca; internet www.psc.gov.yk.ca.

Women's Directorate: Unit 1, 404 Hanson St, POB 2703, Whitehorse, YT Y1A 2C6; tel. (867) 667-3030; fax (867) 393-6270; e-mail brenda.barnes@gov.yk.ca; internet www.womensdirectorate.gov.yk.ca.

Yukon Energy Corporation: 2 Miles Canyon Rd, Box 5920, Whitehorse, YT Y1A 6S7; tel. (867) 393-5300; e-mail communications@yukonenergy.ca; internet www.yukonenergy.ca.

Yukon Housing Corporation: 410H Jarvis St, Whitehorse, YT Y1A 2H5; tel. (867) 667-5759; fax (867) 667-3664; e-mail ykhouse@gov.yk.ca; internet www.housing.yk.ca.

Yukon Liquor Corporation: 9031 Quartz Rd, Whitehorse, YT Y1A 4P9; tel. (867) 667-5245; fax (867) 393-6306; e-mail yukon.liquor@gov.yk.ca; internet www.ylc.yk.ca; Pres. MARC TREMBLAY.

Yukon Workers' Compensation Health and Safety Board: 401 Strickland St, Whitehorse, YT Y1A 5N8; tel. (867) 667-5645; fax (867) 393-6279; e-mail worksafe@gov.yk.ca; internet wcb.yk.ca; Pres. and CEO VALERIE ROYLE.

Legislative Assembly

(September 2008)

Speaker: TED STAFFEN (Yukon Party).

Clerk: FLOYD MCCORMICK.

Election, 10 October 2006

	Seats at election
Yukon Party	10
Liberal	5
New Democratic Party (NDP)	3
Total	18

Index of Statistical Tables

THE USA

CANADA

160°
120°
80°
40°
0°
ARCTIC OCEAN
Beaufort Sea
Baffin Bay
GREENLAND (DENMARK)
JAN MAYEN (NORWAY)
Arctic Circle
ALASKA (USA)
Davis Strait
Denmark Strait
ICELAND
Reykjavík
Norwegian Sea
FAROE ISLANDS (DENMARK)
Hudson Bay
Gulf of Alaska
CANADA
UNITED KINGDOM
North Sea
ISLE OF MAN (UK)
NORTHERN IRELAND
GREAT BRITAIN
IRELAND
Dublin
London
Amsterdam
BELGIUM
CHANNEL ISLANDS (UK)
Paris
FRANCE
Ottawa
SAINT PIERRE AND MIQUELON (FRANCE)
ANDORRA
UNITED STATES OF AMERICA
Washington DC
PORTUGAL
SPAIN
Madrid
Lisbon
GIBRALTAR (UK)
MELILLA (SP)
Algiers
NORTH ATLANTIC OCEAN
Rabat
CEUTA (SP)
BERMUDA (UNITED KINGDOM)
MOROCCO
ALGERIA
Gulf of Mexico
BAHAMAS
Tropic of Cancer
MEXICO
Havana
WESTERN SAHARA
HAWAII (USA)
TURKS AND CAICOS ISLANDS (UK)
DOMINICAN REPUBLIC
PUERTO RICO (USA)
CAYMAN ISLANDS (UK)
CUBA
BRITISH VIRGIN ISLANDS (UK)
US VIRGIN ISLANDS (USA)
SAINT-BARTHÉLEMY (FRANCE)
SAINT CHRISTOPHER AND NEVIS
ANTIGUA AND BARBUDA
HAITI
Santo Domingo
Port-au-Prince
JAMAICA
Kingston
ANGUILLA (UK)
SAINT-MARTIN (FRANCE)
MONTSERRAT (UK)
GUADELOUPE (FRANCE)
MAURITANIA
Nouakchott
MALI
Mexico City
GUATEMALA
BELIZE
Belmopan
HONDURAS
Guatemala City
Tegucigalpa
San Salvador
EL SALVADOR
NICARAGUA
Managua
COSTA RICA
San José
PANAMA
Panamá
NETHERLANDS ANTILLES (NL)
ARUBA (NL)
DOMINICA
SAINT LUCIA
MARTINIQUE (FRANCE)
BARBADOS
SAINT VINCENT AND THE GRENADINES
GRENADA
TRINIDAD AND TOBAGO
CAPE VERDE
Praia
SENEGAL
Dakar
GAMBIA
Banjul
Bamako
GUINEA-BISSAU
GUINEA
Conakry
Freetown
SIERRA LEONE
Monrovia
LIBERIA
CÔTE D'IVOIRE
Yamoussoukro
Abidjan
GHANA
Accra
TOGO
BENIN
BURKINA FASO
Ouagadougou
Caracas
VENEZUELA
Georgetown
Paramaribo
GUYANA
SURINAME
FRENCH GUIANA (FRANCE)
Bogotá
COLOMBIA
Quito
ECUADOR
EQUATORIAL GUINEA
SÃO TOMÉ AND PRÍNCIPE
São Tomé
PERU
BRAZIL
ASCENSION (UNITED KINGDOM)
PACIFIC OCEAN
Lima
Brasília
SOUTH ATLANTIC OCEAN
SAINT HELENA (UNITED KINGDOM)
FRENCH POLYNESIA (FRANCE)
La Paz
BOLIVIA
Sucre
PARAGUAY
COOK ISLANDS (NEW ZEALAND)
Tropic of Capricorn
Asunción
CHILE
PITCAIRN ISLANDS (UNITED KINGDOM)
Santiago
URUGUAY
Buenos Aires
Montevideo
TRISTAN DA CUNHA (UNITED KINGDOM)
ARGENTINA
Africa South of the Sahara
Central and South-Eastern Europe
Eastern Europe, Russia and Central Asia
The Far East and Australasia
The Middle East and North Africa
South America, Central America and the Caribbean
South Asia
The USA and Canada
Western Europe
FALKLAND ISLANDS (UNITED KINGDOM)
SOUTH GEORGIA AND THE SOUTH SANDWICH ISLANDS (UNITED KINGDOM)
Antarctic Circle
www.europaworld.com